# MICHAEL BROADBENT'S

# *Vintage Wine*

*This book is dedicated to Daphne*
*who, for fifty years, has aided and abetted my career in wine: as a co-packer of very old wines in*
*very cold cellars, travelling companion to the world's vineyards and wine events,*
*sitter in and amanuensis at my endless talks and tastings,*
*draft and proofchecker — and critic.*

*Happily, she also loves wine. What more can one ask!*

# MICHAEL BROADBENT'S

## *Vintage Wine*

FIFTY YEARS
OF TASTING
THREE CENTURIES
OF WINES

**HARCOURT, INC.**

NEW YORK   SAN DIEGO   LONDON

Requests for permission to make copies of any part
of the work should be mailed to the following address:
Permissions Department, Harcourt, Inc.,
6277 Sea Harbor Drive, Orlando, Florida 32887-6777.

www.HarcourtBooks.com

Library of Congress Cataloging-in-Publication Data
available upon request
ISBN 0–15–100704–7
First U. S. edition
K J I H G F E D C B A

Created and designed by
Websters International Publishers Ltd
Axe and Bottle Court, 70 Newcomen Street, London SE1 1YT
www.websters.co.uk

Printed and bound by Brepols Graphics Industries NV, Turnhout, Belgium

*Editorial Director and Chief Editor*   Fiona Holman
*Designer*   Nigel O'Gorman
*Assistant Editors*   Lorna Bateson, Deborah Hamer-Acquaah, Julie Ross
*Desktop Publishing*   Keith Bambury, Lesley Gilbert
*Index*   Dawn Butcher
*Managing Editor*   Anne Lawrance
*Production*   Sara Granger

## AUTHOR'S ACKNOWLEDGEMENTS

Apart from my wife, Daphne, to whom this book is dedicated, I am particularly
grateful to two 'heroes', or rather heroines, who have shouldered the largest share of
the burden: Rita Mackintosh who, over 12 months, has typed and put on to computer
all my manuscripts, and Fiona Holman who has edited the work with great patience
and tremendous thoroughness. Also Adrian Webster for his unbridled enthusiasm and
encouragement, and, of course, the full Websters team.

Other key players include Rosemary Ward, my long-suffering secretary, who re-
indexed my tasting books by subject, a crucial start (see Introduction), Susan Keevil
for research and initial 'box' drafting, and assistance from Dorothee Schneider and
Janet Stansfield.

Many notes have been made at trade tastings and at events at home and overseas,
virtually all mentioned in the text. Acknowledgements to many of my generous hosts
and dining companions can be found on page 536.

Last and certainly not least, a very special thanks to Dieter Bock for most
generously providing an office and secretarial facilities in St James's Place. Our
relationship is somewhat like 'Papa' Haydn (me) to the Esterhazys!

# Contents

Introduction 6

Notes for Readers 8

Red Bordeaux 9

White Bordeaux 169

Red Burgundy 215

White Burgundy 273

Rhône 302

Loire 315

Alsace 326

Mas de Daumas Gassac 338

Germany 342

Italy 392

Tokaji 410

Spain's Unique Vega Sicilia 417

Two Portuguese Rarities 418

Chateau Musar 419

Champagne 421

Vintage Port 449

Madeira 495

California 506

Australia 529

New Zealand 534

South Africa 535

Appendices 536

People, Organisations and Events mentioned in the Text 536
Glossary of Words and Expressions used in the Tasting Notes 542
Level/Ullage Descriptions and Interpretations 545

Index of Wines 546

# Introduction

*'What terms will convey an adequate notion of a wine, when duly mellowed by age and which is only developed by long keeping … to tell us that it is penetrant, volatile, transient and so forth is nothing to the purpose. The only satisfactory and intelligent way is when the description can be given in comparison with some other known sensation of taste.'*
Dr Alexander Henderson, A History of Ancient and Modern Wines, *1824*

Well, the reader, by looking over my shoulder at the notes in my tasting books, will see that I try.

## Background
I was not born with a silver *tastevin* in my mouth; I came into the wine trade exactly 50 years ago, quite fortuitously. My lengthy architectural training was interrupted by military service and ended through sheer idleness. At the age of 25 a drastic change was called for. My mother, who was an avid reader of André Simon and T A Layton, spotted the latter's advertisement for a wine trainee in *The Times*. I applied and was taken on. With unaccustomed energy and enthusiasm I spent a year with Laytons sweeping the cellars, taking and delivering orders (see box page 54), followed by Saccone & Speed (page 467) and Harvey's of Bristol (page 469). Happily, I was in my element and so for eleven years had a thorough grounding in wine and the wine trade. Then, seeking pastures new, I took the plunge and, having heard on the grapevine that Christie's were thinking of restarting wine auctions, approached the Chairman and, to cut a long story short, was taken on in 1966 to head up a completely new wine department. It was extraordinarily well timed and, as they say, 'right up my street'. The international market for fine and rare wine as we know it today simply did not exist. It was a challenge. I travelled widely, met collectors, attended and conducted tastings, the outcome of which can be seen in this book. I have loved every minute and consider myself very lucky.

## The purpose of the book and my source material
My aim, through the use of tasting notes, is not only to illustrate the style and quality of individual wines, but also to trace their development. And, importantly, to rate vintages and, where appropriate, to describe the weather and market conditions which make one vintage year more successful and significant than another. The main text is based on my handwritten tasting notes, in excess of 85,000, in small, identical red books – 133 to date. Since September 1952 I have used the same format, inserting notes in order of tasting with date, occasion and place, the name of the wine and a brief description under columns headed 'appearance', 'nose', and 'taste'. Each book is indexed with the relevant page number of wine and vintage. All this takes time and has become something of a fetish, but it has stood me in good stead.

## The contents and scope of the book
I make no apology for the preponderance of French wines. I regard France as the cradle of fine wine, for with the honourable exceptions of Germany and its Riesling and Italy with Sangiovese and Nebbiolo, virtually every major grape variety and style of wine can be traced back to France. Here, the world's classic grape varieties are most at home: the now ubiquitous Cabernet Sauvignon and Merlot in Bordeaux; Pinot Noir and Chardonnay in Burgundy; Sauvignon Blanc in Sancerre and Pouilly-Fumé; Chenin-Blanc in Anjou and Touraine; Gewurztraminer in Alsace (the German Gewürz is different, just as Alsace Riesling is different) and Syrah in the Rhône. This is not to say that all the French wines from these grape varieties and regions are better than those grown elsewhere, but that, at their best and most typical, they set the standards that others seek to emulate.

And if Bordeaux dominates the book, it is not just because I am partial to claret (and Sauternes), or that from the beginning of my career it has played a major part. Bordeaux is unquestionably the largest and most important fine wine region in the world. For centuries it has dominated the market; it has a long proven track record. Its reputation rests not only on the major brands (Château Lafite and Pétrus are entities, individual vineyards, nevertheless they are, in effect, brands). Few other wines have such ability to keep and develop, both in maturity and price.

Next, perhaps less easy at first sight to justify, why is the book mainly devoted to top quality wines? Two paragraphs on the facing page will, I hope, answer this very valid question.

## My approach to wine
For half a century, from my wine merchandising days to my time as a wine auctioneer, I have dealt with the consumer and have always had the consumer's interest in mind rather than the producer's.

There is no such thing as 'objective' tasting. Tasting wine is subjective: what I think and what you think of a wine is important. Less and less these days do I labour with tortured descriptions, I am more concerned with the wine's quality and its state of development. Moreover, I do not claim to be a 'great' taster, merely a fairly conscientious one. What I can claim, though it was never originally intended, is that my notes now cover an immense gamut of wines and vintages, the method of notation being totally consistent over my half-century involvement in wine. I am concerned less with knowledge than with understanding and perspective.

It would be most convenient for a wine to have a once-and-for-all rating. In practice, the taste, or one's perception of a wine, can differ depending on the context: the temperature of the wine and the room, the fitness, alertness and experience of the taster, the conditions in which the wine has been stored, the cork, the ullage, its relationship with other wines tasted alongside, with food, the ambience and the company.

One can only record what a particular wine was like at the time of tasting.

## Why are so many other wines not included?

This, I can assure readers, is not pure snobbery. I do not just taste and make notes. My wife, Daphne, and I drink wine every day. Life is short, we do not waste our time on bland indifferent wines; we would rather share a half bottle of something with character and quality than drink six bottles of plonk.

As I state in various chapters, the vast majority of white wines, certainly dry white wines, are for drinking while young and refreshing. Only the classic sweet wines (of Bordeaux, Germany and the Loire, for example) and a handful of great dry wines such as Montrachet and Haut-Brion Blanc, benefit from bottle-ageing. Most wines are produced and moved through the distribution chain as quickly as possible. Moreover, the vintage, if noted at all, has little significance. They are bought, listed and drunk, to be immediately superseded by the next vintage.

Another good reason is that, as I explain below, the number of wines on the market has proliferated to such an extent that no one book, whatever its size, could cope. The world is now awash with wine. It is impossible to keep up, nor is there much point. One has to specialise. Why publish tasting notes on wines decent enough for drinking but which lack definable character? Most have no future anyway; they are ephemeral.

My one regret is not to have space to comment more on the many very good wines I have tasted from Chile, from important areas in North America, Washington, Oregon and New York State for example. Austria is another major omission – I admire the wines enormously, though they are largely in the fleeting white wine category; and the excellent new 'Pannobile' reds have, as yet, little track record. For sins and omissions I hope to be forgiven.

Perhaps next time.

## The ever-expanding world of wine

Fifty years ago, a wine merchant would offer for sale what now appears to be a remarkably limited range of wines. Heading the list would be 'claret' or red Bordeaux, for laying down and for drinking, followed by a fairly limited selection of white Bordeaux, reasonably extensive red and white Burgundy sections, a surprisingly large selection of 'Hock' and 'Moselle', few Rhône, fewer Loire, some Alsace; then sherry, port, champagne and spirits. The New World had not been invented.

Now, it seems that all the world is making wine. Not just the New World, but European countries which previously produced wines solely for domestic consumption are now seeking export markets. Every US state seems to be making wine. New Zealand, once known only for lamb and butter, is dominated by wine – huge plantings of vines to meet the world demand for Sauvignon Blanc and Chardonnay, and to develop with increasing successful Cabernet blends and, now, Pinot Noir. It would seem to be a wine consumer's paradise. We are spoilt for choice but, I suspect, we have never been more confused.

## 'Red alert': the Gold Medal syndrome

Oscar Wilde defined fox hunting as 'the unspeakable in full pursuit of the uneatable'. A propos certain 'cult' wines and modern 'global' reds I am inclined to change the last word to 'undrinkable'.

Like much else, things have gone too far. Red wines are being produced which seek primarily to impress. The current vogue is for deep-coloured reds, full of fruit and flesh, sweet and easy to taste. They win gold medals. They are written about by wine writers who are always on the lookout for something new. The 'critics' on both sides of the Atlantic heap praise on monumental, small production, over-priced wines which are scarcely drinkable. The newer cult wines have no track record; will they ever come round? As for the producers, I am torn between admiration for their toil, dedication and the risks they take and, frankly, dismissal of what seems like a monumental ego trip.

Alas, it is even happening in Bordeaux. Dare I say it, the wines of many châteaux are becoming more alike in style, and the once stark differences between the various appellations are less distinguishable. European classics should be appreciated for their variety, their finesse, their ability to age gracefully and their sheer drinkability. Instead, we are being knocked off track by the outrageous, the obvious, the fashionable and the bland.

## People, places, dates

My work has always involved a great deal of travel, to visit clients, to inspect and even to pack their wines; to conduct auctions and attend pre-sale tastings; charity wine auctions and dinners; to 'moderate' wine tastings and seminars. Not just overseas. Much the same on home territory.

A bare tasting note is a bit stark and clinical. The where and with whom puts various and varying occasions into perspective. Risking the accusation of 'name dropping', I hope the name and context add interest; they also serve, however skimpily, to acknowledge the generosity of hosts and efficiency of organisers. If some names crop up more frequently than others, Hardy Rodenstock for example, it merely serves to emphasise the number of his events which are of a scale, comprehensiveness and eye for detail without equal.

The tasting dates are more crucial. In relation to the different dates of tasting a particular wine, my aim is to trace and describe its evolution. The 'last tasted', of necessity repetitive, is even more important. The more recent the note, the more valid my comments. Having said this, a ten-year-old note of a major wine is better than no note at all; and a 30-year-old note of a century-old wine can still be relevant (assuming another bottle is in the same condition). The star rating and when to drink are explained below.

## Postscript

This is a very personal, somewhat idiosyncratic, book; I praise and admonish, I mix unconcealed adulation and quirky dislikes. The reader does not have to agree with me, but perhaps what I have to say will stimulate some original thoughts. On the subject of tasting, which is what the book is mainly about, it is difficult, at times well-nigh impossible, to put the smell and taste of a wine into words. Happily it is not essential to describe a wine in order to enjoy it.

I am, however, concerned with the quality and state of maturity of a wine, what it was like, whether it is drinkable now, or, in the case of a young vintage, its future, my opinions being based on first-hand notes.

I do recommend note-making, for a note, however brief, acts as an invaluable *aide mémoire*; it concentrates the mind, and if, like mine, the notes become a wine diary, they will be fascinating to look back upon. But better than a notebook is a glass in the hand!

Michael Broadbent
2002

---

### NOTES FOR READERS

**VINTAGE ASSESSMENTS** Each vintage or year is given a star rating (see right); where relevant I describe the weather conditions during the growing season. (v) indicates a variable vintage.

**WINE NOTES** Below each vintage heading, the wines, in **red type**, are listed in ascending vintage order and then within alphabetical order (in the case of Bordeaux, preceded by the first growths; in Red Burgundy, by DRC; and in White Burgundy by Montrachet). Also, whenever appropriate, the name of the wine is followed by that of the producer, estate or domaine in **bold type**. This is followed by my tasting notes (each culled from my tasting books), with dates of tasting if tasted more than once, and my star rating. At the end of the tasting note *information in italics* gives the occasion and date of the last time I tasted the wine, and tells you when to drink if appropriate.

**PUNCTUATION** Semi-colons are used to divide 'appearance' of the wine from its 'nose' (aroma, bouquet) and 'palate' (taste in the mouth). In my tasting books these three elements are noted in vertical columns; in the text these have been translated into semi-colons.

**WINE ASSESSMENTS** Within each chapter the quality and state of maturity of individual wines are assessed. Throughout the book, I have used the 'broad brush' 5-star rating system I use in my tasting books. Although I occasionally use a 20-point system at blind tastings to supplement my notes they relate only to a particular wine tasted at a particular time. In my opinion, the 100-point rating system is flawed because it is inflexible and does not allow for bottle variation and context.

**STAR RATINGS**

| | |
|---|---|
| ★★★★★ | Outstanding |
| ★★★★ | Very good |
| ★★★ | Good |
| ★★ | Moderately good |
| ★ | Not very good, but not bad |
| No stars | Poor |

**QUESTIONMARKS WITH THE RATINGS** These indicate that I am uncertain about a wine's future or feel I need to retaste it. The same applies to the rating of a particular vintage or year, especially one where the wines are too young to assess properly.

**BRACKETS** To give the reader an indication of the present drinkability, and a prediction of the ultimate quality of a young wine, I use brackets, for example:

A wine rated ★(★★★) means 1 star for drinking now: (the wine is immature, unready); but the 3 additional stars show that its potential at full maturity is 'very good'.

A wine rated ★★★(★★) can be drunk with pleasure now but should be 'outstanding' after further bottle age.

**WHEN TO DRINK** For certain wines I offer a rough and ready guide to drinkability based on the quality of the vintage, the 'pedigree' of the producer and my own first-hand notes and experience.

For example: '*Now–2008*' means that I consider the wine is ready for drinking but will continue on its plateau of maturity until around 2008. This does not mean, however, that the wine will suddenly drop off its perch. Unless the cork and storage conditions are bad, wines tend to decline relatively slowly.

# Red Bordeaux

W hy, when the whole world is awash with new wine, do I spend so much time evaluating and re-evaluating the wines of the past, especially those of Bordeaux? I am tempted to start at the beginning, historically; but to be realistic, Bordeaux still dominates the fine wine market. The names of its châteaux are the best known, the most revered and, particularly over the past few decades, the most traded in wines in the world.

A knowledge and understanding of what lies behind the label, the wine name and the vintage, is vital. The way one château differs from another and, as crucially, one vintage from another, is of more than superficial interest. Moreover, the way each wine has evolved or is likely to evolve over a period of time is of very much more than purely academic interest.

Let's dwell briefly on size: in area, Bordeaux is the largest fine wine region in the world, with nearly forty separate districts. It has more individual producers – many thousands – than any other region in the world and more people directly involved in the wine trade.

The greatest influence on the region is Bordeaux's maritime climate. The endlessly unpredictable fluctuations of weather during the growing season are mainly responsible for the style and quality of the wine. This is why I summarise the weather conditions of each vintage. Add to this the differences of microclimates and geology, not to mention the ministrations of individuals, and one starts to become aware of the endless permutations.

That is only the beginning. Almost uniquely in France, the wines of Bordeaux are made not just from one vine variety but from several, and it is the proportions in which the *cépages* are planted and used in the final blend by each château, that creates the unique complexity of this wine.

Then there is time. Most well-made wines will keep for a period although all have a finite life. The red wines of Bordeaux not only keep but – and this is the crucial point – are capable of evolving in bottle, being transformed from fruit-dominated young wine to something fragrant, harmonious, mature and infinitely subtle. Tracing the evolution of a vintage, of a wine, as it ages is one of the main themes of my book, and of this chapter in particular.

I am English. My half century in wine has been dominated by Bordeaux because it has been my major occupation and because it is endlessly fascinating. Not that I taste and drink it exclusively, as my tasting books will testify, but I always 'come home' to Bordeaux. Its top wines set the standards.

While it is easy to be diverted by the rich, red, sweet and easy 'gold medal' award wines from other areas and from other countries, and to be taken in by the glib specious global taste so prevalent in modern offerings, I would like to point out that red Bordeaux or claret, good claret, is not 'old hat'; it remains the best of all beverages. Its colour is not only entrancing by candlelight but, more usefully, tells us much about its content and, very accurately, its maturity; its nose – smell, fragrance, you name it – gives not only sensual pleasure but awakens the salivary glands; it is rarely too heady, too alcoholic; its acidity refreshes, its tannin, obtrusive when the wine is tasted alone, does several jobs. Tannin leaves the mouth clean and dry between one forkful of food and the next. It is an anti-oxidant, preserving the wine and, the medical world agrees, helps keep our arteries clear. Claret aides the digestion, calms the soul, stimulates civilised conversation.

Claret works on so many levels, appealing to both intellect and the senses. What more can one want?

# Late 18th to the end of the 19th century

An immense spectrum of events encompassing wars, political shenanigans, booms and busts, through which the English, unlike the French, sailed relatively unscathed. And for the whole of this period for which I have notes, red Bordeaux, claret, dominated the fine wine market. Claret, of course, had been a staple drink of the English since the Middle Ages, but it comes as a surprise that the first growths were already firmly established and recognised in the latter half of the 18th century. We can thank the inexhaustibly enquiring mind of Thomas Jefferson and his copious correspondence for very precise reports on the quality of the wines, made during his travels through the wine districts of Europe at the time he was the American 'Minister Plenipotentiary' to France.

Jefferson, among many other attributes, was a noted wine connoisseur with very catholic tastes. During his term of office as ambassador he took time off to tour many European wine districts. In May 1787 he went to Bordeaux, visited several major châteaux, noting on his return to Paris that 'of Red Wines, there are 4. vineyards of first quality, viz. 1. Chateau Margau (*sic*) ... 2. La Tour de Segur (Latour) ... 3. Houtbrion (*sic*) and Chateau de La Fite', citing the owners and average production of each. Incidentally Jefferson also noted that the top of the second growths was 'Mme Rauzan's' (a formidably efficient lady whose two brothers were guillotined, despite protesting that they were not aristocrats); Ch Mouton, then known as Branne-Mouton, lagged behind.

Apart from Pepys' reference to Ho Bryen (*sic*) in his diaries, it was a century later before the now well-known châteaux names would put in an appearance. Happily, Christie's archives survived the complete destruction of their premises during the London Blitz in the early 1940s and the first vineyards to be named in a catalogue were Lafete (*sic*) and Chateau Margau (*sic*), both in 1788, the year after Jefferson's visit to Bordeaux. Despite the intervention of the Napoleonic wars and the relatively high taxes on French wine imports, red Bordeaux continued to be the staple drink of the English upper classes. It was shipped in cask and sold by merchants under their own name simply as 'claret'.

The importance of the Bordeaux châteaux and the growth of the Bordeaux trade increased through the 19th century, despite being knocked off balance by a severe attack of oidium in the 1850s, just five years before the famous Classification. It was during this period of great prosperity that rich bankers and the wealthy elite of Bordeaux bought vineyards and built prettily pretentious châteaux of which Palmer and Pichon-Longueville (Baron) are prime examples. In England, sales were boosted when the Prime Minister Gladstone lowered the taxation on 'light' wines; though this hardly affected the top growths which, thanks to prosperity and some superb vintages, continued to fill the cellars of the aristocracy and newly prosperous middle-classes. But then, not for the first or last time, the market became overheated; by 1870 the prices reached untenable levels and though some very good wines were made, a new and disastrous pest, phylloxera, was beginning to make itself felt in the vineyards. The last top-class pre-phylloxera vintage was 1878, for by 1879 the deadly aphid had taken a hold, with no cure in sight.

The next blow was mildew, which affected the vines in the mid-1880s; phylloxera affected the quality, mildew the quantity. It was a dire period: trade was at a low ebb, and prices were uneconomical for the producers. Eventually it was discovered that spraying the vines with copper sulphate combated mildew (it still does) and grafting native fruiting varieties on the American root stock enabled vineyards to recover. Nevertheless mildew is still a problem today and the phylloxera is endemic. The 1893 vintage was the brightest spot in this otherwise fairly dismal late 19th-century period, though the decade did end on a high note with the 1899 vintage.

## Vintages at a Glance
**Outstanding ★★★★★**
1784, 1811, 1825, 1844, 1846, 1847, 1848, 1858, 1864, 1865, 1870, 1875, 1899
**Very Good ★★★★**
1791, 1814, 1861, 1869, 1871, 1874, 1877, 1878, 1893, 1895, 1896
**Good ★★★**
1787, 1803, 1832, 1863, 1868, 1887, 1888, 1892 (v), 1898 (v)

## 1784 ★★★★★
The most renowned vintage of the period. *Entre deux révolutions*, between the American War of Independence and the French Revolution, the year that Thomas Jefferson, later to become President, was appointed the American Minister Plenipotentiary to France.
**Ch Lafitte** (*sic*) An ullaged bottle tasted two centuries later. Alas, but unsurprisingly 'over the top', oxidised: colour dark brown; nose like pure balsamic vinegar; despite the rich

components – undrinkable. *The oldest vintage at Lloyd Flatt's memorable Ch Lafite tasting in New Orleans, Oct 1988.*

**Ch Margaux** One of the most renowned wines of this great vintage. Letting a friend have two hampers containing 124 bottles at cost from his own stock, Jefferson wrote to explain the high price: 'This indeed is dear, being three *livres* a bottle, but it is Ch Margau (*sic*), of the year 1784, bought by myself on the spot (in 1787) and therefore genuine'. Jefferson did not trust wine merchants, insisting on the wines being bottled at the château, arranging for his agent in Bordeaux to supply bottles engraved (*étiquetté* was his instruction) for identification, with the vintage, name of château and his initials – more ordinary wines just had the initial scratched – he called this *diamanté* – on each bottle, for example, 'F' for 'Frontignan'.

A half bottle of the '84 Margaux bought by Marvin Shanken, proprietor of the *Wine Spectator*, at Christie's auction at Vinexpo, Bordeaux, in 1987 and, at his request, recorked by me at the château – a fairly delicate operation witnessed, apprehensively, by Paul Pontallier and the *maître de chai*. The bottle itself had a tall neck, its body straight sided and engraved '*1784 Ch Margau Th.J*'. The level was just below top-shoulder, the blackened cork surprisingly long. A little was poured into a glass, all three of us having a good sniff and tiny taste. Despite its oxidation, the colour was a fairly healthy orange-rimmed red brown, with just a whiff of what clearly might once have been a marvellously rich wine. There was no point in topping it up so I gently inserted a new tapered cork and dipped the top of the neck into hot wax – risky with old glass which tends to crack easily. The end of the story is that, at Marvin Shanken's expense, I carried it to New York by Concorde. *Recorked and tasted Aug 1987.*

---

## Lloyd Flatt

*An American aviation consultant, and a major buyer at Heublein and Christie's in the 1970s. Lloyd was one of the earliest and most generous givers of tastings, in New Orleans (where he had two homes in the French Quarter; one exclusively as his cellar). These tastings were all 'vertical' and held over two or three days, covering such major topics as: Ch Mouton-Rothschild, 75 vintages (in 1986); Ch Ausone, 56 vintages (in 1987); and Ch Lafite, 116 vintages, beginning with 1784 (in 1988). A most distinguished, striking-looking fellow, Lloyd is very tall: he always wears a white suit and an eye-patch. On one occasion a little boy at an airport asked him if he were a pirate. He responded: 'Yes, now go away'.*

## 1787 ★★★

**Ch Lafitte** (*sic*) A wine of some notoriety. It was the first of the 'Jefferson' wines to come on to the market when a single bottle was sold at Christie's in December 1985. Unsurprisingly, I well recall the occasion, for in advance of the sale no one had any idea of its worth, so the owner agreed to let it go without reserve. Instead of the usual estimate in the catalogue, I coined the phrase 'inestimable'. Starting at around £2000 the bidding went quite speedily up to £7000, then to £10,000 until eventually two bidders were left in the running. I finally brought the hammer down at £105,000, still a world record auction price for a single bottle of wine. The successful bidder was Christopher Forbes, the underbidder being Marvin Shanken. Flown in the Forbes private jet to New York that

evening, it had pride of place on Jefferson's dining table in the Presidential Memorabilia section of the Forbes Museum. Not long after, I received an agitated telephone call from the curator. Due to the heat of the spotlights, the cork had fallen in! As it was for display and not for drinking, I merely advised her to insert a stopper.

Regarding tasting, I have two notes, both made under laboratory conditions. The first I opened in Munich in 1987. Both wax seal and cork looked old, the wine was brown-tinged and the nose and taste distinctly old. Yet, after a very long delay, the laboratory reported that the wine contained an unspecified amount post 1960. Shock, horror and much publicity. Subsequently in August 1992 a half bottle from the original collection was analysed by the two pre-eminent men in the field, Dr Bonani in Zurich and Professor Edward Hall in Oxford (best known for their work on the 'Turin shroud'). Once again I was charged with cork drawing and tasting, witnessed by Dr Bonani, the owner and a lawyer. No question about the bottle. It was correct and, subsequently, after a long and expensive process, the cork and the wine were also found to be absolutely correct. My tasting note: tawny, no red, a dark brown flaky sediment; nose restrained and though oxidised opened up quite richly with residual fruit traces; a touch of sweetness on the palate and acidic, acetic, finish. *Last tasted in Zurich, August 1992.*

**Ch Margaux** Similar bottle to the Lafitte. Slight ullage, wizened black cork, thick, gritty, puce-coloured sediment, the wine itself deeper than expected; little nose at first but exposure to air revived it quite sweetly; richly flavoured, well balanced. *In Wiesbaden, Sept 1987* ★★★★

**Ch Branne-Mouton** (its name until the Rothschild purchase in 1853 when it became Mouton-Rothschild). A bottle of similar provenance opened at Mouton in the company of the technical director, the *maître de chai*, and some German collectors. Jancis Robinson and I were the only English present. There was nearly a disaster. Instead of shaving off the wax capsule the German sommelier used a small hammer. The glass cracked and the wine started to leak. (Old hand-blown bottles are friable, the sides varying from eggshell thin to finger thick. Incidentally it is risky, often impossible, to try engraving on very old bottles.) A bowl was put under the bottle and the wine, which had been in the cellar at Mouton for some months to settle, was quickly decanted. Its colour was deep amber; nose, initially non-existent, opened up quite remarkably. Not a trace of oxidation or acidification. Fairly rich and, what little we had to taste, perfectly drinkable. The veteran *maître de chai* had absolutely no experience of wine of this age. Jancis and I just looked at each other, shrugged and, frankly, enjoyed the experience. *Tasted at Ch Mouton-Rothschild, June 1986* ★★★★

## 1791 ★★★★

James Christie in his wine sale catalogue of 23 May 1797 offered for sale six hogsheads of first growth claret of the 1791 vintage 'considered the best that France has produced for many years'.

**Ch Margaux** A contemporary bottle with striated neck and 19th-century label '*Claret Margaux*'. Pale, little red. As with the other wines of the period tasted, the bouquet was strange, ethereal, opening up attractively, the flavour and balance quite remarkable. *At Bipin Desai's Margaux tasting in Los Angeles, May 1987* ★★★★★

## 1799 ★★

Harvest began 5 October. Fairly big, unremarkable crop.
**Ch Lafite** From the château, recorked 1953. Fragrant, faded but fascinating. *The oldest vintage in Dr Marvin Overton's landmark Lafite tasting, 'moderated' by Elie de Rothschild and myself, in Fort Worth, Texas, May 1979* ★★★★

## 1803 ★★★

Average sized crop; good wines.
**Ch Lafite** From the château: warm amber; sound, fragrant; dry, lean but firm. *At the Overton Lafite vertical, May 1979* ★★★

## 1806 ★★

Average crop of no particular reputation.
**Ch Lafite** In the mid-1950s it was the policy of Lafite to supply the most prestigious French restaurants with equally prestigious old vintages. In the 1970s and 1980s quite a few bottles of 1806 Lafite came back on the market, Christie's handling several from the Restaurants Darroze in Villeneuve-de-Marsan, Caviar-Kaspia in Paris, Le Coq Hardi at Bougival, and elsewhere. They fetched very high prices.

Just one note: warm amber, orange-gold highlights; lovely bouquet, firm and fragrant. Probably recorked at the château around 1953. *One of the most beautiful of all the old wines at Flatt's Lafite tasting, New Orleans in Oct 1988* ★★★★

## 1811 ★★★★★

The most famous 'comet' vintage. Early harvest starting 14 September. Fairly abundant crop of very good wines.
**Ch Lafite** Labelled '*CHÂTEAU LAFITE grand Vin, JJ Van der Berghe, Bordeaux, recorked at the château in 1980*'. On the pale side with vestiges of red; immediately forthcoming old bouquet reminding me of spearmint, then Chartreuse; a touch of sweetness on the palate, distinctive, minty flavour, vestiges of sustaining tannin and acidity, good length. *The oldest vintage in Wilfred Jaeger's pre-phylloxera Lafite tasting at his hillside home south of San Francisco, June 2001* ★★★

---

### Wilfred Jaeger

*I had not previously met Mr Jaeger and was unaware of his quite extraordinary collection of great wines. A top San Francisco chef provided a meal which started at 3pm and ended roughly three hours later, the ten men present tasting and drinking Lafite of the vintages 1811, 1832, 1858, 1864, 1865, 1870 and 1877, to which he added as an afterthought, to compare, Latour 1864 and 1865, plus one or two other wines including Mouton 1945, Yquem 1847 and Taylor's 1870 port — all duly and appropriately noted elsewhere in this book. For range, condition, and sheer brilliance, the most unbelievably good late lunch of my entire career.*

---

## 1814 ★★★★

Average crop of very good wines.
**Ch Lafite** From the château, recorked in the 1950s. Colour faded; little nose at first but, typical of Lafite, opened up over a period of two hours. Old, interesting. *At the Overton Lafite tasting, May 1979* ★★

## 1825 ★★★★★

Extremely early start of harvest: 11 September. A crop of fairly ordinary size, producing wines which, though initially tough and tannic, developed well over a long period of time.
**Ch Lafite** Recorked at the château. Beautiful colour; 'ravishing' bouquet and flavour to match. *At the Overton Lafite tasting, May 1979* ★★★★★
**Ch Gruaud-Larose** A most memorable bottle. From the château, bought at Christie's by Len Evans, hand-carried by me from London to serve at a dinner being given in my honour, on my first visit to Australia. The plane was delayed so there was no time for the wine to settle. Yet it survived: very rich, mulberry-like bouquet; and lovely flavour. *In Sydney, Feb 1977* ★★★★

## 1832 ★★★

Very small crop following a very hot summer. Moderately good wines.
**Ch Lafite** Four notes. First, a bottle recorked at the château in June 1987 and served at Rodenstock's annual tasting that autumn: it was very good indeed. Next, a bottle bought at Christie's in 1979 and noted at Lloyd Flatt's Lafite tasting in October 1988: positive, powerful, with a sort of singed grape flavour caused by the heatwave. Thirdly, in 1995, faded but lively; scented; delicate, delicious, yet slightly astringent. I described it as 'arsenic and old lace'.

Most recently, a superb bottle, recorked in 1980, neither pale nor delicate but deep and rich-looking; a faultless, spicy, almost eucalyptus bouquet; full-bodied, excellent flavour, lots of grip and still tannic. *Last tasted at Wilfred Jaeger's, June 2001* ★★★★★

## 1844 ★★★★★

An early harvest, from 15 September. There was a small crop and high prices.
**Ch Lafite** I have two notes, both bottles recorked in 1953. The first a remarkably good bottle at a Heublein VIP pre-sale tasting in New Orleans in 1976. The second very similar: beautiful colour; opulent, almost overripe bouquet; fairly sweet, lovely flavour, good tannin and acidity, great length. This was the first wine that made me realise what sensationally good wines were made well before the commonly accepted 'pre-phylloxera' period 1858–1878. *Last noted at Lloyd Flatt's Lafite tasting, Oct 1988* ★★★★★

## 1846 ★★★★★

Hot summer, early harvest (from 14 September) and a fairly abundant crop of very good, sturdily constituted wines.
**Ch Lafite** Two excellent notes, the first, with a '*Harvey's Selection*' slip label at Lloyd Flatt's in 1988 and, a year later, an equally impressive bottle: fabulously deep colour; good, fragrant, sustained bouquet; soft, ripe, velvety tannins. *Last noted lunching at the château, June 1989* ★★★★★

## 1847 ★★★★★

A very abundant crop harvested and the wines were contrarily described as 'full-bodied yet exquisite'. However, the English trade, despite low prices, apparently found these wines too delicate for their customers' coarser taste. Not so the Cruse family, the pre-eminent of the Bordeaux 'merchant princes' of the period who made huge purchases (always from Médoc châteaux, rarely if ever from St-Émilion or Pomerol).

**Ch Margaux** Its '*Cruse et Fils Frères Bordeaux*' label reminding us that by no means all the first growths were bottled at the château. An anything but exquisitely delicate magnum at Desai's Margaux tasting: deep, intense; sweet, fruity, almost jammy bouquet; full-bodied, powerful. Almost too good to be true. *Tasted in Los Angeles, May 1987* ★★★★

**Ch Rauzan** Perhaps worth mentioning again that Jefferson reported that Mme Rauzan's wine was the top of the *deuxième cru* wines of the Médoc, the 'super second' of the period, and well ahead of Mouton.

Two notes, both of bottles from the private cellars of Lafite, the first tasted on the spot: a remarkably harmonious wine, delicate and charming; the second bought by Rodenstock at Christie's in 1986: a bit rubbery on the nose but also very sweet with a singed fruit flavour and good length. *Last tasted at Rodenstock's 16th annual 'Weinprobe', Sept 1995. At best* ★★★★

## 1848 ★★★★★

Similar sized crop and quality of wine to 1847.

**Ch Lafite** Three notes. First, a deeply coloured magnificent bottle at the Overton tasting in 1979, then a dried-out bottle with attenuated flavour in 1986 and one labelled 'R *Galos, Gérant*', recorked in 1986. Almost indescribably good despite a touch of residual tannic bitterness. *Last noted at Lloyd Flatt's Lafite tasting, Oct 1988. At best* ★★★★★

**Ch Margaux** Reported to have started picking very early, on 4 September, its production 12,000 cases. A bottle from the private cellars at Lafite and bought by Bipin Desai at Christie's for his Margaux marathon. Appearance lively and lovely (the wine and Bipin's wife); amazing fragrance, the hallmark of Margaux; perfect weight, flavour and acidity. A really delicious drink. *Los Angeles, May 1987* ★★★★★

### CIRCA 1848

**Ch Bel-Air-Marquis d'Aligre** Famous in its day but though this has appeared at auction on several occasions, the precise vintage was never found on the labels. Three notes in the mid-1980s and five bottles tasted in the mid-1990s, varying from oxidised to pale but lively. 'A faded beauty with twinkling eyes.' *Last tasted Sept 1995. At best* ★★★

## 1849 ★★

Average crop, producing average wines. Only one note.

**Ch Ausone** Recorked: autumnal colour; smoky, raisiny, high-toned; dry, complete though faded. *Sept 1987* ★★★

## 1852 ★

Average crop, light wines.

**Ch Rausan-Ségla** From the cellars at Lafite. Showing its age, its bouquet volatile yet delicate; sweet, a touch of caramel, acidity taking over. *At the annual Rodenstock tasting, Sept 1995* ★

## 1854–55

Mentioned because this was probably the lowest point of the first of the three disasters which affected the vineyards of

Bordeaux: *Oidium tuckerii*, a disease which attacks young vines causing the leaves to drop off. The effect severely curtailed production: for example, a total of only 22 *tonneaux* was produced by the four first growths in 1854 compared with 254 *tonneaux* two years previously. With such a scarcity, prices rocketed. Paradoxically, 1855 was the year of the famous Médoc classification.

### 1855 Classification

*The 1855 classification of Bordeaux châteaux is still largely in use today. It was originally demanded by Napoleon III for the Universal Exhibition in Paris, to ensure that French dignitaries could recognise easily the most impressive of the region's wine properties. The leading châteaux in the Médoc and Sauternes were grouped according to the prices their wines fetched. A similar classification was developed about 100 years later in the Graves and St-Émilion regions. Pomerol has never been classified. Note, these rankings referred to the finest vineyards. Today, it is the wines themselves that are more often judged.*

## 1858 ★★★★★

By 1858, an effective anti-oidium treatment had been discovered and applied and, as if to make up for the five previous poor vintages, a hot summer led to a healthy harvest towards the end of September. This year marked the start of an extremely prosperous period, particularly for the Bordeaux merchants.

**Ch Lafite** Seven notes. This was the oldest vintage of Lafite from the cellars of Lord Rosebery, which featured in Christie's landmark sale of 'Finest and Rarest Wines' in May 1967 (see box page 422), a single lot of four magnums which sold for 5300 shillings per six. At the pre-sale tasting it was crisp, fragrant but thinning. Two years later, a very good bottle from the château at Overton's Lafite tasting. Other bottles variable but all remarkably flavoury, some with a prickle of acidity made up for by the wine's scent. In all seven notes, the last recorded: a warm amber colour; a short burst of exquisite, quintessentially Lafite fragrance; lean, clean, delicious. *Last noted at Lloyd Flatt's Lafite tasting, Oct 1988* ★★★★★

**Ch Mouton-Rothschild** Three notes. Each bottle labelled '*Mouton, Bn de Rothschild, Proprietor, 1858 R Galos Gérant, Bordeaux*', and all with original corks and good levels. Baron Nathaniel had purchased Branne-Mouton in 1853 in the middle of the oidium blight and too near to the 1855 classification for quality (and price) to be elevated. It remained a *2ème cru classé*. First tasted at Mouton: the colour of faded tiles; harmonious; rich. The second with teeth-gripping tannin. The third like creosote. Too horrible to taste. *Last noted Sept 1987. At best* ★★★★

**Ch Rauzan** Two bottles, both recorked, unbranded, from the private cellars at Ch Lafite and the first tasted there in 1986: an unhealthy amber; 'refined linoleum and barley sugar nose'; faded. The second with a sweet start and finish on the palate, despite leathery old tannin. *Last tasted Sept 1995. At best* ★★★

## 1861 ★★★★

Heavy frost on 6 May devastated the vineyards. Very small crop. Good, 'elegant' wines. They were however very expensive and started to overheat the market.

**Ch Latour** Labelled '*Café Voisin*', a fashionable Paris restaurant. Remarkably good: delicate, fragrant bouquet and flavour. *At Kerry Payne's Fête du Ch Latour, June 1981* ★★★★

# 1862

Fair-sized crop of modest to middle quality.

# 1863 ★★★

Small crop which had a moderate reputation at the time.
**Ch Latour** Only tasted once, though a bottle at a Christie's Latour tasting in New York a couple of years ago was reported to be the star of the show. This certainly corresponds to my much earlier note: incredible depth of colour; beautiful, lingering bouquet; touch of sweetness, full body and fruit, soft yet perfectly harmonious. Great wine, perfect drink. *Dining at the château, March 1970* ★★★★★
**Ch Laroze** (Gruaud-Larose) Bottled by a West End wine merchant, Claridge. Of the 24 dozen 'packed' (binned) '1865' many remained. Tasted in the cellars at Bodorgan (see also Ch Lafite and Ch Kirwan 1865) and twice pre-sale. Variable: rich to mushroomy; fruity, piquant to decayed and tart. *Aug 1970–Jan 1971. At best* ★

# 1864 ★★★★★

*Vins complets*. One of the greatest vintages of the 19th century. Despite the heat at vintage time (picking from 17 September), an abundant crop of superbly balanced wines.
**Ch Lafite** I have been privileged to taste, to drink, this wine – reputedly the finest wine of the vintage and the greatest Lafite of the century – on seven occasions. Whether Queen Victoria, a regular sherry and claret drinker, was fully aware of its stellar quality, I do not know, but it was certainly in the royal cellars and being consumed in the mid-1980s.
First noted in 1976: a superb Cockburn and Campbell magnum. The second, and most memorable, a jeroboam from the cellars of Mrs James de Rothschild which, in an American cellar, had suffered cork failure (see below). A perfect bottle from the château, recorked, at the Overton tasting in 1979; again in 1987, and another, recorked by the *maître de chai* in 1986, at Flatt's Lafite tasting in 1988. All superb.
Next, an almost too sweet bottle, labelled '*Lafite Bon (Baron) de Rothschild, R. Galos*' at a Rodenstock tasting in 1995, and,

---

### Château Lafite 1864

*Any chance to taste a wine such as this is going to be eventful, but when asked to speak at a televised charity dinner in Memphis, Tennessee – a $1000-a-head dinner, in fact – I met with a tricky scenario. The bottle, a jeroboam, was badly ullaged to low-shoulder level and judging by the smell of the cork, the content was likely to be pure vinegar. On decanting, it became obvious that the wine was indeed 'pricked'. In order to save the situation, I smelled the wine and nodding sagely, handed it to my host, John Grisanti, for the first sip. He nodded as if approvingly. I then said: 'This is a very old wine. The grapes for this wine were picked during the autumn of 1864 which was when General Sherman, whose troops were based in Memphis, went marching across Georgia leading his Union troops into battle with the Confederates.' I added: 'Tonight you are tasting not just wine, but history.'*

---

very recently, perfection, complete, harmonious. *Last tasted at Wilfred Jaeger's, June 2001* ★★★★★
**Ch Latour** The Windsor Castle cellar book reveals that when the 1864 Lafite ran out, around 1874, the royal butler went on to the 1864 Latour.
One old and two very recent notes. Overpowering, almost sickly sweet at Payne's Latour tasting in 1981. An exquisite bottle at the Wine Dinner hosted by Carl Geisel and Hardy Rodenstock at the Königshof in Munich in March 2001: fabulous, spicy, eucalyptus-scented bouquet; perfect flavour, weight and balance. Still tannic. Most recently, brought cool from his cellar to compare with the Lafite: a bottle with a pictorial label, '*Château Latour 1864 Grand Vin Bordeaux*': similar colour to Lafite; spicy bouquet, creaking a bit after 40 minutes; exceedingly flavoury, delicious. Distinguished. Venerable. *Last noted at Wilfred Jaeger's tasting, June 2001* ★★★★★
**Ch Margaux** Two notes, both bottled by Cruse, the dominant *négociant* in Bordeaux. At Desai's Margaux tasting in May 1987, emitting a glorious blackcurrant fragrance but slightly acetic. Four months later: original cork, good colour – but not an old lady, a little tart. *Last noted at Rodenstock's tasting, Sept 1987. At best* ★
**Ch Mouton-Rothschild** '*R. Galos Gérant*' on capsules and labels. One rich wine reduced to sourness thanks to a loose, greasy cork. Another miraculously surviving a crumbly cork and mid- to low-shoulder ullage: pale but with a healthy glow; nose remarkably sound with vestiges of fruit. Delightful. *At Heublein pre-sale tastings, in 1974 and 1975. At best* ★★★
**Ch Léoville** (*sic*) Wax seal embossed 'Claret. Greenwell Hutchinson'. A superb bottle from one of the greatest cellars of old wine ever handled by Christie's, at Fasque in Scotland. The wine, not moved since purchased by Sir Thomas Gladstone Bt around 1868, was in perfect condition despite a diminution of colour; sweet bouquet, with not a trace of decay. A sweet and gentle wine that held well in the glass for three hours. In my enthusiasm I gave it 7 stars. *Tasted May 1972* ★★★★★

# 1865 ★★★★★

Another great vintage, sturdier than the 1864 and, in my experience, the most dependable vintage of this period. Another very abundant crop harvested early, from 6 September. A boom time: the highest prices of the century, lead by Ch Lafite and Ch Latour (the former selling exclusively to six *négociants*) while Ch Margaux, tied to a contract, lagged behind.
**Ch Lafite** First encountered in the cellars at Bodorgan, the seat of the Meyrick family in Anglesey, North Wales: 104 bottles not moved since binned, capsules embossed '*Lafite*' but unbranded cork. Levels, and overall condition, perfect (just five 'slightly ullaged'). First tasted in the cellar: medium pale but lovely colour; bouquet wholesome but fading; drying out and thinning though very much alive (one of the 'slightly ullaged' bottles – halfway down the neck! – was sweeter but slightly more acidic). Two other notes, one at the pre-sale tasting. Lafite, a bottle from Lord Rosebery's cellar at Overton's tasting in 1979: amazingly youthful, good, rich. Perfectly balanced. At Rodenstock's in 1995: embossed glass 'lozenge' with name of wine on shoulder of bottle, '*R. Galos*' on label. Alas, nose like blancmange, medicinal, tinny. Volatile, oxidised with grubby aftertaste. Most recently, a bottle recorked at the château in 1980: medium-dry, lovely colour, amber rim; showing its age

and slightly malty at first but after an hour had got its 'second wind'. Dry, a hefty style, very tannic. Very impressive. *Last noted at Jaeger's tasting, June 2001. At best* ★★★★

**Ch Latour** First, a deep rich and remarkable bottle from the château in 1977 and a year later, dining at the château: virtually opaque and younger looking than the 1920 alongside; very fragrant, high-toned; some sweetness, lovely flavour, silky texture; fabulous despite twist of acidity. More recently at Rodenstock's March 2001 tasting, a bottle from the Café Anglais: lovely, rich, faultless bouquet; amazingly sweet, perfection despite its 1865 tannic bite. Three months later, as with the 1864s, a bottle recorked in 1980, casually brought out from Jaeger's cellar to compare with the Lafite: still fairly deep, with a good mature rim; eucalyptus noted yet again on the nose; good flavour, balance, condition, length. Faultless, even allowing for a slight touch of the vintage's tannic astringency. *Last noted at Jaeger's tasting, June 2001. At best* ★★★★★

**Ch Gruaud** From a large stock salvaged in 1991 from a ship sunk in 1972. Some horrible, one quite good, a third drinking surprisingly well. *At Arlberg, Austria, Sept 1993. At best* ★★

**Ch Kirwan** This is one of the most surprising and remarkable wines of my long career at Christie's. It was a find that nearly never happened.

To try to cut a long story short, friends of ours had built a holiday cottage on land belonging to Sir George Meyrick at Bodorgan, in North Wales, so my wife and I killed two birds with one stone – a weekend staying with them combined with work in the Bodorgan cellar. By teatime on the Sunday we had checked, listed and packed the wines. Just before leaving I spotted a wine bin with 25 ordinary-looking bottles, unlabelled with plain capsules. My first reaction, being somewhat tired, was that after packing all the great wines it seemed a waste of time to bring these anonymous bottles to London; my second reaction was of curiosity, so I drew the cork: it was clearly branded '*1865 Kirwan*'. I then noticed the faint remains of the by then familiar oval Claridge shoulder labels. The wine still had a marvellously deep colour, a lovely old nose, was rich with a fine flavour and finish. This was at 4pm. In the kitchen upstairs I decanted the wine, leaving half for Sir George's supper and almost literally hopping over the wall with the rest for our friends to taste. What was left in my glass was drinking well up to six hours later. This was in August 1970. It was the outstanding wine of the pre-sale tasting that October. Simply no signs of age, no off odours or acidity. Perfection. It was all bought by Peter Palumbo, one of my oldest friends and clients. One or two bottles were subsequently sold on also via Christie's. Bought by Hardy Rodenstock, it gained top marks in his 1995 tasting. A second bottle more recently, though impressively deep was, because of its slight ullage, at last showing its age. *Last tasted March 2001. At best* ★★★★★

**Ch Rausan-Ségla** A curious mid-shoulder bottle with medicinal nose and taste, otherwise flavoury (at Lafite 1983). More recently, just labelled '*Rausan*': good colour; sound, fruity nose; flavoury, citrus-like acidity. *Last tasted Sept 1995. At best* ★★

SOME OLDER NOTES ON THE 1865s **Ch Giscours** Warm-hued; fragrant; a charmer with tolerable acidic finish. *1986* ★★★; **Ch Gruaud-Larose** autumnal but healthy; rich, powerful, astringent. *1976* ★★★; and **Ch Laroze** (*sic*) probably Gruaud-Larose, not St-Émilion. Cork like charcoal yet good colour; spicy nose and sweet, flavoury but medicinal iodine-like tannic finish. *1987* ★★★★

## 1866

Average-sized crop of terrible wines.

## 1867 ★★

Moderate-sized harvest of fairly ordinary but over-priced wines. Now rarely seen.

**Ch Mouton-Rothschild** Provenance: private cellars at Lafite, sold at Christie's, recorked at Lafite. Feeble amber; high-toned, malty, a whiff like amyl acetate; lean, clean but 'pricked'. *At Lloyd Flatt's Ch Mouton tasting, New Orleans, April 1986.*

**Ch Ducru-Beaucaillou** Recorked at Lafite, bought at Christie's. A very attractive wine: lively appearance, gloriously rich, ripe bouquet; drying out but clean as a whistle. *At Rodenstock's tasting, Sept 1987* ★★★★

## 1868 ★★★

Great heat then heavy rain in August. Heat again either side of an unusually early vintage (7 September). Over-priced wines; big, hard, without charm. Nevertheless, some first-growths showing well in the 1980s.

**Ch Lafite** Money flowed. This was the year Baron James de Rothschild paid a colossal price (over 4 million francs) for Lafite. But the 'merchant princes' were also at the height of their power with even first growths selling wine in *barriques* to them for bottling. The first note I have is of a badly ullaged bottle labelled '*Lafitte*' and bottled by Cruse, the most successful of the *négociants*. It was still richly coloured and surprisingly good for its poor level and age (at a Heublein pre-sale tasting in 1978). More recently, a bottle with original cork and perfect level: rich rosehip colour; bouquet opened up beautifully in the glass; despite its reputation, a charmer. *Last noted at Flatt's Lafite tasting, Oct 1988* ★★★★

**Ch Margaux** 14,000 cases produced. A lovely bottle with an interesting bouquet, its trajectory peaking after 45 minutes in the glass, fading after 90. In between, richly flavoured (at Lafite 1983). Four years later, two bottles, slight variation. Both good-looking, one smelling of a venerable *chai*, the other dusty and slightly sour-nosed. But both sweet and flavoury, one complete, tannic, the other more piquant. *The last two noted at Desai's Margaux tasting, May 1987. At best* ★★★★

**Ch Latour** From the château, recorked. Noted as 'not bad' despite nose 'varnishy' combining 'mustard and manure'. Spicy, acidic. *At Kerry Payne's Latour tasting, June 1981.*

**Ch Rausan-Ségla** Short, original, branded cork. Château-bottled label. Fairly deep, rich; immediately forthcoming bouquet, rich but a hint of bananas and worse to come. After ten minutes 'bizarre', very medicinal; strange taste, fair sweetness and body, in fact quite flavoury, with quite a bite at the end. *Sept 1995* ★ *(just).*

## 1869 ★★★★

Yet another top-notch pre-phylloxera vintage. A super-abundant crop picked fairly early, the wines being sturdy, complete and, in my experience, fairly dependable even in their old age. However, I have no recent notes so I shall recapitulate briefly:

**Ch Lafite** Excellent. First tasted a century after the grapes were picked. Peter Palumbo flew us over to Paris for a lunch where, from his private bin at the Coq Hardi, Bougival, he produced a magnum that was fragrant, 'soft, languorous' despite its greasy, old, original cork. Next, a bottle recorked at the château: again, rich, ripe, spicy. *Last noted at Lloyd Flatt's Lafite tasting, Oct 1988* ★★★★

**Ch Margaux** On the day I recorked a bottle of the 1784 at the château, the *maître de chai* was topping up (with some 1970 I noted) and recorking a mid-shoulder bottle of the 1869. Before he did so I had a quick taste. Despite the ullage and some diminution of colour it still had a bouquet which exhibited all Margaux's delicacy and charm. *Aug 1977* ★★★

**Ch Mouton-Rothschild** Three bottles all recorked at Lafite in 1980. Frankly, both in 1983 were variable, malty and decayed, ullaged and decadent, the third 'faded and faint' at first but bouquet and flavour rallied round. Sweet, fragrant. *Last noted at Flatt's Mouton tasting, April 1986* ★★★

OTHER 1869S **Carruades de Ch Lafite** Variable, both 'gamey', one fragrant, rose-scented, the other over-acidic. *At Lafite, 1988. At best* ★★★; **Ch Marquis de Terme** excellent. *Also at Lafite, 1986* ★★★★; and **Ch Montrose** of the 25 dozen bought from Claridge's (not the hotel) and 'packed' in the Meyrick's Hinton Admiral cellar, over 18 dozen remained in the bin at the time my wife and I packed them. Four notes, two in the cellar, good level and mid-shoulder, and two pre-sale. Still deeply coloured, the best had a rich, old, leathery (tannic) nose and remarkably good flavour and aftertaste, though tannin still much in evidence. *April and Oct 1970. At best* ★★★

# 1870 ★★★★★

Together with 1864 and 1865 one of the most magnificent of all the classic pre-phylloxera clarets. But by now the prices had reached an unsustainable level. As in 1945, spring frosts reduced the potential crop and a bakingly hot summer escalated the sugar content leading to an early (from 10 September) harvest of super ripe, concentrated wines.

**Ch Lafite** One of the all time greats and, at its best, a powerhouse, massively endowed with every conceivable component. In fact, in such a powerful and tannic wine that it was virtually undrinkable for half a century. Nevertheless, bottlings varied, and, as always, provenance plays a part. I have had the opportunity to taste, and drink the 1870 Lafite on sixteen occasions starting, however, with an untypical pale and astringent bottle which nevertheless, as if it was conscious of letting the side down, emitted a sweet bouquet which lingered in the glass long after it had been emptied. This was in 1966.

Unquestionably the most magnificent were (and still can be), the Coningham-bottled magnums from Glamis Castle. Of the 48 originally binned in 1878, 41 magnums had remained undisturbed until I and a friendly wine merchant in Perth packed them up for a great sale at Christie's in 1971. Naturally, to make sure that the wine was all right, I opened one at a dinner in the boardroom before the sale attended by a dozen or so wine luminaries. The cork was sound, the level high, the colour so impressively deep that it could have been mistaken for a 1970; nose flawless, the bouquet blossoming in the glass. Perfect on the palate too. A lovely drink. Thank goodness the 13th Earl of Strathmore, who had originally bought it, didn't take to it; it must have been swingeingly tannic. Like the 1928 Latour, it took 50 years to become drinkable. It was in 1934 that his luncheon host asked André Simon, the founder of the Wine and Food Society, for his first reactions to the wines.

They 'evoked memories of Berkshire', the 1870 Lafite 'of the Majesty of the Royal Oak'. That's wine writing for you! No toasty new oak; no gobs of glycerin, oodles of sweet black fruits; awesome…

Then there was a bottle I opened in Sir John Thompson's cellar at Woodperry House to see if the cork was branded. It was: '*Pfungst 1870*'. A fabulous colour, still tannic (in 1976). Later, also Bordeaux-bottled, this time by Cruse, five bottles from the Ten Broeck mansion in Albany (New York), noted at Heublein pre-sale tastings in 1978 and 1979. Purchased in 1879, the wine was still in original cases, wrapped in tissue paper on which was printed *Cruse et Fils Frères*. Each bottle had a glass button on the shoulder embossed *Château Lafite Grand Vin*. They varied, the best being superb. Even those with mid-shoulder levels (caused by cork shrinkage) were surprisingly good. Low-shoulder: oxidised of course. Around the same time a perfect magnum from Woodperry served by Lenoir Josey at a great wine dinner in Houston, and an equally delectable bottle despite being mid-shoulder at the Overton Lafite tasting.

Not all were good: an oxidised Day & Watson London bottling, another ullaged and poor Cruse bottling, and even two below-standard magnums at Rodenstock's *Raritäten Weinprobe* as recently as 1996. Even the Glamis magnum was high-toned and over the top, its twin better, though with a sour/cheesy tannic finish.

Most recently, rising to the occasion, a bottle recorked in 1980: still fairly deep with a fine mahogany-mature edge. Just after decanting, it emitted a deliciously Mouton-like spicy scent. After 30 minutes in the glass it reminded me of Heitz Martha's Vineyard Cabernet: pure eucalyptus on the palate; dry, its fine flavour matching the bouquet, wonderful length, still buoyed up by its original tannins. *Last noted at Wilfred Jaeger's in the hills south of San Francisco, June 2001. At best* ★★★★★

**Ch Latour** First noted in 1969 and unquestionably 5 star then: deep, richly coloured; nose and palate of great depth; beautifully balanced. Then a faultless Scottish bottling, its bouquet glorious, harmonious; distinctly sweet, full-bodied yet soft on the palate as was the earlier bottle. 'An aftertaste like warm toast.' The best wine at Payne's 'Homage to Latour'.

Most recently a superb magnum: still intensely deep; low keyed but rich; touch of sweetness, perfect weight, soft texture noted again. *Last tasted at a Rodenstock event, Sept 1996* ★★★★

**Ch Margaux** Not tasted recently. Three notes in 1987. A very good, fragrant yet powerful English bottling, the wax seal impressed *Monkhouse & Anderson 1st growth claret*, served alongside a somewhat decayed and acidic bottle recorked at the château. The last, with a *Sèze Fils Frères* label had not survived its mid-shoulder ullage. Rich – but oxidised. *Last noted at the château, Aug 1987. At best* ★★★★

**Ch Mouton-Rothschild** A superb bottle at Lloyd Flatt's Mouton tasting: richly coloured; a switchback bouquet, singed and tarry at first opening up sublimely, seeming to be at its summit after 40 minutes, fading then reviving to continue

---

## Tasting old wines

*It is surprising how good old wines can be, but one has to make allowances. First, it is very important to taste an old wine with its age in mind. Second, bear in mind the quality of the vintage. Third, and most importantly, the provenance: how long and how well has the wine been cellared? (See also box page 19.)*

tantalisingly for two hours in the glass. Dry yet rich, tarry, spicy – cinnamon – powerful, lovely. *Noted April 1986* ★★★★★

OTHER 1870S LAST TASTED IN THE MID-1980s **Ch Cos d'Estournel** lovely tawny-red; magnificent bouquet, complete, harmonious; incredibly sweet, and a massive wine as one might expect from a St-Estèphe in a vintage of this calibre. *1983* ★★★★★; **Ch Gruaud-Larose** recorked in the cellars at Lafite. Similar warm amber; gloriously sustained bouquet, ginger and arrowroot; fairly sweet, spicy, complete. *1983* ★★★★★; and **Ch Montrose** two bottles, virtually faultless: autumnal colour; sweet, rich bouquet and flavour. *1986* ★★★★★

## 1871 ★★★★

Following the coldest winter since 1829–30 the growing season was uneven, a fairly small crop being harvested. The wines were elegant but considered too light by the English trade, which, in any case, had bought heavily of the previous vintage. Nevertheless, the Scots, always great claret drinkers, were still in the market. But, as Professor George Saintsbury observed in his seminal *Notes on a Cellar-Book* published in 1924, Bordeaux prices had reached such levels that some of his fellow academics in Edinburgh were turning to port as an after dinner drink (see Ch Lafite below).

**Ch Lafite** From Sir William Gladstone's cellar at Fasque, Scotland, one of 46 bottles remaining in 'Bin 49 Claret/after dinner/Château Lafite 1871'. The coldest cellar my wife and I have ever worked in but its dank chill had preserved the wines laid down by the first baronet, brother of the Prime Minister, remarkably well. The bottles had the typical short Lafite capsules, no labels but fully branded corks. Levels were extraordinarily high, the bottle I opened a mere 1/4 inch below the cork. The cork itself was 'puffy and rather wet' – I quote from the note made pre-sale – 'fine deep colour; lovely bouquet which developed beautifully; medium (dry), medium-light body, excellent flavour, lovely long finish. Perfect'. I gave it 6 stars! *Tasted May 1972* ★★★★★

**Ch Léoville-Las-Cases** Bottled by Bell Rannie's of Perth. Also from the Fasque cellar, its wax seal impressed 'BR Claret', level 2 inches below its branded cork. Less deep in colour, showing more age on the nose, some sweetness and weight but lacking the length of the Lafite. *May 1972* ★★★

**Ch Léoville-Barton** Original capsule and cork. High level. Deep; sound, cedary; crisp, drying out, lean but good. *At a Rodenstock tasting, Sept 1987* ★★★

## 1872 ★

Although not late by modern standards, the start of picking on 22 September was the latest since 1863. The growing season would certainly be familiar to growers in the early 1990s: good weather until the heavy rain in the middle of the harvest. Fairly small crop of ordinary wines.

**Ch Lafite** Tasted on four occasions, each bottle from a different cellar. All fairly pale and very dry but varying from decayed and varnishy to fragrant, flavoury but acidic. *Last noted at Lloyd Flatt's tasting, Oct 1988. At best* ★★

## 1873

Vines severely damaged by a very heavy spring frost which destroyed three-quarters of the crop. Poor wine.

## 1874 ★★★★

Complete recovery: an abundant crop picked early. Very good wines, now variable.

**Ch Lafite** Tasted on 14 occasions starting in 1967 with a maderised recorked bottle from Lord Rosebery's cellar. In the early 1970s a large stock of magnums, bottled by Cockburn's of Leith, with attractive glass buttons or seals embossed '*Brancepeth*', the former seat of Lord Boyne, the vendor. Variable conditions. Two opened for tasting, one with a touch of death, the other faded but which recovered its breath and opened up fragrantly. A good drink. The most important stock came from Woodperry House near Oxford: 23 dozen bottles, fulsomely described by his wine merchant as 'of *Le tout première qualité* bottled at the château full brand on cork', had been purchased by Sir John Thompson's grandfather and 'laid' (binned) July 1877. Five years later, following a flood, he and his butler rebinned the wine on layers of sawdust. By the time my wife and I came to pack up the wine, the sawdust was black and when we came out of the cellar – after unbinning 132 bottles – we looked like miners. Two of the bottles that I catalogued as 'Firsts' (high level) had a lovely brick red colour; not a trace of decay, gentle, fragrant, cedary nose and taste. The 'Seconds' (mid-shoulder) were variable, one with a black and greasy cork: not bad but acidic; the other a touch of sourness. We did not pack or sell the low-shoulder bottles.

Another bottle from the same cellar was opened at the Overton tasting in 1979. Not only was it good but it got better in the glass. Most recently, a bottle from the Woodperry cellar, losing colour and showing its age; still tannic, lean but very drinkable. *Last noted at the Lenoir Josey pre-sale tasting in New York, Nov 2000. A variable performer. At best* ★★★★

### Woodperry House

*Sir John Thompson's 18th-century Oxfordshire home. Sir John was keener on the ownership of racehorses than he was, perhaps, on fine wines. When he was an old man and about to sell Woodperry, the most marvellous old cellar, originally laid down by his grandfather, came to light. (A Master of Wine friend of mine told me at a dinner that Sir John had offered him its entire contents for £300 but he thought he'd better speak to me first...) Sir John's grandfather had originally purchased and laid down the wine, but his son had shown no interest. Thereafter, when Sir John offered the old vintages to his guests at dinner parties the wines were too long in the tooth, and the squirearchy rarely appreciated them. The cellar itself was divided into three parts. When Daphne and I went to pack up the wines for sale in 1976, we found the area near the foot of the stairs was filled with bottles from the local off-licence which Sir John had bought for entertaining, the old wines had just been left in bins undisturbed. These were some of the greatest clarets Christie's has ever handled.*

**Ch Latour** Not tasted recently. A superb bottle from Lord Rosebery's cellar, pre-sale 1967, but a sickly and tart bottle at the Kerry Payne tasting. *Last noted June 1981. At best* ★★★★★

**Ch Mouton-Rothschild** Coincidentally, two notes in May 1974, both bottles with '*R. Galos gérant*' on capsules and labels, both with unbranded, soft, spongy corks and good levels. The first at a Heublein pre-sale tasting, a touch of sourness on nose and overripe sweetness on palate, the second at another 'centenary' lunch given by Peter Palumbo at the Coq Hardi,

Bougival. A far better bottle: excellent colour; rich, no decay; soft, velvety, still full of fruit, long finish. Next, lunching at Lafite, and recorked there: too deep; chocolatey; drying out, tailing off, and its twin, in much better condition, its bouquet beautiful, better than its palate, dry with 'stuffing' taken out of it. *Last noted at Flatt's Lafite tasting, April 1986. At best* ★★★★★
**Ch Ausone** Few, if any, wines from St-Émilion or Pomerol were shipped to England. Médocs only. The oldest vintage of Ausone I have tasted. Excellent colour; very good 'cedar, classic' nose; medium sweet, perfect weight, balance and flavour. *At the Rodenstock tasting in Sept 1995* ★★★★★

FOUR OTHER 1874S (all at a Rodenstock tasting in 1987)
**Ch Gruaud-Larose** once a big wine, still richly scented despite mid-shoulder level; **Ch Léoville-Barton** good level. Intense; nose malty, meaty, rich, and raisiny. Good wine despite high acidity ★★★; **Ch Léoville-Poyferré** merely mentioned to demonstrate the risks of poor levels. A completely oxidised, low-shoulder magnum; and **Ch Pichon-Baron** excellent level: deep, ruby-shaded; sound; perfect flavour, extract and balance ★★★★

# 1875 ★★★★★

An even more abundant crop than 1874 and reputed to be the biggest from the start of records until 1960. Perfectly ripe grapes producing wines of great elegance and finesse. Apparently, however, too light for the British market which had, in any case, bought copiously the 1874. Nevertheless, rather like the 1929 and 1953, the 1875s were sweet and charming when young and, despite their comparative delicacy, and low tannin levels, those that remained (most were consumed young) were superbly drinkable for a century.
**Ch Lafite** Over a dozen notes, all except one emanating from Sir George Meyrick's cellars. All had lead capsules embossed Lafite and a very distinctive oval shoulder label '*Geo Claridge 24 Rood Lane London*' with, in the centre, '*240*'. The bin label was explicit '*Claridge Claret No 240 (Chat Lafite), 40 dozen packed (binned by) Mr Taylor June 1881. Price 75 shillings*' (per dozen) – of which 15 dozen remained untouched, in one bin. Mainly excellent levels but 'Seconds' (which I defined in the catalogue as 'between top and bottom of shoulder' – nowadays we would be fractionally more precise: mid-shoulder, upper-shoulder etc) also tasted. My first note (in May 1970), was made in the Meyrick cellar at Hinton Admiral: lovely colour, 'faded but alive and interesting'.
   A month later I opened a bottle in my office to taste with the late Jack Rutherford, the Cruse agent and one of England's finest palates. Given the wine blind he unhesitatingly identified it. It was lovely, mellow-looking; a faded old lady when first poured but a bouquet that developed richly, with the gingery wholemeal biscuit scent often emitted by the finest mature clarets. A soft, gentle style, silky textured and very rich. Delightful. A lovely drink. Another Meyrick bottle at the Overton tasting in 1979 was rather drab, its initial banana skin nose recovering, a rich raisiny fruitiness remaining after four hours. Most recently, same provenance, but vinegary and undrinkable. *Last noted in the pre-phylloxera 'flight' at Rodenstock's tasting, Sept 1995. At its best still* ★★★★★

LAST NOTED AT RODENSTOCK'S 1875 FIRST GROWTH 'FLIGHT' AT HIS EVENT IN 1987 **Ch Latour** two magnums, both recorked at the château in 1980 and both very odd with

a smell of medicated shampoo; **Ch Margaux** a double magnum, ullaged mid-shoulder yet with excellent, tannin-gripped flavour. I described its nose as 'crystallised violets and clean bandages' ★★★; **Ch Mouton-Rothschild** three poor bottles. Then two magnums, this time recorked in 1982. A lovely wine but, unlike Lafite, its bouquet, initially sweet and harmonious, started to crack up after 35 minutes. A beautiful butterfly, short-lived. A*t best* ★★★★; and **Ch Haut-Brion** two magnums, both mid-shoulder. Earthy, chocolatey. *At best* ★★★

TWO OTHER, OLD NOTES A delicious **Ch Desmirail** from Fernand Woltner's cellar in Paris: pretty colour; sweet, gentle then ethereal old bouquet; flavoury, piquant. *Sept 1987* ★★★★; and **Ch Pichon-Lalande** from Fasque. Fine, fully-branded cork. High level. Sheer perfection. *May 1972* ★★★★★

# 1876 ★

Poor weather, small crop, poor wines.
**Ch Lafite** This was the year that *Phylloxera vastatrix* appeared at Lafite. A portent of things to come. One bottle suffered from cork drop, the other, also château-bottled, turned out to be lovely. I cannot resist quoting part of what I wrote at the time of tasting: 'initial whiff of banana being quickly overtaken by gardenia, then roses – floral' etc. There; you have it. *Noted at Flatt's Lafite tasting, Oct 1988* ★★★

# 1877 ★★★★

Average crop, of light, charming wines – but phylloxera was rapidly spreading through the vineyards of Bordeaux.
**Ch Lafite** An archetypal Lafite, fullish ruby; a bouquet which opened up beautifully in the glass; sweetish, full flavoured yet silky (a magnum from the château in 1967). Then at Flatt's tasting in 1988 a bottle, recorked at the château: pale, bright, appealing; nose fragrant, slightly smoky, again blossoming in the glass. A lovely, sweet old wine with good length.
   Most recently it was the youngest (!) vintage at Wilf Jaeger's tasting: palish, with a rather weak, open, amber rim; at first a touch of liquorice but within ten minutes developing a rich, rather meaty bouquet which had definitely come to its end, not very surprisingly, after 90 minutes. Nevertheless on the palate it was very flavoury and had good length. I wrote 'Cracking up but delicious with the cheese'. *Last tasted June 2001. At best* ★★★★
**Ch Latour** Not tasted recently but at 104 years old intense and fragrant with a touch of decay but lovely. *June 1981* ★★★★
**Ch Ausone** First tasted in 1983, a recorked bottle: perfect weight combined with fragility, lovely texture. More recently with Ch Lafite-like delicacy and in perfect condition. *Last noted at Flatt's Ausone tasting, Oct 1987* ★★★★★

TWO OLDER NOTES **Ch Haut-Bailly** superb magnums served at André Simon's 90th birthday dinner in 1967. At this period, André told us, the château was awarded a gold medal for the finest vineyard in the Gironde ★★★★; **Ch Branaire-Duluc-Ducru** from the 'old wine' cellar (the 'young wine' cellar was full of Burgundy, vintages ranging from 1919 to 1929) of Mme Teysonneau's mansion overlooking the Parc Bordelais. Calvet label, cork branded *Château Duluc*. A pretty, delicate, rosy colour; sweet, gentle yet immensely fragrant bouquet and flavour. 'Lavender and old lace.' Served at a Bordeaux Club dinner. *1979* ★★★★★

# 1878 ★★★★

When the so-called 'pre-phylloxera' period began is debatable, but no question about when it ended. This was the last vintage, the end of an era. A moderate-sized crop of very good wines. Though over 20 1878s tasted, only one relatively recently.
**Ch Branaire-Ducru** A warm, ruddy colour; ripe, spicy bouquet like withered violets, good in its way but cracking up; sweet, lightish, attractive flavour but acidity overtaking. One of my 'arsenic and old lace' wines. *Just one of the 94 very notable wines at Hardy Rodenstock's most generous three-day event at the Arlberg Hospiz, Austria, Sept 1993* ★★

THE FOLLOWING WERE LAST NOTED IN THE MID-1980S
**Ch Lafite** bottled by de Luze: mid-shoulder, basically rich but unclean. Should be better bottles than this; **Ch Latour** similar level but far more attractive: bouquet of ripe mulberries; lovely aftertaste ★★★★; **Ch Mouton-Rothschild** several bottles in the late 1970s but poor levels. A low-shoulder magnum at Flatt's Mouton tasting: surprisingly good on the palate ★★; **Ch Cos d'Estournel** a faded old lady, more of a tart though fragrant and clean ★★; **Ch Gruaud-Larose** another de Luze bottling: high-toned; full-bodied. Just misses; **Ch La Mission Haut-Brion** the oldest of 66 vintages at Bipin Desai's La Mission tasting. Recorked. Fragrant, sweet, lightish, good length ★★★; and **Ch Pontet-Canet** pale, no red but lively; gloriously decadent, overripe bouquet; delicate, delicious ★★★★

AND SOME GOOD CENTURY-OLD 1878S **Ch Mouton d'Armailhacq** bottled by Harvey's. Good colour; complete, firm fruit, developed and held well ★★★; **Ch Peyrabon** very attractive ★★★; and **Ch Rausan-Ségla** with '*Café Voisin*' (Paris) label. Recorked and though mid-shoulder remarkably good: fine colour; no decay; a very rich, pure flavour and fragrant aftertaste ★★★★

# 1879 ★★

On the slippery slope. A late (9 October) vintage, small and ordinary. Despite the poor weather and its dismal reputation some appealing wines have survived, including **Ch Lafite** recorked at the château; dry light, fragrant, gentle. *At Flatt's Lafite tasting, Oct 1988* ★★★; **Ch Ausone** palish amber; bouquet low-keyed and delicate at first then surged richly, redolent of mushroom soup and raisins; light yet rich, soft, delightful. *At Flatt's Ausone tasting, Oct 1987* ★★

# 1880 ★

Poor spring, followed by uneven flowering and a small crop harvested. Mediocre wines.

I HAVE FEW NOTES FROM THIS VINTAGE **Ch Lafite** quite good 'though a bit screwed up' on the finish. *At Lloyd Flatt's Lafite tasting, Oct 1988* ★★; and **Ch Mouton-Rothschild** I have five variable notes, all bottles from the Ten Broeck mansion, some I described as 'oxidised', meaty and malty, and some smelling of smoky bacon rind, yet some a remarkably good old Cabernet Sauvignon. Usually better on the palate; the survival rate much higher. Lightish, flavoury, some quite pleasant though acidity was on the rampage. *At Heublein pre-sale tastings in San Francisco, Atlanta and New Orleans, 1978–1980. At best* ★★

# 1881 ★

Uneven growing season. Hot summer, late harvest (from 2 October). Small crop of mediocre, 'green', tannic wines.
**Ch Lafite** Lovely colour; gamey nose; some fruit and grip. *At Flatt's Lafite tasting, Oct 1988* ★★
**Ch Latour** If you see any collector with this wine in his cellar, or in an auction catalogue, it might well have come from Hinton Admiral, the Meyrick estate in Hampshire, for, of the 30 dozen '*Claridge Claret No 1 Chat Latour 1881*' costing 100 shillings (£5) a dozen and '*packed May 1894*', 27 dozen remained in the original bins, untouched. An exceptionally hard tannic wine. I dare say that Sir George's grandfather liked the wine as little as the Earl of Strathmore at Glamis liked his 1870 Lafite (see page 16).

Though there were no body labels (for, like vintage port, wines laid down in cool and often damp country house cellars were rarely if ever labelled), the short capsules were embossed '*Château Latour 1881 Grand Vin*', so no identification problems. I tasted an ullaged bottle in the cellar in April 1970: good colour but too tart. Another noted with good level at the pre-sale tasting six months later: more than deep, positively opaque; dry, a huge wine with a pungent tannic finish. Reminded me of some 1948s. Eleven years later I tasted one from the château at Kerry Payne's Latour tasting: a faultless old bouquet; 'a big dry wine though still tannic'. *Last noted June 1981. At best* ★★★

TWO OTHER NOTES MADE IN THE MID-LATE 1980S
**Ch Mouton-Rothschild** recorked by Whitwham's, a Cheshire merchant noted for their recorking: spicy nose, excellent flavour ★★★★; **Ch Cantenac-Brown** also recorked, but not by Whitwham: not a bad nose but dried-out ★; and **Ch Gruaud-Larose** sound but astringent ★

# 1882 ★

A double whammy in the vineyards: phylloxera settling in and a severe attack of mildew. Nevertheless, despite a reduced crop, the wines were elegant enough though very light. They are rarely seen nowadays.
**Ch Lafite** Slip labelled by Balaresque, one of the leading *courtiers* (Bordeaux brokers – not a bit like the British 'brokers' of today – see box page 139). Poor condition, poor taste. *One of the dreariest wines at Flatt's Ch Lafite tasting, Oct 1988.*

## Provenance

*Provenance, particularly in relation to old wines, is crucial. Where do the wines come from? How have they been cellared? Have they been moved? Temperature and humidity are vital. When I was head of Christie's wine department, I would insist on seeing the wines myself, in situ, to inspect their condition and later to assist at their packing. It was all a matter of reassurance, that the rarities I catalogued were correctly described for potential buyers.*
*The wines from the cellar at Glamis Castle had 'perfect provenance': they hadn't been moved for generations (see 1870 Ch Lafite page 16) and were kept in what I called pristine cellar conditions. Lord Rosebery's pre-phylloxera bottles, virtually untouched, in the perfect cellars at his two houses, Mentmore and Dalmeny, were another example of perfect provenance, just left to mature quietly (see box page 422).*

# 1883

Uneven growing conditions, a smallish crop and light, thin, fairly poor wines.

**Ch Lafite** Recorked at the château. Pale, not a hint of red; a strange though rather attractive bouquet 'like crystallised pineapple', I noted; dry, light, short, washed out. *At Lloyd Flatt's Lafite tasting, Oct 1988.*

# 1884–1885

The run of poor vintages continued, mildew wreaking havoc and necessitating a two-tier harvest, though phylloxera was said to be 'wearing itself out'. Misleading, for the louse remained active in many vineyards well into the 20th century; indeed, it is still endemic. It was also a lean time for the trade. Only one note, the 1884 **Ch Giscours** Harvey's-bottled. A gentle, undecayed and charming wine tasted in the early 1970s ★★★

# 1886 ★★

A combination of spring frosts and mildew reduced the crop, necessitating, again, a two-tier harvest. A lean period.

**Ch Lafite** Original cork, good level. Good looks; sweet and spicy bouquet; good flavour, balance and finish. *At Flatt's Lafite tasting, Oct 1988* ★★★

**Ch Mouton-Rothschild** A tired off-taste, mid-shoulder bottle. *At Flatt's Mouton tasting, April 1986.*

# 1887 ★★★

A relatively early harvest; mildew under control, only a half-sized crop. The best vintage between 1878 and 1893.

**FOURTEEN NOTES**, the following last tasted in the mid to late 1980s: **Ch Lafite** from a Rothschild family cellar, tasted in 1976: fragrant and attractive; next in 1985, noting a glorious 'old ivy' and coal-tar nose, sweet, soft, delicate. But an ullaged, oxidised bottle at Flatt's tasting in October 1988. *At best* ★★★; **Ch Margaux** two memorably fragrant bottles, from the cellars of Glamis Castle in 1971. I was told by Bernard Ginistet that the scent of 'old ivy' I again noted was caused by mildew-affected grapes. Two bottles tasted, coincidentally, a century after the vintage, were, alas, oxidised. The last pair at Desai's tasting, May 1987. *At best* ★★★; and **Ch Latour** ullaged and lacking fruit in 1970. Later, dining at Ch Lafite: a fine, deep, intense appearance; lovely bouquet, vanilla, cedar, tangerine; sweet entry, dry finish. Good wine. *Last tasted 1983* ★★★★

**TWO OLDER NOTES Ch Durfort-Vivens** traces of richness; an old chap, decent but in his dotage ★★; and **Ch Gruaud-Larose** in excellent condition though astringent ★★

# 1888 ★★★

Rather like 1878, a poor summer was saved by a brilliant September. Though later (2 October), this was an abundant and good quality vintage, the style and elegance of its wines not unlike the 1887s.

**Ch Lafite** Larose & Co Bordeaux label, cork branded 1888. A charming half-bottle from a Scottish cellar in 1972. Another bottle had barely survived being incarcerated in the cellars of a Swedish count (in 1980). The most recent, recorked at the château, pale, no red; curious, charred fragrance; dry, light and faded 'as though skinned alive or charcoal filtered'. *The last at Flatt's tasting, Oct 1988. At best* ★★★

**Ch Mouton-Rothschild** Just one note. Recorked by Whitwham's in 1980: murky; overblown, spicy nose and taste. *At Flatt's Mouton tasting a century after the vintage, May 1988.*

**Ch Haut-Brion-La Mission** (*sic*) From the cellars of the Woltner family who, in 1918, purchased the château, reversing its name to La Mission Haut-Brion. At first it was hard to judge whether the coffee-like nose was the result of oxidation or had the idiosyncratic Graves character. But it settled down with a good flavour despite slightly intrusive acidity. *At Karl-Heinz Wolf's La Mission tasting in Wiesbaden, June 1990* ★★★

**EARLIER NOTES Ch Latour** fragrant, 'ivy' bouquet; light, charming and lovely. *At Ch Lafite, March 1983* ★★★; and much earlier, allowing for the fact that they were around 70 years old: **Ch Margaux** from Glamis Castle, two notes: both fragrant, gentle, lovely ★★★; **Ch Léoville** (*sic*) well constituted ★★★; **Ch Gruaud-Larose** delicate, delicious ★★★

# 1889 ★★

Despite late flowering an abundant crop. Reasonably good, elegant wines.

**Ch Lafite** In 1975: palish but healthy; with a rosy glow; an enchanting bouquet reminding me of a pink-cheeked, bright-eyed old lady; delicate and lovely. More recently: a similar appearance; an extraordinarily scented nose and taste, yet firm with a dry finish. *Last noted at Flatt's Lafite tasting, Oct 1988* ★★★

**JUST ONE OLDER NOTE Ch Mouton-Rothschild** similar appearance to the Lafite; gentle, flavoury, a touch of mint; light, faded, short but delightful. *At Coq Hardi, Bougival, May 1974* ★★★

# 1890 ★★

Cold spring, lovely September but a mediocre crop of full-bodied wines.

**Ch Lafite** First tasted in 1976: château-bottled, original capsule, branded cork, from a Rothschild cellar in Paris: beautiful colour; ripe, exquisite bouquet; rich, positive, attractive but a touch of acidity. A similar bottle, same provenance and equally appealing, at Lloyd Flatt's tasting. *Last noted Oct 1988* ★★★

**Ch Latour** A bottle from the château tasted in 1977. Bouquet sweet and noted as *gibier* (gamey), like a well-hung pheasant. And as good to drink. Two later notes, both plummy-coloured wines; rather vegetal, mace and old ivy. Despite the reputation of the vintage, not a big Latour though tannic. A good drink. *Last tasted Nov 1990* ★★★ *(just).*

**OLDER NOTES Ch Margaux** a white cloth was put over the billiards table at Ch de la Fot so that I could taste a selection of wines brought up from the very cold cellars beneath a cow shed. Despite the hospitality of the Marquis de Vasselot my wife and children complained. It was our Easter holiday, and it was snowing. The Margaux, despite original cap, label, cork and good level, did not live up to its customary charm, lacking in fruit and somewhat austere. *April 1975* ★★; and **Ch Léoville-Poyferré** a beauty, almost as deep as a 1945. Full-bodied, good flavour, retained sweetness. *March 1970* ★★★

# 1891 ★

Poor spring and summer, the vineyards suffering from yet another pest, *cochylis*, severely reducing the harvest, which, though late (2 October), took place in good conditions.
**Ch Lafite** First tasted in 1976, a bottle recorked in 1957. It had an elegant cedary, tea-like bouquet. Attractive. Later from the same Rothschild cellar in Paris, a fruity, honeyed strawberry-scented bottle; sweet, fuller-bodied. *Last noted at Lloyd Flatt's Lafite tasting, Oct 1988* ★★★

AN OLDER NOTE **Ch Léoville-Poyferré** overripe but fragrant bouquet and taste. Delicate yet some richness and attractive flavour. *1978* ★★★

# 1892 ★ to ★★★

Who would be a *vigneron*! Crop reduced by two severe spring frosts, the remainder scorched by a 43°C sirocco wind on 14 August. Then hailstorms. A small crop harvested. Irregular, variable quality, some elegance.
**Ch Lafite** From the cellars of the Caviar Kaspia restaurant in Paris, recorked in 1957: light colour and style; sound, delicate fragrance; elegant (1976). Later, another charmer, Bordeaux-bottled, slightly sweet, feminine, long dry finish with refreshing acidity. *Last noted at Lloyd Flatt's Lafite tasting, Oct 1988* ★★★
**Ch Margaux** Three notes. The first, with original cork, had a ripe, almost exotic scent. The next, at Desai's Margaux tasting in 1987, believed to be recorked: attractive appearance; fruity old nose; sweet, light, faded yet delicious. Most recently, from a large stock, purchased by Whitwham's at a Christie's auction in Geneva and recorked by them in 1979: very sweet though faded, and surprisingly attractive. I also used my old expression 'arsenic and old lace'. *The oldest of 50 vintages at Manfred Wagner's Margaux tasting in Zurich, Jan 1997* ★★★
**Ch Canon** An old note but, I think, worth mentioning. Bottled by Calvet, to whom my hostess, Mme Teysonneau was related, and served by her at a Sunday lunch in between my dirty hands-and-knees stocktaking in her 'old wine' cellar. This contained the widest range of pre-1900 châteaux ever handled by Christie's. Totally delicious, its style reminding me of the 1887 Margaux: a warm tawny colour; very perfumed nose, high-toned, very forthcoming; a light, charming ivy-leaf flavour, perfect acidity, delightful. In fact, a little like Madame: old lace (without the arsenic). *In Bordeaux, April 1979* ★★★★

ANOTHER OLD NOTE **Ch Latour** at 99 years of age, rich in colour, nose and flavour. *1981* ★★★★

# 1893 ★★★★

An extraordinary year, after a string of poor to middling vintages. Warm spring followed by early flowering. The summer was bakingly hot. The exceptionally ripe and abundant harvest was picked from 15 August.

TO MY SURPRISE I HAVE 50 NOTES, but only two 1893s tasted in the 1990s: **Ch Dauzac** a jeroboam; astonishingly deep; malty, plausible, surprisingly good; sweet yet still tannic. Remarkable. *In Munich, Sept 1993* ★★★; and **Clos L'Église-Clinet** magnums: citrus-like scent; soft, attractive, unusual flavour. *One of Rodenstock's discoveries, Sept 1990* ★★★ *How Hardy manages to source these rarities, I do not know.*

I SHALL DIVIDE THE REST OF MY NOTES ON THE 1893S, as briefly as possible, into tasting periods.

LAST TASTED IN THE LATE 1980S
**Ch Lafite** First, in 1972, a bottle from a Scottish cellar with a *'Larose & Cie'* label: deep, rich. Apart from two sour and oxidised bottles, the key word is rich. Then a very sweet, singed, raisiny bouquet and almost caramelly rich flavour at Overton's landmark Lafite tasting in 1979, leading me to the conclusion that the grapes must have been almost like raisins when picked. In 1987 I noted a faultless *impériale*. The most recent note is of a bottle recorked by Whitwham's in 1974, full and fruity but touched by volatile acidity. *The last of eight notes at Lloyd Flatt's Lafite tasting, Oct 1988. At best* ★★★★
**Ch Margaux** This was first brought to my attention in 1971; it was immensely deep, though with beads at the rim which are often the harbingers of trouble; indeed its lovely, silky texture was somewhat marred by acidity. Ten months later, an incredibly rich, fabulously complete 20/20 6-star bottle.
   Probably the most perfect, however, was from the cellar of Woodperry House, château-bottled, long cork, good level: sweet, soft, violet-scented bouquet, no signs of decay; soft, almost creamy texture (in 1976). The following year, an opulent *impériale* that I could not fault. Most recently, purchased at the Woodperry House cellar sale, a lively ruby colour; fragrant bouquet – surely the hallmark of Margaux; beginning to lose weight but still beautifully balanced. A most lovely drink. *Last tasted dining at David d'Ambrumenil's, Nov 1989* ★★★★★
**Ch Cheval Blanc** An incredibly deep, positively exotic double magnum. As previously recorded: *hors classe*. *With Jacques Hébrard who was practically reduced to tears at Walter Eigensatz's tasting of 1893s and 1929s in Wiesbaden, June 1987.*
**Ch Pétrus** Another double magnum at the same tasting. Coffee-like nose; chunky, high extract, spicy tannic finish. Provenance unknown but impressive. *Wiesbaden, June 1987* ★★
**Ch Cos d'Estournel** Two magnums, recorked. One faulty, the other lively, gamey, lovely to drink. *At Rodenstock's wine event, Sept 1987* ★★★★
**Ch Montrose** Original cork. Faultless, fragrant; soft fruitiness but a dash of volatile acidity. *At the Cercle de Vingt, Versailles, May 1988* ★★

LAST TASTED IN THE EARLY TO MID-1980S **Ch Latour** two disappointing, one rich and gamey on the nose; dried-out, fragrant, faded but very drinkable. *Last tasted at the château, 1981. At best* ★★; **Ch Mouton-Rothschild** four notes, two ullaged yet fascinating and just surviving, two excellent, with the opulent, spicy Mouton character, lovely, rounded and in wonderful condition. *Last tasted in 1981. At best* ★★★★★; **Ch Brane-Cantenac** lovely. *1985* ★★★; and **Ch Pichon-Lalande** one oxidised, the other fragrant; soft, lovely texture. *1981. At best* ★★★

OTHER WINES NOT TASTED SINCE THE 1970S **Ch Figeac** rich yet delicate ★★★★; **Ch Gruaud-Larose** opaque; austere ★★; **Ch Léoville** (*sic*) bottled by Chalié Richards and Holdsworth: amber-hued; overripe fruit but attractive; gamey, flavoury, sound ★★★; **Ch Léoville-Poyferré** bottled in Bremen, tired but holding on ★★; and **Ch Pape-Clément** another wonderful wine from Woodperry House: lovely colour, mahogany-tinged; gentle, cedary bouquet; soft, easy-going, sound, very attractive ★★★★

# 1894 ★

The wines had suffered from the previous year's excessive heat. Humid conditions encouraged *coulure* (poor fruit set), then rain was followed by a small, late (5 October) harvest.

LAST TASTED IN THE LATE 1980S **Ch Lafite** recorked: pale, fragrant, 'lacy' old bouquet; faded, frail. *Oct 1988* ★; **Ch Ausone** ullaged and earthy, but some delicacy in 1977. More recently, a tawny rose colour; spicy though slightly varnishy nose and taste. *Oct 1987* ★; **Ch Kirwan** double magnum: ruby core; chocolate, oak and vanilla; full, chewy, very tannic, marked acidity. *Sept 1988* ★

# 1895 ★★★★

Not easy for the growers: wet until end of July, too dry in August and September with excessive heat at vintage time. The first vintage in which some growers learned how to make wines when the grapes have been brought in under excessively hot conditions. In such circumstances too much sugar stops the fermentation and causes volatile acidity. In the days before consultant oenologists made the rounds, not all châteaux sought, received or benefited from advice. Lafite was one of the few châteaux that did, the manager asking a scientist friend how to cope with the high temperature. He was advised to draw the juice off the must, cool it for one night in another vat and then return it to continue fermenting. On another occasion, the *maître de chai* was obliged to put lumps of ice into the overheated vats. Today, of course, more sophisticated cooling devices are in use.

**Ch Lafite** The results were successful. I had never come across *T. de Vial & Fils, Bordeaux* (on capsule) before but their corks, branded *Vial*, had survived 80 years: a good, fairly deep colour; a lovely old cedar bouquet which opened up deliciously; flavour to match, soft, excellent finish. More recently, a bottle recorked by the *maître de chai* in 1987 (it would not have been château-bottled originally, for in the phylloxera-affected period, from 1885 vintage to the 1906, Lafite did not bottle its own wine at the château: the wine was all supplied in *barriques* for merchant-bottling). The recorked bottle was equally good: deep; sweet, lively but rich; good fruit and length. *Last noted at Flatt's Lafite tasting, Oct 1988* ★★★★
**Ch La Mission Haut-Brion** First noted dining with Jean Delmas at the château during the 1978 harvest, a bottle recorked in 1950. On the pale side but very attractive; fragrant old bouquet reminding me of ivy leaves and vine roots; delicate, charming, delightful, its slightly edgy end acidity dealt with by the food. More recently, also from the Woltner cellars, a deliciously scented bottle; light, stylish, very drinkable. *Last noted at Karl-Heinz Wolf's La Mission tasting, June 1990* ★★★

# 1896 ★★★★

An abundant crop; fine and delicate wines.
**Ch Lafite** Did the château bottle their own wine for the use of the family, or was it bottled for them by just one favoured *négociant*? The bottle I tasted in 1976 came from Baron Guy de Rothschild's Paris cellar and had been recorked at the château: very attractive with a sweet, ripe bouquet; dry, lightish, touch of piquancy. More recently, a bottle recorked by the *maître de chai* had a less healthy brown rim, malty nose, and was more acidic. *Last noted at Flatt's Lafite tasting, Oct 1985. At best* ★★★

OF THE OTHER OLDER NOTES The best were of **Ch Brane-Cantenac** fragrant, one-dimensional, clinging to life. *At Lafite, 1983* ★★; **Ch Giscours** bottled by de Luze: delectable bouquet; somewhat faded but sound. *1981* ★★★; **Ch Montrose** palish but healthy; old cedar and residual fruit; dry, on the light side, gentle, the tannins that had preserved it for over 80 years 'having relinquished office'. *1976* ★★★ *(just)*.

# 1897 ★

A reminder that Bordeaux has a maritime climate, the Atlantic being only a fast hour's drive west of Pauillac. In 1897 the beneficial sea breezes turned into strong on-shore salt winds which scorched the vines. The smallest crop between 1863 and 1910 harvested in good weather conditions. Mediocre wines.
**Ch Lafite** Despite specialising in fish, the restaurant Caviar Kaspia in the Place Madeleine in Paris had an incredibly good cellar of red Bordeaux including many old vintages of Lafite, back to 1806 (several sold at Christie's and, later, in America at the Heublein auctions). The best 1897 tasted in 1976 came from this cellar: a pretty, pleasing, dry and elegant wine recorked at the château in 1957. Two subsequent bottles suffering from lower levels though one, despite a sort of well-hung game bird overripeness, was very flavoury; the other tart. More recently, palish, faded, feeble but sound. *Last noted at Flatt's Lafite tasting, Oct 1988. At best* ★★
**Ch Latour** From the château, recorked: healthy colour; pear-like nose; dry, light and delicate for Latour. *Last tasted 1981* ★

# 1898 ★★ to ★★★

Half the normal sized crop. Tannic wines needing considerable bottle age, some of which have survived.
**Ch Lafite** Two consistent notes 12 years apart. Both recorked. A ruddy-tawny colour. Apart from a curious tarred rope element to the nose and taste, quite nice, light and flavoury. Life supporting tannins still in evidence. *Last noted at Flatt's Lafite tasting, Oct 1988* ★★★
**Ch Margaux** Recorked. Tawny-hued; rich, slightly pungent nose. Still tannic. *At Desai's Margaux tasting, May 1987* ★
**Ch Le Curé-Bon-La-Madeleine** Typical of Hardy Rodenstock to find a magnum from this very small and little

---

## André Tchelistcheff and the 1898 Lafite

*The great annual Heublein wine auctions that I conducted (from 1969 to 1982) were preceded by mammoth tastings attended by upwards of 500 potential buyers and 'wine buffs'. In 1971, André Tchelistcheff, the doyen of Napa Valley winemakers, turned up at a pre-sale tasting in San Francisco and we asked him to open and comment on one of the old wines. At the top table we always had a range of old and rare bottles for people to taste. André chose a bottle of Lafite, vintage 1898. This was a period when Americans were not all that knowledgeable but avid. After opening and decanting, André, with the microphone full on, but as if to himself in his charming French-Russian accent, took a sip and said: 'Tasting old wine is like making love to an old lady.' The whole room went silent; he paused. 'It is possible.' Another pause. 'It can even be enjoyable.' Sip and pause again, adding: 'But it requires a leetle bit of imagination.' This caused a sensation. Not only was it very amusing (some were shocked), it was so apposite. One has to make allowances when tasting old wine.*

known château next to Ch Ausone. A good, deepish colour; initially a smell of overripe bananas, though the fruit lurking beneath surfaced after 20 minutes. On the palate, dried out, lean, but good length. *Sept 1988* ★★

OTHER WINES TASTED IN THE MID- TO LATE 1980S
**Ch Latour** beautiful colour; on the verge of decay but perfumed; surprisingly sweet and light, soft, spicy and fragrant. *Dining at Ch Lafite, July 1985* ★★★★; **Ch Brane-Cantenac** autumnal colour; fragrant, rich, toasted nose; fading, piquant, flavoury. *Also at Ch Lafite, March 1983* ★★★

THE BEST LAST TASTED IN THE MID-1970S **Ch Mouton-Rothschild** a very ripe, rich, complex old fellow on nose and palate. Firm, holding well at nearly 80 years of age. *At the château, 1975* ★★★; **Ch Villemaurine** the first old vintage of this château that I have ever come across. The château has the most spectacular of all the underground, Roman-quarried *caves* in St-Émilion. A delicious wine if you like sweet decadence. Very delicate, with a flavoury aftertaste. *1977* ★★★

# 1899 ★★★★★

The first of the renowned *fin de siècle* twin vintages. A well-nigh perfect growing season culminating in an abundant harvest. Wine of stature to match, yet with a certain delicacy and great finesse. Buoyant prices. To my surprise I have 45 1899 notes dating from 1967.
**Ch Lafite** Eight notes. Even in a vintage like this, Lafite sold their wine in bulk (by the *tonneau*, four *barriques* yielding approximately 100 dozen bottles) to Bordeaux *négociants* for bottling or shipping on to other merchants. The first I tasted, in 1971, had been bottled by Louis Mortier: light, refined, beautiful flavour. The same year, 'Château Lafite Grand Vin' could have been a Harvey's of Bristol bottling. It was a lovely, gentle, cedary and elegant wine. In 1978 at a Heublein pre-sale tasting, two bottles from the Ten Broeck mansion, New York, curiously labelled 'mise d'A.G. & E. Rothschild', one low and 'blown', the other quite good, 'a little tart, but clean'! An exquisite bottle at the Overton tasting in 1979 and a rather varnishy one at Lloyd Flatt's in 1988. More recently, a spectacular, recorked, double magnum: fragrant, gentle, beautifully balanced. *Last noted at Walter Eigensatz's tasting, May 1999. At best* ★★★★★
**Ch Margaux** Two bottles tasted at the château in 1972, both pale, with a faint, ruddy glow; one with a rich, fascinating, high-toned bouquet, its initial sweetness punctured, drying out; the other very scented and fragrant, though it turned rather sickly sweet, it had rather more bite on the palate. Not a very thrilling start. Jumping 15 years to a couple at Desai's tasting, one, with a Pillet-Will label (Count Pillet-Will had bought the château in 1879) distinctly unhealthy, the other revealing, at its most seductive, Margaux's feminine allure. It displayed a lively and lovely colour and a beautiful bouquet; distinct sweetness, by no means full-bodied, fragrant, lovely. In 1989 an *impériale* with original cork. A richly coloured wine with shapely 'legs'. Its bouquet, sweet and fragrant, collapsed within 30 minutes. Exotically flavoured but in the end, a superannuated *diva*. *Last tasted blind, a jeroboam, at Aarlberg, Austria, Sept 1993. At best* ★★★★★
**Ch Latour** First tasted in 1967, impressively coloured; a bit of bottle-stink soon cleared revealing remarkable fruit; not a big wine but soft and full-flavoured. Frankly variable — more to do

with storage and provenance. None matched the first tasted. *Last noted March 1987. At best* ★★★★★
**Ch Mouton-Rothschild** A bottle in 1969 did not live up to its rich, velvety appearance. Nose 'as dry as dust'. Making an effort to be rich. The next was agreeable, silky, faded but complete. The best was a bottle recorked by Whitwham's in 1974: a lovely, lively appearance; fragrant; slightly minty bouquet; perfect weight, lovely flavour, firm, dry finish (at Lloyd Flatt's Mouton tasting in 1986). More recently, a double magnum, far more opulent, chocolatey; dry, crisp, good length, highish acidity. *Last noted at Eigensatz's big bottle tasting, May 1989. At best* ★★★★★
**Ch Ausone** Very rich, raisiny, slightly maderised. *Oct 1987* ★★
**Ch Le Curé-Bon-La-Madeleine** A magnum alongside the 1898. It looked tired, its old nose trying not to submerge, though it made a last gasp effort – like the Duke of Clarence just before he drowned in the butt of Malmsey. Not bad fruit but raw finish. A curiosity. *At Rodenstock's tasting, Sept 1998.*
**Clos L'Église-Clinet** Another Rodenstock curiosity, a magnum, tasted blind: soft, jammy fruit on the nose, though showing its age; sweetish, soft and attractive though unusual flavour on the palate. *Sept 1996* ★★★
**Ch Léoville-Barton** Epitomising the gentleness, delicacy and finesse of the '99 at its best. First tasted in 1976, a very attractive, mature appearance; fragrant, delicious, lightly fruity bouquet which opened up richly, biscuity, in the glass. Medium-dry, medium-light (weight), gentle and appealing, with a good, dry finish. Next, dining at Ch Lafite in 1982, I gave it 6 stars, and the following year, also at Lafite, noting its intense, beautiful, limpid appearance; forthcoming bouquet with an almost powder-puff sweetness; drying out with a gentle sigh. Most recently, palish; a rich singed, slightly tangy nose which reminded me, somehow, of bracken; dried out, refreshing. Clearly past its best but more than a spectre at the feast. *Last noted at the Josey pre-sale tasting in New York, Nov 1990. At its best* ★★★★★
**Ch Brane-Cantenac** A rich, refined bottle from Glamis Castle, bottled by Nathl Johnston, tasted in 1971. Later, full, firm, nice texture, well balanced. A good period for this château. *Last tasted at Ch Lafite, from the 'exchange stock' cellar, March 1983* ★★★★

ALSO TASTED IN MARCH 1983 **Ch Cantenac-Brown** a really beautiful wine: sweet, delicious, good acidity ★★★★★; **Ch Léoville-Poyferré** Lafite-like, beautifully evolving scent. Lovely flavour, slightly acidic ★★★★

MANY OTHER CHÂTEAUX TASTED IN THE LATE 1960S TO MID-1970S Among the best were: **Ch Beychevelle**; **Ch Gruaud-Larose**; **Ch La Lagune** ('even better than Mouton'); **Ch Moulin-Riche** the second wine of Poyferré, incorrectly bin-labelled 'Mouton-Riche' in the Glamis Castle cellar; **Ch St-Pierre-Bontemps** (now called just St-Pierre).

---

## Exchanging wines

*From time to time readers will notice comments on quite a few wines from different châteaux from the cellars at Ch Lafite. It was certainly the practice of top châteaux – not just the first growths – to exchange wine, out of courtesy and, I suppose curiosity. These wines tended to accumulate, for, as can be imagined, hosts prefer to serve mainly their own wines at luncheons and dinners.*

# 1900–1919

Wealth, power then war and its aftermath. The Edwardian era conjures up flamboyance, opulence and splendour. But, as they say, 'it was alright for some'. Wine merchants, importers on both sides of the Atlantic were doing well as, in Bordeaux, were the *négociants*, in particular the 'merchant princes' who had the whip hand in their dealings with the producers. The result of World War One was to suck able-bodied men into the conflict, many never to return, as witnessed by the memorials to the fallen in every British and French city, town and village. The shortage of both labour and materials made life difficult for the producers. The weather conditions did not help, 1915 being a complete disaster. Some people profited by the war; wine merchants from northern France and the Low Countries were able to move to Bordeaux and to buy châteaux: Cordier for example, Ginestet and the Woltners. But generally, post-war recovery was slow, the Volstead Act of October 1919 heralding the end of a prosperous era for the US wine trade.

## Vintages at a Glance
**Outstanding ★★★★★**
1900
**Very Good ★★★★**
1904, 1911
**Good ★★★**
1905, 1906, 1914, 1918, 1919

## 1900 ★★★★★

The second of the renowned twin vintages. Whereas the 1899s had finesse and delicacy, the sort of feminine charm later associated with the 1929s and 1953s, the 1900s were more structured – to use a fashionable expression – well balanced and more obviously impressive. But it was also a superabundant vintage following perfect weather conditions and the wines were uniformly excellent. That is to say, those that were capable of making top quality wines did. But, paradoxically, the producers did not profit. The trade had taken up the 1899s at good prices; they had a surfeit and put pressure on the châteaux proprietors to reduce their prices.

**Ch Lafite** Tasted on six occasions. Variable, mainly because of provenance, storage conditions and cork failure; and possibly because Lafite at the time sold mainly in bulk, relying on either the various *négociants* to do the *élevage* and bottling, or, having sold on in *barrique*, for their overseas customers to bottle – not any Tom, Dick or Harry, but dependable importers and merchants.

First tasted at Dr Marvin C Overton's tasting of Lafite, representing every decade from the 1790s to 1970s. With high fill, its appearance was warm and attractive, not deep; the bouquet opened up in the glass magnificently. A rich, full-flavoured wine, its life-supporting tannins and acidity still in evidence. I gave it a rare 20/20. In the early 1980s, an exciting *Réserve du Château*, its overripe *gibier* (gamey) bouquet like an old cedar cigar box – or singed hair. 'Over the hill', it cracked up but was fun while it lasted. Skipping over the ullaged and oxidised, including a very disappointing bottle at Lloyd Flatt's marathon (116 vintages of Lafite, 1784 to 1986), an excellent magnum, recorked at the château in 1991: still very sweet, rich, good flavour and length, delicious. *Last tasted in 'flight' 5 of Hardy Rodenstock's wine weekend, Sept 1996. At best ★★★★★*

**Ch Latour** One of Latour's great vintages, its condition now of course depending on provenance and cork. First tasted dining at the château – a great privilege – in 1970. At 70 years of age the appearance of the wine was magnificently deep, with palate to match, still pretty massive with lots of grip. A delicious and memorable mouthful. I shall pass over an ullaged, though interesting, magnum in 1978 and a disappointing, oxidised and woody bottle at Kerry Payne's 'Homage to Latour' in 1981. More recently, two very good magnums at a Latour tasting I conducted for my German publisher, Hallwag, and the Zurich wine merchants, Reichmuth, at one of my favourite hotels, the Baur au Lac. Both magnums still surprisingly deep and healthy. No holding back, the bouquet was fully formed and raring to go. A sweet, ripe, harmonious thoroughbred, which after 75 minutes in the glass, soared opulently and exotically. On the palate the sweetness of impending decay but still with ripe, rich fruit, extract, tannin and acidity, and fragrant aftertaste. *Last tasted in Zurich, Oct 1994. At best ★★★★★*

**Ch Margaux** The finest Margaux of the century. I first tasted it in 1969, its bouquet reminding me, among other things, of deep, rich Burgundy. A couple of years later, shipped by de Luze but château-bottled, noting its impressively deep colour; deep yet delicate and 'velvety' fragrance; silky, beautifully balanced: a perfect wine. Two equally perfect bottles in 1987, then a curious dried-out double magnum in Hamburg (1993), and, more recently, three virtually flawless bottles all tasted on totally different occasions and all, coincidentally, with Barton & Guestier labels, two stating clearly that they were '*reconditioned and recorked*' by B & G. The first, in January 2000, at a spectacular dinner given by Joshua Latner at the Lanesborough Hotel in London, the second at Manfred Wagner's Margaux tasting in Zurich, the last at a Rodenstock dinner at the Königshof Hotel in Munich. No point in describing each of them, they were all superb, with the same surging fragrance, Margaux at its very best; sweet, still perfectly balanced, the flavour many-layered. The loveliest of drinks. *Last tasted March 2001. All ★★★★★ except one example. It is perhaps worth noting here that the Geisel family's Königshof is superb in every way despite its plain exterior facing Munich's main square.*

### Château Margaux
*When I was lunching with Mme Teysonneau in Bordeaux in 1979, after spending Sunday morning on hands and knees in her cellar (see 1892 Ch Canon page 21), she casually remarked that she had used up all her Château Margaux 1900, some 11 dozen bottles I seem to recall, at her daughter's recent wedding. What a waste.*

**Ch Margaux Deuxième Vin** Worth mentioning because a small stock of this wine was purchased by the château, catalogued simply as Château Margaux, at an auction in Paris. The error was discovered when it was delivered. So beware. It was in fact quite good, rich, ripe, '*gibier*', velvety, with a good finish. *Lunching at the château, April 1975.*

**Ch Mouton-Rothschild** Half a dozen notes, none recently. Variable, starting with an excellent bottle in 1970 and an acetic one a few months later. A bottle from the private cellars at Lafite good though acidity creeping up. A rich though faded mouthful at Flatt's Mouton tasting and a sweet, full, fat and chewy bottle a few months later. If only Philippe de Rothschild had been around at the time. *Last tasted June 1986.* At best ★★★★

**Ch Branaire-Ducru** Holding its fruit but drying out at the end. *Sept 1992* ★★★

**Clos L'Église-Clinet** Fairly deep ruby; curious, slightly stalky nose and old spicy (cloves) flavour. A magnum. One of Rodenstock's discoveries. *Sept 1996.*

**Ch Pichon-Longueville, Lalande** First tasted in 1987. Extraordinary scent, whiff of excess volatile acidity; rich, full, lovely flavour spoiled by a hot acidic finish. Most recently a jeroboam. Original cork which broke on extraction. Fairly deep; showing its age, a citrus touch, cracking up; yet on the palate sweet, full, rich. With lovely flavour and good tannin and acidity, the last uppermost. *At the same Rodenstock tasting, Sept 1996* ★★★★

LAST TASTED IN THE MID- TO LATE 1980s **Ch Ausone** lacking excitement. *1987* ★★; **Ch Pétrus** bottled in Scotland, the vintage and name of the wine merchant in Leith partly visible: no red left; decayed yet fragrant; acidic yet clean. Spicy aftertaste. *1986* ★★; **Ch Brane-Cantenac** autumnal; sweet, soft, delicate. *1985* ★★★★; **Ch Figeac** fragrant, pomegranate; very sweet, lively, like faded rose petals. *1988* ★★★★; **Ch Gruaud-Larose** richly coloured; dry, fullish, lively. *1984* ★★★★; **Ch La Mission Haut-Brion** from a Woltner cellar, slight ullage. 'Pricked' (acidic) but flavoury. *1985* ★★; **Ch Mouton d'Armailhacq** orange rose; spoiled by mercaptan (broken-down sulphur), like old rubber tyres. *1985*; and **Ch Tertre-Daugay** a deep, plummy yet soft, mellow and delicate double magnum. *1987* ★★★

THE BEST OF EARLIER NOTES **Ch Léoville-Las-Cases** from Glamis Castle, de Luze label. Excellent level, lovely colour; fragrant, cedary; soft, lovely flavour, refined, elegant. Superb from eyes to mouth. *1971* ★★★★★; **Ch Pape-Clément** good level, colour; sound; good long flavour. *1973* ★★★★; **Ch Rausan-Ségla** variable. *1981.* At best ★★★★★

# 1901 ★

A large harvest of very uneven quality. Just one fairly old note.
**Ch Latour** Rich 'coffee beans' bouquet; dry, faded. *1981* ★★

# 1902 ★

Moderately large crop of ordinary wines.
**Ch Lafite** First noted at the Overton tasting in 1979: well preserved, exquisite bouquet and taste. Fairly light, fragrant, delicate, good acidity. At Flatt's Lafite tasting, a similar appearance, pale but ruddy; fragrant spicy but dry, light and thin. *Last tasted Oct 1988* ★★

**Ch Ausone** Several bottles, all mid- to top-shoulder and with a palish, healthy glow; fragrant, delicate but gamey bouquet; dry, light, lean, losing fruit but lovely acidity. *Aug 1987* ★★★

**Carruades de Ch Lafite** The oldest Carruades to come my way and drunk on four occasions, starting shortly after I purchased it in 1981. Recorked. Nose like mushroom stalks; dry, twisted, short but very drinkable. A touch sour in 1982, the best at a Bordeaux Club dinner in 1984: a healthy glow; herbaceous nose, faded; delicate old flavour. Edgy acidity. Most recently, unsurprisingly, showing its age. Very dry. Tart. *Last tasted Oct 1988. At best* ★★★ *(just).*

# 1903

The third dreary vintage in a row. Freezing April, sunless summer. Small crop of poor wines.
**Ch Lafite** More notable for the glass lozenge on the shoulder optimistically embossed *Grand Vin 1903 Château Lafite.* These bottles would *not* have been supplied by the château but by a *négociant* for his customers. Alas, oxidised. *Oct 1988.*
**Ch Latour** Pale and tart. *Nov 1977.*

# 1904 ★★★★

Return to good times and, by a small margin, the best vintage between 1900 and 1920. Excellent growing season, abundant crop of very good wines. A surprising number of wines tasted.
**Ch Lafite** First tasted in 1970. A poor start. Fragrant but astringent. Next, two in 1976 both oxidised. An excellent bottle in 1982 and, more recently, a good bottle at the Lloyd Flatt Lafite tasting. *Last tasted Oct 1988. At best* ★★★★

**Ch Latour** Just one note: deep and still youthful-looking; intriguing nose, sound, cedary, sweaty socks (tannin!) developing into old cigars, then, after 25 minutes, pungent, like old stables. Palate less complicated, somewhat sweet, smooth tannins, very easy to drink. *At Harry Waugh's Bordeaux Club dinner, April 1987* ★★★★

**Ch Malescot-St-Exupéry** Plummy coloured; cheesy, spicy, soft, lacking length. *At Rodenstock's Malescot tasting, Sept 1990* ★

**Ch La Mission Haut-Brion** Noted at two La Mission tastings: at Desai's in 1985, surprisingly good despite poor level. Distinctly better at Karl-Heinz Wolf's tasting: crisp, fragrant nose and taste. Very dry, light, good acidity. *Last tasted in Wiesbaden, June 1990. At best* ★★★★

---

## Harry Waugh

*He made his name and reputation in the late 1940s and 1950s as a brilliant wine buyer – and salesman – for Harvey's of Bristol. Born in 1904, he died at the age of 97 with all his faculties intact. He was the most generous and likeable of men, and a brilliant natural taster. He didn't try to describe a wine effusively. It was something that just happened: a kind of instinctive recognition. His judgement was impeccable. I edited three or four of his wine diaries, and in my own time too – it wrecked many of my summer weekends. He dictated the notes into a machine and Prue, his wife, typed them up. When I read them through, I remember at first being horrified. Everyone he met was 'charming', 'delightful', the places 'beautiful', the wines 'gorgeous'. I said: 'Harry, I can't publish all of this! Nobody will believe you, it's too good to be true!' But I now think of it as a sort of 'Queen Mum' syndrome. Harry radiated warmth and generosity and everyone responded in equal measure.*

THE BEST OF THE 1904S TASTED IN THE 1980S
**Ch Brane-Cantenac** at its old, rustic (almost) best. *At Ch Lafite, 1982* ★★; and **Ch Moulin-Riche** the second wine of Poyferré and recorked by Lalande, the owners at the time. Remarkably good. Surprisingly rich though faded, delicate, attractive. *From Mme Lawton's cellar, inherited from the Lalandes, 1982* ★★★★

THE BEST OF MY OLDER NOTES **Ch Cheval Blanc** a superb bottle, from Eduard Kressmann's private cellar (both about the same age, 73). Gentle, lovely. *1977* ★★★★; and **Ch Cantemerle** coincidentally bottled by Kressmann's: fragrant, delicate, attractive. *1976* ★★★★

## 1905 ★★★

A large crop of light, moderately elegant wines, now variable, faded but flavoury. A dozen or so notes, all made in the 1980s.
**Ch Lafite** From a Rothschild family cellar in Paris: finely graded colour, sweet, gentle stem ginger bouquet; dry, delicate, attractive flavour (in 1976). More recently, probably from the same cellar and with a similar note. *Last tasted at Flatt's Lafite tasting, Oct 1988* ★★★★
**Ch Latour** My first note, from 1981, is to demonstrate that the air in a low-shoulder bottle can sometimes be benign. Despite its too brown shading, this wine had a gentle and remarkably unscathed nose. It was faded, but what little was left was quite good to drink.

My next note is a bottle from an old-money mansion in upper New York State. There was a vast, well-stocked cellar with a range of magnificent wines, well looked after – except that when recorking the butler had filtered each wine through loose powdered asbestos. Though the wines had survived, we could not in all honesty (and to avoid future litigation) put this in a Christie's sale so, hugely disappointed, we had to leave the treasures *in situ*. The '05 Latour we tasted in the cellar was in fact quite good, though the filtration had reduced the colour and some of its pristine body. Too bad. *March 1985.*
**Ch Margaux** A superb bottle tasted in 1969: decanted 6.45pm, poured at 8.45pm and still lingering fragrantly in the glass at 10.30pm. A wine of immense charm; silky textured, acidity checked, most enjoyable. At Desai's tasting in 1987, also flavoury but more acidic. More recently, similar, 'delicately poised'. *Last noted at Lloyd Flatt's Ch Margaux tasting, Oct 1988. At best* ★★★★
**Ch Cos d'Estournel** From the château, re-corked 1983: no red left; faded and creaking. *In Miami, Jan 1990.*
**Ch Figeac** A controversial magnum. An over the top, scented taste, vanilla and raspberries, the latter could just have been from very ripe Cabernet Franc grapes. *The oldest wine in Desai's Figeac tasting in Paris, Dec 1989 rating?*

THREE OTHER WINES LAST TASTED IN THE 1980S
**Ch Mouton-Rothschild** Delicate, 'fine but lacking' in 1977. Fabulously rich colour; the smell of a wet pedigree dog, delicious. Dry, lean and, again, lacking. *At Lloyd Flatt's Mouton tasting in April 1986* ★
**Ch Brane-Cantenac** Rich, rustic, farmyard character very similar to the wine in some more recent years. Something of an acquired taste. *March 1983* ★★★★ *in its way.*
**Ch Gruaud-Larose** One from the château stringy and tart, the other marvellously fragrant, lively, refreshing. *At Heublein pre-sale tastings in 1980 and 1981* ★★★★ *(at best).*

## 1906 ★★★

The season started wet but the vines suffered from excessive heat and drought in August, reducing the yield and producing robust wines of good quality. Although I have made only one note of this vintage in the last decade, those notes made of wines either side of 80 years of age are still relevant as some of these wines are remarkable survivors.
**Ch Lafite** First tasted in 1970. Very rich nose, lovely flavour. A good looking bottle with impeccable provenance: more 'medicinal', flavoury but with a touch of tartness (1976). More recently, a palish, ruddy-amber colour; nose sweet, biscuity, evolving quickly and precariously, overripe, stably, smelly butyric acid? Yet on the palate fairly sweet, soft and flavoury. Exotic. Living dangerously, so take care. *Last noted at Flatt's tasting, Oct 1988. At best* ★★★
**Ch Margaux** The best wine of the vintage. A dozen notes, varying from oxidised to superb, starting with a rather too brown, austere bottle in 1970, then a mahogany-rimmed, most attractive wine in 1971. Another beauty, elegant though with touch of astringency (1975). In 1982, four bottles with descending levels, from the cellars of Prunier Traktir in Paris, the best, upper-shoulder; fairly deep, richly coloured; sweet, old, gorgeously perfumed bouquet; soft, gently rich and harmonious. Most recently, recorked by Whitwham's: fragrant nose, holding well; sweet and delicious in its dotage. Almost decrepit but a survivor. *Last noted at Manfred Wagner's Margaux tasting, Nov 2000. At best* ★★★★

SOME SLIGHTLY OLDER NOTES **Ch Latour** better colour and nose than taste. Acetic. *June 1981* ★; **Ch Mouton-Rothschild** recorked 1965. Lively, attractive, lovely flavour, dry finish. *April 1986* ★★★; **Ch Haut-Brion** a pale, somewhat sickly, rich but decayed (1972), and an excellent bottle from the Dillon cellar. *Dec 1979* ★★★★ *(at best)*; **Ch Ausone** despite level, fragrant and flavoury. Good wine. *June 1982* ★★★; **Ch Brane-Cantenac** from the Prunier cellar in Paris, with different levels, the high being very good, but even the mid and low-shoulder bottles surprisingly drinkable. Moral: better an ullaged bottle from a perfect cellar, undisturbed, than a high level bottle which has done the rounds. *Autumn 1982. At best* ★★★; **Ch Figeac** a rosehip colour; unassuming bouquet that rose splendidly to the occasion; dry, flavoury, a little tart (after all, we were in Paris) *1989* ★★; and **Ch Marquis de Terme** two bottles, both from the Paris cellar of Fernand Woltner, and both drunk in the same month. The first at my country house, a lovely bottle, very complete, rich, finishing well, the second creaking a bit like my host, George Rainbird (publisher and former chairman of the Wine & Food Society) at his 80th birthday dinner. *March 1985. At best* ★★★

## 1907 ★★

An abundant crop but of little interest now.

FOR THE RECORD **Ch Lafite** delicate, fragrant but marked by sourness. *Oct 1988*; **Ch Margaux** the first bottled in Vienna and with some Viennese charm (1975), and a recorked bottle, good-looking but acetic. *May 1987*; **Ch Mouton-Rothschild** two similar bottles, same provenance, bouquet trying hard. Drinking well, though lean and tame for Mouton. *April 1986*; and **Ch Haut-Brion** earthy, tobacco leaf nose. Dry, light, short. Idiosyncratic. *March 1983* ★

# 1908 ★★

An average year, though tannins have helped some of the wines to survive.

**Ch Lafite** Recorked and from a good Paris cellar. Prettily coloured; cedary, both gentle and rich but no middle. Decent finish (1976). A maderised, grubby bottle at Lloyd Flatt's tasting. *Last noted Oct 1988. At best ★★*

**Ch Latour** A superb bottle from the Comtesse de Beaumont's cellar in Brittany: 1974 saw yet another Easter holiday spent packing up a cellar with a wife and children who were beginning to complain. The wine was still tannic but delicious.

I had another excellent bottle at Marvin Overton's seminal Ch Latour tasting in 1976, and a deep, soundly based bottle with leathery tannins in 1981. Most recently, two bottles, one oxidised, the other losing colour but lively; there was a very good old thoroughbred stables nose; dry, faded yet still retaining vestiges of fruit and refreshing acidity. *Last noted at a Last Friday Club dinner at Ranji's in Memphis, Tennessee, Dec 1987. At best ★★★★*

**Ch Margaux** Three notes. Two at the Desai tasting in 1987 and, as bottles can vary, they did, one fairly sweet and attractive, the other unknit and edgy. Most recently, with Pillet-Will label, recorked in 1991: on the pale side; old, quite good cedary nose; semi-sweet, an appealing flavour and holding its own. *Last noted at Manfred Wagner's tasting in Zurich, Jan 1997. At best ★★*

**Ch Mouton-Rothschild** Two bottles with original *Bn de Miollis* labels, recorked 1980. First noted in 1985: autumnal colour; a fleetingly rich bouquet; crisp, flavoury, with a touch of acidity. Then an identical bottle at Lloyd Flatt's tasting. *Last noted Oct 1988 ★★*

**Ch Cheval Blanc** In magnums. One with mushroomy nose, the other superb, sweet singed flavour and marvellous acidity. *At the château. At best ★★★★*

**Ch Pétrus** Red-tinged; exotically fragrant yet rustic; sweet, decadently overripe opulence. *The oldest vintage at Hans-Peter Frerick's remarkable Pétrus tasting in the Margrave's Palace, Munich, April 1986 ★★★*

# 1909

Stormy August and hail badly damaged a healthy crop. The vintage was saved by late September sun. Average crop of light wines which are long past their best.

**Ch Lafite** Four notes from 1955. Faded and thin. *1969.*

**Ch Margaux** Decayed (1987), oxidised. *Nov 1990.*

**Ch Mouton-Rothschild** Recorked 1980, one not bad, the other like a smelly cheese. *April 1986.*

**Ch Haut-Brion** The best so far. Rich, idiosyncratic, cracking up but quite enjoyable. *March 1982 ★★.*

**Ch Cheval Blanc** One of the very few bad bottles from this château. Oxidised. *Sept 1997.*

**Ch Léoville-Las-Cases** Something of a novelty. A surprisingly deep-coloured wine; over the hill yet some fruit. Depraved but interesting. *A half-bottle at Michael Le Marchant's farm in Somerset, June 1995.*

TWO WINES SHOWING WELL, BEARING IN MIND THEIR AGE, IN THE MID-1970S **Ch Palmer** a charming old lady ★★★; and **Ch Léoville-Poyferré** fairly light, gentle, faded but sound ★★

# 1910

Poor weather, mildew and a late harvest.

FOR THE RECORD **Ch Lafite** decadent bouquet; lean, faded, piquant. *Oct 1988*; and **Ch Haut-Brion** reputed to be the best of the year. Only tasted once, in 1971: light, charming, forthcoming bouquet; a dryish gentle wine, faded but clinging to life ★★

# 1911 ★★★★

A small but good crop having somehow survived storms, mildew, pests, summer heat and drought.

**Ch Lafite** Remarkably attractive. A bottle recorked in 1987 at Lloyd Flatt's tasting. For its age, no faults. *Oct 1988 ★★★★*

**Ch Latour** Four old but relevant notes. Two, with the same provenance as the Margaux tasted in 1976 (see below) and both recorked, one minty with a touch of tartness, the other, four months later, with gentle, sweet, fragile old nose; lightish for Latour, fading but fragrant. Later I tasted a short, acidic Berry Bros bottling, and another with the original château cork: it was flavoury, short and with tingling acidity. *Last noted June 1981. At best ★★*

**Ch Margaux** Six notes. Another charmer though there has been some variation. First tasted in 1976, from a Rothschild cellar, recorked: flowery rim, fragrant; short, dry finish. A year later, same provenance. A fine, deep colour for its age, also fragrant and complete, though seemed more austere. Then two bottles at a tasting in 1985, one with original château capsule and Pillet-Will label, feminine and attractive, the other with a plain capsule but excellent label overprinted '1911', with a slightly mushroomy nose and touch of decay. A similar looking bottle two years later, pre-sale. Though a fraction too brown and a rich bouquet becoming a bit overblown, it was piquant and very flavoury. Most recently, a delicious bottle, still sweet, rich, with good tannin and acidity. *Last noted at the Josey pre-sale tasting in New York, Nov 1999 ★★★★*

**Ch Mouton-Rothschild** First tasted in 1972, it was light, gentle, faded but sound. In 1983 a whiff of amyl acetate spoiling an otherwise attractive wine. Four years later I tasted two really poor bottles. Oxidised. *Last tasted Sept 1987. At best ★*

**Ch Ausone** Only one note. Sweet, elegant, spicy bouquet; nicely evolved, lean and long. *At Lloyd Flatt's Ausone tasting in New Orleans, Oct 1987 ★★★*

**Ch Cheval Blanc** Small *rendement*: 12 hl/ha. Five notes, the first two, in 1976 and 1977, from a distinguished Paris cellar. Both with the original cork and both light, one meaty, malty, but with a rich and interesting texture, the other was dried out. A decade later, two Cruse-bottled magnums, both sweet and fleshy. Most recently: pale, very little red; delicate, fragile old bouquet and flavour. *Faisandé. Last noted the second oldest of 50 vintages of Cheval Blanc at Karl-Heinz Wolf's tasting overlooking the Attersee in Austria, Sept 1997. At best ★★★*

OTHER 1911S LAST TASTED IN THE 1980S **Ch Gruaud-Larose** two totally oxidised bottles (1976). Later: fragrant but faded. *1983 ★★*; **Ch Léoville-Poyferré** sweet, fragrant, light and mild. *1983 ★★*; **Ch La Mission Haut-Brion** variable, some elegance and crisp. *1987. At best ★★★*; and **Ch Rausan-Ségla** fragrant and arboreal. *1977.* More recently: autumnal colour; fabulous bouquet, glorious flavour and length. *1985. At best ★★★★*

**THE BEST OF THE OLDER NOTES Ch Cos d'Estournel** delicate; attractive flavour and enough richness to mark its piquant acidity. *1976* ★★; **Ch Figeac** from the château: spicy, scented, silky texture. *1979* ★★★

## 1912 ★★

Not the easiest of vintages from the growers' point of view, but few are. Unsettled weather: heat in May and a cold wet August made up for by a fine warm September. An abundant crop of light wines.

**Ch Lafite** Though all recorked and with good provenance, as variable in condition as the growing conditions. The first three, all from Baron Alain de Rothschild's cellar in Paris. I recall my initial visit in December 1969. In my ignorance I telephoned to ask the number in the street. The reply was to ring at the big, black door on the left. The house and garden occupied the whole of one side of the street! Of the three, the palest, with little red left was dried out, the other two, tasted in the early 1970s, were fragrant though fading. Delicious to drink. Two very good bottles, one recorked in 1957, gentle, cedary; the other with fabulous bouquet, minty (eucalyptus), gingery. Lovely (1971). Another, from the château, floral and flavoury. *The last at Flatt's tasting, Oct 1988. At best* ★★★★

**Ch Latour** Just one note. Bouquet surprisingly like the Lafite. A flavoury but faded old lady. *June 1981* ★★★

**Ch Margaux** Recorked 1990. Pillet-Will label. Sweet and sour. Not bad for its age. *At Wagner's tasting, Jan 1997* ★★

**TWO WINES AT LLOYD FLATT'S TASTINGS Ch Mouton-Rothschild** alas: acetic. *April 1986*; and **Ch Ausone** glowing amber; trying hard – appealing but, not surprisingly, long past its best. *Oct 1987.*

## 1913

One of the worst vintages. A disaster because of pests and miserable weather.

**Ch Margaux** Original château capsule and Pillet-Will label. Smelled of seashells and old ivy though it improved with air. Acidic. Could have been worse. *At Wagner's tasting, Jan 1997.*

**A DODGY LINE UP Ch Lafite** poor bottle, but even if recorked I doubt if it would have been much good; **Ch Latour** two, both from the château, recorked. Fragrant (1977); sweet and spicy. *1981* ★★; **Ch Ausone** freshly picked mushrooms, lean, losing fruit but flavoury. *1984* ★

## 1914 ★★★

August was hot; on the 14th war was declared. The first crop of the war was small but of good quality.

**Ch Lafite** Two very consistent notes in the mid-1970s: prettily coloured; delicate, fragrant, cedar-like nose and flavour. Dry. Lacking length. More recently maderised, short. *Last noted at Flatt's Lafite tasting, Oct 1988. At best* ★★

**Ch Margaux** Healthy colour; its first whiff was reminiscent of a Spanish loo but the bottle stink cleared after three minutes, opening up attractively; fairly sweet, surprisingly good though one of my congregation of faded old ladies. *At Manfred Wagner's tasting in Zurich, Nov 2000* ★★★ *(just).*

**Ch La Mission Haut-Brion** Showing well at two La Mission tastings, Desai's in 1985 and, more recently: almost

creamy fragrance; sweet, attractive. *Last noted at Karl-Heinz Wolf's tasting in Wiesbaden, June 1990* ★★★

**OTHER NOTES BOTH LAST TASTED AT LLOYD FLATT'S TASTINGS Ch Mouton-Rothschild** a decayed fragrance, dried out. This one joins my 'arsenic and old lace' collection. *April 1986* ★; **Ch Ausone** a fragrant charmer. Clearly a good period for the château. *Oct 1987* ★★★

**ONE OLDER NOTE Ch Gruaud-Larose** London-bottled, lovely colour, sound nose and flavour. Despite touch of end acidity, very drinkable. *July 1980* ★★★

## 1915

Every conceivable problem: rain, humidity, mildew. Shortage of labour and materials caused some vineyards to be abandoned.

## 1916 ★★

Wet spring, warm August and fine weather for harvest. Hard, tannic, long-lasting but charmless wines. Only two wines tasted in the last decade, several in the 1980s and noted only briefly.

**Ch Cantemerle** Four notes, all from the cellars of Mme Binaud, an old friend, whose family had been the proprietors. The oldest of a dozen vintages from her cellar in Bordeaux, tasted *in situ* and at her country house (1983) and much later selecting for sale. Those showing well, lovely flavour and texture, delicate, attractive, one horribly oxidised. *Last noted at the pre-sale tasting, April 1996.*

**Ch La Mission Haut-Brion** Fragrant, powerful (at the château in 1978); leathery (1985); fragrant, fully evolved, rich – like Castrol XL motor oil; rich, gnarled cedar and of characteristic tobacco taste. *Last tasted June 1990* ★★

**Ch Siran** Pale; smelly; rich but tart. *Last noted at the pre-sale tasting, Sept 1993* ★

**LAST NOTED IN THE 1980s Ch Lafite** (Woltner cellar) rich, overripe, good fruit, tannic. *Oct 1998* ★; **Ch Latour** first tasted 1974, drying out, leathery; at the château, initial sourness cleared but stalky and short (1975); a recorked bottle very flavoury; very tannic (1977); holding in 1981; sound but so-so. *Last tasted April 1987* ★; **Ch Mouton-Rothschild** lean, scrawny, dried out. *April 1986*; **Ch Ausone** excellent for age. *Oct 1987* ★★★; and **Ch Léoville-Poyferré** astringent (1970); then rich and delicious. *Last tasted Oct 1981* ★★★ *(at best).*

**JUST ONE CURIOSITY WORTH MENTIONING**
**Ch La Lagune** Bottled by Moll & Moll which I unearthed, almost literally, in 1967, at Castlemilk in Scotland, once famed for its great cellar of wines. Seven fairly consistent notes, *in situ* and subsequently, pre-sale and lastly at a dinner party. Holding well but my guests didn't like it. I used to think that any of this wine appearing at auction or in collectors' cellars must have been from Castlemilk. It had a very distinctive pictorial label, London-bottling; but I was confounded by a rich, roasted, austere château-bottling tasted in 1973. *At best* ★★

## 1917 ★★

Good weather conditions, early harvest picked with a workforce consisting mainly of women, children and very old men. Charming wines, now fatigued and risky.

**Ch Latour** First tasted in 1973 at Joseph Berkmann's first-in-the-field 'dinner tasting' (we each had four ranks of four glasses in front of us – and food. But it worked): deep, youthful appearance (Joseph at that time, and the 1917); nose like old parchment but rich on the palate. Seven subsequent notes including a soft Berry Bros bottling. Most recently, tasted blind at lunch at Lafite: nose gamey, rich, attractive; touch of sweetness, nice weight, delicious flavour. *Last tasted Sept 1998. At best* ★★★

OTHER '17S LAST TASTED IN THE 1980S **Ch Lafite** variable. *Oct 1988. At best* ★★★; **Ch Margaux** attractive, nice fruit. *Two bottles May 1987* ★★★; and **Ch Pétrus** pungent, overripe, sharp. *April 1986.*

OLDER NOTES **Ch Léoville-Barton** over half a century old, silky, firm, good length. *1969* ★★★★; **Ch Gruaud-Larose** rich, ripe but tart finish. *1976–77* ★★; and **Ch Durfort-Vivens** two notes, variable. *Both in 1978. At best* ★★

# 1918 ★★★

A good summer with ripe grapes harvested, still with labour shortages, just before Armistice.

**Ch Latour** First tasted in 1974, a bottle from the de Beaumont cellar, alas, sour and stringy, yet, a couple of years later, an excellent, deep, perfectly balanced bottle from the same cellar. Next, an oxidised magnum, then a raw austere bottle. More recently, four all with good levels: lean, pinched, *gibier* nose and taste. Piquancy elevating its fragrance but drying out. *Last noted at the Hallwag and Reichmuth Latour tasting at the Baur au Lac, Zurich, Oct 1994* ★★

**Ch Mouton-Rothschild** Two recorked bottles at the Flatt tasting. One drab, the other with overripe sweetness on the nose but drying out (1988). Most recently, recorked in 1985: soft ruby; fragrant; showing its age but drinking well. *Last tasted Dec 2000. At best* ★★★

**Ch La Mission Haut-Brion** Light, peppery, thinning out (at the château in 1978); flavoury, short (1985). Most recently, a corky acidic bottle. Which just serves to remind us that when tasting old wines, one is tasting individual bottles. Provenance and condition are vital. *Last noted June 1990. At best* ★★

**Ch Siran** Very sweet, flavoury, good for its age. *At the pre-sale tasting at Christie's, Oct 1983* ★★

OTHER '18S TASTED IN THE 1980S **Ch Lafite** first tasted in 1969 'dried out … passé'. Variable notes through the 1970s, from two oxidised to two old, rich, fragrant, crisp and holding well. A recorked bottle similarly described at the Flatt tasting. *Last noted Oct 1988. At best* ★★★; **Ch Margaux Grand Vin** deep; rich, attractive. *May 1989*; **Ch Margaux 2ème Vin** aged but fragrant, holding well (1973), lean, pine-flavoured. *May 1987*; **Ch Ausone** a recorked magnum from the always

dependable Nicolas cellar, Paris. Richly coloured; glorious bouquet; excellent despite teeth-gripping astringency. A good period for Ausone. *Oct 1982* ★★★★; **Ch Calon-Ségur** faded but passable. *June 1987* ★; and **Ch Léoville-Poyferré** producing exceptionally good wines, weather permitting throughout the teens and twenties. A silky, perfect bottle from Jean Calvet's cellar in Bordeaux (1974). Then another sound and flavoury bottle. *Oct 1981* ★★★★

1918S SHOWING WELL IN THEIR FIFTIES **Ch Certan 'Mme Demay'** ★★; **Ch Gruaud-Larose** ★★★★; and **Ch Haut-Bailly** ★★

# 1919 ★★★

Not an easy year for the growers. Good flowering conditions boded well for the vintage, but this was dashed by a damp humid July which fostered mildew, including the more serious 'powdery mildew' (oidium) followed by scorching heat in August. Those who could cope with the hot grapes made good wines, others suffered from excess volatile acidity on the threshold of vinegar.

**Ch Lafite** An abundance of good wines thanks to the efficient control of fermentation temperature. First tasted in 1976: flavoury, dry; and a fragrant, spicy, stylish wine at Flatt's tasting. *Last noted Oct 1988* ★★★

**Ch Haut-Brion** Four variable notes in the 1970s. A delicious bottle at a Heublein pre-sale tasting in 1980: full flavoured, fruity, tolerable acidity. 'A very good 1919.' More recently, the colour of a deep walnut, tawny-green at the rim; a touch of iron, almost rusty, then a clover-like spicy bouquet that was retained until the end of the meal; very dry, full-bodied, a rich, curious medicinal flavour – these were notes when tasting blind. My first reaction had been Graves, without Haut-Brion elegance. *Last tasted lunching at Berry Bros, Sept 1993* ★★★

**Ch La Mission Haut-Brion** Five notes, variable from oxidised to rich, ripe, *faisandé*. Sweet, yet some bitterness and noticeable acidity. *Last tasted Oct 1992. At best* ★★

**Ch Gruaud-Larose** A magnum at the château in 1976, its bouquet redolent of damp leaves; rich yet still tannic, twist of acidity, good aftertaste. Three more magnums: all with good colour; bouquet with sweetness of decay; drying out. *Last noted Sept 1993. At best* ★★

**Ch Siran** Very sweet, flavoury, attractive. *At a pre-sale tasting, Oct 1993* ★★★

1919S LAST TASTED IN THE LATE 1970S TO EARLY 1980S **Ch Latour** three notes, of different provenance, 1971–1976. Some decomposition and astringency, but surviving, just. Pale and pretty, light yet rich. *Last noted Jan 1981. At best* ★★; and **Ch Margaux** mid-low shoulder, palish yet lively looking; decaying but fragrant; the sweetness of well hung game – and still a good drink! *Dec 1980* ★★

# 1920–1929

The two most successful decades ever for red Bordeaux, certainly in the 20th century, were the 1920s and 1980s, for though each one had slightly fewer great vintages than in the 'pre-phylloxera' period, the best vintages then were spread over four decades.

The 1920s tend to be associated with 'flappers', cocktails and general fun and games – and industrial unrest. Wine continued to be the prerogative of the prosperous upper classes. What they drank was limited strictly to the well tried and familiar European classics (America was in the throes of Prohibition). They were well served by Bordeaux, not just for the plethora of splendid vintages but, despite some hotting up in the late 1920s, prices, even for the best, were well within reach. There was a cosy relationship between the *négociant*, his importing agent, the 'shipper', and the myriad family wine merchants – somewhat at the expense of the producers.

The decade ended on a high note, winewise, with the renowned – but unalike – twin vintages, 1928 and 1929. They exemplify what is so endlessly fascinating about Bordeaux: that wine from the same vineyard, same grape varieties, made in the same way, in the same *chai*, can be so different in style from year to year and, thanks to Bordeaux's maritime climate, the infinitely variable weather conditions during the growing and ripening season.

## Vintages at a Glance
**Outstanding ★★★★★**
1920, 1926, 1928, 1929
**Very Good ★★★★**
1921
**Good ★★★**
1924

## 1920 ★★★★★

A great start to one of the best-ever decades in the history of Bordeaux. But it nearly didn't happen, as rot-inducing weather during an exceptionally cold July and August caused problems and a reduction of crop. Saved by a sunny September. Small production, high quality.

**Ch Lafite** In 1967 described by my mentor, Harry Waugh, as 'probably the most perfect claret now' (and he was a director of Ch Latour!). First noted at the Overton tasting in 1979: a warm and lovely odour; gentle, fragrant flavour. Nine years later, a nose initially like mushroom soup but emerging valiantly, fragrantly, but with a touch of maltiness. Better on the palate: elegant, stylish, good length but not quite right. *Last noted Oct 1988. At best ★★★★★*

**Ch Latour** Amusingly, Harry Waugh, a year earlier (1966) said that it 'surpasses Lafite', and Eduard Cruse proclaimed it 'the best of all first growths'. My own first note was made in 1970: 'soft, velvety, with Mouton-like Cabernet scent; opulent wine at its peak'. Two more excellent notes in the mid-1970s but only one since then, a superb 6-star bottle at Kerry Payne's tasting: very sweet, marvellous depth, length and aftertaste. *Alas, not tasted since June 1981 ★★★★★*

**Ch Margaux** A fairly monumental Margaux, anything but feminine and fluttery. Only two notes: rich, holding well; huge, severe, very dry finish – but good (1971). Next, a recorked magnum: complete; delicate and 'mildly opulent' bouquet. Good length, austere, dry finish again noted. *Last tasted Oct 1988. At best ★★★*

**Ch Mouton-Rothschild** Very rich, spicy, magnificent bouquet in 1972, just showing a trace of age. A dry, medium-light, well balanced and lovely wine. Alas, only one more note:

colour of faded brick; an explosion of scents, gingery, tangy, tea, and an amalgam of flavours; soft, rich, oaky, perfect balance and length. *One of the top wines at Lloyd Flatt's Mouton tasting in New Orleans, April 1986 ★★★★★*

**Ch Haut-Brion** 'Héritiers Larrieu' on the label. Orange-tinged; old vanilla – for André Simon it evoked 'the magnificence of the purple beech'; fullish, supple but a touch of malt. *April 1987 ★★*

**Ch Cheval Blanc** Great, but wait until we get to the 1921! First, in 1978, spoilt by its low level. Good, but a whiff of volatile acidity in 1984. Then a superb magnum: with gloriously evolved bouquet and flavour. Very sweet, full-bodied, fragrant (at the château in 1986). Most recently: impressive colour; initial whiff of freshly picked mushrooms; distinctly sweet, a characteristic of Cheval Blanc in the 1920s, good body, flavour much better than nose. *Last noted at Karl-Heinz Wolf's tasting overlooking the Attersee in Austria, Sept 1997. At best ★★★★★*

**Ch La Mission Haut-Brion** Roasted and rich (1978). Bottles of different provenance in 1985, one a charmer, the other, though browner, extraordinarily fragrant. More recently a double magnum: lovely, gamey; citrus touch; 'creaking and crumbly' but still delicious. *At another of Karl-Heinz Wolf's tastings, this time in Wiesbaden, June 1990. At best ★★★★*

**Ch Cantemerle** Warm red brown; nose conjuring up old oak (tree not cask); sweet, lightish, very attractive flavour but touch of sourness on finish. *From the Binaud cellar, Oct 1955 ★★★*

**Ch Olivier** Danish-bottled (Schalburg). Several notes, all from Baron Raben's well-filled, well-preserved, cool, dry cellar at Aalholm Castle. Slightly variable, two described as 'faded old ladies, sweet in the middle, but with wrinkles'. Mainly fragrant and charming, some a bit acidic. Interesting to see the Olivier labels depicting the beautiful turreted château in which the Black Prince was born in 1330. *Last tasted May 1992.*

SOME OTHER 1920S SHOWING PRETTY WELL WHEN LAST TASTED IN THE 1980S **Ch Brane-Cantenac** first tasted in 1976: very good for its age. Then again, when a sexagenarian. *Oct 1986 ★★★*; **Ch Gruaud-Larose** good in 1976. Rich, flavoury but starting to crack up. *March 1983 ★★*; **Ch Palmer** rich, fine (1973). Later more overripe, very sweet and burgundy-like. *Oct 1984* ★★★; and **Ch Pichon-Lalande** medium pale, soft garnet red; lovely, rich, delicate, old cedar bouquet; flavoury, refreshing. *On two occasions in 1980* ★★★★

AND SOME OF THOSE TASTED ONLY IN THE 1970S **Ch Branaire-Ducru-Sarget** (*sic*) ★★; **Ch Certan** ★★; **Ch Durfort-Vivens** ★★★; **Ch Léoville-Las-Cases** Belgian-bottled ★★; **Ch Léoville-Poyferré** ★★★; **Ch Petit-Village** ★★★; **Ch Phélan-Ségur** ★★★; **Ch Rauzan-Gassies** ★★★; and **Ch Rausan-Ségla** ★★

## 1921 ★★★★

The hottest summer and earliest harvest since 1893, with attendant problems: singed grapes, overheated vats. But some magnificent wines, laden with alcohol, extract, tannins.

Breaking the pattern, I propose to start with an unprecedented tasting of 1921s at Hardy Rodenstock's wine weekend, September 1995. All the wines, in magnums, were tasted blind and the following is a summary of my notes made before the names of the wines were revealed. In order of serving, starting with a sound, quite attractive *bourgeois* Médoc, **Ch Parempuyre**; next an oxidised **Ch Montrose**; and a charming, lovely **Ch Gruaud-Larose**. Then the main 'flight', also blind, also in magnums: **Ch Lafite** recorked. Old nose which, typically, blossomed in the glass; good but somewhat astringent – went better with the food; **Ch Margaux** my second highest mark: earthy, fragrant bouquet; sweet, complete, lovely flavour, weight and length; **Ch Haut-Brion** a bit too brown and a touch of oxidation – but had I known I would have made allowances for the idiosyncratic Graves nose, for on the palate it was much more recognisable with its earthy, tobacco taste. Good length. It improved on acquaintance; **Ch Latour** deep; scented, touch of resin; strangely sweet, very flavoury but uncharacteristic. Good mark though; **Ch Mouton-Rothschild** similar nose (to Latour) but minty, eucalyptus; spicy flavour reminding me of a Heitz Martha's Vineyard. Astringent; **Ch Cheval Blanc** very deep, opaque core; old, oaky, leathery nose; full-bodied, powerful, excellent tannins, a touch of astringency. High mark; **Ch Pétrus** almost opaque, browner rim than Cheval Blanc; its initial restrained oaky, tannic nose opened up fabulously; very sweet, very rich, lovely flavour from entry to end. My highest mark; **Ch Ausone** a characteristic Ausone nose, rather Graves-like, always reminds me of brown paper and old tea; nice weight but raw; and **Ch L'Église-Clinet** deep, rich; low-keyed then opened up beautifully; nice weight, good flavour, dry finish and that elusive element, charm. High mark.

BRIEFER NOTES, IN THE USUAL ORDER, FIRST GROWTHS FIRST **Ch Lafite** Only one note prior to 1990. Sweet, assertive, leathery tannins. *At Flatt's tasting, Oct 1988* ★★
**Ch Latour** Poor bottles in 1976 and 1986. Extremely good (at Payne's tasting in 1981); showing age but good fruit; very sweet, touch of decay yet attractive. *Sept 1994. At best* ★★★★★
**Ch Margaux** Touch of death, cracking up (1970); almost Pétrus-like thickness of fruit; a sweet, rich, hot, singed character; great length and finesse (magnum in 1987). Most recently, recorked 1988, sweet, full, delicious. *Last noted at Wagner's tasting, Jan 1997. At best* ★★★★★
**Ch Mouton-Rothschild** Several notes, no duds, starting with two in 1972; rich, lovely; strapping, tannin-laden wines. Three more good notes in the mid-1980s. Most recently a

jeroboam: ripe nose like well-hung pheasant; sweet, gamey, flavoury too, full, rich, soft yet firm finish. Deteriorated after 20 minutes. *Last tasted at the château, Baroness Philippine rising to the occasion, as always, at a dinner with my rich and distinguished friends, the Palumbos, Mark Birley, the Lloyd-Webbers, Olga and Dieter Bock and some lovely ladies, Sept 1998* ★★★★★
**Ch Haut-Brion** First noted, gentle, sound (in 1974). A very good bottle from the Dillon cellar: fragrant, delicate bouquet, sweet, good texture, elegant; complete (1974). Showing its age but rich (Dec 1992). (See also 1995 tasting above.) *At best* ★★★★
**Ch Ausone** Two very good earlier notes: full-bodied, rich, beefy, excellent. *Oct 1988* ★★★★
**Ch Cantemerle** First tasted in 1971: a fruity old man, faded, acidic. More recently: tawny red; sweet, 'warm', bouquet of caramel and truffles, then singed violets (well, that is what I wrote at the time). Good flavour. Dry finish. *From Mme Binaud's cellar, Oct 1995* ★★★
**Ch Cheval Blanc** Unquestionably the 'star' of the vintage and which made its reputation. No early notes but five totally consistent notes in the mid-1980s. Perfection. *And see the tasting in 1995 below* ★★★★★
**Ch Cheval Blanc** Belgian-bottled by Vandermeulen. Alas: 'oxo'dised, rich bananas. Pity. The other Vandermeulens were better. *The oldest claret at Frans de Cock's spectacular wine weekend in Paris, Dec 1995.*
**Ch Latour-à-Pomerol** Labelled modestly *Grand Vin* and *Premier Grand Cru*. Immensely deep; far too sweet, thick, rich and chewy. As so often with Pomerols, impressive but lacking finesse. *In Munich, March 2001* ★★
**Ch Pétrus** In addition to the magnum in 1995, two bottles in the 1980s, one concentrated sweetness, beautiful flavour, the other more subdued and with higher acidity ★★★★★
**Ch La Mission Haut-Brion** Incredibly rich, roasted, toasted bouquet; excellent (1978) and later, two magnums, the first browning at rim; rich, soft, chewy (1985). More recently: fragrant, tangy, singed; sweet, lovely, very rich flavour, good length. *Last noted June 1990* ★★★★
**Ch Siran** Deep; rich, malty; good length, still tannic. *At a pre-sale tasting, Oct 1993* ★★

THE BEST OF MY OLDER NOTES, ALL THE WINES AROUND HALF A CENTURY OLD **Ch La Lagune** very attractive ★★★; **Ch Léoville-Las-Cases** sound ★★; **Ch Léoville-Poyferré** untypically baked and earthy ★★★; **Ch Marquis de Terme** rich ★★★; **Ch Palmer** overripe ★; **Ch Pichon-Lalande** at its best charming ★★★; and **Ch Rauzan-Gassies** very good, holding well ★★★

## 1922 ★

Good spring and early summer but spoiled by cold wet September. Huge crop but variable. Late pickers did best. Not worth seeking. Only one recent note.
**Ch Siran** Dry, fragile, flavoury. *Pre-sale Oct 1993* ★★

LAST TASTED IN THE 1980S **Ch Lafite** a faded old lady with a sharp tongue (1984), and an oxidised bottle (1988); **Ch Latour** ranging from oxidised to surprisingly nice (1975 and 1977). Doubtless late picked, and the best of the year. Fragrant, flavoury. *Last tasted 1981. At best* ★★★; **Ch Pétrus** two magnums, Bordeaux-bottled, with Kressmann capsules. One chocolatey, the other like strawberry jelly, and acidic. *Sept 1987*; and **Ch Beychevelle** a dismal half bottle. *Jan 1989.*

# 1923 ★★

Another late harvest. Moderate quality.

**Ch Lafite** The first, bottled by Barton & Guestier: mature tawny; good flavour but becoming tart. A strange, unprepossessing looking bottle at the Flatt tasting which turned out to be surprisingly attractive (1988). Most recently, original capsule, level upper-shoulder: a palish orange colour; old, smoky nose; dry, light, 'cheesy'. *Last noted at a pre-sale tasting in New York, Dec 1997. At best* ★★

**Ch Latour** Almost as deep as the 1926; strange, old chocolate; sweet, rich enough but short dry finish (1973); a virtually opaque magnum showing its age, more mushrooms than fruit; better on palate. Rich. Chunky. *Not tasted since June 1981. At best* ★★

**Ch Latour** Belgian-bottled, Vandermeurlen. Much better preserved than the château bottling. Surprisingly sound. Delicate (for Latour) with light fruit on nose; attractive flavour, lightish, refreshing acidity. *At de Cock's tasting, Paris, Dec 1995* ★★

OTHER PASSABLE OR AT LEAST FAIRLY INTERESTING 1923S LAST NOTED IN THE 1980S **Ch Margaux** a delicious and charming wine. First tasted, a magnum, in 1960: aromatic; light, sweet, velvety. A decade later, a finely graded colour leading to a rich mahogany rim; bouquet of raspberry and cedar; rich, silky, but faded. More recently, probably recorked: lovely; sound; lightish, short. *Last tasted Oct 1988. At best* ★★★; **Ch Haut-Brion** an almost deathly double magnum in 1969 rising from the grave supported by its richness, extract. A sickly bottle in 1976. And a too-sweet, gamey bottle; delicate, flavoury but tart. *Last noted in Florida, May 1981. At best* ★★; **Ch Cheval Blanc** pale; fragrant, old, but not decayed. Firm and sound. *At the château, Sept 1986* ★★; **Grand Cru des Carruades, Près Château Lafite** on the label *Ginifers, Proprieteur* and diagonally, in red, *Mise Bouteille authentique*, a rare curiosity. I had bought several half bottles catalogued as Carruades de Château Lafite. I assume this was a presumptuous look-alike. Not very good either. *At lunch, Chippenham Lodge, April 1992* ★★ *(for cheek)*; **Ch Larose** (sic) probably St-Émilion. One of a large stock competently bottled in the cellars at Aalholm Castle in Denmark: lovely, lively; sweet, light, soft, pleasing. *At pre-sale tasting, Nov 1989* ★★★; **Ch Pétrus** Bordeaux-bottled labelled *1er grand cru F. Laport fils Négociant*. Surprisingly fragrant and unusually elegant despite its overripeness. Tinny edge. Dry finish. *April 1986* ★★; and **Ch Siran** neutral nose; soft, quite attractive. *Oct 1993* ★★

# 1924 ★★★

An abundant crop of attractive wines despite the poor spring and wet summer. Saved (as in 1978) by a flawless September. 'Divinely decadent; advancing age but opulent charms' to quote me, not Parker. I have an astonishing number of notes, just short of one hundred, many dating from the 1970s, partly due to the number coming on to the market. I see from a Christie's catalogue of 1973 that we listed a range of 21 '24s from one French cellar, including all the first growths.

**Ch Lafite** When it is at its best, one of my favourite old vintages of Lafite, with all the lightness of spirit, charm and elegance of, say, a 1953. A bad start, however, with two poor bottles, with Lafite capsules and Cruse slip labels, in 1971 and 1977. Then a tawny coloured, 'arboreal', attractive bottle in 1979, and a super 6-star bottle from the Dillon family's cellar

in New Jersey. This, I decided, was Lafite at its most exquisitely delicate best. Sheer perfection. Next, fragrant and delicious in 1986 despite crumbly cork; a magnum in 1988, faded but gently fruity; and later that autumn yet another lovely bottle. Most recently, an austere *Marie-Jeanne* and three bottles brought by Eric de Rothschild to a luncheon at Christie's in Paris to celebrate the publication of the French edition of my *Great Vintage Wine Book*, one attractive, ethereal, light; the second seemed drier; the third warranting my 'arsenic and old lace' description, but better on the palate; soft, very easy to quaff. *Last noted Nov 1993. At best* ★★★★★

**Ch Margaux** Another charmer. First a soft, ripe, long flavoured bottle with the Ginestets at the château in 1975. A fully evolved, delectable bottle at the Desai tasting. Next, dining at Dom de Chevalier, a fascinatingly curious magnum decanted at 7pm, served at 10.30pm. It had been recorked in 1978, labelled '*1924*', but the cork was branded 1920! Deeply impressive colour; a rather singed, *faisandé* bouquet and flavour – the sweetness of decay but dry finish. Full-bodied, still fruity. On balance, looking back, this might well have been Margaux 1920. More recently, and more reliably because of its original cork, a deeply disappointing bottle due to some ullage and doubtless poor storage. *Last noted at Wagner's tasting, Jan 1997. At best* ★★★★★

**Ch Latour** An excellent, rich, tannic bottle recorked in 1968 at Overton's first growths tasting in 1976. Two, variable, at Heublein tastings. The following year: a lovely but near its end bottle in 1980. Showing well in 1981; an oxidised magnum in 1996. Most recently, recorked in 1966 and drinking well: an amazingly deep colour; excellent, spicy, cedar nose, with a touch of eucalyptus, then, as the air got to work, like ground coffee. Good fruit and flavour, though drying out a bit. *Last tasted, coping well with 'Abergavenny Rarebit' at the 50th anniversary dinner of the Bordeaux Club, at Christie's, Feb 1999. At best* ★★★★★

**Ch Mouton-Rothschild** Philippe de Rothschild was just 20 years old when in 1920 he took in hand the administration of Mouton. By 1924 he was finally in the saddle and this vintage displays all of his brilliance and excitement. Two superlative notes; first a jeroboam at Rodenstock's in 1985, the second at Flatt's Mouton vertical the following year: lovely colour; delicate, harmonious bouquet that blossomed in the glass; luxuriant flavour, great length and finish. A lovely wine. (It was

## Baron Philippe de Rothschild

*The staid and conservative Bordelais were shaken out of their lethargy by a presumptuous playboy, Philippe de Rothschild, who, in 1922, aged 20, had been put in charge of the somewhat neglected family estate, Ch Mouton, which had been purchased by the English branch of the Rothschilds in 1853. The first thing to alarm the establishment was his decision, right from the word go, to bottle his own wine exclusively at the château – not many of the grands crus were doing this. The second was to commission an artist friend, Carlu, to design a most untraditional art deco label for his first successful vintage, 1924. (Shades of things to come.) This had Bordeaux in shock. Mouton had long been neglected, to the extent that at the time of the 1855 Classification it was not considered good enough to become a premier cru classé. Clearly this rankled, as right from the start Baron Philippe worked assiduously to improve and promote the wine until, at last, in 1973, Ch Mouton-Rothschild achieved first growth status. He was a brilliant, charming and innovative man.*

a double magnum of this wine that Peter Morrell, a New York wine merchant, paid the then 'huge' price of £230 at Christie's in 1973. He flew to London overnight, attended the auction and returned that afternoon to a blaze of publicity.) *Last tasted March 1986* ★★★★★

**Ch Mouton-Rothschild** Belgian-bottled by Vandermeurlen. Fragrant, tea-like, a bit metallic, with peppery fruit. Very 'medicinal' Pauillac. Rich, crisp, good flavour, touch of tartness. *In Paris, Dec 1995* ★★★

**Ch Cheval Blanc** Just one note: pale, healthy glow; scented old *gibier* bouquet that opened up sweetly. Smoky taste, attractive in its decadent way. *At Karl-Heinz Wolf's tasting in Austria, Sept 1997* ★★★

**Ch Batailley** A dependable wine even at 70 years of age. Dry, fragrant, nice weight and bite, refreshing acidity. *Bordeaux Club at Hugh Johnson's, Saling Hall in Essex, July 1995* ★★★

**Ch Branaire-Duluc-Ducru** Flavoury but short. *Oct 1992* ★★

**Ch Dauzac** A faded but charming old lady. *Sept 1990* ★★★

**Ch Ducru-Beaucaillou** Variable, austere and astringent when first tasted in 1967. Then a surprisingly lovely half-bottle. More recently a jeroboam: deep; scent of oysters; dry, mushroom taste. *Last tasted Sept 1993. At best* ★★

**Ch Gruaud-Larose** Jeroboams: overripe, exotic in 1990. Another more recently, decayed, dried out. *Last noted at Rodenstock's mammoth Gruaud tasting, Sept 1993.*

**Ch Larose** Like the 1923, bottled at Aalholm and first noted at lunch in August 1987 with Baron Raben-Levetzau to discuss the sale of his wines. Several notes since, including bottles I bought at the subsequent auction. All really pretty good. *Last noted at a vinous Sunday lunch, Aug 1994* ★★★

**Ch Palmer** Several notes in the mid-1970s, including an *impériale* which I described as 'like a sexy *demi-mondaine* of uncertain age but opulent charm'. More recently: more of a sour-natured old man, better on nose than palate – yet a certain tattered elegance. *Last tasted Sept 1994. At best* ★★★

SOME OTHER 1924S LAST TASTED IN THE 1980S
**Clos Fourtet** slightly variable. Overripe acidity mollified by food. *Dining with Peter Wallenberg after checking his cellar at Drottningholm, March 1987* ★★; **Ch Léoville-Las-Cases** an astringent but flavoury *impériale* in 1962; a magnum recorked by Whitwham's after it had been opened by Customs and Excise! It had survived: beautiful bouquet; lovely, deft, flavoury. *Last noted May 1980. At best* ★★★; **Ch La Mission Haut-Brion** variable. Beautiful bottle from the Woltner cellars (1978); screwed up at Desai's tasting (1985). A 'dumb and dusty' magnum and a more impressive double magnum with good fruit but a bit woody. *The last two at Karl-Heinz Wolf's La Mission tasting and dinner, June 1990. At best* ★★; **Ch Nenin**

---

### Château-bottling

*A procedure adopted as recently as the mid-20th century, bottling having virtually all been in the hands of négociants and merchants. It was Baron Philippe de Rothschild, in the early 1920s, who decided that enough was enough. In the wake of phylloxera, the resultant dramatic wine shortages meant the temptation to blend and 'stretch' a wine once away from the eyes of the growers was too great an attraction for less scrupulous merchants. The young Baron successfully persuaded the Bordeaux first growths that bottling their wine at origin would guarantee authenticity and quality. Other châteaux followed quickly after them.*

variable. At best silky and firm. *May 1989* ★★★; and **Ch Tertre-Daugay** rich, but drink before it fades away. *March 1983* ★★

SELECTED 1924S SHOWING WELL IN THE 1970S
**Ch Chasse-Spleen** a piquant charmer ★★; **Ch Desmirail** delicious ★★★; **Ch Duhart-Milon** spicy, flavoury ★★; **Ch Giscours** fading but attractive. And a very good Justerini & Brooks bottling: deep, firm, rich ★★★; **Ch Pape-Clément** a light, hard, earthy Graves ★★; **Ch Pichon-Lalande** a lingering thoroughbred. Refined. Silky ★★★★; and **Ch Rausan-Ségla** overripe, flavoury ★★

## 1925

Upstaged by the flanking '24s and '26s and, despite abundance, ignored by the Bordeaux trade. Too old now.

BRIEFLY **Ch Lafite** variable notes. A poor wine. *Last tasted Oct 1988*; **Ch Latour** late picked and, as always, managing to make a decent wine even in a poor year. *June 1981* ★; **Ch Mouton-Rothschild** variable, from drab and oxidised to a sneaking fragrance and astringency. *Last tasted April 1986*; **Ch Ausone** a quite good magnum. Chewy, chunky. *Oct 1987* ★; and **Ch Calon-Ségur** Bordeaux-bottled by Eschenauer. Surprisingly good. *Dec 1992* ★★

## 1926 ★★★★★

Great vintage. Long, hot summer, small crop of high quality wines put on the market at commensurate prices in the buoyant late 1920s (the US was in the throes of Prohibition).

**Ch Lafite** Quite distinctly a hot year wine, first tasted lunching at Berry Bros, in 1975. Opulently ripe, magnificent. Another, recorked in 1987, rich, fragrant but with a touch of astringency (1977). Alas, a disappointing, over-the-top bottle at the great Overton tasting in 1979 and not much better at Lloyd Flatt's. More recently, a couple of bottles very generously brought by Éric de Rothschild for my *Decanter* 'Man of the Year' dinner. Slight bottle variation but both delicious, fragrant, with lingering aftertaste. *Last tasted March 1993. At best* ★★★★

**Ch Latour** Half a dozen consistently admiring notes, the first made the month I joined Christie's – an empty office and no secretary, July 1966. Three excellent bottles in the 1970s, 'silky, fabulous, developed well'; perfect bottles, twice, at the château 'delicate, *à point*', 'not showing its age'. Most recently, high level; fairly deep rich ruby; faultless bouquet; eucalyptus; medium-dry, not as full-bodied as expected, spicy, really lovely. *Last tasted with Paolo Pong, Dec 2000* ★★★★★

**Ch Margaux** From mid-1970s to late 1980s, consistently good with Margaux's inimitable fragrance blossoming in the glass. Flavour to match. Rich yet delicate. *Last noted at Desai's tasting in Los Angeles, May 1987* ★★★★★

**Ch Mouton-Rothschild** Once again, consistent notes, all good, in bottle, in magnum and from a jeroboam. All very deep with an opaque core; rich, ripe, fragrant, spicy 'medicinal'. Sweet, soft, lovely, still fairly tannic. *Last, the magnum, at Flatt's Mouton tasting, April 1986* ★★★★★

**Ch Haut-Brion** In my opinion, the best Haut-Brion until we reach the 1945. Noted in different contexts and sizes, bottle, magnum and jeroboam. The most notable, indeed the ones that first impressed me, were from the Dillon family cellar at Dunwalke in New Jersey, sold at Christie's in 1979. Among their other great wines were 9 dozen magnums and

13 dozen bottles of the 1926 Haut-Brion, all in perfect condition. But Haut-Brion is first and foremost a Graves and its nose and taste are very distinctive, totally unlike its peers, the *1er cru* Médocs, save for its finesse. The bouquet is usually more earthy, sometimes gingery, tobacco-like, 'singed fern' I noted. Most recently still almost opaque; harmonious, rich nose; fairly sweet, full flavoured, powerful, verging on the '28 in style. *Last tasted at Len Evans' 'Single-bottle Club' dinner in the Hunter Valley, Australia, Sept 2000* ★★★★★

**Ch Ausone** Two bottles, slightly varying levels at Flatt's Ausone tasting. Deep, rich; at best spicy, scented; soft and fleshy for Ausone. *Last tasted Oct 1987* ★★★★

**Ch Cheval Blanc** One of the greatest wines I have ever tasted, preferred to the '21, even the '29, and, dare I say it, the '47. At any rate it was when I first tasted it in 1967, lunching at Berry Bros. Although not deep in colour, mahogany tinged, it was the most complete, the richest, certainly the sweetest and most harmonious wine imaginable. Two bottles had been decanted four hours before serving. I couldn't believe it was from Bordeaux and, rather rudely, took my glass to the window overlooking St James's Street to have a better look at the colour, to concentrate on the honeyed nose and rich taste. I thought it was a great Burgundy. More good notes in the 1970s. More recently, showing well, a magnum, delicate and fading but with finesse and great length. *Last tasted May 1987* ★★★★★ *It should still be superb.*

**Ch Pétrus** Two notes, in bottle (1986) and double magnum. Deep, rich, intense; opulent, ripe figs, mulberries, musk; sweet, hefty, spicy, still tannic. *Last tasted in 1987* ★★★★★

**Ch Cantemerle** Pale, faded but bright; curiously rich and sweaty; sweet, delicious. *From the Binaud cellar, March 1996* ★★★

**Ch Dauzac** A double magnum: velvety purple; switch-back nose and flavour, rising and falling, sweet entry, dry finish. Fragrant but short. *At Hardy Rodenstock's closing dinner, Sept 1990* ★★★ *(just).*

**Ch Ducru-Beaucaillou** Deep, fine, cedary, drying out in 1975 and one could say more or less the same about an *impériale* 21 years later. Bouquet of gnarled oak; a bit stalky, stably old flavour, fragrant, good length. *Last tasted blind in Munich, Sept 1996* ★★★

**Ch Léoville-Poyferré** An *impériale*, palish, sound, gentle bouquet; lovely weight, flavour, balance. Elegant. Poyferré reaching the end (in 1929) of a long run of beautiful vintages. *Sept 1990* ★★★★

**Ch La Mission Haut-Brion** Fabulous colour, but a bit of a dusty old man in 1973. A superb bottle, silky and elegant – not what I normally expect of the usually masculine La Mission (1978). Its change of character noted again in 1985, from the Woltner cellar which, however, soured in the glass. Most recently, same provenance (via Christie's Woltner cellar sale), a touch of cork on the nose, minty, recovered, then a scent of fresh *cèpes*. Drying out, losing weight, but a characterful and memorable magnum. *Last tasted dining at Christan Sveass', Oslo, April 1996. At best* ★★★★

**Ch La Tour Haut-Brion** I am not a fan of La Mission's younger and coarser brother. Interesting nose though, fine rich tea, then smoky and after 25 minutes reminding me of the smell of an old steam train. Rich, smoky Graves flavour, showing its age, very tannic, raw. *March 2001* ★★

SOME OTHER 1926S SHOWING QUITE WELL IN THE 1980S
**Ch Calon-Ségur** despite three poor notes in the 1970s, two good magnums: opaque; chunky; full, tannic, no decay. *May*

1981. *At best* ★★★★; **Ch Cos d'Estournel** sound, sweet, perfect flavour, balance – finish. *March 1982. At best* ★★★★★; **Ch Duhart-Milon** rich in every way. Vanilla and leather. *Nov 1983* ★★★★; **Ch Figeac** fragrant, warm, biscuity; drying out but attractive. *Dec 1989* ★★★; **Ch Olivier** Danish-bottled. Lovely. *July 1989* ★★★; and **Ch Rauzan-Gassies** surprisingly good though drying-out. *July 1993* ★★★

# 1927

Rather like me, despite being conceived at the time of the excellent 1926 harvest and born in a pleasant and balmy May it was downhill from then on. Cold, wet and windy weather lead to an atrocious harvest and very poor wines. At least I survived.

**Ch Latour** Known for its ability to make good, or at least passable, wines even in poor vintages, proved to be the case in 1927. Two good bottles from the cellars of the de Beaumont family, then a pale, washed out and skinny bottle at a tasting in San Francisco. *Last tasted June 1981. At best* ★★

**Ch Margaux** An old note but it was far more attractive than the Romanée-Conti alongside. *April 1971* ★★

**Carruades de Mouton-Rothschild** It is not commonly known that both Ch Lafite and Ch Mouton have vines on the adjoining Carruades plâteau. Lafite had already used the name but Philippe de Rothschild appropriated it for this, his first poor vintage (there was no *grand vin*). What attracted me was not just my birth year but the beautiful Carlu labels. Very scarce though I managed to buy two magnums, one badly ullaged, the other I gave to the Baron when he saw it in my office. Later I bought a lot which included several half-bottles. They turned out to be surprisingly delicious. *Last tasted May 1990* ★★★

**Ch Ducru-Beaucaillou** An anonymous-looking magnum. Lovely colour; some residual fruit; lean, acidic. *Sept 1990* ★★

# 1928 ★★★★★

The first of the famous twin vintages; both great but of totally contrasting weight and style. What produced these massively tannic wines? Summer heat thickened the skins from which were extracted deep colouring matter and tannin. The exceptionally good ripening conditions were responsible for the richness and substantial alcoholic content. This is the longest lived vintage of the decade.

Because they came on to the market just before the slump, large quantities remained unsold. Stocks remained in some merchants' cellars until well after World War Two and were on merchants' lists even in the mid-1950s, which is one of the reasons I have so many notes, almost 200, for I tasted quite a lot in my early retailing days, from 1953–1959. The rest of my notes, indeed most, were made during my time at Christie's, from 1966, and at many tastings.

**Ch Latour** I am putting this first, for it was, and still is, the star of the vintage. Like the 1870 Lafite, so dense, powerful and bitterly tannic that it was a full half century before it was mellow enough to be enjoyed. I have been privileged to taste this wine on 16 occasions following its progress from 'enormous, too full of tannin' in 1953. Very austere, yet tannin cloaked and velvet and opening up in the 1970s. I considered it at its peak in the 1980s: intensely deep; spicy, cinnamon, cedary bouquet; surprisingly sweet and velvety despite its tannin, masculine, with great concentration and length. But on it goes. Four impressive bottles, fabulous bouquets but still very tannic, even harsh (in Zurich 1994). An oxidised bottle then an impressive bottle, fragrant, drinking perfectly. *Last tasted at Joshua Latner's dinner, Jan 2000. At best* ★★★★★

**Ch Lafite** Frankly not a patch on the Latour; indeed both the '28 and '29 like undernourished twins. Poor notes in the 1970s, 'thinning', 'mushroomy', 'astringent' and just plain 'dull'. Some Lafite fragrance straining to emerge. Most recently, a very odd tasting, minty, sharp bottle at the 1928s tasting in San Juan. *Last tasted Nov 1998. At best* ★★

**Ch Margaux** Eight notes. Slight bottle variation but mainly very good: deeply coloured; sweet, singed, cedary, fragrant bouquet; 'sweet, tanned and tannic'. This was the first time (in 1976) I used the expression 'iron fist in velvet glove'. To demonstrate that not all the 1928s in San Juan were below par, the Margaux was superb, a 'mouthfilling powerhouse'. Most recent: rather too sweet and caramelly; rich yet still very tannic. *Last noted at Manfred Wagner's tasting in Zurich, Nov 2000. At best* ★★★★★

**Ch Mouton-Rothschild** Four poor bottles in the 1960s and 1970s made up for more recently: fragrant, sweet, crisp, attractive in San Juan, and, despite its age remarkably sweet on the palate, lighter than expected. Delicious. *Last noted at Paolo Pong's dinner at Jancis Robinson's, June 2000. At best* ★★★★

**Ch Mouton-Rothschild** Belgian-bottled by Vandermeurlen: opaque; almost sickly sweet but opened up fragrantly; full of fruit, crisp, tannic. *At de Cock's in Paris, Dec 1995* ★★★★

**Ch Haut-Brion** A strange period for Haut-Brion. Weird winemaking. Not even one pleasant bottle from 1970 to the most recent. I am surprised that the Dillon family wanted to buy the château (in 1935) after tasting the '28 and '29 let alone the '30, '31 and '32s. Nearly a dozen notes ranging from oxidised to curiously impressive, via 'stewed opulence'. Screwed up at the Latner dinner in January 2000 and, five months later, thick, 'cooked', very tannic. *Not rated.*

**Ch Ausone** By the early 1980s it had lost a good deal of colour yet, despite fungi on the nose, was fairly harmonious. Three variable, mainly poor bottles at Flatt's Ausone tasting. Most recently, a lovely colour showing perfect maturity; bouquet that always reminds me of dried leaves, fragrant in its way; and on the palate surprisingly full and rich, with good length and acidity. *Last noted in San Juan, Puerto Rico, Nov 1988. Not my favourite '28 but, at best,* ★★★

**Ch Cheval Blanc** Nothing like as good as the 1929. Seven critical notes from 1955. Some fragrance and charm but faded. 'Arboreal' – bad flower scent more appropriate: geraniums (sorbic acid). *Last tasted June 2000. At best* ★★

**Ch Cheval Blanc** Belgian-bottled by Vandermeurlen. Two notes: glorious, reminded me of the '26 (in Paris 1995). Later: rich, meaty, and with none of the château-bottled faults – but, of course, it was bought at Christie's! *At a Rodenstock dinner, March 2001* ★★★

**Ch Pétrus** Two notes, the first, in 1984, jammy, like late-harvest Zinfandel. More recently: opaque; concentrated; molasses nose, on verge of oxidation; strange flavour, severely tannic. *A magnum, last noted at a Rodenstock tasting, Sept 1996.*

**Ch Brane-Cantenac** A lovely bottle, sweet yet still tannic. *At the Josey pre-sale tasting, Nov 2000* ★★★★

**Ch Calon-Ségur** A château whose wines were much liked by the British trade and its customers, which is why I have many notes, starting in 1954. I was working for Saccone & Speed, at that time top-class 'carriage trade' wine merchants. The '28 was listed at 26 shillings (now £1.30p) a bottle.

Consistently deep, mouthfilling, tannic. Most recently showing its age, though still deep. 'Old oak and mocha' nose; austere. An old-fashioned St-Estèphe. *Last noted in Nov 1998. At best* ★★★★

**Ch Cantemerle** In 1985 and 1988 described as a 'faded old lady'. Both were from the Binaud cellar, the more recent recorked by Whitwham's. In fact it was a very fragrant, stylish, pretty wine. Indeed charming if a bit tart. *Last tasted at Dr Thomas's tasting in Puerto Rico, Nov 1998* ★★★

**Domaine de Chevalier** Two notes made dining at the Domaine, first in 1981 with the charming Claude Ricard (we played the piano after dinner, alternating for two hours. I had drunk enough wine to lose my inhibitions but not to lose my concentration). More recently with the new owner Olivier Bernard. After 27 years in bottle it had lost some of its opacity; showing age as before, but sweet and fragrant, with good body and length. *Last noted April 1998* ★★★★

**Ch Ducru-Beaucaillou** Surprised to find only two recent notes: both luminous and lovely; high-toned yet faded; sweet, lively, some charm, soft entry, tart finish. *In Nov 1998 and at Paolo Pong's in June 2000* ★★★

**Ch Montrose** A big black, lovely, vigorous, tannic wine when first tasted in 1955. Creaking a bit, a lean and austere bottle in 1990. Most recently, still fairly deep; faultless nose; full body and flavour, rich extract. Still tannic. *Last at Paolo Pong's, June 2000* ★★★★

**Ch Mouton d'Armailhacq** Losing colour, fruit and weight but soft and delicious. *At dinner, May 1993* ★★★

**Ch Trotanoy** Magnificent. *Sept 1986* ★★★★★

THE 70TH ANNIVERSARY TASTING OF 1928S I conducted this extraordinary event in San Juan, Puerto Rico, in November 1998. All the wines were donated by Dr Charles Thomas of Nashville, Tennessee. The following notes cover the 33 châteaux not already commented on above:

**Ch Carbonnieux** dead. This wine has never been made to last; **Ch Cos d'Estournel** Nicolas, Paris label. Full flavoured; very good. Consistent with earlier notes ★★★★; **Ch Desmirail** Réserve Nicolas. Holding well. Firm. Tannic ★★★; **Ch Durfort-Vivens** some Margaux charm, dried fruit, astringent ★★; **Ch L'Évangile** despite low-shoulder surprisingly fragrant, with silky Pomerol texture. Earlier, in 1996, a magnum with an unusual strawberry nose and taste ★★★; **Ch Gruaud-Larose** several earlier notes, starting with a good though leathery bottle in 1956. Lastly, with Nicolas label, recorked: deep; sound; dry and lean ★★; **Ch Léoville-Las-Cases** spicy, eucalyptus; complete, delicious. Also consistent with many earlier notes. Almost luscious for a '28 ★★★★; **Ch Lynch-Bages** surprisingly, considering the popularity of this château among British consumers, only one note. Bordeaux-bottled; very Pauillac-oyster nose, but on the palate raw and teeth-gripping; **Ch La Mission Haut-Brion** several variable notes, some very good, no faults. At the 1928 tasting, a fine bottle with original 'long long cork'. A powerhouse. Still loaded ★★★★; **Ch Nenin** faded fruit. Refreshing but tart; **Ch Pichon-Lalande** château-bottled, Nicolas label: fragrant, good flavour, length. Some astringency but not enough to spoil its charm ★★★; **Ch Rauzan-Gassies** quite good; rich but tart ★; **Ch Rausan-Ségla** well bottled by The Wine Society, London: convincingly deep, sound; good chewy flavour ★★★★; **Ch Rouget** recorked in the 1950s. Beautiful colour; very good sweet bouquet; full-bodied, singed flavour ★★★; and, finally, **Ch Talbot** Bordeaux-bottled by Kressmann. Finished.

## Re-corking

*A sometimes necessary but worrying procedure. During prolonged cellaring corks have a tendency to dry out and lose their elasticity, running the risk of letting in air leading to oxidation. It is a normal procedure for many châteaux to re-cork their own wines every 15 or 20 years, to ensure both uninterrupted maturation, and the longest possible lifespan. Sometimes the bottles are topped up at this stage, ideally with wine of the same vintage. In the case of older and rarer wine the château will top up with a younger vintage. Although a bottle recorked at or by the château will give the owner or eventual buyer reassurance, I personally prefer wines with their original corks. After all, if the bottle is ullaged, the wine really should be drunk – or rejected.*

OLDER NOTES INCLUDE **Ch Bouscaut** earthy, masculine *1984* ★★★; **Ch Lascombes** magnum: austere, tannic *1981* ★★; and **Ch Duhart-Milon** firm, austere, sound *1983* ★★

# 1929 ★★★★★

A wonderful vintage. At its best it was the epitome of elegance and finesse, and the end of an era.
**Ch Lafite** Variable. Not Lafite at its best. Only one really admiring note, a bottle in 1988, attractive forthcoming bouquet, sweet, very appealing flavour, somewhat acidic. *Last tasted, an opulent over-the-top jeroboam, in 1989. At best* ★★★ *(just).*
**Ch Latour** Superlative. Softer and more amenable than the '28. Sixteen notes, almost all 5 stars, dating from December 1955. (I had moved that autumn from Saccone & Speed to Harvey's of Bristol, and was based in London.) Always deeply coloured, its bouquet variously described – mainly inadequately – as rich but restrained old cedar, spicy (eucalyptus once again, cloves and sage), 'medicinal' Pauillac, and so forth. On the palate generally sweet, soft and luscious for Latour – a complete contrast to the monumental and tannic '28 – velvety, elongated. More recently a perfect magnum in a 'flight' of Latours at a Rodenstock weekend. *Last noted Dec 1995* ★★★★★
**Ch Margaux** Ten notes. A variable performer, but at its best characteristically fragrant and bursting with charm. Of the more recent notes, an extraordinarily rich bottle at Manfred Wagner's tasting in 1997, and an excellent bottle in the Margaux 'flight' at a Rodenstock weekend: attractive colour, not deep; delicious bouquet, Margaux's crystallised violets; sweet, very rich, fragrant. A lovely old flavour. *Last tasted Nov 2000. At best* ★★★★★
**Ch Mouton-Rothschild** In the latter half of the 1960s and through the 1970s this was the 'star' of the sale room. I described the wine as 'like a great *diva*, world renowned but not unsullied'. I have over 20 notes. It always seemed on the brink. Fleshy, often corrupt, always exciting. And always with the inimitable Mouton Cabernet fragrance. *Last tasted May 1989. At best* ★★★★★
**Ch Haut-Brion** Very strange. Len Evans and I nearly came to blows over it at the first-ever 'single bottle club' dinner in Sydney – with the best palates of Australia and the Prime Minister. Len loved it; I did not. A curiously, consistently, stewed character. Heated must? More like black treacle or port. Clearly a matter of taste. *Many notes, last tasted May 1989.*
**Ch Cheval Blanc** One of the great '29s. Several admiring notes from 1971. A rich, rosy-hued tile red with globular 'tears' or 'legs'; indescribable bouquet, perfect fragrance. A gentle, soft, glorious wine. Perfection. *Last tasted May 1989* ★★★★★
**Ch Pétrus** Two notes, the first at Walter Eigensatz's *impériale* tasting in 1989, and then a double magnum at a Rodenstock tasting. I inspected the latter in the cellar. It had the original château capsule but provenance unknown. The wine was most impressive, '28ish in weight, deep amber-brown with meaty, chocolatey rim and a rather course texture which I described as a 'yeoman farmer with mud on his boots'. None of the subtlety of the top Médocs. *Last tasted Sept 1998. At best* ★★★

**Ch Beychevelle** Orange-tinged; sweet, vanilla nose and taste. An agreeable old lady. *At a pre-sale tasting, May 1993* ★★★
**Ch Calon-Ségur** A delicious magnum: fruit and violets; excellent crisp flavour, balance and length, one of Calon's peak periods. *Tasted Sept 1996* ★★★★★
**Ch Cantemerle** Fragrant, charming, lovely flavour somewhat marred by its swingeing finish. *At the Binaud cellar, Oct 1995* ★★★
**Ch La Mission Haut-Brion** Eight notes. A magnificent '29, one of the best ever La Missions, certainly the richest. Variable though, the best, from the original Woltner cellars. (Henri and Fernand, the sons of Frédéric who had purchased the estate, were the sole partners from 1926 until they died in the 1970s. They were brilliant innovative winemakers and managers.) *At its best* ★★★★★ *Last tasted June 1990.*

TWO RENOWNED '29S **Ch Léoville-Poyferré** the last gasp of a wine of great finesse, alas not tasted at its zenith; and **Ch Pontet-Canet** magnificent when I first tasted it at Harvey's in 1956. Lesser bottles since. *Last tasted March 1987. At best* ★★★★★

OTHER '29S LAST NOTED IN THE 1980S **Dom de Chevalier** a château-bottled magnum and a Danish-bottled from Aalholm Castle, both superb. Delicate, fragrant, perfect balance. *Last noted Oct 1982* ★★★★★; **Ch L'Enclos** beautiful colour; soft, very rich, fleshy. *July 1989* ★★★★; **Ch Figeac** consistent notes over 20 years apart. Rich, almost roast beef; full, rich, tangy and tannic. *Last noted Dec 1989* ★★★; **Clos Fourtet** many notes from 1954. Probably the best ever Fourtet. Positive. Delicious. *Last tasted Oct 1983* ★★★★; **Ch Gruaud-Larose** sweet and sour; ripe, soft, but an acid edge. *Last tasted Nov 1986* ★★★; **Ch Haut-Bailly** an astonishingly rich Graves. *June 1988* ★★★; **Ch Léoville-Las-Cases** sweet, full, rich, fleshy, tannic. *Oct 1984* ★★★; **Ch Marquis de Terme** sweet, rich, still fruity. *Last tasted July 1988. At best* ★★★★; and **Ch Rauzan-Gassies** variable, but the best, from Aalholm, bottled by Kjaer and Sommerfeldt, still the top traditional wine merchants in Copenhagen. *Last tasted July 1989* ★★★★

# 1930–1939

One of Bordeaux's most difficult decades, both for grower and merchant. It opened with three atrocious vintages: poor wines for which there was no market. It was the Great Depression. Growers were in despair, producers lost money, châteaux changed hands at give-away prices, including, among the best known, Ch Haut-Brion, bought in 1935 by Clarence Dillon, of the wealthy American banking family. (It is said that he actually wanted to buy Ch Cheval Blanc but it was a foggy day and Haut-Brion, in a suburb of Bordeaux, was easier to get to.)

The end of Prohibition in 1933 coincided with somewhat better growing conditions and trade, but the American market was slow to recover, and the British merchants and their customers were awash with '28s, '29s and earlier vintages. 1933 was the year that the *Guide Michelin* introduced its star rating system (its rosettes). Among the few restaurants in France to receive the coveted three rosettes was the famous Chapon Fin in Bordeaux.

In 1935 the French took steps to improve their wine quality and protect names by introducing the *appellation contrôlée* system. There was some recovery by 1937 and that vintage was welcomed though, as the following notes show, these wines never really threw off their astringency.

## *Vintages at a Glance*
**Outstanding** ★★★★★
None
**Very Good** ★★★★
1934
**Good** ★★★
1933

## 1930

Poor weather, execrable wine, no market and generally hard times for everyone.
**Ch Latour** The only '30 I have tasted but on two occasions. In 1983, at first glance, it had quite a good ruby colour; a light, spicy bouquet trying to lift off but the palate was thin and acidic. More recently, a similar note, but seemed chunkier and more chewy, ending on a sour note. *Last tasted dining at the château, Nov 1990.*

## 1931

A moderate-sized crop of poor wines though fractionally better than 1930. Slump. No market.
**Ch Lafite** Recorked. Pale, dull; a curious 'soft fluffy' nose which opened up in a straggly sort of way. Flavour not all that bad but raw and acidic. *At Flatt's Lafite tasting, Oct 1988.*
**Ch Latour** Despite its reputation for making the best of a bad job, three notes consigned it to oblivion. Varnishy, skinny, unbalanced. *Last tasted Sept 1981.*
**Ch Margaux** A better than expected bottle at Wagner's Margaux tasting. Curious fragrance fading away; slightly sweet, light, flavoury but short. *Nov 2000.*
**Ch Haut-Brion** Despite the black treacle, molasses character of the wine at this period, it could have been worse. Rich, malty nose; dry, drinkable, but varnish and acidity on the finish. Several notes. *Last tasted at Mutsuo Okabayashi's (and my wife's) birth year dinner in Tokyo, June 1989.*
**Ch La Mission Haut-Brion** Certainly the best surviving '31. Several notes. Deeply coloured; surprisingly sound; singed rich tobacco nose and taste. Dry, acidic finish. The Woltner brothers doing their best. *Last noted at Karl-Heinz Wolf's La Mission tasting in Wiesbaden, June 1980.*

**Ch Pichon, Lalande** Showing its age and condition: old banana skins. Palate better than nose. Refreshing acidity – went quite well with roast lamb. *At another Okabayashi tasting and dinner in Tokyo, Oct 1995.*

## 1932

The third and probably the worst of the terrible trio. Very late and uneven harvest, poor crop, dreadful wines. It would be interesting to know whether, with modern methods of crop control and winemaking, better wines could have been made. However, no-one would, or could afford to buy the wine in this period of great depression, anyway.
**Ch Latour** As always doing its best. Despite its impressive colour it was creaking at the joints. Dried out and tart. *Served out of curiosity, dining at the château, Nov 1990.*

## 1933 ★★★

Another small crop but this time because of high winds during the flowering period. Fairly light, attractive wines. However, apart from La Mission, no '33s tasted during the last decade. For me the lightness and charm of the vintage was epitomised by **Ch Margaux** which I drank in the 1950s and 1960s and **Ch Cheval Blanc** in the 1970s.
**Ch La Mission Haut-Brion** Rich, ripe but crumbling even in the 1970s. Variable. Even the Woltners' bottle, though flavoury, had edgy acidity. *Last noted June 1990. At best* ★★

LAST NOTED IN THE 1980s **Ch Lafite** light, delicate, delicious when first tasted in 1955. A similar note in 1980. More recently, a whiff of 'bottle stink' clearing beautifully; rich, flavoury, fragrant. *Last tasted Oct 1988. At best* ★★★★; **Ch Latour** soft and almost overripe in the 1960s and 1970s. Beautifully coloured; cedary; fullish body for a '33, good flavour but

---

### Berry Bros

*Charles Walter Berry, writing in* In Search of Wine *(published in 1934), mentions, casually, that Berry Bros bought the entire 1933 crop of Ch Beychevelle and Ch Rausan-Ségla, the latter having only 11% alcohol.*

always seemed on the verge. Living dangerously. *Last tasted June 1981. At best ★★★*; **Ch Mouton-Rothschild** rather briefly and condescendingly noted as 'dry, crisp, fine and drinkable' in 1955. A jump of over 30 years to Lloyd Flatt's tasting: two halves, one decayed, the other delicious though gamey. *Last tasted April 1986. At best ★★★*

# 1934 ★★★★

The decade's best vintage. The grapes were saved from a two-month drought by September rain. An abundant harvest, very good wines. Now risky, but the best kept still drinking well.
**Ch Lafite** Variable. In the 1950s and 1960s I noted a hardness though even then a touch of age. Curiously, better notes in the 1970s. Very mature looking, the bouquet variously described as rich, fragrant, complex; attractive flavour, charming. Two poor bottles in the 1980s, but a superb magnum at Lloyd Flatt's tasting. Very sweet, richly flavoured, in excellent condition but constant over-maturity noted. *Last tasted Oct 1988. At best ★★★★*
**Ch Latour** Also typical of the mid-1930 vintages. Prematurely aged though very flavoury and appealing. First tasted in 1955. I then (in 1958) noted it as 'very big yet soft… nearing its peak'. Some tart bottles in the 1970s. In 1980, a scent of 'old cellars and boiled fennel', overripeness noted again. Four bottles at the Latour tasting in Zurich. Despite their lovely mahogany colour, and exciting though over-the-top scents, a let-down on the palate. I wrote 'curling like fallen leaves'. Fragrant but piquant, astringent. *Last tasted Oct 1994. At best ★★★ and not getting any better.*
**Ch Margaux** Fifteen notes. Despite some poor, doubtless badly cellared bottles, my favourite '34. So very Margaux. Yet, and yet, the decay of the '30s noted quite early, even in the mid-1950s, certainly by the early 1970s. But it soldiers on. More recently at Wagner's first Margaux tasting in 1997: rich, biscuity bouquet – though *faisandé*. Sweet, assertive fruit, very tannic. Most recently, a richly flavoured bottle. Bouquet very attractive but just misses greatness. A high mark at *Manfred Wagner's second Ch Margaux tasting, Nov 2000. At best ★★★★*
**Ch Mouton-Rothschild** Harry Waugh, before I joined him at Harvey's in 1953, described it simply as 'a beautiful bottle, reaching its apogee'. Two years later, under his wing, I was somewhat more down to earth: 'very full' (appearance); 'deep and fine' (bouquet); 'very, very, dry tannins still, (yet) soft taste, fine but no frills'. Both I and the wine matured over the years for there were more appreciative notes in the 1960s. In the 1970s, five mainly critical notes, almost all mentioning highish acidity. The very best, and most recent, a '*Rés du Baron*' jeroboam recorked in 1953: lively, intense; initially restrained but complete, opening gradually. Lovely and – for Mouton – relatively low-keyed. Sweet, fairly full-bodied, delicious fruit, excellent tannin and acidity. 'A perfect drink.' *Last tasted Sept 1987. Risky, but at its best ★★★★★*
**Ch Cheval Blanc** Arguably the finest, certainly – in my experience – one of the most reliable of the 1934s. First noted 'rich, delicate, ethereal, exquisite' in 1978, and several admiring notes since, including a glowingly coloured magnum in 1986, its beautiful bouquet, ripe, subsiding gently but not decayed. Well constructed. All the component parts in balance. Most recently another magnum with upper-mid-shoulder level, a bit hazy; nose disappointingly neutral though much better on the palate; sweet, complete, fading gracefully but still drinking well. *Last tasted Dec 2000. At best ★★★★★*

**Ch Pétrus** Deeply coloured, very rich, 'thick' reminding me in some ways of Haut-Brion '29. A bottle, acidity taking over, and, later, an *impériale*. Where Hardy Rodenstock finds these wines I know not. There are simply no records of production, of stock or sales prior to 1945. All I can say is that the big bottle was delicious. *Last tasted Sept 1990 ★★★★*

**Ch Cantemerle** Two notes. Very good wine. Perfect colour; sweet, sound and fragrant. Never a heavy wine, its light elegant style appealing to Philippe de Rothschild who told me he preferred Cantemerle as a drink to his more potent Mouton. *From the Binaud cellar. At this period the château was owned by Henrÿ (sic) Binaud's wife's family. Tasted Oct 1995 ★★★★*
**Dom de Chevalier** Making allowances for age, almost faultless. Three notes in 1981: fully developed with an entrancing medium deep, mature appearance, its wary bouquet opening up fragrantly as the air coaxed it out of its shell. A similar bottle deliciously sweet, rather like a '47, noted dining at the domaine in 1984. Ten years later, showing its age though complete and harmonious with silky texture, good acidity. *Last noted once again dining at the domaine, April 1994 ★★★*
**Ch Duhart-Milon** Fading, but gracefully. *Nov 1992 ★★*
**Ch Gruaud-Larose** Unusually for Gruaud, normally so full of fruit, and for a '34, rather austere. I certainly noted it as dry, even harsh at 30 years of age and, most recently, a magnum, teeth-grippingly dry, with edgy acidity rather a let-down after its tantalising bouquet. *Last noted at Len Evans' great wine dinner in the Hunter Valley, Sept 2000 ★★*
**Ch Gruaud-Larose-Faure** Shipped by de Luze, bottled by Chr Stausholm and removed for sale from the excellent cellar at Aalholm Castle. Two points: one that the bottling experience and skills of the top Danish wine merchants were on a par with the best of the British, and often better than at the château, and that a wine stored, since original purchase, in a perfect cellar, has the best chance of survival. *Tasted with the packing team (Daphne and Brian Ebbeson), July 1989 ★★★*
**Ch La Mission Haut-Brion** The Woltners at their brilliant best. One of the finest '34s and holding well. Deep, richly coloured; rich, ripe, fragrant, cedary, fruit-packed bouquet; sweet, powerful but not heavy, lovely flavour and finish. *Last tasted June 1990 ★★★★★*
**Ch Rausan-Ségla** A plummy-coloured, fragrant jeroboam. Good flavour and grip. *Sept 1990 ★★★★*
**Ch Siran** Delicious flavour, good length. *At a pre-sale tasting in Oct 1993 ★★★*

OTHER 1934S LAST TASTED IN THE 1980S **Ch Haut-Brion** variable, but an improvement on the '28 and, particularly, the '29. Half a dozen notes, the best in 1955 'extraordinarily alert, magnificent fullness; earthy tang'. Later a bottle with a taste of syrup of figs. *Last tasted May 1981. At best ★★★*; **Ch Ausone** probably at its best in the early 1940s. Deliciously scented but drying out in 1983, and two overripe, rich but decaying bottles at Flatt's tasting. *Last noted Oct 1987. Never tasted at best. Now just ★*; **Ch L'Angélus** a very crisp attractive Kjaer & Sommerfeldt bottling from Aalholm. *July 1989 ★★★★*; **Ch Beychevelle** lovely bottling by Chr Stausholm, also from Aalholm. Translucent; delicate; fragrant. A delicious drink. *Last tasted Sept 1989 ★★★★*; **Carruades de Ch Lafite** ripe, chocolatey bouquet; lean; more austere on palate. *Oct 1988 ★★*; **Ch Cos d'Estournel** with an old-fashioned St-Estèphe character, a bit austere and disappointing when first noted in 1955 and consistently so ever since. *Last tasted with*

Bruno Prats at Ch Marbuzet, May 1986 ★★ *(just)*; **Ch Figeac** idiosyncratic, intense, rich, a bit over-the-top and variable. Several notes. *Last tasted Dec 1989 ★★ a matter of luck and personal taste*; **Ch Palmer** unconvincing and long after its sell-by date. *In Oct 1984 ★*; and **Ch Talbot** from Aalholm Castle, but this time, château-bottled. High-toned, good flavour. Touch of end acidity. *May 1988 ★★★*

## 1935 ★★

Abundant vintage of moderate quality. The British wine trade had stocked up with '34s so few wines were bought, and I have only tasted a few.

**Ch La Mission Haut-Brion** Three notes, all bottles from the Woltners' cellars. At its best a vanillin, blancmange, lactic nose; fairly sweet, flowery flavour. *Last noted at Wolf's La Mission tasting, June 1990. At best ★★★*

TWO OTHER 1935S **Ch Latour** two notes: flavoury but acidic at the de Beaumont pre-sale tasting in 1974. A lively looking, very dry and piquant bottle at the Fête de la Fleur. *Last tasted June 1981 ★*; **Dom de Chevalier** deathly colour; malty nose; faded but interesting. *July 1987.*

## 1936

Not much better than 1935 and largely ignored by the British wine trade. Nevertheless, I have over two dozen notes, mainly tasted in the 1960s and 1970s.

**Ch Margaux** Tasted only at the two Manfred Wagner Margaux tastings. At the first, in 1997, a bottle recorked in the early 1980s, distinctly old, dried out. At the second, a rather better bottle: an attractive colour with a yellow tinge to its maturity; curious nose and flavour, unknit, 'holding on for dear life'. Tart finish. *Last tasted Nov 2000. Give it a miss.*

**Ch La Mission Haut-Brion** Four notes. Uneven but, at its best, healthy, well-developed; cheesy nose but charming. The most recent tasted was most unattractive. *Last noted June 1990. At best ★★*

OTHER 1936S LAST TASTED IN THE 1980S **Ch Latour** contrasting notes in the mid-1970s, one fragrant, flavoury and charming, another bottle 'green' and tart. A reasonably good bottle from the de Beaumont cellar and later a delightful bottle which matched my 1976 note. *Last tasted June 1981. At best ★★★*; **Ch Mouton-Rothschild** variable. Mainly fragrant but faded. *Last tasted April 1986. At best ★★*; **Ch Ausone** despite lacking depth of colour, nose and taste, a warm, open knit delicate and charming wine. *Oct 1987 ★★★*; **Ch Cheval Blanc** flavoury but lacking flesh. Dry, acidic. *Magnum, Sept 1986*; **Ch La Fleur-Pétrus** showing age but retaining fruit; soft, some flesh, surprisingly flavoury. *At Corney & Barrow, Helmet Row (a quaint corner of the City of London), Dec 1984 ★★★*

## 1937 originally ★★★★, now only ★★

At the time rated as highly as the 1934 and though undoubtedly the second best year of the 1930s, now one of my least-liked major vintages of red Bordeaux. The problem stemmed from the weather. Though there was no rain, neither was there much sun. It was cool from May to mid-September though the grapes were harvested in good conditions. Bottled early in the war, the wines that survived were pounced upon by the wine-starved trade and largely consumed in the late 1940s. Incidentally, I have my marked-up Saccone & Speed's Winter 1954–55 price list. We still had some '26s, '28s, '29s and '34s though rather more of the '37s. 'Some wines of this excellent vintage are still not ready' wrote Sir Guy Fison Bt, the distinguished buyer, 'but the following have developed perfectly' including Ch Branaire-Ducru at 18 shillings and six pence (83p!) a bottle, and Ch Margaux at 35 shillings. Curiously, when I moved to Harvey's, their 1954–55 list included only one '37, Ch Lynch-Bages, but also quoted a few '47s and '49s.

So what went wrong? The wines were tannic from the start but, in time, this turned into astringency.

My dislike was confirmed when I was tasting 60 '37s accumulated by Hardy Rodenstock, occupying one day of his wine weekend in 1988. How long it took Hardy to accumulate so many I do not know. Even allowing for some wines with less than good levels, it was an invaluable exercise.

Apart from Rodenstock's 60 I have almost exactly a hundred other notes, stretching from my retailing years in the mid-1950s, to the mid-1960s and also many in the 1970s.

I shall be brief. First some châteaux tasted in the 1990s:

**Ch Latour** Not my favourite Latour, for despite certain attractions virtually every single one of my 14 notes, starting in 1955, uses the word 'astringent'. Of the three most recent, some mahogany coloured, 'surprisingly not bad, rich but astringent' bottles generously provided by the late Peter Sichel at a dinner held at Ch Palmer in June 1995 to celebrate the 40th anniversary of the first visit by my wife and I to Bordeaux. Most recently, at Hugh Johnson's Bordeaux Club dinner, an almost Mouton-like spiciness, fragrant exciting – but the context made all the difference. *Last noted at Saling Hall in Essex, Aug 1999. At best ★★★*

**Ch Haut-Brion** One of the best '37s. First tasted in 1975, noting a curious tea-like nose and, surprise surprise, 'astringent'. Another with a deep concentrated appearance and nose; not bad but with an 'obtrusive teeth-gripping tannic–acid' finish. Appropriately, one of the best bottles was from the Dillon cellar (1979). Most recently, a surprisingly youthful-looking magnum, leathery, old tobacco, showing its age on the palate. Raw. *Last noted Sept 1995. At best ★★*

**Ch Cheval Blanc** Another good '37 first noted in 1960. Consistent: a soft, quite good middle palate ending with tannic grip. The most recent, a magnum, a bit mushroomy on the nose, fairly sweet and mellow – apart from a kick in the teeth. *Last tasted Sept 1997 at Karl-Heinz Wolf's excellent 'Weinart' Cheval Blanc tasting in Austria, Sept 1997 ★★★*

**Ch La Mission Haut-Brion** Unsurprisingly, one of the best '37s. Consistent notes: virtually opaque; massively full and fruity nose and palate. Fragrant, idiosyncratic Graves bouquet and 'tobacco' taste. Very sweet. Complete. Impressive but laden with tannin and acidity. *Last tasted June 1990 ★★★★*

**Ch Mouton d'Armailhacq** Apart from one oxidised magnum, an attractive wine with characteristic spicy Cabernet aroma and flavour, not unlike its senior cousin, the Mouton *Grand Vin*, or Lynch-Bages. Stylish, but still a '37. *Last tasted Sept 1994. At best ★★★ (just).*

**Ch Canon** A spicy, fragrant bouquet; sweet, crisp, fruity, elegant. An excellent '37. *In magnum, Sept 1988 ★★★★*

**Dom de Chevalier** Richly coloured; very fragrant; sweet, earthy. I thought it was a '47. A very good magnum in 1988 and another on top form. *Tasted most recently at the domaine, Sept 1998 ★★★*

OTHER FIRST GROWTHS LAST TASTED IN 1988 Ch Lafite first tasted in 1974 and, believe it or not, 'astringent'. Thereafter some excellent magnums, a gentle, fragrant, cedary bottle in 1979. Several in the 1980s, variously described as tart but exciting, lean, stringy, ungracious but sound. *Last noting 'Lafite delicacy', at a Christie's boardroom lunch, Oct 1988. At best ★★★;* Ch Margaux a good '37. A pretty colour, charming and fragrant, its '37 acidity hardly noticeable in the 1970s. Maturing reasonably elegant, its body, fruit and extract holding the tannic/acid grip at bay. *Last tasted Sept 1988 ★★★;* Ch Mouton-Rothschild massive and tough looking; 'scented old boots' (!), rich, but some decay, with 'swingeing acidity' in the early 1970s. Variable, to say the least, in the 1980s. A medicinal, caramelly, overripe bottle and a lovely looking magnum with sweet, beautifully evolved, cedary, Cabernet bouquet; good fruit surviving its vice-like grip. *Last tasted Sept 1988. At best ★★★;* Ch Ausone one thing one can say about Ausone: it is different. I often note a strange dried leaf: 'bracken'-like taste. Its bouquet is equally curious but can open up fragrantly, the '37 being no exception – but for the acidity. *Last tasted, a magnum, Sept 1988. At best ★★★;* and Ch Pétrus a corked, tart jeroboam and a plummy-coloured, fairly sweet magnum. Flavoury but lean for Pétrus. *Both tasted Sept 1988. At best ★★★*

A LINE-UP OF VARIABLE 1937S LAST TASTED IN 1988 Ch Beychevelle rich, fragrant though drying out and faded. *At best ★★★;* Carruades de Ch Lafite a fragrant, delicately poised magnum and a murky, dried-out bottle. *At best ★★★;* Ch Ducru-Beaucaillou magnum. Delicious ★★★; Ch La Fleur-Pétrus ripe bouquet, very flavoury, pasty acidity ★★; Ch La Gaffelière fruity but tart ★★; Ch Léoville-Barton a charming, delicate Corney & Barrow bottling, and, more recently, a lean tannic magnum ★★; Ch Marquis de Terme four notes. Rich, crisp, flavoury. *At best ★★★;* Ch Montrose overladen with tannin even in the mid-1950s, but some fragrant bottles and a substantial magnum. *At best a good '37 ★★★;* Ch Palmer very rich but past it, though one of the least astringent of the '37s. *At best ★★;* Ch Pichon-Baron excellent bouquet, good fruit, very tannic ★★★; Ch Pichon-Lalande recorked. High-toned, very flavoury, fragile, acidic ★★; Ch Pontet-Canet attractive despite acidity ★★★; Ch Rausan-Ségla lean but not bad ★★; Ch Trotanoy magnum. Delicious fruit but harsh finish ★★; and Vieux Ch Certan good flavour but slightly volatile ★★

Of the many other 1937s tasted, many had poor levels, risky at best, oxidised at worst. Avoid this vintage, unless the wines have high levels and a dependable provenance.

## 1938 ★

Cold, stormy summer. Large but late vintage. Mediocre wines bottled during the early days of World War Two.
Ch La Mission Haut-Brion First several notes from 1978. Once again the Woltners managed to produce a good wine in a difficult year. Showing well at Bipin Desai's tasting in 1985: lively, attractive, spicy, masculine and 'like a lesser '48'. Surprisingly pleasant and easy at Karl-Heinz Wolf's tasting in Wiesbaden. *Last tasted June 1990 ★★★*

FIRST GROWTHS LAST TASTED IN THE 1980S Ch Lafite in a pale green wartime bottle. Delicate spicy bouquet; lean, firm and sound. *Oct 1988 ★★;* Ch Latour first tasted in 1966: 'neither corked, oxidised or acetic, but poor'. It was variable in the 1970s. The most recent bottle I have tasted was light for Latour, pleasant but fading. *Last tasted June 1981 ★;* and Ch Mouton-Rothschild overripe, creaking, dry and acidic. *April 1986.*

ONE OR TWO OLDER NOTES the best being Ch Cheval Blanc; Ch Calon-Ségur and Ch Rausan-Ségla.

## 1939

An abundance of light but fragrant wines.
Ch La Mission Haut-Brion Once again as with the '38, demonstrating the Woltners' care of vineyard and winemaking skills in difficult conditions, this time the war. Two good bottles, first at Desai's La Mission tasting in 1985 and, most recently, at Karl-Heinz Wolf's tasting in Wiesbaden, from the Woltner cellar sales at Christie's. A spicy, fruity wine, touch of vanilla and iodine – very Graves, very La Mission. Surprisingly delicate and flavoury though not without a touch of end acidity. *Last tasted June 1990 ★★★ (just).*

LAST TASTED IN THE 1980S Ch Lafite pale; bouquet evolved fragrantly; light, lean but flavoury. *Oct 1988 ★★★;* Ch Latour in 1964 interesting but tired. Touch of rot but hint of elegance in 1978. More recently – in a clear glass wartime bottle: dead brown, oxidised. *Last tasted in 1981. Avoid unless good level and provenance;* Ch Mouton-Rothschild in 1978: acceptable though acidic. A decade later, in wartime bottle, healthy colour but anything but healthy nose and taste: overblown and sour. *Last tasted April 1988;* Ch Figeac first in a green wartime bottle, good level but a whiff of banana, cracking up. Next, a few months later: sweet, almost chocolatey nose; touch of edgy acidity. *At Desai's, Paris, Dec 1989. At best ★*

# 1940–1949

Five wartime vintages, some, as will be seen, quite good, and five post-war vintages, three being of almost unsurpassed quality. Although Bordeaux was well away from the war zones, following the collapse of France it was governed by the Vichy régime and under German occupation until the war's end. It could have been worse. Wine was needed; wine was produced, the main problems being lack of labour and materials.

The *négociants* were in an invidious position. They were obliged to trade with the Germans which, unsurprisingly, left them open to the charge of collaboration. There were uncomfortable moments for them when the war ended. But the main problem was to reconstruct the trade. Many traditional markets were badly dislocated and economically weak. British post-war restrictions lasted well into the 1950s. But, as if to make up for this, along came the '45s, '47s and '49s. Wine merchants everywhere restocked at what now looks like give-away prices, aided by Stafford Cripps, the austere Labour Minister who, with unexpected foresight, reduced the British import duties on wine.

## Vintages at a Glance
**Outstanding ★★★★★**
1945, 1947, 1949
**Very Good ★★★★**
None
**Good ★★★**
1943, 1946, 1948

## 1940 ★★
Distinctly better than 1939 but tough wartime conditions, shortage of labour and materials. Average-sized crop. Some attractive wines though uneven.
**Ch Lafite** Very good level. Deep, rich red brown; low-keyed but harmonious. Flavoury. *Oct 1988* ★★
**Ch Latour** Nine notes. A strong classic Cabernet Sauvignon nose and flavour, raw edged and still immature in 1967. In the mid-1970s (the short wartime corks noted) surprisingly nice, velvety and flavoury. Very forthcoming, fragrant bouquet, rich, chunky. More recently, still deep in colour and laden with fruit and tannin. *Last tasted at a pre-sale tasting in Chicago, Sept 1990* ★★★
**Ch Margaux** Only tasted in half-bottles, the last pair at Manfred Wagner's Margaux tasting. Both with top-shoulder levels: palish, orange-tinged colour; scents of mocha and toffee. Better on palate: sweet, attractive, very flavoury despite slight acid edge. Holding well. *Last tasted in Zurich, Jan 1997* ★★★
**Ch Mouton-Rothschild** Three bottles, one mid-shoulder, at Lloyd Flatt's tasting. The top-level wines had a beautiful colour; gushingly fragrant bouquet; sweet, soft, and lovely, with a very dry finish. *April 1986. At best* ★★★★
**Ch Cheval Blanc** A fragrant, flavoury magnum. *Tasted at the château, Sept 1986* ★★★★
**Ch La Mission Haut-Brion** All from the Woltner cellars. First noted at the pre-sale tasting in 1978, then at Desai's, and later at Wolf's La Mission tasting. All in excellent condition. Not a big La Mission but very fragrant, rich, firm. Virtually perfect. *Last tasted June 1990* ★★★★
**Ch La Tour Haut-Brion** Sweet, fragrant but short. *Tasted June 1990* ★★★

OTHER GOOD 1940s TASTED IN THEIR TWENTIES AND THIRTIES Ch Haut-Brion, Ch Calon-Ségur and Ch Palmer.

## 1941 ★
Small crop harvested under difficult conditions. It had a poor reputation, which is not entirely borne out by my notes on the few tasted.
**Ch Lafite** A wonderfully evolved bouquet and flavour, spicy, fragrant, crisp and clean. *Oct 1988* ★★★★
**Ch Latour** 'Austere' noted in 1969 and 1978, though light for Latour, flavoury, some charm and a surprisingly fragrant aftertaste. *Last noted 1981. At best* ★★
**Ch La Mission Haut-Brion** Consistent notes at the pre-sale tasting in 1978, at Desai's in 1985 and at Wolf's. All from the Woltner cellars. Plummy brown colour; rich, coffee-like bouquet; lightish, lean, with a touch of end acidity. *Last tasted June 1990* ★

## 1942 ★★
Better spring and summer conditions spoilt by a poor September. A small crop of 'useful' wines. Now variable.
**Ch Margaux** Only one note. Wartime green bottle. Plain capsule. A healthy, glowing, luminous appearance; light, gentle fragrance with crisp fruit; sound, delicate, flavoury but with tart finish. *At the Wagner tasting, Nov 2000* ★★★ *(just)*.
**Ch La Mission Haut-Brion** Slight variations at the two major La Mission tastings. Desai's in 1985: a light, gentle fragrance but some decay. More recently at Karl-Heinz Wolf's tasting: a pretty looking wine, but sweeter and in better condition. An uncharacteristically feminine La Mission. *Last tasted June 1990. At best* ★★★
**Ch Palmer** Rich mahogany; dry, on the light side, tart but drinkable. *Pre-sale, May 1991* ★★

OTHER MAJOR 1942s TASTED IN THE 1980s Ch Lafite several non-committal notes in the 1970s. A good bottle at Flatt's tasting: healthy, attractive, pleasantly evolved, fruity. *Last tasted Oct 1988. At best* ★★★★; Ch Latour as a 20-year old it was opaque and 'loaded' but subsequently noted, 'ageing', the wine short and lacking any vestige of charm. *Last tasted June 1981* ★; Ch Mouton-Rothschild also short but at least positively, perhaps precariously, fragrant and flavoury. *March 1983* ★★; Ch Ausone extremely good, one of the best '42s. Richly mature colour; harmonious bouquet, fragrant, refreshing. *At Flatt's Ausone tasting, Oct 1987* ★★★★; Ch Cheval Blanc pricked. Should be better than this. *Dec 1987;*

Ch Figeac attractive, fragrant though faded. *Dec 1989* ★★★;
Ch La Fleur-Pétrus overall lean and dry but with good
flavour. *Dec 1980* ★★★; Ch Lascombes body sagging like the
belly of a superannuated footballer. Good colour though and
decent fruit. *Feb 1985* ★★; and Ch Petit-Village owned at
the time by the Ginistets, later given by Pierre to his sister,
Mme Prats, and her son Bruno of Ch Cos d'Estournel.
Deeply coloured; harmonious Cabernet Franc bouquet; good
sturdy wine. *Dining with Bruno Prats at his Ch Marbuzet, May
1986* ★★★

## 1943 ★★★

The best of the war vintages. Overall, wines with richness and
fruit but short, the best still drinking well. Of over 50 notes:
Ch Lafite Tasted only at Lloyd Flatt's spectacular tasting:
healthy sound nose and, a feature of Lafite, evolving into a
beautiful, delicate bouquet. However noted as 'a bit screwed
up' on the palate, but flavoury. *Oct 1988* ★★★
Ch Margaux First noted in 1975 as deep; with delicate
bouquet and taste, in good condition; an abrupt finish noted
consistently. Nevertheless, even when it 'teeters on the brink',
always interesting. *Last tasted Feb 1988. At best* ★★★★
Ch Latour I have just looked up my original note, made in
April 1954 when I was still at Saccone's: 'full' (appearance)
'unspectacular at first, but laden with overtones' (the nose), a
'trifle hard and might not improve much. Peculiar but fruity
and super taste'. A 'strapping' (strong, burly) note in the mid-
1960s and, by the 1970s, changing colour, to paler but lovely
autumnal red. I thought its bouquet was as good as the '45,
beautifully developed, 'delicate but concentrated'. Rich, crisp
and flavoury but lacking length. *Last tasted July 1981. At best*
★★★★ *Should still be good.*
Ch Mouton-Rothschild In the Baron's absence, the château
was assiduously looked after by an old lady retainer. Baron
Philippe, whose wife died in a concentration camp, was not at
the château during the war. The '43 Mouton had to wait until
August 1946 to be bottled, and they were still having to use
relatively poor quality wartime corks. I first tasted the wine, a
bottle from a good private cellar in Australia, in 1975. It was
unappealing. It is curious that I have drunk so many good
bottles of Mouton at Ch Lafite, the '43 being no exception. At
a Sunday lunch in March 1983: uncorked at 10am and poured
at 1.30pm to accompany soft brown eggs presented on a
wicker-work tray and served with 'soldiers' of toast by a white
gloved man servant, the Mouton was undeterred: a
magnificent vibrant colour; a whiff of bottle stink which soon
cleared to reveal a wonderful spiciness, subsiding by 3.30pm,
the end of lunch. A lovely, flavoury mouthful. Three years later,
another attractive bottle, its nose opening up, positively
belching, a Mouton characteristic *cassis* fragrance and
inimitable flavour. *Last tasted April 1986* ★★★★★
Ch Haut-Brion First tasted in 1959, at that time a soft, very
pleasant wine, not unbalanced like some '43s. Showing well in
the 1970s but not tasted since 1978. Should still be good ★★★
Ch Cheval Blanc Tasted twice. Well developed in 1974.
More recently: rich, mature-looking; harmonious; sweet,
perfect weight and flavour. *Last noted lunching at Berry Bros,
May 1993* ★★★★
Ch Ausone Lively, sweet, appealing, good, rich and rounded.
Like other '43s, a bit short. *Oct 1982* ★★★
Ch Beychevelle Pale; crisp; dry slightly woody. *At a pre-sale
tasting, May 1993* ★

Ch Cap de Mourlin A creaking but attractive St-Émilion,
the oldest of the 11 (red) vintages served at the fifth
anniversary of the Académie du Vin de Bordeaux in the city's
Grand Théâtre. *Last tasted June 1998* ★★
Ch Cos d'Estournel Four notes since 1974. Cedary, very
attractive nose, rich on the palate but a touch of acidity and
the usual '43 bluntness. *Last tasted June 1988. At best* ★★★
Ch Figeac Historic. The first vintage vinified by Thierry
Manoncourt when he was allowed to return to the château.
The young man made a good job of it, producing a wine of
extraordinary strawberry-like sweetness and exciting flavour,
yet well balanced. *A bottle brought by Thierry from his cellar to
Desai's Figeac tasting in Paris, Dec 1989* ★★★
Ch Gruaud-Larose An extremely good note in 1975: very
ripe, scented bouquet; fine flavour and balance though a bit
austere. More recently: rich, vegetal nose; crisp, good fruit but
raw finish. *Last tasted in magnum, Sept 1993. At best* ★★★
Ch La Mission Haut-Brion Three good notes, at Desai's
and Wolf's tasting, packed with flavour, rich and ripe. Most
recently: a pale green wartime bottle: still fairly deep; an earthy,
freshly picked mushroom, arboreal, autumnal bouquet and
flavour. Showing its age but sweet, with tannins. *Last noted
dining with Danielle and Christian Pol-Roger in Épernay, June 1997.
At best* ★★★★
Ch Siran Fragrant nose, flavour and aftertaste. *Oct 1997* ★★★★

## 1944 ★★

Forgotten and rather underrated. A fairly big crop of light
wines of irregular quality. Some charmers.
Ch Lafite One of the charmers, particularly in its youth. First
tasted in 1986; a long note which I can boil down to 'refined,
soft, silky on the palate, its bouquet the best feature'. And at
Flatt's tasting, again better on the nose with touch of maltiness
on palate. *Last noted Oct 1988. Variable, risky. Depends on cellaring.*
Ch Latour Five notes, from the mid-1950s. Not a big Latour
and with some charm. Pungency and piquant acidity also
noted. *Last tasted June 1983. At best* ★★
Ch Mouton-Rothschild Like the 1943, late-bottled, this
time in 1947. An inimitable spicy, rich, high-toned bouquet;
sweet, flavoury but with a touch of rawness. *April 1986* ★★★
Ch Haut-Brion Surviving half-bottles with variations of
level, yet delicate and healthy (in 1979). Most recently, a low-
shoulder bottle with old, honeyed, spicy nose; sweet, chewy,
touch of vanilla, excellent acidity. The air in this ullaged bottle
must have been very benign. *Drinking surprisingly well at a
British Airways seminar at Mosimann's, April 1998. At best* ★★★
Ch La Mission Haut-Brion Fairly pale, fully mature but a
bit lactic in 1977. Most recently, a Woltner cellar bottle with an
attractive bouquet but curious overtones. Sweet, lightish, aged
but pretty. Short. *Last tasted June 1996* ★
Ch Pontet-Canet Shipped by Cruse, the owners, and
bottled by their London agent: ripe, delicious (in 1979). A
decade later, colour tile red shot with ruby; glorious flavour
with light, silky, leathery tannins. A charmer. *Last tasted at a
dinner party at home, May 1989* ★★★★

## 1945 ★★★★★

Arguably one of the greatest vintages of the 20th century, and
in my opinion eclipsing the 1961. An early harvest yielded
magnificent, long-lasting wines of the highest quality. The very
small crop size was the result of severe frosts in May, when the

vines were literally nipped in the bud. The wines' exceptional ripeness, concentration and power were due to a summer of drought and excessive heat. The vines and the winemaking also benefited – though it may not have been appreciated at the time – from some fortuitous circumstances: first, old, or at least fully mature, vine stock as there had been little replanting during the war; second, traditional winemaking methods. New oak barrels were a thing of the future as was the influence of the consultant oenologist. The best, and best kept, are still superb. I think I was born and entered the wine trade at the right time for I see I have over 200 notes covering a wide range of châteaux of this great vintage.

**Ch Lafite** I didn't have the opportunity to taste this wine in cask; I was in the army, and by the time I had entered the wine trade in 1952, most merchants had by then sold their top '45s. I have certainly made up for it since. My first note of the 1945 Lafite was made in 1967 towards the end of my first season at Christie's. Nearly 30 notes have been logged since, and in varying sizes of bottles from halves to double magnums. Yet despite the varying occasions and contexts, what is remarkable is the relatively little bottle variation. It is important to realise that even the 1945 Lafite does not have the depth of colour, weight or intensity of Latour and Mouton. It is Lafite, and from the start I recorded its medium depth and already mature appearance, also, more importantly, its refined and delicate bouquet, flavoury richness and extended finish.

My most recent notes include a flawless magnum at the Eigensatz tasting in 1993 and an extraordinarily good magnum, despite its mid-shoulder level, at Christan Sveass' great dinner in Oslo. The cork was sound so the air in the ullage must have been benign. The wine had a beautiful colour; medium deep, with rich 'legs' but not intense, unlike the flanking Margaux and La Mission, the colours of which seemed to press the sides of the glass. Just about every note over the years refers to a glorious fragrance which seems to unravel itself after 15 or 20 minutes in the glass. Also noticed at the Sveass dinner, and previously, its sweetness to which one adds, unoriginally, rich, soft with masked tannins. A glorious mouthful. *Last noted April 1996* ★★★★★

**Ch Latour** A great wine. Surely one of the best ever Latours, drinking beautifully now but with many years more life. As with Lafite, not tasted in my early years in the trade. My first note was made in October 1967: 'deep'; very rich, 'packed' (bouquet); dry, extremely vigorous and youthful for a 22-year old, with plenty of tannin and acidity. 'A good strapping drink'. And so on for another 28 notes through the next three decades. What I have noticed, as it matured further, is its increasing sweetness. An amalgam of notes gathered at dinners and tastings: always deep, with an opaque core; spicy bouquet, eucalyptus, cedar, smoky tea (Lapsang), cheesy – not smelly cheese but a sort of sweaty tannin. Full-bodied, rich, complete, silky, tannins, complex, great length. The very best: a double magnum from Lenoir Josey's cellar at a Wine and Food Society dinner in Houston in 1983. Served last it trounced the preceding 'stars', including Lafite and Margaux '53, the exquisite Mouton '49, and others. *Last noted dining at a charming lakeside restaurant in Pfäffikon near Zurich, following Manfred Wagner's Ch Margaux tasting, Nov 2000* ★★★★★

**Ch Margaux** A magnificent wine. Nothing fragile and feminine about this '45, at least not in its early years. From the start, very deep in colour with a beautiful richness and intensity; and in the 1970s with Latour-like massiveness and

tannin. Its fragrance, the hallmark of Margaux, being variously described as ripe mulberry, crystallised violets, cedar cigar box, creamy – and always glorious. On the palate its initial tannins ameliorating, now soft and velvety. The climax of two Bordeaux Club dinners (at Caius, Cambridge, 1996, and at John Jenkins' Jacobean Childerley Hall, Oct 2000). A vivacious and fabulously fragrant bottle at the Sveass dinner and showing at its magnificent best at both of Wagner's Margaux tastings, in 1997 and 2000. *Last tasted in Zurich, Nov 2000* ★★★★★

**Ch Mouton-Rothschild** Baron Philippe was back in time for the harvest. His label appropriately headed *L'Année de la Victoire*. In this great but small vintage he produced 151,744 bottles (and halves), 2091 magnums and just 116 *grands formats* (which embraces double magnums, jeroboams and *impériales*). I originally coined the phrase 'a Churchill of a wine', meaning larger than life, immediately recognisable, complex, endlessly fascinating, unforgettable. The only first growth I tasted in its (relative) youth. In July 1954 I wrote 'dark, deep, (yet) translucent; amazing nose. Quite unlike *any* other claret, spicy, Indian mango chutney(!). Loaded with tannin, acidity and all the good things. Full and flavoury'. Apart from the chutney, it still applies. The first thing to notice is its extraordinary colour. I have on more than one occasion recognised the wine by this alone. And its bouquet is equally distinctive, in fact one of the most astonishing smells ever to emerge from grapes grown out of doors. The power and spiciness surges out of the glass like a sudden eruption of Mount Etna: cinnamon, eucalyptus, ginger, 'Friars Balsam' (noted once!). Impossible to describe but inimitable, incomparable, and, because of this and its appearance, several times 'guessed' blind. There is simply no other wine like it. Its taste is a component of smell, its fragrance is reflected on the palate. Still lovely, still vivacious. Seemingly tireless – indeed another half century anticipated. *Last tasted blind, and immediately recognised, at Wilfred Jaeger's mountain-top late lunch, June 2001* ★★★★★★ *(6 stars)*

**Ch Haut-Brion** Again, a superb wine, possibly the best ever Haut-Brion. That great taster Harry Waugh merely wrote 'Really good, heavenly wine'. This was in 1953, and as always, his judgement was unerring. In 1959 I noted its earthy richness, full yet soft, 'a great wine of a great year'. Later, in 1974, 'at peak' – but on it goes! Again, some two dozen notes, mainly bottles, just one magnum, and a couple of Belgian-bottled (Dimets & Lyssens). What this wine manages to do is to combine concentration with elegance and, despite being laden with 1945 tannin, it is relatively unobtrusive – or at least, it fits in. To describe all its virtues and nuances is impossible: consistently deep in colour, 'warm ruby' quite recently noted, with a rich, mahogany, mature rim; its bouquet fragrant of course. Scanning my notes, 'vanilla chocolate', tobacco, earthy,

---

## Lenoir Josey III

*Oil man from Houston, Texas. Connoisseur, collector and senior member of the Wine & Food Society. One of the earliest buyers at Christie's (from the early 1970s), he began accumulating wine in his twenties and like all of his acquisitive ilk, he did not know when to stop! (He also has a worldclass collection of toy soldiers, for example!) In recent years he found his cellar building up enormously so had a sale through Christie's in November 2000. This was one of the best single-owner sales ever held in the USA: lots included wines previously cellared at Glamis Castle in Scotland and not moved for three generations.*

harmonious, honeycomb, touch of liquorice; silky texture, crisp fruit, luscious, perfect weight, great length. A gentle giant. But all the time, remembering it is a *1er cru classé* Graves, not a Médoc. *Last tasted Dec 2000* ★★★★★

**Ch Ausone** First tasted in April 1955. 'Big and black. *Corsé.* Finely knit but nowhere near ready.' Twenty years later, still astringent, and, in 1986, noting its fine, deep colour and powerful, idiosyncratic 'dried leaves' flavour. Unfruity and very tannic. No recent notes, the last, at Flatt's tasting, a screwed-up magnum. *Last tasted Oct 1987. At best probably* ★★★★, *hard to say.*

**Ch Cheval Blanc** It was over 20 years old when I first tasted it: 'fragrant, forthcoming, a trace of highish volatile acid enhancing its richness' and on the palate some sweetness, not a heavyweight, fine consistency and long dry finish. A total contrast to the uniquely mammoth '47. A more typical Cheval Blanc in its fragrance, deft touch and elegance. Alas, not recently tasted, but noted as gently faded in 1987, and a flavoury but acetic-edge magnum at the great Eigensatz tasting. Clearly some problems with vinification. *Last noted May 1993. At best* ★★★★

**Ch Pétrus** A great disappointment when first tasted in 1974. Half a dozen much better notes in the 1980s upholding its formidable reputation and (now) outrageous price. Dining with a dear old friend, the late George Reece, in Los Angeles I noted it as the 'Noval '31 of claret, though really, I don't think of it as claret at all; indeed, the conventional British claret drinker thinks more in terms of the leaner and, dare I say it, more subtle Médocs. Having said that, this wine is hugely impressive, with a lively depth of colour; a bouquet that opens up gloriously. No question: sweet on the palate, full of fruit, flavour and, for a big wine, elegant. Almost too rich at a tasting in 1986, showing perfectly at Arthur Hallé's wonderful tasting in 1987 despite the sommelier opening and decanting the wines in the wrong order. In fact it worked out well. We were confounded, its bouquet perfection, evolving fabulously; mulberries, blackberries, deft touch of ginger, and powering out effortlessly. Two hours in the glass and only starting to fade. All the components in the mouth. 'Almost too nice' and 20 out of 20 awarded by me at one tasting. My last note happens to be one of the most unbelievable ever made. Karl-Heinz Wolf intended to serve a Belgian-bottled jeroboam at dinner (in the middle of a J J Prüm tasting). Labelled '*Château Pétrus/1er des Grand Crus (sic) de Pomerol and bottled by Aug. Delgouffre & Co*'. It had of course been standing for some hours, but when the cork was drawn at 4pm it was pure vinegar. My host promptly substituted magnums of '82 Ch

---

## Jean-Pierre Moueix

*Jean-Pierre Moueix must be one of the shrewdest men in the entire Bordeaux trade. His company operates from modest offices in Libourne and specialises in the wines of the Right Bank. Jean-Pierre, now retired, can take a great deal of credit for putting Pomerol on the map, this relatively small district being unimportant in the Bordeaux scheme of things until after World War Two. In 1945 he befriended the owner of Ch Pétrus, Mme Loubat, and arranged to market the wines of this property exclusively. On Mme Loubat's death in 1961, he gained a half-share of the property when her nephew sold him his part of the inheritance. Pétrus became the first 'cult wine'. Jean-Pierre's son Christian, who has inherited his father's old world courtesy and charm, now very effectively runs the Moueix properties and businesses.*

Pichon-Lalande. However, at 9.30pm, out of curiosity, the jeroboam was poured. It still had vinegary overtones, yet, to everyone's astonishment, an hour later it started to recover and develop sweetly on the nose. It was, of course, tart yet curiously refreshing and went well with sweetbreads and braised asparagus! *Last noted overlooking the Attersee, April 1999. At best* ★★★★

What is so extraordinary is that each of these top '45s is unquestionably great yet each is so distinctly different. I suspect that not one of the proprietors, and certainly not his *maître de chai*, was looking over his shoulder to see what the others were doing. They just got on with it, uninhibited and totally uninfluenced by outside factors. No smart consultant oenologists, no talk of 'global' taste, and not a 'wine critic' in sight! 1945 was particularly successful in Pomerol. In fact, the post-war vintages put Pomerol on the map; at least, the English map. Hitherto, these wines had mainly been appreciated by denizens of the Low Countries.

**Ch Gazin** One of the first great Pomerols I ever tasted: 'powerful stuff' in 1964, 'silky; perfectly balanced' in 1967, 'velvet over iron' in 1969. Eight notes between 1964 and 1974, retaining its lovely colour; sweet, old cedary bouquet; still rich, velvety, perfection. *Last tasted Nov 1992* ★★★★★

**Ch La Conseillante** Another superb wine. In fact I have always admired the wines of this slightly underrated but never underpriced château. First in 1977; two ripe, rich Harvey's bottlings in 1986, and a good Danish bottling (Schalberg) from Aalholm Castle, losing weight but still soft, delicate and lovely. Most recently a superb magnum at Len Evans' 'Single-bottle Club' dinner: fabulous fruit, perfect balance, complete. *Last noted in the Hunter Valley, Australia, Sept 2000* ★★★★★

Deliberately out of order, a magnificent Graves:

**Ch La Mission Haut-Brion** Vying with the '29 as the greatest vintage of La Mission. I had hardly heard of the Woltners when I first tasted it, but many notes later, through the 1970s and 1980s, confirmed its status. Three notes in the last decade: a deeply coloured; vigorous and 'stably' bouquet, gloriously tangy and high-toned, dining with the Lloyd-Webbers in 1994; at 50 years of age, a gloriously rich, fragrant bottle; full-bodied, fabulous flavour, still tannic at Peter Ziegler's in 1995. Lastly a magnum, displaying its characteristic tobacco-like, gravelly flavour, very sweet, full, rich, spicy. *Last noted at Christan Sveass' dinner in Oslo, April 1996* ★★★★★

OF THE MANY CLASSED GROWTH MÉDOCS TASTED RECENTLY

**Ch Batailley** First tasted in 1957: characteristically good fruit through the 1970s, and a particularly good note in 1986. Now showing its age, rather vegetal and fading. *Last noted at Hugh Johnson's Bordeaux Club dinner, July 1995. Once* ★★★, *now* ★★

**Ch Calon-Ségur** The post-war vintages of Calon were probably the best ever, and still extremely good. I think it was the first '45 I ever tasted: 'well-rounded. Pleasing in every way.' Too young in October 1952. Many good notes in the 1960s and 1970s. 'Fruity but austere' in 1966, packed with fruit and flavour. Three recent notes: a deep, velvety, rich mahogany colour; mature nose, touch of vanilla and coffee, fleshy, cedary; rich though drying out a bit. Still tannic; still impressive. *Last tasted Dec 1995. At best* ★★★★

**Ch Cantemerle** A lovely wine. Typically fragrant and gentle for a '45. Notably lovely bottles at Desai's in 1986 and a low-keyed but soft, rich and lovely wine from Mme Binaud's cellar. *Last tasted Oct 1995* ★★★★

**Ch Gruaud-Larose** Many noted. Just starting to become drinkable in 1954. I suppose fruitiness is the hallmark of Gruaud, and it displayed this, and other virtues, at its best in the 1970s. But from start to finish, tannic. In the 1990s a full, fruity, very fragrant but very dry tannic magnum in 1994, an unusually named *Dame-Jeanne* in 1996, an impressive, very flavoury bottle at a British Airways dinner, though acidity beginning to catch up and, more recently, a sensational jeroboam, deep ruby, multi-dimensional, full of fruit but after 30 minutes drying and dying. *Last tasted Sept 1998. At best* ★★★★

**Ch Langoa-Barton** A wonderful wine. Bordeaux-bottled by Barton-Guestier: attractive, rich, intense (1974, 1981); fragrant, crisp (1986), and most recently fully mature looking; glorious, rich bouquet; excellent cedary flavour and dry finish. *At lunch with Liliane, Eva and Anthony Barton, Sept 1998* ★★★★★

**Ch Léoville-Barton** Raw, tannic and totally unready in 1954. Softening in the 1960s, excellent Berry Bros and château-bottling superb in the early 1970s; Corney & Barrow's noted. Most recently a lovely, fragrant, cedary, château-bottling. *Last tasted April 1991. At best* ★★★★

**Ch Léoville-Poyferré** Bottled by Saccone & Speed and tasted there as a 27-year old 'junior' in 1954 and 1955. Beautiful bouquet but austere; equally applying to bottles tasted in 1986. Most recently, a magnum, château-bottled, showing its age, fading, losing fruit, but attractive. *Last tasted at the Rodenstock weekend in Sept 1996. At best* ★★★★*, now* ★★

**Ch Lynch-Bages** Noted in the 1950s and 1960s, at best in 1986, displaying its characteristic, almost exaggerated blackcurrant Cabernet Sauvignon nose. Most recently, superb Belgian-bottled (bought at Christie's): luminous, lovely bouquet, glorious, spicy, eucalyptus flavour. Delicious but we did not linger as it cracked up within 20 minutes. *Dining at the Weiser's beachside villa on St Bart's, Feb 2000* ★★★★

**Ch Talbot** The always dependable, leaner fourth growth 'cousin' of Gruaud. Nothing but glowing notes from the start – well not quite the start, for I first tasted it lunching with Pierre Cordier, when he lived in splendid semi-isolation (his wife Pierrette lived in grand style in Bordeaux), at the château in 1976. A very ripe, *gibier* and amazingly sweet and delicious magnum at a Last Friday Club Lunch at Raji's in Memphis (1997), a fine 'bricky', still tannic jeroboam in 1998 and, most recently, a beautiful double magnum as guest of Pierre Cordier's daughters, owners of Talbot, dining at the Mirabelle in London. *Last noted April 2000* ★★★★★

OTHER 1945S LAST TASTED IN THE 1980S AND EARLY 1990S **Ch Cos d'Estournel** perfect flavour, texture, balance. *Feb 1986* ★★★★; **Ch Croizet-Bages** good flavour. Touch of acidity. *Aug 1991* ★★★; **Ch Ducru-Beaucaillou** the first '45 I ever tasted; in Sept 1952: 'too dry and too rough'! In short, a stern, tannic '45. Variable notes, flavoury but still a bit raw on the finish. *Last tasted Dec 1990. At best* ★★★; **Ch La Dominique** undrinkable, tannic in 1954; still unready in 1961, a rich exciting wine through the 1980s. *Last tasted July 1988* ★★★★; **Clos L'Église** variable. Rich but raw. *Last tasted Feb 1986. At best* ★★; **Ch L'Enclos** the lightest and driest Pomerol shipped by Cruse in the late 1940s. Silky, rich but dry finish. *Last tasted Feb 1986. At best* ★★★; **Ch Figeac** extraordinarily sweet, almost Mouton-like peach and fragrance. Overtaken by tannins. *Dec 1989* ★★★; **Ch La Fleur-Gazin** variable. A lovely note in the early 1970s. Later, its

fragrance and silky Pomerol-texture failing to materialise. *Last tasted Feb 1986. At best* ★★★; **Ch Le Gay** variable but some bottles fabulously rich, with great concentration. Tannic though superb aftertaste. *Last noted July 1990. At best* ★★★★★; **Ch Grand-Puy-Lacoste** slight variation, one marred by poor cork. Then an opaque, intense bottle with crisp, classic Pauillac nose, full-bodied, concentrated, well preserved. Long life. *Last tasted June 1988* ★★★★★; **Ch Léoville-Las-Cases** several very variable notes but mainly excellent, the best from Aalholm Castle, shipped by Cruse and Danish-bottled by Kjaer & Sommerfeldt: fabulous colour; rich, blossoming bouquet but still very tannic. *Last tasted July 1989. At best* ★★★★★; **Ch Malescot St-Exupéry** several notes. Exuding the characteristic Malescot cassis Cabernet aroma; lovely crisp fruit. *Last tasted Feb 1986. At best* ★★★★; **Ch Montrose** unsurprisingly tough in its early days but, though rich and spicy, lean and leathery. Good wine so long as it does not dry out completely. *Last tasted Feb 1986* ★★★ *(possibly* ★★★★*)*; **Ch Mouton d'Armailhacq** always a charmer, even in 1945. Several notes: piquant, stylish, flavoury, at best delicious. *Last tasted Feb 1986. At best* ★★★★; **Ch Nenin** variable, chewy, sweet, chocolatey, coarse texture. *Last tasted Sept 1996. At best* ★★★; **Ch Palmer** various bottlings, variable notes. Some excellent but though crisp and with good fruit, lacking the intrinsic richness of a fine '45. *Last tasted Dec 1986. At best* ★★★★; **Ch Pichon-Baron** several very variable notes, from dried out to rich and penetrating. *Last tasted Feb 1986. At best* ★★★; **Ch Pontet-Canet** Cruse-owned, Cruse-bottled (in Bordeaux). Basically an excellent '45, understandably hard in 1954 yet very rich aroma. Retained its severity well into the 1960s, but the best bottles, sweet, rich and more mellow, in the late 1970s to mid-1980s. *Last tasted June 1990. At best* ★★★★; **Ch Rausan-Ségla** many notes, various bottlings, in various conditions, the best being three château-bottled magnums in the mid- to late 1970s. *Last noted July 1988. At best* ★★★★; **Ch Rauzan-Gassies** the start of a long underperforming period. Several notes. Not good. *Last tasted Feb 1986*; **Clos René** Cruse, associated mainly with classic Médocs, greatly appreciated the post-war Pomerols. This was a favourite of their London agent and introduced to Harvey's customers by Harry Waugh in the 1950s though my first note 'magnificent nose; fabulous flavour, perfect balance. Perfection' appears in 1974. Later described as a 'rosy-cheeked peasant'. *Last tasted Feb 1986. At best* ★★★★; **Ch La Tour Haut-Brion** raw and coarse. *Last tasted June 1990* ★; **Ch Trotanoy** magnificent, incredibly rich, fully evolved. *Last tasted Feb 1986. At best* ★★★★★; and **Vieux Ch Certan** a mammoth wine. Excellent in mid-1970s. Variable. *Last noted Feb 1986. At best* ★★★★

THE MOST IMPRESSIVE '45S OF THE OTHERS TASTED ONLY AT BIPIN DESAI'S MARATHON IN 1986 **Ch Brane-Cantenac** ★★★★; **Dom de Chevalier** ★★★; **Ch La Fleur-Pétrus** ★★★; **Ch La Gaffelière** ★★★★★; **Ch Haut-Bailly** ★★★★; **Ch Kirwan** ★★★★; **Ch La Pointe** ★★★★; **Ch Pichon-Lalande** ★★★; and **Ch La Tour de Mons** ★★★★★

# 1946 ★★★

Good enough summer but first half of September very wet. Late, hot harvest. In fact it was not a bad vintage at all but, sandwiched between the great '45s and '47s, largely ignored.

**Ch Lafite** Just two notes, showing surprisingly well at Lloyd Flatt's Lafite tasting in 1988: good colour and soft fruit nose, not bad flavour, 'chewy', but lacking length and Lafite elegance. Most recently, at a disposal of unwanted stocks from a Rothschild family cellar, pale, woody–nosed and tart. *Last noted at a pre-sale tasting, March 1996. At best ★★★ (just).*

**Ch Latour** Five notes between 1964 – laden with tannin – and 1976, probably at its best around then though showing a touch of raw acidity. Sound but short in 1981 and a subsequent oxidised bottle. *Last tasted June 1990. At best ★★*

**Ch Mouton-Rothschild** Remarkably good when first noted in 1971, impressively deep colour; rich, fruity, typically Mouton Cabernet nose. A big wine that, at the time, was more drinkable than the '45. Another good note in 1988: no signs of decay but lean. By 1986 though still deep and spicy, a bit austere – yet a high mark. The most recent, still rich and fruity though acidity noted. Tasted blind I thought it was a '47 or a '49. *Last tasted March 1989 ★★★★*

**Ch La Mission Haut-Brion** Four notes, all bottles from the Woltner cellars. First tasted in 1978: lovely colour, flavoury, acidic but good for the year. At Wolf's tasting in 1981, flavoury, lean but some astringency. Then an oxidised bottle. *Last tasted June 1990. At best ★★*

OTHER 1946s **Ch Lascombes** 1985 ★★★ and **Ch Baret** opaque, marvellously rich nose and fabulous old Graves flavour. *Part of a large stock from the château, Sept 1983 ★★★★*

# 1947 ★★★★★

The second of the three great post-war vintages. An increasingly hot summer followed by harvesting in almost tropical conditions. The grapes had an exceptionally high sugar content but the heat caused serious fermentation problems, resulting in quite a few wines suffering from high volatile acidity. On the whole, exceptionally rich almost voluptuous wines, though some living dangerously.

**Ch Lafite** Combining richness and charm. Tasted on nearly 20 occasions, first in 1958. Then, and in 1959, I noted it as faultless: really lovely, full flavoured, perfectly balanced. Yet in the mid-1960s and some noted through the 1970s, I detected a 'prickly', slightly tart acid edge, though it was still delicious. And in the 1980s 'charm and power', a gloriously rich, fragrant, lovely wine. At the great Eigensatz first growth magnum tasting in 1993 I thought the Lafite was the most perfect of the 'flight'. More recently, very good flavour, but edgy acidity creeping in at the Sveass dinner (1996). The most recent, its appearance mellowing as was its bouquet. Still fairly sweet, soft, drinking well but acidity trying to catch up. *Last noted at the Rodenstock wine weekend, Sept 1998 ★★★★ Drink up.*

**Ch Latour** Predictably a big wine, but judging from quite a large number of notes, something of a roller coaster. First tasted in May 1954: 'a very big wine', and a decade later 'as dry, full, big and raw'. In short it was going to need time.

---

## Académie du Vin de Bordeaux

*The great and the good. Founded in 1947 with the aim of maintaining standards and monitoring the quality of wine from its illustrious members – all growers of great distinction who have the finest traditions to uphold. The academy also organises frequent lectures and presentations to honour literary figures. I have been a membre d'honneur since 1973. Comte Alexandre de Lur Saluces is the president.*

---

Volatility noted in 1966, a certain austerity in the 1970s. Richness combined with noticeable acidity as it developed. Variable notes, though many good, fragrant and flavoury in the 1980s, and just a couple of notes in the last decade. A hefty, lively magnum in 1993 and, most recently, losing its pristine depth of colour; nose 'classic' but showing age; rim, still full-bodied, tannic with fragrant aftertaste. *A magnum, last noted Sept 1996. At best ★★★★*

**Ch Margaux** I noted this in September 1958 as 'big yet soft. Almost ready, lovely flavour', but as I and the wine developed, a decade later, noted 'its lack of Margaux's feminine charm, even a touch of coarseness and acidity'. However 'velvet' appears several times, so does 'a towering and rather unyielding wine' (1977). In 1987 two Hankey Bannister London bottlings, one oxidised, the other mellow and attractive; and at de Cock's tasting a very sweet, sound but souped up Vandermeurlen bottle. Three variable notes made in the last decade. Two at Manfred Wagner's Margaux tastings, an 'almost mammoth', highly impressive bottle from the dependable Nicolas cellar, recorked in 1998 but, at the second tasting, a very flavoury but tart mid-shoulder bottle. A sound, harmonious, well-constituted magnum though a bit 'four-square' at Kaplan's '1947s' dinner in 1997. *Last tasted Nov 2000. Variable, not the usual Margaux brilliance, but at best ★★★★*

**Ch Mouton-Rothschild** Youthful when first tasted in 1961. A 'wonderful vintage' wine, ecstatic notes through the 1970s remarking on its magnificent fragrance, concentration, depth, fabulous flavour and lovely aftertaste. Towards the end of the decade 'acidity noticeable'. A gloriously rich, soft, fleshy, elliptically perfect bottle at the Flatt tasting (1986). And so on. More recently, at the Sveass dinner in Oslo, an almost caricatured Mouton spiciness on the nose, with a very sweet, exotic flavour and aftertaste. Most recently, another recorked Nicolas bottle with exquisite bouquet. It was a glorious mouthful. Despite the lurking acidity, it was not showing its head over the parapet. *Last noted at a Rodenstock dinner, March 2001. At best at least ★★★★★ This is one of the great '47s.*

**Ch Haut-Brion** Only four notes. At ten years of age 'beautiful bouquet and flavour but far too strong to drink with enjoyment'. Stylish, hard and steely in 1971. Yet, time the healer – in the case of wine, the developer: a superb magnum at the Eigensatz tasting in 1993. More recently: an earthy, sweet, soft, fabulous bottle. *Last tasted Sept 1995. Not exactly from rags to richness, but at best ★★★★*

**Ch Ausone** Only three notes, in magnum and bottles, all very good. *Last tasted May 1993 ★★★★*

**Ch Ausone** Belgian-bottled by Vandermeurlen. Tasted blind: very fragrant; well balanced, with citrus-like fruit and acidity. Very attractive wine. *At Frans de Cock's tasting, Dec 1995 ★★★★*

**Ch Cheval Blanc** This should have headed my list of 1947s for it is not only the most impressive, famous (and expensive) '47 but is unquestionably one of the greatest wines of all time. It did not put Cheval Blanc on the map – it was already there – but it was, and is, a terrific eye-opener. First noted in March 1959 'very full flavoured, soft on the palate yet with very dry almost bitter finish. Great quality'. More ecstatic notes in the mid-1960s 'full, *very* rich, silky, perfect' and in the margin 'knocked Lafite and Margaux out of court'! Three extremely good Harvey's bottlings interspersed with magnificent château-bottlings, including an incredibly rich, fat, ripe, magnificent magnum with high alcohol. But I could go on, and on, for I have been privileged to taste, to drink, to note the '47 Cheval Blanc on well over two dozen occasions. I confess to describing its mammoth concentration and sweetness as 'port-like' and, dare I say it, prefer the elegance of the 1966! My best notes were made in the 1980s when it appeared to me to be at its zenith: 'huge, soft, complete, rounded, fabulous, concentration' and so forth, but also 'lacking charm'. Its original opacity is now medium or fairly deep. It was at its best at the Latner dinner: lovely bouquet; losing its positive sweetness, though very rich and powerful (14% alcohol) with a slightly tarry taste. Still impressive. Most recently, faultless yet – dare I say it – unexciting. *At the Russian National Orchestra Patrons dinner at Spencer House, London, May 2000* ★★★★★

**Ch Cheval Blanc** Belgian-bottled: two in 1977 labelled 'J van der Meulen-Decannière' both rich, very flavoury but with marked acidity. The other more recently, I think just labelled 'Vandermeurlen', at de Cock's tasting in Paris: intensely deep; sound bouquet, lots of fruit on nose and palate, rich with an attenuated slightly acidic finish. *Last tasted Dec 1995* ★★★★

**Ch Pétrus** Unsurprisingly magnificent. Not tasted until it had nearly and effortlessly reached its quarter century. It was fabulous: deep, rich, rounded, more than faultless, impregnable. I had to wait 15 years to have the chance of tasting it again, blind. I thought it must have been a '45, '47 or '49, plumping for the latter. I was wrong, but not all that far out. Opaque, rich, ripe, sweet, full, chunky. More recently, in 1990, noting its mature rim, somewhat malty nose which sat in the glass, not budging. Incredibly sweet though so full-bodied that the alcohol was positively burning. High extract, with tannin and acidity. I hate to be condescending but this is not my style of wine. Perhaps just as well as one has to be a multimillionaire to buy it. Though I have to admit noting a perfect magnum at the Eigensatz tasting. *Last noted May 1993* ★★★★★

**Ch Pétrus** Three Vandermeurlen bottlings, first in 1977, sound but missing the size and fat of the château-bottling, then twice in Paris; slight bottle variation – or was it me? A magnificent, powerful, mouthfilling bottle at the tasting, then chunky, impressive but charming and tannic at dinner the same day. *Last tasted in Dec 1995. At best* ★★★★★

A RANGE OF OTHER '47S **Ch Batailley** I have always liked this, from the first taste in 1955. Deep and rich in 1989 and still drinking well. *Last tasted 1992* ★★★★; **Ch Calon-Ségur** first tasted in 1954 and on Saccone & Speed's retail list, château-bottled, at 16 shillings (80p) a bottle. Not cheap at the time. But it was a 'lovely big wine'. Several notes, including an excellent Danish-bottling and, rather curiously, six consistently good bottles through the 1990s. Now fully mature; lovely bouquet and flavour. Still surprisingly tannic but otherwise perfect. *Last noted at a Grands Crus dinner at Christie's, Sept 1997* ★★★★★; **Ch La Croix-de-Gay** rasping. *March 2001*; **Dom de Chevalier** an elegant crisp and fragrant magnum. *Sept 1996* ★★★★; **Ch Ducru-Beaucaillou** despite its sweetness, acidity noted from the start. Most recently, rich but edgy double magnum with coffee-like oxidation. Not a particularly good Ducru. *Last tasted Sept 1996. At best* ★★; **Clos L'Église** (sic) so many similar and confusing names congregate in Pomerol. Two rich, chunky 'male' magnums in the 1970s ★★★; **Ch L'Église-Clinet** a fascinating double magnum with a back slip label 'Jacobus Boelen', one-time distinguished wine merchants in Amsterdam. Opaque, plummy; very sweet, slightly caramelly nose; very full, rich, laden with fruit. Excellent though acidity lurking (this wine had been made by M P Lasserre of Clos René, the man who also made the great

1947 Ch Cheval Blanc). *A brilliant Rodenstock find, tasted Sept 1998* ★★★★★; **Clos L'Église-Clinet** (very confusing!) this was bottled by Jean Terrioux, Pauillac. Intensity, taste better than nose. Good length. *March 2001* ★★★; **Ch Figeac** at its opulent best. It is often almost over the top, but always manages to keep its balance. Several good notes in the 1980s. Most recently, two bottles with original corks, one dried out yet beguiling, the other sweet, positive and attractive. *Last tasted April 1997. At best* ★★★★; **Ch La Fleur** from the start (1955) an admirable wine and several bottlings since, including an excellent Schalburg bottling from Aalholm Castle. Incidentally, Baron Raben's favourite wine. Most recently, a gloriously rich, fragrant Vandermeurlen bottling. *Last tasted Dec 1995* ★★★★★; **Ch Gruaud-Larose** starting with three notes in 1954 when it was already rich, ripe and fruity, 'fairly advanced for a '47'. Much more recently, two bottles, one recorked in 1993, dry with good flavour and grip, the second sweeter and more richly evolved, with good Gruaud fruit. *Last tasted at a Kaplan '47s dinner in Chicago, April 1997. At best* ★★★★; **Ch Haut-Bailly** very popular in Scandinavia. Of the four bottles tasted, three were Swedish-bottled from Peter Wallenberg's cellar. All were very pale, but the bouquet expanded like Mouton. Sweet. Good length. The fourth was Danish-bottled, from Aalholm Castle, but served at a Commanderie de Bordeaux dinner in Oslo. Much deeper in colour; a scented, vanilla fragrance; full, rich, with good fruit and excellent acidity. *Last tasted April 1996. At best* ★★★★; **Ch Latour-à-Pomerol** very deep, opaque core; bouquet like rich tea; sweet, excellent flavour, extract, tannin and acidity. *March 2001* ★★★★; **Ch La Mission Haut-Brion** seven consistent notes since 1973, including two magnums, one at Desai's tasting, the other more recently: a deeply coloured wine with very distinctive nose and taste 'dried leaves', 'tobacco', 'cedar'. I even noted 'peat' on the palate. An extraordinarily rich, idiosyncratic Graves brilliantly handled by the Woltners. *Last tasted at Stephen Kaplan's '47s dinner in Chicago, April 1997* ★★★★★; **Ch Mouton d'Armailhacq** orange-tinged maturity; showing its age; a 'medicinal' Pauillac flavour but tart. *From Stuart Lever's cellar – a barn in Oxfordshire – and served at an alfresco lunch in great heat, July 1994*; **Ch Nenin** an opaque magnum; strawberry-like fragrance; decent flavour but severely tannic finish. *Sept 1996* ★★; **Ch Pavie** one London-bottled by Cruse's agents: a charming wine, lovely and long (1974) and two bottled by Vandermeurlen. With a good flavour and balance (1977) and most recently rich but tired out. *Last noted at Rodenstock's '47s dinner in Munich, March 2001. At best* ★★★; **Ch Pichon-Baron** three poor bottles in 1974 and 1977, an excellent Danish-bottled wine from Aalholm and a *Marie-Jeanne* bought at Christie's and tasted in a 'flight' of '47s: deep, mahogany; classic, oaky, harmonious bouquet; lovely flavour, in excellent

---

## Bordeaux Club

*Founded in 1947 by the late Allan Sichel, Professor Sir John (Jack) Plumb and Harry Waugh (the latter two died in 2001 aged 88 and 97 respectively). There are currently six members: Dr Neil McEndrick, Master of Gonville & Caius College (referred to in the text as 'Caius'), Cambridge; John Jenkins, farmer of Childerley Hall in Cambridgeshire; Hugh Johnson (Saling Hall, Essex); Dr Louis Hughes (Harley Street specialist in male fertility); Simon Berry of Berry Bros, and myself. We take it in turns to host dinners and produce our very best bottles.*

condition. *Last noted Sept 1996. At best* ★★★; **Ch Pichon-Lalande** several notes between 1954 and 1969. Rich and ripe but volatile acidity noted. More recently, a lean but flavoury and acidic magnum (1996) and a better magnum, with original cork at Stephen Kaplan's '47s dinner: good fruit, bricky, plummy fruit; very flavoury, very tannic. *Last tasted at the Ritz Carlton, Chicago, April 1997. At best* ★★★; **Ch Pontet-Canet** half a dozen notes. Deliciously soft and flavoury in 1956, a marvellously preserved jeroboam, bottled by Cruse (they never château-bottled) in 1973, a couple of the 1980s including a double magnum accompanying baked Brie – ugh! *Last tasted Oct 1992. At best* ★★★★; **Ch Rouget** quite a lot of wines of post-war vintages from this Pomerol estate found their way on to the British market but I can only find one recent note. It had been bought at auction by Lenoir Josey: a very rich autumnal colour; slight touch of woodiness; sweet, rich, tannic, sound. *At the Josey pre-sale tasting, Nov 2000* ★★★; **Ch Siran** soft, rich, sweet, lovely. *At a pre-sale tasting Oct 1993* ★★★★; and **Vieux Ch Certan** two bottles with slight variation at Kaplan's '47s dinner, one softer, with more vinosity, both rather stern and austere for '47s, but each a good mouthful. *Last tasted April 1997. At best* ★★

# 1948 ★★★

A good enough vintage though largely ignored by the trade as it sat so uncomfortably and inconveniently between the great 1947 and 1949. It could have been worse because although there was an exceptionally good spring, the summer was cold and the vines suffered from *coulure* (fruit drop). This reduced the crop which, however, was harvested in good September weather. Some of the wines had an aggressive masculinity and lacked charm, others had a more dextrous fragrance.

**Ch Lafite** I thought that it was a lovely wine when I first came across it in December 1954. Harry Waugh, at whose feet I was to sit, summed it up as 'good. Quite reasonably priced' (meaning cheap). I later noted it as mellow but lacking length, and it seemed to go through a dumb period. Two decades later it was showing its age, overripe, rich and exciting (at a splendid lunch at Leeds Castle, Kent 1974). Slightly variable but mainly good notes in the 1980s: 'perfect now', 'delicate', 'crisp', 'delicious' and which opened up with air, as Lafite so often does. *Last noted at Jack Plumb's Bordeaux Club dinner at Christ's College, Cambridge. At best* ★★★★

**Ch Latour** 'Green' and completely unready in 1956. Later, it was spicy, zestful but astringent. Frankly not a very well-balanced wine. Raw, tannic and unappealing. *Last tasted March 1989. At best* ★★★

**Ch Margaux** Happily not a beefy '48. More charm, though when first tasted in 1975, its richness was stalked by high acidity. A good bottle at the Coq Hardi in Paris in 1980: fragrant, harmonious, better balance and not showing its age. A jump of nearly 20 years: very fragrant; sweet, rich, lovely flavour, good length. An elegant '48. It paid to wait. *Last noted at another Kaplan dinner, Feb 1998* ★★★★

**Ch Mouton-Rothschild** A characteristically rich and exciting wine, 'green' when young, and needing well over 20 years to show its true paces. A well-developed magnum at Flatt's Mouton tasting in 1986, similarly attractive at a Latour/Mouton tasting in Wiesbaden. *Last noted March 1989* ★★★

**Ch Haut-Brion** Only two notes: an assertive – I nearly wrote pig-headed – tobacco-flavoured bottle in 1990, made up for a decade later by a well nigh perfect magnum: rich,

mature; sweet, harmonious bouquet; lovely flavour and weight, though I thought drying out a bit. *Last tasted at a Rodenstock dinner, March 2001. At best* ★★★★

**Ch Cheval Blanc** For some reason or other many notes, at least well over a dozen, sometimes alongside the '47 (I well recall Edmund Penning-Rowsell preferring it to the '47 at a dinner at the Travellers' Club in London in the 1970s). First tasted in 1961, a big wine, lots of fruit but unready. In the next two years noted as 'blackstrap', 'not very attractive but interesting'. In fact it took about 20 years to come into its own. I have seven good notes in the 1980s, by no means all château-bottled, including a singed-raisiny port-like Averys' bottling (English merchants were bottling Cheval Blanc as late as the 1960s), and four excellent Danish-bottled wines shipped *en barrique* by Eschenauer and bottled by K Dorph-Peterson. There were 182 bottles in three bins at Aalholm Castle. I can be precise because Daphne and I, with Brian Ebbeson, fortuitously Danish but working in Christie's wine department in London, packed up the vast cellar over one weekend: a hard and dusty job. Some 18 years later a deep, intense, still red, magnum; rather peppery but sweet, with crisp fruit. *Last noted alongside the '47 at Karl-Heinz Wolf's Cheval Blanc tasting in Austria, Sept 1997. At best* ★★★★

**Ch Pétrus** Just two notes: a black, plummy-coloured bottle with singed, ripe, rather sweaty and sickly nose, huge, tough and tannic in 1986. A less overtly aggressive bottle, sweeter, softer, more fleshy at the 'Stockholm' tasting in London. *Last noted April 1990. At best* ★★★★

**Ch Beychevelle** Hard, tough. *May 1993* ★

**Ch Calon-Ségur** Undrinkable in 1960s. Still tannic but good. Not a patch on the '47 and '49. *Last tasted Dec 1992* ★★

**Clos L'Église-Clinet** Opaque, astringent, very tannic. A magnum. *Sept 1996* ★

**Ch L'Évangile** Opaque; crisp fruit; lovely texture, silky tannins. Magnum. *Sept 1996* ★★★★

**Ch La Fleur** In 1996, a magnum. Deep, velvety; little nose; indefinable, but decent fruit. Then another magnum at Rodenstock's La Fleur tasting: rich and attractive. *Last tasted Aug 1998. At best* ★★★★

**Ch Latour-à-Pomerol** Magnum: rich, almost molasses on the nose; sweet, full, rich, chewy. *Sept 1996* ★★★★

**Ch Léoville-Barton** One of the most exquisite wines ever tasted. By far the most attractive '48 and, in fragrance and delicacy, on a par with Mouton '49. First tasted in 1971 dining with an old wine trade friend, Rob Kewley, one of the first MWs, who died later in a plane crash (the pilot had not filled up with fuel at the small airport in Dijon because it was expensive. It ran out and crashed en route home). The wine had a lovely mature garnet red colour, a fabulously sweet, ripe bouquet and flavour, rich, perfect tannin and acidity, balance and elegance. My host made the mistake of bringing up another bottle cool from his cellar. It was good, but like a second cup of tea, not as fresh. Anthony Barton must have read my note at some time or other because he served it blind at lunch. It was beautiful, inimitable, and I said it could only be his '48. *Last noted languishing at Ch Langoa, June 1992* ★★★★★

**Ch La Mission Haut-Brion** A great '48. Fabulous bouquet, lovely smoky flavour in 1966. 'Fabulous' used yet again at the age of 30, bolstered by a spicy, earthy flavour and fragrant aftertaste. A couple of bad bottles in the mid-1980s. A beautiful, still opaque, sweet, fleshy bottle with silky leathery tannins at Wolf's tasting in 1990. Most recently, losing some of its colour but a rich velvety appearance; showing its age but very fragrant; very Graves, very dry but with lots of fruit and character. *Last noted dining at Domaine de Chevalier (all the vintages ending in the figure 8), April 1998. At best ★★★★★*

**Ch Nenin** One of the most attractive magnums in Rodenstock's Pomerol 'flight'. Rich, gentle, vanilla, tannic, with attractive aftertaste. *Sept 1996 ★★★★*

**Ch Siran** Toasted character. Still tannic. *Oct 1993 ★★★*

**Ch Palmer** A 'big fruity wine' in 1954. Laden with tannin (1970). Most recently: lively ruby colour; rich, biscuity then stably – a tangy, verging on pungent, smell of a thoroughbred stables. Rich, quite a bite. Slightly tart finish but went well with beef. *At Kaplan's '48s dinner at the Four Seasons, Los Angeles, Feb 1998 ★★★★*

THE BEST OF THE OLDER NOTES WITH GOOD POTENTIAL
**Ch Cantemerle**; **Ch Chasse-Spleen**; **Dom de Chevalier**; **Ch La Dominique**; **Ch Haut-Bailly**; **Ch Léoville Las Cases**; **Ch Lynch-Bages**; **Ch Malescot-Margaux**; **Ch Pape-Clément**; **Ch Pavie**; and **Ch de Pez**.

# 1949 ★★★★★

The third of the great trio of post-war vintages. Stylistically quite different from the concentrated '45s and the ripe and more opulent '47s. At their best, and there were many wines of great style, avoiding some of the constraints and excesses of the two other vintages just mentioned.

What on earth were the growing conditions to produce wines like these? Certainly not predictable, perhaps not even understandable. The year started with the driest January and February all round. The always crucial flowering period took place in cold, rainy weather which caused the worst *coulure* ever remembered and, consequently, a much reduced crop. Hot weather followed, increasing to an almost unprecedented heat wave, 43°C recorded in the Médoc on 11 July. Then storms and, finally, a late harvest in fine weather.

It was a very popular vintage with merchants and their customers, prices being very reasonable: Lafite 'for laying down' (in 1954) a mere 24 shillings a bottle, unsurprisingly sold out by the following year.

The best are still superb but living precariously; storage and provenance are vital.

**Ch Lafite** I think I would describe this as capricious, certainly inconsistent, judging by over 20 notes spanning over 45 years, from a most disappointing first tasting in March 1955 to a spicy, exciting and excitable bottle in September 2000. But I am jumping. Astringency, fading but with a piquant flavour in the early 1970s. 'Nothing like the charm of Mouton or the balance of Latour' noted at a Saintsbury Club dinner in 1979, and a fully mature *impériale* at Marvin Overton's 50th birthday dinner in Fort Worth. Completely mature in the early 1980s, more than a trace of overripeness later in the decade. This is not to say that it was not attractive to drink. I noted variously delicacy, smooth texture, a touch of leanness, citrus-like (acidity), skinny, *gibier* – some better, some worse. Never boring. Most recently: high-toned, tea-like, spicy; sweet entry; dry slightly raw finish, but very flavoury. *Last noted at Len Evans' 'Single-bottle Club' birthday dinner, Sept 2000. At best ★★★★★*

**Ch Latour** No question, an extremely good wine. Well over two dozen notes with only one or two duff bottles. First tasted in December 1954: 'very dark. Full (flavoured), big and raw'. In fact it was still 'green' and raw in the mid-1960s, laden with tannin, though a fine classic cedary nose and magnificent

flavour noted, also its great length. Ten notes tracing its development through the 1970s and a dozen in the 1980s. Towards the end of this decade it started to reach its 'plateau of perfection' though several times noted a touch too much acidity. More recently, a perfect bottle, rich, complete at the Four Vintages dinner in 1993 and in 1996 a magnum, tasted blind, noting a still very deep appearance yet a mature mahogany rim; classic Pauillac nose showing some age; rich, full-bodied, extremely tannic, but with fragrant aftertaste. Most recently: lovely colour; perfect nose, rich, perfect balance. Fabulous. *Last noted at the Josey pre-sale tasting in New York, Nov 2000 ★★★★★ if well stored, a long life ahead.*

**Ch Margaux** An archetypal elegant Margaux, exceedingly fragrant. I shall never forget the first time I had this wine: it was in 1958 at an after-wedding dinner party for the younger guests in the Lake District. Asked to choose the wine and not wishing to land ourselves with something too expensive, I ordered four bottles of 'Margaux' at 15 shillings a bottle. When the waiter brought it and showed me the label, I noticed that it was not the generic Margaux I ordered, but Ch Margaux 1949, château-bottled. After I queried this, the waiter returned to say that the manager confirmed that this was what we had ordered. Ignorance is bliss. I noted it as 'very fine, full, soft and rounded'. As a corollary, the food and service were so bad that, after complaining, we only had to pay for the wine!

Ch Margaux, sometimes, like Ch Cheval Blanc, shipped its wine in hogsheads for bottling by English wine merchants. Generally this was done well but I noted a sharp and austere Chalié Richards bottling in the early 1970s and, in 1986, a very good one bottled by the very upper crust merchants, Block Grey and Block from the cellars of the Earl of Dundee. Château-bottled, it seemed to me to be at its best in the late 1980s. Three notes in the last decade: lost a great deal of colour; on the nose it was faded but charming and, more importantly, evolved most fragrantly in the glass; on the palate almost caramelly sweet, on the light side but with a fraction too much acidity (in a 'flight' of '49s, tasted blind, I thought it was the Cheval Blanc). The last two at Manfred Wagner's Margaux verticals, the best in 1997, level upper-mid-shoulder, a lovely autumnal colour; touch of fungi bottle stink due to its ullage but which cleared, exuding rich fruit. On the palate, pleasant sweetness, lovely texture, but showing its age and not as great as expected. There were two bottles at the second event, the one with similar level to the bottle just described which was very sweet and flavoury, good but with noticeable acidity. The other was red brown, oxidised. I didn't bother to taste it. *Last noted Nov 2000. At best ★★★★★ but watch out.*

**Ch Mouton-Rothschild** Unquestionably the finest '49. A wine that, at its best, has an inimitable fragrance and deftness of touch. It was Baron Philippe's favourite. I have been fortunate enough to taste this wine on 18 occasions, starting in March 1963 when I noted its fabulous, unbelievably rich, ripe Cabernet Sauvignon bouquet and flavour: 'very rich, soft, fabulous' again on the palate though I only gave it a 4 stars. The fifth appeared in the mid-1970s: a perfect bottle with flavoury Cabernet nose and, though very rich, displaying its '49 hallmark, delicacy. A lovely wine. Nine notes in the 1980s, all 5 star, two wines even awarded 6 (and one corked), redolent of Mouton's cassis fragrance, charm and delicacy. This was when the wine was at its best. When last noted it looked fully mature but lively, its bouquet gushing exotically; exciting, I thought, drying out. *Last noted at Farr Vintners' Ch Latour and Mouton dinner tasting, Sept 1993. At best ★★★★★★ (6 stars).*

**Ch Haut-Brion** A curious wine. It often is: in 1954 I wrote 'difficult to place, looks like a '47, lighter (on the palate) than it looks'. Dry. 'A trifle green.' Its greenness had disappeared by the late 1950s: 'soft' noted, and, in the mid-1960s, nice flavour, balance, refreshing and 'good to drink'. Haut-Brion, though customarily elegant, has a very distinctive taste, more earthy than its peers in the Médoc, with a touch of coffee, tobacco leaves on the nose. I thought it was at its best in the mid-1980s. Only one recent note: still very deep and fairly intense; relatively (compared, say, to Mouton) low-keyed nose; touch of honey; a wine of great power and length with an end taste of singed heather (and I should know. I was brought up in the Yorkshire moors!). *Last noted dining at the château with the family and Jean Delmas, Sept 1998* ★★★★

**Ch Ausone** A strange style of wine. First tasted, and liked, in the 1950s, but noting its austere, brackish '48-like taste in the 1970s. One has to adjust for Ausone, and at Lloyd Flatt's vertical he had secured a perfect bottle: magnificent colour; rich, very spicy bouquet; fairly sweet, soft, fleshy, good length. *Ending on the high note, Oct 1987. At best* ★★★★

**Ch Cheval Blanc** Another wonderful wine which along with the Ch Mouton-Rothschild and Ch Margaux, having the most perfect expression of the vintage. I don't know why but I have tasted this on almost three dozen occasions, starting in August 1954, and spread throughout the 1960s, 1970s and 1980s, including a Justerini & Brooks and two Corney & Barrow bottlings, all excellent. It seemed to be on the top of its form in the mid–late 1970s, variously described as fabulous, deep, magnificent, mature (appearance); 'crushed ripe mulberries' (twice), plummy fragrance and scented Cabernet Franc; on the palate medium sweetness and weight, rich, 'calm', soft, ripe – you name it. Some variable bottles in the 1980s but, on the whole 'fabulous'. Four notes in the 1990s: beautiful, intriguingly attractive magnums, complete, harmonious, fleshy at Rodenstock's tastings in 1993 and 1994, and a convincingly deep, classic, lovely bottle with sustaining tannins and acidity at Wolf's vertical in 1997. (Incidentally, Jacques Hébrard, whose wife's family owned the château, told us that 1949 was a 'no problem' vintage harvested between 26 September and 9 October of low yield, 24hl/ha and using old *barriques*. Most recently, from my own cellar, alas a bit cloudy but with a soaring nose-filling bouquet. Sweet enough, but

---

### Emile Peynaud

*Renowned Bordeaux oenologist and educator whose studies had a profound impact on the world of wine from the 1950s onwards. It all began in 1949 when Peynaud teamed up with Jean Ribéreau-Gayon at the Institut d'Oenologie at Bordeaux University. Of all the practical oenologists he is the daddy of them all. Peynaud's innate attention to detail drove him towards seeking an understanding of winemaking processes where previously there had been mere acceptance. His researches focused on the production of clean-tasting wines, derived from controlled fermentation and eradication of bacterial spoilage. Peynaud was the first to leave nothing to chance in the cellar and chai, right from the selection of healthy grapes, to spotless conditions at the bottling line. He greatly resented wines being described as 'Peynaudised' – though the term was, and is, often used. He said that you can't change the soil, and the wines speak for themselves. He once commented to me, wryly, that I have the easy time of it, because I talk and write about the 'lovely ladies'. He had to work with the squalling brats.*

frankly a bit disappointing. *Last noted at my Bordeaux Club dinner at Christie's, Feb 1998. At best* ★★★★★

**Ch Pétrus** Hard to fault. Five notes. All the component parts *in excelsis*! Impressively deep; ripe, fleshy, mulberry-like nose; sweet, mouthfilling, velvety and soft despite its life-preserving tannin. *Last tasted May 1993* ★★★★★

**Ch Pétrus** Belgian-bottled (Vandermeurlen). Apparently late bottled and certainly not as deep as the château-bottling. Spicy, eucalyptus-like nose; sweet enough but lacking flesh. Lean dry finish. *At Frans de Cock's event in Paris, Dec 1995* ★★

**Ch Calon-Ségur** An indication of how rapidly these post-war vintages were bought by the British trade and as speedily resold: the very popular Calon-Ségur made particularly good wine in 1945, '47 and '49 but none of these vintages was to be seen by the early 1950s. On the other hand, Saccone & Speed, even in 1954, listed Calon-Ségur '28s and '37s.

I suppose this is the reason that I got neither sight nor smell of the great post-war trio until very recently. When I finally tasted Calon '49 it was showing gloriously well; indeed perfection, in 1994, and a slightly leaner but elegant magnum the following year. *Last tasted Sept 1993* ★★★★ *If it is not too ridiculous to say: still worth looking out for at auctions. You never know where you might find some.*

**Ch Cantemerle** Always a favourite château, at least until more recent years. The '49 had a particularly beautiful colour and, in its early days (1977 to 1983) an exquisitely perfumed bouquet. One tart and one superb half-bottle before the sale of Mme Binaud's cellar in 1996 and, later the same year, bought by Hardy Rodenstock, a very attractive *Marie-Jeanne*. *Last tasted Sept 1996. At best* ★★★★

**Ch Figeac** One of Thierry Manoncourt's early successes, but he did have the benefit of a perfect growing season. It was only seven years after this that I first tasted it: a 'full, smooth big wine' (I didn't waste words. Perhaps I had still not got the hang of it!). A particular feature is its extravagant fruitiness, glorious fragrance, and at Desai's Paris tasting, a taste I described as like raspberries and cream. Happily quite a few notes, including a lovely, fragrant, elegant magnum in 1994 and, most recently, sheer perfection: surprisingly deep in colour though a fully mature rim; a sweet, rich, totally delicious bouquet and flavour. A wine combining the original, I nearly said eccentric, certainly characterful Thierry and the vivacious and charming Marie-France. *Last noted at the opening dinner of a '5-star group's' week in Bordeaux, hosted by the family at Figeac, Sept 1998* ★★★★★

**Ch La Fleur** One of the very best of 32 vintages of La Fleur presented by Rodenstock: a fragrant, opulent magnum. Sweet, full, rich, lovely fruit, balance and finish. And for a wine of such blatant magnitude, great charm. *Sept 1998* ★★★★★

**Ch Léoville-Las-Cases** An old bottle from my own cellar. Level upper-shoulder. Surprisingly sweet, lovely fruit and delicacy but with a sharp, 'pricked', dry finish. *At my Bordeaux Club dinner, Dec 1995* ★★★

**Ch La Mission Haut-Brion** The high peak of the Woltners' long stint at La Mission and said by them to be the best-ever La Mission, on a par with their '29. A dozen notes from 1971 on, all, I am fairly certain, emanating from the original cellars – we had two major Woltner stock sales at Christie's in the 1970s. All outstanding except a double magnum with high though tolerable volatile acidity and creaking a bit. At its best, always consistently more masculine and assertive then its *1er cru* neighbour, deep in colour, its bouquet distinctive, strong with whiffs of cedar, liquorice,

molasses, spice and mocha. On the palate sweet, rich, earthy with marvellous velvety texture, 'toasted bracken, dry leaves and tobacco'. *Last tasted Sept 1998. With one exception* ★★★★★
**Ch Rausan-Ségla** Several notes from 1954. Variable. The most recent a 'ripe powerhouse of fragrances', rich, lovely but tannic. *Last tasted Jan 1991. At best* ★★★★
**Ch Siran** Better flavour than nose. Richness and Margaux charm. *At a pre-sale tasting, Oct 1993* ★★
**Vieux Ch Certan** Deep; 'old cedar'; classic flavour and weight, sweet mid-palate, rich, tannic. *At Frans de Cock's dinner in Paris, Dec 1995* ★★★

OTHER 1949S LAST TASTED IN THE 1980S
**Ch Beychevelle** on top form. As elegant as the façade of the château, one of the loveliest in Bordeaux. Many notes. *Last tasted March 1983* ★★★★★; **Ch Certan** a soft, velvety, fragrant charmer. *Last tasted Jan 1989* ★★★★; **Ch La Conseillante** certainly a Pomerol year. One beautiful bottle, one maderised.

*Last tasted April 1982. At best* ★★★★; **Ch Cos d'Estournel** first tasted in 1954, several since. *Last tasted March 1984. At best* ★★★★; **Ch Grand-Puy-Lacoste** consistently well-run château, highly dependable. The '49 superb. *Feb 1988* ★★★★; **Ch Lynch-Bages** many notes over the years. A spicy, Mouton-like Cabernet character, vivacious. *Last tasted April 1988. At best* ★★★★; **Ch Montrose** on top form and most impressive; massive, tannic, needing at least 20 years bottle age. Now sweet, ripe, spicy with silky tannins. *Last tasted April 1985* ★★★★; **Ch Palmer** somewhat precocious. It was very forward when first tasted in July 1954, then most memorably lunching with Peter Sichel at the château on our first visit to Bordeaux in July 1955; unforgettable too for Daphne, for she disturbed a wasps' nest after lunch on the roof. They sought refuge in her hair, then a rich auburn. *Last tasted, showing its age but with wonderful richness and ripeness, Nov 1986* ★★★★; and **Ch Talbot** variable. More masculine than its 'cousin' Gruaud. An aged classic. *Last tasted Oct 1984. At best* ★★★

# 1950–1959

A period of recovery. In Bordeaux the châteaux proprietors struggled to renovate and replant, the merchants to restock. *Négociants* still ruled the roost and, with the cosy relationships resumed, British shippers (importers) and their wine merchant customers had a head start. A period when gentlemen sold to gentlemen who in turn sold to gentlemen. (This all changed when I came into the trade in 1952!) Moreover, competition was limited. The Americans, despite the efforts of Alexis Lichine and Schoonmaker, were only starting to appreciate – and drink – good Bordeaux; and the Australasian market simply did not exist. It was in 1950 that some enterprising and far-sighted producers and *négociants* founded *La Commanderie de Bordeaux* which, after half a century, still flourishes, with active 'chapters' worldwide.

In Britain, virtually every town, certainly every county town, had at least one good wine merchant, usually family-owned, just as each used to have a tailor, shoemaker, saddler, and so forth. It was a period when brewers still brewed, and sold, beer, and retail licences were hard to obtain. But it was also in the 1950s that things started to change. Shortage of working capital and the threat of death duties caused family wine merchants to sell out to the breweries who, in turn, developed off-licence chains mainly selling less expensive wines. Yet Bordeaux still dominated the wine merchants' lists, followed by Burgundy and German wines, plus, of course, sherry, port and champagne. Rarely anything else. For the comfortably off in Britain, it was the last period in which they could drink decent claret everyday, and first growths at the weekend. Perhaps at the expense of the producer: château proprietors made very little money. But there were some lovely wines and more than the decade's fair share of really good vintages including my favourite, 1953, and the 1959, not only the most impressive of the decade, but one of the greatest of the century.

**Vintages at a Glance**
**Outstanding** ★★★★★
1953, 1959
**Very Good** ★★★★
1952 (v), 1955
**Good** ★★★
None

## 1950 ★★

Abundant, the crop nearly double that of 1949, but of uneven quality and imported by the British wine trade as useful, inexpensive 'fillers' or everyday clarets. Best in Pomerol, Margaux and Graves. Some wines surviving well.
**Ch Lafite** At nine years of age: lovely nose, attractive, supple, a pleasant drink. Over the next four decades very similar notes, flavoury, some charm. Most recently a magnum showing its age, fully evolved, fragrant; characteristic Lafite flavour, a touch of acidity making it merely a refreshing drink. Not a great '50. *Last tasted at the château, June 1988* ★★
**Ch Latour** Many notes. Aged 10, surprisingly soft and drinkable for Latour. 'Completely satisfying', full flavoured. But not as good as Ch Margaux (in 1968 and 1970). Probably at its best in the mid-1970s, but prettily coloured, fragrant, complex and flavoury but with no great length in 1988. Quite a good bottle the following year but recently noted a horribly oxidised bottle. *Last noted Sept 1996 at best* ★★
**Ch Margaux** The best '50. I tasted this when it was being bottled in late April 1953. Even at that stage I recorded it as 'charming, elegant. Should be ready early'. Many notes in the 1950s and 1960s, considering it at its peak in 1973. Always an attractive drink, with Margaux femininity and style. Most recently, a gentle fragrance, fading a little; still with some sweetness and charm. *Last tasted May 1987* ★★★★ *Should still be good, though becoming frail.*

**Ch Mouton-Rothschild** First tasted in 1956. Like the others, soft, forward, a wine to drink not to keep. My best note was in 1975 when it seemed to have got its act together: quite a good colour, lovely – though not very Mouton-like-nose, flavoury and quite a lot of grip. But by the mid-1980s, I noticed a touch of austerity, even asperity. More recently, a spicy but quirky magnum, lean and tart-ended. *Last noted at a Commanderie de Bordeaux dinner in Oslo, April 1996. At best* ★★★ *but on decline.*
**Ch Haut-Brion** Undeveloped and so-so in 1955; two decades later quite pleasantly evolved with a pleasingly rich flavour. But not tasted since. *Last noted June 1975.* ★★★ *Could have survived.*
**Ch Ausone** Better in its youth. Fragrant and pleasant to drink at seven years of age, but hardly surviving a quarter of a century. Unbalanced though not ungainly. *Last tasted Oct 1987.*
**Ch Cheval Blanc** For once, not on best form. Twenty notes over 30 years and little consistency, partly due to being bottled by several British wine merchants, by *négociants* in Bordeaux as well as at the château. Uncharacteristically 'raw', 'austere', 'disappointing', 'tart', even 'varnishy' interspersing the less frequent 'elegant', 'lovely', and so forth. My best notes in the 1970s though richly textured showing its age (Bordeaux Club 1995) and, most recently, surprisingly deep in colour but fairly similar note. *Last noted at Karl-Heinz Wolf's Cheval Blanc tasting, Sept 1997. At best* ★★
**Ch Pétrus** Only one note. Powerful, spicy. *At the Stockholm tasting. April 1990* ★★★★
**Ch L'Évangile** A deep, sweet, chewy wine bottled by Reidemeister & Ulrichs, distinguished wine merchants in Bremen. *March 2001* ★★★
**Ch La Fleur** Three notes. The first two at one of Dr Arne-Curt Berger's 'Parker 100' tasting at Le Canard in Hamburg in October 1993. One bottle, obtained in the USA, turned out to be oxidised, the other 'ex-château' from Mouiex: an immensely deep appearance; low-keyed yet massive, sweet,

slightly singed nose; very sweet, immensely powerful, very high extract, packed with fruit and tannin. Enormously impressive to taste but hardly suitable to accompany a meal. The third a magnum at Rodenstock's monumental La Fleur tasting. A similar note and similar reaction: opaque; sweet, singed, black treacle nose; full in every way, high extract noted again, not unlike a Guigal Côte-Rôtie in character. Concentrated, and certainly very impressive. But who wants to go to bed with a wrestler? *Last tasted Sept 1998* ★★★★★ *for sheer monumentality,* ★ *for drinking.*

**Ch La Mission Haut-Brion** Unsurprisingly, with the Woltners in such brilliant form, one of the best '50s. Quite a few notes, four earning my 5 stars in the early 1970s: wonderful mahogany-edged colour; extremely firm, deep, spicy, earthy 'first growth calibre' nose; lovely silky flavour, very rich, beautifully and fully developed. Later, sweet, harmonious bouquet and flavour, wonderful fruit and balance. A peppery but surprisingly rich, plump, fleshy bottle in 1990, 'smoky', somewhat aggressive in 1996. Most recently, touch of iodine on nose, vegetal on palate. Much more enjoyable than it sounds: good texture and fruit. Definitely a good '50. *Last tasted June 2000* ★★★★

---

### The Woltners

*Frédéric Woltner bought Ch La Mission Haut-Brion in 1918 but it was his two sons, Fernand and Henri, who became the great innovators there. Henri took the helm in 1921 and remained the guiding influence until his death in 1974. The Woltners were the first to introduce stainless steel vats which were initially lined with glass. The first of their great wines was made in 1929, but it was during the post-war period that they were at their peak, culminating, of course, in the stunning 1959 vintage.*

---

OTHER MAJOR 1950S LAST TASTED IN THE 1980S
**Ch Beychevelle** *April 1989* ★★★; **Ch Figeac** *Dec 1989. At best* ★★★; and **Ch Le Gay** *April 1984* ★★★★

# 1951

Appalling weather conditions, execrable wines: thin, acid, decayed. Avoid. Not even **Ch Latour** or the Woltners at **Ch La Mission Haut-Brion** could beat the elements. **Ch Lafite** pale, thin, curled up and acidic; and **Ch Mouton-Rothschild** surprisingly flavoury though hollow and short.

# 1952 ★★ to ★★★★

The British wine trade went to town with this vintage. Both Harvey's and Saccone & Speed, both of which I was connected with at this period, each listed a wide range of 1952s for 'laying down', the latter prefacing their offer by stating that 'We hold a further extensive range of the fine wines of the 1945, 1947 and 1949 vintages. These will be offered at their maturity' (having, I suspect, sold the best to favoured customers when first put on the market).

Most clarets were bottled by merchants, classed growths such as Ch Calon-Ségur averaging 12 shillings a bottle – roughly half the price of château-bottled first growths. Prices were reasonable which meant, really, that they were not very profitable for the producers. The resurgence of interest in wine in the USA was only in its relatively early stages and markets

for quality wine outside (impoverished) Europe did not exist. We had Bordeaux to ourselves.

The actual growing season was very satisfactory up until September which was cold and unsettled. The harvest was fairly early and I suspect the unripeness of some of the crop is responsible for its variability: best in the Graves and on the Right Bank, harder, more unyielding in the Médoc.

I was too junior in the trade when the 1952s were being bought, so most of my considerable number of notes were made in the 1960s when the wines were considered mature enough to list. At that time I was also on Harvey's table wine-buying committee, which gave me a good view of both sides of the business.

**Ch Lafite** In common with many wines from the Médoc, a rather ungracious and unsatisfactory wine though it was agreeable enough in the early to mid-1960s. My best note is of a flavoury magnum in 1980. More recently (in 1998) two more magnums, each recorked at Lafite in 1983, variable and both cracking up. My last note is of another magnum served at a rather grand dinner in 'The Dairy' at Waddesdon Manor, the Rothschild mansion in Buckinghamshire. I was informed later that Eric de Rothschild had suggested serving the (exquisite) 1953, but the 1952 was selected instead. As I had been invited to speak about the wine, I had to choose whether to be truthful or kind as Jacob (Lord) Rothschild was present. What I actually wrote on the menu and later in my little red book was 'fairly deep, slightly drab, with open (weak) rim; showing its age, scent of something like beetroot and living dangerously; medium sweet, medium (body), mushroomy, drying out and tannic'. But it managed to hold its own with *gougères and salade persillée. Last tasted Dec 2000. At best* ★★

**Ch Latour** The combination of Latour and a vintage like 1952 did not augur well, and my earliest note, in 1962, was 'raw and unready'. It was austere and tannic through the 1970s, and variable, mainly due to provenance, in the 1980s. In 1990, dining at the château, lamb didn't ameliorate the rawness though it was still quite impressive in appearance, and fragrant. Most recently, my 21st note, a magnum maturing nicely; bouquet fully evolved; sweet, very rich but still tannic. Will it do a '28? I doubt it. *Last tasted Sept 1993. At best* ★★★

**Ch Margaux** Reputed to be one of the best '52s though this hardly applies now. A dozen notes. Behind hand and severe in the first 20 years of its life. One of my best notes is also the unlikeliest: Danish-bottled, bought by an English merchant who sold it on to a New York importer, whence to Tokyo where in 1989 I had the pleasure of drinking it with a good Japanese client at the Imperial Hotel. More recently 'cheesy' noted on three quite separate occasions. Last but not least: sweet, crisp, good flavour but astringent. *Last noted at Manfred Wagner's vertical tasting, Nov 2000* ★★

**Ch Mouton-Rothschild** Six notes but none in the 1990s. Nevertheless, looking at these notes I am left with the impression that it has the vivid colour, fragrance and flavour to more than make up for the hard tannins. Worth looking out for. *Last tasted April 1986* ★★★★

**Ch Haut-Brion** This is definitely one of the best surviving. Seven notes in the 1960s and 1970s, the earlier ones good; later, despite its characteristic earthy Graves character, showing signs of cracking up. A nondescript note in 1987 but showing well at a recent Haut-Brion/La Mission tasting. Deeper than the '53; distinctive, slightly chocolatey, earthy bouquet which opened up well. Predictably tougher than the '53, with citrus-like fruit, good flavour but very tannic. I thought it would go on and on. *Last noted at a tasting I conducted for the London wine merchants, La Réserve, June 2000* ★★★★

**Ch Ausone** Many notes, château-bottled, Belgium-bottled and English (Averys and Harvey's). Basically very good though strange, with its curious overmature colour and idiosyncratic nose. Variable of course, and I would have said better in the early 1960s had it not been for a very good Vandermeurlen bottle (one of several previously noted) at de Cock's Paris tasting: not deep but richly coloured; nice gentle fruit, 'singed', good depth, perfect weight, its tannin and acidity serving to preserve and refresh. *Last tasted Dec 1995. At best* ★★★

**Ch Cheval Blanc** Definitely one of the best '52s, almost from start to finish – except that it is nowhere near finished. Well over a dozen notes starting somewhat unenthusiastically in July 1954, but perking up when in 1960 I tasted a very attractive, very drinkable, Scottish-bottling (Gloag's of Perth, better known for their 'Famous Grouse' whisky). Either side of 1970 noting lovely, silky texture, perfect balance, and two equally good notes, amongst others, in 1987 and 1990. Most recently: very deep, mature-rimmed; very good classic Cheval Blanc nose and taste, very sweet, good body, nice weight (12.6 % alcohol) and tannic grip. Relatively small *rendement,* 31hl/ha. *Last noted at Wolf's vertical, Sept 1997. At best* ★★★★

**Ch Pétrus** Six notes including one poor bottle. Characteristically deep in colour; finely textured, combining power and flesh; its sweetness and high alcoholic content masking its sustaining tannin. *Last tasted April 2000* ★★★★★

**OTHER '52S TASTED IN THE 1990S**

**Ch Canon-La-Gaffelière** Flavoury, sweet and lively but showing its age and acidity lurking. Dining at the château with Stefan Graf von Neipperg who would have made a better job of the '52. *April 1998* ★★

**Ch Cantemerle** A good period and a much better than average Médoc. Three notes, the most recent from Mme Binaud's cellar: good colour; very attractive bouquet; a stunning lively wine, fruit holding hands with tannin. *Last tasted April 1996* ★★★★

**Ch L'Evangile** Bordeaux-bottled by Eschenauer. Fully mature but remarkably sound with good old fruit and mellow tannins. *At a big tasting conducted for* Vinum *magazine in Zurich, April 1998* ★★★

**Ch La Fleur** Nose unknit and showing its age though it revived a little. Drying out. Disappointing. *August 1998.*

**Ch La Mission Haut-Brion** Ah! The ever dependable Woltners. Another successful vintage though not all the bottles were in top condition. Showing well, I gave it 5 stars at Karl-Heinz Wolf's tasting in 1990. A surprise to be served it by the Schÿler family dining at their Ch Kirwan in 1998: very sweet,

**Laytons**

*I was not born with a silver* tastevin *in my mouth. My career in wine started at the bottom of the ladder in 1952, when I spent a year as a trainee with Tommy Layton in Duke Street, London. This involved sweeping cellars, taking orders and delivering the orders by van to smart houses in Mayfair. These tasks were far from highly paid. I remember receiving my first tip – I was given only two during that first year – it was from an Aberdonian lady and it was six pence. The second was from a Jewish gentleman. So perhaps I was lucky from the start? I learnt a lot and made many useful contacts in the trade.*

rich, earthy, with a touch of iodine on finish. 'Holding well and drinking well' (*and* I guessed the vintage). Most recently a similarly good bottle noted, spicy but less aggressively masculine than usual. Crisp, very good fruit. Delicious. 'A broader-shouldered wine' than Ch Haut-Brion. *Last noted at the La Réserve tasting, held, curiously, at the Irish Club in Eaton Square, June 2000. At best* ★★★★★

**OTHER '52S, SHOWING WELL IN THE 1980S Ch L'Angélus** a well-nigh perfect Danish bottling from Aalholm Castle. *July 1989* ★★★★★; **Ch Beychevelle** a peak period. *May 1986* ★★★★; **Dom de Chevalier** a good '52 but lacking usual Chevalier charm. *March 1982* ★★★; **Ch Figeac** dry for Figeac but flavoury, with lots of grip. *Dec 1989* ★★★; **Ch Langoa-Barton** bottled by Barton & Guestier. Masculine. *Nov 1989* ★★★; **Ch Léoville-Las-Cases** not showing well – for me at any rate – in the 1960s and 1970s, and there were some unreliable bottlings. By far the best a Danish bottling from Aalholm: cedary, soft, fleshy. *At best* ★★★★; **Ch Léoville-Poyferré** not a good period, partly because made from young vines following extensive replanting. Seemed best in the mid-1970s. Most recently lacking fruit and charm. *Oct 1985* ★; and **Ch Montrose** I much admired Montrose in the 1950s. Classic, fruity, tannic wines needing plenty of bottle age. Good wine though with teeth-gripping tannin. *Oct 1986* ★★★★ *Will keep.*

# 1953 ★★★★★

One of my all-time favourite vintages, combining fragrance, finesse and charm, epitomising claret at its best, the antithesis of some latter day blockbusters. As so often with the Bordeaux maritime climate and changeable weather conditions, not an entirely perfect growing season. A hot, sunny summer and propitious ripening period was rudely interrupted by heavy rain mid-September. However, the subsequent late harvest produced wines which were easy, lovely to taste even in cask: beautiful babies, no problems at puberty, well-behaved teenagers, elegant, lively and charming in their prime, middle-aged without crises, ageing gracefully. Unless treated badly.

**Ch Lafite** A lovely wine, Lafite at its beguiling best. Not a thruster, not a show off, a wine of exquisite charm and finesse. I have been fortunate enough to taste this wine some three dozen times, in bottles varying from halves to jeroboams, in an extraordinary variety of places and contexts. It was said to have been bottled over a period of nine months, so one might have expected some variations. All I can say is that I have never had a bad bottle (had, not tasted: one does not spit out a wine like this). Most recently, despite its maturity and delicacy, I felt it would survive, like the 1875. This is not a wine to describe. Words simply cannot do it justice. If you are ever fortunate to share a bottle, just let it speak for itself. *Last noted, a perfect magnum at Walter Eigensatz's big bottle tasting in Wiesbaden, May 1993* ★★★★★ *Having said this, it is now past its peak and one can expect some frailty unless a perfect bottle from an ideal cellar.*

**Ch Latour** The consensus is that this is not a great '53, the '52 having more character, the '55 better balance. However, having scanned nearly 20 notes, most warrant 4 stars despite its leaking tannic finish. Some exotic nasal descriptions in the 1980s, including 'oysters, ozone and clams' – a good Pauillac smell. After all it is only an hour's drive to the sandy beaches – 'striking eucalyptus Cabernet' and, using the immortal André Simon's phrase (about a mature Latour) 'with the majesty of the Royal Oak'. Anyway, recent notes include a very deep, fairly intense magnum, good but not great (Sept 1996), and the following month a horribly oxidised bottle at a BYOB dinner in New York. Misguided: a stupid bottle to bring. Most recently, an immediately forthcoming bouquet, mature, even aged, bricky, slightly medicinal (Pauillac again); a sweet, ripe entry, a touch of decay yet a rich drink and still tannic. *The last accompanying braised rib eye in Pomerol sauce at a Crédit Suisse wine dinner at the Shangri-La Hotel, Hong Kong, Oct 1999. At best ★★★★*

**Ch Margaux** Now here's a wine. One of the loveliest of all vintages of Margaux and, incidentally, with the great 1959 and 1961, putting paid to the received nonsense that good wine was made at Margaux only after the Mentzelopoulos purchase in 1977. I recall Harry Waugh, Harvey's wine buyer, writing in 1954 'lovely, deep, altogether a splendid wine, too good to spit out'. A great taster, with impeccable judgement. I didn't taste it until 1961, and on a couple of occasions found it condensed and unready. It opened up in the late 1960s, and in the early 1970s I used very similar descriptions: rich, smoky, lovely, silky, soft, velvety, glorious, etc. By the 1980s a rich charmer, with perfect balance, great length. Six of my more than 20 notes made in the 1990s: one (in Florida) 'delicate, fading old lady' though not borne out by more recent notes. At the two Manfred Wagner verticals, the first sheer perfection, a glorious mouthful the next, alas, oxidised. One of the most perfect was a bottle I had bought at a Christie's auction in 1994 and served at my Bordeaux Club dinner in Feb 1998 (cork drawn at 4pm, decanted at 6pm and poured at 8.20pm). It had a lovely, cedary bouquet which, after over an hour in the glass exuded tea-like fragrance. Sweet, delicious, still with a firm core, easy to drink, dry finish. Lovely but fading a little at Josh Latner's dinner in January 2000 and, two days later, surprisingly, a lovely bottle at the annual III Form Club dinner at Boodle's Club. *Last tasted (Wagner's bad bottle), Nov 2000. At best ★★★★★*

**Ch Mouton-Rothschild** First tasted in its tenth year and from then on a most lovely wine. I have nearly 20 notes, not one of them less than sensationally good – I see that in 1972 I went over the top and awarded it 6 stars for sheer perfection, and I described its appearance as 'deep and crisp and even', but this was being playful as it was never more than fairly deep. But, as always with Mouton, it is glittering, dazzling bouquet and flavour, its spiciness, its zest which attracts. Never a dull moment – just like Baron Philippe himself and, nowadays, epitomised by his daughter Philippine. The most recent notes include a perfect though by now more restrained bottle, but lovely, at de Cock's *Dîner du samedi* in Paris, and a glorious bottle, displaying Mouton's inimitable blackcurrant aroma, and fragrant, many-layered flavours. Fascinating, great length. *Last noted at the Josey pre-sale tasting at Christie's in New York, Nov 2000 ★★★★★*

**Ch Haut-Brion** This was one of the first wines I ever had an opportunity of tasting in cask, on my first visit to Bordeaux in July 1955. Despite being three years into my wine trade career I had not much experience of tasting very young wines, and, like many others, found that it was just that, an experience: black violet liquid puckering the mouth and staining the teeth (though probably good for the bowels). Anyway I was not too impressed. It was 11 years later that I noted its lovely bouquet, rather earthy taste, silky tannins, fruit and 'vinosity'. More recently and amusingly, opening and tasting a bottle in the kitchen of Prince Rupert Löwenstein's house at Ham in Surrey in 1996. Fully mature, ruddy; an extraordinary whoosh of fragrance, slightly raisiny; dry, tannic,

good though. The following year, sadly, an undrinkable bottle at my own Bordeaux Club dinner. Lastly a delicious bottle at the La Réserve tasting: lovely colour, luminous, nice gradation; beautiful bouquet slightly marred by a touch of something like varnish; delicious, singed, hot, earthy flavour. *Last noted June 2000. At best ★★★★★*

**Ch Ausone** Only five notes, none very recent. In its youth (1956) very appealing. A good '53. A particularly good note in the mid-1950s when it seemed fully developed. Swingeingly dry at the Flatt tasting. *Last noted Oct 1987. At best ★★★★*

**Ch Cheval Blanc** Basically, and should have been predictably, a charmer though not all were château-bottled and not all – though most – in good condition. Exactly two dozen notes starting with trade samples in 1956 and spanning its progress from flavoury but 'green' youthfulness to its ripe maturity in the early to mid-1970s. The notes include four variable Harvey's bottlings, the best, silky perfection in 1987. Several more recent: in 1995 at Barry Phillip's 'Silver Jubilee Dinner', a very sweet, soft, elegant bottle from his renowned Chilgrove cellar – the sort of claret I would be happiest to drink by itself, though it went perfectly with the fillet of Aberdeen beef. A superb bottle at Wolf's vertical in 1997: never very deeply coloured, a soft, mellow brick red with shades of ruby; the sort of fragrance that can't wait. Mocha, a touch of lime blossom; a most lovely wine with perfectly integrated component parts. Light in style and only 12% alcohol. Most recently, two bottles from a private cellar in California, one oxidised the other, bottled by Vandermeulen, sound but lacking '53 charm. *Last tasted March 1999. At best ★★★★★*

**Ch Pétrus** At that time jointly owned by the formidable Mme Loubat who had met her match in Jean-Pierre Moueix. To quote Harry Waugh once more, tasting from the barrel: 'Fine in every way, supple with much breed. A beauty'. And so it was: I have not one bad note amongst the eighteen made since 1956. It was an early developer, easy to drink but I think achieving perfection in the 1970s including pretty good but not great Harvey's bottling in 1976 (see Ch Calon-Ségur below for the price). By the mid-1980s, the normal château-bottled wine had maturity, a fairly deep appearance but was showing orange-tinged maturity, its nose and flavour being fully developed. Around this time I noted vanilla, fennel, cedar, spice on the nose. It was not as sweet as expected but full and fleshy. However after the top Médocs, relatively four-square and lacking finesse. In 1990 a lively fragrance, firm though beginning to show a touch of end acidity. Most recently, a perfect magnum at the Eigensatz tasting in Wiesbaden. *Last tasted May 1993. At best ★★★★★*

OTHER '53S TASTED FAIRLY RECENTLY (IN THE 1990S)

**Ch Beychevelle** From the start, one of my favourite '53s. A cask sample in 1954: a light, fruity, charmer. However, I think it was at its best in the early 1970s for it did not have the stamina for long life. Nevertheless, it was a 'warm', cedary and still pleasing drink when last tasted. *At a pre-sale tasting, May 1993. At best ★★★★ Drink up.*

**Ch Calon-Ségur** Very popular with British wine merchants and their customers at this period, and making very good wine. Harvey's, in 1956, had 32 of their own bottlings 'for laying down'. Calon-Ségur was 11 shillings (55p) a bottle retail (Ch Pétrus also bottled by Harvey's was of course more expensive: 16 shillings – 80p!). As this was our main stock-in-trade, I have many notes starting in February 1955. The Calon was big and fruity and drinking well by the early 1960s. Then a gap of 20 years: a superb château-bottled magnum, deep colour for a '53; marvellous old, cedary nose; by now (1983) soft, velvety, with complete roundness and harmony. At its peak. Most recently, still drinking quite well. *Last noted dining at Camilla and Alistair Sampsons', Jan 1997. At best* ★★★★★

**Carruades de Ch Lafite** A minor mirror image of the *grand vin*. Bought for home drinking. Variable. At its best a soft, light, easy charmer. *Last tasted March 2001. At best, but not often* ★★★

**Ch Cos d'Estournel** Another pretty popular wine at the time, and an early developer. Many notes, the most recent being superb: 'surprisingly deep for a '53; glorious, fragrant bouquet. Claret at its very best, delectable flavour, weight and balance'. *Last noted dining with an old wine trade friend, David Rutherford, Feb 1999. At best* ★★★★★

**Ch Figeac** Excellent wine. Sweet, fat, lovely and well-developed by the early 1960s and powering on through the 1970s. In 1986 I thought it had the richness and ripeness of a '59 and the firmness of a '61. More recently, at a Bordeaux Club dinner: bouquet very original, 'slightly caramelly, tea and tobacco' – Hugh Johnson described it as 'balsam and honey'. A soft, easy, earthy wine with a dry finish. Past its best but delicious. *Last noted March 1995. At best* ★★★★★

**Ch Grand-Puy-Lacoste** One of my favourite Bordeaux châteaux, owned at the time by a bachelor, M. Dupin, who made consistently excellent and always dependable wine. This is long before I started to buy a few cases of every vintage, and I did not taste the '53 until it was 20 years old. Nine very good notes. At its superb best in the early 1980s. Most recently, an *impériale*: rich, mature colour; showing a bit of fungi at first but it opened up brilliantly. On the palate, the sweetness of age and ripeness. Fragrant. Good length and aftertaste. A delicious wine though its seams beginning to show. *Last tasted at Rodenstock's wine weekend, Sept 1996. At best* ★★★★★

**Ch Gruaud-Larose** Yet another fragrant and fruity '53. My best note made in 1985 when I thought it was at its peak of perfection: lovely glowing colour; a fabulously ripe bouquet redolent of hot tiles, cedar; perfect weight, flavour and balance. Most recently a voluptuous *impériale*. *Last tasted, just one of 31 vintages of Gruaud, Sept 1993* ★★★★★

**Ch Lynch-Bages** An enormously popular wine. Again to put that period in perspective: Harry Waugh (in 1954) 'Delicious, beautifully full flavour. A wine to gamble on. Would like at least 40 hogsheads at £30'. Thirty pounds a *barrique* of 25 dozen bottles so just over £1 per dozen ex-cellars. Those were the days for the British wine merchant and his customers, but less so for the château proprietors. When I first tasted it in March 1956, it retailed at ten shillings (half of one pound) a bottle. Certainly one of the most attractive and drinkable '53s. For a start it did not have the usual tannic backbone. In fact, it was fully mature in 1972, my last note before the most recent: a lovely, mellow looking wine with an immediately fragrant bouquet. Ideal weight, sweetness and balance. Perfection. *Last noted in May 1994 at David Carter's, who had bought the wine when he was still at university in the late 1950s. How wise. How patient* ★★★★★

**Ch La Mission Haut-Brion** A predictably good wine. On the subject of prices, in 1954 Harry Waugh noted it as 'lovely, excellent but too expensive at £112 a hogshead' (from Calvet). I tasted it the following July in cask and certainly agreed with his assessment but couldn't comment on the price. Many notes taken, through the later 1950s, 1960s, 1970s and 1980s, not one less than good bottle, though its very distinctive flavours recorded, included singed, burnt, peaty, dried bracken, tobacco

and a slightly aggressive masculinity. Not a lightweight '53, though plenty of fragrance and some elegance. More recently, in bottles and one magnum: still impressive, totally different in character and style to the Haut-Brion at the La Reserve tasting. *Last noted June 2000. At best* ★★★★★, *and will continue.*

**Ch Mouton d'Armailhacq** Another charmer: a really good drink, 'fruit and balance' in 1960, but then not tasted for over 30 years, its bouquet 'lovely old cedar', firm yet delicate but drying out. *Last tasted Nov 1992. At peak* ★★★★

**Ch Pichon-Lalande** A lovely '53. Elegant. Stylish. Nine notes, twice in *Marie-Jeannes* in 1978 and 1986, and on both occasions their silky (texture) noted as well as glorious fragrance. A couple of Réserve Nicolas bottles the same year, one lovely the other suffering from a poor cork. More recently, surprisingly deep and intense, despite its mature rim and an astonishing flavour, spicy but astringent. Next, at a 'Weinart Probe' Pichon-Lalande dinner, a magnum, less deep, fully developed with a gentle, fragrant, harmonious, cedary bouquet and lovely flavour. On the light side, drying out, with attenuated finish. *Last noted Nov 1994. At its best* ★★★★ *Now fading. Drink up.*

**Ch Siran** Recorked. Well developed, very sweet, soft. *At a pre-sale tasting, Oct 1993* ★★★

**Ch Talbot** I was not very taken with this in its youth, and even after ten years in bottle I thought it a bit raw and lacking charm. But this *is* the fascination of good Bordeaux, and shows why it should be cellared and given time to mature. What alerted me was a most attractive Averys' bottling in 1975. A wonderfully relaxed wine, complete, delicately poised. Two excellent notes in the early and mid-1980s, when I thought it at its peak, but two more recent notes: a delicate, fragrant, refreshing and genuinely charming double magnum in 1995 and, the following year, a well nigh perfect *impériale* – I gave it very high marks. Then an understandably good, rich, ripe magnum from the château, delicious but beginning to dry out. *Last tasted at a dinner hosted by the Cordier daughters, Mme Bignon and Mme Rustmann, April 2000. At best* ★★★★

**Ch Trottevieille** Something of a surprise. An almost unrealistically deep appearance; low-keyed but harmonious nose; also surprisingly full and rich, vigorous, but with a certain coarse 'un-'53-like' masculinity. *The ninth wine of 11 St-Émilion Premiers Grands Crus Classés tasted at the Dîner Millésimes de Collection, at the château, June 1995* ★★★?

**THE BEST OF THE 1953S TASTED IN THE 1980S**
**Ch Certan-de-May** lovely wine, many notes. Most recently a fragrant Harvey's bottling. *Last tasted June 1987* ★★★★ *drink up*;
**Ch La Conseillante** always dependable. *Sept 1983* ★★★;
**Ch Ducru-Beaucaillou** it seems extraordinary now that a *2ème cru classé* claret could be bought in *en barrique* for bottling by a private person, in this case by a doctor in Cheshire. Probably bottled as well as at the château; a good wine but not a great Ducru. *Last tasted Feb 1989* ★★★; **Ch Giscours** *Last tasted in March 1981* ★★★★; **Ch Gruaud-Larose** rich, rounded, lovely. *Last tasted Sept 1987* ★★★★★; **Ch Langoa-Barton** several Harvey's bottlings between 1956 and 1983. The best levels good but now fading. *Last tasted Dec 1983. At best* ★★★;
**Ch Léoville-Barton** also interesting to note that very little was château-bottled. Happily Harvey's and Berry Bros' bottlings were very good. A most beautiful wine, at its best in the mid-1970s. *Last tasted July 1988* ★★★★ *but drink up*;
**Ch Léoville-Las-Cases** a luscious wine. *Last tasted July 1988* ★★★★★; **Ch Palmer** memorably tasted from the cask at my

first visit to Bordeaux, July 1955. Fragrant. Harvey's and château-bottlings at peak in the mid-1970s. *Last noted Sept 1986* ★★★; **Ch Rausan-Ségla** various English and Scottish bottlings, the best by David Sandeman. Very rich. *Last tasted Oct 1988. At best* ★★★ *but drink up*; **Ch Rauzan-Gassies** before the château went into decline, quite a good '53. *Pre-sale, Sept 1989* ★★; **Ch Prieuré-Lichine** both Alexis Lichine and his '53 at their most delightful best. *Oct 1988* ★★★★; and **Vieux Ch Certan** harmonious, silky, still perfect. *April 1984* ★★★★★

# 1954

One of the worst summers on record. The British wine trade had indulged in a spending spree with the '52s and '53s and 1955 was waiting in the wings. Fewer than two dozen notes and few of these recent. For the record:

**Ch Latour** Trying to live up to its reputation of producing a decent wine in a poor year. Ten notes did not convince me. Chunky, coarse and blunt. *Last tasted March 1989* ★

**Ch Margaux** Professor Sternby has a habit of challenging one with strange wines. Confusingly this bottle (in 1996) had a 1954 slip label but 1952 branded on the cork. Nils: don't do it again! Sensibly put into perspective at Wagner's vertical. Although pale and orange-tinged, its nose and taste not at all bad. Leathery tannins and short. *Jan 1997* ★

**Ch Mouton-Rothschild** Skinny in cask. Very variable bottles. Flavoury but short. *Last tasted in March 1989. At best* ★

OTHER '54s **Ch Ausone** quite good. *Oct 1987* ★★; **Dom de Chevalier** showing quite well either side of 1970. Variable bottlings since then. *Last tasted March 1990. At best* ★★; and **Ch La Mission Haut-Brion** some charm, flavoury, slightly bitter finish. *Last tasted Feb 1985* ★★

# 1955 ★★★★

A very good, somewhat underestimated yet useful vintage, now undeservingly neglected. On the whole beneficial weather conditions. A warm sunny summer, welcome showers in September and a decent-sized crop harvested in good conditions. It would seem that I have more notes than almost any vintage in the 1950s, literally hundreds, but fewer than 40 made since 1989.

**Ch Lafite** A delightful, well nigh perfect Lafite vintage. Many notes. Misleadingly advanced in the early 1960s but, as so frequently, developing fragrance and nuances of flavour. Beguiling if one has the patience, opportunity and time; and do not let a touch of astringency mar its lingering flavour and aftertaste. In some ways it epitomises all the virtues, that nouveau tasters and writers despise: delicacy, charm, subtlety, length and the sort of weight – or lack of it – that makes this sort of wine such a perfect drink or 'food wine', to use a more vulgar term. A beautiful lady, slow to reveal her charm, needing patience and understanding. *Last tasted Aug 2000* ★★★★★ *Should still be delicious.*

**Ch Latour** Very good wine, more complete and better balanced than the '52 and '53. Totally different in style and weight to the Lafite. From the start a deep purple, tannic wine, packed with fruit. Not remotely precocious but needing bottle age, its bouquet and flavour evolving through the 1960s and 1970s. At the age of 40, coming into its own. Several subsequent notes, slight variations due, as always to provenance and condition, five since the mid-1990s, one of the best

opened on New Year's Eve 1997 with my family. Always reassuring to pull a good long original cork. It was drinking perfectly, with a lovely old flavour, its tannin subdued. Another wonderful bottle at John Jenkins' Bordeaux Club dinner. Still very deep, surprisingly intense and youthful looking; a fully evolved bouquet, classic, cedary, fragrant and ageing a little, but faultless on the palate. A passable but fractionally acidic bottle at a pre-sale tasting in Los Angeles (1999) and an impressive but imperfect magnum with a gravy-like nose and peppery finish at Len Evans' dinner in the Hunter Valley, Australia. Lastly, deep, healthy colour; perfect nose, flavour, balance and length. Complete. Faultless. *Last tasted dining at Jeffrey Benson's, Feb 2001* ★★★★★ *Will go on, and on.*

**Ch Margaux** A lovely wine, with characteristic fragrance and charm. Showing consistently well, half a mark between them, at Wagner's two verticals in 1997 and 2000. Harmonious, fragrant; sweet, perfect weight, delicious flavour (not very original description I agree; but that is how it was). Perhaps the most unusual was opening five half-bottles to select two for Evans' 'Single bottle Club' dinner (Sept 2000). In combination, a soft gentle bouquet and flavour, fading a little and a touch too dry. *Last tasted Nov 2000. At best* ★★★★★

**Ch Mouton-Rothschild** A spectacular wine probably at its opulent best in the 1980s. In fact it was a bit of a slow starter, and in 1961, I described it as 'loaded', needing time, and 'very expensive' at 36 shillings (£1.80) a bottle. The 16 notes I made in the 1960s and 1970s followed its evolution, in particular the build up of its intense characteristic cassis fragrance. Most recently, a richly coloured, fully mature magnum with good crisp fruit, vivacity and dry finish. *Last noted at Peter Ziegler's outstanding tasting at the Schlosshotel Erbach, Germany, Dec 1995* ★★★★★ *(Not to be confused with Rheingau's Erbach.)*

**Ch Haut-Brion** A wide spread of notes starting in 1961, observing a fairly speedy development. Indeed noted as 'v. mature' at 10 years of age. Extremely good notes through the 1970s, with a particularly lovely, 'easy, elegant' bottle from the Dillon cellar in 1979. A touch of austerity noted in 1983. More recently, at Ziegler's tasting, a richly fragrant magnum with a distinctive tobacco-like flavour, dry and somewhat unbending. The taste conjured up embers in a drying fire. Next, a refreshing but raw-edged bottle with, initially, a lovely singed-bracken bouquet. And, most recently, alas, a bad bottle in Balham, south London. *Last noted Feb 2001. At best* ★★★★

**Ch Ausone** Not tasted.

**Ch Cheval Blanc** Still being shipped in hogsheads to English wine merchants, some excellent Berry Bros' bottlings drinking beautifully at 30 years of age: rich, soft, earthy, completely rounded – no sharp edges, a touch of Cheval Blanc iron (from the soil) on the finish but noted as *à point*. But some château-bottled variations, the following noted in 1978: a deep, brick red double magnum, medium sweetness, soft, lovely, and a brown-rimmed bottle with a 'calm' cedar-caramel nose, both colour and caramel anticipating a touch of decay and strange descriptions such as 'velvety and rusty nails' and 'too smooth, too round, too rotten'! The latter must have been due to hot storage. To demonstrate that the latter was an aberration, a fabulous bottle in its fortieth year at Ziegler's tasting. I gave it 19/20. The following year a good but not flawless magnum at Wolf's vertical: more meaty, more chewy but refreshing. *Last noted Sept 1997. At best* ★★★★★

**Ch Pétrus** Five notes, from a tannin-laden magnum in 1967; 'huge', 'velvety', 'suede textured' through the 1970s. 'Magnificent but not Médoc' in 1983 – which shows my old school bias! A good, powerful bottle at John Jenkins' Bordeaux Club dinner in 1993. More recently, less deep in colour, more mature, more evolved – yet, despite its richness, still tannic. *Last tasted at Ziegler's memorable Saturday tasting in Dec 1995* ★★★★

OTHER MAJOR '55S LAST TASTED IN THE 1990S

**Ch Batailley** Delicious, bricky, cedary, bottled by G F Grant. (Heaven knows where we found this. It must have fallen off the back of a lorry.) *At a Christie's lunch, July 1995* ★★★

**Ch Beychevelle** The sort of vintage which used to suit Beychevelle. Several notes, lightish and easy drinking at only four years of age; attractively developed by 1986. More recently, rich 'milk chocolate' bouquet, drinking pleasantly. Will be tiring now. *Last tasted May 1993. At best* ★★★★

**Ch Calon-Ségur** A good '55. First tasted in 1959. Full, fruity, and, for a St-Estèphe, not too tannic. Drinking well through the 1960s and 1970s, but acidity creeping up in the 1980s. Only once tasted recently: showing its age. *Last tasted March 1999. At best* ★★★ *But risky now.*

**Carruades de Ch Lafite** A surprisingly raw, tannic *impériale*. *Oct 1992* ★

**Ch Ducru-Beaucaillou** I first tasted a cask sample at Harvey's in March 1956. It was lovely. Several *barriques* had been shipped to Bristol and I witnessed the bottling – one cellarman seated at the tap, handing the filled bottle to his mate for corking. This was on 18 December 1957. (I have a note that the château bottled their '55 in April 1958.) Despite this, surprisingly little variation and 'silky', 'smooth', 'refined', 'top class' dot the ten notes I made in the 1970s. Then a gap of nearly 20 years: a magnum, from the château, recorked, given by Xavier Borie for the dinner following Eigensatz's big bottle tasting. Richly mature; harmonious bouquet, cedar, 'warm tiles'; sweet, perfect flavour, weight and balance, though its aftertaste hinted at fatigue. *Last tasted July 1995. At best* ★★★★

**Ch La Fleur** Fragrant, 'warm'; perfectly balanced, lively, holding well. *At Rodenstock's major vertical tasting of La Fleur in Munich, Aug 1998* ★★★★

**Ch Gruaud-Larose** A lovely wine, perfect in the 1960s and 1970s including good bottlings by Harvey's and Dolamore's (a family owned firm which started to slip off the map when it moved from Baker Street). Losing colour, but a fragrant, beautifully mature bottle in 1981, fading in 1986, latterly a horrible over-the-hill double magnum in 1998. However, an overripe and deliciously drinkable jeroboam in September 1993. *Last tasted Sept 1998. At best* ★★★★ *But risky now.*

### The Sichels

*There are two main branches of the Sichel family. On the Franco-British side, there were Allan Sichel, of Sichel & Co of Bordeaux, and his son Peter. Peter and I were great friends and contemporaries. It was he who escorted Daphne and I on our first visit to Bordeaux in 1955. The Sichels became part-owners of Ch Palmer in 1938 and still have a minority shareholding, and in 1961 Peter bought Ch d'Angludet. His sons (all five of them) now ably run the properties as a family business. The great thing about Peter was that he was the most honest, quietly influential and highly respected member of the Bordeaux trade. Very sadly, he died in 1998; we all miss him. The other branch of the family, best known for its Liebfraumilch Blue Nun, is headed by the urbane and ubiquitous (fellow cyclist) Peter M F Sichel who is based in New York.*

**Ch Lagrange** (St-Julien) Variable. At its best in the 1970s. Most recently, not bad flavour but overmature. *Last tasted Oct 1996. At best* ★★ *Avoid.*

**Ch La Lagune** Always the odd man out, with a scent and sweetness of its own. Mocha, lightish, refreshing. *Donated by Peter Sichel for our 50th Anniversary dinner at Ch Palmer, June 1985* ★★★ *Holding up, just.*

**Ch Lanessan** Better known for its carriage museum. Danish-bottled: just good enough. *Pre-sale, Amsterdam, Nov 1996. Avoid.*

**Ch La Mission Haut-Brion** Not a gentle, easy '55. Despite its richness and vinosity, aggressively tannic in 1966, bitterness marring its finish in the early 1970s. By the end of that decade its bouquet had achieved perfection and, despite a bit of a bite, was lovely. Fully opened up, softer, sweet and ripe in the mid-1980s. Most recently, with an astonishing spicy bouquet, eucalyptus, raspberries – almost like '45 Mouton. Very exciting wine, crisp fruit but a bit tart on the finish. *Last noted at the La Réserve tasting, June 2000. At best* ★★★★★ *Should still be very good.*

**Ch Mouton d'Armailhacq** 'Baron Philippe' on label. An agreeable château-bottling in 1963 and a rather unexpected British Transport Hotels bottling in 1968 (at that time BTH ran some of the top hotels in England and Scotland, and had an excellent cellar). Scented and overripe by the mid-1980s and most recently. *Last tasted Jan 1993. At best* ★★ *Give it a miss.*

**Ch Palmer** 'Luscious for claret' in 1961, some less complimentary notes soon after, and in the 1970s, including 'sharp', 'touch of volatile acidity', 'rather dull'. A better note in the mid-1980s: 'elegant but not great'. Most recently, a 'light, easy, charming middle-aged lady with her slip showing'. *Last noted, another bottle kindly provided by Peter Sichel, dining at the château in January 1995. At best* ★★★ *Over the hill now.*

**Ch Pavie** Strange? Only one note. Continuing my sexist comments, the bouquet reminded me of expensive, once fashionable dresses in a dowager's wardrobe. Dry, lean, strangely flavoured but easy to drink. *A double magnum, Sept 1998* ★★★?

**Ch Pichon-Lalande** 400 cases, château-bottled, landed at Bristol docks in April 1958. I first tasted the wine five months later. 'Very firm, excellent flavour, expensive' (it appeared on Harvey's list for 'laying down' at 19 shillings (95p) a bottle, just under half the price of '47 Latour on the 'drinking list'). A couple of desultory notes until a recorked *Marie-Jeanne* in 1993, well developed, well balanced. Fully mature, of course: 'soft, rich, perfect now'. *Last tasted dining at Ch d'Yquem, June 1998. At best* ★★★★ *Clearly still good if well cellared.*

**Ch Siran** Nice weight, sweet, soft, lovely. *At a pre-sale tasting, Oct 1993* ★★★

**Ch Talbot** Eight consistently complimentary notes from 1959 to 1978, both Harvey's-bottled and château-bottled: quality, balance, rounded. Declining in depth of colour but not in flavour. Then a jump of 20 years. Bottled by Nicolas, Paris, its appearance now a bit weak, but the sort of bouquet that has been dying to be released, flaunting all its charm. Harmonious, soft, sweet. Held well in the glass. *Last noted at a tasting of 'Premier Bordeaux wines' I conducted at the Palm Beach International Food and Wine Fair, Feb 1998. At best* ★★★★★

# 1956

Atrocious. On a par with 1951. Meagre, thin, yet some faintly drinkable wines. Mainly as a penance. Avoid.

**Ch Lafite** Put in to his Lafite vertical in 1988 by Lloyd Flatt, for completeness. Chaptalised of course, light, pleasant – though short. More recently, recorked in 1992 (although '1991' was on the cork itself). No red left; nose surprisingly rich and lively – but aged. *Last tasted pre-sale, March 1996.*

**Ch Latour** Half a dozen notes and making a serious effort to live up to its reputation for producing a passable wine in a poor year. Surprisingly deep in colour, and quite good, though short in 1970. Flavoury but tart Cabernet character in the later 1970s; 'raw', 'flavoury', 'subdued', 'acidic' in the 1980s. Most recently, a jeroboam, an aberration. *Last tasted Oct 1992.*

**Ch La Mission Haut-Brion** Contrasting notes: light, dry, lean and short – in fact, un-Mission-like at Desai's vertical in 1985. Most recently, a bottle from the Woltner cellars sold at Christie's: surprisingly dry, rich and chewy, though with a strange sweaty nose. *Last tasted June 1990. At best ★★*

## 1957 ★

Fairly highly regarded at the time and misguidedly bought by the British trade. Weather, as always, principally responsible: hot in March, the precocious buds hit by April frosts, poor flowering, 'the coldest August on record', unripe grapes picked in an early October heat wave. Aggressive, astringent wines, though some flavoury and drinkable, particularly when young.

**Ch Lafite** An attractive Cruse sample in October 1958, but I noted its piquancy in the 1970s. Allowing for its marked yet tolerable acidity, which I often allude to as 'refreshing', I rather enjoyed (five) bottles spanning the 1980s, though 'meagre', 'creaking', 'vanilla and varnish' crop up. And I must repeat a jolly occasion in 1984 when Eric de Rothschild served it with oysters and sausages, apparently customary at Sunday luncheons at Lafite. *Last tasted March 1990 ★*

**Ch Latour** One of my least-liked vintages of Latour. As astringent as the '37. Colour impressive, though misleading. Two poor bottles in the late 1980s. *Not tasted since March 1989.*

**Ch Margaux** Noticeably bitter in cask (August 1958). 'Screwed up', 'tart', 'uninteresting' in the 1970s; raw and unbalanced' noted in 1981. I predicted that it would turn out like the '37. Most recently: sour nose; flavoury but lean and very acidic. *Last tasted at Wagner's vertical, Nov 2000. Avoid.*

**Ch Mouton-Rothschild** In 1961 lovely fruity Cabernet flavour, but not cheap at 32 shillings (£1.60) a bottle; richness masking its acidity in the 1970s. Fragrant, flavoury, charming with raw '57 acidity. *Last tasted March 1989 ★*

**Ch Haut-Brion** A good '57 as '57s go. Noted that it was a '47 *tonneau* crop'. Not much selection in those days. In cask, October 1958, flavoury and well balanced save for its 'bite'. Mixed notes in the 1970s and 1980s, 'leathery', 'earthy', 'loose knit' – also 'lovely' and 'silky'. Just a couple of 'raw', 'spicy', notes in 1985. Most recently, at the La Réserve tasting, a pleasant colour with the orange rim I associate with maturity and high tannins, yet surprisingly appealing on the nose: touch of vanilla, harmonious, refreshing – but changed for the worse, smelly, after an hour in the glass. Nevertheless, quite good flavour despite tannin and high acidity. *Last tasted June 2000 ★*

**Ch Ausone** Rather to my surprise, quite a few notes, starting with an almost burgundy-like, soft, chocolatey Cruse cask sample in 1958. Varying from severe to quite attractive, though end acidity almost always noted in the 1960s and 1970s. A moderate note at Flatt's Ausone vertical in 1987. Most recently: fully mature, weak rim; sweet 'old oak' (an arboreal analogy); sweet entry, raw finish. *Last noted at a pre-sale tasting in New York. If you see it again, don't bid.*

**Ch Beychevelle** Two very good, yet fairly acidic Army & Navy Stores' bottlings. Most recently from the château: a nose

like hot chocolate (Cadbury's I assume); old wood, attractive but of course with '57 acidity. *Last tasted May 1993 ★★*

**Ch Cheval Blanc** The vines had been almost completely destroyed by a most severe (–4°C) frost, in February 1956. Some recovered but both quantity and quality were severely reduced. Cheval Blanc 1957 (and 1956) not tasted.

**Ch Cissac** I have always had a soft spot for Cissac and its owner, Monsieur Vialard, ever since tasting his '53 competently bottled by a Dr Snell in Cheshire. The '57 was the oldest of 20 vintages at a pre-promotional-sale tasting. Alas, it was showing its age and couldn't hide its sourness. *April 1996.*

**Dom de Chevalier** The oldest of the vintages ending in 7 (save for the wonderful Warre's '27 vintage port see page 458): rich 'legs', thick; the smell and almost the weight of a pile of bricks. Sweet. Interesting. *At the domaine, Sept 1998 ★*

**Clos Fourtet** Jeroboam, lean but supple, tannic. *Oct 1992 ★★*

**Ch Lynch-Bages** My favourite '57, the volatile acidity merely enhancing its bouquet and flavour. Typical blackcurrant aroma and flavour in cask. Then good notes in the 1960s and 1970s, including a very good Harvey's and a very bad British Transport Hotels bottling (I recall recommending that it should be destroyed). The best was Bordeaux-bottled: excellent aroma, dry, chunky and very flavoury in 1972, and a similar bottle in 1985. More recently, also Bordeaux-bottled, from David Carter's pristine cellar: now dried-out (the wine not the cellar!). *Last tasted May 1994. At best ★★★*

**Ch La Mission Haut-Brion** The best of all the '57s, thanks to the Woltners' skill and Woltner provenance. I cannot resist quoting the note I made at the Desai vertical in 1985: 'almost '61 opacity; attractive bouquet – calm sea, hot pebbles, sacking (sack cloth. I am surprised I didn't add 'ashes') and iodine. Flavour to match'. More recently, rich fruit, peppery, tannins. *Last noted at Wolf's vertical, June 1990 ★★★★ Worth looking out for.*

**Ch Pétrus** Orange-rimmed; 'cheesy', spirity; sweet and mild with tolerable acidity. *Pre-sale, New York, Oct 1996 ★*

**Ch Pichon-Baron** Five notes from a cask sample in 1957 to 1983 when it seemed to be at its 'surprisingly attractive' best; refreshing but not over-acidic. Most recently, a deep, brown-rimmed magnum, with sweet, ripe, earthy nose and taste. Tolerable acidity, though the finish turned to astringency. *Last noted at lunch at the château, Sept 1998. At best ★★★*

OTHER PASSABLE '57S LAST TASTED IN THE 1980s
**Ch Beychevelle** elegant, flavoury. *1987 ★★★*; **Ch Gruaud-Larose** magnum fruity but acidic. *1983 ★★*; and **Ch Léoville-Las-Cases** raw but flavoury. *1985 ★★*

## 1958 ★★

A pleasant, late-harvested, easy vintage completely trumped by the excellent and high-priced '59s. British claret connoisseurs appreciated its understated qualities and reasonable price. The trade, however, had bought heavily the '57s and held back to buy the '59s. Although only predicted to be quick maturing 10-year span wines, the best lasted far longer but are now fading or faded.

**Ch Lafite** I did not like this in its (and my) youth, but by 1975 described it as 'gentle, feminine, ripe and attractive'. A nice bottle and a spectacular *impériale* at the Flatt tasting in the 1980s. Only once since: medium pale, fully mature, attractive appearance, nose and taste. I liked it. *Last noted, one of eight borderline vintages from a Rothschild cellar, at a pre-sale tasting in March 1996 ★★*

**Ch Haut-Brion** Ten notes. A relatively dull, uninspired '58. Seemed at its not bad best in the mid-1970s. Later, a touch of rawness. *Last tasted, a jeroboam, in Oct 1992. At best ★★ Declining.*

**Ch Cheval Blanc** Late picked (October 6–19). The first decent vintage after the great frost. Mainly good notes from the 1970s to mid-1980s: soft, agreeable, no harsh edges, 'scented cedar'. Alcohol a modest 11.6%. Most recently, an unknown English bottling, fairly deeply coloured; a touch of 'linoleum' on the nose; sweeter, fuller, richer than expected. *Last noted at Wolf's vertical, Sept 1997. At best ★★★ Fading.*

**Ch Pétrus** Would not have achieved its present fame with this vintage, though impressive – up to a point. Sweet but 'edgy'. *Last tasted April 1990 ★★ Unlikely to do any better.*

**Ch La Mission Haut-Brion** Consistent notes. Mocha-like nose, rich enough but short. Most recently, surprisingly impressive colour, fairly red; sweet, harmonious but clearly chaptalised nose; chewy fruity flavour. A very good '58. *Last noted dining at Dom de Chevalier, April 1998 ★★*

**Ch Beychevelle** Strange: dried-out. *May 1993.*

**Ch Giscours** Sweet, harmonious, fully developed nose; interesting wine with curious uplift of flavour. Drying out. *Sept 1995 ★★*

OTHER '58S LAST TASTED IN THE 1980S **Ch Margaux** by no means a *grand vin*. Not bad, but drying out. *Last tasted May 1981 ★*; **Ch Latour** stodgy in its youth; spicy but short. Some fragrance but uninteresting. *Last tasted March 1989 ★*; **Ch Mouton-Rothschild** tried its best to be exciting in the 1970s. Latterly hollow and short. *Last tasted March 1989 ★ on its way out*; and **Ch Ausone** richly scented, good flavour though now light and lean. *Last tasted Oct 1987. At best ★★★*

# 1959 ★★★★★

A great vintage. Hugely popular with the British wine trade, proclaimed by the pundits as 'the vintage of the century' and *très grands vins* by the Bordelais, the optimists were not far out despite some talk of lack of acidity. Apropos, the eminent Professor Peynaud states that if a wine has an abundance of all the major component parts, alcohol, extract, fruit and tannin, an equally high level of acidity is not only not essential, it is not necessary. The 1959 vintage was blessed with a very favourable growing season, in particular a fine, warm summer, with rain mid-September to swell the grapes; the harvest followed a week or so later.

**Ch Lafite** One of the best-ever Lafites, quite different from the more delicately fragrant '53s, and keeping well.
I did not have the opportunity to taste it in its youth; indeed, I see with some surprise that my first note was made at a Heublein pre-auction tasting in May 1975 when it was already well developed yet, clearly, with many years of life. I have since been fortunate to catch up, with just short of three dozen neatly spread notes. Ignoring an occasional poorly kept bottle, admirable. It has always had an impressively deep colour, though now, of course, showing some mahogany-edged maturity; always a magnificent mouthful too. One of the most interesting and salutary tastings was organised in 1994 by Weinart at Aschau, south of Munich, to compare the top 1959s and 1961s (blind). Though the '61 Lafite was very fragrant, I observed that the '59 had a deeper, mulberry colour, a rich, harmonious nose and was sweeter, fuller, more complete. Though I say it myself, I managed to produce a perfect bottle at my Bordeaux Club dinner in 1996, drawing the cork

(having stood the bottle up for 24 hours) at 5.45pm, decanting an hour later, and pouring at 8.20pm to give it plenty of time to open in the glass – which it did. Then, in 1998, an excellent magnum, among other magnificent wines, from N K Yong's cellar, dining at his home in Singapore. It had everything in abundance except, perhaps, charm. Well, what has it got? The extraordinary ability to exude not only an immediate cedary perfume but, very much a Lafite speciality, the way it opens up further avenues of fragrance and subtle by-paths, lingering in the mouth. Each time you pick up your glass you notice another facet of scent and taste. It also happens to be a good drink, still a perfect beverage. *Last tasted Dec 2000 ★★★★★*

**Ch Latour** A glorious, mammoth wine. It just goes from strength to strength. Forty notes from July 1963. Initially a black purple colour, nose packed with fruit, full-bodied, its extract and sheer power seeming to absorb, partially to disguise its tannic intensity. To quote André Simon once again, it has 'the majesty of the Royal Oak!' In the late 1960s I thought it was going through a dumb period, its austerity very noticeable. Through the 1970s 'huge', 'massive', 'bottled velvet'; and not much change in colour, nose or power in the 1980s. Still opaque, fragrant but peppery with marvellous fruit though still hard and tannic at the Hallwag tasting in 1994, and, another magnum, even more so at the Weinart blind tasting later the same year. Next, it more than held its own against the '45 and '61 in a Rodenstock 'flight' of Latours (in 1995). Outstandingly the finest at a dinner for 'the international press' at Latour, and, despite its mid-shoulder level, still mouthfilling at Hugh Johnson's Bordeaux Club dinner later that year. A pretty tough bottle with Len Evans in the Hunter Valley in Australia. More recently, showing no signs of flagging, its opacity merely prefacing its beautifully developed bouquet, excellent flavour and perfect balance – perfect enough to keep up the maturing process for another quarter century. *Last noted at the Russian National Orchestra dinner at Hatchlands, Surrey, Dec 2000 ★★★★(★★)!*

**Ch Margaux** Despite its deep appearance, already ripe and lovely when first tasted in the early 1960s. Margaux's inimitable perfume and charm noted through the 1970s, no lack of acidity noted. Almost all warranting 5 stars in the 1980s, when it started to look less intense and show more maturity. In 1994, tasted alongside the '61 in Aschau, both were fully mature-looking with a touch of orange at the rim. On this occasion I found the '61 more fragrant and charming, though I think the '59 was not at its best; nor was it at Wagner's first Margaux vertical. However, at the second, a bottle recorked in 1986 was superb, one of my highest marks, ahead of the '61. By now a medium depth of colour; a lovely 'warm', rich, well-tempered, complete, harmonious bouquet; sweet, full, rich and rounded. However, looking back, of my 29 notes, about half a dozen have been disappointing to poor, mainly due to less-than-good levels and poor corks. *Last tasted Dec 2001. At best superb ★★★★★*

**Ch Mouton-Rothschild** 'Magnificence piled upon magnificence' is what I wrote in 1991, and it still applies. Tasted on over two dozen occasions starting in March 1963, only one less than first rate. Initially deep but not as black or vivid as Latour, it held its colour unwaveringly until the 1990s, yet always rich, with touch of ruby. But hang the colour, it is the bouquet and flavour which makes this one of the most exhilarating, one of the greatest, vintages of Mouton. At Weinart's blind tasting in 1994 it just beat the '61 and earned my highest marks of the entire tasting, particularly noticing its harmony and 'tea chest of spice' on the nose, and fabulous flavour. Spice, eucalyptus, noted again, and its crisp vivacity aiding and abetting the bouquet – the finest wine at pre-sale tastings in New York in 1996 and 1999. (Christie's wine-buff clients are treated to seriously fine wines before each auction.) Jousting with Latour '59 at the Hatchlands dinner in Surrey, it had a glowing immediacy of bouquet and fabulous intensity of flavour. A bravura performance in aid of the Russian National Orchestra. Most recently, a perfect bottle at yet another superb Hardy Rodenstock event. *Last tasted March 2001* ★★★★★ *and will go on.*

**Ch Haut-Brion** There is a world of difference between the wine of Haut-Brion, arguably the oldest great-wine château in the Bordeaux region, and its peers in the Médoc. The mesoclimate is different, but above all – perhaps I should write beneath all – is the soil, the deep Graves-gravel. The wine is most distinctively different in appearance, nose and taste – yet it has elegance and finesse. For a start, and at the start – my first of three dozen notes made in October 1964 – it is totally different in colour to the three '59 Médocs mentioned above. Not as deep but brown, its edge displaying a somewhat misleadingly mature rim. Its bouquet also has a soft earthiness, which evolved steadily through the 1970s, a sort of warm brick – hot Provençal tiles – scent with deep cedar and tobacco, invariably opening up in the glass, fragrant, lingering on the palate, its initial austerity softening. One of the best bottles was tasted in May 1984: its initial 'tobacco leaf' nose developing a delicate, 'old bracken' scent, finally, after 50 minutes, sweet, pure harmony and fragrance. On the palate, full of fruit, loose knit yet with concentrated, fabulous, flavour and good length. A decade later, vying with the '61 though less deep, more mature looking; slightly singed, chocolatey but fragrant; a fairly sweet powerful wine and very alcoholic. Perfection at a tasting in 1995, a beautiful, fully mature, brown-rimmed wine with bouquet surging out of the glass. Very sweet – with that distinctive earthy, tobacco-leaf taste, lunching at Ch Langoa. Most recently, by a short head the best wine at La Réserve's Haut-Brion/La Mission tasting: a wonderful gradation of colour; showing age but sweet and mellow, with a lovely edge-of-honeycomb scent after an hour in the glass. A positive, sweet entry and soft. All the component parts working in harmony. *Last tasted June 2000* ★★★★★

**Ch Ausone** Only five notes: when first tasted in 1971 showing well. Then tasting in pairs in 1994, the '59 had a slight resemblance to Haut-Brion on the nose: mocha, spice, peppery, opening up, 'cold tea and coffee'; an equally strange flavour, brown paper, autumn leaves. Dry and austere, the '61 more complete. Most recently, medium deep; autumn leaves again, but very fragrant, opening up richly. This time, it seemed to be extraordinarily sweet and rich, chunky, chewy, still tannic. *Last noted at the 1er grand cru St-Émilion dinner, June 1997. A very good Ausone* ★★★★

**Ch Cheval Blanc** Hot, difficult vinification, but the end result was a lovely wine, sweet and soft in the 1970s, though curiously, alongside the '61, it appeared to be dry and somewhat austere. It must have been a below-par bottle (1994), for at the same dinner, following the '59 Ausone noted above, a deliciously lively bottle, bouquet slightly singed, with faintly raisiny fruit and, once again, very sweet on the palate, rich, glorious with perfect tannin and acidity. A very similar bottle at Wolf's vertical. *Last tasted Sept 1997. At best* ★★★★★

**Ch Pétrus** Not tasted in its youth but predictably sweet and fleshy when first noted in 1972. Showing well in 1990 and

1993, and, the following year at the very useful Wolf/Weinart paired tasting when, though a big, rich wine, fully mature, it did not quite match the magnificent splendour of the '61. *Last tasted Nov 1994* ★★★★★ *Time in hand.*

THE BEST OF THE REST

**Ch Beychevelle** Several English bottlings, the best from the most dependable Army & Navy cellars. It was a harmonious, fully evolved, velvety mouthful. Probably at its best (1983). A decade later a good château-bottling. *Last noted May 1992. At best* ★★★★ *But fading now.*

**Ch Brane-Cantenac** Mature but drying-out. *At the château, April 1998* ★★

**Ch Calon-Ségur** Confusing to have so many English-bottled wines but they were mainly good. Most recently, a superb jeroboam, château-bottled of course, at the Gala dinner following the Weinart tasting: sweet, full-bodied, concentrated like a '61, and very tannic. It did not go well with the turbot. *Last tasted Nov 1994. At best* ★★★★

**Dom de Chevalier** Showing well in 1983 and, more recently, a most excellent magnum, blackberry coloured, nose restrained yet rich and fruity, opening up superbly in the glass. Full-bodied, fragrant, very tannic. Claude Ricard at his masterful best. *Last noted in Aschau, Nov 1994* ★★★★

**Ch Cissac** To demonstrate what a relatively minor Médoc can do in a vintage like 1959. Several notes, including Dr Snell's home bottling in 1967. And three, impeccable, since. Sweet, full, rich, tannic. *Last noted dining with the Vialards at their château, Sept 1995* ★★★★

**Ch La Conseillante** Limpid, with shades of cherry; lovely fragrance; rich silky Pomerol texture. First rate. *Dinner at Aschau, Nov 1994* ★★★★

**Ch Cos d'Estournel** In its prime an excellent '59. Well made, beautifully balanced, very tannic. Charm and bite. Most recently, autumn colour, overripe bouquet, good flavour, still tannic. *Last tasted Jan 1990* ★★★★★ *But past its best.*

**Ch Ducru-Beaucaillou** Several notes. Initially deep and tannic and all but one good – a 'chicken droppings', guano nose (a phenolic problem I was told), rich but tainted. More recently, its original deep colour simmered down, mature; spicy fruit, a touch of rusticity; dry, with a cold, standoffish flavour and lingering tannin. *Last tasted Nov 1994. At best* ★★★

**Ch L'Église-Clinet** Two recent notes: still with opaque core; very sweet, full, rich and fleshy (1995). Next bottled in Belgium in 1961, with very distinctive nose and flavour, opening up, finally delicious. The Belgians were traditionally the great appreciators of the wines of Pomerol at a time when they were generally considered too insignificant by the British trade and their principals in Bordeaux. Only a 6-ha vineyard, average production 1200-plus cases a year. Not worth bothering with! Now a cult wine! *Last noted at a Rodenstock vertical, July 1998. At best* ★★★★

**Ch Figeac** Only one note, at the blind tasting of paired '59s and '61s already referred to. 'Impressively deep but browning rim; bouquet open, grassy, 'tea and mothballs', idiosyncratic; sweet, with a touch of iron from the soil and a hot spicy finish. A roller coaster of a wine. *Nov 1994* ★★★

**Ch Grand-Puy-Lacoste** A big, serious, tannic, slowly maturing wine, tough in the 1960s and 1970s, evolving in the 1980s, at its zenith in the mid-1990s. A superb classic cedary nose, opening up sweetly. On the palate, well clad though leaner than expected, yet with good fruit. Complete. *Last tasted Sept 1995* ★★★★ *And will still be good.*

**Ch Gruaud-Larose** Many notes, many bottlings, all good, for this was still a period when experienced British merchants were at their most dependable, the Army & Navy Stores' bottlings particularly notable. I must confess that at the Weinart blind tasting I would have bet heavily that the '59 was the '61. The '59 was so dry, severe and tannic, though fully mature-looking, sweet and spicy on the nose. *Last tasted Nov 1994* ★★★★ *Will still be good.*

**Ch Guillot** Another Pomerol little known in England but favoured by other northern Europeans, this one Danish-bottled. Mahogany colour; austere. *Oct 1995* ★★

**Ch d'Issan** Raw and unready when first tasted. Developed well. Last tasted Bordeaux-bottled by Cruse. The Cruse family still own this beautiful moated castle tucked out of sight in Margaux. A good chunky wine and drinking well. *The oldest of three d'Issan vintages at a Saintsbury Club dinner, April 1994* ★★★

**Ch Langoa-Barton** Strangely, I would have expected the '59 to be made of sterner stuff. But it had a wonderful fragrance. *Last tasted June 1992* ★★★★

**Ch Latour-à-Pomerol** Very deep. As often, with even top Pomerols, the palate more interesting than the nose. Certainly the case here. A classic fullness and flavour. Complete and on the palate only, a grudging 5 stars. *Sept 1998* ★★★★★

**Ch Léoville-Poyferré** Not too inspired by the various English bottlings tasted in the 1960s. Seemed much more harmonious, château-bottled, in the 1970s. Most recently, a soft, sweetened, complete and delicious flavour. In short, Poyferré, almost at its very best. *Last tasted in New York, Feb 1997* ★★★★

**Ch Lynch-Bages** Uncharacteristically tough and uncharming in its early days. The wine of two other highly dependable bottlers, Berry Bros and IECWS (The Wine Society) tasted well, either side of 1970. Most recently, mature, orange tinged; its bouquet fully evolved, in fact with the typical high-toned, spicy, Pauillac Cabernet nose hurtling out of the glass. 'The poor man's Mouton' I condescendingly observed. Lovely and will keep. *Last tasted Nov 1994* ★★★★

**Ch Malartic-Lagravière** To demonstrate yet another superb bottling, this time by Christopher's (before its sad demise, claiming to be the oldest-established wine merchant in London). A deep, uplifting, delicious red Graves. 'Now living dangerously.' *Jan 1992* ★★★

**Ch Malescot-St-Exupéry** A full, fruity *impériale* tasted in 1992. More recently, I had a rich, ruby-tinged bottle, with wonderful mulberry-like fruit. Dry finish. *Last tasted Sept 1999. At best* ★★★★

**Ch La Mission Haut-Brion** The Woltners at their peak. The wine took 20 years to shrug off some of the tannin. Initially restrained but perfectly evolved by the early 1990s. Very sweet, tobacco-like Graves flavour and a perfect elliptical shape (1994). Most recently a superb bottle at La Réserve's tasting: deep, more intense than the Ch Haut-Brion, tinged with cherry red; more scented too, 'earthy', 'cheese rind', 'singed tobacco', 'pebbly', its crisp fruit opening up richly; more astringent than the Ch Haut-Brion, crisper fruit, more aggressive, with excellent tannin and acidity. *Last tasted June 2000* ★★★★★ *And will keep.*

**Ch Montrose** Very popular with merchants at this period and a fine Justerini & Brooks' bottling, among others, in the 1970s. In 1979, 'broad-shouldered', 1983 'rock of ages'. A substantial wine with all the component parts evolving simultaneously. Two recent notes, the most memorable at

Hugh Johnson's: still deep and velvety though with a fully mature rim; a classic cedary nose that opened up deliciously; some ripe sweetness, fairly but not too full-bodied, fleshy, complete, with tannin and acidity to keep it going for years. *Last tasted Aug 1999* ★★★★★

**Ch Palmer** Also very popular, and not just because of its English name, bottled extensively by merchants. A superb, ripe, fleshy, spicy well-muscled magnum in 1989; alas, in 1994, a corked bottle which, in any case, would have been thrashed by the '61. Most recently, medium deep, fully mature; classic, cedary bouquet; superb sweetness and ripeness, lovely flavour, gloriously rich and harmonious. *Last noted at the Farr Vintners/Mähler-Besse dinner at Ransome's Dock, Feb 2001* ★★★★

**Ch Pape-Clément** Not its best period, but some charm and fragrance, provided by different bottlings in the 1960s and 1970s. A good château-bottling tasted in 1983 and a poor woody bottle a year later. Only one more recent note: an outrageous *impériale* at a modest 31-wine dinner with Dr Schiele, a former President of Germany, as guest of honour. Also typical of Rodenstock's generosity, a wonderful intermission listening to Bocelli, the now famous blind tenor. Oh, the wine? Bouquet vegetal but bursting forth sweetly; a very earthy Graves flavour, and tannic. I disliked its aftertaste. *Last noted at the Königshof hotel, Munich, Sept 1996. At best* ★★★★

**Ch Pichon-Baron** Deep, tannic. Impressive. At its magnificent best in the 1980s. Still tannic but drying out. *Last tasted Feb 1992. At best* ★★★★

**Ch Pichon-Lalande** Mixed notes due to different bottlings in its early days. I would have thought the '59 an archetypal Lalande and happily, judging by two recent notes, it has turned out well: a lovely, fruity, fragrant, spicy bouquet; dry, perfect weight and flavour, rich yet lissome (provenance Nicolas, Paris) at a Rodenstock tasting in September 1994, and two months later, a really spectacular *impériale*: almost opaque; fruity, chunky, peppery, bouquet conjuring up its *terroir* and *chai*. *Last noted at Karl-Heinz Wolf's Pichon-Lalande dinner in Aschau, Nov 1994. At best* ★★★★★

**Ch Trotanoy** Impressively deep; good fruit; sweet, very good flavour but a surprising touch of rawness. *Sept 1995* ★★★

**Ch La Tour Haut-Brion** Initially a tough nut and a coarser version of Ch La Mission though fragrant, with good fruit, tannin and acidity. *Last tasted June 1990. At best* ★★★ *Will keep but will it improve?*

**Vieux Ch Certan** Started and ended somewhat austerely, seemed at its best in the mid-1970s, exhibiting a velvety Pomerol texture. Most recently, fully mature; nose better than palate, for, despite showing its age, it was rich and fragrant. Dry, somewhat austere, very tannic though opening up to leave one with a sweet impression. In the end, I gave it a very high mark. *Last tasted Sept 1994. At best* ★★★★

SOME OF THE BEST '59S NOTED IN THE 1980S (with star ratings when last tasted) **Ch Batailley** good fruit, attractive, lacking length. *1983* ★★; **Ch Canon** glorious bouquet, lovely wine. *1985* ★★★★; **Carruades de Ch Lafite** good fruit and flavour. *1983* ★★★; **Ch La Lagune** rich, lovely flavour, fruit and weight. *1983* ★★★★; **Ch Léoville-Barton** rich, deep, sweet to the finish. A charmer. *1989* ★★★★★; **Ch Léoville-Las-Cases** claret at its best. *June 1986* ★★★★; **Ch Pontet-Canet** various bottlings. *1987. At best* ★★★★; **Ch Rausan-Ségla** rich but tannic. *1983* ★★?; and **Ch Talbot** various bottlings. Impressively rich. *1987. At best* ★★★

# 1960–1969

This decade saw some of the best and some of the worst-ever claret vintages. I regard this as a transitional period in wine, with changes of emphasis, though Bordeaux continued its dominant role.

In 1961 the abolition of resale price maintenance in the United Kingdom immediately resulted in a period of feverish price cutting. Although retail licences were still strictly controlled, by the mid-1960s supermarkets, with superior tactics and finance, fought to obtain licences. Tesco led the way, with my former colleague, Jimmy Duggan, at the helm. This became another nail in the British retailers' coffin, though the survivors, the remaining 'carriage trade' merchants, continued to thrive. By this time, the entire structure of the wine trade had fragmented. This timely situation was particularly fortuitous for Christie's. It led to the resumption of wine auctions which had ceased during the war and had not been able to restart straight away due to post-war restrictions. It was also fortuitous for me. I had reached the dizzy height of UK sales director of Harvey's of Bristol and was ripe for pastures new. In the summer of 1966 I resigned from Harvey's and joined Christie's to establish a new, specialist wine auction department. The first sale was held on 11 October that year. Among the 32 wine auctions in the first season was a ground-breaking 'Finest and Rarest' wine auction held on 31 May 1967. It put Christie's firmly on the map. The auction included a splendid array of great wines, including Lord Rosebery's two cellars of pre-phylloxera Lafite, and attracted, for the first time, collectors from overseas – for the international fine wine market, as we know it today, did not exist prior to 1966. Christie's first season was the watershed. And then, as now, Bordeaux dominated the saleroom scene.

## Vintages at a Glance
**Outstanding ★★★★★**
1961
**Very Good ★★★★**
1962, 1964, 1966
**Good ★★★**
None

## 1960 ★

It is much easier to be wise after the event, but after the magnificent 1959 vintage no one, at the time, could have anticipated yet another blockbuster, the 1961. The 1960 vintage was considered at the time a light, relatively inexpensive wine to drink while waiting for the '59s to mature. In fact the weather conditions were not at all bad though a cold summer hindered the ripening of the grapes. Few tasted in recent years and, thank goodness, rarely seen.
**Ch Lafite** Many notes, mainly in the 1960s. In many ways they typified the weakness of the vintage. Had it been port, the vintage would not have been 'declared'. Nevertheless, it was fragrant though lacking colour (no sun, thin grape skins, little extraction). It hardly warranted the honour of filling an *impériale* recently tasted. *Last noted Sept 1990.*
**Ch Cheval Blanc** In August 1960, the vines looked like 'wilted roses'. A small, late harvest of light wines, pale from the start and premature. Autumnal but flavoury. Most recently, not a bad colour, still red but with weak rim. A whiff of vanilla on the nose which opened up without rhyme or reason, and a touch of iron on the palate. Not a bad flavour, but acidic. *Last noted at Wolf's vertical, Sept 1997.*
**Ch Beychevelle** Magnum: pale, light. Expired. *May 1993.*

SOME OTHER '60S TASTED LAST IN THE '80S, all in decline: **Ch Margaux** astringent in its youth. Light, scented, chaptalised, drinkable. *July 1984 ★★*; **Ch Latour** initially fragrant though piquant. Not a bad colour, cedary nose but short and sharp. *March 1989 ★★*; **Ch Mouton-Rothschild** one of the most attractive, piquant, quite appley, through the 1970s and quite good notes since, despite its shortness and acidity. *March 1989*; **Ch Haut-Brion** drinking quite well in the mid-1960s, but prematurely aged by the early 1970s. Light but sound, quite attractive. *May 1985 ★★*; **Ch Ducru-Beaucaillou** light, stylish, but touch of bitterness. *Feb 1980 ★*; **Ch Figeac** variable and risky. At its best quite flavoury. *March 1985*; **Ch Lafon-Rochet** light, flavoury, sound but not much character, and short. *July 1985 ★*; **Ch La Lagune** so often an odd man out and bucking the trend. Really surprisingly sweet, fleshy and well balanced. *June 1985 ★★*

## 1961 ★★★★★

A great vintage often compared to the 1945 for the two have several things in common. First of all, nature did the pruning: frosts severely reducing the potential crop in 1945 and heavy rain washing away the pollen in 1961. Though there was persistent rain in July, there was a drought in August, followed by a very sunny September, which resulted in a harvest of small, thick-skinned, well-nourished grapes in turn producing deeply coloured, ripe but concentrated and tannic wines.

Opinions vary, some sure of the '61s superiority, some – as I do – considering the '45s greater. The risk is that the tannin will outlive the fruit. Nevertheless some fabulous wines made.

With well over a thousand individual notes on '61s, I have to be ruthless in my selection. I shall begin with one of the greatest '61s, and unquestionably the best-ever Palmer.
**Ch Palmer** The senior staff at Palmer have generations of experience but I wonder if they can pinpoint the precise reason for the success of their '61. Despite, perhaps because of, the perverse growing conditions, the wine had achieved an unusual balance of sugar and acidity, and perfect ripeness. I confess that the first time I tasted it, a Berry Bros' bottling, I described it as having a deep, fine, velvety appearance, 'slightly austere yet rich on the palate' and 'frankly disappointing', more to do with me than the London bottling. This was in January

1972, so then it already had some maturity. I am glad to say that the subsequent (two dozen) notes, all château-bottled, made up for this initial slight. Indeed, in 1973, I noted its very rich, remarkably concentrated nose and taste, awarding it 5 stars, and at Dr Taam's epoch-making horizontal tasting of 1961s in 1978, gave it 20/20 for its 'Burgundian richness, mulberry-ripe fruit. Complex, fragrant' etc. etc. Sixteen similarly glowing notes spanning the 1980s. More recently, among the more memorable at Wolf's Aschau tasting in 1994, my highest mark of all the top '61s and '59s. The following year a superb bottle at a Saintsbury Club dinner, its silky and harmonious bouquet accelerating like Michael Schumacher from the starting grid. Full-bodied yet elegant, fleshy yet lissome. In 1998 an old wine trade friend, Jim Hood, recklessly opened two bottles at dinner in Bristol, and I think there were only six of us, including wives, and one with a cold. Most recently at Len Evans' 'Single Bottle Club' dinner in the Hunter Valley in Australia. Now of course, less deep but an indescribably lovely bouquet and flavour. Perfection. *Last tasted Sept 2000* ★★★★★ *Will go on.*

**Ch Lafite** I first tasted Lafite '61 in June 1975: 'fine, dry, lovely, refined, long'. Through the 1980s I noted the typical Lafite understatement and its ability, indeed need, to open up in the glass, lacking the immediate impact of Mouton or Latour, or, for that matter, a top California Cabernet. Nevertheless many 5-star notes – gentle, spicy, silky tannins, a certain delicacy and always great length. By the early 1990s, though still richly coloured, showing some maturity. At Wolf's Aschau tasting in 1994 its bouquet, initially fragrant, rich and cedary, opened up in the glass, providing extra dimensions, half a point ahead of the '59 though the latter was sweeter and more complete. Typical of Rodenstock to arrange a 'flight' of five vintages of Lafite, all in *impériales*, the bouquet as previously described though I noticed a rather dry finish. The first tasting I conducted for La Réserve was a horizontal of '61s in March 1999, and my most recent detailed note was made there. The level was excellent, into the neck. An attractive, rich, convincing colour with perfect gradation from the bowl of the glass to its rim. It was poured and tasted at 8pm, ripeness and bottle age noted. Exactly 30 minutes later it had gained complexity and a rich, spicy 'biscuity' bouquet. It had the sweetness of fully ripe grapes and alcohol, a mouthfilling flavour, very good tannins and acidity. Complete. It is a food wine, and needed food. My wife, who always takes my notes whenever I conduct a tasting, usually chips in her own remarks, this time 'slight Fernet Branca taste'. Whatever next! *Most recently noted at a pre-sale tasting in New York, May 1999. At best* ★★★★★ *Will keep. Give it time to breathe.*

**Ch Latour** Immensely impressive, beautifully balanced but, not surprisingly, 'still severe' when first tasted in the autumn of 1968. Its great depth of colour, concentrated magnificence, richness and length noted throughout the 1970s – but slow to evolve. On two occasions in the 1980s, I gave it 6 stars, 4 for its impressiveness, 2 for future splendour. Of the eight recent notes, its depth of colour is the first thing one notices, and its nose, rather like Lafite's, is a bit slow to open up. Surprisingly sweet too yet a very tannic finish (at Aschau in 1994). In 1997, a corky, woody bottle at a Saintsbury Club dinner. It was helped along by the cheese soufflé. At the La Réserve tasting, despite its extraordinary sweet, nose-filling bouquet, a mammoth wine, all the component parts excessively represented. Most recently, a superb bottle at Josh Latner's dinner. *Last tasted Jan 2000* ★★★★(★★). *Another half century of life.*

**Ch Margaux** Another splendid '61 first tasted in the autumn of 1964. It was lovely wine then though 'green' and, of course, unready. First really noted its fragrance and elegance developing through the 1970s. In 1981, rich, complex, harmonious, wonderful 'sap' – '20 years of development' ahead. Not long after I thought it a 5-star 'perfect drink', fragrant and refreshing, later noting its richness and concentration. Indeed, 5 stars appear with monotonous regularity in the 20 notes spanning the decade of the 1980s. Nine noted more recently, one (of several bottles) opening up at a Christie's wine-tasting in 1989, and at the American Club in Tokyo. A magnum showing its age but sweet and fleshy presented by Corinne Mentzelopoulos at the Margaux dinner at Brooks's in London, March 1990. At Wagner's vertical in November 2000, losing some of its pristine depth of colour and with a fully evolved bouquet; sweet entry, dry finish, excellent body, fruit and flavour. Great length, still concentrated. A very similar description at a Rodenstock dinner in March 2001. Most recently, perfect magnums lunching with the Bacchus Society of America. The bouquet leapt out of the glass, sweet, brambly fruit, singed, fragrant; amazingly sweet, showing a little age but beautiful. It demonstrates that superb wines were made at Margaux long before the Mentzelopoulos purchase in 1977. *Last tasted June 2001* ★★★★★ *At peak but will soldier on.*

**Ch Mouton-Rothschild** I first tasted the '61 around the time of bottling in July 1963. It was high in extract and packed with tannin. Had it been softer it would have been described fulsomely, with 'gobs of fruit' and so forth and won a gold medal. Deservedly, of course, but not for drinking. Happily, these days were before 'wine critics' had been invented and amateur professionals and professional amateurs let loose in print! Nevertheless, it had amazing richness and ripeness; unusual concentration and length noted though remaining unready through the 1970s. Then, towards the end of the 1980s, the soft, fleshy qualities were in evidence, the best bottle (one was oxidised) being described as perfect at Lloyd Flatt's tasting in 1986.

However, I have only four notes from the 1990s: no longer opaque, mature; lovely, fragrant, spicy bouquet and flavour. Drier and crisper than the fully developed '59 which I thought the greatest at Aschau. The last two occasions in New York. Bouquet with Mouton-like 'grace and fragrance', superb, drinking well, at a Zachys/Christie's charity dinner and, thanks to an astonishingly generous guest at a BYOB dinner at Christie's, Park Avenue. Whether it had been brought 'double-decanted' – back in the same bottle after rinsing – I know not. It was fine, crisp, with a notably dry finish. *Last tasted Feb 1997* ★★★★★ *but I would enjoy it – if you can – while at its peak. However, it will not fade away for quite a time.*

**Ch Haut-Brion** First tasted in July 1963 around the time of bottling. Red Graves tend to develop quite quickly, even top-quality wines like Haut-Brion, though this can be misleading. However, judging from my notes, the nose certainly evolved fragrantly, and even at six years of age, the wine was an attractive and refreshing drink, though basically unready. A decade later showing maturity and displaying what I think of as characteristic Haut-Brion scents: hot, pebbly, deep, earthy, singed; on the palate a lovely texture, 'gentle but firm'. At a Bordeaux Club dinner in 1980, 'rounded but not ready'. Despite its unremitting depth of colour, by the mid-1980s I noted 'elegant', 'well mannered', 'beautifully balanced' – on two occasions 'elliptical'. Only four more recent notes. Sweet, with perfectly assimilated tannins and acidity; a superb magnum: rich, complete, harmonious, good length and a very high mark at the Aschau blind tasting (1994). Most recently, a magnum, and easily the best wine at a very weird tasting in the Musée Baccarat, Paris. It could only have been Haut-Brion and despite showing some age, excellent. *Last tasted May 2000* ★★★★★ but it will never be as great as the '45.

**Ch Ausone** Invariably I have a dearth of notes when it comes to Ausone. Frankly it has never been an English favourite. Its taste is idiosyncratic and, over the years, its quality has varied. Its vineyard site on the slopes on the outskirts of the medieval town of St-Émilion could not be more different from the Médoc first growths near Pauillac. The *cépage* mix is also different, as are its mesoclimate and soil, so perhaps it is understandable if my first note, made when it was 10 years old, while commenting on its style and elegance, adds 'not as great as most '61 Médocs'. Yet by the mid-1980s, it had a rich but mature appearance, well developed bouquet and correct but curious 'dried leaves' flavour. At the Aschau tasting in 1994 it had a lively colour, a light but harmonious, slightly spicy, fragrant bouquet; complete but austere, with a lean, dry, tannic finish. A jeroboam served at the gala dinner afterwards seemed distinctly sweeter (perhaps it was the food), concentrated but with a slightly sandpapery texture. Most recently, an excellent bottle produced by Neil McKendrick at his Bordeaux Club dinner: rich but mature; the familiar (to me) 'dried leaves, brown paper' bouquet but with great depth; positively and surprisingly fleshy and rich despite its unremitting tannin and acidity. *Last noted at Caius, Cambridge, June 1998* ★★★★

**Ch Cheval Blanc** I am a huge admirer of the wines of Ausone's non-identical-twin (they are the only two St-Émilion châteaux classed as *1er grand cru classé A*). Noted in 1967, simply as a 'nice, rich, velvety wine'. A decade later at Dr Taam's tasting I first noticed a hint of '47 port-like richness on the nose, more loose knit and less obviously dramatic than its peers in the Médoc. In 1983, an unqualified 5-star note. Fabulously deep colour, again another reference to port – this time more specific: Fonseca's! sweet, soft, perfectly ripe and right. I see in the margin a reference to its price, it had been bought from the IECWS (The Wine Society) in 1963: 30 shillings a bottle. Fourteen other mainly adulatory notes in the 1980s and just five notes, but all good, in the last decade, its sweetness reiterated, also its perfect harmony. Quite the best wine *hors classé* at an extraordinary dinner in 1996, brilliantly good at Wolf's extensive vertical in 1997, its many layered, almost exotic bouquet growing even richer in the glass. Good length, a slightly nutty, walnut flavour and aftertaste. Most recently, three bottles, two with a touch of oxidation (storage) but the third very good indeed. *Last noted at the Russian National Orchestra dinner at Spencer House, London, March 2002. At best* ★★★★★

**Ch Pétrus** For some time, and understandably, one of the stars of the saleroom. Though I first tasted it in 1967, I only awoke to its magnificent, amazing fruit, and velvety richness in 1978 and made eight glowing notes through the 1980s. Colour 'black as Egypt's night', opulent, 'rich, rich, rich', spicy, even peppery (alcohol), chunky yet velvety, with soft ripe mulberry-like fruit, fleshy, 'almost cloying', a 'railroad chairman's wine' – which sounded a rather old-fashioned expression: well, an oil-rich potentate or tycoon's wine, for the reason that you do not have to be an expert to appreciate this wine, you wallow in it; and you have to have that sort of wealth to have it in your cellar, let alone to order it in a restaurant. But I must stop being condescending. It is a superb, almost unbeatable

## The Bacchus Society of America

*An annual 'Bacchus' weekend organised by 'Mr Gourmet' elect. Founded in 1959, these are events at which luminaries in the wine world are honoured, the most recent being Alexandre de Lur Saluces (of Yquem) and the Egon Müllers (from the Saar). I am also an honorary member by virtue of receiving their Lifetime Achievement Award in 1992. The current members are drawn together by their love of food and wine; more to the point, all possess substantial collections of fine wine – which they show off to perfection.*

mouthful. Of my two most recent notes, one will have to be dismissed as it was presented at a dinner party in January 2000 as 'believed to be Pétrus 1961'. It had a phoney-looking wax capsule and cork branded 1988! Back to 1994 for a superb bottle, sweet, exceedingly full – body and fruit. A luscious mountain of a wine. *Noted, blind, at Wolf's tasting of '61s and '59s in Aschau, Nov 1994* ★★★★★ and no end in sight.

SELECTED CLASSED GROWTHS AND OTHER UNUSUALLY FINE '61S TASTED IN THE 1990S

**Ch Batailley** Bottled by Justerini & Brooks: intensely deep; initially a rather dusty nose, then muted blackberry; full of fruit and flavour. *At Hugh Johnson's Bordeaux Club dinner, July 1995* ★★★★

**Ch Beychevelle** Quite a few notes and though many are highly complimentary, including some excellent Berry Bros' bottlings, it seemed at its best in the 1980s. More recently, an *impériale*, in Aschau, with a bland, vanillin nose and touch of sourness and two bottles, one oxidised the other with an over-mature, varnishy nose; better on the palate, dried out, bitty, unconvincing. *Last noted at La Réserve's 1961 tasting, March 1999. At best* ★★★★ but be wary now.

**Ch Calon-Ségur** A wide spread of notes, 22 since 1967. Surprisingly, it developed relatively quickly though, to quote myself 'like a successful marriage, improved with age'. It was at its best in the mid-1980s. Coincidentally, my most recent note is of a Gloag's of Perth bottling first tasted in 1985. Now fully mature with a warm orange tinge, and a deliciously cedary flavour and good length. *Last noted Feb 1994. At best* ★★★★ but doubtless tiring now.

**Ch Canon** A beautifully rich, earthy, fragrant bottle, pre-sale in New York in 1984 and, 13 years later, a medium-deep, ruby-tinged magnum with harmonious bouquet and a full, rich flavour masking its tannin. Faultless. *Last noted at the 1er grand cru St-Émilion dinner at the château, June 1997* ★★★★

**Dom de Chevalier** Several notes. It seemed to grow in stature through the 1980s and I have an extraordinary ★★★★(★★) rating of a bottle in 1986: its bouquet developing 'fabulous spice' and on the palate 'fine, perfectly packed extract, concentration'. A superb magnum in Aschau (1984), restrained yet delicious, strawberry-like nose; shapely, good flavour, texture and length. A very high mark. More recently served with Beaufort and Minolette cheeses at Hugh Johnson's Bordeaux Club dinner. It seemed to have gained extra dimensions; the bouquet becoming sweeter, tea-like, smoky, very tannic though (which coped with the cheeses). But is it drying out? *Last tasted at Saling Hall, Essex, Dec 1997* ★★★★

**Ch Ducru-Beaucaillou** A superb '61, endorsed by nearly forty notes well spread over 22 years. Excellent from the start. Five stars through the 1980s. More recently, a superb magnum in Aschau, fully developed, rich, lovely, complete. At the La

Réserve tasting of '61s in 1999, a ruddy, orange-rimmed maturity; the most beautiful bouquet, copy-book classic, perfectly mature; sweet, cedary cigar box scent, mellow, understated. At its peak. Most recently, showing its age but delicious. Extended flavour, still with tannin and acidity. *Last noted lunching with Anthony Hanson at the Carlton Club in London, July 2001* ★★★★★ *The sommelier, being generously offered a taste, proceeded to pour himself a glassful!*

**Clos L'Église** Fragrant and fleshy in the 1980s. Still deep. Extraordinary goat's cheese and chocolate bouquet! Sweet. Firm. *Last tasted Feb 1992* ★★★?

**Ch L'Évangile** Beautiful wine. Herbaceous, spicy nose; sweet, fruit packed, lovely texture. *Last tasted Feb 1992* ★★★★★

**Ch Figeac** High Cabernet Sauvignon content noted in the 1960s, a Burgundy-like opulence in the 1980s. Consistently sweet but now showing some maturity. Lovely bouquet; soft, chunky, good flavour and grip. *Last noted at the Aschau tasting, Nov 1994* ★★★★★ *Will last.*

**Ch La Fleur** A magnificent magnum. Not as deep as expected but a very fragrant bouquet, sweet, spicy, biscuity; full-bodied, crisp, tannic finish. *Last noted at a Rodenstock lunch, Aug 1998* ★★★★★ *Long life.*

**Ch Grand-Puy-Lacoste** Four English bottlings including Saccone & Speed and Berry Bros, all good in the late 1960s, the latter in 1980. The rest château-bottled. A first-rate classic though understated Pauillac. Still tannic. *Last tasted Feb 1992* ★★★★★ *Plenty of life left.*

**Ch Gruaud-Larose** One of the most attractive '61s. Just under 20 notes over a 30-year span. All except the last, which was a bit below par, showing well, notably at the Aschau tasting in 1994: ripe, expansive bouquet; sweet, soft, rich, rounded, with good length and lovely finish. Another fleshy bottle in 1998 lunching in Albany, Piccadilly, with Michael Edwards and Hugo Kindersley. *Last noted at the La Réserve tasting of '61s, March 1999. At best* ★★★★★

**Ch Léoville-Las Cases** Followed for nearly four decades, and all pretty impressive, the exception being curiously variable bottles at Dr Taam's seminal 1961 horizontal in 1978, and a 'gnarled oak', mellow but tannic bottle at a New York Wine Society's 'exponential' tasting (1998). Most recently, two superlative bottles, one at the Irish Club in London in 1999, the other dining in Pfäffikon, near Zurich, after Wagner's Margaux vertical. *Last noted Nov 2000. At best* ★★★★★

**Ch Lynch-Bages** Over 30 notes starting with two good Lupton's bottlings in 1967 (a most respectable family merchants in Bradford which went into liquidation not long after), also Hay & Sons, Sheffield, (once renowned, long defunct), Saccone's – not as good as the château-bottling; a good Dutch bottling, a vinegary Wine Society's, all in the 1970s and 1980s, and a superb Berry Bros' bottling in 1990.

### Dr John Taams

*A doctor in the small country town of Groot-Ammer in Holland, John Taams was unwittingly the pioneer of what is now known as a 'horizontal tasting' (one vintage, several châteaux). The event, held in May 1968, was entitled* Comment se Developpent (sic) Les Grands Crus 1961 de Bordeaux, *and was attended by a group of international tasters, amateurs and professionals. Marvin Overton was to follow with spectacular 'vertical' tastings (one château, several vintages) some time later (the first, of Ch Latour, was held in Fort Worth, Texas in 1976). (See page 89.)*

But these were just a representative sample of the scores of English bottlings of a very popular château. Seven notes since 1990, all but one good – a delicious but fagged out bottle at the La Réserve tasting (1999). Lastly – a great surprise – a magnum bottled by Findlater Mackie, bought in the early 1960s and well cellared since: richly coloured, still impressively deep; beautiful nose with characteristic though toned down Lynch-Bages 'cassis', a touch of sweetness, nice weight, soft, rounded, harmonious, with well assimilated tannins. A perfect drink. *Last noted at a Sunday lunch in Gloucestershire at Clare and David Carter's, May 2001* ★★★★★ *At peak.*

**Ch Malescot-St-Exupéry** Curiously, this classed-growth Margaux has something in common with Pauillac's Ch Lynch-Bages: a distinctive, blackcurranty Cabernet nose. Once quite popular, and now taking on a new lease of life. Well over 30 fairly consistent notes, the two most recent exhibiting Malescot's distinctive fragrance; very deep, very 'Cabernet'; concentrated, complete, with a glorious, spicy flavour (Bordeaux Club dinner 1996) and equally distinctive bottles at a Saintsbury Club dinner. *Last tasted April 1998* ★★★★ *Will continue.*

**Ch La Mission Haut-Brion** Many notes over two decades. A monumental multi-dimensional wine, very impressive at the Klassische Weindegustation in Zurich: opaque, intense, concentrated; harmonious bouquet with distinctive Graves earthiness, fragrant, liquorice; sweet, powerful, sandy-textured, tannic. And, six months later, a magnum showing more maturity in appearance and more than age on the nose than either the wine just noted or the '59 alongside. Mocha, chocolate also noted, and great power. Ripe yet with a touch of bitterness. Frankly I preferred the '59. *Last noted at the Weinart tasting in Aschau, Nov 1994* ★★★★★ *And will go on.*

**Ch Pape-Clément** Good but not great. Fairly consistent notes from the late 1970s. Very rich, very earthy, and distinctive 'tobacco'-like flavour and good length – at lunch in boiling sun in Stuart Lever's garden in Gloucestershire, 1994. More recently, mature looking; very sweet, soft. *Last noted at a pre-sale tasting in New York, Oct 1996* ★★★ *Drink soon.*

**Ch Pichon-Baron** My earliest notes, from mid-1960s to mid-1970s, all English-bottled, were good, but of three château-bottlings in the 1980s, two were decidedly 'pricked', with high volatile acidity which left, literally, a sour taste in my mouth. Saved by a decent bottle in 1992 and, most recently, impressively deep, its nose a pleasant surprise: fruit, vanilla, a fragrant jamminess matched by its flavour. Overall lean, spicy, with good grip but not too tannic. *Last noted at the La Réserve tasting conducted March 1989* ★★★★ *Drink soon.*

**Ch Pichon-Longueville-Lalande** Many notes, starting with a good but unready Grant's bottling in 1967 and a 'stewed' J Lyons' bottling in 1973 – mentioned because, of all the London bottlings, Lyons' were the least reliable, mainly, I suspect, because they were kept too long in cask. Most recently noted at the Weinart blind tasting: though richly coloured, a touch of orange at the rim; crisp, fragrant bouquet with more to come; mouthfilling, complete, very tannic. *Last noted in Aschau, Nov 1994. At best* ★★★★★

**Ch Talbot** Consistently good since the mid-1970s. Most recently: now medium deep, with a lovely gradation to an almost tawny rim; intriguing bottle-aged bouquet, *gibier*, liquorice, and, after 90 minutes, a delicate, floral fragrance; sweet, nice weight, good acidity, masked tannin. A charmer. *Last noted at the La Réserve tasting of '61s, March 1999* ★★★★★ *Lovely now. Why wait?*

**Ch Smith-Haut-Lafitte** I was not too conscious of this well-sited Graves estate, one of the region's largest, before the dynamic Cathiards took over in 1990. Happily, they unearthed a magnum of the scarce '61 vintage to wind up an eight-wine vertical. As the wine had not had long to settle I decanted it about 15 minutes before tasting. It had a fully mature, mahogany rim; showing age on the nose though rich and spicy. Sweet, oxidising in a relaxed way. Dry finish. Nice wine. *At a masterclass for the Chaîne des Rôtisseurs at La Caudalie, June 2000 ★★★★ (just). Drink up.*

OTHER GOOD TO EXCELLENT '61S, ALL LAST TASTED IN FEBRUARY 1992 **Ch Boyd-Cantenac** a specious charmer ★★★; **Ch Branaire-Ducru** delicious but not great ★★★; **Ch Brane-Cantenac** variable. A soft, attractive magnum. *At best* ★★★; **Ch Cantemerle** delicacy and charm. *At best* ★★★★; **Ch Clinet** coffee-like nose. Powerful ★★★★; **Ch Cos Labory** deep; fragrant; lean, flavoury ★★★; **Ch Haut-Batailley** almost exaggerated Pauillac blackcurrant fragrance, crisp, silky, delicious ★★★★; **Ch Latour-à-Pomerol** two notes, both excellent. Sweet, fleshy, a fabulous mouthful. Pomerol at its best ★★★★★; **Ch Léoville-Barton** a dozen notes. Apart from two poor bottles, a rich yet elegant wine. *At best* ★★★★★; **Ch Léoville-Poyferré** various bottlings, all uniformly good. Seemed at best in the mid-1980s. *At best* ★★★★; **Ch Montrose** though noting its quality in the mid-1960s, I did not wake up to its massiveness until the mid- to late 1970s, predicting a long life, '30 years'. By the mid-1980s, I described it as an archetypal Montrose, soft yet tannic, velvety yet dry, with wonderful '61 concentration. Sinewy, mouth puckering ★★★(★★) *Another 20 years*; **Ch Mouton-Baron-Philippe** fragrant. Cabernet cassis, 'strawberry and gardenia'. Lean. Flavoury. Not a *grand vin* but agreeable ★★★ *drink soon*; **Ch Rausan-Ségla** penetrating bouquet; full-bodied, rich, long, still tannic ★★★★; **Ch St-Pierre** rich, mature, cedary nose and taste ★★★; and **Vieux Ch Certan** variable but on the last two occasions good: bouquet of coffee and ginger; sweet, soft, fleshy, good fruit and acidity ★★★★

NOT ALL 1961S WERE SUCCESSFUL. The following were poor to not very good when tasted in the 1990s: **Ch Belgrave** (Pauillac); **Ch La Cabanne**; **Clos Fourtet**; **Ch Fourcas-Hosten**; **Ch Gazin**; **Ch Giscours**; **Ch Lafon-Rochet**; **Ch Lagrange** (St-Julien); **Ch La Pointe**; **Ch Prieuré-Lichine**; **Ch Rauzan-Gassies**.

LASTLY, FAIR TO MAGNIFICENT '61S LAST TASTED IN THE 1980s and worth looking out for: **Ch Chasse-Spleen** ★★★★; **Ch La Gaffelière** ★★★; **Ch Le Gay** ★★★★; **Ch d'Issan** ★★★★; **Ch Kirwan** ★★; **Ch Langoa-Barton** ★★★; **Ch Pontet-Canet** ★★★★; and **Ch Trotanoy** ★★★★★

---

### Louis Skinner MD

*Former dermatologist, a close friend, and the most knowledgeable food and wine connoisseur of my acquaintance. We first met in 1969. Lou founded the Miami Chapter of the Wine & Food Society, the Commanderie de Bordeaux and other wine societies. He was also the host of memorable tastings, some of which I helped organise and conduct — notably '61 clarets at 20 and 25 years of age. Long retired, he lives in a timewarp 1930s home in an elegant park-like residential area, Coral Gables (Florida).*

---

# 1962 ★★★★

Thoroughly upstaged by the quality, the sheer bravado of the preceding year. But because the 1961 vintage was very small and, in the light of the times, very expensive, the abundant crop of the very good '62s following a satisfactory growing season, proved useful. I have always liked this now somewhat underrated and largely overlooked vintage. It was particularly successful in Pomerol.

First tasted in October 1964; the bulk of some very considerable notes were made in the 1970s and 1980s. Most were at their best in the ten years straddling these two decades but many are still drinking well, and, because they are largely forgotten, and relatively inexpensive, are worth looking out for at auction or from specialist merchants and brokers.

I am concentrating my comments on wines tasted *since* the mid-1980s.

**Ch Lafite** Many notes. It has a shade of red that is typical of many '62s, indicating highish – but usually tolerable and refreshing – acidity. Several recent notes including in 1996 an *impériale* with a herbaceous, vegetal nose that opened up beautifully, and even better flavour though with citrus-like acidity on the finish. Two years later a double magnum also displaying the distinctive '62 redness; dry, lively, berry-like, crisp. Most recently, several bottles now showing colour loss and age on the nose, lean and pinched. *Last noted at Christie's tasting at the American Club, Tokyo, prior to the annual wine auction, Nov 1995. At best lean, elegant ★★★★*

**Ch Latour** Not long after bottling, deep purple, packed with fruit, but raw and tannic. Developing well through the 1970s and 1980s, on several occasions warranting 5 stars. More recently, a still deeply coloured magnum with good fruit though showing signs of cracking up on the nose. Surprisingly sweet yet tannic. A bit stalky (tasted blind in 1996). Most recently, similar depth, with reddish tinge; a classic Médoc nose and very good flavour, body and finish. *Last noted at a dinner hosted by David Orr at Ch Rausan-Ségla, Sept 1988. At best ★★★★*

**Ch Margaux** Tasted in cask, October 1964. A light style but raw, the rawness noted until the early 1980s. In the meantime its fragrance evolved and was fully developed by the mid-1980s. In 1998, a bottle decanted on the spur of the moment at La Turpina, Bordeaux, a small fashionable restaurant in the old town, famed for its local dishes: colour a soft cherry red; fragrant, correct, but with '62 bite. The bouquet opened up 'like well hung meat' – but this might just have been the open-hearth cooking! Last noted at Wagner's second Margaux vertical, and showing well: this time ruby-coloured; a fragrant, biscuity bouquet of considerable depth, lean, flavoury, but with a touch of tartness. *Last tasted Nov 2000 ★★★★*

**Ch Mouton-Rothschild** Distinctive blackcurrant Cabernet aroma when first tasted in May 1965, and which continued through the 1970s. Lovely flavour, some delicacy, tannic enough in the 1980s. Tasted on just three occasions during the last decade, including deliciously fragrant bottles with lovely, crisp fruit at a Mouton tasting conducted for the Hollywood Wine Society (1998). Most recently, still quite richly coloured, sweet and fragrant. *Last noted at a pre-sale tasting, New York, May 1999 ★★★★*

**Ch Haut-Brion** First tasted in cask, October 1964. Perhaps a little more than youthful astringency, its deep, earthy and richly attractive flavour developing through the 1970s. 'Soft', 'velvety', 'lots of grip', 'long life'. Sweetness, elegance and lovely texture noted in the 1980s. A magnum drinking well at Rodenstock's opening dinner in 1995: sweet, refreshing. My 19th note made at Michael Edwards' lunch in Albany: still fairly deep and youthful for a 36 year-old (wine not Edwards) with typical earthiness and Haut-Brion elegance. Acidity but refreshing and not obtrusive. *Last tasted Aug 1998* ★★★★

**Ch Ausone** I have just five notes, starting off slowly in 1971. At Lloyd Flatt's vertical in 1987: fully mature, light, delicate, fragrant, with good length. 'One of the most attractive Ausones I have ever tasted' I wrote at the time. *Not tasted since 1987* ★★★★

**Ch Cheval Blanc** Over 20 notes. It was on the light side despite its youthful severity in October 1965, but opened up quite quickly in the 1970s, lovely but lean and perhaps lacking length. Only one recent note, its colour noticeably red; bouquet low-keyed but in under 30 minutes had opened up beautifully; medium-sweet, lovely flavour, well balanced. The '62 acidity hinted at by its red tinge not particularly noticeable. *Last tasted at Karl-Heinz Wolf's vertical in Austria, Sept 1997* ★★★★ *Might as well get on drinking it. A fraction of the price of the '59, '61 or '82.*

**Ch Pétrus** I have consistently good notes from 1967 apart from a 'woody' magnum in the mid-1980s. Medium depth, hint of ruby though mature; lovely, rich bouquet; drier than expected with a touch of end acidity, but very attractive. *Last noted lunching in grand company at the Lefevre Gallery, London, Nov 1994* ★★★★

**Ch Beychevelle** A slow starter which developed beautifully in the mid-1980s. Rich, spicy 'almost 1961 quality'. *Last tasted May 1993* ★★★★

**Ch Calon-Ségur** Quite a few notes, from a raw, bitter Harvey's bottling tasted in 1966, to various other bottlings through the 1970s when it began to shrug off its St-Estèphe austerity. By the 1980s well developed with a particularly lovely nose, excellent body, extract and flavour, yet still youthful. *Last tasted Oct 1992* ★★★

**Ch Figeac** Unlike the Calon, much more appealing in its youth (March 1966), opening up fairly quickly, 'attractive, well made'. As always, full of fruit and character yet some rusticity. Most recently, a well developed ruby; a minty, fragrant bouquet with a whiff of caramel. Lovely, lively, excellent finish. *At my Bordeaux Club dinner, Nov 1995* ★★★★

**Ch Gruaud-Larose** Many notes. From the start, one of my favourite '62s. In one sense the Médoc equivalent of Figeac: it is almost always full of fruit, with rich character, though in this vintage a bit leaner than usual. A sweet, fleshy, very fruity double magnum slightly marred by its '62 acidic finish (in 1994). Most recently, and surprisingly, served at dinner after Le Pin '86 and '88 by Armin Diel. Decanted at 10pm its bouquet was getting tired by 10.45pm, as was I (it was the sixth wine, following a tasting of Armin's own wines). But it was, unquestionably, a marvellously sweet and fleshy mouthful. *Last tasted at Schlossgut Diel in the Nahe Valley, Nov 1995* ★★★★

**Ch Léoville-Las-Cases** An outstanding '62. Many notes. Making a good start in October 1965 and four years later 'a well balanced, understated classic', bottled by Berry Bros. Lovely through the 1970s and 1980s. Only one recently, a well nigh perfect magnum: soft ruby; harmonious, bricky bouquet; with sweetness, weight, flavour and balance. As good as they come. Just starting to dry out. *Last noted dining at La Turpina in Bordeaux with Norman Rush's group of Jackson, Mississippi doctors, Sept 1998* ★★★★★

**Ch Magdelaine** Rich, velvety, silky tannins. *Last tasted May 1991* ★★★

**Ch Malescot St-Exupéry** Savoury, but tannin and acidity rather over-egging the omelette. *Last tasted Sept 1990* ★★

**Ch La Mission Haut-Brion** Any reader who has followed my notes in chronological order will have had a surfeit of my paeans of praise of the Woltner brothers and their wines. However, although it is impressive I am less enthusiastic about their '62. Powerful, high alcohol, crisp, very flavoury but acidity omnipresent. Most recently, bouquet forthcoming but pungent; a rich, earthy, bricky, iron flavour. Acidic. *Last noted at BYOB dinner in New York, March 1999* ★★

**Ch Palmer** Quite a few notes, consistently attractive, from a good Harvey bottling noted in 1965, peaking I thought in the early 1970s. In 1976, a deeply coloured bottle; cedary, vinous bouquet; touch of sweetness leading to a dry, tannic finish. Rich and flavoury. Then a gap of nearly a quarter of a century. A double magnum with plain capsule, slip label, but fully branded cork from the cellars of The Saintsbury Club at Vintners' Hall, and won in a raffle, much to the chagrin of other members! However, as it is my son's birth year, I opened it for his 40th birthday dinner at Brooks's. It was still quite deep though autumnal. There was a welcome surge of cedary fragrance as I decanted it and, when poured, had a flavour to match, old but retaining fruit and drying out a bit. It went down well. *Last noted 11 Jan 2002* ★★★★

**Ch Pichon-Lalande** Slightly to my surprise, not many notes. A desultory London bottling in 1969 and, the following year, a much more interesting Christopher's bottling: 'raw, fruity, needs time'. Yet developing well in the mid-1970s. A 'not very interesting' *impériale* in 1987. Most recently, a more attractive jeroboam, 'good for its age'; good flavour, nice weight. Crisp, dry, acidic end. *Last noted at Bob Dickinson's Bacchus Society dinner at Norman's Restaurant, Coral Gables, Nov 1997* ★★★★

**Ch Rauzan-Gassies** Still going through an underperforming period, quite unworthy of second growth status. Thick, jammy, lacking length. *Last tasted Sept 1990. Avoid.*

**Ch Talbot** A reassuringly reliable wine and on the whole consistently satisfactory notes, starting with a Harvey's bottling in April 1966, just three months before I left to join Christie's. Good bottling also by Paten's of Peterborough, a particularly attractive Saccone bottling in 1976, a Kinloch's with too much volatile acidity and in the late 1980s, almost the best of all, Danish-bottled by Kjaer & Sommerfeldt. Also, of course, château-bottled. Overall, cedary, quite complex, flavoury, with '62 piquancy. *Last tasted, a double magnum, Oct 1992* ★★★★

**Ch La Tour de Mons** For long a very dependable *bourgeois supérieur* from Soussans in the 'greater Margaux' area and, at the time, owned by the Héritiers Dubos of Cantemerle. Several fairly recent notes, all from the cellars of Mme Binaud, *née* Dubos. I bought quite a bit for drinking at home. Most recently, my last bottle, pleasantly, openly mature; ripe, slightly chocolatey bouquet with whiff of citrus; easy drinking, refreshing touch of '62 acidity. *Last tasted Jan 2001* ★★★ *Autumnal, on the turn.*

THE BEST OF OTHER '62S LAST NOTED AT RODENSTOCK'S EXTENSIVE HORIZONTAL TASTING IN SEPTEMBER 1987 unless otherwise indicated: **Ch Batailley** chunky, rich château-bottling ★★★; **Ch Beauséjour** firm, fruity ★★★; **Ch Belair** with some of Ausone's dried-leaves character. Fragrant, elegant, easy ★★★; **Ch Brane-Cantenac** curiously rich ★★ *drink up*; **Ch Canon** firm, rich, fully evolved ★★★★; **Carruades de Ch Lafite** a sweet charmer.

Oct 1988 ★★★ *drink up*; **Ch La Conseillante** soft, rich, high quality. *July 1988* ★★★★; **Ch Cos d'Estournel** variable. A particularly fragrant J & B bottling. *At best* ★★★; **Ch Croizet-Bages** delicious ★★★; **Ch Ducru-Beaucaillou** many notes. Sweet, crisp, lovely. *June 1988. At best* ★★★★ *drink up*; **Ch La Fleur-Pétrus** sweet, ripe yet tannic ★★★; **Ch La Gaffelière-Naudes** attractive, flavoury but acid-etched ★★ *drink up*; **Ch Gazin** agreeable, flavoury, drying-out. *At best* ★★★ *drink up*; **Ch Grand-Puy-Lacoste** many notes, several bottlings. Fragrant, good fruit, classic. *At best* ★★★★; **Ch Haut-Batailley** fragrant, spicy, flavoury, some flesh but overall lean ★★★★; **Ch Langoa-Barton** various bottlings, very fragrant, good fruit, nice weight, crisp. *Nov 1989* ★★★; **Ch Lascombes** a good '62. Shapely, sweet, complete – with refreshing acidity. *At best* ★★★; **Ch Léoville-Barton** initially austere. Richly coloured, classic cedary nose, lean and elegant ★★★; **Ch Léoville-Poyferré** light style, easy charm ★★★ *(just)*; **Ch Lynch-Bages** a typically exuberant wine but acidity catching up ★★; **Ch Montrose** several notes. Lovely wine, flavoury, lean, dry finish ★★★; **Ch Mouton-Baron-Philippe** lively, fragrant, easy ★★★ *drink up*; **Ch Pape-Clément** many notes, few recent. Once one of my favourite '62s. Fragrant and charming but passed its peak. *At best* ★★★★; **Ch Pavie** rich, ripe, rustic ★★★; **Ch La Pointe** one of the best La Pointes I can recall. Lovely colour, rich nose, silky texture punctured with perfectly tolerable acidity ★★★★; **Ch Pontet-Canet** very many notes, various bottlings (never at the château). High toned, attractive, 'acidic tail wagging the dog' ★★; **Ch Rausan-Ségla** many notes. Initial 'greenness' now softened. Some delicacy and stylishness ★★★; **Clos René** a wine more or less 'discovered' by Harry Waugh and well bottled by Harvey's. Rich, meaty, earthy with twist of lemon on finish ★★★ *drink up*; **Ch de Sales** a more silky Harvey's bottling. Sweet and easy ★★★ *drink up*; **Ch Smith-Haut-Lafitte** intense, fragrant, elegant ★★★★; and **Vieux Ch Certan** iron fist in velvet glove. Full yet with lean dry finish ★★, *possibly* ★★★ *now*.

# 1963

Cold summer with rot in the vineyards. Light acidic wines. Pretty abysmal but, following so many great vintages, there was no necessity to buy them.

**Ch Lafite** Even the few selected *cuves* nowhere near *grand vin* standard. Pale, watery; fragrant in a tinny sort of way. Thin, short. *Last tasted Oct 1988.*

**Ch Margaux** Several notes. Most recently, at the two Wagner verticals: palish, tawny-hued; very light, tinny seaweed nose and taste to match (1997). Most recently, a horrible fishy smell and dreadful taste. *Last tasted Nov 2000.*

**Ch Mouton-Rothschild** Mild and inoffensive at Flatt's vertical in 1986 and surprisingly sweet but tinny and skinny at Frérick's in 1989. Fragrant but medicinal and faded. *Last tasted Sept 1990.*

# 1964 ★★★★

Dismiss the idea that this was anything other than a very good vintage; yet it is tarnished merely because of very heavy but localised rain in the middle of the harvest, mainly in Pauillac and St-Estèphe, which caught out some major châteaux. Ch Latour picked early and made a top-class wine. Ch Lafite, Mouton-Rothschild, Lynch-Bages and Calon-Ségur were all caught with their pants down. But as will be seen, even the

rain-soaked vineyards managed to produce some very flavoury wines. Nevertheless, it must be admitted that the very best '64s were made to the south of the Médoc, in the Graves, and on the Right Bank some outstanding Pomerols and St-Émilions.

I link 1962 and 1964 in my mind. Both of equal quality, both of quite different styles, the '62s, as we have seen, lean, lively, acidic, the '64s, as I hope I can demonstrate with my notes, chunkier, rounder, fruitier. As always, variations in the two growing seasons were responsible. In 1964 a pleasantly warm spring was followed by a very satisfactory flowering which promised, all being well, a big crop. The hot dry summer and ideal ripening conditions in September led most of the châteaux to start picking around the third week of September. In the Médoc most were more than half way through, some finished by 8 October, when it rained incessantly for two weeks. Those who had not finished picking either continued or waited. Some châteaux, Lynch-Bages for example, finished harvesting as late as 24 October. The reason the Right Bank got off lightly is because Merlot is an early-ripening variety. I have noted some of the Médoc picking dates below.

I have several hundred notes on over 250 châteaux. Many were, of course, tasted in the late 1960s and most were drunk from the mid-1970s to mid-1980s, when they were at their best. The following is a selection of the more frequently encountered wines.

**Ch Lafite** Picking started 26 September, ended 16 October, the last nine days caught by the rain. Despite this, not at all bad. Quite a few flimsily fragrant bottles, two most recent being in *grands formats*, an overripe jeroboam, with ivy leaf scent and taste, quite attractive but astringent (1994), and an *impériale* with better nose than taste. Faded – prematurely old – lady. Cracking up. *Last noted Sept 1998* ★

**Ch Latour** Vying with Ch Pétrus as the finest '64. Picking started 25 September and was completed before the rains came on 7 October. A large number of notes, over 30, starting with a very attractive 'sweet fruity' cask sample in April 1965. Good but still austere and unready in the early 1970s, though later 'like a '59', and in 1978 'will probably develop like the '43s' – by which I meant rich but blunt. Its nose and taste opened up, demonstrating its flesh and rich character through the 1980s. Tasted or drunk on a dozen occasions in the 1990s, all very good indeed save for an oxidised bottle. If anything goes to show what an immense difference bottle age can do to a top-class claret, the continuing evolution of the '64 Latour is the perfect example. It goes on and on gaining extra dimensions. On the last three occasions a marvellous mouthful, plump, perfectly balanced, rounded and sweet yet still with a tannic finish (Bordeaux Club dinner 1997). Then a tasting for the Bär Bank in Zurich in 1998, losing its pristine depth of colour. A bouquet of cedar and old oak (the tree not the cask). Fully mature, lovely flavour. Most recently showing well at Paolo Pong's dinner tasting. *Oct 2000* ★★★★★

**Ch Margaux** Picking started 21 September and ended 15 October, a week into the rain. And it shows. Cask sample first tasted April 1965 and its soft, feminine qualities soon apparent. If anything, I found it too easy in the early 1970s; nor was I much impressed on the couple of occasions I tasted it in the 1980s. Both my more recent notes made at Wagner's tastings, a sound, surprisingly firm but unspectacular wine in 1997 and, at the second, a bottle recorked in 1994, deeper, more convincing, sweeter, richer, more chewy and holding well. *Last tasted Nov 2000* ★★

**Ch Mouton-Rothschild** Late picked, starting 1 October ending 16 October. When first tasting a cask sample in May 1965, I noted it as light and pleasant but lacking the usual Cabernet Sauvignon aroma and taste. Over a dozen notes since, many in the 1970s and 1980s, the flavour not unattractive but invariably qualified 'no length', 'skinny', 'no flesh'. Not tasted since the Frérick/Wodarz Mouton tasting in Wiesbaden in March 1989 when it was light, flavoury, unconvincing. *Last tasted March 1989. At best* ★★

**Ch Haut-Brion** Several notes through the 1980s, and five in the last decade. A fully mature yet intense appearance; nose like cream cheese; smoky, very earthy, dry at a dinner at Christie's in 1997 to honour Jack (Sir John) Plumb. Most recently, a very harmonious, earthy bottle. *At Paolo Pong's dinner held at Jancis Robinson's (Nick, as always, doing the cooking), Oct 2000* ★★★★

**Ch Ausone** Soft and sweet in cask (1965) for such a young wine. Developed attractively through the 1970s. I often noticed a tobacco-like scent which reminds me of Graves. Fine quality. Drinking well, some charm. A good '64. *Last tasted June 1989* ★★★★

**Ch Cheval Blanc** Picked between 22 September and 9 October. One of the loveliest of all the '64s. Fine and fruity cask sample and steady, invariably pleasant development, 'full, soft, velvety, stylish and rounded' in 1973. Fully evolved, glorious in the mid- to late 1980s. Four more recently: perfection at the Lefevre Gallery in London in 1994; sweet, rich, perfect dining in 1995 with Dr Lou Skinner, one of the unsung heroes of the American wine and food scene; a rather disappointing magnum at the Weinart vertical in 1997 – Jacques Hébrard told us that the wine was difficult to vinify. The *rendement* being 37hl/ha, and the alcoholic content quite low (12%). At Paolo Pong's in 2000, showing its age though attractively evolved; fairly sweet but now lean and drying out. Then a well-nigh perfect bottle: harmonious, *à point*, dry finish at Hugh Johnson's Bordeaux Club dinner, December 2001. Most recently, a red tinge hinting at volatile acidity; ripe, 'bricky'; sweet, rich, good fruit, still some tannin and a bit of a bite. *Last noted at a Russian National Orchestra supporters dinner, Spencer House, London, April, 2002. At best now* ★★★★

**Ch Pétrus** Although representing Pétrus exclusively from 1945, Jean-Pierre Mouiex bought a half share from the redoubtable Mme Loubat in 1964. From the start a wonderful wine, almost indecently packed with fruit and all good things; fleshy, fragrant – a whiff of volatile acidity noted on a couple of occasions. A very sweet, very rich, well-balanced bottle at a pre-sale tasting in New York in 1999. Most recently, a superb double magnum from Tom Black's cellar at a dinner for the Russian National Orchestra: impressively deep and still youthful; low-keyed but harmonious and complete nose (but I never consider the bouquet of Pétrus, or of quite a few other Pomerols, is as interesting as the taste and feel in the mouth). In fact, I found it straining my imagination to use the expression bouquet at all. But what a glorious mouthful and mouth feel. Deep. Rich. Yet not overpowering. *Last tasted at Mosimann's, London, Dec 2000* ★★★★★

SOME OTHER '64S LAST TASTED IN THE 1990S

**Ch L'Angélus** A spectacular jeroboam said to be the best ever made. A glorious mouthful but fully mature. *Sept 1998* ★★★★ *But peaking.*

**Ch d'Angludet** Faultless: soft, mature, lovely. *June 1992* ★★★★

**Ch Beychevelle** Remarkably sweet, soft, superb. *Last tasted May 1993. At best* ★★★★

**Ch Canon** A lovely wine, vying with Cheval Blanc '71 as the best wine at a *Dîner Millésimes de Collection* at Ch Trottevieille: richly coloured; harmonious, fragrant; a warm character, fullish, rich, lovely. *Last tasted June 1995* ★★★★

**Ch Canon-La-Gaffelière** Absolutely at its peak. Could not evolve any more. A lovely mouthful. *Dining at the château, April 1998* ★★★★ *but not for long.*

**Ch Cantemerle** Good, flavoury magnum but lean for a '64. *March 1996* ★★

**Dom de Chevalier** Several notes, mainly excellent. At its best in the mid-1980s: smooth, perfectly balanced, soft, fleshy. Most recently two bottles, shipped to London by Schröder & Schÿler, bottled by Berry Bros, bought at Christie's and served blind at dinner at the domaine. I should have stuck to my first impression, for at least I was 'in' Bordeaux. Its twigginess made me think of Italy so I had to backtrack. There was a certain woodiness and austerity, not the usual charm. Drying out. *Last tasted April 1994. At best* ★★★★ *But on the downhill slope.*

**Ch Figeac** The Bordeaux *négociant* de Luze habitually jumped the gun by bringing cask samples for London merchants to taste as early as the February after the vintage, as in this case. Showing quite well though my notes record 'disappointing' and 'too easy' in the early to mid-1970s. In 1980, however, an incredibly dark *impériale* was broached at a dinner at Gravetye Manor in Sussex, and the following year a double magnum that I described as a 'gentle giant'. Even better at Desai's Figeac tasting in Paris: it really had filled out, rich, fig-like. Which is why, shortly after, I said it was 'like Concorde': bumpy take off, steep climb, then supersonic (the wine) reaching cruising speed in the mid-1970s. Never a dull moment with Thierry Manoncourt's wines. In fact, whenever I think of Figeac I think of Thierry. *Last tasted Dec 1989. At best* ★★★★ *and should still be excellent.*

**Ch La Fleur** Should have been magnificent. It was woody. *Sept 1998.*

**Ch La Fleur-Pétrus** Better than La Fleur but tannin-laden, severe. *Sept 1994* ★★

**Ch La Mission Haut-Brion** Several notes. Not for the first time I noticed a whiff of excess volatile acidity creeping into the Woltner wines though it often served to enhance the flavour. Nevertheless, a very good magnum in 1999 dining with the David Rutherfords: not as austere as it can be, in fact a pleasing mellow nose, with the typical earthy/tobacco finish. More recently, a tarry, spicy-nosed, very 'gravelly' flavour and dry finish. *Last noted at Paolo Pong's '1964s' dinner, Oct 2000. At best* ★★★★ *but I am inclined to downgrade it.*

**Ch Moulinet** Confusingly, there is a Ch Moulinet in both Pomerol and in St-Émilion. The latter I liked and drank with pleasure in its early days. An odd bottle cropped up and with its lovely mellow appearance, sweet fruit and good flavour it was drinking well – though with a '62-like astringent finish. *At home Dec 1994* ★★★ *(just).*

**Ch Pavie** Many notes. Variable bottlings. On the whole, certainly in the late 1970s and early 1980s, fully mature, sweet, rounded. Only tasted once recently, a jeroboam with a strong mocha, coffee shop smell; dry, showing its age, touch of sourness. Some sour remarks made about poor grapes used and old barrels. But I think it was more due to the state of the bottle. *Last noted Sept 1998. At best* ★★★★

**Ch Pichon-Lalande** Picked from 23 September to 12 October. Good wine. Even in its early years (1967) soft and agreeable. Several other notes, all 'attractive' including a deep, peppery *impériale* with a touch of aniseed. Fully evolved, opulent in 1985. Most recently, its appearance reminded me of my father's old Labrador, lying on its back waiting to be tickled: soft, mature, a warm open-rimmed rosehip and orange colour; an instantly forthcoming bouquet, soft, lovely, gently singed, cedary; on the palate a reasonable touch of sweetness with a clean dry finish. Somewhat faded but holding up. *The oldest vintage at Christie's Pichon-Lalande masterclass, March 1995* ★★★★ *But drink soon.*

**Ch Rauzan-Gassies** Why this was among the nine rather good wines served at a dinner for the international press I do not know. It was a poor period for the châteaux and the '64, though drinkable, did nothing for its reputation. It was upstaged by the magnificent '59 Latour, which was served later. *Last tasted at Ch Latour, June 1999* ★

**Vieux Ch Certan** What a contrast: the Gassies (above), a poor representation of Margaux, and the 'Vieux', a dependable Pomerol. Only two notes: in 1980, very complete, well balanced, fully mature but 'lacked a little zing', drunk with a *noisette* of overdone English lamb: and more recently, a lovely, soft, rounded magnum absolutely at its best for drinking. *Tasted blind at a Rodenstock dinner, Sept 1994* ★★★★

SOME OF THE BEST (AND WORST) OF THE OTHER '64S, last tasted in the 1980s. It was an impossible task to cull the 250 notes, so here is a small selection. **Ch Croizet-Bages** rich, ripe, lovely. *March 1986* ★★★; **Ch Gazin** earlier very good but though still rich, showing its age. *Dec 1985* ★★★; **Ch Gruaud-Larose** picked 24 September to 17 October. Variable and not just because of the different bottlings. *Feb 1989. At best* ★★★; **Ch Langoa-Barton** ungracious, austere, cracking up. *Dec 1985*; **Ch Léoville-Las-Cases** picked 24 September to 9 October. Many notes, mainly good – but not great. *1989* ★★★; **Ch Léoville-Poyferré** many notes, variable in the 1960s and 1970s. Most recently 'soft, ready and waiting'. *Feb 1986* ★★★ *drink up*; **Ch Montrose** picked 21 September to 2 October, well before the rains. First tasted in cask and distinctly good. Montrose at its sturdiest best. Lovely, classic, tannic, long lasting. *April 1987* ★★★★ *and more to come*; **Ch Palmer** picked 21 September to 8 October, also before the rain. Yet, disappointing. Noted as inelegant and chunky. *Not tasted since 1981* ★★; **Ch Pape-Clément** quite good, with characteristic Graves taste. But not as good as the '62. *Oct 1989* ★★; **Ch Rouget** this often creeps out of the woodwork and can be very attractive. A good, rounded Pomerol. *July 1984* ★★★; **Ch de Sales** in a district of very small vineyards, de Sales is a giant (40ha) and generally produces agreeable, early-maturing wines at a reasonable price. The '64 was open knit, with a lovely flavour but lacking the class of a top Pomerol. *June 1983* ★★★ *drink up*; and **Ch Trotanoy** I expected better from this usually immensely impressive vineyard. *Sept 1987* ★

A SPRINKLE OF NOTES ON OTHER '64S, which I would love to try again: **Ch Grand-Puy-Lacoste**; **Ch Lafon-Rochet**; **Ch Léoville-Barton**; **Ch du Tertre**; and **Ch La Tour de Mons**.

# 1965

A wet, miserable summer resulting in a meagre crop of mean, short, acidic wines. Few tasted recently. Don't bother.

**Ch Lafite** At its early best a light luncheon wine. Slightly better than the '63 though this is not saying much. *Last noted at a pre-sale tasting, July 1988.*

**Ch Latour** Some fragrance, raw, still some tannin. Making the best of a bad job. *Last tasted March 1989* ★

**Ch Mouton-Rothschild** Pale but pretty. Trying hard to be Mouton. *Last tasted March 1989.*

**Ch Haut-Brion** Good colour; dry, light, passable. *Last tasted May 1985.*

**Ch La Mission Haut-Brion** Surprising wine in many ways with depth of colour and fragrance. A tolerable '65. *Last tasted Sept 1990* ★★

**Ch Montrose** Only old notes but, with Ch Latour and Ch La Mission, the best of the '65s ★★

**Ch Margaux** *non-millésime* A botched though understandable attempt to make a drinkable wine by making a blend of the 1963, 1964 and 1965, marketed in 1966. The trade did not take to it and the experiment was not repeated. One recent note: palish with tarry rim; nose of weak tea and treacle but faded fast. Light. Astringent. *At Wagner's Margaux vertical, Nov 2000.*

# 1966 ★★★★

One of my favourite vintages which I have always described as a 'lean, long-distance runner'. Growing conditions: early flowering, cool and fairly dry summer but a very hot, sunny, ripening September, with the harvest starting in good conditions on 6 October.

As with the 1964 vintage, I have several hundred notes on well over 200 châteaux so the following is just the tip of the iceberg. Hardly surprisingly, at well over 35 years old, many of the minor wines are well past their best and not the kind that remain long on the shelves or in the cellars.

**Ch Lafite** This is the sort of wine that, if not treated with care and concentration, might pass for – well, a decent drink but nothing special. There is simply no doubt in my mind that it needs plenty of air, plenty of time in decanter and glass. It is like an exceptionally shy person who has to be gently courted to bring out his or her true qualities. I have well over two dozen well-spread notes. At its best it is the epitome of my 'lean, long-distance runner'. But not all notes have been brilliant. Just to deal with the more recent. In 1995 a fragrant bottle from the Nicolas cellar in Paris mischievously thrust, blind, by Rodenstock, into a 'flight' of pre-phylloxera châteaux. To be honest it was more than lean. It was a bit raw. The next year, in New York, a tasting of 1966 first growths to celebrate the 30th anniversary of Christie's wine department: the Lafite was elegant but again a bit 'edgy'. The following week, on the precise anniversary (11 October 1966), of my first sale, at a very grand dinner in the Great Room in King Street, London, no fewer than three *impériales*, one magnificent, the others as I shall describe. The best had a good level and a deeply coloured, velvety-ended cork. Bouquet with the fragrance that only Lafite can exude. Lovely flavour, lean, good length. A jolly good drink. I don't know where the other '*imps*' came from but one had a rough sort of cork and old weevil traces. Somewhat oxidised but seemed to gain its second breath. We drank it last. The third imperial was a disaster. Upon removing the capsule, the slightly depressed cork was seething with live weevils, yet after removing the crumbly cork, it was, surprisingly, better than No. 2! Most recently, a classic jeroboam, harmonious, refreshing but with fading fruit, at a tasting I conducted for *Vinum* magazine in Zurich. *Last tasted April 1998. At best* ★★★★ *but it has passed the finishing post.*

**Ch Latour** Around a dozen notes but none prior to 1976. By that time an unsurprisingly magnificent depth of colour, its core opaque. Enormous, well stacked, velvety, unready. In fact the slowest maturing of all the '66s. Seven notes in the 1990s, all highly satisfactory. For example, vigorous, excellent balance and flavour at the Bär Bank in Zurich (1998). The following spring a lovely 'old oak' bottle, its tannin tamed but very much at work, and a month later, Christie's 'Tasting of the Century', all top 1966s, not just Bordeaux, at Vinexpo, Bordeaux, conducted by myself and Christopher Burr who had organised it. The Latour was perfection: fine colour; fragrant cedary bouquet, unblemished flavour and condition. In October 2000, drinking well at a Saintsbury Club dinner. A flavoury, beautifully textured wine, with time in hand. Most recently: opaque core; sweet old cedary bouquet, starting to show some age; very rich mouthful, dry finish. 'Lovely now.' *Last tasted at Hugh Johnson's Bordeaux Club dinner at Saling Hall, Dec 2001* ★★★★★

**Ch Margaux** Noted as elegant, fruity, slim yet with (firm) core in the mid-1970s. A decade later displaying its inimitable fragrance, beautiful elliptical shape, flesh and length. Yet, a certain leanness and dry finish. It was also showing well at the 1966 Wine Experience gala dinner in New York, a bit restrained on the nose until it decided to relax and open up. Still tannic. The most instructive events were Manfred Wagner's two Margaux vertical tastings in Zurich, my notes and ratings not dissimilar, in both instances (1997 and 2000) it was interesting to see how well the bouquet developed – about 45 minutes to reach perfection. Both were in good condition with fine flavour, texture and length. *Last tasted Nov 2000* ★★★★ *Time in hand.*

**Ch Mouton-Rothschild** A typically dramatic wine though in its (relative) youth after seven years in bottle, while very flavoury, austere, with a touch of coarseness yet gentle, unready, at the Krug Award for Excellence dinner at Inigo Jones' Banqueting House in Whitehall. Its bouquet and flavour noticeably holding up in the 1980s. More recently, well-nigh perfect bottles also in London at a Mouton dinner at Brooks's Club hosted by Philippine de Rothschild in 1994, its fragrance surging out of the glass, all signs of coarseness ironed out. Yet I thought it fading, though very gracefully. Next a splendid bottle, its bouquet similarly restrained but opening up beautifully: full, rich and tannic, at the gala dinner referred to in the previous entry. Most recently, showing more maturity, brown-rimmed, some age on nose but rich and perfectly delicious on the palate. *Last noted at lunch with Hervé Berland at 'Grand Mouton', Sept 1998* ★★★★ *But don't wait too long.*

**Ch Haut-Brion** To my surprise, a couple of dozen notes starting with an impressive cask sample in November 1967, and drunk on all conceivable occasions. With the late Dr King (a great cellar) in Atlanta, with my friend Sr Morales Doria in Mexico City, and elsewhere, mainly in the 1980s, and without exception showing well, 'elegance', 'complete', 'perfect fruit', 'marvellous flesh' cropping up in my notes. More recently, an excellent bottle I served at my Bordeaux Club dinner at Christie's in 1994: level into the neck, perfect cork pulled at 5.45pm, decanted an hour later and served at 8.15pm. Still deep and richly coloured; typical Haut-Brion scent of tobacco and iron, opening up deliciously, tea-like, very sweet, fullish body, lovely flavour, earthy tannic finish. Then a remarkably good double magnum at the Christie's 30th anniversary dinner: the grapes were being picked and the wine fermented at the time of the department's first auction. For the sake of historical accuracy I report an overmature, somewhat oxidised bottle in New York. *Last tasted Oct 2001. At its best* ★★★★

**Ch Ausone** Good wine. Idiosyncratic as always. Stylish and elegant in the early 1970s; very fragrant and flavoury at Flatt's tasting in 1987, but not tasted since. *Last noted Oct 1987* ★★★★

**Ch Cheval Blanc** I have always preferred the '66 to the great '47 for though the latter is hugely impressive, the '66 is the epitome of elegance. Apart from a cask sample in November 1967, with an understandable touch of greenness and tannins, evolving splendidly through the 1980s, 5 stars appearing several times. Five encounters during the last decade including a bottle served alongside the other first growth '66s at my Bordeaux Club dinner in 1994. Despite its poor crumbly cork it was delectable, frankly the best of the lot. No holding back the bouquet, an immediacy about its fragrance yet opening up even more gloriously. Very sweet, a lovely cedary flavour, good flesh and weight. Totally harmonious. A 5-star bottle at the centenary tasting in New York in 1966 and two splendid bottles provided by Dick Edmunds to celebrate his 30th year at Boodle's and mine at Christie's. The following year an elegant magnum with a scent so lively, fragrant, that I described it as 'dancing' out of the glass. This was at Karl-Heinz Wolf's Cheval Blanc vertical, Monsieur Hébrard told us that the *rendement* was very low, 20hl/ha, and the alcoholic strength equally modest (12.2%). What a contrast to the clumsy, packed with fruit, obvious wines so fashionable today in certain quarters, not only on the other side of the Atlantic. *This* is what claret is all about. *Last tasted Sept 1997* ★★★★★

**Ch Pétrus** Well, I suppose this is the style of wine they all try to imitate. But I must admit, it was enormously impressive, from a 'hefty' cask sample in 1967, followed by some impressive tastings in the 1980s. Deep, the wine's extract almost visible it is so thick looking. An equally rich nose, almost malty yet developing a lovely fragrance. Sweet, full-bodied, yet tannic. Made as if the grapes had not been pressed but allowed to drip their sugar-laden juice. *Last tasted April 1990* ★★★★★ *Long life.*

### OTHER '66S TASTED IN THE 1990S

**Ch Batailley** Always dependable, certainly very good, possibly at its very best in 1966 because its comfortably fruity style enriches the leanness of the vintage. Still fairly deep; a leafy arboreal nose – or perhaps it was the influence of Hugh's arboretum – which opened up deliciously. Rich and moderately mouthfilling, with attractive Cabernet Sauvignon touch to the end taste. *Last noted at Hugh Johnson's Bordeaux Club dinner, July 1995* ★★★★

**Ch Beychevelle** I liked it in cask and have liked it consistently since then. It developed misleadingly early, its style suiting the vintage. *Last tasted May 1993* ★★★★

**Ch Calon-Ségur** Many notes. Raw and tannic in 1969 but by the mid-1970s had developed a classic cedary nose and flavour, firm and dry. Continuing to shed its pristine St-Estèphe austerity through the 1980s. Most recently, a superb Avery's of Bristol bottling: lovely colour, bouquet of flavour. Soft, *à point*. A perfect claret. *Last noted at a Saintsbury Club dinner, Oct 2001* ★★★★★

**Ch La Conseillante** A wonderful wine. Most memorably noted in solitary splendour at Sandricourt, John Goellet's estate north of Paris, after grubbing around on my hands and knees sorting out his cellar. Still deep; shows its age, an attractive, bricky, rich bouquet and flavour. Perfect body (like the maid who looked after me, running the bath and so forth) and lovely texture (not the maid. *Ne touchez pas.*). *Last noted May 1995* ★★★★ *Still tannic.*

**Ch Cos d'Estournel** From the start a splendid wine, the start being February after the vintage, so it was probably de Luze jumping the gun again. Ten consistently good notes through the 1970s and 1980s, hitting a high (5-star) spot in 1990. Since then just a couple of notes. A bottle recorked in 1988, bought at one of Christie's auctions in 1996 and served at my Bordeaux Club dinner in 1998. I see that I gave it a lot of air, drawing the cork at 4pm, decanting at 6pm and pouring at 8.20pm. It was really worth it for the bouquet was wonderfully fragrant, cedary, tea-like; sweet, delicious, easy and charming yet with a sustaining core. Last tasted a fortnight later at my 'Réserve Tasting of Premier Bordeaux Wine' in Palm Beach. It was extremely good: mellow for a '66, lovely fruit, delicious. Claret at its best. *Last tasted Feb 1998* ★★★★

**Ch Ducru-Beaucaillou** Roughly two dozen notes spread through the 1970s and 1980s. Although very good, lacking the immediacy of Cos, rather stern and unyielding. Five stars appear frequently (★★★ for drinking, ★★ for further development). Silky texture, fine flesh, a wine with class yet a bit tight-lipped. *Last tasted Feb 1992. Still* ★★★(★)

**Ch Figeac** Another cask sample prematurely presented but already soft and attractive, and consistently so through the 1970s and 1980s. On the last two occasions, quite independently, I described the bottles as typical Manoncourt wines, full of fruit and character. It was showing well at the *1er grand cru* tasting in May 1997, most attractive, most distinctive, its fragrance reminding me of privet. Five months later, a bottle straight from Bob Dickinson's fabulous cellar and which took time to open up. But good. *Last noted at a tasting at Jodi and Bob's home in Florida, Nov 1997* ★★★★★

**Ch L'Église-Clinet** *'Élevé by A & R Barrière Frères'* and probably bottled in Belgium. Most fulsomely described on the label and, in fact, pretty good. Lovely, meaty fragrance; perfect maturity, rich with dry finish. At best before its time: now one of the most fashionable of Pomerol châteaux. *April 1997* ★★★

**Ch La Fleur** Another now very fashionable and expensive Pomerol but, as with many, probably most, of the small vineyards in this tight-packed district, hitherto mainly shipped to and appreciated by the Belgians. Unquestionably a beautiful wine. Still deep and fairly youthful looking; one of the loveliest of Pomerol scents; good flesh, balance, its richness masking considerable tannin. One of the best of 32 vintages of La Fleur presented by Hardy Rodenstock in 1966, over lunch. *Last tasted Sept 1998* ★★★★★

**Ch Gazin** Yet another surprisingly soft and agreeable cask sample tasted in London in Feb 1967. Velvety but very tannic, fully developed in its 20th year. Most recently a jeroboam which put me in mind of the excellent '45 tasted in my early days in the trade. An amazingly sweet nose, the ripe raspberry-like Cabernet Franc oozing out. Good fruit, flesh, complete. Drinking deliciously. *Sept 1998* ★★★★

**Ch Grand-Puy-Lacoste** This always is a long-distance runner, and a château whose wine I now buy every vintage. My first taste of the '66 was a pleasant, piquant Justerini & Brooks' bottling in 1971. At a *Decanter* tasting in 1979, softer than Ducru; a well developed, characteristically sinewy classic in the mid-1980s. *Last tasted April 1993* ★★★★ *and still developing.*

**Ch Gruaud-Larose** Although drinking well in the late 1970s, noted several times as unready during the early part of the next decade. Also various bottles 'fully evolved', 'full of fruit and extract', 'crisp', 'still tannic' – a bit of a hotch potch of notes. A fragrant, rich, cedary double magnum at the château in April 1994, notably full-bodied and laden with fruit, extract

and tannin. Two months later a most attractive bottle, stylish, mature, drinking well. *Last noted at lunch with Meg and Eddie Penning-Rowsell, at Chippenham Lodge, June 1994* ★★★★

**Ch Haut-Batailley** Six very good notes. Its style is as consistently elegant as neighbouring Batailley's is dependably chunky and fruity. Not really ready in the mid-1970s but a decade more bottle age transformed it. Yet another delicious meal, this time lunch at Sandricourt, after another dusty and grimy few hours in the cellar. Asked to choose a wine, I brought up a bottle of the Haut-Batailley: it had a deep, rich, mahogany-mature colour; perfect bouquet and lovely cedary flavour. Marvellously refreshing – perhaps because I earned it! Noted 'claret at its best'. *Last tasted May 1995* ★★★★

**Ch d'Issan** I like it but it can vary, as with their bottlings of this '66. Several notes, a particularly memorable bottle in 1983 lunching with Lionel Cruse and his mother at d'Issan, their lovely moated château. It seemed at its best in the mid-1980s, but, most recently a very good Berry Bros' bottling at a Sainsbury Club dinner (Anthony Berry, until recently, was the 'cellarer', which helps!). Lovely vinosity, nice texture and weight. Crisp. It mitigated the tough medallions of veal. *Last tasted April 1994* ★★★

**Ch La Lagune** This Haut-Médoc château lies between the southern end of Margaux and the city of Bordeaux and so its soil is more like that of Graves. Often burgundy-like, the '66 was distinctly sweet and fragrant. Several consistent notes, the most recent a deeply impressive double magnum tasted blind. I didn't know what it was but it had a good shape, fruit and finish and I added 'a perfect wine'. *Last tasted at a Rodenstock dinner, Sept 1998* ★★★★

**Ch Lascombes** My first note, in 1971, was simply 'delicious'. Several variable notes in the 1980s, impressively deep, palate better than nose. Most recently, though deep, a rather deathly mahogany rim; bouquet of fragrant old oak; ripe sweetness, gnarled fruit, teeth-gripping tannin. *Last noted at a Lascombes pre-sale tasting, Sept 2001. Now* ★★ *Best to avoid.*

**Ch Léoville-Las-Cases** A promising cask sample in February 1967 and a string of pretty good notes since, apart from two uncharacteristically poor Army & Navy Stores' bottlings. Much liked in the early 1980s, svelte, with 'silky tannins, perfect length'. Three recent notes, one bottled by Nicolas, Paris: an impressive, hefty 'masculine' wine, hopelessly and inappropriately accompanying 'Santa Barbara Channel Spot Prawns with Ravioli of French Black Winter Truffles' at the Four Seasons in Los Angeles. Our generous host Stephen Kaplan should have known better, but perhaps it was the chef: they always want to show off and rarely understand wine! Most recently, on our annual winter holiday in St Bart's, a perfect bottle dining with the Weisers at their beachside villa. Faultless. *Last tasted Feb 2000* ★★★★

**Ch Léoville-Poyferré** Attractive but not up to Léoville-Las-Cases. *Last tasted Oct 1992* ★★★

**Ch Lynch-Bages** I thought Lynch-Bages and '66 would be a classic combination. Well, at its best it is, with inimitable verve and spiciness. The oldest of 13 vintages of Lynch-Bages commented on at a meeting of the '33 Club in The Wine Bar, Brussels, not the ideal spot – too cramped. The wine was good; surprisingly sweet yet drying out at the end. Good weight, balance and flavour. *Last tasted Nov 1995. At best* ★★★★

**Ch Lynch-Moussas** Also surprisingly sweet and lovely though still tannic. *Feb 1993* ★★★

**Ch La Mission Haut-Brion** For me, the last great wine of the Woltners and which I have been privileged to drink on

20 occasions. They called it 'a no problem' vintage. Through the 1970s, a rich, plump, well-knit though many-layered wine. Yet despite its stature I could not help commenting on its acidity, notably at a wine dinner at Gidleigh Park in Devon (in 1996). This is not to damn with faint praise; quite the opposite. It *is* impressive. One of the great '66s, though the volatile acidity a bit high. Most recently, showing its age, with rich 'legs' but watery rim; nose creaking, mocha and iron, slightly stewed tobacco. Lots of grip, lovely fruit and length. Refreshing. *Last tasted Sept 1998. Should be ★★★★★ but really I found it hard to justify more than* ★★★

**Ch Montrose** A classic of its kind. Two variable and premature cask samples. Every subsequent note mentioning tannin. But that is what the old Montrose used to be. I will jump straight to a perfect example, a bottle alongside the Cos, and bought at the same sale, at my Bordeaux Club dinner in 1998. Now medium deep, richly coloured, mature; a rather hard-to-get nose; dry, somewhat austere, massive, still tannic. It will come round, eventually. *Last tasted Feb 1998* ★★★(★★)!

**Ch Mouton-Baron-Philippe** Despite being unserious and utterly charming, a stayer. Most recently, served in magnums by Philippine de Rothschild after Opus One '87 and before the jeroboam of the 1921 Mouton *grand vin* at an appropriately grand dinner at Mouton. The wine was a sheer delight. Elegant, delightful flavour, a touch of pepperiness on the finish. *Last tasted Sept 1998* ★★★★

**Ch Palmer** Exceptionally good, not quite the '61 but superbly balanced. Thanks partly to my longstanding friendship with the much-missed Peter Sichel, many notes, in fact exactly 22. All good including excellent Army & Navy Stores, Berry Bros and Quellyn Roberts (of Chester). Several recently including an interesting pair at a dinner hosted by Jim Hood in Bristol, one château-bottled, the other by The Wine Society. They differed, the latter looking more mature, its nose taking ages to open up. It was sweet, rich, straightforward and tannic. I actually preferred The Wine Society bottling, finding the bouquet more attractive and spicy; a fraction too sweet but a very interesting flavour, lovely, stylish. A very good bottle noted at a pre-sale tasting in New York (1999) and, best of the lot, the fourth and oldest vintage of Palmer served by Michael Le Marchant: it was fully mature-looking with slight orange tinge; a fabulous – no other word – bouquet; sweet, lovely flavour, balance and finish. *Last noted at the Le Marchants', Aug 1998* ★★★★★

**Ch La Pointe** Drinking perfectly. *Jan 1993* ★★★★

**Ch Rausan-Ségla** A cask sample, February 1967: raw but with good potential. Surprisingly soft but firm – if this is possible – and flavoury in the early 1970s; certainly well balanced. A couple of very good notes in the mid-1980s: delicious, elegant, perfect weight, dry finish but no bitter tannins. Most recently a delicious bottle, fairly sweet, good texture, 'vinosity' (well I know what *I* mean) and perfect state of maturity. A most stylish '66 and very Margaux. *Last noted dining at Ségla with David Orr, April 1997* ★★★★

**Ch Talbot** Consistently lovely, sweet, rich and ready. *Last tasted Dec 1990* ★★★★

**Ch La Tour Haut-Brion** I do not normally care for the number two wine of La Mission, finding it coarse. However, on the couple of occasions I have had the '66 I found it surprisingly sweet and soft. *Last tasted June 1990* ★★★

**Ch La Tour de Mons** You can't win them all. I used to regard this *cru exceptionnel* on a par with the excellent Ch Chasse-Spleen, but it was the middle of three less than

impressive clarets at a Saintsbury Club dinner. Bottled by Averys and somehow unconvincing, showing age, too loose knit. And it further demonstrates that most red Bordeaux wines below *cru classé* quality do not age as well. They just become older and do not develop those important extra dimensions. This wine should not have been served at 30 years of age. Ten years maximum. *April 1996* ★

SOME OTHER '66S LAST TASTED IN THE MID- TO LATE 1980s **Ch L'Angélus** at peak in the mid-1970s. *Nov 1986* ★★★ *drink up;* **Ch Boyd-Cantenac** pleasant, easy, lacking length. *Nov 1986* ★★; **Ch Branaire-Ducru** just three notes. 'A surprise and a delight.' Fragrant. Touch of spice and elegance. *Nov 1986* ★★★★; **Ch Brane-Cantenac** ten very mixed comments, flavour, agreeable in the mid-1970s but overblown in the 1980s. *Nov 1986. Better to avoid;* **Ch Canon** several good notes. Chunky yet elegant, glorious fragrance. *Sept 1986* ★★★; **Ch Canon-La-Gaffelière** not its best period. Light and easy in the early 1970s. Mixed reception latterly. *Nov 1986* ★★★ *(giving it the benefit of the doubt). Best drink up;* **Ch Cantemerle** always elegant and stylish. It needed time to come round. Fragrant, crisp. *Nov 1986* ★★★, *possibly* ★★★★; **Ch Cantenac-Brown** 'fulsome', rarely elegant but drinking well. *Sept 1986* ★★★; **Carruades de Ch Lafite** a wine of faded charm. *Nov 1986* ★★★; **Dom de Chevalier** classic Graves, beautifully made by Claude Ricard. Fragrant and firm. *Oct 1989* ★★★★; **Ch Croizet-Bages** never great, always agreeable. Hunky fruit, ripe and ready. *Nov 1986* ★★★ *drink soon;* **Ch Duhart-Milon** now soft, ripe agreeable. *Nov 1989* ★★★ *drink soon;* **Ch Fourtet** unexciting. Lean. Dry finish *Nov 1986* ★★; **Ch La Gaffelière** a bit of a roller coaster but by the mid-1980s, soft, rich, complete. *1986. At best* ★★★ *drink up;* **Ch Giscours** several notes. Never seemed to shed its initial greenness, my best note February 1986. Excellent nose. Dry, lean. *Nov 1986* ★★; **Ch Haut-Bailly** always well made, ahead of the pack. A charmer. Sweet, fragrant. *Nov 1986* ★★★★; **Ch Lafon-Rochet** I always found this wine rather austere and lacking fruit and flesh but the '66 is quite good, might even develop further. *Nov 1986* ★★(★)?; **Ch Lanessan** variable. If you find any, drink it. *Nov 1986* ★★; **Ch Langoa-Barton** lean, refreshing, good length. *Nov 1986. At best* ★★★; **Ch Léoville-Barton** 'a textbook '66' – my original lean, long-distance runner. Fragrant, firm, elegant. *Nov 1989* ★★★★; **Ch La Louvière** another consistently well made Graves that deserves to be better known. Lovely colour, fragrance, flavour. *March 1987* ★★★; **Ch Magdelaine** lovely wine. I can't fault it. *June 1989* ★★★★; **Ch Malescot-St-Exupéry** a rather specious hollow yet flavoury wine. *Nov 1986* ★★; **Ch Marquis de Terme** variable bottles. Deep, rich, chunky. *Jan 1987. At best* ★★; **Ch Nenin** classic Pomerol in the mid-1970s. Very pleasant weight and style. Extremely elegant. Fully developed. *Nov 1986* ★★★★ *drink up;* **Ch Pape-Clément** many notes including a quartet of Berry Bros bottlings in the 1970s. Not its best period, but flavoury. *Nov 1986* ★★?; **Ch Pavie** the '66 on the light side and mature by the early 1980s. Latterly I much enjoyed a fully developed, shapely, nice-textured bottle. *Nov 1986;* **Ch Pichon-Baron** one tends to think that the deep, concentrated, big-boned Baron is a recent trait. Not so. Impressive but lacking finesse and grace. *Nov 1986* ★★★; **Ch Pichon-Lalande** totally different style to its almost namesake above. Lalande is softer, more scented. Lovely fruit. *Nov 1986* ★★★★; and **Ch Trotanoy** marvellous wine. Packed with fruit but well ordered and fragrant. *Sept 1987* ★★★★

OTHER VERY GOOD '66 POMEROLS ALSO TASTED IN THE 1980s Ch La Croix-de-Gay; Ch La Fleur; Ch La Fleur-Pétrus; Ch Latour-à-Pomerol; Ch Petit-Village; Ch de Sales; and Vieux Ch Certan.

# 1967

A peroxide blonde of a vintage; initially attractive but the black roots soon began to show. Not the fault of the winemakers who, because of unripe grapes, had to chaptalise the wines heavily.

**Ch Lafite** Several notes. Surprisingly deep but raw in cask, March 1969; an effort at fragrance and charm in the early 1970s but lacking middle. Most recently, colour lost; thin and tinny. *Last noted at a pre-sale tasting, March 1996.*

**Ch Latour** Initially a deep plummy purple and doing as well as can be expected in a vintage like this, its nose really very attractive in the mid-1970s; soft, generous, not refined. Surprisingly agreeable at a Saintsbury Club dinner in 1997, still fairly deep-coloured, its nose opening up quite fragrantly. Rather better than the inedible medallions of veal served with it. Then, very appropriately accompanying a hog-roast barbecue in Memphis, Tennessee, though very variable, mainly dried out, some woody. *Last noted Sept 1999. At best* ★★

**Ch Margaux** Well made, soft and pleasing in the 1970s. Seemed at its best at a Madeira Club dinner in Savannah (1980). The last two notes made at Wagner's Margaux verticals. In 1997 sweet but raw, and acidity catching up. At the second tasting, a nose like cream cheese, slightly woody; better flavour than nose, fairly light, acidic. *Last tasted Nov 2000* ★ *Forget it.*

**Ch Mouton-Rothschild** In fact, quite pleasant in its 'dyed blonde' early 1970s. Lack of balance and some tartness as chaptalised effect started to wear off. Still, it survived. Most recently, a pale rosy glow; somewhat singed nose; surprisingly sweet and flavoury though light and short. *Last noted at a pre-sale tasting in New York, Sept 1997* ★★

**Ch Cheval Blanc** A surprisingly early harvest, starting with the Merlot on 7 September, and *not* chaptalised. Seven variable notes in the 1970s, probably at its softest and most drinkable best in the mid-1980s. At the New York pre-sale tasting in 1997, distinctly superior to the Mouton. Sweet but short. A week later, in Austria, at Wolf's vertical, an unconvincing appearance; crisp, tangy, spicy nose; seemed much drier, raw, coarse textured, touch of vanilla, short. *Last tasted Sept 1997* ★★ *A rare, vapid Cheval Blanc.*

**Ch Pétrus** Clearly, Pomerol did better in '67 than the Médoc, thanks to early picked Merlot. Rich, but qualified by 'shapeless' and 'lacking cohesion' at tastings in the mid-1970s and 1980s. Most recently, at another pre-sale tasting at Christie's in New York, on the pale side for Pétrus, orange-tinged, tangy, 'old stables' nose. Sweet. Quite a good '67. *Last tasted in May 1999* ★★

**Ch Beychevelle** Sweetish nose; flavoury but tart. *Last tasted March 1993.*

**Ch Cantemerle** Well over a dozen notes. A good '67. Some fruit and charm though raw edged. *Last tasted – a bottle from Mme Binaud's cellar, March 1996* ★★

**Dom de Chevalier** Delicious though short in the early 1970s. Probably at its best then though some richness, and noted in 1992 as 'one of the best' 67s. More recently, fully mature; nose muffled, but no harsh edges; initially sweet but with touch of astringency. *Last noted at a dinner at the domaine, all the vintages ending in the figure 7, Sept 1998* ★

**Ch Cos d'Estournel** Fragrant, thin. *Last tasted May 1992* ★

**Ch Ducru-Beaucaillou** Seven notes. A pretty good '67, luminous, dry, crisp, flavoury. *Last tasted May 1992* ★★

**Ch La Gaffelière** Faded, and showing its age; and 'edgy', but quite a good '67. *At the La Fleur vertical, Sept 1998* ★★

**Ch Larcis-Ducasse** When journalists visit Bordeaux *en masse* for the spring tastings we are billeted at various châteaux. I had never visited this château before (it is near Pavie) and my host served a range of his wines at dinner. Although not up to his superb '85 and very good '70, the '67 made quite a good showing. Sweet, rich, fragrant, vanillin nose; creaking a bit but some sweetness. *At the château, April 2000* ★★

**Ch Léoville-Las-Cases** First tasted in June 1969. Light for Las-Cases but well handled by Monsieur Delon. Six pretty good notes covering the 1970s: 'cedary', 'elegant', 'easy'. Probably at its best after ten years. Then a jump of 14 years: rich, nose; relatively soft, a moderately good '67. *Last tasted May 1992* ★★ *(almost* ★★★*)*

**Ch Lynch-Bages** Only three notes. In June 1969, flavoury, piquant. In the middle of the 1970s, I was baffled and off course: I thought it was a poor burgundy! Most recently I just wrote 'mediocre'. The Cazes failed to make the most of this admittedly not very inspiring vintage. *Last tasted May 1992* ★

**Ch Malescot-St-Exupéry** 'Green', with edgy acidity, twice in the mid-1970s. Most recently a lean, crisp, quite pleasant *impériale*. *Last noted Sept 1990.* ★ *Drink up.*

**Ch La Mission Haut-Brion** One of the best '67s starting off well with a deep, rich, earthy flavour. Touch of sourness – a sort of pasty acidic finish though well disguised by its relative richness. By the mid-1980s considerable colour loss. Good flavour though. *Last tasted June 1990* ★★

**Ch Montrose** A dozen notes. Severe, raw, ungracious, 'no future'. Then a very dry jeroboam with high volatile acidity in 1986, and another, four years later, decidedly better, rich, with leathery tannins. Not bad but lacking the body and Charmolüe charm. *Last tasted May 1992* ★ *Avoid.*

**Ch Palmer** Over a dozen notes, mainly in the 1970s. Various bottlings including two dire specimens by Corney & Barrow, one oxidised, two other with a nose I described as 'like a gas leak', prickly, tart. Berry Bros' bottling not much better, more fruit but with tart finish. The Palmer seemed at its best in 1980, though not much middle or length. Half a dozen notes in the 1990s: the oldest vintage in a vertical of Palmer at a Christie's wine course in 1994, château-bottled: a nose like linoleum and stale cheese (my wife, who takes my notes when I am lecturing – and adds her own – wrote 'marzipan'). Unbalanced, refreshing but completely upstaged by the marvellous 1970. Rather unfair really. Most recently, a tolerable Berry Bros' magnum at a Christie's Bordeaux lunch. Showing its age. Dry, lean, fragrant, but … (I never finished it. The wine or the note). *Last tasted July 1998. At best* ★

**Ch Pichon-Baron** Not a very good wine. Noting, in 1978, some fruit but a molasses sort of sweetness on the nose; light, insubstantial. In the mid-1980s a strange nose, dry, skinny. Most recently, a woody, malty nose; poor. *Last tasted May 1992. Avoid.*

**Ch Siran** Surprisingly attractive; silky. *Last tasted Oct 1993* ★★

SOME OTHER '67s LAST TASTED IN THE 1980s
**Ch Ausone** chocolatey, chaptalised nose; lacking middle, but a pleasant if lactic flavour. *Oct 1987* ★; **Ch Brane-Cantenac** quite agreeable but short and acidic. *May 1987* ★; **Ch Calon-Ségur** light, forward, pleasant enough in the mid-1970s to mid-1980s. More recently, dry, clean, crisp, short. *June 1987* ★;

Ch Prieuré-Lichine sweet, flavoury, tolerable acidity. A good '67. *Oct 1988* ★★; and Ch Rausan-Ségla some charm, flavoury but little to it in the 1970s. More recently, showing its age, little red left, more of an amber-mahogany. Despite its sweetness, a wine 'with its stuffing taken out of it'. *April 1989.*

# 1968

Not since the 1930s were there so many bad vintages in one decade. Atrocious; entirely due to a cold spring, uneven flowering, not bad July but the coldest and wettest August for many years. An abundant crop of unripe grapes were picked in fine weather starting 4 October.

Ch Lafite Should have taken a leaf out of Cheval Blanc's book and de-classified, for this pale pink, shallow and short wine did nothing for its reputation. *Last noted Oct 1988 'skeletal but drinkable'.*

Ch Latour Displaying in cask its bitterness, lack of both body and length. Later, not undrinkable. Most recently, a fragrant magnum, some fruit, but lean and dry. *Last tasted Sept 1990.*

Ch Haut-Brion A tolerable '68 but not quite right. *Last tasted May 1985.*

Ch Pétrus Stewed, chunky and raw in 1979. 'Heavily chaptalised' noted in 1988, but most recently a surprisingly good bottle. Brown-rimmed though; a nose like old tea leaves; sweet, lovely flavour and almost silky Pomerol texture. *Last tasted April 1990* ★★? *I wouldn't bank on it. Perhaps this is the only vintage of Pétrus to which the Taiwanese are justified in adding Coca-Cola.*

Ch Beychevelle Not unattractive in the early 1970s, but soon left high and dry, skinny and tart. Most recently: pale, chocolatey; sweet, rank. *Last noted May 1993.*

Dom de Chevalier The much admired Claude Ricard had to decide whether to become a concert pianist or take over the domaine. I think this wine was made by a concert pianist. Not surprisingly showing its age, and short. At one of Olivier Bernard's dinners, all the vintages ending in the figure 8. *Last noted April 1998.*

Ch La Mission Haut-Brion I must give Fernand and Henri Woltner marks for trying in this terrible vintage. Two notes: light, dry, short, slightly raw but flavoury, in 1985. Most recently though it had some fragrance, there was a strange pasty taste. *Last tasted June 1990.*

## International Wine & Food Society (IWFS)

*Founded by André Simon in 1933, the 'Wine & Food Society' held its first event in 1934 – an Alsace lunch. The aim of the society was to improve the dismal standards of English food and foster the understanding of wine. Regular dinners and tastings were held with gastronomic civilisation in mind. I was invited to join the committee in the early 1950s. I became president at a time when the Americans, very active, seemed intent on taking over the Society. We had the most amazing rows (the US committee members were most surprised I could be so aggressive!) and I think I managed to hold them off. It is now an international society, and certainly very strong in the States. They hold regular meetings, or 'chapters', which are usually themed.*

*André died in 1970 aged 94. I well recall his shock of white hair, pink complexion and extraordinary memory. He was proof enough that wine is good for you. He was the 'Churchill' of wine and food. Nobody has come near him since. A great man.*

JUST TWO OTHER '68S LAST TASTED IN THE 1980S

Ch Ducru-Beaucaillou sweet, chaptalised, short. *June 1982*; Ch Gruaud-Larose quite a good effort. Soft, flavoury but raw. *Oct 1983* ★

## III Form Club

*Sometimes written as 'Third', usually III, the club was founded just after World War Two by mainly London-based members of the wine trade. There are generally four wine tastings a year and an annual dinner at Brooks's Club. I joined in 1968. Happily the club thrives thanks to the introduction of younger members whose tasting abilities put one to shame!*

# 1969

Another unripe and acidic vintage due to very uneven weather conditions. But, allowing for the often sharp and omnipresent acidity, some quite flavoury wines in the early days. Despite this, rampant inflation and a spurious demand was beginning to push up the prices. Then 1970 came along.

If my memory, and notes, serve me right, this was the first of Edmund Penning-Rowsell's 'first growth' tastings, at which Ch Lafite, Latour, Margaux, Mouton-Rothschild, Haut-Brion, Ausone, Cheval Blanc and Pétrus were tasted and drunk at dinner ten years after each vintage. These were fascinating and salutary experiences; and fair, because all the bottles had been maturing undisturbed in Eddie's perfect stone-flagged cellar since first acquired. More about these tastings as the notes progess. See also box facing page.)

Ch Lafite Fragrant, charming, 'amusing' and flavoury, though piquant bottles in 1974 and 1976. Later, intriguing, some complexity but a bit thin. At ten years of age with the Penning-Rowsells; fragrant; iron and seawater, its medicinal nose reminding me of the smell of Dr Gilchrist's surgery in my Yorkshire boyhood days. Piquant, flavoury, intriguing but a bit thin. Almost a decade later, surprisingly attractive, with refreshing acidity. *Last tasted Oct 1988* ★★ *but no future.*

Ch Latour Starting in 1974, seven notes, every one incorporating the word 'raw'. At ten years of age, the deepest of the first growths, a big mouthful but dull. More recently, some semblance of fragrance but stalky, tannic – and raw. *Last tasted March 1989* ★

Ch Margaux Six notes in the 1970s. At Eddie's '10-year' tasting: very light, delicate nose but 'cold' and peppery; piquant, flavoury, short, flat yet acidic. A leap to Wagner's useful Margaux verticals, first in 1997: palish, fully mature; initial scent of tangerine but then weedy; better than expected though with teeth-gripping, citrus-like acidity. At the second, more fragrant; light style. Dry, lean, acidic. *Last tasted Nov 2000.*

Ch Mouton-Rothschild In cask, soft and forward. Untoward acidity not apparent. But though light and quite flavoury, an un-Mouton-like, rather dull character. At 10 years of age, very 'green', with decent length but with peppery and swingeing finish. Seemed more tolerable in the 1980s, fragrant though lean, dry and acidic. *Last tasted March 1989* ★

Ch Haut-Brion Raw and astringent in cask, May 1970. Its characteristic earthiness and some softness in the mid-1970s. At all Penning-Rowsell's dinners I always insisted on tasting the Haut-Brion first as it is so different in character to the first growth Médocs. It was showing quite well, with a good colour; sweet, iron-earthy nose; nice, firm flavour but, though not hard, austere. Just one other note: dry, flavoury, tolerable acidity but short. *Last tasted May 1985* ★

**Ch Ausone** I am not sure what happened to the Ausone at the 1979 tasting but of the four notes in my books it was bucking the trend: quite a good '69. Light, lean but flavoury. *Last tasted Feb 1993* ★★

**Ch Pétrus** Slow to evolve but in 1974 the most complete and rounded of the first growths. I remember sitting beside Christian Mouiex, enjoying a magnum and dipping into a huge tin of caviar at Frérick's extraordinary Pétrus evening in the Margrave's Palace in Munich. In the interval we were entertained by a dancing bear. Both Christian and I preferred the Beluga to his '69. *Last tasted April 1986* ★★

**Ch Cheval Blanc** Just one note, made at Karl-Heinz Wolf's Weinart tasting in Austria. We were informed that it was a very small crop (19hl/ha). Surprisingly high alcoholic content for the vintage: 13% (the 1962 was 11.5%, the 1960 12%). Curious nose, hard to get to grips with. Lean, acidic, sharp finish. Better with food. *Sept 1997.*

---

## Eddie Penning-Rowsell

*The 'dean' of Bordeaux wine writers, author, journalist, scholar, and owner of a remarkable private cellar accumulated over half a century. Eddie began his lifetime love of wine in 1937 as a sideline to his career as a book publisher, when his wife's employer, the BBC, gave her some non-vintage Beaujolais as a leaving present. This somewhat modest start progressed to a detailed, meticulous knowledge, particularly of the wines of Bordeaux – a region to which he became a regular visitor at vintage time. Eddie is best remembered by me for hosting, with his wife Meg, a series of annual 10-year-old first growth claret dinners (with Jancis Robinson and respective spouses) at his country house in Oxfordshire. The spouses were often far better tasters than the experts. The first dinner took place in 1969. Sadly, Eddie died in March 2002, just short of his 88th birthday.*

---

### SOME OTHER '69S LAST TASTED BETWEEN THE MID-1980S AND 1990S

**Ch Beychevelle** A cask sample was rushed to London by de Luze in February 1970 and offered to the trade at £228 a hogshead (approx. 25 dozen bottles). It was stalky but stylish. Rival offers were made much later yet still 'ex-cask' (August 1971). Not the usual elegance, a touch of coarseness and a flat, dry end noted in the mid-1970s; pleasant, but short and thin. 'Unknit' and high acidity noted in 1981. A similar magnum tasted 12 years later. *Last tasted May 1993* ★

**Ch Cantemerle** Pale; light; dry, thin, acidic. *April 1996.*

**Ch Cos d'Estournel** Dumb, then peppery cask samples. Offered at £204 per hogshead, and not worth the price. Some swingeing acidity noted in the mid-1970s and ill-advisedly served at a big dinner to celebrate Lord Pritchard's 70th birthday. He was a former chairman of Allied, then probably England's most important brewers. The wine was raw; on the other hand Derek Pritchard had some of that Lancashire rawness. Most recently: medicinal, thin and tinny. *Last tasted May 1992. Avoid.*

**Ch Ducru-Beaucaillou** Showing very well in cask, but the '69 piquancy and acidity tinkering with its development. Raw and lacking charm in the late 1970s. A jump of over 20 years: just 'good for a '69'. *Last tasted May 1992* ★★

**Ch Gruaud-Larose** Again, I have many notes from the 1970s: It started off well, but 'tart', 'scraggy', 'raw' noted, reaching its most damning in 1979. Yet a decade later it seemed to have got its second breath, surprisingly sweet, its acidity on hold. *Last tasted Nov 1989* ★★

**Ch La Mission Haut-Brion** Light weight for La Mission. Quite good bouquet but on the palate 'lean, mean and acidic'. *Last noted June 1990.*

### SOME OTHER TOLERABLE '69S LAST TASTED IN THE 1980S

**Ch Batailley**; **Ch Branaire-Ducru**; **Ch Dauzac**; **Ch La Gaffelière** (Naudes); **Ch Magdelaine**; **Ch Montrose**; **Ch Pichon-Lalande**; and **Ch La Tour Haut-Brion**.

# 1970—1979

In retrospect, this was one of the worst decades for red Bordeaux: overheated market, poor weather, the mid-1970s slump, and a major wine scandal.

Why was the market overheated? Inflation and a secondary, false market. In the UK there had been little change in the retail price index between the wars, and well into the 1950s. Inflation started in earnest in the 1960s and soared towards the end of that decade. By 1970, not only was inflation well into double digits, resulting in a flight from money into property and commodities, but, in the case of wine, specifically Bordeaux, it coincided with a big natural increase in demand and the emergence of 'wine investment' schemes. The 1970 vintage was seen as a perfect vehicle for the speculators and, even more happily, it was good enough and big enough to cope. But the new two-part market was bound to cause serious overheating. The wine trade was obliged to keep up the pace, and the Bordeaux *négociants*, with one or two honourable and cautious exceptions, added fuel to the fire. The 1971 vintage, as will be seen, was far smaller though of good quality. By then, prices had reached their peak. When the poor 1972 vintage came along at even higher prices, the market faltered, the oil price hike having devastating effects: secondary banks and the property and wine markets collapsed. This slump continued with two more poor vintages, '73 and '74. The net result was a disastrous fall in demand, and for over two years there was no cash flow in Bordeaux. Producers and *négociants* were in dire straits. And even the largest and most important stockholders, British and French, unloaded. Auctions provided a convenient outlet, and, during the mid-1970s, Christie's held their biggest-ever sales, for Bass Charrington, for Delor, for the Cordier châteaux and others. The quantities in these sales were vast, the prices low. For example, one auction included 2000 cases of 1970 Ch Mouton-Rothschild selling at an average price of £74 per case. Two one-hundred case lots fetched £54 and £55 per case respectively. It was a dream world for bargain hunters. Every lot found a buyer. Happily, Ch Lafite and Mouton, in unprecedented collaboration, timed *their* sale just as the market was about to recover. This was in 1976, the year that the *vin de garde* '75s came on to the market.

The wine scandal would not have so much as made a paragraph in the local press had it not been for the carelessness of the perpetrators, Cruse et Fils Frères, one of the most distinguished of the 'merchant-princely' houses. They were caught switching paperwork relating to some very ordinary red and white wine. Nothing to do with fine wine or major châteaux. There was some talk of arrogance in their initial dealing with the authorities, but in 1974 the end result was ignominy. They lost face and reputation, and a senior member of the Cruse family committed suicide. Coming in the middle of the Bordeaux slump, this affair sounded the death knell of the old-school *négociants* who had dominated the Bordeaux trade for so long. There was gradual recovery, and the next decade, as will be seen, took the Bordeaux market to greater, and more stable heights.

## Vintages at a Glance
**Outstanding** ★★★★★
None
**Very Good** ★★★★
1970, 1971, 1975
**Good** ★★★
1976 (v), 1978

## 1970 ★★★★

A highly important vintage in many ways: its fine quality (initially overrated) and its timing provided a jump start to the wine boom which was already hotting up during the dreary 1967, 1968 and 1969 vintages.

There was every reason to believe that it was going to be a highly satisfactory vintage, and as important in its way as the 'millennium' vintage three decades later; the weather conditions, despite ups and downs, were conducive to greatness: successful flowering, great heat and drought in July followed by an August in which coolness and hot sunny intervals were tempered by rain; then a long, hot, ripening period leading to a large and successful harvest which began in early October. Unusually, all the major grape varieties, Cabernet Sauvignon, Cabernet Franc, Merlot (usually the first) and Petit Verdot (usually the last) ripened fully around the same time. In theory splendid, but with such a big crop it was tricky to get all the grapes fermented concurrently and 'housed'. All the vats were full.

There was rampant inflation, and I well recall that it was around this time that the 'bright boys' jumped on the investment (speculation) band wagon. I was invited by more than one specious investment company to lend my name and advice. It has happened before and it will happen again. Invariably it all starts at the top of the market and is followed by a slump.

But what about the actual wines?

I do not wish to show off, but from the spring of 1971 to the present day, my little red books have been bursting with tasting notes of the '70 Bordeaux. I shall have to be more selective than ever. The following notes trace the development of the most important '70s over the past three decades.

**Ch Lafite** My first taste of the wine in cask almost never happened. It was in August (1971). I made the mistake of turning up without a prior appointment. I was not quite given the brush off but told to join a group and wait. The portly, immensely important, *maître de chai* then unlocked the doors and we all followed him, sheep like. As we shuffled past the first-year *barriques* I explained to the *maître* that I was only there to taste the 1970; to which he replied that if he gave *everybody* a taste of the wine, Lafite would not have anything left to sell! Being thus rebuffed, I continued to perambulate. At the top of the steps, alongside the dusty iron gates to the *cave privée*, the private cellar, our guide gave us an idea of the immense value of the dusty old bottles by telling us that one single bottle of the 1844 had recently been sold at auction for $5000. I tapped him on the shoulder and somewhat diffidently added that it had taken place in San Francisco that May, and that I was the auctioneer. It galvanised the old fellow for he then made a great fuss of me, even to the extent of giving me a booklet on the history of Lafite. Oh, and I was allowed to taste the '70. The wine was very impressive: deep; full of young fruit; rich, already showing some elegance.

Some 26 notes have helped put it into perspective. I hope the following summary will help.

The '70 Lafite was anything but a slow developer, its nose and taste opening up through the 1970s. By 1979 it was showing its paces at Dr Marvin Overton's grand Lafite tasting. My notes were as follows: (appearance) medium deep, rich, attractive, still undeveloped; (nose) intense, very fruity, exhibiting more of a Cabernet Sauvignon aroma (than its flanking vintages), evolving richly, biscuity; medium dry, fairly full-bodied, with 'ripeness and roundness'.

Wonderful development through the 1980s. In 1981 'really with the richness of a '34 or a '20'. Opulent bouquet. A soft velvety texture. 'Absolutely delicious', 'perfect now'. And so it went on. Not a blockbuster, but flavoury, savoury, cedary. All 5-star. By the mid-1980s, 'surprisingly drinkable', its great length, what the French call *persistence*, so admirable, also its aftertaste. I think that it was at its best around that time.

Half a dozen notes during the last decade. In 1996, a tasting event, fabulous even by Rodenstock's own standards, we tasted – blind – a whole 'flight' of great wines in magnums. It might seem a bit over the top but I preferred the 1870 from Glamis Castle to the 1970. The latter had a touch of sourness on the palate. Still tannic. Very distinctive. Later that autumn a very good bottle at the annual Wine Committee dinner at the Athenaeum (club not hotel). From a low-keyed start its bouquet opened up beautifully, as only Lafite can. Rich, but quite a bit of acidity. The following year, a most disappointing dried out jeroboam at a Bacchus Society Installation Dinner in Coral Gables; but this must have been bad cellaring, sometime in the past. Most recently, medium pale, fully mature, slightly orange-tinged; very mature, cheesy, with a medicinal Pauillac bouquet; surprisingly sweet, attractive, with very noticeable tannin and acidity. It needed food. *Last noted at a pre-auction tasting in Geneva. At best ★★★★, it is very much on the decline.*

**Ch Latour** An immensely impressive wine, and 30 notes which seem hardly to vary from tasting in cask as early as January 1971, and again in April 1972. Even making allowances for its understandably tannic grip, it refuses to budge. Tasted and drunk – more like chewed – in every conceivable circumstance. Like 'the Lion King' it visibly proclaims its power and importance. More recently, one can just detect a touch of maturity; its nose is almost impossible to describe because, unlike the Lion King, it hardly shows its head above the parapet. It needs days of decanting time and hours in the glass. Mouthfilling, concentrated, still very tannic. At the Rodenstock blind tasting of great wines, as with the Lafite, I preferred the 1870 – it was so much more drinkable. Perhaps one of the more bizarre combinations was its accompanying 'Sorgham molasses–roasted elk with sweet potatoes and huckleberry sauce', at Hal Lewis's Installation dinner, a Bacchus Society annual binge, in Memphis, Tennessee (September 1999). Most recently noted at Zachys/Christie's Millennium Wine Dinner in New York. *Last tasted May 1999* ★★★★★ *It will still be teasing some of you in 50 years' time.*

**Ch Margaux** A big wine but, unsurprisingly, much more approachable than the Latour. Not as many notes, and not tasted in cask. It was deep, rich, complex in 1974 and ploughed steadily through the 1980s, beefy for Margaux, and, in 1987, I wrote 'a bit four-square' and 'holding back'. Fragrant but not the captivating variety. The two most useful notes, and the most recent, once again made at Wagner's verticals, first in 1997, the second three years later. Almost identical notes. Now medium-deep, a lovely colour; nose low-keyed but harmonious, sweet, good fruit, slow to open up; medium sweetness and body, rich, good fruit, grip and balance, its sustaining tannins and acidity under control. *Last tasted Nov 2000* ★★★★ *Drink or keep.*

**Ch Mouton-Rothschild** No matter its popularity and the price it fetches (the autumn 2001 auction price was £920 a case; Haut-Brion £800, Lafite £820 and Latour an astonishing £2600), I think Mouton '70 is flawed. Read on. First tasted in 1974, fairly deep and solid but not excessively so, with both its nose and taste exhibiting a pleasant, sweet fruitiness. I first started to note a certain leanness and austerity in the late 1970s. Through the 1980s my notes include 'scraggy', 'swingeing upturned acidity', 'high-toned' (nose), 'a bit edgy', more acidity than tannin, 'a bit lean', though flesh and good fruit also commented on. My last four notes consistently remark upon this edge of acidity. Higher than usual volatility at a pre-sale tasting (1994); a raw, tannic *impériale* 'but good with chicken cassoulette' (1996); 'very fragrant, tea, cedar, holding well', but a touch of acidity (at the Hollywood Wine Society's Mouton tasting in 1998). Most recently, deep but something lacking, fairly fragrant, with Mouton intensity; on the lean side and a bit raw, though with zestful Mouton cassis. *Last noted at Hal Lewis's Installation Dinner in Memphis, Sept 1999* ★★★ *Fine if you want a flavoury drink but, unlike the Latour, I would not cellar it in the hope of it shrugging off that acidity.*

**Ch Haut-Brion** Far more consistent, ploughing a steady furrow, not excessively deep or exaggerated in any way. Overt is the word. Twenty notes from the mid-1970s. Fairly powerful and tannic initially, starting to show some maturity by the early 1980s, and consistently exhibiting its characteristic - and difficult to describe, without giving offence – smell and taste: 'gravelly', 'iodine', 'tobacco', caramel occasionally, 'smoky'. Among my recent notes a splendid bottle generously produced by my old friend Geoffrey de Luze, dining at Paveil in 1995. It had a fabulous colour and nose; fairly sweet, full-bodied, 'a smoky character but not tobacco', à *point*, drinking perfectly. Also, now looking fully mature, 'excellent' at the Khoury cellar pre-sale tasting (1997). Most recently; served by Neil McKendrick at his Bordeaux Club dinner: sweet, soft, fleshy but a suggestion of dried leaves and a tart finish. *Last tasted at Caius, Cambridge, June 1998* ★★★★ *My conclusion is that this was at its best in the mid-1980s.*

**Ch Ausone** Only six notes. Never very deep in colour, plummy rather than purple. Good 'legs' though, and its own strangely attractive scent, vanilla, strawberry, an earthy touch; singed, soft yet austere, lacking length. *Last tasted at a St-Émilion 1er grand cru classé event, June 1995, helped by the cheese* ★★★

**Ch Cheval Blanc** More than first rate. I recall it coming top in a blind tasting of '70s organised by a Danish wine journal in Bordeaux. I did manage to taste this in cask, April 1972. It clearly had a good future. 'Elegance' and perfect balance are dotted through my notes. *Not a blockbuster*. Most of my notes were made in the 1980s, only two recently. Showing well, perfectly evolved at a pre-sale tasting in New York (1997), and later the same year at Wolf's tasting in Austria: a lovely mellow colour; bouquet sweet, 'singed', fragrant, classic, great depth; medium sweetness and body. A good ripe flavour. Most recently, soft, rich, delicious aftertaste. Very good but 'past its perfect best'. *Last tasted at the Russian National Orchestra dinner, Spencer House, London, April 2002* ★★★★★

**Ch Pétrus** Fine, rich but not all that deep in April 1972, a glorious mouthful though. Quite quick to develop, soft, nicely balanced in 1976, then, in the early 1980s, an astonishing flavour of ripe mulberries, pretty high alcohol, impressive, lovely. More than just fleshy yet not fat. However a rather cool note in a Pétrus 'flight' in 1990: very sweet yet restrained and, I thought, lacking fruit. Only three notes in the 1990s. Most recently a double magnum, fairly full, chunky, austere and lacking in expected length. *Last tasted Sept 1995* ★★★ *Does this warrant its stratospheric price? (£7200 a case at Christie's in June 2001. For drinking I hope.)*

I HAVE AN IMMENSE NUMBER OF NOTES on other châteaux, so I shall have to be selective. My overall impression is that the quality of this vintage was much exaggerated and that its 'perfect balance' was not all that it seemed.

**Ch Batailley** Nine consistently good notes since 1974. Most recently: classic claret, excellent flavour and balance. *Last noted dining at the Jonathan Lyons', July 1998* ★★★ *Ready.*

**Ch Beauséjour-Bécot** Also reliable. Most recently, pleasantly coloured, mature; sweet, slightly jammy fruit; sweet, soft, chewy, very agreeable, yet still tannic. Last noted at the Hotel Pulitzer, Amsterdam after conducting a tasting. *April 1998* ★★★★

**Ch Belair** Beware of the Belairs and Bel-Airs. There is a minor Bel-Air in Pomerol, (Bel Air) Marquis d'Aligre (rarely seen) in the Médoc, and *this* Belair, a neighbour of Ch Ausone and at this period under the same family ownership. Having said all this, I have only one note: it was raw, woody and horrid. *At an important dinner in St-Émilion, June 1997.*

**Ch Beychevelle** Good wine. Rich, purple, stylish, tannic cask samples in 1971 and 1972. Well developed in the late 1970s, fully developed late 1988. Beginning to creak a little in 1997 though still attractive. Now fully evolved, perhaps lacking definition and character. *Last tasted Sept 1999* ★★★

**Ch Branaire-Ducru** Soft and chocolatey in cask. Something of a charmer but acidity creeping up. Recently a dull and dusty jeroboam, showing its age. *Last tasted at the Christie's Wine department Christmas dinner, Dec 1994* ★★ *Drink up. (We did.)*

**Ch Brane-Cantenac** Lots of flavour and good fruit but a strange though not unpleasant rustic, farmyard, overripe character. *Last tasted Feb 1993* ★★★

**Ch Calon-Ségur** Fragrant and fruity in cask. Evolving pleasantly through the 1980s. Most recently, a good mature colour, distinctly sweet, sound, drinking well. *Last noted at an office tasting at Christie's, June 1998* ★★★

**Ch Canon** Ten consistently good notes since 1974. Rich, well knit, well balanced, crisp, very attractive. Perhaps just a touch of coarseness. Harmonious nose, easy, pleasant, fully developed. *Last noted dining at Ségla with David Orr, also president of Canon, Sept 1998* ★★★★ *At its best now.*

**Ch Cantemerle** The 1970 weight and style did not suit this former charmer. Untypically austere but not bad. *Last tasted Feb 1993* ★★ *I do not envisage much improvement.*

**Ch Cantenac-Brown** From start to not yet finished. A pleasant if inelegant wine. *Last tasted Feb 1993* ★★★

**Ch Chasse-Spleen** I normally admire this well run château. But, though good, unusually severe, tough and tannic in its youth. A leap of 25 years and a double magnum showing its age, dry, crumbling a bit. To be hard on it, it demonstrated that even the best *bourgeois* Médoc only gets older, not necessarily better. *Last noted at lunch at the château, March 2001* ★

**Ch Carbonnieux** Best when young and fresh, the '70 more serious but, frankly not all that good. *Last noted dining at the château, Feb 1993* ★

**Dom de Chevalier** Very good wine. My notes mainly between 1974 and 1986. Fairly deep ruby; rich, spicy fragrance and flavour. Most recently, tasted blind, still deep but mature; classy and classic nose which arose gracefully, good texture, length, fruit. My top mark in a select range of 1970s. *Last tasted Sept 1994* ★★★★

**Ch Cissac** A wine for drinking not for collecting. I have tasted a very wide range of vintages, all decent working wines, and have 14 notes of the '70, so I really ought to mention it. But the '70 was not particularly good. Presented by Louis Vialard and showing well at a Cissac tasting for the Prince of Wales's Trust at Sherborne in Dorset. *Most recently at a Cissac vertical at the Savoy Hotel, April 1996* ★★★

**Cos d'Estournel** Bruno Prats' first vintage at Cos. A mass of notes, all good, though tannin very much in evidence; several in the 1990s, most detailed at a Cos Master Class at Christie's: lovely rich colour; serenely mature bouquet, 'candlewax'; despite its self-evident tannin, gentle, lovely, crisp and no sign of decline. Most recently, an *impériale*, rich, fairly complex, nice weight, drinking well and 'as good as it will ever be'. *Last tasted at a Saintsbury Club dinner, Oct 2000* ★★★★

**Ch Croizet-Bages** Crisp and fruity. *Last tasted Feb 1993* ★★★

**Ch Ducru-Beaucaillou** Leaving aside Latour, I rate Ducru and Cheval Blanc as the best of the '70s. Over two dozen notes from a classic, concentrated cask sample in April 1972. Slow to develop but by the mid-1980s complete, balanced, 'well clothed', 'magnificent', 'almost of Latour weight and class'. Extended finish. 'Perfect.' Ten notes over the last decade. The most recent include a superb, sweet nosed, harmonious *impériale*; classic St-Julien weight and taste (Coral Gables, 1997), perfect flavour and balance but, as an afterthought, drying out (at Jean Ramet's in Bordeaux, 1998). Most recently, a very good bottle, 'correct – but not with local spicy foods'. *Last tasted, somewhat bizarrely, 'Rollin' on the River' on board the Memphis Queen III, Sept 1999. At best* ★★★★★

**Ch Duhart-Milon** Fruity but raw and acidic. *March 1992* ★

**Ch L'Évangile** Rich, chewy, chunky. Lacks charm. *Last tasted May 1991* ★★ *Might have opened up.*

**Ch Figeac** An excellent 1970. At Figeac, the *cépage* mix is more or less equally divided between Merlot, Cabernet Franc, and, unusually in St-Émilion, Cabernet Sauvignon. Figeac featured pretty prominently in my notes in the mid-1970s. It almost made my equal top marks at the 'great Danes' tasting of '70s and I noted its glorious, uplifting fragrance and taste throughout the 1980s. An amalgam of conflicts, delicacy and rip-roaring fruit, vigorous, ripe tannins. Beginning to show signs of gentle decline at Gidleigh Park in Devon in 1994, yet the following year almost rumbustious, very earthy, touch of iron and supporting tannin. *Last tasted June 1995* ★★★★★

**Ch La Fleur** One of my highest marks at Rodenstock's 32-vintage La Fleur tasting. Amazingly fresh and fragrant for a 28-year old; full-bodied, concentrated fruit, very impressive. But not a food wine – too powerful. Incidentally, no new wood used. *Sept 1998* ★★★★★

**Ch La Fleur-Pétrus** A serious wine. Rich, ripe, noticeable acidity in the early 1980s when I first tasted it; also inimitable Pomerol texture. On the last two occasions a touch of malt or caramel on the nose which then opened up spicily. A fairly sweet, fleshy, chunky mouthful, excellent with venison. *Last tasted June 1995* ★★★★

**Les Forts de Latour** Delicious, spicy. A good mouthful. *Last tasted Nov 1990* ★★★

**Clos Fourtet** A rather dreary period. Not a good '70. Acidic. Then four Berry Bros bottles: though showing its age, drinking well. *Last noted, dining with Jean and Yuri Galitzine at Holywell Hall, July 1996. For the weekend* ★★★★★, *for the wine* ★★

**Ch La Gaffelière** Combining a certain rustic exuberance and gutsy fruits charm, often noticeably highish acidity. A decent flavoury mouthfiller. Drinking well but now showing some age. *Last tasted June 1995* ★★★ *just. Will not improve.*

**Ch Giscours** A most un-Margaux-like wine. No feminine charm or delicacy, more of a rugger player. Nonetheless, very impressive. Intensely deep from the start. Hefty, packed with fruit, perhaps compressed is a better word. Yet fragrant. Tasted on 20 occasions, the last an oxidised bottle at home. In any case beginning to show its age, good crisp fruit jousting with now raw tannin (1998), yet a remarkably youthful looking bottle with good fruit, its nose beautifully open and fragrant after an hour in the glass; sweet, full, attractive, a touch of tar and quite a bite, at Louis Hughes' first Bordeaux Club dinner at the Saville Club in London. Two months later, still astonishingly opaque, concentrated, dry, full, peppery, tannic. I added 'a great '70'. *Last tasted March 2001, the sort of wine I am impressed by but do not much like. If you do, then* ★★★★★

**Ch Gloria** The creation of Henri Martin. At its best in the 1980s. Now though pleasantly mellow and flavoury, very dry on the finish. *Last tasted Jan 1994* ★★★

**Ch Grand-Puy-Lacoste** Another serious wine, this time from Pauillac. Concentrated in cask and slow to mature, I have some 20 notes monitoring its progress. Yet though a devotee, I have been disappointed with the '70. It tried to 'lift off' in the 1980s but it remained obstinately grounded by its tannin. On the last four occasions, at my own dinner parties and at a masterclass at Christie's, it was almost port-like and well past its best, cracking up in the glass, leaving it high and dry. Some bottles quite good. I prefer the younger vintages. *Last tasted April 1999. Sadly* ★★

**Ch Gruaud-Larose** Literally dozens of notes, mainly from the mid-1970s to the late 1980s. As usual, full of chunky fruit, like Oxford marmalade, yet unrelentingly tannic, some even tart. Yet when last encountered, sweet, still full of fruit and drinking well. *With tournedos of beef at a Saintsbury Club dinner, April 1999. At best* ★★★

**Ch Haut-Bailly** A good, earthy Graves cask sample. But I really became hooked in 1978: it was so fragrant and ripe, soft and well-balanced. Not less than delicious since. A lovely mature colour, soft, harmonious bouquet and flavour. Spicy

finish. Drinking well. *Last noted at a pre-sale dinner at Christie's, June 1997* ★★★★

**Ch Haut-Batailley** A slow developer and now fully fledged, mature-looking, rich bouquet and good depth. *Last tasted Feb 1993* ★★★★

**Ch Larcis-Ducasse** Tasted blind dining at the château. Mature, clearly a good vintage though the quite harmonious and fully evolved nose was not very distinctive. Better on the palate. Nice weight, good flavour. Not a great '70 but a good drink. *April 2000* ★★★

**Ch Lascombes** Not my favourite château but five good notes, rich, fleshy (up to 1986). Touch of coarseness noted in 1994 but showing quite well at a pre-sale tasting: deep; fragrant; ripe, full-bodied, good fruit, pretty well-balanced. *Last noted Sept 2001. At best* ★★★

**Ch Léoville-Barton** Still unready and untypically 'chunky' when I first tasted it in 1979. Four unsatisfactory notes in the 1980s and bottle variation, some soft, some with high acidity in 1991. Most recently, a magnum that, despite its good mature appearance, nose of prune, figs and walnuts; quite good fruit and texture, was lean and, I added, 'about to fall apart'. *Not a charmer. Last noted dining in Austria, April 1999* ★★

**Ch Léoville-Las-Cases** An austere cask sample but soon opened up. Fifteen well spread notes, all good. A gentlemanly classic, marvellous fruit, impressive yet despite its flesh, still tannic. Now mature; typical cedary nose, very good balance and flavour. *Last noted dining with my old Christie's boss Guy Hannen, July 1996* ★★★★

**Ch Léoville-Poyferré** I seem to have only two notes, but recent. A strange, chocolatey, poor bottle in 1993 and a fairly attractive bottle with muffled cedary nose, taut, dry and rather acidic finish. *Last tasted at lunch in New York, Feb 1997. At best* ★★ *Give it a miss.*

**Ch Lynch-Bages** Opaque, concentrated Cabernet, very flavoury in cask, its usual fairly cassis character developing quite quickly, cinnamon, fruit and tannin – delicious in the late 1970s, and on into the 1980s. Half a dozen consistently good notes through the 1990s including at a blind tasting of '70s *impériales*. Thought to be Mouton-Rothschild! Savoury, flavoury, delicious. *Last tasted in Memphis, Sept 1999* ★★★★

**Ch Magdelaine** Lovely colour; fabulous bouquet; sweet, delicious. *Feb 1993* ★★★★

**Ch La Mission Haut-Brion** Like Mouton, flawed: too acidic. It started with a bottle: opaque, highly concentrated, magnificent (April 1972) and continued to dazzle and impress but it was in 1978 that I noted a 'raw finish' with a question mark. In the next decade, seven notes made in a variety of circumstances all referring to what I put down as high volatile acidity. Most recently, still deep ruby; fruity but 'peppery' and acidic nose; dry, full, lively and lusty. Interesting but unbalanced. *Last tasted dining in Chelsea, July 1994* ★★

**Ch Montrose** The sort of vintage to suit Montrose. Rather like La Mission, intensely deep and packed with fruit and tannin. 'Magnificent but too heavy for (a City) lunch' in 1980! Massive, Latour-like, rich, mouthfilling but tough. Five recent notes: exciting, rich, glorious flavour but still very tannic. 'Good but not great' a jeroboam in 1997. High toned, raw tannic finish. *Last tasted at a Bordeaux Club dinner in June 1998* ★★(★★) *I suppose it will come round, eventually.*

**Ch Mouton-Baron-Philippe** Fifteen notes. Once a charmer, not always a charmer. Probably at its modest zenith in the early 1980s: 'Drinking well.' Most recently, drying out. *Last noted Sept 1997* ★★

**Ch Marquis d'Alesme-Becker** A couple of peppery, Dutch-bottled examples, and two château-bottled, one in Barbados, most recently in Geneva. Rarely seen in England and I can see why. *Last tasted May 1992* ★

**Ch Palmer** A very good '70 and a top vintage for this château. Although not tasted until 1979, I have masses of notes since – nearly 20 in the last decade. They are so consistent that there is no point in repeating even a fraction of the comments. At a Palmer dinner we were given the *cépage* mix – starting with Cabernet Sauvignon at 30.5%. Most unusually the Merlot was higher, but either the Cabernet Franc and Petit Verdot numbers did not add up or I got the figures down wrong. Though now showing some maturity it is a lovely, rich, well-balanced wine and drinking superbly. *Last noted at lunch with the Detroit Commanderie de Bordeaux at the château, May 2001* ★★★★★

**Ch Pape-Clément** Several notes in the 1970s, showing well in the early 1980s. *Last noted lunching al fresco, July 1994* ★★ *Still very tannic.*

**Ch Pavie** Never a big '70 but 'drinking perfectly'. *Last tasted at a post-auction supper in New York, March 1997* ★★★

**Ch Pichon-Baron** Five mainly critical notes. Disappointing. *Last noted Feb 1993.*

**Ch Pichon-Lalande** Delicious cask sample in 1972 and quite a few good notes since. Certainly very flavoury, showing at its best in the mid- to late 1980s. A jeroboam in 1994 with a rich, tangy bouquet but with strange tarry taste. More recently, a bottle showing its age (like me). Very drinkable. *Last tasted at a lunch given by Decanter magazine to celebrate my 20th anniversary as a columnist and my 70th birthday, May 1997* ★★★

**Ch Pontet-Canet** Bottled in Bordeaux by Cruse, and not a good wine. Stalky, lacking character. Variable. Uninspiring. *Last tasted Feb 1993. Avoid.*

**Ch Rausan-Ségla** A pretty good wine. Firm, fleshy, good fruit. Still tannic. *Last tasted dining at the château, Sept 1998* ★★★

**Ch de Sales** Delicious. Light and easy for a '70. *Last tasted March 1991* ★★ *Drink up.*

**Ch St-Pierre-Sevaistre** I have several notes in the mid-1970s to mid-1980s, and, to my surprise, they read 'lovely, rich, biscuity', 'softness, ripeness, flesh, perfect now' (1985). Most recently, chewy, full of fruit, still tannic, a squeeze of tangerine and drinking well. *Last tasted, with pheasant, at the 25th anniversary of the Northampton Branch of the IWFS at one of England's top country house hotels, Hambleton Hall, Nov 1995* ★★★★ *Worth looking out for.*

**Ch Talbot** Always very popular but I can never quite understand why. Clearly a richly rustic, hen-coop, gentleman farmer's claret, also popular with British Airways First Class passengers. Chunky, usually leaner and more masculine than Gruaud. A ripe though borderline '70. Most recently: 'deep; farmyard, dry finish' necessarily briefly noted, the 17th of 20 wines at 'The Imperial Dinner' in Pokolbin, New South Wales. The nearest thing to a Hunter Valley 'sweaty saddle' Shiraz. *Last tasted Sept 2000* ★★★

**Ch La Tour Haut-Brion** Many notes in tandem with La Mission; but very odd, with a nose like the singed top of rice pudding and, most recently, like a wet dog. *Last tasted Feb 1993. On balance I prefer rice pudding to wet dogs.*

**Ch Trotanoy** First noted in 1977 when it was opaque, mouthfilling, rich, and had length. Then there was a jump of nearly 20 years. Not distinctive but its bouquet faultless and palate perfection. Velvety. Very fleshy. *Last tasted dining with N K Yong in Singapore, Jan 1998* ★★★★(★)

Of the very many '70s showing well in the mid- to late 1980s Ch L'Angélus *Oct 1985* ★★★★; **Ch d'Angludet** *March 1986* ★★★; and **Ch Latour-à-Pomerol** deep, rich, tannic. *April 1987* ★★★(★)

Earlier notes, but good potential **Ch Canon-La-Gaffelière**; **Ch La Conseillante**; **Ch Clerc-Milon**; **Ch Citran**; **Ch Coufran**; **Clos René**; **Ch La Louvière**; and **Ch Siran**.

# 1971 ★★★★

A relatively small but good quality, very high priced vintage. Coming at the top of the overheated market, it was overrated by the Bordelais and has been underrated by the British. Many wines have turned out better than the '70s. The weather conditions appeared to favour producers on the Right Bank, especially Pomerol, and in the Graves. Some top growth Médocs have turned out poorly, yet they were the most expensive wines of the period.

**Ch Lafite** *Not a grand vin.* Weak-rimmed, lacking fruit and substance noted in its early days, yet managed to scrape up a *soupçon* of elegance and fragrance in the early 1980s. Described as 'grubby', 'over the hill', 'living dangerously', but also 'lean but flavoury'. Frankly, 20 not very complimentary notes. Most recently, a tart bottle at Brooks's, a strange nose, feeble but pleasant enough. Fortunately we had something better to follow. *Last tasted June 1996* ★

**Ch Latour** Again, 20 notes. Totally different in weight and style to its first-growth Pauillac neighbours. More substance, better balanced but simply not inspiring. Raw and dumb in cask, struggling to open up in the 1980s, a bit four-square and unyielding. Half a dozen notes in the last decade, the most unexpected in 1984 sandwiched between an 1892 Perrier Jouët (with *foie gras*) and Belle Époque rosé '85 (*tarte tatin aux poires*) at the Maison Belle Époque in Épernay. Later a fragrant, crisp but austere *impériale*, an understated 'good' '71 but, most recently, upstaged by both Ausone and Cheval Blanc. Tannic. Astringent. *Last tasted Sept 1999* ★★★? *I really can't make it out.*

**Ch Margaux** Distinctly more attractive than Lafite or Latour. Though not as many notes, well covered from the mid-1970s and a decade later displaying considerable charm with a delicate, fragrant bouquet and crisp fruit and, though fully mature-looking, almost identical comments at a dinner in 1996. The following year, at the first of Wagner's verticals,

---

### Joseph Berkmann

*Joseph Berkmann was responsible for organising a series of excellent wine dinners – the first, to my knowledge, ever to feature a wide range of vintages of one wine over a meal. Berkmann (then a notable London restaurateur) started his events in 1971: 'an English Dinner with a selection of 1945 clarets', which included all the first growths. Subsequently, a wide range of vintages of a single château would be served – I think I attended the entire series which consisted of: Ch Mouton-Rothschild, 12 vintages from 1893 to 1955 (in 1972); Ch Latour, 14 vintages from 1917 to 1962 (in 1973); Ch Haut-Brion and Ch La Mission Haut-Brion (1974). Each one was attended by the owner of the château in question. Fellow guests included Harry Waugh, Edmund Penning-Rowsell, Quentin Crewe and other leading English wine writers and tasters. Joe Berkmann is now a very active wine importer.*

sweet, flavoury, refreshing, some charm but just misses. Now fully mature-looking with a ruddy amber colour and a nowhere-to-go orange rim. Initially an attractive 'leaf mould' nose which opened up richly. Fairly sweet, nice weight and shape, lean yet fleshy. *Last tasted Nov 2000* ★★★ *No need to wait.*

**Ch Mouton-Rothschild** Concentrated fruit in 1974; well constituted, but 'raw' and 'lean' interspersing 'easy', 'attractive', and fully evolved bouquet by the end of the 1980s. Only one note since. Colour less deep but good, fully mature. Fragrant. Full of flavour and surprisingly rich, chunky fruit and good length. *Last tasted Nov 1990* ★★★★ *Worth keeping an eye on.*

**Ch Haut-Brion** Good wine. Showing better and better, particularly good note in 1990 'soft, fleshy, elegant'. The following year a lovely double magnum, silky 'perfect now' but on the verge of drying out a little. Most recently, a rich, meaty, gravelly, bottle-age bouquet; sweet, 'elegant', distinctive, good length. *Last noted at a pre-sale tasting in London, Jan 1999* ★★★★

**Ch Ausone** Tasted from the cask, 15 days after racking in February 1972. A fascinating, clove-like flavour. Deeper in colour than the '70, nice texture, silky tannins (mid 1980s). Bouquet evolved by 1990 and its distinctive, curious, singed leaf taste, asserting itself. Most recently a fairly intense colour with velvety sheen; rich, unmistakable bouquet. Fairly sweet, powerful, 'burnt brown paper' taste but drinking well. *Last tasted dining in Memphis, Sept 1999* ★★★★ *Probably at peak.*

**Ch Cheval Blanc** For me, this is the star wine of the vintage, from a fragrant cask sample and effortless trajectory through the 1980s. 'Lovely flavour and texture', perfect balance, seemingly effortless development. Ten notes, tasted in Munich, Luzern, and at Wolf's vertical in Austria, a jeroboam; yet again in Memphis; memorably dining at the Kröne in Assmannshausen on the Rhine in the company of two brilliant and eccentric winemakers, August Kesseler (from the Rheingau) and Jim Clendenen (of Au Bon Climat in California). Every note virtually identical: sweet, fragrant, elegant, stylish, lovely. Most recently, my top wine at a Cheval Blanc dinner (including '47, '59, '61, '64 and '70) for the Russian National Orchestra. *Last noted at Spencer House, London, April 2002* ★★★★★

**Ch Pétrus** Rich, full-bodied (13.5% alcohol), laden with tannin in cask. My best notes in the mid-1980s, its power and tannin tamed by its velvety Pomerol texture and flesh. More restrained in the nose, more meaty than the Cheval Blanc, which after all is just a stone's throw away. Impressive, fragrant but more of a blunt instrument. *Last tasted at the Josey cellar pre-sale tasting, New York, Nov 1990. At best* ★★★★

**Ch Beauséjour-Bécot** Funny how the names of some wines ring a bell, this one conjuring up old Monsieur Bécot, a conscientious winemaker who survived a tussle with the local wine authorities. A long story, long since ended. A fleshy wine, quite substantial. Most recently: 'sweet, very distinctive and attractive, nice flavour and grip'. One of my top marks at a *1er grand cru* tasting. *Last noted June 1997* ★★★★

**Ch Beychevelle** Good notes. Elegant, well rounded. Fully mature. *Last tasted May 1993* ★★★

**Ch Calon-Ségur** Quite attractive but, when last noted at a Saintsbury Club dinner, it had a brown-sugary nose; mild flavoured, rather dull. *An unknown English bottling, April 1996* ★★

**Ch Cos d'Estournel** Not a brilliant '71. From its early days lean but easy. Eight notes, including a fragrant *impériale* bought at Christie's which, mercifully, went well with food (1994). More recently, again better nose than palate. Lean and drying out. *Last tasted Sept 1997* ★★

**Ch L'Église-Clinet** Rich, touch of toffee; sweet, high extract, impressive. *March 2001* ★★★★

**Ch La Fleur** Just two recent notes: youthfully tinged; fabulous bouquet; rich, lissome and lovely, well sustained by its tannin and acidity. *Last noted at Christie's tasting in the American Club, Tokyo, Nov 1999* ★★★★★

**Ch Gruaud-Larose** I have many notes. The customary chunky fruit was apparent in the early 1970s, although it appeared leaner and more sinewy. Rather tannic but quite stylish. *Last tasted Sept 1993* ★★★

**Ch Kirwan** Two notes, not much more than ordinary in 1976. Recently an *impériale* not quite living up to its size. Quite good fruit though a bit astringent. *Last tasted Sept 1994* ★★

**Ch Lascombes** Sweet, attractive nose; silky/leathery tannic texture, good length. *At a pre-sale tasting, Sept 2001* ★★★

**Ch Léoville-Las-Cases** Slow to evolve. Good flavour and texture. *Last tasted March 1992* ★★★

**Ch Palmer** Upstaged by the magnificent '70 and struggling initially. It needed time and was showing well at a Palmer vertical at Christie's: colour of gnarled mahogany; harmonious nose that opened up fragrantly; curiously sweet entry leading to a very dry finish. Good fruit, texture, lean but charming. *Last tasted July 1994* ★★★★

**Ch Pichon-Lalande** Early maturing. Total contrast in style to Baron. Open knit, fully mature, still very attractive. *Last tasted Jan 1998* ★★★

**Ch Siran** Feeble colour; light but sweet nose and taste. *Last tasted Oct 1993* ★★ *Drink up.*

**Ch Trotanoy** Eight notes, from a rich stylish mouthful in the mid-1970s and, a decade later, seeming almost to outdo Pétrus in its rich, velvety appeal. A further ten years on, combining richness and elegance. Now mature-looking; lovely nose, perfect harmony, flavour, balance. *Last noted at a splendid wine dinner with Melina (an exquisite cook) and N K Yong, in Singapore, Jan 1998* ★★★★★

A WIDE RANGE OF MAJOR '71S, ALL LAST NOTED IN NOVEMBER 1990

**Ch Brane-Cantenac** To my surprise, lovely scent; silky, gentle, fragrant ★★★

**Ch Branaire-Ducru** Now fully mature. Very distinctive bouquet; richly flavoured ★★★

**Ch Canon** Lovely wine. Fragrant, sinewy for Canon, lively and interesting ★★★★

**Ch Cantemerle** The sort of vintage that suits Cantemerle. Even elegant in cask. Delicious fragrance, lovely flavour, well clad. Almost exotic ★★★ *Should be at peak now.*

**Ch Certan-de-May** Made at L'Évangile. One of these maltily rich Pomerols. Certainly lots of fruit and flesh. For those who like the style ★★★★

**Dom de Chevalier** Now fully evolved yet still with tannic sustenance ★★★

**Ch La Dominique** Rich, silky, tannic ★★★★

**Ch Ducru-Beaucaillou** Firm, flavoury, easy and elegant in its youth, but later found a bit overripe, with raw finish ★★?

**Ch L'Enclos** Another successful Pomerol. Sweet, rich ★★★★

**Ch L'Évangile** And another, this one very tannic ★★★(★)

**Ch Figeac** One of Thierry Manoncourt's favourite wines. Typically exuberant. Best, I think, in the early 1980s. But fun ★★★★ *Drink up.*

**Ch La Fleur-Pétrus** Sometimes Pomerols are better in the mouth than on the nose (if you see what I mean). Over a 12-year span, rich, appealing and lots of grip ★★★★

**Les Forts de Latour** Lacking, of course, the *gravitas* of the *grand vin* but a decent wine. A bit lean ★★★

**Ch Grand-Puy-Lacoste** Stylish, firm, flavoury from the late 1970s. Then a gap of ten years. Not much change. Crisp, lean, good ★★★(★)

**Ch La Grave Trigant-de-Boisset** Now known simply as Ch La Grave. Bought by Moueix in 1971. Not an easy year. The vines badly damaged by hail. Taking a risk, he kept the tainted wine in cask for three years. When last tasted, the bouquet and taste quite sensational ★★★★★

**Ch Haut-Bailly** Very good indeed. Developing steadily and almost harmonious. A rich, earthy Graves, drinking well. Should be perfect now ★★★★

**Ch La Lagune** Different. Neither Médoc nor Graves (whose soil it shares). Touch of coarseness ★★

**Ch Latour-à-Pomerol** Fragrant, rich, attractive ★★★★

**Ch Magdelaine** Developed well. Rich. I liked it ★★★

**Ch Malescot-St-Exupéry** Better nose than palate. Flavoury but will more bottle age smooth its rough edges? ★★?

**Ch La Mission Haut-Brion** Much better than the '70: fragrance, harmony, length. Lovely ★★★★

**Ch Montrose** Many notes. Relatively lean and rather disappointing ★★

**Ch Pape-Clément** Demonstrating the superiority of '71 Graves over Médocs. Now mature, distinctive ★★★★

**Ch Pavie** Many notes. More elegant than the '70 ★★★

**Ch Pichon-Baron** Piquant fruit, assertive, very tannic ★★

**Ch Talbot** Somewhat unenthusiastic notes in the 1970s. 'Dry, rather raw', 'good with food' in 1983 and 1984. Lovely colour, lean but flavoury ★★★

**Ch La Tour Haut-Brion** An improvement on the '70. Fragrant, dry and lean ★★★

**Vieux Ch Certan** What can you expect in a copybook Pomerol vintage, but a delicious example? Rich but a lighter style than some of the big guns. Silky tannin ★★★★

SOME OTHER '71S SHOWING WELL IN THE MID- TO LATE 1980S **Ch Batailley** very drinkable, lacking finesse ★★; **Ch La Gaffelière** soft and delicious ★★★; **Ch Giscours** not unlike the '70, a pretty massive mouthful. Rich, fleshy, tannic. ★★★★; **Ch Haut-Batailley** elegant. Beautifully balanced ★★★★; **Ch Langoa-Barton** a charmer ★★★; **Ch Léoville-Barton** fragrant, nice weight. Class and style ★★★★; **Ch Lynch-Bages** rich, flavoury but relatively insubstantial ★★; and **Ch Rausan-Ségla** I am tempted to use the word 'specious', but silkily delicious. Hint of acidity ★★

## 1972

Cataclysmic. Known to be a poor vintage yet prices were out of all proportion. In combination with the other problems already described, it broke the market. Cold spring, late flowering, some July warmth followed by a miserably cold and wet August, although September and October were reasonably fine. It was one of the latest vintages on record, resulting in a fairly large crop of immature grapes of uneven quality. Avoid.

**Ch Lafite** Not as totally deficient as '63s, '65s or '68s, an insubstantial early developer. By dint of some selection, some quite fragrant wine emerged but not enough to warrant its *grand vin* description. Drinkable. *Last tasted June 1990* ★

**Ch Latour** Hardly living up to its reputation of making a tolerably good wine in a poor year. 'Dry, short, undistinguished.' *Last tasted March 1989.*

**Ch Margaux** It at least tried. Quite impressively deep in its youth, attractive though bitter tannins. A pretty good double magnum in 1983, fragrant bouquet, somewhat hard on the palate. Two notes at the Wagner verticals, the first in 1997, substandard: lean, twisted, yet drinkable. Palish, weak-rimmed; nose and flavour better than expected. Some sweetness, a dash of fruit, tolerable acidity. *Last tasted Nov 2000* ★★ *(just).*

**Ch Mouton-Rothschild** Wishy-washy colour; a spurt of characteristic blackcurrant; unbalanced. Like an ugly sister danced by Robert Helpmann. *Last tasted March 1989* ★

**Ch Haut-Brion** Very pale. Losing its battle with unripe almost green grapes. *Just one note: Aug 1985.*

**Ch Ausone** Also encountered only once, at Lloyd Flatt's vertical. Not bad nose, light, highish acidity. *Oct 1987.*

**Ch Cheval Blanc** Prettily coloured, light, pleasant in 1975. Just over 20 years later, an orange-rimmed magnum, unknit, fungi, its nose and taste reminding me of a superannuated 'dried-leaves' Ausone. *Last noted at Wolf's vertical, Sept 1997.*

**Ch Pétrus** Several notes. Frankly poor. *Last tasted April 1987.*

FEW '72S TASTED IN THE 1990S They include **Ch Beychevelle** ten notes. Chaptalised, raw – but vestiges of Beychevelle fragrance and charm. *May 1993* ★; **Ch Cantemerle** surprisingly fragrant and fruity in cask. Prettily-coloured and still lively looking. Dry, a bit raw. *April 1996* ★; and **Ch Gruaud-Larose** two notes: quite good fruit but short in 1975. Not much difference: a *mélange* of fruit and raw sourness. *Sept 1993.*

SOME OTHER '72S TASTED IN THE MID- TO LATE 1980S **Ch Calon-Ségur** not as bad as it looked. Dry, light, piquant. *May 1986*; **Ch Ducru-Beaucaillou** one of the better '72s. Quite fragrant and flavoury. A 'tinny' finish. *May 1987* ★★; **Ch La Lagune** not bad fruit in its early years. Some sweetness let down by rasping finish. *Sept 1989*; **Ch Montrose** not bad. Fragrant, dry, lean, raw. *Oct 1985*; **Ch Palmer** tolerably drinkable up to its eighth year. Nose 'browned off' in several senses. *Oct 1984*; **Ch Talbot** a tolerable '72. Dry, light, some fruitiness. *March 1982*; and **Ch La Tour-Haut-Brion** preferred to La Mission. Quite attractive. *Nov 1986* ★★

## 1973 ★★

The producers, the châteaux proprietors, must have lost heavily, for although the growing season was quite good – in fact a fine summer and ripening period with a wet July intermission – there was neither the incentive, nor cash, to work hard in the vineyards let alone green prune. This resulted in an abundant crop of wines that were not bad but could have been better; and by the spring of 1974, there was no market. Instead of blaming the growers, we should sympathise.

I find I have a fairly large number of notes, mostly made in the late 1970s to early 1980s. Those noted in the 1990s follow. **Ch Lafite** Like quite a lot of '73s, Lafite was quite attractive in its early days, particularly its (chaptalised) bouquet. The adjective 'fragrant' appears in all my notes made in the 1980s, 'delicious', 'perfect light luncheon wine' and so forth. However, by the mid-1990s, distinctly on its way out. A magnum (1994) had a smell that reminded me of a public swimming pool, seaweed and iron; very dry with its tinny Cabernet taste unassisted by strains of fishiness, oysters. Most recently pale; faded nose; no more to come. 'Needs drinking.' *Last noted at a pre-sale tasting in 1996* ★

**Ch Latour** Deep, 'plummy coloured' and surprisingly 'charming' for a youthful Latour and at its best in the early 1980s, its lack of fruit, a touch of rawness and stalkiness, and shortness, becoming more noticeable in the 1980s. My most recent note was made over a decade ago: 'lacking fruit but light and easy for Latour'. *Last tasted Dec 1990* ★★

**Ch Margaux** Only three notes. Remarkably forward by the late 1970s, medium pale; fragrant and charming on nose and palate. At Penning-Rowsell's '10-year' tasting in 1993, the Margaux fragrance its best feature, otherwise lacking. It was not in Wagner's first vertical. In the second it was a bit odd on the nose, James Suckling describing it as 'gravy'. Better on the palate. 'Sweet, light, acidic, drinkable'. *Last tasted Nov 2000* ★

**Ch Mouton-Rothschild** No recent note but in 1977 light, 'refined' nose, quite nice, rather acidic. What was predictable was its unpredictability. At ten years of age, a surprisingly low-keyed nose, tinny acidity. Easy going at Flatt's tasting (1986). Most recently, fully evolved, chaptalised nose; lightish, easy. Short. *Last tasted March 1989* ★

**Ch Haut-Brion** A paucity of notes. It was the second best of the first growths line up in 1983. More recently, fuller-bodied than expected, soft yet assertive 'iron-tobacco' Graves tasting, good texture and aftertaste. *Last tasted July 1987, then* ★★★

**Ch Ausone** Only one note, at Flatt's Ausone tasting. Palish, already brown-tinged; not bad bouquet; overall dry and a bit acidic. *Last tasted Oct 1987* ★

**Ch Cheval Blanc** Quite a good '73. Showing well in the mid-1980s, soft, gentle, flavoury. A good magnum at the château in 1986 and another at Wolf's vertical in Austria. Orange-tinged, rich 'legs'; whiff of fresh mushrooms, medicinal nose; better on the palate, easier to drink than the '72 and the '74 but one-dimensional. Low alcohol content (11.8%). *Last tasted Sept 1997* ★

**Ch Pétrus** Sacrifices were made to maximise richness by severe selection of grapes, resulting in an even smaller production than usual. Did it pay off? Certainly impressively purple in cask (1974) but loose-knit and bitter. A bit four-square and unexciting in the mid-1980s. More recently, less deep; good crisp Merlot-based aroma; fullish, 'meaty', quite stylish (1994). And at a pre-sale tasting in New York; attractive colour; honeyed nose; touch of caramel, dry finish. *Last tasted Dec 1997* ★★ *A fairly good '73 but will not improve.*

OTHER '73S LAST TASTED IN THE 1990S
**Ch Beychevelle** A dozen notes. Nondescript. *Last tasted May 1993. Ignore.*

**Ch Brane-Cantenac** Prematurely aged, 'rustic', quite flavoury, acidic. *Last tasted March 1990.*

**Ch Cos d'Estournel** A typical '73 Médoc. Quite appealing in its youth but a noticeable astringency. A pleasant, easy drink despite tingle of acidity. *Last tasted Jan 1990* ★

**Ch Ducru-Beaucaillou** A slow starter. Latterly quite attractive but lacking stuffing. *Last tasted Sept 1993* ★★

**Ch La Fleur** Showing the advantage of a small vineyard able to select its best ripe Merlots. Light, crisp, attractive, lacking length but refreshing. *Last tasted Aug 1998* ★★★

**Ch Grand-Puy-Lacoste** Many consistent notes in 1976: a light (for Lacoste) chaptalised character, drinking agreeably, fragrant and some delicacy. At its best in the early 1980s. Most recently, touch of cherry-red, weak rim; fragrant but showing its age. A strange oyster-shell taste. *Last noted at the launch of the third edition of the Danish edition of* Wine Tasting *or* Vin Smagning *at Gyldendals in Copenhagen, March 1999* ★

**Ch Gruaud-Larose** One of the top '73s. Convincing colour, vigorous and tannic in the mid-1970s. At best in the mid-1980s. Latterly, fleshy but a bit dull. *Last tasted Jan 1990* ★

**Ch Malescot-St-Exupéry** Bland but well chaptalised and still a very pleasant drink. *Last tasted Sept 1990* ★★★

**Ch La Mission Haut-Brion** Flavoury, fragrant, fairly light for La Mission. Pleasant, easy, short. *Last tasted June 1990* ★★

**Ch Palmer** flavoury in the late 1970s, a decade later running out of steam. Most recently, pleasant, some charm. *Last noted, a bottle from the château, May 1991* ★★ *Drink up.*

**Ch Talbot** After an innocuous start, showing quite well in the early 1980s. Now fairly pale; fragrant; easy but piquant. *Last tasted June 1991* ★★ *Drink up.*

OTHER '73S LAST TASTED IN THE MID- TO LATE 1980S
**Ch Batailley** uninspiring. 'Peroxide' wearing off. Acidic. *July 1987;* **Ch Branaire-Ducru** a pleasant, lightish, flavoury wine. *May 1984* ★ *probably still quite drinkable;* **Ch Calon-Ségur** initially showing well. Fairly good notes in the early 1980s. Became 'overblown', quite attractive but on last legs. *June 1987;* **Ch Croizet-Bages** quite good. Stylish but tails off. *March 1986* ★; **Ch d'Issan** my idea of an easygoing light lunch wine. *June 1985* ★★; **Ch La Lagune** more richness than most '73 Médocs and good notes, particularly in the early 1980s. Very sweet, chocolatey, flavoury. Not bad. *Jan 1987* ★★; **Ch Lascombes** still initial depth and concentration soon dissipated. Opulent but odd. Fulsome and flavoury, but risky. *April 1988* ★; **Ch Léoville-Las-Cases** Monsieur Delon not on top of his '73. Chaptalised. Slightly bitter. *Jan 1984;* **Ch Léoville-Poyferré** not bad but advanced maturity. *Last tasted Jan 1984;* **Ch Lynch-Bages** a tolerably good '73. At least interesting, with piquant fruit. *April 1987* ★★; **Ch Montrose** mediocre. *April 1988;* **Ch Pichon-Baron** in its early days, delicate bouquet; pleasing. When last tasted quite flavoury and attractive. *April 1988* ★★; **Ch Prieuré-Lichine** a plausible charmer. Fragrant, piquant, flavoury. *Oct 1988* ★★; **Ch Rausan-Ségla** a good start and pleasing development. Some fruit, a bit raw but flavoury. *May 1986* ★★; **Ch Smith-Haut-Lafitte** a callow youth yet stylish. Rather vegetal (beetroot) nose and taste. Chaptalised of course but a silky charmer. *Oct 1987 almost* ★★★; and **Ch La Tour Haut-Brion** rich-looking for a '73, fragrant and very flavoury. More recently, fairly assertive, characterful, very dry finish. *April 1987* ★★★

# 1974

Bordeaux was at its lowest ebb, and the wines seemed to reflect this. As always, it was the weather that dictated the quality and quantity. The year began well with good flowering to launch a substantial crop. The summer was fine and dry, thickening the skins. Ripening was hampered by rain in the latter part of September and it continued cold and wet throughout the harvest in October. The grapes swelled in firm thick skins. There was no green pruning, little selection of grapes or vats. The quantity of wine was prodigious, its quality mediocre. Many wines tasted mainly in the mid- to late 1970s have been omitted. Those that were poor in the early to mid-1980s will be terrible now. The following, except for most of first growths, are notes mainly last made in the 1990s. About the most dismal set of notes in my entire collection.

**Ch Lafite** Not tasted in its formative years, the first useful note being made at the Penning-Rowsell '10-year' tasting delayed until March 1985. Surprisingly fragrant, in fact intensely so, but eventually it gave me a whiff of chlorine and, after 90 minutes or so in the glass, I described it as 'opulent but depraved'. (At these first growth tastings, I usually decanted the wines around 6pm and they were served at dinner one by one, but fairly speedily, the glasses remaining on the table.) It was certainly fully evolved by the end of 1988 but my notes were always qualified by 'a bit hollow', 'tinny and overripe', 'short'. Not a wine to cellar. *Last tasted Oct 1988.*

**Ch Latour** First tasted just after bottling. 'Raw', 'skinny', 'twisted (acidic) finish', 'scrawny' appearing in my notes from the end of the 1970s to early 1980s. Its colour was pretty good at Penning-Rowsell's in March 1985, though its nose scarcely got off the ground. Fairly full-bodied, good if undemonstrative flavour. The first growth with the best future. But, literally, it is not a flyer. 'Passable flavour. Tannic. Short' at the Frérick's/Wodarz tasting. *Last noted March 1989* ★

**Ch Margaux** Four notes. Palish pink, quite fragrant and flavoury in 1980. At just over ten years old, more of a ruby colour; a tight, high-toned but gentle fragrance. Dry, short, crisp, very flavoury and some charm but finished raw and short. My next two notes made at Wagner's tastings. In 1997, a not bad, 'medicinal' singed fragrance; not bad flavour but lean, austere, edgy finish. At the second, a drab, dreary, weak-rimmed appearance; medicinal and dreadful taste. Less of a shooting star, more of a damp squib. *Last tasted Nov 2000.*

**Ch Mouton-Rothschild** A quick developer, quite attractive fruit but raw in the late 1970s. Ruby-coloured: fairly good – some of Margaux's fragrance, but on a par with Latour at the Penning-Rowsell tasting. Later in the 1980s, a depraved Cabernet aroma and a tinny, medicinal taste. Drinkable but … *Last tasted March 1989.*

**Ch Haut-Brion** One of the better '74s. Light yet chunky and short in 1976. In 1985 quite a good ruby colour, low-keyed, hard though unmistakable Haut-Brion flavour. Medium length. Most recently, some sweetness, silky tannins, a pleasant easy drink. *Last tasted June 1990* ★★

**Ch Ausone** Once again, better on first acquaintance: some fruit, and at least interesting (1978). Speedy evolution. Pale, orange-tinged; little nose; dried leaves taste. *Last tasted Oct 1987.*

**Ch Cheval Blanc** I have a couple of notes. The wine was trying hard at the Penning-Rowsells' but I preferred the Haut-Brion and the first growth Médocs. Flavour was not bad though hollow. At Karl-Heinz Wolf's three-day, 50-wine Cheval Blanc tasting, it was put firmly in its place: a ruby-tinged magnum; some crisp fruit, vanilla; modest fruit, short, raw finish 'scraggy'. *Last tasted Sept 1997.*

**Ch Pétrus** By far the best of the '74 first growths at the Penning-Rowsell tasting in March 1985: deeper, fuller, richer. But a relatively poor magnum, leaner, tannic at Frérick's Pétrus tasting in Munich. *Last tasted April 1986* ★

OTHER '74S LAST TASTED IN THE 1990S
**Ch Beychevelle** Vanillin nose, dry, quite good texture. *Last tasted Aug 1993* ★
**Ch Cantemerle** First tasted flying on Concorde to New York in 1981. It was not a good choice: grubby nose, short, dull and dry. Who selected this inappropriate wine for British Airways 'flagship' I do not know. Not I; because I didn't join the British Airways wine-tasting panel until 1984! Only one subsequent note: slightly better than the '72, which is not saying much. *At a pre-sale tasting, March 1996.*
**Ch La Fleur** Sweet, not bad nose; unbalanced, with raw, dry, hard tannic finish. One of the least good wines of this otherwise excellent Pomerol château. *Last noted Aug 1998.*
**Ch Malescot-St-Exupéry** Pure iodine. Dry, raw, awful. *Last tasted Sept 1990.*

A SMALL RANGE OF OTHER '74S TASTED IN THE MID- TO LATE 1980S **Ch Brane-Cantenac** sulphur had failed to prevent a poor wine from deteriorating. *Oct 1985;* **Ch Calon-Ségur** not bad: quite pleasant, but how it managed to be raw and soft I know not. Short. *June 1987* ★; **Ch La Conseillante** orange-tinged; positive flavour, some length. *Oct 1985* ★★; **Ch Ducru-Beaucaillou** several notes. Light but chunky, tannic, uninspiring. *Oct 1985;* **Ch Duhart-Milon** once again exhibiting the rusty orange-tinged overmaturity. Sweet, odd taste, tart finish. *Oct 1989;* **Ch Figeac** piquant nose; unknit but an agreeable drink *Oct 1985* ★★; **Les Forts de Latour** some fruit and flesh clinging precariously to a decimated body. A bit raw; but not bad. *April 1987* ★; **Ch Gazin** some fruit but lean and tannic. *Oct 1985;* **Ch La Grave-Trigant-de-Boisset** a good '74, ruby coloured; decent, positive nose and taste: marron and spices. *Nov 1985* ★★★; **Ch Gruaud-Larose** a good firm and fruity cask sample followed up quite well. Agreeable flavour. A tart but tolerable '74. *Oct 1988* ★★; **Ch Léoville-Poyferré** just tolerable. *Last Oct 1985;* **Ch Lynch-Bages** many notes. By 'medicinal' I mean, in this instance, the smell of lint, bandages and iodine – a grotesque caricature of the Lynch-Bages Pauillac fragrance. Taste of rot too. Perhaps they tried to put it in splints. *Tasted Nov 1985;* **Ch Montrose** plum pudding: plummy colour, a pudding of a wine, but one cooked by a superannuated prep school matron: dry, stern, forbidding; **Ch Smith-Haut-Lafitte** in fact very fragrant and spicy for a '74. They must have been able to afford new oak casks. More 'Hammersmith' than Haut-Smith and certainly not Lafite. *Nov 1986* ★★; **Ch Talbot** it seemed to fly regularly and frequently on British Airways transatlantic flights and not all bad. *Last tasted, supersonic at 57,000 feet, Jan 1986* ★★; and **Ch La Tour Haut-Brion** sweet though crude; this curiously medicinal smell again, but at least fruity and drinking well. *Nov 1986.*

# 1975 ★★★★

Despite being pronounced optimistically a *vin de garde* in the somewhat better trading conditions in the spring of 1976, the wines have turned out to be irregular; indeed, for some time now it has been a controversial vintage. Unquestionably better than the three preceding vintages and certainly interesting, not to say challenging. Initially, I must confess, I was impressed by the '75s, but over the last decade I have noticed an imbalance between both the châteaux and the wines.

The weather conditions also were much more conducive: a mild spring, favourable flowering conditions, a hot and dry summer with some welcome rain to swell the grapes before the end of September harvest. But the summer heat and dryness, whilst helping the sugar content, thickened the skins. It resulted in wines of good fruit with high alcoholic content, dark colour and high tannins. It was, still is, the latter which has caused the controversy.

**Ch Lafite** Curiously, picking at Lafite began on exactly the same date as in 1959. It certainly started off well, with positive fruit and a lovely spicy flavour when first tasted in cask twelve months later. It opened up beautifully, positively swelling in the glass, gaining complexity but its tannin not quite masked by its richness – this was in the late 1970s. Showing pretty well at Penning-Rowsell's '10-year' tasting (though rarely did it ever come top). It was a question whether the fruit and extract could keep the tannin at bay. At Nils Sternby's tasting of 1975s (not just Bordeaux) in Malmö (1995), his magnum was very distinctive, very fragrant on nose and palate. Tannin very noticeable. I gave it the same mark (tasted blind) as the Latour, but fractionally below Mouton. Most recently, a rather disappointing bottle at a rather grand dinner party: mature looking; nose – to me – of 'iron' underpinned by liquorice. I added 'oh dear, not very nice'. *Last noted at Lafite, Sept 1998. At its best ★★★ but I now doubt if it will improve.*

**Ch Latour** Well over two dozen notes. Positively opaque a year after the harvest. Immense complexity compared with other '75s tasted in the late 1970s, but it simmered down in depth though not youthfulness, with lovely middle palate. Tannic, but well clad and the best balanced just beyond its tenth anniversary. Eight fairly consistent notes over the last decade: 'delicious'. Better than the '78 (in 1990), though 'too tannic, too astringent' at a tasting in 1995. Better with food – it positively *needs* food. Certainly helped cope with the fillet of lamb at a Vintners' Company Installation Dinner (1997). Last noted at John Jenkins' Bordeaux Club dinner. His wife is a wonderful cook and her duck needed no underpinning. The Latour was fragrant, a bit leathery but with good fruit and flavour. Still tannic of course. *Last tasted at Childerley Hall, Sept 1998 ★★★ Not only a keeper but might well have more to offer.*

**Ch Margaux** One of the better '75s. Four notes in the 1980s: flavoury, flavoury, flavoury, some Margaux charm but very tannic. Three notes over the past decade. At the first Wagner tasting, an attractive bouquet but a strange (though I frequently notice it in the Médoc) oyster shell, metallic whiff. Sweetness and extract masking its tannin. 'A good '75'. Showing well though a similar 'sea breeze' fragrance reflected on the palate. Soft. Good length – one of my highest marks in Sternby's tasting of '75s. Most recent note made at Wagner's second tasting. This time 'tea leaves', 'slightly sour but not unattractive'. Better than expected. Fair fruit masking tannin. *Last tasted Nov 2000 ★★★*

**Ch Mouton-Rothschild** Like a fully-primed bomb waiting to go off, at a tasting in 1979. Packed, concentrated, with promises of things to come. They did. Just short of 20 notes most of which dwell upon its spicy fragrance – but also teeth-gripping tannin. Of the seven weird and wonderful occasions over the last decade, including a highly marked magnum, 'very

attractive but a bit astringent' (just part of a note made at a major tasting in 1994). Another magnum in 1995: still deep and impressive, crisp flavour, full body and flavour, soft, mouthfilling with a powerful finish. Slightly below par, mocha nosed, chewy, chunky, 'inelegant' bottles hopelessly paired with *foie gras chaud* (in New York 1996). Now browning at the rim; crisp, good flesh but, again, with teeth-gripping tannin. Most recently, no longer deep in colour; nose 'OK', but 'unattractive, unstable' and put off by its end bite. One might have thought it could cope with *fromages affinés*, but it didn't. *Last noted at the Fête de la Fleur dinner at Ch Pontet-Canet, June 1999. At best ★★★★ (just). I think it worth requoting my Jane Mansfield analogy: 'mean, moody and magnificent'.*

**Ch Haut-Brion** A dozen notes. Not all that impressive in cask (Sept 1976) but a quintet of mainly admiring notes in 1978–79: 'well knit', 'gentle fruit', 'rich, fragrant', tannin referred to only once. If anything, it seemed to gain in colour through the 1980s, and in other ways, but 'raw tea', 'very dry tannic finish', 'severe', cropping up to qualify its fragrance and flavour. The last three notes all being made at major tastings, an austere, earthy magnum in 1994 (tasted blind I thought it must be Ch La Mission); nose like Ambrosia creamed rice pudding and flavour of tobacco and autumn leaves, good length and aftertaste – I liked it! – at a tasting of '75s in 1995. Most recently, now with an orange-brown mature rim; a rich, attractive, slightly smoky bouquet; good flavour and body. 'Complete'. *Last noted at a pre-sale tasting, Jan 1999 ★★★★*

**Ch Ausone** Idiosyncratic and contradictory as usual. In March 1979 its sweet, almost jammy and chocolatey nose was a complete contrast to the severity of its taste. A very elaborate note, too long to quote, made at Desai's tasting of '75s at Sotheby's in 1984. Certainly an intriguing bouquet and taste, 'singed', its richness tussling with its rawness. Most recently at a very wide range tasting of '75 clarets I conducted in Malmö: my favourite 'dried leaves' simile – nose and taste. Quite good length – but *tannic*. *Last tasted April 1995 ★★★*

**Ch Cheval Blanc** Over three times as many notes as Ausone, not because I avoid the latter but because I am more exposed to Cheval Blanc. However, I much prefer the 'white horse' to the Roman poet (Ausonius). A relatively elegant '75 though by no means immune to the ever-present '75 tannin. Several recent notes. One of my highest marks at the Malmö tasting in 1995: rich 'legs', 'opening up agreeably' (the nose not the 'legs'); very much a Right Bank wine though *tannic* (Frans de Cock's dinner in Paris, 1995). An extraordinary explosion of sweetness after 20 minutes of shyness; sweet, rich, high extract, chewy and tannic (at Wolf's vertical in 1997). Next, in Tokyo, 1999: the same uplift of richness on the nose reflected on the

---

### Michel Bettane

*The most influential journalist/wine taster of France. He and I found ourselves perplexed with the 1975 Médocs, in the sense that they seemed to us out of balance. We didn't know whether they would turn out well, or badly. A special tasting was arranged for us in June 1993, in the new chai at Ch La Tour-Carnet, and we tasted, blind, a wide range of Médoc châteaux, afterwards comparing notes. We came to the unsurprising conclusion that those wines which were well made with good concentration, good extract would last, but those badly made (scraggy and poor) would not. Perhaps that applies to every vintage! Coincidentally, Ch La Tour-Carnet turned out to have produced the worst wine of the tasting!*

palate. 'A very good '75 but very tannic.' Most recently, a jeroboam at Eigensatz's 'Red Wine' gala dinner: soft, mature cherry-tinged rather than the rusty orange I associate with '75s. Low-keyed, slightly varnishy, but opened up richly; better on palate, lean fruit, dry finish. *Last tasted at the Hotel Eden-Parc, Bad Schwalbach, Nov 2001. At best* ★★★★

**Ch Pétrus** A deep, rich, fleshy and impressive mouthful from my first encounter on its tenth birthday – and since. How I managed to conduct, to 'moderate', 118 '75s at a one-day event in Malmö (in 1995) I do not know. All I do know, from my notes, is that I awarded the three top marks to Ch Pétrus, La Fleur and Mouton. The same year I was equally impressed: thick, velvety, full of fruit, chewy, – you name it. *Last tasted at de Cock's dinner in Paris, Dec 1995* ★★★★★

There is no question of my quoting from the surprisingly detailed notes of the 118 '75s at the Malmö tasting mentioned above. They were presented by district and, not surprisingly, covered a wide range of qualities from minor *bourgeois* to many of the classified growths and all the firsts. An important feature of the tasting was that we were able to taste two bottles of each wine, virtually all consistent. Here is a selection of the most important and interesting (not necessarily the same thing), all last noted in March 1995 unless otherwise stated:

**Ch Batailley** A good '75. Typical Batailley, easy, fruity style. Tannin effectively masked ★★★

**Ch Beauséjour-Bécot** Rich, chunky fruit. Tannic. *Last tasted Nov 1985* ★★★

**Ch Belair** Dry. No flavour or finish. All tannin. Pre-sale, *Dec 2001. (But it had been shipped from the Argentine.)*

**Ch Beychevelle** Quite good. Many notes. Sweet. Good fruit but very tannic. *Last tasted May 1993* ★★

**Ch Boyd-Cantenac** Moderately good. Soft yet piquant ★★

**Ch Branaire-Ducru** Almost too sweet. Attractive fruit. Noticeable tannin and acidity ★★

**Ch Brane-Cantenac** Somewhat exaggerated, 'medicinal', fruit but attractive flavour. Noticeable tannin and acidity ★★

**Ch Calon-Ségur** Classic nose; surprisingly sweet, nice weight and length. Tame tannin and acidity ★★★

**Ch Canon** Colour loss. Reservations. Muffled tannin ★★

**Ch Cantemerle** Several notes, some quite recent. Soft ruby matching soft fruit. Fragrant. Fleshy. Surprisingly harmonious despite noticeable tannin. *Last tasted Dec 1995* ★★★

**Ch Cantenac-Brown** Many notes. Peppery fruit. Raw ★★

**Ch Carbonnieux** Fragrant. Flavoury. Easy ★★ *Drink up.*

**Dom de Chevalier** Nose like creamed rice pudding. Very flavoury. Attractive. Good length. Acidity noticeable ★★★

**Ch La Conseillante** Lovely bouquet. Full. Rich. Touch of liquorice. Tannic. Astringent ★★★

**Cos d'Estournel** Bitterly tannic in cask. Opened up well. Soft, harmonious bouquet but, though good flavour, in the end too tannic. *Last tasted June 1993. Allowing for tannin* ★★★

**Ch Coufran** Very dependable. Unusually for St-Estèphe, 100% Merlot. Good if not great '75. Sweet and easy ★★★

**Ch La Croix** Rich, rustic, flavoury but astringent ★★

**Ch Ducru-Beaucaillou** Many notes. Good colour; classic cedary nose; fruit and extract almost succeeding in masking its silky-leathery tannin. *Last tasted June 1999* ★★★

**Ch Duhart-Milon** In 1984 I described it as the Pétrus of Pauillac with an aftertaste like La Tâche. Well, not quite: certainly Pauillac. Fragrant ★★★?

**Ch Durfort-Vivens** Piquant, a bit over the top; but attractive. ★★ *Drink up.*

**Clos L'Église** Sweet, good fruit and grip ★★★★

**Dom de l'Église** Almost exotic, meaty, bouquet. Very sweet, rich but touch of astringency ★★★

**Ch L'Église-Clinet** Lots of Clinets in fairly close proximity to Pomerol's hideous church. Lean. Raw fruit. Disappointingly tannic. *Sept 1998* ★★

**Ch Figeac** Even more eccentric than usual, and a batch of poor bottles encountered at a big *Rotwein* event in Frankfurt. More recently, orange-tinged; 'thick' but fragrant and much better on palate though astringent at the extensive Malmö tasting. Most recently, a corky, powerful, tannic *impériale. Avoid.*

**Ch La Fleur** In 1993: very deep but orange-tinged; 'seaweed'; dry, raw, powerful but not very attractive. Apparently a 'Parker 100'. Not for me. More recently: rather neutral nose which was too disinterestedly proud to open up. Touch of citrus to its dense fruit. Austere. Very tannic. I hope that Robert Parker, whom, incidentally, I admire, will be around in another 20 years to see if, like Rip van Winkle, the wine eventually wakes up. *Last tasted Dec 1995* ★★★★?

**Ch La Fleur-Pétrus** Much preferred to its almost namesake above. Two recent notes: deep; gloriously sweet, uplifting bouquet; full-bodied, very rich, almost perfect – but very tannic ★★★(★★) *I would rather bet on this than the La Fleur.*

**Ch Gazin** Fully developed. Attractive bouquet but lacking depth. Easy. Touch of astringency ★★ *Drink up.*

**Ch Giscours** Many notes. Impressive colour; surprisingly good bouquet when it opened up. Lots of fruit. Good grip. Tannic. *Last tasted April 1995* ★★★

**Ch Grand-Puy-Lacoste** Several notes. An extremely attractive magnum at the Malmö tasting, good texture, lovely fruit. Tolerable tannin and acidity. Last tasted June 1993 ★★★(★)

**Ch La Grave** Elevated bouquet; elegant, silky tannins but some astringency ★★★

**Ch Gruaud-Larose** Impressive in cask. Slow to evolve. A tinge of orange; excellent nose; surprisingly sweet entry leading to a very dry astringent finish by way of attractive fragrance and flavour. *A magnum went well with beef at a Bordeaux Club dinner for Jack Plumb, June 1997* ★★★★

**Ch Langoa-Barton** Mellow, almost overripe. Yet lean. Certainly interesting. *Last tasted Feb 1992* ★★ *Drink soon.*

**Ch Lascombes** Several notes with mixed reception, including mouth-puckering astringency. Most recently: opaque; hard, leathery, almost woody nose; full-bodied, very tannic, fair extract but drying out. *Last noted at a pre-sale tasting, Sept 2001*

**Ch Latour-à-Pomerol** Rich but not very distinctive. Chunky, chewy fruit. Touch of astringency ★★★

**Ch Laujac** Better flavour than nose. Nice fruit. Good length and texture ★★★

**Ch Léoville-Barton** Much liked in its early days but an untypical rusticity on nose and palate. Sweet enough, mature but slightly tinny and tannic. *Last tasted Oct 1993* ★★

**Ch Léoville-Las-Cases** Several notes. Decidedly better than the Léoville-Barton above – richer, fuller, good fruit, length and extract managing almost to mask its tannin. Most recently, fragrant and drinking well. *Last noted at a Saintsbury Club dinner, Oct 1997* ★★★★

**Ch Léoville-Poyferré** Not a particularly good '75 or good Poyferré. 'Medicinal' nose. Quite rich and flavoury but 'edgy'. *Last tasted Dec 2001* ★★

**Ch Magdelaine** Weak rim, sweet yet lean. Tolerable tannin. *June 1997* ★★

**Ch La Mission Haut-Brion** Many notes. As distinctive as always. Could *only* be La Mission. Rich, crisp, surprisingly sweet finish and aftertaste despite more than a touch of astringency which coped well with a cheese soufflé. _Last tasted at a Bordeaux Club dinner at Caius, Cambridge, June 2000_ ★★★★

**Ch Montrose** Understandably hard in cask and, as usual, slow to develop. Classic. Lovely flavour and texture. Spicy. Silky tannins and slightly astringent ★★★★(★) _This has a future._

**Ch Meyney** Fairly deep magnum, good fruit ★★★

**Ch Les-Ormes-de-Pez** Rich. Good fruit and balance ★★★

**Ch Pichon-Lalande** Many notes, far superior to the neighbouring Pichon-Baron from the start. Tasted nine times in the last decade, the last two dining at the château. Remarkably good for a '75 – rich, flavoury, full of fruit, its tannin completely submerged. _Last noted at May de Lencquesaing's 75th birthday celebration, June 2000_ ★★★★

**Ch Pontet-Canet** Now almost a borderline case; some richness, marked tannin and acidity ★★★ _(just)._

**Ch Prieuré-Lichine** Orange-rimmed; enough fruit; a quite attractive drink. Piquant. _Last tasted June 1993_ ★★ _Drink up._

**Ch Rausan-Ségla** Several notes. Distinctive. Nice firm flavour and weight, with '75 grip ★★★

**Ch de Sales** The ideal club claret. Never expensive, always drinkable. Many notes. Rich, rounded, easy ★★★ _Drink up._

**Ch St-Pierre-Sevaistre** Classic. Good flavour, good weight and balance ★★★

**Ch Smith-Haut-Lafitte** Very fragrant and flavoury but with teeth-gripping tannins ★★

**Ch Talbot** Quite a few notes, the best in the mid-1980s. More recently, good nose, ripe flavour – but astringent ★★★

**Ch Trotanoy** Impressively rich from start to not yet finished. Colour now medium-ruby and mature. Fairly sweet, its rich fruit masking high tannin content. _Last tasted at Christie's pre-sale tasting in Tokyo, Nov 1999_ ★★★★

**Vieux Ch Certan** Sweet, fullish, good fruit, attractive ★★★★

Some decent '75s, among the many that were too astringent or piquant and raw or simply below standard: **Ch Bouscaut; Ch La Cabanne; Ch de Camensac; Ch Chasse-Spleen; Ch Le Crock; Les Forts de Latour; Ch de Fieuzal; Clos des Jacobins; Ch Lynch-Bages; Ch Malartic-Lagravière; Ch Malescot-St-Exupéry; Ch Moulinet-Lassere; Ch Mouton-Baronne-Philippe; Ch Nenin; Ch Palmer; Ch Pape-Clément; Ch Pavie; Ch Petit-Village; Ch de Pez; Ch Pichon-Baron; Ch Poujeaux; Ch Siran; Ch La Tour Haut-Brion;** and **Ch La Tour de Mons.**

# 1976 ★★ to ★★★

A vintage of undoubted charm; after a quarter of a century, many still delightful but most wines well past their best.

It is worth remembering that most red Bordeaux wines do not have the structure to compete with the better sited and better suited. Many are best from four to seven years of age; in a good vintage perhaps up to ten or twelve. But beyond that, perfectly decent claret, the so-called _petits châteaux_, do not develop extra facets and nuances with age: they just get older.

Well, what sort of growing conditions were responsible for the charming '76s? First of all, it was a year of exceptional heat in north-west Europe: a summer of alarming drought in England which was ended by rain towards the end of August and which dragged on to the following spring. In Bordeaux, the warm conditions persisted. Because of early budding and flowering everything was advanced, resulting in the earliest harvest of the decade, beginning on the 15 September. One might assume that the resulting wines would be dark, alcoholic and tannic. It was a lack of rain which resulted in a lack of flesh, the wines being more lean than supple. But they were undoubtedly attractive, well timed and reasonably priced.

**Ch Lafite** Once a charmer, nearly always a charmer though some of the patina wearing thin. It could almost have been a '53 so easy and flavoury from weaning in cask through the 1980s, when most of my notes were made. Over six in the last decade, ignoring a corked bottle but including bottles drinking perfectly at a Bacchus Society dinner (in 1997): a fragrance that reminded me of orange blossom. Very sweet, enough flesh, delicious. At a pre-sale tasting in New York (1999), my impression was that it was losing its charm. Magnums presented at a Domaines Barons de Rothschild dinner at Brooks's in London: though not, as at past dinners a co-commentator, I was quietly enjoying myself in a corner of the Great Subscription Room, one of the loveliest rooms in London, when Éric de Rothschild called for a comment. I duly obliged. The '76 was deeper than expected; its bouquet, mature and totally harmonious; good fruit, good drink yet with keen-edged tannins. Very drinkable. Went well with the Welsh rarebit. _Last tasted Nov 2000_ ★★★★ _but past its peak._

---

## Marvin Overton

_Neurosurgeon from Fort Worth, Texas. His seminal Latour tasting in 1976 covered 47 vintages (1899 to 1972); another, of Lafite, in 1979 took in 36 vintages from 1799 to 1979. Alas, wine now takes a back seat to his missionary zeal and Bible texts…_

---

**Ch Latour** Nearly 20 notes. Understandably opaque and severe in cask, its deep purple _robe_ hanging on as it developed. A rather dour wine in the mid-1980s. Only three notes in the past decade, the best, fully evolved; the sweetness of ripe grapes and fairly high alcohol. A really delicious mouthful (at an Athenaeum wine dinner, 1976), but less impressive, 'unexciting' at a recent dinner in Memphis. _Last tasted Dec 1997_ ★★★

**Ch Margaux** I would have imagined that the combination of Margaux and 1976 would have been a marriage made in heaven. Alas, at best a registry office matrimonial agreement. It was towards the end of the Ginestets' tenure; they were in financial trouble and simply could not afford a benchful of even old ladies to do the sorting. The last two notes made at Wagner's useful vertical tastings. At the first, in 1979, it exhibited a faded fragrance and some charm; fairly sweet, nice weight, quite good flavour but an acidic tendency. At the second, a very mature, open appearance with '75-like orange tinge. Bouquet fragrant, offering itself like an eager divorcee. Walter Eigensatz thought it had 'the sweetness of death'. There was a certain decayed charm. It needed drinking, and I was quite happy to help it along. _Last tasted Nov 2000_ ★★★

**Ch Mouton-Rothschild** I would have expected more from this, too. In the 1980s, crisply fragrant, spicy but almost the wrong sort of length: attenuated, pointed. Now medium deep, a browning rim; a sweet, lively Cabernet nose; dry, crisp (1997). 'Faded but fragrant' bouquet, lean, pleasant enough but no more. _Last noted at a Mouton tasting for the Hollywood Wine Society, March 1998_ ★★

**Ch Haut-Brion** Good in cask and a dozen notes since, showing particularly well in the mid- to late 1980s, well developed, harmonious. Most recently, a true earthy tobacco nose and flavour, its dry finish now tinged with a touch of bitterness. *A good lunch wine though, July 1999* ★★★★ *Drink soon.*

**Ch Ausone** An uneven performer despite its ancient repute and imminent renaissance: Pascal Delbeck's first vintage as winemaker. Alas few notes but rich, attractive, spicy (sage) forthcoming bouquet; lively yet taut. *Last tasted in 1985* ★★★★ *Probably still holding well.*

**Ch Cheval Blanc** The iron in the soil often very noticeable, as when first tasted in the spring of 1978. The top of the first growths at Penning-Rowsell's '10-year' tasting (Ch Ausone not represented). At its best in the late 1980s and early 1990s: sweet, lovely texture, delightful. Amid all the great and less great at Wolf's great tasting in 1997 it was very stylish with some charm but beginning to dry out; this was confirmed at a pre-sale tasting a few months later. Attractive though. *Last tasted Dec 1997* ★★★★ *Drink soon.*

**Ch Pétrus** Good but by no means great. Nine notes from its rich mulberry coloured *début* – for me – at five years of age. Critical notes in the mid-1980s, perhaps because I was expecting more. Yet, much more recently though drinking well, with good weight and flavour I felt its bouquet, initially pleasing, faded a little in the glass. My most recent note I shall write off as it was a bit corky and austere. *Last noted briefly at a pre-sale tasting in New York, Dec 1997* ★★★? *Future?*

**OTHER '76S TASTED IN THE 1990S**

**Ch Beychevelle** Ten notes up to 1984. Only one since. Unusually lean and tannic. *Last tasted May 1993* ★★ *Drink soon.*

**Ch Batailley** Mature. Good nose and flavoury. Soft. Well balanced. *Dining at the château, June 1995* ★★★

**Ch Cantemerle** At its delightful and delicate best in 1980. Still a pleasing drink but acidity creeping up. *Last tasted April 1990* ★★ *Drink up.*

**Ch Cantenac-Brown** Distinctive 'chocolatey' fruit. Sweet. Soft. Ready. Just a touch of tannin and acidity warning. *April 1994* ★★ *Drink up.*

**Ch Chasse-Spleen** In the early 1980s our everyday claret at home – not an extravagant indulgence I can assure you. 'Delectable, delicious'. Now fully ripe and on a gentle decline. *Last tasted April 1990* ★★ *Drink up.*

**Ch Cissac** Showing well at a Cissac tasting at the Savoy Hotel, London and at a pre-sale tasting. Rich and fragrant, warranting its *cru exceptionnel* status. *Drinking well April 1996* ★★★

**Ch La Dominique** An old favourite of mine. Fully mature. Fairly sweet. *June 1998* ★★★

**Ch L'Église-Clinet** Luminous, mature; incredibly sweet blossoming of fragrance; as good as it looked. Rich, fruity, dry finish, *à point. At a Rodenstock wine weekend, Sept 1998* ★★★★

**Ch Figeac** Expecting this to be like a rush to the head it was surprisingly severe after bottling and for the next few years seemed at its – now characteristic – best, its flavour spreading in the mouth like the proverbial Burgundian 'peacock's tail'. Most recently, very forthcoming, attractive, fully developed. Extraordinary flavour. *Last noted Sept 1993* ★★★★★ *Drink soon.*

**Ch Grand-Puy-Lacoste** I am writing this just as I have confirmed my order for the vintages 1999 and 2000 – I buy it every year. 'Uncompromising' is the expression which comes to mind whenever I think of Lacoste. Even in an amenable vintage like the '76. But undoubtedly stylish. Perfect now. *Last tasted Jan 1992* ★★★★

**Ch Gruaud-Larose** Frankly and surprisingly variable notes. Drinking well in the mid-1980s, but despite its customary fruit, a bit lean for Gruaud. *Last tasted May 1990* ★★★

**Ch La Lagune** Many notes, showing particularly well at comparative tastings of '76s in the early 1980s. Very mature. Rich appearance and nose. Very sweet, delicious. Near to perfection in the late 1980s. Most recently, a double magnum, drinking well. *Last tasted Sept 1993* ★★★★

**Ch Langoa-Barton** Nearly 20 notes since 1980. Chunkier, more masculine than the Léoville yet quite quick to develop. I thought it needed drinking in the mid- to late 1980s, lacking length, and acidity catching up. *Last tasted Jan 1992* ★★

**Ch Léoville-Barton** Fragrant: cedar and fruit; nice weight, agreeable, refreshing. *Last tasted March 1992* ★★★ *Drink now.*

**Ch Léoville-Las Cases** Consistently good notes from 1984 though I was recently slightly disappointed with some double magnums. (I realise that this sounds a bit *blasé*. But there you are.) Now a lovely, soft, ruby colour; firm, still tannic. Excellent with food. *Last tasted Sept 1993* ★★★★

**Ch Lynch-Bages** First tasted, a cask sample, in 1977: very characteristic Cabernet Sauvignon noted, still raw. Later notes in the late 1970s and early 1980s, a superficial charmer, attractive. Most recently: fully mature; still flavoury, packing half a punch, dry finish. Possibly not the best of sample bottles but needs drinking. *Last tasted Dec 2001* ★★ *Drink up.*

**Ch La Mission Haut-Brion** Fragrance, character, charm. Nothing but hugely admiring notes through the 1980s. If anything perhaps lacking the length of a *grand année* and a touch of bitterness in the finish. *Last tasted June 1990* ★★★★

**Ch Montrose** Rather like Lacoste, an uncompromising sort of wine. At its worst stolid, at its best unselfconsciously sure of itself. Good fruit, good grip, silk-clad tannins. Now mature; slightly sweaty tannin on the nose but sweet and rich. *Last tasted Sept 1996* ★★★★ *Will continue.*

**Ch Petit-Village** Low-keyed in cask but opened up quite quickly, deliciously fragrant by the early 1980s. By 1986 well developed, soft, fleshy though with tannic bitterness. Most recently, a double magnum: elegant; fully evolved, Merlot softness, flesh and texture. *Last tasted Sept 1993* ★★★★

**Ch Pavie** Less of a charmer than anticipated. Sweet then sharp. Lean. Quite good with the fish. *At a 1er grand cru dinner, Jan 1997* ★★

**Ch Pichon-Lalande** Almost too eager to reach the table and certainly a delight to drink in the early 1980s. In 1985 I wrote 'Claret at its most beguiling'. Most recently, drinking well at a dinner of managers and secretaries of the 'Most distinguished clubs of the world'. *Last noted at the Carlton Club in St James's Street, Oct 1997* ★★★★

**Ch de Sales** The easiest of wines. *Last tasted March 1992* ★★

**Ch Talbot** Several notes. Now ripe, stylish, flavoury, drinking well though acidity catching up. *Last tasted a sample bottle from an excellent Parisian cellar at Christie's, Sept 1996* ★★★★ *Drink soon.*

**Ch Latour-à-Pomerol** Distinctive. Very attractive. Good. Dry. Sound. *Pre-sale tasting Dec 1997* ★★★

**OTHER '76S TASTED IN THE MID- TO LATE 1980S**

**Ch Calon-Ségur** agreeable flavour but a bit faded and short. *June 1987* ★★; **Ch Cos d'Estournel** a good '76. Agreeable weight and flavour. *June 1988* ★★★; **Ch Ducru-Beaucaillou** frankly very contradictory notes. Certainly not a shrinking violet: mouthfilling, surprisingly tannic. *Feb 1988. Probably* ★★★ *but second opinion needed;* **Ch Duhart-Milon-Rothschild** prettily coloured; fragrant, piquant. An after-theatre supper wine. *Nov 1986* ★★; **Ch Giscours** constantly surprises me. One of the darkest coloured, chunkiest and most tannic '76s. Yet revealed fruit and flesh, drinking well. *March 1988* ★★★;

**Ch Grand-Puy-Ducasse** always completely different in style and, frankly, quality, to Lacoste. Already overmature, a bit over the top but a curiously attractive drink. *July 1989* ★★; **Ch Léoville-Poyferré** not a patch on its neighbours. *Nov 1986* ★★; **Ch Magdelaine** a lovely wine. Ripe to the edge of opulence; a wine in full bloom. *Not tasted since July 1987. At best* ★★★★ *I just hope the bloom has not faded;* **Ch Palmer** a delicious wine. *Oct 1986* ★★★★ *(and probably still is);* **Ch Pape-Clément** got off to a flying start but lacked the stamina to stay the course. *Oct 1989* ★★ *drink up;* **Ch Troplong-Mondot** pretty reliable. A wine I enjoy drinking, particularly in an easy vintage-like '76. *March 1985* ★★★ *drink up;* and **Ch Trotanoy** probably deserves better notes but certainly deep, thick, rich and fleshy. *Sept 1988* ★★★★? *But doubtless still going strong.*

## 1977

The worst vintage of an uneven – to say the least – decade. Spring frosts, rain throughout the summer followed by the driest (but not sunniest) September on record. It didn't have a hope really. After gorging ourselves with the two preceding vintages they were unwanted anyway.

Few tasted, the most salutary being the '10-year' tasting of seven first growths at the Penning-Rowsells' in 1987.
**Ch Lafite** Could be a dashed sight worse. An effort at fragrance and flavour but dry, lean and tart. *Last tasted Sept 1989* ★ *Not worth pursuing even out of curiosity.*
**Ch Latour** The top of the seven first growths in 1987. Well chaptalised but not managing to convince. Fairly light for Latour. A bit austere but not unpleasant. *Last tasted Sept 1989* ★
**Ch Margaux** First tasted when it was already six years old and surprisingly like La Tâche '75, a terrible vintage in Burgundy. Some fragrance, delicacy and grip in 1987, but two recent notes have put it firmly it its place. The first at Wagner's Margaux vertical in 1997: palish, orange-tinged; a light, singed, chocolatey nose and taste. Light, lean, edgy but not unattractive – 'a light lunch wine'. But that was before the second tasting: a weakling with brown sugar nose, and flavour of withered autumn leaves. *Last tasted Nov 2000.*

### The Mentzelopoulos family

*André Mentzelopoulos, a very wealthy Frenchman, bought Ch Margaux, arguably the most prestigious château in Bordeaux, in 1977. His first vintage was the '78. He immediately instituted immense improvements in the vineyard and chais, also renovating the historic château itself. Since his untimely death in 1980, his daughter Corinne, with great charm and determination, has headed up a first-rate team.*

**Ch Mouton-Rothschild** Probably at its best in 1978, the fleshiest and richest of the seven, but lacking length. When last tasted, pale; a watered-down version of Mouton aroma. Dry, light, easy, short. *Last noted at the Frerick's/Wodarz tasting in March 1989* ★
**Ch Haut-Brion** Tasted only once, at Penning-Rowsell's, with the other 10-year old first growths. Almost a caricature, with its smoky tobacco and autumn leaves smell and taste. Short. Touch of bitterness. A sad ending. *Last tasted Dec 1987.*
**Ch Ausone** One note again, also aged 10, but at Lloyd Flatt's Ausone vertical, not with Penning-Rowsell – he rarely had Ausone in his cellar. Not bad: soft, easy, short. *Oct 1987* ★

**Ch Cheval Blanc** It always did well at Penning-Rowsell's '10-year' tasting. In 1987 it was rated second. A decade later, the opening wine but by no means the oldest at Karl-Heinz Wolf's monumental three-day vertical. We were informed that there were many problems. Not only was the harvest late, but it was miserably small and short – just five days. Although with a somewhat unhealthy overmature orange tinge, it was not bad. Its nose was rich, smoky and opened up like a dusty old carpet. Some sweetness. Bitter finish. *Last tasted Sept 1997.*
**Ch Pétrus** Surprisingly, or perhaps not surprisingly, deep looking. Better nose than taste. Prune-like fruit. Consistently dry, gritty texture, very tannic. *Last tasted Sept 1988* ★

A FEW OTHER '77S TASTED IN THE 1990S
**Ch Beychevelle** Heavily chaptalised nose like blancmange on toast. Dry and tart. *May 1993.*
**Ch Chasse-Spleen** Warranting its reputation of one of the best non *cru classé* wines of the Médoc. Certainly making an effort: surprisingly deep; sweet, fruity; not bad flavour but short and with an acidic finish. *Jan 1993* ★
**Ch Ducru-Beaucaillou** Not bad in cask. Most recently, now fairly pale, orange-tinged maturity; more vegetal than fruity; quite good flavour. *Last noted Dec 1990* ★
**Ch La Fleur** I can't help admiring Hardy Rodenstock's patience and persistence, locating wines – often over long periods of time – to build up collections to let his friends taste. He did not miss out the '77. It looked unusually weak and vapid; but both nose and flavour surprisingly sweet. Attractive though not fully knit. Short, *à point* – as good as it could ever be in such an appalling vintage. *Aug 1998* ★★
**Ch Gloria** Not exactly *in excelsis* but trying hard to be fragrant. Light, lean, flavoury. *Sept 1990* ★
**Ch Gruaud-Larose** Well, if anyone can pull it off, Gruaud can; and it nearly did. Positive nose; adequate body, quite pleasant flavour and texture. Short of course. *Jan 1988* ★★
**Ch La Mission Haut-Brion** The last of the two brilliant Woltner brothers, Fernand, died. It was the end of an era. It was also about the best '77 showing well at various tastings, all emanating from the Woltner cellars and mostly sold through Christie's. *Last tasted, and drinking quite well, in June 1990* ★★★

SOME OTHER '77S TASTED IN THE MID- TO LATE 1980S
**Ch Léoville-Poyferré** pale; light but fragrant; flavoury, dry finish. Tolerable acidity. *June 1986* ★★; and **Ch Pichon-Baron** rotten grapes. Heavily chaptalised. Crisp but raw nose; spicy but hollow tannic end acidity. *April 1987.*

## 1978 ★★★

Almost the mirror image of 1976. Appalling growing season. At the end of August châteaux owners were in despair. Complete disaster loomed. Then, suddenly, the weather improved with a September blessed with cloudless skies and unbroken ripening sunshine through to the start of the harvest just after the first week in October. It was, in the many times repeated words of Harry Waugh, 'the year of the miracle'.

But could a last minute reprieve make up for the previous miserable conditions? Well, up to a point it did, though I have always had my doubts about the balance of the wines. The best are very good but most are in decline.
**Ch Lafite** Just eight notes. First at an MW tasting of '75s in May 1982. Not bad but unimpressive. By the mid-1980s, loosened up and attractive, even assertive with good length

and finish. Trying hard to hold on to its fleeting fragrance. And certainly managing to be flavoury and elegant though lean. Now fully open and mature looks; distinctly 'Lafite', correct but with edgy acidity. *Last tasted in the wine department of Christie's in New York, June 1998* ★★★ *Get on with it.*

**Ch Latour** The first of 14 well-spaced notes first made at Harvey's en primeur tasting in June 1980, priced, incidentally at £159 per case: 'opaque', 'dumb', concentrated, intense. Despite this, it seemed to lose colour and opened up quite quickly. Peppery Cabernet aroma and tannic before Christie's first and only wine auction in Washington (1981); spicy, cinnamon-nosed, showing quite well at the MW tasting in 1982. Rated equal with Lafite at Penning-Rowsell's '10-year' tasting, but soon to dry out, lacking conviction in the early 1990s. A relatively weak magnum at a Latour tasting in 1996 and 'unconvincing' a year later. Showing its age though some richness dining with Paul Bowker at The Square. In May 1998, and a month later, quite soft and agreeable. Most recently, a rather tired bottle, showing its age at The Wine Experience Grand tastings. *Last noted in New York, Oct 2001* ★★

**Ch Margaux** An important vintage in several respects but first and foremost because it was the first vintage following Margaux's purchase by André Mentzelopoulos. Although he expended a great deal of money on improvements – drainage to give just one example, I think it is a mistake to dismiss the quality of the wine previously made by the Ginestets, for the wine of any châteaux could have been disparaged had it been acquired after the dreary vintages of the mid-1970s. One has only to turn to the 1961, tasted recently, to be reminded that, pre-Mentzelopoulos, great wines were made.

I first tasted the '78 in April 1979. Even then soft and supple, but it was a Merlot *'ensemble'* before the final *assemblage.* The following January, opaque, ripe and fragrant at Harvey's en primeur tasting (price to the trade £133.50 per case). Showing well, a magnificent, intense purple, with good flesh, fruit and balance at a tasting I conducted at the Madison Hotel in Washington (1981). Spicy and silkily tannic at Desai's vertical in 1987. More recently, at further verticals, less deep, more mature; fully developed bouquet, nice texture but tannic and showing its age (Hollywood Wine Society 1995) and lastly at Manfred Wagner's Ch Margaux tastings. Very consistent notes, quite good nose, a sort of static fragrance. Some sweetness, medium-full body and a tingle of end-acidity. *The last notes made in Jan 1997 and Nov 2000* ★★★ *Good wine but past its best.*

**Ch Mouton-Rothschild** Plummy-coloured, very flavoury at the MW tasting in 1982. Murky, muffled and moderate at Flatt's vertical in 1986 and lacking excitement at Penning-Rowsell's '10-year' tasting. Not unlike the '76 alongside and quite attractive at a lunch in 1994. Most recently, not exactly well-paired with *homard du Maine aux ceps et au curry* at a charity dinner in New York. It survived. Stylish. Drinking agreeably. *Last tasted Dec 1996* ★★★ *(just). Not a brilliant Mouton.*

**Ch Haut-Brion** Immediately forthcoming and agreeable at Harvey's en primeur tasting in January 1980 (Price £158.50). 'An early developer?' Its distinctive Graves nose and taste evolving in the early 1980s and pleasingly mature at 10 years of age. Two bottles from the cellars of a Scottish castle noted in 1994. They varied slightly, one 'old and edgy', its nose clearing but still tart, the other better, firmer. Most recently, now orange-tinged; nose strange, a bit cardboardy and a taste which led me to think of brown paper. Well, either the wine is deteriorating or the last few bottles have been unrepresentative. *Last noted at a pre-sale tasting, Jan 1999* ★★?

**Ch Ausone** Thinking of brown paper brings me to Ausone, for although it was said to be in a renaissance period, I recently used the expression 'dried leaves', not for the first time, though it did emit some fragrance. It was 'dry' at the start, swingeingly tannic and lean in the mid-1980s, distinctive and intense at 10 years old but – dried leaves again. *Last tasted June 1998* ★★ *Drying out.*

**Ch Cheval Blanc** One of the most satisfactory '78s, its richness and good fruit noted in the early 1980s, soft and spicy, lovely texture. My best description was made in 1988 'crisp fruit, lively … combining roundness and fair length. Elliptical is the word'. Three more recent notes – its Cabernet Franc fragrance noticeable at Wolf's vertical in 1997, also sweet, quite good fruit but a dry, surprisingly raw finish. That December, a much more attractive bottle at Hugh Johnson's Bordeaux Club dinner at his shop in St James's Street: a lovely colour; soft, bricky, unrestrained bouquet; perfect weight, complete, delicious. Also very fragrant and distinctive at a pre-sale tasting in Los Angeles though a trace of acidity which would not have been noticeable with food. *Last tasted March 1999* ★★★★

**Ch Pétrus** For rather obvious reasons, I tend to taste and drink less Pétrus than most other wines. On the eight occasions I have been exposed to the '78, I am convinced that it is not all that good. It is certainly peculiar, combining exotic fruit with a curious meatiness. Even so, it is fragrant and attractive in its wilful way.

Having donated a case of magnums to the Saintsbury Club, I later suggested to the 'cellarer', Anthony Berry, that as it was fetching such a ridiculous price at auction, we might sell and spend the proceeds on a good young Lafite and other wines. Which we did! But when this was announced at a subsequent dinner at Vintners' Hall, there were loud complaints from members who had never had an opportunity of tasting Pétrus. I was rounded upon but explained that I had given the case to the club in the first place, and had I kept it, I would have made a handsome but undeserved profit for myself! Recent notes: dining with the Suffolks in 1993, drinking quite well despite competition from ripe Vacherin cheese. A meaty *impériale* in 1995, fragrant, sandy-textured and drying out. *Last noted at Donald Kahn's dinner at Mosimann's for the supporters of the Russian National Orchestra, Dec 2000* ★★★

NOT ALL THAT MANY '78S TASTED IN THE 1990S but among the most interesting and salutary were the following:

**Ch Beychevelle** Distinctly uneven. Two variable bottles at a Beychevelle vertical commented on for The Tasting Club at Buck's Club in Mayfair. Palish, mature; both a bit smelly, cheesy; one sweet and chewy, the other crisper, cleaner. *Last tasted Dec 1997* ★ *Not recommended.*

**Ch Bonnet** A very pleasant surprise. Produced by André Lurton towards the end of lunch: deep, lively colour though mature; very sweet, ripe bouquet and flavour, its nose opening up, tea-like. Rich, silky, remarkable length. *At Grézillac in the Entre-Deux-Mers, Oct 2001* ★★★

**Ch Branaire-Ducru** Initially deep ruby, quick to evolve. Speciously attractive bouquet, spicy, light, a very pleasant drink. *Last noted at a state banquet at Buckingham Palace, April 1993* ★★★ *Drink soon.*

**Ch Brane-Cantenac** A pretty good, at least very drinkable '78. Fairly sweet, soft, chewy and ripe (there often seems to be a ripeness, even overripeness, *fermier*, particularly on the nose of Brane). Tannic finish but lots of character. *Last tasted March 1990* ★★★ *Drink soon.*

**Ch Cantenac-Brown** Bertrand du Vivier had a big stock which he asked me to dispose of. Though not a great fan of Cantenac-Brown, I found it not at all bad, fully mature, uncharacteristically lean, with a light dry tannic end. *Sample bottle tasted Sept 1995* ★★ *Some might turn up.*

**Ch Chasse-Spleen** I normally look out for this usually dependable wine. But the '78 a bit raw. *Last tasted April 1994* ★

**Dom de Chevalier** A youthful cherry red and initially raw but maturing well by the late 1980s. A distinctive and distinguished, scented bouquet; stylish, nice weight, lean Graves earthiness, fragrant aftertaste. *Last tasted, in magnums, Sept 1992* ★★★★ *Drink fairly soon.*

**Ch Clarke** Baron Edmond de Rothschild bought the château at the nadir of Bordeaux vintages. Its *1er cru classé* cousins must have been alarmed lest the Rothschild name and money could work a fairy godmother transformation on this *bourgeois*. They need not have worried. This was probably drinking quite well in the early 1980s. *Dried-out when last tasted Aug 1999.*

**Ch La Conseillante** Six notes. It started off well, with all the lovely characteristics of this admirable property. I judged it at its best around 1985, since then having noticed some excess volatile acidity. Its richness has been pricked, fruity but leaner than expected. *Last tasted Feb 1990. At best* ★★★

**Cos d'Estournel** Many notes. Variable. At Bob Paul's tasting of '78s at 10 years of age, it was showing well; indeed, so were quite a lot of other '78s. Looking back they were probably at their peak. Since the end of the 1980s, one corked bottle at that Conservative bastion, the Carlton Club (sign of things to come?), mellow, fragrant but faded; losing fruit, drying out but refreshing at one of my annual tastings at Lyford Cay (1997). A year later at an 'exponential' tasting in New York, some charm and fruit, nice weight but with lip-licking acidity and tannin. *Last tasted Dec 1998. At best* ★★★ *Drying out.*

**Ch Coufran** Memorably at the Fête de La Fleur banquet, at Ch Coufran when I had the honour to preside, June 1988. At 10 years of age it was at its very pleasant best. Still quite nice. *Last tasted June 1991* ★★★

**Ch Ducru-Beaucaillou** Quite a lot of notes, 16 to be precise, from cask samples in June 1979. As previously mentioned, most of the '78s, even this class of wine, were probably not at their best at 10 years of age. Certainly my best notes were in the latter part of the 1980s. More recently, apart from a corked bottle from my own cellar, 'drinking as well as can be', 'just a touch hollow' at the *ban de vendanges* dinner at Ch La Tour-Carnet in 1995. A rather more complimentary note made at a Bacchus Society dinner: 'a good '78', attractive fruit. Slightly raw finish. *Last tasted Nov 1997. At best* ★★★

**Ch L'Église-Clinet** Mature, brown rim; sweet fruit on nose and palate but showing age, edgy, past its best. *Sept 1998* ★

**Ch L'Évangile** Fragrant and lovely in the early 1980s. Showing well at Bob Paul's '10-year' horizontal: deep, stylish, intriguing, fleshy. Just a touch of '78 piquancy. *Last noted Aug 1991* ★★★★. *But I would not wait much longer.*

**Ch La Fleur** Rather disappointing. Sweet enough but a curious pasty texture. Better with food. *At Rodenstock's La Fleur vertical, Sept 1998* ★★?

**Ch Fombrauge** A relatively minor St-Émilion that I have usually found very agreeable and modestly priced. This particular bottle was found in a drinks cupboard at a friend's weekend house at Bosham in West Sussex. Expecting nothing much, I opened it for their Sunday lunch. Now autumnal with 'sear and yellow' rim it was light but sound and, to my surprise, it opened up very pleasantly in the glass – probably to

the surprise of the wine itself which had become accustomed to standing (not lying) undisturbed for so long. And it went well with delicious cold salmon. *Last tasted Aug 1999* ★★

**Les Forts de Latour** I described this, initially, as 'a thick stemmed sort of wine'. Charm neither present nor expected. Several notes, the most recent drunk at 56,000 feet high on Concorde. Still fairly deep and intense but the sediment was rather a problem as it was not decanted. Interesting nose; soft, a bit corky (not corked), tannic but in fact drinking quite well. *Last tasted Dec 1997* ★★

**Ch Giscours** Not 'thick-stemmed' exactly but on the whole thick, substantial, well endowed with everything but finesse and charm. Stuffed with fruit. Almost chewable. Quite a few notes. In 1995 at the Savoie in Margaux. Used to be rather a joke, 'dining at the Savoy'. But it always has been excellent value and for long patronised by Bordeaux proprietors and trade. Bouquet sweet, harmonious, fully developed but drying out a bit. Most recently at an annual III Form Club dinner: still remarkably deep, almost opaque, rich, jammy, slightly tarry nose. Sweet. Attractive. A good '78. *Last noted at Boodle's, London, Jan 2001* ★★★

**Ch Gruaud-Larose** Nearly 20 notes, consistent in the sense that the characteristic Gruaud fruit is omnipresent though, in this vintage, uncharacteristically lean and raw. Having said that, my most recent note, admittedly at a Christie's wine department Christmas dinner, with one's critical faculties, one's colleagues and fare. 'Drinking quite well'. 'But I did notice its bouquet, ripe with a touch of manure' – present company excepted. *Last tasted Dec 1998.*

**Ch Haut-Bailly** Pale; faded; easy, dry finish. Rather disappointing. Just the bottle? *Pre-sale tasting, Dec 2001* ★

**Ch Haut-Batailley** I like the style; in fact, at the time of writing I have just ordered four cases of the lovely vintage 2000. Anyway, the '78 started off well with pleasing cask samples, though some hesitant notes in the mid 1980s. Perfection, sweet, soft and lovely at a tasting in 1989 but, most recently, seemingly on its way out: palish, fully mature; an uncharacteristic rustic, even smelly nose. Better on the palate but surprisingly tannic and raw. *Last noted with the Tasting Club at Berry Bros, April 2001. Would have been better with food* ★★

**Ch Kirwan** Plummy-coloured, stewed fruit and vanilla; some softness and flesh but unconvincing. *Last tasted Dec 1990* ★★

**Ch Lagrange** (Pomerol) An often overlooked Pomerol (its St-Julien namesake being so much better known). A sweet, easy, attractive '78. *May 1992* ★★★

**Ch La Lagune** A very dependable '78. Over a dozen notes, from a sweet, chunky cask sample, subsequent tastings and dinners, all drinking well. More recently, still surprisingly deep in colour; sweet; soft – yet highish alcohol 'a good '78' at dinner for Citibank clients at Christie's (1995), and also sweet, soft and ready at an IWFS St James's branch dinner at the unobtrusive yet classy Cadogan Hotel in London. *Last tasted April 1997* ★★★

**Ch Langoa-Barton** The wine rarely achieves the class and sheer perfection of the Léoville-Barton. (The château itself, however, combines the best of French elegance and inimitable British country-house perfection.) But it has a good shot at it with the '78. It reached its zenith towards the end of the 1980s: spicy, flavoury, pleasant and easy. Two more recent notes: now fully mature, with orange rim; showing maturity on nose and palate. Dry, crisp but still flavoury (1996) and, most recently, magnums at a Saintsbury Club dinner. Plummy coloured; again showing some age though it appeared to

sweeten in the glass. Needs drinking. *Last tasted April 1997.*
*At best* ★★★

**Ch Léoville-Barton** Frankly disappointing. Not unnaturally, in its early days it had some puppy fat. Quite a few subsequent notes have referred to its noticeable though not too worrying acidity, and, more recently, to a hard tannic edge. Only tasted twice in the last decade, most recently 'medium, mature, cheesy, so-so'. *Last noted at a pre-sale tasting, Jan 1994* ★★

**Ch Léoville-Las-Cases** Impressive in cask, June 1979 and January 1980, developing steadily and well, reaching what I believe to be its peak at the end of that decade. A wine, as so often, with extra dimensions and, in 1991, described after tasting as 'a political performance'. Showing well at a pre-sale tasting in 1993 – in fact fairly high marks – but very recently, spicy nose but hard to get to grips with. Dry, now losing body weight, not bad but unexciting. *Last tasted Nov 1999. At best* ★★★★ *but in decline.*

**Ch Léoville-Poyferré** Showing its age but sweet and quite attractive. *Dec 2001* ★★

**Ch Lynch-Bages** With fruit and flavour yet lacking the usual flair. More than that, a stalky/woodiness noted on several occasions. Most recently an attractive luminous colour; lively and interesting bouquet but which was not sustained. Flavoury of course but on the lean side, with a slightly tart, raw finish. *Last tasted Dec 2001* ★★

**Ch Malescot-St-Exupéry** Its style being almost carelessly brash: distinctive fruit, a sort of coarse cassis fragrance. Not unattractive but not quite a wine one would ask to dinner. Lean, unnecessarily aggressive. *Last tasted Sept 1990* ★★

**Ch La Mission Haut-Brion** I stayed at La Mission during the '78 vintage. Unbroken blue sky. La Mission has some of the brash self-confidence of Malescot but that is just the starting point: it has so much else to offer, and though in the earlier notes I had reservations, my two most recent notes didn't mention any. A still deep, most attractive, fully developed tobacco flavour (Bordeaux Club 1995) and superb magnums at an opening 'flight' of La Missions: almost opaque, ruthless; sweet fruit, still youthful fragrance; full, fleshy, a glorious mouthful. A great wine; an amusing '78. *Last tasted at a Rodenstock wine weekend, Sept 1998* ★★★★★

**Ch Montrose** A dozen notes. Predictably closed but with depth and potential. Flesh and texture then noticeable. Three recent notes, deep but with a surprising amber-coloured rim. Good drink though (Christie's boardroom lunch 1994); the most interesting, though I say it myself, at a very vinous dinner

### Andrew Lloyd-Webber

*Now a good friend, despite a distinctly shaky start. A terrible misunderstanding occurred halfway through an important sale of wine I was conducting, when I decided not to accept any more of Andrew's bids because I had no idea who he was! He and his two companions (they were 'casually dressed', to say the least) were not at all pleased. This was at a time he was busily preparing to stage Jesus Christ Superstar and, of course, his name was not yet well known. But, having admitted to a terrible gaffe, I invited him to lunch at Christie's two months later to apologise for and explain my actions. I had been concerned that one person, unknown to Christie's, was buying up all the best wines. He very generously understood my predicament. It would have been better if he had introduced himself before the sale. Looking back, it was undoubtedly the most embarrassing moment of my career as an auctioneer.*

party at home alongside Portugal's greatest red, Barca Velha, also of the '78 vintage. They had quite a bit in common but again I noticed that the Montrose had this orange mature rim – reminded me of a baboon's bottom. Very good. At or a little past its best, finishing very dry. *Last tasted July 1999* ★★★★ *(just).*

**Ch Palmer** A lovely wine and a very good 1978. Many notes, seven during the course of the last decade. Seductively rich, ripe, mulberry-like fruit; full, soft and fleshy in its early days. To the extent that I thought that (in 1985) it could not possibly get any better. Apart from an odd 'drying out' note, proving a fascinating companion to '78 Sassicaia and Cheval Blanc at Hugh Johnson's (in 1997) rather vegetal, Merlot-like, distinctive, touch of liquorice', needs drinking. Fully mature, delicious but fading and slightly raw at lunch (1999). Most recently, sweet, attractive, quite good length and residual tannin and acidity. Otherwise *à point. Last noted at the Ch Palmer dinner at Ransome's Dock in London, Feb 2001* ★★★★ *Best to drink soon.*

**Ch Pavie-Decesse** Fragrant, original, good flesh, attractive. *Nov 1990* ★★★ *Drink soon.*

**Ch Pichon, Baron** Showing well at tastings in the mid-1980s, powerful, spicy. Marvellous components but perhaps a trifle coarse. Most recently: rich, ripe, mature appearance; old, oaky nose; flavoury but tart. Even though this last bottle was perhaps not of the best, the '78 Baron is sure to be on the downward slope. *Last tasted Dec 2001. At best* ★★★

**Ch Pichon Longueville, Comtesse de Lalande** This was the year, hence the full title, that Mme de Lencquesaing took over the château from her brother Alain Miailhe, literally by drawing the short straw. One is tempted to describe Mme de Lencquesaing as *formidable*, but she is warm, approachable, with boundless energy. Anyway, she seemed to put her stamp on her first vintage: a good, rich, fruity, spicy wine. Many notes, half a dozen during the last decade. Yet, like almost all the '78s, now failing to a certain extent to live up to expectations. At random: cedary, correct; sweet mid-palate, but not rich or convincing enough (with duck, Gidleigh Park, Devon 1997); a minty, fleshy *impériale* holding up well (Bacchus Society 1997); rich, ripe but touch of cork (1997). Surprisingly deep; good rich bouquet but disappointing. Raw finish. *Last noted pre-sale in Geneva, May 1999. At best* ★★★★ *Variable.*

**Ch Siran** Drinking well. *Sept 1995* ★★★

**Ch Talbot** Many very consistent notes, but it is my constancy that is in question. I admire Talbot but find its overripe, 'superior rustic' smell and taste, as seen in its '78, hard to fathom. A matter of personal taste. *Last tasted Jan 1993* ★★★

**Ch Trotanoy** A wonderful wine. It manages to be impressively mouthfilling and also to exude charm. Quite 'silky, sweet, rich, round, delicious'. *Last tasted May 1991* ★★★★

OF THE MANY '78S TASTED IN THE MID- TO LATE 1980S nearly all are past their best and should be drunk soon. (The star ratings apply at that time.) **Ch Boyd Cantenac** delicious. *Jan 1987* ★★★; **Ch Canon** rich. All the component parts. *May 1985* ★★★★; **Ch Canon-La-Gaffelière** rich, earthy, pleasing. *July 1989* ★★★; **Ch Cantemerle** variable. *June 1986. At best* ★★★; **Ch Certan-de-May** lovely wine. *1988* ★★★★; **Ch Clerc-Milon-Mondon** fleshy but bitter tannic finish. *Sept 1989* ★★; **Ch Durfort-Vivens** extraordinary fruit and spice. *Sept 1986* ★★★★; **Ch Figeac** gushing, almost exotic. *Dec 1989* ★★★; **Ch Le Gay** luscious. *April 1988* ★★★★★; **Ch Gazin** fleshy, spicy, velvety tannins. *Feb 1988* ★★★★; **Ch Grand-Puy-Ducasse** unimpressive. *July 1989* ★; **Ch Grand-Puy-Lacoste** fragrant, elegant, crisp, good texture. *Feb 1989* ★★★★; **Ch Haut-**

Bailly rich. Good. *March 1988* ★★★; **Ch d'Issan** soft, fleshy, elegant. *Feb 1988* ★★★; **Ch Lagrange** (St-Julien) flavoury, lean, very tannic. *Nov 1989* ★; **Ch Lascombes** quite good. *Jan 1988* ★★; **Ch Latour-Martillac** quite nice. *Oct 1989* ★★; **Ch Lynch-Moussas** surprisingly fruity and attractive. *Oct 1988* ★★; **Ch Malartic-Lagravière** quite flavoury. *July 1989* ★★; **Ch Mouton-Baronne-Philippe** lean, deft, easy. *Oct 1989* ★★★; **Ch Pontet Canet** not very good. *Jan 1989*; **Ch Prieuré-Lichine** rich, ripe, attractive. *Oct 1998* ★★★; **Ch Rauzan-Gassies** poor. *April 1989*; **Ch La Tour-Carnet** not good enough for its class. *June 1988* ★★; and **Ch La Tour Haut-Brion** deep, rich, good. *Oct 1986* ★★★

# 1979 ★★

An abundant crop, the biggest since 1934, small, thick-skinned grapes resulting in a very tannic wine, lacking flesh. Because the British merchants were overstocked with '75s, '76s, and '78s, it was hard even to give the '79s away despite their cheapness – this was the last really inexpensive Bordeaux before prices once again began to take off when the 1982s hit the market (and the headlines).

The wines were generally at their best in the mid-1980s, particularly those from the Right Bank, but since then the paucity of fruit, flesh and extract has left the tannin high and dry. Except for the great Pomerols, give the vintage a miss.

**Ch Lafite** Like a bad-tempered baby pulled out of its cot by a doting father it was presented on its first birthday prior to a Lafite dinner at Boulestin's in London. Raw and raucous. By the early to mid-1980s, it was hard and very tannic but with good length. At Penning-Rowsell's '10-year' dinner its nose and taste beginning to demonstrate Lafite fragrances, though touch of astringency.

I have just four notes over the past decade: peppery, high-toned; firm, flavoury but dry (Stockholm 1994). In a 'flight' of four Lafite *impériales*, spicy, good fruit but raw, very tannic (1996). Yet another *impériale*: attractive, enough fruit and in particular enough extract and tannin to cope with black truffle and mascarpone-crusted Brie (Bacchus Society 1997). Most recently, Jamie Guise's last magnum (see also the 1867 Ch Yquem from his father's cellar): still deep, rich, lovely; distinctly good, distinctly Lafite – it opened up fragrantly; pretty good yet still very tannic. *Last noted at a Sunday lunch, July 1999* ★★★

**Ch Latour** I look back on some pretty appalling notes made throughout the 1980s. Indeed I cannot recall one wine, let alone Latour, being so rudely referred to: smelling of 'old socks', 'sweaty fat' (at a subsequent tasting), 'animal fat, pork and boot polish', 'very cheesy, bandages' – whether mint, lint or over sores not elaborated upon – 'dung'. 'Happily a better flavour than nose', which is at least something. Most recently, a much kinder note at a pre-sale tasting in London: (now) medium-deep, still youthful; nose very rich though very tannic, opening up quite agreeably; dry, good flavour, on the lean side and with tannic finish. On the whole I am not too keen and doubt if it will ever rise above the character of a dour Scotsman. *Last tasted Jan 1999* ★★

**Ch Margaux** M. Mentzelopoulos' second vintage. Well over a dozen notes from autumn of 1981, fragrance frequently reiterated. Also flavoury, but the raw '79 tannin hard to get away from. The last three notes all, coincidentally, at vertical tastings; the first, in 1995, during a Hollywood (Florida) Wine Society weekend: cherry red; bouquet quickly opening up; crisp, surprisingly attractive for a '79. Next at Wagner's tasting

in 1997: still very deep and intense; also fragrant, sweet, slightly 'meaty' bouquet and flavour. Very tannic and, I thought, a vinegary whiff. Not much change, sweeter than expected, good flavour, lean and with leathery tannic texture. *Last tasted Nov 2000* ★★★ *I doubt if it will change much.*

**Ch Mouton-Rothschild** Lots of fragrance and flavour but tarred with the same '79 tannic tar brush. Good flesh, fair fruit, spicy. An attractive if lean mouthful. A bit raw and very tannic. *Last tasted Oct 1990* ★★★

**Ch Haut-Brion** First noted at a French Wine Farmers' trade tasting in April 1980. They were quick off the mark. The main impression, throughout, was austere, raw tannins and relatively low prices. Two fairly recent notes: deep, rich looking; ripe 'bricky' nose; good flavour; fairly tannic (pre-sale New York 1997). Next, to help celebrate the fifth anniversary of the Académie du Vin de Bordeaux in the city's Grand Théâtre, mature-looking, 'tannic', and little else to say. The 12 other wines and very distinguished table companions included Philippine de Rothschild and Monsieur Beaumarchais (fascinating to meet a descendant of the famous author). Most recently: deep, dark cherry-red tinge, rich legs; alas, unexciting except for the high acidity hinted at by the redness just noted. A touch of liquorice, opening up with a whiff of caramel; surprisingly sweet on the palate, but spoiled by its astringency, leaving the mouth puckered and dry. Nice try Hugh, but … *Last noted at Hugh Johnson's, Saling Hall, Dec 2001. At best* ★★

**Ch Ausone** As usual, the odd man out, firstly in appearance: pale, pink-tinged; second, the nose 'hints of strawberry and chocolate', distinctive and attractive; third, in some ways more appealing than its peers, at any rate those from the Médoc. Crisp fruit, silky tannic texture. *Last noted at Penning-Rowsell's '10-year' tasting, Feb 1989* ★★★

**Ch Cheval Blanc** One of the best '79s, outstanding at a major MW horizontal in 1984. At 10 years of age, richly coloured with a beautifully evolved bouquet, 'cloves, cinnamon and honey'; svelte, elegant. A decade later dining with Matts Hanson at Le Coq Blanc, Stockholm: pleasant sweetness and weight, easy, slightly chaptalised style (chaptalisation was first used at the château in 1978, or so I was told). Most recently, a magnum: very mature looking; noticeable vanillin on nose; surprisingly pleasant, its 'leathery-harsh silk texture' with *coq au vin* (the *vin* being Cheval Blanc of course). *Last noted at the Wolf/Weinart vertical in Austria, Sept 1997* ★★★★

**Ch Pétrus** Ten notes. Slow to develop. For ten years or so a heavily laden but not perfectly balanced wine, heftily imbued with tannins and acidity. At the start of the last decade, in bottles, starting to shed some of its colour, fragrant though peppery, but in *grands formats* still deep with youthful ruby colour, the first, a jeroboam in 1994 tasted blind with other top '79 Pomerols: a 'powerhouse', full of fruit and tannin. A year later, between the '78 and '88, all in *impériales* like some praetorian guard: crisp fruit on nose and palate, 'classic', tannic – it was better with food. *Both at Rodenstock wine weekends, the last in Sept 1995* ★★★★

**Ch Beychevelle** First tasted in cask, April 1980: virtually opaque; good fruit, sweaty tannins; stylish even at that stage. Developed well. Still fairly deep; rich, cedary nose; full-bodied for Beychevelle, fleshy and tannic. *Last tasted May 1993* ★★★

**Ch Boyd-Cantenac** It would be understandable if you wished to avoid Boy in a vintage like '79 but it turned out to be pretty good: still deep, 'thick' (extract), quite good fruit; surprisingly sweet, rich – and tannic. *Last noted at a pre-sale tasting, Jan 1998* ★★★

**Ch Calon-Ségur** Intense purple in the spring after the vintage, full of fruit. Its bouquet evolving attractively, its best feature, for though at first sip sweet, there is a touch of leanness and astringency. Needs food. *Last tasted Feb 1990* ★★★

**Dom de Chevalier** Most notes made in the mid-1980s: deep, bouquet slow to develop, good texture, rich but a bit raw. *Last tasted Sept 1993* ★★★

**Ch La Croix-de-Gay** Magnums: deep, well developed bouquet, soft, velvety tannins. *Speaking on the 'Wines of Pomerol' at a Commanderie de Bordeaux dinner to honour the Hospitaliers de Pomerol, in Bristol, May 1995* ★★★

**Cos d'Estournel** A heavy fairly localised storm during flowering severely reduced the crop. In cask (April 1980) even tougher than Ch Montrose. It ameliorated through the 1980s. Its bouquet needs a little coaxing, but fragrant. Crisp fruit. Good wine. *Last tasted Jan 1990* ★★★

**Ch Ducluzeau** Couldn't resist this. This Listrac wine sounds like Peter Sellers' French detective. The first taste surprisingly sweet and 'not unattractive'. *At a pre-sale tasting Sept 1996* ★★

**Ch Ducru-Beaucaillou** The truth is that however much we all liked and admired the late Jean-Eugène Borie, Ducru could be rather stodgy and lacking zest. From an austere cask sample no enthusiastic notes, stalky, woody and, the last, alas, corked. *Last tasted Sept 1997. Might just be my luck.*

**Dom de L'Église** A not very impressive double magnum. The least deep. Its dry-leaves taste and austerity reminded me of a poor Ausone. Nose much better. *Last tasted Sept 1994* ★

**Ch La Fleur** In the same group of top '79 Pomerols but this time in bottles (four): very deep; fragrant bouquet, citrus whiff of acidity, touch of mocha; some sweetness, wonderful texture, richly flavoured. *Last tasted Sept 1994* ★★★★★

**Ch La Fleur-Pétrus** The second of the four great '79s; deep, intense, lively looking, rich 'legs'. Crisp, 'soft fruit' character; rich, rounded, fleshy, tannic. *Last tasted Sept 1994* ★★★★

**Ch Giscours** Most notes in the mid-1980s and very consistent: packing a punch, rich, assertive yet elegant. One more recent note: nose needed coaxing, but within minutes opened up well. *Last tasted April 1995* ★★★(★) *Still needs time.*

**Ch Gruaud-Larose** An 'all things to all men' sort of wine. Many notes. Characteristically full of fruit. Deep, plummy. Rich, ripe Médoc scents. A mouthfiller! Sublimating tannins. Most recently: still richly coloured, very good, slightly caramelly nose; good fruit, curious 'mucked-out stables' endtaste exposing raw tannins. Needs food. *Last noted at a pre-sale tasting, Dec 1997.*

**Ch Kirwan** A good '79, but one is biased when dining with the proprietors. Nice weight and flavoury. Very refreshing. *Last tasted Sept 1998* ★★★

**Ch La Lagune** Ruby; spicy; agreeable. Amenable tannic/iron end. *Last tasted Jan 1993* ★★★

**Ch Lascombes** Variable notes. Richly coloured; some ripeness and sweetness but with teeth-gripping tannin and acidity. *Last tasted April 1992* ★★

**Ch Léoville-Barton** I wish I could say more. It is very drinkable but it is as if all its component parts have been through a sieve. Fragrant, yes; lean yet some flesh; refreshing. Admittedly not tasted very recently. *Last tasted Jan 1990* ★★★

**Ch Léoville-Las-Cases** Nearly 20 notes and very impressive from the spring of 1980 to the mid-1980s, after which I noted more pedestrian qualities, cedary but earthy, quite good fruit but, of course, tannic. My penultimate note made at a British Airways wine committee tasting when it was deemed 'ready to

fly!'. Ironic therefore when at the annual British Airways wine committee dinner, at the Waterside Inn, Bray, the wine was decidedly woody and earthy. *Last tasted Nov 1996* ★★?

**Ch Lynch-Bages** Also many notes, from a not too exciting cask sample. It developed a more recognisable Lynch-Bages-Cabernet spiciness in the mid-1980s but was lean and severe. At a vertical tasting for the '33 Club in Brussels my comments were brief: still deep; tannic; not bad. Holding well. *Last tasted at a pre-sale tasting Dec 1997* ★★★(★)

**Ch Palmer** Continuing its run of well above average wines. Half a dozen consistent notes from the mid-1980s: glorious colour; fleshy ripe fruitiness on both nose and – for a '79 – on palate. Endorsed by my most recent note though its tannin now laid bare – a lean, attenuated, spicy, teeth-gripping finish. Good length. Needs food. *Last noted at the 'exponential' (I keep having to look this word up) tasting in New York, Dec 1998* ★★★

**Ch Pape-Clément** Brown-orange-rimmed maturity; 'bricky' Graves nose; earthy, gravelly on palate. Tart finish. *Last tasted at a pre-sale tasting, Sept 1997* ★★★

**Ch Pavie** A very good '79. Crisp fruit; rich extract masking sustaining tannins and acidity. *At the Millésimes de Collection dinner in St-Émilion, June 1998* ★★★★

**Pavillon Rouge de Ch Margaux** Interesting to see what the second post-Mentzelopoulos Pavillon would be like. Fragrant, vigorous, lean, attractive. 'An overpriced adolescent.' *Not tasted since Nov 1990* ★★

**Ch Pichon-Longueville-Lalande** Over a dozen mainly admiring notes, full of crisp fresh fruit and excitement, from cask to the early 1990s. Two recent more studied notes very briefly summarised, made at Lalande verticals, the first an *impériale* in 1994 at the Weinart Probe dinner: very deep, still youthful looking; nose hard to get to grips with; sweet enough flavour relatively (after the '85) lean and tannic. Lastly at Christie's Pichon-Lalande masterclass, palate more interesting than nose but lack of balance. *Last tasted March 1995. At best* ★★★★ *Drink soon.*

**Ch La Tour Haut-Brion** Complex, rather strange; dry, its austerity mellowing, crisp, fruity. *Last tasted June 1990* ★★★

**Ch Trotanoy** From the start, an impressive wine, deep, 'rich' is a feeble understatement, with the inimitable silky Pomerol texture. The last of eight notes, this time two magnums, a sweet, fleshy mouthful, yet not 'pushy'. Good fruit and flavour. Glorious. *Last tasted Sept 1994* ★★★★★

A SELECTION OF THE MANY '79S TASTED IN THE 1980S, good, bad and indifferent and making allowances for the subversive tannin and diminishing fruit: **Ch d'Angludet** ★★★; **Ch Batailley** ★★; **Ch Branaire-Ducru** ★★★; **Ch Brane-Cantenac** ★★★; **Ch Canon** ★★★★; **Ch Canon-La Gaffelière** ★★★; **Ch Cantemerle** ★★; **Ch Chasse-Spleen** ★★★; **Ch Croizet-Bages** ★★★; **Ch Dassault** ★★★; **Ch Figeac** ★★★; **Ch La Fleur-Gazin** ★★★★; **Ch Les Forts-de-Latour** ★★★; **Ch La Gaffelière** ★★; **Ch Gloria** ★★★; **Ch Grand-Puy-Ducasse** ★; **Ch Grand-Puy-Lacoste** ★★★★; **Ch La Grave-Trigant** ★★★; **Ch Haut-Bailly** ★★★; **Ch Haut-Batailley** ★★★★; **Ch Lagrange** (St-Julien) ★; **Ch Lanessan** ★★; **Ch Langoa-Barton** ★★★; **Ch Latour-à-Pomerol** ★★★★; **Ch Léoville-Poyferré** ★★★; **Ch La Louvière** ★★★; **Ch Magdelaine** ★★★; **Ch Marquis de Terme**; **Ch Montrose** ★★★★; **Ch Mouton-Baronne-Philippe** ★★; **Ch Pavie-Decesse** ★★★; **Ch Petit-Village** ★★★; **Ch Pichon-Baron** ★★; and **Ch La Pointe** ★★★

# 1980–1989

Unquestionably this was a great decade, matching the 1920s for the number of high quality vintages. Unlike the early 1930s and the mid-1970s, when poor weather and a severe recession coincided, the 1980s reversed the process: there was, allowing for the natural variations described below, overall a vast improvement in weather conditions, and, even more happily, a renewed demand to match. The wine trade, if not exactly licking its wounds, did not re-enter the market and stock up. The big brewers in Britain had burnt their fingers once and, since then, have been more or less out of the market, private customers being the main buyers of *en primeur* wines. In the United States and further afield, the 1982 vintage hit the button. Prices had recovered and the benefits of the new prosperity are plain to see: the châteaux proprietors had the means to renovate, to install new vats, to increase the use of new barrels, even to rebuild vineyard walls. But the most important result for the consumer was the increasing care in the vineyards: pruning and green pruning to reduce yields and increase quality, and the selection of only the best vats for the *grand vin*. The other noticeable thing about the 1980s is the increasing number of 'second wines' made from the less fine vats and wines made from young vines. This was a contrast to the depression in the mid-1970s, when this sort of care and selection could not be afforded.

In the 1950s, consultant enologists hardly existed. The precursor was Professor Ribereau-Gayon, but the best known became Emile Peynaud. His influence was considerable. He always averred that his job was to prevent or rectify mistakes and that the accusation that Médoc châteaux were being 'Peynaudised' was more than unfair. However, by the 1980s, there appeared a new breed of consultants employed to advise on and, hopefully, to improve the quality of wine. Happily, though, 'designer' wines had not yet arrived.

*Vintages at a Glance*
**Outstanding ★★★★★**
1982, 1985, 1989
**Very Good ★★★★**
1986, 1988
**Good ★★★**
1981, 1983

# 1980 ★

If the decade ended with a bang, it certainly opened with a whimper. Cool spring, late and uneven flowering, June cold and wet, a moderate summer and early autumn prolonged the ripening process. A very late harvest, well into October, resulted in an average-sized crop of less than average quality.

**Ch Lafite** The epitome of a light luncheon wine, indeed fulfilling precisely that purpose on the last six occasions in the mid-1990s, all from a case of magnums in my own cellar and consumed pleasantly at three successive boardroom luncheons (Christie's never thanked me) and three at home. Identical notes too: medium, touch of mahogany, mature; modestly fragrant bouquet opened up nicely, touch of iodine, light style, flavoury, refreshing. Hardly a '59 or a '61, but a pleasant enough drink. (And one's guests are always impressed by the label!) *Last tasted May 1996* ★★

**Ch Latour** Though considered 'more serious' than Lafite, not half as pleasing as a drink though I confess I haven't tasted it since 1990. Its best feature at Frérick's tasting, and at the Penning-Rowsells', was the emergent bouquet. Otherwise, despite its fruit, astringent. It might have become a bit more amenable. *Last tasted March 1990* ★★?

**Ch Margaux** One of the few first growths tasted in cask (Oct 1981), deeper in colour than expected for the vintage, and fragrant. The most interesting was tasted at the château in

1984 in the company of Émile Peynaud who informed us that the grapes were picked from 17 October, the latest harvest of the century. Showing well at Desai's tasting (1987) and at Penning-Rowsells' '10-year' review: ruby-coloured, peppery at first but opened up spicily. Silky tannins, crisp, short. The first of my more recent notes was made at Wagner's tasting in 1979s (when Paul Pontallier confirmed the late harvest but told us that it started on 4 October): dry, quite good flavour, very tannic. A modest mark. Next at a pre-sale tasting 'nondescript' appearance and nose. On the light side, drying out, with a 'leaking end'. At Wagner's second vertical a rather more generous note: fragrant, chaptalised; some sweetness, lacking flesh, an easy, 'light lunch wine'. *Last tasted Nov 2000* ★★

**Ch Mouton-Rothschild** I was flattered to be asked by Baron Philippe to provide the tasting notes for his first label exhibition catalogue which was published in 1983. It gave me a good excuse to request sample bottles of the most recent vintages that I had not yet tasted. The '80, I was told, had been bottled in June 1982 so was pretty fresh. At Penning-Rowsells' '10-year' tasting it did not look very convincing, nor was its bouquet quite as exciting as one might expect even in a light vintage. A pleasant enough drink, just enough fruit but a bit raw. If Philippine is planning yet another label book, I hope she will give me an opportunity to update my note. *Last tasted March 1990* ★★

**Ch Haut-Brion** One or two unimpressive notes, then in 1990 at Penning-Rowsells' 10th-anniversary dinner/tasting, given time in the glass, the bouquet unravelled fragrantly. On the palate, fairly light, with the unmistakable Pessac bricky, tobacco-like taste. A bit short. Most recently, one of 20 wines at Len Evans' fancy dress 'Imperial Dinner' at Robert's Restaurant in Pokolbin, New South Wales. We were all given our marching orders: precisely which character each guest was to assume. For example, an Australian lady made a remarkable look-alike Queen Victoria in appearance and deportment; one poor chap had to go as Hitler (quite good too. I suspect that Len didn't like him). Daphne and I had to dress up as Marie-Antoinette and Louis XVI. I wanted to do it on the cheap, with tomato sauce down my T-shirt, but I was tempted to show off my legs in white hose. We would have looked magnificently regal had it not been for the cotton wool wigs. The wine was quite good. *Last tasted Sept 2000* ★★

**Ch Ausone** Only two notes. At Lloyd Flatt's in 1987: pale, thin, tinny, unknit and short. Better on its tenth birthday. Quite pleasant though loosely knit. *Last tasted March 1990* ★ *Drink up.*

**Ch Cheval Blanc** In cask, a good note. At Penning-Rowsell's, voted best of the 10-year-old first growths. Better on palate than nose; sweet, silky texture, elegant. Most recently, the second wine of the first 'flight' of Wolf's three-day Cheval Blanc marathon. A healthy appearance; attractive bouquet, touch of iron, sweet; gentle fruit, dry finish. Good to drink now. Unlikely to get any better. *Last tasted Sept 1997* ★★★

**Ch Pétrus** In 1986, Hans Peter Frericks gave a lavish Pétrus tasting/dinner in the Margrave's Palace in his home town of Munich. A magnum of the '80 was produced for the tasting and an *impériale* for the dinner. It was a bit over the top, spicy, specious but an attractive drink. And drink it we did, accompanied by caviar dished out like porridge. I was sitting next to Christian Mouiex who agreed that 'the beluga was sensational but did nothing for the Pétrus'! Next, in 1990, a more modest-sized bottle at the Penning-Rowsells': ripe, mulberry, specious. This, effectively, was my last note as a double magnum at Rodenstock's opening dinner was oxidised. *Last sniffed at, Sept 1995. At best* ★★

**OF THE OTHER '80s LAST TASTED IN THE 1990s**

**Dom de Chevalier** Not tasted in its youth and, 16 years old, at the château, already orange-tinged; rather chocolatey, vanillin nose. Chaptalised, earthy, tannate of iron finish. Most recently, an odd bottle 'liberated' from the wine department cellar, decanted in my office and trotted along for an important dinner at my club with Christa and Bob Paul. It was pale and pretty; a pleasant nose and taste; some sweetness, on the light side and with the same slightly bitter iron taste at the end previously noted. *Last tasted Oct 1998* ★★

**Ch La Fleur** Already mature and fairly light in 1987. Unimpressive, to say the least at Rodenstock's vertical: fully mature, weak-rimmed, quite good only. Next, a sweetish, attractive but lean, crisp and slightly 'edgy' bottle in Rodenstock's vertical in 1998. The following year a fairly similar note, lean and a little tart (certainly not a *geisha*). *Last tasted at the American Club in Tokyo, Nov 1999* ★

**Ch Figeac** Only one note. A 'pale and interesting' 17-year old, sweet, surprisingly attractive, but lacking length. *Last tasted Sept 1997* ★★ *Drink up.*

**Ch Les Forts de Latour** Several notes. Most recently: a good, mature colour; spicy Cabernet Sauvignon nose; good flavour but touch of astringency. *Last tasted Nov 1998* ★★

**Ch Lynch-Bages** Several notes. A lively, lightly fruity wine. Most recently, palish, weak-rimmed but on the palate lean but fragrant, a pleasant after-theatre supper wine! *Last tasted at the '33 Club tasting in Brussels, Nov 1995* ★★

**Ch La Mission Haut-Brion** Fairly good colour; dry, light, austere. Several notes. *Last tasted June 1999* ★

**AMONG THOSE TASTED IN THE MID- TO LATE 1980s**

**Ch Brane-Cantenac** alright if you like hen droppings; **Ch Calon-Ségur** ★★ *drink up*; **Ch 'Certan, De May de**

**Certan'** (*sic*) more of a mouthful than the wine itself ★★; **Ch Croizet-Bages** raw edge ★; **Ch Duhart-Milon** flavoury, acidic, short ★; **Ch Grand-Puy-Lacoste** raw, tannic ★; **Ch Langoa-Barton** attractive lunch wine ★★; **Ch Léoville-Las-Cases** one of the best '80s ★★★ *but drink up*; **Ch Léoville-Poyferré** lacking character. Short. **Ch Mouton-Baronne-Philippe** light, thin, short, 'yet a certain delicacy and not without flavour ★★; **Ch Palmer** one of the best '80s ★★★; **Ch Pichon-Lalande** almost a charmer ★★; **Ch Pontet-Canet** light, dry, tart; and **Vieux Ch Certan** bottle varnish. *At best* ★★

# 1981 ★★★

A good claret vintage, the sort that the British buy for drinking not for display or investment. The weather conditions were advantageous: the early flowering in hot, dry weather which continued throughout the summer with a sprinkling of rain in September to swell the grapes and which cleared for the harvest on 1 October. Particularly successful in Pomerol.

**Ch Lafite** It encapsulated the vintage, at least as far as the Médocs are concerned. Showing well on its tenth birthday 'soft, gentle fragrant; good fruit, flavour, texture' (noted at the Penning-Rowsells' in 1991). Just five notes since, most unexpectedly in Chile dining with Maria Ignacia and Jorge Eyzaguirre on their reclaimed Los Vascos estate. Dry, lean, very drinkable in March 1994; identical note a couple of years later at a BYOB dinner in New York – needed food, which, happily, was provided. And at two pre-sale tastings, the first in London: mature, open appearance; fully developed nose, cedary, fragrant; nice weight, crisp, delicious flavour. And four months later, its dryness and leanness noted. *Last tasted in Geneva, May 1999* ★★★ *Drink soon.*

**Ch Latour** Neither big nor charming. In fact rather pedestrian by Latour standards. Perhaps not the sort of vintage that suits. Having said that, fairly full-bodied; nose of some depth, cedary, biscuity; a decidedly good flavour and crisp fruit, but lacking length and with a swingeingly tannic finish. Not tasted recently and will doubtless have opened up and softened a little. *Last tasted June 1991* ★★(★★)?

**Ch Margaux** Showing well in cask, September 1982. But when I tasted it the following May, I was forcibly struck by the all-pervading smell of wet concrete at the château. They had recently completed the new second-year cellar by digging a huge hole across the road just outside the main *chai*'s perimeter, lining it with concrete and, when finished, planting grass seeds so that now it just looks like a lawn. But I certainly thought that this pungent smell must infiltrate the oak *barriques* and affect the smell and taste of the wine. However, reviewing my notes, I cannot trace any evidence in the wines, though on my annual visits I still found the smell of concrete very pervasive. In its early years, sinewy and tannic. At the age of ten, still deeply coloured; crisp fruit, lean, raw but flavoury. Next, at the first of Wagner's 'definitive' (I hate the word) verticals in 1997, fairly fragrant, a bit vegetal; better on palate. Sweet, lean, crisp. The following year at L'Académie du Vin de Bordeaux event, displaying a well-developed Margaux fragrance; surprisingly sweet and fleshy though with a curiously dry, slightly acidic finish. The following year, in New York, 'lean and flavoury'. At Wagner's most recent tasting, its bouquet soft, mature, with a citrus touch but fading in the glass, and as previously described. Attractive though and *à point*. *Last tasted Nov 2000* ★★★ *Drink soon.*

**Ch Mouton-Rothschild** A dozen notes, clearly at its – very attractive – best in its first ten years, notably at the Penning-Rowsells' '81s tasting in June 1991. It really was delicious, particularly its flavoury, spicy bouquet and crisp, fruity flavour. Just enough flesh but some tannic bitterness. Lovely fruit and flavour, from a Scottish cellar, pre-sale in 1994, but a couple of years later lunching at Chippenham Lodge, joined by the Penning-Rowsells and the Averys, it was showing considerable maturity, though richly coloured; fragrant though slightly vegetal nose; crisp, flavoury but with a rather screwed-up acidic finish. The next note hosting a gourmet dinner at the Grand Bay Hotel, Coconut Grove, Florida, when it appeared still to be youthful and intense with a typically spicy Mouton Cabernet Sauvignon nose. But it was raw and very tannic. Pan-seared supreme of squab did not help much. Another bottle from my country cellar, 'ready now' but querying its future. Most recently, crisp, lean, flavoury and acidic. *Last noted at a pre-sale tasting, Jan 1999* ★★★ *but not improving.*

**Ch Haut-Brion** A very good '81, but in its own very individualistic way. Elegance and vinosity come to mind. More harmonious, less dramatic than La Mission across the road. By its tenth birthday richly coloured, maturing; high-toned fragrance; with '81 leanness but good structure. And of course, 'tobacco', earthy (I also wrote 'brick dust' which sounds awful but was somehow trying to get its character). Then in 1997, conducting an auction talk, something of a speciality of mine, with Joan, Duchesse de Mouchy and Jean Delmas, in the main auction room at Christie's, Park Avenue. We and the audience all had a glass of the '81 which though good, and in most appropriate company, was not the sort of wine I like to drink without food. Most recently, outshining some other top '81s, with excellent flavour, good length, tannin and tolerable acidity. *Last noted at a pre-sale tasting in London, Jan 1999* ★★★★

**Ch Ausone** Ausone is on a different wavelength. Just a couple of notes. Definitely a good wine. Touch of malt, tobacco, dried ferns, earthy – not all that different from Graves but distinctively different. *Last tasted June 1991* ★★★

**Ch Cheval Blanc** No problems here, no damning with faint praise, no excuses. First tasted in cask in September 1982. Very good. Its natural sweetness noted through the 1980s. Showing well on its tenth birthday: fragrant, powerful, attractive. A lovely gradation of colour, maturing well; good fruit and grip; slightly smoky taste, harmonious though rich tannin (at the Baur au Lac, Zurich, 1994). Drinking perfectly at Christie's wine department's Christmas dinner the same year, and an impressive *impériale*: opaque core; sweet, good flavour, perfect weight (alcohol 12.6%), touch of iron. Dry finish. *Last noted at the Wolf/Weinart Cheval Blanc vertical, Sept 1997* ★★★★ *overlooking the Attersee in Austria.*

**Ch Pétrus** At one year old, advanced puppy fat, amazingly full, fleshy, rich, complete. Developing a spicy bouquet by the mid-1980s. As an early nine-year-old adolescent, playing hard to get yet teasing. On its tenth birthday, having decanted it four hours before taking it to the Penning-Rowsells', it was really showing off unashamedly. Opulent but blunt. A splendid pairing with the Ch Cheval Blanc at my *Klassische Weindegustation* in Zurich, surprisingly less deep, less intense; with mulberry-ripe richness; fleshier, rounded, powerful finish but lacking the subtlety and finesse of the Cheval Blanc. Most recently, one of a really terrific line-up of over 50 top wines at a Christie's pre-sale tasting in New York. Sweet. Delicious. *Last tasted Dec 1997* ★★★★

A RANGE OF '81S TASTED IN THE MID- TO LATE 1990S to demonstrate their current state of play:

**Ch Brane-Cantenac** Not my favourite wine in a vintage like this. Clearly chaptalised and showing an orange-tinged maturity early on. A more than usually over-the-top nose, but, I admit, lots to taste. In 1990 I recommended 'Drink now to 1996'. Three years after this 'deadline' certainly fully developed but lean and acidic. *Last tasted Jan 1999* ★★ *Drink up.*

**Ch Canon** A good wine. Drinking well in 1989. Seven years later perfectly evolved, sweet, harmonious, nice fruit. Delicious. *Last tasted March 1996* ★★★★ *Drink soon.*

**Ch Chasse-Spleen** Just shows how good husbandry and winemaking pays off. From its deep-coloured youth, maturing evenly, light style but constantly attractive. Certainly endorsed recently and much more appealing than the classed growths alongside. *Last tasted April 1994* ★★★ *Drink up.*

**Dom de Chevalier** Several notes. Spicy, scented, rich but tannic. A taste-provoking experiment lunching at the domaine. One bottle was decanted at 12.30pm and poured at 2.10pm, the other was decanted immediately before pouring. There was a difference. The first showed a touch of oxidation, was sweet, soft, pleasant, easy but showing its age (13 years); the freshly decanted with much less aeration was more closed on the nose, appeared firmer, dryer, spicy and surprisingly tannic. Six at table preferred the aerated, nine preferred the freshly poured. *Last tasted April 1994* ★★ *to* ★★★

**Ch Cos d'Estournel** A 70/30/30 wine (Cabernet Sauvignon, Merlot, new oak). A delicious cask sample brought by de Luze to London the April after the vintage. Continuing to show well. Michèle Prats, at my tasting in Florida (1990) informed us that there had been a violent rainstorm during the harvest 'which caused some lack of concentration and charm', not that we noticed. It was delicious. Most recently, actually showing considerable charm, with lip-licking acidity at the exponential tasting. A very attractive wine, far better than the '78 that followed. *Last noted at the 'exponential' tasting in New York, Dec 1998* ★★★★ *Drink soon.*

**Ch La Croix du Casse** Mentioned because not often seen, and where I found it I know not. Deliciously sweet and *à point. At home, Dec 1994* ★★★ *So you never can tell!*

**Ch L'Église-Clinet** Hardy Rodenstock was one of the first fully to appreciate the outstanding quality of a wine relatively unknown to the great wide world, and overshadowed by the likes of Pétrus and, more recently, Le Pin. The '81 was in a range of 15 vintages and demonstrated that the leanness of the vintage seeped through to the Pomerols. Also, like some other leading Pomerols not very interesting on the nose. Lots of grip. Hopefully a long life ahead. *Last tasted Sept 1998* ★★★(★)?

**Ch Figeac** Not my favourite Figeac vintage. 'Stalky', 'hard', 'woody though very flavoury'; 'rusty coloured rim', 'dry', 'leathery'. These were between 1984 and 1990. Rather better magnums in 1996 at a BYOB dinner in New York, quite attractive to drink by itself but 'a slightly woody finish'. More recently, a distinctive, flavoury sample at a pre-sale tasting in Los Angeles. *Last tasted Feb 1998* ★★ *Variable.*

**Ch La Fleur** Also at the same Los Angeles tasting as above, and also a bit dry and raw for a top Pomerol. It went down better with calves' kidneys. *End of August 1998* ★★(★)?

**Ch Giscours** Managing to be a sweet, chunky wine, none of the '81 leanness. By 1995, still very deep; big and fleshy. Most recently, quite good flavour and extract, with a sort of Médoc-medicinal taste that I had noticed on a previous occasion. *Last tasted June 1998* ★★★ *A good '81 but totally lacking charm or finesse.*

**Ch Grand-Puy-Lacoste** I mentioned earlier, apropos some of the older vintages, that Lacoste is, in effect, one of the unsung heroes of the Médoc, Pauillac in particular, always uncompromisingly well made. It was with the 1981 vintage that I started seriously to buy several cases each year; for this reason I had many notes and have been able to follow its progress more closely than other wines, from my first taste of it in cask in April 1982. (Incidentally, it amuses me that a leading wine critic has taken so long to discover its virtues though, to be fair, he was new to the game in the early 1980s and very recent vintages have been more obviously good.)

Always slow to evolve, its bouquet started opening up in the late 1980s, though still lean and dry. The 16 notes made since have always been at home, either at weekends or at dinner parties. It started to look mature by the mid-1995s though, being an '81, it had only just started to soften yet I have a note made at dinner in 1996 – 'perfect now'. I believe it to be a pretty good example of this class of wine (5ème cru classé, the same as the more heart-on-sleeve Lynch-Bages) in this rather lean vintage. *Last tasted Sept 2001* ★★★

**Ch Gruaud-Larose** Interesting to see how a fleshy fruity Gruaud can cope with a lean vintage like 1981. Well it coped well. A wine rich, soft, chewy and 'rustic' in its earlier days and, by 1995, still a fairly impressive, youthful ruby colour; an immediate belch of fragrance though I thought it rumbled uneasily in the glass. Fairly sweet, fleshy, medicinal iron/tannins, and lacked length, particularly after drinking some '70s at Neil McKendrick's, excellent as usual, Bordeaux Club dinner. Most recently, richly coloured but fully mature. Assertive nose. Flavoury but a sort of ripe farmyard character and rustic finish. *Last tasted at the Josey pre-sale tasting in New York, Nov 2000* ★★★★ *Drink soon.*

**Ch Kirwan** The sort of vintage that helped give this 3ème cru classé an 'underperforming' reputation. Like a pendulum swinging too far in very recent vintages. But even though many if not most '81s were lean, Kirwan was 'pinched' and lacking. The oldest red at the opening dinner of La Cité Mondiale du Vin in Bordeaux: weak-rimmed; a bit corky; not bad, 'nice weight, citrus touch'. *Last tasted April 1994* ★★ *Forget.*

**Ch Latour-à-Pomerol** Fairly deep; drinking well. Good tannins. Neither lean nor particularly fleshy. *With Mogens Nielson at Caviar House, London, Dec 1999* ★★★ *Will continue.*

**Ch Léoville-Las-Cases** Intense purple, cedary, not a big wine – indeed a certain delicacy – tasted in cask in September 1982 with the shrewd and capable Monsieur Delon. Though lacking the usual extra dimensions, it developed well through the 1980s, restrained but attractive, with good fruit and flesh. My recent notes, despite a now more mature appearance, illustrate its leanness and leathery tannins (1993) though it was drinking pretty well at a Wine Club dinner at Hambleton Hall: velvety appearance; touch of mocha. Most recently, merely noted as 'austere' at Len Evans' Imperial Dinner. *Last tasted Sept 2000. At best* ★★★ *Drying out.*

**Ch Lynch-Bages** In my notes on Grand-Puy-Lacoste I referred to Lynch-Bages' heart-on-sleeve character. Well, in 1981, its heart was in the right place. A stream of admiring notes, its flavour and vivacity making up for its less robust components and slight lack of length. In 1996, crisp, fragrant fruit, not a big wine. Ready. Showing well in 1997 at a tasting in Brussels, and a year later a magnum lunching at Pichon-Baron. Still fairly deep though maturing; surprising richness and extract on nose and palate masking its tannins. *Last tasted Sept 1998* ★★★★ *A good '81. Should keep well.*

**Ch La Mission Haut-Brion** Spicy but aggressive in its youth but rich, ripe fruit on the nose, crisp flavour and bitter tannins noted towards the end of the decade. An 'austere' bottle at a pre-sale tasting in 1997 and a somewhat more explicit note at auction: fairly deep; rich, arboreal, oaky nose with touch of iron; some sweetness, full-bodied, fairly well equipped with tannin and acidity. Typically masculine. *Last tasted Jan 1999* ★★★(★)

**Ch Montrose** I imagined that Montrose in 1981 would be not only lean but austere and was surprised by a fragrant cask sample and its relatively relaxed development. Recent notes indicate that its bouquet is as seductive as before, sweet and meaty; also on the palate, though the tannin not sublimated by its extract (1996). A more recent tasting endorsed this view. *Last tasted in Los Angeles, Feb 1998* ★★★★

**Ch Palmer** Fragrant and spicy in its youth. By the mid-1980s, sweet and fleshy – but not a big wine. Fair length, some charm. Probably at its best in 1990, judging by an admiring note. Most recently, fully mature in appearance, nose and taste. A touch of amber orange at its rim. Some sweetness, rich, but with quite a bite. *Last tasted lunching at the château, May 2001* ★★★★ *but should be drunk soon.*

**Ch Pichon-Longueville, Baron** To give it its – then – full title, jousting with La Comtesse. No love lost between these grandees. Curiously, the cask sample in the spring of 1982 had almost appropriated the Comtesse's fruit. Consistently attractive though lacking length and touched by acidity. Most recently, a bottle from a good Scottish cellar, despite its rather peppery nose was both surprisingly sweet and not lean for an '81. *Last noted at a pre-sale tasting, Jan 1999* ★★★

**Ch Pichon-Longueville, Comtesse** (Having dropped, temporarily, Lalande.) Deeper colour, more fragrant, with 'taut, spicy eucalyptus flavour and excellent aftertaste'. Eight notes since. Well evolved bouquet, lovely flavour in 1990. My next note a magnum at a serious dinner at home: maturing, classic nose and flavour, good tannin (1994). The following year, at Le Canard in Hamburg: still a touch of ruby and noticeably rich 'legs'; lovely, ripe mulberry-like aroma, which opened up beautifully; though gloriously rich and fleshy, its fairly high tannin content cleaning the palate between mouthfuls of roe deer! Most recently, still rich and ripe: full flavoured, masked tannin. *Last noted at a pre-sale tasting, Jan 1999* ★★★★

**Ch Prieuré-Lichine** Not the sort of vintage to suit Prieuré. Light, easy, plausible. *Last noted Dec 1993* ★★ *Drink up.*

**Ch St-Pierre** Two bottles, deeper than expected but one poor and bitter, the other with harmonious nose; softer and quite pleasant. *Jan 1994* ★ *I wouldn't risk it.*

**Ch de Sales** Fully mature, looking ten years older and showing its age. Drying out. Lacking the class and stamina to ride out a vintage like '81. *April 1995* ★

**Ch Talbot** What did the good old stand-by make of the '81 vintage? Well, I have a dozen notes. Incidentally, a fairly high percentage of Cabernet Sauvignon (71%). Consistently deep, thick, intense for an '81; typically ripe, slightly smelly Talbot aroma; rich yet very tannic. Similar notes through to the 1990s. By 1994, at a Christie's Bordeaux wine course, though still deep, a mature mahogany rim; 'singed', sweet, harmonious bouquet with that curious ripe smell, iodine this time. Hefty, alcoholic, slithery tannins; very dry finish. And similar notes at the same course later the same year. *Last noted Nov 1994* ★★★★

**Ch La Tour Haut-Brion** Tannic. Good weight and flavour (1986). Eleven years later: rich, earthy, and better than the La Mission alongside. *Last tasted Dec 1997* ★★★ *Will keep.*

**BRIEF NOTES ON OTHER '81S LAST TASTED IN THE LATE 1980S AND VERY EARLY 1990S** Ch L'Angélus soft and fleshy for an '81. *July 1990* ★★★; **Ch Beauregard** Pomerol. Indeterminate. Lean. Short. *Sept 1990* ★; **Ch Beychevelle** spicy but hollow and dry. Bitter finish. *March 1991* ★; **Ch Branaire-Ducru** mature. Crisp fruit. Light easy style. *June 1991* ★★; **Ch Calon-Ségur** moderate lean. Very tannic. *Sept 1990* ★; **Ch Canon-La Gaffelière** touch of sweetness. Fairly light, lean, flavoury. *Jan 1991* ★★; **Ch Cantenac-Brown** sweet, jammy, chunky for an '81. *Jan 1988* ★★; **Ch Croizet-Bages** crisp, fruity, piquant. *July 1990* ★★★; **Ch Ducru-Beaucaillou** wholesome, refreshing fruit and acidity. Restrained: an Englishman's claret. *Oct 1987* ★★★; **Ch Duhart-Milon** good bouquet; overall dry but with some flesh. Well made. Flavoury. *Sept 1990* ★★★; **Ch L'Évangile** distinctive, rounded Pomerol style, with extract. Oaky. *Sept 1989* ★★★; **Les Forts de Latour** massive, raw with tannic acid finish. *Jan 1988* ★★?; **Clos Fourtet** sweet, soft fruit. Flat and tannic. *Sept 1990* ★; **Ch La Gaffelière** attractive. Crisp, fragrant. *June 1991* ★★★; **Ch Gazin** beguiled by its youthful charm. Soft, fruity and fleshy yet leaving a very dry impression. *Oct 1990* ★★★; **Ch La Grave-Trigant-de-Boisset** good wine. Chewy, rich. *June 1988* ★★★★; **Ch Haut-Bailly** very deep. Spicy. Crisp, very refreshing. *Oct 1989* ★★★★; **Ch d'Issan** deep, fleshy for an '81. Very agreeable. *April 1989* ★★★★; **Ch Lafon-Rochet** Lean at the best of times, more so in 1981. *Nov 1989* ★; **Ch La Lagune** a plausible drink both uplifted and downgraded by a whiff of volatile acidity. *July 1990* ★; **Ch Lascombes** slight but well formed. *Nov 1990* ★★★; **Ch Léoville-Barton** lean, unyielding. Time will tell. *March 1991* ★★?; **Ch Léoville-Poyferré** firm fruit but teeth-gripping tannins and acidity. *July 1989* ★★; **Ch La Louvière** sweet, soft fruit, rounded though short. *May 1988* ★★★; **Ch Mouton-Baronne-Philippe** a normally elegant and lean wine, the '81 rather emphasises the latter. Yet some flesh to go with its attractively crisp fruit. *Aug 1987* ★★★; **Ch Nenin** fully evolved, sweet, flavoury, a touch of acidity. *Sept 1990* ★; **Ch Pape-Clément** fairly sweet, good flavour and length. More acid than tannin. *Dec 1990* ★★; **Ch Pavie** Fragrant. Lovely flavour. Good fruit, length and aftertaste. *Sept 1990* ★★★; **Ch Pontet-Canet** spicy; soft, rich, good acidity. *July 1989* ★★★

# 1982 ★★★★★

A milestone. A sign of the complete recovery of the market; more, that the combination of richness and perceived quality matched the economic climate. It was the first really important, and well-timed, *vin de garde* since 1970, and perhaps the first universally touted ripe-for-investment vintage of the post war period. But how have they turned out, and what is their future?

First though, the climatic conditions preceding the birth of this vintage. Ideal growing conditions. Flowering early and evenly. Hot and dry summer, harvest from 14 September in great heat, the early-ripening Merlot with very high must weight. There was then a change, two days of heavy rain. I was there and thought it presaged another '64. The sun and fresh breezes enable the Cabernets to ripen more normally. Rich tannic wines resulted. The big guns still have fire power and length of trajectory.

**Ch Lafite** Although not tasted prior to 1985, even at that stage I gave it, unhesitatingly, a potential 5 stars. Roughly two dozen notes spread pretty evenly over the years since. One thing is certain, it is not a delicate wallflower. Over the 1980s, the Lafite bouquet developed beautifully. At Penning-Rowsell's '10-year' first growth tasting it was still markedly deep, intense; nose spicy, quite powerful, nowhere near levelling off. The most detailed and useful notes were made at three subsequent comparative tastings of first growths. What has been apparent is the closeness in depth and quality. At Kaplan's 1982 evening in Chicago in 1997, it was well evolved with an extraordinary flavour, full of fruit, fragrant. At Rodenstock's wine weekend in 1998, 'tasted blind', it seemed high-toned and crisp, half a point below the other first growth Médocs, its length and fragrance a major feature at a mixed tasting of '82s in Hamburg (March 2000). Most recently, still impressively deep and comparatively youthful; a well developed, sweet and harmonious bouquet. Mouthfilling, so much on show, so much left to show. *Last noted at the La Réserve tasting of '82 Pauillacs, April 2001* ★★★★(★) *Another effortless 20 years?*

**Ch Latour** I have a note that 17,054 cases of the *grand vin* and 7832 of Les Forts were produced. Half my notes made in the 1980s, starting in September 1984 at the time of the bottling: an opaque, dumb, massive wine. At Penning-Rowsell's '10-year' tasting I described it as 'a mouth and fork wine', so big and chewy. Lovely fruit and fragrance at Kaplan's (1997) – tasted blind I put it down as the Mouton. High mark and hefty, again blind (1998). Starting to shed some of its colour and to mature in appearance and nose: a lovely cedar pencils bouquet; sweet, full of fruit, lots of tannin and still 'chewable' (Hamburg 2000) and, most recently, emitting 'warm', ripe, cedary and redcurrant scents. Surprisingly sweet, very amenable despite its tannic grip. Delicious. *Last noted at the La Réserve tasting, April 2001* ★★★(★★) *Twenty glorious years ahead.*

**Ch Margaux** First tasted in cask in May 1983, and again in September 1984, two months before the *grand vin* was to be bottled. On each occasion dazzled and beguiled, as so often, by its aroma and mouthfilling ripeness. Jumping to Penning-Rowsell's '10-year' tasting, I gave it a pretty high mark in that exalted company, its bouquet opening up gloriously in the glass over the course of dinner; lovely, berry-like fruit, crisp. Delicious. At Kaplan's tasting of '82s in 1997 at least I guessed it *was* the Margaux and it was voted top; and I am pleased to say I recognised it in the Rodenstock 'flight' in 1998, its recognition signal being the blossoming of its bouquet. The two Wagner verticals were particularly interesting as it was always next to the '83. At the 1979 tasting I referred to the '83 as feminine and the '82 as masculine, the latter having more power and less elegance. In between, in Tokyo (1999), I noted 'loose knit', good fruit, very tannic (still). Most recently, at the second Wagner tasting: very fragrant, hot-vintage scent; sweeter than the '83, high alcohol, extract and a very dry, tannic finish. *Last tasted Nov 2000* ★★★(★★) *Long life.*

**Ch Mouton-Rothschild** Magnificent, the higher than normal percentage (80%) of Cabernet Sauvignon very noticeable. Exactly two dozen notes from 1985 and not a dud among them. At ten years of age, still opaque and youthful; a massively spicy nose and flavour, yet lots of flesh, my No 2 to Pétrus by half a point. And on, and on. By 1996 at the tasting of '82s in Brussels, a mulberry ripe Cabernet nose; intense, dramatic, silky-leathery tannins. Unready. Excellent at Kaplan's '82 event, hefty, thick, very tannic. Still stylish at Hollywood Wine Society's Mouton tasting (1998). A somewhat less enthusiastic note at the Athenaeum House and Wine Committee dinner: 'touch of tar' on the nose 'stolid, impressive but unexciting' (April 2001) but reprieved three days later though 'tarry' again added to its rich, ripe, Cabernet Sauvignon bouquet; 'better this evening than last Monday'. Open knit, 'coarser on finish' (than Lafite). *Last noted at the La Réserve tasting of 1982 Pauillacs, April 2001* ★★★★(★)

**Ch Haut-Brion** 12,000 cases made, far fewer than the other *1er crus classés*. Almost as many notes. So different in style, so good – and a totally different *cépages* mix, roughly 50/50 Cabernet Sauvignon and Merlot, on the deep Pessac soil. At Penning-Rowsell's '10-year' first growth tastings, I have always insisted on serving the Haut-Brion first as it is so distinctive, as on this occasion, and, although good, it got my lowest mark. The word 'distinctive' used again at a tasting of first growth '82s, for Christie's in Hong Kong, sweet, earthy (1995). The top wine at the Fête de la Fleur dinner in 1997: very sweet, good fruit, rich, characterful. At Rodenstock's blind tasting it was unmistakable, now mature, fully evolved bouquet, lovely flavour (1998). Curiously, noted as very tannic, with a metallic touch happily transformed by rather fatty lamb cutlets (dining at the château, 1998), 'needs time' at Latour (1999). Most recently: a glowing, mature, tile-red; sweet, now very soft, rich, complete. Tannin assimilated. *Last noted at the MW Haut-Brion tasting, Jan 2000* ★★★★★ *Superb.*

**Ch Ausone** Another 50/50 *cépages* mix, this time Merlot and Cabernet Franc. The heat at harvest time was intense, the grapes being brought in with exceptional ripeness, and though the sugar was high, the acidity was low. The *Wine Spectator* reported that Pascal Delbeck had added 'a tiny' amount of tartaric acid. Certainly not noticeable to me when I tasted it in cask in May 1983. Some notes and five years later I gave it fairly good marks at the Penning-Rowsell tasting: a harmonious nose that reminded me of Daphne's rice pudding; very sweet and I thought already fully mature. An impressive magnum, full of fruit, tasting of 'autumn leaves and brown paper' (which is how I recognise Ausone) at Kaplan's '82s dinner (1997); delicious, drinking well (New York, later the same year). Most recently, also in New York, very attractive. *Last tasted May 1999* ★★★★ *Drink whenever it suits you.*

**Ch Cheval Blanc** Worth mentioning the curious *cépage* mix: Cabernet Franc 60%, Merlot 34%, Cabernet Sauvignon only 1%, but Malbec 5%. First tasted in cask with the always friendly and helpful but somewhat lugubrious Jacques Hébrard, whose wife and sisters-in-law had inherited the property. A charming, winsome wine but more to it than is revealed at first glance. Totally different in weight and style to the Médocs, or to Ch Pétrus for that matter. In 1995 a major horizontal of '82s in Hong Kong, the lightest (comparatively) of the first growths, a lovely wine. The next horizontal (1996) in Brussels, two bottles of each, just in case: an undramatic but harmonious nose. More interesting on the palate: sweet, elegant, stylish. At Kaplan's event (1997), among a wide variety of '82s, my joint highest mark, with Ch Pétrus and Le Pin. Later that summer, in Austria, at the very extensive Cheval Blanc tasting, a magnum, the wine by now showing considerable maturity with an orange edge and 'legs' as impressive as the arches of Durham Cathedral; rich, bricky bouquet; well evolved with extract but with a slightly bitter tannic-iron finish. Monsieur Hébrard, who was present, informed us that the production had been enormous, the *rendement* 55hl/ha. Incidentally I noted the same bitter iron finish, teeth-gripping, this time at Rodenstock's, also a magnum (1998). The following year, showing well with lovely flavour, still tannic. *Last noted at Christie's tasting in Tokyo, Nov 1999* ★★★★(★) *Good life ahead.*

**Ch Pétrus** For long one of the stars of the saleroom, and one can see why. Curiously, first tasted in 1985 at the Simi Winery in Sonoma with Thelma Long, the star winemaker well known in California. Very courageous of Thelma to pitch her 'regular' (not reserve) Cabernet Sauvignon alongside some '82 first growths. The Simi came out well, only half a notch below Pétrus. My first comparative tasting was with the other 10-year-old first growths. My highest mark, a rare enough 19/20. Just so sweet, rich, fleshy, fruit packed, rounded. Next, a massively impressive double magnum, showing a bit of maturity; sweet, fragrant, harmonious nose and taste to match. Lots of grip, lovely wine, needs time (Rodenstock dinner 1995). And, the following month, in Hong Kong, a similar note: lovely, rich, fleshy. In Brussels in 1996, a similar velvet-lined mouthfiller but, I thought, lacking subtlety and finish. Most recently, at Kaplan's '82s dinner, with noisettes of Virginia lamb, by now less deep in colour; bouquet fully evolved and justly deserving about every praise one could heap upon it. *Last tasted April 1997* ★★★★★ *Life everlasting.*

The problem now is how to do justice to the wines of 250 châteaux – not including the minor ones, consumed in the mid-1980s – a third being of classed growth or equivalent standard. I shall just have to be highly selective, giving precedence to those most recently tasted.

**Ch Batailley** Dependable as always. Now fully mature, its bouquet unravelled deliciously; sweetish, chewy, good length, dry finish. *April 2001* ★★★★

**Ch Beauregard** A remarkably good magnum, rich, forthcoming, chunky fruit. *April 1994* ★★★★

**Ch Belgrave** (Pauillac) Deservedly modest. *Oct 1998* ★★

**Ch Belgrave** (St-Laurent) New owner splashing out with new oak. *June 1999* ★★

**Ch Beychevelle** Many notes. Impressive, even elegant in cask (May 1983) but a bit slow to get off the ground. In 1999, a lovely colour; surprisingly floral; distinctly sweet, delicious, with power and length. Most recently: opened up slowly but fragrantly, both on nose and palate. Truthfully, I thought it a bit stolid and lacking finesse and not quite living up to the occasion. *Last noted accompanying 'The Upper's Reward', Fillet of Beef, at the annual Swan Feast at Vintners' Hall, Nov 2001* ★★★

**Ch Boyd-Cantenac** Chunky, fruity, tannic. *Aug 1990* ★★★

**Ch Branaire-Ducru** Eight notes. All good. Soft, stylish, attractive in cask and steady development. Still holding its colour, ruby, intense; fragrant, spicy, eucalyptus nose; sweet, mouthfilling, glorious flavour. *Last tasted in Amsterdam, April 1998* ★★★★

**Ch Brane-Cantenac** A rural, rustic sort of wine from cask to middle age. A mature orange tinge even a decade ago. Full, fleshy mouthful though still tannic. *Last tasted June 1991* ★★★?

**Ch Calon-Ségur** A chunky, tannic wine in cask. Two recent notes, both at dinners, a month apart in New York and Chicago. A good colour with '82 density; a *mélange* on the nose, oak, liquorice, even camphor. A good Calon of the old style, nice fruit, not caring too much about pleasing, still tannic. *Last tasted April 1997* ★★(★) *Hard to predict.*

**Ch Canon** Started in cask the way it meant to go on. Not the usual soft, relaxed wine. Sterner stuff. Ten notes. Fully evolved appearance and lovely nose, rich; sweet. But dry finish (1996). The following year, an attractive magnum; herbaceous, rich, then meaty; ripe sweetness, very good fruit and extract masking its considerable tannin content, leaving a slightly bitter finish. *Last noted at Kaplan's '82s dinner, April 1997* ★★★★

**Ch Cantemerle** Mixed thoughts about this. Intense, fruity in cask. Seemed seamless at six years of age but three later notes emphasise the tannin which belies its maturity. Good rich flavour, texture and length. Despite the *filet* of beef, tannic. Certainly lacking the charm and elegance of the wine's best period (the mid-1950s). But it is, after all, an '82. *Last tasted at lunch, Nov 1995* ★★★(★) *Giving it the benefit of the doubt.*

**Ch Cantenac-Brown** Unimpressive from the start. Threadbare and tannic. *Last tasted Oct 1993* ★

**Ch Certan-de-May** Half a dozen fairly consistent notes. Deep, firm; impressive, harmonious nose of the sort which gets more interesting as one goes back to it. Sweet, fleshy, excellent consistency (texture), complete – at a Bordeaux Club dinner at Caius, Cambridge (1996), endorsed at Kaplan's '82s dinner (1997) and again quite recently: soft, chewy. *Last noted at a pre-sale tasting in Los Angeles, March 1999* ★★★★ *Lovely now.*

**Ch Chasse-Spleen** Masses of notes as I bought it for drinking at home. Rich: colour, nose and taste. Living up to its reputation. And, unlike many *bourgeois* clarets, not only holding on but, after 15 years, still with bouquet which opens in the glass. *Last tasted at lunch in the country, May 1997* ★★★★ *I wouldn't wait any longer, and haven't any left anyway.*

**Ch Cissac** Demonstrating again that, in a vintage like 1982, some very good *bourgeois* wines can keep well. Quite a few notes. Good fruit and grip. *Last tasted April 1996* ★★★

**Ch Clarke** Another Médoc hinterland château, this one owned by Baron Edmond de Rothschild. Satisfactory, no more. *April 1998* ★★

**Ch Clerc-Milon** Another Rothschild wine (this time Baron Philippe). Several notes. Mature; ripe, good depth; full rich flavour; good dry finish. *Last tasted May 2000* ★★★★

**Ch La Conseillante** A magnificent wine. I recall having to rush home to provide a substitute for one of three, my last three, magnums of Ch Lafite, which was undrinkable, corked. The two bottles of Conseillante, hastily decanted, turned out to be more than a standby; it was so much better to drink. The Lafite was totally unready. Many notes. My last bottle served at my Bordeaux Club dinner. Why try to describe it? Both it and my favourite '85 Cheval Blanc were perfect. *Last tasted Dec 1999* ★★★★★

**Ch Cos d'Estournel** Fourteen notes tracing its progress from a surprisingly easy-going cask sample in May 1983. It then seemed to stiffen its resolve. Recent notes include bottles which though good were upstaged by quite a few of the 30 or so of Kaplan's '82s in 1997. Later the same year, a pretty powerful jeroboam, siphoned into decanters in Bob Dickinson's cellar at 12.30pm for the Bacchus Society dinner that evening. My best and most recent note: good colour, mature red brown rim; well nigh perfect bouquet, gentle, harmonious; surprisingly sweet though finishing dry, good fruit. Attractive. *Last noted at a comparative tasting of '82s and '89s at the Hotel Louis C Jacob, Hamburg, March 2000* ★★★★

**Ch Ducru-Beaucaillou** I was at the château on 21 September, just six days after the picking had started, the Merlot being brought in first. Jean-Eugène Borie told me that the must weight was exceptional, as high as the '47. I first actually tasted the wine the following spring. Clearly good potential. Most of my notes were made in the 1980s, just four since. A rather unshowy '82, leaner than some. Rich nose, though, at Kaplan's '82s dinner (1997), good texture, dry finish. Later that autumn one of three Ducru *impériales* ('70, '78 and '82) at Bob Dickinson's installation dinner at the Biltmore, Coral Gables. Spectacular setting, all at one very long table, like

a state banquet at Windsor Castle. The '82 was still enormously deep; a very good rich mouthful, leanness not noted but still very tannic. Most recently: showing its age; good but now creaking a bit. *Last noted coping with tournedos of Scottish beef at a Vintners' Court luncheon, Nov 2001* ★★★

**Ch L'Église-Clinet** Just three fairly recent notes. Very good but rather severe. Texture rough rather than Pomerol-silky. Tannic. Most recently, a sweet, ripe-nosed almost creamy magnum; fairly full-bodied, very fruity. Tannic. *Last tasted Sept 1998* ★★★★(★) *Needs more time.*

**Ch L'Évangile** Consistently good. Eight notes from 1989. A lovely fleshy Pomerol, mouthfilling, rounded, loads of fruit and tannin but not as mouthfillingly fat as some (1996). Very distinctive fragrance, crisp fruit, grip, a lean touch (1997). 'Quite punchy, good length'. *Last tasted at a pre-sale tasting in New York, Dec 1997* ★★★★

**Ch Feytit-Clinet** Two notes. First with the proprietor. It had a job to follow the perfect '71 Climens and *foie gras* in the company of the 'Veuve Clicquot Femme du Vin 1992'! Somewhat rustic. Meaty, earthy. *Last noted at lunch in the country, June 1995*

**Ch Figeac** I could never accuse Thierry Manoncourt of making boring run-of-the-mill wine. Fourteen notes, more at dinners and luncheons than at tastings, which is as it should be. I enjoyed them all. The past three or four encounters including served with freshly picked asparagus and smelly French cheeses dining at the château; naturally I did not complain (1998). Later that autumn drinking well at a *Decanter* magazine vintage dinner; in strange company at the restaurant Che, very distinctive, fully mature (1999). Most recently, effortlessly following Lafite '90 and '88 at another Bordeaux Club dinner at Caius, Cambridge. Sweet, rich, chewy, ready. *Last tasted June 2000* ★★★★ *Drink soon.*

**Ch La Fleur** Two recent notes. A noticeably ripe Cabernet Franc raspberry-like aroma; good fruit, great length but with a lean tannic finish. *Last tasted, a magnum, at Rodenstock's La Fleur vertical. Sept 1998* ★★★(★)

**Clos Fourtet** Several notes from its early days. Mixed reviews recently. Unimpressive, drying out (a dinner in St-Émilion in 1995). Most recently, showing quite well, with an attractive bouquet; some sweetness and good tannin and acidity. Not thrilling. *Last noted at an '82 tasting in Amsterdam, April 1998* ★★

**Ch Le Gay** A fearsomely opaque magnum; youthful fruit still, and peppery. Spoiled for me by its raw, bitter, biting finish. *Sept 1998* ★★★? *A bruiser. I wouldn't wait.*

**Ch Giscours** Notes spanning 15 years. Strangely low alcohol for an '82 (12%). Quite fragrant, crisp fruit, very tannic (April 1998). Later that autumn, well developed fruit but with a raw tannic finish. *Last tasted Sept 1998* ★★

**Ch Grand-Puy-Lacoste** Once again, masses of notes for I bought several cases for home drinking and entertaining. As always, enormously impressive in cask but a slow developer. I rather regret drinking mine too early. The few bottles I have

## Union des Grands Crus

*An association of the leading châteaux in Bordeaux, whose first tasting in the UK for the trade and wine journalists was organised by Steven Spurrier and myself at Christie's in 1982. The UGC has in the last few years been holding important vintage-assessment tastings in Bordeaux the spring after the harvest, with an important reassessment in London the next year.*

## Robert Parker

*It was for his enthusiastic pronouncements concerning the 1982 Bordeaux vintage that he originally made his name. Parker trained as a lawyer in Baltimore (USA) and is now the most influential of all the wine commentators and critics. He is noted for his very detailed assessment of wines and vintages and his controversial 100-point marking scale.*

left will probably see me out. The most recent notes made at tastings: crisp, taut, long term (Brussels 1996). The oldest vintage, a bottle from my own cellar at a Grand-Puy-Lacoste vertical at a Christie's masterclass (March 2000): showing well, impressively dense appearance; beautiful bouquet (though Daphne unkindly added to my notes 'like a dodgy Figeac's'). Lots of fruit and flesh, but I have to admit, drying before its full blossoming. Most recently, a hard, stalky-nosed bottle (Daphne said 'corked'. I think she was right this time), with teeth-gripping astringency. *Last noted at the La Réserve tasting of '82s, March 2001. At best* ★★(★★)

**Ch Gruaud-Larose** Many notes. It started off well, with the fruit and flesh and excitement I normally expect. In fact it had all the component parts, but several recent notes have included the word 'stodgy'. 'Good, but …' At the extensive tasting of '82s in Brussels it had an impressive colour; fruity, cedary nose; mouthfilling and tannic, 'good life ahead'. At Kaplan's it was loaded but very tannic. Most recently, understandably upstaged by Mouton '85. Rather stolid in comparison. So, I am not too thrilled with '82 Gruaud. *Last tasted Dec 1997. At best* ★★(★★)?

**Ch Haut-Bailly** Distinctive, rich, earthy, sweet. *Last tasted Dec 1993* ★★★★

**Ch Haut-Batailley** As '82s go, it is rather lean without the customary elegance, but dependable as always. Crisp. Refreshing. *Last tasted March 2001* ★★★

**Ch Lagrange** (St-Julien) Still immensely deep, distinctive nose and flavour, still fruit-packed. Hard tannic finish. *Last tasted April 1997* ★★(★) *I slightly doubt if this will come round.*

**Ch La Lagune** A large number of notes covering 15 years. Apart from a bottle at a Bordeaux Club dinner that one of the members quaintly described as *sous bois* and that I decided was corky, its finish 'pinched'. A magnum definitely corked at Kaplan's '82s event (1997). A sweet, soft, fleshy, most attractive bottle at my tasting in Brussels (1996). Two years later, showing perfect maturity and some age on the nose but a delicious taste, soft, good length, marked tannin. Most recently, slight yet noticeable bottle variation despite being brought up from a good country house cellar. The best of four bottles had pleasing sweetness, good body, some flesh though still tannic. *At the Guises', Jan 2002. At best* ★★★★

**Ch Langoa-Barton** First tasted in cask September 1983, opaque touch but fleshy. Developed fragrantly, my best note in 1993: surprisingly sweet, fairly full-bodied, chewy, chunky fruit. Ready for drinking. Most recently, a rather woody, very tannic bottle. *Last tasted Sept 1995. At best* ★★★ *It might dry out.*

**Ch Latour-à-Pomerol** Medium-deep; very sweet, meaty almost chewy bouquet; dry, well constructed, tannic. *At Kaplan's '82s dinner, April 1997* ★★(★)

**Ch Léoville-Barton** In cask, totally different from the Langoa. Lovely flesh, flavour and length, but with a lean touch. Half a dozen recent notes, all good but all with tannic grip. Coincidentally the previous two notes made dining (always in rather grand company) at the Laidlaws in Chelsea Square,

London, still fairly deep; in each instance I merely described its bouquet as 'classic'; a fairly substantial wine, still tannic but drinking well. Most recently, Anthony Barton played a splendid – indeed astonishing – trick on his guests, mainly Bordeaux *négociants* and *courtiers*, serving the same wine, his '82 Léoville, in two sizes of bottle, standard and double magnum. Both were very good; both were distinctly different, to the extent that I thought the first wine (in bottles) was the '59 and the second (double magnum) the '61, the latter appearing firmer, less mature, tannic. Only Pierre Lawton suspected the trick; and correctly guessed '82 in different-sized bottles! An eye-opener. *Last noted lunching at Ch Langoa, Oct 2001* ★★★★(★)

**Ch Léoville-Las-Cases** A rare opportunity, for me at any rate, to taste from the vat the autumn of the vintage. Astonishing that anything so powerful can simmer down into something drinkable. In fact it was slow to evolve. With nine notes made over the past decade it has been interesting to observe its progress at tastings and dinners. Even in the mid-1990s I thought that it was still unready and very tannic. At Kaplan's tasting in 1997 its bouquet was surprisingly forthcoming, rich, no harsh edges; its texture was good, also its length. But still a fairly lean, tannic finish. Most recently, still impressively deep with rich 'legs'; fairly concentrated, top quality, 'delicious but …' (for the tannin). *Last noted at the '82s and '89s tasting in Hamburg, March 2000* ★★★(★), *hopefully* ★★★★ *in time. But when?*

**Ch Léoville-Poyferré** I was not impressed by cask samples and thought something was lacking. It has in fact developed a fragrant bouquet and I noted it as surprisingly sweet, with great flavour but with vice-like grip (magnum 1997). Most recently, almost opaque in the glass yet mature nose, the sweetness noted again, a slightly tarry flavour and very tannic. *Last tasted at a Commanderie dinner in Bristol, Jan 2000* ★★(★) *Not a great '82. I doubt if it will shed the tannin.*

**Ch Lynch-Bages** From start to by no means finish a deliciously flavoury mouthful. Its virtue, if not virginity, intact. Many notes, all really rather repetitive so I will jump to the most recent: now medium-dry, with a core of cherry red, its colour positively pushing the sides of the glass; a bouquet that could hardly wait, toasty, lovely fruit; sweet entry, delicious flavour, velvety texture, dry but overly tannic. *Last noted at the La Réserve tasting of '82s, March 2001* ★★★★(★)

**Ch Magdelaine** 'Meaty' on the nose; very sweet, lovely fruit, slight touch of iron. *Last tasted June 1995* ★★★★ *Delicious now.*

**Ch Malescot-St-Exupéry** I occasionally 'damn with faint praise' the more specious vintages of Malescot. Not the '82. Fruity from the start, drinking well in 1990 and, most recently, deliciously fragrant; very sweet, soft, chewy fruit, well balanced, dry finish. *Last tasted hosting a rather grand black tie 'Club' dinner at Hambledon Hall, an extremely comfortable country house hotel overlooking Rutland Water, Dec 1998* ★★★★

**Ch La Mission Haut-Brion** Many notes, first, two months after bottling, September 1984. A meaty mouthful. Through the 1980s displaying just about every feature common to La Mission at its best, though bottom-heavy with tannin. My most recent notes, both made at tastings in the mid-1990s draw attention to its predicable depth of colour though its amber-brown rim hinting at maturity; also a typically earthy, tobacco-like, slightly malty nose and taste. Laden with tannin. *Last tasted April 1997* ★★★(★) *I suppose it could eventually turn into a 5-star wine; in any case it is a matter of taste.*

**Ch Monbousquet** I do not often come across this *grand cru* St-Émilion but, presumably from Christie's directors' reserves, I drank it with great pleasure – and some surprise – three times within three weeks. *Last tasted Dec 1999* ★★★

**Ch Montrose** A serious combination, Montrose and the 1982 vintage. And so it proved to be. Although not tasted recently, harmonious, excellent flavour but its ripe sweetness hardly denting its tannic astringency. *Last noted Feb 1992. Then* ★(★★★★) *Now likely to be* ★★★(★★) *A long haul wine.*

**Ch Mouton-Baronne-Philippe** Six, consistent, notes during the last decade, none previously. Rich, now mature; very good, fully developed Cabernet fragrance; dry, lean for an '82. Drinking well. A bottle from my own cellar, to introduce Julie and Tubby Bacon to our local Lebanese restaurant, 'Mes' Amis' (*sic*). From Chicago, but with a pied-à-terre in London, the Bacons' hobby is eating out. They publish the best private guide to London restaurants which my wife and I find invaluable. *Last tasted October 1999* ★★★★

**Ch Palmer** Strangely, not a very good '82. First tasted with Franck Mähler Besse (whose family firm of *négociants* own roughly two-thirds of Palmer) in May 1983, just over a month after they had made the *assemblage*. Interesting, too to taste the nearly assembled wine out of new and 'old', probably second-year, casks. Neither was as impressive as I had expected; nor were two cask samples tasted that autumn. In 1985 'a bit watery and lacking'. Later noted as 'short'. More recently, overall dry, severe and length queried (at Kaplan's tasting in 1997). Then a deeply coloured *impériale*, quite good bouquet, tarry, then fruit; chalk, chewy (a very typical '82 characteristic), full-bodied, impressive, probably partly due to the size of bottle and grandeur of the occasion, but lacking finesse and charm. *Last noted at Bob Dickinson's investiture dinner at the Biltmore Hotel, Coral Gables, Florida, Nov 1997* ★★(★)

**Ch Pavie** Several good notes, pleasing from the start. Most recently: mature; bouquet nicely evolved. Sweet, soft, attractive and the most ready to drink of the 'flight' of Right Bank '82s at Kaplan's tasting. *Last noted April 1997* ★★★★ *Drink soon.*

**Pavillon Rouge de Ch Margaux** Ruby; spicy; lean. Quite a good drink. *Last tasted March 2000* ★★★ *Drink soon.*

**Ch Petit-Village** Fully developed, fragrant, familiar Pomerol Merlot fragrance. Sweet, fairly substantial. Delicious to drink by itself. *Last tasted Jan 1996* ★★★★ *(just, just) Drink soon.*

**Ch Pichon-Longueville-Baron** Consistent notes. Most recently: now mature; rich nose, curious combination on palate; surprisingly sweet yet with a searingly dry finish. *Last tasted April 2001* ★★(★) *Worth keeping? Not by me.*

**Ch Pichon-Longueville, Lalande** With and without food. Masses of notes – well, 20 to date, most over the past decade: prettily coloured, well-upholstered, delectable. Sweetness and fruit. Being an '82, dry finish. *Last noted at the La Réserve tasting of '82s, April 2001* ★★★★ *Just tuck in.*

**Ch Le Pin** Little did I think that the rich, fruity half-bottle sample from Richard Walford, the importer, tasted in November 1983 was going to be one of the shooting stars of the saleroom; nor did the Thienpont family anticipate, when they first experimented with a tiny parcel of land, situated near Ch Petit-Village and their own Vieux Château Certan, that Le Pin would become a super-expensive cult wine, upstaging even Pétrus. Two more admiring notes in the 1980s. Most recently: very good. A very high mark at the Kaplan '82s event. Glorious nose, very fruity, very distinctive; sweet, soft, velvety, full of fruit. Fragrant. *Last tasted April 2001* ★★★★(★)

**Ch Pontet-Canet** In 1988 I wrote 'need to retaste'. I have. And still don't like it: slightly tarry, Gripfix nose; piquant fruit, harsh. Astringent. *Last tasted April 2001.*

**Ch Prieuré-Lichine** I was a friend of the flamboyant and charming Alexis Lichine and stayed at Prieuré regularly. Dining with him on Thursday, 23 September, he told me that his Merlot, which had started to be picked on the Monday, was all in and the Cabernet Sauvignon was under way. The point of mentioning this is that on the Right Bank, in conditions of great heat, most of the super-ripe Merlots had been picked prior to the previous weekend when the weather broke. On the Monday evening I drove from the city of Bordeaux to Prieuré in torrential rain. Though the sun and sea breezes dried the grapes 'like washing on the line', there had been a change in the weather. I think Alexis had got his timing wrong for his wine is a bit weak for an '82. Just a refreshing drink. *Not tasted recently, last in Dec 1992* ★★

**Ch Rausan-Ségla** Masses of notes but none very recently. Not a great '82. Lean and piquant. *Last tasted May 1991* ★?

**Ch Rauzan-Gassies** Rather like its non-identical twin, lean and very tannic. *Last tasted June 1999.*

**Ch Rochemorin** One of André Lurton's many properties, assiduously and thoughtfully renovated like all the others – an AC Graves from Martillac: fully mature, orange-tinged; rich, bricky nose, harmonious, spicy; full, rich flavour, mature, substantial (13.5% alcohol), good length but still tannic. *Lunch at Ch Bonnet, Oct 2001* ★★★

**Ch Sociando-Mallet** This *bourgeois* Médoc has received high praise in recent vintages. Hardy Rodenstock wickedly inserted a bottle between Haut-Brion and Ch Margaux, tasted blind of course, hoping both to catch us out and, I suppose, to demonstrate the quality of Sociando. It didn't quite work because the latter has a distinctly strange, high-toned nose and equally curious flavour. Crisp and good length though, with citrus-like acidity on its finish. *Sept 1998* ★★★ *in its way.*

**Ch Talbot** Impressive in cask, developing into a full and fleshy wine. Quite a few notes in the 1990s, the last two both in magnums, first lunching at the château: mature; ripe; sweet, rich, à point, 'no point in keeping it', and a fortnight later dining with the proprietors at the Mirabelle: deep, velvety, sweet and chunky. *Last tasted April 2000* ★★★★ *Drink soon.*

**Ch Trotanoy** To demonstrate the extraordinary almost tropical heat at vintage time, on 16 September the temperature in the vat was 33°C, on 19 September it was 21°C, on 20 September it was 23°C. On 21 September it rose to 25°C in the morning and up to 26°C in the afternoon. On the day of my visit, 22 September, it was 29°C. By 1989, the wine was very distinctive, full of flesh, fruit and of course tannic. Most recently, with the Bachmanns in San Francisco. It was very good. No signs of 'baking'. Just a perfectly rich drink. *Last tasted Dec 2000* ★★★★

**Vieux Ch Certan** While the Thienponts were playing with their tiny sideline, Ch Le Pin, they were busily coping with the heat at 'Vieux'. To be frank, when first tasted in 1989, I did not find it very appealing, and most recently found its finish marred by bitter, teeth-gripping tannin. By its own standards and '82 Pomerols, comparatively mean and pinched. Disappointing. *Last tasted Jan 1996* ★(★)?

**Ch Violette** Not a shrinking violet. A deep, powerful, very tannic Pomerol. *At a tasting for* Résidence *magazine, Amsterdam, April 1998* ★★★(★)

**BRIEF RATINGS OF SOME OTHER '82S, ALSO LAST TASTED IN THE 1990S:** Ch de Camensac ★★; Ch Capbern-Gasqueton ★★★; Ch Coufran ★★★; Ch Dauzac ★★★; Ch Desmirail ★★; Ch Durfort-Vivens ★★; Ch Ferrière ★★;

Ch Fombrauge ★★; Ch Gazin ★★★★; Ch Grand-Puy-Ducasse ★★; Ch d'Issan ★★★; Ch Kirwan ★★?; Ch Labégorce-Zédé ★★★; Ch Lascombes ★★★; Ch Malartic-Lagravière; Ch Marquis d'Alesme ★★★; Ch Marquis de Terme ★★; Ch Les Ormes-de-Pez ★★★; Ch Pape-Clément ★★★; Ch Plince ★★; Ch Pouget ★★; Ch Phélan-Ségur ★★; Clos René ★★★; and Ch Trottevieille ★★

# 1983 ★★★

I usually link in my mind the 1983 and 1981 vintages. They certainly have quite a bit in common, in style and weight for example. Both are, or at least were, considered more characteristic of Bordeaux than the widely different and somehow 'un-English' 1982 claret, by which I mean the sort of claret which *we* liked to drink. The other thing they now have in common is that they should be drunk and not hung on to. The trouble is that for people of my age, 1983 is not thought of as an old wine, yet, let's face it, it will soon be 20 years old.

Even in the very good vintages and ideal circumstances, minor wines, the *petits châteaux*, are best consumed at any time from four to eight years. Some of the better made, more firmly structured might be good for ten or 12 years. But after that they rarely evolve further, they just become old.

What shocked me however was that even the classed growth Médocs of this vintage were showing distinct signs of age and tiredness at 16 years of age. This was at a *Decanter* magazine tasting of 23 châteaux in December 1999 (though not including the first growths).

The weather conditions were quite good, for though there was a poor start it improved in time for the flowering and the summer was hot and dry. The harvest, which started towards the end of September, took place in ideal conditions resulting in a large crop of good quality wines. Perhaps too large a crop, too diluted: one thing everyone agreed about was that the most successful district was Margaux. But perhaps I should let my notes speak for themselves.

**Ch Lafite** This started off in its charming fragrant way; I even reckoned it was level pegging with the 1985 at Lloyd Flatt's monumental Lafite tasting in 1988: good colour; attractive fruit on nose and palate. Good weight. Fairly tannic finish – after all it was only a child. A couple of years later I thought it was swingeingly dry. 'Needs food' (but Lafite is, after all, the archetypal food wine). Four more recent notes, one of the most detailed made in April 1995 at Christie's first masterclass in New York: double-decanted, it had a good rich colour and mature red-brown rim; bouquet light and fragrant but with a hard core, slightly varnishy and not much development in the glass. Lean, with a touch of that curious Pauillac oyster shell taste. The following year, in a 'flight' of five Lafite *impériales*, dumb at first, but this time the bouquet opened up beautifully. It seemed a fairly powerful wine, rich, tannic with a dry citrus touch on the finish. Most recently, helping to celebrate the 50th anniversary of L'Académie du Vin de Bordeaux: fragrant, touch of sweetness, with 'edgy acidity' and overall dry. Most recently, at the 19th annual dinner of the Commanderie de Bordeaux at Bristol memorable more for my speech which contained more rude stories than the occasion demanded. Like Queen Victoria, the dressed-up ladies were not amused and the be-medalled Bristol gentlemen thought I had gone over the top. After my speech at their first dinner all those years ago, I thought I would not be asked again. This time I knew it. The Lafite, which surprisingly survived the blue cheese, was rather disappointing. No charm. In short a moderately good Lafite, but drying out. *Last tasted Jan 2000. At best ★★★★ But now I would settle for ★★★*

**Ch Latour** First tasted in the *chai* in September 1984. Intense purple but not its usual opacity. But it was fairly full-bodied and stuffed full of youthful fruit. Then not noted again for five years, at the Frericks/Wodarz tasting in Wiesbaden. Not a heavyweight but rich, fleshy and fine. Several more recent notes: deep, velvety; fragrant, cedary bouquet opening up richly. Sweeter than expected, good fruit and flavour (at a Bordeaux Club dinner at Caius, Cambridge, 1998). The same year, at the Christie's wine department's Christmas dinner – we never stinted ourselves (I never asked where the wines had come from). Bouquet well developed. Again surprisingly sweet which, with its flesh and good fruit, masked the tannin and acidity. I added 'the most amazingly ready and drinkable Latour'. *Last tasted Dec 1998 ★★★★*

**Ch Margaux** This was the wine of the vintage. Could it be just a coincidence that this was the much admired Paul Pontallier's first vintage at Margaux? I usually find Margaux exceptionally appealing in cask, its vivid purple, its fruit-driven aroma and dramatic taste. One takes for granted the accompanying tannins, one leaves inspired, but with blackened teeth! So it was with the '83 when I first tasted it twelve months after the harvest. On several occasions I have tasted it alongside the '82 and, at Lay & Wheeler's Margaux evening in 1990, judged the '82 to be better. However, on a more recent occasion, though both enormously impressive, I finally came down on the '83 – it just had that extra touch of finesse. I have been fortunate enough to taste the wine on well over a dozen occasions over the last decade, three drinking superbly at our various Bordeaux Club dinners, but not showing at its best (dozens of bottles opened for the thousand or so participants) at a Wine Experience tasting in New York in 1995. Later at highly educational vertical tastings, one of the earliest of those in 1995, with the Hollywood Wine Society, and on each occasion tasted in the same 'flight' as the '82, the '83 tending to have a more glorious bouquet and crisper flavour. The total difference in style noted again at the two Wagner tastings in Zurich, the first in 1997. A double treat at the Château Margaux dinner at Brooks's in London (March 2000) for the wine and our one lady guest, Corinne Mentzelopoulos, who bowled over the elderly members: she is as witty as she is attractive. If I were to sum up the '83 Margaux, it would be as noted at John Jenkins' dinner (Oct 2000): a beautiful colour, medium deep and still youthful; the unbeatable Margaux fragrance soaring out of the glass; sweet, soft and rich. It fills the mouth with flavour and seems to last forever. *Last tasted at Manfred Wagner's Margaux vertical in Zurich, Nov 2000 ★★★★★*

**Ch Mouton-Rothschild** First tasted with the late and legendary *maître de chai* Raoul Blondin in his lair, a tiny tasting room. This was in September 1984 and they had just finished bottling the '82. A good lively colour but not deep. Very Cabernet cassis. Its fragrance already enticing at Flatt's Mouton tasting in 1986 after which it continued to evolve, with great depth of fruit and flavour to match, but some austerity. Just four notes over the last decade, the penultimate at a first growth tasting I conducted at Christie's for the Citibank in 1995. Richly evolved and with a mature mahogany rim; a peppery, very fruity, blackcurrant Cabernet Sauvignon scent; sweet and exciting but I noticed very high acidity and its tannin now laid bare. Most recently, at another Hollywood Wine Society tasting of nine vintages and preceding the '82. Unquestionably a most attractive wine, its tannin and acid finish not out of line. One was tantalised by its flavour. I added 'more or less ready' for drinking. *Last tasted March 1998* ★★★★

**Ch Haut-Brion** A quintet of notes: first at the château in September 1984. Good wine, texture and length. Curiously, its youthful nose reminded me of thoroughbred stables. Quite independently in 1997 and 1998 I described it as sweet, rather caramel-like and 'brown sugar' respectively. The usual earthy-tobacco flavour, fairly tannic. The most recent and useful note was made at a MW tasting moderated by Clive Coates, with Jean Delmas and Robert Luxembourg. Delmas informed us that the vineyard had suffered hail damage on 4 and 5 July and though August was hot it was also humid causing botrytis problems. At 17 years of age the '83 had an open, mature, orange-brown rim; a fully developed, slightly smelly and stalky nose, showing its age. More vegetal than the '85 and, I thought, drying out. *Last tasted Jan 2000* ★★★ *Not a great Haut-Brion. Needs drinking.*

**Ch Ausone** A good Ausone: more of a rich, elegant Pomerol style, silky textured, good length. This was in 1987. More recently, at Penning-Rowsell's '10-year' tasting: now fully mature, rather weak rimmed; its bouquet fully evolved, sweet, soft, vanillin, reminding me of curling autumn leaves. Sweet, soft texture, open knit, chewy. *Last tasted June 1993* ★★★★

**Ch Cheval Blanc** A really lovely wine. Intense, fleshy, tannic in 1985. My top marks at the Penning-Rowsells' '10-year' first growth tasting. Perfect to drink – as a drink; a rare claret that does not need the assistance of food though I see it went well with Explorateur cheese at one of John Jenkins' Bordeaux Club dinners (in 1995) and again, for he must have had quite a few bottles in his cellar, three years later. A superb double magnum, scented, sweet, full of fruit, good length but noticeably tannic at a Rodenstock tasting in 1994, and in 1997 fragrant, crisp, beautiful flavour with tannins and more noticeable acidity. This was at Wolf's famous vertical and I noted that at 13% only the '90 had a higher alcoholic content (13.6%). Most were between 12 and 12.5%. At the most recent John Jenkins' Bordeaux Club dinner at Childerly Hall it was beyond description. It had such a sweet, lovely, 'melting charm'. *Last tasted Sept 1998* ★★★★★

**Ch Pétrus** First noted at Frerick's Pétrus *extravaganza* in 1986: an intense ruby magnum, almost jam-like sweetness and richness though still hard on the palate. Starting to show some maturity in 1990 but, I have to say, my lowest mark of the eight first growths at Penning-Rowsell's '10-year' tasting and dinner in 1993. I thought it was surprisingly lean and tannic even (slightly) preferred the Ausone. Most recently, an impressive double magnum with crisp and agreeable fruit on nose and palate, good texture but very dry finish. *Last tasted at Rodenstock's opening dinner, Sept 1995* ★★★★

**MASSES OF '83S IN MY NOTES** A selection of the most interesting and important ones follows. I hope they give the feel of the vintage, then and now.

**Ch L'Angélus** Attractive cask sample in the spring of 1984 and that autumn 'dazzled by its fragrance' at the first tasting in London for the Union des Grands Crus held at Christie's. Seemed to have shown its all by 1987 for when last tasted at seven years of age, thinning, noticeable colour loss; a bit too

sweet and easy (the style has much changed recently). *Last tasted May 1990* ★★★ *But drink up.*

**Ch Batailley** Several notes, the most recent at two Christie's boardroom luncheons within a month of each other: pleasant, easy, soft fruit, ready. *Last tasted Jan 1995* ★★★

**Ch Beauséjour-Duffau-Lagarosse** Sweet, rich, attractive. *Oct 1993* ★★★

**Ch Beychevelle** On the whole, a good '83. Originally spicy and very tannic, still rather aggressive, fruity and flavoury but with 'swingeing finish' (dinner at Athenaeum, London, 1996), less so at a Beychevelle vertical in 1997, in fact 'sweet, delicious, drinking well', and one of the drying-out Médocs at the *Decanter* tasting. *Last tasted Dec 1999* ★★★ *Should continue.*

**Ch Branaire-Ducru** Appeared pale (probably chaptalised) and a quick maturer but, though not all that impressive, holding its own and quite attractive at ten years of age. A touch of raw fruit. *Last tasted Dec 1993* ★★ *Drink up.*

**Ch Brane-Cantenac** Fragrant and delicious in cask. By 1990 fully mature 'rich coffee-like nose', ripe but with raw finish, and not dissimilar notes a decade later: 'sweet, mature, rather chocolatey nose', 'interesting flavour, attractive, but finishes raw'. *The last note, tasted blind, Dec 1999* ★★★ *Drink soon.*

**Ch Calon-Ségur** Just three notes from an unimpressive cask sample, flavoury but tannic four years later. At ten years of age its superficially attractive, chaptalised nose and flavour 'but raw finish' bearing an uncanny resemblance to the two preceding châteaux. Fully mature. *Last noted at a pre-sale tasting, Dec 1993* ★★ *Drink up.*

**Ch Canon** A lovely wine, all the component parts showing well in the fall of 1984. By 1996 (at the Canon v. Lynch-Bages tasting) a lovely, soft, polished, mature appearance; very sweet, somewhat rustic, chocolatey, fully evolved nose; lovely ripe tannins and crisp acidity, light style but good length. Yet three months later, from my own cellar, though extolling its colour and nose, added 'a bit bland'. *Last noted at a Sunday lunch, June 1996. At best* ★★★★ *But drink up.*

**Ch Cantemerle** Uncharacteristically chunky, lacking charm in October 1984. Quite good nose developing by 1987 but, 12 years later the latter had diminished. It was drying out. *Last tasted, blind, Dec 1999* ★

**Dom de Chevalier** A charmer. Eight notes. Fragrant, elegant, though tannic from the cask up to its 'middle age'. Now mature, drinking well. *Last noted at the Fête de la Fleur dinner held at the domaine, 1993* ★★★ *Drink soon.*

**Ch Cos d'Estournel** Well over a dozen notes, from a very 'medicinal', even 'smelly' and very tannic cask sample, and variations on this throughout the 1980s. This was one of my home-drinking clarets so I was able to drink it regularly, my last bottle being polished off in 1997; my best note. Then, a couple of years later, tasted blind, fully mature colour, nose and taste. Touch of sweetness, attractive but very tannic and astringent. Last tasted Dec 1999. *At best* ★★★ *Will not improve.*

**Ch La Croix du Casse** Owned by the proprietors of the better-known Clinet. Distinctly Pomerol, ruby, rich, good body and flavour. A sort of up-market *rince bouche* at a Commanderie de Bordeaux dinner near Oslo. *April 1996* ★★★

**Ch Desmirail** At its best at a tasting of '83 Margaux. Flavoury, elegant. My estimate of its best drinking span was from then (1990) to 1998. I was more or less spot on because the following year it was more than fully mature, showing its age with an astringent finish. *Last tasted Dec 1999* ★★ *Drink up.*

**Ch Ducru-Beaucaillou** A very good '83 from a correct, purple and tannic cask sample, and half a dozen bottles since.

The best of nine of its peers in 1993, its bouquet fully developed, fragrant, a touch of figs, very sweet, chewy, attractive in 1998 and showing well at the *Decanter* tasting: mature, good flavour, good length – for an '83. *Last tasted Dec 1999 ★★★★ Drink while the going is good.*

**Ch Duhart-Milon** A lean but always fragrant style and the '83 very much so. Eight consistent notes over a 12-year period. Flavoury but acidic at the *Decanter* blind tasting in 1999. Most recently: drinking well but its tannin and acidity upstaging the fruit. *Last noted at a Christie's boardroom lunch, June 2000 ★★★ Drink up.*

**Ch L'Église-Clinet** Very deep, fairly intense; a rich though rather malty, molasses nose; better on palate. Full of all the component parts. *Last tasted Sept 1998 ★★★, possibly ★★★★*

**Ch L'Évangile** Someone flippantly described it as 'like port without sugar' in 1991. It was quite sweet, as red wines go. It certainly harboured a great deal of colour, depth of fruit and tannins. A couple of years later noticing more maturity; harmonious; rich, mature, tannic. Not my favourite style of wine but an impressive '83. *Last noted at the London Wine Trade Fair, May 1993 ★★★, possibly now ★★★★*

**Ch Figeac** A delicious wine. Three notes in the late 1980s, deep, plummy; rich, spicy, enticing; a mouthful of flavour, tannic but wonderful aftertaste. And four notes over the past decade. In April 1994, the high (for St-Émilion) Cabernet Sauvignon element very prominent on the nose, sweet, firm, iron/earthy flavour. Five months later, a very fragrant double magnum, good length, silky Pomerol type of texture. Most recently, a delicious drink at the opening dinner of the Union des Grands Crus week of tastings. *Last noted in the spectacular candlelit cellars at Ch Villemaurine, April 1997 ★★★★*

**Clos Fourtet** Within a stone's throw of Villemaurine and with similar old quarried cellars hewn out of the rock and, coincidentally, the first château I ever visited: it was very chilly and foggy inside. Two cask samples of the '83 the following spring and autumn, the first not ready, the second not very inspiring. Then a jump of 23 years: surviving the leap, pleasant, well developed nose; quite good flavour but with a curious dry, 'singed' finish. *Last tasted June 1997 ★★ Drink up.*

**Ch Giscours** I have been so accustomed to the dark and chewy Giscours that it came as a surprise to find the '83 so delicious, with a hint of delicacy in cask – then, latterly, realising that, as mentioned in the introduction, the Margaux district was successful. At five years of age flavoury and fleshy. My most detailed notes, too long to transcribe, have been made at three Bordeaux wine courses, my overall impression though fruity and flavoury, the gooseberry-like acidity is

---

**Bipin Desai**

*A physicist of Indian extraction living in southern California. Bipin is a very active and energetic organiser of important tastings. The first I attended was a tasting of 1959 claret from 31 châteaux in 1983. This was followed by a tasting of 1945s, then, as commentator, vertical tastings of Ch La Mission Haut-Brion, Ch Margaux, and Ch Figeac. Though semi-commercial, in that people pay to attend, they are of interest and often of great benefit to the owners of the châteaux in question. For example, the de Mouchys attended the tasting of La Mission Haut-Brion in 1987, enabling them to taste a wide range of vintages and compare wines they hadn't tasted before side by side. Corinne Mentzelopoulos and Paul Pontallier came to the vertical of Ch Margaux in 1987.*

becoming a little more than 'refreshing'. Certainly fully mature, a mahogany tinge though deeper than some '83s. *Last noted June 1995. A good Giscours, a pretty good '83 ★★★ Drink soon.*

**Ch Grand-Puy-Lacoste** This was the third vintage that I bought seriously, so I have masses of notes. Alas, all consumed, though unlike quite a few '83 Médocs, it had plenty of life left. At this time, the wine was underappreciated and underpriced so it was not all that much of an extravagance. Not only did I have the pleasure of following its progress, dipping into my own cellar, but we were able to drink, and offer to our guests a really good claret bought early.

Not quite as slow to mature as in the bigger vintages, it was developing well in its tenth year though still rather tannic, and I found that even at 15 years it benefited from a fair amount (almost half a day) of decanting time. I think I eventually timed it right for my last bottle was consumed with friends at dinner a couple of days after my birthday: the wine was aged 17, I was 73. The wine, at any rate, was still fairly deep but had a ripe, mature, immediately forthcoming bouquet; sweet, flavoury, charming, and with a lovely aftertaste, *à point. Last noted at a dinner party at our flat in London, May 2000 ★★★★*

**Ch Gruaud-Larose** Started off with a bang. Alongside the '81 positively opulent. Then it seemed to go through a stage of puberty, finally emerging as a fully fledged, and fleshed adolescent. A good, rich and ripe bottle showing at its best, for example, at a Bordeaux Club dinner in 1995. Fully developed, sweet, attractive, pretty well balanced at the 1999 *Decanter* tasting. By the late 1990s, fully developed. Most recently, typically fruity and flavoury but with quite an end bite. *Last noted at a Saintsbury dinner, Oct 2001 ★★★ Lively but drink soon.*

**Ch Haut-Bailly** A delicious cask sample in April 1984, then a gap of 12 years, fully mature, very 'Graves', surprisingly chunky for an '83. Four more consistently good notes. The thing about red Graves is that it tends to develop quickly yet cruises more effortlessly on its 'plateau of perfection' than one might expect. Most recently, rich, mature looking; with the difficult-to-describe earthy, mocha, cigar leaf bouquet and flavour. It seemed to get sweeter in the glass. *Last noted at a Christie's masterclass, April 2002 ★★★★ Lovely now.*

**Ch Haut-Batailley** One of my favourites. The '83 exuded elegance and charm even in cask. Seemed an early developer, but for no good reason I did not come across it again for 16 years, by which time it was certainly fully mature, an easy style of wine, the tannin so noticeable at a tasting bench would be unnoticeable with food; it would merely serve to refresh, leave the mouth clean and dry – an aid to the digestion. That is what good claret is for. *Last tasted, blind, Dec 1999 ★★★★ but, as with the Haut-Bailly, I am biased.*

**Ch d'Issan** Tasted in 1984, 1987, 1990 and at the 1999 *Decanter* Médoc tasting: not bad, lean and, most recently, still raw. A mediocre '83. *Last tasted Dec 1999 ★*

**Ch Kirwan** Tasted in 1984, 1990 and a decade later. Not the best period for this Schröder & Schÿler-owned château, but distinctly better than the nearby d'Issan, demonstrating that not all the '83 Margaux were brilliant. Now fully mature, but not offering a particularly interesting nose or taste. Not a bad drink. *Last tasted lunching at Ch Talbot, April 2000 ★★*

**Ch Labégorce-Zédé** Owned by the Thienpont family. Only two notes. A dashed sight better Margaux than the previous two listed above. Very high marks in 1990, and surprisingly deep; very fragrant; with a slightly sweet, delightful style and finish. *Last noted with Jacques Thienpont, whose family owns the château, in Brussels, March 1999 ★★★★*

**Ch La Fleur** Superb magnum: cedary, Cabernet Franc fragrance. Rich, spicy, lovely. *Sept 1998* ★★★★

**Ch Lafon-Rochet** Only one note, thank goodness. Strange. Drying out. Had it ever been otherwise? *Dec 1999.*

**Ch Lagrange** (St-Julien) Three quite good notes in 1988. Variable recently. Some fragrance, dry finish. *Last noted at the* Decanter *tasting of '83s, Dec 1999* ★

**Ch La Lagune** A surprising number of notes from May 1984: spicy, good flavour. Two critical notes in 1988. Seemed at its ripest best, ready for drinking in 1990. Most recently, very disappointing, drying out. *Last tasted as sort of curtain-raiser at a 'Cigar and Port' evening at Brooks's Club in London, Oct 2000* ★★

**Ch Langoa-Barton** A bit pedestrian. *'About right now' at a tasting in Copenhagen, March 1999* ★★

**Ch Lascombes** Certainly living up to the '83 Margaux reputation. Still in cask when I first tasted it in Feb 1985 and brilliantly good. In 1990 and 1998 its almost '82-like richness and extract noted. Now fully mature, bouquet with several dimensions; distinctly sweet, attractive flavour and good length. *Last tasted, blind, at the* Decanter *tasting of '83s. Dec 1999* ★★★★

**Ch Léoville-Barton** A lean and tannic wine from the start. Seemed at its best either side of 1990 but still a bit raw. Only one note since: undemonstrative, severe, still too tannic. *Last noted at dinner, March 1997* ★ *Disappointing.*

**Ch Léoville-Las-Cases** A different ball game. Though tannic at least with a fully supporting cast. Most recently, ruby coloured, crisp, spicy fruit; some intensity and, for an '83 St-Julien, many layered. *Last tasted in New York, Dec 1998* ★★★(★)

**Ch Léoville-Poyferré** Several notes from a lean but supple cask sample. Developing steadily, fragrant but quite a bite around the 1990s. Most recently, very straightforward. A copybook claret (but I confess, tasting blind, I thought it was a Margaux). *Last tasted Dec 1999* ★★★ *Drink now.*

**Ch Lynch-Bages** I started off by writing 'if only they can be all as easy and delightful as this'. No fewer than four cask samples in 1984, all beguiling, equally so in the mid- to late 1980s: cassis scent, charm, rich and easy. Yet noted in 1994, 1995 and 1996 'disappointing'. Then, delicious and 'a charmer' reappearing at a dinner in Brussels. *Last tasted April 1997. I'll chance it and give it at least* ★★★

**Ch Malescot-St-Exupéry** As so often, a bit over the top, plausibly attractive, specious. But I am being condescending. Notes all around 1990. Most recently, 'drinking fairly well' (with my chairman). *Last tasted Oct 1998* ★★

**Ch Marquis de Terme** Good enough in 1990. Now showing its age, unknit, sweaty, stalky, raw finish. *Not showing well at the* Decanter *tasting of '83s, Dec 1999.*

**Ch La Mission Haut-Brion** Very good wine. Spicy, crisp, full-bodied from the start. Good notes in 1990. Most recently, still very deep though with maturing edge; a rather hard, spirity nose; full, rich, assertive – a fragment of rusty iron! *Last tasted at a charity dinner in New York, Dec 1997* ★★(★★)?

**Ch Montrose** It started out well. Continued typically spicy, tannic. In 1990 though impressive I thought it should be given far more bottle age but at the recent *Decanter* blind tasting, it looked fully mature and though quite fragrant, was drying out. *Last tasted Dec 1999* ★★(★)? Risk keeping?

**Ch Mouton-Baronne-Philippe** Richly flavoured but lean, fragrant as always, and some charm. *Last tasted Dec 1993* ★★★

**Ch Palmer** I was originally informed that it had an unusually high percentage of Petit Verdot but the current managing director told us that it was only 2.4%. Well, whatever, I thought it was hard and stalky in its early days and somewhat raw well into the 1980s. Eight subsequent notes, the best in 1995 at a tasting for Wein & Co in Vienna: a charmer, fully developed – yet a hard tannic, chewy texture. I was expecting more but found it wanting (1999). Most recently, variable bottles, one corky, the other a bit of a mixture, full, sweet entry but very tannic. And, I thought, drying out. *Last tasted at the Palmer/Farr Vintners' dinner, Feb 2001* ★★ *A disappointing Palmer.*

**Ch Pichon-Longueville, Lalande** Many notes, twice in 1984, rich, ripe fruit but of course tannic, maturing well, gaining extra dimensions. Tasted on ten occasions through the last decade and, frankly, not wholly consistent. I think it was at its best in the first half of the 1990s. 'Very drinkable now' (1994), 'lovely flesh … a joy' (1995), flavoury but with touch of astringency (April 1999), and later that year, straightforward, not mind blowing. Most recently, a jeroboam: still youthfully plummy coloured; surprisingly deep, rich, slightly mocha nose; sweet entry, rich extract, dry finish. *Last noted at the Eigensatzs', Bad Schwalbach, Oct 2001* ★★★ *Drink soon.*

**Ch Prieuré-Lichine** Five notes. Consistently disappointing from the spring of 1984. *Last tasted in July 1999* ★

**Ch Rausan-Ségla** Good wine. Firm, good flesh, stylish. Gentle fragrance. Good flavour and grip. Best I think in the early to mid-1990s. *Last tasted Dec 1999* ★★★★ *But not improving.*

**Ch St-Pierre** Smelly cheese; astringent. *Dec 1999.*

**Ch Talbot** From the start, rich, rustic – always reminds me of a deliciously pongy farmyard. Can't think why I like it. Now over-developed, with a distinctly acidic finish. *Last noted at the* Decanter *tasting in Dec 1999* ★★

**Ch Tertre-Roteboeuf** I think this was my first exposure to this new 'cult' wine. Quite nice. Consumed by my wife and me, sandwiched between two of our favourite everyday wines, Charles Heidsieck Brut Réserve and Graham's 10-year old tawny. *The Sunday before Christmas, Dec 1994* ★★

**Ch La Tour-de-By** I first visited this fine mid-19th century mansion in 1995. The tower is a bit phoney – built in 1825 on the site of an old Dutch mill; the owner Marc Pagès, is slightly aloof, dignified, distinguished, and (he will not like me to mention this) the recipient of the Croix de Guerre. More to the point, he makes one of the best and most dependable *bourgeois* wines of the northerly (Bas) Médoc. I tasted a range of wines, the oldest being the 1983, fully mature, harmonious, light style, pleasing. I have followed his vintages ever since. *Last tasted Sept 1995* ★★★

**Vieux Ch Certan** Lovely wine. Surprisingly deep, with well developed nose; sweet, soft, lovely, 'at best now' (in 1995). Yet, four years later more good features noted, rich 'legs, extract and velvety tannins. *Last tasted March 1999* ★★★★ *No hurry.*

---

### Commanderie de Bordeaux

*Founded in 1950 to promote the wines of Bordeaux, and now highly successful, with 60 branches worldwide holding dinners and tastings. I became an honorary member, then a full member (in 1983), of the New Orleans chapter. The Commanderie is particularly active in the USA, less so in England with one branch in Manchester, one in Bristol – at which I recall making two cringe-making speeches on grand occasions, one at the opening dinner and one on their 10th anniversary. The newest branch is in London. I have particularly happy memories of speaking at or co-hosting American chapter events, the most recent with the Detroit chapter in Bordeaux, two delightful days in delightful company squeezed in between engagements elsewhere.*

BRIEF ASSESSMENTS OF SOME OF THE MANY OTHER '83S (with year last tasted): Ch d'Angludet delightful. *1997* ★★★; Ch Beauregard elegant. *1995* ★★★; Ch Belair *1990* ★★★; Ch Boyd-Cantenac *assez bien*. *1996* ★★; Ch Chasse-Spleen extraordinary for its class. *1997* ★★★★; Ch Coufran *1995* ★★; Ch Dauzac *1990* ★★; Ch Durfort-Vivens *1990* ★★; Ch La Gaffelière *1993* ★★; Ch Gazin *1996* ★★★; Ch Larcis-Ducasse *1999* ★★; Ch Malartic-Lagravière *1993* ★★★; Ch Pichon-Baron *1988* ★★★; Ch Le Pin *1988* ★★★★; Ch Pontet-Canet *1988* ★★★; Ch Rauzan-Gassies *1990* ★?; and Ch Siran *1990* ★★

# 1984 ★ to ★★

The key element of this vintage is the failure of the Merlot which resulted in serious problems, shortages and imbalance on the Right Bank and caused the over-domination of the Cabernets on the Left. The situation was exacerbated by the wines coming on the market at too high a price, in some instances higher than the '83s, even '82s. The weather, as always, was largely to blame though not for the prices. April was warm and advanced the vegetation. May was cold and – this is when it all happened – an incomplete flowering during an excessively hot and dry June caused *coulure*, the Merlot vines being worst affected. Summer, reasonably warm, was succeeded by a humid September. The wet October was rudely interrupted on the 5th by the hurricane Hortense.

The Merlot-dominated vineyards in Pomerol were particularly badly affected, Ch Pétrus for example, planted with virtually 100% Merlot, having a minuscule crop. The failure of the Merlot in the Médoc was less catastrophic because it is very rarely the dominant variety. But it did result in an even higher than usual percentage of Cabernet Sauvignon. What with that and the dismal ripening and harvesting periods, the wines lack balance. Once more, I am indebted to Hardy Rodenstock for the opportunity of tasting a wide range (18) of top '84s, blind of course, just one session during his 13th Raritäten Weinprobe in October 1992.

## Hardy Rodenstock

*A Munich resident, Hardy began buying fine and rare wines at Christie's in the 1970s. He is the most lavish giver of major wine events, to which he invites his close friends, among whose number I am lucky to count myself. Hardy spends about a year organising each tasting, and the extraordinary quantity and quality of the wines presented have been recorded frequently in these pages. His attention to detail is phenomenal. The first of his annual tastings, of about 40 wines, was held in 1980, but the first that I was able to attend, at the Restaurant Fuente in Mülheim, was in 1984: a black tie event, 75 wines, eight courses. We sat down at 12 midday and got up again at 12 midnight (with a splitting headache!). These later developed into two- and three-day weekend events held at Wiesbaden, then at the Arlberg Hospiz in Austria, one at Ch d'Yquem, and latterly at the excellent Hotel Königshof in Munich. Each event must cost Hardy a fortune, not to mention the time and trouble taken to organise it. Hardy is a remarkably modest man, but jealous of his sources, though many of his rare wines have been bought at Christie's. Through his immense generosity I have not only had the opportunity to taste an enormous range of great and very rare wines, but have met a very wide circle of enthusiasts and collectors, becoming one of the privileged fixtures at Hardy's events.*

**Ch Lafite** Raw and tannic at four years of age. By 1985, a silky texture noted but a very dry finish. At Rodenstock's blind tasting of '84s, it came out moderately well: vanillin, chaptalised nose which opened up. Classic flavour but lean and tannic. Though deep-coloured its tell-tale rim was a bit weak and lacked intensity. Just four notes, all magnums, from my own cellar, in the first half of the last decade, none since. At a Christie's board lunch – providing my own wine, not for the first time – in 1995, it was satisfactory as a drink but not notable. A couple also drunk the same year, on Christmas Eve at home and on Christmas Day with all the family at a friend's house in Somerset. It went quite well with the candles, crackers and sparklers. A year later and somewhat more interesting, a magnum I had decanted for a CD-ROM tasting. It was fortunate that we had all the time in the world, for it took nearly two hours for its bouquet to emerge. Most recently, another magnum at Daphne's 65th birthday dinner. Though fairly deep and showing some maturity, like the birthday girl, it was overall dry and hard with just enough fruit. Happily I have no more left. *Last tasted July 1996* ★★

**Ch Latour** First tasted in cask and, unsurprisingly, raw and tannic. In 1989 at the Frericks/Wodarz tasting its Cabernet-dominated spiciness developed quite well. Unknit though and with a touch of bitterness. In 1992, tasted blind alongside the other first growths, it had a fragrant, vegetal nose ('boiled cabbage' – it was a bit smelly). Chunky. Raw fruit. The following year, at a Bordeaux Club dinner at Childerley Hall with *salade tiède rustique* and *noisette de chevreuil*: very deep, a lovely ruby colour. Much better on the nose, very Cabernet Sauvignon aroma and flavour. Dry, crisp – but spoilt by a finish like hen droppings. *Last tasted May 1993. Not recommended.*

**Ch Margaux** In 1987 raw end. Very tannic. At Rodenstock's, blind, in 1992, half a point beneath Mouton. Opaque; plenty of blackberry-like fruit on nose and palate. Quite sweet too. Then at the two Wagner verticals, the first in 1997. We were informed that it was almost 100% Cabernet Sauvignon – just 5% Merlot. Better than I had expected with quite decent fruit and grip. But unbalanced, twisted, a bit cheesy. Cheese noted again, though Cabernet Sauvignon lurking beneath. Not a good bottle. Lean, slightly woody, even a touch of cork. *Last tasted Nov 2000* ★★ *but I should give this a miss too.*

**Ch Mouton-Rothschild** It is perhaps as well that a high percentage of Cabernet Sauvignon and Mouton are compatible. The Cabernet Sauvignon element being even more dominant, on nose and in taste, in 1984, but its overall rawness due to a lack of maturity. Several notes from a cask sample in April 1986: lots of fruit but raw. In 1984, hard, flavoury 'but ungracious'. For me the best wine, by a short head, at Rodenstock's blind tasting: a very deep cherry red; rich, chunky, biscuity, Cabernet nose. A massive wine, full of fruit and tannin. *Last tasted Oct 1992* ★★★ *(just).*

**Ch Haut-Brion** Tasted only once, blind: frankly poor, with a rustic, hen shit nose though spicy. Later it had the smell of cast-off cigarette paper though its bottle stink did eventually wear off. Some sweetness, very flavoury in an obscure sort of way. Raw dry finish. *Last tasted Oct 1992. Not recommended.*

**Ch Ausone** Not tasted.

**Ch Cheval Blanc** Attractive colour its best feature. Bitter tannins managing to cope well with lamb cutlets (1990). Under more clinical conditions – one has to concentrate at blind tastings – its appearance was not particularly notable, its nose a bit odd, quite attractive in its way (I wrote 'Cheval

Blanc'?). Sweet, not bad fruit, silky/leathery tannins and quite good length. *Last tasted Oct 1992* ★★ *One of the better '84s.*
**Ch Pétrus** In the early autumn of 1984, walking round the vineyard, scarcely a grape could be seen; the Merlot almost completely wiped out. Not quite though, for the enterprising Rodenstock placed a bottle at the end of his blind tasting. Its bouquet, low-keyed at first, was leafy, herbaceous and opened up fragrantly. Some sweetness, combining soft fruit and crispness. Tannic-iron finish. *Last tasted Oct 1992* ★★★

OTHER '84S LAST TASTED IN THE 1990S
**Ch L'Évangile** Not bad nose. Light, dry, tart. *May 1991* ★ *Drink up.*
**Ch Fieuzal** Normally a well-made Graves. Though Cabernet Sauvignon fairly prominent, a very strange, slightly scented flavour. *Served at the closing dinner of the Union des Grands Crus, April 1994* ★
**Ch La Fleur** Moderate colour; some fruit but no development. Dry, lean, raw. *April 1998* ★
**Ch Grand-Puy-Lacoste** This is one vintage of Lacoste that I did *not* buy. Although quite fragrant it was lean, with taut fruit and citrus-like acidity. *One of the least good of 14 vintages ranging from 1981 to 1994, tasted at the château, June 1995.*
**Ch Kirwan** At nine years of age a fully mature appearance, high-toned, boiled sweets (candies) scent and poor flavour. Probably heavily chaptalised. *At a pre-sale tasting, Dec 1993. Drink up.*
**Ch Léoville-Barton** At the same tasting as the Kirwan and identical low marks for appearance, nose and taste. This time, caramel scented. Dry. Raw. *Dec 1993.*
**Ch Liversan** Unusual to see old vintages on fairly ordinary French restaurant lists, but I soon found out why. Pretty deadly colour, too orange; poor, over the top nose; raw, woody, dried out, Just drinkable. *At the Restaurant des Yachts, Pauillac. Sept 1998, Liversan? Liver salts would have been more enjoyable.*
**Ch Montrose** I was curious to see the 11-year old '84. There were two bottles, one with a nose like brown sugar, dry, tannic, the other sweeter and more flavoury. *At Anthony Byrne's trade tasting, April 1995. At best* ★★ *I wonder if anyone bought it?*
**Ch Pichon-Lalande** For some reason or other five notes, a jeroboam showing quite well at the tasting of '84s in 1992. Two years later 'not bad, raw fruit' and, shortly after 'softer and mellower than expected' – which was not saying much. Most recently, with May de Lencquesaing (had she provided the wine?) at the *Decanter* magazine millennium dinner at the opening of Vinopolis in London. Still deep, some flesh and Cabernet grip … but, alas, not rising to the occasion. *Last tasted July 1999* ★

THE FOLLOWING WERE LAST NOTED AT RODENSTOCK'S BLIND TASTING OF '84S IN OCT 1992 (in order of tasting)
**Ch Branaire-Ducru** (jeroboam) Sweet, chaptalised nose; nice weight, fruity but raw ★
**Ch Léoville-Barton** (*impériale*) Deep cherry red; crisp fruit, fragrant; some depth and 'meat' but raw and tannic. Fair length ★★ *I doubt if time will help.*
**Ch Léoville-Las-Cases** (jeroboam) Deep, one of the most intense; vanillin, quite good cedary nose and flavour. Tightly bound fruit, too dry; tannic and bitter ★★
**Ch Beychevelle** (magnums) Translucent; sweet, jammy, chaptalised nose which opened up quite well. A strangely attractive fragrance. Some plausible fruit. The food helped blunt the bitter tannin ★★★

**Ch Ducru-Beaucaillou** (jeroboam) Good colour and 'legs'; sweet, attractive nose, touch of caramel, opened up fragrantly. More severe on palate. Dry, leathery tannins, raw without food. Quite a bite ★★★ *(just).*
**Ch Cos d'Estournel** (jeroboam) Deep; low-keyed; dry, leathery tannic texture. Quite attractive (with pork!) but a bit raw and diminishing ★★★ *(just).*
**Ch Lynch-Bages** Opaque in cask. Rather common and stalky, rough textured (1988). Several previous notes. At the tasting of '84s in 1992, a jeroboam, very deep, intense; with a distinctive flavoury Cabernet fruit and flavour. Dry, at bit raw but refreshing. An attractive '84 ★★★
**Ch Margaux** and **Ch Haut-Brion** Previously noted – see page 110.
**Ch La Mission Haut-Brion** Earlier notes: plummy colour; quite good nose; fleshier than expected but lacking length (noted in 1990). More or less repeated in 1992: crisp fruit, chunky, 'medicinal' flavour, characteristic 'tobacco' finish ★★★
**Dom de Chevalier** Harmonious bouquet; good fruit and flavour. Tannin and acid in balance. A satisfactory '84 ★★★★
**Ch Lafite**, **Mouton**, **Latour** and **Cheval Blanc** Already noted – see page 110.
**Ch Figeac** Unusually for St-Émilion, a relatively low percentage of Merlot (roughly 30%), the rest being Cabernet Franc, so less affected by the small Merlot crop. My early notes point to advanced maturity, not borne out in 1992. Quite lively bouquet, a touch of volatility, opening up well. Very flavoury but a very dry, austere, acidic finish ★★

# 1985 ★★★★★

I have been much looking forward to reviewing this vintage, hoping that a reappraisal of my notes would confirm my perceptions. It seems to encapsulate all that is good about Bordeaux, the wine, not the city: its weight, its balance, its character. It is certainly my favourite vintage of this splendid decade typifying claret at its best.

But why, and how? Quite simple really: after one of the coldest winters on record, happily when the vines were dormant, but with considerable frost damage in some districts, there was an early and successful flowering which anticipated an early and substantial crop. Following a long, hot summer, the harvest took place in ideal conditions. Only the unlucky or incapable made a mess of their '85s.

Having re-read all my notes, I am more than ever convinced that this is one of the most perfect vintages, both for drinking now and for keeping.
**Ch Lafite** I am, of course, fortunate. It is my job, my hobby, my pleasure, to have the opportunity so frequently to taste wines of this quality and not, I can assure you, always at someone else's expense. I have just short of two dozen notes of the '85 Lafite, tracing its progress not from cask but from October 1988. It crops up at least once in a dozen of my tasting books since 1992, and in a wide variety of contexts. Of the more recent: masterclasses (New York 1995); luncheons at Christie's 1999 and (also in 1999) rather appropriately at New Court, the Rothschild Bank in the City of London. Several wine dinners: James Beard Foundation, New York, 1995; for the Crédit Suisse, at the Shangri-La in Hong Kong, 1999; at yet another Kaplan event, this time devoted to the great '85s (in Chicago, April 2000). Then at home the following month (a magnum), and so on. With the exception of straightforward lunches and dinners, my job is frequently, to conduct or

'moderate' tastings. And I am almost invariably obliged to sing for my supper, which happily is always a pleasure.

Well, what is the '85 Lafite like? At Lloyd Flatt's monumental Lafite tasting in 1988 I gave it one of my highest marks (19/20). At the age of three it had a very deep, lovely purple colour; sweet, rich, very fragrant nose and, on the palate, good fruit, with all the component parts in place. Not *too* massive, not *too* dry, not *too* anything; just with excellent potential. It has progressed steadily, with scarcely a note out of place. It is, however, like so many good vintages of Lafite, if not actually withdrawn, certainly not an extravert. It is a wine that does a sort of slow striptease, revealing more each time one sniffs and sips. It is still fairly deep in colour, with a dark velvety core; still a fairly youthful 15-year old, with the inimitable bricky, oyster shell nose which unravels in the glass. Perfect weight, balance, texture and control. Still fairly tannic and though it makes a delicious drink, still needing more time. My penultimate note: a delicious magnum at a dinner party at home, but still with time in hand. Most recently, a surprise – to say the least – bottle brought by my friend Christian Sauska from his cellar in New York via his apartment in Budapest, and drunk with his winemaker, Zanos Arvay in a roadside restaurant between Tokay and Saraspatak. It had travelled well. *Last noted (in Hungary) August 2000* ★★★★(★) *Delicious now but another effortless 20 years.*

**Ch Latour** Not quite as many notes but well spread, the first, just before fining in September 1986. Unsurprisingly, an intense purple, loaded with blackcurrant fruit, full, tannic yet surprisingly fleshy. In its fifth year, still very deep of course but its nose evolving well: chocolate, coffee, biscuity, tobacco – a whole raft of sweet, interesting aromas; sweet ripeness on the palate, a feature continuously noted, fairly massively constructed, highish alcohol and tannin, yet leaving one with a feeling of warmth. A rich, broad-shouldered wine. Of the several notes made in the mid- to late 1980s, I shall just pick out two. A 'Réserve tasting of Premier Bordeaux Wines' I conducted at the first, and the last, Palm Beach International Food and Wine Fair, in February 1998: medium deep and mature-looking, with a mahogany rim; bouquet low-keyed at first but which opened up marvellously; gloriously sweet and full of fruit. Good length and finish. Still tannic. Most recently, in first-growth company at Stephen Kaplan's 1985 vintage event: bouquet by now ripe, almost meaty, opening up beautifully in the glass and after an hour, fully evolved, 'biscuity'. I do not leave the wine untouched. By the time that hour has elapsed, little remains in the glass! On the palate a full, rich, almost mocha-flavoured wine, with an excellent dry finish. *Last tasted at the Four Seasons in Chicago, April 2000* ★★★★(★) *Lovely now but so much more to come.*

**Ch Margaux** Tasted twice in cask, June and August 1987: a deep, already fragrant, fleshy wine though mouthfilling with mouth-puckering tannins. At five years of age, those tannins were soft and silky, the wine already displaying Margaux's inimitable scent and elegance. Bottled velvet. Nine notes tracing its development through the 1990s, the most revealing at Manfred Wagner's two verticals, the first in 1997, an excellent 'flight' which enabled us to compare the virtues of the decade of the 1980s. For example, the Margaux '85 was less deep and softer looking than the '86, but much more evolved on the nose. In fact a glorious, fruity charmer, confirmed on the palate. One of my highest notes in this 48-vintage tasting. Identical marks at Wagner's next, in November 2000. If anything even more fabulously evolved: sweet, full,

rich, with perfect fruit and balance. Dipping back to Kaplan's '85s event in April 2000, it was almost beyond description. 'Soft, feminine yet determined'. *Last tasted Nov 2000* ★★★★★ *Lovely now, many beautiful years ahead.*

**Ch Mouton-Rothschild** I also had the pleasure, and always the privilege, of tasting this in cask in June 1986. At Mouton, one does not taste directly from the cask. In this instance from a cask sample in the small tasting room of the *maître de chai*. The wine was marvellously deep of course, but not opaque; glorious young fruit superstructure above a firm foundation. A touch of leanness but fleshy. Already by December 1990 it had started to mature, its nose inimitably Mouton, spicy Cabernet, glorious; showing some elegance, lovely texture and aftertaste. Eighteen subsequent notes, and even if space permitted, some would be repetitive if not tedious. I have therefore looked up notes made in 1995, when it was at an interim stage of maturity. Alas at the 15th Grand Awards banquet in New York I found it 'surprisingly chunky and uncharming. Expected better'. The *filet mignon* was excellent, so it must have been all the chatter and noise in the Marriott Marquis ballroom. Or it might just have been me, because at my Bordeaux Club dinner in January 1996 I described the bouquet as 'exotic, lovely Cabernet Sauvignon, and at 9.40pm very fragrant'. Note the time: I had drawn the cork at 4.30pm, decanted it at 5.40pm and served it at 8.50pm. I also served Pol Roger '34 and '88; Laville-Haut-Brion '89; Cheval Blanc, Lafite and Mouton – all '85s; Lafite '59 (the best of the lot) and Suau, an '85 Barsac. Oh, and Hine Grande Champagne '66, landed '67, bottled '82. Just odd bottles. I don't have a great cellar.

Back to Mouton, briefly. At exactly 15 years of age, two bottles both medium deep, one still a bit hard but fragrant, with a lovely texture, soft, fruity. The other, strangely, with a lovely sweet bouquet but a touch of woodiness and acidity. Both at a wine dinner at home, November 2000. Most recently, another Bordeaux Club dinner, this time hosted by Dr Louis Hughes, a new member. It had all the exotic Mouton fragrance; soft, flavoury, crisp but, I noted, with a touch of astringency. *Last noted at the Savile Club, London in Jan 2001* ★★★★★ *An exciting wine at the top but not yet over it. Will continue recklessly for another ten years or more.*

**Ch Haut-Brion** Not tasted in its youth, and not much liked in the autumn of 1992. When I first put my nose in it, it was rich but raw. Then subsequent notes to put it in perspective. First, at Edmund Penning-Rowsell's '10-year' first growth dinner in July 1995: fairly deep, still youthful; initially restrained but opened up. Lovely, spicy, gingery, well nigh perfect. And a high mark on the palate too, despite its initial austerity. Good earthy flavour and balance. A lot to it. Later in the year, noted at a tasting of first growth '85s at Gidleigh Park in Devon. Certainly distinctive – Haut-Brion is different; on the palate a 'minerally' hot pebbles taste – swingeingly dry, with bitter tannin. 'Needs time.' Showing its class however at a rather dreary boardroom lunch I hosted in December 1998. At 15 years of age a more interesting note at the MW Haut-Brion tasting at which Jean Delmas informed us that 1985 was 'a drought year, one of the hottest of the century. Some fog in September that helped the ripening at Haut-Brion', which seems strange. But the wine was showing well, still with youthful good looks; sweet, delicious, very good length. Most recently, at Kaplan's evening of '85s, I noted a rather vegetal nose which opened up fragrantly; wonderful elegance and texture, 'tobacco taste and finish'. *Last tasted April 2000* ★★★★★ *Lovely now but will continue.*

**Ch Ausone** As usual, a paucity of notes. Just four. First, an attractive two-year old at Lloyd Flatt's Ausone tasting in New Orleans; plausible, sweet. Next, at ten years of age, the second of the eight in Penning-Rowsell's first growths line-up: maturing well; good but curiously 'singed brown paper' nose and taste; yet soft and appealing. Most recently, at the opening dinner of Kaplan's 1985 vintage weekend: now looking fully mature; bouquet of caramel, then tea leaves and, after two hours, a distinctive ripe Cabernet Franc scent. On the palate less exciting. The usual 'autumn leaves'. *Last noted at the (excellent) restaurant Tru in Chicago, April 2000* ★★★ *Ready now.*

**Ch Cheval Blanc** One of my absolute favourite wines. For me, perfection. A plethora of notes – well, 20 to be precise, several from my own cellar. I have just two precious bottles left. Too expensive to replace. First tasted in cask in September 1986, probably in the second-year cellar. Deep purple; nose low-keyed, taut; good shape, good fruit, cinnamon/spicy new oak. To be truthful, though impressive it gave me no inkling of the beauty to come. However, by the time of my next taste in March 1991, the first bottle I opened after I had bought a couple of cases, had changed out of all recognition. I didn't decant it, just poured (a Sunday lunch in the country). Its initial whiff of iron, clover and mint, then, with air, rich, almost pungent. Distinctly sweet on the palate. Full of fruit, and delicious to drink by itself. With almost '82 richness and extract. At ten years of age, with the seven other first growths, not my top mark despite its lovely nose, flavour and texture. Several bottles, all drinking perfectly at subsequent luncheons and dinners at home and, of course, with Bordeaux Club members. Unsurprisingly, showing perfectly at Kaplan's 1985s event. Most recently, sandwiched between the excellent and rare '78 Barca Velha (Ferreira's 'Douro Lafite') and '62 La Tâche, at a wine dinner at home. Decanted at 7.45pm, served two hours later: now medium deep, rich, with mature rim; a lovely, fully evolved bouquet; perfect sweetness, body, flavour, tannin and acidity. *Last tasted June 2000* ★★★★★ *Perfect now but balanced sufficiently for, say, another ten years.*

**Ch Pétrus** First noted on its fifth birthday at Johann Björklund's Pétrus tasting. Still ruby, but seemed to be already fully evolved: ripe, rich, mulberry sort of fruit. At ten years of age, alongside the other first growths, positively opulent, fantastically full of fruit, concentrated, mouthfilling. Equal top with Mouton, which had a fractionally finer bouquet, and Pétrus, the slightly better palate. Most recently, at 15 years of age, now mature looking, rich, complete. *Last tasted at Stephen Kaplan's '85s event, April 2000* ★★★★★ *Perfect now. Another 20 years of life.*

**Ch Batailley** Archetypal Batailley, enjoyable fruit rather than finesse. Many notes. Probably at its best either side of ten years old. Certainly by 1994 it already looked pretty mature, its nose being its best feature. On the palate, despite a sweet entry, a touch of peppermint and, despite softness, an edgy acidity. (Noted at a Christie's Bordeaux wine course. It really needed food.) More recently, a perfectly pleasant fruitiness, perhaps slightly 'tarry', which I have noted in some Pauillacs. *Last tasted dining with the Conseil des Crus Classés du Médoc at Ch Haut-Brion, June 1997* ★★★

**Ch Beychevelle** A couple of not very impressive cask samples in May 1986, and again in August shortly after bottling (which had finished 11 July : 25-26% Merlot I was informed) when it seemed surprisingly soft and easy. In its fifth year I noted it as opaque with good depth of bramble-like fruit, agreeable sweetness and flesh. Beautifully evolved though more tannic than expected at a Beychevelle tasting in 1997. At 15 years of age now less deep, more open and relaxed; extraordinarily vivid fruit; sweeter and softer than expected and an unexpected touch of rusticity. Nice though. *Last noted at Kaplan's 1985 event, April 2000* ★★★★ *Drink soon.*

**Ch Branaire-Ducru** Aged two: pleasant enough but not very impressive. Aged five: fragrant, agreeable, but no more. Next, and most recently, in magnums exactly ten years after the harvest, a positive, still ruby colour; a light fruity bouquet which seemed to deteriorate in the glass. Crisp, touch of blackcurrant but mediocre finish. Probably never 'at best'. *Assez bien. Last noted at Christie's 'Dinner with Michael Broadbent' in Hong Kong, Oct 1995* ★★ *Drink up.*

**Ch Brane-Cantenac** In April 1987, very typical, very distinctive, sweet, rich, spicy. By 1990, fully evolved 'biscuity' bouquet; sweet, full, rounded, fleshy (sounds like the mistress of a wealthy Victorian gentleman, ensconced in a discreet villa in St John's Wood). More recently, an above-average mark at an extensive *Decanter* tasting of 1985 Médocs. Fully mature, touch of orange; open, warm, enveloping scent ('I'm only a bird in a gilded cage'). Rich. Good fruit, flavour and length. *Last tasted Sept 1994. A generous* ★★★★ *Enjoy while it lasts.*

**Ch Calon-Ségur** The trouble with a cask sample is that one rarely knows when it is drawn. A distinctly odd sample in May 1986. Much better, tasting from the cask, that September. Also the problem with Calon-Ségur is that it can be a bit of a stern St-Estèphe. However, in April 1987, its sweetness and extract masked the tannin, and a couple of years later it had all the component parts. Three subsequent notes, the most recent an odd bottle from my country cellar showing well at a small luncheon party. By now fully mature in appearance, nose and taste. Lovely, soft, ready, but showing its age. *Last tasted May 2000* ★★★★ *But drink soon.*

**Ch de Camensac** A little seen and sometimes under-performing classed growth, yet up to scratch in this vintage. For some reason I have roughly a dozen notes, mainly between 1988 and 1991, and all surprisingly good. A sweet, soft, easy wine. It was also showing quite well at the *Decanter* tasting in 1994: fully mature; harmonious; soft fruit, fairly mouthfilling. Alas, most recently, a corked bottle at a rather grand tasting in Bordeaux. *Last noted June 1997. At best* ★★★

**Ch Canon** Masses of notes because I bought a few cases and enjoyed drinking the wine over a number of years. In cask though (May 1986), it seemed to be quite a full, chunky, tannic wine. Yet after a matter of 11 months had speedily evolved, for despite a still rather hard, taut nose, it was fairly sweet, fleshy and nicely put together. It was its sweet, rich, singed fruit, soft entry, fleshiness and lightly refreshing acidity that I liked best, and its best was, I think, in the mid-1990s, for on the last few occasions I noted the acidity catching up. *Last noted in Aug 2001* ★★★ *Drink up.*

**Ch Canon-La-Gaffelière** Good wine, from April 1987 to date, drinking perfectly in its fifth year and, more recently, a magnum, now fairly mature. Sweet, with a surprisingly full, rich, chewy character. *Last noted lunching at Ch Beauregard, April 1994* ★★★ *Drink soon.*

**Ch Cantemerle** I was prepared to write 'how the mighty have fallen', for I have always had memories of its exquisite character in the 1950s, particularly the '55, one of the best wines of that vintage. However, looking at my notes, starting with a good, chewy, tannic cask sample in April 1987, the owners clearly rose to the occasion and made a decent '85, in fact, remarkably good in its fifth year. At the *Decanter* tasting of

'85s its nose was a bit bland, and though with good fruit, leaner than expected. A similar note in March 1997 and, though some bottle variations noted, a fully mature, soft, sweetish, very agreeable flavour. *Last tasted at a dinner at Wilton's in London on Daphne's birthday, July 1991. At best ★★★ Drink soon.*

**Ch Chasse-Spleen** Though rarely if ever underrated, it is definitely overdue for re-classification, the '85 being a prime example. Superb in cask and showing steady development. Most recently, still surprisingly deep in colour, with good nose, weight, flavour and balance. Went well with *Suprême de Faisan Bonne-Femme* in the Lord Mayor's apartment at Mansion House. Sir John Chalstrey, a surgeon, was Shrieval Sheriff when, as candidate for Lay Sheriff, I was defeated in the deciding ballot by just 16 votes. Perhaps as well. A whole year of lunching and dining in fancy dress would have been daunting – unless all the wine had been as good as the Chasse-Spleen. *Last noted Oct 1996 ★★★*

**Dom de Chevalier** For a domaine of such modest size (production then averaged only 4500 cases) it has a consistently good reputation, as demonstrated with their excellent '85. Deep and fragrant in cask. Evolving well. Most recently, now a medium-deep, warm, mature colour; harmonious, slightly spicy bouquet. A most agreeable mouthful. *Last noted lunching at a neighbouring Pessac-Léognan château, March 2001 ★★★★ Good now. Will keep.*

**Ch La Conseillante** This must be one of my favourite Pomerols, yet the '85 only tasted once. At seven years of age, impressively deep; rich, classic nose; sweet, crisp, marvellous fruit. *Last noted June 1992. Then ★★★(★) Should be perfect now.*

**Ch Cos d'Estournel** A lovely wine. For me a perfect Cos, even from the start: one could spot its elegance in cask, and fruit and, of course, youthful spiciness. At five years of age still a rich ruby; sweet, harmonious nose; perfect balance and harmony – with these qualities one can't go wrong. My eleventh note made at Kaplan's '85s dinner at the Four Seasons: still youthful looking; touch of iodine on nose but rich, ripe and lovely. Fleshy, complete, delicious. Most recently, hosting the annual wine dinner at the Knickerbocker Club, New York. In appearance confusingly similar to the '90 Cos served first; also a similar nose and character, but a fraction lighter (12.5% as opposed to 13% for the '90), softer yet still with tannic support. *Last tasted Oct 2000 ★★★★★ This is what claret is all about. Drink now or keep five–ten years.*

**Ch Ducru-Beaucaillou** Alas, I hate to say it, but not up to standard. Pedestrian, and some poor bottles. Dry, lacking length in cask, and a not dissimilar note at a tasting in 1989. At the second *Decanter* tasting of '85s, in 1994, one bottle poor, the other 'so-so'. A disastrously corked bottle at Kaplan's '85s event (April 2000) but showing quite well at Farr Vintners' recent tasting. *Last noted Oct 2001. At best ★★★ Drink soon.*

**Ch L'Église-Clinet** Deep for an '85. Velvety. A beautifully developed bouquet with some of the soft character of the '89; fairly sweet, lovely flavour, figgy fruit, some grip and a lot of charm. *At Rodenstock's L'Eglise-Clinet vertical, July 1998 ★★★★★ Lovely now. Long life.*

**Ch L'Évangile** A charmer. Just two notes: a glorious bottle in the elegant setting of Spencer House in London in May 1991. Recently: deep, velvety appearance; good fruit, expanding in the glass; sweet, rich, ripe, silky tannins. Complete. *Last noted at Kaplan's '85s dinner, April 2000 ★★★★★ Drink now or keep.*

**Ch Feytit-Clinet** '*Cuvée de la Comet*'. Old vines. Lunching with the proprietor who cooked for us at his extraordinary house near Poitiers. A seriously attractive wine, pleasant

flavour, drinking well. *A pleasant stop en route to Vinexpo in Bordeaux, June 1999 ★★★*

**Ch de Fieuzal** I am very fond of red Graves. They make easy and attractive drinking in a vintage like 1985. It was good from the start in May after the vintage, and the following April. Four notes since. A rather rustic, unusual flavour, sweet, rich and perfect lunchtime weight (only 12%), at Gidleigh Park in Devon in 1997. More recently: a bouquet and flavour with the sweet, warm, earthy glow of mature Graves. Crisp. Holding well. *Last noted lunching at the château, April 2000 ★★★★ Ready now.*

**Ch Figeac** A very good palate-tantalising Figeac. Enticing in cask: fragrant and full flavoured, combining fruit and oak in 1989. Next at a comparative tasting of '85 clarets at Gidleigh Park: now fully mature, the palest of the range, with a warm red-brown rim; bouquet fully developed, very distinctive, original, with a touch of caramel and 'singed brown paper', opening up fragrantly. A very idiosyncratic wine, but almost always attractive and charming. *Last noted Nov 1997 ★★★★*

**Ch La Fleur** Three recent notes. At Rodenstock's vertical (1998), tasted blind, I thought that because of its touch of rawness it was the '88. At an otherwise excellent wine dinner in Hamburg, the '85 did not have the same competition. It was lovely, harmonious, sweet, silky textured, yet with a dry, tannic finish. *Last noted March 2000 ★★★★★*

**Ch La Fleur-Pétrus** An *impériale*. Sweet – touch of caramel – good fruit and depth; excellent on palate, classic, touch of 'cream cheese', and slight astringency which, however, was sublimated by the food (some meat dish, in German, so I forget). *At Rodenstock's 15th 'Raritäten Weinprobe' at the Arlberg Hospiz in Austria, Sept 1994 ★★★★*

**Ch Gazin** Just one note: 'rich, impressive, fleshy, good tannin and acidity'. *June 1992 ★★★★ Drink soon.*

**Ch Giscours** Aged two, quite appealing, but in 1989, sweet fruit tempered by very slight maltiness on the nose, though good grip. This strange 'virol' nose noted again the following year when it seemed bland and chaptalised, the latter noted again more recently. By now fully mature; high toned, unknit. Frankly, a disappointing '85. *Last tasted April 1996 ★★*

**Ch Grand-Puy-Ducasse** A good Ducasse but a middling '85. A fragrant spicy cask sample (May 1986). Unknit, tannic (1989). 'Quite a good mouthful' the following year. Most recently at the *Decanter* tasting of '85 Médocs. Good colour, now mature; minty, unharmonious nose. Flavoury but with citrus-like acidity on the finish. *Last tasted Sept 1994 ★★*

**Ch Grand-Puy-Lacoste** Many notes because I bought some and still have a few bottles left. Tracing its evolution – Lacoste is always slow – from an excellent, firm, spicy cask sample. An 'opaque no tricks' bottle the following year. By 1989 impressive but holding back. At ten years of age noted at a 14-wine line up at the château. My third highest note (the '82 and '90 were each a point higher), but it was rich, complete, classic. Subsequent notes, save for one I put into a Christie's Grand-Puy-Lacoste vertical masterclass in March 2000, all at home. At 15 years of age it had mellowed yet was still intense with a fairly mature rim; a fragrant, cedary, refreshing nose that opened up beautifully in the glass; sweet entry, soft, rich, good fruit mid-palate. Delicious. A charmer. And a similar note at lunch the following month. *Last tasted Dec 2001 ★★★★★ Lovely now. Another 10–15 years.*

**Ch Gruaud-Larose** Strangely, no early notes. But by its fifth year Gruaud at its best: fragrant, good flesh and length. Aged nine, an interim note at the first *Decanter* tasting of '85s: sweet, rich, very pleasant. Wines of this style and quality do not 'come of age' at 21 but more like 15. Its appearance was no longer 'impressively deep' but a softer, luminous garnet; fully evolved bouquet and flavour, rich, good fruit, expansive, fleshy. *Last noted April 2000* ★★★★ *On the verge of 5-star. No signs of fading away.*

**Ch Haut-Bages-Libéral** Not a wine I normally go in for but, apart from a poor cask sample, seven notes, all good. In short, a lovely wine, perfectly balanced. *Last noted at a Distillers' Company lunch, June 1998* ★★★★ *Drink soon.*

**Ch Haut-Bailly** Another wine I bought and enjoyed. Most recently, medium deep, maturing rim; sweet tea-like fragrance; sweet, nice weight, lovely flavour, gentle, well-tempered tannin and acidity. *Last noted at a Christie's masterclass, April 2002* ★★★★★ *Perfect now.*

**Ch Haut-Batailley** So different from Haut-Bailly, each encapsulating the best of its class, Pauillac and Graves. Usually lean, crisp and elegant, the '85 is incredibly sweet and fleshy. Good, ripe fruit. Very attractive. One of my highest marks at the *Decanter* blind tasting of '85 Médocs. *Sept 1994* ★★★★★

**Ch d'Issan** This could not be mistaken for either Graves or Pauillac. A somewhat hidden-away Margaux, literally and metaphorically. Fragrant, as Margaux should be, in cask. Somewhat slow to get off the ground but, by its fifth year, harmonious, lovely. Tasted blind in 1994 it showed considerable maturity; its bouquet and flavour soft and 'warm', with ripe fruit. More recently, its bouquet surging out of the glass, somewhat loose knit, and upstaged by the altogether more powerful Gruaud. *Last noted dining at Ch Haut-Brion, June 1997* ★★★★ *just. Drink soon.*

**Ch Lafon-Rochet** Not my favourite St-Estèphe but this was well put together and much less austere than usual. Several notes, but none since the blind tasting of '85s in 1994. Showing maturity in appearance and on nose. Rich, cedary; nice weight and style. Unusually elegant. *Last tasted Sept 1994* ★★★ *Drink soon.*

**Ch La Lagune** Rich, very spicy the spring after the vintage. Developed richly, nose and flavour. One 'slightly disappointing', lacking Lagune's 'burgundy' appeal' – but it was wedged between Ch Gruaud and Cheval Blanc ('85s at Gidleigh Park in Devon in 1997). Most recently, 'distinctive, attractive'. *Last noted at the Christie's wine department's Christmas lunch at restaurant Che, Dec 2000* ★★★ *Ready.*

**Ch Langoa-Barton** Tends to be a touch raw when young, but at its best in a vintage like 1985. Several recent notes. Showing well, blind, in 1994, rich fruit, good balance. Most recently: delicious, perfect weight, good flavour. Ready. Perhaps as well, as I was at the same table as Liliane and Anthony Barton at the opening dinner of a week of tastings. *At Ch Gazin, March 1999* ★★★★ *Will keep.*

**Ch Lascombes** Several well spread notes. Sweet, agreeable weight, flavour and balance. *Last noted at a pre-sale tasting, Sept 2001* ★★★

**Ch Léoville-Barton** Despite a couple of less than admiring notes, a classic. Deep, rich, sweet and easy, its nose particularly good at the *Decanter* tasting in 1994. More recently (March 2001): good depth of colour still, yet with a mature tawny rim; beautiful bouquet, fragrant, well knit. Lovely on palate, lightish style, refreshingly dry finish. Most recently: still deep, its lovely texture, wonderful flesh. *Last noted lunching at Langoa, Oct 2001* ★★★★★ *For me the perfect claret. Drink now–2015.*

**Ch Léoville-Las-Cases** I was privileged to taste this wine in cask with the courteous but reticent Monsieur Delon in May

1986. It has all the component parts in place poised to embark on its inexorable journey towards maturity. Deep, rich, intense. But even aged ten, still not ready. Aged 15, showing well, complete, beautifully balanced (Kaplan, April 2000). Very recently: appearance still impressively deep and rich; a many-layered bouquet – there seemed to be so many things going on – tea, autumnal leaves, black treacle – and still evolving; sweet, with substantial Latour-like character and weight (their vineyards are next to each other, separated only by a small *jalle*, more of a ditch than a water course). High in alcohol, almost chewable. Still unready. *Last noted at Christie's masterclass, March 2001* ★★★★(★) *Say 2010–2020.*

**Ch Léoville-Poyferré** Somewhat more easy going and amenable than the two other Léovilles, though in 1996, at a pre-sale tasting in Amsterdam I noted 'surprisingly dry, a bit austere'. The trouble with these pre-sale tastings is that there are too many wines and too many eager tasters. No chance for an in-depth tasting let alone the time to allow a wine to open up. Most recently, with two hours to enjoy the company of the three Léovilles (like 'the three tenors') of four vintages, no excuse. Deeper and richer colour than the Barton; a 'cedar pencil', singed, earthy nose which opened up after only 20 minutes: lovely, harmonious. A wonderfully sweet approach, good mid-palate and mouth-drying astringency. *Last tasted March 2001* ★★★★(★) *Perhaps best between 2005 and 2015.*

**Ch Lynch-Bages** Nearly 20 notes from an opaque, fleshy, spicy pipette-full followed by a cask sample in May 1986. Fragrant and well clad the following April and an early almost startlingly virile development. At five years of age: deep, black cherry intensity; crisp, minty, pure blackcurrant aroma; overall dry, fairly concentrated. 'A masculine '85. Needs time and food'. This was at a tasting I conducted for Cathay Pacific in Hong Kong. The managing director, also at the tasting, being Rod Eddington, now the boss of British Airways! Then, by the age of 15, the wine was fully evolved, fragrant, sweeter, very positive. Most recently: still pretty deep, its bouquet almost too extravert and trying too hard to live up to expectation (and price). But good. *Last noted at dinner with a Japanese wine expert Rie Yoshitaki and three Chinese wine enthusiasts in the Cassia restaurant, Berkeley Square in London in Dec 2000* ★★★★★ *Now–2020.*

**Ch La Mission Haut-Brion** Just four notes over a 10-year period. Gloriously ripe fruit. Bouquet variously described as mulberry, brick dust, iron, iodine and tobacco. Full-bodied. Masculine. *Last tasted April 2000* ★★★(★★) *2010–2020 to beyond my lifespan!*

---

## Vinexpo

*An enormous, biennial wine fair held on the outskirts of the city of Bordeaux and first held in 1985. It is the only event to successfully gather together the world's wine trade under one, kilometre-long roof. Each fair exceeds the previous one in size, and provides an impeccable excuse for meeting old friends and tasting alongside a gamut of different wine palates. The most fun of all is to be had at the numerous parties held at the surrounding châteaux during the evenings. Each château takes it in turn to host the Fête de la Fleur, a sumptuous dinner for visiting wine friends – and, needless to say, each one attempts to outdo its predecessor in largesse. I was approached before the first Vinexpo took place to see if Christie's would hold a fine wine auction there in return for a free stand. Of course I said yes.*

**Ch Montrose** Seven notes. Hardly surprising: impressive in cask. My top mark (19/20) at the *Decanter* blind tasting of '85 Médocs in 1994. No longer opaque, medium deep, mature; classic fragrance in 2000. Most recently: now medium deep though richly coloured with an open, mature rim; nose redolent of old oak (tree not cask), sweet, great depth opening up, floral, complex; good wine though still stern, austere and tannic. *Last tasted at home, Jan 2002* ★★★(★) *Perhaps 5 stars in time.*

**Ch Mouton-Baronne-Philippe** Several notes. Chunkier than expected. Seemed at its best at ten years of age with a particularly good note at Christie's Bordeaux wine course: a soft red, rich, maturing; very agreeable harmonious black fruit aroma – touches of raspberry and strawberry; stylish, perfect weight, quite good length. Delicious (Jan 1995). Most recently: good, but upstaged by the *grand vin*. *Last noted at a Hollywood Wine Society Mouton seminar, March 1998* ★★★★ *Now–2010.*

**Ch Palmer** A dozen consistently good notes, from 'fragrant yet tannic' (1989); 'high-toned fruit, still tannic' (1994); 'still a hint of ruby, fragrant, perfect weight, more astringency than expected' (1997), and variations on the same theme in between. Most recently: soft, ripe, open, vanillin bouquet which held well. Richly flavoured. A good but not great Palmer. *Last tasted April 2000* ★★★★ *Now–2015.*

**Ch Pichon-Longueville, Baron** A dozen notes. Two recent, each within a month of each other at my so-called masterclasses. The first at Cordeillon-Bages, Pauillac, the second at the luxurious medieval Ch de Bagnols in Beaujolais. Both bottles from the château, one disastrously corked, the other sweet with rich fruit; soft, a rather hefty '85, though well balanced. Delicious. *Last tasted Sept 1998. At best* ★★★★ *Now–2010.*

**Ch Pichon-Longueville-Lalande** A mass of notes from 'fruit-packed' in cask, rich and fleshy at five years of age, and almost identical notes around its – her (La Comtesse) – tenth birthday. Really in its element at a tasting in 1999: it even *looked* fleshy; a distinctive, scented, elegant, soft, ripe, earthy nose, explosively lovely after 30 minutes in the glass. The same later in the month. 'Ready'. Most recently, lunching with May de Lenquesaing and her nephew Gildas d'Ollone 'drinking perfectly'. *Last noted at the château, Oct 2000* ★★★★★ *Now–2020.*

**Ch Le Pin** My oriental friends must be a bit tired of this by now. I have only tasted it once. Not very deep, mature, relaxed; a very strange, high-toned scent of crystallised violets. Equally strange flavour. Ripe Cabernet Franc? Finishes a bit raw. *Last noted at Kaplan's '85s event, April 2000 rating?*

**Ch Pontet-Canet** Variable notes, from a fruity, tannic, cask sample to most recently, sweaty nose; very odd, gravelly, earthy flavour and a tart, astringent finish. *Last tasted, blind, at the Decanter tasting of '85s, Sept 1994* ★★?

**Ch Prieuré-Lichine** 'Zestful' is the word. Fragrant, piquant, lean but fruity. My most recent two notes within two months of each other. Rich, red, maturing; most appealing soft fruit – Merlot, mulberry, nose and taste. Good length. Dry finish. *Last tasted Nov 1994* ★★★★ *Should be delicious now.*

**Ch Rausan-Ségla** Ten notes from a typically tight-knit cask sample. Not a 'speedy Gonzalez' but lots of scent and flavour. A high mark at the *Decanter* blind tasting in 1994. More recently, glorious fragrance, crisp, but a touch of rawness. Needs air, and time. *Last tasted April 2000* ★★(★★). *Say 2010–2015.*

**Ch Rauzan-Gassies** Half as many notes as its superior neighbour. A good Gassies as Gassies goes. But why it was chosen by the Conseil des Crus Classés du Médoc to march alongside the other seven very good clarets I do not know.

Not bad, a touch of austerity. Little else. *Last noted dining at Ch Haut-Brion, June 1997* ★

**Clos René** One of the '85s I bought for drinking at home. A velvety, very rich, harmonious Pomerol. Full, fruity, dry finish. *Last noted Jan 1996* ★★★★ *Drink up (I have).*

**Ch Talbot** I have a love-hate relationship with Talbot. It has such a rustic farmyard character, mainly on the nose. But I can't help liking the '85. I thought it had reached its plateau of – if not perfection – easy, charming drinkability on its tenth birthday (at a Christie's wine dinner in Hong Kong): deliciously deep, velvety looking; soft, sweet, ripe. *Showing well at a pre-sale tasting in Geneva, May 1999* ★★★★ *Drink now–2010.*

**Ch du Tertre-Roteboeuf** A relatively new 'cult' wine. Impressive but not my type. On both occasions 'unknit' noted, one in relation to its nose, the other to its palate. Rich. Alcoholic; too spicy; thick, coarse tannic finish. *Last tasted 2000* ★(★★★)? *Needs time though I am not prepared to wait.*

**Ch La Tour-de-By** It was about this time (vintage) that I began to notice this consistently well made, relatively inexpensive *cru bourgeois*. The '85 perfect at 10 years of age. Ripe. Flavoury. *Last noted lunching at Chippenham Lodge, Dec 1995* ★★★ *Why keep it longer?*

**Ch Trotanoy** A predictably impressive, silky textured *impériale* in 1994. Next, a rich ruby, sweet, chewy bottle at a Christie's Park Avenue boardroom lunch (I didn't know that they treated their guests so well in New York. We also had the '89). Once again, *grace à* Stephen Kaplan, a very interesting bottle with a soft, milky sort of bouquet and gentle fruit which, after 20 minutes, exploded with an extraordinary Cabernet Franc fragrance. Powerful. A bit inky. *Last noted April 2000* ★★★(★) *2010–2020.*

**Vieux Ch Certan** Soft gentle and rich to look at, smell and taste. Fragrant. A lovely wine. *April 2000* ★★★★★ *Now–2015.*

FAR TOO MANY '85S TO NOTE IN DETAIL – the following have all been tasted since 1995: **Ch d'Angludet** ripe, mature ★★★; **Ch L'Arrosée** fragrant, lean ★★★★; **Ch Beauséjour-Duffau-Lagarosse** ★★★; **Ch La Cabanne** at school there was a poem in French. It began *'ma Cabanne est pauvre'* (I could never remember more than the first line, and understood even less). Soft. Fully mature ★★★; **Ch La Cardonne** delicious. I cannot think why the Domaines Rothschild sold the châteaux ★★★; **Ch Certan-de-May** ★★★; **Ch Clerc-Milon-Mondon** beguiling but acidic ★★★; **Clos du Clocher** ★★; **Ch Fourcas-Dupré** ★★★; **Ch Larmande** ★★★; **Ch Larcis-Ducasse** ★★★★; **Ch Marquis de Terme** ★★; **Ch du Tertre** ★★★; **Ch La Tour-Carnet** for a change: ★★★; and **Ch La Tour-Figeac** ★★★

SOME OTHER '85S SHOWING PROMISE IN THE EARLY 1990S (as usual, my rating at the time) **Ch Beauregard** ★★★; **Ch Bon Pasteur** ★★★; **Ch La Croix-de-Gay** ★★★(★); **Ch La Croix-Toulifaut** ★★★; **Ch L'Enclos** ★★★; **Ch Fourcas-Hosten** ★★; **Clos Fourtet** ★★(★); **Ch Gloria** ★★★; **Ch Moulinet** ★★★; and **Ch Plince** ★★★

# 1986 ★★★★

I must confess, my first, second and most recent impressions of this vintage have varied. At first I didn't know quite what to make of it. Then, after the 1988s came along I saw a certain similarity, linking the '86s and '88s as firm, relatively slow off the mark. But can the most prolific crop since World War Two,

15% bigger than 1985, produce wines of real quality? The '85s managed it, but the weather conditions were slightly different. In 1986 bud break was delayed, though the weather improved and the flowering was successful. The summer was hot and dry until the latter part of September when, after a useful sprinkling of rain, there was a violent storm which dumped 10cm of rain on the city of Bordeaux and its immediate surroundings. The harvest began at the very end of September and continued into October in glorious weather.

Having read through a large number of notes, my impression of the vintage has become more clarified, and I think I can answer the question posed above.

On the whole, 1986 produced hard, tannic wines which at best, given time, might – just might – turn out well. But I would not bank on it, except for Mouton and just one or two others. They are of course good 'food wines' and are unlikely to go 'over the hill' without plenty of notice.

**Ch Lafite** First noted at the Union des Grands Crus tasting at Christie's in 1988. It showed well. Good depth of fruit, long but lean and taut. Four recent notes: trying to mature; fragrant but hard; crisp, citrus-like fruit, and tannic. Refreshing. Unready (1996). Still fairly intense; low-keyed, slightly peppery, just waking up; some sweetness, but with teeth-gripping tannins (tasted blind 1998). Most recently, a magnum, still very deep, thick (extract) but with a surprisingly mature orange rim that I associate with tannins dominating the fruit (like some '75s). Very 'medicinal', iron, typically Lafite nose; more amenable than I expected, good mid-palate fruit but hard edged. Something like a '62 or '66. *Last noted at a combined children's birthday lunch party at home, Jan 1999 (★★★★) I propose to leave my children Emma and Bartholomew two magnums each in my will – if Daphne hasn't drunk them!*

**Ch Latour** I expected this to be mammoth and undrinkable, but from the start (a cask sample in September 1987), though clearly a long haul wine, it had lovely fruit and flesh. Yet, very tannic in its formative years, it was always a fascinating mouthful. Only one recent note, tasted blind, level pegging with Mouton but, surprisingly, less deep, more amenable and attractive than the Lafite. Well balanced. Crisp fruit. *Last tasted, just for a change, on the fifth day of Rodenstock's week-long Yquem marathon in Munich, Sept 1998 (★★★★) 2015–2025.*

**Ch Margaux** Always such a joy to taste in cask. I was fortunate enough to have three dips, first in the June after the vintage, bowled over by the fruit, flesh and spice which tended to make one overlook a certain austerity and tannic content. A masculine Margaux. Half a dozen recent notes, two at the Wagner Margaux vertical. At the first (1997) raw, hard, spicy; assertive, concentrated. In 1998, blind, nose like wet cobnuts; distinctly raw again. In March 2000 at a Margaux dinner at Brooks's: though very fragrant, severe on the palate and hard-edged, lean and pinched. The roast beef did not do much for it. Eight months later at Wagner's second tasting, a distinctly better note. Still opaque and youthful looking: crisp fruit, opening up beautifully; sweet, lovely fruit, attractive but very tannic. *Last tasted Nov 2000 ★(★★★)? Give it lots of time.*

**Ch Mouton-Rothschild** Deserving its reputation as outstandingly the best '86. Certainly a spectacular wine from my first encounter in 1989: vivid purple; intense varietal fragrance; packed tight with fruit. Of my most recent notes: impressive bottles at the Mouton dinner at Brooks's in 1994. Nose peppery at first, then it sprang to life; on the palate the sweetness of ripe grapes and alcohol. Full-bodied, full flavoured, fabulous fruit, very dry finish. Deep but no longer

opaque; ripe Cabernet scents; 'deep, rich, tannic, long life' (Mouton event in 1998). Most recently, tasted blind: intense, still youthful; high toned, fragrant; earthy, fleshy, good flavour and length. Very tannic (I preferred the '82). *At Rodenstock's, Sept 1998 ★★(★★★) 2012–2030.*

**Ch Haut-Brion** Just three notes. First tasted with Jean Delmas at La Mission in 1990. Impressive, chewy, tannic and at that stage, astringent. Next, rich, soft-centred, developing a mahogany rim; vanilla, earthy, spicy; sweet, fleshy, yet lean and very tannic (at a first growths tasting for Citibank in 1995). Most recently, once again in a blind line-up of '82s and '86s: opening up; but a smelly, iodine nose. I thought it was cracking up. On the palate, earthy, thick-textured and a bit raw. In limbo. *Last tasted Sept 1998 ★★? I am sure it will pull round but your guess as to when is as good as mine.*

**Ch Ausone** Not tasted.

**Ch Cheval Blanc** Two notes: lean and rather raw in 1990. Next, a magnum at the Wolf/Weinart vertical: very deep, fairly intense but 'only thinking about' maturing; fragrant but more peppery than the '85 on nose and palate (more Cabernet Franc). Good firm fruit though, and went well with the beef. *Last noted, March 1997 ★★(★★) Should turn out well – 2010–2020.*

**Ch Pétrus** Only tasted once. Very impressive: crisp ruby; sweet nose, opening up beautifully; very sweet, rich, full-bodied, caramel flavour and aftertaste. *April 1990. Then (★★★★★), now ★★★★(★) but should be very drinkable now. Long life.*

**Ch L'Angélus** The first four notes date from 1988 to 1990. In essence the wine was sweet, fleshy, astringent. Recently: fairly impressive, a touch of '86 leanness, but substantial. Tannic. *At a reception for a German delegation at Christie's, May 1999 ★★(★) A mid-term wine.*

**Ch Batailley** This château has a better chance than many Médocs of producing a fruity, amenable '86. Recent notes, one demonstrating this (dining at the château, 1997), the other noticing some coarseness and very tannic. *Last tasted Dec 2000 ★★★? Clearly context comes into this. Nevertheless, it has a future.*

**Ch Beychevelle** Ten notes, from cask onwards. Nine not too complimentary, 'lean', 'sinewy', 'astringent' cropping up. Alas, my two most recent notes somewhat contradictory. At a tasting of nine vintages in 1997 I noted 'surprisingly sweet, good fruit, yet astringent and teeth-gripping'. Then, on Concorde en route to New York, though deep and still youthful-looking, softer than expected. Must have been the height, speed and dizzy expectations. *Last tasted Oct 1999 ★★(★) Not bad but I wouldn't put my money on it.*

**Ch Branaire-Ducru** Two brief notes, both recent. Plummy; low-keyed; unexciting, tannic. *Last tasted Oct 1999 ★★*

**Ch Canon** Several notes. Most recently, looking fairly mature; caramelly-chocolatey nose; spicy, lean and quite a bite for Canon. *Last tasted March 1996 ★★(★)?*

**Ch Chasse-Spleen** Yet again top of its class. Well made. Rich, chewy 'chocolate with a tannic coat'. *Last tasted April 1998 ★★★*

**Ch Cos d'Estournel** First noted at Michèle Prats' presentation in 1990. The first vintage in which Cabernet Franc grapes used – but only 2% (Cabernet Sauvignon 67%, Merlot 33%). Nine notes. A good deal of fruit, fragrance and astringency. However, a surprisingly attractive double magnum recently served at Cos: still deep, lively but maturing; very sweet, 'chewable'. Very 'un-St-Estèphe', rich, with silky tannins. *Last noted at the closing lunch of the week of press tastings in Bordeaux, March 2001 ★★★(★)*

**Ch Desmirail** Five notes. Surprisingly attractive at tastings (*Decanter* 1996) and dinners. Most recently: quite good fruit, sweet on nose and palate though leading to a tannic finish. *Last noted April 1997* ★★★ *Drink while the going is good.*

**Ch L'Église-Clinet** Four notes. Opaque, intense. Low keyed, a touch of greenness. Drier than expected, spicy but raw and tannic. Most recently, a bottle and a double magnum, one of the least appealing of the 'flight', 1982–1994. *Last tasted Sept 1996* (★★)? *Time will tell.*

**Ch L'Évangile** Deep, fairly intense; good rich fruit and flesh. More advanced than the '86 Médocs. *Last noted dining at Ch Lafite, where the already distinguished party had been joined by the Bartons and Nicholas Soames who managed to cope effortlessly with a second pheasant. Sept 1998* ★★★★

**Ch de Fieuzal** I cannot think why I have so many notes but they are all pretty favourable. Nice fruit, lightish style, crisp, a fair amount of tannin. Most recently, now medium deep, maturing, a sweet, earthy Graves nose; good flavour, but with gripping, leathery, tannins. 'Still some way to go.' *Last noted dining with the Union des Grands Crus at Ch Lagrange, March 1998* ★★★

**Ch La Fleur** Deep; sweet fruit; fairly full-bodied, rich, fleshy. Very satisfactory. (Tasted blind I thought it must be the '85.) *One of the 32 vintages presented by Hardy Rodenstock (in 'flights' alternating with 15 vintages of Ch L'Église-Clinet, and 125 vintages of Yquem), Munich, Aug–Sept 1998* ★★★(★)

**Ch Giscours** Initially 'port and prunes'. Strangely rich fruit. More recent notes, include 'unknit' (nose), 'light style', which I now find hard to believe, and 'unconvincing' (*Decanter* 1996). Yet an odd half bottle with quite pleasant flavour and crisp fruit. *Last tasted at home, April 1996* ★★

**Ch Grand-Puy-Lacoste** An impressive '86, in fact one of the best if you are prepared to wait for this sinewy wine to mature. Several notes in its early days. Only one recently: a convincing spread of colour, starting to mature; fresh, interesting nose with a column of fruit round a hard core. An exciting wine, crisp, fruity with good, drying tannins. *Last noted at a Grand-Puy-Lacoste masterclass, March 2000* ★★(★) *2010–2020.*

**Ch Haut-Bailly** Unusually, 100% Cabernet Sauvignon as the Merlot completely failed in 1986. In 2001 a fairly deep though mature-looking double magnum at the château which opened up well. Most recently: very fragrant bouquet; earthy, minerally, 'hot tiles'. Needs time. *Last noted at a Christie's masterclasss, April 2002* ★★★

**Ch d'Issan** Showing well at *The Worshipful Company of Distillers' Millennium Dinner in the Painted Hall, Greenwich, May 2000* ★★★

**Ch Kirwan** A somewhat specious new style. Still very deep and youthful; certainly fragrant; sweet and very 'new-oaky'. *Last tasted lunching at Ch Chasse-Spleen, March 2001* ★★(★)

**Ch Langoa-Barton** First tasted in 1988 – very spicy. And described in 1990 as 'a lanky, somewhat raw-boned youth'. After a further seven years the youth was maturing quite well. Fragrant, fine with lamb. *Last noted at a Christie's boardroom lunch, Nov 1997* ★★★

**Ch Lascombes** Fairly mature; fragrant nose; good fruit and spicy aftertaste. Masked tannin. *Last tasted, blind, Jan 1996* ★★★

**Ch Léoville-Barton** Initially deep, spicy with 'well-clad tannins'. Certainly so at the tenth anniversary *Decanter* tasting; I preferred the Langoa at that stage. Most recently, still virtually opaque; a nose of 'iron'; good fruit, but tight-lipped, lean and tannic. *Last noted lunching at Ch Yquem with the Palumbos, Lloyd-Webbers, Mark Birley and ladies, Sept 1998* ★★(★★) *Followed by the '86 Yquem, which, somewhat sweeter, also needed 10–20 years to mature fully!)*

**Ch Lynch-Bages** A wine that positively swooshed out of the cask to meet you. Packed with flavour, its vigour and fruit taking one's mind off the tannins. Several recent notes, three made within as many weeks. First: rich but swingeingly tannic dining at the excellent restaurant Jean Ramet; the next two at masterclasses conducted at Ch Cordeillan-Bages and at Ch de Bagnols (in southern Beaujolais): impressively deep though a misleadingly mature rim; fleshy, ripe, leathery, cedar and 'cheese rind' bouquet – quite exciting; nice fruit but a lean touch. An agreeable drink despite its teeth-gripping finish. *Last tasted Oct 1998* ★★(★★) *2008–2018*

**Ch Palmer** Early notes: muffled mulberry, fragrant, tannic. In 1995, at a tasting conducted for Wein & Co, Vienna, the nose was very sweet and seemed fully developed; soft, ready (only 12 per cent alcohol), with bitter-sweet finish. 'An untypical '86.' Most recently, lunching with Julia and Guy Hands (the wizard of Nomura) and two Christie's colleagues at Che. I had double decanted the bottle at 11.45am. Nose a bit hard but quite nice fruit, refreshing, not over-tannic. *Last tasted Sept 1999* ★★★ *Now–2015.*

**Ch Paveil de Luze** A very handsome family-owned château making dependable wine but rarely a long-keeper. So I was interested to see how a 13-year-old Paveil had survived. Well: now mature, indeed probably at its optimum; good, firm, not too tannic. *Lunching with Patricia and (Baron) Geoffroy de Luze, June 1999* ★★★ *(just). (Geoffroy was doing a stage when I was a junior at Saccone & Speed in the mid-1950s.)*

**Ch Petit-Village** The opening wine of The Tasting Club: a lightish, mature-looking ruby; almost Graves-like earthy character with a touch of tar on the nose. Sweetish, soft, ready. *At Berry Bros, April 2000* ★★★ *Drink soon.*

**Ch Pichon-Lalande** A dozen notes. Good, rather high toned fruit. Then, on its tenth anniversary, plummy coloured, taut brambly fruit on nose and palate. Relatively forthcoming, though tannic. More recently, dining at the château (June 2000): sweet, rich, mouthfilling, its extract masking tannic finish. Four months later, the oldest of six vintages of Lalande: sweet, rich, 'touch of molasses' nose; crisp, lean, dry, drinking well. *Last noted at a masterclass at Les Prés d'Eugénie, Christine and Michel Guérard's exquisite spa-hotel-restaurant, Oct 2000* ★★★ *(almost 4-star). Could possibly attain that level.*

**Ch Talbot** A slow starter though in its tenth year very amenable: deep, velvety; good rich fruit, sweet and not blatantly tannic. Most recently, at the closing lunch for wine journalists: fairly mature appearance; rich, a touch of Talbot 'iron', sweet, attractive, with a touch of bitterness on the finish. *Last noted at Ch Cos d'Estournel, March 2001* ★★★ *Now–2015.*

**Ch du Tertre** Not a Margaux I come across often. Now mature with a shade of orange; attractive fruit, 'sweaty' tannin; fairly sweet, crisp, good flavour and grip. *Pre-sale, Jan 1999* ★★★ *(just). Drink soon.*

---

### Anthony Barton

*The Barton family, of Anglo-Irish descent, has been present in the region since the early 18th century. Anthony has brilliantly managed châteaux Langoa and Léoville-Barton since his uncle died in 1986. What I like about his approach is its consistency: the wines are excellent yet never overpriced. Anthony is a no nonsense chap; he doesn't like pomposity and hates waffle and humbug. Ch Langoa, where he and Eva live, combines the very best of French and English taste, both in the gardens, and its beautiful interior.*

THE FOLLOWING WERE TASTED, OR LAST TASTED, AT *DECANTER*'S TENTH ANNIVERSARY BLIND TASTING OF '86 MÉDOCS, JANUARY 1996

**Ch Brane-Cantenac** Rich, cedary bouquet; surprisingly sweet, good extract, tannic (1992). At the *Decanter* tasting, very attractive fruit and flavour. One of my highest marks ★★★

**Ch de Camensac** Fully mature, open knit. Early drinking ★★

**Ch Cantemerle** Surprisingly sweet and forthcoming in its second year. Quite attractive ★★★ *Drink soon.*

**Ch Clerc-Milon** Two notes. 'Syrup of figs' nose. Good fruit but austere, tannic. *Last tasted Jan 1996* ★★(★)

**Ch Cos Labory** Rich, mature; fruit and oak; fairly sweet, full-flavoured ★★★

**Ch Croizet-Bages** Singed, caramel, chaptalised sort of smell and taste. Untypical of the vintage ★★

**Ch Durfort-Vivens** Impressively deep yet fairly mature; sweet, spicy, attractive bouquet; dry, lean, quite good fruit. Tannic ★★(★)

**Ch Gruaud-Larose** Several very good notes particularly in its earlier stages, full of colour, ripe fruit, sweetness. In its tenth year I thought the nose was holding back a bit, but on the palate, sweet, pleasing, amenable, not over-tannic, refreshing acidity. Nice wine ★★★(★) *Now–2015.*

**Ch Lagrange** (St-Julien) Four notes. On its tenth anniversary a lovely, rich, velvety colour; harmonious bouquet though tannin detectable; surprisingly sweet, good fruit, lovely texture and flavour. Complete. Without wishing to be condescending, an unpredicted high mark ★★★★ *Now–2012.*

**Ch Léoville-Poyferré** Several earlier notes. By 1996 the 'sweaty feet' tannic smell had become merely sweaty, to which I added 'a touch of vanilla'. Some sweetness, taut, lean but attractive and quite a lot to it ★★★

**Ch Lafon-Rochet** Indeterminate nose which after over two hours in the glass opened up deliciously; for Lafon, in a vintage like this, more fruit and more interesting than expected ★★★

**Ch Lynch-Moussas** I was also surprised when this was revealed (a reminder that all these 10-year old Médocs were tasted blind). Quite a well developed nose; straightforward, fullish body, good-enough fruit, lean, tannic. *Better than* ★★, *not good enough for* ★★★. *Should soon be as good as it will ever get.*

**Ch Malescot-St-Exupéry** Four notes including an undrinkably austere *impériale* in 1990. By its tenth year, maturity; chunky fruit; agreeable enough, reasonable balance. Not as exotically flavoured as usual ★★★ *Say 2005–2015.*

**Ch Montrose** As always, a serious wine, slow to mature. At ten years of age still very deep and youthful-looking; a nose that hinted at great depth, things to come; fairly sweet on entry, very good fruit though straight-laced. Pretty dependable, long term ★★(★★) 2015.

**Ch Mouton-Baronne-Philippe** Not the usual feckless charmer. Good firm fruit, but very tannic ★(★★) *2005–2015.*

**Ch Marquis de Terme** Better flavour than nose, which is not saying much ★★

**Ch Marquis d'Alesme-Becker** Another 'aristocrat' from Margaux. Better than its 'cousin', the Marquis de Terme, but not altogether convincing ★★

**Ch Pontet-Canet** Unknit, but interesting bouquet; surprisingly sweet, full and fruity. Very tannic ★★(★)

**Ch Rausan-Ségla** Opaque, plummy fruit; sweet, fullish, lots of oak, stylish. Very appealing ★★★(★)

**Ch St-Pierre** (Bontemps et Sevaistre to give it its former title.) Old oak; distinctly *un*appealing.

OTHER '86s TASTED ON DIFFERENT OCCASIONS

**Ch Léoville-Las-Cases** Just two notes. Immensely impressive at the MW tasting in 1990. Equally so, but more developed, at the Wein & Co tasting in Vienna: most attractive, fragrant though still peppery, with cedary nose; a fine, firm, dry wine. *Last noted Nov 1995 then* ★★(★★) *Now doubtless further evolved. Say 2010–2020.*

**Ch La Mission Haut-Brion** Several notes but none recent. Undoubtedly a good '86, its glorious fruit suppressed by its tannins. All, I hope, will be revealed. *Last tasted Nov 1990. Then* (★★★★) *Say 2010–2020.*

**Ch Pichon-Baron** A very good '86. Eight pretty good notes, the last two within three months of each other. Plummy coloured, full of fruit, some austerity but with attractive aftertaste. A mouthwatering nose, its 80% Cabernet Sauvignon very noticeable. Impressive on the palate, fairly full-bodied, soft fruit but crisp. Delicious but not ready. *Last noted at a Commanderie de Bordeaux tasting in Oslo, April 1996* ★★★(★) *2005–2015.*

**Ch Le Pin** After an afternoon tasting his Nahe wines, at dinner Armin Diel served us with a very good Meursault and two half bottles of Le Pin, of which the '86 came first. An extraordinary, sweet, velvety, mulberry-rich character; fullish and fleshy. *At Schlossgut Diel, Nov 1995* ★★★★

**Ch de Sales** Good fruit; chunky, maturing pleasantly. *With the Hospitaliers de Pomerol in Bristol, May 1995* ★★★ *Drink soon.*

**Ch Smith-Haut-Lafitte** Sweet, easy, refreshing. *Last tasted Nov 1990. Then* ★★(★) *I suggest early drinking.*

**Ch Sociando-Mallet** Craftily inserted into a blind tasting of first growths in the hope of both fooling us and to demonstrate the quality and style of this Médoc *cru exceptionnel.* It was deeply coloured and still immature; a 'classic nose', Cabernet, slightly peppery, good but no development in the glass; dry, crisp fruit, good length, complete but *very* tannic – but so was the '86 Margaux. On the palate I gave it identical marks to the Margaux and the Haut-Brion ('86). Being wise after the event, the clue to its class was its inability to develop extra nuances. *One of the 'flights' at Rodenstock's wine week, Sept 1998* ★★★ *But no point in keeping it longer.*

OTHER '86s WORTH LOOKING OUT FOR **Ch Canon-La-Gaffelière**; **Ch Coufran**; **Ch Haut-Bages-Monpelou**; **Ch La Louvière**; **Ch Les Ormes-de-Pez**; and **Ch Prieuré-Lichine**.

# 1987

A rather shaky middle span of a 'bridge' supported by the firm, not to say hard, supports '86s and '88s at either end, enabling the claret lover to cross from the delectable '85s to the glorious '89s.

Climatically not a very good start: long, cold winter and spring, humid June resulting in prolonged and uneven flowering. July and August dull and cool. Some rain early in an otherwise fine, sunny September. However, this was succeeded by an unsettled October, the grapes being harvested in dreary, wet conditions. Despite this, there was an average-sized crop producing sound-enough wines.

In the early to mid-1990s these were mainly considered to be easy, quaffable luncheon wines, available in restaurants, at prices as modest as their quality. Now faded curiosities.

**Ch Lafite** A none-too-impressive start. Half a dozen notes, mainly in the mid-1990s. Dipping, out of curiosity, into a case of magnums, the first with quail at a dinner party in 1995: lean, flavoury, a touch of tartness. The following January, at a boardroom lunch: soft ruby colour; agreeable nose, dry and on the lean side. A year later Jancis Robinson and I approached Eddie Penning-Rowsell's '10-year' first growths tasting without enthusiasm but, of course, curious to see how they compared. Lafite turned out to have a surprisingly deep, plummy colour, already showing some maturity; nose not bad at all; medium sweetness and body, lean fruit, loose knit, attenuated yet blunt ended. *Last noted June 1997* ★★

**Ch Latour** Bottled in May 1989 and first tasted the following April. It seemed to be a quick-developer, an opinion I endorsed later. Aged ten, it lacked the customary depth and intensity; low-keyed nose; trying to put on a show but weak for Latour. *Last noted at the Penning-Rowsell tasting, June 1997* ★★ *Decent mid-term drinking.*

**Ch Margaux** Raw and lean in cask, April and June 1988 and again, very spicy, in April 1989. My lowest mark at the tenth anniversary tasting. It seemed to me to have highish volatile acidity, and was skinny and very astringent. At the two Wagner tastings, straddling Penning-Rowsell's, the first was not unattractive, with a surprisingly harmonious nose, though its fragrance faded. Some sweetness and softness. Raw finish. At the second Margaux vertical it was showing a fair amount of maturity. Though with some sweetness and softness on the palate, I found the nose well below Margaux's standards noting it as 'nvn' (not very nice). *Last tasted Nov 2000* ★★ *Drink up.*

**Ch Mouton-Rothschild** Just three notes: attractive mid-term drinking (1990). And, on its tenth birthday, prettily coloured; attractive, biscuity, fruity nose which, after 50 minutes in the glass powered out, as if impatient to join the '86. Easily the best bouquet. On the palate, spicy, distinctive, singed, chaptalised sort of flavour, but departing with a bitter finish. *Last tasted June 1997* ★★

**Ch Haut-Brion** Also just two notes. Fairly well developed after only three years. Aged ten, quite a good colour and characteristic Haut-Brion nose: warm tiles, biscuity and which, like the Mouton, opened up deliciously. Sweet, chewy, agreeable, spicy tobacco flavour, dry finish. I liked it. *Last noted June 1997* ★★★ *But don't wait.*

**Ch Ausone** Edmund Penning-Rowsell was not the greatest fan of Ausone. It was not in his commodious cellar and his guests had difficulty in locating any to bring with them. **Ch Cheval Blanc** First tasted at the château in 1989: fragrant, light and easy. At Penning-Rowsell's, an attractive colour, mature rim; caramel nose. Very sweet, slightly singed, earthy flavour. The easiest to drink. Five months later, at Karl-Heinz Wolf's vertical of 96 vintages of Cheval Blanc, the caramelly nose noted again though it opened up quite richly; light style, crisp fruit, smoky taste. Not bad at all. *Last noted in Austria, Sept 1997* ★★★ *Drink soon.*

**Ch Pétrus** Just one note, at Penning-Rowsell's. A fine ruby colour; low-keyed nose but good fruit. Equal high marks with Ch Haut-Brion on the palate. Very fragrant. Crisp fruit. Bitter finish. June *1997* ★★(★)

THE MAJORITY OF MY OTHER NOTES OF THE '87S were made in the early 1990s when, in any case, they were best for drinking. But, to give an idea of what some were looking like in the latter part of the 1990s, I proffer the following:
**Dom de Chevalier** Still with a touch of plummy youthfulness but a weak, open rim; surprisingly good fruit on nose and palate. Very rich. Touch of iron and astringency. *At*

one of Olivier Bernard's dinners, this time all the (seven) wines with vintages ending in the figure 7 ★★ *Drinkable.*
**Carruades de Ch Lafite** Light. Fragrant. Pleasant easy drinking. At dinner in the 'Dairy' at Waddesdon Manor in Buckinghamshire after a Christie's/Domaines Rothschild wine course. *Sept 1998* ★★ *for quality,* ★★★ *as a drink.*
**Ch L'Église-Clinet** Weak rim; vegetal, chaptalised nose; interesting taste, touch of liquorice, crisp, citrus-like fruit. *At the Farr Vintners' tasting with Denis Durantou, whose great-grandfather had, in 1882, combined the different plots of Clos L'Église and Dom de Clinet: a total of 4.5ha surrounding the church, St-Jean-de-Pomerol. Tasted July 1998* ★★
**Ch Lynch-Bages** Well, if anyone can do wonders with a vintage like the '87, Jean-Michel Cases can; and he almost succeeded, for his initial cask samples in October 1988 and May 1989 were spicily appealing with quite good fruit, though not the finish. It was firmly put in its place at a vertical tasting of 13 vintages: lean, medicinal nose; surprisingly sweet but short, with sandpapery tannin and tart finish. *Last noted at the '33 Club tasting in Brussels, Nov 1995* ★ *Drink up.*
**Pensées de La Fleur** The first vintage of the second wine of La Fleur: caramelly, chaptalised; easy, agreeable, slightly chocolatey flavour with peppery finish. *Aug 1998* ★ *A curiosity.*

BRIEF NOTES ON SOME OTHER '87S, TASTED IN THE EARLY 1990S **Ch Beychevelle** spicy. Oil of cloves. *1991* ★★; **Ch Cantemerle** surprisingly attractive. *1994* ★★★; **Ch La Conseillante** very good for an '87. *1990* ★★★; **Ch Cos d'Estournel** one poor note. *1990*; **Ch Duhart-Milon** easy. *1990* ★★; **Ch L'Évangile** sweet, easy. *1991* ★★; **Ch de Fieuzal** agreeable. *1990* ★★; **Ch Grand-Puy-Lacoste** curious, fishy, metallic nose and unpleasant finish. *1995*; **Ch Gruaud-Larose** sweet, easy. *1994* ★★; **Ch Léoville-Las-Cases** not bad but undistinguished. *1990* ★★; **Ch La Mission Haut-Brion** distinctive. *1990* ★★★; **Ch Palmer** 'green' but attractive. *1991* ★★; **Ch Pape-Clément** 50% new oak which was too much for the wine. Curiously rich; smoky oaky nose. Quite nice. *1992* ★★; **Ch Pontet-Canet** medicinal lint nose, tarry taste. *1991*; and **Ch Prieuré-Lichine** light luncheon wine. *1990* ★★

MANY '87S TASTED IN 1989 WERE REALLY QUITE AGREEABLE but even if I had an up-to-date note, they should, by and large, have been consumed in the early 1990s.

# 1988 ★★★★

The first of a trio of very good vintages and the penultimate vintage of a more than interesting decade. Rather like the '86s, with which, at one time, they seemed to be level pegging, I now think that the '88s, initially somewhat overrated, are now just about coming into their own as serious long-term clarets.

Climatically, for this has the greatest influence on quality and quantity, the spring of 1988 was more than usually wet, necessitating much spraying; the later flowering conditions were uneven. The summer, from July to September, was drier than usual, monthly temperatures being average. The grapes were ripe and thick-skinned, resulting in deep colours and high tannins following a late harvest in satisfactory conditions.

My conclusion is that 1988 is a very good vintage and currently undervalued; but in the end, time and tannin will be jostling for supremacy.

**Ch Lafite** It is not only unpleasant but self-defeating to taste young wine from the cask in cold glasses in a cold cellar; and with relatively tough wines like the '88s, even more difficult. My more useful notes therefore stem from the mid-1990s, the first detailed note being made at a tasting I organised and conducted in March 1995 at the millionaires' retreat in the Bahamas, Lyford Cay. The Lafite, in magnums, crisp, blackcurrant aroma. On the palate surprisingly agreeable (for a tough vintage) and less severely tannic than expected. Fleshy but unready of course. Next an austere bottle in 1997, then, at Penning-Rowsell's '10-year' tasting of first growths, fairly deep; a fragrant, mild tea, well-developed nose; sweet, 'rather strange flavour', and soft tannins. Most recently, at a Bordeaux Club dinner (decanted at 5.45pm, served around 8.30pm): very deep, opaque core; attractive, very vanillin nose; surprisingly sweet, lean, with good flavour and masked tannin. *Last noted in the Master's Lodge, Caius, Cambridge, June 2000* ★★(★★) *At its best, say, 2010–2025.*

**Ch Latour** My early tastings were not very well timed. First shortly after fining in April 1989, next not long after bottling in September 1990. It was of course very deep: 'mulberry centre, purple rim'. Loads of unsettled fruit; powerful, aggressive and astringent. Two months later, the colour of cherry brandy, more intense than the '89, its nose already settling down, scented cedar and Cabernet Sauvignon. Good fruit, with flesh round its muscles. It is always interesting to see how the first growths compare in style and development ten years after the vintage. Latour was still impressively deep and intense; nose low-keyed but harmonious; delicious flavour, full-bodied of course, with good length and a somewhat hot, crisp finish. Complete. *Last tasted with Jancis Robinson and Eddie Penning-Rowsell and our spouses, all good tasters, July 1998* ★★(★★) *A good, medium-term wine, say 2012–2020.*

**Ch Margaux** Tasting at the château in April 1989, Paul Pontallier informed us that the vines, from July (1988) were under stress which slowed their maturity. The vat sample was opaque, with intense violet rim; fragrant with fruit and spicy new oak. It was bottled late August – early September 1990 and I next tasted it mid-October. Still very spicy but lovely. At Manfred Wagner's first vertical in 1997, the '88, a double magnum (which we drank in our 'light lunch' break) had what I call an 'Italianate' nose, still very spicy and oaky; fairly sweet, a big, fruity, tannic wine. The following July it was Penning-Rowsell's turn, this time alongside its peers: crisp fruit, developing a scent which reminded me of a wet retriever after a day on the moors (actually I don't shoot, but was brought up on the now notorious Saddleworth Moor in Yorkshire). Delicious on the palate, with an interesting texture. I happened to be at Margaux, with friends, at vintage time, September 1998, lunching at a long table with the pickers. However, our simple but hearty fare was craftily supplemented with bottles of the '88. Though unready, with loads of grip, it 'went down a treat'. Most recently, noted at Wagner's second Margaux vertical: still pretty deep; crisp and fragrant, its nose this time reminding me not of damp dogs but thoroughbred stables (I don't ride these days either; but you know what I mean). What did surprise me was that it was softer and more fragrant than I had expected, though lean and astringent after the '89. Nevertheless, a very good wine with considerable length, and future. *Last tasted Nov 2000* ★★(★★) *Possibly 5-star when fully mature. Say 2010–2020.*

**Ch Mouton-Rothschild** First tasted in Nov 1990, roughly four months after bottling. It looked younger than the '89, its nose muffled as if in the cold (which it was). Yet surprisingly sweet, very tannic of course and fleshier than expected. Not

tasted again for eight years: the bouquet by now opened up and spicy; rich, singed flavour. This was at the Hollywood Wine Society's Mouton Seminar, March 1998, followed four months later by the Penning-Rowsells' '10-year' first growth tasting at which it showed off its richness of bouquet and flavour. Yet still youthful looking, with a rich, toasty nose which then reminded me of warm tea and, after an hour, 'sodden wholemeal biscuits'. Palate full of fruit, delicious flavour, easy to drink (all the wines at these '10-year' tastings were served during dinner), very rich but a slightly bitter finish. *Last tasted July 1998* ★★★(★) *2008–2020.*

**Ch Haut-Brion** First tasted 26 November 1990, three days before it was due to be bottled. Full of colour, fruit, extract, velvety yet very tannic. Next tasted dining at 'Nick's' (quite posh) after my son Bartholomew's port tasting in Jackson, Mississippi, April 1997: fleshy but unready. The following year at the Penning-Rowsells', still fairly intense and immature. Decanted at 7.10pm it was, as always, the first of the eight first growths to be poured (at 7.55pm). It took half an hour for the nose to start opening up, and a further half hour to settle into its harmonious, warm, bricky tea-like routine. Slightly singed flavour, good length, dry and a bit raw on the finish. Most recently, at the MW Haut-Brion tasting: a thick core but maturing; a floral, citrus-like nose, but the lowest key of the trio, '88, '89 and '90, and nothing like as splendid as the '85 and '82. Nevertheless, a silky tannic texture and mocha-like flavour. Astringent with teeth-gripping tannin and acidity. *Last tasted Jan 2000* ★★(★) *but might shed its astringency.*

**Ch Ausone** There was a major error in the 1991 edition of *The Great Vintage Wine Book*. The Cheval Blanc notes appeared under the heading of Ausone. In fact, my first note of the '88 Ausone was made at the Penning-Rowsell '10-year' tasting. As usual, less deep than the other first growths and with the most mature rim; a strange, low-keyed 'dry' nose that reminded me of oyster shells. Finally, after an hour in the glass, attractive, open and relaxed; an equally strange (well, compared with the Pauillacs) mild, 'dried leaves' character. On the lean side with gritty texture. The following January, medium depth, touch of cherry red; extraordinarily sweet and nutty. I gave it a very high mark. Excellent body, flavour, balance and length. Incidentally, I find it interesting to compare notes on wines studied for two hours over dinner with those made speedily 'on the hoof' at a big pre-sale tasting. They can differ substantially. And they did. *Last noted at Christie's pre-sale tasting in London, Jan 1999. To give it the benefit of the doubt* ★★★★ *2005–2015.*

**Ch Cheval Blanc** Just three notes. First, the April after the vintage: virtually opaque and, despite its youthfulness, remarkably forthcoming with lovely fruit and extract. Six years later, at the Citibank tasting: still impressively deep; hard nose though sweet, with a hint of vanilla and tobacco; soft yet tannic, refreshing, harmonious. The following year (1997), at Wolf's big vertical, it was trying to mature. It had a crisp Cabernet Franc fruitiness. (Cabernet Franc was 65% of the blend in 1988) but I felt it lacked the usual Cheval Blanc charm. 'Needs time.' More recently, at Penning-Rowsell's '10-year' tasting, much less deep in colour, and showing some maturity. The tobacco-like taste I previously noted (in 1996) was repeated. But overall a sweet and lovely wine. *Last tasted July 1998* ★★★(★) *Now–2015, possibly longer.*

**Ch Pétrus** Just two notes, firstly, in 1995, an *impériale* packing a punch. Intense, concentrated fruit. Mightily impressive. Next at Penning-Rowsell's '10-year' first growth tasting. A lovely, medium deep, fairly intense appearance; very attractive, ripe, mulberry-like fruit; a bit of a 'best foot forward' wine with hot, alcoholic finish. A very good mouthful but totally lacking in charm and finesse. *Last tasted July 1998* ★★(★) *Perhaps I am being mean.*

**Ch L'Angélus** Very much of a relatively new state-of-the-art St-Émilion. I tasted it twice in the spring of 1989. New oak was very much to the fore, but there was still a lot of fruit. Exactly 12 months later, developing quite nicely, rich-looking; sweet, slightly chocolatey nose; attractive but unready. Most recently, the opening wine of a *1er grand cru* St-Émilion tasting: fairly deep ruby; well endowed with fruit and extract, but the tannins and acidity levels very high. *Last noted June 1997* ★★(★) *I felt it was trying too hard in an unsympathetic vintage. Probably drinking well now.*

**Ch Beychevelle** In 1989, decidedly cedary and spicy. Within a year the nose had opened up, with sweetness noted on the palate, both confirmed at a mammoth British Airways tasting in 1995: high mark for its bouquet, and one of the highest for its rich, fruity, singed flavour all of which masked the '88 tannins. Two years later, at a Beychevelle vertical (The Tasting Club at Buck's) I was pretty impressed but its leathery tannin more noticeable. Yet sweeter and richer than I had expected. I opened my last bottle recently at a small Sunday lunch with guests. Now medium deep; a lovely 'old oak', slightly cheesy bouquet; fairly sweet, soft, chewy, ready for drinking. A good '88. *Last tasted May 2001* ★★★ *Now–2010.*

**Ch Branaire-Ducru** Five notes, from its opaque, 'dumb', unready start. An easy-style fruitiness developing. In 1995, at the Fête de La Fleur banquet, a somewhat herbaceous nose and curious scented flavour, sweet, very tannic and 'a bit clumsy'. Then a more detailed note at a Christie's Bordeaux wine course: attractive colour and gradation; a touch of varnish, 'like highly polished new casks' – except that new *barriques* are not varnished! But I go on: lovely, crisp fruit, touch of chocolate and tar. Surprisingly sweet for an '88 – but so was its neighbour, Beychevelle. Thick and tannic. In the end, I didn't like it, for I had added 'ugh'. *Last tasted March 1997* ★★ *Interesting. But I doubt if it is going anywhere.*

**Ch Beauséjour-Bécot** Fennel scent delicious. *Sept 1998* ★★★

**Ch Calon-Ségur** Although not overly impressed at the Grands Crus tasting in Bordeaux in April 1989, it was showing well at the customary and useful follow-up tasting 12 months later: opaque, intense, well-balanced, lovely nose. Next noted on its tenth birthday: still very deep, with rich 'legs'; very good nose. Surprisingly sweet entry, good body, fruit and flavour. Still tannic. *Last noted at a 'classic claret' dinner at the Bath Spa Hotel, Dec 1998* ★★(★) *2005–2015.*

**Ch Canon** Six notes. Opaque, full of fruit, very tannic in April 1989. Expanding, expansive but not expensive the following April. A jump to 1996, and a fascinating tasting at Gidleigh Park in Devon: six vintages of Canon and Lynch-Bages, contrasting and complementary. The '88 Canon softer, sweeter than Lynch-Bages, and more tannic than the '89. In April 1997, elegant but lean for Canon. A very good '88, a note repeated at a board luncheon: 'a bit stern for Canon' (1999). Most recently, dining at home, now less deep, maturing; curious nose, slightly sour, tea-like, but easy on the palate. Dry finish. *Last noted May 2001* ★★★ *Forget the tannin. Drink soon.*

**Ch Canon-La-Gaffelière** First tasted in April 1989 and then in 1990. The initial bitter tannins struggling with loads of fruit. Dining at the château in April 1998 with the meticulous

and dynamic Stefan von Neipperg, his charming countess and their brilliant winemaker, Stéphane Derenoncourt – a novel combination for parochial St-Émilion; a German Graf and Gräfin and a young man from, I think, Brittany with no previous wine experience! But it works. The nose of the '88 was still peppery and reminded me of asparagus. Sweet, fleshy, a good '88. Thank goodness I did not have to drive home after the '89 Bollinger, seven clarets, not all his, an Austrian Trockenbeerenauslese, and an Eiswein from the Pfalz. I slept well, and as normal in these situations, woke up with a clear head to face the next day of tastings. More recently, at the Union des Grands Crus lunch at the Mairie, Bordeaux: still fairly deep; tarry nose; powerful and tannic. *Last noted April 1999* ★★★(★) *2006–2015.*

**Ch Carbonnieux** First tasted in April 1989, and then in 1990. A very consistent, unpretentious wine, light in style and rarely at its best with age. Better on palate than nose. Showing quite well at a Christie's Bordeaux wine course in 1995. Already maturing, with a rather weak rim; crisp blackcurrant nose; light (12% alcohol) and dry, 'pinched' but refreshing. Most recently, lean and tannic. *The last a hasty note made at a pre-sale tasting in Los Angeles, March 1999* ★★ *A light luncheon wine, not for laying down.*

**Carruades de Ch Lafite** 'In cellar cool' sounds evocative but it is not easy to taste when the wine is frigid: vivid, purple, dumb and tannic. It was better in London the following year (1990). Eight years later, still a fairly deep but soft cherry red; fragrant, cedary; attractive weight, flavour and flesh. Elegant perhaps, but, being an '88, lacking Carruades charm. *Last noted at the Bath Spa 'Classic Wine Dinner', Dec 1998* ★★(★) *2005–2012.*

**Ch Clinet** I don't much like Clinet – it is a 'Parker wine' – but I was in the minority when first tasting the cask sample of this curious, appley, Rhône-like wine. A week later, in London, without looking at my previous tasting notes, I described its nose as 'stewed apple and cloves', with 'strange, stalky, Rhône flavour'. In April 1990, this time 'cress and spice' and a more attractive blackberry flavour. More recently, dining in the quarried *caves* at Ch Villemaurine, I noted it as 'crisp, lean and elegant', 'a very good '88'. So perhaps the majority, and Mr Parker, were right after all! *Last tasted April 1997* ★★★ *2005–2012.*

**Ch Clerc-Milon** Deep, velvety; very sweet, fleshy. A good mouthful. *Dining at Brooks's Club in London, Feb 1998* ★★★

**Ch Cos d'Estournel** Cos was one of the standoffish châteaux (including Ducru and Las-Cases), which did not deign to submit sample bottles for the international journalists to taste at the annual Union des Grands Crus tastings, so my first sniff of the '88 was in January 1990 at a Cos tasting in Florida. Opaque, vigorous, attractive. Three months later, in London: lovely fruit, very tannic. The most recent notes both made at Christie's masterclasses, the first, in 1996, at a Cos vertical: the '88 very impressive, still immature, violet-tinged; nose crammed with fruit and mouthwatering acidity, opening up, like Concorde reaching cruising altitude, attaining rich fragrance and depth. But quite a bite, and raw. Next, two years later, the opening wine at a horizontal tasting of '88 red Bordeaux. Ten years had not alleviated the rasping tannin. The colour was less deep, mauve rimmed. Good flesh, fruit and flavour. *Last tasted July 1998* ★★(★★) *2008–2016.*

**Ch La Croix-de-Gay** Consistently good notes from its youth to the most recent. Never very deep, now less so, and mature looking; its original 'ensemble of cherries and raspberries' (presumably the ripe Cabernet Franc) 'spiced up with new oak', noted as merely sweet and attractive, with taste to match. Delicious and easy, though not without tannin. *Last noted at a pre-sale tasting, April 1996 ★★★★ Now–2012.*

**Ch Ducluzeau** A chunky, tannic wine, adequately accompanying an *entrecôte* at the Maison du Vin in Sauternes. It was very late, and Brigitte Lurton and I had just finished tasting 30 vintages of her Ch Climens. Coincidentally, at the next table was Jean Borie who owns and had been born at Ducluzeau. I think he was in the area to buy wines for our favourite, traditional, Bordeaux aperitif, Lillet. *Oct 2001 ★★*

**Ch Ducru-Beaucaillou** As with Cos, the mountain has to come to Mohammed. Spurning the organised tastings, one has to make private arrangements to taste at Ducru (and the first growths). So, in April 1989, a classic, understated Ducru, but astringent. In 1990 I noted that it would need a good deal of bottle age. Nine years later, though less deep, with a rich, biscuity, fully developed nose and good flavour, its initial astringency now noted as 'a bit edgy'. Doubtless better with food. *Last noted Jan 1999 ★★(★) 2006–2015.*

**Ch Duhart-Milon** Two early notes. Good fruit, but shy. Hard and restrained. In its tenth year, deep, still intense and unready; very Pauillac aroma; powerful, punchy. A long distance runner. *Last tasted at Waddesdon Manor in Buckinghamshire, Sept 1998 ★(★★) 2010–2020.*

**Ch L'Église-Clinet** Three recent notes. First at a vertical blind tasting in 1996: opaque, velvety; sweet, soft, vanillin nose. Full-bodied, high alcohol (I thought it must be the '90) but overall dry and a bit raw. Next, in July 1998, at a Farr Vintners' vertical: still velvety; peppery, uplifting tannic nose; firm, lean, tannic. Two months later, served from an *impériale*, continuing the dinner tasting after the musical interval – I think this was the year Hardy Rodenstock invited the gifted, blind tenor, Andrea Bocelli, to perform. The wine was as full and rich as the maestro's arias. Good fruit, flesh masking the tannins. *Last tasted Sept 1998 ★★★(★) Now–2015.*

**Ch Fieuzal** Very attracted to this in its early years, though almost too specious and spicy. Most recently, 'rustic' nose, fairly sweet, 'an agreeable '88'. Drinking well. *Last tasted at dinner, April 1997 ★★★ Drink soon.*

**Ch Figeac** Many notes. Initially opaque, dumb and concentrated. Later, richly perfumed Cabernet Sauvignon and new oak, pleasing texture noted. More recently, now medium deep but impressive; fruit and charm; sweet, distinctive, a very amenable '88 lunching with the hospitable Monsieur Fourcroy at his Ch Franc-Mayne. Before lunch – 2 April 1997 – all his guests were basking in June-like sun: cloudless blue sky, no breeze, temperature above 21°C and with our backs to the wall of the château, it had reached over 26°C. The châteaux proprietors in St-Émilion were, however, worried that the precocious buds would be nipped by frost. Three months later, the Figeac had nice, crisp fruit, its oakiness very noticeable, as was the very dry, slightly bitter finish. *Last noted dining at home, July 1997 ★★★(★) I hope the fruit survives the tannins.*

**Ch La Fleur** Full of rather raw fruit. Crisp. Short dry finish. *Tasted blind (I thought it was the '86), Aug 1998 ★(★★) 2005–2012.*

**Ch Grand-Puy-Lacoste** Uncompromising, virtually immovable in April 1989 and 1990. Several notes since, as I buy Lacoste every year. At a Christie's masterclass in 2000, pretty deep and intense; unwilling to more than hint at its intrinsic fragrance. Though sweet and with lots of fruit, still unyielding. Most recently, making an effort to mature; lovely, classic, bricky nose; full-flavoured, soft flesh mid-palate but a dry tannic finish. Needs food, needs time. I will hang on to the rest of my bottles. *Last noted Sept 2001 ★★(★★) 2010–2020.*

**Ch Gruaud-Larose** Dumb, tannic and bitter in April 1989 but 12 months later I noted Gruaud's characteristic fruit, chunky and, of course, tannic. In 1994 opening a vertical tasting at the château: bouquet now rich, ripe and spicy, complete but very tannic. Almost identical notes three years later. *Last noted at the Marques & Domaines tasting, Jan 1997 ★★(★★) Will be a good mouthful, but unlikely to throw off the underpinning tannin. Say 2007–2014.*

**Ch Haut-Bailly** Deep, velvety; rich 'bricky' Graves. Fleshy, earthy, extract masking tannin. A very good '88. *Dinner at Hambleton Hall, Rutland, Dec 1998 ★★★★ Now–2015.*

**Ch Haut-Batailley** Deep, crisp and not very even. The last two notes made dining at Brooks's in London. It needed plenty of decanting time but, for an '88, was drinking well. Later the same month a similar note, adding dry, lean, and lacking its usual charm. *Last noted April 1997 with my son, his wife and in-laws ★(★★) 2010–2020.*

**Ch d'Issan** I liked this from the start; and 'tannin' not mentioned once. In 1994 a well-developed bottle at home. Surprisingly sweet, with good grip (well, grip is the tannic element). *Last noted April 1994 ★★★*

**Ch Kirwan** Hesitant from the beginning. Mid-life crisis or seven-year itch? Unconvincing. Tannic. *At a British Airways tasting, Jan 1995 ★(★) Move on.*

**Ch Léoville-Barton** 'An understated classic' at the two opening tastings. Lovely fruit, flavour and fragrance. Showing well at a tenth anniversary horizontal masterclass of '88s: luminous, fine but understated, a touch of sweetness, long tail, delicious. A few months later, masculinity noted; but a fine wine. *Last noted, coping with smoked chicken at the Bath Spa 'Classic Wine Dinner', Dec 1998 ★★(★★) 2008–2016.*

**Ch Léoville-Las-Cases** Three fairly recent tastings. Frankly unimpressive, possibly a poor bottle (at a British Airways tasting for first class in 1995). Good, nicely evolved nose, soft fruit, but contradicted by its unyielding palate. Good extract battling with tannin (at a Farr Vintners' tasting, January 2000): most recently, despite its youthful appearance, showing some age on the nose; fleshy, tannate of iron finish. It needed the beef. *Last noted at the Wine Committee dinner at the Oxford and Cambridge Club in London, April 2001 ★(★★★) Assuming it pulls itself together.*

**Ch Lynch-Bages** Seven notes. Toasty, spicy, mouthfilling fruit in its formative years. Aged eight, at Gidleigh Park in Devon alongside Ch Canon: deeper, more intense, still youthful; crisp, lean, refreshing but with teeth-gripping tannin. Unready. Similar a year later. Most recently, not 'sweet and sour' but sweet and soft, yet tannic. Still finding its way. *Last noted lunching at Ch Cos d'Estournel, March 2001 ★★(★★) I live in hope.*

**Ch Mouton-Baronne-Philippe** Decanted at 7.45pm, it opened up rapidly and had a rather mocha-like nose and flavour. Fullish, soft yet tannic. A deliciously rich drink. *At dinner, Aug 2000 ★★★ Soon–2010.*

**Ch Palmer** Quite good, rich, toasty nose and fleshy fruit in cask. Less impressive a year later but striving to open up in 1990 and 1991. The most useful note made at the horizontal of '88s at Christie's: richly coloured but with a mature red-brown edge; soft, sweet, 'brown sugar' scent which opened up attractively. Sweet, good fruit, hot, slightly bitter finish. Pleasant to drink, but not living up to its 'super second' reputation. *Last noted July 1998 ★★★ Drink soon.*

**Ch Pavie** Lean, oaky, tannic in April 1989. Opening up deliciously a year later. Tasted at lunch with my old friend, the late Jean-Paul Valette, at the start of the 1995 harvest. The '88, though deep, already showing some maturity. Vanillin nose. Dry, attractive but very tannic. Served at Ch Yquem on its tenth birthday. Exactly the same note, word for word. *Last tasted June 1998 ★(★★) Just. Give it another two to three years.*

**Ch Pavie-Decesse** Jean-Paul made a better job of Decesse. It was one of my everyday clarets, bought from Justerini's in half bottles. Apart from one, hopelessly oxidised, a fair amount of extract, and pleasant to drink. But not up to my original prognosis. *Last tasted Oct 1996 ★★ Drink up.*

**Ch Pichon-Baron** Half a dozen notes: purple and tight-knit in the spring after the vintage. Evolving well a year later, and, soon after, deliciously full and fleshy. At ten years of age tasted at the château with Monsieur Matignon: fairly sweet, rich, very good fruit. Showing well. Most recently: maturing; crisp, ripe berry nose; good length and tannic grip. *Last tasted at Farr Vintners', Oct 2001 ★★★(★) Now–2015.*

**Ch Pichon-Lalande** This was about the time of the 'battle royal', with May de Lenquesaing complaining that by dropping its title, Baron, Pichon-Longueville might lead people to think that La Comtesse de Lalande was its second wine! Or words, cross words, to that effect. To make matters worse, the new boys across the road were making rather good wine. Although Lalande was not at first as immediately impressive as Baron, my most recent three notes have been consistently complimentary, each one ending 'a good '88'. Two notes in its tenth year, first lunching at Ch Brane-Cantenac and, three months later, at the Christie's '88s masterclass: richly coloured; good fruit, a whiff of lavender and 'sea breeze'; mouthfilling, sweet, masked tannin. Two recent notes: mahogany-rimmed maturity; sweet, fleshy. A good ripe '88. 'Delicious now'. *Last noted at Farr Vintners', Oct 2001 ★★★★ Now–2012.*

**Ch Le Pin** Just one half bottle. Drier, more oaky, with citrus-like acidity. Crisp fruit. Not a bad drink. *With the '86 at Schlossgut Diel in the Pfalz in Nov 1995 ★★★★*

**Ch Prieuré-Lichine** From the start, most attractive fruit and flesh. On its tenth birthday, still youthful; fragrant; characteristically lean, but flavoury and refreshing. A good Prieuré and a pleasing '88. *Last noted at the Bath Spa Claret Dinner, Dec 1998 ★★★ Now–2010.*

**Ch Rausan-Ségla** Just three notes. First, at a Rauzan-Ségla (the château changed its name from Rausan to Rauzan in 1994) dinner at Brooks's Club in London in 1995: opaque, good fruit but immature. Five years later, within five months of each other. Crisp 'good with cheese'! (Lunching at Ch Talbot.) A complete contrast to the Ch Pichon-Lalande alongside: deeper, more ruby; lovely, crisp, refreshing bouquet; an elegant, lean Margaux managing to equate soft fruit and fairly obtrusive tannin. *Last noted at the France in Your Glass tasting, Sept 2000 ★★(★★) 2008–2020.*

**Vieux Ch Certan** First noted in Brussels at a tasting of two Thienpont wines, Vieux Ch Certan and Labégorce-Zédé. The Pomerol deeper, rather more four-square, the Margaux crisper, harder and more tannic (1999). Next, a surprising and spectacular *impériale* with the Bacchus Society, en route to present a Lifetime Achievement award to the Egon Müllers at Scharzhofberg in the Saar. Deep, still with youthful edge; fragrant; lean, very tannic, but loads of flavour. *Last noted dining at the Zur Traube restaurant at Grevenbröich. The only reason for visiting this small, provincial, unpronounceable German town is to experience Dieter Kaufmann's cooking, to plunder his extensive and very high quality cellar and, after dinner, to stagger up to the quietest and most comfortable rooms imaginable.*

OF THE MANY OTHER '88S LAST TASTED IN THE LATTER HALF OF THE 1990S, most of the Médocs and Graves can be summed up in four words: 'good fruit, lean, tannic', the Right Bank tending to be fleshier but – as has been noted – also very tannic. As can be imagined, those that I only tasted in their youth were, understandably, even more tannic, but among the many, the following had good potential (star ratings as noted at the time): **Ch d'Angludet** ★★(★); **Ch Brane-Cantenac** ★★★; **Ch Chasse-Spleen** ★★★; **Dom de Chevalier** ★★★(★); **Ch Durfort-Vivens** ★★(★); **Ch L'Évangile** ★★(★★); **Ch Gazin** ★★(★); **Ch Giscours** ★★(★★); **Ch Labégorce-Zédé** ★★(★); **Ch Lafon-Rochet** ★(★★); **Ch La Lagune** ★★(★); **Ch Langoa-Barton** ★(★★); **Ch Lynch-Moussas** ★★★; **Ch Malartic-Lagravière** ★★★; **Ch La Mission Haut-Brion** ★★(★★); **Ch Montrose** ★(★★★); **Ch Pape-Clément** ★★★; **Ch de Pez** ★★(★); **Ch La Pointe** ★★★; and **Ch Talbot** ★★(★★)

# 1989 ★★★★★

Unquestionably a great vintage and one which brought the decade to a resounding close.

I originally considered extending this section to end with the 1990s, as 1988, '89 and '90 are such a formidable trio, each different in its own way. However, I might as well stick to plan, ending on a high and starting the next with a kick start as with the earlier twins, 1899 and 1900.

First, the weather conditions. In May, growth was three weeks ahead of normal. Early flowering in excellent conditions, followed by the hottest summer since 1949 and the earliest harvest since 1983. However, though the grapes were fully ripe the tannins were not, though later-picked grapes did have softer tannins, but at the expense of acidity.

When youthful, the wines almost without exception were extraordinarily appealing. I personally thought we were in for another '85 but with extra dimensions; perhaps even an early developer. In fact what seems to have happened is a sort of reversal of roles, the tannin becoming more noticeable, turning the '89 into a much longer-haul vintage than I had anticipated. Nevertheless, many superlative wines.

**Ch Lafite** I think it almost superfluous to describe what Lafite, in a vintage like 1989, looked and tasted like in the spring and autumn of 1990. From time to time I am asked how one judges a young Bordeaux in cask; equally I should like to have posed the same question to my mentor, Harry Waugh, whom I have previously referred to as one of the finest judges of claret. Harry was, at the time of writing, aged 97, extraordinarily fit and lean, but a bit forgetful. In any case, his was a natural gift; his senses were almost on autopilot. So, briefly, the most important factors are appearance: depth, richness of colour, intensity, and palate, the degree and balance of component parts and its length. The wine should smell good of course, it should have a recognisable aroma and an unforced fragrance. But its virtues and beauty become more apparent as the wine matures. When I tasted the '89 Lafite in the spring of 1990, it was opaque, intense, vividly purple; nose, crisp young fruit but unyielding; full, firm, fleshy, mouth-puckeringly tannic. Six months longer in *barrique* and not much noticeable difference. It was in the following spring, April 1991, that its fruit components, tempered by the spiciness of new oak (cloves, cinnamon, vanillin) started to take shape, its completeness and length promising a good, indeed, pretty extended future. It has only just occurred to me that if one could accurately measure what the French call persistence, one might, by extension calculate the length of its life.

My next exposure to the '89 was in March 1995 at a vertical of Lafite, all in magnums, I conducted at Lyford Cay in the Bahamas – and what a vertical: '89, '88, '85, '83 and '82. It was deep, having lost its pristine opaqueness, a soft ruby colour with the thickness and richness I associate with high extract. On the nose it was 'unobvious', when first poured out, yet it had an attractive cedary scent, harmony (no harsh edges) and depth (it clearly had much more to reveal). After 30 minutes, it started to open up. Very rich, with the sweaty smell that more than hints at the tannin content, and lots of fruit which provided a sort of fig leaf to hide its masculinity. Definitely not a shrinking violet: a wine of substance with great future. Two months later, at my first masterclass at Christies in New York, this time a horizontal of '89s: spicy; sweet, with fullness of fruit but not of alcohol which is – for claret – the ideal 12.5%.

I shall jump to the always fascinating and informative Penning-Rowsell tasting of '10-year' old first growths. They were all decanted at about 6.30pm and served in fairly short order from 8pm, and we were able to sip and savour (and drink) them at dinner over the next two hours. They were all good. The Lafite was beginning to show some maturity. For me, on the palate it was equal top with Latour and on the nose with Mouton (7/7) – Jancis Robinson, Eddie Penning-Rowsell, and spouses, all use a 20-point scale 3-7-10 (for appearance, nose and palate). Anyway, a lovely wine, complete, with a very fragrant aftertaste. My next and most recent note was made at a dinner party at home. Despite a warm rich mature colour with a tinge of orange at the rim, the wine had an extraordinary attack, a very rich 'entry', nice weight, good fruit, plenty of tannin and acidity. Very good but unready. And the nose? I had the advantage of smelling and tasting when I decanted it (a magnum) at 4.30pm: very rich, impenetrable depth and concentration. At 6.10pm, sweeter, richer, more fragrant, and after my guests had gone home – leaving me to rinse, steam and polish the Riedel glasses – it was still gloriously fragrant, tea-like. *Last tasted May 2001* ★★★★(★) *Forget it for another ten years: say 2010–2030, or beyond.*

**Ch Latour** Also tasted in the spring and autumn of 1990: black as Egypt's night, its 100% new oak very apparent. Never easy to taste when immature and even the following November, though it had a tantalising cedar and Cabernet Sauvignon scent, and on the palate all the components in abundance, one might as well 'shut up shop' – cellar it and forget it. At the masterclass in New York (April 1995), it was certainly impressive and though a big wine, like Lafite, only had 12.5% alcohol. Nose strongly Cabernet, mouthwatering, extensive; crisp lovely flavour with refreshing acidity and a bitter tannic finish. At the Penning-Rowsells' in 1999, less deep, a luminous ruby; very fragrant nose; distinctive, full-flavoured, crisp, complete. The bitterness not noted but it had more acidity than the other first growths. Most recently, one of eight *grands formats*, all *1er cru* except Figeac (and the Lafite turned out to be a '95) served by larger-than-life Walter Eigensatz at dinner. A jeroboam: my notes uncannily similar to the bottle at Penning-Rowsell's two years before. A marvellous mouthful despite its edgy tannic finish. *Last noted at the Eigensatzs' Hotel Eden-Parc, Bad Schwalbach, Oct 2001* ★★★(★) *Possibly 5-star if the astringency mellows. Say 2010-2025.*

**Ch Margaux** First tasted at the château in April 1990. One does not have to have been born in Seville to be tantalised by the provocative blouse, swirling skirt and haughty demeanour of a flamenco dancer. So it is with the scent and verve of a young Margaux, particularly if, as almost always, tasting with the infectiously enthusing Paul Pontallier who makes even statistics fascinating: an early harvest, starting 10 September; a blend of 77-78% Cabernet Sauvignon, 'about' 15% Merlot, 5% Petit Verdot and 2-3% Cabernet Franc, all of which ripened fully about the same time; alcohol 12.7%. He extolled the soft tannins which add sweetness and lower the acidity. My next note was made at a vertical in March 1995, more flesh than the '90, but marked tannins, and another, eight months later at a first growth tasting: 'sweet, lovely fruit yet with a kick in the tail'. At the first of Wagner's Ch Margaux tastings in 1997 it had a deep, velvety colour and wonderful fruit, my equal highest mark, with the '85 and '45, of the 48 vintages tasted that day. At the Penning-Rowsells' in June 1999, it was still fairly deep and youthful. Its nose was very forthcoming, a sort of minty fragrance, level pegging in marks with Mouton and, believe it or not, Ausone. But there was a leanness on the palate and very dry finish. At Wagner's second vertical in Nov 2000, I rated it second only to the '45. Sweet, soft, rich – a lovely wine. Last tasted, blind, from a jeroboam: very deep, almost opaque, cherry-tinged but maturing; singed spicy bouquet; drier than expected, stern, firm but with very good flavour (I thought it was the Mouton). *Last tasted at the Eigensatzs', Bad Schwalbach, Oct 2001* ★★★★(★) *2010–2025.*

**Ch Mouton-Rothschild** Also exciting in its youth, with Mouton's inimitable, spicy, cassis aroma, flesh and fruit. Twelve months after the harvest, peppery, vigorous, its tannins on the bitter side. The following spring (1991), I found it so much more exotic than the '90. Sweet. Fabulous. Rodenstock produced an *impériale*, prematurely, in September 1995: very dry. But a couple of months later, bottles (I think we had two) with wonderful mouthfilling fruit at a tasting I conducted for Goldman Sachs at Christie's in Frankfurt. No longer opaque, a deep, black cherry colour. Superbly fragrant, minty, peppery fragrance and lovely crisp Cabernet Sauvignon flavour. Most recently, this time in Hamburg at a comparative tasting of '89s and '82s, I noted its 'legs', fantastic bouquet and flavour. A touch of iodine, lovely mid-palate fruit, its high Cabernet Sauvignon content (about 76%) having provided the exclusive Mouton flavour and character. Leaner than expected and still very tannic. *Last noted at the Hotel Louis C Jacob's wine event in Hamburg, March 2000* ★★★(★★) *2010–2030.*

**Ch Haut-Brion** A wonderful wine. Deep, rich and spicy, sweet, fleshy, well endowed (November 1990). The following spring, alongside La Mission, superb. Not tasted for another nine years, less deep of course, fairly well developed; a singed, toasted, ripe nose and flavour: 'roasted coffee beans'. A touch raw and earthy (in a blind tasting of '89s in 1998). At the '10-year' tasting: ruby colour; soft, fragrant, spicy; '89 sweetness and richness, elegant. A slightly tarry, dry finish. 'Richness' is the word, noted again (Tokyo 1999). Two notes in 2000, with almost identical descriptions: medium-deep, maturing, its colour soft and mellow; warm, rich, slightly earthy nose and taste. Bouquet opening up beautifully; soft mellow repeated, sweet, full, rich, lovely flavour but with teeth-gripping acidity. Most recently, a double magnum: rich, fruity but with a slightly astringent finish already noted. *Last tasted at the Eigensatzs' Hotel Eden-Parc in Bad Schwalbach, Nov 2001* ★★★(★★) *2010–2025.*

**Ch Ausone** Deep; oaky; good fruit, spice, aftertaste – and future (at a tasting of '89s in St-Émilion, November 1990). Nine years later at the Penning-Rowsells' one of my highest-ever marks at these '10-year' tastings. Fine, misleadingly mature looking; its harmonious though strangely attractive 'tea leaves and brown paper' fragrance; delicious flavour but its silky leathery tannins giving it quite a kick. Most recently, in magnum: very distinctive flavour, lean but fragrant, curiously soft and chewy but with astringent finish. *Last tasted at the Eigensatzs' Hotel Eden-Parc in Bad Schwalbach, Nov 2001 ★★★(★★) 2008–2020.*

**Ch Cheval Blanc** First noted at a tasting arranged for me by the late Jean-Paul Valette at the Maison du Vin in St-Émilion. Alongside the other *1er grand cru* St-Émilions it had extra dimensions. Interestingly, though 'not remotely the weight of the first growth Médocs', its alcoholic strength is higher, 13%. A wine of distinctive charm and elegance. At the New York masterclass in 1995 I couldn't help noticing its 'legs' (a habit of mine); a refreshing wine on nose and palate. Deliciously sweet, 'not a blockbuster'. Two years later, at the Wolf/Weinart Cheval Blanc tasting, it was showing much more maturity than the '90; sweet, ripe, soft tannins, 'charm' noted again. We were informed that it was a very early harvest, between 7 and 27 September and a very big crop. Next noted in its tenth year: mature looking; perfect harmony; the lightest in style, easiest of the eight first growths. A lovely wine though. Most recently, in jeroboam, tasted blind: rich, chocolatey, mocha nose – could only be Right Bank; soft, chewy, elegant, lovely. *Last noted at the Eigensatzs' Hotel Eden-Parc in Bad Schwalbach, Oct 2001 ★★★★★ Now–2015.*

**Ch Pétrus** First tasted November 1990: a seriously big wine: opaque, intense, purple; packed and powerful (13.5%, a whole degree more alcohol than the first growth Médocs) – said to be the result of a rigorous 'green harvest' to thin out the bunches and concentrate the grapes. Tasted again from the cask in June 1991: disarmingly sweet but very tannic. Next, a double magnum served at Rodenstock's opening dinner in 1995: still very deep and intense, but it had developed a marvellous scent; sweet, chunky, oaky, spicy. And three years later, teasingly in a blind 'flight', incorrectly noted as 'not Pétrus', level pegging with the odd-man out, Gaja's Darmagi.

At Penning-Rowsell's '10-year' first growth tasting in 1999 it was still deep, youthful with opaque core; and a slightly chocolatey nose. As so often, even with these top Pomerols, far more interesting on the palate: sweet, rich, full of fruit, rounded – but a slightly rough texture ('raw tannin' in 1998) noted again. Most recently, a double magnum: still virtually opaque; good fruit, truffles; fairly full-bodied, a touch of austerity, good texture (which should have alerted me), great length. Tasted blind I thought it was the Latour. *Last noted at the Eigensatzs' Hotel Eden-Parc in Bad Schwalbach, Nov 2001 ★★(★★★) 2015–2030.*

**Ch Batailley** Agreeable in cask, very agreeable after seven years, doubtless delicious now. Lovely deep soft cherry red; crisp 'black fruit' nose; refreshing acidity. *Last tasted at a Christie's Bordeaux wine course, March 1996 ★★★ Now–2010.*

**Ch Beychevelle** The words 'fleshy' and 'spicy' used in November 1990 and in its tenth year. Sweet, ripe, attractive. *Last noted at a buffet supper at the now sadly soulless château, March 1999 ★★★ Now–2012.*

**Ch Bonnet, de Cruzeau** and **Rochemorin** All André Lurton's wines, each with its own character, each very good. *At Ch La Louvière, March 2001 ★★★*

**Ch Branaire-Ducru** One of the two Médoc châteaux to start picking in August, a plot of young Merlot vines, at 9am on the 31st. First tasted in November 1990 and reeking of new oak, fruit, spice, chunky tannins. In its eighth year still youthfully tinged; a low-keyed, gentle fragrance that opened up attractively. The sweetness of ripe fruit, but still tannic. *Last tasted dining at Ch Branaire, April 1997 ★★★ 2005–2015.*

**Ch Canon** A fulsome note at the time of my first tasting, November 1990. Even then, fragrant, shapely (elliptical, swelling and subsiding gracefully). Good nose; soft, chunky fruit, easy style, delicious. *Last noted at a Gidleigh Park tasting in Devon, March 1996 ★★★★ Now–2012.*

**Ch Cantemerle** Initially opaque, with all present and correct. In its eighth year still deep; good fruit and flesh, but unready. *Last noted dining at Brooks's Club ★★(★) 2005–2015.*

**Ch Cantenac-Brown** In cask I thought it lacked conviction. Drinking well though at the Fête de la Fleur (at the château) in June 1997, also, most recently, at the Union des Grands Crus lunch in Bordeaux: touch of coffee on the nose; good texture, a refreshing citrus squeeze. 'Surprisingly attractive' I noted with an air of condescension. *Last tasted April 1999 ★★★ Now–2010.*

**Ch Chasse-Spleen** A dependable 'club claret'. Just about right. Good fruit. Drinking well. *Feb and May 1998 ★★★ Drink soon.*

**Ch Clinet** Three notes. First a double magnum in 1995, very tannic, very oaky but with good nose. Next in 1997 over-extracted and too tannic. Not my favourite style of wine. More recently, deep, medium intensity, a bit smelly (tannins?); unusual, distinctive flavour, hefty, rich, raw. Its raw tannic finish tamed by spicy beef. *Tasted blind, at dinner, on the fifth day of Rodenstock's Yquem marathon, Sept 1998 ★(★★)*

**Ch La Conseillante** Another Pomerol but much more my style of wine. An opulently fruity bouquet; fabulously flavoured magnum in 1994. Cloves, cinnamon, tannin, but high mark and good future. The following year, this time in double magnum, also at a Rodenstock event, its bouquet fully evolved; but rather more open knit though still very oaky and tannic. *Last tasted Sept 1995. Then (★★★★) now likely to be ★★★(★)*

**Ch Cos d'Estournel** First noted in 1995 with other '89s at two tastings in New York: black cherry; a 'warm' toasty nose which opened up well; good fruit, rounded, substantial (13% alcohol). Four subsequent notes, losing colour, mature rim; its nose, we thought, tainted by the smell of the cardboard carton the glasses came from; better on the palate but touch of bitterness, something lacking. In 1999, it featured in the Grand Awards '89 'Super-seconds' tasting in New York when it was medium deep, velvety but with a slightly weak mature rim; sweet but sweaty nose and surprisingly sweet on the palate. Lovely fruit. Very amenable but a touch of bitterness. Good, but 'super'? Most recently, a double magnum: deep; very fragrant; dry, crisp, firm, elegant. Tannic finish. *Last noted in Bad Schwalbach, Oct 2001 ★★★(★) Soon–2015.*

**Ch Ducru-Beaucaillou** Only two notes. Unsurprisingly opaque, understated but complete (November 1990). Next, now medium deep, 'luminous'; rich nose though a touch of edginess; sweet, good fruit, tannin and acidity. *Last noted at a pre-sale tasting, Jan 1999. Good but not inspiring ★★(★) 2008–2018.*

**Ch Durfort-Vivens** Rather satisfactory to taste a wine selected from a range of 35 red Bordeaux at a British Airways tasting for first class in January 1995, to know that it was on board by the end of 1996, and to taste it first hand (actually second hand – a friendly cabin services director brought it from the front cabin; I was travelling Club) on BA 299 to Chicago the following spring. In the space of a couple of years it had matured agreeably, its masked tannin at last unmasked.

Sweet, soft, flavoury, mildly gripping, coping well with British Airways fare – if not fares. *Last tasted at a great height, April 1997* ★★★ *Drink soon.*

**Ch L'Église-Clinet** One of Rodenstock's pet wines and unleashed on his guests at fairly regular intervals: double magnums in 1995 and 1996. My notes ranging from a rather strange nose but very good texture, opaque, immature looking; spicy, severe; very dry bitter tannins, to the two most recent in magnums: deep, plummy; scent of privet, a slightly smelly, overripe nose; sweet, soft, fleshy to the point of opulence (no new oak used). On balance, a delicious mouthful. 'Decadent' (to use one of Robert Parker's favourite expressions). *Last tasted Sept 1998. A wine for hedonists* ★★★(★)

**Clos L'Église-Clinet** Very deep but a brownness around the rim; chocolatey, static nose; fairly sweet, chunky, stodgy, unexciting. *In Bad Schwalbach, Oct 2001* ★★

**Ch Figeac** At its fragrant, mouthfilling, flavoury best. Displaying its sweetness, spiciness and charm even in cask. Most recently, at a most delightful dinner party given for a group of friends and hosted by Marie-France and Thierry Manoncourt with Comte Éric d'Aramon, their son-in-law, who is now running the estate: even the colour is luscious; glorious fruit, evolved, rounded; á full, fleshy mouthful with masked tannin. Most recently, idiosyncratic as ever, it was by no means flawless (I thought its rim was a bit weak, its nose almost sickly sweet and a touch of woodiness); the double magnum was voted 'top', much to Thierry Manoncourt's delight, at the blind tasting of *1er cru '89 grands formats* (big bottles) at Bad Schwalbach. It was irresistibly rich and fragrant with good length and spicy finish. *Last noted Oct 2001* ★★★★.

**Ch La Fleur** In magnums, still opaque, sweet, full, fleshy. Glorious. *Sept 1998* ★★★★★ *Now–2025.*

**Ch La Fleur-Pétrus** Bought by Mouiex in 1952. 80% Merlot, 20% Cabernet Franc. Now mature looking; rich yet, somehow, lean, with good Pomerol texture and lovely flavour. A good drink. *Noted at a Bordeaux Index tasting in the cellars of the Stafford Hotel in London, Nov 1999* ★★★★ *Now–2015.*

**Clos Fourtet** A very deep, plummy purple in the spring and autumn of 1990 but good, rich, soft fruit. By 1997, maturing, rather rustic character, very sweet and ripe. Drinking well (lunch at Ch Franc-Mayne). Two years later, rich and chewy (at the château with André Lurton, one of his many estates), finally a bottle at home, now fairly mature with a fully developed nose and taste. Once my least favourite St-Émilion but delicious in 1989. *Last tasted Feb 2000* ★★★ *Drink soon.*

**Ch Le Gay** Two notes two days apart, the second blind which is a useful if somewhat salutary experience: less to do with identifying the wine, more to do with one's notes concurring. Happily they were near enough! The wine has a lovely, deep, rich colour; ripe mulberry, a hint of mint; very distinctive, full of fruit, some finesse and elegance, spicy tannic finish. *Last noted Sept 1998* ★★★(★★) *2005–2025.*

**Ch Gazin** Also rising to the occasion in 1989 and showing well the following autumn: crisp, rich, tannic. In its tenth year, deep, velvety; a rich, 'meaty' nose; sweet and pretty massive. *Last noted dining with the von Neippergs at Ch Canon-La-Gaffelière, April 1998* ★★★(★) *2005–2015.*

**Ch Giscours** I have been a Mousquetaire d'Armagnac for many years but have only managed to get to one event, the 36th Grand Chapitre, in 1994. It was a spirited occasion. After Armagnac as an aperitif, they served a strange local red, then Ch Filhot with *foie gras*. Next this full, fleshy, tannic, Giscours with *magret de canard*, followed by eau de vie and champagne –

in that order. I slept well. A year later, when dining at the Savoie (in Margaux) a tall Dutch gentleman, who turned out to own three-quarters of the restaurant, passed a bottle to our table. A fully developed nose with a curious uplift to the flavour but, I thought, beginning to dry out. *Last tasted Sept 1995* ★★

**Ch Grand-Puy-Ducasse** Dry, crisp fruit but I didn't notice any obvious '89 richness or quality. *Noted at a pre-sale tasting, May 1998* ★★

**Ch Grand-Puy-Lacoste** A really lovely wine. Opaque; rich Pauillac character; full of all the good things. I bought a few cases and am still drinking it. Many notes, not all at home. I shipped some to Lyford Cay in the Bahamas and it opened my tasting in 1995. Deep, lovely colour; masses of fruit and extract. Normally a slow developer, the '89 exudes good health and drinkability. The very evening I wrote this note (and for this note, I decanted a bottle): beautiful to look at, sweet bouquet and flavour. Perfect with Daphne's roast beef and Yorkshire pudding. *Last noted Sept 2001* ★★★★★ *Now–2015.*

**Ch Gruaud-Larose** A vintage tailor-made for Gruaud. Five notes, from opaque, packed with fruit in November 1990 to a softer, more mature, ripe-nosed, fleshy mouthful eight years later and, most recently, though with a rich, now mature appearance and ripe, spicy bouquet, it had surprising grip and tannin. *Last noted, albeit superficially, at a Farr Vintners' tasting, Oct 2001* ★★★(★) *Soon–2020.*

**Ch Haut-Bailly** Faultless in cask and beyond criticism on its tenth birthday: a deep, rich, soft, characteristically earthy Graves, its flesh masking considerable tannin. Most recently: still impressively deep; very sweet, rich yet perfect weight. A typically lovely '89. *Last noted at a Christie's masterclass, April 2002* ★★★★(★) *Now–2025.*

**Ch Lagrange** (St-Julien) Fairly deep; rich; chewy, touch of coarseness but good extract, tannins and acidity. *Lunching at Ch Cos d'Estournel, March 2001* ★★★ *Now–2015.*

**Ch Lascombes** Two recent notes. Richly coloured but coarse texture (1999). Curious tannic bitterness. *Last tasted Sept 2001* ★★ *I must retaste.*

**Ch Léoville-Barton** Usually there is a considerable difference in content and style between the two *2ème cru* St-Juliens, the Barton, very correct, very English (despite its Irish ancestry) and the Gruaud noted above, more French: the gentleman versus the well-endowed young matron, except that in 1989 the stiff upper lip relaxes. A somewhat fleshier and riper wine than usual, with extra dimensions, body, fruit, texture, length of course. Several notes from cradle to the age of consent. *Last noted at the Grand Awards '89 'Super-seconds' tasting in New York, Oct 1999* ★★★★(★) *2005–2025.*

**Ch Léoville-Las-Cases** One is not often able to taste Las-Cases in its extreme youth. Monsieur Delon was always unwilling to put his wine in with others or to provide cask samples. The first of half a dozen notes made in 1995: immensely impressive, already perfectly harmonious, a 5-star wine in the making. Jumping five years, showing well at Farr Vintners: sweet, fully aroused. Rich yet tannic. *Last tasted Jan 2000* ★★★(★) *2005–2030.*

**Ch Léoville-Poyferré** Reputed to have the finest vineyard site in the whole of the Médoc and making wine of the highest quality from the mid-19th century to 1929. 1989 sees it back on form. Immaculate, 'copybook' in cask and after five years still opaque, packed with brambly fruit. A classic waiting in the wings. *Not tasted since Jan 1995. Then* (★★★★) *Now probably* ★★★★(★) *Say 2005–2030.*

**Ch La Louvière** Five recent notes, four at home. Rich fruit and extract. Drinking well. Totally delicious. Most recently, maturing well; soft, fleshy, *à point* yet some grip. *Last noted lunching with André Lurton, Oct 2001* ★★★★ *Now–2015.*

**Ch Lynch-Bages** Usually outperforming its *5ème cru classé* status; 'the poor man's Mouton' – or so it was condescendingly referred to. In fact it is no longer, in price, accessible to the sort of buyer who lapped up Lynch-Bages prior to the mid-1960s. It is 'its own man', invariably packed with exciting fruit and flavour. But I wonder if in 1989 it was trying too hard. Among many notes, I have stated more fruit than charm. At the Hotel Louis C Jacob in Hamburg in 2000: still deep, intense, vibrant fruit, whiff of raspberry; a big, mouthfilling wine, though I noticed a trace of bitterness on the finish which, I am sure, will wear off in time. Most recently, a jeroboam: almost opaque, still youthful; spicy; full of flavour, quite a bite. *Last noted at Bad Schwalbach, Oct 2001* ★★★(★) *2008–2020.*

**Ch Mouton-Baronne-Philippe** Ruby in cask. Ruby aged seven. More flesh than usual but tight-knit and tannic. *Last tasted Dec 1996. Then* ★★(★★) *Drink now–2015.*

**Ch Palmer** At its best. Many notes from glorious, generously endowed in cask to the Grand Awards 'Super-seconds' tasting in New York. Now maturing; rich, ripe (52% Merlot in '89), open, biscuity; sweet, delicious fruit and flavour. Still tannic. *Last noted in Oct 1999* ★★★★(★) *Now–2015.*

**Ch de Pez** A consistently good St-Estèphe *cru exceptionnel* and I can see why Monsieur Rouzaud of Champagne Roederer decided to exploit its potential further. He must have been impressed with the '89: surprisingly fruity and tannic. *Last noted at a pre-sale tasting, April 1996* ★★(★) *Now–2010.*

**Ch Pichon-Baron** This would never have been in any list of 'Super-seconds' prior to AXA ownership and Michel Cazes' supervision. It certainly showed excellent potential in cask and my only subsequent note, at the Grand Awards tasting in New York: still virtually opaque; rich, slightly tarry nose; a big, ripe, fleshy wine. *Last noted Oct 1999* ★★★(★) *2005–2025.*

**Ch Pichon-Lalande** After a shaky start, a poor cask sample, eight subsequent notes, all good, from a really lovely mouthful, luscious *and* elegant (Christie's masterclass, March 1995). Later the same month at a comparative tasting in Brussels, softer, richer, more mouthwatering than Palmer. Most recently, still deep but mature looking; marvellous, rich, ripe fruit on the nose and palate. Fleshy, even plump, soft tannins. *Last noted at a vertical for France in Your Glass, at Eugénie-les-Bains, Oct 2000* ★★★★★

**Ch Le Pin** A 'mystery' magnum served blind: very sweet, mocha-like, rather unsophisticated; powerful, rich, tannic (Michel Bettane thought it 'sexy'). At lunch on the third day of Hardy Rodenstock's five-day Ch d'Yquem marathon. The chef at the Königshof hotel in Munich, managed to produce six lunches and six dinners, all brilliantly inventive, with appropriate dishes for the extraordinarily diverse wines Hardy had produced. It was tiring, but we all survived. *Sept 1998* ★★★(★★) *2010–2030.*

**Ch La Pointe** There could hardly be a greater contrast between this Pomerol and Ch Le Pin in size, style and price! I have several notes: fully mature; pleasant, slightly minty nose; very sweet, easy, good acidity. Short. *Last tasted lunching at the château, Sept 1998* ★★★ *Drink soon.*

**Ch Talbot** First, a strange cask sample, which had a fig-like nose. At a tasting in 1995 I described the wine as 'vegetal' and though it had good fruit I queried the finish. More recently, its bouquet was now more recognisably normal, cedary, 'old oak' (trees not casks); a fairly rich mouthful. *Last tasted at my auction talk in New York, March 1997* ★★★ *(some might rate it more highly). Now–2015.*

**Ch Tertre-Roteboeuf** An extraordinary St-Émilion 'cult' wine which has become very fashionable since the 1980s. Whether it was its name having a subliminal influence, my first note (in 1998) referred to its meaty nose, then more like 'boiled ham'. Full, rich, singed aftertaste. Most recently, still deep, rich, intense, unusual, curiously sweaty (tannic) nose; sweet, delicious, rich texture – more like vintage port. *Last noted at a tasting conducted by the owner, François Mitjavile, in London, March 2001* ★★(★★★)? *Now–2025?*

BRIEF RATINGS ON SOME OF THE MANY OTHER '89S TASTED IN THE MID- TO LATE 1990S **Ch d'Angludet** ★★★; **Ch d'Armailhac** ★★★; **Ch Bon-Pasteur** ★★★★ ready now; **Ch Bouscaut** ★★★; **Ch Canon-La Gaffelière** ★★★(★); **Dom de Chevalier** ★★★★; **Ch Clerc-Milon** ★★(★); **Ch La Dominique** ★★★(★); **Ch Duhart-Milon** ★★★; **Ch La Gaffelière** ★★★; **Ch La Grave-Trigant-de-Boisset** ★★★; **Ch Haut-Batailley** ★★★; **Ch d'Issan** ★★★★; **Ch Labégorce-Zédé** ★★★; **Ch Langoa-Barton** ★★★(★); **Ch Latour-à-Pomerol** ★★★(★); **Ch Magdelaine** ★★★(★); **Ch La Mission Haut-Brion** ★★★(★); **Ch Montrose** ★★(★★); **Ch Moulinet** ★★; **Ch Pape-Clément** ★★★(★); **Ch Pavie** ★★★; **Ch Pontet-Canet** ★★?; **Ch Prieuré-Lichine** ★★★; **Ch Rausan-Ségla** ★★★(★); **Ch Siran** ★★★; and **Ch La Tour-de-By** ★★★

# 1990–1999

There are two ways of looking at the 1990 vintage: the end of an era or the bright start to a decade of dashed hopes, near misses, good but less glamorous years. Even the best vintages of this decade, and some are very good, tend to be compared with the 1990, just as a younger child looks up to the 'Captain of School'. What is certain is that the euphoria and general satisfaction with the 1980s, ending up with the magnificent twins of '89 and '90, made the 'rain-stopped-play' years of '91 to '93 less attractive. Anyway, by then everyone was sated with stock. The 1995 vintage was fairly well-timed. It gave the trade in Bordeaux and in London the impetus it needed.

Who were 'the trade'? Almost gone were the *négociants-éleveurs,* the big companies, the stockholders. All – well, almost all – were now brokers, selling on, not sitting on stock. In England, only the old-fashioned but surprisingly go-ahead Berry Bros and a handful of other London and provincial wine merchants supplied from stock. Though the auctioneers, Christie's and Sothebys, continued to thrive, the brokers had captured a good deal of the trade, Bordeaux continuing to be a major part of their portfolio, their clients worldwide. Only in the United States was the wine trade still structured: importers, wholesalers and retailers keeping more or less to their own patch.

The only trouble with Americans is that so many of them, both trade and private buyers, are too influenced by wine critics, by the otherwise admirable Robert Parker in particular. How important is America and its taste preferences? To put this in perspective, in 1999 the United Kingdom and Germany each imported more Bordeaux by value and by volume than the United States. We would not mind so long as the producers took less notice of American-led global taste and stuck to what they do best: produce good, well-established, food-wine claret. Horses for courses, I say. Just one more thought: wouldn't it be boring if every vintage was of equal quality and style? Bordeaux, thanks to its maritime climate, produces great wines for long keeping *and* good value wines for everyday drinking.

## *Vintages at a Glance*

**Outstanding** ★★★★★
1990

**Very Good** ★★★★
1995, 1996 (v), 1999 (v)

**Good** ★★★
1993 (v), 1994, 1997, 1998 (v)

## 1990 ★★★★★

An excellent vintage with similar attributes to the '89 but certainly not an identical twin.

First, the growing conditions. January to March unusually warm and sunny, up to 25°C on 24 February, advancing vegetation. Beneficial rain in April followed by a very hot, dry and sunny May. The flowering was uneven and prolonged, satisfactory for the Merlots, less so for Cabernet Sauvignon. July was excessively hot, up to just short of 39°C on the 21st. This heat had a reverse effect, hindering maturation by impeding the rising of the sap. August was warm and dry. Unlike 1989 this did not deter the ripening, as a well-timed beneficial sprinkling of rain in September enabled the grapes to be harvested from around mid-month. In general, the Merlots were in remarkable condition with some of the highest levels of sugar ever recorded. The later ripening Cabernet Sauvignon grapes were small and thick, with a concentration of juice and colouring matter.

**Ch Lafite** Despite its deceptively purple hue, surprisingly soft and easy though I much preferred the '89 alongside (at the château, April 1991). This attractive, easy, fragrant style noted again at the MW tasting of '90s in November 1994. A huge vote for elegance but low for power at Eigensatz's amazing blind tasting of 144 of the very best 1990 reds from around the world. Lafite's fragrance seemed to be self-generating, its fleshy ripeness exemplified by a magnum produced, not for the first time, at one of Rodenstock's annual wine weekends (1998). The Penning-Rowsell '10-year' first growth tasting was much looked forward to by Jancis Robinson and me. We were not disappointed. All the wines were within a point or so, Lafite level pegging with Margaux and Latour. The Lafite was still fairly deep, plummy coloured but maturing; bouquet evolving well; soft, fleshy, good length; complete – all that was needed was time, more bottle age. Its unreadiness for drinking was demonstrated at a Lafite dinner with Eric de Rothschild at Brooks's in London. The roast grey partridge was unable to compete. Nevertheless, the penetratingly lovely bouquet and flavour were appreciated. Strange though how a wine so beguiling and easy in its youth can close up. Its second wind eagerly awaited. *Last noted Nov 2000* ★★★(★★) *2015–2040?*

**Ch Latour** Fewer notes. Tasted at the château the same day as Lafite, the contrast was marked. Not an attractive and easy style the April after the vintage. Big and black; severe; teeth-blackening; very tannic. 'Magnificent' in 1993. At the MW tasting of '90s a year later, its nose had developed well; on the palate surprisingly sweet. In 1996, however, at the Eigensatz marathon, I noted its opaqueness and intensity; its full body and its raw tannin and acid finish. Yet later that year, tasted also blind, at a Rodenstock dinner alongside the other first growths, its bouquet I noted as earthy and spicy, opening up beautifully. Despite its tannin it had a delicious flavour, by no means the mammoth I would have expected. Most recently, also alongside all the first growths, I noted it as having wonderful depth and resonance; a classic, cedary Pauillac nose; some ripe sweetness, full flavoured, leathery, tannic texture, good length and dry finish. *Last noted at the Penning-Rowsells',* *June 2000* ★★★★(★) *Not a long-lasting '28 but a long haul, well balanced wine, say 2010–2030.*

**Ch Margaux** As many notes as Lafite. Crop thinning was severe in 1990 – 30% of the new vine grapes were culled. Also first tasted in April 1991. The usual intense purple, new oak, lean, stylish, supple. Two years later, at a Ch Margaux masterclass at Christie's: ripe, rounded, with raspberry-like aroma. Elegant. Impressive. Lovely fruit noted at the MW tasting (1994) and perfect balance (1995). Rather easy going when hemmed in by some of the New World big guns in Eigensatz's tasting of '90s (in 1996). Later that year, also blind, noting an almost Pomerol-like texture but touch of bitterness, its bouquet developing as only Margaux should (I nearly said 'can'), and wonderful fragrance in the mouth (blind again, 1998). But rather like the Lafite '90, though very fleshy, it was unready. Not even the charm of Corinne Mentzelopoulos, and certainly not the chicken consommé, could entice it fully out of its shell (Margaux dinner at Brooks's in London, April 2000). Five months later, at Manfred Wagner's vertical in Zurich: rich, biscuity nose, great depth; sweet, fleshy, full of fruit, excellent length. I rated the '89 fractionally higher. But the '90 was very good indeed and approaching cruising altitude. *Last tasted Nov 2000* ★★★—★★★★(★) *2010–2025*.

**Ch Mouton-Rothschild** In 1991 I preferred the '89 which, of course, had a head start, being a year older. Yet, a matter of two years after bottling it had generated an almost explosively rich, spicy nose; very sweet, full and packed with goodies. Leaping over the next two notes (poor bottles at the Eigensatz tasting), its bouquet was fully developed and its fine texture and length noted (Hollywood Wine Society Mouton presentation, 1998) and a further jump of two years to Penning-Rowsell's '10-year' tasting. Here, alongside its first growth peers, it was still fairly deep coloured; bouquet clamouring to get out, opening up rapturously, though I was too aware of the new oak spiciness – attractive but oak, like garlic, should be present but not overdone. Sweet, rich, lively, a touch of leanness and pinched tannin and acidity. Impressive but needs time. *Last noted June 2000* ★★★(★★) *2005–2020*.

**Ch Haut-Brion** In April 1991, this and the above first growths were each tasted at the respective châteaux. (One has to be there in person and by appointment. No use airily summoning a cask sample.) It was opaque, hard yet fragrant, fleshy and elegant. By the time I had got round to it there was little left at the MW tasting (Nov 1994) but what little there was, was lovely. Unmistakably Graves with its soft, earthy character. Also unmistakable at a Rodenstock tasting of first growth '90s: easy fruit, slightly sandy texture (1998). More recently, at the MW Haut-Brion tasting (January 2000): now medium-deep with a relaxed open mature rim; rich, chocolatey, mocha nose, opening up beautifully; sweet, soft, firmer than the '89, perfectly balanced with a rich, fragrant yet dry finish. Finally, at Penning-Rowsell's '10-year' tasting, very similar to the previous note. Surprisingly sweet, lovely flavour, shape and texture yet with life-supporting grip (my highest mark, with Margaux and Lafite). *Last tasted June 2000* ★★★★(★) *2005–2025*.

**Ch Ausone** Superb. Highly impressive tasting in April 1991 with Pascal Delbeck who knows exactly how to handle the idiosyncratic Ausone. Only two other notes. It did not fare too well in unsympathetic company, opening up 'flight' 7 at the Eigensatz tasting of '90s. It was up against Allegrini's La Poja from Italy, Lloyd Reserve Coriole Syrah from Australia and other outlandish but interesting wines – all tasted blind. It was good, however, despite 'nil votes'. In a far fairer context, at Penning-Rowsell's '10-year' first growth tasting, it was still an odd-man out. Now mature-looking; low-keyed, attractive bouquet; a soft, sweet entry, crisp, fragrant and a very dry 'autumnal' finish. *Last tasted June 2000* ★★(★★) *2005–2015*.

**Ch Cheval Blanc** Six notes, first at the château in April 1991, this time with all the 60 or so international wine journalists. A most attractive wine, perfectly balanced and easy to appreciate. Immediately forthcoming, very sweet, very rich – a glorious wine - at the MW '90s tasting in 1994. Similar note and showing well in relatively sympathetic company at the Eigensatz marathon though I rated Ch La Conseillante top, half a point higher (blind, 1996). Quite the best, easily 5 stars, at a Union des Grands Crus opening dinner in the spectacular underground cellars (lit by hundreds of candles) at Ch Villemaurine (1997). A magnum at the Wolf/Weinart vertical in 1997: deeper than the '89; a very sweet, open, slightly caramelly nose; sweet, full, rich (we were told it had a high percentage of Merlot) and with a very oaky finish. Most recently, a deep, velvety colour with mature rim; bouquet open and relaxed, perfect harmony; sweet, earthy, silky texture, spicy oak and good dry finish. *Last noted at the Penning-Rowsells', June 2000* ★★★★(★) *Soon–2015*.

**Ch Pétrus** First tasted from the cask in June 1991. Dense, full of fruit and flesh. Less tannic than the '89. Twelve months later, a week before bottling, a potential 5 stars. Next tasted blind, at the frequently mentioned Eigensatz tasting of 144 of the world's top '90s. It was in good company, including La Tâche, Pavillon Ermitage, Latour, La Turque (easily top of the 'flight') and so forth. It had nothing to be ashamed of. Coincidentally it was again set against La Turque in a Rodenstock 'flight' (also blind) of '90s in 1996. Only half a point separated them, the Pétrus tough and tannic. The following year at the Union des Grands Crus dinner, before Christie's best-ever one-owner sale: deep and velvety; full of fruit and flesh. Very impressive, very tannic. Most recently, the last of Eddie Penning-Rowsell's '10-year' first growth tasting of the '90s: still very deep; thick, chunky, fleshy nose but one could smell the sweaty tannins; fairly sweet, full, rich, complete but with a dry, rather coarse finish. Well, I suppose it is gilt-edged and will soften with time. A matter of taste. *Last noted June 2000* ★(★★★)? *2015–2025*.

---

## Walter Eigensatz

*A big man in all senses. A Swiss national and married to Karina, the proprietor of three clinics and the Hotel Eden Parc in Bad Schwalbach. I first met Walter at the Rodenstock tastings in the early 1970s and thereafter as a generous host in his own right. His tastings are in as grand a format as he is: the great 1893 and 1929 claret vintages, for example, were all in jeroboams; 'The 144 top 1990 red wines of the world', and, most recently, the fascinating White/Red events at Schloss Johannisberg and Bad Schwalbach.*

AN ALARMING NUMBER OF '90S TASTED, so I am afraid I shall have to be very selective, which will not make me too popular with some proprietors. Moreover, this book is not meant to be a gazetteer of every châteaux of every vintage. Apart from space consideration, it would be too mammoth a task, and not all that enlightening. In any case, some other wine writers and critics give fairly comprehensive coverage. Perhaps this is the moment to remind readers of my purpose: to demonstrate the progress of wines from cask to bottle, thence to maturity.

Except where otherwise stated, all the following wines were first noted in April 1991 at the annual Union des Grands Crus tastings which take place in each of the major Bordeaux districts over a concentrated four-day period.

**Ch L'Angélus** Very much a modern and up-front style of St-Émilion. Dark and tarry, 'black treacle' noted. On the other hand, it did show well at the Eigensatz worldwide '90s tasting: good fruit though not wholly knit; taut, crisp, fairly concentrated, with a biting tannic finish. *Last noted June 1996* ★★(★) *or 4 stars if it is to your taste.*

**Ch d'Armailhac** (Note the change of name from Mouton-Baronne-Philippe.) First tasted in June 1992: fruit still 'green'; yet surprisingly sweet, soft, rich and rounded. Seven years later: still a rich ruby; sweet, singed nose; agreeable weight (12.5% alcohol) and flavour. Still tannic. Most recently: now medium-deep, a soft, lovely colour with mature rim; an immediacy of bouquet, ripe, rich, leaping out of the glass; crisp, refreshing fruit, still sweet though finishing dry. *Last tasted, dining at home, Nov 2001* ★★★(★)

**Ch Batailley** My first note made in March 1994 shortly after buying a quantity, mainly in half bottles for casual drinking at home. (I do not just write about wine; my wife and I drink wine with every meal.) But it also featured in a Christie's Bordeaux wine course in 1997. No seven-year itch or hitch here: richly coloured; well put together nose, mellowing, reminding me of squashed, ripe raspberries; distinctly sweet, rich, fruity tannins present but unobtrusive. My stock soon ran out and my last note was made at a Distillers' Company lunch. Nice wine. *Last tasted June 1998* ★★★ *Drink soon.*

**Ch Beauséjour-Bécot** Mature. Drinking well. *March 2001* ★★★ *Drink soon.*

**Ch Beychevelle** Just four notes, first at a British Airways 'futures' tasting for Concorde: opaque; good depth of fruit on nose and palate. Fragrant, tannate of iron, oaky aftertaste. Most recently, still deep; wonderfully ripe fruit and flesh. Tannin not particularly noticeable. Very drinkable now. *Last noted at The Tasting Club's Beychevelle vertical, Oct 1997* ★★★★ *Now–2015.*

**Ch Canon-La-Gaffelière** Good wine. Still richly coloured, maturing; cedary, blackcurrant pastille nose; very sweet on the palate, high alcohol (14%), good fruit, dry finish. *Last noted at a Christie's Bordeaux wine course, March 1997* ★★★(★) *Now–2015.*

**Ch Cantenac-Brown** An extraordinary, almost sickly rich nose but good flavour and grip in the mid-1990s. Most recently, seemed a bit unyielding. *Last noted March 1998. I will settle for* ★★★ *Drink soon.*

**Dom de Chevalier** A good note in April 1991. Extra-dimensions. A Cabernet-dominated vintage. Crisp, surprisingly tannic in the mid-1990s. More recently, its bouquet like singed brown sugar; sweetish, soft yet with drying finish. Elegant. *Last tasted June 1996* ★★★(★) *Now–2015.*

**Ch Certan-de-May** Surprisingly mature looking for a seven-year old; pleasing, harmonious bouquet; misleadingly gentle entry but departing with a teeth-gripping tannic finish. Silky texture. *To represent the Pomerol district at a Bordeaux tasting at Lyford Cay in the Bahamas, Feb 1997* ★★(★★) *Probably ready now but a long life predicted.*

**Ch Clerc-Milon** Ripe, rustic, chunky fruit in 1994. Seven years later: medium-deep; the same 'rustic', farmyard smell reminding me of Ch Talbot, many-layered; very sweet, almost chocolatey on the palate, soft, chewy, aromatic, drinking well. *Last noted lunching at home, Nov 2001* ★★★★ *Now–2010.*

**Ch Clinet** In cask, black, malty, plummy. I didn't care for it. Two recent notes, the most detailed at a Christie's Bordeaux

wine course in March 1999: still deep, velvety; good ripe nose with strawberry-like fruit, yet strange; sweet, giving the impression of power though only 12.5% alcohol. A month later, lunching in Bordeaux, I found it very tannic. Really not my style of wine. *Last tasted April 1999. For those who are Clinet fans* ★★★(★) *Probably a long life.*

**Ch La Conseillante** Now this is my type of wine. Of course, in this vintage, opaque in cask but harmonious and classy. At the marathon blind tasting of the world's best '90s in 1996, I thought it had a lovely Pinot flavour – it turned out that 'flight' 10 was devoted to Merlot! Jumping over another good note to the most recent: still very deep; a huge, rich, fleshy mouthful, sweet, balanced. *Last noted dining at Ch de Malle, March 1999* ★★★★ *Now–2015.*

**Ch Cos d'Estournel** Sixteen months in 100% oak. First noted in March 1993: rich fruit, 'good future'. Next at the MW tasting of '90s in 1994: strong mocha, toasted, fragrance; lighter style than the Ch Montrose, attractive. Half a dozen subsequent notes. Starting to mature in the mid-1990s; touch of vanilla, exciting and delicious nose; its initial sweetness terminating in a swingeingly dry finish, but good, rich middle palate. In 1998, lively nose noted again, evolved, ginger and chocolate bouquet; attractive, with charm. 'Coming round'. Most recently, drinking well but tannic. *Last noted at the Knickerbocker Club, New York, Oct 2000* ★★★(★) *Now–2015.*

**Ch Ducru-Beaucaillou** First noted in October 1994 at a British Airways tasting for Concorde: opaque; unknit, slightly woody; full but severe – a long haul wine in both senses. Two months later, at the MW tasting, slight woodiness noted again but easier on the palate. At a pre-sale tasting in January 1999, still 'unknit', good body, tannic. Four months later, still deep and intense, but its cedary nose a bit raw, 'not on top form'. Nevertheless, on the palate quite shapely, 'well-mannered', but something missing. A rather disappointing Ducru. *Last noted at a tasting at the Richemond in Geneva, May 1999* ★★

**Ch L'Église-Clinet** Four notes, first in June 1996. Wedged between Spottswoode Cabernet Sauvignon and Le Pergole Torte at Eigensatz's blind tasting of '90s, I noted it as bland, with a touch of malt, then brown sugar; sweet, specious. Next, three months later at Rodenstock's first vertical 'flight', and at another in 1998. Happily my notes coincide: deep, intense plummy purple but starting to mature; rich, crisp fruit; fairly sweet, full, fleshy, dry finish. Most recently, at a Bordeaux Index Right Bank tasting: still with youthful good looks; touch of asparagus on the nose and 'unimpressive' – but it was tasted blind, between Ch La Fleur-Pétrus '89 and the wonderful Vieux Ch Certan '61. Nevertheless, it had a good flavour though a touch raw and very tannic on the finish. *Last tasted Nov 1999* ★★(★★)? *Needs time.*

**Ch L'Évangile** Three notes. A glorious, golden youth. So rich that one could almost spread it on toast (May 1991). Jumping another five years: maturing, elegant 'legs'; milk chocolate, vanillin nose; fleshy, good fruit, masked tannins. *Last tasted June 1996* ★★★★★ *Now–2015.*

**Ch de Fieuzal** In cask, April 1991, distinctive, smokey, oaky nose, good fruit and length. Next, though full and fleshy, tannic bitterness on the finish. (Daphne's birthday dinner at The Waterside Inn, Bray in 1998.) Most recently: still youthful; 'distinctive' noted again, a whiff of tangerine. Very good but desperately needs food. *Last noted dining at Gidleigh Park, Devon in April 2001* ★★★(★) *2005–2015.*

**Ch Figeac** A 5-star cask sample and four subsequent notes, the most recent at comparative tastings. Now fully mature with an open, relaxed, red-brown rim; soft, sweet, biscuity bouquet. No harsh edges. On the palate, sweet, fruity, a touch of earthiness, totally delicious. *Last noted at a France in Your Glass event at George Blanc's restaurant in Vonnas in Oct 1999* ★★★★★ *Now–2010.*

**Ch La Fleur** One note. Tasted blind, against competition. Medium deep, rich 'legs'; vegetal, cedar-like nose with strange underbelly; too sweet, earthy, very tannic. *At the Eigensatz marathon, June 1996. I suppose it will turn out well. Probably* ★★(★★) *now. Say 2008–2015.*

**Ch Le Gay** Are Fleur and Gay just good friends? Because at the blind tasting of Right Bank wines I noted a very strange vegetable smell and touch of spearmint. Attractive, slightly minty flavour, though lean with good length, dry finish. *Last noted at the Bordeaux Index tasting, Nov 1999* ★★(★★) *2006–2012.*

**Ch Gazin** Opaque, tannic in cask. One of the best wines at one of the most cold and miserable tastings I have ever conducted: very deep; very fragrant, lovely fruit and good texture (North Carolina, Oct 1995). Lovely at the 20th anniversary of *Decanter* lunch, 1997. Most recently, still deep; sweet, rich, meaty. *Last tasted lunching at Ch Yquem, June 1998* ★★★★ *Now–2012.*

**Ch Grand-Puy-Lacoste** Masses of notes. First admired at the MW tasting of '90s in 1994: sweet, glorious fruit, masked tannins. I had already bought several cases by then, but my next note was at a vertical tasting kindly arranged at the château in 1995 by Xavier Borie. After the '82, my highest mark of the range: opaque, intense, immature; intense fruit too on the nose, rich Cabernet Sauvignon, spicy; full of fruit, tannin and iron. Next, at the first-ever tutored wine tasting in South Korea (October 1995), the most impressive of the seven '90 Bordeauxs at the event. A wine which has all the component parts for the long haul. I recently opened a bottle just to see how it was getting on. Still hard and unyielding, a big contrast to the '89 we enjoyed at dinner the previous evening. *Last tasted at home, Sept 2001* ★(★★★★) *2010–2020.*

**Ch Haut-Bailly** First from a cask sample, then from the cask at the château in April 1991. Extraordinary scent; rich, taut, tannic, good fruit and length. Seven subsequent notes. In the mid-1990s, lovely flavour, texture and grip. I must have bought some for the next few notes were made dining at home in the late 1990s: starting to show maturity, but a rich, thick concentration of colour; lovely tarry, earthy Graves bouquet; full-flavoured, a dry, cutting finish. Most recently, a similar description: sweet, spicy, touch of leanness. Needs more time. *Last tasted April 2002* ★★★(★) *2005–2015.*

**Ch Labégorce-Zédé** Two notes, both in Belgium eight months apart. Perfect colour, fairly deep, convincing; fragrant, fruit, mellow; ripe, excellent fruit and balance. *Last tasted in Brussels, Nov 1999* ★★★(★) *Now–2010.*

**Ch Lafon-Rochet** Unknit, somewhat astringent at the MW tasting in 1994. The opening wine at my tutored tasting in South Korea: dark cherry; nose opened up well; fair fruit, lean, tannic. A bit meagre. *Last noted at the Hotel Shilla, South Korea, Oct 1995* ★★(★) *Now–2010.*

**Ch La Lagune** Also first noted in 1995 at the first tutored tasting in South Korea. It had travelled well. Spicy, tannic. More recently: deep, rich, well put together. Dry finish. *Last noted at the (excellent) restaurant Le St-Julien, in that commune, Sept 1998* ★★★(★) *Now–2010.*

**Ch Lanessan** A couple of notes: fairly deep and rich; herbaceous; some sweetness, attractive flavour, silky tannins. *Last noted at a blind tasting of 1990s in Bordeaux, May 1995* ★★(★)

**Ch Larcis-Ducasse** I was pretty unfamiliar with this château, situated on the lower slopes below St-Émilion, until I stayed there. At dinner we were served with the '90 which impressed me, to the extent that on leaving I found a magnum in my car which I disposed of agreeably at a wine dinner at home six months later. It was rich, wholesome, crisp, delicious. Most recently, drinking well at a Union des Grands Crus reception and dinner. *Last noted in the chais at Ch d'Yquem, March 2001* ★★★ *Ready now.*

**Ch Lascombes** Five notes: showing well at a British Airways tasting for Concorde in October 1994, and ripe, very sweet, chunky fruit a month later. Most recently showing some age; drinking well but unexciting. *Last noted lunching with journalists at Ch Talbot, April 2000* ★★★ *Drink soon.*

**Ch Latour-à-Pomerol** Showing only moderately well in mixed company (Eigensatz's monumental tasting of 1990s in 1996) but the following year, hugely impressive in an equally impressive *impériale*: thick looking; sweet, meaty, harmonious but static bouquet; sweet, full-bodied, rich, fleshy. *Last noted hosting a Christie's wine dinner at the Übersee Club, Hamburg, June 1997* ★★★★ *Now–2010.*

**Ch Léoville-Barton** First tasted April 1993: lovely colour, excellent potential. Showing well at the MW tasting in 1994: rich, good balance and flavour. Six subsequent notes. Of the more recent: harmonious, no harsh edges despite tannic finish. Perfect weight (12.5% alcohol), at a France in Your Glass Bordeaux tasting at Vonnas (1999). The following year: deep ruby; 'classic'; remarkably good with the 'Wild Duck Paprika' (Bordeaux Club at Childerley Hall). Not showing at its best at Christie's Three Léovilles tasting in March 2001: old oak, fag ends and singed brown paper. Hopefully, definitely, untypical for it was most impressive seven months later: deep but mature looking; sweet, classic nose evolving richly; equally sweet on the palate, complete, its richness masking the tannins. *Last noted at the château, Oct 2001* ★★★(★) *2008–2020.*

**Ch Léoville-Las-Cases** First tasted at the château in June 1992: deep; dumb; sweet fruit, high extract, oaky. High marks at the MW tasting in 1994. More than holding its own at the blind tasting of 1990s in Luzern in 1996: fragrant, silky texture. Most recently: wonderfully deep, rich but mature (needed decanting); restrained but harmonious; a powerful, fleshy wine, tannins both silky *and* swingeing. *Last noted at Christie's Three Léovilles tasting, March 2001* ★★★(★★) *2010–2030.*

**Ch Léoville-Poyferré** First tasted at the château, June 1992: very deep; too much oak; very tannic. Different, though with identical marks to the Léoville-Barton at the MW tasting (1994). In 1999: intense, velvety; blackcurrant fruitiness, lovely, spicy, great depth; the sweetness of ripe grapes and alcohol (13%), good length. Still very deep but maturing nicely; similar notes on nose and palate. Sweet yet swingeingly tannic on the finish. Yet I added 'perfect' and 'good future'. *Last noted at Christie's Three Léovilles tasting, March 2001* ★★★(★★) *2010–2025.*

**Ch La Louvière** An agreeable cask sample in April 1991. 'An easy early developer'. Holding well though. Richly coloured; mature nose; sweetish. Soft, attractive, *à point. Last noted lunching at Ch Smith-Haut-Lafitte, March 2001* ★★★ *Drink soon.*

**Ch Lynch-Bages** Fragrant and spicy at the MW tasting in 1994. Nine very consistent subsequent notes, except for one corked bottle, through the mid- to late 1990s. The opening vintage of a Lynch-Bages vertical (for the '33 Club, Brussels, 1995): deep, rich, velvety; sweet nose and taste; firm, crisp, mulberry-like ripe fruit, perfect balance. The highest number of votes in its 'flight' – all top 1990s from around the world

(Luzern, 1996). Honeysuckle scent; very attractive flavour and texture (at the Maison du Cygne, Brussels, 1997). Most recently, still deeply coloured; a whiff of menthol; good flesh and flavour. *Last tasted at the château, May 2001* ★★★(★) *Soon–2015.*

**Ch La Mission Haut-Brion** First tasted at the château, April 1991: opaque; lovely fruit, depth; crisp, very good length, great potential. Sweet, recognisably Graves, earthy, singed (blind tasting of '90s in 1996). By 1999 no longer intense, maturing well; taut, singed nose; impressive, masculine, teeth-gripping tannins. Most recently, decanted 5.45pm, first noted at 7.15pm: deep, rich, opaque core; earth and iron. By 8.45pm it was 'showing its all': fairly sweet, rich, touch of iron, dry finish, drinking well. Two hours later, the remains in my glass exuded a soft, rich mocha. *Last noted at Neil McKendrick's Bordeaux Club dinner at Caius, Cambridge in June 2000* ★★★★(★) *Now if you like, but better 2010–2025.*

**Ch Montrose** Only two notes. At the MW tasting in 1994 I noted a sweet, cheesy, distinctively manure-like nose; powerful, packed with fruit, tannin and acidity. Two years later at the blind tasting of top 1990s from around the world, I gave it my lowest mark of the 144 wines for, despite its deep, velvety appearance, I disliked intensely its barnyard smell and taste. It was not just one bottle; I went round the room sniffing all six bottles. Others marked it modestly too. Yet it has been given critical accolades. It must have been going through a sick period. I keep meaning to retaste it. *Last noted June 1996 rating?*

**Ch Les Ormes-de-Pez** Opaque core, struggling without avail to mature. Nose, unknit, raw. Swingeingly tannic. Would have been better with food. *Tasted in the chai at Ch Lynch-Bages, May 2001* (★★★)? *2008–2015.*

**Ch Palmer** Cask sample in April 1991, and in June tasted at the château. It clearly had great potential: deep, sweet, soft fruit, good length and soft tannins. Also showing well at the MW tasting of '90s (in 1994): attractive, fragrant. The following year, in Brussels, though good, the Ch Pichon-Lalande was more impressive. At the mammoth tasting of '90s in Luzern, it was top equal with Ch Haut-Brion in a 'flight' which included Ornellaia and two excellent California Cabernets, Grace Vineyards and Dunn. At a Christie's wine course tasting of '90s in 1999 I noted it as 'a charmer but relatively light weight', Daphne then spotting that its alcoholic strength was a modest 12%. Two subsequent notes made within a couple of days: still fairly deep and intense, with rich 'tears' or 'legs'; nose noted, twice, as 'cheesy', rich, chocolatey; 'incredibly sweet' on the palate, lots of fruit, spice – lovely to drink by itself. In fact, it accompanied 'Warm confited Trelough duck salad'. *Last noted at a Farr Vintners' Mähler-Besse luncheon at Ransome's Dock, London in Feb 2001* ★★★★ *Now–2015.*

**Ch Pape-Clément** At the first tasting in April 1991 we were informed that because of irregular ripening, great care had had to be taken to sort out the grapes. Vats were 'bled', removing 12% of the juice. Opaque, impressive, more Médoc than Graves in style, its 75% new oak giving the wine a spicy, tannic finish. Rather conflicting notes in the mid-1990s: sweet, earthy, delicious at a blind tasting of 35 '90s (in Bordeaux 1995), but though there was considerable concentration and good fruit, it led to a bitter end. *Last tasted, also blind, in June 1996. Should have softened a little by now. Say* ★★★(★) *2006–2015.*

**Ch Pichon-Baron** Ten notes over a period of five years. Very deep and very sweet, but with an easy style despite its richness at the MW tasting in 1994. Several notes in the mid-1990s, contexts varying. It seemed full and austere in a mixed 'flight'

of '90s Cabernets in 1996, 'rather tarry' noted several times, even 'creosote and liquorice' alongside Ch Lynch-Bages the following year. My most detailed note made at a Christie's wine course tasting of '90s in March 1999. Briefly, still looking mouthfillingly deep, its crisp black-fruit aroma opening up voluptuously. Very fruity yet with good grip, 'needs six more years'. All the wines in this tasting had been purchased from Farr Vintners. The Baron cost £65 a bottle, the same as Palmer. Poyferré was £62, La Mission £75 and Clinet £85. *Last tasted lunching at the Mairie in Bordeaux, April 1999* ★★★(★) *2005–2020.*

**Ch Pichon-Lalande** First tasted in cask, Oct 1991: opaque; beautifully ripe fruit and flesh. Always interesting to taste and compare these neighbouring rivals, the opposite side of the road, literally and metaphorically. Alongside the Baron at the MW tasting (1994), much less deep in colour, with attractive mocha-like fruit on nose and palate. Delicious. Also lower in alcohol, 12.5% as opposed to 13%. Several other notes, with continual references to mocha, and in a variety of contexts, at Lyford Cay in February 1996 – bought from Zachy's, list price $59.95. Showing well at the Frankfurt tasting later that year: beautiful nose, great depth; a fleshy and exuberant wine. Most recently: still very deep but mature looking; coffee, ginger and wholemeal nose with flavour to match. But still tannic. *Last noted at a France in Your Glass tasting at Les Prés d'Eugénie, Sept 2000* ★★★★(★) *Now–2015.*

**Ch Pontet-Canet** I dislike this wine intensely. Six notes: 'unknit nose, horrible tarry taste' in 1994; rich, curious, tarry (1995); musky nose, dry, austere, 'very odd flavour', touch of tar and farmyard with a terrible iron finish. This was on a British Airways flight to Miami in 1999. But it was very popular and there was not a bottle left (I had been upgraded to first class!). Four months later 'an unpleasant tarry taste'. *Last noted, ironically, at the Fête de la Fleur dinner at the château, June 1999.*

**Ch Prieuré-Lichine** One of the best-ever Prieurés. Crisp, purple fruit in April 1991. Most recently, from a 14-litre balthazar, still virtually opaque, rich, harmonious bouquet; sweet and fleshy. *At the Decanter millennium dinner at Vinopolis in London, July 1999* ★★★★ *Now–2015.*

**Ch Rausan-Ségla** Half a dozen notes starting with an impressive cask sample in April 1991: opaque; rich fruit; elegant, good texture. Evolving steadily over the 1990s with particularly sweet, fleshy, 'fabulous' bottles served at a Rauzan-Ségla dinner at Brooks's in London hosted by David Orr in 1995. Two more recent tastings, now relatively forward, soft and chewy. Well balanced. Nice to drink by itself. *Last noted at Eugénie-les-Bains, Sept 2000* ★★★★ *Now–2015.*

**Ch Sénéjac** A family estate at Le Pian in the Haut-Médoc taken over by Comte Charles de Guigné in 1973. Decent wine though a bit astringent. A handy Leclerc supermarket nearby to fill the car's tank with low-price fuel. *May 1999* ★★

**Ch Smith-Haut-Lafitte** First tasted in April 1991: soft fruit but seemed to lack length. Over half a dozen notes since. Chunky, complete (1995). Later the same year: some of the firmness of the Médoc, the delicacy of Margaux. But this was in Seoul! Fragrant, sweet, ripe, pleasant (at Vonnas, 1999). Most recently, an impressive magnum. Lovely colour, still deep; spicy, scented; sweet, mouthfilling, with good fruit and extract. *Last noted at a Smith-Haut-Lafitte masterclass for the Chaîne des Rôtisseurs at the château, June 2000. I gave it an over-generous* ★★★(★★) *but, a truer perspective would be* ★★★(★)

**Ch Sociando-Mallet** A newly-fashionable *bourgeois* Médoc first noted at one of Rodenstock's blind tastings tucked, wickedly, between the '90 Mouton and Haut-Brion. I didn't know what it was but it was my lowest mark of the 'flight'. Next, at a Farr Vintners' tasting in 1999: strange, interesting, sweet but, I thought, trying too hard. The following year, in Hamburg, harmonious, impressive but unsubtle. Most recently, tasted at David Peppercorn's insistence: certainly rising well above its class, in a rather modern way but I prefer real Médocs to Pomerol-style Médocs. *Last noted also at Farr Vintners in the customarily cramped conditions, Oct 2001* ★★★(★)

**Ch La Tour-de-By** I asked the distinguished but reticent owner, Marc Pagès what the rosette was in his lapel: '*Croix de Guerre*' he replied. I first bought this wine from James Seely: it was so reasonably priced, I have had most vintages since. Half a dozen consistent notes of the '90, mainly at home. Rich fruit, lovely flavour, extract coping with new oak. *Last tasted at lunch at the Mairie in Bordeaux, April 1999* ★★★ *Drink now–2010.*

**Ch La Tour-Carnet** A chronically underperforming classed growth but quite a good '90. Several somewhat unenthusiastic notes, its sweet nose better than palate. Not a big wine (12% alcohol). Touch of oak and austerity. *Last tasted Feb 1998* ★(★) *Might as well drink up.*

OTHER WINES LAST TASTED IN THE MID-1990S

**Ch Patache d'Aux** Just goes to show that there are many other useful clarets below the rank of classed growth. First tasted blind and showing well at an extensive British Airways wine tasting in 1994: deep, already maturing; ripe nose; good flavour, body, length, and 'some elegance'. We selected it for Club World and I next came across it the following autumn, heading for New York on BA 117. Happily, still showing well. Attractive though still tannic. More recently, tasted in a different 'Club' connection: lunch at Pratt's Club in St James's with the managers and secretaries of 'The Distinguished Clubs of the World' following a tasting of top clarets I conducted for them at the 'true blue' Carlton Club. Definitely a good 'club claret' though still somewhat immature. *Last tasted Oct 1997* ★★(★) *Despite its tannin, best drunk while still holding its fruit.*

**Ch Pavie** A ripe, well-balanced cask sample tasted in April 1991. Showing well, nose opening up richly, with good silky tannins at the MW tasting, 1994. Soft, darkish cherry colour starting to show some maturity though contradicted by its dry, somewhat bitter, tannic finish. Good, raspberry-like fruit on the nose, spicy too (at the tasting for Goldman Sachs at Christie's in Frankfurt, 1995). It performed far better with food. Lean for a '90, refreshing, ending sweetly. *Last noted at the opening Union des Grands Crus dinner in the caves of Ch Villemaurine, April 1997* ★★★

**Ch de Pez** Another well made and usually very dependable *cru exceptionnel* and showing its paces in this vintage. Sweet, rich, attractive nose, and all one needs on the palate. *Noted at a pre-sale tasting, April 1996* ★★★ *Now–2010.*

**Ch Plince** Four notes, its plausible, fragrant nose and soft fruitiness accompanied by bitter tannins. *Last tasted 1996* ★★(★)

**Ch Le Pin** My second highest mark in a 'flight' which included Ch Pétrus, Latour, La Fleur and La Tâche at the world's top '90s blind tasting in June 1996: sweet, lovely nose, perfect weight and flavour, well integrated tannins and acidity (Guigal's La Turque beat it by half a point). Later that year, showing well but again trounced by La Turque and another Hermitage wine, Ermitage Le Pavillon. *Last noted at a Rodenstock blind tasting, Sept 1996* ★★★★ *Now–2012.*

**Ch Talbot** Three notes. An attractive, even exciting wine. Agreeably drinkable in 1995. Lovely colour; sweet, chewy, with almost '82 extract. *Last noted at Ch Villemaurine, April 1997* ★★★(★) *Now–2012.*

**Ch Tertre-Roteboeuf** Spicy oak; sweet, soft, chewy. *Last tasted Sept 1996* ★★★★ *Now–2012.*

**Ch Troplong-Mondot** Appealing in its youth. Not at all bad, with good brambly-fruit but outclassed at two recent blind tastings. *Last tasted Sept 1996* ★★(★) *Drink soon.*

**Ch Trottevieille** Three notes. On Christmas Day in 1996 despite double-decanting, 'needed air'. It certainly got it, for it was next drunk picnicking with the family at Badminton. A fairly decent, drinkable wine, no more. *Last tasted watching the equestrian 'eventers' at Badminton, May 1997* ★★(★★)

THE FOLLOWING WERE TASTED BETWEEN NOVEMBER 1994 AND JANUARY 1995 (the stars indicating the quality and potential) **Ch d'Angludet** easy style ★★(★); **Ch Branaire-Ducru** good fruit ★★(★) plus?; **Ch Brane-Cantenac** very attractive ★★(★★); **Ch Calon-Ségur** positive, mouthfilling ★★★★; **Ch Canon** attractive ★★★, *possibly* ★★★★; **Ch Cantemerle** plausibly attractive ★★(★★); **Ch Duhart-Milon** lean, fruity, very tannic ★(★★) plus?; **Ch Giscours** rich fruit. Lighter style than expected ★★(★); **Ch Grand-Puy-Ducasse** ★★(★); **Ch Gruaud-Larose** glorious fruit. Long finish ★★★(★); **Ch Haut-Batailley** sweet, easy, charming ★★★; **Ch d'Issan** fragrant, charming ★★★(★); **Ch Kirwan** deep, rich, tannic ★★(★); **Ch Lagrange** (St-Julien) good fruit ★(★★); **Ch Langoa-Barton** firm ★★★; **Ch Loudenne** usually weak and uninspiring. The best ever ★★★; **Ch Malartic-Lagravière** light style, lacking length, edgy ★★; **Ch Malescot-St-Exupéry** fragrant, herbaceous, crisp fruit ★★(★) (*just*); **Ch Marquis de Terme** some richness. Tannic ★(★)?; **Ch Millet** (Graves) very attractive. Early developer ★★★; **Ch Olivier** soft, fruity. Early developer ★★★; **Ch Petit-Village** rich. Tannic ★★(★★); and **Ch Siran** very fragrant. Light style though tannic ★(★★)

THE FOLLOWING WERE TASTED ONLY ONCE, in June 1992, but showed good potential: **Ch La Fleur-Pétrus** curious style, delicious flavour (★★★★); **Ch La Grave-Trigant** ripe, rural, distinctive (★★★★); and **Ch Magdelaine** very distinctive character, crisp fruit, good length (★★★★)

# 1991 ★ to ★★

This was something of a comedown after the magnificent 1990 vintage, thanks to the vagaries of Bordeaux's weather. January and February were dry, with a few days of frost and snow which did not affect the dormant vines. March was also dry and mild, encouraging growth. The first major setback took place in April, for though the month was mainly mild, with average rainfall, a severe frost hit the region on the nights of the 21st and 22nd, the temperature plummeting to -8°C. Vines were frozen, new shoots destroyed overnight. The immediate and long-term effect was seriously to reduce the crop. It would be a small harvest.

The cold continued into May. The first half of June was reasonably warm and dry, the second half wet. This delayed and extended an uneven flowering. July was hot but rainy, causing rot worries. August was dry and hot – the hottest August since 1926 – to the extent that there was hope of a repeat of 1961 – small, ripe, concentrated grapes. Alas, towards the end of that otherwise encouraging September, eight days of rain before the harvest dashed these high hopes.

From time to time I have noticed a tendency to blame the châteaux in Bordeaux for making less than top-class wine when, as I have stated over and over again, the vagaries of a maritime climate are the chief culprit. The Gironde is not like hotter regions such as California, the Cape or the Hunter Valley – thank goodness. For would it not be tedious – for the intelligent consumer – for every Bordeaux vintage to score 90-plus? Surely variety is the spice of life, and this one great region produces wines of infinite styles and quality – and price; wines for drinking not for medals.

Though I have not tasted many, I have found the '91 a useful vintage. Wines to drink now while waiting for the '95s and the big guns, '89s and '90s to mature. Most of the following notes were made at the MW tasting of '91s at Painters' Hall in London, November 1995.

**Ch Lafite** First noted at the MW tasting of '91s in November 1995: a not very deep ruby; gentle, fragrant, concealing, some depth; surprisingly sweet, light style, lean, attractive. One of my highest marks of the tasting. More recently, a magnum served at a dinner party at home: still an attractive ruby; crisp fruit; some sweetness, pleasing flavour, tannins and acidity. It sounds very condescending, even arch, to repeat that I found it 'really remarkably drinkable'. *Last noted Dec 2000* ★★(★) *Now–2010.*

**Ch Latour** November 1995: richly coloured; strange, 'medicinal', very alcoholic nose; cedar and fruit, taste reminiscent of oak bark, great length. Next, cedar noted again; sweet, very pleasant flavour; ready now despite its grip. *Last noted at the château, Sept 1998* ★★★ *Now–2015.*

**Ch Margaux** The potential spoiled by rain. Small crop, 18hl/ha, picked quickly at the beginning of the rainy period. In November 1995: fairly deep; good depth; medium sweetness and body. Very attractive fruit. Relatively high mark. Five years later: starting to mature; nose initially chocolatey but within 30 minutes had opened up fragrantly; later a touch of tar and caramel, and after two hours in the glass, completely faded. Decent flavour, reasonably complete, drinking quite well. *Last tasted at Wagner's vertical, Nov 2000* ★★★ *(just).*

**Ch Mouton-Rothschild** Philippine de Rothschild asked me if I would write some notes for the new edition of the Mouton labels book and sent bottles to taste. The 5-cm cork was too hard and crumbly for my Screwpull so I had to use the broad-bladed corkscrew I normally reserve for old corks. On the nose a bit stalky, some spice, opening up a little. On the palate more depth than I had expected. Overall lean and dry (tasted February 1995). Only nine months later, a much better note at the MW tasting. Nose much more evolved, rich, gingery; quite powerful, surprising tannins and acidity. Two years later: a luminous cherry red; singed, biscuity, mocha nose; crisp, quite good with veal which ameliorated the slightly better finish. *Last noted hosting a Christie's dinner at the Übersee Club, Hamburg, June 1997* ★★★ *(just). Drink fairly soon.*

**Ch Haut-Brion, Ch Ausone, Ch Cheval Blanc** Not tasted.

**Ch Pétrus** Below standard in 1991 and so not marketed.

OTHER 1991s, MORE RECENT NOTES

**Ch Duhart-Milon** The opening wine, dining at Ch Lafite: lean, quite good fruit, coping manfully with *homard Breton, Sauce Don Carlo*, but not half as interesting as the company, the Anthony Bartons, Mark Birley, Lynne Guinness, the Palumbos, Serena and Nicholas Soames. *Hosted by Eric de Rothschild, Sept 1998* ★★ *Drink soon.*

**Ch L'Église-Clinet** Fairly deep, starting to mature; very pleasant fruit; more body and flesh than expected. Good dry finish. Stephen Browett (of Farr Vintners) told us that it was originally 60 francs a bottle but no-one wanted to buy it. It certainly went well with air-dried ham, leek and white truffle oil vinaigrette. *With Denis Durantou at Farr Vintners' 'A night in Pomerol heaven', July 1998* ★★★ *Drink soon.*

**Les Forts de Latour** Fairly deep, mature rim; sweet, easy, very drinkable. *At the château, Sept 1998* ★★★ *Drink soon.*

**Ch Grand-Puy-Lacoste** I have been tucking into the '91 for some time. However, I did not actually taste it until June '95 when, at the château, Xavier Borie laid on a tasting of ten vintages. It was already evolving well; nose very forthcoming, lean, 'medicinal', herbaceous; sweet, medium full body, easy fruit and flavour. Later that autumn, drinking pretty well (at home) though I decided to leave it for a bit. Next drinking it at lunch in August 2000, it seemed remarkably deep and youthful; chunky, good fruit, firmer than many '93s. Several more bottles enjoyed at lunches and dinners, showing more maturity, 'muffled' though with a well developed Cabernet nose. Most recently, opened for lunch in the country to see how it was coming along. Happily drinking well. Sweet and rich for a '91. Good fruit. *Last noted Sept 2001* ★★★(★) *A seriously good '91. Now–2012.*

**Ch Haut-Bages-Averous** A dependable Cazes wine. Attractive fruit, firm, a touch of iron. *Sept 1996* ★★★ *Drink now.*

**Ch Labégorce** A lot of money has been spent here. Perhaps as well. Already mature; a rather woolly scented nose and taste. *Served at lunch at Ch Chasse-Spleen, March 2001* ★★ *Drink up.*

**Ch Labégorce-Zédé** A different ball game. The opening wine of a tasting of Thienpont (a Belgian family) wines, appropriately served at the hotel and catering college in Bruges. Flattering to have a packed audience of professors and alumni, but the lighting was not good. Initially low-keyed, the nose opened up with a cedary Margaux fragrance, then like singed coffee. Touch of fruit, medium weight, refreshing acidity, with a bitterness on the finish that would not have been noticed with food. *Nov 1999* ★★ *Drink soon.*

**Ch Léoville-Barton** Medium-deep, weak-rimmed, maturing; a trifle medicinal, crisp fruit, opened up with a leafy but lean fragrance; medium-dry, light style, lean, refreshing bordering on astringency, dry finish. *At the château (Langoa), Oct 2001* ★★ *For drinking not keeping.*

**Ch Léoville-Las-Cases** Offered in 1994 by Sichel & Co for Concorde. It was very impressive for an unfashionable vintage and the offer was taken up. I see that I tasted it the following year, flying to New York. Stylish. Well balanced. Alas not tasted since the MW tasting of '91s: a really good classic, cedary nose; intriguing flavour, but lean. *Last noted Nov 1995* ★★★ *Should be very drinkable now.*

**Ch Lynch-Bages** Just one brief note. Very good colour, crisp fruit. *At an Anthony Byrne tasting, April 1995* ★★? *Should be a decent drink now.*

**Ch Marsan** Consisting mainly of the de-classified Ch La Fleur-Pétrus, whose production had been reduced to some 650 cases from the normal 3500. It is said that it included some Pétrus but Christian Moueix has not confirmed this. A one-off. Youthful, intense, a bit corky; crisp fruit but very tannic. *Lunching at Corney & Barrow, Nov 1995. A curiosity. Drink soon?*

**Ch Palmer** Showing well at the MW tasting of '91s in 1995: ruby; superficially attractive nose; fairly penetrating flavour. More recently, maturing; sweet, spicy, oaky nose; nice fruit, reasonable extract, lightish weight (12% alcohol), good acidity.

_Last noted at a tasting to promote Meine Lieblingsweine in Mannheim, Germany, April 1998_ ★★ _Drink soon._

**Ch Phélan-Ségur** Never a great St-Estèphe but the '91 was surprisingly agreeable and drinking well. _At the Union des Grands Crus lunch at the Mairie in Bordeaux, April 1995_ ★★ _For drinking not keeping._

**Ch Pichon-Baron** Only one note. 'A bit thin and unimpressive'. _An ungracious note made at lunch after a Cazes tasting at the Cavalry Club, London in April 1996_ ★★

**Ch Pichon-Lalande** Three fairly recent notes, all made at the château. First at a buffet lunch following a tasting of '98 Pauillacs in March 1999. Already with mature colour and nose; distinctly sweet, singed, chewy. Next at dinner in June 2000 around the time of May de Lenquesaing's 75th birthday. 'Chocolatey, surprisingly sweet'. Most recently; ruby sheen; more classic and cedary than expected; drinking well though a touch of iron and tannin. _Last noted at dinner with May and her nephew Gildas d'Ollone, March 2001_ ★★★ _Now–2010._

**Ch Le Pin** An _impériale_, the only one made, brought by Jacques Thienpont and his wife Fiona, née Morrison – a MW. It had two hours to settle before being served at a dinner following my tasting of Thienpont wines at La Maison du Cygne in Brussels. The wine was remarkably deep for a '91, with opaque core; a curious nose, a touch of 'virol' (the malty restorative). I well recall the pre-war advertising placard 'Virol. Anaemic girls need it'. On the palate, rich, fleshy but a stringy finish. Still, it was a rare treat. My colleague David Elswood then auctioned the empty bottle for _Docteurs sans Vacances. In Brussels, March 1999. Probably_ ★★★

**Ch La Tour-de-By** Our everyday (more or less) claret at home, mainly consumed between 1994 and 1998, though I have a few bottles left. I do not usually make a detailed note, just the date. It's for drinking not discussion. Briefly: ruby; surprisingly sweet on nose and palate, attractive fruit. Touch of tannic bitterness. _Last noted at Sunday lunch at Chippenham Lodge, May 1998_ ★★

THE FOLLOWING '91S WERE LAST NOTED at the MW tasting of '91s in November 1995, unless otherwise stated (with rough and ready star rating at the time):

**Ch Beauséjour-Duffau-Lagarosse** ★★; **Ch Beychevelle** very forthcoming, fragrant nose, easy, oaky style ★★★; **Ch Branaire-Ducru** very forthcoming, touch of caramel; intriguing flavour, lean, lightish style ★★; **Ch Brane-Cantenac** open, developed, spicy, tender dry finish ★★★; **Ch Cantenac-Brown** chocolatey; dry, lean, tannic ★★; **Ch Dauzac** easy style. Flavoury. New oak ★★; **Ch Desmirail** chaptalised. Sweet, light. Short ★; **Ch Ducru-Beaucaillou** very attractive fruit and flavour ★★★; **Ch Durfort-Vivens** lean ★; **Ch La Fleur-de-Gay** sweet, full, rich, fruity. Very oaky ★★; **Ch Giscours** curious nose, attractive fruit. Light style ★★★; **Ch Gruaud-Larose** deep, velvety; rich, rustic; packed with fruit. A good '91 ★★★; **Ch d'Issan** classic nose; good fruit. Very oaky ★★★; **Ch Langoa-Barton** classic, cedary; soft fruit, nice weight, very attractive ★★★; **Ch Lagrange** (St-Julien) fragrant, cedar, slightly stalky; dry, spicy, new oak, lean ★★; **Ch Marquis d'Alesme-Becker** sweet but raw ★; **Ch Pavie** rich, chewy, nice fruit ★★★; **Ch Petit-Village** ★; **Ch Prieuré-Lichine** ★★; **Ch Rauzan-Gassies** chaptalised, easy, screwed-up finish ★; **Ch St-Pierre** very spicy, new oak; nice weight and flavour. Lightish style ★★; and **Ch Talbot** rich, full of fruit, a good '91 ★★★

## 1992 ★

Highly respected, wise and experienced, the late Peter Sichel observed in his early report on the vintage: 'Thirty years ago 1992 would have been a disaster'. Rot control, costly and time-consuming elimination of unripe and unhealthy grapes, severe selection of vats and more recent technical winemaking advances enabled the well-run châteaux to make consumable wine after execrable growing and harvesting conditions: the wettest summer for over half a century, rainfall roughly double the average (and well in excess of 1987 or 1984) and the fewest hours of sunshine since 1980. But the rot, almost literally, had set in earlier. Heavy rains in June delayed and extended flowering, leading ultimately to uneven ripening. Finally, weather conditions before and during the harvest were well below average, the soil saturated, grapes diluted and with uneven ripeness. The Merlot suffered least, Cabernet Sauvignon most. Overall production in Bordeaux was even higher than the previous all-time record, 1990. But there the comparisons end.

**Ch Lafite** Just one note: an odd magnum taken on Christmas Eve to my daughter and son-in-law's and consumed at lunch on Christmas Day. It had a light sediment so I decanted it at 11.15am into an open jug to give it plenty of air. The family were eventually seated around 2.30pm. Not deep, maturing; a bricky sort of nose which survived the crackers and sparklers; a light, chaptalised and refreshing drink. _At Saintsburyhill Farm, Dec 1999_ ★★ _(just). Drink up._

**Ch Latour** Knowing Latour's reputation for making good wine in a bad year, their '92 should be better than average. Alas, I have not yet put it to the test.

**Ch Margaux** Two notes, both made at Manfred Wagner's verticals. First in 1997. Weak rimmed; loose knit, vegetal, some delicacy, opened up sweetly; softer than expected but lean and lacking fruit. Three years later its nose faded in the glass, touch of liquorice, unknit; semi-sweet chaptalised taste, short and raw. _Last tasted Nov 2000_ ★ _(just)._

**Ch Mouton-Rothschild** In February 1995, I was sent a bottle to annotate for the updated book of Mouton labels. An even shorter cork than the '91. Clearly no point in using what the trade used to call 'long longs' for a vintage not destined for a long life in the cellar. Plummy purple; a brambly Cabernet aroma, quite sweet on nose but its nasal trajectory, to use a clumsy expression, was relatively short-lived. It had a lightish, fruity style, quite attractive. Lean. Oak on the finish and very tannic. The following year it was handed out on trays to the audience at my auction talk with the witty and sparky Philippine de Rothschild. The wine was deeper than expected, still youthful looking. Both nose and palate raw at first and very tannic – in short, not an ideal wine to serve without food but towards the end of our duologue, it had opened up and sweetened into a refreshing drink. _Last noted at Christie's, Park Avenue, Dec 1996_ ★(★) _Drink while still refreshing._

**Ch Haut-Brion** Deeper and somewhat richer looking than I expected; quite good fruit; touch of sweetness but with a curious, rough, chewy texture and noticeable acidity. _At Anthony Byrne's tasting, April 1995_ ★ _Drink up._

**Ch Cheval Blanc** A magnum at the Wolf/Weinart vertical in Austria. We were informed that it had rained throughout the harvest which finished 9 October. Medium, already well developed colour; curious nose, touch of chocolate; dry, spicy new oak laid bare, hardly recognisable as Cheval Blanc. _Sept 1997, scarcely_ ★ _Drink up._

**Ch Pétrus** In a blind 'flight' of five magnums, four top Right Bank Bordeauxs, the fifth Chapoutier's Ermitage Le Pavillon. It was later revealed that wine No 1 was Pétrus. It had what I often describe as a 'Parker 100' depth of colour; nose hefty, peppery, with a touch of stalkiness; initially dry and surprisingly complete, crisp and tannic. Though severe, it sweetened up with the food. *'Flight' 2 at Rodenstock's dinner in Munich, Sept 1996 (★★) A good '92 but future hard to predict.*

OTHER SIGNIFICANT '92S

**Ch d'Armailhac** First noted at a British Airways blind tasting in December 1994: deep, youthful; crisp fruit, vanillin; pleasant flavour, complete, stylish but astringent. A year later, a similar note at an extensive blind tasting which included ten '92s. Another 12 months elapsed: still deep and youthful but unpleasantly raw. The tough breast of Norfolk duck did not help. *Last noted at a Wine Trade Benevolent Society dinner at Vintners' Hall, London, Nov 1996 ★ beyond the first flush of youth, now a pimply adolescent.*

**Ch Calon-Ségur** Spicy, chocolatey nose; quite good fruit and texture. The finish questionable. *Last tasted, blind, Nov 1995 ★★ Drink soon.*

**Ch Cantemerle** First noted at the extensive Union des Grands Crus tasting in London in April 1994. An average mark: not bad colour; dull nose; medium body and fruit. Next, at a blind tasting of 64 clarets, including many '92s and '93s. It showed rather better: decent colour; oaky, brambly, slightly 'stewed' nose and taste. A fairly big wine. It was short-listed with three other '93s. *Last tasted Nov 1995 ★★ Not a bad '92. Probably drinking well enough now.*

**Ch Cos d'Estournel** Noted at two mammoth blind tastings in 1995 and 1997, either side of a smaller trade tasting in 1996. Impressively deep yet somehow unconvincing. And that goes for the nose and palate too, yet some body and better than expected taste. *Assez bien. Last tasted June 1997 ★★ Drink soon.*

**Ch La Dauphine** I have always had a soft spot for the wines of this elegant château close to the banks of the Dordogne and not just because it was there that, with Harry Waugh, I was enthroned as a *gentilhomme d'honneur de Fronsac* for organising the first-ever promotional auction of Fronsac wines (Christie's 1970). A decent '92 served at the launch of Hubrecht Duijker's excellent *Bordeaux Atlas and Encyclopaedia of Châteaux. Oct 1997 ★★ Drink soon.*

**Ch Ducru-Beaucaillou** Only one note. Open knit chaptalised nose; 'sour flavour', slithery tannins. *Blind tasting, Jan 1995. Perhaps it has improved a bit, but I wouldn't bother.*

**Ch L'Église-Clinet** Hardy Rodenstock and Farr Vintners have been working hard to promote the wines of this tiny château, but even the brilliant Durantou could not make much of the '92. A magnum, first tasted blind in 1996 alongside the Pétrus: stalky nose; austere, bitter. Bitterness noted again at Farr's in July 1998, and a jeroboam, this time at Rodenstock's five-day marathon in Munich. Still deep; lean, tannic. 'Not drinking too well at the moment' was an understatement. *Last noted Sept 1998 ★ Will it ever?*

**Ch Grand-Puy-Lacoste** Partly loyalty, partly curiosity. I think I only bought a couple of cases of the '92. Perhaps I should not have let my heart rule my brain, for it was one of the least good of the range tasted at the château. Nose not bad, 'touch of seaweed' but distinct Cabernet fruit; but on the palate lean, metallic, teeth-gripping astringency. *June 1995. Lacoste is always a slow developer but I do not hold out much hope for the '92.*

**Ch Haut-Batailley** Distinctly more appealing than the other Borie family's '92s, Lacoste (above) and Ducru. Fairly mature appearance; open, brambly fruit, though a whiff of rubber noted. Better on palate. Some richness and fruit. *Tasted blind Nov 1995 ★★ Drink soon.*

**Ch Lascombes** Weak-rimmed; light, cheesy, chaptalised nose; teeth-gripping tartness. Avoid. *Last noted at a pre-sale tasting, Sept 2001.*

**Ch Léoville-Barton** Showing quite well at the Union des Grands Crus tasting in April 1994: sweet, oaky, decent length. Next noted on an American Airlines flight to Miami in 1998, en route to Puerto Rico. It had a fragrant farmyard smell (the wine not the cabin); a bit raw with a bitter, tannic finish, though not bad with the beef. Most recently clearly the least good of the decade: nose of dried leaves and black treacle; dry, lean with teeth-gripping astringency. *Last noted at the château, Oct 2001.*

**Ch Léoville-Las-Cases** Decidedly better than the Barton (see above): good colour and fruit; positive flavour, oaky, very tannic. *At a trade tasting, April 1995 ★★ Drink soon.*

**Ch Rausan-Ségla** Showing quite well at the Union des Grands Crus tasting in 1994 but in a blind tasting which included '85s, '89s and '90s, the following year, it was completely out-classed; strange nose, volatile acidity; tinny metallic taste. *Last noted Jan 1995. Avoid.*

**Ch Tertre-Roteboeuf** I am not sure how this cropped up in a pre-sale tasting but it was very attractive and appealing in its too-sweet sort of way. *April 1996 ★★ Drink soon.*

**Ch de Valandraud** The second vintage of this St-Émilion cult wine first tasted blind in a 'flight' of Right Bank wines. Opaque, intense; broad, sweet, brambly, harmonious nose; fairly sweet, rich, fruity, good flavour (Rodenstock, 1996). Most recently, at another Right Bank blind tasting. Similar looking; very forthcoming, exaggerated, rich, chocolatey-mocha nose; on the palate far too chocolatey. For eating not drinking. *Last noted at the Bordeaux Index tasting at the Stafford Hotel, London, Nov 1999. Simply not my style of wine though an impressive '92.*

THE FOLLOWING IS A SELECTION FROM THE 58 '92S noted at the Union des Grands Crus tasting in London, April 1994 and not tasted since. The star ratings are those assessed at the time of tasting. Some wines will have improved since then, many will be drinkable now, very few much of a future. Allowance must be made for an element of puppy fat and the early attraction of chaptalisation. Like a peroxide blonde, eventually the black roots show. **Ch L'Angélus** impressively deep; good fruit, fair flesh, very tannic ★★★; **Ch d'Angludet** restrained; very pleasant, early developer ★★; **Ch Beauregard** very deep; sweet, lots of fruit, good oak ★★★; **Ch Beychevelle** surprisingly sweet, quite attractive ★★; **Ch Brane-Cantenac** feeble colour; very sweet, open, easy, unconvincing ★; **Ch Branaire-Ducru** sweet and easy. ★★; **Ch Canon** unknit; better on palate. Some sweetness, quite nice fruit, an early developer ★★; **Ch Cantenac-Brown** impressively deep; attractive fruit and oak ★★★; **Ch Chasse-Spleen** surprisingly sweet, chewy, light style. No fireworks here. ★★; **Ch Citran** very deep; good fruit and oak. Quite rich yet tannic. ★★★; **Ch Clinet** immensely deep; idiosyncratic; plausible, easy to taste yet tannic. Too oaky. ★★★; **Ch Coufran** unyielding; sweet fruit; acceptable extract. Very tannic. ★★; **Ch Croizet-Bages** unconvincing. Some sweetness. Touch of iodine. ★; **Ch Dauzac** sweet, soft, bland. ★★; **Ch Durfort-Vivens** forthcoming nose; sweaty tannins; very sweet, open, easy. ★★;

**Clos Fourtet** deep; good fruit; beguiling oak, easy. ★★★; **Ch Figeac** attractively evolved fruit. Light easy style ★★; **Ch Fourcas-Hosten** nice wine. ★★ (the Fourcas-Dupré samples all woody); **Ch Gazin** meaty; sweet, rich, also plausible ★★★; **Ch Grand-Mayne** very deep; good fruit; lots of oak. ★★; **Ch Grand-Puy-Ducasse** unknit, hard; not bad fruit but astringent ★; **Ch Gruaud-Larose** deep; good fruit; soft, attractive. A good '92 ★★★; **Ch Kirwan** very deep. Good fruit. Peppery finish ★★★; **Ch Labégorce** hard nosed; dry, lean, flavoury but far too much oak ★★; **Ch Lafon-Rochet** deep; hard; lean ★; **Ch Lamarque** better known for the car ferry which plies across the Gironde to and from Blaye. Handsome château but minor wine ★★; **Ch Langoa-Barton** very sweet. Flavour of dark chocolate ★★★; **Ch Léoville-Poyferré** some woodiness; dry, severe, tannic ★; **Ch Loudenne** pretty château, dreadful wine; **Ch Lynch-Bages** richly coloured; quite good nose; sweet, open knit ★★★ *probably drinking agreeably now*; **Ch Malescot-St-Exupéry** rich colour, meaty, tannic; not bad fruit ★★; **Ch Monbrison** horrible. Tannate of iron?; **Ch Montrose** deep; classic; medium sweetness and body. Good fruit and length. A good '92 ★★★; **Ch Les Ormes-de-Pez** deep; sweaty tannic nose; surprisingly sweet, fruity and attractive ★★★; **Ch Palmer** good flavour and length. Lean. Not enough fruit to cover the oak ★★★; **Ch Pavie** sweet, rich for a '92, attractive ★★★; **Ch Petit-Village** drinkable ★; **Ch Phélan-Ségur** farmyard and seaweed; **Ch Pichon-Baron** deep; good fruit; sweet, surprisingly good. Better than the '93 ★★★; **Ch Pichon-Lalande** deep, rich; fruit and brown sugar smell; fairly full-bodied, straightforward. A good '92 ★★★; **Ch Pontet-Canet** rich appearance, nose and taste. Very sweet. Fleshy. A good '92 ★★★; **Ch Prieuré-Lichine** open knit; oaky and tannic ★; **Ch Rauzan-Gassies** palish; chocolatey; sweet, bland ★; **Ch Siran** pink, feminine and stylish ★★; **Ch Talbot** very sweet, open knit, easy ★★; **Ch La Tour-de-By** remarkably good. Well made ★★(★); **Ch La Tour-Carnet** *assez bien* ★; **Ch Troplong-Mondot** surprisingly attractive. Speciously sweet, with fruit, flesh and oak ★★★; and **Ch Villemaurine** refreshing, citrus-like. Open. Easy ★★

# 1993 ★★ to ★★★

Variable, the results depending, as suggested by Peter Sichel in his report on the previous vintage (see page 136), less on good luck than on good management, care and selection. The problem once again was rain. Unlike 1991, when the rains arrived at an inopportune time after an otherwise excellent growing season, or 1992 which skirted the edges of a complete washout, 1993 had more rain than either – 160 days out of the 365 – but the growing season was unusual in that the first three months were abnormally dry with the burgeoning vines dying for a drink, the next four months quite the opposite, with the heaviest rains in September.

Yet, despite those vagaries, the vines were in much better shape than might have been expected, the Merlots in particular being almost perfectly ripe by mid-September. The effect of rain is juice dilution, and the later-ripening Cabernet Sauvignons were susceptible, which is where the care and selection came in.

I was able to taste a wide range of '93s organised by the Union des Grands Crus de Bordeaux, at the opening tasting for international wine writers in Bordeaux in April 1994 (1)

and, 12 months later, for the trade at the Merchant Taylors' Hall in the City of London (2). The latter is a one-day tasting with tables manned by the proprietors, their wines ranged by district. This is not the ideal set up but at least enables me to follow up, however superficially (because of the limited time and crowded attendance), the previous tasting which takes place in more leisurely, structured and seated conditions over four days in Bordeaux. There was also a useful MW tasting of '93s in November 1997 at Stainer's Hall in the City (3).

**Ch Lafite** First noted in November 1997 at the MW tasting of '93s: medium-deep; a surprisingly well developed nose, sweet and soft. Attractive. Decent length. Five years later, there was not much change. Most recently, a 'trial' magnum at lunch and three more served at Bartholomew's 40th birthday dinner three days later: fragrant; soft-enough, easy, straightforward, lean. Seemed to go down well. *Last noted Jan 2002* ★★ *Will keep but will not turn into more than an agreeable drink.*
**Ch Latour** First tasted in April 1997 with Christian Le Sommer, then the manager, at the château: still immature; attractive, cedary nose; overall dry, on the lean side but good. Just six months later: less deep than expected; an open, very attractive, cedar and Cabernet nose; seemed sweeter, not a heavyweight Latour. *Last noted at the MW tasting, Nov 1997. Then* ★★★ *Should be drinking reasonably well now.*
**Ch Margaux** A quartet of notes starting in January 1997. At the opening wine of Manfred Wagner's first vertical: my initial impression was 'green', with hard, crisp fruit, its nose opened up quite attractively; not bad fruit but lean, with raw finish. Later the same year, at the MW tasting, it seemed sweeter, soft and complete. Next tasted at the château with Paul Pontallier: plummy colour; quite nice fruit but unexciting (September 1998). Last bottle noted in more detail at Wagner's second vertical: soft fruit noted again, on nose and palate; a slightly watery, chaptalised character, but drinking quite well. Not a very notable Margaux. *Last tasted Nov 2000* ★★ *Drink soon.*
**Ch Mouton-Rothschild** First noted in April 1995: deep, youthful ruby; fruit and oak with strange minty, herbal, honeyed, rustic smell; lightish style, attractive. The following November at the opening of Les Arts du Vin Exhibition in Brussels, some flesh but very tannic and absolutely unready for drinking. After a further two years, settling down to be a good mouthful, developing some of its inimitable spicy nose and sweetness. But not a long-haul wine. *Last noted at the MW tasting, Nov 1997* ★★★ *Drink soon.*
**Ch Haut-Brion** Just one fairly recent note: medium, open-rimmed, maturing; nose a rich *mélange* of coffee and fruit (cold coffee and chocolate powder someone said); distinct citrus character, easy style but dry finish. *At the MW Ch Haut-Brion tasting, Jan 2000* ★★ *Drink soon.*
**Ch Cheval Blanc** Tasted in the *chai* in April 1994: very deep, fine violet rim; very good, fresh young fruit; dry, medium-full body, rounded tannins. Next, a magnum at the Wolf/Weinart vertical. Monsieur Hébrard informed us that it was very cold for the harvest. The Merlot picking finished on 20 September, and the Cabernet Franc five days later, the final *cépages* mix being 50-50. Still fairly deep and intense; good young fruit; dry; surprisingly assertive, tannic. *Last tasted Sept 1997* ★★(★) *Now–2012.*
**Ch Ausone** and **Ch Pétrus** Not tasted. The reader might well ask why. Alas I did not discover this major omission until the book was about to be delivered to an anxious printer and even more anxious publisher. Next time…

OTHER '93S TASTED

**Ch d'Angludet** Cabernet Sauvignon 45%, Merlot 35%, Cabernet Franc 15%, Petit Verdot 5%. (1) An agreeable youth and on the last three occasions at Christie's Bordeaux courses. Detailed and consistent notes. Lovely, rich, cherry red; fragrant fruit. Soft yet refreshing. *Last tasted Feb 1998* ★★★ *Drink soon.*

**Ch d'Armailhac** Cabernet Sauvignon 49%, Merlot 26%, Cabernet Franc 23%, Petit Verdot 2%. First noted at a British Airways tasting in November 1995: good hard fruit, very tannic and leathery. Two years later, good depth of colour; spicy aroma; attractive, chunky fruit (3). More recently, at a tasting of Pauillac wines from the Domaines Barons de Rothschild, at which the above *cépages* mix was noted. A deep, polished garnet; lovely, smooth, minty, eucalyptus nose; already showing some bottle age, 'with nice trajectory across the palate'. Firm. Medium length. *Last tasted at Waddesdon Manor, Buckinghamshire, Sept 1998* ★★(★) *Now–2010.*

**Ch Batailley** Among the several châteaux not showing their wines at either of the Union des Grands Crus tastings though perfectly willing to provide sample bottles for the MW tastings. In November 1997: opaque centre; sweet and, as usual, fairly fruit-laden and attractive. Most recently, representing Pauillac at a Christie's Bordeaux wine course. Detailed notes taken down by my wife who patiently attends all my lectures/tastings and confirming its substantial fruit and good flavour. Batailley is a very consistent wine and always moderately priced. *Last noted May 1999* ★★★ *Now–2010.*

**Ch Beychevelle** Four notes, first in April 1994 (1): very dry, spicy, 'dried blackcurrant'. The following year (2), rather raw with bitter tannins. Opening up somewhat and quite pleasantly scented at the MW tasting (3). Most recently, medium deep, open-edged; sweet, sweaty, rustic nose, not bad flavour but unimpressive. *Last noted at a buffet supper at the château, March 1999* ★★ *Drink rather than keep.*

**Ch Cantenac-Brown** Four notes. Initially a fairly good note among the Margaux: easy style, lacking intensity. Well developed, with its characteristic chunky, chocolatey character, attractive, easy. *Last noted lunching at the château with Henri Lurton, April 1998. A generous* ★★★ *but get on with it.*

**Ch Clerc-Milon** Cabernet Sauvignon 50%, Merlot 34%, Cabernet Franc 13%, Petit Verdot 3%. First noted at the MW tasting (3): spicy Pauillac fruit; very flavoury, 'for mid-term drinking'. Next noted in January 1998 at the gala French dinner, cruising off the coast of Sumatra on the *Seaborn Spirit*. Taut. Needed more maturity 'but OK with steak'. Later that autumn, still fairly youthful; good cedary-iodine nose; soft yet with firm dry finish. 'A food wine'. *Last noted at the Waddesdon Manor tasting in Buckinghamshire, Sept 1998* ★(★★) *2005–2012.*

**Ch Clinet** Initially deep violet; tight oaky nose; firm, fleshy. Most recently: still opaque, intense, rich 'legs'; bramble and tar;

---

## Farr Vintners

*The first and certainly the most successful of the new breed of British wine brokers which didn't exist before I started wine auctions at Christie's in 1966. Farr differs from other brokers in that it carries stocks of wine. Over the last 20 years Stephen Browett and Lindsay Hamilton have built up their company to its current considerable standing and have a well-deserved international reputation. Bordeaux (both old and new) makes up around 70% of the company's business, but its range of burgundy, Rhône and other classic wines is also much sought after.*

at first I thought it a very good mouthful, though it had a coarse finish. The more I sipped it the less I liked it. *Last noted at the Rheingauer Giganten dinner at the Wagnerian Gothic hotel at Assmannshausen, in the Rheingau, Nov 2000* ★★?

**Ch La Dominique** A 45-acre vineyard next to Cheval Blanc. Showing well at the two earlier tastings, its deep, velvety colour particularly notable. My most detailed note made at a tasting conducted for the Nassau 'Baillage' of the Rôtisseurs. Still deep, intense, with mauve edge; crisp, raspberry-like mouthwatering fruit, 'thoroughbred stables'; on the sweet side, full of fruit and flavour yet only 12% alcohol. Soft tannins, fleshy. *Last tasted Feb 1998* ★★(★★) *Now–2010.*

**Ch L'Église-Clinet** Just one note: deep, still immature; rich nose, depth; slightly sweet, good fruit and flesh. Crisp, dry finish. *With Farr Vintners, July 1998* ★★★ *Now–2012.*

**Ch L'Évangile** Despite its very deep colour and tannins, surprisingly easy and open on the palate (1). A similar note at the MW tasting (3) and most recently, a fleshy wine, drinking well. *Last noted at dinner, May 2000* ★★★ *A very attractive '93 for early drinking.*

**Ch Feytit-Clinet** A mix of 85% Merlot and 15% Cabernet Franc. A normal 12.5% alcohol. Not a wine I normally come across but selected by Steven Spurrier, Christie's wine course co-founder, for a couple of my Bordeaux sessions to represent the district Pomerol. Certainly impressive, its nose particularly interesting, dense, wholesome, lovely after an hour in the glass. Rather like Burgundy, the wine appeared to open up, to develop, in the mouth. But very tannic. Needs time and/or food. *Tasted in July 1997 and Feb 1998* ★(★★) *Worth pursuing.*

**Ch La Fleur** Deep; lively but static nose; good fruit and flesh. *At Rodenstock's vertical, Aug 1998* ★★★★ *(just). Now–2010.*

**Ch La Fleur-Pétrus** The tiny compact Pomerol district is full of châteaux with confusingly similar names – Fleurs, Pétruses and masses of Églises, mostly very good, as is this spicy, Mouiex-owned, wine. *On the Corney & Barrow table at The Bunch tasting in London, Jan 1998* ★★(★) *2003–2012.*

**Ch Fombrauge** A mix of 60% Merlot, 30% Cabernet Franc, and 10% Cabernet Sauvignon. A good old standby used at three recent Christie's Bordeaux wine courses. Four-square, dependable, agreeable. Lacking intensity. *Last noted May 1999* ★★ *Drink up.*

**Ch Grand-Puy-Lacoste** First impressions: lean and raw at the Union des Grands Crus tasting in London, April 1995 (2). Only two months later showing surprisingly well at a useful vertical at the château which gave me time to make a more detailed note: deep ruby; attractive Cabernet aroma with oak; good fruit, fair extract, leathery tannins. In June 1997, at the closing France in Your Glass dinner at Ch de Bagnols: the nose opened up well; good flavour but with mouth-drying tannins. More recently, another more detailed note at a Lacoste masterclass at Christie's (April 1999), which can be summarised as still fairly deep and youthful; nose not very clear cut but which opened up spicily, with touch of ginger and mandarin. Surprisingly sweeter than the '95, chunky but with a slightly coarse texture and bitter finish. Most recently, a bottle from my own cellar, again still youthful looking but a good rich nose and fine with food. *Last noted at a Sunday lunch at Chippenham Lodge, Dec 2000. A good '93 which will improve – up to a point* ★★(★) *2005–2010.*

**Ch Gruaud-Larose** A wine to suit a wealthy East Anglian farmer, for I found it had a rather over the top smell of manure at the London tasting, April 1995 (2), and a 'touch of farmyard' on the palate at a Maisons, Marques & Domaines tasting in 1997. Later that year, ripe fruit, 'slightly *fermier*' on the nose; sweet, good fruit, complete and with an attractive aftertaste. Most recently, just a glass at an Easter Saturday dinner at Gidleigh Park in Devon. Despite its rustic character, I like it. *Last tasted April 2001* ★★★(★) *Now–2012*.

**Ch Haut-Bailly** Cabernet Sauvignon 65%, Merlot 25% and Cabernet Franc 10%. Masses of notes. Showing well at the opening Union des Grands Crus tasting in April 1994 (1). The next eight notes, made at a series of Christie's wine course Bordeaux tastings between April 1996 and March 1999, providing a useful opportunity to see, from my detailed notes, how the wine had developed. In appearance, the colour changed from ruby with a mauve rim to a nicely graduated dark cherry; its nose fragrant, fruity, initially with a touch of hardness but evolving into a more mellow, wholesome, slightly earthy/biscuity Graves bouquet; on the palate from mouthfilling fruit with tannin lightly gripping the teeth to a well-structured sweetness, ready for drinking. Most recently, a pleasing richness, nice weight (12.5% alcohol) and flavour. *Last noted at a vertical tasting of the vintages of the 1990s at the château, June 2001* ★★★(★) *Now–2010*.

**Ch Kirwan** Cabernet Sauvignon 40%, Merlot 30%, Cabernet Franc 20% Petit Verdot 10%. As much as I like my old friend Jean-Henri Schÿler and his family, their *3ème cru classé* Kirwan has been an uneven performer. My four rather unenthusiastic notes: 'opaque; specious, very oaky, no charm' – April 1994 (1); 'disappointing' – April 1995 (2); 'smell of tobacco and new oak' and 'very fruity but harsh finish' – April 1996, at a tasting for the Commanderie de Bordeaux; and finally, 'thick fruit; so-so, drying on palate'. *Last noted lunching at Ch Cos d'Estournel, March 2001* ★(★) *Drink up*.

**Ch Labégorce-Zédé** Cabernet Sauvignon 50%, Merlot 35%, Cabernet Franc 10% and Petit Verdot 5%. Following Ch Haut-Bailly at three Christie's Bordeaux wine course sessions between December 1998 and the following May and demonstrating what quality the Thienpont family can produce from a *bourgeois* Margaux. Detailed notes, consistent, which I précis: fairly deep, soft, velvety cherry red; very fragrant, sweet, distinctive nose; crisp fruit, touch of leanness, quite a bit of tannin, good acidity. *Last tasted May 1999* ★★(★) *Now–2010*.

**Ch Langoa-Barton** Cabernet Sauvignon 70%, Merlot 15%, Petit Verdot 8%, Cabernet Franc 7%. I seem to have given this a pretty good going over: the two Union des Grands Crus tastings in April 1994 and 1995, the MW tasting of '93s and two Christie's Bordeaux wine courses at which I always make the most detailed notes simply because I go through the various facets of each wine with the classes. There is another good reason; a seated tasting with nearly two hours to taste and discuss eight wines provides an opportunity not only to compare like with like but, also most importantly, time for the nose of the wine to open up over a period of at least 30 minutes – my wife times my comments. At both the Bordeaux wine courses the evolution of the Langoa in the glass was significant, its initial cedar and crisp fruit opening up beautifully. On the palate it also showed its class: shapely but tannic. *Last noted at Christie's Bordeaux wine course, Feb 1998* ★★★(★) *2005–2012*.

**Ch Léoville-Barton** A good '93, showing well at the opening tasting in April 1994 (1) and at the MW tasting (3): classic, cedary; good length. In between the two, the first wine at a tasting for Goldman Sachs at Christie's in Hamburg and, most recently, and most usefully, in a vertical of the decade at the château: still surprisingly deep and youthful; slightly singed,

open fruit, unknit nose with a touch of tar; not too dry, nice texture – silky tannins, fair length. If the latter note sounds over-critical, the description enabled me to recognise the wine when my wife handed me glasses in random order to taste blind. In the final analysis, a fairly straightforward, decent wine for interim drinking. *Last tasted Oct 2001* ★★(★) *2005–2012*.

**Ch Lynch-Bages** Context is everything, well almost everything. Good notes at the opening tastings in 1994 (1) and 1995 (2): good, crisp. Twelve months later, the first wine at a Lynch-Bages/Pichon-Baron tasting in Brussels, flavour slightly marred by bitter tannins. Next, for the Chaîne des Rôtisseurs in Nassau: delicious crisp Cabernet nose; sweet, soft, overall tannic. Most recently, a disappointing bottle in rather noisy company at the very popular Lion d'Or, Arcins. *Last noted June 2000. At best* ★★(★) *2005–2011*.

**Ch Palmer** From the start (April 1994), a very attractive '93. Distinctly sweet, complete. The opening wine at my Bordeaux tasting for the Chaîne des Rôtisseurs in Nassau: rather thick set, plummy colour; low-keyed, soft, fleshy nose and 'wonderful depth'; rich fruit, a good mouthful despite its modest alcohol content (12%). *Last tasted Feb 1998* ★★(★★) *Now–2010*.

**Ch Pavie** Merlot 60%, Cabernet Franc 30%, Cabernet Sauvignon 10%. In 1994 rich, soft, easy and attractive. Most recently at a Christie's Bordeaux wine course: good, deep colour; lovely nose, touch of strawberry and pepper; chunky fruit, mouth-drying tannins. Nicer than expected and much preferred to very recent vintages. *Last tasted July 2001* ★★★

**Ch Pichon-Baron** Eight notes starting with the early tasting (1): initially a raw youth but soon opened up, 'rich, full', and a good mark in 1995 (2) and at two tastings in 1997, the word 'chunky' appearing a couple of times, but a more complete note made in Frankfurt: impressive colour; extra-dimensional nose, fruit, tar and chestnuts; a convincing, mouthfilling wine. (13% alcohol). Another two notes in 1998. Showing some maturity, good fruit, chewy. *Last noted at the château, Sept 1998* ★★★(★) *2006–2012*.

**Ch Talbot** A citrus touch and silky tannic texture (1). Sweet, firm fruit (2). Impressive colour; forthcoming, rustic yet floral nose; full of fruit, attractive (3). Most recently, at the Fête de la Fleur dinner, its nose becoming less floral and more farmyard, its touch of astringency coped well with the *poitrine de canneton*. *Last noted at Ch Pontet-Canet, June 1999* ★★(★) *Now–2010*.

**Ch Trotanoy** A couple of fairly recent notes: nose forthcoming, ripe and harmonious; very sweet, full of fruit, delicious. Also tannic. *Last noted at The Bunch tasting, Jan 1998* ★★(★★) *Now–2010*.

A LARGE NUMBER OF NOTES, some 350 in total, not including some *petits châteaux* bought for drinking at home in the 1996–97 period. The following are my most recent notes of some of the principal châteaux, and in many cases first tasted in April 1994 (1), the spring of 1995 (2) and at the MW tasting in November 1997 (3).

**Ch L'Angélus** (1) Opaque, intense; nose hard to define: a combination of fruit, tar and wood. Static but fragrant; also some sweetness and richness, rather austere with hard tannins. Next was a tasting at the Ritz in April 1996, at which several growers were exhibiting their wines. Monsieur Hubert de Bouard presented three vintages including his '93, which I noted as sweet, fleshy, with lovely flavour and texture. The following year, a good note but tannic. *Last noted at the MW tasting (3), Nov 1997* ★(★★) *Probably best between now and 2012*.

**Ch Branaire-Ducru** All three notes at tastings (1), (2) and (3) conveniently placed with the St-Juliens. Deeper colour than Ch Beychevelle; a touch of raw stalkiness noted initially; quite good fruit and weight. Tannic grip. Lacks length. *Last tasted at the MW tasting (3), Nov 1997* ★(★) *2005–2012.*

**Ch Brane-Cantenac** Among the Margaux at all three tastings. Initially fairly deep with an open fruit and oak nose and spiciness. Somewhat exaggerated piquant fruit on the nose; 'specious' noted once, 'attractive' on all three occasions. Fairly well developed and easy. *Last noted at the MW tasting (3), Nov 1997* ★★★ *Now–2010.*

**Ch Canon** Also in all three tastings referred to in the introduction. My best note at the opening tasting, in fact positively eulogistic: soft, rich, full, fleshy, and so on. Certainly not shy, but a poor woody bottle at the MW tasting (3). *Last noted at the MW tasting (3), Nov 1997. At best* ★★(★★) *Now–2010.*

**Ch Chasse-Spleen** As usual, a cut above its class. At the opening tasting (1), quite nice fruit, a touch of elegance though with youthful bitter tannin. A touch of sweetness, crisp, clean, agreeable, with refreshing acidity. *Last noted at a tasting for clients of Christie's, Frankfurt, Nov 1997* ★★★ *Now–2010.*

**Dom de Chevalier** Surprisingly sweet, open and rounded nose at the opening tasting (1), though less impressive on the palate. Equally forthcoming nose; sweet, attractive at the MW tasting (3) and later the same month, more detailed notes made at the Christie's tasting in Frankfurt, to which I had added 'charm' and 'pleasing weight' (only 12% alcohol). *Last noted at the MW tasting (3), Nov 1997* ★★★ *Drink now–2010.*

**Ch Cos d'Estournel** Another classed growth château that remains aloof from the Union des Grands Crus tastings, so first noted at a Dent & Reuss presentation in March 1996: very attractive ruby; sweet, soft but sweaty (tannins); stylish, crisp fruit, very attractive – noted again at the MW tasting (3), sweet yet lean with a tannic finish. Nice wine. *Last noted at the MW tasting (3), Nov 1997* ★★(★) *2006–2015.*

**Ch Ducru-Beaucaillou** The Bories do not show their wines at the early Union des Grands Crus tastings, so I have only one, not very helpful note made briefly at the MW walk around tasting (3): deep; oaky, tannic; dry, some spice, peppery finish. Not overly impressed. Perhaps it has both opened up and settled down. *Last noted at the MW tasting (3), Nov 1997* ★★? *Judgement reserved.*

**Ch Duhart-Milon** Nice wine. Spicy, good fruit at the MW tasting (3). More recently served with partridge at a Domaines Barons de Rothschild dinner at Brooks's in London. Sweet (chaptalised) nose; 'chewy' noted on both occasions. A very pleasant drink. *Last tasted Nov 2000* ★★★ *Drink soon.*

**Ch de Fieuzal** Red Graves of this ilk mercifully (for people who actually drink wine) escape the attentions of the speculator. At the opening tasting (1) opaque, intense; unknit; despite good fruit notably tannic. Exactly a year later, it had shaken off some of its youthful excesses (April 1996) and by October 1997 – at a France in Your Glass gala dinner at Ch de Bagnols – coped pretty well with *filet de boeuf*, yet though soft and sweet on the nose, the raw tannin lingered on. Less than a month later, simmering down, relatively easy and attractive. *Last noted at the MW tasting (3), Nov 1997* ★★(★) *just. Now–2008.*

**Ch Figeac** An unusual *cépages* mix for St-Émilion: Cabernet Sauvignon 35%, Cabernet Franc 35%, Merlot 30%, the first being responsible for the distinct blackcurrant aroma at the opening tasting (1). Twelve months later, at the second Grands Crus tasting, crisp fruit, delicious. In February 1997 the opening wine at a Bordeaux/Burgundy tasting at Lyford Cay.

A *mélange* of fruits; plummy colour; soft fruit, touch of strawberries and cherries which blossomed in the glass. Nice wine. Nine months later: sweet, attractive, easy fruit. *Last noted at the MW tasting (3), Nov 1997, almost* ★★★★ *Now–2018.*

**Ch Lafon-Rochet** Cabernet Sauvignon 70%, Merlot 30%. Next door to Ch Cos d'Estournel and overlooking Ch Lafite, Lafon-Rochet makes an austere wine, at times a caricature of the St-Estèphes of old though it was showing well, better than expected, at the opening Union des Grands Crus tasting (1), also at the second (2), when I noted good fruit and tannin. Selected to represent its district at the Bordeaux wine course previously referred to, and with more time to taste 'in depth' (a CNN news expression I try to avoid): deep, velvety, black cherry; good nose, touch of menthol, tannic; raw, hard, 'blatant fruit', the sort of tannic finish which reminds me of concrete. *Last noted at the MW tasting (3), Nov 1997* (★★) *Say 2005–2010.*

**Ch Larmande** Well over a dozen notes because I bought some from Justerini's for dinner parties. However, I first tasted it at the two Union des Grands Crus tastings and, each time, in the company of other St-Émilions it showed well: an impressively deep colour; concentrated, brambly, new oak, tannin and acidity. Looking back, I can hardly believe this. Anyway, it must have been the following year that I bought and tasted the wine, commencing with several lunches and dinners in December 1996. It had started to lose some colour the following year and although an agreeable drink, I noted acidity catching up. A bottle opened for lunch was better in the evening. Anyway, I have none left. The sort of wine for which Shakespeare might have coined the phrase 'gather ye rosebuds whilst ye may'. *Finally consumed Nov 1997. Perhaps as well* ★★ *Drink up.*

**Ch Léoville-Las-Cases** How the Institute of Masters of Wine managed to persuade Monsieur Delon to part with three bottles, I do not know. Fragrant, cedary; firm, convincing fruit. *Last noted at the MW tasting (3), Nov 1997* ★★(★) *2005–2012.*

**Ch Léoville-Poyferré** Five consistently good notes, at tastings (1), (2), (3), and the last at a Christie's tasting in Frankfurt. The nose went through three phases: marvellous fruit, syrupy-honeyed, very agreeable; a moderately sweet, soft, fruity wine with correct dry finish. *Last noted at the MW tasting (3), Nov 1997* ★★(★★) *2005–2012.*

**Ch Pichon-Lalande** Three notes, two at the tastings I refer to as (1) and (2), the third for Goldman Sachs in Frankfurt. Less intense than its rival, the 'Baron'; sweeter and more fleshy too. An attractive food wine. *Last tasted Nov 1996* ★★★ *Should be ready for drinking now to around 2010.*

**Ch Rausan-Ségla** Notes at all three tastings, (1), (2) and (3): a seriously good '93. Suave, quite a bit of new oak; complete, impressive. *Last noted at the MW tasting (3), Nov 1997* ★★(★★) *Now–2010.*

**Ch Smith-Haut-Lafitte** A lot of money and effort has been put into this now major Pessac-Léognan estate. Perhaps over-oaked but if I were to use one word, it would be vivacious. Five notes: my top rating in the opening Graves 'flight'. In 1997 delicious, with spicy chicken at the château. Crisp, sweet, exciting at the Hallwag press conference in Frankfurt to publicise Hubrecht Duijker's *The Bordeaux Atlas and Encyclopedia of Chateaux*. Most recently, at a Chaîne des Rôtisseurs lunch at the château. Spicy, lean, very flavoury. Went well with the *lapin rôti*. *Last tasted June 2000* ★★★ *Now–2010.*

**Vieux Ch Certan** Initially tangerine-like finish and acidity. Attractive. Most recently: lovely, sweet, harmonious bouquet;

soft, nice texture, good finish. Very attractive. *Last noted at a Christie's tasting in Frankfurt, Nov 1997* ★★★★ *Now–2008.*

SOME COMMENTS ON OTHER '93S noted mainly at the early Union des Grands Crus tastings in Bordeaux in April 1994 (1) and in London in 1995 (2); also at the MW tasting of '93s in London in November 1997 (3) and on other occasions. Arranged in alphabetical order: **Ch Beauregard** (1) Merlot 55%, Cabernet Franc 45% – Cabernet Sauvignon not used in 1993. 60% new oak. Oak apparent but good fruit and extract. 'Singed caramel' nose. Fair fruit *1998* ★★ *drink soon;* **Ch Canon-La-Gaffelière** (1) initially opaque; delicious soft blackberry nose; sweet, good fruit and grip ★★★? *drink now;* **Ch Cantemerle** a decent '93, softer than expected ★★★ *drink soon;* **Ch Carbonnieux** good wine. Tends to develop early ★★ *drink up;* **Ch Certan-de-May** (3) fragrant, attractive; lean, dry finish ★★ *drink soon;* **Ch Clarke** (1) dry, oaky, spicy ★★ *drink soon;* **Ch La Conseillante** lovely wine. Forthcoming, scented blackberry; open knit; fleshy yet very tannic ★★★★ *now–2008;* **Ch Cos Labory** (1), (2) and (3): spicy, fragrant, lean, dry ★★ *drink soon;* **Ch Coufran** (1) youthful, attractive, but hard ★★ *nevertheless, drink soon;* **Ch Dassault** (1) and (2) sweet, open, fragrant, forthcoming. Crisp, flavoury ★★★ *drink soon;* **Ch Dauzac** a promising start. Firm fruit. Quite good flavour. ★★★ *drink soon;* **Ch Durfort-Vivens** (1) overoaked, hollow, chaptalised ★ *drink up;* **Ch Ferrière** lots of fruit, sweet, attractive ★★★; **Ch Fonréaud** (1) brambly, specious, spicy ★★★ *drink up;* **Ch Fourcas-Dupré** (1) raw fruit; **Ch Fourcas Hosten** (1) good consistency ★★; **Ch Fourtet** curious citrus-like piquancy. Less concentrated than its initial opacity suggested. *Probably* ★★ *drink soon;* **Ch Franc-Mayne** (1) initially a taste of unripe pears. Drinking quite well ★★ *drink up;* **Ch Grand-Mayne** (2) sweet, chewy fruit, attractive ★★★ *drink soon;* **Ch Grand-Puy-Ducasse** very tannic. Lean ★★ *drink soon;* **Ch Haut-Bergey** (1) opaque, very spicy, oaky ★★ *drink soon;* **Ch d'Issan** (3) sweet, attractive ★★★ *drink soon;* **Ch Lagrange** (St-Julien) oaky, severely tannic (★★?); **Ch Larrivet-Haut-Brion** (1) ripe, rustic, citrus nose; lean but very flavoury ★★ *drink up;* **Ch Lascombes** (1) after a poor start, attractive, easy ★★ *drink soon;* **Ch La Louvière** (1) fragrant; overall dry, lean fruit ★★ *drink soon;* **Ch Magdelaine** as one might expect of Mouiex, exceptionally attractive fruit, flavour and style ★★★★ *now–2008;* **Ch Malartic-Lagravière** (1) very oaky. Modest fruit. Something lacking ★; **Ch Malescot-St-Exupéry** (1) and (2) initially closed, peppery; (3) spicy, chunky. ★★; **Ch Malescasse** good flesh. Complete ★★ *drink up;* **Ch Marquis de Terme** (2) speciously oaky. Quite appealing ★★ *drink soon;* **Ch Maucaillou** well made. Lean, spicy, tannic ★★ *drink soon;* **Ch Montrose** (1) the best St-Estèphe, well constructed, surprisingly sweet ★★★★ *now–2009;* **Ch Nenin** (1) opaque, velvety; sweet, fat, soft; fleshy but lacking structure ★★ *drink up;* **Ch Les Ormes-de-Pez** (1) good fruit, well made, hard tannins *1998* ★★★; **Ch Pape-Clément** (1) very good nose. Distinctive. Relatively pale now; pleasant, fragrant; surprisingly sweet, soft, easy *1998* ★★ *drink up;* **Ch Pavie-Decesse** (1) rich though restrained. Good wine ★★★; **Ch Petit-Village** (1) Merlot 80%, Cabernet Franc 10%, Cabernet Sauvignon 10%. Initially very deep; rich, gloriously figgy fruit; flesh; yet lean. More recently, good, nice texture and flavour *1998* ★★★ *drink soon;* **Ch Phélan-Ségur** (1) started off quite well but raw and undistinguished in mixed company *1998* ★★; **Ch La Pointe** (1) Merlot 80%, Cabernet Franc 20%. From the start, very sweet, pleasant, easy style *1998*

★★★ *drink up;* **Ch Pontet-Canet** four notes. Good fruit. Convincing ★★★ *now–2008;* **Ch Prieuré-Lichine** (1) specious oak and fruit ★★★ *doubtless drinking well now;* **Ch Rauzan-Gassies** (1) poor wine. Lacking body. 'Horrible'; **Ch Siran** five notes. Some elegance, nice fruit and texture, ripe fruit, lean ★★★; and **Ch La Tour-Figeac** weak. The worst wine at the St-Émilion session (1). Only moderately decent, chewy, very tannic *Avoid.*

# 1994 ★★★

Despite another rainy September, a surprisingly good vintage which was, however, upstaged by the '95s.

The winter of 1993–94 was one of the warmest on record, the year opening with mild temperatures and normal rainfall. Budding took place at the end of March but the beginning of April was cold, with heavy rain. This was followed, on the 15th, by heavy frost across the whole region. Overall this reduced the potential crop by about 50%, in some vineyard plots from 70 to even 100%. Warm weather returned with temperatures of up to 20°C continuing into May. This encouraged re-budding. June and July were hot, a heatwave inducing a rapid flowering. The warm weather continued through August. Everything was set, as in 1993, for a fine, early harvest but from 7 September, heavy rains soused the region. Picking, which had started on the 9th, was resumed around the 19th, most grapes being picked around the 24–25th after which there was more rain. Some châteaux chose to wait until fine weather resumed on the 28th, some Cabernet Sauvignons being picked up to 7 October.

Because of the frosts, the yields were small but the early-picked Merlot and Cabernet Franc were of good quality, the later-picked Cabernet Sauvignon uneven.

Who would be a grape grower?

**Ch Lafite** Showing well in its youth: fairly deep, good fruit, 'early developer' (MW tasting November 1998). Subsequent notes not quite as flattering. Dry and a different ball game to the lovely, fleshy '99 tasted alongside at the château in June 2000. Most recently, tasted blind, I noted it as 'trying to mature'; a classic Médoc nose which opened up attractively in the glass, but on the palate dry, raw and tannic. I think it needs to get its second breath, but will not make a great bottle. *Last tasted in a 'flight' of first growth '94s at the Rodenstock wine event, March 2001* ★★(★) *Say 2006–2015.*

**Ch Latour** First tasted at the MW tasting of '94s, November 1998: not as deep as expected; positive, fragrant; surprisingly sweet, rich, attractive flavour but of course tannic. The only other note made at Rodenstock's blind tasting of '94s: though richly coloured the most mature looking of the first growths; chunky fruit; some sweetness, chewy, marked tannins. The scores were very close, mine three points ahead of the average for Latour. *Last tasted March 2001* ★★(★) *2005–2012.*

**Ch Margaux** As always, interesting to taste with and listen to Paul Pontallier. My first note of the '94 was made in his tasting room in September 1995. Apropos the harvest, Paul told me that after several days of torrential rain there had been some sun and drying wind. The Merlot was very ripe, like the '82, with potential alcohol of 13%. The young wine was a medium-deep ruby; the nose, as so often at this stage, already had a typically attractive Margaux scent; good fruit, fair extract and length but high tannins, like the '88 and almost as high as the '86. At the MW tasting in November 1998, I noted a strong coffee-mocha nose with the sweaty smell I associate with tannin. Rich though. Exactly two years later, at Manfred Wagner's vertical, the nose seemed unknit, hard edged and it was swingeingly tannic. Lastly at Rodenstock's, tasted blind: while still youthful looking, I noted a slightly chocolatey scent, and, despite its omnipresent tannin, gave it a high mark for fragrance. *Last tasted March 2001* ★(★★) *2006–2015*.

**Ch Mouton-Rothschild** Finding myself with some odd bottles in my country house cellar, I put four '94s together, two of Kendall-Jackson's Cabernets (from California), one rather unfairly, of Ch La Tour-de-By, and the Mouton which I am happy to say had a deep, rich, velvety *robe*; crisp, intense, spicy Cabernet Sauvignon aroma; 'great length', very tannic. This was in March 1998. A few days later I tasted it alongside the '95 bottle sent to me by Philippine de Rothschild to provide notes for the Mouton labels book. It didn't stand the comparison: lean, whereas the '95 was rich. It showed much better a few months later at the MW tasting, mainly because so many of the other '94s were mediocre. Another old bottle consumed at home: very fragrant in my big Riedel glasses, good fruit, dry finish (February 2000) and, most recently, tasted blind, with the other first growth '94s. My score was on a par with Ch Lafite, finding it leathery and lacking Mouton's flair. *Last tasted March 2001* ★(★★)? *Time will tell.*

**Ch Cheval Blanc** 'Cold year, much rain', Monsieur Hébrard told us at the mammoth Wolf/Weinart vertical in September 1997. The magnum was typically sweet on entry, lean, with an astringent finish. Showing far better in comparison to the other '94s at the MW tasting the following year. In fact my highest mark. Attractive fragrance, lovely flavour. My second highest mark at Rodenstock's blind tasting: a well developed, sweet and chocolatey nose and flavour. I did not note any excess tannin. Clearly evidence of the Right Bank's success in 1994. *Last tasted March 2001* ★★★(★) *Now–2012*.

**Ch Pétrus** One note, at the Rodenstock tasting: deeper than the Ch Cheval Blanc, its nose rather hard and uninteresting though a good flavour, its tannin masked. *March 2001* ★★(★) *Perhaps it is going through its 'seven-year itch'.*

I did not attend the opening tasting in Bordeaux organised by the Union des Grands Crus in the spring of 1995 but managed to get along to the follow-up in London in April 1996 and the MW tasting of '94s in November 1998. More detailed notes were made at British Airways tastings (always blind), at Christie's wine courses and on other occasions.

**Ch Beychevelle** First noted in April 1996: rather coarse and chewy. The following year, showing quite well at British Airways blind tasting of '94s, '95s and '96s to see if any were suitable for the first class and Concorde cellars: plausibly attractive fruit and oak. Later the same year (1997), the youngest in a line-up of Beychevelles: low-keyed, dry, lean, so-so. At the MW tasting: surprisingly pale: rather hollow, chaptalised nose; lightish style, chewy. Unimpressive. *Last tasted Nov 1998* ★★ *Drink up.*

**Ch Branaire-Ducru** First impression, nice texture and fruit endorsed at the British Airways tasting a year later. Tannin noted. An odd bottle at a Sunday lunch in August 1998: surprisingly sweet, chunky fruit. We drank it. Later that year: muffled, spicy nose; fruit and some bite. Not bad, but no more. *Last noted at the MW tasting, Nov 1998* ★★ *Drink up.*

**Ch Cantemerle** A moderate note at the MW tasting, weak rim; mediocre nose; sweet, soft, chunky. The next two notes made on board the *Crystal Symphony* (an excellent cruise liner incidentally) on one of the rare occasions I sailed as a lecturer.

It was already showing quite a bit of maturity; not very distinctive; some fruit, touch of sweetness. Disappointing. *Last noted afloat, Sept 1999* ★★ *Drink up.*

**Ch Certan-de-May** First noted in February 1998 at a Bordeaux tasting for the Chaîne des Rôtisseurs in Nassau: lean, hard, pinched and tannic. Not ready. Not a very good start. Showing better later that autumn, noting fairly good fruit and depth though too oaky. *Last noted at the MW tasting, Nov 1998* ★★(★) *2005–2011*.

**Ch Cos d'Estournel** First tasted at the château in September 1995. We were informed of the 'bleeding' to remove water from the vats before fermentation (bleeding was also used in the previous three vintages, up to 15% if there had been heavy rain). The Merlot was harvested before the rain, finishing on 15 September; the Cabernet Sauvignon five days later. The result was an impressively deep appearance; tight-knit nose; mature though intense tannins, quite good fruit. At the MW tasting in 1998 it was amongst the deepest in colour of all the Médocs. Good nose: tobacco and fruit; curious flavour, good length. More recently, noted at a Bordeaux tasting for the Nassau chapter of the IWFS: quite good fruit, some flesh. A respectable '94. *Last tasted Feb 1999* ★★(★) *Now–2009*.

**Dom de L'Église** Stalky; fairly sweet and soft though with a bitter iron tannic finish. *At a British Airways tasting, June 1997* ★★? *Not good enough.*

**Ch L'Église-Clinet** First noted in 1996 at a Rodenstock wine weekend, tasted blind in a random vertical of eight vintages: deep, intense, immature; attractive Pétrus-like fruit but more metallic. Hard. Bitter. I thought it an older more tannic vintage. Farr Vintners then organised a vertical in July 1998: slightly chocolatey; not bad fruit but raw, with bitter end. Most recently, craftily inserted into a blind 'flight' of first growths: I must confess I had no idea what it was. Quite fragrant; some charm but grippingly tannic. *Last tasted at a Rodenstock weekend, March 2001* ★(★★) *2006–2010*.

**Ch Giscours** First tasted at the Union des Grands Crus tasting in 1996: low-keyed; better flavour than nose. A touch of tar. The following year tasted blind: vanillin (oak); brambly fruit, tannic. Sweetened up a bit with more bottle age. Some richness. 'Tannic' undertone again. *Last noted at the MW tasting, Nov 1998* ★(★) *It ought to smooth out a little but not worth keeping.*

**Ch Gruaud-Larose** Noted only briefly at the perambulatory tastings of the Union des Grands Crus in April 1996 and the later MW tasting. If Gruaud can't produce a decent fruity, mouthful, no-one can. Happily it did. Fragrant, rich; very sweet, enough fruit, not over-tannic. An early developer. *Last tasted Nov 1998* ★★★ *Now–2008*.

**Ch Haut-Bailly** Light, fruity style, somewhat astringent finish (1996). A good note at the MW tasting, silky, attractive. Most recently, at a vertical of the decade at the château. The bottle had been opened the previous evening: a very earthy Graves nose; some sweetness, good fruit but, in the chill of the *chai*, tannin uppermost. *Last tasted with Véronique Sanders, the gérante, June 2001* ★★(★) *Give it a bit more time.*

**Ch Lascombes** At the Union des Grands Crus (1996) and MW tasting (1998) I gave a poor note to the nose: woody, corky. Rather better on the palate but very tannic. Still youthful looking; firm fruit, surprisingly pleasant texture. *Last noted at a pre-sale tasting, Sept 2001* ★★ *No point in keeping.*

**Ch Léoville-Barton** One of the best wines in the Union des Grands Crus tasting of '94s in April 1996: some sweetness; perfect weight, good length, fruit and oak. 'Classic'. The same word 'classic' applied to the nose at the MW tasting (1998), also length. Fairly tannic. The best of the St-Juliens. Almost identical notes, though extended, the following year: still impressively deep and youthful looking: unshowy, crisp, cedary nose. Firm. Complete. Most recently: deeper and richer than the '93; dry, oaky, firm noted again. A good '94. *Last tasted at the château, Oct 2001 ★★★(★) 2006–2012.*

**Ch Léoville-Las-Cases** At the MW tasting (1998): good colour; tannin on the nose – a sort of sweaty smell but masked by sweetness on the palate. Quite good body and fruit. On a par with the Léoville-Barton at the Lyford Cay tasting in the Bahamas. Beautiful cedary nose: fairly massive and concentrated despite the very normal 12.5% alcohol. Most recently, still plummy coloured; low-key nose; nice fruit, the tannin on the raw side. Needs food. *Last noted, fleetingly, at a Farr Vintners' tasting, Jan 2000. A good '94 ★★(★★) 2006–2012.*

**Ch Léoville-Poyferré** Two notes in April 1996, the first on Monsieur Cuvelier's stand at The Ritz (London), and a similar note the following day at the Union des Grands Crus walk around: initially a touch 'green' and raw though quite attractive fruit. Lighter than I had expected. Next, at two British Airways wine committee blind tastings the following year at which the wine was selected for First Class. Showing quite well at the MW tasting: spicy, good fruit, oaky (1998). Rather pleasing to drink the wine one had helped to select on two flights: BA 008 Tokyo to London, November 1998 and on BA10 from Sydney to Bangkok. It helped pass the time and aid the digestion. Three consistent notes at recent Christie's Bordeaux wine courses: still intensely deep; fragrant, cedary, quite a lot to it; touch of sweetness, fleshy yet raw, very dry finish. Not at all bad! *Last tasted March 2002 ★★★*

**Ch La Louvière** Cabernet Sauvignon 64%, Merlot 30%, Cabernet Franc 3%, Petit Verdot 3%. First tasted April 1996: dry, very stern and unyielding. Interesting to note what four more years can do. We used it to represent the Graves district at three Christie's Bordeaux Wine Courses within the space of seven months. Though still very deep in colour, it had started to mature; a chocolatey, smokey, oaky nose; first sip sweet but finishing dry with fair-enough soft fruit mid-palate. Well made – but needs more time. *Last noted Oct 2000 ★(★★) 2004–2009.*

**Ch Lynch-Bages** A couple of quick notes within a year of each other: remarkably forthcoming, high-toned nose; very distinctive flavour, slightly Pauillac, 'medicinal'. *Assez bien. Last tasted July 1995 ★★ Drink now–2008.*

**Ch Malescot-St-Exupéry** 'Coarse' noted at both the Grands Crus (1996) and MW (1998) tastings yet with a good dose of Malescot fruit. The nose its best feature. Some sweetness, very flavoury Cabernet nose and piquant flavour. Agreeable. *Last noted lunching at Ch Chasse-Spleen, March 2001 ★★★ just. Drink soon.*

**Ch Montrose** First tasted with Monsieur Lemoine at the château in September 1995. Like so many wines tasted from the cask, surprisingly sweet and spicy. In fact delicious. Two years later, almost too sweet on the nose. A good wine but the tannin very noticeable. Showing well at the MW tasting. Still very deep; good nose, fruit and coffee; well made. Complete. *Last tasted Nov 1998. A good '94 ★★(★★) 2006–2012.*

**Ch Palmer** In April 1996: vanillin; surprisingly sweet and chewy. Two years later, at the MW tasting, losing some colour; sweet, easy, attractive. Then at two Palmer tastings within four days. Just to show one should not take *too* much notice of *cépages* statistics. The Sichel family informed us that the '94 was a blend of Cabernet Sauvignon 54%, Merlot 36.8%, Cabernet

Franc 7.6% and Petit Verdot 1.6%; at the Mähler Besse tasting (they own roughly 70% of Palmer) the managing director quoted: Cabernet Sauvignon 50%, Merlot 47%, Petit Verdot 2% and Cabernet Franc 1%. Never mind: a chunky, chewy, rather raw wine, a bit lean and mean when served between the '95 and '90. *Last tasted Feb 2001 ★(★) 2005–2010.*

**Ch Pape-Clément** Nice fruit but very oaky (April 1996). Sweet but a touch of coarseness and rough, tannic grip noted on the Vintex stand (Vinexpo 1997), but opening up pleasantly just four years after the vintage. Noted as sweet, very attractive, with smokey, oaky finish. *Last tasted Nov 1998 ★★(★) Now–2008.*

**Ch Pavie** First tasted from the cask with my old friend, the late Jean-Paul Valette at the château in September 1995: deep of course; very pronounced fruit; dry, firm, a fair amount of acidity. At the MW tasting (1996): sweet, soft, easy, forward. A similar note at Vinexpo the following year. *Last tasted June 1997 ★★ Drink soon.*

**Ch Pichon-Baron** 'Surprisingly sweet' noted on the first three occasions. Rich, chewy (1996). Minty, chocolatey nose; touch of tar, raw, leathery (May 1997) and the following month, tasted blind: tarry noted again, but much more attractive fruit on the palate. Four years after the vintage, developing well; forthcoming, 'medicinal' Pauillac nose and flavour, tight Pauillac fruit on the palate. *Last noted Nov 1998 ★★★ 2005–2010.*

**Ch Pichon-Lalande** Half a dozen notes, all good, its length – not a feature of many '94s – at the Union des Grands Crus tasting (1996), its fruit and flesh (1997), a good combination of fruit and oak (1997); sweetness, rich fruit – a fairly high mark at the MW tasting (1998). Most recently, shown at two France in Your Glass tastings at Eugénie-les-Bains: opening up with an almost farmyard animal richness. Surprisingly sweet. A good '94. *Last tasted Oct 2000 ★★★★ 2006–2012.*

**Ch Rauzan-Ségla** (Note the change of spelling, from 'Rausan' to 'Rauzan' from the '94 vintage.) Five good notes. A sweet, lovely flavour at the opening tasting of '94s but following the '95, a touch of rawness though good texture and flavour (Frankfurt 1997). Back in the company of '94s (1998), it shone once again, its appearance showing some maturity; well evolved nose and flavour. Spicy. Good, dry finish. A similar note in the company of four '94s at Lyford Cay (1999) but tannin more noticeable. Most recently, at my Rauzan-Ségla/Pichon-Lalande tasting at Eugénie: crisp fruit, restrained at first but intriguingly evolved after an hour; nice flesh and fruit, well made, excellent flavour but still very tannic. *Last tasted Sept 2000 ★★(★★) 2006–2012.*

**Ch Smith-Haut-Lafitte** I think I preferred this in its youth, noting a Merlot-like fleshiness and richness. High marks, April 1996. The next year at Vinexpo, sweet, chunky, its earthy Graves character emerging. Attractive. Next, in 1998, a magnum lunching at the château with Florence and Daniel Cathiard. It seemed to have a somewhat singed nose and taste. Most recently, in a vertical conducted at La Caudalie, not bad but outflanked by the better '95 and '90. *Last noted June 2000 Verging on ★★★ Drink soon.*

**Ch Talbot** Five somewhat uneven notes, I also preferred it in its youth: deep; spicy; crisp fruit, attractive, tannic (April 1998). A year later, evolving well, rich, chewy. Next, tasted blind, a rather dismal bottle among 17 other '94s: raw nose; rustic and rusty (tannin) on the palate. A much more favourable note at the MW tasting: spicy, rich. Most recently, the opening wine at a Talbot tasting followed by dinner. The event was elegantly hosted by Nancy Bignon and Lorraine Rustmann, daughters of the late Jean Cordier, owners of Talbot. *Last tasted at the Mirabelle, London, April 2000* ★★(★) *Now–2009.*

**Vieux Ch Certan** Once again, a good start: fairly sweet, soft and attractive (cask sample 1996). Also showing well at the MW tasting of '94s. But at the tasting of Thienpont wines in Brussels in March 1998, it was totally outclassed by the other vintages: 'somewhat unexciting' I noted. Later the same year, also in Belgium, another tasting of the two Thienpont wines, Vieux Ch Certan and Labégorce-Zédé. It showed better: 'not half bad', with nice, mouthwatering fruit; quite good flavour and length. A convincing wine, much better than the reputation of the vintage. *Last tasted Nov 1999* ★★(★) *2005–2010.*

A SELECTION OF OTHER '94s noted at the Union des Grands Crus tasting in Bordeaux, April 1996 (1), the London MW tasting of '94s, November 1998 (2) and at other times.

**Ch L'Angélus** At the Ritz (London) in April 1996: hard and fairly full-bodied. At four years of age still deep; laden with thick, hefty fruit. Impressive, a good '94 but not my style. *Last noted Nov 1998 (2)* ★(★★) *2004–2010.*

**Ch d'Armailhac** First noted at Ch Mouton-Rothschild, September 1998: muffled mulberry; delicious fruit. *Last noted Nov 1998 (2)* ★★ *To drink not to keep.*

**Ch Batailley** Interesting to see what other airlines fly. Drinking quite well on SQ 143, Bali to Singapore, in January 1998. Ten months later, a rather better note: deep; very fragrant; sweet, positive fruit. A good, very drinkable '94. *Last tasted Nov 1998 (2)* ★★★ *Now–2016.*

**Ch Brane-Cantenac** Dry, tannic, undistinguished (1). Mature; coffee and spice; dull. *Last tasted Nov 1998 (2)* ★

**Ch Calon-Ségur** Very forward, evolved in appearance, nose and taste. Surprisingly sweet. Chunky. Firm. Attractive. *Last tasted Nov 1998 (2)* ★★★ *Drink soon.*

**Ch Cantenac-Brown** Seemed better first time round. Some sweetness, positive, good grip (1). Tar and tinny on the nose; raw tannin. Time the healer? I wonder. *Last tasted Nov 1998* ★?

**Dom de Chevalier** Attractive though very tannic and too much oak (1). The following year: jammy, oaky nose; plenty of fruit, some class but raw finish. *Last noted at a British Airways blind tasting, June 1997. Should have softened a little by now* ★(★)?

**Ch Clerc-Milon** Good fruit, very tannic (2). Immediately appealing, fragrant, mouthwatering Cabernet aroma; dry, lean, crisp, stylish. *Last noted at the tasting for the IWFS, Lyford Cay in the Bahamas, Jan 1999* ★★★ *Drink while crisp and still fresh.*

**Ch La Dominique** Rather disappointing. Poor nose, moderate palate, June 1997. Most recently: some fruit (Daphne noted 'rotten eggs'); very dry, sandpapery texture. *Last tasted at Lyford Cay, Feb 1999. Use up at a shooting party.*

**Ch L'Enclos** Merlot 82%, Cabernet Franc 16%, Malbec 2%. Selected to represent Pomerol at a couple of recent Christie's Bordeaux courses. Beautiful, honeyed, mellow nose evolving sweetly, like wholemeal biscuits; shapely, elegant, no harsh edges until its teeth-gripping tannic finale. *Last noted March 2000* ★(★★) *2005–2010.*

**Ch Grand-Puy-Lacoste** The youngest wine in the vertical at the château in June 1995. Showing well; good, intensely spicy/oak Cabernet Sauvignon nose and flavour. Most recently, having shed its youthful appeal, rather stern and unyielding. Needs time. *Last tasted from my own stock, Nov 2001* (★★) *2006–2012.*

**Ch Kirwan** Rich, biscuity nose and flavour. Much oak (1). Almost identical note two years later. Sweet, crisp tannin and acidity. *Last noted Nov 1998 (2)* ★★★ *Now–2008.*

**Ch Lafon-Rochet** Crisp fruit, characteristically tannic (1). Surprisingly attractive fruitiness. Tannin omnipresent. Will it ease enough over time to make a pleasing drink? *Last tasted Nov 1998* (★★)?

**Ch Lagrange** (St-Julien) Sweet, rich, appealing (1). Losing some of its puppy fat at a tasting in 1997. Hard nosed though with pleasant sweetness to moderate the tannin. *Last tasted Nov 1998* ★★★ *2005–2010.*

**Ch Langoa-Barton** Whiff of tar; fruity, chunky (1). The second time round noting a touch of 'green' stalkiness; good, but austere finish. Masculine version of Léoville. *Last tasted Nov 1998* ★(★) *2005–2010.*

**Ch Larmande** More wood than oak; almost corky. Severe (1). Next, a bottle from the château consumed with not much pleasure (or gratitude) at a Sunday lunch at Chippenham Lodge. Nose not too bad but coarse and woody on the palate. *Last tasted Feb 2001. Alas, not recommended.*

**Ch Lynch-Moussas** Despite its impressive appearance, a simple wine lacking length. A somewhat better note at a blind tasting, some fruit noted. *Last tasted June 1997* ★

**Ch La Tour-de-By** Average *cépages* mix: Cabernet Sauvignon 55%, Merlot 40%, Cabernet Franc 3% and Petit Verdot 2%. First tasted in September 1995 at the well-sited 19th-century château overlooking the Gironde. Marc Pagès thought his '94 was like his '88. Though it had crisp fruit, I found it very tannic. But he kindly sent me a case which my wife and I have been ploughing through since 1997. Good fruit, surprisingly sweet but still on the raw side. *Last tasted May 1998* ★(★)

BRIEF IMPRESSIONS OF THE '94s, tasted only once, either at the Union des Grands Crus tasting, April 1996 (1), the MW tasting, November 1998 (2), or on other occasions. **Ch Canon** woody, raw (1) ★; **Ch Canon-La-Gaffelière** fleshy, attractive (1) ★★★; **Ch Carbonnieux** pale; attractive; early developer (1) ★★; **Ch Clinet** deep, crisp, very tannic. *At the Ritz, April 1996* ★★★; **Ch La Conseillante** herbaceous; fragrant, oaky, very attractive (1) ★(★); **Ch le Crock** curious, cheesy nose; raw tannins. *At the Ritz, April 1996* ★; **Ch Croizet-Bages** on the pale side; crisp fruit; light style, raw (2) ★(★); **Ch Desmirail** advanced appearance and taste. Light style (2) ★★; **Ch Ducru-Beaucaillou** crisp fruit; tannic. Not inspiring (2) ★(★); **Ch Duhart-Milon** richly coloured; positive fruit; very attractive, for early drinking (2) ★★★; **Ch Durfort-Vivens** forward; chaptalised; sweet, soft, easy (2) ★★; **Ch L'Évangile** very good fruit, depth, length and bite (2) ★★(★★); **Ch Figeac** surprised only to have one note. Spicy nose; sweet, attractive, touch of bitterness (2) ★★(★); **Ch La Fleur-Pétrus** good, crisp fruit (2) ★★★; **Ch La Gaffelière** forward. Sweet, stewed character. (2) ★★; **Ch Gazin** meaty nose; rich fruit, attractive (1) ★★★; **Ch Haut-Batailley** pleasant, easy, open, agreeable. Not 'serious' (2) ★★★ *drink soon;* **Ch Larcis-Ducasse** oaky; stewed, hollow, touch of bitterness *At home, July 2000* ★; **Ch Marquis de Terme** very deep; unripe cherry; sweet, chunky, chewy, coarse (2) ★; **Ch La Mission Haut-Brion** luminous; stalky fruit opening up well; positive, attractive, tannic. Good wine (2) ★(★★) *2005–2010;* **Ch Pavie-Decesse** strange. Almost malty (1); **Ch Paveil-de-Luze** chaptalised nose; light style, unconvincing. A light lunch wine, which was exactly how we drank it. *Dec 1998* ★ *drink up;* **Ch La Pointe** surprisingly deep; some sweetness and depth, shapely, complete (1) ★★★; **Ch Pontet-Canet** dense; hard; full and richer than expected (1) ★★★;

**Ch Prieuré-Lichine** plummy; crisp, fragrant, very tannic (1) ★(★); **Ch Rauzan-Gassies** better nose than palate. Quite good strawberry-like fruit but raw tannic finish (2) ★; **Ch Siran** rich fruit, extract, tannin and acidity (1) ★★★; **Ch Sociando-Mallet** not a vintage to help its new reputation. Good nose but raw tannic finish. *Pre-sale tasting, May 1998* ★; and **Ch Trotanoy** very good wine. Cherry-like fruit; sweet, attractive (2) ★★(★)

# 1995 ★★★★

After the previous less inspiring four vintages, 1995 was much welcomed by trade and consumers alike. It was the first major *en primeur* vintage sales campaign since 1990; perhaps overhyped, with prices to match. Yet it has turned out well, to the extent that I am tempted to add an extra star. But let's see.

The growing season started well, early and consistent, following a very mild winter with substantial rainfall to help replenish the water level. Bud break was regular, with rapid flowering before the end of May. The driest summer for 20 years; unusually hot too, up to 30°C. *Véraison* was also early. In short, all was set for an exceptional vintage. Picking started early, on 11 September, but was almost immediately interrupted by heavy rain which then subsided into light showers. These lasted until the 20th, after which most châteaux resumed picking in increasingly warm weather ending with an Indian summer.

Some Merlots were caught by the early rain but Cabernet Franc and Cabernet Sauvignon were very successful, the latter achieving almost unheard of sugar levels. Overall, the wines are ripe, firm, with considerable charm and a good future.

**Ch Lafite** First noted and showing well at a major pre-sale tasting, including a dozen top '95s in New York, November 1997. Exactly two years later, at the MW tasting of '95s: deep and richly coloured; nose equally rich with rather gingery scent, sweaty tannins and considerable depth; sweet, good fruit, soft mid-palate, distinctly tannic. More recently, tasted blind, one of my top marks in a 'flight' of first growth '95s. In fact, all scored high, averaging between 93 and 96 points. The Lafite was still youthful looking; its nose deep, classic, rich and opening up well; sweet, good extract and fruit, the tannin and acidity more integrated. Elegant, firm, good future. Most recently, tasted blind at the end of a 'flight' of '89 double magnums. No wonder I found it different. Expecting an '89, a '95 Lafite had been delivered in error. Lacking the sweetness and richness of the first growth '89s, even a touch of astringency but firm, elegant, good future. *Last noted at the Eigensatz dinner, Nov 2001* ★★(★★★) *2007–2025*.

**Ch Latour** 100% new oak noted when first tasting the '95 at the château in April 1997. As expected, very intense, with opaque core; gloriously sweet and fragrant nose; good consistency, well integrated, very dry tannic finish. Next, in November 1997, at the pre-sale tasting mentioned above, with more flesh and fruit than the Lafite. Very good but colossally tannic at the MW tasting in 1999. At Rodenstock's blind tasting of first growth '95s, the nose somewhat chocolatey, also a whiff of tar; sweet, ripe, very dry but seeming less oppressively tannic. A fine wine. Long life predicted. *Last tasted March 2001* (★★★★★) *2020–2030 or beyond*.

**Ch Margaux** Five notes, the first in April 1997, seven months before it was due to be bottled. Tasted alongside the '96, there was a tremendous difference in style, the '95 seeming to have more of the elusive, indefinable vinosity; complete,

with gloriously mouthfilling young fruit, well integrated tannins and perfect balance. Again at the château, a year after it had been bottled: nose ripe, harmonious; good extract and fruit. At the MW tasting in 1999, losing some of its pristine depth of colour; sweet, distinctive Margaux fragrance; lovely flavour and length. Next, at Manfred Wagner's vertical in November 2000: bouquet fully developed; a touch of citrus fruit and dry finish. Most recently, tasted blind, my second highest mark of the first growth '95s. Maturing nicely; singed mocha nose and flavour, very tannic. I confess I did not recognise it as Margaux and even put 'not my style'. Dear me: it *is* a lovely wine and will continue to develop well. *Last tasted March 2001* ★(★★★) *2007–2020*.

**Ch Mouton-Rothschild** Also five notes, the first two in New York, December 1997. Crisp fruit and peppery at the pre-sale tasting, but quite unready for drinking at dinner the same evening. The following spring, making a note for the Mouton label book: opaque, velvety; nose like cedar pencils, opening up fragrantly; sweet, full, good extract, exciting flavour – 12.5% alcohol noted. In November 1999, beginning to open up at the MW tasting, its nose distinctly and characteristically spicy blackcurrant; deliciously crisp flavour and glorious end taste. My highest mark, though tied with three other first growths, at Rodenstock's blind tasting. *Last noted March 2001* ★(★★★★) *2007–2025*.

**Ch Haut-Brion** First noted in December 1997 at a pre-sale tasting in New York: deep, velvety; harmonious; very dry finish. Next, the opening wine at the MW Haut-Brion tasting in September 1998: nice texture and weight (13%), elegant. 'Delicious flavour, great length' among other facets noted at the MW tasting of '95s in November 1999, and, three months later, at yet another MW tasting, a vertical of Haut-Brion. Very detailed notes made: deep, crisp ruby with maturing rim; somewhat cherry-like fruit developing richly over 30 minutes in the glass; attractive fruit, chewy, shapely, good dry finish (Monsieur Delmas observed that the '95 was softer, smoother and rounder than the '96, with fleshier, mellower tannins). An equal top mark at Rodenstock's blind tasting of first growth '95s. Lovely wine. *Last tasted March 2001* ★★(★★★) *2005–2020*.

**Ch Ausone** The first year with Alain Vauthier in control. A paucity of notes as usual, though I do have two; both made the same month. At the MW tasting far less deep than the other first growths; an assertive, singed, mocha and oak nose and taste. Very sweet and attractive, though I had reservations. Shortly after, tasted blind: fragrant nose, mocha noted again, plus vanilla; nice weight and pleasant flavour. Stylish. Dry finish. *Last noted at the Bordeaux Index Right Bank blind tasting, Nov 1999* ★★(★★) *2005–2015*.

**Ch Cheval Blanc** A surprisingly sweet, chocolatey, rich, spicy magnum at the Wolf/Weinart vertical in September 1997. Three months later: delicious flavour and aftertaste. The following autumn, with Pierre Lurton at the château, its sweetness almost gamey; rich and chewy (64% Merlot I was informed). Equally admiring notes at the MW tasting of '95s in November 1999 and, later the same month, more detailed at the Bordeaux Index Right Bank blind tasting, including 'far too chocolatey' with a (pleasant, nostalgic) whiff of a thoroughbred stable; lean but flavoury. Although 'chocolatey' noted again at Rodenstock's blind tasting, I awarded it equal top mark, adding 'sweet, easy', 'maturing quickly' and 'great charm'. *Last tasted March 2001* ★★★(★) *Now–2015*.

**Ch Pétrus** In 'flight' two of Rodenstock's blind tasting of first growth '94s, '95s, '96s and '97s: medium deep, lovely colour, maturing; good nose, a bit stalky at first but a class act; sweeter than expected (I did not know it was Pétrus), good flavour, extract and assimilated tannin. It received the highest overall (average) mark though the level was remarkably uniform, only 2 points out of 100 separating them, mine being at the lower end. *Tasted in Munich, March 2001* ★★★(★★) *2006–2020*.

OTHER '95S I did not attend either of the Union des Grands Crus tastings, the widest range of notes being made at the MW tasting of '95s in November 1999. Other notes include lunches and dinners at our flat in London or our weekend retreat near Bath. Whenever a bottle is opened, I taste and make notes before, and then with, the meal.

**Ch L'Angélus** Merlot 50%, Cabernet Franc 47%, Cabernet Sauvignon 3%. Deep, velvety, intense, impressive; attractive fruit; very sweet, fleshy, lovely flavour and texture. A 'quick maturing wine'. Will certainly progress. Coincidentally the next two notes made within a fortnight of each other, the first at the MW tasting in November 1999: very sweet, full, rich, with teeth-gripping tannins. A more critical note made at the Bordeaux Index Right Bank blind tasting. I preferred the nose (mocha, chocolatey, good depth) to the palate which though hefty, impressive, full of fruit and extract, lacked charm. *Last noted Nov 1999* ★★(★★) *2005–2015*.

**Ch d'Armailhac** First noted at the Hollywood Wine Society's Mouton seminar presented by Robin Kelly in March 1998: good fruit. A charmer. Next, a bottle from the château: starting to mature, good rich 'legs'; sweet, very fruity; perfect weight, crisp flavour. *Last noted before and during Sunday lunch at Chippenham Lodge, May 2001* ★★★(★) *Now–2015*.

**Ch Batailley** Over half a dozen notes. 'A copybook Batailley' from the start: Freddie Price's trade tasting in May 1996 at Davy's wine bar, conveniently close to Christie's. Next, at an extensive British Airways blind tasting in June 1997. Of the 44 clarets, 15 were '95s. Batailley performed well, certainly one of the runners up: sweet, full, chunky. Almost too good to be true at the MW tasting, November 1999: speciously delicious. Most recently, at a France in Your Glass masterclass at Eugénie-les-Bains, partnering Ch Lynch-Bages. Still a youthfully mauve appearance; archetypal nose, lovely flavour. Still tannic of course. *Last tasted Dec 2001* ★★★(★) *2005–2015*.

**Ch Beychevelle** Cabernet Sauvignon 60%, Merlot 28%, Cabernet Franc 8% and Petit Verdot 4% – a good spread of classic Médoc grape varieties. First noted at the British Airways tasting in June 1997, in fact one of my three highest marks of the entire range ('92s to '96s): pleasing texture and flesh, nice weight, easy style. More recently, and most interestingly, at a tasting of all the classed growth St-Juliens of the '95s vintage at Vinopolis in London: middle of the road colour, touch of mahogany, trying to mature; fragrant, refreshing, 'cedar pencils' nose; rich fruit, agreeable body (12.5% alcohol), a touch of grittiness mid-palate, dry finish. *Last tasted March 2000* ★★★(★) *2004–2015*.

**Ch Branaire-Duluc-Ducru** (to give it its full title). Cabernet Sauvignon 70%, Merlot 22%, Cabernet Franc 5% and Petit Verdot 3%. First tasted at the MW tasting in June 1997: very sweet, lots of fruit to balance the usual Branaire oakiness. Next at the Union des Grands Crus opening dinner in Bordeaux, March 1999: drinking well, crisp, nice style. Most recently, at the St-Julien tasting of '95s at Vinopolis: thick core, long 'legs', slightly weak rim; fragrant, crisp, mouthwatering fruit; touch of sweetness, good body (13% alcohol), dry finish. An easy 'food wine'. *Last noted March 2000* ★★★(★) *2005–2015*.

**Ch Clerc-Milon** Spicy, tannic, crisp yet a quick developer (tasting at Christie's in 1997). The last of eight wines at the Bordeaux tasting at Lyford Cay in the Bahamas in 1999: ignoring Daphne's 'mothballs' for I found the nose soft, sweet, somewhat strawberry-like; interestingly only 12% alcohol. Chewy, chocolatey, nice wine. A bottle from the château and rather disappointing: a sweet, fleshy, 'thick' Cabernet nose and taste spoiled by a raw dry finish, an astringency so pronounced that even the lamb could not disguise it. *Last tasted at lunch, Chippenham Lodge, May 2001* ★★★ *Might sober up.*

**Ch Cos d'Estournel** First noted in June 1999 at a comparative tasting of Cos and Ch Pichon-Lalande of four vintages. Interesting contrast of styles, the Cos fairly deep and intense; dumb at first, fruit emerging; almost too sweet and ripe on the palate, and by no means a lightweight (13% alcohol). Four months later, attending James Suckling's 'Super-seconds' tasting at the New York Wine Experience, commentary by Jean-Guillaume, Bruno Prat's son: lovely rich velvety colour; broad, tea-like, gingery nose; rich, 'tobacco' spice. 'Fresh, with good balance of sugar and acidity'. Finally noted at the MW tasting and once again noting its sweet, too mocha nose and taste. An American taste? *Last noted Nov 1999* ★★★(★) *2005–2015*.

**Ch La Dauphine** I have always liked this wine; so did Christian Moueix when in the 1990s he made a surprise move buying this Fronsac château and some others in the same district. Not long after – in 2000 – he sold them, telling me frankly that he had had an offer he could not resist. Anyway, I bought some halves of the '95 from Justerini & Brooks for drinking at home. It was delicious at five years of age. *Last noted supping at Chippenham Lodge, Oct 2000* ★★★

**Ch Dauzac** Very deep, velvety, intense; fragrant, some oakiness; agreeable weight, flavour, consistency and flesh. *Dining at Ch Bonnet with André Lurton who has been advising Dauzac since 1992, Oct 2001* ★★★(★)

**Ch Ducru-Beaucaillou** Cabernet Sauvignon 65%, Merlot 25%, Cabernet Franc 5%, Petit Verdot 5%. At the MW tasting rich but very tannic. Four months later at the Vinopolis St-Julien tasting: 'thick', singed, whiff of petrol, mocha and toast; sweet, rich, very good mid-fruit, 13% alcohol, toasted, oaky tannic finish. *Last tasted March 2000* ★★(★★) *2006–2015*.

**Ch Durfort-Vivens** Rather reassuring to drink a wine selected for British Airways in 1997 – stylish but raw and tannic at that stage – on a British Airways flight: very flavoury but still pretty tannic. *Last noted on BA 10, Sydney to Bangkok. (Len Evans' story is that if you take your wife to Bangkok, you have to pay corkage.)* ★★(★) *Now–2012*.

**Ch L'Église-Clinet** Hardy Rodenstock can be credited with first drawing attention to Denis Durantou's genius, endorsed by Farr Vintners. My first note however was at a tasting of '95s, before a charity dinner at Christie's in New York. Then two verticals within two months of each other in 1998, first with Farr Vintners in July: alas, horribly corked. Next, tasted blind in Munich: very good though the '82, '85 and '89 got higher marks. Most recently, not for the first time, craftily inserted by Hardy into the blind tasting of first growth '95s: still a very deep, immature appearance; nose slow to rise from the glass but enormously impressive on the palate, full and rich. I had no idea what it was, awarding it equal highest marks with the '95 Cheval Blanc, Mouton and Haut-Brion. *Last tasted March 2001* ★★(★★) *2005 –2015*.

**Ch L'Enclos** Representing Pomerol at two recent Christie's Bordeaux wine courses. Merlot 82%, Cabernet Franc 17% and, unusually, Malbec 1%. Deep, red-brown rim; delicious soft fruit scent which comes up to meet you halfway; sweet, silky texture, fleshy fruit, dry finish. *Last tasted March 2002* ★★★(★)

**Ch La Fleur-Pétrus** Merlot 90%, Cabernet Franc 10%. Almost too sweet at the MW tasting in November 1999. Convincing, maturing; harmonious – a bouquet of real quality; rich, full-bodied (13.5% alcohol), soft, fleshy fruit, extract masking tannin. Lovely wine. *Last noted at a Bordeaux tasting at Eugenie-lès-Bains, July 2001* ★★★(★)

**Ch Figeac** First noted in September 1998 dining in style at the château with Mark Birley, the Lloyd-Webbers, the Palumbos, and Olga and Dieter Bock. The '95 was the first of four delicious vintages to be served: stylish though youthful and drinking well. Next, in October 1999, at a tasting of '95s and '90s for France in Your Glass guests at Vonnas, the tiny French village which is totally dominated by Georges Blanc's luxurious eating-hole. The Figeac typically fragrant, touch of raspberry (ripe Cabernet Franc?), well evolved and more dramatic than the '90. Sweet, fleshy, 13% alcohol. More recently, at the MW tasting, a nice uplift of crisp fruit but still tannic. *Last noted Nov 1999* ★★★(★) 2006–2016.

**Ch Giscours** Sweet, fair fruit, oaky tannin (June 1997). A moderate note in June 1999. Five months later, more not-too-generous comments: spicy; not bad fruit, leaner than expected. *Last noted at the MW tasting, Nov 1999* ★(★)?

**Ch Grand-Puy-Lacoste** Bottles from my own stock provided for Grand-Puy-Lacoste masterclasses, April 1999 and March 2000, with the MW tasting in between. Typical, archetypal, a wine in a vintage like this which, to me, epitomises the best, understated, unshowy Pauillac – all it ever lacks is time. It is a leisurely developer, as if waiting for all the component parts to feel comfortable with each other: fruit, the sweetness of ripe grapes, good flesh, a touch of leanness, and elegance. Most recently, a bottle for supper at Chippenham Lodge to see how it was coming along. Beginning to drink well. *Last noted Dec 2001* ★★★(★) 2010–2020.

**Ch Gruaud-Larose** Cabernet Sauvignon 60%, Merlot 30%, Cabernet Franc 7%, Petit Verdot 3%. In May 1997, deep, ripe, minty, rich. Two months later at the MW tasting: plummy, smooth textured. At the St-Julien '95s tasting: starting to mature; mint noted again, its nose opening up beautifully; soft, fleshy fruit, peppery finish. Very typical Gruaud mouthful. *Last tasted March 2000* ★★★(★★) Now–2015.

**Ch Haut-Bailly** At the MW tasting, November 1999: fully evolved nose; surprisingly sweet, rich, lovely fruit and oak. Two years later, at the château: perfect weight and balance. Still tannic. Most recently, very fragrant; sweet, shapely, lovely. *Last noted at a Christie's masterclass, April 2002* ★★★(★★) Now–2012.

**Ch Labégorce-Zédé** Earlier vintages of this consistently well made *bourgeois* Margaux have been mainly noted at Thienpont tastings. Later, until we finished it, the '95 was a good home consumption standby. Perhaps I should have kept it longer. Deep, velvety; a touch of stalkiness; rich, full of fruit. *Last noted at Chippenham Lodge, Oct 1999* ★★(★) 2005–2010.

**Ch Lagrange** (St-Julien) Cabernet Sauvignon 66%, Merlot 27% and Petit Verdot 7%. The biggest classed growth vineyard in St-Julien and well managed. Just two notes, good fruit and grip (June 1997) and a detailed note at the St-Julien tasting of '95s: beautiful colour, touch of mauve; lovely, cedary nose, fragrant, quite a lot of oak; dry, good wine, a tannic bite on the finish but not harsh. Needs food – and time. *Last tasted at Vinopolis, 'City of Wine', beneath monumental brick-vaulted arches south of the Thames, March 2000* ★★(★★) 2006–2016.

**Ch La Lagune** In the past, this château produced 'the burgundy of the Médoc'. Seems to toe the line now. First tasted in April 1999: fair sweetness though very tannic. Quite a lot to it. The next occasion was, in a sense, more amusing. The 80 or so wine writers who congregate in Bordeaux for a week in April are generously accommodated at various châteaux. La Lagune's guest quarters are rather bleak, and after an exhausting day of tastings, the three of us allocated to the château were dying for a refreshing drink – and food. Champagne was on the cards and it is fortunate that La Lagune is owned by Ayala. A bottle was brought. There was no white wine so I brought out a bottle I had been given by André Lurton. One bottle of claret was provided: the '95: deep ruby; sweetish, soft, very oaky, agreeable. To stimulate further our witty and wicked chat I then sacrificed my last bottle of '94 Broadbent port which had been intended for our (absent) host. In the end, a good time was had by all three of us. At least we weren't charged corkage. *Last tasted March 2001.* ★★★

**Ch Lascombes** Deep, still youthful looking; pleasant enough fruit, a very slight touch of stalkiness; better on palate. Still tannic. *At a pre-sale tasting, Sept 2001* ★★(★)

**Ch Léoville-Barton** Cabernet Sauvignon 72%, Merlot 20%, Cabernet Franc 8%. Nine notes starting with a good cask sample in May 1996. Lean but fragrant the following year. Three in October 1999, the first at George Blanc's restaurant in Vonnas, the next at the annual wine dinner at the Knickerbocker Club in New York: impressive, substantial. The following day at the 'Super-seconds' tasting, as correct and gentlemanly as Anthony Barton who introduced his wine. One month later at the MW tasting: delicious, mouthfilling, spicy. Even more so at Vinopolis and the opening wine at Christie's Three Léovilles/three vintages tasting in March 2001: refreshing, charming, overall dry. Most recently in a line-up of the decade: deeper than the '90, rich, dense; fragrant, harmonious nose with quite different character to the '91, '92 and '93; lovely flavour and texture. Mocha, oaky, tannic finish. Classic. *Last tasted at the château, Oct 2001* ★★★(★★) 2005–2020.

**Ch Léoville-Las-Cases** Cabernet Sauvignon 65%, Merlot 19%, Cabernet Franc 13% and Petit Verdot 3% – usually a higher percentage of Petit Verdot. Fragrant but swingeingly tannic at the MW tasting (November 1999). The value of a seated tasting proving itself on the next two occasions, though there is only space here for a fraction of my notes. In essence: a strikingly impressive appearance; sweet rich nose, full of fruit. (In March 2000 I see my wife added – for she takes notes when I am lecturing – 'mumble mumble'. Someone once said that listening to me was 'a triumph of mind over mutter'.) On the palate its natural sweetness and rich extract masking the tannin. The first note made at Vinopolis, the most recent at Christie's Three Léovilles tasting: no harsh edges, harmonious nose; mouthfilling; smooth despite its tannin. *Last tasted March 2001* ★(★★★★) 2008–2020.

**Ch Léoville-Poyferré** Cabernet Sauvignon 65%, Merlot 25%, Petit Verdot 8%, Cabernet Franc 2%. Half a dozen notes from a very good, fleshy cask sample in April 1996. Two good notes in 1997: surprisingly sweet, attractive despite immature raw tannin. Less deep; citrus whiff; appealing fruit and refreshing acidity (MW tasting 1999). Very convincing, immediate impact, mouthfilling (Vinopolis, March 2000). Most recently, velvety, fragrant, blackcurrant plus a whiff of singed peat; shapely, moderately substantial, lean, dry and austere. 'Needs another five to ten years'. *Last noted at Christie's Three Léovilles tasting, March 2001* ★★(★★) 2006–2016.

**Ch Lynch-Bages** Ten notes, three in 1997, a totally predictable wine. Clearly unready when first tasted in July but starting to evolve later that autumn. Its appearance almost opaque. Shortly after, in October 1997, a touch of sweetness and flesh, with a whiff of sea breeze. Used at three France in Your Glass masterclasses between 1997 and June 2000, gradually changing colour and opening up, with the inimitable Lynch-Bages fragrance and vivacity. Showing well at the MW tasting. More recently, the best wine – sweet, delicious – opened for the Chaîne des Rôtisseurs at the Lion d'Or in the Médoc. *Last tasted June 2000* ★★★(★★) *Now–2015.*

**Ch La Mission Haut-Brion** First tasted in December 1997 at a pre-dinner tasting in New York: totally unready, masculine, raw dryness. Two years later: showing some of its characteristic mocha nose; very good crisp fruit, extended tannic finish. *Last noted at the MW tasting, Nov 1999* ★★(★★) *Say 2008–2020.*

**Ch Montrose** At the MW tasting in November 1999: not as deep but certainly as tannic as expected. Nose undeveloped. Packed with fruit. Most recently, its nose now crisp and ripe, with concealed depth; lovely flavour and grip. *Last tasted at Farr Vintners, Oct 2001* ★★(★★★) *Will prove a winner 2006–2020.*

**Ch Palmer** An unusually high percentage of Merlot for the Médoc: 50.8%, the rest being Cabernet Sauvignon. Quality apparent from a half bottle cask sample in May 1996 and the wine never looked back. One of the 'Super-seconds' at the Wine Experience in New York, October 1999: fairly deep, velvety, crisp fruit; very tannic. Totally delicious at the MW tasting in November 1999. Most recently, four days apart, at the Sichel and Farr Vintners/Mähler-Besse tastings: still very deep; the nose needed time to come out of its shell. A lovely wine, for me a cross in style, weight and quality between the '59 and '66. *Last tasted Feb 2001* ★★★(★★) *2005–2015.*

**Ch Pichon-Baron** First noted at the Cazes AXA tasting at the Cavalry Club in London in April 1996: even then some elegance but dominated by oak and tannin. The other half dozen notes show slow progression, including three 'correct but slightly astringent' noted in 1997 and two at masterclasses in 1998. Teeth-gripping tannin. Frankly I did not think it fully deserved its place among the 'Super-seconds' and was still a bit raw at the MW tasting. *Last tasted Nov 1999* (★★★)? *Frankly disappointing.*

**Ch Pichon-Lalande** Cabernet Sauvignon 45%, Merlot 40%, Cabernet Franc 15% (no Petit Verdot this time – usually there is about 8% – because its growth was arrested by the summer heat). Many notes. A total contrast to neighbouring Baron. Softer, sweeter, more fragrant, though still with leathery tannins in June 1997. Steady development yet the bottles presented by May de Lencquesaing for the *Decanter* millennium and 'Man of the Year' dinner in July 1999 (the 'man' was Jancis Robinson!), though full of fruit was bitterly tannic. Nevertheless, that autumn I think it warranted its place among the 'Super-seconds. Distinctive, scented; sweet, rich, chewy at the MW tasting and equally fragrant, almost gamey at a Lalande tasting at Eugénie-les-Bains. *Last tasted Oct 2000* ★★(★★) *2008–2020.*

**Ch Smith-Haut-Lafitte** Quite a few notes made either at the château or nearby at La Caudalie, the Cathiards' elegantly rustic hotel/restaurant and spa. Certainly a well made and attractive '95. Surprisingly sweet, good mid-fruit and dry finish. *Last tasted March 2001* ★★★(★) *2005–2015.*

**Ch Talbot** Cabernet Sauvignon 66%, Merlot 24%, Cabernet Franc 5%, Petit Verdot 2% and, unusually, Malbec 3%. Showing well at a British Airways tasting in June 1997: fragrant, cedary; good fruit. At the MW tasting, a touch of Talbot *fermier* – ripe,

rustic smell; attractive sweetness but of course still tannic (November 1999). Four months later, a detailed note at the Vinopolis St-Julien tasting of '95s. Not as deep as some of the '95s but a very polished appearance; a really beautiful fragrance, cedar pencils (farmyard not noted this time); interesting texture, crisp fruit, straightforward, a bit four-square, dry finish. *Last tasted March 2000* ★★(★★) *2005–2015.*

A SELECTION OF THE MANY OTHER '95S, TASTED BETWEEN 1997 AND 2002 **Ch d'Angludet** very good nose, extract and flavour ★★★; **Ch d'Arcins** a minor Médoc but agreeable ★★; **Ch Beauséjour-Duffau-Lagarosse** (and one thought that only German names were complicated), one of many half bottles for recent home drinking ★★★; **Ch du Bosq** more halves from Justerini's. Very good fruit. A perfect vintage for this class of wine ★★★; **Ch Brane-Cantenac** loose knit, coffee bean flavour ★★; **Ch Canon** sweet, spicy; delicious though tannic ★★★(★); **Ch Canon-La-Gaffelière** a strawberry-like charmer ★★★; **Ch Cantemerle** sweet, gingery; good flavour and weight ★★★; **Ch Cantenac-Brown** good fruit, agreeable ★★★; **Ch Certan-de-May** touch of liquorice; Unusual flavour and style ★★★?; **Ch Certan-Guiraud** very deep; curiously sweet, interesting ★★?; **Dom de Chevalier** lively, nose opening quickly; a bit raw but should be very good now ★★★?; **Ch Cissac** opaque; good but time in hand ★★(★); **Ch Clinet** opaque; idiosyncratic, tarry; fairly sweet, concentrated. Very good in its way ★★★; **Ch La Croix-du-Casse** yet another Justerini & Brooks half. Rustic nose and taste. Fleshy. 'Toasted iron tannins' ★★(★); **Ch Desmirail** quite good Margaux fragrance and fruit. Chunky and somewhat coarse. More bottle age should smooth the edges ★★(★); **Dom de L'Église** (not to be confused with L'Église-Clinet.) Easy style. Lacking class ★★; **Ch L'Étoile** lesser known Graves of a vintage like this are usually very good value ★★; **Ch L'Évangile** alas only one (very recent) note: attractive fruit; lovely flavour, texture and length ★★★★; **Ch Feytit-Clinet** *Cuvée de la Comète* (very old vines). Good chunky flavour ★★★; **Ch La Fleur** suave, stylish, tannic (Rodenstock vertical) ★★★★; **Ch Gazin** chocolatey; attractive, lighter style to the 'flowers' above. ★★★; **Ch Grand-Puy-Ducasse** dreadful nose; medicinal, bitter; **Ch Kirwan** 'a good Merlot vintage'. Lots of new oak but richness and flesh to compensate ★★★(★)?; **Ch Lafon-Rochet** typically hard, oaky, lean but good flavour ★★(★); **Ch Langoa-Barton** deep, still youthful; beautiful cedar nose which opened up attractively; good fruit. Dry finish ★★★; **Ch Larmande** fruit and flesh. Bitter tannic finish ★★(★); **Ch Lynch-Moussas** good wine. All the components neatly arranged ★★★; **Ch Magdelaine** very distinctive. Sweet. Good length ★★★; **Ch Prieuré-Lichine** surprisingly sweet. Fruity. Attractive. ★★★; **Ch Rauzan-Ségla** spicy, oaky, rich, stylish ★★★(★); **Ch Rauzan-Gassies** sweet, chewy but not up to 2ème cru standard ★★; **Clos René** lovely, harmonious nose; beguiling, fleshy, soft tannins ★★★(★); **Ch Roc-de-Combes** François Mitjavile and his son have transformed this modest Côtes de Bourg château and the wine is now rich, unusual, very distinctive ★★★; **Ch de Sales** easy, agreeable. ★★★; **Ch St-Pierre** sweet, chocolatey; toasted oak, a bit overdone. Touch of vulgarity and coarseness ★★; **Ch du Tertre** strange overtones; good fruit but raw metallic tannins (old note) (★★)?; **Ch Tertre-Roteboeuf** deep; rich; sweet, and chewy ★★★★; **Ch La Tour-Figeac** deep; good extract and flavour ★★★; **Ch Tronquoy-Lalande** one of my 'everyday' half bottles.

Still opaque. Very tannic but good with Daphne's shank of lamb stew! ★★; **Ch Troplong-Mondot** good fruit and grip ★★; and **Ch Trotanoy** last but certainly not least: sweet, fruit-laden ★★★★★

# 1996 ★★ to ★★★★

Though upstaged by the attractive '95s, this vintage is better than it was first made out to be, and improves greatly on acquaintance. Indeed, after looking through my notes, I think it is a seriously underrated vintage.

First, the vital (growing) statistics: the occasional bouts of frost in February and March were too early to do any damage though the bud break was delayed until mid-April. The all important flowering was quick and even, finished by the 20th day of a very hot June. It continued warm until August which started cool but ended with hot sun and cold nights. High expectations were initially dampened, pre-harvest rain affecting the early-ripening Merlots which diluted and reduced the crop size in Pomerol and St-Émilion. The Médoc fared better with roughly half the rainfall, though towards the end of September, it rained again. The late-picked Cabernets were of high quality resulting in rich, fairly concentrated wines. This vintage is worth watching.

**Ch Lafite** There are some cellars I feel able to taste in, but Lafite is not one of them (too cold), so the first whiff of the '96 was *en passant* before dinner at the château. I merely and inadequately noted that it was deep, complete and had good length. Next, a couple of years later, it was showing very well at the MW tasting of '96s in November 2000: still plummy and immature; more earthy than expected but fragrant and with depth. On the palate, crisp, lovely flavour and length. Last noted at Rodenstock's blind tasting of first-growth '94s, '95s, '96s and '97s. Slight bottle variation. Both bottles (of the '96) with opaque core, the first a bit vegetal though a classic Cabernet; rather raw; the second seemed to have better fruit, tannin and acidity. I was interested to note, when all had been revealed, that the average score of the pretty experienced tasters only slightly varied, ranging from 92 to 95 points, most 93 and 94. Lafite was the latter though my own rating was one point less. As so often, a wine that needs time, and patience. *Last tasted March 2001 (★★★★) Possibly 2012–2030?*

**Ch Latour** The *grand vin* first tasted at the château in September 1998. After the delicious '97, it was low-keyed and stern. Very tannic. Only a couple of years later, at the MW tasting of '96s, though deep, it appeared advanced. At first sniff, it seemed very similar to the Lafite – overall I gave it identical marks (18/20). I do not use the 100-point scale unless my host insists and the context is appropriate. Surprisingly sweet, too. Chewy. Good fruit, very dry finish. But at the Rodenstock blind tasting of '96 first growths I gave it my second highest mark, two points above the average. Lovely colour; touch of mocha, fragrant; stylish, very good flavour, silky/leathery tannic finish. *Last tasted March 2001 (★★★★) 2015–2030.*

**Ch Margaux** The *grand vin* was 85% Cabernet Sauvignon and Cabernet Franc, Merlot 10% and Petit Verdot 5%. It is always a joy to taste at Margaux and in April 1997, I tasted the '96 alongside the '95, which was totally different in style. The '96 was opaque, of course; low-keyed but with classic fruit; lovely flavour, lean, spicy tannic finish. I added 'clearly a wine of finesse, like a champion lady swimmer, sinewy, streamlined, shapely, with firm, rippling pectoral muscles'. Next tasted in September 1998, a month after it had been bottled, prior to

lunch with the pickers. Dark cherry; crisp, tight, taut fruit; lean, with elegance as well as power. Good potential. Next, in April 2000 at the château where Paul Pontallier told us that it was one of his favourite vintages. Mouthfilling, very tannic, great potential. Later that autumn, extremely high marks at the MW tasting. Perfect colour; nose developing sweetly and on the palate a soft entry and fragrant finish. At the second of Manfred Wagner's Margaux verticals, once again, it proved a foil to the '95, being different, with a touch of tar, spice and citrus fruit on the nose. Very tannic. The following spring, at Rodenstock's blind tasting of first growths it earned, with Ch Cheval Blanc, my highest mark. But what was extraordinary was the closeness of everyone's points. I noted it as the sweetest of all, wonderful fruit, masked tannins. *Last noted March 2001 (★★★★) 2010–2020.*

**Ch Mouton-Rothschild** As with the other first growth Médocs, one has to book a precise date and time to taste. I usually fall in with Steven Spurrier, so in September 1998, we were allowed to taste their Médoc 'stable', d'Armailhac, Clerc-Milon and the *grand vin* of the two vintages, '96 and '97. We discussed the wines with Hervé Berland who told us that the *cépages* mix of the '96 *grand vin* was Cabernet Sauvignon 77%, Merlot 13%, Cabernet Franc 10%. It had an extraordinary nose, toasted mocha; sweet, full, rich, lovely Cabernet flavour and end taste. Indeed I gave it my top mark at the MW tasting in November 2000. Rich extract; a ripe, wonderfully fragrant, 'manifold' nose. Lovely. The following spring, 'mocha' noted again; sweet, chunky, a touch of tannic bitterness. But a fine wine. *Last tasted March 2001 (★★★★★) 2012–2030.*

**Ch Haut-Brion** Just five notes starting in September 1998 at the château with Jean Delmas: medium deep; plummy coloured; softer and more harmonious on nose and palate than the '97 alongside. Nice texture, moderate length. Next, at the MW Haut-Brion tasting in January 2000. Still with youthful good looks; very fragrant, earthy, mocha – Delmas said 'very characteristic Pessac, burnt jam and (can't read my writing!) wine with a high level of residual sugar and high acidity'. Certainly a rich, chunky wine, with a tannic, iron finish and aftertaste. Ten months later, at the MW tasting of '96s, I wrote: 'totally different ball game'. High mark. Lovely richness and texture. Most recently, tasted blind against six other first growth '96s. Now medium-deep with rich 'legs'; nose packed with fruit, fragrant; sweet, fairly full body masking the tannin and acidity, complete, lovely flavour. My mark was higher than the average. I rated it on a par with Ch Margaux. *Last noted at one of Rodenstock's wine dinners, March 2001 (★★★★) 2008–2025.*

**Ch Cheval Blanc** First tasted at the château in April 1997. Neither very deep nor intense, but rich; a lovely, young scent, extraordinarily peachy; flavour to match. Chewy, attractive. At the MW tasting in November 2000, it looked as though it would be fairly quick maturing; very fragrant, this time 'soft raspberries'. Perfect balance. 'A charmer'. At the Rodenstock blind tasting mentioned above, much the same. Developing well. A lovely wine. *Last tasted March 2001 ★★★★ 2006–2018.*

**Ch Ausone** First tasted in the most impressive *cave* – literally a cave, a Roman underground quarry in St-Émilion – in April 1998: impressively deep, fairly intense, a certain leanness and masculinity. More recently, at the MW tasting of '96s: very forthcoming nose and, I thought, pretty alcoholic; medium dryness and medium-full body. Very straightforward. Once such an uneven performer, Ausone seems to have taken on a new lease of life without losing its distinctive character. *Last tasted November 2000 (★★★★) Say 2008–2020.*

**PREFACE TO THE FOLLOWING '96S** A young red Bordeaux starts life with a purple tinge but the depth of colour and intensity varies. The nose will combine a young fruit aroma and oak to a greater or lesser degree. All will be tannic. In the case of wines tasted in the spring after the vintage, only the exceptions will be noted: exceptionally deep or pale; exceptional oakiness and hard tannins, plus a general comment on overall quality and style. The opening tastings were all held in host châteaux in their respective districts in April 1997 and the '96s comprehensive tasting took place in London in November 2000. Apart from the first growths, the wines are lined up district by district very fairly and democratically in alphabetical order.

**Ch L'Angélus** The first wine of the opening tasting in April 1997 of Right Bank wines – 12 St-Émilions, 11 Pomerols – at Ch Franc-Mayne. Incidentally all the bottles here were very cold, which made it rather hard work. Opaque; muffled, indistinct nose; fair fruit but harsh tannins. Three and a half years later, some colour loss though still pretty deep; hefty, fruit-laden on nose and palate. Very dry finish. Impressive. *Last noted at the MW tasting of '96s, Nov 2000* (★★★★) *2006–2015.*

**Ch d'Armailhac** Cabernet Sauvignon 55%, Merlot 25%, Cabernet Franc 20%. Several notes: muffled mulberry; sweet, delicious fruit and flavour. Tannic of course. Most recently: fairly deep, with a thick midriff; lively, interesting nose; crisp fruit, refreshing, still a bit raw. *Last noted at Christie's Bordeaux wine course, July 2001* ★★(★) *2004–2012.*

**Ch Batailley** At a British Airways tasting in June 1997: opaque; slightly charred scent and touch of caramel; sweet; full, rich fruit, attractive. More recently: intense, still with a youthful mauve rim; lovely nose, 'well put together'. 'A good mid-term drink'. *Last noted at a France in Your Glass masterclass at Eugénie-les-Bains, June 2000* (★★★) *2006–2015.*

**Ch Beauregard** In April 1997: brambly fruit; dry, a quite impressive youthful Pomerol. Next, not a very deep colour; slightly chocolatey, appealing, easy-going. *Last noted Nov 2000* ★★★ *Now–2012.*

**Ch Beauséjour-Bécot** Positive, good fruit and texture, vivacious (April 1997). Harmonious; sweet, soft, easy but complete (Nov 2000). Most recently, still youthful; rich nose but, I thought, far too oaky on the palate. *Last noted at the opening Union des Grands Crus dinner at Ch d'Yquem, March 2001* ★(★★) *2006–2015.*

**Ch Bernadotte** A *cru bourgeois* bought by May de Lencquesang in 1995 and run by her nephew Gildas d'Ollone. First tasted at Pichon-Lalande in September 1998: good, crisp, spicy fruit. Then, supping with Gildas after a session accompanying him on the flute: sweet, rich, drinking well. *Last noted Oct 2001* ★★★

**Ch Beychevelle** Quite good fruit, mocha-like nose. A moderately good mark, tasted blind at a British Airways tasting, October 1999. An almost identical mark at the MW tasting though the description was slightly less complimentary: a slightly smelly, earthy, rustic nose. Better on the palate. *Last tasted Nov 2000* ★★? *Room for improvement.*

**Ch Branaire-Ducru** Just one note: an attractive ruby colour; crisp, fragrant nose and taste. Oak very noticeable, as always. Lean. Raw tannins. *Nov 2000* (★★★) *2008–2016.*

**Ch Brane-Cantenac** A Lurton family château. In April 1997 I tasted the range of Margauxs blind. Impressive looking; some fruit but sweaty tannins, later 'privet', and a citrus touch; agreeable flesh and fruit. More recently: plummy colour; fairly sweet, rich, with crisp fruit. The wine of this once 'farmyard'-reminiscent château has taken a distinct turn for the better. *Last tasted Nov 2000* ★★(★★) *2006–2016.*

**Ch Calon-Ségur** First noted at a British Airways blind tasting. I gave it only moderate marks. Not very impressed at the MW tasting. Not very deep; a pleasant-enough, sweet, easy sort of wine though with a touch of coarseness. *Last tasted Nov 2000* ★(★) *Now–2012.*

**Ch Canon** The château was having problems around this time because fungicide applied to the new wooden beams of the *chai* installed in the 1980s was leaching out, affecting the casks. At the tasting in April 1997, I noted a slightly sickly nose; strange flavour, like a Douro red. Others I talked to also noted something not quite right. But later, it seemed to have got its second breath, its nose had opened up, fully developed; sweet, open, easy style – just a curious crushed stem taste on the finish. *Last tasted Nov 2000* (★★?) *Drink soon.*

**Ch Canon-La Gaffelière** April 1997: opaque, intense; closed, later rather sickly; positive, 'Italianate', very tannic. I can't say that I took to it, but the following April it seemed to have simmered down: good fruit; a substantial wine. *Last noted at the château, April 1998* ★(★★) *possibly 4 stars. Say 2006–2016.*

**Ch Cantemerle** First tasted in April 1997: full flavoured, rich fruit, specious spicy oak. Most recently, a brief note *en passant* at Farr Vintners': 'attractive but …'. A decent drink, no more. *Last tasted Oct 2001* ★★ *Now–2000.*

**Ch Cantenac-Brown** April 1997: pleasant enough, chewy, a bit lacking. Developing well. A touch of earthiness, easy, attractive. 'Medium life expectancy'. *Last noted Nov 2000* ★★(★) *2006–2015.*

**Ch Les Carmes-Haut-Brion** April 1997: a fragrant immediacy about the nose; distinctive, quick maturing. Touch of Graves 'tobacco', good flesh. Nice wine. *Last noted at a Union des Grands Crus dinner in March 2001* ★★★ *Now–2012.*

**Ch Chasse-Spleen** Once again, well above its class. In April 1997: deep velvety violet; good flavour, cedar and citrus finish. Nice weight, 12.8% alcohol. *Last noted supping at Chippenham Lodge, June 2000* ★★★ *Now–2012.*

**Dom de Chevalier** April 1997: plenty of fruit, complete but I thought a bit heavy-handed and lacking charm. A better note at the MW tasting: distinctive, good flavour. All there. *Last noted Oct 2001* ★★(★★) *2006–2016.*

**Ch Clerc-Milon** Cabernet Sauvignon 60%, Merlot 30%, Cabernet Franc 10%. First tasted at Mouton, September 1998: opaque; low-key nose but marvellous entry and texture. Tannic of course. Also showing well at the MW tasting. Fullish, complete. *Last tasted Nov 2000* ★(★★) *2006–2016.*

**Ch La Conseillante** April 1997: touch of leanness; very fragrant, oaky. One of my highest marks at the MW tasting: 'a completely satisfactory flavour, weight, balance. Excellent tannin and acidity'. *Last tasted Nov 2000* ★(★★★) *2006–2016.*

**Ch Cos d'Estournel** A high percentage of Cabernet Sauvignon, long maturation. An acidic vintage. Still very tannic and raw though with good fruit at a British Airways tasting in June 1997. Leaping into prominence at the 'Top Ten' tasting at the New York Wine Experience, October 2000. Similar in colour to the '96 Barossa Estate from South Australia alongside; a very good, broad, fragrant nose which opened up richly in the glass. A dry wine, full of Cabernet fruit. 'Needs time'. The following month, the nose similarly well-developed. Nice flavour, style, weight, tannic texture. Still deep and plummy; sweet, sweaty, tannic nose; rich and rustic, rather surprisingly. Interesting mouthful. *Last noted fleetingly, Oct 2001* ★★(★★) *2004–2015.*

**Ch La Croix-de-Gay** In April 1997 and November 1990: unusual fragrance which I thought might be the Cabernet Franc, but only 10% in the mix (80% Merlot, 10% Cabernet Sauvignon), ripe fruit, attractive flavour. Most recently: trying to mature but still with mauve rim; suave, harmonious nose; silky texture, soft, drying finish. *Last noted at a Christie's Bordeaux wine course, July 2001* ★★★(★) *2004–2015*.

**Ch L'Église-Clinet** First tasted in the *chai* with Denis Durantou in April 1998: marvellous fruit with violets overtone; sweet, fullish, delicious. Next, also in the company of Denis at a Farr Vintners' vertical in July 1998: 'a real Pomerol vintage' we were told. Certainly a lovely magnum. Fleshy, small berry flavour. Two months later at another vertical, this time presented by Durantou's earnest admirer, Hardy Rodenstock. It really was a lovely, fleshy wine. More recently, and yet again, placed by Hardy in a blind tasting of first growth '96s, all seven of which were showing almost equally well. L'Église-Clinet pegged level with the flanking Latour and Mouton. Being wise after the event, I noted the Pomerol hallmark, a silky tannic texture. *Last tasted March 2001* ★(★★★) *2006–2016*.

**Ch de Fieuzal** One of several consistently well-performing Pessac-Léognan wines which deserve to be better known. Four consistently good notes from April 1997, at a British Airways tasting two months later noting a beguiling, spicy scent and taste, with mulberry-like ripe fruit. Very attractive. At the MW tasting, still very deeply coloured with a rich, creamy nose and most appealing flavour. Five months later, a very forthcoming, earthy Graves bouquet; sweet, soft, very distinctive. Definitely recommended. *Last noted with The Tasting Club at Berry Bros, April 2001* ★★(★★) *Now–2015*.

**Clos Fourtet** April 1997: opaque; subjugated fruit, impressive but hard. Colour simmering down; fragrant; good length; very attractive; 'a great improvement over the old days'. *Last tasted Nov 2000* ★★(★★) *just. 2006–2012*.

**Ch Giscours** Quite a change in style from the big and beefy wines produced in the 1970s. Certainly not opaque and dense, quite the opposite. Though fragrant with a soft entry, it was on the lean side and fairly acidic (April 1997). Later that autumn, unknit, fruit akin to pears and apples, but soft and fragrant on the palate. Fellow members of the British Airways wine committee will be familiar with my favourite expression 'specious'. More recently, opening up nicely: sweet, easy, an early developer. *Last noted Nov 2000* ★★★ *Now–2010*.

**Ch Grand-Puy-Lacoste** First tasted with Xavier Borie at Ch Ducru, June 1997. Distinct blackcurrant Cabernet Sauvignon aroma; concentrated, full of fruit. More recently: less deep – 'perfect colour', 'perfect fruit' on nose and palate. Perfectly balanced too. One of my top marks at the MW tasting of '96s. I am glad I had already bought some of it. *Last noted Nov 2000* (★★★★) *possibly 5 star in due course. 2008–2025*.

**Ch La Grave Trigant-de-Boisset** Medium, relaxed; very attractive wine, light grip. *Oct 2001* ★★★(★) *Soon–2015*.

**Ch Gruaud-Larose** On typically top form. Briefly: opaque; distinctive, spicy, good fruit (April 1997). Showing well at a British Airways blind tasting in October 1999. Now a lively ruby colour; multi-layered fruit on nose and palate. Masked tannins. My highest mark of the St-Juliens at the MW tasting. *Last noted Nov 2000* ★(★★★★) *2006–2020*.

**Ch Haut-Bailly** First noted at the opening tasting of Graves, April 1997: velvety, convincing; sweet, slightly honeyed nose; already supple with good fruit and extract. Also showing well at the MW tasting (2000): rich, complete, well made. In 2001: still fairly deep, shade of blackberry on colour and, curiously

similar, on the nose. Touch of vanilla. Most recently: sweet fruit; rich, crisp Graves character. Needs bottle age. Very attractive wine. *Last tasted at Christie's, April 2002* ★★(★★)

**Ch Haut-Batailley** Richly coloured; ripe; rich yet tannic. Stylish. Needs time. *Oct 2001* ★★(★★) *2005–2015*.

**Ch Kirwan** The new style of Kirwan thanks to the ubiquitous Michel Rolland. First tasted in the Margaux line-up in April 1997: deep, rich; nose and palate rich and concentrated, the Cabernet Sauvignon more like figs and prunes. Oaky. Specious. At the MW tasting I found the nose very evolved, chocolatey; a full, rich, very tannic wine. It has been awarded high marks by certain critics and sales have greatly improved. *Last tasted Nov 2000* ★(★★★) *if you like the style. Say 2006–2015?*

**Ch Labégorce-Zédé** First noted at a tasting of the two major Thienpont family's châteaux (the other being Vieux Ch Certan) I conducted in Brussels in March 1999: medium deep, luminous, attractive colour; crisp, young, varietal nose, opening up fragrantly; crisp, lightish style, spicy fruit. I subsequently bought some half bottles from Justerini's for drinking at home. Plummy coloured; fresh, crisp fruit. Pleasant. *Last noted July 2001* ★★(★) *Now–2012*.

**Ch La Lagune** Very deep; full of rich, chunky fruit. With roast breast of duck. *About right for a Distillers' Installation Dinner, Nov 2001* ★★(★) *Soon–2010*.

**Ch Larcis-Ducasse** A fairly quick-maturing wine; fragrant enough; sweet, soft fruit – I suspect much Merlot – nice but a little unconvincing (April 1997). The next two notes made at home: easy drinking. *Last noted Jan 2001* ★★★ *Now–2010*.

**Ch Larrivet-Haut-Brion** Cabernet Sauvignon 55%, Merlot 45%. In 1997: lean, flavoury but too oaky. A more detailed note made at a Christie's Bordeaux wine course. Briefly: opaque core; good fruit, opened up well; crisp, nice wine, overall dry. *Last tasted July 2001* ★★(★) *2004–2010*.

**Ch Lascombes** Three notes. Frankly unimpressed. Lean fruit; loose knit (April 1997); equally low-keyed and unconvincing nose though flavoury, 'some charm' (MW 2000 tasting). Curious, malty nose; a rich, singed, mocha taste. *Last noted at the Lascombes pre-sale tasting, Sept 2001* ★★ *2004–2010*.

**Ch Léoville-Barton** Showing well at the opening Union des Grands Crus tasting, April 1997: opaque; cedary; good flavour, silky-leathery tannic texture; fragrant. Classic fragrant, similar texture, good length but acidity noted (MW tasting November 2000). Most recently: now a plummy purple; mocha, coffee nose, more meaty than the '95; crisp fruit, lean, good but rather tart. *Last tasted at a vertical of the 1990s decade at the château, Nov 2001* ★(★★) *2008–2016*.

**Ch Léoville-Poyferré** Vivid purple; touch of tar; attractive; very tannic (April 1997). Showing well at the British Airways tasting two months later: fragrant; good fruit, classy but a bit too oaky. More recently: still impressively deep; ripe, a little more rustic than expected; sweet, fullish fruit, tannin and acidity. Nice wine. *Last tasted Nov 2000* ★★★(★) *2005–2015*.

**Ch Lynch-Bages** April 1997: fairly intense purple; touch of tar; sweet, good fruit and grip. Next, at a Lynch-Bages/Batailley masterclass (June 2000). Though still impressively deep, starting to mature; nose and palate now well developed, sweet, delicious, fairly full-bodied (13% alcohol), masked tannins. Five months later, harmonious, soft fruit, attractive wine. *Last noted at the MW tasting of '96s, Nov 2000* ★★(★★) *2006–2016*.

**Ch Montrose** The Charmolüe family's centenary vintage. Cabernet Sauvignon 65%, Merlot 25%, Cabernet Franc 10%.

Traditional fermentation in oak vats and 20% new oak *barriques*. At the opening tasting, April 1997, it was top of the St-Estèphes: low-keyed nose but exceptional richness, flesh and fruit on the palate. Next, at the *Wine Spectator* 'Top Ten' seminar in New York, bouquet now enriched, great depth; sweeter and fleshier than its neighbour and rival, Ch Cos d'Estournel. Crisp, dry finish. A month later, at the MW tasting: lovely colour, cherry-red core; rich, full, chunky, complete, impressive. *Last tasted Nov 2000* ★(★★★★) *2006–2026*.

**Ch Palmer** Five notes. My top mark of the Margauxs tasted blind in April 1997: spicy, new oak, good flesh. 'A feminine Palmer' noted after the names were revealed. In 1999, showing well at a blind tasting for British Airways First Class and Concorde (very prudent of British Airways to buy for future service). Of the 19 Margauxs in the MW tasting of '96s (November 2000) it was my top mark, along with Ch Margaux: rich, fragrant bouquet with extra dimensions; lovely flavour, miles ahead of the pack. Most recently, at the Sichel tasting in February 2001 and later that month with Farr Vintners, Bernard de Lange, managing director of Palmer, informed us that it was a very ripe Merlot vintage. Though it had a lot to offer, I found it at this stage very tannic, with a citrus-like touch of acidity. Will doubtless get its second breath. *Last tasted Feb 2001* ★★(★★) *2008–2018*.

**Ch Pape-Clément** I gave this fairly high marks at the opening Graves tasting (April 1997): spicy; full of fruit and extract. Rich. Interesting. At a British Airways blind tasting in 1999: though deep, it was beginning to mature, its distinctive Graves flavour and style very noticeable. A bit raw and earthy. More recently, its nose fully evolved, open, rich; complete, very tannic. *Last tasted Nov 2000* ★★(★★) *2008–2016*.

**Ch Pichon-Baron** In April 1997: good fruit, well balanced though a touch of tartness. The following September at the château, dry, crisp, firm, tannic. Cabernet Sauvignon 76%, the rest Merlot. No Cabernet Franc or Petit Verdot used in the *grand vin* in 1996. Two years later: rich though muffled fruit, toasty, some ginger on nose and palate. Very flavoury, spicy oak. *Last tasted Nov 2000* ★★(★★) *2006–2015*.

**Ch Pichon-Lalande** Cabernet Sauvignon 46%, Merlot 34%, Cabernet Franc 12% and Petit Verdot 8%. An interesting *cépages* mix: 30% less Cabernet Sauvignon than the neighbouring Baron, and it tastes sweeter, more fleshy. However, all the '96 Pauillacs were showing well in April 1997, the Lalande, opaque of course, already very fragrant; rounded. Next at a vertical in October 2000, now a velvety dark cherry colour; crisp, cedary; leaner than the '95 but good fruit and extra dimension. The following month, alongside 13 other Pauillacs, on a par with Ch Grand-Puy-Lacoste though of contrasting style. Rich fruit and flesh. Attractive. *Last noted Nov 2000* ★★(★★) *2006–2018*.

**Ch Prieuré-Lichine** Attractive Cabernet flavour, spicy, softer than expected (April 1997). High-toned, stylish (1999), on the lean side, fruit and oak, dry finish (2000). Still fairly deep; sweet, good fruit. A good Prieuré. *Last noted lunching at Ch Chasse-Spleen, March 2001* ★★(★) *2005–2015*.

**Ch Rauzan-Ségla** Showing very well at the 1997 and 2000 tastings: lean but elegant, crisp fruit ★★★(★) *2005–2015* (Ségla, *2ème vin*, was also remarkably good at Christie's wine courses in 2001.)

**Ch Rol Valentin** My one and only note of this 1.9-ha St-Émilion cult wine. Raw, severe, tannic. I suppose this will develop into something more interesting. *At the Bordeaux Index Right Bank 'À la mode vs traditionelle' tasting, Nov 1999. I don't like it now and find it difficult to predict its future.*

**Ch Smith-Haut-Lafitte** The Cathiards are always keen to show the results of their investment and hard work. The '96 red, Cabernet Sauvignon 60%, Merlot 30%, Cabernet Franc 10%, (they also make a good 100% Sauvignon Blanc dry white) I first tasted with them in March 1997: impressively deep; complex, fragrant; crisp, lean and vivacious – which description might apply to both Florence and Daniel. The following month it made a creditable showing in a line-up of 18 red Graves though it had the slight tartness I had noted in other '96s. In October 1999, in a British Airways blind tasting, a very sweet, open, slightly strange nose; coffee-like flavour and somewhat coarse texture. The following year, like many new reds, overoaked. *Last tasted Nov 2000* ★(★★) *2006–2012*.

**Ch Sociando-Mallet** A substantial vineyard north of St-Estèphe brought to virtual *cru classé* standards by Jean Gouffreau and commanding a commensurate price. Certainly impressive: rich, mature; hefty but sweet and delicious despite tannin. *At Farr Vintners, Oct 2001* ★★★(★) *2006–2012*.

**Ch Talbot** Cabernet Sauvignon approximately 60%, Merlot 26%, Petit Verdot 5%, Cabernet Franc 3%. I nearly said 'a good old stand-by', traditionally popular in England. First tasted with its peers in April 1997. Its initial scent was of peppery sawdust but good fruit emerging. Nice weight, though too oaky at that stage. In a blind tasting for British Airways in October 1999 it had high marks and was selected for first class. The two sisters who own the château presented it for selected wine writers and I found it deliciously sweet and fruity (at the Mirabelle in London in April 2000). Seven months later, now a medium-plummy colour; very typical, ripe and rustic – the punters like this, – sweet, fleshy for a '96, good flavour, soft fruit. *Last noted Nov 2000* ★★(★★) *2005–2018*.

**Ch Trottevieille** It was showing quite well at a British Airways blind tasting in November 1997, with its attractive, youthful fruit. Much later, Philippe Castéja, an old friend, sent me a case out of the blue. A nice wine, quite good fruit and weight, on the lean side (1999 and subsequent), though, I confess, I have not been too keen on it recently: dry, rather strange piquant acidity. I doubt if he will send me more. *Last tasted March 2001* ★(★) *Drink up.*

**Ch Trotanoy** Rich and fragrant. Complete. Good length. Excellent wine. *Last tasted Nov 2000* ★★★★

**Vieux Ch Certan** Two recent tastings, first in Brussels, March 1999: crisp, spicy Cabernet fragrance and flavour. Eight months later: glowing colour; harmonious and more to come; vigorous, tannic, good texture and future. *Last noted for Wijngustatic, Alumni Hotelexi OLV, Bruges, Nov 1999* ★★★★

THE FOLLOWING NOTES BRIEFLY COVER SOME OF THE MANY '96s I tasted in April 1997 in Bordeaux (1) and/or November 2000 in London (2) and on other occasions: **Ch d'Angludet** curious *mélange* of fruits; rich texture and flavour (1) ★★★; **Ch Balestard-La-Tonnelle** (1) ★★; **Ch Belair** light, easy style (2) ★★★; **Ch Belgrave** (St-Laurent) a wine undergoing renaissance under Michel Rolland – dense; good, rich fruit, full and spicy (2) ★★★; **Ch Bouscaut** (1) and (2) ★★; **Ch Boyd-Cantenac** fully developed; sweet, chewy, coarse (2) ★★; **Ch La Cabanne** good fruit and flesh (1) ★★★; **Ch Camensac** Unexciting (1) ★★; **Ch Cap de Mourlin** (1) ★★; **Ch Carbonnieux** piquant. Light style. Fragrant finish (1) and (2) ★★; **Carruades de Ch Lafite** very fragrant,; lean, attractive. *Sept 1998* ★★★; **Ch Chantegrive** much new investment here, and it shows. Light style, elegant, and like most Graves of this class, an early developer (1) ★★★;

**Ch Citran** I have a feeling that there was a South African winemaker at the château around this time. Certainly a new style: very deep, vivid; attractive nose, citric, tannic; very Cabernet, very spicy, lots of new oak, lean. Trying too hard? (1) ★★★; **Ch Clarke** superficially floral, scented nose and flavour. Quite attractive. Light style. Despite the Rothschild ownership, still a *bourgeois* Listrac (1) ★★; **Ch Clinet** less deep, lower-keyed than expected though more punch on palate. For a change, a Clinet I like (2) ★★★; **Ch Cos Labory** certainly trying harder. Surprisingly sweet, ripe fruit, yet lean and tannic (1) and (2) ★★★; **Ch Coufran** well made wine. Fragrant, spicy, nice texture. Crisp fruit (virtually 100% Merlot) (1) and *July 1998* ★★★; **Ch Croizet-Bages** initially pure cassis. Irresistible. (1). Less enthusiastic. (2) ★★★?; **Ch Dassault** sweet, extracted, plausible (1) ★★; **Ch Dauzac** improvements here. Rich, ripe, piquant fruitiness; fairly sweet, fleshy, distinctive, attractive – yet something missing. (1) and (2) ★★★; **Ch Desmirail** (1) and (2) ★★; **Ch La Dominique** good wine (1) ★★★; **Ch Ducru-Beaucaillou** for some reason or other only one note. Surprisingly sweet entry; dry, slightly coarse finish (★★?); **Ch Duhart-Milon** piquant, stylish, easy ★★; **Ch Durfort-Vivens** attractive flavour. Early developer (1) and (2) ★★; **Ch L'Évangile** fruit and flesh. Good length (1) ★★★; **Ch Ferrière** light, easy, short. (2) ★★; **Ch Figeac** alas, only one note. Distinctive of course. Mellow, light style, attractive but unconvincing. (1) ★★?; **Ch La Fleur-de-Gay** rich fruit and oak (2) ★★★; **Ch Fonréaud** (1) ★★; **Les Forts de Latour** restrained; surprisingly sweet, fruit and grip (1) and *Sept 1998* ★★★; **Ch Fourcas-Dupré** similar nose to Hosten. A bit raw (1) ★★; **Ch Fourcas-Hosten** Touch of rawness on the nose but an easy drinkable wine (1) and *July 1998* ★★; **Ch Franc-Mayne** big wine. Very tannic (1) ★★; **Ch La Gaffelière** attractive nose; sweet, slightly harsh tannins. Needs time. ★★★; **Ch Gazin** deep, rich; sweet, fragrant finish (1) and (2) ★★★; **Ch Grand-Mayne** dry, spicy, good length (1) ★★; **Ch Grand-Puy-Ducasse** a good Ducasse. Fairly developed, ripe fruit; chewy, touch of coarseness (1) and (2) ★★★; **Ch Haut-Bages-Libéral** rich, rustic, chunky fruit yet lean, crisp, attractive (1) and *April 2001* ★★★; **Ch d'Issan** crisp fruit. Attractive (2) ★★★; **Ch Lafon-Rochet** sweet, fleshy, open knit (1) ★★★; **Ch Lagrange** (St-Julien) crisp, fragrant, agreeable (2) ★★★; **Ch Latour-Martillac** soft, sweet and easy (1) ★★★; **Ch Lynch-Moussas** impressively deep; fragrant, spicy; distinctive, citrus touch, good ripe fruit. Oaky. April and *June 1997* ★★; **Ch Malartic-Lagravière** deceptively big though initially understated, settling into a light, easy style (1) and (2) ★★★; **Ch Malescot-St-Exupéry** initially raw, unready. Developed fragrance and flavour. Crisp. Touch of tartness (1) and (2) ★★ possibly ★★★; **Ch Marquis de Terme** well made.

---

### Institute of Masters of Wine

*Supervisors of the world's toughest, most demanding wine exams. On passing them, one becomes a 'Master of Wine' – an achievement I managed in 1960; I then became chairman of the Institute in 1970. The exams began in 1953, their aim to maintain a parallel trade qualification to those of other professions. That there are still fewer than 250 Masters of Wine at large today says something for the rigour of the examination, and successful candidates tend to be great assets to the trade. The Institute holds regular tastings, both by region and by producer (or château), many of which are recorded in these pages.*

Broad, soft, fleshy (1) and (2) ★★★; **Ch La Mission Haut-Brion** only one note: very distinctive, spicy; less aggressively masculine but still fairly tough and tannic. A long haul wine (2) ★★★★; **Ch Monbrison** crisp. Attractive ★★★; **Ch Nenin** (1) ★★; **Ch Olivier** distinctive. Surprisingly good sweetness, flavour and length (1) and (2) ★★★; **Ch Pavie** Scent of box hedge; lightish style, charm (1) ★★★; **Ch Pavie-Decesse** almost rasping. Too tannic (1) ★; **Ch Petit-Village** attractive scent. Pleasant enough. Dry finish (1) and (2) ★★; **Ch Phélan-Ségur** good fruit. Austere but attractive. Long life (1) ★★★; **Ch La Pointe** deep, full, fleshy. Good wine (1) ★★★; **Ch Pontet-Canet** very good – tempted to say surprisingly good. Attractive nose; lovely crisp fruit, lean but lissome (1) ★★★; **Ch Rauzan-Gassies** surprisingly deep at first, less impressive in its fourth year. Good nose however, rich, spicy; positive on palate; crisp, touch of coarseness and slight astringency. A good Gassies (1) and (2) ★★★; **Ch Siran** fairly sweet, full flavoured, good flesh and positive (1) ★★★; **Ch La Tour-Carnet** a new broom at the château. I thought it was too spicy – cinnamon – oaky though speciously attractive. Better than in older times (1) ★★★?; **Ch La Tour-de-By** one of my favourite clarets for drinking at home – surprisingly good fruit and flesh (1) *Last tasted Feb 2001* ★★★; and **Ch La Tour Haut-Brion** sweet, distinctive; much softer and sweeter than expected (2) ★★★

# 1997 ★★★

On the whole, this was a surprisingly useful, very drinkable vintage though it was launched on to the market at too ambitious a price. Looking at my notes on the weather, so crucial for crop size and quality, the phrase 'early and long' recurs: an unusually warm February and the hottest spring for half a century caused premature but prolonged bud break and uneven conditions. Flowering was also very early, usually good news for it is normally the harbinger of an early harvest – but this was also extended and uneven. May was cool and wet which caused *coulure* and *millerandage*, which are both difficult to prevent and both reduce potential crop size. Rain in May and late June with rot problems. Fortunately it was hot and sunny for the second half of August and through the unusually early and – once more – prolonged harvest. Some châteaux picked early and some held on for more phenolic ripeness, late-picked Cabernet Sauvignon being particularly successful.

I have around 300 notes on 135 châteaux, many first tasted at the Union des Grands Crus tasting in Bordeaux in the spring after the vintage and in London a year later; also there was a useful MW tasting of '97s in November 2001 which filled in a few gaps and confirmed my earlier opinions. In addition I have enjoyed drinking many minor clarets of this vintage on social occasions.

Once again, I am indebted to Hardy Rodenstock for a salutary blind tasting, in March 2001, of first growths of this and three other Bordeaux vintages: we were not told which four vintages they were, nor the order of châteaux within each vintage. Overall it is an attractive vintage for drinking now. **Ch Lafite** The *grand vin* was bottled in May 2000. First tasted, fairly superficially, from the cask before dining at the château in September 1998. It was not as good as the '96 but still had quite nice flesh.

At Rodenstock's blind tasting in March 2001, it had a good colour, intense, youthful; a 'classic tea and mocha' nose, which opened up quickly, lovely, fragrant. In short, showing well.

Medium-dry entry leading to a dry, very tannic finish. Good but as yet a bit raw. It was my second highest mark which also turned out to be identical to the group's average. Very straightforward, a good mid-term future. At the MW tasting: sweet, singed, herbaceous. Most recently: 'drinking surprisingly well' at lunch with the family (a magnum) on Christmas Day. *Last noted Dec 2001* ★★★ *Now–2010.*

**Ch Latour** No Petit Verdot used in the blend because of rot. First tasted alongside the '96 at the château in September 1998: deep, fairly intense; a whiff of liquorice; surprisingly sweet, in fact delicious with pleasant, oaky endtaste. Again the following March. I liked it enormously, recording an aroma of raspberry and cedar. Sweet again. 'Lovely fruit. Complete'. At Rodenstock's blind tasting I thought the flavour was better than the nose which I described as sweet, slightly chocolatey, rich and chewy. A bit lean. Good mark but a couple of points below the consensus. *Last tasted Nov 2001* (★★★★) *Not a blockbuster Latour but I liked its sweetness. Say 2010–2020.*

**Ch Margaux** First noted at Wagner's vertical in November 2000 and described by Paul Pontallier as 'a difficult year – strict selection for the *grand vin*'. A pleasant, medium-deep appearance. Attractive colour, nose and taste. More forward than the '98, the nose fully developed, slightly chocolatey and after three hours in the glass still rich, attractive with hint of coconut. Touch of sweetness. Fragrant. And at Rodenstock's blind tasting, March 2001, its nose and taste reassuringly similar. Full flavoured. My equal top mark. Most recently, at the MW tasting: cherry-like fragrance; dry, touch of coffee/mocha. *Last tasted Nov 2001* ★★(★★) *Now–2012.*

**Ch Mouton-Rothschild** Cask sample first tasted in September 1998 with Hervé Berland: a small crop, 55% selected for the *grand vin*, the smallest percentage ever. The *cépage* mix was Cabernet Sauvignon 77%, Merlot 13%, Petit Verdot 6% and Cabernet Franc 4%. Five weeks macerating, six in wooden vats, only 80% new oak. At this stage still opaque, intense; muffled though with crisp Cabernet Sauvignon aroma; surprisingly fleshy, good extract and tannins. Next noted in March 1999: nose like freshly sawn wood, spice; crisp fruit. In March 2001, tasted blind: still deep; nose low-keyed, but peppery at first, opening up gradually; a 'lean edge' noted. My score was identical to that of Ch Latour, two points below the consensus. Most recently: fragrant, crisp, dry finish. Most recently: fragrant, crisp, dry finish. *Last noted at the MW tasting, Nov 2001* (★★★★) *Needs time. 2010–2020.*

**Ch Haut-Brion** The *cépage* mix was Cabernet Sauvignon 43%, Merlot 43% and Cabernet Franc 14%. Three notes, first, the full range of their '97 Brions with Jean Delmas and Jancis Robinson at Ch La Mission in April 1998: fairly deep, velvety colour; 'meaty', distinctive fruit; sweet, fairly full-bodied, very rich, but very tannic, with chewy Graves character. Next, in the tasting 'room with a view' at the château. New oak, very fragrant, crisp, blackcurrant fruit. Good wine. Tasted blind in March 2001: still very immature looking; frankly the least good nose – better on palate, flavoury but with teeth-gripping tannins. I must be honest, it was my lowest score, four points below the consensus. However, it was showing very well at the MW tasting: soft, attractive fruit, good length. *Nov 2001* ★★★★ *2007–2015.*

**Ch Ausone** First tasted in cask. Hugely impressive: very deep, intense, fabulous colour; at this stage low-keyed but spicy (new oak); sweet fruit mid-palate, massively tannic. Most recently, still very tannic but very good crisp fruit. A very good Ausone. *Last noted at the MW tasting, Nov 2001* ★★★(★★) *2008–2020.*

**Ch Cheval Blanc** I am totally seduced by the wines of Cheval Blanc. First tasted at the château with Pierre Lurton in April 1998 and again in September. We were informed that the wine (a blend of 60% Cabernet Franc and 40% Merlot from 35ha of vines) spent an average of 18 months in medium-toasted new oak supplied by five different coopers. Racked by gravity every three months and fined after 15 months using fresh egg whites with a pinch of salt. As usual, not as deeply coloured as the first growth Médocs; slightly vanillin and raspberry nose; surprisingly sweet, with good fruit, extract and soft tannin. A fairly similar, though more fragrant, note made at the château in June 2000. My highest mark at Rodenstock's blind tasting, March 2001, one point above the average: intensity, stylish, good length. Sweet, delicious. A delight to drink by itself. *Last noted at the MW tasting, Nov 2001* ★★★★★ *2004–2018.*

## Karl-Heinz Wolf

*A German, living in Austria. Creator of some of the most memorable tastings I have attended – Ch Latour and Ch Mouton-Rothschild (in 1986); Ch La Mission Haut-Brion (in 1990); 1959 versus 1961 red Bordeaux at Aschau (in 1994); the 50-wine Ch Cheval Blanc tasting (in 1997), and 70 Mosel wines with J J Prüm (in 1999). His wealth stems from his food business which he sold for a considerable sum in the 1980s, but his first love is dealing in wine and in contemporary art through his company Weinart. Private collectors attend the many tastings he holds in Germany and in Austria.*

**Ch Pétrus** Only one note, at Hardy Rodenstock's blind tasting of first growths: not as deep as expected (after it was revealed) and plummy coloured; better flavour than nose which I had given my lowest points. Medium-sweet, rather coarse fruit. My score: five points above the consensus which, in turn, was the third highest of the fairly consistent vintage notes. *Last tasted March 2001* (★★★) *2010–2020?*

OTHER '97s TASTED ON THE FOLLOWING OCCASIONS at the Union des Grands Crus in Bordeaux in March and April 1998 (1); in London, April 1999 (2); at the MW tasting of '97s in November 2001 (3); or as otherwise indicated. (Star ratings and probable 'plateau of maturity' at the date of last tasting.)

**Ch L'Angélus** Very deep, rich; good fruit, depth; sweet, chewy, very fruity, very tannic (2) and (3) ★★(★) *2005–2012.*

**Ch d'Angludet** Cabernet Sauvignon 58%, Merlot 35%, the rest Cabernet Franc and Petit Verdot. A very crisp, attractive, fragrant, berry-like wine (1) ★★★ *Drink soon.*

**Ch d'Armailhac** Cabernet Sauvignon 55%, Merlot 22%, the rest Cabernet Franc. Four weeks macerating, 45% new oak. Tasted at Ch Mouton-Rothschild, first in September 1998. Then in March 1999, fairly deep, luminous ruby; delicious fleshy fruit, Cabernet Sauvignon and oak. Initially sweet, soft fruit, light style, a bit loose-knit. (3) ★★★ *Now–2010.*

**Ch Balestard-La-Tonnelle** Fragrant. Light style (1) ★★ *Early drinking.*

**Ch Batailley** Usually dependable and consistent. *June 2000* ★★ *Early drinking.*

**Ch Beauregard** Sweet, port-like Pomerol nose. Distinctive flavour, nice texture. (1) ★★ *Drink soon.*

**Ch Beauséjour-Bécot** Deep; elegant, oak, fine fruit. Last tasted at the château, good fruit, delicious. (1) ★★★ *Now–2008.*

**Ch Belgrave** (St-Laurent) Fairly fragrant, attractive fruit (1). *Last tasted at Vinopolis in London, Sept 1999* ★★ *Now–2008?*

**Ch Bernadotte** The first vintage made since May de Lenquesaing's purchase of this *cru bourgeois* château in 1995. A valiant effort. Raspberry-like fruit, crisp, peppery, good tannins. *Tasted at Ch Pichon-Lalande, Sept 1998* (★★) *Now–2008?*

**Ch Beychevelle** Very oaky, speciously attractive; sweet, lightish style (2) and (3) ★★★ *Now–2010.*

**Ch Branaire** (formerly called Branaire-Ducru – 'new broom sweeps clean'.) Attractive appearance; sweet, fragrant, herbaceous – privet; sweet, good fruit, very flavoury. Plenty of new oak. (1) and (2) ★★★ *2005–2010.*

**Ch Brane-Cantenac** I used to have mixed feelings about the wine from this château but under one of the ubiquitous Lurton sons it is now making nice wine. Three reasonably consistent notes: still fairly deep and youthful; new oak but harmonious nose and taste. Good, soft fruit flavour, masking tannin. Delicious. *Last noted at a British Airways tasting, Aug 2001* ★★★ *2005–2012.*

**Ch La Cabanne** A rich, figgy 92% Merlot Pomerol. Distinctive, crisp fruit and texture (1) ★★★ *Now–2008.*

**Ch Calon-Ségur** Just like old times: a fragrant Cabernet aroma, dry, crisp, good. *Last noted at a tasting for the Detroit chapter of the Commanderie de Bordeaux (a most delightful group) at the Relais de Margaux, May 2001* ★★★ *2007–2012.*

**Ch Canon** English-managed, owned by Chanel. Sweet, fruity nose; soft, loose-knit, dry finish. Delicious. (1) and (2) ★★★ *Now–2008.*

**Ch Canon-La-Gaffelière** Unusual to have a German count (Stéphan von Neipperg) fully integrated in what one suspects might be a rather parochial district like St-Émilion. But he and his wine have an excellent reputation, though I find it a bit too concentrated. The 1997 has fig-like fruit and good length. (1) and (2) ★★★ *2005–2015.*

**Ch Cantemerle** A touch of coarseness, very tannic. Very sweet nose and specious fruit. Lacking the charm of its mid-1950s zenith. (1), (2) and (3) ★★ *Now–2007.*

**Ch Cantenac-Brown** A large, somewhat unprepossessing château, like an English girls' boarding school. Fragrant, slightly rusty; good texture, extract and flavour (1) ★★★ *2005–2008.*

**Ch Cap de Mourlin** One of the myriad of smallish but good St-Émilion properties. Open knit, touch of tangerine; piquant, flavoury (1). *Now–2010.*

**Ch Carbonnieux** Always a dependable light-style, early drinking red Graves: crisp fruit. Quaffable (1) ★★ *Now–2008.*

**Carruades de Ch Lafite** Nice flesh. Flavoury. *Sept 1998* ★★★ *Now–2010.*

**Ch Chasse-Spleen** Consistently well made, always above its *bourgeois* station in life. Evolving well in the year between the two tastings. (1) and (2) ★★★ *2005–2015.*

**Dom de Chevalier** Very fragrant; good flavour and substance. (1) and (3) ★★(★) *2005–2012.*

**Ch Citran** Another well made *bourgeois* Médoc. Lovely nose; attractive style, good flavour. (1) and (2) ★★★ *2005–2015.*

**Ch Clarke** A Listrac *cru bourgeois* owned by Baron Edmond de Rothschild. The wine has an attractive fruity flavour. (1) ★★★ *Drink soon.*

**Ch Clerc-Milon** I confess that I always have to think hard about which of the Rothschilds this belongs to. Tasted at Mouton in September 1998 and March 1999: fairly laden with new oak, spicy, but fragrant and attractive. Then, at a France in Your Glass masterclass at Eugénie-les-Bains in July 2001: fresh, fruity, distinctive, blackcurrant nose; elegant, feminine, the oaky

tannins settling down. Most recently, I noted fresh, varietal aroma; crisp, lean and flavoury. *Last tasted Nov 2001* ★★★ *Now–2010.*

**Ch Clinet** Deep; rich and figgy; very distinctive, sweet, concentrated. Impressive but not my style of wine. (1) and (2) ★★★★ *2006–2016.*

**Ch La Conseillante** For long a consistently well made wine. An immediacy about this nose, tangerine-like fragrance; fairly sweet, nice fruit and balance. A delicious wine. (1), (2) and (3) ★★★★ *2005–2020.*

**Ch Cos d'Estournel** I was taken by the wine's glorious young fruit in April 1998. Crisp. Oaky. Most recently, one of the deepest and most intense of the '97s at the MW tasting. Nose a bit unknit but rich on the palate, with dry finish. *Last tasted Nov 2001* ★★(★★) *2005–2012.*

**Ch Cos Labory** Spicy, herbaceous; good flavour, raw tannin (1) ★★★? *2006–2015.*

**Ch Coufran** This has long been one of my favourite *bourgeois* clarets. Unusually for St-Estèphe, the wine is virtually 100% Merlot. Impressively deep; fragrant; noticeably sweet, good fruit and flesh. Tannic (1) and (2) ★★★ *2005–2012.*

**Ch La Croix-de-Gay** Deep, rich, figgy fruit; rich, nice texture (1) ★★★ *2005–2012.*

**Ch Croizet-Bages** Fragrant, attractive; light, refreshing style (1) and (3) ★★★ *Now–2008.*

**Ch Dassault** Distinctive fruit; good extract, chewy, a bit four-square. (1) ★★★ *2004–2010.*

**Ch La Dominique** Fragrant, spicy; nice fruit and flesh but rather bitter tannic finish. (1) and (2) *Last tasted April 1999* ★★★?

**Ch Ducru-Beaucaillou** First tasted at the château, September 1998. Quite good fruit, unaggressive (30% reduction of tannins during the first year in cask). An easy Ducru. *Endorsed at the MW tasting* (3) ★★★ *Now–2008.*

**Ch L'Église-Clinet** Denis Durantou has something of a reputation and his wine is certainly impressive. First tasted at the château in April 1998: an intense, youthful violet; flavoury aroma; full of fruit, extract masking the tannin. Hardy Rodenstock has done a lot to draw attention to Durantou's brilliance and constantly included the wine blind in the company of the first growths. In this vintage, it achieved the highest overall vote though my score was 4 points below this and 1 point ahead of Ch Latour. *Last tasted March 2001* ★★★★ *2008–2020.*

**Ch L'Évangile** Strong, Rhône-like character. Chocolatey. Chewy. Soft, yet acidic finish. (1) and (3) ★★★ *just. Now–2008.*

**Ch Figeac** Fragrant, light style, delicious, forward. (1) and (2) ★★★★ *2004–2015.*

**Ch La Fleur-Pétrus** Good extract, crisp fruit, refreshing acidity, dry finish. (3) ★★★

**Ch Fonroque** Impressive. Soft. *At a CIVB dinner and tasting, Dec 2000* ★★ *Now to 2010.*

**Les Forts de Latour** First tasted in cask September 1998. Seemed sweet and easy. An astonishing raspberry-like nose; good fruit, attractive. *Last tasted at the château, March 1999* ★★★ *2005–2012.*

**Ch Fourcas-Hosten** Light style, soft, flavoury (preferred to Fourcas-Dupré) (1) ★★ *Now–2010.*

**Clos Fourtet** Intense. Citrus-like fruit and acidity (1) ★★ *Nov–2012.*

**Ch Franc-Mayne** Conflicting notes. Good, rich fruit and texture at the opening tasting (1) (and preferred to Ch Grand-Mayne) but, sandwiched between an '89 and a '90 (of other châteaux), it seemed rather lean and raw. Context is all! *Last* tasted March 2000 ★★★ *To give it the benefit of the doubt, say 2007–2012.*

**Ch Gazin** Rich 'legs'; figgy nose, evolved sweetly; distinctive flavour, fullish, chunky, dry finish. (1) and *(2)* ★★★ 2005–2015.

**Ch Giscours** Easy, sweet, chewy, short. (1) and *(3)* ★★ *Now–2008*.

**Ch Grand-Puy-Lacoste** High percentage of Cabernet Sauvignon. Fleshy, mouthfilling (with the Detroit chapter of the Commanderie de Bordeaux, May 2001). Five months later, at the Hôtel St James, Bordeaux: now a relatively soft, gentle colour with nose to match. Most recently, tried out at home from the three cases I lugged from Bordeaux. More advanced than I had anticipated but tannins lurking. *Last tasted Oct 2001* ★★★ *Now–2012.*

**Ch Gruaud-Larose** Sweet, rounded, delicious second time round. (1) and *(2)* ★★★★ 2007–2015.

**Ch Haut-Bages-Libéral** Better flavour than nose. Surprisingly sweet and soft when last tasted. (1) *and with 'The Tasting Club' at Berry Bros, April 2001* ★★ 2005–2010.

**Ch Haut-Bailly** Crisp fruit, vanillin; lacking the depth of the '96 and '98 but attractive and easy (1). *Last tasted at the château, June 2001* ★★ *Now–2010.*

**Ch Haut-Batailley** Now maturing quite well. Always stylish. Sweet, agreeable. *Last tasted (3)* ★★★ *Now–2010.*

**Ch Kirwan** In 1993 a new winemaker from Clinet changed the style of wine. An unusual 1997: opaque; strange, rich, spicy, oaky nose; fairly powerful, dry tannic finish. We will have to see how it turns out (1) (★★★)?

**Ch Lafon-Rochet** Only 55% of the normal crop selected. Two notes in April 1998: good fruit; just enough flesh. Tannic. Most recently, the opening wine in a horizontal tasting of '97s: dark cherry, surprisingly intense; lovely nose; quite flavoury. A good Lafon. *Last noted at the Hôtel St James in Bordeaux, Oct 2001* ★★★ 2005–2012.

**Ch Lagrange** (St-Julien) Japanese owned and well managed. Three notes, one I thought slightly tart. Complete, flavoury, spicy, new style. *Last tasted June 1999* ★★★ 2007–2015.

**Ch La Lagune** *Assez bien*. Dry finish. *Oct 1999 and (3)* ★★ *Now–2008.*

**Ch Langoa-Barton** Nice wine. Seemed sweeter and fuller than the Léoville (see below). Good fruit, complete. Tannic. (1) and *(2)* ★★★ 2008–2018.

**Ch Larcis-Ducasse** I had not taken much notice of this St-Émilion château, not far from Ch Pavie, until I went to stay there during one of the Union des Grands Crus tastings. M. Gratiot gave me a couple of bottles of his '97 which was attractive and drinking well. (1) and at home, July and *Sept 2000* (★★) *Now–2010.*

**Ch Larmande** Rich, assertive, impressive. Very tannic. *(1)* ★★(★) 2008–2012.

**Ch Larrivet-Haut-Brion** Attractive fruit; silky-leathery texture, Graves flavour. (1) ★★★ *Now–2012.*

**Ch Lascombes** High toned, meaty; lightish, forward. *Last tasted Sept 2001* ★★ *Now–2012.*

**Ch Latour-Martillac** Good fruit. (1) ★★ *Now–2008.*

**Ch Léoville-Barton** Seemed masculine and raw in the April 1998 line-up, but a year later, surprisingly sweet and delicious. *Last tasted at the château, Oct 2001* (★★★★) 2007–2018.

**Ch Léoville-Las-Cases** Fairly deep; a very forthcoming nose, deep and sweet; rich, fairly substantial. Masked tannin. A good '97. *(3)* ★★★★ 2004–2012.

**Ch Léoville-Poyferré** Making good wine these days. Four notes, all good. Despite its youthful looks, a very forthcoming,

'warm' cedary nose; light, some charm, oaky, good length. Dry finish. *(3)* ★★★★ 2006–2012.

**Ch Lynch-Bages** Six notes. From the start one of the most attractive of the '97s. Typical Lynch-Bages blackcurrant fruit, complete, refreshing. *(3)* ★★★(★) 2005–2012.

**Ch Lynch-Moussas** Herbaceous. Flavoury but light style *(1)* ★★ *Now–2010.*

**Ch Magdelaine** Raspberry-like aroma and flavour. Crisp. Appealing *(3)* ★★ *Drink soon.*

**Ch Marquis de Terme** Very spicy, Cabernet varietal nose, aroma and taste. Flavoury and feminine. *(1)* ★★★ *Now–2010.*

**Ch La Mission Haut-Brion** At the château, April 1998: soft, easy, attractive flavour, like a young port. Most recently: singed oaky mocha nose; full-flavoured, chewy, quite a bite. *(3)* ★★★ 2006–2015.

**Ch Monbousquet** Despite being from 'the wrong side of the tracks', down towards the Gironde, this is a notably successful St-Émilion. Deep and still youthful; fleshy, ripe, open nose; sweet, weighty. Despite very dry finish, drinking quite well. *Last noted at a horizontal tasting of '97s with a small group attending a France in Your Glass weekend at the Hôtel St James in Bordeaux, Oct 2001* ★★★ *Drink now–2010.*

**Ch La Mondotte** Very deep, rich, massive, impressive. Owned by Stéphan von Neipperg, made by the talented Stéphane Derenoncourt. *At Ch Canon-La-Gaffelière, April 1998* (★★★?) 2007–2015.

**Ch Montrose** The dependable Charmolüe family made a good '97. Classic. Complete. (1) ★★★(★) 2005–2015.

**Ch d'Olivier** The Black Prince, born here in 1330, would have approved. (1) ★★★ 2005–2012.

**Ch Les Ormes-de-Pez** Attractive. Light style. Easy, short. (1) ★★ *Now–2010.*

**Ch Palmer** Noted on five of the six occasions as having a chocolatey-mocha nose. A touch of leanness yet chunky, and very dry finish. Some charm. An attractive '97. *Last tasted after Edmund Penning-Rowsell's funeral, March 2002* ★★(★) *Soon–2008.*

**Ch Pape-Clément** A new broom at the oldest *vignoble* in Bordeaux. Very rich, good flavour, complete. Very drinkable. *Last noted at a British Airways tasting, Aug 2001* ★★★ *Now–2012.*

**Ch Pavie** Very fragrant and attractive. Much preferred to more recent vintages. *(2)* ★★★ *Now–2010.*

**Ch Pavie-Decesse** Sweet. Delicious. *(2)* ★★★ *Now–2010.*

**Ch Petit-Village** Nice texture, flavour, depth. Touch of piquancy but a surprisingly good mouthful. *Last noted with 'The Tasting Club' at Berry Bros, April 2001* ★★★ *Now–2010.*

**Ch Phélan-Ségur** Light style. Not as pretty as the proprietor's wife *(1)* ★★ *Now–2007.*

**Ch Pichon-Baron** Consistent notes. Fragrant, sweet, soft, easy. *Last tasted Aug 2001* ★★★ *Now–2008.*

**Ch Pichon-Lalande** Six notes. Fairly good fruit and flesh, attractive but leaner than expected with a touch of astringency. *Last tasted Nov 2001* ★★? 2006–2012.

**Ch Pontet-Canet** One of the largest vineyards in the Médoc with 78ha of vines. Only 36% of the crop used for the *grand vin*. Four notes. Initially taut and tannic, crisp fruit but raw. Opening up, sweet, good fruit. Easy. More tart than taut. *Last tasted June 1999* ★★(★)? 2007–2012.

**Ch Rauzan-Gassies** Good colour and fruit. Great improvement on past performance (1), (2) and *(3)* ★★★ 2003–2008.

**Ch Rauzan-Ségla** A stylish '97. Fragrant immediacy, refined. Delicious; fragrant, crisp fruit; lean, firm, good length. *(3)* ★★★★ 2007–2012.

**Ch Siran** Better flavour than nose. A sweet, soft, easy character buffeted by a raw, tannic finish. (1) and *(2)* ★★(★) *2007–2012.*

**Ch Smith-Haut-Lafitte** Florence and Daniel Cathiard have certainly put all their energy, enthusiasm (and money) into this estate. And it shows. Three notes. Rich, oaky, fleshy, modern style Graves. *Last tasted at La Caudalie with the Chaîne des Rôtisseurs from Detroit, June 2000* ★★★ *Now–2010.*

**Ch Talbot** Three consistent notes. Initially very tannic; delicious fruit; sweet, ripe, relatively easy. *Last tasted Nov 2001* ★★★ *Now–2010.*

**Ch Tertre-Roteboeuf** One of these modern, chocolatey, very sweet, very fleshy, over the top wines. Frankly awful. *At the 'Alles über Wein' Millennium Gala in Mainz, May 2000. But for those who admire the style* ★★★

**Ch La Tour-Carnet** Sweet, flavoury. A big improvement in recent years. It used to be one of the worst-performing of the Médoc classed growths. *(1)* ★★ *2005–2010.*

**Ch La Tour-de-By** I have been following this excellent Bas-Médoc château for some time. Attractive. Drinking well though tannic. *Last tasted March 2002.* ★★ *Now–2008.*

**Ch La Tour Haut-Brion** Soft, easy, sweet, like young port. *At Ch La Mission Haut-Brion, April 1998* ★★★ *Now–2010.*

**Ch Troplong-Mondot** Impressive colour; good Merlot fragrance; soft and fleshy, 'Italianate', yet very dry finish. *Tasted May and July 2001* ★★ *2005–2010.*

**Ch Trotanoy** Richly coloured; creamy, vanilla and mocha nose; sweet, chewy and easy despite its tannins *(3)* ★★★(★) *2004–2012.*

**Vieux Ch Certan** Very distinctive aroma; good fruit, attractive flavour. *(1)* ★★ *Now–2012.*

# 1998 ★★ to ★★★

Variable, like so many recent Bordeaux vintages; but, as always in less than perfect weather conditions, so much depended on the foresight and skill of individual châteaux proprietors and/or their winemakers. Moreover, the increasing use of consulting enologists is having a unifying effect on the style of wine produced.

Mild rainy winter; dry sunny warm spring, encouraging early bud break. April cold and wet, but early May, having been spared dangerous frosts, was beneficial, resulting in one of the earliest flowerings this decade. June was erratic while August was too dry and too hot with scorching temperatures, up to 39°C on 10 and 11 August. This shrivelled the vine leaves and grilled the grapes, inhibiting sap rise. September was a roller coaster: good weather, storms and sunshine in the second half followed by heavy rain in October. Merlot, almost always early ripening, was picked before the heavy rains, Pomerol and St-Émilion benefiting. The Médocs were uneven with high Cabernet tannins. Overall, the second largest crop this century. I made around 200 notes on a score of châteaux, mainly at the annual spring tastings of the Union des Grands Crus in Bordeaux and London, in 1999 and 2000 respectively. Stars in brackets indicate my quality rating when the wine has reached its plateau of maturity.

**Ch Lafite** Cabernet Sauvignon 81% and Merlot 19%. No Cabernet Franc or Petit Verdot used. Tasted only once. Very deep, intense; low-keyed but good flesh; complete. Frankly I found it hard to assess at such an early stage, particularly as it was only 9.30 in the morning (preceded by Mouton at 9). But it has to be done! *Tasted at the château, April 1999.*

**Ch Latour** Opaque; dumb at first then lovely fruit; dry, full-bodied, on the lean side, good length. I preferred the '97 but time will tell. *At the château, March 1999* (★★★) *2010–2025?*

**Ch Margaux** First tasted in the *chai* in April 1999: fairly deep, plummy-purple; sweet entry, dry finish, good fruit. Next at Wagner's vertical, similar description though, given time in the glass, a great whoosh of fruit and oak, within an hour a touch of caramel, after three hours positively exotic. Crisp, dry and fruity. *Last tasted in Zurich, Nov 2000* (★★★★) *2010–2025.*

**Ch Mouton-Rothschild** Classic Mouton *cépage* blend – Cabernet Sauvignon 86%, Merlot 12% and Cabernet Franc 2% – and 57% of the crop used for the *grand vin.* In March 1999, opaque, intense; complete; more flesh and fruit than the '97. More recently, with Patrick Léon: spicy, fragrant, very 'Mouton' aroma; good fruit and length. Very tannic yet fleshy. *Last tasted at the château, April 2000* (★★★★) *2012–2025.*

**Ch Cheval Blanc** Just one note: very deep, velvety; fragrant, spicy, rich, tannic, good length. Good but not exactly a charmer at this stage. *From the cask at the château, March 1999* (★★★?) *I really need to retaste.*

**Ch Haut-Brion** Merlot 55%, Cabernet Sauvignon 35%, Cabernet Franc 10%. Deep, still plummy-purple; nose initially sweet, vanillin but with considerable depth, developing a touch of rich tarryness; pleasant sweetness and weight, mouthfilling, with fragrant fruit, good length and grip. Considered the best since the '89s and '90s. *Tasted at the château, Oct 2001*(★★★★). *A fairly long-haul wine, say 2012–2025.*

**Ch Ausone** and **Pétrus** not yet tasted.

SELECTED CHÂTEAUX OF THE '98 VINTAGE Noted at the Union des Grands Crus tastings in Bordeaux in March-April 1999 (1) and in London in May 2000 (2) or as otherwise stated.

**Ch Angélus** (This was the year the L' was dropped from the name.) Very deep; a spicy, oaky, tannic wine but full of fruit. *Last tasted Jan 2000* (★★★) *2005–2012.*

**Ch d'Angludet** Cabernet Sauvignon 58%, Merlot 35%, Petit Verdot 5% and Cabernet Franc 2%. Deep, distinctive, crisp, flavoury. (1) and (2). Still tannic, with oaky aftertaste. *Last noted at the Sichel tasting at Searcy's, London, Jan 2001* (★★★) *2007–2015.*

**Ch d'Armailhac** Deep, velvety; crisp, oaky; lean, flavoury, overall dry, softer tannins. *At Ch Mouton-Rothschild, March 1998 and April 2000* (★★★) *2007–2015.*

**Ch Batailley** Fragrant; sweet, soft, chewy. *Aug 2001* (★★★) *2004–2012.*

**Ch Beauregard** (Pomerol) Floral; attractive, open knit. *(1)* (★★) *2004–2010.*

**Ch Beauséjour-Bécot** Deep, velvety; attractive fruit and sweet, light style. (1). *Last tasted Jan 2000* (★★★) *2004–2010.*

**Ch Beychevelle** Fragrant, cedary; lean, firm, positive yet unexciting. (1) and *(2)* (★★★) *Time will tell.*

**Ch Bouscaut** Good nose; nice flesh and flavoury. Silky tannins. (1) and *(2) 2004–2012.*

**Ch Branaire** Touch of liquorice, cedar, rich, chunky, oaky, tannic. (1) and *(2)* (★★★★) *2007–2015.*

**Ch Brane-Cantenac** Curiously fragrant; attractive, lean, spicy, silky tannins. (1) and *(2)* (★★★★) *2007–2015.*

**Ch Canon** Fragrant; good flesh and length. Very tannic. (1). *Last tasted Jan 2000* (★★★) *2005–2012.*

**Ch Canon-La-Gaffelière** Deep velvety-purple in its youth; fascinating nose, touch of violets and sweetness. Nice weight. Lean and aristocratic like its owner, the Count von Neipperg. *(1)* (★★★★) *2006–2015.*

**Ch Cantemerle** Always shown under the general heading 'Haut-Médoc' at tastings. In fact, this is one of the nearest classed growth châteaux to the city of Bordeaux and the soil is more akin to Graves, just to the south. *(1)* (★★★) *2007–2015*.

**Ch Cantenac-Brown** No longer chocolatey. Fragrant, spicy; good fruit, crisp, a touch lean. (1) and (2). *Last tasted Aug 2001* (★★★) *2007–2015*.

**Ch Cap de Mourlin** Very deep, velvety; rich, forthcoming nose; open knit, good fruit and flesh. *(1)* (★★★) *2005–2010*.

**Ch Carbonnieux** Normally a light style, firmer than usual. Good wine. (1) and *(2)* (★★★) *2004–2010*.

**Ch Chasse-Spleen** Always dependable, interesting, good fruit and grip. *(1)* (★★★) *2005–2012*.

**Dom de Chevalier** Distinctive, stylish; fairly sweet and rich, flavoury, tannic. (1) and *(2)* (★★★★) *2006–2015*.

**Ch Citran** Fruit, flesh, lean but good flavour and length. *(1)* (★★★) *2005–2012*.

**Ch Clarke** Opaque, concentrated, stern, tannic. *(1)* (★★)? *2008–2015*.

**Ch Clerc-Milon** Fragrant, oaky; sweet, fleshy, attractive. *At Ch Mouton-Rothschild, March 1999 and April 2000* (★★★★) *2006–2012*.

**Ch Clinet** Rich, malty, tarry; full, rich, spicy. Very tannic. Many are impressed by Clinet but it's not my style. *(1)* (★★★) *2006–2012*.

**Ch La Conseillante** Most attractive fruit and flavour, well put together, good texture and elegance. *(1)* (★★★★) *2005–2015*.

**Ch Cos Labory** Unusually deep and impressive. (1) and *(2)* (★★★) *2005–2012*.

**Ch Coufran** Merlot fruitiness, well made, complete. *(1)* (★★★) *2005–2012*.

**Ch Couvent des Jacobins** Deep, plummy; youthful; some sweetness and softness, dry finish. Needs time. *Aug 2001* ★★(★) *2004–2012*.

**Ch Croizet-Bages** Dependable Cabernet Sauvignon fruit and flesh. *(1)* (★★★) *2005–2012*.

**Ch La Dominique** Two notes. Rich 'legs'; distinctive fragrance, slightly metallic; fruity, chewy, good flesh, tannic. *(1)*. *Last tasted Aug 2001* (★★★) *2005–2012*.

**Ch Duhart-Milon** Lean, flavoury. *At Ch Lafite, March 1999* (★★★) *2007–2015*.

**Ch Durfort-Vivens** Rich, chewy, tannic. *(2)* (★★★) *2007–2015*.

**Ch Ferrière** Now in the capable family hands also owning Ch Chasse-Spleen, Citran and Haut-Bages-Libéral, so improvements noticeable. Very oaky, fragrant, attractive. (1) and *(2)* (★★★) *2006–2012*.

**Ch Figeac** Distinctive, flavoury and fragrant as always; sweet, easy, some delicacy and charm. (1) *Last tasted Jan 2000* ★★★(★) *Soon–2012*.

**Les Forts de Latour** Spicy. Not unlike the '97 which I slightly preferred. Needs more time. *At Ch Latour, March 1999* (★★★) *2007–2015*.

**Ch Fourcas-Dupré** Oaky, lean, tannic. *(1)* (★★) *2006–2012*.

**Ch Fourcas-Hosten** Coarser fruit, early developer. *(1)* *2004–2010*.

**Ch Fourtet** Fragrant, complete, good texture. (1) *Last tasted Jan 2000* (★★★) *2006–2015*.

**Ch Franc-Mayne** Intense. Impressive, fullish fruit. *(1)* (★★★) *2004–2010*.

**Ch La Gaffelière** Classic. Complete. Oaky, spicy. (1) *Last tasted Jan 2000* (★★★) *2004–2012*.

**Ch Gazin** Curious, tea-like, minty nose; soft fruit, silky textured. *(1)* (★★★) *2005–2015*.

**Ch Giscours** Fragrant, spicy (cloves), touch of tar and mandarin, very sweet, rich, dominated by a lean, dry, oaky finish. Needs time. (1) and (2) (★★★★) *2008–2020*.

**Ch Grand-Mayne** Strange, malty nose; rich yet coarse texture, bitter tannins. Needs time. *(1)* (★★)?

**Ch Greysac** One of the most dependable of the (Bas) Médocs. Good flavour, early drinking. *(1)* (★★★) *Now–2009*.

**Ch Gruaud-Larose** One of the best '98s: full, rich, fragrant, fairly sweet. Easy drinking yet still tannic. (1) and (2). *Last tasted Aug 2001* (★★★★) *2007–2020*.

**Ch Haut-Bailly** Long one of my favourite wines. The best ever crop of Merlot (41% in the final blend). Medium deep, rich, lovely crisp strawberry-like fruit; lovely flavour, sweet yet a touch of austerity. (1). *Last tasted at Christie's masterclass, April 2002*. (★★★★) *2005–2015*.

**Ch Kirwan** Some might say 'renaissance', certainly new style and impressive; deep; oaky, concentrated; sweet, full of fruit, chewy. More masculine assertiveness than Margaux feminine charm. (1) and *(2)* *2009–2015*.

**Ch Lafon-Rochet** A change here too, much more amenable than the austere style which used to remind me of its concrete cellar. Curious privet like nose but attractive flavour. (1) and (2) (★★★) *2005–2012*.

**Ch Lagrange** (St-Julien) Three notes. Curious fragrance; very oaky, astringent. Needs time. (1) and (2). *Last tasted Aug 2001* (★★★)? *2008–2015*.

**Ch Langoa-Barton** Fragrant; good fruit and grip. Always rounder and a touch coarser than Léoville. (1) and *(2)* (★★★) *2007–2015*.

**Ch Larcis-Ducasse** Sweet fruit and oak. Attractive. *(1)* (★★★) *2003–2010*.

**Ch Larmande** Very fragrant, fruity, spicy. Speciously attractive. *(1)* ★★★ *2003–2012*.

**Ch Larrivet-Haut-Brion** Opaque; full, rich, fruity, soft, yet raw finish. *Aug 2001* ★★(★) *2004–2010*.

**Ch Latour-Martillac** Good fruit but austere. *(1)* (★★★) *2004–2010*.

**Ch Léoville-Barton** Initially very deep, velvety; dry, sinewy, good length. Always a class act. (1) and (2). Most recently: rich purple robe; initially subdued but opened up, rich, with almost butterscotch sweetness on palate and finish. Tannic, oaky. *Last tasted at the château, Oct 2001* (★★★★) *2008–2020*.

**Ch Léoville-Poyferré** Lots of new oak, scent of freshly sawn wood; good fruit and style. (1) and *(2)* (★★★) *2005–2020*.

**Ch La Louvière** A most dependable Lurton family property. Good fruit, flesh, flavour, intensity. Initially astringent. *(1)* (★★★) *2005–2015*.

**Ch Lynch-Bages** Very deep; rich, brambly Cabernet Sauvignon aroma; full of fruit and character, but new oak rather intrusive. However tempting, give it breathing space. (1) and *(2)* (★★★★) *2007–2015*.

**Ch Lynch-Moussas** Sweet, soft, open knit, early developer. (1) and (2). *Last tasted Aug 2001* ★(★) *Now–2010*.

**Ch Magdelaine** Soft, chewy, easy. *Jan 2000* (★★★) *2004–2010*.

**Ch Malescot St-Exupéry** Distinctive blackberry-like Cabernet Sauvignon, austere, tannic. Needs time. *(1)* (★★★)? *2007–2015*.

**Ch Marquis de Terme** Surprisingly sweet, light style (1) and *(2)* ★(★) *Now–2010*.

**Ch Maugey** As if to prove what can be done in the middle of the large Entre-Deux-Mers region, this is a somewhat self-conscious, semi-cult wine called Le Jean-Marc (the owner, Monsieur Maugey's Christian name); there is also a New

World-style back label detailing the *cépages* (Merlot 68%, Cabernet Franc 17%, Cabernet Sauvignon 10% and Malbec 5%) and production in 1998: bottles (3600), magnums, doubles etc. including 7 'Nabuchodonozors' (*sic*): still youthful, long 'legs'; red berry, coffee and liquorice; rich, ideal weight (12.5%), full of fruit, tannin masked by extract. *A bottle from Hardy Rodenstock, at home, March 2002* (★★★) *Now–2010?*

**Ch La Mission Haut-Brion** Merlot 65%, Cabernet Sauvignon 35%. Youthful; fragrant, good fruit and depth, became more tarry in the glass; substantial, full of fruit, oak, good length, dry finish. *At the château, Oct 2001* (★★★★) *2010–2025.*

**Ch Monbrison** Deserves to be better known. Deep, rich, crisp fruit, tannic, good length. (1) and (2) (★★★) *2007–2012.*

**Ch Olivier** Attractive, spicy, too much new oak. (1) (★★) *2005–2015.*

**Ch Les Ormes-de-Pez** Reliably attractive. (2) (★★★) *2005–2012.*

**Ch Palmer** Only one note: deep, plummy; spicy, chocolatey; sweet, rich, approachable. *At the château, April 1999* (★★★) *2007–2015.* (I have also tasted Palmer's new Alter Ego which is meant for early consumption; though fairly sweet, it was very raw and tannic in Feb 2001).

**Ch Pape-Clément** A perfect vineyard site, slightly uphill from Ch La Mission Haut-Brion and with the distinctive taste of tar and tobacco associated with wines from the Talence commune. Fragrant. Once again making good wine. (1) (★★★★) *2006–2015.*

**Ch Pavie** Opaque, intense; too sweet; full, fleshy, toasted. New style. (1) *Last tasted Jan 2000* (★★) *for me,* (★★★★) *for some. 2006–2012?*

**Ch Pavie-Decesse** Same new owner as Ch Pavie. Nose like brown sugar, fragrant in its way; attractive flavour and weight but very tannic. (1) (★★★) *2005–2012.*

**Ch Petit-Village** Rich, soft texture, attractive. (1) (★★★) *2005–2015.*

**Ch de Pez** Dependable, particularly under the meticulous ownership of Claude Rouzaud (of Champagne Roederer). Sweet, fleshy, short. *Cask sample, Jan 1999* (★★) *2004–2010.*

**Ch Pichon-Baron** Taut, spicy fruit and oak; powerful, condensed fruit, impressive but lacks charm; touch of tar. (1) and (2) *2008–2016.*

**Ch Pichon-Lalande** Four notes. A total contrast to Ch Pichon-Baron, the AXA-owned competitor across the road. Good fruit, very agreeable, still tannic of course. (1), (2) and *at the château, April and Oct 2000* (★★★) *2008–2016.*

**Ch La Pointe** Rich, very flavoury, good texture, loose knit. (1) ★★ *2004–2014.*

**Ch Pontet-Canet** Still with that distinctive whiff of tar on the nose but rich, complete, good wine. (1) and (2) (★★★), possibly (★★★★) *2007–2015.*

**Ch Prieuré-Lichine** Deep; sweet scented; not as lean as in the past but still a touch of piquancy. Good fruit, flavoury. (1) and (2) (★★★) *2005–2012.*

**Ch Quinault** Alain and Françoise Raynaud bought the property in 1997. This has now become a new cult wine classed as St-Emilion, but from vines planted on (less good) low ground close to Libourne and the river Dordogne. Nevertheless the vines are old (planted between 1930 and 1961). I like and admire Dr Alain Raynaud, a recent president of the Union des Grands Crus, but find this new wine very contrived. Opaque, intense; rich figgy fruit; sweet, full, very spicy oaky aftertaste. *Cask sample, April 1999* (★★)?

**Ch Rauzan-Gassies** Big improvement. For so long underperforming. Fragrant, attractive, some leanness and astringency. (1) and (2). *Last tasted Aug 2001* (★★★) *2007–2015.*

**Ch Rauzan-Ségla** Deep, intense; immediately forthcoming, spicy oaky fragrance; some sweetness, delicious flavour, good firm fruit, taut finish. Class act. (1) and (2) (★★★★) *2008–2018.*

**Ch Respide** The sort of easy-going minor Graves I like: sweet, soft fruit, light (alcohol 12%), attractive. *At home, Feb 2002* ★★ *Drink soon.*

**Sanctus** Yet another new cult wine, created by Patrick Baseden and his Chilean cousin Aurelio Montes de Baseden, whose wines are already famous in their own right. Predictably deeply coloured; sweet bramble and oak nose; a full, rich, soft, fleshy mouthful, with oaky end taste. *From a sample drawn in May 1999* ★★★? *No track record. Small production. Will any be left to pronounce judgement?*

**Ch Siran** Good mouthful, positive, spicy oaky flavour and aftertaste. (1) and (2) (★★★) *2006–2012.*

**Ch Smith-Haut-Lafitte** Redolent of mocha, chocolate, tobacco; rich extract. (1) (★★★) *2005–2012.*

**Ch Talbot** Very much in the customary Talbot style, rich but rustic; very attractive fruit, flesh, silky, leathery tannins. Good wine. (1) and (2) (★★★★) *2007–2015.*

**Ch Tertre-Roteboeuf** Another cult wine made by a passionate winemaker, François Mitjavile. An average of 2200 cases made a year. I cannot help admiring him and his concentrated, fruity wine. *At a Corney & Barrow presentation, March 2001* (★★★★)

**Ch La Tour-Carnet** With a new *maître de chai* this wine has much improved. Crisp fruit, plenty of new oak, attractive but very tannic. (1). *Last tasted Aug 2001* (★★★) *2007–2012.*

**Ch La Tour-de-By** Three recent notes. My favourite (Bas) Médoc wine for everyday drinking. Well made, sweet, fragrant, crisp fruit. Agreeable. *Last tasted at home, Aug 2001* ★(★) *Soon–2008.*

**Ch La Tour Haut-Brion** Deep, youthful; oak and blackberry; fragrant, lots of fruit, oak and grip. *Oct 2001* (★★★) *2005–2015.*

**Vieux Ch Certan** Sweet, soft, spicy; somewhat light character, attractive, dry finish. (1) (★★★) *2005–2012.*

# 1999 ★★ to ★★★★

Less and less can one generalise about a vintage save to say that the care, skill (and, occasionally, a bit of luck) of the *maître de chai*, winemaker, or proprietor – aided and abetted by consultant-enologists – can make the difference between a poor wine and a good wine. Over the past few years far more attention has been given to vine management for, as they say, good wine can only be made from good grapes.

That good grapes could be produced at the end of a growing season like 1999 is little short of a miracle. For some it was one of the most difficult years in memory, difficult and costly. The wet winter of 1998 topped up the water table. January and February were cool and abnormally dry but bud burst took place in equally abnormal heat. April and May were also very hot, but humidity necessitated early spraying. Exceptional heat in the latter part of May encouraged early flowering. Early June was stormy and caused some *coulure*, but the rest of the month was again very hot right through to the end of July. August variable, delaying *véraison* (colour change), but the three weeks which led up to 5 September were ideal, dry and warm. This was rudely interrupted by a severe thunderstorm and a swathe of devastating hail from Libourne to St-Émilion. Who would be a *vigneron*! And which of them made good wine? Those who sprayed in time, green pruned, sorted the grapes and selected the best vats. On the whole, some very agreeable wines though the market held back a little, to see how the 2000 would turn out.

**Ch Lafite** The scale of Lafite's operation can be judged from the number of pickers: 420, starting with the Merlot on 20 September and Cabernet Sauvignon on the 27th; and of the severe selection of vats, only 40% of the crop used for the *grand vin* (a blend of Cabernet Sauvignon 74%, Merlot 18.5%, Cabernet Franc 6% and Petit Verdot 1.5%). The result is, in the words of a respected English wine merchant, 'a spectacular Lafite'. Just two notes so far, both cask samples tasted at the château, first in April 2000, the second two months later. A deep, intense, convincing appearance with an almost opaque, velvety core; lovely, sweet, fleshy, youthful aroma; some sweetness, undemonstrative with but good mouthfeel and silky tannins. An attractive future. *Last tasted June 2000* (★★★★) 2015–2030.

**Ch Latour** Deep, plummy; fragrant – hint of violets and oak; sweet, full-bodied, a soft ripeness, attractive, classic Latour. *Tasted at the château, March 2001* (★★★★★) 2015–2025.

**Ch Margaux** Cabernet Sauvignon 77%, Merlot 15%, Cabernet Franc and Petit Verdot 8%. First tasted from the cask March 1999, still vivid purple, very sweet, fleshy, lovely fruit – softer and sweeter than the '98 though not as concentrated. Next, the opening vintage of Manfred Wagner's vertical in Zurich, November 2000: attractive fruit and oak nose; after three hours positively exotic, full of fruit and oak but well integrated. Most recently at the château, an amazing fragrance; very sweet, chewy but alongside the 2000, a touch of rawness. The '99 was being bottled at the time of my last visit, 25 June 2001: 200,000 bottles, the *grand vin* being 40 per cent of the production. *Last tasted at the château, March 2001* (★★★★) 2015–2030.

**Ch Mouton-Rothschild** Cabernet Sauvignon 78%, Cabernet Franc 4% and Merlot 18%. First tasted with Patrick Léon at the château, alongside the '98 – a similar colour, more fleshy fruit, ripe Cabernet and oak, less spicy. Very sweet, hovering between lissom and plump ripeness. Next, with Hervé Berland: deep, velvety; 'toasted' Cabernet aroma that opened up beautifully. 'Fleshy' noted again, dry finish, and charm. (★★★★) *An attractive wine – say* 2012–2030.

**Ch Haut-Brion** Considered the best since the '89s and '90s. Merlot 55%, Cabernet Sauvignon 35% and Cabernet Franc 10%. Tasted alongside the '98 and, in comparison very forward in appearance; a spicy, very fragrant nose; touch of sweetness, silky tannins, lovely texture, good acidity. Very attractive but lacking the drive of the '98. *Oct 2001* (★★★★) 2008–2025.

**Ch Ausone** and **Ch Pétrus** not yet tasted.

**Ch Cheval Blanc** Merlot 55% and Cabernet Franc 45%. Pierre Lurton gave us some interesting information, particularly about the harvest that followed a stress-free growing season for the vines. The grapes were physiologically ripe from 13 September, the Merlot being picked between 14 and 18 September. Harvesting was interrupted by heavy rain, from 19–21 September, the Cabernet Franc being picked between the 22nd and 28th. 'Very healthy grapes, the best looking since 1989'. Unusually deep, virtually opaque; low-keyed, but fragrant and oaky on nose and palate. Ripe, fleshy, dry finish. Impressive. *At the château, April 2000* (★★★★) 2010–2030.

THE MAJORITY OF MY '99 NOTES were made at the Union des Grands Crus tastings in Bordeaux in April 2000 (1), in London in May 2001 (2) and on a few other more recent occasions. Of the roughly 150 wines tasted, the following notes cover the best, or at least most interesting:

**Ch Angélus** Packed with fruit and flavour. Very tannic. (2) (★★★★)

**Ch d'Angludet** Cabernet Sauvignon 50%, Merlot 45% and Petit Verdot 5%. Three notes. Very distinctive; riper and sweeter than the '98, good flesh and fruit. Silky leathery tannins. Once again above its *cru bourgeois* level. (1), Jan 2000 and (2) (★★★)

**Ch d'Armailhac** Deep, cedary, fleshy; very good fruit. Always a deliciously flavoury wine with flair. *Last tasted at the château, March 2001* (★★★★) 2008–2015.

**Ch Batailley** Two notes. Dependable, easy style. Packed with fruit, good texture, early drinking. *Last noted Aug 2001* (★★★) 2004–2010.

**Ch Beauséjour-Bécot** My relationship with the Bécot family goes back some 20 years when we had a promotional sale for the château at Christie's. The new generation in charge is consistently making one of the most agreeable and stylish St-Émilions. Good flavour, length and tannins. (1) and (2) (★★★) 2006–2012.

**Ch Bernadotte** I nearly said May de Lenquesaing's new plaything but I really mean another string to her bow. Although not far from Ch Pichon-Lalande, the château is difficult to find but worth it as it is a comfortable place to stay and play (accompanying May's nephew Gildas d'Ollone, a talented flute player). Several notes, mainly made at Ch Pichon-Lalande. Attractive fruit. *Last tasted March 2001* (★★) 2003–2008.

**Ch Beychevelle** A pity that this most beautiful of châteaux is so bleak inside. The Achille-Fould family and their period furniture left ages ago. But despite this, some attractive wines are being made, the '99 sweet and fruity. (1) and (2) (★★★★) 2008–2016.

**Ch Bouscaut** A fragrant, sweet and easy Graves. (1) and (2) (★★★) 2004–2012.

**Ch Branaire** Three notes. A great deal of investment here, new *chais* and equipment. Perhaps too much new oak. Blackberry-like fragrance. Good fruit. A bit lean. Very tannic finish. (1) and (2). Most recently, holding back but good power. *Aug 2001* (★★★) 2006–2015.

**Ch Brane-Cantenac** Style continuously evolving. Reminds me of the former chocolatey character of Cantenac-Brown (see below) – no relation. Full of fruit, oak and tannin. Should make a good bottle. (1) and (2) (★★★★) 2008–2015.

**Ch de Camensac** Impressively deep; good fruit; sweet, nice flesh but astringent. *Tasted blind, Aug 2001* ★(★★) 2004–2010.

**Ch Canon** 50% Merlot, resulting in a sweet, easy style, reminding me of the '85. (1) and (2) ★★★ 2004–2012.

**Ch Canon-La-Gaffelière** Extraordinarily high-toned, unusual scent, touch of tea; sweet, good flavour, but lean, no more than a hint of elegance but certainly impressive. (1) and (2) 2006–2015.

**Ch Cantemerle** Attractive but lacking the elegance it had in its heyday (mid-1950s). (1) ★★★ 2006–2015.

**Ch Cantenac-Brown** Sweet fruit; oak and tannin. (1) (★★★) 2006–2015.

**Carruades de Ch Lafite** Cabernet Sauvignon 69% and Merlot 31%. A shade of the *grand vin* but still stylish. A forthcoming, cedary nose; soft ripe fruit. (1) ★★★ 2005–2012. *Should make a pleasant drink.*

**Ch Chasse-Spleen** Would certainly be upgraded to at least *5ème cru classé* if there was ever a reclassification of Bordeaux châteaux. Good fruit, and with the length so often lacking in *bourgeois* Médocs. *(1)* ★★★★ *2006–2012.*

**Dom de Chevalier** Admiring Olivier Bernard as I do, I confess that I was worried when I learned of the increase in the vineyard acreage and the state of the art new *chai*, but despite the absence of Claude Ricard's artistry, some very attractive wines being made. The '99, an easy style, lighter than expected, also (tasted blind recently) a bit lean, good but with a touch of astringency. Time will tell. (1), (2) and *Aug 2001* (★★★) *2006–2015.*

**Ch Citran** Fruit, good follow through and finish. *(1)* (★★★) *2005–2012.*

**Ch Clinet** Characteristically dark; tarry; rich but with swingeingly teeth-gripping tannins. This Pomerol château has many adherents but I am not one. *(2)* ★ or ★★★★ *(a matter of taste) 2008–2012.*

**Ch Clerc-Milon** Sweet, fleshy fruit. Attractive. *At Ch Mouton-Rothschild, April 2000 and May 2001* (★★★) *2006–2012.*

**Ch La Conseillante** As Pomerols go, this wine could hardly be a bigger contrast to Ch Clinet (see above). Not deep in colour, not overladen with extract, much easier yet with refreshing tannin and acidity. (1) and *(2)* (★★★★) *(just) 2006–2012.*

**Ch Coufran** With the aid of 100% Merlot, the wine is soft, fruity and fleshy. *(1)* (★★★) *2005–2012.*

**Ch Dassault** I only have a nodding acquaintance with this airplane tycoon's wine but am impressed by his '99. *(1)* (★★★) *2005–2012.*

**Ch Dauzac** A bit of money spent here too. Very sweet, fruit, extract and lashings of oak. *(1)* (★★★) *2002–2012.*

**Ch La Dominique** Despite an opaque core, open knit and distinctly soft. Sweet, fruity. Distinctive, with extra nuances. Easy, forward. (1) and *Sept 2001* ★★(★) *Now–2012.*

**Ch Ducru-Beaucaillou** Hard to pin down in its early days in cask yet showing class. Elegant future predicted. *(1)* (★★★★) *2008–2020.*

**Ch Duhart-Milon** Cabernet Sauvignon 90% and Merlot 10%. Very fragrant, saplings and greengages; ripe fruit and grip. *At Ch Lafite, April 2000* (★★★) *2005–2012.*

**Ch Durfort-Vivens** Fairly good fruit and flesh but a bit too sweet and easy. (2) and *Aug 2001* ★(★) *Now–2009.*

**Ch de Ferrande** A somewhat underestimated Graves. Attractive *(1)* (★★★) *2004–2010.*

**Ch de Fieuzal** Good, crisp, flavoury Graves. *At the château, April 2000* (★★★) *2004–2010.*

**Ch Figeac** Some problem here. Strange overtones which, hopefully, will wear off. (1) and *(2) rating? Must retaste.*

**Les Forts de Latour** Forthcoming; sweet, soft, already developing attractively. *At Ch Latour, March 2001* ★★★ *2005–2012.*

**Clos Fourtet** Once such a dull, stiff, cardboardy wine, now fragrant, fruity and soft. *(1)* ★★(★★) *Now–2010.*

**Ch La Gaffelière** Fragrant, fruity, 'singed and sooty'. Sweet. Soft with that touch of acidity which, over the years, I have often noted. (1) and *(2)* ★(★★) *Now–2010.*

**Ch Gazin** Haunted by its magnificent '45. I have always had a soft spot for this château. Deep, velvety; sweet, attractive, forward. *(1)* ★(★★) *Soon–2010.*

**Ch Giscours** The wine seems to have lost the dense aberrations it showed during the 1970s. It is now richly coloured, sweet, attractive. Citrus-tinged acidity. Fair potential. (1) and *(2)* (★★★) *2007–2015.*

**The Grand-Puy châteaux** Year after year there is no contest – **Grand-Puy-Lacoste** has substance and style and usually needs bottle age, **Grand-Puy-Ducasse** limps along, the '99 distinctly odd with no finish. So Lacoste *(1)* (★★★★) *2010–2020* whereas Ducasse is ★ *don't bother.*

**Ch Gruaud-Larose** A delicious '99. Fruit, flesh and spice which will develop into a very satisfying mouthful. (1) and *(2)* (★★★★) *2007–2020.*

**Ch Haut-Bailly** Bottled Easter 2001. First, a cask sample in April 2000, next at the château. A consistently well made, stylish wine, one of my favourite Pessac-Léognans – no exaggeration, no speciousness, just extremely good. *Last tasted at the château, June 2001* ★★★★ *2006–2016.*

**Ch Haut-Batailley** Easy to mix up the names but not the wines. The most consistently elegant and charming of the Borie family's Pauillacs, exemplified by their '99. *At Ch Ducru, April 2000* ★★★★ *2006–2016.*

**Ch Kirwan** Rich, tarry, black treacle nose. Sweet, fleshy, intense. Very good in its way but a bit over the top. (1) and *(2)* (★★★)? *2006–2015?*

**Ch Lafon-Rochet** Mint and privet; soft, fruity, oaky, tannic. *(1)* (★★★) *2007–2015.*

**Ch Lagrange** (St-Julien) Interesting flavour, crisp fruit, very dry finish. Needs time. (1), (2) and *Aug 2001* (★★★) *2007–2015.*

**Ch La Lagune** Run by an experienced and fairly formidable lady called Mme Jeanne Boyrie. The wine no longer as idiosyncratic as in the past when it was known as 'the burgundy of the Médoc'. The '99 will make an attractive bottle. *(1)* (★★★) *2006–2015.*

**Ch Langoa-Barton** Unyielding in its youth. A wine of substance yet a touch of leanness, and very dry. (1) and *(2)* (★★)? *2008–2016.*

**Ch Larcis-Ducasse** Having drunk an excellent '90 and beautiful '85 on a recent first visit, I have woken up to this slightly neglected château in St-Émilion, bordering Ch Pavie. Like so many wines tasted from the cask in the spring after the vintage, young fruit has winning ways. (1) and *(2)* (★★★) *2005–2015.*

**Ch Larmande** A charming little property in St-Émilion. The results of new outside investment are plain to see – and taste. Now impressively rich. An agreeable mouthful. (1) and *(2)* (★★★) *2004–2010.*

**Ch Lascombes** A rather soulless château. This is the first vintage of the new *régisseur*, Bruno Lemoine (previously at Ch Montrose). Certainly a very positive wine, with lots of grip but a touch of rawness which will wear off. (1) and *(2)* (★★★)? *2007–2015.*

**Ch Léoville-Barton** A superb '99. At the two earliest tastings described as 'deep, velvety', and even after only 18 months in cask with a glorious nose and delicious flavour. (1) and (2). Most recently: very good, rich mocha nose and flavour. Good flesh, very oaky and tannic. *Last tasted at the château, Oct 2001* (★★★★) *2006–2020.*

**Ch Léoville-Poyferré** Once again approaching the style and elegance of the days of former glory (see 1929 page 36). By no means a big wine, a shapely copybook St-Julien. (1), (2) and *Aug 2001* (★★★★) *2006–2020.*

**Ch Lynch-Bages** One is rarely disappointed; indeed I usually have a tingle of anticipation. Typically spicy fruit. (1). *Last tasted at the château, May 2001* (★★★★) *2006–2020.*

**Ch Lynch-Moussas** Deep, mature rim; taut but fragrant, scent of Pauillac 'oyster shells'; straightforward, dry finish. *Last noted in a British Airways tasting (blind), Aug 2001* (★★) *2002–2009.*

**Ch Malescot-St-Exupéry** Continued improvements here. Interesting. 'Very Malescot' blackcurrant aroma; somewhat specious fruit but a lot of flavour. Very tannic. *(1)* (★★★) *2007–2016.*

**Ch Maucaillou** Very dependable. Good fruit and spice. *(1)* ★★ *Soon–2007.*

**Ch La Mission Haut-Brion** Merlot 50%, Cabernet Sauvignon 42%, Cabernet Franc 8%. Dumb at first but opened up; touch of sweetness, nice weight, fruit and grip, relatively easy. Less substantial than the '98. *Last tasted at the château, Oct 2001* (★★★★) *2008–2015.*

**Ch Palmer** Half the crop declassified. The *grand vin* gloriously velvety; intensely fragrant; surprisingly sweet, spicy. *At the château, April 2000* (★★★★) *2006–2020.*

**Ch Pape-Clément** Full use of a superb vineyard site and now, once again, one of the stars of Pessac-Léognan. The *régisseur*, Monsieur Larramona, informed us that the Cabernet Sauvignon was very ripe, with a natural strength of 13.5–14%. *(1)* and *(2)* (★★★★) *2005–2015.*

**Ch Pavie** All the talk is of the huge transformation made here by the new owners. Frankly I preferred the perfectly agreeable wine made by the much-liked Jean-Paul Valette. But this is the 100-point Côte-Rôtie style of Bordeaux much, well somewhat, in vogue. Opaque; tarry, liquorice; fairly powerful, concentrated, singed with a finish of tar and tannin. It will be most interesting to see how this turns out. *(1)* (★★) *for me,* (★★★★) *for some.*

**Pavillon Rouge de Ch. Margaux** Fragrant, quite different to the *grand vin*, lean but flavoury. *(1)* (★★) *2004–2010.*

**Ch Pichon-Baron** Sugar levels higher than '98. Initially I was quite impressed, also the following year, but recently, tasted blind, I noted a touch of coarseness and 'rusticity'. Very tannic. *(1)*, *(2)* and *Aug 2001* (★★★)? *We will see.*

**Ch Pichon-Lalande** A higher percentage of Merlot (47%) than Cabernet Sauvignon (37%) – unusual for a Pauillac wine – soft, yielding fleshy fruit which masked considerable tannin and acidity. *(1)* and *(2)*. *Last tasted Aug 2001* (★★★★) *2006–2016.*

**Ch Pontet-Canet** Good fruit but extremely tannic. *(1)* and *(2)* (★★★) *2009–2020.*

**Ch Prieuré-Lichine** Stéphane Derenoncourt moved here recently from Ch Canon-La-Gaffelière in St-Émilion with a brief to change the previous lean but fragrant style to something richer. It still is a Médoc wine, still Prieuré. Happily the St-Émilion soil and microclimate don't travel! Nice wine though. *(1)* and *(2)* (★★★) *2005–2012.*

**Ch Rauzan-Gassies** Changes continue here too. At first I disliked the tarry, molasses nose, but the following year I thought it had simmered down. Crisp. Very tannic. *(1)* and *(2)* ★★★ *(just) 2006–2015.*

**Ch Rauzan-Ségla** Continuing its renaissance: a fragrant, spicy, sweet, crisp wine. *(1)* and *(2)* (★★★★) *2006–2020.*

**Ch Talbot** Initially impressively deep. Very oaky, crisp Cabernet fruitiness; sweet for Talbot and settling down nicely. Possibly an early developer. *(1)* and *(2)*. *Last noted at a Talbot tasting in London* (★★★★) *2005–2015.*

**Vieux Ch Certan** Very good wine, soft ruby; very rich, fragrant nose; sweet, surprisingly easy despite tannin. Good length. *(1)* and *(2)* (★★★) *2005–2015.*

# 2000 and the future

Unsurprisingly, the 2000 vintage was anticipated with a combination of hope and anxiety; merchants anticipated substantial trade to mark the millennium, unless of course the wine turned out to be unbelievably awful. In the event, most people were reasonably satisfied, particularly in the light of the uneven 2001s.

And the future? As always, all depends on the weather and the market. They are linked. As we have seen, the former dictates the overall quality and style, and a healthy market is essential to keep the wheels of trade in motion. Putting it more bluntly, unless consumers and collectors are prepared to pay an appropriate price, the producer cannot afford to make a fine wine. If any reader doubts this, compare conditions between the mid-1970s and mid-1980s. There is another factor: competition. It seems that all the world is making wine. Bordeaux grape varieties such as Cabernet Sauvignon and Merlot are ubiquitous; Cabernet Franc less so but increasing; and even Petit Verdot and Malbec are used to produce wines for the table, and with increasing success. Although some of these Cabernet-based wines, particularly the cult ones are beginning to price themselves out of the market, most, notably those from Australia and Chile, are very good value. Incidentally, I have just used the expression 'wines for the table' because in France 'table wine', ridiculously in my opinion, has the lowest connotation whereas *vino da tavola* in Italy is a term that can nowadays be used for blends, often including Cabernet Sauvignon, which are in fact out of the ordinary and some are very good indeed. One thing that many of the New World and 'new' Old World Bordeaux look-alikes have in common is that they are not, in practice, ideal wines for the table; they are too rich, they dominate the food, they do not refresh; indeed, they are often best drunk without food, whereas decent red Bordeaux is made to accompany food and is best *with* food.

A word about investment and speculation. Only wines of high quality and of top vintages are suitable, which limits the range. Moreover, as one is always reminded when buying any financial product, prices, values, can go down as well as go up. To a certain extent, investment is justifiable but speculation, by its nature, is risky. But there is nothing new about speculation, it has been a feature of the Bordeaux market as long as there has been a market, the difference between the 1860s and 1960s is that the speculators then were trade, whereas in the early 1970s and 1980s, it was non-trade.

The sensible thing is to follow the more traditional pattern, for claret drinkers to buy their favourite wines when young and cellar them so that, after ten years or more, they can drink them when mature and at cost. Mature wine of good quality surplus to requirements can then be sold at an enhanced price on the open market. As wine is a consumable commodity, its value increases as it matures and available stocks decrease.

I am an optimist. I am of course biased. One of the reasons that claret has been so successful over the centuries is that it is the perfect beverage: its multifarious shades of red are appealing and informative, its nose is refreshing and, as it opens up, it can reveal endless nuances; it tastes good and, when sipped, the wine cleans the palate between each mouthful. The tannin, often harsh when young, is an antioxidant. It not only preserves the wine, but is said to help keep our arteries clear. Claret, particularly fine claret, is subtle and intriguing. It appeals to all our senses – and aids the digestion! Bordeaux is *good* for you.

## 2000 ★★★ to ★★★★★

The growing season, as always in Bordeaux, was by no means straightforward. The New Year and spring were more than mild, with above-average temperatures in March, resulting in early bud burst. However, though the warmth continued in April and May, it was wet, flowering starting at the end of the month. The damp conditions continued through a depressingly cloudy and humid June and July. What saved the day (rather like 1978 though the heat and sun arrived a month earlier) was almost unbroken sunshine without rain from August through September, resulting in fine ripening conditions favouring the Merlot and, for those who waited and timed it right, the late-ripening Cabernet Sauvignon.

Unquestionably, this was a very good year, fairly uniform in quality with some really outstanding wines. No serious cellar should be without some decent 2000s.

**Ch Lafite** An astonishingly high percentage of Cabernet Sauvignon (93.3%) with Merlot 6.7%, the final *assemblage* including 10% press wine. The *grand vin* was just 36% of the total harvest. Cask sample tasted March 2001: opaque, intense purple rim; crisp, fragrant, pronounced Cabernet Sauvignon aroma and flavour; sweet, wonderfully ripe, fleshy, extended, with dry leathery tannic finish. (★★★★★) *Great wine with a long life ahead.*

**Ch Latour** Cabernet Sauvignon 77%, Merlot 16%, Cabernet Franc 4% and Petit Verdot 3%, the *grand vin* representing 48% of the crop. Cask sample tasted March 2001 at the château: very deep, velvety, opaque core, with intense purple rim; dumb at first, rich, spicy, violets, very Cabernet; full, hard, spicy, tannic. Denser tannins and higher acidity than the '99. (★★★★★) *Long life.*

**Ch Margaux** The *grand vin* was 40% of the crop; Cabernet Sauvignon 80%, Merlot 10%, Petit Verdot an unusually high

7% and Cabernet Franc 3%. Cask sample first tasted in March 2001 with Paul Pontallier who described his Cabernet Sauvignon as 'out of this world …, a new benchmark … top vintage'. Fairly deep, black cherry, mauve rim, rich 'legs'; as usual, nothing shy about the scent of the young Margaux, it exuded raspberry-like fragrance; sweet, fullish, concentrated, dense, firm, with lovely fruit – yet even more tannin than the '86. Next, tasted in the first-year *chai*. To be brief: it was impressive. *Last noted perambulating before lunch at the château with the Bacchus Society, June 2001* (★★★★★) *Classic, long haul wine.* (The '99s were being bottled at the time of our visit.)

**Ch Mouton-Rothschild** The *grand vin* comprised Cabernet Sauvignon 86% and Merlot 14% (no Cabernet Franc as it was too unripe to use). Cask sample at the château, March 2001, with Hervé Berland: very deep, velvety; dark bramble colour; scent of bitter violets, taut fruit and iron; dry, full, hard, concentrated. Impressive but not as sensuously exotic as the '89 or '90 at the same stage. *Tasted at Ch Mouton* (★★★★★) *A long life ahead.*

**Ch Haut-Brion** Opaque; rich, great depth; excellent fruit, complete, richly textured, velvety tannins, great length. *At the château, March 2001* (★★★★★) *Classic. Long life.*

**Ch Ausone** Cabernet Franc 55% and Merlot 45%. Tasted from the cask, June 2001, in the underground *cave* with Alain Vauthier who told me that in future he was going to include Cabernet Sauvignon, Petit Verdot and Carmenère in the blend. Very deep, velvety, intense; glorious fruit and spice; very good indeed, the oak giving the wine a distinct taste of cloves, good length. A superb Ausone. (★★★★★) *Long life.*

**Ch Cheval Blanc** Merlot 53% and Cabernet Franc 47%. Very successful vintage, natural strength as high as 14.9%, average alcohol of the Merlots being 13.7%, and no vats under 13.2%. Strict selection with the *grand vin* only 55% of the crop: opaque, intense, immensely impressive; low-keyed, subdued fruit on the nose but mouthfillingly full, fruity, and fleshy on the palate. A delicious wine. *March 2001* (★★★★★) *Long life.*

**Ch Pétrus** Cask sample tasted June 2001 with Christian Moueix at the J P Moueix offices in Libourne: very deep, fairly intense; sweet, rich, somehow totally unique; very sweet on the palate, with lovely fruit and flesh. Complete. Potentially a great Pétrus. (★★★★★) *Long life.*

UNLESS OTHERWISE STATED, the following very broad cross-section of 2000s were noted at the tastings at various host châteaux organised by the Union des Grands Crus de Bordeaux in March 2001 and attended by a wide cross section of international wine writers.

What came over very clearly was the depth of colour of the wines: many were quite opaque at the core, with intense violet rims. Like all young red Bordeaux in a vintage of this quality, the wines, almost without exception, were – are – liberally endowed with tannins. Therefore, to save endless repetition, I have only referred to the appearance of the wine if it is exceptionally dark or lacking depth of colour, and only if excessively tannic – for the use of new oak seems very prevalent – or lacking tannin.

Most of these wines have good mid-term prospects of 8–15 years unless otherwise suggested.

**Ch Angélus** Intense, very oaky, appealing violets scent; sweet, full, rich, concentrated fruit and oak. Out to impress, and it does. But where is the finesse? (★★★)

**Ch d'Angludet** Very deep; fragrant, distinctive, almost floral; hard to pin down but a good wine. (★★★)

**Ch d'Armailhac** Immensely deep, almost black; aroma of bramble and coffee; full, fleshy but very tannic. *At Ch Mouton-Rothschild, March 2001* (★★★★)

**Ch Beauséjour-Bécot** Crisp, intense, oaky nose and taste. full-bodied, as yet unknit, with very oaky, spicy finish (★★★)

**Ch Belair** (St-Émilion) Medium-depth and intensity, mauve rim, rich 'legs'; initially a smell of pure sawdust, then sweet, fragrant fruit; similar on palate. Lean. Very dry, hard finish. *Tasted with Christian Moueix in Libourne, June 2001* (★★★)?

**Ch Beychevelle** Startling Cabernet and oak nose; bramble and spice; very positive flavour, good fruit, attractive. Quite different in style to the Beychevelles of old. (★★★★)?

**Ch Bouscaut** Deep, velvety; good flesh and fruit, developing a tangerine-like scent; dry, good grip and length, tannin and citrus-like acidity. (★★★)

**Ch Branaire** Pleasant, straightforward, whiff of raspberry, opening up with pronounced vanillin scent; good fruit, nice weight, piquant finish – a bit tart. (★★★★)?

**Ch Brane-Cantenac** Medium deep; good flavour and length. (★★★★)

**Ch Canon** Unknit, sweaty, almost smelly; hefty, blunt, very tannic, bitter finish. One of my favourite St-Émilions, usually dependably fruity and charming. I just hope this develops as it should. (★★)?

**Ch Canon-La-Gaffelière** Rich 'legs': fragrant, spicy; very sweet, fruity, rich but not overconcentrated. Very tannic. (★★★★)

**Ch Cantemerle** Whiff of tea (not Earl Grey), sweet, rich on nose and palate. Chewy fruit, easy style. (★★★★)

**Ch Cantenac-Brown** Broad, meaty; silky tannins, chewy, very good length. (★★★★)

**Ch Carbonnieux** Ruby colour; closed at first but a touch of tangerine; firm, lean but in 2000 good fruit and flesh. (★★★) *Good wine, but often an early developer.*

**Ch Les Carmes-Haut-Brion** Very distinctive, whiff of onions and citrus; fairly sweet, very flavoury. (★★★) *An early developer.*

**Carruades de Ch Lafite** Cabernet Sauvignon 51.4%, Merlot 42.3%, Cabernet Franc 4.9% and Petit Verdot 1.4%: fresh, crisp fruit. *At Ch Lafite* (★★★★)

**Ch Certan-Marzelle** Hard, scent of freshly sawn wood, touch of black treacle; very sweet, very distinctive. Not my style of wine. *At the J-P Moueix offices in Libourne, June 2001. For me* (★★★), *for the glib and global* (★★★★)

**Dom de Chevalier** Rich, toasted oak, mocha nose and flavour; medium- to full-bodied, rich, good length. One cannot help noticing the difference between this modern style of Chevalier, with the increased plantings and state of the art stainless steel winery, and the more delicate and fragrant wines produced by Claude Ricard, the previous owner who sold the domaine in 1983. The current owner, Oliver Bernard, however, has inherited Ricard's passion for this still quite small Pessac-Léognan estate, despite moving with the times. (★★★★)

**Ch Clerc-Milon** Cabernet Sauvignon 67%. Distinct Cabernet aroma, curious fragrance, sweaty tannins; dry, good fruit but hard tannic finish. *At Ch Mouton, March 2001* (★★★)

**Ch Clinet** Opaque, intense; sweet, fig-like richness and oak; fairly sweet, certainly rich, almost 'pressed', concentrated fruit and very tannic. I can see the attractions, but I have rarely liked the style. *For me* (★★★), *for admirers of Clinet* (★★★★)

**Ch La Conseillante** A 12-ha vineyard owned by the Nicolas family and which has long been one of my favourite Pomerols. I first tasted the 2000 in March 2001: Merlot 80%, Cabernet Franc 20%, when the average age of the vines was between 40 and 45 years: very deep, almost opaque, open mauve edge; brambly fruit, fragrant, oaky, tannic; sweet, rich, very flavoury, masked tannin. Next, visiting at short notice in June and received by Arnaud de Lamy who joined the château, as manager, in January 2000. Similar note, good concentration, spicy oaky finish. A few days later on the tasting room bench at the J-P Moueix offices in Libourne, the nose reminded me of cold roast beef. Clove-like spice. Good wine. *Last tasted June 2001* (★★★★)

**Ch Cos d'Estournel** Subtle, fragrant but low-keyed and harbouring sweaty, leathery tannins; sweet, almost fruit salad – delectable. Tannic of course. (★★★★★) *Will keep well.*

**Ch Cos Labory** Fragrant, citrus touch; straightforward. Dry finish. (★★★)

**Ch La Croix-de-Gay** Deep, velvety; low-keyed, hard, slightly stalky; sweet, flavoury but taut and tannic. Impressive. (★★★★) *Needs time.*

**Ch Croizet-Bages** Bottle variation, neither very appealing, one with tinny meat-extract nose, dry, raw. The other so unpleasant on the nose that I did not bother to taste it. They should have been more careful on their cask samples.

**Ch Dassault** Lovely violet rim; intense, taut, brambly fruit; sweet, full-bodied, attractive flavour. (★★★)

**Ch Dauzac** Lean fruit, bitter oak; lean but flavoury. (★★★)

**Ch Dominique** Rich, brambly, sweaty tannins; fairly sweet, full, rich, loaded with all the right components. (★★★★).

**Ch Duhart-Milon** Low-keyed, hard, unyielding; dry curious tarry/iron flavour, very tannic. *At Ch Lafite, March 2001* (★★★)?

**Clos L'Église** Merlot 70%, Cabernet Franc 15% and Cabernet Sauvignon 15%. Concentrated nose and palate, sweet, packed with fruit, masked but bitter tannins (★★★★)

**Ch Ferrière** Fragrant, violets, oaky; touch of sweetness, good fruit but lean. (★★★)

**Ch de Fieuzal** There has been a substantial amount of new investment here. The 2000 was deep, fairly intense; slightly toasted oaky nose but overall scented and attractive; rich, plenty to it, dry finish. (★★★★)

**Ch Figeac** Very deep, though medium intensity; soft, fragrant fruit, scent of raspberry and violets; sweet, amenable, attractive, dry finish. Original and very flavoury as always. (★★★★)

**Ch La Fleur-Pétrus** Deep, richly coloured; taut fruit, citrus whiff, opened up beautifully; sweet, lovely fruit, very tannic. *At the J-P Moueix offices in Libourne, June 2001* (★★★★★) *A beautiful mid- to long term wine.*

**Ch Fonplégade** My main memory of Armand Moueix, the owner who died recently, is of getting up in the middle of the night, wandering, lost, down a long unlit passage into his bedroom. I think this was his last vintage. One of his best too: very attractive fruit and depth. (★★★★)

**Forts de Latour** Cabernet Sauvignon 65% and Merlot 35%; 40% of the crop. Medium intensity; crisp, a bit stalky but opened up well; surprisingly sweet, moderate flesh, but overall lean and very tannic. *At Ch Latour* (★★★★)

**Clos Fourtet** Huge improvement over the old days but, alas, the Lurtons who had effected the improvements recently sold the property. André Lurton told me that this was to provide his children with some cash! (Difficult when all one's wealth is tied up in vineyards and property.) A dry, powerful wine with good fruit and bitter tannic finish. (★★★)

**Ch Franc-Mayne** Belgium-owned, producer of 'Mandarin Napoléon'. Comfortable place to stay (no dark corridors, unlike at Ch Fonplégade, see above): spicy oak; attractive fruit, fairly sweet but rather raw finish. (★★★)

**Ch Gazin** Sweet, open-knit, blackberry-like fruit; sweet, broad, open style, good fruit, oaky finish. *At the J-P Moueix, offices in Libourne, June 2001* (★★★★)

**Ch Giscours** Low-keyed but good fruit; medium sweet, fleshy. Quite a lot to it. (★★★★)

**Ch La Gaffelière** I used to recognise this wine easily in the old days as it reeked of volatile acidity. Not so now. Lean – for St-Émilion – spicy nose; dry, very distinctive, drying finish. Not sure that I don't prefer the more fleshy, exotic and less flawless Gaffelière. *Tasted at the J-P Moueix offices in Libourne, June 2001* (★★★)

**Ch Grand-Mayne** Fragrant, taut oak, depth; interesting and attractive fruity flavour. (★★★)

**Ch Grand-Puy-Ducasse** Alas, this wine never measures up to Ch Grand-Puy-Lacoste (see below). Slightly tinny, tarry nose; not bad fruit, reasonable length and finish, but with mouth-searing tannin. (★★)

**Ch Grand-Puy-Lacoste** Cabernet Sauvignon 78%, Merlot 20% and Cabernet Franc 2%. Lovely dark velvety core, fairly intense; very fragrant, ripe, very Pauillac Cabernet aroma; medium-dry, firm, loads of fruit and tannin. Because of my long friendship with Xavier Borie and the fact that I have, for many years, bought several cases of his wine every vintage, I managed to squeeze some of the '00 out of him – he had more or less pre-sold the lot! *Tasted at Ch Ducru, March 2001* (★★★★★) *A long haul wine.*

**Ch La Grave** (formerly called La Grave-Trigant-de-Boisset) Medium intensity; sweet fruit, whiff of raspberry (ripe Cabernet Franc, though it is only 15%). Sweet, amenable, attractive. *At the J-P Moueix offices in Libourne, June 2001* (★★★★)

**Ch Gruaud-Larose** Vivid mauve rim; interesting aromas of spicy fruit; very distinctive flavour, flesh and fruit. (★★★★★)

**Ch Haut-Bailly** Only 50% of crop used for the *grand vin*. First tasted March 2001: taut, fragrant; good fruit and flavour. Next, very deep; good young fruit; dry, oaky, spicy. One of my favourite red Graves. *Last noted at the chai, June 2001* (★★★★)

**Ch Haut-Batailley** Cabernet Sauvignon 75% and Merlot 25%. Very deep, velvety, fairly intense; fresh, exuding taut, discreet oak; surprisingly sweet and soft, fleshy, masked tannin, good acidity. I was enchanted with this wine and, on my return, ordered a few cases. *Tasted at Ch Ducru with Xavier Borie, March 2001* (★★★★★) *A medium-term charmer.*

**Ch Haut-Bages-Libéral** A lesser-known 5ème cru classé Pauillac in the capable hands of Claire Villars: almost opaque; strange style, slightly cheesy fruit (my mentor Harry Waugh used the expression cheesy not in a derogatory sense. Probably a tannic emanation), opening up, touch of tar; medium-dry, impressive, ripe fruit and extract, very flavoury, perhaps lacking a little length. An optimistic (★★★★)

**Hosanna** (formerly Ch Certan-Giraud) Very bizarre new name though I confess to being entranced by its deliciously crisp fragrance; sweetness on palate and most agreeable fruit. Yet very tannic. Christian Moueix explained the reason behind its new name – but I forget. *At the J-P Moueix offices in Libourne, June 2001* (★★★★★)

**Ch d'Issan** Cabernet Sauvignon 69% and Merlot 31%. Final *assemblage* made January 2001, 60% used for the *grand vin*, 50% new oak: mauve rim; curious, as yet unknit, soft, spicy (cloves), better on palate, oaky, attractive, citrus touch. (★★★)

**Ch Kirwan** Virtually opaque; rich, brambly fruit, distinct vanillin as it opened up; rich, chocolatey, a touch of coarseness on the palate, plenty of new oak. A Michel Rolland-inspired renaissance. Is it still Margaux, though? (★★★★)

**Ch Lafon-Rochet** Medium intensity, rich legs; high-toned, whiff of citrus and tar; medium-sweet, bramble-like fruit, very flavoury. A good Lafon. (★★★★)

**Ch Lagrange** (This one is St-Julien and there are four other Lagranges in Bordeaux.) Initially hard, earthy, then mocha-like; dry, very toasted mocha flavour, hefty, chewy texture. (★★★)

**Ch La Lagune** Deep, velvety, mauve edge; initially hard and dusty but good fruit emerged; sweet, rich, fruity, easy, dry finish. (★★★)

**Ch Langoa-Barton** Opaque, intense; vivid; fragrant, initially slightly stalky, then a touch of tar and black treacle, opening up sweetly, almost caramelly; medium-dryness and weight, straightforward fruit and oak. (★★★★)

**Ch Larcis-Ducasse** Very forthcoming fruit and oak; attractive but lean, very oaky, bitter finish. Needs time to settle down. (★★★)

**Ch Larmande** Curious nose, quite good fruit and flesh. (★★)

**Ch Larrivet-Haut-Brion** Deep; firm, very toasted Graves nose and taste, complete, sweet, impressive. (★★★★)

**Ch Lascombes** Low-keyed, hard edge but interesting fragrance; very distinctive, slightly medicinal-Médoc flavour, taut dry finish. (★★★★)

**Ch Latour-à-Pomerol** Distinct blackcurrant fruit (despite Merlot 90% and Cabernet Franc 10% and not a smidgen of Cabernet Sauvignon); fairly sweet, good fruit, with typically silky texture and leathery tannic finish. *At the J-P Moueix offices in Libourne, June 2001* (★★★★)

**Ch Latour-Martillac** Sweet, chocolatey, mocha Pessac-Léognan nose; good fruit and grip, lean, very tannic. (★★★)

**Ch Léoville-Barton** Very deep; low-keyed, correct, touch of cedar, evolving fragrantly, sweetly; medium sweetness and body, very straightforward flavour and style, delicious though a bit obviously oaky on the finish. Utterly dependable and never overpriced. (★★★★★)

**Ch Léoville-Las-Cases** The *grand vin* was 35.19% of the crop; the final blend was Cabernet Sauvignon 76.8%, Cabernet Franc 14.4% and Merlot 8.8% - no Petit Verdot or press wine. Aroma of deep bramble and cedar, touch of raspberry (ripe Cabernet Franc); surprisingly sweet, ripe fruit, good length, fragrant, tannic and acid finish. Fabulous wine. It was difficult enough in Monsieur Alain Delon's day to gain access to his *chais*. His son has inherited this curious obstinacy, though I perfectly understand how tiresome endless interruptions can be, particularly if there are trippers just doing the rounds. Steven Spurrier and I rely on Isabelle Bachelard to get us in! Worth the effort. *At the château (or rather, in the office; there is no château), March 2001* (★★★★★) *A great future.*

**Ch Léoville-Poyferré** Fragrant fruit and oak, opening up beautifully; medium sweet, soft, lovely fruit, delicious flavour, with a dry, slightly bitter finish. (From the mid-19th century to 1929 some of the very best clarets were made at Poyferré which is said to have one of the most perfect vineyard sites in the Médoc. Happily, the past few years have seen a return to that form.) (★★★★★)

**Ch La Louvière** André Lurton's pride and joy in the Graves. Harmonious, good fruit on nose and palate, sweet, slightly toasty, fleshy, well-balanced, dry tannic finish. (★★★★)

**Ch Lynch-Bages** Good fruit but not the characteristic overt Cabernet Sauvignon aroma, though opening up almost like boiled sweets, candy fragrance; sweet, very attractive. Dry finish. No problems here. (★★★★★)

**Ch Lynch-Moussas** Sweet – too sweet, attractive, rather specious fruit. (★★★) *Early developer.*

**Ch Magdelaine** I have always liked this St-Émilion which deserves to be far better known. Deep, fairly intense; cedar (Daphne said like 'daffodils' – they are all out at the time of writing so I must do some sniffing); sweet, agreeable fruit and flesh. *At the J-P Moueix offices in Libourne, June 2001* (★★★★)

**Ch Malartic-Lagravière** Fragrant, toasted Graves nose with underlying 'onion skin' richness; sweet, fullish, fleshy, good fruit and extract. (★★★★).

**Ch Malescot-St-Exupéry** Malescot has always had a recognisably Cabernet Sauvignon varietal nose, its edge this time a bit tinny, metallic; dry, lean, very varietal flavour. Interesting developments here. (★★★★)?

**Ch Marquis de Terme** Plummy purple; nose of newly sawn wood, very oaky, attractive fruit and flesh but searing dry finish. (★★★)

**Ch La Mission Haut-Brion** Opaque core, velvety, intense; rich, brambly aroma and flavour. Lovely taste. More grip than Haut-Brion. *At the château, March 2001* (★★★★★) *Great future.*

**Ch Monbrison** Velvety ruby; good fruit on nose and palate. Agreeable texture. Decent mouthful. (★★★★)

**Ch Monbousquet** A St-Émilion on the 'wrong side of the track', on low ground between the long straight D670 and the river Dordogne. Gérard Perse makes impressive wine here: almost black; smell of crushed bramble, pressed caviar and tar; sweet, jam-packed, very oaky. Impressive but frankly not my style of wine. *Tasted at Ch Pavie* (★★★)?

**Ch d'Olivier** A magnificent turreted castle in the woods near Léognan, birthplace of the Black Prince in 1330,. He would have liked this wine: rich 'legs'; good fruit and depth; medium-sweet, lean, tannic, citrus-fruit acidity (★★★)

**Ch Les Ormes de Pez** Opaque; curious mixture of citrus and meat on nose and palate. Very flavoury. (★★★)

**Ch Palmer** The *grand vin* was from Cabernet Sauvignon 53% and Merlot 37% (though the *cépages* planted are Cabernet Sauvignon 47%, Merlot 47% and Petit Verdot 6%). I first tasted a cask sample in the *chai* in March 2001: deep, velvety; low-keyed, mainly spicy oak; raw fruit but with good flesh and length, fairly high acidity. *Tasted again in May, no change.* (★★★★★) *Long life.*

**Ch Pape-Clément** The very characteristic, tobacco-like Pessac nose, refreshing citrus-fruit – marmalade to go with the toast! Very rich, flavoury, but with a very oaky (too oaky?) end taste. Impressive though. (★★★★)

**Ch Pavie** Merlot 70%, Cabernet Franc 20% and Cabernet Sauvignon 10%. Very deep, velvety; tobacco-like, sweaty tannins; sweet, full-bodied, charred and tarry taste. Impressive – but I much preferred the late Jean-Paul Valette's Pavie, which was so much more drinkable. *Tasted in the chai. For me ★★, for wine competitions and our American cousins* (★★★★★)

**Ch Pavie-Decesse** Concentrated, tarry; fairly sweet, full-bodied, good flavour but overextracted. Not for me. *At Ch Pavie* (★★★)

**Pavillon Rouge de Ch Margaux** Sweet, fragrant, fleshy with Margaux charm. More dense, and totally different from previous Pavillon vintages. (★★★★)

**Ch Petit-Village** Opaque; very distinctive, lean, oaky, fragrant, with charm; sweet, citrus-like refreshing fruit, very drying finish. (★★★★)

**Ch Phélan-Ségur** Strange, cheesy nose; dry, distinct fruit but raw. I wish I could be kinder because we all like the proprietors and, if I can be bold, to a man simply adore Mme Gardinier, the epitome of French prettiness and charm. (★★) *I am longing to be asked to lunch.*

**Ch Pichon-Lalande** An unusually high percentage of very ripe late-picked Cabernet Sauvignon. Alcohol 12.8%, acidity 3.5g/l. Sweet, good, crisp, ripe fruit. *At the château with May de Lencquesaing and her nephew, Gildas d'Ollone, March 2001* (★★★★★)

**Ch Pichon-Longueville** Vivid mauve edge; rich, spicy Cabernet aromas; sweet, good fruit, extract, flesh, very Cabernet, lots of oak. Attractive. (★★★★)

**Ch La Pointe** Opaque; distinctive, peppery, curious tinny edge; very dry, bitter tannins. Needs time. (★★★)

**Ch Pontet-Canet** This is a very large, well-sited vineyard and château adjoining Ch Mouton-Rothschild in Pauillac. Over the years an uneven performer, and even a decade ago I noted, and did not like, its strong tarry character. Though still a touch of 'tar' on nose and palate, a rich, well-constituted wine with depth and length. (★★★★)

**Ch Prieuré-Lichine** Very deep, intense; spicy, minty fragrance; not the usual lean fruit but surprisingly rich, with chewy Cabernet character. (★★★★)

**Ch Quinault** I do not admire this style of wine: blatantly opaque, intense; black treacle and tar; sweet, concentrated, impressive but quirky, and not what the British expect of that excellent beverage, claret. *Tasted at Ch Pavie* (★★)?

**Ch Rauzan-Gassies** The improvement continues. Elegant fruit on the nose, touch of orange rind, then fragrant, tea-like; sweet, chewy Cabernet mid-palate. Nice wine. (★★★★)

**Ch Rauzan-Ségla** Continues its successful run of stylish, well-made wines. Very forthcoming aroma, good fruit, sweaty tannin underlay; excellent weight, style, elegant with fragrant, oaky finish and aftertaste. (★★★★★) *A good, long-term wine.*

**Ch Siran** Virtually opaque; positive, attractive fruit; pleasant sweetness, texture, stylish richness, oaky finish. Deserves to be more highly regarded. (★★★★) *Almost 5-star.*

**Ch Smith-Haut-Lafitte** Sweet, very toasted oaky nose and flavour. Rich, fairly full-bodied, very tannic. (★★★★)

**Ch Talbot** Very oaky, citrus whiff, sweet bramble; good fruit and weight. Oak very noticeable and a touch of tartness on the finish. Needs to settle down. (★★★★)

**Ch La Tour-Figeac** Strange fragrance and flavour of freshly sawn wood and twisted violets; sweet. (★★)? *Early developer.*

**Ch La Tour Haut-Brion** After the Dillons purchased the Mission estate in 1983, they replanted with a good deal of Merlot. The mature vines have certainly produced a slightly less aggressive La Tour. Though the 2000 unsurprisingly was opaque and intense, with characteristic tautness, it is fragrant, with lovely flavour and aftertaste. One of the best that I can recall. *At Ch La Mission Haut-Brion* (★★★★)

**Ch Troplong-Mondot** Freshly sawn wood again; sweet, interesting, rich fruit, masked tannin. (★★★)

**Ch Trotanoy** Very deep, opaque core, intense; rich blackberry and cedar nose of considerable depth; sweet, chewy fruit. As magnificent as expected. *At the J-P Moueix offices in Libourne, June 2001* (★★★★★)

**Vieux Ch Certan** Another favourite Pomerol of mine, long owned by the Thienpont family from Belgium. Merlot 70%, Cabernet Franc 20%, Cabernet Sauvignon 10%. Cask sample first tasted March 2001: opaque; rich, spicy, oaky, attractive; dry, rich though with a lean touch. Next, tasted from the (Séguin-Moreau) casks a week after fining: deep, velvety; sweet, relatively easy yet, of course, tannic. A sample, from a half bottle, before fining, was quite different, richer, with excellent soft tannins. Tasted with Alexandre Thienpont who told me they sell at one price, not in tranches as in the Médoc. *At the château, June 2001* (★★★★).

OTHER 2000S, mainly *cru bourgeois* wines from cask samples tasted at host châteaux in Bordeaux, March 2001:

**Ch d'Agassac** an incredibly pretty, historic, moated and turreted bijou château that I could not resist sketching while staying at nearby Ch La Lagune. Intense, mauve; rather speciously fragrant vanilla and raspberry-like scents; fullish body and flavour, moderate length, tannic (★★★); **Ch Balestard-La-Tonnelle** sweet, caramelly; a quickly evolving 'heart on sleeve' wine (★★★); **Ch Beauregard** (Pomerol) deep mauve; complex nose, fresh, young, stalky, very oaky; sweet, rich, fairly packed with fruit and tannin (★★★); **Ch Bernadotte** spicy, speciously attractive (★★★); **Ch Cap-de-Mourlin** two notes: opaque; tar and black treacle; touch of coarseness, very tannic (★★)?; **Ch Chasse-Spleen** velvety, flavoury, complete (★★★★); **Ch Clarke** good flavour and flesh (★★★); **Ch Fourcas-Dupré** hard (★★); **Ch Fourcas-Hosten** fragrant; taut, tannic (★★★); **Ch Fonréaud** good mouthful (★★★); **Ch de France** open, fragrant, sweet and toasty on nose and palate. Nice weight, very dry finish (★★★); **Ch Greysac** nose like newly sawn wood, lissome; **Ch Haut-Bergey** very forthcoming toasted nose; dry, lean, oaky finish (★★); **Ch Labégorce** deep, velvety; surprisingly harmonious, even creamy; good fruit, chewy (★★★★); **Clos du Marquis** (this is Ch Léoville-Las-Cases' *2ème vin*) Cabernet Sauvignon 68%, Merlot 24.5%, Petit Verdot 4.9% and Cabernet Franc 2.6% (40% of crop). Virtually opaque, low-keyed but good; surprisingly sweet, ripe fruit (★★★★); **Ch Maucaillou** crisp fruit, spicy (★★★★); **Ch Pique-Caillou** light, refreshing, open, easy style (★★) *for early drinking;* **Ch Potensac** attractive, understated fruit; very sweet, delicious flavour, crisp. I just queried its length (★★★); **Ch Poujeaux** hard, oaky (★★★); and **Ch La Tour-de-By** lean, spicy (★★★)

# White Bordeaux

Currently only about 14% of the wines of Bordeaux are white – these are mainly dry, some 70% being of the lowly Bordeaux *appellation*. The only sweet wines of note are made in Sauternes and Barsac, enclaves of the Graves region, and in Ste-Croix-du-Mont and Loupiac on the opposite (right) bank of the Garonne.

The reason why the sweet wines dominate this chapter is their longevity and their ability, in common with the higher grades of Tokaji Aszú and the finest German wines, to improve with age, whereas dry white Bordeaux, with very few exceptions, is made for early consumption. For practical purposes, therefore, my notes on dry white Bordeaux appear mainly among the most recent vintages, the exceptions being the few very high-quality wines from Pessac-Léognan, the northernmost and best part of the Graves region nearest to the city of Bordeaux. Traditionally, dry white Bordeaux was made from a blend of Sémillon and Sauvignon Blanc grape varieties, though nowadays Sauvignon Blanc is often used entirely on its own.

The Sauternes *appellation*, consisting of five communes, Sauternes, Bommes, Preignac, Fargues and Barsac, covers a relatively small and compact area nestling in the southern part of the Graves, near Langon. These five communes benefit from a unique microclimate resulting from the confluence of two rivers, the broad, tidal, warm-water Garonne and the tiny Ciron, whose cool waters spring in the Pyrenees. At certain times in the autumn morning mists arise which are then burned off by the warm, ripening, afternoon sunshine. The mist encourages the formation of botrytis (known in France as *pourriture noble* or 'noble rot'), its effect on ripening grapes being to concentrate natural sugar content and (tartaric) acidity. In some years such as 1970 wines can be made without the onset of botrytis but, though sweet, they lack the extra dimension. The principal *cépages* are Sémillon, a broad, dependable variety happily susceptible to botrytis, and the more acidic Sauvignon Blanc which adds zest and balance. Sometimes a small percentage of the grapey, aromatic Muscadelle is used.

Barsac is the largest Sauternes commune and because of its lower-lying situation produces a distinctive style of wine. It is entitled to its own *appellation* as well as that of Sauternes and many of the top châteaux here choose to use the Barsac name rather than that of Sauternes. Incidentally, there is no such thing as a 'dry Sauternes'. Sauternes, traditionally and legally, is sweet. Though dry white wine can be made in these five communes it usually has a distinctive name, Ygrec in the case of Ch d'Yquem, and 'R' for the dry white of Ch Rieussec, both sold as straightforward Bordeaux AC.

One has only to visit Ch d'Yquem to see why it is so special. The ancient château sits in a commanding position with its vast rows of vines spreading down the slopes below: a perfect combination of site, soils, drainage and *cépages*. Equally dominant, since the 18th century, is its wine, both in quality and price. From the 1780s until quite recently, the château was owned and run by the Lur Saluces family; the present Comte Alexandre de Lur Saluces continues to manage the estate.

Yquem, along with Tokaji Aszú Eszencia and the finest madeira, develops well in bottle and is famed for its longevity. For long it has been the pride of connoisseurs and collectors – among the latter, the intrepid Hardy Rodenstock whose extraordinary five-day tasting in September 1998 of 125 vintages of Ch d'Yquem dominates the following notes.

# 1784–1899

It is not known precisely at what period sweet wines started to be made in the Sauternes district; the use of late-picked grapes, even the understanding of botrytis, could well have predated the Hungarians in Tokaj (see page 497) or the Germans in the Rheingau (see page 342). What is certain is that sweet wines were made in the 1700s and that the reputation of Yquem was well established long before the end of that century.

Two events are worthy of note: the transfer of ownership of Ch d'Yquem in 1785 from the Sauvage family to the aristocratic Lur Saluces and the correspondence between Thomas Jefferson and the new owners, followed by his subsequent visit to Bordeaux in May 1787. Jefferson, then the American Envoy (Ambassador) to France, wrote (in French) from Paris on 18 December 1787 to Monsieur Diquem (*sic*):

'Not having the honour of making your acquaintance, I trust in your good faith to excuse me the liberty of writing to you directly. I will have need for some small provision of white Sauternes for my own use during my residence in France… I know that yours is of the best crus of Sauterne and I would prefer to receive it directly from your hands because I would be sure it is genuine, good and sound. Permit me then Sir, to ask if you still have some of the Sauterne, first quality, of the year 1784, and if you would kindly let me have 250 bottles…'

The reply, also in French, 'Chateau d'Yquem, 7 June 1788. As Mr D'Yquem's son-in-law, Sir, and the owner of all his assets, I have the honour to reply to your letter to him. I have drawn and bottled [the 1784] with the greatest care …..Your very humble and obedient servant/Comte de Lur Saluces.' The consignment of 'Cinq Caisses de vin de Cinquante Bouteilles' was handled by Jefferson's agent in Bordeaux and shipped via Rouen to Paris.

The full provenance of several of these old vintages is not known and I have described their condition and, to a necessarily limited extent their colour, smell and taste, as I have found them. As can be seen, many of these ancient wines appear to have been remarkably well preserved and, by any standards, are most lovely wines. It is worth mentioning that the cellars of Ch d'Yquem contain relatively few old vintages; also, alas, that I have discovered that the wines recorked and probably topped up at the château are often less good than those not tampered with. Some recorking is done to establish the authenticity of the wine in order to preserve its value; my firm recommendation is for owners of these rare and lovely wines never to have them recorked, no matter what the level.

Regarding vintages of this period, these roughly follow the pattern described in the Red Bordeaux chapter (see page 9), with pockets of excellence: the outstanding pre-phylloxera period, and recovery in the 1890s.

## Sauternes Vintages at a Glance
**Outstanding ★★★★★**
1784, 1802, 1811, 1831, 1834, 1847, 1864, 1865, 1869, 1875, 1893
**Very Good ★★★★**
1787, 1814, 1825, 1828, 1841, 1848, 1858, 1871, 1874, 1896, 1899
**Good ★★★**
1818, 1822, 1851, 1859, 1861, 1870

## 1784 ★★★★★
The most renowned vintage of the late 18th century and well documented thanks mainly to the original copies of the letters of Thomas Jefferson (see above and facing page).
**Ch d'Yquem** Bottled at the château in January 1788. Sloping shouldered bottles with contemporary wheel engraving 'Ch d'Yquem ThJ 1784'. First noted at a Rodenstock Raritäten Weinprobe in Wiesbaden in 1985 in the presence of Comte Alexandre de Lur Saluces. Magnificently deep amber gold in the decanter. Bright; scented, vanilla; still sweet, creamy, delicious. Most recently, at Rodenstock's week-long tasting of Yquem in Munich. I removed the short, crumbly, original cork, the level of the wine being mid-shoulder. The wine had a warm mahogany-amber colour with a pronounced yellow-green rim. Initially, the nose, unsurprisingly, was creakingly old but, after 15 minutes settled down to reveal a remarkably rich, tangy, honeyed scent, and after a further 30 minutes opened out: very sweet, like black treacle. After a further 15 minutes it seemed to me (as I wrote at the time) 'like a thoroughbred horse peeing on clean straw'. Happily, it did not taste like that: medium sweetness and body; it was really very drinkable with a lovely old flavour and good finish. *Last noted at the Rodenstock Yquem tasting in Munich, Sept 1998 ★★★★*

## 1787 ★★★★
**Ch d'Yquem** A slightly more bulbous bottle, with an extended neck. Level top-shoulder. Engraved with name of wine, year and Jefferson's initials. Deep amber-brown with apple-green rim; bouquet of singed raisins, attractive, considerable depth. Still drinkable, its marvellous acidity cutting through a black treacle-like flavour and thickness. *Tasted – sharing a glass with Michel Bettane, arguably France's most renowned taster, and Helmut Romé of Austria's Falstaff magazine – at the Rodenstock Yquem tasting in Munich, Sept 1998 ★★★*

Footnote: From 1789–1855 the wine was known as 'Yquem', and as 'd'Yquem' before and after this period.

## Thomas Jefferson

*Jefferson, later to be the third US President, was Envoy (Ambassador) to France from May 1784 to October 1789. He once wrote 'Good wine is a daily necessity for me.' He was a noted connoisseur and, visiting Bordeaux in May 1787, he ordered on the spot the 1784 vintage of Ch Margaux and other first growths. Jefferson did not trust wine merchants and insisted that the wines be bottled at the château, his agent in Bordeaux providing bottles engraved for identification (labels were not in use at that time, nor the convenient 12-bottle boxes we are accustomed to. Wine was customarily transported in wicker hampers usually containing 50 bottles). He also ordered more top growths and other wines for himself and the President, George Washington, instructing his agent in Bordeaux to have the wines étiquetté with the name of the wine and the initials TJ and GW so that the content and ownership of the bottles could be identified.*

*The 1784 Ch d'Yquem and Ch Margaux and the 1787 Ch Lafite and Ch Branne-Mouton referred to in this book are from a small cache of wines claimed to be originally in the possession of, or at least ordered by, Thomas Jefferson. Though the present owner is reticent about the provenance, there is a considerable body of evidence supporting their authenticity. The bottles themselves, examined independently by two Christie's glass experts, are unquestionably of the period, and a distinguished expert from the British Library confirms the contemporary style of the engraved letters and figures.*

*On a recent visit to Ch d'Yquem I was permitted by Comte Alexandre de Lur Saluces, to inspect the original ledger in the archives relating to Jefferson's purchase.*

## 1802 ★★★★★

**Ch Yquem** Labelled '*Château-Yquem, Perrault, Chalon s/Saône*'. Picking started 23 September. Good colour for age though not star bright; slightly maderised but otherwise rich with shades of caramel and vanilla. Better flavour than expected. Rich yet dry finish. Good acidity. *In Munich, Aug 1998* ★★★

## 1811 ★★★★★

The most famous 'Comet' vintage.
**Ch Yquem** First tasted at the château in 1986. Contemporary hand blown bottle, labelled '*Château Yquem, Marquis A M de Lur Saluces, 1811, Grand Vin Sauternes*'. Blackened cork. Wine a lovely colour, raisiny, still sweet. Nine years later, at Rodenstock's 16th annual rare wine tasting. Worn label. Gold; high-toned apricot; barley sugar flavour with aggressive acidity. Most recently, similar label to the bottle noted in 1986: sweet scent. It reminded me of raspberries and cream. Considerable depth and length. Dry finish. *Last tasted Sept 1998* ★★★★

## 1814 ★★★★

**Ch Yquem** Picking commenced 29 September. First tasted in 1995: palish orange gold; vanilla 'blancmange' nose; good flavour but edgy acidity. Most recently, labelled '*Château Yquem, Lur Saluces, 1814*'. Original soft dark cork. Level upper shoulder. Lovely colour; rich, peachy, perfection – almost too good; chocolatey flavour, fragrant aftertaste. Michel Bettane and I looked at each other in wonder. But we both agreed: it really was delicious. *Last tasted in Munich, Sept 1998* ★★★★★

## 1818 ★★★

**Ch Yquem** Picking commenced 17 September. Similar label to the 1814. Original dried-out cork. Level into neck. Nose showing its age, singed but fragrant; sweet, full, fat, tangy, with positive raisiny flavour. *Tasted in Munich, Sept 1998* ★★★★

## 1822 ★★★

Exceptionally hot, dry, year.
**Ch Yquem** Unusually early harvest, picking started 27 August. Labelled '*Château Yquem, Lur Saluces, 1822, Grand Vin*'. Original short, slightly spongy cork. Fairly deep amber; good fruit, slightly singed bouquet; losing sweetness and touch of fungi, rot, on the finish. *Tasted in Munich, Sept 1998* ★★

## 1825 ★★★★

**Ch Yquem** Picking commenced 11 September. Four notes: the first, Bordeaux-bottled by the *négociant* Chabeau. Level upper-mid shoulder. The highlight of Bud Moon's Yquem tasting in Chicago in 1988. Next, with Brossault, Chalon-sur-Saône label, a bottle bought at Christie's and tasted in 1994. The colour of tea; marvellous old caramel-vanilla bouquet; very rich, great length. A similar bottle tasted a year later: *crème brûlée*, dry finish. Most recently, with lead capsule embossed '*1825 G Paillère & Fils, Bordeaux*'. Original cork, level top-shoulder. Unclean nose, grubby, oily, dried-out. *Last noted Sept 1998. At best* ★★★★

## 1828 ★★★★

**Ch Yquem** Picking commenced 15 September. Fully labelled. On the pale side; muffled, 'so-so' nose; moderate flavour, caramelly, dry finish. Disappointing. *Noted Sept 1998* ★

## 1831 ★★★★★

**Ch Yquem** Picking commenced 14 September. Original cork. Level upper-shoulder. Palish, light-green edge; raspberries and cream again, too sweet, over the top. Very sweet on palate, nice weight. In excellent condition. *Noted Sept 1998* ★★★★

## 1834 ★★★★★

**Ch Yquem** Early harvest. Picking began 9 September. Similar label to the 1814, but with '*Sauternes*' added. Short pale gold capsule, short, wizened cork. Level top-shoulder. Beautiful colour with orange highlights; rich, fragrant bouquet of great depth; very rich, clean, attractive. *Tasted Sept 1998* ★★★★

## 1838 ★★

Mediocre for reds, better for Sauternes.
**Ch Yquem** Harvest commenced 29 September. Similar label, capsule and cork to the 1834. Level upper-shoulder. Brown tinged amber; malty, varnishy, oxidised nose; grubby finish. *Tasted with no great pleasure, Sept 1998.*

Footnote: The 125 vintages of Yquem at Hardy Rodenstock's monumental five-day event in September 1998 were not tasted in strict chronological order but grouped in appropriate 'flights' of eight (see box page 211).

## 1840 ★★

**Ch Yquem** Picking commenced 17 September. Original cork. Level upper-shoulder. Appearance warm amber, not bright; old nose but some fragrance. Much better on palate: rich, classic, good acidity. *Tasted Sept 1998 ★★★ (just).*

## 1841 ★★★★

**Ch Yquem** Picking commenced 18 September. Original cork. Level upper-shoulder. Colour of amber-mahogany; alas, oxidised, its departing richness overcome by the smell of overripe bananas. Palate spoilt by twisted, acidic, unclean finish. *Noted Sept 1998. Can't win them all!*

## 1846 ★★

**Ch Yquem** Picking commenced 14 September. Original cork. Level upper-shoulder. Bright, quite attractive varnishy yellow; nose neither distinctive nor good; strange flavour, rich – yet austere. *Noted Sept 1998.*

## 1847 ★★★★★

Unquestionably the greatest-ever Sauternes vintage. Sauternes was well-liked by the Polish and Russian courts and aristocracy, and it was this wine that smashed all records when, in 1859, the Grand Duke Constantine, the brother of the Tsar, paid 20,000 francs for a 900-litre tun of the 1847 Yquem.
**Ch Yquem** Picking commenced 25 September. Tasted on eight occasions. Three times in April and once in September 1986, all amazingly good, wines with astonishing power and concentration. One, with a Cruse, Bordeaux, label, a disaster at Bud Moon's Yquem tasting in 1988. Thickly coloured; raisiny; intensely sweet with great length in 1995. At the great Yquem tasting in 1998 an attractive amber-gold; overpoweringly sweet nose ('*dragée*' was Michel Bettane's comment); immensely sweet, fabulous flavour, incredible finish. Most recently, a superb bottle with short gold capsule and original cork: faultless bouquet, harmonious, glorious evolution in the glass; very rich, excellent flavour, perfect acidity, length and finish. *Last tasted at Wilfred Jaeger's remarkable pre-phylloxera Bordeaux tasting, June 2001 ★★★★★★!*

## 1848 ★★★★

**Ch Yquem** Picking commenced 20 September. Bearing the label of a Bordeaux merchant, '*L Tampier*', and with original cork, tasted at Yquem in 1987: very sweet; creamy, honeyed, vanilla and orange blossom bouquet and flavour to match. Next, château-bottled, at Bud Moon's tasting: buttery yellow colour; gentle, soft, creamy bouquet; good flavour and acidity. Most recently, original cork branded '*Yquem Grand Vin*'. Level upper-shoulder. Very good colour, gold highlights; slightly varnishy nose, but rich, with great depth. Powerful, full-bodied, complete, good acidity. *Last tasted Sept 1998 ★★★★*

## 1851 ★★★

**Ch Yquem** Picking commenced 27 September. Original cork. Level upper-shoulder. Warm orange-amber; honeyed, fudge-like, fragrant bouquet; drying out a little, singed barley sugar flavour and good acidity. *Tasted Sept 1998 ★★★★*

## 1858 ★★★★

**Ch d'Yquem** Picking commenced 27 September. Following the 1855 classification of Bordeaux's top sweet white wines, when Yquem was classed as the only *1er grand cru classé* château, the d' was reintroduced to the name. Interesting to note, also, is how frequently the Lur Saluces sold their wine *en barrique* for bottling by Bordeaux *négociants* though never, to my knowledge, by British wine merchants.
First tasted in 1981, a half bottle labelled '*Ch Yquem Sauternes, Keyl & Co, Bordeaux*', capsule '*K & C*', cork branded '*Yquem 1858*'. Also, low-shoulder and therefore oxidised though I noted 'sweet old Sémillon nose'. However, I have a note that around the time of the 1855 classification only Sauvignon Blanc grapes were used. I find this hard to believe. Next, a bottle from a Scottish cellar with glass shoulder button embossed '*Château Yquem, Haut Sauternes, Grand Cru*', tasted at the château in 1986. Despite slightly shrunken cork and a nose like Tokaji Eszencia, delicious, rich, concentrated. Most recently; short capsule quite common in Bordeaux at the time, badly bin-soiled label with vintage slip label, upper-shoulder level. Another too-good-to-be-true bottle, very fragrant raspberries and cream nose and taste. Angelo Gaja, who was also at the tasting, wondered if this was an ice wine (hardly if picked at the end of September). *Last tasted Sept 1998 ★★★★?*

## 1859 ★★★

**Ch d'Yquem** Picking commenced 23 September. Recorked at the château in 1994. New label. High level, doubtless topped up. Showing its age though, slightly varnishy, caramelly but held well. Rich, tangy. *Tasted Sept 1998 ★★★*
**Ch Rieussec** Château-bottled, good level. The only other 1859 tasted. The colour of brown sherry; bouquet and flavour of amazing power, richness and depth preserved by its high madeira-like acidity. *Sept 1987 ★★★★★*

## 1861 ★★★

**Ch d'Yquem** Picking commenced 22 September. Two similar notes, first tasted in 1985. Most recently, original cork. The colour of black treacle, bouquet and flavour to match. A sort of 'essencia' created by high sugar content, low alcohol, very high acidity keeping maderisation at bay. I gave it high marks. *Last tasted Sept 1998 ★★★★*

## 1864 ★★★★★

One of the greatest Bordeaux vintages, both red and white.
**Ch d'Yquem** Picking commenced 17 September. Tasted twice, both labelled '*Château Yquem, 1864, Bottled by Cruse & Fils Frères, Bordeaux*'. Original short unbranded corks. Despite the cork falling in (a not infrequent problem with old Sauternes), well-nigh perfect when tasted at Yquem in 1987. Most recently, surprisingly pale; smoky caramel bouquet; dried out, not very clean. *Last noted Sept 1998. At best ★★★★★*

## 1865 ★★★★★

Another great pre-phylloxera vintage for both red and white Bordeaux.
**Ch d'Yquem** Picking commenced 15 September. First noted, a label similar to the 1864, in 1987. Bouquet evolved

beautifully in the glass; sweet, soft, delicate, perfect. Most recently, recorked at the château in 1992, showing its age on the nose, caramelised yet somehow correct. Alas, dried out, like a superannuated athlete. *Last tasted Sept 1998. At best* ★★★★★

## 1867 ★★

**Ch d'Yquem** Picking commenced 18 September. An old but memorable note: a seriously ullaged bottle, three-quarters full, from an otherwise excellent cache I packed up and later sold for Sir Anselme Guise Bt. (pronounced Ansem Guys!) of Elmore Court, Gloucestershire. Opaque, virtually black; seriously maderised, caramelly but clean, its high concentration of sugar and extract bolstered by equally high acidity. Surprisingly delicious. Most recently, a Barton & Guestier bottling, on the pale side; corky though not corked nose but delightful taste. *Last noted Sept 1998* ★★★

## 1868 ★★

**Ch d'Yquem** Picking commenced early – 7 September. Two notes: a dried-out bottle in 1971 and, most recently, with similar label to the 1867, '*Château Yquem, 1868, Barton & Guestier, Bordeaux*'. Colour a bright yellow gold, really too pale for its age (possibly preserved with a hefty – original – dose of sulphur dioxide). Curious ethereal, spirity, beery nose. Neither very sweet nor full-bodied. Interesting though, acidity keeping it on its feet. *Last tasted Sept 1998* ★

**Ch Coutet** Pfungst & Co labels, from Sir John Thompson's cellar (see box on Woodperry House page 17): two bottles, both perfection. In remarkable condition thanks to a cool country house cellar and wine not moved since Sir John's grandfather bought the wine. *Tasted June and Sept 1977* ★★★★

## 1869 ★★★★★

A great vintage.

**Ch d'Yquem** Picking commenced 15 September. Five notes, first amoroso coloured, magnificent *crème brûlée* bouquet and flavour in 1969. Next a superb magnum to celebrate its centenary with Peter Palumbo at the Coq Hardi, Bougival; a good bottle in 1984, and one four years later with a Cruse label and bouquet like 'apple crumble, peaches and *crème brûlée*'. Most recently, with an oily original cork, also with a Cruse label and its contents mimicking the ostentatious brass wire criss-crossing the bottle: warm amber with orange-gold highlights; enticing, creamy, well-tempered *crème brûlée* and orange blossom bouquet that opened up, exotically. Sweet, assertive, raspberry-vanilla flavour, very fragrant but quite a bite. How was this achieved? No matter, I thought it was delicious. *Last tasted Sept 1998* ★★★★

**Ch La Tour-Blanche** Incredibly deep colour. By candlelight looked like a red wine; intensely rich, vanilla fudge nose; still sweet, like the caramelised top of *crème brûlée*. Surprisingly like the Ch d'Yquem just described. Glorious. *Dining at Ch Lafite, 1982* ★★★★★

## 1870 ★★★

Great for red, less so for white.

**Ch d'Yquem** Picking commenced 26 September. Just one disappointing note. Original cork. Slight ullage. Little nose, better flavour, on the lean side. *Sept 1998* ★★

## 1871 ★★★★

**Ch d'Yquem** Picking commenced on 26 September. First tasted in 1985: château-bottled, dark tawny; rich though somewhat sharp bouquet, old, 'deep honey', held well; sweet, assertive, pasty flavour, backbone of acidity. Next, level upper shoulder: an attractive amber-coloured, rich, toasty-nosed, sweet, powerful, concentrated wine at Bud Moon's Yquem tasting. *Last noted Feb 1988. At best* ★★★★

## 1872

Clearly these were bad times for the family for it was in this year that the 'whole of the stock remaining in the cellars of the Marquis de Lur Saluces' were sold for 'a lump sum' to Monsieur Jules Clavelle, comprising 240 *barriques* of the 1871 Yquem, 440 *barriques* of the 1870 and 20 of the 1865, plus 40 *barriques* of Coutet 1868 and 32 (in bottles) of the 1861, and 28 *barriques* (in bottles) of Filhot 1865, all three châteaux owned by the Lur Saluces family at that time.

Not even Rodenstock could find a bottle of the 1872 Yquem for his marathon tasting (see box page 211).

## 1874 ★★★★

A very good pre-phylloxera vintage.

**Ch d'Yquem** Picking commenced 25 September. Several notes made in the 1970s. Variable, depending on the levels, from syrup of figs to *crème brûlée*. Most recently, recorked at the château in 1994: opaque, too brown; nose of old caramel; rich though dried out. Why owners of old Yquem request recorking, and why the head cellar man at Yquem recorks wine past the sell-by date, I do not know. If not pointless, then risky. *Last noted Sept 1998.*

## 1875 ★★★★★

A vintage noted for its delicacy and elegance.

**Ch d'Yquem** Picking commenced 24 September. All four notes are of Yquem bottled by Bordeaux merchants. Despite its low level a Brandenburg Frères bottling excellent in 1978. Two Cruse bottlings tasted in the late 1980s, one well-nigh perfect, rich, harmonious, the other upper-mid-shoulder level, paler, sour, dried out. Most recently, another Cruse bottling palish amber-gold; quite good but hard to pin down bouquet; rich, assertive. *Last tasted Sept 1998. At best* ★★★★★

---

### Botrytis cinerea

*Botrytis, called* pourriture *in France, is a grape mould which can either be disastrous for the crop, or highly beneficial. Most commonly appearing as grey rot, it is a sworn enemy, but as 'noble rot' (*pourriture noble *in France and* Edelfäule *in Germany), its onset can be particularly lucrative – notably for the lucky growers in misty parts of Sauternes and Barsac in Bordeaux, the Loire Valley, or the vineyards of the Mosel. Botrytis mould saps the moisture from the grape until what's left inside is a concentrated sugary essence, which when fermented, produces an exceptionally sweet, focused wine. Thin-skinned grapes, such as Sémillon, Chenin Blanc and Riesling, are particularly susceptible to noble rot and each of these has the necessary acidity to balance the intense sweetness of the botrytised juice. The wines have tremendous ageing potential.*

## 1876 ★★

**Ch d'Yquem** Picking commenced on 26 September. The bottle we tasted still had its original, branded cork. Low-keyed nose; creamy, good flavour, no signs of age, dry finish. *At Rodenstock's marathon tasting, Sept 1998* ★★★

**Ch Coutet Lur Saluces** Original capsule, label and cork. Mid-shoulder level. Colour of an old Sercial madeira; touch of malt and drying out. *Tasted 1988* ★★

**Ch La Tour-Blanche** Recorked 1987. Nose of 'sugar and sour honey'. Completely dried-out. *At Maurice Renaud's six-hour luncheon in Versailles, May 1988.*

## 1878

Good in the Médoc, poor in Sauternes.

ONLY ONE OLD NOTE **Ch Filhot Lur Saluces** Pale and brown; oxidised, madeira-like; dried-out, faded and acidic *1976.*

## 1880 ★

**Ch Filhot Lur Saluces** Original capsule, label and cork. Excellent level. Lovely colour; rich old bouquet and flavour but completely dried-out. *1987* ★

## 1881 ★

A dreary period for Bordeaux, red and white. Phylloxera wreaking havoc and its antidote still being frantically sought (but see 1899 Ch d'Yquem).

ONLY ONE OLD NOTE **Ch d'Arche** Can you imagine dry black treacle? *1983.*

## 1884

To add to the growers' woes, mildew followed in the footsteps of phylloxera.

TWO OLD NOTES **Ch d'Yquem** Surprisingly attractive. Despite the wine being on the verge of extinction, holding up well. *1984;* **Ch de Rayne-Vigneau** lovely but short. *1970* ★★

## 1886

Mildew now serious throughout the region.
**Ch d'Yquem** Late harvest from 1 to 28 October. Original cork, high level. Rather drab appearance; rich but slightly varnishy; very sweet, surprisingly positive and attractive flavour but I suspect that the 'crystallised violets' and high-toned acidity had much to do with the mildew. *Tasted Sept 1998* ★★★

## 1887

Another season spoiled by mildew.
**Ch d'Yquem** Harvested late: 10–28 October. Recorked 1996. Weak-looking; old banana skins, tart, finished. *Noted Sept 1998.*
**'Ch Sauternes'** Strangely named wine shipped by Brandenburg Frères, Bordeaux. Short hard cork. Slight ullage. Very good golden colour; old, sweet, botrytis crème caramel nose; still sweet, good flavour, dry finish. *An amazing half bottle at a pre-sale tasting, Chicago, Feb 1992* ★★★

## 1888 ★

**Ch d'Yquem** Extended harvest, 27 September – 30 October. Drying out, austere (1977). More recently, recorked in 1996: high-toned, hard edged, Bual madeira-like nose; dry, assertive, molasses aftertaste. *Last noted Sept 1998.*

## 1890 ★★

**Ch d'Yquem** Several old notes in the early to mid-1970s. Variable levels. At its best, soft and lovely (1975). Most recently: richly coloured; caramelised nose, rich, but became almost sickly sweet after 80 minutes in the glass (I always try to hold on to my glass to note the effect of air on its evolution). A sweetish, old barley sugar flavour. *Last tasted (a magnum), Sept 1998. At best* ★★★

## 1891 ★★

**Ch d'Yquem** Two notes, the first bottle recorked in 1988: amber-gold; very rich but malty; totally dried-out. Unclean finish. The oldest vintage of Manfred Wagner's Yquem tasting in Zurich, 1992. Most recently, level into neck, but poor nose, 'cold', fishy, slightly scented, then sweet, finally faded. Also dried out, raw and grubby. *Last noted Sept 1998.*

## 1892 ★

**Ch d'Yquem** Four notes, variable bottles: quite good in 1975. Sound and still fairly sweet – the oldest vintage of Yquem at the Schloss Johannisberg tasting in 1984. A cloudy, murky, oxidised bottle in 1988. Most recently, despite its very good level, corked, its palate better than its nose. Still rich, lean, flavoury – but spoiled. *Last tasted Sept 1998. At best* ★★

## 1893 ★★★★★

At last, a change for the better, both weather and market, but not without problems: one of the hottest summers on record in Bordeaux, difficult for the reds but, like 1921, better for Sauternes, and common to all, problems in controlling fermentation temperatures.
**Ch d'Yquem** Tasted on three occasions, all memorable. First, in 1995 at Peter Ziegler's outstanding rare wine tasting at the Schlosshotel Erbach: warm orange-amber; deep, rich, honeyed bouquet reminiscent of ripe apricots, peaches and overripe grapes; very rich, powerful, fairly high volatile acidity, alcoholic, impressive. Next, in 1996, served with *foie gras* at a great wine dinner in Oslo hosted by a major collector of wine, Christan Sveaas (see below): a similar description to the bottle tasted in 1995: incredible power, almost pungent, in perfect condition (I gave it 6 stars!). Most recently, on the fourth day of Hardy Rodenstock's Yquem marathon in

### Christan Sveaas

*Christan Sveaas is a Norwegian wine collector of international stature. Ch d'Yquem 1893 was the opening wine with foie gras at a wonderful dinner of great wines he gave in Oslo in 1996. The sheer quality of the vintages tasted that night would be hard to beat. Incidentally, his 11-wine dinner, all first growths, ended with another Yquem, the superlative 1921.*

### Château de la Fot

*Over a period of several years, the family's Easter holidays were spent in France, packing up wine in old cellars. Daphne and the children made up the cartons while I sat in the sun — or so my wife avers. One memorable packing expedition was to Ch de la Fot. The owner, the Marquis de Vasselot — I seem to recall that he was president of France's pig breeders' association — stored his old wines in a cellar underneath the cow sheds. It happened to be snowing that Easter which made the work doubly uncomfortable and very chilly. However, we did have the rare privilege of enjoying the Marquis' hospitality. One evening we covered the billiard table with a sheet and tasted the whole of his range, including the Filhot 1896 and ending with some superb old cognacs.*

Munich, a bottle recorked at the château in 1996 and, frankly, not as good, more mahogany in the colour, whiff of 'varnish' on the nose and with bitter caramelised orange aftertaste. *Last noted Sept 1998. At best* ★★★★★ *plus.*

OTHER, OLDER NOTES **Clos Haut-Peyraguey** remarkably good at my Bordeaux Club dinner in *1981*; **Ch Suduiraut** despite mid-shoulder level still sweet and delicious in *1985*.

## 1894

A dismal reversion to poor conditions.
**Ch d'Yquem** Top-shoulder; palish yellow amber; strange coffee-like nose and taste that reminded me of singed heather (I was brought up on the Yorkshire moors. The heather was 'sweated' annually). Dry. *Tasted Sept 1998.*

## 1895

**Ch d'Yquem** In 1981, mid-shoulder level, dried out, yeasty, acidic. Most recently, despite very good level, too pale, also dried out though quite fragrant. *Last noted Sept 1998.*

## 1896 ★★★★

**Ch d'Yquem** Three notes: showing magnificently well, with my top marks at the Yquem/Schloss Johannisberg tasting in 1984, its richness verging on unctuous. Not quite blemish free at the Rodenstock marathon in 1998, more ethereal despite its richness, very good acidity and dry finish. Most recently, an odd bottle, pale amber; bouquet of old apricots and honey; pure caramel flavour, excellent acidity. I don't know where this came from. *Last noted Jan 2000. At best* ★★★★★

OLDER NOTES **Ch Filhot** two notes: drying out, faded. *Tasted at Ch de la Fot, April 1975*; **Ch Sigalas-Rabaud** fine colour; honeyed bouquet; rich, tangy. *1975* ★★★

## 1899 ★★★★

**Ch d'Yquem** Harvested between 19 September and 21 October. Up until the end of the 19th-century Yquem vines were still ungrafted. Four notes: old but interesting in 1973; a wretchedly ullaged and caramelised bottle in 1985 but showing well the previous year at Schloss Johannisberg: bouquet of 'scented ferns' that opened up creamily in the glass; not a heavyweight like the '93, more gentle and charming. Most recently: warm amber; pleasant, sweet nose that started to fade; medium-sweet, good flavour and acidity. Dry finish. *Last tasted Sept 1998. At best* ★★★★

**Ch Coutet** Medium-deep amber; very rich, barley sugar and *crème brûlée*; no longer sweet yet very rich. Excellent in its way. Dry finish. *At Wilfred Jaeger's wine dinner in San Francisco, March 2002* ★★★

**Ch Filhot** Alas, corked. Nevertheless, despite this handicap it was still sweet and had very good length. *At Jaeger's wine dinner in San Francisco, March 2002.*

OTHER, OLDER NOTES **Ch Suduiraut** two notes: caramel cream (1981), orange blossom, glowing. *1985*; **Ch La Tour-Blanche** showing well. *1981.*

# 1900—1929

Generally speaking, economic and weather conditions match those described in the Red Bordeaux chapter (see page 24). The quality of individual vintages speak for themselves, with 1915 as the nadir and the end of the 1920s triumphant. The following chart lists the best vintages of the period. Any wine of high quality and unimpeachable provenance in my 4- to 5-star range should still be excellent.

A practical tip: levels of ullage up to 7cm below the cork are not abnormal; for, unlike old red Bordeaux wines with an equivalent level, the wine can still be sound.

### Sauternes Vintages at a Glance
**Outstanding ★★★★★**
1906, 1921, 1929
**Very Good ★★★★**
1900, 1904, 1909, 1926, 1928
**Good ★★★**
1914, 1918, 1920, 1923, 1924

## 1900 ★★★★

The second of the *fin de siècle* twin vintages, perhaps less successful for the whites than the reds.
**Ch d'Yquem** Harvested over an extended period, 19 September – 29 November. Four notes, very variable dependant as always on level, condition (and provenance). A beautiful bottle in 1972; a low-shoulder, maderised yet still sweet and surviving bottle in 1984. The most interesting, bottled in Bordeaux by H Wulffe, had a bouquet of nutmeg and old honey, concentrated but lacking length (in Chicago 1988). Most recently, a bottle recorked in 1990: fragrant; good flavour, assertive but dried out and a bit tart on the finish. *Last noted at the Rodenstock marathon, Sept 1998. At best ★★★*
**Ch d'Arche** A surprise and delight. Amber gold; lovely orange blossom fragrance reminding me of Yquem '45 or '53. Still sweet, wonderful flavour, good length, finesse and perfect acidity. *At Rodenstock's 17th Weinprobe, Munich, Sept 1996 ★★★★*

## 1901 ★

**Ch d'Yquem** Harvested 13 September – 5 October. Recorked 1996. Singed, caramelised nose, rich, fragrant; medium-dry, floral, clean. *At Rodenstock's tasting Sept 1998 ★*

## 1902

**Ch d'Yquem** Harvested 30 September – 31 October. Recorked 1996. Cunningly placed alongside the 1802, but infinitely inferior: oxidised, smell of rice pudding and banana skins; dried-out, almost rasping. *Noted Aug 1998.*

## 1903 ★★

**Ch d'Yquem** Harvested 24 September – 30 October. Recorked 1996. A green tinge; caramel, peaches, blossom; still sweet, good flavour, strength and length. *Rodenstock's five-day Yquem tasting in Munich, Aug/Sept 1998 ★★★*

## 1904 ★★★★

The best vintage between 1900 and 1906.

**Ch d'Yquem** Harvested 17 September – 14 October. Recorked 1994. Good colour; strange, light, Manzanilla-like nose; lean, uninteresting flavour, dry finish. *Noted Aug 1998 ★*

**OTHER, OLDER NOTES Ch Coutet** deeply coloured, very rich, perfect condition. *1979 ★★★★*; **Ch Filhot** deep amber; very fragrant; caramelised but delicious. *1987 ★★★*; **Ch de Rayne-Vigneau** a good period for this château; two notes, high extract, glorious. *Last tasted 1981 ★★★★★*; **Ch La Tour-Blanche** creamy bouquet with hint of tangerine; powerful, tangy, attractive though drying out. *1985 ★★★*

## 1905

**Ch d'Yquem** Harvested 13 September – 16 October. Recorked 1993. High-toned, rich, 'oily' (like a ripe Riesling) nose. Almost too sweet. Good grip. *Aug 1998 ★★ (just).*

## 1906 ★★★★★

A classic Sauternes vintage, still good if kept well.
**Ch d'Yquem** Harvested 11 September – 24 October. Two notes, the first, in 1985, outstanding: amoroso-like colour; intensely rich, ambrosial bouquet; silky texture, great length. Most recently, original cork, soft, poor. Deep amber-brown – not a good sign; high-toned, madeira-like nose that settled down, making me think of squashed sultanas. Immensely sweet and powerful, good grip but slightly maderised. Bought from a US retailer. *Last noted Aug 1998. At best ★★★★★*

**OTHER, OLDER NOTES Ch d'Arche** opaque, malty. *1985*; and **Ch Lafaurie-Peyraguey** fabulously rich. *1976 ★★★★*

## 1907

**Ch d'Yquem** Harvested 4 September – 31 October. Recorked 1995. Corky, but not altogether bad; dried-out though flavoury. *Noted Aug 1998 ★*

## 1908

**Ch d'Yquem** Harvested 16 September – 22 October. Recorked 1995. The colour of black treacle or Pedro Ximenez; nose reminding me of an 1863 Malmsey, hard-edged, tangy, pure *rancio*; flavour of dried prunes and burnt raisins. *Aug 1998.*

## 1909 ★★★★

What a depressing roller-coaster of weather conditions the poor Sauternes growers had to endure during this period; a risky business, made up for by vintages like the '06 and '09.

**Ch d'Yquem** Harvested 21 September – 12 November. A superb bottle tasted at Schloss Johannisberg in the Rhiengau in 1984: rich, positively hefty, with a flavour of *marron glacé*. Most recently, a bottle recorked in 1995 and simply not up to scratch. Why, I wondered, after so much recorking at the château, have there been so many less than satisfactory bottles? Probably far better to leave them with the cork they are long used to, and drink them. Anyway, despite its lovely colour and fragrance it had dried out, with a flavour more like an old Tokaji Aszú Eszencia. *Last tasted Aug 1998. At best* ★★★★

ANOTHER, OLDER NOTE **Ch Lafaurie-Peyraguey** superb. *This was one of a range of vintages from the château tasted prior to the big Cordier sale at Christie's, Sept 1976* ★★★★

## 1911

**Ch d'Yquem** Two notes. First in 1992, top-shoulder level: strange, high-toned nose; dried-out, virtually no fat or flesh, but finishing cleanly. More recently, a bottle recorked in 1996, tasted blind against the 1811 – no comparison. The really old wine was better. Hefty boiled sugar nose; varnishy flavour, moderate finish. *Last tasted Sept 1998.*

## 1912

**Ch d'Yquem** Harvested 29 September – 13 November. Two notes, first in 1988, misleadingly youthful vanilla and pear aroma but dry, raw and unclean. More recently, a bottle recorked in 1996 rather better, amber; touch of corkiness and slightly caramelised on nose; still fairly sweet, quite appealing caramel and apricot flavour. *Last tasted Aug 1998* ★
**Ch Lafaurie-Peyraguey** Original cork and label: '*Fred Grédy, Proprietor*' (the Cordier family acquired the château after World War One). Luminous *oloroso*; caramelised but quite good. *April 1985* ★★

## 1913 ★★

**Ch d'Yquem** Harvested 18 September – 30 October. A strange pale, completely dried-out bottle at the Moon tasting in 1988. Most recently: yellow amber-coloured; curious neutral nose; fairly dry, uninteresting. *Last tasted Aug 1998.*

ONE OLDER NOTE **Ch Lafaurie-Peyraguey** lovely bouquet; medium-sweet, zestful. From the château cellars. *At the Cordier pre-sale tasting, Sept 1976* ★★★

## 1914 ★★★

**Ch d'Yquem** Harvested 14 September – 8 November. Three notes: two fine and rich (1969 and 1973). Most recently, recorked in 1994. Lively and lovely colour; very curious, highish tone nose, chocolatey, then slightly sickly vanilla; equally odd peach-skin flavour. Very dry finish. *Last noted Aug 1998. At best* ★★★★

OTHER OLDER NOTES **Ch Caillou** an attractive Barsac, very good for its age; flavours of honey and mint. *1988* ★★★; **Ch Filhot** its richness overcame its amber-brown colour and unmistakable maderisation. *1984*; **Ch Lafaurie-Peyraguey** beautiful. *1976* ★★★★; **Ch de Rayne-Vigneau** sound but drying out. *1975* ★★

## 1915

A wretched wartime vintage. Ch d'Yquem not made.

## 1916

**Ch d'Yquem** Harvested with difficulty 30 September and 12 November. Recorked 1995. Surprising richness overcoming touch of corkiness and grubby finish. *Tasted Aug 1998.*

## 1917

**Ch d'Yquem** Harvested 13 September – 24 October. Recorked 1996. Richly coloured; quite good bouquet, old vanilla and orange blossom; just enough sweetness, otherwise tired. *Tasted Aug 1998* ★

## 1918 ★★★

One has only to look at the memorials to the fallen in every town and village in France to be reminded of the carnage in the trenches of World War One. In the vineyards, work was devolved on the women, the very young, the old and the lame. There were shortages of materials as well as labour.
**Ch d'Yquem** A late harvest started 1 October and ended 8 November, three days before the Armistice. Pale green wartime bottle. Recorked 1993. Astonishingly pale, with a fine bitty sediment; attractive, fragrant bouquet; fairly sweet, on the light side, good flavour, dry finish. *Tasted Aug 1998* ★★★
**Ch Climens** Two good notes: in 1984 richly flavoured 'reminiscent of lanolin, Vaseline and lemon curd'. Did I write that? More recently, at Frans de Cock's outstanding wine weekend in Paris: lovely colour; heavily botrytised nose; rich *crème brûlée,* bouquet and flavour. Very sweet. Penetrating aftertaste. *Last tasted Dec 1995* ★★★★
**Ch Lafaurie-Peyraguey** Lovely lime-shaded amber; glorious bouquet and flavour. Still sweet, soft with good length and fragrant aftertaste. *Noted Sept 1990* ★★★★

## 1919 ★★

**Ch d'Yquem** Although the harvest in Sauternes started around 20 September the pickers at Yquem waited until 3 October and continued until the end of the month. Two fairly similar notes, first at Moon's tasting in Chicago in 1988. Unexpectedly pale lemon yellow colour; low-keyed but quite good nose; medium sweetness, good, clean, positive flavour and good acidity. *Last tasted Aug 1998* ★★

---

### Handling old Sauternes

*Sauternes keeps very well. The wine's richness forms a protective barrier round the cork, thus keeping it moist and in working order – like engine oil in a car – and very rarely do the corks deteriorate. However, because of this, great care is needed when opening. Over-enthusiasm with the corkscrew can push the cork down into the wine. It's best to hook the point into the cork and then twist with as little pressure as possible. I disapprove strongly of recorking Sauternes. It is very rarely necessary and adds no new dimensions to the wine. In fact, tasting recorked and original bottles side by side, the recorked are usually less good. Longevity? Good vintages will keep for 50 years or more, lesser vintages 10 to 15 years.*

## 1920 ***

A first rate Sauternes vintage though upstaged by the great '21.
**Ch d'Yquem** Picking began 17 September, more or less in line with the rest of Sauternes, ending exactly a month later. Only two notes, well apart. In a state of decline but not bad (1955). Most recently, original cork: palish amber-gold; quite good spicy fragrance, dried-out, short. *Last tasted Sept 1998* ★
**Ch Doisy-Dubroca** Three half bottles from the cellars of Prunier-Traktir, Paris, the first couple at the pre-sale tastings in October and December 1982 and showing well: fragrant, touch of caramel, good fruit, excellent acidity, and another half more recently: despite mid-shoulder level and deepish colour, still sweet and attractive. *Last noted in the office, May 1998* ★★★
**Ch Lafaurie-Peyraguey** Rich, plump and magnificent, tasted twice in 1976. More recently: amber orange; peach blossom and honey; fairly sweet, glorious, assertive; great length, toffee-like finish. *Last tasted at Rodenstock's 15th Raritäten-Weinprobe at the Arlberg Hospiz, Austria, Sept 1994* ★★★★

## 1921 *****

Unquestionably the greatest vintage of the 20th century, Yquem in particular being legendary. Following the hottest summer since 1893, grapes were harvested with a tremendously high sugar content which, after fermentation, resulted in high levels of alcohol and residual sugar.
**Ch d'Yquem** A colossus. Perhaps the most staggeringly rich Yquem of all time, certainly since the towering 1847. A word of advice: do not be put off by the dark colour. This is correct and the same applies to a slightly lesser extent with Yquem 1929 and 1937.

I am of course spoiled. But it is my job; and I have had the privilege and pleasure of tasting – of drinking (even I do not spit out the '21 Yquem) the wine – at last count – over 30 times, from magnums as well as bottles. Not all have warranted 5 stars for, as always, provenance, storage, and state of the cork has a bearing. But most have been unforgettable.

One of the most unusual had been bottled in Switzerland (1921 was the last vintage to be sold by Lur Saluces in cask). It was in a green glass bottle with pictorial label and short cork. Apart from the (harmless) tartaric acid crystals – after all, Switzerland can get pretty cold in winter – it was excellent.

One thing I have noticed is that the differences are more due to bottle variation rather than the wine's evolution which, at least for the past 30 or so years, seems to be relatively static.

Rather than give a blow by blow account I propose to mention two tastings and three fairly recent dinners, the first in Germany at Peter Ziegler's tasting, in the eighth and final 'flight'. It was placed between the 1893 and 1945 Yquems, ending with von Schönborn's Marcobrunner *feinste* TBA. I gave the 1893 and 1921 equally high marks but actually preferred the exquisite 1945 Yquem.

Coincidentally, Christian Sveaas' dinner in 1996, which opened with the 1893, ended with a superb (6-star) 1921. At the Rodenstock Yquem marathon in 1998 I gave it my highest marks, fractionally above 1869 and 1937 (out of a total of 125 vintages tasted that week). It was voluptuous at Josh Latner's dinner at the Lanesborough Hotel in London, January 2000 and, when last encountered it was sheer perfection.

Finally, I shall endeavour to describe the elements and variations in appearance, nose and taste. Certainly not dark, but in my last five notes varying from fairly deep, at best a warm amber-gold, on one occasion reminding me of an old *oloroso* sherry, on another Bual madeira-like, with a pronounced apple-green rim. The bouquet, very rich, honeyed of course, peachy, barley sugar (boiled and spun sugar), intense yet fragrant, 'custard cream', *crème brûlée* yet again, but very true. On the palate from sweet to very sweet, depending I think on context, unquestionably rich, powerful, even assertive, great length and intensity, and supported by life-preserving acidity. One of life's sublime experiences. *Last tasted a bottle brought by Paolo Pong to a dinner at Jancis Robinson's, Dec 2000* ★★★★★
**Ch Lafaurie-Peyraguey** A bottle in 1968 from Sir Gerald Kelly's cellar: a bouquet 'beyond ripeness'; lovely old flavour but losing pristine sweetness. More recently: singed, Tokaji-like, rich raisiny bouquet; tangy, burnt toffee taste, its richness coping well with its teeth-gripping acidity. *Sept 1990* ★★★★

OTHER '21S, OLDER NOTES **Ch Climens** two notes, the first lacking richness (1977), the second hefty (1985) – not as good as the '29, '37 or great post-World War Two vintages; **Ch Coutet** two consistent notes, magnificent, lovely acidity, a very good Coutet. *1971, 1976* ★★★★★; **Ch Guiraud** London-bottled by Geo Tanqueray, madeira-like nose, 'surprisingly nice' on palate. *1969* ★★★; **Ch de Rayne-Vigneau** one bottle oxidised with yeasty finish, the other superb, its bouquet initially buttoned up, blossomed beautifully, powerful, fine. Two occasions in 1976. *At best* ★★★★★; **Ch de Ricaud** (Loupiac) very good flavour and balance. *1982* ★★★; **Ch Suduiraut** just one note. Excellent. *1975* ★★★★★; **Ch La Tour-Blanche** four notes, the first perfection, one corked, two very good. All in *1987. At best* ★★★★★

## 1922 *

The harvest was plentiful but the wines light and lacking.
**Ch d'Yquem** Picking started early, 12 September (some said too early) but finished 14 October. Three notes, first in 1971: tired looking; lacklustre nose; losing sweetness and body – probably never had much. Then a mediocre drying-out bottle in 1976. Most recently, a bottle recorked in 1992: showing age but good, later very caramelly; not bad, though its aged taste somewhat spoiled by a raspingly dry, acidic finish. I thought (we were tasting blind, in pairs a century apart) it was the 1822! *Last tasted Aug 1998. At best* ★★ *(just)*.
**Ch de Myrat** An older note of a relatively minor Barsac, a half bottle with a mid-low shoulder which turned out to be surprisingly rich. 'An unexpected pleasure'. But so it should have been because Myrat, at the time of the 1855 classification, was considered the finest wine in Barsac after Climens. Unhappily the vineyard was grubbed up by its aristocratic owner because it simply did not pay. The amiable Comte Xavier de Pontac, scion of one of Bordeaux's oldest families, owners of Ch Haut-Brion and other properties in the 17th century, bravely replanted in the late 1980s but had the ill fortune to hit the worst set of vintages in recent years, 1991–1994. He and his wine are recovering. *Tasted June 1988* ★★

OTHER '22S, OLDER NOTES **Ch Lafaurie-Peyraguey** light, quite nice, short. *1976* ★; **Ch de Rayne-Vigneau** sound, good flavour, gently balanced. *1994* ★★

## 1923 ***

Moderately good vintage.

**Ch d'Yquem** Harvested 26 September–10 November. Several notes in the 1970s all quite good but drying out. Most recently, recorked in 1995: weak colour; mediocre nose; vanilla chocolate, lacking conviction. *Last tasted Sept 1998. At best* ★★

**Ch d'Arche** Fairly deep amber; caramelised nose; sweet, with high acidity propping it up. *At Christie's, May 1998.*

**Cru d'Arche-Pugneau** Not to be confused with the *2ème cru classé* Ch d'Arche (above). A surprisingly delicious wine, still sweet. *Last tasted March 1992. At best* ★★★★

**Ch Filhot** Barley sugar nose but, despite good flavour, dried-out. *Dining with the Schÿlers at Ch Kirwan, Sept 1998* ★

OLDER NOTES **Ch Coutet** a remarkably good Schröder & Schÿler half bottle. Nose like an old Coteaux du Layon Chenin from the Loire. Rich and fine. *1971* ★★★; **Ch Guiteronde** to demonstrate the importance of storage, a couple of very attractive half bottles from Prunier's in Paris. *At pre-sale tastings, Oct and Dec, 1982* ★★★★

## 1924 ★★★

Wet summer saved by glorious ripening September sun. Underrated.

**Ch d'Yquem** Harvested 26 September – 10 November. Four variable notes: a superbly luscious bottle in 1977 but disappointing at the Schloss Johannisberg 'match' in 1984. A far better bottle two years later at a Christie's pre-sale tasting in Chicago: orange-tinged old gold; beautifully fragrant bouquet; well nigh perfect. Most recently, another recorked bottle, in 1996: its bouquet, poor at first, opened up quite richly after 10 minutes in the glass but not for long. Better on the palate – in fact, quite rich. *Last tasted Sept 1998. At best* ★★★★

**Ch Guiraud** Four half bottles, variable in 1976 and 1988. On the whole remarkably good. Deep coloured; caramelised but delicious. Still fairly sweet, ripe, rich, tangy. Good length. *Last tasted at Neil McKendrick's Bordeaux Club dinner, Cambridge, June 1997. At best* ★★★★

**Ch de Rayne-Vigneau** Original cork. Good level. Lovely golden colour; lanolin-like bouquet which opened up sweetly in the glass; by no means with pristine sweetness but in excellent condition, a touch of tangerine, good length and aftertaste. *Dinner at Chippenham Lodge with house guests, Christa and Bob Paul and Jill Priday, New Year's Day 1994. (This was some weekend. We must have been in a perpetual haze for I served eight wines on New Year's Eve, seven for lunch on New Year's Day, ending with 1962 Noval Nacional, and six wines that evening.)* ★★★★

**Ch des Tastes** Not the first but the oldest delightful Barsac look-alike from Ste-Croix-du-Mont, across the Garonne from Sauternes. Creamy, honeyed, orange blossom fragrance and taste. Excellent acidity. *Perfect with Daphne's chicken liver pâté, Sunday lunch at Chippenham Lodge, August 1994* ★★★★

OLDER NOTES **Ch Climens** despite loose cork, lovely. *1977* ★★★★; **Ch Filhot** drying out though very rich overall. *1979* ★★★; **Ch Guiteronde** more halves from Prunier cellar, curiously not as good as the '23s though quite attractive. *1982* ★★; **Ch Lafaurie-Peyraguey** a magnificent, succulent wine though it took two hours to recover from its initial bottle stink. *1977. At best* ★★★★; **Clos du Pape** Bordeaux-bottled by Turpin, one rich and tangy, the other with fabulous colour, acidity a bit rasping but holding well. *Both in 1972* ★★; **Ch Rabaud-Promis** powerful, classic. Drinking well. *Also from the Prunier Traktir cellar in Paris, 1982* ★★★★; and

**Ch St-Amand** two, both excellent in 1974, then several bottles with variable levels and in variable condition at a wine weekend dinner at Studley Priory, near Oxford. *Last tasted 1979. At best* ★★★

## 1925

**Ch d'Yquem** Harvested 7 October – 24 November. A couple of notes, 30 years apart yet almost identical. Terrible wine: twisted, sharp, dried-out, bitter spirity end. *Last tasted, a bottle recorked in 1996, Sept 1998. Avoid.*

## 1926 ★★★★

**Ch d'Yquem** Harvest 29 September – 27 October. Half a dozen notes, starting in 1975 – a lovely bottle, but considerable bottle variation in the mid-1980s. Most recently, recorked in 1996, too pale, little nose, poor flavour, short. Most disappointing. One of my lowest notes in the entire five-day tasting of Yquems in Munich. *Last tasted Sept 1998. At best* ★★★

**Ch de Rayne-Vigneau** Two bottles in 1969, one fabulously golden in looks, smell and taste, the other not as fresh. Still rich and lovely. *Last tasted November 1990. At best* ★★★★

**Ch St-Amand** A minor property in Preignac. Many notes, variable. Two good Prunier bottles: sweet, rich and attractive in 1982 and again over a decade later. *Last tasted Feb 1993* ★★★

OLDER NOTES **Ch Climens** seven consistently good notes between 1957 and 1960, none since. 'Nectar'. *Last tasted 1960* ★★★★★; **Ch Filhot** variable, poor bottle in 1976, fairly good half in *1988*; **Ch Rabaud-Promis** two notes, dull, disappointing (1976), bouquet rich but a touch of resin, drying out but lovely (*1977). At best* ★★★

## 1927

Appalling season, disastrous for reds and dry whites, but Sauternes enjoyed an Indian summer. Sauternes and port are the only possible wines to celebrate my birth year.

**Ch d'Yquem** Picking started, possibly in desperation and while the going was good on 29 September and finished up, probably with more grey rot than *noble*, on 27 October. Tasted first at the Rodenstock marathon in 1998, recorked 1996: a very deep, warm, amber-mahogany; nose slightly oxidised (though pedants insist that, just as a woman cannot be slightly pregnant, a wine either is oxidised or it is *not* oxidised), its smell – unworthy of the term 'bouquet' – like slightly fishy, oily, burnt honey. Complete. In 1998 I preferred it to the '24 and '26. Most recently, with original capsule, branded cork and fully labelled. Originally shipped from Bordeaux by André Maurois and imported by Vintage Wines Inc., New York, a second slip label bearing the name '*D R Recher & Co, Chicago*', then on to Tawfiq Khoury's cellar in San Diego. Back to New York for the spectacularly successful Khoury sale at Christie's in December 1990 and bought by my son as a birthday present on condition that he was there when I opened it. Despite its peripatetic background it turned out to be in surprisingly good condition, deep as the previous bottle and nose caramelised, but rich and delicious. *Last tasted at home with all the family in Jan 1999* ★★★

**Ch de Rayne-Vigneau** Delicious bouquet of peaches, apricots, honey and spices. Still rich but finishes abruptly. Two

consistent notes. *Last tasted on my birthday, May 1990* ★★★
OTHER '27S, OLDER NOTES **Ch Climens** remarkably good
for the year. Three notes in 1977 ★★; **Ch Doisy-Védrines**
the best of the lot. Rich. Well balanced. *1981* ★★★★;
**Ch Filhot** dried-out. *1981*; **Ch Lafaurie-Peyraguey** rich
nose but acidic. *1976*; **Ch La Tour-Blanche** drunk six times
and consistently good for the year. *Last tasted 1984* ★★

## 1928 ★★★★

The first of a pair of Sauternes vintages of outstanding quality
but of different weight and style. Also excellent for the major
dry white Bordeaux wines, some of which have survived.
**Ch d'Yquem** Harvested from 24 September –
8 November. Tasted well over a dozen times in different
contexts through the 1970s and 1980s, almost all 5-star though
colour variation noted, from lemon gold to rich warm amber,
but never as dark as the '29. Most interestingly, indeed
uniquely, a pair of '28s at the Rodenstock Yquem tasting in
1998, one recorked, one with original cork which bore out
my criticism of recorking already mentioned in these notes.
To be specific, the nose of the bottle recorked in 1990, despite
being very sweet and rich, was unknit and caramelised, its full
rich flavour marred by a touch of rawness. The un-recorked
bottle had a better colour, infinitely better bouquet, very
harmonious, great depth, and was distinctly sweeter, with
glorious flavour, length and aftertaste. Most recently and less
happily, not good: deathly brown, a nose reminiscent of
Malmsey and butterscotch, and toffee-like taste. The provider
of this bottle, an American wine buff, admitted to recorking
and topping up the bottle (with what?) in his own cellar. *Last
noted conducting a '70th anniversary tasting of the 1928 vintage' in
San Juan, Puerto Rico, Nov 1998. At best* ★★★★★
**Ch Caillou** A delightful magnum, surprisingly full, rich,
tangy, its excellent acidity not only life-preserving but 'cutting'
the cheeses with which it was appropriately served. *At a
Rodenstock dinner tasting in Munich, Sept 1996* ★★★★
**Ch Climens** Nine consistently good notes mainly in the
1970s and 1980s. Most recently, a gorgeous amber-gold;
intriguingly complex botrytis nose that unravelled in the glass;
still fairly sweet, with '28 crispness and acidity giving it a dry
finish. *The 16th of the 17 wines (including claret and burgundy)
served at the San Juan tasting of '28s, Puerto Rico, Nov 1998* ★★★★
**Ch Filhot** Several notes. At its best crisp and flavoury. *Last
tasted Sept 1990* ★★
**Ch de Rayne-Vigneau** Admittedly this is a *1er cru* while Ch
Filhot above is *2ème*; but the difference in class shows, over and
over again. A couple of notes: exquisite bouquet, fragrance and
taste, losing its sweetness but otherwise perfection in 1985.
More recently, very rich, tangy, but a bit tired. *Last noted, a
bottle from the 'natural' cellar of a noted California connoisseur, at the
San Juan tasting of '28s, Nov 1998. At best* ★★★★
**Ch Suduiraut** Three notes. A superb wine. Orange-tinged,
amber-gold; fabulous bouquet, crisp, fragrant, dried apricots;
still sweet, immense depth and complexity. In 1984, 1988 and
in San Juan in 1998, a bottle from the perfectly maintained
cellar of Ben Ichinose, one of the earliest of latter-day
American collectors, and, incidentally the finest wine in the
line-up of 17 '28s. *Last tasted Nov 1998* ★★★★★

DRY WHITE **Pavillon Blanc de Ch Margaux** Two notes,
first in 1987: bright yellow; dry fullish body, excellent length
and acidity. More recently, a similar description but, after

tasting it in the office, I took it to Brooks's for dinner, and
finding the '86 Pavillon Blanc on the list added it to the glasses
of the '28 50-50. The result was superb, the old wine providing
character and the young one stability. *Last tasted May 1993* ★★★

## 1929 ★★★★★

Magnificent. The finest Sauternes vintage between 1921 and
1937. Like these two vintages, the wines were deep in colour.
Some good dry whites have survived.
**Ch d'Yquem** Harvest 20 September – 9 October. Sheer
perfection on all but one (the recorked bottle below) of several
memorable occasions. To summarise, slight colour variation
though mostly a deep, rich amber, some a rose-tinted tawny;
peaches and cream ride uppermost, also apricots (sorry to drag
this out again, but it is so apposite), peeled sultanas, sometimes
slightly chocolatey, always richly penetrating. Also always sweet,
never seeming to dry out, its flavour being a concentration of
all the fragrances just mentioned, with great length and
exquisite aftertaste. The odd man out was the bottle recorked
in 1994 which, despite its attractions (notably a hint of
crystallised violets, which reminded me of a fine old cognac or
perhaps a refined Bual madeira), was less sweet, its finish dry
and raw compared with the un-recorked bottle tasted
alongside. *Last noted Aug 1998. At best* ★★★★★
**Ch Climens** Five notes from 1965. Softer and creamier than
the '28. 'Perfect. Won't improve' (in 1980). Though not tasted
recently, this is unquestionably one of the greatest vintages of
one of the most consistently well made Sauternes (*1er cru*
Barsac to be more precise). As I last noted, far more *crème* and
far less *brûlée* than most old Sauternes. Perfection. *Last noted
March 1983* ★★★★★
**Ch Doisy-Daëne** Belgian-bottled by Vandermeulen. Superb.
Colour positively glowing; rich bouquet of lemon curd and
apricot; sweet, full – almost hefty and very fragrant. One of my
top marks at Frans de Cock's astonishing tasting of 33
Vandermeulen bottlings, including first growths and great
vintages. *Noted in Paris, Dec 1995* ★★★★★
**Ch Filhot** Hurrah! One of the better Filhot vintages. Several
consistent notes in the 1960s and 1970s. More recently, rich,
meaty, caramelly bouquet and flavour. Fairly sweet, positive
flavour, lovely texture at finish. *Last tasted Sept 1995* ★★★★ *(just)*.

OTHER '29S, OLDER NOTES **Ch Bastor-Lamontagne** a
superb half. *1973* ★★★★; **Ch Guiraud** one of the best ever –
soft, rich, ripe. *Watching wrestling with Peter Palumbo in his box at
the Albert Hall, 1981* ★★★★; **Ch Laville** both Bordeaux-bottled
by Eschenauer. The first, in 1978 was high-toned and acidic.
The other bottle, six years later had fabulous colour; intense
yet soft botrytis bouquet that held well in the glass for two
hours; perfect flavour and balance. *At my Bordeaux Club dinner,
1984* ★★★★; **Ch de Ricaud** (Loupiac) half bottles from the
Prunier cellar: herbal fragrance, assertive, lovely flavour, just
lacking the length of the classy wines on the opposite bank of
the Garonne. Several notes, *1982* and *1986* ★★★; and
**Ch Rieussec** caramel and cream – lovely. *1977* ★★★★

DRY WHITES **Ch Laville Haut-Brion** faultless.
Harmonious honeyed bottle-age bouquet, excellent flavour,
flesh, balance. *From the Woltner family cellars, tasted June 1999*
★★★★; **Pavillon Blanc de Ch Margaux** colour of an old
armagnac; smoky fragrance; showing its age but agreeable all
the same. *Sept 1990* ★

# 1930–1949

The world depression hit Bordeaux as elsewhere, white wine production and sales being affected as much as red. Weather conditions in the 1930s were equally disastrous, only the '34s and, in particular, the '37s having real quality. Well-kept Sauternes of these two vintages can still be in remarkable condition. The miracle of the post-war vintages cannot be explained, merely appreciated.

In this section, one or two of the top dry whites have been included, to exemplify the quality and staying power of the wines of the major châteaux and best vintages. The market for dry whites was steady, bearing in mind economic conditions, but it has to be said that it was mainly cheap sweet wines, in essence imitation Sauternes, which sold well, interest in the great Sauternes languishing despite their quality.

### Sauternes Vintages at a Glance
**Outstanding ★★★★★**
1937, 1945, 1947, 1949
**Very Good ★★★★**
1934, 1942, 1943
**Good ★★★**
1935, 1939, 1944

## 1930
Descent into the abyss. Appalling weather conditions. Ch d'Yquem not made.

## 1931
Nearly as bad, weather *and* market.
**Ch d'Yquem** Harvested 22 September – 5 November. Tasted on half a dozen occasions. Why? I know I should not say this, but it is my wife's birth year. Both of us were born in execrable vintage years – except, of course, for port. (Our children were better served: born in 1959 and 1962). A surprisingly healthy bottle in 1968 though with a curious piquancy. Acidity consistently noted. Variations in colour from fairly pale to deep amber (which looked more like a red wine in the decanter); sickly sweet, malty nose; still rich, with dry acidic finish. Most recently, another pointlessly recorked Yquem, this time 1997: mushroomy, sour nose; dried-out, sharp and unclean. *Last tasted in Munich, Sept 1998. At best ★*

## 1932
The third of a disastrous trio and in the depths of the world depression. Strange how bad weather, bad vintages and bad times sometimes coincide.
**Ch d'Yquem** Harvested 14 October – 21 November. Just one note, a bottle recorked in 1991. Mahogany core; hefty, singed, chocolatey nose which, to my surprise, opened up quite fragrantly. Sweeter than expected, too. Taste of old barley sugar and caramel. Could have been worse. *Noted Sept 1998 ★*

## 1933 ★
**Ch d'Yquem** Harvested 18 September – 14 October. My first encounter (1990) discouraging as the cork fell in. Blancmange-like nose; still fairly sweet, its acidity keeping the wine – and the cork – afloat. A dried-out bottle in 1992. Six years later, a bottle recorked 1991: somewhat pale; poor unknit nose that faded into nothing. Again, completely dried-out. Raw. *Last noted Sept 1998. At best, being charitable, ★*

OTHER, OLDER NOTES **Ch Filhot** glorious colour but dried-out and acidic. *1978*; **Ch Lafaurie-Peyraguey** two notes, one oily, not good, the other quite rich. *From the château 1976. At best ★★★*

DRY WHITES **Ch Laville Haut-Brion** lovely colour; nice fruit; almond-kernel taste, acidic. *June 1990 ★★*; and **Ch La Louvière** fragrant, waxy, old Sémillon nose; lean, good acidity. *March 1988 ★★★*. I have recently tasted a range of Louvières with the present owner, André Lurton, and have been impressed by how well it ages.

## 1934 ★★★★
Encouraging signs of recovery though still a very lean time.
**Ch d'Yquem** Harvesting early 7 September – 4 October. Two encouragingly consistent, well-nigh identical notes, first at the Moon tasting in 1988. Both 'medium-deep, warm looking'; bouquet fragrant, 'classic, honeyed', opening up in the glass. Fairly sweet, full body and flavour, rich. *Last noted – not recorked – at Rodenstock's Yquem tasting, Sept 1998 ★★★★*
**Ch des Tastes** (Ste-Croix-du-Mont) Four consistently good notes in the 1970s (when I must have bought it) and quite recently, proving a delightful surprise to members of the Bordeaux Club at my dinner at Christie's, served with *foie gras*. A rich amber with apple-green rim; honeyed lanolin bouquet; medium-sweet, delicious ripe apricot flavour and excellent acidity. I had decanted it shortly before serving mainly to show off its ruddy colour. I had a backup bottle of an excellent 1996 Loupiac and even tried the old champagne trick of blending the two wines in one glass, the old wine providing the character, the young wine the vigour. It was interesting but we unanimously decided to drink them both 'straight up'. *Last tasted Dec 1999 ★★★★*

OTHER, OLDER NOTES **Ch Coutet** perfect bouquet; lively, stylish. *1983 ★★★★★*; **Ch Filhot** nice but second rank. *1987 ★★*; and **Ch Lafaurie-Peyraguey** several excellent half bottles. *1978 ★★★★*

DRY WHITES An excellent vintage. **Ch Laville Haut-Brion** virtually faultless. *June 1990 ★★★★★*; **'Vin de Château Lafite'** with Carruades cork. Attractive but one-dimensional. *1978 ★★*

# 1935 ★★★

**Ch d'Yquem** Harvested 16 September – 31 October. Quite a few notes in the 1970s and 1980s. Bottle variation, from an unhealthy pale yellow to one smelling of sweat. But in between times some very attractive bottles, 'delicacy' and 'elegance' recurring in my notes. Most recently, a bottle recorked in 1996: richly coloured; fragrant, with a high-toned, crystallised violets bouquet that reminded me of a refined old Sercial madeira. Good flavour, sweet entry leading to a distinctly dry finish. *Last tasted Sept 1998. At best* ★★★

**DRY WHITES Ch Laville Haut-Brion** Bottle age gave the wine the colour and bouquet of a Barsac. Dry throughout, of course, but still excellent. *From the Woltner cellars, at Karl-Heinz Wolf's tasting in Wiesbaden, June 1990* ★★★★

# 1936 ★★

**Ch d'Yquem** Harvested 21 September – 23 November. Not a great Yquem. At Bud Moon's in 1988: orange-tinged; strange nose, reminding me of poached salmon, others of wild cherries; flavoury, lean. Most recently, recorked 1995: similar appearance; scent of squashed raisins and old Sercial; medium-sweet, not bad flavour, lean but clean. *Last noted Sept 1998* ★

**OLDER NOTES Ch d'Arche** Consistently attractive. An inexpensive find. Many notes. *Last tasted in 1985* ★★★

**DRY WHITES Ch Laville Haut-Brion** raw, acidulous, lime blossom bouquet. Very dry, stalky, teeth-gripping acidity. *At the Wolf tasting of Woltner wines, June 1990* ★

# 1937 ★★★★★

One of the great Sauternes vintages, on a par with the top pre-phylloxera years and 1929, but perhaps not as monumental as the 1921.
**Ch d'Yquem** Harvested 21 September – 6 November. Around a dozen notes, mainly in the 1980s. If well cellared, then certain still to be superb. Although a naturally deepish coloured wine, generally less dark than the Yquem '21 and '29. If it is amber-brown then expect a maderised, malty character. At its normal best, a glowing amber-gold with dash of orange; its bouquet will have all the component parts so frequently repeated in past vintage notes, the difference being the endless succession of these scents, their depth and abundance. Still sweet, concentrated, ambrosial, untiringly persistent. A magnum (in 1988) I described as having 'an explosive bouquet and almost exaggerated flavour'. Most recently, a superb bottle despite a rather varnishy, singed, raisiny fragrance; very sweet, tremendously rich, fleshy, almost fat … and so on. It had survived a West Coast importer, a California private cellar and a final trek, probably not direct, to Munich. *Last tasted Sept 1998. At best* ★★★★★
**Ch Coutet** Several notes, all consistent, mainly in the 1970s, one, excellent, in 1981, and very recently: a fairly deep old gold colour, once again, served from decanter, looking almost like a red wine; old nose, apricot skins and caramel; now medium-sweet but with a good rich flavour, quite powerful, with a hot alcoholic finish and crisp '37 acidity. *The last from Paolo Pong's cellar and consumed at Nick Lander and Jancis Robinson's, June 2000* ★★★★

**OTHER VERY GOOD WINES LAST TASTED IN** 1988
**Ch Climens** six notes. A superb Climens, creamy, rich, lovely ★★★★★; **Ch Gilette, Crème de Tête** rich 'tears' or 'legs' like Gothic arches; honey, straw, vanilla and mint; very sweet, high acidity ★★★★; and **Ch Lafaurie-Peyraguey** I have many good notes. Full flavoured, honeyed. Drying a little but still superb ★★★★★

**EARLIER NOTES Ch de Ricaud, Crème de Tête** (Loupiac) superb, perfectly balanced, glorious flavour. Three occasions in 1979 ★★★★; **Ch Suduiraut** bottle variation 1980. *At best* ★★★; **Ch Voigny** Charming, fragrant. *1983* ★★★

**DRY WHITES** These also had an excellent reputation but the acidity, which so unbalanced the reds in 1937 too, started to take over. **Ch Bouscaut blanc** Amber; creamy, honeyed; dry, a bit short. *At the château in 1988 and June 1992* ★★★

# 1938 ★★

A mediocre vintage bottled in the early days of the war.
**Ch d'Yquem** Harvested 12 September – 29 October. Only tasted once. Recorked 1990. High-toned, showing its age; drying, lean but flavoury. *Noted Sept 1998* ★

# 1939 ★★★

Moderately good.
**Ch d'Yquem** Harvested 24 September – 22 November: five notes, variable levels. Fine flavour, long, rapier-like finish in 1972. Excellent in 1983: lovely colour, rich bouquet; rich, fat, good length. Some more 'medicinal'. Most recently, a resin- (not raisin!) like overtone to its quite rich caramel and raisiny character. Still sweet, fleshy. *Last tasted Sept 1998. At best* ★★★★

**OLDER NOTES Ch Rabaud-Promis** lovely colour; sweet and gentle bouquet, good flavour though acidic. *1976* ★★; **Ch La Tour-Blanche** very good though dry finish. *1976* ★★★

# 1940 ★

Poor wartime vintage.
**Ch d'Yquem** Harvested 30 September – 6 November. A perfectly respectable bottle at the Moon tasting in 1988, less good more recently, recorked in 1991: palish and tired looking; nose could have been an old Bual madeira; drying out, faded but hanging on. *Last noted Sept 1998. At best* ★

**ONE VERY GOOD DRY WHITE Ch Laville Haut-Brion** rather Loire-like Chenin Blanc aroma with a touch of *citronelle*. Good body, firm, fine condition. *June 1990* ★★★★

# 1941

A difficult wartime year.
**Ch d'Yquem** Harvest 13 October – 22 November. In 1992, completely dried-out. More recently, a bottle recorked in 1995. Good colour; singed, raisiny, tangy nose; drying out yet rich and assertive. Short dry finish. *Last noted in Munich, Sept 1998* ★

**ONE DRY WHITE Ch Laville Haut-Brion** dry, firm, lean, acidic. But in excellent condition. *June 1990* ★★★

# 1942 ★★★★

On the one hand very good weather conditions, on the other hand, there were wartime problems of labour and equipment shortages. Results were excellent, however.
**Ch d'Yquem** Harvested 5 September – 19 October. Three notes, slight variation, overall pretty good. First tasted in perfect condition in 1980 and showing well at the Schloss Johannisberg/Yquem tasting in 1984: gentle, fragrant bouquet belying its body and power. Most recently, original cork and level into neck: fairly deep colour; very rich, heavily honeyed, toffee-like nose. Holding its sweetness with attractive raisiny flavour not unlike a mature 5 *puttonyos* Tokaji Aszú, with similar acidity. *Last tasted Sept 1998. At best ★★★★*

**DRY WHITES** A good vintage. **Ch Laville Haut-Brion** well balanced and in excellent condition. *June 1990 ★★★*

# 1943 ★★★★

Overall the most satisfactory wartime vintage.
**Ch d'Yquem** Harvested 14 September – 12 October. Good though drying out in 1972. Four consistently good notes since: warm amber, orange-tinged; classic bouquet, very forthcoming; sweet enough, rich and positive, with fairly high volatile acidity (noted in 1984) merely uplifting its fragrance. Most recently, with a Danflou New York slip label, original cork, very good level: hefty old-fashioned style, bouquet and palate, sweet, good length and acidity. *Last noted at the Rodenstock marathon, Sept 1998. At best ★★★★*
**Ch Climens** First tasted in 1963: old gold, assertive, firm. Lovely wine, perfect balance in 1970. Most recently: good level. Attractive, waxy buttercup yellow; fragrant, honey and vanilla; some sweetness loss but fine flavour and in excellent condition. *Last noted dining with Jane and Barney Wilson in Hungerford, April 1996 ★★★★*
**Ch Coutet** Rich, fine but losing its sugar in 1958. Most recently: bottled in Belgium (a wartime pale green bottle). Warm amber; old apricots – frankly over the top; not bad flavour but dried-out. *Last tasted alongside the '37 at Jancis Robinson's, June 2000 ★★*
**Ch Rabaud** Marigold gold; old honey and caramel; losing its pristine sweetness. *At a Christie's luncheon, May 1997 ★★★*
**Ch Suau** Yellow, drying out, disappointing. *Dec 1992 ★*

**DRY WHITES** A 5-star vintage; though few wines now left as most were consumed in the deprived and thirsty immediate post-war period. **Ch Haut-Brion** first whiff distinctly stale probably due to greasy cork and slight sediment. However it opened up richly, its bottle-aged bouquet remaining fabulous for three hours. Sweet for a dry white, full-bodied. *At a Bordeaux Club dinner, April 1990 ★★★★*; **Ch Laville Haut-Brion** full-bodied, firm, good but not in the class of '45 and '49. *June 1990 ★★★*

# 1944 ★★★

Good but variable now.
**Ch d'Yquem** Harvested 19 September – 14 October. First tasted in 1981. Three good and consistent notes: amber gold, orange-tinged, vivid apple-green rim; lovely 'honeyed bouquet', 'lanolin', 'orange blossom' repeated; very attractive flavour, good length, dry fragrant finish. The most recent bottle

had its original cork, level just into the neck and had effortlessly survived transportation to and from Chicago. *Last tasted in Munich, Sept 1998 ★★★★*

# 1945 ★★★★★

A small crop produced in difficult post-war conditions but of superb quality. Also excellent dry whites.
**Ch d'Yquem** Harvested 10 September – 20 October. A considerable number of notes starting in 1969, none less than magnificent. But not an opulent Yquem, rather an elegant yet concentrated 'honey and flowers' Yquem. 'Clover honey' and 'orange blossom' recur in my notes, perhaps rather unoriginally and certainly repetitive. The loveliest of colours, warm gold, pure gold; bouquet perfection, opening up in the glass like a water lily; still sweet, intense, great length. Perfection at Peter Ziegler's tasting of great wines in 1995; equally so, despite the bottle enduring two transatlantic crossings at Rodenstock's Yquem marathon. *Last tasted in Munich, Sept 1998 ★★★★★ Another quarter of a century of life.*
**Ch Doisy-Daëne** Two consistent notes, most memorably at the 1945 dinner at the British Embassy in Paris in 1995. Served alongside *Glace à l'Orange et Fromages* it performed well above its *2ème cru* Barsac classification, its bouquet redolent of peaches, apricots, barley sugar, bottle age and botrytis. Drying out a little but rich, with excellent length and finish. Twelve months later excellent with *Terrine de foie gras légèrement fumé et confit de coing*. Most recently, a similar note though paler. *Last noted at a British Airways meeting (and dinner) at the Waterside Inn, Bray, Nov 1996. At best ★★★★★*
**Ch Lafaurie-Peyraguey** Four consistently good notes, first, fabulous, refined, in 1976; fragrant, concentrated, superb in 1984. A glorious bottle and one of my highest marks at Peter Ziegler's monumental tasting in 1995: perfect amber-gold; lovely clover honey bouquet; still sweet and rich with glorious flavour. Most recently an astonishingly good bottle bought by one of the Jackson, Mississippi, group at the Maison du Vin in Bordeaux en route to dinner at the restaurant La Tupina, where it was quickly decanted (because of the slight powdery sediment) and consumed with great satisfaction. Bouquet assertive, very rich, singed raisins. Perfect flavour, weight and counterbalancing acidity. *Last noted Sept 1998 ★★★★★*
**Ch Rieussec** I suspect that few regular visitors to the island of St-Barthélémy in the Caribbean maintain a cellar of great wines. Ron Weiser, now US Ambassador to Slovakia, does. This was the penultimate of an eight-wine dinner (four warranting 5 stars, four 4 stars): glorious colour, bouquet and flavour, its superb acidity keeping the 55-year-old Sauternes alive. *At the Weiser beachside villa, Feb 2000 ★★★★★*

**DRY WHITES** A superb vintage for the top Graves.
**Ch Laville Haut-Brion** Several notes, all from the Woltner family cellars. Thanks to honeyed bottle age, the scent of Yquem, yet on the palate dry, firm, steely. *Last noted at the Wolf tasting in Wiesbaden, June 1990 ★★★★★*

# 1946

After much rain and rot, the harvest was saved by very hot weather at vintage time. Rarely seen – thank goodness.
**Ch d'Yquem** Harvested between 9 September and 19 November. Two notes, first in 1988. Original cork, level upper-mid shoulder. Poor colour, Striving to clamber out of

the grave. Most recently, yet another bottle which hardly survived surgery (re-corking, in 1997). Whiff of old banana skins; medium sweet, caramelised. *At Rodenstock's Yquem marathon tasting in Munich, Sept 1998.*

## 1947 ★★★★★

Hot summer with the harvest beginning early in intense heat on 15 September. Superbly ripe, rich wines.

**Ch d'Yquem** Harvested 13 September – 13 October. First tasted in 1954: 'incomparable, luscious', and 14 times since. Never a poor bottle. Perfect, glowing amber-gold with apple-green rim; bouquet – well, the usual thing only more so, yet totally harmonious; still remarkably sweet, mouthfilling with a singed hot-vintage character. Always decant a wine like this. It looks the purest glowing gold in a decanter by candlelight. The most recent bottle had been imported many years ago by Browne-Vintners, New York, survived cellarage and the recent journey back to Munich. *Last noted Sept 1998* ★★★★★

**Ch Climens** A dozen notes. Perfection in 1965, losing some of its initial sweetness in the early 1980s. One of the most magnificent of all Climens vintages. Once again, a glowing amber shot, like taffeta, with pure gold highlights; despite its richness, crisp, minty, ripe nectarines, *crème brûlée*; perfect flavour, weight and balance with creamy texture and infinite aftertaste. *Last noted at Barry Phillips' 'Silver Jubilee Dinner' at the White Horse, Chilgrove, Jan 1995* ★★★★★

**Ch Climens** Belgian-bottled by Vandermeulen. Orange-tinged; hefty, caramelised; not as sweet as the château bottling and perhaps lacking length. Still pretty good though. *At Frans de Cock's Vandermeulen tasting in Paris, Dec 1995* ★★★

**Ch Coutet** Many notes, not all château-bottled. Even in the mid-1960s and early 1970s showing signs of drying out though still rich. At best, full, fat, rich and soft. A good Coutet. Lebègue's London-bottling tasted in 1990 had all the component parts. In 1993 peaches and honey. Most recently, Vandermeulen's Belgian-bottling, despite a bouquet that opened up beautifully in the glass, was overall lean and acidic, lacking '47 richness and sweetness. *Last noted in Paris, Dec 1995. At best* ★★★★

**Ch Doisy-Daëne** Only one note, Belgian-bottled by Vandermeulen. Very high marks indeed. A lovely wine, still sweet, rated by me far higher than its *2ème cru* classification. *In Paris, Dec 1995* ★★★★

**Ch Farburet** An unknown Barsac not tasted before or since. With plain capsule, cork and slip label and despite its mid-shoulder level it was remarkably good. Clearly a high percentage of Sémillon. Fragrant, sweet and crisp. *Found in Christie's cellar and consumed with unexpected pleasure at a boardroom lunch, July 1994* ★★★★

**Ch Rieussec** The finest Sauternes to appear in the first of my little red tasting books: 'liquid gold, rich and strong…' (November 1952) though 'drying out' appearing consistently in seven notes in the late 1960s. A delicious soft and fat Lebègue London-bottling in 1990 and, more recently, cork pulled at 5.50pm and decanted at 9pm (glorious colour in decanter), 'sheer perfection, creamy yet crisp' but it did not stand up to the pear soufflé. *The tenth wine at my Bordeaux Club dinner, May 1994* ★★★★★

OTHER '47S, OLDER NOTES **Ch Doisy-Védrines** scent like orange sorbet; drying out though rich. Really lovely. *1971* ★★★★; **Ch Filhot** showing its age, even in *1965* ★★;

**Ch Gilette** disappointing nose; very sweet, 'oily and assertive'. *1990* ★★; **Ch Lafaurie-Peyraguey** superb. *1976* ★★★★★; **Ch Suduiraut** deep, rich, lively. *1970* ★★★★; and **Ch La Tour-Blanche** glorious flavour, silky texture *1990* ★★★★

DRY WHITES **Ch Laville Haut-Brion** amber; pure honeycomb bouquet; dry, assertive, rich but a disappointing finish, probably lacking acidity. *June 1990* ★★★

## 1948 ★★

Quite good but lacking richness. Commercially uninteresting because it was sandwiched between two great vintages and wines are rarely seen now.

**Ch d'Yquem** Harvested 24 September – 13 November. At six years of age full and fruity but not as rarefied as expected. By 1961 it already had a deep amber-gold colour and considerable richness, 'not cloying' noted. Ten years later losing some of its sweetness, holding back and lacking the length of a vintage like '49, endorsed in 1987. Two bottles showing well at the Kaplan dinner in 1998: 'singed butterscotch'. Most recently, a bottle recorked in 1993: slightly drab appearance; nose almost too sweet, 'orange peel extract'; crisp, good flavour and condition. Acidity high. *Last noted Sept 1998. At best* ★★★

OTHER, OLDER NOTES **Ch Climens** orange-tinged; fabulous bouquet and flavour but 'needs drinking' (half bottles tasted in 1981 and *1986* ★★★★; **Ch Coutet** my first-ever taste of Coutet, bottled by Christopher's, rich, delightful. *1953* ★★★; and **Ch Doisy-Védrines** pale gold; drying out but agreeable. *1977* ★★

## 1949 ★★★★★

A great vintage, still superb.

**Ch d'Yquem** Picking between 27 September and 17 October (the driest October on record). Over a dozen notes, lovely, soft, complete in the 1960s. Four lovely bottles in the 1970s and at peak of perfection in 1984. Rich bottle age and botrytis honey and apricots at Carré des Feuillants, Paris, in 1995. Most recently: original cork, with 'Kobrand Corp. New York, via Delor' on the label. By now paler but lovely; exquisitely floral, orange blossom bouquet; still sweet and fleshy, dry finish. A wine of style and charm. One of my top marks at Rodenstock's tasting in Munich, 1998. Most recently: 'gorgeous' (the wine not our host). *Last tasted at Len Evans' 70th birthday 'Single bottle club' dinner in the Hunter Valley, Sept 2000* ★★★★★

THE BEST OF THE OLDER NOTES from the late 1970s to late 1980s **Ch Climens** nearly as many notes as Yquem dating from 1962 though none recently. One of the best vintages of this consistently good château. Less deep in colour than Yquem, leaner, but creamy and superbly balanced. *1977* ★★★★★; **Ch Coutet** good vintage for Coutet too. A fine Sichel bottling in 1956. 'Old gold', rich and ripe a decade later. Most recently, a half bottle: excellent flavour, harmonious. *1983* ★★★★★; and **Ch de Rayne-Vigneau** perfection. *1987* ★★★★★

DRY WHITES A good vintage. **Ch Laville Haut-Brion** slightly variable but at best yellow-gold; lovely ripe 'waxy' Sémillon nose; dry, highish acidity but delicate and fragrant. *Last noted at Karl-Heinz Wolf's tasting, June 1990* ★★★★

# 1950–1969

The dry whites, particularly decent quality Graves, sold steadily, albeit at near to uneconomic prices. However, much commercial Graves was poorly made, often oxidised, mostly 'protected' by the overuse of sulphur; the sweet wines were somewhat better, but I well remember them, for the whole of this period, being offered blatantly by *négociants* as 'Sauternes No 1, 2 or 3' with slight variations in quality and sweetness. This harmed genuine Sauternes just as Liebfraumilch undermined the fine German estates. Nevertheless, there were some superb vintages of Sauternes, and several are still glorious to drink now.

### Sauternes Vintages at a Glance
**Outstanding ★★★★★**
1955, 1959, 1967
**Very Good ★★★★**
1953, 1962
**Good ★★★**
1952, 1961, 1966

## 1950 ★★
Damp conditions compensated for by an Indian summer. Interestingly all my early notes were of Harvey's of Bristol bottlings. Only Yquem was château-bottled.
**Ch d'Yquem** Harvested 20 September – 27 October. Comte Alexandre de Lur Saluces likes the '50 – I don't. I am put off by its nose described variously as 'oily', 'varnishy', 'almond kernels' (the latter noted consistently, eight times, between 1961 and 1984), but less critically in 1988 and a decade later (original cork), leaner than the previous great vintages but flavoury. *Last noted in Munich, Sept 1998* ★★

OTHER, OLDER NOTES **Ch Climens** rich yet refreshing. *1965* ★★★★; **Ch Coutet** a dozen notes from 'magnificently well balanced' in 1954, a lovely, rich Harvey's bottling in 1955 (it retailed at 17 shillings and 9 pence per bottle). High strength: alcohol 16% and 6° Baumé. Soft, perfect harmony noted in the 1960s and 1970s. David Peppercorn produced one bottled by his family firm, Osborne's of Margate, at his dinner party in 1981: vanilla cream flavour, drying out a little. A good château-bottling, deep, rich, honeyed, and still fairly sweet. *Last tasted 1983. At best* ★★★★; **Ch Doisy-Védrines** a delightful Harvey's bottling. *1955* ★★★★; **Ch Gilette 'Crème de Tête'** 20 years in tank, no wood used. Rich, fat, idiosyncratic but excellent. *1984* ★★★★; **Ch Roumieu** crisp, excellent. *1958* ★★★★; **Ch de Tastes** (Ste Croix-du-Mont) fine colour; lovely botrytis and honey bouquet; medium-sweet. Light style. *1977* ★★★; and **Ch La Tour-Blanche** 'vast', cumbrous, fruity and luscious in 1954. A less over-the-top description though still full-bodied. *1958* ★★★

## 1951
Disastrous year. None tasted. Ch d'Yquem not made.

## 1952 ★★★
A better vintage. Picking started early, 17 September, with variable success, the crop at Ch d'Yquem destroyed by hail. This was the first Sauternes vintage I tasted in cask on our first visit to Bordeaux in July 1955. I have tasted few '52s recently.

OLD NOTES **Ch Climens** a 'so-so' sample in 1954 and, at the château, tasted ex-cask, it was good but I preferred Coutet. Nine far more complimentary notes between 1959 and 1982, and different bottlings. Good but not great, though without much room for improvement. *1982* ★★★; **Ch Coutet** in July 1955 my wife expressed her first taste eloquently: '*Comme miel*', which pleased the cellarmaster. An old gold, attractive but drying out Harvey's bottling. *1972* ★★★

DRY WHITES A good vintage for the top Graves, with some of the firmness and masculinity of the Médoc reds.
**Ch Haut-Brion blanc** extraordinarily good in the mid-1970s, delicate, rather like a fine white Burgundy but more fragrant and spicy. *1975* ★★★★. *Could still be good, if well kept*; and **Ch Laville Haut-Brion** austere, interesting. *1990* ★★

## 1953 ★★★★
Lovely wines, the best still drinking well.
**Ch d'Yquem** Harvested between 2 October and 10 November. First tasted at the château in cask in July 1955: 'extremely rich and full though I preferred Coutet' ('53) at this stage! In the early 1970s I also preferred the '55 though appreciating its delicacy and lovely aftertaste. Accompanying, complementing, with 'dancing fruitiness' and a light touch, *foie gras* in Germany in 1983 and a honey and blossom charmer surviving the *millefeuille à la crème légère* at a Marin County Wine & Food Society dinner in California in 1985. A perfect bottle, harmonious, crisp in 1988 and most recently my eighth note: though always on the pale side it was taking on a shade of mahogany with age with a sort of hefty fragrance, good length, sweet. It is still one of my favourite Yquems though thoroughly upstaged by the three great post-war vintages ('45, '47 and '49). *Last noted at Rodenstock's marathon tasting in Munich, Sept 1998* ★★★★

### My first tasting of Yquem
*This takes me back to around 1950 and the home of Dr Thomas Kerfoot, a family friend who lived near us in Cheshire, a man of great taste. (He owned an important manufacturing chemists in Lancashire.) We sat in his garden on a lovely summer evening and drank Yquem with nectarines. I'd just come out of the army and was studying architecture; I knew nothing about wine – as a family we drank it with meals, but nothing special – but this was the first really great wine I'd ever tasted. I was also, at this stage, introduced to Ch Lafite. I have always been grateful to Thomas Kerfoot, long since departed, for I think my first sip of these first growths must have lingered in the back of my mind, a sort of delayed spark which brought me eventually into wine.*

**Ch Filhot** Rather light in style, nice but not outstanding in 1970. Two decades later orange and lime – not flavour, colour; frankly disappointing. Rather hard and caramelly. *Last tasted Oct 1990* ★★

OTHER, OLDER NOTES **Ch Climens** and **Ch Coutet** both lovely in cask; **Ch Doisy-Daëne** perfect peaches and cream, melted barley sugar bouquet *1986* ★★★★; **Ch Gilette 'Crème de Tête'** '*doux*': fabulous, unusual raspberry piquancy; medium sweet, peachy end taste. Charming. *1987* ★★★★; and **Ch Roumieu** perfection. *1979* ★★★★

DRY WHITES Some good Graves but most will be over the top by now: **Ch Haut-Brion** attractive fruit, honeyed bottle age, dry, distinctive, unusual – magnum tasted blind alongside the '55. *In Munich, Sept 1996* ★★★

# 1954

Late vintage, unremitting rain. Only Ch d'Yquem tasted.
**Ch d'Yquem** Harvested 9 October – 16 November. Variable: unknit and acidic in 1971, a surprisingly rich bottle in 1983. Most recently: vanilla, burnt sugar; hefty, assertive, lip-licking acidity. Difficult times, but marketing this was bad for Yquem's reputation (see also 1963). *Last tasted Sept 1998* ★

# 1955 ★★★★★

To make up for 1954, a perfect growing season and well-nigh perfect Sauternes. Still lovely.
**Ch d'Yquem** Harvested 17 September – 28 October, 14%, 4.5° Baumé. First tasted in cask, October 1958: pale, fruity but strong whiff of preservative sulphur; starting to take on colour, sweet, smooth, fat yet with good counter-balancing acidity (early 1960s). Beautiful, opening up in the late 1960s, early 1970s. By 1980, a deep orange-gold reminding me of the '29; intensely rich, very sweet – but killed stoned dead by a sugary *crème brûlée* at the Jubilee Dinner of the Institute of Masters of Wine! Four other notes in the 1980s: 'an astonishing orange-rose-amber with pale lemon rim', still very sweet, very rich, good length and lovely aftertaste. Sustained and refreshed with high acidity (including a level of volatile acidity which the quality control of the Quebec Liquor Board in Montreal found unacceptable). A glorious bottle, lunch in the sun in 1994. Most recently: seemed too deep for a vintage of the 1950s; hefty, classic, caramelised nose; sweet, full, complete, masked acidity, excellent finish. *Last tasted at the Yquem marathon event in Munich, Sept 1998* ★★★★★

### The 1950s

*The marvellous Sauternes vintages of this decade – 1952, 1953, 1955 and (best of all) 1959 – went largely unnoticed. Nobody wanted these wines. This might have had to do with the heavy-handed way in which the négociants tried to sell them, without regard to the finer differences between châteaux, or purely because the fashion then was for reds and dry white wines. Although cheap Sauternes lookalikes were popular, the sort of people who should have appreciated the real thing, from top class châteaux, rather despised sweet wines. Perhaps the British could not place them and, unlike the French, did not serve them with pâté or with cheese; and as for an apéritif, heaven forbid!*

**Ch Climens** Two ripe, rich Harvey's bottlings in the mid-1960s. Very fragrant, spicy, spearmint and crème caramel bouquet; lovely, fullish, harmonious - coping with *foie gras* in 1988. Most recently: glorious, ripe bouquet and flavour. Not too plump, just right. Perfect. *Last noted at the Christie's Wine department's Christmas dinner, Dec 1998* ★★★★
**Ch Gilette 'Crème de Tête'** 25 years in cement tanks. After five years in bottle wonderfully rich. A decade later liked it less. Lacking the evolution of bouquet of a classic Sauternes. Powerful. Rather hard finish. *Last tasted June 1990* ★★?
**Ch Lafaurie-Peyraguey** A couple of notes: fabulously rich, tingling acidity in 1976. More recently somewhat overwhelmed by the '59. Higher tones, less sweet but good length and acidity. *Last tasted Sept 1994* ★★★★
**Ch Sigalas-Rabaud** A good Scottish bottling in 1969 but superior, château-bottled, in 1977: distinctive yellow; magnificent bouquet, concentrated flavour. A lovely bottle at a British Airways Catering and Wine dinner at the Waterside Inn, Bray: now amber-gold; waxy Sémillon-orange blossom nose; sweet though with a dry, caramelly finish. Most recently, at the Sigalas-Rabaud pre-sale tasting, drying out, powerful, caramelised. *Last noted March 1997* ★★★

OLDER NOTES **Ch Coutet** 'feeble' in 1959; in 1960 preferred the '57 but a good, fat, strong yet soft Harvey's bottling in 1967 (a retaste necessary!); **Ch Doisy-Védrines** nearly a dozen notes between 1959 and 1973, all good despite the various bottlings (Cruse, The Wine Society). Palish at first but gaining amber-gold. Beautiful bouquet. Despite losing some of its pristine sweetness, lovely wine. *Last noted 1973* ★★★★; **Ch Filhot** hurrah: a pretty good Filhot, ripe, flavoury, lovely finish. 1964, 1968 and *1971* ★★★; **Ch Liot** a discovery of Harry Waugh's and excellent for its class and certainly good value at 12 shillings and 6 pence per bottle (in 1958) – Yquem '50 was three times the price! Fat almost syrupy. *1959* ★★★; **Ch de Rayne-Vigneau** lovely wine. Four notes 1963 to *1978*, deepening in colour, still sweet ★★★★; and **Ch Suduiraut** many notes in the early 1970s: old gold; notable botrytis and bottle age; perfect flavour and balance. Classic. *Last tasted 1972* ★★★★ *(probably still very good)*.

DRY WHITES A good year for these wines. **Ch Haut-Brion** five notes: a very dry strong-flavoured wine, clearly unready in 1958. By the mid-1970s it had deepened in colour, developing a rich, complex bouquet and flavour. Most recently, a pure yellow gold, rather austere magnum. *Last tasted Sept 1996* ★★★★; **Ch Laville Haut-Brion** perfection in the mid- to late 1970s; showing well in the early 1980s. More recently, similar colour to Ch Haut-Brion but somewhat overdeveloped on the nose. Plateau of maturity either side of 20 years. *Last tasted June 1990. At best* ★★★★★

# 1956

An appalling vintage. Bad weather at all the critical times though a last minute reprieve enabled producers to pick desultorily.
**Ch d'Yquem** Late and extended picking from 8 October to 21 November salvaged a few usable grapes resulting in 14% alcohol and 4.5° Baumé. Five notes, first in October 1958, the wine still in cask, fruity but acidic and sulphury. By the early 1960s opening up, smoothly, crisply attractive, lightish, Barsac-like. By the late 1980s a deep orange amber, flavoury but raw

and short. Most recently, weak-rimmed; curiously fragrant nose, surprisingly sweet but lean. *Last noted in Munich, Sept 1998* ★★

## 1957 ★★

Perverse weather conditions, the coldest summer and hottest October on record, the latter advantageous for Sauternes, less so for the dry whites.

**Ch d'Yquem** Picked 30 September – 31 November. Disappointing though not unattractive in the mid-1960s, perfect with *foie gras* in 1969. By the late 1980s fairly deep orange amber; whiff of mercaptan which cleared when it opened up in the glass. Consistently sweet, assertive, toffee-like flavour, marked '57 acidity, lacking length. Most recently: seemed paler and weak-rimmed; unknit nose; still sweet and powerful but not a great Yquem. *Last tasted in Munich, Sept 1998* ★★

OTHER, OLDER NOTES **Ch Coutet** a dozen notes from a nicely balanced cask sample in 1958, crisp, clean, attractive in the early 1960s and a string of very good Harvey's bottlings up to the early 1970s, medium sweet with refreshing Barsac bouquet and acidity ★★★ *Could still be good*; **Ch Rieussec** five consistently good notes between 1958 and 1971 ★★★; and **Ch Suduiraut** excellent flavour and balance. *1970* ★★★★

## 1958 ★★

Good summer, late harvest. Wines *assez bien* but upstaged, rightly, by the great 1959s.

**Ch d'Yquem** Five notes. Rich and ripe in 1964. Five years later, touch of old gold, surprisingly good for the vintage, fully mature. Very sweet, assertive, better flavour than nose at 30 years of age. Noted in 1995 as 'a bit obvious' and somewhat 'clumsy' managing to compete with 'Brandy Snap *millefeuille*' at Barry Phillips' 'Silver Jubilee Dinner' at the White Horse, Chilgrove. Most recently, singed caramel nose and taste, some fat, hot finish. *Last tasted in Munich, Sept 1998. At best* ★★★

THE BEST OF THE OTHER OLDER NOTES **Ch Coutet** *1978* ★★★; and **Ch Suduiraut** *1983* ★★★★

## 1959 ★★★★★

A great vintage. Monumental Sauternes following a long hot summer with some rain just before the harvest to flesh out the heat-concentrated grapes, retaining their high sugar content.

**Ch d'Yquem** An almost indecent number of notes, coincidentally at almost regular intervals. Richly coloured from the start, a deep, somewhat musky nose, soft ripe and luscious at five years of age – in fact not long after bottling. Blossoming beautifully through the 1970s, concentrated, magnificent. Colour deepening, a warm old gold, fabulous *crème brûlée* bouquet, high extract (with *Brie de Meaux* at a Lafite dinner at the old Boulestin's in 1980). Fifty years of life predicted in 1983, a scent reminding me of my grandmother's duck egg custard. On through the 1980s, paeans of praise, a doubly memorable bottle dining in Eaton Square with Madeleine and Andrew Lloyd Webber in 1994. By 1998 a fairly deep gold with a touch of orange; high-toned peach-skin bouquet; still very sweet with marvellous flesh and fat, great length and finish. Most recently: a rich, apricot and

lime blossom bouquet of great depth; sweet, powerful, its flesh and fat balanced by its excellent acidity. A hot, dry finish with a touch of caramel. *Last noted, blind, at Wilfred Jaeger's second dinner in San Francisco, March 2002* ★★★★★ .

**Ch Climens** Only two notes, the first in 1972: an excellent, firm, heavyweight Barsac. Most recently: a lovely, medium-pale, orange-yellow with an open, lime-shaded edge; showing its age on the nose, a whiff of caramel; fairly sweet, powerful yet lean with a touch of vanilla and good acidity. *Last noted, blind, at Wilf Jaeger's, March 2002* ★★★

**Ch Doisy-Daëne** A *2ème cru* Barsac at its best in '59. Distinctive yellow; fragrant bouquet, vanilla, 'duck egg custard' again; sweet, crisp fruit, grapey, good acidity. *At Weinart's gala dinner at the Residenz, Aschau, Nov 1994* ★★★★

**Ch Gilette 'Crème de Tête'** Amber orange, waxy sheen; lovely ripe apricots bouquet and flavour, crisp, excellent acidity, long caramel aftertaste. *At Bob Dickinson's 'Mr Gourmet' dinner, Miami, Nov 1997* ★★★★

**Ch Guiraud** Many notes, mainly in the mid- to late 1960s, including five rather indifferent J Lyons' bottlings. Château-bottlings all good but not great. In the mid-1970s honey and vanilla, less fat than expected, a bit abrupt. More recently, following a great madeira tasting at Bill Baker's in Somerset: fairly deep amber-gold; barley sugar and lemon curd, dry finish. *Last tasted April 1994. At best* ★★★

**Clos Haut-Peyraguey** Flowery bouquet; sweet, tangy, assertive. *Sept 1993* ★★★★

**Ch Lafaurie-Peyraguey** Two good Percy Fox (Cordier's agents) bottlings in the mid-1960s. Probably at its best in the mid-1970s, noting fabulous Beerenauslese-like bouquet, very rich, marvellous fruit and acidity. More recently: low-keyed nose; very sweet and full-bodied with surprising acidity for a '59. *Last tasted Sept 1994* ★★★★

**Ch Rieussec** Two really lovely half bottles, shipped by Sichel and bottled by my old firm Saccone & Speed, in 1984 and 1985. Superb, château-bottled, with barley sugar nose, marvellously rich, perfect balance at my Bordeaux Club dinner, July 1992. Most recently, tasted cursorily and inadequately at Farr Vintners. *Last noted Jan 1990. At best* ★★★★

**Ch Sigalas-Rabaud** Perfection in mid-1980s. Two recent notes: 'apricots' on nose and on taste. A lovely, fairly substantial wine. Vanilla and 'barley sugar' noted twice. *Last tasted at Karl-Heinz Wolf's Landart Restaurant in Austria, April 1999* ★★★★

**Ch Suduiraut** Over a dozen admiring notes: 'classic', 'heavyweight', fat, rich and lovely in the 1970s. Warm amber gold; fabulously rich ripe bouquet and flavour, fragrant, perfection in the 1980s. At the Dickinsons' in Miami (1997): floral, orange blossom, creamy bouquet; sweet but not as fulsome or fat. Great length. Lovely wine. Most recently: orange-amber; perhaps with auto-suggested orange blossom bouquet and flavour. Sweet, fat, concentrated. A wine of considerable power, good length. When tasted blind alongside the Yquem and Climens, most of the tasters rated this even better than Yquem. Both magnificent. *Last tasted at Jaeger's second dinner, March 2002* ★★★★★ *Will keep another 20 years.*

**Ch La Tour-Blanche** Superb. Richly coloured, very sweet, glorious flavour, excellent acidity. *At Aschau, Nov 1994* ★★★★★

DRY WHITES Rather too hot and too ripe in 1959 for dry white Bordeaux and most wines were consumed in the early 1960s. Volatile acidity was a problem.

**Ch Laville Haut-Brion** Burnished gold; honeyed; medium dry, fullish body, lovely flavour. *June 1990* ★★★★

**Ygrec** Fabulous, richly coloured; high volatile acidity merely enhancing its flavour. *The oldest and best of a vertical of Ygrecs at Ch d'Yquem, Sept 1986* ★★★★

# 1960 ★

Cold wet summer which suited the dry whites better.

**Ch d'Yquem** In 1964 I over-optimistically thought the nose, 'green' but attractive, was like the '62. Palate, light, 'poignant' and slightly astringent. Seemed to have got its second breath by 1972, though with a hard, slightly bitter finish. Fragrant, spicy, classic flavour, citrus-like acidity in 1988 and a decade later, despite its faded *pelure d'oignon* colour, surprisingly sweet on the nose, quite good flavour, bite at the end. *Last tasted in Munich, Sept 1998* ★★ *but I wouldn't bother.*

**DRY WHITES** Quite a few 1960s tasted, mainly uninspiring, the best was – as so often – **Ch Laville Haut-Brion** fresh and attractive in *1978* ★★

# 1961 ★★★

Poor flowering, drought in August and sunny September reduced the size of the crop. Sauternes good but lacking the lusciousness of the '59s.

**Ch d'Yquem** Picked 9 September – 26 October. A dozen notes, four in the 1960s, starting creditably in 1964. 'Packed with flavour, needs time' in 1967. Contrasting notes in the mid- to late 1970s, 'rather hard and ungracious' then 'full, rich, concentrated'. Somewhere in between about right! Caramel and barley sugar noted fairly consistently from 1987 to the present day. Also sweet, rich, powerful, with dry finish. At Rodenstock's Yquem tasting, bottle variations, one with singed raisin taste and very dry acidic end, the second crisp, attractive, not great. Frankly a mixed bunch of notes, possibly bottle variations. *Last tasted Sept 1998. At best* ★★★

**Ch Climens** Nine notes. Rich and lovely in mid-1960s to mid-1970s. Nicely mature by 1980 and 'probably at peak' noted in 1986. Showing some age in colour and on nose in 1990 and 1993 though ripe, honeyed, fleshy, with marvellous acidity. Most recently: soft, fragrant, drying out a little but very good. *At Hugh Johnson's Bordeaux Club dinner, July 1995* ★★★

**Ch Coutet** Seven good notes from 1964. Not a heavyweight but lovely from the start, reaching full maturity, rich, well-knit by 1980. Then a jump of 14 years to an interesting comparison of Lovibond's London-bottling and a château-bottled wine. Both had a similar colour, Lovibond's rather scented, with a raspberry-like, slightly artificial taste. The château-bottling was far superior, sweet, honeyed, soft, harmonious, fleshy. *The latter pair provided by Belle and Barney Rhodes at Jancis Robinson's, May 1994* ★★★

**Ch Doisy-Védrines** Fresh young fruit in 1964, opening up, attractive but lacking depth in 1975 and, recently, an intriguing Averys' bottling, a lovely amber-gold; bouquet of chocolate and barley sugar, touch of caramelisation; tangy. Good acidity. *Dining with the redoubtable Bristolian, Jim Hood, Jan 1998* ★★★

**Ch Rieussec** Attractive, Barsac-like weight and crispness in 1965, showing well in the late 1960s and early 1970s, including a very good Harvey's bottling. Yet I felt something was lacking. Recently, sweet, soft, curiously caramelly with a trace of peach kernels which I never like. And it was destroyed by the pudding. I protested, as usual! *Last noted at Hugh Johnson's, Saling Hall, Aug 1999. At best* ★★★

**OTHER, OLDER NOTES Ch Guiraud** many notes, varying bottlings, all good. *Last tasted in 1976* ★★★; **Ch Lafaurie-Peyraguey** *1983* ★★★; and **Ch La Tour-Blanche** *1987* ★★★★

**DRY WHITES** On the whole, better Graves than Sauternes though most by now tired or consumed.

**Ch Laville Haut-Brion** I have many notes. I am reminded of the 1989 which, like this wine, at four years of age I considered 'the best ever' Laville. Good notes through the 1970s and 1980s, gaining in complexity. Two poor bottles at a tasting in 1990. Most recently: lovely yellow gold colour; soft, rich, ripe Sémillon nose; excellent, rather nutty flavour and good acidity. *At a pre-sale dinner in honour of Tawfiq Khoury in New York, March 1997. At best* ★★★★

**OLDER NOTE Pavillon Blanc de Ch Margaux** Almost on a par with the *grand vin* for quality. Lovely colour; fragrant, dry yet richly flavoured and with excellent acidity. *1987* ★★★★ *Probably still good.*

# 1962 ★★★★

Far superior to the 1961s, superb, elegant, but lacking the richness and body of the great 1959s. A cold wet spring delayed the flowering which was nonetheless successful and, after a warm, fairly dry summer, a sprinkling of rain and sun both ripened the grapes and encouraged 'noble rot' for a successful Indian summer harvest.

**Ch d'Yquem** Picking 2 October – 15 November. Many notes, from a cask sample in October 1964, through the late 1960s and 1970s to seven in the 1980s, but only one recently. The progression from excellent but undeveloped (early 1970s) to its full blossoming (mid-1980s) was steady and consistent. 'Honey and flowers' (sounds like an aftershave), 'barley sugar and orange blossom', 'mandarine *(sic)* and ripe peaches'. Throughout an elegance to temper its sweetness. Perhaps one should not be surprised that at 36 years of age its colour was a too deep ruddy-amber; nose singed, prune-like; raisiny, almost tart. In fact disappointing, but perhaps it was the bottle or the context. *Last noted at the marathon Yquem tasting in Munich, Sept 1998. At best* ★★★★ *Drink soon.*

**Ch Climens** Many consistent notes from 1964. The most recent: perfect, harmonious, creamy bouquet; sweet, fullish, apricots, wonderful acidity. *Last tasted Jan 1993* ★★★★

**Ch Coutet** Ten consistently good notes. Rich yet crisp in 1967, plump for a Barsac (1968). Firm and still youthful at ten years of age. Never very sweet, always with good, almost lemon-like, acidity. Gaining in colour yet never deep: a bright yellow gold; floral bouquet; lovely flavour and aftertaste. Most recently: beautiful bouquet, apricots, vanilla. An exceptionally good Coutet with Barsac finesse. *Last noted at Hugh Johnson's Bordeaux Club dinner at Saling Hall, Aug 1999* ★★★★

**Ch Doisy-Védrines** Full, rich, remarkably good though a touch of coarseness alongside Ch d'Yquem. *At a BYOB dinner in New York, Feb 1997* ★★★★

**Ch Guiraud** A poor bottle in 1973. Then, two really good notes in the early 1980s, ripe, rich yet crisp. More recently: orange amber; lovely barley sugar nose; still sweet, good flesh, almost fat, with orange blossom flavour and marvellous acidity. *At Harry Waugh's Bordeaux Club dinner, Jan 1995* ★★★★

**Ch Sigalas-Rabaud** Glorious colour; sweet, silky, harmonious bouquet; rich, powerful. Just a little four-square, lacking the quintessential finesse. *Last tasted in April 1990* ★★★★

OLDER NOTES **Ch Doisy-Daëne** *1978* ★★★; **Ch Rayne-Vigneau** *1973,* potential ★★★★; **Ch Rieussec** fragrant but lacking middle palate. *1982* ★★; and **Ch Suduiraut** consistently lovely wine. An old-fashioned style. Fully mature yet with years of life when last tasted in *1982* ★★★★(★)

DRY WHITES Some attractive wines, now mainly over the hill even if they can be found. **Ch Haut-Brion blanc** keeping better than Laville but not tasted since *1988* ★★★; **Ch Laville Haut-Brion** delicious at five years of age and, up to *1982*, I made 14 good notes: gaining colour, a full, firm, mouthfilling wine. Always dry. Variable, perhaps tiring by the mid-1970s. *Last noted at Wolf's La Mission/Laville tasting in Wiesbaden, June 1990. At best* ★★★; and **Ygrec** spicy, fragrant, elegant and ageing gracefully. *1986* ★★★★

# 1963

Abysmal. The first of three poor vintages. Hardly the fault of the unhappy proprietors. Dreadful weather conditions from start to finish.

**Ch Yquem** Picking in terrible conditions between 4 October and 20 November. This should never have been put on the market. An aberration or economic necessity on the part of the Marquis de Lur Saluces (his nephew, Comte Alexandre's first vintage was the 1967). First tasted in 1969: an unhealthy brown-tinged amber; prematurely aged with oily nose and taste. Trying to dig itself out of the trench in the early and mid-1970s: flat, short. Some was certainly sold into the British trade and I well recall the Savoy Hotel unloading their stock at Christie's. Two bottles tasted at Rodenstock's marathon. One labelled 'bottled 1972'. Quite different in colour and taste: one palish yellow, lightish style, faded. The other deeper, more orange; nose of dried-out old apples yet sweet and quite powerful. Not bad in fact. *Last tasted in Munich, Sept 1998. Avoid.*

# 1964

A promising year with a hot summer and ripe grapes; the early pickers (i.e. the dry whites and the reds) benefited but torrential rain ruined the Sauternes harvest.

**Ch d'Yquem** Not made. Perhaps, this is why the old Marquis was obliged to sell his '63.

**Ch Climens** First tasted in 1968: 'surprisingly good for its age'. By the mid-1970s I was damning it with faint praises. Most recently: weak rim; nose better than expected, but dried-out and caramelly, with a hot finish. *The oldest and weakest (alcohol 13.3%) of 30 vintages tasted with Bérénice Lurton at the château, Oct 2001* ★

**Ch Sigalas-Rabaud** Orange-gold; caramelised; not bad. *Dec 1992* ★

OLDER NOTES, NONE WARRANTING MORE THAN I STAR **Ch Guiraud** *1982* ★; **Ch Lafaurie-Peyraguey** Jaundice yellow but not bad nose and taste *1978* ★; and **Ch La Tour-Blanche** A curious wine, rich though acidic. *1970* ★

# 1965

The third disastrous vintage in a row due to appalling weather conditions: heavy rains and rot-inducing humidity. Moreover no-one wanted sweet wines. The château owners in despair.

**Ch d'Yquem** Picked with great difficulty 22 September – 30 October. Lebègue's showed a cask sample in 1967. Not bad in fact. However two bottles decanted in 1988 had a pale, pure yellow-gold colour, one with an oily, petrolly nose that I didn't bother to taste, the other faded, odd, dried-out. A decade later: deeper amber; apricots – much better nose than expected. Touch of sweetness, singed, toffee-like taste. Dry finish. Oh dear! *Last tasted in Munich, Sept 1998.*

**Ch Climens** Not marketed.

ONE OTHER NOTE **Ch Suduiraut** surprisingly rich. Good character thanks to highly selective (expensive and uneconomical) grape-picking and an experienced *maître de chai* – the term 'winemaker' was not used in those days! *1978* ★★

# 1966 ★★★

A return to better times, vintage-wise, but still a difficult Sauternes market. An unusually cool dry summer with no real warmth until September, resulting in wines with lean, firm and sinewy character.

**Ch d'Yquem** Picking 15 September – 9 November. A dozen notes, beginning with a cask sample in October 1967: showing well, rich, beautifully balanced. For me its prime feature, 'balance', appeared in my notes in 1972 but subsequent comments somewhat variable. The problem with Sauternes is that it is so often served with killingly rich desserts. In the mid-1970s I noted some sharpness (acidity) yet one 'lacking zest and finesse'. But good notes through the 1980s, a slight but noticeable deepening of colour, lovely classic honeyed 'barley sugar' bouquet, quite assertive, somehow managing to be plump as well as lean. More recently, overpowering and caramelly after tasting a string of Ch Lafaurie-Peyragueys (1994), distinctly overtaken by the 1967 at Rodenstock's Yquem tasting (1998) and losing some of its initial sweetness. Most recently, noting its surprisingly deep orange-amber colour; caramelised barley sugar bouquet; rich flavour. *Perfect with the terrine of foie gras at Hal Lewis' 'Mr Gourmet' Investiture dinner at the Peabody Hotel, Memphis, Sept 1999* ★★★★

**Ch Climens** Unimpressive in its youth but better as it developed, its bright yellow noticeable. Flavoury, touch of bitterness (in 1982). Most recently, an odd half bottle found in the cellar: now a deep orange; heavily caramelised nose and taste. Sweet. Hefty. *Last tasted at the château, Oct 2001* ★★

**Ch Sigalas-Rabaud** Startlingly bright yellow and surprisingly dry. Good acidity. *Noted at the Sigalas-Rabaud pre-sale tasting at Christie's, March 1997* ★★

OTHER '66S LAST TASTED IN THE 1980S **Ch Bastor-Lamontagne** *Jan 1987* ★★; **Ch Guiraud** *June 1982* ★★★; **Ch Lafaurie-Peyraguey** *May 1983* ★★★ *(just);* and **Ch Suduiraut** *July 1985* ★★★★

DRY WHITES Rather better conditions for the dry whites. Some firm dry Graves, but of little interest now.

**Ch Laville Haut-Brion** Just 1500 cases bottled eight to nine months after the vintage. Showing well at five years of age, an archetypal Laville. A not unusual period of puberty in the late 1970s, well-mannered but a bit four-square. At the age of nearly 25 the wine seemed to me as perfect as it was ever likely to get. *Last tasted June 1990* ★★★★

**Ygrec** One of the best vintages in a range tasted at Ch d'Yquem in 1986 and subsequently confirmed: a fragrant, honeyed nose, not unlike the sweet *grand vin*, dry enough, shapely, good length. *Last tasted Sept 1990* ★★★

# 1967 ★★★★★

A superlative vintage, the best since 1959. The crucial flowering period was late, which always leads to a late harvest. That and a wet September made life difficult for grapes destined to make dry white and red Bordeaux but sunny conditions at the end of September, together with beneficial botrytis, were doubly favourable in Sauternes resulting in fine, stylish wines, the best of which are still superb.

**Ch d'Yquem** Picking 26 September – 25 October. This was Comte Alexandre de Lur Saluces' first major vintage and one of which, understandably, he is inordinately proud.

Like a fine mature first growth Médoc or a classic Montrachet, its bouquet opens up and blossoms in the glass. When it is first poured: honey; after ten minutes, pineapple; after 30 minutes, an almost indescribable scent, 'ambrosial' always come to mind. After an hour, sublime. I am of course privileged but I hope not spoiled. I do not take a wine like this for granted. On each of the almost 50 occasions I have tasted the '67 Yquem I have relished its qualities, though there have been some very noticeable variations, of colour and more particularly of taste, which I put down either to condition (storage) or more often the food context.

I first tasted the '67 at the château in the spring of 1973, Alexandre de Lur Saluces opining that it was 'one of the best Yquems this century'. Glorious, I thought, but early days. Initially its colour was a medium pale gold, deeper than the '66, but from the start with a fascinating nose. Many notes around ten years of age: 'magnificent', 'mint and muscat', 'lanolin' (the Sémillon element), 'honeyed botrytis' of course. *Botrytis cinerea* or noble rot always adds several dimensions to the bouquet and flavour. In the late 1970s the '67 was a more buttery gold. Always sweet, of course. I noted in 1981: 'seems now fully on its plateau of perfection', well knit, harmonious, perfect balance and the essential counter-balancing acidity.

Perfection with *feuilleté au foie de canard frais et truffe* at the dinner at the Dolder Grand in 1983 to launch, in Switzerland, my first *Great Vintage Wine Book*. And a year later Prinz Metternich and Comte Alexandre jointly hosted at Schloss Johannisberg an unprecedented dual vertical tasting, opening with 1967 Ch d'Yquem and Schloss Johannisberg's Trockenbeerenauslese of the same vintage. Each was perfect in its own way, Yquem having, in Walter Eigensatz's words, the colour of burnished gold; fuller and heavier on the nose which, however, unravelled itself gloriously, perfection after 90 minutes in the glass. Continuing through the 1980s, deepening in colour, amber, old gold; orange blossom and ripe peaches noted several times; rich, ripe, great length, superb aftertaste.

More recently, the oldest and by far the most concentrated and impressive at an Yquem vertical in Aspen (1994), '5 star' (1995), a fragrant, 'dancing', lime blossom bouquet; perfect weight and finesse at Rodenstock's Yquem marathon and gracing a grand dinner at Ch Haut-Brion (both in 1998); the best wine at a strange tasting in Paris and, most recently, a magnum at Len Evans' 70th birthday 'Single-Bottle Club' dinner in the Hunter Valley, showing a bit of age, caramelly and crusty like our host (actually magnificent). *Last noted Sept 2000* ★★★★★

**Ch Climens** Alcohol 14.1%, 84g/l residual sugar. Typically rich and positive in its youth. Most recently: medium-deep

yellow gold, lime rim; strangely unknit nose, slightly minty, creamy, touch of resin, then opened up, fragrant barley sugar. Fairly sweet, very distinctive, spicy, dry finish. Charming but not great. *Tasted at the château, Oct 2001* ★★★

**Ch Gilette 'Crème de Tête'** Despite its ancient origins, the Médeville family having owned the château since the 18th century, it has been described by Stephen Brook as 'the most bizarre Sauternes of them all'. Why? Only produced in outstanding years, the wine is aged for up to 25 years in large tanks, not wood. I have one note: buttercup yellow; minty nose; very assertive. Hard end. *Tasted with pear and hazelnuts, Oct 1990* ★★

**Ch Guiraud** Many notes, consistent, good not great, from a rich start in 1974, ranging, as it matured, from yellow gold, through amber to old gold. Showing well throughout the 1980s, its bouquet honeyed botrytis, with whiff of spearmint; sweet, touch of caramel, good long flavour and finish. 'Another 20 years life' noted in 1984. Most recently, colour of brass, with a slight tartrate deposit; 'old gold' nose and flavour. Drying out a bit but rich with very good acidity. Truthfully, past its best. *Last noted lunching with the David Carters in Gloucestershire, May 2001* ★★★★

**Ch Sigalas-Rabaud** Three notes. Nose of passion fruit and pineapple; excellent flavour, balance and finish (1981). Very good in 1992. More recently the best of nine vintages (1955 to 1984): very fragrant, perfection; medium-sweet, good length, excellent acidity. *Last noted at a pre-sale tasting, March 1997* ★★★★

**Ch Suduiraut** One of my favourite Sauternes, making consistently good wines under the aegis of Mme Frouin and family. The 1967 said to be better than Ch d'Yquem, but I have had them both together and the latter has the edge, just. Nearly 20 notes: good colour, excellent nose flavour and balance throughout the 1970s. In the 1980s they include 'celestial marmalade' (oh dear), minty barley sugar, creamy apricot, crème caramel – well, perfect honeyed botrytis; and on the palate, consistently sweet, rich, powerful yet not remotely too heavy or cloying.

More recently, a bottle I decanted because it had a slight sediment, but it was worth doing so if only for the fabulous colour in the decanter. Beginning to lose some of its pristine sweetness but a beautiful wine. The same month a glowing warm gold; bouquet that blossomed in the glass; very fragrant but losing flesh. Virtually perfect (all in 1996). *Last noted at a Saintsbury Club dinner – glorious still, at least when sipped before the 'Baked Figs with Mascarpone Ice-Cream', London, March 1997* ★★★★★

**Ch La Tour-Blanche** Two, both, coincidentally, bottled by Dolamore's: pure gold; light, waxy, oyster shells (I think) nose; ready now (1986). Fairly sweet and rich, good tangy flavour. *A rare event in the annals of the Bordeaux Club. Jack Plumb invited the ladies. Dinner at Christ's College, Cambridge, Jan 1994* ★★★

MANY OTHER '67S TASTED over the years but none recently. **Ch Coutet** I have many notes. Perfect with strawberries and cream. *Last tasted 1983* ★★★; **Ch de Fargues** a Lur Saluces property. First seduced by the '67 at the Asher Storey sale in 1974, and consumed with the greatest pleasure several times in the later 1970s: golden; ripening beautifully; lovely flavour and balance. Drying out a little but still worth seeking out. *Last tasted 1985* ★★★★; **Ch Lafaurie-Peyraguey** Lovely in the mid- to late 1970s, thanks to perfect botrytis ★★★★; and **Ch Rieussec** a fine classic flavour, rich and long. *Last tasted 1984* ★★★★

**DRY WHITES** Not a bad vintage and happily a few survive.
**Dom de Chevalier** Olivier Bernard loves fooling his guests with blind tasting vintages ending with the same figure – on this occasion the figure 7 His '67 *blanc* had a touch of astringency but was very drinkable. *Sept 1998* ★★ (However – unsurprisingly – the '27 Warre eclipsed the lot.)
**Ch La Louvière** A somewhat under-appreciated Graves and often very good in old and 'off' vintages as was this. *Served in magnums at the Fête de la Fleur, Bordeaux, June 1991* ★★★

# 1968

The less said about this year the better. Cold, sunless, unripe grapes.
**Ch d'Yquem** You can't say they don't try. It must have been difficult to find any suitable grapes and it was still in cask in April 1973. Not surprisingly they were reluctant to let me taste the wine – even out of curiosity: it was a deep amber with watery rim; sweet though, even a touch of richness but high acidity and bitterness. 20 years later: mahogany; harsh, medical, caramelly nose; dry, with a taste that reminded me of singed bracken. Most recently: a sort of fishy, caramel taste, probably the worst wine at Rodenstock's Yquem marathon in Munich. *Last tasted Sept 1998.*

# 1969 ★

Wet spring, poor flowering – in short, dismal. Growers in Sauternes were saved by the Indian summer.

**Ch d'Yquem** I first tasted this in cask in April 1983. Rather pale, crisp, fairly marked acidity. Five years later, lanoliny, yet with lemon-like acidity. Later, I found it had an assertive nose and, most recently, it was still palish and weak-rimmed; but with a far more attractive bouquet and taste then I expected. Sweetish, light style, acidity propping it up. *Last tasted Sept 1998* ★★ *(just).*
**Ch Climens** Harvested 10 October–5 November. Hail in July reduced the crop, yield of only 5hl/ha and 19,500 bottles produced. Alcohol 14%, residual sugar 76g/l. Climens was 'making the best of a bad job' with hints of class in 1973. Grassy, lightish in 1976, piquant but flavoury in 1984. At 32 years of age, amber-gold, the deepest of all the Climens vintages tasted from 1964 to 1999; sweet, rich, caramelly nose and taste; medium-sweet, crisp fruit, good acidity. *Last tasted at the château, Oct 2001* ★★

**OTHER, OLDER NOTES Ch Coutet** light, not bad. *1975* ★; **Ch Doisy-Védrines** Berry Bros should not have bottled this; **Ch Guiraud** a touch of harmony. *1984* ★★; **Ch Lafaurie-Peyraguey** golden amber; almond paste nose and taste. Succumbed to *mousseline of almonds* but recovered slightly afterwards. *1986* ★; **Ch Rieussec** five notes from 1976. Initial touch of bitterness but a decade later fragrant and lovely. Pale in colour for Rieussec; gloriously rich nose but a bit over the top. A good '69. *Last tasted pre-sale in 1986* ★★★; **Ch Sigalas-Rabaud** not bad ★★; and **Ch Suduiraut** like Ch Climens and Avis 'we try harder'. Good colour, fairly sweet, taste of toffee apples. *1978* and, in Palm Beach, *1988* ★★

# 1970–1989

Two totally contrasting decades, the 1970s starting reasonably well; then came the oil price hike, instant recession and a complete collapse of the Bordeaux market which affected the speculative reds more than the whites. Prices for Sauternes still remained uneconomically low. Interestingly, as I hope my notes will indicate, each of the pairs of good Sauternes vintages, 1970–71 and 1975–76, could not have been more different. The next decade was more successful for reds than sweet whites, both in quality and market value, though the '83 Sauternes were, and still are, excellent. The end of the 1980s was blessed with the first two of an outstanding trio of vintages. In the mid-1980s there was also a development of considerable advantage to those Sauternes châteaux that could afford it: the process of *cryoextraction* or freeze concentration. In a less good vintage, crop savings can be made by chilling the grapes for 20 hours before pressing. This process reduces the water content. Introduced in 1985, it was first used at Ch d'Yquem in 1987.

It was very noticeable in the 1980s that the making of dry whites improved enormously: much of the credit going to Professor Denis Dubourdieu of Bordeaux University. However, I believe that the pendulum began to swing too far, from the drab, heavy-handed Graves of old to the fresh, lean, fruity and acidic. In my view Sauvignon Blanc and new oak are not compatible bedfellows: too much of either one is superficially attractive but specious. Balance is all.

## Sauternes Vintages at a Glance
**Outstanding ★★★★★**
1971, 1975, 1983, 1989
**Very Good ★★★★**
1976, 1985 (v), 1986, 1988
**Good ★★★**
1970, 1979, 1982

## 1970 ★★★

A turn for the better but ripe grapes more generous in alcohol than acidity. In Sauternes an Indian summer increased the sugar content of the grapes but inhibited the development of botrytis. In my opinion this is an overrated vintage producing some stodgy, four-square wines lacking the botrytis richness and zest of the '71s.

**Ch d'Yquem** A cask sample tasted in April 1973: pale, lemon-tinged, though rich, a touch of bitterness in the finish. However it rounded out in the mid- to late 1970s with a ripe lanolin-like nose, richness and balance. It deepened in colour in the 1980s, but despite its overall harmony it lacked botrytis. In 1990 I first used the expression 'four-square', 'very good though uninspired'. A magnum in 1996 assertive but drying out at the end. A similar note in Miami a year later. Most recently, amber-gold, still fairly sweet, hefty, alcoholic, touch of caramel. *Last noted in Munich, Sept 1998 ★★★ Drink soon.*
**Ch Climens** Alcohol 14%, residual sugar 79g/l. Several notes between 1970 and 1985: medium-sweet, no *pourriture*. Now medium-deep yellow; minty, slightly varnishy, unknit nose that deteriorated slightly in the glass; some sweetness, better flavour than nose, somewhat stodgy, 'four-square' though with good acidity. From its youth, completely upstaged by the '71. *Last tasted at the château, Oct 2001 ★★*
**Ch Filhot** Pale, lemon-tinged with a lovely though 'green' fragrance when first tasted in 1974. Then there was a gap of nearly a quarter of a century to the eight-wine Sauternes and Barsac dinner at Brooks's organised by Christie's, hosted by Comte Xavier de Pontac, whose forbears were selling their wine at 'the Pontac's Head' in Pepys' time. Alas, the Filhot, now a fairly deep amber-gold, was dried-out and caramelised. *Last tasted May 1998 ★*

**Ch de Rayne-Vigneau** Six notes in all. In 1981 'nice wine but not up to the former classic standards'; in 1983 'kerosene and peach kernels, unimpressive'; in 1984 unenthusiastic and three very variable bottles tasted on Mud Island, Memphis, Tennessee: all deep in colour, one with a mushroomy nose, the next not bad, the third softer, sweeter, creamier, caramelly. Even making allowances for condition, it was not very good. *Last tasted Sept 1999. At best ★★*
**Ch Rieussec** Not the usual golden colour but with a mild, gentle honeyed nose and fairly rich on the palate in 1975. Good but lacking botrytis, its colour palish, distinct whiff of spearmint, less dense and hefty than some '70s. Nice acidity in the mid- to late 1980s. More recently, having gained more colour, still sweet with a lovely flavour. *Last noted at a Christie's wine department Christmas dinner, Dec 1995. At best ★★★★*
**Ch Suduiraut** If anyone could have made a great '70 in this period it was Suduiraut. Initially surprisingly pale though both bouquet and flavour were attractive in the mid-1970s to early 1980s. 'Four-square' appeared twice including my most recent note: more colour; scented vanilla nose; still fairly sweet but with a hard finish. *Last noted at dinner before and after* Grand Marnier Soufflé glacé, *Nov 1990 ★★★*

OLDER NOTES **Ch Bastor Lamontagne** unexceptional. *1982 ★;* **Ch Coutet** many notes between 1974 and 1978. Pleasant enough but I noted 'the more I see the 1970s the less I like them'. Did the owner lose heart before he sold the château? More recently, still on the pale side with scented bouquet and lovely flavour. 'Delightful now'. *Last tasted at a Commanderie de Bordeaux dinner in 1986 ★★;* **Ch Guiraud** five notes in the mid- to late 1970s, none since. Initially I thought it good but by no means a heavyweight; later considering it too pale; no great development on the nose, touch of peach kernels on the palate. Overall disappointing. *Last noted 1979 ★;* and **Ch Lafaurie-Peyraguey** six notes, all in the mid-1970s, none since. Seemed at best in 1975. Pale yellow, Sémillon uppermost, lacking flesh, not very sweet. *Last noted 1977 ★★*

OTHER OLDER NOTES **Ch Brousset** hollow. *1976;* **Ch Doisy-Védrines** attractive. *1978 ★★;* **Ch Roumieu-Lacoste** fat, creamy, powerful. *1983 ★★★;* **Ch Sigalas-Rabaud** *1976 ★★;* **Ch La Tour-Blanche** attractive not classic. *1977 ★★*

**DRY WHITES** A substantial year for the top-quality Graves. **Dom de Chevalier** lovely flavour, texture, balance. *Last noted 1988* ★★★★; **Ch Haut-Brion** powerful, steely, long life though only tasted in its infancy. *1973*; **Ch Laville Haut-Brion** fragrant, intense, mouthfilling. *1986* ★★★★

## 1971 ★★★★★

An excellent Sauternes vintage thanks to a pleasant, sunny summer, ideal ripening conditions and botrytis.
**Ch d'Yquem** The best vintage between 1967 and 1975. Good throughout the 1980s, the lovely, floral, honeyed botrytis bouquet a prime feature, also its power and richness, length and acidity. A fraction below my expectations at the Munich marathon in 1998, including a corky bottle, but this might have been in the context of so many great Yquem vintages. Most recently, coping well with *'Blue cheese crème brûlée'*(!): richly coloured; barley sugar and caramel nose; sweet and rich, a glorious powerhouse of a wine with perfect counter-balancing acidity. Time in hand. *Last tasted at the 'Mr Gourmet' dinner in Memphis, Sept 1999* ★★★★★
**Ch Climens** Ambrosial. In the class of '29 and '49. Grapes with perfect *pourriture noble* were harvested in four *tries* between 8 October and 3 November. *Rendement* 12hl/ha, long – six weeks – fermentation *en barrique*, approximately 33,000 bottles of the *1er vin*, alcohol 13.9%, residual sugar 99.5g/l.
    I often think of Climens in the same context as Ch Cheval Blanc: each has a long, consistent, invariably good reputation, wines with style, finesse and of the highest quality, amply demonstrated by this wine. I have nine notes spread mainly through the 1980s, 'every one a winner' as the fairground barker would say! A lovely, lively, waxy yellow shot with gold; nose and palate in perfect harmony. Although fairly assertive, still an ideal weight. As it evolved, the colour seemed to become even more beautiful, its palate even more extended. Sheer perfection in 1988. Next in 1995, with *terrine de foie gras* in the country kitchen of the somewhat eccentric owner of one of the finest cellars in France, a pure yellow gold; faultless, seamless bouquet, 'cream of fruit'; drying out a little yet rich, elegant, creamy texture. Most recently: now a rich gold with green rim and orange and lime highlights; as soon as poured, an amazingly rich, almost too rich, buttery bouquet, lanolin, fudge (soft caramel), great depth; very sweet, full-body and glorious flavour, richness and depth. *Last tasted at the château, Oct 2001* ★★★★★ *Will continue to enchant for another quarter century.*
**Ch Coutet, Cuvée Madame** The top *cuvée* marketed only in great years. Unquestionably good: golden colour; a bouquet of sweet ripe peaches that leaps out of the glass; sweeter than the standard blend, wonderful style and life, great length, superb aftertaste. Totally blissful magnum with further evolution in store. *March 1992* ★★★★★
**Ch de Fargues** Comte Alexandre Lur Saluces' '71 showed at its superb best at a tasting I conducted for the Bär Bank in Zurich: yellow-gold, orange highlights; risking yawns I must repeat the well worn honey, *crème brûlée* description; sweet of course, excellent flavour, body and acidity. Well-nigh perfect. *April 1998* ★★★★★
**Ch Filhot** I have rarely been impressed by this *2ème cru* Sauternes, owned by a branch of the Lur Saluces family, despite its imposing château and the knowledge that Jefferson, who visited Bordeaux in 1787, ranked it number two after Ch d'Yquem. Yet, despite its run-down state in the early 1970s, the

1971 rose to the occasion, showing well, unusually fleshy. *Dining at Ch Latour, June 1999* ★★★★
**Ch Sigalas-Rabaud** Bright buttercup yellow; glorious, fragrant bouquet but less sweet than expected. Good length. *Noted at a pre-sale tasting, March 1997* ★★★

**SOME OTHER SAUTERNES LAST TASTED IN THE 1980S** and worth looking out for: **Ch Coutet** (normal, not Cuvée Madame) ten consistently good notes from the mid-1970s to mid-1980s: stylish, well-balanced. *Last tasted 1986* ★★★★; **Ch Rieussec** not a heavyweight, stylish, attractive. Three good notes. *Last tasted in 1984* ★★★★; and **Ch Suduiraut** two notes. Less sweet and not as great as I expected. *Last noted 1980* ★★

**OTHER OLDER NOTES Ch Doisy-Daëne** too pale, too grassy; some richness and fat but not serious. *1979* ★★; **Ch Lafaurie-Peyraguey** at five years of age curious autumnal nose, leaves and nuts; not very impressive. A palish, new, light style, medium-sweet, not unattractive but not good enough. *1978* ★; and **Ch Sigalas-Rabaud** fresh mint leaf and honey; soft, fleshy, nice acidity. *1979* ★★★

**DRY WHITES** A highly successful year, particularly for the top Graves which, if kept well, can still be superb, allowing for bottle age which, of course, changes the character of the wine. **Ch Laville Haut-Brion** impressive in 1978 and 1979. A very interesting wine. As an experiment Henri Woltner left bunches on the vine far longer than usual, indeed as long as possible. As a result the must had a very high sugar content which converted into 13.5% alcohol. The resulting wine had a startling brilliant amber colour; a bouquet like a ripe Barsac, full, rich, honeyed; ripeness giving the wine a touch of sweetness, superb length and aftertaste. *Last tasted June 1990* ★★★★★; **Dom de Chevalier** dry. Perfectly balanced. *1985* ★★★★; and **Ygrec** Rich, firm yet elegant. *1986* ★★★★

## 1972

Poor year. Unsuitable weather conditions. Many wines, including Yquem declassified. Two châteaux who made the effort are noted below. All made a loss, for no-one wanted the wines when they came on the market.
**Ch Climens** Late harvest, two to three *tries* between 8 November and 5 December. Alcohol 14%, residual sugar 76g/l. Ten notes, nine in the 1980s. Heavily sulphured nose though not bad. Spoilt for me by my much disliked pasty peach kernel taste. Most recently, showing its age though still sweet and better than expected. *Last tasted at the château, Oct 2001* ★ *Drink up or avoid.*
**Ch Suduiraut** Six notes, first in 1978, no length, twist of acidity. Seemed to get its second breath through the 1980s though I did note Gripfix on the nose. The best of the '72s with moderately sweet, barley sugar flavour. Hot acid finish. *Last tasted 1989* ★★

## 1973 ★★

An indifferent growing season and Bordeaux was still in a depressed state. Some modestly passable wines made. I have tasted few recently and in any case most of them should have been consumed by the mid-1980s.
**Ch d'Yquem** Just three notes. At 11 years of age, a lovely golden colour; surprisingly rich nose and flavour. Elegant and

with a surprisingly good length. Four years later the bouquet opened up and reminded me of strawberries. Very flavoury. Deft touch. Most recently, high-toned fragrance; sweet, opened up in the middle but with a slightly raw unusual finish. *Last tasted in Munich, Sept 1998* ★★★ *(just).*

**Ch Climens** Harvested in three *tries* between 15 October and 10 November in very good weather. There was very little botrytis but *beaucoup de rôti*, resulting in high alcoholic content (14%) and residual sugar 94g/l. I first tasted it in 1997, when I noted it as being quite good but unexciting. Then, a series of notes straddling the decade of the 1980s. The wine opened up, somehow enriching itself. It became, at 12 years of age, somewhat sweeter and fuller-bodied than expected. Far from drying out it seemed to taste sweeter though towards the end of the 1980s, despite its fragrance, it seemed not wholly knit. By 1991, a waxy yellow; buttery, almost oily nose; rich, Caramac (toffee fudge) flavour and flesh. Most recently: a light, quite good, creamy fragrance; still sweet, rich, assertive, with caramel aftertaste. Probably at its best towards the end of the 1980s. *Last tasted with Bérénice Lurton at the château, Oct 2001* ★★★ *Drink soon.*

A SELECTION OF OTHER WINES, noted mainly in the 1980s: **Ch Caillou** sweet, lean, flavoury. *1982* ★★; **Ch Coutet** ripe Sémillon noted, assertive flavour and acidity. *1981* ★★; **Ch Doisy-Dubroca** one can not expect much from a *2ème cru classé* Barsac in a year like this. Assertive though, with good acidity. *1981* ★★; **Ch Filhot** the same applies. Lacking fat but not without charm. Perfect with *foie gras. 1981 and 1983* ★★; **Ch Nairac** good but no finesse. *1979 and 1982* ★★; and **Ch de Rayne-Vigneau** three notes. Variable bottles. Amber-gold. Sweet, some fat. Quite good. Not up to its usual standard. *1981* ★★

DRY WHITES Some quite good Graves made which were at their best around 1977. Too late now.

## 1974 ★ at best

Cold damp and dismal. A washout everywhere except for one or two passable Barsacs. I have tasted none recently and they are not worth seeking out. Ch d'Yquem not made.

**Ch Climens** Uneven harvest with four *tries* carried out between 12 October and 18 November. Initially there was much botrytis but there were problems with rain. Alcohol 14%, low sugar, 62g/l. Not tasted in its early days but quite good 14 years later. Waxy Sémillon nose, honey sweet plus acidity; mouthfilling and assertive, respectable balance, refreshing acidity. Most recently: palish, hefty, clumsy, low-keyed nose; drying out a little but better than expected. *Last tasted at the château, Oct 2001* ★ *Drink up.*

**Ch Coutet** Grassy, hefty; clumsy, slightly caramelised. Fishy finish. *Last tasted in 1982.*

## 1975 ★★★★★

An outstanding vintage in Sauternes, among the finest wines of the decade. Spring frosts, hot dry summer, some welcome rain in September, followed by good harvest conditions including excellent botrytis and sustaining acidity.

**Ch d'Yquem** Fourteen notes. Unquestionably a lovely wine. First tasted dining at Ch Margaux in 1981 when its youthful acidity was very noticeable. Progressing from a pale golden colour in the early 1980s to a richer gold, its bouquet fragrant but immature, slightly raw, becoming more floral, peachy, the common denominator being its sweetness, flesh, life and length. Notable bottles with illegal ortolan – *même sous la serviette, c'est interdit* – at Frans de Cock's fabulous wine weekend in Paris. With its sheer deliciousness showing up the 1970 at the Bacchus Society Installation Dinner in Coral Gables, and on a par with the 1959 but a different style at the Munich tasting. Most recently, sheer perfection: creamy, honeyed, orange blossom bouquet of impenetrable depth; rich, perfect weight, flavour, balance and length, with another 20 years to go. *Last tasted at the Josey pre-sale tasting in New York, Nov 2000* ★★★★★

**Ch Climens** Extremely good, almost up to the '71 in quality, combining power with finesse. Harvested between 27 September and 22 October, four *tries*, excellent botrytis, small crop (7.2hl/ha), high quality. Very high alcoholic content (14.6%) and residual sugar (96g/l), 90% of crop made into the *1er vin* and some 25,000 bottles produced. Eight good notes: first in 1982. Most recently: medium-gold; floral, honeyed bouquet, wonderful richness and depth revealing extra dimensions; sweet, full-bodied, wonderful concentration and length. *Last tasted at the château, Oct 2001* ★★★★★ *Another 20 years in hand.*

**Ch Coutet** Just three notes. Hefty, a bit grassy nosed, very rich and tangy soon after bottling. The most memorable at a Christie's boardroom lunch with the late H. M. Queen Elizabeth the Queen Mother in 1982. Most recently, now golden in colour; the Sémillon honey and spice, Sauvignon contributing the whistle-clean acidity. Very rich, assertive yet not fat and with gooseberry-like acidic finish. *Last tasted at a Gidleigh Park wine dinner in Devon, Feb 1994* ★★★★

**Ch Guiraud** Curious nose, piquant on the palate in 1978. Fragrant but unknit with Sauvignon 'cats' pee' aroma uppermost, attractive though and flavoury (1982). Most recently, considerably deepened in colour, orange gold, settling down to a honeyed bottle age and botrytis bouquet; very agreeable flavour. *Last noted at a Christie's wine department Christmas dinner, Dec 1999* ★★★

**Ch Lafaurie-Peyraguey** Cloudy and unrecognisable cask sample, but lovely acidity noted (in April 1976). Two years later no great development, nose of 'lightly stewed grass', rather dull. By 1991 some improvement. Most recently: lovely colour; cream of *crème brûlée* bouquet; sweet, rich, hefty, with hot alcoholic and acidic finish. Attractive though. *Last noted at a Decanter Wine Encounter masterclass, London, Nov 1998* ★★★

**Ch de Malle** Alas not as beautiful as the château itself or as elegant as the Comtesse de Bournazel. Too pale, too green; rich but almond flavour (1982). Most recently, one bottle

---

### Tries

*A trie is a sortie into the vineyard to select fully ripe individual bunches or individual botrytised grapes. At Ch d'Yquem, for example, in a modest vintage such as 1973, there might be anything up to a dozen forays through the vineyard to collect effectively a few bottles' worth of grapes. Very experienced picking teams are needed, as in many years botrytis affects separate parts of the vineyard differently; conditions will even vary from vine to vine. One vine can have a lower alcohol potential than another. Similar sweeps apply in Germany, Alsace and the Loire, where botrytised grapes are selected for their sweet wines.*

corked, the other almost, but not very good, with vanilla on nose and the same kernelly finish. *Last tasted at Odette Ryan's 30th anniversary dinner at Christie's, Dec 2000* ★

**Ch Rieussec** Showing promise at three years of age though with a hot dry immature finish and raisiny aftertaste. Good evolution in early 1980s. The odd man out because of its deep highly distinctive orange-tinged amber, hefty Beerenauslese-like nose and concentration. 'Magnificent in its way', I wrote in September 1982. Evolving well, having to cope with *Charlotte au chocolat* and raspberry soufflé en route. Positively luscious in the early 1990s, full, fat with silky acidity. More recently, singed, caramelised bouquet; intensely rich yet drying out a little. A hefty, almost Bual madeira-like nose and taste. Idiosyncratic. *Last noted at Mentzendorf's tasting, Feb 1996* ★★★★

**Ch Sigalas-Rabaud** At three years of age, Sauvignon seemed dominant, length lacking. Very odd, still raw and immature with Sauvignon aftertaste at the *Decanter* tastings in 1975 and in 1982. Most recently, fresh, forthcoming, with a touch of meat, lemon curd, peaches and 'the smell of a new tennis ball' (really!). Good flavour though lacking intensity and with a hot, hard, dry finish. *A brief encounter at* Decanter's *Wine Encounter, Nov 1998* ★★

**Ch Suduiraut** A superb wine from start to whenever it will finish. The start, for me, tasting the wine at the château in April 1978. Good colour, a botrytis nose, flavour and acidity. A touch of bitterness on the finish. Within four years a deep gold, rich, classic bouquet and flavour. (Unmistakable. Correctly identified at the *Decanter* blind tasting.) Two equally admiring notes in 1988: harmonious, fully evolved, fragrant, peach and blossom; very sweet, yet with dry finish, great length, power and vivacity. *Last noted at a pre-sale tasting in New York, Sept 1997* ★★★★★

BRIEF NOTES ON THE VERY MANY LAST TASTED IN THE 1980s **Ch d'Arche** nothing special. 1978, 1982 ★; **Ch Doisy-Védrines** positive, stylish. 1978, 1982, *1986* ★★★★; **Ch de Fargues** pure gold; very flavoury, good spiky acidity. *1983* ★★★★; **Ch Filhot** too pale; grassy style 1978, *1982* ★★; **Ch Guiteronde** pale, too much sulphur; fat, rich. 1982–1983 ★★; **Clos Haut-Peyraguey** buttercup yellow; fairly powerful, hard finish. 'Needs time'. *1982* ★★★; **Ch Liot** agreeable and good value. 1979, 1980, 1981 and *1982* ★★★; **Ch Nairac** like a Graves with bottle age. Somewhat artificial flavour. *1982*; **Ch Rabaud-Promis** deep yellow; mint, raisins, 'syrup of figs'; very sweet, rich, attractive, headache-inducing. *1987* ★★★; **Ch de Rayne-Vigneau** not up to former standards, fulsome, plausible, soft, pleasing. 1981–*1982* ★★; **Ch Romer du Hayot** pale, herbaceous; fuller and more bitter than expected. 1982–1983 ★★★; **Ch Suau** unimpressive. 1981, 1982 and *1983*; and **Ch La Tour-Blanche** several notes, light style, generally not impressed. 1976 in cask, 1982–83 and *1987* ★

DRY WHITES Some excellent wines, dry with some austerity, but only the best are still worth seeking out.
**Ch Haut-Brion** Pale, vanilla, Chardonnay-like nose; dry, firm, unready in early 1980s. Most recently, deepening in colour; very distinctive iron-earthy nose and taste clearly related to the red *grand vin*. Dry, fairly full-bodied, stern. When I was a guest lecturer on the *Seabourn Spirit* the sommelier brought me this wine following a passenger's complaint. It was sound, but I could see why the 'punter' had not liked it. Not the easiest of wines, and too old. *Last noted in the South China Seas, Jan 1998. A matter of taste.*

# 1976 ★★★★

These were lovely wines from the word go but, in the final analysis, only the best 1976s will stay the pace. A year of excessive heat and drought; thoroughly ripe grapes, well nigh perfect in Sauternes.

**Ch d'Yquem** Harvested speedily between 21 September and 13 October because of the swift onset of botrytis. A dozen notes, first tasted at the château in 1983: creamy, rich, fat, intense and fabulous. Good notes throughout the 1980s noted highish acidity – a higher level of volatile acidity than would be acceptable to the Quebec Liquor Board. More tasted and drunk in the 1990s, on three occasions at Saintsbury Club dinners in 1995, 1998 and 2000. (We must have a big stock!) At one dinner, describing it as a bit 'stodgy and four-square', but it might have been the raspberry soufflé. Otherwise nothing but admiration, the wine all the time deepening in colour, and the usual, rather repetitive descriptions of bouquet and flavour throughout, noting in Dec 2000 its sweetness and length though a touch of bottle age (caramel) was observed. Fully developed. Most recently: orange-gold; scent of old apricots and *crème brûlée*; sweet, full, rich, some caramelisation. *Last tasted with Tarte Frangipane aux figues at Hugh Johnson's Bordeaux Club dinner, Dec 2001* ★★★★★ *Though I think it is on the decline.*

**Ch Climens** A hot, dry summer, beautiful grapes, but over four *tries* between 1 and 23 October, and although the grapes changed colour, from golden to almost chocolate, no botrytis appeared. Large crop with 30,000 bottles of the *1er vin*. Fairly high alcohol (14.3%) and very high residual sugar (114g/l). Superb throughout the 1980s, rich and fat for a Barsac. Golden colour, 'legs' or 'tears' like Gothic arches, imbued with every possible fragrance and flavour, rich but crisp. Most recently: low-keyed, very slightly varnishy nose, but with good depth; sweet, crisp, full-bodied, slightly spicy finish, *à point*. *Last tasted at the château, Oct 2001* ★★★★ *At its best now.*

**Ch Coutet** Slightly variable notes, improving with maturity. Attractive but underdeveloped in 1983. Three less good notes between then and 1990: 'too pale', 'not sweet enough', high (volatile) acidity, a feature of the '76s due to the very hot weather at vintage time, touch of peach kernels. Much liked at Bordeaux Club dinners in 1996, 1998 and 2000, its colour more golden, but not deep; herbaceous, grassy, cress-like; lovely flavour and its acidity both propping it up and adding vivacity. Enjoyable, good but by no means great. *Last noted at Childerly Hall, Oct 2000* ★★★ *Drink soon.*

**Ch Doisy-Védrines** Four notes, the first in 1978. Noticeable botrytis. Most recently: good colour; nose a bit unyielding; medium-sweet, soft, barley sugar flavour and aftertaste. Fairly high acidity. *Last tasted July 1992* ★★★

**Ch Guiraud** Always rather deep in colour, an old amber-gold in the mid-1980s, a beefy style, already caramelly. Most recently, the honeyed bottle age bouquet of a good vintage, powerful, its taste reminding me of an Eiswein, alcohol and acidity noted. Not bad but not good enough. *Last tasted Sept 1998* ★★ *Drink up.*

**Ch Lafaurie-Peyraguey** Curiously only one note. I am not a great fan of Lafaurie but I found the '76 astonishing: immensely rich, with a varnishy high-toned nose, toffee-like, fruity but after 30 minutes in the glass reminding me of old apples in a hayloft. Hefty, good length, dry finish. *Tasted at the 'Decanter Encounter' masterclass, at the rather opulent Landmark hotel, Marylebone (London), Nov 1998* ★★★ *Drink soon.*

**Ch Rieussec** Nearly a dozen notes, its characteristic and very recognisable depth and opulence of colour throughout, also its almost exotic bouquet and flavour. Very rich, some caramel, somewhat over the top but most enjoyable. The Tchaikovsky of Sauternes. The most recent note at Sir John Plumb's Bordeaux Club dinner at Christ's College, Cambridge. *Last tasted Jan 1997* ★★★★

**Ch Sigalas-Rabaud** A couple of notes. Lovely mellow bouquet, plump yet Barsac-like in style (1980). Most recently at the *Decanter* tasting totally different to the Ch Lafaurie-Peyraguey, sound, brighter and fresher despite the touch of brown in the gold; grassy grapiness; drying out but refreshing, minty, hard finish. *Last noted at the* Decanter *Wine Encounter masterclass, Nov 1998* ★★ *Drink up.*

**Ch Suduiraut** I well remember tasting this at the château in April 1978. It was extraordinarily delicious, but I also recall Mme Frouin telling me at the time that her 1975 would eventually turn out to be the better wine; indeed, at a Suduiraut tasting in 1983 she said that the '76 was going downhill and again praised the '75. I had always admired Suduiraut (now owned by AXA), its colour, its richness and power combined with zest. *Last noted at the end of my presentation of 1928 clarets in San Juan, Nov 1998* ★★★★

SOME OTHER BARSACS AND SAUTERNES MAINLY TASTED IN THE 1980s **Ch Bastor-Lamontagne** many notes. Agreeable. Good value. 1981 and *1984* ★★★; **Ch Doisy-Daëne** light style, pleasant, nicely made. *1980* ★★★; **Ch de Fargues** matured in old Yquem casks. Honeyed, powerful, high volatile acidity but attractive. *1985* ★★★; **Ch Filhot** an early developer. At Terence Conran's 50th birthday in October 1981 'some plumpness, quite nice' (both wine and my host!). Grassy. Good in its way. *Last tasted 1993* ★; **Ch Liot** light style. Unimpressive. *1982* ★; **Ch Menota** a less well known Barsac. Deeply coloured, incredibly concentrated nose; very sweet, rich, a bit 'four-square'. Will be interesting to see how it has developed: superb or a falling star? *1982* ★★★?; **Ch Nairac** hard, lean, alcoholic, swingeingly dry finish. *1989*; and **Ch Romer du Hayot** pale but plump. A touch grassy. *1983* ★★★

DRY WHITES Some very attractive Graves but, though still drinkable (**Ch Haut-Brion, Ch Laville Haut-Brion** and **Dom de Chevalier**), they are now well past their best.

# 1977

Poor crop, poor wines, the result of an cold summer and the driest September on record.

**Ch d'Yquem** Amid the real rot, after much gleaning, some usable berries must have been picked. On the two occasions I have tasted the wine, first in 1983, 'surprisingly' appears in relation to its colour, and at the Munich marathon 'surprisingly fragrant' and 'surprisingly good'. Overall its initial rawness and hardness translates into quite a bite. Certainly different. *Last tasted Sept 1998* ★ *(just).*

**Ch Climens** As on previous occasions, like Avis, tries harder. Hit by frost, small crop (4hl/ha) harvested in two *tries* between 10 and 24 October. Alcohol 14% and residual sugar 101g/l. A couple of notes in 1987: 'not at all bad'. Most recently, surprisingly sweet (less surprising, had I seen the analysis), rich, caramelly with quite good dry finish. *Last tasted at the château, Oct 2001. At best* ★★ *Drink up.*

**Ch Sigalas-Rabaud** Putting this into a promotional sale did the château no good. At the pre-sale tasting it had a strange smell and taste reminding me of an old stables. *March 1997.*

# 1978 ★★

Cold spring, wet summer and a long sunny autumn that ripened the crop but did not allow *pourriture* to form on the grapes in Sauternes.

**Ch d'Yquem** Frankly, a poor Yquem. Only 15% of the crop, just under 60,000 bottles, sold under the Yquem label. The palest in a line-up at the château in 1983, not bad nose and flavour but lean, acidic. At ten years of age buttercup yellow, curious soapy nose, but raw and short. A further ten years later now orange and not bright; hefty, unknit nose; dryish, caramelly toffee-like taste. Clumsy. *Last tasted Sept 1998.*

**Ch Climens** Once again rising to the occasion. A late harvest, 30 October to 23 November, little botrytis, modest *rendement* (10hl/ha) but substantial production of 40,000 bottles. Alcohol 14.2% and residual sugar 106g/l. Two fairly good notes in the mid-1980s: fragrant, easy, lacking length. In April 2000, dining at Dom de Chevalier in Pessac-Léognan, very yellow, surprisingly good. Even more recently, slight bottle variation: the first harmonious, waxy, touch of meatiness and kernels, the other more creamy. Both still fairly sweet, crisp, with good flavour, the second cleaner. *Last noted at the château, Oct 2001. At best* ★★★ *Drink up.*

**Ch Coutet** As usual paler than Ch Climens. In 1984 a warm crusty smell, well made, a waxy fruitiness, crisp acidity. Unready. Most recently, completely upstaged by a jeroboam of 1921 Ch Mouton-Rothschild. Still pale, grassy, light style. Quite nice. *Last tasted at a great dinner for some very distinguished guests hosted by the Baronne Philippine de Rothschild at Ch Mouton-Rothschild, Sept 1998* ★★

**Ch Rieussec** One note: deep amber – as usual; vanilla, *crème brûlée* nose, sweet, excellent counter-balancing acidity. Attractive, *à point. At the Domaines de Rothschild dinner at Brooks's Club, London in Nov 2000* ★★★★

**Ch Sigalas-Rabaud** Minty; medium-sweet, kernels, raw, pasty. *At a pre-sale tasting, March 1997* ★

**Ch Suduiraut** Sémillon 80%, Sauvignon Blanc 20%. Relatively pale and not an old-style heavyweight. Still immature and a touch of sulphur dioxide in 1983. In 1986 its nose reminded me of asparagus and nectarines: delicious, harmonious, the two *cépages* still distinguishable, yet it seemed at its best. Two years later a less complimentary note. *Last tasted June 1988. At its best* ★★★

DRY WHITES Successful vintage but most wines tiring now.

**Ch Haut-Brion** This wine usually benefits from bottle-ageing and it was certainly better in 1987 than in 1985 – the former a lovely wine with considerable potential. A decade later sound as a bell, impressive but not exciting. Most recently: still fairly pale with just a tinge of straw; dry, assertive, touch of vanilla, very good acidity. Important to serve this wine not too cold, and give it time to breathe. *Last tasted at a BYOB dinner in New York, March 1999* ★★★

**Ch Laville Haut-Brion** Initially pale, fragrant, dry but lean. More recently a lovely, buttery nose; fairly dry but rich, soft, with fragrant aftertaste. This wine should still be excellent. *Last tasted April 1990* ★★★★

**Ch Carbonnieux** Never great, always dependable and best drunk young. Nevertheless at 13 years of age drinking well:

gentle bouquet, honeyed bottle-age and lemon. Dry of course, good acidity. *Last noted dining at the château, April 1991* ★★

**Dom de Chevalier** Easy and attractive in 1982. Somewhat unknit, its nose faded; dry but rich. I noted 'improved on acquaintance' (1986). Most recently, low-keyed but honeyed bottle age on nose; very dry, lean, good length, highish acidity. Well preserved – by sulphur – for a 20-year old. *Dining at the Domaine, April 1998* ★★

**Pavillon Blanc de Ch Margaux** The first vintage after its purchase by Monsieur Mentzelopoulos and I think the best I have ever tasted. Though not tasted recently, my notes are full of praise, both at three and ten years of age. A fascinating nose, in part reminding me of both a ripe Loire Chenin Blanc or of a good Napa Chardonnay; dry, firm, harmonious. Should still be delicious. *Last tasted April 1988* ★★★★

**Ygrec** Sémillon 50%, Sauvignon Blanc 50%, 100% new oak. Bottled March 1981. Six notes, the first a year after bottling when the wine was not ready. Well developed by 1987 but two less appealing notes since. Interesting to see how this wine has evolved. *Last tasted Sept 1990. At best* ★★★

# 1979 ★★★

Better for Sauternes than for dry white Bordeaux because of the late harvest following a cold and showery growing season.

**Ch d'Yquem** Extended picking, the first *trie* 15 September and the last very late, 29 November. Eleven notes, first tasted (a half bottle) in February 1983, yet in September, with Alexandre de Lur Saluces I noted 'bottled 4 months'. Perhaps they bottled the halves first. But it does indicate how long Yquem is matured *en barrique*. After five years, gaining colour; complete, attractive; assertive, good length. By 1990 a touch of barley sugar and caramel. Somewhat outshone at a tasting of ten vintages in Aspen (1984), pale and on the lean side pre-sale (1995), acidity noticeable (magnum 1995), sweet, flavoury (pre-sale again 1997). Most recently: now a pure yellow gold; sweet, creamy bouquet and taste. Nice flesh. Dry acidic finish with none of the peach kernel character I had noticed earlier. *Last tasted in Munich, Sept 1998* ★★★

**Ch Climens** Harvested in very good weather, three *tries* between 15 October and 10 November. Too dry, so little botrytis. Alcohol 14% and residual sugar low, 72g/l. Five notes: 'peach kernels' noted consistently, a taste I do not like though I am told it is correct. Most recently: medium-pale yellow gold; two-part nose, touch of caramel and peach kernels but opened up fragrantly; sweet, caramelly flavour, waxy textured. Herbaceous but not a top Climens. *Last tasted at the château, Oct 2001* ★★ *Drink soon.*

**Ch Coutet** Sémillon 80%, Sauvignon Blanc 15%, Muscadelle 5%. Elegant but not ready at five years of age. Nose still unknit in 1987 but a year later it seemed all-of-a-piece and delicious. A highly polished appearance; fragrant, mouthwatering nose; good length, good acidity, though in the company of Ch d'Yquem and Ch Rabaud-Sigalas, still comparatively pale; fragrant, with a strange vanilla whiff which reminded me of duck-egg custard. Not very sweet, light style but quite a bite. *Last tasted at Rodenstock's 15th Raritäten Weinprobe, Sept 1994* ★★★

**Ch Guiraud** Six notes. Rich, almost chocolatey in 1983. Quite good development. Most recently: positive, classic nose; sweet enough, pleasant flavour and very good aftertaste. *Last noted Jan 1991* ★★★

**Ch Rieussec** Elaborate notes made during a visit to the Quebec Liquor Board's shop in Montreal in 1983. Price

Canadian $19.55, and a good buy. Needed more time though. A rich, powerful wine despite lacking finesse, with short hot finish. *Last tasted Oct 1991* ★★

**Ch Sigalas-Rabaud** The smallest of the *1er cru* Sauternes estates. A couple of notes. At five years of age surprisingly pale; pleasantly forthcoming nose, lanolin and honey; sweet but with lean touch and slightly pasty acidic end. Most recently, showing well at the château's pre-sale tasting. *Last tasted March 1997* ★★★

### OTHER SAUTERNES TASTED IN THE 1980s

**Ch de Fargues** rich, positive. *1983* ★★★; **Ch Filhot** Sémillon 65%, Sauvignon Blanc 33%, Muscadelle 2%. Not my favourite château and often fully deserving its *2ème cru* rating but the '79, really quite nice: surprisingly fragrant, lively, crisp acidity, the Muscadelle giving it just a whiff of grapiness. 1986 and *1987* ★★★; **Ch Lafaurie-Peyraguey** sweet, attractive flavour and flesh. Good length. *1987* ★★★; **Ch de Malle** pale and unexciting in its youth. Whiff of Gripfix on the nose; curiously interesting taste. Not bad. *1983* and *1986* ★★; **Ch Raymond-Lafon** good wine, plump, warm rich finish. *1986–1987* ★★★; **Ch Rayne-Vigneau** grassy, fairly sweet, crisp, very kernelly. *1985* ★★; and **Ch Suduiraut** several notes spanning the 1980s, but none recently. Initially fullish and fat but lacking botrytis, flair and finesse. A rich rather obvious wine. *Last tasted 1988* ★★★

### DRY WHITES Somewhat diluted though flavoury wines.

**Ch Laville Haut-Brion** six notes, none up to the usual high standard. Most recently, pale for its age; distinctive, quite good fruit; soft and, I thought, lacking acidity. *Last noted at a pre-sale tasting in New York, Dec 1997* ★

# 1980 ★

An inauspicious start to one of Bordeaux's best decades. Cold dismal weather early in the year resulted in poor flowering conditions. Then a hot dry August before the weather broke, September being cold and wet. Sauternes was saved by sunny weather from the end of September.

**Ch d'Yquem** Picked late between 20 October and 18 November. Five notes all confirming the below average quality of the wine. Probably at its best in 1991, with intriguing scents, mint, fig, quince, orange blossom; rich, but with hot, loose end acidity. My lowest mark at the Yquem tasting in Aspen (1994) and similarly low mark at Rodenstock's marathon tasting in Munich: a strange minty nose; medium sweet, lean, lip-licking acidity. *Last tasted Sept 1998. Barely* ★

**Ch Climens** Late harvest in mainly fine weather, 27 October – November 13, three *tries* with rain towards the end. Once started, botrytis formed rapidly, 85% of the crop made as the *1er vin*, approximately 25,000 bottles. Alcohol 14.2% and residual sugar 76g/l. Six notes, five in the mid- to late 1980s: bouquet 'a sort of opulence', richer than expected. Most recently: a deep amber-gold; curious nose, strawberry larded with furniture polish and caramel; it appeared far sweeter than its (subsequently noted) analysis, powerful, touch of ginger and pepperiness. *Last noted at the château, Oct 2001* ★ *Long past its modest best.*

**Ch de Fargues** Much better than its famous cousin Ch d'Yquem. Attractive nose and taste. *Feb 1990* ★★

**Ch Liot** Pale and wan. Hard, grassy, unknit nose; sweet, not bad. *At a pre-sale tasting, April 1994.*

OTHER SAUTERNES TASTED IN THE 1980s **Ch Filhot**
grassy, herbaceous, crisp fruit. Quite good but no great life
ahead. *1984* ★★; **Ch Guiraud** a half bottle bought for
cooking. Tasted first, of course. Minty, caramelly, short. Best for
the pot. *1989* ★; **Ch de Rayne-Vigneau** very pale, poor nose,
little to it. *1985*; **Ch Rieussec** I was lucky enough to be in the
right place at the right time, tasting at the château with Eric
de Rothschild and Professor Peynaud shortly after the
Rothschild purchase. But not a good start, vintage-wise.
Curiously I preferred the *2ème* vin to the *crème de tête*, the
former richer and flatter, the latter though rich, raw. *Sept 1984
★★, I wonder?*; and **Ch Suduiraut** only one youthful note.
Usually dependable and the '80 better than expected. Quite
well balanced. *1980* ★★?

DRY WHITES Insubstantial wines and now *passé*.

# 1981 ★★

Hot, dry summer resulted in good grapes and autumn rainfall
and an Indian summer encouraged *pourriture noble*.
**Ch d'Yquem** Harvested 5 October – 13 November. Half a
dozen notes. Certainly a rather untypical Yquem. My notes
include 'odd, scented, petrolly, boiled salmon', 'spicy, curious,
macaroon', later 'pineapple husk' and of course barley sugar.
On the palate, high acidity, hot, spicy, lean, 'strangely scented'.
But, in fact, better than it sounds! 'Different', lean and lacking
length in Aspen. In Munich, old straw gold, weak-rimmed;
full, rich but strange. Most recently, refreshing, better than
expected. *Last noted dining at Ch Rauzan-Ségla, Sept 1998* ★★
**Ch Climens** Harvested 6–20 October, three *tries*, mainly in
lovely weather with a little rain towards the end. Although
quite a big crop, only 37% low-yielding (7hl/ha) for 22,000
bottles of the *1er vin*. Alcohol 14% and residual sugar 76g/l. Six
notes from mid-1980s to 1991. Fragrant, herbaceous, 'mustard
and cress'. Next, a decade later, bottle variation, the first
medium-deep yellow gold; four-square, touch of *noisette*;
medium-sweet, rather hard, caramelly finish. The other paler;
touch of clover honey; dry finish, something lacking. *Last noted
at the château, Oct 2001. At best* ★★ *Move on*.
**Ch Coutet** Tasted only once. Very attractive nose and flavour.
I thought it (then) better than Ch Climens. *July 1989* ★★★
**Ch Filhot** Light, gentle, nice. *At a Bordeaux Club dinner, May
1989* ★★
**Ch Lafaurie-Peyraguey** Three good notes. Fragrant,
creamy, barley sugar and pineapple. Sweet. Some fat and flesh.
Well made. *Last tasted July 1990* ★★★
**Ch de Malle** Surprisingly good for the château and the year.
Lovely colour; light, honeyed; sweet, some richness though a
bit lean. Reasonable length. *July 1990* ★★
**Ch de Rayne-Vigneau** Pale; scent of watercress; fairly
sweet, *assez bien*. Sensibly accompanying *fromages de France*. *Oct
1989* ★★★
**Ch Rieussec** Seven recent notes. As usual, old gold; good
nose, sweet, honeyed, but 'cress' on four quite separate
occasions, coincidentally noted, also grass and celery. Sweet
and unusually good for an '81, a lovely emerging flavour.
Assertive. Most recently, showing well despite being paired,
quite inappropriately, with *tarte fine au pommes caramelisées*.....
*At my 70th birthday and Decanter's 20th anniversary lunch at Les
Jardins des Gourmets in Soho, London, May 1997* ★★★
**Ch Romer du Hayot** Mediocre. Acidic end. *Last tasted,
twice, July 1990*.

**Ch Sigalas-Rabaud** Fragrant; good flavour and acidity.
Some delicacy. *At the pre-sale tasting, March 1997* ★★★

ONE OTHER SAUTERNES TASTED IN THE 1980s
**Ch Guiraud** mediocre. *1983* and *1987* ★

DRY WHITES Some fairly good wines now well past their
'sell-by' date. Three possible exceptions (**Ch Haut-Brion**
never tasted) – **Ch Laville Haut-Brion** three good notes.
*Last tasted Oct 1988* ★★★; **Dom de Chevalier** not tasted since
the mid-1980s but a stylish, elegant wine. *Last tasted May 1985*
★★★; and **Pavillon Blanc de Ch Margaux** attractive, smoky,
fruity and fragrant nose and taste; Good acidity. *Last tasted Nov
1990* ★★★

# 1982 ★★

As if to demonstrate the fickleness of Bordeaux's maritime
climate, a bountiful crop of fully ripe grapes, thanks to a sunny
summer and exceptionally hot September, turned sour for the
vineyards of Sauternes. The welcoming showers which
encouraged the *pourriture noble* turned into heavy rain which
washed it all away.
**Ch d'Yquem** To take advantage of the ripeness, high sugar
content and early signs of *pourriture*, picking started
16 September but after the 24th, the weather changed for the
worse and later grapes were not used despite the continuation
of *tries* until 5 November. Yquem, one of the biggest vineyards
in Bordeaux, around 102 hectares, yielded in 1982 just 3hl/ha.
The relatively small amount of wine made was kept in cask
until March 1986. The *cépages* mix I noted were Sémillon 80%
and Sauvignon Blanc 20%. I first tasted the wine in 1988,
twice. It had a gloriously golden colour, nose somewhat
unsettled, better on the palate. At the tasting in Aspen, the
1982 was served from a double-magnum. It combined a rich,
creamy nose with very refreshing acidity. In fact I noted it as
delightful. It was the last served of the 16 Bordeaux wines of
the 1982 vintage at a tasting I conducted for the Banque
Communale in Brussels. I soon became accustomed to the
un-British, somewhat unruly audience! The wine was better
mannered – waxy, smoky, full, intense. Most recently, marked
by me not much higher than the '81 and, of course
considerably less good than the '88, '89 and '90. Having said
this, it wasn't bad – but do not align it with the great *1er cru*
Médocs. *Last tasted in Munich, Sept 1998* ★★
**Ch Climens** Harvested from beginning of October to early
November. First two weeks fine, with botrytis but rain in the
third week washed the botrytis away. Two *tries*, the latter very
speedy. Overall a good vintage and very big crop for Climens,
23hl/ha overall, with 66% at 15hl/ha producing 60,000 bottles
of *1er vin*. Alcohol 13.8% and residual sugar 84g/l. In the mid-
1980s, fragrant, sweet, fleshy though stolid. Most recently,
medium pale; low-keyed at first, then fragrant, floral; still
sweet, touch of peach kernels, hard and lacking charm. *Last
tasted Oct 2001* ★★★ *No improvement likely.*
**Ch Nairac** Golden; hollow, grassy; fairly sweet, assertive but
mediocre. *July 1992* ★
**Ch Raymond-Lafon** Sweet, full, alcoholic in 1986. Basking
in warm summer evening, candlelight and the terrace: good
colour (as it should be by candlelight); soft 'warm', peachy
bouquet; pleasingly plump and rich with a dry finish. *Last
noted, with distractions, at an al fresco tasting and supper for
Christie's VIP clients in Coconut Grove, Florida, March 1995* ★★★

**Ch Rieussec** Just three pretty good notes. Complete, soft, gentle, good length; more solid than zestful. *Last noted at a Christie's boardroom luncheon, May 1991* ★★★

**Ch Suduiraut** Roasted grapes picked exceptionally early, 16 September. Alcohol 14%. First tasted in 1988: sweet, hefty; minty, spicy; good length and acidity. More recently: waxy yellow; rich bouquet; very sweet, full-bodied. Showing well. *Last noted at the Martin Bamford Memorial Dinner in the Dorchester, London, Nov 1992* ★★★★

**Ch Suduiraut, Cuvée Madame** Grapes picked 26 September. Richer, more powerful than the above. Wonderful harmony. *June 1988* ★★★★★ *Should be perfect now.*

SOME OTHER BARSAC AND SAUTERNES, TASTED IN THE 1980s **Ch St-Amand** pure barley sugar. Sweet, pleasant though a minor powerhouse. *1986* ★★; **Ch Lafaurie-Peyraguey** sweet, sugary, clumsy. *1985* ★★; and **Ch Lamothe** not often seen. Sweet, powerful, good length but with a hot alcohol and acid finish. *1986* ★★

DRY WHITES Successful vintage for dry white Bordeaux and the top wines are certainly worth pursuing.

**Ch Haut-Brion** First tasted in May 1983. An impressive, powerful wine though clearly needing considerable bottle ageing. A 'wonderful mouthful' in 1990, 'will develop further'. Indeed after nearly ten more years, though still fairly pale, a magnificent bouquet, fragrant, nutty, opening up in the glass like a great Montrachet, pineapple, vanilla, peaches. Medium dry – certainly not dry, with delicious flavour and length. *Last noted at a pre-sale tasting in London, Jan 1999* ★★★★(★)

**Ch Laville Haut-Brion** First tasted in 1984. Unready but impressive. An assertive and distinctive bottle in 1990, drinking well but more to come. Most recently, still pale; low-keyed though harmonious nose; dry, somewhat austere, good flavour and acidity. Still developing. *Last noted at Karl-Heinz Wolf's charming Landart Restaurant in Tangleberg, Austria, April 1999* ★★★(★)

**Ch Laville Haut-Brion, Crème de Tête** Very ripe grapes picked 10 September and kept *en barrique* until May 1983. Sold after one year in bottle. Minty, fresh, *nerveux* in 1984. An impressive, fleshy wine. Inappropriately opened as an aperitif and it needed fish. *Last noted at a Ch Margaux dinner at Brooks's Club, London in April 1988* ★★★(★)

ALSO VERY GOOD **Dom de Chevalier** only 200 cases made, so hard to find. *1985. Then* ★★★(★★)

# 1983 ★★★★★

Almost ideal growing conditions resulting in a fairly abundant – for Sauternes – crop of grapes producing the best vintage between 1975 and 1989. A wet spring was followed by hot dry weather in June and July. Rain in August and early September caused some anxiety but misty mornings and warm days proved ideal for the development of botrytis.

**Ch d'Yquem** A plethora of admiring notes so consistent that it is pointless to repeat every description. As always, the wine was noted on varying occasions, formal tastings including 'verticals' in Chicago in 1988 and in Munich, the Yquem marathon a decade later. Also at lunches and dinners in Chicago, New York and Caius College, Cambridge and one at the château when it was overpowered by very salty Roquefort. Never very deep in colour, now an attractive orange-gold, its

bouquet emitting the usual scents, but with great intensity, apricots, honeyed botrytis, *crème brûlée*; a sweet, creamy wine masking considerable power and assertiveness. Superb yet still evolving. *Last noted in jeroboam at the white/red summit at the Hotel Eden Parc, Bad Schwalbach, Nov 2000* ★★★★★

**Ch Climens** Superb. On a par with the 1971. Harvested 6 October–4 November, three to four *tries* in very good weather. Fairly large crop with over 60,000 bottles of the *1er vin*. Alcohol 14.4% and residual sugar 96g/l. First tasted exactly a year after the grapes were picked: enormously impressive, with the power and firmness to indicate a long life. But, even at that stage, a bright yellow-gold, its nose exuding a honeyed Sémillon aroma. Showing well at the Peppercorns' Climens tasting in 1987, a wine of charm and finesse which would equally apply to Serena Sutcliffe at that time (before becoming a competitor!). A decade later, dining at Ch Bouscaut: glorious colour, 'lemon curd' and highly polished gold; apricots and cream, lanolin and honey; a lovely sweet flavour but leaner than expected. Stylish, excellent acidity. Most recently: still fairly deep, richly coloured; rich, honeyed bouquet that opened majestically; very sweet, full-bodied, rich yet firm, good length and good life. *Last tasted at the château, Oct 2001* ★★★★★ *Lovely now and another quarter century of perfection.*

**Ch Coutet** Just two notes, both made at Neil McKendrick's Bordeaux Club dinners, first in 1995. Pale for a rich vintage; a grassy style but fragrant; first described as medium-sweet, on the second occasion very sweet – not so unusual as so many external conditions have a bearing, including the weather and time of year, (March and June respectively) and the accompanying sweet dishes which, in the elegant, indeed sumptuous Master's Lodge, tend to be a trifle exotic. Gaining some colour however, now fully developed, soft and rich with a touch of caramel on the end-taste which is better than the Gripfix I had noted early. *Last tasted June 1998* ★★★

**Ch Doisy-Daëne** Pale tropical fruits; sweet, light style, crisp. *Feb 1993* ★★★★ *Drink soon.*

**Ch Doisy-Védrines** First tasted in cask, October 1984. Unknit, with intrusive sulphur and acidity. Then a jump of 13 years, a 'delicious but not serious' bottle from my own cellar at a dinner hosted by Christie's and the Bordeaux Club honouring Jack (Sir John) Plumb. This was followed, six months later, by an excellent bottle sensibly served with 'Gallantine of *foie gras*', though not cold enough, at a Wine and Food Society dinner in Memphis. Shortly after, a bottle, with cheese, at my own Bordeaux Club dinner. Now golden; vanilla, orange blossom; sweet, light Barsac-style but still sweet and well-balanced. *Last tasted Feb 1998* ★★★★

**Ch Filhot** At four years of age the components very discernable, the blackcurrant and acidity of Sauvignon Blanc and gentle honeyed waxiness of Sémillon. Good flesh and flavour. The next two notes made at the III Form Club annual dinners at Boodle's Club in London, the first in 1994, delicious, fully developed. Most recently, very sweet, lovely flavour and flesh, citrus-like acidity, noting 'not a great '83 but a very good Filhot'. *Last tasted Jan 2000* ★★★

**Ch Lafaurie-Peyraguey** In 1985, nose like toasted marshmallows; sweet, full, crisp, good length. More recently; golden; creamy bouquet; good barley sugar flavour and acidity. *At a Commanderie de Bordeaux dinner in Miami, Feb 1992* ★★★★

**Ch de Malle** Alas, not a notable 1983. *April 1991* ★

**Ch Nairac** Fragrant, light, crisp. *April 1991* ★★

**Ch de Rayne-Vigneau** Over half a dozen notes, first in October 1984 and even at that stage lovely. Showing well in

1987, first at a pre-sale tasting: fragrant, beautiful flavour and length. Next with the powerful bite to cope with '*Foie gras et sa gelée au Porto*' and, later the same month, with '*Symphonie de Sorbets*', a less suitable bedfellow. A glorious honey and custard half bottle in 1990 and, in 1999, showing well: beautiful colour, harmonious nose, nice weight and flavour 'fleshy but lissom', very good acidity. *The last two identical notes at Saintsbury Club dinners, the most recent in Oct 2001* ★★★★

**Ch Rieussec** Sémillon 75%, Sauvignon Blanc 22% and Muscadelle 3%. An astonishing number of notes (over 20), starting at the château in 1984 tasting the new wine with Professor Peynaud and Eric de Rothschild and lunching equally memorably at Ch Lafite afterwards. Then a steady parade of bottles, all good, on several grand occasions, curiously served with *tarte tartin* before Ch Pétrus '78 with *vacherin* at the Mickey Suffolks' in 1993; struggling with '*Gelée de groseilles rouge*'; with apple tart and green apple sorbet; with raspberry soufflé (the Vintners' Company) and so on. I always taste the wine before whatever has been created in the kitchen turns nectar into 'dry dross'.

It is a curious characteristic of Rieussec to have an unusually deep colour, amber shaded with orange, both nose and flavour being equally rich, almost exotic. The '83 was fully evolved by the late 1990s. At the 19th annual dinner of the Commanderie de Bordeaux in Bristol, preceding one of my less successful speeches, it was delectable. It will continue to enrich and enchant. *Last noted at the Russian National Orchestra's benefit dinner at Hatchlands, Surrey in Dec 2000* ★★★★

**Ch Suduiraut** Here picking began on 26 September, its sugar content 306g/l. Despite this, and though an old (elderly!) admirer, I have had reservations, noting my pet dislikes of peach kernels and almond paste on both the nose and the palate. Now a light gold, fragrant, nutty; on occasion not as sweet as expected. *A good note, however, when last tasted at The Distillers' Company Millennium dinner in the Painted Hall, Greenwich, May 2000* ★★★

OTHER SAUTERNES TASTED IN THE MID- TO LATE 1980S
**Ch Guiraud** pallid, grassy, sulphury; better on palate. *Last tasted Oct 1987* ★★, *retaste*; **Ch Haut-Peyraguey** soft, sweet, mustard and cress flavour. *May 1987* ★★; **Ch Rabaud-Promis** good wine. *Last tasted Sept 1989* ★★★; and **Ch Romer du Hayot** waxy-sheened gold; smooth waxy texture. Attractive bouquet; sweet, crisp acidity. *Oct 1989* ★★★

DRY WHITES
**Ch Haut-Brion** In the mid-1980s pale; charred oak nose; dry, firm, distinctive. 'A great future'. Most interestingly, at a Bacchus Society dinner alongside Laville (see below). It had more depth and vinosity and far more power than the latter. Mouthfilling (13.5–14% alcohol) and impressive. *Last tasted in Memphis, Tennessee in Sept 1999* ★★★★

**Ch Laville Haut-Brion** First tasted in cask, September 1984, six weeks before bottling. Unknit but exciting. Most recently, with the Haut-Brion, very pale, lemon-like, mouth watering, opening up after an hour in the glass with amazing honeyed fragrance. Distinctly dry, firm, elegant, lean, a touch of austerity. *Last tasted Sept 1999* ★★★★(★)

**Pavillon Blanc de Ch Margaux** 100% Sauvignon Blanc, fermented and aged in new oak *barriques*. Waxy yellow-green; many-faceted fragrance; fairly light with crisp acidity. Attractive but not in the same league as Ch Laville Haut-Brion above. *Last tasted Nov 1990* ★★★

## 1984 ★ to ★★

Erratic weather conditions, with uneven flowering. A fine summer was followed by heavy rain in September which delayed the Sauternes harvest until the middle of October, botrytis helping to save the day. Not for keeping.

**Ch d'Yquem** Picking 15 October to 13 November. First noted at the château five years after the vintage and I was surprised by its unexpected attractions. After a further five years and halfway through the line of up to ten vintages in Aspen in 1994 I gave it moderate marks, finding the nose a bit oily, caramelly, but again better than expected. Sweet, touch of fat, hot dry finish. More recently, on the fourth day of Rodenstock's marathon in 1998 awarding similar marks. A medium-sweet, assertive, rather hefty wine. Caramel noted again. *Last tasted in Munich, Sept 1998* ★★

**Ch Climens** Declassified.

**Ch de Fargues** As noted on one or two previous occasions, this Lur Saluces château at times makes more attractive wine than Ch d'Yquem. I liked the nose, taste and acidity of this wine. *June 1989* ★★★

**Ch de Rayne-Vigneau** Specious, vanilla nose; medium-sweet, hot and horrible. *At a British Airways blind tasting of 41 dessert wines, 16 of them Sauternes, July 1992.*

**Ch Suduiraut** Seems to be getting more like Ch Lafaurie-Peyrauguey with its mint-leaf nose and taste. Sweet, quite good. *Only one early note, June 1988* ★★★?

**Ch Sigalas-Rabaud** Very pale; mint and cress. Medium-sweet, good flavour but short. Much preferred the '81 tasted alongside. *March 1987* ★★

DRY WHITES Unripe and acidic wines. **Dom de Chevalier** oaky, spicy, austere, full-flavoured at three years of age. Green, grassy, fragrant enough. Very dry. Acidic. Interesting only. *Last tasted Sept 1996.*

## 1985 ★ to ★★★★

Harsh winter followed by fine and dry weather throughout the spring, summer and autumn, September being one of the driest on record. In Sauternes the drought resulted in high concentrated sugar levels but there was insufficient moisture to encourage *pourriture noble*. Variable wines.

**Ch d'Yquem** Picking was late, selective and prolonged between 1 October and 19 December. Half a dozen notes starting in 1989: attractive, harmonious, good acidity, and consistently good notes since: in Aspen (1994); dining with the Pauls at Coral Gables (1996), impressive yet a complete contrast to the delicate Scharzhofberg Auslese, both in magnums in Luzern; fragrant and pleasant, the best of the 1980–1987 'flight' in Munich and, most recently, with 'Sautéed Hudson Valley Duck *foie gras*', its bouquet blossoming and penetrating, lovely flavour, weight and charm. *At Stephen Kaplan's 1985 vintage event in Chicago, April 2000* ★★★★

**Ch Climens** Late harvest, 23 October–15 November, four *tries*, botrytis too little and too late. *Passerillage*: raisin-like grapes high in sugar. Big crop, 56,000 bottles of the *1er vin*. Alcohol 14%, residual sugar 101g/l. First tasted only recently, at my Bordeaux Club dinner in 1999. Pale gold; floral; lovely flavour and balance, nice flesh, touch of caramel but drier finish than expected. Two years later: forthcoming floral bouquet, whiff of lime; very sweet, powerful, fat, rich, toffee-like. *Last tasted at the château, Oct 2001* ★★★★ *Now–2015.*

**Ch Doisy-Daëne** Very pale; uneven, grassy-minty nose; rich, almost malty. *At a pre-sale tasting, April 1994* ★

**Ch Guiraud** First tasted (two notes) April 1987: minty, fruity, sweet, crisp. More recently: lovely gold colour; harmonious, toffee-like; lacking fruit, powerful. *July 1992* ★★★

**Ch de Malle** Pale yellow; forthcoming nose; sweet, fairly full-bodied, peach kernel aftertaste. *April 1994* ★

**Ch Rieussec** Scent of walnuts and barley sugar; rich, good texture and acidity (1989). Two years later: pure gold; vanilla, honey; sweet, very attractive. *Last tasted at Waterstone's, Manchester, Dec 1991* ★★★

**Ch Suau** A little seen *2ème cru* Barsac. Light gold; rich, somewhat oily nose; sweet, agreeable scented flavour. It went well with both the apricot tart and the English cheeses. *At another of my Bordeaux Club dinners, at Christie's, Jan 1991* ★★

**Ch Suduiraut** Disappointing period. First in 1988. Next, blind: palish; grassy nose, poor flavour, short. *July 1992* ★

**DRY WHITES** Some nice wines made and with staying power. If only the top names are noted below it is because most dry whites are made to be consumed within two to four years.

**Ch Haut-Brion** Served far too young in an *impériale* in 1987 but impressive, and its potential noted. In 1991, though it opened up in the glass, it was still immature. Most recently, still pale; forthcomingly fragrant; dry, nutty flavour, considerable body and good finish. But I expected better. *Last tasted at the 50th anniversary dinner of the Bordeaux Club, Feb 1999* ★★★

**Ch Laville Haut-Brion** Curious scent of camphor, pure vanilla and face powder. Overall dry and lean, with good acidity. As so often, an interesting, somewhat idiosyncratic wine. *At Stephen Kaplan's 1985 vintage dinner at the Four Seasons, Chicago, April 2000* ★★★

**Dom de Chevalier** First tasted in cask in 1985, 'like a precocious child, impatient, trying to talk and walk'. Aromas of pineapple, apricots, pears, with the spiciness of new oak. Four years later, fragrant; ideal weight, balance and lovely flavour. *Last tasted Sept 1990* ★★★ *Should still be good.*

**Pavillon Blanc de Ch Margaux** Pale, lime-tinged; pronounced aroma of Sauvignon Blanc 'tom cats', spearmint, and (I noted) 'armpits'; lean, scented, grapey, acidic. Certainly not a shy shrinking violet. *Sept 1990* ★★★ *but for early drinking.*

**Ygrec** First tasted in September 1986, its youthful acidity uppermost. Three years later this acidity cutting the wine's richness and fat. In 1990 gaining colour; clover honey bottle age developing a scent of 'blancmange' then 'marshmallow'; dry, a strange flavour, hefty but harmonious in 1994. Two years later the Sémillon now uppermost, but with a whiff of kerosene reminding me of a Riesling. A good rich flavour. A good Ygrec but … *Last tasted Sept 1996* ★★

# 1986 ★★★★

The year got off to a good start with a fine spring, successful flowering and perfect summer. However, as occurred in 1990, heavy rains came at harvest time, followed by humid, misty conditions which encouraged the development of botrytis. Variable quality.

**Ch d'Yquem** Picking 5 October to 10 November. First tasted in 1992: cream and mint; powerful, good potential. Next, in Aspen (1994). Still immature. Half a dozen notes since, mainly in 1998–89, all good but not spectacularly good. Rather pale for Yquem; an assertive nose, mint, honey, apricots – the usual. 'So so' at the 50th anniversary dinner of the

Académie du Vin de Bordeaux, 'showing well', as well it might, lunching at Yquem in the company of the Lloyd Webbers, the Palumbos, the Dieter Bocks, Mark Birley and other friends. Next, better still in Hong Kong, very fragrant, time in hand. Then, a modestly decent note in Munich. Most recently, a lovely, blossomy bottle, stylish with good acidity. *Last noted at the American Club in Tokyo, Nov 1999* ★★★ *maybe will attain* ★★★★

**Ch d'Arche** Medium sweet, crisp, dry, acidic finish. At tastings in 1992, 1994 and 1996. *Last noted – and not selected – at a British Airways tasting in April 1996* ★★

**Ch Climens** Harvest 6–23 October, much botrytis, three *tries*, 40,000 bottles of *1er vin* (50% of the crop), 10,000 bottles of *2ème vin*, the rest declassified. Alcohol 14.5% and residual sugar 101g/l. I noticed bottle variation in 1990 and, a decade later, despite its attractive golden colour, I didn't like the nose and didn't bother to taste it. A year later, at the château: a rather hard though honeyed nose; sweet, firm, some flavour, finishing both caramelly and dry. Disappointing. *Last noted Oct 2001* ★★

**Ch Coutet** Fairly sweet and full for Coutet. In 1990 I thought it would 'probably improve with bottle age'. I can't say it has. Another minty half bottle lacking length in 1994 but quite a nice bottle recently, honeyed nose, decent flavour and acidity. *With the Pauls at their London flat in Nov 1999* ★★

**Ch Doisy-Daëne** Lovely gentle fruit, harmonious nose but short, tails off. *Last tasted June 1991* ★★

**Ch Filhot** In 1990: grassy, herbaceous. Next, blind: ordinary, unknit; assertive, touch of caramel. *July 1992* ★★

**Ch Guiraud** A lovely floral fragrance, 'delicately poised' shortly after bottling. A touch of Muscadelle noted in 1990 but its flavour was not a patch on its nose. Fairly sweet, though less appealing at a more recent line-up of dessert wines. *Last tasted in April 1996* ★★

**Ch Lafaurie-Peyraguey** An improvement on the earlier, light grassy styles. In 1990: very sweet, full of body and flavour. My top wine in a tasting of 24 '86s. More recently: punchy, delicious, 'one of best-ever Lafauries'. *Last tasted Dec 1991* ★★★★★

**Ch Lamothe-Guignard** Rarely seen in the UK and, judging by the '86, understandably so. Nose, though quite rich, had a whiff of apple core; hefty, slightly woody (*not* new oak), powerful finish. Not exactly the most gracious of Sauternes. *At a pre-sale tasting, April 1994* ★

**Ch Liot** I have always had a soft spot for the unpretentious Liot. The '86 decent but not very exciting. Some flesh. 'Somewhat obvious'. *At a pre-sale tasting in April 1994* ★★

**Ch Nairac** Another modest Barsac, Sémillon 90%, Sauvignon Blanc 6% and Muscadelle 4%. My early notes very variable to

---

## Tasting with Jancis Robinson at Yquem in 1986

*One of Hardy Rodenstock's great annual tastings took place at Ch d'Yquem in 1986. Most of Hardy's guests were German, quite a clique. Jancis and I were the only British tasters and we duly joined the party (in black tie and long dresses) at 12 noon to be bussed from our hotel in Bordeaux to Yquem. None of the Germans ever spit out at these tastings. The sommeliers at the usual Rodenstock venues know me and always bring over a silver bucket. At Yquem, though, we had to be more enterprising. Jancis and I found an antique Chinese bowl big enough for two to spit into amicably. A somewhat unorthodox use for such a rare ceramic masterpiece.*

say the least. More recently, despite its pallid and not very bright complexion, quite a nice waxy (Sémillon) nose; sweet with nice delicate fruit. In fact it was delicious. But perhaps I was making allowances for the context. *Last noted at a tutored tasting at the Hotel Shilla in South Korea, Oct 1995. Probably* ★★

**Ch de Rayne-Vigneau** One of the best '86 Sauternes. I have over half a dozen pretty good notes, starting with a lovely cask sample in June 1987. Herbaceous, very sweet the following year, its colour warming up in 1990, and showing well in 1991, 1992, 1994 and 1997, the latter at a Conseil des Crus Classés du Médoc dinner at Ch Haut-Brion, the first and last wines not being from the Médoc at all.

By the most extraordinary coincidence no sooner had I headed up this paragraph (in July 2001) than I had to leave my office to conduct a Christie's Bordeaux wine course session. Coincidentally, the '86 Rayne-Vigneau had been selected to represent Sauternes. Here is what I said, and my wife wrote: 'Beautiful colour, Tutankhamun gold with a touch of lemon; lovely mature waxy Sémillon bouquet, honey (of course), the Sauvignon element being mouthwatering, and considerable depth. Sweet entry with the vital counter-balancing acidity. Good. Slightly minty flavour, still very fresh, nice length'. Similar notes at two subsequent wine course lecture-tastings. *Last tasted in March 2002* ★★★★

**Ch Rieussec** Several notes throughout the 1990s. Peachy and a slightly oily nose noted twice, also 'like Turkish delight', but on every occasion kernelly almond paste on the palate. Nevertheless a sweet fleshy wine. My most complimentary note being made at a Commanderie de Bordeaux dinner on the outskirts of Oslo. Briefly: fragrant, rich, lovely flavour but with the same kernelly finish. Pretty good with bread and butter pudding at Brooks's Club in 1997 but considerable bottle variation at a recent III Form Club dinner: colours ranging from pale yellow to warm orange, the paler wines crisp and fresh. All were sweet, with good acidity. *Last noted Jan 2002. At best* ★★★

**Ch Sigalas-Rabaud** Palish, tinge of green; Sauvignon mintiness on nose; moderately sweet, light style. *At a pre-sale tasting in April 1994* ★★★ *(just).*

**Ch Suduiraut** Showing well at two years of age. Floral, honeyed though pale and on the lean side. Then a fairly detailed note four years after the vintage. More recently: distinctive fragrance, soft peach and apricot with flavour to match. Fleshy yet delicate. *Last tasted Dec 1991 but with plenty of time still in hand* ★★★★

OTHER BARSACS AND SAUTERNES TASTED only once, or last tasted, in 1990: **Ch Broustet** ★★; **Ch Caillou** herbaceous, sweet, soft ★★; **Ch Doisy-Dubroca** rich, good length ★★★; **Ch Doisy-Védrines** 'sublimated honey', good flavour ★★★★; **Ch Clos Haut-Peyraguey** light, sweet, fat and short ★; **Ch Rabaud-Promis** harmonious, delicate style and a good finish ★★★★; **Ch Romer du Hayot** lovely wine ★★★★; **Ch Suau** pleasant with good acidity ★★★; and **Ch La Tour-Blanche** a one-off note: otherwise it was sweet, full and fat ★★★

DRY WHITES A successful vintage for early pickers. However at **Ch Haut-Brion** the crop was too abundant and diluted so none marketed. Of the other dry whites most were, rightly, drunk young and are unlikely to have survived; **Ch Carbonnieux** dry, straightforward and unexciting. *Last tasted Feb 1992* ★; and **Ygrec** dry, acidic. *Last tasted Sept 1992* ★

# 1987 ★

Cool spring with uneven flowering. Summer generally warm and dry but the Sauternes harvest was marred by heavy storms in early October. In any case it was completely upstaged by the following three vintages.

**Ch d'Yquem** Picked 30 September to 6 November. First noted June 1992: rich, soft but lacking length. Next: brass coloured; fragrant but unknit; touch of marzipan, hard finish at the Aspen tasting in 1994. More recently, to my surprise, about the best vintage in the 1980–1987 'flight', still unknit but sweet, with surprisingly good weight and flavour. *Last tasted in Munich, Sept 1998. At best* ★★★ *(just).*

**Ch d'Arche** Pale gold; fragrant, light style, short. *July 1992* ★★

**Ch Climens** Declassified.

**Ch de Fargues** Lovely colour; strange nose; sweet, fairly full-bodied, barley sugar flavour. Hard. Pasty acidity. *At a British Airways tasting in April 1996* ★★

DRY WHITES Altogether the dry whites enjoyed better conditions than the sweet wines as the grapes were picked before the storms. Few wines remain and I have tasted only one recently: **Dom de Chevalier** nose quite harmonious, lanolin and vanilla. Dry, classic Graves, fragrant, drinking well. *Lunch at the Domaine, Sept 1998* ★★★

# 1988 ★★★★

The first of an unprecedented trio of highly successful Sauternes vintages. The early autumn weather, following a hot summer with storms, encouraged the spread of *pourriture noble* and provided ideal harvesting conditions. My original assessment of this vintage was 5 stars, outstanding, but while unquestionably good I think it doesn't quite stand up to the two following vintages, particularly the 1990.

**Ch d'Yquem** Half a dozen notes. First tasted in June 1992, just after bottling. Then a double magnum at Farr Vintners' dinner (1993). Next, the youngest of a vertical of ten vintages, in Aspen in 1994, my marks equalling the oldest of the range, 1967. Already golden in colour; intense bouquet, harmonious, creamy. Fresh, delightful, with good length – what the French call *persistence*. Next, in 1995, crisp and refined, alongside the powerful '89 at the opening dinner of Rodenstock's 16th annual tasting. Two years later, its creamy bouquet opening up beautifully in the glass; perfect weight. At ten years of age at the Yquem marathon, and from a double magnum, paler than I expected with low-keyed nose. But very sweet, intensely rich, fleshy. Time in hand. More recently (2000) at Len Evans' 'Imperial Dinner' preceding the '83, very sweet, good flesh and finish. The following year, honeyed depth, fairly powerful, perfect acidity. *Last noted at the white/red summit at Schloss Johannisberg, Nov 2001* ★★★★★ *Long life.*

**Ch Climens** Excellent vintage, grapes heavily botrytised and picked in three *tries*, some parcels four times, 17–29 October, in perfect autumn sunshine. Overall 18hl/ha, but the *1er vin* (67% of the crop) at only 12hl/ha. High alcohol and residual sugar: 14.4% and 106g/l respectively. First tasted in cask in April 1989. A rather hefty, buttery, nose; very sweet, full, rich, intense. Most impressive. Seven years later at a Bordeaux Club dinner displaying more of its Barsac origin, cress-like, minerally, crisp bouquet, seemed not as sweet, powerful though with expanding finish. At ten years of age fully fledged, perfectly balanced, glorious. More recently, at Neil

McKendrick's Bordeaux Club dinner: paler than expected, bouquet fragrant, privet-like; creamy, excellent flavour, perfect acidity. Lastly, very rich, fragrant, nutty bouquet; now tight, closed, with marzipan-like taste, good acidity. Perhaps in a menopausal state. *Last tasted at the château, Oct 2001* ★★★(★)?

**Ch Coutet** First tasted in 1996 at a Bar Guest night dinner hosted by my daughter in the Inner Temple: good but with more to come. In 1998: a typical Coutet minty cress-like nose, crisp, showing well. Then with chicken liver *parfait*: light gold; very good bouquet, a *mélange* of botrytis Sémillon and refreshing Sauvignon. Nice weight, very good flavour, crisp dry finish. Most recently, perfect with *foie gras*: lovely, floral nose; sweet, equally flowery flavour and good acidity. *Dining in patrician style with Carol and Jamie Guise at Sherston, Wiltshire Jan 2002* ★★★★

**Ch de Fargues** Lovely colour. Sweet, good acidity. Better flavour than nose. *Tasted in April 1996* ★★★

**Ch Filhot** Surprisingly pale; good botrytis nose. Very sweet, full, rich, good fruit, flesh and acidity. Might have been the occasion but it seemed an unusually good Filhot. *With local foie gras at the 36th Grand Chapitre de la Compagnie des Mousquetaires d'Armagnac in Sept 1994* ★★★★

**Ch Guiraud** Despite a cloudy cask sample, April 1989, glorious nose, immense sweetness, its potential confirmed the following year. Crisp, good in 1994. In 1997 very good but needing more time. Most recently, coping surprisingly well with profiteroles and fresh raspberries at a Distillers' Installation Court dinner: yellow gold; lovely, scented, orange blossom bouquet; sweet, very good indeed. *Last tasted Nov 2001* ★★★★

**Ch Lafaurie-Peyraguey** Very good though 'unknit' cask sample in April 1989. Five years later, richly honeyed bouquet, well constituted. Most recently, this time with 'Stem ginger and Macadamia Nut Soufflé' at the annual Swan Feast at Vintners' Hall: yellow gold; vanilla, touch of honey, whiff of grapes; sweet, fullish, assertive flavour, very good acidity. Still a bit harsh on the finish. *Last noted Nov 2001* ★★★(★)

**Ch Lamothe-Guignard** Very attractive colour, sweet, nice weight. *Nov 1998* ★★(★)

**Ch Liot** Half a dozen consistently good notes in 1997 and 1998 all at Christie's Bordeaux wine course sessions. Good colour, waxy sheen; fragrant, touch of spice; a harmonious wine of considerable charm. Excellent for its class and will develop further. *Last noted Dec 1998* ★★★(★)

**Ch de Malle** Cloudy cask sample, good but short. Most recently, rather pale; fragrant, minty nose and flavour. Lean and light. *Last tasted dining at Domaine de Chevalier, April 1998* ★★

**Ch Nairac** Cloudy cask sample in April 1989. Pleasant enough the following April. Very sweet, But very much a *2ème cru*. *Last tasted April 1994* ★★

**Ch Rabaud-Promis** Strange, slightly malty nose; very sweet, full, rich. *April 1994* ★★, *possibly* ★★★ *now*.

**Ch Raymond-Lafon** Good colour, fragrant nose and pleasing flavour, good acidity. *Dec 1997* ★★★

**Ch de Rayne-Vigneau** Immensely impressive cask sample, confirmed 12 months later. Lovely honeyed bouquet; very sweet, high extract, glorious. *Last tasted April 1999* ★★★★

**Ch Sigalas-Rabaud** Two notes, first in 1994. Grassy cress-like nose; sweet enough, good enough. Expected more. *Last noted at a charity dinner at Christie's, Dec 1997* ★★

**Ch Suduiraut** In April 1994 it was cloudy and bitter but impressive with great potential. Twelve months later, the chrysalis had turned into a butterfly, tinged with gold,

forthcoming, exuding power and beauty. More recently, lightly honeyed, settling down, self-assured, not too sweet. *Last tasted dining at La Maison du Cygne, Brussels, April 1997* ★★★★

**Ch La Tour-Blanche** Just one note. Curious, slightly kernelly, oily nose. Very sweet, fat, rich. *April 1994* ★★★? *Need to retaste.*

DRY WHITES The wet and humid September was not conducive to good wines. Early pickers did best. I have tasted few recently. **Ch Haut-Brion** and **Ch Laville Haut-Brion** I have not tasted the two top Graves since 1990 but both were excellent then and probably drinking well now; **Dom de Chevalier** cask sample showing well in April 1989: good fruit, fragrance and flavour. Oak noticeable. More recently, classic, waxy, creamy nose; fairly dry, full flavoured, the spice of new oak, good length. *Last noted dining at the Domaine, April 1998* ★★★; and **Ygrec** rather neutral nose. Dry. Frankly not much to my liking. *Sept 1996*.

# 1989 ★★★★★

Extremely hot summer assured the grapes' full ripeness and very high sugar content, added to which misty mornings provided the highly desirable botrytis. Magnificent Sauternes. The best vintage of the decade.

**Ch d'Yquem** No longer can one taste the wine in cask but only on release. My first eulogistic note was made in September 1995: superb, powerful yet not excessive. Two months later at the Wine Experience 'Grand tastings', unquestionably lovely. A creamy fleshy magnum at the Königshof, Munich in 1996. More recently, also *grace à* Hardy Rodenstock: a medium yellow-gold with visibly rich 'legs' or 'tears'; an immediacy about the bouquet as if it had been frustrated and couldn't wait to surge out of the bottle. High-toned, honey, peaches, apricots; very rich, full-bodied, complete, quite a bite to it and extended flavour. A long life ahead. *Last tasted Sept 1998* ★★★★(★)

**Ch Bastor-Lamontagne** A big vineyard (Sémillon 78%, Sauvignon Blanc 17% and the balance, I presume, to be Muscadelle) and a relatively minor *cru bourgeois* yet capable of producing some very attractive wine. First tasted and much enjoyed at lunch, probably with *foie gras* – I did not note the menu – in St-Émilion in 1994. Subsequently selected by Steven Spurrier for three of the Christie's Bordeaux wine course sessions I conducted in 1996. It had an impressively rich appearance, an attractive bouquet variously described as ripe peaches, vanilla, milk chocolate, a touch of gooseberry (acidity), waxy, lanolin, pure honey – you name it! Sweet, slightly grapey flavour, not insubstantial, fleshy, high alcohol (14.5%), good counter-balancing acidity. In short, consistent and, as always, good value. *Last tasted Nov 1996* ★★★

**Ch Climens** Magnificent. Considered a precocious harvest, three *tries* from 25 September–9 October. Modest *rendement*, 11hl/ha. Only two weeks' fermentation *en barrique* (normally three), 42,000 bottles of the *1er vin* with one of the highest levels of alcohol and residual sugar (14.5% and 123g/l). Five notes, the first in 1991: shimmering colour; luscious, honeyed, great length. Developing well by 1993, then a jump of eight years: deep yellow-gold; lovely, deep, orange blossom nose and flavour. Very sweet, full, rich yet elegant. *Last noted part way through a glorious and instructive morning's tasting of 30 vintages, with Bérénice Lurton at the château, Oct 2001* ★★★★★ *Glorious now, generations of life ahead.*

**Ch Doisy-Daëne** A *2ème cru* Barsac which not surprisingly in 1989 produced a very attractive wine. First tasted in June 1991: delicious. Next in 1994: showing well at a pre-sale tasting, creamy nose, rich, well made. Even more impressive at a tasting I conducted at Christie's in Frankfurt: pure Tutankhamun gold; delicious nose, honey sweet, mouthwatering acidity. Sweet of course – 'a charmer'. Most recently, with cheese. *Last noted at a Wine & Food Society St James's branch dinner at the Halcyon hotel, London, May 1998* ★★★★

**Ch Doisy-Védrines** This is the largest of the three *2ème cru* vineyards which were originally all part of the Doisy estate (the third is Dubroca). Luscious and juicy, notably sweet in April and June 1991. Three years later sweet and honeyed, 'not too heavy' at the opening dinner of La Cité Mondiale du Vin, Bordeaux's ill-fated version of London's Vinopolis. Now an amber-gold, showing some honeyed bottle age, not quite as sweet as the Daëne, a touch of caramel but with gorgeous flavour and good length. *Last tasted April 1998* ★★★★

**Ch Lafaurie-Peyraguey** Showing well in April and June 1991: fragrant, floral, clover, *fraises des bois*, high-toned honey; pretty good to taste, too. Rich, good texture, assertive at a dinner at Christie's in New York. More recently, pale gold, rich, tangy bouquet. In words of the popular song 'sweet and lovely'. *Last noted at a pre-sale tasting in Geneva, May 1999* ★★★★

**Ch Liot** First tasted in April 1994: 'sweet, very good for its class'. The following year, like the 1988, used very satisfactorily at Christie's Bordeaux wine course sessions: crisp, honeyed melon, fleshy, herbaceous. *Last tasted March 1996* ★★★★

**Ch Nairac** Mixed reactions. In April and June 1991: very scented, 'hyacinth'; 'extraordinary, unclassic', attractive but tailed off. Three years later, my notes more down to earth: crisp, vanilla; very sweet, fleshy (for Nairac) quite good. Next a horrible sample bottle submitted by a usually on-the-ball importer for a British Airways (blind) tasting. Rejected of course. *Last tasted April 1996. At best* ★★★

**Ch Rieussec** First tasted in March 1991: herbaceous, rich, good length, as yet hard on the finish. Four months later admiring its fragrance and flavour. In 1994, though unusually pale for Rieussec, very sweet and packing a velvet-lined punch. Similar notes, repeating 'powerful', nutty flavour. Good not great but might develop reasonably well. *Last noted at Mentzendorf's Rieussec seminar in Feb 1996* ★★★

**Ch Suduiraut** Eight notes, a superb start in 1995 at a tasting conducted for Goldman Sachs in New York. Beautiful bottles, served not cold enough, at a Fête de la Fleur banquet in Bordeaux in 1997. Several, indeed mostly, at various dinners. Always superb. *Last tasted at the Fête de la Fleur dinner, this time suitably cool, at Dom de Chevalier, April 2000* ★★★★★

**Ch Suduiraut, Crème de Tête** Cork branded *'Madame de Suduiraut'*. 14.5% alcohol and 146g/l sugar: orange-gold; the orange scented bouquet and candied orange flavour. Powerful yet soft. Superb. *At Ch Suduiraut, Sept 1998* ★★★★★

SHORT NOTES ON OTHER SAUTERNES LAST TASTED IN 1994 **Ch d'Arche** Light style, straightforward ★★; **Ch Broustet** pale, distinctive, flowery, a bit short ★★★; **Ch Guiraud** pale, lighter than expected, crisp ★★★; **Ch Lamothe-Guignard** sweet, quite rich, hot, hard finish. Needs bottle age ★★?; **Ch de Malle** rich. A touch of hardness ★★(★)?; **Ch Sigalas-Rabaud** very fragrant; very sweet, crisp, taste of oak. A 'curious but attractive' wine ★★★; and **Ch La Tour-Blanche** very sweet, fat, rich ★★★

SAUTERNES TASTED ONLY IN 1991 **Ch Coutet** unusual to have the alcoholic content to the second decimal place (13.54%), residual sugar 102g/l, acidity 4.6g/l. A lovely wine, melon and youthful grapefruit; very sweet, 'puppy fat' peaches, good length, aftertaste and potential. I must see if I can find any; **Ch Filhot** Crisp and lean. Not a great '89, possibly ★★; **Ch Rabaud-Promis** Alcohol 13.8%, residual sugar 110g/l, acidity 4g/l. Not very impressed. Lacked conviction. ★★?; and **Ch de Rayne-Vigneau** attractive, a certain delicacy of flavour. Good length, and potential ★★★★

DRY WHITES An extraordinary year and some astonishing wines made. Because of the intense summer heat the grapes ripened precociously, with too much natural sugar and too little acidity. To forestall these problems the grapes were picked in August and early September.

**Ch Haut-Brion** A small crop, very small *rendement*, picked in August. First tasted in November 1990, the yellowest colour of a range of recent vintages. The nose, initially 'cool', opened up explosively. Surprisingly sweet for a dry Graves. In April 1991, two months after bottling, its extraordinary character and quality confirmed. Six years later, admittedly tasted in difficult conditions, it was lovely, creamy on the nose but, I felt, a bit austere. *Last tasted at a pre-sale tasting in New York, Dec 1987* ★★★(★)

**Ch Laville Haut-Brion** I well remember being bowled over by this wine when I tasted it at La Mission with the imperturbable Jean Delmas in November 1990. It was easily the most beautiful young wine – from anywhere – that I have ever tasted. Exotic youthful aromas, voluptuous on palate. Confirmed a year later. Aromatic. 'The best Laville ever.' The production was small, hard to find and expensive but I happened to notice some Laville '89 on O W Loeb's list at a rather steep price per case, then discovered it was a 'case' of *six* bottles. Nevertheless I ordered a case but found myself rationed to three bottles! The first bottle I opened at my Bordeaux Club dinner in January 1996. We were entranced by the wine. Next, triple exposure in December 1997 at a pre-sale tasting, a charity dinner and after-sale dinner in New York: consistently seductive, golden, creamy, gloriously mouthfilling.

In September 1998, dining grandly at Ch Haut-Brion with the Duc and Duchesse de Mouchy, he an old Etonian, she, formerly the Princess de Luxembourg, the granddaughter of Clarence Dillon who bought Haut-Brion in 1935, and her son Count Robert de Luxembourg, recently appointed managing director, with of course Jean Delmas: I thought it was beginning to dry out. It had certainly lost its puppy fat though the bouquet was as creamy and peachy as ever. Turbot partnered it beautifully. Most recently, I produced my second bottle but although very good it was a bit of a let down, like a second cup of tea. It seemed more oaky and austere. *Last tasted hosting a Bordeaux Club dinner, Dec 1999. At its best* ★★★★★

SHORT NOTES ON OTHER DRY WHITES **Dom de Chevalier** two notes, the first at the Domaine a year after the vintage. Butter, vanilla topping delicious fruit. Most recently, good flesh body length and enough acidity. *Last tasted March 1998* ★★★★; and **Pavillon Blanc de Ch Margaux** 100% Sauvignon Blanc. Oaky, ripe attractive nose; medium-dry, assertive, delicious with steamed halibut (at a Ch Margaux dinner at Brooks's Club in London, with the delightful Corinne Mentzelopoulos at the helm). *March 2001* ★★★★

# 1990–1999

This was a roller coaster decade for Sauternes, whereas the dry whites had few problems. There is no doubt that those châteaux in the Graves region which produce both red and dry white wine have a distinct advantage: the whites are quickly bottled and soon sold, providing useful cash flow. Alas, however one respects and admires Sauternes, the prices they command hardly compensate château proprietors for the risks and costs of production. Happily, but controversially, those producers in Sauternes who installed the expensive *cryoextraction* equipment, were able to avoid complete disaster in the poor years of the early 1990s.

## Sauternes Vintages at a Glance
**Outstanding** ★★★★★
1990, 1996
**Very Good** ★★★★
1995, 1997, 1998, 1999
**Good** ★★★
None

## 1990 ★★★★★

The third of the outstanding Sauternes trio of vintages. As in 1989 a hot dry summer brought the grapes to full ripeness, (overall the highest sugar levels since 1929). The worry that it was too dry for botrytis to set was remedied by adequate rain in August and September, inducing early evidence of noble rot and well-nigh perfect conditions for the production of great sweet wines.

In retrospect, and after looking through all my notes, I think 1990 is the best Sauternes vintage for decades. The conditions were such that virtually no-one made a poor wine and even the habitual underperformers did well.

**Ch d'Yquem** Picking 28 September – 10 October. Bottled in 1994. The biggest crop since 1893. The first opportunity that I, and a group of international wine writers, had to taste the wine was just prior to its release in April 1997. It already had a rich golden colour. The next thing I noticed was a surprising touch of caramel on the nose, then on the finish, with a hint of what I now just refer to as *noisette*. Overall impressive, powerful, yet only 13% alcohol. Later that autumn, at a *Decanter* tasting (blind) of 16 1990s, I confess I did not rate it as highly as some of the others. Nothing like a glimpse of the label! But a year later, the 122nd wine of Rodenstock's Yquem marathon tasting, sandwiched between the '83 and '91 at the closing dinner, it was sheer perfection. Shortly afterwards Anthony Barton served the '90 at a luncheon at Ch Langoa and in December it featured as one of the *Wine Spectator's* 'top 10' wines of the year. An amalgam of my most recent notes: limpid yellow-gold; perfect richness and ripeness on the nose; 'classic'; very sweet, full, fleshy, velvety, richly flavoured, perfect balance. 'Perfect now, yet great future'. *Last tasted at the Wine Experience, New York, Dec 1998* ★★★★★

**Ch Climens** Another superb wine, botrytis-laden grapes picked with just three *tries* over an unbroken period of heat and sun, 17 September–4 October. The *rendement* after selection was 10hl/ha. Because of the richness of the must, fermentation was unusually prolonged, lasting 2½ months in small oak *barriques*. Nearly 37,000 bottles of the *1er vin*, alcohol 13.6% and exceptionally high residual sugar, 130g/l. First noted in 1997 at *Decanter* magazine's blind tasting of 1990s. I gave it high marks, retasting carefully after all was revealed. No

question, this is a lovely wine, floral, privet on the nose; sweet, rich, full-flavoured, excellent balance and finish. Most recently: a rich amber-gold; deep, ripe, rich, harmonious nose and flavour. Very sweet of course, lovely fruit, complete. *Last tasted at the château, Oct 2001* ★★★★★ *Glorious, but better to give it another five to ten years. Almost infinite life.*

**Ch Coutet** Good wine. Also high marks tasted blind. Full, rich, flesh and fat. *At the* Decanter *tasting, Sept 1997* ★★★★★

**Ch de Fargues** Delicious with West Country cheeses taming its youthful aggressiveness at Gidleigh Park in Devon in 1997. Pale gold; fragrant, lanolin and mint leaf; sweet but on the lean side, delicious vanilla and honey flavour. *Last noted dining at the Hotel Eden Parc, Bad Schwalbach, Nov 2001* ★★★(★)

**Ch Lafaurie-Peyraguey** Impressive cask sample in April 1991, heady, assertive, not the old, light, minty style. Rich, yet unknit at the 1997 *Decanter* tasting but, more recently, a much better note: good colour, flavour and balance. *Last tasted at the Hong Kong Wine Society's annual dinner, Oct 1995* ★★★★

**Ch de Malle** Four notes. Luscious, fleshy, assertive, 'surely the best ever' in cask. High marks tasted blind in 1997: 'opulent', complete. More recently: amazingly rich, apricots and peaches. *Last noted dining at the château, classified as one of France's monuments historiques, with the Comtesse de Bournazel and her son, March 1999* ★★★★

**Ch de Rayne-Vigneau** Also tasted in cask, April and June 1991. Nose subdued, palate full, alcoholic, hard, lacking charm. Better flavour than nose, crisp, decent length. After only 13 months, settling down to face a good future, very sweet, honeyed, high acidity. *Last tasted July 1992. At least* ★★★★ *now*

**Ch Rieussec** Twenty months *en barrique* and 14.5% alcohol. First tasted in June 1991: pure gold, not the deep orange of some earlier vintages; rich, ripe, crisp, flavoury. Next, at one of the most miserable tastings of my life, outside, in the hills of North Carolina on a chilly October afternoon in 1995. The wine, though, was lovely. Next, at the château in 1996, opening up nicely, and on another strange occasion – a wine tasting I conducted for the Count von Schönborn at Pommersfelden, a vast German palace in the middle of a field! Very sweet, dry finish. For some reason or other it reminded me of raisins in rum. Attractive but 'a touch of clumsiness' at the *Decanter* tasting. Yet another exotic location, lecture-tasting on the most luxurious of all cruise ships, the *Seabourn Spirit*, in January 1998 somewhere off Sumatra, and a month later in another exotic location, equally effusive notes: now a beautiful pure gold; bouquet variously noted as 'lychees and rose petals', almost Gewürztraminer-like, peaches, apricots and, as usual, honey; sweet of course, with lovely flesh and flavour, good length, long life predicted. *Last noted conducting a Bordeaux tasting for the Chaîne des Rôtisseurs in Nassau, Feb 1998* ★★★★★

**Ch Suduiraut** Half a dozen notes: impressive at its first showing, a good cask sample in March 1991, particularly its depth of colour, fat and power due to its high alcoholic content, 15%. Three notes later, at a British Airways wine committee blind tasting in 1996: I thought it was very good but hefty, almost pungent and needing much more bottle age. Fragrant but a hot finish noted again at the *Decanter* blind tasting of 1990s.

That autumn a far more fulsome note, perhaps reflecting the ambience, the Ch de Bagnols, one of the most luxurious castles in France: by then it was a fairly deep orange-gold; honey and flowers (sounds like Truefitt and Hill's hair oil), certainly very fragrant; sweet, plump, full-bodied, slightly caramelly, floral, good acidity, and again, a year later, a masterclass, same time same place. *Last tasted at Ch de Bagnols, near Villefranche, Oct 1998* ★★★★★

**Ch La Tour-Blanche** Consistently good notes from its then rather hard assertive youth; lovely, honeyed; very sweet, great length at Walter Eigensatz's gala dinner at the Palace Hotel, Luzern, in 1996. Twelve months later it fully justified a place in Hugh Johnson's 'luxurious sweet wines' presentation at a Hallwag book launch in Frankfurt. More recently, I noted it as retaining its fat, flesh and sweetness at the *Decanter* tasting of '90s. *Last noted Sept 1997* ★★★★★

**OTHER BRIEFER NOTES OF WINES** mainly last tasted in 1997: **Ch d'Arche** harmonious and very good *Tasted only in cask, June 1991* ★★★★; **Ch Bastor-Lamontagne** similar note to Ch d'Arche; very sweet and intense. *For its class* ★★★★★; **Ch Broustet** lovely, honeyed, lightish style and delicious. *For its class* ★★★★; **Ch Doisy-Daëne** in cask: powerful, impressive, lacking finesse. Later: harmonious nose, sweet, hefty, dry finish ★★★; **Ch Doisy-Védrines** fragrant, good acidity in cask. Yellow, substantial, the more so in the company of pale and light Rhine wines at Vinexpo in June 1997, yet surprisingly dry. Later that autumn: touch of orange; sweet, suave; 'hefty' used again ★★★; **Ch Filhot** in cask, it was lean and flavoury. Later, I noted it as very fragrant, sweet, distinctive, its dryness embodying fairly high volatile acids, otherwise very good ★★★; **Ch Clos Haut-Peyraguey** fragrant, assertive, hot finish ★★★; **Ch Lamothe-Guignard** richly coloured, sweet, powerful ★★★★; **Ch Nairac** tasted in cask both in April and June 1991. I noted it as being nicely scented. 'Pineapple and boiled sweets … a good Nairac'. Then very sweet but hard in 1994. Botrytis, fat on finish ★★★; **Ch Romer du Hayot** grassy cress-like style. Quite good but needs time. *Tasted only in cask, June 1991* ★★; and **Ch Sigalas-Rabaud** very sweet, rich, powerful. Similar notes when next tasted in 1997, adding spicy, honeyed bouquet. Good wine. ★★★★

---

## Sauternes and food

*When should you drink Sauternes? The classic combination is with foie gras or pâté at the beginning of a meal – though this rich combination tends to ruin the appetite for the rest of the menu. I personally prefer to serve it at the end with cheese. Most people, unfortunately, want to serve Sauternes with dessert. Unless all the ingredients are slightly less sugary, this simply doesn't work. What is the point of going to all the trouble of making this super-sweet wine – one glass per vine (at Yquem) – if you then turn it into a dry wine after one mouthful of a pastry chef's sweet confection? The important thing, when presented with a difficult combination, is to taste the wine first. Incidentally, I positively hate the expressions 'pudding wine', and, even worse, the girlish 'stickies' (ugh!).*

**DRY WHITES** Despite the hot summer the dry whites turned out to have a better balance of acidity and alcohol than the '89s. All except the top growths should have been consumed by now.

**Ch Haut-Brion** First tasted at the château in April 1991. A lovely wine, full, firm, with great potential. Six years later, a good colour; rather idiosyncratic style, waxy, touch of vanilla, distinctive; firm dry finish, a bit four-square. Try more bottle age. *Last noted dining at the château, June 1997* ★★★(★)

**Ch Laville Haut-Brion** Sémillon 60%, Sauvignon Blanc 40%. Distinctive yellow-gold; gently scented youthful aromas, pineapple and oak. Sweeter than Ch Haut-Brion. This was in April 1991. Six years later: creamy nose, slightly kernelly at a pre-sale tasting in New York. The following year, tasting with Jean Delmas: a very confident yellow colour; low-keyed, waxy bouquet, Sémillon very evident. Medium-dry. A class act. *Last tasted Sept 1998* ★★★(★)

**Dom de Chevalier** Cask sample, March 1991: a lovely, forthcoming, well-balanced wine. More recently, good colour, nose and flavour but unexciting. *Last noted, briefly, at a Union des Grands Crus opening dinner, March 1999* ★★★★

# 1991

Back to the bad old days. A see-saw of growing conditions, the Sauternes district affected by April frosts even more severely than the red wine districts to the north and the east. Summer was wet, August in particular afflicted by very heavy rain. Some improvement in September with a burst of exceptional heat on 21 September, yet within a week the temperature had plummeted to 10°C. Picking in Sauternes was the earliest in recent years, most ending by 17 October. In between, the pickers had the unenviable task of separating the grey rot from the *pourriture noble*. No spring (1992) tastings and just two wines noted from both ends of the scale.

**Ch d'Yquem** Picking started 2 October and ended mid-November. The 125th vintage of Yquem, small production, 90,000 bottles, and the last to be tasted at Rodenstock's Yquem five-day marathon in Munich in September 1998. It was served with the final course of the closing gala dinner at the excellent Königshof hotel. With considerable ingenuity and advance planning our host and the chef had devised six 'light' lunches and six dinners, each of which was original, appropriate and delectable. Each dinner consisted of half a dozen courses, each of which was accompanied by four to eight wines, some tasted blind.

Alas, the 1991 ended this unrepeatable event with not a bang but a whimper. Having said this, it was not wholly bad and there were bottle variations. At my table it had a palish yellow colour with a touch of straw; a curious, slight nose with a whiff of old apples; on the lean side and high acidity. Later that month, at Yquem with Mme Garbay, the young, attractive and down-to-earth *maître de chai*, the 1991 benefited from being tasted solo rather than being upstaged by the great 1990 in Munich 12 days prior. Its bouquet was of ripe melon with a surprising touch of honey; reasonably sweet, spicy, a flavour of hot honey and caramel, high acidity. *Last tasted at the château, Sept 1998* ★

**Ch Climens** The harvest started surprisingly early on 17 September, because of the precociousness of botrytis, which saved the vintage, for rain fell from the 25th until the bitter end on 9 October. There were just two *tries*. Moreover, because of earlier frost, the crop was small, a mere 5hl/ha producing 20,000 bottles. Alcohol was a normal 14% and residual sugar low at 67g/l. The colour was fairly pale: heavily caramelised, kernelly nose; surprisingly sweet and sugary, hefty style. *At the château, Oct 2001 ★ for drinking, not keeping.*

**Ch Nairac** Yellow-gold; medium-sweet, somewhat loose knit but surprisingly attractive flavour. Acidity. *March 1998 ★*

**DRY WHITES** Picking began on 15 September and those who picked early did best. A very small crop. I have tasted few of these wines and none recommended for drinking now.

## 1992 ★

Another wet and sunless year, particularly disastrous in Sauternes due to lack of sunshine, cold and damp conditions which hampered the development of beneficial botrytis.

**Ch d'Yquem** Only 60 *barriques* made. Declassified.

**Ch Climens** As on previous occasions, by dint of careful and expensive grape selection, a more-than-passable wine made. A medium pale yellow-gold; an extraordinary nose and taste which reminded me of mandarins. Minty and surprisingly attractive for such a meagre vintage. *Served with the first course at the Union des Grands Crus opening dinner at Ch Gazin, March 1999 ★★ (for trying).*

A QUARTET OF BARSACS AND SAUTERNES TASTED IN APRIL 1994 **Ch Doisy-Védrines** a curious two-part malt and lime nose; sweet, lean, grassy but attractive in its way ★★; **Ch Lafaurie-Peyraguey** golden-tinged; honey and mint; sweet, surprisingly good for the year, sweet, full, rich, fruity ★★★; **Ch Nairac** only a meagre 300 bottles produced per hectare and the last third of the vintage in '92 wiped out. With the surviving grapes the Heeters managed to make a medium-sweet, crisp and not unattractive wine ★★; **Ch de Rayne-Vigneau** another tryer, and another one that succeeded against all odds; lightly honeyed nose; sweet, delicious, peachy flavour. Doubt if it has the components with the right balance to keep. *Interesting to see ★★★*

**DRY WHITES** The grapes were harvested during the first fortnight in September before the deluge. Light, fresh and fruity wines made, commercially useful for early drinking.

**Ch Laville Haut-Brion** Very bright yellow; unknit, butter and caramel; much better on palate, firm, fragrant, good acidity and surprisingly good length. *At James Lawther's tasting of whites at Ch Cordeillan-Bages, Pauillac, Sept 1998 ★★★*

**Dom de Chevalier** The first wine served at the opening Graves dinner at Ch Malartic-Lagravière in June 1999: pale; agreeable nose; surprisingly attractive. Ten months later, nose little and lean as was the flavour but some length and good acidity. *Last tasted at the Domaine, April 2000 ★★*

## 1993

Another wet season and the mid-autumn weather was disastrous in the Sauternes areas; one of the worst ever sweet-wine vintages, black or grey rot dominating. Nevertheless the wines of ten courageous, or optimistic, châteaux were shown to wine journalists at Ch La Tour-Blanche (where the spring Sauternes tastings are presented) in April 1994. One or two have been tasted since. Frankly I felt sorry for the growers. Even allowing for the unreadiness of some of the cask samples, it was not much of a vintage for them to sell.

**Ch Climens** Declassified.

**Ch Doisy-Védrines** Cask sample not too bad, minty nose; just sweet enough, lightish, hot peppery finish. Exactly two years later, nose still 'green' and unknit; seemed to be drying out, certainly too dry and hard for dessert wine purposes. A good strong cheese wine! *Last tasted April 1996 ★ for trying.*

**Ch Lafaurie-Peyraguey** The best of the bunch at the opening tasting: a scented, slightly unusual character. Crisp, quite good flavour. A year later some fat and flesh, hard finish. Way below standard. *Last noted at the Union des Grands Crus tasting of '93s in London, April 1995 ★★ (just).*

**Ch Romer du Hayot** Sweet, soft, surprisingly powerful. *April 1996 ★★*

OTHER BARSACS AND SAUTERNES noted only at the opening cask sample tasting, 6 April 1994: **Ch Broustet** quite good ★★; **Clos Haut-Peyraguey** terrible; **Ch Lamothe** two woody bottles; **Ch Lamothe-Guignard** good nose; not very sweet but not bad ★; **Ch Myrat** strange oily, kerosene nose and taste; **Ch Nairac** not really ready to taste. Cloudy; chlorine-like nose which evoked a public swimming pool; touch of bitterness. Hardly had a chance but it might have recovered; **Ch Rabaud-Promis** taste of rot, bitter, alas not 'Promis-ing'; and **Ch Rieussec** good colour; nose quite rich; unexciting but a good effort ★

**DRY WHITES** The vintage was certainly more successful for the dry whites than the sweet wines, the grapes being picked hastily after the official start on 10 September. Four wines tasted, one worth noting: **Ch Laville Haut-Brion** just one note. Very pale; gentle, scented nose; dry and light for Laville, touch of lemon, very attractive – for the short term. *Dining at Ch Rauzan-Ségla, Sept 1998 ★★★*

## 1994 ★

Far better season though the rains in mid-September affected the vines in the Sauternes area. The harvest was prolonged and hazardous. The weather eventually improved but it was touch and go, a battle between botrytis on the one hand and ruination on the other. Those who harvested late achieved the best results. Nevertheless I well recall, at the opening tasting at Ch La Tour-Blanche in the spring following the vintage, seeing all the proprietors almost in despair after such a string of dismal vintages.

**Ch d'Yquem** Picked late, bottled in the spring of 1998 and tasted 12 months later. Orange gold; low-keyed; sweet and somewhat underpowered. *At the château, April 1999 ★★*

**Ch Climens** Harvested between 21 September and 15 October in wet conditions. Three *tries*, small production further reduced by severe selection. Alcohol 14%, residual sugar 76g/l, 34,000 50-cl bottles produced. Distinctly pale in colour; a light, fragrant but superficial nose; fairly sweet, strange barley sugar flavour, lacking length. Bérénice Lurton told me later that it was better in the afternoon and though still 'unprepossessing' it 'needs to be forgotten for a few years'. *At the château, Oct 2001 ★★ Possible improvement, say 2004–2010.*

THE FOLLOWING '94s were mainly last tasted, or only tasted, in April 1996: **Ch Broustet** very strange flavour. Touch of ginger; **Ch de la Chartreuse** hefty, quite good flavour though unexciting ★; **Ch Doisy-Védrines** not bad ★★; **Ch Lafaurie-Peyraguey** better than expected, sweet, a touch of fat ★★; **Ch Liot** much better than expected. *Last tasted in 1999* ★; **Ch de Malle** also surprisingly attractive, mint and honey, touch of caramel ★★; **Ch Nairac** little nose, medium-sweet, not at all bad ★★; **Ch Rayne-Vigneau** creamy, positive, rich, good acidity, hot finish. One of the best '94s ★★★ (*just*); **Ch Roland** rarely seen. I've stayed there but the château is as dismal as the wine, though the '94 was better than expected ★; **Ch Suduiraut** (in 1995) bright; attractive; fairly sweet, assertive, good acidity ★★★; and **Ch La Tour-Blanche** (in 1995 and *1996*) initially cloudy, grassy, immature, assertive. Developed quite well: good colour; creamy, vanilla; very sweet, rich ★★★

**DRY WHITES** The grapes benefited from highly favourable growing conditions and were mainly picked before the start of the rains in mid-September.
**Ch Haut-Brion** Two notes, the first at a pre-sale tasting, the second at a charity dinner: pale green gold; very fragrant bouquet that opened up attractively; dry, lovely flavour, fresh, fairly powerful, good acidity. As so often, somewhat austere. *At Christie's in New York, Dec 1992* ★★★(★)
**Ch Laville Haut-Brion** Very pale; light, subdued nose; medium dry, on the lean side and surprisingly oaky. Went well with 'Fillet of Wild Sea Bass'. *At a Bordeaux Club dinner in the Master's Lodge, Caius, Cambridge, June 2000* ★★(★)?
**Pavillon Blanc de Ch Margaux** Palish, slightly green tinge; fragrant, spearmint; medium – not dry, pleasantly aromatic with slightly spicy finish. *Went well with a light (fishy) lunch between 'flights' two and three of Manfred Wagner's 50-vintage vertical of Ch Margaux in Zurich, Nov 2000* ★★★

# 1995 ★★★★

A return to better times. Beneficial growing conditions until mid-September, then blessed with an Indian summer after the rains ceased on 20th. Although some proprietors made small first *tries* between 6 and 13 September, most waited until later, three-quarters of the crop remaining on the vine and botrytis spreading rapidly. As the grapes were by then suitably ripe there was an urgency to start picking which was completed in record time by the second week in October.
**Ch d'Yquem** After tasting other '99 Sauternes cask samples, the large group of international wine journalists was privileged to taste the just released Yquem '95, accompanied by *pâté de fois gras* 'finger food'. Comte Alexandre de Lur Saluces introduced his young lady *maître de chai* who reminded some of us that the vineyard, one of the largest in Bordeaux, consisted of 103 hectares planted with 80% Sémillon and 20% Sauvignon Blanc, and the wine spent 3½ years in wood. The '95 had a good colour and a fragrant, rich, peachy nose with much more to come; sweet, of course, rich but certainly not plump. Hot alcohol (13.8%) and good acidity, verging, not unusually, on the highish volatile side. Attractive. Considerable future. *Tasted April 2000* ★★★(★) *Say 2015–2035.*
**Ch Climens** Another wet harvest with very rapid botrytis and picking between 18 September and 24 October. Two *tries* carried out, severe selection, alcohol 14%, residual sugar 74g/l: 45% of crop selected for the *1er vin* and 30,000 bottles produced. Pale gold; honeyed yet 'green' and unknit; fairly sweet, moderate extract and length. Disappointing, though Bérénice Lurton reported that, like the '94, it had settled down, showing much better in the afternoon. 'Give it time'. *Tasted at the château before a very late lunch, Oct 2001* ★★★?

**Ch Coutet** Light, rather delicate minty nose; sweet, crisp, attractive. *Sept 1998* ★★★ *Ready for drinking.*
**Ch Lafaurie-Peyraguey** First noted at a *Decanter* masterclass in 1998: bright and beautiful warm yellow gold; totally convincing 'cream of *crème brûlée*', honeyed bouquet; sweet, rich, full-bodied, hot alcohol and acidic finish. Attractive. Could do with bottle age. Most recently – just very good. *Last tasted April 1999* ★★★(★) *Now – 2015.*
**Ch Rabaud-Promis** Pale; minty grassy style; sweet from start to finish. Nice wine. *May 1998* ★★★(★)? *2003–2015.*
**Ch Rieussec** Quite good colour; rich bouquet; slightly odd flavour, but good potential. *May 1998* ★★(★)? *2003–2015.*
**Ch Sigalas-Rabaud** An appealing green gold colour; very fresh, attractive, forthcoming; good honey-peachy flavour but a hot, hard, dry finish. Needs time. *Nov 1998* ★★(★) *2005–2015.*
**Ch Suduiraut** First noted and much liked at a trade tasting in 1996. Very pale, certainly paler than expected; good fruit and depth; sweet, fat, full of fruit, delicious flavour. More recently, similar, bouquet particularly attractive, very fragrant, scented, orange blossom; light style but flavoury with somewhat hard dry finish. Will benefit from more bottle-ageing. *Last tasted at the annual wine dinner at the Knickerbocker Club, New York, Oct 1999* ★★★(★) *2003–2020.*
**Ch La Tour-Blanche** Bright yellow-gold; honey and cress; fairly sweet, crisp, appealing flavour, lively acidity. *At a 'Weinprobe Bordeaux 1995' in Cologne, April 1998* ★★★★ *Now–2015.*

**BRIEF NOTES ON** *DEUXIÈME CRU* **AND MINOR BARSAC AND SAUTERNES CHÂTEAUX Ch Broustet** touch of something like iodine on the nose; very sweet but unattractive flavour. *1997;* **Ch du Dragon** an expensive Cordier wine, fragrant, not sweet enough, hard finish. *1996* ★; **Ch Lamothe** very pale; sweet, caramelly, dry finish. Rather pedestrian. *1998* ★; **Ch Liot** remarkably good for its class: fragrant, sweet, mouthwatering nose, opened up nicely. Two notes. *1999* ★★★; and **Ch de Malle** pale; fragrant, flowery; medium-sweet, crisp. Attractive. *1998 and 1999* ★★★

**DRY WHITES** Good conditions for the dry whites, a considerably larger crop than 1994 and picked early, mainly between 28 August and 4 September. The minor wines will have been consumed. Most of the rest are probably at their best now but the top wines have class and stamina.
**Ch Haut-Brion** Attractive nose, opening up in the glass, whiff of vanilla and touch of peach kernels on the palate. Good length and aftertaste. *The first – and best – wine at the Fête de la Fleur banquet, Ch Pontet-Canet, June 1999* ★★★(★) *2003–2015.*
**Dom de Chevalier** Very pale; low-keyed, some spicy oakiness; dry, complete, all-of-a piece, firm. *Tasted at the Domaine, April 2000* ★★★ *Now–2010.*
**Ch Smith-Haut-Lafitte** Palish but positive; very fragrant; medium dry, spicy, touch of melon and pineapple. *Last tasted at La Caudalie, June 2000* ★★★

# 1996 ★★★★★

An interesting year, particularly successful in Sauternes due to a confluence of distinctive and almost fortuitous conditions. In fact, fluctuating weather during the growing season was responsible for long, slow ripening of the grapes which in turn produced wines with wonderful aromas, particularly the

Sauvignon Blanc which had been picked before the seemingly inevitable September rains. Botrytis first appeared on the Sauvignon Blanc grapes towards the end of August which necessitated some thinning as some had shrivelled before the harvest began. The first two *tries* were erratic because of the rain but the third *trie* on 4 October, which happened to be the first *trie* at Ch d'Yquem, and the fourth, after a final burst of botrytis on 17 October, were picked in perfect conditions, resulting in richly constituted wines.

I first tasted a wide range, some 23 châteaux from Barsac and Sauternes, in April 1997. As usual at this early stage, many wines had the haziness, sometimes cloudiness, of wines that were still in their early stages of evolution. Some were simply not ready to taste. Nevertheless, even a too-early tasting does give one a feel for the potential quality of the vintage.

**Ch d'Yquem** Not tasted. Not yet released (as at 2002) but from all accounts promises to be exceptionally fine.

**Ch Climens** Harvested 24 September–24 October. Rapid and intense botrytis. Despite the rain it was a very good crop with two *tries*: *'Pure et d'une grande concentration'*, according to Bérénice Lurton; 66% of the crop was used for the *1er vin* (36,600 bottles) and 34% for the second wine, Cyrès de Climens. Slightly longer fermentation than normal followed by one month *en barrique*. Alcohol 13.9% and residual sugar 104g/l. As with Yquem, Climens stands aloof, never showing its wines with the other châteaux at the usual April tastings following the harvest because it is considered premature, well before the final *assemblage*. So I first tasted it at the château in June: paler than expected; classic, beautiful shaped nose with a dash of acidity which called to mind greengages; sweet, nice fat, good length, dry with hard finish. Most recently, peach kernels on nose and palate, its considerable sweetness confirmed by later analysis. Richly textured. Needs time. *Last tasted at the château, Oct 2001* ★★(★★) *2006–2030.*

**Ch Lafaurie-Peyraguey** Already a touch of gold colour at the opening tasting; *pourriture* was very evident, apricots, hefty style; sweet, assertive good flavour, length and acidity. Two years after the harvest, now highly polished; very distinctive, forthcoming, herbaceous mint and cress, mouthwatering nose; very sweet, full-bodied (14% alcohol), positive, peachy on palate with lip-licking acidity. Delicious but more to come. *Last tasted at my Decanter masterclass, Nov 1998* ★★★(★) *Ready soon–2020.*

**Ch Liot** Attractive, positive, distinctly sweet and impressive in its way in June 1997 and showing well at two recent wine courses at Christie's: lovely colour, buttery yellow, shades of green and gold; gentle, sweet, minty, honeyed nose with mouthwatering acidity; sweet, nice weight (14% alcohol), delicious flavour, refreshing acidity. *Last tasted Oct 2000* ★★★ *or* ★★★★ *for its class. Drink now–2010.*

**Ch Nairac** Initially hazy and hard. A matter of months later, creamy, fleshy, good flavour. Most recently, colour deepened, a lovely gold; honeyed *pourriture* evident on nose; sweet, lovely, very good finish. *Last tasted March 2001* ★★★★ *for its class. Now–2010.*

**Ch Rieussec** Sémillon 90%, Sauvignon Blanc 7% and Muscadelle 3%, yield 25hl/ha, slightly higher than average for Rieussec. Residual sugar 100g/l. Positive colour but, initially, not star bright; nose unknit, peppery but underlying quality. Better on the palate. Honey and spice. More recently: yellow gold; very pronounced bouquet, oak and honey; fairly sweet and plump, assertive, good texture. *Last tasted with Charles Chevalier at the château, Sept 1998. Probably* ★★(★★★)

**Ch Sigalas-Rabaud** Alcohol 14%, sugar 118g/l, total acidity 4.5g/l, volatile acidity 0.90g/l. Lightly honeyed, classic nose even in the early stages; good flavour, some charm, honeyed finish. Eighteen months later: bouquet first low-keyed, creamy, touch of mint and honeycomb edge, good acidity. Sweet, similar style to the neighbouring Lafaurie, in fact the same winemaker. *Last noted at the Decanter masterclass, Nov 1998* ★★★(★★) *soon–2020.*

**Ch Suduiraut** Initially hard and unforthcoming, good but 'rather masculine'. Two months later, settled down but nose still low-keyed. Sweet, good flavour, hard finish. Needed time. More recently, its nose, minty, grassy, agreeably evolved; medium-sweet; lean, elegant, with good acidity. The *maître de chai* informed me that the yield was 'quite large', 20 hl/ha. Bottled June 1998, the final blend having only a small amount of Sauvignon Blanc. *Last tasted at the château, Sept 1998* ★★(★★★) *2005–2020? We shall see.*

THE FOLLOWING '96s were mainly noted at the opening Sauternes tasting at Ch la Tour-Blanche in April 1997: **Ch Coutet** palish, bright; youthful gooseberry and pineapple, *pourriture* and *pâtisserie*! Sweet, good length and aftertaste but not wholly convincing. Early days. Should be fine ★★(★); **Ch Guiraud** hazy; low-keyed but emerging fragrance; fairly sweet, more of a Barsac weight and style, some finesse, dry finish. Good potential ★★(★★); **Clos Haut-Peyraguey** slightly hazy at the opening tasting but showing its power and class on nose and palate. Low-keyed, peach at first, but blossomed in the glass; very sweet, full, powerful but not too assertive, finished richly. ★★★(★★) *deserves to be better known;* **Ch Rabaud-Promis** youthful rather 'acetone' pineapple nose; medium-sweet, high-toned, noticeably acidic. Premature. ★★(★) *should develop well;* **Ch de Rayne-Vigneau** initially hazy; flowery nose; sweet, powerful, richly honeyed. Two months later, it was more settled, good flavour and grip. *Last tasted June 1997* ★★★(★★) *should be excellent. 2005–2020;* and **Ch La Tour-Blanche** Still hazy; very good nose which opened up in the glass; fairly powerful yet elegant, with good length and potential ★★(★★★)?

A SELECTION OF *DEUXIÈME CRU* AND LESSER GROWTHS OF BARSAC AND SAUTERNES not tasted since April and June 1997: **Ch d'Arche** sweeter and fatter than expected ★★★; **Ch Bastor-Lamontagne** hazy, sharp, assertive but acidic at first. Better on acquaintance: pale, minty, on the lean side but a pleasant flavour ★★★; **Ch Broustet** strange nose, assertive. Not a sound sample ★★?; **Ch Caillou** hazy and unready but some potential ★★?; **Ch Doisy-Daëne** delicious, very sweet, fragrant, on the lean side ★★★★; **Ch Filhot** pale, lime-tinged; fresh, young, grassy nose; sweet enough, assertive, hard, lean ★★?; **Ch Lamothe** green, unready, assertive, reasonably good future ★★★; **Ch Lamothe-Guignard** honey and mint; sweet, plump, touch of caramel. Attractive ★★★; **Ch de Malle** good colour; *pourriture* honey tempered with gooseberry-like acidity. Some ripe fat, dry finish ★★?; **Ch Romer du Hayot** strangely scented nose and taste, Sauvignon uppermost. Hard to predict. But the '96 vintage quality should have a bearing ★★?; and **Ch Suau** sweet, straightforward, youthful acidity, good potential ★★★

Finally I would like to draw attention to the very good sweet wines made on the right bank of the Garonne in Ste Croix-du-Mont and, in particular, in Loupiac.

**DRY WHITES** The wines were good but not as great as the Sauternes. The picking of Sauvignon Blanc started on 12 September, most proprietors picking before the rain came. The Sémillon crop was more variable. Nevertheless the blending of the two worked and the best wines will keep well.

If Sauternes are in varying states of evolution and drinkability at the far-too-early spring tastings following the harvest, the dry whites are even worse. They appear hazy, cloudy, milky and are anything but wholesome. I do not enjoy tasting them at this stage. Most will, of course, develop fairly quickly. In any case the vast majority are short-haul wines, dry, refreshing, for early consumption. For this reason I am only listing a couple.

**Ch Haut-Brion** Despite a 'cold', austere, nutty nose, not as dry as expected, nice weight, lovely flavour and great length. *At the château, Sept 1998* ★★(★★) *Now–2010.*

**Dom de Chevalier** Served somewhat prematurely at dinner at the Domaine in June 1997: it was still cloudy but dry, firm, crisp and good on the palate. Three years later, it had changed almost out of recognition: whiff of new oak and 'arboreal' piquancy; still distinctly dry of course, Sauvignon very apparent, attractive, acidic. *At the Domaine, April 2000* ★★★

# 1997 ★★★★

A roller-coaster of a year, as in the rest of Bordeaux, starting with an unusually warm February and the hottest spring for 50 years. Yet there was frost in Sauternes in April. Bud break was premature, flowering three weeks early and also long. May was cool and wet but the rain in late June and August was not a problem. The harvest was difficult, the good grapes and rotten ones being dotted around each vineyard, making selection or *tries* labour-intensive and time-consuming, and yields were especially low.

**Ch d'Yquem** Not yet released (as at 2002).

**Ch Climens** An early start, 11 September, followed by a prolonged harvest which ended 30 October, the latter part blessed with magnificent hot and sunny conditions, and very good botrytis. Four weeks fermentation *en barrique*. The *rendement* for the *1er vin* was 8hl/ha and 80% of the crop, roughly 32,000 bottles, was selected. Alcohol was 14.2% and there was moderate residual sugar, 77g/l. Medium-pale yellow gold; very forthcoming nose, with rich, spicy, clove-like new oak fragrance; medium-sweet, very peachy-nutty flavour and aftertaste, leaner than the '98. Considered *'un très grand millésime'* by Bérénice Lurton. Certainly worth watching. *At the château, Oct 2001* ★(★★), *possibly 4-star future. Say 2007–2020.*

A RANGE OF '97 SAUTERNES AND BARSACS tasted somewhat prematurely as usual, at the beginning of April 1998 at Ch La Tour-Blanche. On the whole, class showed, the *1er cru classé* wines being superior to the *2ème classé* and *crus bourgeois*. Usefully, at the spring Sauternes tastings we are told the size of vineyard and *cépages*.

PREMIER CRU SAUTERNES AND BARSACS first tasted in April 1998 or as otherwise stated:

**Ch Coutet** 38.9ha; Sémillon 75%, Sauvignon Blanc 23% and Muscadelle 2%. Two years in wood. Good colour nose, flavour and finish. Very good wine. *Potential* ★★★★ *say 2004–2015.*

**Ch Guiraud** Big vineyard, 100ha; Sémillon 65%, Sauvignon Blanc 35% and the wine spent 2½ years in *barrique*. Cloudy at first but fragrant and positive. I was less confident about this

## Labelling of high quality wines

*Ch d'Yquem was one of the first properties to use labels which could not easily be faked, or removed. Special features are incorporated that will show only under ultraviolet light.*

the following spring: curious apricot and peach skin flavour and bite. *Last tasted April 1999. Time will tell.*

**Clos Haut-Peyraguey** Only 15ha; Sémillon 83%, Sauvignon Blanc 15% and Muscadelle 2%. Two years in *barrique*. Hazy but good botrytis, grapey-minty nose; assertive, still harsh, good potential ★(★★) *2004–2015.*

**Ch Lafaurie-Peyraguey** 40ha; Sémillon 93%, Sauvignon Blanc 5% and Muscadelle 2%. Pronounced yellow colour but hazy at opening tasting. Good botrytis nose; sweet, fleshy, good flavour. Confirmed 12 months later. Pale, sweet, creamy, good grip. *Last tasted April 1999* ★★(★★) *Say 2004–2020.*

**Ch Rabaud-Promis** 33ha; Sémillon 80%, Sauvignon Blanc 18% and Muscadelle 2%. Two years maturation, half in vats, half in *barriques*. Fragrant, grapey; fairly sweet, quite attractive but unexciting. Good acidity ★(★★) *2003–2015.*

**Ch de Rayne-Vigneau** 80ha; Sémillon 75%, Sauvignon Blanc 23% and Muscadelle 2%. Usually between 18 and 24 months in *barrique*. Cloudy, and unready nose yet on the palate sweet, full, fat, slightly minty, good length and acidity ★★(★★), *possibly 5-star in due course. 2004–2020.*

**Ch Rieussec** 75ha; Sémillon 90%, Sauvignon Blanc 8% and Muscadelle 2%. Two years in *barrique*. Initially a strange nose that reminded me of condensed milk. Very sweet, fat, rich, curious finish. Later that autumn bright yellow gold; expansive, well-balanced, peachy and creamy nose and flavour to match. Very sweet (120g/l sugar), excellent counter-balancing acidity, good length and finish. *At the château, Sept 1998* ★★(★★★) *2004–2020.*

**Ch Sigalas-Rabaud** Only 14ha; Sémillon 85% and Sauvignon Blanc 15%. Two years in *cuves* and *barriques*. Not star bright initially but impressive: fragrant; very sweet, full-bodied, good finish, attractive ★★(★★★) *2003–2015.*

**Ch Suduiraut** Bottled June 1999. 86ha; Sémillon 80% and Sauvignon Blanc 20%; 18–24 months in barrique, 20% of which are replaced each year. Impressive even at the first showing; classic botrytis honey; good flesh and acidity. Later the same autumn remarkably advanced and forthcoming. Sweeter than the '96, excellent acidity. More recently, developing well, fairly powerful and assertive. *Last tasted April 1999* ★★(★★★) *2004–2020.*

**Ch La Tour-Blanche** State-owned and an agricultural school, hence the rather academic *cépage* percentages (I had slightly *expected* them to go to two decimal places but they don't quite add up anyway!) – 30ha; Sémillon 77.5%, Sauvignon 19.5% and Muscadelle 2.7%. Fermented for 15–21 days in new wood followed by two years in *barrique*. Good nose and flavour, honeyed botrytis, creamy, vanilla, mint and oak. Not as sweet as some, but good body, flesh and taste. ★★(★★★) *2004–2020.*

*DEUXIÈME CRU AND LESSER SAUTERNES AND BARSACS* first tasted in April 1998:

**Ch Bastor-Lamontagne** 50ha, of which 7ha are leased; Sémillon 78%, Sauvignon Blanc 17%, Muscadelle 5%. 18 months in *barrique*. Initially cloudy; clover honey, sweet, crisp good fruit. Two years later the clouds had lifted, the colour lime with gold highlights; nose that conjured up milk chocolate; very sweet, quite attractive with some flesh and fat. An inexpensive unassuming wine, clearly quite good in this vintage. *Last tasted April 2000* ★★★ *Drink now–2010.*

**Ch Broustet** 16ha; Sémillon 68%, Sauvignon Blanc 20% and Muscadelle an unusually high 12%. Very minty, herbaceous, sweet, assertive ★★★ *Drink soon.*

**Ch Caillou** 13ha; Sémillon 90%, Sauvignon Blanc 10%. Unready, raw, but good straightforward flavour. Should turn out quite well ★★★ *Say now–2010.*

**Ch Doisy-Daëne** 15ha; Sémillon 70%, Sauvignon Blanc 20% and Muscadelle 10%. Two years in *barriques*. Classic, spicy; very sweet, full-bodied, good flavour. Oaky aftertaste ★★★ *possibly* ★★★★ *2004–2015.*

**Ch Doisy-Védrines** 27ha; Sémillon 80%, Sauvignon Blanc 20%. Two years in *barriques*. Already honeyed, grapey; good flesh and flavour. Well balanced. Showing well 12 months later: very forthcoming nose and fragrant aftertaste ★★★★ *2004–2015.*

**Ch Filhot** 16ha; Sémillon only 55%, Sauvignon Blanc 40%, Muscadelle 5%. Unready but quite fragrant; medium-sweet, dry finish ★★? *2003–2010.*

**Ch Lamothe** The smallest of the Sauternes classed growths at 7.5ha; Sémillon 85%, Sauvignon Blanc 10% and Muscadelle 5%. Good colour, undeveloped but some charm. Interesting flavour ★★★ *2003–2010.*

**Ch Lamothe-Guignard** 17ha. Sémillon a very high 90%, Sauvignon Blanc 5% and Muscadelle 5%. A hefty style of wine, very sweet, somewhat caramelly ★★★? *2005–2012.*

**Ch de Malle** 27ha; Sémillon 75%, Sauvignon Blanc 23% and Muscadelle 2%. Fairly sweet, fat for de Malle, touch of caramel ★★★ *(just). 2003–2010.*

**Ch de Myrat** 22ha; Sémillon 88%, Sauvignon Blanc 8% and Muscadelle 4%. Two years in *barriques*. Fragrant botrytis; medium-sweet, initially hard. Will it open up? ★★? *2007–2010.*

**Ch Nairac** 16ha; Sémillon 90%, Sauvignon Blanc 6% and Muscadelle 4%. Positive colour; fragrant; very sweet, full, fat, dry finish. A good Nairac ★★★ *2003–2012.*

**Ch Romer du Hayot** 16ha; Sémillon 70%, Sauvignon Blanc 25% and Muscadelle 5%. Nice weight and style, barley sugar flavour ★★★ *2003–2012.*

**Ch Suau** 8ha, Sémillon 80%, Sauvignon Blanc 10% and Muscadelle 10%. Grassy; strange rather varnishy flavour. I hope it will get its second wind ★★?

**DRY WHITES** Less good than the sweet wines, for though the harvest had an early start on 18 August, those Sauvignon Blanc grapes with a high sugar content lacked acidity. The later-ripening Sémillon tended to dominate, giving the Graves blends a broader style with good depth of fruit but lacking Sauvignon Blanc vivacity.

**Ch Haut-Brion** First tasted at the château in the spring of 1998. Delicious young nose, spicy, sweet and soft, like blancmange; a combination of ripe grapes and alcohol resulting in surprising sweetness. Full-bodied, attractive, touch of astringency. Should have a good mid-term future. *Tasted April 1998* ★★★(★★) *2005–2015.*

**Ch Laville Haut-Brion** Sémillon 80%, Sauvignon Blanc 20%. Picking commenced 18 August. Good colour; young pineapple aroma and flavour; rich but less sweet than Ch Haut-Brion. Oaky. Dry finish. Should turn out well. *Tasted at Ch La Mission-Haut-Brion, April 1998* ★★★(★★) *2005–2015.*

**Dom de Chevalier** First noted in April 1998. Very pale; fragrant, piquant Sauvignon Blanc uppermost; medium-dry,

delicious fruit. Minty. Two years later: a vivacious aroma, attractive, perhaps lacking a little length. *Last tasted at the Domaine, April 2000* ★★★ *Now–2010.*

**Ch Talbot Caillou Blanc** One of the few white Médocs produced. Fairly pale, touch of green; very distinctive, not remotely like its Graves cousins; dry enough, fullish flavour, vanilla and peardrops. Might possibly benefit from more bottle age. *In magnum, dinner at home, May 2001* ★★? *Now–2005.*

# 1998 ★★★★

The third good but not great Sauternes vintage in a row, to some extent making up for the disheartening harvests earlier in the decade. The growing season got off to a good start, warm and sunny, with early bud break. April was cold and wet but after the first week in May it was dry and sunny with quick, even flowering from the end of the month. June was normal, July erratic but August extremely hot, the vines literally scorched with temperatures up to 39°C. September was cooler and fine, some storms, sunny from mid-month. Then heavy rain from the beginning of October. The best Sauternes were made from the very ripe botrytis-infected first *tries* between 16 and 29 September and again from 10 October, well after the worst of the rains.

**Ch d'Yquem** At the time of writing (April 2002) not available for tasting.

---

### Rodenstock's 1998 Ch d'Yquem marathon

*When Hardy Rodenstock first told me about his plan to taste 125 vintages of Ch d'Yquem over a period of five days, my first reaction – well, second – was how on earth, even with over six months prior notice, could anyone write off a week in the early autumn to taste a range of wines from just one château – and sweet wine at that! Naturally, I put the date in my diary: arrival in Munich on Sunday 30 August (1998), departure after the customary 'gala dinner', on Saturday 6 September. And of course I turned up. As always, the event was immaculately organised and the tastings were well paced. We were given plenty of time to taste and reflect; some of the wines were served blind, others in vintage 'flights'. To drink blind, wines which were exactly 100 years apart in age, surely concentrates the mind.*

*The morning's tastings were followed by a meal. The chef at the Hotel Königshof presented a masterly array of lunches and dinners, different every day, and each with appropriate wines. In addition to the Yquem, two other verticals were slotted in: 32 vintages of Ch La Fleur (1945–1995) and Ch L'Église-Clinet (15 vintages, from 1947 to 1996). Plus wines with lunch and with dinner. My notes dominate Volume 118 of my tasting books. A total of 284 wines, all of the highest quality. There were two dozen tasters, mainly European, but including a contingent from Hong Kong. It was memorable to say the least, and I'm horrified to think what it cost our host! A unique event. I hate to use the word 'definitive', but that is as near as it gets.*

---

**Ch Climens** Picking began here on 25 September in very good weather, with very rapid botrytis but the rest of the harvest, ending 16 October, enjoyed mixed conditions. Three *tries*, yield of 13.3hl/ha, four to six weeks fermentation *en barriques*, *élevage* 19 months in *barriques* from different *tonneliers*. 64% of the crop went into the *1er vin* and 36,650 bottles produced. Alcohol 14.2% and residual sugar 86g/l. Along with

Ch d'Yquem, Climens does not show its wine with the other châteaux at the usual opening spring tasting at Ch La Tour-Blanche, and for a very good reason – at this time the wines are still in their original *barriques* and unblended. The '98 had been 'mainly assembled' in September 1999 but was still in cask when I first tasted it the following spring: pale in colour and still not star bright; very fragrant though, with considerable depth. Very good indeed. Exactly a year later: lovely nose, fragrant orange blossom, after 1½ hours in the glass, like a sweetshop; very sweet, very rich, slightly chewy confectionery, spicy (cloves, new oak), good length and aftertaste. *Last noted at the château, Oct 2001* ★★(★★) *Lovely wine with a good future, say 2010–2025.*

MOST OF THE NOTES THAT FOLLOW were made at the Sauternes opening tasting on April Fool's Day, 1999.
**Ch Coutet** Fragrant, easy, attractive yet not overly impressive. Should turn out well though ★(★★)? 2005–2015.
**Ch Guiraud** Not ready. Touch of toffee. Medium sweet. Unexciting. Must retaste ★★
**Ch Lafaurie-Peyraguey** Ignoring its cloudy appearance a complex, minty, botrytis nose with tangerine-like acidity. Sweet, powerful. Impressive ★(★★★) 2006–2015.
**Clos Haut-Peyraguey** Pure yellow-gold; very good nose, opening up attractively. Reminded me of privet. Very sweet, rich, honeyed, good length and acidity. Just slightly cloying; but good future. Deserves to be better known ★★(★★) 2004–2015.
**Ch Rabaud-Promis** Low-keyed, minty, acidic; not very sweet, dull finish and caramelly acidic aftertaste ★★?
**Ch de Rayne-Vigneau** Cloudy; nose so creamy that it reminded me of a milking parlour; a touch of hardness and a bit four-square. Not one of my top marks. Yet, it's early days (★★★)?
**Ch Rieussec** The best of the bunch at the tasting. Although not bright, a distinctive yellow gold; sweet, creamy, vanilla, classic; very sweet, very rich, honeyed botrytis flavour, ★(★★★) 2005–2020.
**Ch Sigalas-Rabaud** Rich, honeyed; very sweet, lovely flavour, classic ★(★★★) 2006–2015.
**Ch Suduiraut** Very sweet, crisp, attractive. Queried its finish. Retaste. *Probably* ★(★★★)
**Ch La Tour-Blanche** Barley sugar botrytis nose and taste. Firm. Good length ★(★★★) 2005–2015.

*DEUXIÈME CRU* AND LESSER SAUTERNES AND BARSACS briefly noted 1 April 1999 (all the wines for drinking between now and, say, 2012): **Ch d'Arche** good weight and flavour ★★★; **Ch Bastor-Lamontagne** ★★; **Ch Broustet** very sweet, teeth-gripping acidity ★★; **Ch Caillou** honeyed botrytis; hefty, some length but lacking acidity? ★★; **Ch Doisy-Daëne** rich, good depth; touch of toffee, rich, lacks the deft touch of Védrines ★★; **Ch Doisy-Védrines** scented, attractive; crisp Barsac style, decent length ★★★★; **Ch Filhot** piquant Sauvignon aroma, fragrant; pedestrian on palate, short, acidic ★; **Ch Lamothe** rich, some depth, hefty style ★★★; **Ch Lamothe-Guignard** caramelly, crusty, dry finish ★★; **Ch de Malle** despite high percentage of Sémillon, very much a Sauvignon Blanc aroma; very sweet, light style, crisp, grapey flavour. Good acidity ★★★; **Ch de Myrat** floral, attractive; sweet, hefty style ★★★ (*just*); **Ch Nairac** not ready for tasting. Unusually rich nose yet lean on the palate. Youthful acidity ★★, *possibly* ★★★; and **Ch Suau** pure gold colour, more appealing than nose or taste ★★

DRY WHITES Because of the excessive heat in August, fully ripe grapes were picked early, Sauvignon Blanc first, either side of the beginning of September. The wines were not dissimilar to the '97s, tending to lack acidity, perhaps somewhat better.
**Ch Haut-Brion** Sémillon 50%, Sauvignon Blanc 50%. A hefty, stolid but very rich, full-bodied wine. Impressive but I preferred the '99. *At the château, Oct 2001* ★★(★★) *2004–2015.*
**Ch Laville Haut-Brion** Sémillon 78%, Sauvignon Blanc 22%. Rich, youthful, pineapple aroma, greater depth than the '99. More substantial, more fruit, more of a bite, complete, oaky, good acidity. *At Ch Haut-Brion, Oct 2001* ★★(★★) *2004–2015, possibly longer.*

OF THE WIDE RANGE OF PESSAC-LÉOGNAN WINES at the opening tasting on 31 March 1999, most were cloudy and many simply not in a fit state to taste. Showing well, however, were **Ch Chantegrive** (making very good wines following recent improvements), **Dom de Chevalier**, **Ch Haut-Bergey** and **Ch La Louvière**.

TASTED MORE RECENTLY, in March 2001: **Ch Latour-Martillac** dry, lean and far too oaky; and **Ch Smith-Haut-Lafitte** as vivacious as Madame Cathiard.

# 1999 ★★★★

A satisfactory and more uniform growing season, an Indian summer inducing excellent botrytis which helped produce the fifth very good Sauternes vintage in a row. A small harvest with excellent potential.
**Ch Climens** Localised rain on 25 September. Harvested between 29 September and 18 October with rapid and intense botrytis. Early picking excellent, after the first *trie* the weather was less clement and after the second *trie 'moins intéressant'*. Four weeks fermentation *en barrique*. 63% of the crop was used for the *1er vin* and some 23,000 bottles produced. Alcohol 14.2% and residual sugar 91g/l.

As already mentioned, Climens does not provide sample bottles at the customary open tasting for the fairly large gathering of international wine journalists. Tasting is very much by appointment. Casual visitors are not welcome; in any case the absence of directional signs, in common with Ch d'Yquem, makes the château difficult to find in low-lying Barsac. But on 4 April 1999 Bérénice Lurton, a member of Bordeaux's most prolific wine family, demonstrated to a small, privileged and very serious group precisely why she does not show her wine the spring after the vintage. At this time, the wine is in *barriques* made by different *tonneliers*, including the well-known Demptos and Séguin-Moreau, and is still very much in a state of evolution. Bérénice then selected barrels to enable us to taste the considerable variations on a theme; and they did vary, except for a general haziness. In the first cask the wine was fragrant and flowery, sweet, crisp, with quite a bite, the second spicier, richer and fatter, a third less sweet, a fourth grapey, rich, powerful, and so forth. The last sample shown, from the best cask, was the most fragrant, buttery, sweetest and richest. All Sémillon and no Sauvignon Blanc at Climens, the differences being due to the different 'parcels' in the vineyard and, as mentioned, the casks. The wines were nowhere near finished, the final *assemblage*, a crucial selection, being made later on, in this case around September 2000.

Most recently, youthful aroma still unknit, but fresh, floral, very attractive with mouthwatering acidity; sweet, very fragrant, still very oaky, very pleasant flavour, good length and future. *Last tasted at the château, Oct 2001 (★★★★) 2010–2025.*

**Ch Guiraud** At the first tasting a minty Sauvignon character; medium-sweet, dry spicy finish. Just over a year later, a whiff of mandarin on the nose; very sweet, very rich mouthful. Hot finish. *Last tasted May 2001 (★★★) 2006–2020.*

**Ch Lafaurie-Peyraguey** Fragrant, reminding me of camomile; sweet lean and firm at the opening tasting. A year later it was, I thought, the sweetest of the group, if anything too sweet, too rich. Impressive. *Last tasted May 2001 (★★★★) Say 2006–2020.*

**Ch de Rayne-Vigneau** A good start: very fragrant, peaches, ripe orange, honeyed; very sweet, assertive, complete, lovely. More recently: a limpid pale gold, its earlier promise confirmed. *Last tasted May 2001 (★★★★) 2006–2025.*

**Ch Sigalas-Rabaud** Preferred it first time round. Confectionery. *Need to retaste.* Rating?

**Ch Suduiraut** Opened well: melon and honey; sweet, good flavour, flesh, fat, length and aftertaste. Seemed not as dramatic but clearly good. *Last tasted May 2001 (★★★) 2006–2020.*

**Ch La Tour-Blanche** Low-keyed, peachy acidic nose; very sweet, rich, high extract and good acidity. Next, still with a youthful pineapple aroma, appearing less sweet but hefty with a rich texture and slightly caramelly finish. *Last tasted May 2001 (★★★) possibly 4 stars. 2006–2020.*

THE FOLLOWING *PREMIER CRU* BARSACS AND SAUTERNES were tasted on 1 April 2000: **Clos Haut-Peyraguey** unusual spearmint scent and flavour. Attractive though (★★★)?; and **Ch Rieussec** cloudy but rich looking; very good nose, spicy, buttery, honeyed; very sweet, complete, good length and aftertaste, fairly high acidity (★★★★)

THE FOLLOWING *DEUXIÈME CRU* AND LESSER GROWTH SAUTERNES AND BARSACS tasted only in April 2000, unless otherwise stated: **Ch Bastor-Lamontagne** good fruit, quite a bite; developing well, vanilla, ripe melon, lanolin; nice fruit and grip. *Last tasted May 2001 (★★★)*; **Ch Broustet** very sweet, clove-like spiciness – new oak. *Probably (★★)*; **Ch Caillou** quite good (★★); **Ch Doisy-Daëne** not very sweet, crisp (★★); **Ch Doisy-Védrines** showing very well: good colour; sweet buttery Sémillon, botrytis; rich, mouthfilling, complete. *Last tasted May 2001 (★★★★)*; **Ch Lamothe** spicy, sharp, assertive. Will settle down (★★)?; **Ch Lamothe-Guignard** Sémillon uppermost, sweet, some flesh (★★★); **Ch de Malle** quite good depth; very sweet, attractive (★★★★); **Ch de Myrat** gold colour; caramelly nose; surprisingly dry, full-bodied (★);

## Ch Climens

*I have always been a huge admirer of Ch Climens. For consistency, reliability and quality it is – in my opinion – unmatched. And it is in good hands. I am indebted to Bérénice Lurton(-Thomas) for arranging a unique tasting of 30 vintages, from 1964 to 1999 (and for 2001 as it was bubbling in the vat) in October 2001. It helped put the vintages in perspective.*

**Ch Nairac** surely one of the best Nairacs: lovely apricot and lanolin nose; surprisingly sweet, excellent flavour, body and finish. *Last tasted May 2001 (★★★★)*; and **Ch Romer du Hayot** very minty, Sauvignon Blanc uppermost; medium-sweet, quite a bite. Should improve (★★★)

DRY WHITES An equally satisfactory year for the dry whites. Harvesting took place in great heat in Pessac on 30 August, Sauvignon Blanc was picked first, as usual. However – paradoxically – the Sauvignon Blanc provided the power and the later-picked Sémillon the fruit, both attaining natural alcohol levels over 12%.

**Ch Haut-Brion** Sémillon 65%, Sauvignon Blanc 35%. Medium-pale, very bright, youthful lime tinge; initial scent of spearmint, then the more 'waxy' Sémillon. Medium – a touch of sweetness, perfect weight, lovely young pineapple flavour and finish. More bite than the '98. *At the château, Oct 2001 (★★★★) Good potential.*

**Ch Laville Haut-Brion** Sémillon 75%, Sauvignon Blanc 25%. Fairly pale; youthful lemon and pineapple, opening up attractively; medium-dry, a medium-light character, stylish, pleasant flavour, dry finish. *At Ch Haut-Brion, Oct 2001 (★★★★) probably drinking deliciously in its youth, a possible 'closure' or dumb period from 2005–2010, lovely thereafter. It will be interesting to see.*

**Dom de Chevalier** Two notes, both emphasising the very Sauvignon Blanc zestfulness and flavour. Will be *à point* now. *Last tasted April 2000 ★★★*

**Aile d'Argent** the relatively new dry wine produced by Philippine de Rothschild's excellent team. Having said that I still found the '99 a bit boring. Pricey too ★★★ *for those that can afford it.*

OF THE '99 PESSAC-LÉOGNAN WHITES noted at the opening tasting in April 2000 I preferred the quietly consistent **Ch La Louvière**, the 'modern' **Ch Smith-Haut-Lafitte** and **Ch Bouscaut**. The other wines were not in a fit condition to taste. But all are for early drinking anyway.

# 2000–2001

The dry whites look after themselves; it is Sauternes one should care more about, to understand the disappointment, in some cases despair, following a poor harvest, and its financial implications, and to join in the welcome relief provided by the fair enough 'Millennium' vintage of 2000 and the truly magnificent 2001. And it is worth reminding ourselves that unlike their counterparts in the Loire, the Rhine and Mosel, who can choose whether to delay picking a part of their crops, having already made their more commercial, run-of-the-mill dry or medium-dry wines, the Sauternes producers, who mainly make only one style of wine, face an almost all-or-nothing situation.

## 2000 variable, at best ★★★

The millennium vintage in Sauternes was something of a damp squib. Results were very mixed, with Ch Nairac in Barsac, for example, unable to make any wine.

The Union des Grands Crus annual opening tasting of Sauternes for journalists was held on 26 March 2001 at Ch La Tour-Blanche as usual, a somewhat bleak and unprepossessing winery and agricultural school situated at a high point on the far western side of Sauternes.

It was well organised, with the option to taste blind. Most of the proprietors were present, anxious as always, about their 'babies'. This year they were a mixed bunch (the wines). Held even earlier than the last year, far too early in the opinion of most of the professional visitors; the wines were not easy to taste and assess. For example 12 of the 20 châteaux's wines ranged from hazy to cloudy, only six being bright, the 'nose' varied from unfinished though hard to creamy and fragrant. All were sweet, some very sweet.

**Ch Climens** Tasted in cask – not the final blend; pale yellow; fragrant, spicy; medium-sweet, lovely flesh but not fat. Should turn out well. Only 10,000 to 11,000 bottles of the *1er vin* likely to be produced. *At the château, Oct 2001.*

OF THE *PREMIER CRU* SAUTERNES, the following wines showed the best potential: **Ch Lafaurie-Peyraguey** grapey; very sweet, mouthfilling, lovely; **Ch de Rayne-Vigneau** excellent; **Ch Rieussec** with astonishing colour, like unpolished brass; but equally amazingly sweet, fat and full; **Ch Sigalas-Rabaud** good though on the lean side; and **Ch Suduiraut** good enough.

OF THE SLIGHTLY LESSER MORTALS **Ch Broustet**, **Ch Bastor-Lamontagne**, and **Ch Doisy-Védrines** were all good; **Ch Filhot** surprisingly good; **Ch Lamothe-Despajols** (new to me) and **Ch de Malle** also good.

DRY WHITES The Pessac-Léognans were tasted on 27 March 2001. My group of journalists was tasting at Ch Smith-Haut-Lafitte. Only at the Sauternes tasting at Ch La Tour-Blanche do all the (nearly 100 in 2001) journalists taste in one place. For all the other wines we split into small groups which usually works well.

The young dry whites usually look even worse than the Sauternes, most being hazy and unfinished, to the extent that I find tasting them at this stage unhelpful. The best time, though one can very rarely taste a complete range, is in June or

perhaps October (the year after the vintage) or, better still, after bottling. But of course, it is always interesting to taste them while they are young in order to trace their development.

**Ch Haut-Brion** Though still slightly hazy on the nose, the wine was showing considerable character and depth. Not the often austere style but sweeter, softer and fleshier than the Ch Laville Haut-Brion. Attractive. Considerable potential. *Tasted in the company of Count Robert de Luxembourg, Joan de Mouchy's son (now managing director) and the imperturbable 'rock-of-ages' Jean Delmas at Ch La Mission Haut-Brion, March 2001 (★★★★) Say 2005–2020.*

**Ch Laville Haut-Brion** Also slightly hazy; fragrant nose, youthful pineapple and oak; dry, very good. But I missed the excitement of the almost overpowering '89. *Also tasted at Ch La Mission Haut-Brion, March 2001 (★★★)? A good excuse to taste again.*

DRY WHITES Having mentioned the relatively untastable dry whites I can now say the following Pessac-Léognans were showing quite well in March 2001: **Dom de Chevalier** as usual; **Ch Pape-Clément** a wine to look out for; and **Ch Smith-Haut-Lafitte**.

## 2001 (★★★★★)

I was fortunate to be in Barsac during the vintage. Picking had started around 10 October and on the day I arrived at Ch Climens for the remarkable vertical tasting, there was a clear blue sky and the pickers were busy. The following day, as Daphne and I were about to leave the Hôtel St James which overlooks the Garonne, there was a heavy morning mist which was burnt off by the sun around midday. Perfect conditions for botrytis, perfect vintage weather for all Sauternes. Watch out for these wines and lay them down for your grandchildren!

**Ch d'Yquem** Comte Alexandre de Lur Saluces was ecstatic; perfect conditions for harvesting. Alas, no-one will be able to taste this wine – unless his policy changes – until around 2006.

**Ch Climens** I had a quick taste of the must before fermentation but my judgement must be circumstantial and I will defer to Bérénice Lurton who confirmed the ideal weather conditions and the botrytis superb – 'the most beautiful I have ever seen'. Her *chef de culture* and enologist, Christian Bronstant, compared it to the 1989.

At the time of writing, no '01s ready for tasting but clearly this is a great vintage in the making and as already stated a must for all lovers of Sauternes.

# Red Burgundy

Although the preponderance of Bordeaux notes in this book might give the impression that I do not rate the wines of Burgundy as highly, I must preface the following observations by stating, unequivocally, that I *like* Burgundy, the wine and the region. Compared to Bordeaux it is so much easier to visit and I challenge anyone not to experience a thrill when, driving south from Dijon – but not on the *autoroute* – they see on their right signs to a string of villages with a roll-call of evocative names: Gevrey-Chambertin, Chambolle-Musigny, Vougeot, Vosne-Romanée, then, skirting the little town of Nuits-St-Georges, on to the old walled city of Beaune; thence to Pommard, Volnay and beyond. The vineyards are continuous and contiguous, the *côtes*, the slopes, looking like one neat carpet of vines.

Unlike Bordeaux, with its maritime climate and range of *cépages*, Burgundy, 400 miles or so (and a tedious, over 6-hour drive) to the north-east, has a continental climate and, for the reds, uses just one grape variety, Pinot Noir. But the other principal difference is the subdivision of land. Unlike Bordeaux, Burgundy is not a myriad of châteaux surrounded by their own vineyards but blocks and strips of vines tended by a multiplicity of owners, some grand, mostly modest. The way the owners tend their vineyards, make and look after their wines, makes for infinite variations on a theme.

This is no place for a history lesson, but there is evidence of viticulture preceding the arrival of the Romans. After the decline, and the dark period of the barbarians, monastic institutions began to develop viticulture, though it was not until the early Middle Ages that the Benedictines and Cistercians, followed by the Dukes of Burgundy and the aristocrats, established what were to become the great vineyards. By the time of Jefferson's visit in the 1780s there already existed a vineyard hierarchy but there was no classification in the Bordeaux sense except an unofficial one in an important treatise by a Dr Lavalle published (coincidentally, in the same year as the Bordeaux classification) in 1855 and which formed the basis of an official classification of *grands crus*, Burgundy's top-ranking vineyards, in 1861.

The next rank is *1er cru*, followed in descending order by village, regional and generic Bourgogne appellations. For example, 'Chambertin' is a *grand cru*; 'Gevrey-Chambertin, Clos St-Jacques' is a *premier cru*, 'Gevrey-Chambertin' alone is a village wine. (In Bordeaux the tip of the hierarchy is *premier cru classé*, whereas *grand cru*, as used in St-Émilion, for example, is distinctly less grand). In the following pages I have not singled out the *grands crus* from the *premiers crus* – the wines are grouped by vintage year alphabetically.

But it is not enough to know the village and vineyard names; more important in Burgundy is the name and reputation of the producer. And this is what makes the region so challenging and fascinating. There can be some disappointments *en route*, as my notes will indicate, but burgundy at its best is sublime, unbeatable. Moreover, this is not a gazetteer of burgundy, my notes being used, as elsewhere in the book, to describe the background, quality, style and state of development of wines of a given vintage as and when I have come across them. Alas, my work at Christie's precluded the luxury of three month stints in Burgundy.

I list the wines of the Domaine de la Romanée-Conti (DRC) before the others in each vintage, not just because they epitomise – arguably – red burgundy's best, but more importantly because they provide a benchmark of the character, quality and state of development of a given vintage. For, although there are other great estates, there is not one domaine, at least not one familiar to me, which can give such a good overall view of each vintage.

# 19th century

Burgundy, as elsewhere, was not immune to the dreaded louse phylloxera, but it arrived later than in Bordeaux and was first recognised in the Côte de Beaune in 1878. It caused havoc. It was not until 1887 that grafting onto American root stock was reluctantly accepted as the only solution; this ended the age-old and haphazard system of *propinage* or 'layering', bending a vine shoot to take root.

It is a pity that the British upper classes of the time were not as appreciative of the fine wines of Burgundy as they were of Bordeaux. This had more to do with history and custom than with quality and ability to age for, contrary to common belief, the best burgundy keeps well and it is sad that more examples have not emerged from the ideal cellars of British country houses to prove the point. The few 19th-century burgundies I have tasted have come mainly from France, from Burgundy itself, or from patrician cellars in the USA. I have listed the major 19th-century vintages below on the off chance that a cobwebbed bottle or two might turn up, even though my notes only cover a few of these years. For similar reasons, I have recorded very briefly notes of wines a century or more old when tasted, particularly those from the cellars of the Domaine du Château de Beaune which still occasionally come on to the market.

## Vintages at a Glance

**Outstanding ★★★★★**
1811 (Comet), 1846, 1865, 1875

**Very Good ★★★★**
1802, 1806, 1815, 1819, 1822, 1825, 1834, 1848, 1859, 1864, 1869, 1870, 1878, 1887

**Good ★★★**
Post-1850 only: 1858, 1877, 1885, 1886, 1893, 1894, 1898

## 1858 ★★★

**Corton, Clos du Roi** Labaume-Aîné From the family cellars: faded though sound and attractive. *1967* ★★★

## 1864 ★★★★

A very good pre-phylloxera vintage.

**Beaune, Clos de la Mousse Dom du Ch de Beaune** Three notes, two made at Heublein pre-sale tastings. On the last occasion dining with Lloyd Flatt, one of the principal purchasers: deep colour for age, lovely old Pinot nose; lacking flesh but otherwise faultless. *Last tasted Oct 1987* ★★★★

## 1865 ★★★★★

A magnificent vintage producing deep, firm, flavoury wines.

**Beaune, Première Cuvée, Grizot Bouchard Père** Four notes between 1977 and 1987, mainly at Heublein pre-sale

### The Heublein wine auctions

*Noting Christie's success in London, Heublein decided to follow suit optimistically announcing 'The First Premier National Auction of Rare Wines'. After quelling some trade objections the first was held in Chicago in May 1969. Resplendent in morning coat, sporting a carnation – but somewhat nervous – I took the rostrum. Happily, Heublein's optimism was fully justified and it soon became the most prestigious annual event in the USA. It also gave me the opportunity to meet the new breed of wine buffs like Lloyd Flatt and to taste many rare wines including those from Bouchard's cellars beneath the ramparts of Beaune.*

tastings. All good: lovely colour, rich; good fruit, intense flavour, still retaining tannins. *Last noted dining with Lloyd Flatt, Oct 1987* ★★★★★

**La Romanée, Tête de Cuvée Bouchard Père** Fragrant; sweet, soft yet firm. Glorious. *At the Heublein pre-sale tasting, May 1981* ★★★★★

**Volnay, Santenots Bouchard Père** Three notes, two at Heublein tastings. Very good smoky Pinot nose; good, light Volnay character. More recently: surprisingly deep colour; sound, rich, slightly 'stewed' vanillin bouquet; very good flavour, complete, touch of tar, excellent tannin and acidity. *Last noted lunching with Joseph Henriot, the new owner of Bouchard Père, Nov 1995* ★★★★

**Clos Vougeot Bouchard Père** Made before the Clos was split into small parcels (see box page 218). Last recorked in 1960. Beautiful colour; sweet nose, no signs of decay, ripe sweetness on palate, assertive yet languorous flavour. Good fruit, extract, alcohol, tannins and acidity. *Last noted at the Heublein pre-sale tasting, May 1981* ★★★★★

**Romanée-Conti** Labelled 'S. Guyot, Masson & fils & J. Chambon Petits fils de J.M. Dufault-Blochet'. Medium-pale, warm amber with a ruddy core, good colour for its age; sweet, low-keyed, virtually faultless bouquet despite showing a bit of age, opening up fragrantly after only 15 minutes and holding well; on the palate medium-dry, good length and acidity. In remarkable condition. *The oldest vintage in Wilfred Jaeger's unprecedented burgundy tasting, San Francisco, March 2002* ★★★★★
(See also Vosne-Romanée Cuvée Duvault-Blochet page 270.)

## 1893 ★★★

**Pommard** (probably English-bottled.) A half bottle from the cellars of the Duke of Beaufort at Badminton House. Still retaining good colour, sweet on nose and palate. Remarkably drinkable. *Tasted with Ch Lafitte 1787 in Zurich, Aug 1992* ★★★

## 1898 ★★★

**Bonnes-Mares Faiveley** Three bottles, all tasted in the early 1980s. Good levels; remarkably deep colour; sound bouquet, no faults; touch of sweetness, full-bodied, high alcoholic content and extract, meaty, singed, rounded flavour, dry finish. *Last tasted dining at home, Aug 1981* ★★★★

# 1900—1929

This section covers three highly interesting decades, bisected by World War One.

The early part of the 20th century saw continuing concerns with the problems of phylloxera and vineyard restructuring. Modern times also arrived with the foundation of the Station Oenologique in Beaune, followed by the enactment of the first legislation in France to eliminate wine fraud and protect names of origin. In 1919 further laws were enacted, concerning village and vineyard boundaries and, in 1929, the outlawing of hybrid and other inappropriate vines. Most burgundies were shipped *en barrique* for bottling locally by wine merchants. In Burgundy itself the trade was dominated by merchants in Beaune and Nuits-St-Georges, few individual domaines being known by name. Most of the burgundies I have tasted from this period have emanated from France, most notably from the incredible Barolet cellar.

Upon Dr Barolet's death, his two elderly sisters sold the entire stock to the Swiss-owned *négociant* de Villamont. The first *tranche* of nearly 1500 cases (vintages 1911–1959) being auctioned at Christie's ex-cellars Beaune to promote the name which was previously known only to the Barolet father and son's private customers in Belgium, and to establish prices. The sale in December 1969, which I entitled the *'Collection du Dr Barolet'* was a great success, with prices well above normal levels, thanks to the remarkable condition of the wines. Unknown to the public, this was only a fraction of the stock – for example, there were some 2000 bottles of 1921 Clos de la Roche in three large 'bins' – which were subsequently recorked and distributed on to the market through the trade in the 1970s. The original bottlings which I tasted on the spot and at pre-sale tastings in Paris, Geneva and London were excellent.

The other major collection belonged to Mme Teysonneau in Bordeaux. After I had spent all one Sunday sorting out her pre-phylloxera clarets, the widest range ever handled by Christie's, the good lady asked if I would like to see the 'young wine' cellar. Despite being cold, grubby and tired, I could hardly refuse and it turned out to be full of Calvet burgundies, the youngest vintage of which was 1929!

I have listed the best vintages of the period and any wine of high quality and unimpeachable provenance in the 4- to 5-star range could still be excellent. A practical tip: levels of ullage up to 7cm below the cork in bottles of old red burgundy are not abnormal; and, unlike the equivalent level in old claret bottles, they are not necessarily a danger signal. As always, however, the provenance, storage and condition of cork are important.

## Vintages at a Glance
**Outstanding ★★★★★**
1906, 1911, 1915, 1919, 1929
**Very Good ★★★★**
1904, 1920, 1923, 1926, 1928
**Good ★★★**
1914, 1916, 1918, 1921, 1924

## 1900 ★★
Heavy rain at vintage time increased volume but reduced quality. Just two old notes.
**Chambertin, Tête de Cuvée F Chauvenet** Amazingly rich, almost overblown. *From a New England cellar, May 1977* ★★★
**Nuits-Calvet** From Mme Teysonneau's cellar in Bordeaux. I have two notes. Good colour; rich; sweet, soft. Tasted 1978 and *1979* ★★★

## 1904 ★★★★
The first very good vintage after 1887. Hot dry summer. Early harvest, from 15 September.
**Chambertin Jules Regnier** Lively though very little red; aged but attractive; fading yet flavoury. *At a Christie's pre-sale tasting, Chicago, June 1984* ★★★

**Grand-Musigny Faiveley** Bought at auction and served at a couple of dinner parties. Fairly pale; nose showing its age at first, a touch of vanilla, overmature, fragrant; distinctly sweet, light, elegant, delicate yet rich. *Last noted at home, July 1981* ★★★
**Richebourg J Calvet** Magnificent rosy-hued colour; nose developed a rich, singed, old Pinot fragrance and flavour. Silky perfection. *Tasted at Christie's, May 1986* ★★★★

## 1906 ★★★★★
Great vintage. The growing season was perfect, the hot summer increasing the sugar content but reducing the yield by concentrating the grape juice. The harvest was early.
**Chambertin, Clos de Bèze Faiveley** A jeroboam served at a Rodenstock dinner for 50 people: palish, open-rimmed but attractive, rich 'legs'; interesting, rich, many-layered, slightly piquant fruit; medium-sweet, rich, soft yet tangy. Excellent for its age. *In Munich, Sept 1996* ★★★★★
**Richebourg** Another jeroboam. From a Belgian cellar, bought at Sotheby's. Handwritten label with signature 'Krug'. Small unbranded cork so probably bottled in a private cellar – normal practice among connoisseurs in Belgium. Similar appearance to the Chambertin, above. Initially old, faded, ivy and privet bouquet that opened up fragrantly; also slightly sweet, rich, very flavoury but with a dry 'bracken-like' finish. *At the same Rodenstock dinner in Munich, Sept 1996* ★★★

**Romanée-St-Vivant Dufouleur** An amazingly good half bottle. A rosehip tawny hue with pale yellow rim; lovely, fragrant old beetroot-like Pinot bouquet that opened up in the glass, sweet, glorious, mulberry-like fruit; sweet, beautiful smoky flavour, good length and intensity, excellent finish. Opened on the spur of the moment and poured, undecanted. *At dinner at home, April 1990* ★★★★

## 1911 ★★★★★

A great classic Burgundy vintage. Weather conditions similar to 1906. None tasted recently.

**Chambertin, Clos de Bèze Guichard Protherot** Despite its very considerable ullage, surprisingly good. *Oct 1981* ★★
**Corton, Clos du Roy** (*sic*) Firm unbranded cork. Pale orange-tinged amber; gentle bouquet, faded but lovely; amazingly powerful wine, laden with sweetness and alcohol. *From Lady Birley's cellar in Sussex, Nov 1980* ★★★
**Clos de Vougeot Lupé-Cholet** Crumbly cork. Good level for age. Autumnal colour, mahogany centre, amber rim; rich smoky old Pinot nose – beetroot and cold tea. Fine, rich old flavour. *From a cellar near Biarritz, tasted Nov 1987* ★★★★
**Santenay Dr Barolet** The oldest vintage in the Barolet cellar. Variable. Little colour left, somewhat sour. Other bottles reported to be better. *Last tasted pre-sale, Dec 1969.*

## 1914 ★★★

Seldom seen wartime vintage.

**Romanée-St-Vivant Marey-Monge** A rare pre-DRC vintage: very rich rosehip tawny; sweet, very vegetal root-like old Pinot nose of considerable depth, then showing a touch of sourness, later earthy, singed bracken; extraordinarily sweet, full-bodied, magnificent flavour with length and depth. A great wine. I thought it was a '37. A bottle from Mme Marey-Monge's cellar given to André Noblet, the former DRC *maître de chai. Served blind by Aubert de Villaine at the end of the St-Vivant tasting reported later, Nov 1995* ★★★★★
**Clos de Tart** Recorked. Still very richly coloured, with an amber-brown rim; an old farmyard smell, then soft leather; very sweet, good old smoky Pinot flavour and aftertaste. Acidity nibbling at the edges. *Tasted with Patrice Noyelle of Mommessin at Clos de Tart, Oct 1990* ★★ (*My old friend Patrice is now managing director of Pol Roger champagne.*)

---

### Clos de Vougeot and its multiplicity of owners

*Clos de Vougeot is the largest grand cru of the Côte d'Or, and one of the few Burgundian clos that is still really a clos (a vineyard enclosed by four walls). It was assembled by Cistercian monks in the 12th, 13th and 14th centuries from pieces of land received as donations to the church. The final 50-hectare plot was walled up in 1336 and remained in the careful hands of the monks until after the French Revolution, when the Clos was sold to Julien-Jules Ouvrard in 1818. (The wines, over this time, steadily gained in reputation.) Clos de Vougeot remained under single ownership until 1889 but since then, through the complex French inheritance laws, it has become further and further sub-divided until its owners now number over 80, each proprietor with only a few rows of vines. Since the land within the clos varies considerably in its geology, the style and quality of the burgundies from the many growers varies also, despite their common grand cru name.*

## 1915 ★★★★★

The weather in 1915 was good throughout the growing season resulting in a large crop of superb early-harvested grapes. None tasted recently, but I live in hope!

**Bonnes-Mares** Possibly London-bottled. Beautiful colour; rich old Pinot bouquet and flavour. Powerful yet silky. *May 1967* ★★★★
**Chambertin, Vieux Cépages Labaume-Aîné** Super-ripe, old Pinot, rich, honeyed, fading but delicious. *From the Labaume cellar sold at Christie's in the late 1960s* ★★★
**Musigny** Shipper unknown. Level high, and good, long, unbranded cork. Palish, little red but very healthy glow. At first fairly light, delicate and faded on both nose and palate, but after its 'second breath' developed richly in the glass. Crisp, clean and refreshing on the palate. Dry, slightly acidic finish. *At the pre-sale tasting of Lady Birley's cellar, Oct 1980* ★★
**Musigny Labaume-Aîné** Orange-tinged; opulent bouquet reminding me of well-hung pheasant. Delicious, though near the edge. *Before the Labaume cellar sale, Dec 1968* ★★★★
**Musigny, Tête de Cuvée Bouchard Père** Very pale; old, refined, sound. *From the Bouchard cellars in Beaune at a Heublein pre-sale tasting, May 1973* ★★
**Nuits, Cailles Morin** Exquisite. *June 1977* ★★★★

## 1916 ★★★

Rare wartime vintage. Originally 'light and stylish' but faded now. Just three old notes.

**Aloxe-Corton Labaume-Aîné** Surprisingly fine, extended bouquet for age and class; palate rich but lacking balance. *Aug 1967* ★★
**Gevrey-Chambertin** Probably bottled in Burgundy. Sweet, rich, old roasted Pinot bouquet and flavour. *From a private Dutch cellar, tasted pre-sale, Amsterdam, Oct 1980* ★★★

## 1917 ★★

Small crop of mediocre wines. Rarely seen. I only have one old note.

**Beaune, Clos des Avaux Labaume-Aîné** Lovely colour though faded; old, earthy nose; better on palate, attractive, piquant, refreshing. *May 1968* ★★

## 1918 ★★★

Fine harvest, above average quality. Rarely seen.

**Chambolle-Musigny, Charmes Labaume-Aîné** Thanks to Mme Labaume, whose cellar Christie's sold in 1968, I have tasted a wide range of these scarce vintages. Even though the notes are old, an idea of quality and condition is helpful. Odd bottles do crop up from time to time. As charming as its vineyard name: delicate bouquet; yet remarkable richness on the palate. Elegant. Firm. Well balanced. *Aug 1967* ★★★

## 1919 ★★★★★

Great vintage. Below average production of magnificently ripe wines. Over two dozen notes, though I hae only four in the 1980s and just one more recent one.

**Beaune, Clos des Avaux Dom du Ch de Beaune** Lovely colour; initially the nose reminded me of cold seawater but it developed a lovely fresh fragrance; slightly sweet, beautiful flavour and acidity. Perfection. *At Lloyd Flatt's, New Orleans, Oct 1987* ★★★★★

**Chambolle-Musigny Dr Barolet** One of the most beautiful and dependable of all Barolet burgundies. Several pre- and post-sale notes dating from 1969–1970. Most recently: medium-pale, healthy glow; sound nose and flavour, holding well. In fact remarkably good. *Last noted at the Josey pre-sale tasting in New York, Nov 2000* ★★★★

**Hospices de Beaune** (Cuvée unknown) **Calvet** From Mme Teysonneau's 'young wine' cellar in Bordeaux. A perfect bottle in 1979. The following year a good deep colour; rich, singed Pinot, gamey nose; rich and velvety, firm, dry, slightly acidic finish. *Last tasted at lunch with Peter Palumbo, Feb 1980* ★★★★

**Musigny de Vogüé** Medium-pale, pink-cheeked; a most extraordinary fragrance, cherries and *poire Williamine*; sweet, delicately flavoured, with cherry-like fruit, positive, good length and aftertaste. *A lovely wine: one of the most attractive of the 55 remarkable burgundies from the cellars of Wilfred Jaeger tasted over three sessions, two dinners and a Sunday lunch, March 2002* ★★★★★

**Nuits-St-Georges Faiveley** Deep-stained, unbranded cork with wizened and crystalline end. Medium colour, fully mature of course; slightly old mushroomy nose that evolved richly in the glass; medium sweetness and weight. As so often, high in alcohol yet lightish in style. Elegant, smooth, good dry finish. *Dining at Houston House, near Edinburgh, May 1982* ★★★★

**Richebourg C Marey Liger-Belair** Oh dear: a smell of ripe Stilton and with stewed old Pinot taste. Absolutely not delicate; quite a bite. *At Jaeger's, for the record only, March 2002.*

**Volnay, Fremiets, Clos de la Rougeotte Dom du Ch de Beaune** Very heavy bottle, original pictorial label. Fairly deeply coloured; dry, over-the-hill but drinkable. *At Wilfred Jaeger's, March 2002.*

## 1920 ★★★★

A good start to the best-ever burgundy decade. Too little sun in July and August slowed development of the grapes in an otherwise good growing season. The late September harvest took place in perfect conditions. Small production.

**Chambertin Héritiers Latour** Medium-pale but bright and beautiful; a whiff of the 'fishy' Pinot I associate with Chambertin, slightly smoky, waxy bouquet of great style and quality; medium-dry, very crisp, flavoury, with a lean sinewy character. Perfection. *Bought at Christie's sale of Fernand Woltner's Paris cellar, Oct 1980, and served at dinner, June 1981* ★★★★★

**Charmes-Chambertin** Cork branded with a difficult to read restaurant name, '*Foyot*'? First noted dining at home. Breaking Burgundian tradition I decanted the wine and served it four hours later. Even then, the bouquet evolved even more fragrantly in the glass. Delicious. More recently, similar cork, 9-cm ullage – (this is good for its age and rarely a problem with burgundy). Palish but very good colour; sound, rich, hefty and, as before, opened up and held well; some sweetness, very rich – possibly reinforced with a sturdy Rhône wine or cognac, who knows? Touch of tartness, otherwise drinking well. *Last noted at a Christie's lunch, March 1994. At best* ★★★★

**Pommard Pierre Ponnelle** Extremely good level and colour; showing its age, *faisandé*, whiff of tar and fungi; touch of liquorice, drying-out. One cannot expect great things from a *négociant's* village wine of this age, but one never knows. The pursuit of old wines is fun, an occasional revelation, sometimes leading to deep despair. *Dining with Camilla and Alistair Sampson, antique dealer and odd-bottle magpie, March 2000.*

**THREE CALVET BURGUNDIES FROM MME TEYSONNEAU'S CELLAR** tasted prior to the sale, August 1979: **Aloxe-Corton** sweet, light, complete but short ★★; **Chambertin** tile red; rich bouquet; sweet, fairly full-bodied, sustained flavour. Perfect condition ★★★★; and **Chambolle-Musigny** orange mahogany; soft, rich, fragrant; sweet, complete, lovely ★★★★

## 1921 ★★★

Exceptionally hot summer. Early harvest.

**Romanée-Conti** Labelled '*de Villaine & J Chambon Petits fils de J.M. Dufault-Blochet*'. Impressively deep yet soft, warm red; nose a bit dusty at first, with a touch of cork or wood, though after only five minutes had evolved richly; very sweet, very good flavour, considerable power though showing some decay. Extended finish, more acidity than tannin. *At Wilfred Jaeger's rare burgundy tasting, March 2002* ★★

**Charmes-Chambertin Dr Barolet** Magnificent colour; bouquet evolved fabulously; a full, rich, harmonious wine 'with the angel of death hovering overhead'. *Tasted with Harry Waugh in the original cellars, Beaune, Oct 1969* ★★★★★

**Richebourg** Belgian-bottled by **Vandermeurlen** Medium-deep; an almost '28-like firmness, thick, stewed, slightly maderised but exuding hefty fruit; very sweet, curiously scented flavour, very fragrant, vanilla. More than just interesting. *At Frans de Cock's Vandermeurlen wine tasting at Le Carré des Feuillants, Paris, Dec 1995* ★★★

**Clos de la Roche Dr Barolet** As mentioned in the introduction, three large stone bins housed around 2000 bottles of this wine alone. Half a dozen notes, first tasted with Harry Waugh in the courtyard above the cellars (the smell in the cellars was too pungent) in October 1969 and subsequently at the pre-sale tastings and on other occasions. Frankly variable, some differences being between the original unrecorked bottles and those recorked by the Swiss-owned *négociant*, de Villamont, the latter pale, pink-tinged; very fragrant; dry light weight, pleasant enough, the ones (alongside in 1985) with original corks more richly coloured though fully mature; a more pungent, tangy nose; fairly full-bodied, drying out but assertive. Most recently: palish but glowing with health; very good, slightly singed nose; excellent flavour, still tannic. *Last noted at the Josey pre-sale tasting, New York, Nov 2000. At best* ★★★★

**Clos de Tart** Belgian-bottled by **Vandermeurlen** Palish, open; showing its age, touch of oxidation but cleared a little; raw but coped with food. *At Frans de Cock's, Paris, Dec 1995* ★

**Volnay L Grivot** Served blind: medium-deep, beautiful colour, fully mature; sound nose but showing some age, whiff of mushroom, slightly vegetal – which put me on to burgundy; sweet, clearly a big-vintage wine but soft and a most lovely drink. Remarkable for its age. *Dining with Danielle and Christian Pol Roger, in Épernay, June 1997* ★★★★

## 1922 ★

An abundance of mediocre wines squeezed out of the market by the two very good adjacent vintages. None tasted.

## 1923 ★★★★

Small but high quality vintage.

**Santenay-Volnay** (sic), **Hospices, Cuvée Gauvin Berry Bros & Rudd label** Lively colour; trace of fungi which cleared;

touch of sweetness but drying out. With air, a charmer. *A rare half bottle produced by Mutsuo Okabayashi at the end of his great wine dinner in Tokyo, June 1989* ★★★

SOME OLDER NOTES **Beaune Dr Barolet** already mentioned: beware. There was a big stock of this wine that I did not consider good enough for the original Barolet sale. Variable. *Last tasted 1981. At best* ★★; **Musigny Calvet** three, all from Mme Teysonneau's cellar, and all good, retaining Musigny femininity and elegance. *1981* ★★★; **Romanée, La Tâche** (*sic*) **Berry Bros** original cork, good level. Ruddy glow; fragrant, sweet vanilla and old oak, with fringe of decay; high extract, good flavour, touch of rawness. *1984* ★★★; and **Savigny, Hospices, Cuvée Fouquerand Dr Barolet** bought, *élevé* and bottled by Dr Barolet's father who started this extraordinary business. Lovely colour; distinguished bouquet; refined flavour and texture. One of the best wines in the Barolet sale. *Dec 1969* ★★★★

## 1924 ★★★

Despite inclement weather, some pleasant wines were made. None tasted recently. The best of my old notes was a 45-year-old **Volnay, Santenots Labaume-Aîné** Mahogany; sweet; soft, most agreeable. *Tasted 1968* ★★★

## 1925 ★

Its poor reputation (the crop was halved by cochylis) was not borne out by several wines tasted in the 1960s and 1970s, including a surprisingly attractive **Santenay Dr Barolet**, and in the early 1980s an excellent **Chambertin Héritiers Latour**.

## 1926 ★★★★

Cold weather inhibited flowering and a long summer drought reduced the crop, but some extremely good wines made. **Corton, Clos de la Vigne au Saint L Latour** Warm, toasted, privet-like bouquet; medium sweetness and body, lovely smoky old Pinot flavour, feminine, excellent acidity. *One of the best of 16 old burgundies from a Swiss cellar tasted at Corney & Barrow, May 1995* ★★★
**Ch Corton-Grancey L Latour** The most interesting facet was its very long cork which nevertheless failed to prevent some oxidation, doubtless due to poor cellarage. Attractive colour, then rosehip orange. *At Corney & Barrow, May 1995.*
**Corton, Clos du Chapitre L Latour** What a pity. A disappointment, too, for Louis-Fabrice Latour who had come to London to taste rare wines produced by his grandfather

### The Burgundy market

*At this period, in common with most other wines, burgundy was shipped in cask for bottling by merchants or even by private customers in the traditional market, Belgium, and also to Holland, Switzerland, Denmark, like England, there were many high-quality wine merchants. Most of the wines were handled by the big Burgundian négociants, who had close business relations with importers who, in turn, sold to merchants for bottling. Their bottling was proficient and dependable; the quality depending on what the Burgundian négociants chose to ship. Transatlantic shipments were in bottles.*

Louis Latour Snr (aged 91 at the time of the tasting). Not good. *At Corney & Barrow, May 1995.*
**Nuits-St-Georges Belgian-bottled by Vandermeurlen** Palish, wings spread, mature of course; whiff of Pinot's characteristic beetroot aroma which blossomed attractively; lovely fruit, flavour, condition, tannin and refreshing acidity. *Equal top of the eight very good Vandermeurlen burgundies at Frans de Cock's wine event in Paris, Dec 1995* ★★★★

## 1927

Cold wet summer, poor harvest, the worst vintage of the decade. Avoid.

ONLY FOUR NOTES, all old, two of **Romanée-Conti** better than expected though variable, both pale, little red; one mushroomy, the other old but sweet on the nose, light and sound, thin. Not much of a drink to celebrate my birth year. *Last tasted 1971*; and two of **Faiveley**'s **Gevrey-Chambertin** equally variable, from lively to acetic. *Last tasted 1981.*

## 1928 ★★★★

Frost in the spring, rain and hail in June, a bakingly hot August followed by more hail conspired to reduce the crop size. But what remained was of high quality. Lacking the '29 elegance these wines were sturdy, dependable and long-lived.
**Romanée-Conti** Recorked at the Domaine. Similar label to the 1921. Medium-deep, lively colour with cherry and ruby highlights and mature tawny rim; very sweet, harmonious bouquet, rich, almost meaty which held well; fairly sweet on the palate, excellent, crisp taste, touch of spice resembling iodine (iron, from the soil), very good flavour which seemed to get sweeter in the glass. *At Wilf Jaeger's, March 2002* ★★★★★
**Pommard-Epenots Dr Barolet** Originally one of the best of all the Barolet wines. Many notes, all but two very good. One of the recent less good, recorked by de Villamont, had little red left; nose high-toned, varnishy, like nail polish; drinkable, but not correct (at the '28s tasting, San Juan, 1998). More recently, a bottle from the original Barolet sale, medium-pale, mahogany-tawny mature rim; an intriguing *fraise des bois* fragrance; dry, good flavour but on the lean side and still with '28 tannin. Most recently: medium-deep, attractive colour; initially a rather cheesy old nose, then meaty, gravy-like; clearly some oxidation but very flavoury despite its hot, edgy acidity. A disappointment though, for Barolet's '28 Epenots and Rugiens were top class at the original 1969 sale. *The first of two pairs, '28s and '29s, at Wilfred Jaeger's second evening dinner tasting, March 2002* ★
**Clos de Tart Belgian-bottled by Vandermeurlen** Open, attractive, rich 'legs'; strange, sweet, very forthcoming strawberry-like fragrance, just a touch jammy; fairly sweet, fullish body, very good flavour, length, condition. *Equal top with the '26 Nuits-St-Georges at Frans de Cock's tasting in Paris, Dec 1985* ★★★★
**Clos de Vougeot Pasquier-Desvignes** 'aux domaine du Marquisat depuis 1420' Fair depth and intensity; a demonstrative but sound nose; sweet, complete, touch of meatiness but surprisingly good flavour. *At Wilf Jaeger's, March 2002* ★★★
**Vosne-Romanée C Marey Liger-Belair** Medium-deep; old, whiff of cheese; sweet, fullish, dry finish. *Coped quite well with 'Seared Pinder Farm pheasant' at a gourmet dinner in New York, Feb 1993* ★★★

# 1929 ★★★★★

This was a glorious vintage, combining abundance and high quality. Refined, ripe, elegant; wines of immediate appeal, some of which, if well cellared, have stayed the course.

**Aloxe-Corton, Les Brunettes** L Latour No-one seemed to know what or where 'Brunettes' was, and it hardly mattered. Long 'legs', pale and no red left; tight, meaty nose and taste. Well, not entirely bad. *From the fairly disastrous Swiss cellar, at Corney & Barrow, May 1995.*

**Beaune, Clos du Roi** L Latour Even worse. Oxidised. What a let-down and entirely due to poor storage. *May 1995.*

**Chambertin, Cuvée Héritiers** L Latour No red; fruit lurking under banana skins; flavoury but acidic. Beery finish. *At Corney & Barrow, May 1995.* See above.

**Chambertin** Belgian-bottled by Vandermeurlen Lively colour, hint of cherry; flowery, fruity, whiff of old apples but overall attractive; sweetness etched with raw, tart acidity. Rather aggressive. *At Frans de Cock's tasting in Paris, Dec 1995* ★

**Chambolle-Musigny, Amoureuses** Seguin Manuel Good colour, red core; sweet bouquet; sound, flavoury, more than interesting. *Served, curiously, in the wake of Taylor '55, at Stephen Kaplan's magnificent dinner in Los Angeles, Feb 1998* ★★★

**Pommard, Rugiens** Dom du Ch de Beaune Fairly deep; fragrant, whiff of vanilla; there was attractive sweetness but also hot, gum-gripping acidity. *At Wilfred Jaeger's burgundy tasting, March 2002* ★

**Romanée-St-Vivant** Marey-Monge Lively warm rosehip colour; showing its age initially but quickly settled down, sweet, soft, scented, then after 30 minutes the tanginess of a thoroughbred stables; very sweet, a lovely, rich, chocolatey flavour, good length and acidity. Complete. *At Aubert de Villaine's St-Vivant tasting at the Domaine, Nov 1995* ★★★★★

**Romanée-St-Vivant, Les Quatre Journaux** L Latour Oxidised. What is the point of hanging on to old wine in poor condition? Corney & Barow must have regretted providing the venue for what could have been such an exciting tasting. *May 1995.*

**Volnay, Caillerets, Ancienne Cuvée Carnot** Dom du Ch de Beaune Medium-deep, still ruby-tinged; meaty nose; fullish, dry, singed, tarry, sweet mid-palate and good finish. I enjoyed it. *At lunch in the Bouchard cellars, Nov 1995* ★★★

**Vosne-Romanée, Les Beaumonts** Dr Barolet Deep, rich, mature; two-part nose, touch of malt; taste of tarry old oak. Drinkable, but, alas, had deteriorated (storage, I think) since originally tasted at the time of the Barolet sale (1969). *Last noted at a pre-sale tasting at Christie's, New York, Feb 1992.*

**Clos Vougeot** Faiveley Agreeable bouquet though a slightly oily richness; sweet, an initial taste of old mushrooms but better the second time round. *At Wilfred Jaeger's, just for the record, March 2002.*

**Clos Vougeot, Ch de la Tour** Moreau Very good level; palish but healthy glow; the sweetness of well-hung pheasant, slightly tart. But we drank it. *At the Sampsons', March 2000* ★

# 1930–1949

The same pattern as elsewhere: economic slump, war and a series of miraculous post-war vintages. Burgundy in the 1930s was more successful than Bordeaux, the 1937 being outstanding.

Although there was legislation in the previous two decades, it was not until 1930 that Pinot Noir was finally designated as Burgundy's 'noble' red grape; in 1935, most importantly, the *Appellation d'Origine Contrôlée* (AOC) laws were enacted. Domaine-bottling was pioneered by a few major growers in the 1930s, a step not popular with the local *négociants* who were, however, in no position financially to do much about it.

In order to awaken Burgundy from the torpor of recession, leading producers got together in 1934 to create the *Confrèrie des Chevaliers du Tastevin*. Ten years later the imposing Château de Clos Vougeot became the site of its festivities, notably the spectacular and lengthy banquets to which celebrities, including foreign royalty, famous performers, artists and connoisseurs, were – and still are – invited to form a worldwide circle of burgundy enthusiasts.

## *Vintages at a Glance*
**Outstanding ★★★★★**
1937, 1945, 1949
**Very Good ★★★★**
1933, 1934, 1943, 1947
**Good ★★★**
1935, 1942

## 1930 ★
Execrable harvest. Pale, thin and unbalanced wines.
**Beaune, Clos des Mouches Dr Barolet** Perhaps, after the famous English landscape gardener, we should refer to 'Capability Barolet' for he had a nose for a decent wine and knew how to *élever* it. First tasted with Harry Waugh in the courtyard above the cellars in October 1969: it was not a fine wine, but sound. As there was a big stock of decent-looking bottles, I put 20 cases in the sale. It sold. I bought some myself and last served it at a dinner party at home: a lovely rosehip colour (orange-shaded tawny); delicious nose; very flavoury, delicious, refreshing acidity. It surprised even John Avery. *Last tasted at Chippenham Lodge, April 1995 ★★★ (Averys of Bristol have long been renowned for their burgundies.)*
**Morey St-Denis Dr Barolet** This was rich, silky but a touch astringent. *At the pre-sale Barolet tasting, 1969.*

## 1931
Uninterrupted cold and rain from July to mid-September. Then, sun for a late harvest. But there was no market and little incentive. Light, astringent wines. However, Dr Barolet did his best and 13 cases of magnums and bottles of his not too bad **Chambolle-Musigny, Charmes** were all sold, albeit at low prices in 1964.
**Richebourg DRC** First tasted in 1995 at a dinner to honour my wife Daphne given by Mutsuo Okabayashi in Tokyo. The bottle had been recorked at the Domaine in 1988: a lovely warm autumnal colour; excellent old scented Pinot bouquet; sweet, palish, soft; fleshy – clearly chaptalised – with a smoky end taste. Next, a bottle I served at Daphne's 65th birthday dinner at Christie's: excellent level, very good original cork. I decanted it at 6.30pm and the wine was served at 8.30. It was very pale, no red left; smoky old nose with touch of liquorice; sweet, surprisingly lovely flavour, rich, refreshing acidity. *Last noted July 1996 ★★★*

## 1932
The growing season was not as bad as all that: normal flowering 25 June, poor July but warm and dry throughout August to the last week of September, after which violent storms. The harvest was extremely late and, as with the two previous vintages, no market; at least none imported into the UK as the trade still had a surfeit of '28s and '29s. None tasted.

## 1933 ★★★★
A very good but very small vintage. Stylish, elegant wines, several tasted and enjoyed prior to the 1980s, none since. Of those tasted at the peak, between 35 and 40 years of age, outstandingly the best was **Ponnelle's Romanée-St-Vivant** bottled in Brighton; followed by **Damoy's Chambertin, Clos de Bèze**, **Labaume-Aîné's** velvety **Volnay** and **L Latour's Beaune, Vignes Franches**; and of the several **Barolet** wines, **Bonnes-Mares** and **Corton, Clos du Roi**.

## 1934 ★★★★
Perfect growing conditions. The biggest vintage of the decade; ripe, well-constituted wines. Nowadays, the too rapid growth and overabundance of bunches would have been countered with crop-thinning. Also exceptional heat at vintage time caused some fermentation problems, again more easily controlled nowadays. What could have been great was merely very good. The small growers were anxious to make up for lost time and money by selling as much as possible to merchants who, in turn, needed to have decent stocks of wine for a slowly reawakening market.
**La Tâche Berry Bros & Rudd** A most interesting bottle from the cellar of a Vanderbilt mansion in upper New York State. Bottled by Berry Bros: good classic nose, whiff of lemon; very sweet, delicious flavour and finish. Back in London I visited Berry Bros and, in their archives, noted that this was listed in 1937 as 'La Tache Romanee' at 118 shillings per dozen for credit, 108 shillings (just over £5) per dozen for cash! *The first of four '34s at Wilf Jaeger's second dinner tasting in San Francisco, March 2002 ★★★★★*
**Grands-Echézeaux DRC** Also from the Vanderbilt cellar, with 'Berry Bros & Co' pictorial label, sub-headed 'Domaine de la Romanée-Conti, Bourgogne': low-keyed, meaty nose; full, rich, singed flavour, with power and length. *At Wilfred Jaeger's, March 2002 ★★★★*

## Domaine de la Romanée-Conti

*The Domaine de la Romanée-Conti, referred to in the text as DRC, has long been described as the 'central pearl' of the Côte de Nuits. For several centuries now, its wines have been treasured for their strength, finesse and longevity. The domaine's records go back to 1512 and the monks of St-Vivant. The current owners, the de Villaine family, acquired the estate in the 1870s.*

*The Domaine consists of two monopole wines, Romanée-Conti (1.81ha) and La Tâche (6.06ha), with major holdings in the grands crus of Richebourg, Grands-Echézeaux, Romanée-St Vivant and Echézeaux. 1934 was the first vintage in which DRC could claim sole ownership of La Tâche, the completing portion of the vineyard which had been purchased from the Liger-Belair family the previous year. DRC also has a minuscule holding in Le Montrachet – 0.68ha. Because of the high quality and necessarily small production, there is always insufficient wine to meet the demand of the world's wealthy elite, hence DRC's high prices.*

*Since 1953 the Domaine has numbered every bottle enabling them to trace its distribution back to the original barrel if necessary. Throughout this chapter I do not add DRC after the solely owned Romanée-Conti and La Tâche.*

**Chambolle-Musigny Poulet** Medium, open-rimmed, pale mahogany; slightly chocolatey, pre-war commercial burgundy; nevertheless in very good condition, not classy but pleasant to drink. *Dining at the Bensons' in London, Feb 2001* ★★★
**Chambolle-Musigny, Les Amoureuses Dr Barolet** First tasted in 1969 before the Barolet sale: rich, ripe, *faisandé* bouquet, lovely wine. Palish, pleasant colour; gentle, harmonious bouquet; touch of sweetness, perfect weight, crisp, delightful flavour. Virtually faultless. *Last tasted at Len Evans' 'Single-bottle club' dinner in the Hunter Valley, Sept 2001* ★★★★
**Chambolle-Musigny, Les Charmes** 'Collection du Dr Barolet, shipped by François Martenot, négociant-éleveur à Savigny-Lès-Beaune'. I also noted that this was imported by 'Copel Ltd, Algonquin, Illinois', a company I knew in the 1970s. I suspect that Martenot was a *sous-nom* of de Villamont, and the shipment must have been after the 1969 Barolet sale at Christie's: a strange, curiously attractive nose and taste, rather artificial, touch of strawberry-like fragrance, with sharp but refreshing finish. *At Wilfred Jaeger's, March 2002* ★★
**Pommard, Les Epenots Dr Barolet** Variable at the Barolet pre-sale tastings, ageing but rich. Medium-pale, orange rim; meaty nose; very flavoury but with hot, slightly acidic end. *Last noted at the Josey pre-sale tasting, New York, Nov 2000* ★★★
**Romanée-St-Vivant J Drouhin** *'Vin des Anciens Celliers des Rois de France et Des Ducs de Bourgogne'*, slip labelled *'1934/tirage d'Origine'*, the bottle emanating from H Graf-Lecocque, Drouhin's sole agent in Belgium. Well, all this might even have impressed the Vanderbilts; it certainly impressed me: a ripe but low-keyed bouquet; meaty, fractionally malty, rich, good length, clean finish. An enjoyable mouthful. *At Wilfred Jaeger's, March 2002* ★★★★

OF THE OTHER DR BAROLET '34S **Chambolle-Musigny** very good ★★★★ (though a recorked bottle in 1992 was orange and decayed); **Chambolle-Musigny, Charmes** (45 dozen in the sale sold at high price) variable. *At best* ★★★★★; **Grands-Echézeaux** touch of astringency, but otherwise very good. *Last tasted in 1986* ★★★★; **Pommard Rugiens** very good indeed; **Volnay** and **Volnay, Clos des Chênes** all good.

OF THE OTHER '34S TASTED IN THE 1980S, the following were excellent: **La Tâche**, **Labaume Aîné**'s **Chambolle-Musigny**; **Clos des Lambrays** magnificent; **de Vogüé**'s **Musigny** and **Bouchard Père**'s **Volnay, Caillerets, Ancienne Cuvée Carnot** could still be delicious.

## 1935 ★★★

Some say this was a very good vintage; at the time of the harvest it was noted as 'clean and sound' and abundant. But the British trade, once again, found themselves stocked up and few wines were bought. Clearly it was more popular in Belgium as Dr Barolet had eight different '35s in his cellar, some in large quantities. One older note is worth a mention.
**Grands-Echézeaux 'Du Domaine de la Romanée-Conti'** *'George Thienpont à Etichove'*, presumably Belgian-bottled. (Thienpont are old-established Belgian wine merchants and current owners of Ch Vieux-Ch-Certan and Labégorce-Zédé in Bordeaux.) Deeply coloured; attractive bouquet; sweetish, fairly full-bodied, sound but unsubtle, with a spirity finish. *Dining at Arnaud's in New Orleans, April 1986* ★★★★
**Savigny, Hospices, 'Cyrot'** believed to be **Cuvée Fouquerand Dr Barolet** One of the two very best Barolet wines: a hot-vintage depth of colour, nose and 'sunburnt' taste. Fairly full-bodied, dry finish. *Tasted pre-sale, Dec 1969* ★★★★

## 1936 ★

Small crop and variable, being mainly well below average quality. Totally ignored by the British trade. The quality of the '37 vintage then banished the '36s into obscurity. None tasted.

## 1937 ★★★★★

Close run by the '34 now, but unquestionably the outstanding vintage in this difficult decade. Growing conditions near to ideal thanks to warm weather from May throughout the summer. If anything, there was too much sun and too little rain, the welcome sprinkling in September being insufficient to swell the grapes. The harvest began on the 27th in excellent conditions. The crop was small, roughly half that of the '34, the grapes more concentrated and tannic; this enabled the best wines to keep extraordinarily well.

Eagerly awaited by the trade, they proved useful in the wine-starved immediate post-war years. With other pre-war vintages they were still on the Saccone & Speed list when I joined the company in 1952, the '45s, '47s and '49s still being offered 'for laying down'. Because of this, I had opportunities to taste many '37s and even more of high quality after I joined Christie's in 1966, particularly in the 1970s and 1980s. Alas I have tasted few of these wines recently.
**Romanée-Conti** A great wine. First noted in 1957 dining with a customer, a fruit farmer in Cheshire with a marvellous cellar. I quote from my tasting book volume 3: 'Big and black, taut and concentrated; sweetish, packed with flavour. Same class as Mouton '45. Good for ten years or more' (I had been in the wine trade five years!). Next at Christie's in 1972, then seven years later at a boardroom luncheon: 'still fairly deep … overripe and gamey on the nose, but opulently rich and attractive … flavour seemed to extend and get richer in the glass'. More recently, a magnum, spectacularly upstaging a range of over 60 '37 red Bordeaux at a Rodenstock wine weekend: a fairly deep, warm, autumnal colour; ripe, rich,

classic Pinot 'beetroot', fragrant, sustained; very sweet, full, fleshy. Like the dance of the seven veils, each gentle inhalation and sip revealed more. Most recently, an unrecorked bottle from the Vanderbilt cellar: not as deep as expected, ruddy coloured with a light tawny rim; a touch of sourness and iodine on the nose though open and harmonious; sweet, good flavour, somewhat pinched and lean and with '37 edgy acidity. I have had more perfect bottles and think this is on its final downhill slope. *Last noted at Wilf Jaeger's tasting, March 2002* ★★

**Richebourg DRC** First tasted (a magnum at a Rodenstock dinner) in 1988: magnificent, very sweet, great depth of flavour and more grip than Romanée-Conti itself. Most recently, undiminished. Original lead capsule, long cork, very good level, with added slip labels. '*Red Burgundy wine*' – a good start! – '*Imported by National Wine & Liquor Importing Company*' (USA). Still impressively deep, a rich mature mahogany rim; bouquet sweet, excellent, with a citrus note – '37 acidity, after 30 minutes mocha, after two hours in the glass still good but fading a little; on the palate, extraordinarily sweet, rounded, perfect flavour, richness masking supportive tannins, great length. Great surprise too. *One of three fabulous bottles discovered by Fritz Hatton in a Pacific Palisades cellar and tasted at Christie's in Los Angeles, March 1999* ★★★★★

**Corton Doudet-Naudin** Behind the walls of a mansion in Savigny-Lès-Beaune, this firm had a considerable following in Britain well into the 1960s. The wines were instantly recognisable and had a chocolatey character. Many, if not most of the post-war burgundies on the list of one of London's most reputable wine merchants were sourced from Doudet-Naudin. And I have to say that of the very many D-N burgundies I have tasted over the years, no matter how old the vintage, I cannot recall one in less than very drinkable condition. The '37: a lovely, palish, fully mature, autumnal colour; an attractive, singed nose; unusual but appealing taste though drying out. *At Christie's pre-sale tasting, Dec 1996* ★★

TOP '37S LAST TASTED IN THE 1980S
**La Tâche** Magnificent, expansive, unforgettable aftertaste. *Last tasted March 1980* ★★★★★
**Gevrey-Chambertin Leroy** Ripe, elegant, lovely wine. *Tasted with Lalou Bize, 1984* ★★★★
**Clos des Lambrays** Well-stacked, crisp, aromatic. *Last tasted Sept 1988* ★★★★
**Mazis-Chambertin Leroy** Lovely flavour, soft, dry finish. *1980* ★★★★
**Nuits-St-Georges, 1er Cru Thomas-Bassot** Smoky Pinot; sweet, lovely flavour, length. *Sept 1988* ★★★★
**Volnay, Hospices, Cuvée Blondeau C Giroud** Magnificent bouquet; excellent flavour, soft, fragrant, dry finish. *1980* ★★★★

## 1938 ★★

Variable weather, late harvest and wartime bottling, though due to shortages, some wine remained in cask until after the war. I have only nine notes, only one recent.
**Romanée-St-Vivant Marey-Monge** A rare bottle from the cellar of Mme Marey-Monge given to the previous DRC *maître de chai*. One of three old vintages following a St-Vivant vertical, 1994 to 1966 vintages. Palish, rosehip tawny orange; showing its age but fragrant, whiff of violets, taking on meaty, singed scents; a distinct touch of rot, lean, good length but very acidic. *At Aubert de Villaine's St-Vivant tasting, Nov 1995* ★

ANOTHER MAJOR '38 NOTED IN THE 1980S
**La Tâche** Warm, expansive, autumnal; extraordinary, chocolatey nose; sweet, 'exquisite, incandescent' I noted, and lingering flavour. *A glass generously brought to our table by James Halliday, dining at La Pyramide, Vienne, Sept 1984* ★★★★★

EARLIER NOTE **Dr Barolet's Corton** Tasted with Harry Waugh in the courtyard above the Barolet cellars just outside the city walls of Beaune, its colour matching the filtered autumn sunlight and golden leaves. Rich, firm nose and taste. Twenty-five dozen out of a very large stock selected for the Barolet sale. *Tasted Oct 1969* ★★★

## 1939 ★★

Average-sized crop, delayed harvest. Good wines made by those who had the labour and means to select the best grapes. Wartime bottling. Not shipped, rarely seen.

ONLY ONE TASTED Surprise, surprise, **Dr Barolet's Morey-St-Denis**, recorked by de Villamont: good colour; light, short but adequate length, pleasant enough. *Dec 1971* ★★

## 1940 ★★

Hard winter, beautiful spring, then mildew almost decimated the crop. Those who coped made some very good wine.

FOUR OLD NOTES, three **DRC**s, all tasted at the Coq Hardi, Bougival in *1980*: **Romanée-Conti** opulent bouquet, rich palate, lovely finish ★★★★; **La Tâche** ripe, 'roasted', rich, appealing ★★★; and **Richebourg** surprisingly gentle and delicate, fading but with charm and elegance ★★★; and one other wine, from Maxim's, Paris tasted *1978*: **Thomas-Bassot's Chambertin, Tête de Cuvée** mushroom-scented ★★

## 1941 ★

Some mildew. Unripe grapes were picked with difficulty in cold, damp conditions. Slaked wartime thirsts. Despite its poor reputation, the only two '41s I have tasted have been surprisingly good. **Dr Barolet's Corton** showing well pre-sale and subsequently. *Last tasted in 1971* ★★★; and **Drouhin's Chambolle-Musigny** a sweet, soft, spicy, fragrant magnum. *Dining with Drouhin's agent, Parry de Winton, Feb 1983* ★★★

## 1942 ★★★

An unusually early vintage of undoubted quality.
**La Tâche** A bottle from Prince Rupert Löwenstein's cellar in 1996: lovely warm, glowing mahogany; low-keyed at first, rich, slightly malty vegetal nose, good depth; medium dryness and body, crisp, tangy, good length, sweet finish. Next, in a wartime green bottle: palish, healthy glow; fragrant old Pinot soon developing a mocha-like, brown sugar scent; sweet, fading gracefully, good firm dry finish. *Last noted in Zurich, April 1998, the oldest wine in Wagner's La Tâche tasting. At best* ★★★★
**Richebourg DRC** From ungrafted pre-phylloxera vines. Pale green wartime bottle. Long, fully branded cork with deep stained velvety end. Medium-pale, attractive; low-keyed at first, soon emerging a good ripe Pinot aroma, then perfect sweetness; sweet on the palate too, rich, singed, powerful, good length. *At Prince Löwenstein's, Ham, Surrey, July 1996* ★★★★

**Chambertin-Ruchottes** **Thomas-Bassot** Emanating from Maxim's Paris and first noted at a Heublein pre-sale tasting in 1981. Next, in 1990, pale but healthy; attractive bouquet reminiscent of smouldering leaves; soft yet a touch of acidity. Most recently, bottles from Benno Friedman's cellar, originally bought at a Heublein sale in New Orleans. One bottle corked, the backup palish; smoky vanilla nose and 'ambrosial beetroot'; excellent flavour, quite a bite. *Last noted at a Last Friday Club dinner at Raji's, Memphis, Dec 1997. At best* ★★★

**Grands-Echézeaux** **Leroy** Wartime bottle, Leroy slip labels; long cork. Soft, palish mahogany with greenish rim; touch of liquorice, revealing a deep, ripe, meaty Pinot fragrance; dry, medium body, sound singed flavour, good length and grip. *In the Löwenstein cellar, July 1996* ★★★

## 1943 ★★★★

The best wartime vintage, following a well-nigh perfect spring, summer and autumn. Good quality though the crop was reduced by frosts in May and localised hail in July. If well kept, the wines should still be remarkably good.

**Romanée-Conti** Still from ungrafted vines. Original embossed wax seal, label, branded cork, fairly good 5-cm level. Medium-pale texture with orange rim and ruddy glow; low-keyed at first but sound, after 30 minutes rich, biscuity, meaty, an hour later fully evolved, a perfect old Pinot, fading after two hours. Distinctly sweet, ripe flavour, perfect maturity, fairly good length and attractive finish. *From a fine private cellar in San Francisco, tasted at Christie's, Los Angeles, March 1997* ★★★★

**La Tâche** First tasted in Melbourne, 1977: a bottle taken by car from my host's cellar to a Chinese restaurant. It just survived the journey and the 'sweet and sour'; a pity though. Sometime in the 1980s, this friend, a virtuoso violinist as well as a knowledgeable wine collector, sold quite a few of his old burgundies at Christie's in London (we would not have handled them had I not actually visited his excellent cellar). Quite coincidentally bought by Barney Wilson who served the wine at an excellent dinner party in Hungerford. In fact, two bottles were opened, the first richly coloured with a flowery bouquet floating over a typical vegetal, beetroot Pinot aroma; very rich, very meaty, very good. Perhaps, as a '43, lacking some La Tâche panache. The second bottle was rich and tangy but showing its age on nose and palate. *Both last noted at Jane and Barney Wilsons', April 1996. At best* ★★★★

**Chambolle-Musigny, 1er Cru** **Thomas-Bassot** Another Maxim's cellar wine tasted before the Heublein auctions I conducted round the USA between 1969 and 1981. This particular wine was in the 1971 sale and bought by Lloyd Flatt, then the best known and most generous collector, whose second house in New Orleans was devoted to his wines. Following his divorce, he had to dispose of his entire cellar, which must have been heartbreaking. This wine was one of 49 of his fabulous wines opened at the tasting prior to one of our best-ever one-owner sales in America. In common with all of them, it was in very good condition, not very deep in colour; a smoky Pinot nose, dry with good flavour. *Last tasted at Christie's in Chicago, Sept 1990* ★★★

**Richebourg** **Leroy** From the same Australian cellar as the La Tâche. Also two bottles opened. Slight variation. The first lovely, soft, luminous red: dry, hefty, alcoholic but lean, very fragrant, the other slightly deeper; very forthcoming; vanilla scented; sweeter, elegant, stylish, good length; dry finish. *At the Wilsons' in Hungerford, April 1996* ★★★★

SEVERAL OTHER GOOD '43S TASTED but not recently, the finest being a magnificent **DRC**'s **Richebourg** 'with uplifting and expanding second phase of flavour' ★★★★★; **Lejay-Lagoute**'s **Vosne-Romanée** ★★★★; **Thomas-Bassot**'s **Clos St-Denis** ★★★; and two very good **Bouchard Père**'s: **Beaune**, **Grèves** and **Clos de la Mousse** both ★★★

## 1944 ★

A wash out, literally. Light wines, little colour. A pity because the growing season had been exemplary until 8 September, the very day Beaune was liberated by the Allies, when the rains came down and continued detestably until the end of October, spoiling the delayed harvest.

ONLY ONE TASTED a watery **Romanée-Conti** in 1959.

## 1945 ★★★★★

A great vintage. Though the war in Europe had ended earlier in the year, labour problems and shortages continued. In the vineyards, the major setback was severe frosts in March and April, otherwise the unaffected vines benefited from a beautiful spring with flowering beginning 20 May (the earliest start between 1940 and 1977) and completed rapidly. On 21 June a sudden and severe cyclone ravaged ten of the principal villages in the Côte de Beaune. The ensuing summer was hot but dry. The result of 'nature's pruning' and low rainfall resulted in a small crop of high quality, concentrated grapes.

Because of the small production and the post-war thirst, few '45s remain and though I noted many in my early days in the trade, I have tasted relatively few recently.

**Romanée-Conti** From the last of the ungrafted vines. Total production 600 bottles – no record of magnums or jeroboams. The magnum presented at the 'Tasting of Rare Wines' at the Musée Baccarat, Paris, in May 2000 was said to be made up of two bottles. Alas, like several other wines of this tasting, it was a great let-down. Medium-deep, correct mature rim and bitty sediment; showing age on the nose, reminding me of old lamb chops; certainly powerful, tannic, and probably *was* the '45, but not well kept. As a matter of interest, a jeroboam (which, in Burgundy, is a double magnum) brought into Christie's the following morning had an old capsule, convincing body and vintage neck label, but the Domaine had refused to authenticate it. So that was that. Most recently: ullage a not serious 4.5cm (all the others were around 3cm): medium-deep,

---

#### Manfred Wagner

*A reticent Swiss, now retired from a local bank, whose hobby and abiding passion is wine. He continues to collect wine for his astonishingly good vertical tastings – which, in my view, are exceedingly important for putting each vintage in perspective. Wagner's tastings are usually held to celebrate his birthday, and to each of them he invites a small group of mainly Swiss and German friends, both trade and amateur. They are always one-day affairs, held at the Zurich Airport Hilton. I have attended four: two major verticals of Ch Margaux, the first to celebrate his 50th birthday in 1987, the second in 2001; one of Ch d'Yquem (held in 1992) and in 1998 a La Tâche vertical with Aubert de Villaine, beginning with the '42 vintage, all of which I refer to in the text.*

richly coloured; amazingly sweet bouquet, after ten minutes black truffles and a whiff of liquorice, and after 30 minutes unspeakably glorious, reminding me of fresh raspberry crumble; sweet, firm, spicy, richly textured, perfect crisp fruit, great length. *The outstanding wine of the three-day burgundy tasting, and in perfect surroundings, a bright early spring day on a hilltop overlooking San Francisco Bay. With thanks to Wilf Jaeger, our super-generous, knowledgeable, yet modest and self-effacing host. Last tasted March 2002* ★★★★★★ *(6 stars).*

**La Tâche** Though the note is old, it was such a superb wine that I feel it worth mentioning. First noted in 1961 at a dinner at home I gave for Alain de Vogüé (of Veuve Clicquot) and my then chairman, George McWatters. It was hugely impressive, but only starting to open up. Twenty-two years later, the oldest and outstandingly the greatest of 26 vintages of La Tâche arranged by Aubert de Villaine for a book Christie's were proposing to commission. The most noticeable facet was its depth of colour, not the usual unconvincing mature Pinot; more importantly, its extraordinary volume of scents, exuding power, unravelling relentlessly; rich, great length and the great burgundy hallmark, the 'peacock's tail' opening up in the mouth. *Not tasted since May 1983 but unforgettably* ★★★★★

**Richebourg DRC** Medium-deep; deliciously ripe, earthy bouquet that was still excellent after 2½ hours; a sweet powerhouse of a wine, lots of grip, tannin and acidity. Just the slightest touch of sour old age. *At Wilfred Jaeger's second tasting dinner in San Francisco, March 2002* ★★★★★

**Chambertin J Drouhin** Very good colour but nose and palate disappointing, woody, on the verge of corkiness, some decay. Alas… Even Wilf Jaeger can't win them all. *March 2002.*

**Ch Corton-Grancey L Latour** Two notes, first at a pre-sale tasting in New York in 1996. Lovely, singed mature Pinot; a powerful wine in excellent condition. Most recently, a bottle from Nicolas in Paris: soft, rosy-cheeked; sweet, rich, ripe; dry, touch of mocha, very singed but enjoyable. *Last noted at Jaeger's dinner tasting, March 2002* ★★★★

**Grands-Echézeaux Grivelet** Bernard Grivelet, a big man with a somewhat chequered career, produced some speciously convincing wines for Harvey's in the 1950s and I well recall meeting him at his Ch de Chambolle-Musigny with Harvey colleagues in 1957 – a very agreeable tea on the lawn. This particular magnum had a decent colour, sound, somewhat meaty nose, was drying out but not bad. A case of six magnums fetched $2000, at a time when $300 would have secured a dozen bottles of superb Scharzhofberger Goldkapsel Auslese. *Noted at a pre-sale tasting in New York, Dec 1996* ★★

**Pommard, Rugiens François Gaunoux** A lovely colour; very good bouquet; touch of ripe sweetness, deliciously crisp flavour, dry finish. *At Wilf Jaeger's, March 2002* ★★★★★

OF THE TWO DOZEN OR SO OLDER NOTES, the following stand out: **Clos des Lambrays** great richness and depth; reminding me of '47 Pétrus, amazingly sweet, seven notes, last in *1987* ★★★★★; de Vogüé's **Musigny, Vieilles Vignes** on my first visit to Burgundy in 1958; a magnum 'very strong, huge, outsize – but fine'. Later a magnificent silky magnum and excellent bottle, but a badly and sadly recorked bottle in *1985*. *At best* ★★★★★; de Vogüé's **Musigny** there was a very strange cellar mix-up: the wine was labelled Bonnes-Mares but the cork branded Musigny, so it must have been the latter: soft, velvety, refined (1960); boundless life. *1984* ★★★★★; Faiveley's **Chambolle-Musigny** a powerhouse of fragrance. *1985* ★★★★★; and **Leroy**'s **Gevrey-Chambertin** *1984* ★★★★

## 1946 ★★★

Unfairly dismissed despite its quality. A tolerably good sunny growing season with an abundant crop until hail in August, followed by a cold rainy period. The last half of September was warm, prior to a decent harvest. However, sandwiched between the '45 and '47, very few wines were purchased.
**Chambertin A Rousseau** Quite good colour, very heavy sediment; nose and palate still sound and very good for age and vintage. *At the Josey pre-sale tasting, New York, Nov 2000* ★★★

THE ONLY OTHER '46S TASTED a deep, rich **Dr Barolet Beaune, Hospices, Cuvée Rousseau-Deslandes** ★★★ *(1969)*, and a lovely **Thomas-Bassot Chambertin** at Heublein tastings in the late 1970s to early 1980s ★★★

## 1947 ★★★★

A wonderfully rich vintage following an excellent growing season: warm summer, fully ripe crop picked early, from 16 September. Despite the problems encountered when the grapes are picked and fermented in very hot weather, the '47 burgundies seem, in retrospect, more stable than their counterparts in Bordeaux. Nevertheless, even the best are fully evolved. 'Gather ye rosebuds whilst ye may' – except that these glorious roses are turning brown at the edges. I was fortunate to have started my wine trade career in the early 1950s when these '47s were imported, mainly *en barrique*. The quality of wine and of merchant bottling in the UK was reassuringly high, allowing for some commercial 'stretching' at either end.
**La Tâche** In 1987: medium-pale; fragrant, singed, slightly malty bouquet, very sweet. Great power and length. More recently, despite its 7-cm ullage, a similar colour – a nice glow; more than overripe, *gibier* on the nose and sweet banana skins on the palate. Could have been worse. *Last noted at Wagner's La Tâche vertical, April 1998. At best* ★★★★

**Chassagne-Montrachet Bouchard Père** Rich colour, bouquet and flavour. Very sweet. Touch of toffee. *At the Flatt collection pre-sale tasting, Sept 1990* ★★★★

**Clos Vougeot Dufouleur** Deep, rich; vanilla, prunes; strange flavour, very tannic. *Feb 1993* ★ *Interesting only.*

**Beaune, Clos du Roi P Monnieux** Good varietal nose, crisp, delightful; agreeable sweetness, weight, flavour, length and refreshing acidity. *At Corney & Barrow, May 1995* ★★★

**Beaune, Grèves Ropiteau-Mignon** Alas, more than showing its age. Aftertaste like dried bracken. *July 1995.*

**Chambertin, Clos de Bèze Labègue-Bichot** Trust Hardy Rodenstock to find a '47 jeroboam for his closing dinner (for 50) in Munich: medium-pale, healthy, attractive; nose sound; very flavoury but with edgy acidity. *Sept 1996* ★★

**Corton Belgian-bottled by Vandermeurlen** Quite good colour but, sadly, oxidised. *In Paris, Dec 1995.*

**Pommard, Les Grands-Epenots Louis Poirier** Deep; very rich smoky Pinot nose and taste though spoiled by its finish. *At a III Form Club tasting at Boodles, July 1995.*

**Romanée-St-Vivant Bottled by Reidesmeister & Ulrichs, Bremen** (Still one of Germany's leading wine merchants.) Recorked. Very good colour; lovely bouquet, fragrant ripe Pinot; sweet, fairly full-bodied, rich, good grip. *At the Breuers' rare wine dinner in Rüdesheim, Nov 1997* ★★★★

**Romanée-St-Vivant Seguin Manuel** Rich *robe*; hefty, somewhat 'stewed' but held well and seemed to become more refined; sweet, full, meaty. *At Corney & Barrow, May 1995* ★★

**Vosne-Romanée** Belgian-bottled by **Vandermeurlen** Good colour, warm, attractive; initially light, pleasing fruit on the nose immediately followed by a curious sickliness from which it recovered, after 30 minutes rich, hefty; pleasant ripeness, sweetness, body, fruit, flavour and balance. *At Frans de Cock's wine event, Paris, Dec 1995* ★★★

OLDER NOTE **Musigny** de Vogüé first tasted (the Vieilles Vignes) in 1957: a fine, delicate bouquet and intriguing flavour. Lovely wine. One of the most superb '47s, the domaine at its zenith. In 1982 served blind at Laytons' towards the end of lunch when I was expecting port. I thought the colour and nose not quite right, but the taste brought me back in the right direction. Decanted because of its heavy sediment. Colour perfect. Very distinctive, smoky bouquet. Marvellous flavour. Rich. Still very tannic. Two years later: one low level, oxidised, the other gloriously rich and ripe at Khoury's de Vogüé tasting. Fragile bouquet, 'arsenic and old lace'. Fabulous warmth and length. *Last tasted Oct 1984. At best* ★★★★★

OTHER '47S SHOWING WELL IN THE 1980S **Bouchard Père's** rich, ripe **Beaune, Marconnets** in *Memphis, 1983* ★★★★; **C Giroud's Corton** sweet, full, soft, rounded. *Dec 1980* ★★★★; **Morin's Grands-Echézeaux** variable but at best, soft, ripe, lovely. *1981* ★★★★; **Mazis-Chambertin** bottled by Averys of Bristol, opulent, singed, vegetal, walnut-flavoured. *With Len Evans in the Hunter Valley, 1985* ★★★

### Frans de Cock

*A Belgian businessman and wine connoisseur with a great cellar. He organised one of the most memorable wine events I have ever attended, held over a weekend in Paris, in December 1995. Among a remarkable array of great wines were some outstanding top quality Bordeaux and burgundies of the great 1947 vintage, Belgian-bottled by Vandermeurlen.*

## 1948 ★★

Fairly good, somewhat idiosyncratic wines. Like the '46s, they were largely bypassed by the British trade, which wisely focused on the flanking '47 and '49 vintages. Variable weather conditions, the late spring and early summer too cold and wet though it was good from mid-August to the early October harvest. Quality will range from tired to very good.
Both **DRC's La Tâche** and **Richebourg** were immensely impressive in their youth, 'big and black' even at ten years of age, the La Tâche being at its perfect best in 1980. If well cellared, the DRC '48s should still be richly mouthfilling.

## 1949 ★★★★★

The most perfect end to the decade. One of my favourite of all burgundy vintages. The vital flowering took place in worryingly unsettled rainy conditions but thereafter the climate behaved admirably, warm and dry to ripen and concentrate, sufficient rain to swell the grapes prior to picking from 27 September. Elegant, well-balanced wines, the best the epitome of burgundy. The '49s filled both private British cellars and the merchants' coffers. As part of my stock-in-trade, I tasted many of these wines in the late 1960s, a dozen or so excellent ones in the 1970s but, alas, not many recently.

**La Tâche** Very good colour, soft ruby core with perfect gradation to mature autumnal rim; rich, smoky bouquet and flavour, good medium fruit, quite a bite, showing its age on the finish. *At Manfred Wagner's La Tâche vertical, April 1998* ★★★
**Chambertin** A **Rousseau** Great wine: rich, fully evolved, vegetal Pinot, penetrating, sinus-clearing nose; very powerful and penetrating, amazing texture, flavour and aftertaste. *At the Marcobrunn and Chambertin dinner at Schloss Reinhartshausen, Nov 1995* ★★★★★
**Chambolle-Musigny, Les Charmes** Doudet-Naudin First tasted in 1988: bouquet of pickled walnuts and wet straw; sweet, delicious flavour, good length. Most recently, and surprisingly, following La Tâche '69 and '61 at Len Evans' 70th birthday marathon: still quite a good colour; typical Doudet-Naudin sweet, chocolatey nose; agreeable sweetness and body and, as I would have predicted, reliably sound if lacking the charm of its name. *Last tasted Nov 2000 in the Hunter Valley* ★★★
**Corton** L Jadot Very deep; meaty, almost volcanic earthy nose, sound as a bell; very sweet, full-bodied, high extract and alcohol, and fairly high acidity. Impressive. *Lunching with André Gagey and his son, Pierre-Henry, at the Hostellerie de Levernois, near Beaune, Oct 1990* ★★★★
**La Romanée** Dom de la Romanée With Thomas-Bassot slip label. Level 4cm. A 'ringer' slipped in blind between the Romanée-Conti '59 and '52. Medium-deep (I thought it was a '45); low-keyed yet rich; showing some age, a touch of fungi and tannic. *At Wilfred Jaeger's burgundy tasting, March 2002* ★★
**Volnay, Santenots** Camille Giroud Deep but amber-rimmed; deliciously ripe *gibier*, singed, chocolatey bouquet; sweet, still vigorous, lovely. *At the closing dinner of the Hollywood Wine Society's wine weekend, Jan 1990* ★★★★
**Vosne-Romanée** François Gros Good colour; rich, slightly stewed Pinot nose with a whiff of raspberries; sweet, pleasant singed flavour, well-balanced, complete. *Dining at Gidleigh Park in Devon with Len Evans and Brian Crozer, Nov 1997* ★★★★

SOME INTERESTING '49S TASTED IN THE 1980S de Vogüé's **Bonnes-Mares** a great period for this domaine though a disappointingly faded, acidic magnum. *1984* ★; Leroy's **Chambertin** bouquet expired after a 'fluttery fragrance and perfume', yet powerful on the palate, sharp yet scented. *1988* ★★★; **Charmes-Chambertin** Paris-bottled by **Prunier** two notes: still a fairly big wine, attractive. *1982* ★★; and three more Leroy wines: **Gevrey-Chambertin, Les Cazetiers** very deep though aged; sweet; chocolatey bouquet and flavour. Elegant but a whiff of volatile acidity and bitter finish. 'Otherwise great'. *1984* ★★★★; **Mazis-Chambertin** opaque, massive, tannic but showing its age. *1984* ★★★★; and **Richebourg** remarkably deep; a lovely old bouquet and flavour though past its best, creaking. *1985* ★★★; and two from **Charles Noëllat**: **Nuits-St-Georges** fragrant, charming, flavoury. *1984* ★★★★; and **Clos Vougeot** healthy glow; vanilla; lovely flavour, firm, still tannic, good finish. *1984* ★★★★

FINALLY, THE TWO GREATEST '49S TASTED IN THE 1970S de Vogüé's **Musigny** this epitomised the finesse and elegance of both Musigny and the vintage. Superb colour which glowed in a Georgian decanter; opulent bouquet and a scent rarely achieved by any wine; rich yet firm, beautiful sustained flavour ★★★★★; and **Marey-Monge's Romanée-St-Vivant** fabulous, almost exotic bouquet; powerful yet perfectly formed. Burgundy at its very best ★★★★★

# 1950–1969

Apart from some excellent vintages, the early part of the 1950s was much concerned with the replanting and regeneration of old vineyards and clearing out pockets of poor vine stocks; this was followed in the mid-1950s by important, long-term clonal research.

In parallel, however, the AOC laws were being sidelined by the 'stretching' of *le vrai* burgundy with wine transported by road tanker from the Rhône, the Midi and elsewhere. I joined the wine trade in 1952, first with Laytons, then Saccone & Speed, and, from 1955 to 1966, Harvey's of Bristol. I soon came to realise that a good deal of the burgundy shipped to the UK was not 100% what it purported to be. Around this time only about 15% of burgundy was domaine-bottled. The trade was dominated by the *négociants*, merchants who provided the importer with what the latter and his wine merchant customers wanted: well known names at commercially acceptable prices. I recall organising, for my young contemporaries' tasting club, a horizontal of the best known Côte d'Or village wines: Santenay, Pommard, Volnay, Beaune, Nuits-St-Georges and Gevrey-Chambertin – all from one reputable burgundy house, which turned out to be, in ascending order of price, variations on a theme. Moreover, British wine merchants, skilled and experienced bottlers, were also not immune to 'stretching' and blending. By and large, one got what one paid for and there were few complaints.

I have literally hundreds of notes, most of which are now, of course, out of date. As these wines were bought for drinking, few for ageing and never as an investment, hardly any survive, but the '52s and '59s are particularly well worth looking out for, as are the '62s, '64s, '66s and '69s, perhaps from an abandoned cellar, or at auction.

## Vintages at a Glance
**Outstanding ★★★★★**
1959, 1962, 1969
**Very Good ★★★★**
1952, 1953, 1961(v), 1964, 1966
**Good ★★★**
1955, 1957

## 1950 ★

Burgundy is susceptible to hail and the vineyards suffered more than their fair share in July, August and September, the latter two months being wet. Nevertheless, the harvest began relatively early, on the 18th, the rain-swollen grapes producing an abundance of light wines of modest quality. Once again, having gorged themselves with the '49s and not exactly flush with cash, the British trade gave the '50s a miss.

None tasted recently, nine last noted in the 1960s and 1970s, just two quite good wines in the 1980s: **Volnay, Hospices, Cuvée Jehan de Massol** from the Quancard family cellars, two bottles with a 5-cm ullage: pale but attractive *pelure d'oignon* (the colour of much burgundy in the Middle Ages); slightly vanilla-scented Pinot bouquet; light but with good length and acidity. *1989. At best ★★★*; and **Pierre Ponnelle**'s **Vougeot, Clos du Prieuré** two similar notes: medium colour; gentle but rich bouquet that opened up in the glass, holding its fragrance over a long period; soft, rather short but lovely flavour. In good condition. *Last tasted 1984 ★★★*

## 1951

Dismal summer, harvest delayed until 15 October. None imported, few tasted, none recently – yet, of my half dozen or so notes, some surprises: **Poulet Frères**' **Grands-Echézeaux** good colour, rich 'legs'; lovely, clean-cut Pinot, holding well; sweet, soft, lovely, with excellent acidity. The clue provided by my host Bernard (Barney) Rhodes: the wine was made from young declassified grapes from the newly planted Romanée-Conti vines. *1986 ★★★*; **Clos des Lambrays** palish; remarkably attractive nose, toasted, chocolatey, chaptalised Pinot; lacking length and acidic but 'not at all bad'. *1981 ★★*; **La Tâche** lively, rosy colour; sound 'beetroot' Pinot nose; dry, crisp, sound. *1985 ★★*

When Harry Waugh and I first visited the Barolet cellars in Beaune in 1969, we began by tasting some of the 'off' vintages and were intrigued to assess the results of the good Doctor's ministrations. We tasted his '51 **Chambolle-Musigny.** Consistent notes then, before and after the sale, and the following year. Colour not bad but watery rim; a surprisingly sound and attractive flavour, ripe, slightly peppery.

## 1952 ★★★★

One of my favourite vintages of the decade; firm well structured dependable wines worth looking out for. Many notes, particularly in my Harvey's of Bristol days, but now they are half a century old. It would have been a great vintage had it not been for a cool September following a June drought mitigated by some rain in an otherwise very hot July and August. Fairly late harvest – 7 October.
**Romanée-Conti** Bottles not numbered. By 1945, the production from the ungrafted old vines had become uneconomical and a decision was finally made to uproot and replant with American root stock. 1952 was the first major vintage to be harvested from the young vines. A medium ruddy-amber colour; spicy, slightly minty, soft, harmonious bouquet which soon developed a meaty, gravy-like smell and after an hour had become degraded. Initially, on the palate, it was very sweet, very 'warm', very rich yet it was showing some age and the finish was twisted and slightly sour. A less than good bottle? *At Wilfred Jaeger's unprecedented Romanée-Conti extended lunch, March 2002 ★★*

**Richebourg DRC** First tasted in 1967: austerely rich. Next in 1979, still deeply coloured; well developed nose; a deep, velvety wine with rounded flesh over firm bones. Most recently, a magnum produced by Aubert de Villaine, after the St-Vivant vertical. Autumnal colour and bouquet, the latter low-keyed at first but opening up dizzily with many facets; on the palate sweet, firm, excellent flavour, balance, length and finish. Showing its age yet full of life. *At the Domaine, Oct 2001* ★★★★★
**Romanée-St-Vivant Shipped by Jadot, Belgian-bottled by Vandermeurlen** Good colour; rather jammy nose; very sweet, rich, delicious. In excellent condition. The last of the Vandermeurlens served at Frans de Cock's closing dinner. *At Carré des Feuillants, Paris, Dec 1995* ★★★★

OF THE TOP '52S, LAST TASTED IN THE 1980S
**Romanée-Conti** A great wine by any standards. Several notes, bottles and a magnum: ripe, opulent, complex – burgundy at its best. *Last noted at the Khourys, 1982* ★★★★★ *Will still be superb.*
**Musigny de Vogüé** Fragrant, lively, massive and masculine for Musigny yet soft and lovely. *At the Khourys, 1984* ★★★★★
**Nuits-St-Georges, Clos des Porrets H Gouges** Deep; truffles; rich, firm, tannic laden. *At the Domaine, 1981* ★★★★★
**Richebourg Lebègue-Bichot** Jeroboam: broad, expansive, rich, ripe, excellent balance, complete. *1985* ★★★★

OF THE MANY OLDER NOTES, these wines stand out:
**La Tâche** ★★★★★; **J Drouhin's Grands-Echézeaux** ★★★★★; **Averys' bottling of Pommard, Grand Epenots, Clos des Citeaux** ★★★★; and **L Latour's Romanée-St-Vivant** ★★★★

# 1953 ★★★★

A most attractive vintage following a growing season that could hardly have been more different from 1952 for, following a mild spring, June and July were cold and wet. Happily, August and September were warm and dry, a 'no problem' harvest of ripe grapes from the 29th.

Less sturdy but with more charm than the '52s, the wines were instantly appealing and very popular. I well recall, with Harry Waugh, organising a tasting for Oxford colleges at All Souls in May 1956: there were 13 '53s, all bottled between June and December 1955 by Harvey's, ranging from a Côte de Beaune-Villages at 110 shillings per dozen to Richebourg at 218 shillings, the latter, I noted 'a lovely full wine. Great pedigree'. Those were the days. I might even have bottled it from the cask myself for I did my first stint in Harvey's Bristol cellars in the summer of 1955. Few 53s to be seen now and in any case I think they were at their best in the mid-1970s to mid-1980s.
**La Tâche** Astonishing how these DRCs, when young, can vary in depth of colour, from the impressively deep (the '45) to the misleadingly pale, as was this '53. By 1966, fully mature-looking, delectably fragrant, lovely but seemed at its peak. Yet in 1983, it was ploughing on steadily, with archetypal La Tâche scents; mouthfilling flavour yet light in style, with unobtrusive sustaining tannin and acidity. Most recently, at Wagner's La Tâche vertical, its best feature being its sweet, richly developed bouquet. Strangely assertive. Not as inspiring as expected. *Last tasted April 1998. At best* ★★★★
**Chambolle-Musigny Patriarche** Something of a surprise: lovely sweet Pinot nose; very sweet, a beautifully souped-up flavour. *At a III Form Club tasting, July 1995* ★★★

**Richebourg R Bouillon, M Rossin** Rich but open-rimmed, orange tinge; very fragrant, correct Pinot bouquet that drooped in the glass; flavoury but a bit lean, and with tart finish. *At the strange Burgundy tasting at Corney & Barrow, May 1995* ★★? *A 'don't call me, I'll call you' wine.*

A FEW OF THE BEST WINES LAST TASTED IN THE MID-1980S **Héritiers Latour's Chambertin** 1984 ★★★★; **Leroy's Mazis-Chambertin** 1984 ★★★★; and **L Latour's Romanée-St-Vivant, Les Quatre Journaux** 1985 ★★★★

And if you ever come across **DRC's Romanée-Conti** and **Grands-Echézeaux**, do let me know. I am dying to renew their acquaintance.

# 1954 ★★

Vintages have a habit of being leap-frogged or by-passed, but understandably so, for importers and wine merchants had, wisely, bought heavily of the two preceding vintages, and the quality of the '55s was known before the '54s were due to be bottled. The summer was wet but the harvest was saved by a warm and sunny autumn: quantity not quality.
**Romanée-Conti** Palish, 'warm', open rim; a fully evolved, chaptalised but fragrant bouquet with an amazing, muscatelle-raisiny scent and aftertaste. Sweet, singed. Something of a surprise. *One of a range of curious vintages from Prince Rupert Löwenstein's cellar, tasted in his kitchen with Charles Hawkins, Ham, Surrey, July 1996* ★★★
**Richebourg DRC** My understanding was that the Domaine declassified all but their **Romanée-Conti** and **La Tâche** (the latter tasted at the Domaine in 1983). However the '54 Richebourg was No 4 in a line-up of DRC reds at the New York Wine Experience: palish, orange-rimmed; a strange overripe scent; very sweet, rich, odd but attractive. *Oct 1991* ★★

# 1955 ★★★

Unquestionably good, the best with finesse, but lacking the masculinity and staying power of the '52s and ripe charm of the '53s. Popular with the trade. Harvey's in their autumn 1957 wine list described the vintage as 'most irregular', yet it was to feature exclusively in the 'laying down' section in 1959.

Despite a cold June and late flowering, by August the vines were in excellent condition. Well-ripened grapes were picked early October 'in the best conditions for 20 years'. I have described it as 'the Indian summer of English bottling', the bottling being reliable, indeed, more reliable than the wines that emanated from Burgundy, 'stretching' and the blatant abuse of village names being commonplace. But the British consumer was perfectly happy, and the prices were attractive.

Harvey's in fact were right first time, for, with notable exceptions, the wines were not suitable for laying down, the Côte de Nuits lacking length and flesh, the Côte de Beaune reds light and at their best in the mid-1960s.
**Chambertin Leroy** Fairly pale, very mature-looking; sweet, vanilla nose, 'very Leroy'. Its colour misleading for it was fairly powerful, flavoury, good not great. *At the curious Baccarat tasting in Paris, May 2000* ★★
**Latricières-Chambertin Belgian-bottled by Vandermeurlen** Fairly deep; thick, 'stewed', over the top, whiff of raspberry; sweet, jammy fruit, fragrant, dry finish. *At Frans de Cock's tasting in Paris, Dec 1995* ★★

Of the seriously good '55s tasted in the 1980s de Vogüé's **Bonnes-Mares** 1984 ★★★★; **Leroy**'s **Chambertin, Clos de Bèze** ★★★★; **Louis Latour**'s **Chambolle-Musigny** and **Ch Corton-Grancey** both in 1984 and ★★★★, all of which should still be delicious.

I have not tasted any of the very many English-bottled '55s since the 1970s, but the best bottlings of the grander names might well have survived.

## 1956

Execrable. Not only the worst vintage of the decade but one of the worst ever. But 'don't blame the pianist': the exigences of the climate were the problem, principally cold and incessant rain throughout July and August which caused the vines to suffer from pests and diseases. The hot sunshine in September was too late for recovery and the decimated late harvest was an unmitigated disaster. Perhaps with modern know-how something could have been saved. But the trade and the consumer do not need a vintage like this.

**La Tâche** Strangely, four notes, first at the Domaine in 1981: variable bottles, both short; again in 1983 at the vertical, researching for a DRC book: a bit too thick and brown; smell of rot; lean, acidic. Most recently at Wagner's vertical, not as pale as expected, lively, with a touch of green at the rim; an astonishing bouquet, like a genie out of the bottle, old beetroot, intriguing and, after an hour in the glass, positively opulent and seemingly effortless – it reminded me of the last piano recital of Horowitz. Palate still sweet, flavour of fragrant brown paper, attractive singed finish. *Last tasted in Zurich, April 1998. At best* ★★

Only two other '56s tasted **DRC**'s **Romanée-Conti** pale; surprisingly ripe old nose but dry, thin and gristly. *1972* ★; **Leroy**'s **Gevrey-Chambertin, Cazetiers** pale, pink-tinged; rot on nose and palate. *1984*.

## 1957 ★★★

Of little interest now though the '57s were quite well liked in the early 1960s to mid-1970s. Those with sufficient fruit and body to cope with the high acidity were flavoury and zestful. The imbalance was caused, as always, by the weather which was fine during the first half of the season 'with a crescendo of heat' in June; early July was warm, but thereafter it was cool and rainy. A fairly big vintage of unripened grapes, lacking sugar and over-endowed with acidity.

I have a large number of notes, most made before 1970 and over half prior to 1965. In any case, most of the English-bottlings are now irrelevant. I have tasted few recently.

**Charmes-Chambertin E Brocard** An oddment lurking in Christie's cellars and first brought to light by my colleague, Duncan McEuen, for a III Form Club burgundy tasting in 1995: a rather strange citrus, boiled candy nose and unmistakable '57 acidity. A second bottle, the following year, part of a motley collection I was tasting for a CD-ROM video: quite a good colour for its age; a harmonious mocha-like nose which after two hours in the glass became surprisingly sweet and delicious; nice weight, positive, 'warm', a tolerable acidic edge. *Last tasted Jan 1996* ★★

**Charmes-Chambertin Chanson** Richly coloured albeit an orange rim; very characteristic 'fishy', oyster shells Chambertin

nose, in fact very attractive, some vanilla, held well; some sweetness, good body, good length and crisp acidity. Surprisingly good for its vintage and age. *At the weird tasting of old burgundy at Corney & Barrow, May 1995* ★★

**Clos de Tart** Appropriately named though its tartness, high toned and fragrant, was attractive in its fifth year. But after 28 years, palish and weak-looking; not much nose; good flavour though and dry finish. *Last tasted March 1990* ★★

Of the few '57s last tasted in the 1980s, two stand out: **La Tâche** at three years of age, light, ripe, fragrant, most attractive and immediately drinkable. 25 years on, a jeroboam, still fairly pale, mature-looking; lovely ripe Pinot-beetroot aroma, almost too exotic. Dried-out but with intriguing flavour, with piquant '57 acidity. *1985* ★★★★; and **Roumier**'s **Musigny** delicious, sweet bouquet and flavour. *1980* ★★★

## 1958 ★★

The British trade had bought too many of the '57s and by the time the '58s were ready, the quality of the '59s was apparent. No '58 burgundies were bottled, listed or even referred to in Harvey's retail lists of the early to mid-1960s. Only two '58s ever tasted, both DRCs.

**Echézeaux DRC** A strange, meaty, not very distinctive nose though it sweetened up; not wholly convincing on the palate either. Dried-out and rather short. *July 1996* ★

And one older note **La Tâche** a warm, ruddy colour; sweet, somewhat caramelly nose and taste. Substantially, but well, chaptalised. *1983* ★★

## 1959 ★★★★★

At last, a top class vintage, one that I have always thought of as the end of an era. The weather conditions were ideal for blossoming in June; July and August were hot and dry followed by some rain to swell the grapes prior to an early harvest from 14 September in hot weather. A record crop of high quality wine.

I have more notes on this vintage than on any other except 1964, but of course the largest number were in the 1960s when I was not only on the Harvey's Wine Committee but busy organising Harvey's 'shops within shops' (retail outlets in department stores); then several dozen good notes in the 1970s, just over two dozen in the 1980s and, as time passes, less than a dozen notes in the last decade.

**Romanée-Conti** Production 9607 bottles. First noted at the big Lebègue annual tasting in the monumental arches beneath London Bridge Station in 1964: amazingly rich and concentrated. Still totally unready in 1979 but 15 years later wonderfully evolved: medium-deep; soft, velvety, fleshy, harmonious bouquet with mulberry-hint of fruit; full, rich, mouthfilling. Dry finish. Most recently, bottle number 0929: Fairly deep, richly coloured; sweet, harmonious nose, rich fruit, almost jammy – strawberry, raspberry – great depth, faultless; lovely flavour, still with excellent tannin and acidity, typical Romanée-Conti persistence of flavour. One of my highest marks of the entire range. *At Wilf Jaeger's Romanée-Conti luncheon, March 2002* ★★★★★ *Perfect now, yet years of life left.*

**Richebourg DRC** Low-keyed but ripe and correct; sweet, soft, rich, complete, with good grip. *One of the seven '59s at Jaeger's second burgundy dinner in San Francisco, March 2002* ★★★★★

**Beaune, Hospices, Cuvée Nicolas Rolin F Protheau**
Rich colour, nose and taste. *March 1990* ★★★★
**Chambolle-Musigny Dr Barolet** An interesting wine. When Harry Waugh and I made our preliminary tastings of the Barolet wines in Beaune in October 1969, the '59s were still in cask – and they were in beautiful condition even though there had been some colour loss over the ten years. My pre-sale note read 'fine, mature, heavy bead (rich 'legs'); sweet, beautiful, biscuity nose; medium-dry, soft and delicate, on the light side for a '59'. I gave it high marks and the 50 cases sold well. By this time, the Swiss-owned *négociant*, de Villamont had bought the entire cellar – many thousands of dozens – for marketing later and many bottles were recorked.

The most recent note is of a recorked bottle. Its colour was good; rich, smoky nose and flavour. A decent but uninspiring drink. *Last noted at the Lloyd Flatt pre-sale tasting, Chicago, Sept 1990. At best* ★★★★
**Chambolle-Musigny L Latour** In 1971: rich, chunky flavour. More recently: very deep; good nose; rich, excellent balance. *Last noted at a III Form Club tasting, July 1995* ★★★★
**Ch Corton-Grancey L Latour** A cloudy, chocolatey, soft, chewy but stewed bottle in 1995. Happily far better magnums at Latour's bicentenary dinner: fine, deep colour; surprisingly gentle nose, earthy root-like Pinot; rich and powerful, full of fruit and vigour. Years of life ahead. This dinner was a nerve-wracking occasion for I had to wait until 12.30am to deliver my speech. Coincidentally, I had to make another, same place, same time, the following night, this time at the Chevaliers du Tastevin banquet. Sunday was a welcome day of rest! *Last tasted at Ch de Clos Vougeot, June 1997* ★★★★
**Chambertin Leroy** Pale; stewed beetroot yet rich and ripe, holding well; a strange, singed, overripe taste. Showing its age and a trifle tart. *At Wilf Jaeger's dinner tasting, March 2002* ★
**Corton Dom du Ch de Beaune** Better on nose than palate: ripe, singed, good mature Corton bouquet; 'sweet and sour', very drinkable but a bit edgy. *At Wilf Jaeger's, March 2002* ★★★
**Grands-Echézeaux Gros Colette** I must confess some confusion. There are several members of the Gros family but on the label of this wine, Colette followed Gros. Anyway, the wine was richly coloured; nose correct, ripe, singed, harmonious; dry, lean, quite good flavour though a little tart on the finish (nothing personal). *At Jaeger's, March 2002* ★★★
**Grands-Echézeaux Leroy** Two notes, first in 1994 at the Weinart Gala dinner at the Residenz, Aschau: very good, fully evolved bouquet; rich, full, smoky flavour. Quite a bite. A couple of years later at a dinner party at Lyford Cay in the Bahamas: rich, chocolatey nose opening up later with a scent of 'old honey' and tobacco. A lovely, sweet, minty flavour, mocha end taste. *Last tasted Feb 1996* ★★★
**Le Musigny L Jadot** Dark cherry, mature rim; scented nose developing a bit of caramel; sweet, meaty, hot, peppery, still tannic, good in its way but only a shade above '*bonne cuisine*', the sort of burgundy the English used to prefer. *At Wilfred Jaeger's first burgundy dinner, March 2002* ★★★
**Richebourg Viénot** First noted in 1980 at a pre-sale tasting in London: deep, mature; good wine, full-bodied, soft, richly flavoured. Nearly 20 years later, time and probably storage resulted in a pale, strange, tired old wine. *Last noted at another pre-sale tasting, this time in Geneva, May 1999. At best* ★★★★
**La Romanée Dom du Ch de Vosne-Romanée** Palish, open; ripe, meaty, sweet vegetal nose; sweet on palate, attractive, quite an end bite, with the charm of an old *roué*. *At Wilf Jaeger's burgundy tasting, March 2002* ★★★

**Ruchottes-Chambertin Louis d'Armont** New to me. A rather hard, sharp-edged, medicinal nose that opened up well; better on palate, its flavour spoiled by its acidic finish. *From a Swiss cellar, May 1996* ★
**Clos Vougeot J Drouhin** Of the 50ha of this vast walled vineyard, Droubin own 0.6ha in the middle section and 0.3ha in the lower part. Sweet, rich, rounded, lovely. *Jan 1993* ★★★★
**Clos de Vougeot Jacques Prieur** Orange-tinged; good smoky Pinot nose; firm, dry, tannic finish. *July 1995* ★★

AMONG THE VERY BEST '59S LAST TASTED IN THE 1980S
**La Tâche** supreme. *1985* ★★★★; **Berry Bros** magnum of **Beaune, Hospices, Cuvée Rousseau-Deslandes** powerful, austere 'good for 20 years'. *1988* ★★★★; **Doudet-Naudin**'s **Corton** predictably deep, sweet, solidly impressive. I felt that it could almost be cut like cake and will last for ever. *1983* ★★★; and **Mazis-Chambertin** full, firm, loads of grip. Long life. *1984* ★★★★; **Marquis de Villeranges**' **Mazis-Chambertin** full flavoured, still tannic. *1987* ★★★★; **Faiveley**'s **Musigny, Tasteviné** rich. *1987* ★★★★; **de Vogüé**'s **Musigny, Vieilles Vignes** magnificent. *1984* ★★★★★; **Lupé-Cholet**'s **Nuits-St-Georges, Ch Gris** rich, ripe. *1984* ★★★★; **L Latour**'s **Pommard, Epenots** *1983* ★★★; **Leroy**'s **Richebourg** assertive, needed time. *1988* ★★★; **Viénot**'s **Richebourg** richly flavoured. *1980* ★★★ and **Romanée-St-Vivant** fragrant, stylish. *1984* ★★★★; **Bouchard Père**'s **Volnay, Caillerets** elegant, fragrant. *1987* ★★★★; and **Clair-Daü**'s **Volnay, Caillerets** lovely wine. *1981* ★★★★★

AND THE BEST OF THE EARLIER NOTES **DRC**'s **Echézeaux** and **Grands-Echézeaux**.

# 1960

Yet another by-passed vintage thanks to a poor summer. A large crop of uneven and mainly unripe grapes. I have only ever tasted two: **Jadot**'s **Beaune Vignes Franches** stewed and tart in *1980* and a young, light but not unattractive **Ropiteau**'s **Volnay** *1966*.

# 1961 at best ★★★★

Over and over again it is mistakenly assumed that a great vintage in Bordeaux will be an equally great vintage in Burgundy and vice versa, forgetting that the former has a maritime climate, the latter continental – among other factors. 1961 is a case in point.

The growing season started off most encouragingly. A warm spring, with, by May, vegetation well in advance of normal. The difficulties started with an exceptionally long and uneven flowering followed by a poor summer. September was, however, fine and warm, the harvest taking place in good conditions from the 25th. The crop was well below average and the quality, though better than originally anticipated, simply not of an overall level of excellence to demand and get, prices 50% above those of the magnificent '59s. I have tasted many '61s but relatively few since 1990.
**Romanée-Conti** Only one fairly recent note: deep in colour with noticeably thick 'tears' or 'legs'; a marvellously rich, brambly, harmonious Italianate nose which was evolving after nearly an hour in the glass; sweet, a big wine. *In the pickers' dining room at the Domaine, Nov 1995* ★★★★

La Tâche DRC First tasted at the big annual Lebègue event in 1964. These tastings were the high point of London's annual trade calendar. My 49 notes made that October included a full range of DRCs, some of four vintages, Ch Margaux and Haut-Brion each of six vintages, Ch d'Yquem of five, and other wines, all glamorously deployed by the 'ringmaster', Harvey Prince, in candlelit alcoves in the cavernous cellars beneath London Bridge Station. However, my note of the '61 La Tâche was: 'dry, lightish, thin and green'. (The Echézeaux, Grands-Echézeaux and Richebourg have not been tasted since; I preferred the latter). In 1972 though, 'rich, acidity noticeable' whereas in 1983 I considered it fully mature though criticised its 'raw spiky finish' adding 'not a patch on the '62'. Quite right.

More recently, a fragrant, assertive and impressive jeroboam at a big Rodenstock tasting with dinner in 1996. Fragrance noted again at Manfred Wagner's vertical in 1998, adding 'firm core, hard, hot finish', and a not too dissimilar note at Len Evans' 70th birthday celebrations though I found it attractive, dry, with some delicacy, despite it being completely upstaged by the '69. *Last noted at Len Evans' 'Single-bottle Club' dinner in the Hunter Valley, Sept 2000* ★★★ *or, at a squeeze,* ★★★★ *depending on the occasion.*

Romanée-St-Vivant Marey-Monge Distinct orange tinge; a curious, slightly fishy/malty nose but soft, silky and attractive on the palate. *At a pre-sale tasting in Chicago, Feb 1992* ★★★

Chambertin A Rousseau A magnum: warm, mature, tawny-orange rim; curious minty, arboreal, 'ivy' nose; very sweet, soft, lovely; 'vegetal' this time: good length, masked tannin. *The oldest vintage in a session devoted to the domaine of Armand Rousseau and well presented by Roger Bohmrich MW, at the tenth Hollywood Wine Society weekend seminar, March 1995* ★★★★

Ch Corton-Grancey L Latour First tasted in 1971: deep, rich, meaty Pinot nose and taste. Lovely wine. More recently, the oldest of ten vintages I presented at a Hollywood Wine Society seminar: sweet, crisp, delicious. *Last tasted March 1998* ★★★★

Clos de la Roche P Ponnelle This was about the time I nearly left Harvey's to join Ponnelle's British agents. I let them down, ungraciously, at the last minute. Perhaps as well as I then would never have joined Christie's. Luminous; crisp, fruity nose that opened up gloriously; very sweet, fairly full-bodied, good flavour and length. *At the Hollywood Wine Society's closing dinner, Jan 1990* ★★★★

Clos de la Roche Remoissenet Its smell evoked memories of the Tame Valley Tennis Club, tennis shoes, dusty hard courts, the wooden Club house — a shed; paper mill effluent in the Tame river, the viaduct. A meaty, slightly stale taste. *At a III Form Club tasting, July 1995.*

Clos de Vougeot, Le Prieuré Pierre Ponnelle Good colour; sweet, slightly jammy nose; rich, sound, a certain pepperiness and hard finish. *A jeroboam at Hardy Rodenstock's closing dinner Munich, Sept 1996* ★★

OF THE MANY '61S LAST TASTED IN THE 1980S Bouchard Père's Beaune, Grèves, Vigne de l'Enfant Jésus two lovely magnums: mature, ripe, opulent; charred taste, touch of hard acidity. *Sept 1982 At best* ★★★★; de Vogüé's Bonnes-Mares garnet; ripe, sweet, velvety (1971), harmonious, shapely. *1989* ★★★★; and their Musigny, Vieilles Vignes variable, at best spicy, fragrant. *1984* ★★?; J Drouhin's Chambertin, Clos de Bèze gorgeously velvety (1971), a powerhouse (1973), magnificent colour; incredibly rich, ripe 'yet somehow

unready' nose; enormous, high quality. *1980* ★★★★(★); Bouchard Père's Le Corton rich, wholesome, masculine. *1981* ★★★★; and Noëllat's Clos Vougeot warm, lively, fragrant. *1984* ★★★★

# 1962 ★★★★★

Unquestionably a superior vintage to 1961 but I believe this was not fully recognised at the time — the trade complained that the prices were at the level of the '61s.

Among other virtues (this is very subjective), 1962 harbours one of my rare 6-star assessments: La Tâche.

There was a cool spring with good flowering conditions in June, followed by a fair July, fine and warm August with some welcome rain in September. The belated harvest of sound, fully ripe grapes began on 8 October. Fairly understandably, not many of these wines are seen these days, but they are well worth looking out for.

Romanée-Conti Dry, raw, tannic, unpalatable at the Lebègue tasting in 1964. Still closed and hard in 1977. A decade later, a quarter of a century after the grapes were on their last lap of ripening, a jeroboam, now medium-deep, richly coloured but mature-looking; its still reluctant bouquet took 20 minutes to unwind but after half an hour in the glass displayed a toasty richness. Still full-bodied, assertive, mouthfilling — and another quarter century of development. Most recently, bottle number 047465: imported by Frederick Wildman. Medium-deep, open, fully mature rim; sweet, harmonious nose with marvellous richness and depth, opening up with beautiful scent, sweet, smoky fragrance, fully evolved after an hour and holding well for another; on the palate sweet, excellent flavour, great length, good grip. *At Wilfred Jaeger's third session, the DRC lunch, March 2002* ★★★★★ *Perfection, yet more to come. Let this be a lesson. Do not make the mistake of 'condemning' an immature Romanée-Conti. Had this been an easy, obvious fruity wine in its extreme youth it would not have developed into a magnificent state of maturity.*

La Tâche As so often, in their extreme youth DRCs can be disarmingly unimpressive, sometimes pale, often very hard. At the Lebègue tasting in October 1964, previously referred to, it seemed rather light in character but within eight years had opened up well. In 1973 gaining depth, sweeter, more opulent and at a late supper in 1976, filled the entire room with fragrance. Two hugely admiring notes in 1983, its hallmarks being an almost exotic bouquet and multi-faceted flavour expanding — 'the peacock's tail' — in the mouth. Most recently, at a dinner party at home: level 4cm below cork; medium-deep, open, fully mature colour; 'scented beetroot' nose; rich, fabulous, perfection. Among my guests were Len Evans who rightly prides himself on his palate and (Lord) Rudolf Russell. All the wines were served blind — they included a typically idiosyncratic '49 Château-Chalon, L Latour's '85 Corton-Charlemagne, the great '78 Barca Velha, my favourite '85 Ch Cheval Blanc and '35 Taylor. To Len's chagrin, he was trounced every time by Rudolf and had to resort to suggesting that a duke's son had had an unfair flying start, being brought up with this class of wine! *Last tasted at our London flat, June 2000* ★★★★★★ *(6 stars).*

Richebourg DRC Once again, curiously dry, light and lacking substance in 1964 but even at that stage, dramatically different in style to La Tâche, despite the vines being only a stone throw away and being harvested and vinified in the same cellars. After three years it had got over the shock of its first exposure, developing richly. More recently tasted alongside the Romanée-Conti (see left): deeply coloured;

fragrance more immediate and totally different; a good mouthful with time in hand. *Last noted Sept 1997* ★★★★(★)

**Grands-Echézeaux DRC** Also first noted at the Lebègue tasting in 1964 when it seemed more approachable and appearing more advanced at another Lebègue tasting in 1987. Two notes in 1972: deep, richly coloured; complex bouquet; fabulous flavour – 'saffron', 'cloves', perfect balance. Perfection. Still sweet and plenty of grip in 1986. Next at Corney & Barrow in 1995: very fragrant, elegant, with the slightly fishy Pinot scent I had noted in 1972; very sweet, gloriously rich flavour which expanded in the mouth and left an unmatchably fragrant aftertaste. Most recently: full and forthcoming, sweet, old-Pinot root-like bouquet; ripe and rich, tangy, considerable power and great length. *Last noted at Wilfred Jaeger's opening dinner tasting in San Francisco, the first of three '62s tasted blind, March 2002* ★★★★★

**Bonnes-Mares de Vogüé** Richly coloured; crisp, fine, mature bouquet; excellent flavour, with mature fruit, body, length and elegance. Sweet finish. *At Wilfred Jaeger's tasting, San Francisco, March 2002* ★★★★★

**Chambertin Camus** Medium-pale; low-keyed nose that deteriorated in the glass; showing its age, drying out. *At Wilfred Jaeger's first dinner in San Francisco, March 2002.*

THE FOLLOWING WERE THE BEST OF THE VERY FEW '62s last tasted in the 1980s: de Vogüé's **Musigny, Vieilles Vignes** purest expression of Pinot; fine, scented, fragrant. *Sept 1984* ★★★★★ *will still be excellent*; and **Leroy**'s **Mazis-Chambertin** lovely. *Sept 1984* ★★★★ *but probably past its best now.*

OF THE THREE DOZEN OR SO NOTABLE WINES NOT TASTED SINCE THE 1970s, outstandingly the best, and likely stayers were: **J Drouhin**'s **Beaune, Hospices, Cuvée Maurice Drouhin** ★★★★ and **Clos de la Roche** ★★★★; **Clair-Daü**'s **Bonnes-Mares** ★★★★; **Bouchard Père**'s **Chambertin** ★★★★; **L Jadot**'s **Corton** ★★★★; **Leroy**'s **Nuits-St-Georges, Argillières** ★★★★; **Berry Bros**' bottling of **Volnay, Hospices, Général Muteau** ★★★★; and **H Lamarche**'s **Vosne-Romanée, La Grand-Rue** ★★★★

# 1963 ★

I gave a grudging 1 star to this vintage. The first half of the year was perfectly normal, with some rain in July and a fairly wet August. From 18 September and through October it was warm and sunny. A late, protracted harvest ending in sunshine on 2 November resulted in an enormous crop of pale, acidic, mediocre wines. Wisely, the vintage was barely touched by the trade and I have only tasted six wines.

**La Tâche** I have three notes on La Tâche: dry, lean, not bad fruit and at least interesting. *Last tasted Oct 1983* ★

# 1964 ★★★★

Very good vintage indeed, producing rich, meaty and fairly substantial wines of a contrasting style to the '62s and '66s. Following an exceptionally hard winter, perfect flowering in June, a hot, almost too hot, summer with some drought conditions reducing the crop but perfect ripening weather, alternating rain and sun, for an excellent harvest from 18 September. It was immediately recognised as a first-rate vintage and record prices were reached at the Hospices de Beaune auction.

I have more notes on burgundies of this vintage than on any other but mainly dating from their youth until the mid-1970s. Alas, I have tasted surprisingly few since the late 1980s.

**Romanée-Conti** First tasted in October 1967 alongside the '66 at Lebègue's annual trade tasting. Not unusually at this stage, lacking colour, very undeveloped though fairly sweet, with lovely flavour and potential. Then a quantum leap of nearly 30 years: still on the pale side of medium, fully mature-looking; its nose just sat there, undemonstrative, complacent but good. Much more to it on the palate, fairly sweet, full-bodied, rich, powerful, tangy, still with silky tannins. *Last noted in Prince Rupert Löwenstein's cellar, Ham, July 1996* ★★★★ *At its zenith but will continue to please.*

**Grands-Echézeaux DRC** Strangely, not shown at Lebègue's 1967 tasting though the '61, '62 and '66 appeared. Pale and undeveloped in 1971, and a sweet, piquant, light style 'that could develop well', 1972. Nearly 20 years later: medium-pale; luminous, mature; sweet, meaty nose with a touch of 'damp cardboard'; fairly sweet, good flavour and length, still with grip though fully mature. *Last tasted at a DRC tasting at the New York Wine Experience, Oct 1991* ★★★★

**Aloxe-Corton, Vieilles Vignes Michel Couvreur Sélection** In fact made by Thévenot from 20-year-old vines and first tasted in the delightfully named village Bouze-Lès-Beaune, in 1972. After nearly 20 years, still very agreeable, lively, good grip. *Last tasted Sept 1990* ★★★ *Will continue to make a good drink.*

**Chapelle-Chambertin Leroy** The first of a 'flight' of six Leroy '64s: very fragrant bouquet; sweet, soft, very rich, good length. Delicious. *At Jaeger's tasting, March 2002* ★★★★ *Drink up.*

**Ch Corton-Grancey L Latour** I expected more when I tasted it at 10 years of age in the London shipper's offices but it seemed to show better two years later at a Louis Latour dinner; plum-coloured; sweet, rich, some silkiness but unrefined and, I thought, a bit 'stewed'. However, at the Louis Latour vertical I conducted for the Hollywood Wine Society, it had good, cherry-like fruit on the nose; sweet, soft, rounded, 'warming', delicious but not great. *Last tasted March 1998* ★★★

**Corton, Hospices, Cuvée Charlotte Dumay Leroy** Medium-pale, touch of cherry; initial whiff of age which soon cleared, slightly singed '64 heat, sweet fruit; good, rich, nutty flavour. Dry finish. *At Wilfred Jaeger's tasting, March 2002* ★★★

**Moulin-à-Vent, Vieilles Vignes L Latour** Imported by Frederick Wildman. Good colour; slightly sour; better on the palate, dry, touch of rawness and sandy texture. This was Wilf's 'ringer', inspired by my notes on a couple of very good Moulin-à-Vent '47s tasted in the 1970s, one of which had begun to resemble a firm ripe Pinot. *This* was unquestionably (wise after the event) a tired Gamay. Good try though. *At Wilf Jaeger's tasting of great burgundies, March 2002* ★

**Musigny J Drouhin** The first of seven '64s Musignys tasted blind: medium-pale, pinkish hue, open, mature rim; sweet, attractive, gently fragrant, opening up spicily and holding well (for 2½ hours); fairly sweet on the palate, fair body (alcohol 13%), slightly gritty texture, dry finish. *At Wilfrid Jaeger's, March 2002* ★★★ *Drink soon.*

**Musigny, Vieilles Vignes Coron** Labelled '*produced by de Vogüé, owner, at Chambolle-Musigny .. bottled and shipped by Coron Père et fils ... exclusively imported for Esquin Imports*'. Esquin I knew well: they were early buyers at Christie's in the late 1960s and 1970s. Medium-deep; fairly high-toned 'boiled beetroot' Pinot, this time noting a strawberry-like development; dry, stern, fair body (alcohol 13%), a touch of tartness but delicious flavour. *At Wilfrid Jaeger's, March 2002* ★★★

**Musigny Faiveley** Pleasant appearance; sweet, very attractive, fully mature, eventually strawberry-like, agreeable sweetness and flavour, rich, straightforward. *At Wilfred Jaeger's tasting, March 2002* ★★★

**Musigny Leroy** (Labelled 'Le Roy'). Good colour; touch of sourness at first, low-keyed yet within 45 minutes an exotic strawberry jam scent completely contradicted by its dry, somewhat coarse and short palate. *At Jaeger's, March 2002* ★

**Musigny J Prieur** Imported by Wildman. Deep but rather unattractive colour; very sweet, slightly malty nose, sweetening up in the glass like fudge or butterscotch also becoming outrageously over the top; medium-sweet, chunky, not bad fruit but an odd man out. *At Jaeger's, March 2002* ★

**Musigny, Vieilles Vignes de Vogüé** Attractive colour; distinctly floral bouquet, slightly singed, developing an almost Cabernet Franc raspberry scent; dry, most delightful flavour and great length. Though the alcoholic strength was only 11.5% I was told that this was just a routine regulatory figure at this period and had no significance. *At Wilfred Jaeger's Leroy 'flight', March 2002* ★★★★ *Drink soon.*

**Pommard, Epenots Leroy** Fragrant though not very forthcoming; initially sweet and showing its age but good flavour, tannin and acidity, rather lean and with a slightly raw, dry finish. Quite a good drink. *At Wilfred Jaeger's, March 2002* ★★ *Creaking a bit.*

**Clos de la Roche J Drouhin** Most elegant, beautifully balanced in 1975. More recently, showing age in appearance, nose and taste but stylish. Its bouquet developed well, then faded; powerful but needed drinking. *Last noted at a Saintsbury Club dinner at Vintners' Hall, April 1992* ★★★ *Drink up.*

**Clos de la Roche Leroy** Palish, soft; good fruit, like quite a few of those old burgundies, 'sweet and sour', classic flavour, lean, dry, good length. *At Wilfred Jaeger's, March 2002* ★★★

**Romanée-St-Vivant Leroy** Dash of cherry red; very sweet, attractive, vanilla nose, opening up, mocha-like; very sweet also on the palate, chewy, slightly singed, lovely aftertaste. *At Wilfred Jaeger's, March 2002* ★★★★

**Savigny-Lès-Beaune Leroy** Very sweet, crisp fruit, vegetal; rich, good body, a touch of rawness and quite a bite. *In the Leroy 'flight' at Wilfred Jaeger's tasting, March 2002* ★★★

**Volnay, Clos des Chênes Ropiteau** Palish, soft, mature, rosehip – orange-tawny; distinct whiff of stewed beetroot, *le vrai* Pinot; sweet, pleasant, fully mature, flavour verging on *gibier*, good acidity, attractive. An oddity found in my cellar. *It enlivened a modest supper at home, March 2000* ★★★

---

### Grands and premiers crus

*In Burgundy the rank of premier cru (first growth) comes below that of grand cru (great growth) which is reserved for 34 prime vineyard sites (in Chablis, the Côte de Nuits and Côte de Beaune). Premier cru holdings are far more numerous.*

*This is somewhat confusing for those more familiar with the classification in Bordeaux where premier cru is the highest rank (in the Médoc and Sauternes). St-Émilion is even more confusing, with premier grand cru classé, followed by grand cru classé, then a lower-ranking mass of grands crus. In Bordeaux the vineyard of a premier cru classé like Ch Lafite is exclusively owned, tended and the wine made by Lafite whereas a grand or premier cru vineyard in Burgundy can be owned by more than one producer whose wine might well differ in style and quality to that made from his neighbour's portion of vines.*

OF THE MANY '64S LAST TASTED IN THE 1980S, the following stand out: **DRC**'s **Richebourg** ★★★★; **Leroy**'s **Chapelle-Chambertin** ★★★, **Grands-Echézeaux** ★★★, **Mazis-Chambertin** ★★★★, **Nuits-St-Georges, 1er Cru** ★★★★ and **Clos des Corvées** ★★★★; **Musigny** from **Pierre Ponnelle**'s private cellar ★★★★; **Averys**' magnum of **Musigny** ★★★★; **H Gouges**' **Nuits-St-Georges, Porrets-St-Georges** ★★★★ and **Nuits-St-Georges, Les Pruliers** ★★★★; **L Latour**'s **Romanée-St-Vivant** ★★★★; and **Le Pousse d'Or**'s **Volnay, Caillerets** ★★★★

AND THE BEST OF EARLIER NOTES **La Tâche**; **de Villamont**'s bottling of **Beaune, Hospices, Clos des Avaux**; **de Vogüé**'s **Bonnes-Mares**; **A Rousseau**'s **Chambertin**; **Trapet**'s **Chambertin**; **Roumier**'s **Chambolle-Musigny, Amoureuses**; **Thévenot**'s **Corton, Bressandes**; **J Regnier**'s **Latricières-Chambertin**; and **H Gouges**' **Nuits-St-Georges**.

## 1965

Literally and metaphorically, a washout. Arguably the worst-ever post-war vintage. In some districts, the hours of sunshine were the lowest since 1910. By early September, the vineyards were waterlogged. *Véraison* had not taken place, and rot appeared quickly in the small, jam-packed bunches. Then, on 8 September, Burgundy was struck by the most appalling storm in living memory; soil was washed down the slopes and vineyards were swept away. There was belated sun at harvest-time, 12 October. Nonetheless the Domaine de la Romanée-Conti, habitual late pickers, did manage to make some wine.

*The Wine & Spirit Trade Record*, an old-established monthly, was ill-advised and reported that: 'The wines of the 1965 vintage show excellent qualities for the most part'; presumably the same correspondent who stated that 1963 was 'without any manner of doubt a good year'. This once-distinguished trade journal folded not long after. The editor, my old friend Hector King, was the first to appreciate and publish, in 1963, my *Wine Tasting*, but whether it was the grandiloquence of my unprecedented treatise or the *Record*'s glowing reports of Burgundy's two worst vintages that put it out of business, I shall never know.

Of the four '63s tasted, two are **DRC**'s: **La Tâche** first served as a light luncheon wine following a DRC tasting at Christie's in 1972, and at the Lebègue/DRC tasting at Quaglino's in 1974: fairly pale, minty, raw and acidic. Next, out of curiosity, in a vertical at the Domaine when it seemed to have deepened in colour, though it was too brown; a strange fragrance; light, crisp, flavoury but still acidic. *1983*; and **Grands-Echézeaux** also at the tastings in *1972* and *1974*: stringy, raw, thin, unbalanced.

## 1966 ★★★★

Good quality and quantity. Not great but stylish. My sort of wine. The growing season began rockily with some hail damage in the spring. The summer was not particularly good though the weather improved at the end of August. September was sunny and balmy, with a little rain to swell the grapes, the harvest starting at the end of the month in exceptionally fine conditions. Alas, I was not in on the start as I was busy preparing my first wine auction which took place at Christie's on 11 October (see page 452).

**Romanée-Conti** One of my favourite burgundy vineyards, Romanée-Conti, certainly deserves its title of 'the central pearl of the Côte de Nuits necklace'. At the unusually early presentation in 1967, richer and bigger than the other '66 DRCs. A decade later, less deep, more mature; rich, ripe, still packing a punch. Soft, classic, in 1984 and in 1984. Most recently, bottle number 07054. Imported by Wine Warehouse, Los Angeles. Medium-pale, 'warm', slightly weak, open, yellow-amber rim; low-keyed but harmonious nose; sweet, excellent, crisp flavour, weight, length and tannic finish. Not untypical, a disarmingly un-deep, unconvincing colour yet performing well. *Last tasted at Wilfred Jaeger's DRC session, March 2002* ★★★★

**La Tâche** Unlike its performance in certain earlier vintages already recorded, the youthful La Tâche was already aromatic and exciting at the big Lebègue tasting in the autumn of 1967 and five years later, one of the stars of the Christie's/DRC tasting. Certainly not pale and loitering but deeply coloured and positive in the mid-1970s, almost over-opulent, exuberant, velvety yet zestful at a DRC tasting in 1977.

In May 1983, with Christopher Fielden and the late John Arlott – cricket commentator, wine bibber and wine writer – I went to the Domaine to discuss a book about DRC. We were treated to a vertical of La Tâche. The '66 deep; fragrant; crisp, rich, perfectly balanced (and the DRC '66 Montrachet served at a very simple lunch afterwards, was more than memorable: the greatest dry white wine I have ever drunk). Only a matter of months later, beginning to show maturity at the rim and its bouquet and flavour in full flower, indeed in full flood. Glorious in 1992, and three notes since: superb, assertive, 'vast and tannic' at Prince Rupert Löwenstein's in 1996, and early the following year, within a day of each other in New York, a slightly woody, tannic bottle brought to a restaurant for lunch but not given enough time to open up. A fully mature-looking, hefty, spicy, sweet and powerful bottle from Tawfiq Khoury's cellar, with quite a bite and remarkable acidity. *Last tasted in New York, Feb 1997. At best* ★★★★★

**Grands-Echézeaux DRC** Already showing its richness when first presented to the trade in October 1967. In 1971, at dinner, its nose and flavour beautifully developed. By 1972, at the Lebègue/Christie's tasting, I preferred it to the '62 and also to the '66 La Tâche – which was high praise indeed. By 1977, it had lost quite a bit of colour but was very rich, displaying the inimitable DRC 'peacock's tail'. More recently, a recorked bottle: ruddy, tawny, mature; an extraordinary 'fish skin' Pinot nose that opened up fragrantly; full-bodied, very sweet, excellent length, tannic. *Last noted at Prince Rupert Löwenstein's, July 1996* ★★★★(★) *Will continue to evolve.*

**Romanée-St-Vivant Marey-Monge/DRC** It was in 1966 that the Marey-Monge family granted DRC a lease of their share of this major vineyard. First noted at the pre-sale tasting of the 'Fifth Anniversary Premier National Auction of Rare Wines' I conducted in Atlanta, Georgia, in 1973. It was part of a large cellar of burgundies from Le Pavillon restaurant in New York: a fine, rich wine; drinking well. Two years later: fabulously rich, 'high flavoured', with long, dry finish. Four more recent notes: first, dining at the Domaine in November 1995 and demonstrating the curious unwillingness of the Burgundians to decant, a slightly cloudy bottle; sweet, powerful, with enough tannin to cope with destructive cheeses and, the following day, noted again at a vertical tasting of St-Vivants: almost sickly sweet nose, raspberry, rose-like fragrance; rich and heavenly flavour. The following month at a pre-sale tasting in

---

## The Burgundian tradition of not decanting

*A mature red Burgundy will usually have some sediment, so it is a mystery to me why Burgundians don't decant! I personally remain in favour of decanting, whatever the traditionalists may say. If you choose not to, then you need a very steady hand, and to bring all the glasses to the bottle (not the other way round). It is of course essential that the pouring stops before the sediment reaches the upper neck. I once witnessed a magnum of Richebourg, I forget its vintage, being spoiled by my host, a noted connoisseur, who, wisely standing at his sideboard with eight large glasses line up, poured steadily into the glasses, continuing round and round to the bitter end, giving everyone's glass a final* coup de grâce *of sediment! Decanting is far safer.*

New York: exuberantly flowery nose; very ripe, delicious. Most recently, at lunch, after a 'follow-up' vertical tasting: now medium-deep, mature but healthy colour; fragrant, 'refined beetroot' nose; sweet, ripe, lovely flavour but still with quite a bite. *Last noted at the Domaine, Oct 2001* ★★★★

**Echézeaux DRC** First noted at the Lebègue tasting in 1967: purple-tinged of course; very rich aroma and taste. Sweet, zestful. 30 years after the vintage, medium-pale, tawny edged, with a lovely warm glow; fragrant 'fishy Pinot' nose; full-flavoured, assertive, good length, tannic. Two notes the following year, now described as rosehip-coloured; glorious, soft, singed beetroot; seemed very sweet, with excellent acidity. And the following day, in the same New York restaurant, with La Tâche, much more forthcoming and, again, very sweet. A month later, March 1997, its gloriously ripe Pinot fragrance deteriorated after half an hour though its lovely, ripe flavour expanded in the mouth. Though delicious, now showing a trace of decadence. Most recently: very fragrant, distinctive, forthcoming bouquet and flavour. Perfect weight and state. Dry finish. *Last noted at Christie's 'Tasting of the Century', all '66s, conducted by Christopher Burr and myself at Vinexpo, Bordeaux in June 1999* ★★★★★

**Bonnes-Mares A Ligneret** Good colour; slightly stewed, chocolatey nose but sweet, fullish and quite good flavour. Still tannic. *From a Swiss cellar, Geneva, May 1996* ★★

**Corton P de Marcilly** Fully mature, no red left; showing its age, dry finish. *At a pre-sale tasting, Amsterdam, Nov 1996* ★

A HOST OF SUPER '66S LAST TASTED IN THE 1980S
**DRC's Richebourg** noted simply as 'rich' in 1967. Less deep in colour by 1972 but rich, assertive. By 1984, bouquet 'fully aroused'; dry, full but lean. Fabulously fragrant. *Sept 1984* ★★★★★ *Will still be excellent – if kept well (the usual proviso);* **A Rousseau's Chambertin** at his and its best. Glorious. Power and character. *Oct 1987* ★★★★★; **Leroy's Chambolle-Musigny** still ruby; evolved fragrantly; sweet, good fruit and flavour, lovely acidity. *Jan 1984* ★★★; **L Latour's Corton, Clos de la Vigne au Saint** a 'welter-weight' Corton, a lovely wine. *Last tasted Aug 1989* ★★★★ *Will keep;* **Remoissenet's Corton, Bressandes** first noted at an Averys' tasting in 1974: rich, meaty and, despite the oil crisis, expensive. Still deep and intensely coloured in 1980 and, two years later, a scented 'chocolate cake' nose; sweet from start to finish. A heavyweight Corton. *Last tasted Aug 1982* ★★★★; and **de Vogüé's Musigny, Vieilles Vignes** at Khoury's de Vogüé tasting: classic, perfect harmony, fine, flavoury, balance and length. Touch of '66 leanness but a class act. *Oct 1984* ★★★★★

OF THE EARLIER NOTES, the following were outstanding: **Chandon de Briaille's Corton-Bressandes; Dzikowsky's Gevrey-Chambertin; Trapet's Latricières-Chambertin; H Gouges' Nuits-St-Georges, Les St-Georges; Bouchard Père's Romanée-St-Vivant;** and three excellent **Clos Vougeot: Drouhin-Laroze, Moreau-Fontaine** and **Morin's Ch de la Tour.**

## 1967 ★★

From the sublime to the not so hot. But it could have been a good vintage. First of all, nature did the pruning with widespread frost on 4 May. The summer was warm and sunny, lulling growers into complacency – or short-sighted economy – by seeming to cut out the need for the customary 'dusting' to protect the vines against disease. They were caught out by ten days of rain in September, with disastrous results, though good weather returned in time for the vintage on 2 October. Some wines were particularly high in alcohol and there was much variation in quality – not just because of affected vines but also because of the tendency of some winemakers to speed up the fermentation stage.

The market was, however, very active, though in Britain, the effects of the credit squeeze had dampened demand. It was noticeable that more wine was shipped in bottle, less in bulk, to UK wine merchants.

I have as many notes of the '67s as of the '66s but they were mainly made in the 1970s. I have relatively few from the 1980s, and only one recent one.

**Romanée-St-Vivant** I shall ignore a corked bottle I tasted in the 1980s. Next, the second oldest vintage tasted in the 18-vintage weekend at the Domaine in 1995. To my surprise, it was a lovely, rich colour, still red (though this is often a sign of high volatile acidity); equally surprising, it had a rich, harmonious nose and flavour; good depth, medium-sweet, attractive, on the lean side but with a 'hot', dry, acidic finish. *Last tasted Nov 1995* ★★

OTHER '67S SHOWING WELL IN THE 1980S **La Tâche** in 1972: pale, pink-tinged and piquant. Then tinged with orange; sweet, superficial; lean, firm and wiry. *May 1987* ★★; **Leroy's Chambertin** autumnal brown; now surprisingly rich and meaty; good flavour but austere and lacking length. *April 1985* ★★; and **Mazis-Chambertin** richly coloured; ripe nose; firm, crisp, decent flavour, length and aftertaste. A good '67. *Sept 1984* ★★★; **Jean Grivot's Vosne-Romanée** very sweet, velvety texture, good tannin and acidity. *Sept 1984* ★★★★; and **Clerget's Vosne-Romanée, Tastevinée** in 1972 light, lean, fragrant, later looking pale and fully mature; vanilla-scented; bitter sweet, but very drinkable. *Last tasted Aug 1983* ★★★

OF THE VERY MANY '67S TASTED IN THE 1970S, the following showed particularly well: **L Jadot's Bonnes-Mares; A Rousseau's Chambertin; Bertagna's Gevrey-Chambertin, Clos de la Justice; de Vogüé's Musigny; Faiveley's** and **Misserey's Clos Vougeot;** and a notable **Averys'** bottling of **Chambolle-Musigny.**

## 1968

Poor wines. Thin, unripe. Though the growing season started well, June was excessively hot, followed by too little sun and too much rain in July and August. Picking started at the end of September but the damage had already been done. The market considered the vintage a catastrophe and, a rare event (or non-event): the Hospices de Beaune auction was cancelled.

APART FROM SOME BEAUJOLAIS, I have tasted only three wines: **Pierre Ponnelle's Vosne-Romanée, Beaumonts** twice in 1983: pale, orange tawny; spicy, medicinal nose; heavily chaptalised so some specious sweetness, lacking body but quite flavoury. And in the 1970s **Romanée-Conti** surprisingly deep but overblown; and **G Berthaud's Fixin, Les Arvelets** a light 'quicky'.

## 1969 ★★★★★

I think it took a little time to realise that this was by far the finest of the unusually good trio: '69, '70 and '71, and I suspect that claret lovers, only too aware of the scraggy and tart red Bordeaux, half-dismissed the '69 burgundies, though it happens to be the excellent acidity which made, and has sustained these wines.

The growing season opened with a cold, rainy spring, followed by late flowering which was happily countered by very fine ripening weather in July and August. This enabled well-developed grapes to survive a cold, wet September and, in exceptionally good weather, produce from 5 October a small sound, ripe crop.

I tasted a quite large number of these wines in the 1970s and 1980s and an unusual proportion were of high quality. Happily, I have tasted some delicious '69s fairly recently.

**La Tâche** I have nine notes, starting with an early presentation at Lebègue's in 1972, the wine's appearance belying its fullness and richness. In 1974, though its colour was deeper than the '70, it was starting to show some maturing at the rim, a strange state of limbo which was hard to explain to an American client. Firm, flavoury, lean but well-balanced at the La Tâche tasting at the Domaine in 1983, but later that autumn I found it completely lacked the flair of the '62 or the fine '66. It took another half-dozen years to open up and by 1990 was beautifully evolved, its bouquet fabulous, its flavour exciting, attenuated.

At Manfred Wagner's La Tâche vertical in 1998, it had an open, mature colour; its nose initially showing its age but soon opening up very fragrantly, with hints of tea, and strawberries; medium-sweet, full, rich, lovely texture and delicious flavour, firm, dry, still tannic. (Aubert de Villaine told us that La Tâche suffered from hail in July just before *véraison* which reduced the crop.) Most recently a magnum, immediately preceding bottles of the '61, at Len Evans' 'Single-bottle club' dinner: a very good colour; a perfectly harmonious bouquet with, I thought, a whiff of vanilla; glorious flavour, fragrant aftertaste. Perfection. *Last tasted Sept 2001* ★★★★★ *At its summit but still with years of life.*

**Grands-Echézeaux DRC** In 1972 palish and pink, not nearly as deep and purple as I had expected; fresh, youthful, intensely fragrant aroma; dry, misleadingly light in style, yet firm and with life-enhancing youthful acidity. Not tasted again for another 23 years: fully evolved; a lovely scented varietal nose with touch of meatiness; fairly sweet, medium weight, fragrant, dry finish. Just astonishing how these great DRCs can be so disarming, often misleading, teasing, until – like the last stretch of the fairground roller coaster – they glide effortlessly on to the last stretch. *Last tasted at Barry Phillips' 'Silver Jubilee Dinner' at the White Horse, Chilgrove, Jan 1995* ★★★★★

Romanée-St-Vivant **DRC** Fairly deep, richly coloured; complete, harmonious nose but a harder edge and less evolved than the '71; fairly sweet, full-bodied, firm, very good, refreshing and life-sustaining acidity. Fine wine. *Last noted at the St-Vivant vertical at the Domaine, Nov 1995* ★★★★(★) *A long, immaculate life ahead.*

Bonnes-Mares **de Vogüé** A wonderful wine which had survived effortlessly its journey from Ann Arbor in Michigan to the isle of St Bart's in the French West Indies. I noted it had a slight powdery sediment in the bottle after (wisely) decanting: lovely colour; the real thing – a beautiful ripe, elegant 'beetroot' Pinot; excellent flavour, great length though with a curious upturned tannic finish. Very refreshing. *At Ron Weiser's dinner on St Bart's, Feb 1999* ★★★★

Bonnes-Mares **Clair-Daü** Magnums: one oxidised, the other rich, a touch of spearmint; soft, initially attractive but disintegrated after a little time in the glass. The wine, or the provenance? *Both tasted in Boston, March 1992. At best* ★★

Bonnes-Mares **Drouhin-Laroze** Fairly deep; quite good; soft, pleasant, drinking well but I noticed a bit of an end-bite. *At a Saintsbury Club dinner, London, Oct 1998* ★★★

Bonnes-Mares **A Ligneret** Medium-deep, mature-looking; fairly sweet, quite attractively rich nose and taste. It was drinkable but certainly not a class act. *Tasted pre-sale in Geneva, May 1996* ★★

Corton, Clos Fiètres **E Voarick** The eighth of a 15-wine 'East Meets West in the South' banquet at River Terrace, Mud Island: I tasted two bottles, one a bit screwed up, although it improved in the glass. The other was better, more fragrant. But both disappointing. Badly stored. One cannot be too careful. *In Memphis, Tennessee, Sept 1999.*

Ch Corton-Grancey **L Latour** I seem to recall I found this the best of a range of Corton-Granceys shown by the importers in the late 1970s but cannot find the note. Anyway, it was certainly one of the best of a vertical of eight vintages: good fruit; dry, firm, good length presented at a Hollywood Wine Society seminar. *Last tasted March 1998* ★★★★

Echézeaux **Leroy** An open, fully mature rim; somewhat 'stewed' Pinot nose; fairly sweet, attractive flavour, good acidity. A trifle, specious, and hopeless accompanying 'Upstate New York Egg Farm Dairy Cheese'. *At a Stephen Kaplan dinner in Chicago, Feb 1998* ★★★

Gevrey-Chambertin, Clos St-Jacques **Fernand Pernot** Incredibly deep, fragrant, complex in 1977. An impressive magnum in 1984. More recently: still fairly deep; bouquet evolved fragrantly in the glass; distinctly sweet, soft despite its full complement of tannins and acidity. Delicious. This is what '69s are all about. *Last noted dining with the Peppercorns, Jan 1990* ★★★★ *Probably still good.*

Musigny, Vieilles Vignes **de Vogüé** Reputed to be the Count's favourite wine. At Khoury's de Vogüé tasting in 1984 it was orange-tinged and though distinctive and elegant, was a bit tart. Much better bottle in 1987. A year later, again a very mature orange tinge, honeyed bouquet but showing its age. More recently: an attractive colour; very rich varietal nose; very sweet on the palate, glorious in its way but now almost over-mature and 'almost tart'. *Last noted at a pre-sale tasting in New York, Sept 1997* ★★ *Possibly there are better bottles in British cellars but otherwise the wine is living on borrowed time.*

Nuits-St-Georges, Les Argillières **Thomas-Bassot** Once again, from an American cellar: palish, mature, orange-tinged; curious nose, meaty, old straw; flavoury but – again – a bit tart. *At a pre-sale tasting, New York, Oct 1996* ★★

Volnay, Caillerets **Bouchard Père** Medium-deep, mature; smoky Pinot nose; dry, rich, excellent flavour, very good acidity. *At the annual III Form Club dinner at Boodle's Club in London, July 1995* ★★★

Clos de Vougeot **Drouhin-Larose** Crisp, lively ruby colour; very good crisp bouquet, flavour, tannin and acidity. This time from a good English cellar (beneath Vintners' Hall in London). *At a Saintsbury Club dinner, Oct 1994* ★★★★ *Probably needs drinking up now.*

SOME OF THE BETTER '69S LAST TASTED IN THE 1980S
**DRC**'s Richebourg *1986* ★★★★; Beaune, Hospices, Clos des Avaux (unknown bottler) *1986* ★★★★; **Leroy**'s Chambertin *1989* ★★★★; **Trapet**'s Chambertin *1989* ★★★★; Echézeaux **DRC** *1983* ★★★★★; **Leroy**'s Chambertin ★★★★ and Gevrey-Chambertin, Cazetiers *1984* ★★★; **Clair-Daü**'s Gevrey-Chambertin, Clos St-Jacques *1985* ★★★; **Dujac**'s Clos de la Roche *1981* ★★★★; **Felix Clerget**'s Clos Vougeot *1986* ★★★; **Jean Grivot**'s Clos Vougeot *1989* ★★★; **Henri Lamarche**'s Clos Vougeot *1984* ★★★; and **Mugneret**'s Clos Vougeot *1987* ★★★★

# 1970–1989

If not exactly a turbulent period, it was certainly one of great contrasts: economic, stylistic and in quality.

The 1970s started off well, but the almost unhealthily buoyant market quickly evaporated. This coincided with poor growing conditions, which had a disastrous effect on the '73s, '74s and '75s. The atrocious 1977 vintage obliged the best estates to take great care with grape selection and it was not until the 1980s that fermentation control in difficult conditions was mastered. (Though the '78s were superb.)

An important factor not much mentioned these days (perhaps conveniently forgotten) was the effect of the United Kingdom entering the Common Market. Until 1971, instead of wine over the permitted yield being declassified, an unquantifiable amount was 'massaged': any surplus was conveniently exported to the United Kingdom, which required only a shipping invoice, keeping the statutory *acquit vert* for European customers. The British trade took some comfort in the thought that they were importing the real thing while their counterparts on the continent 'enjoyed' lesser wines under the protection of the official permits. But when *le vrai bourgogne* arrived, the English had a shock, for instead of the deeply coloured, meaty, chocolatey reds they were used to, they received almost unrecognisable wines, often much paler and quite different from the good old days of crafty blending, so much so that some experts assumed that the producers had changed their winemaking methods, speeding up fermentation for quick consumption. Perhaps there was more than a grain of truth in this for vinification still tended to be haphazard.

Importantly, domaine-bottled wines were beginning seriously to bypass the *négociants* even though the vast majority of the growers did not have the necessary incentive or ability to market their wines direct. The move towards more bottling at the estate was accelerated when, in 1976, the *autoroute* from Paris, with an exit conveniently near Beaune, opened up the Côte d'Or to an ever-increasing number of cellar-door buyers.

Looking back, the decade of the 1980s was not as successful as in Bordeaux; though, for me, two vintages epitomised burgundy at its most delightful best. There was considerable improvement in overall quality and commerce, with two of the most appealing vintages of recent times: 1985 and 1988.

What was noticeable to me was a sea change in attitudes, particularly among growers. The younger generation of *vignerons*, though lacking the experience of their forebears, tended to be not only more qualified, technically, but more innovative and conscious of quality. While their fathers tended to go their own way, the next generation were interested to see what their contemporaries were up to; they even compared notes and tasted each other's wines. The period ended with the establishment, in 1989, of the Bureau Interprofessionnel du Vin de Bourgogne (BIVB).

## Vintages at a Glance
**Outstanding ★★★★★**
1978, 1985, 1988
**Very Good ★★★★**
1971, 1986, 1989
**Good ★★★**
1972, 1976, 1979, 1980 (v), 1983 (v), 1987

## 1970 ★★

Another of those vintages about which which one can say it 'came in with a bang, left with a whimper'. It was conveniently sandwiched by the superior '69s and '71s and, not for the first time, the British, at any rate, had in mind the '70 clarets (which have also turned out to be overrated).

Apart from a poor spring, the growing conditions were well above average with a successful flowering, sunny July and good weather through to the harvest which began at the end of September, running on into early October, producing a large (too large) crop of ripe grapes. There was a certain amount of euphoria, prices at the Hospices de Beaune auction that November breaking all records. But the wines lacked grip and, though initially attractive, also lacked stamina. It might

seem unfair to generalise from relatively few recent notes, but I am convinced that most '70s are not worth pursuing.

**La Tâche** Half a dozen fairly well spread notes, the first at Lebègue's tasting in 1974: distinctly pale but flavoury, with a youthful tingle. Next in 1983 at the La Tâche vertical at the Domaine: very fragrant but a touch of hardness, and dry. At 20 years of age, a magnum displaying richness, ripeness and complexity, assertive, good length. Harmonious though perhaps 'lacking a little zest'. Next, a bottle at a dinner in the country on New Year's Day 1994. The level I noted was 4.5cm below the cork. It looked fully mature with a rosehip colour, hint of orange and lemon tawny rim, lovely, rich, singed Pinot; distinctly dry, nice weight, attractive 'beetroot' flavour and aftertaste. Four years later at Wagner's La Tâche vertical: palish, lovely, open; 'singed' noted again, sweet, harmonious bouquet that, after an hour in the glass, had faded; not bad flavour but now lacking fruit, rather hard, with a dry finish. Most recently: fragrant bouquet; flavoury but a hot alcoholic finish, surprisingly edgy and raw before the 'Squab *en vessre* (*sic*) with southern grains'. *Last tasted at Hal Lewis's 'Mr Gourmet' Installation dinner, Memphis, Sept 1999* ★★★ *Drink up.*

**Grands-Echézeaux DRC** Only one not very up-to-date note: fairly deep; spicy; impressive. *Dining in San Juan, Jan 1990. Then* ★★★(★) *Probably still drinking well.*

**Chapelle-Chambertin Bouchard Père** Several notes over a period of ten years. In 1980 a palish, pretty colour; some richness about the nose but overall dry and lacking the style and flavour expected. A decade later, pale, orange-tinged; 'damp cardboard', dry, not bad but not good enough. *Last tasted Jan 1990 ★ Not worth bothering about.*

**Corton Dom du Ch de Beaune** Middling everything: colour, nose, sweetness and weight. Nose fully developed, a bit 'fluffy'; soft, needs drinking. Which is precisely what happened to it, accompanying a haunch of venison. *At a Saintsbury Club dinner, Oct 1994 ★★*

**Morey-St-Denis L Latour** Several notes, first in 1977: dry, elegant, good flavour, firm. More to come. Most recently: now soft, but enough tannin and acidity to hold it together. Attractive but not thrilling. *Last tasted Aug 1990. Then ★★★ but drink up.*

**Musigny Dom Jacques Prieur** Medium-deep; stewed beetroot; sweet, rich, very drinkable but no Musigny elegance or charm. *At Hal Lewis's 'Mr Gourmet' dinner, Memphis, Sept 1999 ★★★ (just).*

AND TWO DISAPPOINTMENTS **Chambolle-Musigny, Les Amoureuses Réserve des Taillandiers** good colour but not much else: stewed nose; not bad flavour, touch of tartness. *In Geneva, May 1996;* and **Morey-St-Denis L Latour** 5-cm ullage and poor cork – not the best of signs. And so it turned out. Oxidised. A disaster. I had had the wine for some time, immaculate storage conditions – of course – but I used my backup bottle of '70 Giscours instead. You can't win them all. *Prior to dinner at home, May 2001.*

SOME OF THE '70S LAST TASTED IN THE 1980S **de Vogüé's Bonnes-Mares** quite attractive in the mid- to late 1970s: attractive colour; classic nose and flavour but lacking the touch, elegance and style of Bonnes-Mares at its best. Soft and completely mature. *April 1980. Then ★★★ drink up;* and his **Chambolle-Musigny, Amoureuses** disappointing. An exaggerated scent, described by my wife as 'fish glue and paraffin'. *Oct 1984 ★;* **Pierre Ponnelle's Corton, Clos du Roi** ripe, singed, pleasant, dry, commercial. *May 1986 ★★;* **Mérode's Corton, Marechaudes** several notes. Though pale, quite fragrant up until the late 1970s, but by the mid-1980s fading, losing its colour – no red left, and eventually an oily, over-done nose and yeasty finish. *May 1986;* **L Jadot's Corton, Pougets** rich and powerful in 1977, 12 years later: paler, sweet nose, delicious flavour. *April 1989 ★★★ probably still good to drink.* **L Latour's Gevrey-Chambertin** fully mature in 1977. Aged 18, little nose, lacking interest. Only a village wine and commercial (in the best sense). *April 1988 ★ forget it;* **Leroy's Gevrey-Chambertin** so pale that I thought it must be the '77 though the bouquet opened up beautifully. Dry, open knit, yet firm. Good length. *Sept 1984. Then ★★★ probably just hanging on;* **Faiveley's Gevrey-Chambertin, Combe aux Moines** orange tinge; almost sickly sweet nose and flavour. Nice though. *Sept 1988. Then ★★★ probably way over the top now;* **de Vogüé's Musigny, Vieilles Vignes** pink-cheeked; sweet, chocolatey, scented bouquet; drying out and a bit hard for a '70, but 'probably more to come'. *Oct 1984. Then ★★★(★) probably drinking well now;* and **Bertagna's Vougeot, Clos Perrière** pale, rosy-hued; low-keyed, lightweight, dry, quite nice. *Nov 1986 ★★*

Looking at other notes made in the 1970s, a few wines stand out, but not many, and there is no point in recalling them.

# 1971 ★★★★

The firmest and, judging by my own notes, infinitely the most dependable of the '69, '70 and '71 trio, for though it has had the reputation of being somewhat hard, unyielding and 'untypical' it is these very factors which have so effectively developed the best over the past 30 years. There was some unevenness at the time of flowering and a severe hailstorm in August, affecting in particular the Côte de Beaune, otherwise the growing season was satisfactory. The weather during the first half of September was lovely and a small crop of ripe grapes was harvested from the 16th. The major estates and top *négociants* produced wonderful wines which are still delectable. As always, avoid the middle-of-the-road commercial wines.

**Romanée-Conti** Misleadingly advanced in 1974, deepening in colour and filling out after a further nine years. Opulent and exuding fragrance; a sweet, vast, complex and complete wine in May 1983. Most recently, bottle number 02835, '*Imported by W&S Specialty, Kansas City*'. Paired with the '78. Medium-deep, warm, soft, open; more restrained than the '78 but very good, with a true classic Pinot character opening fragrantly; very sweet, very rich and complete – all the components fully represented and in place, extract masking tannin (alcohol 13%). Outstanding. *At Wilfred Jaeger's incomparable Romanée-Conti tasting in his hillside home south of San Francisco Bay, March 2002 ★★★★★*

## Blending and stretching

*It was fairly common practice prior to the UK's entry into the EEC in 1971, for négociants in Burgundy and British merchants to engage in stretching and blending, 'improving' wine, particularly, of course, the well-known Côte d'Or village names, from Gevrey-Chambertin in the north to Santenay in the south, and virtually all the marketable wine appellations in between. There were several commercial reasons: to supply, say, Pommard which, with Nuits-St-Georges, was in the greatest demand, at a cheaper price than the competition; also, ingeniously, to provide the consumer with the sort of burgundy he had been accustomed to for generations.*

*Here are two examples: I recall discussing blending and adulteration, over lunch in the 1960s, with a well-known and highly regarded négociant in Beaune. My host gave me a typical example of the sort of problem he faced: a big British hotel group had placed an order for a substantial number of barriques of wine from a famous grand cru far in excess of the average production of that cru. The négociant, not wishing to lose a good customer, met the order, blithely telling me that if he had not done so, some other merchant would have supplied an inferior wine.*

*In 1957, when I was with Harvey's, Harry Waugh and I took to Burgundy three samples of Santenay which had been purchased from two importers, one direct. We invited a local broker and three or four Santenay producers to taste the wines blind. Without hesitation they described wine number one – the wine preferred by Harvey's customers as 'bonne cuisine', a well cooked-up blend, probably with a decent Côtes du Rhône; the second, a deeply coloured, dense, sweet wine, they called 'Goût Américain', implying that it had been 'souped up' with wine from the Midi or even Algeria. The third, rather pale in colour, and with an unfamiliar taste, was, unanimously, 'le vrai Santenay'.*

*The British also got up to a bit of blending and stretching; some of the best-regarded wine merchants adding port, even brandy, to beef up their much admired burgundies.*

**La Tâche** Nine notes, the first, pink-tinged and high toned at Lebègue's opening trade tasting in 1974, still holding back in 1977, but by its 10th year, opening up fragrantly. Then, magnums, in 1982: 'ambrosial beetroot', rich but still tannic. In 1983, at the Domaine, I had the rare pleasure of what some Americans describe as a 'double cross' tasting, meaning vertically and horizontally, with all the other DRC '71s, against which it seemed rather restrained. Hardy Rodenstock produced a jeroboam in 1989: it had sweetened up despite its tannic bite, with good colour and wonderful fragrance. Another jeroboam in 1992 at a Bacchus Society dinner in Boston held in my honour: a wonderful wine with 'extra dimensions', fruit, flesh, length, and tannin. Most recently at Manfred Wagner's vertical: still with good colour; gloriously fragrant, sustained Pinot bouquet, sweet, superb balance. *Last tasted in Zurich, April 1998* ★★★★★ *Plenty of life left.*

**Richebourg DRC** It always astonishes me to note how different these DRC wines can be despite the proximity of the vineyards and the same winemaking in the same cellars. At the opening Lebègue tasting in 1974, the 'roasted' Richebourg could not have been more of a contrast to the La Tâche. In 1977 it was soft and rounded, and at the horizontal tasting in 1983 it had deepened in colour (DRC wines have this extraordinary ability to take on colour with bottle age) – in fact, the darkest and most intense of the DRC '71s, with an expansive, rich, Pinot nose and flavour. More recently, a magnum: still richly coloured but showing some maturity; glorious bouquet; sweet ingress, flavour of violets, great length. *Last tasted Sept 1990. Then* ★★★★(★) *Doubtless perfection now.*

**Grands-Echézeaux DRC** Expensive, even in 1974, yet half the price of Romanée-Conti. In a state of puberty in 1977, but by 1980 a well-developed energetic adolescent. In 1983 stylish, elegant, fragrant, its otherwise deep colour starting to show some maturity. At 'sweet 17', refined, superb with much more to come, February 1988. Most recently a magnum at Wilf Jaeger's DRC tasting: brownish, mature rim; very sweet, fully ripe 'boiled beetroot' nose of great depth and which held magnificently (though one distinguished guest described the bouquet as 'dying flowers' – as a result of the hail). Sweet entry, lovely flavour but a fairly swingeingly dry finish. *March 2002* ★★★★

**Romanée-St-Vivant DRC** I have always had a soft spot for the St-Vivant, yet of all the DRC 'stable', it does not command quite the attention that some of the others do. I align it with their Grands-Echézeaux. Perhaps more of an immediate impact than the bigger guns, certainly delightful at

---

### The Hospices de Beaune auction

*The famous wine auction which takes place on the third Sunday in November in Beaune. As it is a charitable (and publicity motivated) event, the prices fetched for wines from the Hospices' own vineyards usually considerably exceed the normal market value, but serve as a barometer of those to be expected of the new vintage. The proceeds go to the charitable organisations of the Hôtel Dieu, founded by Nicolas Rolin in 1443. I well recall my first attendance in 1971. Having been used to conducting auctions which averaged 220 lots per hour, I was appalled at the amount of time taken, each lot being auctioned by candle, with the successful bid being the one taken as the flame flickered out – all very medieval. The celebrations either side of the auction are occasions of much pomp and glamour, and mark a significant event in the Burgundian calendar.*

its first showing in 1974 and typically fragrant and elegant in 1983. In 1989 beginning to show full maturity; glorious bouquet; assertive and nevertheless well supported by tannin and acidity. Another good note in 1991, 'stylish'. More recently: very attractive colour, rich 'legs'; fully evolved bouquet surging out of the glass, sweet, fragrant, singed, great depth; now very sweet on the palate, full-bodied (14% alcohol), rich flavour, touch of citrus zest and still tannic. *Last noted at a St-Vivant vertical at the Domaine, Nov 1995* ★★★★★

**Beaune, Hospices, Cuvée Brunet bottled by Covins** Fully mature; 'beetroot' aroma; good flavour, dry finish. *At a pre-sale tasting, Amsterdam, Nov 1996* ★★★

**Beaune Grèves, Vignes de l'Enfant Jésus Bouchard Père** Lovely wine, mulberry-ripe fruit in 1977. A decade later: excellent, mouthfilling. More recently, still showing well. *Last tasted Sept 1990. Then* ★★★★ *Should still be good.*

**Bonnes-Mares, Vieilles Vignes Clair-Daü** Mature; nose both earthy and flowery, vegetal and violets, opening up marvellously; sweet, full, soft yet assertive, rich yet dry finish. *Dining at the Peppercorns', Jan 1990* ★★★★★ *Will still be good.*

**Bonnes-Mares G Roumier** Correct, open, mature rim; lovely, well-developed Pinot opening up sweetly; soft, sweet, attractive texture, very dry finish. *At Wilf Jaeger's dinner tasting in San Francisco, March 2002* ★★★★ *Now–2010.*

**Charmes-Chambertin L Latour** Fairly pale, very little red; palate better than nose, which is not saying much. *At a BYOB dinner, New York, Oct 1996* ★

**Corton, Clos des Fiètres E Voarick** Two bottles: medium, brown-rimmed; both good; one more luminous and more delicious. Touch of strawberry. *At an 'East meets West in the South' dinner, Memphis, Sept 1999* ★★★

**Echézeaux Leroy** What I had hoped would be a fun and relaxed evening with my son in the French Quarter turned out to be a seven-wine dinner at the fashionable Emeril's: excellent food, lovely wines, solicitously supervised by *maître de chai* Leo Verde and somewhat ungraciously appreciated by me. The wines were pretty good. This one was cloudy though the nose opened up wide, soft, and spicy. Good flavour. Dry finish. *In New Orleans, Nov 1997* ★★★

**Morey-St-Denis A Lignier** One of nine '71s from a Swiss cellar, this being the best of five middle-of-the-road Lignier wines. *At a pre-sale tasting in Geneva, May 1996. At best* ★★

**Musigny de Vogüé** Palish, soft and pretty; initially a singed, chocolatey, mocha nose but good fruit; palate disappointing, a combination of overripe, decayed sweetness and very dry, tart finish. *At Jaeger's tasting, March 2002* ★ *Should be better than this.*

**Volnay, Les Taillepieds H de Montille** Fully mature, open rim; sweet, ripe 'beetroot' varietal nose opening up and holding fragrantly; sweet, rich, excellent flavour. *The first wine at Wilf Jaeger's three-day great burgundy tasting, March 2002* ★★★★ *Drink now–2012.*

**Vosne-Romanée Jean Bridron** Fully mature; unknit; not bad – merely dull; **Bridron**'s **Gevrey-Chambertin** and **Chambolle-Musigny** also mediocre. Same provenance, same pre-sale tasting. They should not have been accepted for sale. Let this be a lesson. *All tasted May 1996. At best* ★★

**Clos Vougeot Hudelot** Rich, toasted; powerful, assertive yet harmonious. Impressive. *At Becky Wasserman's Hollywood Wine Society's Burgundy seminar, Jan 1990* ★★★★

THE FINEST '71S LAST TASTED IN THE 1980S **Beaune, Hospices, Cuvée Nicolas Rolin** bottled in Beaune for Hedges & Butler: richly coloured; exciting bouquet;

marvellous flavour, elegance, length. Not tasted since 1980. *Then ★★★★★ light years ahead of so many run-of-the-mill, shippers' burgundies and should still be lovely;* **L Jadot**'s **Bonnes-Mares** but to demonstrate the quality and dependability of a major *négociant*'s burgundy: toasted, rich, and fragrant. *March 1985 ★★★★;* **de Vogüé**'s **Bonnes-Mares** deep, rich, substantial; and their **Musigny, Vieilles Vignes** elegant, gorgeous. *Both Oct 1984, both at least ★★★★ both should still be fine;* **J Drouhin**'s **Chambertin, Clos de Bèze** another supremely good burgundy house: after 14 years still rich and ruby; a glorious surging flavour. Perfect. *Nov 1985 ★★★★★ will still be good;* **de Vogüé**'s **Chambolle-Musigny, Les Amoureuses** a full-bodied rather than feminine Chambolle, *'Les Amoureuses' hard at it. Oct 1984 ★★★★;* **A Rousseau**'s **Charmes-Chambertin** opulent. *July 1982 ★★★★ and should be, still;* **J Drouhin**'s **Echézeaux** lively, firm, fragrant, elegant. *Nov 1985 ★★★★;* and **Trapet**'s **Gevrey-Chambertin** sweet, rich, chunky, dry finish. *Nov 1983 ★★★★ Only a village wine but with 1971 substance.*

## 1972 ★★★

A vintage largely misunderstood by the British and somewhat over-regarded by the French, though neither view is of much relevance now. I tasted quite a lot of '72s in that decade. They were positive, flavoury, firm, very drinkable though not stylish, and I frequently detected a telltale bitterness on the finish.

It was an unusual growing season following a severe winter with snow in January and February, a warm spring, but a cold and dry summer. A warm rainy September saved the day and a huge crop, well over the permitted yield, was a problem. Despite this, and the British trade's lack of interest (few wines shipped for bottling), there was no let-up in price. The habitually late-picking Domaine de la Romanée-Conti wines were outstandingly the most successful. Few other wines now worth looking out for.

**La Tâche** Seven notes, a microcosm of the vintage: at the Domaine in September 1975 and in London in November, rich and powerful. By 1980 well in advance of the '71, forthcoming nose, rich, good texture. In the mid-1980s, good fruit and depth and in 1989 showing maturity, 'dramatically sweet', inimitable La Tâche scent. Eight years later, losing colour and fully mature; very rich, forthcoming bouquet; good flavour, rich but tannic. But more recently, tasting it alongside the '69, '70 and '71, I felt it had run its course: medium-deep, luminous, slightly singed nose, after 90 minutes in the glass 'refined beet' – whatever I meant by that; slightly caramelly taste, not bad but edgy. *Last noted at Wagner's La Tâche vertical, April 1998 ★★ Hanging on (just).*

**Chambertin, Clos de Bèze J Drouhin** Pale, very little red; lean, dried out. *At a pre-sale tasting, New York, Dec 1997 ★*

**Gevrey-Chambertin, Lavaux-St-Jacques Leroy** Medium-deep, a dull plum colour; crisp but low-keyed Pinot nose; positive, crisp, a touch of *gibier* overripeness, very dry finish. *At the Marcobrunn/Chambertin dinner tasting at Schloss Reinhartshausen, Germany, Nov 1995 ★★*

**Musigny, Vieilles Vignes de Vogüé** Showing well in the mid-1980s though lacking length. More recently: good colour; scented Pinot aroma; dry, crisp, fruity. Good acidity and grip. *Last tasted Jan 1990 ★★★ Probably holding on.*

**Pommard, Rugiens, Tasteviné Gaunoux** Palish, fully mature; good ripe Pinot smell which reminded me of the shoe repair shop at Hammersmith Station; sweet, earthy, ripe, refreshing acidity. *In Singapore, Jan 1998 ★★★*

**Clos St-Denis Dujac** A jeroboam: gloriously ripe, fragrant; Pinot nose and taste. Dry. Slightly bitter finish. *April 1993 ★★★*

SOME OF THE RELATIVELY FEW '72S LAST TASTED IN THE 1980S **DRC/Marey-Monge**'s **Romanée St-Vivant** pale but with firm backbone in 1975, rich, elegant in 1980, beautifully evolved. *Sept 1989 ★★★★ should still be lovely;* **de Vogüé**'s **Bonnes-Mares** good wine. Not a trace of '72 bitterness. *Oct 1984 ★★★;* **L Latour**'s **Ch Corton-Grancey** rich but austere in 1975. An off-bottle more recently. *May 1986. At best ★★★ and probably drinking quite well;* **Leroy**'s **Gevrey-Chambertin, Cazetiers** rich, distinctive, good flavour and balance ★★★ and **Mazis-Chambertin** pink and pretty, stylish. *Both Sept 1984 ★★★;* **J Grivot**'s **Nuits-St-Georges, Boudots** deep, rich, then very tannic. *Sept 1984 ★★★ Should have survived;* and **Dom de la Romanée**'s **La Romanée** dry, good length, nice wine. Fully mature. *Dec 1987 ★★★*

OF THE MANY '72S TASTED MAINLY IN THE MID- TO LATE 1970S, the following were outstanding: **DRC**'s **Romanée-Conti, Richebourg** and **Grands-Echézeaux**; **Leroy**'s **Nuits-St-Georges, Clos des Corvées**; **A Rousseau**'s **Clos de la Roche**; **Dujac**'s **Clos St-Denis**; and **R Engel**'s **Vosne-Romanée, Brûlées**.

## 1973

Eminently forgettable. As in Bordeaux, there was a combination of unsuitable weather conditions, poor quality and overproduction, which coincided with a drop in demand. Had the market been more propitious and had vineyard management and winemaking been of today's standards, something could have been made of this vintage.

In fact, the growing season started off well, with flowering in good conditions; a substantial early harvest was envisaged. Until mid-July, the summer was the hottest since 1945. Then the rains came, continuing through September; the harvest extended to 18 October. The third largest crop in four years, an over-abundance of light, watery wines, lacking acidity. They were relatively cheap, but what little charm and drinkability they had was short-lived.

**La Tâche** The only '73 tasted since the 1980s. Unimpressive in 1977, dry, light style, touch of bitterness, but at least trying. Three more years in bottle and it had taken on more colour despite premature ageing, a brown edge. Nevertheless, an open, appealing bouquet, gentle fruit and attractive aftertaste. Most recently, put into perspective at Wagner's vertical: slightly drab appearance; initially the nose was not bad, a touch of brown sugar, no depth though after 1½ hours in the glass, it had opened up with a whiff of fragrance like a faded bouquet stolen from someone's grave. Fairly dry, light and not very interesting. *Last tasted April 1998 ★*

THE OTHER DRCS were well below standard: **Romanée-Conti**'s 'peacock's tail' had quite a few feathers missing; **Richebourg** pale, pink and modest; **Grands-Echézeaux** weak and watery. The only other decent wine tasted in the 1980s was **L Jadot**'s **Beaune, Theurons** sweet, surprisingly assertive and quite likely a survivor.

I was about to say 'pass on to the '74s' but, as will be seen, the dreary succession continued until Burgundy came out of the doldrums in 1976. But for the record …

# 1974

I do not want to compare Bordeaux and Burgundy endlessly, but it is almost uncanny how some vintages have such a similar character and quality, while others, '61 and '62 for example, have reverse roles. The '74 burgundies, along with the '74 Bordeauxs, lacked grace, to say the least.

The flowering was uneven but the summer was warm and sunny. September was marred by cold and rain, the grapes being harvested in the third week in dismal, wet and windy weather. The economic gloom continued, the Hospices de Beaune prices were down 25% and there were virtually no overseas buyers.

**La Tâche** Although I have not heard it said, DRC wines have something in common with Ch Latour in that – by dint of late harvesting and severe selection – they can be quite good even in a poor vintage. 'Quite' is the operative word here. In this case, a good deal of chaptalisation which has the effect of disguising raw and immature grapes and providing a disarming sweetness which, like an insincere smile, cannot be sustained. My notes made in the 1980s were consistent: strange, stewed fruit fragrance; superficially appealing but raw and acidic, with a pasty texture. Put into perspective again by Manfred Wagner, whose tasting was attended by Aubert de Villaine; after all, it is not every day that a producer has the opportunity of tasting over 30 vintages of his own wine. Appearance medium, open, luminous, fully mature; a touch of sourness which though eventually fading in the glass, had shaken itself clear. On the palate, dry and tart. *Last tasted in Zurich, April 1998.*

**Clos de Tart** Brown-tinged; earthy, vegetal 'Irish stew and malted milk'; surprisingly sweet, assertive, malty and acidic. *At the domaine, Oct 1990.*

OF THE OTHER '74S LAST TASTED IN THE 1980S, the best of a fairly dreary bunch were **DRC's Grands-Echézeaux** flavoury but acidic; and **Richebourg** fragrant vinosity; **Ropiteau's Chambertin, Clos de Bèze** scented, elegant, well balanced; **Prince de Mérode's Pommard, Clos de la Platière** 'fabulously ripe Pinot nose and flavour'.

LOOKING BACK, I SEE THAT I TASTED QUITE A FEW '74S IN THE LATE 1970S, but the only ones remotely notable were the young Jacques Seysses' **(Dujac) Gevrey-Chambertin, Combottes** and **Clos de la Roche**, and a predictably plausible **Doudet-Naudin Pernand-Vergelesses** 'Méthode ancienne', fairly deep and meaty.

---

### Chevaliers du Tastevin

*Established during the 1930s Depression to stimulate and revive interest and trade in the wines of Burgundy. Banquets are held regularly for Chevaliers and their guests at its headquarters the Château du Clos de Vougeot. They are very elaborate, colourful and long drawn out affairs – all that time helps one digest the several courses and wines. I have had the honour of presiding over two chapitres at Clos Vougeot. The first was in the elegant footsteps of Catherine Deneuve!*

*The Chevaliers du Tastevin now has branches all over the world. The frequent meetings are always very entertaining. I suppose I first went to one of the dinners as a guest in the 1960s, and in 1975 I was unexpectedly dubbed a Chevalier of the New Orleans chapter – having gone to a dinner there on the spur of the moment.*

# 1975

The third cold and wet harvest in a row. A pity because the growing season started well with a fine, late spring and early summer, and a hot end to July. Ignoring the hail, which is endemic in Burgundy, striking unpredictably and indiscriminately, the crucial ripening period from the latter part of August and into September was humid, wet and stormy. There was widespread rot. A crop of poor, thin and rotten wines, two-thirds that of 1974 and half the size of the 1973 vintage. The market in 1974–75 was at its lowest ebb for a very long time. Very few wines tasted even in the early days and those I did taste were poor and of little interest now.

**La Tâche** The palest of the DRC's '75s at the opening trade tasting in 1980; one could smell the rot and the wine lacked firmness and grip. However, the following autumn, it was at least recognisable though its nose reminded me of 'damp ferns' and its taste smacked of liquorice. In 1983, it had gained a sort of second wind, the La Tâche fragrance struggling to surface; sweet, light, flavoury but short. More recently, yet again put into perspective at Wagner's vertical: fairly pale, weak-rimmed, orange-tinged; a light beetroot nose which, after an hour, developed an almost exaggerated, citrus-edged, fragrance which lasted for quite some time. On the palate, mediocre, medicinal, with dry finish. *Last tasted in Zurich, April 1998.*

THE REST OF THE DRC 'TEAM' TASTED IN THE EARLY 1980S None were really worthy of the name though not wholly unattractive: **Romanée-Conti** prematurely orange-tinged, nose distinctive and packing a surprising punch; **Richebourg** a shadow of its normal ebullient self; **Grands-Echézeaux** open knit, edgy acidity; **Romanée-St-Vivant** initially acidic, at a later tasting sweeter and fuller than expected, flavoury and stylish but with a bitter finish; and **Echézeaux** the tail end of the range had a clean-cut colour; caramelly, chaptalised nose; hollow, loose knit, some fragrance but with edgy end acidity. Even knowing the recuperative powers of the DRC wines, I doubt if any are now of more than academic interest.

# 1976 ★★★

I have demoted this vintage to 3 stars for, despite its considerable virtues, it produced unbalanced wines, over-endowed with tannin from the start and they still are.

What was the problem? Northern Europe first enjoyed an exceptionally hot summer, then worried about the drought. The grapes were baked, and the thick sunburnt skins, fermented following the early September harvest, produced not just an unusual amount of colouring matter but hard tannins as well.

Nevertheless, the market, recovering from the recession and the effect of three dreary vintages, bought heavily though there was some resistance in the New Year to the high prices. At the moment, and for the next – say – five to ten years, it is a race against time for this vintage. Will the impressively constituted but still very tannic wines become more amenable, or will they continue to dry out?

**Romanée-Conti** In 1979: intense, concentrated, but as yet undeveloped nose and flavour, very rich and with a fabulously penetrating aftertaste. The deepest of the DRC range in 1982. Five years later: noticeably powerful. By 1989 fully evolved, heavenly 'almost theatrical' Pinot fragrance; sweet, mouthfilling yet still hard. Most recently, rich, harmonious nose; sweet, full, very rich and powerful. *Last tasted Feb 1992* ★★★★

**La Tâche** Nine notes, the first in the spring of 1980 at the London agent's opening tasting. Good colour and fruit; flavoury, elegant but with quite an end bite. The following autumn, hard, tannic, no signs of yielding, yet by 1982, La Tâche's inimitable aroma was clawing its way out of the glass; powerful, perfumed. Showing well but unready at the vertical tasting of La Tâche at the Domaine in 1983, its ethereal quality and 'peacock's tail' spreading in 1985. By 1987, it was beginning to show some maturity and its bouquet was immediately forthcoming. A wonderful flavour, but lean. Two notes in New York in 1992, first at a pre-sale tasting and the other a bottle brought in by an American client who, seeing an Australian slip label and Leroy's neck label was — fairly understandably — suspicious. I happened to know the vendor, Berek Segan, owner of Emerald Wines in Melbourne, the agent for both Leroy and DRC. He had an excellent cellar. Happily, my notes made the same day, the first at the pre-sale tasting (wines from an American cellar), and later, in the office, with the 'offending' Australian bottle, were identical: palish, fully mature; soft, sweet, open, with a characteristic 'beetroot' fragrance; sweet, soft, good fruit but, though long, finishing noticeably tannic and acidic. Most recently: fragrant but fading; medium sweet but with a hot, tannic finish. *Last noted at Wagner's vertical, April 1998* ★★ *It really should warrant a potential 4 stars but whether the fruit will survive the tannin, I do not know.*

**Richebourg DRC** The most premature looking of the DRC's '76s in 1980, nose also undeveloped but a good, firm, broad-shouldered flavour which opened up in the mouth. However, within a couple of years, both nose and taste had evolved well, sweet, lovely by any standards; well endowed. A decade later, still on the pale side and unquestionably mature; sweet, fragrant bouquet; soft mid-palate but very tannic and good for another decade or so. *Last tasted Feb 1992* ★★★★ *Will be interesting to see how this has developed.*

**Romanée-St-Vivant DRC** In 1980, dry, assertive. By 1982, beginning to open up, with silky texture but abrupt, astringent finish and, the following summer, the St-Vivant fragrance and richness making one ignore its tannin. Most recently: lean, dry, tannic and, alas, slightly corky. *Last tasted Feb 1992. At its best* ★★★★ *Probably still drinking well, assuming it is not drying out.*

**Grands-Echézeaux DRC** Warm, mature colour; ripe, elegant, slightly scented 'squashed cherry bouquet'; pure Pinot flavour, good texture, dry finish. *At Wilfred Jaeger's dinner tasting in San Francisco, March 2002* ★★★★ *Drink soon.*

**Beaune, Grèves, Vignes de l'Enfant Jésus Bouchard Père** A couple of recent notes: showing quite well at a pre-sale tasting in 1997 and the following year, now fully mature with good ripe nose and flavour. I did not notice the usual '76 tannin, probably because it accompanied strong cheese. *Last tasted dining with the Tim Stanley-Clarks, Sept 1998* ★★★

**Bonnes-Mares G Roumier** Medium-deep, still a hint of cherry; very sweet, ripe and delicious nose but a warning — smelly — overtone; very raw, dry, good length but not in prime condition. *At Wilfred Jaeger's tasting, March 2002* ★

**Chambertin A Rousseau** Now palish, open, rosy-hued; sweet, mature, slightly smoky aroma; sweet, rich, but by no means hefty. The '76 tannin present but merely leading to a good, dry finish. *May 1999* ★★★

**Corton, Clos du Roi** Terres Vigneuses New to me. Good colour, some ruby; attractive, fullish, mature nose and flavour. Still tannic. *Dining at Porcelli's, New York, Oct 1996* ★★★

**Corton, Clos du Roi** Voarick Two very different bottles served, not very helpfully, with turbot at a British Airways wine committee dinner at The Waterside Inn, Bray. The first had a touch of ruby; harmonious nose, good fruit, slightly smoky; dry, crisp, still tannic. The other looked deeper and richer, with a velvety sheen; softer and richer on the nose but with a sweaty tannin smell and touch of liquorice; sweeter, fuller — totally different. *Nov 1996* ★★★

**Corton, Hospices, Cuvée Dr Peste** Very deep, in fact quite dark, though with a mature rim; meaty nose; fairly sweet, full-bodied, rich, concentrated but with a slight coarse tannic end. *Lunching at Bouchard Père in Beaune, Nov 1995* ★★★

**Corton, Hospices, Cuvée Charlotte Dumay** The highly esteemed André Gagey of Jadot was very concerned about the very high tannin content of the '76s and gave the wine extra time to soften. This was put into magnums 2½ years after the vintage. At 14 years of age, its nose was soft and harmonious, with vanillin picked up from the oak; a good, rich mouthful, but still stubbornly tannic. *Jan 1990* ★★★★

**Musigny J Drouhin** My most admiring note: lovely deep colour; rich, yet elegant nose; fabulous flavour, assertive, good length, dry finish, tannin relatively unobtrusive. *Oct 1990* ★★★★ *Should still be delicious.*

**Clos de Tart** Five notes. A perverse wine, first tasted in 1980: pricked with high volatile acidity which gave its appearance a pink-red tinge and nose high-toned with a citrus edge. Flavoury but tinny. The same in 1983; better in magnum in 1985, plummy-coloured, jammy on the palate, managing to be both soft and raw. Five years later, its volatile acidity imparting a liveliness to its colour, elevating its bouquet and bringing out the flavour. Tannin throughout. Perverse it might be but I enjoyed it. *Last tasted Oct 1990* ★★★ *Probably a bit scraggy now.*

**Volnay, Les Taillepieds de Montille** Paired with the '71. Medium-deep, misleadingly youthful cherry red which, however, turned out to be an indication of things to come: a sour overripeness, almost amyl acetate on the nose, tart on the palate. *Poor bottle at Wilfred Jaeger's burgundy dinner, March 2002.*

MANY '76S LAST TASTED IN THE 1980S, without exception tannic, among the best: **DRC's Grands-Echézeaux** several notes: intense, a marvellous core of fruit but (then) unyielding. *1982* ★★★★; then three **Echézeaux**: **DRC's** lively and fragrant. *1982* ★★★; **Moillard's** richly coloured, flavoury. *1988* ★★★; and **Mongeard-Mugneret's** the best. *1989* ★★★★; **de Vogüé's Bonnes-Mares** laden with hard tannins and acidity. 'Needs time'. *1984* ★★★?; **Dom de Varoilles' Gevrey-Chambertin, Varoilles** interestingly the wine was vatted quickly 'to prevent the tannin eclipsing the fruit'. Sweet, toasted Pinot; dry, very rich, yet raw. I don't think it quite worked. *1985* ★★★ *(just)*; **Dujac's Morey-St-Denis** the ever-questing Jacques Seysses tried it both ways. He opened two bottles from the same *cuvée*, one which had had one year *en barrique*, the other two. For me, the latter was better, deeper, richer-looking, more fragrant, more opulent with richness of texture. But they were both only four years old. *1981. At best* ★★★ *possibly 4-star*; and **d'Angerville's Volnay, Champans** elegant but by no means a light, feminine Volnay, in fact quite powerful — and tannic. *1986* ★★★

AND OF THE '76S TASTED ONLY IN THE LATE 1970S, few stood out, the best being three **Cortons**: **Bonneau du Martray's** ★★★, the **Bressandes** of **Chandon de Briailles** ★★★ and **Latour's Ch Corton-Grancey** ★★★★; and a well-constructed village wine, **A Rousseau's Gevrey-Chambertin** ★★★

# 1977

Thanks to the perverse weather, this was a most difficult vintage; despite a flicker of optimism in the early days, it was wisely avoided by the trade which had bought the '76s heavily and kept whatever resources remained for the excellent '78s.

The growing season started well with an ideal, frost-free spring and flowering in perfect weather with the promise of a substantial crop. Then the rains set in, daily in July, a fine break in the first half of August, then thunderstorms. All this necessitated a great deal of anti-rot spraying – 13 times by DRC compared with seven in 1976. The weather improved in September and continued warm until a fairly late harvest, early October, when the rains came again. But there were other, unpublicised problems, one being the effect of overfertilisation and excessive nitrogen. One major grower in Gevrey-Chambertin had enormous problems which he put down to lead in the glass bottles. But this was not the reason. A full range of his wines, including Chambertin and Clos de Bèze, were adversely affected, as for a time was his reputation. I was able to taste them all, but they were mainly not in a fit state to be put back on the market. Those estates who could afford to wait and to pick selectively, were able to produce wines with a fairly good colour, high acidity and good levels of alcohol.

The DRC, always late harvesters, waited until the third week in October, taking immense pains to pick only the most sound grapes, the malolactic fermentation in December reducing high acidity. All in all a costly business and, frankly, not justified by the results though the early tastings were interesting, **La Tâche**, **Richebourg** and **Grands-Echézeaux** being the best. One cannot accuse the domaine of not trying.

OF THE OTHER '77S TASTED few warranted more than 1 star. Among the best of a bad bunch: **Leroy**'s Gevrey-Chambertin, Cazetiers ★★; **Barrault-Lucotte**'s Grands-Echézeaux, Tasteviné ★★; **George Roumier**'s Morey-St-Denis, Clos Bussière ★★; and **Bertagna**'s Vougeot, Clos de la Perrière ★★

# 1978 ★★★★★

At last, a great vintage. Yet, weather-wise it was touch and go: spring and early summer cold, retarding vegetation and flowering. Around the third week in August, the sun came out and superb weather through September and into October saved the vintage which started in the Côte d'Or, around 11 October, resulting in a small but healthy crop, producing wines with good colour, alcoholic content, and notably aromatic. Opening prices surged, 100% up in the same period as 1977. Some members of the trade were concerned about the expense, and whether the consumer would be able to accept this new level of prices. They need not have worried.

Thanks to high extract and tannins, the best are still drinking well and some have yet to attain their peak. No good burgundy cellar should be without a bottle or two!

**Romanée-Conti** Magnificent. First tasted at the Domaine in 1983. Two bottles, slight variation due to the temperature, one just brought from the cool cellar. Fairly deep; harmonious but restrained; rich, massively constructed, the colder bottle seemed drier and spicier. Development scarcely budging after a further two years, fragrant, complete, fruit-packed. More bottle age needed. Then a leap of 15 years, less

deep; a 'classic', singed leather, 'beetroot' Pinot nose which, after only 20 minutes in the glass, opened up fragrantly and flagrantly, great richness and depth; sweet, wonderful, mouthfilling flavour, elegant, dry finish. Years of life ahead. At Loggerheads, Len Evans' impressive erection in the Hunter Valley, in September 2000: a deep, yet exotic bouquet; medium sweet, full, soft – a wine with extra dimensions. Most recently, bottle number 001256: imported by Domaine Chandon. The first and youngest of 11 classic vintages of Romanée-Conti: medium-pale, lively looking, open yellow-amber rim; sweet, rich, lovely fragrance, pure mature 'beetroot' varietal bouquet that opened up in the glass, soft fruit, whiff of raspberry; also sweet on the palate, full-bodied (yet a moderate 13% alcohol), interesting texture, peppery acidity and an upturned, almost spritz, finish. *Last tasted at Wilfred Jaeger's Sunday DRC lunch, March 2002* ★★★★★ *Drink now–2012.*

**La Tâche** The vineyard is separated from Romanée-Conti by only a narrow track, but the wine is always totally different in style. If the latter has the concentration, extra dimensions and grandeur, La Tâche, for me, is more approachable, more Tchaikovsky than Beethoven, elegant, opulent, fragrant. Eight notes, first in 1981, wrapped in its vivid purple robe; already opulent; fruit-laden, rich, elegant. Two bottles in 1983, fragrant, scented but much more to come; shapely, slender, flowery but firm. A decade later, dining at Schloss Ramholz, its bouquet was in full bloom; fairly sweet, rich of course, but a touch of bitterness on the finish. A 'definitive' note (how I hate that word) – at least to put it in perspective – at Wagner's vertical in 1998: an immediate surge of scent, powerful, variable, then strange 'fishy' (anchovy) Pinot whiff which, after gaining its second wind, continued to outpour a deep, rich fragrance. Some sweetness, hefty – high alcohol. More recently: mature rim; a ripe and lovely nose which after 20 minutes positively gushed out of the glass; soft, beautiful flavour, good length, dry finish. *Last noted at Len Evans' 70th birthday extravaganza at Loggerheads in the Hunter Valley, Sept 2000* ★★★★★

**Grands-Echézeaux** DRC First tasted at the Domaine in 1983: fairly deep, rich and plummy-coloured; fragrant, refined; sweet, mouthfilling, firm, great length and future. Most recently: some colour loss, tailing off to a somewhat weak rim; almost sickly sweet, jammy even, on the nose yet the finish dry and a bit raw. The bottle? Should have been finer. *Also last noted at Loggerheads in the Hunter Valley, Sept 2000. At best* ★★★★★

**Romanée-St-Vivant** DRC First noted at the Domaine in 1983: impressive colour, still youthfully purple at the rim; nose somewhat restrained, peppery, firm, unyielding at first though it opened up well, overall dry, crisp, with rich varietal aftertaste. Next, tasted at the St-Vivant vertical at the Domaine in 1995: distinctly deep, still ruby; very rich, singed, fragrant bouquet that opened up further in the glass until, for an hour, it was almost chocolatey sweet; the palate has sweetened up too though it had a dry, extended finish. Full of flavour. My second highest mark, after the '71, of the entire range (up to the '94). Most recently: bouquet fully evolved , surging out of the glass; sweet entry, dry finish, elegant. The essence of burgundy. *Last tasted in the Hunter Valley, Sept 2000* ★★★★★

A SELECTION OF OTHER MOST RECENTLY TASTED '78S **Beaune, Cent Vignes** Ch de Meursault Very good, mature Pinot; sweet, good fruit, flavour and weight. Ready. *At the tasting conducted for* Vinum *in the historic Zunfthaus z. Meisen in Zurich, April 1998* ★★★★ *Drink now.*

**Bonnes-Mares Clair-Daü** 'Legs' wide open; ripe, fragrant but a rather 'stewed Pinot' character; soft yet lean. Disappointing. *At a Memphis Wine & Food Society dinner, Dec 1997* ★★

**Bonnes-Mares J Drouhin** Showing well in the early 1980s. Still very deep, with a dark cherry core; glorious bouquet, with a sort of cherry-like fruit; perfect sweetness, fairly hefty yet not obtrusively so, lovely flavour, with mulberry-ripe fruit. All the component parts perfectly balanced. *Last noted dining with Claude and Frédéric Drouhin in Savigny, Oct 2001* ★★★★★

**Chambolle-Musigny, Charmes Remoissenet** Deep, intense; meaty, full of fruit; an old-fashioned style, rather plausible but an attractive drink. *At a Burgundy dinner in Florida, Jan 1990* ★★★ Not great, but will have survived.

**Ch Corton-Grancey L Latour** Showing well, good future in 1981. By 1990, some colour loss, palish and pink-tinged; a 'warm' distinctive Pinot aroma; fullish, firm, still dry and tannic. A disappointing bottle at an eight-wine vertical: nose old and cheesy; stewed and tart. *Last noted at my Louis Latour seminar for the Hollywood Wine Society, March 1998. At best* ★★★?

**Musigny Clair-Daü** Soft, ripe, varietal nose; rather vegetal, earthy. Touch of bitterness. Lacking Musigny style, charm and femininity. *In Memphis, Dec 1997* ★

**Richebourg J Drouhin** Rich, mature; equally rich, ripe nose expanding in the glass; sweet, mouthfilling, great to drink though still tannic. *Before a packed audience at Wine Japan, Tokyo, May 1990* ★★★★★ Should be perfect now.

**Clos de la Roche Dujac** Superb. First noted in 1995, dining at Le Montrachet in New York: fabulous, surging bouquet, sweet, fragrant with matching flavour. Perfect weight and acidity. Most recently: medium-deep, mature; scented 'beetroot' Pinot, glorious fragrance; lovely flavour, touch of leanness and quite a tannic bite. *Last noted at the Josey pre-sale dinner in New York, Nov 2000* ★★★★

**Clos de la Roche A Rousseau** Sweet, hefty, mature Pinot; sweet, rich; delicious Nuits. *In Geneva, May 1999* ★★★★

**Clos de Tart** Opulent in 1987. By 1990 well developed, brown rim; smell of ripe Pinot and grilled sausages, evolving exotically; rich, ripe fruit. Described then as 'an attractive, buxom, nubile, highly scented tart'! More recently, retiring gracefully; still plenty of scent though; spicy, dry finish and something lacking. *Last noted in 1992 at a Bacchus Society dinner in Boston* ★★

**Volnay, Caillerets Pousse d'Or** Complete, harmonious bouquet; glorious flavour, very fragrant, touch of leanness, tannin and rather high acidity. *Jan 1990* ★★★★

**Vosne-Romanée, Beaumonts Remoissenet** Mature; good varietal nose; some sweetness, singed Pinot flavour, good tannin and refreshing acidity. *At Michael Ruger's seminar at the Winefest, Sarasota, Florida, April 1997* ★★★

**Vosne-Romanée, Aux Brûlées H Jayer** Very deep, richly coloured, dark cherry core, rich 'legs'; initially low-keyed but expanded in the glass; medium-sweet, full-bodied, rich, concentrated, perfect flavour, balance, grip, acidity – and life. Fully endorsing Jayer's remarkable reputation. *At Frans de Cock's lunch at Carré des Feuillants, Paris, Dec 1995* ★★★★★

**Vosne-Romanée, Cros Parantoux H Jayer** Even better: deep, hefty, richly coloured and bouquet to match. Laden but not inhibited with extract, the nose opening up wonderfully; amazingly sweet, concentrated, glorious length and aftertaste, still tannic. It reminded me of a DRC Richebourg at its best. *At the same lunch (see above) in Paris, Dec 1995* ★★★★★ Years of life.

**Clos Vougeot Coron** Palish, fully mature; quite good scented Pinot nose and taste. Sweet. *Pre-sale, New York, Sept 1997* ★

**Clos Vougeot Noëllat** Excellent in the mid-1980s. Most recently: still fairly deep; a classic, ripe Pinot nose and flavour. *With lamb at a Saintsbury Club dinner, April 2000* ★★★★

OF THE MANY '78S LAST TASTED IN THE LATE 1980S, the following should still be drinking well: **Mongeard-Mugneret's** Echézeaux fragrant, crisp, wonderful flavour. *1989* ★★★★; **R Monnier's** Pommard, Vignots very sweet, rim, lovely mouthful. *1989* ★★★; **L Latour's** Romanée-St-Vivant, Quatre Journaux very rich, deep, great future. *1987* ★★★★; **Lafarge's** Volnay, Clos des Chênes full of fruit, very tannic, great class. *1989* ★★★★; and **Jean Grivot's** Vosne-Romanée, Beaumonts a rich, mouthfilling wine of great length and silky tannins. *1989* ★★★★

AND SOME CHOICE '78S WITH POTENTIAL FROM THE MID-1980S: **DRC's** Richebourg massive scale ★★★★★; **Tollot-Beaut's** Beaune, Clos du Roi fragrant, very tannic ★★★; **Dubreuil-Fontaine's** Corton, Perrières luscious, harmonious, high alcohol, tannic ★★★★; **Leroy's** Mazis-Chambertin fabulous flavour, well stacked ★★★★; **de Vogüé's** Musigny, Vieilles Vignes elegant ★★★★; and **Noëllat's** Clos Vougeot excellent, firm flavour. *1984* ★★★★

# 1979 ★★★

A good, healthy, prolific vintage. Low temperatures in March and April delayed vegetation; budding and frosts coincided in early May. But apart from three major hailstorms, the most severe in June, cutting swathes between Nuits-St-Georges and Chambolle-Musigny, the summer weather was favourable and a large harvest of healthy grapes took place around the end of September. Prices at the Hospices de Beaune auction eased by 18%. Though less well-balanced than the '78s, there were some attractive wines which are still holding well.

**Romanée-Conti** Only one note, but memorable, a jeroboam: medium, expansive but open and fully mature in its 15th year; a sensational, indescribably glorious bouquet; sweet, full of vigour and power, fabulous flavour, length and aftertaste. Almost ruined, however, by *Kässpätzle*, a drain-smelling cheese dish. *At the opening dinner of Rodenstock's 14th Raritäten-Weinprobe, Arlberg, Sept 1994* ★★★★★

**La Tâche** First tasted at the Domaine in September 1981. The wine had had three months in bottle and was beginning to show a little bottle sickness. Nevertheless, it had good fruit and was very fragrant with an excellent flavour. Lalou Bize told me it would be at its best in 20 years time, Aubert de Villaine said 'ten'! Showing well in 1991 at a DRC tasting in New York: bouquet fully developed and 'fantastic'; impressively sweet, fullish, very flavoury with good grip and fabulous aftertaste. Most recently at Wagner's vertical. Aubert de Villaine told us that hail in June reduced the yield to a mere 12hl/ha. Now a palish, pretty coloured wine; very distinctive fragrance with a touch of malt, which Aubert put down to the tannins; very sweet, very rich, meaty character; great length, very dry finish. *Last tasted in Zurich, March 1998* ★★★★

**Romanée-St-Vivant DRC** At the Domaine in November 1995: attractive colour, open, mature; a sweet, 'warm', singed and slightly raisiny nose which evolved fragrantly; extraordinarily sweet, positive, vegetal, on the lean side, good despite moderate finish. Two years later at a pre-sale tasting in New York: not much red left but a 'lovely DRC' bouquet and flavour, powerful, scented. *Last tasted in Sept 1997* ★★★★ (just).

**Beaune, Grèves** Averys A lovely wine, fragrant, good fruit, weight and texture. *Dec 1990* ★★★★

**Beaune, Clos des Mouches** J Drouhin In 1981, at Drouhin, though deeply coloured, I thought it lacked length. Nine years later, also in Drouhin's tasting room, little red left, a fully developed bouquet; sweet, rich, fruity and ready for drinking. *Last tasted Oct 1990. Then* ★★★ *Drink up.*

**Beaune, Clos des Ursules** L Jadot Good ripe nose; nice weight, a bit lean, attractive. *April 1991* ★★★

**Chambertin, Cuvée Héritiers Latour** L Latour Medium-deep; good, sweet Pinot fragrance; dry, good body, though on the lean side and extremely tannic. *At the Marcobrunn and Chambertin dinner, Schloss Reinhartshausen in the Rheingau, Nov 1995* ★★★? *Possibly 4-star if the tannins have ameliorated.*

**Chassagne-Montrachet** Gagnard-Delagrange Good wine. *Sept 1990* ★★★

**Corton, Clos des Cortons** Faiveley Rich, colour bouquet and flavour. Full. Complete. *Jan 1993* ★★★★

**Ch Corton-Grancey** L Latour Over half a dozen notes, first in October 1980: stalky, raw, immature but good flavour. Unenthusiastic notes in 1981 and 1983, but had opened up by 1987. Showing well at a Corton-Grancey vertical in 1990: fully mature appearance; gloriously ripe, fully evolved scent; soft, spicy, rich fruit but a touch of end bitterness (which would not be noticed with food). My next note somewhat contradicts the last statement for it was at a dinner in 1996 that I noted a slightly tart finish. The following year, the oldest vintage in a 10-wine vertical: fully mature; a rather meaty, figgy scent; good flavour and grip. *Last tasted in the open air below the vineyard at Latour's 200th anniversary tasting, June 1997* ★★★ *Holding on.*

**Clos de la Roche** Dujac Mixed notes. First tasted in 1981: rich, spicy finish. By 1985, I noted a certain muskiness and slightly bitter end and, in 1990, a bottle from my own cellar again noting a bitter tannic-iron finish though the bouquet was fabulously rich. Was Dujac hit by the hail? *Last tasted Nov 1990* ★★?

**Clos de Tart** A touch more red (acidity?) than the '78; fruitful nose that opened up fragrantly; sweet, harmonious, very pleasant. *At the domaine, Oct 1990* ★★★

**Vosne-Romanée, Cros Parantoux** H Jayer Medium, with ruby at its centre; showing some age but glorious bouquet, ripe, exciting; medium-dryness and body, still very crisp, fragrant, dry finish (some minor bottle variation). Jayer's Parantoux is now the star of the sale room, the best vintages commanding outrageous prices. *Noted at Rodenstock's dinner, Sept 1994* ★★★★

OTHER '79S SHOWING QUALITY AND CONSIDERABLE POTENTIAL WHEN TASTED IN THE LATE 1980S L Jadot's **Chambolle-Musigny, Charmes** rich, flavoury, tannic. *March 1989* ★★★; Jean-Louis Laplanche's **Pommard, Ch de Pommard** sweet, spicy, mouthfilling with an expansive 'peacock's tail'. *Feb 1986* ★★★★; Ponsot's **Clos de la Roche** opulent, elegant, lovely texture. *Nov 1987* ★★★★; and Hubert de Montille's **Volnay, 1er Cru** stylish, copybook Volnay. Palish, youthful, nicely made. *April 1986* ★★★

# 1980 ★★ to ★★★

Uneven quality and the market still in recession, Hospices de Beaune average auction prices were down 17%, the second price drop in a row. The cold New Year and spring delayed

bud break. Cold in June led to an extended and uneven flowering; a late, probably small and uneven crop predicted. Summer temperatures, August in particular, were above average and continued into September. There was some rain before the harvest which started around 10 October. Late pickers fared best. Some surprises, but alas few wines tasted in the 1990s. If well kept, they could be fun.

**La Tâche** Late picked. First tasted in cask in 1981: a sweet, chocolatey, chaptalised nose, fair body, quite good length. Next, at the La Tâche vertical at the Domaine in 1983: palish pink; a somewhat stewed fruitiness; deceptively light style. As so frequently quoted, Manfred Wagner's La Tâche vertical in 1998 put the '80 in perspective – a bottle from the DRC cellars: fairly pale and open; an immediacy of fruit switching into something more meaty, sweet, quite rich. Medium sweetness and body, on the lean side but very flavoury. Most recently, and surprisingly, a glorious burst of fragrance; light style yet heady, lovely flavour, slightly lean noted again. *Last noted at a BYOB dinner in New York, March 1999* ★★★ *Drink while the going is good.*

**Romanée-St-Vivant** DRC Also late picked. A fairly pale, youthful mauve, decent flesh and good fruit, better balance than expected and spicy aftertaste when tasted in cask in 1981. Showing surprisingly well in its 15th year: a mature rim of course; its nose rather like Concorde taking off: a surge of fragrance, sweet, soft fruit, iodine, then a shut down of the booster followed 15 minutes later by another burst of fragrance as it continued its climb to cruising altitude; very sweet, complete, fully evolved, rich, slightly chocolatey. Very attractive. *Last noted at the St-Vivant vertical at the Domaine, Nov 1995* ★★★★ *Drink before it touches down.*

**Beaune, Clos des Mouches** J Drouhin Alcohol 12.4%, total acidity 3.6g/l. The opening vintage of the 1980s tasting kindly laid on for me by Robert Drouhin, in order to put the decade into perspective. Already ten years old, it was showing some maturity; a fully evolved nose which, rather like the St-Vivant, paused, then gathered momentum, opening up beautifully. Firm, a touch of hardness, good acidity, dry finish. *Oct 1990* ★★★ *Drink soon.*

**Gevrey-Chambertin, Cazetiers** H de Villamont Fully mature; nose slightly faded; sweet, light, pleasant enough. *At Christie's pre-sale tasting in Tokyo, Nov 1999* ★★ *Drink up.*

**Gevrey-Chambertin, Clos St-Jacques** A Rousseau Rich, mature colour; glorious Pinot scent, fragrant; sweet, medium weight, very flavoury and with a most attractive 'peacock's tail'. *At a Rousseau session conducted by Roger Bohmrich, now one of the several American MWs, at the Tenth Anniversary Great Wine Seminar in Florida, March 1995* ★★★★ *Drink soon. (Despite the pompous title, these annual wine weekends were superbly organised by my old friend Robert Maliner, with many truly great wines. I was privileged to 'moderate' quite a few. 2002 was said to be the last.)*

A SELECTION OF THE MOST SUCCESSFUL '80S NOTED IN THE LATE 1980S Jacques Prieur's **Chambertin, Clos de Bèze** fragrant, crisp, touch of bitterness on the finish. *1986* ★★★; Philippe Leclerc's **Gevrey-Chambertin, Cazetiers** spicy, nutty, crisp fruit; piquant acidity. *1989* ★★★; G Serafin's **Cazetiers** lovely fragrance and depth; sweet, soft, good grip. *1989* ★★★; and de Vogüé's **Musigny** spicy; good weight and fruit, tannin and acidity. Dry slightly bitter finish. *1989* ★★

OTHERS SHOWING WELL IN THE MID-1980S Tollot-Beaut's **Aloxe-Corton** ★★★; H Jayer's **Vosne-Romanée, Cros**

**Parantoux** the winner of a gold medal in Mâcon in 1982. Certainly impressive ★★★★; **Morin**'s **Clos Vougeot, Ch de la Tour** ★★★; **A Rousseau**, **Dujac** and **H Gouges** also produced some above average wines. Most others warranted only 1 or 2 stars – they were not unattractive but lacked staying power.

# 1981 ★★

Regarded as a poor vintage in Burgundy but it was not all that bad, at least in the earlier years. It would appear that only the most conscientious, selective, late pickers made passable wine. The growing season opened with a warm spring, but frost nipped the buds, automatically reducing the potential crop. From then until a modicum of sun in August, conditions were poor and the main, late, harvest from 24 September to 5 October, was continually interrupted by rain. This was followed by a slight improvement in the weather that favoured late pickers. I do not have many first-hand tasting notes to offer the reader but it is a vintage of little interest now.

**La Tâche** The youngest vintage of an array of La Tâche going back to the great '45 tasted at the Domaine in May 1983: noted merely as 'fresh, light style'. Two years later, at the agency tasting in London, already fairly forward, an easy fruitiness, soft, loose-knit, quite mature. Most recently, at Wagner's vertical, at which Aubert de Villaine reminded us that it was a very wet and most difficult year and that even the customary late-picked grapes were very small, as was the overall crop. Predictably fairly pale and fully mature in appearance; a sweet open, fairly well evolved nose, fragrant but breaking up within 40 minutes and malty after an hour or so. However, sweet and easy on the palate, fragrant and with some delicacy. *Last tasted April 1998 ★★ Drink up.*

**Romanée-St-Vivant DRC** Just two notes, first at the agency tasting in London in November 1985: a sweet, earthy, one-dimensional nose; open, loose knit. A decade later at the Domaine, placed neatly in the middle of the St-Vivant vertical: though by no means deep, richer looking and not as pale as the '82; quite good nose; soft, sweet, harmonious and complete with a whiff of mocha, becoming low-keyed after 15 minutes and then, in the curious way that DRC wines have, after a further 15 minutes, settling down to a gentle, light, fragrant long haul. Crisp, berry-like flavour, interesting tannic texture, far better than expected. *Last tasted Nov 1995 ★★★ (just). But drink soon.*

**Beaune, Clos des Mouches J Drouhin** The second vintage in the 1980s decade line-up in Drouhin's tasting room. Surprisingly low alcoholic content, 12%, with acidity 3.6g/l. Already, after nine years, fully mature looking with a weak, watery rim; sweet, not very clear cut nose which oxidised – malty – after an hour in the glass; on the light side, short, with hard, slightly acidic finish. *Oct 1990. Then ★ and not tasted since, but I doubt if it will have improved.*

**Clos des Lambrays Dom des Lambrays, Saier** Pale, chocolatey, very sweet but showing its age. *Tasted pre-sale in Geneva, May 1992 ★*

**Morey-St-Denis L Jadot** 'Vegetal' Pinot nose; 'nutty', pleasant enough, dry finish. One could always rely on André Gagey to make the best of a bad job: a drinkable wine, not completely washed out by the rain. *June 1990 ★★*

**Musigny de Vogüé** Tasted twice, on neither occasion noting 'Vieilles Vignes'. First at the domaine in October 1990, the day after visiting Drouhin; the same purpose, to compare vintages of the decade. It had an immediately forthcoming, fully evolved, high-toned fruitiness, which developed fragrantly in the glass; medium sweetness and weight, soft yet lean, rather short, some tannin. Nine years later, on the pale side but still lovely looking; a rich, meaty Pinot nose with a whiff of malt; good flavour and surprising end bite. *Last noted at a surprisingly extensive pre-sale tasting at Christie's in London, Jan 1999 ★★ Certainly flavoury but not a stayer.*

I TASTED THE FULL RANGE OF **DRC** WINES IN 1985 BUT ONLY TWO SINCE, AS NOTED ABOVE. Of the others, **Romanée-Conti** itself had, as usual, more stuffing than the rest, with quite a bit of tannin and acidity to support its soft fruit flavour; the **Richbourg** was not its usual broad-shouldered self and its acidity was very noticeable. I preferred the **Grands-Echézeaux**, advanced and flavoury, and the **Echézeaux**, usually a step or so below, was pleasant, spicy, with a touch of bitterness. My experience of the DRC wines is that they can be very misleading; even pimply girls can change into attractive young ladies – but not grand matrons.

OF THE RELATIVELY FEW OTHER '80S I TASTED IN THE MID- TO LATE 1980S, I quite liked the following: **Bernard Bachelet**'s **Charmes-Chambertin** rich, rustic, sweet, fullish, agreeable despite touch of bitterness. *1986 ★★*; **Bachelet-Ramonet**'s **Chassagne-Montrachet, Clos de la Boudriotte** misleadingly pale, fragrant. *1987 ★★*; and **A Rousseau**'s **Gevrey-Chambertin** fragrant, attractive, noticeable acidity. *1987 ★★*

# 1982 ★★

The first thing to say is that 1982 in Burgundy was nothing like its equivalent in Bordeaux, either in terms of quality or market excitement. The growing season was good: warm early spring, early flowering, fine summer, hot September, a healthy crop of ripe grapes harvested from the 20th, continuing warm weather into October. So what went wrong? Overproduction or a bumper crop resulting in lack of concentration?

The very noticeable feature of these '82s is that they scarcely qualify as *red* burgundy as they are often so feeble, pale, with little red and a weak open rim. But red wine, red burgundy, does not have to be deep in colour to be good; Pinot Noir grapes have thin skins and only when they are suntanned in a hot ripening period can a good deal of colour be extracted during fermentation.

**La Tâche** At the opening trade tasting in November 1985: spicy, varietal aroma; dry, firm, already with inimitable La Tâche aftertaste. Eleven months later: very fragrant, harmonious nose; perhaps a touch sweeter, lasting Pinot flavour, good acidity. I gave it a minimum of 3 stars. Next noted at Wagner's vertical: the same medium-pale, but now a warm rose colour with dreary rim. Alas, it was corked and 'screwed up'. So judgment must be reserved. *Last noted April 1998 ★★★? Probably best to drink soon.*

**Romanée-St-Vivant DRC** In the autumn of 1985: fairly pale, still with an immature purple tinge; very fragrant 'fruit and root' aromas; assertive, good length, tannin and acidity. Five years later, it appeared, in isolation, to have gained a bit of colour, but was sweet and full flavoured. Early in 1991, I thought this time it was losing colour – but of no great consequence as all depends on the light at the time of tasting. Attractive. Very drinkable. More recently noted at the St-Vivant vertical at the Domaine (vintages 1967–1991).

Appearance open, fully mature with an attractive glow; soft, fragrant, slightly singed nose, developing sweet and easy and returning a light (shallow?) fragrance. On the palate sweet, very characteristic, very burgundian (no mistaking this for Bordeaux), but appeared to have a chaptalised character and though with tannic grip, lacking length. *Last tasted Nov 1995* ★★★ *(just).*

**A SELECTION OF OTHER '82S LAST TASTED AND BRIEFLY NOTED IN THE 1990S**
**Beaune, Clos des Mouches J Drouhin** First at dinner in 1989, but a more considered note the following year at the decade-of-the-1980s vertical at Drouhin's: medium-pale; already fully mature looking and, as with so many burgundies, a rather weak, open rim. The nose was also fully developed, settled down harmoniously and held well; some sweetness, middling weight (alcohol 12.8%), ready for drinking, some tannin, moderate acidity (3.5g/l). *Last tasted Oct 1990. Then* ★★★ *These regular 'decades' tastings are very useful. They throw each vintage into perspective. Not a wine to keep.*
**Bonnes-Mares L Jadot** Paler, vegetal and alas, not living up to its *grand cru* status and distinguished *négociant*: vegetal. *July 1990* ★ *It surely cannot have gained in stature in the intervening years.*
**Bonnes-Mares G Roumier** A leading grower with 1.8ha of this very *grand cru* (de Vogüé owns 1.5ha). Only one note: a decent colour, attractive, ripe, varietal nose and flavour. Drinking pleasantly. *At Christie's wine course dinner at Boodle's Club in London, Oct 2000* ★★★ *Drink soon.*
**Chapelle-Chambertin Trapet** Two bottles, both pale, one with a faint red tinge, the other with not a vestige of red; open with a sweet, stewed Pinot nose, the other more chocolatey, one soft and short, the other with a bit more of a bite. Yet neither was out of condition. *Feb 1991. Depressing really.*
**Corton, Clos de la Vigne au Saint Amance** Quite good nose and flavour, crisper than expected. A small hurrah! *June 1991* ★★★
**Ch Corton-Grancey L Latour** First tasted in 1990: palish, open; slightly stewed nose; sweet, soft, touch of bitterness. More recently, one of a range tasted just below the vineyard *en plein air*, not the best of conditions for a critical note, but the orange tinge was not due to the — very welcome — sunlight; otherwise it was not dissimilar to the first bottle I tasted. Positive flavour, more grip than expected. *At Latour's 200th anniversary tasting and lunch, June 1997* ★★★ *Pleasant but not for long keeping.*
**Gevrey-Chambertin A Rousseau** Admittedly one of his village wines, not a *grand cru* but if Rousseau cannot make a decent '82, who can? Pale, virtually *pelure d'oignon*; little nose 'just a dusty old Pinot'; minimal fruit, stewed — chaptalised — taste, dry finish. *Jan 1991* ★ *Of little interest then, surely of no interest now.*
**Musigny de Vogüé** I do not think this was from *vieilles vignes* and I was distinctly unimpressed at the domaine's vertical in 1990, meaty, cheesy, lacking the charm, elegance and finesse of Musigny. *Oct 1990* ★
**Musigny, Vieilles Vignes de Vogüé** Tasted alongside the '81, its nose far more evolved; sweet, rich, ready. *At a Musigny pre-sale tasting in London, Jan 1999* ★★★ *Drink soon.*
**Nuits-St-Georges L Jadot** This eminent firm tended to hold their annual tastings at the Savoy Hotel, always a hot day, always hot overcrowded participants, followed by a slap up, doubtless very costly, lunch. Not the best conditions for a critical tasting, at least not for me. I noted at the time that the wine was vegetal and sweaty, like most of the tasters; sweet, broadly based, slightly acidic. Not bad in the circumstances. *June 1990* ★★ *Ready then.*
**Clos de Tart** A weak-rimmed, pink-tinged, three-year-old, fairly fragrant and piquant, yet juggling lightness of style and character with some weight of alcohol and the charm of a frigid smile. After five years pristine piquancy, now raw and somewhat astringent. *Last tasted Oct 1990* ★★?
**Clos Vougeot, Tastevinage** Bottler unknown. Labels bearing a reference to *Tastevinage* indicate that the wine has been honoured in its youth at a tasting at the Château de Clos Vougeot; at least a seal of approval by a motley array of professional and serious lay tasters. I have taken part and must have been given a bottle which we consumed at lunch on New Year's day: a bright rosehip colour; very little nose; dry, fairly nondescript (the '82 Veuve Clicquot was better, as was the '70 La Tâche!). *Jan 1994* ★★

**A SELECTION OF OTHER '82S** showing as well as could be, or with good potential in the latter part of the 1980s: **DRC**'s **Grands-Echézeaux** powerful, spicy fruit and good length at the opening tasting in 1985. In its fourth year, a healthy ruby red sheen; agreeable weight, fruit and fragrant aftertaste. *1986* ★★★★; **L Jadot**'s **Beaune, Clos des Ursules** cherry red in 1984, dry and spicy. Three years later: well developed, good nose, stylish. *Last tasted 1987* ★★ *probably still drinking well*; **Bouchard Père**'s **Beaune, Teurons** (*sic*) two notes. Pleasant and probably approaching its peak at six years of age. *1988* ★★; **A Rousseau**'s **Chambertin, Clos de Bèze** happily, with the extra dimensions of a *grand cru*; gloriously rich nose; oaky spice flavour and aftertaste. *1987* ★★★; **Philippe Bouzereau**'s **Corton, Bressandes** from his 0.15ha of vines in the Bressandes, and nicely made: scented Pinot nose; pleasant weight, flavour and finish. *1989* ★★★; **Daniel Rion**'s **Nuits-St-Georges** the colour of a 30-year-old tawny port; very ripe Pinot nose and flavour, with very dry oaky finish. *1989* ★★★; **H Gouges**' **Nuits-St-Georges, Vaucrains** at least some ruby; brambly varietal nose; fairly powerful, full-flavoured. *1988* ★★★ *probably holding on nicely*; **Chandon de Briailles**' **Savigny-Lès-Beaune** made, of course, from old vines on his own doorstep and one of the perennial surprises of Burgundy in that even in the spring after the vintage it seemed completely ready for drinking, deliciously forthcoming. Six years later, still a charmer, flowery, flavoury. *1989* ★★★★ *might well still be*; **Simon Bize**'s **Savigny-Lès-Beaune** at that time an up-and-coming grower with an excellent reputation. A brown-tinged maturity even at five years of age, soft, low-keyed nose that, after 30 minutes had developed a marvellous scent; surprising body, alcohol and power, and very good flavour. *1987* ★★★; **H de Montille**'s **Volnay** another star performer. Despite its pallid '82 appearance, a skilful balance of high alcohol and delicacy of flavour, with noticeable tannin and acidity. *1987* ★★★ *almost 4-star. A survivor I suspect*; **La Pousse d'Or**'s **Volnay, Caillerets, Clos des 60 Ouvrées** a *monopole*, a solely owned *clos* within Caillerets, of which this domaine owns one-third. Fairly pale; very sweet, somewhat caramelly nose; light style but fairly alcoholic. Pleasant flavour. *1987. Then* ★★★ *I suppose it might have survived*; **J Grivot**'s **Vosne-Romanée, Beaumonts** a different ball game: some intensity of colour; a rich, warm 'cassis and cobnuts' nose and taste. Sweet, fairly full-bodied, good tannin and acidity. Attractive. *1988* ★★★★; and **Grivot**'s **Nuits-St-Georges, Boudots** from 60-year-old vines, and **Clos Vougeot** both very impressive in their youth ★★★

THE OTHER DRC '82S only noted at the initial trade tasting in 1985: **Romanée-Conti** was seriously impressive, extraordinary rich, scented nose; powerful and penetrating, far superior to the '81. I gave it a potential 4 stars; **Richebourg** sturdy, aromatic; **Echézeaux** luminous; vegetal, fragrant, assertive. All 3 stars and with an interesting future.

# 1983 ★★★ (variable)

'Don't shoot the pianist, he is doing his best'. A difficult and highly controversial vintage, the growing season punctuated by disasters – frost, hail, excessive heat, wet and rot; excessively hard and tannic wines; with hindsight, crass premature marketing and a verging on scandalous report on the DRCs in a major American wine journal. Not for the first time, some of our American cousins have a tendency to blame the producer for problematic wines, blithely forgetting (if they were aware of it in the first place) that unpredictable and uncontrollable weather conditions are primarily responsible.

So, first of all, what *were* the problems during the growing season and what were the results? A cool, wet, dreary spring with localised hail storms in May that cut swathes through the Côte de Nuits – the vineyards of Chambolle-Musigny and Vosne-Romanée were badly affected and lost one-third of their potential crop. However, the subsequent flowering was satisfactory and the months of June and July were exceptionally hot, advancing the grapes' development, concentrating the flesh and thickening the skins. The weather then deteriorated; it was dull and wet from the end of August to mid-September, causing considerable rot problems. Then mixed weather for the harvest. Those who picked late and highly selectively did best.

Undoubtedly, one of the two major problems was rot, for unless every single affected grape is discarded, rotten grapes in a bunch can affect the taste of the wine. The thick, tanned, pigment-laden skins certainly resulted in wines with an impressively deep colour – a complete contrast to the wishy-washy '82s, but on the down side, they also caused the other major problem: excessively harsh tannins.

Aound this period, Drouhin were in the habit of showing their wines early, in the spring after the harvest, and I recall the shock of these dark hard tannic wines – I nearly wrote 'dark satanic' – in fact, it was not a bad description.

Tannin was also a problem for the wines of the Domaine de la Romanée-Conti. Because of this they decided to bottle late, between March and May 1986. One cannot criticise this decision, but a big mistake was made, possibly at the request of their American importers, by shipping the wines soon after bottling, for they were on retailers' shelves by that autumn. Totally unready, totally undrinkable. The retailer and consumer are accustomed to American wine producers deciding on a 'release' date for their wines which, in any case, tend to be more amenable, fruity and drinkable far earlier than bordeaux and even burgundy of the same age. Presumably it was assumed that the DRC '83s, having been distributed to merchants and restaurants in the States, had also been 'released' and were ready for drinking. This was proven not to be the case when, in the autumn of 1986, the scathing article appeared, damning the entire DRC range.

I happened to be in San Francisco at the time and the importers, well-known to me, rushed over a bottle of each of the DRCs to taste. On my way to London, the British importers also brought the full range of '83 DRCs to retaste.

They were harsh, tannic, and at that stage quite unready for drinking. But the folly had been to put them on the market so prematurely and risk equally premature criticism.

**Romanée-Conti** Either this will need half a century in bottle to come round or the tannin will continue inexorably to dominate. I am afraid that I am unlikely ever to know. First tasted in San Francisco on 2 November 1986; the deepest of the '83 DRCs: purple core and intense violet rim; deep, classic Pinot aroma evolving opulently, bramble-like fruit; massive, concentrated and tannic, yet soft and chewy. A similar note a month later in London (I never refer to previous notes, preferring to taste afresh and compare my notes afterwards): a vast, velvety, fruit-packed wine, its extract just about masking its tannin and acidity. 'Great potential'.

I had been given two magnums as an unsolicited fee by the Domaine for writing a strong letter on their behalf which lambasted the earlier American critical review. The first of these magnums I took to Christie's in 1991, and after giving it a few days to settle, decanted it around 12.30pm for a lunch I was hosting in the boardroom. On decanting, I noted a fairly deep colour, more ruddy than red; its aroma was subdued but on the palate massive and dry. Served at 1.20pm, it was really huge and unyielding, tough but with a very fragrant aftertaste. I kept some back: the bouquet after three hours had opened up richly but the wine was still unyielding on the palate. Frankly, disappointing as a drink and still far too immature. I shall hold on to my last magnum as long as possible. *Last tasted March 1991* ★★(★★★) *In 15 to 50 years? Wait and see.*

**La Tâche** Noted at each of the tastings in November 1986: richly coloured; an urgent surging aroma, hard-edged at finish, but evolving gloriously in the glass; crisp, fragrant, lean, penetrating and expanding in the mouth. Hard. Tannic. Most recently at Manfred Wagner's La Tâche vertical, a magnum at lunch between the two sessions. Medium-deep, attractive colour, maturing; a flowery varietal nose, with, I thought, a whiff of rot but not on the palate. After half an hour, 'tea'. Sweet, by no means massive, soft, chewy, with a dry, citrus-like finish. *Last tasted April 1998* ★★★(★) *with slight reservations.*

**Grands-Echézeaux DRC** At both November 1986 tastings: a classic Pinot aroma, firm, good flavour and length, spicy, tannic finish. Three years later, starting to show some maturity at the rim; bouquet very attractive; sweet, well balanced, shapely, good flesh. More recently: mature though still a touch of ruby; rich nose; fullish; very appealing and I did not notice any rot or excessive tannin. As a matter of interest, its price to the trade was £502.52 per dozen 'dpd' (duty paid and delivered). *Last noted at a DRC tasting in London, April 1992* ★★★(★)

**Romanée-St-Vivant DRC** A lovely limpid colour in 1986 but looking like an early developer; delicate, herbaceous bouquet; elegant but firm with very assertive tannins and acidity. Four years later, noticeable colour loss and maturity; very good bouquet; now sweeter and softer, attractive flavour and aftertaste though a touch of bitterness on the finish. Next, in April 1992, seemed low-keyed but full and rich on the palate and still noticeably tannic (price, incidentally, £582.52 per dozen). More recently at the St-Vivant vertical at the Domaine: ruddy coloured; rich, singed flavour, harmonious, then, after an hour sagging a little; distinctly sweet, interesting, lovely, still quite a bite. I rated it fractionally below the '80. *Last tasted Nov 1995* ★★(★)

**Echézeaux DRC** This was the weakest of the range, and in 1986 bottle variation (in San Francisco), more or less matched in London: 'stewed' Pinot, volatile and a biting edge. Bottle variation again in 1990, both fragrant but on nose I thought there was a touch of rot. Distinctly below standard. Two years later, bottle variation again: distinctly mature looking; noses initially sweet and appealing though one bottle a bit corky – or was it rot? Sweet, soft, dry finish – and, as always, in a comparatively modest – for DRC – price range. £382.52 dpd *Last tasted April 1992* ★★?

**Chambertin A Rousseau** Two notes in the mid-1990s. Ripe; sweet, good flavour, 'hopeless with cheese' at Neville Abrahams' 20th anniversary dinner at Soho-Soho in 1994. The following spring, fully mature looking; subtle, complex nose, almost too sweet; good flavour, power, length, tannin and acidity. *Last noted at a Rousseau tasting in Florida, March 1995* ★★★★ *Should be excellent now.*

**Chambertin, Clos de Bèze A Rousseau** Fairly deep, rich; soft, harmonious, high alcohol; fairly sweet, full-bodied. An expanding flavour. *At the same Hollywood Wine Society event, Florida, March 1995* ★★★★ *Good life predicted.*

**Chambertin, Héritiers Latour L Latour** At ten years of age: medium-pale, open, mature; sweet, very attractive nose and lovely flavour. *High marks at a pre-sale tasting of 'An Outstanding Cellar of Fine and Rare Wines', Dec 1993* ★★★★

**Chambolle-Musigny, Charmes Moillard** Mediocre nose; swingeingly dry, very hard tannic end. No 'charm' in evidence. *Dinner after a tasting at Lyford Cay in the Bahamas, Feb 1997* ★ *I do not think that this will benefit from bottle ageing.*

**Charmes-Chambertin A Rousseau** The biggest *grand cru* vineyard in Gevrey and one of the biggest in Burgundy. Lovely colour, gentle gradation; equally gentle, harmonious nose, more scented than varietal; some sweetness, elegant, crisp, good tannins. *At the Rousseau tasting, Florida, March 1995* ★★★★

**Charmes-Chambertin Taupenot-Merme** The 66th wine and the oldest vintage at a British Airways red burgundy tasting for Concorde. Deep, too brown; correct old Pinot, attractive in its way, but it wouldn't fly. *June 1999* ★

**Ch Corton-Grancey L Latour** A good, deep, chewy cask sample in October 1985. Four years later, considerable colour change, mature, rosehip-hued; fully developed, very sweet, good, rich flavour, noticeably tannic. Most recently, now a deceptively orange tawny colour; attractive, gentle, subdued, mature Pinot nose; lean, good flavour but certainly lots of grip, hard and acidic. *At the bicentenary opening tasting, June 1997* ★★? *I cannot see the fruit surviving the tannin. Will be interesting to see.*

**Corton, Hospices, Cuvée Charlotte Dumay Lupé-Cholet** 'Warm', mature appearance; stewed Pinot, hard; frankly unattractive, 'brackish', dry finish. *Office sample. Not accepted for sale, Sept 1994.*

**Corton, Hospices, Cuvée Dr Peste Rossignol** Sweet, powerful, very tannic. *Sept 1991* ★★(★)? *The odds are in favour of this opening up and softening, but there is no guarantee.*

**Echézeaux Pierre Bourrée** Stewed Pinot; sweet, flavoury, good length but teeth-gripping tannins. *At a pre-sale tasting, Dec 1993* ★★(★)

**Gevrey-Chambertin, Les Cazetiers A Rousseau** Rich, mature; 'beetroot' Pinot opening up beautifully, whiff of raspberry; sweet, powerful, very tannic. *At Rousseau's tasting, Florida, March 1995* ★★★(★)? *All depends on tannins ameliorating.*

**Gevrey-Chambertin, Clos St-Jacques A Rousseau** First noted at the Rousseau tasting in Florida, 1995: rim, mature; crisp, fragrant; very flavoury but crisp, citrus-like acidity. Eight months later, in the company of Charles Rousseau at the Marcobrunn and Chambertin dinner at Schloss Reinhartshausen in the Rheingau: in the candlelight looked

very deep; a nutty, penetrating varietal scent; chunky, chewy, powerful, aggressive and swingeingly tannic. Not even the rich food tamed it. *Last tasted Nov 1995* ★★★★ *for impressiveness,* ★★ *for drinking then. What of its future? Well, I hope for the best.*

**Clos de la Roche A Rousseau** Fairly deep, ruddy-hued; rich, earthy nose that opened up well but with sweaty tannic overload; powerful, rounded, and teeth-gripping tannins. *At the Rousseau tasting in Florida, March 1995* ★★(★★)? *A typical '83 conundrum. Which way is it heading? It might turn out well but I would not bank on it.*

**Ruchottes-Chambertin A Rousseau** Deep; rich, high extract, attractive now; fairly sweet, full-bodied, lovely fruit and tannin. *At the Rousseau tasting in Florida, March 1995* ★★★(★) *Once again, a tannic overload but it will, I think, turn out impressively.*

**Volnay, Clos des Angles Prosper Maufoux** Unimpressive, very tannic. Not even tamed or improved by *filo borek* (cheese in a pastry roll). *At a Saintsbury Club dinner, unusually dominated by burgundy, and with two California Pinot Noirs, Oct 1996. Better for us old fellows to stick to claret.*

### SOME OTHER '83S, ALL LAST TASTED IN 1990

**Beaune, Clos des Mouches J Drouhin** Showing well at the opening tasting in 1984, purple-tinged of course and oaky. After six years: looking fully mature; touch of strawberry and liquorice; assertive, good fruit and flavour. One of the best of the decade. *At Drouhin, Oct 1990* ★★★★

**Beaune, Toussaints René Monnier** Very pronounced varietal aroma; good flavour, body, fruit and extract but a fairly hard tannic finish. *March 1990* ★★★

**Beaune, Clos des Ursules L Jadot** Deep yet mature; bouquet opened up fragrantly; full of fruit, extract and velvety tannins. *With André Gagey at Jadot, Oct 1990* ★★★★

**Chambertin, Clos de Bèze Damoy** Sweet, rather smelly old beetroot nose, tannic and overripe. Dry, leathery, tannic finish. *Feb 1990* ★★?

**Chambertin, Clos de Bèze L Jadot** Rich nose but with sweaty tannins like old socks – and as old socks do, improved with air; very distinctive 'fishy' Chambertin Pinot flavour. Distinctive. A bit hollow. Perhaps better than my comments. *Oct 1990* ★★★?

**Gevrey-Chambertin, Estournelles St-Jacques Clair-Daü** Smell like a singed doormat; sweet, chewy, flavoury but rather bitter tannic finish. *Jan 1990* ★★

**Pommard Thomas-Bassot** Palish, rosy-hued; hard, stewed Pinot nose and taste. Very dry tannic finish. *Jan 1990* ★

**Clos de Tart** Lively colour; fragrant, cherry-like, then strange off-scents like lead-free petrol – the effect of hail I was told. Full-flavoured but very astringent with an aggressive stalky end. *At the domaine, Oct 1990* ★

**Vosne-Romanée J Grivot** Pale; bramble-like Pinot opening up pleasantly; fairly sweet, flavour of sweet beetroot, good length. Tannic, of course, but not aggressively so. *At Le Gavroche in Mayfair, Feb 1990* ★★★★

### SOME OTHER '83S, LAST TASTED IN THE LATE 1980S

**L Latour's Gevrey-Chambertin, Cazetiers** a deep, brambly cask sample, opening up in the autumn of 1985. Four years later: considerable colour loss, a palish, warm tawny; sweet, good flavour but tannic. *Last tasted Nov 1989* ★★★?; **P Leclerc's Gevrey-Chambertin, Cazetiers** crimson sheen; almost Pauillac oyster shell scent, a version of Chambertin's 'fishy' Pinot; sweet, soft, fleshy, fruity, delicious. *Feb 1989* ★★★★; and

H **Magnien's** Gevrey-Chambertin, **Cazetiers** brick red; gentle, floral, walnuts and dried raisins nose; powerful, good length, extremely tannic (I noted that Magnien believes in long fermentation. His wines tend to be austere). *Feb 1989. Then ★★(★★)*; **L Latour's** Pommard, **Epenots** cask sample looking prematurely aged; huge, very tannic. Later, a gentle rosy glow; ripe bouquet; sweet, less massive, soft despite its tannins. *Nov 1989 ★★★*; **L Latour's** Romanée-St-Vivant, **Les Quatre Journaux** elegant cask sample, good length and future. Four autumns later: glowingly mature; fragrant; sweet, fullish, lovely flavour, elegance noted again. *Nov 1989 ★★★★*; and **Mongeard-Mugneret's** Vosne-Romanée, **Orveaux** fully mature looking; good, 'vegetal' Pinot nose that became richer and smoother as the air got to it. Flavour to match. High alcohol and needing bottle age. *Feb 1988 ★★★★*

# 1984

One of the most lacklustre vintages of the decade. Eminently forgettable. But, once again, not the fault of the growers who had to contend with a poor spring, late flowering and *millerandage*; a respite with heat and sun in July but a stormy August and very rainy September, one of the wettest on record. Late, damp and dismal harvest.

**La Tâche** Fairly pale and orange-tinged at the importers' tasting in 1990, nose also fully evolved but loads of tannin. Lacking the flair and elegance of La Tâche at its best, but fairly impressive. Two years later at a DRC tasting in London: chocolatey nose; sweet, chewy, good flavour. Ready. More recently at Wagner's La Tâche vertical: now pale, amber-orange and with a tired brown edge – like an autumn leaf. Nose more interesting, fragrant, ripe, touch of malt, opening up richly, but after 30 minutes seemed to turn in on itself; medium sweetness and body, decent enough flavour but lacking its usual length. *Last tasted April 1998 ★*

**Romanée-St-Vivant** DRC Also orange-brown-rimmed in 1990; a singed, chocolatey, chaptalised nose; chunky, agreeable. At the DRC tasting in 1992, the bouquet seemed soft and pleasantly up-turned; sweet, 'agreeable' again, dry slightly acidic finish (half the price of the '83). Most recently, at the Domaine, served with *faisan en cocotte lutée*. Unusually in Burgundy, the wine had been decanted: a lovely rich colour and nose, first a bit chocolatey, then minty; sweet yet tannic, some power and grip though lacking length and with a slightly coarse finish. *Last tasted Nov 1995 ★★*

**Grands-Echézeaux** DRC Only one note. Fairly deep; good fruit; sweet and drinking well. *At the DRC tasting at Painters' Hall, London, April 1992 ★★★ Drink up*.

**Echézeaux** DRC At eight years of age: pale and luminous; rich, 'stewed fruit' nose; sweet, adequate fruit, touch of pepperiness and dry, slightly bitter finish. Almost half the price of the '83 and half the price of the '84 La Tâche. *At Painters' Hall, London, April 1992 ★★*

THE FOLLOWING WERE ALL TASTED IN THE EARLY 1990S

**Beaune, Clos des Mouches** J Drouhin Low alcohol: 12.3%, acidity 3.8g/l. Rather weak and watery-rimmed; light, floral nose; raw fruit and acidic. After the '81, the least satisfactory vintage of the decade. *At Drouhin, Oct 1990*.

**Gevrey-Chambertin** L Trapet Pale, pink highlights; unknit; strange, piquant, beetroot flavour. *March 1990*.

**Musigny** de Vogüé The palest and most developed looking of all the Musignys of the decade. Nose sweet, vegetal, high-

toned, developing in the glass, pleasantly scented; earthy, touch of liquorice. *At the domaine, Oct 1990 ★★ (just)*.

**Beaune, Grèves, Vignes de l'Enfant Jésus** Dom du Ch de Beaune Harvested from 2 October. Unattractive, sweaty, fungi nose; dry, mediocre, raw. *At Bouchard Père, Nov 1994*.

**Chapelle-Chambertin** L Trapet 'Surprisingly agreeable for an '84'. Good, rich Pinot nose and flavour. *With Salmis de Faisan at Le Jardin des Gourmets, London, Nov 1994 ★★★*

**Echézeaux** H Jayer It was with eager anticipation that I approached this Jayer wine. It was corked. *At a pre-sale tasting, Los Angeles, Feb 1998*. I am sure it would have been the best '84.

**Vosne-Romanée** Gerard Mugneret Rosehip tawny; a mild stewed Pinot nose; dry, some grip, unimpressive. *April 1990 ★*

AND, FOR THE RECORD, three Hospices de Beaune wines *élevés* and bottled by Rossignol for a Swiss gentleman, and all tarred with the same brush: **Beaune, Hospices, Cuvée Dr Peste** full of fruit but taste of young port. *Sept 1991*; **Corton, Dr Peste** – the old doctor was very generous in his donations to the Hospices – some fruit, flavoury, but raw. *July 1992*; and **Mazis-Chambertin, Cuvée Madeleine-Collignon** dry, lean – oh dear. *Sept 1991*. They had one common denominator: a poor nose, varnishy, malty sometimes with a dollop of jam. Was this the vintage *élevage* or poor storage?

# 1985 ★★★★★

One of my favourite burgundy vintages. Certainly some of my most consistently glowing notes.

The weather conditions were interesting: unprecedented low temperatures in January, snow in February delaying budding but minimising the risk of late frosts. Delayed flowering; June and July were fairly normal but, from the first week in August, heat and drought, then hail storms; 25% of the crop in Aloxe-Corton was destroyed, but surviving vines produced excellent wines – see the several Corton notes below. From 1 September constant sunshine. A ripe, healthy crop and one of the best vintages in most growers' memories.

A wide range of '85s tasted and noted below. They demonstrate the superiority and extra depth of the *grands crus*, the quality of *1ers crus* as well as, even in a vintage like this, the variations between village wines. Add to this classification system the variations between domaine- and French-bottled (note, however, no English bottlings).

**Romanée-Conti** Alas, only one note: concentrated nose; very sweet, rich, multi-dimensional. *Tasting a client's stock in New York, Feb 1996 ★★★★★*

**La Tâche** First tasted at the Domaine, October 1990: deep, rich, intense yet showing some maturity; extraordinary aroma, back to its brilliant self after the preceding dreary vintages, spreading and fluttering its wings like a bird after rain. The sweetness of ripe grapes and alcohol, assertive, great length, dry finish. Six years later, from an American cellar, showing well. Also in New York, at a BYOB dinner in 1997 – what deliciously extravagant wines our American friends bring to these informal events. The wine was lovely. The following year at Wagner's vertical: now medium-pale, attractive; a light, fragrant Pinot aroma, then opened up beautifully and within 30 minutes fully evolved. Believe it or not, after four hours in the glass (I only left a little!), lovely, still exuding charm, and an hour after that reminding me of a shop dispensing aromatherapy oils. On the palate sweet, nice weight, lovely flavour, perfect balance. One of the best of Wagner's 60 vintages. Most recently: beautiful in all respects. At its most gloriously fragrant best. *Last noted at the closing dinner of Stephen Kaplan's 1985 vintage event in Chicago, April 2000* ★★★★★

**Richebourg DRC** First tasted in 1996: hefty; very dry finish. Most recently: still deeply coloured; 'hefty' used again to which I also added 'glorious'; a massive wine with loads of grip. Tannic. Superb but not a heart-on-sleeve wine. It needs time. *Last noted at Kaplan's closing dinner at the Four Seasons, Chicago, April 2000* ★★(★★) *Say 2006–2020.*

**Grands-Echézeaux DRC** Lunching at the Domaine in 1990: still youthful; good fruit but unready; a confident entry, great style, silky tannins. In 1996, lined up with all the other '85 DRCs, seemed relatively low-keyed though very good. Most recently: excellent, mature Pinot bouquet and flavour. Great length, marvellous fragrance. *Last noted at a Christie's pre-sale tasting at the American Club, Tokyo. Nov 1999* ★★★★★

**Romanée-St-Vivant DRC** My highest overall mark at the St-Vivant vertical (1978–1991) in November 1995: exuberantly fragrant, soft mocha, then walnuts and autumnal berries; expanded quickly in the mouth, glorious flavour and finish. Three months later: very sweet, rich, delicious. *Last tasted Feb 1996* ★★★★★ *Drink now or keep another 5 years or so.*

**Echézeaux DRC** Scented, sweet and attractive. *Feb 1996* ★★★★

**Beaune, La Mignotte Leroy** Ruby and still youthful for a mature '85; good fruit; soft, fleshy, penetrating flavour. *At a Christie's pre-sale tasting in Tokyo, Nov 1999* ★★★★

**Beaune, Boucherottes L Jadot** One of the eight '85s tasted blind at the Haberdashers' Company in the City of London: mature; good, ripe, varietal nose; sweet, crisp, good flavour, a bit hard on the finish but recommended 'drink'. *Jan 1993* ★★★ *Doubtless fully evolved now.*

**Bonnes-Mares Clair-Daü** All I got on the nose was a good deal of vanillin. It became too sweet. On the palate, crisp, very flavoury. *At a Bacchus Society dinner in Memphis, Sept 1999* ★★★

**Bonnes-Mares L Jadot** Rich, harmonious 'stewed' Pinot nose; fairly sweet, fullish, punchy tannins and acidity. Recommended 'hold'. *At the Haberdashers' Company in the City of London, Jan 1993* ★★(★) *then. Should be ready now.*

**Chambertin A Rousseau** At a burgundy tasting for 'Wine Japan' in 1990: tremendous power and depth; sweet, mouthfilling, lovely aftertaste. 'Worth flying to Tokyo for'. Most recently, now medium depth, lovely colour, mature rim; excellent bouquet; magical, highly sensitive fruit, elegant, perfect condition. *Last noted dining with Andrea and Christian Sauska in his apartment with fabulous views over Budapest, Aug 2000* ★★★★★

**Chambertin, Clos de Bèze A Rousseau** Medium, rather a weak rim; quite good classic 'fishy' Pinot nose; very flavoury but a lot of oak. Recommended 'hold'. *At the Haberdashers' Company in the City of London, Jan 1993* ★★(★★) *then. Doubtless fully evolved now.*

**Corton J Drouhin** Fairly deep; perfectly harmonious, gentle, touch of spice; medium sweet, matching flavour, smooth, lovely. Perfection. *Two bottles, dining with Kate and Bill Baker in Somerset, Jan 2001* ★★★★★

**Corton Dom Sénard** Still a touch of ruby; brambly fruit and 'roast beef'; a powerful, tannic wine, good potential. Sénard was a delightful old man who spoke flawless English. Much missed. *Last noted dining at the restaurant, De Biggarden on the outskirts of Brussels, Jan 1996* ★★(★)

**Corton Tollet-Beaut** Sweet, fudge-like (soft toffee); sweet, rich, easy, very agreeable. *Noted at a pre-sale tasting, New York, Nov 2000* ★★★

**Corton, Clos des Cortons Faiveley** In 1993: sweet, rich, delicious. A year later: medium-deep, ruby core, maturing; lovely varietal aroma and taste; fairly sweet, chewy, spicy and tannic. *Last noted dining with Freiherr von Kühlmann at Schloss Ramholz, Germany, before packing his wines, June 1994* ★★★

**Corton, Maréchaudes de Mérode** Deep, earthy, almost meaty Pinot nose. Frankly not very interesting. Why mention it? Not all '85s are sublime. *At a pre-sale tasting, Feb 1992* ★★

**Ch Corton-Grancey L Latour** Four notes. The best of an interesting range at a Latour tasting in 1990, still fairly deep and youthful; immature blackberry-like aroma; 'nutty' Corton flavour, good length. Seven years later at Latour's bicentenary tasting, then at the dinner in Beaune, still fairly deep; very mature fig/prune-like nose and taste. Hefty, fleshy, high extract, old fashioned type of wine. Good flavour. More recently at a Latour seminar I conducted for the Hollywood Wine Society, one of the best of eight vintages from 1961–1995: sweet, good fruit, nicely evolved. *Last tasted March 1998* ★★★★

**Echézeaux Jacques Cacheux et Fils** Fully mature though a touch of hardness on the nose; fairly sweet, good crisp fruit. Cacheux was new to me, so I looked them up in Hanson's *Burgundy*. Out of six parcels totalling 4.57ha, they own 0.66ha of the *grand cru* Echézeaux. *Pulled out of Bob Dickinson's excellent cellar in Miami, Nov 1997* ★★★

**Echézeaux Thomas-Bassot** Fairly pale, rosy-hued, very mature appearance but better flavour and more bite than expected. *Pre-sale tasting, Los Angeles, March 1999* ★★★ *(just).*

**Gevrey-Chambertin, Combe aux Moines P Leclerc** Mature; fragrant; attractive fruit. Very drinkable. *At a pre-sale tasting, March 1999* ★★★ *Drink soon.*

**Gevrey-Chambertin, Clos St-Jacques L Jadot** Glorious fruit and flesh. *Last tasted Feb 1993* ★★★★★

**Gevrey-Chambertin, Clos St-Jacques A Rousseau** Mature; an exciting surge of fragrance, fully evolved, basking in perfect maturity; sweet, gorgeously lush flavour. Pinot at its best. *At the Rousseau St-Jacques vertical, Florida, March 1995* ★★★★★ *Perfection now.*

**Clos des Lambrays** Fairly deep, lively; lovely, rich, singed Pinot; perfect weight, good grip, responsive. *Lunch at Bill Baker's, April 1994* ★★★★

**Latricières-Chambertin L Ponsot** Glorious fragrance; excellent flavour, body and balance. *With Filet of Beef at the Josey pre-sale dinner, New York, Nov 2000* ★★★★ *Fully evolved now.*

**Mazis-Chambertin J Faiveley** Probably the least known *grand cru* of the immense Faiveley holdings. Good colour, surprisingly intense; very good vegetal Pinot aroma; fairly sweet and full, lovely flavour, touch of bitterness on the finish. *At Gidleigh Park, Devon, Feb 1995* ★★★★ *Should be at peak now.*

**Mazis-Chambertin, Hospices, Cuvée Madeleine-Collignon Leroy** Fairly deep; 'warm'; scented, vanillin; sweet, fragrant, a light rein, delicious. *In New York, Feb 1996* ★★★★

**Musigny, Vieilles Vignes de Vogüé** Showing well, fully mature, very rich and attractive (New York, 1996). A very similar note two years later, adding 'good but not great'. *Late supper at Christopher Burr's after music making, Aug 1998* ★★★★

**Nuits-Meurgers H Jayer** Surprisingly deep; almost Italianate brambly fruit, opened up well; medium sweetness, by no means light (13% alcohol), lovely flavour, good grip. *Lunching with Jo Gryn in The Wine Bar, Brussels, March 1995* ★★★★

**Nuits-St-Georges R Ampeau** Not bad. Not good enough. *At Lyford Cay in the Bahamas, March 1996* ★★

**Nuits-St-Georges Leroy** Should have been decanted. Well made, lots of flavour, ready. *At Lyford Cay, Feb 1998* ★★★

**Nuits-St-Georges, Clos des Argillières L Latour**
Unconvincing appearance; slightly 'stewed' Pinot nose; quite
good flavour, some grip. Would not inspire me to bid high. *At
a pre-sale tasting, London, Dec 1993* ★★
**Nuits-St-Georges, Clos de la Maréchale Faiveley** Good
nose; medium sweetness, fullish body, rich, crisp, good length,
tannic. *At the Haberdashers' Company in the City of London, Jan
1993* ★★★★ *(just). Should be fully evolved now.*
**Nuits-St-Georges, Les Poirets R Arnoux** Good, rich,
singed Pinot nose; sweet, medium weight, pleasant easy style –
yet Arnoux' old-fashioned reputation is for powerful wines. *At
a Sunday wine lunch at Chippenham Lodge, Aug 1994* ★★★
**Pommard Olivier Leflaive** Sweet, crisp, good acidity. *At the
Haberdashers' Company in the City of London, Jan 1993* ★★★
**Richebourg J Gros** Smell of gravy (meaty Pinot); sweet,
attractive. *At the Josey pre-sale tasting, Nov 2000* ★★★
**Clos de la Roche A Rousseau** Mature; good, rich, varietal
nose and flavour. Fairly sweet and full-bodied. Nice weight
and balance. *Lunch at Bill Baker's, April 1994* ★★★★
**Romanée-St-Vivant, Les Quatre Journaux L Latour** In
1992: full of fruit and tannin. Good length and finish. Three
years later: sweet, rich, vanillin; very sweet, fruit, a bit 'stewed'
but attractive. *Last noted at a Gidleigh Park wine dinner in Devon,
Feb 1995* ★★★★ *Doubtless fully developed now.*
**Savigny-Lès-Beaune, Les Lavières R Ampeau** Not much
red left; true Pinot aroma, subtle, soft, harmonious; almost a
caricature of Pinot. Verging on liquorice. Very good in its way.
*At my Lyford Cay burgundy tasting in the Bahamas, Feb 1998* ★★★★
**Volnay Lafarge** I admire the Lafarge family's Volnays but
found this a bit unconvincing, certainly unexciting, dry and
tannic. *At the Haberdashers' Company, Jan 1993* ★★
**Volnay, Clos des Chênes Lafarge** Vastly superior to their
village wine. Lovely, rich ruby; crisp, delicious nose; flavour
lively and lovely, perfect acidity. *Dining with my agent, Bob
Lescher, at Montrachet, New York, Feb 1996* ★★★★
**Vosne-Romanée, Suchots Thomas-Bassot** Dry and
uninteresting. Why mention? Read between the lines. *At a pre-
sale tasting, New York, Sept 1997* ★

OTHER '85s SHOWING WELL WHEN LAST TASTED
BETWEEN 1990 AND 1992 A Morot's Beaune, Bressandes
★★★★; J Drouhin's Beaune, Clos des Mouches ★★★★★;
L Jadot's Beaune, Clos des Ursules ★★★★; G Roumier's
Bonnes-Mares ★★★★; L Latour's Chambertin, Héritiers
Latour ★★★★★; Bouchard Père's Le Corton, Dom du Ch
de Beaune ★★★★; J Drouhin's Echézeaux ★★★★★;
J-F Mugnier's Musigny ★★★★; de Vogüé's Musigny ★★★★★;
H Gouges' Nuits-St-Georges, Porrets-St-Georges,
Nuits-St-Georges, Les Pruliers and Nuits-St-Georges,
Les-St-Georges all ★★★★; Boissot's Pommard, Hospices,
Cuvée Billardet ★★★★; Dujac's Clos de la Roche ★★★★★;
Clos de Tart ★★★★★; and J Drouhin's Vosne-Romanée,
Suchots and Clos Vougeot, both ★★★★★

# 1986 ★★★★

I was tempted to demote this vintage to 3 stars but felt this
would be unfair, particularly in the light of insufficient
evidence of the current drinkability of so many wines tasted
only in the early 1990s. The growing season was reasonably
satisfactory with a mild spring, excellent flowering in a warm
and sunny June, conditions continuing, with occasional storms
in late August and early September causing rot problems. A
late harvest, from 28 September, enjoyed good weather. Late
pickers made the best wines. This has turned out to be a
largely forgotten vintage, and I for one will look out for any
wines that come on to the market.
**La Tâche** Even in the very early 1990s, beginning to show
some maturity; very good, rich, vegetal fragrance; ripe
sweetness, full-bodied, touch of bitterness, inimitable aftertaste.
Most recently noted at Wagner's very useful La Tâche vertical.
Now mature, singed, spicy Pinot, seeming unknit at first but
opened up fragrantly and the small amount left in my glass
holding well for over four hours. Good, firm, fullish, flavoury.
*Last noted April 1998* ★★★★ *Now–2010.*
**Richebourg DRC** First tasted in 1989: misleadingly pale
appearance for a powerful, tannin-laden wine. The following
year: a soft, autumnal red-brown; lovely, gentle, open nose;
silky, leathery tannins. *Last tasted Jan 1990. Then* ★(★★★)
*Probably at its best from 2006 onwards.*
**Grands-Echézeaux DRC** First tasted in 1990: sweet, rich,
tannic. The following year, fairly deep yet browning at rim;
rich, soft, harmonious, but still very tannic. *Not tasted since Nov
1991. Then* (★★★). *Doubtless fully evolved now but with a future
well into the first decade of the current century.*
**Romanée-St-Vivant DRC** In spite of the close proximity of
the vineyards, a totally different style to the Richebourg. Tasted
twice in 1990: coffee, mocha, truffles on the nose though
tannic, verging on raw. A jump of five years to the DRC St-
Vivant vertical: surprisingly pale, open, weak-rimmed, orange-
tinged; a fully evolved, singed, mature nose, fragrant, vegetal.
Rich but no development though settled down harmoniously;
medium-dry, attractive flavour and style, lean, dry, tannic finish.
*Last tasted Nov 1995* ★★★ *Say now–2010?*

THE FOLLOWING ARE THE BEST, or the most salutary, tasted
between 1990 and 1993. None tasted recently.
**Beaune, Clos des Mouches J Drouhin** Alcohol a modest
12.6%, acidity fractionally higher, at 4g/l. Showing well at the
vertical of the decade: a rosy glow; forthcoming, fragrant;
distinctive, assertive, high tannin content. *Oct 1990* ★(★★★). *Will
be fully evolved now.*
**Beaune, Hospices, Cuvée Hugues et L Bétault** Varnishy
overtone, like an old tobacco pouch, and **Cuvée Maurice
Drouhin**. Both dry and lean, the latter softer and with better
length. Swiss stock. *Sept 1991* ★★
**Beaune, Teurons Dom du Ch de Beaune** In 1988, palish with
youthful tinge. In 1990 not much red left. A year later, rosy-
hued; sweet and attractive with more power and bite than
expected. Last tasted Feb 1991. *Then* ★★★(★) *but I think this was
overrated on my part.*
**Beaune, Close des Ursules L Jadot** The enologist told me
that such is the peculiarity of Pinot Noir that it would gain
colour. A soft, very scented nose; lightish style but good
supporting tannin and acidity. *Oct 1990* ★(★★★) *Probably drinking
well now.*
**Bonnes-Mares L Jadot** Another misleadingly pale Jadot wine;
Sweet nose but very tannic. *June 1990* (★★★) *But has probably
grown in stature and certainly in drinkability.*
**Le Corton Dom du Ch de Beaune** The opposite to the two
Jadot wines. After two years less deep, but with a not dissimilar
scented, vanillin nose; fullish Corton body. Very agreeable. *Last
noted Oct 1990. Then* ★(★★★) *Probably delicious now.*
**Corton, Clos du Roi Prince de Mérode** Fruit overruled by
tannins. *At a pre-sale tasting, Feb 1992* (★★) *Hopefully will have
shed its hardness.*

**Gevrey-Chambertin, Cazetiers** J Drouhin Weak; stewed; unconvincing. *Dec 1990* ★★

**Gevrey-Chambertin, Estournelles-St-Jacques** L Jadot Alcohol 13.2%. Lovely, rich, biscuity nose; good flavour, very tannic. *At Kobrand's Jadot tasting in New York, Feb 1993* ★★★

**Musigny** de Vogüé Fragrant, scented – like an Oregon Pinot Noir – lean, spicy, good future. *Oct 1990. Then* ★(★★★) *Doubtless drinking well now.*

**Nuits-St-Georges, Porrets-St-Georges** H Gouges Fragrant, full, firm ★★★(★); **Les Pruliers** fragrant, touch of bitterness, needs time (★★★); **Les St-Georges** hefty, fruity, lots of grip (★★★★). *All tasted Aug 1991.*

**Clos de Tart** Two notes in 1990: immature; brambly, smoky; good flavour, firm, tannic. Two years later, the oldest of four vintages: lovely, fragrant nose; good flavour but very tannic, quite a bite. *Last tasted at Mommessin's, March 1992* ★(★★) *Possibly 4 stars but not guaranteed.*

**Clos Vougeot, Musigni** (sic) Gros Frères Good colour; very good Pinot nose and flavour. 'Perfect now'. *Lunching with Bill Baker and Terence Conran at Le Pont de la Tour, London, Jan 1993* ★★★★ *Hard to see how this could improve.*

The best, those with the most promise, tasted in the late 1980s Lafarge's Beaune, Grèves ★★★★ and Volnay, Clos au Ch des Ducs ★★★★; Bouchard Père's Beaune, Grèves, Vignes de l'Enfant Jésus ★★★★; André Mussy's Beaune, Montremenots ★★★; G Roumier's Chambolle-Musigny ★★★; Alain Burguet's Gevrey-Chambertin, Vieilles Vignes from Burguet's 4ha and 'his most dependable wine' (according to Hanson) ★★★; Faiveley's Mazis-Chambertin ★★★★; Monthelie-Douhairet's Pommard, Champans ★★★; and from J-F Mugnier Chambolle-Musigny, Amoureuses ★★★, Fuées ★★★ and Le Musigny ★★★★

# 1987 ★★★

Good, but not as good as the early reports indicated for though it was indeed a small crop, with grapes with a high ratio of skin to juice, my notes indicate that there was a good deal of chaptalisation. Chaptalised wines are often very attractive when young, but do not retain their appeal.

The growing conditions were not easy though budding was early enough. However, heavy rains in May and June hampered flowering, resulting in poor fruit set and – later – a small late harvest. The summer was changeable. The late harvest, from 5 October, took place in warm sunshine. Late pickers, as so often, fared best.

**La Tâche** Not for the first time, a 'contrary Mary'. At the opening tasting in February 1990: nose refined, fragrant; sweet, lean and long. Eleven months later 'richly coloured though not deep'; more assertive and tannic than expected. The following spring (1992), at Painters' Hall, neither deep nor pale; characteristic Pinot nose; good fruit but austere (and a 'shocking' price: £937 per case, nearly twice the price of the '84). Put into perspective at Wagner's vertical in 1998: then fairly pale, weak amber-tawny rim; the smell of a wet retriever, sweet, caramelly and unconvincing; medium sweet, on the light side, quite an attractive development but short. A year later: pale, 'unconvincing' applied to its appearance; sweet, slightly singed, fully developed nose; richer and more body than its colour led one to anticipate. *Last noted at a pre-sale tasting in New York, May 1999* ★★★ *But unenthusiastic.*

**Romanée-St-Vivant** DRC Slight bottle variation at the opening tasting, February 1990: indeterminate appearance; low-keyed, vegetal. The second bottle better, more grip and elegance. A year later: mature; soft, rather chocolatey; sweet, very flavoury, good follow through. 'My style of wine'. In 1992, the same chocolatey nose noted, and elegance. Dry, powerful, tannic. Next, at the DRC St-Vivant tasting: softly coloured, open, mature; sweet, 'chocolatey' noted yet again; the second bottle was almost sickly sweet, both with notable vanillin. One bottle dry, lightish, clearly chaptalised and with a short, coarse, dry finish. The second was horribly sweet, also coarse and tannic. All these bottles noted above came from the DRC cellars. *Last tasted Nov 1995* ★★

So what is one to think of the DRC '87s? I have not tasted the rest of the range since the early 1990s.

**Romanée-Conti** Pale; low-keyed but genuinely complex; assertive, considerable length, tannin, acidity. *Feb 1990* (★★★)?

**Richebourg** Slight bottle variation in 1991. Both paler than expected, both full-bodied and dry. One seemed more fragrant. The following year it seemed sweeter, flowery for Richebourg though good, rich and meaty round the waist. Dry finish. (High price: £852.) *Last noted May 1992* (★★★★)

**Grands-Echézeaux** In 1990, low-keyed, bitter tannins. The following year: palish, open, luminous; chocolatey (chaptalised), slightly stewed nose; soft fruit, adequate tannin and acidity. *Last tasted Jan 1991 (not available for tasting in 1993)* ★★★ *Seemed a quick developer.*

**Echézeaux** Slight bottle variation in 1990, better at the opening DRC tasting. Rather scented, delicious flavour but tannic. In 1991, a pale plummy colour, browning; soft fruit, like crushed strawberries. Fairly lean and tannic but lacking the thrust of its elder brother, Grands-Echézeaux. The following year, surprisingly sweet, strawberry noted again; overall drier and more powerful than expected. *Last noted April 1992* ★★★

Of the few '87s tasted in the mid-1990s

**Beaune, Grèves, Vignes de L'Enfant Jésus** Dom du Ch de Beaune Grapes picked 29 September. Weak-rimmed; singed, stewed, chaptalised nose and flavour. Raw tannins. *In the cellars of Bouchard Père, Nov 1995. Not very good.*

**Le Corton** Dom du Ch de Beaune Medium-deep, maturing; not bad nose or flavour but not up to *grand vin* standards. *In Bouchard Père's cellars, Nov 1995*

**La Romanée 'Grand Cru Exclusivité'** Dom du Ch de Vosne-Romanée Picking from 22 September. Open, mature; very scented, chaptalised nose and flavour. Sweet, short. *In Bouchard Père's cellars, Nov 1995* ★

**Vosne-Romanée, Champs Perdrix** Perrin-Rossin Palish, maturing; slightly vegetal nose; medium sweet and body, quite good flavour. More interesting to see how it tasted in different shaped glasses. Seriously better in a Riedel burgundy glass. (Hanson states that the controversial Guy Accad was involved from the 1982 to 1988 vintages though, because of the mixed results with the 1987, there was a change of advisor.) *Magically presented by Georg Riedel, at Christie's, April 1996* ★★★

Of the many other '87s tasted in the very early 1990s, most were fairly consistently in the 3-star range, including J Drouhin's Beaune, Clos des Mouches pink-cheeked, quite attractive, more acidity than tannin (Robert Drouhin told me that he preferred his '87s to '86s, even in the Côte de Nuits); L Jadot's Chambertin, Clos de Bèze deep, aggressive, much tannin due to a 26-day maceration; **J-F Mugnier**'s **Chambolle-Musigny** well balanced; **R Groffier**'s **Chambolle-Musigny, Sentiers** delicious, spicy; **Fontaine-Gagnard**'s **Chassagne-Montrachet, 1er Cru** meaty, powerful, tannic; **Chandon de Briailles**' **Corton-Bressandes** powerful ★★★★; **Faiveley**'s **Corton, Clos des Cortons** ★★★★; **J Drouhin**'s **Morey-St-Denis, Clos des Ormes**; **Dujac**'s **Clos de la Roche**; **D Rion**'s **Vosne-Romanée** powerful, good mouthful ★★★★; and **J Drouhin**'s **Clos Vougeot**.

# 1988 ★★★★★

With the '85, one of the two best vintages of the decade. But whilst the '85s had an easy – misleadingly easy – charm, the '88s were less flattering, firmer and with a long life predicted. But, however high the overall standard, the common denominator is tannin. Most are tannic, some heavily laden.

Mild winter, wet spring, continuing cool and damp though the flowering was satisfactory. The important feature of the growing season was an exceptional summer: three hot, dry months from the end of July through to October, happily interspersed with refreshing showers. The result of this heat was thick skins, ripe and concentrated flesh, deep colour, fairly substantial alcohol and a great deal of tannin. All the signs are that this is a long-term vintage but, as always, with this amount of tannin, there is a worry that the tannin will outlive the fruit. Happily, the intrinsic richness, the extract and complexity will, I am fairly sure, make these wines a rare pleasure to drink through the first two decades of the 21st century.

**Romanée-Conti** First tasted at the Domaine, October 1990: very deep, richly coloured; opulent, all-pervasive aroma, fairly sweet and full-bodied, high extract masking tannins, rounded. Next, at the London importer's tasting in London (at that time, Percy Fox), January 1991: similar note; and again two months later: a powerhouse with great future. *Last tasted March 1991. Then (★★★★★) Not tasted since.*

**La Tâche** At the opening tasting, 1990: deep, fairly intense; full of exotic Pinot aromas and flavours. Elegant. Great length, silky tannins. In January and March 1991: bright cherry red; crisp, fragrant; concentrated, spicy, intense, very tannic. Most recently at Wagner's vertical: now less deep, showing some maturity; vegetal Pinot aroma, sweet, like caramel with an upturned edge; sweaty tannins, but after an hour rich, great depth, and after four hours in the glass, strawberry-like fruit, later still spicy. Fairly sweet, assertive, piquant fruit and some astringency. *Last tasted April 1998 ★★(★★★) Say 2008–2020.*

**Richebourg** DRC Also very deep two years after the vintage and two good notes the following New Year and spring. A full, chunky, tannic wine, dry with silky textured tannins, fragrant aftertaste. 'Great future'. *Last tasted March 1991 then (★★★★★) and not tasted since. Should be a stayer.*

**Romanée-St-Vivant** DRC An immediately attractive wine when tasted at the Domaine two years after the vintage, spicy yet harmonious, rich and rounded. In January and March 1991, ruddy colour, cherry-tinged; penetrating DRC Pinot aromas; powerful yet elegant, good length – all the virtues. More recently at the St-Vivant vertical at the Domaine: now medium-deep, bright, open, rich 'legs'; sweet, harmonious nose with whiff of vanillin, its initial harsh edge softening and opening up. Almost sickly sweet after an hour or two in the glass. Medium-sweet entry leading to a very dry, tannic finish, full-bodied, crisp, firm. Fine wine, needs time. *Last tasted Nov 1995. Then ★(★★★★) Probably fully evolved 2008–2020.*

**Grands-Echézeaux** DRC In 1990, deep purple; crisp fruit; assertive, great length. Two notes later: packed with fruit, wonderful fragrance, stylish, lovely aftertaste. Great future. *Last tasted March 1991. Then (★★★★★) Now probably ★★★(★★) Say 2008–2020.*

**Echézeaux** DRC Plummy coloured; sweet, 'boiled beetroot' Pinot aroma, dry, lively. Five months later; pink-tinged; crisp fruit; dry, firm, very tannic. Never up to the Grands-Echézeaux in style and depth, but should develop well. *Not tasted since Oct 1991. Then (★★★) Possibly 4-star, and best between now and 2010.*

**Beaune-Chouacheux** **Héritiers L Jadot** Ruby; scent of cherries and oak; still tannic. *Feb 1993. Then an optimistic (★★★★) Probably drinking quite well now, at least 3-stars.*

**Beaune, Clos des Fèves** **Chanson** Noted at two Distillers' Company wine committee tastings, first in 1995: not very impressive; dominated by new oak. Twelve months later: neutral nose; flavour neither bad nor good. Raw finish. I hope we took a decision not to serve this at our dinners. *Last tasted Sept 1996. Frankly, this sort of négociants' wine is not the best advertisement for burgundy.*

**Beaune, Montrevenots** **J M Boillot** In 1990: good colour; deep, rich, scented; powerful, complete, fairly dominant tannin and acidity. Most recently, at a tasting I conducted at Lyford Cay, I noted that picking began 26 September, fermentation temperatures up to 32°C, alcohol 13%. Now medium-deep, cherry red with maturing rim; very fragrant, spicy, lovely scent, 'true burgundy'; 'powerful' and 'complete' noted again. A very well made wine. *Last tasted Feb 1998 ★★(★★) 2005–2012.*

**Beaune, Clos des Ursules** **L Jadot** Bottled and tasted June 1990: fruity, fragrant; good flavour and grip. Later that autumn: impressive, good future. Most recently: some colour diminution, attractive nose and taste. Drinking fairly well but I was not as enthusiastic as I thought I should have been. *Last noted at a Distillers' Company ladies banquet at the Mansion House in the City of London, Sept 1997 ★★★*

**Beaune, Toussaints** **Mathouillet-Besancenot** A domaine previously unknown to me but it was recommended by the young sommelier at Cliveden. It was pretty impressive: fairly deep; a lovely, soft, fragrant Pinot; richly flavoured but with quite a bite and slightly bitter, tannic finish that even the excellent beef could not quite constrain. *July 2000 ★★(★★)*

**Chambertin, Clos de Bèze** **L Jadot** Bottled in June 1990 and first tasted that October: deep; strong scent of oysters and iodine (from the anthocyanins, pure vegetal aroma, very characteristic of Chambertin Pinot – I was glad to be told this for I had long since noticed and noted the 'fishy Pinot' of Chambertins); dry, powerful, lots of fruit, great length, the tannin a bit metallic. More recently, at a pre-sale tasting in New York just noted 'very tannic'. *Last tasted Sept 1997 ★(★★★) Well, when will it come round? At a guess between 2005 and 2016.*

**Charmes-Chambertin** **Taupenot Merme** A relatively big 1.5-ha plot in a 9-ha domaine. The last but one tasting for Concorde. Alas, it was more than mature looking; too brown; nose a hefty old Pinot, slightly cheesy. Frankly it was so dreary that I didn't bother actually to taste it. Why this had been submitted, I do not know. It was the price of some other very good *grand cru* younger wines. *June 1999.*

**Le Corton** **Dom du Ch de Beaune** First tasted in 1991: fairly deep, purple sheen, weak rim; harmonious; sweet, full, firm, tannic. More recently: not dissimilar, colour now plummy, starting to mature, minerally, slightly medicinal nose; a big wine, meaty, with plenty of tannic grip. *Last noted lunching at Bouchard Père, Beaune, Nov 1995 ★★(★)*

**Corton, Bressandes Chandon de Briailles** Two notes in the mid-1990s: medium-deep ruby; lovely rich nose; fairly sweet, soft and full (alcohol 13%). I gave it 4 stars at a British Airways tasting at Hugh Johnson's in 1994. Nearly 12 months later, served at dinner following a British Airways meeting: slightly scented nose; lovely Pinot flavour, quite a bite. *Last noted at Mosimann's, Jan 1995* ★★★(★) *Should be fine right now.*

**Ch Corton-Grancey L Latour** First noted at a Latour tasting in 1990: not as deep coloured as expected; attractive light fruitiness; sweet, soft but, I thought, for a Corton of this vintage, slightly lacking substance. A year later, further evolved, scented, agreeable. Most recently noted at a Corton-Grancey vertical: now fairly pale and fully mature looking; pure Pinot nose; leaner and drier than the '90 or '85, crisp, good flavour but very dry, tannic finish. *Last noted at my L Latour seminar in Florida, March 1998* ★★★(★) *Approaching its best but still tannic.*

**Corton, Maréchaudes Prince de Mérode** Pink; sweet, soft, harmonious nose; dry, crisp, attractive. *Feb 1992. Then* ★★★(★) *'For early drinking' which is out of character for a Corton of this vintage.*

**Corton, Pougets L Jadot** Lovely, soft, ripe. *June 1992* ★★★(★) *But this contradicts my last statement. Perhaps some of these tannic '88s were relatively advanced.*

**Echézeaux René Engel** Fairly well developed; rich, meaty Pinot; tannic, impressive. *Pre-sale, Los Angeles, March 1999* ★★★(★)

**Gevrey-Chambertin, Cazetiers Faiveley** Medium, hint of cherry red; low-keyed; better flavour than nose, crisp fruit. *Pre-millennium sale, New York, May 1999* ★★★

**Gevrey-Chambertin, Clos St-Jacques L Jadot** Two notes in the early 1990s. In 1991: nutty, fragrant; surprisingly soft and fleshy, with silky tannins. Two years later at a Jadot tasting at the Savoy Hotel: palish; sweet, rather stewed Pinot; 'soft' noted again, good flavour, slightly bitter finish. *Last tasted June 1993* ★★★ *Probably drinking very well now.*

**Gevrey-Chambertin, Clos St-Jacques A Rousseau** Medium, maturing; soft, earthy, slightly smoky, harmonious; good flavour, crisp, with a citrus-like acidic touch to accompany its tannins. Attractive. *At Rousseau's St-Jacques vertical at the Hollywood Wine Society seminar, Florida, March 1995* ★★★(★) *Should be drinking very well now.*

**Nuits-St-Georges, Clos de la Maréchale Faiveley** Colour and nose similar to Faiveley's Cazetiers; dry, considerable grip, needs time. *May 1999* ★(★★)

**Nuits-St-Georges, Vaucrains H Gouges** In 1991, lovely, crisp, youthful fruit. Five years later, maintaining a good colour, Pinot aroma and flavour. Fair tannin and acidity. *Last tasted Nov 1996. Then* ★★(★) *Doubtless drinking well now.*

**Pommard, Grands Epenots L Jadot** 0.6ha: not domaine-owned; Jadot have a long-term arrangement with the same grower. Medium-deep, mature rim and rich 'legs'; good fruit, noticeable tannin on the nose, considerable depth; medium sweetness and body, fragrant, as rich as it looked, opening up gloriously in the glass, spicy, dry finish. *Paired with the '96 at the 'Transformations' seminar, conducted with Matt Kramer's customary verve and flair at the New York Wine Experience, Oct 1999* ★★★★(★) *Now–2010.*

**Clos de Tart** Four notes, first at Mommessin's London tasting in March 1990: immature; lightly scented aroma; lean, flavoury, piquant. Later that autumn: dash of cherry red; 'oil of cloves' spiciness; fairly full-bodied, complete. Noted as 'a tart with a heart'. Next, at the Mommessin vertical in 1992: still immature, paler than expected; spicy nose noted again; dry, medium full (13% alcohol), firm, good length. Most recently:

soft cherry; lovely, ripe, hen droppings' scent; sweet, delicious flavour, the end bite – more than a peck – very noticeable. *Last noted dining at home, Sept 2001* ★★★(★) *Perhaps overrated, but an enticing drink.*

**Clos Vougeot Méo-Camuzet** Good colour, luminous, rich 'legs'; compared with the New World wines, understated nose and flavour. Medium sweetness, soft, good length. *One of only two burgundies, the rest American Pinot Noirs, in a 15-wine tasting in Florida, March 1998* ★★★ *Holding its own quite well.*

SOME OTHER '88s SHOWING WELL IN THE EARLY 1990s with potential rating at the time of tasting: **J Drouhin's Beaune, Clos des Mouches** very sweet, very tannic (★★★★); **L Latour's Beaune, Vignes Franches** full, fleshy (★★★★); **de Vogüé's Bonnes-Mares** glorious nose; soft tannins (★★★★★); **L Trapet's Chambertin** austere (★★★); **Bouchard Père's Chambertin, Clos de Bèze** assertive (★★★★); **L Trapet's Chambertin, Vieilles Vignes** laden, fragrant (★★★★★); **J Drouhin's Chambolle-Musigny, Les Baudes and Hauts Doix**, both new to me, both (★★★); **A Guyon's Chambolle-Musigny, Clos du Village** fragrant, powerful (★★★★); **Chandon de Briailles' Corton, Clos du Roi** scented, very rich (★★★★★); **Philippe Rossignol's Gevrey-Chambertin** (★★★★); **Clos des Lambrays** classy (★★★★); **L Trapet's Latricières-Chambertin** full flavoured (★★★★)?; **Jacques Prieur's Musigny** (★★★★); **de Vogüé's Le Musigny** superb, concentrated fruit, very tannic (★★★★); **Alain Michelot's Nuits-St-Georges** fabulous flavour, sweet, spicy, very tannic (★★★★), his **Cailles** impressive (★★★★) and his **Chaignots** marvellously rich and fragrant (★★★★★); **H Gouges' Nuits-St-Georges, Porrets-St-Georges** firm, full, tough and tannic (★★★★) and his **Pruliers** 'violets', crisp fruit, lean and austere (★★★★); **Ch de Meursault's Pommard, Epenots** (★★★★); **J-M Boillot's Pommard, Sausilles** oaky, sweet, tannic (★★★★); **Dujac's Clos de la Roche** lovely fruit, assertive (★★★★); **Ch de Meursault's Volnay, Clos des Chênes** flavour, intensity (★★★★); and **Bouchard Père's Volnay, Hospices, Jehan de Massol** fruit, power, length (★★★★)

# 1989 ★★★★

Not as tannic as the '88s but well constructed and, on the whole, very satisfactory wines, the best and best-kept drinking well into the first, even the second, decade of the present century. And so it should have been, for the growing season was favourable: a mild winter and an early spring encouraging growth, two weeks in advance of normal. A long hot summer resulted in an early harvest of healthy ripe grapes picked in perfect conditions from 13 September.

**Romanée-Conti** First tasted at the Domaine with Lalou Bize-Leroy, Aubert de Villaine and his father in October 1990. At 12 months: a deep velvety purple; good rich nose; full-bodied, substantial fruit and extract. 'Great potential'. Next, at a Bin Club tasting in June 1992: fairly deep, lovely, soft, vanillin nose; intense, assertive, great length – earning an exceptionally high mark (appropriate for the price: £3588.66 per dozen in bond duty free. And that was 10 years ago). *Feebly and maddeningly my most recent note mis-indexed. Then* ★★★(★★)

**La Tâche** At the opening tasting in 1990: good colour; sweet yet tannic nose; lean, crisp fruit, tannic finish – clearly not as luscious as I had expected. In 1992 its bouquet restrained but very fragrant and a much more in character note on the palate: sweet, full, rich, lovely fruit, an attack of tannin and acidity and great length (very high mark. Bin Club price £1188.66 in bond). Six years later at a Zachys/Christie's dinner at Spago's in Los Angeles: now medium-deep; ripe, fleshy nose, a touch of pepper and somehow evoked 'tea and toast'. On the palate, sweet, full, luscious but still with tannic grip. Most recently at Wagner's vertical in Zurich: fairly mature appearance; less intense, more open than expected, a somewhat chocolatey fragrance which after a long time in the glass took on a strawberry-like fruitiness, still spicy after six hours. Fairly sweet, full, still assertive, notably tannic and with a long piquant fruity extension. *Last tasted April 1998* ★★★(★★)

**Richebourg DRC** Only two notes. Predictably deep colour; soft, rich, meaty nose; well stacked, indeed laden with alcohol and fruit, its extract masking substantial tannin. An extremely high mark at the Bin Club tasting: soft, lovely nose; (surprisingly) elegant, stylish, good flavour and length (price then: £868.66 in bond). *Not tasted since June 1992. Then ★(★★★★) Should be lovely now.*

**Romanée-St-Vivant DRC** Five notes, first in 1990: a really lovely wine, soft and sweet but in 1992 noted its depth of colour, full body, crisp, punchy flavour and substantial tannins. At the St-Vivant vertical at the Domaine in 1995, it was now medium-deep, more advanced than the '90 and with a glorious nose: fleshy, soft fruit, fragrant, with flavour to match except that I noted a slightly 'hollow' acidic finish. Its next surprising appearance was with the '90, both jeroboams, at Karl-Heinz Wolf's dinner between the Weinart tasting of J J Prüm's 83 Mosels in April 1999: rich, muffled, 'boiled beetroot' Pinot nose; a big wine, loads of fruit but a certain coarseness. (I rated the '90 higher). Most recently, at the follow-up St-Vivant vertical: still fairly deep, dark cherry; vegetal nose, 'broccoli', sweet, rich, high alcohol, assertive and more grip than the '90. *Last noted at the Domaine, Oct 2001* ★★★(★★) *Could still do with more bottle age.*

**Grands-Echézeaux DRC** Just two early notes: richly coloured; a hard, spicy, youthful aroma in 1990, yet sweet, chewy with lots of fruit. Two years later, a high mark on the palate, soft fruit yet well endowed with tannin and acidity. (Price: £568.66 in bond). *Last tasted June 1992. Then ★★(★★★)*

**Echézeaux DRC** In 1990: rich, luminous; youthful scented fruit; sweet yet very tannic. At the Bin Club in 1992: appealingly fragrant, very varietal; fullish, good fruit, and above standard (it is usually good, but often a gulf between it and its 'Grands' elder sister. Price in 1992: £408.66 in bond). Most recently: though its nose was ripe it seemed still to be unready. A fairly big wine, with a touch of tannic bitterness. *Last noted at a Wine & Food Fair in the Cask Hall at Rothbury in the Hunter Valley, Sept 2000* ★★(★★) *Give it time.*

**Beaune, Clos de la Chaume, Gauffroy** Hippolyte Thévenot/Guyon Heaven knows where I found this – at least, it was new to me. Sweetly scented; fairly substantial yet light in style. *Lunch in the country, Dec 1992* ★★★

**Chambertin, Clos de Bèze A Rousseau** Misleadingly palish and pink-tinged; its nose initially fairly delicate and elusive but unravelled and after 90 minutes reminded me of milk chocolate; sweet, very firm, good wine, needed time. *At my Klassische Weindegustation in Zurich, May 1994* ★★★★(★)

**Corton, Bressandes Chandon de Briailles** A stock offered to the British Airways tasting committee at a remarkably reasonable price: scented Pinot; very flavoury, lean, fragrant. I liked it. *Feb 1994* ★★★★ *(just).*

**Corton, Clos du Roi Chandon de Briailles** Coincidentally, a

month later and also at a British Airways meeting: light ruby; lovely ripe Pinot; fairly sweet, lovely flavour but with a '72-ish bitterness in the finish. *March 1994* ★★★

**Ch Corton-Grancey L Latour** A sensationally attractive, purple-tinged cask sample in October 1990: fragrant, rich, firm aftertaste. Next, in 1996, at a tasting and lunch at Latour's London office: now surprisingly pale yet packing a punch (alcohol 14%) and still tannic. The following year *au dehors*: now showing a touch of orange; curious nose; crisp fruit, full, notable grip and tannin. *Last noted at the Latour bicentenary tasting in the vineyard, June 1997* ★★★ *better with food.*

**Gevrey-Chambertin, Vieilles Vignes Dom Bachelet** Noted sitting in on Christie's Burgundy wine courses, two months apart. An old-fashioned, unfiltered wine. Reassuringly consistent notes: soft, sweet, 'warm' though a touch of smelly hydrogen sulphide from which it recovered; a sweet, rich, full-flavoured wine, passable tannin. *Last tasted March 1993.* ★★★

**Musigny de Vogüé** Drawn from the cask in October 1990, the youngest in a line-up of Musigny vintages of the 1980s: even at that stage, a lovely wine, fragrant, soft and supple. Next in the mid-1990s: showing some maturity; delicate, floral nose which evolved gloriously in the glass with hint of raspberries; though fleshy, still with a touch of youthful hardness. Refreshing acidity, tannic bitterness. 'Needs five years'. *Last noted at my tasting in Zurich, May 1994. Then ★★★(★★) Doubtless ready now but more to come.*

**Pommard, Fremiers** (*sic*) **de Courcel** A family estate based for four centuries in Pommard. They aim for maximum extraction, no destalking, long vatting. Two years in new wood and bottle age accounted for its relatively pale colour, though a lovely, soft gradation and luminosity; smoky vanillin nose; sweet and soft on the palate too, yet with a tannic finish. *At my burgundy tasting in the Bahamas, Feb 1998* ★★★(★)

**Richebourg Méo-Camuzet** Sweet, full, very rich. *Oct 1992. Then ★★★(★★) Should also be lovely now.*

**La Romanée Dom du Ch de Vosne-Romanée** Palish; sweet, vanillin, soft fruit; rich, rounded yet with good grip. *Tasted in the Bouchard Père cellars, Beaune, Nov 1995* ★★★(★)

**Romanée-St-Vivant, Les Quatre Journaux L Latour** Nice wine. Touch of bitterness. Very good with a Burgundian speciality egg dish. *Served at refreshing cellar temperature at L Latour's bicentenary dinner at Ch de Clos Vougeot, Jan 1997* ★★★ *(as one of the speakers, I did not have much appetite).*

**Clos de Vougeot, Tastevinée** Fairly deep and, as it should have been, rich and very attractive. *At a Chevaliers du Tastevin dinner, Nov 1995* ★★★★

SOME OTHER VERY GOOD '89S, TASTED IN THE EARLY 1990S with potential rating at the time of tasting: **J Drouhin**'s **Beaune, Clos des Mouches** lovely wine (★★★★) and **Epenottes** rich (★★★★); **L Jadot**'s **Beaune, Clos des Ursules** deep, oaky, fragrant (★★★★); **de Vogüé**'s **Bonnes-Mares** described as the 'great uncle' of Comte Georges de Vogüé's family of wine. Nevers oak used (Allier for the Musigny). Glorious wine (★★★★★); **L Jadot**'s **Chambertin, Clos de Bèze** rich, '89 charm (★★★★★); **L Latour**'s **Chambertin, Cuvée Héritiers Latour** brilliant colour, full-bodied (★★★★★); **de Vogüé**'s **Chambolle-Musigny, Amoureuses** lean but supple (★★★★); **J Drouhin**'s **Chambolle-Musigny, Haut-Doix** rich (★★★★); **Bouchard Père**'s **Le Corton, Dom du Ch de Beaune** (★★★★); **Dujac**'s **Clos de la Roche** flavoury, with charm (★★★★); and **Clos de Tart** fragrant, crisp fruit (★★★★)

# 1990–1999

Surely one of the best decades in Burgundy, certainly starting off with a bang with the 1990. Better still, fuller awareness of quality among both the producers and consumers. There seemed to me to be a renewed confidence in Burgundy, the shortcuts and grey areas of the past left firmly in the past. Moreover, the price paid for good burgundy – and the best has never been available in substantial quantities – was more directly based on quality and demand, the latter being not the fickle inflationary demand of secondary 'investment' in a speculative market.

## Vintages at a Glance
**Outstanding** ★★★★★
1990, 1999
**Very Good** ★★★★
1993, 1995, 1996, 1997, 1998
**Good** ★★★
1992, 1994 (v)

## 1990 ★★★★★

A superb vintage. In common with the '89 vintage, there was a hot summer, but there were important differences. The winter was unusually warm, with temperatures up to 23°C in February and March, encouraging vegetation. But April to June was much cooler with a good deal of rain. Flowering was later than usual and the potentially large crop was reduced by *coulure* and *millerandage*. The summer was hot and too dry, with near drought conditions. Nevertheless, ripening was advanced and the harvest began early, on 17 September in the Côte d'Or. Grapes were small and healthy with thick skins resulting in concentration of flesh and high sugar levels, good colour extraction and tannins.

I well remember Justerini & Brooks' major tasting of the youthful '90s in January 1992. It was an eye-opener. No puny, wishy-washy, colourless wines here. The following notes summarise my early impressions of the wines, next in the mid-1990s, and, of course, more recently. The lesser wines, the good value reds from southern Burgundy and the lower-priced shippers' village wines should have been drunk by now. I am therefore concentrating, as usual, on the major domaines and top *négociants'* wines.

This was unquestionably an outstanding red wine vintage worldwide and burgundies showed well at the extraordinary, six 'flight' blind tasting of 144 of the world's best wines at a tasting hosted by Walter Eigensatz, Johann Willsberger and Jürg Reinshagen at the Palace Hotel in Luzern in June 1996.
**La Tâche** Not tasted until the mid-1990s, first at the Luzern tasting. La Tâche was in the 12th and last 'flight' which included Ch Latour, Ch Le Pin, Ch Pétrus, La Turque, Giacosa's Barbaresco Riserva Speciale and a super Syrah from Australia, Roman Bratasiuk's Clarendon Hill. It showed well: fairly deep, rich 'legs'; curiously exotic; sweet, fruit-laden, 'beetroot' Pinot grip (I did, after a struggle, identify it). Two years later, at Wagner's La Tâche vertical in Zurich: richness, extract, noting an earthy fragrance, opening up perfectly; sweet, full-body, fruit and all the component parts. *Last tasted April 1998* ★★★(★★) *Approaching full maturity, but long life predicted.*
**Romanée-St-Vivant DRC** Noted at the first St-Vivant vertical at the Domaine, November 1995: fairly deep, soft yet firm and rich looking; a wonderfully harmonious nose, complete, touch of vanillin and 'sweaty' tannins, considerable depth, becoming floral and, as I have noted before with DRC, after an hour, a whiff of strawberry. Fairly full-bodied, crisp yet soft, rounded, with richness masking the tannins. Great length. 'Great potential'. Four years later, a jeroboam (with the '89 previously described) at Karl-Heinz Wolf's villa overlooking the Attersee: a powerhouse, fairly sweet, yet very tannic, very fragrant, 'needs ages'. It gave the braised beef a tough time. Most recently, at the second of the St-Vivant verticals: still deep, fairly intense; perfect Pinot, harmonious; sweet, mouthfilling, rich, complete, masked tannin – the easiest to drink of the younger vintages. Aubert de Villaine told our very small group – which included *Le Meilleur Sommelier de France* – that the yield was 33.86hl/ha and 24,026 bottles, the biggest by far between 1989 and 2000. *Last tasted Oct 2001* ★★★(★★) *Great wine. Now–2012.*
**Beaune, Clos des Mouches J Drouhin** First tasted, fresh from the cask, in October 1990. Because of the natural tannins, the grapes had been destalked but Robert Drouhin said there would be no need to use new oak. Showing well at a Bin Club tasting in 1992. Then in 1994, at a Gidleigh Park wine weekend tasting of 1990 burgundies. An almost Oregon-like Pinot Noir aroma (Robert Drouhin's charming daughter, Véronique, runs their Oregon estate), fragrant, immediately appealing. A lovely wine, agreeable now. Most recently, at Drouhin's, their oldest vintage of Clos des Mouches in the decade of the 1990s: never very deep, now fully mature with a touch of orange at the rim; surprisingly little nose, slightly jammy; sweet, good fruit but a bit raw. Disappointing. The bottle? Storage (at Drouhin's)? I suspect it would have been better from a good cold British cellar. *Last tasted Oct 2001. Benefit of the doubt* ★★★ *Possibly 4 stars. Drink now.*
**Beaune, Clos des Ursules L Jadot** First noted at a Distillers' dinner in September 2000: good but I felt that it was fully mature, needing drinking. Most recently at Jadot, the oldest vintage of the decade. A most useful session. Anthony Hanson and I tasted separately, then we compared notes with Pierre-Henry Gagey and his brilliant winemaker, Jacques Lardière, who told us that the wine had had 33–35 days maceration. Still a dark cherry red; good fruit, rich extract, brambly, touch of tar; sweet, complete, masked tannin, good length. *Last tasted Oct 2001* ★★★★ *Drink now–2008.*
**Beaune, Hospices, Cuvée Domaines Hospitaliers** First noted dining at Mosimann's Centre in Battersea after a British Airways wine committee meeting, a magnum: lovely wine, 'will keep'. The next two occasions on BA 001 (Concorde). Very good, certainly impressive but very tannic, 'unready'. The following year showing better: sweet, harmonious nose, good flavour and length, but still pretty tannic. *Last noted at 50,000 feet, October 1995* ★★★★ *Now–2008.*
**Chambertin, Clos de Bèze Faiveley** Frankly noted as 'stewed' when tasted at a pre-sale tasting in New York in 1997. Most recently, still firm and tannic at the Seventh 'Tour de

France' evening at Domaine de Chevalier. *Last noted, but only briefly, June 2001. The jury is out. It should be first rate.*

**Chambertin, Clos de Bèze A Rousseau** Buried in the middle of 'flight' 3 of Eigensatz's worldclass reds – six burgundies, six other Pinot Noirs. Tasted blind, as all were, I found it had a curious low-keyed nose and flavour. Sweet yet very tannic. Though it was in the top four, the number of votes cast, including mine, were modest. Perhaps needing more time to shake off its tannic overcoat. *June 1996* ★★(★)?

**Chassagne-Montrachet, Clos de la Boudriotte Ramonet** Delicate, fragrant, delicious; fairly full and sweet, lovely flavour, length and aftertaste. *In Luzern, June 1996* ★★★★ *Ready now.*

**Corton Bonneau du Martray** The King of Corton: medium; sweet, harmonious, varietal; soft, rich, fleshy and fragrant. Perfect with roasted veal tenderloin. *Hosting a Christie's dinner at the Grand Hyatt, Hong Kong, Oct 1995* ★★★★★ *Lovely now.*

**Corton, Hospices, Cuvée Domaines Hospitaliers** Lovely wine, 'will keep'; and the **Cuvée Dr Peste** deep; scent of violets; full, tannic, magnificent. ★★★★★ *Both tasted after a British Airways wine meeting at Mosimann's, Jan 1995.*

**Corton, Clos Rognet Méo-Camuzet** Appealing fruit, depth, fragrance; very sweet, lovely fruit and flavour. *In Luzern, June 1996* ★★★★ *Drink now–2008.*

**Ch Corton-Grancey L Latour** Tasted in the vineyard in 1997: harmonious, rich, full (alcohol 14%). Next, in 1998, at a Latour domaine seminar: wonderful nose, great warmth, concentration; sweet, mouthfilling, good length and components. One of the best ever. Most recently: less deep, a light tawny edge tinged with orange; perfect harmony; rich, complete, oaky aftertaste. Despite its mature appearance, it has time in hand. *Last tasted at the 10th Anniversary of L Latour's London office, July 2000* ★★★★ *Now–2008.*

**Gevrey-Chambertin, Combottes Leroy** Deep; very good bouquet and bouquet. *At the Josey pre-sale tasting, New York, Nov 2000* ★★★★ *Drink soon.*

**Gevrey-Chambertin, Clos St-Jacques L Jadot** Good rich appearance; vegetal, opened exotically; full-flavoured, excellent fruit, length and aftertaste. Very tannic. *In Luzern, June 1996. Then* ★★★(★) *Should be softening by now.*

**Nuits-St-Georges, Clos des Argillières Dom du Clos St-Martin** Rich colour, nose and taste. Full. Good grip. *At Bouchard Père, Beaune, Nov 1995* ★★★ *Drink soon.*

**Nuits-St-Georges, Ch Gris Lupé-Cholet** Whenever I see this estate's name I remember enjoying tea and gossip with the Lupé sisters, wonderful characters but totally different from each other, in their old town house. They had a passion for vintage port. Fragrant; crisp fruit – not blatantly Pinot Noir, nor speciously burgundian, but pretty good. *At Gyldendal, my Danish publisher, in Copenhagen, March 1999* ★★★ *Drink now.*

**Pommard Coste-Caumartin** Very old family domaine and even older house and cellars, but new to me. Very deeply coloured; good fruit; impressive, very dry. *At a Christie's tasting for VIP clients in Florida, March 1995* ★★★ *Drink soon.*

**Pommard, Clos des Epéneaux Comte Armand's 'Monopole'** First noted in 1994 at Gidleigh Park: impressively deep, intense; nose hard at first but opened up, whiff of tangerine; good fruit but laden with tannin. Next, among the Eigensatz 'best reds': high-toned fragrance, reminding me of boiled sweets; crisp, scented fruit, tannin dominant. *Last tasted June 1996* ★★(★★) *Still needs time.*

**Pommard, Rugiens Gaunoux** A very traditional estate where the wines are given *barrique*- and bottle-ageing before release. Deep, rich, impressive; one could smell the warmth of

the summer, wonderful but restrained fruit, an old-fashioned burgundy nose opening up gloriously. Sweet, fullish, delicious. *At Lyford Cay in the Bahamas, Feb 1997* ★★★★(★) *Now–2008.*

**Clos de la Roche Dujac** Good colour though with orange-tinged maturity; soft, harmonious, varietal nose; full, complete, rich, perfect balance. *At the domaine with Jeremy Seysses, Oct 2001* ★★★★★ *Lovely now.*

**Romanée-St-Vivant Leroy** Deep ruby; brilliant fruit; lovely wine, still tannic. *At a pre-sale tasting, New York, Oct 1996* ★★★(★)

**Ruchottes-Chambertin Duvergey-Taboureau** Old company but new to me. A bit raw even with *confit* of pigeon. *At the Champagne Academy annual dinner, the Ritz, May 1995* ★★(★)?

**Volnay, Taillepieds d'Angerville** Dark cherry; low-keyed fruit; good flavour, silky tannins. *In Luzern, June 1996* ★★★

**Vosne-Romanée, Beaumonts Leroy** Almost opaque; very fragrant, extraordinary in its way; sweet, its fruit a bit too scented, almost artificial – but popular with a large and very experienced group of tasters, including Mme Bize-Leroy (and her dog). It gained the highest number of votes of the Pinot 'flight'. *In Luzern, June 1996* ★★★★ *Now–2008.*

**Vosne-Romanée, Les Beaux-Monts** Tastevinage label (1994) **Clavelier Brosson** Good colour; nose holding back but not on the palate: sweet, firm, high extract, loads of fruit, marvellously complete. *Lyford Cay, Feb 1998* ★★★★★ *Having noticed the price, £26 from Howard Ripley, remarkable value.*

**Vosne-Romanée, Cros Parantoux H Jayer** Very deep, richly coloured; strangely sweet, then fragrant, spicy; very sweet, marvellous fruit and flavour, very distinctive. I thought it was a bit over the top but, before its identity was revealed, it received a large number of votes for the top wine of the range. *In Luzern, June 1996* ★★★★ *Drink now.*

A SUPERB RANGE AT A TASTING OF 1990 BURGUNDY at Gidleigh Park in Devon in February 1994 (some wines already mentioned in the main text above). A précis of more detailed notes: **Michèle and Patrice Rion's Chambolle-Musigny** ruby; rich and rustic; sweet, elegant, nice texture ★★★; **Tollot-Beaut's Corton, Bressandes** intense; smooth, elegant; substantial (alcohol 13.5%), attractive, tannic ★★★(★); **Jean Mongéard's Les Echézeaux** palish, orange-tinged; soft, 'boiled beetroot', harmonious; surprisingly assertive, tannic ★★(★★); **A Rousseau's Gevrey-Chambertin, Clos St-Jacques** singed, vegetal, Pinot aroma; very sweet, soft yet light character, refreshing, lovely ★★★★; **Dujac's Morey-St-Denis** very appealing, scented nose and flavour. Tannic ★★★(★); **Daniel Rion's Nuits-St-Georges, Vignes-Rondes** very deep; exotic Oregon-like Pinot; very sweet, hefty, old-fashioned style ★★(★); **Anne et François Gros' Richebourg** deep classic Pinot, very scented; substantial (alcohol 13.5%). Rich 'copybook' burgundy, lovely now, masked tannin ★★★(★) *will keep;* **J Drouhin's Savigny-Lès-Beaune, Serpentières** wholesome, undramatic; pleasant (the lowest alcohol 12.5%) ★★★; **Y Clerget's Volnay, Clos du Verseuil** gentle, fragrant; light style, charming, feminine, not for long keeping ★★★; **Méo-Camuzet's Vosne-Romanée** delicate, scented; stylish. Mid-term drinking ★★★ and their **Clos de Vougeot** initially dumb, lovely fruit, strawberry-like, elegant; mouthfilling extract, new oak, delicious but 'needs time' ★★★(★); and **Gros Frère et Soeur's Clos Vougeot, Musigni** (*sic*) deep, pink and polished; richly scented Pinot; suave, silky, elegant ★★★★

OF THE OTHER '90S TASTED IN THEIR YOUTH, the following had outstanding potential: **Drouhin-Laroze's**

Bonnes-Mares; Clos de Tart; J Drouhin's Musigny, Mazis and Griottes-Chambertin; R Arnoux's Clos Vougeot; Haegelin-Jayer's Echézeaux; R Engel's Grands-Echézeaux; and Anne et François Gros' Clos Vougeot.

# 1991 ★★ very variable

Judging by a cross-section of notes, not a very inspiring vintage and, apart from the extraordinary DRCs and one or two others, best forgotten.

The growing conditions could not have been more contrary and difficult: April was warm with early bud burst and May and June cold, delaying flowering and causing *coulure* and *millerandage* which reduced the crop size. The summer was hot and dry, but at the end of September heavy rains fell on the mature grapes just before the harvest, followed by more rain. Those who timed their picking and were selective were able to make wines with fair colour and concentration.

As the auction season is hectic, I did not visit Burgundy as much as I would have liked, so the opening tastings of Corney & Barrow, London's DRC agent, were particularly helpful. My notes have an extra dimension because, arriving late (about 12.45pm), I found that wine just poured into a standard ISO tasting glass was hard to smell and taste whereas wine which had been poured at around 10am into a broad-bowled burgundy glass had opened up so much that it could have been a completely different wine. (Corney & Barrow now use small burgundy glasses for tasting.)

**Romanée-Conti** Yield 22hl/ha, total production 224 cases. Duty-paid price per bottle £411 in 1994. Medium-deep, soft colour, touch of orange; subdued but rich (after three hours in a burgundy glass); dry, massive, concentrated, tightly knit. Impressive for a '91. *At Corney & Barrow, Feb 1994 ★★★★?*

**La Tâche** 23hl/ha, 1428 cases. First noted at the opening tasting in London, February 1994. £341 per bottle duty paid. Deep, far more intense than Romanée-Conti or Richebourg; rich, earthy Pinot aroma, sweet, spicy – after three hours, fragrant but elusive; very assertive, concentrated, good balance,

impressive and with charm. Next at Wagner's vertical in 1998: deep, fine colour; sweet, rich, varietal. After an hour, delicious strawberry-like fruit, after four hours, rich, jammy fruit; medium sweet, fullish, astringent finish but held well. The following year, a magnum (served blind – I thought it was Richebourg): lovely colour, touch of cherry red; fragrant and rather cherry-like Pinot nose; deliciously sweet, glorious fruit, lissome, dry finish. Excellent with cheese, but needs time. *Last noted dining with Karl-Heinz Wolf at his Landart restaurant in Tanglberg, Austria in April 1999 ★★★(★★) Astonishingly attractive, both the wine and the setting.*

**Richebourg DRC** 24hl/ha, 937 cases; opened at £90 per bottle. Richly coloured; initially subdued but, after three hours in the open glass, fully evolved, very fragrant; positive, good flavour, loads of tannin, acidity and oak. *Feb 1994 ★★★*

**Romanée-St-Vivant DRC** 27hl/ha, 1548 cases, £60 per bottle at the opening tasting in 1994: not deep but richly coloured; meaty, hard, rather low-keyed; positive, assertive; crisp fruit, fairly tannic, fair aftertaste. Next, the following autumn at the first St-Vivant vertical at the Domaine: ruby sheen; soft, vanillin, brambly fruit, fragrant; surprisingly stylish, attractive, crisp, loose-knit. In 1999 at a Christie's pre-sale tasting in Tokyo: appearance still youthful; a touch of bitterness and 'one hell of a bite'. Most recently, at the second St-Vivant vertical: rich, jammy, strawberry nose; pretty sweet, good texture but crumbly fruit, 'something lacking', astringent. *Last noted at the Domaine, Oct 2001 ★★(★) I think I preferred it young.*

**Grands-Echézeaux DRC** 23hl/ha, 799 cases, £70 per bottle. Appearance and nose soft and rich, noted great depth in open glass; distinctly sweet, good fruit, tannin present but not overt. *Feb 1994. Then ★★★ Probably drinking well between now and 2010.*

**Echézeaux DRC** 30hl/ha, 1474 cases, £48 per bottle. Palish, youthfully pink; hard and closed when first poured but had opened up nicely after three hours; assertive, lean, spicy new oak, very dry tannic finish. *Feb 1994 ★★★ Now–2006.*

**Beaune, Clos des Mouches J Drouhin** Alcohol 13%, acidity 3.9g/l. Described by Frédéric Drouhin as 'an overlooked vintage'. Disregarding a corked bottle, a fully mature appearance, open, slight orange tinge when freshly poured, a pleasant varietal scent but shortly after seemed to have a rather smelly overtone; better flavour than nose, touch of sweetness, 'lacked mature tannin'. So so. Like the '90, a bit disappointing. *Tasting the decade of the 1990s at Drouhin, Oct 2001 ★★ Drink up.*

**Beaune, Grèves, Vignes de l'Enfant Jésus Dom du Ch de Beaune** Harvest started 25 September. Deep; curious, singed, cedary scent; sweet, good fruit, crisp, dry finish. *Tasted in the cellars to assess its quality for Joseph Henriot, the new owner of Bouchard Père et Fils. Nov 1995 ★★★ For early drinking.*

**Beaune, Marconnets Dom du Ch de Beaune** A modest half bottle noted in May 1995 dining on Brittany Ferries – the French line with quite the best cross-channel food – between Portsmouth and St Malo: plummy colour; 'Italianate', brambly nose; quite good. And another, a month later, same ship, same crossing, en route to Burgundy and tasted in Bouchard Père's cellar. Later *assez bien. Last tasted Nov 1995 ★★ Not bad, but not good enough. Drink up.*

**Beaune, Clos des Ursules L Jadot** Jacques Lardière informed Anthony Hanson and me that they had a small crop because of hail and bad weather. 18 days maceration. Fairly deep, maturing; a leafy sort of fruit, black treacle and, after 20 minutes, tar; sweet, soft, treacley flavour but with tannin and stiletto sharp acidity. Raw finish. *At Jadot, Oct 2001 ★★ Will the sharpness ever become blunted?*

## Tasting red burgundy

*Perhaps the most misunderstood feature of red burgundy is its colour or, more specifically, its not infrequent lack of colour. On occasion, as with some 1982s, the heading 'red burgundy' seems inappropriate. The principal reason for this is the grape variety: the skin of Pinot Noir is thin, with less colouring matter to be extracted during fermentation. But although it might sometimes look unconvincing, the wine itself is often remarkably high in extract and alcohol. Next, the nose: the smell of burgundy is often difficult to grasp and will not necessarily evolve in the glass. Do not anticipate the pronounced aroma of New World Pinot Noir: the smell is often neither fruity nor flowery; more frequently it is earthy, beetroot-like, more vegetal, even bush-like, reminiscent of bramble, hawthorn. In my experience burgundy's major feature is taste.*

*The difference between tasting burgundy and Bordeaux is that Burgundy happens in the mouth. They call it the 'peacock's tail'. It has the peculiar ability to expand, the flavour filling every part of the palate, and, after swallowing, releasing a fragrant aftertaste. It is sweeter than claret, less obviously tannic due partly to the nature of the Pinot Noir grape, partly to chaptalisation (quite normal in Burgundy) and to the resulting high alcohol content. For me, at its best, burgundy is sublime.*

**Bonnes-Mares de Vogüé** Deep; surprisingly malty; rich, stewed, very strange. *Oct 1993 Rating? Retaste.*

**Chénas L Champagnon** Classic jammy Gamay fruit; medium-dry, lightish, positive flavour, refreshing acidity. My style of village Beaujolais. *Last tasted Nov 1993 ★★★ Drink up.*

**Chambolle-Musigny de Vogüé** Deep; curious, muffled, stewed Pinot nose and flavour. *Oct 1993 ★★?*

**Echézeaux J Drouhin** Low-keyed fruit; loose knit, dry finish. *Oct 1993 ★★?*

**Gevrey-Chambertin, Clos St-Jacques A Rousseau** The youngest vintage in Rousseau's St-Jacques vertical tasting: ruby; rich, brambly nose, opening up agreeably, touch of raspberry; medium-sweet, crisp, good grip and attractive. *Tasted in Florida, March 1995. Then ★★★ Doubtless it is drinking well now, but not for long keeping.*

**Grands-Echézeaux J Drouhin** Cherry red; lovely fruit; rich, oaky, very tannic. *Oct 1993 ★(★★) Needs time.*

**Mazis-Chambertin Sélection des Jurés-Gourmets de la Confrérie des Chevaliers du Tastevin** to which, of course, I belong. All great fun. A couple of bottles given to me by the Grand-Connétable following my Presidency at one of the Clos Vougeot banquets, and first noted dining at home in the country in 1997: an attractive, luminous appearance; crisp fruit, very fragrant; remarkably sweet, hefty yet soft and fruity with dry finish. The second bottle consumed, at lunch this time, two years later: now showing more maturity; 'stewed Pinot' nose and taste; still sweet and soft though a touch of bitterness on the finish. *Last noted May 1999 ★★★ to be kind.*

**Morey-St-Denis, En la Rue de Vergy Bruno Clair** A vineyard just above Clos de Tart, newly planted in 1980. Light, stylish, tannic. *At a Heyman, Barwell & Jones trade tasting, March 1995 ★★(★) At £12 per bottle plus VAT somewhat more affordable than the DRC '91s.*

**Musigny de Vogüé** Very deep, intense, purple; rich, tannic. No elegance or femininity. Give it time. *Oct 1993 (★★)? Retaste.*

**Nuits-St-Georges, Les Pruliers H Gouges** Still youthful cherry red; low-keyed, vanilla, slightly earthy, pleasant fruit; dry, crisp; refreshing, touch of bitterness. 'Needs food'. *At the France in Your Glass dinner at Ch de Bagnols, June 1997 ★★★ Now–2005.*

**Clos de la Roche Dujac** Palish, soft ruby; an intriguing scent of *merde* and *betterave*; boiled beetroot flavour and good, dry finish. (Daphne's note reads: 'Pinot nose and aftertaste. A decent weekend wine'.) *At the Domaine, Oct 2001 ★★★*

## 1992 ★★★

A vintage that was acceptable, commercial and drinking well in its own decade. I would rate it 'good' overall but have the feeling that it has lost its lustre. Though, as will be seen, some wines have given me great pleasure.

The growing conditions started optimistically following an exceptionally mild winter and spring which advanced vegetation. Flowering was also early, at the end of May and beginning of June, with some *coulure* and *millerandage* stepping in to lower the potential crop which, nevertheless, looked alarmingly abundant; some of the better growers green-pruned. August was hot and sunny which advanced ripening, leading to an early harvest, from 12 September in the Côte de Beaune and from the 18th in the Côte de Nuits, mainly completed by the third week when rains set in.

**La Tâche** Just one note, made at Manfred Wagner's vertical in Zurich: medium-deep, forward – already looked fairly mature; light, vegetal Pinot aroma speedily opening up, fragrant, crisp

and, even after four hours in the glass, still a light charmer; dryish, relatively light body and style but with teeth-gripping acidity. *April 1998 ★★★ But just misses. Drink soon.*

**Romanée-St-Vivant DRC** First noted at the St-Vivant vertical at the Domaine in 1995: palish, open, prettily coloured, advanced; soft fruit nose, touch of citrus, then low-keyed, 'medicinal', after 40 minutes attractive, harmonious but no further development; a pleasant soft fruit flavour, a bit hollow. Next, alongside Jayer's '92 Echézeaux at a dinner party at home, January 2000: now fully mature looking; an immediate burst of fragrance; fabulous, soft, very varietal; its appearance misleading for it had surprising power, bite and length, a lovely crisp flavour, later becoming astringent. Most recently, at the follow-up vertical: open, mature; when first poured, a very vegetal nose, stewed beetroot, cabbage, but after less than 30 minutes, very fragrant and sweet; firm fruit, lean, fair length, dry, somewhat astringent finish. *Last noted at the Domaine, Oct 2001. By DRC standards ★★, by other yardsticks ★★★ Now–2006.*

**Echézeaux DRC** Late-harvested. First noted in the pickers' dining room (with *homard grillé*) in November 1995: palish, youthful pink; stewed, vegetal nose that opened up attractively; light style, good length, scented, crisp, refreshing acidity but very tannic. Later the same month, lunching at Corney & Barrow: very fragrant; lovely entry at mid-palate, good length, acidity rather than tannin noted. Delicious. *Last tasted Nov 1995 ★★★ Drink soon.*

**Beaune, Grèves, Vignes de l'Enfant Jésus Dom du Ch de Beaune** Early picking: 12 September. Two notes, a day apart, both in the Bouchard Père cellars: neither pale nor deep; cedary, sweet, slightly stewed nose; nice weight, lean touch, fair length. Not a bad drink. *Nov 1995 ★★*

**Beaune, Clos des Mouches J Drouhin** Christmas Eve at Gidleigh Park in Devon, 1998: maturing nicely; sweet, strawberry-like fruit; sweet, fair body (alcohol 13%) but light style, attractive, a soft touch, drinking well. I have never been known as a big spender – £26 a half bottle – but we did have three other wines and went to bed reasonably sated. More recently, at the 1990 decade line-up at Drouhin's: ruddy coloured, open rim; jammy, strawberry Pinot nose and taste; nice fruit. Pleasant enough. *Last tasted Oct 2001 ★★★ Drink soon.*

**Chambertin A Rousseau** Two months after bottling: good colour, ruby, cherry; opened up very fragrantly, crisp fruit; dry, fullish, lean, considerable grip and tannin which 'cut the calf's foot' admirably and went quite well with the fish. *The opening red at the remarkable 'Marcobrunn and Chambertin' dinner at Schloss Reinhartshausen in the Rheingau, Nov 1995. Then ★★(★) Not perfectly balanced yet probably drinking very well now.*

**Corton Bonneau du Martray** Palish yet youthful for its age; very sweet, very good, rich, crisp Pinot nose and flavour. An excellent '92. *At a British Airways annual wine and food 'summit' tasting and dinner at Mosimann's, April 1998 ★★★★ Drink now.*

**Ch Corton-Grancey L Latour** Latour celebrated their bicentenary in 1997, first with a tasting in June. Happily it was a fine day, for they had arranged a vertical tasting of Corton-Grancey and Corton-Charlemagne vintages, each on a barrel top leading up a path between the vines: the '92 Grancey had very developed colour, touch of orange; warm, stewed Pinot nose and flavour, full-bodied (alcohol 14%), sweetish. Next, at the 10th anniversary of Louis Latour's London office: still pink-tinged, weak about the rim; very forthcoming, ripe, varietal nose; far more punchy than its colour led one to expect and with a hot, hard finish. *Last noted July 2000 ★★(★) Should soften a little.*

**Echézeaux G Jayer** *'Produit vinifié, élevé et mis en bouteille par Henri Jayer'* (George's brother). One of over 30 '92 burgundies at a Bibendum tasting in January 1994, and I fell for it, ordering it on the spot, since when I have served it several times at lunches and dinners at home. Has it changed over the past nearly nine years? Having looked through my notebooks, the answer is, not much. It was sweet, powerful, marvellous, complete with good length and finish when first tasted and the same still applies. Perhaps more mellow. The most detailed note was made at a dinner in 1997: only 13% alcohol though it seemed more, heady, spicy, and a deft use of oak. A misleadingly unconvincing open-rimmed appearance, but that is common to many burgundies. A lovely wine. The real thing. *Last noted Nov 2001* ★★★★ *I shall continue to enjoy it.*

**Echézeaux E Rouget** Coincidentally, also first noted at the Bibendum tasting in 1994, though I didn't buy it: decent colour; straightforward, slightly spicy nose and flavour, good tannins and aftertaste. Next, tasted three years later in Miami, a bottle extracted from Bob Dickinson's excellent cellar: pleasant; soft, sweet, touch of cloves (oak). Attractive wine. *Last noted Nov 1997* ★★★★ *Drink up.*

**Beaune, Clos des Ursules L Jadot** In the line-up of the decade tasted with Anthony Hanson at Jadot. Jacques Lardière told us that 15% was *saigné* (bled, to concentrate the must). Mature; sweet, chaptalised nose, hint of raisins; soft, quite rich, brambly tangy taste. Relatively easy style though with refreshing grip. *Noted Oct 2001* ★★★ *Drink soon.*

**Chambertin, Clos de Bèze L Jadot** Good colour; strawberry and ruby; good fruit, lots of new oak; dry, assertive, tannic. *At Jadot's tasting, Feb 1993* ★★(★) *Now–2008.*

**Mazis-Chambertin 'De noble lineage'** With *bons fromages de Bourgogne* at the 'Chapitre de la Vigne en Fleur', the June banquet of the *Chevaliers du Tastevin*: Good colour; attractive vanillin scent; sweet, crisp, fragrant and positive. *Last noted at Ch de Clos Vougeot, June 1997* ★★★(★) *Then 'could do with more time'. Should be more fully evolved now.*

**La Romanée Dom du Ch de Vosne-Romanée** Picking started early, 12 September: rich, fully evolved, spicy nose; very attractive but too much oak. *In the cellars of Bouchard Père, Nov 1995* ★★★ *(just). Drink up.*

**Savigny-Lès-Beaune Chandon de Briailles** On the pale side; light, crisp, over-oaked for its weight but a reasonably priced charmer. *At a Heyman, Barwell & Jones' tasting, March 1995* ★★ *Easy and early drinking.*

**Volnay, Vendanges Sélectionnées Lafarge** 'A blend from mainly *1er cru* vines, all older than 30 years'. Also tasted in 1994. It was a good colour, very fragrant with fabulous fruit – and half the price of Jayer's Echézeaux, so I bought some for home drinking. Several notes since: not great, no outstanding features but a good Sunday lunch party wine. *Last noted Jan 1999* ★★★ *Drink soon.*

**Volnay, Hospices, Cuvée Général Muteau** Bought at the Hospices auction in November 1992 by Don Zacharia (of Zachys, a leading New York retailer) and Marvin Shanken (of the *Wine Spectator*), *élevé* and bottled by L Jadot. Rarely does one have the name of the auction purchaser or that of the merchant in whose cellars the *barriques* were looked after until finally bottled. A most attractive wine. *Noted at lunch at Christie's, Park Avenue, April 1995* ★★★★ *'good future'. Don and Marvin must be pleased with their purchase.*

OTHER '92S TASTED (ONLY) AT BIBENDUM'S BURGUNDY TASTING IN JANUARY 1994 **Luc Camus'** Beaune, Clos du

Roi unknit, whiff of Gripfix; touch of bitterness ★?; **Ghislaine Barthod's Chambolle-Musigny, Aux Beaux Bruns** pleasing weight and style ★★★; her **Charmes** dry and tannic ★★★; and her **Les Fuées** attractive fruit; sweet, light and charming ★★★; **Denis Mortet's Gevrey-Chambertin, Les Champeaux** good fruit, soft, some depth, appealing ★★★; **Méo-Camuzet's Nuits-St-Georges, Aux Murgers** deep, thick appearance, scent of celluloid; assertive, tannic ★★?; his **Vosne-Romanée, Aux Brûlées** a similar smell, plus oak; very good flavour but spicy and very tannic; his **Cros Parantoux** rich, spicy, delicious ★★★★; and his **Richebourg** lovely but an outrageous price ★★★★; **J-M Boillot's Pommard, les Jarollières** piquant acidity ★★; and **Volnay, Les Pitures** fairly deep ruby; stalky, spicy; rich, lively, attractive ★★★

# 1993 ★★★★

I had forgotten how attractive the '93s were, still are, until assembling notes to give a sort of overview.

The growing season began well: early budding and successful flowering. However, the summer was warm and wet with mildew threats which had to be countered with a great deal of care and attention. Happily, August was hot and dry, with good ripening conditions which thickened the skins – fortuitously, as the grapes needed protection from the effects of fairly heavy rains in the third week of September. Most wines are ready but the most tannic still have a little way to go.

**Romanée-Conti** I first tasted the full range of DRC '93s when the wines were shown to an always rather small – but I don't know how select – group of merchants and wine writers by Aubert de Villaine at Corney & Barrow, March 1996. I try not to miss the opportunity of tasting them at this stage, though I do not always find it easy to appraise them. A second look, smell and sip is always helpful to put the wine and vintage in perspective. The Romanée-Conti had a very flowery and surprisingly soft nose; on the palate, full, packed, good length. Totally unready of course. *March 1996* (★★★★)

**La Tâche** At the opening tasting, holding back on the nose but also packed with flavour with a surprisingly tough, masculine finish. Almost exactly two years later, a more detailed and leisurely note: fairly deep; an immediately forthcoming nose, very rich, fragrant Pinot, sweet, vanillin, then a touch of caramel, still rich after four hours and even after six hours in the glass, a strawberry-like fruitiness. On the palate, sweeter and softer than the '94 and more amenable than the '92. I liked it. *Last noted at Wagner's vertical, April 1998* ★★★(★) *Evolving well, good mid-term.*

**Richebourg DRC** Very forthcoming, open, fragrant, flowery nose; a substantial wine with a long, dry finish and good aftertaste. *March 1996. Then* ★(★★★) *Doubtless evolving well now.*

**Romanée-St-Vivant DRC** First noted at the Domaine in November 1995, supping in the pickers' dining-room with the de Villaines and a dazzling array of great palates including Michel Bettane, Luigi Veronelli, Armin Diel and others: plummy colour; nose initially muffled, fruit and vanillin but soon opened up attractively; sweet, medium weight, loose-knit, attractive but early days. Three months later, noticing a touch of meatiness but crisp, a wine of great style and length. Most recently: deepish, plummy; bottle variation, one chocolatey, the other cherry-like; sweet, crisp, mouthfilling, tannic. *Last noted at the second St-Vivant vertical at the Domaine, Oct 2001* ★★(★★)

**Grands-Echézeaux DRC** Very singed, fragrant, flowery nose; sweet, rich, flavourful. *March 1996* ★★(★★)

**Echézeaux DRC** Bright ruby; an open-topped sort of nose, lovely fruit, opened up well. Crisp, tannic, refreshing. *March 1996* ★★★ *An early developer.*

**Beaune, Clos des Mouches J Drouhin** Detailed notes made at a Burgundy and Bordeaux tasting at Lyford Cay in the Bahamas in 1996: good colour, soft, black cherry, youthful rim; sweet and fragrant at the morning's pre-tasting and good, crisp fruit and vanillin which seemed to sweeten in the glass; dry, tannic yet glorious flavour, later noting its lively, earthy, delicious flavour and wonderful taste. An attractive mid-term wine. Most recently, at the decade of the 1990s line-up: less deep, distinctly pinker; pleasant raspberry-like fruit; relatively high acidity (4.1g/l) noted but good fruit and sustaining tannins. Nice wine, but I was not as enraptured by it as I was in the Bahamas! *Last tasted at Drouhin, Oct 2001* ★★★ *Say now–2008.*

**Beaune, Clos des Ursules L Jadot** At the tasting of the decade of the 1990s, the day after Drouhin's range. Dark cherry, some intensity, still immature (at eight years old); thick, chocolatey, rich, brambly nose with hard edge; sweet, powerful, distinctly tarry taste, mouthfilling and fairly well endowed with tannin and acidity. Curiously (and I realise it sounds pretentious), there was a whiff that reminded me of the 1887 Ch Margaux. *At Jadot, Oct 2001* ★★★ *Needs time but not much.*

**Corton Bonneau du Martray** Fairly deep; very fragrant, good fruit support; sweet, attractive, nice texture, length and aftertaste. Tannic and 'needs time'. *At a British Airways tasting, June 1999* ★★★(★)

**Ch Corton-Grancey L Latour** Faint violet tinge; very scented, cherry-like fruit; good positive flavour, substantial (alcohol 14%) and showing quite well in the Grancey line-up alongside the vineyard. *June 1997* ★★★ *Drink soon.*

**Gevrey-Chambertin Antonin-Guyon** By Burgundy standards a very big estate with vineyards dotted along the Côte d'Or. Fairly deep; rich and fragrant; very attractive fruit, its sweetness almost overdone and effectively masking its tannins. *At a British Airways tasting, June 1999* ★★★ *Drink soon.*

**Gevrey-Chambertin, Clos St-Jacques A Rousseau** Rousseau is one of Gevrey's most important domaines. Their St-Jacques is 2.5ha which, in 1993 yielded 22 *pièces (barriques)*. Medium-deep and still youthful, with an open, mauve tinge; lovely scent, copybook Pinot Noir, sweet, rich, crisp fruit, delicious flavour. *Sipped in Charles Rousseau's office after tasting with his daughter, Corinne, a range of his 2000s, from his village wine up to Chambertin, Oct 2001* ★★★(★) *Still time in hand.*

**Musigny J Drouhin** From their 0.70-ha vineyard. Pre-tasted in the morning: scented; elegant, glorious flavour and texture; and at the evening tutorial: delicate scent, crystallised violets; sweet, feminine, enchanting – 'a real beauty'. *At Lyford Cay in the Bahamas, Feb 1996. Then* ★★★(★) *Should be delicious now.*

**Clos de la Roche Dujac** Mature; ripe, soft, harmonious Pinot; fairly sweet, lovely, silky tannins. *One of my top marks in the vertical tasting at the domaine, Oct 2000* ★★★★ *Now–2008.*

**Savigny-Lès-Beaune Simon Bize** Not very distinctive but most agreeable nose; light style, almost Bordeaux-like weight, tannin and acidity. *A bargain from Zachys in New York, at a Lyford Cay tasting, Feb 1997* ★★★

**Clos de Tart Mommessin** Good, ripe, varietal aroma that opened up gloriously; spicy Pinot, surprisingly tannic, excellent aftertaste. *Noted at a tasting with Christopher Burr for Crédit Suisse, Hong Kong, Oct 1999* ★★★(★) *Now–2006.*

**Vosne-Romanée J Gros** Low-keyed, slightly vegetal, touch of tar, despite sweetness, very tannic. Good flavour though and needs food. *At a tasting of Club to Concorde class wines for very receptive British Airways cabin crew staff, Oct 1998* ★★★ *2004–2006.*

**Clos Vougeot J J Confuron** From a 0.52-ha vineyard at the upper end of this huge multi-ownership Clos: deep but maturing; fragrant, crisp, delicious, excellent tannin and acidity. *At a Hollywood Wine Society Pinot Noir seminar, March 1998* ★★★★

**Clos Vougeot D Rion** 50% new oak, *en barrique* about 18 months, alcohol 13.5%. Amazingly deep – almost Ch Latour-like – youthful, plummy; sweet, harmonious, toasted, mocha nose; a masculine wine, packed with fruit, marvellous but very tannic. Needs food. *At my Lyford Cay, Bahamas, tasting, Feb 1996* ★(★★★) *Preservative tannins should have started to ameliorate.*

**AND A RANGE OF '93S NOTED AT THE POL ROGER/ FAIVELEY TASTING IN MARCH 1996**, all the wines hand-bottled without filtration: **Chambertin, Clos de Bèze** very rich, good length ★★★★; **Corton, 'Clos des Cortons'** predictably big, tannic wine ★★(★); **Latricières-Chambertin** fragrant, whiff of privet and violets; sweet, rich, very attractive ★★★★; and **Mazis-Chambertin** luminous ruby; crisp, refined; mouthfilling, fragrant ★★★★ *Mostly ready now.*

# 1994 ★ to ★★★

Frankly, I do not know what to make of this vintage. Some growers, some domaines, made a fairly spectacular start yet my most recent notes are less than enthusiastic. Could it have been a damp squib? Jadot, in a Côte de Beaune context, reported a terrible vintage. But the growing conditions were not all bad. After a cold spring, May was pleasant and flowering took place in early June in very favourable conditions. Hot weather continued through July and August and a good, healthy crop was anticipated. However, the optimistic early start to the harvest was almost immediately interrupted by rain. Rot was a problem and though by 20 September sunny weather had returned, some damage had been done. Late pickers fared best.

Apart from the DRCs, the most enlightening tastings were the verticals of the decade of the 1990s kindly laid on by Drouhin, Jadot and, without forewarning, Dujac. They helped put the 1990s in perspective and in each case and place, the '94s were the least attractive. Nor have they much of a future.

The complete range of DRCs was first tasted at the Domaine in November 1995. All were in François Frères casks, 'bung up'. Next in London at Corney & Barrow in February 1997. All the wines, I noted, had the same alcoholic strength, 13%, on the labels but there is usually a bit of leeway.

**Romanée-Conti** I counted 14 *barriques* in the main cellar and 14 in the St-Vivant cellars across the road, but cannot vouch for my accuracy. Initially dumb though fruit remained in the drained glass, yet in the mouth a wine of enormous power and length. 15 months later, in London, far less deep, in fact surprisingly forward; still dumb but rich, easing itself out of the glass reluctantly; assertive, tannic. *Last noted Feb 1997* ★(★★)? *Will need a good deal of bottle age.*

**La Tâche** 61 *barriques* plus 58 in the St-Vivant cellar. Nose of fruit and oak; masked tannins, though touch of bitterness, 'neither feminine nor flowery'. Next, in London (1997), far deeper in colour than the Romanée-Conti, virtually opaque; nose far more evolved in the open glass, four hours after pouring; sweet, assertive, piquant fruit, good length, very tannic. A year later, at Wagner's La Tâche vertical: only noted as 'fairly deep' but its nose almost a caricature of Pinot: 'boiled beetroot'. It opened up, vanilla, meaty, then a touch of caramel.

After over four hours in the open glass, fragrant, and after six hours, an astonishing explosion of fruit. On the palate (tasted just after it was poured), very dry, tannic, slightly astringent. This is a wine that needs time and air to bring out its flavour. *Last tasted April 1998* ★(★★)? *(Possibly over-optimistic.)*

**Richebourg DRC** From the cask: low-keyed but distinctive; dry, big, severe. In London: not as deep as expected; a broad, meaty, spicy nose, spice and depth; powerful, intense, spicy, long, dry, tannic finish. *Last noted Feb 1997* ★(★★)? *Time will tell.*

**Romanée-St-Vivant DRC** Yield 25.94hl/ha, 11,425 bottles. First tasted at the Domaine cellar in November 1995 and the following day from the cask in the St-Vivant cellar. In both instances far more forthcoming and advanced, both nose and taste. Sweet, fragrant, glorious flavour and aftertaste – though very tannic. In London, three months later, very good though I was not quite as enraptured, yet good crisp fruit and intensity. Most recently, at the St-Vivant vertical: initially chocolatey, fruit and oak, then a *mélange* of strawberry and liquorice; medium sweet, lean, loose-knit, dry, slightly raw finish. It had lost its bloom of youth without showing any of the benefits of maturity. *Last tasted at the Domaine, Oct 2001* ★★?

**Grands-Echézeaux DRC** In cask: pretty abrasive, hard and tannic. Much more forthcoming in bottle: rich, spicy; fairly sweet and full-flavoured, good fruit and length. Distinctly tannic. *Last tasted Feb 1997* (★★)? *Slow start, early decline?*

**Echézeaux DRC** In cask, crisp, good fruit, lean, very tannic. Next, from bottle, poured 9am, nosed at 1pm: gentle fruit. But in freshly poured glass a bit smelly. Sweet, flavoury but harsh, very tannic finish. *Last tasted Feb 1997* (★★) *Not liked.*

OF THE RELATIVELY FEW OTHER '94s TASTED RECENTLY
**Beaune, Clos des Mouches Chanson** Brambly, oaky, elegant and quite attractive nose and flavour though dry and a touch too tart. *June 1999* ★★

**Beaune, Clos des Mouches J Drouhin** Soft, mature, curious, slightly stewed; curiously ambivalent, placid entry, 'green' tannic finish. One of the least attractive at the 1990s vertical. *Tasted Oct 2001.*

**Beaune, Clos des Ursules L Jadot** Pierre-Henry Gagey and Jacques Lardière were unanimous: a terrible vintage. Not a bad colour though and showing some maturity; brambly Pinot nose, touch of tar, unknit, clearly chaptalised; better on palate, fragrant, fair length, leathery tannic finish. *At Jadot, Oct 2001* ★

**Corton Bouchard Père** Appealing fruit and style; good fruit and oak but astringent. *Tasted June 1999* ★★ *Doubtless better with food. But do not keep.*

**Corton, Pougets Pierre André** This estate, housed in an imposing château in Corton with a Burgundian diamond-patterned roof, like the Hospices de Beaune's, regularly sends me reports though I am sorry to admit that I rarely come across their wines; also sorry to say that I did not think much of this: stewed, boiled beetroot nose, whiff of spearmint; sweet, unknit, coffee-like taste and rather acidic. *Tasted June 1999.*

**Nuits-St-Georges Méo-Camuzet** Méo is a business graduate whose mentor is Henri Jayer. From my own stock, bought from Berry Bros, the first bottle corked. A month later, a second bottle showing well: medium-deep, maturing nicely; fragrant, brambly Pinot nose, touch of hardness; decent sweetness, body (alcohol 13%), good flavour and acidity. First tasted 12 noon, drinking pleasantly though understated at 1.30pm. *Lunch at Chippenham Lodge, Dec 2000* ★★★

**Clos de la Roche Dujac** Soft, open, garnet; *merde* smell; sweet, almost overripe in a well-hung game sense, touch of

caramel, raw. Oh dear, if Jacques Seysses can't pull this rabbit out of the hat, who can? *At the domaine, Oct 2001.*

**Vosne-Romanée, Les Beaux-Monts Leroy** Very flavoury, touch of caramel, good grip. *At the first pre-auction wine tasting following Christie's move to the Rockefeller Center, New York, May 1999* ★★★ *Now–2005.*

**Clos de Vougeot Leroy** Very open and relaxed appearance; meaty Pinot; good flavour, body and grip. *At a pre-sale tasting, May 1999* ★★★ *Drink soon.*

# 1995 ★★★★

Unquestionably an attractive vintage but, judging by my notes, well endowed, possibly over-endowed with tannin. Overall: small vintage, high quality.

Growing conditions were not all that easy: the winter was mild, March cool, delaying bud break to mid-April. Low temperatures led to frost and the subsequent flowering was slow and irregular. Happily, the summer was hot and the grapes matured speedily. Rain during the first half of September threatened rot problems though the weather improved for a satisfactory end of vintage. Yet again, late pickers fared best.

Among the best producers of the Côte d'Or I have noted fair consistency of quality and style. Certainly a vintage to keep one's eye on. Alas, I could not attend the opening presentation of the DRC '95s.

**Romanée-St-Vivant DRC** At least I was able to taste this at the recent vertical at the Domaine. I was also able to record their production of St-Vivant and yield, 12,221 bottles, 17.92hl/ha – and that it is a most attractive wine, in appearance, nose and taste. Maturing nicely; loose-knit, yet fragrant nose which, after an hour, yawned, stretched its legs, and exuded a slight whiff of strawberries; pleasing sweetness, good flesh; delicious flavour and charm. *At the Domaine, Oct 2001* ★★★(★) *Say now–2010.*

**Beaune, Clos des Mouches J Drouhin** First tasted in 1999 at a Bahamas Wine & Food Society dinner at Lyford Cay: good, deep colour, attractive nose and flavour but as tannic as the '94 claret at the preceding tasting. Most recently, at the decade of the 1990s line-up: a soft garnet; vanillin. Good fruit; attractive flavour, flesh, body (alcohol 13%) but with highish tannins. *Last tasted Oct 2000* ★★★(★) *Could benefit by another handful of years.*

**Beaune, Clos des Ursules L Jadot** 'Very small crop, very slightly chaptalised, needs another five years'. Good colour, still youthful; sweet, discreet touch of vanillin, lovely brambly Pinot aroma; sweet, soft, fair flesh, good length. Complete but very tannic finish. *Tasting the decade of the 1990s at Jadot, Oct 2001* ★★(★★) *2006–2010.*

**Chambertin A Rousseau** In Los Angeles, March 1999: 'Michael Broadbent into the 21st century' … 'A tutored tasting of fine wine' beneath which was printed 'Mean, Moody and Magnificent' – not me but, it turned out, my one-time reference to Ch Mouton '75. Anyway, of the 30 *barriques* produced in 1995 from the estate's 2.5ha of this *grand vin* I have helped to consume a bottle or two. At four years of age, starting to mature; a very distinctive, vegetal Pinot aroma, whiff of mothballs and singed raisins, no harsh edges; good flavour, soft centre yet refreshing acidity but surprisingly tannic. Most recently, generously opened by Charles Rousseau in his office after lunch on a Saturday: rich 'legs'; sweet, harmonious brambly nose; rather like our host, a big wine in every sense, colourful, characterful, fairly full-bodied (alcohol in excess of 13%). All the component parts, rich extract, well modulated tannins and acidity. *Last tasted at the domaine, Oct 2001 ★★★★(★) Lovely now but will really benefit from more bottle age.*

**Corton L Jadot** Deep, rich, maturing; slightly scented, singed, brambly; very sweet, rich, full-bodied (yet alcohol only 13%), fairly tannic but under control. *At a Jadot tasting in London, April 2001 ★★★(★) Say 2006–2012.*

**Corton, Bressandes Ch de Citeaux, Philippe Bouzereau** Good colour; harmonious; fairly sweet, fleshy, attractive flavour, crisp dry finish – in fact a noticeable end-bite. *Dining at Ch de Bagnols, near Villefranche, Oct 1998 ★★★(★) 2004–2010.*

**Ch Corton-Grancey L Latour** First tasted in the vineyard at the 200th anniversary celebrations in 1997: soft red; good texture and body (alcohol 14%), considerable grip. Next, the following year, at the Corton-Grancey vertical in Florida: low-keyed, undramatic Pinot but good fruit; warm, crisp flavour, like biting a cherry, noticeable acidity. July 2000: good colour, pink-rimmed; nose now well developed, rich, deep Pinot; mouthfilling, loads of tannin. Most recently: mature; lovely ripe bouquet; very sweet, 'warm' – totally delicious. *Last tasted March 2001 ★★★★ Now mature but plenty of life ahead.*

**Gevrey-Chambertin L Latour** The occasion more interesting than the wine. It happened to coincide with a staff tasting at Butler & Sands, the leading wine merchant in Nassau – an amazingly keen and knowledgeable group, young, mature, black, white, male and female. The wine was pleasant enough, no harsh edges, mature for its age but with '95 teeth-gripping tannin. *Feb 1999 ★★(★)*

**Clos des Lambrays Dom des Lambrays, Saier** Mature; stewed. So poor that I didn't go on to taste it. *Submitted by a very respectable merchant for a British Airways tasting, June 1999.*

**Nuits-St-Georges, Les Porets-St-Georges Faiveley** Mature; curious, slightly meaty nose; sweet, soft, berry-like flavour, dry finish. *April 2001 ★★★ Now–2008.*

**Savigny-Lès-Beaune, Les Haut-Jarrons Ecard** A 2-ha vineyard in this 21.5-ha Savigny estate. On the pale side of medium; not bad, just misses. I am always interested in the unfamiliar but I didn't much care for its peach-kernelly finish. But it did not disgrace the occasion. *Hal Lewis' hog roast 'bar-B-que' in Memphis, Sept 1999 ★*

**Savigny-Lès-Beaune, Les Vergelesses Simon Bize** Palish; good, fresh, acidic Pinot aroma; dry, crisp fruit but astringent. *At The Square, London, Feb 2002 ★★*

BRIEF NOTES ON A RANGE OF '95S AT JUSTERINI & BROOKS' TASTING IN JANUARY 1997 **Tollot-Beaut's Beaune, Grèves** which I always like, good fruit, opened up in the mouth ★★★; and their **Corton, Bressandes** 'nutty' Corton character powerful and very tannic ★★(★★★); **Bonneau du Martray's Corton** fairly deep; so nutty, almost woody; surprisingly sweet, good flavour and texture ★★(★★); **Bruno Clair's Chambertin, Clos de Bèze** undeveloped; sweet, impressively mouthfilling but clearly needing plenty of time ★(★★★); whereas his **Gevrey-Chambertin, Cazetiers** was much more amenable. Nice wine ★★★; **Ghislaine Barthod's Chambolle-Musigny, Les Fuées** light but very sweaty (tannic) nose; crisp, attractive flavour ★★(★); and her **Les Véroilles** also strangely sweaty and extremely tannic. Justerini & Brooks regularly show Barthod's wines but I didn't know what to make of these tannins; **Rollin's Pernand-Vergelesses, Ile de Vergelesses** had a very sweet, attractive nose and flavour but, at around 16 months of age, quite a tannic bite;

**d'Angerville's Volnay, Champans** (the Marquis was pouring) had an easy appealing nose; very sweet yet tannic ★★★(★); and his **Clos des Ducs** nutty, sweet but very tannic ★★(★★); **R Chevillon's Nuits-St-Georges, Vaucrains** was impressively sweet and powerful ★★(★); and his **Les St-Georges** very rich, with good extract ★★(★★); however, **Emmanuel Rouget's Vosne-Romanée, Cros Parantoux** at a fiendish price was raw and totally unready to be shown.

AND TWO YEARS AFTER THE VINTAGE, at a Berkmann tasting, though I was principally interested in the white burgundies, I noted a quartet of very good reds: **Vincent Giradin's Volnay, Santenots** modest body (alcohol 12.5%), excellent flavour, good acidity and oaky finish ★★★; **Alain Michelot's Nuits-St-Georges** a most reasonably priced village wine, with good rich fruit ★★★; **Perrot-Minot's Chambolle-Musigny, Vieilles Vignes** another example of what makes burgundy such a minefield, a 10-ha estate with less than a handful of small *climats* mainly in the Côte de Nuits, 0.5ha in Chambolle: good soft fruit, the requisite '95 tannin ★★★; and **Mugneret-Gibourg's** excellent **Echézeaux** made by the widow and two daughters of the well respected Dr George Mugneret: very fragrant, dry, crisp fruit, powerful grip ★★(★★★)

# 1996 ★★★★

A good vintage, quantity and quality, the lesser wines for early drinking, those from the best producers need bottle age.

The growing conditions could hardly have been better: cold winter, cool spring and wet May which forestalled late frost problems; June was warm with an ideal quick and early flowering. The summer was long, cool rather than hot but with ripening sunshine and a cooling north wind to help maintain acidity levels. The harvesting of healthy grapes took place in bright, but not warm, conditions in late September and early October. The overall lack of real warmth was responsible for the evident tannin and acidity which, as in 1995, sometimes verges on astringency.

**Romanée-St-Vivant DRC** Production 19,031 bottles, the biggest in recent years, yield 27.15hl/ha. According to Aubert de Villaine the grapes missed full maturity by three to four days. Medium-deep, trying to mature; crisp, lean, firm fruit, complete, silky-leathery tannins, great length, powerful finish. Plenty of tannin. *At the St-Vivant vertical, Oct 2001 (★★★★)*

**Beaune, 1er Cru, Cuvée Famille Chanson** Palish; crisp oaky nose and flavour. *At Chanson Père et fils' 250th anniversary tasting at the Savoy Hotel in London (and which also marked the company's new ownership by Bollinger). June 2000 ★★ Drink soon.*

## Élevage

*Means 'schooling' in French! But also the 'bringing-up' of the wine after it first emerges from the fermentation vat, to the time when it is bottled and ready for sale. This is a crucial period. The number of times the wine is racked, how often the barrels are topped-up (because of evaporation), the length of time in cask and its origin (French oak from the Tronçais, Nevers or Allier forests), the method of fining (by egg white for the best wines), and the duration of time in bottle before release. All these things have a tremendous effect on the end result. Yet every producer will have a slightly different approach, which is what makes Burgundy particularly fascinating. The permutations are endless.*

**Beaune, Clos des Mouches J Drouhin** Medium, pink-tinged; good nose, harmonious, slightly smoky; sweet, lean but attractive flavour, decent fruit, its originally high acidity simmering down. *In the 1990s vertical at Drouhin, Oct 2001* ★(★★)

**Beaune, Clos des Ursules L Jadot** A big crop, 32 days maceration and no chaptalisation needed. Deep, richer looking than the '95; whiff of raisins, sweet, opened fragrantly; sweet, rich yet lean and with good flesh. Crisper than the '95. Extended and very dry finish. *At the tasting of the decade of the 1990s at Jadot, Oct 2001* ★★(★★) *2004–2008.*

**Charmes-Chambertin C Dugat** Very deep, thick, plummy; hefty and coarse nose and palate, sweetish, meaty, lacking charm. *With the Joseys at Annie's, Houston, Aug 2000* ★★

**Charmes-Chambertin A Rousseau** 'The easiest of the *grands crus*' according to Charles Rousseau. Touch of privet and caramel; hard, thanks to thick skins – and quite unready. *At the domaine, Oct 2001* (★★★) *Say 2005–2010.*

**Chassagne-Montrachet, Vieilles Vignes Colin-Deléger** Was it because most people think this is white that the red Chassagne sales are a bit sluggish? I jumped at Berry Bros' special price offer of £13.60 and bought some for home-drinking: a soft, youthful ruby; Italianate brambly Pinot which developed a lovely fragrance; moderately sweet, alcohol 13% on the label but I think this was an understatement; pleasant fruit, good texture, a citrus touch. *Sunday lunch, Nov 2000* ★★★

**Ch Corton-Grancey L Latour** First tasted *en plein air*, the youngest vintage at Latour's 200th anniversary tasting (1997): attractive colour, youthful violet rim; crisp fruit on nose and palate, (alcohol 14%), good acidity. Three years later at the 10th anniversary of Latour's own company in London: colour less deep, now pink-tinged; low-keyed but complete, tannic. Quite a bite to it. *Last tasted July 2000* ★★★(★) *2004–2010.*

**Echézeaux Chanson** Very distinctive, scent like violets; somewhat stewed taste, oaky, spicy, decent length. *June 2000* ★★★ *(just). Not for keeping.*

**Richebourg A F Gros** Just 12 *barriques* made: good cherry-ruby colour; an immediacy of fragrance settling down to a serious nuttiness; a mouthfilling wine with the extra dimensions of a *grand cru*. Very dry finish. *At Charles Hawkins' dinner tasting with the proprietors at Ransome's Dock, Jan 2002* ★★(★★) *Probably best between 2006-2015.*

**Santenay, Clos de Malte L Jadot** I am afraid I associate Santenay with a rather dreary health spa and casino. A couple of notes both cruising and lecturing on board the *Crystal Symphony*. Dependable Jadot but a light style, nose fair enough lacking definition, hard to pin down. Well made and a decent drink. Cruise liners, in my limited experience, have rather undistinguished wine lists though *Crystal* is clearly one of the best. I was also struck by the keenness of the sommeliers with whom I had private after-hours tastings. *Afloat in the Mediterranean, Sept 1999* ★★★ *(just). Drink soon.*

**Volnay, Cuvée Sélectionnée Lafarge** Fairly deep; good nose and flavour. Overall dry, lean but shapely. Refreshing acidity. *Dining at Au Gourmet, Beaune, Oct 2001* ★★(★) *Dependable but could do with a bit more bottle age.*

**Volnay, Les Caillerets, Clos des 60 Ouvrées Dom de la Pousse d'Or (monopole)** This was the last vintage of Gérard Potel, winemaker and past owner. I bought it from Berry Bros for home-drinking. Still youthful; good flavour, length and crisp dry finish. *At lunch, Oct 2000* ★★(★) *I shall give it another three to four years.*

**Vosne-Romanée, Aux Réas A F Gros** Deepish ruby; good depth; pleasant sweetness, good body and length. A full, rich,

stylish wine. Still tannic. *At Hawkins' dinner at Ransome's Dock in London, Jan 2002* ★★★(★) *2005–2010.*

**Vosne-Romanée, Les Chaumes Daniel Rion** Fairly deep, intense and still immature; sweet, brambly aroma, sappy and somewhat green underlay; good fruit and flavour, new oak evident, quite a bite, somewhat astringent finish. *The only burgundy in a Pinot Noir blind tasting at the New York Wine Experience, Nov 1998. Then* ★★(★) *Doubtless more evolved now but needs time.*

THE BRITISH AIRWAYS TASTING PANEL on which I served for many years, produced many surprises, good and not so good. BA uses dependable suppliers, does not look for the cheapest and always tastes blind. But I was frequently appalled by the quality of wines, no matter what their names, status or price, submitted by merchants. Of the 66 burgundies entered for tasting in 1999 for Concorde, exactly half were so poor on the nose alone that I didn't bother to taste them, and of the 14 '96s, 11 *1ers crus* and three *grands crus*, nine were simply not good enough even to contemplate. Merchants' wines, *négociants'* wines, no domaines mentioned on the label and none inexpensive. They are the wines which give burgundy a bad name. At the tasting I rated the following wines as above average: **Bichot's Volnay-Champans** delicious fruit; **Chanson's Beaune, Clos des Mouches** needed time; **Parisot's Pommard, Les Chanlains** though too oaky; from **Michael Morgan Pommard, Rugiens** and only one of the *grands crus*, also from **Morgan 'La Grande Famille des Domaines' Corton** spicy and attractive.

# 1997 ★★★★

The third very good year in a row and judging by my rather arbitrary selection of notes, I found these wines appealing.

Apart from a cold and wet July, growing conditions were favourable. Vegetation was advanced by a warm and dry spring and the weather continued fine for the ever-crucial flowering. Late June saw the arrival of unseasonably cool, damp weather continuing into July. August, however, was hot, with no rainfall though there was some worrying humidity. Apart from a sprinkling of rain, which conveniently stopped before the early harvest, September was also hot. It was a smaller crop than in 1996 but of very good quality.

**Romanée-Conti** All six DRC reds tasted, courtesy of Corney & Barrow and Aubert de Villaine who is always present to discuss his wines. Although the wines are listed in order of importance (quality and price), they are always tasted in reverse order, starting with Echézeaux. To quote from information provided, a reminder that Romanée-Conti itself is small, just 1.8ha, the average age of the vines is 52 years, the yield in 1997 was 21.85hl/ha and production was below average, 401 cases (of 12 bottles). Often I am more seduced by La Tâche, but this had a rich immediacy on the nose and was fuller and sweeter, its hallmark being multi-dimensional and relatively concentrated. A mouthfiller. Good fruit. *Feb 2000* ★(★★★) *Will last well into the second decade of the 21st century.*

**La Tâche** The vineyard is 6.06ha. The average age of the vines is 46 years, In 1997 the yield was very low: 19.60hl/ha. production was 1272 cases, two-thirds of the average. The wine had a pronounced, brambly Pinot aroma; drier than expected, lean, firm, flavoury of course, teeth-gripping tannin but delicious end taste. *Feb 2000* (★★★★) *2008–2016.*

**Richebourg DRC** The vineyard is 3.51ha, the average age of the vines is 39 years. In 1997 the yield was 29.16hl/ha, production was 1015 cases. Medium deep, relatively open rim, forward; rich, round, meaty; fairly sweet, broader character – as always – powerful, good length, very dry, tannic finish. *Feb 2000 (*★★★★*) For the long haul.*

**Romanée-St-Vivant DRC** The vineyard is 5.28ha, the average age of the vines is 33 years. In 1997 the yield was 22.27hl/ha, production was 792 cases, half the average. In February 2000 the wine was fairly deep, plummy blackberry-like colour; sweet, whiff of privet; stern but elegant, very tannic. More recently I was told that the yield was only 13.60hl/ha, which seems more likely bearing in mind the small production: the wine appeared less deep. But it was still mauve-edged; sweet, slightly singed, raisiny nose which opened up beautifully, sweet, honeyed; crisp fruit, lightish in style but well endowed with tannin and acidity. *Last tasted at the Domaine, Oct 2001* ★★(★★) *Good life ahead.*

**Grands-Echézeaux DRC** The vineyard is 3.52ha, the vines are old, with an average age of 51 years. In 1997 the yield was 20.98hl/ha and production was 673 cases, well under half the average. The wine was fairly deep, purple-tinged; the initial impact was somewhat disappointing but it opened up, deep, rich, mulberry-like; good concentration and length, oak, quite a bite, well endowed with tannin and acidity. *Feb 2000 (*★★★★*)*

**Echézeaux DRC** Although also a *grand cru*, Echézeaux is usually considered very much a *younger sibling* to the next door *grands crus* and the wine is often more amenable. The vineyard is 4.67ha and the average age of the vines is 31 years. The yield in 1997 was 26.03hl/ha and production was 1240 cases, only 100 cases below average. The wine had a misleadingly palish, open appearance; very fragrant; crisp, very oaky, very spicy, delicious flavour. Dry finish but refreshing acidity. *Feb 2000* ★(★★) *A relatively early developer.*

**Beaune, Les Cras Sélection Jean Germain** Ruby; jammy; straightforward but lacking zest. *A Christie's hosted dinner at The Square, London, Feb 2002* ★★

**Beaune, Clos des Fèves Chanson** A *1er cru* from Chanson's own domaine shown at their 250th anniversary tasting. Lovely crisp fruit on nose and palate. Some sweetness but very oaky. *June 2000* ★★(★) *Possibly 4 stars when fully evolved, say 2005–2010.*

**Beaune, Grèves, Vignes de l'Enfant Jésus Bouchard Père** Good colour, low-keyed but stylish and drinking well. *Nov 2000* ★★★ *Now–2007.*

**Beaune, Clos des Mouches J Drouhin** First tasted in London in April 2001: crisp, some depth; notably sweet, soft, good flesh, dry finish. Very attractive. Six months later in Beaune: still showing traces of purple; combination of oak and fruit; the sweetest of the 1990s decade, character almost overripe, low acidity, very oaky. *Last tasted at Drouhin in Beaune, Oct 2001* ★★★ *Drink now–2007.*

**Beaune, Clos des Ursules L Jadot** Yield 26hl/ha. Very deep though maturing; sweet, brambly aroma, good depth, showing well; fairly sweet, perfectly ripe (as in 1996, no need to chaptalise), crisp fruit, very tannic. *At Jadot in Beaune, Oct 2001* ★★(★) *2005–2010.*

**Beaune, Vignes-Franches L Latour** Medium, maturing; very sweet, soft toffee nose and flavour. Delicious. *In London, April 2001* ★★★ *Drink now–2007.*

**Bonnes-Mares de Vogüé** Medium-deep, immature; when first poured, very sweet, classic, considerable depth but, after 90 minutes, had opened up fully, with 'thick' extract, and a touch of caramel; dry, complete, lovely flavour, considerable length. *In*

*'flight 2', Pinots, at the 'Club 50' tasting in Düsseldorf, March 2000* ★★★(★) *2005–2015.*

**Charmes-Chambertin J Drouhin** In June 1999: immediately forthcoming and very fragrant nose, a fair amount of new oak; very sweet and appealing, touch of chocolate, almost too obviously attractive. Most recently: I have to confess that this note doesn't concur with the earlier one. Either it had lost its coy young charm or I did not give it the attention it deserved. Nice wine though, lightish style, dry. *Last noted, only briefly, at the lunch following the fairly exhausting Dreyfus Ashby tasting of Hugel, Jaboulet and Drouhin wines, Jan 2002. Giving it the benefit* ★★★(★) *Drink soon.*

**Ch Corton-Grancey L Latour** The youngest vintage at the Latour, London, 10th anniversary vertical. Palish and pink; sweet, pleasant, very slightly stewed Pinot nose; delicious flavour, touch of raspberry, Corton body (alcohol 14%), good tannin and acidity. *July 2000* ★★(★) *Say 2005–2012.*

**Gevrey-Chambertin, Combes aux Moines Chanson** Palish, open rim; a bit jammy; mouthfilling, oaky, dry. *At Chanson's 250th anniversary tasting, June 2000* ★★★ *Drink soon.*

**Nuits-St-Georges, Clos de la Maréchale Faiveley** Palish; low-keyed, scented beetroot; sweet, soft, attractive fruit, agreeable weight (alcohol 13%), dry finish. *At the London House burgundy tasting, April 2001* ★★★ *Now–2007.*

**Clos de la Roche Dujac** Medium-pale, light style, mauve-tinged; ripe Pinot-beetroot nose; sweet, most attractive varietal flavour and good dry finish. *In the 1990s decade vertical tasting at the domaine, Oct 2001* ★★(★) *Say 2005–2012.*

**Vosne-Romanée, Cros Parantoux E Rouget** A wonderful luminosity and richness without being deeply coloured; ripe, flowery; a wine of charm and style. *Dining at Annie's, Houston, with the Joseys after a day spent checking their cellar. Aug 2000* ★★★★ *Delicious with dinner but a good life ahead.*

**Vosne-Romanée, Les Chaumes Méo-Camuzet** Youthful, enticingly open; immediately fragrant when first poured but gained in sweetness and depth after time in the glass; good flavour 'in a modern style', appealing but I questioned its length. *'Club 50' tasting, Düsseldorf, March 2000* ★★★?

A WIDE RANGE OF '97S TASTED, mainly in London, between January and June 1999. Here is a small selection:

**Beaune, Belissand J Garaudet** A grower new to me who, it is reported, aims for power, extraction and high tannin levels needing long ageing. His '97s reported to be 'amongst the best ever made'. Certainly pretty solid looking; good richness and depth; fairly full-bodied, good fruit and components. *At Laytons, London, Jan 1999* ★(★★★)

**Chambolle-Musigny, Les Sentiers R Groffier** Robert Groffier is one of the few *vignerons* who can remember the 1947 harvest. Symptomatic of the changes for the better in Burgundy, Groffier, in the 1990s, has been pruning more heavily which has resulted in a major reduction in yields and more concentrated quality. Deep, youthful; rich 'warm' Pinot, whiff of strawberry, certainly rich, very good flavour, complete. *At Laytons, London, Jan 1999* ★★★(★) *2007–2015.*

**Echézeaux D Bocquenet** Another producer new to me. He uses stainless steel and long maceration: the result is opaque wine with a purple rim; a gloriously big mouthful. *At Laytons, London, Jan 1999* ★★(★★) *2006–2012.*

**Gevrey-Chambertin R Groffier** A deep-coloured wine; meaty, hard yet rounded. Medium-sweet, hefty style. *At Laytons, London, Feb 1999* ★★(★★) *2005–2010.*

**Gevrey-Chambertin Dom Humbert** New to me. Apparently M Humbert is a keen rugby player. In between games, he manages to make very attractive wine. In fact, I fell for it in a big way: gloriously opulent Pinot aroma and flavour to match. *At Laytons, Jan 1999* ★★★★ *Drink now.*

**Gevrey-Chambertin, Estournelles-St-Jacques J-P Marchand** Sweet, attractive, youthful fragrance. *June 1999* ★★★★ *Drink now.*

**La Grande-Rue (Monopole) François Lamarche** This *grand cru* vineyard is sandwiched between La Tâche and, on the opposite side of the track, Romanée-Conti and is solely owned by Lamarche. I well recall meeting Henri Lamarche, a perky bird-like old man, in the 1960s and 1970s and admiring his 'High Street' wine. The '97 is very deep, weak-rimmed; a very strange, certainly distinctive, scent and taste. Dry, lean and vegetal. Interesting but not worth its exorbitant price. *At the Laytons' tasting, Jan 1999* ★★?

**Richebourg Anne Gros** Looked fairly advanced; well evolved, vegetal (beetroot Pinot) aroma and flavour. Good length. Small crop. Extremely high price. *At Laytons', Jan 1999* ★★★(★) *2007–2015.*

**Savigny-Lès-Beaune, Les Pimentiers Maurice Ecard** Maurice Ecard, one of Savigny's 'most serious' growers, said that his '97 grapes were the best since 1947 and comparable with his '59, '71, '85 and '90. Rich, soft, oaky Pinot nose with good depth; firm, good flavour, no frippery, touch of tannic bitterness. His **Narbartons** is even better, deeper; very positive, crisp Pinot flavour. *At the Laytons' tasting, Jan 1999* ★★(★★)

**Volnay, Clos des Chênes Fontaine-Gagnard** These family estates are very complicated and, for me, confusing. Richard Fontaine came into wine in 1985 through marriage. His father-in-law is Jacques, of the ubiquitous Gagnard family. Fairly deep colour; still hard, good fruit and oak; complete. *At Laytons', Jan 1999* ★★★(★) *2004–2008.*

**Vosne-Romanée, Les Hautes Maizières R Arnoux** Robert Arnoux had the reputation of making uncompromising wines destined for long keeping, not quick drinking. His son-in-law, Pascale Lachaux, now runs this large (12ha) estate. The '97s were bottled early, by gravity, unfined and unfiltered – which must reassure some wine writers. I found the wine fragrant, with a whiff of freshly sawn wood; firm, good flavour. *At Laytons', June 1999* ★★★(★) *Now–2010.*

**Vougeot Bertagna** This is a *1er* not *grand cru* wine but nonetheless it is still satisfactory despite its weak rim and rather specious oaky nose. Sweet and flavoury though with mouth-drying tannins. *June 1999* ★★(★) *Probably now–2010.*

OF OTHER '97s, THE FOLLOWING WERE *ASSEZ BIEN* OR FAIR ENOUGH **Mestre-Michelot's Santenay, La Comme** ★★★; **Bouchard Père's Volnay, Les Caillerets, Cuvée Carnot** ★★★; and **F Lamarche's Vosne-Romanée, Les Chaumes** ★★★

# 1998 ★★★★

A remarkable vintage. The best are very good which really makes the run of vintages in the mid- to late 1990s quite exceptional. It was astonishing how the growers managed to juggle with such varying conditions. The winter of 1997–98 was wet but relatively mild. Budding occurred towards the end of March but there were widespread frosts over the Easter weekend, hitting the lower slopes of the Côte d'Or. Early May saw a change to sun and high temperatures which resulted in an explosion of growth. Flowering started early, as in 1996 and 1997, but was unevenly spread over three weeks. By early June, all was on course but the second week was cool, and unwelcome oidium appeared. July swung between spells of cool and very hot weather (up to 38°C on the 14th). There was a second heatwave in August. Dryness and heat stressed the vines and singed the grapes: there was welcome rain in the first half of September, then sun for a week, and rain again. But the grapes were healthy and the harvest successful.

**Romanée-Conti** Bottled June–July 2000, 422 cases of 12 bottles or equivalent. Not a very impressive colour, but DRC wines are often misleading and actually gain colour in bottle. Arriving late at Corney & Barrow's tasting, I took advantage of smelling the wine that had been sitting in a large burgundy glass for at least three hours. Fully awakened by the air, it was lovely, whereas freshly poured in my glass it was tighter, harder, spicy and concentrated. On the palate fairly sweet, a full, rich wine with abundant fruit and length. As always, multi-dimensional. *Feb 2001* (★★★★) *A long haul wine.*

**La Tâche** 1410 cases produced. In the open glass, flowery, lovely. Surging with fragrance and fruit when freshly poured; medium-sweet, full, rich, a powerful statement, glorious flavour and length. Spicy aftertaste. *Feb 2001* (★★★★)

**Richebourg DRC** The wine had not benefited from aeration. Freshly poured I found it reclusive, low-keyed though complete; more interesting on the palate, fairly sweet, fleshy, rounded, shapely. Richness masking considerable tannin. *Feb 2001* (★★★★)

**Romanée-St-Vivant DRC** Moderate yield: 18.60hl/ha, 1085 cases produced. At the Corney & Barrow opening tasting: fairly dark; in the glass poured at 8.15am and sniffed nearly four hours later, it had a wonderfully deep, velvety scent, but in the freshly poured glass, it was totally different, more brambly, Italianate; medium sweet but with coarser texture than the others, quite a bit of grip, in fact very tannic. More recently, at the vertical of St-Vivants, an attractive colour, slightly less deep, soft and with medium intensity; when first poured out, exactly the same descriptions as before, Italianate again, with brambly fruit that opened up spicily and, in the end, had 'a scrape of honey'; a rougher texture than the '99 and with a relatively harsh, immature, tannic finish. *Last noted at the Domaine, Oct 2001* (★★★★) *Needs time.*

**Grands-Echézeaux DRC** In the long-poured glass, totally different, well evolved, 'more serious' than the Echézeaux which opened the tasting. Distinctive fruit in the freshly poured glass. On the palate, surprisingly sweet, fullish, rich, complete, good length. I have always liked the elegant Grands-Echézeaux style. *Feb 2001* (★★★★) Say *2008–2016.*

**Echézeaux DRC** Medium, mauve rim; delightful, fragrant, lovely in the long-poured glass but hard, spicy, comparatively unyielding when freshly poured. Sweet, soft entry, crisp, very spicy, oaky flavour, finish and aftertaste. *Feb 2001* (★★★★) *Very good but will not have the extra facets and long life of the five senior DRCs. Say 2006–2012.*

**Beaune, Clos des Epenottes Parent** First noted December 2000: moderate colour; soft, warm nose; agreeable flavour though something lacking. Six months later, pink-tinged; nose as described but not very varietal. I found the finish surprisingly dry. *Last tasted Jan 2001* ★★★ *(just). Not very exciting.*

**Beaune, Grèves, Vignes de l'Enfant Jésus Bouchard Père** Still virginal pink; sweet, gently stewed nose and flavour. Light grip. Pleasant enough. *March 2001* ★★★ *Early drinking.*

**Beaune, Clos des Mouches J Drouhin** Youthful mauve-purple; pronounced varietal aroma and oak; very good flavour overcoming the initial tannic impression. Nice wine, good future. *At Drouhin, Oct 2001* ★★(★)

**Beaune, Clos des Ursules L Jadot** Medium deep, open-rimmed, early maturing; open-knit, slightly chocolatey (chaptalised), sweet, vanillin, opened up attractively; sweet, brambly fruit, easy, very sweet finish. *Nice but rather propped up. At Jadot, Oct 2001* ★★(★)

**Corton, Clos des Cortons Faiveley** Medium deep, still mauve-tinged; crisp, brambly nose and taste. Sweet. *April 2001* ★★★, *perhaps* ★★(★) *Very agreeable mid-term drinking.*

**Corton, Clos des Fiètres** Medium deep, soft cherry tinge; unable to smell much – food, candles and so forth, but a good powerful wine aptly chosen to accompany *'Les Bons Fromages de Bourgogne et d'Ailleurs'* (I was not a 'big cheese' on this occasion. No speech). *At the Chevaliers du Tastevin dinner at Ch de Clos Vougeot, Oct 2001* ★★★★

**Nuits-St-Georges, Les Cailles Bouchard Père** Gentle fruit; sweet, very attractive, some grip. *April 2001* ★★★ *2005–2010.*

**Pernand-Vergelesses, Ile de Vergelesses Tastevine** Served with *oeufs en meurette vigneronne*, a Burgundian speciality frequently served at Tastevin dinners, which, to my surprise, works. The wine was crisp, attractive and had the right acidity to cope with the poached eggs in rich brown gravy. *At Ch de Clos Vougeot, Oct 2001* ★★★ *Drink soon.*

**Volnay, Clos des Chênes Bouchard Père** Low-keyed, not very distinctive; very dry, tannic rawness. None of Volnay's femininity and charm. *Tasting at London House, April 2001* ★★

OF THE RELATIVELY FEW '98S NOTED AT THE JUSTERINI & BROOKS TASTING, JANUARY 2000 **Tollot-Beaut**'s **Beaune, Grèves** as attractive as usual – a good old J & B standby! Delicious upfront fruit on nose and palate, good length, very oaky ★★(★); and **Corton, Bressandes** powerful ('whew!'), very tannic, very oaky (★★★★). Of the three **d'Angerville** Volnays, his **Champans** unknit but very attractive, with lots of grip ★★(★★); **Taillepieds** nutty, hard, very tannic ★(★★★); and **Clos des Ducs** more forthcoming, good length ★★(★★)

# 1999 ★★★★★

A great vintage and, for ripeness and finesse, exceeding even the 1990. This vintage is a must.

It also demonstrates the total unpredictability of the weather, for the year started pretty miserably with an unusually wet spring, raining almost incessantly, clogging the earth between the vines. The wet conditions continued through April and May, though the first half of June was brilliantly hot and sunny with unusually high temperatures, 34°C – to quote from the DRC report – on 1, 2 and 4 June, and 28°C on the 13th and 14th which provided perfect flowering conditions. However, the weather during the rest of June and through July was indifferent, variable. Happily the crucial ripening periods, August and September, were both hot and dry, 'luxuriant' leaves creating, by photosynthesis, substantial sugar content, and the moisture reserves resulting from the earlier heavy rains preventing any ill-effects of drought, particularly vital when temperatures soared to 37°C for the first three days in August, and almost as high (up to 36.5°C) towards the end of that month. And 36°C from 9 to 15 September for the main harvest which followed. A generous quantity, one of the biggest ever, and high quality.

The ripeness was exceptional; all in all, a 'no problem' vintage. Quite naturally I jumped at the opportunity of tasting this and the full range of DRC reds with Aubert de Villaine at Corney & Barrow and, as always, found the wines fascinating and challenging. Starting this time with their new and unprecedented *1er cru* Vosne-Romanée, next the Echézeaux and on up through the range. Romanée-Conti, as always, was tasted at the end. I first smelled all the wines in the large, long pre-poured glasses, then tasted them freshly poured.

**Romanée-Conti** The main harvest took place between 20 and 27 September, with a second picking 27 to 29 September. The yield from this 1.8-ha vineyard was a respectable 31.5hl/ha, the 576 dozen bottles produced being comfortably above average (and the price stratospheric). The nose was spicy, clove-like, the new oak very apparent. Although not dramatic, a wine of great depth. Distinctly dry, masculine, concentrated, chewy and of course tannic. Like an unexploded bomb. *Tasted Feb 2002* (★★★★★) *A great future for the lucky – and very wealthy – few, and a disastrous waste for those who might buy it for almost immediate drinking – alas, this does happen, and unwittingly harms the reputation of the Domaine. This is a serious problem, particularly in the USA. Drink 2020 and beyond.*

**La Tâche** The last of all the *grands crus* to be picked. Yield 22.6hl/ha, 1387 dozen bottles, well below average. In the long-poured open glass: glorious fruit, floral nose and, when freshly poured, an impatient aromatic upsurge. Spectacular and indescribable. On the palate a marvellous ripe softness, yet very spicy, with excellent tannin and acidity. Great length. A lovely wine. Surely one of the greatest ever La Tâches. *At Corney & Barrow, Feb 2002* (★★★★★) *Probably best from 2012 and unquestionably 40-plus years of brilliant life.*

**Richebourg DRC** Yield 35.2hl/ha, 1231 dozen bottles, 25% above average: very deep, plummy rim; a very distinctive though underplayed nose; sweet, powerful. A broad, brooding wine with lovely spicy finish. *Feb 2002* (★★★★★) *A long haul wine, lacking the panache of La Tâche but magnificent in its way. From 2012, almost indefinitely.*

**Romanée-St-Vivant DRC** The second last DRC vineyard to be harvested: low yield: 18.2hl/ha, 1071 dozen, two-thirds of the average. First tasted at the Domaine in October 2001: deep, intense, dark cherry; immediately fragrant, redcurrant aroma plus liquorice; very sweet, full, fleshy, lovely flavour, length and soft, very sweet finish. Most recently: a touch more iron to its fruit and spice. Lovely, rich flavour and long, dry finish. Exotic and ethereal. Superb. Probably one of the best-ever St-Vivants. *Last tasted Feb 2002* (★★★★★) *2012–2030.*

**Grands-Echézeaux DRC** Yield 28hl/ha, only 839 dozen. Medium deep cherry red; spicy, almost chocolatey in the open glass, crisper when freshly poured. Medium sweet, lovely flavour, noticeable tannin and perfect acidity. Combines power and elegance, finesse and great length. Magnificent wine. *Feb 2002* (★★★★★) *2012 to beyond 2030.*

**Echézeaux DRC** Yield 31.4hl/ha, production 1221 cases, slightly down on average. Fairly deep. In open glass, herbaceous though, after four hours, simmered down. More vivid, crisp and varietal, when freshly poured; sweet, delicious, a relatively easy charmer but well endowed with tannin and acidity. Echézeaux can sometimes lag behind, but it is, of course, always a fraction of the price of its older siblings, two-thirds the price of Grands-Echézeaux, its production half that of Romanée-Conti and roughly 12% of the price. A very good Echézeaux. *Feb 2002* (★★★★) *Should be drinking deliciously between 2005–2015, doubtless longer.*

**Vosne-Romanée, 1er cru, Cuvée Duvault-Blochet**
DRC It was something of a surprise to see this *1er cru* hanging on to the coat tails of the *grand cru* DRCs. Aubert de Villaine explained that due to the *surmaturité* of the crop he and his colleague, H–F Roch, decided to create a second wine using the remarkable grapes from young vines from all the Domaine's five *grand cru* sites. The name Duvault-Blochet is that of Aubert de Villaine's ancestor who purchased the Domaine in 1865.

I was very taken by it: fairly deep with an immature violet rim. In the long-poured glass it had a glorious nose, meaty, chocolatey, spicy and, freshly poured, pleasant sweetness, weight. Despite its 'second wine' implication, attractive and elegant. *At Corney & Barrow, Feb 2002* ★(★★★) *Say 2004–2012. (I secured a small allocation and can't wait.)*

SELECTED '99S, TASTED RECENTLY (When to drink: broadly speaking 3-star wines from now–2009, 4- and 5-star, and Côte de Beaune before the Côte de Nuits, 2005–2015.)
**Beaune, Boucherottes Dom Héritiers Jadot** Fragrant, great depth; sweet, fullish (13.5%), attractive. Tannic. *Feb 2001* (★★★)
**Beaune, Cent Vignes L Jadot** Luminous; scented; delicious. *At Jadot's '99 en primeur tasting at the Mandarin Oriental Hotel, Knightsbridge, Feb 2001* (★★★)
**Beaune, Clos de Mouches J Drouhin** Initially pure mauve; well constituted fruit and oak on the nose, and most attractive flavour. Dry. Tannic. Frédéric Drouhin stated that this was one of those rare enough vintages that combined quantity and high quality. *At Drouhin, Oct 2001* (★★★★)
**Beaune, Teurons Dom Jadot** Tank fermented, aged *en barrique* 12–15 months. Medium-deep, plummy-coloured; pleasantly scented; very sweet, complete, rich yet firm with perfect tannin and acidity. *At Jadot's tasting, Feb 2001* (★★★★)
**Beaune, Clos des Ursules (Monopole) Héritiers Jadot** Bought by Louis Henry Denis Jadot in 1826 and the jewel in the Dom Héritiers Jadot portfolio. First noted at Jadot's *en primeur* tasting in February 2001. The biggest-ever crop, double that of 1998. Very fragrant, oaky nose and taste. Plenty of grip. Later that autumn I noted its lovely, youthful colour; crisp yet soft, berry-like fruit; very sweet, rich, spicy – cinnamon – flavour and aftertaste. *Last noted at Jadot, Oct 2001* (★★★★)
**Bonnes-Mares L Jadot** 1.6-ha vineyard; sweet, very fragrant, lovely wine. Length and finesse. *At Jadot's tasting, Feb 2001* (★★★★★)
**Chambertin, Clos de Bèze Dom Jadot** A really beautiful nose yet with curious walnutty character; sweet, grip, great length. *By far the most expensive wine at Jadot's tasting, Feb 2001* (★★★★★)
**Chambolle-Musigny Géantet-Pansiot** A little known 11-ha estate. A high quality cask sample showing both depth and breadth; rich, attractive. *At Howard Ripley's opening tasting at the St James's Club which very conveniently backs onto my office, Jan 2001* (★★★)
**Chambolle-Musigny Roumier** Charming, correct, very tannic. *Jan 2001* (★★★★)
**Chambolle-Musigny, Les Fuées Dom Jadot** Crisp, fragrant, stylish. *At Jadot's tasting, Feb 2001* (★★★★)
**Charmes-Chambertin Géantet-Pansiot** Rich, meaty; good wine. *Jan 2001* (★★★)
**Chassagne-Montrachet, Clos St-Jean Guy Amiot** Not very deep; soft, fragrant, strawberry-like; dry, crisp, on the lean side but a wine of considerable charm. Tannic. *Jan 2001* (★★★★)

**Chassagne-Montrachet, Clos St-Jean Ch de Maltroye** Extraordinarily pungent but loads of fruit; sweet, on the soft side, moderate weight (alcohol 13%). *Jan 2001* (★★★)
**Corton, Pougets Héritiers Jadot** A 1.5-ha plot bought in 1914. Fairly deep; distinctly sweet, meaty, Corton character; sweet on palate too, full-bodied, well built. *Feb 2001* (★★★★★)
**Échezeaux L Jadot** Fragrant, elegant, classic, tannic. *At Jadot's tasting, Feb 2001* (★★★★★)
**Gevrey-Chambertin, Vieilles Vignes Géantet-Pansiot** Fairly deep; rich fruit; sweet, attractive. *Jan 2001* (★★★★)
**Gevrey-Chambertin, Cazetiers Dom Jadot** Full, crisp fruit; sweet, powerful, fine flavour, tannic. *At Jadot's tasting, Feb 2001* (★★★★)
**Gevrey-Chambertin, Aux Echézeaux Dom Fourrier** Pale; light raspberry-like and too oaky cask sample. *Jan 2001* ★★?
**Gevrey-Chambertin, Clos St-Jacques Dom Jadot** This is a 1.5-ha vineyard which came with the purchase of Clair-Daü majority holding in 1985. Open-rimmed; equally open and generously fragrant nose, touch of vanillin; sweet, almost chocolatey richness. *At Jadot's tasting, Feb 2001* (★★★★)
**Griottes-Chambertin Dom Fourrier** Hefty Pinot aroma; delicious wine. *Jan 2001* (★★★★★)
**Clos des Lambrays** Almost Mouton-like nose, fruit and freshly sawn wood; very rich, lovely flavour, length. *Jan 2001* (★★★★★) *Seems to have taken on new life.*
**Nuits-St-Georges, Les Boudots Dom Gagey** A half-hectare parcel in the 6.5-ha Boudots purchased by the Gagey family (of Jadot). A firm, 'serious' nose; surprisingly sweet, fair length, very attractive. Tannic of course. *Feb 2001* (★★★★)
**Nuits-St-Georges, Chaines Carteaux L Jadot** Not tasted before. From a 3-ha vineyard just above Les St-Georges on the border of Prémeaux: good colour; fascinating crystallised violets scent and flavour. *At Jadot's tasting, Feb 2001* (★★★★)
**Clos de la Roche Dujac** 'Bullet-proof wines' is how young Jeremy Seysses describes their '99s. Good brambly fruit; very positive, still closed but marvellous potential. *At the domaine, Oct 2001* (★★★★) *Possibly 5-star future.*
**Savigny-Lès-Beaune, La Dominode Dom Jadot** A soaringly attractive, sweet, spicy scent and flavour. Quite a bite. *At Jadot's tasting, Feb 2001* (★★★)
**Savigny-Lès-Beaune, Les Guettes Dom Gagey** Good, sweet fruit but raw finish. Needs time. *Feb 2001* (★★★)?
**Volnay, 1er Cru de Montille** Deep; very good varietal aroma; dry, powerful, good length, considerable potential. Not a feminine Volnay. (De Montille's village wine much paler, with raspberry-like fruit; firm.) *Jan 2001* (★★★★)
**Volnay, Clos de la Barre (Monopole) L Jadot** Appealing colour, pink-tinged; sweet, fragrant, very vanillin nose and flavour. Most attractive wine. *At Jadot's tasting, Feb 2001* (★★★★)
**Volnay, Clos des Chênes J M Gaunoux** Sweet, fragrant; crisp, lovely. *Jan 2001* (★★★★)
**Volnay, Taillepieds d'Angerville** Low-keyed; delicious flavour but some bitter tannins which will need a bit of time to simmer down. *Justerini & Brooks, Jan 2001* (★★★)?
**Vosne-Romanée, Les Beaux-Monts L Jadot** Fairly deep; meaty style, good serious fruit; very sweet, body, alcohol 13.5%, good balance. Attractive. *At Jadot's tasting, Feb 2001* (★★★★)
**Vosne-Romanée, Aux Réas A F Gros** Cherry red; very fragrant, whiff of strawberry, lovely fruit; medium sweet, rich, good flavour, tannin and acidity. Refreshing but unready. *Dining with the proprietors at Ransome's Dock in London, Jan 2002* (★★★★)

# 2000 and the future

It is still early days, but on the face of things burgundy is continuing to go through a successful period, both in terms of the market and of vintages. I detect healthy attitudes in the producers and the trade and a good deal more respect from consumers – a far cry from the cynical and frankly not good enough days of yore. I am an optimist. There is an absence of the unhealthy and distorting secondary demand from speculators and 'investors'. The international demand for the small supplies of the very best is another thing altogether. For example, if the world demand for the wines of the Domaine de la Romanée-Conti continues, as it always has, to be high, prices will remain in the stratosphere; this applies equally to other major estates. There is no point in bleating about this, for the finest burgundy has always been expensive; it has always – historically – been the prerogative of the wealthy and influential. What we must all be concerned about is that, below these most exalted levels, burgundy should be honest and good, that it should live up to its reputation. But, in the final analysis, you get what you pay for. The essential tool is knowledge of dependable producers and merchants. Read; try to find your way through the burgundian minefields. You will be rewarded.

When it comes to burgundy I do not place too much reliance on professional wine critics, some of whom, particularly Americans (I might be wrong), seem to taste all red wine, even Bordeaux, with hefty and obvious Cabernet Sauvignons in mind. I think one must accept that burgundy is very beguiling in its extreme youth; that the almost startling fruitiness in the spring after the vintage has by the autumn been transformed, and by the time it is put in bottle it sometimes bears little relation to the initial exposure; the first is fruit, in bottle it is wine.

This is why I prefer to take advantage of the many trade tastings traditionally held early in the second year after the vintage, the specialist importers and merchants having tasted and selected prior to presentation to restaurateurs and consumers. Or perhaps I am just lazy. Fair warning, my impressions and star ratings are perhaps optimistic.

## 2000 ★★★

Although some are bold enough to rate the 2000s as highly, if not more highly, than the excellent '99s, while this certainly applies to the white burgundies, the consensus of opinion is that the reds are more variable and less successful. The season started off well with a mild spring and almost summer-like May. Warmth in June enabled the flowering to be speedy and successful. July, however, was cold and wet though August sun and heat enabled the ripening process to catch up. Rain returned in September with a big storm mid-month, immediately preceding the *ban de vendange*, particularly affecting the Côte de Beaune. The threat of rot was serious, leading some growers to pick the Pinot Noir as soon as the rain had eased, leaving the Chardonnay until later. The later-picked Côte de Nuits reds are likely to be the most successful.

Quality, as always, depends on the level of pruning and, at harvest time, selection. There were few vinification problems. Generally the ripe tannins are lower than in the '99s.

I have tasted relatively few 2000 reds. The full DRC range will not be presented until Feb 2003 and the general (UK) trade tastings will also take place at roughly the same time. The following represents my first preliminary, and arbitrary, view of the 2000 vintage, some from tasting in cask in October 2001, but mainly notes made at its first presentation in London, January and February 2002. At these I concentrated on the better and more interesting estates, those which have a future rather than the quite attractive lesser generics and village wines which will be bought by restaurants and retailers for relatively quick consumption. I am indebted to the following importers and merchants: Howard Ripley, Justerini & Brooks, Dreyfus Ashby (J Drouhin) and Louis Jadot. What emerged clearly was the extra dimensions of the *grand cru* wines, so I have decided to list these first.

THE *GRAND CRU* WINES
**Romanée-St-Vivant DRC** Low yield, 19.83hl/ha, producing 1160 cases, two-thirds of the average. A barrel sample opening the St-Vivant vertical at the Domaine: medium–deep, plummy colour, pale mauve rim; when first poured fragrant, spicy, then a touch of immature stalkiness, fragrance returning and after 90 minutes gorgeous. Distinctly sweet, medium – full body, good flesh, very pleasant fruit, fair finesse, touch of bitterness on the finish. *At the Domaine, Oct 2001* (★★★★) *Say 2006–2012.*
**Bonnes-Mares J Drouhin** Deep, tangy nose; fairly assertive, good length, touch of bitterness and acidity noticeable. *Jan 2002* (★★★★) *Needs time to settle down.*
**Chambertin A Rousseau** 2.15ha; Charles Rousseau told us that unlike the '99 it was an irregular vintage. Powerful, spicy and tannic. *From the cask, Oct 2001* (★★★★) *Needs time.*
**Chambertin, Clos de Bèze Bruno Clair** Very good, sweet, oaky nose; good length. *Jan 2002* (★★★★) *2008–2015.*
**Chambertin, Clos de Bèze J Drouhin** Fairly deep; good nose; very rich, chewy, powerful, good length, tannin and acidity. *Jan 2002* (★★★★) *Classic. 2008–2015.*
**Chambertin, Clos de Bèze A Rousseau** The oldest of the Gevrey vineyards, planted by monks of the Abbaye de Bèze circa 630AD 1.41ha; very peppery, spicy – eucalyptus-like – aroma; impressive persistence in the mouth. *Tasted from the cask, Oct 2001* (★★★★)
**Le Corton J Drouhin** Medium deep, lively, cherry-tinged; powerful, rich, meaty nose; fairly full-bodied, good, 'singed' Corton flavour, dry finish. *Jan 2002* (★★★) *2008–2015.*
**Le Corton Follin-Arbelet** Medium, plummy; low-keyed nose, difficult to get to grips with; very dry, powerful, raw. *Jan 2002* (★★★) *Needs time. 2010–2015.*
**Corton, Bressandes J Drouhin** Sweeter, not as full-bodied, more charm than Le Corton, rich, lovely flavour. (★★★★) *2006–2012.*

**Corton, Bressandes Follin-Arbelet** Medium-deep; fragrant, nutty; very sweet, richness masking tannins. *Jan 2002* (★★★) *2006–2012*.

**Corton, Bressandes Tollot-Beaut** Medium-deep; plummy-coloured; rich, nutty; lovely tangy flavour, very tannic. *Jan 2002* (★★★) *2006–2012*.

**Echézeaux E Rouget** Nose and flavour of great power and depth. *Jan 2002* (★★★★) *2010–2015*.

**Gevrey-Chambertin, Clos des Ruchottes (Monopole) A Rousseau** 1.06ha; spicy, complex; very rich and powerful. Hint of eucalyptus. Corinne Rousseau reckoned it needed five to seven years. *From the cask, Oct 2001* (★★★★) *2005–2012*.

**Grand-Echézeaux R Engel** Cask sample: low-keyed, aroma of raspberry and figs; very good flavour and length. Very tannic. *Jan 2002* (★★★) *2008–2015*.

**Grands-Echézeaux J Drouhin** 0.50ha; cherry tinge, open rim; strawberry-like scent, considerable depth; sweet, good flavour, quite a lot of grip. *Jan 2002* (★★★★) *2008–2012*.

**Griottes-Chambertin J Drouhin** Floral, fragrant, harmonious; very sweet, lovely flavour, great length. Sweet throughout. *Jan 2002* (★★★★) *2006–2012*.

**Clos des Lambrays** Cask sample: hard but fragrant, raspberry-like young fruit, touch of bitterness; dry, good length. *Jan 2002* (★★★) *2006–2012*.

**Mazis-Chambertin A Rousseau** 0.53ha; 'Mazis' branded on the cork, 'Mazy' on the label. An impressive mouthful, needing long cellaring. *From the cask, Oct 2001* (★★★★) *2008–2015*.

**Musigny J Drouhin** Good colour; lower-keyed, more elegant than Drouhin's Bonnes-Mares; also sweeter, softer. Rich, very fragrant, delicious. The most expensive of the range. *Jan 2002* (★★★★★) *Glorious future. 2006–2012*.

**Romanée-St-Vivant Follin-Arbelet** Very nutty, brambly nose; very oaky, immensely sweet with price to match. *Jan 2002* (★★★) *hopefully. 2006–2012*.

**Clos de Tart** Good colour; spicy oaky nose, crisp fruit, depth; amazing power, very oaky, very tannic. *Jan 2002* (★★★★) *Long haul wine. 2008–2015*.

**Clos Vougeot J Grivot** Cask sample. Youthful raspberry-like aroma; lean, crisp, long, very oaky. *Jan 2002* (★★★★) *2006–2012*.

**Clos de Vougeot J Drouhin** Fairly deep, dark cherry core; rich, a touch of the 'fishiness' I associate more with Chambertin; surprisingly sweet, silky tannins, dry finish. *Jan 2002* (★★★★) *2006–2012*.

### THE PREMIER CRU WINES

**Aloxe-Corton, Les Vercot Follin-Arbelet** New to me; a good colour, nose unknit; better on palate but very dry and raw. *Jan 2002* (★★)? *2005–2010*.

**Auxey-Duresses Comte Armand** Cask sample: deep; earthy, raw. *Jan 2002* (★★★)? *2005–2010*.

**Beaune, Grèves Tollot-Beaut** Medium-deep; sweet, rich, brambly nose; very sweet, delicious. *Jan 2002* (★★★) *2004–2005*.

**Beaune, Clos des Mouches J Drouhin** I make a point of following Drouhin's 'Mouches' year after year to put the vintages of one domaine into perspective. First tasted October 2002. It had been in bottle for one week: mauve; good, young fruit but unknit. Four months later: medium pale, touch of cherry red; cherry-like fruit too, and violets, on the nose; sweet, very attractive, fragrant with pleasant end taste. *Last tasted Jan 2002* (★★★) *2005–2010*.

**Chambolle-Musigny, Les Amoureuses J Drouhin** Touch of meatiness, bramble and cold ashes; sweet, soft fruit yet good tannin and acidity. *Jan 2002* (★★★) *2006–2010*.

**Chambolle-Musigny, Les Veroilles Ghislaine Barthod** Very fragrant, sweet but quite a bite. *Jan 2002* (★★★) *2006–2010*.

**Chambolle-Musigny, Les Fuées Ghislaine Barthod** Sweet, slightly meaty, caramelly nose; sweet, delicious, silky tannins (★★★★) *2006–2010*.

**Gevrey-Chambertin, Cazetiers A Rousseau** 0.75ha; two-year-old *barriques* used for all Rousseau's wines except the *grands crus*. Cask sample: plummy colour; dry, spicy. Some elegance. *Oct 2001* (★★★)? *2006–2010*.

**Gevrey-Chambertin, Clos St-Jacques A Rousseau** Cask sample; good colour, powerful aroma; very tannic. *Oct 2001* (★★★★) *2008–2012*.

**Gevrey-Chambertin, Clos St-Jacques Bruno Clair** Nutty, fragrant; lovely fruit, good length. *Jan 2002* (★★★★) *2005–2010*.

**Morey-St-Denis Dujac** Vanillin; attractive flavour, soft, spicy, good tannins. *From the cask, Oct 2001* (★★★★) *2005–2010*.

**Nuits-St-Georges, Les Corvées Pagets R Arnoux** Cask sample. Assertive fruit; very sweet, oak, good length. *Jan 2002* (★★★★) *2006–2012*.

**Nuits-St-Georges, Les Perrières R Chevillon** Fragrant; very sweet, spicy, oaky. *Jan 2002* (★★★) *2005–2010*.

**Nuits-St-Georges, Les Cailles R Chevillon** Fairly deep; very sweet and very oaky. *Jan 2002* (★★★) *2005–2010*.

**Nuits-St-Georges, Les St-Georges R Chevillon** Deep, 'thick' (extract); nutty, Italianate, brambly; sweet, good flavour but dry sandy texture. Very tannic. *Jan 2002* (★★★★) *2006–2012*.

**Pernand, Ile de Vergelesses Rapet** Cask sample. attractive strawberry-like fruit; soft fruit, dry finish. *Jan 2002* (★★★) *Now–2006*.

**Pommard, Les Rugiens de Courcel** Cask sample. Raw. Unfinished. *Jan 2002?* Too early to assess.

**Savigny-Lès-Beaune, Aux Vergelesses Simon Bize** Cask sample: caramel and raspberry nose and flavour, agreeable, good finish. *Jan 2002* (★★★) *Now–2006*.

**Savigny-Lès-Beaune, La Dominode Bruno Clair** fragrant; dry, crisp, good flavour. *Jan 2002* (★★★) *Now–2006*.

**Volnay, Champans Marquis d'Angerville** Low-keyed, crisp fruit, moderately priced, classic. *Jan 2002* (★★★) *2005–2009*.

**Volnay, Clos des Ducs Marquis d'Angerville** Fairly deep; sweet, rich, chewy. Attractive wine. *Jan 2002* (★★★) *2005–2009*.

**Volnay, Taillepieds Marquis d'Angerville** Fairly deep; 'nutty'; sweet, delicious. *Jan 2002* (★★★) *2005–2009*.

**Volnay, Clos des Chênes J Drouhin** Medium deep colour; pleasant scent; some sweetness. *Jan 2002* (★★★) *Now–2008*.

**Vosne-Romanée, Les Hautes Maizières R Arnoux** Cask sample, low-keyed nose but good fruit; pleasant sweetness and weight, very good flavour, well balanced. *Jan 2002* (★★★★) *Should 'make a good bottle'; drink, say, 2006–2012*.

**Vosne-Romanée, Aux Brûlées, Vieilles Vignes Bruno Clavelier** Cask sample. Extraordinary high-toned nose; very acidic. *Jan 2002* (★★) *Hard to see how this will turn out.*

**Vosne-Romanée, Clos du Château (Monopole) Vicomte Liger-Belair** The young Vicomte was at the J & B tasting to pour and talk: medium-deep; pleasant fruit; sweet, good flavour and grip. *Jan 2002* (★★★★) *2006–2010*.

### THE VILLAGE WINES

**Gevrey-Chambertin A Rousseau** 2.26ha; the least grand wine of the Rousseau range: palish cherry red; raspberry-like fruit on nose and palate. Crisp but destined for early drinking. *From the cask, Oct 2001* (★★) *Say 2004–2010*.

**Morey-St-Denis-Villages Dujac** Medium-pale mauve; light style, elegant. *From the cask, Oct 2001* (★★★) *2004–2008*.

# White Burgundy

If, as I have already written in my Introduction to this book, France is the cradle of fine wine, Burgundy has long set the standards for the world's dry whites. For Burgundy's white grape variety, the Chardonnay, has spawned a global flood of look-alikes, or at least attempted look-alikes, ranging from very good indeed to grotesque. Happily, the one word one can never use in relation to white burgundy is grotesque. It is not. It is often understated and subtle, and, at its best, is a wine of finesse and refinement. As we all know, the grape variety does not appear on the label. I hope it never will, for white burgundy would lose face value if it ever had to compete in the burgeoning world Chardonnay market. On the other hand, let me hasten to add that the wide availability of Chardonnay has taken some of the pressure off the white wines of the Côte de Beaune, though the demand for the relatively small quantities of the very best will continue to strain the purse.

I think of white burgundy as being divided into three main parts: Chablis, the Côte de Beaune and southern Burgundy. It is a very extended region. Chablis, situated roughly halfway between Beaune and Paris, is quite separate; the only thing it has in common with Burgundy proper is the dry style of the wine and the Chardonnay grape. Chablis lovers, if they scan this chapter, might query the comparative paucity of my notes. The reason is that despite the development potential of *grands crus* in suitable years, most Chablis is consumed young and fresh, and my subject is wine that is not only capable of, but which will benefit from bottle age. I have always preferred the classic, steely, bone-dry Chablis to the speciously oaky, which I personally find out of character, though these wines have, in this day and age, the sort of character that sells.

Southern Burgundy, the Côte Chalonnaise and Mâconnais, with good but moderately priced wines such as Montagny, the Mâcon-Villages wines and Pouilly-Fuissé, produce dry white wines almost entirely for everyday drinking. They are not my subject matter. Which leaves the principal communes of the Côte de Beaune, in effect those of Corton-Charlemagne, Meursault, Puligny-Montrachet and Chassagne-Montrachet. These are the touchstones; at their best inimitable.

## 19th century–1949

Even if one manages to come across a bottle of white burgundy of an old vintage, it is virtually impossible to judge what it was like in its early days. Even a comparison of growing conditions is not very helpful, save for a general, overall indication of quality, for the vine husbandry and, in particular, winemaking methods have changed.

This first section of older vintages is merely to put white burgundy into a historical perspective, the following chart indicating the quality of vintages based on reasonably well-documented reports and, to a lesser extent, on (my) subjective judgement which, in turn, is based on fairly arbitrary tastings of old wines, observing that, as with pre-phylloxera claret, if they are remarkably good now – for their age – they must have been remarkably good in their youth and heyday. Of course, all depends on provenance and condition and, in the case of the Bouchard pre-phylloxera and more recently revived Barolet wines, upon recorking policy.

It is hardly necessary for me to add that the condition of bottles of old vintages is likely to be risky, and, even at best, they do not drink like their modern, certainly post-1980s, counterparts. Expect the wine to be deeper in colour, preferably a glowing yellow-gold rather than a drab tawny yellow, with a sweet, honeyed bottle-age bouquet; also sweeter on the palate and more substantial – the light, squeaky clean and lean wines either did not exist or, if they did exist, will not have survived. But old wines can be delicious even if only of passing interest.

## Vintages at a Glance

**Outstanding ★★★★★**
1864, 1865, 1906, 1928, 1947
**Very Good ★★★★**
1899, 1919, 1923, 1929, 1934, 1937, 1945, 1949
**Good ★★★**
1941

# 1864 ★★★★★

**Le Montrachet Dom du Ch de Beaune** The oldest authenticated white burgundy I have ever tasted. From Bouchard's cellars beneath the ramparts, regularly recorked. First noted at a Heublein pre-sale tasting in 1981 and an identical note at a Lloyd Flatt event (Lloyd was one of the earliest and most important buyers of old burgundy). Though not recent, worth recording: bright straw gold; no faults, opening up in the glass; full-body, wonderful, honeyed – bottle age, taste and life-sustaining acidity. *Last tasted at Lloyd Flatt's tasting in New Orleans, Oct 1987* ★★★★★

# 1865 ★★★★★

Another great pre-phylloxera vintage. Two old notes: **Bouchard Père's Meursault** 'warm straw'; varnishy, *vin jaune*-like bouquet; dry, pungent, high acidity. *1987* ★★; and their **Meursault, Charmes** bright, buttery gold; smoky old Chardonnay nose; dry, sound, delicious. *1981* ★★★★★

# 1899 ★★★★

A good *fin de siècle* vintage.
**Montrachet Audibert & Delas** Fairly deep amber; sweet, caramelised, maderised; better on palate, medium dryness and body, good acidity. *Tasted blind at the opening Rodenstock dinner in Munich, March 2001* ★ *Interesting only.*

# 1906 ★★★★★

Great vintage.
**Le Montrachet 'Quancard Collection'** From a private cellar of old wines in Burgundy sold at Christie's in 1978, bought by Peter (Lord) Palumbo. This is an old note, but made in an unusual setting. Yellow straw; excellent bouquet and flavour. *Picnicking in Palumbo's box at the Royal Albert Hall, watching wrestling, London, Feb 1981* ★★★★★

# 1919 ★★★★

**Clos Blanc de Vougeot Jules Regnier** Not only extremely rare, but the oldest white burgundy I had ever tasted at the time (until the 1864 Montrachet see above). Bought from Berry Bros to serve blind at a dinner party at which Barney (Dr Bernard) Rhodes demonstrated his brilliant palate by identifying the wine. Old gold; great depth; ripe, sweet, honeyed. *At home, Jan 1965* ★★★★

# 1923 ★★★★

**Montrachet Bouchard Père** Two fairly disastrous bottles at one of the most disappointing rare wine tastings I have ever attended, organised by Arnaud Canoen van Oudendyche at the Musée Baccarat in Paris. The first bottle the colour of old *amontillado*; maderised, fudge-like nose; very sweet, rich but with teeth-gripping acidity. The other bottle was cloudy and with the smell of ancient apricots. *May 2000.*

# 1928 ★★★★★

A great, firmly constituted vintage.

ALAS, I HAVE TASTED ONLY ONE '28 **Meursault Cuvée Réservée au Restaurant Les Fevriers** from a French nobleman's cellar sold at Christie's in the 1970s and bought by Peter Palumbo and Lloyd Flatt, the first served at lunch in Paris, the second dining in New Orleans, both in the 1980s, mentioned not as a name dropping exercise but to demonstrate how fortunate I have been to auction rare wines to great collectors and be involved in sharing them at their tables. Both bottles were remarkably drinkable. *Last tasted May 1981. At best* ★★★★

# 1929 ★★★★

**Bâtard-Montrachet L Poirier** Plain lead capsule, labelled. Very good, bright gold; first, a whiff of old age, then clearing richly, deeply honeyed; fairly dry, full-bodied, very good acidity, like an old but dry Sauternes. *Tasted in the office, July 1994* ★★★
**Bâtard-Montrachet Seguin-Manuel** Two bottles: fairly deep amber gold; nose of bottle age and smoke, old apples; amazingly sweet, fullish, good – if old – flavour and length. *Chosen to open a Bâtard 'flight' at Rodenstock's gala dinner, Sept 1994* ★★★
**Corton-Charlemagne L Latour** Bright orange-gold; sweet, creamy, peach-like, surprisingly good; dry, firm, very good acidity but touch of oxidation. *At a tasting of old burgundies at Corney & Barrow, May 1995* ★★
**Corton-Charlemagne Seguin-Manuel** Original bottle, new labels. Initially, fungi on the nose yet quite good, but soon cracked up; dry, austere, full-bodied, very good acidity. *The oldest of six Corton-Charlemagnes at Rodenstock's 15th Raritäten Weinprobe opening dinner, Sept 1994* ★

# 1934 ★★★★

The second best vintage of the decade, but I have not tasted any wines recently. The best 1934s I have ever tasted were two **Dr Barolet** wines: **Meursault** several notes, all good, starting with the original pre-sale tasting in 1969. *Last tasted in 1981;* also the **Meursault, Charmes**, a dozen variable but many good notes: yellow gold; scent of old apples; well past its best but acidity holding it together. *Last noted at Jancis Robinson's Wine Programme tasting, Dec 1982. At best* ★★★

# 1937 ★★★★

**Meursault Jacques Sourdillat** Very pale for its age, lemon-lime tinged; still fresh and youthful with a scent of lemon curd, 'lemon cheese'; dryish, soft, light acidic finish. *At Rodenstock's pre-dinner tasting, Sept 1998* ★★
**Puligny-Montrachet, Combettes Leflaive** Amber orange; nose initially low-keyed but opened up like Cointreau, then old pears; bone-dry, full-bodied, good flavour, length and acidity. *At Rodenstock's wine weekend, Austria, Sept 1990* ★★★★

# 1941 ★★★

A good wartime vintage lost to the British market until the Barolet cellar came to light in 1969.

**Meursault, Charmes Dr Barolet** Fairly deep yellow gold, very good for its age; sweet, surprisingly good, varietal scent and bottle age; remarkably good flavour and acidity. *At Duncan McEuen's III Form Club tasting at Christie's, July 1995* ★★★

# 1945 ★★★★

Small vintage producing firm wines. Only the best and best kept wines still survive.

**Bâtard-Montrachet Thévenin** Yellow gold, touch of orange; maderised, old toffees; dry, old appley flavour and grubby finish. The oldest of four great vintage Bâtards. Alas … *At Rodenstock's in Munich, Sept 1998.*

**Chablis, Grand Cru, Les Preuses Simonnet-Febvre** Pale for its age, presumably a good dose of carbon dioxide; bread, dough-like, slightly meaty, touch of lemon; nutty flavour. Did not live up to the occasion. *At the 1945 vintage dinner at the British Embassy in Paris, Dec 1995* ★★

TWO OLDER AND BETTER NOTES **Meursault, Hospices, Cuvée Jean Humblot** from Claridges, Paris, sold at Christie's late 1970s. Eight notes since, slightly variable, from yellow gold to deeper gold; bouquet from old straw to rich and nutty; dry yet rich, firm, spicy. Elegant. *Last noted 1982. At best* ★★★★; and **Leroy's Meursault, Perrières** pale, dry, firm. *1984* ★★★

# 1947 ★★★★★

Rich, rounded wines which, slightly surprisingly – judging from the dozen or so notes I have – survived better than the firmer '45s. Buy only from impeccable cellars, otherwise avoid this vintage.

**Montrachet Thévenin** Very bright, gold highlights; creamy, honeyed bottle age; dry, austere, good for its age. *At a Rodenstock tasting, Sept 1998* ★★★

**Le Montrachet Belgian-bottled by Vandermeurlen** Pure gold, rich 'legs'; clean, 'lemon curd' opening up like blancmange, white chocolate with sweet pineapple chunks; medium-dryness and body, a bit four-square, touch of caramel,

otherwise sound. *The first of Vandermeurlen's white burgundy bottlings at Frans de Cock's tasting in Paris, Dec 1995* ★★★

**Meursault, Charmes Leroy** Slight variation: one yellow gold, the other more orange-tinged; the latter creamy, harmonious; assertive, mint, spice, excellent acidity. The first with unclean finish. *At Stephen Kaplan's event in Chicago, Sept 1990. At best* ★★★

**Meursault, Perrières Seguin-Manuel** Surprisingly pale; soft, harmonious, smoky, a whiff of honeyed bottle age and fungi; bone-dry, austere, good acidity and overall excellent condition for its age. *At Rodenstock's 15th Weinprobe, Sept 1994* ★★★★

OF THE SEVERAL OTHER '47S LAST TASTED IN THE 1980S **Averys' Bâtard-Montrachet, Cuvée Exceptionnelle** rich in every sense. *1984* ★★★★; **Dr Barolet's Chassagne-Montrachet** dry, firm. *1981* ★★★; and **L Violland's Corton-Charlemagne** almost too good to be true. *1985* ★★★★

# 1948 ★★

By-passed by the British wine trade. And to my surprise, I did not taste any wines from this vintage in the mid-1950s when I was with Saccone's and Harvey's.

ONLY ONE NOTE **Chevalier-Montrachet Bouchard Père** Bought by Lloyd Flatt at a Heublein auction. A rich, powerful wine. *Noted at the Flatt pre-sale tasting in Chicago, Sept 1990* ★★★

# 1949 ★★★★

An outstanding white burgundy vintage. I have tasted few of these wines recently but they are worth looking out for, even though most of the wines may be tiring now.

**Corton-Charlemagne Ancien Dom du Ch Grancey, London-bottled by Dolamore** Warm gold; toasted coconut; full-bodied, wonderful flavour, good acidity. *Dining with Jack Plumb at Christ's, Cambridge, Nov 1989* ★★★★★

OTHER OLDER, MEMORABLE NOTES **Baron Thénard's Le Montrachet** similar colour; sweet, fading but good; warm, nutty flavour. *At a Heublein pre-sale tasting in Las Vegas, 1975* ★★★★; and **Ch de la Maltroye's Chassagne-Montrachet** old gold; lovely old bouquet; rich, fine depth of flavour. *Lunching at Justerini & Brooks, 1975* ★★★★

# 1950–1979

Three decades, during the course of which some remarkably good wines were made, but with a big gulf between the relatively few top wines from old-established domaines and the great mass of commercial wines which, at the time, were accepted as the norm.

Judging by my own experience, for my formative years in the wine trade date from the first of these decades, white burgundy was the wine that preceded claret at dinner parties. It was taken for granted, bought by price and name, by which I mean that it was generally assumed that a wine at a pound a bottle would be better than one at 15 shillings, and that a wine with Montrachet on the label would be better than a Meursault, and infinitely better than a Mâcon Blanc. Individual names of domaines were surprisingly little known, though there was an awareness that some *négociants* and merchants' names were better, and their wines more reliable, than others.

In the gentlemen's clubs of Pall Mall and St James's, and their equivalents in the provinces, white burgundy was taken for granted, most club whites being called 'Chablis' which, I suspect, had little to do with the produce of the vineyards of the Yonne. The word 'Chardonnay', of course, never appeared on a label nor in a wine list. Even if the British were aware of this grape variety, it was never mentioned: white burgundy was white burgundy. 'Chardonnay', as pioneered in California in the middle of this period, was just something on the horizon.

On the subject of Chablis, despite its ubiquitousness, I see that in 1951 Saccone & Speed, a major retailer, listed only one, among a meagre eight whites, compared with 40 red burgundies and Harvey's in 1955 listed 24 whites of which only seven were domaine-bottled, including Laguiche's '52 and '53 Montrachet. The rest were imported in cask and bottled in Bristol, including a '52 Chablis against which I noted 'a good wine (but) not Chablis'! It is worth stressing that splendidly hot years like 1959 and 1964 were marvellous for the red burgundies but far less so for the whites which tended to suffer from flabbiness. White burgundies thrive on the acidity of cooler vintages.

**Outstanding** ★★★★★
1962, 1966
**Very Good** ★★★★
1952, 1953, 1955, 1961, 1967, 1969, 1971, 1973, 1976, 1978, 1979
**Good** ★★★
1950, 1957, 1959, 1964, 1970

## 1950 ★★★

At the time considered a good, 'useful' vintage.

NONE TASTED RECENTLY, but an excellent **Laguiche Montrachet** noted at the Restaurant Darroze in Villeneuve-de-Marsan, in whose cellar my wife and I packed, for sale at Christie's, some magnificent wines. *1978* ★★★★

## 1952 ★★★★

As with the red burgundies, a very good, firm, well-structured vintage.
**Corton-Charlemagne J-M Garnier** Good wine. First noted lunching at Crockfords in 1987, both steely and nutty. More recently, a bottle brought by Stephen Kaplan for lunch at The Park Avenue, New York: attractive yellow; waxy bouquet, touch of caramel; good flavour, showing some age and a bit four-square despite its acidity. *Last tasted Feb 1997* ★★★

## 1953 ★★★★

Lovely wines, deservedly popular in the late 1950s and early 1960s. I have tasted many, the majority English-bottled, but few recently. Likely to be flabby and tired now.

## 1954 ★

Because the '53s and '55s were so good, the '54s were understandably neglected. Few wines were shipped.

## 1955 ★★★★

Well balanced and very popular in their heyday.

SOME OUTSTANDING WINES TASTED between the late 1960s and very early 1980s but none since; including three **Corton-Charlemagnes**, **L Latour**, **Bouchard Père** and **J Drouhin** all warranting ★★★★

## 1957 ★★★

Like their red counterparts, well endowed with acidity, the sort that either makes or breaks a wine. This vintage popular with the trade. The Serein valley and slopes around the town of Chablis have always been susceptible to frost, and in 1957 the major part of the Chablis harvest, including most of the finer growths, was wiped out.

I tasted quite a few of wines of this vintage in the early 1960s, and some have survived 20 years quite effortlessly, the best being a **Labaume-Aîmé Bâtard-Montrachet** drunk in 1977 at lunch in Sydney with Len Evans.

## 1959 ★★★

Hot year, grapes too ripe and lacking in acidity. High alcohol. Few tasted recently, and none inspiring enough to pursue.
**Puligny-Montrachet L d'Armont** Bright buttercup gold; a sort of rich waxy, vanilla bottle-age nose; quite good. *Tasted in Geneva, May 1996* ★★

**Puligny-Montrachet, Clos de la Mouchère H Boillot**
Palish straw yellow; smoky Chardonnay; dry, touch of rot and old sulphur dioxide. *The worst in a 'flight' of interesting old vintages at a Rodenstock tasting in Austria, Sept 1994.*

# 1960 ★★

Unripe grapes and poor wines.

# 1961 ★★★★

White burgundies did better than the reds but they were showing at their best in the mid-1960s.
**Corton-Charlemagne Berry Bros & Rudd** Pale gold; richly evolving old bouquet; bone dry, steely, good drink but lacking character. *At home, Sept 1990 ★★★*
**Meursault, Genevrières L Jadot** Very bright warm gold; nose of fresh peeled mushrooms, peaches and pineapple; dry, very good acidity. The second bottle very acidic. *At the Musée Baccarat tasting in Paris, May 2000. At best ★★★*

# 1962 ★★★★★

Excellent vintage but the best, such as **L Latour**'s **Corton-Charlemagne**, were superb in the 1980s. Only one wine tasted recently but top wines are worth looking out for.
**Chevalier-Montrachet Dom du Ch de Beaune** Deepish yellow gold; low-keyed but harmonious nose; medium-dry, full-bodied, rich, touch of vanilla and good acidity. *At lunch in Bouchard Père's cellars, Beaune, Nov 1995 ★★★*

# 1963 ★★

Mediocre wines.

# 1964 ★★★

As in the case of 1959, a hot summer and very ripe grapes. The wines tended to lack suppleness and zest. Be wary.
**Le Montrachet Laguiche** A well-below standard, oxidised bottle as early as 1968, a dull and flabby bottle in 1972. More recently, surprisingly pale (sulphur?) but not bright; maderised nose reminding me of a stale dry Tokaji Szamorodni and taste of an old *amontillado. Last tasted Sept 1990.*
**Bâtard-Montrachet Camille Giroud** Giroud was noted for his cellar of mature wines. This had a pure Tutankhamun gold colour; a honeyed rich bottle-age fragrance that opened up in the glass; fairly dry, lovely texture and good length. *Presented by Becky Wasserman, the highly regarded American courtier (broker), at a Hollywood Wine Society weekend, Jan 1990 ★★★*
**Musigny blanc de Vogüé** Rare enough at the best of times: good colour for its age; attractive buttery, smoky-oaky nose, with some honeyed bottle age; agreeable sweetness, body and flavour. *At a Christie's pre-sale tasting in New York, Dec 1997 ★★★★*

# 1965

Atrocious vintage. Thin, acidic wines.

# 1966 ★★★★★

Excellent vintage. All the component parts in balance but few to be seen now and only the very best, well kept, will be more

than just interesting. I tasted quite a few '66s in the mid- to late 1970s when most were at their peak, but only five in the 1980s, most of them Montrachets and all magnificent. I wouldn't hesitate to acquire a bottle or two if any came on to the market.
**Le Montrachet DRC** Although an old note, its background and extraordinary quality are worth repeating. It was, I believe, the first vintage made at the Domaine in combination with the old de Moucheron parcel of vines. First tasted in 1976: 'magnificent power, fragrance and future'; next with Herbert Allen, the inventor of the Screwpull corkscrew, who was to become a good friend. We drank it after visiting his workshop and cellar in Houston in 1980. Then, most memorably, after the La Tâche vertical at the Domaine, accompanying a simple tasting room lunch: yellow gold; fabulous bouquet which soared, with an equally amazing expansive and expanding flavour. The finest dry white I have ever drunk. *Last noted, and never forgotten, May 1983 ★★★★★*
**Chassagne-Montrachet blanc Louis d'Armant** To show that only the very best, of impeccable provenance, are worthwhile, this was stewed and fatigued. *Geneva, May 1996.*
**Meursault C Marey Liger-Belair** Pure gold; honeyed but showing its age; dry, fullish body and flavour. Good acidity. *In the office, Sept 1996 ★★*
**Puligny-Montrachet E Sauzet** Pronounced yellow; smoky, vanilla; touch of peach kernels on nose and taste, assertive, caramelly finish. *Sept 1998 ★★*

# 1967 ★★★★

Very good, zestful, best in the mid-1970s, and many warranting 4 stars. Several in the late 1980s still showing well.

# 1968

With 1965 one of the two worst years of the decade.

# 1969 ★★★★

A very good vintage with firm, well constituted, vibrant wines. I have tasted many '69s, which were at their best in the 1970s, but only three recently.
**Le Montrachet Leroy** Lovely colour, medium yellow gold; smoky-oaky nose that reminded me of a bonfire, smooth, harmonious, whiff of pineapple. Held well. Very powerful, assertive, good length and delicious flavour. More life. *With Brie de Meaux at a wine luncheon I hosted at the Louis C Jacob hotel on the outskirts of Hamburg, March 2000 ★★★★*

---

### The temperature to serve white burgundy

*A common fault is to serve good white Burgundy chilled. It is almost always better at room temperature. If served too cold, it will close up and lose all its expression, unlike most dry white wines – such as Sauvignon Blanc – which should be served at lower temperatures. Why? The nature of the wine, I suppose. I once tasted the excellent DRC Montrachet 1969 served almost ice-cold. It was crisp and refreshing at first, but as the chill eased off its bouquet opened up. I kept some in my glass and went back to it an hour later. Its bouquet had completely transformed, becoming sweeter and more forthcoming. I handed round my glass so that my fellow tasters could realise what they had missed!*

Meursault **Leroy** Pronounced yellow gold colour; oaky, nutty; very assertive, very oaky, hard but fragrant, good acidity. *At a Rodenstock lunch in Munich, Sept 1998* ★★★

Meursault, Charmes **Leroy** A bottle purchased direct from Leroy in 1999 and served at a wine luncheon: very pale for its age; a distinctive, sweet, meaty, nutty nose, whiff of lime blossom and flavour to match. Adequate acidity, dry finish. *With Bresse-Poulard at the Louis C Jacob hotel, Hamburg, March 2000* ★★★

## 1970 ★★★

The wines were soft but agreeable, mainly lacking the acidity to sustain any interesting life beyond its own decade. Of those tasted in the 1980s, few wines warranted more than 2 stars, outstandingly the best being the Montrachet from the Domaine de la Romanée-Conti.

Le Montrachet **Laguiche** An underwhelming magnum. Palish; mild-nosed; dry, fairly full-bodied, soft, lacking zest. *At Jack Plumb's 80th birthday dinner at Christie's, June 1991* ★★

Bâtard-Montrachet **Geisweiler** Lanolin yellow; meaty, peach kernels nose; 'dry, raw, horrid'. *At a III Form Club tasting, Boodle's Club, London, July 1995.*

Corton-Charlemagne **Bonneau du Martray** Pale for its age; curious *mélange* which after 15 minutes exuded a strange array of farmyard scents plus banana and mango; full-bodied, firm, austere, with dry, acidic finish. I cannot think why I gave it, in the end, a high mark. *The oldest of six in a Corton-Charlemagne 'flight' at Rodenstock's 15th Raritäten Weinprobe opening dinner at the Arlberg Hospiz, St Anton, Austria, Sept 1994.*

## 1971 ★★★★

One of the best vintages of the decade. Drinking well through the 1980s, the best surviving into the 1990s.

Chevalier-Montrachet **J Drouhin** Lovely colour; toffee-like scent; dry, good despite a degree of maderisation. *At a pre-sale tasting, New York, Dec 1997* ★★★

Corton-Charlemagne **Ancien Dom des Comtes de Grancey, L Latour** Fabulously rich with extended flavour in 1976, lemon-tinged and characteristically nutty nose and taste a couple of years later. Next, in 1982, a smoky, almost salty taste and, despite its body, some delicacy. Most recently: palish gold; very good bouquet, an underpinning of vanilla and crisp fruit; perfect weight and flavour. *Last noted at lunch on board the Carnival Destiny, docked in Miami, as a guest of Bob Dickinson, the managing director of Carnival Cruise Lines who also happened to be 'Mr Gourmet', Nov 1997* ★★★★★ *Impressive, but all the same I am glad we were able to disembark.*

Meursault, Charmes, Hospices, Philippe le Bon **P-A André** Bottle variation, one buttery, almost Corton nose and flavour, the other charmless, *pas bon. Sept 1990. At best* ★★

Meursault, Perrières **Leroy** Golden; buttery, nutty, powerful yet suave. Excellent with stone crabs – my idea of a banquet. *At Bob Dickinson's opening Bacchus Society dinner at Joe's Stone Crabs, Miami, Oct 1997* ★★★★

## 1972 ★★

Many producers chaptalised in order to balance excessive acidity in the wines. Quite a few wines got away with it during that decade. Several warranted my 3-star rating but it is best to forget this vintage now.

## 1973 ★★★★

At its best, delicate, fragrant and attractive with sustaining acidity. The consensus at the time was that the '73s were better than the '70s but not as good as the '71s. At its least good, unbalanced and too acidic.

I SEEM TO HAVE ONLY ONE NOTE OF A '73 TASTED IN THE LAST DECADE

Le Montrachet **Baron Thénard/Remoissenet** Raw and unready in 1974, 'mouthfillingly glorious' in 1979. Three years later, a pure yellow gold; smoky, spicy, expanding bouquet and perfect weight, classic, elegant. More recently: medium-pale yellow; rich, slightly meaty nose; good flavour but showing its age. *Last noted, with Morecambe Bay shrimps, at Edmund Penning-Rowsell's 80th birthday dinner at the Travellers' Club, London, March 1993* ★★★★ *(A modest prelude to '61 Palmer and '45 Latour.)*

OF THE MEMORABLE '73s TASTED IN THE 1980s the following were the best: **Laguiche/Drouhin**'s Montrachet *1989* ★★★★; **L Latour**'s Chevalier-Montrachet, Les Demoiselles I have always liked the story of the proximity of the Le Chevalier (vineyard) to Les Demoiselles which resulted in a Bâtard out of bedrock, as the Chinese might say. *1983* ★★★★★; **Delagrange-Bachelet**'s Criots-Bâtard-Montrachet superb. *1981* ★★★★★; **L Latour**'s Corton-Charlemagne *1984* ★★★★; and **Leroy**'s Meursault, Les Narvaux and Meursault, Poruzots both *1988* ★★★★

## 1974 ★

Poor weather, recession and a lack of quality in the wines. The vintage was virtually ostracised.

Chevalier-Montrachet **L Latour** From L Latour's own vines: buttercup-yellow; surprisingly sweet, soft, rich and buttery, with a pleasant smoky-oaky nose and taste. *At lunch to celebrate the 10th anniversary of Louis Latour's London office, July 1996* ★★★

Puligny-Montrachet, Les Combottes **P Matrot** Touch of straw; vanilla, slightly malty and kernelly nose and taste. Well past its moderate best. *At a pre-sale tasting, Amsterdam, Nov 1996.*

THOSE TASTED IN THE 1980s INCLUDED **Comtes Lafon**'s Le Montrachet the Lafon family told me that they loved all their '74s. 'To convert sugar into alcohol takes six months, then two years in cask' and the aniseed, liquorice nose I noted 'never occurs in a ripe vintage'. It had a fennel-flavoured finish. Idiosyncratic. *Sept 1984* ★★★★; and **Leflaive**'s Bienvenues-Bâtard-Montrachet golden; rich, meaty, malty. *June 1986* ★★

## 1975

Not a good vintage. The wines were lacklustre and short. Of the two dozen or so notes made in the late 1970s, most were below par, only one wine warranting 3 stars. I tasted even fewer in the 1980s and only one wine during the last decade.

Corton-Charlemagne **Bonneau du Martray** After '75 Bollinger, the first of 15 '75s from around the world served blind at Professor Nils Sternby's 65th birthday dinner: golden colour; smoky old Chardonnay developing a glorious honeyed bottle age scent; very dry, fullish, meaty. Very good despite its age. Like our host. *In Malmö, April 1995* ★★★

# 1976 ★★★★

Very good vintage but variable due to the excessive heat of the summer, overripeness and some lack of acidity. However, a most welcome one after the dreariness of the wines, and economic climate, of the previous four vintages. I made dozens of notes in the 1970s and 1980s and fewer in the 1990s. The top wines can still be very good.

**Montrachet Sélection A Lichine** From vines owned by Milan and sold to Delagrange-Bachelet, bottled by Lichine. Very complicated. Good colour, medium-pale gold; smoky then sweet, blancmange-like nose, a touch of fungi (old cask?); positively dry, fullish, with lip-licking acidity. *At a Rodenstock evening session, August 1998* ★★

**Montrachet R Thévenin** Medium-deep orange gold; touch of oxidation; very dry, taste of old apples, grubby finish. *The worst of five disappointing Thévenin Montrachets (1945–1979) at a Rodenstock tasting in Munich, Sept 1998.*

**Corton-Charlemagne Bouchard Père** Somewhat unknit; better on palate, medium dryness and body, 'warm' finish. *At a pre-sale tasting, New York, Dec 1997* ★★

**Corton-Charlemagne L Latour** First tasted autumn 1977: an appealing youth, slow to develop though nutty and fragrant by 1980. In 1986 noted great penetration of flavour and, the following year, still pale with a fresh lemony nose that preceded a harmonious richness. Mouthfilling, oaky, glorious flavour and aftertaste. Most recently, still pale for its age; good bouquet, length and flavour. *At a pre-sale tasting in New York, Dec 1997* ★★★★

I TASTED MANY FIRST-RATE '76S IN THE 1980S, the best included the following: **DRC**'s **Montrachet** several notes from 1979, latterly fragrant but lean, needing time. *1987* ★★★★; **Jean Bachelet**'s **Bâtard-Montrachet** and his **Chassagne-Montrachet, La Romanée** *1987*, both ★★★★; **Ramonet-Prudhon**'s **Bâtard-Montrachet** superb. Expanded in the mouth. *1983* ★★★★★; **G Déléger**'s **Chevalier-Montrachet** powerful, impressive. *1989* ★★★★; **L Latour**'s **Chevalier-Montrachet** also powerful, and with a lovely texture. *1989* ★★★★ and their **Corton-Charlemagne** many notes, gloriously mouthfilling. *Last noted 1987* ★★★★; **Leroy**'s **Meursault, Les Narvaux** delicious. *1988* ★★★★; and **Leflaive**'s **Puligny-Montrachet, Les Pucelles** steely, charred, lovely acidity. *1983* ★★★★

# 1977 ★

This was a damp and dismal vintage with torrential rain throughout the summer. Because of small stocks and a seemingly insatiable demand for white burgundy, the prices were out of all proportion to quality. Of the few dozen wines I tasted up to the mid-1980s, only nine warranted 2 stars. I have tasted only one of these wines in the 1990s.

**Corton-Charlemagne Bonneau du Martray** Ripe, rich, 'calf's foot jelly' nose; medium-dry, classic flavour and dimensions. *At a Rodenstock tasting, Arlberg, Austria, Sept 1994* ★★★

LAST TASTED IN THE MID-1980S **DRC**'s **Montrachet** unknit, flowery but acidic. *Oct 1987* ★★; **Guy Roulot**'s **Meursault-Perrieres** creamy, attractive Chardonnay; nutty, toasty fragrance. Refreshing tartness. *Oct 1985* ★★; and **de Vogüé**'s **Musigny Blanc** a whisper of style and elegance. *March 1982* ★★

# 1978 ★★★★

At last, a major white burgundy vintage. The wines were supple, well constituted and of surprisingly high strength. I recall Drouhin's top white, ranging from 13.8 to 14.2% alcohol. Don't confuse 'white' with 'light'. Quite naturally, there are variations, more to do with the quality of the producer than provenance. As always, the minor wines, from minor districts, or the middle of the road (at best) commercial wines should all have been drunk by the mid-1980s. Happily, I have many notes of the top wines.

**Montrachet DRC** Strangely, two exemplary notes both made at events in Australia, first, in 1985 at a tasting conducted in Melbourne for Emerald Wines, the DRC/Leroy agents: yellow gold; 'nose-filling smoky-oaky richness', toasted, buttery; full, rich, flavoury, with fabulous aftertaste (5 stars). Almost too rich for supper afterwards. Alas a corky, stewed bottle from an American cellar in 1996. Most recently, two bottles served at Len Evans' 70th birthday reception, one of which, most regretfully, I noted as 'dull', the other pale for its age; very sweet, rich, vanilla nose of unplumbed depth; dry, crisp, nutty. Not at all bad! *Last tasted Sept 2000. At best* ★★★★

**Montrachet A Ramonet** Yellow gold, pendulous 'legs'; nose low-keyed at first, but at room temperature it opened up, sweet, nutty, lemon-curd, classic, oaky-smoky, then further elevation, pineapple and vanilla; medium-sweet, very full-bodied, a mammoth wine, with power, length, excellent life-guaranteeing acidity and '20 years to go', I noted. *At Frans de Cock's lunch at Carré des Feuillants, Paris, Dec 1995* ★★★★★ *Will still be fabulous.*

**Montrachet Baron Thénard/Remoissenet** One of a range of badly stored wines with too easy corks: straw-coloured, orange- and brown-tinged; stewed, acidic. *Office tasting, New York, Feb 1996. Let this be a lesson.*

**Montrachet Thévenin** Bright yellow, gold highlights; low-keyed, creamy; very dry, moderately good, acidic. *One of a disappointing Rodenstock range in Austria, Sept 1998* ★

**Bâtard-Montrachet L Latour** Two notes, one at the Khoury pre-sale tasting and another bottle the same evening: glorious lime gold; rich, meaty bouquet; sweet, full, rich, lovely flavour, excellent acidity and a similar note, 'smoky, nutty' added. *New York, Feb 1997* ★★★★★

**Bâtard-Montrachet Leflaive** In 1982 good to look at; its flavour expanding in the mouth like La Tâche. In 1987: a magnum, yellow gold; oaky, evolving; powerful (alcohol in excess of 13.5%) and, the following year 'a gusher', rich, buttery, ripe, great length. *More recently, lunching in Meursault with Vincent Leflaive and his daughter, Oct 1990* ★★★★★

**Bienvenues-Bâtard-Montrachet A Ramonet** Frans de Cock is an enormous admirer of Ramonet and I can see why: lovely positive colour, hint of lime; creamy, rather Sémillon-like nose opening up richly, sweet, blissfully fragrant; fairly sweet, full-bodied, very rich, perfect touch of oak, good length and acidity. Elegant despite its power. Years of life. *In Paris, Dec 1995* ★★★★★

**Corton-Charlemagne Bonneau du Martray** In the mid-1980s: pale yellow-gold; fragrant, scented, time in hand. More recently, still pale; honeyed bouquet of great depth; dry, nutty, assertive, good length, fairly high acidity. *Last tasted July 1990. Then* ★★★★ *Will still be good.*

**Puligny-Montrachet, Les Pucelles Leflaive** Yellow, waxy sheen; deceptively mild, smooth, calm but very good length and acidity. A fine, understated wine. *Nov 1990* ★★★★

OF THE VERY MANY 5-STAR '78S I WAS FORTUNATE TO TASTE AND DRINK IN THE MID- TO LATE 1980s, the following were the most notable **Montrachets**: **Laguiche** intense; **L Latour** mouthfilling, magnificent; and **Baron Thénard** very rich; and two of the most notable **Bâtard-Montrachets**: **Bachelet-Ramonet** rich, powerful; and **J Drouhin** intense.

OF THE 4-STAR WINES (AT LEAST): **Gagnard**'s **Chassagne-Montrachet, La Boudriotte** perfection; **L Latour**'s **Chevalier-Montrachet** great style, **Corton-Charlemagne** and **Meursault, Genevrières** extraordinarily rich; **L Jadot**'s **Corton-Charlemagne** lovely; and **H Boillot**'s **Puligny-Montrachet, Clos de la Mouchère** steely, well balanced, good length.

# 1979 ★★★★

Vying with the '78s, the '79s had an early, easy charm yet fine structure. Most were at their best by the mid- to late 1980s but the top wines have stayed the course.

**Montrachet** **A Ramonet** Lovely colour, pure gold highlights, rich 'legs'; served too cold, its nose initially slightly fishy with a touch of lemon but as it gained room temperature it opened up, biscuity, spicy, and, after an hour, fabulous and after nearly two hours in the glass 'pure pineapple'; medium-dry, assertive, incredibly powerful, vanilla flavour and aftertaste, excellent acidity and length. Great wine. *At Frans de Cock's opening dinner in Paris, Dec 1995* ★★★★★

**Montrachet** **Bouchard Père** Medium pale; cress-like nose; kernelly flavour. *Noted quickly at a pre-sale tasting in New York, Dec 1997* ★★?

**Bâtard-Montrachet** **Bachelet-Ramonet** Two close, but not very recent notes: glorious smoky-oaky nose, hint of lime, toasted coconut and marshmallow; pleasing sweetness, very rich, assertive, fruit-laden. Magnificent. *Last tasted Sept 1990.* Then ★★★★★ and still will be.

**Bienvenues-Bâtard-Montrachet** **Leflaive** Palish, lime-tinged; served too cold, touch of walnuts but after 30 minutes opened up, rich, biscuity, smoky; fairly dry, fullish, still powerful but slightly harsh finish. *Dining at The White Hart, Chilgrove, Jan 1995* ★★★

**Beaune, Clos des Mouches** **J Drouhin** Fruity, high acidity in the autumn of 1981; developing well in the mid-1980s, taking on some colour by 1988, nose more buttery, fruit, oak; positive, assertive but a slightly hard, acidic finish. *Last noted at Drouhin, Beaune, Oct 1990* ★★★★

**Corton-Charlemagne** **Bonneau du Martray** Bright yellow; initially hard but opened up, gently honeyed clover; full-bodied, very good flavour, vanilla, appley acidity, years of life. *At Rodenstock's 15th wine weekend at the Arlberg Hospiz, Austria, Sept 1994* ★★★★★

**Meursault, Tasteviné** **Jaffelin** Deep yellow; strong, slightly caramelised vanilla, opening up with a classic oaky-smoky nose and taste. Fullish but not in prime condition. *From Adrian Miles' cellar at Lyford Cay in the Bahamas, Feb 1996* ★★

**Puligny-Montrachet, Clavoillon** **Leflaive** Deep, rich, toasty, vinous; medium sweetness, full flavour and body, in short, rich and lovely. *Lunching at Corney & Barrow, Leflaive's importers, Nov 1995* ★★★★

**Puligny-Montrachet, Les Pucelles** **Leflaive** 'Out chardonnaying Chardonnay', gloriously honeyed nose; steely, firm, crisp acidity (1985). By 1990 it had deepened to a distinctive shade of yellow; waxy, buttery, spicy bouquet that opened up fabulously in the glass; dry, crisp, nutty aftertaste. More recently: seemed fairly pale, but probably it was the lighting; very oaky, dry, lean. *Last tasted at a BYOB dinner at the Tribeca Grill, New York, Feb 1996* ★★★★

**Puligny-Montrachet, Les Pucelles** **H Moroni** A magnum and two bottles: a fraction too deep, gold; very soft, oaky-smoky pronounced vanilla nose and taste. Medium-dry, full-bodied. A bit too hefty and lacking Puligny steeliness. *At the Arlberg Hospiz, Austria, Sept 1994* ★★★ *(just).*

SOME OF THE TOP '79S TASTED IN THE 1980s with my ratings at the time: **DRC**'s **Montrachet** instantly lovely yet all set for a long life. *1983* ★★★★★; **L Latour**'s **Montrachet** dry, full-bodied, toasted oak, very good acidity. *1983* ★★★★★; **Blain-Gagnard**'s **Bâtard-Montrachet** soft, rich, lovely ★★★★; **L Latour**'s **Bâtard-Montrachet** full-flavoured ★★★★; **E Sauzet**'s **Bâtard-Montrachet** delicious ★★★; **Leflaive**'s **Bienvenue-Bâtard-Montrachet** very dry, lovely. *1989* ★★★★; **A Ramonet**'s **Bienvenue-Bâtard-Montrachet** *pain grillé* nose, full but firm, hefty yet delicate. *1988* ★★★★★; **Leflaive**'s **Chevalier-Montrachet** delicate, subtle, good length ★★★★; **M Amance**'s **Meursault, Charmes, Hospices, Cuvée Albert Grivault** many notes, all fabulous. Gentlemanly, stylish. *1989* ★★★★; **de Moucheron**'s **Meursault, Ch de Meursault** crisp, classic, refined. *1986* ★★★★★; **Leroy**'s **Meursault, Perrières, Réserve Personnelle** lovely, buttery nose; dry, fullish, austere. *1988* ★★★★; **Leflaive**'s **Puligny-Montrachet, Combettes** lovely expanding flavour. *1988* ★★★★; and **Sauzet**'s **Puligny-Montrachet, Combettes** variable, some softness, vanilla and oak. *Oct 1985* ★★

# 1980–1999

These are the two decades which are the most relevant to those who deal in and drink white burgundy, apart, of course, from the wines being made and marketed at the beginning of the present millennium.

Once again, I feel I must say that what follows is not a gazetteer, for the complexity of this region makes it impossible to do justice to the wines of just one vintage let alone a couple of decades.

We are fortunate to be living in a period following a spate of remarkably, indeed uniquely, good vintages. The hallmark of a fine white burgundy is its subtlety, length and finesse: with a rare, sometimes inexplicable ability to be intensely satisfactory, which means I often find them hard to describe.

**Outstanding ★★★★★**
1986 (v), 1989 (v), 1996, 1997
**Very Good ★★★★**
1982 (v), 1983, 1985 (v), 1990 (v), 1995, 1998, 1999
**Good ★★★**
1988, 1991(v), 1992, 1993 (v), 1994 (v)

## 1980 ★★

An inauspicious start to the decade. Lacklustre and now of little interest. Few tasted and none within the past ten years.
**Montrachet Laguiche/Drouhin** From the Laguiche estate, the wine made, *élevé* and bottled by Drouhin. Fragrant, pleasant, good length and acidity. *At Drouhin, Beaune, Oct 1990* ★★★ *Not a long-haul wine.*
**Beaune, Clos des Mouches J Drouhin** Spicy, acidic, 'green' though some fragrance, crisp and flavoury. 'Pasty acidity.' *Tasted at Drouhin, Beaune, Oct 1990* ★★

## 1981 ★

Mediocre. Yet, for some reason or other, many more notes but few of real interest then and even fewer of interest now.
**Chassagne-Montrachet, Première Cuvée Ch de la Maltroye** Pale; nondescript nose; not bad flavour and length, good acidity. *Pre-sale, New York, Feb 1996* ★★
**Puligny-Montrachet, Combettes R Ampeau** Very pale, green-tinged; soft, grassy, minty nose; dry, light style yet substantial alcohol (13.5%). Good for its age. *At a Gidleigh Park wine weekend dinner in Devon, March 1996* ★★
**Puligny-Montrachet, Les Folatières Remoissenet** Palish; good vanilla nose, touch of *noisette*; vanilla-custard flavour, oaky aftertaste. *At Michael Ruger's seminar at the Wine Fest, Sarasota, April 1997* ★★★★ *(just).*
**Puligny-Montrachet, Les Pucelles Leflaive** Still fairly pale in 1990, smoky nose and flavour but lacking length. More recently, similar appearance but I found the nose very attractive, developing well in the glass; relatively substantial (alcohol 13.5%) with excellent flavour and acidity. *At Gidleigh Park, Devon, March 1996* ★★★

OF THE OTHER '81S I TASTED IN THE 1980s the following were the best: **Laguiche**'s **Montrachet** the lowest strength of the decade (alcohol 12.4%), weak, watery and woody. *At Drouhin, 1988*; **Drouhin**'s **Beaune, Clos des Mouches** chaptalised, soft, pleasant enough but no future. *1988* ★; and their **Corton-Charlemagne** fairly full and rich but acidic. Not good. *1987* ★; **L Latour**'s **Meursault, Genevrières** no nose, assertive but verging on woody. *1987* ★; **de Vogüé**'s **Musigny Blanc** bright yellow gold; pineapple and vanilla, then bread crust; crisp, flavoury, moderate length. A good '81 but no more. *1987* ★★. No other wines were more than 2 star, and none are worth recording now.

## 1982 variable, up to ★★★★

Like the little girl in the nursery rhyme: when she was good, she was very very good but when she was bad, she was horrid. In the beginning, it was a ripe and attractive vintage but if not exactly flaccid, the wines had inadequate acidity to provide any zest and life. One well-known *négociant* originally described his '82 as 'a smashing success'. Another that 'it was even more successful in Chablis'. I wonder what they think of the vintage now? My recommendation is to avoid shippers' wines or drink up.

Even though most of my notes are not recent I shall start with the Montrachets as they should, in effect, represent the best of the vintage.
**Montrachet Bouchard Père** At 5½ years of age, it was a plump, yellow-gold colour; fat, buttery nose; full-bodied (alcohol 14%). Impressive but lacking zest. *March 1988* ★★★★ *(just).* Drink soon.
**Montrachet L Jadot** Lovely, wax-sheened yellow colour; creamy, vanilla, harmonious nose; lovely, full, rich and buttery flavour. *Sipped while admiring the fine collection of 18th-century American furniture in the home of Frank Hohmann II, New York, Oct 1995* ★★★★
**Montrachet Comtes Lafon** I first tasted this in the autumn of 1984: warm, crusty, lovely but lacking ultimate length. Then five years later: straw gold; glorious, creamy, almost custardy bouquet; full, fat, rounded, oaky, touch of bitterness. *Last tasted at the domaine, Meursault, Sept 1989* ★★★★

### Vineyard sizes in Burgundy

*Many of Burgundy's vineyards are very small in size – Le Montrachet, for example, is a mere 8 hectares. It is shared between ten fortunate owners, each of whom makes wine from what must be only a few rows of vines – the Domaine de la Romanée-Conti owns just 0.68ha, for example, Comtes Lafon a mere 0.31ha and Domaine Leflaive 0.8ha. The tricky thing with such small-scale production is catering for a world demand! Just how many bottles of Montrachet can you squeeze out of one small vineyard? I tasted six different 1982 Montrachets through the late 1980s and early 1990s – they really did vary in quality and style, and made fascinating comparisons.*

Montrachet **Laguiche/Drouhin** Fairly pale; high toned, still youthful pineapple, opening and holding well; some sweetness, fairly full-bodied (alcohol 13.5%), intriguing flavour, decent length, moderately good acidity (3.8g/l). *At Drouhin, Beaune, Oct 1990* ★★★★ *Ready now.*

Montrachet **Jacques Prieur** Fairly pale, lime-tinged yellow; fragrant; sulphur dioxide noted and a smell that, when opened up, reminded me of Italian vanilla ice-cream. Sweetish, soft yet assertive, austere yet lacking acidity. *At a Rodenstock wine weekend dinner in Austria, Sept 1990* ★★★

Montrachet **DRC** Surprisingly pale, lemon-tinged gold in its youth; extraordinary nose, crusty bread, brown sugar and toast, a full-bodied, nutty, spicy wine. *At an early DRC trade tasting at Corney & Barrow, Nov 1985* ★★★★

Bâtard-Montrachet **E Sauzet** Buttery, waxy; richly flavoured, touch of bitterness. *Lunch at Christie's, London, Oct 1990* ★★★★ *Drink soon.*

Beaune, Clos des Mouches **J Drouhin** First noted in 1990 at Drouhin's line-up of the 1980s: palish; rich, forthcoming nose, butter, vanilla; soon to evolve an extraordinary confection; moderately full-bodied (alcohol 13.3%), positive, (acidity 3.9g/l) with a hard, dry finish. Despite its exotic nose I did not rate it highly. More recently: waxy lime-yellow; harmonious, vanilla nose; dry, pleasant, oaky/vanilla taste and quite good length. *Last noted lunching at Bill Baker's after his old madeira tasting, a hard act to follow, in Somerset, April 1994* ★★★

Chevalier-Montrachet **Leflaive** First tasted in 1986. Low-keyed, slow to emerge, sulphury, muffled nose; better on palate but soft and lacking. Next: palish, lime-tinged, creamy but not very distinctive nose or flavour, with a scented aftertaste. Though it grew on me, it lacked the Chevalier's expected panache. *At Hugh Johnson's Bordeaux Club dinner, Jan 1995* ★★★

Corton-Charlemagne **Bonneau du Martray** Positive yellow; luscious, bread-crust nose; rich, full-body and flavour, surprisingly good acidity for an '82. *Dining with Karina Eigensatz in Wiesbaden. In Walter's absence I was allowed to plunder his cellar, July 1994* ★★★★

Corton-Charlemagne, Hospices, Cuvée François de Salins **Jaboulet-Vercherre** Fairly deep yellow; waxy, buttery Chardonnay nose; moderate length. Spoiled for me by whiff of almond kernels on nose and palate. *Jan 1990* ★★

Meursault **Ch de Meursault** Pale gold; soft, showing its age; meaty, touch of caramel. 'Needs drinking'. *White burgundy tasting, New York, Dec 1996* ★

Meursault, Clos de la Barre **Comtes Lafon** In the cellar: lemon-tinged; attractive (all Lafon's wines are unfined, unfiltered and bottled by hand, two *barriques* a day). Most recently: pale for its age, still lemon-tinged; sweet, crusty (bread), lovely bouquet; medium-sweet, delicious flavour and excellent acidity. *At a Christie's wine course team dinner to celebrate our 18th anniversary, at Boodle's Club, London, Oct 2000* ★★★★

Meursault, Blagny **L Jadot** Pale; not showing its age; a bit austere. Minor and overpriced. *June 1990* ★★ *Drink up.*

Meursault, Genevrières **Bouchard Père** Two notes. Waxy yellow; oaky, vanilla nose; rich, like an old-fashioned California Chardonnay – very attractive flavour and aftertaste. *Last tasted Sept 1990* ★★★★ *Drink soon.*

Meursault, Genevrières **Jobard** Very dry, oaky, austere, almost woody. Drying out? *Treating my agent to dinner at Montrachet, New York, Feb 1996* ★

Puligny-Montrachet, Les Pucelles **Leflaive** Palish; broad, too meaty for Pucelles; curious flavour. Not a patch on the Clos de la Barre above. *At Boodle's Club, London, Oct 2000* ★★

SOME OTHER '82s SHOWING WELL IN THE MID- TO LATE 1980s A Ramonet's **Bâtard-Montrachet** pale and delicate; fabulous bouquet, fragrant, harmonious. Medium-dry, medium-full, soft yet crisp enough. A promising start but seemed to tail off. *1986* ★★★; **L Jadot**'s **Chassagne-Montrachet** excellent. *1987* ★★★; **L Latour**'s **Bâtard-Montrachet** nutty, oaky, richly flavoured. *1985* ★★★★; **J Drouhin**'s **Corton-Charlemagne** fragrant, nutty, oaky; lively, good length. *1986* ★★★★; and **Ch de Meursault** made from Charmes and Perrières: purest Chardonnay, excellent flavour and aftertaste. *1985* ★★★★

# 1983 ★★★★

Vast improvement over the '82s. Well endowed whites with body, flesh and good acidity. The best still drinking well.

Montrachet **Laguiche/Drouhin** Distinctive yellow; nose deep, rich, with spicy fragrance after two hours in the glass; sweet, rich, full-bodied (alcohol 14.1%, higher even than the great '78), good acidity (3.7g/l), like the '86 but, oddly, slightly lower than the '82. Lovely wine. *At Drouhin, Beaune, Oct 1990* ★★★★★ *Drink now–2010 or thereabouts.*

Montrachet **Jacques Prieur** Palish gold; hefty, toasty, oaky nose and flavour. Unknit. Fairly high acidity. *At a tasting dinner on the first evening of Rodenstock's marathon five-day Ch d'Yquem tasting in Munich, August 1998* ★★

Montrachet **DRC** Palish yellow; low-keyed nose; far more interesting on the palate, fairly sweet, full of flavour, fruit, body. Impressive but still hard. 'Needs time.' *The oldest of a flight of Montrachets at Rodenstock's gala dinner, Sept 1995. Then* ★★(★★★) *Probably a fully fledged 5-star now. A long-haul Montrachet.*

Bâtard-Montrachet **Leflaive** Palish; wonderfully fragrant, nutty, oaky bouquet and flavour. Rich, fullish, yet lean and steely. Lemon-like acidity. Very high mark. *Preceding the DRC Montrachet (see above), Sept 1995* ★★★★★

Beaune, Clos des Mouches **J Drouhin** First tasted in the spring of 1984: a cask sample, at Drouhin's opening tasting of '83s. Then very pale; youthful 'acetone' nose; dry, expanding flavour, lovely aftertaste. At seven years of age, a deeper yellow; vanilla nose opened up beautifully; pleasing flavour, its richness masking its high alcoholic content (13.7%) the highest of the decade, and the acidity (3.8g/l) completing the balance, adding zest and a good lifeline. *Last tasted at Drouhin, Beaune, Oct 1990* ★★★★ *Should be excellent now but drink soon.*

Bienvenues-Bâtard-Montrachet **Leflaive** First noted lunching with Vincent Leflaive in 1990: then still green-tinged; slightly scented; more powerful than the eye or nose predicted. Rich, shapely, mouthfilling. More recently: palish, waxy sheen; low-keyed, a bit oily and though it started to lift itself, a touch of caramel maderisation held it down; dry, full, nutty, powerful but no charm. *Magnums at Bob Dickinson's 'Mr Gourmet' Investiture dinner at the Biltmore, Coral Gables, Nov 1997. At best* ★★★?

Chassagne-Montrachet **J Drouhin** Lovely. *May 1991* ★★★

Chevalier-Montrachet **Leflaive** First noted in 1987 dining at Domaine de Chevalier. 'A great wine.' Deft touch of oak, refined, long lemony flavour and long life predicted. More recently, in magnums: still pale; very oaky-smoky bouquet; very dry, lean but assertive. Served too cold but delicious. *Last noted at Bob Dickinson's 'Mr Gourmet' dinner, Nov 1997* ★★★★

Chevalier-Montrachet, Les Demoiselles **L Jadot** Bouquet showing some age but good; medium-dryness and body, smoky flavour, elegant, ready. *Dining with Madeleine and Andrew Lloyd-Webber, Sept 1994* ★★★★

**Meursault, Les Chevaliers Guy Prieur** Opened up nicely; good flavour and very good acidity. Another '83, but livelier, at a Saintsbury Club dinner. *April 1995* ★★★

**Meursault, Poruzots F Jobard** Bright yellow; attractive, minty nose and taste. Medium sweetness and body. Touch of lanoline. Good acidity. *At the Dickinsons', Miami, Nov 1997* ★★★

**Puligny-Montrachet L Jadot** Knockout drops! Astonishingly high alcohol (14.6%) and acidity (4.6g/l – but which is, of course, low by German Riesling standards). Yellow-hued; very rich bouquet; the sweetness of ripe grapes and substantial alcohol; plump for Puligny. *With André Gagey, at Jadot, Oct 1990* ★★★★★ *If any left, should still be an amazing mouthful.*

**Corton-Charlemagne Bonneau du Martray** First tasted in 1987, beautifully constructed, good future. More recently: yellow gold; an immediacy of fragrance, grassy, scented, lively, positive; very attractive, minty rather than Corton nuttiness, leaner than Latour's, good acidity. *Dining with Jancis Robinson, May 1994* ★★★★ *Her husband, Nick, did the cooking as usual. Belle and Barney Rhodes (from the Napa) supplied the wines from their London cellar. In all, we had ten wines and the '55 port was so good that I had two glasses. I was stopped on the way home by the police who asked me if I had had a drink that evening. I said I had just been out for dinner. He said he would not book me for doing 35 mph in a 30 mph area but would I step out and have my breath tested. I blew long and hard into the bag but nothing happened. I was allowed to drive on. 'Low blood pressure', said Daphne. Faulty testing kit thought I, or Divine intervention.*

**Corton-Charlemagne L Jadot** Glorious. Lovely fruit and vinosity. *At Jadot, Oct 1990* ★★★★★ *Should still be excellent.*

**Corton-Charlemagne L Latour** Around seven notes, first in 1989: a luminous grape green; lovely nose; full, rich, nutty, dry finish. Next, alongside the Bonneau du Martrays at Jancis's modest little dinner party (see above). Deeper than the Bonneau, pure gold; nose and palate stolid and stodgy at first but more uplifting after time in the glass. Showing well at Latour's bicentenary tasting in 1997, fragrant, sweet. Later that autumn: hefty, nutty, a tingle of acidity (Bacchus Society dinner). The following year: rich nose but 'stewed', like apples in a hayloft; sweet, fat, powerful. *Last tasted at my Hollywood Wine Society Latour seminar, March 1998* ★★★ *Frankly, a bit stodgy.*

**Meursault, Charmes Prosper Maufoux** Pale for age but unimpressive. Needed drinking. *With filet 'moneybags' of monkfish at a Saintsbury Club dinner, London, Oct 1994* ★

**Meursault, Charmes, Hospices, Cuvée Bahezres de Lanlay** (Unknown bottler.) But this is what Meursault is all about. Rich, colourful, ripe, lovely. *Feb 1990. Then* ★★★★ *Should still be good but drink up.*

OF THE MANY '83S TASTED IN THE MID- TO LATE 1980S, the following stand out: **Jean-Paul Gauffroy's Meursault, Chevalières** wonderful colour, toasted coconut, macaroon nose, hefty yet fine and crisp. *1987* ★★★★; **Philippe Bouzereau's Meursault, Les Grand Charrons** gloriously rich, powerful, with acidity. *1988* ★★★★; **Javilliers' Meursault, Tillets** assertive, good fruit and acidity. *1987* ★★★; **de Vogüé's Musigny Blanc** a splendid youth, all the component parts. *1997* ★★★★, *possibly 5-star*; and **H Clerc's Puligny-Montrachet, Folatières** mouthfilling yet crisp. *1985* ★★★★

# 1984 ★

A distinctly poor vintage, entirely due to one of the worst Septembers on record, when it rained ceaselessly well into October. The growers had to deal with unripe, albeit fairly healthy grapes (July and August were warm but with drought conditions), necessitating considerable chaptalisation which countered the high acidity and made the resultant wine fairly passable in its early years. The few notes that follow clearly demonstrate the mediocrity of the wines and, by and large, their sorry state. Avoid.

**Montrachet Laguiche/Drouhin** A curiously artificial 'boiled sweets' nose, plus vanilla; dry, medium-weight (alcohol 13.2%); dry, positive though hard, acidic (total acidity 4.2g/l) due to lack of full ripeness of the otherwise healthy grapes; raw, with a strangely scented aftertaste. *At Drouhin, Beaune, Oct 1990. Then* ★★ *No improvement likely.*

**Montrachet DRC** Medium-pale yellow; hefty, slightly caramelised fruit; fairly sweet, full-bodied, rich, a touch of coarseness but quite good length. Provenance unknown. *Tasted at Christie's in New York, Feb 1996* ★★?

**Bienvenues-Bâtard-Montrachet Remoissenet** Not bad colour, nose and taste, which is not saying much. Curious taste, scented, somewhat acidic. *New York, Feb 1996* ★

**Chassagne-Montrachet L Latour** Stewed, vanilla, lemon-tinged acidity. Mediocre. *March 1991* ★

**Chassagne-Montrachet Olivier Leflaive** Pale; fragrant; a bit 'pasty' and oaky but quite attractive. *Dining at Domaine de Chevalier, Bordeaux, June 1999* ★★

**Chassagne-Montrachet, Morgeot G Déléger** Strange, unattractive nose and flavour. Acidic. *Feb 1996.*

**Meursault, Charmes Pierre Morey** Many notes. In its youth fairly pale with a touch of lemon and pineapple on the nose and flavour, some soft fruit and oak but distinctly dry. Later, its leanness and austerity noted. 'Lacking length.' Aged six: rich vanilla nose, dry enough, moderately decent flavour. *Dining with James Halliday, at home. It impressed neither of us. July 1992* ★ *Certainly no good now.*

**Puligny-Montrachet, Les Folatières L Jadot** Deep gold; fat, scented, vanilla nose. The must heated and the wine heavily chaptalised, its rawness due to immature grapes. *With André Gagey, Oct 1990. Forgettable wine, unforgettable person.*

NOTES ON A SELECTION OF '84S TASTED IN THE LATE 1980S **Ramonet's Montrachet** lemon gold; lemon-like acidity and oak on the nose, hollow, tinny; dry, a soft, not bad, flavour despite its lean austerity and acidity. *1989* ★ – *if Ramonet could not make a good wine that year, no one could*; **J Drouhin's Beaune, Clos des Mouches** noted merely to indicate the basic elements in such a vintage: alcohol 13.6% after chaptalisation, pH 3.34, total acidity 3.9g/l comprising 0.9° tartaric, 0.44 volatile. The net result not at all bad ★ *cask sample tasted in London, March 1986*; **L Jadot's Meursault, Charmes** passable. *1989* ★★; and **Leflaive's Puligny-Montrachet** dry, assertive, a good domaine doing its best in a poor year. *1989* ★★★

# 1985 variable, at best ★★★★

This should have been an exemplary vintage. It was certainly promising, but it was not until I began assembling my notes that I realised how uneven the wines were – and are. The harvest was good, if a little late; the grapes were ripe. Perhaps some of my 4-star wines, from the description, should have been elevated to 5-star. Most probably the wines had a seven- to ten-year span with exceptions at either end. The minor wines were for quick and enjoyable drinking, the well made classics are still holding on. But on balance, drink up.

As mentioned earlier, it is a constant surprise to me that so many growers and merchants can put their name to a vineyard of only 7.68ha yielding between 4000 and 5000 cases a year. Five Montrachets open up this quite interesting vintage.

**Montrachet Dom du Ch de Beaune** Picking began 25 September. At ten years of age, palish with touch of lemon; lemon and vanilla on the nose; fairly sweet, soft, dry finish (the tasting was to see if Bouchard Père's top wines were of *grand cru* quality. This was below standard but whether it was then declassified to *1er cru*, or lower, I do not know). Next, noted at a Rodenstock's gala dinner: colour now gold, a sort of tarnished gold; very old smell, buttery, oily, minty, tinny; on the palate 'rather flat'. *Last tasted Sept 1998. Poor wine.*

**Montrachet Chartron et Trébuchet** Pale yellow, waxy sheen; nose minty at first then smoky, spicy, vanilla; dry, fairly full-bodied, good length, austere. *July 1990. Then* ★★★(★)

**Montrachet Laguiche/Drouhin** First noted at Drouhin's opening tasting in London, March 1986: very pale; immature, unknit, raw pineappley nose; very oaky. Next, in 1990: bottle variation, first in the tasting room, one lacking fruit and woody, the second more fragrant with lovely flavour and a third bottle, to clinch matters, produced by Robert Drouhin to drink at lunch. It was superb: bright; delicate, oaky fragrance; perfect weight and balance (alcohol 13.3%, acidity 3.4g/l), rich, buttery flavour – thank goodness. Eight years later, *grace à* Diane Klat at the next table: very fragrant, slightly smoky bouquet which developed well but positively explosive on the palate, eager to show its paces, marvellous length and aftertaste. *Last tasted at The Waterside Inn, Bray, a dinner to celebrate Daphne's birthday, 22 July 1998* ★★★★

**Montrachet Baron Thénard** Really far too premature, a jeroboam opened at dinner two autumns after the vintage. But it was very impressive, with a smoky, lemony nose that opened up as if to order, displaying attractively youthful fruit; long on the palate, spicy, combining power and elegance. Eleven years later, in the first flight of a tasting, in bottle this time: pale, still retaining a hint of youthful green; served too cold, though fragrant, opening up as it reached room temperature, nutty, vanilla; very good, clean, fresh flavour and length with a lovely lemony, oaky finish. *Last tasted at dinner on the fourth evening at Rodenstock's Ch d'Yquem marathon, Sept 1998* ★★★★

**Montrachet DRC** A substantial wine with a convincing appearance; rich, round, soft, bread-like – more dough than crust, with touch of pineapple. Full-bodied (I thought about 13.8%; our hosts, who should have it at their fingertips, said it was 14 to 14.5%), certainly very rich, nutty flavour, good acidity. A lovely wine. *Served (at room temperature; Aubert de Villaine considered 15°C best) after the DRC tasting of 1994s and before dinner, at the Domaine, Nov 1995* ★★★★

**Beaune, Clos des Mouches J Drouhin** Five notes, first at Drouhin's opening tasting in March 1986: mild, pleasant young fruit, fairly substantial (alcohol 13.3%); good acidity (3.7g/l). The following year I noticed the way the flavour swelled in the mouth, always a good sign. Very detailed notes in 1990, briefly its crisp fruit opening generously, broad, peach-like, and ending with a soft, discreet vanilla scent; the sweetness of ripe grapes, soft yet assertive. 'Needs time.' At ten years of age, it appeared to have a satin sheen; gloriously evolved bouquet; delicious oaky-Chardonnay flavour, rich, perfect balance and lovely oaky aftertaste. *Last noted at Hugh Johnson's Bordeaux Club dinner at Saling Hall, Essex, July 1995* ★★★★ One of the best-ever Drouhin Clos des Mouches, brought out at the right age, served at the right temperature and appreciated by like-minded companions.

**Bienvenues-Bâtard-Montrachet Remoissenet** Surprisingly pale; perfect, harmonious, slightly crusty (bread) nose; rich, full-body and flavour, perfect balance, very good acidity. *Dining as the guest of Ron Weiser at the smart English-owned (and expensive) Eden Roc Hotel, St Bart's, Feb 1999* ★★★★

**Chassagne-Montrachet, Les Vergers Delauney** Lemon-gold; nose and taste attractive but showing its age, not high class, saved by its good acidity. *When guest speaker at a nine-wine dinner at the Athenaeum, Pall Mall, Nov 1996* ★★

**Chevalier-Montrachet Dom du Ch de Beaune** At the 'trial by jury' tasting in the Bouchard Père cellars. Oily, grubby nose; drab, hefty (alcohol 13.5%), short. 4000 bottles produced. How many in stock, and their fate, unknown. *Nov 1995.*

**Chevalier-Montrachet Leflaive** Palish; vanilla, touch of maltiness; rich, fairly full-bodied, lacking finesse. *At my Bordeaux Club dinner at Christie's, July 1992* ★★

**Chevalier-Montrachet, Les Demoiselles L Latour** Palish straw yellow; light, honeyed but 'stewed' nose; not bad but not crisp enough, poor finish. *At an exploratory tasting in New York, Feb 1996. (I thought this might have been provenance – poor storage – except that Latour's Chevalier-Montrachet '85, not Demoiselles, noted in 1989 developed a sweet, malty character and lacked zest.)*

**Corton-Charlemagne Bonneau du Martray** Two notes, six months apart, neither good. First at a pre-sale tasting: bright, highly polished lime-edged yellow; touch of lanolin and oiliness on the nose. Some Corton meatiness but not up to standard. Next, from a private English cellar: not bad but spoilt for me by a touch of almond kernels and end bitterness. *Last noted in Christie's tasting room, March 1994.*

**Corton-Charlemagne Dom du Ch de Beaune** Picking began 25 September, 8500 bottles produced. Rich yellow gold; oily, even after ten years 'green' on the nose and, frankly, a bit smelly; dry, horrible almond kernel taste. *In the Bouchard Père cellars in Beaune. Clearly due for declassification. Nov 1995.*

**Corton-Charlemagne L Latour** Several notes, first at the bicentenary tasting in the vineyard, June 1997: attractive colour; vanilla nose, oily, nutty, but spoiled for me by a strong peach kernels flavour. A far better note that autumn at one of Bob Dickinson's 'Mr Gourmet' dinners (at Norman's, a fashionable restaurant in Coral Gables. Norman, the chef, was clearly addicted to salt). My note reads 'rich, nutty, creamy' (nose); medium sweet, hefty, complete. Perhaps the grilled 'Gulf escolat with chanterelles with a malanga(?) purée in a smoked salmon something or other' (I can't read my note) helped. But at my Domaine Louis Latour seminar the following year I liked it least of the seven Corton-Charlemagnes: peachy, appley, unknit; kernelly, with dry acidic finish (Hollywood Wine Society, 1998). Nor did I like it much at one of my own dinner parties. *Last noted June 2000. On balance, thumbs down.*

**Meursault, Perrières Leroy** Disappointing, fullish, nutty, so-so flavour. Not a patch on the '71. *With stone crabs at Joe's, Miami, Oct 1997* ★

**Puligny-Montrachet, Les Folatières L Jadot** Late-picked, early October, the juice one day on its lees, fermented in 20% new oak, then 14 months *en barrique*, fined with skimmed milk. First tasted in 1988: pale but pure yellow gold; rich, oaky-smoky, buttery nose; dry, powerful, firm, needing bottle age. The following year: fragrant, evolving but still a bit raw on the palate. Yet, only three years later, I noted it as soft, very oaky, 'needs drinking'. *Last noted lunching with Jadot's London agents, Hatch, Mansfield in March 1992* ★★★ I suspect it will be tired by now.

**Puligny-Montrachet, Les Truffières L Latour** Glorious, rounded, mouthfilling and delicious in 1989. Also drinking well three years later: very good nose; sweet enough, fairly full-bodied, rich, excellent flavour. *Last noted at Jean-Pierre Louqiaud's, Bordeaux, June 1992* ★★★★ *Could still be excellent.*

**SOME GOOD '85S, TASTED IN 1990** Olivier Leflaive's **Meursault, Charmes** pale, lovely, crisp, dry and delicious. *June 1990* ★★★★; **Leroy's Meursault, Genevrières** flowery, attractive, considerable length; and their **Les Narvaux** spicy, dry, assertive. *Both wines tasted Sept 1990* ★★★★; and **de Vogüé's Musigny blanc** despite its comparative youth, a lovely jeroboam from Hardy Rodenstock's cellar: pale; exquisite bouquet, aniseed, vanilla; subtle, delicately balanced, elegant. *At the Arlberg Hospiz, Austria, Sept 1990* ★★★★★

# 1986 up to ★★★★★

Unquestionably a very attractive and successful white burgundy vintage: dense, well-structured, firm and with excellent acidity. Most, inevitably, were drunk while young and fresh; some – also inevitably – not as good as they should have been, but the best are still lovely to drink.

Once again, my notes open with half-a-dozen Montrachets. At its best, Montrachet epitomises the best expression of the now ubiquitous Chardonnay, the finest dry white wine in the world. So how did the well-structured vintage '86s perform?

**Montrachet Dom du Ch de Beaune** Interestingly, not put on trial at the tasting in Bouchard's cellar in 1995. My only note was made on the second day of a Rodenstock weekend: not bright (I had a look at other bottles and they were the same); apart from vanilla I noted something that I cannot effectively describe, for it reminded me of my grandmother's dye works in Delph (my mother's mother, a widow, owned a mill where I spent many happy hours as a child, fascinated by the immense coal-fired boilers and the pungent wet-blanket smell. She also had a Bechstein I loved to play). On the palate, though reasonably full and firm, unexciting. *Sept 1996* ★★

**Montrachet Laguiche/Drouhin** Only tasted in its youth: nose low-keyed, slow to emerge; medium-dry, medium-full body (alcohol 13.3%), good length, teeth-gripping acidity (3.7g/l). Needed considerable bottle age to open up and simmer down. *At Drouhin in Beaune, Oct 1990.* Then ★(★★★★) *Probably on its plateau now and with more time in hand.*

**Montrachet L Latour** In a 'flight' of two Bâtards and four Montrachets at one of Rodenstock's gala dinners in Munich. Very pale, touch of lemon; moderately attractive nose and taste and good acidity. I was not enchanted. *Sept 1995* ★★

**Montrachet Jacques Prieur** Yellow, touch of straw; nutty, beginning to show some bottle age; dry, firm, fairly full-bodied and good acidity. Many bottles, for it was at another Rodenstock dinner for 50 people. *Munich, Sept 1996* ★★★

**Montrachet A Ramonet** Bob Dickinson upstaging even Hardy Rodenstock with a salmanazar – one imagines that it used up almost all of Ramonet's ¼ hectare of vines! Very pale; rich, toasty bouquet that spread its wings magnificently; distinct sweetness, full-bodied, nutty flavour – what a pathetic, inadequate description; rich of course and with very good acidity. 'Needs time'. Served with 'Fresh White Truffles and Pan Seared Lobster with a Boniato Vichyssoise'. There is style for you. *At Bob's 'Mr Gourmet' Investiture dinner, Coral Gables, Nov 1997* ★★★★★ *Will keep for ages.*

**Montrachet DRC** Palish; scent of toasted coconut, opening up beautifully; mouthfilling, in fact quite a bite, coping well with a far less exotic fish dish than the above Ramonet wine: 'Escalope of Hake with Colcannon, Tomato Velouté'. My guest was the possessor of one of America's most extensive cellars, coincidentally, in Coral Gables. *At a Saintsbury Club dinner, Oct 1997* ★★★★★

**Bâtard-Montrachet Marc Jomain** New to me, a *négociant-éleveur* in Puligny. Pale; little nose; taste of strong Gripfix (marzipan-smelling glue) and appallingly acidic. Two bottles, identical. *Sept 1996.*

**Bâtard-Montrachet Pierre Morey** Classic young Chardonnay ensemble: nutty, oak, vanilla and raw pineapple; dry, crisp, firm, fragrant. *Jan 1990.* Then ★★(★★) *Should be fully formed by now.*

**Beaune, Clos des Mouches J Drouhin** This is always my vintage yardstick. Of the entire range of white Mouches from 1979 to 1989 tasted at Drouhin in 1990, I rated this the highest. It was well endowed with alcohol (13.5%) and acidity (3.9g/l). Two years prior to this, Hugh Johnson and Colin Anderson MW placed this top of 26 *grand cru* and 1er *cru* white burgundies of varying vintages at a British Airways blind tasting. Naturally we wanted to see what it would be like at 50,000 feet, so the British Airways wine committee flew by Concorde to Barbados. Ah those were the days! The wine, and the team, survived. In its youth I did in fact find it a bit too oaky, but this always appeals to British Airways' passengers. It exuded power as well as fragrance. Most recently, fully mature, its original pale yellow now medium-gold; its nose conjured up woodland thoughts – after all, we were only yards from Hugh's arboretum – and fresh picked mushrooms. After 15 minutes, it developed a subtle fragrance and, a quarter of an hour after that, a lovely *mélange* of vanilla and pineapple chunks; medium sweet, perfect weight and flavour. Immaculate balance, fully mature. It blossomed in the glass. *Last noted at a Bordeaux Club dinner at Saling Hall, Essex, August 1999* ★★★★★

**Bienvenues-Bâtard-Montrachet Leflaive** Very pale, lime-tinged; crisp, spicy, lemon-like acidity; fairly dry, fragrant, stylish, acidity flapping in the wind. *Wine dinner at Gidleigh Park, Devon, Feb 1995* ★★★ *Should be drinking well now.*

**Chevalier-Montrachet Leflaive** Palish, star bright, a touch of lemon, medium dryness and weight, crisp, elegant. *Lunch at 47 Park Street, the Roux brothers' service apartment, July 1992* ★★★

**Chevalier-Montrachet, Les Demoiselles L Jadot** Lemon-tinged yellow; rich, good depth, flavour, length and aftertaste. *July 1992* ★★★★

**Chevalier-Montrachet, Les Demoiselles L Latour** Very nutty nose and flavour. Fairly sweet, certainly very rich and still developing. *At Latour's bicentenary dinner at Ch de Clos Vougeot, June 1997.* Then ★★★(★) *Doubtless fully mature now.*

**Corton-Charlemagne Bonneau du Martray** First tasted in 1995 at John Jenkins' Bordeaux Club dinner, with *Coquilles Saint Jacques, au Sauce d'Esau*, noting the refreshing '86 lemon-like acidity on the nose, and oak; fairly sweet, mellow (character, not acidity) and mouthfilling, fully evolved, excellent acidity. Several notes since: in full bloom, 'almost New World' (heaven forbid!) at *Decanter's* 20th anniversary lunch (1997); and a return to Childerly Hall, accompanying a very similar dish to the one in 1995, 'Scallop Mousse with a Mussel Sauce' (excellent – Chloë Jenkins is a gifted cook). And the wine: a very good, positive colour; very rich, minty bouquet; indeed richness the operative word. Perfection. *Last noted Oct 2000* ★★★★★ *At peak now.*

**Corton-Charlemagne L Latour** The third of three vintages served at Bob Dickinson's dinner at Norman's, in Coral Gables: pale, green-tinged; fragrant but unknit, grassy, almost Sauvignon Blanc-like; dry, a strong almond flavour, lean and slightly tinny. Much preferred the '85. *Nov 1997* ★★

**Corton-Charlemagne Remoissenet** Very good, full-flavoured, perfect (then), good acidity. *Lunch with the Stuart Levers in Lechlade, outside, under a hot sun, July 1994* ★★★★

**Meursault, Charmes Comtes Lafon** Lovely gold sheen; smoky, citrus touch; sweet, richly flavoured. *The oldest vintage in a Hollywood Wine Society Lafon 'flight', March 1995* ★★★★

**Meursault, Charmes, Hospices, Cuvée Albert Grivot** bottled by **Prosper Maufoux** At a pre-sale tasting in 1995 I found its unknit, oily nose off-putting so did not taste it. Coincidentally served a couple of years later at a Saintsbury Club dinner. Bottle variation: colours ranged from pale to deepish yellow; vanilla, lemony nose; dry, mediocre flavour, good acidity but at best unexciting. *Last noted April 1997. Not recommended.*

OF THE SEVERAL OTHER MEURSAULTS TASTED IN 1990 AND 1991 **J-P Gauffroy**'s I found rather heavy and chewy, but it sold out! ★★★; **F Jobard**'s stylish, archetypal, just good ★★★; **H Bouzereau Greure**'s **Charmes** richly flavoured, firm, good acidity ★★★; and **P Javillier**'s **Clos du Cromin** delicious ★★★★

FEW PULIGNY-MONTRACHETS TASTED RECENTLY. Of those wines noted in 1990–91: **E Sauzet**'s disappointing ★★; **Bouchard Père**'s **Folatières** rich, nutty, long ★★★; **L Jadot**'s very good indeed ★★★★; and **Leflaive**'s **Perrières** copybook ★★★★

# 1987 ★★

Less satisfactory for the whites than reds. Quite attractive and commercial at the time but terrifically variable as just a glimpse of the following notes will indicate.

**Montrachet Dom du Ch de Beaune** Alas, a bad period for Bouchard. Picked late, 5000 bottles produced and distinctly substandard, much below *grand cru* quality: appearance too deep; an oily, caramelly nose and flavour. Almond kernels. Terrible. *In the Bouchard Père cellars, Beaune, Nov 1995.*

**Montrachet Laguiche/Drouhin** Tasted only in its youth. Already yellow, lightly tinged with gold; attractive though unknit nose, with most of the components waiting to join hands; mouthfilling (alcohol 13.4%), rounded, quite good acidity (3.7g/l), 'perhaps lacking length'. *At Drouhin in Beaune, Oct 1990. I gave it ★★★ and 'drink soon'. Doubtless tired of waiting.*

**Montrachet A Ramonet** Interesting to see what 'the master' made of his '87: a slightly too-deep yellow, though bright; scent of jelly babies and fruit gums; fairly full-bodied but not up to scratch. I thought it might have been the provenance but now believe it was the vintage. *In New York, Dec 1996. But see also the Ramonet wines below.*

**Beaune, Clos des Mouches J Drouhin** Two early notes, in August 1989: light fruit and oak, opened up pleasantly. Next, at a vertical at Drouhin: distinctive yellow; vanilla and spice but fruit emerging; full-bodied (alcohol 13.7%), good acidity (4.1g/l), rounded, delicious. *Last noted Oct 1990. Then ★★★, almost 4-star, but I suspect that it will be more than ready now.*

**Bienvenues-Bâtard-Montrachet A Ramonet** I was informed that Bâtard's and Bienvenues' low-yielding, old vines were vinified together, then put in individual *barriques*, 35% new and lightly charred, lees not stirred (no steel tanks). The

end result was extremely good: palish; lovely, rich, soft, oaky nose, quick to open up and quite dramatic; fairly sweet and full-bodied (13.5%), very rich, oaky Chardonnay with excellent aftertaste. *Noted at a Gidleigh Park wine weekend dinner, Devon, Feb 1995* ★★★★ *A very good '87 and probably best by now.*

**Chassagne-Montrachet J-N Gagnard** Very good, rich, nutty, almost 'New World'; very good flavour and balance. Drinking well. *Dining with Colin Harris in Chelsea, London, July 1994. Then* ★★★★ *Now, I suspect, past its best.*

**Chassagne-Montrachet A Ramonet** Very pale, lime-tinged, immediately forthcoming, a delicious, oaky-smoky swoosh and, after over an hour, some remained in my glass, fabulously rich; drier than expected, substantial (13.5% alcohol), but very good flavour and aftertaste. *With grilled red mullet at a Gidleigh Park dinner, Devon, Feb 1994* ★★★★

**Chassagne-Montrachet, Morgeot Gagnard Delagrange** Though fairly rapturously commented on by our 'cellarer', I did not find this very impressive. Dry, 'moderately passable'. *At a Saintsbury Club dinner, London, Oct 1996* ★★

**Chevalier-Montrachet Dom du Ch de Beaune** Picking from 29 September and 6900 bottles produced. This was even worse than the '85: hefty, though 'only' 13% alcohol, oily, chaptalised nose; flavour of almond paste. Horrible. *At Bouchard Père, Beaune, Nov 1995.*

**Corton-Charlemagne, Fourget** (*sic*) **Bouchard Père** The oldest, 25th and last in a line-up of variable, to say the least, white burgundies in a British Airways' tasting for First Class and Concorde. This wine never left the ground. *Feb 1999.*

**Meursault, Charmes L Jadot** Old vineyard, old vines, small crop. Jadot once again doing their best to rise to the occasion with a decent, passable '87, nose open, creamy, touch of oil and malt; better on the palate, sweet, soft, ready. *At a Lafon tasting of Charmes, March 1995* ★★★ *Just, but doubtless* passé *now.*

OF THE FAIRLY LARGE NUMBER OF '87S TASTED EITHER SIDE OF 1990, I rated few as 3-star and most wines would be long since over the hill.

# 1988 ★★★

A good vintage and deservedly popular when it came on to the market. But the yield was high and the wines of those producers who did not prune hard or select diligently tended to lack concentration. But there were quite a few ripe, fresh, well-balanced wines. As always, the lesser wines will have long since been consumed, few surviving on lists beyond the mid-1990s, but the finest are still drinking well.

**Montrachet DRC** Only tasted in its youth, but even then a very attractive mouthful, good nose, fairly full-bodied, good flesh, fruit and acidity. *At the Domaine, Oct 1990. Then* (★★★★) *Doubtless drinking well now.*

**Montrachet Laguiche/Drouhin** In its third year, fragrant, lovely. *March 1991* (★★★★)

**Montrachet Dom du Ch de Beaune** Picking from 20 September. The best of a chamber of Bouchard horrors: medium-pale yellow; pleasant, pineapple, Chardonnay, very rich but a trifle too hefty and clumsy; sweet, full, rich, oaky, mouthfilling. *In Bouchard Père's cellars, Beaune, Nov 1995* ★★★

**Montrachet Lionel Bruck** Now part of the large Boisset empire. Glorious colour, waxy sheen and dash of green; low-keyed, smoky, honey and touch of lime; dry, fairly full-bodied, reasonably firm but, after all that, unexciting. *Opening the first 'flight' of Rodenstock's wine weekend tasting, Sept 1996* ★★★ *(just).*

**Beaune, Clos des Mouches J Drouhin** My 'vintage yardstick' wine but only tasted in its youth: then pale; immature, pineapple and oak; medium-dry, pleasant acidity. Moderately good. *At Drouhin. Then (★★★) Doubtless fully mature by now. Do not expect time to have increased quality or drinkability.*

**Chablis, Montmain J-M Brocard** The Brocard estate is huge by burgundy standards. This *1er cru*, in magnum, was served at a British Airways' seminar dinner at Mosimann's. It was highly polished, palish, with a touch of still youthful green; nose sweet, soft, smoky with a lemony underbelly; dry enough, lean yet fairly hefty, very good acidity – as if it were a Sauvignon Blanc-imbued Chardonnay. It went well with steamed halibut. *April 1998 ★★★ A good 10-year old.*

**Chassagne-Montrachet Ch de la Maltroye** Palish yellow straw; good nose, Chardonnay with some bottle age; excellent flavour and length. *A modest lunch at Wiltons with Taylor Thomson, a wine collector extraordinaire. Nov 1994 ★★★★*

**Chassagne-Montrachet, Les Chevenottes Ch de la Maltroye** Yellow gold, the second bottle paler; harmonious; dry, taste of marzipan, Gripfix, and with tinny acidity. Not as bubbly as the supple, energetic 'champagne for health' Joan Oliphant-Frazer, lunching at the Café Royal in London, to reward me for my foreword to her book. *Jan 1995 ★*

**Chevalier-Montrachet Dom du Ch de Beaune** A decent, well-balanced, mouthfilling and flavoury wine in its youth (1990). The best of an underperforming range only five years later: now yellow gold; a hefty (alcohol 13.5%) wine, frankly rather dull and lacking the crisp, stylishness of a really good Chevalier. *Last tasted in Bouchard's cellars, Nov 1995 ★★★ (just).*

**Corton-Charlemagne Bonneau du Martray** After 36 previous wines, all of younger vintages and tasted blind, this did not show well. It had a 'stewed' nose and was dry, raw and acidic. For its high price it should have been better. *April 1994.*

**Corton-Charlemagne J-F Coche-Dury** How fortunate of Caius College to have such a far-sighted and discerning don; or perhaps this was only purchased for Neil McKendrick's cellar (he is now Master), for this is a 'cult' wine though Coche-Dury himself would, I am sure, dispute the term. Not one but two vintages at McKendrick's Bordeaux Club dinner, the '88 first: fairly pale; an appealing, fragrant, smoky, vanilla nose that took on a hint of chocolate; fairly sweet, delicious flavour, substantial (alcohol 13.5%) but not overdone, with a good, clean, dry finish. *At Caius, Cambridge, June 1998 ★★★★*

**Corton-Charlemagne L Latour** Good wine. First tasted in March 1991: pale but anything but insipid: lovely, nutty, scented, new oak nose and full, soft, spicy taste. Next, one of the best in the '83 to '96 vertical tasted in 1997: fairly sweet, full-bodied (alcohol 14%) and good grip. More recently, at an almost identical vertical I conducted at a Hollywood Wine Society weekend: almost meatily rich, good acidity, oaky aftertaste. Ten years old; perfect for drinking. *Last noted March 1998 ★★★★ Will keep.*

**Corton-Charlemagne E Voarick** One of a 'flight' of six: very pale; an odd, cheesy, oily nose; dry, austere, firm and very good with food. In fact, despite its nose I gave it a fairly high mark. *At Rodenstock's tasting, Arlberg, Austria, Sept 1994 ★★★?*

**Meursault, Charmes Comtes Lafon** Smoky, vanilla and a touch of honeyed bottle age; medium-sweet, full-bodied, mouthfilling, firm, even a touch of austerity, high acidity. *At a Lafon Charmes vertical, March 1995 ★★★*

**Puligny-Montrachet Leflaive** Picked 27 September. At two years of age: pale; grapey, spearmint and youthful pineapple; soft yet firm, but with a touch of peach stones. The latter confirmed at a tasting of '88s in 1993, 'cool', dry, peach-kernelly finish. Not at all to my taste. Miserably endorsed by a bottle returned to Christie's by a well-known broker: the wine was unusually pale even for Leflaive, kernelly nose and a taste like cyanide. *Last tasted Feb 1996. What went wrong? Bad fining?*

**Puligny-Montrachet Prosper Maufoux** Dry, crisp, not very attractive. *July 1995 ★*

**Puligny-Montrachet, Les Folatières H Clerc** Touch of gold; strange toasted nose reminding me of Gentleman's Relish and grilled bacon; fairly full-bodied, very oaky, spicy – crispy bacon! Dear me. *Sept 1996 ★★★*

**Puligny-Montrachet, Les Folatières Prosper Maufoux** Touch of caramel, dry, full, crisp, not bad. But really, simply not good enough. *At a pre-sale tasting, Christie's, July 1995 ★★*

**Puligny-Montrachet, Les Pucelles Leflaive** Pale, star bright, lime yellow, making one salivate just to look at it; firm, fresh, lemon and vanilla; surprisingly sweet – served with salmon – and still youthful. *A surprise bottle at Sara and Esmée Johnstone's harvest-time kitchen dinner at Ch de Sours, in the Entre-Deux-Mers, Bordeaux, Sept 1995 ★★★★*

OF THE VERY MANY '88S TASTED IN THEIR YOUTH, both **L Latour**'s and **Leflaive**'s **Bâtard-Montrachet ★★★★**; no Chablis above ★★★ and, in fact, most well below; **Gagnard-Delagrange**'s **Chassagne-Montrachet, Boudriotte** classic **★★★★**; and **Bouchard Père**'s **Corton-Charlemagne ★★★** *(just).*

AND OF THE LARGE NUMBER OF MEURSAULTS, **Boyer-Martenot**'s very flavoury but a bit austere **★★★★**; **Bouchard Père**'s and **L Latour**'s **Les Charmes ★★★★**; **F Protheau**'s **Genevrières, Hospices, Cuvée Baudot** superb **★★★★★**; **René Manuel**'s **Poruzot** fragrant **★★★★**; and a superb **J Drouhin**'s **Puligny-Montrachet, Clos de la Garenne ★★★★★**

# 1989 up to ★★★★★

Burgundy is a complex region and its wines vary enormously, depending not so much on the vintage as the skill, perseverance, conscientiousness and, frankly, intent, of the individual producers and merchants. In 1989, the grapes were ripe, the harvest early. The wines were immediately attractive, most were at their best in the mid-1990s though, as will be seen, some of the top wines are still drinking beautifully.

Quite apart from the fact that they feature in my most recent notes, the reason for so many Montrachets, Bâtards, Chassagnes and Corton-Charlemagnes is to demonstrate how varied the styles and qualities are. Alas, what is shocking is how unforgivably bad so many white burgundies are. They let so-called New World Chardonnays in at the front – and back – door. But what a revelation the best white burgundies can be.

**Le Montrachet DRC** It is very rare for a sample bottle to be produced, even at the fairly exclusive trade and select press tasting at Corney & Barrow; even rarer to be allowed to sample this wine in cask. When I saw the ten small barrels – the total production – it brought home to me the scarcity and impossibility of meeting even a fraction of the demand of the world's wealthy. Well, I was allowed to taste it just 12 months after the wine had been made: a distinctive lime yellow in the glass; an impact of rich, waxy, spicy, vanilla and, within minutes, the scent of freshly ground coffee; touch of ripe sweetness, carrying its weight effortlessly, with fragrance and lovely acidity. *At the Domaine, Oct 1990 (★★★★★) Superb then, will be fabulous now and still evolving.*

**Montrachet Laguiche/Drouhin** First, a cask sample at Drouhin in October 1990: good colour; already fragrant, full of fruit tempered with oak; fairly sweet, beautiful flavour and follow through. My highest mark at a tasting in 1992: fragrant, crisp, delicious. Then, at four years of age: excellent, gently toasted, classic, opening up further; outstandingly the best of a range of top white burgundies at a Rodenstock tasting. How can one describe perfection? *Last tasted in Arlberg, Austria, Sept 1993. Then ★★(★★) Will be perfect now.*

**Montrachet Baron Thénard** First noted in 1995 at Jardine's Cellar Club tasting dinner in Tokyo: richly coloured; very pronounced oaky-smoky nose and flavour, full, assertive, superb. The following year, at a Rodenstock dinner in Munich: almost too oaky, very, very rich, toasty, powerful, fabulous flavour; and at Rodenstock again in 1998 – a sort of 'Hardy' perennial. But wait, listed as *Remoissenet* but with *Thénard* on the label, served with 'Sable fish with *tat soi*, water chestnut and ginger-soy-hijiti broth' at an extravagant Zachys/Christie's millennium dinner in New York (owner/chef Charlie Trotter and his entire brigade had been especially flown over from Chicago – an extravagance not to be repeated, however superb the fare). The *tat soi* somewhat overpowered the Montrachet. The following day Christie's eager clients could taste it among the 28 seriously good wines at the millennium pre-sale tasting. Impressive, remarkably sweet, very flavoury but too much oak. *Last tasted at the Rockefeller Plaza, May 1999 ★★★★*

**Montrachet Dom du Ch de Beaune** First tasted from the cask, October 1990: a vast improvement on some of the underperforming wines of the mid-1980s: fragrant, oaky; fairly sweet and full-bodied; soft but lovely. Two years later, simply described as 'classic' nose and taste. Very good indeed and a high mark. *Last noted at a monumental Bin Club tasting in Gloucestershire, June 1992 ★★★★★ Alas not tasted since.*

**Montrachet L Jadot** Malty, meaty. Very poor nose so not tasted. Surely a poor bottle. *At the Bin Club tasting, June 1992.*

**Montrachet L Latour** Good colour; classic fruit and vanilla; too oaky. A moderate mark. Rather disappointing. *At the same Bin Club tasting as above, June 1992 ★★*

**Bâtard-Montrachet Bouchard Père** Surprisingly deep gold; creamy vanilla, touch of caramel and smoke; unusually low alcoholic content for its class and vintage: 12%. Rich but a bit flabby. Over the top but drinkable. *A bottle from a temperature-controlled cellar in the Bahamas brought to New York for me to report on. Which I did after consuming most of it over dinner at the Knickerbocker Club, Dec 1996. I assumed that it had experienced a touch of sun at some stage of the supply line but, after my experiences with some of Bouchard's grands crus of the 1980s, I wonder?*

**Bâtard-Montrachet L Latour** In cask, October 1990: very correct. A most attractive, powerful wine. Somewhat less effusive at the Bin Club tasting: soft, rich, quite good only. *Last tasted June 1989 ★★★ (just).*

**Bâtard-Montrachet Niéllon** Excellent: a most attractive, smoky nose and flavour, soft, rich, long smoky finish. *Dining at Le Montrachet, New York, Oct 1995 ★★★★*

**Bâtard-Montrachet Leflaive** Fairly pale; far too oaky on nose and palate, and not enough fat for a Bâtard of a vintage like 1989. *At the Grands Crus pre-sale dinner at Christie's, London, Sept 1997 ★★★*

**Bâtard-Montrachet Olivier Leflaive** Just six *barriques*, but, tasting from the cask, much more attractive than his uncle's wine. Delicious. Mouthfilling. *At Olivier Leflaive's, Oct 1990. I gave it an exuberant 5 stars and suggest it will be drinking well, fully mature now, but perhaps ★★★★?*

**Chassagne-Montrachet A Ramonet** A class act. Rich, fairly powerful, good acidity. *At Gidleigh Park, Devon, Feb 1994. Then ★★★★ Should still be lovely.*

**Chassagne-Montrachet L Latour** Coincidentally served two months apart, first at Gidleigh Park, then at a Court Dinner at Saddlers' Hall in the City of London. Happily identical notes: nose low-keyed at first but opened up fragrantly; lovely flavour and balance. *Last noted March 1994 ★★★*

**Chassagne-Montrachet, La Boudriotte Gagnard-Delagrange** 20 to 25% new oak, usually bottled after 15 to 16 months. Pale, lime-tinged; a most delicious, smoky, lemony nose and mouthful. Fragrant aftertaste. *At Gidleigh Park, Devon, Feb 1995 ★★★★★*

**Chassagne-Montrachet, Les Caillerets A Ramonet** Highly polished, pale gold; sweet, smoky-oaky nose and flavour, full-bodied, very good acidity. *Dinner after the second day of tasting Ch Cheval Blanc, by the Bodensee, Sept 1997 ★★★★*

**Chassagne-Montrachet, Les Chaumées Colin-Déléger** A 2-ha vineyard out of a 12-ha estate, half red, half white; subdued nose that opened up well; drier and more austere than expected for such a ripe vintage, powerful though only 13% alcohol. *At the Gidleigh Park wine dinner, Devon, Feb 1995 ★★★★ Should be superb now.*

**Corton-Charlemagne Coche-Dury** Fabulous, and well deserving his starry reputation: indescribably sweet, 'full cream', surging bouquet; fairly sweet, soft, rich, heftier than the '88 – well, one could go on. *At Neil McKendrick's Bordeaux Club dinner, Caius, Cambridge, June 1998 ★★★★★*

**Corton-Charlemagne L Latour** An attractive cask sample brought to London in 1990, softer than the '88, richer, more beguiling. Next, in 1997, at the open-air bicentenary tasting: substantial body – they were all 14%, but with deftness and flair. Then at the Latour seminar vertical, a wonderfully sweet, soft, full, rich wine. *Last noted at a Hollywood Wine Society weekend, March 1998 ★★★★★*

**Corton-Charlemagne E Voarick** As strange and austere as his '88: smell of vanilla, meat and cheese rind; dry, too severe. *Sept 1994 ★★*

**Meursault, Charmes Comtes Lafon** The estate reckoned the 1992 and 1989 their best vintages. The '89, a small crop of ripe, healthy grapes. At the Lafon vertical in 1995: a touch of pure gold; delicious butter and oaky nose – hardly an original description – like a Labrador on its back waiting to be scratched; sweet, very full-bodied, with toasty, oaky flavour and lemon-like acidity. The following year, showing superbly in unfamiliar surroundings: positively opulent on the nose and almost too powerful (but it did follow some far lower-strength Nahe wines). *Last noted dining with Armin Diel at Schloss Diel in the Nahe, Nov 1996 ★★★★★*

**Meursault, Genevrières Chauvenet** Vanilla and whiff of caramel; dry, nutty, good acidity but not in the same league as Lafon's. *Dining at Chippenham Lodge, May 1997 ★★*

**Meursault, Perrières Comtes Lafon** Distinctive yellow; a harmonious subtle nose; lovely, full-flavoured, smoky, oaky. *At the Dîner Classique V, Baur au Lac, Zurich, Oct 1994 ★★★★*

**Pouilly-Fuissé, Vieilles Vignes Ch Fuissé/Vincent** I first fell for his wine when I tasted Vincent's beautifully fragrant and delicate '83, so when I saw that the '89, clearly a better vintage, was coming up for sale at Christie's, I bought some. Naturally, I have many notes, starting in June 1995: yellow gold; full, rich, lime and oak; hefty (alcohol 13.5%), very attractive. The '89 is anything but fragrant and delicate, it is a big wine, high alcohol and extract. In fact, almost knockout drops. A couple of notes (though I have more) in the autumn of 1996: palish though distinct yellow; a good though not particularly distinctive nose; far more impressive on the palate, a wine of considerable depth. No longer inexpensive, Monsieur Vincent's wine is well worth looking out for. *Last tasted Oct 1996* ★★★

**Puligny-Montrachet, Grand Champs** Sélection Jean Germain Distinctive mustardy yellow; positive, oaky, vanilla which, after time in the glass, was like Ambrosia Creamed Rice; on the sweet side, plump, fleshy, running to fat – like a 40-year-old barmaid who knows what's what but verging on blowsiness. *Dining with the wine committee of the Athenaeum Club, Nov 1996* ★★★ *(just).*

**Puligny-Montrachet, Les Pucelles** Leflaive First tasted from the steel vat in October 1990 (it had been in oak until the end of the malolactic fermentation): surprisingly harmonious despite its youth. Then a jump of eight years to a strange, fishy, kernelly bottle, flabby with a poor finish at lunch between the Ch d'Yquem 'flights' in 1998. Two months later: it was fragrant but I thought it too old on the nose and with a trace of peach kernels and rich, oaky end taste. However, it went well with potted shrimps (at the Boot & Flogger in London, entertaining an amusing, voluble Russian, Boris Voladarsky, and my wife). *Most recently, drinking well with halibut at the Saintsbury Club dinner, London, April 1999* ★★★ *Good but no better that that.*

## 1990 ★★★★ but variable

I was expecting better. The variations in quality are, frankly, surprising to say the least. Yet some of the wines, the top names, are magnificent. The growing season was good, but the heat and drought favoured the reds. There was a surprisingly large, too large, crop of whites which, while rich, often elegant and mainly well balanced, were best for early drinking.

**Montrachet** Laguiche/Drouhin First tasted in Drouhin's cellars in October 1990. Despite its unfinished state, clearly great potential. Next, in 1994: pale; subdued at first but then opened up magnificently, after 90 minutes gloriously evolved; dry, nutty, oaky, austere but attractive (full marks). Two years later: very fragrant, toasty, smoky nose; appeared to be fairly sweet, certainly rich, fat, higher acidity than the '89 but masked. *Last tasted at the Montrachet/Laguiche tasting at the Institute of Directors, London, Feb 1996* ★★★(★★)

**Montrachet** Comtes Lafon At a combined vertical and horizontal tasting conducted by Dominic Lafon: initially low-keyed but after 20 minutes developed glorious richness; marvellous flavour, great length and aftertaste, with light but tingling acidity. *March 1995.* Then ★★(★★★) *Will be lovely now.*

**Montrachet** Thénard/Remoissenet First tasted just after fermentation: great power and potential. In 1994 seemed very pale; nose sustained but low-keyed; dry, full-bodied, good oak,

### Domaine Comtes Lafon

*Lafon is famed for its white burgundies; but then being based in Meursault this is hardly surprising. The unusual thing about Lafon is that they traditionally keep their wines far longer on their lees (nearly two years) than does any other domaine, and they bottle late. Their aim is to make white wines that will last. Nothing is rushed, and the wine is allowed to develop at its own pace – an approach which has been tremendously successful.*

classic, excellent aftertaste. A year later, soft yet lively and fairly assertive, the aftertaste noted again. The last two notes made at Rodenstock's gala dinners. Most recently: pale, very oaky nose; good flavour and grip. *Last noted, speedily, at the Millennium pre-sale tasting, New York, May 1999* ★★★★★ *Fully developed. Will keep.*

**Bâtard-Montrachet** Fernand Coffinet New to me. Very sweet, over the top, smoky, toasted coconut nose; full-bodied, a broad-based decent mouthful. *Sept 1995* ★★★ *Fully mature now.*

**Beaune, Clos des Mouches** J Drouhin First tasted in its cradle, October 1990: sweet, crisp, loads of fruit. A jump to two recent notes, first at a Saintsbury Club dinner in 1999: a mature, soft yellow; fully developed vanilla nose; medium-sweetness/and body, attractive but, I thought, lacking acidity. Next, the oldest in the decade line-up: distinctly yellow, rich 'legs'; showing a lot of age on the nose, honeyed, slightly caramelly – residual sulphur? Flavour to match. Chewy. Tired and disappointing. *Last noted at Drouhin, Oct 2001* ★★ *Drink up.*

**Chassagne-Montrachet** L Latour Palish; neutral nose; dry, fairly full, firm and mouthfilling. Good length. *At a Lyford Cay tasting in the Bahamas, March 1994* ★★★ *Drink soon.*

**Chassagne-Montrachet** A Ramonet Pale; good nose though not distinctive; very satisfactory flavour and acidity. Classy. *Lunching with Carol and Jamie Guise, July 2000* ★★★★ *(Jamie's aged father, Sir Anselme, had a stash of old wines in the cellars of Elmore Court including the 1867 Ch d'Yquem, see page 173).*

**Chevalier-Montrachet** Leflaive Hardly any colour, just a tinge of lime; curiously meaty nose and horrible almond kernelly taste. *In Los Angeles, March 1999. Wine or storage?*

**Chevalier-Montrachet, Les Demoiselles** L Jadot Very good indeed. Perfect blend of fruit and oak. *At Christie's wine department's Christmas dinner, Dec 1997* ★★★★

**Corton-Charlemagne** Bonneau du Martray Coincidentally, two recent notes, both in the Far East: with 'Wonton of Boston Lobster' at a Crédit Suisse dinner in Hong Kong. Served too cold and, though good, the bouquet was infinitely better after 30 minutes in the glass (as usual, I left a little to taste later); dry, medium-full (alcohol 13%), very good fragrant flavour. A few days later (in half bottles) at a buffet dinner at the American Club in Tokyo. Delicious nose, like supercharged vanilla ice cream; distinctly sweet, a perfect blend of fruit and oak, smoky, elegant, good finish. *Last noted Nov 1999* ★★★★★ *Can't get much better than this.*

**Corton-Charlemagne** L Latour Their harvest completed 10 October, the last grower to finish. Natural sugar reached 14%. A colossal number of notes, starting in March 1995 at a gourmet dinner in Florida: rich, oaky; very good flavour and balance but 'needs time'. A few months later in Hong Kong – flavour enhanced by swordfish; at the Latour bicentenary tasting and dinner in 1997, well developed, its richness coping with *foie gras*. And so on – consistently good. Someone described the taste as 'yellow plum', at the vertical in 1998. It was quite the best, its nose now toasted pineapple and peach. Coping with stone crabs in 1999.

Most recently, with an enormous *Petit Choux farci au Crabe* at Hugh Johnson's Bordeaux Club dinner (I seem to be the only person to produce white Bordeaux at these events): now a waxy yellow gold; sweet, rich, creamy, vanilla bouquet and a wonderfully rich, mouthfilling flavour. Very good acidity. *Last tasted Dec 2001* ★★★★★ *One of the best ever 'LL' Charlemagnes. Fully developed by now.*

**Meursault, Clos de la Barre** Comtes Lafon A 2.1-ha plot of vines, big for Burgundy. Full-bodied, good fruit, firm acidity. *At the Lafon tasting in Florida, March 1995* ★★★★

OTHER MEURSAULTS AT THE ABOVE LAFON TASTING in March 1995 **Charmes** lovely colour; heavenly fruit, plump, pineapple; fairly sweet and full-bodied, fine, rich flavour, tingling acidity ★★★★; and their **'Desirée'** planted in the Santenots area of Meursault. A very big crop. Positive yellow; positive, firm, attractive. The first wine at the Lafon Meursault horizontal ★★★; **Perrières** lovely, dry, firm, fragrant ★★★★★

OTHER MEURSAULTS, CHARMES **J Monnier** creamy, good flavour and length. *1994* ★★★; **J Drouhin** bottle variation: some too yellow, too orange or too drab; dull; almost flabby, even though from a good cellar (Vintners' Hall). *1998*; and **C Viénot** good colour, nose and flavour. *1994* ★★★

**Meursault, Genevrières F Jobart** Palish yellow; fragrant, walnut-like, dry (why do restaurants serve white burgundies so cold?); dry, classic. *At Tanglberg, Austria, April 1999* ★★★
**Meursault, Genevrières L Latour** Developed quite well, butter and oak on nose and taste. Attractive but a bit four-square. *At a Vintners' Company Installation Dinner, July 1997* ★★★
**Meursault, Perrières Coche-Dury** Frans de Cock really did push the boat out in Paris, serving the '78 Coche-Dury Ruchottes with *truffe fraiche rapée* at lunch and this magnificent wine at dinner, accompanying oysters on a bed of cream, topped with caviar. It really was awfully good! Gentle yet assertive, fairly sweet, full, rich – a big buttery flavour and splendid finish. *At the Carré des Feuillants restaurant, Paris, Dec 1995* ★★★★★
**Pouilly-Fuissé, Vieilles Vignes Manciot-Poncet** A 13-ha domaine previously unknown to me. I normally associate Pouilly-Fuissé Vieilles Vignes with the admirable Monsieur Vincent, but this was a pleasant surprise, and in the cellars of my own club. Good colour; very pleasant, creamy nose; fairly dry, nice weight, very attractive, as was Laetizia, Georg Riedel's daughter who was doing a traineeship at Christie's at the time. *At Brooks's Club, London, June 1995* ★★★

PULIGNY-MONTRACHET To my surprise, I cannot find one really good note, both **Leflaive**'s and **Sauzet**'s were disappointing: the former austere with nutty, kernelly taste. (*1997* ★), the latter also for me spoilt by the touch of peach kernels (*1999* ★★); **Leflaive**'s **Puligny-Montrachet, Clavoillon** was also disappointing. *1995* ★★; and the best of a poor bunch at a British Airways tasting in *1994*: **G Chavy**'s **Puligny-Montrachet, Folatières** creamy, rich; positive, verging on aggressive, good length ★★★

# 1991 ★★★ but variable

An appalling growing season. Louis Latour reported that the first weeks of July were like 1989, very hot, retarding development. The grapes should have been picked (at Corton-Charlemagne) on 20 September though the *ban de vendange* was set for the 25th. Heavy rain fell from the 29th, the vines were thirsty because of the drought and the leaves fell. The result was wines 'like '82s'. Take care.
**Montrachet Laguiche/Drouhin** Bottled early, October 1992. First noted at Drouhin's London tasting in October 1993: toasted vanilla; full, assertive, good length, hot finish. Next, *en passant* at the Wine Experience Grand Tastings in New York in 1995: pale; good; stylish, great length. The following year at the Montrachet Laguiche tasting: good 'legs' – which I always admire; nose relatively low-keyed yet intense and slightly spicy;

medium sweetness and fullish body. Rich, rounded, good length and acidity. I was surprised. *Last noted Feb 1996* ★★★
**Montrachet DRC** Lovely yellow gold; immediately rich, minty, caramelly vanilla, greengage undertone, opening up fragrantly; almost malty richness, assertive, crisp acidity. *At lunch, between Wagner's La Tâche 'flights', April 1998* ★★★
**Montrachet Thénard/Remoissenet** Whiff of peach kernels; fairly sweet, very flavoury, oaky, powerful. *At the Christie's Millennium pre-sale tasting in New York, May 1999* ★★★
**Montrachet Verget** Palish; I seem to recall Hugh Johnson saying the smell reminded him of watered cognac; after that I recorded extraordinary power, yet lean and flexible with good length. At Hardy's tasting dinner, the only Rodenstock event ever attended by Hugh and by Robert Parker who was surprisingly self-effacing, acknowledging modestly in his subsequent newsletter that this was one occasion when he was not the star turn, or words to this effect. *Sept 1995* ★★★
**Bâtard-Montrachet Niéllon** Bright yellow green; immature, acidic, later flowery; 'shockingly dry', lean. Far too much new oak for its style and weight. Too slight to accompany a meat dish. *At a Rodenstock dinner, Sept 1994* ★★
**Beaune, Clos des Mouches J Drouhin** First noted at a Drouhin tasting in London in 1993: very fragrant; attractive but slightly soapy feel, youthful pineapple and vanilla, good acidity, oaky finish. One of the top wines at a British Airways blind tasting in 1994. Most recently, in the decade line-up at Drouhin (all had 13.5% alcohol and 30% new oak): still fairly pale; unknit gooseberry and caramel nose, smoky vanilla; medium sweet, better flavour than nose; light end acidity. *Last tasted Oct 2001* ★★ *It seemed to have lost its initial impetus.*
**Bienvenue-Bâtard-Montrachet A Ramonet** Magnums served at Rodenstock's dinner for 50, many distinguished guests, as customary, joining the tasting team, including Dr Schiele, an ex-President of Germany. During the weekend, 88 wines were tasted, many recorded in this book. The wine was pale with a slightly green tinge; oaky, scented vanilla nose, lean, almost sharp; lovely crisp oaky flavour, good length, lemon-like acidity. *At the Königshof hotel, Munich, Sept 1996* ★★★★ *Probably at its best now.*
**Chassagne-Montrachet, Les Caillerets A Ramonet** 0.40ha of vines out of a 14-ha estate. Old vines, one-third new oak, *en barrique* 12 to 15 months. Pale; buttery; astonishing flavour, rich attack, full-bodied (13.5%) yet I queried its length and finally decided it was a bit raw and disappointing. *At Gidleigh Park, Devon, March 1997* ★★ *(But the '91 Kistler, Durell vineyard Sonoma Chardonnay was infinitely better – rich and exciting ★★★★)*

OTHER CHASSAGNE-MONTRACHETS **Fontaine-Gagnard** three notes: stodgy, lacking zest; scented, soft, buttery, slightly better. *1996* ★★; **Laguiche/Drouhin** 'toasted' nose; dry, too much oak. *1993* ★★; **Niéllon** soft, oaky flavour and 'warm', dry finish. *1998* ★★★; **La Boudriotte Gagnard-Delagrange** rustic, poor nose. *1994*; **Morgeot L Latour** nice weight and flavour. *2001* ★★★; and **Morgeot, Clos de la Chapelle L Jadot** an attractive mouthful, good acidity. *1994* ★★★

**Chevalier-Montrachet Leflaive** Curious mintiness; dry, fairly powerful, oaky, cloves-like spice, lean finish. *April 1998* ★★
**Chevalier-Montrachet Dom du Ch de Beaune** Picking started 25 September. Very forthcoming, nutty, vanilla nose; fairly sweet, fairly full-bodied (alcohol 13.5%), oaky, spicy flavour. Much better than expected. *In Bouchard Père's cellars, Beaune, Nov 1995* ★★★

**Chevalier-Montrachet, Les Demoiselles Niéllon** Full, fairly assertive, good enough. *Boardroom lunch, Nov 1995* ★★★
**Corton-Charlemagne Dom du Ch de Beaune** Good colour; sweet, totally dominated by oak. Lacking length. *In Bouchard Père's cellars, Beaune, Nov 1995* ★

OTHER CORTON-CHARLEMAGNES **L Latour** several notes. Very pronounced oaky nose that opened up fabulously though a touch of caramel (1996); the following year at dinner: rather obvious, too sweet, plausible. Most recently: very pale; low-keyed; sweet but lean, vanilla and a trace of kernels, dry finish. *July 2000* ★★; **Bonneau du Martray** good nose, correct but no more. *May 1999* ★★; and **J Drouhin** full-bodied, nutty, moderately good. *Oct 1993* ★★★

**Meursault, Charmes Comtes Lafon** Old vines. Very small crop. Rained before harvest. Touch of caramel and vanilla; lovely, buttery flavour (1995). Five years later: served too cold but nose opened up well, sweet, vanilla; fullish, assertive flavour, good length for a '91. *At a dinner to honour Lenoir M Josey – using his own wines!, New York, Nov 2000* ★★★
**Puligny-Montrachet, Champs-Canet E Sauzet** Dry, lean, oaky, crisp acidity. *July 1995* ★★★
**Puligny-Montrachet, Clavoillon Leflaive** Good colour, fragrant, honeyed; initially powerful (alcohol 13.5%) and assertive but tailed off. Served with pike which brought out the flavour. *A Hallwag tasting lunch,* Präsentierung *by me at Le Canard, Hamburg, May 1995* ★★
**Puligny-Montrachet, Clos de la Mouchère H Boillot** Selected out of a very mixed bag of 37 white burgundies for Concorde, tasted blind of course, in April 1994. The following February, after an extensive tasting of German wines, enjoyed with British Airways' very good sandwiches (much needed after a long and concentrated tasting). Next, lo and behold, or rather high and behold, enjoyed on Concorde: medium pale; no nose, partly because of the height and cabin air, also because of the hopeless glasses (at that period), but positively exotic on the palate, slightly sweet, very attractive. *Last tasted en route to New York, March 1997* ★★★

OTHER PULIGNY-MONTRACHETS **Dom Chartron's Clos du Cailleret** acceptable. *1994* ★★; **L Jadot's Champs-Gains** spicy, good enough. *1994* ★★; **J Drouhin's Folatières** neutral nose; grapey, oaky. *1993 and 1994;* **Maroslavac-Léger's Folatières** attractive nose; not bad, hard finish. *1994* ★★; **J Drouhin's Perrières** take away the oak, no nose, little taste. *1993* ★; and **Laroche's Ch de Puligny-Montrachet** positive, lean, attractive. *1994* ★★

# 1992 ★★★

A remarkably good growing season. Ripening took place under perfect conditions as August temperatures were high. Glorious sunshine lasted virtually throughout the relatively early harvest. The white grapes were fully ripe and rounded, the problem being enough fruity acidity to balance the sweetness and body. On the whole there were some attractive wines, with the usual surprises and disappointments. The best are drinking well now.
**Montrachet Laguiche/Drouhin** Very forthcoming nose, oaky, minty, some depth; fairly assertive, flavour of pineapple, teeth-gripping acidity. *At the Montrachet/Laguiche tasting at the Institute of Directors, London, Feb 1996* ★★★

**Montrachet Bernard Morey** Two bottles, one corky the other with a light, immature, pineappley aroma; good flavour and acidity. A marvellous finish, oaky, smoky aftertaste. Much to my surprise one of my top marks in a flight of Montrachets and Chevaliers, though the others were all '94s. *At Rodenstock's, of course, Sept 1996* ★★★★
**Montrachet Thénard/Remoissenet** Very pale; meaty, caramelly; lean, gripping acidity. *At Christie's Millennium pre-sale tasting, New York, May 1999. By far the least good of a vertical of Thénard '89 to '93.*
**Bâtard-Montrachet Blain-Gagnard** Gooseberry-like acidity but quite good length. *An early note at Bibendum's tasting of '92, Jan 1994* ★★★
**Bâtard-Montrachet L Latour** Dry, hot, acidic finish. Even allowing for tasting out of doors, not very good. *June 1997* ★
**Bâtard-Montrachet Leflaive** Vanilla, scented, opened up; mild mid-palate yet steely and nutty. *At Hardy Rodenstock's opening dinner in Munich, Sept 1995* ★★
**Bâtard-Montrachet A Ramonet** First tasted in 1994: lovely, classic nose; full-bodied, good flavour though very oaky, spicy. The following year: lemon-tinged, star bright; lovely, gently scented; glorious flavour (Hugh Johnson said 'mirabelle'), very oaky, but elegant and with excellent acidity. *Last tasted at Rodenstock's gala dinner, Sept 1995* ★★★★
**Bâtard-Montrachet E Sauzet** Totally different style to Ramonet's: mild, slightly vanilla, harmonious; dry, full, assertive, oaky, smoky flavour and aftertaste. Good acidity. *Rodenstock, Sept 1994* ★★★ *(just). One feels that the oak is used like a pit prop – to keep the roof from falling in.*
**Beaune, Clos des Mouches J Drouhin** Palish; acidic, unknit pineapple and vanilla but not unattractive; surprisingly sweet and rich, well plied with fruit and oak. *In the decade vertical at Drouhin, Oct 2001* ★★
**Bienvenues-Bâtard-Montrachet J-C Bachelet** From 80-year-old vines. Yield 18–20hl/ha. Even in its youth, the wine was straw-coloured; slightly appley, young nose; rich and powerful with good grip and acidity. *At Bibendum, Jan 1994* ★★★ *Some potential. Would be interesting to see how it has shaped up.*
**Bienvenues-Bâtard-Montrachet Leflaive** Preceded by 1893 Ch d'Yquem (with *foie gras*) and followed by '26 Ch La Mission Haut-Brion, a rather bold, in fact essential divider. Served very cold. Light, malty, and opening up as it approached room temperature, revealing vanilla and a touch of honey; dry enough, firm, oaky Chardonnay flavour. It seemed to get sweeter on nose and palate. Almost too sweet. *At Christan Sveaas' great wine dinner in Oslo, April 1996* ★★★

THE FOLLOWING '92 CHABLIS HAVE BEEN SELECTED ARBITRARILY AND ARE OF VARYING INTEREST. First the *grands crus:* **William Fèvre's Bougros** gooseberry-like acidity, dry, some quality and length. *1995* ★★★, and **Le Clos** fuller and more meaty; dry, good fruit and flavour, positive, quite a bite, good length. *1995* ★★★; **J-M Brocard's Les Clos** very scented; buttery and oaky – not my style of Chablis but quite attractive. *1995* ★★; and **J-P Droin's Valmur** grassy, assertive. *1994* ★★★. Next the *premiers crus:* **William Fèvre's Vaulorent** very pale; scented, vanilla; dry, crisp, positive. *1995* ★★; and **L Moreau's Mont de Milieu** good fruit; firm, holding well. *At a Taste of France, Palm Beach, Feb 1998* ★★★

**Chassagne-Montrachet, Les Chevenottes J-N Gagnard** Palish, green-tinged; rich, full, oaky, mouthfilling. *With Georg Riedel after his 'glass tasting', Christie's, April 1996* ★★★

OTHER CHASSAGNE-MONTRACHETS **Blain Gagnard**'s **Clos St-Jean** unknit, green; dry, good fruit, gooseberry-like acidity. For refreshing early drinking. *At Bibendum, Jan 1994* ★★; **M Niéllon**'s **Clos de la Maltroye** complete, harmonious; medium dryness and weight, nutty, good aftertaste. *At Rodenstock's, Munich, Sept 1995* ★★★; and **Clos St-Jean** fragrant, lovely flavour but austere. *At Rodenstock's 16th* Raritäten Weinprobe *in Munich, Sept 1995* ★★★

**Chevalier-Montrachet Leflaive** Pure buttercup-yellow shot with gold highlights. In Riedel glass: lovely vanilla nose; sweet, soft, a touch of fat, lovely; in Baccarat's 'Grands Blancs' glass it seemed a touch more raw, coarser and caramelly; but a bit more to it on the palate. Both at an N K Yong dinner in Singapore, 1998. More recently: floral; attractive. *Last noted with supreme of guinea fowl at a dinner hosted by Anne-Claude Leflaive at Vintners' Hall, London, June 1999* ★★★★

## N K Yong

*Singapore surgeon – head of a large hospital. Known to all as 'NK'. The best known wine man in the region, and far beyond. He has a brilliant cook in his wife Melina, to match his exceptional cellar. He has been very active on the council of the International Wine and Food Society. NK is very serious about his wine and I have enjoyed many a fabulous bottle while dining at his home with his family and very knowledgeable friends.*

**Chevalier-Montrachet Dom du Ch de Beaune** Gold colour; touch of oiliness, otherwise very good; dry, interesting texture, some flesh, very slight touches of caramel, kernels and nuttiness. *Lunch in the country, Jan 2000* ★★★ *(just).*
**Corton-Charlemagne L Latour** As usual, several notes, first in May 1995 at a James Beard Foundation Dinner at Christie's in New York: smoky-oaky nose; hefty style, good length – but not good with caviar. Less impressive in the open air (1997), hot and rather acidic. Showing quite differently at the vertical in 1998: full, open, buttery, spicy nose with a touch of gooseberry-like acidity. 'Hefty' noted again, toasty, dry finish. Most recently: assertive, full-bodied, touch of rawness. *Last tasted July 2000. On the whole* ★★★ *but I would get on with it.*
**Meursault, Charmes Comtes Lafon** 1.7ha of vines producing 5000–8000 bottles a year. Dominic Lafon told us that the '92 was outstanding for white, and it was certainly well demonstrated by this, the youngest vintage in a vertical back to the '86: medium-pale yellow, with touch of lime; gentle, youthful pineapple aroma, becoming pleasantly scented; crisp, good length, glorious flavour. *At a Hollywood Wine Society weekend in Florida, March 1995* ★★★★

OTHER MEURSAULTS **J Drouhin**'s **Charmes** very pale; all oak – scent and taste. Speciously attractive. *1995* ★★★; **Alain Coche**'s **Charmes** buttery; fairly sweet and full, positive, good length, vanilla finish. *1994* ★★★; and his **L'Ormeau** fragrant, acidic. *1994* ★★

**Pouilly-Fuissé, Vieilles-Vignes Ch Fuissé/Vincent** Picked early. The harvest in the Mâconnais started 10 September. Fresh, attractive; dry enough, delightful flavour and style. It reminded me of the '83. I much prefer drinking this class of Pouilly-Fuissé to most Chablis. *Dining at Miriam and Jonathan Lyons', July 1998* ★★★

**Puligny-Montrachet, Les Referts J-M Boillot** Jean-Marc's Referts was once part of Etienne Sauzet's estate. Crisp, spicy, fragrant, lightly honeyed; medium-dry, nutty, oaky flavour, lip-licking, fresh lime acidity, very fragrant aftertaste. *At a Gidleigh Park opening dinner, Devon, March 1997* ★★★★

OTHER PULIGNY-MONTRACHETS **Dom Chartron**'s **Clos du Cailleret** young, appley; full-flavoured, acidic and very oaky. *1994* ★★; **Remoissenet**'s **Champs Gain** dry, lean, not good enough. *1994*; **Leflaive**'s **Clavoillon** not very distinctive; better on palate, rich, good length, interesting flavour. *1995* and *1996* ★★; **J Drouhin**'s **Folatières** positive, good nose and flavour, attractive lanolin and oak. *Dinner after Dow's vintage vertical, Oct 1998* ★★★; **Maroslavac-Léger**'s **Folatières** unknit, almost too rich; full-flavoured. *1994* ★★; and **J-C Bachelet**'s **Sous les Puits** a vineyard next to Blagny and similar in character to St-Aubin. Surprisingly sweet, rich yet austere and assertive. Could develop well. *1994* ★★★

## 1993 ★★★ variable

A useful vintage, but one needing great care in selection. There was overproduction of generic white burgundy and higher than average acidity – and the time of picking, whether before, during or after the rains is crucial.

The leading producers of *grands* and *premiers crus* picked before the rain and made some excellent wines, many not only drinking well now but with more to come. Most wines from the generic and *négociants'* village wines should have been consumed well before the end of the decade.
**Montrachet Laguiche/Drouhin** Bottled at the end of April 1995. First noted at the Montrachet/Laguiche tasting in Feb 1996: pale; light fragrant style, spicy, some depth; dry, lean, acidic. Next in 1998 at the big tasting for *Vinum* magazine in Zurich: gaining colour, now more yellow; low-keyed at first but, like all good white burgundies, opened up beautifully in the glass and held its own for the entire length of the tasting; dry, firm, positive, excellent finish. Needed time. Two years later at the *Primum Familiae Vini* dinner at Vinopolis, distinctive yellow; classic bouquet and flavour, fullish 'well-tuned'. Most recently, dining with Claude and Frédéric Drouhin: crisp, inimitable Montrachet nose, glorious flavour, length and aftertaste. Full-bodied (alcohol 14%) and exuding power as well as beauty. *Last tasted Oct 2001* ★★★★★ *Lovely now. Good for another ten or more years.*
**Montrachet Fleurot-Larose** Tiny production. Medium-pale gold; lovely, fragrant, fully opened bouquet, touch of vanilla blancmange; medium sweet, full, rich, oaky, nutty flavour and fragrant aftertaste. *Opening the first 'flight' of Rodenstock's wine weekend at the Königshof hotel, August 1998* ★★★★★
**Montrachet Chartron et Trébuchet** This *négociant* in Puligny was said to have bought the wine for Fleurot-Larose. I thought the latter would have had too little to sell, but at least Chartron would market it well. It is therefore not very surprising that my note made (the day after the wine above) was pretty similar, perhaps more unknit, slightly metallic and peppery at first on the nose but then opened up, 'blancmange' noted once again. I also noted the 'lean Chartron style' but now think I must have merely reacted to the name. *At dinner at the Königshof hotel, Munich, August 1998* ★★★★
**Montrachet Thénard** Very pale; little nose, fairly dry, attractive but with slightly caramelly aftertaste. *At a pre-sale tasting, New York, May 1999* ★★

**Bâtard-Montrachet A Ramonet** First tasted in 1987: star bright, hint of green; less developed nose than the preceding '89 Caillerets but slightly sweet, very full-bodied, lovely flavour, texture and balance though a touch of youthful rawness. More recently, a Methuselah: smoky, oaky, biscuity bouquet and flavour, rich, substantial. *With Maine lobster at River Terrace on Mud Island, Memphis, Sept 1999* ★★★★

**Beaune, Clos des Mouches J Drouhin** Youthful acidity, slightly charred nose, opening up richly; fairly sweet but teeth-gripping, sharp, raw acidity. *At Drouhin, Beaune, Oct 2001* ★★?

**Chablis** A good, more even vintage in Chablis: **Dom Laroche's** very pale, very light on the nose, very dry, steely, scented and acidic. *1995* ★★; **Parisot's Vaudésir** steely; good length and flavour. *1999* ★★★; and, the best of my notes, a delicious **Montée de Tonnerre** but, alas, I failed to note the grower. *1996* ★★★

**Chassagne-Montrachet, La Boudriotte A Ramonet** Star bright as usual; hefty, smoky, rich and attractive nose; fairly dry, full-bodied (13.5%), rich and powerful like my host, with good acidity. *With a very secretive friend, in Florida, Dec 1996* ★★★★

**Chassagne-Montrachet, Vergers A Ramonet** Broader, richer, soft pineapple and wholemeal biscuits; sweeter, softer (than the Boudriotte), rich, rounded, attractive. *Same place, Dec 1996* ★★★★

**Chassagne-Montrachet, 'La Grand-Montagne' Fontaine-Gagnard** Lovely bright yellow; spicy, oaky, fragrant; attractive, smoky, okay flavour, good length, tingling acidity. *Sample bottle from Laytons, Sept 1996* ★★★★

**Chevalier-Montrachet Leflaive** Far better than the '92: vanilla nose; lovely, rich, nutty taste. Very appropriately tasted at the Domaine de Chevalier in Bordeaux – with other members of the same group, which includes Paul Jaboulet and Zind-Humbrecht – who get together one evening each Vinexpo. *June 1997* ★★★

**Chevalier-Montrachet E Sauzet** Compared in Riedel glasses, in which it seemed more flowery, and in Baccarat 'Grands Blancs' glasses, the nose appearing rather raw and palate more of a bite. Nice wine though. *Jan 1998* ★★★

**Corton-Charlemagne Bonneau du Martray** Rich but unknit; some sweetness, good flavour and certainly interesting. But, tasted blind, though good it was not among the runners up. *At a British Airways tasting, May 1999* ★★★ *Doubtless will taste better when I see the label!*

**Corton-Charlemagne Coche-Dury** Fairly pale; very good indeed, its nutty vanilla bouquet opening up fabulously in the glass; dry, assertive, a powerhouse. *At a dinner in honour of Lenoir M Josey, New York, Nov 2000* ★★★★

**Corton-Charlemagne L Latour** Green-harvested in July. The *ban de vendanges* was proclaimed 15 September but Latour began picking here on the 20th, just before the rains which started the eve of the 22nd and continued until 4 October. First tasted in the vineyard in June 1997 on Latour's 200th anniversary: pale with tinge of lemon; low-keyed, correct; good flavour, body (alcohol 14%), length and acidity. Most recently (served far too cold; it deadened the nose): dry, steely, powerful, impressive. *Last tasted July 2000* ★★★(★)

**Meursault, Ch de Blagny L Latour** An attractive, practical, dependable and reasonably priced wine. First tasted blind in 1995. Good nose, length, acidity. *Last noted at lunch at Latour's London office, July 1996* ★★★

**Meursault, Sous la Velle Dom Michelot** A 2-ha plot in an important 23-ha domaine. At 15,700 metres, Mach 2, 1380 mph, outside temperature –58°C. I was glad to be inside,

sipping contentedly. Unusual in an aeroplane, the nose had immediate impact, very fragrant, oak; fairly dry but rich and buttery – almost belonged to the 'New World' that I was speeding to – good length, acidity and aftertaste. *On Concorde, Dec 1997* ★★★★

**THREE MORE MEURSAULTS** from **Domaine Michelot**, all tasted blind in May 1999: **Clos du Cromin** positive yellow; rich, buttery nose and flavour but a slight touch of Gripfix, almost, marzipan ★★★ *(just)*; **Grand Charrons** colour a bit too deep, straightforward ★★★; and **Clos St-Felix** the best of the trio; substantial, positive, complete, good potential ★★★★

**Puligny-Montrachet, Clavoillon Leflaive** Once again, served too cold but sweet and soft vanilla emerged; crisp yet buttery, oak, good length and acidity. I liked its vivacity and it went well with grilled scallops. *At a St James's Branch dinner of the IWFS at the Halcyon hotel in London, May 1998* ★★★

**Puligny-Montrachet, Les Folatières Leflaive** Pale; sweet, fragrant, whiff of spice, touch of caramel; dry, lean, acidic, kernelly aftertaste – and expensive. *Dec 1996* ★★★

**Puligny-Montrachet, Les Pucelles Dom Verger** Good bouquet, touch of oak; dry, crisp Puligny character and very good acidity. *At Christie's wine department's Christmas dinner, Dec 1996* ★★★

**A WIDE RANGE OF** mainly *négociants'* '93 Chablis, Meursaults and Pulignys tasted in 1995. They ranged from ordinary to acceptable – few of the wines were actually bad but not many were above average: the latter included three **Chablis** *grands crus*: **La Chablisienne's Grenouille**, **Henri Dupas' Les Preuses** and **Fèvre's Bougros**. Most of the importers' Meursaults and Puligny-Montrachets were depressingly mediocre.

# 1994 ★★★ variable

Louis Latour's comments, which I précis under his Corton-Charlemagne below, sum up the difficulties the growers had, and what a gamble making wine can be: do you pick early, pick hurriedly at the onset of rain, or hope the weather will clear up enough to pick later? 1994 presented a classic dilemma. And, at the risk of repeating myself, those who cared and who could afford to take endless pains in the vineyard and winery managed to make a good job of their wines. Anything less can safely be by-passed.

**Montrachet Laguiche/Drouhin** A barrel sample brought to London around the time of bottling. Distinctive yellow; very fragrant, with twist of lemon, touch of oak, youthful vanilla and pineapple; fairly sweet, full-bodied, 'hot' rich flavour, very good teeth-gripping acidity. A big mouthful, quite unready. *Feb 1996* ★★★, *or* ★★★★ *star potential.*

**Montrachet Fleurot Larose** Very small production: just one *barrique* in 1994. Curious, unknit, slightly oily nose; medium-sweet, full-bodied, hefty yet soft touch, 'buried oak' (I think I meant the considerable taste of oak was masked by the other components). High, hot, end acidity. *In Rodenstock's opening 'flight' of Montrachets, August 1998* ★★ *Worth trying, but I did not regard it very highly.*

**Montrachet L Jadot** Pale, green-tinged; low-keyed nose, twist of lemon, a smidgen of fruit; more positive on palate, dryish, medium full-bodied, lean, very acidic. *At lunch on the fifth day of Rodenstock's Yquem marathon, Sept 1998* ★★★ *Needed more bottle age, but can it aspire to 4-star?*

**Montrachet E Sauzet** Two notes, both at Rodenstock tastings, first in 1996: pale; positive, vanilla, touch of caramel and oak, almost too assertive with the fish dish, needed time. Next, two years later, in a blind 'flight' opening the dinner on the third day of the Yquem marathon (to give some idea of the scale of Hardy Rodenstock's events and his incredible generosity, in 1998 in addition to 125 vintages of Ch d'Yquem tasted over five mornings, each day there was lunch with at least four wines, a dinner tasting with an average of 20 wines and a gala dinner on the last night with 37 wines. The tastings and lunches were attended by 24 people and 50 or 60 the gala dinner). The wine seemed more fully developed the second time round, nose more powerful, full, rich, surging out, smoky pineapple; dry, power and flavour, length and good acidity. *With sucking pig, 'shaved' carpaccio, Sept 1998* ★★★★

**Beaune, Clos des Mouches J Drouhin** Muffled, still youthful, pineappley nose; fairly dry, a bit stolid (Daphne 'quite liked it'). *At Drouhin, Oct 2001* ★★★ *(at most).*

**Chassagne-Montrachet Laguiche/Drouhin** Bottled September 1995. Palish; fragrant, high toned yet soft blancmange nose; fairly sweet, surprisingly mouthfilling, very agreeable. *At the Institute of Directors, London, Feb 1996* ★★★★

**Chassagne-Montrachet, Les Vergers Marc Morey** Fairly pale; quite attractive fruit; distinctly sweet, good body (alcohol 13.5%) and flavour. *At a Haynes, Hanson and Clark tasting, Sept 1996.* Then ★(★★) *Will be fully mature now* (**Morey**'s **Chassagne-Montrachet, Virondot** – a 0.6-ha vineyard new to me, less sweet but full, fruity and attractive ★(★★)

**Chevalier-Montrachet E Sauzet** Pale; high-toned, spicy (cloves), good fruit but coarser style and more acidity than Leflaive's; earthy, assertive, severe – good with fish (1996). Next, still youthfully minty, acidic; served too cold, dry, firm, oak on finish, acidity verging on tartness. *Last noted blind, at Rodenstock dinner tasting, Sept 1998* ★★★

**Chevalier-Montrachet Leflaive** Pale; light, fragrant, slightly minty, both open and harmonious, later surging vanilla; dry, firm, steely, good acidity. A delicious drink. Top of a small flight of '94s. *Rodenstock, Sept 1996* ★★★(★) *Should be perfect now.*

**Corton-Charlemagne Bonneau du Martray** A half bottle wedged between six excellent wines at Emeril's, the 'in' restaurant in New Orleans. Palish yellow; a creamy rather than nutty Corton-Charlemagne. Showing well. *Nov 1997* ★★★★

**Corton-Charlemagne L Latour** After an exceptionally warm summer, the weather broke on 31 August. Two weeks of torrential rain. Starting on 19 September, Latour employed 70 pickers at Corton-Charlemagne. Four well-spaced notes, first at their London office: very pale; agreeable oaky nose and flavour. Full-bodied (14% alcohol). It went well with pan roast cod at a dinner at Christie's in honour of the great collector Tawfiq Khoury and his friends (1997) but was less satisfactory tasted in the open air later that summer – a nice idea to taste alongside the vineyard, but not ideal. Most recently: now 'sear and yellow'; slightly caramelised; some sweetness, presumably chaptalised to achieve 14% alcohol, vanilla flavour and raw finish. *Last noted at Latour's London office, July 2000. At best* ★★★

**Meursault F Jobard** A small, 4.5-ha estate including 1.87ha in Meursault: good acidity and vanilla; austere, *assez bien*, fair length, dry finish. Selected from the ship's stock for a comparative tasting of white wines. *On the Seabourn Spirit, the Rolls-Royce of cruise ships, in the Malacca Straits, Jan 1998* ★★

**Meursault, Perrières Ropiteau-Mignon** Fresh, still youthful; distinctly dry, oaky, positive and attractive. *Drinking well on BA 001 (Concorde) en route to New York, Sept 1997* ★★★

**Pouilly-Fuissé G Duboeuf** A miserably memorable occasion when this modest wine was served to a fairly large party of Americans at Paul Bocuse's restaurant in Lyon. Not only was there bottle variation, some pale and bright and fresh (though too oaky), some deeper and in less than good condition, some drab, straw-coloured and oxidised. The wine waiters seemed neither to notice nor care. The wine was not old; the estimable Monsieur Duboeuf would not have sold Bocuse duff stock, so the wine must have been badly stored. It resulted in my highly critical article in *Decanter*, entitled 'Paul who?' I doubt if Maître Bocuse saw it but it caused great amusement among my French friends. *No-one had ever been so outspoken about one of France's icons. Tasted at Bocuse, in Lyon, 1997.*

**Puligny-Montrachet, Les Champs-Gain Remoissenet** Palish; light 'bread basket' nose; touch of sweetness, soft, not too much oak, good enough for Concorde. *At a tasting for very receptive British Airways cabin crew staff at Heathrow, Oct 1998* ★★★

**Puligny-Montrachet, Les Pucelles Leflaive** Pale; floral nose, lime and pineapple, lively; medium-dry, lovely flavour, oaky finish. *At the annual 'Bunch' tasting at the Groucho Club, Soho, Jan 1999* ★★★; also **Puligny-Montrachet, Les Clavoillon** Quite good too, a touch of gooseberry on the nose, more solid, peppery finish ★★

**Santenay Vincent Girardin** I think this was the first time I had drunk a white wine from the southern end of the Côte de Beaune: a very attractive yellow gold; very good, slightly oaky nose; medium-dry, full-bodied (alcohol 13.5%), very attractive, well-rounded flavour, deft use of oak and good acidity. *Tasted as a guest of John Wheeler, whom I first met in Bordeaux in 1955, at a Broderers' Company Court Dinner, March 1997. I gave it 4 stars (not because the dog could sing so well but because it could sing at all). Well, say* ★★★★ *but it will be tired by now, even out of tune.*

# 1995 ★★★★

A most attractive and largely very successful vintage despite its temperamental growing season: grapes ripening well during a hot summer and early vintage hampered by rain and risk of rot during the first half of September. One of the growers told me that it was a three-stage harvest due to morning mists, afternoon sun and botrytis, both beneficial and harmful. Yields were down 30% but a touch of noble rot gave wines more richness and concentration with increased sugar levels and good acidity. A case of 'all's well that ends well'. The best wines are lovely now.

**Montrachet DRC** Total production 150 cases. Very pale; poured 8.30pm (too cold), scented by 8.45, fully evolved vanilla and touch of caramel by 10pm; amazingly powerful, deft oak, spicy. *At a Zachys/Christie's dinner at Spago's, Los Angeles, Feb 1998* ★★★(★★)

**Montrachet Laguiche/Drouhin** Meeting up with Len Evans and Brian Croser at Gidleigh Park in Devon, I was asked to taste blind from two glasses. I had simply no idea what they were. In my right hand glass the wine was very pale, with a green tinge; clearly still very youthful; medium-sweetness, pineappley, on the lean side, far too much spicy oak and a touch of bitterness on the finish. My conclusion was that it was rather an obvious 'New World', and, knowing them, Australian Chardonnay. Their faces dropped. The wine in my left hand glass was pale; firm, steely; the same sort of sweetness, fairly full-bodied, better balanced, more complete. 'A good quality classic white burgundy.' They were not pleased. The first was Croser's '96 Petaluma Chardonnay, just bottled; the first Australian $60 Chardonnay; the second was Laguiche's '95 Montrachet. I next tasted it in 1998, finding it high toned, smoky, very rich; lovely flavour, good acidity, very high mark. Most recently, a jeroboam: touch of youthful lemon, almost grapefruit-like; very good indeed, clinging reluctantly, patiently, to the sides of the glass. *At Hal Lewis' Bacchus Society investiture dinner at the Peabody Hotel, Memphis. Sept 1999 ★★★★(★) Will be even better, say 2005–2020.*

**Montrachet** L **Latour** Very pale; hefty; taste of peach kernels, disappointing. *At dinner following Mikhail Pletner's recital on historic pianos (Chopin's, Beethoven's, Liszt's) at Hatchlands, Surrey, Dec 2000 ★★*

**Montrachet** Thénard/**Remoissenet** A jeroboam: pale; touch of vanilla but shapely, harmonious nose; medium-dry, fairly powerful, good flavour, spicy. *Accompanying John Dory at the Peabody, Memphis, Sept 1999 ★★★(★) Still time in hand.*

**Montrachet** Bouchard **Père** Eleven *pièces*, equivalent of 275 dozen bottles produced. Tasted from the cask: still cloudy (we were told that the whites were taking a long time to settle). Surprising depth and persistence of youthful aroma; frankly hard to judge but potential apparent. *In Bouchard Père's cellars, Beaune, Nov 1995. Then (★★★★)?*

**Montrachet** Fleurot-Larose Medium-pale, highly polished; not dissimilar to the '94 nose; much better on the palate: medium-dry, fairly full-bodied, touch of lanolin-like fat and plumpness, more forthcoming than the '94, with lip-licking acidity. Rare, good but not sensational. *At Rodenstock's tasting, in Munich, August 1998 ★★★*

**Bâtard-Montrachet** Leflaive Fullish, nutty, minty with 'green' youthful acidic undertone, opening up fragrantly; medium-sweet, full-bodied, good flavour, extract and oak. Starting to spread its wings. High mark. *Sept 1998 ★★★(★★)*

**Bâtard-Montrachet** E Sauzet First tasted in January 1997: positive, full-flavoured. Twenty months later: palish, touch of green; delicious nose, lean yet full-bodied, delicious flavour, good length (Jancis Robinson – I think her second Rodenstock event – added 'nervy'). *Sept 1998 ★★★★(★)*

**Bâtard-Montrachet** L Jadot Magnums: palish, star bright; low-keyed – served too cold but opened up well as it approached room temperature; rich entry but overall dry, smoky-oaky finish. Rather lean and ethereal. *With Bresse-Poulard at the Louis C Jacob hotel, Hamburg, March 2000 ★★★(★)*

**Bâtard-Montrachet** J-N Gagnard Lovely, oaky; glorious, power-packed, fragrant aftertaste – and so it should have been for the price – nearly £1000 per dozen. *Jan 1997. Then ★★(★★★) Doubtless evolving magnificently now.*

**Bâtard-Montrachet** Albert Morey Fabulous mouthful. *Oct 1997 ★★(★★★)*

**Beaune, Clos des Mouches** J Drouhin Medium-pale, rich 'legs'; good vinosity, whatever I mean by that, initially harmonious but then I thought it a bit unknit, with some meatiness; better on the palate, fairly sweet, rich, assertive, full-bodied (labelled 13.5% but alcohol actually 14%). *At Drouhin, Beaune, Oct 2001 ★★(★★) I think it will pull through.*

**Chablis, Valmur** J-P Droin Pale; very attractive nose and flavour, distinctive, unusual, good texture. *Caviar dinner at the Sampsons' – we take it in turn, Feb 1998 ★★★★ Probably at peak.*

**Chablis, Vaulignot** (sic) **Louis Moreau** A Chablis *1er cru* vineyard unfamiliar to me. Much enjoyed the wine though. Exceptionally pale; touch of vanilla; bone dry, slightly steely as, I believe, Chablis should be, delicate fruit, good length. *With M Moreau at 'A Taste of France' which I hosted at the very* smart Mar-a-Lago Club, Palm Beach. *(I knew it first as the Merryweather Post's house – she was the Post Toasties heiress, and this was the family's seaside 'cottage' - before Donald Trump turned it into a club.) Feb 1998 ★★★*

**Chablis, Les Preuses** Simonnet-Febvre Pale; almost meatily rich; a steely, powerful, scented *grand cru*. *At Ponti's annual Wine Fair, Hong Kong, Oct 1999 ★★★★*

**Chassagne-Montrachet, Morgeot** L **Latour** Very pale; low keyed; medium-dry, fairly full-bodied. *With seared pepper tuna at the Swan Feast at Vintners' Hall, London, Nov 2001 ★★★*

THE FOLLOWING CHASSAGNE-MONTRACHETS were all noted at opening tastings in 1997: **Jean-Noël Gagnard**'s **Chevenottes** fragrant; positive, 'warm', nutty ★★★; and his **Caillerets** also good but with extra dimensions, dry, full-bodied, excellent acidity ★★★★; **Marc Colin-Déléger**'s **Chaumées** powerful, assertive, very good acidity ★★★; his **En Rémilly** neutral nose but positive flavour, crisp, very high acidity ★★★; and his **Les Vergers** soft, creamy nose; rich flavour, oak, good length, hard finish; needed bottle age ★★★; **Bernard Morey**'s **Les Embrazées** distinctive; crusty, charred, mouthfilling, delicious flavour, good length ★★★★; and his **Les Caillerets** sweeter, lovely flavour, oak and acidity ★★★★

**Chevalier-Montrachet** Dom du Ch de Beaune A Methuselah: pale; initially restrained by serving too cold but after 30 minutes floral and fragrant; lean, flavour of vanilla and pineapple, good length and acidity. With almost the leanness and elegance of a Leflaive Chevalier at its best, and a style of wine that cannot be emulated outside Burgundy. *Served at the Bacchus Society 'East meets West in the South' dinner in Memphis, Tennessee, Sept 1999 ★★★(★) Still youthful. Needs more time.*

**Chevalier-Montrachet** L **Latour** Very pale; 'a Leflaive look-alike'; medium-dryness and weight, strange flavour, very raw at first – too cold – but later was pleasantly crisp and 'nutty'. *At Hatchlands, Surrey, Dec 2000 ★★★*

**Corton-Charlemagne** L **Latour** Green pruned, good fruit, low yield. Half a dozen notes, the first in 1997 at Latour's bi-centenary tasting: pale lemon yellow; nose forgivably evasive as the tasting was in the open next to the vineyard. Some ripe sweetness, soft and, I thought, a bit soapy. At home later that autumn, much more positive on the nose, oak and vanilla, this time 'a bit austere'. Showing much better at the vertical – the youngest Charlemagne – in 1998: smoky Chardonnay, some sweetness, crisp, fresh, lovely flavour and acidity. And so forth, until most recently, still pale; crisp, pleasant fruit, attractive. Good but by no means great. *Last tasted July 2000 ★★★*

EARLY NOTES OF CORTON-CHARLEMAGNE **Bouchard Père**'s: tasted soon after fermentation and, though cloudy, sweet and fruity on the nose; rich, good acidity. Morning mist, afternoon sun – picked in stages to avoid the risk of rot. *Nov 1995 ★★★*; **Bonneau du Martray**'s fairly deep colour, nose still youthful; positive, powerful, good length, glorious potential. *Jan 1997 ★★★★*; and **Dom Rollin**'s: a 0.7-ha holding in a 12-ha family estate new to me but very impressive: good fruit, fragrance and depth, powerful, oaky. *Jan 1997 ★★★★*

**Mâcon-Clessé, Dom de la Bon Gran** Jean Thévenot He is passionate about his unique (I think) sweet wines. His '95 'Levouté' had a pale gold colour; honeyed, peachy nose which reminded me of Robert Weil's *Auslesen*; medium-sweet, rich, packing a punch (alcohol 14.5%), with a hard, dry finish.

Needed bottle age. And his 'Bon Gran', 4000 bottles made from 100% botrytis-affected grapes: a pale gold; lovely, rich nose; very sweet, rich, peachy flavour, excellent length and acidity. *At the winery, Oct 1999* ★★★★★ *Hors clessé!*

THE FOLLOWING MEURSAULTS WERE ALL TASTED IN 1997 **Albert Grivault**'s **Les Perrières** fragrant, still pineappley; medium-dry, good flavour ★★★; and his **Clos Les Perrières** though neutral on the nose, more positive on the palate, delicious flavour, good length ★★★★; **J Drouhin**'s **Perrières** crisp, touch of oak; lovely fruit and acidity ★★★; **F Jobard**'s **Genevrières** fairly sweet, powerful, oaky, good length (tasted blind I thought it was an Australian Chardonnay) ★★★★; and **Vincent Girardin**'s **Les Narvaux** very attractive, nutty, oaky, moderate weight (alcohol 12.5%, most were 13.5%) ★★★

**Pouilly-Fuissé, Vieilles-Vignes Ch Fuissé/Vincent** Another lovely wine from the king of Pouilly-Fuissé: palish yellow, good 'legs', rich, nutty, vanilla, some oak; very good flavour, balance and acidity. Quite a mouthful (alcohol 13.5%). *At a France in Your Glass gala dinner at Ch de Bagnols, Oct 1997* ★★★
**Puligny-Montrachet, Clavoillon Leflaive** A 4.8-ha plot out of a total domaine of 22.37ha. Vincent Leflaive died in 1993 and the estate was taken over by his daughter Anne-Claude. Stainless steel is used for freshness of fruit. The '95s were bottled between February and April. Very pale, lime-tinged, star bright; pure, understated Chardonnay, youthful pineapple and vanilla, slight smokiness, mouthwatering acidity; unmistakable lean style, full-bodied yet unobtrusive (alcohol 13.5%); delicate, subtle, good acidity. Classic. *At a tutored tasting I conducted in Los Angeles, March 1999* ★★★(★)
**Puligny-Montrachet, Perrières E Sauzet** Pale, bright; crisp, smoky, dry, lean but assertive. *At Annie's in Houston, with the Joseys, Aug 2000* ★★★ *Excellent sommelier and wine list.*
**Puligny-Montrachet, Les Folatières H Clerc** Pale; vanilla, oak; dry enough, straightforward. *Memorable more for the occasion, a special Vintners' Company court luncheon for the Bishop of London and myself following the 'Court of Binding' when his Lordship and I were elected members of the Company, 'Honoris Causa', Nov 2001* ★★★

## Tasting white burgundy

*As with most of the world's dry white wines, white burgundy is made to be drunk while still young and fresh. However (unlike most other dry whites), the finest will not only keep but will positively benefit from a certain amount of bottle-ageing. Optimum cellaring time depends on the quality of the vintage, and the following are indicators to look out for. Colour (relatively unimportant) in young wines can be greenish, whereas in 'big' vintages the likes of Meursault and Le Montrachet can be a deeper buttery yellow in hue. As they age, the wines become more and more golden in colour. As with red burgundy, the nose is often quite hard to get to grips with. Don't expect the exaggerated waxy, buttery smell of Australian Chardonnay, rather a more low-keyed, toasty, slightly bread-like smell, which, however (if not served too cold), will open up in the glass. On first sipping it will range from dry to medium-dry (never sweet). It can be surprisingly high in alcohol, its taste nutty, oaky, toasty and, with bottle age, quite honeyed. Acidity should be refreshing but not tart. Quality can be measured by length of flavour, and the way it expands in the mouth and lingers on the palate.*

I TASTED THE FOLLOWING PULIGNY-MONTRACHETS IN 1997 **E Sauzet**'s **Combettes** positive, fragrant; assertive ★★★★; and **Garennes** far sweeter than expected, good flavour and aftertaste ★★★★; **Philippe Chavy**'s **Les Folatières** good colour; fragrant; crisp, good flavour and acidity ★★★; **Vincent Girardin**'s **Perrières** yellow; lean, rapier-like, high acidity, good length ★★★★; and **B Morey**'s **La Truffière** nutty; rich, powerful ★★★★

# 1996 ★★★★★

If the '95s were good, the '96s were even better, wines with extra dimensions, about as good as white burgundy can get. Louis Latour reported very good growing conditions, low rainfall, long ripening period, healthy clusters with sugar levels and acidity high following the coldest September on record.

However, having assembled my notes, I am shocked at how few of the '96s I have tasted. I am even more appalled at the number of horrid, raw, poor wines that I come across at trade tastings. Stick to the best *négocants* and serious domaines.
**Montrachet Thénard/Remoissenet** Perhaps it was the morning 'flight' of 21 Yquems that made the opening wine at lunch appear more than usually acidic and austere. Not so: it was its immaturity. Palish, green-tinged, very bright – it actually looked youthfully mouthwatering; nose surprisingly minty, oaky, good but only on the fringes of harmony; medium, fairly full-bodied though on the lean side, raw, pasty, pineappley acidity. *Sept 1998* (★★★★) *possibly 5 star in due course.*
**Montrachet Parisot** Very fragrant; some sweetness and softness, attractive but a touch of spice and oak. Far too young and right out of our price range. *At a British Airways tasting for Concorde, May 1999* (★★★★)?
**Bâtard-Montrachet DRC** Just one barrel made 'for family use'. Beautiful colour, yellow with green gold highlights; fragrant, charred Chardonnay, smoky oak and fruit; sweet, soft, full-bodied, lovely rich fruit, excellent and fabulous acidity. *Served blind during the lunch at the Domaine following the St-Vivant tasting, Oct 2001* ★★★(★★) *We were all fooled.*
**Beaune L Latour** Rather a nice surprise: good colour; very attractive and interesting mint and oak nose; positive flavour, good acidity. *Feb 1999* ★★★, *or* ★★★★ *for its class.*
**Beaune, Clos des Mouches J Drouhin** Good colour; attractive and deep combination of fruit and oak; harmonious; medium-sweet, good structure, weight (the normal 13.5%), leaner, crisper and more acidic than the riper, fuller '95. *One of the best at the 'Decade of the 1990s' tasting at Drouhin, Beaune, Oct 2001* ★★(★★) *A good middle-distance runner.*
**Chablis, Les Clos J-M Brocard** Very bright; intriguing raspberry-tinged aroma; dry, good acidity, and, thank goodness, not a speciously oak-laden Chablis. *Feb 1999* ★★★
**Chablis, Vaillons William Fèvre** A very respectable *1er cru.* Pale yellow; very good nose, flavour and body. *Most refreshing after tasting 24 vintage ports, at Fells' offices, Nov 2000* ★★★
**Chablis, Valmur J-M Brocard** First noted at a British Airways tasting in February 1999, not dissimilar to Brocard's Les Clos. It seemed to gain stature with air – not so much in the glass as up in the air: positively attractive and refreshing nose; not too dry, good flavour and length. *Last noted on BA 15, London to Singapore, Aug 2000* ★★★
**Chassagne-Montrachet, Les Caillerets J-N Gagnard** Almost as pale as many '96 Mosels; young, fruity; medium-sweet, lovely flavour, oaky, spicy, excellent weight. *Trouncing six older Montrachets at a Rodenstock lunch, Sept 1998* ★★★★(★) *Now–2010.*

**Corton-Charlemagne L Latour** Fermented in 100% oak casks from the domaine's own *tonnellerie*. Several notes. Good old standby. The youngest vintage at the bicentenary line-up in June 1997: palish, lemon tinge; mildly spicy, pleasantly youthful; some sweetness on entry but overall dry, still hard and a touch of bitterness on the finish. Next at Stephen Kaplan's 'informal tasting' in Chicago, April 2000: crisp, scented nose; ripe sweetness, the usual full body (14% alcohol though in balance and not hefty). Very good flavour and acidity. Three months later, showing its best with a lively fragrance; noted again as 'overall dry', firm, crisp, good length and finish. *Last tasted at Louis Latour's office lunch in London, July 2000* ★★★★(★)

**Mâcon-Clessé, Dom de la Bon Gran Jean Thévenot** Thévenot is always the last to pick, but the '96 did not have the same beneficial botrytis as the '95. A pale wine; soft nose combining honey and asparagus; medium – neither dry nor sweet, powerful, complete, good length and acidity. *At the winery, Oct 1999* ★★★

**Mâcon-Uchizy Gallet** Palish; clean, appealing nose; not too dry, pleasant weight, good acidity. A very attractive drink. *Lunching at The Square, London, Nov 1999* ★★★

**Puligny-Montrachet L Jadot** Good colour, nose and delicious flavour, distinctly oaky, good acidity. *Lunching with Anthony Hanson at the Carlton Club, July 2001* ★★★ *(I find Anthony's book on Burgundy immensely helpful.)*

**Puligny-Montrachet, Les Referts L Latour** A couple of notes, both in Hong Kong: very good indeed with Chinese food. *At the restaurant China Lan Kwai Fong, after the Crédit Suisse tasting, Oct 1999* ★★★

# 1997 ★★★★★

A very satisfactory vintage. Thanks to a hot summer and favourable ripening conditions a decent sized harvest of very attractive wines. Judging by my notes, the overall quality is unusually even and though there was a deficit of acidity in some quarters, I have found the wines well balanced, their ripeness and flesh very appealing. Most are perfect now, while the firmer, more acidic '96s are taking their time.

**Montrachet DRC** Medium-pale yellow; low-keyed at first but soon opening up sweetly, then after an hour far too exotic, with pronounced scent of vanilla and soft toffee; fairly sweet, full-bodied, nutty, oaky, spicy flavour, a prickle of carbon dioxide on the finish. *Dining at the Seerose hotel, Pfäffikon, with Manfred Wagner after his Margaux vertical in Zurich, Nov 2000* ★★★

**Montrachet Thénard/Remoissenet** Palish yellow; some sweetness, powerful, meaty, good vinosity and length. *Jan 2000* ★★★? *Say now–2010.*

**Montrachet A Ramonet** Pale yellow; smoky, vanilla, whiff of coconut; dry, full-bodied, powerful (alcohol probably over 14%), crisp, wonderful flavour and acidity. *At Rodenstock's opening dinner at the Königshof hotel, Munich, March 2001* ★★★★(★)

**Montrachet Jacques Prieur** Pale gold; lovely, rich, nutty, toasted coconut; fairly sweet, full-bodied, hefty style, deliciously rich flavour. *At the Königshof hotel, Munich, March 2001* ★★★★

**Bâtard-Montrachet Leflaive** Very powerful, very fragrant, buttery – immediately proclaiming its *grand cru* status; rich, massive without being overwhelming or clumsy, wonderful flavour, terrific length, nutty/vanilla finish. *At a Domaine Leflaive dinner hosted by Anne-Claude Leflaive and Corney & Barrow, Vintners' Hall, June 1999* ★★(★★★) *I suggest 2005–2015.*

**Beaune, Clos des Fèves Chanson** Lovely crisp fruit, but very oaky. *June 2000* ★★★

**Beaune, Clos des Mouches Chanson** Good flavour, oak dominating. Dry finish. *June 2000* ★★★

**Beaune, Clos des Mouches J Drouhin** Extremely good. One of the best in an impressive line-up of the decade. Youthful, oaky nose, yet after minutes, creamy, harmonious; fairly sweet, very rich, still a bit raw on the finish. *At Drouhin, Beaune, Oct 2001* ★★(★★★) *Soon–2008.*

**Chablis, La Fourchaume Guy Mothe** Pleasant, scented; dry, pretty good. Adequately accompanying fillet of 'Sea bass *vierge*' – not sure how one can tell if a fish is *virgo intacto*. Lunching in great style, at the presentation of their new wine list at Spencer House, St James's, Sept 2000 ★★★

**Chablis, Montmains, Vieilles Vignes Dom des Malandes** Flavour not as long as its name but went down well at the Distillers' Company millennium dinner. *In the spectacular Painted Hall, Greenwich, May 2000* ★★

**Chablis, Vaillons, Vieilles Vignes Laroche** Very pale; good, open but not exceptional; dryish, very fragrant, delicious flavour. Paired with four different dishes and presented by Daniel Boulud of the restaurant Daniel, and Jean-Luc Le Du, his sommelier, two luminaries of the wine and food scene in New York. *At the Wine Experience, New York, Oct 1999* ★★★

A RANGE OF '97 CHABLIS GRANDS CRUS TASTED IN 1999 All the wines were fairly consistent – good but by no means exceptional, the best from **Moreau** and **William Fèvre**. Details, alas omitted. Most of these wines are for early drinking.

**Chassagne-Montrachet, Les Chevenottes Marc Morey** Pale; rich, meaty nose; full-flavoured and very attractive. *At Laytons, London, Jan 1999* ★★★(★) *Now–2004.*

**Chassagne-Montrachet, La Maltroie Fontaine-Gagnard** Pale yellow; rich, nutty nose and taste. Firm, teeth-gripping. *Jan 1999* ★★★(★) *Needs time.*

**Chevalier-Montrachet Leflaive** Very pale, lime-tinged; 'classic'; sweeter than expected, refined though still raw and youthful. Very dry finish. Will benefit from bottle age. *At Donald Kahn's dinner at Mosimann's, London, Dec 2000* ★★★(★)

**Corton-Charlemagne Coche-Dury** Pale yellow; lemon-like acidity; dry, lean. Very good but will benefit from more bottle age. *At Josey's pre-sale dinner, New York, March 2001* ★★(★★)

**Corton-Charlemagne Louis Latour** Flinty, smoky nose, slightly metallic (chalk soil); ripe entry, very dry finish, vanilla flavour, raw acidity. Needs bottle age. *Before the Louis Latour lunch in London, July 2000* ★★★(★) *Say now–2010.*

**Mâcon-Viré, Dom Gillet Jean Thévenot** An interesting wine, late-harvested – 5 to 10 October: pale; nose still youthful, pears and apples; medium-sweet, (residual sugar 4.5g/l), full-flavoured, rich, delicious. *Oct 1999* ★★★★

**Mâcon-Clessé, Dom de la Bon Gran Jean Thévenot** More honeyed; sweeter, rich, pineappley flavour, good acidity. *In Thévenot's cellar, Oct 1999* ★★★★

**Meursault, Charmes, Hospices, Bahèzre de Lanlay Chanson** Fragrant, oaky; attractive flavour, dry finish but too much oak – and what a colossal price. *At Chanson Père et fils' 250th anniversary tasting co-hosted by the English agent Richard Banks and Bollinger, Chanson's new owner, June 2000* ★★★

**Meursault, Les Genevrières Dom Michelot** Spicy, oaky, unusual nose and taste. Good weight and mid-palate fruit, excellent acidity. *At Laytons in London, Jan 1999* ★★★(★)

**Meursault, Les Genevrières, Tasteviné** Dry, raw, acidic yet coped with *les suprêmes d'empereur au verjus*. *At the Chapitre des Vendanges, Ch de Clos Vougeot, Oct 2001* ★★

**Pouilly-Fuissé, Tête de Cuvée Verget** Almost colourless; nutty nose, positive, very good, crisp, dry flavour and good length. Interesting to see a name like Pouilly-Fuissé, disregarded in the 1950s and 1960s, then suddenly fashionable (and overpriced) on the American market, now finding its true level, particularly successful yet not overpriced in a vintage like '97. *At Farr Vintners, Jan 2000* ★★★ *Ready for drinking.*

**Puligny-Montrachet, Clos du Cailleret** (**Monopole**) **Dom Chartron** Very pale; attractive, deft touch of oak; slightly fatter than expected, good fleshy fruit mid-palate and excellent acidity. *At Laytons in London, Jan 1999* ★★★(★)

# 1998 ★★★★

Despite a difficult growing season a remarkably good vintage for the whites. Some Côte de Beaune producers considered them superior to the '97s. By and large, firm, elegant, fragrant wines and some good aromatic Chablis. These are classic white burgundies for mid-term drinking. Alas, I have not yet tasted any Montrachets and I can't think why. But there is still plenty of time …

**Bâtard-Montrachet J-N Gagnard** Pale; wonderful 'toasted' nose; slightly sweet, delicious flavour, length and acidity. The real thing, but what a price. *At Justerini & Brooks' tasting of '98s, and later at Farr Vintners, Jan 2000* ★★(★★★) *Say 2005–2015.*

**Bâtard-Montrachet** Nutty nose; rich and powerful – as a buyer has to be (over £1000 per dozen). *At Justerini & Brooks, Jan 2000* ★★(★★★) *2005–2015.*

**Beaune, Clos des Mouches J Drouhin** Palish but positive yellow; youthful, pineapple nose, opening up fragrantly; medium-dry, mouthfilling fruit and oak (alcohol 13.2% though the label stated 13.5%). Delicious flavour, perfect balance. *At Drouhin, Beaune, Oct 2001* ★★★(★) *2005–2010.*

CHABLIS However, with the exception of a wide range of William Fèvre's Chablis tasted in June '99, I am sorry to record that most '98s I have tasted have ranged from poor through to not very interesting. Naming names: **J-P Droin**'s **Montmains** palish; minty; touch of caramel, acidic. *Wine & Food Society supper at Bibendum, Dec 2001* ★; **Jean Durup**'s **Vieilles Vignes** dry, mild, uninteresting, adequate. *At Brown's Hotel, March 2001* ★★; **William Fèvre**'s **Bougros** one oxidised (February 1999), on the next occasion: oaky apple juice. *British Airways tasting, May 1999* ★★; and **Pinson**'s **Mont de Milieu** nondescript nose; not bad flavour, good acidity. *May 2001* ★★

WILLIAM FÈVRE The energetic and enterprising Joseph Henriot, having acquired Bouchard Père in Beaune, then turned his attention to Chablis, purchasing Fèvre, the largest owner of Chablis *grands crus* (15% of the total, according to Hanson). At Vinexpo in June 1999 Henriot hosted a tasting of the full range of the top Fèvre wines. All the *premier cru* wines were very pale, almost colourless: the first, the **Montmains** I found attractive but too oaky – but Fèvre is a dab hand with oak; the **Vaillons** with youthful pineapple immature scent which always reminds me of ping pong table tennis balls, very flavoury; the **Montée de Tonnerre** lovely fruit but with a hot acidic finish. I did not taste the **Fourchaume**.

There was no question, however, that all of Fèvre's *grands crus* had extra dimensions: the **Blanchots** spicy, good flavour and length; **Bougros, 'Côte de Bougerots'**, a 6-ha vineyard, would have been my idea of a steely Chablis had it not been for the whiff of Gripfix and peach kernels. The

**Valmur** (1.66ha), fragrant, firm, steely, attractive; **Vaudésir** (1.2ha) ping pong balls – like acetone - on the nose, spicy, very good, full flavour and length; **Grenouilles** (0.57ha) more yellow; immature nose but quite powerful; **Les Preuses** (2.4ha) medium-dry, very positive flavour, length and acidity, ready soon; finally **Les Clos** Fèvre owns 3.5ha out of a total of just over 26ha, the biggest Chablis *grand cru*: very fragrant; good fruit and excellent acidity. Will benefit from bottle age.

When are these Chablis best to drink? I suggest the *premiers crus* at two to four years after the vintage, the *grands crus* at perhaps three to five years. By and large, Chablis (like Sancerre) is best drunk young and fresh.

**Chassagne-Montrachet** Just as I picked on William Fèvre's Chablis wines above, perhaps I might be permitted to let **Jean-Noël Gagnard**'s '98s represent some of the Côte de Beaune's *premiers crus*, all, incidentally made by his daughter, Caroline Lestiné. For convenience and to put them in perspective, I have listed them in a (slightly) ascending price order: **Les Chevenottes** very pale, delicious, nutty, good fruit; medium-dry, attractive, touch of citrus-like acidity; **Les Champs-Gain** light, walnutty nose; very good, full flavour, assertive; **Clos de la Maltroye** (a tiny *climat* of 0.33ha), spicy; touch more vanilla, positive flavour, fairly full-bodied (alcohol 13.5%) with slightly pasty acidity. Needs bottle age; **Morgeot** (they have just 0.8ha) hard to pin down on the nose but very good quality and length; and **Les Caillerets** (1ha) a beautifully flavoury aroma and taste, spicy, delicious – I ordered some on the spot. *All tasted at Farr Vintners in London, June 2000. I would rate them all around* ★★★★ *They all need some bottle age, say 2005–2010, or longer.*

**Corton-Charlemagne L Latour** Noted at the bicentenary tasting: pale, unusual, interesting, punchy, pineappley; touch of immature 'acetone'; distinctly dry, crisp, full-bodied (alcohol 14%) and still relatively immature. *July 2000* ★★(★★) *2005–2010.*

**Mâcon, Monbellet 'Wen en Pattes' Jean Rijckaert** A somewhat idiosyncratic and out of the ordinary white Mâcon with very distinctive nose and flavour and good length. *At Farr Vintners, London, Jan 2000* ★★★ *Drink soon.*

**Mâcon-Viré André Bonhomme** An interesting visit to a 9-ha domaine that must, at one time, have been through a tough time. Monsieur Bonhomme is very proud of what he is doing. He uses 25% new oak for his old vines and top wines, the remaining wines are aged in two- to four-year-old *barriques*, or no oak at all. The first I tasted was his '98 from young vines and no oak (to my surprise, he has a customer in Philadelphia who doesn't want oak): pale, of course; clean, fresh, minty nose; medium-dry, medium-full (alcohol 13%), attractive, youthful, pineapple, a bit short. His **Cuvée Spéciale** from 20- to 50-year-old vines spent seven months in oak and was bottled at the end of August (1999): also pale; better fruit, more depth, whiff of spearmint; good flavour, more body, hot finish. It seemed he produces almost single-handed between 50 and 60,000 bottles a year. *At the domaine, Oct 1999. At best* ★★★ *His wines are for drinking at between two and five years.*

**Pouilly-Fuissé, Vieilles Vignes Ch Fuissé/Vincent** Very pale; very rich, powerful wine (alcohol 13.5%) reminding me of the '89, good length. Now becoming expensive, well into the Côte de Beaune price league. *Jan 2000* ★★(★★)

**Puligny-Montrachet J Drouhin** A relatively modestly priced village wine. It had something to be modest about. 'Fulsome.' A perfectly decent drink. *In a line-up of 47 white burgundies at a British Airways blind tasting, March 2001* ★★

**Puligny-Montrachet, Clos de Cailleret** Chartron et Trébuchet An interesting partnership. Jean-Louis Chartron a grower in, and one-time mayor of, Puligny, and Louis Trébuchet a Beaune politician. I have usually found their wines, all white, rather lean and steely but this '98, from their 2.45-ha vineyard, very attractive: decent colour; sweet-nosed and positive flavour. *May 1999* ★★★(★)

**Puligny-Montrachet, Les Combettes** E Sauzet Powerful (and high-priced). *June 2000* ★★(★★) *Say 2005–2010.*

**Puligny-Montrachet, Clos de la Garenne** E Sauzet Very pale; touch of immature 'celluloid'; medium-dry, full flavoured, very acidic. Needs bottle age. *Jan 2000* ★(★★★) *Say 2005–2010.*

# 1999 ★★★★

Not *another* good vintage? Burgundy has had a remarkable run of good vintages recently though the whites are perhaps not quite as remarkable as the reds. Thanks to sunny conditions in the late summer and early autumn, there were record levels of maturity, with particularly high sugar levels for Chardonnay, averaging 180g/l, and substantial tartaric acidity at 7.5g/l, both the highest at the start of the harvest for ten years which resulted in wines with substantial alcohol, extract and balancing acidity. These are wonderful wines, the lesser ones for drinking soon while young and fresh and the classics destined for good, even long term, drinking, unless otherwise stated. All these '99s tasted in London, unless otherwise noted.

**Montrachet** L Jadot Very pale indeed; fragrant, squeeze of lemon; fairly sweet, rich, full-bodied (13.5%), lovely flavour and length. *At Jadot's* en primeur *tasting, Feb 2001* (★★★★★) *and already sold out!*

**Bâtard-Montrachet** L Jadot Vinified in new oak *barriques*. Very pale, tinge of lime; crisp, fragrant, vanilla from the casks; medium sweet, fairly full-bodied (13.5%), very good, positive flavour. Hard finish. Needs bottle age. *At Jadot's* en primeur *tasting, Jan 2001* (★★★★) *2006–2016.*

**Bâtard-Montrachet** E Sauzet Very pale; meaty; powerful, nutty, oaky. *At Justerini & Brooks', Jan 2001* (★★★★) *2006–2016.*

**Bâtard-Montrachet** P Jomain Extremely pale, almost colourless; fragrant, whiff of lemon; dry, firm, fine, steely. *At Howard Ripley's tasting, Jan 2001* (★★★★)

**Bâtard-Montrachet** Lequin-Colin Tiny parcel (0.12ha) from a domaine new to me. Very pale; very meaty; rich, tough finish. Needs time. *At Howard Ripley's tasting, Jan 2001* (★★★★)

**Bienvenues-Bâtard-Montrachet** Paul Perrot A 0.38-ha holding in a 19-ha estate which has regularly sold wines to J Drouhin: rich, tangy nose; fairly sweet, very rich, very powerful. *At Howard Ripley's tasting, Jan 2001* (★★★★★) *I have always liked the power combined with elegance of Bienvenues. It will be interesting to see how this wine turns out.*

**Chablis, Grenouilles** L Jadot Grenouilles is a 9-ha *grand cru* vineyard, east-facing and with light soil. Jadot's is vinified in oak. Palish, attractive colour; still young and appley; surprisingly sweet, full-bodied (13.5%), touch of blancmange. A substantial Chablis which will benefit from some bottle age. *At Hatch Mansfield's, Feb 2001* ★★(★★) *Say now–2006.*

Notes on various '99 Chablis A major blind tasting (in London, March 2001), of 14 Chablis (seven *1er cru* and seven *grand cru*) which I rated fairly highly. Among the better wines were **Long-Depaquit's** Vaillons pleasant though unexciting (★★★); **William Fèvre's** Côte de Lechet fragrant; good fruit, attractive flavour and good acidity (★★★★) and his

Montmains ordinary young nose but pleasant and easy (★★★); **Bouchard Père's** Bougros pleasant enough (★★★); and their 'La Grande Famille des Domaines' Vaudésir buttery, oaky; not my style but good length and decent flavour (★★★)

**Chassagne-Montrachet** Morin Quite attractive nose and taste, fairly alcoholic and acidic. *March 2001* ★(★★)

**Chassagne-Montrachet, Les Benoites** Chartron et Trébuchet Grassy and none-too-clean on the nose; better on palate, hefty, alcoholic and acidic. *March 2001* ★★ *Possibly 3-star with more time in bottle.*

**Chassagne-Montrachet** Ch de la Maltroye Virtually colourless; fragrant, floral; very positive impact (alcohol 13%), quite a bite and marked acidity. Needs bottle age. *At Howard Ripley's tasting, Jan 2001* ★★(★)

**Chassagne-Montrachet, Clos du Ch de Maltroye** Ch de Maltroye I do find all these Maltroyes very confusing. But this wine warranted its higher price. Also virtually colourless; good depth; fairly sweet, glorious flavour, oaky, good length. *At Howard Ripley's tasting, Jan 2001* ★★(★★)

**Chevalier-Montrachet Dom des Héritiers**, Jadot A 1.04-ha parcel bought in 1794 by the first members of the Jadot family to arrive in Beaune from Belgium. Now equally owned by Jadot (0.5ha) and L Latour. Pale; effusive, crisp; sweet, lovely flavour and lip-licking acidity. *At Jadot's tasting, Feb 2001* ★★★★

**Corton-Charlemagne Dom des Héritiers**, Jadot A 2-ha holding. Good, characteristically nutty, vanilla nose; surprisingly sweet, full-bodied of course, rich. *At Jadot's tasting (the wine not yet bottled), Feb 2001* (★★★★) *Good life ahead.*

**Corton-Charlemagne** L Latour Medium slight lemon tinge; great swoosh of vanilla, good fruit; medium sweetness, very rich, mouthfilling. *At a Latour tasting, April 2001* ★(★★★)

**Corton-Charlemagne** Rapet Père et fils Major 2.5-ha parcel in very old 19-ha family estate. Classic nutty, oaky nose; fairly sweet, certainly very rich, substantial (13.5%), very oaky, lovely. *At Howard Ripley's tasting, Jan 2001* (★★★★) *2000–2015.*

**Meursault, Charmes** L Jadot Very pale; a lot of vanilla (new oak) fulsome verging on specious; extraordinarily sweet – for a 'dry' white burgundy; oaky, flavourful. Attractive. *At Jadot's, Feb 2001* ★★(★★) *A rich mid-term drink, if you can get hold of it. The UK trade allocation already sold out!*

**Meursault, Genevrières** L Jadot Very pale indeed; surprisingly sweet, full-bodied (13.5%), fragrant, new oak, very attractive. *At Jadot's, Feb 2001* ★★(★★) *Only 15 cases left by the time of the tasting.*

**Meursault** At a comparative blind tasting of 47 white burgundies at British Airways in March 2001, there were 11 '99 Meursaults. They were largely uninspiring though, when revealed, there were some surprises. Among the better wines were **Chartron et Trébuchet's** well made, good finish (★★★); **Vincent Girardin's** speciously oaky but attractive; hefty, astringent – needing bottle age (★★★); **Patriarche's** ★(★★) (better than their Ch de Meursault); and **Pierre André's** positive, hefty, flavoury (★★★). The rest were mediocre though all drinkable.

**Puligny-Montrachet** Leflaive Very pale; slight green tinge; good nose; very flavoury, still hard, steely and acidic. *At Dom de Chevalier, Bordeaux, June 2001* ★(★★★) *Needs time.*

**Puligny-Montrachet, Les Combettes** E Sauzet Very pale; immature, powerful, oaky. *At Justerini's, Jan 2000* ★★(★★)

**Puligny-Montrachet, Les Folatières** L Jadot Very pale; immediately appealing, scented, vanilla nose and flavour; 'curiously lovely', a hint of violets in the aftertaste. *At the Jadot tasting, Feb 2001* ★★(★★)

# 2000 and the future

Allowing for the ever variable and totally unpredictable growing conditions in Burgundy, it would seem that the future is rosy thanks to improved quality and the seemingly insatiable demand for the best wines. Although the great growths of the Côte de Beaune are, and will remain sublime, even more care and attention in the vineyard and more efficient winemaking could improve things even further.

Even so, Burgundy continues to be let down by small producers whose vineyard is almost a sideline; by overproduction; and by the depressingly poor commercial wines which open up the opportunities for New World Chardonnays to step in even though some of these are no longer as inexpensive as they used to be.

You only have to drive south, beyond Chagny to the Côte Chalonnaise and the Mâconnais, to realise how much wine is being produced in these attractive areas of southern Burgundy. Wines such as Montagny, from the Côte Chalonnaise, and the various Mâcon-Villages can take up the slack, taking the pressure off Meursault and Puligny from the Côte de Beaune by producing perfectly decent white burgundy and selling it at a price which enables the smaller and less well-off producers to make increasingly good wine and consequently to enjoy a better livelihood.

## 2000 ★★★

Not the easiest of weather conditions, as reported in the Red Burgundy chapter (see page 271). The whites of the Côtes de Beaune were picked after the Beaune reds, roughly at the same time as the Côte de Nuits, the grapes being dried by a cold north wind. Chablis, considerably to the north of the Côte d'Or, usually harvests later, and picked ripe and healthy grapes under a blue sky.

**Montrachet Laguiche/Drouhin** Cask sample: very pale of course; low-keyed but very fragrant; sweet entry, powerful, youthful 'captured pineapple' flavour, teeth-gripping acidity. *At a Drouhin tasting in London, Jan 2002* (★★★★)

**Montrachet L Jadot** Almost colourless; nutty; splendid wine, notable persistence of flavour – worth having a stop watch, good acidity. Great potential. *Jan 2002* (★★★)

**Bâtard-Montrachet L Jadot** At 11.5ha, Bâtard is the largest of the Côte de Beaune white *grand cru* vineyards but with piecemeal ownership, the largest holding being 1.9ha. It produces an average of 53,000 bottles (approx. 4400 cases). Extremely pale; soft mid fruit, masking acidity. Impressive (prices confusingly quoted in Euros!). *Feb 2002* (★★★★)

**Bâtard-Montrachet Dom Vincent/François Jobard** Very impressive nose and taste though I did not take to its touch of peach kernels. With Bâtard power. Should turn out well. *Jan 2002* (★★★★)?

**Bâtard-Montrachet Ch de Maltroye** Assertive, impressive but far too much oak. Also pretty expensive. *At Howard Ripley's tasting in London, Jan 2002* (★★★★)

**Beaune, Clos des Mouches blanc J Drouhin** Youthful pineapple; touch of sweetness, rich, soft, fullish body and oaky fruit. *Jan 2002* (★★★★) *Nice wine. Probably at best 2004–2007.*

**Bienvenues-Bâtard-Montrachet Dom Paul Pernot** A 0.38-ha *climat* in a 19-ha estate, with over a dozen small parcels dotted around the Côte de Beaune. The Pernot family regularly sell their white grapes to Drouhin. The wine was lean and nutty. Needs time to show its 'very welcome' charm. *Jan 2002* (★★★)

**Chablis, Grenouilles L Jadot** Vinified in oak. Slightly more 'meaty' than Les Preuses, whiff of violets; soft, oaky, lemon-like acidity. Attractive. *Feb 2002* (★★★) *I do not think I would keep this for more than five or six years. And I dare say it will all be consumed, with pleasure, long before that.*

**Chablis, Les Preuses L Jadot** Preuses is a 8-ha *grand cru* vineyard with light soil. Wine vinified in oak. Almost colourless though with a slight stain of youthful green; an immediacy of fruit and vanilla; pleasantly fruity entry, young but not raw, pineapple and a good deal of oaky vanilla. Good acidity. 'Will keep for more than 10 years': Jadot's opinion, not mine. Who am I to disagree? *Feb 2002* (★★★)?

**Chassagne-Montrachet, Les Caillerets Dom Guy Amiot** Tinge of straw; lean, acidity a bit tinny. I queried its length. *Jan 2002* (★★★)?

**Chassagne-Montrachet, Les Chaumes, Clos de la Truffière Dom Vincent/François Jobard** Virtually colourless; dry, good length, acidity and future. *Jan 2002* (★★★★)

**Chassagne-Montrachet, Les Grandes Rouchottes Ch de Maltroye** A 0.5-ha holding in a 16-ha estate. Slightly minty, nutty nose and flavour. Medium-dry, good length. *Jan 2002.*

**Chassagne-Montrachet, Clos du Ch de Maltroye, Monopole Ch de Maltroye** A 2.5-ha holding producing red and white wines. Rich nose and flavour, powerful, oaky. *Jan 2002* (★★★★)

**Chassagne-Montrachet, Morgeot, Vignes Blanches Ch de Maltroye** Whiff of celluloid; dry, acidic. *Jan 2002* (★★)

**Chevalier-Montrachet, Les Demoiselles Dom des Héritiers, Jadot** Deliciously forthcoming, the Chevalier clearly aroused by the proximity of Les Demoiselles, oaky; medium sweet – as white wine goes – lean and fit, good acidity. *At the Jadot tasting in London, Feb 2002* (★★★★)

**Corton-Charlemagne J Drouhin** Deep, fairly rich, meaty/fruity, unknit; fairly full-bodied, good flavour that needs sorting out. Lovely acidity. *Jan 2002* (★★★★)

**Corton-Charlemagne Dom des Héritiers, Jadot** Very meaty; medium sweet, full, soft, nutty. What Corton-Charlemagne is all about. *Feb 2002* (★★★★★)

**Criots-Bâtard-Montrachet L Jadot** The only *grand cru* vineyard wholly within the commune of Chassagne, its pale stony soil producing a wine with more delicacy than the broad-shouldered Bâtard-Montrachet. It was very pale; crusty; very mouthfilling, touch of lemon-like acidity, dry finish. *Feb 2002* (★★★★)

**Mâcon-Azé, 'Chardonnay' Dom de Rochebin** This wine is mentioned because it was the first 2000 white burgundy I tasted and because, unusually for Burgundy, and indeed for most French wines, it mentioned the grape variety on the label. I am not sure I approve of this: on the one hand, it panders to the uninformed public, and, on the other, it merely exposes a pleasant enough wine to the already overcrowded global Chardonnay market. It was pale; fresh but nondescript; a light and dry wine with refreshing acidity. *In the interval at the Royal Opera House, Covent Garden, Aug 2001* ★★

**Mâcon, Lugny L Latour** A decent club standby. Nothing much to this wine but it takes the strain off, and saves the expense of, the classic Côte de Beaune whites that one used to drink as a matter of course. *Dining at Brooks's Club, St James's, Nov 2001* ★

**Meursault, Charmes L Jadot** Bought from contract growers from a vineyard with richer and heavier soil than Meursault-Perrières, further up the slope. Pale; touch of lemon and oak; some richness, touch of oak and mouth-drying acidity. *Feb 2002* (★★★)

**Puligny-Montrachet, Les Folatières J Drouhin** Very pale; touch of gooseberry-like acidity on nose which translated to grapefruit on the palate. Lovely flavour, good length, smoky-oaky aftertaste. *Jan 2002* (★★★★) *2005–2010.*

**Puligny-Montrachet, Les Folatières L Jadot** Almost colourless; broad, open, crusty (bread) nose with a slight whiff of celluloid; rich, well integrated oak, very hard acidic dry finish. *Feb 2002* (★★★★) *Needs time, say 2004–2008.*

**Puligny-Montrachet, Clos de la Garenne (Monopole) Duc de Magenta** – a perfect name for a writer of purple prose. The wine was virtually colourless; low-keyed, crisp, vanilla; broader, richer style, very good flavour and length. *At the Jadot tasting, Feb 2002* (★★★★) *Good wine and needs time.*

**Puligny-Montrachet, Les Referts L Jadot** Very pale; deliciously fragrant, crisp, oaky nose, flavour and aftertaste. Soft yet lean. *Feb 2002* (★★★)

# Rhône

I have always been intrigued by the wines produced in the regions bordering France's two greatest rivers, the mainly light white and acidic wines from the Loire and, quite the opposite, the mainly sturdy reds, from the Rhône. To talk about the Rhône, one of France's greatest rivers, as a vinous entity is misleading because there is a great north and south divide. The steep slopes of the Côte-Rôtie *appellation* commence on the right bank of the river at Vienne, not far south of Lyon, whereas way down river south of Orange the vineyards south of Châteauneuf-du-Pape spread themselves on a broad plain with a near-Provençal climate and 'feel' where vines swelter under the sun. In the North, from Côte-Rôtie to Hermitage, the wines are usually made from one variety and Syrah rules supreme whereas in the South, though Grenache is the dominant variety, in Châteauneuf up to 13 different varieties are permitted for the red wine.

The best white wines, all dry, are made in Condrieu, a very small *appellation* near Vienne where the Viognier grape holds sway, in Hermitage and further south in Châteauneuf. However, the following notes are entirely concerned with the red wines, for the same reason as elsewhere: virtually all the whites are best consumed while young and fresh. Even the classic Condrieu is generally considered at its best in the second or third year though white Hermitage is capable of developing interesting traits with bottle age. I have also had some white Châteauneuf drinking well up to ten years after the vintage.

The contrast between the northern and southern Rhône could not be more dramatically illustrated than by the comparison between the following red wines: Guigal's Côte-Rôtie, a 100% Syrah, new oak-aged wine, Ch de Beaucastel's Châteauneuf-du-Pape which uses all 13 permitted grape varieties and is bottled early, and Jaboulet's classic Hermitage La Chapelle (principally Syrah though a small amount of Marsanne and Roussanne can be used in Hermitage) acting as pivotal 'referee' between the North and the South. A red Rhône for all seasons!

## Two centuries to 1977

It must be admitted that though Rhône wine has been shipped to England from – well almost – time immemorial, it has never had a strong showing, as Christie's archives reveal. It certainly appeared in some gentlemen's cellars, Coti Roti (Côte-Rôtie) as early as 1768 and Hermitage in 1773. By the early 19th century the reputation of Hermitage was such that it was often transported to Bordeaux to add body and substance to the red wine in weak vintages. There are even reports of Lafite being 'Hermitaged' and as late as 1850 a Christie's catalogue included 'Hermitage blended with claret' – under Bordeaux. Few old Rhône wines have survived, though in the late 1960s a quantity of 1825 Lanerthe (a renowned estate in Châteauneuf) and 1832 'Ermitage' was found in a cellar near Lyon. It appeared in several Heublein auctions, and bottles of each were opened at pre-sale tastings. They varied from sour to surprisingly drinkable.

Rhône wines appeared to be no more popular in the prosperous Victorian times. However, the only vintage of this period I have tasted, an 1871 Hermitage (in 1990), was more than just interesting. I also notice that Rhône wines did not feature at all in a Saccone & Speed price list of the 1920s. In the 1950s there was a small selection of Rhône wines in Harvey's retail lists, mainly Tavel, Hermitage and Châteauneuf-du-Pape. Côte-Rôtie made its first appearance in 1958 (the 1955 vintage) which is a reflection of the lack of interest in and scarcity of the wines of this *appellation*, whose steep vineyards have always been uneconomical to tend.

In 1984 Yapp Brothers persuaded Gérard Chave to bring some of his old Hermitage vintages to London: the 1929 was remarkably good (★★★) as was the 1942 (★★★). I have listed the best vintages between 1929 and 1977 in the chart (see facing page), even though I only give tasting notes for a selection of post-war vintages.

## Red Vintages at a Glance
NORTHERN RHÔNE (CÔTE-RÔTIE, ST-JOSEPH, HERMITAGE, CROZES-HERMITAGE, CORNAS)
**Outstanding ★★★★★**

1929, 1945, 1949, 1959, 1961, 1969, 1971

**Very Good ★★★★**

1933, 1937, 1943, 1947, 1952, 1953, 1955, 1957, 1962, 1964, 1966, 1967, 1970, 1972 (v) (except Côte-Rôtie)

**Good ★★★**

1934, 1942, 1976 (v)

SOUTHERN RHÔNE (MAINLY CHÂTEAUNEUF-DU-PAPE)
**Outstanding ★★★★★**

1929, 1945, 1949, 1952, 1959, 1961, 1970

**Very Good ★★★★**

1934, 1937, 1947, 1955, 1957, 1962, 1967, 1964, 1969, 1971

**Good ★★★**

1939, 1944, 1953, 1966, 1972 (v)

The vintage rating stars relate to the entire region, North and South, unless otherwise indicated.

# 1945 ★★★★★

Great vintage. Small production. Hermitage particularly fine though not tasted since *1973* (when La Chapelle was magnificent).

# 1947 ★★★★

Hot vintage. Ripe, rich, alcoholic, voluptuous wines. Fully if not overmature now. Few wines to be found now.
**Hermitage, Rochefine** Jaboulet-Vercherre Seemingly ageless, great charm. *1989* ★★★; and **Châteauneuf-du-Pape A Establet** hefty, commercial. *1989* ★★

# 1949 ★★★★★

Well-nigh perfect growing season throughout the Rhône. Very rare. The best and best kept wines can still be excellent.
**Hermitage, La Chapelle P Jaboulet Aîné** Perfect balance and condition. *1985* ★★★★★

# 1952 ★★★★ North ★★★★★ South

Firm, long-lasting wines.
**Hermitage Chave** Rich, lovely. *1984* ★★★★

# 1961 ★★★★★

Superb conditions throughout the region, Hermitage said to be the best of the century. La Chapelle now virtually priceless.
**Hermitage Jaboulet-Isnard** Fairly deep, mature; opulent fruit; sweet, rich, excellent flavour. *Tasted Feb 2000* ★★★★
**Hermitage, La Chapelle P Jaboulet Aîné** Huge in 1967; fruit-laden in 1983. Magnificent in 1990. One of my top scores at the 'Parker 100' tasting in Hamburg. *Last tasted Oct 1993* ★★★★★

# 1966 ★★★★ North ★★★ South

At their best in the mid-1980s but a superb Chapelle recently.
**Hermitage, La Chapelle P Jaboulet Aîné** Mature; harmonious, sweet, fairly soft, very fragrant. *At the Hollywood Wine Society Grange/Chapelle tasting in Florida, March 1995* ★★★★

# 1967 ★★★★

Good conditions throughout the region, Châteauneuf now considered to be on a par with 1978 but mainly at their best in the late 1970s. Some wines showing well in the mid-1980s, in particular **P Jaboulet's Côte-Rôtie, Les Jumelles**, lovely texture, elegant *Dec 1984* ★★★★ *but none tasted since.*

# 1969 ★★★★★ North ★★★★ South

Good to very good in Châteauneuf, better in Hermitage, and a small but outstanding crop in Côte-Rôtie.
**Hermitage Chave** Magnificent in *March 1984* ★★★★★
**Hermitage, La Chapelle P Jaboulet Aîné** Wonderful vinosity and stemmy fruit; silky but showing its age. *At the MW Grange/La Chapelle tasting in London, May 1992* ★★★

# 1970 ★★★★ North ★★★★★ South

An excellent year in the south and very good in the north. Good vintage in Châteauneuf, better still in Hermitage and a small but outstanding crop in Côte-Rôtie. Long winter, some frost in the north, very warm summer, large crop in Hermitage. These wines are still worth looking out for.
**Hermitage Jaboulet-Isnard** Fairly deep; fair quality, very tannic. *Pre-sale, New York, Sept 1997* ★★★
**Hermitage, La Chapelle P Jaboulet Aîné** Huge and tough – a hot vintage wine – in 1972. By 1989, tasted in magnums: glorious fragrance; good flavour, texture and balance. More recently: richly coloured; ripe, almost claret-like nose; sweet, full-bodied, rich fruit, harmonious. Great power and length. Lovely a decade ago. Will still be superb. *Last noted at the MW Grange/Chapelle tasting in London, May 1992* ★★★★★

## Chapoutier

*Large and important merchant house based in Tain L'Hermitage. For several decades after World War Two Chapoutier's agent in the UK was a company called Hellmers, run by the avuncular Mr Scott (whom no one called Ronald, let alone Ron or Ronnie) who, when I drove Tommy Layton's van – in 1952 – to pick up wine from Hellmers' cellars, always had some wine for me to taste.*

*Thereafter, for many years, he invited me to his annual tastings, modest affairs but always interesting. In 1961, out of the blue, while I was working for Harvey's of Bristol, he invited me on a four-day trip (by train) to visit Chapoutier. Mr Scott brushed aside my offer to pay my share of the travel, saying that instead I could thank Harvey's who, craftily buying direct from Chapoutier to cut out the agent, had in fact been paying the full price, Chapoutier crediting Hellmers with their normal commission. Very gentlemanly, I thought, and served Harvey's right!*

# 1971 ★★★★★ North ★★★★ South

Particularly successful in Côte-Rôtie, full-bodied wines with ageing potential.

**Hermitage, La Chapelle P Jaboulet Aîné** Tough and huge in 1972. In 1989 fragrant, glorious. More recently: herbaceous bouquet that developed well; silky, leathery tannins, 'surprisingly attractive'. *Last noted at the MW Grange/Chapelle tasting, May 1992* ★★★★★

OLDER NOTES **Jaboulet**'s **Côte-Rôtie, Les Jumelles** an outstanding example, 'amazingly rich and powerful' I wrote in 1984 and probably lovely now. **Hermitage** produced typically harmonious wines: **Chave**'s (also tasted in 1984) superb. In the south, the wines of **Châteauneuf** were good but had lower levels of acidity, nevertheless, **Ch Rayas** was excellent at ten years of age and **Paul Avril**'s **Clos des Papes** rich though tannic in the mid-1980s.

# 1972 ★ to ★★★★ variable

Cold spring, moderate summer. Attractive wines in Châteauneuf-du-Pape, excellent in the mid-north, Cornas and Hermitage (small crop); mediocre in Côte-Rôtie: acidic and hard wines.

**Crozes-Hermitage, Dom de Thalabert P Jaboulet Aîné** Singed vanilla; fairly sweet, full, fleshy, good acidity. *Dining at the Sloane Club, London, Nov 1991* ★★★

**Hermitage, La Chapelle P Jaboulet Aîné** Very small crop due to hailstorm on 14 July. Palish, fully mature; herbaceous; surprisingly attractive. *At the MW tasting, May 1992* ★★★

# 1973 ★ to ★★

Heavy rain in early September resulted in a huge crop of variable quality wines throughout the region. Avoid this vintage. I have tasted only one wine.

**Côte-Rôtie, Les Jumelles P Jaboulet Aîné** Chaptalised; weak, easy. An after-theatre wine. *Tasted at the Sloane Club, London, Nov 1991* ★

# 1974 ★ North ★★ South

Abundant but moderate quality in Châteauneuf-du-Pape, mediocre in Hermitage – I have not tasted any wines since the mid- to late 1980s – poor in Côte-Rôtie. Only one tasted in the 1990s. Drink up.

**Côte-Rôtie, Les Jumelles P Jaboulet Aîné** Chaptalised, weak though flavoury. *Nov 1991*.

# 1975 ★ to ★★

Mediocre quality throughout the Rhône, particularly in the south which suffered from heavy rain in August and a hot, dry sirocco in mid-September. I have tasted one odd half bottle recently.

**Châteauneuf-du-Pape** Bottled by **Berry Bros**. An odd half: good level; palish soft ruby; sound, gentle, slightly earthy fruit; rather sweet, unusual, slightly boiled candy flavour, good acidity. Attractive. *At Rosebank, Feb 2000* ★★

# 1976 ★★★ North ★★ South

Variable quality in Châteauneuf-du-Pape due to rain at vintage time. The northern Rhône faired better – a hot, dry summer producing ripe, concentrated wines though autumn rain was also a problem. I tasted some good wines from the 1980s, also some quite good Hermitage, the best being Chave's in 1984. I only have one more recent note.

**Hermitage, La Chapelle P Jaboulet Aîné** Palish open appearance; strange, lean yet malty nose; sweet, silky texture, fair length, hot finish. *At the MW tasting, May 1992* ★★★ *(just). No future.*

# 1977 ★ to ★★

Bad weather in the northern Rhône resulted in thin, acidic wines. A fine autumn in the south enabled growers to produce some quite attractive wines. I tasted some passable wines in the mid-1980s – Jaboulet in Hermitage and Chapoutier in Châteauneuf. Of no interest now.

# 1978–1999

In addition to grouping together the decades of the 1980s and 1999s I have deliberately broken the pattern by starting this section with the 1978 vintage, not just because it struck an exceptionally high note in the wake of the variable, mainly pretty dreary vintages of the 1970s, but because there seemed to be a change of gear: a new optimism, better times ahead. 1978 gave the Rhône a kick start.

Through the 1960s and 1970s, the interest in Rhône wines had been lacklustre. The relatively few producers known to the British, and I suspect American, trade and consumer, were the merchant-growers like Paul Jaboulet Aîné and the occasionally uneven Chapoutier (happily, now back on track). English importers included the then youthful specialist Robin Yapp and, well-known to my contemporaries, Mr Scott of Hellmers, Chapoutier's agent (see box page 303). In 1978 Côte-Rôtie was re-discovered and burst into life. Guigal, partly due to the enterprising Robert Parker, became famous and fashionable.

If the 1980s were, in effect, the breeding ground, the 1990s moved ahead, taking advantage of better vintage weather here than in Bordeaux. To a certain extent, the interest in Rhône and Italian wines has grown in parallel, as has the quality. Also, in common with other French regions, some younger producers are making their name, and enologists, as elsewhere, have been pandering to the taste for easy, fruity, amenable wines.

However, apart from Guigal's Côte-Rôtie and Jaboulet's La Chapelle, prices remained at sensible drinking levels.

## Red Vintages at a Glance
NORTHERN RHÔNE (CÔTE-RÔTIE, ST-JOSEPH, HERMITAGE, CROZES-HERMITAGE, CORNAS)
**Outstanding** ★★★★★
1978, 1983, 1985, 1990, 1998, 1999
**Very Good** ★★★★
1979, 1982, 1988, 1989, 1995
**Good** ★★★
1981 (v), 1986 (v), 1991, 1992 (v), 1996 (v), 1997

## 1978 ★★★★★

Despite the terrible weather conditions, this was unquestionably a great Rhône vintage and said to be the best since 1911. It seemed to herald a much welcomed renaissance in the region.
**Châteauneuf-du-Pape Ch de Beaucastel/Perrin** In 1991 still a very deep ruby; crisp fruit; full, very positive, good tannin and acidity, but with a ripe, rustic hen droppings' finish. Most recently: now fully mature, ripe, singed bouquet; sweet, showing its age. *Last noted at Paolo Pong's Beaucastel v. Rayas tasting, May 2001* ★★★★
**Châteauneuf-du-Pape Ch Rayas** Medium-deep, soft ruby; also singed – mature, hot, vintage bouquet; attractive fruit and flavour. *Tasted May 2001* ★★★★★ *Time in hand.*

### Paolo Pong

*The young man with this delightful name is Chinese, the scion of a wealthy Hong Kong family. Passionately interested in wine, he has accumulated a substantial cellar of top growths and rare vintages. He has brought wine to dinners at our flat in London but the tastings I have attended have mainly been held at the London home of Jancis Robinson and her husband Nick (Lander) who nobly does the cooking. Not just old and great claret but, as noted, Rhône wine from two top estates: Ch Beaucastel and Ch Rayas, both leaders in Châteauneuf-du-Pape.*

SOUTHERN RHÔNE (MAINLY CHÂTEAUNEUF-DU-PAPE)
**Outstanding** ★★★★★
1978, 1983, 1985, 1989, 1990, 1995, 1998
**Very Good** ★★★★
1982, 1999
**Good** ★★★
1979, 1980, 1981 (v), 1986 (v), 1988, 1992 (v), 1996 (v), 1997

**Côte-Rôtie, Brune et Blonde Guigal** At five years of age, the heat of the vintage seemed to shimmer through the wine. Hefty. Unready. In 1988, still very deep coloured; rich, meaty, singed nose; sweet, full bodied, a gloriously expansive flavour, good length and superb aftertaste. Probably at its peak in the early 1990s for when last tasted, though still deep, velvety and very good I felt that it was beginning to dry out. *Last tasted a bottle from my son's cellar, San Francisco, Dec 2000* ★★★★
**Côte-Rôtie, Les Jumelles P Jaboulet Aîné** Les Jumelles means 'the twins' but these – Côte Brune and Côte Blonde – are not identical. At ten years of age, perfect bottles. Medium-deep, richly coloured; deep, very ripe nose and taste. Medium sweetness, fairly full bodied, lovely flavour, dry finish. More recently, a 20-year old magnum, now medium-deep and mature; seemed overripe but settled down pleasantly. Rich, full, lovely. *A perfect drink at a Christie's board lunch, Oct 1998* ★★★★★
**Côte-Rôtie, La Landonne Guigal** This was the first vintage after Marcel Guigal had unified the La Landonne vineyard on the Côte Brune slope. The vines had been planted in the birth year of Philippe, Marcel's son. Immensely impressive. In 1988 different from his La Mouline. Enormous weight, power, extract. Totally unready at ten years of age. A 5-star wine. Most recently, tasted in the cellars with Philippe: still fairly deep; something of a shock after tasting the '98s and '99s: most unusual, slightly fig-like (Syrah), medicinal liquorice bouquet and flavour; very rich, fairly full bodied, fabulous old flavour, still tannic yet finishing sweetly. *Last tasted Oct 2001* ★★★★★ *But past its peak.*

**Côte-Rôtie, La Mouline Guigal** At ten years after the vintage: opaque, making the Brune et Blonde look feeble. Close knit, harmonious; rich, complex and concentrated. Tannin laden. Glorious fruit. Alas, nine years after that I had the misfortune of tasting this in the wrong order and in the wrong ambience – a BYOB dinner, where guests snatch other guests' bottles. Unsurprisingly it seemed rather raw and tasteless after Ch d'Yquem. *Last tasted in New York, Feb 1997. At its best* ★★★★★

**Hermitage Guigal** Fairly deep, rich; figgy, smoky; medium sweet, rich, ripe, still packing a punch. Very good. *At a pre-sale tasting, New York, Dec 1997* ★★★★

**Hermitage, La Chapelle P Jaboulet Aîné** So massive that it was given an extra year in cask. First tasted in its third year: opaque, purple; peppery; packed with fruit. Tannic. Next a jump of eleven years: 'perfection now'. Three years later (1995) at the MW tasting of Penfolds Grange against La Chapelle: the latter was softer and somewhat overwhelmed by the Australian classic. Next, at the Jaboulet seminar in 1998: now medium-deep, still retaining a hint of youth; very fragrant bouquet; rich, perfect weight and state. A velvety magnum, powerful (alcohol 15%) in Paris. Most recently, with boned saddle of lamb: still ruby-shaded; lovely bouquet; sweetish, soft, perfect balance. *Last noted at a Saintsbury Club dinner, March 2001* ★★★★★

**Hermitage, La Sizeranne Chapoutier** A soft burgundy red, mature, open; perfectly harmonious bouquet, opening up fabulously, reminiscent of ripe figs; very sweet, richly flavoured, still with peppery grip, dry finish and scented aftertaste. *In Copenhagen, March 1999* ★★★★★

## 1979 ★★★★ North ★★★ South

Variable weather conditions and quality: Côte-Rôtie in the north enjoyed an abundant harvest beginning in late September; rain delayed harvesting in Hermitage until early October. In the South, the wines of Châteauneuf were successful, fragrant and soft.

**Châteauneuf-du-Pape Ch de Beaucastel/Perrin** Gently coloured, fully mature; ripe, citrus touch; flavoury, more acidity and looser knit than Rayas. *At Paolo Pong's Châteauneuf tasting, at Jancis Robinson's, May 2001* ★★★

**Châteauneuf-du-Pape Ch Rayas** Medium-deep, mature; very open, scented; medium-sweet, very good flavour and grip. *Paolo Pong's tasting, May 2001* ★★★★

**Côte-Rôtie, La Mouline Guigal** Medium, fully mature; low-keyed but harmonious; peppery, with teeth-gripping finish yet ready for drinking. *At the big Vinum tasting in Zurich, April 1998* ★★★

OTHER CÔTE-RÔTIES SHOWING WELL IN THE MID- TO LATE 1980S **Guigal's** Côte-Rôtie, Brune et Blonde *1988* ★★★★; and **Jaboulet's** Côte-Rôtie, Les Jumelles *1983* ★★★

**Crozes-Hermitage, Dom de Thalabert P Jaboulet Aîné** Medium-deep, misleadingly youthful looks; warm, sweet, harmonious bouquet; sweet, very tannic showing its age. *At the Hollywood Wine Society's Jaboulet seminar, March 1998* ★★★

**Hermitage, La Chapelle P Jaboulet Aîné** In 1992, fragrant, open knit; dry, lean, slightly acidic. Most recently: medium-deep; cherry-like fruit; supple, delicious flavour, well balanced. Clearly a survivor – and also survived avocado sorbet with pickled ginger. *Last noted at the Hollywood Wine Society's gala dinner, Coconut Grove, Florida, March 1998* ★★★★

OTHER HERMITAGE WINES SHOWING WELL IN THE MID- TO LATE 1980S **Chave's** Hermitage *1984* ★★★★; and **Guigal's** Hermitage *1985* ★★★★

## 1980 ★★ North ★★★ South

Big contrast between the North and the South, due as usual to weather conditions. Côte-Rôtie suffered from a poor spring and flowering, finally improving for a late vintage. Châteauneuf and the south enjoyed much better weather, the largest crop ever recorded harvested from 25 September. By and large, these were early-maturing wines mostly tasted in the mid- to late 1980s and largely irrelevant now.

## 1981 ★★ to ★★★

In the north, rain interrupted flowering and harvest though some good wines were made in Côte-Rôtie; in the South the flowering was also uneven but, after a summer drought there was a moderately good vintage and rich, concentrated wines.

**Châteauneuf-du-Pape Ch de Beaucastel/Perrin** Two notes in the late 1980s described their surprisingly deep colour and intensity, and mouthfilling components. I have two notes in 1997: still fairly deep; well-developed fruit; sweet, rich, drinking well. Most recently: medium-deep, a shade of pink; mature, slightly singed; less sweet and softer texture than the Rayas, with good length, tannin and acidity. *Last noted at Paolo Pong's Beaucastel v. Rayas tasting, May 2001* ★★★

**Châteauneuf-du-Pape Ch Rayas** Medium but intense; fragrant; sweet, soft, attractive, dry finish. *At Paolo Pong's tasting, May 2001* ★★★★

**Côte-Rôtie** None tasted recently but **Guigal's** La Mouline was rich and fully evolved. *In 1988* ★★★★ *Should still be drinkable.*

**Hermitage** Both **Chave's** and **Jaboulet's** La Chapelle were showing good potential in the mid-1980s.

## 1982 ★★★★

Even by Rhône standards, the summer was excessively hot and dry. Despite heavy rains in August, it was an early harvest, winemakers having to cope with sun-baked grapes, hot fermentation and reduced acidity. It was not an easy time though the more competent producers made very good wine.

**Châteauneuf-du-Pape Brunier/Dom du Vieux Télégraphe** Alas I have tasted few of the '82s and I have only one representative note in its youth. Tasted at a Christie's wine course: deliciously soft and sweet but with an upturned touch of tannic bitterness. *1985* ★★★★ *Probably surviving.*

**Côte-Rôtie, Les Jumelles P Jaboulet Aîné** Medium-deep, youthful red though with a mature rim; very meaty, slightly caramelly; sweet, rich, a good mouthful for its age. *At a Saintsbury Club dinner, London, April 2002* ★★★

**Hermitage Chave** Several notes. Showing good potential in 1984. A decade later, magnums opened at Yapp Brothers' 25th anniversary lunch in Mere: richly coloured, fully mature; singed, hot vintage scents; a sweet rich mouthful, drinking perfectly. (Gérard Chave, a mutual friend, was delighted, as we all were.) Next recently, at the MW Hermitage tasting in London, at which Jean-Louis Chave told us of the difficulty in controlling the temperature during fermentation. Colour now 'broad' and fully mature; a glorious 'old oak', rich, soft, singed bouquet; fairly full bodied, soft, ripe. Rather an old-fashioned rustic style, getting a bit gamey. *Last tasted May 1999. At its peak* ★★★★ *Now past its best but a good ripe mouthful* ★★★

**Hermitage, La Chapelle** P Jaboulet Aîné In its youth (1987) impressively deep; rich, evolving beautifully in the glass; full, fleshy, meaty. Still mouthfillingly attractive. *Last tasted in May 1992. Then* ★★★★ *Doubtless fully mature and tiring now.*

## 1983 ★★★★★

A magnificent summer, one of the hottest and driest on record. The North and South were equally successful – the wines were initially rich and concentrated with hard tannins. If 1978, as it were, set the wheels in motion, 1983 sped the Rhône on its way. The reds are still drinking well.

**Châteauneuf-du-Pape** Ch de Beaucastel/Perrin In 1997, fully mature; sweaty (tannic), singed, hot vintage nose, dry, over mature, with a rustic-barnyard, tannic acid flavour and aftertaste. Drinking well in magnums at a Saintsbury Club dinner in March 2001. Two months later at Paolo Pong's tasting: weak rimmed; agreeable fruit but with one hell of a bite. Later that autumn: medium-mature, soft, lovely colour, slightly orange edge; very fragrant, soft spicy – needs air I was told; pleasant sweetness and weight (alcohol 12.5%), a lovely coffee-bean flavour and 'very good' tannin and acidity. *Last tasted in the cellars at Ch de Beaucastel, Oct 2001* ★★★★

**Châteauneuf-du-Pape** Ch Rayas Two notes in the early 1990s. The 1995, fragrant, flavour seeming to spread its wings in the mouth. Next, lunching at Brooks's in 1993 I noted its orange tinge and stewed nose and taste – owing, I found later, to it being stored in the club's dispense area at about 24°C for two or three years! My comments to the Club Secretary were noted. Most recently: pleasant, sweet, ripe bouquet; fragrant, attractive, hot finish and quite a bite. *Last noted at Paolo Pong's tasting, May 2001* ★★★(★)

**Cornas** Auguste Clape (I have added his Christian name to add dignity to an unfortunate surname.) Rustic, farmyard and sweet yet with a tart, tannic finish. *At an IWFS St James's branch dinner in London, April 1999* ★★

**Cornas** P Jaboulet Aîné Grown on a granite slope south of Hermitage. Soft red, almost mahogany maturity; touch of singed caramel but otherwise harmonious and mature; sweet, soft, very agreeable, gentle tannins. Complete, ready. *At a Syrah tasting for the Singapore chapter of the IWFS, Jan 1998* ★★★

**Crozes-Hermitage, Dom de Thalabert** P Jaboulet Aîné Medium-deep, maturing nicely; lovely fruit, subtle fragrance; sweet, singed, earthy, dry finish. *At the Hollywood Wine Society's Jaboulet seminar, Florida. March 1998* ★★★★

**Hermitage, La Chapelle** P Jaboulet Aîné In 1987: intense, impressive; hot singed nose; flavour of figs, prunes and chocolate. 'Needs time: still taut' in 1992. Eleven years later, two notes: an attractive luminous quality, sweet, drinking well, at Maliner's Jaboulet seminar: soft red; very fragrant finish, touch of sharpness and, later, tarry, treacly; very flavoury; with cherry-like fruit, spoiled by an astringent finish. Most recently: developing an orange rim; better flavour than nose, good length, somewhat acidic. *Last noted at lunch at home* ★★★ *Drinking quite well, but get on with it.*

**Hermitage, La Sizeranne** Chapoutier In 1989: fig-like fruit, flavoury, very tannic. Next, accompanying boiled beef and dumplings at 'The Installation Lunch' given by the Lord Mayor and Lord Mayor-elect: rich, mature (the Lord Mayor has to be both). Very distinctive fragrance and flavour, touch of malt. *Last tasted at Mansion House, London Nov 1993* ★★★★

## 1984 ★★

Small crop of largely mediocre wines. Though the flowering took place in good weather, conditions became increasingly cold and wet. Three weeks of rain put on the final dampener, the vintage extending from 16 September to 11 October. Nevertheless, some strict selection enabled some a certain amount of good wines to be made, though I have tasted few.

**Hermitage, La Chapelle** P Jaboulet Aîné Medium-full, fair length and tannic in 1989. Three years later: rich, drinking well, with the balance to improve and survive. *Last tasted at a Rodenstock event in Germany, Oct 1992* ★★★

THE FOLLOWING WERE SHOWING REASONABLY WELL IN THE LATE 1980s Châteauneuf-du-Pape: Jaboulet's Les Cèdres *1987* ★★★; and Dom de Marcoux's *1987* ★★★; Côte-Rôtie: Guigal's Brune et Blonde *1988* ★★★; and Jaboulet's Les Jumelles *1987* ★★★; and finally, Guigal's Hermitage *1988* ★★★

## 1985 ★★★★★

Outstanding, despite a cool spring and late flowering; it was a hot, dry and sunny summer with no rain in the South until after the vintage. I have many notes.

**Châteauneuf-du-Pape** Ch de Beaucastel/Perrin Roughly one-third Syrah, Mourvèdre and Grenache with small quantities of the other 10 varieties. Several notes, the first in November 1988: very deep; opulent; earthy, high extract, silky tannins. Next at a dinner in January 2000: high-toned; gorgeous flavour, touch of mocha, dry finish. Most recently, at Paolo Pong's tasting alongside the '85 Ch Rayas: still a touch of ruby; meaty, alcoholic nose; fairly full-bodied and firm. *At Paolo Pong's tasting, May 2001* ★★★★★

**Châteauneuf-du-Pape** Ch Rayas Attractive colour; soft, open, harmonious bouquet; sweeter than the Ch de Beaucastel (above), very agreeable flavour. I just queried its length. *At Paolo Pong's tasting, May 2001* ★★★★★ *Completely ready.*

**Châteauneuf-du-Pape, La Bernadine** Chapoutier Sweet, pleasing. *Sept 1990* ★★★ *Drink up.*

OTHER CHÂTEAUNEUF-DU-PAPES SHOWING WELL IN THE LATE 1980s Boiron's Châteauneuf-du-Pape, Le Bosquet des Papes *1988* ★★★★; and Jaboulet's Châteauneuf-du-Pape, Les Cèdres *1987* ★★★★

**Cornas** Some hugely successful '85s but I have few recent notes. Outstanding were Robert Michel's La Geynale *1990* ★★★★★; A Clape's *1987* ★★★★★; and Jaboulet's *1987* ★★★★

**Côte-Rôtie, Brune et Blonde** Guigal At four years of age: very deep; glorious bouquet, fleshy, fig-like fruit, spicy; substantial yet refreshing. Excellent but needing bottle age.

---

### Châteauneuf-du-Pape

*The 'new castle' (or châteauneuf) is said to have been built by Pope John XXII between 1318 and 1333 as a summer residence to escape the heat of Avignon. The castle remained standing until 1944, when the German forces (who had been using it as an ammunition dump) blew it up. The ruins have undergone some restoration and stand today as a focal point for the region's growers. One of the peculiarities of the region is that red Châteauneuf can be made from up to 13 permitted grape varieties.*

Most recently, still surprisingly deep, black cherry with youthful edge; very good fruit on nose and palate. Sweet. Delicious. *Last noted at a St James's branch IWFS dinner, London, April 1999 ★★★★(★) Drinking well but more to come.*

**Côte-Rôtie, La Landonne Guigal** The most fully developed of Guigal's '85s. Fragrant; shapely. *Oct 1993 ★★★★ Now–2005.*

**Côte-Rôtie, La Mouline Guigal** Opaque, harmonious, demure; very sweet, full bodied, lovely fruit, silky texture, good length. *At Arne Berger's 'Parker 100 tasting', Hamburg, Oct 1993 ★★★★★ Drink now–2010.*

**Côte-Rôtie, La Turque Guigal** In 1993: opaque; meaty, singed Syrah nose; sweet, full-bodied, lovely texture, powerful yet elegant. Most recently: still deep, immature, intense; rich, figgy nose opening up gloriously; heavenly beetroot-like fruit and flavour, dry fragrant finish. *Last noted at Kaplan's outstanding 1985 vintage dinner, Chicago, April 2000 ★★★★★ Say 2005–2025.*

OTHER CÔTE-RÔTIES SHOWING GREAT PROMISE IN THE LATE 1980S **Emile Champet's** 1987 ★★★★★; **Robert Jasmin's** 1997 ★★★★★; **Vidal-Fleury's Chantillonne** 1988 ★★★★; and **Jaboulet's Les Jumelles** 1987 ★★★★★

**Gigondas** This *appellation* in the hills just to the north-east of Châteauneuf is noted for its agreeable, fruity, good-value reds and does not come into my remit as the sort of wine that both needs and benefits from bottle-ageing, for it is normally bought for early drinking. However, Robin Yapp produced for lunch in his garden the '85 **Dom St-Gayon** which after 15 years was looking very mature, with a tinge of orange; a strangely attractive, minty, eucalyptus nose and taste; medium-sweet, good acidity. *Tasted Aug 2000 ★★★ to prove a point but, I suspect, it was better when young.*

**Hermitage, La Chapelle P Jaboulet Aîné** Macerated for three weeks. No new wood: 12 to 18 months in two- to three-year-old burgundy *barriques*. Ten notes, from a spicy, tannic two-year old with great future. Warm flesh and richness noted in 1988 and again in 1992. A series of good notes from deep, velvety at Gidleigh Park (1997) – the year that the well-liked Gérard Jaboulet suddenly died; at the Bär Bank tasting (Zurich 1998); elegant, complete, lovely (at Kaplan's '85s event in 2000) and, most recently, at the Primum Familiae Vinum annual dinner: still fairly deep, very fragrant; richly textured, substantial. *Last tasted at Vinopolis, London, Nov 2000 ★★★(★) Lovely now and still with time in hand.*

**Hermitage Guigal** Medium-deep; sweet, tannic, figgy; rich, good flavour but slightly astringent. *At a Gidleigh Park wine dinner, Devon, Nov 1997 ★★★★*

TWO MORE HERMITAGE WINES SHOWING WELL AT THE TURN OF THE DECADE **Chave's** 1989 ★★★★; and **Chapoutier's La Sizeranne** 1990 ★★★★

## 1986 ★★★ South

Uneven and difficult, much selection needed. Warm dry weather during the summer followed by rain at the end of August; September was mainly dull, then rain diluted the crop, spreading rot in the North. The South enjoyed better weather and its late vintage from 4 October lasted a month with large crop of uneven quality. Few tasted.

**Côte-Rôtie, Les Jumelles P Jaboulet Aîné** Totally different to Guigal's style of wine. For a start, it had spent less time in cask. Already, aged five, it was soft and mature-looking; fig-like fruit; dry, brambly flavour, more assertive than its appearance. Tannic. *Feb 1991 ★★★*

**Côte-Rôtie, La Landonne Guigal** In 1990 deep, immature; hefty, the smell of roast beef; very rich, mouthfilling, laden with fruit, alcohol and tannin. Most recently: still very deep, immature, opaque core; very distinctive fragrance, floral, figgy; dry, massive, very tannic and totally unready. I dare say it would win a gold medal and score 100 points. But not for me. *Last noted at Christie's pre-sale dinner in honour of Lenoir Josey, New York, Nov 2000 (★★★★)?*

**Côte-Rôtie, La Mouline Guigal** First tasted in October 1990: richly coloured but not deep; slightly stalky, nutty nose; crisp, brambly fruit, distinctly tannic. More recently: strange, its nose had a whiff of tar and black treacle; 'hot' yet lean, still tannic. Disappointing. *At the Josey pre-sale tasting, New York, Nov 2000 ★★ Hard to assess. On balance, give it a miss.*

**Côte-Rôtie, La Turque Guigal** Formerly a Vidal-Fleurie vineyard, on the Côte Brune. Tasted only in its fourth year: opaque; tremendously rich, harmonious, with vanilla and strawberry scents; well stacked, very oaky, lovely. *At a French Wine Farmers' tasting in London, Oct 1990. Then (★★★★)*

**Hermitage, La Chapelle P Jaboulet Aîné** In its sixth year although still dumb and very tannic, it was crisp and flavoury. *At the MW Grange/Chapelle tasting, May 1992. Then ★★(★★)*

## 1987

The worst weather of the decade. Northern Rhône suffered persistent rain in August and conditions were even worse in the South. Best forgotten. **Guigal** made a passable **Côte-Rôtie** and **Hermitage**; **Jaboulet** made a stewed **Hermitage, La Chapelle** but made no wine in Châteauneuf.

**Châteauneuf-du-Pape Dom de Mont-Redon** The only decent '87 tasted: harmonious, silky texture. Drinking well. (Ah, but what would it be like now, ten years on?) *Harrod's Gourmet Club tasting, March 1992 ★★★*

## 1988 ★★★★ North ★★★ South

On the whole this was an excellent vintage, particularly in the north. The Côte-Rôtie vineyards were severely hit by two hailstorms during flowering which reduced and concentrated the crop. Humidity problems in the South were countered by spraying and early picking, avoiding later rain.

**Châteauneuf-du-Pape Ch de Beaucastel/Perrin** In 1993, in double magnums: ruby; hard, peppery; good fruit. Tannic. Most recently, in magnums: new soft, mature-looking; strange, dried-out nose, dried leaves, old wood(?); better on palate. Sweet, richly flavoured, cheesy, masked (soft) tannins. *Last noted at Stephen Kaplan's 'Informed Tasting', Chicago, April 2000 ★★★*

**Châteauneuf-du-Pape Ch Rayas** Soft, open, mature; sweet, easy, agreeable nose; attractive flavour. Mouth-drying tannin. *At Paolo Pong's tasting, May 2001 ★★★★★*

**Hermitage Chave** 'Round and soft tannins' in 1988. Still youthful; lovely crisp fruit; pleasantly sweet and full, soft fruit, lovely flavour. *Last tasted at the MW Rhône tasting, Painters' Hall, London, May 1999 ★★★★*

FIVE OTHER '88 CHÂTEAUNEUFS TASTED IN THEIR EXTREME YOUTH (IN 1990) **Guigal's** ★★★; **Chapoutier's Petite Cuvée** – just that, *petite!* ★★; **Dom de Beaurenard's** ★★★; **Clos de Brusquières'** ★★★; **Dom de Mont-Redon's** ★★★★; and **Ch de Vaudieu's** ★★★

**Côte-Rôtie, La Landonne Guigal** At six years of age: opaque; curious nose, spicy new oak; very sweet, full-bodied, attractive, impressive. More recently, with 'Matsuzaka-Beef' at Zachys/Christie's millennium dinner in New York: deep ruby; good nose; a strangely Bordeaux-like style, good flavour, firmness and austerity. *Last tasted May 1999* ★★★(★)

**Côte-Rôtie, La Mouline Guigal** Spicy nose; sweetly elegant, new oak, raw tannin. Austere. Undeniably impressive. *At 'The Parker 100' tasting in Hamburg, Oct 1993* (★★★★)

**Côte-Rôtie, La Turque Guigal** In October 1993: very deep, intensive; sweet, rich, very flavoury. Speciously *spritzig* new oak. Most recently: still opaque and youthful; tar-like nose; very much a 'Parker 100' sort of wine. Could not even cope with the cheese. *Last noted at the Russian National Orchestra dinner at Hatchlands, Surrey, Dec 2000* (★★★★)

**Crozes-Hermitage, Guiraude Dom Graillot** A newcomer, Alain Graillot, whose first vintage was 1985. Medium-deep, maturing; baked nose; medium sweetness and body, some softness, good flavour. *At the MW Rhône tasting, Painters' Hall, London, May 1999* ★★★

**Crozes-Hermitage, La Petite Ruche Chapoutier** Sweet, jammy, sweaty (tannin); rather tinny fruit, bitter tannins and rather acidic. *May 1990* ★★

**Crozes-Hermitage, Dom de Thalabert P Jaboulet Aîné** Intense, dark cherry; a massive whiff of black treacle; ripe yet tannic. An *osso bucco* wine. *Nov 1991* ★★★★

**Hermitage, La Chapelle P Jaboulet Aîné** In 1992, one bottle woody, poor, rich, spicy. Six years later: good tannic texture. Still very deep, rich and fairly intense. Most recently, at Paolo Pong's tasting: now medium-deep, ripe, rich, fruity; despite soft entry, very tannic finish. *Last noted May 2001* ★★★(★★) *I am sure it will continue to improve.*

## 1989 ★★★★ North ★★★★★ South

A drought year. The older vines with a deep and complex root formation coped best – this was particularly noticeable in the Côte-Rôtie; Hermitage produced a crop of rich wines. An early vintage in Châteauneuf produced rich, complete reds.

**Châteauneuf-du-Pape Ch de Beaucastel/Perrin** Several notes. Unusually opaque in 1993 yet sweet, full, fruity, elegant – and tannic. By 1999 deep but mature; touch of liquorice; very sweet, lovely rich fruit, meaty, glorious flavour (tasting for Credit Suisse, Hong Kong). Shortly after, at Christie's pre-sale tasting in Tokyo: lovely wine. Most recently, at the Paolo Pong tasting at Jancis Robinson's: now medium-deep with a touch

### Mont-Redon

*The most distinctive feature of vineyards in parts of the southern Rhône is the soil, not soil as we gardeners know it, but large, sandy-coloured, weather-rounded pebbles or galets which act like night-storage heaters, absorbing the sun's rays during the day and emitting its heat during the night. This accelerates the natural ripening process. For many years my wife and I, later with the children, spent our summer holidays touring wine areas. It was in 1960 that we first drove down the valley of the Rhône, and the first vineyard in the south that we visited was Mont-Redon, as it happens the biggest estate in Châteauneuf. As a souvenir I purloined a few large pebbles, one of which I used as a doorstop in my office for years, much to the irritation of my secretary, Rosemary, who kept stubbing her toes.*

of cherry; lovely chunky fruit, on nose and palate, with a touch of ripe softness. *Last tasted in London, May 2001* ★★★★★

**Châteauneuf-du-Pape Ch Rayas** Open knit, mature, weak pink rim; almost over-sweet, mulberry-ripe fruit; sweet, lovely, though a dry finish. *At the Paolo Pong tasting at Jancis Robinson's, May 2001* ★★★★★

Two early notes **Châteauneuf-du-Pape, Les Cèdres Jaboulet** lovely, great potential *1991* ★★★★; and **Châteauneuf-du-Pape, La Bernadine Chapoutier** showing well with good future. *1990* ★★★★

**Côte-Rôtie, Les Jumelles** Both **Chapoutier's** and **Jaboulet's** had very good potential in the early 1990s.

**Côte-Rôtie, La Mouline Guigal** Lovely colour; sweet and soft – and burgundy-like (why not? Côte-Rôtie is nearer to the Côte de Beaune than to Châteauneuf); rich, delicious. *At the Josey pre-sale tasting, New York, Nov 2000* ★★★★★

**Crozes-Hermitage, Dom de Thalabert P Jaboulet Aîné** Three notes, from an opaque cask sample in May 1990 with extraordinary aroma, fulsome and flavoury. The following year spicy, soft, agreeable. By the mid-1990s, drinking well and good value! *Last noted at our annual grouse dinner at Wilton's in Jermyn Street, Aug 1999* ★★★

**Hermitage Chave** Medium-deep, rich; very good, slightly meaty and singed nose; medium-sweet, well balanced, lovely flavour. In fact, delicious. *Pre-sale, New York, Nov 2000* ★★★★★

**Hermitage, La Chapelle P Jaboulet Aîné** Several notes, first in 1991: distinctive nose and taste; rich, tannic. Next, in 1998, at the Hollywood Wine Society's Jaboulet seminar: fine, deep; low-keyed but crisp fruit, harmonious; very sweet (the sweetest in the range), excellent flavour, complete and tannic. More recently, in magnums: still fairly intense but maturing; gorgeous outpouring of bouquet; warm, rich – yet still struggling to harmonise, so much going on. Fairly sweet, full-flavoured, very good fruit, excellent tannin and acidity. *Last noted at Stephen Kaplan's wine event in Chicago, April 2000* ★★★★★

## 1990 ★★★★★

A splendid year throughout the Rhône. Mild spring, early flowering, hot dry summer, though not as baking as in 1989, and an early harvest – mid-September in the North and from the 9th in the South. The wines were firmer and with more power than the '89s.

**Châteauneuf-du-Pape Ch de Beaucastel/Perrin** First in magnums in 1993: opaque, rich, full, silky tannins. In 1998 Daphne and I treated ourselves to a quiet Christmas away from the family. On Christmas Eve we settled down to dinner with three decent half bottles, preceded by a whisky sour and with Moscato d'Asti with the pud. Though it was against the grain to pay £36 for a half bottle of the Beaucastel, it was extremely good. Most recently, at Paolo Pong's Beaucastel v. Rayas tasting: now much less deep, mature; a ripe open nose which reminded me of melon and parma ham; good flavour, hot dry finish. Quite a bite. *Last noted at Jancis Robinson's, May 2001* ★★★★(★) *More to come.*

**Châteauneuf-du-Pape Ch La Nerthe** An historic property and one that is very nostalgic for me – it reminds me of the cache of 1825 'Lanerthe' referred to in the introduction (see page 302). The '90 was deep, rich, oaky, with good fruit. Noted on another occasion, receiving the *Rame d'Honneur*, a rather ridiculous oar with a tassel, at *Le Verre et L'Assiette* award ceremony. I was interested to see that the other five recipients were all personalities also noted for paddling their own canoes: Serena Sutcliffe, Jancis Robinson, Georges Lepré (from Paris) and the Roux brothers, Albert and Michel. *At the Royal Agricultural Hall, London, May 1994* ★★★

**Châteauneuf-du-Pape Ch Rayas** Tough to be pitted against 144 of the world's best '90s (at Eigensatz's tasting in 1996). The Rayas acquitted itself pretty well. Tasted blind I noted a piquant high-toned, bilberry-like fruitiness; very sweet, immensely rich, full of fruit. 'Most unusual' – in the context of the flanking La Turque and Giacosa's Asili. Most recently, alongside Ch de Beaucastel: rich, spicy; soft, full, fleshy, with fairly swingeing tannic finish. *Last noted May 2001* ★★★★(★) *Will benefit from another five years in the cellar.*

**Châteauneuf-du-Pape Clos des Papes/Paul Avril** First noted at the INAO dinner at the Vintners' Hall in London in 1995: opaque; strange, very tannic. I did not like it. More recently, at the closing France in your Glass tasting dinner at Ch de Bagnols: it was still impressively deep; but this time it had a good, rich, ripe nose; fairly sweet, full, ripe fruit, rich, mouthfilling flavour. *June 1997* ★★★★

**Châteauneuf-du-Pape, Homage à Jacques Perrin Ch de Beaucastel/Perrin** A special *cuvée* first released in 1989 by François and Jean-Pierre Perrin in honour of their father, *'un grand homme'*, who died in 1978. (It is not made every year.) Very deep, opaque core, intense; low-keyed, great vinosity, slightly malty; the 'Latour' of Paolo Pong's tasting of Châteauneuf vintages from '78 to '98: enormously impressive. *May 2001* ★★★(★★) *2005–2020.*

**Cornas A Clape** Deep, very fragrant; sweet, lovely fruit, soft tannins. *Tasted July 1992* ★(★★★★) *Probably excellent now.*

**Cornas, Les Ruchets Jean-Luc Colombo** Strangely scented, violets, over the top. Rather unreal flavour to match. *One of my lowest marks at Eigensatz's 'top 144 1990s of the world' blind tasting, June 1996* ★?

**Côte-Rôtie R Jasmin** Intense purple; scent of syrup of figs; very sweet, powerful. Like port. *At Robin Yapp's, July 1992. Then* (★★★★★) *Doubtless delicious now.*

**Côte-Rôtie, La Turque Guigal** My highest mark in a flight of 12 wines, including Ch Pétrus, Ch Le Pin and Penfold's Grange at Eigensatz's 'top 144 1990s of the world' blind tasting in 1996: the most dashingly flowery, scented nose, yet below that seeming superficiality, great depth; glorious flavour, heavenly fruit, fragrant aftertaste. A few months later, totally coincidentally, I marked it the highest in a 'flight' of ten 1990s, once again including Ch Pétrus, Le Pin, Ch Margaux and Latour, tasted blind in random order. I made a virtually identical note. *Last tasted at Rodenstock's wine dinner at the Königshof hotel, Munich, Sept 1996* ★★★★★

**Crozes-Hermitage Guiraude Dom Graillot** 100% new oak, usually bottled in December of the following year. Deep; sweet, rather Richebourg-like; positive, earthy, vegetal flavour. Well balanced. *At the MW Rhône tasting, May 1995* ★★★★

**Crozes-Hermitage, Les Launes Delas** Medium-deep; not very distinctive; fullish, straightforward but nothing special. *At the 1990–91 Past-Masters' dinner held at the Innholders' Hall, London, Oct 1994* ★★

**Crozes-Hermitage, Dom de Thalabert Jaboulet** Deep; low-keyed, figgy; sweet, big, attractive wine with singed flavour. *At the Hollywood Wine Society's Jaboulet seminar in Florida, March 1998* ★★★★

**Hermitage Chave** Rich, medium intensity, good 'legs'; curious smell of an empty hearth, smoky, beefy, touch of liquorice; too sweet and with strange leathery tannins. *At the Eigensatz 1990s tasting in Luzern, June 1996* ★★?

**Hermitage, La Chapelle P Jaboulet Aîné** Several notes. In 1996: opaque, intense; muffled, figgy, touch of malt; sweet, full, hefty – high marks for power. Next, at a Syrah tasting in Singapore (1998): more homogenous bouquet, very distinctive flavour, touch of raw tannin. Shortly after: magnificent, complete, sweet, full (alcohol 13.9%), delicious, at the Jaboulet seminar in Florida. Most recently: still impressively deep; delicious flavour and crisp fruit. *Last noted at Christie's millennium pre-sale tasting, New York, May 1999* ★★★★★

**Hermitage, Monnier de la Sizeranne Chapoutier** Deep rich ruby; sweet, good fruit – but dried out after spicy beef. *Dining at The Good Earth, a Chinese restaurant in London, June 1995* ★★★★ *(tasted pre-spice).*

**'Ermitage', Le Pavillon Chapoutier** I first came across this at Eigensatz's 1990s tasting in Luzern. It sounds rather affected, like Americans pronouncing herbs as 'erbs – all very French I'm sure. It was opaque, intense and rich; low-keyed but earthy (not 'h'earthy) and distinctive; sweetish, full bodied, very good fruit and flavour. I gave it a higher mark for palate than nose, and higher than the Ch Pétrus. *Tasted blind, June 1996* ★★★★★

**St-Joseph Grippat** Gentle fruit; dry, stylish, good acidity. *Tasted July 1992* ★★(★) *Probably passing its best now.*

# 1991 ★★★ North ★★ South

This was an uneven year. The Rhône was the only major region in France not severely hit by spring frosts; July and August were both hot and dry but mid-September rains spoiled the chance of a top-class vintage. In the South, the Grenache which had suffered from *coulure* during flowering, had ripening problems; late summer storms and humidity in September caused some rot. There was a small crop of light wines in Châteauneuf and it was somewhat more successful in the North for those who picked before the rain.

**Châteauneuf-du-Pape Guigal** Medium-deep; not very distinctive. *Dining at the Stanley-Clarks', Sept 1998* ★★

**Cornas, Les Ruchets Jean-Luc Colombo** Worth mentioning that Cornas has a total of 100 ha of vines. Like Côte-Rôtie, the vineyards, mainly on porous granite behind this small village, are on a steep slope and dotted around a very wooded area. Medium-dry, maturing; fairly rich, open fruit; dry, lean, sappy with dry lightly acidic finish. *At the MW Rhône tasting in London, May 1999* ★★★ *Drink up.*

**Côte-Rôtie, La Mouline Guigal** Medium deep, maturing; harmonious; medium sweet, nice weight, attractive flavour. Some charm. *With 'Rosemary Roasted Quail' at the pre-sale dinner in honour of Lenoir Josey, New York, Nov 2000* ★★★ *Drink soon.*

**Côte-Rôtie, La Turque Guigal** Deep, rich, impressive; sweet, soft, burgundy-like; rich, delicious. *At the Josey pre-sale tasting in Nov 2000* ★★★★ *(which just goes to show what Guigal can do in a mediocre vintage).*

**Hermitage, La Chapelle Jaboulet** I first tasted the '91 Chapelle at Dom de Chevalier during Vinexpo in June 1995 and again in 1997. My notes were identical: deep ruby; curious *marrons* nose; powerful for a talked-down (not by Jaboulet) vintage. Next in 1998 at the Jaboulet seminar in Florida: deep, still youthful; cherry-like fruit, fully evolved; sweet, soft, excellent texture; maturing nicely. Jumping a couple of years to a jeroboam at a French wine dinner in Hamburg: complete, no harsh edges, a copybook Hermitage. *Last tasted March 2000* ★★★★ *Drink soon.*

**Hermitage, La Sizeranne Chapoutier** Fairly deep, still youthful. Good nose and palate. An agreeable lunchtime wine. *With Don Zacharia, Christie's wine auction partner in New York, at Daniel's, July 1998* ★★★

**St-Joseph Grippat** Bought from Yapp's for home-drinking in 1994. Fairly deep though light style. Lovely, uplifting fruit and flavour. Touch of sweetness. Next, dining de luxe at the Troisgros restaurant in Roanne. Good deep fruit. Ready. *Last tasted Oct 1998* ★★★

## 1992 ★★★ South

A moderate year. Though conditions started well, with successful flowering, this was followed by six weeks of wet weather which caused rot problems and uneven ripening. August was hot but September wet and stormy. Small crop in the north and, despite all the problems, some quite good wines were made though I have tasted few. Early drinking.

**Châteauneuf-du-Pape M Bernard** Medium-deep, soft ruby; quite good fruit, easy, fair length. Agreeable. *Dinner at home, March 1995* ★★★

**Châteauneuf-du-Pape A Brunet** Deep; fairly sweet and full. Quite good flavour. *On my preferred New York to London day flight, BA 178, April 1995* ★★★

**Cornas Chave** Rich appearance but not a very distinctive nose, agreeable enough. *At Yapp's tasting, Sept 1995* ★★★

**Hermitage Chave** First noted at Yapp's tasting, September 1995. Medium, open, maturing; attractive fruit, medium-sweet, rich, lovely flavour, perfect fruit and oak. I must have bought some for my next three notes were with meals at home in 1996, 1998 and, last, in 1999. By then it was showing some maturity; lovely, slightly burgundian nose; rich, earthy, distinctive. Most enjoyable. *Last tasted at Chippenham Lodge, May 1999* ★★★★

## 1993 ★★

Continuing a fairly dismal period, between 1991 and 1994, the good summer conditions were washed away by heavy rains, with serious flooding in the South, from mid-September. Mainly lightish wines. Chaptalisation was widespread. This was fine as a sort of stop gap, not for cellaring.

**Châteauneuf-du-Pape Ch de Beaucastel/Perrin** Medium, fully mature; sweaty, singed barnyard scents and flavours to match. Very much in its strange in-between stage. Perrin's wine is best drunk young or after, say, seven years. (The '83 was tasting much better). *At Michael Ruger's tasting at the Winefest in Sarasota, April 1997* ★★

**Cornas, Les Ruchets Jean-Luc Colombo** 100% Syrah. Jean-Luc, whose wines were new to me, told us that the vintage in general was not very good though, thanks to green harvesting, he made a decent wine. I agree: a sweetish wine with agreeable fruit and good length. Soft yet lean. *At the MW Rhône tasting at Painters' Hall, May 1999* ★★★

**Côte-Rôtie Jasmin** Medium-deep, youthful, rich 'legs'; a touch of rather common stalkiness; medium sweetness and weight. Quite nice only. *At the Yapp tasting, Sept 1995* ★★★

**Côte-Rôtie, Brune et Blonde Guigal** Fairly deep youthful ruby; swingeingly raw and tannic at first but improved and sweetened in the glass. Paul Bocuse's food helped. *Oct 1997* ★★

**Hermitage Chave** Misleadingly pale; attractive nose; fairly sweet, rich, powerful. A big wine needing time. *At the Yapp tasting, London, Sept 1995. Then ★★★, probably at peak now.*

**St-Joseph Dom de Chèze/Rostaing** Fairly deep; medium dryness and fullness, good flavour. *At our annual grouse dinner at Wilton's, Sept 2000* ★★★

## 1994 ★★ North ★ South

Once again, high hopes were dashed by heavy mid-September rains. 'High hopes' because, despite earlier *coulure* problems around flowering time, the summer was exceptionally hot, up to 42°C being recorded and a 'vintage of the century' prayed for. (Alas, how many times have we seen pious hopes dashed.) Steep, sloping vineyards were able to shed excess water but some vineyards were waterlogged. The grapes were not ripe enough, lacked acidity and had to be chaptalised.

The market was not thrilled with the '94s, nor, frankly, did I take much note. Some growers, however, managed to produce decent wines.

**Châteauneuf-du-Pape Guigal** Very popular in British Airways' Club Class on the transatlantic routes: most drinkable. *Noted Oct and Dec 1997, and Feb 1998* ★★★ *Then it ran out.*

**Châteauneuf-du-Pape, Homage à Jacques Perrin Ch de Beaucastel/Perrin** Fairly intense dark cherry; very distinctive, figgy, tarry nose; fairly sweet and full bodied, chunky fruit, a touch of raw tannin. *At Paolo Pong's Beaucastel v. Rayas tasting, May 2001* ★★(★)

**Côte-Rôtie Rostaing** Mature, unexceptional; with a good dry finish. Did not quite rise to the occasion. *At a lunchtime presentation of the new wine list at the beautifully restored Spencer House in St James's Place, London, Sept 2000* ★★

**Crozes-Hermitage, Guiraude Dom Graillot** Decent colour; a distinctly sweet, fragrant, oaky slightly vegetal nose that almost sang like a Domaine de la Romanée-Conti wine; lean and green, vegetal, slightly metallic, oaky tannic finish. A brave try. *At the MW Rhône tasting, London, May 1999* ★★★ *(just).*

**St-Joseph, La Grande Pompée Jaboulet** Deep, youthful, plummy-coloured; strange, hard nose; a bit raw, 'so so'. *At a Sainsbury supermarket tasting, Sept 1997* ★

## 1995 ★★★★ North ★★★★★ South

After the less than successful four previous vintages – blame the weather not the growers and winemakers – 1995 was a very satisfactory vintage. As so often, the North and South were affected in somewhat different ways. In the North *coulure* and *millerandage* during the flowering reduced the potential crop by 20% but the reds were – are – elegant and charming. In the South the late September Mistral wind had a drying effect, resulting in very ripe, fairly concentrated grapes, with good levels of tannin and acidity and said to be comparable to the '90s. The wines are worth cellaring and lovely to drink. What more can one want?

**Châteauneuf-du-Pape Ch de Beaucastel/Perrin** Medium depth and intensity; attractive fruit, very distinctive; a delicious mouthful, good fruit, still tannic and a citrus-edge adding to its refreshing acidity. *At Paolo Pong's enlightening Beaucastel v. Rayas tasting over dinner at Jancis Robinson's, London, May 2001* ★★★★(★)

**Châteauneuf-du-Pape Ch Rayas** Dark cherry, still youthful; unknit and a bit sharp; sweet, fascinating fruit, good grip. *May 2001* ★★★(★★)

**Châteauneuf-du-Pape, Homage à Jacques Perrin Ch de Beaucastel/Perrin** Very deep ruby, intense, still youthful; very sweet ripe, fig-like fruit; rich, fleshy, dry finish. I queried its length. *At the Paolo Pong tasting, May 2001* ★★★(★★)?

**Châteauneuf-du-Pape Dom du Vieux Télégraphe** Deep, mature rim; low-keyed, meaty; sweet, rich, ripe, berry-like fruit. Drinking well. *Lunch at The Square, London Oct 2001* ★★★

**Cornas, La Louvée Jean-Luc Colombo** A single-vineyard wine from 60–70 year-old vines. 100% new oak. Medium-deep, rich core, long 'legs'; rich, plummy fruit, sweet, scented; good fruit and flavour. *At the MW tasting, May 1999* ★★★(★)

**Cornas, Les Ruchets Jean-Luc Colombo** Jean-Luc informed us that the average age of his vines was 50–60 years, and, surprisingly, they were ungrafted - the original vines, not clones. He uses 30% new oak. Medium-deep; plummy; rich Italianate fruit and oak; richer, rounder than La Louvée, with slightly singed, figgy fruit and good length. *At the MW Rhône tasting, London, May 1999* ★★★(★)

**Côte-Rôtie P Jaboulet Aîné** Medium-deep, soft red though with youthful violet rim; gentle, low-keyed but harmonious; an intriguing softness, full flavoured but not hefty (alcohol 12.5%), good length, crisp, needs time. *At a Syrah tasting for the IWFS, Singapore, Jan 1998* ★★★(★)

**Côte-Rôtie, Ch d'Ampuis Guigal** Comprising six vineyards, two in the Côte Brune, three in the Côte Blonde. Aged in 75% new *barriques* of 222 litres, known locally as 'tung'. Fairly deep, immature, rich 'legs'; crisp, oaky, spice with deep fig-like fruit; sweet, full, rich fruit and oak flavour and aftertaste. Dry finish. (We were informed by Marcel Guigal at the time that Syrah is known as 'Sirène' in Côte-Rôtie, but as 'Sirèné' or 'Durif' in Hermitage – and Petite Sirah in the Napa. Perhaps I should add that it can be spelled Sirah in the Hérault and elsewhere, not to mention 'Hermitage' in Australia). *At the MW Rhône tasting, London, May 1999* ★★★★★

**Côte-Rôtie, Brune et Blonde Guigal** 30% new oak. Medium, youthful; sweet, crisp, bilberry-like fruit; medium sweetness and body, lean and long. *At the MW Rhône tasting, London, May 1999* ★★★

**Côte-Rôtie, La Turque Guigal** Made with Syrah from the Côte Brune with 5% Viognier added. Three years' ageing in 100% new oak, unfined and unfiltered. Deep, attractive, rich 'legs'; rich, fig-like brambly fruit; sweetly fruitful, concentrated yet soft, soft yet tannic. *May 1999* ★★★(★★)

**Crozes-Hermitage, Dom de Thalabert Jaboulet** Deep; not much nose but deliciously sweet with good fruit. Complete. *At the Jaboulet seminar in Florida, March 1998* ★★★(★)

---

### The hill of Hermitage

*Hermitage, or Ermitage, gained its name, some say, from the presence of a hermit who took up residence on the hill. Stories abound as to how this came about; one is that he was a knight, Gaspard de Stérimberg, wounded in the 13th-century Crusades, who sought refuge, planting vines and living the rest of his days there. The addition of the 'H' is another mystery, although it is likely, given the wine's frequent mention in 17th-century literature, that this was a result of its constant translation into English. The wine of Hermitage met favour with the nobility, and at one time commanded a higher price than most of the châteaux of Bordeaux (first growths excepted, as these were in any case occasionally 'assisted' by Hermitage wine up to the mid-19th century). The wine was renowned for its power and balance; and also its ability to mature and evolve for more than 30 years. Phylloxera in the 1880s, followed by the two world wars, took its toll. It was not until the 1970s that the fashion for Hermitage wine, both red and white, began to return, spearheaded by Chapoutier and Jaboulet.*

**Hermitage, La Chapelle Jaboulet** In January 1998 in Singapore: rich, classic, well evolved, spicy. Two months later: deep, still youthful, rich 'legs'; low-keyed but fragrant, opening up spicily in the glass; tight-knit, concentrated, crisp, very good fruit, tannin and acidity. *Last tasted in Florida, March 1998* ★★(★★★)

## 1996 ★★ to ★★★

Similar to 1994, with rain. But there were more problems in the South – demonstrating again that you cannot generalise about the Rhône because there is so often a north-south divide. The season started well with satisfactory flowering. Early August was cool and wet which inhibited sugar development. Happily, in the North late August was sunny and conditions were good until the harvest end. The crop was healthy and abundant. In the South, the rain continued into September though the Mistral wind saved the crop from rot.

**Châteauneuf-du-Pape Ch de Beaucastel/Perrin** Medium-deep ruby; a meaty, farmyard smell – I was told that Mouvèdre needs oxygen in its early stages; medium-sweet, ripe, good fruit, a touch of $CO_2$, lovely acidity. *In the cellars at Beaucastel, Oct 2001* (★★★★) *Needs bottle age.*

**Châteauneuf-du-Pape, Les Cailloux Alain Brunet** Lively, lovely but surprisingly mature-looking; very good nose; lovely flavour, very pleasant dry finish. Nice now. *At the Wine Experience, New York, Oct 1999* ★★★★

**Cornas, St-Pierre Jaboulet** A 3-ha vineyard purchased in 1993: pleasant fruit; nice weight, delicious flavour. Some oak. Refreshing. *At Vinexpo, Bordeaux, June 1999* ★★(★)

**Côte-Rôtie Jasmin** Deep, immature; amazing scent of violets, privet and Persian cats; very distinctive: I liked it. Apparently Robert Jasmin now destalks to improve the colour of the wine. *On the Yapp table at The Bunch tasting at the Groucho Club, Jan 1998* ★★(★★) *Will be interesting to see how this develops.*

**Côtes-du-Rhône, Coudoulet de Beaucastel Ch de Beaucastel/Perrin** Always agreeable. *Good value at Monkeys, Daphne's favourite London restaurant, Sept 2001* ★★

**Crozes-Hermitage, 'Famille 2000' Jaboulet** Opaque, tough. Nowhere near ready. *At the Vinexpo supper at Dom de Chevalier, Bordeaux, June 1999* (★★★)

**Crozes-Hermitage, Dom de Thalabert Jaboulet** Cask sample at the Jaboulet seminar in Miami: deep purple; nose closed; dry, crisp, fruit, tannic, austere. *March 1998* (★★★)

**Hermitage Chave** Jean-Louis Chave aims to make a good *appellation* wine, not a 'Chave' wine. It is a blend of *lieux-dits*, from seven different types of soil and blended for fruit and tannin. In 1996 he used grapes from old vines from slopes with good exposure. Medium-deep, plummy, noticeably rich 'legs'; sweet, slightly muffled nose, bramble-like fruit; medium-sweet, good balance and body, crisp fruit, dry finish. Finesse. *At the MW Rhône tasting, London, May 1999* ★★(★)

**Hermitage, La Chapelle Jaboulet** First tasted in March 1998 at the Jaboulet tasting in Florida: opaque, intense; extremely figgy Syrah aroma; flavour to match, a powerful peppery wine. By 1999 losing some colour; good depth, length and tannins. Most recently, still youthful with a rich, singed taste. Very tannic. *Last tasted at Dom de Chevalier, Bordeaux, June 2001* ★★★(★★) *Needs more bottle age.*

## 1997 ★★★

A useful and attractive vintage. Both the North and the South experienced early budding and a prompt start to flowering.

The summer was relatively cool until a heatwave hit the entire region at the end of August. Apart from a couple of storms, the ripening and harvesting proceeded in favourable conditions. In the North the red grapes were picked from 25 September, the only complaint being that the extreme heat had 'burnt' some of the grapes. This resulted in deep colour and, at best, suggests wines with a long life. The picking in the South was much earlier and the wines are easier and very pleasant for current drinking.

**Châteauneuf-du-Pape** Ch de Beaucastel/Perrin Richly coloured; very good, raspberry-like fruit; slightly sweet, lovely flavour – delicious. *At Farr Vintners, London, Jan 2000* ★★★ *For relatively early easy drinking.*

**Châteauneuf-du-Pape** Ch Mont-Redon Very deep; pleasant fruit; sweet, rich, very drinkable. *Dinner at the somewhat pretentious Près du Moulin, near Orange, Oct 2001* ★★★

**Châteauneuf-du-Pape, 'Le Crau',** Dom du Vieux Télégraphe Medium, soft cherry, starting to mature; pleasant, easy, soft brambly fruit; sweet, soft, rich fruit, pleasant flavour with refreshing, up-turned end. *Part of a batch of agreeable half bottles for home drinking (Daphne always has the lion's share whatever the size of bottle) bought from Berry Bros, Feb 2002* ★★★

**Côte-Rôtie, Ch d'Ampuis** Guigal From six vineyards around La Turque and La Mouline. Informed by Philippe, Marcel's highly competent son and heir, that it was a long, hot, late harvest. The wine spent 38 months in new oak. Very deep, very rich colour and spice; also very sweet, full-bodied, fruit-packed, very tannic yet with a velvety texture. Impressive. *In the cellars, Oct 2001* (★★★★)

**Côte-Rôtie, Les Jumelles** Jaboulet Fairly deep; sweet, 'warm', lovely fruit; fairly sweet, slightly singed, raisiny flavour. Attractive. *At Dom de Chevalier, Bordeaux, June 1999* ★(★★)

**Côtes du Rhône** Reds from this *appellation* are destined for early drinking, as are most of the delightful, fruity and very quaffable wines such as Gigondas from areas in Châteauneuf's hinterland. But the simple AC Côtes du Rhône, though very variable, can be excellent, as I was reminded by Guigal's '97, consumed with great enjoyment by the family at Christmas 2001 – about the right age for this sort of wine and the Ch de Beaucastel wine below.

**Côtes-du-Rhône, Coudoulet de Beaucastel** Ch de Beaucastel/ Perrin First tasted in Jan 2000 at Farr Vintners and ordered on the spot – excellent value for home-drinking, and at my daughter's: richly coloured, extraordinary nose, like a whiff of fine cognac and crushed raspberry; delicious, and ready to drink. We soon tucked in, finding it fullish, soft, very fruity and delicious. *We finished it off pretty quickly for I cannot find any notes after March 2000* ★★★

**Crozes-Hermitage, Réserve** Perrin Youthful; very curious nose and flavour. Touch of tar. Neither expensive nor liked. *At Farr Vintners, London, Jan 2000*

# 1998 ★★★★★

Great vintage. Uniformly good growing season (except for severe April frosts in Côte-Rôtie). The summer was hot and dry, a touch of rain then intense heat in August, stressing the vines. Happily, well-timed rain fleshed out the parched grapes which was followed by dry and sunny conditions. Sun-tanned skins produced deeply coloured reds and a high sugar content with substantial levels of alcohol.

**Châteauneuf-du-Pape** Ch de Beaucastel/Perrin First tasted May 2001. Medium-deep; fully open; crisp fruit but tannic.

More recently, plummy; almost overripe, smelly; raw, tannic. Needs bottle age. *Last tasted at Farr Vintners, Oct 2001.* (★★★★)

**Châteauneuf-du-Pape, Homage à Jacques Perrin** Ch de Beaucastel/Perrin Five grape varieties used, Grenache uppermost – 60%. First tasted blind, May 2001: opaque core, intense, velvety; peppery fruit which opened up sweetly; rich, soft, fleshy, complete. Five months later, 'thick', dense, almost port-like nose; sweet, full fruit flavour, high alcohol (circa 15%), slightly figgy flavour, masked tannin, great length. A great classic in the making. *Last tasted in the cellars, Oct 2001* (★★★★★)

**Châteauneuf-du-Pape** Dom de la Mordorée/Dom de la Reine des Bois Deep, plummy, good 'legs'; very sweet, fragrant; almost too sweet though with good grip. Full bodied. A rich mouthful. *Lunch at the Stafford Hotel, London, Oct 2001* ★★★(★)

**Châteauneuf-du-Pape** Ch Rayas Medium-pale, open rim, light style; soft fruit; a bit lean, sweet, gamey, curious flavour, swingeingly tannic. *At Paolo Pong's tasting, May 2001* ★★(★★)?

**Côte-Rôtie, Brune et Blonde** Guigal Aged in 30% new oak and bottled end July 2001. Dark cherry; sweet, bramble-like fruit, tannic. *At Guigal's, Oct 2001* (★★★)

**Côte-Rôtie, La Landonne** Guigal Opaque core, velvety; more meaty and less oaky than their La Turque (below); firm, minerally, fullish (alcohol 13.5%) peppery finish. Long life. *From the cask, Oct 2001* (★★★★★)

**Côte-Rôtie, La Mouline** A lighter wine from the Côte Blonde which contains approximately 12% of Viognier. Opaque; a lovely wine, very fragrant, very spicy. *From the cask, Oct 2001* (★★★★)

**Côte-Rôtie, La Turque** Guigal From the Côte Brûne. Opaque; brambly-blackberry fruit; medium-sweet, totally different flavour and character to La Mouline. *From the cask, Oct 2001* (★★★★★)

**Côtes-du-Rhône, Coudoulet de Beaucastel** Ch de Beaucastel/Perrin Grenache 30%, Mourvèdre 30%, Syrah 20% for colour and tannin and Cinsault 20% for finesse, or so I was told by Mike Rijken who kindly showed us round. Fairly deep, soft, velvety ruby; fruit, figgy, sweaty tannin; dry, good fruity pleasant flavour, natural tannin from the skins (no new oak). *In the cellars, Oct 2001* (★★★★) *For early and easy drinking.*

# 1999 ★★★★★ North ★★★★ South

This was particularly successful in the northern Rhône, the grapes in Côte-Rôtie ripening early and reaching record sugar levels. Some growers claimed their wines were as good as their '98s, at least one stating that it could be compared to the best of the 20th century. It was slightly less successful in Châteauneuf due to heavy rains at the end of September.

**Châteauneuf-du-Pape** Ch de Beaucastel/Perrin Fairly deep, ruby; crisp, spicy, gamey, Mourvèdre noted; lovely young fruit, crisp, good length, tannic. *In the cellar, Oct 2001* (★★★★)

**Châteauneuf-du-Pape** Dom de Père Pape Very deep; very sweet, chewy, chocolatey, smothered with oak. *On BA 285, London to San Francisco, Feb 2002* ★★

**Côte-Rôtie, La Landonne** Guigal Opaque; intense; sweaty tannin and figs; medium-sweet, full-bodied, meaty, touch of liquorice. *In cask, Oct 2001* ★★(★★★)

**Côte-Rôtie, La Mouline** Guigal Opaque, vivid purple; full-bodied (Syrah attaining 14.7% alcohol), firm but fleshy and a velvety feel despite the tannin. *In cask, Oct 2001* ★★(★★★)

**Côte-Rôtie, La Turque** Guigal Deep; wonderful vinosity, plus a scent of fresh sawn wood; very sweet, fullish (alcohol 13.5%), lovely flavour. *At Guigal, Oct 2001* ★★(★★★)

# 2000 and the future

After the fairly desperate time in the not so distant past, when to most people the only familiar Rhône wine name was Châteauneuf-du-Pape, much of which was possibly not genuine and certainly not up to today's standards, and then more recently, when the steep slopes of Côte-Rôtie had been largely abandoned because the price paid for the wine was not worth the labour, things have certainly changed in the Rhône, and for the better. The main competition, on export markets at any rate, is from outside France, from Australia and more recently California where Syrah is 'the flavour of the month'. 'Imitation is the sincerest form of flattery' is all very well…. It is, however, always consoling for the growers that the soil and climate of the hot valley of the Rhône is rather special. The future bodes well.

## 2000 ★★★

A good vintage but not without its problems. New Year and the spring were abnormally dry with, generally, above average temperatures. April to June was wetter and July was exceptionally cool. August was quite the opposite, with very high temperatures and dry. The month of September was more equable with fine warm days interspersed with occasional showers.

**Châteauneuf-du-Pape Le Bosquet des Papes/Boiron** Slightly cheesy and spirity; sweet, soft entry, chewy, adequate tannin and acidity. *At the Loeb tasting, London, March 2002* ★★(★★)

**Châteauneuf-du-Pape Clos Val Seille** Medium deep; sweet, brambly fruit; very flavoury, mouthfilling (alcohol 14%), good tannin and acidity. *At the Loeb tasting, March 2002* ★★(★★)

**Châteauneuf-du-Pape Dom de la Vieille Julienne** Cask sample: floral, fragrant; very sweet, lovely flavour, good length, well integrated tannin and acidity. *March 2002* ★(★★★)

**Cornas, Dom de Rochepertuis Dom Lionnet** Pleasant sweetness, crisp fruit, good depth. *March 2002* ★★★(★)

**Cornas, Dom St-Pierre P Jaboulet Aîné** Jaboulet's 3-ha vineyard. Their first vintage was in 1994. Medium-deep; very forthcoming, fruity, figs and fudge (soft toffee); sweet, fullish (alcohol 13.5%), attractive flavour, light tannin and acid finish. I much enjoyed this. *At the Dreyfus Ashby tasting at Vintners' Hall, London, Jan 2002* ★★(★★)

**Côte-Rôtie Dom Daubrée** Medium deep; fragrant, nice fruit, youthful acidity; medium sweetness and body (alcohol 12%), a lean touch and with very oaky, spicy aftertaste. Moderately impressive. *March 2002* ★★(★★)

**Côte-Rôtie Dom J M Stephan** Very deep; fragrant, oaky; attractive, moderate weight, lean, tannic. *March 2002* ★★(★★)

**Côte-Rôtie, Les Jumelles P Jaboulet Aîné** Deep, fairly intense; rich, hefty, though only 13% alcohol; full fruit nose and palate. Figgy. *At the Dreyfus Ashby tasting, Jan 2002* ★(★★★)

**Crozes-Hermitage, Les Armandiers Dom de Murinais** Deep; rather ordinary, raspberry scent, better flavour than nose. Very oaky. Moderately priced. *March 2002* ★★(★)

**Crozes-Hermitage, Les Jalets P Jaboulet Aîné** Fairly deep; high-toned, rather common Syrah; very fragrant, moderate weight (alcohol 13%), very tannic. *March 2002* ★(★★)

**Crozes-Hermitage, Dom de Thalabert P Jaboulet Aîné** Fairly deep; very sweet, meaty, touch of caramel, leathery; very strange flavour reminding me of a young vintage port (though alcohol only 13%). *London, Jan 2002* ★★?

**Hermitage, La Chapelle P Jaboulet Aîné** Jaboulet's flagship wine: deep; figgy, Syrah aroma; medium-sweet, fullish body; good fruit, touch of leanness. *Jan 2002* ★★(★★)

**Hermitage, Le Pied de la Côte P Jaboulet Aîné** From roughly 50% wine not put into the La Chapelle blend and 50% bought-in grapes. Medium-deep, luminous ruby; unknit nose; fairly sweet, very rich, (alcohol. 13%), figgy fruit. Half the price of Jaboulet's La Chapelle above. *Jan 2002* ★★(★) *For early drinking.*

**St-Joseph Dom du Cornilhac** Very deep; extraordinary scent of violets; dry, 'boiled candy' fruit and very tannic. *March 2002* ★★★

**St-Joseph Dom du Mortier** Medium-deep; attractive, fragrant, whiff of raspberry; soft, very pleasant weight and flavour. Oaky. *March 2002* ★★★

# Loire

I have always wondered at, and admired, the totally contrasting styles of wine made close to the banks of France's two great rivers, the turbulent Rhône which empties itself into the Mediterranean, and the Loire, the longest river in France, which flows at a more leisurely pace from the Massif Central to the Atlantic coast. Roughly halfway, not far from Orléans, where the Loire changes direction from due north to flow due west, two major wine areas face each other: close to the right bank is Pouilly-sur-Loire, home to Pouilly-Fumé (not to be confused with Pouilly-Fuissé in the Mâconnais), and Sancerre is on the opposite bank of the Loire on slopes above the river. Both areas produce archetypal Sauvignon Blanc, white, dry and zestfully acidic, neither warranting bottle age, in common with most other Sauvignon Blanc wines. Much of it is of moderate quality but there are a few quite exceptional producers. Much further down river, almost at the mouth, near Nantes, is the Pays Nantais or Muscadet region, named after the grape from which the dry white wine is made. These wines are best drunk young and fresh. Though I like, and drink, them, they are not the subject of this chapter. Nor are the refreshingly delightful dry wines from Anjou and Vouvray.

Chenin Blanc produces a huge range of wines in its homeland of Anjou-Touraine, from dry, medium-dry, semi-sweet to sweet, and both still and sparkling. The following notes, however, are confined mainly to the medium-sweet and sweet wines of good vintages, particularly ones made from botrytis-affected grapes as in Sauternes and Barsac. It is doubtful whether any but a limited few of the dry whites, such as a top-class Savennières, will actually benefit from bottle age.

First, though, here is an approximate definition of the levels of sweetness used on the labels of the white wines of Vouvray and Anjou. *Sec* is dry; *demi-sec*, literally half-dry, can vary according to the vintage; *moelleux*, which sounds pleasingly like mellow, also varies between medium-dry and fairly sweet; and *doux* is definitely sweet though the acidity, a marked feature of all Loire wines, can give it a dry finish. The sweetest of all are often described as *liquoreux*. Virtually all the richer, sweeter whites not only keep well but evolve in bottle.

Lastly, and frankly for me least, are the Loire reds, Chinon, Bourgueil and Saumur-Champigny. Made mainly from Cabernet Franc, some from Pinot Noir and Gamay, they tend to be very acidic and in my experience only those made in a top (warm) vintage are worth pursuing and capable of development in bottle. They are best drunk on the spot, in a restaurant, on the banks of the Loire.

## The older, classic vintages: 1928–1959

It was not just the depression of the 1930s; the consensus was that the wines of the Loire, light and acidic 'did not travel'. As far as the British were concerned they were local wines, holiday wines: Muscadet, cheap and innocuous in Brittany, Sancerre in Paris bistros – both of course excellent with oysters which, in France, are consumed year round, not just when there is an 'R' in the month. The post-war period was much the same. Few merchants imported any Loire wines though I notice that, thanks to their erudite buyer, Sir Guy Fison, Saccone & Speed in 1951 listed three, a '45, '46 and a '47, the latter 'Clos le Mont Vouvray', price 16 shillings and 6 pence, one shilling more than château-bottled '47 Léoville-Lascases. Harvey's listed Loire wines for the first time in the spring of 1957, just four, ranging from Muscadet at 8 shillings a bottle to 'Pouilly Fumé (Château du Nozet)' at 22 shillings, well over the price of even the best Bristol-bottled claret and just 3 shillings less than Latour '50.

In the hot summer of 1959, having parked our five-month-old daughter, my wife and I first explored the Loire on one of our regular annual busman's holidays. It was later to prove a useful stopping off place, outward bound or returning from wine regions in the south.

## *Sweet Vintages at a Glance*

**Outstanding** ★★★★★

1928, 1937, 1947, 1949, 1959

**Very Good** ★★★★

1934, 1945

**Good** ★★★

1933, 1953, 1955

## 1928 ★★★★★

A great vintage. Well-structured wines with excellent acidity. Now scarce. A few sweet wines have survived.

**Anjou, Rablay** **Caves de la Maison Prunier** A wonderful wine, tasted over a dozen times, first in 1982 when, at the suggestion of Mme Prunier, whom I knew when she ran her famous restaurant in St James's Street, I visited the Prunier-Traktir cellars in Paris. There, to my astonishment, among old Sauternes was a colossal quantity of the '28 Rablay. It had been bought after the vintage during one of Mme Prunier's father's annual visits to the Loire and shipped to his cellars in the spring of 1929 for bottling. Then came the Depression, followed by the war. In the post-war period not only was the wine considered too old but the taste then was for Chablis and the dry acidic wines of Sancerre.

After I had taken stock, Monsieur Barnagaud-Prunier suggested that I try a half bottle of the '28 at lunch with his Dover sole. And I drank the lot! Not like me. What first struck me was the bottle itself, a heavyweight with wire over the top of the cork, presumably – as it was a sweet wine – in case of secondary fermentation. It was relatively pale in colour, sound as a bell, with honeyed bottle age, still fairly sweet (I think it had been *moelleux* rather than *doux* – Monsieur Prunier told me that a medium-sweet Loire wine was traditional with Dover sole), with lovely flavour, body, and sustaining acidity. It was outstanding. The problem was how to market 100 dozen bottles and as many halves. I decided to put it all in one sale, with a tasting note and samples for tasting. At the subsequent auction at Christie's (December 1982) I bought some for the wine department's boardroom luncheons, and a few bottles and halves for myself. Although there was some variation of condition in the halves, every bottle I have since tasted has been consistently good, so there is no point in a blow-by-blow description of one.

Between 1991 and 1993 I served it at boardroom luncheons. When I poured this golden-coloured wine, guests wondered what it could be, but all agreed it was perfect with sole Véronique. The rest I drank at meals at home. At random, a note made at a Sunday lunch in the country, August 1997: fabulous amber-gold with apple-green rim; lovely, very Chenin Blanc honey, with a refreshing whiff of 'lemon curd' acidity; medium-sweet, glorious flavour, good body and perfect acidity – even better after two hours in the glass. Most recently, still gloriously rich on the nose, with perfect acidity. *Last served at a wine dinner at home, May 2001* ★★★★

**Moulin-Touchais** One of the largest Loire estates, with 145ha of vines, of which this Coteaux du Layon is a fraction of its production. Though an old note, mentioned because it was the oldest vintage of an extremely large cache from the cellars of the Touchais family which found its way to England in the 1970s. Yellow, gold highlights; the smell of damp straw in a thoroughbred stable; medium-sweet, rich, sustaining acidity. *Tasted 1981* ★★★★

## 1933 ★★★

A good vintage, scarce and not tasted recently. The once omnipresent **Moulin-Touchais** and **Ch de Fesles** from Bonnezeaux were both good in the early 1980s.

## 1934 ★★★★

The second-best Loire vintage of the 1930s. **Poniatowski's Vouvray, Clos Baudoin** tasting well in the early 1980s.

## 1937 ★★★★★

Vying with 1921 and 1928 as the greatest pre-war Loire wine vintage of the century. Again, no recent notes but **Arrault's Saché** excellent at 40 years of age and **Moulin-Touchais**, thanks to botrytis, (not all the sweet Touchais wines were thus blessed) like Tate and Lyle Golden Syrup in the 1980s.

## 1945 ★★★★

Small crop of excellent wines. **Ch de Breuil**, **Marc Bougrier's Coteaux du Layon** and **Moulin-Touchais** were all good.

## 1947 ★★★★★

The greatest post-war vintage. Beautiful wines made and jealously hoarded, yet over the past few years odd bottles have been culled from the original estates, in particular fine well-preserved Vouvrays which had benefited from a gloriously hot summer and early autumn with perfect conditions for the growth of *Botrytis cinerea* or 'noble rot'.

**Moulin-Touchais** First tasted in 1982: a Beerenauslese-like nose, lovely flavour, crisp finish. Most recently, the first of a trio of '47s, two bottles of each just to make sure, at one of Stephen Kaplan's wine dinners. Slight bottle variation, both with an attractive, rich, yellow-gold colour; one with a whiff of gravy, the other of linoleum; both medium-sweet, one on the hefty side with a flavour of barley sugar and caramel, the other more assertive. *Last tasted in Chicago, April 1997* ★★ *Intriguing but past their best.*

**Vouvray, Colnot** **Marc Brédif** From his 20-ha estate based in Rochecorbon. Several notes, showing well in the 1980s, golden; honeyed; medium-sweet, complete. More recently, at Kaplan's dinner in 1997: two bottles which, I noted from the labels, had been 'selected by Fenton Wines'. Colin Fenton and I had been contemporaries at Harvey's in the mid-1950s. He had impeccable taste and after he left, in the early 1960s, he imported Salon champagne and other fine wines. Two bottles, two glasses, helpfully differentiated by coloured discs: 'on my left', as the referee would announce, in the blue (glass) corner: slightly hazy amber; sweet, rich blackberry-like nose; sweet, lean, lovely flavour and acidity. The red disc wine was a bright amber-gold; crisp, minty; less sweet, crisp with dry finish. No honeyed botrytis noted. Most recently, served by Robin Yapp, a long-time friend and specialist in Rhône and Loire wines, at a lunch in his garden. 'Carte Noir' appeared on the label and though the bottle had an 11-cm ullage and the wine was slightly cloudy, its amber-gold, apple-green rim was glorious in the sunlight; nose sound; now medium-dry – perhaps it had never been *doux* – good body, delicious old-gold taste and crisp, dry finish. Daphne and I were on our way to a funeral in Dorset and Yapp's village was en route. Unfortunately we were late, got lost and arrived at the wake just as everyone was leaving. *Last tasted Aug 2000* ★★★

**Vouvray Bourrillon-Dorléans** Also from Rochecorbon. One of two '47s presented by the distinguished Professor Jacques Puisais, one of the world's great tasters, living in Tours – the heart of the Loire Valley – and Jacques Coulis, at a tasting in London of 'some of the top vintages of the Loire produced this century'. Amber-gold; a nose and taste like freshly picked mushrooms, acidity holding it up and a surprisingly good finish. *June 1999* ★★

**Vouvray Jean-Pierre Laisement** Extraordinarily rich bouquet of raisins and old apples; sweet, delicious. *At the Puisais' Loire tasting in London, June 1999* ★★★★

**Vouvray, Le Haut-Lieu, moelleux Huët** Superb wine from the famous *clos* on the slopes above the small town of Vouvray. Whether the venerable and venerated Gaston Huët, now well into his 80s, made this wine or just stood by, I do not know. Four recent notes, the first a pair at Kaplan's dinner in April 1997, both had a glorious, warm, orange-gold colour; the 'blue label' with an excellent albeit hefty nose; sweet, with a nice blend of fat and acidity, the 'red label' sweeter and richer, a powerful wine with excellent acidity – both were outstanding with cheese. Showing well that October at Bob Dickinson's opening Bacchus Society dinner at Joe's Stone Crabs restaurant in Miami, more than one bottle. No faults. Coincidentally, just a month later: medium-deep warm amber with gold highlights; a deeply honeyed bouquet, dried apricots and vanilla; still deliciously sweet, rich, like *crème brûlée*, excellent acidity and overall condition. It cut the terrine of duck *foie gras* effortlessly. *Last tasted, with immense pleasure, at a Gidleigh Park wine weekend, Devon, Nov 1997. At its best* ★★★★★

**Vouvray Caves de la Maison Prunier** Both bottles emanated from the Prunier sale at Christie's. But one had a scent of apricot, fairly sweet, high acidity, and the other was slightly cloudy with a Tokaji-like, appley nose but despite its maderisation was strangely richer. *At a Bacchus Society dinner in Memphis, Sept 1999. At best* ★★

**Vouvray Foreau** A brief mention for I had always regarded this as the best '47. *Last tasted in 1986* ★★★★★

## 1949 ★★★★★

Excellent vintage, not as luscious as the '47 but with good fruit and firm structure. Two very good 4-star wines, when last tasted in the early 1980s: **Ch de la Guimonière**'s **Chaume**, the best of the seven designated Coteaux du Layon communes, and the ubiquitous **Moulin-Touchais**.

## 1953 ★★★

Good but lacking the richness and class of the '47 and '49. Probably insufficient botrytis.

**Vouvray, Le Mont Huët** Le Mont is one of Huët's three best vineyards. Medium-yellow gold; a curious Tokaji dry Szamorodni-like nose – it reminded Daphne of an old kitchen J-cloth. An effort at sweetness but with a very dry finish. *At Joe's Stone Crabs restaurant, Miami, Oct 1997* ★

## 1955 ★★★

The summer lacked heat though botrytis helped. Three old notes, all in the early 1980s. By far the best: **Ch de la Guimonière**'s **Chaume** ★★★★; **Moulin-Touchais** not at its best

★★; **Brédif**'s **Vouvray** dry, austere but drinking quite well ★★★
**Chinon, Clos de L'Olive Couly-Dutheil** Soft, mature, rich; unusual, very distinctive fragrance; flavour of dried raspberries and *fraises des bois*. Dry, acidic finish. *At the Vins de la Loire tasting, at Searcy's, London, June 1999* ★★★ *Rare and remarkable.*

## 1959 ★★★★★

Magnificent vintage, following an exceptionally hot summer, the best since 1947.

**Bonnezeaux Ch des Gauliers, Foarlinne-Boivin** Jean Boivin was behind the moves to make Bonnezeaux, south of Angers, the first district to be awarded *cru* status by the INAO. (Jean's son describes the difference between Bonnezeaux and Quarts de Chaume with French felicity in Jacqueline Friedrich's book on the Loire: 'The two are brothers, not twins. The first is nervier, the Quarts fatter. A good Bonnezeaux is a vivacious stand-up wine. It does not recline like Mme Récamier. Quarts is more languorous'). Boivin's '59 has a good golden colour; rather caramelly, 'calf's foot jelly' nose; medium-sweet, hefty, excellent acidity, dry finish. *At Yapp's sunlit lunch, Aug 2000* ★★★

**Coteaux du Layon, Chaume Ch de la Guimonière** First tasted in 1982: perfect colour, nose and taste though austere, probably no botrytis. More recently, a creamy Chenin nose; fairly sweet and assertive, with lovely flavour and weight. Drinking perfectly and no signs of fatigue. *At a splendid wine dinner with my old friend Lou Skinner in his timewarp house in Coral Gables, Florida, March 1995*

**Moulin-Touchais** Seven notes: the youngest and most impressive vintage at an Imperial College line-up in 1991. Certainly a highly distinctive wine albeit with considerable variations; on the whole very good in its way. Most recently, medium-pale gold, good colour for its richness and age; ripe Chenin nose with slightly varnishy overtones (noted on previous occasions); fairly sweet, fullish, firm, with a singed butterscotch flavour. 'Very good in its way' repeated. *Last noted at a Kaplan dinner in Los Angeles, Feb 1998* ★★★★

**Vouvray Marc Brédif** Not star bright, a sliver of sediment, so decanted to enhance its shimmering yellow-gold colour; good nose; medium-sweet, correct weight, original flavour, good acidity. *Went well with Daphne's chicken liver pâté at a vinous dinner party, May 2000* ★★★

**Vouvray Foreau** A flat yellow; very good honeyed nose; medium-dry, good flavour and plenty of life. *Oct 1982* ★★★★

**Vouvray, Clos Naudin, moelleux Foreau** Though old notes, a wonderful four-star wine 'with ten to fifteen years' more life when tasted in the early 1980s. Probably still good.

---

### Quarts de Chaume and Bonnezeaux

*These two enclaves within the Coteaux du Layon appellation south of Angers produce superior sweet wines from botrytised Chenin Blanc grapes. Vineyards here benefit from autumn mists rising from the Layon, a minor tributary of the Loire, which encourage the production of botrytis or noble rot, as in Sauternes. Production of these wines is very small, and not guaranteed every vintage, as it is totally dependent on the onset of noble rot. Chenin Blanc's naturally high acidity makes the perfect foil for the intense sweetness of the concentrated, botrytised juice, and these delicious golden, viscous wines can last (and improve) for many decades. I first visited the area in 1959 and well recall picnicking on the banks of the Layon.*

# 1960–1989

With travel and currency restrictions eased, the 'Garden of France' became a popular destination, its main attractions being the glorious châteaux. Nothing like fresh trout with the local wine. But back home the wines did not taste the same; the modest Anjou Rosé, I noted, was less appealing.

Restaurants offered the same old – or rather young – Muscadet, Sancerre and Pouilly-Fumé. However, one small company frequently mentioned in my notes, Yapp Brothers, was more innovative. Robin Yapp, an ex-dentist, recognised what would now be called a 'niche market' for two taken-for-granted wine areas, each coincidentally bordering France's great rivers, the Loire and the Rhône. Based in Mere, a village roughly halfway between London and 'the West Country', he sourced wines from small but high quality producers. Yapp's have long been the main supplier of our 'elevenses', the perfect time to drink the sweeter whites from Anjou and Touraine. Even the older wines of the best vintages can still be delectable.

## Sweet Vintages at a Glance
**Outstanding ★★★★★**
1964, 1989
**Very Good ★★★★**
1962, 1971, 1976, 1985, 1986, 1988
**Good ★★★**
1966, 1969, 1975, 1978, 1982

## 1960
A poor start to the decade, but also the vintages '63, '65, '67, '68 (particularly awful) '72, '74 and '77 not worthy of mention. The wines are of no interest now.

## 1961 ★★
Good for dry Loire wines, but not for sweet. Even **Moulin-Touchais** was below par. *1982* ★★

## 1962 ★★★★
I am surprised I haven't more notes, for it was a very good vintage despite being overshadowed by the rich '64s. **Moulin-Touchais** *1981* ★★★★

## 1964 ★★★★★
The best vintage of the decade for the *demi-sec, moelleux* and *doux* wines. The dry whites lacked acidity and have long since departed. Many of the sweeter wines were drunk with enjoyment in the 1970s and were at peak in the early 1980s.
**Bonnezeaux Ch des Gauliers** So good in the early 1970s that I bought some from Robin Yapp in 1973. For the next seven years it was delightful: bright, lively yellow; medium-sweetness which seemed to spread itself in the mouth, yet very refined for a ripe Loire wine, and with enough acidity to balance its richness. More recently, at 21 years of age: a deeper straw-gold; beyond bottle age, slight maderisation; now medium, drying out, but a good old apricots flavour and supporting acidity. *Last noted at Lou Skinner's, March 1995* ★★
**Vouvray, moelleux Marc Brédif** Lanolin yellow; lanolin on the nose too. Mature Chenin, reminding me of lemon cheese cake. Now dry but with a lovely flavour. *At Jodi and Bob Dickinson's, Miami, Nov 1997* ★★★

**OTHER GOOD '64S IN THE 4-STAR CATEGORY**, last tasted between 1982 and 1984: **Ch de Fesles'** Bonnezeaux a heavily bemedalled wine; **Ch de Guimonière's** Coteaux du Layon and **Moulin-Touchais** plump yet shapely, 'strangely attractive'.

## 1966 ★★★
Better for dry wines than for sweet.
**Bonnezeaux Ch de Fesles** Dryish, lacking zest. *1982* ★★

## 1969 ★★★
Quite the opposite to 1966, better for sweet than for dry, the acidity providing a good sustaining backbone for the richer Anjou and Vouvray wines. However none tasted recently. In the early 1980s the best were **Ch de Fesles'** Bonnezeaux, **Brédif's** Vouvray demi-sec, and **Moulin-Touchais**.
**St-Nicolas-de-Bourgueil, Vignoble de la Jarnoterie Mabileau-Rèze** The only red '69 tasted recently: very mature, brown-tinged; harmonious, soft brown sugar nose and taste. Good in its way. *At the Vins de la Loire tasting, June 1999* ★★

## 1970 ★★
This was a vintage of abundance, not class. Some decent *demi-sec* made but it was not a sweet wine year.

## 1971 ★★★★
A very good vintage. Stylish, elegant, with zestful and sustaining acidity. The best of the sweet wines still very good.
**Quarts de Chaume Dom Baumard** Surprisingly pale for its age (then nearly 20 years old), lovely waxy Chenin aroma that so often reminds me of Sémillon without its attendant acidity. Lovely wine. Perfect acidity. *From a Marie-Jeanne at a Wine & Food Society dinner, Aug 1989* ★★★★
**Vouvray, Clos du Bourg, sec Huët** An unusual opportunity to taste a 26-year-old quality dry wine from a leading producer: remarkably pale for its age and very bright; dry, good length, flavour and acidity. *'Dining with wine' at Gidleigh Park, Devon, Nov 1997* ★★★
**Vouvray, Clos du Bourg, moelleux Huët** If Gaston Huët's dry was good, the soft and sweet wine was bound to be excellent. And so it was: palish; most attractive, honeyed

botrytis nose; fairly sweet, lovely flavour, perfect acidity. I must take my hat off to Paul Henderson for finding such fascinating wines for his wine weekends. He and his chef do all the work. I am merely 'the performing monkey'. *At Gidleigh Park, Devon, Nov 1997* ★★★★

## 1973 ★★

Better for dry wines but some Vouvrays and Layons attractive in their early years.
**Quarts de Chaume Dom Baumard** Fragrant, medium sweet, its richness beginning to be touched by malt. *April 1989* ★★

## 1975 ★★★

Good vintage for dry and sweet. Now mainly *passé*.
**Moulin-Touchais** In the early 1980s: sweet, rich, powerful, almost pungent. More recently, a palish yellow-gold; very strange nose, scented Chenin, vanilla, violets, and almond paste; equally strange taste, raw, artificial, acidic. Oh dear! *My old friend Nils Sternby scoured the world for '75s for his 65th birthday and retirement dinner. Last tasted April 1995. At one time* ★★
**Quarts de Chaume Dom Baumard** Creamy, good fruit, crisp. *Aug 1985* ★★★

## 1976 ★★★★

An extremely hot summer, a drought year in northern Europe. An early harvest of super-ripe grapes. I enjoyed many of these sweet whites in the 1980s but, to my surprise, I have tasted none since. These hot years produced the best reds though they are now, of course, hard to find.
**Bourgueil, Cuvée Ploquin, Dom du Chêne Arrault Christophe Deschamps** Fairly deep, soft, red, rich core; soft yet hefty fruit, showing some age; extremely good for its age on the palate. Still very tannic. *At the Vins de la Loire tasting at Searcy's, London, June 1999* ★★★★

## 1978 ★★★

A good dry white vintage. Of no interest now.

## 1979 ★★

Another good year for dry Loire wines, by which I mean wines from the extreme west (Muscadet) and the extreme east (Sancerre and Pouilly-Fumé), as well as the good dry Vouvrays from Touraine in between. There were also some attractive sweet Coteaux du Layon wines too, but these have now gone the way of all flesh!

### Gidleigh Park

*A secret wine hideaway at the end of a long, winding country lane in Chagford, Devon. Not only is this the most deliciously calm, tranquil hotel, with superb views over the surrounding countryside, but Paul Henderson's wine list is unequalled. Estimable old Bordeauxs, burgundies and Rhônes are accompanied by ancient Loires and classics from Italy, Spain and California. Gidleigh has proved the most delightful setting for a number of memorable tastings. For some years I hosted annually one of Paul's wine weekends. Many wines tasted there are dotted about these pages.*

## 1980 ★★

The worst summer of the period: six weeks of uninterrupted rain, a disaster for the dry whites. A late harvest, the second week in October, the sweet, botrytised grape-picking rudely interrupted by snow! Despite these handicaps, some pleasant *demi-secs* including **Brédif**'s **Vouvray** *Tasted Oct 1989* ★★★

## 1981 ★★

Small harvest and mediocre wines.

## 1982 ★★★

A large crop of ripe grapes. The dry wines, though lacking acidity, were popular in their youth. Excellent for reds. I have no record of tasting any sweet wines.
**St-Nicolas de Bourgueil, Dom Les Quarterons Clos des Quarterons** Good colour, rich, ruby with mature rim; ripe Cabernet Franc nose; unusually rich and fleshy, good flavour. Holding well. *At the Vins de la Loire tasting, June 1999* ★★★★

## 1983 ★★

Very mixed weather conditions and some mediocre wines. Only one sweet '83 ever tasted.
**Moulin-Touchais** Lovely colour; a heavy, oily, curious goaty-scented nose; sweet, hefty, coarse. One of an astonishing array of sweet wines at a British Airways tasting, 31 in all, including Sauternes, Alsace, German, Austrian and Tokaji. How I survived, I do not know. *July 1992* ★★

## 1984 ★

This turned out to be the last of a batch of very uneven, mainly mediocre Loire vintages. I felt sorry for the growers. A **Saumur-Champigny** was good with sausages!

## 1985 ★★★★

A great improvement. In particular, the central Loire vineyards of Anjou and Vouvray enjoyed unbroken hot and dry weather from the third week in August right through to early November. Also particularly good year for the reds, Chinon, Bourgueil and Saumur-Champigny. (Unless you have a penchant for tart wines, it is better to buy and drink Loire reds only in really good – hot – years.)

I have tasted few sweet wines and only one in the 1990s.
**Coteaux du Layon, Chaume Ch de la Roulerie** Waxy yellow; scented, honeyed Chenin nose and flavour. Good acidity. *June 1991* ★★★★ *Wine of this quality should still be good.*

## 1986 ★★★★

A very good, indeed ideal, year for the dry whites – Sancerre and Pouilly-Fumé the best of the decade. Only one sweet wine noted.
**Quarts de Chaume Dom Baumard** Palish; medium-sweet, lovely flavour, good acidity but showing its age. Needed drinking. *Pub supper at The Nobody Inn at Doddiscombsleigh, near Exeter. A tiny village whose only raison d'être is this remarkable establishment with one of the best wine (and Scotch whisky) lists in England, Aug 1992* ★★★

# 1987 *

Dry wines only. Now long past their sell-by date.

# 1988 ★★★★

A very satisfactory all-round vintage for reds and dry and semi-sweet whites. Several *demi-sec* '88s noted in the early 1990s, not for keeping.

**Bourgueil Dom de la Closerie** Raspberry red, weak rim; aroma of squashed raspberries; *medium-dry, soft, earthy, rustic character. At the Vins de la Loire tasting, London, June 1999* ★★★

# 1989 ★★★★★

Exceptional winter conditions: early budding, flowering advanced by three weeks and a very hot summer. A superb vintage for the semi and sweet whites, a quintessential Chenin year, on a par with 1947. The Chinon and Bourgueil reds were excellent, the dry whites from Sancerre and Pouilly-Fumé being atypical, a bit too plump, alcoholic and lacking acidity.

**Bonnezeaux Ch de Fesles, J Boivin** Pale; lovely, sweet, minty nose and flavour. Perfect acidity. Still immature though its hard finish proved excellent with cheeses. *Also noted at The Nobody Inn, Devon, Aug 1992. Then* ★★★(★★) *Probably perfect now.*

**Coteaux du Layon Ch de la Roulerie** Buttercup yellow, honeyed; sweet, quite assertive, very attractive. *Lunch in the country, Sept 1993* ★★★★ *Lovely now, will keep for another ten years.*

**Coteaux du Layon, Clos Ste-Cathérine Baumard** Surprisingly pale; a very original scent, ripe melon and peach; fairly sweet, good flesh, fabulous flavour, perfect balance and acidity. Still a touch of immature hardness. *With caramelised pear tarte tatin at an IWFS dinner at the Cadogan – a quiet, very characterful and traditional hotel in Sloane Street, April 1997* ★★★★(★)

**Jasnières, Les Truffières, moelleux J-B Pinon** A small producer at La Chartre-sur-le-Loir (Le Loir is a tributary of La Loire). One of a range bought on two occasions from Yapp Brothers – Robin Yapp's lists are temptingly informative. First tasted in July 1994, shortly after the first purchase, noting incidentally that it had been described in the list as a 'rare Comet year *moelleux*': palish yellow still with a youthful green tinge; sweet, lightly honeyed Chenin nose; medium-sweet, soft, delicious flavour, complete but still a bit harsh. Also I thought it lacked a little charm and decided to give the rest some bottle age. Two bottles broached six years later, both opened for our weekend elevenses at Chippenham Lodge. Medium-pale, waxy yellow; fragrant, classic, grassy, cress-like Chenin blanc; moderate weight (alcohol 12.5%), pleasant flavour, adequate acidity, its finish softer but still a bit unexciting. *Last noted Dec 2000* ★★★ *I have more but doubt if it will be more than an agreeable mid-morning drink, or perhaps with cheese.*

**Quarts de Chaume Ch de Suronde, Zuffourade** On the pale side; fairly sweet, perfect weight and acidity, creamy texture, lovely flavour. *At Lou Skinner's, Coral Gables, March 1995* ★★★★

**St-Nicolas de Bourgueil, 'Les Harquerets' Dom de la Cotelleraie, Maison Gérald Vallée** Medium-pale, soft red, pink rimmed; a ripe and most appealing raspberry-like (Cabernet Franc) nose; sweeter and richer than normal. Delicious. I am not a huge fan of Loire reds, but in a ripe vintage like this they can be most attractive. *At the Vins de la Loire tasting at Searcy's, London, June 1999* ★★★★

**Vouvray, demi-sec Bourillon-Dorléans** Many notes, from just after purchase in 1992: palish, medium-dry as indicated, with cheese, and as a mid-morning drink in the country. Better as it gained even a little bottle age, its nose becoming more honeyed, rather like a waxy Sémillon. Alas, all consumed. *My last note made at home, April 1994* ★★★

**Vouvray, moelleux, réserve Daniel Jarry** Another Yapp purchase, first tasted in July 1994: bright yellow; waxy nose, leafy Chenin; medium-sweet, lovely 'clover leaf' flavour, agreeable weight (alcohol 12.5%), very good acidity giving it a hard but refreshing finish. Perfect mid-morning refresher – and the next day. Four years later, between Jarry's *demi-sec* '96 and Prunier's Anjou '28: grassy nose, bottle age and botrytis honey undertone; touch of caramel developing at its edge. *Last tasted at lunch, Aug 1998* ★★★ *Probably at its best.*

**Vouvray, doux/liquoreux Daniel Jarry** Distinctive yellow with lemon gold highlights; very good, honeyed, waxy Chenin nose and flavour, not much sweeter (or more expensive) than the *moelleux* but with a soft, rich mid-palate and counterbalancing acidity. Also bought from Yapp Brothers. *A perfect summer drink. July 2000* ★★★★

**Vouvray, Clos Baudoin Prince Poniatowski** The prince's great, great-uncle was the last King of Poland. The family came to France in 1855 and, liking the wine, Philippe Poniatowski's grandfather bought the estate, Clos Baudoin being the 'signature' wine (according to Jacqueline Friedrich). First noted at a British Airways tasting in June 1992: pale; grassy, minty nose; medium-sweet, very good flavour and acidity but unsuitable as a dessert wine. Most recently, at Jacques Puisais' top Loire tasting: now a slightly deeper yellow; low-keyed but ripe nose; medium-sweet, lovely flavour and length with crisp, dry finish. Delicious. *Last tasted June 1999* ★★★★ *Perfect now or keep for another 10 years.*

**Vouvray, Cuvée Florent Duplessis-Maury** Good classic Chenin nose and flavour. Probably *demi-sec*, certainly medium-dry. A perfect cheese wine. *Dinner at The Lodge, Lanai (Hawaii), Sept 1992* ★★★

**Vouvray, Le Haut-Lieu, moelleux, 1er trie Huët** A lovely wine first tasted in May 1991; then a waxy yellow-green; honeyed botrytis nose; medium-sweet (residual sugar 100g/l), fairly substantial (alcohol 12.9%) and excellent acidity (5.70g/l). Glorious flavour but still a bit hard. Most recently: now a yellow-gold; harmonious bouquet; delicious flavour, perfect balance. *Last noted at a pre-sale tasting in Geneva, May 1999* ★★★★ *Good for another five to ten years.*

OTHER VERY GOOD '89s all tasted in May 1991 and which should still be drinking well: **Bonnezeaux, La Montagne Dom de Petit Val** medium-sweet, full-bodied, good fruit and acidity ★★★★; **Coteaux du Layon, Beaulieu, Clos des Ortinières Dom d'Ambinos** lovely, soft yet excellent acidity ★★★★ long life; **Quarts de Chaume Ch de Bellerive** full-bodied, good acidity, 'needs time' ★★★★; **Vouvray, Clos du Bourg, moelleux Huët** fairly deep yellow; 'butter mint' nose, wonderful flavour, length and aftertaste ★★★★★; and **Vouvray, Cuvée Constance, moelleux Huët** made from botrytis-affected grapes from Huët's three vineyards, Le Haut Lieu, Le Mont and Le Clos du Bourg. Yield only 5hl/ha, 390g/l sugar in the juice, long fermentation in barrel just achieving 10.9% alcohol, leaving 162g/l residual sugar. A sort of Loire Beerenauslese. Even at scarcely two years old, it was a rich, golden colour; pure honeyed botrytis nose and flavour. The most perfect Loire wine I have ever tasted. ★★★★★★ *(6-stars). Will be lovely now but will probably stay delicious for at least another 20 years.*

# 1990–1999

A decade blessed with more than its fair share of good vintages and lovely wines, as my somewhat arbitrary selection of notes will indicate, some peaking, some which will benefit from further bottle age.

## Vintages at a Glance
**Outstanding** ★★★★★
1990, 1997
**Very Good** ★★★★
1995, 1996
**Good** ★★★
1993, 1998 (v), 1999

## 1990 ★★★★★

Another excellent vintage for early-picked dry whites, for reds and the medium-sweet to sweet wines. Weather conditions not easy for the flowering which, though early, was uneven. Drought and scorching sun tempered by later rains. Early morning mists in October enabled superb and sweet wines to be made. I was much taken with this vintage. Firmer and less luscious than the '89s; I bought and drank a lot.

**Azay-le-Rideau, moelleux G Pavy at Saché** Surprisingly pale; lightly honeyed Chenin nose; drier than expected, light (alcohol 11.5%), pleasant, easy style, good acidity: a perfect mid-morning weekend summer drink. *July 1993* ★★★★

**Coteaux du Layon, Chaume, Les Aunis, Cuvée Louis Ch de la Roulerie** First tasted at lunch on Christmas Day, 1993: most attractive wine but no good with plum pudding! A month later at a less stressful family lunch: already a pronounced yellow gold; glorious nose; remarkably sweet, full-bodied (alcohol 14%), fat, delicious. Another half bottle greedily shared by Daphne and me. *The last two notes made at after-theatre suppers in 1996; ideal* ★★★★★

**Coteaux du Layon, Ch La Tomaze, Cuvée Les Lys Lecointre** First tasted in June 1994 at Yapp Brothers' 25th anniversary lunch: palish, touch of youthful green; grassy, scented, medium-sweet, very enjoyable. I must have bought some, for my next note was the following month: better as a mid-morning drink than with a meal. Delicious. A few months later, noting its very minty, peach-like scent; touch of almonds. Most recently: now a luminous, lanolin and buttercup yellow; curious waxy bouquet, raw apricot and honey, 'powdery blancmange'; but still sweet, fat, full and rich, with very good acidity and finish. *Last noted at elevenses, Jan 2001* ★★★★ *Seemingly years of life left.*

**Montlouis, Grains Nobles Michel et Laurent Berger** First noted at a Yapp tasting in September 1995. Before that, few of even the best bottles purchased from Yapp had been over £10, but this was a more serious £273 per dozen. A sweet, rather raspberry-like scent; rich of course, lovely flavour and with the customary Loire acidity. I next dipped into it in 1998. By now it was a more distinctive, waxy yellow but still had a delightful, delicate, lime-blossom and honey bouquet and flavour like ripe melons and peaches. Next, at elevenses: a ripe melon-yellow; sweet, peachy, raisiny; lovely fruit and flesh, glorious mid-palate, perfect weight (alcohol 13%), richness masking Loire acidity. Delicious with ripe apricots. *July 1999* ★★★★★

**Quarts de Chaume Dom Baumard** Medium-pale yellow; waxy peach-skin, Chenin nose; medium-sweet, good flavour

and acidity. Harsh finish. *Dining with the Josey family in Houston, Aug 2000* ★★★(★) *Even after ten years, still not fully developed.*

**Quarts de Chaume Ch de l'Echarderie** First noted in December 1993: fairly pale; lovely, sweet Chenin aroma (best not to serve these wines too cold); excellent flavour and balance. Many bottles tasted since – I must have been one of Robin Yapp's best customers. In 1997 I noted it drier than expected, more *demi-sec* than *moelleux*. Most recently, noting its smooth texture, rich flavour and good length. *Last tasted at Sunday morning elevenses, July 2000* ★★★★ *Happily I still have a few bottles left.*

**Savennières, Clos du Papillon Joly** A famous property and my favourite Loire dry white. I had forgotten this bottle so opened it to see how it had survived. Now a distinct touch of yellow; nose low-keyed, bottle age but sound; bone dry (as are most Savennières), austere, firm, distinctive flavour and holding well. *Tasted at Chippenham Lodge, March 2002* ★★★★

**Vouvray, Trie des Grains Nobles Dom des Aubuisières** A delectable half bottle shared by Daphne and me on BA 244 from Santiago to London, following our visit to Chile as guests of the Trade Commissioner. I think they only had one half bottle on board – the other First Class passengers didn't know what they were missing. A lovely waxy-sheened gold; gloriously sweet nose and taste, 'honey and flowers' (sounds like a gentleman's hair dressing). This was in March 1994. *The following January, this time with cheese at a British Airways wine committee dinner at Mosimann's. Perfection* ★★★★★

**Vouvray, Clos Naudin, moelleux Foreau** Outstandingly lovely nose, immensely fragrant; sweet, fat, soft – only 9.5% alcohol – perfect acidity. *At the De Biggaarden restaurant, Brussels, Jan 1996* ★★★★★

**Vouvray, Clos Baudoin, moelleux Prince Poniatowski** Paler than his '89; minty, acidic nose; curiously sweet. Good but lacked the fat of the '89. *Tasted June 1999* ★★★

## 1991

An atrocious growing season. The Loire, of all French regions, most affected by severe frosts which decimated many

---

### 'Elevenses'

*The term 'elevenses' may not be familiar to readers outside the UK. It refers to a mid-morning drink. In the office, rather than coffee, I would offer visitors madeira. At home, particularly in the spring and summer, it is almost invariably a semi-sweet Loire or German wine, the sort not dry enough to serve as an aperitif or with a meal (except as an accompaniment to cheese) and not sweet enough to qualify as a dessert wine.*

*So, for our 'elevenses' at Chippenham Lodge, we indulge – modestly – in either an estate-bottled Auslese from the Rhine or, more frequently, a moelleux from Vouvray or the Coteaux du Layon. Opened on the Saturday morning, we enjoy a couple of glasses, put the bottle back in the fridge alongside the milk, and continue on the Sunday morning in lieu of communion wine!*

vineyards. Despite a hot summer, rain spoiled the harvest. There was some botrytis which enabled a few sweet wines to be made, but I haven't tasted any.

# 1992 ★★

Growing season good until the end of July, thereafter variable sun, rain and humidity. Some good – much welcomed after the previous year's frosts – dry whites. Muscadet and the Sauvignon Blanc of Sancerre and Pouilly-Fumé of little interest now. The reds from Chinon and Bourgueil were also quite successful, the best of which will have survived. Some sweet whites.

**Coteaux du Layon, La Roche Ch de la Genaiserie** Attractive nose; some sweetness, very acidic; and **Les Simonelles** neutral nose; hard, slightly medicinal. *Both tasted at home – weekend wines – April 1999* ★★

**Vouvray, demi-sec Daniel Jarry** Palish yellow, lime-tinged; crisp, acidic, young fruit; more *sec* than *demi*. Dry, gooseberry-like acidity. A pleasant enough, youthful refresher. Not our idea of an elevenses, better with trout. *July 1994* ★★ *Too old now.*

SEVERAL REFRESHING DRY '92S ENJOYED IN THE EARLY 1990S, among the best Sancerres: **A Vatan's Cuvée St-Francis** fragrant. *1994* ★★; **Paul Millerioux' Clos du Roy** good fruit and acidity. *1994* ★★★; and **Pierre Bonnet's Les Roysiers** white currant and tomcats. *1994* ★★★; but most wines, like **Pabiot's Pouilly-Fumé**, merely adequate ★★

# 1993 ★★★

Seemingly better weather conditions than the rest of France. Sancerre and Pouilly-Fumé did not start picking until 8 October and were caught by the rain. However, the later botrytis-affected grapes made some good, sweet wines.

**Bonnezeaux Cuvée Mathilde Marc Angeli** First noted at a Yapp tasting in 1995. Then palish; honeyed; sweet, lovely apricot flavour. Again in 1996, noting its power and length. By 1998 gaining colour; peaches and apricots on the nose. Most recently, orange-tinged amber; very good, sweet, honeyed bouquet – bottle age and botrytis; medium-sweet, delicious flavour, with tinglingly acidic finish. Hopeless with stewed pears. *Dining at home, Oct 1999* ★★★★

**Coteaux du Layon, La Roche Ch de la Genaiserie** Strange nose; sweet, crisp, not bad. *At a British Airways tasting for First Class dessert wines, April 1996* ★★

**Vouvray Dom des Aubuisières** Sweet nose; medium-sweet, attractive flavour and good acidity. *April 1994* ★★★ *Youthful then – should be fully evolved now.*

# 1994 ★★

The region was badly hit by frosts in mid-April. However, it was very hot from June to mid-August, then wet. There was a change for the better after 26 September, when sun and botrytis enabled some sweet wines to be made. The dry whites were totally unmemorable.

**Coteaux du Layon, Sélection de Grains Nobles Philippe Delesvaux** Medium-deep amber-gold; a curious, oily edge though some honeyed botrytis, just missed being very good; fairly sweet, fullish body, not bad but not quite right. *Hosting a post-tasting dinner at La Maison du Cygne, Brussels, March 1999* ★ *Disappointing.*

# 1995 ★★★★

Successful throughout the Loire, from Muscadet to Sancerre and Pouilly-Fumé though the latter neighbouring *appellations* were untypically rich. The reds were good and the sweet whites, where there was careful grape selection, were very good indeed – the sort of wines I like.

For interest, I mention one or two Sancerres which, on the whole, were best drunk around two years after the vintage. These were certainly not wines to hang on to.

**Coteaux du Layon, Ch la Tomaze Lecointre** A perfect spring mid-morning drink in 1999: medium-pale, straw-yellow; low-keyed, slightly grassy, 'hard honey'; medium-sweet, medium body (alcohol 12.5%), a flavour that reminded me of my favourite Bassett's Liquorice Allsorts coconut wheels. Good acidity. A really pleasant straightforward Layon and modestly priced (I paid Yapp £6.50 per bottle. A year later, the price had gone up to £7.25). I noted an unusually soft lanolin, Chenin Blanc taste, with some fat and flesh. The same again the following spring, always mid-morning. On both occasions the nose had opened up, sweet, floral and seemed sweeter on the palate. *Last tasted March 2001* ★★★★ *I hope it will go on improving, for I have a few bottles left.*

**Sancerre Ch de Sancerre** Very good, crisp Sauvignon Blanc; bone dry, austere. *May 1997* ★★★

**Sancerre, Cuvée Pierre J Balland-Chapuis** Palish, lime-tinged; rich, flowery, not too dry, soft, speciously attractive flavour. About maximum age, not for keeping. *May 1999* ★★★

**Sancerre, Clos La Néole A Vatan** Pale, green-tinged; very fragrant, minty; not too dry, spicy taste, good acidity. *Correctly preceding the Meursaults and Vouvrays at the Bacchus Society opening dinner at Joe's Stone Crabs restaurant, Miami, Oct 1997* ★★★ *Perfect then. Not a wine to keep.* (Some of the locals regard Joe's as a tourist trap; it is in fact extremely good. But I hate to think how many thousands of crabs lose one big claw for our delectation.)

**Sancerre, Les Roches Dom Vacheron** Very pale; minty, refreshing Sauvignon Blanc; dry, lean, crisp, good length. A copybook Sancerre, perfect for drinking young and fresh. *At Gidleigh Park, Devon, Nov 1997* ★★★★

**Quincy Denis Jaumier** Crisp, fragrant; dry, minty, distinctive, good acidity. A bit austere. *Tasted at the Bluebird Club, Chelsea, Aug 1997* ★★★

**Vouvray, moelleux Dom des Aubuisières** Pale; grassy; not very sweet, mild, short. And their **Le Marigny** quite attractive. Both too young and lacking fleshy fruit and acidity. *April 1996* ★★(★)

**Vouvray, Le Clos du Bourg, 1er trie Huët** Palish; pure cress; medium-sweet, relatively lightweight (alcohol 12%), delicious flavour, perfect acidity. A seemingly effortless wine from the old master. *At a tasting for the 'Star Group' at Christie's, June 1999* ★★★(★) *My idea of a copybook Vouvray.*

**Vouvray, sec Huët** Little nose, dry, light, rather neutral flavour, good acidity. A decent fresh drink but lacking the attractiveness of the sweeter Huët wines. *Dining at Le Pont de la Tour, London, July 1999* ★★

# 1996 ★★★★

A good growing season though uneven in the spring. Growth caught up, the flowering in late June being very successful though the potentially large harvest was curtailed by drought conditions throughout the summer. Welcome rain in

September swelled the grapes and the harvest proceeded from the end of the month. However, though autumn winds helped keep rot at bay it also prevented the onset of beneficial botrytis. Nevertheless some really lovely sweet white wines were made, which should survive well into the present decade.

**Bonnezeaux Ch de Fesles** Glorious yellow; mint and honey; fairly sweet, rich, good fruit, lovely, slightly gingery flavour, good length and finesse. So much for the missing botrytis. I think this *did* benefit from noble rot. *Dec 1997* ★★★★

**Coteaux du Layon, Beaulieu Pierre-Bise** Touch of mint and caramel; fairly sweet, lovely. We didn't order this but the ever-enthusiastic Jean Luc Le Du, probably the best sommelier in New York, insisted that we taste it. *At Daniel's, New York, June 1998* ★★★(★) *Could have benefited from a bit of bottle age.*

**Coteaux du Layon, Chaume, Les Aunis, Ch de la Roulerie Ch de Fesles** The label is getting as complicated as a German wine, but it is worth every inch: palish, waxy yellow; gloriously rich nose, like dried apricots and honey; very sweet, full, rich, mouthfilling, with an unusual but good oaky-acid finish. *Elevenses, Chippenham Lodge, Dec 1997* ★★★★

**Coteaux du Layon, Chaume, Les Julines Ch de Fesles** Medium pale yellow; lovely, honeyed – pure expression of ripe Chenin Blanc; very sweet, rich, fairly powerful (alcohol 13%), lovely fruit – youthful pineapple and melon. *Elevenses at noon (we had breakfast late), at Chippenham Lodge, Dec 1997* ★★★★★

**Coteaux du Layon, Dom Pierre Blanche Lecointre** Pale, lime-tinged; sweet, rich, buttery nose and taste. Some agreeable fat, acidity completely integrated. *Elevenses, March 2002* ★★★(★) *From Yapp Brothers. Good value at under £6.*

**Coteaux du Layon, Les Omnis, Dom des Forges Dom Banchereau** A substantial estate: 35ha, of which roughly 25ha produces its sweeter wines. All hand-harvested by *trie* – combing the vines for the best ripe and botrytis-affected grapes. Fermented in steel vats. Lovely nose, honey and mint; fairly sweet, lightish style, absolutely glorious flavour with a lively touch and excellent acidity. *Showed by Tanners of Shrewsbury at The Bunch tasting, London, Jan 1998* ★★★★

**Jasnières, Dom de la Charrière, Sélection de Raisins Nobles Joël Gigou** Palish yellow, lime highlights; grassy – rather like the '95; medium-sweet, pleasant enough, fair flesh, light end acidity. Twice the price of the Domaine Pierre Blanche Coteaux du Layon above and not worth the extra. *Elevenses, at Chippenham Lodge, March 2002* ★★★ *(just).*

**Pouilly-Fumé Ch de Ladoucette** Unquestionably the most important property in Pouilly-sur-Loire, with a vast, imposing rather Victorian mansion that Daphne and I have visited only once, way back in the mid-1950s. But I have tasted the Baron de Ladoucette's wines many times, the '96 first in the Bahamas at a tasting I conducted in February 1999 for the staff of the wine merchants, Butler and Sands, and the following month at dinner in Brussels: very pale, star bright, slight green tinge which already started to make the mouth water; delicate, subtle, slightly minty Sauvignon Blanc aroma with raw gooseberry-like acidity; dry but by no means bone dry, nice weight (alcohol 12.5%), lovely fresh flavour, some flesh, excellent acidity. Perfection though perhaps a bit short. *Last tasted March 1999* ★★★★ *Will still be refreshingly attractive.*

**Pouilly-Fumé, Dom Berthiers J-C Dagueneau** Very pale; a fuller, broader style of wine to the Vacheron Sancerre, less acidic, very good in its way. *At Gidleigh Park, Devon, Nov 1997* ★★★ *I was uncertain whether this wine was best drunk at one year of age or whether another year or two might have opened it up a little more. Anyway, it's just a theoretical exercise, as these Loire Sauvignon*

*Blancs tend to be drunk almost the minute they come on to the market.*

**Pouilly-Fumé, Ch de Tracy Comtesse A d'Estutt d'Assay** Pale, green-tinged; very floral, fragrant Sauvignon Blanc; the merest touch of sweetness, fair body (alcohol 13%), but overall dry, with lip-licking acidity. One of the oldest estates in the district, celebrating their 600th anniversary in 1996. *Taken to Glyndebourne for our picnic supper, Aug 1998* ★★★

**Quincy Jacques Sallé** Jacques, a somewhat maverick journalist and publisher, happens to own a vineyard in Quincy; a district whose main distinction is that it was the second viticultural region in France, after Châteauneuf-du-Pape to be granted AOC status (I am grateful to Jacqueline Friedrich for this and other Loire tidbits): a characteristic melon yellow; crisp, Sauvignon Blanc, fairly dry, youthful grapefruit and pineappley fruit, good acidity. *At lunch at home, Jan 1999* ★★

**Sancerre, La Porte de Caillou H Bourgeois** Correct but unspectacular Sauvignon Blanc. A bit over-scented. A good food wine. *Feb 1998* ★★

**Vouvray, demi-sec Daniel Jarry** Very pale; almost Sauvignon Blanc-like acidity. More *sec* than *demi*. I added blackcurrant cordial and made a Kir. *Lunch in the country, Aug 1998* ★★

**Vouvray, moelleux Daniel Jarry** This time more *demi-sec* than *moelleux*, a pleasant, soft ripeness but very dry acidic finish. *At home, April 2001* ★★★

**Vouvray, Clos Naudin, sec Foreau** Pale; light, delightful Chenin aroma; dry, clean, crisp. Frankly I much prefer a good dry Vouvray to the run-of-the mill Sancerres and can never understand why they are so little-known outside the region. *With Don Zacharia at Daniel's in New York, June 1998* ★★★

**Vouvray, La Gaudrelle, Réserve Personnelle Alexandre Monmousseau** A 14-ha estate, concentrating on 'off-dry' wine. Certainly interesting, certainly not 'off': orange-tinged gold; peachy nose; sweet, unusually modest weight (alcohol 11.5%), very attractive honey and apricot flavour. *At a British Airways dinner at the Chelsea Garden restaurant, London, June 2001* ★★★★

# 1997 ★★★★★

The third remarkably good Loire vintage in a row. Superb wines, honeyed botrytis much in evidence. As in Sauternes and with German sweet wines, botrytis adds an extra dimension to the super-ripe grapes. Yet there were worrying moments, for despite good flowering, the end of June was the coolest and wettest for 30 years. Happily, the summer was long and hot, punctuated by rainstorms which served to refresh flagging grapes. Muscadet was picked at the end of August, Chenin Blanc from early September to the end of October for the super-ripe botrytised grapes. Adequate acidity balanced the ripe Sauvignon Blancs of Sancerre and Pouilly-Fumé. An excellent vintage for the reds, Chinon, Bourgueil and Saumur-Champigny.

**Azay-le-Rideau, moelleux G Pavy** Pale, slight spritz; pleasant, young, grassy nose; medium-sweet, light (alcohol 10.8%), quite good fruit, tingling acidity. *July 2000* ★★★ *(The most exquisite château in the Loire is at Azay.)*

**Bonnezeaux Ch de Fesles** First noted in 1998 at the *Decanter* magazine Vintage dinner: distinctive buttercup-yellow, waxy sheen; lovely ripe botrytis-affected Chenin Blanc; sweet, perfect weight and flavour, excellent acidity. Accompanying Red Pippin and Bramley apple tart, with cinnamon ice cream! Two years later, a similar description, adding 'fleshy botrytis' nose; heavenly flavour. *Last noted Jan 2000* ★★★★(★) *Long life.*

**Coteaux du Layon, Les Aunis Ch de la Roulerie** First noted in November 1999 on BA 008, Tokyo to London. Once again, I think Daphne and I were the only passengers to try it; the cabin staff were won over. Beautiful golden colour; crisp, honeyed; sweet, lovely flesh, flavour and texture. Most recently, sensibly and conveniently in a 50-cl bottle: lime blossom, gloriously rich, perfect acidity. Superb. *Last noted (mid-morning), Feb 2001* ★★★★(★)

**Coteaux du Layon, Le Clos du Bois Jo Pithon** Straw yellow; fairly sweet. Delicious. Now working just over 4ha of vines, Pithon concentrates on quality Chenin. I had a feeling this was from his *grains nobles. Farr Vintners, Jan 2000* ★★★★

**Coteaux du Layon, Chaume Ch de la Guimonière** Bright yellow; honey and clover; sweet, lovely flesh and flavour. Very good – and very necessary – acidity. *At Chippenham Lodge, Sept 2001* ★★★★★ *A delectable half bottle.*

**Sancerre, La Grande Cuvée Pascal Jolivet** From 1ha of 40-year-old Sauvignon Blanc vines. From the first pressing, full malolactic fermentation. 'Needs two to five years'. Palish; scented, minty Sauvignon Blanc; medium–dry, delicious young pineapple fragrance. *At the Maison Marques et Domaines tasting, London, Jan 2000* ★★★

**Sancerre Rouge, 'Génération ★★★' Alphonse Mellot** Crisp fruit with raspberry-like Cabernet Franc aroma; dry, lovely crisp fruit and acidity. Most refreshing. 'Perfect for a warm evening supper'. *At Domaine de Chevalier, June 1999* ★★★★ *Mellot is one of the group of independent growers who co-hosts a supper tasting each Vinexpo at Domaine de Chevalier, Bordeaux.*

**Sancerre, La Grande Cuvée Rouge Pascal Jolivet** From 40-year-old Pinot Noir vines. Medium pale red; very fragrant; light style, very pleasant fruit and good acidity. *Jan 2000* ★★(★) *Give it more bottle age.*

# 1998 variable. At best ★★★

A very uneven growing season: mild-spring, heavy rain in April and frost. May and June just warm enough, though not for the flowering. August very hot, then rain set in, easing enough in the second half of September for the Sauvignon blancs to be harvested. The later ripening Cabernet Franc (for the reds) and Chenin Blanc were picked in variable weather in October. The late-harvested wines were more successful.

**Coteaux du Layon, Chaume, Les Aunis Ch de la Roulerie** A conveniently sized 50-cl bottle of *Grand Vin Liquoureux* from Ch de Fesles. Yellow; honeyed Chenin; certainly sweet, slightly raisiny flavour, rich and attractive, good acidity. *At home, Aug 2000* ★★★★

**Montlouis, Vieilles Vignes Dom des Liards** Medium-sweet; really lovely flavour. Mouthfilling but not heavy (alcohol 12.5%). *At Yapp Brothers, Aug 2000* ★★★

**Pouilly-Fumé Ch de Ladoucette** Dependable as ever: very pale; good crisp Sauvignon Blanc aroma and flavour. Crisp. Refreshing. Perfect with oysters. *At Wilton's, 'the Establishment's' restaurant, London, June 2000* ★★★

**Pouilly-Fumé, Les Griottes Pascal Jolivet** Apparently a unique site. Long fermentation. Very pale; still youthful but, I thought, a touch of woodiness; appropriately named for I noted a cherry-stone flavour. (I preferred his lesser-priced village wine). *Jan 2000* ★★

**Pouilly-Fumé** I have tasted fewer of these wines than Sancerre but they were distinctly better, the best being **Michel Redde**'s **La Moynerie** ★★★; **Guy Saget**'s **Les Logères** ★★★ and **Pascal Jolivet**'s ★★★

**St-Nicolas-de-Bourgueil Dom de la Rodail** Fairly deep cherry-red; still very youthful, good fruit, jammy Cabernet Franc; dry, crisp fruit, good acidity. An unripe Bourgueil. Desperately needing food. *Dining at Ardres, near Calais, May 2000* ★★

**Sancerre, Cuvée François de Montigny Henry Natter** Very pale; a great swoosh of scented Sauvignon Blanc; dry, most unusual, soft not acidic, attractive in its way. *At Bibendum, the wine merchant, not the restaurant, London, Dec 2001* ★★★

**Sancerre, Dom la Moussière Alphonse Mellot** Piquant, varietal aroma and flavour. Dry of course. A good expression of Sancerre. *At Dom de Chevalier, Bordeaux, June 1999* ★★★

**Sancerre, Les Roches Dom Vacheron** Pale, fresh, dry, crisp. *Dec 2000* ★★

**Vouvray, Le Mont, demi-sec Huët** Palish; a bit hard and underdeveloped; more *sec* than *demi*, lightweight (alcohol 12%), decent flavour, good acidity. *At an IWFS Caviar and wine evening at Bibendum, London, Dec 2001* ★★★

I TASTED A VERY WIDE RANGE OF '98S FROM SANCERRE IN MARCH 1999 Out of 19 wines tasted most were mediocre and some were downright poor. No wonder New Zealand's Sauvignon Blancs are popular. Of the best: **Michel Redde**'s **Les Tuilleries** elegant but very acidic ★★★; and **Monmousseau**'s not ready but with decent potential ★★★

# 1999 ★★★

The year started well: an ideal spring, no frosts, successful flowering and a beautifully warm summer. However, the rains came: from mid-September, with just ten days break in early October. The dry whites, from Muscadet to Sancerre, fared best but the growers of Chenin Blanc struggled, needing many expensive *tries* to find ripe and botrytised grapes to make their sweet wines.

The dry whites should have been, and mostly have been, drunk by now. I have not tasted enough of the sweet wines to advise, but I doubt if there are many of more than adequate quality.

**Chinon, Jeunes Vignes C Joguet** Astonishingly deep, black cherry, almost opaque, with immature mauve rim; very pronounced aroma, more like a jammy Gamay than raspberry Cabernet Franc; dry, a decent if acidic mouthful (Joguet's Cuvée Terroir was less convincing in both appearance and nose; lacking conviction). *Dec 2000. At best* ★★ *Something of an acquired taste, except in a good hot ripe vintage.*

**Coteaux du Layon, Les Clos Dom Leduc-Frouin** Yellow-gold; lovely ripe Chenin; sweet, assertive (alcohol 13.5%), good flavour. A delightful surprise! *Lunch on Brittany Ferries, Santander-Plymouth, July 2001* ★★★ (Brittany Ferries, French-owned, has by far the best food on any cross Channel routes – particularly the huge bowls of prawns.)

**Menetou-Salon Henri Pellé** An agreeable, reasonably priced Sancerre look-alike, near Bourges: pale; an attractive, crisp, varietal aroma (Sauvignon Blanc); fairly dry, light, very pleasant flavour, good acidity. *In New York, Oct 2000* ★★

**Muscadet Dom de la Grange** The only time I drink Muscadet is at a quayside restaurant of a Channel port, or during our winter holidays on the isle of St-Barthélémy in the French West Indies. The wine must be drunk young and chilled, and varies from fairly neutral to more than adequate. Pale; very little nose; dry, light, clean, short. *Perfect with newly flown-in mussels at the restaurant La Marine, Gustavia, Feb 2001* ★★

**Muscadet de Sèvre-et-Maine, Dom de Noë Guy Saget**
Saget must be one of the principal suppliers to St-Barthelémy. Pale, fresh, dry, very pleasant – a wine destined to accompany *crabe farcie. At our favourite beachside restaurant, La Gloriette, St-Barts, Feb 2001* ★★★
**Sancerre, La Chapelle, Ch de Thauvenay Henri Bourgeois** Another island standby. So pale, practically colourless; very distinctive Sauvignon Blanc aroma and taste, delicious flavour and excellent acidity. Perfect with 'sashimi thon and spicy poulet'. *At our other regular quayside haunt, Maya's, St Barts, Feb 2001* ★★★

**Sancerre, 'Edmond' Alphonse Mellot** Extremely good, fragrant, touch of oak, good length. *At Domaine de Chevalier, Bordeaux, June 2001* ★★★
**Sancerre Rosé, Cuvée Moulin Bèle André Vatan** Very pale, rather insipid metallic pink; attractive, fresh, young fruit (Pinot Noir), refreshing; dry, firm, medium (alcohol 12.5%) but light in style and very acidic. A better than average rosé, ideal for summer picnics. *At Chippenham Lodge, July 2000* ★★
**Sancerre Rouge Alphonse Mellot** Medium deep cherry red; good fruit; very acidic, too raw. *June 2001* ★★? *Needs a couple of years of bottle age.*

# 2000 and the future

The encouraging thing is that there has been a distinct improvement in quality. This, I believe, has less to do with competition from the New World wines than a welcome French phenomenon, a new breed of *vigneron* whose aim is simply to produce the best wines of their type, weather permitting. Although I recently tasted an excellent Chenin Blanc from Monterey in California, I really do not think that this will ever impinge on the best that this underrated grape can produce in the Loire. Nor, strangely, does the New World flood of Sauvignon Blanc seem to dent the sales of the neighbouring *appellations* of Sancerre and Pouilly-Fumé, the progenitors of this now ubiquitous grape variety – but, as mentioned left, they ought to watch out.

I have a recurrent (aren't they always?) New Year's resolution: to spend more long spring holidays touring this region. After all, most parts of the Loire are little more than a couple of hours drive from a Channel port. Jacqueline Friedrich, an American based in Paris, whose book (*A Wine & Food Guide to the Loire*) I have much enjoyed, has promised to take me by the hand, to revisit the traditional and to meet proponents of the Loire *nouvelle vague*. In between sketching the numerous beautiful châteaux of course.

## 2000 ★★★

Heavy rains throughout the spring were followed by moderately successful flowering in early June. July was cool with more rain-inducing mildew. Happily, August was dry and warm. Grapes for the dry wines were picked early; Muscadet, Sancerre and Pouilly are good but only a few intrepid growers managed to make sweet wines from grapes picked in late November, none of which I have yet tasted.
**Bourgueil, Dom Chesnaies Lamé-Delisle-Boucard** Fairly deep purple; good, fresh, raspberry-like, Cabernet Franc varietal aroma; on the dry side, medium weight (alcohol 12.6%), good flavour and acidity. *On Brittany Ferries, July 2001* ★★(★) *Perhaps it needs a bit more bottle age.*
**Menetou-Salon** Producer unknown. A surging, full, raw, varietal (Sauvignon Blanc) aroma; dry, yet rich, full and flavoury. Distinctive. *At a British Airways tasting, April 2001* ★★★
**Pouilly-Fumé** Very variable wines, ranging from raw and tinny to characteristic and refreshing. The best was **Pascal Jolivet**'s floral nose; crisp fruit, well balanced, good, dry finish. *April 2001* ★★★
**Quincy Joseph Mellot** Fulsome, fragrant; good, flavoury, very dry acidic finish. *April 2001* ★★★

**Quincy, Les Victoires Henri Bourgeois** Sweet, blackcurrant scent; touch of sweetness and richness but with raw, hot, acidic finish. *March 2001* ★★
**Quincy, Les Belles Dames H Quancard** Very pale; raw but fragrant 'tomcats' aroma; not too dry, attractive, floral flavour, raw, acidic finish. *April 2001* ★★
**Sancerre Henri Bourgeois** Lunching with my publishers at Pétrus in St James's Street. Very straightforward; pale, dry, refreshing. However it was followed by Pommard not Pétrus. We had to draw the line somewhere! *August 2001* ★★
**Sancerre, La Croix au Garde Henry Pellé** Palish; a most unusually scented nose and flavour. Fairly dry, attractive flavour and noticeably not acidic. *Lunch at the Stafford Hotel, London, Dec 2001* ★★★
**Sancerre** A range of other Sancerres, at a British Airways tasting in April 2001, showing considerable variation from poor to tinny and drab and just plain uninteresting. The best of the bunch: **Pascal Jolivet**'s very pale; floral, tinny overtones, acidic; surprisingly sweet, richly flavoured, good mid-palate, the customary acidic finish ★★★; and **Henry Pellé**'s hefty, raw but rich Sauvignon Blanc aroma; fulsome, surprisingly rich and soft; flavoury, raw finish ★★★

# Alsace

I am a fan of the wines of Alsace. Sticking my neck out, I would say they are about the most honest and dependable I know. If you buy a Riesling, it is a Riesling and nothing else. They are never overpriced.

Alsace is an odd man out: the region is most definitely French, yet it has many Germanic overtones. This includes the wines; it is the only classic French wine region producing varietal wines sold under the grape name. The best wines come from four 'noble' varieties – Riesling, Gewurztraminer (spelled in Alsace without an umlaut over the 'u', unlike Germany), Pinot Gris (still often labelled as Tokay-Pinot Gris) and Muscat. As well as these four Sylvaner and Pinot Blanc are also used. Inexpensive 'Zwicker' is a blend (of 'noble' or other local varieties).

If the following all too brief notes contain a preponderance of Hugel wines, there is more than one reason for this. The family are old friends. I met Jean Hugel when, in the 1950s, he came to London with Ronald Barton annually to present their very contrasting yet complementary wines. His son, popularly known as Johnny, has long been a close friend and, like me, though semi-retired, he is still very active, keeping an eye on his nephews Etienne and Marc. Hugel wines, with their distinctive yellow labels, were the pioneers of Alsace wine, not only in post-war England but also in the USA through Dreyfus Ashby and their Welsh super-salesman, Parry de Winton.

Despite their quality and dependability, Alsace wines have not been the easiest to sell, and it is largely thanks to the efforts of a handful of major firms and gifted individual winemakers that the fine wine horizons have been widened. The introduction of *grand cru* classifications (in 1985) has been responsible for an increasing awareness of what can be achieved. Giving credit where credit is due, Robert Parker has drawn attention to the superb wines made in Alsace, notably from the Zind-Humbrecht estate. I myself have also long admired Trimbach, which makes a more delicate style, and also some of the monumental wines of Schlumberger. But there are so many other dependable producers, such as Domaine Weinbach run by the Faller ladies.

Although I enjoy drinking the many excellent and good-value everyday wines from Alsace, limited space means that my notes are devoted to the better, richer, age-worthy wines and to those vintages which *were* good, still *are* good, and those with an enviable future.

# 1865–1970

Alsace has had a chequered history – first it was German then French, German again from 1871 until after World War One. In 1918 Alsace became French again but only for 22 years until World War Two and finally French again at the end of the war. This confused history left a legacy of very ordinary wine. It was not until the 1930s that the producers were encouraged to 'pull their socks up' and uproot poor vines. The Hugel family was heavily involved in this renaissance and the tightening up of regulations. They were also the first to introduce two styles of wines now associated with Alsace: *Vendange Tardive* and *Sélection de Grains Nobles* (from botrytis-affected grapes and referred to in my notes as 'SGN'). As can be seen, old Alsace wines do exist, and, unbelievably, can survive.

**Outstanding ★★★★★**
1865, 1900, 1937, 1945, 1959, 1961
**Very Good ★★★★**
1921, 1928, 1934, 1964, 1967
**Good ★★★**
1935, 1953, 1966

## 1865 ★★★★★

**Tokay d'Alsace Hugel** The Hugel family have been living in Riquewihr for over 350 years. In the family cellars is a small collection of very old wines, and this 1865, one of their few remaining bottles, was opened by Johnny Hugel late at night after Peter Ziegler's all-day tasting of some of the greatest-ever wines at Burg Windeck: deep warm amber; honeyed, grapey bouquet – no signs of decay. Sweet. The Hugels thought it must have been over 200° Oechsle – rich, perfect flavour and acidity. *Tasted at Hugel's in Riquewihr, May 1983* ★★★★★

## 1900 ★★★★★

**Riesling Hugel** Palish amber-brown with sediment; surprisingly good old-Riesling nose, not oxidised as the colour suggested; dry but losing its punch and zest. *The oldest wine at the dinner at L'Auberge de l'Ill to celebrate Hugel's 350th anniversary, June 1989.*
**Riesling SGN Hugel** Old amber; very rich and intense bouquet but dried-out. High acidity. *Tasted Sept 1985* ★★

## 1921 ★★★★

Great vintage but Alsace scarcely on its feet after nearly half a century of German occupation. None tasted.

## 1928 ★★★★

**Riesling Kaefferkopf Albert Schoer** Deep yellow-gold; fragrant, grapey; medium-dry, harmonious, good acidity keeping it sprightly. *At lunch in Bordeaux with Mme Teysonneau, April 1979* ★★★★ *The youngest white wine in her cellar!*

## 1934 ★★★★

One of the best inter-war vintages.
**Riesling Mittelbergheim Stein E Boeckel** Lovely amber colour; rich, yet dry. Good length. *Tasted pre-sale, March 1985* ★★
**Traminer Réserve Exceptionnelle Hugel** (Would now be labelled *Sélection de Grains Nobles*) Made from botrytis-infected

grapes from the *grand cru* Spoerren (*sic*) vineyard. Alcohol potential 18.6%, 190° Oechsle and 55g/l residual sugar. Two notes. Both excellent: lovely old gold; sweet, old barley sugar and butterscotch fragrance; once very sweet, now drying out but rich and powerful with marvellous acidity. *Last noted at Hugel's 350th anniversary SGN tasting in Riquewihr, June 1989* ★★★★★

## 1935 ★★★

**Riesling Vendange Tardive Hugel** Amber gold; very good, honeyed bottle age bouquet; now dry, assertive, sound (alcohol 13.2%) and very good in its way. *At Peter Ziegler's rare wine lunch/tasting at the Schlosshotel, Erbach, Dec 1995* ★★★

## 1937 ★★★★★

Great vintage but I have only tasted one wine. It was dry and acidic, as well as being a poor bottle, dried-out or badly stored.

## 1945 ★★★★★

Hot summer, small crop. This was a difficult period in Alsace, following considerable destruction in the battle of the Ardennes late in the war. Johnny Hugel once told me that there had been no electricity from November 1944 to September 1945.
**Gewurztraminer SGN Hugel** Nose like Tokaji Eszencia; flavour of dried raisins, excellent acidity. *Tasted at Hugel's, Riquewihr, June 1989* ★★★★
**Riesling Vendange Tardive Hugel** Medium amber-gold; vanilla, peachy, some maderisation reminding me of a Tokaji dry Szamorodni; medium-sweet, rich and substantial. *Tasted at Peter Ziegler's tasting, Schlosshotel Erbach, Dec 1995* ★★★

### Vendanges Tardives and Sélections de Grains Nobles (SGN)

*Vendange Tardive means 'late harvest' and, in terms of Alsace wines, refers to wines made from late-picked grapes with high natural sugar levels, strictly without the use of chaptalisation. Vendange Tardive wines can vary between fully dry and rich styles, through to very sweet, without there being any indication of the amount of sweetness on the label. While this can be very irritating, the term Vendange Tardive is always a measure of good quality. Sélection de Grains Nobles wines are made not merely from late-harvested fruit, but from individually selected, late-ripened, botrytis-affected berries: these wines are invariably sweet, rare and expensive.*

## 1953 ★★★

Good summer. Ripe grapes though the lesser wines were quick maturing and lacked acidity.

**Riesling Vendange Tardive Hugel** Originally labelled *Réserve Exceptionnelle Auslese*. Harvested 15 October, alcohol 13%, residual sugar 6.0g/l, acidity 6.3g/l. Three notes, the first in 1980, lacking the acidity to counterbalance the sugar. A much better bottle at Ziegler's in 1995: pure gold; very distinctive, fragrant; dry, assertive with very fragrant vanilla aftertaste. Most recently, in magnum: paler than expected; slightly spicy, then 'smokey'; very dry, slightly peachy flavoured, almost steely, with rapier-like acidity. Remarkable vivacity for its age. *Last noted at Hugel's Vendange Tardive tasting, the Cinnamon Club, London, April 2002* ★★★★

## 1959 ★★★★★

Hot summer. As in 1953 quick maturing, the richer wines best. This vintage was well represented in the price lists of my Harvey's of Bristol days. At that time most Alsace wines were shipped in cask, even Hugel's Gewurztraminer Réserve Exceptionnelle being bottled by Harvey's.

**Gewurztraminer SGN Hugel** Bottled by Hugel. Still magnificent, still sweet, firm, soft and spicy. *At Hugel's 350th anniversary SGN tasting, Riquewihr, June 1989* ★★★★★

**Riesling Vendange Tardive Hugel** Pure gold; classic Riesling, almost creamy in its richness; medium-sweet, full, rich, fleshy with a 'warm', nutty finish. Perfect expression of a great vintage with a quarter of a century's bottle age. *At Peter Ziegler's rare wine lunch/tasting at the Schlosshotel, Erbach, Dec 1995* ★★★★

**OTHER, OLDER RATINGS Schlumberger's** Riesling Sélection Spéciale 'Cuvée 27' ★★★ and their **Gewurztraminer** 'Cuvée 37' ★★★; and **Beyer's Traminer Cuvée Exceptionelle** ★★★★

## 1961 ★★★★★

**Gewurztraminer Vendange Tardive Hugel** Tawny with orange tinge; high-toned, peachy nose and taste. Drying out with a touch of bitterness on the finish. *Tasted at Len Evans' 'Single Bottle Club' dinner, Hunter Valley, Sept 2000* ★★

**Riesling Vendange Tardive Hugel** Picked 28 October, alcohol 12.85%, residual sugar 8.2g/l, acidity 5.8g/l. In magnum at Ziegler's, 1995: fragrant, whiff of melon and mint, opening up, more peachy and very harmonious; medium-sweet, full-bodied, marvellous power and class. Most recently: old gold; initially low-keyed but opened up, grapey, honeyed;

medium-dry, rich, fairly assertive, in excellent condition. *Last noted at Hugel's Vendange Tardive tasting, London, April 2002* ★★★★

**OTHER '61S Hugel's Gewurztraminer SGN** perfectly balanced. *1989* ★★★★; and **Beyer's Gewurztraminer Cuvée Exceptionnelle.** *1973* ★★★★

## 1964 ★★★★

Another hot year. Excellent for late-harvest wines. I have many notes of this vintage dating from the late 1960s and early 1973s. All were good and the most outstanding was **Hugel's Gewurztraminer Vendange Tardive Réserve Exceptionelle Auslese** *Tasted 1966. Then* ★★★★, *it might well have survived.*

## 1966 ★★★

Good year. Well-structured whites with good acidity.

**Riesling Vendange Tardive Hugel** Picked 25 October, alcohol 13.3%, residual sugar 7.4g/l, acidity 5.2g/l. First tasted at Christie's Tasting of the Century at Vinexpo (in 1991): palish gold; mature Riesling with classic kerosene nose and touch of honeyed bottle age; rich but surprisingly dry, fullish, firm, good acidity. Most recently: pale for its age; initially a whiff of bottle age, then minty, opening up vividly with a sort of raw, greengage acidity; very dry, lean, more acidic than the (tartaric) analysis indicated. Holding well. *Last tasted April 2002* ★★★

**OTHER '66S MAINLY TASTED OR CONSUMED IN THE MID-1970S** Among the top wines **Hugel's Gewurztraminer Vendange Tardive** stood out.

## 1967 ★★★★

A very good vintage with some top-quality, late-harvest wines as in Germany's Pfalz region, just north of Alsace. Notably, two excellent **Hugel** wines, both **Réserve Exceptionelle Vendange Tardive**, one Tokay, the other Gewurztraminer tasted in the mid-1970s, one recently.

**Gewurztraminer SGN Hugel** Warm gold; old but soft, peachy and Tokaji Aszú-like bouquet; medium-sweet, full-bodied. *Tasted June 1989* ★★ *Doubtless dried out by now.*

## 1970 ★★

The period ended on a mediocre note. There was an abundant crop of ripe grapes, but they lacked zest. I mainly tasted these wines in the early 1970s and none of them are worth recording now.

# 1971–1989

On the whole, this was a successful period with a plethora of well made dry wines which, with few exceptions, will have – and should have – been drunk within three to six years after each vintage.

Once again, I am concentrating on the sweeter wines of higher quality which not only survive bottle age but actually benefit, developing extra nuances and complexities of bouquet and taste.

**Outstanding** ★★★★★
1971, 1976, 1983, 1988 (v), 1989
**Very Good** ★★★★
1981, 1985, 1986 (v)
**Good** ★★★
1975

## 1971 ★★★★★

An excellent vintage for the richer wines, but the smallest crop of the decade due to *coulure* in June and, overall, a very dry growing season. A burst of heat in the autumn resulted in some overripe, high-quality, late-harvest wines of which I have been fortunate to taste and drink quite a range, all without exception very good. I start with a recent note.
**Gewurztraminer SGN Hugel** Sweet, fat, earthy style. *Last tasted June 1989* ★★★★ *Fully developed.*
**Riesling Cuvée Particulière Beyer** Dry; delicate, held in trim by its excellent acidity. *At Michael Druitt's 'Vintage Dinner' in London, Sept 1989* ★★★
**Riesling Vendange Tardive Hugel** Picked 15 October, alcohol 12.3%, residual sugar 10g/l, acidity 7.6g/l. Paler than expected (at Ziegler's in 1995), but with classic ripe Riesling bouquet which opened up in the glass. Also drier than expected, full body and flavour but somewhat austere. Most recently, seemed to have gained colour, now a brassy gold; rich from start to finish, with whiff of classic kerosene, then smokey, grapefruit; combining dryness with richness, wonderful extract, full, complete. *Last noted at the Hugel Vendange Tardive tasting, London, April 2002* ★★★★★

## 1975 ★★★

This was a good summer and followed by a late October harvest. Few wines tasted.
**Riesling Clos Ste-Hune Trimbach** Highly polished; pure Riesling kerosene with scented bottle age. Beautifully made as always, medium-dry, firm, refreshing prickle, fragrant finish. *With Cassoulette d'Homard Breton at Carré des Feuillants, Paris, Dec 1995* ★★★★ *A superb 20-year-old.*

## 1976 ★★★★★

A great year, particularly for the richer wines. Good flowering during hot, dry weather in mid-June. Well-nigh perfect summer, with an occasional shower to flesh out the grapes. An average size crop picked from early October and ideal conditions for late-harvested wines. Many of the latter have more than survived and not infrequently appear at auction. I have many notes, mainly Hugel's.
**Gewurztraminer Vendange Tardive 'SGN par Jean Hugel', Fût 20 Hugel** Old Jean Hugel told his son 'Johnny'

that he had never in his life seen better grapes and 'he had better not make a mess of them'! Fût 20 is Hugel's greatest cask. 135° Oechsle, alcohol 13.7%, residual sugar 53g/l, 100% botrytis-affected grapes. Several notes: golden sheen; ambrosial syrup of figs, intensely rich and fragrant. *Last noted at the Hollywood Wine Society's Hugel tasting, Jan 1990* ★★★★★
**Riesling Clos Ste-Hune Trimbach** Palish gold; very pronounced Riesling character, slightly appley bottle age; bone dry, firm, good flavour and acidity. *Prior to a Rodenstock wine dinner, in Munich, Sept 1998* ★★★★
**Riesling SGN Hugel** One of Hugel's greatest Rieslings. Picked 20 October, 142° Oechsle, fermentation from 20 October to mid-July (1977), alcohol 12.8%, residual sugar 51g/l, acidity (tartaric) 7.2g/l. 5500 bottles produced. Probably at its peak in 1989: buttercup yellow; grapey, ripe, fragrant; medium-sweet though rich with a marvellous uplift of acidity. In 1997 at Gidleigh Park, a half bottle: good colour; fabulously honeyed bouquet of great depth; fairly sweet, still quite a bite. Most recently, at a masterclass conducted by Étienne Hugel at Vinopolis: now with a pink-gold orange tinge; hefty, concentrated sultana-like fruit; drying out but still rich and ripe; sustained by very good acidity. Now a brassy touch to its old gold, but very bright; perfectly harmonious, creamy nose; very sweet, lovely texture, peachy flavour, complete, well balanced. *Last noted at Hugel's Vendange Tardive tasting, London, April 2002* ★★★★★
**Riesling Vendange Tardive Hugel** Picked 20 October, alcohol 13.05%, residual sugar 13.6g/l, acidity 6.1g/l. First noted at Peter Ziegler's in 1999: palish; classic Riesling fragrance; medium-sweet, full-bodied, rich, lovely flavour, complete. 'Yet more to come'. Most recently: medium-gold with orange-gold highlights; broad, harmonious, touch of caramel; dry, strange, slightly spicy flavour, fairly powerful, finishing hard. *Last noted at Hugel's Vendange Tardive tasting, London, April 2002 At best* ★★★★
**Tokay-Pinot Gris SGN Hugel** Hugel's first Pinot Gris SGN produced since the 1865, noted earlier. In 1989: bouquet of spicy peach skins, rose-cachou and crystallised violets; very sweet, rich, soft, rounded, marvellously gentle. Five years later, labelled *Tokay d'Alsace, Grands Nobles, Sélection Jean Hugel*. Fairly stolid, concentrated and a bit four-square, with good finish. *Last tasted, from my cellar, dining with the family, July 1994* ★★★★

## 1978 ★★

Small crop due to late and unsatisfactory flowering though some quite good wines made.
**Riesling Clos Ste-Hune Trimbach** First tasted in 1984: typically delicate and fragrant; dry, crisp. Nine years later: dry and drinkable at lunch with Magnus von Kühlmann, at Schloss Ramholz, an imposing Wagnerian pile, to discuss the disposal of his wines. Subsequently my 'mate' Daphne and a young colleague packed up his extensive cellar, a dusty, tiring

job more than made up for by a stay in rather grand surroundings. *Last noted Dec 1993* ★★

**Tokay-Pinot Gris Clos St-Urbain Zind-Humbrecht** Although an old note, this is the first wine I can recall tasting from this now highly renowned family estate, probably because Olivier Humbrecht was the first Frenchman to sit and pass the MW examination and also this wine was possibly the finest made in the '78 vintage: 105° Oechsle, alcohol 14.3%: buttercup gold; 'milk and honey' bouquet; fairly dry though rich and substantial. *Tasted Sept 1986* ★★★★ *And will have survived.*

# 1979 ★★

Large crop of largely 'commercial quality' wine.

**Riesling Clos Ste-Hune Trimbach** Noted in 1985 as 'an ideal light luncheon wine'. Most recently, tasted blind alongside the '79 Petaluma Rhine Riesling. A complete contrast: the Australian wine spicy, attractive, mouthfilling, with decent acidity and good length; Trimbach's more steely but whose bouquet developed exotically in the glass. Dry, rich yet austere and complete. *Last tasted with Brian Crozer and Len Evans at Gidleigh Park, Devon in Nov 1997* ★★★

**Riesling 'Jubilee' Hugel** Pale; very forthcoming, 'oily' varietal aroma; dry, good but unexciting, with quite a powerful tang. *At Johnny Hugel's 70th birthday lunch at the Savoy Hotel in London, Nov 1994* ★★★

**Riesling Mambourg, Cuvée Centenaire Sparr** Very pale, still green-tinged; crisp, floral, lightly grapey bouquet; fairly dry, fragrant, elegant, clean cut, very good aftertaste. *At yet another 70th birthday party, this time Len Evans', Sept 2000* ★★★

# 1981 ★★★★

Very satisfactory year with quantity for the market and quality for the connoisseurs. Good flowering, sunny summer and an early harvest yet conditions were also well nigh perfect for late-harvest wines.

I have tasted a surprisingly large number of these wines, many in the mid- to late 1980s. Here are some of the better and more interesting of my recent notes.

**Gewurztraminer SGN Hugel** Fairly sweet, rich, spicy. Classic. *Tasted June 1989. Then* ★★★★(★) *Should be at peak now.*

**Pinot Noir** Alsace reds around this time as uninspiring as the Germans'. **Hugel** and **Kuentz-Bas** not bad.

**Riesling Réserve Personnelle** (now called 'Jubilee') **Hugel** Pale; a ripe bottle-age kerosene Riesling; dry, remarkably good for its age. *A surprise magnum at lunch after the Hugel tasting in London, Jan 2002* ★★★

**Riesling Vendange Tardive Hugel** Picked late, 16 November, alcohol 12.6%, residual sugar 8.0g/l, acidity 7.2g/l. A very untypical *Vendange Tardive*: medium-pale yellow; low-keyed, grassy, minty nose; extremely dry, almost raw, melon-like flavour, lean and acidic. *At Hugel's Vendange Tardive tasting, London, April 2002* ★★

**Tokay-Pinot Gris Vendange Tardive Hugel** Just 100 cases produced. A most lovely wine. Beautiful colour; cress-like nose; flavour of grapes and ripe melons. *At a Hollywood Wine Society seminar, Jan 1990. Then* ★★★★ *Should still be perfect.*

TWO GRAND CRU RIESLING '81S TASTED IN 1990 **Zind-Humbrecht's Rangen** flat, peach kernelly, not liked; and **Dopff au Moulin's Schoenenbourg** dry, crisp, fruity ★★★

# 1982 ★★

A huge crop of largely unexciting wines, all noted without much enthusiasm in the mid-1980s.

# 1983 ★★★★★

Excellent vintage, abundant and of high quality; many of the top wines are still superb. The growing season followed 'the warmest winter, wettest spring and driest summer on record'. Extended harvest from early October to mid-November for the late-picked wines. I have many notes, the most recent:

**Gewurztraminer Cuvée Seigneurs de Ribeaupierre Trimbach** First tasted in 1987: distinctive yellow; copybook Gewurz; spicy, grapey, 5 star. More recently: glorious, soft, ripe, rose-cachou-scented; medium-dry, fullish, rich yet mild. *Last noted dining at the Walnut Tree, Abergavenny, after a cycle ride over the Black Mountains (I had to change from my hot pants in the loo, Daphne having followed in the car), Aug 1994* ★★★★

**Gewurztraminer SGN Hugel** Perfection. *At the Loeb/Hugel tasting in London, Feb 1991* ★★★★★

**Riesling Clos Ste-Hune Trimbach** Magnum: pale; flowery, sweet, peachy, whiff of vanilla; fairly dry, full-bodied (95° Oechsle but fully fermented out), magnificent but a bit austere. *At Peter Ziegler's rare wine lunch/tasting at the Schlosshotel, Erbach, Dec 1995* ★★★★★

**Riesling Vendange Tardive Hugel** Even in a good vintage this wine was only 1% of Hugel's production. Held for six years before release. Three notes, first in 1990: very pronounced yellow gold; harmonious, honeyed, crisp, grapey; not as sweet as expected. Spicy. Rounded. Again in 1992. Next, at Peter Ziegler's alongside the Trimbach: classic Riesling nose; medium-sweet, full-bodied, lovely flavour, soft touch and elegant. At peak. Most recently: at Étienne Hugel's masterclass at Vinopolis in London. Only 5% botrytis we were informed: medium gold colour; subtle, honeyed nose, waxy, spicy, touch of peach kernels; rich but not as sweet as the '89 or '95, but all the component parts lined up. Good acidity. A wine to accompany turbot. *Last tasted Nov 1999* ★★★★

**Riesling Vendange Tardive, Cuvée Frédéric Emile Trimbach** Very pale, lime-tinged; classic ripe kerosene Riesling, delicate, touch of melon; surprisingly dry, delicate yet firm. *Superb with cheeses at Gidleigh Park, Devon in Feb 1994* ★★★★

**Tokay-Pinot Gris Réserve Personnelle Kuentz-Bas** Fragrant, creamy, full-flavoured, grapey, lovely. *Last tasted June 1993* ★★★★

**Tokay-Pinot Gris SGN Hugel** 192° Oechsle, an astonishing 220 g/l residual sugar: fairly deep yellow; smoky, harmonious, 'Williamine pears'; fabulous, sweet, rich, fat, fleshy, perfect – and very necessary – acidity. *At Hugel's 350th anniversary SGN tasting, Riquewihr, June 1989* ★★★★★ *This wine will still be superb.*

**Tokay-Pinot Gris Vendange Tardive, Sélection Jean Hugel** Pale; lovely, spicy, grapey nose; a bit four-square – needed a touch of botrytis, but good flavour. Alcohol 13.5%. *Last tasted at the Loeb/Hugel tasting in London, Dec 1999* ★★★

OTHER SUPERB '83S TASTED IN 1989 AND 1990 and likely still to be superb. **G Lorenz's Gewurztraminer Altenberg** ripe, lovely. *1990* ★★★★; **Zind-Humbrecht's Gewurztraminer Gueberschwir Vendange Tardive** dry, assertive *1990* ★★★; **Hugel's Gewurztraminer SGN** great length. *1989* ★★★★★; and their **Tokay-Pinot Gris Réserve Personnelle** fairly dry and very distinctive *1990* ★★★★

# 1984 ★

There was a late spring, followed by uneven flowering and a cool, wet summer. A dry and sunny October saved the day – just. Few wines tasted and they are of little interest now. Zind-Humbrecht displayed their abilities in this dismal year and, by dint of selection, made two *grand cru* Rieslings, a decent one from the Rangen site and a good one from Brand.

# 1985 ★★★★

An abundant crop of good wines followed a fine and dry summer. Picking began in early October and, for the SGN wines, continued into December. There were attractive wines in each quality range. I tasted many of them when they were young, and few were of less than very good quality.

The new Alsace Grand Cru *appellation* took effect from this vintage. It is not as straightforward as one might imagine. The only permitted grape varieties were Gewurztraminer, Riesling, Tokay-Pinot Gris and Muscat, specific varieties being linked to designated *grand cru* vineyards. For example, Gewurztraminer could not be designated as *grand cru* if grown in a Riesling *grand cru* vineyard. If the grapes came from a single *grand cru* vineyard, the vineyard could be named on the label; however, if the grapes came from more than one *grand cru* vineyard – which is permitted – the vineyards could not be named. No blends were allowed and the permitted yields were restricted. (Alas, these complications are ongoing.)

**Gewurztraminer Clos St-Landelin Muré** A 1.6-ha terraced vineyard which takes me back to my first year in the wine trade, though Tommy Layton did not have a blockbuster like this: rich, earthy, scented Gewurz; almost too powerful to drink (alcohol 15.8%!). *Tasted Sept 1988 ★★★★★ Will have simmered down now.*

**Muscat Rangen Zind-Humbrecht** Splendid combination of good *grand cru*, good year and gifted winemaking. Medium-dry, assertive. *At an all-embracing Zind-Humbrecht tasting, London, June 1990 ★★★★★*

**Muscat Rothenberg Vendange Tardive Zind-Humbrecht** Rich, spicy. *Tasted in London, June 1990 ★★★★★*

**Riesling Rangen Grand Cru Zind-Humbrecht** Austere but high quality. *At a Zind-Humbrecht tasting in London, June 1990. Then ★★★(★) Probably drinking well now.*

**Riesling TBA Hugel** Medium-pale yellow; youthful kerosene Riesling aroma; not as sweet as expected, full body and flavour. Hot finish. *At Peter Ziegler's rare wine lunch/tasting at the Schlosshotel, Erbach, Dec 1995 ★★★★★*

**Riesling Vendange Tardive Hugel** An unusually delicate wine, crisp, Hugel Riesling at its best. *At the Loeb tasting, Feb 1991 ★★★★ Will be fully mature now, needs drinking.*

## Alsace grands crus

*Superior Alsace wines from named vineyard sites. The wine must also come from a single vintage and one of the four 'noble' Alsace grape varieties (Riesling, Muscat, Gewurztraminer and Pinot Gris). There are also yield restrictions and regular tasting tests to pass. The original list of 25 grands crus (declared in 1983) has now been upped to over 50. While these sites are undoubtedly some of the finest, not every grower wishes to declare his wine a grand cru as the appellation restrictions – particularly on yield – are often felt to be too limiting.*

**Tokay-Pinot Gris Comtes d'Eguisheim Beyer** Earthy, slightly grapey; dry, yet rich, full-bodied (alcohol 14.5%), very fragrant but with a long, harsh finish. Perfect with *foie gras* and *timbale de brochet*. *Tasted at a Diners Club International Vintage Evening at the Waterside Inn, Bray, Oct 1994 ★★★★*

**Tokay-Pinot Gris Vendange Tardive Hugel** Hefty, very good. *At the Loeb tasting, Vintners' Hall, London, Feb 1991 ★★★★*

# 1986 variable, at best ★★★★

A poor start to the growing year but by June the weather was ideal for the flowering. Late summer was cold, encouraging rot, followed by ideal weather again. Picking began 9 October, morning mists encouraging botrytis followed by ripening sun. There were many very good *Vendange Tardive* wines which I tasted in the late 1980s and early 1990s. Here are some of my most recent notes.

**Gewurztraminer Kitterlé Grand Cru Schlumberger** Sublime bouquet; medium-dry, powerful, glorious scented flavour. Long life. *Tasted Feb 1991 ★★★★★ Probably beginning to reach its peak.*

**Gewurztraminer SGN Zind-Humbrecht** Pure gold; exotic bouquet; fairly sweet, delicious flavour and a fabulous future. *At Domaine de Chevalier, Bordeaux, June 1999 ★★★★(★)*

**Riesling Cuvée Frédéric Emile Trimbach** Surprisingly pale; perfect bouquet, slightly peachy; a most unusual and delicious wine, medium-dry, good length, firm but perfectly mature. *With baked red mullet, at an IWFS St James's Branch dinner, at the Cadogan Hotel, Sloane Street, April 1997 ★★★★*

**Riesling Clos Ste-Hune Trimbach** First as an aperitif in September 1998 before a Rodenstock dinner: pale; flinty, minerally; very dry, crisp, firm, an excellent expression of Riesling. Recently, still pale for its age; austere, touch of peach kernels. Trimbach have mastered the art of making a bone dry wine interesting. *A very expensive half bottle (one of several) last noted at a Christmas Eve dinner at Gidleigh Park in Devon, Dec 1998 ★★★★*

**Tokay-Pinot Gris 'Jubilee' Hugel** Dry, full-bodied (alcohol 14.3%), good fruit, harmonious. *At Johnny Hugel's 70th birthday lunch, at the Savoy Hotel, London, Nov 1994 ★★★*

# 1987 ★★

Variable, both weather and wine, the most unusual feature being a five-day period when all the vine varieties flowered simultaneously. Then it was hot; August was cold and wet, followed by a heatwave in September through to early October. Harvesting took place in mid-October in variable weather. I have tasted relatively few '87s, mainly between 1989 and 1991. None worth reporting now.

# 1988 ★★★ to ★★★★★

A glorious spring and summer spoiled by heavy rains before the harvest. Hot November and botrytis enabled some high quality late-harvest wines to be made. The best are still superb.

**Gewurztraminer Cuvée Anne Schlumberger** Harvested mid-November after late-autumn sun. The first to be made from '100% botrytis grapes' since 1976: just one 60-litre cask. Yellow gold; heavenly honeyed botrytis nose; full-bodied. Perfection. *The last wine in an impressive Schlumberger line-up at the London Wine Trade Fair (they had sold out so I ordered the '89), May 1991 ★★★★★ Drink now–2010.*

**Gewurztraminer SGN Hugel** In 1991: honeyed; fabulous flavour and aftertaste. More recently: palish; fragrant, grassy, minty; sweet, good flavour but with a hot, hard finish. April 1996 ★★★(★★) *Now–2010.*

**Riesling 'Jubilee' (formerly Réserve Exceptionnelle Personnelle) Hugel** Honeyed Riesling; very dry, assertive, austere. *Feb 1991* ★★★★ *Should be on top form now.*

**Riesling Vendange Tardive Hugel** (Picked late, 9 November, very high potential alcohol 14.7%, actual alcohol 13.5%, residual sugar 19.5g/l, acidity 6.6g/l). First noted in 1991: glorious peachy nose; medium-dry, lovely, soft, like the flesh of a ripe grape, with fragrant aftertaste. Most recently: medium-yellow gold; touch of lime, green acidity, opening up, more honeyed; surprisingly dry, firm, good acidity but lacked a bit of excitement. Will benefit from even more bottle-ageing. *Last noted at the Hugel Vendange Tardive tasting in London, April 2002* ★★★

**Tokay-Pinot Gris Cuvée Tradition Hugel** In 1991, nose hard to define (I have always found it difficult to describe Pinot Gris, totally different to Riesling and Gewurz). Lightly grapey, a touch of melon; firm, fragrant. More recently: fairly dry, full-bodied, good fruit and acidity. *Last noted lunching at Chippenham Lodge, with the Averys and Penning-Rowsells, Aug 1996* ★★★

OTHER TOP CLASS '88S TASTED IN THEIR YOUTH
GEWURZTRAMINER **Zind-Humbrecht**'s **Goldert Grand Cru** lovely wine. *1990* ★★★★; **Hugel**'s **'Jubilee'** powerful. *1991* ★★★★; **Kuentz-Bas**' **Cuvée Tradition** delicate and fragrant. *1991* ★★★★; and **Zind-Humbrecht**'s **Clos Windsbuhl** rich and fragrant. *1990* ★★★★
RIESLING **Hugel**'s **SGN** astonishing wine: hefty; minty; sweet, crisp, spicy. *1989* ★★★★★ *will still be superb.*
TOKAY-PINOT GRIS **Zind-Humbrecht**'s **Clos Jebsal** scented; full-bodied; lovely, needs time. *1990* ★★★★ *should be fully mature now;* **Hugel**'s **'Jubilee'** dry, spicy, good length and aftertaste. *1991* ★★★★; and **Vendange Tardive** fabulous flavour and fragrance, though hard. *1991* ★★★★★ *Doubtless perfect now.*

Lastly, **Hugel**'s **Vin de Paille du Jubilee** Rare and only 200 half bottles produced. Pale gold; glorious scent – a *mélange* of Muscat, Gewurz and Riesling; slightly sweet, delicate, lovely. *Served at the end of Hugel's 350th anniversary dinner at L'Auberge de l'Ill, Alsace, June 1989* ★★★★★ *I was presented with one of these half bottles after my closing speech. It will see me out.*

# 1989 ★★★★★

Superb vintage, combining abundance and overall high quality. A hot and dry summer, ripening advanced well ahead of normal. An unusually early harvest from 29 September, with the largest-ever production of late-harvest and SGN wines with great richness and keeping qualities.

**Gewurztraminer, Clos des Capucins, Cuvée Théo Dom Weinbach/Faller** Very distinctive, subtly scented rose-cachou; medium-sweet, full-bodied, fairly solid yet rounded, excellent but plodding. *After stone crabs at the Pauls' in Coral Gables, March 1995* ★★★★

**Gewurztraminer Heimburg SGN Zind-Humbrecht** Glorious bouquet of scented roses; fairly sweet, very rich. An incredibly beautiful wine. *Tasted at the annual Vinexpo buffet/tasting at Dom de Chevalier, Bordeaux, June 1997* ★★★★★ *Glorious now. Will keep and evolve over another 20 years.*

**Gewurztraminer Réserve Willm** Lovely, scented, harmonious; medium-sweet, soft, deliciously ripe flavour. Trace of peach kernels. *Dining at Rosebank, London, April 1994* ★★★★
**Gewurztraminer SGN 'S' Hugel** First tasted in 1994, the most fabulous wine served at Johnny Hugel's 70th birthday lunch at the Savoy: yellow; deliciously rich, 'ripe melon'; breathtaking, mouthfilling. Most recently, introduced by Etienne Hugel at the *Primum Familiae Vini* dinner: now a fairly deep gold; glorious bouquet and flavour. Full, rich, superb aftertaste. *The Hugel family's 350th vintage, last tasted at Vinopolis, London, Nov 2000* ★★★★★
**Gewurztraminer Vendange Tardive Hugel** Perfectly matching 'Burger of Fresh Duck Foie Gras' at a gala dinner in 1994 for the Fifth Annual Rare Wine Auction of the American Institute of Food and Wine, New York: creamy nose; fairly sweet and full, soft texture, glorious flavour, years of life. ★★★★
**Muscat Rolly Gassmann** Remarkably pale for its age and vintage; vivid scents, flavoury, grapey tomcats, blackcurrant candy and refreshing acidity. Like all Alsace Muscats, after the exotic nose always surprisingly dry on the palate. Very flavoury though austere. Fragrant aftertaste. *Tasted pre-dinner at Ch de Bagnols in southern Beaujolais, Oct 1998* ★★★
**Riesling Comtes d'Eguisheim Beyer** True Riesling aroma; very dry, yet rich, with good flavour and length. Complete. *At a British Airways catering and wine meeting at the Waterside Inn, Bray, Nov 1996* ★★★★ *(Those were the days!).*
**Riesling 'Quintessences de Sélection des Grains Nobles' Dom Weinbach/Faller** Golden colour; immensely rich kerosene Riesling aroma, with a touch of caramel and honeyed botrytis; sweet, rich, perfect weight (alcohol 13.5%), length, finish. *At the Faller tasting at Justerini & Brooks, London, Sept 1997* ★★★★★ *Years of life ahead.*
**Riesling Clos Ste-Hune Vendange Tardive Trimbach** Surprisingly pale; pure Riesling, with oily kerosene aroma; dry, firm, full (alcohol 14%), well constructed. Clearly from very ripe grapes fully fermented out. *Excellent with cheeses at Gidleigh Park, Devon, March 1997* ★★★(★)
**Riesling Vendange Tardive Hugel** Picked 26 October, 30% botrytis, alcohol 13.8%, high residual sugar 25.7g/l, normal acidity 6.4g/l. Over 1000 cases produced. First noted at Etienne Hugel's masterclass in 1999: deep gold; lovely, harmonious, pure Riesling; disappointing on palate after the '95. Positive, assertive, rich but dry finish. Next January 2002: soft, rich nose but drier than expected. Most recently: warm gold; fully evolved, harmonious, slightly scented, honey and mint; medium-dry, hefty, four-square, good acidity, and dry finish. *Last noted at Hugel's Vendange Tardive tasting, in London, April 2002* ★★★★
**Riesling Clos Windsbuhl SGN Zind-Humbrecht** Surprisingly low-keyed nose; sweet, amazingly rich and full for its surprisingly modest strength (alcohol 11.9%). Hot, biting finish. *After dinner at Gidleigh Park, Devon, Nov 1997* ★★★(★★) *Needs more time.*

OTHER '89S SHOWING GREAT PROMISE IN 1991
GEWURZTRAMINER **Dopff au Moulin**'s **Brand Grand Cru** ★★★★; and **Schlumberger**'s **Cuvée Christine** ★★★★★
MUSCAT **Schlumberger**'s **Réserve** dry; piquant ★★★★
RIESLING **Zind-Humbrecht**'s **Brand Grand Cru** steely ★★★★; **Schlumberger**'s **Princes Abbés** ★★★★ and **Saering Grand Cru** powerful ★★★★; and **Dietrich**'s **Schloss** austere ★★★★
TOKAY-PINOT GRIS **Schlumberger**'s **Kitterlé Grand Cru** ★★★★★; and **Zind-Humbrecht**'s ★★★★

# 1990–1999

This ranks as the most successful decade ever experienced by the growers in Alsace; only one vintage was ranked less than good, with the proviso, of course, that with wine there are always exceptions and some are less good than others. This will always be so. But, as I wrote in my introduction, in Alsace dependability is the name of the game.

**Outstanding ★★★★★**
1990, 1995 (v), 1997
**Very Good ★★★★**
1992 (v), 1993, 1996, 1998
**Good ★★★**
1994 (v), 1999 (v)

## 1990 ★★★★★

The second of the exceptional twin vintages, similar in style and quality to 1989, but with a considerably reduced volume. The only blip (a major one): the growing season was cold with wet weather during flowering which caused both *coulure* and *millerandage*, reducing the crop by some 25% compared with 1989. Most affected were the more delicate Gewurztraminer, Muscat and Tokay-Pinot Gris. Conditions during the rest of the summer were excellent and a crop of healthy grapes was harvested from 4 October.

Sugar content was high and many *Vendange Tardive* wines were made but, because of the lack of botrytis, there were only a few SGNs. The best were outstanding, but there were some disappointments too. The very good dry wines should have been drunk by the mid-1990s.

**Gewurztraminer, Cuvée Anne Schlumberger** Fairly sweet, full, rich, scented flavour, excellent finish and aftertaste. *At the BBC Food Awards, Sept 1996* ★★★ *Drink now to beyond 2010.*

**Gewurztraminer Fronholz Ostertag André Ostertag** Ostertag ('Easter Day') is a controversial winemaker based in Epfig with something of a cult following. He owns a 12-ha vineyard. He makes very little Gewurz: bright yellow; scented; medium-dry, comparatively light (alcohol 11%), unusual style and violet-shaded flavour. Short. *At the press reception for Les Arts du Vin exhibition in Brussels, Nov 1995* ★★★ *Not a very good choice or position, for it followed Philippine de Rothschild and her '93 Ch Mouton-Rothschild.*

**Gewurztraminer SGN Dopff au Moulin** Lovely yellow-gold; heavy botrytised nose of considerable depth; sweet, full-bodied, very good flavour. *April 1996* ★★★★

**Gewurztraminer Vendange Tardive Dopff au Moulin** Very pale – too pale; very good, fragrant, spicy nose; medium-sweet, disappointing flavour. *Tasted April 1996* ★★★

**Gewurztraminer Vendange Tardive Wolfberger** Palish, lime tinged; unusual, interesting nose; too dry, poor flavour. *April 1996* ★

**Riesling, Cuvée Frédéric Émile Trimbach** Tasted only in its youth. Crisp, grapey; dry, full-bodied, soft, good flavour and length. *Tasted May 1993* ★★★★ *Should be at peak now.*

**Riesling Grand Cru Saering Schlumberger** Very good, rich, ripe nose; classic flavour but lacking excitement. *Tasted March 1993. Then* ★★★ *but should have been drunk by now.*

**Riesling Vendange Tardive Hugel** Harvested 23 and 26 October, alcohol 12.8%, residual sugar 16.5g/l, acidity (tartaric) 7.0g/l. Palish yellow, pure gold highlights; forthcoming,

harmonious, lime blossom, touch of spice; bone dry, steely, extended finish. A supercharged food wine! *At Hugel's Vendange Tardive tasting in London, April 2002* ★★★(★) *Not everyone's 'cup of tea' but will keep and develop extra nuances.*

**Tokay-Pinot Gris Vendange Tardive Caves de Ribeauvillé** One of the oldest co-operatives in France with about 90 member-growers. Medium-pale yellow; rather (Hungarian) Tokaji-like; medium-sweet, full-bodied, overall somewhat austere. Unexciting – but not expensive. *April 1996* ★★

**Tokay-Pinot Gris Vendange Tardive Dom Weinbach/Faller** Slightly minty, indefinable but good nose; sweet, soft, lovely flavour, full-bodied yet with delicacy and fragrance. Which just shows what these brilliant ladies can do! Perfect with *millefeuille de foie gras. At the Biggaarden restaurant, Brussels, Jan 1996* ★★★★★ *Perfection then and will keep.*

## 1991 ★★

The one really poor vintage of the decade. After three very dry years, rain was needed, but it was badly timed. The only good thing in 1991 was that Alsace did not suffer the severe frosts which affected most of France's vineyards. Hail in August did considerable though localised damage. Then heavy rain and yet more rain in September, delaying the harvest.

There were some dreary wines and even the better dry wines should have been consumed by the mid-1990s. However, there are some surprises from producers who picked late, risking all to make more-than-interesting wine. A limited cross section of my notes follows.

**Gewurztraminer Grand Cru Mamburg Sparr** Palish; correctly scented; neither dry nor sweet, fullish body and fairly powerful with a typical Gewurz blunt finish. *On BA 255 to Barbados before settling down to rum punches on holiday, Oct 1994* ★★★ *Will be well past its best now.*

**Riesling Turkheim Zind-Humbrecht** Palish, star bright; attractive varietal aroma; bone dry, somewhat austere, very good but – to my surprise - unsuitable for spicy food. *At Vong restaurant, London, Jan 1996* ★★★

**Tokay-Pinot Gris Blanck** Medium-dry, fullish body (alcohol c. 13.5–14%), a good, solid, well-made wine though hardly inspirational. (At the time I rather favoured the then not very well known Pinot Gris but now find them too heavy at lunch time.) *Tasted May 1994* ★★★ *(just)*

**Tokay-Pinot Gris 'A 360 P' Ostertag** His barrel-fermented Muenchberg Pinot Gris was denied its rightful *grand cru* status so he marketed it as 'A 360 P' after its cadastral designation. Surprising colour; medium-dry, very good flavour, consistency (texture) and balance. Now here is an interesting winemaker adding an extra dimension. *Lunch at Sally Clarke's in Kensington, Dec 1994* ★★★★ *But for drinking then, not now.*

**Tokay-Pinot Gris Patergarten Blanck** Palish; excellent flavour and liveliness of style. Good acidity. *Lunch with my Norwegian fellow pianist and wine-writing friend, Stig Lundberg, at my local wine bar, Balls Bros, London, Feb 1994* ★★★

**Tokay-Pinot Gris Clos Jebsal SGN Zind-Humbrecht**
A small production from late-picked, selected botrytis-affected berries. A half bottle at Le Montrachet in New York: rich gold; gloriously honeyed, peachy, bouquet and flavour. Sweet, rich but with a crisp, acidic touch giving it a refreshing finish. *Oct 1995. Surprised and exuberant I gave it* ★★★★★

## 1992 ★★ to ★★★★

Once again, with its sheltered position along the lower slopes of the Vosges facing the Rhine valley, the growers in Alsace enjoyed well-nigh perfect conditions. Early budding, frost-free, excellent flowering, followed by a warm, dry summer and the hottest August since 1921. Their good fortune continued with a perfect September, picking commencing on the 30th, avoiding the torrential rains which plagued the rest of France.

I enjoyed some decent dry wines in their youth and, as noted below, one of the finest-ever Pinot Gris. No other sweet wines have come my way.

**Tokay-Pinot Gris Grand Cru Kitterlé Schlumberger**
Extraordinary colour, medium-deep, amber-gold; very rich, honeyed bottle-age bouquet, almost Gewurz fragrance; medium-dry, full-bodied (alcohol 14%), a bit four-square but with excellent flavour. Good length. Very impressive. *With Coquilles St Jacques aux Truffes at the annual wine tasting and gourmet dinner at the Knickerbocker Club, New York, Oct 2000* ★★★★★ *Which goes to show how a top class Pinot Gris will not only keep but take on new dimensions with bottle age.*

**Tokay-Pinot Gris Patergarten Blanck** I found that this was a follow on for the '91 I had been drinking and becoming bored with. It was, in fact, distinctly better than usual: a positive, waxy yellow; good nose; dry, fairly full-bodied, very distinctive and attractive flavour, good length. Several notes on this pretty dependable type of wine, best drunk with something like turbot. *At Balls Bros, London, Jan 1995* ★★★ *Not for long keeping though.*

## 1993 ★★★★

Once again the lofty Vosges mountains protected Alsace from the heavy early autumn rains that affected the rest of France. Despite uneven conditions prior to the harvest, which began on 23 September, the earliest date since 1976, all varieties were successfully gathered in – albeit between showers. The crop was smaller than the '92 but quality was higher, with ripeness almost reaching '88 and '89 levels. However, late pickers were hampered by rain and few sweet wines were made. All except the very best dry wines should have been consumed by now.

**Gewurztraminer Vendange Tardive Sparr** Medium-pale, touch of spritz; lovely, gently spicy Gewurz varietal fragrance; medium, not sweet, excellent flavour. Hard to place a wine like this. Not a dessert wine. Probably good with turbot but best with cheese. *At a British Airways blind tasting, April 1996* ★★★

**Riesling Clos des Capucins Cuvée Théo Dom Weinbach/Faller** Beautifully made. Dry, full-bodied. What an Alsace Riesling is all about. *In Coral Gables, Feb 1996* ★★★★

**Riesling Cuvée Frédéric Émile Trimbach** Two notes within a few days. Palish; crisp, steely nose; very good, firm, dry and stylish. Excellent flavour and marvellous length. *Tasted Dec 1998* ★★★★

**Riesling Grand Cru Kirchberg de Barr Willm** Dry, distinctive, a touch of peach kernels which I never like, and lacking zest. *Tasted Jan 1996* ★

**Riesling Clos Ste-Hune Trimbach** Very good varietal aroma; dry, clean as a whistle, with a hard, dry finish. Rather unexciting. *At a Rodenstock lunch in Munich, Aug 1998* ★★★

**Riesling Grand Cru Schlossberg Cave de Kientzheim** The Schlossberg slopes overlook the little town of Kaysersberg, noted for being, among other things, the birth place of Dr Albert Schweitzer, organist and Bach authority who eventually ran a hospital in darkest Africa. It was where Daphne and I spent our first-ever night in Alsace. Our bedroom was at the inn which overlooked the square and the church. The noise of the fountain and the quarter-hour chimes kept us awake all night. The château of Kientzheim is also the headquarters of the Confrérie St-Étienne. The Cave is a co-operative, and pretty good too. *Noted Jan 1997* ★★ *For early drinking.*

**Tokay-Pinot Gris Kuentz-Bas** Cress-like fragrance; mature dry finish, attractive. *Tea-time with Lou Skinner, Coral Gables, Feb 1996* ★★★

## 1994 ★★ to ★★★

A difficult year for the growers. Cold, wet spring, flowering following a rainy period which ended 8 June. Summer reasonably warm and dry but followed by 30 days of rain, persistent and heavy, in September. Rot was prevalent, Riesling being most affected. The only crop that remained healthy throughout the deluge was Gewurztraminer. Those growers who held out took advantage of the returning fine weather.

There were some good ripe Gewurztraminers of a generally higher quality than the '93s, both late-harvested and botrytis-affected. These are the only wines which were, and still are, of interest.

**Gewurztraminer B H Geyl** Medium-pale yellow; very distinctive rose-cachou fragrance; medium-sweet, copybook flavour. *Selected to demonstrate the Gewurz varietal characteristics at Christie's wine course, London, Jan 1997* ★★★

**Gewurztraminer Cuvée d'Or Quintessences de SGN Dom Weinbach/Faller** Gold; gloriously ripe, honeyed, spicy botrytis; sweet, full (alcohol 14%), soft and long. Glorious wine. *Tasted Sept 1997* ★★★★(★) *Now to beyond 2010.*

**Gewurztraminer Goldert Vendange Tardive Zind-Humbrecht** Luxuriously rich yet a soft and spicy Gewurz; fairly sweet, superb flavour and balance. *At Hal Lewis' Bacchus Society 'Bar-B-Que', Memphis, Sept 1999* ★★★★ *Lovely then. Will keep.*

**Gewurztraminer SGN Rolly Gassman** Slightly hazy straw gold; glorious lychees; fairly sweet, very rich, honeyed botrytis flavour reminding me of a 6-putt Tokaji. *At a France in your Glass dinner at Ch de Bagnols near Villefranche, Oct 1998* ★★★★

## 1995 ★★★★ to ★★★★★

Late bud break, damp spring, uneven flowering with *coulure* which limited the eventual production. September was rainy and cool but there was a long Indian summer in October. Late pickers did best. Whereas it was the Rieslings that suffered in 1994, they were regarded as perfect in 1995, generally superior to Gewurztraminers, though, as always, there were exceptions. Also there were some superlative Pinot Gris (the name 'Tokay' was being dropped, at long last, because of the confusion with Tokaji from Hungary).

The better wines of all grapes and classes can still be drunk with enjoyment – but don't wait. The top sweet wines will positively last.

**Gewurztraminer Grand Cru Furstentum SGN Dom Weinbach/Faller** Yellow; opulent aroma, rose-cachou, lychees; very sweet, luscious, moderate weight (alcohol 12%), richness and fat cut by unusual (for Gewurz) acidity. A brilliant wine. *Sept 1997* ★★★★(★) *Lovely now, will keep and develop.*

**Riesling Grand Cru Schoenenbourg de Riquewihr Dopff au Moulin** Pale, bright; hard-nosed; fairly dry, distinctive flavour, good acidity. Classic. Yet I was expecting something greater. *Tasted June 1997* ★★★

**Riesling Muhlforst Caves de Ribeauvillé** Dry, hot and hard. A none-too-brilliant co-operative wine. *Tasted Jan 1997* ★

**Riesling Vendange Tardive Hugel** Harvested 26 October, 60% botrytis, alcohol 12.6%, tremendously high residual sugar 45g/l, fairly high acidity 8.7g/l. Production 250 cases. First noted at Etienne Hugel's masterclass in 1999. Deep gold; glorious, fresh, very fragrant clover honey bouquet; deliciously sweet with counterbalancing acidity. Most recently: pure gold; substantial grapey, grassy, honeyed nose; sweet, rich, beautiful texture and balance. Totally delicious. *Last noted at Hugel's VT tasting in London, April 2002* ★★★★

**Tokay-Pinot Gris Altenbourg Cuvée Laurence Dom Weinbach/Faller** Made by Colette Faller and daughter. Palish, bright yellow; hefty, peach and mint nose; fairly sweet, full-bodied (alcohol 14%), superb flavour, perfect acidity. *During my live chat on Decanter magazine's website, Dec 2001* ★★★★

**(Tokay) Pinot Gris Clos Jebsal SGN Zind-Humbrecht** Golden colour; gloriously exotic, honeyed botrytis fragrance; very sweet, immensely rich yet not cloying, lovely flavour, great depth, perfect acidity. Outstandingly the best wine at the VIIème Tour de France des Appellations. *At Dom de Chevalier, Bordeaux, June 2001* ★★★★★ *Great now but will continue to dazzle well beyond 2010.*

**Tokay-Pinot Gris Vendange Tardive Dom Weinbach/Faller** Very good fruit, greengages; medium-sweet, rich, more peach-like on palate, light weight for Pinot Gris (alcohol 12%), very good acidity. The Faller ladies had just the right touch. *At the Justerini & Brooks tasting, Sept 1997* ★★★★ *Should be perfect now.*

## 1996 ★★★★

In many ways this was an ideal vintage, with vivacious dry wines. For me the Rieslings were particularly attractive, a trio of the most appealing being noted below. Growing conditions: spring late, bud burst uneven. June mainly warm and dry, flowering from 6 June and Gewurztraminer affected by *coulure*. The rest of the summer was warm and dry, the harvest beginning in cool conditions in early October, continuing – for the late-harvest wines – almost to the middle of November though the dry weather prevented the formation of botrytis.

Most wines were consumed in the late 1990s but the better wines are still delicious.

**Riesling Cuvée Ste Cathérine II Dom Weinbach/Faller** From the lower part of the Schlossberg vineyard and known under this *cuvée* designation before Schlossberg was classified *grand cru* (in 1975). All rather confusing. Totally different appearance to the Schlossberg II below: positive yellow; still hard though with considerable depth; sweeter, spicy, higher extract though same strength, good length, 'hot', dry finish. *Tasted Sept 1997* ★★★(★★) *Probably at its best 2003–2008.*

**Riesling Grand Cru Schlossberg II Dom Weinbach/Faller** The family owns 8ha of the Schlossberg. Almost colourless; good, light, fragrant Riesling aroma; fairly dry, excellent flavour,

pleasant weight (alcohol 13%), firm, crisp, long, dry finish. *At the Justerini & Brooks tasting, London, Sept 1997* ★★★★

**Riesling 'Les Princes Abbés' Schlumberger** Pale; good, fresh, varietal aroma; crisp, delicious, light style and weight (alcohol 12.5%), and very good value. *At a Maison Marques et Domaines tasting, London, Jan 2000* ★★★

**Riesling Vendange Tardive Hugel** Harvested 14 and 17 October, alcohol 12.6%, residual sugar 25g/l, very high acidity 10.2g/l. Two recent notes: touch of yellow; very rich nose, fat and fleshy; yet surprisingly dry, excellent flavour and length. Two months later: lovely, honey and orange blossom, almost Pinot Gris-like; swingeingly dry (no malolactic fermentation) but good flavour and penetrating length. Fully fermented out reminding me once again of a fine Rheingau Auslese trocken (though the Hugels might disapprove of the comparison). *Last noted at Hugel's Vendange Tardive tasting at the Cinnamon Club in London, April 2002* ★★★★

## 1997 ★★★★★

Yet another superb vintage despite some early problems with an uneven bud break and *coulure* due to rain in June and July. August and September were hot and sunny, with record overall hours of sunshine, double those of 1995. Fully ripe grapes were harvested from 1 October: the Riesling was excellent with excellent with very high ripeness levels, but Gewurztraminer, once again hit by *coulure*, suffered crop losses. Early morning mists in October generated some botrytis, but not everywhere. The harvest ended on 4 November.

Ideally this is a dry wine vintage and many of the wines should have been, quite rightly, consumed while young and fresh. I have quoted a handful of notes to illustrate the richer styles of the three major grape varieties.

**Gewurztraminer 'Jubilee' Hugel** Medium pale yellow; lovely mellow lychees and rose-cachou; medium-sweet, rich, mildly spicy. *At lunch after Hugel's Vendange Tardive tasting at the Cinnamon Club in London, April 2002* ★★★★

**Gewurztraminer SGN Hugel** Potential alcohol 22%, 165° Oechsle, alcohol 13.5%. Two recent notes: yellow gold; gorgeous, deliciously scented Gewurz; very sweet, incredibly rich, substantial and complete. Two months later, at lunch after the special Hugel Vendange Tardive tasting: pure gold; perfect harmony, quintessence of Gewurz; fabulously rich, power yet with finesse. One of Hugel's greatest. *Tasted April 2002* ★★★★★

**Riesling Rangen Clos St-Urbain Zind-Humbrecht** Positive yellow; very good classic Riesling; medium-dry, lovely flavour, touch of youthful pineapple; very good acidity. Copybook. *At Dom de Chevalier, Bordeaux, June 1999* ★★★★ *Refreshing then and should be perfect now.*

**Riesling Vendange Tardive Hugel** Harvested 2 November with very little botrytis. Alcohol 12.75g/l, acidity 6.6g/l. Palish yellow; harmonious, slightly waxy almost Chenin nose, crisp, grapey; medium-sweet, delicious flavour, fragrant, good finish. *At Hugel's Vendange Tardive tasting, April 2002* ★★★★ *Lovely. Will keep. At peak probably 2005–2010.*

**Tokay-Pinot Gris Altenbourg Cuvée Laurence Dom Weinbach/Faller** Bright yellow; hefty, minty, peachy nose; medium-sweet, full-bodied (alcohol 14%), rich, superb flavour and perfect acidity. *During my live chat on Decanter magazine's website, Dec 2001* ★★★(★★) *Lovely now but even better with further bottle age. I am pretty sure that Decanter had no idea how long it would take, and the cost of setting up a website. And I, in my ignorance, thought this chat really would be live!*

# 1998 ★★★★

Four really good – indeed unprecedented – vintages in a row. Yet the weather conditions throughout the growing season were very up-and-down: cool April, hot and dry May, uneventful flowering. July was wet but from early August to mid-September, there was exceptional heat. An early harvest, 25 September, in sunshine but a short, sharp burst of rain put off most picking until early October. As always, the minor dry wines for drinking soon, with many good Gewurztraminers and zestful Rieslings. But the gap between the merely decent and the really good is continuing to widen.

**Gewurztraminer Schléret** Used for some time to illustrate the distinctive Gewurz scent and style at Christie's Wine Course introductory sessions. Very consistent and typical Gewurz aroma combining rose-cachou and lychee; medium-dry, good, slightly spicy-flavoured, typically rather short and blunt ended, lacking the zestful acidity of a Riesling. *Last noted Nov 2001* ★★★ *For early drinking.*

**Gewurztraminer Vendange Tardive Hugel** Pale, lime tinged; beautifully scented Gewurz; medium-sweet, lovely flavour, easy (alcohol 12%), a touch of blandness. *Jan 2002* ★★★

**Riesling Schoenenbourg Vendange Tardive Hugel** Harvested 21 October, alcohol 12.35%, high residual sugar 43g/l, acidity 7.1g/l. Two recent notes: pale, lime-tinged; herbaceous, floral, reminding me of a ripe Saar Riesling; fairly sweet, glorious, apricot-like fruit but hard acidic finish. Needs time. Two months later: pale, faint green tinge; very eager to perform, flowery fragrance, greengages and lime; medium-sweet, lovely, delicate, crisp, with tingling acidity. *Last noted, the youngest of 13 vintages, at Hugel's VT tasting at the Cinnamon Club, London, April 2002* ★★★(★) *Delicious now. Will keep and develop.*

**Tokay-Pinot Gris 'Jubilee' Hugel** Pale; floral, delicious; medium, neither dry nor sweet, full-bodied (alcohol 13.5%), delicious flavour. *Jan 2002* ★★★(★)

A TASTING OF ZIND-HUMBRECHT '98s held in London, March 2000, The tasting, 14 of Zind-Humbrecht's '98s, a perfect vintage to display the varietal and quality differences, was an eye opener and I found it by far the most interesting Alsace tasting for some time. I summarise the wines briefly below.

**GEWURZTRAMINER Heimbourg** (limestone soil) relatively low-keyed; fairly sweet (14.5%) ★★★(★); **Clos Windsbuhl** spicy; medium, lovely flavour (14%), dry finish ★★★★; **Grand Cru Hengst** 127° Oechsle, 40g/l residual sugar, an astonishing 16% alcohol. Medium-dry, rich, spicy, intense. Hard finish. Nowhere near ready. Olivier Humbrecht told me that it would need at least ten years ★(★★★★); and **Goldert Vendange Tardive** lovely aroma, mint and orange blossom; fairly sweet, still hard. *June 2001* ★★★(★★)

**RIESLING Gueberschwihr** in bottle for ten weeks at the time of tasting. Pale, unusually spicy; lovely flavour, (alcohol 13%), lacking length (the least expensive of the range) ★★★; **Grand Cru Brand** fermented for one year, 8g/l residual sugar, alcohol 14.8%: medium pale; full, ripe melon; dry but very rich, with peachy flavour. Rather like an Auslese trocken

from the Rheingau ★★(★★★); **Grand Cru Rangen de Thann, Clos St-Urbain** good colour; low-keyed but with ripe melon and honey – touch of botrytis; medium sweet, full-flavoured, 'warming' (alcohol 13.5%). Glorious ★★★(★★); **Clos Hauserer** pale; grapey, 'greengage' acidity; distinctly more powerful though only 0.5% more than the Gueberschwihr and the Turkheim. *Needs time* ★★(★★); **Clos Heimbourg** medium pale; more melon-like, fragrant; medium-sweet, delicious flavour (alcohol 13%), good finish ★★★(★); **Herrenweg** very pale; lively, fragrant, slightly spicy; dryish, very pleasant flavour, good acidity. A copybook, reasonably priced, refreshing wine ★★★; and **Turkheim** bottled in February 2000. Positive colour; good crisp Riesling aroma; medium-dry, soft yet hot (alcohol 13%) finish. *Needs time* ★★(★)

**PINOT GRIS Heimbourg** Oechsle 118°, 49g/l residual sugar, alcohol 13.5%. Pale; subtle, honeyed botrytis nose; medium-sweet, glorious flavour. Drink by itself, also perfect with selected cheeses. ★★★(★★) *will gain momentum with bottle age;* **Rothenbourg** unusually for Alsace, a west-facing vineyard catching the late afternoon sun, favourable for botrytis: pale; honeyed bouquet; medium-sweet, rich, extra dimensions because of botrytis ★★★★(★); and **Clos Windsbuhl** ripe quince jelly and marmalade scents; medium-sweet, substantial but not hefty, delectable botrytis ★★★(★).

# 1999 variable, at best ★★★

Well, the run of really good vintages in Alsace could scarcely continue and the weather conditions saw to it in 1999. The season started well enough with a pleasant spring, hot May and relatively early flowering which, however, was extended until mid-June owing to humid conditions. Mildew was a problem and was exacerbated by mixed weather to the end of July. August was equally mixed but from the middle of the month to the third week in September, the weather was hot and dry. Then came the rain. It lasted for five weeks during what should have been an ideal harvesting period. It was a question of picking between wet spells, and selection. Some growers were harvesting to the very end of November. Yet, overall, growers reported some good wines with racy acidity. I think this is understandable optimism; after all, it is their living. Those buyers who laid in earlier vintages can count themselves lucky.

**Pinot Noir 'Les Neveux' Hugel** I have never thought much of red Alsace wines. In the past, not unlike German Spätburgunder, they lacked definition with colours ranging from *pelure d'oignon*, a sort of feeble-tinted tawny, to plummy and weak-rimmed. Produced at lunch following the Hugel tasting, this one was surprisingly deep and impressive; distinct Pinot aroma; dry, full-bodied (alcohol 14.5%) and with remarkably good flavour. *Jan 2002* ★★(★) *Serious, agreeable. It would be interesting to see how this takes bottle-ageing.*

**Riesling Cuvée Ste-Cathérine II Dom Weinbach/Faller** Palish yellow; steely, whiff of lime blossom; dry, firm fruit, good aftertaste. *Tasted Jan 2001* ★★(★)

**Riesling Rangen Zind-Humbrecht** Flowery; dry, good flavour and aftertaste. *Tasted in London, June 2001* ★★★ *Drink soon.*

# 2000 and the future

Looking back helps me to look forward. For over the past decade in Alsace, better and better, more individualistic wines have been made by a handful of intelligent, diligent – well, brilliant – grape growers and winemakers setting new standards. In the middle remain the good, well-established, merchant growers; while the stubbornly ordinary producers plod along. But it is rare to come across a really bad Alsace wine.

My hope, and I am sure it is the hope of the producers, is that the market will more and more appreciate these wines for, despite the intense world competition for shelf and cellar space, the best Alsace wines are inimitable.

A final word. Go to Alsace. It is one of the most attractive of all wine regions with, without question, the prettiest villages, a mass of good local restaurants and decent places to stay.

## 2000 a cautious ★★★, possible ★★★★

Uneven weather conditions: early bud break, very hot May and June, satisfactory flowering; very cool July, warm and sunny in August and early September. Then mixed weather. The harvest started unusually early in the third week of September. The main problem was not ripening but, at the lower level, overproduction.

On a more positive note, some beneficial botrytis formed, and some interesting late-harvest and SGN wines have been made, albeit in small quantities. Few were available for tasting at the time of writing.

**Gewurztraminer Hugel** Very pale, lemon-tinged; fresh, youthful, minty nose with characteristic lychees aroma; medium-dry, delicious, dry finish. *Perfect with the Cinnamon Club's spicy food, London, April 2002* ★★★★ *for freshness and charm.*

**Gewurztraminer Cuvée Laurence Dom Weinbach/Faller** Glorious varietal aroma, but with a hard core; sweet, rich, lovely. *At Justerini & Brooks annual tasting, Jan 2002* ★★(★★)

**Riesling Grand Cru Schlossberg Cuvée Ste-Catherine 'L'Inédit' Dom Weinbach/Faller** Very pale; lovely pineappley nose; medium-sweet, rich, soft, 'crusty' flavour. *Jan 2002* ★(★★★)

A RANGE OF HUGEL WINES TASTED IN ASCENDING QUALITY ORDER JANUARY 2002
**Riesling 'Hugel'** Vinified from 95% bought-in grapes. Very pale, lime tinged; delicious, forthcoming, floral, minty nose; dry, light (alcohol 11.5%), still young and raw. Good acidity. Inexpensive. (★★★)
**Riesling 'Tradition'** Selection of the best bought-in grapes. Almost colourless; touch of almond kernels or marzipan on nose and flavour. Dry, fragrant (alcohol 12%) (★★)?
**Riesling Grand Cru 'Jubilee'** From Hugel's own *grand cru* vineyard. Very pale; good depth; medium dry, alcohol 12%, greater length and depth ★★(★★)
**Tokay-Pinot Gris 'Jubilee'** Palish; slightly nutty, good fruit, gooseberry-like acidity; medium-sweet, full-bodied (13.5%), good flavour; melon and grapes ★★(★★)

# Mas de Daumas Gassac

Why devote a chapter to this one relatively small domaine? First because it exemplifies what two people, Aimé and Véronique Guibert, can do with vision, courage, enterprise, tenacity – and a bit of luck, together with the sage advice of two eminent professors; secondly, because I have had the unusual opportunity of following the progress of their wine from the very first vintage in 1978 to the present day.

Aimé Guibert, whose family was in the leather business for generations, came from Millau, long the centre of glovemaking in France. When he and his wife bought the farm (the *mas*), they had considered making a local wine though they suspected that the little valley of the Gassac, a tributary of the Hérault, had its own peculiar microclimate. This was confirmed by Henri Enjalbert, Professor of Geography at the University of Bordeaux, who also suggested that the geological structures were capable of producing a wine of *grand cru* quality. Rock, scrub and tree clearing began in 1971 and the first vines, principally Cabernet Sauvignon, were planted on a 1.6-ha plot. (The domaine has now expanded to 40ha, with 28ha planted with red varieties and 12ha with white.) Through other friends the Guiberts got in touch with Professor Emile Peynaud who, though initially reluctant to be involved, was eventually persuaded to advise and, to their surprise and delight, turned up in time for the Guiberts' first vintage, 1978.

Aimé Guibert first made a white wine in 1986 and I have been able to taste this and all other vintages to date. Although dry whites wines do not feature much in this book, I think that Guibert's experimentation with *cépages* and winemaking is interesting. Some are, of course, too old, some as yet immature, some – like the superb 1998 which I served at my 75th birthday dinner – fully and deliciously developed.

It is not my job, nor is there space, to comment on the choice of vine varieties or early marketing problems and how they were overcome. I shall confine myself to my own very subjective notes, frequently made at home with food, which after all is the ultimate purpose of the wine, but also at the major vertical tastings, one at Gassac on my first visit in 1994 and on the complete range of all Guibert's vintages tasted at home with Alastair Mackenzie, Jancis Robinson and Freddie Price in September 2001. In 1992, writing to the Guiberts, Peynaud observed that 'vertical tastings are like family photographs; they date quickly and one must constantly bring them up to date'. Well, here goes.

## Mas de Daumas Gassac (Red)

**1978** From young vines, and the first vintage to be put on the market. Despite the label stating *pur Cabernet Sauvignon*, the blend was Cabernet Sauvignon 87%, Tannat 8%, Malbec 4% and Syrah 1%. First tasted in December 1989 – at home, with steak and kidney pie: deep, attractive, still youthful; rather medicinal Ch Talbot-like nose; good fruit, tannic. Next, at an extensive vertical tasting in London in 1990: low-keyed, not much development, but with a certain piquancy. Then, at the complete vertical at Gassac in September 1994: nose opened up fabulously but tannic and austere. Showing its age yet still some sweetness and fruit in London in 1998. Most recently, tasted at home: now, understandably, showing its age, its colour lacking definition; nose oxidising and tarry, 'singed black treacle', with sweaty old tannins enabling it to cling to life. Dried out and a bit tart. *Last tasted Sept 2001. Now over the hill. At best* ★★

**1979** From a blend of Cabernet Sauvignon 80%, Tannat 15%, Syrah 3%, Malbec 2% (again labelled *pur Cabernet Sauvignon*). Also first tasted at lunch in 1989: plummy; sweaty, tannic nose

but good fruit; dry, lean, silky tannins and austere. A year later at the vertical tasting: low-keyed nose, showing some age, leathery tannic texture. Next, the oldest of five vintages consumed, well partially consumed, at a Sunday lunch at home. Very dry, tannic, austere even with food (1990). Then at Gassac (1994) brambly, blackcurrant aroma; silky tannic texture. Lean and austere. Most recently: rich yet nebulous; rich, cheesy nose that held well – vanilla and 'old oak' after nine hours. More power and flesh than the '78. Good flavour but tannin and acidity firmly in charge. *Last tasted Sept 2001* ★★

**1980** First tasted in May 1987, the oldest of six vintages, from the importer, Mistral Wines. Although said to be '100% Cabernet Sauvignon', in fact it was a *mélange* of varieties, in this case Cabernet Sauvignon 80%, Malbec 10%, Syrah 6% and Tannat 4%. However, we were also provided with more detailed information about its make-up: alcohol 12.9%, dry extract 27.00g/l, pH 3.45, volatile acidity 0.52g/l and total acidity 3.5g/l. Thickly coloured; sweaty tannins: wet leather and armpits; medium-dry, raw, tannic. No great length. Next, at lunch in 1990: richly coloured; rustic nose; some sweetness, fruit laden but tannic. Similar note a month later, adding lean, 'lots of grip'. At Gassac in 1994, crisp fruit, well-evolved nose: nice weight, overall dry but fragrant. Most recently: still fairly deep and intense; nose hard, tannic but with crisp fruit, 'singed bracken', tarry overtones; notably good fruit, some soft flesh, sweetness battling tannin, a bit tart. *Last tasted Sept 2001* ★★

**1981** This was the first vintage of Daumas Gassac I ever tasted. I had already heard of Monsieur Guibert's wine but he later kindly sent me a bottle for my comments. Emile Peynaud was advising at this stage and, what with his expertise and the dominance of Cabernet Sauvignon, the style of the wine leaned towards Bordeaux. Monsieur Guibert must also have sent a sample bottle to the Danish magazine, *Alt om Mad* (All about Food) for it was shortly afterwards, in March 1984, that I tasted it again at a lunch for the press at Le Cocotte restaurant in Copenhagen: purple, intense; spicy; very taut and tannic but good fruit (as my contribution I had brought a bottle of 1928 Anjou Rablay). Next at Mistral Wines' tasting in 1987: showing well: lovely bouquet, Cabernet dominant (100% on the label but contents only 81%, with Malbec 12%, Syrah 6% and Tannat 1% – I won't bore readers with all the other statistics – it was not dissimilar to the '80); lean but shapely, still with youthful tannin. A good wine with a good future. Next, twice, in 1990: fleshy, firm, tannic. Yet at the Gassac vertical (1994) I thought it relatively light and easy, lacking length. I much looked forward to retasting it. Alas, the bottle was corked. *Last sniffed Sept 2001. At best* ★★★

**1982** It was at a Christie's pre-sale tasting in July 1986 that the wine really made me sit up. First of all, I was surprised to see it in a Fine Wine sale. But it was immensely impressive: distinctive, intense, purple; excellent nose which I thought must be Cabernet Sauvignon or Cabernet Franc; 'a ripe alcoholic sweetness', rich, fruity, tannic. Quite coincidentally, a month later, staying with Hugh Johnson; my host produced a decanter and challenged me to name the wine. It was one of those rare occasions when, with just a glance at the colour, it clicked. Without smelling or tasting I said 'Mas de Daumas Gassac', and added '82'. HJ was taken aback. There was no more blind tasting that weekend!

Next, in July 1988, at a 'works outing' – my annual picnic lunch for the Christie's wine department at Chippenham Lodge: good soft flesh. A very high mark at the vertical in 1990: softening, delicious; and again, twice, later that year, though at lunch, despite being impressive, 'no charm'. My highest mark (with the 1990) at the complete vertical at Gassac in 1994: full, rich, soft, spicy, *à point*. Most recently: rich, velvety, mature brownish rim. The blend of Bordeaux varietals (Cabernet Sauvignon dominating, plus Merlot, Malbec, Cabernet Franc) giving it a most distinct Bordeaux nose, bricky, forthcoming, a touch of iron, great depth and, even after nine hours in the glass, very fragrant. On the palate, soft, fleshy, its richness masking the tannins. Freddie Price said this was the first vintage to show its *terroir* character whereas I put it down to the *cépages*. It was excellent. The second best wine of the 23 vintages. *Last tasted Sept 2001* ★★★★★ *Drink soon.*

**1983** By this time, the grape varieties were reasonably mature and the winemaking mastered. First noted at the Mistral vertical in 1987. No contradictions here: Cabernet Sauvignon 80% yet, unlike the '82, with Pinot Noir and Syrah but no

Tannat. Higher alcohol and extract than even the '82. Fragrant, vigorous, exciting fruit, spicy; lovely flavour, elegant, good texture. Next, in 1990, two notes, both also very good if not quite as rapturous. At Gassac (1994): open, harmonious, *cerise*. Sweet, Pomerol-like flavour and texture. Fully evolved. Most recently: still a wonderfully deep velvety colour; rich, bricky, high-toned nose, then tarry and after an hour, sweet and herbaceous. Held well for nine hours. On the palate, soft, fleshy, still tannic. My top mark of the tasting. *Last noted Sept 2001* ★★★★★ *Drink soon.*

**1984** Cabernet Sauvignon 80%, the rest Malbec, Merlot, Cabernet Franc, Pinot, Syra (*sic*) and Tannat. First tasted 1987: nose stalky, citrus, celery; dry, fullish, austere, raw tannins, no great length. At the vertical in 1990 rich 'legs' noted, tannins again; touch of bitterness. Unknit but attractive at Rodenstock's wine weekend (also 1990) and at Gassac (1994) muffled, flavoury but tart. Most recently: mature; warm, rich, singed bouquet, sweet, very flavoury but slightly bitter and tart. *Last tasted Sept 2001* ★ *Drink up.*

**1985** It is interesting to follow the progress of a wine from cradle to full maturity: a cask sample drawn in January, tasted in May (bottled in April) 1987: 60,000 bottles, 1000 magnums, 30 jeroboams, 12 methusalems (*sic*): opaque, of course: spicy, cinnamon, new oak, sweet raw, blackcurrant (Cabernet Sauvignon) fragrance, figgy, almost port-like, lovely flavour, length and finish. Elegant though lean. A good start. Exactly three years later: sweet, full, very rich, velvety. Next, at lunch in 1991: still very deep, full, soft, fleshy, lovely. With the 1983 my second highest mark at the vertical tasting at Gassac in 1994. A really lovely wine, complete, good future. Most recently: still richly impressive, fragrant, harmonious; some sweetness, good flavour, fruit, tannins and acidity. One of my three top marks. *Last tasted Sept 2001* ★★★★★ *Lovely now. Why wait?*

**1986** The Cabernet Sauvignon element lowered to 75%, the rest Cabernet Franc, Merlot, Malbec, Syra, Pinot Noir, Tannat. In May 1990 still intense, fragrant, spicy new oak; fresh crisp fruit, tannic. Good wine. Laden with fruit and tannin at Gassac (1994). Next, over a decade later: strange though attractive fruit, opening up fragrantly; very positive, lovely flavour, leathery tannins. Might well develop further. *Last noted Sept 2001* ★★(★) *Now–2006?*

**1987** Cabernet Sauvignon reduced to 70%, the rest of the blend made up of six other varieties. By now, the alcoholic content was lower, around 12.7%. Three verticals, the first in 1990. Plummy purple; sweet, soft, pleasant. The next at Gassac in 1994, very sweet, chocolatey, 'Caramac' fudge; chunky, spicy, tannic, but 'ready soon'. Drinking well, soft and fleshy in 1998. Most recently: fully mature, weak-rimmed; very sweet, caramelly nose, 'black treacle'; sweet, its softness losing the battle with raw tannic grip. After time in the glass nose and taste of mocha and chocolate. *Last tasted Sept 2001* ★★ *Drink up.*

**1988** A great vintage. A similar blend to to the '87. In May 1990 opaque; very rich; fairly sweet, full bodied, good fruit, tannins and acidity. Two months later, a similar note, adding high extract, spice, flesh. At Gassac (1994): rich 'legs'; verdant, vegetal, medicinal nose; full flavour, lean touch; still a lovely colour; bouquet emerging fragrantly and holding well; sweet, crisp fruit, firm, still tannic. In September 2001 Freddie Price observed that Daumas Gassac was building up to a crescendo with the '88, '89 and '90. *Last tasted May 2002* ★★★★★ *At peak.*

**1989** First tasted the spring after the vintage. Rather rough texture yet good potential. At Gassac (1994): alcohol 13%, more varnish than fruit but opened up well; silky yet teeth-gripping tannins. Now fairly deep, still youthful; nose singed, bricky, spicy; very sweet, with a warm ripe fruitiness. Lovely wine. *Last tasted Sept 2001* ★★★★★ *Now–2009.*

**1990** Settled down to a *cépage* mix similar to the '87 and '88. Tasted at Gassac in 1994: very high mark, deep, fairly intense; very rich, deep, 'tea and chocolate' nose: good fruit, flesh, extract. Most recently: very good nose, distinctly sweet, distinctive fruit; nice weight 12.7%, similar to the previous four vintages. *Last tasted Sept 2001* ★★★(★) *Now–2010.*

**1991** First tasted at home in December 1993: assertive, fruit-laden, not ready, of course. The Cabernet Sauvignon had clearly reached full maturity and 90% of the Cabernet Sauvignon in this blend was from old vines, the rest was Cabernet Franc, Malbec and Syra. At Gassac (1994) surprisingly deep, intense, well-evolved nose, rich, biscuity; crisp good extract but very tannic. By 1997 good fruit and flesh. At ten years of age, a fragrant, herbaceous nose that opened up beautifully; however, though sweet, I found it slightly woody and astringent. *Last noted Sept 2001* ★★(★)

**1992** Over half a dozen notes, first at Gassac in September 1994: good 'legs'; open knit, youthful fruit – a quick developer? Curious, chunky. Next in 1997: youthful, raw, astringent. Yet only a year later drinking well though tannic. In 1999, picnicking at Glyndebourne – 'alright on the night'. Preceded by the '94 *blanc*, quaffed with the family at another picnic, 'The Fourth of June' at Eton – colourful but hardly ideal conditions. Most recently: still deep, rich, plummy, well developed nose, mocha, then caramel, dry, crisp, good length and, bypassing the edgy tannin, a rich aftertaste. *Last noted Sept 2001* ★★★ *Drink soon.*

**1993** Roughly similar *cépage* mix to the '91 but this time with Tannat added. First tasted in cask at Gassac in September 1994: purple, very pleasant young fruit and easy style, highish acidity. Then two notes in 1998: medium-deep, soft, plummy, crisp attractive fruit; touch of sweetness, integrated tannins and acidity though the latter very noticeable (both with meals at Chippenham Lodge). Labouring under picnic conditions, 'The Fourth of June' again, May 2000, but drinking well exactly a year later. Now with the look of an early developer; nose of strawberries and raisins; sweet, very fruity, good grip and finish. *Last tasted Sept 2001* ★★★(★)

**1994** Similar varietal mix to 1992. Although I had met Aimé Guibert several times before, mainly at Vinexpo, and we had corresponded regularly, this was the year of our first visit to the estate. It was well timed: we joined the family and pickers at the harvest supper, very jolly and musical (Véronique Guibert has a lovely voice). Just a slight problem: after weeks of hot dry weather there was torrential rain the day before we arrived and they had not closed the skylight in the guest bedroom. That September the wine was still fermenting so I first tasted it at the London Wine Trade Fair the following May with Aimé (he thought it was his best ever): opaque, of course, very

good fruit and flavour. Next at home in 1992: lovely, lively, fragrant; rich, thick texture, chewy, tannic. Then at four years of age and, though youthful in appearance, drinking well. However, at the recent line-up, I found it disappointing: a strange, milky, corky nose; tart and astringent. I hope it was just the bottle. (I feel I should add that Alastair Mackenzie thought it showed well in the mouth, with good balance and structure.) *Last noted Sept 2001. At best* ★★★★★

**1995** In May 1997, though sweet, almost caramelly on the nose; very dry, oak and tannic grip on the palate. A couple of years later: good fruit, delicious, flavoury, discreet oak and tannin. Most recently: still very deep; bricky, Bordeaux-like nose (Cabernet Sauvignon 'ancien' now 90% of the blend) which opened up richly; fairly sweet (Alastair Mackenzie thought it was black treacle and old leather), good soft fruit and dry finish. *Last tasted Sept 2001* ★★★(★) *Now–2010.*

**1996** Four notes. Initially full of colour, fruit and extract. In 1998 still virtually opaque; very rich sweet nose and taste, but tannic. Now looking mature; tangy; good flesh but very tannic. *Last tasted Sept 2001* ★★(★) *Probably at its best 2005–2010.*

**1997** A sweet, chaptalised sort of fruitiness. Left in the glass I thought it had a touch of mercaptan. Rich, but very tannic texture. Mackenzie and I had reservations about its potential. *Last tasted Sept 2001* ★?

**1998** Cabernet Sauvignon now 80% of the blend. A couple of notes in May 2000. Touch of tar on the nose; fairly full-bodied (13% alcohol). Packed with ripe fruit. Richness masking tannins. Most recently: deep, velvety; nose assertive, very tannic, good acidity. *Last tasted Sept 2001* ★★★(★) *2006–2012.*

**1999** First tasted May 2001, but it needs time. Alcohol 13%. Less deep, softer lighter style than the '98, delicious nose, raisins, plums and figs; open knit, easy, very fruity. An early developer. *Last tasted Sept 2001* ★★★ *Now–2006.*

**2000** First tasted 12 months after the vintage: dark cherry; fruit full and fruitful; powerful, concentrated, tannic of course. Most recently, after the end of barrel *élevage* and before going back into steel tank 'to digest the wood taste', prior to bottling in mid-February (2002): fairly deep, plumy; rich, strawberry-like nose, sweet, harmonious; medium full-bodied (alcohol 13%), rich, soft tannins, good length. Good wine, good future. *Last tasted May 2002* (★★★★)

**2001** The Gassac valley experienced incredible thermal shocks in September, which Guibert says led to 'a fabulous extraction of colours and tannin'. Following its first three months of barrel *élevage* it was fairly deep, dark cherry; low-keyed, bramble-like, good depth; nice flesh, soft tannins, still a bit raw. To be bottled March 2003. *Jan 2002* (★★★★) *Time will tell.*
**Cuvée Emile Peynaud** A new super-blend and a totally different ball game: 100% Cabernet Sauvignon from 30-year old vines from Peyra Fioc, a small vineyard planted on the poorest Gassac soil: opaque core, intense purple rim; and equally intense aroma; perfumed oak – at this stage difficult to get through the oak to the clearly abundant fruit; fairly sweet, full body, high extract, velvety richness masking soft tannins and acidity. Clearly a 'tour de force'! *Jan 2002* (★★★★★) *Watch this space.*

# Mas de Daumas Gassac (White)

**1986** Aimé Guibert's first white. The original *cépages* blend was 80% Viognier (from cuttings given by Georges Verney of Condrieu, and planted in 1981), 10% Chardonnay and 10% Muscat de Frontignan. The wine spent two months in oak. I first tasted it in June 1987. Then it was pale waxy yellow; youthful pineappley nose and some $CO_2$; medium-dry, good fruit, excellent acidity, spicy oaky finish. Not tasted since.

**1987** Viognier reduced to 60%, Chardonnay increased to 30% and Muscat remained at 10%. In Aug 1989: pale, green-tinged; fragrant; dry, firm, vanilla and oak, steely but fragrant. More recently: straw-coloured; unusual meaty, waxy nose; flavour of fennel. Attractive but tailed off. *Last tasted April 1991. Then ★★★ Probably faded now.*

**1988** Back to 60% Viognier, 20% Chardonnay, 5% Muscat plus 15% Petit Manseng (a grape that does well in Jurançon in south-west France). From this vintage I could follow its ageing. When first tasted in June 1989 it already had a rich, positive, straw colour; slight scented vanilla and walnuts nose: medium dryness and body, rich oaky flavour and good length. More recently: gold-tinged; and flavour richer, softer, oaky. Most recently: amber-gold; rich honeyed bottle age; like Barsac but dry. *Last tasted Sept 2001 ★★★ Good for its age but at the edge.*

**1989** A noticeable shift of *cépages* mix: Chardonnay now 40%, Viognier down to 25% with 25% Petit Manseng, 5% Muscat and 5% mixture of local white varieties such as Marsanne, Roussanne and others. First tasted May 1990: raw, young pineapple husk nose; slightly sweet, full bodied, rich. Most recently: still palish yellow; rich ripe fruit; sweet and lovely. *Last tasted Sept 2001 ★★★★★*

**1990** Chardonnay 30%, Viognier 30%, Petit Manseng 30%, Muscat 5% and other varieties 5%. Two notes in 2001: fairly pale; forthcoming – the usual youthful 'pineapple'; medium dry, fruity, attractive but short. *Last noted Sept 2001 ★★ Drink up.*

**1991** Similar *cépages* blend. As bad luck would have it, the bottle sent by Aimé for the vertical tasting in September 2001 was oxidised. The replacement was better: pure gold highlights; nutty, wax, vanillin, whiff of apricot and honeyed bottle age. After 90 minutes, honey and caramel: on the palate dry but rich (alcohol 13%), a bit stolid – a halfway house between the freshness of youth and serenity of age. *Last noted Jan 2002 ★★★*

**1992** The blend had more or less settled down – Viognier 35%, Chardonnay 30%, Petit Manseng 30% and other varieties 5%. First tasted March 1993: lovely young aroma and flavour. Good fruit, acidity and aftertaste. By 1995 a lemony-waxy Chardonnay and vanilla nose: fairly hefty, interesting but not thrilling. Perfect with chicken liver pâté. Most recently: creamy, unusual, attractive, 'like a mild Hock'. *Last tasted Sept 2001 ★★★*

**1993** First tasted at the harvest supper at Gassac in Sept 1994: very good nose; medium-dry, attractive flavour, body and balance. 'Should be even more delicious with bottle age'. Endorsed exactly seven years later: fairly sweet, good acidity. Very attractive wine. *Last tasted Sept 2001 ★★★★ Drink soon.*

**1994** The yield of each vine reduced. Several notes. The must tasted at the time of the harvest: smell of pure pineapple juice; sweet, delicious, not as concentrated as expected. Next in the spring after the vintage: surprisingly attractive and drinkable 'but will improve'. By June 2000 it had neither the excitement of youth nor the benefit of benign maturity, like me! However, showing well recently: still pale, lime-tinged; nose an amalgam of Vaseline, pineapple and fresh-peeled pears. A lovely wine. *Last tasted Sept 2001 ★★★★*

**1995** First tasted in the spring of 1996: fabulous youthful aromas; surprisingly sweet (8g/l residual sugar), lovely rich flavour, good body (alcohol 13%), highish acidity, oaky aftertaste. Like '89 Ch Laville Haut-Brion in its youth. By May 2000 distinctly yellow; sweet, soft, rich, very oaky, attractive. Similar note at the September 2001 tasting, though I found it acidic. *Most recently at a lunch party at home, Jan 2002 ★★★*

**1996** The blend for the '96, '97, '98 and '99 white was virtually identical: 30% each Viognier, Chardonnay and Petit Manseng, with 10% maximum of other varieties. In May following the vintage it was showing a touch of $CO_2$, with raw pineappley nose, very oaky; good flavour but with a touch of what I probably incorrectly describe as acetone. At five years of age: rich nose; meaty, creamy, too sweet. Most recently: very rich and seemed to get richer in the glass. Impressive. *Last noted dining at home, Jan 2002 ★★★*

**1997** First noted at lunch, August 1998: fairly pale; immature apple, grapefruit and pineapple husk aromas; medium-dry, peachy, mixed fruit flavours and slightly bitter oaky finish. Most recently, curious, high-toned nose; fairly rich, minty – not a very helpful note. *Last tasted Sept 2001 ★★ Might benefit from a year or more bottle age?*

**1998** At the vertical tasting in September 2001: pale; very fragrant, piquant fruit; very good flavour, sweet but with dry finish. Most recently, served at my 75th birthday dinner at Vintners' Hall. Delicious. *Last tasted May 2002 ★★★★ At its peak.*

**1999** Five notes, the first in May following the vintage: palish, hint of green and a prickle of $CO_2$ clinging to the sides of the glass; very assertive young aromas and oaky taste. At the tasting in September 2001: showing well though still youthful, a characteristic 'pineappley' nose and oak. Most recently: taken to our local Lebanese restaurant: perfect with spicy food. Good length, totally satisfying. *Last tasted at Mes Amis, Fulham, London, Jan 2002 ★★★(★)*

**2000** Now really complex: '*environ 15 cépages traditionnels*', consisting of 25% each Petit Manseng, Viognier and Chardonnay and 25% of 15 other varieties, some of which represent between 1 and 3% of the total, the others less than 1%. In May 2001 it was relatively pale; all the appeal of youth; medium-dry, fruity, attractive but short yet with good fruit and acidity, 'should develop well'. *Last tasted May 2001 ★(★★)*

**2001** Good colour, lime-gold highlights, immature pineappley aroma; medium-dry, soft fruit yet youthful acidity. *May 2002. Needs time to settle down, say 2003–2006.*

# Germany

I happen to like German wines; by this I mean the quality wines mainly from well-established estates, with extraordinarily varied styles, ranging from bone dry to exquisitely sweet, and certainly not the cheap, sugar-and-water sort masquerading in traditional 'flute' bottles. Quality German wines have two advantages for the consumer. First, price. Because German wines are considered a niche market, demand is limited and there is little speculative or investment element, and so even the quality wines tend to be good value. Second, of all the major classic wines of Europe these are, in my opinion, the easiest to enjoy. You do not have to be an expert to appreciate the smell and taste of a really good German wine despite the initially complicated looking label. Those people – and there are quite a few – who purport not to like sweet wines or who at first glance find German wine labels incomprehensible are missing out on one of the joys of wine. It really does not take long to understand the logic behind the very informative names.

And in common with many others whose judgement I respect, I regard the Riesling, the grape that produces so many of Germany's top wines, as the most interesting and most versatile of all white wine grapes. Though the Riesling is grown elsewhere, only in Germany does it combine such charm and delicacy with deftness of touch.

Why do I list and describe so many old wines, ranging from feine Auslese to TBA quality? Mainly to demonstrate their extraordinary quality and longevity; to share – albeit inadequately – my love and admiration of such wines. For most readers, my notes will provide purely vicarious pleasure but I should point out that though the wines are rare they are not entirely beyond reach for, from time to time, bottles emerge from private and estate cellars to appear at auction. However, whereas notes on old and rare wines are my tribute to the great and the good, both wines and producers, those relating my experiences of recent vintages should prove more practical.

Producers of quality German wine are ideally seeking a perfect balance of fruit and acidity. These low alcohol *fruchtig* wines are delightful drunk by themselves. The initial attempts to make *trocken* (dry) wines for food were not wholly successful. Removing the 'fruit' reduces the flavour. They just need food to bring out the taste. However, some extremely good *Erstes Gewächs*, first growth, dry wines are now being produced.

Most of my notes over the years have been made at home, with friends, at trade tastings, and at the various estates. As conductor of the annual wine auctions for the VDP, Rheingau, I have been exposed to many tastings of the best young vintages. I am indebted to the Breuer brothers for invitations to their rare wine dinners, to the ubiquitous Hardy Rodenstock, and to Schloss Johannisberg, Schloss Reinhartshausen, Weingut Robert Weil, the Müllers at Scharzhofberg, and many others all mentioned in the text.

---

### Abbreviations used in the text for the German wine regions

(Rg) Rheingau: the historic heart of German wine, on the right bank of the Rhine east and west of Wiesbaden, with the highest number of *Erstes Gewächs* or first growth vineyards. Firm, from dry, steely to the finest TBAs.

(M) Mosel-Saar-Ruwer: the Mosel Valley along with two important tributaries, the Saar and the Ruwer. The most northerly of Europe's classic wine regions. Light, fruity, acidic wines, ranging from very dry to the finest TBAs.

(N) Nahe: geographically and by wine style between the Mosel and the Rheingau. Wines with distinctive fruit.

(Rh) Rheinhessen: on the left bank of the Rhine, with a handful of great estates overlooking the river. Inland, a lake of ordinary wine made from Müller-Thurgau and other easier, early-ripening grapes.

(P) Pfalz: historically, called the Palatinate in English. Just north of Alsace and producing the best Gewürztraminers.

(F) Franken: historically, called Franconia in English. Steely wines from Silvaner and the acidic Rieslaner.

There are four other regions occasionally mentioned in my notes:

(B) Baden: the most southerly region. Very large production, both white and red wines.

(W) Württemberg: white and red.

(HB) Hessische Bergstrasse: little exported.

(A) the Ahr Valley: north of the Mosel, specialising in red wine.

# 18th and 19th Century

Not as a history lesson, but to demonstrate that 'it has not always been so', it is perhaps worth reminding ourselves that the English have been importing Rhine wines, or 'Rhenish', for a thousand years. Not only were the wines palatable but transporting them was relatively safe and easy: down the Rhine, pausing only to pay robber barons a toll, and a short hop across the North Sea. From the Middle Ages, from Shakespeare's time to the 18th and early 19th century, 'hock', the English term for Rhine wine, particularly 'old Hock', was fashionable and expensive. Christie's unique archives are helpful. As a matter of interest, 'Hock (fine old)' first appeared in an auction catalogue of February 1767, just two months after James Christie's inaugural sale, appearing frequently thereafter. The first 'vintage' of *any* wine to appear in a wine catalogue was the 1748, at Christie's in 1772; and to give some indication of its value, a dozen bottles of 'Very Old Hock' sold in 1808 for over £10, the highest price for any wine at auction between 1766 and the 1880s.

'Old Hock' bore no resemblance to the light fruity wines of today. My note on the 1727 (below) gives some idea. The 1653 Rüdesheimer tasted in 1977 from the cask in the Bremer Ratskeller (see box page 344) was like an old dry madeira, pungent and very acidic (if it had not been it would not have survived at all), interesting to smell and sip but no more. But it was in Victorian times that good German wines, from the Rheingau and Franken mainly, achieved a high level of popularity.

## Vintages at a Glance

**Outstanding ★★★★★**
1748, 1749, 1811, 1822, 1831, 1834, 1846, 1847, 1857, 1858, 1861, 1865, 1869, 1893

**Very Good ★★★★**
1727, 1738, 1746, 1750, 1779, 1781, 1783, 1794, 1798, 1806, 1807, 1825, 1826, 1827, 1942, 1959, 1862, 1880, 1886

**Good ★★★**
21 vintages in the 18th century of which in the text 1748
20 vintages in the 19th century

## 1727 ★★★★

**Rüdesheimer Apostelwein** (Rg) This wine comes from a large cask in the famous '12 Apostles' cellar beneath the Town Hall or *Ratskeller* in Bremen (see box page 344). The first time this appeared in a Christie's wine catalogue was in 1829 when it sold for £5 per dozen, a high price at the time. An occasional half bottle has appeared at auction since that date, mainly over the past 30 years. The wine is drawn from the mother cask, which is then topped up with a young Rüdesheimer of appropriate quality. In this way the large volume of the old wine is kept refreshed. I first tasted the 1727 at Schloss Vollrads in 1973 at a tasting of wines of the world to celebrate Count Matuschka's 80th birthday (see box page 259).

Another memorable occasion took place at a dinner in Sydney on the evening of my first visit to Australia in February 1977. By way of welcome, my host, the irrepressible Len Evans, had invited the Prime Minister and a group of the best 'palates'. Among other fine and rare wines was this 250-year old Hock. Just as it was about to be served, there was a shattering crash followed by an agonised Australian voice 'Gee Len, sorry; we'll just have to have the 1728'! (The 'waiter', Anders Ousbach, who had dropped a handful of spoons, was a wine expert and opera singer known for his practical jokes.)

On my second visit to Bremen, in 1981, I was able to taste the wine from the cask. It had an amber straw colour, the smell of old apples and a nutty, appley taste. Dry. Good length. High acidity. More recently, from a half bottle '*Réserve du Bremer Ratskeller*': it was paler than I had previously noted, Sercial madeira-like colour; bouquet also reminded me of an old madeira, then more like a raya sherry. After two hours in

---

## A Note on German wines

**GRAPE VARIETIES** On the wine label and in my notes these always follow the village and vineyard name. The main varieties are Riesling, Silvaner or Sylvaner, Gewürztraminer, Spätburgunder (Pinot Noir), Grauer Burgunder (Pinot Gris) and Weisser Burgunder (Pinot Blanc). Important 'crosses' are Müller-Thurgau, Scheurebe, Rieslaner, Ruländer and Siegerrebe; others that feature only occasionally in this chapter are Bacchus, Huxelrebe, Optima and Ortega.
**STYLES AND QUALITIES** German wine is classified according to the natural grape sugar content at harvest time, measured in degrees of Oechsle or must weight.

*QbA:* 'quality' wine from a designated region but in fact, pretty ordinary and for early drinking.
*QmP:* 'quality' wine with distinction (addition of sugar not permitted). The levels are (in ascending order of ripeness): *Kabinett:* dry to medium-dry, usually light wines; *Spätlese:* literally late-picked. Ripe grapes, with moderate natural sugar content; *Auslese:* selected ripe bunches. Higher sugar content; *Beerenauslese* (or BA): selected fully ripe berries. Always sweet; *Eiswein:* sweet wines made from grapes frozen on the vine, with concentrated grape sugar. Now always BA level. *Trockenbeerenauslese (*or TBA): overripe

berries affected by *botrytis* (noble rot) or *Edelfäule* in German. Rare, exceptionally sweet, concentrated wines.

Prior to 1971 growers could additionally qualify their better wines, usually from particularly successful casks, prefixing *Auslese* for example with *feine, feinste, allerfeinste, edel*. Now these superior wines are often identified by the capsule's colour and length: *Goldkapsel, lange Goldkapsel*, or by specific cask or *Fuder* numbers. *Trocken* (less than 9 grams per litre of residual sugar) means dry; and *halb trocken* (between 9 and 16g/l residual sugar) half dry. *Erstes Gewächs* means first growths. These are high quality, dry wines.

## The Ratskeller of Bremen

*Bremen, in north Germany, one of the old Hanseatic trading cities, is not exactly on any wine lover's itinerary. Perhaps it should be. For over five centuries the vaults beneath the Ratskeller or town hall have housed great casks of wine. The Twelve Apostles are huge ornate barrels, still containing wine, with elaborately carved heads, but the Rose Cellar, at the far end, is the most venerable. Here, casks of wine date back to the 1653 vintage – very sharp and not very nice – and the famous 1727 Rüdesheimer noted in the text which I tasted on my first visit in 1973. Afterwards one repairs to the Weinstube (wine tavern) to contemplate, and dip into, an astonishing range of German wines and vintages. If it was in France the Michelin Guide would award the Bremer Ratskeller three stars, indicating* Vaut le voyage*!*

the glass, a smell of rich old stables and an hour after that, an amazing pungency lingered in the empty glass. On the palate medium-dry, lightish weight, a soft, gentler, slightly toasted old straw flavour, tolerable acidity, and clean finish. *Last noted at a dinner to mark the publication of the German edition of my* Great Vintage Wine Book *in Zürich, Oct 1983* ★★ *for pleasure,* ★★★★★ *for interest.*

## 1748 ★★★

**Schloss Johannisberger Riesling Cabinet Wein** (Rg) Original 'flute' bottle with the oldest label in the castle cellars. Original short, blackened cork. Decanted. Very bright and warm old amber, with a rosy glow, almost like a faded old red wine; smell of wet hazelnuts and walnuts; intolerably high acidity and not drinkable. *From the cellars of the Schloss Johannisberg and presented at Hardy Rodenstock's annual tasting in Wiesbaden, Oct 1985.*

## 1846 ★★★★★

**Schloss Johannisberger Blaulack** (Blue label) (Rg) The oldest vintage at the memorable Schloss Johannisberg/Yquem tasting. Prince Metternich told us that, from the castle's records, picking began on 12 October. Medium amber-gold; light but sound when first poured, touch of linoleum and faded fruit, but fragrant, resembling charcoal and sultanas, cracking up after ten minutes; dry, positive flavour, like a refined old amontillado, with good length and remarkable for its age. *At Schloss Johannisberg, Nov 1984. As a drink* ★★★, *for its age* ★★★★

## 1862 ★★★★

A very big crop of fine wines which were shipped in quantity to Britain.
**Schloss Johannisberger Riesling Goldblaulack Auslese** (Rg) Warm amber; slightly smoky, minty, raisiny bouquet, developing a rich, old straw nose, like a 5-putt Tokaji Aszú, then charred, akin to an old fire in a grate. Medium-sweet, very assertive, high acidity, fragrant, exciting. *At the Schloss, Nov 1984* ★★★★
**Schloss Johannisberger Riesling Goldlack TBA** (Rg) The oldest vintage in the tasting at the Schloss to celebrate the estate's 900th anniversary: medium-deep amber; concentrated,

toffee-like bouquet of considerable depth, slightly malty, reminding me of 'calf's foot jelly', then old stables, finally – after an hour – rich old straw; still fairly sweet, certainly rich and powerful, its flavour extending into a dry finish with biting acidity. *Nov 2001* ★★★

## 1870 ★★

**'Castle Johannisberg'** (Rg) According to Schloss Johannisberg's archives, there was a modest crop (312hl) of 'mediocre' quality but it was presumed good enough for the English market. The anglicised label was an impressively useful sales aid: '*1870 Prince Metternich's Castle Johannisberg/First Growth*', flanked either side '*By special appointment to H.M. the Emperor of Germany*' and '*By appointment to H.R.H. Prince Georg of Prussia*' and, in large letters, '*MANNSKOPF & SONS FRANKFURT °M*'.

I had recently bought the wine at Christie's and I opened it at a boardroom lunch. By chance an old friend of mine, Hermann Segnitz, a distinguished Bremen wine merchant, was in London and came as a last-minute guest. To his, and everyone else's surprise, the wine was pale for its age, fairly dry and drinking well. *Oct 1979* ★★★

## 1893 ★★★★★

After 1811 and 1865, this was the best vintage of the 19th century. There were very high levels of botrytis.
**Assmannshäuser Spätburgunder Auslese** (Rg) **N Sahl Weinhändler** Paler than expected, a tinge of tawny-red, bright and healthy; gentle, sound nose which opened up, varnishy, with strawberry-like fruit; dry, austere, singed flavour. *At a Breuer rare wine dinner in Rüdesheim, Nov 1998* ★★
**Erbacher Marcobrunn Riesling BA** (Rg) **Schloss Reinhartshausen** Deep amber with touch of orange, and pure gold highlights; no faults; still sweet, a singed 'barley sugar' flavour with dry, raisiny finish. *At Schloss Reinhartshausen, Nov 1995* ★★★★
**Schloss Johannisberger Riesling Goldlack** (Rg) Very ripe grapes, very high sugar content: 130° Oechsle. Surprisingly pale for its age; initially a scent of cold tea and slightly powdery Muscat. After 30 minutes spicy, complex, honey, sultanas; medium-dry, fading to a very dry finish. Too lean and austere despite its fleeting fragrance. *At the Schloss, Nov 1984* ★★
**Marcobrunner Cabinet Riesling feinste Auslese** (Rg) Glorious, bright, rosehip colour; bouquet of sultanas and apricots; dry, rather meaty flavour and high, pasty acidity. *One of three bottles from an English private cellar, bought by Hardy Rodenstock and tasted at Ch d'Yquem, Sept 1986* ★★

## 1897 ★★

**Stein Auslese** (probably Silvaner) (F) **Bürgerspital zum Heiligen Geist** Colour of strong tea, cloudy and deathly; oxidised yet with a fragrance of spicy old pears. Nosed only, not tasted. *Bought at Christie's, noted at Ch d'Yquem, Sept 1986.*
**Steinberger Riesling Cabinet Wein** (Rg) **Staatsweingut (Eltville)** Bright yellow-gold colour; fabulous, unusual and distinctive honeyed bouquet; rich yet dry, with very good flavour, depth and length. *At the Breuers' rare wine dinner, Rüdesheim, Nov 1997* ★★★

# 1900–1939

The reputation and demand for the finest Rhine wines reached its zenith in the period before the outbreak of World War One. Prices at the Kloster Eberbach auctions reached stratospheric levels and there was some concern about winemaking methods and authenticity, to the extent that in 1909 a wine law was enacted, introducing the concept of *Naturwein* or *Naturrein* for the unsugared wine, and stipulating that wine should come from the vineyard actually named on the label. German wines were immensely popular in Britain in Victorian times and, to my surprise, the interest was not totally snuffed out by World War One. Indeed, Mr Rudd joined the eminent retailers, Berry Bros, in 1920 on the strength of his knowledge of German wines, and at Berry's boardroom luncheons in St James's, German wines would occasionally be served throughout.

World War One and particularly the devastatingly inflationary 1920s had a catastrophic effect, not so much on the actual quality of the wine made but on its traditional market. There was a timely boost in 1921, unquestionably the greatest German vintage of the 20th century and a vintage incidentally which finally endorsed the high quality of the wines of the Mosel. But in Germany, the beneficiaries were the nouveau riche rather than the traditional wine drinkers of the now ruined middle and upper classes. Raging inflation in Germany in the 1920s had a disastrous effect on the wine trade though the wealthier estates survived. Although there were some good vintages in the 1930s, because of the activities of Hitler's National Socialist Party which came to power in 1933, the market was greatly affected by the internment or flight of the Jewish merchants who had ably handled so much of the German wine trade.

The quality of winemaking was high throughout the 1920s and 1930s though consumption in Britain dropped in the Depression. And, in the final analysis, one either liked and drank Hock, or one didn't. With the exception of the great estates, most imported German wine was shipped in cask for bottling by English wine merchants. I well recall, in the late 1970s, buying a dozen or so bottles of 1933 Erbacher Honigberg *Naturrein* bottled by Block, Fearon which had come from a cold damp cellar of a Cambridge college. Every bottle I consumed was delicious. It was as fresh as a daisy after some 45 years.

## *Vintages at a Glance*
**Outstanding ★★★★★**
1911, 1921, 1937
**Very Good ★★★★**
1904, 1915, 1917, 1920, 1929, 1934
**Good ★★★**
1900, 1901, 1905, 1907, 1926

## 1904 ★★★★
**Geisenheimer Mäuerchen Riesling BA** (Rg) **Friedrich v Lader** Very short cork. Very deep brown; an amazing scent, fresh, assertive, muscatel-like; very rich, singed grapes flavour. *At the first annual Rodenstock tasting I ever attended, at the Fuente Restaurant, Mülheim, Oct 1984* ★★★

## 1911 ★★★★★
Magnificent vintage, the best between 1900 and 1921.
**Erbacher Marcobrunn Riesling TBA** (Rg) **Schloss Reinhartshausen** 182 Oechsle, 106g/l acidity. Rich amber; lovely, fragrant, floral, harmonious; still sweet, intense with clean barley sugar flavour and fantastic life-preserving acidity. *From the remarkable Schatzkammer of old vintages at Schloss Reinhartshausen, Nov 1995* ★★★★★
**Steinberger Riesling Cabinet BA** (Rg) **H Sichel Söhne** Colour of orange pekoe tea; very powerful, but 'blown', mercaptan; medium-sweet, pungent but with a fragrant uplift. *At Rodenstock's tasting in Mülheim, Oct 1984.*

## 1915 ★★★★
Big harvest and very good quality.
**Berncasteler Doctor Riesling** (M) **Deinhard** Just surviving a poor ullage level. Grubby finish. *From an old Scottish cellar, Sept 1994* ★
**Berncasteler Hintergraben** (M) **Kgl Frevich** Surviving a 21-cm ullage. Dry. Clean. *From the same Scottish cellar as the previous wine, Sept 1994* ★
**Erbacher Marcobrunn Riesling Auslese Cabinet** (Rg) **Schloss Reinhartshausen** 110° Oechsle. Rich amber with orange-gold highlights; very sound, touch of honey; medium-sweet, good flavour, dry, rather austere acidic finish but overall in good condition. *At Schloss Reinhartshausen, Nov 1995* ★★★
**Hochheimer Stein Riesling TBA** (Rg) **Weingut Kroeschell** Recorked, $SO_2$ added, resulting in a trace of mercaptan. Showing age despite good 'lemon curd' colour and light, creamy, honeyed old bouquet. Drying out. *The first wine in the 8th 'flight' (Gang), a total of 52 wines, at Peter Ziegler's outstanding rare wine tasting, at the Schlosshotel, Erbach, Dec 1995* ★

## 1920 ★★★★
**Erbacher Honigberg Riesling Auslese** (Rg) **Schloss Reinhartshausen** Filtered, with $SO_2$ added, and recorked in 1981. Bright orange tawny gold; lovely old honeyed botrytis bouquet; dried-out but rich. Slight whiff of old fungi and sourness on the finish. *At the Schloss, Feb 2002* ★★★ *for age.*
**Forster Ungeheuer Riesling Auslese** (P) **v Bühl** Colour of dried apricots; bouquet of sultanas, honeyed botrytis and

bottle-age; medium-sweet, fairly full-bodied, lovely old barley sugar flavour, good extract, length and aftertaste. *Bought at Christie's, then served at dinner at home, Oct 1988* ★★★★

**Schloss Johannisberger Riesling Goldlack Auslese** (Rg) Late-bottled. Unusual varietal blend, 55% Riesling, 45% Sylvaner. 115° Oechsle. In oak until bottled in 1930. Amber gold; lovely, honeyed, grapey – no signs of old age, holding well; medium-sweet, very assertive flavour and acidity. Dashing and fragrant, some charm but, after the nose, a bit austere. *At the Schloss, Nov 1984* ★★★★

## 1921 ★★★★★

The greatest vintage of the century. Small crop of extremely ripe, healthy grapes picked early after a scorching summer. Exceptionally rich wines.

**Assmannshäuser Höllenberg Spätburgunder** (Rg) **Staatsweingut** An amazing colour; bouquet of strawberries and smoked cheese; showing age, raw, still tannic. *At the Breuer rare wine dinner, Rüdesheim, Nov 1996* ★

**Erbacher Honigberg Riesling Auslese** (Rg) **Schloss Reinhartshausen** Very deep tawny, similar to a Bual madeira; very sweet bouquet and flavour, old honey and toffee, considerable power and wonderful aftertaste. Of Beerenauslese quality. *At the Schloss, Feb 2002* ★★★★★

**Erbacher Rheinhell Riesling Auslese** (Rg) **Schloss Reinhartshausen** Warm gold; sound, harmonious but initially unrevealing, opening up gently, honeyed; distinctly dry, firm, in excellent condition but lacking flavour and charm. *At the Schloss, Nov 1995* ★★

**Erbacher Siegelsberg 'Original'** (Rg) **Schloss Reinhartshausen** Medium yellow gold with pale, pure gold highlights; slightly caramelised old Riesling, corked, then, after 45 minutes – definitely corked. Yet when first tasted, dry, clean and fresh, despite showing its age. A conundrum. *At the Schloss, Feb 2002* ★★?

**Schloss Johannisberger Riesling Cabinet** (Rg) 105° Oechsle. Pure burnished gold; lightly grapey nose, remarkably fresh for this age, though after 30 minutes tiring, with touch of resin; dry, fairly assertive, 'kerosene' (Rieslings quite often have a slightly oily, petrolly smell and taste). Good acidity. *At the Schloss, Nov 1984* ★★★

**Liebfraumilch feinste Auslese** (Rh) **B M & J Strauss** (London) Amber shot with gold,; amazing scent of lilies, of raisins, slightly Tokaji-like and varnishy; medium-sweet, with good, rich, singed-grape flavour which tailed off (included as a rare early 'Liebfraumilch'). *Bought at auction, served in Mülheim, by Hardy Rodenstock, Oct 1984* ★★

**Nackenheimer Rothenberg Riesling TBA Naturrein** (Rh) **Staatsweingut** Amber; fabulous raisiny bouquet; very sweet, exquisite peachy flavour, wonderful acidity, great length. *Served alongside 1847 Ch Yquem at Rodenstock's dinner, March 2001* ★★★★★★ *(6 stars, as was the Yquem).*

**Niersteiner Auflangen Riesling Auslese** (Rh) **Franz Karl Schmitt** Marvellously rich colour, nose and taste. Pure gold, honeyed, barley sugar nose, then spearmint; medium-sweet, fairly full-bodied yet gentle, soft, good length, perfect acidity. *From the Aalholm Castle cellars, Denmark, Aug 1989* ★★★★★

**Wehlener Sonnenuhr Riesling Auslese** (M) **J J Prüm** Made by Manfred's grandfather (see box right). The oldest vintage at the Weinart/Prüm tasting in Austria. Despite its lovely colour, the bouquet was faint and the wine dried out. Strange and disappointing. *April 1999* ★

## 1927 ★★

Small production, below average quality.

**Deidesheimer Hohenrain Riesling TBA** (P) **Bassermann-Jordan** A birthday present from the estate after conducting the great VDP auction in Wiesbaden, 1999. Level up to original crumbly cork: very deep brown with yellow-green rim, like an old Malmsey; deliciously sweet, heavenly, its bouquet like an old Australian Muscat, butterscotch, crust of *crème brûlée*; still very sweet, Muscat and a touch of malt, with excellent life-preserving acidity. *At Chippenham Lodge with Daphne and the children three days after my 75th birthday, May 2002* ★★★★

**Erbacher Marcobrunn Riesling Kabinett** (Rg) **Schloss Reinhartshausen** Colour of old polished brass; honeyed bottle age, touch of caramel but really very good; bone dry, fruit dissipated but excellent acidity. *At the Schloss, Feb 2002* ★★

**Kiedricher Gräfenberg Riesling Spätlese** (Rg) **Robert Weil** Served blind: colour of an Aszú-Eszencia; low-keyed, reminiscent of apples in a hayloft; dry, slightly caramelly but with very good acidity. Showing its age - like me. I should have guessed. *The last wine at a press dinner hosted by Wilhelm Weil and my publisher, Falken, Kiedrich, April 1998* ★

## 1929 ★★★★

A lean decade in Germany, the 1929 vintage being the next best after 1921. These ripe and appealing wines were virtually all consumed in the 1930s. I have only three recent notes.

**Erbacher Marcobrunn Riesling Auslese** (Rg) **Schloss Reinhartshausen** Fairly deep old gold with lime rim; lovely old honey and apricots bouquet; sweet but, unsurprisingly, showing its age yet a rich old grapey flavour, good acidity and aftertaste. *At the Schloss, Feb 2002* ★★★★

**Nierstein** (*sic*) **Riesling** (Rh) **H Sichel Söhne** Golden colour; rich, slightly smoky bouquet; very dry, very good flavour for its relatively lowly status and age. *From an American cellar, at the Christie's pre-sale tasting in Chicago, June 1983* ★★★

## 1930

The first of two very poor vintages.

**Erbacher Marcobrunn Riesling Cabinet** (Rg) **Schloss Reinhartshausen** Labelled 'Kabinett trocken'. Deep old gold; nose like soft brown sugar, sweet, peach, vanilla; fairly dry, more body and better flavour than expected, old but clean finish. *At the Schloss, Feb 2002* ★

---

### J J Prüm

*The Weingut Joh Jos Prüm, known familiarly as 'JJ' was founded in 1911 by the grandfather of the highly respected Dr Manfred Prüm. Although the estate produces wine from Berkasteler Lay, Graacher Himmelreich and Zeltinger Sonnenuhr, it is best-known for its Wehlener Sonnenuhr. From the terrace of the Prüm family home on the opposite bank of the Mosel, visitors have a panoramic view of the broad sloping sweep of vines and the famous sundial, even better with a glass of Manfred's wine in hand. There are several mentions of JJ's wines in the text, most notably the unprecedented range of 125 wines presented by Manfred Prüm at Karl-Heinz Wolf's Weinart tasting in Austria in April 1999, beginning with the Wehlener Sonnenuhr Riesling Auslese 1921 and ending with his most perfect – 6-star – '71 TBA.*

# 1931

**Erbacher Rheinhell Riesling Kabinett** (Rg) **Schloss Reinhartshausen** Medium-deep orange tawny with a very pale lime edge; good, deep, honeyed bouquet; sweet, rich, good length. A great surprise. Clearly of Auslese quality. *At the Schloss, Feb 2002* ★★★

# 1933 ★★

An abundant vintage and pleasant wines. I have tasted several 3 and 4 star wines, but I have only one recent note.
**Rauenthaler Baiken Riesling TBA** (Rg) **Staatsweingut, Eltville** Palish gold; touch of mushrooms; drying out, flavour of singed sultanas, good acidity. *At Peter Ziegler's Club lunch/tasting at Burg Windeck, May 1983* ★★

# 1934 ★★★★

Very satisfactory vintage. I have several older good notes, with the wines ranging up to 5 stars in quality and condition. I have only tasted three wines recently.
**Erbacher Hohenrain Riesling Spätlese** (Rg) **Schloss Reinhartshausen** Medium-deep, bright orange-tawny; slightly singed, smoky old sultanas nose; fairly dry, showing its age, austere, with teeth-gripping acidity though quite good, honeyed aftertaste. *At the Schloss, Feb 2002* ★★
**Schloss Johannisberg Riesling Dunkelblaulack** (Deep blue capsule) (Rg) The picking started on 4 October, the earliest for their Auslesen for 30 years. Pure gold, pale for its age; delicate, smoky, but a bit smelly – cracking up. Medium-dry, lightish, an odd oily taste, with a twist of lime and a touch of bitterness. *At the Schloss, June 1983* ★★★
**Niersteiner Pettental und Auflangen Riesling TBA** (Rh) **Franz Karl Schmitt** Prune-like amber; very powerful bouquet and flavour, bottle age and botrytis. Still sweet, immensely rich, flavour of peaches, apricots and caramel. Magnificent. *At Rodenstock's wine weekend, Sept 1996* ★★★★★
**Piesporter Goldtröpfchen Riesling Auslese** (M) Bottled by Berry Bros. Pale gold; almost Semillon-like, buttery, waxy nose; medium-dry, excellent flavour and acidity. *At the pre-sale tasting, Chicago, June 1983* ★★★

# 1935

**Hattenheimer Wisselbrunnen Riesling Spätlese** (Rg) **Schloss Reinhartshausen** Bright orange-tawny; a whiff like a damped down wood fire, some honey. Very dry, tart sour. Oh dear… *At the Schloss, Feb 2002.*

# 1937 ★★★★★

A great vintage in Germany, as for white wines elsewhere in Europe. The best wines will still be excellent if well stored. Unquestionably this is my favourite German vintage.
**Brauneberger Juffer-Sonnenuhr Auslese** (M) **Fritz Haag** Orange-gold; lovely, honeyed, orange blossom; drying out, taste of peach skins, firm, earthy, marvellous acidity. *June 1992* ★★★★
**Erbacher Marcobrunn Riesling TBA** (Rg) **Schloss Reinhartshausen** Two notes. First tasted in 1988 at Rodenstock's *Festival des Jahrgangs 1937*, Arlberg: lovely colour; perfect peach blossom fragrance; fairly sweet, lovely flavour. And, more recently, a fairly similar note: rich amber with apple-green rim;

delicious bouquet, raisins, butterscotch, 'last rose of summer', not unlike a refined old Verdelho; rich but drying out, very high acidity, slightly short. It opened up in the glass, holding well. *Last noted dining at Schloss Reinhartshausen, Nov 1997* ★★★★
**Schloss Johannisberger Riesling Auslese** (Rg) Bottled after two years in oak. Perfectly polished gold; an old Riesling bouquet, its oak and smoke reminding me of a venerable Chardonnay; sweeter than expected, with very lively fresh, fruity flavour and good length. Just lacking the persistence and aftertaste of a truly great wine. *At the Schloss, Nov 1984* ★★★★
**Rauenthaler Baiken Riesling TBA** (Rg) **Staatsweingut** A deep, almost tawny colour; perfect *crème brûlée* bouquet, very Sauternes-like; sweet, mouthfilling flavour, fresh, raisiny style, perfect condition and acidity. Magnificent. *At Peter Ziegler's, Burg Windeck, May 1983* ★★★★★
**Steinberger Riesling TBA** (Rg) **Staatsweingut** Colour of Bual Madeira; glorious, chocolatey, raisiny bouquet; very sweet, soft flesh, apricots, perfect acidity. *A break between vintages at Wagner's Margaux tasting, Jan 1997* ★★★★
**Wachenheimer Goldbächel-Gerümpel Riesling allerfeinste Goldbeeren TBA** (P) **L Wolf-Erben** Beautiful tawny with amber-green rim; glorious concentrated essence of honey and raisins; very rich, very concentrated and with intense extract and flavour. Touch of prune. Fabulous length. *At Rodenstock's annual tasting, at Ch d'Yquem, Sept 1986* ★★★★★
**Wachenheimer Mandelgarten Natur** (P) **Winzerverein Dürkheim** Imported by Kjaer and Sommerfeldt, Copenhagen. Amber-gold; rich, honeyed bouquet, apricots and lanolin, no faults; medium-dry, yet rich, soft, honeyed, bottle-age flavour. Good, dry finish. *From the Aalholm Castle cellars, Denmark, Aug 1989* ★★★★

# 1938 ★★

Average vintage; some good wines made but rarely seen.
**Assmannshäuser Höllenberg Rot-Weiss Riesling Auslese** (Rg) **Staatsweingut** Colour of 10-year-old tawny with ruddy glow; deliciously rich strawberry jam, then raisiny bouquet like a 5-putt Aszú. Sweet, glorious, fabulous aftertaste. Remarkable for a 60-year-old German red. *At the Breuers' rare wine dinner, Rüdesheim, Nov 1998* ★★★★

# 1939 ★

**Erbacher Marcobrunn Riesling** (Rg) **Schloss Reinhartshausen** Very good nose; medium-dry, positive flavour, holding well. *The oldest of the 'ending in 9' vintages presented by Bernhard Breuer at a Christie's dinner, Feb 2000* ★★

## Benedictines and Cistercians

*Some of the finest of Germany's vineyard sites today originated from the monastic holdings of the Benedictines (followers of Saint Benedict) and the subsequent, stricter branch, the Cistercians (set up in 1098). Schloss Johannisberg (founded circa 1100), Kloster Eberbach (founded 1136) and Karthäuser Hofberg (founded 1335) are some of the most notable. The current vineyard patterns of the Rheingau, for example, were mostly set out during the stewardship of the monasteries at this early time. The monks also kept extensive records from this period detailing viticultural and winemaking improvements. Much of their dramatic architecture, notably Kloster Eberbach, also survives intact.*

# 1940–1959

Worderld War Two was as difficult for the German wine estates as for those of occupied France, with shortages of labour and materials. The lack of labour, general collapse and depredations of Allied troops, particularly the French who had more than one reason for the pillaging of German wines, made life intolerable. It is a wonder that any wine managed to be made in 1945. Only grim determination enabled the producers to take advantage of the great post-war vintages, notably the 1949, which coincided with the establishment of the Federal German Republic.

This period saw the start of technological changes and viticultural experiments with new grape varieties; the aim was to produce easier to grow, earlier ripening and more prolific varieties in these difficult northerly regions. However understandable an aim that might have been, it would lead to an undermining of quality and image.

By the mid-1950s, most leading British wine lists featured a wide range of German wines serviced by specialist importers, many of whom were new companies started up by the German Jewish traders who had managed to escape to Britain before the war. 1959 was one of the greatest vintages of the second half of the 20th century.

## Vintages at a Glance
**Outstanding ★★★★★**
1945, 1949, 1953, 1959
**Very Good ★★★★**
1947
**Good ★★★**
1942 (v), 1943, 1946, 1952

## 1940
**Hattenheimer Wisselbrunnen Riesling Kabinett** (Rg) **Schloss Reinhartshausen** Pleasant old gold; a surviving old Riesling, touch of caramel; dry, showing its age and of historic interest only. *At the Schloss, Feb 2002.*

## 1941
**Erbacher Hohenrain Riesling Kabinett** (Rg) **Schloss Reinhartshausen** Pale old gold; floral, herbaceous, old honey; bone dry, clean, sound, lacking depth, very high acidity. *At the Schloss, Feb 2002 ★★ for its age and vintage.*

## 1942 ★★ to ★★★
Average to good wartime vintage.
**Erbacher Marcobrunn Riesling TBA** (Rg) **Schloss Reinhartshausen** Warm orange-gold; peach blossom and apricots; still fairly sweet, lovely flavour. *At Rodenstock's annual tasting, Arlberg, Austria, Sept 1988 ★★★★*

## 1943 ★★★
As in France, the best of the wartime vintages.
**Assmannshäuser Höllenberg Spätburgunder** (Rg) **Staatsweingut** Medium, soft red; rich, high-toned scent of squashed strawberry and crushed cherry; very flavoury, fresh for its age, accompanying well the next dish. *At the Breuers' rare wine dinner, Rüdesheim, Nov 1998 ★★★*
**Deidesheimer Kieselberg Riesling Auslese** (P) **Bassermann-Jordan** Bottle variation. The first amber-gold; honeyed bottle age; residual sweetness, good fruit. The second dried-out, but good length. *Presiding over The Taste of Germany weekend, Banff Springs, Canada, Oct 1998 ★★*

**Schloss Johannisberger BA Fass Nr 92** (Rg) Lively gold; bouquet opening up beautifully, exuding an almost *Gewürztraminer* spiciness which, even after two hours, had a heavenly rose cachou and lychees-like scent; medium-sweet, good, but rather one-track and lacking fat. *At the Schloss Johannisberg/Yquem tasting, Nov 1984 ★★★★*
**Schloss Johannisberger Riesling Goldlack BA** (Rg) 900 litres made. Re-corked 1973. Rich gold; floral bouquet, scented ripe Riesling. Medium-sweet, rich yet delicate – alcohol only 5.5%. Easy to drink, but touch of earthiness, even rot. *Lunch at the Eigensatzs', Wiesbaden, June 1987 ★★★★*
**Wehlener Sonnenuhr Riesling feinste Auslese** (M) **J J Prüm** Pure gold; spicy, honeyed; fairly dry, good but unusual flavour, perfectly mature but a bit blunt, like '43 red Bordeaux. *At Peter Ziegler's Burg Windeck, May 1983 ★★★★*

## 1945 ★★★★★
A great but pitifully small vintage thanks to a hot, dry summer and lack of labour. Few shipped, few seen. I have been fortunate to taste – and drink – over a dozen, six since 1990.
**Deidesheimer Kieselberg Riesling BA** (P) **v Bühl** Deep amber; very *crème brûlée* Sauternes-like nose and taste; meaty, assertive, full, rich flavour. *At Peter Ziegler's tasting, the Schlosshotel, Erbach, Dec 1995 ★★★★*
**Deidesheimer Kränzler Riesling BA** (P) **Bassermann-Jordan** We were informed by our host, Peter Ziegler, that this wine had been 'refreshed' with 3% of the '83 vintage at the estate. No matter: the end result was stupendous, one of the top marks of the entire tasting. How can one describe perfection? Richness, yet delicacy, the most fragrant of aftertastes. *At the Schlosshotel, Erbach, Dec 1995 ★★★★★*
**Erbacher Marcobrunn Riesling Auslese** (Rg) **Schloss Reinhartshausen** Rich orange colour, pale lime rim; very rich, soft, sweet orange peel and barley sugar bouquet; fairly sweet, powerful, tangy. Good dry finish. *At the Schloss, Feb 2002 ★★★*
**Erbacher Marcobrunn Riesling Auslese** (Rg) **Schloss Reinhartshausen** Rich gold; lightly honeyed, no signs of age, a charmer; a touch of sweetness managing to carry the fairly high acidity, sound, its flavour good though not very distinctive. *At the Schloss, Nov 1995 ★★★*
**Johannisberger Mittelhöle Riesling BA** (Rg) **v Mumm** Pale for its age; completely dried-out. *At Peter Ziegler's tasting, the Schlosshotel, Erbach, Dec 1995.*

**Schloss Johannisberger Riesling Auslese Fass Nr 62**
(Rg) Dull amber, weak rim; nose muffled at first, dough-like, lacking fruit support, rich, yet a touch of decay. After an hour, white chocolate, after two, appley, Tokaji-like. Surprisingly sweet on the palate, an old smoky flavour, crisp dry acid finish. *At the Schloss, Nov 1984* ★★★

**Schloss Johannisberger Riesling Rosagoldlack BA** (Rg) After producing three for the *Welt-Raritätenprobe*, 'only 180 bottles' remained in the cellar. Frankly disappointing: historic yet not exciting. Concentrated, but dried-out and showing its age. *At the Schloss, Nov 2000* ★

**Marcobrunner Riesling feinste TBA** (Rg) **v Schönborn** What a way to spend a Saturday! Krug '76 around noon, then eight flights accompanying eight courses. We departed at 6.45pm, dazzled but not dazed. This superb wine was the last of the 56 magnificent wines: heavenly, still sweet with highish but inspired acidity. *At Peter Ziegler's tasting, the Schlosshotel, Erbach, Dec 1995* ★★★★★

**Schloss Vollrads Riesling Kabinett** (Rg) Bright gold; sound, low-keyed, soon opening up; sweeter than expected, lovely flavour, crisp acidity, finally left with a taste of apricots. *At the Breuers' rare wine dinner in Rüdesheim, Nov 1996* ★★★★

## 1946 ★★★

Curiously, this was reported to be a 'good' vintage. The production was roughly double that of the meagre 1945. The wines are rarely seen.

**Assmannshäuser Höllenberg Riesling Spätburgunder Kabinett** (Rg) **Staatsweingut** Tired, tawny, hint of orange-red; whiff of *fraise des bois*; dry, of course, lean, touch of rot. *Another Breuer rarity, Rüdesheim, Nov 1997* ★

**Steinberger Riesling naturrein Fass Nr 58** (Rg) **Staatsweingut** 'Low pH, accounting for its pale (for age) gold colour'. Nose nutty, woody, fungi; dry, raw. A curiosity. *At the Breuers' rare wine dinner, Nov 1996.*

## 1947 ★★★★

A very hot year with half the normal rainfall. Very rich, soft wines of high quality.

**Eltviller Sandgrub Riesling** (Rg) **Fischer Erben** A most extraordinary, high-toned, penetrating scent, so sharp that it tickled the nose. Dry. Assertive. Well past its sell-by date. *Served at midnight when the magnificent Breuer wine dinner was still ongoing, Nov 1998.*

**Schloss Johannisberger Riesling Goldlack TBA** (Rg) Medium-deep amber-gold highlights, lime rim; perfectly harmonious, scented, peaches, apricots; sweet, perfectly formed, lovely flesh, flavour, acidity. Great wine. *At Schloss Johannisberg's 900th anniversary tasting, Nov 2001* ★★★★★

**Schloss Johannisberger Riesling TBA Fass Nr 163** (Rg) 155° Oechsle. Amber-gold; honeyed, touch of spice. After an hour, developing a lemon *eau-de-cologne*-like scent. Now medium-sweet but with excellent flavour, a deft touch and lip-licking acidity. *At the Schloss, Nov 1984* ★★★★★

**Niersteiner Orbel Silvaner Riesling Auslese** (Rh) **Guntrum** Surprisingly pale for its age, still lime-tinged; malted honey, old and slightly 'oily'. *A surprise bottle produced at Vinexpo, Bordeaux, by Hajo Guntrum, June 1997* ★

**Schloss Vollrads TBA** (Rg) Deep amber with apple-green rim; very powerful bouquet of great depth, singed raisins and honey; sweet, full-flavoured, high extract yet delicate. Glorious

length and aftertaste. Great wine. *With Graf Matuschka and other members of the Vintners Pride group of estates, at the Schloss, Sept 1988* ★★★★★

## 1948 ★★

Rated average to good. Infrequently seen as few shipped to the UK. The following three wines served by Bernhard Breuer at the brothers' Hotel Rüdesheimer Schloss in November 1998.

**Hattenheimer Mannberg Riesling** (Rg) **Staatsweingut** Orange-gold; very forthcoming, nutty, madeira-like nose; very dry, austere, quite a bite. ★★

**Mittelheimer Edelmann Riesling Auslese** (Rg) **G Bäumer** Three notes, all at the Breuers' rare wine dinners. The first two bottles, variable, in 1996 (went well with eel!): colours orange, cloudy; one maderised, both austere. Two years later, better colour; very rich, heavy, creamy, smoky, 'old Sauternes' nose; strange meaty taste, rich texture. This time with crayfish. *At best* ★★

**Steinberger Riesling naturrein Staatsweingut** (Rg) Yellow-gold; rich, mushroomy – rather like the 1727 Rüdesheim; bone-dry, firm, 'old Hock' flavour, quite a bite. ★

## 1949 ★★★★★

A beautiful vintage. Perfectly balanced wines. By 1949 the vineyards had recovered, and so had the trade. A very popular vintage, many of my notes starting in 1954. Most of the notes I made in the mid-1950s to early 1960s are no longer relevant as the wines are now past their best, although ten of the best, tasted between 1961 and 1973, were reported in the 1980 edition of my *Great Vintage Wine Book*.

**Erbacher Bühl Riesling Auslese** (Rg) **Schloss Reinhartshausen** (Bühl is now Schlossberg) Medium-deep orange-tawny; whiff of muscatelle raisins and citrus, honeyed depth; medium-sweet, rich, flavour and aftertaste of candied orange peel. Dry finish. *At the Schloss, Feb 2002* ★★★★

**Freiherr v Fahnenberg Auslese** (B) **Nepomuk Steiert** Trust Bernhard Breuer to bring a really rare and complicated Baden wine to the tasting of vintages ending in '9'. Freiherr v Fahrenberg is the vineyard, Steiert the grandfather of Wolf Sellweg, the wine 80% Pinot Gris, 20% Riesling. Strength an unusual 13%. Mocha nose; dry, good length, its background more interesting than its taste. *At Christie's, Feb 2000* ★

**Hattenheimer Hassel Riesling BA** (Rg) **Adam Albert** An old private estate which still exists: pure yellow-gold, some elegance but lacking the honeyed bottle age and botrytis I was expecting. Vanilla, marshmallow flavour, drying out. *An interesting rarity at the Breuers' rare wine dinner, Nov 1996* ★

**Schloss Johannisberger Riesling Auslese** (Rg) **Schloss Johannisberg** 110° Oechsle. Whiff of old apples; fairly rich, holding well. The oldest vintage at a rare wine tasting I conducted for the VDP Rheingau. At the previous year's auction, my hammer had come down at DM2200, roughly £700 a bottle. *At the Krone, Assmannshausen, Nov 1998* ★★★★

**Niersteiner Ober Rehbach Riesling BA** (Rh) **Geschwister Schuch** Bright yellow straw; melon scent; alas dried-out, yet rich, with good acidity. *With* Flan de Thé *at Manfred Wagner's post-Ch Margaux dinner, Pfäffikon, Nov 2000* ★

**Steinberger Riesling Auslese** (Rg) **Staatsweingut** Orange gold; touch of fungi; fairly sweet, rich, distinctive, creamy. *At Bernhard Breuer's dinner 'ending in '9 vintages' at Christie's, Feb 2000* ★★★★

**Wehlener Sonnenuhr Riesling Auslese** (M) **J J Prüm**
Pure gold; lovely, floral, honeyed bouquet and flavour; perfect
harmony. Medium-sweet. *June 1992* ★★★★★
**Wehlener Sonnenuhr Riesling feine Auslese** (M)
**J J Prüm** Lovely amber-gold; a rich mouthful though showing
its age. 'Old Riesling', touch of tartness. *At the Weinart/Prüm
tasting, April 1999* ★★★

## 1950 ★★

Harvey's of Bristol, in their autumn 1954 retail price list,
equated the 1950 with the 1947, stating that both 'proved to
be excellent vintages'. Despite this rash statement, the quantity
they listed was comparatively modest, and most disappeared
without trace in the mid-1950s. Yet, at the time, an estate-
bottled Schloss Johannisberger Spätlese was more expensive
than any '50 first-growth red Bordeaux, and an Auslese from
Deidesheim over twice the price. As a matter of interest,
J J Prüm's Wehlener Zeltinger Sonnenuhr BA fetched around
DM6500 in the Grosser Ring auction in October 2000. I have
tasted few of these wines since the late 1950s and only three
since the late 1980s.
**Hochheimer Domdechaney Riesling Auslese** (Rg)
**Aschrott** The oldest of 38 Aschrott wines tasted with Professor
Michael Jaffé and his managers. Warm gold; bouquet of
spearmint, honey and pine; on the palate dried-out though
rich, showing its age. *At the British-owned estate, June 1994* ★★
**Steinberger Riesling naturrein** (Rg) **Staatsweingut**
Oechsle 75°, very high acidity 12.5g/l. Pale, bright; rich,
smoky bouquet; dry, stalky, positive flavour, surviving
swingeing acidity. *At the Breuer rare wine dinner, Nov 1996* ★
**Wehlener Nonnenberg Natur** (M) **S A Prüm** Nice fruit,
honeyed bottle-age; distinctly dry, lean, austere, a bit tart. *With
Raymond Prüm in Wehlen, Sept 1988* ★

## 1951

Poor thin wines. Few exported. Only one fairly old note.
**Graacher Humberg Riesling Natur** (M) **S A Prüm**
Humberg is now part of the Himmelreich vineyard. Buttery
gold; slightly earthy, honeyed bottle age; medium-dry, lightish,
tasting older than nose. How they managed to make this
without chaptalisation I do not know, but it had evidently -
from its taste - been sustained by sulphur. Not bad though.
*At S A Prüm's, Wehlen, Sept 1988* ★★

## 1952 ★★★

A good vintage. Harvey's, in 1954, listed no fewer than 18
wines, over half bottled in Bristol. I have tasted many, which
were mostly sold and consumed in the mid- to late 1950s. I
have only one recent note.
**Hattenheimer Stabel Riesling Spätlese Schloss
Reinhartshausen** (Rg) Pure gold; musty at first, then
honeycomb, lovely, creamy; rather stern '52 Rheingau
character, good body, clean dry finish. *March 1991* ★★★

## 1953 ★★★★★

Wines of enormous charm and appeal, deservedly popular
when put on the market. In those days vintages tended to be
first listed by wine merchants in the spring of the second year
after the vintage. I tasted masses at the time and many since.

One word of warning: the quality of corks used by the
Germans in the mid-1950s was variable, often poor; on the
other hand, the wines were mainly expected to be drunk
young, not cellared for 10 or 20 years. Having said that, the
best can still be lovely to drink now.
**Eitelsbacher Karthäuserhofberg Burgberg Riesling
feinste Auslese** (M) Fresh, peachy bouquet; medium-dry,
light weight yet full of flavour. Rather short, blunt-ended. *At
Peter Ziegler's tasting, Burg Windeck, May 1983* ★★★
**Erbacher Herrenberg Riesling Auslese Cabinet** (Rg)
**Schloss Reinhartshausen** The Herrenberg vineyard is now
called Schlossberg. An astonishing warm, orange-gold; honey
and raisins; fairly sweet, caramelised flavour, touch of chocolate
orange, dry finish. Really a *feinste Auslese* and, in some ways,
not unlike Ch d'Yquem '53. *At the Schloss, Nov 1995* ★★★★
**Hochheimer Kirchenstück Stielweg Riesling Auslese**
(Rg) **Aschrott** Golden; fairly sweet, rich, touch of caramel and
cream. *At Aschrott's, June 1994* ★★★
**Maximin Grünhäuser Herrenberg Riesling BA** (M) **v
Schubert** Yellow gold; touch of vanilla, heavenly ripe peaches;
medium-sweet, full, even assertive flavour. Powerful, years of
life though drying out. *At Peter Ziegler's tasting, Burg Windeck,
May 1983* ★★★★
**Niersteiner Ober Rehbach Riesling BA** (Rh) **Heyl zu
Herrnsheim** The best site on the banks of the Rhine. Steep
slope. Red slate. Five notes made at different sessions at the
excellent 'The Taste of Germany' weekend at the Banff
Springs Hotel. Oechsle 122°. 8.1g/l acidity. Slight bottle
variation. Beautiful pale yellow with highlights; fragrant, floral,
delicate bouquet and flavour. Drying out a little, fading
gracefully. *Oct 1998. At best* ★★★★
**Niersteiner Rehbach Riesling BA** (Rh) **Heyl zu
Herrnsheim** The oldest vintage at a pre-auction tasting
conducted by Prinz Salm, the head of the VDP, and myself at
Christie's. 'King Tut' gold; creamy, honeyed; strange, smoky,
slightly caramel flavour with lovely aftertaste. *Oct 1997* ★★★★

### Tommy Layton and my first tasting note

*As a result of applying for the position of 'trainee' advertised in
The Times, I joined Laytons Wine Merchants in September 1952.
(I later read in one of his books that he took me on because of my
Italianate handwriting!) Aged 25, I was a late starter. My duties
ranged from sweeping the cellar to taking and processing orders and
delivering the wine.*
*Tommy Layton was a prolific wine writer, an underappreciated
post-war innovator, an eccentric and tempestuous autocrat. He was a
'free vintner' (i.e. he could sell wine without a licence) and, in
Duke Street, Manchester Square, had a wine bar – novel in those
days – a wine restaurant, a retail business and ran The Circle of
Wine Tasters. During my year with Tommy I learned a lot, from
how to taste wine to how not to run a business. From the start,
'TAL' encouraged me to make notes and the first entry in my little
red tasting book is dated 17 September 1952: 'Graacher (Moselle)
Deinhard 107/- per dozen. Full honeyed bouquet and flavour to
match'. Other wines in this tasting of trade samples were a '46
Luxembourg Riesling, a '49 Liebfraumilch and inexpensive Alsace.*
*Later that month I was able to taste wonderful old vintage port
('20 Graham, 1896 Tuke) and good claret including 'Ch Palmer
Margaux 1949 English-bottled. Could do with a long rest'. Cost
price 110/-, only three shillings more per dozen than the non-
vintage Graacher! Those were the days.*

**Rauenthaler Baiken Riesling TBA** (Rg) **Graf Eltz** Amber-gold; orange blossom, – rather Yquem-like; rich though drying out. Firm finish. *At the Breuers' rare wine dinner, Nov 1997* ★★★★

**Rauenthaler Pfaffenberg Riesling TBA** (Rg) **Staatsweingüter, Eltville** Pale orange tawny; creamy, perfection; sweet, fat, fabulous length, balance and flavour. On a par with the '37 Baiken though lacking the latter's intensity. *At Peter Ziegler's, Burg Windeck, May 1983* ★★★★★

**Russelheimer Riesling Spätlese** (Rg) **Aschrott** A historic vineyard said to be the home of Riesling. For its age and quality, rich, remarkably good. *At a VDP pre-sale tasting in the Rheingau, Oct 1996* ★★★

**Steinberger Riesling edel BA** (Rg) **Staatsweingut** The oldest of ten Steinberg vintages presented by Dr Serbé in 1994: rich orange-gold; glorious barley sugar (botrytis and bottle age) bouquet; very sweet, almost syrupy richness, heavenly flavour. Most recently: similar note, singed toffee, excellent flavour, acidity and length. Great wine. *Last noted at the Raritätenprobe at Schloss Johannisberg, Nov 2000* ★★★★★

**Steinberger Riesling Spätlese naturrein** (Rg) Harmonious, honeyed bottle age; dry, firm, fairly assertive. Holding well. *At the Breuers' rare wine dinner, Nov 1998* ★★★

**Wehlener Sonnenuhr Riesling BA** (M) **J J Prüm** Two notes, first at Peter Ziegler's tasting in 1984: yellow; fabulous bouquet, like ambrosial lemon curd; flavour to match. Fairly sweet, fleshy, buttery texture. Lovely. Most recently, similar though slightly less ecstatic. *Last noted at the Weinart/Prüm vertical tasting, April 1999. At best* ★★★★★

# 1954

Disastrous weather. Only one ever tasted, in the New Year of 1955. It hadn't aged well!

# 1955 ★★

A moderately good vintage that made a modest appearance in British retail wine lists around the autumn of 1957, the high water mark for German wines at Harvey's. All the wines were sold for quick consumption and I have only tasted one since the late 1950s.

**Durbacher Schlossberg Clevner Traminer** (B) **Wolff-Metternich** Great rarity, only 300 bottles produced. Unusually a mix of red and white grapes, combining to produce an astonishing 200° Oechsle. Rich, touch of tawny; very floral (our host Peter Ziegler just said 'roses'); very sweet, glorious flavour but, to quibble, lacking a bit of length. *Dec 1995* ★★★★★

# 1956

Even worse than 1954. Frost damage, miserably cold wet summer - my first visit to Germany in June: cold and rain every day (see box right). Damp-induced rot, vineyards largely abandoned. No wines tasted.

# 1957 ★★

Moderate quality. Heavy frost damage in early May, mid-summer was warm and sunny but there was almost continuous rain throughout August and September. Some wines were bought in 1959 to succeed the '55s and were mainly consumed by the early 1960s. Most of my notes were made between 1958 and 1967. I have just two notes since.

**Graacher Domprobst Riesling Natur** (M) **S A Prüm** Mint leaf and honeyed bottle-age; unknit; dryish, clean, attractive but lacking acidity and with a touch of bitterness. *With Raymond Prüm in Wehlen, Sept 1988* ★

**Wehlener Sonnenuhr Riesling BA** (M) **J J Prüm** Orange-gold; very sweet, raisiny nose; much drier on the palate. A touch of rot but dry, fragrant finish. Tasted blind – no one could identify it! *At the Weinart/Prüm tasting, April 1999* ★★

# 1958 ★★

Mediocre but abundant vintage. After a shaky start, a fine August and September augured well. Rain during an exceptionally prolonged harvest swelled the grapes but diluted the quality. Had the British wine trade followed the more recent practice of buying wines the spring after the vintage, more wines would have been imported. Happily, the quality of the 1959 vintage was recognised before major purchases of the '58s had been made. I have tasted only a few.

**Graacher Himmelreich Riesling Natur** (M) **S A Prüm** Yellow-gold; soft, lactic nose, settling down to a cool fragrance; fairly dry, still reasonably fresh and attractive. Flavour reminded me of Vaseline and vanilla. Firm dry finish. *With Raymond Prüm in Wehlen, Sept 1988* ★★

# 1959 ★★★★★

At last, to end a mixed and mainly disappointing decade, a magnificent vintage, though the excessively hot summer created unusual, indeed unprecedented, winemaking conditions. However, glorious wines were made from sun-enriched grape juice with an extraordinarily high sugar content and there was a record number of Beeren and Trockenbeerenauslesen wines in the Mosel-Saar-Ruwer.

Once my favourite vintage after the 1937 but the wines are now variable and mainly past their best. The top wines can still be beautiful.

**Assmannshäuser Hinterkirch Spätburgunder Kabinett** (Rg) **Staatsweingut** Soft, mature red; harmonious, opening up richly, dry, good, firm finish. Still some tannin. Went well with pheasant. *At the Breuers' rare wine dinner, Nov 1996* ★★★

**Berncasteler Doctor Riesling feine Auslese** (M) **Dr H Thanisch** Pale for age; curious, minty, kerosene; drying out, earthy, disappointing. *June 1992* ★

**Brüssele Lemberger Auslese** (W) **Graf Adelmann** Lemberger is an old red grape variety grown only in Württemberg. Attractive colour, weak rim; very sweet, almost

---

## My first visit to Germany

*In the early days of our marriage, every summer holiday was spent in a different wine region. Our first visit to Germany was to the Mosel. We went all the way from London and back on our Vespa motor-scooter. This was in June 1956, and for two weeks it rained every day. It was a memorable trip because Daphne had to carry the luggage when we went uphill. It was also our (well, my) laudable ambition at that time to make love — necessarily furtively, and at night — in a famous vineyard. I well recall one such occasion. It was the Bernkasteler Doktor vineyard, conveniently opposite the small hotel at which we were staying. As mentioned, it was unusually cold and wet, so a bit muddy. The experience somewhat dampened my ardour...*

overpowering nose, like strawberry jam, sweaty; dry, fullish, firm. Flavour more neutral. *Another curiosity, at Peter Ziegler's tasting lunch at Burg Windeck, May 1983* ★★★ *in its way.*

**Erbacher Marcobrunn Riesling Spätlese Cabinet Fass Nr 59/24** (Rg) **Eberhard Ritter** und **Edler v Oetinger** Bottled in Denmark by Kjaer & Sommerfeldt. Unusually pale for a 30-year-old; nose still very fresh and youthful, mint leaf; dry, mild, touch of peach kernels. *From Aalholm Castle, Denmark, Aug 1989* ★★

**Erbacher Marcobrunn Riesling Auslese Cabinet** (Rg) **Schloss Reinhartshausen** First tasted at Rodenstock's Arlberg weekend in 1988: sweet, glorious flavour, ripe, rich, perfectly balanced. Most recently: warm gold, orange highlights; similar bouquet and flavour, almost word for word, adding singed raisins. Good length and flavour but drying out a little. *Last tasted at the Schloss, Feb 2002* ★★★

**Erbacher Marcobrunn Riesling TBA** (Rg) **Schloss Reinhartshausen** Warm amber; orange Muscat scent; lovely singed, Tokay-like flavour with wonderfully honeyed aftertaste. More recently: similar in many ways, very rich, fragrant; sweet and powerful. Very good acidity and aftertaste. *Last tasted at the Welt-Raritätenprobe at Schloss Johannisberg, Nov 2000* ★★★★★

**Hallgartener Schönhell Riesling TBA** (Rg) **Löwenstein** A delicious half bottle to round off a stone-crab supper at Bob Paul's in Florida: deep amber-gold; glorious, slightly singed raisiny, smoky bouquet and taste. Still fat and fleshy though drying out. *Feb 2001* ★★★★

**Hattenheimer Wisselbrunnen Riesling BA** (Rg) **Schloss Reinhartshausen** In 1959 Wisselbrunnen was judged to be better than Marcobrunn. First tasted in the cellars in 1995: amber-gold; honeyed, floral, fragrant; very rich though lighter in style and drier than expected. A charmer, good length, lovely finish. Most recently, an almost identical note, adding touch of spearmint and marmalade, with fabulous acidity. *Last noted at the Schloss, Feb 2002* ★★★★★

**Schloss Johannisberger Riesling feine Spätlese** (Rg) Warm gold; richly forthcoming, old apricots; a bit four-square. *At Bernhard Breuer's 'The '9s dinner' at Christie's, Feb 2000* ★★

**Schloss Layer Pittermännchen Riesling Cabinet TBA** (N) **Schlossgut Diel** Orange-amber; lovely caramelised apricots nose; rich but drying out a bit. A hefty, old-fashioned style, lacking zest and acidity. *Made by Armin's father, it had been awarded the Bestes Fass der Jahrhundert-Ernte 1959. Dining with Armin Diel at Schlossgut Diel, Nov 1996* ★★ *A departed glory long past its best.*

**Maximin Grünhäuser Riesling Herrenberg** (M) **v Schubert** Though no indication on the label, of at least *feinste Auslese* quality: medium-orange; raisins, rose petals, touch of lime; very sweet, perfect weight and excellent acidity. *At Len Evans' 'Single-bottle Club' dinner, Hunter Valley, Sept 2000* ★★★★

**Oestricher Lenchen Riesling Auslese** (Rg) **Wegeler** Drying out. Disappointing. *At my Fine Wine auction tasting, at the Krone, Assmannshausen, Nov 1998.*

**Oestricher Lenchen Riesling hochfeine Auslese** (Rg) **J Spreitzer** Yellow-gold; honey and cress; medium-sweet, quite a bite for a '59. *At the VDP pre-sale tasting, Nov 1999* ★★

**Rauenthaler Baiken Riesling TBA** (Rg) **Staatsweingüter** An astonishing 248° Oechsle, 13° total acidity. Rich gold;

intense bouquet, singed raisins; high extract, concentrated, raisiny, wonderful acidity. Magnificent. *The best of an outstanding range of wines produced by Peter Ziegler at Burg Windeck, May 1983* ★★★★★★ *(6 stars).*

**Rauenthaler Herrberg Riesling Spätlese** (Rg) **v Simmern** Just to prove that a '59 Spätlese can keep well. Touch of orange; medium-dry, good structure, condition and length. *At Breuer's 'The '9s' dinner at Christie's, Feb 2000* ★★★

**Scharzhofberger Riesling Auslese** (M) **Egon Müller** First tasted with the Müllers, father and son, in 1996. It was drying out a little and lacking zest. A similar note four years later. We were told that though the grapes were very ripe, they lacked botrytis. *Last tasted at the estate, May 2000* ★★

**Steinberger Riesling BA** (Rg) **Staatsweingut** Two bottles, one corked, the second, though with good flavour and length, was drying out. Surprisingly high acidity for a '59. Not a patch on the TBA. *At the Breuers' rare wine dinner, Rüdesheim, Nov 1997* ★★

**Steinberger Riesling TBA** (Rg) **Staatsweingüt** First tasted in 1987: rich amber with pronounced apple-green rim; fabulously rich, raisiny, like Tokay essence; very sweet, mouthfilling, glorious barley-sugar flavour, great length, excellent acidity. 231° Oechsle, 148g/l residual sugar. The sugar content was so high that the sluggish fermentation continued into March. Three notes. Two years later a memorable bottle at Michael's Restaurant, Santa Monica, a similar note. More recently at a 'VDP auction bests' tasting (in 1991 it had sold for DM3000). Amber-gold; bouquet of singed *crème brûlée*; still sweet, intense, glorious muscatel-like flavour, length and acidity. Great wine. *Last noted at the Krone, Assmannshausen, Nov 1998* ★★★★★

**Wehlener Sonnenuhr Riesling Spätlese** (M) **J J Prüm** Sitting in the sun, overlooking the Attersee with our host, Karl-Heinz Wolf, Manfred Prüm and our wives waiting for other guests to arrive, the afternoon prior to the 83-wine, two-day Prüm marathon. Truthfully, showing its age: buttercup yellow, overall dry, touch of oxidation. On the Sunday, from the best cask, *Fuder 38*: golden; classic Riesling nose; spicy, long past its best. *April 1999* ★★

**Wehlener Sonnenuhr Riesling feinste Auslese** (M) **J J Prüm** Three notes. First at a Hollywood Wine Society dinner in 1985. A remarkably pale yellow colour for a '59, still retaining a youthful green tinge; lightly herbaceous, grapey; medium-sweet, fleshy, soft, perfect flavour, just enough acidity. Then I nade a surprisingly similar note 14 years later though one bottle was smelling of mushroom soup. *Last tasted April 1999. At best* ★★★★

**Wehlener Sonnenuhr Riesling feinste Auslese** (M) **S A Prüm** A similar *feinste Auslese* by another Prüm. Mild, then an eruption of fragrance; medium-sweet, plump, good length and acidity. *Tasted in Wehlen, Sept 1988* ★★★★

**Wehlener Sonnenuhr Riesling TBA** (M) **J J Prüm** The last wine of the last flight of Prüm's 83-wine tasting. Manfred told us that his father, Sebastian, had made the '59s. Rich orange-amber; the smell of damp towels, 'calf's foot jelly' and whiff of vinegar. A most extraordinary taste (Daphne: 'like vanilla ice cream with fudge sauce'), a touch of raspberry. Alas, completely outclassed by the '76 and '71 TBAs. *April 1999* ★★★

# 1960–1979

The emphasis on new technology, techniques and experimental grape varieties continued apace, led by the famous Institute of Viticulture and Oenology at Geisenheim. My own view is that too much attention was given to productivity and not enough to quality with the emphasis being on early-ripening varieties such as the prolific Müller-Thurgau rather than the noble Riesling. Other varieties were introduced more for their sugar content than any character, and when planted on alluvial soil on flat land – so much easier to manage than the steep slate slopes of the Mosel Valley – the production of easy, fairly sweet, less costly to make wines took off. The 'rationalisation' of vineyards and their names introduced by the 1971 German wine laws, ostensibly to simplify the marketing of the wines, had disastrous effects. Cheap, sugary and watery wines were marketed under familiar wine names, for example Niersteiner Gutes Domtal and Piesporter Michelsberg. There emerged a flood of cheap Spätlese and Auslese wines from non-traditional varieties and less good districts. All this harmed the image of German wines and undermined the old-established quality-wine estates.

### Vintages at a Glance
**Outstanding ★★★★★**
1967 (v), 1971, 1973 (v)
**Very Good ★★★★**
1964, 1975, 1976
**Good ★★★**
1961 (v), 1963 (v), 1966, 1969, 1970, 1979

## 1960 ★

A return to poor weather. An abundance of mediocre wine, not unlike 1958. Only one tasted recently.
**Hattenheimer Wisselbrunnen Riesling Kabinett** (Rg) **Schloss Reinhartshausen** Palish lemon with gold highlights; fresh 'lemon curd' nose and flavour. Very acidic. *At the Schloss, Feb 2002* ★

## 1961 ★ to ★★★

Another poor summer in Germany sandwiched between an encouraging spring and an extraordinarily hot September which saved the day. Wide variations, from fairly ordinary to Spätlese quality; no great sweet wines. None tasted recently.

## 1962 ★ to ★★

A moderate vintage, best known for its Eiswein. Another difficult growing year: late, cold spring, uneven blossoming. Extremes, dry but hot, grapes unripe, and, after all seemed lost, there was a change in early October, harvesting continuing well into November, the last grapes being picked in early December in below-freezing temperatures. I have few notes.
**Forster Mühlweg Riesling Auslese** (P) **Bürklin-Wolf** The Mühlweg vineyard no longer exists. Good colour for its age; slightly oily nose; distinctly dry, peach stones flavour, raw. *At the estate, Sept 1980.*
**Wehlener Sonnenuhr Riesling feine Auslese** (M) **S A Prüm** Picked in November and initially classed as *feinste Auslese* though it should, I was told, have been an Eiswein: plump, by no means super. Coincidentally, six years later, at the estate: lime gold; harmonious, grapey, lightly honeyed touch of kerosene; medium-sweet, lovely flavour, soft yet firm, perfect, understated acidity. *Last tasted in Wehlen, Sept 1988* ★★★

**Wöllsteiner Äffchen Sämling Auslese Eiswein** (W) **Weingut Wirth** A prize-winning wine; straw gold; ripe, rich nectarine fragrance, touch of 'petrol'; very sweet though light in style and a bit of a let-down on the palate, straw-flavoured. *Sept 1987* ★★★

## 1963 ★ to ★★★

Amazing how any decent drinkable wines could be made after such a growing season: the Rhine frozen, cold spring, late flowering, sunny July then rain through to an abrupt Indian summer at the end of October. Yet I have a surprising number of good notes, though few made recently.
**Casteller Schlossberg Rieslaner Spätlese** (F) **Fürst Castell** A rarity produced at an extemporised tasting at the Schloss between tea on the terrace and the ducal procession down the sloping lawns to the annual Castell *Weinfest* attended by estate workers and families and visitors. All very 'umpah' band jollity. The wine was surprisingly good for an off vintage, dry but full and fragrant. *Sunday, 7 July, 1997* ★★★
**Schloss Johannisberger Riesling Rosalack Auslese** (Rg) I can't think why this wine was entered for sale. A curiosity perhaps. It was cloudy; so-so; dry, hard finish. *At the VDP pre-auction tasting at Schloss Reinhartshausen, Nov 1995.*
**Rüdesheimer Berg Mauerwein Riesling Auslese** (Rg) **v Schönborn** From a terraced section of the Berg. Peachy botrytis; sweet, rich, but touch of ignoble rot. *At the VDP auction tasting at the Krone, Assmannshausen, Nov 1998* ★★

---

### Eiswein

*Eiswein, German for icewine, is made in certain years from grapes picked – usually in November or December and often at around 4 or 5am – while still frozen on the vine. They are then transferred directly to the presses, where they are crushed so that their water content, in the form of ice crystals, is separated from the super-sweet concentrated juice. Eiswein grapes do not have noble rot, which makes their flavour very clean-cut, their sweetness balanced by their refreshing acidity. Under German wine law, Eiswein has its own Prädikat category which is now at Beerenauslese level. Although Eiswein is extremely attractive, I personally prefer Beerenauslese (and, of course, Trockenbeerenauslese), wines which I find more subtle and multi-layered.*

**Wachenheimer Rechbächel Riesling Cabinet** (P)
**Bürklin-Wolf** Bright Tokaji-like amber; very fragrant, remarkably fresh, slightly grapey, spicy, like a sea breeze; dry, lightish, firm, fresh but kernelly. *At Peter Ziegler's tasting, Burg Windeck, May 1983* ★★

# 1964 ★★★★

A rich, ripe vintage following an almost too good summer, the hottest and sunniest year ever, hours of sunshine even exceeding 1959, though the resulting wines not so massively structured. The same problems however; tricky winemaking in hot conditions, ripe grapes, high sugar content and low acidity.

Undoubtedly most successful in the northerly Mosel-Saar-Ruwer where the naturally high acidity of the Riesling grown on steep slate slopes counterbalanced the unusually ripe sweetness. Popular, attractive, the best vintage between 1959 and 1971, some still lovely, others tired.

**Bernkasteler Badstube Riesling Auslese Fuder 9** (M)
**J J Prüm** Burnished gold; sweet, fragrant old Riesling, fudge and mint; showing its age, overall dry now and tailing off. *At the Weinart/Prüm tasting, April 1999* ★ *Well past its best.*

**Bernkasteler Doctor Riesling Spätlese** (M) **Thanisch**
Thanisch is one of the three owners of the renowned Doctor vineyard, the muddy slopes of which Daphne and I struggled to ascend on a wet June evening in 1956. Noted at a pre-sale tasting in New York. It was still delicious. *Dec 1997* ★★★★

**Eitelsbacher Karthäuserhofberg-Kronenberg Riesling feinste Auslese** (M) **Rautenstrauch** Curious bouquet, still lively; medium-sweet, still fresh. Lacking length. *June 1992* ★★★

**Erbacher Hohenrain Riesling Spätlese Cabinet** (Rg)
**Schloss Reinhartshausen** Prior to 1971 the 'Spätlese Cabinet' bottling, the equivalent of Gold Capsule, was for the Schatzkammer, the private reserve cellar for special occasions or for Spitzenwein auctions. The bottles were opened, poured into a small vat, filtered, sulphur dioxide added, then rebottled with new corks. Pale yellow (I wrote 'surprisingly', but doubtless due to the sulphur dioxide); light, clean, raisiny nose; medium-dry, rich, mid-palate, grapefruit-like end acidity. *In the tasting room at the Schloss, Feb 2002* ★

**Erbacher Marcobrunn Riesling Spätlese** (Rg)
**Staatsweingut** Pale; ripe, harmonious; fairly dry, mild, fully developed but tailed off. *At the VDP pre-sale tasting held at Schloss Johannisberg, Nov 1999* ★★

**Johannisberger Hölle Riesling Auslese** (Rg) **Johannishof Eser** Lime yellow; fairly sweet still, good for its age. *At the VDP pre-sale tasting, Nov 1995* ★★★

**Niersteiner Hipping u Rehbach Riesling TBA** (Rh)
**Reinhold Senfter** Bright yellow; honeyed, rather raisiny; medium-sweet – very disappointing. *Oct 1980* ★★

**Rauenthaler Baiken Riesling Auslese** (Rg) **Schloss Eltz**
I met the charming Graf Eltz before he was ruined by a disastrous business venture. The family's principal castle, dramatically overlooking the Lower Mosel, is well worth seeing. This '64 had a perfect colour for its age, lovely flavour, 'drying out elegantly'. *Dining at the Krone, Assmannshausen, June 1996* ★★★

**Scharzhofberger Riesling Auslese** (M) **Egon Müller**
Tasted on our first visit to this beautiful estate tucked away off the Saar Valley. This was a wet harvest with the lowest acidity in Egon Müller senior's experience: yellow-gold; buttery, creamy nose; fairly dry and, I had the temerity to think, a touch of rot. *May 2000* ★

**Dom Scharzhofberger Riesling Fass Nr 7** (M) **Hohe Domkirche** Good, rich, yellow; buttery, fragrant, harmonious; dry, lovely flavour, excellent acidity. *July 1983* ★★★★

**Steinberger Riesling feine Spätlese Kabinett** (Rg)
**Staatsweingut** Bottle variation at the Steinberg dinner. One dull, lacking zest, the other fresher, perfect with pheasant. *Nov 1994. At best* ★★

**Steinberger Riesling BA** (Rg) **Staatsweingut** Half bottles: fairly deep amber; 'calf's foot jelly', smooth, caramelly nose and aftertaste; sweet, flavour of quince, good acidity. *At the Welt-Raritäten tasting, Schloss Johannisberg, Nov 2000* ★★★★

**Steinberger Riesling TBA** (Rg) **Staatsweingut** Old gold; toffee, liquorice, pure old Riesling which blossomed in the glass; still very sweet, fat, lovely flavour and aftertaste. *One of the finest wines at the Breuers' 23-wine dinner, Nov 1997* ★★★★★

**Wehlener Sonnenuhr Riesling Spätlese** (M) **J J Prüm**
Still remarkably pale and green-tinged; very gentle fruit; dry, lightish, mild, a bit faded but well-balanced. *A sunny Sunday lunch at Chippenham Lodge, guests Herbert 'Screwpull' Allen and Ted Hale, June 1983* ★★★

**Wehlener Sonnenuhr Riesling feine Auslese Fuder 15** (M) **J J Prüm** Orange-gold; sweet, peachy, caramelly bottle age and botrytis nose and taste. For a '64 a bit lacking though drinking pleasantly. *April 1999* ★★ *Drink up.*

# 1965

Vying with 1956 as one of the worst vintages of the century. Growth uneven and retarded, cold wet summer. Harvest delayed until November, then largely abandoned. I tasted some just drinkable wines between 1966 and 1974 and none since.

# 1966 ★★★

Good but totally different in style to the '64: the wines were paler, firmer, more steely, with good sustaining acidity. A relatively small crop, harvested late due to cold and rain at the end of an otherwise well-balanced growing season. Due to cold, wet weather in early November few sweet wines were produced, save for some very late-picked grapes made into Eiswein with some success.

The notes I made in the late 1960s and early 1970s were remarkable for the evenness of quality: the wines had considerable style. I have tasted few recently, the following being a representative cross-section.

**Bernkasteler Doctor Riesling Spätlese** (M) **Thanisch**
Classic 'oily' Riesling; medium-sweet. Touch of peach kernels. *At a pre-sale tasting, New York, Dec 1997* ★

**Erbacher Langenwingert Riesling Kabinett** (Rg) **Schloss Reinhartshausen** This vineyard is between Erbach and Kiedrich. Palish, like a fine sherry, with lime gold highlights; low-keyed, lime blossom; some sweetness, melon-like flavour, fresh, refreshing acidity. *At the Schloss, Feb 2002* ★★★

**Erdener Prälat Riesling feinste Auslese** (M) **Dr Loosen**
90–94° Oechsle, from 100% ungrafted Riesling planted in red sandstone soil. Wines matured in 1000-litre *Fuder*. Palish yellow; fairly hefty, slightly malty nose; dry, medium-full weight and flavour. Bracken-like endtaste. *The oldest vintage of a wide range of Loosen's wines introduced by Stuart Pigott in London, Sept 1988* ★

**Hochheimer Domdechaney Riesling Spätlese** (Rg)
**Werner** An earthy Hochheim showing its age. *At a major VDP Rheingau tasting prior to a promotional sale at Christie's, Sept 1996* ★

**Lorcher Krone Riesling Auslese** (Rg) **v Kanitz** Graf v
Kanitz is the major proprietor in the Mittelrhein, downstream
from Bingen. Deserves to be better known. Lean and
attractive. Rich but not sweet. *At the VDP pre-sale tasting, Nov
1995* ★★★

**Wehlener Sonnenuhr Riesling Auslese** (M) **J J Prüm**
Bright yellow-gold; medium-sweet – I thought a touch of rot,
but it went well with the *foie gras*. Some finesse. *April 1999* ★

**Zeltinger Schlossberg Riesling feine Auslese** (M)
**J J Prüm** As if to remind us that he has other strings to his
Wehlen bow: a similar colour to be the above; nose initially a
waxy kerosene Riesling character that seemed to spread itself,
creamily; good, flavour and length, dry finish. Also served with
*foie gras. At the Weinart/Prüm event in Austria, April 1999* ★★★

## 1967 ★ to ★★★★★

Fairly ordinary in the lower quality range but some excellent,
late-picked, botrytis-affected sweet wines due to the
switchback climatic conditions: very variable spring, retarded
growth, lovely summer but high hopes dashed by heavy rains
in September which washed out many vineyards. Those estates
that hung on for the late autumn sunshine made superb TBAs.

Not much note was taken of the '67s by the British trade
which, apart from specialists in German wine, seems
psychologically affected by what happens in French districts,
and 1967 was not particularly notable in Bordeaux. I tasted
many '67 German wines prior to and during a tour in 1969,
most notably at a fine wine auction in Wiesbaden that spring
which really opened my eyes to the quality of the top wines
of this vintage. Forget the lesser wines but look out for the big
guns: much underrated.

**Binger Scharlachberg Riesling TBA** (Rh) **Villa Sachsen**
Dark barley sugar, apple-green rim; powerful, honeyed,
caramel; sweet yet fruit drying out, low alcohol, slightly
tobacco-like flavour. Very good. 'Shades of Yquem'. *At a pre-
sale tasting, Christie's, Oct 1997* ★★★★

**Casteller Hohnart Silvaner Natur** (F) **Fürst Castell** Palish;
broad, milk-and-honey nose; dry, powerful, strange, unfamiliar
but attractive Franconian wine. *Tasted with other wines of the
'Pride of Germany' group of estates hosted by Graf Matuschka at
Schloss Vollrads, Sept 1988* ★★★

**Deidesheimer Leinhöhle Riesling TBA** (P) **v Bühl** First
tasted in 1973, then a medium-pale lemon-gold with a rich yet
delicate and grapey Pfalz nose; very sweet. Several notes since
then. Aged 22, rich amber-gold; bouquet now heavier, toffee-
like, with singed raisin fruitiness, great depth; still very sweet,
full, fat, with high volatile acidity and caramelly aftertaste. *Last
tasted Sept 1988* ★★★★★ *Magnificent then, but needs drinking.*

**Hattenheimer Hassel Riesling BA** (Rg) **H Lang** 140°
Oechsle, 9g/l acidity. Two notes a day apart, both at the
German wine weekend in Banff. Yet almost identical
descriptions including 'very Germanic', 'very Wagnerian',
'almost unctuous'. A beautiful burnished gold; syrup of figs,
'butterscotch'. I liked it! *Last noted Oct 1998* ★★★★

**Hattenheimer Schützenhaus Riesling Auslese** (Rg)
**Balthasar Ress** As President of the VDP Rheingau in the mid-
1990s, Stefan Ress was very active in the efforts to open up
and 'internationalise' their annual wine auctions. I was invited
to take over as auctioneer and to produce a Christie's
catalogue for the first joint sale in the autumn of 1994. In
addition he involved me in the related wine activities during
the annual week of wine. Naturally I tasted many Ress wines

including this powerful, honeyed wine of *feine Auslese* quality
on a couple of occasions. *Last noted pre-sale, Sept 1996* ★★★★

**Schloss Johannisberger Riesling Auslese** (Rg) Straw
gold; crisp, toffee-like, later reminding me of parchment used
in book-binding; full flavoured, raisiny. Past peak. *At the VDP
pre-sale tasting, May 1996* ★★

**Schloss Johannisberger Riesling TBA** (Rg) This was
paired with Ch d'Yquem '67 at the opening of the
unforgettable Johannisberg/Yquem marathon at the Schloss in
November 1984. Both wines were superb. Each distinctive in
its own way. I knew, the moment I had tasted them, that it was
not going to be a competition, more a comparison of styles.
The following autumn, quite coincidentally paired again with
the Yquem. As both the notes of the TBA were similar, I
combine them: medium-deep, lovely amber-gold with a hint
of orange; glorious bouquet, refined, orange blossom and a
rich, crisp, sultana grapiness developing in the glass, intense
spiciness, cinnamon, tea; sweet and rich yet delicate, fabulous
acidity, touch of caramel, fragrant finish. *Lasted noted at
Rodenstock's annual rare wine tasting, Wiesbaden, Oct 1985* ★★★★★

**Schloss Johannisberger Riesling Goldlack (TBA)** (Rg)
Amber; rich, tangy; sweet, crisp, lovely flavour, assertive,
caramelly aftertaste. Clumsy after the great '47. *At the 900th
anniversary tasting at the Schloss, Nov 2001* ★★★★

**Schloss Layer Goldloch Riesling Edel BA** (N)
**Schlossgut Diel** Said to be the best wine made by Armin Diel's
father. First tasted dining at the Schloss in 1996: a glorious
amber-gold; *crème brûlée* nose; sweet, Sauternes-like, high
(12g/l) acidity. Next, presented at the *Welt-Raritäten-Probe* at
Schloss Johannisberg: rich, powerful but drying out and with a
dry, slightly bitter finish. *Last tasted Nov 2000. At best* ★★★★

**Marcobrunner Riesling edelbeeren Auslese** (Rg)
**v Schönborn** Warm gold; rich, classic 'oily' ripe Riesling,
stewed apples, *crème brûlée*; rich but drier than expected. Now
too dry for its high acidity. *The penultimate wine at Breuer's
Rheingau Wein-Raritätenprobe in Rüdesheim, Nov 1998* ★★★

**Rauenthaler Herrberg Riesling Auslese Cabinet** (Rg)
**v Simmern** Palish yellow gold; lovely ripe honeyed bouquet,
with Rauenthal richness; fairly sweet, fat, but not heavy,
exquisitely balanced: perfect fruit and acidity. *At Christie's pre-
sale tasting, March 1980* ★★★★★ *Could still be lovely.*

**Wachenheimer Rechbächel Riesling TBA** (P) **Bürklin-
Wolf** Grapes picked 12 November, Oechsle 184°, acidity
9.3g/l. Three experiences of this extraordinary wine, first at
H Sichel's 'Tasting of the Century' in 1975: glorious, but
almost too fat and cloying. Most recently, at Sichel's re-run of
the original tasting: tawny gold; the sweetness and
concentration of brown treacle! *Last noted at the Royal Society of
Arts, London, Sept 1992* ★★★★

**Wehlener Sonnenuhr Riesling feinste Auslese** (M)
**S A Prüm** My host told me that, despite 50–60% rot in his
vineyards, the late-picked grapes were excellent. I noticed a lot
of tartaric acid crystals at the bottom of the bottle (perfectly
harmless of course). Medium yellow; low-keyed at first, with
an underlay of wax and 'greenness' that reminded me of
Sauvignon Blanc; medium-sweet, lively gooseberry-like
flavour and acidity. *With Raymond Prüm, Sept 1988* ★★

## 1968

A poor year in virtually every European wine region, due
entirely to weather conditions (cold, wet and black rot, not
'noble' rot) that makes life an unrewarding misery for the

grower. Mainly thin, raw wines of low quality and short life. One or two drinkable wines in the early 1970s, only one tasted since.

**Rüdesheimer Berg Lay Riesling Cabinet** (Rg) **Scholl v Hillebrand** I well remember visiting this company on the first German tour of Masters of Wine in, I think, 1969. If I cannot quite remember the date, I shall never forget the exceptionally pretty flaxen-haired *Mädchen* handing out glasses of wine. The Breuer brothers left the company, Bernhard to concentrate on their vineyards and brilliant winemaking and Heinrich on their Rüdesheimer Schlosshotel. This off vintage wine must have been nostalgic for them. The result of the cold, wet harvest was a pale colour; creamy then tinny nose; soft, open-knit, poor flavour, drab finish. *At the Breuers' dinner, Nov 1998.*

## 1969 at best ★★★

Reasonably good, firm, acidic wines. A good growing season spoiled by lack of rain, then, at the crucial ripening period, three weeks of thick fog obscured the sun. The Pfalz and Rheinhessen districts suffered most, particularly the early ripening varieties, but estates in the Rheingau and Mosel, with their classic later-ripening Rieslings, were able to take advantage of the late October and early November sun.

After the '71s came along, the '69s were largely forgotten. Many tasted when young, several showing well in the mid- to late 1970s. The best can still be very agreeable to drink.

**Eltviller Kalbsflicht Riesling** (Rg) **Fischer Erben** Palish yellow-green; lime blossom, glorious; dry, better nose than flavour. Lip-licking acidity. *At Bernhard Breuer's 'The '9s' dinner at Christie's, Feb 2000* ★★

**Erbacher Marcobrunn Riesling** (Rg) **Staatsweingut** Yellow gold; rich, flowery bouquet and flavour. Medium-dry. Soft. Very pleasant. *Also at the Breuer dinner, Feb 2000* ★★★

**Erbacher Rheinhell Riesling Kabinett** (Rg) **Schloss Reinhartshausen** Pale gold; sweet yet touch of rawness; medium-sweet, positive flavour but peach kernels aftertaste. *At the Schloss, Feb 2002* ★

**Erdener Prälat Riesling hochfeine Auslese** (M) **Dr Loosen** Natural sugar content of grapes 100–105° Oechsle, close to Beerenauslese, hence the *hochfeine* suffix. Nowadays 83–110° entitles the grower to the Auslese category. It is the abolition of these fine distinctions, and the changing of vineyard boundaries and names by the German Wine Laws of 1971, that have done so much to handicap the great estates in order to give others, and the ignorant public, an equal opportunity! Back to the wine: an attractive yellow colour; honeyed bottle-age and ripe grapes; medium-sweet, fairly full-bodied for a Moselwein, even fat, but with very good acidity. Touch of bracken on the end taste. *At the Loosen tasting in London, Sept 1988* ★★★

**Erdener Treppchen Riesling feinste Auslese** (M) **Mönchhof** Yellow gold; rich, ripe, kerosene grapiness; medium-sweet, full, rich, creamy, honeyed. Dry finish. *June 1992* ★★★★★

**Graacher Himmelreich Riesling Eiswein hochfeine Auslese** (M) **J J Prüm** Golden; hard to pin down; not as sweet as expected, creamy, dry finish. *April 1999* ★★

**Hallgartener Deutelsberg Riesling** (Rg) **Engelmann** A vineyard parallel to Steinberg which used to be Hallgarten's best. Pale for its age; low-keyed, cress-like, opened up nicely; medium sweetness and body, curious flavour, lovely acidity. *At Bernhard Breuer's 'The '9s' dinner at Christie's, Feb 2000* ★★★

**Kallstadter Saumagen Riesling BA** (P) **Koehler-Ruprecht** Medium amber; rich, honeyed, slightly caramelly; medium-sweet, assertive, 'oily' Riesling. *At Breuer's dinner, Feb 2000* ★★★

**Oberemmeler Hütte Riesling feinste Auslese** (M) **v Hövel** Yellow; peachy, soft, sweet bouquet; sweet entry, firm dry finish. Honeyed. *June 1992* ★★★★

**Wachenheimer Mandelgarten Scheurebe BA** (P) **Bürklin-Wolf** Gold; heavenly, honeyed, high-toned, with whiff of Scheurebe's grapey 'tom-cats'; sweet, rich, its fatness cut with high (12g/l) acidity. *Sept 1980* ★★★★

**Wehlener Abtei Riesling hochfeine Auslese naturrein** (M) **Michel Schneider, at Zell** I first tasted this in 1997 and again two years later. Brilliant buttercup yellow; waxy, honeyed botrytis and bottle age with a touch of peach kernels; fairly sweet, rich, some fat, good acidity. *Last tasted Oct 1989* ★★★

**Wehlener Sonnenuhr Riesling feine Auslese** (M) **J J Prüm** This and the next two wines served together, and with each I had reservations, undecided as to whether the common factor was just bottle age or rot. And it was not the lobster! If this wine was only moderately good, what were the lesser quality '69s like? *At the Weinart/Prüm tasting, April 1999* ★

**Wehlener Sonnenuhr Riesling feinste Auslese** (M) **J J Prüm** Similar colour, nose and taste but extra dimensions. Some sweetness. *April 1999* ★★

**Wehlener Sonnenuhr Riesling hochfeine Auslese** (M) **J J Prüm** Warm gold; fragrant old honey; less sweet than expected, fairly powerful and with good length. *April 1999* ★★★

**Winkeler Jesuitengarten Riesling Spätlese Joseph Hamm** Yellow-gold, slightly hazy; smell and taste of old oily Riesling. Ordered out of curiosity to see how a '69 Spätlese had survived. It hadn't. *At the Schlosshotel Krone, Hattenheim, May 2000.*

## 1970 ★★★

Definitely not comparable with the best French districts. Rather plodding wines due to late blossoming, dry summer and moderate autumn. Early pickers made passable wine for quick consumption. Some growers took advantage of the late summer sunshine; one or two even picked as late as 6 January, 1971! Among the survivors are the extraordinary, and rare, Strohwein, benefiting from perfect cellaring.

**Erbacher Rheinhell Riesling BA Strohwein** (Rg) **Schloss Reinhartshausen** To make this, the individually picked, very ripe, grapes were spread out on corrugated asbestos roof panels! Of the 280 bottles made, I have consumed just two with, I must confess, slightly different descriptions - either me or bottle variation. The first (May 1982) a deepish straw gold; bottle-age botrytis; fairly sweet, excellent flavour, texture, balance and aftertaste. Developed well in the glass. Slightly pasty end acidity. Eighteen months later, a pure yellow-gold; very fragrant, Muscat-like; some sweetness though light style. The original acidity appears to have settled down. Perfect. *Last tasted Oct 1983. At best* ★★★★★

**Forster Pechstein Riesling Auslese** (P) **Bürklin-Wolf** The sulphur content kept low because the grapes were in cask three and a half hours after picking. An incredible yellow; glorious, broad, buttery, slightly peachy, honeyed and raisiny bouquet; medium dryness and body. Lovely flavour. *At the winery, Sept 1980* ★★★

**Geisenheimer Kirchgrübe Riesling feinste Auslese** (Rg) **Schumann v Horadam** Pale for its age; lovely, honeyed bouquet and flavour. *At Christie's in Chicago, June 1985* ★★★

**Graacher Himmelreich Riesling BA** (M) **J J Prüm**
Orange-gold; honeyed; rich but drying out, with a touch of
leanness. Apricots and acidity. *At the Weinart/Prüm tasting, April
1999* ★★★

**Hattenheimer Hassel Riesling Kabinett** (Rg) **Schloss
Reinhartshausen** Warm yellow-gold highlights; interesting
cedary, lime honey nose; touch of sweetness, pleasant, positive,
quite rich, with a clean, dry finish. *At the Schloss, Feb 2002* ★★

**Schlossböckelheimer Kupfergrube Riesling Kabinett**
**Deinhard** Yellow, tinged with gold; buttery, harmonious, dry,
four-square, with just enough acidity to survive. *Aug 1986* ★★

**Trierer Thiergarten Unterm Kreuz Auslese, Weihnachts-
Eiswein-Edelwein** (M) **Fritz v Nell** A remarkable wine
made from grapes picked on 24 and 25 December. Palish;
bottle age and Eiswein honey; fairly sweet, good acidity. I am
ashamed that my pre-sale tasting note is shorter than the name
of the wine. *At Christie's, July 1983* ★★★

**Wehlener Sonnenuhr feinste Auslese Eiswein** (M)
**J J Prüm** Frozen and still unripe grapes picked 24 December.
Brought by Manfred Prüm to Ziegler's tasting in 1995: lime
yellow; raw, with 'Saar-like' acidity. Next at the Weinart/Prüm
tasting, its lovely yellow colour its best feature. Rot noticed on
both occasions and, despite fragrance, an attenuated, sharp
finish. *Last tasted April 1999* ★

**Wehlener Sonnenuhr Riesling BA** (M) **J J Prüm** Orange-
gold; 'calf's foot jelly'; fairly sweet, honey and lime blossom.
Excellent acidity. *April 1999* ★★★

# 1971 ★★★★★

A magnificent vintage. More on a par with the '49 and '53,
rather than the heavy weight '59 and the sweet ripe '64. Early
flowering, well formed; a fine summer, with sunshine and
warmth from early July through to the autumn, the lack of
rain concentrating the flesh. Perfectly healthy, fully mature
grapes picked in ideal conditions. Arguably the most perfect in
the Mosel and its tributaries: the best Saar and Ruwer wines
for decades, the early morning mists providing moist
nourishment and burning off to continue the ripening.
Overall the quality was high, almost too high for the bigger
commercial houses.

Drink up the Spätlesen and lower quality wines, but look
out for Auslesen from the better estates. Most are woefully
undervalued at auction even though they have been off
merchants' lists for years. The scarcer and more expensive
Beeren and Trockenbeerenauslesen are still magnificent. Of the
many dozens tasted since the early 1980s I have made a
selection to illustrate development, quality, and condition.

**Bernkasteler Doctor u Graben Riesling Auslese** (M)
**Thanisch** The original famed Doctor vineyard was a mere
1.52ha but at a meeting in Trier in 1970 it was extended to
15ha by including other vineyards. Thanisch, which initially
made its reputation with their 1921 TBA, the first ever TBA in
the Middle Mosel, had stretched the availability by
incorporating wine from their Graben vineyard, while
Lauerberg, owners of only a minute part of Doctor, added
Bratenhöfchen. Initial whiff of kerosene; drying out and
showing age though very good acidity. *After Florida Stone crabs
with the Pauls, March 1995* ★★

**Casteller Trautberg Silvaner Riesling TBA** (F) **Castell**
Picked 22 November. 212° Oechsle. Pure amber; immensely
deep honey, malted caramel nose; very rich but avoiding being
cloyingly rich. Glorious wine. *At Castell, July 1997* ★★★★★

**Casteller Trautberg Silvaner TBA** (F) **Castell** Grapes
picked at 212° Oechsle. The Dukes of Castell have lived at
Castell for over 800 years. Their charming, 18th-century
mansion overlooks their vineyards, with the ruined Schloss
atop the hill. The wine was the colour of Verdelho or sweet
sherry; lively, delicious bouquet of toffee and cream with
flavour to match. A tingle of acidity. *At the VDP pre-sale tasting,
Christie's, Oct 1997* ★★★★

**Eltviller Sonnenberg Riesling Auslese** (Rg) **Schloss Eltz**
Four notes on a classic Rheingau. Buttery yellow in the
summer of 1980, with honeyed nose, very good fruit, perfect
balance. By 1989 the colour of Beerenauslese, deep warm
gold; rich, honeyed botrytis bouquet; medium-sweet, lovely
and lively, with very fragrant aftertaste. Prior to the 1971 wine
laws this would surely have been a *feinste Auslese*. Most
recently, a shade of orange noted; glorious bouquet of peaches
and peach skins; heavenly wine, ill-matched with *crème brûlée*.
*Last tasted Sept 1991* ★★★★

**Eltviller Sonnenberg Riesling BA** (Rg) **v Simmern** Fairly
deep orange-amber; deep, honeyed bouquet; sweet, holding up
well, lovely flesh, flavour and balance. *Brought out by Bob Paul
following the disappointing 'Doctor' (see above), March 1995* ★★★★

**Erbacher Hohenrain Riesling Spätlese** (Rg) **Schloss
Reinhartshausen** Palish; rich, deep, classic 'kerosene' Riesling;
sweet, soft, lovely peachy flavour and good follow through. Of
*feinste Spätlese* quality. *At the Schloss, Feb 2002* ★★★★★

**Erbacher Hohenrain Ruländer Spätlese** (Rg) **Schloss
Reinhartshausen** Medium-deep old gold; delicate, floral, lemon
and honey reminding me of Fürmint; medium-dry, caramelly
flavour, showing age, flat finish. *At the Schloss, Feb 2002* ★★

**Erbacher Marcobrunn Riesling Auslese** (Rg)
**Staatsweingut** Some interesting comparisons. Bouquet similar
to the Steinberger Spätlese but richer than the wine above.
Very good fruit and acidity. *At Breuers' dinner, Nov 1997* ★★★★

**Erbacher Marcobrunn Riesling Auslese** (Rg) **Schloss
Reinhartshausen** Harmonious, gently honeyed; rich, just a
touch of bitterness, at a very novel 'Marcobrunn and
Chambertin' dinner. *At the appropriately named Marcobrunn
restaurant at the Hotel Schloss Reinhartshausen, Nov 1995* ★★★

**Erbacher Schlossberg Ruländer TBA** (Rg) **Schloss
Rheinhartshausen** Alcohol 10%, 147g/l of sugar, 8.9 acidity.
One of the few and probably the last Ruländer (Pinot Gris)
TBA. Two virtually identical notes, the first, memorably, at a
dinner in 1983. The second the following year: orange tawny
with lemon-green rim; bouquet out of this world: high-toned,
honeyed, sultanas; very sweet, richly concentrated, fabulous
flavour and caramelly aftertaste. *July 1984* ★★★★★

**Erbacher Siegelsberg Spätburgunder Weissherbst BA**
(rosé) (Rg) **Schloss Reinhartshausen** Powerful bouquet;
intensely sweet but lacking length. *At the Schloss, Oct 1992* ★★★

**Geisenheimer Kläuserweg Riesling Spätlese** (Rg)
**H H Eser** A lovely minty wine though some $SO_2$
conservation noted. *At a pre-sale tasting, Christie's, Sept 1996* ★★

**Graacher Domprobst Riesling Auslese** (M) **Weins-Prüm**
Melon yellow; deep, rich, honeyed; good, ripe, grapey flavour.
Hard dry finish. *Grosser Ring tasting, London, June 1992* ★★★(★)

**Graacher Himmelreich Eiswein BA** (M) **J J Prüm**
Mouthwatering apricots; sweet, ripe, lovely peachy flavour.
Dry finish. *At Peter Ziegler's marathon, Dec 1995* ★★★★★

**Hattenheimer Engelmannsberg Riesling Auslese** (Rg)
**G. Müller-Stiftung** Floral; rich, assertive, honeyed, lovely. Dry
finish. *At the tasting prior to the promotional VDP auction at
Christie's, Nov 1995* ★★★★

**Hattenheimer Engelmannsberg Riesling TBA** (Rg)
**Balthasar Ress** Deep amber; rich, caramelly; very sweet, rich, full, creamy, shapely. *At the VDP mammoth, 46-wine pre-sale tasting, May 1996* ★★★★

**Hattenheimer Nussbrunnen Riesling Auslese** (Rg)
**Balthasar Ress** Honeyed; rich yet surprisingly dry. *At the VDP pre-sale tasting, Nov 1995* ★★★

**Hattenheimer Nussbrunnen Riesling BA** (Rg)
**v Schönborn** First tasted in the 500-year-old cellar with Paul Graf v Schönborn and his manager Gunter Thies in 1997. Then three notes, all connected with the excellently organised 'The Taste of Germany' weekend I hosted in Banff. This wine was among the range for me to pre-taste and approve, then at the 'History in a Bottle' sessions. Oechsle 130°, residual sugar 73.8g/l, total acidity 7.7g/l, alcohol 12% and winner of several medals. Yellow gold; fragrant, minerally; not over-sweet, though fairly hefty, with lip-licking acidity. *Last tasted Oct 1998* ★★★★

**Hattenheimer Pfaffenberg Riesling BA** (Rg)
**v Schönborn** Honeyed *Edelfäule* and lime blossom; a rather 'oily' Riesling but a wine with great charm and finesse. *At the Breuers' wine dinner, Rüdesheim, Nov 1996* ★★★★

**Hattenheimer Wisselbrunnen Riesling TBA** (Rg)
**Schloss Reinhartshausen** Alcohol 11%. Noted at one of Christopher York's wine dinners, in April 1982: an extraordinary orange-red colour, warm, clearly due to extraction of pigment from the shrivelled, sun-baked grape skins during fermentation. Very bright, with a light tartrate deposit; ambrosial bouquet, touch of muscatelle grapiness; sweet, lightish in style though with typical '71 fat and marvellous acidity. Still with years of life ahead. *Last noted Oct 1992* ★★★★(★)

**Schloss Johannisberger Riesling BA** (Rg) First tasted at a Rodenstock wine event in Wiesbaden, 1985: yellow-gold, rather like '67 Ch d'Yquem; gloriously honeyed bottle age and botrytis; touch of sultanas; sweet, pleasantly light in style, like an exquisite ballet dancer. Eleven years later served blind at a Breuer rare wine dinner. Rich but beginning to lose some of its pristine sweetness. High acidity noted. Perfect with cheese. *Last tasted Nov 1996* ★★★★ *Passing its peak.*

**Schloss Johannisberger Riesling Rosalack Auslese** (Rg)
Warm orange gold; kerosene, honeyed botrytis and bottle age; fairly sweet, delicious flavour, good acidity. Perfect with *foie gras. At Walter Eigensatz's 60th birthday dinner, Bad Schwalbach, March 1999* ★★★★

**Schloss Johannisberger Riesling Rosagoldlack BA** (Rg)
Gloriously honeyed, rich but very dry finish. *At the VDP pre-sale tasting, Nov 1995* ★★★★

**Kallstadter Saumagen Huxelrebe TBA** (P) **Gerhard Schulz** Very deep amber-gold; the Huxelrebe raisiny nose and taste. Very sweet still, good acidity. Should keep well. *In the most unlikely surroundings, Hal Lewis' al fresco 'hog roast' in Memphis, Tennessee, Sept 1999* ★★★★

**Kiedricher Gräfenberg Riesling Auslese** (Rg) **Robert Weil** 125° Oechsle. Buttercup yellow; showing some age and drying out a little. But good, ripe flesh. Lovely. *At 11.30am, on arrival at the winery, Nov 1999* ★★★★

**Kreuznacher Steinweg Riesling BA** (N) **Ludwig Herf** Palish; fruit salad; medium-sweet, pleasant weight, delicious flavour. *Dec 1992* ★★★ *Drink soon.*

**Lorcher Bodental-Steinberg Riesling Spätlese** (Rg)
**v Kanitz** Very distinctive Rheingau, honey, kerosene, peppery, touch of peach kernels. *At the Raritäten Weinversteigerung Vorprobe (pre-sale tasting in short), Nov 1999* ★★

**Oestricher Lenchen Riesling Auslese** (Rg) **Bernhard Eser** Pure kerosene Riesling with bottle age and botrytis; powerful, assertive, drying out. *At Schloss Johannisberg, Nov 1999* ★★★

**Oestricher Lenchen Riesling BA** (Rg) **Jos Spreitzer** Two notes, first in 1983: golden colour with hint of orange; a lovely calm, harmonious, honeyed combination of botrytis and bottle age; fairly but not very sweet, medium body, very good flavour and acidity, the latter a bit hard, with a lemon peel twist. Reassuringly similar note at the rare wine tasting at Schloss Johannisberg. *Last tasted Nov 2000* ★★★★

**Rauenthaler Baiken Riesling Spätlese** (Rg) **Staatsweingut** Aged ten: yellow, slight *spritz*; rich, almost meaty at first, developing honey and fruit – touch of pineapple; medium-dry, light style, the trace of carbon dioxide giving the finish a refreshing uplift. After over a quarter of a century a deeper amber tinged with orange; slightly caramelly and now distinctly dry. Past its best. *Last noted at the Breuers' dinner in Rüdesheim, Nov 1997. Now* ★★

**Rauenthaler Baiken Riesling Auslese** (Rg) **Schloss Eltz** Golden; lovely, honeyed bouquet and flavour. Medium sweetness and body, fragrant aftertaste. *At lunch with Stefan Ress to discuss my first VDP auction, Sept 1994* ★★

**Rauenthaler Baiken Riesling Auslese** (Rg) **Staatsweingut** Warm gold; rich, hefty, old honeyed bouquet; sweet, custard-like flavour, quite high acidity. *Last tasted at a dinner in Miami after Bob Paul's great tasting of 1970 red Bordeaux, Feb 1993* ★★★★

**Rauenthaler Berg Riesling Auslese** (Rg) **Schloss Eltz** Orange tinge; attractive, kerosene; medium sweetness and body, good flavour, lovely. *April 1991* ★★★ *Drink up.*

**Rauenthaler Rothenberg Riesling BA** (Rg) **Eser** Served blind. Unmistakable Rauenthal richness, very forthcoming; all the components in balance. Perfect acidity. A long life ahead. *At the Breuers' wine dinner, Rüdesheim, Nov 1996* ★★★★(★)

**Rüdesheimer Berg Rottland Riesling Kabinett** (Rg)
**Scholl & Hillebrand** Very attractive, pure varietal; less good on palate. Raw kernelly finish. *At Breuers' wine dinner, Nov 1998.*

**Schloss Saarstein Riesling BA** (M) Yellow-gold; very rich, warm, peaches and honey; not as sweet as expected, powerful, good acidity. *At the Grosser Ring tasting, London, June 1992* ★★★★

**Scharzhofberger Riesling Auslese** (M) **Egon Müller** Rather like a nobleman dropping his Christian name when signing a letter, Egon Müller, the sole owner, does not prefix

### Egon Müller

*The pinnacle: the top Saar estate, in Wiltingen, with 27 hectares of vines on some of the steepest slate slopes imaginable. The estate's most famous sites are Scharzhofberg and their solely owned Wiltinger Braune Kupp.*

*One of the oldest and most distinguished wine families, the Müllers live in a handsome manor house at the foot of the Scharzhofberg. Across a small yard are the cellars which are considered sacrosanct – prying visitors are not encouraged. However, in 1996 my wife and I were graciously received by Egon 'senior' and 'junior' and, before lunch, I was permitted a glimpse of the old cellars. Nothing 'state of the art' here; what emerges from the low-ceilinged vaults are the masterpieces which regularly command the highest prices at the annual Grosser Ring auctions in Trier.*

*Egon Müller 'senior' died shortly after our last visit, and the modest, diffident but charming Egon 'junior' continues in his father's footsteps. I suppose he is now 'senior' because, recently married, his wife has produced a new Egon 'junior'!*

his estate name with the village, Wiltingen. First sipped with Egon Müller and his son in 1996 after a brief glimpse of the cellars (a rare privilege. Few are allowed anywhere near!) Fabulous colour, warm gold; perfect in every way, sweetness, balance of fruit and acidity. Next, a tasting for the Bacchus Society. We were informed by the Müllers that the yield was low. Like the '83, there was no botrytis, the '71s were 'hard and inaccessible when young' – as were their '90s. Not much change in four years: peachily perfect. *Last noted at the estate, May 2000* ★★★★★

**Steinberger Riesling Spätlese** (Rg) **Staatsweingut** After a quarter of a century still fairly pale with a bouquet and flavour reminiscent of crystallised violets. Medium-dry. Complete. Well balanced. *At the Breuers' marathon dinner, Nov 1997* ★★★

**Steinberger Riesling Eiswein Auslese** (Rg) **Staatsweingut** Old gold; fabulous, honeyed, sweetness balanced by perfect acidity. *At the Staatsweingüter auction tasting, Nov 1994* ★★★★

**Wehlener Sonnenuhr Riesling Spätlese** (M) **J J Prüm** Floral, lovely; drier than expected but holding well. The first of the range of J J's '71s. *At the Weinart/Prüm vertical, April 1999* ★★

**Wehlener Sonnenuhr Riesling Auslese Goldkapsel** (M) **J J Prüm** Lovely golden colour; fragrant, creamy, harmonious bouquet; medium-sweet, lovely flavour, balance, length and fragrant finish. Two notes, first tasted blind. *April 1999* ★★★★★

**Wehlener Sonnenuhr Riesling BA** (M) **J J Prüm** Medium-deep warm gold; honey, lime blossom, cream; very sweet, wonderful flavour and length. Perfect balance of fruit and acidity. *April 1999* ★★★★★ *Perfection now.*

**Wehlener Sonnenuhr Riesling TBA** (M) **J J Prüm** The penultimate wine at the Weinart/Prüm tasting and my highest rating of the entire weekend. Golden; a fragrance and flavour that defy description. Sweet but not oversweet and with dry finish. *April 1999* ★★★★★★ *(6 stars).*

**Winkeler Hasensprung Riesling TBA** (Rg) **v Hessen** Warm autumnal tawny; hefty, caramelised and very concentrated nose and taste. Very sweet still and with lovely aftertaste. *At the Breuers' wine dinner, Rüdesheim, Nov 1997* ★★★★

BRIEF NOTES ON SOME OF THE 28 REMARKABLE '71S shown at H Sichel's in London September 1992, repeating their 'Tasting of the Century' in 1975. All were magnificent. **Eitelsbacher Marienholz Riesling Spätlese** (M) **Bischöfliches Konvict** peaches and cream; medium-sweet, excellent acidity. Delicious; **Forster Kirchenstück Riesling Auslese** (P) **Bürklin-Wolf** toasted honey; very rich, powerful; **Hattenheimer Pfaffenberg Riesling TBA** (Rg) **v Schönborn** harmonious, honeyed botrytis; outrageously lovely petroly Riesling, intensely sweet, concentrated, not of this world; **Iphöfer Julius-Echter-Berg Silvaner BA** (F) **Juliusspital, Würzburg** deep orange-gold; an astonishing bouquet; very sweet, like golden syrup; **Münsterer Dautenpflänzer Riesling Auslese** (N) **Staatsweindomäne** lemon yellow; perfect 'fruit salad' bouquet and flavour; **Niersteiner Pettenthal Riesling Auslese** (Rh) **F K Schmitt** complete; ripe; very rich, fragrant; **Niersteiner Spiegelberg Silvaner TBA** (Rh) **Bezirks-Winzergenossenschaft** incredibly sweet, perfect acidity. Will last forever; **Piesporter Goldtröpfchen Riesling Auslese** (M) **Tobias** rich bouquet; medium-sweet, perfection; **Piesporter Goldtröpfchen BA** (M) **Tobias** very sweet, peachy, glorious flavour; **Rauenthaler Baiken Riesling Spätlese** (Rg) **Graf Eltz** rich, oily Riesling; assertive with balancing acidity; **Rüdesheimer Berg Rottland Riesling Auslese** (Rg)

**Staatsweingut, Eltville** straw gold; classic, full, peachy, firm; **Saarburger Rausch Riesling Auslese** (M) **Forstmeister Geltz** yellow; soft, peachy, pure Riesling; medium-sweet, full flavoured, ripe fruit, marvellous acidity of *feine* quality; and **Wachenheimer Luginsland Riesling BA** (P) **Bürklin-Wolf** deep gold; raisiny; sweet, powerful, great length.

# 1972 ★

Unimportant and not notable though it did supply the trade with a quantity of lesser wines after the quality, and costliness, of the '71s. I have tasted a couple of dozen, mainly in the mid-1970s and only one recently.
**Erbacher Siegelsberg Riesling Eiswein BA** (Rg) **Schloss Reinhartshausen** Trust Bernhard Breuer to find this rare half bottle, but it might well have come from the Schloss' cellars as the latter contains an almost unmatched collection of vintages back to the 1890s. The colour of cognac; surprisingly fragrant, but with a slightly fishy, rubbery (mercaptan?) nose and taste. Interesting only. *At the Breuers' long and fascinating wine dinner, Rüdesheim, Nov 1998.*

## Schloss Vollrads – eight centuries of wine

*I have several memories of this great Rheingau estate: my first visit was in May 1973 to attend Graf Matuschka-Greiffenclau's 80th birthday celebrations. I then stayed overnight in the gloomy, cavernous Schloss to take part in the following day's international tasting. (I had been requested to bring a couple of bottles, not of English wine but Chinese. They were execrable.)*
*My next visit was in 1988 when I went to advise, heaven forbid, the 'Vintners' Pride' group on how to promote the awareness of fine German wine; as a final sweetener, literally, Erwein, the old Count's son produced a superlative bottle of his '47 TBA. Erwein was the most indefatigable promoter of German wine and cuisine and we met on many occasions, memorably as speakers at a Castle Hotel wine weekend in Taunton, Somerset. But tragically he committed suicide in 1997, effectively bringing to an end 800 years of the Greiffenclaus' winemaking at Vollrads.*

# 1973 ★★ to ★★★★★

Abundant – in fact the biggest crop on record – and some charming light wines made for early consumption. Late spring; almost tropical summer heat made up for the late flowering, and rain in late September for the near drought conditions. Despite this, disappointing wines, diluted through overproduction and the more ordinary wines lacking acidity made up for by a few of outstanding quality.
**Erbacher Michelmark Riesling BA Eiswein** (Rg) **zu Knyphausen** Picked at −16° C. 12g/l acidity. Gold medal winner 1974. First noted dining at home with the Khourys in 1999: surprisingly deep orange; caramel; intensely sweet, fat, muscatelle-like taste, wonderful acidity. An identical note at Schloss Johannisberg. *Last tasted Nov 2000* ★★★★★
**Mittelheimer Edelmann Riesling Auslese** (Rg) **Engelmann, Nass label** The estate celebrated its 300th anniversary in 1987. Originally managed separately, the estates of Karl-Franz Engelmann and Adam Nass were united in 1985. The history more interesting than the very straightforward but unexciting wine. *At the VDP pre-sale tasting at Schloss Reinhartshausen, Nov 1995* ★★

**Scharzhofberger Riesling Auslese Eiswein** (M) **Egon Müller** Old gold; floral, Sauternes-like; sweet, full-flavoured, glorious acidity. *At the Grosser Ring tasting of rarities at the Victoria & Albert Museum, London, June 1992* ★★★★★

**Wallhäuser Mühlenberg Grauer Burgunder Eiswein** (N) **Salm-Dalberg** These Grauer Burgunder (Pinot Gris) grapes were picked in early December. Prinz Michael Salm's first vintage at the 800-year-old family estate. Palish buttery yellow; delightful peach and melon bouquet; sweet, lovely flavour and acidity. *At the Schloss, Sept 1988* ★★★★

**Wallhäuser Mühlenberg Ruländer Eiswein TBA** (N) **Salm-Dalberg** Very positive yellow; distinctly minty, fragrant bouquet; sweet, rich but not fat, with a pleasantly light delicate touch and delicious apricot flavour and lovely acidity. Half bottle: a perfect after-theatre dessert wine. *At Chippenham Lodge, Oct 1988* ★★★★★

# 1974

Weather conditions the opposite to 1973: a dismal summer with one of the wettest autumns in memory. I tasted a few lacklustre wines in the 1970s but none since.

# 1975 ★★★★

A good vintage but, as soon as the immediately attractive '76s appeared on the market, buyers seemed to lose interest. But the firm, slightly more acidic '75s have now overtaken the softer, more plausible '76s.

There was a late spring but warm, speedy flowering. An extremely hot late summer and heavy rain in early September were followed by ripening sunshine. Some very good wines were made though there were variations of style and quality due to conflicting winemaking approaches: the old-fashioned and the sweeteners.

Looking back at my notes it also seems to be a period when experimentation – mainly, it seems, in the Pfalz – with strange grape varieties and crossings was coming to a head: Ehrenfelser (Riesling x Sylvaner), Kanzler und Perle, Optima, Ruländer, which I always like, the older-established Müller-Thurgau (Riesling x Sylvaner) and, of course, the Silvaner or Sylvaner which is really at its best in Franken. All of which appear in my notes for '75s. Conspicuous by its absence is the Traminer or Gewürztraminer, a scented, exotic grape I used to associate with the rustic, sometimes goaty Pfalz wines.

Good '75s are incredibly undervalued and those of genuine Auslese quality are still lovely. First a selection of wines mainly tasted recently.

**Assmannshäuser Höllenberg Spätburgunder Weissherbst Auslese** (Rg) **R König** Colour of warm straw with orange highlights; rich, slightly toffee-like nose and taste; medium sweetness and body, very rich, lovely aftertaste. *At the VDP pre-sale tasting at Christie's, Sept 1996* ★★★

**Bernkasteler Johannisbrünnchen Müller-Thurgau BA** (M) **S A Prüm** Palish lemon-gold; lovely, fragrant peachy ripe bouquet with incredible depth of fruit, more flowery than a straight Riesling; fairly sweet, rather light and a bit lean for a Beerenauslese, elegant, flowery with a slightly kernelly finish and raisiny aftertaste. *At the estate, Sept 1988* ★★★

**Brauneberger Juffer Riesling Auslese** (M) **F Haag** Bright yellow; creamy 'fudge' (soft toffee) nose; an old Riesling character. Tired. *The oldest vintage in a tasting of Schloss Lieser and Fritz Haag wines at the Schloss, May 2000* ★

**Erbacher Siegelsberg Riesling Kabinett** (Rg) **Schloss Reinhartshausen** Bronze-tinged yellow; strange nose, like a dentist's surgery (Daphne wrote 'acorns?'); dry, some richness yet austere. Needs food. *At the Schloss, Feb 2002.*

**Erbacher Siegelsberg Riesling Auslese** (Rg) **v Oetinger** Most attractive wine. Not too sweet. Good '75 acidity. From the estate of Eberhard Freiherr v Oetinger who doubled up as the renowned VDP wine auctioneer until, after his retirement in 1994, I took over. *At the VDP pre-sale tasting, Nov 1995* ★★★

**Johannisberger Klaus Riesling Auslese** (Rg) **Prinz v Hessen** Pale; surprisingly dry and acidic. *At the VDP pre-sale tasting, Nov 1995* ★

**Schloss Johannisberger Rosagoldlack Riesling BA** (Rg) Four notes, first in August 1998 on the balcony of our flat overlooking the Thames, its colour as dramatic as the view. Lanolin gold; intensely sweet. Then at lunch at Chippenham Lodge. Next, a hefty classic at a German Wine Institute tasting at Vinopolis in April 2000. Similar note seven months later, touch of spearmint and '75 acidity noted after the '76. *Last tasted at the Schloss, Nov 2000* ★★★(★)?

**Oestricher Lenchen Riesling Auslese Eiswein** (Rg) **Deinhard** Pale gold; sweet, botrytised Riesling scent; medium-sweet, attractive, good acidity yet lacking length. Tasted blind at Nils Sternby's 65th birthday dinner in Malmö; I thought it could be an Icewine from almost anywhere. *April 1995* ★★★

**Scharzhofberger Riesling Kabinett** (M) **Egon Müller** The wines of the Saar can be very acidic in the lower Qualitäten levels. This one certainly was, and it is interesting to compare it with the sweeter, riper levels that follow. *Dec 1996* ★

**Scharzhofberger Riesling Spätlese** (M) **Egon Müller** Ripe fruit, medium-dry, good acidity. *At the pre-sale tasting, Dec 1996* ★★★ *Doubtless still delicious.*

**Scharzhofberger Riesling BA** (M) **Egon Müller** Warm orange-amber; soft, harmonious barley-sugar bouquet which spread its wings; very sweet and rich but lacking the concentration of their TBA. A deep grapey, honeyed flavour. *At Peter Ziegler's great wine tasting at the Schlosshotel, Erbach, Dec 1995* ★★★★★

**Scharzhofberger Riesling TBA** (M) **Egon Müller** An amazing colour, amber with apple-green rim; rich, fragrant, raisiny; very sweet, fat, fleshy, simply glorious. *Dining with the Bacchus Society at the Müllers', May 2000* ★★★★★

**Serriger Würtzberg Riesling Auslese** (M) **Bert Simon** A 'monopole' vineyard, the most southerly (upstream) in the Saar Valley. Low-keyed, peachy; the lemon-tinged Saar acidity on the lips toning down its sweetness. Lively, interesting. *At the Grosser Ring VDP rarities tasting, June 1992* ★★★ *At peak now.*

**Ürziger Würzgarten Riesling Auslese** (M) **Christoffel-Berres** Peaches and fruit salad; medium sweetness, despite mild mid-palate, quite powerful. Hard dry finish. *June 1992* ★★★

**Wehlener Sonnenuhr Riesling Spätlese** (M) **J J Prüm** Classy; medium-sweet, delicious crisp, creamy flavour. Good acidity but lacking length. *April 1999* ★★★ *Drink up.*

**Wehlener Sonnenuhr Riesling Auslese lange Goldkapsel** (M) **J J Prüm** At 14 years of age, demonstrating the perfect time to drink a wine of this vintage quality. A beautiful, uplifting floral bouquet; perfect balance of sweetness and acidity. Lively and lovely. *April 1999* ★★★★★

**Wehlener Sonnenuhr Riesling BA** (M) **J J Prüm** Unusually pale; rather raw apples and pears nose; medium-sweet, crisp, quite attractive but completely upstaged by the Scharzhofberg BA. *At Peter Ziegler's tasting at the Schlosshotel, Erbach, Dec 1995* ★★★

Some other very good '75s tasted in the mid-1980s and probably at their best now in 2002: **Canzemer Altenberg Riesling Auslese** (M) **Bisch. Priesterseminar** two notes; amazingly rich despite its sulphur; soft, rich yet more delicate than the '76. Very pleasant light fruit ★★★; **Forster Schnepfenflug an der Weinstrasse Ruländer Auslese** (P) **Winzer Forst** a massively impressive co-operative wine worthy of its gold medal for its name alone! Several notes: a deep, orange-tinged, amber-gold; a rich, heavily honeyed nose with typical Ruländer (Pinot Gris) grassiness and grapiness, very Beerenauslese-like; medium-sweet, hefty, assertive flavour. A wine for Wagnerian Rhine maidens ★★★★; **Hochheimer Königin Victoria Berg Auslese** (Rg) **Pabstmann** grapes picked at 106° Oechsle. Rich, grassy, honeyed, old-fashioned style; medium to dry finish, some fat, exciting flavour. Superior and will last ★★★★; **Kallstadter Kobnert Silvaner Kabinett** (P) **Eduard Schuster** an interesting, bronze medal-winning wine made from Silvaner grown on limestone soil. Very distinctive yellow; almost Traminer spiciness, with strawberry and honey-rich depth of fruit; lightish, clean fresh, firm and dry ★★★; **Niersteiner Klostergarten TBA** (Rh) **H F Schmitt** straw colour; sweet, sultana-like nose and taste, yet (despite its fat) a light style and nice acidity ★★★★; and **Ruppertsberger Linsenbusch Ehrenfelser Spätlese** (P) **v Bühl** palish; light, fragrant, unusually scented bouquet; medium-dry, easy, attractive, perfect ★★★★

# 1976 ★★★★

A gloriously ripe vintage with soft, fleshy, extremely attractive wines, the only handicap being a certain lack of acidity in some of them. This was a year of great heat and drought throughout the summer in northern Europe. However, in southern Germany, with its mild continental climate, the weather was pleasantly warm from mid-September to early October, dampness returning to encourage the formation of *Edelfäule* (noble rot).

This was the sort of year that brings out the best in the Mosel and, in particular, in the Saar and Ruwer, which normally produce fairly acidic wines. This vintage had more than its fair share of lovely Auslesen and fabulous Beeren- and Trockenbeerenauslesen wines. On the whole, these are still lovely, some past their peak, some with time in hand. Most Kabinett and Spätlese wines should have been drunk by now.

Although in terms of depth of quality 1976 ranks below the firmer, greater, all-round 1971, there are few German vintages which have given me more pleasure.

**Berncasteler Doctor Riesling Auslese** (M) **Thanisch** Vaseline gold; flowery fruit, greengages, privet; a lovely rich 'oily' Riesling, but with a curiously hard finish. *Lunching at the Smag & Behag office in Copenhagen, Aug 1996* ★★★★

**Bischoffinger Steinbuck Ruländer TBA** (B) **W G Bischoffinger** Three notes, all at tastings before and during the German wine weekend at Banff Springs, Canada. An astonishing wine, 235° Oechsle, 270g/l residual sugar, acidity 10.2g/l, alcohol 6.51%. The colour of Bual madeira; its hefty toffee and raisins nose and flavour offset by its vital acidity. Immensely sweet (one of my notes said 'cod-liver oil and malt'!). Great length. Delicious. *Oct 1998* ★★★★★

**Brauneberger Juffer-Sonnenuhr Riesling TBA** (M) **Fritz Haag** Orange amber; singed raisins; sweet, incredibly rich and concentrated, superb aftertaste. Great wine. *At Schloss Lieser, May 2000* ★★★★★

**Burghornberger Wallmauer Traminer Auslese** (W) **v Gemmingen-Hornberg** Wallmauer is a very steep, terraced, south-facing vineyard; the Traminer grapes were picked on 4 November. At 12 years of age a very positive yellow colour; scented, spicy nose, a bit earthy, slightly malty; medium dryness and weight, soft, open flavour and texture. Hard rather than acidic finish – a Traminer trait. *Sept 1988* ★★★ *Probably still drinking well.*

**Erbacher Hohenrain Riesling Spätlese** (Rg) **Schloss Reinhartshausen** Lovely orange-tinged gold; ripe, honeyed botrytis bouquet; medium-sweet, lovely flavour, sweet fruit and upturned acidic finish. Perfection. *At the Schloss, Feb 2002* ★★★★★

**Erbacher Marcobrunn Riesling Auslese** (Rg) **Schloss Schönborn** Gold medal winner. Amber-gold; bouquet of old peaches; rich but caramelised with touch of bitterness. *Dining at the Krone, Assmannshausen, May 1996* ★★★ *Long past its best.*

**Erbacher Siegelsberg Riesling Spätlese** (Rg) **Schloss Reinhartshausen** Golden; waxy, honeyed; surprisingly sweet, more like a *feine Auslese*. *At a Berry Bros lunch, Sept 1993* ★★★★

**Erbacher Siegelsberg Weissherbst TBA** (Rg) **Schloss Reinhartshausen** Amber; rich, raisiny; sweet, toffee-like, powerful, dry finish. *Oct 1992* ★★★★

**Forster Jesuitengarten Riesling Auslese** (P) **Bassermann-Jordan** Four notes, first in 1988 when it seemed at its best: old gold; very perfumed, with citrus-like zest; rich, flavoury, with a touch of lemon and cayenne pepper on the finish. The next three, with Harvey's of Bristol slip labels, noted at elevenses, the best time to drink an Auslese, in 1996, 1999 and 2000. But now showing its age and, though smooth, a bit four-square. *Last polished off at Chippenham Lodge, Sept 2000. At best* ★★★

**Graacher Domprobst Riesling Auslese** (M) **Max Ferd. Richter.** Rich, kerosene Riesling nose with honeyed *Edelfäule* and bottle age; medium-sweet. *March 1992* ★★★★ *Drink soon.*

**Graacher Himmelreich Riesling Auslese** (M) **J J Prüm** Yellow-gold; ripe; not as sweet as expected. Sound but lacking acidity. *At the Weinart/Prüm tasting, April 1999* ★★ *Drink up.*

**Graacher Himmelreich Riesling Auslese lange Goldkapsel** (M) **J J Prüm** Fairly sweet, super-ripe, lovely, honeyed, peachy flavour. Assertive. *April 1999* ★★★★

**Hallgartener Jungfer Riesling BA** (Rg) **Engelmann** Lovely mellow, perfect acidity. *VDP pre-sale, Nov 1994* ★★★★

**Hattenheimer Engelmannsberg Riesling TBA** (Rg) **Balthasar Ress** Amber; spicy, verbena, spearmint, creamy; very sweet, raisiny, slightly caramelly flavour and aftertaste. *At the VDP pre-sale tasting, May 1996* ★★★★

**Hattenheimer Heiligenberg Riesling Auslese** (Rg) **H Lang** Straw gold; honeyed, fairly sweet and ripe, but now a bit tired. *Sept 1997* ★★ *Drink up.*

**Hattenheimer Nussbrunnen Riesling Auslese** (Rg) **v Simmern** Several notes: perfection aged ten. Still lovely: a glorious buttercup yellow; soft, rich, peachy bouquet with hint of barley sugar; medium-sweet, ripe, fleshy, good length and acidity. To be drunk by itself, not with food and emphatically not a 'pudding wine'. *Last tasted June 1988* ★★★★ *Drink soon.*

**Hattenheimer Nussbrunnen Riesling BA** (Rg) **Georg Müller-Stiftung** Two similar notes, first in May 1996, the next four months later. Soft yellow-gold; lovely, fragrant bouquet; very rich but with surprisingly hot end acidity. *Last noted at the VDP tasting, Sept 1996* ★★★

**Hattenheimer Wisselbrunnen Riesling Auslese** (Rg) **Balthasar Ress** 'Kunst edition' (artist's label). Two notes. First at Ress' 'Cabaret dinner' in 1994. Fairly deep gold; good honeyed botrytis nose; rich, dry finish. Similar note a year later. *Last noted at the VDP pre-sale tasting, Nov 1995* ★★★

**Hochheimer Hölle Riesling Auslese** (Rg) **Künstler**
Clover honey; medium-sweet, crisp, lovely. *At the VDP pre-sale tasting, Nov 1995* ★★★★

**Schloss Johannisberger Riesling Goldlack (TBA)** (Rg)
Surprisingly deep, lime rich and very rich 'legs'; rich, touch of malt; sweet of course, the most alcoholic of the TBAs, toffee-like taste, good acidity. *At the 900th anniversary tasting at the Schloss, Nov 2001* ★★★

**Laubenheimer Karthäuser Riesling BA** (N) **Tesch**
A gold medal winner from young (six-year-old) vines. Golden; honey and greengages; sweet, ripe, creamy, soft Nahe character yet combining honeyed botrytis and lip-licking finish. *At Schloss Johannisberg, Nov 2000* ★★★★★

**Lorcher Bodental-Steinberg Auslese** (Rg) **v Kanitz** An historic, steeply sloping 23-ha vineyard just downstream from Assmannshausen. Wonderful colour; crisp fruit; very distinctive flavour, peachy, high acidity for '76. *At the Fine Wine Auction Tasting I conducted at the Krone, Assmannshausen, Nov 1998* ★★★★

**Lorcher Bodental-Steinberg Riesling BA** (Rg) **v Kanitz**
First tasted in 1988: already a fairly deep, orange-gold resulting from the overripe botrytised grapes: peaches, apricots and honey; fairly sweet, perfect *Edelfäule* flavour, but, I thought a bit lacking in acidity. Eleven years later, a similar description though this time I considered the acidity high, and predicted a long life. It is probably perfect now. *Last tasted Nov 1999* ★★★★

**Lorcher Pfaffenwies Riesling Auslese** (Rg) **v Kanitz**
Yellow; rich, medium-sweet, ripe, 'oily' Riesling. *At the VDP auction tasting, Nov 1994* ★★

**Maximin Grünhäuser Abtsberg Riesling Spätlese** (M) **v Schubert** Historic estate, basically one steep 32-ha hillside vineyard on the Ruwer: Abtsberg (11ha) on the upper slopes, Herrenberg in the middle, Bruderberg (4ha) on the lower. The Abtsberg and Herrenberg Auslesen were both rich and lovely in the late 1980s. The '76 Spätlese: beautiful gold colour; fairly sweet, very good flavour, some flesh. Attractive wine. *At Gidleigh Park in Devon, Feb 1995* ★★★ *Now at or just past peak.*

**Neipperger Schlossberg Riesling Auslese** (W) **Graf v Neipperg** 126° Oechsle; 8.1° acidity; 29g/l sugar. Interesting, for Neipperg's brother, Stephan, owns Ch Canon-La-Gaffelière in St-Émilion. Colour: very deep brown gold; raisiny, botrytis and bottle age; very dry, almost bitter, touch of caramel. *At a pre-sale tasting, London, Oct 1997* ★★

**Niersteiner Hölle Gewürztraminer BA** (Rh) **Senfter**
Strikingly yellow; distinctive rose cachou and lychees scent; fairly sweet, rich, distinctive Gewürztraminer exotic flavour. *At my Falken book launch in Rüsselheim, April 1998* ★★★

**Ockfener Bockstein Riesling TBA** (M) **Forstmeister-Gelz Erben** Unusual bouquet; very sweet, full-flavoured, glorious. *Sept 1992* ★★★★★

**Oestricher Lenchen Riesling BA** (Rg) **Querbach** Orange-amber; raisiny, dried-out, disappointing, its once firm bosom now sagging. *The final wine at the Rheingauer Giganta dinner, Hotel Krone, Assmannshausen, Nov 1995* ★

**Oppenheimer Sackträger Riesling BA** (Rh)
**Staatsweingut** *Goldene Kammerpreismünze* in 1979, *Grosser Preis DLG* in 1980. Warm orange colour; cream, honey and apricot bouquet; sweet, soft, ripe, lovely. Lacking acidity. *Dec 1991* ★★★★

**Rauenthaler Baiken Riesling Auslese** (Rg) **v Simmern**
Orange-tinged gold; shapely, complete, fragrant; medium-sweet, touch of Rauenthal rich earthiness. *At the VDP pre-sale tasting, May 1996* ★★★★ *At peak now.*

**Rüdesheimer Berg Schlossberg Riesling Auslese** (Rg)
**Gruensteyn** Lightly honeyed; medium-sweet, crisp, attractive. Perfectly mature. *At the VDP pre-sale tasting, Nov 1995* ★★★

**Rüdesheimer Klosterlay Riesling BA** (Rg) **Ress** Glowing amber-gold; harmonious, peach blossom; sweet, good acidity, firm. Needed time. *At the VDP pre-sale tasting, May 1996. Now at least* ★★★

**Scharzhofberger Riesling Kabinett** (M) **Egon Müller** To demonstrate the keeping quality of a '76 made at a top estate in the Saar: initially pale, now a distinctive yellow; pure Riesling aroma with a whiff of lime; dry, firm, remarkably fresh. *At the estate, May 2000* ★★★ *But drink up.*

**Scharzhofberger Riesling Spätlese** (M) **Egon Müller** The '99 Spätlese we tasted was virtually colourless, the '76 now a medium-pale yellow; nose with good depth; medium-dry, still fresh, dry finish. Delicious now. *At the estate, May 2000* ★★★

**Scharzhofberger Riesling Auslese** (M) **Egon Müller** Four notes, first at a pre-sale tasting in 1996: ripe, medium-sweet, slightly pasty acidity. Next at the German Embassy in London in 1999, honeyed bottle age very apparent, ripe, peachy character. A really lovely wine. Its creaminess and length noted dining at Dieter Kaufman's, Grevenbröich in May 2000, and a couple of days later with the Egon Müllers. By now a beautiful yellow-gold; its rich ripe Riesling fragrance developing a piquant whiff of spearmint. Lovely wine. I think it is worth mentioning at this juncture that the Müllers' Auslese is usually the equivalent of other estates' *Goldcap* (or, prior to 1971, *feinste Auslese*) and their Beerenauslese often up to TBA quality and concentration. *Last tasted May 2000* ★★★★

**Scharzhofberger Riesling Auslese Goldkapsel** (M) **Egon Müller** Two notes, first at a pre-sale tasting at Christie's in 1996: super-ripe kerosene Riesling; sweet, fat, rich (4 stars). More recently at the estate: now deeper in colour, orange-tinged and with a bitty sediment said to be due to calcium affected by botrytis. A bit of a heavyweight. Full, rich. *Last tasted May 2000* ★★★★ *Drink up.*

**Scharzhofberger Riesling TBA** (M) **Egon Müller** One of only nine TBAs made since 1959. Deep tawny, orange highlights, apple-green rim and rich 'legs'; an indescribably lovely bouquet, slightly raisiny, lime honey and acidity (Hugh Johnson just said 'Turkish delight'); tremendously rich, concentrated, dry finish, good length. *At the estate, May 2000* ★★★★★★ *(6 stars) Perfect now.*

**Schlossböckelheimer Kupfergrube Riesling Auslese** (N) **Staatsweingut** Typical ripe Nahe fruit salad, with bottle age; rich, lovely flavour, adequate acidity. *Elevenses at Chippenham Lodge, Jan 1999* ★★★★

**Schloss Vollrads Riesling TBA** (Rg) Fairly deep, orange-tinged; very powerful nose, a bit hard and with the maltiness of Bavarian beer; sweet, full, very rich, meaty, toffee and chocolate, very assertive but also very fragrant with an extraordinary mint leaf aftertaste. *Sept 1990* ★★★★★

**Wallufer Walkenberg Riesling BA** (Rg) **Jost** The Jost family are unusual in having vineyards at the opposite extremities of the Rheingau and Mittelrhein, the grapes from Walluf near Wiesbaden being rushed across to Bacharach for crushing the same evening. This wine was shown at two major rare wine tastings, coincidentally both held at Schloss Johannisberg, the first in November 1999 and the other 12 months later. Peter Jost told us that 1976 was 'a year that growers pray for. Perfect conditions for harvesting during the first week in October in T-shirts, it was so hot!' Certainly a lovely wine. Happily my notes tally: amber-gold; ripe botrytis and honeyed bottle age. Fairly substantial, sweet entry, dry finish. *Last tasted Nov 2000* ★★★★

**Wehlener Sonnenuhr Riesling Auslese** (M) **Berg Prüm** Yet another Prüm, this one in full: Zach. Bergweiler-Prüm Erben. Standing up: manfully (the wine not the family) at Jean and Hal Lewis's 'hog roast' in Memphis, Tennessee. Holding well. *Sept 1999* ★★★★

**Wehlener Sonnenuhr Riesling Auslese Goldkapsel** (M) **J J Prüm** Two bottles, one cloudy with white sediment, a botrytis calcium fault. Tart. The second with lovely colour, nose and flavour. Delicious. *April 1999. At best* ★★★★

**Wehlener Sonnenuhr Riesling Auslese lange Goldkapsel** (M) **J J Prüm** Lovely gold; touch of orange; sweet, rich, gloriously honeyed flavour, good acidity and length. *At the Weinart / Prüm tasting, April 1999* ★★★★★

**Wehlener Sonnenuhr Riesling BA** (M) **J J Prüm** Paler than expected; high-toned, 'greengage' zest; sweet, rich, some softness, adequate acidity. *April 1999* ★★★★

**Wehlener Sonnenuhr Riesling TBA** (M) **J J Prüm** Grapes picked October 29. First noted at the end of Peter Ziegler's 7th 'flight' in 1995: fairly deep amber; perfect harmony; very sweet yet with lovely acidity. Most recently, at the Weinart marathon. Equally lavish notes, a tinge of orange appearing; raisiny, fragrant; fat, soft, barley-sugar flavour and finish. One of Manfred Prüm's greatest wines. *Last tasted April 1999* ★★★★★

**Wehlener Sonnenuhr Riesling TBA** (M) **Maximinhof** Yet another Prüm connection, Gerd Studert of the Studert/Prüm estate. Medium-deep orange; concentrated, raisiny, great depth; sweet, very rich, fat, powerful, good length and excellent acidity. *June 1992* ★★★★★

**Wiltinger Kupp Riesling Auslese** (M) **zu Hoensbroech** Pure ripe Riesling; fairly sweet and soft. Nice wine. *At a pre-sale tasting, Dec 1996* ★★★ *Drink up.*

**Winkeler Hasensprung Riesling TBA** (Rg) **Deinhard** A marvellous golden colour, very sweet, concentrated and, in 1984, needing more time. By 1990, a fairly deep, warm orange-gold; very rich, tangy, almost Tokaji Aszú-like nose; sweet, hefty, assertive, raisiny, great length, fragrant aftertaste. Finishes a little hard. Still 'needing more bottle age'. However, eight years later, despite its lovely *crème brûlée* bouquet and lovely flavour, it was beginning to dry out a little. *Last tasted with Melina's delicious bread and butter pudding, dining with N K Yong in Singapore, Jan 1998* ★★★★

**Winkeler Jesuitengarten Riesling Auslese** (Rg) **Jacob Hamm** 'Winkel, winkel, little star'. And this was. Rich fruit, pleasing sweetness, elegant. *Nov 1995* ★★★ *Needs drinking.*

OF THE 200 OR SO OTHER NOTES OF THOSE LAST TASTED IN THE MID-1980s, the following were well above average: **Bernkasteler Badstube Auslese** (M) **J J Prüm** ripe, lovely ★★★★; **Deidesheimer Herrgottsacker Riesling Auslese** (P) **v Bühl** *Grosser Preis* DMG – a top medal winner. Two notes. Perfection ★★★★★; **Eitelsbacher Karthäuserhofberger Burgberg Spätlese** (M) lovely, complex ★★★; **Essinger Ruländer TBA Eiswein Winfried Frey** 174° Oechsle, sugar 225g/l, acidity 9.1: deep orange-amber stained by shrivelled brown skins; honeyed, scented; very sweet from start to finish yet with a deft touch ★★★★★; **Forster Kirchenstück Riesling Auslese** (P) **v Bühl** winner of the DLG *Grosser Preis* in 1979: deep buttery yellow; ripe fruit and honey. Delicious ★★★★★; **Geisenheimer Mäuerchen Riesling BA** (P) **Basting-Gimbel** glorious, sweet, full, rich – touch of end bitterness ★★★★; **Graacher**

**Himmelreich TBA** (M) **S A Prüm** golden; blissful bouquet, soft, exquisite flavour ★★★★(★); **Hattenheimer Wisselbrunnen Beerenauslese** (Rg) **Molitor** rich. Perfect balance ★★★★; **Hochheimer Königin Victoria Berg TBA** (Rg) **Pabstmann** 164° Oechsle. Only 144 bottles produced: beautiful bouquet; sweet, fabulous flavour that expanded in the mouth, great length ★★★★★; **Kiedricher Gräfenberg Riesling Spätlese** (Rg) **Robert Weil** rich, ripe, honeyed, raisiny, harmonious nose and taste. Lovely shape in the mouth. Dryish, lightish, gentle. More like an Auslese ★★★; **Königschaffhauser Steingrube Spätburgunder Weissherbst TBA** (B) an extraordinary rosé wine made from Pinot Noir by a local co-operative and winner of two top medals. Several notes: a rich, warm, ruddy, tawny colour; fabulous nose, grapey, honeyed, hint of grass and straw; very sweet, immensely rich, marvellously Wagnerian, lovely acidity ★★★★★; **Niersteiner Auflangen Scheurebe TBA** (Rh) **Staatsweingut** several notes: pure yellow-gold; overwhelming yet crisply honeyed bouquet; very sweet, fat, luscious, great length and acidic uplift ★★★★★; **Randersackerer Pfülben Silvaner BA** (F) **Juliusspital** winner of the DLG *Grosser Preis*, 1977, and a Würzburg gold medal. Several half bottles: golden; rich, raisiny, spicy nose; medium-sweet, Sauternes-like flavour, fat but a consistently hard, short, dry finish ★★★; **Rüdesheimer Berg Roseneck Riesling Auslese** (Rg) **Naegler** Beerenauslese-like honeycomb-wax richness, harmonious, like pineapple in syrup, scented, spicy; medium-sweet, plump yet gentle and fragrant. Perfection ★★★★; **Scharzhofberger Riesling Auslese** (M) **v Hövel** medium-dry, excellent ★★★★; **Scharzhofberger Riesling Auslese** (M) **Vereinigte Hospitien** pale gold; gentle, honeyed plus pure lime; medium-dry, ripe, very flavoury – would have been *feinste Auslese* prior to the 1971 wine laws ★★★★; and **Serriger Vogelsang Riesling TBA** (M) **Vereinigte Hospitien** concentrated, syrupy, lovely richness and racy acidity ★★★★★

# 1977 ★

Modest quality wines for early consumption. Late flowering and poor summer were followed by marvellous warmth in early October. Then, in November, conditions were right to enable some Eiswein to be made. Average production and very few quality wines.

I tasted quite a lot of '77s in 1980 and 1981, including far too many raw and acidic Mosel wines. There were some quite passable ones from the more southerly Pfalz. Virtually all these wines should have been consumed long before now. I have just two relatively recent notes.

**Assmannshäuser Höllenberg Spätburgunder Weissherbst Eiswein BA** (Rg) **Staatsweingut** The genius behind this was famous, sometimes controversial, Dr Hans Ambrosi, for long the Director of the State Wine Domaine in Eltville which owns and manages seven estates in the Rheingau. Colour warm amber; very good, sweet, raisiny, appley bouquet; very sweet, fat, great length and very high acidity, its sweetness toned down by the pudding. *At the Breuers' rare wine dinner, Rüdesheim, Nov 1998* ★★★★

**Forster Elster Riesling Spätlese** (P) **v Bühl** Winner in 1978 of an Ehrenpreis ('special' prize), higher than a gold medal. First tasted in Deidesheim in 1980: good flavour. In 1982, lunchtime at home; fairly hefty, grapey nose; medium-dry. Passable acidity and finish. Most recently: a rich, positive, attractive but not altogether harmonious fruit salad bouquet, with bottle age – more mango than honey. Very fruity complex flavour, lively acidity. Michael Hiller, the American who was running the estate at that time, described it as a 'wine with a beard'! _Last tasted at von Bühl's, Sept 1988_ ★★★

# 1978 ★★

Moderate quality. A poor spring, late flowering and wet summer were rescued by lovely, balmy sunshine in September through October. The harvest was late. Small crop of useful, commercial wines. I tasted a reasonably representative range of wines from different regions and estates between 1980 and 1983 but only one, an Eiswein, since the late 1980s. My overall impression of the wines is that they were pleasant enough, mostly mild and gentle, lacking distinction and length.

**Erbacher Hohenrain Riesling Eiswein** (Rg) **Schloss Reinhartshausen** Fairly deep gold with orange highlights; bouquet like golden syrup and 'calf's foot jelly'; sweet, lip-licking honey and acidity, yet with a taste of late season rot. Long acidic finish. _At the Schloss, Feb 2002_ ★★★

# 1979 ★★★

On the whole these were pleasant, light and easy wines. Very severe frosts in January caused widespread damage to the dormant vines. An inclement spring was followed by late flowering and a poor summer but a lovely, sunny, ripening autumn saved the late harvest. There were regional variations, the Rheingau and Pfalz had bigger and better harvests, the Rheinhessen was small but good and the Mosel small and quite good. There was not as much _Edelfäule_ as in 1983 ( the next good year) and there were also problems with an assault by red spiders.

I have a broad spectrum of notes made in the early 1980s. Looking back, I rather liked the wines and my comments were certainly far more agreeable than adverse. They lacked the excitement, grandeur and finesse of a good classic vintage, but were pleasant to drink. Here is a small selection of some unusual and more recent notes.

**Bernkasteler Doctor Riesling Auslese** (M) **v Schorlemer** Part of a batch bought at Christie's. Waxy yellow; low-keyed but harmonious; drying out, its finish verging on astringent. _Last noted at elevenses at Chippenham Lodge, Dec 1994. At best_ ★★ _Now well past best._

**Brauneberger Juffer Sonnenuhr Riesling Auslese Goldkapsel** (M) **Fritz Haag** Three consistent notes while hosting 'The Taste of Germany' weekend at Banff Springs, Canada. Must weight 120° Oechsle, residual sugar 89g/l, acidity 10g/l, alcohol 7.5%. Pale, lime-tinged; delicate, floral, almost minty bouquet; edge of honeycomb sweetness; medium-sweet; delicious flavour, zestful. _Last tasted Oct 1998_ ★★★★

**Dhroner Hofberg Riesling Auslese** (M) **Milz-Laurentiushof** Fresh, delicious, crisp; medium-dry, perfect weight and flavour, delicate grapiness, charm. _June 1992_ ★★★

**Erbacher Steinmorgen Riesling Eiswein** (Rg) **zu Knyphausen** Picked very late – 14 January 1980! Gold prize winner. 122° Oechsle, 11.8g/l acidity. From the 1979 vintage Eiswein had to have minimum Beerenauslese Oechsle levels.

First tasted pre-sale in 1997: amber-gold; almost syrupy nose; sweet, mouthfilling, good flavour. The following year: beautiful, flawless bouquet; not as sweet as expected, good, firm flavour, dry finish. _Last noted at 'The best of VDP auctions' tasting, Assmannshausen in the Rheingau, Nov 1998_ ★★★★

**Graacher Himmelreich Riesling Kabinett** (M) **J J Prüm** Still very pale; very dry, almond kernels flavour. However much I admire 'J J', this was distinctly unexciting and not to my taste. _Tasted with Manfred Prüm, June 1990_ ★

**Kanzemer Altenberg Riesling** (M) **v Othegraven** A most extraordinary wine which, though in effect a _Sekt_, illustrates Bernhard Breuer's genius. He was a consultant to this Saar estate and recently found in the cellars a large stock of '79 Auslesen which he refermented to make a sparkling wine. The bottle, served blind, had been disgorged six months: very pale, lively; rather metallic Saar nose; dry, light, clean as a whistle, excellent youthful acidity. _With tarte aux pommes at Bernhard Breuers' 'The '9s' dinner, Christie's, Feb 2000_ ★★★

**Maximin Grünhaus Abstberg Riesling Spätlese** (M) **v Schubert** Pale for its age; attractive; refreshing. After the tasting to launch the (excellent) English edition of Diel and Payne's _German Wine Guide. An appropriate aperitif before dinner at the German Embassy, London, June 1999_ ★★★

**Niersteiner Auflangen Silvaner BA Eiswein** (Rh) **Guntrum** The grapes were picked on 31 December, yet there was not much botrytis. 148° Oechsle, 1800 bottles produced. Deep gold; beautiful honey-sweet, pure raisin nose; fairly sweet, some plumpness yet still hard. Good acidity. _After lunch at 'Hajo' Guntrum's, Sept 1988_ ★★★★

**Oestricher Lenchen Riesling Auslese Eiswein** (Rg) **Wegeler** Yellow-gold; very good ripe kerosene Riesling nose and flavour. Mouthfilling. Not as sweet as expected. _At the VDP pre-sale tasting, Nov 1999_ ★★★

**Rüdesheimer Berg Roseneck Riesling BA** (Rg) **Staatsweingut** Yellow-gold; musty, mushroomy; sweet, rich, better flavour than nose. _At Bernhard Breuer's 'The '9s' dinner at Christie's, Feb 2000_ ★★★ _(just)._

**Wallufer Walkenberg Riesling Kabinett** (Rg) **J B Becker** Interesting to try a 20-year-old Kabinett wine. Buttercup yellow; rich 'legs'; waxy Riesling nose; fairly dry, surprisingly good. No decay. _Lunching with Jochen Becker-Kuhn and Frau Büchner, the very efficient VDP executive, at the Krone hotel, Assmannshausen, Nov 1999_ ★★

**Wehlener Sonnenuhr Riesling Spätlese** (M) **J J Prüm** Only just surviving 20 years though still fairly pale and with surprisingly youthful nose. Despite its unusual sweetness, it was strange and drying out. Acidity holding it up. _April 1999_ ★

**Wehlener Sonnenuhr Riesling Auslese** (M) **J J Prüm** Also pale for its age, with deeper fragrance, sweeter though light style. _April 1999_ ★★

**Wöllsteiner Ziffchen Optima Ruländer BA** (Rh) **P Müller** An exotic combination of grapes, the full-bodied juicy Ruländer (Pinot Gris) and the newer, grapey Optima. Two notes in 1987: bright yellow-gold; very attractive, scented, peachy flavour; a fairly sweet, plump, muscatelle-flavoured wine with excellent acidity. Most recently, a similar note as above but now a slightly deeper, waxy gold; intriguingly novel bouquet, spearmint; perhaps lacking length but with tingling acidity. _Last tasted Aug 1990_ ★★★

# 1980–1989

An important decade. While the cheap sugar-and-water wines still dominated the German market, the great estates, some of which had, frankly, been under-performing, were revising their ideas. As mentioned before, in respect of Bordeaux in the mid-1970s, if one cannot sell one's wine for a price which reflects its quality, or even recoup the cost of its production, there is a strong temptation to cut costs and make do. The trouble was that the taste for fine *fruchtig* wines had been corrupted by the flood of cheap sweet wines, UK imports reaching the astonishing peak of 17 million cases in 1985. Unhappily the attempt to produce more dry wines, partly as a reaction to the cheap sweet wines, partly to provide wines for the table, resulted in many largely unsuccessful *trocken* and *halb-trocken* wines. The best were made from quality grapes whose sugar content was fully fermented out, the result being generally dry and with naturally higher alcoholic content. The least successful were from immature grapes picked early to preserve acidity. Both tended to be uninteresting. Remove the 'fruit' and one is left with little else.

## Vintages at a Glance

**Outstanding ★★★★★**
None
**Very Good ★★★★**
1983, 1988, 1989 (v)
**Good ★★★**
1985, 1986 (v)

## 1980

A strange and difficult vintage for the grape grower. After a cold wet winter, spring emerged tentatively, though lovely warm weather arrived in May and continued until early June. Then, just as there were hopes for a bumper crop, the weather changed and from mid-June it was cold and wet, resulting in the latest flowering in memory, finishing at the end July, with, on average, only half setting. Moreover, bunches and grapes were of very variable size which made vinification difficult despite the good ripening autumn weather. The harvest was late and meagre, the smallest since 1962.

I have tasted very few of these wines, only one of even Spätlese quality which was quite flavoury with refreshing acidity. *Passé* now. Avoid.

## 1981 ★★

Variable, mainly modest to moderate quality. Somewhat below-average crop. Warm weather induced advance vegetation in April but premature shoots were damaged by frosts at the end of the month. May to mid-June was unusually moist but warm weather induced early flowering of part of the remaining crop, the rest delayed in less than ideal conditions. However, those that flowered early, ripened early. When I visited the Königin Victoria Berg vineyard in Hochheim on 2 September (1981), Mr Hupfeld told me that he had never known such advanced, well-formed and tightly bunched grapes in his life – they were at least a month ahead of normal as his flowering took place earlier than in the Rheingau proper. He expected an average harvest. Alas the weather turned cool and wet at the end of the month. Probably the Pfalz did best.

I have tasted a fairly wide range, mainly in 1983 and 1984, mostly QbAs, few of higher than Spätlese quality, and quite variable. Now of little or no interest.

**Ruppertsberger Linsenbusch Scheurebe Spätlese (P) Deinhard** First noted at Deinhard's trade tasting of '81s: aroma rather like the 'lychee' of Gewürztraminer; a broad fragrant flavour. By the end of the 1980s more yellow; lovely grapey nose, hint of passion fruit; medium – a bit too sweet for food, plump yet crisp and with adequate acidity. A flavoury drink. *Last tasted Jan 1989* ★★★

**Wehlener Sonnenuhr Riesling Eiswein (M) J J Prüm** Pale yellow gold; curious smell, like a clothes washer, and equally odd flavour, toasted and tart. *At the Weinart/Prüm tasting, April 1999.*

## 1982 ★

Yet another mediocre vintage. This time a bumper harvest in quantity if not in quality thanks to heavy rain – to the extent that some growers had storage problems. The wines were as unpredictable as the weather, the latter ranging from deepest winter frosts, through sunshine and drought to the rain at vintage time already mentioned The biggest crop ever recorded in Germany, half as much again as 1973. I tasted a wide range when they came on to the market in the summer and autumn of 1983, but few since 1984. One of the few major growers to make a success of '82 was J J Prüm, his five grades of Wehlener tasted together at the Weinart tasting

**Casteller Kugelspiel Rieslaner Spätlese (F) Fürst Castell** Another grape crossing. Yellow; an extraordinarily flowery aroma plus scent of banana; dry, curiously pungent, with strange apricot skin flavour and aftertaste. *Sept 1988* ★?

**Graacher Himmelreich Riesling Spätlese (M) J J Prüm** Flavour of dried apricot. Austere. *At the Prüms, May 2000* ★

### Königin Victoria Berg

*Prior to a visit by Queen Victoria and the Prince Consort in 1850, this 2-ha vineyard was known as Hochheimer Dechantenruhe. The tradition of royal gifts from the vineyard owners began in 1857 and resumed in 1950 when the Auslese was given as a christening present for Princess Anne (HRH the Princess Royal). When HM Queen Elizabeth II visited Wiesbaden in 1965 she was presented with the wine, and the '75 vintage was drunk at the Silver Jubilee Banquet at the Guildhall in London in 1977. A few years later, the '76 Beerenauslese was presented to HRH the Prince of Wales and Lady Diana Spencer as a wedding present.*

**Graacher Himmelreich Riesling Goldkapsel (M)**
**J J Prüm** Very Riesling: 'oily', kerosene, tempered with peach; rich, a different character to the Wehlens below. A bit of an end bite. *At the Weinart/Prüm tasting in Austria, April 1999* ★★
**Ingelheimer Spätburgunder (Rh) J Neus** A district specialising in soft Pinot Noir reds. A jammy, slightly caramelly nose; medium-dry, quite attractive but with a rusty nails finish like some of the early New World Pinots. *May 1987* ★★
**Johannisberger Klaus Riesling Auslese (Rg) v Hessen**
Rare to find an Auslese in 1982. Palish yellow gold; very unusual 'smoky apricot' scent; medium-sweet, faultless, fragrant aftertaste. Four months later, 'gooseberry' added to my earlier note, and marvellous acidity. A very good '82. *Last tasted Sept 1996* ★★★ *Doubtless peaking now.*
**Wehlener Sonnenuhr Riesling Spätlese (M) J J Prüm**
Two close notes. For a difficult vintage not at all bad: very pale; lively, acidic, fresh for its age; sweeter than expected though with teeth-gripping acidity. *April 1999* ★
**Wehlener Sonnenuhr Riesling Auslese (M) J J Prüm**
In 1996: touch of *spritz*; nose hard but good; fairly sweet, rich, good length, dry finish. Most recently: good but austere for an Auslese. *At the Prüms, May 2000* ★
**Wehlener Sonnenuhr Riesling Auslese Goldkapsel (M)**
**J J Prüm** Meaty, peachy nose and taste. Sweet. *April 1999* ★★
**Wehlener Sonnenuhr Riesling lange Goldkapsel (M)**
**J J Prüm** Certainly an extra dimension here: sweeter, richer, botrytis, length. *April 1999* ★★★★
**Wehlener Sonnenuhr Riesling BA (M) J J Prüm** Not a success: pale; strange fishy fragrance; drying out, touch of rot? *At the Weinart/Prüm tasting, April 1999.*

# 1983 ★★★★

At last, a real vintage, the best since 1976. When I say 'real' I mean natural, unforced, thanks to better growing conditions.

A relatively mild winter with no frost damage was followed by a cool wet spring, with rains in April and May. Good flowering conditions during the latter half of June were followed by a long dry spell in July and August. A judicious combination of rain and sun in September swelled and ripened the berries. However, there was little or no botrytis.

Though highly rated at the time, the overall reputation of 1983 has eased back a little. It was, however, unreservedly successful in the Saar and Ruwer, as well as the Nahe. As always, the best growers made the best wine. I have tasted a wide range and large number, of which the following is a recent cross-section, including some of the most bizarre. A most invigorating vintage, one of my favourites, still well worth looking out for and of course drinking.

**Avelsbacher Hammerstein Riesling Auslese (M)**
**Staatsweingut** Lightly grapey, assertive, still hard at seven years of age. *Sept 1990* ★★★ *Probably at peak now.*
**Berncastler Doctor Riesling Auslese (M) Lauerberg** Pale, lime green-tinged; positive rich, ripe, grapey nose, with honey, melon; medium-sweet yet a nice light style, agreeable grapey flavour. *At a tasting conducted for Shibata, the Japanese publisher of* Wine Tasting, *in Tokyo, Nov 1989* ★★★
**Brauneberger Juffer-Sonnenuhr Riesling Auslese (M)**
**Max Ferd. Richter** A silver prize winner in 1985. Peachy; a perfect (for Daphne and me) mid-morning glass – opened on Saturday, finished off on Sunday. Quicker if we have weekend guests. Soft, flavoury, lacking a bit of zest. *Easy drinking. Last noted July 1998* ★★★

**Brüssele Kleinbottwarer Lemberger Kabinett trocken (W) Graf Adelmann** From a vineyard in Württemberg dating back to Roman times and Lemberger, a red grape, better known as the Austrian Blaufränkish grape. Medium-deep, youthful cherry red; rather green fruit, blackberry-like, plus whiff of fresh banana; slightly sweet, medium-full body, curious earthiness and tinny tannins. Lacking length but at least with more guts and interest than most of the Rhine reds. *At the 2nd Europäisches Wein-Festival in Frankfurt, Sept 1988* ★★
**Casteller Feuerbach Domina Kabinett (F) Fürst Castell**
95° Oechsle. Not chaptalised. Another curious German red wine, this time the grape, Domina, being a Portugieser crossed with Spätburgunder. A surprisingly deep red, a slight *spritz*; crisp, Gamay-like fruit; dry, medium-light, correct balance of tannin and acidity. Attractive. Like a young Chinon without the rasping acidity. Two notes. *Last tasted Sept 1988* ★★★
**Erbacher Marcobrunn Riesling Auslese (Rg) zu Knyphausen** The aristocratic Knyphausen family have a very small plot of Marcobrunn on the north side of the railway line which cuts through this famous vineyard. A very distinctive bouquet – if the Baron will forgive me – of violet-scented furniture polish. But I liked it! *Nov 1994* ★★★ *(just).*
**Essinger Rossberg Spätburgunder Weissherbst BA (P) Manfred Frey** The colour of old gold or unpolished brass buttons; fabulous, deep, creamy bouquet and flavour. Sweet, clover honey, perfect acidity. *Dining with Karina Eigensatz – Walter was away, so I plundered his cellar, July 1994* ★★★★
**Filzener Herrenberg Riesling Eiswein (M) Reverchon**
Three notes, first pre-tasting in London and the next two at the 'Wines of Germany' weekend in Banff. I had not tasted the wines from this very good Saar estate before. The grapes had been picked at –9° C on 15 November. Oechsle 149°, alcohol 10% and amazingly high acidity, 18g/l. Bottled in May 1984 after four months in traditional oak barrels. It deserved its *Goldene Kammerpreismünze (Mosel)*. Bright yellow-gold; scent of lime blossom; sweet, of course, flavour of ripe peaches, with gooseberry-like, teeth-gripping acidity. Delicious. Exciting. *Last tasted Oct 1998* ★★★★
**Forster Jesuitengarten Riesling Eiswein (P) v Bühl**
A delicious half bottle, sweet, delectable. *Dining with Miriam and Jonathan Lyons in Swiss Cottage, London, July 1998* ★★★★
**Hallgartener Schönhell Riesling Eiswein (Rg) Engelmann** Two notes: first in May 1996 at a VDP pre-sale tasting: caramel custard nose; sweet, crisp, lovely flavour, rich yet delicate – but with teeth-gripping acidity. The same autumn in Germany: soft, yellow-gold colour; caramel cream again but showing some maderisation. Acidity noted again. *Last tasted Sept 1996* ★★
**Hattenheimer Nussbrunnen Riesling TBA (Rg) v Simmern** Glorious! *At the VDP pre-sale tasting, Nov 1997* ★★★★★
**Hochheimer Domdechaney Riesling Spätlese (Rg) Werner'schen** First tasted in 1988: pale; low-keyed; fairly dry, lean, crisp, very flavoury, good acidity. Eleven years later: still rich, good fruit, complete. Daphne gave it 5 stars. *Last noted at the Gigantische dinner at the Krone, Assmannshausen, Nov 1999. For a Spätlese of this age,* ★★★★
**Hochheimer Domdechaney Riesling Spätlese (Rg) Aschrott** Probably at its best at ten years of age. Still palish, most attractive, crisp, honeyed, harmonious. Excellent balance of fruit and acidity. *At the estate, June 1994* ★★★★
**Hochheimer Hölle Riesling Auslese (Rg) Aschrott**
Mint and cress; medium-sweet, lovely flavour, at peak. *Sept 1996* ★★★★

**Hochheimer Kirchenstück Gewürztraminer Auslese**
(Rg) **Aschrott** A rare opportunity to taste a Rheingau
Gewürztraminer. Typically spicy; fairly sweet, powerful. Would
be interesting to see how this has turned out. *At the estate, June
1994* ★★★

**Hochheimer Kirchenstück Riesling Auslese** (Rg)
**Aschrott** First tasted at the estate in May 1994: lime-gold; very
pure Riesling nose; medium-sweet, classic. Next at the pre-sale
tasting: gentle, scented; rich yet dry. *Last noted Sept 1994* ★★★
*Probably past best now.*

**Hochheimer Kirchenstück Riesling Auslese** (Rg)
**Künstler** One of my earliest notes on Künstler's wines and
showing its class: deliciously fragrant; perfect fruit and acidity.
*At the VDP pre-sale tasting at Christie's, Sept 1996* ★★★★

**Hochheimer Königin-Victoriaberg Riesling BA** (Rg)
**Hupfeld** A famous vineyard at the eastern end of the Rheingau
with a monument commemorating the visit of Queen
Victoria in 1850 (see box page 365). Hard. Rather earthy – an
acquired taste. *Sept 1997* ★★?

**Hochheimer Königin Victoria Berg Riesling Spätlese**
(Rg) **Pabstmann** First tasted in July 1984. It was fragrant, rather
unusual and unsettled but soft, gentle and agreeable on palate.
Seven years after the vintage it took on an attractive yellow
gold; deep, warm, earthy, grassy bouquet and flavour. Seemed
sweeter. *Last tasted Oct 1990* ★★ *Drink up.*

**Hochheimer Stielweg Riesling Eiswein** (Rg) **Werner**
Dr Michel was Director of the German Wine Institute for
years. His wife inherited the estate, a charming old house in
Hochheim and some top vineyards. Curious, thin, slightly
sickly spearmint nose and taste but perfect with *foie gras. At
Schloss Johannisberg, Nov 2000* ★★

**Hohentwieler Olgaberg Traminer Auslese** (B)
**Staatsweingut Meersberg** Yellow and mellow; bouquet of
peaches and apricots; medium-sweet, glorious flavour, flashy,
grapey, good acidity. *July 1989* ★★★★

**Kreuznacher Krötenpfühl Riesling Eiswein** (N) **Paul
Anheuser** Orange-amber; bouquet of dried apricot skins and
touch of caramel on the palate. Very rich. Marvellous acidity.
*The perfect end to a lunch with Janet and Freddie Price in their sunny
conservatory in Ealing, West London, Aug 1999* ★★★★

**Mülheimer Helenenkloster Riesling Eiswein** (M) **Max
Ferd. Richter** Rich yellow; lovely, stylish; ideal with raspberries
at a Glyndebourne picnic. *Aug 2000* ★★★★

**Ockfener Bockstein Riesling Auslese Goldkapsel** (M)
**Geltz-Zilliken** Palish; grassy nose; medium-sweet.
Disappointing. *April 1993* ★★

**Oestricher Lenchen Riesling Auslese Eiswein** (Rg)
**Wegeler** Straw orange; curiously meaty; sweet, lovely flavour
and aftertaste. *At the VDP tasting at Christie's, Sept 1996* ★★★

**Scharzhofberger Riesling Kabinett** (M) **Egon Müller**
Even a relatively modest Kabinett wine in the hands of the
Müllers can survive age and a hot day on the Mississippi. Pale,
fragrant, dry, light and deliciously refreshing. *'Rollin on the
River', Tennessee, Sept 1999* ★★★

**Scharzhofberger Riesling Auslese** (M) **Egon Müller** The
Müllers told us that it was a hot and very dry summer in the
Saar, producing a big crop: 80hl/ha: typical ripe peachy
fragrance and flavour. Dry finish. *May 2000* ★★★★

**Serriger Schloss Saarsteiner Riesling Auslese** (M)
**Schloss Saarstein** Mild fruit, light (8% alcohol), Saar acidity
making it seem drier than our normal weekend elevenses. *At
Chippenham Lodge, June 1998* ★★★ *(at 12.45pm we switched to our
summer drink, Pimm's).*

**Siebeldinger im Sonnenschein Spätburgunder
Weissherbst Auslese** (P) **Rebholz** An attractive, dry white
from ripe red grapes. In fact, a palish, warm orange amber
gold; lovely, harmonious, honeyed grapey nose; surprisingly
firm, good length and aftertaste. Excellent acidity. Went well
with figs. *Sept 1988* ★★★★

**Traiser Rotenfels Riesling Eiswein** (N) **Dr Crusius** Yeast
added but fermentation stopped at 200g/l sugar. Surprisingly
pale yellow; refined 'soft caramel', very fragrant Nahe 'fruit
salad' nose; very strange, singed richness, lovely acidity. Will
keep. *At Schloss Johannisberg, Nov 2000* ★★★(★)

**Wallhäuser Mühlenberg Riesling Eiswein** (N) **Salm-
Dalberg** 154° Oechsle, 7.9g/l acidity. Pure topaz; barley sugar
and honey; sweet overall though curiously dry mid-palate.
Smooth, delicious. One of Prinz Salm's best wines. *At the pre-
sale tasting conducted by Michael Salm and myself at Christie's, Oct
1997* ★★★★

**Wehlener Sonnenuhr Riesling Auslese Goldkapsel** (M)
**J J Prüm** First noted at Ziegler's tasting in 1995. It might have
been the light but it seemed very pale, not however its nose or
taste, the first heavenly, with still relatively youthful acidity,
'greengage', almost Sauvignon Blanc; on the palate sweet, lean,
crisp, acidic. More recently, a bit more colour developed;
medium-sweet, drier finish than expected. *Last noted at the
Weinart/Prüm tasting, May 2000* ★★★ *Drink up.*

**Wehlener Sonnenuhr Riesling Auslese lange
Goldkapsel** (M) **J J Prüm** For Manfred Prüm his 'long gold
capsule' represents the highest expression of vintage and
vineyard, certainly borne out by his '83: a lovely yellow gold;
fat, rich, creamy nose, fairly sweet, with extra botrytis
dimensions, firm, fragrant aftertaste. Years of life. *At the
Weinart/Prüm tasting, April 1999* ★★★★(★)

**Wehlener Sonnenuhr Riesling BA** (M) **J J Prüm** Two
notes, first at Ziegler's in 1995: heavenly nose, still with
relatively youthful acidity, 'greengage', almost like Sauvignon
Blanc; sweet, lean, crisp, acidic. Next: fragrant, minerally,
aromatic, spicy, lovely flavour, shape, texture, balance and finish.
*Last tasted April 1999* ★★★★★

**Wehlener Sonnenuhr Riesling Eiswein** (M) **J J Prüm**
Orange gold; chocolate, fudge, boot polish, vanilla; most
unusual golden syrup, essencia sort of sweetness. Most
distinctive. *At the Weinart/Prüm tasting, April 1999* ★★★★★

**Winkeler Honigberg Riesling Spätlese** (Rg) **R Nagler**
Noted over a three-year period. Yellow-tinged; grapey, mild yet
fat; medium-dry, a bit four-square, slightly kernelly but
reasonably rich. Needs drinking. *May 1990* ★★

---

## Peter Ziegler

*A German school teacher, and master of a formidable intellect. In
looks he reminds me of Beethoven. I have attended two of his
tastings, which feature wines of the highest quality and rarity, in
their best vintages. The first one was in 1983 at Berg Windeck in
the Black Forest. To get there, I had an amusing drive from Alsace,
with my old friend Johnny Hugel with whom I was staying. We
travelled in his old Citröen, Johnny and his UK agent, Parry de
Winten, in the front and Jane McQuitty, of The Times, and me
in the back. Johnny and Parry both smoked like chimneys. Every
time they lit up, Jane and I would ostentatiously wind the windows
down to let some air in. We behaved like a couple of giggly school
children, and had great fun, coughing and choking, and lurching
from side to side every time Johnny swooshed round a bend.*

I TASTED A HUGE NUMBER OF '83S BETWEEN 1984
AND 1986 and to reel off all my notes would be tedious and
space-consuming. They ranged from QbA, but mainly
Spätlesen and Auslesen. The latter were the most attractive,
whether from the Mosel or elsewhere.

# 1984

Poor, acidic wines; one of, if not the worst vintage of the
decade. Unseasonable weather throughout northern Europe. In
Germany, late budding, late flowering, poor summer, delayed
harvest (from mid-October) in reasonably warm dry
conditions. I have only tasted four wines: only two in the
1990s, both from the top producers in the Saar and Middle
Mosel, but have no burning desire to taste more.

**Scharzhofberger Riesling Eiswein** (M) **Egon Müller**
Orange-amber, apple-green rim; astonishing, apricots, honey;
intensely sweet, waxy fruit, very high acidity. *With Hugh
Johnson at his St James's Street shop, June 1991* ★★★★

**Wehlener Sonnenuhr Riesling Kabinett** (M) **J J Prüm**
Light, easy to drink, fruity, acidic. *After-sale supper at the Cape
Cod Room, Drake Hotel, Chicago, Feb 1990* ★

# 1985 ★★★

An attractive vintage. The long hot summer extended into
autumn, producing ideal ripening conditions – sunny days,
cool nights, hazy mornings. A few welcome showers to
succour the grapes. At best wines of charm rather than
substance. The worst that can be said of some is that they were
a little dull, lacking, short. Most are, or were, very agreeable. I
have a reasonably wide spread of notes from different regions,
mainly at the Kabinett, Spätlese and Auslese level, with rather
too many Trocken wines for my liking. The latter are now all
past their best. Here is a selection of my more recent notes.

**Brauneberger Juffer-Sonnenuhr Riesling Auslese
Goldkapsel** (M) **F Haag** Unusually pale; still very fresh;
medium-sweet leading to a dry slight *spritz* finish. Light (7.2%
alcohol), lean. *Dinner with the Bacchus Society at Dieter Kaufman's
Grevenbroich, May 2000* ★★

**Brauneberger Juffer-Sonnenuhr Riesling Spätlese** (M)
**Willi Haag** Six notes, all at Christie's wine courses. Steely grey
green; subdued, kerosene, grapey aroma but, as one gently
sniffed, a touch of clover honey; medium-sweet, light (alcohol
7.8%) yet with hidden backbone. Elegant wine, fresh and
fruity. A delicious drink. *Last tasted June 1991* ★★★ *Probably still
drinking well.*

**Brüssele Kleinbottwarer Riesling Eiswein** (W)
**Adelmann** The grape sugar had reached 90° before icing, its
final Oechsle over 200°. Just about my highest mark at Peter
Ziegler's great 56-wine tasting (over an extended lunch).
Fabulously sweet and creamy. Graf Adelmann at his most
inspired. *At the Schlosshotel, Erbach, Dec 1995* ★★★★★

**Casteller Bausch Mariensteiner Eiswein** (F) **Fürst Castell**
The first Eiswein made in Franken. Mariensteiner Main
Riesling grapes (a crossing of Sylvaner and Rieslaner, which in
turn is Riesling x Sylvaner) were picked on 31 December 1985
and 1 January 1986. Bright, buttercup yellow; very powerful
honey and spice, with youthful, greengage-like fruit; very
sweet, very rich with high tangy acidity, clean and crisp. *Last
tasted in 1988* ★★★★ *But probably at peak now.*

**Durbacher Plauelrain Riesling TBA** (B) **Winzer. Durbach**
Only Peter Ziegler could lay his hands on a wine like this,

from a Württemberg co-operative, Oechsle 200°: warm amber;
refined, mocha nose; sweet, lovely, raisiny flavour, excellent
acidity. *At the Schlosshotel, Erbach, Dec 1995* ★★★★★

**Eltviller Sonnenberg Riesling TBA** (Rg) **(estate unknown)**
Alongside the Durbacher TBA and, in comparison,
aggressively hot caramelised nose; sweet, hot, assertive, rough
textured. *At Peter Ziegler's tasting, at the Schlosshotel, Erbach, Dec
1995* ★★★ *Perhaps time might smooth the edges.*

**Erbacher Steinmorgen Riesling Auslese** (Rg) **Freiherr zu
Knyphausen** Picked 31 December at 115° *Oechsle*. Surely an
Eiswein? A gold medal winner in 1988. Surprisingly pale;
nutty nose; medium-sweet, touch of pineapple, marvellous
acidity. *At the VDP pre-sale tasting, Nov 1995* ★★★

**Forster Mariengarten Riesling Kabinett** (P) **Bürklin-
Wolf** Soft but still drinking well. *Interestingly, and a reminder of
Queen Victoria's liking for Hock, at a state banquet for the President
of Portugal, Buckingham Palace, April 1993* ★★★

**Hallgartener Jungfer Riesling Auslese** (Rg) **Nass** Very
distinctive nose: vanilla, honey, lime blossom; medium-sweet,
touch of coffee and crisp fruit. *At the VDP pre-sale tasting, May
1996* ★★★

**Hochheimer Stielweg Riesling Spätlese** (Rg) **Aschrott**
Rosehip; sweet, caramelly; dry, earthy Hochheim character. An
acquired taste. *At the estate, June 1994* ★

**Ingelheimer Schloss Westerhaus Riesling Eiswein** (Rh)
**v Opel** Picked 31 December and 1 January 1986. Alcohol
6.1%. Pure yellow-gold; glorious, zestful, grape, peach, mango
and honey; very sweet, delicious crisp fruity flavour, perfect
acidity. It was the best icewine I could recall. *Sept 1988* ★★★★★

**Schloss Johannisberger Riesling Eiswein Blaulack** (Rg)
As the auctioneer at the great VDP *Spitzenweine* wine auction,
I didn't have much time to taste. The Kurhaus in Wiesbaden
was filled to capacity, the sale starting at 1.45pm ending and
going on without a break until 5.15pm. Before the first lot of
each wine was auctioned, a tasting sample was served – for
over 1000 people. This wine preceded lot 340 and, happily, it
was delicious and kept me going. *Nov 1997* ★★★★

**Josephshöfer Riesling Auslese** (M) **v Kesselstatt** The
estate's exclusive vineyard in Graach. 8.5% alcohol. *Silberner
Preis DLG 1988, Silberner Kammerpreismünze 1987*, i.e. two
silver medals. Rich, hefty, goaty nose; medium-dry, richness
balanced by very good acidity. Vanilla aftertaste. *Nov 1990*
★★★(★) *Now to 1995.*

**Verrenberger Verrenberg Lemberger Spätlese trocken**
(W) **zu Hohenlohe-Oehringen** The village and vineyard in
Württemberg bear the same name. An interesting wine,
impressively deep, ruby colour with immature purple rim;
sweaty tannins, vanilla and an explosive depth; dry, raw, tannic
– a strange, rather mouldy taste. Prinz Kraft zu Hohenlohe-
Oehringen, the son of the Duke, thought it might be the soil.
I wondered about the casks. Drink with German sausages or
wild boar. *Red wine dinner-tasting in Frankfurt, Sept 1988* ★? *Hard
to place. Might be at peak now.*

**Wachenheimer Mandelgarten Scheurebe Spätlese** (P)
**Bürklin-Wolf** An extraordinary, exotic bouquet, blackcurrants;
medium dry, very distinctive flavour and aftertaste like
crystallised violets. *April 1993* ★★★★

**Wehlener Sonnenuhr Riesling Auslese** (M) **Dr Loosen**
Palish; very peachy; medium-sweet, light (8.5% alcohol),
delicious flavour but just a little lacking. *Elevenses at
Chippenham Lodge, Aug 1998* ★★ *Drink up.*

**Wehlener Sonnenuhr Riesling Auslese lange Goldkapsel**
(M) **J J Prüm** Frankly not up to the '83 or even the '88. Touch

of wood, even cork, pasty acidity. Its redeeming feature an attractive aftertaste. *At the Weinart/Prüm vertical, April 1999* ★?

**Wehlener Sonnenuhr Riesling BA** (M) **J J Prüm** Pale; floral, gooseberry; sweet, gloriously ripe flesh yet crisp. *One of my best marks at Peter Ziegler's rare wine tasting, at the Schlosshotel, Erbach, Dec 1995* ★★★★★ *Perfect then, doubtless perfect now.*

## 1986 ★ to ★★★

Very mixed results due, as always, to mixed weather conditions. The winter was exceptionally severe, temperatures down to −20°C with some damage to vines. Despite a mild spring, budding was late though conditions caught up for flowering mid–late June. July was exceptionally hot and dry. By August, the ground was parched, light rains doing little to alleviate the situation. Except in the south, September was cold and wet, delaying ripening, the Pfalz in particular benefiting from relatively fine, uninterrupted harvest conditions with excellent botrytis for the higher quality sweet wines. Elsewhere, violent storms in late October made the continuation of picking particularly difficult. In the more northerly regions, good Kabinett and Spätlesen wines were produced but relatively few Auslesen and above, though the best, with firm acidity, are keeping well.

**Assmannshäuser Höllenberg Spätburgunder Kabinett trocken** (Rg) **Robert König** A strange rosehip colour; quite attractive fruit; bone dry. Pinot Noir but not remotely Burgundian in style. A decent food wine, about as good as it would ever get. *Sept 1995* ★★

**Erbacher Hohenrein Riesling Eiswein** (Rg) **v Oetinger** Warm orange-gold; sweet, exotic, mango-like fragrance; let down by a taste of rot and hard, hot, acidic finish. Pity. *At the VDP pre-sale tasting at Schloss Reinhartshausen, May 1996.*

**Hochheimer Hölle Riesling Auslese** (Rg) **Aschrott** A silver prize winner. First tasted at the estate in 1994: still green tinged; a powerful, rich, earthy character. A couple of disappointing notes in 1995, both made mid-morning in the country. Better nose than flavour. The following year, a not very bright yellow; pleasant grapey nose but, again, spoiled by a trace of rot on finish. *Last tasted at home, April 1996. Forget it.*

**Hochheimer Kirchenstück Riesling Auslese** (Rg) **Aschrott** From Aschrott's other top vineyard, also consumed as weekend elevenses. Much better than the Hölle, a lovely, sweet, mid-morning drink. *April 1996* ★★★ *Without wishing to be unkind, the best thing that ever happened to this once great estate was its acquisition by Künstler in 1966.*

**Schloss Johannisberger Riesling Eiswein** (Rg) Waxy yellow; minty, grapey, honeyed; sweet, very acidic. *At a pre-sale tasting, Christie's, Sept 1996* ★★

**Mülheimer Helenenkloster Riesling Eiswein-Christwein** (M) **Max Ferd. Richter** The necessary −10°C occurred on Christmas Day. 145° Oechsle. A heavenly half bottle given to me by my old friend Freddie Price, Richter's importer, and served with cinnamon apples at an after-theatre supper: a lovely yellow-gold though with a cloudy sediment; glorious honey and cream nose and taste. Very sweet. Wonderful acidity. *At Chippenham Lodge, Aug 1994* ★★★★★

**Rüdesheimer Berg Roseneck Riesling Auslese** (Rg) **Heinrich Nägler** Clover honey; lovely flavour but surprisingly dry. *At the VDP pre-sale tasting, Nov 1995* ★★

**Steinberger Riesling Auslese** (Rg) **Staatsweingüter Kloster Eberbach** Kloster Eberbach, founded in 1135, is the biggest of Germany's monastic estates, now owned by the State of Hesse.

Steinberg is one of the largest of the great Rheingau vineyards: 130ha. Three notes, the first two both at VDP pre-auction tastings in May 1996: surprisingly pale; vanilla, cream cheese and 'mouse droppings'; fairly sweet, spicy, minerally, curious uplift. Four months later, a more complimentary note: lovely, grapey classic nose; fairly assertive, touch of caramel on the finish. Well, anyway, I quite liked it. *Last tasted at Christie's pre-sale tasting, Sept 1996* ★★

## 1987

On the whole a poor vintage and I have tasted relatively few wines. Following an unendingly cold and harsh winter, which damaged some vines, a warm spring encouraged growth but a cold May and June had the opposite effect, delaying flowering until July. This was followed by a very wet and sunless summer causing rot problems though from mid-September warm dry weather alleviated some of the growers' distress. There was a very late harvest, Rieslings being picked from the very end of October to the end of November.

The fairly large crop comprised mainly very acidic wines of lowly QbA quality though in certain favoured sites some good, long-lasting Auslesen were made.

**Hochheimer Hölle Riesling Eiswein** (Rg) **Aschrott** Grapes picked 20 December: yellow-gold; creamy, vanilla, 'milk chocolate'; sweet, crisp, lovely flavour, good acidity. *At the estate, June 1994* ★★★★

**Wehlener Sonnenuhr Riesling Spätlese** (M) **J J Prüm** Bone dry. Austere. *June 1990. It is, perhaps, significant that no '87 appeared in the very extensive Prüm tasting in 1999.*

OF THE SEVERAL '87S TASTED IN 1988, only two worth a mention, both 3-star Mosel, **Erdener Prälat Riesling** wines from **Dr Loosen**: **Kabinett halbtrocken** Prälat is the best part of Treppchen (little steps) vineyard, beneath the rocks, facing south: very pale; very scented; a surprisingly warm, rich wine, with broad, dry finish; and **Spätlese** harvested before the rains; mild, grapey, blackcurrant aroma; medium-dry, lightish, nice flavour, very good mouth-drying end acidity.

## 1988 ★★★★

From the spring, through the summer and until the end of September, well-nigh perfect growing and ripening conditions. However pre-harvest rain and fog dampened expectations and there was much hail damage in the Saar and Ruwer. Excellent conditions throughout the Middle Mosel, the Riesling also flourishing well in the Pfalz and the Nahe, the latter district taking advantage of a severe frost on 7 November to make superb Eiswein. The vintage was also good in the Rheinhessen region but, except for estates with the most-favoured sites, perhaps less successful in the Rheingau. On the whole an extremely good yet (as in Bordeaux) perhaps not fully appreciated vintage.

QbAs, *trocken*, Kabinett and lesser Spätlesen should have been drunk by the mid-1990s. Higher quality wines are still drinking well. I have not tasted as wide a range as I would have liked, but, by and large, I have enjoyed them.

**Bernkasteler Badstube Riesling Kabinett** (M) **J J Prüm** Very pale; youthful, grassy, touch of lanolin and harmonious; light, grapey flavour, hard, very dry, slightly metallic acidic finish. Crisp. Refreshing. *March 1991* ★★ *Best at that age. Probably tiring now.*

**Graacher Himmelreich Riesling Auslese** (M) **J J Prüm**
Touch of lime; medium-sweet, soft, nice fruit and flesh but
with gum-gripping acidity. *April 1999* ★★★★ *Now–2012.*
**Hochheimer Hölle Riesling Kabinett** (Rg) **Aschrott**
*Silberpreis.* Crisp, lively, grapey nose and flavour. Probably at its
best at six years old. *At the estate, June 1994* ★★★
**Hochheimer Kirchenstück Riesling BA** (Rg)
**Staatsweingut** Yellow-gold; intriguing, 'hot', lime and grape,
ripe melon bouquet; very sweet, almost a TBA. Excellent
acidity. *VDP pre-auction, May 1996* ★★★★
**Iphöfer Julius-Echter-Berg Huxelrebe Auslese** (F)
**Juliusspital** Deserving its gold medal: pure Tutankhamun gold;
gloriously grapey, raisiny nose; medium-sweet, combining ripe
flesh with Franken steeliness, powerful (unusually high alcohol,
14,5%, for a German wine). *Perfect elevenses at Chippenham
Lodge, May 1999* ★★★
**Königschaffhauser Steingrüble Spätburgunder
Weissherbst Eiswein** (B) **Winzergenossenschaft
Königsschaffhausen** A bit of an oddity, a Baden co-operative
sweet white made from Pinot Noir grapes. Some of the red
grapes' pigment staining its orange-amber colour; glorious
nose, apricots, raisins; sweet, fairly assertive, very good acidity.
*At Rodenstock's opening dinner, Sept 1995* ★★★★
**Oestricher Lenchen Riesling Spätlese** (Rg) **Spreitzer**
Touch of orange; lovely, apricot nose; rich but – perhaps it was
the acidity – drying out a bit. Good flavour. *Dining with the
'musical Bourgeois' family, Nov 1997* ★★★
**Scharzhofberg Riesling Auslese** (M) **Egon Müller**
A magnum at dinner prior to Walter Eigensatz's tasting of 144
red '90s: brilliant colour; lovely, refreshing bouquet; medium-
sweet, delicate, lightly grapey flavour, excellent acidity. A
wonderful contrast of style to the '85 Ch d'Yquem alongside,
but for me, identical marks. *In Luzern, June 1996* ★★★★
**Schlossböckelheimer Felsenberg Riesling Kabinett**
**Paul Anheuser** (N) Extraordinary bouquet and flavour, spicy,
good acidity. *At Vinopolis, London, April 2000* ★★★
**Wehlener Sonnenuhr Riesling Spätlese** (M) **J J Prüm**
The best of the 1980s Spätlesen 'flight'. Extraordinarily fragrant
lime blossom plus 'tom-cats' nose; sweeter than expected, soft.
Lacking length but delicious. *At the Weinart/Prüm vertical, April
1999* ★★★★
**Wehlener Sonnenuhr Riesling Auslese** (M) **J J Prüm**
Palish yellow; well developed, pineapple, grapey; rather four-
square after the '89 but with uplifting acidity and fragrant
finish. *At the Weinart/Prüm vertical, April 1999* ★★★★
**Wehlener Sonnenuhr Riesling Auslese lange
Goldkapsel** (M) **J J Prüm** Acidic, 'greengage' nose; an
interesting conflict of flesh, fat and acidic bite. Rich yet dry
finish. *At the Weinart/Prüm tasting, April 1999* ★★★(★)

THE BEST OF THE '88s TASTED BETWEEN 1990 AND 1993
with their rating at the time: **Bernkasteler Badstube
Riesling Spätlese** (M) **Dr Thanisch** very pale; mild, very
grapey aroma; fairly dry, nice weight, a good, positive flavour,
soft yet very acidic ★★★; **Brauneberger Juffer-Sonnenuhr
Spätlese** (M) **Willi Haag** very pale; touch of kerosene
Riesling, nice fruit, pleasant acidity; medium-dry, light (7.8%
alcohol), fruity, very pleasant end acidity ★★★★ *should still be
lovely;* **Eitelsbacher Karthäuserhofberg Riesling
Spätlese** (M) **Christoph Tyrell** very dry, delicate, firm, good
length and acidity ★★★ *drink up;* **Erdener Prälat Riesling
Auslese** (M) **Dr F Weins-Prüm** earthy, sweaty bouquet;
medium-sweet, rich, ripe, fragrant aftertaste ★★★ *drink up;*

**Forster Ungeheuer Riesling Spätlese** (P) **Deinhard**
lightly honeyed and spicy; medium sweetness and weight,
excellent flavour, violets, good acidity and aftertaste. Replanted
in the rearrangement of vineyard sites that followed the 1971
wine laws, this wine reflects the heavy soil, rich in minerals, of
the Pfalz ★★★★; **Graacher Himmelreich Riesling
Spätlese** (M) **Deinhard** pale; delicate, spicy, acidic,
'gooseberry'; dry, light weight and style, fragrant, good acidity
★★★ *drink up;* **Hochheimer Königin Victoria Berg
Riesling Spätlese** (Rg) **Hupfeld** ripe grapes but curious nose
(sulphur?); medium dryness and weight, touch of fat, very
positive rather earthy Hochheim flavour, very good aftertaste
★★★; **Maximin Grünhäuser Abtsberg Kabinett** (M)
**v Schubert** fairly pale, star bright; lovely fragrant fruit, touch of
melon, pineapple; very light, dry finish. Slight but charming
★★★; **Maximin Grünhäuser Abtsberg Spätlese** (M)
**v Schubert** sweet, plumper, peachy nose; touch of sweetness, a
heavier grapier style, rather hard acidic finish ★★★(★)?;
**Oberemmeler Hütte Riesling Spätlese** (M) **v Hövel**
some depth of fruit; dry, lean, austere, good length. Needs time
★★(★); **Oberemmeler Hütte Riesling Auslese** (M)
**v Hövel** yellow-gold; honeyed, waxy, melon nose, still hard;
rich fruit though still light, refreshingly tart. Needs time
★★(★★); **Oberemmeler Hütte Riesling Eiswein** (M)
**v Hövel** rich, honeyed bouquet; intensely sweet, delicious
balance of fruit and acidity. Almost a TBA ★★★(★★);
**Scharzhofberger Riesling Eiswein** (M) **Egon Müller**
amber; amazing, honeyed sweetness; intensely sweet, very rich,
plump for a Saar wine, good length, fabulous acidity ★★★★★;
**Wehlener Sonnenuhr Riesling Auslese** (M) **Dr Loosen**
several notes: lovely, grapey aroma; medium-sweet, very
attractive fruit and acidity. My style of wine ★★★★; **Wehlener
Sonnenuhr Riesling Auslese** (M) **S A Prüm** very fragrant,
slightly peachy nose; on the dry side of sweet, crisp, good
finish. The *Goldkapsel* version had a rich, honeyed nose; very
sweet, rather obvious ★★★★; **Wehlener Sonnenuhr Riesling
Auslese** (M) **Marienhof** intriguing bouquet of walnuts and
violets; medium sweetness and weight, still hard ★★(★★); and
**Wehlener Sonnenuhr Riesling Auslese Goldkapsel** (M)
**J J Prüm** J J makes several qualities of Auslese, the gold capsule
bottles being superior, the long gold capsules his best.
Deliciously grapey; medium-sweet, good length. Lovely ★★★★

# 1989 ★★★ to ★★★★

On the whole a very good vintage and a large crop thanks to
almost ideal growing conditions. Mild winter, warm spring,
which encouraged early bud break, perfect flowering in June
and a hot, sunny and relatively dry summer. Unsurprisingly, in
these conditions, all grape varieties ripened well and the
harvest began towards the beginning of September. Very ripe
grapes and botrytis made it not the easiest of years for the
lighter styles of wine, lack of acidity being a problem.
Conditions for the richer *Prädikat* styles were very favourable,
boosted by an Indian summer from 10 to 29 October, which
enabled superbly concentrated TBAs to be made.

The lighter, drier wines should have been consumed in the
early 1990s. The higher quality wines are lovely now, and the
best Auslesen, Beerenauslesen and TBAs have life in hand.
**Assmannshäuser Weissherbst Auslese** (Rg) **Allendorf**
Warm amber; crisp, raisiny; medium-sweet, cinnamon
spiciness, good acidity, dry finish. *Dining with Karen and Leo
Gros in Johannisberg, Nov 1999* ★★★ *At peak.*

**Bischoffinger Steinbuck Ruländer TBA** (B)
**W G Bischoffinger** A top-quality co-operative wine: soft tawny; exotic, honey and muscatelle; very sweet, rich, fat, soft. *At Rodenstock's opening dinner, Sept 1995* ★★★★★

**Brauneberger Juffer Sonnenuhr Riesling Auslese** (M)
**F Haag** Pre-tasted in London and, a few days later, featuring in the 'Just desserts' seminar, moderated by Monika Christmann, director of the famed viti/vinicultural school at Geisenheim, and 'presented' by Wilhelm Haag of Fritz Haag. Must weight 99° Oechsle, residual sugar 70.9g/l, total acidity 9.2g/l, alcohol 8%. Happily both my notes were consistent: very pale, lime-tinged, fabulous bouquet, a *mélange* of apricots, peaches, gooseberry-like acidity, vanilla; fairly sweet, tongue-teasing delicacy and acidity. A sheer delight. Fritz Haag well deserves its reputation as, perhaps, the top Middle Mosel estate. *Last tasted at Banff Springs, Canada, Oct 1998* ★★★★★

**Casteller Kugelspiel Rieslaner BA** (F) **Fürst Castell** Scent and flavour like honeyed strawberries and cream. Sweet, glorious, with Rieslaner's heavenly, almost scorching, acidity. *At Castell, June 1997* ★★★★

**Eitelsbacher Karthäuserhofberg Riesling Spätlese trocken** (M) **Tyrell** At six years of age probably at its best. Bone-dry, alcohol 10%, austere yet fragrant. It did not stand up to lobster. *At a dinner tasting conducted for Hallwag at Le Canard, Hamburg, May 1999* ★★ *I prefer a bit of fruit.*

**Eltviller Sonnenberg Riesling Auslese** (Rg) **Belz** Only 550 litres made. Sugar content too high (at 53°) to use SO$_2$ hence the surprisingly deep colour; very rich, very Riesling, floral, thick, honeyed botrytis; fairly sweet, delicious flavour, acidity and aftertaste. *At the rare wine tasting, Schloss Johannisberg, Nov 2000* ★★★★

**Elysium** (Rg) **Breuer** Bernhard Breuer is nothing if not enterprising and innovative. Grape variety not revealed! Aged *en barrique*, presented in a clear glass Bordeaux-type half bottle. Yellow-gold; strange nose reminding me of table tennis balls and marker pens; better on the palate, very sweet, very creamy, good acidity. Good try Bernie! *May 1996* ★★?

**Erbacher Marcobrunn Riesling Auslese** (Rg) **Schloss Reinhartshausen** Amber-gold; violet scented clover honey; medium-sweet, rich, crisp acidity. Excellent with *Vacherin* cheese. *At the Schloss, Nov 1995* ★★★★

**Erbacher Marcobrunn Riesling TBA** (Rg) **Schloss Reinhartshausen** 180° Oechsle, 170g/l residual sugar, acidity 15g/l. A heavily botrytised wine tasted twice. Virtually identical notes. First at Schloss Reinhartshausen in 1995: orange-gold; rich, raisiny; very sweet, rich yet not at all cloying, fabulous acidity. *Last noted, a bottle from my own cellar, at Ronald Holden's dinner at Brooks's Club, April 1999* ★★★★

**Erdener Prälat Riesling Spätlese** (M) **Vereinigte Hospitien** Very pale; youthful, peachy, medium-dry, light, very good acidity. Delicious. *June 1990* ★★★★

**Erdener Prälat Riesling Auslese** (M) **Christoffel-Berres** 96° Oechsle, 11% alcohol: floral, honeycomb, kerosene Riesling; delicious fruit and acidity. *Noted at a pre-sale tasting, Oct 1997* ★★★★

**Erdener Treppchen Riesling Auslese** (M) **Dr Loosen** Pale; flowery, 'greengages'; fairly sweet, soft and rich (9% alcohol). The young master's (Ernie's) touch. *At the St James's Branch IWFS tasting, May 1998* ★★★

**Forster Pechstein Riesling Eiswein** (P) **Mossbacherhof** Gold; fragrant, lime; pineapple, grapefruit and honey flavour. Excellent acidity. *Noted at the VDP pre-sale tasting, Munich, Sept 1997* ★★★★

**Hattenheimer Engelmannsberg Riesling Auslese** (Rg)
**Balthasar Ress** Bright gold; kerosene Riesling, honey and lavender; fairly sweet, over 50g/l sugar. Clean and fresh. *At the 'Riesling Gala', Kloster Eberbach, Nov 1997* ★★★

**Hattenheimer Nussbrunnen Riesling Auslese** (Rg)
**Balthasar Ress** First tasted in 1994 with Stefan Ress: rich, honeyed. Just five months later, lunching with Freddie Price: an amazing colour, deep yellow-gold; bouquet almost overpowering after it had opened up; good consistency and richness. More recently: orange-gold; very exotic beeswax bouquet; a touch of hardness and a bit short. Stefan Ress said that it was his most difficult vintage, the worst for 20 years, and that the wine would probably soften with five to seven years more bottle-ageing. *Last noted at the Falken Press dinner at Robert Weil's, April 1998* ★★★★ *Now–2010.*

**Hochheimer Hölle Riesling Auslese** (Rg) **Aschrott** First tasted in June 1994: bouquet of *feinste Auslese* quality; earthier than the '90. Great power and length. 'Needs time'. Three months later: very rich, very honeyed nose and taste. Dry finish. *At the Aschrott press tasting at Christie's, Sept 1994* ★★★★ *Probably peaking now.*

**Hochheimer Hölle Riesling Auslese** (Rg) **Künstler** 112° Oechsle, 9.9g/l acidity, 10.5% alcohol. Two notes: first at a pre-sale tasting in London, the next a month later. Pure nine-carat gold; rich honey and grapes; powerful. Curious endtaste. *Last noted Sept 1997* ★★★

**Hochheimer Reichestal Riesling Eiswein** (Rg) **Künstler** Perfect gold; distinctive, harmonious, minerally, *fraises des bois*; sweet, refined, perfect length and acidity. *At the VDP auction tasting, May 1996* ★★★★★

**Johannisberger Klaus Riesling Auslese** (Rg) **v Hessen** Winner of a DLG *Grosser Preis*. Glorious buttercup yellow; sweet, 'warm' caramelly; fairly sweet, rich, alcohol 10%, lovely flavour but lacking vivacity. *Elevenses, May 1997* ★★★

**Johannisberger Klaus Riesling TBA** (Rg) **v Hessen** Colour of golden syrup and taste almost to match. Intense. Raisiny. *At the VDP pre-sale tasting, Nov 1995* ★★★★

**Kaseler Kehrnagel Riesling BA** (M) **v Kesselstatt** Classic; not as sweet as expected. A bit short. *At a British Airways blind tasting for First Class dessert wines. April 1996* ★★

**Kloster Eberbach Riesling BA** (Rg) **Staatsweingüt** Deep orange gold; low-keyed; fairly sweet, tangy. At £1000 per dozen rather too costly for the British Airways budget. Not worth it anyway. *April 1996* ★★★

**Kreuznacher Krötenpfuhl Riesling Auslese** (N)
**P Anheuser** Perfect for our elevenses at Chippenham Lodge. An amazing colour; heavenly bouquet; full flavoured, glorious fruit and acidity. More recently: 'honey and roses'; ripe. Lovely. *Last tasted June 1997* ★★★★

**Mülheimer Helenenkloster Riesling Eiswein** (M) **Max Ferd. Richter** Deserving its gold prize. Sweet, glorious flavour, excellent acidity. *A half bottle to wind up a 'light lunch' with Janet and Freddie Price, Oct 1994* ★★★★★ *Will still be delicious.*

**Münsterer Königsschloss Scheurebe TBA** (N)
**M Schäfer** Deep rich amber; fabulous, creamy; very sweet, rich essence of grapes, very good acidity. *Highest mark of the 26 sweet wines British Airways blind tasting, April 1996* ★★★★★

**Oberhäuser Brücke Riesling BA** (N) **Dönnhoff** Half bottles: warm orange-gold; singed, toasted, raisiny nose, opening up fragrantly; intensely rich and sweet, full-bodied, creamy texture, lovely aftertaste. Great wine from an equally great but modest producer. *At the Welt-Raritäten tasting at Schloss Johannisberg, Nov 2000* ★★★★★

**Oppenheimer Kreuz Silvaner Eiswein** (Rh) **Guntrum** Clearly *not* Riesling; disappointing, almond kernels, loose end acidity. *Half bottle at home, Dec 1995* ★

**Roxheimer Höllenpfad Riesling Auslese** (N) **Paul Anheuser** Positive yellow; little nose; rich, yet drier than expected, fairly substantial. *At the Prices', Oct 1994* ★★

**Rüdesheimer Berg Rottland Riesling Auslese** (Rg) **Nägler** Two notes at VDP pre-auction tastings. Assertive, firm, touch of hardness. Needed bottle age. *Last noted May 1996* ★★?

**Rüdesheimer Berg Rottland Riesling TBA** (Rg) **Breuer** The best wine at the 'The year of the '9s' dinner: bright and beautiful; floral, glorious, honeyed 'face powder'; a mammoth, tangy wine. Excellent with cheese. *At Christie's, Feb 2000* ★★★★★

**Rüdesheimer Berg Schlossberg Riesling Auslese** (Rg) **v Schönborn** Glorious lime and orange blossom nose; good, rich, grapey, fair acidity. *Dec 1996* ★★★ *Probably peaking now.*

**Rüdesheimer Berg Schlossberg Riesling BA** (Rg) **v Schönborn** Rich gold; glorious lychee scent; sweet, wonderful consistency, texture, concentration. *At the VDP pre-auction tasting, May 1996* ★★★★

**Salm-Dalberg BA** (N) Assumed to be Riesling. An attractive, ripe half bottle. *Winding up an informal lunch at Schloss Wallhausen, Nov 1996* ★★★

**Scharzhofberger Riesling BA** (M) **v Kesselstatt** Pure lemon gold; classic, honey, botrytis, not too sweet, lovely flavour. And excellent Saar acidity. *April 1996* ★★★★

**Steinberger Riesling Auslese** (Rg) **Staatsweingut** Two notes the same day, first at the VDP pre-auction tasting: lovely. Late – too late – that evening at the Steinberg dinner: rich, gold; fragrant; medium-sweet, beautiful flavour and acidity. It would have gone well with the gorgonzola mascarpone tart, but we left as I had to be fit for the auction the following day. *Last noted at the Kronen Schlösschen, Erbach, Nov 1994* ★★★★

**Wallufer Walkenberg Riesling Auslese** (Rg) **Jost** Fresh, minty; sweet, delicious. *At the VDP auction, Nov 1994* ★★★★

**Wawerner Herrenberger Riesling Eiswein** (M) **Dr Fischer** Spicy, grapey aroma; incredibly sweet yet with a deft touch, power and acidity. *June 1990* ★★★★(★★) *Will still be good.*

**Wehlener Sonnenuhr Riesling Auslese** (M) **J J Prüm** Outstandingly the best of a very good 1980s' Auslesen 'flight': ripe, peachy bouquet and flavour. Lively acidity, lovely wine. *At the Weinart/Prüm vertical tasting, Austria, April 1999* ★★★★★

**Wehlener Sonnenuhr Riesling Auslese** (M) **S A Prüm** Medium-pale; very distinctive, very fragrant, slightly peachy nose; medium-dry, crisp, good flavour and length, dry finish. Needs time. *April 1990* ★★(★★)

**Wehlener Sonnenuhr Riesling BA** (M) **J J Prüm** Surprisingly pale; rich but minerally, unknit; very sweet, fat, luscious with rich 'kerosene' finish. *At the Weinart/Prüm tasting, April 1996* ★★★★★

**Wehlener Sonnenuhr Riesling BA** (M) **S A Prüm** 135° Oechsle, 7.5 acidity, 9% alcohol. Tuthankhamun gold; creamy, slightly minty, honeyed; deliciously sweet, creamy, fabulous flesh and length. *At a pre-sale tasting, London, Oct 1997* ★★★★

**Wehlener Sonnenuhr Riesling TBA** (M) **J J Prüm** Surprisingly pale; floral, minty; sweet yet not overpowering. Lovely. *The oldest vintage and the last lot of the 54-lot, five and a half hour Grosser Ring auction and, at DM1250 per bottle, the highest price in the sale. In Trier, Sept 1997* ★★★★★

**Winkeler Hasensprung Riesling Auslese** (Rg) **v Hessen** Three notes, before and during 'The Wines of Germany' weekend. Oechsle 124°, residual sugar 87.5g/l, acidity 12.25g/l, alcohol 10%. Fermented in old oak barrels, short ageing in stainless steel tanks. Quite deep yellow-gold; orange blossom, dried sultanas, peachy; not as sweet or hefty as expected. Dry finish. *At Banff Springs, Canada, Oct 1998* ★★★★

**Winkeler Jesuitengarten Riesling BA** (Rg) **v Hessen** Rich, raisiny; not as sweet as expected. High acidity. *At the VDP auction tasting, Nov 1996* ★★★

OTHER '89S TASTED IN THE EARLY 1990S **Bernkasteler Doktor Riesling Auslese** (M) **Thanisch** the best *Fuder* (cask). Incredibly rich, ripe, honeyed nose; sweet, great length. Prior to 1971 this would, have been sold as *feinste Auslese* but, thanks to the restrictive wine laws, it can only be sold as Auslese, so this cask is kept for special friends and customers! ★★★★(★); **Casteller Kugelspiel Rieslaner Auslese** (F) **Castell** delicate, honeyed nose; medium sweetness and body, lovely flavour, length and aftertaste ★★★★; **Dalberger Schlossberg Riesling Spätlese** (N) **Salm-Dalberg** immature, peachy, hint of the characteristic Nahe fruit salad nose; medium-dry, flavoury, acidic ★★(★); **Eitelsbacher Karthäuserhofberg Riesling Kabinett** (M) **Rautenstrauch** lovely, delicate bouquet; very dry, fragrant, delicious upturned end of acidity ★★★(★); **Eitelsbacher Karthäuserhofberg Riesling Auslese** (M) **Christoph Tyrell** virtually colourless but will doubtless deepen with bottle age; youthful, grapey, almost Sauvignon Blanc, like 'tom-cats'; medium-dry, surprisingly mild, easy and attractive but, I thought, lacking length ★★★; **Erdener Prälat Riesling Spätlese** (M) **Vereinigte Hospitien** very pale; youthful, peachy; medium-dry, light, very good acidity. Delicious ★★★★; **Oppenheimer Sackträger Silvaner Auslese** (Rh) **Guntrum** another example of a wine that would have been a *feinste Auslese*, had this been permitted: distinctly yellow hue; gloriously rich, honeyed; fabulous flavour, length, toffee-like aftertaste ★★★(★); **Oppenheimer Sackträger Riesling TBA** (Rh) **Guntrum** yellow-gold; most extraordinary nose, spicy, honeyed; great sweetness balanced by high acidity, marvellous concentration, length and aftertaste. And precisely ten times the price of the Auslese! ★★★★(★); **Scharzhofberger Riesling Kabinett** (M) **Egon Müller** virtually colourless; broad, peachy, grassy nose and flavour. Dry ★★(★); **Scharzhofberger Riesling Spätlese** (M) **Egon Müller** pale; peachy, considerable depth; dry, good flavour and length ★★★(★); **Scharzhofberger Riesling Auslese** (M) **Egon Müller** distinct yellow tinge; equally distinctive spicy nose; very rich, honeyed botrytis ★★★(★); **Scharzhofberger Riesling Spätlese** (M) **v Hövel** light, light, grapey nose. Medium-dry, fresh as a daisy, good length ★★★; **Scharzhofberger Riesling Auslese** (M) **Vereinigte Hospitien** sulphury nose; fairly sweet, rich, good length and acidity ★★★(★); **Wehlener Sonnenuhr Riesling Spätlese** (M) **J J Prüm** light, crisp, attractive ★★★; **Wehlener Sonnenuhr Auslese** (M) **Dr Loosen** almost colourless; lovely grapey, peachy nose and taste, medium-sweet, excellent acidity, length, aftertaste. My style of Mosel ★★★★; **Wiltinger Braune Kupp Riesling Spätlese** (M) **Egon Müller** broad, powerful, peachy nose and flavour. Good acidity. Good future ★★(★★); **Wiltinger Hölle Riesling Spätlese** (M) **Vereinigte Hospitien** the Hölle vineyard is wholly owned. Very pale; fresh, light, grapey, touch of youthful pineapple; medium-dry, light weight and style, still a bit hard ★★(★); and **Wiltinger Hölle Riesling Auslese** (M) **Vereinigte Hospitien** pale; surprisingly earthy; medium-sweet, fuller-bodied, very pleasant grapey flavour and nice length ★★★(★)

# 1990–1999

The first thing to say about this period is that growers in Germany were fortunate; on the whole, weather conditions were more favourable than in France; even when the rains came, the growers coped remarkably well.

The market did not fully reflect the quality of wines being made and there seemed to be no end to the demand for sugar and water wines which, in some instances, were not really German at all but EU table wine made from rather neutral Italian white wines spiced up, as it were, by a sprinkling of acidic German wine and marketed in traditional flute bottles with fancy labels and German names. Nevertheless, strenuous efforts were made to improve quality and standing by members of the VDP representing the serious producers and major estates in each region.

One of the ways the VDP Rheingau tackled the problem of image was to introduce an 'international' element. An opportunity arose in 1994 when I was invited to take over as auctioneer, with his blessing, from Baron von Oetinger, the 'von Karajan' of the German wine auction world – a charming old gentleman whom I had first met at one of the big VDP auctions in 1969, and who, in 1994, was well beyond retiring age. The first sale 'in association with Christie's' took place in the historic Kloster Eberbach that autumn. To be frank, the 700-strong audience who were there to taste a large array of wines and enjoy the show did not appreciate an Englishman in a morning coat sporting a carnation; I was not helped by the intransigence of the *Weinkommissäre* (brokers) who had been accustomed to a monopoly of bidding, or the young lady from Christie's Frankfurt office who kindly helped me with numbers – lot numbers, bid steps and bidder numbers – but failed to translate my pleasantries! It was reported that I had no sense of humour...

It was then sensibly decided to split the big young-vintage auction from the smaller fine and rare wine element, so the following November, the first of the VDP/Christie's *Raritäten Versteigerung* was held in more intimate surroundings, with German wine collectors, and bidding from Christie's clients overseas, at Schloss Reinhartshausen. Happily, my relations with the brokers had improved by the time the really big VDP auction took place in Wiesbaden in 1999. The best of the VDP producers from all the major German wine regions took part submitting rarities from their cellars; and all sat in two long ranks behind the auctioneer. I was flanked by an old friend, Professor Dr Leo Gros (despite his formidable title, a man with a great sense of humour), and, on my left, Eberhard von Kunow, the regular Grosser Ring auctioneer from Trier. The whole event was hosted by another good friend, the VDP President, Michael Prinz zu Salm-Salm. Perhaps all this sounds like a lot of puff, but it demonstrated the conscious efforts of the great German estates to make their presence – and the quality of their wines – better known, and to counteract the effects of the flood of cheap imitations which had so undermined their reputation and market. It certainly engendered a good deal of excellent publicity.

## 1990–1999 *Vintages at a Glance*
**Outstanding ★★★★★**

1990, 1993 (v)

**Very Good ★★★★**

1992 (v), 1994 (v), 1995 (v), 1996 (v), 1997, 1998, 1999

**Good ★★★**

1991 (v)

## 1990 ★★★★★

The third good vintage in a row, but totally different to 1989 in several respects. First of all a much smaller crop, below the 10-year average, but firmer, many of the major estates having the highest sugar/acid levels but little botrytis.

Another mild winter and early growth. Well-nigh perfect spring. Flowering early in the Mosel, followed by a hot dry summer, later in Rheinhessen, and some heavy rain. Rather like 1976 in England, the hot summer abruptly ended with serious rain at the end of August, followed by a cool wet September, and rot. The surviving crop benefited from sun and warmth in late September and October. Another classic Riesling vintage, at best the finest wines since 1971.

**Bernkasteler Doctor Riesling Auslese Christ-Eiswein** (M) **Thanisch** Loose cork. Too deep and caramelly yet very rich, with good acidity. Should have been better. *May 1998* ★★
**Bernkasteler Johannisbrünnchen Riesling Eiswein** (M) **J J Prüm** New to me: rich lemon-gold; minty, complete, needs time; sweet, lean, crisp yet lissom fleshiness. A fraction sticky and with youthful bite. *April 1999* ★★★(★)
**Brauneberger Juffer Riesling Auslese** (M) **Richter** Silver medal in 1991. Waxy sheen; grapey nose, minty undertone; medium-sweet, alcohol 8%, good fruit and acidity. Excellent value (bought from Freddie Price for £11.27 including tax). I noted 'perfect spring/summer mid-morning/late morning/teatime'! *In fact, much enjoyed at our elevenses at Chippenham Lodge, April 1995* ★★★★
**Brauneberger Juffer Sonnenuhr Riesling Auslese** (M) **F Haag** Deep, harmonious, rich, complete. Sweet finish. *At Schloss Lieser, May 2000* ★★★ *Fully mature.*
**Burg Ravensburger Dicker Franz Schwarzriesling Spätlese trocken** (B) **Burg-Ravensburg-Freihe** 94° Oechsle, 13% alcohol. What a mouthful (the name, not the wine). Colour of Morello cherry, browning; cherry again on nose; alcoholic; some residual sugar, attractive, clean, dry, acidic end. *Pre-sale tasting, London, Oct 1997* ★★★ *Ready now.*

**Eitelsbacher Karthäuserhofberg Riesling Auslese Nr. 23** (M) **Christoph Tyrell** Nr 23 (no longer the *Fuder* number. Tank number!). First tasted in 1993 on board MV *France* from Strasbourg to Frankfurt: lovely fruit and acidity. Eighteen months later: still very fresh, grapey acidity; fairly sweet, light (9%), glorious flavour. *Last tasted lunching with the Prices, Oct 1994* ★★★★

**Erbacher Marcobrunn Riesling Spätlese Blaukapsel** (Rg) **v Simmern** Old-fashioned, slightly spicy; medium-dry, positive, good finish. *At the VDP pre-sale tasting, Nov 1999* ★★ *Drink up.*

**Erbacher Marcobrunn Riesling BA** (Rg) **v Simmern** Deep, rich, minty, lime blossom; very sweet and fleshy, creamy texture. *At Schloss Johannisberg, Nov 2000* ★★★★★

**Erbacher Marcobrunn Riesling TBA** (Rg) **v Schönborn** Fairly deep amber; very rich bouquet and flavour. Fragrant, great depth. Sweet, powerful, very good acidity and aftertaste. *At Welt-Raritätenprobe, Rheingau, Nov 2000* ★★★★★ *Long life.*

**Erbacher Schlossberg Riesling Auslese** (Rg) **Schloss Reinhartshausen** Prinz von Preussen labels (appropriately Prussian blue) but not living up to Princely expectations. *At the Riesling Gala, Kloster Eberbach, Nov 1997* ★

**Grosskarlbacher Burgweg Scheurebe Auslese** (P) **K & L Lingenfelder** Glorious colour; more honey than Scheugrapiness; medium-sweet, soft, fragrant but disappointing finish – doubtless the grape, it does not have the class of a Riesling. *April 1993* ★★ *then, probably tiring now.*

**Hattenheimer Wisselbrunnen Riesling Auslese** (Rg) **Schloss Reinhartshausen** Lovely wine, classic sweetness balanced by acidity. *Lunch with August Kesseler, Oct 1999* ★★★★ *Perfect now.*

**Hochheimer Domdechaney Riesling Spätlese** (Rg) **Werner** Unusual for me to have tasted so many Hochheimers of such a good vintage, from an area at the eastern end of the Rheingau proper, with a character all of its own, rich, perhaps more earthy. Domdechaney is the top vineyard site, Hölle 'half a point behind' and the Kirchenstück good, but more varied. The Spätlese had a good colour, very fragrant, grapey, ripe melon nose; medium-dry, slightly earthy flavour, not as beguiling as the nose. *At the estate, Nov 1996. Then* ★★★ *Probably peaking now.*

**Hochheimer Domdechaney Riesling Auslese** (Rg) **Aschrott** A gold prize winner first tasted at the estate in 1994. The deepest of the three Auslesen; rich, honeyed; sweet, soft, harmonious, creamy, great length, 7.5% alcohol. A lovely wine. Potential now realised. *Last noted at elevenses, Chippenham Lodge, Sept 2001* ★★★★

**Hochheimer Domdechaney Riesling Auslese** (Rg) **Werner** Fairly distinctive style; botrytis, honey; fairly sweet, perfect weight (7.5%) and acidity. Honeyed aftertaste. *At the estate, Nov 1996* ★★★★ *Should be perfect now.*

**Hochheimer Domdechaney Kirchenstück TBA** (Rg) **Schloss Schönborn** Golden; smoky, tea-like, concentrated grapes; very sweet, fat, lovely, shapely. *With Paul von Schönborn and Günter Thies in the 500-year old cellar, Hattenheim, Nov 1997* ★★★★★ *Will keep.*

**Hochheimer Hölle Riesling Auslese** (Rg) **Aschrott** Gold medal, 1991. Five notes, first at the estate in 1994: green-gold; rich, creamy nose and flavour, assertive, very good acidity. 'Good future'. The next four notes made at elevenses at Chippenham Lodge in 1995; hard honeycomb edge, 'will keep', in 1997 and 1998. Consistently good notes: very sweet, fat, lovely. The perfect mid-morning drink. *Last tasted March 1998* ★★★★ *Will continue.*

**Hochheimer Hölle Riesling Auslese** (Rg) **Künstler** Surprisingly deep yellow-gold; rich, honeyed bouquet and flavour, excellent acidity. *At the VDP pre-sale tasting at Schloss Johannisberg in the Rheingau, Nov 1999* ★★★★

**Hochheimer Kirchenstück Riesling Auslese** (Rg) **Aschrott** Silver prize medal 1991. Five notes, first at the estate in 1994: a really lovely wine, sweet, soft, smooth, elegant (7.5% alcohol). Later at an Aschrott press tasting: greengages/ gooseberry acidity noted. Later, having bought some at Christie's, consumed after the theatre and as elevenses. Consistently enjoyable. *Last tasted Oct 1995* ★★★★

**Hochheimer Riesling TBA** (Rg) **v Schönborn** In fact 50-50 from the estate's Domdechaney and Kirchenstück sites, presumably because not enough was produced to sell separately. A highly successful, much be-medalled wine. Oechsle 176°, residual sugar 240g/l, acidity 8.6g/l, alcohol 7%. Three notes before and during the 'Taste of Germany' weekend. Yellow-gold; peach-like, minty, honey and acidity; very sweet, plump around the waist, delicious. *At Banff Springs, Canada, Oct 1998* ★★★★★

**Johannisberger Klaus Riesling TBA** (Rg) **v Hessen** Orange-gold; extraordinary, singed *crème caramel* nose; very sweet, very rich, very high acidity. *At the Raritäten Weinversteigerung Vorprobe at Schloss Johannisberg, Nov 1999* ★★★★★

**Kiedricher Gräfenberg Riesling Auslese Goldkapsel** (Rg) **Robert Weil** Pale, with a tartrate deposit; crisp, honeyed; fairly sweet, lovely flavour, elegant, good length. A typical Weil style. *At the Rheingauer Giganta dinner, Nov 1995* ★★★(★★)

**Kiedricher Sandgrub Riesling Auslese** (Rg) **zu Knyphausen** Four notes, the first two at VDP pre-sale tastings in 1996. Fairly pale, perfect weight and flavour. The last two at Giganta Riesling dinner at the Krone, Assmannshausen, opening up in 1997. Most recently: piquant, orange blossom and lime; lovely grapes, flavour, delicious and easy drinking. *Last tasted Nov 1999* ★★★★ *Drink soon.*

**Maximin Grünhäuser Riesling Spätlese** (M) **v Schubert** Pale; scented, flowery; medium-dry, alcohol 9%, pleasing fruit and acidity. *Pre-dinner tasting, IWFS St James's Branch, May 1998* ★★★ *Charming and as good as it will ever be.*

**Oppenheimer Herrenberg Silvaner Eiswein** (Rh) **Guntrum** Grapes picked 19 January 1991. Yellow; rich, raisiny, honeyed; very sweet, alcohol 10%. Gloriously penetrating flavour, good acidity. *July 1992. Then* ★★★(★) *Drink soon.*

**Rauenthaler Nonnenberg Riesling Charta** (Rg) **Breuer** The first wine made by Georg Breuer from the exclusive 5-ha vineyard purchased in 1990 and first tasted in 1993. Positive, slightly earthy and spicy, firm and dry. Next, labelled *Spätlese Charta Wein*: delicate, fragrant nose; a really good dry wine, alcohol 11.5%, excellent acidity, good length. *Last tasted at Christie's Wine Dinner at the Übersee Club, Hamburg, June 1997* ★★★

**Rüdesheimer Bischofsberg Riesling BA** (Rg) **Breuer** As if to show Georg Breuer's competence with a more traditional, sweet wine: golden colour; rich, peachy, refreshing bouquet; excellent acidity. *At the tutored tasting of some of the best VDP wines I had auctioned. At the Krone, Assmannshausen, Nov 1998* ★★★★

**Scharzhofberger Riesling Spätlese** (M) **Egon Müller** Two notes, first at the *Alles über Wein* Millennium Gala and, coincidentally served the following evening at the Müllers'. Surprisingly fresh and youthful for a ten-year-old Spätlese thanks to the combination of good vintage and winemaker. *Last noted at the Scharzhof, May 2000* ★★★ *But drink soon.*

**Wallhäuser Mühlenberg Grauer Burgunder Eiswein**
(N) **Salm-Dalberg** Very unusual nose: roses, stewed apples; very sweet, richly textured. Needs bottle age. *June 1991. Then ★★(★★) Probably peaking now.*

**Wehlener Sonnenuhr Riesling Spätlese** (M) **J J Prüm**
The best of an unimpressive 'flight' of Spätlesen ('90s to '95s). The most fragrant and sweetest, with rich, ripe fruit though Stuart Pigott thought it had closed up and needed more time. *At the Weinart/Prüm tasting, April 1999 ★★★ Now–2005.*

**Wehlener Sonnenuhr Riesling Auslese** (M) **J J Prüm**
Interesting to taste this alongside the Spätlesen, all with 7.5% alcohol. Sweeter, more earthy and acidic. *April 1999 ★★★(★) Should develop further.*

**Wehlener Sonnenuhr Riesling Auslese Goldkapsel** (M)
**J J Prüm** Harmonious, honeyed botrytis; fairly sweet, rich, mouthfilling, complete. *April 1999 ★★★★ Now–2010.*

**Wehlener Sonnenuhr Riesling Auslese lange Goldkapsel** (M) **J J Prüm** First tasted in 1993, glorious peach-like flavour. The ultimate Auslese, equivalent to a lesser estate's Beerenauslese. Two close notes. A beautiful waxy-sheened lemon-gold; nose like a great creamy Montrachet; extraordinary flavour. Firm. Crisp. Good length. At the masterclass, perhaps my expectations were too high, but it was hemmed in by two superb Dr Weil wines. *Last tasted Sept 1999 making allowances ★★★(★) Now–2010.*

**Wiltinger Braune Kupp Riesling Auslese** (M) **Egon Müller** Very pale, lime-tinged; medium-sweet, light, pleasing. *At a pre-sale tasting, Geneva, May 1999 ★★★ Drink soon.*

**Winkeler Hasensprung Riesling Spätlese trocken** (Rg)
**Querbach** I am not quite sure what to make of Wilfred Querbach. This particular wine is relatively straightforward: fairly complex, ripe nose; swingeingly dry. Demands food. But I wonder? *At a pre-sale tasting, Nov 1999 ★★ 'Suck it and see'.*

OTHER '90s TASTED IN THE 1990s **Dorsheimer Goldloch Riesling Auslese** (N) **Diel** touch of yellow; lovely honeyed bouquet; medium-dry, nice weight and balance. Positive and attractive. My style of wine! *April 1993 ★★★(★)*; **Eltviller Kalbspflicht Riesling Auslese** (Rg) **Belz** pale; curious white currant, lime, acidic nose; good firm grapey flavour. Acidity high but masked. *At the VDP pre-auction, May 1996 ★★★*; **Eltviller Kalbspflicht Riesling Auslese** (Rg) **Belz** very pale; nose also very acidic, 'tom-cats'; drier than expected, though fragrant. *Sept 1996 ★★★ just*; **Erdener Treppchen Riesling Spätlese** (M) **Dr Loosen** a very agreeable, light (alcohol 8%) luncheon wine. *In Hastings, Aug 1995 ★★★ then, probably tired by now*; **Forster Pechstein Riesling BA** (P) **v Bühl** hazy; ripe, deep, rich, grapey, with gooseberry-like acidity; very sweet, Pfalz fat, 11% alcohol, lovely acidity. *At Chippenham Lodge, Nov 1998 ★★★★★*; **Iphofer Kalb Scheurebe TBA** (F) **Wirsching** very sweet and fleshy, yet with a hard finish. *April 1993 ★★★(★★)*; **Niersteiner Hipping Riesling Spätlese** (Rh) **Reinhold Senfter** from six-year-old vines: a very attractive, flowery aroma and taste. Rich and spicy. I was informed that young vines are more flowery, old vines have more depth – which is logical. *April 1993 ★★★(★)*; **Ockfener Bockstein Riesling BA** (M) **Dr Fischer** full, evolved nose; open knit. Not as sweet as expected. *At the Grosser Ring tasting, June 1996 ★★★ but no more*; **Piesporter Goldtröpfchen Riesling Auslese** (M) **v Kesselstatt** attractive. Lovely fruit and acidity, which is, I suppose, enough. *Dining with the Bourgeois family in Hammersmith, Nov 1994 ★★★ drink up*; and **Rüdesheimer**

**Bischofsberg Riesling BA** (Rg) **Staatsweingut** yellow gold; lively, forthcoming, privet-like nose and flavour. Considerable sweetness and intensity. *At the VDP pre-sale tasting, May 1996 ★★★★(★) Now–2015.*

## 1991 ★★ to ★★★

A mild winter and good start to the spring, rudely interrupted by a severe frost on 20 April and another a week later. The third hammer blow of frost was on 4 June. Despite this, the flowering was successful. Summer was long, hot and sunny. The much needed rain did not arrive until the latter part of September, dampening the harvest prospects.

Frankly, a far from great vintage. The lesser, drier wines were pleasant enough but, by and large, should have been consumed while young and fresh. One or two outstanding wines made by some estates. Pick and choose carefully.

**Erbacher Hohenrain Riesling Eiswein** (Rg) **v Oetinger** Heavenly. Almost too sweet. Remarkable, zestful flavour. *At the Krone Schlösschen, Erbach, Nov 1994 ★★★★*

**Essinger Osterberg Scheurebe Eiswein** (P) **W Frey** Extraordinary, high-toned, intense, exciting but 'green' bouquet; sweet, light style but some flesh. A touch too raw and acidic. *At a Rodenstock weekend, Munich, Sept 1996 ★★*

**Hattenheimer Hassel Riesling Eiswein** (Rg) **H Lang** Oechsle 165°, residual sugar 237g/l, total acidity 12.5g/l, alcohol 8.3%. First pre-tasted in London, noting its teeth-gripping acidity, then at the 'Just Desserts' session in Banff, presented by Gabriele Lang: bright yellow; minerally, harmonious, peachy; an astonishing taste, refined honey and 'lip licking' acidity. *Last noted Oct 1998 ★★★★★*

**Hochheimer Kirchenstück Riesling Auslese** (Rg) **Aschrott** First tasted in June 1994: creamy, lovely flavour and style (7% alcohol). Three months later: fully evolved, noted as sticky yet crisp which is contradictory. But I liked it. *Last noted Sept 1994 ★★★ Probably at peak now.*

**Hochheimer Kirchenstück Riesling Eiswein** (Rg) **Aschrott** Grapes picked 21 December. 162g/l residual sugar, 7% alcohol. Two notes in 1994, first at the estate in June, next at Christie's. Happily consistent notes: surprisingly pale; minty, grassy, 'milk chocolate'; without its excellent acidity its almost sickly sweetness would have been intolerable. More recently, almost Sauvignon Blanc-like nose; lovely grapey flavour, its high acidity coping well with strawberries and cream. *Last noted picnicking in the car park at Royal Ascot, June 1996 ★★★*

**Schloss Johannisberger Riesling Blaulack Eiswein** (Rg) Bright yellow; curious meaty, minty, then wet straw; very sweet, interesting but rustic. Creamy. Good acidity but tailed off. *At the 900th anniversary tasting, at the Schloss, Nov 2001 ★★★*

**Scharzhofberger Riesling Auslese Goldkapsel** (M) **Egon Müller** The equivalent to a *feinste Auslese* pre-1971. Pale; gorgeous, peachy, honeyed, Beerenauslese-like; sweet, honey and grapes, perfect balance. *June 1992. Then ★★★(★) Will be fully developed now.*

**Schloss Vollrads Riesling Eiswein Goldkapsel** (Rg) Pale; honeyed orange blossom; lovely flavour, extremely high acidity. *At the VDP pre-sale tasting, Schloss Johannisberg, Nov 1999 ★★★*

## 1992 ★★ to ★★★★

Swings and roundabouts due, as always, to the constraints of the weather. It started off favourably with a pleasant spring followed by a summer which, though hot, was plagued by rain and humidity – a combination that causes growers to worry about rot. Weather conditions from early October enabled the harvest to proceed satisfactorily but this was rudely interrupted by ten days of rain from the 20th. Those who waited managed to produce some great wines in the Auslese to TBA range. It was also a very successful year for Eiseweins.

**Bischoffinger Rosenkranz Ruländer TBA** (B)
**W G Bischoffinger** Just to demonstrate what a major Baden Co-operative can do. Oechsle 205°, residual sugar 230g/l, total acidity 11.6g/l. Two notes prior to and at the German wine weekend in Banff. A most astonishing colour, pure topaz with apple-green rim; raisiny, like a 6-putt Tokaji Aszú plus a touch of malt; treacle-sweet verging on unctuous, but creamy and with life-saving acidity. *In Canada, Oct 1998* ★★★★★

**Brauneberger Juffer-Sonnenuhr Riesling Auslese** (M)
**Willi Haag** Pale; minty; medium-sweet, grapey, acidic. *May 1999* ★★

**Casteller Kugelspiel Silvaner Riesling Auslese** (F) **Fürst Castell** Gold; caramel cream; rich but not sweet, alcohol 12.5%, high acidity for Silvaner. *At Castell, July 1997* ★★ *Might have softened and evolved by now.*

**Eitelsbacher Karthäuserhofberg Riesling Spätlese** (M)
**Tyrell** Tasted when young. I found the aroma better out of a claret glass though Riedel's German wine glass worked perfectly on the palate, bringing out the flavour and tingling Ruwer acidity. *August 1994* ★★★ *Probably at peak now.*

**Erbacher Marcobrunn Riesling Spätlese** (Rg) **Schloss Reinhartshausen** Over 60g/l sugar. It is said that 'young Marcobrunn puts sweetness into the left pocket' (!?). Grapey; powerful mid-palate, very dry though not acidic. Perfect with cheese. *Dining at the Schloss, Nov 1997* ★★ *Drink soon.*

**Erbacher Marcobrunn Riesling BA** (Rg) **Schloss Reinhartshausen** 330g/l sugar, 7% alcohol. Two notes, first at an auction pre-tasting in 1996. Relatively pale; crisp, fragrant, 'needs time'; very sweet, almost syrupy, glorious flesh. A similar subsequent note except colour deepening, fat and 'flesh' noted again. *Last tasted Oct 1999* ★★★(★)

**Erbacher Michelmark Riesling TBA** (Rg) **zu Knyphausen** Fabulous. But great? *At the VDP auction tasting, Nov 1994* ★★★★ *Probably getting up steam now.*

**Erbacher Siegelsberg Riesling TBA** (Rg) **Schloss Reinhartshausen** Siegelsberg is not a great site but 'it works in all years'. Oechsle 180°; alcohol 8%. Tremendously high extract even without the residual sugar and only 90 litres of the wine produced. Amazing colour, orange-gold; harmonious, honeyed; enormously sweet and concentrated, swingeingly high acidity. Endless life. *Dining at the Schloss, Nov 1997* ★★★★★

**Forster Jesuitengarten Riesling BA** (P) **v Bühl** This is a large, 50-ha, privately owned estate leased out. I first met von Bühl himself at the big Fine Wine auction in Wiesbaden in 1969: he epitomised the wine, hefty, imposing, Wagnerian Germanic with a glimpse of Prussia. At the time of my visit it was being run by an enterprising American, Michael Hiller, who improved and livened up the estate. This must have been one of Hiller's wines. Still a youthful yellow; lovely honey and lime bouquet and taste. Sweet, fleshy, good length. *At one of our country house weekend elevenses, Jan 2000* ★★★★★ *Lots of life.*

**Hattenheimer Wisselbrunnen Riesling Auslese** (Rg)
**Schloss Reinhartshausen** 120g/l residual sugar, 12g/l acidity, alcohol 9%. Two notes within two days, first at the dinner at the Schloss, co-hosted by Jochen Becker-Kuhn and August Kesseler, with another August ('September') Winkler, who was also at the annual Giganten wine dinner where he brilliantly

commented on the wines. Palish yellow-gold; delicate, fragrant; rich, stylish, perfect tingling acidity. *Last noted Nov 1997* ★★★★★ *Should be at peak now.*

**Hattenheimer Wisselbrunnen Riesling Auslese** (Rg)
**zu Knyphausen** Goldene Preismünze 1993. Fairly sweet, hefty style, rich, grapey, good acidity. *Easter Monday elevenses at Chippenham Lodge, April 1998* ★★★

**Hattenheimer Wisselbrunnen Riesling Auslese Goldkapsel** (Rg) **zu Knyphausen** Pure yellow-gold; pure honey; medium-sweet, good fruit and acidity. Fragrant, charming but needed time. *At the Krone, Assmannshausen, Nov 1996* ★★★(★)

**Hochheimer Kirchenstück Riesling Auslese** (Rg)
**Werner** Extraordinary surging aroma of freshly peeled grapes; a touch of apricot on nose and flavour, substantial yet not heavy. Lacking length. *At the Domdechant Werner estate, Nov 1996* ★★★ *Probably peaking now.*

**Hochheimer Reichestal Riesling Auslese** (Rg) **Künstler** When Stuart Pigott published his outspoken *Life Beyond Liebfraumilch* in 1988, Künstler did not even appear in the index. Then Günter Künstler started to make a name for the brilliant detail of his winemaking, of which this is a lovely example. Though not tasted recently, it should be delicious now. *At the VDP auction tasting, Kloster Eberbach, Nov 1994* ★★★★

**Hochheimer Stielweg Spätburgunder Weissherbst Eiswein** (Rg) **Aschrott** Picked 27 December. Residual sugar 135g/l, alcohol 8%. First tasted at Christie's in 1994: quite a mouthful in every respect. Yellow-gold; richly honeyed; exciting acidity coping with its sweetness and richness. A year later, coincidentally tasted not long before the old English-owned Aschrott estate was acquired by Künstler. Delicious, muscatelle-like grapiness. *Last tasted at a caviar supper at our flat in London, Oct 1995* ★★★★

**Kiedricher Gräfenberg Riesling Auslese Goldkapsel** (Rg) **Robert Weil** Wilhelm Weil joined the family firm in 1987, but this was the first year he had total responsibility for the estate. Not a bad start! Only 300 bottles produced. Oechsle 143°. Gloriously rich amber-gold; youthful, peppery, spicy privet; sweet, marvellous flesh and texture, perfect acidity. '20 years of life'. *With Wilhelm Weil, May 1996* ★★★★(★)

**Kiedricher Gräfenberg Riesling BA Goldkapsel** (Rg)
**Robert Weil** Wilhelm Weil informed me that his Goldkapsel level wines were kept back for the VDP auctions. Amber-gold; lime and orange blossom; very sweet, fat, power and beauty combined. Delicious. *The last wine served at the 'Rheingauer Giganta' dinner, Assmannshausen, Nov 1996* ★★★★★

**Mussbacher Eselshaut Rieslaner Auslese** (P) **Müller-Catoir** Palish; youthful, honeyed; a medium-sweet, rich, assertive and spicy wine. Clearly a low yield, high quality producer. *April 1993* ★★(★★) *Doubtless now at its peak.*

**Niederhäuser Hermannshöhle Riesling Auslese** (N)
**Dönnhoff** Another gifted winemaker. First, a bottle given to me by a former colleague and German wine expert, John Boys, which my wife and I consumed in 1995, mid-morning (and the morning after) with great pleasure. Lovely flavour, though not as exciting as its heavenly peach blossom nose. A good but somewhat less eulogistic note – no Nahe 'fruit salad'. Very reasonably priced like so many German wines of this quality. *Last noted at Walter Siegel's centenary tasting in London, March 1997* ★★★

**Oppenheimer Sackträger Gewürztraminer TBA** (Rh)
**Guntrum** Nothing like a good ripe Gewürztraminer for instant appeal. It was not exactly subtle but, in fact, striking:

extraordinary colour, deep orange-amber; raisiny nose coated with caramel and chocolate; concentrated *crème brûlée*. Tokaji-like finish. *Went very well with summer strawberries, at Chippenham Lodge, June 1999* ★★★★

**Oppenheimer Herrenberg Scheurebe TBA** (Rh) **Guntrum** Another bit of exotica from Hajo Guntrum, this time like dried apricots, touch of caramel. Sweet of course. *One of ten fabulous wines served by my son at dinner in San Francisco. I had no idea he had such a good cellar, March 1998* ★★★

**Randersackerer Pfülben Rieslaner TBA** (F) **Juliusspital** Somewhat like the Hospices de Beaune, the Juliusspital is an ancient charitable foundation in the middle of Würzburg, gifted with huge vineyard holdings: 160ha. Rieslaner is very much a Franken grape variety, as is Silvaner, very acidic but a perfect foil for this TBA: Oechsle 254°, 'the highest ever must weight in Germany'. Yellow-gold, orange tinge; fantastically sweet, rich, fat. A new experience. *With Horst Kolesch, the director, July 1997* ★★★★★

**Rauenthaler Nonnenberg Riesling Erstes Gewächs** (Rg) **Breuer** Very pale, dry, austere but fragrant. Alcohol 12%. Very well made and so much better than most *trocken* wines. *Magnum at a Falken Press tasting at Robert Weil's, April 1998* ★★★ *Drink soon.*

**Ruppertsberger Reiterpfad Scheurebe BA** (P) **v Bühl** The combination of grapey Scheurebe and Eiswein at its exotic best, its surging scents a *mélange* of apricots, honey, mint, grapefruit; a 'sweet and sour' flavour. Lovely. *Lunch at Chippenham Lodge with Christopher Burr, May 1998* ★★★★★

**Spätburgunder Rotwein BA** (Rh) **Senfter** No village or vineyard named. Most unusual wine, indeed unique for me. Made from botrytised Pinot Noir, its high sugar content fully fermented out, resulting in a bone-dry red wine with an astonishing 16% alcohol. Warm amber, very little red; slightly malty, prune-like nose; full-bodied, of course. Well, interesting. *Produced for my book launch in a bookshop in Russelheim, April 1998* ★★ *for originality.*

**Steinberger Riesling Eiswein** (Rg) **Staatsweingut** Very pale; gooseberry-like aroma and acidity. Sweet of course (the Spätlese *trocken* was similarly scented but bitterly dry – went well with sweetbreads). *At the Staatsweingüter auction tasting, Kloster Eberbach, Nov 1994* ★★★

**Ungsteiner Bettelhaus Rieslaner TBA** (P) **Kurt Darting** Hard, youthful, slightly sulphury nose; a lovely, very sweet, fat wine with counter-balancing crisp acidity. *At the Hyde Park Hotel, London, April 1993* ★★(★★) *Should be lovely now.*

**Volkacher Karthäuser Weisser Burgunder BA** (F) **Juliusspital** Pinot Blanc. Yellow-gold; lovely, honeyed; fairly sweet, powerful (alcohol 15%), straw-like flavour, very dry finish. *At the hospital in Würzburg, July 1997* ★★★★

**Wachenheimer Rechbächel Riesling TBA** (P) **Bürklin-Wolf** Yellow-gold; glorious aroma and flavour, very sweet despite no *Edelfäule*. Low acidity. Only 60 half bottles produced! *At the Hyde Park Hotel, London, April 1993* ★★★★★ *A Botticelli angel which will be a voluptuous Venus now.*

**Wehlener Sonnenuhr Riesling Spätlese** (M) **J J Prüm** Very pale; little nose; lacking acidity. *At the Weinart/Prüm tasting, Austria, April 1999* ★

**Wehlener Sonnenuhr Riesling Auslese** (M) **J J Prüm** Also very pale; low-keyed; medium-sweet, soft, broader more grapey flavour than the Spätlese. *April 1999* ★★ *Drink soon.*

**Wehlener Sonnenuhr Riesling Auslese Goldkapsel** (M) **J J Prüm** First noted at the Weinart vertical in 1999. One bottle corked, the other: straw colour, mint; light style, some

charm. Nice now. What a difference one year and a different context makes. Still very pale but with lively and lovely nose and flavour. Medium-sweet. Light. Fragrant aftertaste. *Last noted at a Bacchus Society dinner at the superb Zur Traube, Grevenbröich, May 2000* ★★★★ *Drink soon.*

**Winkeler Hasensprung Riesling Eiswein** (Rg) **v Hessen** Picked 30 December. First noted three years after the vintage at a *Rheingauer Giganta* dinner: palish, very bright; delicious, touch of fat, orange blossom and lime. Five years later: still fairly pale ; fragrant, caramelly nose; fairly sweet, rich, with a hard dry finish. *Last noted at Schloss Johannisberg, Nov 2000* ★★★★

## 1993 ★★★★ to ★★★★★

Overall a very good vintage with some outstanding wines produced despite variable weather. The growing season started well, a warm spring leading to an unusually advanced flowering. The summer was very mixed: drought, cool, rainy conditions varying from region to region. There was seriously heavy rain in September and early October when picking started, albeit cautiously. As always in this situation, the better, well-drained, sites and well-managed estates, exercising strict selection, were able to make wines which varied from good to great. Elimination of less than healthy grapes is time-consuming and expensive; and the producer has less to sell. Minor wines should have been drunk by now. The higher quality wines can be a revelation.

**Assmannshäuser Höllenberg Spätburgunder Spätlese** '(★★★)' (Rg) **A Kesseler** Despite being flushed with influenza, August took me to his cellar to taste a range of the Pinot Noirs for which he is rightly famed. This was his late-picked '3-star' wine: lovely deep ruby with rich 'legs'; distinct Pinot Noir varietal character; dry, crisp, considerable depth and length, needing bottle age. *On a cold November evening, 1995* ★(★★★) *Should be very good now.*

**Brauneberger Juffer-Sonnenuhr Riesling BA** (M) **Fritz Haag** Pale; minty, with sharp, gooseberry-like nose, sweet, light style but elegant and with tingling acidity. *The first of Hugh Johnson's 'luxurious' sweet wines at a Hallwag presentation, Frankfurt, Sept 1997* ★★★

**Erbacher Marcobrunn Riesling Spätlese** (Rg) **v Simmern** Rich, spicy nose and flavour. Rather an old-fashioned style. (Alcohol 10%). Touch of almonds on the finish. *April 1998* ★★★ *But drink soon.*

**Hattenheimer Nussbrunnen Riesling Auslese** (Rg) **Balthasar Ress** Two very similar notes exactly a year apart, both as elevenses at Chippenham Lodge: waxy melon yellow; lovely pineapple and greengage fragrance; fairly, but not too, sweet, fairly rich, less acidic than its nose indicated (10% alcohol). Perfect for mid-morning sipping. *Last noted May 2000* ★★★ *Now–2008.*

**Kiedricher Gräfenberg Riesling Auslese** (Rg) **Robert Weil** First tasted at a VDP auction tasting in 1994 and merely noted as 'very very good'. Most recently: glorious gold; still fresh and young; sweet, rich yet light (alcohol 8.5%), ripe botrytis, excellent acidity. Beautiful. Will keep well. Also a perfect weekend mid-morning drink – or at any other time. *At Chippenham Lodge, June 1999* ★★★★ *Now–2010.*

**Kiedricher Gräfenberg Riesling BA Goldkapsel** (Rg) **Robert Weil** A superb wine: Oechsle 186°, 250g/l sugar, 12g/l acidity, alcohol 8.5%. First tasted in 1994, next with Wilhelm Weil in 1996: glorious yellow-gold; minty, spicy, honeyed privet; tremendously rich, full and fat. Then twice in 1998, first ending the Falken press dinner at Robert Weil's, next, six days later, the last of 13 superb wines at a tasting I conducted for *Vinum* magazine. Sheer perfection. *Last noted in Zürich, April 1998* ★★★★★

**Kreuznacher Kahlenberg Riesling Auslese** (N) **Paul Anheuser** One of my favourite wines in my retail days. This '93 had a characteristic peachy fruit salad nose but lacked a little zest. *At the Grosser Ring tasting, June 1996* ★★★ *(just).*

**Lieser Niederberg Helden Riesling Auslese** (M) **Schloss Lieser** Very pale, green-tinged; crisp, fresh, slightly raw gooseberry nose; medium-sweet, light (alcohol 7.5%), refreshing but short. Fritz Haag's son, Thomas, now runs the estate. *At the Schloss, May 2000* ★★

**Lieserer Niederberg-Helden** (M) **Kuntz** An elegant half bottle prominently labelled *Sybille Kuntz Riesling Auslese halb trocken* – clearly a sort of cult wine: very pale; very light (little) aroma; very light style though 11% alcohol. Mild, pure, very acidic – in fact very everything. Definitely better with food. *Dec 1994* ★★ *Should have been drunk by now.*

**Nackenheimer Rothenberg Riesling Auslese** (Rh) **Gunderloch** What a good producer. Preceded by his excellent, fairly dry Spätlese, the Auslese was only slightly sweeter, but firm, lovely, and with a good future. *At Walter Siegel's centenary tasting in London, March 1997* ★★★

**Oberemmeler Hütte Riesling Auslese** (M) **v Hövel** Delicious sweetness, weight, flavour and Saar acidity. Despite its youthfulness, lovely. *At one of the annual Grosser Ring tastings where you get not only delightful wines to taste but a regular opportunity to meet all the vineyard owners, June 1996* ★★★★ *Should be lovely now.*

**Oppenheimer Herrenberg Riesling Auslese** (Rh) **Guntrum** Hajo Guntrum is an old friend and my son is his US importer, so it was appropriate that both my notes were made accompanying Bartholomew's promotional tours. The first note was made in Jackson, Mississippi. The wine was lovely by itself but also a brilliant accompaniment to salmon wrapped in rice paper with a (peppery) citrus vinegrette (*sic*). Next at another joint presentation of (his) 'Broadbent Selections': I thought it very good value at around $12. *Last tasted at the first (and last) Palm Beach International Wine & Food Fair, Dec 1998* ★★★

**Piesporter Goldtröpfchen Riesling Auslese** (M) **Reinhold Haart** The main label 'Reinhold Haart Riesling Auslese', the village and vineyard name, and 'VDP' in support. The real thing, not a cheap sugar-and-water Piesporter: medium-sweet, light (alcohol 7.5%), grapey, slight *spritz*. *St Valentine's Day elevenses with, of course, my wife, Feb 1998* ★★★

**Rüdesheimer Berg Rottland Riesling TBA** (Rg) **Balthasar Ress** Not at elevenses but a half bottle produced at tea time by Stefan Ress: yellow; crisp, honeyed, slightly grassy; sweet, rich, slightly 'oily' Riesling, mouthfilling, good length. *The best tea in Germany. Sept 1995* ★★★

**Rüdesheimer Berg Schlossberg Spätburgunder** (Rg) **Kesseler** Straying from Assmannshausen, where Kesseler is based. A 100 litres of this wine made from stressed (no water), ten-year-old vines; bottled in April 1995. Bramble-like flavour and spicy oak. *In August Kesseler's cellars, Nov 1995* ★(★★★)

**Rüdesheimer Bischofsberg Riesling TBA** (Rg) **Breuer** Lots 465–472 in my first VDP auction in the long refectory at Kloster Eberbach. Every one of the 700 people attending tasted each of the 42 wines before I lifted my gavel. I could only make brief notes: 'very rich, lovely acidity'. *Nov 1994* ★★★★★ *Lovely but then too young. Will last 15–20 years.*

**Scharzhofberger Riesling BA** (M) **Egon Müller** The 53rd of 54 wines tasted during the Grosser Ring auction in Trier. It was exactly 6pm, the sale having started at 1pm. Slow by Christie's standards but the lots were either very big or very high priced: this was over DM1000 a bottle. Well worth it, say I. Yellow; nose shy at first, then deep, peachy, with lovely botrytis; sweet, rich yet elegant, with glorious flavour and perfect acidity. *In Trier, Sept 1997* ★★★★★

**Schloss Schönborn Riesling TBA** (Rg) **Schloss Schönborn** The last of 12 white wines, French versus German, at a tasting I conducted for the Duke and his friends in the middle of a music festival at Pommersfelden, the Schönborn's palace in the middle of nowhere; their idea of a country cottage! Lovely wine: pale gold; raisins, honey and lime blossom, very sweet of course (Oechsle 157°, residual sugar 194g/l, acidity 7.1g/l, alcohol 8.5%). Only 300 litres made. A snip at DM250 a half bottle. *July 1997* ★★★★★

**Steinberger Riesling Auslese** (Rg) **Staatsweingut** The Steinberg vineyard is the Ch Lafite of the Rheingau. A quick taste of youthful perfection, scented, spicy, good future. *At the estate's HQ in Eltville, Nov 1994* ★★★★

**Wehlener Nonnenberg Riesling Auslese Goldkapsel** (M) **S A Prüm** A brave attempt to make a superior wine from not a top site: touch of kernels; distinctive, curious. *Sept 1997* ★

**Wehlener Sonnenuhr Riesling Spätlese** (M) **J J Prüm** Only 7% alcohol. Touch of sweetness. Attractive. *At the Weinart/Prüm tasting in Austria, April 1999* ★★ *Drink up.*

**Wehlener Sonnenuhr Riesling Auslese** (M) **J J Prüm** slight *spritz*; lime, metallic; light, crisp, good acidity. *April 1999* ★★ *Drink soon.*

**Wehlener Sonnenuhr Riesling Auslese Goldkapsel** (M) **J J Prüm** A heavier, meatier style than the '92 or '95; 'slightly Wagnerian', overall drier. *At the Weinart/Prüm tasting, April 1999* ★★ *Drink soon.*

**Wehlener Sonnenuhr Riesling lange Goldkapsel** (M) **J J Prüm** Honeyed; sweet and far richer, fatter, 'broader', than the Goldkapsel. Dry finish. *April 1999* ★★★ *Now–2005.*

**Wiltinger Braune Kupp Riesling BA** (M) **Le Gallais** Owned by Egon Müller: ripe, floral; fairly sweet, lovely, fragrant, dry finish. Lot 51 – which sold at the rate of DM390 per bottle at the Grosser Ring auction. *In Trier, Sept 1997* ★★★★

# 1994 ★★★ to ★★★★

A top class Riesling vintage.

Winter and spring were mild and fairly wet. Both budding and flowering were early; the grapes' potential further enhanced by a warm summer. The crop was large and healthy, perhaps too large for some estates who decided to green prune. Not for the first time, rain in all regions throughout September was heavy, but not disastrously so. Warm, misty weather proved ideal for the development of botrytis, enabling a large quantity of wines of Spätlese quality and above to be made. It is perhaps worth reiterating that in wet weather the flatter, lower-lying land planted with early-maturing vines like Müller-Thurgau does not have the advantage of the well-drained slopes planted with the later-ripening Rieslings.

As always, the minor wines should have been drunk by now but some superb high-quality sweet wines are reaching full maturity and many still have more years in hand.

**Assmannshäuser Höllenberg Spätburgunder Weissherbst Spätlese '★★★'** (Rg) **Kesseler** August Kesseler is the unquestioned genius of the district. The Pinot Noir, in this instance, pressed quickly to separate the (white) juice from the (red) skins. Weissherbst is, strictly speaking, rosé: pale and polished; youthful fruit; long, dry finish. High acidity. *At Kesseler's, Nov 1995* ★★★ *for early drinking.*

**Assmannshäuser Höllenberg Spätburgunder Weissherbst BA** (Rg) **A Kesseler** Picking began on 12 September for Auslesen and Beerenauslese, bunches being separated, even divided, dependant on the quality and ripeness of the grapes. Very pale; fragrant, like mature apples; very sweet (Oechsle 198°) but crisp, glorious. *At Kesseler's, Nov 1995* ★★★★ *Probably at peak now.*

**Assmannshäuser Höllenberg Spätburgunder Weissherbst TBA** (Rg) **A Kesseler** Grapes picked five days later than the Auslesen and Beerenauslesen. Pale; very fragrant, peachy; very sweet (Oechsle 200°), rich but lissom, heavenly fragrance. *At Kesseler's, Nov 1995* ★★★★★

**Brauneberger Juffer-Sonnenuhr Riesling Auslese** (M) **F Haag** Wilhelm Haag, arguably the top producer of the middle Mosel, showed his fairly dry Spätlese, the Auslese being richer, with perfect acidity. *At the Grosser Ring tasting, London, June 1995 – both* ★★★, *the former at peak, the latter now–2006.*

**Brauneberger Juffer-Sonnenuhr Riesling Auslese** (M) **W Haag** Easy to confuse the Haags. This is Willi's wine. His Spätlese I found too lean and acidic, the Auslese richer, with crisp fruit. *June 1995* ★★★ *(Auslese). Probably at best now.*

**Brauneberger Juffer-Sonnenuhr Riesling BA** (M) **F Haag** Oechsle 160°, alcohol less than 7%. First noted at a Grosser Ring tasting in 1997: palish; lovely, minty, floral nose; sweet, lovely fruit, lip-licking acidity. After six years, slightly more colour; glorious bouquet and flavour. Fleshy, with perfectly ripe fruit and acidity. A very successful year for Fritz Haag. *Last noted at Schloss Lieser, May 2000* ★★★★ *Now–2015.*

**Eitelsbacher Karthäuserhofberg Riesling Auslese** (M) **Tyrell** Christoph Tyrell also showed his Spätlese and Auslese the June after the vintage. Both with very acidic Ruwer character, the Spätlese very steely, the Auslese somewhat richer. Far too raw and young. *June 1995* ★★★? *Auslese hopefully softened by now.*

**Erbacher Steinmorgen Riesling Auslese** (Rg) **zu Knyphausen** It is hard for me to criticise a wine made by one of the most charming gentleman in the Rheingau, and an ex-VDP President but I didn't much like this wine: odd flavour of kernels and marzipan. *At the VDP tasting, Sept 1997* ★

**Erdener Prälat Riesling Auslese** (M) **Dr Loosen** From one of the Middle Mosel's geniuses, a lovely, rich wine with good length and future. *June 1995* ★★★★ *Say now–2010.*

**Erdener Treppchen Riesling Auslese** (M) **Dr Loosen** Ernst Loosen produced one of the best Spätlesen at the opening tasting in 1995. His Auslese tasted nine months later was simply delicious, faultless. *Hosting a dinner for my agent, Bob Lescher, at Montrachet, New York, Feb 1996* ★★★★ *Will still be lovely.*

**Forster Jesuitengarten Riesling Auslese** (P) **v Bühl** A typically ripe fleshy Pfalz wine. *An agreeable prelude to Les Arts du Vin exhibition organised by the enlightened Crédit Commercial de Belgique bank, Brussels, Nov 1995* ★★★★

**Forster Ungeheuer Riesling TBA** (P) **v Bühl** An amazing colour, orange-amber; glorious, celestial raisins; incredibly sweet, concentrated, almost overpowering – yet it lacked the charm and fragrance of the preceding 1990 Vouvray Moelleux. *At a memorable dinner at De Bijgaarden, Brussels, Jan 1996* ★★★★

**Fürst Spätburgunder Spätlese** (F) **Rudolf Fürst** Paul Fürst has an excellent reputation in Franken. A soft Pinot Noir colour; very sweet, strawberry-like aroma and flavour. Normal red wine weight (alcohol 13%), and fairly marked acidity. Good in its way but not to my taste. *Lunch at Chippenham Lodge, July 1999* ★★

**Geisenheimer Mäuerchen Riesling BA** (Rg) **Allendorf** Orange-amber; low-keyed; sweet, assertive, touch of peach kernels, good acidity and aftertaste. *At the Rheingauer Giganta dinner at the Krone, Assmannshausen, Nov 2000* ★★★

**Hallgartener Schönhell Riesling BA** (Rg) **Hans Lang** Oechsle 154°, residual sugar 170g/l, acidity 10.5g/l, alcohol 8.5%. Pale gold; floral, forthcoming mint and cress; sweet but lean and attenuated finish. *At a tasting of leading VDP auction wines at Kloster Eberbach, Nov 1998* ★★★ *Now–2010.*

**Hattenheimer Wisselbrunnen Riesling Spätlese** (Rg) **Hans Lang** Classic kerosene Riesling; medium-dry, alcohol 10%, very distinctive flavour and fragrant aftertaste. *May 2000* ★★★ *Drink soon.*

**Hochheimer Domdechaney Riesling Auslese** (Rg) **Werner** Fragrant, lime, floral, privet; fairly sweet, ripe fleshy fruit, lovely flavour and length. (I was glad to note that a well-known St James's Street wine merchant had ordered it.) *At the estate, Nov 1996* ★★★★ *Drink now–2010.*

**Hochheimer Hölle Riesling BA** (Rg) **Künstler** A brilliant wine: pale, lovely, a light-honey BA richness; glorious flavour, crisp acidity, earthy Hochheim aftertaste. *The last of 15 wines at the Rheingauer Giganta dinner, at the Krone, Assmannshausen, Nov 1997* ★★★★

**August Kesseler Riesling Spätlese '★★'** (Rg) **August Kesseler** One of the Rheingau's most brilliant winemakers. A glorious wine, perfect with ragout of calf's head. *This was our first meeting, dining in the Schlosskeller at Reinhartshausen, Nov 1995* ★★★

**Lieser Niederberg Helden Riesling Auslese** (M) **Schloss Lieser** Low-keyed, grapey; medium-sweet but rich flavour and finish. *At the Schloss, May 2000* ★★★

**Monzinger Frühlingsplätzchen Riesling Auslese Goldkapsel** (N) **Emrich-Schönleber** A 250-year-old estate which in the early 1990s sprang into the limelight thanks to the brilliant grape-growing and winemaking talents of Werner Schönleber. The unfamiliar names of the village, to the far west of the Nahe, and of his principal vineyard must be something of a handicap. Considered a great vintage in the Nahe, the '94 has the wonderful, fragrant 'fruit salad' nose and taste that greatly appeals to me. Wonderful flesh and acidity. *At the Welt-Raritätenprobe at Schloss Johannisberg, Nov 2000* ★★★★ *Long life.*

---

## Weingut Robert Weil and the VDP

*Though founded by Dr Robert Weil in 1875, the wines of this estate have really only shot into prominence over the past dozen or so years. Apart from the lovely wines, the estate is visually striking with its extraordinary Victorian villa built by an English aristocrat who also renovated the old church in Kiedrich, and the broad expanse of the Gräfenberg vineyard on the opposite side of the valley. The estate is run by – to me, young – Wilhelm Weil, currently President of the VDP Rheingau, the oldest of Germany's regional associations of leading wine estates. My connection with the VDP goes back to 1994 when I was invited to take over as auctioneer at the VDP sales being organised to promote wines from the great German estates. I shall be conducting this year's VDP Raritäten Weinversteigerung at the time this book (I hope) hits the shelves! And I will not be surprised if Weil's wines once again achieve record prices.*

**Niederhäuser Hermannsberg Riesling TBA** (N) **Staatsweingut** Astonishing richness and power. 267° Oechsle, 400g/l sugar, 108g/l residual. Amber-gold. Whereas the nose struggled to emerge, though refined, there was a positive assault on the palate. Amazingly sweet and rich. *The last wine at the Welt-Raritätenprobe, Schloss Johannisberg, Nov 2000* ★★★★★

**Niederhäuser Hermannshöhle Riesling Auslese** (N) **Dönnhoff** Another top Nahe 'fruit salad' maker. Delicious. *Presented for The Star group at Christie's, June 1999* ★★★

**Oberemmeler Hütte Riesling Auslese** (M) **v Hövel** Rich, grapey; medium-sweet, very attractive flavour, with pleasingly tingling Saar acidity. (Eberhard von Kunow's Spätlese also good.) *At the opening Grosser Ring tasting in London, June 1995. Should be perfect now* ★★★★

**Ockfener Bockstein Riesling Spätlese** (M) **Dr Fischer** Scented; light but with attractive flesh and fruit. *June 1995* ★★★ *Probably at peak now.*

**Ockfener Bockstein Riesling Auslese** (M) **Dr Fischer** Sweeter, richer, touch of fat, good finish. *June 1995* ★★★ *Now–2010.*

**Oestricher Doosberg Riesling Spätlese** (Rg) **August Eser** Pale; minerally; medium-dry, crisp fruit. Curiously, much more attractive than his bone-dry '90. *At the VDP pre-sale tasting, Nov 1999* ★★★ *By itself or with food.*

**Randersackerer Marsberg Rieslaner TBA** (F) **Staatlicher Hofkeller** A remarkable chance meeting with Dr Rowald Hepp, who had spotted me sketching outside the magnificent Residenz in Würzburg. He kindly opened the spectacular vaulted cellars for me and arranged an impromptu tasting. We ended with this wine: Oechsle 222°, a long, cool fermentation used for the first time. Grapes individually picked in late October and early November, and then sorted again: apple gold; fabulous bouquet, deeply honeyed, apricots and *crème brûlée* with flavour to match. Only 6% alcohol. *In Würzburg, July 1997* ★★★★★

**Rauenthaler Nonnenberg Riesling** (Rg) **Breuer** It is not easy to make a dry Riesling which is interesting and totally satisfying; nor does a wine of quality have to be on the sweet QmP ladder (Auslesen, etc.). The genius of Bernhard Breuer is to bridge this gap. One of four '94 dry wines from different villages, tasted blind. Dry, long, distinctive. *Nov 1996* ★★★

**Ruppertsberger Reiterpfad Riesling Auslese** (P) **H Giessen** I do not normally soak off labels, but this had such an attractive drawing of the Giessen house that I stuck it in my tasting book. Rather a hefty Pfalz, ripe, touch of almond kernels. Not great but perfectly agreeable as one of our weekend elevenses drinks. *At Chippenham Lodge, May 2000* ★★

**Ruppertsberger Reiterpfad Scheurebe TBA** (P) **v Bühl** Viscous orange-amber; strange, citrus-like high acidity; alcohol only 6% but the sweetest, fattest, most grapey wine I can recall, the Scheurebe giving it a peculiar sweaty, gooseberry-like flavour. Highly impressive but ... *At De Bijgaarden, Brussels, Jan 1996* ★★★★

**Saarburger Rausch Riesling Spätlese** (M) **Geltz-Zilliken** Restrained, peachy; 'chewy', pasty acidity. *At the Grosser Ring tasting, London, June 1995. Then* ★★ *Drink up.*

**Saarburger Rausch Riesling Auslese Goldkapsel** (M) **Geltz-Zilliken** Not as rich as expected. Very acidic. *June 1995* ★★ *The acidity should preserve and develop the wine. Hard to predict.*

**Saarburger Rausch Riesling BA** (M) **Geltz-Zilliken** Surprisingly pale but still youthful of course; sweet, creamy yet with hard acid edge. Needed time. *Sept 1997* ★★★ *Probably still opening up.*

**Scharzhofberger Riesling Spätlese** (M) **Egon Müller** Youthful apples and peaches; medium-sweet, crisp, very acidic. *June 1995* ★★ *Probably at best now.*

**Scharzhofberger Riesling Auslese Goldkapsel** (M) **Egon Müller** Excellent honeyed botrytis nose, sweet, rich, fabulous flavour and future. *June 1995* ★★★★ *Now–2010.*

**Scharzhofberger Riesling BA** (M) **Egon Müller** Beautiful golden colour; scent of privet and gooseberry; incredibly sweet, glorious flavour and flesh, high acidity. The Müllers informed us that this had been the highest must weight ever in BA and even TBA – so concentrated that no sulphur was needed. It was entered for the important Grosser Ring auction in Trier that autumn and realised DM2300. *With the Bacchus Society, presenting the Müllers with the Distinguished Service Award, May 2000* ★★★(★) *to which I see I added a sixth star. At least a 30-year life span.*

**Schlossböckelheimer Felsenberg Riesling Auslese** (N) **Crusius** Pale, green-tinged; very good, grapey fragrance; ripe, earthy, powerful. *June 1995* ★★★ *Coming round now, good future.*

**Schlossgut Diel Riesling Auslese Goldkapsel** (N) **Diel** Oechsle 130°. Fabulous in its youth, lots of honeyed botrytis. *June 1995* ★★★(★) *Fully developed between 2004 and 2010.*

**Wehlener Sonnenuhr Riesling Spätlese** (M) **J J Prüm** Initially like any young white wine but more to it than at first sniff; attractive, light (8% alcohol), nice now. *At the Weinart/Prüm tasting in Austria, April 1999* ★★ *Drink soon.*

**Wehlener Sonnenuhr Riesling Auslese** (M) **J J Prüm** Pale; low-keyed, minerally; sweeter than the Spätlese, attractive but needs more time. *April 1999* ★★(★) *2003–2008.*

**Würzburger Abstleite Muskat Eiswein** (F) **Juliusspital** Extraordinary smell of cats, mint and mandarin; sweet, rich, lovely flavour and style. *With the Director, Horst Kalesch, July 1997* ★★★★

# 1995 ★★ to ★★★★

Another successful vintage – but mainly limited to later-picked Rieslings, though some decent QbA and Kabinett wines were made for early drinking.

All went well, with an almost idyllically warm summer, but September was depressingly wet with rot problems. Then the weather completely changed for the better, October being the warmest for ten years. Growers who, of necessity, picked early, sorting out their rain-sodden grapes did not do well, but those who waited until October, particularly in the Mosel-Saar-Ruwer, made some superlative wines.

**Brauneberger Juffer-Sonnenuhr Riesling Auslese** (M) **F Haag** Firm, peachy, drier than expected. Raw finish. Needs bottle age. *At the Grosser Ring tasting, London, June 1996* (★★★)

**Eitelsbacher Karthäuserhofberg Riesling Eiswein** (M) **Tyrell** Virtually colourless; there I go again – rich, peachy; sweet, light style, zinging Ruwer acidity, delicious. *At the Grosser Ring auction tasting, Trier, Sept 1997* ★★★★

**Erbacher Marcobrunn Riesling Spätlese** (Rg) **Schloss Reinhartshausen** Pleasant, peachy nose and flavour. Medium dryness and body, nice uplift. *At the Schloss, Nov 1997* ★★

**Erdener Prälat Riesling Auslese Goldkapsel** (M) **Dr Loosen** Late picked after a wet September, first tasted at the opening Grosser Ring tasting in June 1996: rich, fat and fragrant but touch of youthful hardness. Next only 14 months later and already gloriously developed, moving from 4 to 5 stars. Fairly sweet, peachy, perfection. *Last noted at elevenses at home, Aug 1997* ★★★★★ *Now–2015.*

**Erdener Treppchen Riesling Auslese** (M) **Dr Loosen** To demonstrate the versatility of this class of wine, totally delicious at two years of age, yet with the components to keep and develop for a further five to ten years. Delicate peaches and cream; medium-sweet, light (7.5% alcohol), lovely flavour, touch of *spritz*. *The perfect summer wine, at Chippenham Lodge, Aug 1997* ★★★★

**Freinsheimer Musikantenbuchel Scheurebe Auslese** (P) **Lingenfelder** Colour of brass; orange blossom; sweet peachy/tangerine flavour, body (alcohol 9%) and excellent acidity. I preferred the wine to its long mouthful of a name. *April 1999* ★★★

**Graacher Domprobst Riesling BA** (M) **Willi Schaefer** Don't be put off by a hackneyed label showing a monk leaning on a barrel holding a glass of wine. Schaefer has the reputation of making the best wine in Graach, partly because of his two outstanding vineyards of which Domprobst is one. He also happened to make a superb '95: pale yellow; honeyed' sweet, attractive flavour with 'hot' acidic end. Needs time. *Tasted at the Grosser Ring auction in Trier, Sept 1997* ★★★★ *(Fetched a high price).*

**Graacher Himmelreich Riesling Eiswein** (M) **S A Prüm** Rather boring to use the word peachy again, but that is what I note in so many ripe Mosel wines. Harmonious; good fruit and flesh. *July 1997* ★★★

**Hattenheimer Pfaffenberg Riesling Auslese** (Rg) **v Schönborn** Harvested 15 October. Oechsle 113°, residual sugar 71g/l, acidity 9.8g/l. A gold medal winner, and in a sensible 50cl bottle. Very nice too. *At Pommersfelden, July 1997* ★★★

**Schloss Johannisberger Riesling Rosagold (BA)** (Rg) Pure amber; very fragrant clover honey; fairly sweet, very acidic, a long taste in the mouth. Very good with St Felicien cheese. *Dining at the Schloss, Nov 2001* ★★(★) *2005–2020.*

**Johannisberger Vogelsang Riesling Auslese** (Rg) **Johannishof-Eser** Surprisingly pale; fresh, high-toned; delicate sweetness and crisp style. *At the Welt-Raritätenprobe, Munich, Nov 2000* ★★★

**Kiedricher Gräfenberg Riesling Auslese Nr 19** (Rg) **Robert Weil** How do they do it? Faultless, heavenly, fairly sweet but light, with lovely fruit and uplifting finish. *At Christie's in Los Angeles, Feb 1998* ★★★★★ *Will go on.*

**Maximin Grünhäuser Abtsberg Riesling Auslese** (M) **v Schubert** Instantly fragrant, kerosene grapiness; medium-sweet, light (alcohol 8.5%). Charming, with perfect Ruwer acidity. Based in the Ruwer Valley, this is one of Germany's greatest estates and which, I regret, I have not yet visited. *At dinner in San Francisco, Dec 2000* ★★★★ *Will keep.*

**Oberemmeler Hütte Riesling Eiswein** (M) **v Hövel** First noted at the opening Grosser Ring tasting in London in June 1996: crisp, lovely; its incredible richness counterbalanced by Saar acidity. Next, at the actual auction tasting. Its nose had opened up; sweet of course and a nice touch of fat. *Last tasted in Trier, Sept 1997* ★★★★

**Oberhäuser Brücke Riesling Auslese** (N) **Dönnhoff** Low keyed, peachy; medium-sweet, powerful. *At the Grosser Ring tasting, London, June 1996* ★★★ *Considerable potential.*

**Oberhäuser Brücke Riesling BA** (N) **Dönnhoff** First tasted at the opening Grosser Ring tasting; nose pure pineapple, very sweet, fat, assertive, fabulous aftertaste. Next, at a pre-concert supper: my favourite Nahe 'fruit salad'; sweet, fleshy but crisp. Delectable. *Last tasted May 1998* ★★★★ *Another 10–15 years in hand.*

**Ockfener Bockstein Riesling Auslese** (M) **Dr Fischer** Medium-sweet, assertive, firm acidity (his Spätlese had a steely, dry finish). *At the opening Grosser Ring tasting, June 1996* ★★★ *Good potential. Should be developing well now.*

**Piesporter Goldtröpfchen Riesling BA** (M) **Reinhold Haart** Lot 46 in the five-hour Grosser Ring tasting auction. Certainly not any old Piesporter 'golden drops'(*Goldtröpfchen*), but a strange undertone. Sweet, rich of course. A wine to keep. (The brokers paid DM250 a bottle for it.) *At the Grosser Wein auction in Trier, Sept 1997* ★★(★)?

**Rauenthaler Nonnenberg Riesling Erstes Gewächs** (Rg) **Breuer** At the first showing of first growth '95s, to be released in 1997 and previewed Breuers' 'the best of the three'; very pale; minerally, metallic nose, dry, crisp, stylish, good length. Next as a Charta wine, again better than three others. *Opening the Breuers' fine wine dinner, Rüdesheim, Nov 1997* ★★★ *Probably at best now.*

**Rüdesheimer Berg Roseneck Riesling Auslese** (Rg) **Allendorf** Scent like apples in a hayloft; medium-sweet, alcohol 10%, touch of peach kernels but fragrant. Teeth-gripping acidity. Needs more time. *Dining at Leo Gros's home in Johannisberg, Nov 1999* ★(★★)? *(Leo is my co-auctioneer.)*

**Rüdesheimer Berg Schlossberg Riesling BA** (Rg) **Hess'isches Staatsweingut** Very sweet, rich, assertive, very good flavour and acidity. *At the Rheingauer Giganta dinner, Nov 2000* ★★★(★)

**Saarburger Rausch Riesling Eiswein** (M) **Dr Wagner** Well known for his zestful dry white Saar wines, Heinz Wagner also produces outstanding sweet wines and this was one of his best vintages. Lot 45, in the Grosser Ring auction and a brief note made before it went under von Kunow's hammer. Not quite as sweet as expected but first rate. *In Trier, Sept 1997* ★★★★

**Scharzhofberger Riesling Auslese** (M) **v Hövel** A part of this famous vineyard slope owned by Eberhard von Kunow who is also the auctioneer at the important Grosser Ring sales. Not as sweet as expected. A bit hollow. *June 1996* ★(★)?

**Scharzhofberger Riesling Auslese Goldkapsel** (M) **Egon Müller** Surprisingly pale; peachy; firm and not as sweet as expected. Rich though and acidic. Needs time. *At the Grosser Ring tasting, London, June 1996* ★★(★★)?

**Schlossböckelheimer Felsenberg Riesling Auslese** (N) **Crusius** A very old estate based in Traisen, their famous Bastei vineyard being the jewel in the crown, though I have been disappointed with some earlier vintages. Under Peter Crusius, the 1995 vintage saw an improvement in quality and the Bastei Spätlese, though austere, was dry and spicy. This Auslese was very good, with an unusual flavour that I found hard to describe. *Both wines noted at the Grosser Ring tasting in London, June 1996* ★★★ *Both with good potential.*

**Schlossgut Diel Riesling Auslese Goldkapsel** (N) First tasted at the opening Grosser Ring tasting. Oechsle 115°, grapey aroma, lovely flavour, minty, dry finish. Later that autumn, Armin Diel explained that it was a 1200-litre *mélange*, partly from his Goldloch vineyard, partly Pittermännchen, having attempted to make an Eiswein. The mixture certainly worked Nahe 'fruit salad', medium-sweet, with a very dry acidic finish. *Last tasted at Schlossgut Diel, Nov 1996* ★★★

**Schlossgut Diel Riesling Eiswein** (N) Picked early (for an Eiswein), 5 November. Two notes, a month apart. At the June tasting very sweet, fleshy, lovely. Next, at home, surprisingly pale; herbaceous nose; quite a bit of fat and strange flavour like squashed fruit salad. Coincidentally, four months later, another half bottle, fat noted again but fruit salad less oppressed! *Last noted at Schlossgut Diel, Nov 1996* ★★★★

**Serriger Schloss Saarstein Riesling Eiswein** (M) **Schloss Saarstein** First noted at the opening VDP Mosel-Saar-Ruwer estates tasting in London, 1996. Picked 5 November in the middle of the harvest, their earliest Eiswein ever. Oechsle 140°: crisp, glorious. The wine was entered the following year for the big Grosser Ring auction: lot 44. Peachy; distinctive flavour, good fruit, some fat, high acidity. *Last tasted in Trier, Sept 1997* ★★★★ *Will keep.*

**Steinberger Riesling 'First Growth'** (Rg) **Staatsweingut** A dry style that takes some getting used to. This was closed, even the food failed to arouse it. *At the Rheingauer Giganten dinner, Nov 1996* (★)?

**Ürziger Würzgarten Riesling Eiswein** (M) **J J Christoffel-Erben** Virtually colourless; equally 'colourless' nose, perhaps slightly minty. But its sweetness, fruity-acid finish and flesh made up for it. It commanded a fairly good price: DM205 – ex-cellars to the trade. *At the Grosser Ring auction, Trier, Sept 1997* ★★★ *Will open up further.*

**Wehlener Sonnenuhr Riesling Spätlese** (M) **J J Prüm** Picked late October/early November. Pale; nose undeveloped; dry, light (8% alcohol). Manfred said it was too young to drink. *At the Weinart/Prüm tasting, April 1999* ★(★★)

**Wehlener Sonnenuhr Riesling Auslese** (M) **Dr Loosen** Totally and utterly delectable at the opening tasting (1996): marvellous, rich, mouthfilling, with peachy aftertaste (I gave it five stars). My next note made on a bottle I had bought from Loosen's importer: waxy yellow-green, touch of *spritz* which, in the mouth, gave the wine a delicious uplift. Crisp young honey and grapefruit nose; most agreeable fruit and flesh, perfect acidity, length and finish. How can anything like this be made from bunches of grapes grown outdoors! *Last enjoyed at Chippenham Lodge at 11.30am on Sunday, 26 Jan 1997* ★★★★★

**Wehlener Sonnenuhr Riesling Auslese** (M) **J J Prüm** The best of the '90 to '95 Auslesen at the tasting. A very pure statement. Greater depth and length than Spätlese. 8% alcohol. *At the Weinart/Prüm tasting, April 1999* ★★(★★) *2005–2012.*

**Wehlener Sonnenuhr Riesling Auslese Goldkapsel** (M) **J J Prüm** Two notes within five months. First at the vertical, April 1999, with three other Goldkapsels, '90, '92 and '93. Showing well: lovely, honeyed, harmonious nose; medium-sweet, very fragrant but quite a bite and uplifting *spritz*. Happily, an identical note at a Christie's masterclass. *Last noted Sept 1999* ★★★(★) *Now–2010.*

**Wehlener Sonnenuhr Riesling lange Goldkapsel** (M) **J J Prüm** Yellow-gold; hard, minty, complex; fairly sweet, peachy flavour, lovely acidity and finish. Years of life. *April 1999* ★★(★★)

**Wehlener Sonnenuhr Riesling BA** (M) **Studert Prüm** Low-keyed but creamy and harmonious; sweet, rich, ripe, with a rather fishy, oily Riesling finish. *At the Grosser Ring auction, Trier, Sept 1997* ★★ *Potentially higher, perhaps* ★★(★)

**Winkeler Hasensprung Riesling Auslese** (Rg) **v Hessen** A gold prize winner. Slightly higher alcohol than expected (10%), its richness and nice touch of fat cut by good acidity. *Mid-morning at Chippenham Lodge, Jan 1998* ★★★

# 1996 ★ to ★★★★

Unlike the previous few years, rain was not a problem – that is not quite accurate: the problem was no rain. It was an abnormally dry growing season. Cold led to uneven flowering

in June, July was warm and August variable, with some cold and hail. It was cool but sunny in September. By October the sugar was too low and acidity too high. Picking started in early October but those estates that waited benefited from a late Indian summer which happily reversed the sugar/acid ratios. The lesser quality wines picked early are of little interest now but some superb late-harvest wines were made.

It was at the invitation of Wilhelm Haag, the President of the VDP Grosser Ring, that I attended for the first time one of their highly important annual auctions in Trier, at which leading producers put up their best wines for sale; 32 of the 54 lots were the first offering of the '96 vintage. Apart from the wines, I wanted to see Eberhard von Kunow in action, as he was to be my assistant auctioneer at the big VDP auction I was to conduct in Wiesbaden. The auction took five hours because everyone in the packed saleroom was served a tasting sample of each wine, and the *commissaires* (the only bidders) bought huge parcels which they then shared with other brokers. It was a fascinating experience – but I only just managed to catch my flight home from Luxembourg. Incidentally, I asked why so many of these '96 Mosel-Saar-Ruwer wines were so colourless and was told by Herr Haag that it was because the grape skins were so healthy and untarnished.

**Bernkasteler Doctor Riesling Auslese lange Goldkapsel** (M) **Thanisch** The best of the Thanisch Doctors at the Grosser Ring auction, the Spätlese dry and lacking interest, the Auslese better (though it fetched the same price: DM47); the lange Goldkapsel warranting DM112 but no more. Sweetness and flesh and quite attractive. *Trier, Sept 1997* ★★★

**Blauer Spätburgunder 'SJ' Karl** (B) **K H Johner** 'Selection Johner'. Probably Karl Heinz's best-ever wine, certainly a great '96. The estate, in the Kaiserstuhl area, is unusual, in that the wine is never sold under vineyard names, hardly surprising as I read that the Johners have 93 patches of vines in seven vineyards. An attractive red; 'warm' chocolatey nose; sweet, delicious, slightly raspberry flavour with lovely oaky finish (also unusually, all Johner's wines are matured in small wooden barrels). *The first of 'The Wines of Germany' tasting at the German Embassy in London, June 1999* ★★★(★)

**Brauneberger Juffer Riesling Auslese lange Goldkapsel** (M) **W Haag** Grapey; assertive, good flavour, length and excellent acidity. *Lot 4 (sold for DM85 per bottle) at the Grosser Ring auction, Trier, Sept 1997* ★★★(★)

**Brauneberger Sonnenuhr Riesling Auslese Goldkapsel** (M) **F Haag** I would have been perfectly happy with this, had it not been for the next lot, the *lange Goldkapsel*. Grapey nose, depth; fairly sweet, lightish style, quite a bite. *At the Grosser Ring auction in Trier, Sept 1997* ★★(★★) *Say now–2010.*

**Brauneberger Sonnenuhr Riesling Auslese lange Goldkapsel** (M) **F Haag** Unsurprisingly excellent: sweet, with glorious acidity. It sold for exactly twice the price of the 'ordinary' Goldkapsel and nearly three times the price of Willi Haag's *lange Goldkapsel*. *Tasted at the Grosser Ring auction, Sept 1997* ★★★(★) *Possible 5 stars. Long life.*

**Deidesheimer Hohenmorgen Riesling Auslese** (P) **Bassermann-Jordan** Pre-tasting in London, then at 'The Taste of Germany' weekend. Picked 28 October. Oechsle 112°, residual sugar 64g/l, total acidity 9.6g/l, alcohol 10.81%. Pale melon yellow; a glorious, herbaceous, peachy and honey nose with greengage acidity, then rose petals; not as sweet as expected, lovely flavour, clean, dry finish. *Last tasted at Banff Springs, Canada, Oct 1998* ★★★(★) *Now–2010.*

**Erbacher Marcobrunn Riesling Erstes Gewächs** (Rg) **Schloss Reinhartshausen** First growth vineyard, dry wine. Light, fresh, slightly grapey and grassy. Decent flavour, helped by *Zanderfilet* fish. *At the press dinner for* Meine Lieblingsweine *at Robert Weil, April 1998* ★★ *Probably at its best now.*

**Erbacher Michelmark Riesling Eiswein** (Rg) **J Jung** Picked on Christmas Day at −15° C. Oechsle 200°, very high acidity, 19.5g/l. Gold, orange highlights; lime, cress, rather metallic; very sweet of course, quite good flesh, attenuated, lip-licking acidity. *A tasting at the Krone, Assmannshausen, of the top wines of the VDP auction I had recently conducted, Nov 1998* ★★★

**Erbacher Schlossberg Riesling Auslese** (Rg) **Schloss Reinhartshausen** Crisp; sweet, some fat, good acidity. *At the VDP auction tasting, Sept 1997* ★★★

**Erbacher Siegelsberg Riesling Auslese** (Rg) **Schloss Reinhartshausen** Alcohol 10%. Two notes, both recently tasted at home, first as mid-morning elevenses – the perfect time: palish; peachy, minty; fairly sweet, lovely flavour, balance, acidity. *Last noted Sept 2000* ★★★

**Erdener Prälat Riesling Auslese** (M) **Robert Eymael** The first of a surprising number of Prälats at the auction and an interesting comparison of styles and producers. Broad grapey style, medium-sweet, touch of *spritz*. *Lot 5, at the Grosser Ring auction, Trier, Sept 1997* ★★★

**Erdener Prälat Riesling Auslese** (M) **Dr Loosen** Very pale; low-keyed but peachy; medium sweet, excellent acidity. *At Siegel's centenary tasting, March 1999* ★★★(★) *2004–2010.*

**Erdener Prälat Riesling Auslese** (M) **Dr F Weins-Prüm** Very pale; medium-sweet, pleasant, light, grapey, slight whiff of ping-pong balls. *Lot 22, at the Grosser Ring auction, Trier, Sept 1997* ★★★ *(just).*

**Erdener Prälat Riesling Auslese Goldkapsel** (M) **Christoffel-Berres** Pale; grapey, lively acidity; fairly sweet, crisp, attractive. *Lot 10, at the Grosser Ring auction, Trier, Sept 1997* ★★★(★)

**Erdener Prälat Riesling Auslese Goldkapsel** (M) **Dr Loosen** As above but extra dimensions. Three months later, sweet, rich, lovely flavour, acidity and length. Needs time. *Last noted at the 'Masters of Riesling', June 1997* ★★★(★★) *2006–2016.*

**Erdener Prälat Riesling Auslese lange Goldkapsel** (M) **Dr Loosen** Medium-pale yellow; glorious, ripe, creamy; sweet yet light at heart, nice flesh and acidity. *Lot 18 (thrice the price of lot 22, above, and over twice the price of lot 10), at the Grosser Ring auction, Trier, Sept 1997* ★★★★(★) *Long life.*

**Filzener Herrenberg Riesling BA** (M) **Edmund Reverchon** Earthy, fat, sweaty and oily Riesling nose, lanolin and dried apricot; not very sweet though rich, assertive, almost raucous, with teeth-gripping acidity. A bit of a roller coaster. *At Ann Noble's 'It's all in the nose' seminar, Banff, Canada, Oct 1998* ★(★)

**Forster Ungeheuer Riesling Eiswein** (P) **Bassermann-Jordan** A half bottle winding up dinner at Ch Canon-La-Gaffelière in St-Émilion: a most exotic nose; very sweet but perfectly balanced by high end acidity. Alcohol 10.5%. *Followed by a perfect night's sleep, April 1998* ★★★★

**Geisenheimer Rothenberg Riesling Auslese** (Rg) **Wegeler** Medium-sweet, surprisingly dry finish. Pleasing, not great. *Quick note at the VDP tasting, Sept 1997* ★★(★)?

**Graacher Domprobst Riesling Auslese Goldkapsel** (M) **Willi Schaefer** Very forthcoming aroma; one heck of a bite. More like a Saar wine of a less ripe vintage. It fetched the second highest price of the 14 '96s, so someone appreciated it more than I did. *Trier, Sept 1997* ★★?

**Haardter Bürgergarten Rieslaner Auslese** (P) **Müller-Cattoir** Straw gold; distinct peach and apricot; fairly sweet, light style (8.5% alcohol) but rich. A sort of Pfalz renaissance under Müller-Catoir. Delicious flavour, Rieslaner acidity. *At a white wine seminar, Lyford Cay, Bahamas, Feb 1999* ★★★★

**Hattenheimer Pfaffenberg Riesling Spätlese Goldkapsel** (Rg) **v Schönborn** Pale; cress and sulphur dioxide; medium-sweet, good length and acidity. *Sept 1997* ★★

**Hattenheimer Schützenhaus Riesling Goldkapsel** (Rg) **zu Knyphausen** Pale; peachy fruit and flavour. *Sept 1997* ★★★

**Hochheimer Domdechaney Riesling Spätlese** (Rg) **Aschrott/Künstler** The first vintage made by Künstler following his acquisition of the English-owned Aschrott estate. Relatively young, he has put Hochheim back on the map. Very pale; cress-like; ripe, lovely flavour. Which shows what a 'star' winemaker can do with an old estate in a none too easy vintage for the dryer wines. *At the German Embassy, London, Sept 1997* ★★★

**Hochheimer Hölle Riesling BA** (Rg) **Künstler** Almost colourless; glorious fruit, sweetness, length and aftertaste. *At the German Embassy, London, Sept 1997* ★★★(★)

**Hochheimer Kirchenstück Riesling Spätlese** (Rg) **Künstler** 'Künstler's best ever Spätlese'. Lovely fruit and acidity. *Sept 1997. Then* ★★★(★) *Now–2010.*

**Schloss Johannisberger Riesling Rosalack Auslese** (Rg) A particularly successful year at the Schloss. Palish yellow; leafy, herbaceous, spearmint; sweet, crisp acidity, good flavour, length and end taste. Needs time. *At the 900th anniversary tasting, Nov 2001* ★★★(★) *2006–2012.*

**Kanzemer Altenberg Riesling Spätlese** (M) **v Othegraven** Almost colourless; light, slightly peachy, whiff of walnuts; overall fairly dry and with some Saar austerity. *At the Grosser Ring auction tasting, Trier, Sept 1997. Far too young of course. Probably drinking well now* ★★(★)?

**Kanzemer Altenberg Riesling Auslese Goldkapsel** (M) **v Othegraven** Also almost colourless; a broader grapey, peachy, minty aroma; medium-sweet, fragrant but dry acidic finish. *At the Grosser Ring auction, Sept 1997. Potential* ★★★. *Will 'fill out'.*

**Kiedricher Gräfenberg Riesling Spätlese** (Rg) **Robert Weil** Light grapey aroma; slightly sweeter than expected. Lovely flavour, alcohol 8.5%, excellent acidity. Charm personified. *At Chippenham Lodge, Oct 1997* ★★★ *Will be perfect now and up to say 2006.*

**Kiedricher Gräfenberg Riesling Auslese Goldkapsel** (Rg) **Robert Weil** One of the loveliest of wines. Six notes, first at the German Embassy in London in 1997 to celebrate the 100th anniversary of the VDP Rheingau: honeyed botrytis; fabulous flavour and length. Next at a tasting of previous auction highlights and later the same day at the Rheingauer Giganten dinner: very sweet, fleshy, silky, gloriously ripe. At the German Embassy again in 1999, lip-licking acidity. Now a deep amber-gold, perfection. *Last noted at the Welt-Raritätenprobe at Schloss Johannisberg, Nov 2000* ★★★★★

**Kiedricher Gräfenberg Riesling BA Goldkapsel** (Rg) **Robert Weil** In 1997: clover honey; very sweet, glorious. Most recently: pinkish gold; sweet, heady lime blossom and honeyed botrytis; almost TBA richness – almost too sweet. Lovely flavour. Rather harsh end-acidity. Needs time. *Last noted at Christie's masterclass, Sept 1999* ★★★★(★) *2001–2020.*

**Mülheimer Helenenkloster Riesling Eiswein** (M) **Max Ferd. Richter** Picked on Boxing Day, 26 December. Residual sugar 167.3g/l, very high acidity: 16.5g/l, alcohol 12%. Lovely colour; very sweet, delicious, touch of pineapple, uplift of acidity and crisp finish. *With Freddie Price at Vinexpo, Bordeaux, June 1997* ★★★★

**Münzinger 'Antigua' Kapellenberg Spätlese Weissherbst Eiswein** (B) **WG Badischer Winzerkeller** A sample half bottle for my pre-tasting was rich but corky. Happily in better condition at the 'Just Desserts' session. An unbelievable 240g/l residual sugar, total acidity 13.5g/l, alcohol 8.9%. A very Germanic rosé: a pink-gold blush wine; raisiny, caramel and strawberry, very high volatile acidity. A sort of turbo-charged fruit juice. *At Banff Springs, Canada, Oct 1998* ★★★★ *for boldness.*

**Nackenheimer Rothenberg Riesling Auslese** (Rh) **Gunderloch** Lovely nose; medium-sweet, curious fishy flavour, earthy, slightly metallic finish. A much better note, glorious fruit a year later at the pre-tasting and 'Reach for Riesling' session presented by Fritz Hasselbach. Oechsle 100°, residual sugar 65g/l, acidity 9.2g/l, alcohol 9.5%: greengage, gooseberry, steely nose; fairly sweet entry, dry finish, good fruit, excellent balance. It pays to take time tasting. *At Banff Springs, Canada, Oct 1998* ★★★★ *2004–2012.*

**Neumagener Nusswingert Riesling Spätlese** (M) **Milz-Laurentiushof** Lot 1: a sort of aperitif, light, crisp, attractive wine for early drinking. *At the Grosser Ring auction, Trier, Sept 1997* ★★

**Niederhauser Hermannshöhle Riesling Spätlese** (N) **Dönnhoff** Medium-dry, fully ripe for drinking. Good length. *At Justerini & Brooks's tasting, Jan 2002* ★★★

**Niersteiner Hipping Riesling Auslese** (Rh) **Anton Balbach** Hefty pineapple nose though light in style. Earthy, grapey. At £16 a bottle I should have bought some for keeping. *June 1997* ★★★(★)

**Niersteiner Oelberg Riesling Eiswein** (Rh) **Balbach** The Balbach estate is now owned by Gunderloch. Oelberg is a classic, south-facing, sheltered Rheinhessen vineyard comprised of red, sandy soil with clay and a little lime. No botrytis in 1996: Oechsle 168°, residual sugar 225g/l, vital acidity 13.5g/l, modest 7% alcohol. A good note at the pre-tasting in London and a more complete one at the twee 'Just Desserts' session: scent of orange blossom, lime, peaches, later seeming lean, not exactly shrill, like a high note on a violin; sweet, fleshy fruit, good acidity, a joy to drink. *At Banff Springs, Canada, Oct 1998* ★★★★★

**Oberhäuser Brücke Riesling Auslese** (N) **Dönnhoff** Surprisingly pale; Nahe 'fruit salad' and lime fragrance and flavour. Glorious, spicy, excellent flavour and finish. *At Siegel's 'Masters of Riesling' tasting, June 1997* ★★★★(★)

**Oestricher Lenchen Riesling Auslese** (Rg) **Eser** Very distinctive nose and taste, with extraordinary blackcurrant aftertaste. *Quick note at the VDP pre-sale tasting, Sept 1997* ★★★

**Piersporter Goldtröpfchen Riesling Auslese** (M) **Reinhold Haart** Youthful grapiness; sweet, positive, slightly earthy taste and touch of *spritz. Lot 7, at the Grosser Ring auction, Trier, Sept 1997* ★★★

**Rüdesheimer Berg Schlossberg Riesling Spätlese** (Rg) **August Kesseler** The wine had a long fermentation: two months. Very high must weight, 24g/l residual sugar, 11.5g/l acidity. Pale; flowery, spicy; medium-dry, lip-licking tingling acidity. Firm. Needed time. *Dining at Schloss Reinhartshausen, Nov 1997* ★★★ *Ready.*

**Rüdesheimer Berg Schlossberg Spätburgunder Spätlese** (Rg) **August Kesseler** Very small yield, between 6 and 8hl/ha, high acidity, alcohol 12.5%. Fairly deep red, still youthful, rich 'legs'; very good, crisp Pinot Noir aroma; dry,

fragrant, lovely tannin and acidity, slightly smoky. Drinking well with beef. August Kesseler at his best. *At Schloss Reinhartshausen, Nov 1999* ★★★(★)

**Saarburger Rausch Riesling Auslese Goldkapsel** (M) **Geltz-Zilliken** Virtually colourless; light, grassy; fairly sweet, touch of youthful grapefruit. Needed time. *Lot 33 at the Grosser Ring auction, Trier, Sept 1997. Probably* ★★★ *or more now.*

**Scharzhofberger Riesling Auslese Goldkapsel** (M) **Egon Müller** Two wines tasted leading up to the Auslese – the Kabinett had a fresh grapefruit aroma and dry, lean, lip-licking acidity; while the Spätlese was light, minty; medium-dry, delicate and fragrant. The Goldkapsel Auslese was altogether a different ball game: sweet, fleshy, ripe, original – and, at DM330 per bottle, over ten times the price of the Kabinett. *At the Grosser Ring auction tasting, Sept 1997* (★★★★) *for the Goldkapsel.*

**Trittenheimer Leiterchen Riesling Auslese Goldkapsel** (M) **Milz-Laurentiushof** Medium-dry – I expected it to be sweeter. Good, ripe, yet crisp nose and flavour. *Lot 2 at the Grosser Ring auction, Trier, Sept 1997* ★★★(★)

**Ürziger Würzgarten Riesling Spätlese** (M) **Dr Loosen** A well set-up youth. Fairly dry, mouthfilling, excellent acidity. *March 1997* ★★★ *Probably at peak now.*

**Ürziger Würzgarten Riesling Auslese Goldkapsel** (M) **J J Christoffel-Erben** Austere and corky. But it sold. *Lot 9 in the Grosser Ring auction, Trier, Sept 1997.*

**Ürziger Würzgarten Riesling Auslese Goldkapsel** (M) **Christoffel-Berres** No colour at all; pleasant, light, grapey flavour, some charm, lacking length. *At the Grosser Ring auction, Trier, Sept 1997* ★★

**Ürziger Würzgarten Riesling Auslese Goldkapsel** (M) **Dr Loosen** Even Loosen's Kabinett and Spätlese were above average, but the Auslese Goldkapsel, 'over 50% botrytis', was very scented, medium-sweet with steely acidity (at Walter Siegel's centenary tasting in 1997). A few months later, at their 'Master of Riesling' tasting, it was delicious, but needing more time. Excellent value at £24. Alas, an austere, corky bottle at the Grosser Ring auction. *Last tasted Sept 1997. At best* ★★★★ *Say 2006–2016.*

**Ürziger Würzgarten Riesling Auslese lange Goldkapsel** (M) **Eymael** Good wine, good price (DM125). Sweet, fruity, fleshy. *Lot 6, Trier, Sept 1997* ★★★★

**Wehlener Sonnenuhr Riesling Spätlese** (M) **J J Prüm** Unusually minty, like wet privet; fragrant, distinctive. *Lot 19, Trier* ★★★ *Probably at best now.*

**Wehlener Sonnenuhr Riesling Auslese** (M) **J J Prüm** Virtually colourless; fairly sweet, light style, fragrant. *Lot 20 at the Grosser Ring auction, double the price of the Spätlese, Trier, Sept 1997* ★★★★

**Wehlener Sonnenuhr Riesling Auslese Goldkapsel** (M) **J J Prüm** Very distinctive, pronounced nose; drier than expected, touch of *spritz*. Far too young. Needed time. *Lot 21 at DM106, a third higher than the Auslese, at the Grosser Ring auction, Trier, Sept 1997* (★★★)?

**Wiltinger Braune Kupp Riesling Auslese Goldkapsel** (M) **Le Gallais** One can detect the Egon Müller touch, both in respect of style and price: glorious peachy flavour with a deft touch and spritz prickle on the finish. *At the Grosser Ring auction, Trier, Sept 1997* ★★★

**Winkeler Jesuitengarten Riesling Auslese** (Rg) **Jacob Hamm** The Spätlese overall dry. Unexciting. The Auslese a different ball game: lovely, grapey flavour and acidity. *At the VDP tasting, Sept 1997* ★★(★★)

**Zeltinger Sonnenuhr Riesling Auslese** (M) **Vereinigte Hospitien** Light, agreeable. Whatever sweetness there is, is upstaged by the very dry acidic finish. *At the Grosser Ring auction, Trier, Sept 1997* ★(★★)?

# 1997 ★★★★

Despite the vicissitudes of the relatively northern latitude, the German wine regions enjoy a continental climate and, of all the European wine regions, they have had, by any yardstick, a very good run of vintages in recent years – 1997 was one of the best, very small production, ripe grapes, high sugar content though little botrytis and good acidity. All this despite a rocky start with frost in April and flowering hampered by cool weather and localised hail storms. However, very hot weather in August continued into September. Most regions enjoyed some ten weeks of perfect ripening conditions with some rain to refresh the parched grapes on 12 September and on 13 and 15 October. An Indian summer with sun, warmth and clear blue skies enabled harvesting to begin early October. Many growers had completed by the second week in November.

All levels of wine were satisfactory – the Kabinett and Spätlesen for drinking from 1999 into the early 2000s, some superb ripe Rieslings of Auslesen quality and above, though, in comparison to the previous vintages, I have tasted relatively few of these wines.

**Dernauer Pfarrwingert Spätburgunder Rotwein Auslese trocken** (A) **Meyer-Näkel** I first visited the Ahr Valley in June 1956. It is the most northerly of the old classic German wine regions and long famed for its red wines. Meyer-Näkel, whose wines I do not recall tasting before, is now regarded the top producer and his wine, made from fully fermented out Pinot Noir, is an interesting example: medium deep red; strawberry-like aroma and flavour; touch of sweetness, bitter finish. Certainly too young when tasted. Needs time and food. *At the German Embassy, London, June 1999* ★★(★★) *Say now–2008.*

**Erbacher Marcobrunn Riesling Erstes Gewächs** (Rg) **Jacob Jung** One of three first growths (by definition dry), all of which I found austere, some also raw and very acidic. The wines were served with food and certainly needed it. *At the Gigantische Riesling and Spätburgunder dinner at the Hotel Krone, Assmannshausen, Nov 1999. From ★ to ★★*

**Erdener Treppchen Riesling BA** (M) **Dr Loosen** Pale gold; very rich, lovely; a broader style than Robert Weil's, low alcohol (6.5%), and lovely acidity. *At the German Embassy, London, June 1999* ★★★★

**Graacher Himmelreich Riesling Spätlese** (M) **J J Prüm** Rich, grapey, 'goaty'; dry, crisp. We were informed that Graacher is more acidic than Wehlen; it has a slightly different microclimate too, which was very evident to Daphne and me on our motor scooter in June 1956: it rained when we rode through Wehlen but was dry in Graach, and then vice versa! *At the estate, May 2000* ★★★ *Drink soon.*

**Graacher Himmelreich Riesling Auslese** (M) **J J Prüm** Two notes: very pale; nose so dumb that it had to be dragged out screaming! More forthcoming on the palate. More recently an elderberry, minerally blossoming scent; mild, grapey flavour. *Last tasted on Manfred Prüm's terrace, May 2000* ★★★

**Hattenheimer Wisselbrunnen Riesling BA** (Rg) **Eser** Extremely pale, lime-tinged; light, fragrant, whiff of mint and peach kernels; sweet, curious light style but with very fragrant

flavour and aftertaste and good acidity. *At Schloss Johannisberg, Nov 2000* ★★★★ *Now–2010.*

**Hochheimer Hölle Riesling Spätlese halbtrocken** (Rg) **Künstler** Delicate, fragrant, a whiff of $SO_2$; medium-dry, lovely flavour, perfect finish. *At the German Embassy, June 1999* ★★★

**Hochheimer Hölle Riesling Eiswein** (Rg) **Joachim Flick** Palish, lime; lovely peachy fruit and acidity; sweet, very fragrant. *At the Giganten Gala, Nov 1998* ★★★★ *Now–2010?*

**Ihringer Winklerberg Grauer Burgunder Spätlese trocken** '★★★' (B) **Dr Heger** Well: not only novices find this sort of wine name difficult to fathom; yet it is all very logical: from Ihringen in Baden; Grauer Burgunder (a grape variety only recently legalised), Spätlese means 'late picked' of a stipulated minimum ripeness; *trocken* means dry, '★★★' the producer's quality designation. Dr Heger is one of Baden's outstanding estates and probably made the best '97s in all Baden. The wine: attractive, medium-red; 'warm' chocolatey nose; sweet, hefty Burgundian weight (13.5% alcohol), delicious raspberry-like flavour and lovely oaky finish. *At the German Embassy, London, June 1999* ★★★(★) *Now–2010.*

**Ihringer Winklerberg Spätburgunder Rotwein** '★★★' **Auslese** (B) **Dr Heger** Unquestionably a more than 3-star winery, from Ihringen, and a '3-star' Pinot Noir. Very rich varietal aroma which opened up well, scented Pinot, caramel and tar; slightly sweet, very good oaky Pinot flavour, perhaps a bit jammy. *At the 'Club 50' tasting in Düsseldorf, March 2000* ★★★

**Iphofer Kalb Ehrenfelser Eiswein** (F) **Wirsching** Yellow; lovely honeyed nose; sweet, delicious flavour with very dry acidic finish. *April 2000* ★★(★) *Say 2006–2010.*

**Kiedricher Gräfenberg Riesling Spätlese** (Rg) **Robert Weil** A bottle sent to me and consumed (at elevenses of course) less than a year after the grapes were picked. Almost Mosel-like in its lightness and delicacy, touch of flesh, delightful flavour, tingling finish. *Aug 1998* ★★★★ *Now–2006.*

**Kiedricher Gräfenberg Riesling Auslese Goldkapsel** (Rg) **Robert Weil** Wilhelm Weil can hardly put a foot wrong. His trademark is fruity sweetness and charm. Three notes, first a half bottle at a post-theatre supper: scents of melon, greengage and gooseberry-like acidity; sweet, soft, fat, alcohol

---

## The VDP and the great wine auction

*The Verband Deutscher Prädikats–und Qualitätsweinguter e V, VDP for short, is a highly important association of roughly 150 of the finest German wine estates. Its current President is Michael Prinz zu Salm-Salm, the owner of an 800-year-old family estate in the Nahe. It was he who invited me to conduct the Spitzenweinversteirung, an auction held every ten years or so at which participating estates enter their finest and rarest wines. Held 'in association with Christie's' on 15 November 1997 in Wiesbaden, it drew a record attendance of over one thousand, filling the grand hall of the Kürhaus, serried ranks of estate owners behind the rostrum, the important Weinkommissäre (brokers) in commanding positions, with their clients, in the 'front stalls'.*

*My worry was timing, for all participants have an opportunity to taste (a sip) of every wine before the lot is put up for sale. The other potential problem was the possible disruption by the brokers, all of whom I knew and all of whom were accustomed to take their time. With Michael Salm's backing, I had a word with them just before the sale started. I explained that I was not in the Kürhaus for my health, nor was it an ego trip: I was in Wiesbaden to help publicise and promote fine German wines. Happily, it went well.*

8%, glorious fruit and acidity. A peachy, honeyed 5-star wine at 'The Wines of Germany' tasting at the German Embassy. Most recently, the grand finale of the Gigantische dinner: very pale; extraordinary forthcoming bouquet; very sweet, highly original. *Last noted at the Krone, Assmannshausen, Nov 1999* ★★★★(★) *Now–2015.*

**Lieser Niederberg Helden Riesling Auslese '★★★'** (M) **Schloss Lieser** Wilhelm and Thomas Haag told us that it was a very good October and, for them, one of the best vintages of the 1990s. Oechsle 115°, without botrytis, alcohol 7.5%. A sheer delight. Sweet, creamy, peachy. Lovely balance and finish. *At the Schloss, May 2000* ★★★(★) *Now–2010.*

**Riesling Kabinett 'Charta'** (Rg) **Eser Johannishof** Charta wines were by definition dry or at least unsugared. Fresh, minerally; in fact, medium-dry, fragrant, attractive, slightly short. *At the Gigantische dinner at the Krone, Assmannshausen, Nov 1999* ★★★

**Schloss Vollrads Riesling Kabinett trocken** (Rg) So confusing, for 'trocken' is also dry. It developed a spicy nose but was austere and definitely needed the food it was designed for. *At the Gigantische dinner, Nov 1999* ★

**Wehlener Sonnenuhr Riesling Kabinett** (M) **J J Prüm** The opening wine in a 'flight' of '97s: to demonstrate the quality levels. Youthful acidity, minty, white currants; fairly dry, alcohol 8.5%, fragrant. Good with food. Early drinking. *At the Weinart/Prüm tasting in Austria, April 1990* ★★ *Drink now.*

**Wehlener Sonnenuhr Riesling Spätlese** (M) **J J Prüm** Four notes in all, the first one made in April 1999. At that stage it was very pale, low-keyed; firm but needing bottle age. Only two months later, showing great potential among its peers, six '97s, at the German Embassy in London. Glorious fruit but as yet unknit. Similar notes at a Christie's masterclass that September: much more to come. Most recently, opening up, grapey flavoured. *Last tasted at the estate, May 2000* ★★(★★) *Say now–2007.*

**Wehlener Sonnenuhr Riesling Auslese** (M) **J J Prüm** Around 7000 bottles produced. First tasted April 1999. Youthful, lime-tinged, minerally nose; medium-sweet, fragrant, alcohol 7.5%, dry finish. Five months later, much the same. On both occasions slight *spritz*. *Last noted at a Christie's masterclass, Sept 1999* ★★(★) *2005–2010.*

**Wehlener Sonnenuhr Riesling Auslese Goldkapsel Cask 29** (M) **J J Prüm** Top of the range in this vintage. Production only 300–400 bottles. Low-keyed; minerally nose; sweet, soft peachy flavour. Lovely. Alcohol 8%. A different ball game to the straight Auslese. Lovely now and with a great future. *At the Weinart/Prüm tasting, April 1999* ★★★(★)

# 1998 ★★★★

A very good year, at any rate for those well established estates with well-drained vineyards planted with the hardy late ripening Riesling; for there was an abundance of rain which made life more difficult for early-ripening varieties on richer soils and flatter sites.

The growing season started with an early bud break followed by a very wet April. Happily, a hot and sunny May encouraged excellent flowering conditions, two weeks earlier than normal in the Mosel, perfect on the Rheingau, and early – though cool – in June elsewhere. Low temperatures continued, with extensive rain. July was warm and dry though lacking sunshine, and the rest of the summer was extremely hot, with up to 40°C in the Rheingau and an all-time

German record high of 41.2°C in the Middle Mosel. The good ripening weather continued into early September, thereafter there was almost continuous rain. The Mosel enjoyed one week of sun in October followed by storms and floods. Despite the wet, the grapes remained astonishingly ripe and healthy, most harvesting from mid-October. A large, miraculously good crop.

**Dorsheimer Goldloch Riesling Auslese** (N) **Schlossgut Diel** The Nahe valley enjoyed a 'sensational' harvest. Medium-sweet, very good flavour. Dry finish. A broader more earthy style than Mosels. *At the Grosser Ring tasting, London, June 2000* ★(★★) *2005–2015.*

**Erbacher Hohenrain Riesling Erstes Gewächs** (Rg) **Jung** The lesson here is that quality wines do not have to be Spätlese, Auslese or above. *Erstes Gewächs* is not merely first growth but firmly dry, a step up in conception from the Charta wines. Almost colourless; very metallic nose; dry, firm, good length. A perfect food wine – it was served with fish. *At the Rheingauer Giganten dinner at the Krone, Assmannshausen, Nov 2000* ★★★

**Graacher Himmelreich Riesling Kabinett** (M) **J J Prüm** Very pale, distinct green tinge; minerally nose and taste. Medium-dry, light, delicious. *With the Bacchus Society of America on Manfred Prüm's terrace, May 2000* ★★(★) *Now–2005.*

**Hattenheimer Wisselbrunnen Riesling Auslese** (Rg) **Schloss Reinhartshausen** Alcohol 8%; lovely peachy nose; sweet, harmonious. *Nov 1999* ★★(★)

**Hochheimer Kirchenstück Riesling Spätlese** (Rg) **Künstler** Pale; ripe, slightly appley nose; medium-sweet, rich and ripe. *At Justerini & Brooks's tasting, Jan 2002* ★★★ *Now–2007.*

**Hochheimer Stielweg Riesling Auslese trocken** (Rg) **Künstler** Very pale, lemon-tinged; rich, minty, grapefruit; dry, firm, complete. A very well made *trocken* wine. *At the Giganten dinner, Nov 2000* ★★★ *Now–2004.*

**Iphöfer Kronsberg Rieslaner Spätlese** (F) **Hans Wirsching** An estate owned by the Wirsching family since 1630. A typically steely Rieslaner, its prominent acidity kept in check by its alcohol (13%) and ripe fruit. A lovely grapey flavour. *Tasted at Vinopolis, London, April 2000* ★★(★) *Say 2003–2008.*

**Kiedricher Gräfenberg Riesling Auslese** (capsule length not noted) (Rg) **Robert Weil** The last and loveliest wine at the Rheingauer Giganten dinner at the Krone, Assmannshausen: youthful, minerally; an enchanting sweetness, peachy flavour, lovely acidity. *Nov 2000* ★★★(★)

**Kiedricher Gräfenberg Riesling Goldkapsel Auslese** (Rg) **Robert Weil** Very surprising bottle variation in colour, the first pale, the next pure gold, the third amber-gold; the first low-keyed and acidic, the other two more peachy, with extra dimensions; on the palate, the first wonderful richness and texture, the next two more raisiny. *Supplied by Weil for a masterclass at Christie's, Sept 1999. At best* ★★★★

**Maximin Grünhäuser Abtsberg Riesling Spätlese** (M) **v Schubert** Almost colourless; light, fragrant, flowery; medium dry, light (8% alcohol), with delectable flavour, dry finish and lip-licking acidity. *At the annual Gourmet Dinner, Knickerbocker Club, New York, Oct 2000* ★★★(★) *Now–2010.*

**Münsterer Pittersberg Riesling Auslese** (N) **Krüger-Rumpf** Two notes, first at the Grosser Ring tasting in June 2000. Next, five months later: very pale; curious powdery nose; medium-sweet, light, fragrant Nahe style, with dancing acidity. Needs time. *At the Schloss Johannisberg rare wine tasting, Nov 2000* ★★(★★) *Say 2005–2010.*

**Nackenheimer Rothenberg Riesling Spätlese (Rh)**
**Gunderloch** Under Fritz Hasselbach, unquestionably one of
the outstanding estates in Rheinhessen. First his 'Jean Baptiste'
Riesling Kabinett: gooseberry-like acidity; dry, leanish flavoury,
delicious. Then his Rothenberg Spätlese with exactly the right
touch of mild sweetness and refreshing acidity. It all seems so
effortless. *Last tasted at Vinopolis, London, April 2000* ★★(★)
*Now–2006.*

**Nackenheimer Rothenberg Riesling Auslese (Rh)**
**Gunderloch** Two notes, first in April 2000: deceptively pale;
aroma of peaches and greengages; lovely soft, sweet, delicate
grapey flavour. Four months later showing superbly well at
Len Evans' 'Imperial Dinner'. Copybook balance of fruit and
acidity, delectable, delicious. *Last noted in the Hunter Valley, Sept
2000* ★★★(★) *Verging on 5 stars. Can a wine be perfect yet not great?
At best 2006–2012.*

**Niederhäuser Hermannshöhle Riesling Auslese (N)**
**Dönnhoff** One can't help smiling at some of the German
vineyard names. The self-effacing Helmut Dönnhoff,
'Winemaker of the Year' in the 1998 edition of the influential
*German Wine Guide*, lived up to his reputation with this lovely
wine, my ideal Nahe 'fruit salad' wine. *At Vinopolis, London,
April 2000* ★★★(★) *Lovely now but better to let it develop. Say
2006–2012.*

**'Penguin' Eiswein (Rh) Guntrum** Hajo Guntrum is nothing
if not enterprising. Behind the rather obviously commercial
title and label is a most appealing wine. Greenish-tinged
yellow; mint and honey; very sweet, touch of apricot, lovely
acidity. A half bottle, only 9% alcohol, was polished off by
Daphne and me without effort. *At home, Feb 2000. Try it with a
meringue* ★★★

**Piesporter Goldtröpfchen Riesling Spätlese trocken
(M) Reinhold Haart** Theo Haart has an excellent reputation
but must have a constant battle to reassure potential customers
that his is not any old *Goldtröpfchen*. And this was only his
Spätlese *trocken*. Almost colourless, like so many '98 Mosels; a
very flowery aroma positively leaping out of the glass; dry,
fresh, youthful. Delicious. *Dining alone before a Saturday wine
event, at the Hotel Louis C. Jacob, Hamburg, March 2000* ★★★

**Schlossböckelheimer Königsfels Riesling Kabinett (N)**
**Paul Anheuser** An old family estate, founded in 1627. Low-
keyed but very attractive Nahe 'fruit salad' aroma and taste.
Fairly dry. Good acidity. *At Vinopolis, London, April 2000* ★★★
*Early drinking.*

**Wehlener Sonnenuhr Riesling Kabinett (M) J J Prüm**
Very pale, slight tinge of green; spicy; overall dry, 8% alcohol,
touch of austerity, very good acidity. *Though it was agreeable to
taste a range of wines, seated at tables on the terrace of Manfred
Prüm's house overlooking the Sonnenuhr slope, they were not ideal
conditions for tasting, May 2000* ★★ *For early drinking.*

**Wehlener Sonnenuhr Riesling Spätlese (M) J J Prüm**
Extremely pale, a tinge of lime; aroma more grapey than the
Kabinett; medium-dry, pleasant, 'broad' Riesling taste. *At
Prüm's, May 2000* ★★(★) *Say 2005–2010.*

**Wehlener Sonnenuhr Riesling Auslese (M) J J Prüm**
Pale; lovely, fragrant, peachy; medium-sweet, fairly rich, grapey
flavour, very good acidity. *At Prüm's, May 2000* ★★★(★) *Delicious
now but will develop further, say 2005–2012.*

**Wehlener Sonnenuhr Riesling Auslese Goldkapsel (M)**
**J J Prüm** Fairly pale; clearly a good future, and though very
good, the extra 'leg up' of quality designation not all that
obvious. The same sort of sweetness and distinctive 'kerosene'
Riesling flavour. *At Prüm's, May 2000* ★★★(★) *2006–2015.*

**Wehlener Sonnenuhr Riesling Auslese lange
Goldkapsel (M) J J Prüm** More colour, honeyed botrytis;
sweet, lovely flesh, flavour, good length. *The climax of the tasting
at Prüm's, May 2000* ★★★(★★) *2008–2020.*

**Winkeler Hasensprung Riesling Eiswein (Rg) Fritz
Allendorf** Star bright; scent of lime blossom; lovely, lively fruit,
flesh and acidity. *At the Gigantische Riesling dinner at the Krone,
Assmannshausen, Nov 1999* ★★★(★) *Delicious now. Why wait?*

# 1999 ★★★★

This was said to be one of the best vintages since 1976 thanks
to a long, warm and exceptionally sunny summer and despite,
as in 1998, rain throughout the harvest. Once again well-
ripened grapes on the best well-drained sites survived
miraculously. All regions reported very ripe fruit and unusually
low acidity – in fact, this is what makes it comparable to 1976.
The Saar and Ruwer, where very high acidity is often a
problem, were both particularly successful.

As with the other recent vintages, my notes are more
concerned with the quality wines which should develop well.
There are masses of very attractive and inexpensive wines in
the QbA and Kabinett range for early drinking.

**Berncasteler Doktor Riesling Auslese (M) Thanisch**
Minerally, grapey; medium-sweet, austere finish. Needs time.
*At the Grosser Ring tasting, London, June 2000* (★★★) *2005–2010.*

**Brauneberger Juffer-Sonnenuhr Riesling Kabinett (M)**
**F Haag** Very pale; fresh youthful grapiness; not too dry, very
light (7.5% alcohol) and refreshing. *At a tasting for the Bacchus
Society of America of Fritz Haag and Schloss Lieser wines with
Wilhelm Haag and his son, at the Schloss, May 2000* ★★★ *For
relatively early drinking.*

**Brauneberger Juffer-Sonnenuhr Riesling Spätlese (M)**
**F Haag** Pale; attractive, creamy, earthy-fruity Brauneberg
character; medium-dry, light (7.5% alcohol), pleasant, easy
drinking. *At Schloss Lieser, May 2000* ★★(★) *2005–2010.*

**Brauneberger Juffer-Sonnenuhr Riesling Auslese
Goldkapsel (M) F Haag** Crisp, classic; very good, fairly
sweet, rich yet only 7% alcohol and light, grapey flavour.
*At Schloss Lieser, May 2000* ★★★(★) *Say 2006–2012.*

**Eitelsbacher Karthäuserhofberg Riesling Auslese (M)**
First tasted in June 2000: hardly any colour; light, youthful,
spicy nose; medium-sweet, zestful, young flavour. Touch of
hardness on the finish. I was informed by Christoph Tyrell that
his grapes had very little botrytis in 1999 which accounted for
the very pale, unstained colour, and also why he was unable to
produce a TBA. After two years it was beautifully mellow.

## The importance of slate in the Mosel

*The dramatic slate slopes flanking the river Mosel are of critical
importance in the production of this region's fine Rieslings. First,
the slate structure is friable enough and its planes at such an angle
that a vine's roots are able to take a purchase on what are often the
steepest of gradients. Second, its soils hold moisture, important for
quenching the vine's thirst – on other slopes at these angles, water
would just run off, and terracing would be necessary. And third,
slate retains heat and re-radiates the sun's warmth at night, crucial
in assisting the ripening process in this coolish region. Slate's
mineral content is also believed to feed the vines and add character
to their fruit – I certainly find a distinctive minerality to many
Mosel Rieslings.*

*Noted at the Grosser Ring tasting at the RAC Club in London, June 2002 ★★★★ Now–2010. This is an annual tasting to which I always much look forward.*

**Eitelsbacher Karthäuserhofberg Riesling Auslese Cask 22** (M) **Tyrell** A superior cask, price DM36.50 ex-cellars (the standard Auslese DM22.22). Slightly more peachy. Firm. Slatey finish. *June 2000 ★(★★★) 2009–2018.*

**Eitelsbacher Karthäuserhofberg Riesling Auslese Cask 23** (M) **Tyrell** More power, greater length, lovely aftertaste. Price DM43. *June 2000 (★★★★) 2010–2020.*

**Erbacher Marcobrunn Riesling Spätlese** (Rg) **Schloss Reinhartshausen** Very attractive, peachy aroma and taste. Medium-dry, good fruit and acidity. *May 2000 ★★(★) 2003–2008.*

**Erbacher Marcobrunn Riesling Spätlese trocken** (Rg) **Schloss Reinhartshausen** Very pale; gently scented, creamy Riesling opening up in the glass; very dry, and no doubt about it. Refreshing acidity. A good food wine. Most recently: pale, bright; attractive but steely, slightly metallic. I think another year of maturity would be better; however: medium-dry, with a lovely floral flavour. *At the Schloss, Feb 2002 ★★(★)*

**Erbacher Marcobrunn Riesling Spätlese fruchtig** (Rg) **Schloss Reinhartshausen** Pale, bright; distinctive, herbaceous; fairly sweet, crisp, grapey flavour, well balanced, delicious. *At the Schloss, Feb 2002 ★★★ Drink soon.*

**Erbacher Rheinhell Weissburgunder Chardonnay QbA trocken** (Rg) **Schloss Reinhartshausen** Unique. Chardonnay grown in the vineyard on the narrow island in the Rhine opposite the Schloss. Steely, attractive, minerally; dry, firm, austere, Chablis-like. Alcohol 12%. Needs bottle age. *May 2000 (★★★) 2003–2009?*

**Erbacher Schlossberg Riesling Kabinett trocken** (Rg) **Schloss Reinhartshausen** Pale; minerally; dry, alcohol 12.5%, good acidity. A good everyday 'food wine'. Lucky Germans to be able to buy this at the cellar door shop for around DM19 per bottle. *Tasted at the Schloss, May 2000 ★★ For early drinking.*

**Erbacher Schlossberg 'Erstes Gewächs'** (Rg) **Schloss Reinhartshausen** Good colour; still fresh, attractive bouquet; medium – neither sweet nor dry. Soft, mature taste, sweet, fruity finish. *At the Schloss, Feb 2002 ★★(★)*

**Erdener Prälat Riesling Auslese** (M) **Dr Loosen** It is not unfair to say that Ernie Loosen put the Prälat vineyard on the map, at least for us foreigners. It has an exceptional microclimate capable of producing the richest wines of the Mosel. Loosen's winemaker, Bernhard Schug, makes the most of it. The nose of the '99 Auslese, initially like pear drops, has great depth; firm on the palate, with lovely flavour and excellent acidity. *Last tasted June 2000 ★★(★★) 2005–2012.*

**Erdener Prälat Riesling Auslese** (M) **Mönchhof** Robert Eymael's wines are so effortlessly appealing. The ideal wines to sip on a summer's day. This one was colourless; youthful grape and pineapple aroma; medium-sweet, light (alcohol 8%), acidic. *At the Grosser Ring tasting, London, June 2000 (★★★) 2005–2010.*

**Erdener Prälat Riesling Auslese Goldkapsel** (M) **Mönchhof** The often-repeated 'peachy grapey' is not very exciting to read but this, for me, is the character of these Mosel-Saar-Ruwer wines. Interesting to note that this wine had an even lower alcoholic content, 7.5%, so there is no excuse for pussy-footing – drink it with friend, partner, male or female. Fairly sweet, delectable acidity. *June 2000 ★(★★★) 2006–2012 – or earlier.*

**Hattenheimer Nussbrunnen Riesling Kabinett trocken** (Rg) **Schloss Reinhartshausen** Virtually colourless; immature, grapefruit-like acidity; dry, alcohol 11%. Another well-made, versatile food wine. *At the Schloss, May 2000 ★★★ Now–2004.*

**Hattenheimer Wisselbrunnen Riesling Kabinett halbrocken** (Rg) **Schloss Reinhartshausen** Also colourless; a fuller, more forthcoming nose; the 'half dry' an appropriate description, flavour quite good but unexciting. *May 2000 ★★ Drink soon.*

**Hochheimer Reichstal Riesling Kabinett** (Rg) **Künstler** Surprisingly sweet though balanced by crisp acidity, light weight (7% alcohol) and lovely flavour. Incredibly good value for its quality. *At Justerini & Brooks, Jan 2002 ★★★ Now–2005.*

**Iphöfer Kronsberg Silvaner Spätlese** (F) **Hans Wirsching** Silvaner, which can produce lacklustre and mawkish wines in some regions, comes into its own in Franken, and many growers compare their '99s to the excellent '75s, the highish acidity of both vintages adding to Silvaner's vivacity. This wine is pale with a good aroma and dry steely palate. *At Vinopolis, London, April 2000 ★(★★★) 2004–2008.*

**Schloss Johannisberger Riesling Rotlack (Kabinett)** (Rg) Dry, steely, good mid fruit and finish. Why the public shies away from this sort of wine with food, I know not. *Drinking well, dining at the Schloss, Nov 2001 ★★★ Drink soon.*

**Schloss Johannisberger Riesling Goldlack (TBA)** (Rg) The youngest and last of the ten wines at their 900th anniversary tasting: medium-pale, waxy yellow; youthful; very sweet of course, fleshy, creamy, a touch metallic but needs bottle age. Great length and potential. *Nov 2001 (★★★★★) 2015–2040?*

**Kanzemer Altenberg Riesling Auslese** (M) **v Othegraven** Again, like almost all of the Saar and Ruwer wines, almost colourless; a light but delightful aroma like freshly peeled grapes; medium-sweet, much fuller-bodied than its appearance or nose indicated, and with grip. Will benefit from bottle age. *At the Grosser Ring tasting, June 2000 ★(★★) at least. 2006–2012.*

**Kanzemer Altenberg Riesling Auslese Goldkapsel** (M) **v Othegraven** A lovely, ripe, peachy nose, sweeter than the 'plain' Auslese and even more mouthfilling. Under the enlightened and enthusiastic ownership of Dr Heidi Kegel, this great estate is enjoying a renaissance. *June 2000 ★(★★★) 2009–2015.*

**Lieser Niederberg Helden Riesling Kabinett** (M) **Schloss Lieser** Hardly any colour; a strange, 'goaty', cream cheese nose; fairly dry, alcohol 9.8%, light fruity character and good acidity. *At Schloss Lieser, May 2000 ★★ for early drinking.*

**Lieser Niederberg Helden Riesling Spätlese** (M) **Schloss Lieser** Also virtually colourless; touch of fresh grapefruit; medium-dry, fairly light (8% alcohol), mildly grapey, attractive flavour. *May 2000 ★★★ 2004–2009.*

**Lieser Niederberg Helden Riesling Auslese** (M) **Schloss Lieser** Very pale; rich, febrile nose; sweeter, richer more grapey flavour than the Spätlese, alcohol 8%, quite soft for its age. *May 2000 ★★(★★) 2008–2015?*

**Maximin Grünhäuser Abstberg Riesling Spätlese** (Rg) **v Schubert** Almost colourless; extraordinary uplift of fragrance; medium-sweet, lovely acidity though a bit raw – needs time to round it off. *At Justerini & Brooks's tasting of 1999s, Jan 2001 ★(★★)*

**Niederhäuser Hermannshöhle Riesling Auslese** (N) **Dönnhoff** Virtually colourless; another example of Helmut Dönnhoff's seamless winemaking. *June 2000 ★★(★★) 2005–2010.*

**Oberemmeler Hütte Riesling Auslese and Auslese '★'** (M) **v Hövel** Rather like Christoph Tyrell, Eberhard von Kunow makes two grades of Auslese, the superior indicated with a star. Both virtually colourless; both lovely wines, the latter sweeter with zestful Saar acidity. *At the Grosser Ring tasting, June 2000* ★(★★★) *Both from 2008–2020.*

**Oberhäuser Leistenberg Riesling Kabinett** (N) **Dönnhoff** A really lovely fragrant nose, good flavour and aftertaste. A nice deft though slight touch of sweetness. *At Vinopolis, London, April 2000* ★★★ *Now–2006.*

**Piesporter Goldtröpfchen Riesling Auslese** (M) **Reinhold Haart** Piesporter – the real thing. Please refer to my comments on Haart's 1998. His '99 colourless; a steely, slatey, very minerally young nose; medium-sweet, ripe, fairly assertive and that well worn adjective 'peachy' occurring again. *At the Grosser Ring tasting, London, June 2000* ★(★★★) *2006–2012.*

**Saarburger Rausch Riesling Auslese** (M) **Geltz-Zilliken** Not unlike Dönnhoff in the Nahe, Hans-Joachim Zilliken is self-effacing and extremely good at his job as owner-winemaker. A classic Saar wine of an open, ripe style. *At the Grosser Ring tasting, June 2000* ★(★★) *2005–2010.*

**Saarburger Rausch Riesling Auslese lange Goldkapsel** (M) **Geltz-Zilliken** And this proves it: lovely, peachy, fairly assertive. Give it time. *June 2000* ★★★★(★) *2008–2016.*

**Schloss Reinhartshausen Gutsriesling trocken** (Rg) **Schloss Reinhartshausen** Pale, still with a youthful tinge; sweet, flowery, attractive scent; some sweetness on the palate, very attractive flavour and pleasant acidity on the finish. *At the Schloss, Feb 2002* ★★★ *For early drinking.*

**Schloss Saarstein Riesling Spätlese** (M) **Schloss Saarstein** The Ebert family's 11-ha 'monopole' vineyard. I found both their Kabinett and Spätlese attractive, the latter strangely paler, a bit more earthy and with good, teeth-gripping, Saar acidity. *At Vinopolis, London, April 2000* ★★(★) *Now–2007.*

**Scharzhofberger Riesling Kabinett** (M) **Egon Müller** Almost colourless; lovely fresh youthful aroma; slightly sweeter than expected; light style (alcohol 9%), lovely flavour, very acidic. The Müllers have a problem. Though they are supremely successful with their fine, sweet wines, they have a clientele which likes to buy the less pricey, lower quality wines. They can meet this demand by declassifying one rung. Perhaps this is an over-simplification. But the net result is that not infrequently a Müller Kabinett will be in effect a Spätlese,

the latter an Auslese, and so forth. *At the estate, May 2000* ★★★ *Now–2004.*

**Scharzhofberger Riesling Spätlese** (M) **Egon Müller** Also virtually colourless; fresh, youthful, whiff of lime; medium-sweet, a touch of 'baby fat', lightweight (alcohol 8.5%), lovely flavour, glorious acidity. This is the equivalent of many other producers' Auslesen. *At the estate, May 2000* ★(★★★) *2004–2012.*

**Scharzhofberger Riesling Spätlese Fuder 36** (M) **Egon Müller** Very pale; fragrant, delicate; medium – neither sweet nor dry, light, gentle, lovely flavour, violets aftertaste. *At Justerini & Brooks's tasting of wines of the '99s, Jan 2001* ★★★(★★) *2005–2012.*

**Scharzhofberger Riesling Auslese Goldkapsel** (M) **Egon Müller** This was not yet bottled when I first tasted it at the estate in mid-May 2000. Very pale; simply glorious peachy nose and flavour, sweet, rich, alcohol only 8%, perfect acidity. Next presented exactly a month later by Egon Müller junior at the Grosser Ring tasting in London: inimitable, spicy, superb. More recently: sublime ensemble of *Edelfäule* richness and acidity. *At the Primum Familiae Vini reception at Vinopolis, London, Nov 2000* ★★(★★★)

**Scharzhofberger Riesling BA** (M) **Egon Müller** Medium yellow-gold; scent of delectable peach skins; very sweet, of course, lovely plump fruit and perfect acidity. *June 2002* ★★★(★★★) *Lovely now but will develop fabulously.*

**Trittenheimer Leiterchen Riesling Auslese** (M) **Milz-Laurentiushof** *Lage in Alleinbesitz* (sole owners) Although I am familiar with Trittenheim, one of the more upstream villages of the Middle Mosel, I am sorry to say I have never visited this 500-year-old Milz family estate. They are sole owners of the Leiterchen and Felsenkopf vineyard sites and have an excellent reputation. Their '99 Auslese had a curious, slightly appley nose, peachy though; medium-sweet, an attractive mouthfiller. *At the Grosser Ring tasting, June 2000* ★★(★) *2005–2010.*

**Wallhäuser Johannisberg Riesling Auslese** (N) **Schloss Dalberg** An attractive, youthful, minty, grapey aroma and flavour; medium-sweet, touch of pineapple and raw apple. A pleasant summer wine. Needs a bit of time. *At home, June 2000* ★(★★) *Say now–2007.*

# 2000–2001

Riesling has turned full circle. It is firmly back in the saddle as the king of Germany's quality wines, reaching its sublime heights particularly in the Mosel-Saar-Ruwer and the Rheingau regions. This is not to say that it does not thrive in other German wine regions, or that the other classic varieties, Gewürztraminer in the Pfalz for example and Silvaner and the racy Rieslaner in Franken, do not count for anything. Not so. But it seems to me that the well-established workhorse, Müller-Thurgau and more recent fancy grape crossings now know their place, and this place is not in the forefront.

The other interesting thing is that quality is being driven by little more than a handful of great winemakers, some of whom are comparatively young. The previous under-performers must be aware of this and, weather and markets permitting, cannot afford to be left behind. I think the 'stars' and their star prices at auction, for example Weingut Robert Weil's success in New York, serve to demonstrate that world class wine is produced from Riesling.

In contrast to the richer styles are Georg Breuer's brilliant and uncompromising dry wines, excellent with food, and which also benefit from bottle age. Another step in the right direction is the resurrection of *Erstes Gewächs* (first growths), though as in Burgundy with their *grand* and *premier cru* vineyards, it is not without difficulties. Labels are being simplified, with a move to put vintage, estate or brand name, grape and quality on the front label, using the full village and vineyard name for only the estate's top wines. A clearer indication of the sweetness and dryness would help. Above all, let us put firmly in their lowly place the flood of German wine look-alikes. We have had an ABC campaign (Anything But Chardonnay). How about ABS&W (Anything But Sugar and Water)?

## 2000 ★★ to ★★★

'Average to good' is too sweeping; poor to really very good would cover this none-too-easy vintage. Overall a smaller crop than 1999, and 25% down in the Mosel-Saar-Ruwer.

As usual, the weather was to blame, torrential rain occurring in September, three times the average in some districts. The worst hit were the flat vineyards with rich soil and early-ripening grape varieties such as Müller-Thurgau. As so often, the most successful wines were made from the later-ripening Riesling on sloping, well-drained vineyard sites. Those growers who could afford to green harvest in August, later to comb their vines, hand-picking the ripe, discarding the rotten grapes, handling and vinifying them effectively, were able to produce some most attractive wines.

I first tasted a wide range of '00s at the now very large and successful Prowein trade fair in Düsseldorf in March 2001. Even allowing for their youthfulness, few seemed up to the '99s or '98s. Stefan Ress told me that it was his most difficult vintage since 1982. In one instance he had to filter the must before fermentation and later through big filters.

The Kabinett trocken wines and Spätlesen trocken were variable but clearly for early drinking. The most successful dry wine I tasted was made by Georg Breuer who, almost alone in Germany in my opinion, creates naturally bone-dry wines with really impressive structure and length. In view of the success of the 2001 vintage, with a preponderance of fine, rich wines, it is possible that the light dry and lesser 2000s will prove useful, refreshing 'interim' everyday and restaurant wines. A small selection of those tasted follows.

**Paul Anheuser Riesling 'Classic'** (N) **Paul Anheuser** Dry, spicy, crisp. *At the 'Wines of Germany' tasting at Vinopolis, London, April 2001* ★★

**Deidesheimer Paradiesgarten Riesling Kabinett** (P) **Bassermann-Jordan** Mild and pleasant and traditionally more interesting than this classic Pfalz estate's *trocken* wines or their dry austere Blanc de Pinot Gris. *At Prowein, March 2001* ★★

**Dorsheimer Pittermännchen Riesling Spätlese** (N) **Schlossgut Diel** Light, minerally, spearmint nose; medium-dry, crisp, light (7.5% alcohol) and attractive. *At Prowein, March 2001* ★(★) *Drink soon.*

**'Frühlingswein' Riesling Qba trocken** (Rg) **Schloss Reinhartshausen** Aptly named spring wine: fairly dry, lightly spicy and fruity, alcohol 11.5% and – if one lives in Germany – remarkably good value at DM9.90 ex cellars. *At Prowein, March 2001* ★★ *Early drinking.*

**Erbacher Rheinhell Weissburgunder und Chardonnay trocken** (Rg) **Schloss Reinhartshausen** Bright, polished yellow-gold; lively nose – an interesting 50-50 blend of Pinot Blanc and Chardonnay; touch of sweetness, positive, fragrant, good acidity. Tingle of *spritz*. *At the Schloss, Feb 2002* ★(★★)

**Erbacher Schlossberg Riesling Kabinett trocken** (Rg) **Schloss Reinhartshausen** Pale, polished yellow with hint of gold; attractive scented Riesling aroma; medium-dry. Attractive flavour. *At the Schloss, Feb 2002* ★★★ *Early drinking.*

**Erbacher Siegelsberg Riesling Kabinett fruchtig** (Rg) **Schloss Reinhartshausen** Bright, pale, refreshing colour; light but fragrant, slightly minty bouquet; medium-sweet, though light style, fresh, flavoury, rounded, charming. *At the Schloss, Feb 2002.*

**Erbacher Siegelsberg Riesling BA** (Rg) **Schloss Reinhartshausen** An amazing amber-gold colour; sweet, peachy almost raisiny bouquet; less sweet than expected but rich, 'tangy', dry finish. *At the Schloss, Feb 2002* ★(★★★)

**Hattenheimer Nussbrunnen Riesling Spätlese** (Rg) **Balthasar Ress** A fragrant cask vat sample, to be bottled May (2001). *At Prowein, March 2001* ★★

**Hattenheimer Nussbrunnen Riesling Auslese** (Rg) **Balthasar Ress** Despite problems necessitating the charcoal filtration mentioned in the introduction, pleasant sweetness, good fruit and grip. *At Prowein, March 2001* ★★ *Early drinking.*

**Hattenheimer Wisselbrunnen Riesling Kabinett halbtrocken** (Rg) **Schloss Reinhartshausen** Good colour; herbal aroma; medium-dry, attractive young fruit, acidity giving the wine length and finish. *At the Schloss, Feb 2002* ★★

## Hochheimer Kirchenstück Riesling Spätlese (Rg)
**Domdechant Werner** A touch of honey and pleasant flavour but not up to their '99 or '98. *At Prowein, March 2001* ★★ *Early drinking.*

## Iphöfer Julius-Echter-Berg Riesling Spätlese trocken 'S' (F) **Hans Wirsching** The 'S' stands for 'Selection', old vines.
To my surprise, Wirsching's winemaker told me that in Franken they had much better weather in 2000 than in 1999, the harvest taking place from mid-September to mid-October. Although both their Riesling and Silvaner are grown on the same soil, the varietal style is markedly contrasting. More lime on the Riesling nose; dry, crisp (acidity 8.5g/l) and steely. Fully fermented out to 13.5% alcohol. *At Prowein, March 2001* ★(★★) *Now–2006?*

## Iphöfer Julius-Echter-Berg Silvaner Spätlese trocken (F) **Hans Wirsching** Fragrant, crisp, acidic; dry yet rich, very distinctive, slightly scented, powerful (13.5% alcohol), good acidity. *March 2001* ★(★★) *Now–2006?*

## Iphöfer Kronsberg Scheurebe Spätlese trocken (F)
**Hans Wirsching** Scheurebe is just one of over eight different grape varieties grown on this old family estate, one of the largest private wine estates in Germany, with 69ha under vine. Exotic Scheurebe aromas of 'tom-cats' and scent; dry, in some ways rather like Sauvignon Blanc but with very high alcohol (14%). *March 2001* ★(★★)

## Schloss Johannisberger Riesling trocken (Rg) This was
so colourless that I thought it was my water glass. Pleasant enough nose and taste; light, drying. *The opening wine at the Eigensatz's supper prior to the White-Red summit, Oct 2001* ★

## Schloss Johannisberger Riesling Rotlack Kabinett (Rg)
Rotlack is the first premium level Kabinett wine marketed by the estate. A minerally, spearmint nose and taste. Medium-dry. *At Prowein, March 2001* ★ *For early drinking.*

## Schloss Johannisberger Riesling Grünlack Spätlese trocken (Rg) Grünlack is always Spätlese quality but it is
useful for the latter also to appear on the label. First tasted at Prowein in March (it was due to be bottled in May): pale; mild, minerally, with teeth-gripping acidity. Eight months later it seemed to have opened up, its colour more yellow; nose rich but youthful with quite nice fruit; medium-dry, some flesh, pleasant flavour. *The opening wine at Tatiana Fürstin von Metternich's dinner party at the Schloss following its 900th anniversary tasting, Nov 2001* ★★ *Drink soon.*

## Maximin Grünhäuser Riesling Kabinett (M) **v Schubert**
One of my favourite wine labels. Floral aroma, glorious fruit; light (alcohol 7.5%); very high acidity. Good length. *At Justerini & Brooks's tasting, Jan 2002* ★★★

## Maximin Grünhäuser Riesling Spätlese (M) **v Schubert**
Broad grapey nose, some depth; curiously soft, light. Pleasant. *At Justerini & Brooks's tasting, Jan 2002* ★★ *Drink soon.*

## 'Panta Rhei' QbA trocken (Rg) **Schloss Reinhartshausen** Its
contents and presentation as extraordinary as its name: a Traminer, Riesling and Chardonnay blend in a clear glass Bordeaux bottle and with a colourful label. Curious smoky nose; dry, loose knit. An inexpensive food wine. *At Prowein, March 2001* ★★

## Schloss Reinhartshausen Gutsriesling trocken (Rg)
**Schloss Reinhartshausen** Pale and shiny bright; slightly minty 'house Riesling' aroma; medium-dry, good, slightly perfumed flavour, good length. *At the Schloss, Feb 2002* ★★

## Rheingau Chardonnay (Rg) **Fritz Allendorf** From grapes in
his Winkeler Hasensprung and Mittelheimer Edelmann vineyards picked at the end of September and bottled in

November. A faint whiff of ping pong balls (celluloid) but surprisingly delicious flavour though not recognisably varietal. Dry, somewhat pasty acidic finish. Interesting. But why stray from Riesling? *At Prowein, March 2001* ★★

## Rheingau Riesling trocken (Rg) **Fritz Allendorf** Virtually
colourless. Very dry, steely – needs food (alcohol 11.5%, acidity 8.0g/l). *At Prowein, March 2001* ★(★)

## Rüdesheimer Magdalenenkreuz Riesling Kabinett
(Rg) **Joseph Leitz** Mild, grapey, delicious. *At the 'Wines of Germany' tasting at Vinopolis, London, April 2001* ★★ *For early drinking.*

## 'Samarkand' Riesling Qba (B) **Badischer Winzerkeller** This
enormous central co-operative is comprised of 91 co-operatives handling the wine of 25,000 growers. I first visited it in 1968 and wondered how many of us would drown if a 1-million-litre steel tank burst. The title 'Samarkand' is meant to indicate a spicy character. I found it dry, austere, raw and acidic. *April 2001.*

## Robert Weil Riesling Kabinett trocken (Rg) **Robert Weil**
Wilhelm Weil keeps the Kiedricher Gräfenberg label for his higher quality wines – the typical sweet and fruit, charmers. Under the 'Robert Weil' label he produces a range of light and dry wines in a less expensive range for early drinking. These are from a blend of grapes from the Wasserose vines grown on the slatey, minerally soil surrounding the Gräfenberg, also from their Sandgrub vineyard which has a deeper soil, as well as from the slatey Gräfenberg itself, blended according to the year and style. This Kabinett trocken is typically dry, light, with good acidity. *Tasted at the estate, March 2001* ★★

## Robert Weil Riesling Kabinett (Rg) **Robert Weil** Virtually
colourless; peachy now; on the dry side of medium, delicious flavour. I prefer this touch of residual sugar, with its delicately balanced fruit and acidity. *At Prowein, March 2001* ★★★

## Robert Weil Riesling Spätlese trocken (Rg) **Robert Weil**
From riper grapes fully fermented out: attractive, grapey aroma; dry, slightly spicy, touch of violets. *At Prowein, March 2001* ★★

## Weissburgunder und Chardonnay QbA trocken (Rg)
**Schloss Reinhartshausen** Another enterprising blend made from healthy Pinot Blanc and Chardonnay grapes: pale; fragrant; dry, firm, positive finish. Alcohol 11.5%. A really good food wine. *At Prowein, March 2001* ★★★

# 2001 possible ★★★★★

In some ways this vintage is all that the 2000 had hoped to be; the same provisos apply: selective late-picking of Riesling on well-drained sites to obtain optimum results. Yet again, the drawbacks of early-ripening varieties on water-logged soils have been more than apparent.

A cool spring retarded budding but, following a pleasantly warm May, the flowering during the second half of June was very satisfactory. July was warm and humid and August extremely hot. At this stage, maturation was advanced and hopes high. These were dashed by a miserably wet September. Those who had the courage to wait were rewarded by a fabulous October with high temperatures for over a month. The harvest was late in the classic vineyards, from around the third week in October to mid-November.

These are wines of exceptional ripeness, with sweet qualities, notably Auslese, Beerenauslese and TBAs, which some producers compare with the '75s, even the '71s. A great Riesling year. Worth looking out for.

# Italy

Where does one begin? The subject warrants a very large book; even then it would, I think, be impossible to cover the major wine regions, ranging from Sicily in the far south, with its part-North African, part-Mediterranean climate, to the foothills of the Alps and Trentino-Alto Adige and Fruili-Venezia Giulia – I well remember being almost frozen to death there (slight exaggeration) at a big wine seminar one April. Then over to the north-west: to the Valle d'Aosta and Piedmont, down through Lombardy and the Veneto to central Italy, dominated by Tuscany, and on to a host of what might be described as 'midi-south' regions, from Marche, Abruzzo and Puglia on the Adriatic coast to Lazio and Campania on the Tyrrhenian coast.

Most Italian wine is consumed in Italy, and a high proportion never travels out of its home region, whilst many serious drinkers, collectors, top quality merchants outside of Italy – certainly in the UK and US – are mainly concerned with the classics of Piedmont and Tuscany, spearheaded by the so-called 'super-Tuscans'.

What is generally not appreciated, except by people of my generation, is how appallingly bad Italian wines used to be, with the honourable exceptions of those produced by families such as Antinori and Frescobaldi, and the serious producers of Barolo (see the 1997 vintage); and how very recent have been the improvements. Indeed, one can trace the renaissance of Italian wines to the early 1980s. Going back 50 years, as I do, I can well recall the dire image of Italian wines, associated mainly with cheap and cheerful *trattorie* in London's Soho, bottles stacked on warm shelves or strung from the ceiling, the centrepiece of each table an aptly named *fiasco*, straw-covered, with candle protruding from its neck.

In the mid-1950s Italian wines were not taken seriously. I have in front of me the price lists of two major wine merchants for whom, in turn, I worked: Saccone & Speed's 'Winter 1954–55' had one page devoted to 'Italian Wines', four reds, four whites, and one sparkling, all from the larger commercial houses, the best being Chianti Brolio at 17 shillings and 6 pence (no vintage stated). Harvey's of Bristol did not list any Italian wines until the mid-1950s: just two, for the first time, in Autumn 1954, a Chianti Ruffino, red and white, 'bottled in Italy' (coincidentally both at 17 shillings and 6 pence) and in their 1959 list these same two, at 6 pence more per bottle, augmented by one of Harry Waugh's finds, Chianti Nozzole, bottled in Bristol and priced at a modest 8 shillings. Harry was Harvey's' brilliant and innovative table wine buyer and anything he selected sold like hot cakes. But, really, apart from a few specialist importers – Italian restaurants being their main customers – Italian wines were either taken for granted, or not taken seriously, or both.

I happen to love Italy, its landscape, its architecture, its people. I like real Italian food for it manages to be so original, so interesting. I like good Italian restaurants for even at the top end they are different. For me, eating in a top French restaurant is like going to the theatre, in an Italian restaurant like going to the cinema, less of an event, more fun. More to the point, I like – and frequently drink – Italian wine.

The following notes should be treated as less of a critique (I am convinced that one has to live in Italy to really get to know their wines) and more as a commentary on those I have come across and, mainly, liked; it is rather like looking over my shoulder and reading a diary, for this, in fact, is what my tasting books are. My choice of wines may seem capricious which, to a certain extent, it is. I might well seem biased in favour of a small number of producers. My long and close friendship with Angelo Gaja, for example. We actually first met at a wine fair in Germany shortly after I had written an article which suggested that, judging from the small size of the lettering 'Barbaresco', and 'GAJA' in much bigger and blacker type, here was a mammoth ego on the wine scene! He took it well, and my wife and I have enjoyed his company and generous hospitality many times in Piedmont. His alter ego is the immensely charming, likeable and relaxed aristocrat Piero Antinori, equally innovative, equally active in promoting his wines and the wines of Italy.

# Some older, pre-1945 vintages

Despite unification in 1861, individual regions – and producers – continued to go their own way. Efforts were made in the 1920s to define *vini tipici* and the Dalmasso Commission managed to establish the Chianti Classico zone, an important start because of all wine names Chianti was the most abused. Elsewhere, quantity not quality prevailed – Mussolini was no help. Unsurprisingly pre-war vintages are scarce.

## 1930

**Carmignano, Riserva Villa de Capezzana/Bonacossi** Two notes: the first in 1983, re-bottled at the estate in 1960: pale rose tawny; sage-scented; gentle, faded but sound and delicious. The next, re-bottled in 1966: a very similar note, better on palate than nose. *Last noted dining at home, April 1995* ★★★

## 1931

**Barolo, Riserva Speciale Giacomo Borgogno** A great classic from Piedmont. Two notes, first – with '31 Richebourg Domaine de la Romanée-Conti and '31 Niepoort either side – at Daphne's 65th birthday dinner at Christie's (I shouldn't mention the date, but it was 22 July 1996). The bottle had its original, crumbly cork but the level was excellent. The wine had a ruddy-amber colour, no red left; maderised and touch of decay on nose and palate. Yet there was a smattering of charm, its life support, acidity, turning sour.

Most recently, I noted a superbly hefty and handsome bottle with a glass button impressed '*Borgogno Barolo*', embossed lead capsule '*vino Classico Borgogno Barolo*', full body label and neck label '*Riserva 1931*'. The level was very good for its age, 4cm below the very crumbly, original cork. It was in much better condition than the previous bottle: palish, warm tawny with a wide open, yellow rim. On decanting, the nose was slightly sour and cheesy but after 90 minutes it had opened up (rich, meaty, old stables) and after a further hour in the glass, towards the end of dinner, I caught a whiff of old tangerine skin. On the palate medium-sweet, fruit lost with a smoky old flavour, substantial body – seemed nearer to 15% than the 13.5% alcohol stated on the label. All in all, it was delicious. *Last noted at home, May 2002. As a drink, at best* ★★★, *as a rare experience* ★★★★★

## 1937

**Barolo, Riserva Giacomo Borgogno** Palish, orange-tinged; showing its age, 'thoroughbred stables'; sweet, a gentle old lady, good acidity. Delicious. *At a pre-sale tasting of Italian wines at Christie's, July 1996* ★★★

## 1944

**Barolo, Riserva Giacomo Borgogno** Mature, green rim; sweet, developing the 'stables' scent; good fruit. *July 1996* ★★★

# 1945–1979

The end of World War Two was the tentative beginning of a new era. Happily it started with an excellent vintage in 1945. This was also a period when important laws were introduced to try and bring some order to the free and easy world of Italian wine production. The categories of Denominazione di Origine Controllata (DOC) and a higher level aiming at encouraging superior quality, adding 'e Garantita' (DOCG) were enacted in 1963. The first DOCG wines, were Barbaresco, Barolo, Brunello di Montalcino, Chianti and Vino Nobile di Montepulciano, all red wines.

Single-vineyard wines, a new concept, were introduced in Piedmont in the mid-1960s, specifically in Barolo, and, in 1970, in Tuscany by Antinori, the name of his Tignanello wine appearing on the label for the first time in 1971. This was the era of the development of 'super-Tuscans', with enlightened producers such as the Marchese Mario Incisa della Rocchetta and his Sassicaia wine to the fore (see box page 395). These 'super-Tuscans' raised the profile and prices of Italian wine and ushered in the next 'new era', the 1980s.

### Red Vintages at a Glance

**PIEDMONT (BAROLO, BARBARESCO)**
**Outstanding** ★★★★★
1947, 1958, 1959, 1961, 1964, 1971, 1974, 1978
**Very Good** ★★★★
1945, 1952, 1967, 1970
**Good** ★★★
1949, 1955, 1962, 1968, 1969, 1979

**TUSCANY (CHIANTI, BRUNELLO DI MONTALCINO)**
**Outstanding** ★★★★★
1947, 1962, 1964, 1967, 1971, 1978
**Very Good** ★★★★
1945, 1955, 1968, 1975 (v), 1977, 1979
**Good** ★★★
1949, 1952, 1958, 1959, 1961, 1970, 1973

# 1945 ★★★★

Difficult post-war vintage. I have tasted only one wine in the past decade.

**Brunello di Montalcino, Riserva Biondi-Santi** The oldest vintage in a range of Riservas kindly arranged by my good friend Gelasio Gaetani, and hosted by Franco Biondi-Santi and his son Jacopo on my first visit to the estate, Il Greppo, March 1995. The bottle had been recorked twice, in 1970 and 1985: pale, very little red left, a sort of warm rose amber; showing its age but quickly evolving, high-toned and varnishy. After lunch, it smelled of spicy old stables. On the palate, some sweetness, a faded old lady with a waspish tongue. For some reason or other, it reminded me of an 1908 port. A bottle brought to London and stood up for six days to settle had a similar, rather attractive, soft red colour; bouquet with the sweetness of decay; like a very old claret. Very astringent. *Last tasted April 1995. For rarity and value ★★★★★, for drinking ★★*

---

### Biondi-Santi and Brunello

*If only Franco Biondi-Santi's grandfather had registered Brunello, his special clone of Sangiovese, the history of Montalcino – and the family estate, Il Greppo, would have been rather different. Once proudly unique and with a very special, idiosyncratic and unmistakable character, it would have had the market to itself – a similar situation to Vega Sicilia in the Spanish Duero. Now there are over 100 estates in the Brunello di Montalcino zone around the historic hillside town of Montalcino. Most of the wines today bear little resemblance to the original Biondi-Santi style and, it has to be said, are often more amenable, modern and approachable.*

---

# 1947 ★★★★★

Great vintage throughout Italy.

**Barolo, Riserva Giacomo Borgogno** Palish, tint of cherry; sweet, 'cream cheese'; rich, very good acidity. *At a pre-sale tasting, July 1996 ★★★★*

ONE OLDER NOTE **Chianti Rufina Selvapiana** Rich, intense. *1982 ★★★★*

# 1949 ★★★

Moderately good throughout Italy.

**Barolo, Classico E Serafino** Very deep, fully mature; very rich, singed, hot-vintage smell and taste. Excellent. *At a pre-sale tasting, July 1996 ★★★★*

# 1952 ★★★ to ★★★★

Good but better in Piedmont

**Barolo Giacomo Borgogno** An outstanding vintage. The oldest vintage at a Barolo tasting organised for me in November 1994 by Angelo Gaja. He persuaded ten leading growers to bring two wines, their 1990 and an older vintage, to Alba on a Sunday morning. A magnum: pale, scarcely any red, more like a madeira; with the sourness of age on nose and palate, still tannic. Very generous to have sacrificed a magnum for me but it should have been drunk 20 years prior. More recently: fully mature, orange-tinged; strained and strange. *At a pre-sale tasting, July 1996. At best ★★*

# 1954 ★★

Middling quality.

**Barolo, Riserva Giacomo Borgogno** Palish, orange-tinged; sweet, meaty, cheese rind nose and taste. Very rich though. *Pre-sale, July 1996 ★★★*

# 1955 ★★★ to ★★★★

Good in the north, even better in Tuscany.

**Barolo, Monfortino Giacomo Conterno** Palish, very mature, orange-tinged; singed, earthy; very sweet, very rich, very good. *With Gaja at Il Pescatore, near Mantua, Nov 1994 ★★★★*

**Brunello di Montalcino, Riserva Biondi-Santi** Recorked in 1985. Good colour, rich, mature; fascinating nose, when first poured, like a sea breeze, tight, cedary, fragrant, opening up and holding well; fairly sweet and full-bodied, fabulous, 'classic' (I was told) flavour, fruit, grip and length. *At Il Greppo, March 1995 ★★★★★*

# 1957 ★★

Unexciting though early reports of fine wines in Piedmont.

**Barolo, Riserva Giacomo Borgogno** Palish, rosehip; tangy, madeira-like; malty. Attractive despite maderisation. *July 1996 ★*

# 1958 ★★★ to ★★★★★

Great year in Piedmont, good in Tuscany. Few wines remain.

**Barbaresco Gaja** Made by Angelo's father. Palish, rich yet madeira-like, with orange rim; gentle, singed, old nose; better on palate, sweet, 'warm' earthy flavour, (alcohol 14%), lingering tannin and good acidity. *The oldest vintage tasted at Gaja's, Nov 1994 ★★*

**Barolo Giacomo Borgogno** When tasted in 1994 rather madeira-like, warm tawny; unusual violet fragrance; strange but attractive flavour. More than mature. Two years later a better bottle: rich, with lovely glow; low-keyed nose; sweet, rich, crisp, still very tannic. *Last noted at the Italian pre-sale tasting at Christie's, July 1996. At its best ★★★*

# 1959 ★★★ to ★★★★★

Great year in Piedmont, less good in Tuscany.

**Barolo Marchesi di Barolo** Showing its age, yet tannic. *July 1996 ★★★*

**Barolo, Riserva Speciale Torre del Barolo** Palish, open, lovely glow; good spicy bouquet and flavour. *July 1996 ★★★★*

# 1960 ★★

Not particularly good. None tasted recently.

# 1961 ★★★ to ★★★★★

Good in Tuscany. Great in Piedmont, exceptionally hot vintage.

**Barbaresco Gaja** Made by Angelo's father. Two notes, first in 1984, dining at Sparks' Steak House in New York. The late Pat Cetta most generously brought a bottle to my table: it was the most beautiful, faultless, Italian wine I had ever drunk: soft, 'warm', inimitable bouquet; the sweetness of perfectly ripe grapes and a flavour which opened up into an unforgettable crescendo. Over 20 years later, at the end of an Italian wine tasting I was conducting for the Chaîne des Rôtisseurs in Nassau, in the Bahamas, the proprietor, Enrico Garzaroli, opened a surprise bottle and gave it to me to taste blind. It could, I said, *only* be the '61 Gaja: lovely, mature, great-vintage colour; superb, slightly toasted, vanilla bouquet, showing its age; superb flavour and silky 'mouth-feel', great length, still tannic. *Last tasted Feb 1997* ★★★★★

**Barolo Classico Torre dell Barolo** Palish, very attractive colour; spicy bouquet, 'sweaty', tannic underpinning; too tannic. *July 1996* ★★★*, in its way.*

**Barolo, Riserva Giacomo Borgogno** Very little red, brown-tinged; spicy; taste of old oak and old ladies – if you see what I mean. Still tannic. *July 1996* ★★★ *The tannin will remain, leaving the fruit high and dry.*

## 1962 ★★★ to ★★★★★

Although Tuscan wines were said to be superb, I haven't tasted any, except one oxidised Chianti Rufino in the early 1980s. Good vintage in Piedmont but I have only tasted two wines.

**Barbaresco, Riserva Giacomo Borgogno** Good rich bouquet and flavour. *July 1996* ★★★★

**Barolo, Riserva Giacomo Borgogno** Mature, with an apple-green rim rather like an old dessert wine; very sweet, rich, tangy. Showing its age, impressive but again, exceedingly tannic. *July 1996* ★★★

## 1963

Poor year.

## 1964 ★★★★★

Excellent vintage in all regions and the first in which Barolo's individual vineyards were marketed.

**Barbaresco Gaja** First noted at a pre-sale Italian tasting in 1996: sweet, full, rich. Next, the oldest of six Gaja wines at a Rodenstock dinner. Magnum: mellow look; curiously Bordeaux-like, slightly minty, singed nose, touch of mocha; a 'sweet and sour' wine, crisp, lean, perfect balance and condition. Still tannic. *Last tasted Sept 1998* ★★★★

**Barolo, Monfortino Giacomo Conterno** Though an old note, the wine was superb. *May, 1987* ★★★★

**Brunello di Montalcino, Riserva Biondi-Santi** First tasted in October 1994 at the Dîner Classique 'V' in Zürich: a deep, lively cherry red; touch of aniseed, opening up in a most extraordinary way; overall dry, crisp fruit, swingeingly tannic. A curious, young-old taste. The following year at the Il Greppo tasting: intense, still youthfully plummy, with red tinge (usually a sign of high volatile acidity); lovely, fragrant bouquet, slightly lactic; this time noted as sweet, mouthfilling, with rich extract and showing its age on the dry edgy finish. *Last tasted May 1995* ★★★★ *Will have aged further but might well have survived.*

## 1965 and 1966

Poor years.

## 1967 ★★★★ to ★★★★★

Very good vintage, particularly successful in Tuscany.

**Barolo, Riserva Giacomo Borgogno** First tasted in 1983: fine, deep ruby; high volatile acidity; good flavour but tart. Thirteen

years later: fully mature, rich 'legs'; sweet, fragrant, touch of vanilla; sweet. Excellent flavour and condition. *Last noted at a pre-sale tasting, July 1996. At best* ★★★★

**Barolo, Riserva Speciale Torre del Barolo** Very deep; sweet, hefty. *At a pre-sale tasting, July 1996* ★★★

**Barolo, Riserva Speciale (Red Label) Colline Rionda de Serralunga** (Referred to in later notes as 'Rionda'.) **Bruno Giacosa** The oldest vintage at Johann Willsberger's excellent Giacosa vertical at the Hotel Victoria, Bad Mergentheim (Germany): medium-pale, fully mature, soft, autumnal, orange-rimmed. Decanted just before serving, sweet, rich, 'bracken', opening up beautifully, touch of caramel, then a whiff of thoroughbred stables; very sweet, *gibier*, exquisitely decayed, still tannic, extended. Impressive but too old. *Feb 2002* ★★★

**THREE OLDER NOTES Chianti Classico, Riserva Villa Antinori** magnums: good wine. Tannic. *1986* ★★★★; **Chianti Classico, Riserva Brolio Ricasoli** light style, firm texture, tannic. *1982* ★★★★; and **Brunello di Montalcino, Riserva Col d'Orcia** rich yet tannic. *1986* ★★★★

## 1968 ★★★ to ★★★★

Very variable. A limited amount of good wines in Piedmont and very good in Tuscany. Sassicaia made its first appearance.

**Brunello di Montalcino Riserva Biondi-Santi** Fully developed, tinge of orange; immediately forthcoming, slightly meaty and malty; medium-sweetness and body, touch of astringency. *At Il Greppo, May 1995* ★★★★

**TWO OLDER NOTES Brunello di Montalcino Col d'Orcia** rich but bitter. *1982* ★★★★; and **Rubesco Torgiano Lungarotti** one of my favourite Italian reds. Several notes. *1982* ★★★★

---

### Sassicaia and the 'super-Tuscans'

*There is nothing fancy or ostentatious about Sassicaia's winery in the coastal Maremma region of Tuscany, nor its modest and unassuming owner, the Marchese Niccolò Incisa della Rocchetta, whose father planted cuttings of Cabernet vines from Ch Lafite in the mid-1940s. I first visited the San Guido estate in the company of America's Bacchus Society and found no fancy, state-of-the-art trappings. Sassicaia was one of the first of what are now dubbed 'super-Tuscan' wines and is now unquestionably and deservedly of cult status. It started in a somewhat unlikely way. An enormous family estate near the coast, far from the inland Chianti Classico zone, and a vineyard planted with non-Italian vine varieties, principally Cabernet Sauvignon, to make a new, Bordeaux-style wine. It more than worked, breaking rules and regulations to make the once lowly* vino da tavola *respectable. This has had two welcome side effects: it has rekindled an awareness of the wines of Tuscany and – at least in my opinion – has 'raised the game' of the producers of Chianti Classico. These wines have taken off too.*

---

## 1969 ★★ to ★★★

Good crop of sturdy wines in Piedmont. Moderate elsewhere.

**Barbaresco, Santo Stefano di Neive d'Alba Bruno Giacosa** One of the first single-vineyard wines made in Barbaresco. Palish, warm, softly coloured, rich 'legs'; showing its age, whiff of fungi; sweet, 'brackish', lean, very tannic. *At Willsberger's vertical in Bad Mergentheim, Germany, Feb 2002* ★★

Barolo, Rionda **Bruno Giacosa** Similar appearance to the Santo Stefano; sweet, a mixture of chocolate and cabbages, good depth; semi-sweet, lean yet rich, powerful, heady. Raw tannic finish. *Feb 2002* ★★★

**Brunello di Montalcino, Riserva Biondi-Santi** Grapes picked 1 October, ten days too late. Two bottles: fully mature appearance; the first old, gnarled, singed, the second more vinous, both opening up richly, steely, with scent of artichoke; fairly assertive, citrus-like fruit and 'old oak', astringent finish. *Tasted at Christie's, May 1994* ★★

**Chianti Classico, Riserva Ducale Ruffino** Crumbly cork, soft coloured, open orange mature tinge; showing its age but drinking well, warm, fleshy, soft tannins. *A present from Gelasio Gaetani and opened on board the* Crystal Symphony, *Sept 1999* ★★★ *on the verge of 4 stars.*

## 1970 ★★★ to ★★★★

Good vintage in Tuscany and a large crop of very good wines in Piedmont.

**Brunello di Montalcino, Riserva Biondi-Santi** I noted that their Riservas are only produced in perfect years (in the 1970s: '70, '71, '75 and '77) and from vines at least 25 years old. Grapes hand selected and fermented in wood. Aged in large Slovenian oak vats for 4½ years. After all that, (in 1994) the bottle was corked! Better luck at the winery: rich, orange tinge, fully evolved appearance and bouquet. Spicy, tea-like, then a strange sourness, which had recovered when retasted after lunch, three hours after pouring. Far better, open, relaxed, very distinctive, sweet and fruity. On the palate, initially, though showing its age, sweet with very crisp fruit, power and length, but astringent. *Last noted at Il Greppo, May 1995* ★★★

FOUR WINES NOTED IN THE EARLY 1980S **Barolo Riserva F Fiorina** fascinating, ripe, high volatile acidity and tough. Did it ever come round I asked? Yes: it needed three days to breathe. Alas, I couldn't wait. *1982* ★★?; **Barolo, Riserva Speciale Giacomo Conterno** just short of magnificent. *1987* ★★★★; **Chianti Rufina, Nipozzano Frescobaldi** rich, good length and finish. *1983* ★★★★; and **Rubesco Torgiano Lungarotti** deep ruby; rich, powerful, rustic. *1984* ★★★

## 1971 ★★★★★

An excellent vintage. Antinori's single-vineyard wine, Tignanello, marketed for the first time.

**Barbaresco Gaja** A few days after drinking the superb '61 at Sparks in New York (in 1984), I returned to the restaurant and ordered the '71. It was well-nigh perfect. Exactly a decade later: still a lovely colour; not showing its age at all; sweet, fullish, rich, silky tannins, good length. Lovely to drink by itself. *Last noted dining with Angelo Gaja at Il Cascinalenuovo, Isola d'Asti, Nov 1994* ★★★★★

**Barolo, Riserva Prunotto** At ten years old: deep; dumb; massive, laden with everything except fruit. In 1985 'needs 20 years' noted. It was part way there 20 years after the vintage: a softer red, warm, rich; beautifully bricky nose and high-toned fruit and bouquet, developing an amalgam of Verdelho madeira and soft toffee. On the palate it was now sweet and fleshy, tannins softened. *Last tasted Feb 1991* ★★★★★ *I think it will be at its absolute peak now.*

**Brunello di Montalcino, Riserva Biondi-Santi** At Christie's in 1984: deep, mature; initially showing its age, old straw, but

after an hour rich, earthy, Latour-like, evolving further, even after seven hours in the glass. On the palate, some sweetness, full-bodied, soft, chewy, chunky, slightly spicy. Dry finish. A year later, at Il Greppo: richly evolved bouquet, spicy, rich tea, biscuity; lean, slightly stalky, rich yet tannic. *Last tasted May 1995* ★★★★

OTHER TOP '71S LAST TASTED IN THE 1980S **Prunotto's** Barbaresco firm and fine. *1981* ★★★★; **Giacomo Conterno's** Barolo, Riserva Speciale huge, impressive. *1987* ★★★★; **Lungarotti's** Rubesco Torgiano ruby, ripe, elegant. Delicious with or without food. *1987* ★★★★; and **Antinori's** Tignanello first tasted with Piero Antinori, June 1977 and thrice since. Ripe, elegant. A very successful *vino da tavola. Last tasted 1982.* Then ★★★★

## 1972

Disastrous year.

## 1973 ★★ to ★★★

Uneven vintage. Better in Tuscany than in Piedmont. I have tasted only one wine: **Chianti Classico Riserva Antinori** Very good to drink in 1982 ★★★

## 1974 ★★ to ★★★★★

Excellent vintage in Piedmont. Chianti was less reliable and lacked the substance for longevity.

**Barbaresco, Santo Stefano, Riserva Speciale Bruno Giacosa** Palish, lovely; well evolved bouquet of cheese and tea (better than it sounds); very sweet, soft, attractive, great length. *At Willsberger's Giacosa tasting, Bad Mergentheim, Feb 2002* ★★★★★

**Barolo (White Label) Bruno Giacosa** Palish, touch of rose, mature rim; sweet, warm, harmonious which softened and after 80 minutes reminded me of mushroom soup; very rich, singed, good fruit, leaner than the 'red label' (below), good, sweet finish. *Feb 2002* ★★★★ *Preferred it as a drink to the Riserva.*

**Barolo, Bussia Riserva Speciale Bruno Giacosa** Warm tawny; crisp, singed brown paper – it reminded me of Ch Ausone, beginning to show its age but with considerable richness and depth; sweet, tangy, very rich but not enough to mask its mouth-drying tannins. *Feb 2002* ★★★★

## 1975 ★★ to ★★★★

Mediocre in Piedmont, fair in Tuscany though there was some very good Brunello.

**Barolo, Bussia Riserva Speciale Bruno Giacosa** Pale but rich; low-keyed, a modicum of floweriness; very sweet but lean with a somewhat raw, very tannic, finish. *Feb 2002* ★★

**Brunello di Montalcino, Riserva Biondi-Santi** First noted in April 1994: sample bottles sent to Christie's: deep; low-keyed at first, opening up, powerful, peppery, spicy and after nearly two hours, fabulous. On the palate, fairly sweet, fullish (alcohol 13%), crisp fruit, very good.

A year later at Il Greppo. After the '55, the best of all the Riservas: impressive, plummy, rich appearance; immediately fragrant, spicy, with good fruit, holding back then accelerating with fabulous bouquet, more fig-like, great depth; a gloriously rich mouthfiller. Perfect structure and balance. *Last tasted May 1995* ★★★★★

SEVERAL OTHER BRUNELLO DI MONTALCINOS TASTED IN THE EARLY 1980S **Frescobaldi**'s **Castelgiocondo** scented, spicy, elegant. *1982* ★★★(★); **Caparzo** good fruit but severely tannic. *1988* ★★(★★); **Riguardo** acidic. *1983*; **Isabella de Medici** sweet, scented, leathery. *1982* ★★(★)

## 1976 ★★

Few wines worth noting.

**Sassicaia Tenuta San Guido/Marchese Incisa della Rocchetta** Henceforth just referred to as Sassicaia. This seems to be my first note of this incredibly successful wine, the original super-Tuscan first released in 1968 (see box page 395). I noted a 'good flavour, weight and balance'. *At dinner, May 1994* ★★★ *Not tasted since.*

## 1977 ★★ to ★★★★

Small crop of poor wine in Piedmont. Particularly good vintage in Tuscany. The first 100% Sangiovese super-Tuscan (Le Pergole Torte) came onto the market in 1977.

**Tignanello Antinori** Though the first vintage was 1971, it was not until the 1975 vintage that the ever-enterprising Piero Antinori and his enologist, Giacomo Tachis, produced the wine of the style they wanted, blending Tuscany's Sangiovese with about 20% Cabernet Sauvignon. It was – still is – a huge success. This appears to be the earliest vintage of Tignanello I have tasted and then only recently: medium-deep, very mature; bouquet of 'old oak'; some sweetness, perfect weight, rich, soft, *à point* – or whatever the equivalent is in Italian. A lovely wine. *Dining with Jane and Julius Wile at his home in Scarsdale, New York, Dec 1998* ★★★★

## 1978 ★★★★★

The best all-round vintage of the decade, though considered difficult because of the heat in Piedmont. Many notes, so I shall concentrate on the most recent.

**Barbaresco Gaja** First tasted in 1992: dry, full but not heavy. 'Tannate of iron' noted. Next, two bottles, slight variation, both fairly deep, still ruby; neither showing age but one richer, opening up beautifully. Crisp, dry, great length. *Dining with Angelo Gaja in Isola d'Asti, Nov 1994* ★★★★

**Barbaresco, Costa Russi Gaja** First tasted at the winery in November 1994: warm russet with tawny rim; rich, soft, meaty nose; fairly sweet, chewy, still tannic. Lovely wine. *Last noted March 1995* ★★★★(★) *Should be at its peak now.*

**Barbaresco, Santo Stefano, Riserva Speciale Bruno Giacosa** Medium-deep. 'Rich' is the operative word for appearance, bouquet and taste. A nose of vast dimensions. Very sweet, full of fruit, complete, dry, tannic finish. Superb. *At Willsberger's Giacosa tasting, Bad Mergentheim, Feb 2002* ★★★★★

**Barolo Pio Cesare** Using small barrels for the first time. Rich, orange-tinged; strange figgy fruit, violets; rich texture, attractive in its way. Whiff of eucalyptus supposedly from the Yugoslav oak. *In Alba, Nov 1994* ★★★

**Barolo, Falletto Bruno Giacosa** Orange brown, high volatile acidity; very flavoury. *In Los Angeles, March 1999* ★★

**Barolo, Marcenasco Renato Ratti** Fully mature, orange-tinged; attractive bottle age; very sweet, nice weight, easy (alcohol 13%). *In Alba, Nov 1994* ★★★★

**Barolo, Rionda Riserva Speciale Bruno Giacosa** Deep, soft, ruby; smell of mushroom soup, then mulligatawny, with

fruit wedged between; very sweet, very rich, powerful (alcohol 14%). Idiosyncratic. Impressive. *Feb 2002* ★★★★

**Barolo, Serralunga Riserva Giacomo Conterno** Richly coloured, mature; sweet, glorious flavour, still very tannic but excellent with the roast beef. *With Angelo Gaja at Il Pescatore, near Mantua, Nov 1994* ★★★★★

**Sassicaia** First noted when it was ten years of age: opaque, black cherry; perfect harmony on nose and palate. Next, in 1990, the oldest vintage in a Sassicaia vertical: less deep but richly coloured; curious Brie crust nose; some sweetness, agreeable weight and grip. 'Needed drinking.' Most recently, being 100% Cabernet Sauvignon, craftily inserted by Hugh Johnson between '78 Ch Palmer and Cheval Blanc, accompanying steak and kidney pudding at his Bordeaux Club dinner. Deep, fairly intense, still youthful; very curious nose, a touch of tar; some sweetness, touch of liquorice, mouth-drying finish and austere compared with the two '78 clarets. *Last noted at Saling Hall, Dec 1997* ★★★(★)

**Solaia Antinori** Single vineyard next to Tignanello on Antinori's estate (planted with Cabernet Sauvignon 75% and Cabernet Franc 25%; 18 to 24 months in small French oak). The '78 was never released (the '79 was the first to be marketed). Three notes, first in 1988: gorgeously rich nose with unmistakable Bordeaux character, like an '82; spicy, oaky, rich, tannic. Again in 1992. Most recently, dining with Piero and his daughters at the Palazzo Antinori in Florence: now medium-deep, rich (a hefty sediment); distinctly sweet, richness containing considerable tannin, very attractive. *Last tasted April 1999* ★★★★

**Tignanello Antinori** Although not a recent note, I have included it along with Sassicaia and Solaia to round off the super-Tuscan trio. Sweet nose, dry palate, excellent flavour. *Feb 1988* ★★★★ *Probably perfection now.*

SOME OTHER '78S SHOWING PARTICULARLY WELL IN THE 1980S **Aldo Conterno**'s **Barbera d'Alba** admittedly very young but immensely impressive. *1980* ★★★★; **Gaja**'s **Barbaresco, Sorì Tildin** several notes, from 'fennel and walnuts' in 1982. Lean, not an easy wine, in fact daunting. Great though. *1987* ★★★(★) *Probably at its best now*; **Ceretto**'s **Barolo** lovely. *1986* ★★★; **Cavallotto**'s **Barolo, Riserva** glorious. *1987* ★★★★; **Barbi**'s **Brunello di Montalcino** flavoury, tannic. *1988* ★★★★; **Frescobaldi**'s **Chianti Rufina, Nipozzano** great potential. *1988* ★★★★

## 1979 ★★★ to ★★★★

Good, mainly early-maturing wines in Piedmont. Tuscany had a huge harvest, up to high quality.

**Barbaresco, Gallina di Neive Bruno Giacosa** Fairly pale; very good nose; quite a bite. *At a pre-sale tasting in Los Angeles, March 1999* ★★★★

**Barolo, Bussia Riserva Speciale Bruno Giacosa** Palish, fully mature, weak, open rim; chocolatey, soupy, oxidised nose; yet surprisingly good on the palate. Sweet, rich, good fruit, lean but very flavoury, tannic. *At Willsberger's Giacosa tasting, Feb 2002* ★★★ *Very odd.*

**Sassicaia** In its 11th year, outstandingly the best wine of the 1978–1987 vertical: richly coloured, mature – like a top '59 claret; harmonious bouquet; remarkably sweet, rich, fleshy, rounded and with perfectly integrated tannin. *Last noted, drinking well at dinner in the Connaught Grill, March 1992* ★★★★★ *Doubtless perfection now.*

# 1980–1999

If the so-called 'super-Tuscans' spearheaded the changes in the previous decade it was, I believe, in the 1980s that the general renaissance of Italian wine began. This is not to say that in Tuscany itself good wines were not being made – the noble families like Antinori and Frescobaldi set a good example – but some of the larger commercial firms were producing decent but pedestrian wines and the standard of wine from the estates was variable. In the 1990s, the success of the super-Tuscans challenged and re-energised the production of quality Chianti Classico.

In Piedmont there were two schools: one distinctly old-fashioned, producing dark and tannic reds, Barolos in particular; the other, realising that this style of wine needed patience and long cellaring and was far from the popular taste, began making more amenable wines. And in Barbaresco, the influence of Angelo Gaja was of major importance, the quality (and price) of his wines making the international market sit up and take notice.

There could scarcely be a bigger contrast between Piero Antinori the patrician, and Angelo Gaja the thrusting dynamo, both in their own ways enterprising, imaginative and above all representing quality; they have not only been superb promoters of their own regional wines but ambassadors for Italian wines as a whole.

## Red Vintages at a Glance
PIEDMONT (BAROLO, BARBARESCO)
**Outstanding** ★★★★★
1982, 1985, 1988, 1990, 1997
**Very Good** ★★★★
1986, 1989, 1996, 1999
**Good** ★★★
1983, 1987 (v), 1993 (v), 1995, 1998 (v)
TUSCANY (CHIANTI, BRUNELLO DI MONTALCINO)
**Outstanding** ★★★★★
1982, 1985, 1988, 1990, 1995 (v), 1997
**Very Good** ★★★★
1986, 1994 (v), 1996, 1999
**Good** ★★★
1981, 1983, 1987 (v), 1989 (v), 1993 (v), 1998 (v)

## 1980 ★

In Piedmont not a very good start and this was the least satisfactory vintage of the decade. The cool spring continued until June, retarding growth. July picked up and the summer became hot and dry. In late September, the rains came with no let up in October. The result was a very late harvest, some growers still picking in early November with snow on the 4th causing further interruption. In Tuscany, despite similar weather conditions, the grapes were surprisingly healthy.

I have tasted few wines from this vintage.
**Barolo Elio Altare** A small and somewhat idiosyncratic producer: fairly pale; unforthcoming nose and flavour; dry. Not bad for a poor vintage. *At the Sunday morning Barolo tasting organised on my behalf by Angelo Gaja in Alba, Nov 1994* ★
**Sassicaia** Several notes. Drinking quite well in the mid-1980s but in its tenth year 'unknit', nose herbaceous, stalky; lean and short. *The least inspiring of the vertical at the tasting held at Brooks's Club in London, March 1990. Only just* ★★ *then. Of little interest now.*

JUST TWO OTHER OLDER NOTES **Chianti, Nozzole** *1986* and **Badia a Coltibuono**'s **Chianti Classico Riserva** *1987* – both pleasant enough but short.

## 1981 ★ to ★★★

Variable, uneven. Piedmont had the worst of the weather with a hot, humid June and July causing rot problems; it was wet in late August and early September, thereafter cloudy and dry. A late harvest. Tuscany, after a late spring, enjoyed good weather throughout the summer. The harvest, beginning 20 September, was interrupted by rain and those growers who picked early made the better wines.
**Brunello di Montalcino, Riserva Biondi-Santi** First tasted at Christie's in May 1994. It had been put on the market in 1986 and was regarded as of similar quality to their '70. Not very deep; soft fruit, touch of vanilla opening up richly; fair sweetness and body (alcohol 13%), lovely texture and fruit. The following spring at Il Greppo: similar notes, or at least words to the same effect. In fact I gave full marks to the nose, harmonious, nicely evolved, opening up richly and holding well; good flesh, attractive. *Last tasted March 1995* ★★★★ *Probably as good then as it will ever get.*
**Sassicaia** Noted only once at the Brooks's Club vertical: richly coloured; curious nose, rich, slightly cheesy; distinctly sweet, chunky, tannic. *Tasted March 1990. Then* ★★(★) *Would be interesting to see how this developed.*

OF THE RELATIVELY FEW OTHER '81S TASTED IN THE MID- TO LATE 1980S, the following **Chianti**s were interesting: **Castello di Volpaia**'s **Chianti Classico** my first taste of this wine: delightfully fragrant, easy and agreeable. *1986* ★★★; **Badia a Coltibuono**'s **Chianti Classico, Riserva** fragrant, good flavour and length. *1987* ★★★; **Castello di Vicchiomaggio**'s **Chianti Classico, Riserva Prima** elegant, good length. *1987* ★★★; and the best, **Frescobaldi**'s **Chianti Rufina, Riserva Montesodi** *1987* ★★★★

## 1982 ★★★★★

Excellent vintage. In Tuscany it was hot and sunny, but dry. Good quality throughout, particularly the Riservas. Piedmont enjoyed a similar season though there was some rain in late September and early October before the main harvest.
**Barbaresco Gaja** A double magnum flight of Gaja wines at a Rodenstock dinner. Good fruit, hard to define, low-keyed but

fragrant; touch of tar on the palate, teeth-grippingly tannic. *Sept 1998* ★★(★★) *Hard to see this coming round.*

**Barbaresco, Sorì San Lorenzo Gaja** A magnum given to me by Angelo and opened at a dinner party at home. I knew it was a big wine so I double-decanted it over two hours before serving: fairly deep, intense; lovely crisp fruit, a whiff of blackcurrant; swingeingly tannic. Absolutely magnificent but almost undrinkably unready. *Dec 1999* ★(★★★★) *Like the 1870 Ch Lafite or the 1928 Latour it is a wine that will take half a century to come round. Say 2025–2050. Let me know!*

**Barolo Cerequio Michele Chiarlo** Very mature; whiff of bottle stink which cleared, but showing its age on nose and palate. Lean. Tannic. *In Alba, Nov 1994* ★★

**Barolo, Cannubi Marchesi di Barolo** The inheritors of the old Falletti castle, its cellars dating back to 1752. The wine is old style and undergoes long maceration in large oak vats. Still very deep, with opaque core; touch of liquorice, cheesy; sweet, a bit woody (too long in oak?), good old flavour, length and mouth-drying tannin. Holding well. *The oldest wine in an IWFS Barolo tasting conducted by Stephen Hobly, London, March 2002* ★★★★

**Barolo, Ciabot Mentin Ginestra Domenico Clerico** One of Piedmont's new wave small producers. His first vintage was 1979; medium-deep, rich; bricky, fragrant, considerable depth; powerful (alcohol 14.5%), delicious flavour, lovely fruit but still very tannic. *In Alba, Nov 1994* ★★★★(★)

**Barolo, Falletto (White Label) Bruno Giacosa** Palish, soft red, long 'legs'; spicy, totally different to the Rionda Riserva, almost Mouton-like scent and flavour. Sweet, rich. An unusual style. Delicious end taste. I preferred it to the Rionda. Much easier. *Feb 2002* ★★★★

**Barolo, Gran Bussia Aldo Conterno** Only the fourth 'Gran Bussia' made since 1971 and considered the best ever. Low-keyed, showing some age; very attractive, delicious flavour, nice weight (alcohol 13.5%) and style. *At the Barolo tasting in Alba, Nov 1994* ★★★★★ *Well-nigh perfect then. Should still be delicious.*

**Barolo, Rionda Riserva Speciale Bruno Giacosa** Two bottles, the first soft ruby, rich 'legs'; crisp but autumnal fruit; fairly sweet, rich, soft, yet powerful (alcohol 14%), good fruit. Very tannic. The second had a flavour that reminded me of onion soup, its charm dented a little by sandpapery-textured tannin. *Both at Willsberger's Giacosa tasting in Germany, Feb 2002* ★★(★★)

**Brunello di Montalcino, Riserva Biondi-Santi** Very lively appearance, cherry red, intense; slow to emerge but developing a lovely fragrance, rich and spicy over two hours later; fairly astringent, spicy, good length and depth. *At Il Greppo, March 1995* ★★(★★) *Probably, hopefully, a 5-star wine beyond 2025.*

**Sassicaia** At eight years of age: rich, plummy; very sweet nose and palate, plenty of fruit, extract and silky tannins. *Not tasted since March 1990.* Then ★★★(★★) *Should be perfect now.*

**Tignanello Antinori** Fully mature; rather muffled nose, whiff of fungi; soft, ripe, showing its age, drying out. *At a tasting in Antinori's San Casciano cellars, April 1999* ★★★ *Drink up.*

I MUST MENTION FOUR MAGNIFICENT BAROLOS tasted in the late 1980s: **Cavallotto's** packed with fruit and tannin. Needing lengthy cellaring. *1987* ★★★★; **Fontanafredda's** huge, deep, long-term wine. *1998* ★★★★; **Aldo Conterno's Gran Bussia** luminous, lovely, 'legs' like Romanesque arches; an incredible array of fruits on the nose and palate, figs, grapefruit leading eventually to a very tannic finish. *1988* ★★★★★; and **Mascarello's Monprivato** full, soft, fleshy, delicious. *1987* ★★★★

## 1983 ★★★

An uneven year. In Piedmont the growing conditions were less than good: rain during flowering and a humid summer though conditions improved in time for the harvest in October. Growers in Tuscany had a better time of it: good flowering, fine summer, an earlier harvest.

This was the vintage which first awakened my interest in Italian wines, Chianti in particular. Two MWs, Nick Belfrage and David Gleave, with a shop, 'Winecellars', in south London produced an interesting and informative list of Italian wines and I made a point of regularly buying mixed cases – them to select – to drink at home. The '83s were particularly good value, the '85s were better but more expensive, then onward and upward to more recent excellent vintages.

**Barbaresco, Sorì Tildin Gaja** Mature, relaxed; lovely smell, citrus-like fruit, then cress-like, brown sugar; beautifully made; with lip-licking acidity, tannic yet charming. *At the Italian tasting in Nassau, Feb 1997* ★★★★

**Brunello di Montalcino, Riserva Biondi-Santi** Rich cherry red; refreshing fruit, good depth, touch of rusticity, developed richly over a long period; sweet entry, crisp fruit, good length, very astringent. *At Il Greppo. March 1995* ★★(★★) *Totally unready. Will probably need another 20 years.*

**Darmagi Gaja** ('What a pity' – his father's reaction when Angelo Gaja told him that he was making a 100% Cabernet Sauvignon in Barbaresco and which, of course, had to be classed as *vino da tavola*): deep ruby; peppery, spicy nose and taste, though fairly soft and amenable. *Attractive with roast guinea fowl at an Italian dinner, Gidleigh Park, Devon, March 1996* ★★★(★)

**Sassicaia** Dry, lean, Cabernet character in 1989. Not showing well at the vertical tasting at Brooks's Club. Most recently at a Sassicaia tasting in London: now open-rimmed with a soft strawberry colour; sweet, harmonious bouquet; good fruit but with a dry, biting finish. Needs food. *Last tasted May 2002* ★★★

NOTES ON THE THREE '83 CHIANTI CLASSICOS THAT WON ME OVER **Isole e Olena's** soft, easy, delightful and good value. *1987, then* ★★★; **Castello di Volpaia's Riserva** good, assertive. *1988* ★★★; **Melini's La Selvanella Riserva** excellent fruit, rounded. *1988* ★★★; and, finally, one of my favourites of that vintage: **Isole e Olena's** super-Tuscan **Cepparello** from 100% Sangiovese. Crisp and lively. *1987* ★★★

---

### Angelo Gaja

*I have had a long and close friendship with Angelo. His address is very simple: Gaja, Barbaresco, Italy. At least, if not exactly post-office approved, a letter would certainly reach him. His energy and drive would fuel a power station; and like Antinori he is not averse to introducing new international wine varieties.*

*Some years ago, writing about one of his wines, I noted that the name 'Gaja' on the label somewhat dominated that of the wine name (Barbaresco) which was in much smaller type; and suggested that here was a man with a considerable ego. Shortly after that, quite by chance, I met him at a wine fair in Germany. Instead of the expected rebuff I was, to my embarrassment, embraced warmly; since then I have been a fervent admirer. In restaurants he doesn't hesitate to order and praise other people's wines (though some rogueish wit suggested he can't afford to order his own!). My wife and I have happy memories of white truffle-hunting weekends in Alba, of visits and tastings, above all of his incomparable wines.*

# 1984 ★

Poor year except in the north and far south.

**Corvo Duca Enrico Rosso Duca di Salaparuta** The first Corvo vintage from Sicily's best known estate to be enriched by Nero d'Avola, a grape variety introduced from Piedmont by Franco Giacosa, the long-time chief winemaker. At five years of age, impressively deep; hot, spicy; sweet, delicious flavour, rich tannins. *Not tasted since Dec 1989. Then* ★★(★)

**Sassicaia** Produced from my son's cellar for dinner on Christmas Eve: very strange nose, high volatile acidity; nice weight (alcohol 12.5%), flavoury but acidic. *Dec 2000* ★

# 1985 ★★★★★

1983 provided the spark; in 1985 the engine fired. A brilliantly successful and well-timed vintage. Producers rose to the occasion, merchants bought and their eager customers, me among them, fell for them. With the advice of Belfrage and Gleave, I explored a wide range of the best. Unquestionably my favourite Italian vintage.

**Barbaresco Gaja** Three notes, the first two at Gidleigh Park's Italian wine dinners in 1995 and 1997. It is always interesting for me to compare my notes made a couple of years apart, first to see if there are any inconsistencies, second for any indication of the wine's development; but, of course, I have to make allowances for context, with other wines being tasted before and after. Both medium-deep, mature; noses near enough, 'fragrant, bramble-like fruit', spicy; close enough on the palate: soft, full, fruity (the first 'too sweet with rabbit'). The following year at a very vinous family dinner party, noting that the bouquet took two hours to open up. Briefly: sweet, rich extract, good fruit, dry finish. Fair enough. *Last noted March 1998* ★★★★★ *Ready but will keep also.*

**Barbaresco, Camp Gros Marchesi di Gresy** Another of my favourite producers. This wine comes from the Martinenga estate. First tasted in 1989: extraordinarily sweet and full-bodied (alcohol 14%), made from heavily pruned sub-varieties of Nebbiolo and up to three years in oak. Next, in 1994, dining with Angelo Gaja at the famed Guido restaurant in Costigliole d'Asti. A magnum: now mature; lovely bouquet, open, harmonious, sweet and fruity; very sweet on the palate too, its body carried effortlessly and elegantly, with silky tannins and a long, lively finish. Most recently at home. A similar note. Lovely wine. *Last tasted Aug 1999* ★★★★★

**Barbaresco, Gaiun Marchesi di Gresy** A 2-ha subplot in di Gresy's Martinenga estate. First tasted in 1990: softer red than the Camp Gros, but high tannins and acidity. Next, in 1997, at Sunday lunch at Chippenham Lodge: its colour reminded me of old Tudor bricks, mature, russet-tinged; sweet on nose and palate, bouquet opening up, soft, sweet, singed raisins; lovely flavour, full-bodied (14%) losing fruit though, good tannin and acidity. I felt it was at its best. Two years later, in a 'Transformations' seminar – wines paired, young and old – presented by the loquacious Matt Kramer in New York. My notes concurred, compared with the '96 very mature, but a greater vintage anyway. *Last tasted Oct 1999* ★★★★★

**Barbaresco, Santo Stefano, Riserva Speciale Bruno Giacosa** A soft, healthy red; sweet, very full, very rich. Packed with fruit, flavour and malleable tannins. *Alongside his Barolo, at Willsberger's tasting, Feb 2002* ★★★★★

**Barbaresco, Sorì San Lorenzo Gaja** Gaja's top wine served after his 'standard' Barbaresco at the first Gidleigh Park dinner

reported above. The same appearance but very much more to it: sweeter, richer nose, powerful, spicy, lovely fragrance; on the palate firm, multi-layered, greater length, tannins and wonderful acidity. Two years later, also at Gidleigh: 'Pétrus-like' flesh, spice, weight. Great wine. *Last tasted March 1997* ★★★★(★)

**Barbaresco, Sorì Tildin Gaja** Another single-vineyard wine: soft, russet; equally soft, rich, meaty nose; fairly sweet, chewy, still tannic. *At Gaja's, Nov 1994* ★★★(★)

**Barolo Pio Cesare** Fragrant, sweet, fully endowed. *In Alba, April 1990* ★★★★

**Barolo Giacomo Conterno** Fairly deep, rich; a curious brick dust nose, good depth; sweet, full-flavoured, crisp fruit, good length and finish. *In Alba, Nov 1994* ★★★★★

**Barolo, Falletto, Riserva Speciale Bruno Giacosa** Open, mature; far more mature on their nose than his Barbaresco, rich, ripe, powerful (alcohol 14%); very sweet, full flavour, great length. *Feb 2002* ★★★★★

**Barolo, Riserva Bricco Boschis Cavallotto** Fragrant, slight squeeze of mandarin; surprisingly lively, crisp fruit, good length, its acidity cutting the 'local Piedmontese dish of cockscombs and brains'! *With Angelo Gaja and Carlo Petrini in Bra, Nov 1999* ★★★★★

**Brunello di Montalcino La Magia** Deep, rich; soft, 'warm', sweet, full, fleshy. *Dining with Karina Eigensatz, July 1994* ★★★

**Brunello di Montalcino Poggio Antico** Very mature; classic, 'bricky' touch of malt, opening up richly; surprisingly sweet, rich, cherry still tannic. *Christmas lunch at 1915 Pierce Street, San Francisco, Dec 2000* ★★★★

**Brunello di Montalcino, Annata Biondi-Santi** Made from 10–25-year-old vines. The wine spends three years in cask and one year in bottle before release. Mature, slightly tar-like nose; medium dryness and body, agreeable, very good acidity. *Dining with the Biondi-Santis at Il Greppo, March 1995* ★★★

**Brunello di Montalcino, Riserva Biondi-Santi** It seemed to me that all the best vintages ended in a '5'. Evolving well both in appearance and on the nose. Sweet, fragrant, opening up like a classic cedary Médoc; leanish but convincing, high quality and power but with the usual 't & a' finish. *At Il Greppo, March 1995* ★★★★(★) *Should be at its best 2005–2015.*

**OTHER BRUNELLO DI MONTALCINOS**, all tasted in 1990. **Banfi**'s ★★★; **Talenti**'s swingeing tannin ★★★★; **Frescobaldi**'s **Castelgiocondo** ★★★★; and **Il Poggione**'s **Sopozific** ★★★★

**A SELECTION OF CHIANTI CLASSICOS** all tasted between 1989 and 1993. **Castello di Volpaia** ★★★; **San Felice**'s **Poggio** ★★★; **Felsina Berardenga**'s **Riserva** ★★★★; **Rocca delle Macie**'s **Riserva di Fizzano** ★★★; **Cacchiano**'s **Riserva Millennio** ★★★★; and **Fonterutoli**'s **Ser Lapo** ★★★★

**Darmagi Gaja** Three notes within 12 months, two at Gidleigh Park's wine dinners and, in between, at my Italian tasting in Nassau. Summing up: impressively deep, velvety, fairly intense; very good, low-keyed Cabernet Sauvignon nose; 'whew', marvellous flesh and fruit, perfect weight, extract, consistency. *Last tasted March 1997* ★★★(★)

**La Poja Allegrini** The third vintage from a 2.5-ha parcel of vines in Allegrini's La Grola vineyard, matured in small French oak. An island in a sea of Valpolicella commercial mediocrity. Ruby; sweet, slightly chocolatey; full (13.5%) with a richness derived from selected, late-picked (in November), 100% Corvino grapes. Described as a *meditazione* wine. *Last tasted Jan 1993* ★★★★

Sassicaia In 1992 very deep, sweet, full, chewy. Two years later, youthful fruit, developed an agreeable 'biscuity' scent; dry, good flavour, stylish finish, a bit raw and edgy. *At a Rodenstock event, Sept 1994* ★★★(★)

Solaia Antinori Deep, velvety; attractive, citrus-like fruit; silky, leathery tannin, very complete. Fine wine. *At Stephen Kaplan's '85 vintage dinner, Chicago, April 2000* ★★★★

Tignanello Antinori In 1990: deep, intense; good fruit, tannic. Next, noted as aromatic. Attractive wine. *Last tasted at an Italian wine dinner at Gidleigh Park, Devon, Jan 1993* ★★★★

## 1986 ★★★★

Following the success of the small but excellent '85 vintage, producers were filled with a renewed confidence – and put up their prices. The weather was satisfactory overall in Tuscany, and a large crop was harvested after a hot summer. In the north, the heatwave in May was followed by violent, if localised, hailstorms and some top growers, in Barolo in particular, lost up to 40% of their crop. In Piedmont, a small quantity of high-quality grapes was harvested from the last week of September.

Barbaresco Gaja Two bottles: very deep; rather indeterminate, highish toned bouquet; sweet, crisp, very good flavour, moderate weight (alcohol 13%), good, crisp, dry finish. *Dinner with my son in San Francisco, March 1998* ★★★★

Barolo, Falletto Bruno Giacosa Two glasses, tasted completely blind. Both were pretty similar, both mature, the first slightly paler than the other, one 'soft fruit', the other 'crisp fruit'. Both very sweet, full-flavoured, the first seemed very tannic, the other soft and chewy. Well, they were the same wine, one bottle opened the previous evening, the other newly opened before pouring. We were all caught out, though not badly! *At the Giacosa tasting, Feb 2002* ★★★★

Bricco dell'Uccellone Braida di Giacomo Bologna Created by Giacomo Bologna, this famous wine was a *vino da tavola* made from Barbera grapes from the family's hilltop vineyards at Rocchetta Tanaro and matured in small oak barrels. The first vintage was in 1982 and it elevated the taken-for-granted Barbera d'Asti to new heights. It was introduced to me by my first Italian wine mentor, Count Riccardo Riccardi (the translator of my book *Wine Tasting*). Three notes, first in 1989: still immature of course, very fruity, fleshy, spicy (oak), and perfect balance. Next, in 1997, at my Italian seminar in Nassau, a very detailed note summarised: pleasant, open, mature, burgundy-like appearance; soft, chocolatey, singed, with whiff of liquorice I had in fact noted eight years before. Deceptively soft entry leading to a powerful finish, mulberry-like ripe fruit, warm, mouthfilling, tannic. Unquestionably 5 stars. Also showing well at the tasting I conducted for *Vinum* magazine in Zurich. *Last noted April 1998* ★★★★★ *Perfect now.*

Carmignano, Capezzana Bonacossi A super Sangiovese/Cabernet blend. Whiff of liquorice; medium dryness and weight. Soft. Delicious. *Last tasted Oct 1992. Then* ★★★(★) *Doubtless excellent now.*

Sassicaia Only one youthful note. Lovely fruit, showing well but 'lacking the glory and richness' of the '85. *At the vertical, April 1990* ★★★★

Tignanello Antinori First tasted in 1992: deep; soft, rich, ripe fruit, excellent finish. Most recently at Antinori's: now medium deep, with mature rim; more Chianti-like than the others in the vertical. Harmonious. Excellent balance though still tannic. Very attractive. *Last noted April 1995* ★★★★

TWO OTHER EXTREMELY GOOD SUPER-TUSCANS showing well in 1990: Rampolla's Sammarco deep, fleshy, lovely fruit, velvety – expressive ★★★★; and Felsina Berardenga's Fontalloro rich, assertive and with crisp fruit ★★★★

## 1987 ★★ to ★★★

Nice wines, mainly for early drinking. Few worth reporting.

Bricco della Bigotta Braida di Giacomo Bologna The third vintage of another new Barbera produced at the Braida estate: very deep, velvety; rich, fig-like, quite different from his '86 Bricco Uccellone; sweet; full, rich, Rhône-like, powerful. 'Flesh covering Italianate twigs and bushes.' (Well, I think I know what I meant.) *Feb 1997* ★★★

Brunello di Montalcino, Riserva Biondi-Santi Already looking mature; fairly well evolved nose, cellar-like, Spanish root (four hours later, beautifully developed, gingery). Medium sweetness and body, rich, chewy, with silky, leathery, tannic texture. *At Il Greppo, March 1998* ★★★(★)

## 1988 ★★★★★

An excellent vintage but small production: in Tuscany it was the smallest crop for 25 years. The growing conditions in Piedmont either side of a hot, dry summer were anything but ideal: rain caused problems for the Nebbiolo at harvest time but the earlier picked Barberas were very satisfactory. The low crop levels in Tuscany were the result of poor flower set and severe heat and drought in the summer. The best wines were from Montalcino.

Barbaresco Gaja Fairly deep ruby; nutty, brambly, good fruit on nose and palate. Tannic. *At an Italian wine dinner at Gidleigh Park, Devon, Feb 1995* ★★★

Barbaresco, Asili Michele Chiarlo Lovely colour; slightly singed fruit; slightly sweet, full, fruity, nice bite. *At home, July 2001* ★★★

Barbaresco, Santo Stefano, Riserva Speciale Bruno Giacosa In bottle and magnum: lovely, soft, luminous ruby; very good, deep, meaty nose; very sweet, very powerful, lovely flavour and aftertaste but raw, astringent and completely unready. *Feb 2002* ★★(★★★)

Barolo, Falletto Bruno Giacosa A double magnum at dinner hosted by Otto Geisel after Willsberger's Giacosa tasting: soft ruby; harmonious, good fruit; crisp, impressive, very tannic. It 'cut' the rich oxtail beautifully. *At the Geisel family's Hotel Victoria, Bad Mergentheim, Feb 2002* ★★★★

Bricco dell'Uccellone Braida di Giacomo Bologna I tasted this shortly after bottling: black cherry; glorious, raspberry-like fruit; sweet, full-bodied, crisp fruit, spicy, tannic. Alas, the brilliant Giacomo Bologna did not live to see this wine mature. Nor have I, yet. He died the same year. *June 1991. Then* (★★★★)

Brunello di Montalcino Argiano Fragrant; lively, high toned, lovely finish ★★★; Riserva deep, more impressive; low-keyed, spicy; uplifting fruit, rich, powerful, tannic ★★★★ *Both wines tasted in Oct 1994.*

Brunello di Montalcino, Podere Pian di Conte Talenti First tasted in April 1990, very good but still youthful. More recently: glorious colour, mature rim; a 'warm' hot vintage character, soft, harmonious, touch of rusticity; good ripe sweetness and body, misleadingly soft leading to a tannic end bite. Delicious with Daphne's braised lamb shanks. *Lunch at Chippenham Lodge, Nov 2000* ★★★★

**Brunello di Montalcino, Tenuta Greppo** **Biondi-Santi**
Fairly deep, lively; harmonious, whiff of vanilla; medium
sweetness and body (alcohol 12.5%), good extract but four-
square. *Oct 1994* ★★★; **Riserva** fragrant, blackberry-like fruit,
evolving well, biscuity, subtle fruit and spicy, held well. Nice
weight, lovely flavour, rich, spicy. *At Il Greppo, March 1995* ★★★★

TWO MORE '88 BRUNELLO DI MONTALCINOS noted at
the Wine Cellars' tasting, October 1994 **Col d'Orcia** attractive
nose; lean, dry ★★; and **Costanti**'s **Riserva** harmonious, very
appealing fruit, sweet, citrus-like acidity ★★★★

**Cepparello** **Isole e Olena** Soft ruby: gentle fruit, harmonious,
developing a strange port-like scent in the glass; lean, stylish,
good acidity. From the label I see that I paid £9.99 a bottle for
it in 1991. *Dinner at Chippenham Lodge, Dec 1999* ★★★(★)
**Darmagi** **Gaja** Two notes, both in Italian 'flights' at
Rodenstock's wine weekends, first a double magnum in 1994,
between the '89 and '88 Tignanello. Not surprisingly, a totally
different style to the latter, bland, cheesy, harmonious but no
further evolution; delicious, mouthfilling, crisp, tannic. Four
years later: it was still deep, intense and retaining its youth;
crisp, its 100% Cabernet Sauvignon very evident; sweetish,
fairly full, good fruit but lean, 'bell pepper' flavour. *Last noted
Sept 1998* ★★★(★)
**Dolcetto d'Alba, Monte Aribaldo** **Marchesi di Gresy**
Open, mature; soft, 'warm', singed nose and flavour yet
refreshing. Number 28,037 out of the 29,000 bottles produced
– the end of the bottling line! *At Chippenham Lodge, April 2002*
★★★★ *Drink now.*
**Tignanello** **Antinori** Magnum: very good, spicy, red berry-
like nose, then eucalyptus, but after this 30-minute burst,
seemed emptied; crisp fruit, stylish, very good. *At a Rodenstock
tasting, Sept 1994* ★★★★
**Torgiano, Riserva Rubesco, Monticchio** **Lungarotti** First
noted at a pre-sale tasting in New York, November 1990: soft,
rich, ruby; lovely nose; excellent flavour. *Last tasted at supper at
the Peacock Room after a Christie's pre-sale tasting* ★★★★
**Valpolicella Classico, La Grola** **Allegrini** Reputed to be
the only family keeping alive the true quality and style of

## Piero Antinori

*It was 9am on a Sunday morning in San Francisco. Piero and I
found ourselves in an empty hall. We looked at our watches,
simultaneously realising that neither of us had been told that the
clocks had changed overnight and that the Wine Experience
Seminar that we were each to address was another hour ahead. We
shrugged, smiled wryly and repaired to our respective rooms. It could
easily be assumed that a marchese of ancient lineage whose address
was the Palazzo Antinori, Piazza Antinori, Firenze (with the
Capella Antinori conveniently opposite) would be aloof,
unapproachable – or simply a wealthy playboy. Not so.*

*If Antinori wines have an unassailable position in the
international market it is due to the enterprise, initiative and sheer
hard work Piero has put into his family estates and business since
he took control in 1966. He was also the first to break from Chianti
tradition by introducing new (international) grape varieties, such as
Cabernet Sauvignon. Tignanello was the harbinger of what soon
became known as 'super-Tuscans' – its first vintage was 1971. All
in all, Piero Antinori, with relaxed and unpretentious charm, is
Italy's finest ambassador of wine.*

Valpolicella. Palish, bright ruby; very distinctive nose, stalky,
minty; dry, firm, attractive, tannic. *Jan 1992. Then* ★★(★★)
*Doubtless fully evolved now.*

# 1989 ★ to ★★★★

Very mixed fortunes and the smallest vintage of the decade.
Piedmont largely escaped the bad weather and produced some
of the best reds of the decade though yields were down 15%
and some parts of Barolo hit by severe hailstorms. Some areas
in Tuscany had too much rain, others too little. Mainly light
wines and Brunello di Montalcino reputed to be the best.
Alas, I have tasted few Tuscan wines of this vintage.
**Barbaresco** **Gaja** Deepish cherry red; peppery nose, sweaty
tannins; dry, crisp, good body (13.5%) and flavour. Very tannic.
*At my tasting for* Vinum *magazine, Zurich, April 1998* ★★(★) *Needs
more time, say 2005–2012.*
**Barolo, Bricco Boschis, Vigna San Guiseppe** **Cavallotto**
100% Nebbiolo: now mature, long 'legs'; soft, meaty,
harmonious and gentle fruit; ripe sweetness, substantial
(alcohol 14%), velvety, silky tannins. An unforgettable dinner
with Angelo Gaja and Carlo Petrini, the genius behind the
Slow Food movement, at a restaurant, whose name I forgot to
note, in Bra. *Nov 1999* ★★★★
**Barolo, Riserva, Villero** **Bruno Giacosa** First noted
November 1994. Fully mature; sweet, rich, full (14%), 'excellent
now'. With Angelo Gaja at our favourite, extraordinary,
restaurant, Cesare, in a tiny village, Albaretto del Torre on a
hilly ridge in the middle of nowhere. Exactly five years later in
the same place, this time joined by Aldo Conterno (it turned
out that my wife and Aldo share the same birth year. They
arranged to dine again in 2031). A sweet and lovely wine. *Last
tasted Nov 1999* ★★★★★
**Barolo, Sperss** **Gaja** (Sperss is a 'fantasy' name for one of
Gaja's vineyards.) Translucent soft cherry; sweet, red berry-like
aroma; medium sweetness, full-bodied (alcohol 14%), rich,
warming flavour. Tannic, of course. *At Gaja's, Nov 1994* ★★★(★)
**Darmagi** **Gaja** I have four notes. I first tasted it in 1994, at
Rodenstock's 15th *Raritäten-Weinprobe*, a double magnum: it
was very deep; crisp but muffled fruit which sat there without
budging further; mouthfilling, powerful, magnificent (level
pegging with '89 Ch La Conseillante). The following year,
another double magnum served at his opening dinner, the
(100%) Cabernet Sauvignon apparent.

Next, in 1998, craftily, inserted as No 3 in a blind line-up of
mainly top '89 Pomerols. It was still opaque, intense, youthful;
high-toned fruit; sweet, fleshy, good fruit (I thought it was
Ch Pétrus). Most recently, from my own stock, double
decanted at home and taken to Brooks's Club for the annual
Christie's wine course staff dinner. Now a rich ruby; sweet,
and delicious. But it would benefit from more bottle age. *Oct
2000* ★★★(★)
**Rosso di Montalcino** **Biondi-Santi** Their declassified
Brunello. Soft, ruby; very pleasant; lightish, good, clean finish.
Served by the Biondi-Santis at dinner the night of my arrival
at Il Greppo, the most lovely old house and gardens, and at
lunch after the tasting. *In Tuscany, March 1995* ★★★
**Solaia** **Antinori** Rich, distinctly more mature looking than the
'90; very attractive fruit with whiff of blackcurrant and
raspberry, then softer, more restrained, chocolatey, good crisp
fruit but lean and tannic. Less mature than it looked. Citrus-
like acidity. *At the Italian wine tasting conducted for the Chaîne des
Rôtisseurs, in Nassau, Feb 1997* ★★★

**Tignanello Antinori** A reminder: Antinori's *vino da tavola*, 90% Sangiovese, 10% Cabernet Sauvignon and no white Malvasia or Trebbiano (as included in many Chianti blends of the time). Aged in *barriques*. Beautiful colour, touch of mahogany; warm, ripe 'summer heat' bouquet, singed, meaty, good structure and flavour. *At the Italian wine tasting in Nassau, Feb 1997* ★★★(★)

# 1990 ★★★★★

An excellent vintage, one of the best since the end of World War Two. From north to south it was a virtually perfect growing season with a hot, dry summer interrupted with just enough rain to nourish and flesh out the grapes. The harvest was unusually early but yields were low.

My first tasting of 1990 Barolos was helpfully arranged by Angelo Gaja who persuaded ten of the top producers to come to Alba on a Sunday morning, November 1994, each bringing their 1990 and one other, older vintage. Then, in June 1996, Walter Eigensatz organised a two-day blind tasting of 144 of the finest red wines of the 1990 vintage selected from the world's major wine regions. Forty wines were Italian. They, with other wines tasted, are too numerous to describe in detail. I have therefore commented only on the ones I considered the most interesting and outstanding, with a summary of the rest at the end of this section.

**Barbaresco, Asili Bruno Giacosa** First noted in 1996: maturing; earthy, as yet unknit; very sweet, rich, loads of grip, soft yet tannic. 'Needed time.' Most recently: lovely, luminous colour; elegant, sweet, lovely flavour and texture. *Last noted at Willsberger's Giacosa tasting, Feb 2002* ★★★★(★)

**Barbaresco, Costa Russi Gaja** Deep, rich, spicy, tannic. *At Gaja's, Nov 1994* (★★★★)

**Barbaresco, Gaiun Marchesi di Gresy** Fully mature; almost too sweet; almost Pomerol style, pleasant flavour, dry finish. Good wine. Gentlemanly. Did not show up very well in a mixed 'flight' at the Eigensatz marathon. *June 1996* ★★★ *In another context it would, I am sure, be at least* ★★★★

**Barbaresco, Santo Stefano, Riserva Speciale Bruno Giacosa** Fairly deep, dense; rich mocha nose; very sweet, rich; chewy, tannic texture. *Feb 2002* ★★★(★★)

**Barbaresco, Sorì San Lorenzo Gaja** Rich in every way: appearance, nose and taste. Whiff of violets. Fairly sweet, full (alcohol 14%), very distinctive. Fabulous and with a great future. *At Gaja's, Nov 1994* (★★★★)

**Barolo, Cannubi Boschis Sandrone** Fairly deep, velvety, ruby, rich 'legs'; crisp fruit; sweet, full-bodied, very crisp, tannic. *June 1996* ★★★(★)

**Barolo, Ciabot Mentin Ginestra Clerico** Lovely wine, sweet, full of fruit, fleshy, harmonious ★★★(★); and Pajana, an adjacent vineyard: deep, rich, velvety; good fruit; not quite as sweet, laden with tannin ★★★(★★) *Both at Alba, Nov 1994.*

**Barolo, Gran Bussia Aldo Conterno** Ruby; holding back; crisp, fruity, fairly full-bodied (alcohol 14%), lively as well as tannic. *Nov 1994* ★★★★(★)

**Barolo, Monfortino Giacomo Conterno** Giovanni, Giacomo's son, brought his bottles to the tasting. His '90 was quite different from Aldo Conterno's (above): a lovely, soft, warm colour; very sweet, rich nose and flavour. High extract. Beguiling yet tannic. *Nov 1994* ★★★(★★)

**Barolo, Rionda, Riserva Speciale Bruno Giacosa** Lovely, luminous colour; good fruit; very sweet, rich and smooth. *Feb 2002* ★★★★(★)

**Barolo, Sperss Gaja** First tasted at Gaja's in 1994: deep, plummy; lovely vinosity; spicy, tannic. Next, two years later: low-keyed, soft; fairly sweet, fullish, good fruit, good tannin and acidity. Most recently: ruby; assertive fruit, lean, tannic. Very good with beef. *Last tasted at a Rodenstock dinner, Sept 1998* ★★★(★)

**OTHER '90 BAROLOS TASTED ONLY IN ALBA IN NOVEMBER 1994 Elio Altare**'s ruby; lively, crisp, good length ★★★(★); **Marcarini**'s **Brunate** unknit; fresh, crisp, opening up but needing time ★★(★); **Cerequio** (alas, producer not noted; possibly Chiarlo): chunky fruit; sweet, very attractive flavour but coarse, tannic finish ★★(★); **Pio Cesare**'s **Ornato** rich, young fruit, medium-full (alcohol 13.5%), firm first, overall dry ★★★(★); **Paolo Scavino**'s **Rocche dell' Annunziata** fairly deep ruby; full of fruit; sweet, very oaky ★★(★★); and his **Bric del Fiasc** as fine and classic as they come ★★★(★★)

**AND OTHER '90 BAROLOS, NOTED AT THE EIGENSATZ BLIND TASTING IN JUNE 1996 Elio Altare**'s **Arborina** impressively deep, velvety; fragrant; surprisingly sweet, full, lovely fruit, crisp, tannic ★★★(★★); **Michele Chiarlo**'s **Cannubi** fragrant, sweet, open knit ★★★(★★); and **Cà dei Gancia**'s **Cannubi** mediocre ★★

**Brunello di Montalcino Barbi** Ruby; spicy, cherry-like fruit; medium-dry, crisp, good fruit, delicious. Perfect beverage. *At Chippenham Lodge, April 2002* ★★★★

**Brunello di Montalcino, Riserva Quercione Campogiovanni** Very deep, rich core; sweet, very scented oak; immensely rich, chewy with curious scented flavour, hefty, high extract masking tannin and acidity. *At Chippenham Lodge, April 2002* ★★★(★)

**OTHER '90 BRUNELLOS, NOTED AT THE EIGENSATZ TASTING IN JUNE 1996**, most needing more bottle age: **Frescobaldi**'s **Castelgiocondo Riserva** deep, sweet, fruitful ★★★★; **Ciacci Piccolomini**'s **Riserva** full, rich, spicy ★★★; **Val di Suga**'s rich, full, fruity, tannic ★★★★; **Vasco Sassetti**'s crisp, tannic ★★★; **Altesino**'s **Montosoli** tight, tannic ★★★; and **Soldera**'s **Riserva** high volatile acidity.

**Cepparello Isole e Olena** Impressively deep ruby; good fruit, soft, lovely. *Nov 1994* ★★★(★)

**Chianti Classico** To my surprise, I have tasted very few '90s, the best is an old note: **Isole e Olena**'s deliciously soft and drinkable. *Jan 1992* ★★★★

**OTHER CHIANTIS OF THE '90 VINTAGE TASTED IN 1996 Castello di Ama**'s **Chianti Classico, La Casuccia** crisp, oaky, very dry ★★★; **Querciabella**'s **Chianti Classico, Riserva** which received massive votes but not from me. I thought it 'blown' and rustic; and **Galiga e Vetrice**'s **Chianti Rufina, Riserva Villa di Vetrice** fruity but tart ★★

**Fontalloro Felsina** A relatively new super-Tuscan created by Giuseppe Mazzocolin and his enologist from the Veneto, Franco Bernabei. Well-balanced fruit and oak. *June 1996* ★★★★

**Ornellaia Tenuta dell'Ornellaia** (Cabernet Sauvignon 82%, Merlot 14%, Cabernet Franc 4%) First tasted blind in 1996: taut, oaky, with crisp fruit and high acidity. Most recently: rich, rustic, farmyard scents; a sweet and sour wine, fleshy, fruity, still with swingeing tannin. *Last tasted in London, Feb 2002* ★★★?

**Le Pergole Torte Montevertine** This wine was created in 1977 by the wealthy Sergio Manetti from old clones of Sangiovese grown on a 8-ha vineyard in the Chianti zone. Aged in oak barrels, the wine became a new 'super-Tuscan' *vino da tavola*. I was hardly aware of it before attending a tasting conducted by the late Sergio's son, Martino. He told us that 1990 was a perfect growing season. The grapes were harvested in the first week of October, earlier than usual. First noted in 1996 at the Eigensatz tasting of 1990s, finding it somewhat undeveloped and austere though with a good flavour. Next, at the Pergole Torte vertical in London. Pink-tinged, striving to mature; 'smoky', fragrant, opening up richly; fairly sweet and full-bodied, rich, tangy, very good length, tarry tannins. *Last tasted May 2001* ★★★(★★)

**Sassicaia** 4.5ha of vines planted in 1942. 100% Cabernet – both Sauvignon and Franc; 100% barrel-aged. In 1996: crisp, good fruit, austere. A more detailed note the following year: vivid, rich, cherry red yet maturity; lean and hard at first but opened up, silky, harmonious; dry, firm, mouthfilling, nice weight (alcohol 12.5%), good length and future. *Last tasted Feb 1997. Then* ★★★(★) *Probably at peak now.*

**Solaia Antinori** High proportion of Cabernet Sauvignon in this *vino da tavola*. Very deep, velvety; flawless nose and palate; sweet, fleshy, rich fruit, lovely wine and high mark. Great future. *Tasted blind, June 1996* ★★★★(★)

**Tignanello Antinori** First tasted in 1994 at the launch of the *Larousse Encyclopedia of Wine* at Fortnum & Mason, Piccadilly: impressive but very dry (both wine and tome). Rather surprisingly, not among the top 40 Italian wines in the Eigensatz tasting in 1996. Most recently, variable bottles, one woody-corky, the other figgy-nosed, with good flesh and fruit but a whiff of volatile acidity. Perhaps this was the reason. *Last tasted at Antinori's San Casciano winery, April 1999* ★★★

OF THE MANY OTHER ITALIAN '90S AT THE EIGENSATZ MARATHON IN JUNE 1996, the following stood out: **Castel Schwanberg Cabernet** (Sud-Tirol) good fruit, texture, elegance ★★★★; **Allegrini**'s **La Poja** (Valpolicella) spicy, rich, crisp, superb ★★★★★; and **San Giusto a Rentennano**'s **Percarlo** pure Sangiovese 'super-Tuscan', speciously full of fruit and oak but I can see its appeal ★★★★

## 1991 ★

Poor vintage. Poor weather conditions either side of a hot dry summer with heavy rains spoiling the harvest. I have tasted few of these wines. But clearly, with selection, some late-harvested grapes turned out quite well.

**Barbaresco Gaja** Distinctive, brambly, Nebbiolo aroma; lean, oaky, tannic. An 'interim' food wine. Little future. *At Gaja's, Nov 1994* ★★

**Barolo Gaja** I was rather surprised to be told by Angelo that this was not due for bottling until the spring of 1996. I thought it was delicious, with a lovely suave, rich nose and flavour, very sweet, masked tannin. *At Gaja's, Nov 1994* ★★★? *Worth looking out for.*

**Darmagi Gaja** Two magnums, slight variation. Very deep; sweet, ripe fruit – Angelo's team must have selected late-ripening Cabernet; fairly fleshy, full-bodied. The second bottle was deeper, crisper and drier. *In a Gaja 'flight' at a Rodenstock dinner, Sept 1998* ★★★

**Ornellaia Tenuta dell'Ornellaia** Very deep; sweet, tannic, delicious. *Feb 1994* ★★★

## 1992 ★★

A promising vintage, once again spoiled by storms and torrential rain at a critical time – from late September to mid-October. Early pickers with early-ripening grapes did best. Not for keeping.

**Bricco dell'Uccellone Braida di Giacomo Bologna** If not up to the Bologna family's super-Barbera standards, very drinkable and in entertaining company: Aubert de Villaine, Jack Daniels (the Domaine de la Romanée-Conti importer) and Taylor Thomson, a wealthy Canadian collector. *At Prego, an Italian restaurant next door to Christie's in Los Angeles. Feb 1998* ★★

**Chianti Classico Isole e Olena** Despite the rain, Paolo de Marchi's team managed to produce an attractive if rustic and rusty (iron, tannin) wine. Reminded me of an old army joke. Duty officer: any complaints? Bold rookie: tastes like .... Sir. But beautifully cooked! *At the River Café on the banks of the Thames near Hammersmith, Nov 1994* ★★

**Il Chusio Castello di Ama** A *vino da tavola di Toscana*. I first tasted it in 1996 and I decided to give it more bottle age. Most recently: thick, needed decanting; nose still rather hard at first but opened up attractively; surprisingly sweet and spicy though with a dry finish. *At a wine dinner at home, Jan 2000* ★★★(★) *Still time in hand.*

**Le Volte Tenuta dell'Ornellaia** (Sangiovese with Cabernet Sauvignon and Merlot.) Admittedly youthful. A bottle to try from Wine Cellars, then my main Italian wine supplier. Refreshing young fruit, attractive. Easy drinking. Perhaps needing a further year or two. *At home, Dec 1993* ★★

**Le Pergole Torte Montevertine** Perfect summer ruined by two months of rain. Picked 20 October, during a week's break in the weather. 10,000 bottles produced, half the average crop. Dry, lean, raw, with teeth-gripping acidity. *May 2001* ★★

## 1993 ★★★ variable

Yet another rain-sodden vintage following a hot dry summer. Wines mainly for early consumption. I tasted a range of cask samples of Barbarescos with Angelo Gaja in November 1994, his Barolo being the most impressive.

**Dolcetto d'Alba Giacomo Conterno** Very deep, opaque core, purple rim; rather raw and, of course, immature. *But an unforgettable experience at our favourite restaurant, Cesare, at Albaretto del Torre, Nov 1994* (★★)

**Lupicaia Castello del Terriccio** A Merlot and Cabernet blend: deep, velvety; lovely minty, eucalyptus nose and flavour. Ripe sweetness, nice weight (alcohol 13%). Drinking well. *At Chippenham Lodge, May 2002* ★★★★

**Le Pergole Torte Montevertine** Fairly deep, maturing; sweet, tangy with raspberry scent reminding me of Cabernet Franc. Sweet, attractive, good length but with teeth-gripping tannin. *May 2001* ★★★(★)

**San Leonardo Tenuta San Leonardo** A *vino da tavola* blend of Merlot, Cabernet Sauvignon and Cabernet Franc from Trentino in northern Italy and first produced in 1983 by the Marchese Carlo Guerrieri Gonzaga, scion of one of Italy's noblest families – and there are many – with the assistance of the renowned enologist Giacomo Tachis. It was dark and velvety, opaque in the centre; strange nose, like black treacle; dry, mouthfilling (though a moderate 13% alcohol), modern style of wine not to my liking. But, as always in the company of Gelasio Gaetani, enormous fun, in a fashionable outdoor restaurant in Rome. *Sept 1999* ★★★

**Sassicaia** Still fairly deep; fragrant; very good fruit, nice weight, stylish. *At the famous restaurant Gambero Rosso, San Vincenzo, April 1999* ★★★

**Tignanello Antinori** A bit varnishy but fairly harmonious. An early ripener. Drinking well. *At Antinori's, April 1999* ★★

# 1994 ★★ to ★★★★

This vintage showed big differences between the wine regions. Once again, the summer was dry and hot, but in Piedmont growers were affected by heavy frosts and localised hail, with 17 days of heavy rain from mid-September. Tuscany had a far better season and harvest. I have to confess that I have tasted very few '94s. The following wines were the most interesting of a range tasted in their youth in May 1996.

**Chianti Classico: Castello di Volpaia** fragrant, good texture, soft fruit, acidic ★★★; **La Capanne** very deep, good fruit ★★★; **Castello di Brolio** good fruit but too sweet ★★★; **Rocca delle Macìe** fragrant, rich, attractive ★★★★

**Chianti Classico, Riserva Ducale Ruffino** Maturing pleasantly; good fruit and flesh. Whatever is Italian for '*assez bien*'. *Dinner in Florence, April 2000* ★★★ *(just)*.

**Le Pergole Torte Montevertine** Singed, 'bracken'-like nose, lean, attractive and opening up fragrantly; good wine but hard and hampered by its tannic finish. Needs time. *In London, May 2001* ★★(★)?

**Santa Cristina Antinori** I found this Sangiovese and Merlot *vino da tavola* very agreeable at lunch in a modest restaurant in Earl's Court. *May 1996* ★★

**I Sodi di San Niccolò Castellare di Castellina** Supposed to be a 'super-Tuscan'. Positive, good length, on the whole a decent drink. *Supper at the Cantina, Vinopolis, March 2000* ★★★ *(The Cantina has the biggest range of wines by the glass in London.)*

# 1995 ★★★ to ★★★★★

A most difficult and unpredictable growing season. In Piedmont, there was a warm spring leading to optimistic fruit set. This was spoiled by rain which also, later, upset the flowering. Hot July was followed by a cold August with extensive hail damage, particularly in Barolo. Poor weather continued until an Indian summer ended one of the longest growing seasons and latest harvests for two decades. Further to the south, Tuscany suffered similar vicissitudes but from mid-September enjoyed 45 rain-free days and high temperatures. The best, slowly ripened grapes enabled well-structured Chianti Classicos to be made.

Once again, a gap in my armoury. Few wines noted.

**Barolo, Monprivato, Ca' d'Morissio, Riserva Giuseppe Mascarello** Mascarello is an arch-traditionalist – this wine had 25 days' maceration in large oak casks, followed by up to 50 months in 30-year-old Slovenian oak. His '95 was bottled in July 2000. Medium-deep, lovely colour; very rich, crisp, brambly fruit; fairly sweet, full-flavoured, still very tannic. *At the IWFS Barolo tasting, March 2002* ★★★(★★)

**Barolo, Sperss Gaja** Fairly deep, mature; fragrant, oaky, considerable depth; fairly sweet, lovely flavour, spicy, great length. *At Gaja's, Nov 1999* ★★★(★★)

**Brunello di Montalcino Il Poggione** First tasted in April 1999 and so tough that I marked the label 'keep'. But I couldn't resist seeing how it was developing. Fairly deep, soft, fully mature, rich 'legs'; on decanting, brown sugar and cold

tea, an hour later old stables; good fruit, touch of coarseness, very tannic. Years more life. *At lunch, Chippenham Lodge, Jan 2002* ★★★(★★)

**Brunello di Montalcino, Pian delle Vigne Pian delle Vigne/Antinori** I think this was an early Antinori excursion into Montalcino: a lovely ruby colour; crisp fruit, spicy, 'very more-ish'. *At a gala dinner in Wiesbaden, May 2000* ★★★

**Brunello di Montalcino, 'Sugarille' Gaja** Angelo, ever restless, bought a vineyard in Montalcino. This early, 100% Sangiovese made a good start: very deep, rich, plummy coloured; sweet, harmonious nose; delicious flavour, rich, chewy. *At Gaja's in Barbaresco, Nov 1999* ★★★(★)

**Chianti Classico, Riserva Ricasoli/Castello di Brolio** Very deep, opaque core; very fragrant; attractive, bramble-like fruit, lean, firm. *Two notes both on British Airways flights, from New York and to San Francisco, Nov and Dec 2000* ★★★

**Le Pergole Torte Montevertine** Deep, ruby, intense, youthful; black, fragrant, rich; still immature, a lot to it. Tannic bitterness. Good future. *May 2001* ★★(★★★)

**Ornellaia Tenuta dell'Ornellaia** Showing its age on the nose; sweet yet very tannic. While dining, the wine waiter brought me a glass to taste. A customer had found it too tannic. So did I. *In Prego, the Italian restaurant on board the Crystal Symphony, somewhere off Italy, Sept 1999* ★★?

**Rocca di Montegross' Riserva San Marcellino** Velvety ruby; good nose and very attractive flavour. *Perfect at dinner with Robin and Rupert Hambro at their villa in Tuscany, April 2000* ★★★

**San Leone Sonnino** Merlot and Sangiovese: warm ruby; a sweetish, fleshy and very quaffable. *Dinner at the Hambros in Tuscany, April 2000* ★★

**Sassicaia** Still youthful; very rich, singed, hot vintage nose; full of fruit, extract and tannin. Impressive but not ready. *At the Gambero Rosso, San Vicente, after a visit to Sassicaia, April 1999* ★★★(★)

# 1996 ★★★★

A very satisfactory vintage.

**Barbera d'Asti Ceppi Storici** Still youthful with a mauve rim; sweet nose, vanilla and chocolate; perfect weight, crisp fruit, lean style, drinking well. *At dinner at Chippenham Lodge, June 2002* ★★★

**Barbaresco** First, a range of Barbarescos all tasted at Gaja's winery in November 1999. **Barbaresco** sweet, rich, quite a bite, astringent yet lovely ★★★(★); **Costa Russi** the same vineyard as Sorì Tildin but at the bottom of the hill on richer soil. Very deep, rich 'legs'; hefty, chocolatey, harmonious, fig-like fruit; impressive body and flavour. Good fruit ★★★(★★); **Sorì San Lorenzo** wonderful depth of fruit, more amenable than the Tildin, spicy, good length but also swingeingly tannic ★★★(★★); and **Sorì Tildin** long 'legs'; good, tight, brambly fruit; attractive flavour but very stern and with a very dry finish. I felt it was like the month of March, in like a lamb, out like a lion ★★★(★★)

**Barbaresco, Martinenga, Gaiun Marchesi di Gresy** Attractive ruby; initially muffled, jammy fruit but after 20 minutes opened up beautifully, concentrated, figgy; dry, crisp fruit; stylish but still austere and tannic. Good future. *At Matt Kramer's 'Transformations' seminar, New York, Oct 1999* ★★★(★★)

**Barolo, Cerequio Michele Chiarlo** In August 2000: starting to mature; high tone brambly fruit; distinctly sweet, very flavoury but touch of edgy acidity. Three months later high volatile acidity again on the nose and the finish. *Last tasted Oct 2000* ★★

**Chianti Classico Querciabella** Quite good wine, much better company. *Lunch with a charming Japanese lady, at Launceston Place, London, Dec 1999* ★★

**Gagliole Rosso Gagliole/Bär** A new wine, labelled as a Colli della Toscana Centrale, made mainly from Sangiovese with some Cabernet Sauvignon and matured in Slovenian and French oak barrels. Owned and renovated by Thomas Bär of the Bär Bank in Zürich. Daphne and I had lunch at the beautiful estate at Castellina in Chianti in April 1999, during which his wife explained that they had not been buying much fine art at Christie's as their vineyard and winery were eating up so much money! Nevertheless, an idyllic place and decent wine. Recently a magnum: medium-deep, pink-tinged rim; touch of bitterness about the nose but sweet, soft and delicious. *Taken to Brooks's Club for dinner, April 2002* ★★★

**Le Pergole Torte Montevertine** 'An elegant vintage' but not as concentrated as the '95 or '97. Deep, beginning to mature; a slightly singed, tarry nose; lean, good flavour and length, austere and very tannic. *At the Pergole Torte tasting in London, May 2001* ★★(★★) *Needs time and food.*

**Sassicaia** There were originally 6ha of vines and now there are 55ha (Cabernet Sauvignon 85%, Cabernet Franc 15%). The yield was 30 hl/ha, average production 15,000 cases; two years in French *barriques*, 40% new. The '96 was being bottled at the time of my visit in April 1999: crisp, young fruit, lean, stylish. More recently: medium-deep, strawberry-tinted; bramble-like fruit on nose and palate. Low-keyed, a fair amount of grip, hard finish. Needs time *and* food. *Last noted at a Sassicaia tasting in London, May 2002* ★★★(★)

**Seifile** (Means 'six five') **Nada** I never did get to the bottom of this: opaque; very fragrant; dry, modern oaky style. It was a perfect foil for the pig's trotters. *Dinner in Bra, Piedmont with Angelo Gaja, Nov 1999* ★★(★)

**Tignanello Antinori** Deep, fairly intense; rich, figgy, fruit opening up sweetly; good flavour and body. On the lean side, austere finish. Needs time. *With the Bacchus Society of America at San Casciano, April 1999* ★★(★★) *We were spending a very pleasant and instructive four days in Tuscany, the principal object being to present Piero Antinori with the Bacchus 'Lifetime Achievement Award'.*

# 1997 ★★★★★

The sort of vintage to gladden Italian hearts. 'The most successful for half a century' claimed some, but unquestionably good. Piero Antinori even went so far as to say it was probably the greatest vintage of the (20th) century; certainly the best in his 40 years of experience. There is no point in summing up the weather conditions, however responsible they were for the end result. These are wines to cellar.

I find it difficult to make adequate notes at a walk-round tasting, which is why my notes made at the MW tasting of Barbarescos and 19 Barolos in London in September 2001 are brief, and those made at the seated tasting of Barolos organised by the IWFS in March 2002 are more detailed. However, both tastings clearly demonstrated the quality of these '97s.

**Barbaresco Gaja** Fairly deep; crisp fruit, flavour and grip. Immensely tannic. *Sept 2001* (★★★★★) *Will need a good 10 to 20 years in bottle.*

**Barbaresco, Martinenga Marchesi di Gresy** Misleadingly mature-looking; sweet, delicious; and his **Camp Gros** with similar orange tinge and equally delicious. *Both wines noted at the MW tasting, Sept 2001* ★★★(★★)

**Barbaresco, Vanotù Giorgio Pelissero** A producer new to me. Singed, hot vintage nose; sweet, delicious fruit. *At the MW tasting of '97s, Sept 2001* ★★★(★)

**Barbera d'Asti, La Court Michele Chiarlo** Deep, intense; full of rich, crisp 'Italianate' fruit. Delicious. *At home, June and July 2000* ★★★ *Give it another couple of years.*

**Barbera d'Asti, Quorum Hastae** Deep, velvety; oak-laden, tart finish. *Lunch at Chippenham Lodge, Jan 2000* ★

**Barolo, Cannubi Michele Chiarlo** Tinge of orange; exceedingly good fruit, fragrant and of course tannic. *At the MW tasting, Sept 2001* ★★★(★★)

**Barolo, Cannubi Carretta** Deep, fairly intense; good, soft fruit, whiff of tar; fairly sweet, rich, citrus-like acidity, very tannic. *At the IWFS Barolo tasting, March 2002* ★★(★★★)

**Barolo, Cerequio Michele Chiarlo** From a 12-ha vineyard, half of which is owned by Chiarlo. First tasted at Vinexpo, June 2001: sweet, fresh. Maturing; crisp, brambly; rich, alcohol 13.5%, attractive fruit, quite a bite. *Last tasted at lunch, Chippenham Lodge, Aug 2001* ★★★(★★)

**Barolo, Cerequio Roberto Voerzio** A new producer to me. His Cerequio comes from part of the renowned La Morra vineyard. Dark cherry, still very youthful; soft, brambly, chocolatey nose; sweet, lovely fruit, alcohol 14.5%, good length, masked tannin. Delicious – but hugely expensive. *March 2002* ★★★(★★)

**Barolo, Costa Grimaldi Luigi Einaudi** At the MW tasting: touch of tar, impressive. More recently: bottle variation, one woody-oaky. The second with very good fruit, flavour, length and finish. *Last tasted March 2002* ★★★(★★)

**Barolo, Enrico VI Cordero di Montezemolo** A traditionalist producer who has now 'gone modern'. The wine was fermented at 34°C for three days, then racked into 50% new French *barriques* for three years: spicy, oaky, firm, fragrant; very sweet, delicious fruit, attractive but oaky. *March 2002* ★★★(★★)

**Barolo, Falletto Bruno Giacosa** Mild ruby; lovely fruit, evolving sweet, butterscotch scents; fleshy, lovely fruit length and tannic. A magnum at dinner was delicious. *After Willsberger's Giacosa tasting, Feb 2002* ★★★★(★)

**Barolo, Marcenasco Renato Ratti** Gorgeously mouthfilling at the MW tasting in 2001. More recently: dark ruby; slightly singed, chocolatey; fruity, sweet, rich, full (alcohol 13.5%), very good fruit. Delicious. *Last tasted March 2002* ★★★(★★)

**Barolo, Nei Cannubi Luigi Einaudi** Produced by 'a vineyard fanatic' who keeps yields low. Fermented in stainless steel and matured in one- and two-year-old *barriques* for 22 months. At the MW tasting: rich, deep, tangy and fairly sweet. More recently: impressive; fragrant; full-bodied (alcohol 14.5%), crisp fruit, austere and very tannic. *Last tasted March 2002* ★★(★★★)

OTHER BAROLOS NOTED AT THE MW TASTING in September 2001: **Ascheri's Vigna dei Pola** from the La Morra vineyard: surprisingly pale; little nose, very tannic ★(★★); **Luciano Sandrone's Le Vigne** Sandrone is a leading producer of the new school in Barolo, aiming for rapid extraction, the use of *barriques* giving a rich, oaky style. Nose slightly caramelly; very sweet, very good fruit, rich, good length ★★★(★★); and his **Cannubi Boschis** orange-tinged; crisp; sweet, richness masking tannin ★★★(★★); **Giuseppe Mascarello's Monprivato, Riserva** also not as deep as expected, with an orange tinge; an extraordinarily sweet, fragrant, violet-like nose and flavour. Very dry ★★★(★★); his **Ca' d'Morissio** cask sample had biting tannins; **Prunotto's Bussia** deep, fairly intense; very sweet, delicious fruit. Beautiful wine ★★★(★★);

**Parusso's Bussia Rocche** very rich, powerful (14.5%), oaky ★★(★★); **Silvio Grasso's Ciabot Manzoni** – new to me – crisp fruit but teeth-gripping tannin (★★★); **Aldo Conterno's Colonello** single-vineyard wine. Orange tinge; spicy; strawberry-like fruit, extremely tannic. Great future ★(★★★★); and his **Cicala** lovely ★★★(★★); **Fontanafredda's Vigna La Rosa** also with strawberry-like fruit, sweet, powerful, very tannic ★★(★★★); **Oddero's Vigna Rionda** sweet, deep, tarry; full-bodied (14.5%), very rich, well put together ★★★(★★); **Vigna Rionda-Massolino's Parafada** nose like black treacle; tremendously sweet and with teeth-gripping tannin ★★(★★); and **Giacomo Conterno's Cascina Francia** great producer, his 'second wine': one of the palest in the range, with a soft, orange tinge; very fragrant, very tannic ★★(★★★)

**Carmenero Sebino Rosso** Ca' del Bosco Maurizio Zanella, the King of Italian sparkling wines is a great character and a good friend. He also makes excellent Chardonnay in Lombardy, as well as this impressive red: deep, plummy purple, violet rim; sweet strawberry and vanilla nose and flavour. Very attractive fruit. A touch too much oak on the finish. *Lunch at Chippenham Lodge, June 2001* ★★★(★★) *2005–2015.*

**Cepparello** Isole & Olena Presented with charm and humour by Paolo de Marchi at his *Wine Spectator* 'Top Ten' seminar in New York. Long-'legged' ruby, crisp fruit, well balanced, needs more bottle age. *Oct 2000* ★(★★★) *I look forward to drinking this around 2005–2010.*

**Chianti Classico** Antinori This is what I like about Antinori: the company produces very drinkable, very reasonably priced restaurant wines. I always look out for the Villa Antinori label as it is totally dependable. I enjoyed the '97 at two Italian restaurants, Il Falconière in South Kensington, London and Pane & Vino in San Francisco. Deliciously easy drinking. *Nov and Dec 2000* ★★★

**Chianti Classico, Brolio** Castello di Brolio/Ricasoli Drinking well at Vinopolis in 1999. Perfect weight, good fruit. Masked tannin. Good value. *August 1999* ★★(★★★)

**Chianti Classico, Castello di Brolio** Castello di Brolio/Ricasoli Harvested between 30 September and 6 October, 100% Sangiovese, 18 months in 65% new *barriques*. First tasted, a bottle sent to me by Francesco Ricasoli: opaque; citrus-like fruit; lovely flavour, rich dry oaky finish. (At lunch, March 2000.) Most recently, coincidentally, within the space of two days, first at Chippenham Lodge then dining at Boodle's Club after the Ch Haut-Bailly masterclass, with Véronique Sanders and Steven Spurrier: opaque; black cherry, intense; sweet, crisp fruit; lovely rich fruit, intense, good future. *London, April 2002* ★★★★

**Chianti Classico, Pèppoli** Antinori Opaque; crisp, good fruit. *Hosting a large, grand (and expensive) dinner at the restaurant Magna in Siena, April 2000* ★★

**Chianti Classico, Riserva** Rocca delle Macìe Very dependable, very drinkable. *Jan 2000* ★★★

**Chianti Classico, Riserva, Badia a Passignano** Antinori 100% Sangiovese, single-vineyard wine, aged in small *barriques*; rather peppery, youthful aroma; lovely fruit, depth and length. *At Antinori's, San Casciano, April 1999* ★★(★★★) *Later in the day we visited Badia a Passignano, an old monastery noted for a magnificent old mural along one wall of the main chamber. The cellars are filled with casks of Antinori's wines.*

**Chianti Classico, Riserva, Tenute Marchese Antinori** Antinori 100% Sangiovese now permitted for Chianti Classico though 2 to 3% Cabernet Sauvignon used. Very deep, fairly intense; sweet nose, delicious fruit; drier on palate. Very good. *At San Casciano, April 1999* ★★(★★★)

**Dolcetto d'Alba, Cascina Francia** Giacomo Conterno Purple; sweet, raspberry-scented, dry, firm, lean, crisp, oaky and tannic. *At a John Armit tasting, London, April 2000* ★★(★)

**Gagliole** Gagliole A Tuscan *vino da tavola* from 85% Sangiovese with some Cabernet Sauvignon. Opaque, intense: low-keyed, brambly, generously endowed with fruit. *At lunch with Monika Bär at the vineyard, April 1999* ★★(★★) *Drinking well but more to come.*

**Guado al Tasso** Guado al Tasso/Antinori From Bolgheri (Cabernet Sauvignon and Merlot, Petit Verdot 2% and some Syrah, 60% new oak). Cherry-like fruit on nose and palate. Dry, crisp. *April 1999* (★★★★)? *Will be interesting to see how this develops.*

**Monferrato 'Countacc!'** Michele Chiarlo I take my hat off to Michele Chiarlo for his industry, imagination and attractive labels. His wine is quite good, too! First tasted in June 2000: opaque core; fullish, fragrant and flavoury but at this stage too oaky. Four months later, I thought it very good: a lovely, fruity wine, its richness masking tannin. *Last noted supping at Chippenham Lodge, Oct 2000* ★★★(★)

**Nebbiolo d'Alba** Bruno Giacosa Already very mature-looking, palish with orange tinge, low-keyed, arboreal; good fruit but more of a bite than expected. *At a John Armit tasting in London, April 2000* ★(★)

**Ornellaia** Tenuta dell'Ornellaia Cabernet Sauvignon 65%, Merlot 30%, Cabernet Franc 5%. Made by Tibor Gal, a brilliant young winemaker from Hungary – I recall being immensely impressed by his own '97 Egri Bikaver at a lunch in Memphis. Deep, velvety, fairly intense; a veritable cascade of extraordinary fruit, sweet, rich, soft, fleshy. A great wine. *At the Ornellaia tasting at the Groucho Club in London, Feb 2002* ★★★(★★) *Tempting to drink this young and full of fruit but probably at its best from 2010.*

**Le Pergole Torte** Montevertine The youngest vintage at the Pergole Torte tasting: it has extra dimensions: a luminous depth, sweetness, harmony and charm; lovely flavour and length. Delicious. *In London, May 2001* ★★(★★★) *Say 2005– 2015.*

**Romitorio di Santedame Toscana** Ruffino Ruffino's top wine and making a point: deep, velvety, fairly intense; spicy; dryish, good fruit, full-bodied (alcohol 14%) and certainly impressive. *With Gelasio Gaetani at Osteria ar Galleto, Rome, July 2001* ★★★(★★)

**Rosso di Toscano** La Brancaia/Mazzei Maturing nicely; sweet, smoky oak and mocha; rich, deliciously tarry flavour, teeth-gripping tannin and acidity. *At Chippenham Lodge, Feb 2002* ★★(★) *Could well develop agreeably.*

**Sassicaia** Richly coloured, still youthful; sweet, harmonious, good fruit on nose and palate, fleshy, tannic. *Tasted in London, May 2002* ★★(★★★)

**Solaia** Antinori Antinori's single vineyard in Bolgheri. Cabernet Sauvignon 80%, Sangiovese 20%, 100% aged in new French oak. Still in cask. Velvety; crisp fruit; austere yet ripe tannins. *April 1999* (★★★★★)

**Tignanello** Antinori Another single-vineyard wine but this time Sangiovese 80%, Cabernet Sauvignon 20%, so, of course, a different style. A barrel sample: fragrant, spicy; leaner than Antinori's Chiantis, lots of fruit, good length. Delicious. *April 1999* (★★★★★)

**Trinoro** Trinoro/Franchetti Cabernet Sauvignon 80%, plus Cabernet Franc. A relatively new wine, one of its earliest vintages and already making a mark. Very deep, velvety, intense;

very distinctive nose, strawberry and vanilla; sweet, pretty full of fruit; very high alcoholic content (16%) yet not overtly heady, fleshy. Admirable but not exactly my style of wine. *Dining at Naranjas with Gelasio Gaetani, a cousin of Andrea Franchetti, Sept 1999* ★★(★★★)

# 1998 ★★ to ★★★

The previous year was a hard act to follow and uneven weather conditions produced varying results. Briefly, the summer was hot and dry; and the harvest alternated between sun and rain.

Drink the minor reds before the '96s and '97s while the Riserva class wines from both Piedmont and Tuscany will probably be at their best between 2005 and 2012.

**Barbera d'Asti, La Court** Michele Chiarlo I first met Michel Chairlo at a wine fair in Austria, since when I have enjoyed frequent meetings and several of his wines. Although not a subject matter for this book, his Moscato d'Asti Nivole is one of the best – a style of wine I love, perfect for puddings. Also, Chiarlo's labels are most beautifully designed. I first tasted the '98 La Court at Vinexpo in June 2001. Michele told me that Barbera needs to be ripe otherwise it tends to be acidic. In 1998 it benefited from the hot summer and also the autumn heat. The wine spends 18 months in 50% new oak: a lovely, deep, velvety, ruby colour; sweet, rich, distinctive, floral nose and lovely flavour. Enough bite, cherry-like fruit, firm finish. *At home, Sept 2001* ★★(★★)

**Barolo, Cerequio** Michele Chiarlo Maturing; very sweet, rich, pleasantly scented nose; rich, very dry tannic grip. Needs time. *Lunch at Chippenham Lodge* ★★(★★)

**Chianti Classico** Antinori Yet again, an ideal, decently fruity, wine with amenable body (alcohol 13%) – and, as always, reasonably priced. The ideal restaurant wine. *By the quayside in Portofino, July 2001* ★★★

**Cortaccio, Villa Cafaggio** Casa Girelli Cabernet Sauvignon 100%, opaque; full of brambly fruit but with a hard, very oaky finish. I gave it a lot of air, decanting into an open jug and then serving in large glasses. Quite a mouthful but I don't think I would bother to cellar it. *At Chippenham Lodge, Nov 2001* ★(★★)?

**Dolcetto d'Alba, Fontanazza** Marcarini With Angelo Gaja at our favourite restaurant, di Cesari, at Albaretto Torre in Piedmont: deep, velvety; good fruit; attractive despite its youthfulness. *Nov 1999* ★★(★)

**Dolcetta d'Alba, Monte Aribaldo** Marchesi di Gresy Delicious, but more memorable for lunch with Angelo Gaja at Osteria del Boccondivino in a courtyard next to the Slow Food offices in Bra. *Nov 1999* ★★(★)

**Lupicaia** Castello del Terriccio This *vino da tavola* is a Merlot and Cabernet Sauvignon blend: plummy; rich fruit; hefty style though moderate strength (13.5%), plenty of fruit and oak. Excellent with Daphne's risotto. *Lunch at Chippenham Lodge, Aug 2001* ★★★

**Monferrato, 'Countacc!'** Michele Chiarlo An attractive blend of Barbera, Nebbiolo and Cabernet Sauvignon: sweet, lovely, soft fruit, nice weight (13.5%), depth and length. *At Chippenham Lodge, Aug 2001* ★★★ *For early drinking.*

**Nebbiolo Passito, Nepas** Alessandro and Gian Natale Fontino New to me. Very dark cherry; bitter fruit; very dry, concentrated. Probably all right with a very strong hard cheese. *Ending supper at the Hotel Victoria, Bad Mergestheim. Feb 2002* ★★(★★)

**Ornellaia** Tenuta dell'Ornellaia Cabernet Sauvignon 60%, Merlot 35%, Cabernet Franc 5%. Opaque; low-keyed but rich and brambly; very sweet, good fruit, slightly sandy texture, astringent finish. *At the Ornellaia tasting in London, Feb 2002* (★★★★) *Needs time.*

**San Martino, Villa Cafaggio** Casa Girelli Sangiovese 100%. An unsolicited bottle: ruby; very fragrant; crisp fruit, a bit lean and tart. *At Chippenham Lodge, Nov 2001* ★★

**Sassicaia** Fairly deep, rich core, plummy rim; very distinctive nose, newly sawn wood; medium-sweet, full bodied, good length, tannic. *Tasted in London, May 2002* ★★(★★★)

**Scasso dei Cesari** di Valgiano I think this is the first wine from Lucca that I have tasted: deep, velvety, ruby; very attractive fruit, slightly tarry, smoky oak; sweet, fleshy, alcohol 14%, rather coarse tannic finish. Produced for me to taste by Geoffrey Tucker who was clearly impressed. *At home, Feb 2002* ★★(★) *Bottle age will probably smooth the edges.*

# 1999 ★★★★

Overall a very good vintage, the fifth in a row. In Piedmont, despite variable weather conditions and rot-conducive humidity in August, Barolo and Barbaresco were reported to be good – 'on a par with the '95, though not up to the '96s or '97s'. There were high yields in Tuscany; the Sangiovese was outstanding and some producers claimed to have picked their best grapes of the decade.

There was a plethora of decent wines of which I have tasted a niggardly few. In any case, the big guns have yet to show themselves.

**Barbera d'Asti, 'La Court'** Michele Chiarlo The wine spent 12 months in small oak barrels. Very deep, plummy, velvety appearance; brambly, spicy. Oaky nose; ripe sweetness, alcohol 13.5%. Delicious amalgam of fruit and oak, dry finish. *At Chippenham Lodge, May 2002* ★★(★★)

**Barbera d'Asti, Superiore, Cipressi della Court** Michele Chiarlo Fairly sweet, full-flavoured, alcohol 13.5%, rich, touch of tannic iron. Very drinkable. *At Chippenham Lodge, Aug 2001* ★★(★)

**Chianti Classico** Antinori Another vintage of this ideal restaurant wine. Young, nubile, easy. *July 2001* ★★★

**Chianti Classico, Riserva** Rocca delle Macie Not great, but light years better than the commercial Chianti fiascos of yore. *Lunch at Franco's in Jermyn Street, the nearest Italian restaurant to my office, May 2001* ★★

**Cincinnato** Trinoro/Franchetti Only 1800 bottles made by Franchetti from local Lazio grape varieties. Medium-deep – for a change; delicious, cherry-like fruit, fragrant – in fact positively exotic – nose and taste. Hefty (alcohol 15%) but amenable. *Presented by Andrea Franchetti, quite a character, March 2001* ★★(★★)

**Dolcetto d'Alba** Controvento Bava Opaque; dry, firm, fleshy, touch of citrus-like acidity. *A modest birthday dinner at Mosimann's, May 2000* ★★★

**Monferrato, 'Countacc!'** Michele Chiarlo Barbera 35%, Nebbielo 35%, Cabernet Sauvignon 30%. Deep, mauve, rich 'legs'; attractive ripe fruit on nose and palate, crisp, fragrant, tannic. *Tasted at Chippenham Lodge, May 2002* ★(★★★)

**Ornellaia** Tenuta dell'Ornellaia Cabernet Sauvignon 65%, Merlot 30%, Cabernet Franc 5%, 18 months in French oak, 60% new, 40% one year old, 18 months. Opaque; hard, whiff of iodine; sweet, good fruit, lovely texture, silky, leathery tannin. *At the Ornellaia tasting in London, Feb 2002* (★★★★)

Reggiano 'Concerto' Lambrusco Rubino Secco **Medici Ermite** I have never taken to any *Vino Frizzante* but admired its elegant bottle, wired for safety, and elaborate label which makes Germans' look simple. Intense, slightly fizzy purple; high toned verging on vinegary, fruit and raw straw; dry, surprisingly low alcoholic content, 11.5%, blackberry-like taste and a bit of an end bite. Concerto? Not Mozart. But it grew on me after a glass or two. *Pre-dinner at Chippenham Lodge, July 2000 ★★★ in its way.*

**Sassicaia** Fairly deep, plummy red; sweet, minty, spicy new oak; full, rich, very good flavour, flesh and grip. Still at the very beginning of its long career. *May 2002 ★(★★★)*

**Sangiovese, Rosso di Toscana Paolo Masi** Fruity, easy, with a refreshing *spritz* finish. Just for fun. *July 2001 ★★*

**Tassinaia Castello del Terriccio** A Cabernet Sauvignon, Merlot and Sangiovese blend matured in Allier *barriques*. Plummy purple; hard, crisp, blackberry, spicy; sweeter and softer than expected, good fruit, alcohol 13.5%. *A bottle from Paola Gaetani, at Chippenham Lodge, Aug 2001 ★★(★★)*

**Trinoro Trinoro/Franchetti** From 7.4ha of vines in the province of Siena south of Montalcino producing 16,000 cases of Trinoro. Cabernet Franc 70%, Merlot 20%, Cabernet Sauvignon 6%, Petit Verdot 4%. Tasted shortly after bottling: glowing ruby; Cabernet Franc clearly dominant with green, bell pepper fruit; very sweet, strong (alcohol 15%), crisp, lovely flavour with sweet, 'warm', tannic finish. Very distinctive. *At a European cult wines tasting presented by the diffident but very amusing Andrea Franchetti at Corney & Barrow, March 2001 (★★★★) Impressive.*

**Valpolicella Classico Allegrini** Attractive, positive, lively – like my wife. *A surprise birthday holiday for Daphne at the Cipriani, Venice, July 2000 ★★(★★)*

## 2000 and the future

The wines of this great country are on a roll. All that is needed is good weather and a good market. How can they go wrong when Italian food is so much admired!

As I said earlier, Italian restaurants are imaginative and fun, from the huge numbers of bustling *trattorie* which spill on to the pavements in Rome, to the superb restaurants in small towns and villages around Alba. The best are not cheap but the wines are rarely overpriced for their quality – indeed, Daphne and I have had fascinating wines in Florence and Rome at surprisingly reasonable prices, particularly old vintages which the locals and the tourists ignore. It is said that some of the very best Italian restaurants are in New York. I have certainly consumed some of the greatest Italian wines there. London has also come a long way though there is a price gulf between the fair-to-middling and fashionable.

As far as the wines themselves are concerned, I just hope that the major producers in classic regions will not lose sight of their origins by moving into an already flooded international market, sacrificing character for the spurious, if fashionable, 'global' taste. I remain an optimist!

## 2000 ★★★★

From the point of view of the weather it was impossible to generalise about this vintage. As usual I shall concentrate on the growing conditions in Piedmont and Tuscany. The latter enjoyed a mild winter, hot humid spring and high temperatures in June. July was irregular and the second half of August extremely hot, followed by rainstorms. Harvest conditions were very good, Sangiovese being picked from 20 September. Quality was satisfactory with high sugar levels and substantial concentration. In Piedmont, overall quality was sound but the quantity was lower.

**Barbera d'Asti Superiore, Cipressi della Court Michele Chiarlo** Spicy, brambly, new oak scents; delicious for early drinking. *At lunch at Chippenham Lodge, May 2002 ★★★*

**Ornellaia Tenuta dell'Ornellaia** Classed as **Bolgheri DOC Rosso Superiore** Cabernet Sauvignon 65%, Merlot 15%, Cabernet Franc 20%. Barrel sample: opaque, purple rim, rich 'legs'; brambly fruit, opened up sweetly, almost brown sugar; good body, rich young fruit, flesh and texture, though tannic finish. *The youngest vintage at the Ornellaia tasting at the Groucho Club, London, Feb 2002 (★★★★)*

**Trinoro Trinoro/Franchetti** Very small yield, 15 hl/ha, small berries, thick skins. All the Merlot grapes were lost due to heat stress and, in all, a mere 900 cases were made. Astonishing black colour; surprisingly forthcoming nose, sweet, soft toffee, glorious fruit; very sweet, packed with fruit, powerful, high alcohol (in excess of 15%), very oaky, very tannic. *Presented by Andrea Franchetti at Corney & Barrow, March 2001 (★★★★★)? I doubt if I will be around to see it at its peak!*

**Chianti, Colli Senesi Fattoria Sovestro** British Airways dutifully serving Italian wines on their flight to Rome. Deep, slightly sweet, soft, pleasant enough despite its youthfulness – but very oaky. *On BA 557, July 2001 ★★ Decent commercial wine.*

# Tokaji

Tokaj-Hegyalja (the Tokay hills) is a region in the north-east of Hungary, bordering Slovakia and the Ukraine. Though dry white wine is made, the climate, abetted by the confluence of two rivers, the Bodrog and the Tisza, is conducive to the formation of botrytis on the late-ripening grapes and the production of the famous sweet Aszús, which are some of my favourite wines.

## 17th century to 1945

It is safe to say that Tokaji Aszú is the first (since the sweetened and doctored wines of the ancient world) of the great sweet wines, well established as such by the mid-17th century. The beneficial effects of botrytis were noted here almost a century before they were accidentally discovered in Germany. Moreover, the vineyards were the first ever to be classified: in 1700 Prince Rákóczi of Transylvania introduced 1st, 2nd and 3rd class (or growth) quality ratings. Tokaji was the most highly regarded and sought after wine, particularly by Russian and Polish royalty and nobility. The vineyards, mostly owned by the Hungarian aristocracy, were the country's most valuable assets. (Catherine the Great can claim to be one of the first foreign investors; she owned, and protected with her own guards, a major vineyard.) There is much evidence that the wine appealed to English connoisseurs in the 18th and early 19th centuries (Christie's archives reveal that Tokaji appeared in a catalogue dated 1770, only four years after James Christie set up his auction business). Another appreciative connoisseur was Thomas Jefferson who imported and served 'rich Tokay' ('for which I paid a guinea a bottle') at his presidential banquets in the early 1800s. The aftermath of World War One was disastrous for the Hungarian landowners and trade. In 1925 a remarkable cache of old wines was literally unearthed and purchased by Berry Bros. Their 1927 price list includes early 19th-century vintages *from the Princely House of Bretzenheim which became extinct in 1863*. It seems that the family, concerned that the revolutionary forces of 1848 would seize their property, walled up their valuable old wines. Historically the wine and region were called Tokay by the English but the wine is now correctly referred to as Tokaji and the region as Tokaj. In the following notes all the wines included Tokay or Tokaji as part of the name on the label and the producer is indicated where known.

### Vintages at a Glance
**Outstanding** ★★★★★
1834, 1885, 1889, 1900, 1912, 1924, 1937, 1945
**Very Good** ★★★★
1811, 1876, 1901, 1904, 1906, 1935
**Good** ★★★
1865, 1917, 1943

## 1811 ★★★★

The 'Comet vintage' and possibly the greatest vintage of the 19th century throughout the European wine regions.
**Tokay Essence** From the Bretzenheim cellar, mentioned above. I treated myself to an expensive bottle at one of Christie's sales and my wife and I sat up in bed, glasses in hand, on 31 December 1972 to see in the New Year. Its colour was old amber and not very bright, due to the slow-to-settle sediment which can be heavy in old Tokay (which is why it should always be stored upright). Its fragrance and flavour were out of this world, 'ambrosial nectar' I gushingly wrote,

'piquant, crushed raisins, concentrated, luscious'. It is the only wine I have ever tasted which did not have a 'finish'. It just went on, and on. *Tasted 1972–73* ★★★★★★ *(6 stars)*

## 1834 ★★★★★

**Essence** Also from the Bretzenheim cellar: lemon-amber; high-toned, raisiny; like the 1811, but not as concentrated. Acidity resembling an old Sercial madeira. *At Hans Jorissen's tasting of old Tokay in Leiden, Nov 1982* ★★★★★

OTHER 19TH-CENTURY VINTAGES, OLD NOTES:
**1865 Aszú, 5 putts** Windisch-Graetz rich but varnishy. *Leiden, 1982*; **Aszú** (putts unknown) like a soft yet tangy Sauternes, drying, marvellous acidity. *At Hugel's rare dessert wine tasting, 1985* ★★★★; **1876 Tokayer Ausbruch** imported by Lorenz Reich, New York, pre-1914. Three bottles, fully branded corks. Tasted like Bual and Yquem mixed. *Heublein's pre-sale tasting, 1980* ★★★★; **1885 'Imperial Tokay'** two notes: concentrated yet ethereal. *1972 and 1976* ★★★★; from the cellar of Count Potulicki: amber, resinous, rich. *1969* ★★

## Essence

*In documents and on labels the spelling would vary. I have noted Essencia, Eszencia, even Esszencia or Esszenzcia. Whether or not prefixed Aszú, the wine was generally the equivalent of 7 or slightly more puttonyos and rarely marketed in its pure state.*

## 1889 ★★★★★

Essencia **Zimmermann Lipot** Several consistent notes. Most memorably, on my first visit to Budapest in 1972, with Josef Dömöter, head of the Hungarian Wine Trust and Fred May, the UK Monimpex importer (see page 412). Neither had ever tasted an old Eszencia before. I opened it in Herr Dömötor's office, to great wonder and satisfaction, and took the remaining half the following morning to Tokaj, where, in Tarcal, I had lunch with the technical head of the Research Institute for Viticulture. He didn't like it! Briefly: a deep, warm amber; glorious fragrance, rich, chocolatey, spicy; sweet of course, plump, concentrated taste of singed sultanas, excellent acidity. *Last tasted in Leiden, Nov 1982* ★★★★★

## 1900–1904

A RANGE OF OLD TOKAY VINTAGES in the following styles: **Szamorodni, Aszú** and **Ausbruch** (from Austrian merchants). All tasted in the early 1980s in Leiden or at Christie's pre-sale tastings. Among the best: **1900 Ausbruch Adamoviton** from Tolksva: rich, ethereal, perfect ★★★★★; **1901 Szamorodni** (sweet) **Imperial Court Cellars** honey and old apples ★★★★; and **1904 Sweet Szamorodni Borsai Miklos** rich tawny; almost malty, lovely flavour ★★★★

## 1906 ★★★★

Ausbruch **Teringi Henrik** A producer in Tállya. Amber; still sweet, good flavour and acidity. *Tasted Oct 1982* ★★★

## 1912 ★★★★★

Probably the last great vintage of the Austro-Hungarian empire, and the oldest vintage at a small but important Tokaji tasting led by Dr Gábor Rohály, editor of Rohály's (Hungarian) *Wine Guide*, at the Hungarian Embassy in Berlin. **Aszú, 6 putts** Medium-pale amber with lime edge; very rich 'calf's foot jelly' and mature Cheddar nose; fairly sweet, immensely rich, fat, fleshy, powerful, firm with masked acidity. *In Berlin, Sept 2001* ★★★★★

## 1917 ★★★

Aszú, 4 putts **Zimmerman Lipot** As in Germany, much of the Tokaji wine trade was handled by Jewish merchants. Amber; bouquet of old raisins and damp straw; medium-sweet, good flavour and acidity. *Brought to Gidleigh Park, Devon, by Bob Paul where we all stayed after Christmas, Dec 1991* ★★★

## 1924 ★★★★★

Great post-war vintage.
**Essencia** From one of two demijohns from a private cellar in Sarospatac and tasted in the Hungarian Wine Trust's offices.

Scent of rich barnyards. Rich but spoiled by high volatile acidity. *Tasted 1972.*
**Aszú, 6 putts Zimmermann** Oloroso colour; superb bouquet, flavour like ethereal old cognac and Sauternes. *At Hans Jorissen's tasting in Leiden, 1982* ★★★★★

## 1935 ★★★★

Aszú, 6 putts Gentle, fragrant, old straw with a whiff of violets; a lovely wine, toffee-like flavour, perfect acidity, dry finish. *At the Hungarian Embassy in Berlin, Sept 2001* ★★★★

## 1937 ★★★★★

As elsewhere in Europe, a great vintage for sweet white wines.
**Aszú-Essencia** Cloudy amber; scent of squashed raisins, rich, high-toned. *Tasted in Leiden, 1982* ★★
**Aszú, 5 putts** Producer unknown as my cellar flooded and the label was bin-soiled. However, it had its original lead capsule and cork. Level high. To my surprise, for I had left it standing for a long time, just in case, it had virtually no sediment: a lovely, deep, warm amber with pronounced apple-green rim; sweet, rich, deeply honeyed nose and flavour. Its fat cut with excellent acidity. Touch of caramel, very good finish. *Elevenses at Chippenham Lodge, Good Friday, March 2002* ★★★★

## 1942 ★★

A difficult and forgotten wartime vintage.
**Aszú, 6 putts** Showing its age but still meaty, caramelly with hint of squashed horseradish; very assertive, penetrating taste with dry, raw finish. *In Berlin, Sept 2001.*

## 1943 ★★★

A good wartime vintage. Only two old notes. **Aszú, 3 putts Flegmann** Both bottles lovely, medium-sweet with delicate richness. *Tasted March and April 1980* ★★★

## 1945 ★★★★★

A difficult period, but at least it was before the Communists nationalised the Hungarian wine industry.
**Aszú, 5 putts** Imported by Charles Montrose, London. Sweet but of moderate quality. *Tasted 1989* ★★
**Essencia** Richly coloured, viscous; old apples and raisins; very rich, perfect flavour and aftertaste. *At the launch of my* Great Vintage Wine Book *in Zurich, Oct 1983* ★★★★★

---

### Puttonyos, or putts

*The wooden hods used for the measuring of botrytis-affected Aszú berries in the production of Tokaji. The concentrated fruit is kneaded to a paste, then collected in puttonyos (each carrying 20–25 kg); these are then traditionally added to 136-litre barrels or gönci of base wine at a rate of three, four, five or six puttonyos per cask, depending on the required sweetness and quality of the eventual wine. A six-'putt' wine will be the sweetest and best, containing up to 150 grams per litre residual sugar, and expressing a range of complex, intensely concentrated honey and quince characters. In particularly fine vintages, seven-puttonyos Tokaji is made, its sweetness exceeding 200 grams per litre of sugar.*

# 1947–1989

This section covers the period from Communist state control in 1947 to the relaxation and opening up of a free market in 1989. During the long post-war period the Hungarian wine regions were under the deadening hand of The Trust of Wine Enterprises whose headquarters were in Budapest. Each region had its own manager, all exports being handled by the government-controlled Monimpex. 'Control' was the operative word.

When, in 1972, I paid my first visit to Hungary, I met the head of the Trust, Josef Dömötor, who kindly gave me introductions to the main wine regions. In the Balaton region, the manager in charge of production and sales admitted that they were capable of producing Rieslings of Spätlese and Auslese quality but were restricted to just two sorts, one for ordinary consumption and a slightly higher grade for the best restaurants and their Russian clientele, though they did let me taste a 1946 Badacsony Aszú of fabulous quality. To produce finer and more expensive wines, he told me, would involve 'privilege' and 'capitalist' prices. I was told the same in Eger by the local manager (immaculately suited, shooting two inches of cuff, Clark Gable moustache and with his offices in the Bishop's Palace). In Tokaji itself, it was perfectly clear from the abandoned upper slopes and the irrigated lower vineyards that the aim was just to produce wine suitable for export to Russia, but little more.

However, I did in fact taste some very good Tokaji, particularly in the late 1970s to mid-1980s and organised three tastings and promotional sales at Christie's for the Trust. All wines were handled and exported by Monimpex. It is, I think, unfair to condemn this period outright. Though individuality was not allowed to rear its head, some excellent, if old-fashioned, wines were made.

## *Vintages at a Glance*
**Outstanding** ★★★★★
1947, 1952, 1957, 1963, 1968, 1972, 1983
**Very Good** ★★★★
1961, 1964, 1975, 1981, 1988
**Good** ★★★
1956, 1973

## 1947 ★★★★★
The most successful vintage of the post-war period. I have several notes.
**Essencia** First, an Aszú Essencia tasted in Tarcal in 1972: good but not great. Next, in 1974, a bottle from the Hungarian Wine Trust. Taught me a lesson. I did not give it long enough to settle, but it was extremely rich and concentrated, with wonderful acidity. *Last tasted 1974. At best* ★★★★
**Aszú, 6 putts** Pale amber, open rim; hefty, rich, tangy, fragrant bouquet and flavour, fairly sweet, a touch lean but fleshy and elegant, perfect weight, with high, teeth-gripping acidity. An exciting wine. *In Berlin, Sept 2001* ★★★★
**Aszú-Essencia Crown Estates** Deep amber; rich, singed-raisins bouquet; very sweet, lovely flesh, perfect sustaining acidity. *The culmination of the Crown Estates' Castle Island tasting at the Hungarian Embassy, London, Sept 2000* ★★★★★ *(Crown Estates, set up by the government in 1993, is 100% Hungarian-owned. They have the biggest Tokaji cellars and claim to have 25% of the total Tokaji production.)*

## 1952 ★★★★★
**Aszú, 6 putts** Pale amber, open rim; hefty, rich, tangy, fragrant bouquet and flavour, fairly sweet, a touch lean but fleshy and elegant, perfect weight, with high, teeth-gripping acidity. An exciting wine. *At Gábor Rohály's tasting at the Hungarian Embassy in Berlin, Sept 2001* ★★★★

**Aszú, 4 putts Crown Estates** Richly coloured; similar singed raisiny bouquet to the '47 Aszú Essencia, but less intense; medium-sweet, pungent. *Castle Island tasting, Sept 2000* ★★★

## 1956 ★★★
**Aszú, 6 putts Crown Estates** Bottled 1964. Alcohol 12.7%, residual sugar 128g/l, acidity 8.5g/l. Deep amber, lime rim; like an old Verdelho, high-toned, ethereal; sweet, old appley, madeira-like flavour. *At the MW Tokaji tasting, Dec 2000* ★★★

## 1957 ★★★★★
Outstanding vintage and the best since 1947.
**Aszú-Esszencia** (sic) **Monimpex** Several notes, first in 1973. In 1989: warm amber with gold highlights; very rich, baked apples, raisins and honey; TBA-like sweetness and intensity yet not heavy. Soft, fat, glorious flavour. Two notes in 1994, both noting a pale lime rim, great depth, a whiff of caramel, high acidity. *Last tasted (spelled Escenzia) at the Musée Baccarat in Paris, May 2000. At best* ★★★★★

## 1961 ★★★★
**Aszú 5 puttonos** (sic) **Ausbruch Trockenbeerenauslese Cabinet** Fulsomely labelled by Monimpex: deepish amber-gold; rich old-apples nose; not quite as sweet as expected but fine flavour, acidity and aftertaste. *May 1971* ★★★★

## 1963 ★★★★★
**Aszú-Essencia** Warm orange-amber; rich, meaty, raisiny nose and taste. *Showing well pre-sale in Geneva, May 1992* ★★★★
**Muskotàlyos Aszú, 6 putts** Five notes, mainly in the 1980s: fairly deep amber; strange, sweet grapey sort of aroma, raisins and pineapple husk; rich yet lean and crisp. Most recently, a bottle bought at Christie's: now a medium-deep, rose-hip

amber; showing its age with a sort of animal fat, 'calf's foot jelly' and honeyed bouquet; sweet, rich, tangy, unusual orange-muscat flavour and excellent acidity. *Last consumed with great pleasure at an after-theatre supper at Chippenham Lodge, July 1994* ★★★★★
**Muskotályos Aszú, 5 putts** Several notes. Glowing amber gold; spicy, Beerenauslese-like nose; very sweet, intense yet with finesse and flavour of muscatelle and peach. *Last noted Sept 1990* ★★★★★

## 1964 ★★★★

Berry Bros & Rudd, having put great old Tokay Essence on the map in the period following World War One, decided that the time was ripe to relaunch Tokaji by importing Aszú-Eszencia.
**Aszú-Essencia Monimpex** It was good in 1972 but I felt it could do with more bottle age. Indeed, in 1982, it seemed to have developed a more ethereal fragrance; on the palate ambrosial raisins. Possibly at peak in the mid-1980s for by the end of that decade, I got honeyed, old-straw notes. Enjoyable though. *Last tasted in Jan 1989. At best* ★★★★
**Aszú, 6 putts** Rich amber; very penetrating, raisiny, orange-peel bouquet; sweet, immensely rich yet crisp, with 'old appley' taste and long, lean, attenuated, acidic finish. *At the Hungarian Embassy in Berlin, Sept 2001* ★★★★

## 1968 ★★★★★

Warm summer followed by rain, then long sunny spells. Early harvest of heavily botrytised grapes.
**Aszú-Essencia** At 15 years of age, deep orange tawny; rich, old apples and honey, and *crème brûlée* almost like '37 Yquem; sweet, its richness cut by excellent acidity. *Not tasted since Oct 1983. Then* ★★★★★ *Should still be superb.*
**Aszú, 6 putts Crown Estates** Very good, raisiny nose; sweet, medium body, good flavour, length and acidity. *From the Crown Estates' 'Museum Collection', in London, Sept 2000* ★★★★

## 1972 ★★★★★

The top vintage of the (20th) century, for the size and quality of Aszú production across the whole Tokaj region. Long, warm, favourable autumn weather with widespread development of 'noble rot'.
**Essence** John Lipitch, a London importer, gave me a rare opportunity to taste pure unadulterated Tokaji Eszencia. Even after 13 years, it was still 'working'. An immensely rich, raisiny, pervasive, tangy scent remained in the empty glass. Intensely sweet, alcohol only 2% by volume, high acidity, completely masked by incredibly high residual sugar. *March 1985* ★★★★★
**Eszencia** Deep, like PX sherry, almost black treacle with intense apple-green rim; glorious bouquet, mocha and ambrosial caramel; immensely sweet, fat, great length, very high acidity, fragrant aftertaste. (I was informed that Eszencia cannot be vinified in cask as it draws moisture from the wood and causes the staves to split.) *In Berlin, Sept 2001* ★★★★★
**Aszú-Essencia Crown Estates** Amber; nose like freshly-peeled mushrooms in honey; very sweet of course, fat, good length. *From the Crown Estates' 'Museum Collection', London, Sept 2000* ★★★★★
**Aszú, 6 'buttig'** (sic) Amber, green rim; honeyed but corky; sweet, toffee-like, good acidity.

## 1973 ★★★

**Aszú, 5 putts Monimpex** Deep amber; caramelised; sweet, good, old-fashioned style and flavour. Almost coped with excellent pecan pie. *With the Bacchus Society aboard the Memphis Queen III, Tennessee, Sept 1999* ★★★
**Aszú, 6 putts, Svarvas Crown Estates** Warm amber, pale lime rim; restrained but rich, toffee-like; sweet, very rich, 'calf's foot jelly'-like flavour, very good acidity. *Sept 2000* ★★★★

## 1975 ★★★★

**Aszú, 6 putts Monimpex** Orange-gold; raisiny, fragrant; sweet, lovely apricot and raisins flavour, excellent acidity and aftertaste. *Tasted blind but totally unmissable, at Nils Sternby's birthday tasting of '75s from around the world, April 1995* ★★★★

## 1981 ★★★★

**Aszú, 5 putts** Orange-gold; bouquet of honey and straw; fairly sweet, lovely flavour and acidity. *London, Jan 1993* ★★★

## 1983 ★★★★★

Great vintage.
**Aszúeszencia Árvay** Six to seven years in barrel. Two notes, first a bottle sent to me by Christian Sauska, a wealthy Hungarian-American, investing in Árvay's estate, then on a hectic day trip (it is a hard, fast, two-hours' drive each way from Budapest), tasting a range of Árvay's wines in Tokaj in March, 2000: a fairly deep, rich, peachy-gold; warm, harmonious, toasted, smoky mocha, honeyed and floral bouquet; very sweet yet not fat, a touch of caramel, singed apricot flavour and hard acidic finish. Most recently: warm amber; scented caramel; very rich, concentrated, intense acidity and hot finish. *Excellent with Roquefort when lunching with the Hungarian Ambassador in Berlin, Sept 2001* ★★★(★) *More to come.*

## 1988 ★★★★

Warm July and rain in August initiated botrytis. Between 80 and 90% of the crop had noble rot.
**Aszú-Essencia MWB** 80% Furmint, 20% Harslévelü grown in *grand cru* vineyards in Mad-Holdvölgy, produced and bottled by MWB Pince (cellar) in Abaüjszanto. Two bottles given to me by 'MWB', Marta Wille-Baumkauff, at The Wine Trade Fair in London. The wine was lovely: medium, orange amber, gold highlights; hefty, not unlike a chocolatey, meaty Bual madeira; sweet, nice weight (alcohol 10.5%), fairly soft, luscious, raisiny and caramelly. *Last tasted April 1998* ★★★★★
**Aszú, 6 putts MWB** Yellow gold highlights; rich, tangy. Very good with *foie gras. In Berlin, Sept 2001* ★★★
**Aszú, 6 putts Crown Estates** Whiff of old stables; very sweet, very rich, touch of meaty-malted raisins. Delicious. *At the Castle Island tasting, Sept 2000* ★★★★
**Aszú, 5 putts Ch Pajzos** Lemon gold; heavy, honeyed botrytis, tasted more like Sauternes than Tokay; sweet, assertive, lovely botrytised grapey flavour. *At Vinexpo, June 1995* ★★★

## 1989

Judging by the only '89 I have tasted (a 4-putt Aszú from the Hétszélö Estate) avoid this vintage. Or perhaps this is unfair.

# 1990–1999

$S$oon after the market was opened up, outsiders were encouraged to invest, and some serious money moved in. In the vanguard was the enthusiastic Hugh Johnson and what soon became the Royal Tokaji Wine Company; Jean-Michel Cazes (of Ch Lynch-Bages and overseer of the several wine properties of AXA Millésimes) persuaded the insurance company to revive the Disznókő Estate; David Alvarez of Spain's Vega Sicilia built a spectacular new winery at the Oremus Estate, and others started investing too. Their activity, with the practical support of the very experienced István Szepsy has rejuvenated the Tokaj region. The new boys, notably the Royal Tokaji Wine Company, are principally concerned with producing Aszú wines which, like Sauternes, is a risky and expensive business, because growing conditions are not always appropriate. Nevertheless, some lovely wines are being made and I welcome this renaissance.

## Vintages at a Glance
**Outstanding** ★★★★★
1993, 1999
**Very Good** ★★★★
1991, 1992, 1996
**Good** ★★★
1990, 1997

## 1990 ★★★
A good vintage.

**Aszú, 5 putts Royal Tokaji Wine Company** This was one of the first of the new breed of Tokajis I tasted. My first impression was that the wine was more French than Hungarian, more Sauternes than Tokaji and this worried me slightly because of the company's modern approach and up-to-date winemaking, thanks to outside investment. Its colour was canary yellow; soft, low-keyed – not the usual tangy, wet straw; fairly sweet, clean cut, honeyed with very good acidity. *At the London Wine Trade Fair, May 1995. As wine ★★★★, as my idea of Tokaji ★★*

**Aszú, 5 putts, Birsalmas Royal Tokaji Wine Company** Birsalmas is a vineyard classified in 1700 as 'secundae' or 2nd class. Good yellow colour; also very low-keyed, slightly malty; similar sweetness, more assertive, good acidity. More of a classic Tokaji character. And much more expensive. *Also tasted May 1995 ★★★★*

**Aszú, 4 putts Crown Estates** Slightly malty, 'calf's foot jelly'; certainly richer than their 3 putts, with better flavour and acidity. *At the Hungarian Embassy in London, Sept 2000 ★★★*

**Aszú, 3 putts Ch Pajzos** A major 71-ha estate based in Sarospatak. Palish, yellow amber; some of the old appley Tokaji style; medium-sweet, crisp, good length and acidity. *At co-owner Jean-Michel Arcaute's tasting at the Ritz, London, April 1996 ★★★*

## 1991 ★★★★
**Aszú Esszenzcia** (sic) **Szepsy** Orange highlights, long 'legs'; very rich, complex bouquet reminding me of green tea; very sweet, alcohol 9.5%, plump, flowery, good length and acidity. *In Berlin, Sept 2001 ★★★★★ My highest mark of the 14-wine Tokaji tasting (and lunch) at the Hungarian Embassy.*

**Aszú, 6 putts, Szarvas Crown Estates** Amber-gold; slightly malty, tangy, 'raya' nose and flavour. Six years in cask. Fairly sweet (residual sugar 110g/l), relatively lightweight (alcohol, 11.5%) and with good acidity (total 8.5g/l). *At the Castle Island tasting, Sept 2000 ★★★★*

**Aszú, 5 putts Nyulászó Royal Tokaji Wine Company** Warm amber; rich, raisiny, attractive nose and flavour. Lowish alcohol (11%), like a lot of German sweet wines, and with similar acidity. Good, attenuated flavour. Served with a 'crescent of pineapple and mango', quite a novelty for the older members. *At a Saintsbury Club dinner, April 2000 ★★★*

**Aszú, 5 putts, 'Blue label' Royal Tokaji Wine Company** The 'Blue' label wines come from 1st and 2nd growth estates and selected growers. First tasted (with triple chocolate truffle) in 1996: a thoroughly reassuring Tokaji character, definitely not Sauternes! Very sweet. High acidity. Orange amber; slightly malty; sweet, slightly toffee-like flavour and very raisiny aftertaste. *At Waddesdon Manor, Sept 1998 ★★★★*

**Aszú, 5 putts, Szt Tamas Royal Tokaji Wine Company** Szt Tamas is a 1st growth vineyard. I can't help admiring the way Hugh Johnson, who is after all a shareholder, indefatigably promotes the Royal Tokaji wines – I suppose rather as Bob Mondavi does the wines of California, his enthusiasm benefits all Tokaji wines. This single-vineyard wine had a very typical straw and raisins nose; less sweet than expected with a long, dry, acidic finish. *One of 'HJs luxurious sweet wines' at a Hallwag presentation in Frankfurt, Sept 1997 ★★★★*

**Aszú, 5 putts, Botja** sweaty, raisiny, leathery; like taking Virol, the malted, meaty tonic for anaemic girls! *April 1996.*

**Aszú, 5 putts, Birsalmas** a 2nd growth vineyard: glorious colour. Sweet, rich, punchy, excellent flavour. Another, vineyard not stated, was, for me, the strongest in character, the sweetest of the lot, tangy and its acidity, though excellent, a bit too high. *April 1996, and all good in their way.*

**Aszú, 4 putts** from the 40-ha Szarvas vineyard: palish, honeyed, lovely flavour; its alcohol 11.5%, acidity 8.7g/l and residual sugar 110.4 g/l. *At the Tokaji Trading House tasting, Nov 1999 ★★★*

**Aszú, 3 putts** less rich, more alcoholic (13.11%), similar acidity though it seemed raw because of the lower residual sugar (83.2g/l). *At the above tasting, Nov 1999 ★★★*

## 1992 ★★★★
Very good quality Aszús.

**Aszú Disznókő** A range of wines from one of the well-financed new Tokaj companies spearheaded by Jean-Michel Cazes and AXA Millésimes. All had a medium-amber colour: **6 putts** nose low-keyed; sweet, full-flavoured, powerful, good length ★★★★; **5 putts** honeyed, rather Beerenauslese-like nose; also sweet, fairly pungent, good length and acidity ★★★★; **4 putts** honey and melon; medium-sweet, minty, good acidity. *Presented by Jean-Michel Cazes in London, April 1996 ★★★*

# 1993 ★★★★★

The first of the great vintages in which the new wave of producers could show their paces. A veritable explosion of estates and wines of which I have noted a total of 22. I have selected a range of typical wines in descending order of rating, most noted at the excellent MW tasting, December 2000.

**Essencia Ch Pajzos** Bottled 1997. Probably Aszú-Essencia but presumably very high putt value. Certainly glorious, intensely sweet, fat, rich and raisiny. *At Vinexpo, June 1995* ★★★★★

**Aszú-Essencia Royal Tokaji Wine Company** This is an 8-putt wine. First tasted at Zachys/Christie's dinner in Los Angeles: very distinctive, caramel and malt, fat and immensely sweet. Next at the MW tasting: warm, rich, amber-gold into orange highlights; delicious, classic appley, slightly toasty scents; very sweet of course (residual sugar 263g/l), rich and fat yet not heavy (alcohol 7%, like a German TBA), with lovely classic tangy finish. *At the MW tasting in London, Dec 2000* ★★★★★

**Aszú, 6 putts Szepsy** István Szepsy, of Tarcal, is one of the most highly regarded of all the Tokaji producers. I first tasted his wine in Memphis in 1997: totally delicious, fragrant, honeyed, apple blossom. Next: low-keyed with a scent that reminded me of soured cream; light, elegant style, sweet, creamy (alcohol 10.3%, acidity 9.55g/l, residual sugar 206g/l). *Last noted at the MW tasting, Dec 2000* ★★★★

**Aszú, 6 putts Disznókő** Totally different to Szepsy's: sweet, ripe, soft toffee, 'calf's foot', malty-meaty nose; drier than expected (lower residual sugar 154g/l) and higher acidity (10.8g/l) than Szepsy's. Slightly fuller-bodied (alcohol 12%), but spoiled for me by a peach kernelly end taste. *At the MW tasting, Dec 2000* ★★

**Aszú, 6 putts, Szt. Tamas Royal Tokaji Wine Company** Single-vineyard wine. Fairly deep amber; sweet, soft, rich, botrytis; very sweet, fat, fleshy. *Following the remarkable tasting of California cult wines at Waddesdon Manor, Oct 2000* ★★★★

**Aszú, 6 putts, Nyulászó Royal Tokaji Wine Company** Single-vineyard wine. Full, rich, caramelly, old style, 'straw' nose; very sweet, rich, complete, tangy, good acidity (11%, 215g/l, 10.3g/l). *At the MW tasting, Dec 2000* ★★★★

**Aszú, 5 putts Ch Kurucz** (the second label of Oremus Estate, launched by Vega Sicilia and partners): beautiful nose, botrytis and the real Tokaji tanginess. Very high acidity. *Late dinner after a hectic day in Tokaj with Christian Sauska at the restaurant Fortuna on Castle Hill, Budapest, Aug 2000* ★★★★

OF THE OTHER '93 5-PUTT ASZÚS **Crown Estates** two notes: nose like flattened raisins, curious flavour, Hárslevelü uppermost. Next, like old apples in a hay loft. Sweet. Rich. *Tasted Sept and Dec 2000* ★★; **Disznókő** curious, high-toned, fragrant, creamy; medium-sweet, rich, very tangy and distinctive. *Dec 2000* ★★★★; **Oremus** palish, yellow gold; low-keyed; fairly sweet, leanish, taste of apple core, fair length. *Dec 2000* ★★; **Royal Tokaji Wine Company** first noted in 1998 lunching at Wilton's. Hugh Johnson, at a nearby table, brought this for us to taste: lovely gold; touch of molasses; fairly sweet, good acidity. Next at home, in a very handy 25-cl bottle. Acidity giving it a dry finish. *1999* ★★★; and **Tokaji Trading House** rich, raisiny. *1999* ★★★

No '93 4 putts at any of the tastings, but just one 3 putt: **Aszú, 3 putts Crown Estates** warm honeyed nose but upstaged by the sweeter wines and with a feeble, unconvincing finish. *Sept 2000* ★

# 1994 ★★

**Aszú, 6 putts Tokaj Trading House** Warm orange; taste of dried apricot and caramel. Very high alcohol (14.34%), moderate acidity – by Tokaji standards (7.47g/l), residual sugar 182g/l. *At the Farmers' Club, London, Nov 1999* ★★

**Aszú, 6 putts, Szarvas Crown Estates** A very strange madeira-like nose, caramel and rich, damp straw; very sweet, soft, interesting flavour, a touch of 'old sherry' on the finish. *At the MW tasting, Dec 2000* ★★

**Aszú, 5 putts Oremus** Five years in barrel. Fairly rich and fragrant but a touch of almond kernels. We were informed that there was controlled oxidation, with the obvious implication about the old *laissez-faire* attitudes in oxidation. Frankly I am in two minds about squeaky-clean modern vinification. Half the character of Tokaji came from its length of time in small casks and degree of oxidation. Medium-sweet, tangy, lacking length. *At the MW tasting, Dec 2000* ★★

# 1995

**Aszú-Essencia Oremus** Made from 100% Furmint, with astonishingly low alcohol (3%), amazing residual sugar (450g/l) balanced by equally high acidity (17.8g/l). Unquestionably my top mark at the tasting: palish, yellow gold; wonderful fragrance and attractive bouquet, sweet, crisp; incredibly sweet, fat rich, with lip-caressing acidity. *At the MW tasting, Dec 2000* ★★★★★

**Aszú, 6 putts Disznókő** Creamy style, with ambrosial fudge (England's finest soft caramel from The Toffee Shop, Penrith); rich, of course, but with a curious spearmint touch, good length. *Dec 2000* ★★★★

**Aszú, 5 putts Árvay** Colour of old gold; initially creamy, honeyed but became less impressive; fairly sweet, strange flavour, touch of oiliness, caramel and raisins. Normally these rich Tokajis keep reasonably well once opened. This one, after 24 hours, was horrible. *At home, March 2000.*

# 1996 ★★★★

**Aszú, 6 putts, 'Blue label' Royal Tokaji Wine Company** Most imaginatively served at a Saintsbury Club dinner in September 2000 (doubtless Hugh Johnson's idea as it was his wine) with 'Duck liver and Armagnac Parfait' marbled with '*Foie Gras*, Black Truffles and Melba Toast': followed by Chablis and Arbroath Smokies, a '90 burgundy, a '90 claret and '83 Offley Boa Vista. Quite an evening. I am glad my wife, dutifully as always, came to drive me home. The Tokaji was good. Most recently: 'sweet and dry'. *Last tasted in my son, Bartholomew's office in San Francisco, March 2002* ★★★

---

### Furmint and Hárslevelü

*Furmint is the principal grape of Tokaji (making up two-thirds of the crop) and is prized for its lively acidity and its highly desirable susceptibility to noble rot. It is the acidity of this variety which is so critical in counterbalancing the eventual sweetness of the wine, and ensuring that Tokaji lives as long as it does. Furmint's main companion is Hárslevelü (meaning 'lime leaf'), another Hungarian white grape, typically spicy and powerfully flavoured, contributing characteristic aromatics to the Tokaji blend. Furmint and Hárslevelü are occasionally joined by the perfumed Muskotály which has a more raising, grapey taste.*

**Aszú, 6 putts, Königsberg Tokay Classic Winery** Königsberg is a *grand cru* vineyard in the Mäd district. Wonderful colour: yellow gold with orange-gold highlights and light apple-green rim; fragrant; very rich, intensely flavoured, on the lean side but with a good cover of flesh and lovely texture. *Elevenses at Chippenham Lodge, Nov 2000* ★★★★

**Aszú, 6 putts Szepsy** Tasted first in May 2000. Glowing amber-gold; fragrant, orange blossom, yet tangy; fairly sweet, lightish style, some fat but elegant. Most recently: vanilla on nose; rich, assertive, very high acidity. *Last noted at the Hungarian Embassy in Berlin, Sept 2001* ★★★★

**Aszú, '5 or 6' putts Árvay** Árvay János was not sure which this was! Tawny gold, singed, rich, chocolatey nose and flavour. *In the Mayor's parlour, Tokaj, Aug 2000* ★★★

## 1997 ★★★

Small vintage for Aszú wines. I have only tasted two.

**Aszú, 6 putts MWB** I was happy to meet Marta Wille-Baumkauff again. She is a Hungarian who lives mainly in Germany with her German husband. This was the oldest of the four vintages she brought to the tasting. A lovely wine: bright yellow gold with rich 'tears'; peachy, gently honeyed nose; very sweet, glorious peachy flavour. An appropriately feminine style. *With Christian Sauska and Árvay János at Szepsy's winery in Tarcal, Aug 2000* ★★★★

**Aszú, 6 putts Árvay** Two notes, a pre-tasting at home in March and later in Tokaj. Distinctive, meaty, smoky; medium-sweet but fairly fat and fleshy. Lovely flavour but very acidic. *Last tasted Aug 2000* ★★★

## 1998 ★★

I tasted the 1998s and 1999s all in Tokaj or Tarcal in August 2000 in the company of Christian Sauska, to whom I am indebted for a marvellous series of tastings and tours of the remarkably extensive Tokaji vineyards.

**Aszú, 4 putts, Deák MWB** Deák is an old vineyard in the Tarcal area. This wine is 100% Furmint. Sweeter and more acidic than the 3 putt below, reminding me of a *moelleux* Loire wine ★★★

**Aszú, 3 putts, Deák MWB** Also spicy, minty, medium sweet (85g/l and low acidity). For early drinking, but as only 700 bottles were produced, it won't last long ★★

**'Botrytis Selection' Deák MWB** Bottled in 1999. If it had more time in cask it could have been a 5- or 6-putt Aszú (the problem here is small production and shortage of capital). Bright yellow; sweet, plump, fleshy, modest strength (11%) and fair residual sugar (140g/l). Delicious ★★★

## 1999 ★★★★★

Great vintage, rivalling the 1993.

**Natu-essenz Eszencia Hétszölö** Bright yellow; herbaceous, lime honey; very sweet, deliciously fragrant and extended flavour. *At the Hungarian Embassy in Berlin* ★★★(★★)

I have tasted a wide range of Tokajis, including experiments with Furmint and Hárslevelü in American, Hungarian and French oak, as well as some table wines. Of the 6-putt wines, all made by Árvay János, I think I preferred wines from the French oak *barriques* to the young wine in 140-litre Hungarian barrels; both tasting better than the sharp metallic taste from the American barrels. All very complicated. But this is the experimental stage that Tokaji is going through. My favourite of all was a 30% Muskotályos (Muscat Lunel), a future Aszú.

The second batch of extremely interesting '99s were the wines of Kiraly, a joint venture of István Szepsy and a Hong Kong investor, starting with a late-harvest Furmint from a single vineyard, Lapis. The wine is barrel-fermented and then aged in small local Hungarian oak barrels. It is destined for the American market – lucky people. This was followed by a herbaceous, fleshy, 'noble harvest', 4-putt wine, then a 6-putt wine of mixed varietals, and a high quality 6-putt single-vineyard wine which will be 'the most expensive wine on the market – eventually'. Finally I tasted a single-vineyard Eszencia from Lapis. It had a scent of brandy snaps, toffee-like taste and wonderful fat cut by lively acidity. Alcohol? 1%! *All tasted with István Szepsy in Tarcal, Aug 2000.*

# 2000 and the future

I have long enjoyed the rare delights of older vintages and now admire the new. It is wonderful to see one of Europe's great classic wines, long ignored if not completely forgotten, enjoying a renaissance. Nevertheless, despite the influx of new capital and promotional activity, the general perception is that Tokaji is a niche market, confined to the Aszús, in varying degrees of sweetness and quality.

This does pose quite a few problems. The local producers, of which there are many, are undercapitalised, finding it costly to make Aszús, and the market for their less expensive, bread-and-butter dry whites is saturated. The outsiders, bringing in much-needed capital for replanting and investing heavily in state-of-the-art wineries, must be aware that, as in Sauternes, the autumn weather will not always be conducive to the formation of highly desirable botrytis. Even so, thanks to the benign climate, late-harvest wines can usually be made each year. For all these reasons a really fine Tokaji Aszú will never be cheap, but, happily, can be utterly delectable.

## 2000 ★★★★★

Outstanding year, said by some to be one of the greatest ever. Tokaji enjoyed a prolonged Indian summer – endless hot, dry days and balmy nights continuing into the autumn. Just when needed, the botrytis-creating mists arrived. It was a bumper year for Furmint and Muscat. Hárslevelü grapes suffered from the drought, botrytis arriving late. An abundant harvest of rich, high-quality wines.

# Spain's Unique Vega Sicilia

Fifty years ago few self-respecting British wine merchants would have dreamt of importing any Spanish wine other than sherry. Harvey's of Bristol, in the mid-1950s, listed just two table wines: 'Red Rioja' and, simply, 'White'. They were cheap and, frankly, nasty. On holiday in Menorca we would enjoy decent wines, Paternina and Marqués de Riscal come to mind. Paradoxically, it was Rioja, in the 1960s, that, almost by default, made Spanish wines respectable; the trade and consumer did not link 'Rioja' with Spain. Around the same time, the Torres family in Penedès were pioneering quality wine at affordable prices. They shot into prominence overnight when, in 1979, at the second Gault-Millau 'Olympiade' in Paris, the Torres 1970 Black Label came top of the Cabernet Sauvignon class, ahead of Ch Latour and La Mission Haut-Brion.

Since then, new wine regions, new producers and even 'cult' wines have emerged, sometimes in combination. I shall be partial: in Rioja I admire Remelluri, in Navarra Chivite, in Priorat Alvaro Palacios, and Riscal's whites in Rueda. In the Ribera del Duero, Pesquera is renowned, though being up-staged by the 'super-cult', Pingus. There is a clear distinction between table wines which neither need, nor are given, bottle-ageing, and the newly fashionable, small-production and extremely high-priced wines which do not, as yet, have a proven track record. For both these reasons I shall give both a miss and concentrate on the one wine with a legendary reputation – 'the Lafite of Spain': Vega Sicilia.

**Vega Sicilia** The vineyards and winery are situated in the broad, somewhat arid, upland valley of the Duero in northern Spain. The river itself flows west, its name changing to the more familiar Douro as it crosses the border with Portugal.

First produced in the 1860s, Vega Sicilia Único gained an astonishing reputation, despite distribution being largely confined to a wealthy private clientele and the top restaurants of Madrid. It is, or until fairly recently was, extremely idiosyncratic (a novel combination of red Bordeaux grape varieties, exceptionally long ageing in wooden vats and high volatile acidity: something of an acquired taste). Although I came across odd bottles over the years, I first really got to know the wine when, as a prelude to a promotional sale at Christie's, I visited Vega Sicilia in 1989. There, and at the subsequent pre-sale tasting, I was exposed to a range of vintages. At that time the wine was still spending an inordinate amount of time, up to ten years, in large oak casks, and the indelible impression was of intense fragrance battling for supremacy with very high acidity.

OLDER ÚNICO VINTAGES TASTED AT THE BODEGA AND PRE-SALE TASTING IN 1989 unless otherwise stated: 1941 was tart and attenuated; 1942 'a charming old señor'; the 1948 rich and tangy. I have tasted only two vintages from the 1950s: 1953 amazingly powerful and impressive in 1979; a decade later, it had an extraordinary bouquet which evolved richly in the glass, with fig-like fruit on the palate. More recently: 'idiosyncratic', sweet, a touch of oxidation, certainly original. *Last tasted Sept 1994. At best* ★★★★

ÚNICO VINTAGES FROM THE MID-'50S AND MID-'70S and mainly noted in 1989 and 1990: 1957 full, soft and flavoury ★★★★; 1960 very sweet, more earthy ★★★★; 1962 good flavour and texture ★★★; 1964 noted over a ten-year period, initially tannic but eventually beautifully evolved ★★★★; 1965 spicy and dry ★★; 1966 tasted over a decade apart and outstandingly the best: lovely fruit, refined, great depth, stylish. What was apparent, was that when first poured, the wine tended to be somewhat dumb and unyielding, but in every instance, particularly with the '64 and '66, the bouquet gradually opened up and, after an hour in the glass, was indescribably beautiful ★★★★ To appreciate these wines, give them plenty of air, both after decanting and then in the glass.

ÚNICO VINTAGES TASTED MORE RECENTLY
1975 Deep, still youthful; brambly, rather Italianate bouquet; sweet, very fruity, good, dry finish. *Tasted blind during Nils Sternby's 1975-vintage dinner in Malmö, April 1995* ★★★
1981 Magnums: fairly deep ruby; behaving exactly as described above, low-keyed at first but opening up fabulously; medium-dry, fairly full-bodied, soft, lovely texture. Probably the best ever Vega Sicilia. *Presented by the present owner, Pablo Alvarez at the Primum Familiae Vini dinner, at which I acted as 'Ring Master' at Vinopolis, London, Nov 2000* ★★★★
1982 Opaque; initially seemed incomplete, needing air, but 55 minutes later had opened up fragrantly; rich, a bit raw and acidic though it coped admirably with 'Roasted Asian Flavoured Duck'. *At Bill Dickinson's Bacchus Society dinner in Coral Gables, Florida, Nov 1997* ★★★★ *(I rated it equal with '82 Ch Cos d'Estournel and '82 Grange Hermitage.)*
1990 Very deep; immensely tannic. Far too immature. *Hastily noted at the Wine Experience 'Grand Tastings' in New York, Oct 1995* (★★★★)

**Vega Sicilia, Reserva Especial** Vega Sicilia's top wine though its component parts, in terms of vintage and age, are never stated on the label. Very deep, opaque core; spicy, nutty, fig-like fruit, then a whiff of vanilla; a wonderful mouthful but very tannic. *Last noted dining at the Eigensatzs' in Majorca, July 1995* ★★★★★

# Two Portuguese Rarities

The wines of Portugal were very popular in 18th-century Britain, their sales boosted by preferential duty rates, a fraction of those that Britain imposed on French wines. They had slipped out of fashion by the mid-19th century, and Gladstone's sharply reduced taxes on all 'light' wines finished them off. In the 20th century, immediately after World War Two, Portuguese wine sales were spearheaded by the popular and highly successful Mateus Rosé. In parallel came decent reds and whites from Dão, the light acidic Vinho Verde and, somewhat later, good reds from Bairrada. South of Lisbon, the old-established J-M da Fonseca (not to be confused with Fonseca port) produces a range of interesting and characterful wines including their delectable Moscatel de Setúbal. Apart from Buçaco from Bussaco and the 'first growth' Barca Velha (see below), there is, I am glad to say, a singular absence of 'cult' wines. The rest are largely dependable and very good value.

For those who like to explore the wines of historically renowned regions such as Bucelas, Carcavela and Colares, and old vintages, I suggest a visit to one or two of the top traditional restaurants in Lisbon. When I was last there, the wines were almost given away!

**Buçaco** Very much an odd man out. The Palace Hotel at Bussaco and its unique wines appeal to my romantic nature. Originally a palatial royal hunting lodge built in the late 19th century, Bussaco is in the midst of a great forest up in the hills to the east of Coimbra. The wines from their own vineyards are matured in the hotel's cavernous cellars, labelled *tinto*, *branco* and *rosado* (red, white and rosé). The dry whites and rosés are adequate but the reds are far better.

ON OUR FIRST VISIT TO BUSSACO IN 1979 I tasted the following: a 1927 red – my birth year, and a good vintage in Portugal – which was delicious but decadent ★★★; also a 1940 spicy, but acidic ★; 1945 **Reserva Especial** rich and lovely ★★★★; 1951 **Reserva** long past its sell-by date.

OTHER GOOD REDS TASTED IN 1985: 1953 a lovely wine ★★★★★ *but will be frail now*; 1959 great, in its own way like Ch Lafite ★★★★★; 1960 ★★★★; 1963 (a classic port vintage) outstanding ★★★★★ *I predicted another 20 years of life.*

MATURE REDS TASTED ON OUR MOST RECENT STAY AT BUSSACO, OCTOBER 1997: 1982 slightly sweet, good, ripe flavour, extract and flesh, with commendably low alcohol (11%), velvety, burgundy-like ★★★★; and 1983 fairly deep, medium intensity, mature appearance; soft, full-flavoured, 'warm', attractive. *Drinking well* ★★★★ *worth a visit.*

**Barca Velha** Casa Ferreirinha A red wine from the Douro Valley and produced by Ferreira only in suitably good years and in necessarily small quantities. It was the creation of the late 'little Fernando' (Nicolau de Almeida), the charming, twinkle-in-the-eye old gentleman whom I first met some 40 years ago and admired enormously.

THE FOLLOWING INCLUDE MY MOST RECENT BARCA VELHA NOTES
1978 A great wine tasted on half a dozen occasions. In 1996, I bought some at one of Christie's sales, which stood me in good stead. In 1997 I noted a lovely, sweet, warm bouquet –

coincidentally not unlike Buçaco; soft texture, perfect maturity. Three months later, appropriately produced at a buffet supper prior to my presentation of 'The World's Greatest Ports' at a Hollywood Wine Society weekend. The next three occasions dining at home, most recently more than holding its own in good company (wines and guests): medium-deep, still plummy-coloured, good life; sweet, delicious, slightly raspberry bouquet and flavour. Perfect weight and balance. *Alas, my last bottle, tasted May 2001* ★★★★
1983 The oldest of seven vintages presented by Salvador da Cunha Guedes in Ferreira's tasting room in March 1996: deep, plummy though maturing; a gentle, attractive, slightly varnishy nose; dry, with quite a bit of grip. The following year dining with Vito Olazabel at his Quinta do Vale do Meão after an arduous, hair-raising drive from Oporto. It was delicious. *Last tasted Oct 1997* ★★★★

OF THE OTHER SIX VINTAGES TASTED MARCH 1996
1985 Similar character to the '83, nice fruit, good length. ★★★★★ *Should be perfect now.*
1989 Deep, also still plummy-coloured; nose hard, dusty, holding back; a very big, fleshy wine, unready. I was told that they were undecided whether this was to be marketed as Barca Velha or the less exalted Reserva ★★(★★★)
1990 Still youthful, very good fruit but will benefit from bottle age ★★(★★★) *In 1997 on my trip to the Douro the '90 Reserva Especial was served after the '83 Barca Velha at Quinta do Vale do Meão. It was distinctly different, rather more to it, with good length and grip, excellent with a regional lamb dish. This was the last vintage of Especial. Henceforth, it was called just Reserva.*
1991 Opaque core; excellent fruit and finish (★★★★)
1992 Deep, intense, youthful; combination of fruit and oak on the nose; a lovely wine, high extract, good length. Clearly a good future (★★★★)
1994 Another very good port vintage. Still opaque, violet-rimmed; the oak very apparent – Barca Velha spends 6 to 12 months in cask. A lovely wine. *At least 20 years of life* (★★★★★)
1995 Just released before this book went to press. Magnificent. Monumental. *June 2002* (★★★★★)

# Chateau Musar

Why include a wine from Lebanon, and why Chateau Musar? First of all, because the wine is excellent and distinctive, albeit idiosyncratic. Its grapes are grown in the Bekaa Valley, the 'bread basket' of ancient Rome, and transported over the high coastal range to be turned into a great wine by a winemaker who is something of a genius, Serge Hochar. I met Serge and discovered his wine in the late 1970s (see 1967 below) since when he has had, deservedly, a loyal and enthusiastic following.

Serge spent time in, and was inspired by, Bordeaux. But the way he makes wine and the artistry of his blending are all to do with what he feels is appropriate, bearing in mind the surprisingly variable climate and the personality of the individual *cépages*. So do not expect rigid consistency of style or weight; and don't be misled by a palish colour. Musar produce a white and, very recently, a second red. The following notes refer to their classic red, called simply Chateau Musar.

**1956** Made by the pioneer, Gaston Hochar, but bottled by his son Serge in 1959. Good colour for its age; remarkably sound, slightly chocolatey nose; surprisingly sweet, delicious, excellent tannins and acidity. Totally delicious. *At dinner with the Hochar family, Serge, his brother Roland, their wives and Gaston junior on our first day in Lebanon, Dec 1999* ★★★★ *Drink up!*

**1959** The oldest vintage presented by Serge Hochar in London in August 1979: fine, rich, mature; delicious bouquet; sweet, soft, fabulous. Twenty years later: orange-tinged; lovely old nose; still delicious. *Last tasted at Musar in Beirut, Dec 1999* ★★★★★

**1961** I noted a beautiful bottle at Hochar's London tasting in 1979: it had a glow reminiscent of warm tiles. Then at nearly 40 years of age, it was the oldest vintage in the pre-sale tasting: a palish rosehip colour; strange, raspberry-tinged bouquet; but better on the palate, still rich even though acidity catching up. *Last noted at the pre-sale tasting of old vintages of Chateau Musar at Christie's, April 2000* ★★★

**1964** Labelled 'Reserve Rouge', first tasted in August, then in December 1979: nose like Turkish delight, delicious flavour. Four notes in the 1980s: impressive, Bordeaux-style, fleshy, though two 'off' bottles. *Not tasted since Sept 1986* ★★★★?

**1966** Only one note: pale, very mature; sweet, soft, forthcoming; faded but very flavoury. Dry finish. *Tasted pre-sale at Christie's, April 2000* ★★★

**1967** The enterprising Serge Hochar presented his wines for the first time in England at the Bristol Wine Fair in July 1979 which is where I first met him (Christie's were also exhibiting) and tasted his wines: three very dry white and three red. Of the latter, the 1967 was outstanding and in the January 1980 issue of *Decanter* magazine I wrote that it was one of the two top wines of the entire Fair. Dry but rich and fruity later that year and early 1980. A glowing note: luminous, fragrant in 1988, and equally delicious 12 years later: rosehip maturity, still some tannin. *Last tasted pre-sale at Christie's, April 2000* ★★★★

**1969** First noted at the Bristol Wine Fair in 1979: it was already very mature-looking, there was very little red; extraordinary character like an overripe, singed Pinot Noir; dry, surprisingly full-bodied and swingeing tannins. It reminded me of a South African Shiraz. Over 20 years later, orange-tinged; slightly raisiny bouquet; sweet, nice weight. No harsh edges. Delicious. Amazing development. *Last tasted pre-sale at Christie's, April 2000* ★★★★

**1970** In 1983, richly coloured; pine needles and vanilla; soft, velvety, well-balanced, yet powerful and plump like Ch Pétrus. Labelled '*Réserve Rouge Grand Cru*', still deep and rich, complete. *Last tasted pre-sale at Christie's, April 2000* ★★★★★

**1972** In 1979, Serge told me that his red wine was made with a blend of Cabernet Sauvignon, Cinsault, Merlot and Carignan. Already fairly mature, ripe, fullish (13.2% alcohol), reminding me of a South African Cape or soft Coonawarra red. Four notes in the late 1970s to mid-1980s, including a rich, earthy bottle at my daughter Emma's confirmation lunch, and in 1987, in the US with *Le Tournedos de Bison,* of course! A splendid combination. Most recently, attractively coloured, very sweet on the palate, lovely flavour, good length, complete. *Last tasted pre-sale at Christie's, April 2000* ★★★★★

**1975** Very fruity, scented, at Hochar's London tasting in 1979. A whiff of high volatile acidity but flavoury the following summer, with bottle variation. Stylish but acidic at Nils Sternby's birthday tasting of the best '75s from around the world. Yet showing well recently: luminous, lovely glow; lovely nose and flavour, with refreshing acidity. *Last tasted pre-sale at Christie's, April 2000* ★★★

**1977** I have three notes: sweet, assertive, still tannic at *Decanter's* millennium dinner at Vinopolis, London, July 1999. Then next at Chateau Musar that December: singed flavour, long tannic finish. Most recently, sweet, rich, fairly full-bodied despite its misleadingly pale colour. *Last tasted pre-sale at Christie's, April 2000* ★★★★ *(Part of a collection from a neighbouring cellar near Beirut.)*

1978 At the opening tasting in August 1979: palish, mauve-tinged, rather youthful Beaujolais-like appearance, aroma and weight. Dry, light, pleasant. A new experimental quick-fermentation. Not sure I approved of this wine. Next tasted in 1985: 'iron and hen droppings nose'. Pale, 'hot', dry but flavoury in 1988. Two bottles at the Hochars' in 1999, light style (one corked) and another disappointment – the cork fell in at the pre-sale tasting. Not one of Serge's successes. *Last tasted pre-sale at Christie's, April 2000.*

1979 Once again, it was misleadingly pale, fully mature; nose like squashed strawberries; sweet, long, delicious. *Last tasted pre-sale at Christie's, April 2000* ★★★★

1981 The first note made at Chateau Musar in December 1999. Lovely colour; sweet, ripe, rather rustic bouquet; full, rich, good fruit, grip. *Last tasted pre-sale at Christie's, April 2000* ★★★★ *Should be delicious now.*

1983 Good colour; warm, harmonious nose and palate. Very sweet, very agreeable. *At Chateau Musar, Dec 1999* ★★★★

1985 First noted after bottling in June 1987: mostly Cinsault, picked early, long fermentation and no wood used. Lean and lively, with good acidity. Then 12 years later its nose reminded me of a ripe Ch Brane-Cantenac. Very tannic. Raw. Not sure about this wine. *Last tasted at Chateau Musar, Dec 1999* (★★)?

1986 Two close notes: orange-tinged; sweet, chocolatey nose that opened up richly; full, ripe, Pomerol style, with quite a bite. *Last noted pre-sale at Christie's, April 2000* ★★★(★)

1988 Five notes: first in 1996, a half bottle taken to my local Lebanese restaurant 'Mes' Amis' (*sic*), ruby, singed, mouthfilling (14% alcohol). Later that May served at the wedding rehearsal dinner at the Commonwealth Club, Richmond, Virginia, that I gave for my son and future daughter-in-law. It went down very well. Even better at *Decanter* magazine's millennium dinner: very burgundian, perfect with duck. Sweet, soft and, yet again, delicious. An identical note made at my 75th birthday dinner at Vintners' Hall, London in May 2002 and three times since. The most perfectly mature red imaginable: *à point*. I am busily drinking it at its peak. *Last tasted at home, June 2002* ★★★★★

1989 Labelled 'For the Millennium 2000', single-vineyard, predominantly Carignan, not the usual blend. Good colour, sweet, full, rich and uplifting flavour. First tasted at Chateau Musar in 1999. *Last tasted pre-sale at Christie's, April 2000* ★★★(★)

1993 Three notes, the first two made in the cellars and at dinner with the Hochars in Lebanon in December 1999: ruddy-coloured; rich, meaty, mocha nose of considerable depth. Fairly sweet. Good aftertaste. Deft. *Last tasted pre-sale at Christie's, April 2000* ★★★(★)

1994 Hot summer in the Bekaa Valley, 40°C in August and September. One can smell the singed grapes in the wine. Remarkably sweet. Lovely fruit. Two recent notes, identical. *Last tasted Aug 2000* ★★★★

1995 First noted in the tasting room at Chateau Musar, December 1999: deep and rich, high extract. Most recently: good colour; slightly singed, fragrant, high-toned nose; very positive, mouthfilling, good length and acidity. *Last tasted with Serge Hochar at the London Wine Trade Fair at Excel, May 2002* ★★★★ *Drink now–2010.*

1996 Wet year, light vintage. First tasted at Chateau Musar, December 1999. Youthful, weak-rimmed; pleasant, stylish, dry finish. Most recently, distinctly weak, an almost gravy-like nose, soft finish. *Last tasted May 2002* ★ *Drink up.*

1997 First tasted with Serge Hochar in the Chateau Musar cellars, December 1999. The wine was still in individual vats: Cinsault from the *garrigues* of Kefraya in the Bekaa Valley: crisp, fragrant; attractive, some elegance. Carignan from Ana, a little further north: more flesh, nice fruit, very tannic. Cabernet Sauvignon was an incredibly deep colour; green, stalky nose; austere, astringent. It would be another year before blending. Most recently, seemed fully developed, good flavour, lovely aftertaste. *Last tasted May 2002* ★★★★

1998 Tasting of single varietals. In small oak barrels since August (1999). Very distinctive, individual. *In the cellars at Chateau Musar, Dec 1999.*

1999 This is the basic palette from which Serge Hochar, no dry academician, creates his blends: first, a Cinsault from a single, soil-rich vineyard in Ana: deep core, young Provençal scent; delicious flavour, wonderful richness and flesh. Soft tannins. Next, a Cinsault from Ammiq's very gravelly soil: fragrant, lighter style, more charm. Then Carignan from a lighter soil in the Ana district: deep, velvety; spicy *garrigue* scent (I was reminded of Corbières in the Languedoc), flavour more aromatic. Lastly, Cabernet Sauvignon from Kefraya's rocky soil: very deep purple; sweet, lovely crisp flavour, excellent tannins and acidity. End taste of violets and blackcurrants. *In the Chateau Musar cellars, Dec 1999.*

# Champagne

I cannot think of any other wine which automatically, unconsciously, conjures up such a variety of (mainly) happy associations. It is, *par excellence*, the wine of celebration; it has an almost unassailable position in the hierarchy of wine. Naturally I have a glass (of non-vintage) in my hand as I write. We toast the Queen, congratulate couples who, after years of being 'an item', decide to get married; the best man then asks us to raise our glasses. It is the wine of seduction – though the days of stage-door Johnnies and the *Salon Privé* have long since passed (I think). No wine is so deliberately and extravagantly wasted. Like the face of Helen of Troy it has launched (at least) a thousand ships – 'I name thee…' being followed by a bottle breaking over the bows. As for the obscenity of a Formula One winner shaking and spewing the contents over his runners-up on the lower steps of the podium… Ah well. Good publicity?

This chapter is about more serious wine. In fact the whole book is about vintage wine and, unlike many white wines, the best champagne not only keeps but develops in bottle. It is commonly assumed that the grape varieties (Pinot Noir, Pinot Meunier and Chardonnay), the chalky soil and northerly climate are what make champagne champagne. Well yes, but the plus factor is blending. At the top of the pile is vintage champagne made from vineyards classified 100% in the finest districts.

The French think the English are mad to drink and, seemingly, to enjoy old champagne. But there is a moment, when a venerable champagne, its carbon dioxide bubbles congregated in the neck, can, rather like a well-hung pheasant, be richly sublime. With a bit of luck, one can have it both ways, by opening a young vintage, or non-vintage, and mixing the old and young in the glass, 50-50. Quite human really. The young wine (wife) adds vivacity, the old (husband) richness and character. But drink quickly.

## 18th century to 1914

Champagne has always been well regarded, fashionable and expensive. Christie's archives uniquely demonstrate the extraordinarily high regard for it; champagne first appeared in James Christie's catalogues in 1768, two years after the start of his auction house, and customarily commanded prices twice that of the finest claret. It was dry, and still, not sparkling, in those days and Sillery was the most esteemed and expensive.

Despite the Napoleonic wars at the end of the 18th century, which fairly understandably caused shortages and even higher prices, champagne continued to be imported into Britain. The real explosion of demand started in the second half of the 19th century, the trade press reporting an unhealthy pressure on prices culminating with the 1874 vintage, the most renowned of the period, which reached record prices at Christie's.

The *fin de siècle* is associated with extravagant lifestyles in both France and Britain; but, in fact, Chile was the biggest importer of champagne at that period – a period which was not just interrupted but completely knocked off course following the outbreak of World War One.

In May 1967, the 24th wine sale in Christie's first season, three great vintages of Sillery from the cellars of Lord Rosebery appeared in our first Finest and Rarest list: 1857, 1870 and the famous 1874. For the record, I mention them briefly here to indicate the style of the still, dry, champagnes.

## Vintages at a Glance
**Outstanding** ★★★★★
1857, 1874, 1892, 1899, 1904, 1911
**Very Good** ★★★★
1870, 1914
**Good** ★★★
1915, 1919

## 1857 ★★★★★

**Sillery** First noted at the Christie's pre-sale tasting of Lord Rosebery's wines (see box below) in 1967: dry, 'nutty', with a bouquet like an old Château-Chalon (*vin jaune*) from the Jura. A decade later, a similar note: pale yellow amber, 'smoky' – most likely Pinot Noir – bouquet; distinctly dry, assertive yet some delicacy. From which I deduced that it might well originally have tasted rather like a cross between Corton-Charlemagne and dry sherry, firm, with good acidity and probably benefiting from some bottle-ageing. *Last tasted at a dinner party with old wines held at the Travellers' Club, London, Sept, 1977* ★★

## 1870 ★★★★

**Sillery** Also from Lord Rosebery's cellar, a magnum, pale for a century-old white wine, bone dry, firm, described at the time as a cross between a *vin jaune* from the Jura and Montilla with a dash of Sancerre. *At a dinner in Yorkshire hosted by David Dugdale and Tony Hepworth, Jan 1969.*

### Lord Rosebery

*The first-ever sale of 'Finest and Rarest Wines' at Christie's took place on 31 May 1967 and was dominated by wine from the Earl of Rosebery's two great estates, Mentmore in Hertfordshire and Dalmeny in Scotland. In addition to the very rarely seen old Sillery (see page 421) the perfectly maintained cellars contained an unprecedented range of pre-phylloxera claret, mainly Ch Lafite, including – of the 1865 vintage alone – two 'triple magnums', and 15 double magnums, and of the 1874, 40 magnums and 71 bottles, all previously unmoved and in pristine condition. It put Christie's fledgling wine department firmly on the map.*

## 1874 ★★★★★

Alas, I have never seen a bottle of the famous Perrier-Jouët 1874, which achieved the highest price for any wine sold at Christie's between 1766 and 1967.
**Sillery Payne's** One of London's top wine merchants at the time. Straw-coloured; dry, once powerful, fading and not in the best condition. I had to use my imagination. *Tasted pre-sale, May 1967*

## 1892 ★★★★★

Along with the 1874 and 1899 this was one of the finest champagne vintages of the period.
**Perrier-Jouët, Extra** Original corks. Slight bottle variation. The first the colour of warm gold with pin pricks of carbon dioxide; low-keyed but lovely old straw bouquet; medium-dry, fair body; excellent flavour, length and finish. Now more like

an old white burgundy but with a prickle at its edge. The other bottle was a slightly paler yellow gold, totally flat; sweet, sound, good flavour but lacking bite. *Lunching at La Maison Belle-Époque with Thierry Budin and Pierre Ernst (who is credited with the invention of the famous flower bottle which, frankly, put Perrier-Jouët back on the map), Épernay, Feb 1994. At best* ★★★★

## 1899 ★★★★★

Great vintage. Alas never tasted.

## 1904 ★★★★★

Ideal conditions for a great vintage. I have tasted only two wines: a magnum of **Koch** from Glamis Castle *1971* ★★★★ and a freshly disgorged **Moët & Chandon** lovely. *At Moët & Chandon, 1957* ★★★★

## 1907 ★

Not a great vintage but a remarkable survivor.
**Heidsieck** Disgorged 1916. Original foil. Heavy wax seal embossed *Monopole Gout Américain*. Fully branded cork. Pure Tutankhamun yellow gold, pale for its age and surprisingly good mousse when first poured; remarkably good nose: smoky Chardonnay, lanolin and lemon curd; medium-sweet, delicious flavour, assertive, good acidity (responsible for its preservation: that and the air-blocking silt). If I had not seen it – and tasted it – as it was opened, I would have thought it scarcely credible.

The wine has an interesting background. The bottle I tasted was part of a large stock salvaged from the *Jönköping*, a Swedish vessel torpedoed by a German U-boat off the Finnish coast in 1916. Among the 90 tonnes of supplies destined for Russia were 60 of wines, including 50 100-bottle boxes of champagne. For over 80 years, the wine had been preserved at a temperature of 4°C; and, coincidentally, the pressure of the water, at 64m below the Baltic, more or less matched the pressure in the champagne bottles though some, of course, had deteriorated. A trial batch of 24 bottles was sold at Christie's in October 1998 to establish its value: prices ranged from £850 to £2200 per bottle.

Most recently, bottles bought at the 1998 sale and served after a range of Dom Pérignon at Len Evans' 70th birthday dinner; yellow gold; nutty 'sea breeze' nose; distinct sweetness, strange flavour, excellent acidity, good for its age and submerged provenance. *Last tasted Sept 2000. At its best* ★★★★

## 1911 ★★★★★

A great vintage and the best between 1874 and 1921. There was a small crop of excellent wines. However, all was not sweetness and light. The previous year, 1910, had been both the high peak for sales and a disastrous vintage which produced 1 million bottles rather than the normal 30 million, according to Tom Stevenson in his book *Champagne*. The *vignerons* were devastated and furious, their frustration coming to the boil in 1911 with the most serious riots ever experienced. Champagne was on the verge of civil war. Golden times for some maybe; not for most.

Incidentally, 1911 was the oldest vintage and highest-priced champagne on Harvey's of Bristol retail list in 1929, Krug Private Cuvée being 290 shillings per dozen (just under £15 in present day currency).

## Brut and other styles of champagne

Brut *is the term used by champagne producers to indicate a bone dry wine. Literally translated, it means 'raw', in other words with no sugar added at the dosage stage. In reality,* Brut *champagne does have minimal sugar added then – 16 grams per litre to be precise – so* Brut *is rarely as raw as it sounds. General tastes in champagne have become a lot drier since the term was first coined, so* Extra Brut *has been introduced, which has 6g/l residual sugar and very little dosage. The only truly 'raw' champagne, however, is labelled* Brut Natur: *with no dosage, this is the driest style of all.* Sec (dry), *at 17–35g/l sugar, is not notably dry at all.* Demi-Sec (medium-sweet), *has 35–50g/l and is, in effect, fully sweet.* Doux (sweet), *at 50g/l or more is intensely sweet, and is rarely seen.*

*Frankly, I do not take much note of Brut, 'dry', 'extra dry' on labels, whether the champagne is vintage or non-vintage. One is rarely caught out with a 'rich' or* doux *champagne might be served at a champagne dinner, or with a sweet dish in France.*

*Regarding non-vintage, I think it pays not only to buy the best but to give the wines some extra bottle age. Sticking my neck out I have always regarded Louis Roederer as the most dependable but only recently have been pleasantly surprised with a stock of Laurent Perrier non-vintage I bought for my 70th birthday. I used the leftover cases I had forgotten about (I keep my cased stocks in a London bonded warehouse) for my 75th birthday dinner. It had mellowed without losing life.*

*Lastly, there is rosé, pink champagne. Its main virtue is its colour. Yet even the pink is scarcely discernible in some champagnes, Krug for example. I never buy pink champagne, and though some attractive rosés are noted in the text, on the whole I find they lack character and flavour.*

---

**Moët & Chandon, Brut Impérial** Gold, with steadily rising pinpricks of mousse; showing its age; medium-dry leading to a very dry, life-preserving acidity, good fruit. It seemed to unravel intriguingly. *Prior to Hugh Johnson's Bordeaux Club dinner, Aug 1999* ★★★

**Perrier-Jouët, Finest Quality, Extra Brut** Original cork. Medium-deep, very bright old amber with just a prickle on the sides of the glass; bouquet like old madeira, caramelised old walnuts; despite its oxidation, pleasant sweetness, lovely old flavour (once I had got used to it), slight prickle, sherry-like finish. Not a patch on the Pol Roger below but Hugh Johnson's genius to the fore by serving it as an aperitif with *croustadines de noix au mascarpone* which brought out the old wine's taste. *Served in front of a blazing log fire, at Saling Hall, Dec 2001* ★★

**Pol Roger** Probably disgorged in the mid-1950s. First noted at a Pol Roger tasting in 1989: straw gold; soft, nutty, sound old bouquet and flavour, 'rather like a creamy old Chardonnay'. Next and most memorably, a bottle produced by Hugh Johnson for his first Bordeaux Club dinner: sipped

reverentially but with immense satisfaction by the members on a perfect summer evening in Hugh's exquisite garden – I have a happy photograph, taken by Judy Johnson, of Harry Waugh, Jack Plumb (in straw hat), Neil McKendrick, John Jenkins, Hugh and myself. The wine had an excellent colour, very slight prickle, a touch of cloudiness towards the bottom of the bottle – so I declined a top-up; lovely smoky nose; perfect flavour, weight, texture, balance and finish. Perfection. *Last tasted at Saling Hall, July 1993* ★★★★★

## 1914 ★★★★

World War One broke out in August; the German army had reached the champagne vineyards even before the harvest began. It made life difficult for the pickers but good wine was made.

**Pol Roger** Tasted first in 1989, a bottle disgorged in the middle of World War Two. Colour of old straw gold; rich, damp, arboreal nose; rich, good length and acidity. More recently, a bottle also disgorged in 1944 and served at the end of dinner by Danielle and Christian Pol Roger in Épernay: pure amber gold, quite still, no bubbles; soft, old straw nose, slight whiff of *cacao*; full-flavoured, a very slight prickle, remarkably sweet and enjoyable. *Last tasted June 1997* ★★★

OLDER NOTES **Bollinger** disgorged circa 1955, palish; lovely, smoky bouquet and flavour. *1975* ★★★★★; **Delbeck** amber; surprisingly sweet, crisp, slightly *pétillant* finish. *1969* ★★; and **Moët & Chandon** lively, youthful, well preserved. *1958* ★★★

## 1915 ★★★

Fine, well balanced wines. Early harvest. Only one old note; **Moët & Chandon, Dry Impérial** from an old cellar in Devon. Sound, still signs of life, nice old wine. *1968* ★★★

## 1916 ★★

Small crop of unequal ripeness. None tasted.

## 1917 ★★★

Another small crop picked in difficult wartime conditions. Reported to be good, elegant wines.

## 1918 ★

Irregular.

## 1919 ★★★

Peacetime at last but conditions were still difficult. Scorchingly hot summer helped produce firm elegant wines which were all rapidly consumed. I have not tasted any.

# 1920–1944

Two totally contrasting decades followed by World War Two.

The 1920s were well served by six good to outstanding vintages, two, the '21 and '28, vying to qualify as the greatest vintage of the century, although when the latter appeared on the market, the exuberant period of its year of birth had been overtaken by the Great Depression.

Despite prohibition, champagne continued to find its way into the USA, and there were sufficient people of wealth in England to support a de luxe product – mind you, they generally had a cellarful of wines purchased earlier, before the Depression. The trade, however, was overstocked and the early to mid-1930s period was nothing short of disastrous for the champagne producer, a situation exacerbated by the abundant vintage in 1934.

German troops occupied Champagne from May 1940 until liberation in August 1944. One interesting situation materialised during this period: the growers and champagne houses banded together to form the CIVC, the Comité Interprofessionnel du Vin de Champagne, a self-regulatory body to control all aspects of the champagne industry. One of the prime movers was Count Robert-Jean de Vogüé of Moët & Chandon, known to all as Bob. I well recall his brilliant speech when he presided over the annual Wine Trades' Benevolent Banquet in 1967 when, in flawless English, he charmed over a thousand doughty members of the British trade, teasing us about our national foibles, including cricket. It was a rare and memorable occasion.

## Vintages at a Glance
**Outstanding** ★★★★★
1920, 1921, 1928, 1937
**Very Good** ★★★★
1923, 1929, 1934, 1943
**Good** ★★★
1926, 1942

## 1920 ★★★★★

Very good quality. Cold August but followed by a gloriously sunny September. These wines were doubtless consumed rapidly in the middle of the frothy 1920s as none seem to have survived.

## 1921 ★★★★★

As elsewhere in Europe, a long, exceedingly hot summer produced outstanding white wines and champagne was no exception. A small crop was harvested from 19 September. This was the vintage debut of Dom Pérignon, Moet & Chandon's de luxe cuvée.

Although I am an advocate of old champagne with original corks, wines of this age are safer newly disgorged.
**Pol Roger** Pinot Noir 80%, Chardonnay 20%. Harvey's price in 1929 was 150 shillings (£7.50) per dozen. Variable. Half a dozen notes starting with two disappointing, freshly disgorged bottles in 1978. Another two, disgorged in 1974 not much better in 1981. Then, in 1989 a better, more lively bottle disgorged in 1988. Colours varied from pale gold to old brass; bouquets from damp straw to charred wood, but fragrant; mostly less than sparkling but harbouring a refreshing prickle. Most recently, a bottle disgorged in April 1966: surprisingly pale for its age and vintage, pale gold, no mousse; a sweet, creamy, harmonious bouquet with a whiff of coffee; touch of sweetness on the palate, glorious flavour and excellent acidity. 'The best-ever '21'. *At a Gidleigh Park champagne tasting, Devon, March 1997. At best* ★★★★★

## 1922, 1924, 1925 and 1927

Thanks to poor weather, pests, diseases and, curiously, shortage of labour and materials (in 1922), none shipped as vintage.

## 1923 ★★★★

As in Burgundy, a very good vintage but small crop.
**Heidsieck, Dry Monopole** The most ullaged of seven different bottles: drab gold; maderised nose like old apples; slightly grubby finish – too far gone to be given the kiss of life by a nubile non-vintage. Nearly 20 years later a half bottle with a good hard cork. Though amber and sparkle-less and with slightly caramelised bottle age, its very good acidity and vestiges of carbon dioxide keeping it going. Odd halves tasted with my old friend Mutsuo Okabayashi and Isao and Yurie Harada, owner and editor of the *Wine Kingdom* to which I contribute regularly. *At the Imperial Hotel, Tokyo, Nov 1999.*
*(The Japanese are surprisingly keen and well-informed collectors and connoisseurs, many of whom I have met since conducting Christie's first wine auction in Tokyo in 1989. And the sommeliers are in a class of their own, professionally trained, extremely knowledgeable.)*

### Hugh Johnson and the Pol '21

*In 1981, shortly after The Great Vintage Wine Book was published, I arrived at Saling Hall to be greeted by Hugh with 'marvellous; but you are wrong about the '21 Pol Roger' and he promptly brought up a bottle from his own cellar. To his chagrin the wine exactly matched my description! In a gesture typical of his generosity, Hugh opened yet another '21 Pol, different but still by no means a great old champagne.*

*As if, belatedly, to prove Hugh right and to deny my theory that one should not keep disgorged bottles overlong, I happened to taste in 1997 another '21 disgorged by Pol Roger in 1966. It was superb, as noted left. Which also goes to show how tricky and, frankly, unreliable old wines can be. But what fun.*

**Veuve Clicquot, Brut** Several notes: 'Dry England' from Glamis Castle, remarkably good, served before the pre-sale dinner in the boardroom at Christie's at which I opened the first of the magnums of 1870 Lafite. Next, a lively bottle disgorged in 1972 (at lunch 1973), but the most interesting were long-abandoned bottles from the cellars of White's Club, a large cache auctioned at Christie's. Tasted pre-sale, and from a dozen I bought myself. Slightly variable but mainly remarkably good. Some pale for their age, some amber; some with a prickle of carbon dioxide, some flat; all dry, crisp and at best delicious, particularly when revived by adding a non-vintage. Most recently, two bottles, one drab, sweeter and better on nose and palate, the other a lovely gold colour; sweet nose, touch of fungi; dry, firm, remarkably firm and fresh though with swingeing acidity. *The oldest of 12 vintages at Kaplan's Clicquot tasting in Chicago, April 1997. At best* ★★★★

### Stephen A Kaplan

*Retired businessman, now deeply into philanthropic activity; host of many major wine events, and supporter of the American arm of the Institute of Masters of Wine. Spectacularly themed wine tastings are a major distraction for him, as are dinners, mainly hosted in his home city, Chicago, also sometimes in Los Angeles.*

*It is not just the quality and range of wines he amasses and presents at these events, sometimes one day affairs, at others over a weekend, but – as with Hardy Rodenstock – it is easy to take for granted the colossal amount of detailed planning involved; and the way that the various top chefs are persuaded to go out of their way to produce not just the best but most appropriate menus. Guests are mainly American. Daphne and I always feel privileged and flattered to be invited though, as always, 'at the drop of a hat' I am pleased to speak about the wine.*

**Pommery & Greno, Nature** Corks branded '*Pommery Nature 1926*'. Bought at auction. Slightly variable. My last note (though I have more to drink) excellent level, lovely bright orange-amber with gold highlights, still with surprisingly good mousse; pleasant old straw nose and flavour; medium-dry, clean as a whistle. *Last noted lunching at Chippenham Lodge, with Meg and Eddie Penning-Rowsell and Sarah and John Avery, Aug 1996* ★★★, *in its way.*

OTHER OLDER NOTES **Moët & Chandon** 1958 ★★★; and **Pol Roger** consistently good. *Last tasted in 1977* ★★★★★

## 1926 ★★★

Below average crop but good quality wine. I have only tasted two wines and they are very old notes: **Moët & Chandon** light, pleasing 1958 ★★★; **Pol Roger** consistently good. *Last tasted 1977* ★★★★★; and **Pommery & Greno** original cork, cidery but attractive. 1955 ★★

## 1928 ★★★★★

An excellent vintage. Firm, crisp, well-constituted, long lasting wines. But now risky.
**Heidsieck, Dry Monopole** Firm cork, good level. Lovely colour, pure amber; sweet, rich, meaty but maderised; flavour like old sherry or *vin jaune* but very attractive in its way, its acidity giving it much needed support and a dry finish.

Second bottle with slightly more vivacity, creamy old nose, acidic. *Both at Hugh Johnson's Bordeaux Club dinner, July 1995* ★★ or ★★★, *a matter of taste.*
**Perrier-Jouët, Finest Extra Quality, Reserve for Great Britain** The label sounded promising and very good it was, too. Excellent level: bright old gold colour but lacking life; toasted, slightly maderised; by no means 'extra dry', quite a bit of sweetness. Lovely old flavour and pleasant dry prickle on the finish. I then opened a bottle of Perrier-Jouët non-vintage Brut to give it a boost. More recently, a very similar bottle from my own cellar, a better, more honeyed nose and lovely flavour. *Both at my Bordeaux Club dinners at Christie's, in 1994 and 1998* ★★★★
**Veuve Clicquot** First tasted 50 years after the vintage. 'A beauty' ★★★★★. Two bottles at Kaplan's Clicquot tasting in 1997: very similar, both golden, one with a touch more amber but both with rich old flavour and considerable depth; sweet, rich, assertive, good length. The following year, a bottle at home, its level just below the foil: golden, lifeless, not star bright; sweet old straw nose and delicious old flavour, clear, excellent acidity. Sound enough to warrant opening a youthful champagne (in this case, a non-vintage Delbeck) to add 50-50, the old wine providing flavour and character, the non-vintage life. *Last tasted at my son and daughter-in-law's apartment in San Francisco, with Belle and Barney Rhodes, the Itchinoses and Jacques Pepin, the American TV chef, March 1998. At best* ★★★★

OTHER, OLDER NOTES **Krug** first tasted in the autumn of 1957, on the third 'Champagne Academy' in France. Two memorable weeks, the '28 Krug the most magnificent champagne I had ever tasted. It would remain my touchstone until it finally tired (and 1961 Dom Pérignon usurped its position); **Moët & Chandon** perfection in Bougival 1969 ★★★★★; and **Roederer** the first old vintage champagne ever tasted and one of the best '28s. 1978 ★★★★

## 1929 ★★★★

A lovely vintage, abundant, with great charm. Not as firm or acidic as the '28.
**Mumm, Cordon Rouge** Level just below foil indicating that either carbon dioxide, or air, filled the upper neck. In fact the air had got the better of it: old amber, no life; sweet, old straw nose; dry somewhat pungent at first, but made a valiant effort to be the sort of old champagne that some of us like. But its finish was a touch too grubby and it was pointless opening a young champagne to give it a kiss of life. *Pre-dinner at home, Dec 1994.*
**Pommery, Nature** A nostalgic neck label: '*Great Britain and the Colonies*', original fully branded cork, firm though easily extracted, and good level. On pouring: amber gold with very faint pin-prick bubbles; lovely old golden straw nose, sweet, meaty; quite dry, yet mouthfillingly rich, firm, excellent old flavour, length, acidity and finish. *At home, Jan 1994* ★★★★
**Veuve Clicquot, Brut** Several notes, most recently at Stephen Kaplan's Clicquot vertical, served mainly in pairs but the '29 in magnum. As this was 'by appointment to H.M. Queen Elizabeth II' it must have been labelled post-1953 and probably re-disgorged in the late 1960s. It had a certain haziness and a curious minty 'ivy-leaf' scent. By no means *Brut*, with a very distinctive, notably sweet taste, considerable charm, a prickle of carbon dioxide and fabulous acidity. *Last tasted in Chicago, April 1997* ★★★★

ONLY TWO OTHER '29S NOTED, the most memorable being a fine magnum of **Bollinger** enjoyed dining with Peter Palumbo in his box at the Royal Albert Hall, watching wrestling! *London, 1981* ★★★★

## 1934 ★★★★

A very good vintage, perhaps too abundant but timely, for it came on to the market to invigorate those recovering from the depression.

**Pol Roger** I have three notes, the only bottle tasted in the 1990s being from a small stock of old champagne bought at Christie's. It had a heavy wax seal over the original cap but this was like shutting the door after the horse had bolted, for the level was just below the bottom of the foil. The cork seemed firm but it had not kept out the air.

Although the wine had a lovely, palish amber colour it had no life; the nose though powerful was slightly mushroomy and maderised. Yet sweet, rich, and, once one had got used to its creaking character, quite pleasant. The *coup de grâce* was a slightly grubby finish. I had a back-up bottle of the '88 and we all had a glass with the two Pols mixed, 50–50. It worked. Like raising the dead. *At my Bordeaux Club dinner, Jan 1996. Solo ★, but when mixed* ★★★

OTHER '34S, OLD NOTES **Bollinger** creamy, lovely. *1976* ★★★★; **Heidsieck, Dry Monopole** dry, lively. *1978* ★★★; and **Veuve Clicquot** ripe, vinous. *1967* ★★★

## 1937 ★★★★★

Great vintage. Firm, crisp, long-lasting wines taking advantage of the acidity common to all '37s. I have tasted few recently but, if you like old champagne, this is a good vintage to experiment with, but adding the proviso that the wine must have come from a good cellar.

**Mumm, Cordon Rouge** Dry, crisp, good. *At a pre-sale tasting, Dec 1992* ★★★

**Pommery & Greno** An older note, from an old trade cellar in Dublin. Remarkably good: creamy nosed; firm, positive, very good acidity. *Dec 1987* ★★★★

**Veuve Clicquot** Bright yellow; old straw, slightly malty; dry, surprisingly sound. *At a pre-sale tasting, Dec 1992* ★★★ *for its age.*

## 1941 ★★

A moderately good wartime vintage, some bottles of which, having survived the Occupation, were exported after the war.

ONLY TWO NOTES **Pommery & Greno** from the same Dublin cellar as the '37 and in fair condition. *1987* ★★; and **Roederer, Brut** very good, excellent acidity. *1987* ★★★

## 1942 ★★★

Good wines.

**Pommery & Greno** A half bottle from the Dublin cellar mentioned above. Clean, positive flavour, good length and acidity. *Dec 1987* ★★★

**Veuve Clicquot, 'Dry'** First tasted pre-sale in December 1992: good colour, holding well, very good acidity. Next, three bottles at Stephen Kaplan's Clicquot vertical, all bottles bought at Christie's 1992 auction. Slight variation but on the whole, despite showing their age, remarkably good. At best, now more sweet than dry, creamy, lovely flavour, vanillin aftertaste. *Last tasted April 1997* ★★★

## 1943 ★★★★

A very good year, more successful than in any other classic French wine region and the first major vintage to be shipped after the war. Also, freshly disgorged in 1953 it was sold in Britain as the Coronation Cuvée to celebrate the accession of Queen Elizabeth II. These were attractive wines at the time but, in my experience, do not hold up so many years later.

**Delbeck, Extra Sec** One note of an almost 50-year-old half bottle in excellent condition: palish; rich bouquet; medium-dry, good flavour. *At Christie's pre-sale tasting of old champagne, Dec 1992* ★★★★

**Moët & Chandon, Dry Impérial** Another interesting comparison. The first, original bottling: pale; smoky bouquet; dry, fabulous flavour; the second, Moët's Coronation Cuvée 1953 with an odd straw nose and taste. *Tasted alongside the Delbeck above, Dec 1992. At best* ★★★★★

**Veuve Clicquot, Dry** Several notes, two contrasting and salutary in the mid-1970s, one an original bottle in excellent condition, the other a Coronation Cuvée bottle disgorged in 1953 which had lost its lustre nearly a quarter of a century later. Another deeply coloured bottle, propped up by its acidity in 1985. More recently: golden, slight mousse; creamy nose; dry, crisp, delicious. *Last tasted pre-sale, Dec 1992. At best* ★★★

OTHER, OLDER NOTES **Lanson** Lovely wine, beautiful flavour and texture though lacking length. *1985* ★★★★; **Pol Roger** a sprightly 30-year-old. *1973* ★★; **Pommery & Greno** two bottles, slight variation, the least good of the Dublin collection. *1987* ★

# 1945–1979

Despite the superb quality of the immediate post-war vintages, particularly the trio, '45, '47 and '49, there was still a back-log of pre-war stock in the UK. The decades of the 1950s and 1960s each produced a quartet of really good vintages which still, if well kept, will appeal to the British who prefer their champagne calm and characterful like a mature Montrachet.

It is perhaps worth pointing out that unlike every other vintage wine, including port, there is a considerable time lag between the production and launch of a vintage champagne. For example, the delightful '76 Pol was first presented to the British trade in March 1982.

Although Moët's Dom Pérignon, the precursor of the modern spate of de luxe champagnes, was launched pre-war, it was in the post-war period that these champagnes started to take off with Roederer Cristal (in 1945) and Taittinger's Comtes de Champagne in 1952, coinciding with Bernard de Nonancourt's Laurent-Perrier Grande Siècle, a novel blend of three vintages (see Laurent-Perrier page 434).

But I also recall it was around the late 1950s that some major champagne houses were considering dropping vintages altogether, on the specious basis that it would be better to use the best wine of a given year to boost the quality of their (more profitable) non-vintage blends. Think what port would be without its vintage 'standard bearer', I argue. Krug, in 1978, even went the whole hog, producing an undated Grande Cuvée (see box page 436).

## Vintages at a Glance
**Outstanding ★★★★★**
1945, 1952, 1959, 1964, 1971
**Very Good ★★★★**
1947, 1949, 1953, 1955, 1961, 1962. 1966, 1970, 1976, 1979
**Good ★★★**
1969, 1973, 1975

## 1945 ★★★★★

Small crop of excellent wines. The firmness and acidity gave the '45s vigour and a long life. The best, and best kept, will still be delicious if you like your champagne like a lovely old white burgundy.
**Pol Roger** Several notes, including a fine magnum served in the interval between bouts of wrestling at the Albert Hall, its beauty and refinement providing something of a contrast to the bruisers in the ring. Next, also memorably, disgorged ten days before serving, at the 1945 vintage dinner at the British Embassy in Paris hosted by the Ambassador, Sir Christopher Mallaby in 1995. Very little sparkle, more like a Corton-Charlemagne, harmonious, lovely, nutty nose and flavour. More recently, at an 11-wine champagne tasting conducted at Gidleigh Park, the last five being a vertical of Pol, the oldest the '45: medium-pale, yellow gold, a faint prickle; scent and flavour of fresh peeled mushrooms. Delicious, wonderful fruit (a high proportion of Pinot Noir) and length. *Last noted March 1997* ★★★★★
**Ruinart** Good colour; crisp, excellent flavour and condition. *Pre-sale, Dec 1992* ★★★★★

OTHER '45S **Pommery & Greno** several notes from 1955, the last from the Dublin cellar. Removed from the previously unopened metal-banded wooden case, and in perfect condition. *Last tasted pre-sale, Dec 1992* ★★★★; **Roederer** perfect at 30 years of age – I would love to taste it again; and, older still, good bottles of **Heidsieck, Monopole**.

## 1946 ★

Useful wines for non-vintage blends.

## 1947 ★★★★

Very good, thanks to a bakingly hot summer and an unusually early harvest. Production well below average because of the lack of rain.
**Bollinger, Extra Quality** The best of a group of old half bottles tasted with my Japanese friends. Amber-coloured, still – no bubbles; showing its age, a touch of caramel on the nose but very good acidity and the previously hidden prickle just giving it an uplift. How it survived its journey from Christie's South Kensington to Tokyo I do not know. *Nov 1999* ★
**Krug, Private Cuvée, Brut** Straw gold, hazy; wonderful, inimitable old Krug richness; better than it looked, richly flavoured, decent acidity but tired. The opening wine of Kaplan's 14-wine 1947 vintage dinner in Chicago, 1997. A month later at a tasting hosted by Rémi, Henri and Olivier Krug. We were informed that picking started during the last few days of August. The wine, still in its immediate post-war blue bottle, had been disgorged in the mid-1950s: medium straw gold; wonderfully rich, complete, harmonious bouquet and flavour. Medium-sweet, rich, good length, a touch of *crème brûlée* on the finish. *Last tasted with members of the Bacchus Society who were over from the USA to present Rémi and Henri with their Lifetime Achievement Award in Reims, May 1997* ★★★★★
**Pol Roger** Several notes, all excellent, including one bottled in 1948, disgorged May 1981 and tasted a month later; another disgorged in September 1988 and presented at a Pol Roger tasting in 1989. Most recently what appeared to be an original bottling, labelled '*Reserve for Great Britain*'. Lovely bright gold with faint and fine mousse; gloriously full, rich, old straw bouquet; fairly dry, nutty, delicious old flavour. Very good for its age. *As a guest of Stephen Kaplan at Les Nomades restaurant, Chicago, April 1997* ★★★★★
**Veuve Clicquot, Dry** Many notes from 1955. More recently, in 1992: 'Dry': pale for its age, lovely flavour and

excellent length. Then, a magnum (Brut), from Clicquot's cellars, disgorged three months prior: beautiful colour, a sluggish flow of very fine bubbles; nose like freshly peeled mushrooms; uncompromisingly dry, even austere, but complete and drinking well, with a walnut-dry finish. *At Kaplan's Clicquot vertical, April 1997* ★★★★

## 1949 ★★★★

A very good vintage following a long, hot, dry summer. Very well received by the trade and its customers, this vintage figured prominently in my early wine merchant days.

The vintage was first listed by Harvey's in 1955, with prices ranging from 32 shillings and 6 pence per bottle (roughly £1.70 in today's money) for Charles Heidsieck – vulgarly known as 'the tarts' champagne' because it sold well in nightclubs – to 37/6 (under £2 per bottle) for Krug Private Cuvée. Alas I have not tasted any of these champagnes recently though it is worth looking out for for bottles from old cellars, and preferably not 'secondhand' ones on remnant lists.

OF THOSE LAST TASTED IN THE 1980S, AND ONE IN 1990
**Charles Heidsieck** full-bodied and rich. *1990* ★★★;
**Pommery & Greno** dry, firm and in excellent condition. *1987* ★★★; and **Veuve Clicquot** variable but at best it was excellent. *1984* ★★★★

## 1952 ★★★★★

Excellent: firm, long-lasting wines. Worth looking out for.
**Bollinger** First tasted in 1957 and several notes since. By the mid-1980s, taking on colour, touch of orange; lovely, harmonious bouquet; soft and rich. Most recently, 'sheer perfection'. *Last tasted Jan 1991* ★★★★★ *Should still be good – if well cellared.*
**Gosset, Brut** Disgorged 1974. 1% dosage. In 1991 the oldest of eight vintages at a Gosset tasting: pale for its age, moderately lively; nose of dry straw, good depth; dry, quite powerful, good length. Most recently, the second oldest – after the Monopole 1907 – at a Christie's pre-sale tasting: pale, pin-prick bubbles; harmonious old bouquet; dry, clean, considerable delicacy and very fragrant. *Last tasted Oct 1998* ★★★★
**Veuve Clicquot, Brut** Harvested 8 September. A magnum at Kaplan's Clicquot vertical: yellow gold, very fine bubbles; nutty, bottle age straw nose developing creamily; medium-dry, full-bodied, firm, assertive, delicious flavour, lively acidity on finish. *In Chicago, April 1997* ★★★★★

OUTSTANDING '52S LAST TASTED IN THE MID-1980S
**Krug** at its magnificent best in the mid-1960s to mid-1970s, the best being a magnum 'Private Cuvée Extra Sec for Great Britain'. Slight variation since but mainly excellent, including the last tasted: rich, gold, with a continuous stream of fine bubbles; both creamy, richly meaty yet refined; not too dry, rich, firm, good length. A marvellous mouthful. *1987* ★★★★★; and **Pol Roger** also consistently good. Firm and crisp. *Last tasted in 1983* ★★★★★

## 1953 ★★★★

Supple, elegant wines benefiting from a good growing season and early harvest. If anything, the wines were more popular than the firmer '52s.

**Krug** The late Paul Krug, the father of Rémi and Henri, considered this his best vintage between 1945 and 1955. I had the privilege of tasting it with him when I first visited Krug in the autumn of 1957 and was able to follow its progress. It had achieved perfection by the end of the 1960s but continued to develop, gaining colour and bottle age. Alas, not tasted recently but it was perfection in 1983. *Then* ★★★★★
**Perrier-Jouët** Several bottles consumed at the Christie's boardroom luncheons I hosted in the mid-1990s. Frankly variable, but I had back-up bottles for the less good (only one was maderised and at least one I refreshed with a good non-vintage). At least half were very good indeed, fairly lively, with lovely, bright, yellow-gold colour; fine old straw bouquet, good fruit; medium-dry, attractive, gentle mousse, very good acidity. *Last noted at Christie's, March 1995* ★★★
**Veuve Clicquot** Several notes following its progression: soft but refreshing at seven years of age, fully developed at 14, ripely mature aged 24. Most recently, a magnum, Brut, not commercially available but specially disgorged on 31 January 1997, for Kaplan's Clicquot vertical three months later. Fairly pale, its mousse quickly dispersed, yet lingering; its scent reminded me of a swimming pool, slightly minty, good depth (the bouquet not the pool). Not too dry; attractive, nutty flavour, soft yet with a slightly bitter, acidic finish. It went pretty well with 'Sautéed sea scallops, prawns with shellfish sauce and Beluga caviar and sour cream on crouton' – one dish! *Last tasted at the Ritz Carlton, Chicago, April 1997* ★★★★

## 1955 ★★★★

A large crop harvested around the end of September and early October. Very good quality, firm, with refreshing acidity.
**Pol Roger, Brut** For no good reason I appear to have tasted this only once. After 40 years it was pale for its age, a lovely yellow gold with perfect mousse; lovely creamy bouquet; not brut at all, a nice touch of ripe sweetness, perfect flavour, weight, balance and finish. Provided by Pol Roger, and presumably recently disgorged, for the dinner at Ch Palmer on the 40th anniversary of the first visit of Daphne and myself to Bordeaux in the summer of 1955. *Consumed with pleasure and gratitude, June 1995* ★★★★★
**Roederer, Extra Dry** A couple of magnums at the wine department's Christmas dinner in December 1993 – I think we were the only department at Christie's to have held annual dinners in the boardroom; a happy and closely knit team. One magnum was lovely, a 5-star wine, yellow gold with a tinge of orange; glorious, rich, smoky bouquet; slightly sweet, full, nutty-smoky flavour, good acidity. The second magnum was less distinctive. We must have had a few magnums left, for two months later I opened another before a boardroom lunch. It was very good, with a delicious cedary flavour, good length but less sparkle, so I opened a bottle of Sarcey, Justerini & Brooks' house champagne, to enliven it. *Last tasted Feb 1994. At best* ★★★★★
**Veuve Clicquot** Grapes picked the first week of October. I have quite a few notes from 1967 and through the 1970s. I considered the wine fully developed by the mid-1980s. Yet, a decade later, in magnum, bottle age had worked its magic: glorious gold, very slight prickle; very pronounced old straw nose; very good flavour and body, surprising acidity and a touch of froth on the finish. The following year, another magnum, Brut, paler than the previous and more lively; low-keyed, smoky nose with pleasant tanginess; lively, still fresh,

even a little austere, with a dry, frothy finish and just a whiff of mushroom peel. Perhaps a bit wobbly now but never a dull moment. *Last noted at Kaplan's Clicquot lunch in Chicago, April 1997. At best* ★★★★

### OTHER '55S TASTED IN THE 1980S

**Bollinger, RD** I believe this was the pioneer RD, first noted, a bottle disgorged in 1968 and tasted in 1969; the best – supremely fine and rich – in 1982. *Not tasted since* ★★★★

**Dom Pérignon** My only magnum was maderised. *1986.*

**Charles Heidsieck** Quite good in the 1960s and 1970s but three bottles, variable in 1982. *Last tasted 1982* ★★★★

**Krug** Although last tasted in its 25th year and not since, it is worth repeating what Rémi Krug told me about the make-up of their '55 vintage: Krug's final blend, which I was able to note in their tasting room in October 1957, was of 23 different wines of varying styles and from different vineyards. The overall *cépages* mix was Pinot Noir 59%, Chardonnay 26% and Pinot Meunier 15%. It was first shipped to England in 1962 and I enjoyed it on several occasions thereafter though not, alas, since March 1980. *Then, of course,* ★★★★★

**Laurent-Perrier** Not at that time one of the *grandes marques* but showing its potential in 1986. *Last tasted 1986* ★★★

**Pommery & Greno** Best in the early 1960s but still quite good in 1987 ★★★

---

## RD

*A trademark of the Bollinger champagne house, RD is short for récemment dégorgé or 'recently disgorged'. This is used to indicate a vintage wine that has been stored for a number of years but only disgorged (separated from its fermentation lees) when required for sale. This way, it is intended that the wine receives the maximum possible autolytic benefits from prolonged contact with the dead yeast lees. The date of disgorgement is important to note: in my opinion it's best to drink these wines within a year or so of disgorgement as old RDs do not improve with further bottle age.*

---

## 1959 ★★★★★

A magnificent vintage, large and timely, for the British trade's stocks of '52s, '53s and '55s were running out.

**Dom Pérignon** It was around this time that the famous Dom really started to hit the top of the charts. My first taste of it was in a magnum in 1972 when I found it too dry, impressive, but not to my taste (perhaps just as well as it was beyond my means). I preferred it with more bottle age and appreciated it more in the mid- to late 1970s. Most recently, the oldest of four vintages, all disgorged in June 1998, presumably with Len Evans' forthcoming birthday events in mind. In fact, the bottles varied, one very pale with a scent of freshly peeled mushrooms and with a deliciously nutty flavour and very dry finish. The other had a deeper, more golden colour and, though fresher, seemed a bit odd. *Last drunk at Loggerheads, in the Hunter Valley, helping to celebrate Len Evans' 70th birthday, Sept 2000. At best* ★★★★

**Gosset, Brut** Disgorged 1974. Scented vanilla nose; very dry, austere. *Dec 1991* ★★★

**Krug** Medium-deep straw yellow, very fine (meaning very small) bubbles; scent of fresh fungi and walnuts that opened up fragrantly. Flavour to match. Dry. Surprisingly austere. *With the Bacchus Society at Krug, in Reims, May 1997* ★★★★

**Pol Roger** Early harvest, from 10 September. The highest natural sugar and alcohol content since 1893. Fairly recent notes include a bottle disgorged in September 1988 and tasted the following March: pale yellow gold; fresh, crisp, full-bodied, excellent. Then, before a Gidleigh Park wine weekend dinner, recently disgorged: palish, lovely colour but no mousse; rich, old straw scent, great depth; very rich, full-bodied, meaty, good length, dry finish. *Last tasted Feb 1994* ★★★★

**Veuve Clicquot** Harvested from 10 September. Several notes but in 1983, a bottle disgorged in 1980, though very flavoury, was pale and lacking a bit of life. Most recently: a magnum at Kaplan's Clicquot vertical: still fairly pale for its age, yellow with touch of straw, fine bubbles; a lovely, sweet, smoky, very fragrant, nutty – walnuts – bouquet, perfect after an hour in the glass; medium-dry, surprisingly frothy, rich, flavour to match nose. Powerful, attractive, excellent acidity. *Last tasted April 1997* ★★★★★ *A magnificent wine which should still be excellent.*

### OTHER '59S SHOWING WELL IN THE 1980S

**Bollinger** many notes, creamy, smoky, charred flavour, good length. *1983* ★★★★; **Lanson** deep, rich, classic. *Last tasted 1980* ★★★★; and **Moët & Chandon** crisp, good acidity. *1980* ★★★★

## 1960 ★★

Abundant harvest but not of vintage quality.

## 1961 ★★★★

Completely different growing conditions to 1959. Though cold in May, a warm and sunny June enabled flowering to take place in ideal circumstances. July was variable but warmth returned and continued through to the harvest.

Less obvious, less Wagnerian than the '59s, a refreshing style.

**Bollinger, Brut** First tasted at its London launch in 1996. Distinctly lighter and leaner than the '59. Fully developed by its tenth year and much superior to the '62. A good 'mature' note in 1975 and another ten years later 'singed, oaky', soft yet with good, dry finish. Coincidentally, another ten years had elapsed before I drank it again, preceding my Bordeaux Club dinner at Christie's. It was pale for its age with light mousse; slightly fishy (Pinot) nose; very dry, light style for Bollinger, very good acidity. Expected more flavour and depth so I opened another bottle which turned out to be similar, perhaps a bit more lively. *Last tasted Nov 1995* ★★★ *Needs drinking.*

**Bollinger, RD** It was around this time I became a bit disillusioned with the RD. I should have taken more note of the date of disgorgement, for this, I believe, is very significant. By 1982 I had merely noted the '61 RD as dull. A couple of years later, I noted old apples on the nose but unquestionably it had good length. More recently, a magnum, straw-coloured, austere and acidic. *Not tasted since March 1990 and not exactly itching to taste it again* ★★

**Dom Pérignon** A great wine. Several notes. At ten years of age, refined, classic. Another ten years on, a 'Royal Marriage' magnum, disgorged the year of the ill-fated union of Prince Charles and Lady Diana Spencer. Her father, Earl Spencer, was an easy, agreeable man and a regular buyer of old corkscrews and vintage cognac at Christie's wine auctions.

I recall taking a sale once when I suddenly realised that he was bidding against himself. My colleague, Alan Taylor-Restell, had, unknown to me, entered his bid in the auction catalogue, using the name of Earl Spencer's wife, Rayne. When the penny dropped, I had to inform his lordship, who was sitting in the room next to Rayne, of the situation, and start the bidding again. Thankfully he was unfussed and, I think, pleased that I had not inadvertently, stupidly I suppose, let the *faux* bidding continue further.

Anyway, the 'wedding' magnum and another I bought were both consumed that July: dry, firm, taut. By the mid-1980s, it had reached its full maturity: still pale for its age, with a superb, creamy bouquet, opening up beautifully in the glass; a touch of sweetness, perfect flavour, weight, length and acidity. It usurped the position of Krug '28 which, until then, had remained in my memory as the greatest champagne I had ever tasted. On the strength of this, I looked out for more, buying a couple of bottles at subsequent auctions. But, like a second cup of tea, these did not quite reach the previous pinnacle. I noted, in respect of one bottle, that 'it was like trying to rekindle an old love'.

My next bottle I served at a Bordeaux Club dinner in 1994: now yellow gold with very light, very fine, bubbles; slightly smoky, meaty nose, touch of fungi, 'elegant straw' (whatever that meant), hard to explain; very good flavour, length and excellent acidity. A few months later, Harry Waugh produced a bottle for his Bordeaux Club dinner: crisp, nutty, refined. And I think that one word 'refined' sums up a great champagne. Most recently, a magnum, disgorged in 1981: good colour, fine mousse; smoky, showing its age on nose and palate, but still a wonderfully mouthfilling wine. *Last noted at Hardy Rodenstock's opening dinner, March 2001. At its peak, 6 stars. Now a mere ★★★★*

**Gosset, Brut** Disgorged 1983, zero dosage. A lively froth which quickly simmered down; very good bouquet, meaty, nutty, sweet; full-bodied, good acidity. Showing well. *At a Gosset vertical, Dec 1991 ★★★★*

**Krug** Well over a dozen notes. A slow developer, approaching its plateau in the mid-1970s but, for me, probably at its best in 1982, a superb magnum: yellow gold; rich, almost charred bouquet; full-bodied, mouthfilling yet austere. Two poor half bottles – don't waste your time and money on old halves – then a bottle I served alongside the '61 Dom Pérignon. An interesting comparison. Totally different in style but, as I noted in 1986, 'the Krug seemed lumbering and ponderous alongside its rival'. More recently, at Krug in 1997, a bottle disgorged in 1986, straw-coloured with surprisingly big, loitering bubbles; old bouquet of freshly picked mushrooms, meaty, smoky; showing its age. I preferred the '62. Most recently, served by Joshua Latner at a remarkable dinner (the next wine was 1900 Margaux): straw-coloured, a few venturesome bubbles; typical Krug, rich, old straw nose which, interestingly, after one hour in the glass, had a distinct scent of strawberry and vanilla; touch of sweetness, a rich mouthful, good length and acidity. *Last noted at The Lanesborough Hotel, Jan 2000. At best ★★★★★*

**Lanson, Brut** Yellowish but lively; rich, firm, fishy (Pinot) nose and flavour. Very positive but austere. *Oct 1998 ★★★★*

**Moët & Chandon** Disgorged in 1992 for Ursula Hermasinski's birthday. Very fine bubbles but, on the palate, dry, smoky and austere – not at all like the beneficiary. *At a Zachys/Christie's dinner at Spago's, Los Angeles, Feb 1998 ★★★*

**Pol Roger** Several notes with a poor start in 1967, corky, stalky. By 1974, gaining colour, dry, deep, rich. Four years later, dining at Ch La Mission Haut-Brion (I notice that Pol Roger is almost 'by appointment' to many of the top châteaux in Bordeaux): colour of old straw but with a steady stream of bubbles; good nose; dry. Most recently, original cork, a rich

orange gold, a slight fizz when poured but static thereafter; bottle-age bouquet; rich old flavour, good acidity, dry finish. *Last noted at Paolo Pong's wine dinner. At best ★★★★ but tiring now.*

**Pommery & Greno** First notes made in the mid- to late 1960s, still pale of course but with good nose, flavour, balance and finish. Then, for no particular reason, not tasted again until the Dublin-cellared Pommerys came over for sale at Christie's. I bought a case or two for boardroom luncheons and have a dozen or so notes, starting in February 1988. Not unusually, despite pristine appearance, there were bottle variations but it was still pale for its age, with, at its best, a gentle, creamy fragrance and lovely flavour. Last noted at Karl-Heinz Wolf's La Mission tasting in Wiesbaden. He had bought some of the '61 Pommery as well as most of the La Missions at Christie's. It might seem like sacrilege, but after sipping the Pommery, I tipped it into my glass of the '52 to invigorate the older wine. *Last noted June 1990. At best ★★★★ Doubtless tiring now.*

## 1962 ★★★★

This was one of those northern European vintages when a fine, hot, ripening September made up for a mild, sunless summer. The wines were not unlike the '52s, firm, a trifle austere but long-lasting.

**Dom Pérignon** Several notes but none made recently. Consistently noted as very dry, though refined, and with great length. Unquestionably a fine wine. *Last tasted May 1981. Then ★★★★★ Probably still holding well.*

**Henriot** A magnum given to me by Joseph Henriot who had turned his very acute attention to Burgundy, buying – and greatly improving – first Bouchard Père et fils, then William Fèvre in Chablis. Gloriously bright yellow gold with a gentle spread of fine bubbles. Dryish, good flavour, stylish, perhaps lacking length. Yet at nearly 30 years of age, it went down well. *At home, April 1990 ★★★*

**Krug** Disgorged in 1981. Just one note: palish, very fine bubbles; good, fragrant, characteristically 'rich straw' nose, settling down creamily; touch of sweetness, a wonderfully rich mouthful and very good acidity. I preferred it to their '61. *At a tasting in Reims for the Bacchus Society, May 1997 ★★★★*

## 1963

Poor weather, poor wines.

## 1964 ★★★★★

I suppose we – in Britain at any rate – should not be surprised by the many variations in the vintage style, character and weight, indeed in all the vital statistics of different champagnes, for Champagne is a very northerly wine region, only a couple of hours or so down the *autoroute* from Calais. It is almost at the margin of growing grapes successfully in northern Europe. If, in the southern counties of England, we bask in a gloriously sunny summer, the odds are that the growers in Champagne do so too.

The year of 1964 is a case in point. It was an unusually hot summer with heatwaves and the usual panic about drought conditions. However, beneficial showers in Champagne enabled the unusually ripe grapes to flesh out. In short, it was a very good vintage, more like '59 than '61 and '62.

**Bollinger, RD** I have several notes but only in the more recent ones did I note the dates of disgorgement. Dining in

March 1998 with my son and daughter-in-law in San Francisco, we had a magnum disgorged in April 1983: remarkably pale; a slightly fishy (Pinot) aroma; distinctly dry, fresh for its age, with lemon-like acidity. Eight months later, freshly disgorged bottles at a Bollinger tasting at The California Wine Experience: pale gold, a shiver of mousse; very fine bubbles; very fragrant, its age showing – a whiff of walnuts; good fruit, firm, dry, good acidity and a gently frothy finish. *Last tasted Nov 1998 ★★★★*

**Dom Pérignon** First tasted in 1973, though characteristically dry, less austere than usual, doubtless due to the super-ripeness of the grapes. Similar observation in 1976, and in 1977, though pale for its age, bone dry and refined, I found it 'somehow a bit blunt', observing that 1964 and the Dom were not completely compatible. Not tasted again until very recently, a bottle disgorged in June 1998: still fairly pale; a lovely meaty, nutty, bottle-age bouquet; strange flavour, though good acidity, and very dry finish. *At Len Evans' 70th birthday, Hunter Valley, Sept 2000 ★★★*

**Gosset, Brut** Disgorged 1979, dosage 1%. Magnums: modest sparkle; fishy Pinot; dry, surprisingly austere, fair flavour and finish. *Dec 1991 ★★*

**Krug** A rich wine of great character yet not the heavyweight expected. Many notes, first in 1971, finding it fragrant, attractive, well balanced. A magnum in 1973 confirmed my original impression that, despite the vintage, less beefy than one might have expected. It reached its plateau of perfection in the late 1970s: still pale, fine bubbles; rich, smoky, subtle nose; richness balanced by acidity, its flavour opening up majestically. Several more notes in the 1980s, at around 20 years old still relatively pale, with an exceptionally rich bouquet which evolved beautifully in the glass. By 1990, its colour had deepened to a distinct straw gold, bouquet showing age and character, seemed drier but had good length. *Last tasted at Jack Plumb's 80th birthday dinner at Christ's College, Cambridge, August 1991 ★★★★ Should still be drinking well though showing its age.*

**Moët & Chandon, Brut Impérial** First shown at a Champagne Academy dinner in 1970: lively, of course, but surprisingly dry and needing more bottle age. It was much more interesting by the mid- to late 1970s. Then a gap of ten years. Magnums: good colour, very fine bubbles; a very good smoky bouquet and flavour. Seemed quite sweet with delicious flavour and lip-licking acidity. *Last tasted as a prelude to 'A Night in Pomerol Heaven' with Denis Durantou and the Farr Vintners partners, at Ransome's Dock, July 1998 ★★★★ Almost matched the purple prose.*

**Moët & Chandon, Demi-Sec, Grand Crémant Impérial** Well, if not quite as impressive as its title, it was not bad for a 31-year old wine that was originally destined to be drunk in its youth. Rich straw gold, not a sign of bubbly life; good, honeyed, old straw, bottle-age nose, sweet, surprisingly lovely flavour and in very good condition. *Enjoyed before a monumental 12-wine dinner at Lou Skinner's in Coral Gables, Florida, March 1995 ★★★*

**Salon** A magnum, served by Jancis Robinson and Nick Lander after the '73: fine, dry and in excellent condition. *May 1994 ★★★★*

OTHER '64S SHOWING WELL WHEN LAST TASTED IN THE 1980S **Ayala, Brut** 1985 ★★★; **Bollinger** rich, meaty. 1985 ★★★★; **Pol Roger** lovely wine. 1986 ★★★★; and **Roederer, Cristal Brut** multi-dimensional. 1981, *then* ★★★★★

# 1965

Gloomy summer, severe storms, cold and hail. A dry and warm September came too late. The damage had been done.

# 1966 ★★★★

Not the easiest of growing conditions: some vines were killed outright by seriously damaging frosts in the New Year. There was a succession of hailstorms from May through to August, but June hot for the flowering. August itself was wet and lacking sunshine causing mildew problems. The vintage was saved by fine weather in September and early October, resulting in a satisfactory harvest of firm, elegant wines.

I have tasted over two dozen *marques* from this vintage, mainly in the 1970s, less than half that in the 1980s and only half a dozen in the 1990s.

**Billecart-Salmon, Blanc de Blancs** I first came across this in 1980 and was singularly unimpressed, finding it pale, frothy, insubstantial and not particularly harmonious. I was therefore surprised to find that at 30 years of age it was remarkably good: a creamy nose; fairly dry, lovely flavour, excellent life, firm, very good acidity. *At Jane and Barney Wilsons' in Hungerford, April 1996 ★★★★ Should still be excellent.*

**Billecart-Salmon, Cuvée N F Billecart** Reasonably pale for its age; very dry, crisp, excellent acidity – but I found its flavour rather dull. *Also at the Wilsons', April 1996 ★★*

**Bollinger, Brut** The first '66 I tasted, when it was launched on the British market – always well received – in 1971. Even then it had a straw tinge, 'meaty' nose and classic Bollinger style. It gained richness and stature throughout the 1970s, mouthfilling, yet elegant. By the mid-1980s, its straw colour was slightly deeper but with a good, steady stream of what most people pay for, and a good life ahead. A decade later, superb: very fine mousse; buttery, honeyed bouquet; medium-dryness and weight, lovely flavour, very good acidity (at Hugh Johnson's in 1997). Most recently: a very good, rich 'old straw' nose; excellent flavour and acidity. *Last noted dining with Kate and Bill Baker, Jan 2001 ★★★★ Good for another five years at least.*

**Bollinger, RD** Disgorged 1977. I have mixed feelings about these RDs. They are much better drunk freshly disgorged (see 1970). I rarely admire the straw colour, and 30 years after the vintage and 20 years after disgorgement, this wine had no life remaining; its bottle-age straw had come from an old stable and its creaminess was not fresh. Moreover, it was short, with a curious mouth-drying acidity. *At Hugh Johnson's Bordeaux Club dinner, Dec 1997 ★ It should have been drunk in the early 1980s.*

**Krug, Collection** The opening wine of Christie's 'Tasting of the Century' hosted by Christopher Burr and myself at Vinexpo in Bordeaux. Straw yellow, gold highlights, slight prickle of mousse; showing its age on nose and palate but with glorious richness, length and excellent acidity. This was about as far removed from even the best Spanish Cava as the sun is from Glasgow and showed what great champagne is all about. *June 1999 ★★★★★*

**Veuve Clicquot, Brut** Lovely sparkle, firm, dry and elegant in the mid-to-late 1970s. Most recently, a magnum, at Stephen Kaplan's 'Informal tasting' (with three other champagnes prior to his seriously splendid 33-wine dinner): now a medium yellow gold with gentle uplift of mousse; almost Krug-like in its mature richness; not remotely Brut, deliciously rich with a curiously sweet-acidic finish. *Last tasted at the Four Seasons, Chicago, April 2000 ★★★★ But needs drinking.*

# 1967

Not a 'vintage' year, yet until the harvest was ruined by heavy rains the season had progressed well, with satisfactory flowering, hot summer and dry August. September was more than a dampener, the grapes failed to ripen and there was a great deal of rot. I have only tasted one '67 .

**Roederer** Despite showing its age, surprisingly lively, with good flavour and, predictably, noticeable acidity. Clearly Roederer took a good deal of time, trouble and expense to select only the healthiest of grapes. *Jan 1991* ★★★

# 1968

An even more disastrous year than 1967. I doubt if much of the wine was suitable for even non-vintage blends.

# 1969 ★★★

I have always assumed that this was a vintage of convenience; first, after two dreary years to produce a wine which could be marketed as vintage, second, to meet the demand of the hyped-up inflationary period at the time; though this failed to materialise when the wine came on to the market during the 1974 oil price-hike and consequent recession.

My notes reveal that even for a wine known for its acidity the '69 champagnes are generously endowed with the sharp acidity common to all other French wines that year. Happily, this acidity not only suits champagne but aids its longevity.

**Dom Pérignon** In 1989 I gave it 5 stars and suggested that it should continue to improve. It certainly was a lovely champagne, with a steady upwards flow of fine bubbles, a surprisingly scented bouquet, richly flavoured and excellent ('69) acidity. Six years later, in 1995, it had gained more colour and it was showing some age, but was a distinctly dry, classy mouthful, with good life and length. Most recently, medium-yellow straw, slight mousse; rich 'old straw' nose and flavour, but deliciously mouthfilling, with life-sustaining and refreshing acidity. On both the last two occasions the perfect prelude to our annual stone crab supper with the Pauls in Coral Gables. *Last noted Feb 2001* ★★★★

**Alfred Gratien** I always associate this brand with Eddie Penning-Rowsell who died a few days before I wrote up this note. Eddie always gave us vintage Gratien before his wonderful first growth claret dinners and I recall this particular vintage preceding the priceless '45s. For a 21-year-old champagne, it was steady if not vigorous in its bubbly greeting; agreeably mature nose and flavour but with the tartness I associate with the '69 vintage. *At Wootton, June 1990* ★★★

---

### Bready, dough-like smell and taste

*'Autolytic' characters – biscuity, bready notes, and yeast-like flavours – are desirable in all good champagne. Autolysis occurs as spent yeast cells sink into a sediment after the second fermentation has taken place in bottle. The dead yeast lees continue to react with the wine over time, and while champagne can continue to benefit from this contact over several decades, seven years is thought to be the minimum required to see the full benefits. Not every champagne or sparkling wine producer, however, can afford to store his wines this long. As soon as the wine is disgorged, with its sediment removed, autolysis stops.*

**Jacquesson, Blanc de Blancs** *Dégorgement Tardive.* Very lively for its age, doubtless due to its late disgorgement. But was it worth the effort? No, it had a curious dough-like nose and strange taste that reminded me of Madeira cake. I would rather have the cake. *At a pre-sale tasting, Oct 1998.*

**Krug** At ten years of age noticing a lighter style of Krug and more piquancy than usual, but it was a good, refreshing start to Michel Roux's dinner at Le Gavroche at the presentation of The Krug Award for Excellence. Also a couple of years later noted its acidic finish though fragrant and flavoury (1981). In 1989 the Krug Collection was launched, its handsome box including vintage information: 'cold winter, cold rainy spring, summer dry and fine, similar September'. The flowering took place between 16 June and 17 July, the small crop being picked from 1 to 13 October. The 'Collection' was a different ballgame: a lovely rich, nutty wine, though I was surprised by its modest alcoholic content: 10%. Most recently, a Krug Collection magnum served at noon by Wilf Jaeger before his great Romanée-Conti tasting: its colour a pure 'King Tut' gold with fair mousse; low-keyed but gently laced, slightly minerally bouquet with whiff of fresh walnuts; dry – though medium-dry after a rather salty tit-bit – good flavour, length and the '69 trait, acidity. Somewhat idiosyncratic but an elegant start to an unprecedented great burgundy lunch. *In the hills south of San Francisco, March 2002* ★★★★

**Roederer** Several notes, the most memorable being a rare six-bottle Rehoboam preceding a 'double magnum' dinner to celebrate Farr Vintners' 15th anniversary: medium-pale gold with very fine mousse; smoky, like the embers of a wood fire; lovely flavour, good length, marvellous acidity. *April 1993* ★★★★★ *Almost certainly produced for the occasion by decanting an appropriate number of bottles.*

# 1970 ★★★★

Cold spring, late flowering, heavy rain in June, then good conditions through to the harvest. Good, fairly substantial wines and the best keeping well.

**Bollinger, Tradition, RD** First tasted in 1979, the *dégorgement* presumably in 1977 and 1978. Another batch was disgorged in 1980, and all of these early 1970 RDs I liked, noting their lively mousse, creamy, slightly vanillin nose and rich, mouthfilling flavour. Touch of walnuts too. Magnums also disgorged in 1978, and noted the following year, were showing some age, a straw colour but drinking well; dry, firm, nutty – fresh walnuts again – excellent flavour. *Not tasted since June 1991, then rated* ★★★★ *but by now these early disgorged bottles will be past their best ('Tradition' has been dropped from the name).*

**Bollinger, Vieilles Vignes Françaises** Made from ungrafted vines in a 2-ha vineyard. Another not very recent note reported, with my observation that these rare 'VVFs' are the supreme expression of Bollinger, light years ahead of the non-vintage which, quite rightly Cyril Ray said, is best drunk out of silver tankards. I first tasted this nine years after the vintage: it was very pale and frothy, sweeter and richer than the RDs, soft yet mouthfilling. Another admiring note in 1981, then a jump of ten years, by which time it had deepened in colour but was perfection on the palate. Soft, the absence of '69-like acidity apparent. *Last tasted June 1991. Then* ★★★★★ *Past its best now, but probably a deliciously mature drink.*

**Dom Pérignon** An interesting pair of freshly disgorged bottles: first, in September 1996, bottles disgorged the previous month: pale; excellent, lightly oaky-smoky bouquet; dry, crisp, refined. Very good. Next, a bottle disgorged in June 1998: very pale; very rich, smoky nose; sweet approach, dry farewell. Even at this age, a very distinct Pinot character. *Last tasted at Len Evans' 70th birthday, Hunter Valley, Sept 2000* ★★★★

**Charles Heidsieck** Many notes since its first appearance at a Champagne Academy dinner in 1974. A style I like, particularly since its post-war nightclub days, when it craftily pitched itself, pricewise, between other non-vintage and vintage *marques*. (The Heidsiecks are a very distinguished and cultured family whom I first met in 1957, one becoming a concert pianist.) Not tasted recently but the last, a most attractive magnum, disgorged six months previously: slightly sweet, full-bodied, the 56% Pinot Noir dominating its flavour, with good length and aftertaste. *Last noted March 1990* ★★★★ *Drinking perfectly then, probably a bit tired now.*

# 1971 ★★★★★

Now *here* is a vintage! More than good, at its best the epitome of elegance.

It survived all the elements that a northerly *vignoble* – due east of Paris, don't forget – can throw at it: spring frosts, stormy May, hail in June, an uneven flowering in hot but humid conditions. More storms followed in August but mercifully September was hot and dry . A small crop and selection was necessary, but the results – at their best – were fine, crisp, stylish wines. The finest are keeping well – if your taste is for mature champagne.

**Dom Pérignon** On the strength of one note, prior to dinner at Ch Saran, Moët & Chandon's elegant guest mansion in the hills of the Côte des Blancs, it usurped the great '61 (and, earlier, the renowned '28 Krug) as my ideal champagne. Perfection, even at almost 30 years of age, a touch of sweetness, wonderful flavour and length. Refined. And, at 30 years old the same. Perhaps a touch more colour, fine mousse though; a light 'straw' nose; perfect taste, balance, a touch of inner sweetness, great length, excellent acidity. 'Refined' noted again. *Last noted prior to Louis Hughes' inaugural Bordeaux Club dinner at the Savile Club, Jan 2001* ★★★★★ *I see no end to this.*

**Dom Ruinart, Blanc de Blancs** Tom Stevenson in his book *Champagne* reminds us that Ruinart, the oldest sparkling Champagne house, was founded in 1729 by Nicolas Ruinart, nephew of Dom Thierry Ruinart, a friend of Dom Pérignon. In the middle of the 19th century, I see from Christie's archives that Ruinard (*sic*) was the first named champagne house to appear in a wine auction catalogue (in 1840). Dom Ruinart, the brand, was launched in 1959.

The '71 was served by Christan Sveaas at his great wine dinner in Oslo. Still pale, good nose; medium dryness and body, pretty good but, alas, I secretly noted, 'not a patch on the '71 Pérignon'. *April 1996* ★★★

**Krug** Like many '71s, very impressive at the first showings in 1978: pale, lively, 'a good future'. By 1982 'Krug at about its best': palish; very fine, perfectly evolved bouquet; beautifully balanced, excellent acidity, length. After a quarter of a century showing its age, a deeper straw yellow colour, nose and palate to match. Not a Frenchman's taste but laden with character. *Last noted at the Pauls' in Coral Gables, Feb 1996* ★★★

**Lanson, Brut** One brief belated note: 'austere'. *At a pre-sale tasting, Oct 1998* ★★★

**Roederer** On a grand tour of great Bordeaux châteaux with the Palumbos, the Lloyd Webbers, Mark Birley, Olga and Dieter Bock, prior to a dinner hosted by David Orr at

Ch Rauzan-Ségla. At 27 years of age the wine had rich bottle-age colour, nose and flavour. Touch of mature sweetness. Delicious flavour. *At Ch Rauzan-Ségla, Sept 1998* ★★★★

**Roederer, Crémant** Privately imported by Jack Rutherford, whose family firm had represented, for several generations, several of France's major wine houses. Jack also happened to be a great connoisseur of fine classic wines. These old-school wine trade experts, with a lifetime of experience, no longer exist. Crémant is normally drunk young, but this was still lovely, pale for its age; a touch of honey clinging to its mature nuttiness; lovely flavour and finish. *Jan 1990* ★★★★

**Salon** Went surprisingly well with *truffle surprise in Gewürztraminer Aspic, squab feuillette au jus*. Modesty almost forbids me to say that it was at a Society of Bacchus 'Celebration of Spring 1992', 'honoring' (*sic*) myself. The description might almost have applied to me: palish, very little sparkle; showing age; dry, medium-full body, firm and a trifle acidic. Actually, it had a touch of gold and was excellent. Most recently: palish, attractive, very little sparkle; refined, old straw and walnuts; fairly dry, showing considerable maturity but very good, with exceptional persistence of flavour. 'Refined' noted again. *Last noted at a pre-sale dinner in honour of Lenoir M Josey, New York, Nov 2000* ★★★★

# 1972

Late harvest. Not of vintage quality.

# 1973 ★★★

The second biggest champagne vintage of the 20th century. Overproduction tended to reduce firmness and grip but some agreeable, fairly early-maturing wines were made following a hot, dry summer and the dilution of heavy rain in September.

**Bollinger, Tradition, RD** Quite a few notes from 1979 – 'needed bottle age' – to the mid-1980s. All noting its leanness and austerity. Most recently in a line-up of top Bollingers at the Californian Wine Experience in New York. Disgorged two months before the tasting: a lovely yellow gold with lively froth which simmered down to a gentle spray of fine bubbles; very fragrant nose, walnuts and white truffles scent and taste. Quite powerful. *Last noted Nov 1998* ★★★★

**Dom Pérignon** Magnums in 1986: perfect age, perfect drink. Surprisingly sweet and rich (I used to find the Dom dry and austere), with lovely flavour and length. Eleven years later, at a pre-sale tasting in New York: very pale for its age (24) and not much sparkle; sweet, slightly caramelised; also some sweetness on palate, and pleasantly, lightly, frothy. Most recently, the youngest of the Dom vintages, disgorged three months prior to arrival in Australia. Still pale; 'warm' rich nose; soft, sweet, *à point*. A very pleasant drink, holding surprisingly well. *At Len Evans' 70th birthday, Hunter Valley, Sept 2000* ★★★★

**Dom Ruinart, Blanc de Blancs** First 'enjoyed' in 1981, but 'not in the same league' as the other venerable Dom (above). Very pale, lively; creamy nose; dry, light, fresh, flavoury. Perfect at ten years of age 'but not intended to age longer'. But it comfortably survived another 14 years: now medium-pale, surprisingly lively, with a good, steady stream of very fine bubbles. Showing its age on the palate but attractive and 'incredibly sweet really'. *Opened on 31 December with family and house guests, the Pauls from Florida, to see in the New Year, 1998* ★★★

**Gosset, Brut** Disgorged shortly before being shipped. Not good: one strange, one yeasty. *At the London agent's tasting, Dec*

*1991. This is not the first time I have come across poor bottles at a trade tasting. One wonders why they are so lax. Surely they taste the wines to check first? Bad for business …*

**Krug** First tasted in May 1980. We were informed that flowering was 14 to 19 June, picking 28 September to 15 October. It was delicious, deep, nutty, like a great Corton-Charlemagne injected with superfine bubbles. In 1989, Krug released their '73, not freshly disgorged, and packed in individual boxes branded '*Krug Collection*'. Very good: pale; fragrant; full-bodied for a '73. Also shown at the tasting for the Bacchus Society in 1997: now medium-pale with lazy bubbles; sweetish, 'complex' (which means I didn't know how to describe it); unusual but attractive, quite a positive impact. Most recently: now a deeper straw colour and restrained sparkle; showing considerable age on the nose, like old apples in a hayloft, with some sweetness. *Last noted at Paolo Pong's dinner at Nick Lander and Jancis Robinson's, London, June 2000. At best ★★★★ Well past its best now.*

**Laurent-Perrier, Millésime Rare** Chardonnay 55%, Pinot Noir 45%. Magnums: surprisingly pale for its age; a creamy, toasty, bread-like nose; dry, still fresh, complete. Hopeless though with *crème brûlée. At the Champagne Academy annual dinner, May 1994 ★★★★ (just).*

**Pol Roger, Extra Dry** Literally dozens of notes, starting with the first batch I bought in 1983 and the last bottle from my cellar consumed in 1990. I mourned its passing. It was, throughout, delightful and easy-going, changing in colour from pale yellow to straw, its pristine bubbles subsiding over the period. In 1990 Christian Pol Roger brought to a tasting bottles disgorged the previous year. It was quite different. Dry, frothy, fresh. I felt it was cheating a bit. Most recently, recently disgorged, lovely palish gold, bubbles few but fine; lovely, mature, 'golden straw' bouquet; fair body, good flavour and length. *Enjoyed prior to a wine dinner at Gidleigh Park, Devon, Feb 1994 ★★★★*

**Salon** Medium-pale, fine mousse: beginning to show its age, the scent of freshly picked mushrooms; medium-dry, fairly refined. Tired but flavoury. The opening wine in a magnificent eight-wine dinner at Nick Lander and Jancis Robinson's, after which I was caught by the police on the way home doing 35mph in a 30mph zone. Requested to step out of the car, I blew into the bobby's bag – and, happily, the colour refused to change. *May 1994 ★★*

# 1974 ★

A poor vintage at a depressing time. Sales of champagne worldwide (and other luxury goods) were hit by their worst-ever slump due to the oil price crisis. Though there was a good start to the season with a mild spring and early summer, just after flowering it became excessively hot and dry. Welcome rain came in August but then all was spoiled by rain at vintage time. I have tasted only three from this vintage, two in the 1980s.

**Roederer, Cristal Brut** I don't know why Roederer chose to put their de luxe *cuvée* on the market in this undistinguished vintage. It must have been very costly combing the vineyards to find healthy ripe grapes. First tasted in 1982, welcome at the time, but not very good. Then in 1984, pleasant enough. Seven years later in a Cristal Brut vertical, still pale and fairly lively; typical 'old straw' bottle age nose; positive flavour, good acidity. But not de luxe. *Last tasted March 1991 ★★*

# 1975 ★★★

A popular and stylish vintage. Though the summer temperature was above average, lack of sun and a wet second half of September delayed picking until October. The crop was small and the grapes, lacking the benefit of a long ripening period, were acidic, not that this is a grave disadvantage with a naturally acidic wine like champagne.

**Bollinger, RD** About ten notes, first in 1984. Almost from the start a distinctive straw yellow with hint of gold, its other features being a very positive bouquet, rich, complete, considerable depth and scent of fresh walnuts. A classic, meaty Bollinger. A jeroboam in 1986 not up to standard – it would have been 'decanted', probably from bottles. (Bollinger is one of the few houses to mature wine in magnums as well as bottles. But to the best of my knowledge, larger bottles are filled to order.) I must confess that I have not always noted the date of disgorging. A '75 disgorged September 1985 and served at a dinner in 1992, seemed pale for an RD: had a meaty old straw nose and appley acidity. Too long after disgorgement. Another RD, date unknown, had very little life, a curious malty nose, austere with acidic finish; a lacklustre start to Nils Sternby's 1975 vintage dinner in 1995.

More relevant were bottles disgorged two months before shipment to New York for a major Bollinger tasting in 1998. It was a different ball game: very frothy, small and lively bubbles; bouquet sweet, rich, crusty, almost yeasty; interesting but with lean teeth-gripping, sour finish. Most recently, a bottle disgorged in September 1985: warm gold, light mousse; old straw nose and taste. Dry, tired and acidic. *Last noted dining with the Hochar family in Lebanon, Dec 1999. At best ★★ Too old now.*

**Deutz** I rarely come across Deutz. This was at the house of an eccentric (Bordeaux) château proprietor somewhere in the middle of France. The other guest was Corinne Gaudron, '*Veuve Clicquot femme du vin*' 1992! Good colour (the champagne), lemon gold, good mousse, surprisingly fresh (the wine, too); dry, crisp, very good acidity. Refined. *May 1995 ★★★*

**Dom Pérignon** First tasted in 1983: dry, nutty, austere, good length but acidic. Next in 1995, dining at Pied à Terre in London with the American Bacchus Society, recently disgorged bottles: pale, elegant; touch of lemon; fairly dry, good flavour with a smoky, oaky end taste. Five months later an Impériale: pale lemon, a smattering of very fine bubbles; creamy; first reaction glorious, refined, then 'a bit tame', which is rather ungrateful. It must have cost a fortune. *Last tasted at a Rodenstock gala dinner in Munich, Sept 1995 ★★★*

**Jacquesson** Disgorged December 1990. Palish lively; creamy bouquet; dry, good flavour, fair length, '75 acidity. *Supper with the Rudolf Russells after carols at Charlton Park, Dec 1993 ★★★*

**Lanson, Red Label** Around this time the *grande marque* houses were trying almost anything to make their de luxe brands instantly recognisable. Lanson certainly succeeded when this was launched in a simply hideous skittle-shaped bottle in 1984. Good wine, though. Also refreshing magnums tasted in the late 1980s and in 1990. *Most recently, drinking well at a Christie's board lunch in April 1992 ★★★ Looks ain't everything.*

**Laurent-Perrier, Grand Siècle, La Cuvée** Known simply as Grand Siècle, La Cuvée this champagne was the brainchild of Bernard de Nonancourt who decided to blend his best *grand cru* wines of three vintages, roughly 50–50 Pinot and Chardonnay, to make a superlative, perfectly balanced champagne. Magnum, a blend of the '75, '76 and '78 vintages disgorged around 1992. Green-tinged; no signs of age, lean, steely, lemon-scented; full of flavour and character. Excellent acidity. The opening of Kaplan's 'Informal tasting' prior to one of his monumental dinners. *In Chicago, April 2000* ★★★★

**Piper-Heidsieck, Florens Louise** Pale for its age; slightly smoky; dry, excellent flavour and length. A delightful surprise. *Prior to stone crabs at the Pauls, Coral Gables, Feb 2000* ★★★★

**Pol Roger, Cuvée Sir Winston Churchill** Churchill was not only partial to Pol Roger, his favourite champagne, but to the family, especially the courageous and remarkable Odette Pol Roger. It seemed wholly appropriate that Pol's de luxe blend should be named after the great man. I first tasted this new cuvée in 1984, a wine of character and weight, rich and flavoury. Lovely at 12 years of age (my ideal age for vintage champagne). Approaching 20 years, in magnum, it was drinking perfectly, albeit a deeper yellow, retaining a small stream of fine bubbles; lovely, creamy, harmonious bouquet, showing just a hint of bottle age; lovely flavour, perfect length. *Last noted at a boardroom lunch at Christie's, March 1994. Then* ★★★★★ *Doubtless still ageing, gracefully, as was Odette when I last met her in Épernay shortly before her death in December 2000.*

**Roederer, Cristal Brut** First noted, in magnums, at the memorable Josey-hosted Wine & Food Society dinner in Houston in 1983: creamy, elegant, great length, refreshing acidity, the latter being more noticeable a couple of years later. Most recently, alongside the '78, at a dinner party in London, given by Miriam and Jonathan Lyons. At 23 years old, it had taken on a yellow amber colour and lacked sparkle. On the verge of oxidation. I thought it must be a '47, or older. It turned out to have come from Jonathan's father's cellar in Florida. *Last noted July 1998. At best* ★★★

**Taittinger, Comtes de Champagne, Blanc de Blancs** First noted in 1984 at a luxurious supper *à deux* to celebrate our 30th wedding anniversary at Hollywood's Bel-Air hotel, the guests of a kindly old wine lover, George Reese. In 1986 a magnum, though a seemingly light style, was firm to the point of hardness, needing more time. Most recently: pale yellow; slightly minty, lanolin, nose; very good flavour, perfect acidity. *At a pre-sale tasting, Oct 1998* ★★★★★ *Will still be excellent.*

**Veuve Clicquot, Rosé** Almost a coincidental aberration: magnums of the pink-un, both from Stephen Kaplan's cellar but served on different occasions. First at the end of his extensive Clicquot vertical in 1997 with 'fresh berries of the season': palish pink, fine bubbles; neutral nose; very dry, not very distinctive flavour and in any case ruined by the berries. The following year at another dinner at the Four Seasons, this time served as an aperitif: quite a good colour; touch of honeyed bottle age on top of the old straw; good flavour, finish and acidity. *Last noted in Chicago, Feb 1998. At best* ★★★

OF THE OTHER MAJOR '75S LAST TASTED IN THE LATE 1980S **Bollinger, Brut** ★★★★; **Krug** ★★★★★; **Perrier-Jouët, Brut** ★★★★; **Pol Roger, Brut** ★★★★; and **Veuve Clicquot** despite poor weather earlier in the year, one of Clicquot's more memorable vintages. Acidity 8.5g/l, accounting for its — to say the least — refreshing bite! ★★★

# 1976 ★★★★

This vintage was a great favourite of mine, full of flavour and a sheer delight.

It was the year of England's most extended heatwave; and if it is this hot in southern England, it is pretty certain to be hot in northern France. The difference, in 1976, was that the weather broke in England at the very end of August, torrential rain lasting for months on end, ruining an otherwise potentially great English wine harvest, but the good weather continuing in Champagne (and the Loire) to produce a super-ripe harvest. The problem for champagne in these relatively rare hot years is a lack of acidity in the grapes. But let us see how the *champenois* coped.

**Bollinger** Christian Bizot and Bollinger's London agent, Mentzendorff, launched the '76 in June 1982. I described it at the time as marvellously rich, almost a caricature of Bollinger's much admired meaty style of wine, 'with an almost anaesthetising effect on the palate' (on my head, more like!). Several notes since, as it mellowed but, alas, not tasted recently. *Last noted, a rather disappointing bottle, August 1990. At best* ★★★★

**Dom Pérignon** First noted at a reception at Ch Margaux in September 1984 before a grand dinner to celebrate 50 years of trade between Bordeaux and the United States. It turned out to be something of a showcase for Sherry Lehmann. The '76 Dom was dry and long, as was Sam Aaron's speech! Through the 1980s, its colour deepened and I appreciated more its inimitable finesse. More recently: medium-pale straw, very fine bubbles, good for age; deliciously creamy bouquet that almost fought a losing battle against the fumes of a newly lighted stove; dry, firm, a trifle austere, crisp, great length. *Last noted prior to Neil McKendrick's Bordeaux Club dinner, at Caius, Cambridge, a chilly April 1996* ★★★★

**Gosset, Brut** How insular the British are, how habitual our choice of vintage brands. Here we have a champagne from one of the oldest families in the business, producers of wine since 1584, long before bubbles burst on the scene; yet Gosset is not often listed by our merchants and restaurants. Palish yellow, fine mousse; meaty style; excellent acidity, dry finish. *Showing well at a pre-sale tasting, Oct 1998* ★★★★

**Jacquesson** The same might apply (see Gosset above) to Jacquesson, though it was not until the Chiquet family bought this old-established company in 1974 that its flagging reputation was revived. The 1975 must have been their first vintage. After nearly 20 years, it had a very good colour with an agreeable uplift of tiny bubbles; good fruit; a touch of sweetness, very appealing though slightly appley taste. *At home, Jan 1995* ★★★

**Krug** First presented at the Champagne Academy's annual dinner in May 1982. Already a deeper and more yellow colour than the '76 Pol Roger that preceded it, a rich wine needing bottle age. Nevertheless, drinking well, indeed perfectly, through the 1980s, managing, seemingly effortlessly, to combine substance and elegance. In its 19th year, opening Peter Ziegler's tasting at the Schlosshotel Erbach: palish, with a lime-yellow tinge; not very distinctive nose; very good flavour, crisp, lively, fragrant but surprisingly acidic. Most recently served after the '28 Perrier-Jouët at my Bordeaux Club dinner: medium-pale, lively with pin-prick bubbles; delicious smoky nose; dry, mouthfilling, lovely, excellent acidity. *Last tasted Feb 1998* ★★★★ *And will continue to evolve.*

**Lanson, Red Label** Many notes. For some reason or other, Lanson sold a large stock of their '76 through Christie's and I bought some for entertaining, opening bottles at boardroom luncheons between 1992 and 1994. In each instance the wine was pale for its age and very lively; 'good' nose — I didn't try to describe it. 'Good' is good enough. Dry, firm, fullish, very good flavour, balance and length. Guests on two occasions included Jamie Davies of Schramsberg — the Krug of the Napa Valley — Tom Stevenson (perhaps it inspired him to devote his literary

## Dosage

*The tiny amount of sugar added to all champagne (all except Brut Natur) after its second fermentation in bottle. After disgorging, liqueur d'expédition is added to bring the level of the wine up to the cork again. The liqueur contains the sugar, which counterbalances the often high acidity in the young wine. Wines intended to be aged will require lower sugar levels – i.e. a lower dosage – than champagne for younger drinking, as acidity tends to soften with maturity. Dosage is held to be an important factor in adding complexity to the wine.*

life to champagne) and Terence Conran, an old friend. More recently, a magnum, by now a pale old gold but retaining a fair amount of fizz; lovely, rich, bottle-age bouquet; medium-dry, excellent, smoky flavour, good length and acidity. *Last noted dining with Carrie and Chris Foulkes, March 1995* ★★★★
**Laurent-Perrier, Grand Siècle La Cuvée** Blend of '75, '76 and '78 already recorded under 1975 (see page 434).
**Pol Roger** I was enchanted by this wine when it was launched on a bright and sunny spring day in 1982. 'Will be perfect in five years' I noted and bought several cases, which kept us going until we ran out in 1990. It deepened slightly in colour, from pale to straw yellow; a constantly sweet, rich nose; not too dry, well constituted, with character, flavour and length. It had 'come of age', a 21-year-old bottle disgorged about five years prior, produced by Christian Pol Roger – aware of my liking for it – before dinner at his home: still pale for its age, with a steely stream of bubbles; lovely old straw bouquet; medium-dry, lovely, mature taste, good length and dry finish. *Last noted in Épernay, June 1997* ★★★★

OTHER NOTABLE '76S, LAST NOTED IN THE LATE 1980S
**Moët & Chandon** many notes, all good, retaining good colour and life, crisp, firm, good body and excellent flavour ★★★★; **Taittinger, Comtes de Champagne, Blanc de Blancs** refined, stylish ★★★★★; and **Veuve Clicquot, Gold Label** launched with great panache during the Henley Regatta in July 1982 in sweltering heat not unlike the summer of 1976 itself. Needing bottle age, it developed well, with superfine bubbles and excellent flavour ★★★★

## 1977

A damp and dismal growing season.
**Roederer, Cristal Brut** Once again, as in 1974, Roederer Cristal Brut was an odd man out. I don't think that it did Roederer's reputation any good to market Cristal Brut in off-vintages like this. Made from a blend of Pinot Noir picked on 9 October, and Chardonnay on 13 October. First tasted in 1991 and remarkably good for its age and vintage though there was a touch of maltiness on the finish. One more note, quite recent, and in the most unlikely setting, before dinner at Warren Winiarski's home in the Napa Valley, following his tasting 'celebrating 25 years' of Stag's Leap Wine Cellars. Unattractive, maderised. A drab start to an excellent dinner. *Last noted March 1998.*

## 1978 ★★

Almost as poor a growing season as 1977. As in Bordeaux, a bright and sunny September saved the day. **Krug's Grande**

Cuvée launched (see box below). My best notes follow.
**Dom Pérignon, Rosé** Palm Beach's smartest wine. I have only tasted the '78 once, dining with an overindulgent wheeler and dealer. I was neither a fan of the '78s nor, for that matter, rosés, but this was surprisingly lovely, with mouthfilling flavour and excellent acidity. *At Lyford Cay in the Bahamas, Sept 1990. Then* ★★★★
**Laurent-Perrier, Grand Siècle, La Cuvée** The youngest of the three vintages ('75, '76 and '78) making up this very successful blend. See page 434. *Tasted April 2000.*
**Roederer, Cristal Brut** Palish, modest mousse; better nose, flavour and life than the accompanying '75. Still not quite correct and with an acidic finish. I am bound to draw the conclusion that this was not a good period for Roederer, one of my favourite and most consistent champagnes. *July 1998* ★
**Veuve Clicquot** I only have two notes, the first made in 1985 while on board a friend's boat off Bermuda. I enjoyed neither the trip nor the wine. A jump of 14 years to another unlikely venue: a 'Hog wild Bar-B-Que' (*sic*) in Memphis, Tennessee. By now, the bottles were variable, some had good colour and were drinking well. *Last noted at Hal Lewis' 'Mr Gourmet' event, Sept 1999. At best* ★★★

## 1979 ★★★★

A good vintage and a welcome one as it made its appearance in the much healthier wine market of the mid-1980s.

Interesting growing conditions. An exceptionally cold winter through to the spring was followed by severe frosts in May. Happily, flowering was successful and clement weather continued through a warm and sunny summer. A late, but abundant harvest of fully mature grapes, yet with acidity to provide the necessary zest for life.
**Bollinger, RD** I have many notes, mainly from the late 1990s, with considerable variation, both in bottle and magnum, mainly due to the different disgorgement dates and which, with a combination of idleness and ignorance, I failed to note. More recent notes, more pertinent, a bottle disgorged in June 1989 dining at the Coq Blanc in Stockholm in 1994: not much mousse; pleasant, characteristic meaty straw nose; good, positive flavour, body and length. Most recently at the Bollinger presentation at the 'Wine Experience' in New York, bottles disgorged two months prior to the tasting: still pale, lively, small bubbles; good rich nose and rich black truffle flavour. Dry, a trifle acidic and lacking length. *Last tasted Nov 1998* ★★★
**Drappier, Carte d'Or, Brut** Palish straw; showing its age, whiff of fresh fungi; dry, better flavour than nose, interesting only. *At a St James's Branch dinner of the IWFS at the Garrick Club, London, Jan 2000* ★★

### Krug's Grande Cuvée

*As this chapter is devoted to vintage champagne, Krug's renowned and expensive Grande Cuvée does not feature. I recall the family strongly objecting to my cataloguing it for sales under 'non-vintage' so I back-tracked and left it as Grande Cuvée though placing it at the end of a range of vintages. (The only equivalent I can think of is Vega Sicilia's Reserva Especial.) The blend is made up of some four dozen wines from two dozen or so villages and all three varietals, Pinot Noir, Chardonnay and Pinot Meunier, roughly in that order – and up to ten different vintages. Put into one cauldron and stir! The result is, of course, Krug at its most sublime.*

**Gosset, Grand Millésime** First tasted in 1989, very pleasant weight and flavour. Next, a bottle disgorged in 1991, dosage of 1.2%. A smell of tapioca and strange taste. *At a Gosset promotional tasting, Dec 1991. A mistake to show it.*

**Charles Heidsieck, Brut** At 11 years of age, beginning to show its paces with a deep, rich Pinot nose, good, firm, positive flavour and crisp acidity. A good future. Not tasted for another decade but still more than surviving with a vigorously fragrant nose and delicious, mature sweetness, not remotely brut, rich, stylish. *At Kaplan's 'Informal tasting', Chicago, April 2000 ★★★★ Will continue to delight – if you like the style.*

**Krug** Two fairly close notes, one in 1990 at Ch Pétrus with Christian Moueix: distinctive colour and rich, meaty bouquet and flavour. A class act. More recently, the opening salvo at Barry Phillips's 'Silver Jubilee Dinner': a superb magnum, full body, lovely, smoky flavour, excellent length. *Last noted at Chilgrove, Jan 1995 ★★★★★*

**Krug, Clos du Mesnil** The first vintage from the 1.87-ha enclosed vineyard or *clos* in Le Mesnil-sur-Oger in the Côte des Blancs. Planted by Krug with 100% Chardonnay in 1971. and first tasted at the Peppercorns' in December 1984. I thought it fresh and attractive but lacking length and that it probably should have been drunk by the early 1990s. However, it was still very much alive and kicking at the end of that decade: pale for its age; a very steely, rather fishy Pinot nose; dry, yet rich, with an oaky-smoky Chardonnay taste on the palate and teeth-gripping acidity. Lean, austere and a complete contrast in style to the Grande Cuvée. *Last noted at a Krug dinner hosted by Henri Krug at La Caravelle in New York, June 1998 ★★★? A matter of taste.*

**Lanson, Red Label** Two notes, first in 1990: 'lively, firm, excellent, will keep'. And two years later: very pronounced yellow gold; a rich, fragrant, fishy (Pinot) nose; dry, full-bodied, assertive, good length and acidity. A bit austere but with good future. *Last noted at Decanter magazine's Lanson vertical, July 1992. Then ★★★★*

**Mumm, René Lalou** The firm of Dubonnet was one of the major owners of Mumm from the early 1920s. René Lalou married into the Dubonnet family and successfully ran Mumm until 1973. Mumm's new de luxe champagne (launched in 1969) was named after him. Frankly I have never been a fan of Mumm. I must have bought some for Christie's boardroom lunches for I have three notes in a six-month period, all made when entertaining clients and other VIPs. Barring a corked bottle, all were pretty good, not surprisingly showing some bottle age though lively enough, and all had good length and flavour, one noted 'a bit acidic'. *Last noted July 1996. At best ★★★★*

**Pol Roger, Brut** First tasted in May 1985. 'First rate. Dry, lovely, crisp, oaky', and one or two more notes in the later 1980s, one 'rather disappointing'. Then a gap of nine years, now noting a very minty nose; surprisingly rich, with a very original flavour (this was in the context of a range of vintages and *marques*). *Last noted at pre-sale, Oct 1998. At best ★★★★*

**Pol Roger, Cuvée Sir Winston Churchill** Served, appropriately, as an apéritif before we went in to the dinner jointly organised by Peter Sichel and Hugh Johnson and held at the British Embassy at the rue St-Honoré in Paris to celebrate with a glorious array of '45s the 50th anniversary of the end of the war. The '79 Pol Roger Sir Winston Churchill was pale and dry, with good nose, firm flavour and length. Lively enough for its age. Sipped reverently in august surroundings with Christian Pol Roger and other distinguished guests. *One of the most memorable events I have ever attended, Dec 1995 ★★★★*

**Roederer** A magnum before dinner at the Rutherfords' (David's family were Roederer's agents for several generations). Excellent colour; subdued sparkle; a lovely, rich, mellow nose and flavour, rather Krug-like, with good acidity. *Feb 1999 ★★★★*

**Roederer, Cristal Brut** First noted pre-sale in 1998. Surprisingly frothy and, something I rarely notice with champagne, with good 'legs'; sweet nose, beautiful fragrance; wonderful flavour, length and aftertaste. Most recently, superb in every way. Palish, lively; most positive impact on nose and palate. Perfectly mature bouquet and flavour. *Pre-dinner at Spencer House, London, April 2002 ★★★★★*

**Salon** First noted in 1993: creamy nose, with the scent of freshly picked mushrooms; perfect weight, style and flavour. Most recently: very pale though showing some age on the nose; fairly dry, on the lean side. Very good but outclassed by the Roederer Cristal. *At Spencer House, London, April 2002 ★★★★*

**Taittinger, La Française** I am not sure where this champagne comes in the Taittinger hierarchy and I have only come across it once: yellow-tinged, but bright and appealing; stylish nose, ageing well; touch of sweetness, excellent flavour, mellow. *April 1990 ★★★★*

**Veuve Clicquot, La Grande Dame** First launched with the 1973 vintage, La Grande Dame was named after Nicole Barbe-Clicquot-Ponsardin, whose husband died in 1805 only seven years after their marriage, leaving the 27-year old widow in charge of the business. She proved immensely competent and ran Clicquot with flair, authority and drive, dying as 'the uncrowned Queen of Champagne', at the age of 88.

I have two recent notes, first at Mosimann's after a British Airways meeting in 1995: scent of walnuts; touch of sweetness, soft, absolutely delicious. Next, it was surprisingly frothy and vigorous; rich, smoky (Pinot Noir, 60%, Chardonnay 40%); lovely, flavoury, length and good acidity. *Last noted at a pre-sale tasting, Oct 1998 ★★★★ Another ten years of active life ahead.*

**Veuve Clicquot, Rosé** Good colour, positive pink (as opposed to pale and anaemic or orange-tinged, worse still, metallic); fairly rich, touch of honeyed, old straw bottle age; excellent flavour, finish, acidity. One of my rare complimentary rosé notes! *A remarkable 19-year-old 'pink-un', at Stephen Kaplan's dinner with the Khourys in Chicago, Feb 1998 ★★★★*

SOME OTHER '79S TASTED WELL IN THE LATE 1980S and worth looking out for at auction, or wherever: **Bollinger, Brut ★★★; Charbaut, Certificate ★★★★; Charles Heidsieck, Champagne Charlie ★★★★; Lanson, Noble Cuvée ★★★; Pol Roger, Cuvée Blancs de Chardonnay ★★★★;** and **Pommery, Louise ★★★★**

# 1980–1999

I suppose the popular image of champagne is of constancy of sales and quality, with reliance on tried and tested brands. Leaving aside the natural variations due to circumstances beyond the producers' control, notably the weather and growing conditions, the history of champagne is beset with problems, mainly economic, but also a sort of internecine warfare, brand owners versus growers, *grande marque* bickering, and, dare I say it, some cheating. This period at least saw a recovery from the doom-laden mid-1970s and, halfway through, in 1989, enjoyed the second biggest boom in the history of champagne, when, to quote Tom Stevenson, 'a staggering 249 million bottles were sold' which, not surprisingly, resulted in a severe depletion of stocks. It was also a period in which the quality of champagne was queried, with some quite virulent press criticism, some justified. Then, the Gulf War; sales slumped as did prices and by 1993 both were at their lowest ebb (Stevenson). The situation was saved by the approaching millennium.

## Vintages at a Glance
**Outstanding ★★★★★**
1982, 1985, 1988, 1990, 1996
**Very Good ★★★★**
1981, 1989, 1992 (v), 1995, 1997, 1998, 1999
**Good ★★★**
1983, 1986 (v), 1993

## 1980 ★

A small crop and one of the latest harvests on record due to poor, uneven and belated flowering in disastrously cold and wet weather. The wines lacked body and were too acidic. I have tasted only eight '80s, and only three of these during the last decade. Best forgotten.

**Dom Pérignon** Four notes, first around the time of its release, its tooth-tingling acidity uppermost. Acidity more tolerable as it gained bottle age. By the mid-1990s, it had achieved some colour, its bouquet smoky-oaky, sweeter than expected, flavour far too charred but not unattractive. *Last noted, the oldest vintage in a 23-wine de luxe line-up at a British Airways blind tasting for Concorde, Dec 1994* ★★

**Lechère, Grand Cru, Blanc de Blancs** Lechère is a *sous-marque* of Union Champagne, 'a super co-operative' comprising ten individual co-operatives with a total of 1200 growers. This must be their pride and joy. New to me and, to my surprise, a very attractive '80: pale, dry, light, crisp and refined. *Jan 1990* ★★★★

**Pommery, Louise, Rosé** Two notes. Rosehip colour; meaty; some fruit, fair finish. Just for the record. *Last tasted Sept 1990* ★

## 1981 ★★★★

The smallest crop since 1978. Because of this, and despite its high quality, most champagne houses held their fire because the 1982 turned out to be more widely successful. I think it should be borne in mind that whereas, for example, port shippers declare a vintage around the second year, depending on the quality of the wine and state of the market, champagne houses have more time to decide and, in any case, do not release their vintages for four or even seven years.

It is also worth mentioning the reason for the shortfall: mild weather in the new year and spring promoted heavy and premature growth. The vines were literally 'nipped in the bud' by a single night's heavy frost at the end of April. Further

indiscriminate hailstorm damage in May and a cold spell at the beginning of July caused late and irregular flowering. August was hot and sunny, conditions which continued into September so that the grapes were well ripened before the onset of rain at the end of that month. Alas, I have tasted only ten '81s, mainly either side of 1990. Many, however, were of very high quality.

**Krug** A high percentage of Chardonnay (50%) because the poor flowering conditions had particularly affected the Pinot Noir and Pinot Meunier, resulting in a light style of wine. In May 1988, I noted a lime-tinged colour and well developed nose, very distinctive and attractive flavour. Evolved well, and by the end of that decade, had developed a walnut-like fragrance and great length. *Alas, not tasted since Jan 1990. Then* ★★★(★) *Probably delicious now.*

**Krug, Clos du Mesnil** 12,793 bottles produced. At the time of tasting, a pale, lime-tinged, light but steely and rather austere Chardonnay. *Oct 1989. Then* ★★(★★) *but should be perfection now.*

**Lanson** Distinctive yellow; rich, meaty, toasty nose and flavour. Good acidity and length. *July 1992* ★★★

**Pommery, Louise, Cuvée Spéciale** Several notes. By the end of the 1980s, already a golden tinge; crisp, crusty (bread) nose with delicate fruitiness. Good length, excellent acidity. *Last tasted Sept 1990. Then* ★★★(★) *Should be excellent now.*

**Roederer, Cristal Brut** Launched and tasted first in October 1987: frothy like the head on a glass of Guinness. Deliciously refreshing. Later, in magnums, more yellow, mousse less exuberant, nutty bouquet; good length, refined. *Last noted March 1991* ★★★★ *Doubtless perfection, even 5 stars now.*

**Taittinger, Comtes de Champagne, Blanc de Blancs** Several notes, in magnums and in bottle. Dry. Refined. *Last tasted Sept 1989* ★★★★ *Probably still drinking well.*

## 1982 ★★★★★

A highly successful vintage, widely 'declared'. One of those rare years when the growing conditions were well nigh ideal, resulting in the biggest crop on record, three times the size of the 1981, and of uniformly high quality.

**Billecart-Salmon, Brut** Palish gold; attractive nutty-smoky nose; certainly not Brut, with a flavour of oak, mellowed by bottle age. *Lunch at Christie's, New York, Oct 1996* ★★★★

**Bollinger, RD** Pinot Noir 70%, 5% more than normal. Several notes, all made in the 1990s. First, in July 1994, bottles disgorged four months prior, after 12 years on lees: straw-tinged; strange, old apples and straw nose, like a dry Tokaji

Szamorodni; uncompromisingly dry, fairly powerful, austere. Didn't like it, nor did I like another, disgorgement date unknown, served by the indomitable N K Yong in a Chinese restaurant in London (1995). Next, at the Bollinger vertical in New York, disgorged September 1998, two months before the tasting. Still fairly lively; attractive in its quirky way with fragrant *sous bois* (for me: fungi) nose and truffle-like taste. Most recently, disgorged 1996: surprisingly pale; good nose; crisp and youthful. 'The best RD I can recall'. *Last noted at Christie's wine course dinner at Boodle's, Oct 2000. Extremely variable. At best* ★★★★

**Dom Pérignon** Several notes from the late 1980s when it was youthful, crisp, steely, full-bodied, austere, needing bottle age. Showing well in the mid-1990s and a particularly notable magnum in 1997 at Bob Dickinson's 'Mr Gourmet' reception in the sinister-sounding Al Capone suite at the Biltmore, Coral Gables: good colour for its age; very strikingly oaky and smoky nose and flavour. Attractively mouthfilling. Most recently: mild, yet rich, and creamy; soft, lovely, perfect now. *Last noted before John Jenkins' Bordeaux Club dinner at Childerley Hall, Cambridge, Oct 2000* ★★★★★

**Dom Pérignon, Rosé** Perhaps the most over-exposed Dom Pérignon Rosé. First, in magnums, in 1993: palish tawny rose; surprisingly meaty, singed; dry, firm, good, but not inspiring. Just about surviving 'Passion fruit parfait in a champagne soup' at the end of one of Stephen Kaplan's dinners (April 1997). Five months later, pink, dry, not bad, and, one month after that – ignoring a badly corked bottle – opening Bob Dickinson's reception mentioned above. *Last noted Oct 1997. Each time* ★★★ *In short, overrated.*

**Dom Ruinart** Lively, scented; fair length and acidity. *With Calum MacKenna of Drambuie, Jan 1992* ★★★

**Gosset** In the sun-filled yard at Ch Langoa prior to lunch with the Bartons: rich, yellow gold, a touch of straw, good life; rich bottle-age bouquet; slightly sweet, richly flavoured, excellent flavour and finish. Superb. Mind you, the setting and the company helped. *Bordeaux, Sept 1998* ★★★★★

**Heidsieck, Diamant Bleu** Hint of green; very meaty, nutty, smoky nose and taste. *At Mosimann's, London, Jan 1995* ★★★★★

**Krug** A lovely magnum in 1990: good future. Two years later, at the annual Champagne Academy dinner: powerful, coped well with strong cheese. Finding it lightweight alongside the '81 in 1994. Richly flavoured bottles preceding Kaplan's 33 '82s claret dinner in April 1997. The following month, with the Bacchus Society at Krug: now golden; nose deep, rich and smoky, settling down to a soft creaminess; fairly sweet, full flavoured. The sort of wine that glories in a good dose of bottle age. Most recently, an intriguing bottle opening a wine dinner at home: medium-pale straw gold with continuous spray of fine bubbles; bouquet of bitter walnuts; medium-dry, strongly scented old straw flavour, very distinctive, attractive. *Last tasted June 1999* ★★★★★

**Krug, Clos du Mesnil** Just two recent notes. First at lunch at Krug: pale for its age, lively bubbles; nutty, creamy, crusty-bread nose; very good with the cheeses (1997). The following year: similar appearance; very faint whiff of cherry stones; an almost bitter austerity. From Krug's cellars. *Last noted at La Caravelle, New York, June 1998* ★★★ *I prefer the straight vintage.*

**Mumm** Very fresh and fragrant; dry, nutty, good length. *Drinking well prior to a Christie's boardroom lunch, May 1997* ★★★★

**Mumm, René Lalou** Reception on the *Carnival Destiny* cruise liner: very good, mouthfilling. *Tied up in Miami Harbour, Nov 1997* ★★★

**Perrier-Jouët, Belle Époque** Magnum: palish, creamy, nutty, delicious. *Noted briefly prior to a Christie's board lunch, Jan 1997* ★★★★ *(The problem about these luncheons, when I am busy welcoming and introducing guests, is that I have no time to make a proper note of the wines.)*

**Pol Roger** Many notes, first, delicious magnums prior to a Saintsbury Club dinner in 1992, time in hand. By the mid-1990s, opening up. Meaty, lively and lovely (Childerley Hall, 1995). High marks at a Gidleigh Park Pol Roger vertical tasting: still youthfully lemon-tinged; bouquet creamy, harmonious, lovely; wonderfully mature, nutty flavour, good acidity. At its peak (1997). Most recently, again at Childerley Hall, alongside the Dom Pérignon (above). Still lively, nose now ageing a bit, straw and walnutty. Good but upstaged by the Dom. *Last tasted before John Jenkins' Bordeaux Club dinner, Oct 2000* ★★★★

**Pol Roger, Blanc de Chardonnay** Pulled out of my Eurocave to greet Trish and Len Evans: pale for its age; excellent nose; glorious flavour and length. Best I could do. Len is so difficult to please! *At Rosebank, Sept 1996* ★★★★

**Pol Roger, Cuvée Sir Winston Churchill** Half a dozen early notes: a zestful, fragrant, superfine wine. Most recently: magnificent magnums before the Gidleigh Park wine weekend closing dinner: pale gold; rich oaky-smoky bouquet of great depth; medium-dry, glorious flavour, good length, firm, dry finish. *Last tasted at Gidleigh Park, Devon, March 1997* ★★★★★ *(Though hosting, I managed to sneak away to make a brief note.)*

**Pommery & Greno, Super Brut** (no dosage) Recently disgorged: palish, very fine bubbles; fresh, steely, light style for Pommery and '82; bone dry, very austere, good length. *At the Pommery tasting at the Garrick Club, London, March 1993* ★★★

**Pommery, Louise** Slight hint of gold; fresh, surprisingly youthful; also surprisingly dry, austere and steely. More body yet more refined than the brut. *March 1993* ★★★(★) *Probably at best now.*

**Roederer, Cristal Brut** In magnum and bottles; lively; firm, still relatively immature. *Alas, not tasted since March 1991. Then* ★★★(★) *Should be a 5-star mouthful now.*

**Salon** Three notes, all made in the mid-1990s. Curiously unintegrated on the nose but dry and elegant (lunch at Corney & Barrow, 1995; a fellow guest was the late and much missed Auberon Waugh, whose acerbic column in the *Daily Telegraph* gave me endless delight). Next, on the *Carnival Destiny* in Miami harbour, and, a month later, opening the 'Last Friday Club' lunch at Ranji's in Memphis: pure pale gold, moderate mousse; now showing its age on the nose but full-flavoured with very dry, crisp finish. The epitome of refinement and elegance. *Last noted Dec 1997* ★★★★

**Taittinger, Artists' Series** Was this a one-off? It was for me, at any rate. Appropriately tasted opening 'A Celebration of Spring': pale, lively; surprisingly rich and nutty; dry, good quality but if de luxe, only just. *With the Bacchus Society, on receiving their Lifetime Achievement Award, Boston, March 1992* ★★★

**Veuve Clicquot** Many notes, in very different contexts, starting in September 1988, and not a single one less than laudatory. Of the more recent, a magnum of the **Carte d'Or** on New Year's Day 1994: pale gold; 'lovely fish scales' nose; fairly dry, full-bodied, lovely flavour, balance and acidity. In short, a good drink. Then, on 22 July 1996, prior to dinner at Christie's on Daphne's birthday, merely noted, appropriately, as 'refined, mature'. Most recently, at Ch de La Brède in Graves: pale for its age; rich, smoky nose. Perfect. *Last noted with the Montesquieus, June 1998* ★★★★★

OTHER '82S SHOWING GREAT STYLE AND A POTENTIALLY LONG LIFE when last noted in the late 1980s and early 1990s **Bollinger, Grande Année** rich, refined. *1990* ★★★; **Alfred Gratien, Brut** assertive, needed time. *1989* ★★★; **Charles Heidsieck** creamy, fragrant, almost too sweet. *1990* ★★★; **Moët & Chandon** very good flavour, body, length. *1989* ★★★★; **Joseph Perrier, Cuvée Royale** long, rich yet lean, attenuated finish. *1988* ★★★; and **Roederer, Brut** excellent. *1988* ★★★★★ *All probably still drinking well.*

# 1983 ★★★

Another important vintage, and another record crop, in fact the biggest ever recorded in Champagne, the equivalent of 300 million bottles. After a cold, wet spring, flowering took place from 25 June into early July in excellent conditions and presaged a large crop. Thereafter, it was warm and sunny, interrupted by rainy periods. The crucial ripening period in early September was damp, lacking sun and warmth, the harvest taking place from the 24th and lasting well into October.

It was not as good a vintage as originally touted, but it was not at all bad. The wines should now be fully mature and need drinking soon. I have many notes so I shall try to be brief.
**Bollinger, Grande Année** Impeccable comments in the early 1990s. Two more recent notes both made at Christie's luncheons: pale yellow gold; nutty nose and flavour; very dry but mouthfilling, good acidity. *Last tasted Nov 1996* ★★★★
**Dom Pérignon** Totally different in style to the '82, softer, sweeter (in 1990). 'Smoky', medium-dry, lovely (at Dom de Chevalier, Bordeaux, 1994). More recently, pin-prick bubbles; lovely nose; refined, good length. *At Adrian Miles', Lyford Cay, Feb 1996* ★★★★
**Gosset, Grande Millésime** Mixed notes: frothy, scented (1991), 'powerful' (1994). Rather drab appearance; unknit, appley, sweetish. *Last tasted in a line-up of 23 de luxe champagnes, Dec 1994. Not good enough.*
**Alfred Gratien** Still pale and lively, on the light side, with lip-licking acidity. *Preceding eight wonderful '85 clarets at the Penning-Rowsells', June 1996* ★★★
**Charles Heidsieck, Blanc des Millénaires** Fine mousse; firm, excellent balance and length. *Last tasted April 1992* ★★★★
**Charles Heidsieck, Brut** First tasted in 1990 with the winemaker, Daniel Thibault, who told us that the Pinot Noir was slightly botrytised. Delicious. Fragrant. *Last tasted April 1992* ★★★★ *Should be fully mature now.*
**Lanson, Blanc de Blancs** Very distinctive nose; assertive, mouthfilling but odd tart flavour. *July 1993. Probably past it.*
**Lanson, Brut** Several notes in the early 1990s. Pale, quite good, firm. The youngest vintage at a *Decanter* vertical in 1992: quite a lot to it, lean for an '83, refreshing acidity. By the mid-1990s, showing its age in appearance and on the nose; dry, positive, fairly acidic. *Last enjoyed with smoked salmon sandwiches in a box at the Theatre Royal, Bath, Aug 1996* ★★★ *Probably over the edge (of the box) by now.*
**Krug, Clos du Mesnil** Harmonious. Probably at its apogee: more life, froth and richness than the '82. A pleasant mouthful but by no means a top Mesnil. *At La Caravelle, June 1998* ★★★
**Mailly, Cuvée des Echansons, Brut** Unusual: a co-operative, whose members are all Mailly *grand cru* growers. The *cuvée* 75% Pinot Noir and 25% Chardonnay. Fragrant, nutty; dry, fullish body. Fair enough but unexciting. *Tasted blind, in a range of de luxe champagnes, Dec 1994* ★★★

**Moët & Chandon, Brut Impérial** Frothy; fairly high acidity but attractive. *Last tasted Sept 1993* ★★★
**Perrier-Jouët, Belle Époque** Christie's wine department must have secreted quite a stock for I have several notes, starting with a splendidly rich and creamy magnum at our Christmas dinner in 1996. Two more later. Slight bottle variation. Both showing their age, one deliciously ripe and lovely, the second seemed drier and firmer. *Last noted at a Christie's boardroom luncheon, Oct 1998* ★★★★
**Roederer, Brut** A perfect bottle before lunch at the Lefèvre Gallery in very grand company (1994). (Alas, to everyone's surprise, it has now ceased trading.) Two subsequent notes at Christie's, happily still very much in business despite the uncertain times. Lively, dry, firm, crisp. No signs of fatigue. *Last noted Oct 1995* ★★★★ *Should still be drinking well.*
**Roederer, Cristal Brut** Only two notes: fresh, fragrant and most appealing in 1991. Most recently: still very frothy; bouquet of fresh walnuts; dry, lean, holding well. *Last tasted pre-sale, Oct 1998* ★★★★
**Salon** A quartet of notes, three in 1997: lively, sweet, appley nose, 'distinctive but …?' (blind, in January). Showing some age, curious (before dinner at Ch Branaire in April). Bottle variation, one like an old RD, lacking Salon elegance (Memphis, in December). Most recently, among 25 vintage champagnes tasted blind for *Smag & Behag*, the leading Danish wine and food magazine: yellow gold; sweet, rich, creamy nose displaying character and quality; full, rich, but something of an 'acquired taste'. A bit too old. *Last tasted in Copenhagen, March 1999* ★★★ *(just). Drink up.*
**Taittinger, Comtes de Champagne, Blanc de Blancs** Distinctly sweet but with good acidity, smooth, crusty bread (Aschau 1994). Most recently, alongside the '82 and totally different: very pale, 'surprisingly sweet'. *At a pre-sale tasting, Oct 1998* ★★★★ *Drink soon.*
**Veuve Clicquot** Good notes from 1989 to the mid-1990s, a particularly high mark at a Saddler's Company Livery dinner in London, March 1994, and at a Saintsbury Club meeting a month later. Ripe, excellent flavour and length. Probably at its very best. *Last tasted in London, April 1994* ★★★★

ONE OR TWO OTHER '83S, SHOWING WELL IN THEIR EARLY DAYS First the 4-star wines: **Charles Heidsieck, Champagne Charlie** *1990*; **Pol Roger** surprised at having only one note. *1990 – an early developer*; and **Taittinger, Brut** *1989*. Next, the several 3-star wines: **Abel Lepitre** *1989*; **Jacquart, Brut** *1990*; and **Pommery, Brut**.

# 1984

Poor growing conditions. Not a vintage year.

# 1985 ★★★★★

In common with so many other major French wine regions, this was a most attractive, well-balanced, stylish vintage. Certainly one of my favourites.

The weather conditions were far from uniformly good. In mid-January the temperature was down to −25°C, the lowest recorded for 150 years. Fortunately the vines were dormant. Not so in February when a temperature of −15°C destroyed around 10% of the region's vines. The end of April, always a risky period, saw temperatures down to −5°C. Happily, the crucial flowering period took place in good conditions and warm weather continued through July. A hot August and high temperatures in September ensured that the reduced crop of ripe grapes was harvested from the 30th. The quality was high and prices were equally high. I have many notes.

**Billecart-Salmon, Cuvée N F Billecart** I keep wanting to call this wine Billycan. I have two notes: very positive colour, nose and taste, that is to say slightly unusual (blind in 1994). Then, in magnums, good but upstaged by the Bollinger. *Last noted Nov 1997* ★★★

**Bollinger, Brut** Consistently and deliciously good. The two most recent notes: magnums at the Saintsbury Club – surprisingly sweet, 'perfect now', in October, and the following month, 'classic', at the Bacchus Society dinner in Coral Gables. *Last tasted Nov 1997* ★★★★ *For me, one of the best recent Bollingers.*

**Bollinger, RD** I had mixed feelings about this wine at the Bollinger tasting in New York, November 1998. It had been disgorged two months prior and was, I thought, a bit of a mixed-up kid. Perhaps we should have tasted it after it had more time to settle down. It was yellowish, very frothy; rich, slightly yeasty with a very crusty bread-like fragrance. Not dry, certainly interesting but with a lean, sour, teeth-gripping acidic finish. Next, labelled *Extra Brut*, no disgorging date noted, was also youthfully frothy, acidic, dry but attractive. *Last noted blind at the* Smag & Behag *tasting in Copenhagen, March 1999* ★★★?

**Bollinger, Vieilles Vignes Françaises** Showing its age and disappointingly tired on the nose and palate. *At a Saintsbury Club dinner, Oct 1998* ★★

**Bricout, Grand Cru, Arthur Bricout** An old-established company in Avize, originally known as Koch (I recall seeing mid-19th century vintages of Koch in old Scottish cellars), merged with Bricout in the late 19th century. Chardonnay 70%, Pinot Noir 30%. Frankly this '85 was by far the worst of a wide range of champagnes tasted blind in January 1997. No wonder they finally sold out to the phoenix-like Delbeck in 1998. *Tasted 1997.*

**Dom Pérignon** Several notes dating from 1993. Consistently good, reaching its plateau of perfection in 1996, served by John Jenkins at Childerly Hall in 1996: pale, fine bubbles; fragrant, whiff of vanilla; firm and dry but not remotely austere. Long 'smoky' flavour and finish. Last noted at a Bacchus Society dinner on Mud Island, Memphis, memorably coping with 'Arkansas Razorback Caviar on Cork Cake, scrambled eggs and fresh truffles'. Delicious. *Last tasted Sept 1999* ★★★★★

**Dom Pérignon, Rosé** Preceding the Clicquot Rosé and, frankly, superior: rich, complete. *At the Kaplan dinner in Chicago, April 2000* ★★★★

**Gosset, Grand Millésime** Showing well at a combined birthday and *Decanter* magazine 20th anniversary lunch, May 1997. Next, disgorged in 1999: palish, low-keyed but with a distinct appley scent and taste. Rich. Very oaky. *At Stephen Kaplan's 1985 dinner, April 2000* ★★

**Alfred Gratien** I have two notes, both made before Eddie Penning-Rowsell's annual first growth claret tastings. First, in 1995, prior to the '85s, the second prior to the '87s. In each instance the Gratien '85 was in top form: surprisingly pale; crisp, good fruit, good acidity. *Last tasted at the Penning-Rowsells' in June 1997* ★★★

**Heidsieck, Diamant Bleu** Four notes, first accompanying 'warm *ceps* tart' at the Champagne Academy dinner in 1995, again in 1997 and, lastly, at the Bacchus 'Bar-B-Que' in Memphis. On each occasion I ticked its appearance, nose and taste without comment or score. A decent enough drink, *assez bien. Last ticked, Sept 1999* ✓✓✓

**Charles Heidsieck, Blanc des Millénaires, Blanc de Blancs** The first two notes at British Airways tasting, both blind, first in 1993: positive but acidic; next in 1997 and coincidentally word for word 'positive and acidic', adding smoky, classic. Next, strange coincidence, on Singapore Airlines, Bali to Singapore. Steely but opened up sweetly, mouthfilling, frothy acidic finish. *Last tasted Jan 1998* ★★★

**Charles Heidsieck, Brut** Hard, needing bottle age, in 1991. Then two good notes, both on British Airways flights in 1994, one on our return from Chile. Most recently, disgorged in 1999, in numbered bottles: lively; smoky, nutty bouquet and finish. Interesting and attractive. *One of four '85 champagnes at Stephen Kaplan's 1985 dinner, April 2000* ★★★

**Charles Heidsieck, Champagne Charlie** A poor bottle in 1993 made up for seven years later, though very little fizz, a nutty, smoky old straw and chestnuts nose; dry, firm, good flavour. *At Kaplan's line-up of '85s, April 2000* ★★★

**Krug** Pinot Noir 50%, Chardonnay 30%, Pinot Meunier 20%. A final blend of 30 different wines. Ten notes, first made at the launch of the '85 in May 1994 – nine years after the vintage. Already creamy, elegant, perfect weight and flavour. 'Not a heavyweight Krug' I noted. (At a tasting in 1996, I was informed that there had only been 25 vintages of Krug in the 20th century). Tasted, drunk, on several memorable occasions since. At a blind British Airways tasting in January 1997 it was selected by our panel, and I had the pleasure of sipping it on Concorde to New York that September. Bottle variation at Kaplan's '85s tasting but, when last tasted, in magnums, it was excellent. Several times I noted an extraordinary, very individual scented character. The sort of wine that reveals extra dimensions on the rare occasions one is not distracted by the social event at which it is served. *Last tasted at Hatchlands, Surrey, Dec 2000* ★★★★★

**Krug, Clos du Mesnil** Only one note: pale; crusty (bread); fairly dry, lean, steely, excellent acidity. *May 1999* ★★★(★)

**Krug, Rosé** Pale yellow gold, not pink, so I hardly see the point. Curious scent. Not dry. Hugely expensive. *Dec 1994* ★★★

**Laurent-Perrier, Brut** Showing well – 4 stars – in 1992. Less enthusiastic two years later, noting that its mousse dissipated very quickly and, though full-flavoured, it was open-knit, appley and – frankly – so-so. *Last noted July 1994* ★★ *Should have been consumed by now.*

**Laurent-Perrier, Grand Siècle** A totally different ballgame, though sadly I do not know whether this blend included the '82 or '88 or both on the most recent occasion. It was certainly of high quality with a lovely creamy flavour. Last noted in the company of Joan Oliphant-Frazer who exercises in a body stocking and consumes champagne with equal vigour. *At the Café Royal, London, Jan 1995* ★★★★

**Moët & Chandon, Brut Impérial** Hard, lacking length in 1989 but went quite well with the pudding at a state banquet. *Last noted at Buckingham Palace, April 1993* ★★★

**Mumm, Grand Cordon Brut** Pinot Noir 54%, Chardonnay 46%. Yet another fancy brand, and I took against it. Two notes, not too bad except that the attractive nose was, for me, spoiled by a peach kernel flavour and slight soapiness. Which, in the end, says it all. *Last noted at a British Airways tasting, Jan 1995.*

**Mumm de Mumm** It seemed that in this period Mumm, owned by Seagram, were flailing in all directions, with *cuvées* here and there – Cordon Rouge, Vert, de Cramont, René Lalou and now Mumm de Mumm. In April 1991: strange and stalky, blind. The following month prior to the Wine Trades'

Benevolent Banquet (Seagrams in the chair), it was simply not good enough. *Last tasted May 1991* ★★

**Mumm, René Lalou** Immature, acidic in 1989. Softer but unimpressive. *Last tasted, blind, July 1993* ★★

**Perrier-Jouët, Belle Époque** Several notes. As flowery as its bottle design. *Last tasted Nov 1997* ★★★★

**Piper-Heidsieck** It was not my top wine at the British Airways blind tasting in 1996 but I drank it with pleasure, albeit in an inappropriate straight-sided glass, flying Club Class to Miami. The high proportion of Pinot Noir noticeable. Full-flavoured but the finish a bit tinny. *Last noted Oct 1997* ★★★

**Pol Roger, Brut** and **Extra Dry** Several notes, these qualifications confusing. The Brut in 1994 perfectly balanced ★★★★; the Extra Dry certainly was just that, with a distinctly metallic and slight peach kernelly taste. *Last noted April 1998* ★★

**Pol Roger, Cuvée Sir Winston Churchill** Half a dozen notes from 'rich and mouthfilling' in 1992 via superb bottles at a Hollywood Wine Society gala dinner in 1998, combining richness and refinement, to the most recent, very distinctive and perfectly mature. *Last noted at Kaplan's 1985-vintage dinner in Chicago, April 2000* ★★★★★ *Excellent now. Good for another ten years.*

**Pommery, Brut** and **Cuvée Louise** Both good, the first with a classic, rich 50-50 Pinot and Chardonnay blend, the Louise more flowery, greater length. *Both tasted March 1993* ★★★ *and* ★★★★ *respectively.*

**Roederer, Brut** I tend to jump from the always dependable Brut Premier, which I keep 'on tap', to the Cristal Brut, of which I keep odd bottles for special occasions. The vintage Brut is always very good and the '85 (Pinot Noir 66%), only tasted in its youth, was excellent. *Feb 1991* ★★★★★

**Roederer, Cristal Brut** Pinot Noir 55%. Unyielding in 1991. Two superb magnums, one on New Year's Eve and the other on New Year's Day 1994, both glorious, with lip-licking acidity. Most recently, refined and elegant. *Last tasted June 1995* ★★★★★ *Will be approaching its peak now.*

**Taittinger, Comtes de Champagne, Blanc de Blancs** Now pure 'King Tut' gold; lovely flinty nose; excellent flavour, length and acidity. *Last tasted at the Musée Baccarat, Paris, May 2000* ★★★★ *Perfect now. Will keep.*

**Veuve Clicquot** Several very good notes from its first showing, at a Champagne Academy dinner in 1992: stylish, needing bottle age, and, a magnum, disgorged in 1998: a beautifully balanced mouthful. Most recently, at Kaplan's 1985-vintage dinner. *Last noted in Chicago, April 2000* ★★★★★

**Veuve Clicquot, La Grande Dame** From 1989 – which seemed an early 'release' – to the most recent note, a really glorious wine. Initially classic, fragrant, youthfully frothy. Then a warm, pale gold; smoky nose – like a burnt match; perfect fruit, full-bodied, rounded. I had magnums at home and noted, in 1994, its mouth-expanding flavour, excellent length. A sour – 'surprisingly acidic' – note, another magnum, in America (1997) and most recently, at my son's house in San Francisco, still vibrant, firm and seemingly youthful. *Last tasted Nov 1998* ★★★★

**Veuve Clicquot, Rosé** Attractive orange rosé; steely; medium-sweet, crisp, good flavour. With 'Spring bouquet of seasonal berries' at Stephen Kaplan's extensive 1985-vintage dinner. *In Chicago, April 2000* ★★★

AMONG THE OTHER TWO DOZEN OR SO '85S TASTED IN THE EARLY TO MID-1990S, first the 4-star wines: **Billecart Salmon, Brut**; **Binet, Blanc de Blancs**; **Henriot**;

**Jacquart, Cuvée Nominée**; **Jacquesson, Signature**; **Lang-Biemont, Blanc de Blancs**; and **Lanson, Noble Cuvée**. Next, the 3-star wines: **Charbaut, Cuvée de Reserve, Brut**; **Deutz, Blanc de Blancs, Brut**; **Jacquesson, Perfection**; **Lanson**; **Mumm, Cordon Rouge**; **Bruno Paillard, Brut**; **Ruinart, Brut**; **Alain Thienot, Brut**; and **de Venoge**.

## 1986 ★★ to ★★★

The early summer was hot and sunny, but the prospect for a good vintage was dampened by rain in August and early September. Growers who sprayed against rot and picked selectively did best. An extended harvest started on 28 September and lasted, in some vineyards, until November. But one can rely on the better champagne houses to look after their interests in this respect.

The results were variable, as described below. The best champagnes will be at their peak now. I shall comment mainly on those '86s of which I have several notes.

**Moët & Chandon, Brut Impérial** First noted in 1993: agreeable weight and flavour, richness balancing noticeable acidity. Half a dozen notes since. Firm, crisp, refined, would seem to be its hallmark. Last noted at a Champagne Academy dinner. Very French and very inappropriately accompanying 'Pistachio *Crème Brûlée*'. Ignoring the latter, drinking well. *Last noted May 1995. Then* ★★★(★) *Probably at peak now.*

**Pol Roger, Extra Dry** Masses of notes, mainly from my own cellar. First tasted in 1993: firm, crisp, stylish. 'Needs time'. The two most recent notes made in the mid-1990s: magnums – kindly supplied by Pol Roger – at a dinner to celebrate the 30th anniversary of Christie's wine department and, two weeks later, also in magnums at the 129th meeting of the Saintsbury Club when, I confess, I thought it was Pol's White Label, for it was slightly too sweet at first sip and slightly too acidic on the finish. *Last noted, Oct 1996* ★★★ *Drink soon.*

**Pol Roger, Cuvée Sir Winston Churchill** Half a dozen notes, first on Concorde with a horrible salmon and egg dish: touch of sweetness, refreshing, frothy in the mouth, travelling at Mach 2. More recently, on New Year's Eve, unusually in our London flat: lively, attractive, dry, slightly acidic finish. *Last tasted 31 Dec 1997* ★★★ *Will doubtless be drinking well now but not a great* cuvée.

**Taittinger, Comtes de Champagne, Blanc de Blancs** A surprising number of notes, mainly in the early to mid-1990s. Assertive, good flavour and length in 1993. The last two, believe it or not, both on Concorde, outwards to New York (at 51,500 feet, 1230mph, colder than an ice bucket outside: −64°C), arriving in time for a board luncheon at Christie's in Park Avenue, followed by my pre-sale auction talk and, the following day, the auction itself. Returning by Concorde on the Sunday. The cabin temperature on Concorde is normal, quite different from jumbo jets, so drinking the wine is not affected by the altitude or speed. In any case, the Taittinger had enough body to make itself felt. Powerful, mouthfilling, excellent finish. *Last noted Sept 1995* ★★★★

BRIEF NOTES ON OTHER '86S **Billecart-Salmon, Cuvée N F Billecart** smoky flavoured. *1994* ★★★★; **Dom Ruinart, Blanc de Blancs, Brut** in fact four notes, variable, from poor and cardboardy to firm, crisp, with finesse. *Last tasted Oct 1995. At best* ★★★ *So best of luck;* **Krug, Clos du Mesnil** very un-Krug-like, very pale; 'wet straw' though refined. *Dec 2000*

★★★; **Pol Roger, Blanc de Chardonnay** crisp, good length. Best drunk young and fresh. *Nov 1993* ★★★★; **Roederer, Brut, Rosé** *Pelure d'oignon* but very lively; no fruit, more like a damp dishcloth; dry, austere, dull. *At home, Oct 1996* ★; and **Taittinger, Comtes de Champagne, Rosé** very pale pink; dry, refined, length and good acidity. In my opinion, Taittinger makes the best rosés. *Feb 1999* ★★★★

## 1987 ★★

Perhaps, after the excellent '85s and some good '86s, the market was not ready for a third good vintage in a row. Perhaps as well, because it wasn't all that good.

Roller coaster weather – unusually wet spring, an improvement for flowering, then a wet summer, though three weeks of exuberant weather in August was followed by cold and rain. A humid Indian summer with some harvesting on 28 September but other growers waiting until 10 October. A 'useful' crop of reasonably healthy grapes suitable to top up non-vintage stocks. Few wines shipped as 'vintage'.

**Pommery, Louise** Four good notes, all in the early to mid-1990s: pale; dry yet rich and some delicacy (1993). The next year it was showing well in a blind tasting: easy, pleasant, ready but perhaps something lacking. *Last noted Dec 1994* ★★★ *For early drinking.*

THE ONLY OTHER '87S I HAVE TASTED, ALL IN THE EARLY 1990S **Jacquart** straightforward, *assez bien* ★★; **Mumm, Cordon Rouge** austere, short ★; and **Pommery & Greno, Brut** frothy, acidic ★★

## 1988 ★★★★★

Very good vintage. Quantity 10% down on 1987 and both high demand and high grape prices.

Mild spring, good flowering early June, cloudy July and heavy rain before the harvest which began relatively early on 19 September. The average quality was high and the style firm with good acidity. Many champagnes are drinking very well now and many will keep further.

I have tasted roughly 30 *marques* and styles, mainly in the mid-1990s. My more recent notes first.

**Dom Pérignon** Excellent magnums in 1998. A year later, in bottles, an astonishing pale-green gold; deliciously smoky nose; crisp, good length. Very good indeed but will benefit from more bottle age. *Last noted at Hal Lewis' 'Mr Gourmet' dinner at the River Terrace, Mud Island, Memphis, Sept 1999* ★★★(★) *Probably at best 2005–2015.*

**Dom Pérignon, Rosé** Distinct tawny-orange with very fine bubbles; very good, rich but crisp 'wild garlic' nose; medium dry, mouthfilling, complete, excellent flavour leading to a good, dry finish. *At Stephen Kaplan's in Chicago, April 2000* ★★★★★ *Easy to be scornful about Palm Beach's favourite tipple, but it is seriously good!*

**Dom Ruinart, Blanc de Blancs** First tasted, blind, January 1997: palish, bright, green-tinged yellow; fragrant, smoky, complex; surprisingly youthful and acidic, good flavour. Needs bottle age. Next, noted at dinner after a tasting for the magazine *Residence*: comments consistent, would benefit with more maturity though drinking well. *Last noted at the Hotel Pulitzer, Amsterdam, April 1998* ★★★(★)

**Dom Ruinart, Rosé** Palish orange pink; strange scent. Appalling: not like champagne at all. Perhaps the red varietal

element falling apart. Not helped by the dessert. *At the Annual Champagne Academy Dinner May 2002: minus stars!*

**Gosset, Brut** Two good notes: pale, lively; appealingly fresh nose; very pleasant flavour, length and acidity. *Last noted prior to a Saintsbury Club dinner, London, April 1998* ★★★ *Drink now.*

**Henriot, Brut** Magnum: very fine mousse; fragrant, walnuts, lemon tinged; light style, touch of acidity. Good flavour. *At Childerley Hall, Sept 1998* ★★★ *Drink now.*

**Krug, Brut** Excellent wine. Two recent notes. 1999 in Memphis: lovely scent, great length, finesse and future. Most recently, prior to a dinner at Ch Figeac in St-Émilion: a fairly deep straw gold; fine, mature bouquet; fullish body. Classic Krug. *Last noted June 2001* ★★★★(★) *Drinking well but will keep.*

**Moët & Chandon, Brut Impérial** For some reason or other, quite a few notes, first in September 1994, though youthful, drinking well. Must have been a favourite of Hardy Rodenstock's too, for magnums were produced at his big wine events from 1994 to 1998. Good wine. No need to say more. *Last tasted Sept 1998* ★★★ *Will still be at peak.*

**Pol Roger, Extra Dry** Nearly 20 notes, mainly, but by no means all, at my own dinner parties. First, though, at Harry Waugh's Bordeaux Club dinner in January 1995: lively mousse, crisp, nutty, refined, good acidity. It was, however, upstaged by his '61 Dom Pérignon. Consistently good but also consistently noting that it could take more bottle age. My most recent note (none left now) still fairly pale and lively, with splendid flavour and length – and that crucial refinement, finesse. *Last tasted at Chippenham Lodge, Dec 1998* ★★★★

**Pol Roger, Blanc de Chardonnay** First tasted at home, April 1996: lovely flavour, perfect now, excellent acidity. Next 'Brut Chardonnay Blanc' – was this for the American market?: good, crisp, dry, at a Hollywood Wine Society dinner (March 1998). A month later, in Bordeaux: very dry, high acidity. *Last noted at Domaine de Chevalier, April 1998* ★★★ *Good but acidic and needs drinking.*

**Pol Roger, Cuvée Sir Winston Churchill** First noted in June 1997 at Louis Latour's bicentenary dinner at Ch de Clos Vougeot. Then, at ten years of age, at the Champagne Academy dinner. By 1999 one of the two '88s at the 25-wine blind tasting in Copenhagen and holding its own. Most recently, fully mature, in fact beginning to show its age in colour, straw gold, nose – rich 'old straw', and palate, powerful, nutty. *Last noted at the Oxford and Cambridge Club wine committee's dinner, April 2001* ★★★★ *Now–2000.*

**Pommery, Louise** Two recent notes. Dry, firm, needs time. *Last noted at a Champagne breakfast in Hamburg, March 2000* ★★★(★) *Say now–2008.*

**Roederer** A pleasant surprise and drinking beautifully prior to a III Form Club dinner: firm, stylish, good length. The sort of champagne which immediately stands out of the crowd. *Jan 2002* ★★★★ *Perfect now, will keep.*

**Salon** Salon do not produce their champagne every year. In fact, the '88 is only the 31st vintage in 76 years. They had a very good harvest at Mesnil in the Côte des Blancs (100% Chardonnay), all picked on 26 September. Two notes. It suits the vintage: perfect appearance, nose and palate. Trace of walnuts on the nose; dry, firm, excellent flavour, length and acidity. *Last noted at the opening reception of a wine event at the Hotel C Jacob, Hamburg* ★★★★(★) *Could do with another ten years.*

**Taittinger, Comtes de Champagne, Blanc de Blancs** Half a dozen notes, first tasted blind in December 1994, finding it strange and acidic. More recognisable the following year: palish, dry, refined. One of the top wines in another blind tasting of 27 de luxe champagnes in 1997 and getting fully into its stride the following year, its length and refinement noted again. *Last noted at the start of the extensive tutored tasting for* Vinum *magazine, Zurich, April 1998* ★★★(★) *should be perfect now and well into the present decade.*

**Veuve Clicquot** First tasted in July 1994: very pale; rather hard, its 70% Pinot noticeable; dry, excellent flavour and length, still with youthful acidity. Most recently, prior to the Swan Feast at Vintners' Hall. Still pale; not too dry, good flavour and length. Dependable as always. *Last noted Nov 2001* ★★★★ *Perfect for drinking now but will keep.*

**Veuve Clicquot, Grand Dame, Rosé** At the launch of the 1990, there was an interesting tasting of the components of the '88: the Le Mesnil Chardonnay was very fragrant, dry, good length, excellent flavour, very acidic, the Pinot Noir from Verzy very pale, just the slightest hint of pink from the Pinot, dry, firm, fuller body and more rounded than the Ay Pinot Noir which was very dry and steely. The Grande Dame *assemblage* C21 was fairly dry, with good flavour, length and dry finish and the final Rosé blend (*assemblage* C112) was more yellow than rosé, a pale amber gold; nice fruit and bottle age; dryish, firm, mouthfilling, a touch of hardness. As with claret, and vintage port for that matter, the whole was better than the individual parts. *All noted, in London, Jan 2000* ★★★

SOME OTHER '88S TASTED IN THE MID-1990S **Bollinger, Grande Année** needs time. *1996* ★★★★; **de Castellane** rich, mouthfilling. *1997* ★★★; **Gosset, Celebris, Brut** straw gold; distinctive, full flavour, good length. *1997* ★★★; **Heidsieck, Diamant Bleu, Rosé** dreary colour, dull, stodgy nose and taste, acidic. *1994 avoid*; **Jacquart, La Cuvée Nominée** fine mousse; buttery, positive; slightly sweet, good flavour. *Tasted blind 1997* ★★★★; **Lanson, Noble Cuvée** fragrant, appley; very positive, mouthfilling, good length but, on retasting, less than noble. *Tasted blind, 1997* ★★★ *(just)*; and **Perrier-Jouët** firm, good. *1995* ★★★(★)

# 1989 ★★★★

A large crop of very good wines. I must confess that, along with others, I initially over-estimated the quality of this vintage. Having reviewed my notes, I have marked '89 down slightly, from an euphoric 5 to 4 stars. These are rich wines for early drinking.

The growing season was not without its problems, though there were compensations. Severe frosts nipped budding vines, reportedly affecting 20% of Champagne's extensive vineyards. Flowering was interrupted by a cold spell, resulting in two crops and two harvests; one unusually early starting on 4 September, after the exceptionally hot summer; the second from 10 October. The net result was a hefty harvest of ripe grapes, producing some 274 million bottles.

My initial notes will be confined to '89s tasted since 1997.
**Bollinger, Grande Année** Just one note. Lovely wine. *Before dinner at Ch Canon La Gaffelière, St-Émilion, April 1998* ★★★★
**Henriot, Brut** At lunch in the cellars of Bouchard Père in Beaune soon after Joseph Henriot had bought the company: pale, lean and dry. A welcome refresher after tasting all the Bouchard *grands crus*. More recently, dining with neighbours: rich but acidic. *Last tasted Sept 1998* ★★★ *Probably at its best now.*
**Jacquesson, 'Signature'** Despite its relatively new reputation I found it hefty, with a touch of old apples on nose and taste (tasted blind, January 1997), and still not very

appealing, with a strange, smoky, old fungi nose and equally odd flavour. *Last noted July 1999.*
**Krug** Interestingly, Krug released the '89 before the '88, which was considered to be a slower starter with greater potential. First tasted at a Christie's boardroom lunch in November 1997, noticing Krug's basic *cépages*, Pinot Noir for body, Chardonnay for elegance, and Pinot Meunier 'charm and exotic notes'. The following year with *pâté de fois gras* at N K Yong's in Singapore: some of Krug's meaty style, a welterweight (medium-heavy). I scribbled 'frankly I was not too struck. Good length, interesting but lacks zing and finesse'. *Last tasted Jan 1998* ★★★★
**Lanson, Brut** Lively enough; quite good, some character, by no means great. *At a Saintsbury Club dinner, London, April 1999* ★★★ *Drink soon.*
**Bruno Paillard** Perhaps I have been brought up with only the original twelve *grande marque* houses in mind but, as in the case of the Jacquesson, I did not entirely take to this, noticing on both occasions (first in 1997) a rather deep yellow colour; meaty, hefty nose and, though very flavoury on the first occasion, marred by a touch of malty straw. *Last tasted Dec 1998* ★★? *Perhaps I had better adjust my sights.*
**Philipponnat, Grand Blanc Brut** Neither *grand*, nor *blanc*, nor *Brut*: a rich style of champagne with dough (bread) like nose and clumsy flavour. Showing some age. Queried its aftertaste. *At the Julius Bärr Bank tasting, Zurich, April 1998* ★★
**Pommery, Louise** Tasted blind in January 1997: bright, lively, flavoury, complete. Most recently, a disappointing bottle at the Champagne Academy dinner, lacking richness. *Last tasted May 2001* ★★
**Roederer, Cristal Brut** First noted in April 1997 at the 'Winefest' in Sarasota: surprisingly pale with very fine, pinhead bubbles; slightly crusty (bread), refined; medium-dry, firm, fine, long on palate, very good acidity. The following year, gaining colour, similar nose, good, mature flavour. *Last noted in Singapore, Jan 1998* ★★★★ *Well nigh perfect now but time in hand.*
**Taittinger, Comtes de Champagne, Blanc de Blancs** First noted in September 1997 during a break for supper in the middle of the Wolf/Weinart Cheval Blanc tasting. Perhaps it was the refreshing contrast; it went down well. The following autumn it was also showing well after a rather nondescript though clean and dry BYOB at Michael Le Marchant's: good colour, nose and flavour. Slightly sweeter than expected yet a touch hard on the finish. *Last tasted Oct 1998* ★★★(★) *Potentially good but not quite into its stride. Say now–2006.*
**Veuve Clicquot, Brut** Magnum. First noted in April 1997, the youngest vintage in Kaplan's Clicquot vertical: crusty bread-like nose; complete but 'will be more fulfilled in three to five years'. Four notes and three years later: beautifully opened up; perfect flavour and balance. *Last noted at the 136th meeting of the Saintsbury Club, London, April 2000* ★★★★ *Lovely now, will be good for another ten years.*
**Veuve Clicquot, La Grande Dame** Floral, lime blossom but tinny nose; dry, hard and distinctly acidic. Needs time (tasted blind, January 1997). The following year, preceding a marvellous dinner at Ch Mouton-Rothschild, opening up with excellent flavour and, from memory, more rounded than the '88. And a further year on, preceding Hal Lewis' Bacchus Installation dinner just noting good colour, weight and flavour. *Last tasted, with caviar and other distractions, in Memphis, Tennessee, Sept 1999* ★★★★ *A thoroughly satisfactory champagne with another 10 years of active life.*

**Veuve Clicquot, La Grande Dame, Rosé** Including 15% Pinot Noir from their Clos Colin. No discernible pink, more yellow, but a very attractive, fruity flavour, softer than the '88. *At Clicquot's in London, June 2000* ★★★

BRIEF NOTES ON SOME OTHER '89S TASTED IN THE MID-1990S **Ayala, Brut** curiously scented, slightly artificial nose; some sweetness, lightish style and weight, pleasant enough. *1994* ★★★; **Gosset, Grand Millésime** straw tinged; appley nose and flavour, medium-sweet, very positive, fully mature. *1997* ★★; **Lanson, Blanc de Blancs** frothy; very forthcoming yet a hard edge, needs time; positive, even assertive, still with youthful acidity. *1997* ★★(★); **Mumm, Cordon Rouge** two notes. Nothing special (*1990*) and I preferred their undated **Crémant de Cramant** *1997* ★; **Mumm, René Lalou** low-keyed, hard, with an immature, tinny, acidic edge. *1997* ★★; **Perrier-Jouët, Belle Époque** very attractive, presentation and wine. First tasted blind in December 1994 finding it pale, frothy, appealing but too sweet. Next (1996) *'Fleur du Champagne'* in magnums, excellent colour, nose and flavour. Blind again the following year, gaining colour; good fruit, slightly smoky nose; touch of sweetness noted again, but positive and flavoury. *Last tasted 1997* ★★★★ *probably at its best now*; and **Piper-Heidsieck** frothy; tinny; not up to vintage standard. *1998* ★★

# 1990 ★★★★★

An exceptional year, the third largest crop on record, nearly 330 million kilos of grapes producing the equivalent of 288 million bottles (1982 was 295 million, 1983 was 302 million bottles). This despite severe April frosts affecting 45% of the entire region, to some degree. Unsuitable weather during flowering, causing *coulure* and *millerandage*, extended the period from late May to early July. However, by mid-July it was apparent that not only were there large numbers of bunches but the grapes were big. Happily, the summer was hot and dry, causing a not infrequent phenomenon, a second flowering, making up 60% of the crop which was picked long after the first, early, harvest of Chardonnay (on 11 September and from the 24th for the Pinot Noir).

**Bollinger, Grande Année** Christian Bizot said this was a good year, not exceptional but, judging by over half a dozen notes over the past two years, I think he was being unduly modest. I, and the audience at the Wine Experience in New York, were able to taste the first release in November 1998. Pinot Noir 65%, fermentation in (old) oak and maturation in (old) *barriques*, seven years on lees. Palish yellow, very frothy; very fragrant; good flavour and length but austere, needing bottle ageing. In March 1999, I gave it my highest mark of the 25 top champagnes at the *Smag & Behag* blind tasting in Copenhagen; and treated the family to it that Christmas. Two notes the following year, the most recent a magnum at a dinner at Rosebank with the Brounsteins (from Diamond Creek in the Napa) and other friends: fine bubbles; full, nutty bouquet; mouthfillingly rich, wonderful flavour, length and acidity. *Last tasted Nov 2000* ★★★★★ *A well-nigh perfect wine with another ten years to go.*

**Delbeck** This very old champagne house, well known in England around the turn of the 19th century, has taken on a new lease of life, and my son imports it into the USA. So he dutifully provided me with a few cases for my 70th birthday, and I reciprocated, recently, for his 40th, conveniently dating

my first and last note. First at Vintners' Hall, May 1997: pale, lazy bubbles; good nose, touch of vanilla and lemon; dry enough, good flavour, and acidity. *Last noted at Brooks's Club, Jan 2002* ★★★ *Possibly 4 stars with more bottle age.*

**Dom Pérignon** First noted in September 1997 at a Hallwag press conference to celebrate the one-millionth copy of the *Kleine Johnson*, Hugh's annual pocket book, and, with Hubrecht Duijker, the excellent – though I say so myself (I had a hand in it) – *Weinatlas Bordeaux*. The Dom Pérignon suitably honoured the occasion. A lovely wine, unusually rich. Most recently, a magnum welcoming seven guests at Wilf Jaeger's hilltop house south of San Francisco Bay prior to his Romanée-Conti tasting: pale; elegant; noted as 'dry', crisp, very good length, lemon and with smoky aftertaste. *Last tasted March 2002* ★★★★★

**Dom Ruinart, Blanc de Blancs** Dom Pérignon, the better known Dom (also under the LVMH umbrella), is a hard act to follow. Just two notes: three ticks in 1998. A couple of months later: pale, lively, the statutory small bubbles; nose a bit 'stewed', someone mentioned quince; dry, full-bodied (for a Blancs) good length but unexciting flavour. *Last noted at the Decanter magazine Vintage dinner, Nov 1998* ★★★

**Pol Roger, Brut** Many notes, first in June 1997, most memorably, visiting Odette Pol Roger in her elegant home, crammed with memorabilia, opposite the Christian Pol Rogers' in Épernay. I felt like a moonstruck schoolboy hoping to become a disciple. Several notes since. In October 2000 before a Saintsbury Club dinner: bubbles now somewhat subdued; lovely bouquet and flavour, rich, mouthfilling, perfectly mature. *Last tasted at home, Aug 2001* ★★★★ *Will keep.*

**Pol Roger, Brut Chardonnay** At a tasting I conducted in Los Angeles in March 1999: lovely colour, with a gentle, steady, column of bubbles; the epitome of elegance, but still with youthful acidity. Next, the same month, same label, in Copenhagen: more yellow; crusty, fragrant, classic walnuts nose; a high mark. Two months later, this time in London: well nigh perfect. Refined. *Last noted May 1999* ★★★(★) *More to come.*

**Pol Roger, Cuvée Sir Winston Churchill** I think this is worth the extra. First noted on the Pol Roger stand at Vinexpo in June 1999: refined; length, subtlety. Incidentally, Danielle and Christian Pol Roger invariably man their own stand, and it makes all the difference. Also, at most of the earlier Vinexpos, the Christie's stand was adjacent – so we were plied with Pol! Most recently, in magnums, introducing Hubert de Billy, Christian Pol Roger's nephew, at the Primum Familiae Vini presentation at Vinopolis. Went down well. *Last noted Nov 2000* ★★★(★) *More to come.*

## Coulure

*A condition whereby grape bunches fail to set properly. Newly formed berries fall off the vine soon after flowering. To some extent this is a natural regulatory function by which the plant rids itself of the berries it has insufficient carbohydrate reserves to ripen. But more harmful effects are felt in marginal areas of vine growth (such as Champagne) where lower rates of photosynthesis in poor weather conditions – and years of little sunshine – mean the vine is less able to create the energy reserves it needs. Without these reserves it becomes susceptible to coulure and fruit loss. Highly fertile, or excessively fertilised soils also result in coulure as they generate imbalance, the vine putting its energy into leaf-growth instead of fruit formation.*

**Salon** Two notes: pale, lively; somewhat idiosyncratic nose, straw and old mushrooms, good though (June 2001). Next, served the first evening prior to Wilf Jaeger's unprecedented rare burgundy dinner: pale, good colour for age, sauntering bubbles; light, fragrant. Characteristic fresh walnuts bouquet; subtle, perfect yet understated. Elegant. Great finesse. *Last tasted in San Francisco, March 2002* ★★★★

**Veuve Clicquot, Brut** I have many notes, not the least because I bought a case or two from Justerini & Brooks and still have quite a few bottles to keep me going. First tasted, or rather, lunching at Grand Mouton with Hervé Berland: very impressive. I gave it 3 stars for drinking, 5 for future maturity. My second highest mark at the *Smag & Behag* blind tasting in Copenhagen in 1999. Several notes but only a year later, continuing its evolution and immaculately preceding a dinner at home to which Paolo Pong had donated four top-growth '64 clarets. My most recent note, but happily not my last bottle: simply, unquestionably, good. Daphne and I quaffed it by ourselves. *Last noted March 2002* ★★★★★ *Perfect now and could probably see me out.*

**Veuve Clicquot, La Grande Dame** Why pay so much extra for Clicquot's de luxe brand when their Brut is so good? In fact, I gave it a far lower mark at the blind tasting in Copenhagen in 1999. A matter of style: it was more meaty, even appley (acidity) and a bit too sweet. Two subsequent notes. Most recently: pale, refined; superb nose and flavour, this time recording it as 'dry', with good length. *Last tasted in the Dairy at Waddesden Manor, Buckinghamshire, Oct 2000* ★★★★

**Veuve Clicquot, Rosé** Pinker and more frothy than the '89. Perfect for an actress's slipper. An immediate impact (as she took it off?), crisp, good fruit. *Last tasted March 2002* ★★★★★

SOME OTHER '90S TASTED IN THE LATE 1990S **Ayala** *1997* ★★★; **Delamotte, Grand Cru, Blanc de Blancs** champagne house best known a century ago. A good aperitif *1999* ★★★; **Jacquesson, Brut** nothing special ★★; but the **Rosé** was pale pink and quite attractive ★★★ *Both in Memphis, Sept 1999;* **Lanson** to toast the winners of the Lanson Awards. It rose to this sparkling occasion, held at Christie's South Kensington. *1998* ★★★; **Laurent-Perrier, Grand Siècle** good wine. *1997* ★★★★; **Mailly, Grand Cru** full, stylish, mature for age. *1999* ★★★; **Moët & Chandon, Brut Impérial** magnum. *1996* ★★★; and **Piper-Heidsieck** two notes. Unimpressive. *1998* ★★

# 1991 ★★

An abundant vintage of light wines with low acidity levels which were suitable to top up non-vintage stocks during a period of recession which had caused a huge drop in sales worldwide. The problems caused by the failure in 1990 of the growers and *négociants* to renew their joint long term agreements were exacerbated by both the poor market and large crop. Both sides had to review their positions. For the overseas trade and their consumers, the much purchased '90s provided a useful buffer.

Had it not been for the recession, this might have been a vintage year for the growing conditions were not all that bad, even taking into account two damaging spring frosts and a late and uneven flowering. The summer was hot and, until the weather deteriorated suddenly on 21 September causing rot, the rain helped swell the ripe grapes. The harvest eventually got under way when the sun returned on the 30th.

**Pommery** Pale with a faint green tinge, fine mousse; surprisingly good nose, fragrant, crusty (bread), whiff of walnuts; dry, refined, good length and acidity. *At a Pommery champagne dinner in San Juan, Puerto Rico, Nov 1998* ★★★

**Roederer, Brut Rosé** *Pelure d'oignon* colour, not pink; charred character; medium-dry, good length, finish and acidity. *At a trade tasting, Jan 1997* ★★(★)

# 1992 up to ★★★★

A healthy abundant crop, following very favourable growing conditions. Following a spate of disappointing champagnes being released on to the market, the main preoccupation in 1992 was the implementation of new self-regulatory measures to control quality. This was *force majeure* on the part of the growers and champagne houses, for champagne had reeled from some sustained criticism, much of it emanating from the British press and wine journalists.

Despite the quality of the wine, the market was not in a position to take advantage. Even allowing for the fact that it is not my job to taste a wide range critically, few '92s have come my way. Though these by no means represent the whole spectrum, their quality is a pointer. Judging merely from five wines, it is clear to me that those top houses who made a small quantity of high quality wine by dint of very severe selection succeeded, while the larger companies who find such processes uneconomical did not.

**Bollinger, Grande Année** Introduced at the annual Champagne Academy dinner: pale, good mousse; very good bouquet; crisp, high quality and a good finish. It was explained to us that this was by dint of severe grape selection. I think of all Bollinger's various champagnes, Grande Année is my favourite. *Last tasted May 2001* ★★★★

**Dom Pérignon** Not sure where this came from but served in August 1999 before a Sunday lunch, trying it out in three types of champagne flutes. Without going into details, they resulted in slight to distinct differences of liveliness, nose and even apparent acidity. On the whole, it showed well: lively, nutty fragrance, good length and finish. Three months later, noted at the American Club in Tokyo: very pale; shade of lemon-like acidity; firm, with a touch of sweetness to temper its steeliness. I gave it exactly the same rating. *Last tasted in Nov 1999* ★★★(★) *Probably at its best now.*

**Charles Heidsieck, Brut Réserve, mis en cave 1992** Not, strictly speaking, a '92, but their standard non-vintage disgorged in 1992. This was the first champagne labelled with the date of the *mis en cave* and was based on the 1991 Brut Réserve. The labelling also solves the problem of how to know the actual age of a non-vintage champagne, because the labels normally give no indication. It is common knowledge that the better non-vintage champagnes, Roederer for example, benefit from further bottle-ageing. The problem is that one does not normally know, even at the time of purchase, how old the wine is. Charles Heidsieck's new move solves this problem. Incidentally, at the Copenhagen blind tasting, it showed well, one of my highest marks, even in the company of top vintages of de luxe quality. *March 1999* ★★★★

**Moët & Chandon** First noted at the Winefest in Sarasota in April 1997, and fairly impressive. But alongside rather better wines at the Champagne Academy pre-dinner tasting, I found it disappointing. Hollow. *Last tasted May 2001* ★★

**Perrier-Jouët, Brut Millésime** Pale, positively anaemic; little nose; dry, lean, unimpressive. *May 1999* ★

**Pommery, Brut** Pale, fine mousse; good nose, flavour and length. Some finesse. *Noted at the always well-organised Champagne Academy dinner, May 2002* ★★★ *(It is noticeable that the chefs always make a special effort at these annual events.)*

# 1993 ★★★

Despite totally different growing conditions, much the same outcome as 1992: one or two champagne houses, by dint of selection, made some good wine. Most could not.

The season had been largely favourable – there were no spring frosts, localised hail in May which was otherwise hot; almost tropical in June encouraging rapid growth and an early and extremely speedy flowering around the 2nd. Some rain in July but, just before the harvest, torrential and incessant rain set in. The problem was rot and widespread dilution.

**Deutz, Blanc de Blancs** Pale, fine mousse; quite pleasant flavour, its sweetness masking acidity. A stylish wine. A good mark. *Tasted blind in Copenhagen, March 1999* ★★★

**Charles Heidsieck, Brut Réserve, mis en cave 1993** (see Charles Heidsieck 1992 above). Not a straight vintage champagne, just the disgorgement date. Frothy, slightly sweet, positive but acidic. *Moderate marks at the Copenhagen tasting, March 1999* ★★

**Dom Pérignon** Palish, lively; pleasing flavour, very good length and acidity. *On UA 955 London to San Francisco, June 2001* ★★★★ *(To attend, as guest auctioneer, the 20th Napa Valley Wine auction – now more like a fairground and rather different from the sober fund-raising auctions all those years ago.)*

**Dom Ruinart** Lively; surprisingly good nose and flavour. *Lunch at Paveil de Luze, June 2001* ★★★

**Pol Roger, Blanc de Chardonnay** Produced rather unexpectedly before dinner at Scharzhof by the Egon Müllers, father and son, the day they were presented with the Lifetime Achievement Award of the Bacchus Society of America. Egon senior was very ill and, sadly, died not long after; but to everyone's delight, Egon junior, once thought to be a dyed-in-the-wool bachelor, introduced his young bride. Not long after that, a son was born to perpetuate the Müller name. The Pol Chardonnay was very welcome, but it is the Müller family and their Scharzhofberger wine that linger in the memory. *In the Saar Valley, May 2000* ★★★

**Pol Roger, Brut** Every year champagne producers and their agents push the boat out with a tasting in London of just about every brand, non-vintage and vintage available on the market. It is more like a beer garden. The wines are arranged in alphabetical order around the room (in this case, the historic, spectacular, Banqueting House in Whitehall), and by the time I had got to P, I was so fed up with tasting such a lot of below-standard champagnes that arriving at Pol Roger was like reaching an oasis in the desert. I rather recklessly ordered five cases of the '93 on the spot and am slightly regretting it. Despite my loyalty to the Pol Roger family, I think this is one of their weaker vintages: however, it does have some charm; infinitely quaffable. Either I am getting inured to it or it is improving with bottle age. Probably both. *Last tasted at Chippenham Lodge, Feb 2002* ★★★

**Roederer** High quality as always. (Champagne Academy 2001). Later that autumn, tasting the Pinot and Chardonnay blind after trying our hands, and palates, mixing our own '97s, the '93 had a spicy, fruity nose and managed to be round and sharp at the same time. *Last noted in Roederer's tasting room with Martine Larson, Sept 2001* ★★★

**Veuve Clicquot, La Grande Dame** Pale, lively, very good. Served by Comte Alexandre de Lur Saluces at a dinner in honour of the Bacchus Society of America. *At Ch d'Yquem, June 2001* ★★★

# 1994

As with the rest of France, rain again at harvest time dashed all hopes of a great vintage – for the run-up had been promising. Not a vintage year.

# 1995 ★★★★

At last a decent vintage after two very average years. Growing conditions were generally very favourable throughout the summer. There was some alarm when rain caused rot but ideal temperatures returned for an extended harvesting period. After careful selection, some good wines were made.

Some houses 'declared' their '95s in 1999 but most waited. Krug is not due to be presented until this book has gone to press. They should turn out well.

**Billecart, Blanc de Blancs** After an all-day session tasting vintages of Ch Margaux I really felt like an early night, but it would have been churlish to have turned down Manfred Wagner's invitation to dine. His guests were bussed from the Zürich airport Hilton to his home where we were refreshed by the Billecart. Lively; nose slightly metallic, with freshly peeled mushrooms; fairly dry, mouthfilling but very acidic. *On the lakeside at Pfäffikon, Switzerland, Nov 2000* ★★★

**Drappier, Carte d'Or, Brut** Pale and lively; good fruit; touch of sweetness, very attractive flavour, light acidic finish. *At an IWFS St James's Branch dinner at the Garrick Club, London, Jan 2000* ★★★(★) *Could do with another five years of bottle age.*

**Charles Heidsieck, Brut, Réserve, mis en cave 1995** Once again, as with the '93 and '92, not really a vintage wine. But to demonstrate how successful it was, I gave it one of my top marks at the *Smag & Behag* blind tasting of mainly de luxe vintages. Good colour, steady stream of bubbles; fresh, whiff of vanilla and walnut; medium-dry, distinctive, elegant. *In Copenhagen, March 1999* ★★★★

**Perrier-Jouët, Belle Époque** A jeroboam at a Bacchus Society dinner en route to the Mosel: very pale, very fine bubbles; very dry, steely yet light style. The size of the bottle more impressive than its content. *At Dieter Kaufmann's famous Zur Traube restaurant at Grevenbröich, Switzerland, May 2000* ★★★

**Pol Roger, Blanc de Chardonnay** A most welcome glass with Christian Pol Roger at the crowded 'Grand Tastings' in New York. Pale, lively, refreshing. *Oct 2001* ★★★(★) *I shall look forward to cellaring some in due course.*

**'R' de Ruinart** Pale, fine mousse. Drinking well though time in hand. *May 2002* ★★★(★)

# 1996 (★★★★★)

Deemed to be a great vintage, even 'the vintage of the (20th) century'. Producers said that they had not seen the like since 1955; certainly, they said, quality surpassed the '85 and '90 vintages. Unlike so many vintages in the first half of the 1990s, the harvest was not spoiled by rain. In fact, quite the opposite. Heavy rain occurred in August but the perfect ripening conditions which followed in September saved the day.

There has been pressure to put this vintage on the market. We shall see. I can't wait.

## 1997 (★★★★)

Remarkable growing conditions and another successful year in Champagne: after an irregular start, there was perfect weather from August through to harvest time, which resulted in rot-free, healthy grapes with a high degree of ripeness. Another vintage of full rich wines to look forward to.

## 1998 (★★★★)?

Yet another successful vintage, in both quantity and quality. It was assumed that the volume produced would be well timed to top up depleted millennium stocks. In the event, the pre-millennium purchases were over-optimistic, leaving the trade with a post-millennium stock hangover.

## 1999 (★★★★)?

Yet another good – too good – vintage, for, as mentioned in relation to the 1998, it was initially regarded as a timely post-millennium top-up vintage. Whether the '99 will be a vintage year depends on the market, on the economy and, to a major extent, on stock levels. Quality, however, can, as always, be predicted by the success or otherwise of the growing season.

In 1999, the New Year was both warm and sunny; early spring was mild though late April was cooler and held back bud break. May was fine and dry, encouraging vigorous growth. There wer good conditions for flowering in mid-June. The second half of August and early September enjoyed marvellously sunny weather, enabling the grapes to mature quickly and healthily. A potential vintage champagne.

## 2000–2001

The first vintages of the new century opened to mixed feelings. Roughly the equivalent of a year's production had been oversold, resulting in large post-millennium stocks. The outrage of 11 September 2001 had an immediate effect on sales, particularly, of course, in the USA.

'Champagne' has a lustrous ring to it. Its image is something even the best sparkling wines can never emulate. Superficially, the lower-priced sparkling wines made outside the region, however well made some of them they may be, will not only lack the cachet of the champagne name but also the quality – as long as quality is strictly controlled and maintained in Champagne itself. Merely to grow suitable grapes, particularly Pinot Noir and Chardonnay, the two main champagne grapes, to ferment them, induce secondary fermentation in the bottle to produce 'fizz', can result in a passable, enjoyable, even rather good, sparkling wine. But it will never be champagne; it cannot compete with the same principal grape components grown on Champagne's sweeping vistas and vine clad slopes. Above all, the secret is in the blending. And as long as quality is maintained, Champagne's future is assured. I am an eternal optimist.

On what basis, leaving aside price, do we choose one brand over another? A tangled mixture of brand recognition and loyalty comes pretty near the top; how and by whom promoted, a perception of style and quality, the occasion, of course, and the budget and image required. Fashion and prejudices play a leading role. These were brought home to me every time I attended British Airways' blind tastings. Each was interesting, often a revelation, but I particularly looked forward to the champagne (and port) tastings to see, when all was revealed, if my tasting note tied up with my preconceptions of a brand. It was not a game to identify the name, which is perhaps as well as I would not have scored highly. But I was shaken when my unflattering description – strange and scented – turned out to be my long-time favourite non-vintage champagne. Nevertheless, prejudices persist, and mine can be quite easily gleaned from my notes.

Though this chapter is about vintage champagne I am only too aware that non-vintage blends are the motor of the champagne trade. I have my prejudices here too, but as a regular and long-time non-vintage drinker, I think it is not only worth buying the best but – if you have the means and strength of will to give the wine three or four years bottle age. And enjoy it!

## 2000 ?

I will start with the growing conditions for, as always, these are the prelude to the quality and quantity of production.

Winter and spring were mild and wet; May and June were sunny, with the vital flowering stage satisfactory. July was variable; August made a good ripening start but September was the wettest on record with twice the normal rain causing rot problems. The yield was large and quality diluted. It is unlikely to be a vintage year.

## 2001 ?

Champagne experienced the wettest harvest in over a century. Reports are that the crop was huge but quality, unsurprisingly, mediocre. Only growers who had the incentive and means to engage in rigorous selection will have made decent wine. It is very unlikely to be shipped as a vintage year; nor does the overstocked market need it.

# Vintage Port

Portuguese wine was exported to England as long ago as the 12th century, and the Treaty of Windsor, in 1386, consolidated trade between the two countries. Port, as we know it, began life in the late 17th–early 18th century. The trade was often three-cornered: wool shipped from the West Country to Newfoundland, thence cod to the north of Portugal and wine from there to the many ports around the British Isles.

Precisely when port was first 'fortified' has not been firmly established. It is possible that grape brandy was added to shipments of table wine to add strength and stabilise them for the journey by sea. Until well into the 18th century, the wine was probably dry, not sweet. Someone then had the idea of adding brandy to fortify the wine for the sea journey, and – at some unknown later date – of adding it part way through the fermentation, which inhibited the yeasts and resulted in unfermented residual grape sugar. This procedure has been followed ever since. With the exception of dry white ports, it is safe to say that all port is red, strong and sweet.

Some of the well-known port houses were founded in the 17th century, including Taylor which celebrated its tercentenary in 1991, Warre, circa 1670, Croft 1678 and Kopke. The trade was greatly assisted by the Methuen Treaty of 1703 which encouraged shipments from the Iberian peninsula at the expense of the French, the latter's wines being penalised by much heavier import duties; an unfair discrimination that was only remedied by Gladstone in the 1860s.

The shipments of port in the 18th century were colossal and matched by the consumption of 'three bottle' men. Most port shipped in cask was generic, and bottled by wine merchants or privately by butlers in grand houses, its price 'per pipe' indicating its quality. Vintage port, as opposed to 'wood port', ruby or tawny, made its first documented appearance in the middle of that century, the first vintage to appear in a Christie's wine catalogue being the 1765 in 1773.

Vintage port, until recently, tended to be associated with English gentlemen with whiskers and gout, with gentlemen's clubs, and with Stilton; a wine which was, and still is, used to toast the reigning monarch – after which smoking was/is permitted. North America, to our chagrin, has overtaken us. There it is not associated with fuddy duddies and ancient traditions but is regarded more as a dessert wine. I asked my son, whose import company specialises in port, why so much young vintage port was now being consumed in the States? It goes well with chocolate puddings was the answer.

Despite vicissitudes, it is still a wonderful drink.

---

### Vintage and wood port

There are two basic types of port, one is matured in bottle, the other solely in cask or vat. All wine is born – grapes grown, harvested, fermented – in a given year, but in relation to port, 'vintage' has a specific meaning: it represents the tip of the port iceberg, a wine of high quality made in an exceptionally good year, bottled after two years in cask and cellared for further maturation.

Apart from some more, sometimes confusingly, dated ports (see box page 479) all other ports, known in the trade as wood ports, are blended and subdivided into 'ruby' and 'tawny', the latter maturing for longer in cask or vat. Both types are bottled ready for drinking,

the price depending on intrinsic quality and length of maturation. Neither benefits from further ageing in bottle. However, I might add that I regard a fine old tawny as one of the supreme expressions of port and, apart from vintage port which I keep for dinner parties, it is my preferred drinking.

This chapter concentrates almost entirely on classic vintage port which until the early 1970s was mainly shipped in 'pipes' for bottling by wine merchants in the importing country. The name of the bottler, if known, is stated in my notes. Since 1970 Oporto bottling of vintage port has been mandatory, and as from 1997 all port.

# 19th century

Although George Sandeman, dining with the future Duke of Wellington in Torres Vedras in 1809, declared that the vintage 1797 was 'the finest port ever known', it was not until the 19th century that high quality port of a given vintage really came into its own. The Peninsular Campaign certainly had an influence, for the officers would surely have been accustomed to drinking it on mess nights and, after the Napoleonic wars, the famous London military clubs, the 'Senior' (United Services) and 'Junior' were established to continue the traditions. But then, as now, true vintage port, shipped in cask for bottling by UK merchants, was the tip of the iceberg. Another major factor was the availability of straight-sided bottles which enabled port to be binned horizontally until mature. Trade, as always, had its ups and downs but the really staggeringly huge shipments of the 18th century were rarely matched subsequently. Most, I dare say, were rough and ready ports for immediate consumption.

No vineyards are immune to pests and diseases and the Douro suffered severely from the two most serious: the first, in the early 1850s, the fungus oidium which affected quality. Hardly had the growers recovered from this blow, when along came phylloxera, a deadly aphid which attacks vine roots. This pest was first detected in 1868 and, by the late 1880s, had severely affected production in the Douro Valley.

Despite these problems, the 19th century was to see some of the greatest-ever port vintages (see the table below) starting with the 1811, the first of the famous 'comet' vintages (Halley's), the well-timed Waterloo vintage (1815), and perhaps the greatest of all, the 1847. Although most port was shipped by merchants for sale under their own name, the producers' names most familiar to us today first appeared in gentlemen's cellars during the first half of the century. Vintage port was here to stay. Some of my notes are relatively old, but a wine tasted when it was already a century and a half old will be in similar state today assuming, of course, it has been kept well and is in good condition.

## *Vintages at a Glance*
**Outstanding ★★★★★**
1811, 1834, 1847, 1863, 1870, 1878, 1884
**Very Good ★★★★**
1815, 1851, 1853, 1868, 1875, 1896, 1897
**Good ★★★**
1820, 1837, 1840, 1854, 1858, 1869, 1872, 1873, 1877, 1881, 1887, 1890, 1893, 1895

## 1811 ★★★★★

The famous 'Comet' vintage. Alas, I have no tasting notes.

## 1815 ★★★★

Referred to by the British as the Waterloo vintage.
**Ferreira** It is worth mentioning that Ferreira have an unmatched, indeed unique, 'library' of old vintages in their lodge in Vila Nova de Gaia. The two main reasons for the relatively large number of Ferreira wines appearing in my notes, quite apart from a long-standing friendship, is that they have generously donated old wines at charity auctions I have conducted and, more recently, have taken part in tastings for or on behalf of my son, Bartholomew, who happens to be the sole agent and importer of Ferreira's ports in the USA.

Aged in cask for about 50 years, bottled and then recorked every 50 years. (An old port takes two years to recover its bouquet after recorking.) A pale but healthy amber with lemon tinge; woody and acidic at first but settled down after decanting, rich, waxy, still with fruit, slightly estery, like old lace; medium-sweet, medium-light, a wonderful spicy yet soft long flavour, and madeira-like acidity; dry finish. *Four consistent notes, tasted between 1981 and July 1991* ★★★★

**Vesúvio, Qta do Ferreira** An old note but worth recalling. The oldest vintage tasted of the Ferreira family's most famous quinta. Bottled by Ferreira circa 1850 and with original faded old label. My note tallies with those above so probably the same wine. *Tasted May 1978* ★★★★
**Wenceslaus de Souza Guimaräes** Rare bottle, rare experience. Its nose cleared; good flavour – but *old!* At *Christie's Waterloo dinner, Sept 1976* ★★★

## 1820 ★★★

After many poor years, this good vintage was eagerly bought.
**Ferreira** Lovely bright pale amber; rich; high-toned, a bit varnishy; medium sweetness and body, soft, agreeable. *At a pre-sale tasting, April 1981* ★★★
**Shipper unknown** Although this is another old note it is perhaps worth mentioning because the bottle was stoppered with an early example of a fully branded cork (with vintage and, though indistinct, the name of the London bottler), and a reminder that until well into the middle of the 19th century, the (Oporto) shippers' names rarely appeared. Despite mid- to low-shoulder level the wine was not bad for its age. *Tasted July 1974* ★★

## 1834 ★★★★★

One of the most renowned port vintages of the mid-19th century.
**Ferreira** Last recorked 1980. Reputedly made from a single grape variety. Palish, a bit cloudy; high-toned; still sweet. *Tasted in a BBC recording studio for the* Today *programme, April 1981* ★★
**Roriz, Qta do** Kopke's Roriz, 'the giant of the vintage' but withered after a century and a half. *One of 13 bottles from a cellar in Wales, recorked in 1878. Bought at Christie's, tasted Dec 1983* ★

# 1837 ★★★

**Shipper unknown** One of the many remarkable old wines from the cellars at Fasque (see box, right). Original wax seal embossed '*Divie Robertson Port*' (the bottler), '*1837*' on the bin label. Unbranded cork. Pale, dried-out but holding on. *Tasted pre-sale, May 1972* ★

# 1840 ★★★

**Ferreira** Spicy (cloves); a rich wine with very good end acidity. *At a pre-sale tasting, April 1981* ★★★

# 1844

**J & C White & Co.** Pale and faded. *On the David Frost Show in New York, May 1972 (see below).*

---

## The *David Frost* show

*Unquestionably, one of the most embarrassing moments of my professional life. In New York for the annual Heublein wine auction promotions, I was invited to take part in the David Frost show. This was in 1972 and it was live television.*

*I was the last to be interviewed, the intention being for David and his other guests to gather round to sip a rare old vintage port, an English-bottled 1844. This was to take a couple of minutes. But, try as I might, I could not pull the cork which, over time, had become annealed to the neck of the bottle. Using a rather poor corkscrew to bore a hole through the middle of the cork was like root-canal treatment. In the end, I was reduced to sprinkling the wine, like vinegar over fish and chips, into the impatiently awaiting glasses. A shameful episode. (If ever I am faced with this situation again I shall remove the old cork beforehand and just go through the motions.)*

---

# 1847 ★★★★★

Unquestionably the greatest vintage of the period. Roughly 30,000 pipes shipped to England (a shipping pipe contained an average of 110 gallons/500 litres).

**Ferreira** Records show that this was Ferreira's sweetest wine of the century. Still very sweet, and perfectly balanced in 1990. Two more recent notes. Startlingly straw yellow; spicy, grapey, vanilla-like bouquet, slightly varnishy; medium-sweet, ethereal, touch of old straw. Remarkable for its age. *Last noted at Ferreira's pre-sale tasting, New York, Sept 1997* ★★★

# 1851 ★★★★

Prince Albert's Great Exhibition lent its name to this vintage. Very good though many tainted by mildew.

**Ferreira** Amber; fairly sweet and powerful. Marked acidity. *At a pre-sale tasting, April 1981* ★★★

**Stibbart** Tasted twice, one bottle with Freddie Cockburn who could not believe it wasn't a recent post-World War Two vintage despite the clearly embossed wax seal and bin label – and evidence that it had never been moved until my wife and I packed it in the Gladstone cellar at Fasque for the sale at Christie's in 1972. And next, when I recognised it, lunching at Christopher's in 1975. On both occasions, an amazingly deep colour; sound, fruity; sweet, rich, assertive flavour. Still the most

magnificent old port I have ever drunk. *Old notes, but worth recalling* ★★★★★

**Warre** A rather dubious dumpy bottle. Recorked. Dusty old nose, liquorice; not bad flavour and grip though drying out. *In Don Schliff's cellar near Los Angeles, March 1999.*

# 1853 ★★★★

**Hankey Bannister** One of three half bottles from the cellars of Kingston Lyle Park. Clearly rebottled, and with this Sackville Street wine merchant's embossed capsule. Warm amber, spicy scent; fairly sweet, its extract masking fairly high acidity. Its taste reminded me of a lovely old cognac. *Opened rather casually, not expecting much, in May 1988* ★★★★

# 1854 ★★★

Another good 'comet' vintage though only declared by four British shippers, Dow being one.

**Dow** The oldest vintage presented at Dow's bicentenary tasting. Palish, warm amber; meaty, tangy, tar-like nose of considerable depth which opened up fragrantly in the glass; medium sweetness, lean yet rich, good length and acidity. Cracking up. Yet a great treat. *Oct 1998* ★★★

**Ferreira** A cloudy bottle, still sweet, in the early 1980s. Most recently, the oldest of 'The World's Greatest Vintage Ports' at a tasting I conducted for The Hollywood Wine Society's 13th annual seminar in Florida. From Ferreira's cellar. Colour tawny yellow; nose pungent, slightly raisiny and varnishy; still sweet though with madeira-like tang and dry finish. *Last tasted Florida, March 1998* ★★★

# 1858 ★★★

**Chamisso** Capsule embossed '*Chamisso Oporto*'. Good level but short crumbly cork. Pale tawny, no red; high-toned, varnishy, old raisins; on the dry side, better flavour than nose, madeira-like acidity. Could have been an old white port. Interesting only. *From a Christie's client, March 1999.*

---

## The 1851 from Fasque

*Soon after inheriting Fasque, an estate near Montrose in Scotland, Sir William Gladstone Bt managed to find the lost key to the cellar and on opening it discovered a treasure trove of old wines. It transpired that it had never been opened after the third baronet had died in 1927 and the wines, mainly purchased and laid down by the first baronet, brother of the eminent Victorian Prime Minister William Gladstone, consisted of a large quantity of pre-phylloxera claret and even older madeira and port, including the rare 1851. It was quite clear to me that the wine had never been moved; preserved by the low temperature, an unvarying 8°C, and humidity it appeared to be in pristine condition.*

*Over a chilly Whit weekend in 1972, my wife and I, clad in layers of wool and heavy boots, packed up the wine. On arrival in London I extracted one or two sample bottles for cataloguing prior to sale at Christie's later that year. It included 1851 vintage port, bottled by Stibbart, its date, incidentally, clearly identified by the embossed wax capsule (I still have it in my office). It was astonishingly fresh, as described; indeed all the wines were in pristine condition. For range and quality the Fasque cellar was one of the finest ever sold at auction.*

**Ferreira** The first bottle maderised and acidic. The second, a month later: pale mahogany with green rim; sound, gentle, sweet, 'warm'. *Last noted pre-sale, April 1981. At best* ★★★★

## 1860

**Unknown shipper** Not very helpful notes on a couple of 1860s, both palish yellow with very heavy sediment, one acetic the other oxidised, both undrinkable. Which just goes to show you can't win them all; and best to avoid unknown 1860s. *Last tasted July 1997.*

## 1863 ★★★★★

A great vintage.
**Ferreira** Tasted three times, first at the Ferreira pre-sale tasting in 1981, nose a bit mushroomy, sweet, high acidity. In 1988, muscatel and lime bouquet. A lovely old wine, medium-sweet, holding well. Most recently in Ferreira's tasting room. Palish amber, apple-green rim; clearly cask-aged; very rich, high toned, tangy bouquet. Still sweet, powerful. Good length. Raisiny finish. *Last tasted March 1996* ★★★★
**Taylor** Pale; varnishy nose; still some sweetness and with good length but now thin, skeletal. *The oldest vintage at the Taylor tercentenary tasting in London, March 1992* ★★

## 1864, 1865 and 1867

The first two vintages not very good, but some passable wines made in 1867. None tasted.

## 1868 ★★★★

A great pre-phylloxera vintage. Generally declared, with the exception of Croft. Sandeman, 'the biggest ever' and 'very dry', considered the finest.
**Martinez** An old note. The only '68 tasted. Faded, drying out, yet retaining power. Acidic. *From the cellars of Sherborne Castle, Sept 1976* ★★★

## 1869 ★★★

'Total absence of quality' reported by Ridley's trade journal (1870). Shipped only by Croft. None tasted.

## 1870 ★★★★★

Made under most favourable circumstances though 'ravages of phylloxera noted – one quinta, whose production averaged 50 pipes in the mid-1840s, was reduced to 2 pipes in 1870' (*Ridley's Wine Trade Monthly*). Nineteen port houses declared and shipped this vintage, the greatest between 1863 and 1878.
**Cockburn** Dried-out, colour of old tawny. *Oct 1976*.
**Roriz** Perhaps the most renowned of all the old quintas of the Douro, the vineyard was planted in the early 18th century by a Scotsman, Robert Archibald, with wine cuttings from Burgundy he called Tinta de França, later known as Tinta Francisca or Francesa. From 1770 Roriz belonged to the Kopke family whose firm was founded in 1638. Old vintages are very rare. Wax seal embossed with name of bottler 'J Barrow & Sons, 1870 Roriz Port'. Good colour for age, healthy glow; no decay; drying out but lively. Nice finish. *Tasted over a century later, March 1972* ★★★★

**Taylor** Heavy bottle with pronounced old string course around the neck (string made it easier to knock the top off). Level top of neck – ideal for decapitating with the back of a heavy knife – short, unbranded cork. Pale, weak rim, no red left otherwise healthy appearance; exquisite bouquet, touch of liquorice; medium-sweet, remarkably good flavour, sustained by Taylor's backbone and alcohol. Dry finish. *At Jaeger's pre-phylloxera tasting in the hills south of San Francisco, June 2001* ★★★★
**Warre** Labelled 'Warre's 1870 Vintage Port matured, and bottled in 1918'. (An early LBV!) Yellow-tinged tawny; sweet, acetone-edged bouquet; very rich and spicy, but with a medicinal taste, a cross between cough mixture and *Punt è Mes. March 1985* ★★

## 1871

Spring cold and wet, oidium in the vineyards, August intensely hot, heavy rains during the harvest. Not declared.
**Loureiro, Qta de** *See* Serafim Cabral, below.
**Serafim Cabral** An old 'vintage tawny' that has made its appearance under several guises, as Quinta de Loureiro at Christie's in 1972, when I first tasted it, and twice, quite coincidentally, at recent dinners, both with the same label '*Hambledon Special Reserve / Serafim Cabral / imported by the House of Hambledon*' (a brewery in Yorkshire), cork branded '*Porto Cabral 1871*'. First at Jeremy Benson's, a magpie collector of oddities, vinous and otherwise, then at a dinner of the Oxford & Cambridge Club house committee. Pale tawny indicating many, possibly 50 years, in wood; slightly varnishy on the nose but still sweet and delicious. *Last tasted April 2001* ★★★★

## 1872 ★★★

Sixteen shippers. Not tasted but of good repute.

## 1873 ★★★

Shipped by 16 port houses. Only one tasted, **Meyer** drying out though still a good drink. *1972* ★★

## 1874 ★

After all the activity in 1870, 1872 and 1873, only three port houses shipped the 1874. None tasted.

## 1875 ★★★★

Eighteen shippers. Light, fine, elegant wines – as in Bordeaux – but small production. Five old notes made nearly a century after the vintage.
**Noval, Qta do** Very pale; fragrant; refined, great length. *Two consistent notes in the early 1970s* ★★★★

---

### Lot One, 11 October 1966

*I joined Christie's in the summer of 1966 to organise and head up a new specialised wine department. Our first sale was held in October 1966. Lot 1 consisted of six bottles of 1875 Cockburn port, which sold @ 1250 shillings per dozen (everything was offered 'per dozen', except odd bottles, then 'per lot'). The buyer was Peter (Lord) Palumbo who is mentioned frequently in the text. Before 1966, the international fine and rare wine market as we know it today did not exist. How times have changed!*

**Bell Rannie** Perth wine merchant's bottling for the Gladstone family. Lovely colour; touch of sourness; drying, faded, variable. *Three notes prior to the famous Fasque cellar sale in 1972. At best* ★★

# 1877 ★★★

**Ferreira** Good spicy bouquet and flavour, still sweet. Lovely aftertaste. *At a pre-sale tasting, April 1981* ★★★★

# 1878 ★★★★★

Twenty port houses declared and shipped. None tasted recently though I have six remarkably good notes from the mid-1960s to late 1970s, starting with a still powerful and punchy **Dow**: 'one of the best ports of the century' according to Saintsbury (*Notes on a Cellarbook*), two excellent **Cockburn**, a pale but phoenix-like **Martinez**, firm **Kopke**, and a powerful **Harvey's** bottling.

# 1880 ★★

Not a generally declared vintage. Only six shippers.

# 1881 ★★★

Optimistically declared by 20 port shippers but the vintage never lived up to expectations though Thompson & Croft (**Croft**) fragrant, ethereal and charming noted in the mid-1970s and **Martinho's Qta de São** with a fabulous racy flavour in the mid-1980s.

# 1882–1883

Sub-standard vintages. Not declared.

# 1884 ★★★★★

Twenty-one shippers got this right, but I am not sure that Charles Walter Berry did when he described it (in 1935) as 'the last of the classic vintages'. **Cockburn** was still excellent in the early 1970s.

# 1885 ★

Moderate. Only five shippers declared.

# 1886

Not declared.

# 1887 ★★★

Popular and good. Twenty port houses shipped the 1887 to celebrate Queen Victoria's Golden Jubilee. **Cockburn** and **Graham** still delicious in the early 1970s, and five remarkably drinkable English bottlings noted up to the early 1980s.
**Niepoort** Bottled 1897, decanted and re-bottled 1991: liquorice-scented; still fairly sweet, nutty taste, excellent acidity. *A half bottle from Rolf Niepoort enjoyed with lunch at Chippenham, Lodge, May 1992* ★★★★
**Sandeman** Four bottles memorably served at a *Great Vintage Wine Book* dinner: amber-coloured; high-toned liquorice

bouquet which opened up in our glasses; drying and faded but with good length. More importantly, still a good drink. *Provided by Tim and David Sandeman, in Zürich, Oct 1983* ★★★

# 1888–1889

Not declared.

# 1890 ★★★

Tough tannic wines. Twenty shippers. Four notes made in the early to late 1970s, including **Cockburn**, one attractive, one volatile; a refined and fragrant **Dow** bottled by Schofield (up until the 1950s the 'Fortnum & Mason' of Manchester) and a dusty and dried-out **Gilbey**.

# 1891–1892 ★

1891 not declared; 1892: ten shippers. None tasted.

# 1893 ★★★

Number of shippers unknown.
**Dow** Palish tawny, yellow rim; low-keyed but sound; drying out, gentle, faded, but otherwise in excellent condition. *Sept 1983* ★★★★
**Vinho do Porto** A couple of bottles brought in to taste, one labelled '*Vinho do Porto 1893*' with initials V F surmounted by a coronet. Both pale amber with apple-green rim; highish volatile acidity, with madeira-like tang. Yet surprisingly sweet and with good flavour. *From a private cellar in Portugal, Jan 1997* ★★★

---

### Cracking a bottle of port

*It is very difficult to extract a cork from a traditional port bottle in one piece. In order to avoid fiddling around with small pieces of cork broken up in the top of the bottle, a well-tried method is to remove the upper part of the neck altogether.*

*One way is to knock the top off with the back of a heavy knife (not a modern bread knife), the other, simpler, method is to use port tongs. Both have the prime aim of literally cracking the top off the bottle in order to remove it cleanly with the cork still in place. Port tongs work by introducing a sudden change of temperature that will crack the glass: stick the pincers into a fire or a really hot hob, then clamp them round the neck of the bottle for a few seconds to heat the glass; touch the neck with a cloth or a feather soaked in cold water. The neck will crack. Remove it carefully so as not to disturb any glass shards, then decant.*

*Not many people have a cutlass or sabre handy, but the finest performance I have witnessed in cracking a bottle of port was by an old friend, a retired colonel with an excellent cellar, who – quite unselfconsciously – at one of his wine dinners, held a bottle of old port in his left hand and, with his right hand briskly swept the back of a sword upwards, more or less parallel with its neck, catching the underside of the lip of the bottle and removing the neck at one stroke. The bottle received a bit of a jolt but the crust was firmly formed and there was no problem decanting.*

*In the office or at home I use either method, particularly if the bottle is unlabelled and the capsule is not embossed. Once the neck is off, I wrap it in newspaper and break it with a hammer to reveal the name and vintage branded on the cork.*

# 1894 ★★

Moderately good. Thirteen shippers.
**Sandeman** Three old notes. Variable: one musty and bitter, one thinning but good, the third sweet, rounded, lively and lovely. *All in 1966. At best* ★★★

# 1895 ★★★

Good but not declared, probably because the major shippers were aware of the greater potential of the 1896s.
**Niepoort** Bottled 1904. Decanted and recorked 1990. Another interesting half bottle given to me by my old friend Rolf Niepoort. Rich amber; lovely old bouquet, walnuts and muscatel raisins; sweet, clean, lovely flavour. *At Chippenham Lodge, Dec 1994* ★★★★

# 1896 ★★★★

A good, well-received vintage, declared by 24 shippers. Seventeen notes made over an extended period, the first in the autumn of 1952 (see Tuke Holdsworth, below).
**Cockburn** Tasted several times. Consistently good for its age. Pale but rich tawny – a better colour than the 1900; sweet, chocolate, liquorice-like bouquet; still some sweetness and considerable body. A rich and distinctly powerful wine. *Last tasted Feb 1990* ★★★★
**Dow** Remarkably deep for its age, more like a 1945; still sweet on nose and palate, a touch of singed raisins, good acidity, hot finish. *At the Dow bicentenary tasting, Oct 1998* ★★★★
**Eira Velha, Qta da** One of the oldest quintas in the Douro, a vineyard since 1588 and owned since 1809 by the Newman family, traders in wool and wine, established in Oporto in 1735. Confusingly, they traded as Hunt, Roope, their vintage port from Eira Velha being shipped as Tuke Holdsworth.

Two magnums from the Newman family cellars in Devon, and probably the same stock as the magnums of Tuke '96 tasted in 1952 and 1968. At 84 years of age, both had a palish but healthy appearance. The first had a sweet, old, spirity nose, a whiff of mushroom; plummy, peppery but some decay. The second had a soft sweet bouquet with a touch of hardness and spirit lurking beneath. Drying out, lighter than the other magnum, faded but sound. *Both tasted Oct 1980* ★★
**Taylor** Lead capsule embossed '*Skinner & Rook*' (the bottler). Pale, rosehip orange; light, peppery at first, opened up richly,

and after an hour, scented, glorious; still surprisingly sweet, lean yet with good fruit and texture, elegant, excellent acidity. *From Barney Rhodes' cellar, April 1991* ★★★★★
**Tuke Holdsworth** A very old note included because, for me, it is very nostalgic.

Having abandoned my lengthy architectural studies, in September 1952 I joined Laytons Wine Merchants as a trainee (see box page 54). Tommy Layton was an eccentric one-man band and in November 1952 his Circle of Wine Tasters enjoyed a somewhat premature Christmas dinner at which Tuke 1896 was served, a magnum from the Newman family's cellars (see Eira Velha, above). Alas – I quote from the first of my little red tasting books: 'Disappointing. Thin, almost over its life span. Drinkable and pleasant but not unforgettable'. The backup bottle was Croft 1920! Another magnum, in 1967, was rich and holding well. (The same wine and same provenance as the Eira Velha magnums tasted in 1980.) *At best* ★★★

OTHER 1896s, NOT TASTED RECENTLY **Croft** autumnal, fragrant, flavoury. *1984;* **Sandeman** variable, from grubby and yeasty to good. *1967–1982;* and two quite good English bottlings, **Skinner & Rook**, **Hunter & Oliver** and an astringent 'unknown shipper'.

# 1897 ★★★★

Following hard on the heels of the heavily marketed '96, the '97 vintage, though very good, had to take a back seat. Only seven loyal port houses shipped the Queen Victoria Diamond Jubilee vintage.
**Sandeman** Following the prolific 1896 vintage, there was a shortage of brandy to make the '97. Sandeman, in desperation, used Scotch whisky. A tregnum (three-bottle bottle) from Tim Sandeman's cellar was magnificent in 1976, one of the best ports I have ever drunk. The whisky not noticeable!

More recently, from a rather odd-looking bottle with '*Sandeman*' embossed on a raised tablet: still a touch of ruby; sound, meaty but madeira-like nose; medium-sweet, full-bodied, rich, fruity with a strong, tangy finish. *Last tasted Sept 1987. At best* ★★★★★

# 1898–1899

The first year not declared and the second by only one shipper. In any case, the market was saturated and palates sated.

---

## Some of the best traditional British port bottlers

**Army & Navy Cooperative Society** (later, A & N Stores, London)
**Averys** (Bristol)
**Bell Rannie** (Perth)
**Block Fearon Block** (London)
**Block, Grey and Block** (London)
**Christopher** (London)
**Churton** (Liverpool)
**Cobbold** (Ipswich)
**Corney & Barrow** (London)
**Divie Robertson** (Edinburgh?)
**Fearon, Block, Ridges, Routh** (London)

**Grantham** (Sherborne)
**Hankey Bannister** (London)
**Harveys** (Bristol)
**Hawkers** (Plymouth)
**Hay & Son** (Sheffield)
**Hill Thompson** (Leith)
**Hunter, A & E** (Bury St Edmunds)
**Hunter & Oliver**
**IECWS** (London)
**Justerini & Brooks** (London)
**Lupton** (Bradford)
**Muirhead** (Scotland)
**Arnold Perret** (Gloucester)

**Rigby & Evans** (Liverpool)
**C A Rookes** (Stratford-on-Avon)
**Sarson** (Leicester)
**Schofield** (Manchester)
**H & E Selby** (Leeds?)
**David Sandemann** (Glasgow)
**Skinner & Rook** (Leicester)
**Stallard** (Worcester)
**Stibbart** (?)
**Wm Smith** (Bishop's Stortford)

# 1900—1929

$A$s you can see from the table below, and from my notes, this was a wonderful period for port in terms of both quality and sales. Port vintages are relatively easy to remember and the three decades in question open with a splendid quartet of classic vintages at four year intervals. World War One intervened but after starting modestly with the 1919, shipments and sales rose to a crescendo in the 1920s, culminating in the hugely successful 1927 which coincided with the height of the port market and also signalled the end of an era.

### Vintages at a Glance
**Outstanding** ★★★★★
1900, 1908, 1912, 1927
**Very Good** ★★★★
1904, 1920, 1924
**Good** ★★★
1910, 1911, 1917, 1922

## 1900 ★★★★★

The first of four classic vintages declared, rather conveniently spaced, at four-year intervals. Twenty-two shippers.
**Cockburn** In 1966 Wyndham Fletcher, then managing director, said that this was 'the greatest gentleman' Cockburn ever shipped. Tasted once, 80 years after it was bottled. Sweet, vinous bouquet that held well. Palate drying out, elegant, very nice texture, complete and sound. *Tasted March 1982* ★★★★
**Dow** Pale but with a healthy glow; curiously dried-out nose though richly sustained with a hint of liquorice; still very sweet though thinning, with a chocolate flavour and good acidity. *At the Dow bicentenary tasting, Oct 1998* ★★★
**Niepoort** A Colheita, matured in wood, put into demijohns in 1955 and finally bottled in 1972. The colour of a good old 'vintage tawny'; madeira-like; sweet, showing age yet fleshy. *Tasted March 1988* ★★★
**Noval, Qta do** Also late-bottled (*circa* 1940). Palish amber; high-toned, varnishy, fragrant, spicy; still sweet, with good raisiny flavour, excellent depth and aftertaste. High strength and high acidity. *At a Noval tasting at the Portuguese Embassy, London, Nov 1989* ★★★
**Warre** Palish, 'warm', light yellow rim; sweet, fragrant, touch of caramel, fig; drying out a little, lean and spirity but delicious old flavour and good length. *At the Symington tasting in London, May 2002* ★★★★

**OLDER NOTES Croft** sweet, silky. *1966–1982*; **Ferreira** rich, 'plummy'. *1981* ★★★; **Rebello Valente** spirity, but sound. *1971* ★★★; and **Smith Woodhouse** fading gently, complete. *1968–69* ★★★

## 1901—1902

Not shipped as vintage wines.

## 1903

Not generally declared.
**González Byass** Possible Roriz. Bottled in Oporto, 1906. Old note. Avoid. *From the shipper's cellar, Nov 1980. This sherry firm diversified into port in 1896 and secured exclusive marketing rights for Roriz from 1901.*

## 1904 ★★★★

Twenty-five shippers. Though reckoned at the time to be a lighter vintage than 1900, the wines have kept very well.
**Cockburn** Due to the shortage of local brandy, Cockburn used brandy from the Azores for their '04. Tasted twice, old but firm in 1972. A decade later, an Army & Navy Co-operative Society bottling: slightly varnishy nose, brandy laid bare; medium-sweet, elegant, clean, dry finish. *Last tasted March 1982. Could still warrant* ★★★
**Taylor** First tasted in 1974. Excellent level though original cork disintegrated. Very little red; sweet and dusty bouquet, restrained though ethereal; palate sweet, lightish though with a powerful, spirity, dry finish. Sound. Fragrant. *Last noted at Taylor's tercentenary tasting in London, April 1991* ★★★★

**OTHERS LAST NOTED IN THE 1980S Martinez** very pale, fruitless yet rich. *1982* ★★★; **Sandeman** several notes, all good *1985* ★★★★; **Smith Woodhouse** pale, fragrant, powerful. *1984* ★★★★; and five 'shippers unknown' English bottlings, fading but all interesting and very drinkable, from ★★ to ★★★

## 1905

Not declared. None tasted.

## 1906

Not declared though some eventually bottled as vintage.

## 1907

**Terra Feita, Qta da** An obscure Taylor quinta. Old tawny; slightly varnishy nose but still sweet, refined, with a nutty taste. *At a Mentzendorf trade tasting, Feb 1996* ★★

## 1908 ★★★★★

Great vintage, 26 shippers. Early harvest, high must weights.
**Cockburn** Arguably the greatest-ever Cockburn. Tasted several times. At a pre-sale tasting in 1984, one bottled by Skinner & Rook, level just below top-shoulder: palish, orange-tinged, appealing; fragrant, sultana-like, a whiff like turpentine giving away its age; still fairly sweet, assertive, powerful. Most recently, from an old three-part, moulded bottle, top of lead capsule embossed 'Cockburn's 1908 Port', fully branded cork, level top-shoulder. Palish ruddy-hued old tawny; good fruit, touch of mint and liquorice, fully opened out after 40 minutes, sweet, slightly raisiny, glorious, and still excellent the next day. Medium-sweet, full-bodied, very rich, good texture. A very assertive heavyweight, yet ethereal, cognac-like, fabulous flavour. *Last tasted at home, Nov 1990* ★★★★★

**Croft** Four consistently good notes, the first (in 1972) and the fourth, coincidentally, from the same stock. Most recently, a bottle, also coincidentally, bought by Dr John Trotter from me when I was in charge at Harvey's in Manchester and opened to celebrate his 70th birthday. The port had decanted bright (through a matron's silk stocking!) and still had a lovely colour; a touch of age, old liquorice, on the nose; still sweet and fleshy though fading, with a good, dry, somewhat peppery finish. *Last tasted at Wadham College, Oxford, March 1990* ★★★★

**Dow** First tasted in 1971: faded but not decayed. Next in 1990, a bottle originally purchased as an 'Unknown (shipper) '08'. Wax seal crisply and delicately impressed '*Hill Thompson, PORT 1908, Edinburgh*'. Having knocked off and broken the neck to retain the cork in one piece I found it clearly branded '*DOW'S Vintage 1908 bottled 1910*'. The level had been good, well into the neck but the colour was pale, rosy-hued. The nose when first poured smelled of old cork, a bit mushroomy. It remained restrained, low-keyed. Medium sweetness and weight, elegant, very flavoury, good length but with a distinctly dry finish. Another, identical, a year later. Most recently at the Dow bicentenary tasting: positively warm tawny; very good, rich, classic bouquet; very sweet, full body, flavour and grip. Marvellous texture. Hot spicy finish. *Last tasted Oct 1998* ★★★★★

**Ferreira** Rich and lovely in 1981. Eight years later: warm tawny; still sweet, delicious bouquet and flavour. Labelled, old wax seal and original cork, level upper mid-shoulder: palish tawny, lime-tinged rim; high-toned bouquet that reminded me of burnt sealing wax; still sweet, an interesting old taste with dry, peppery, acidic finish. *Last noted dining at home with my son, Bartholomew, Ferreira's agent in the USA. Jan 2002. At best* ★★★★

**Graham** Very good in 1967. More recently an excellent warm ruddy colour; glorious bouquet, spicy, fine brandy; drying out a little, not fleshy but with great length, excellent finish. *Last tasted 1985* ★★★★★

**Offley Boa Vista** Several bottles tasted between 1984 and 1990, all fairly consistent, sound but with varying overtones of age. Two recent notes, both recorked in April 1987 by Whitwhams, the Altrincham wine merchants who specialise in recorking. Original bottles, one heavy, mould-blown, the other a three-part moulded bottle of the period. Both had a warm but palish tawny colour; hard, dried-out nose but still sweet with very good length and lovely warm smoky finish. Highly enjoyable. Both opened at home. *At lunch in May 1997 and dinner in Jan 1999* ★★★

---

## Port lodges

*The port 'lodges', above-ground warehouses, are in Vila Nova de Gaia, on the opposite bank of the Douro to Oporto. The young port is shipped down-river in the spring after the harvest to the lodges. The Upper Douro, where the vineyards lie, is far too hot and dry for the maturation of wine – attempts to do so result in the caramelised flavours and overly brown colour of 'Douro Bake', which is why wines destined for top-quality vintage port have always been transferred downstream.*

*The wine was traditionally transported in barrel, carried by the dhow-like barcos rabelos – flat-bottomed boats that were designed to negotiate the river's treacherous rapids. Today it has a comparatively safer passage by road.*

*The cooler climate and coastal humidity of Gaia ensures that evaporation of the ageing port is minimised and the maturation period gentler and more beneficial.*

**Sandeman** Bottled by A & E Hunter. Original embossed lead capsule, crumbling cork but recognisably branded '*Sandeman 1908*'. Palish warm amber, ruddy, little red left; deep, rich, high-toned bouquet; still sweet, delicious flavour, good length and finish. *Dining at home, July 1999* ★★★

**Taylor** Fine flavour, well balanced in 1970. Old corks can completely disintegrate when pulled though the wine is rarely affected. Such a one (in 1991) had a peppery then almost meaty bouquet, tasting like an old Verdelho. Most recently: pale but richly coloured; lovely spicy nose; still sweet and powerful. *Last noted at the Taylor tercentenary tasting, March 1992* ★★★★

OTHER OLD NOTES **Fonseca** still sound but declining. *1969* ★★★; **Gould Campbell** harmonious, delightful. *1982* ★★★★; **Shipper unknown** recorked by Skinner & Rook in the 1930s: medium sweetness and body but lacking length. *1984* ★★; and **Sandeman's Val de Mendiz** delicate fruit, fading but fine. *1975* ★★★

## 1910 ★★★

Good but not declared. One old note.
**González Byass** Bottled 1913. A blush of red; raisiny bouquet; sweet, light, delicious. *Nov 1980* ★★★

## 1911 ★★★

Good vintage but only one loyal British shipper – it was the year of King George V's Coronation. Other port houses concentrated on shipping the '12.
**Sandeman** Listed by Harvey's in the mid-1950s, price 35 shillings a bottle. Tasted several times in the 1960s, prior to discovery of a remarkable bin-full at Hopetoun House in Scotland, sold by Christie's in 1967. Lovely wine. *Old note (Nov 1964)* ★★★★ *But should still be good.*
**Terra Feita, Qta da** Similar to the '07. Sweet, rich, lovely flavour and condition. *At the Mentzendorf tasting, Feb 1996* ★★★

## 1912 ★★★★★

The last great classic vintage of the period. Twenty-five shippers. Can still be excellent.
**Cockburn** Tasted many times: soft and lovely in 1965; ethereal, refined (1969); bottled in Oporto in 1914 for Alex D Shaw, New York: excellent (1970). Even better than the '08 at a Cockburn tasting (also in 1970). Two useful notes in the mid-1980s, both bottles with fully branded corks. Fairly pale but with an attractive rosy hue; fragrant, forthcoming; still sweet, firm, with the power and backbone I normally associate with Taylor, plus cinnamon spiciness and great length. In 1993 at a Christie's wine department Christmas dinner: pale; old and rather varnishy nose; drying out yet with a curiously sweet finish. Spindly, interesting. Most recently: palish, soft, ruddy-tinged; initially lean, spirity, then rich, tangy and after an hour in the glass ethereal, spicy, lovely; medium-sweet, 'hot', lean, dry finish. But in excellent condition. *Last noted at the Cockburn 'Memories of a Century' tasting at the Travellers' Club, London, May 2002* ★★★★

**Dow** Picking began as early as 12 September. Four notes, the first 'bottled in Oporto, November 1914, for W A Taylor & Co in New York', surprisingly sweet when tasted in 1971. Most recently: colour now settled down to a palish warm tawny; rich, hefty, chocolatey nose; sweet but very 'hot' (combination

of high alcohol and high acidity). A serious old wine with an attractive finish. *Last noted at the Dow tasting, Oct 1998* ★★★★
**Ferreira** Four notes, all bottles from Ferreira's remarkable old-wine cellar. Though pale and fully mature, more plummy-coloured and pinker than the usual amber tawny I associate with ageing in cask; also more prune-like fruit on the nose. Sweet, with good fruit, power, length and aftertaste. *Last tasted March 1988* ★★★★
**Taylor** One of the great classics, tasted a dozen times over a 20-year period from 1968 but, alas, not recently. All but one were English bottlings, notably by Skinner & Rook, including two rare and very good half-bottles. One, Oporto-bottled in the mid-1970s, 'a lively old chap'. After 50 years or so, all were fairly pale but with a healthy glow; drying out but enough sweetness, rich yet fading, firm and fragrant. Most recently, recorked, surprisingly sweet, good length, opened up beautifully. *Last tasted June 1987. At best* ★★★★★

# 1913–1916

The first three years affected respectively by drought, mildew and intense heat. Good in 1916, but, doubtless due to wartime and economic factors, not declared as a vintage.

# 1917 ★★★

A relatively light, supple, elegant and attractive vintage declared by 15 shippers. A dozen notes, few recently.
**Ferreira** First tasted in 1981: pale; sweet and delicate on nose and palate. A curious aftertaste. More recently, pure amber-tawny; high-toned, varnishy, nutty nose and flavour. Sweet though and still tannic. *Last tasted Sept 1997* ★★★
**Taylor** The first, in 1989, believed to be Taylor: old tawny; very old nose; drying out and faded. Next, in 1991, capsule and cork branded '1917'. Surprisingly deep, warm, ruddy; singed, meaty, chocolatey; sweet, fullish, good long rich flavour. *Last noted at the Taylor tercentenary tasting, March 1992* ★★★

OLDER NOTES **Croft** charming and attractive. 1962 and *1970* ★★★; **Delaforce** two good notes, deeper in colour than expected, drying out but fleshy. *1979* ★★★★; **Noval** lovely, lively. *1964* ★★★; **Rebello Valente** peaking in 1968, creaking in *1977* ★; **Sandeman** smooth and silky in the mid-1960s, still sweet, piquant in *1973* ★★; and **Vargellas, Qta de** a faded old lady the same year ★★

# 1918–1919

The first of these years enjoyed a scorching summer and only a small harvest. Vintage not declared. The following year the harvest was abundant but few shippers declared a vintage.
**Offley Boa Vista** 1919, an abundant vintage, reputed to be very good in the late 1940s.

# 1920 ★★★★

Twenty-three shippers. Small production but high quality, good, ripe, fairly robust wines. Sturdy, and if well kept can still be very good.
**Croft** First tasted in 1952, seven notes, variable. Of the three bottles tasted since 1980, one had high volatile acidity. The other two: still sweet and powerful, fleshy, with perfect flavour. *Last tasted Nov 1986. At best* ★★★★

**Graham** Four consistently good notes: a lovely 'fat old wine' (1968), still sweet and lovely in the 1970s. A decade later: good colour, a beautiful red tinge; lively Spanish root bouquet; fairly sweet but losing weight, a bit spirity but delicate and flavoury. *Last tasted Nov 1980* ★★★★ *Should still be good if well cellared.*
**Taylor** I have several notes, the most memorable one lunching at Mentmore with the Earl of Rosebery after checking his cellar prior to Christie's seminal 'Finest and Rarest' wine sale in May 1967 (see box page 422). It was his everyday lunch wine. The wine had a sultana-like fruitiness in the early 1970s and, more recently, bottled by Skinner & Rook: palish warm amber; showing age at first, fragrant, liquorice, opening up beautifully, a whiff like a good Havana cigar; medium sweetness and weight, smooth, refined. *A similar note made at the Taylor tercentenary tasting, March 1992* ★★★★

# 1921 ★

Not declared. The grapes failed to ripen fully. Nevertheless, **Rebello Valente** at 40-years old was delicate and delicious.

# 1922 ★★★

Another small crop though of nice quality. Lightish in style and similar to the 1917s. Eighteen shippers.
**Averys** A mixture of different shippers' wines, bottled in Bristol. Two magnums tasted, one rather spirity, showing its age. In 1981, the second, a lovely wine at Averys' bicentenary dinner. *May 1993. At best* ★★★
**Martinez** Listed by Harvey's in 1954-55 at 30 shillings a bottle. One of the problems of old vintage port is identification. In 1990, a client came to Christie's with a sample bottle from his cellar. He thought this was '19 or '22. It had a plain wax seal. The cork confirmed '*Martinez*' but the vintage was not visible. Level good. Pale, little red left. Showing a lot of age on nose and palate. Spirity, rather acidic but some sweetness and good fruit. We opted for '22. My next note is of a bottle purporting to be from a Scottish cellar and recorked, (but we did not know where and when and by whom?): it was a correct colour for its age and vintage but had a very strange and unpleasant nose and taste. *Last tasted in Don Schliff's cellar, Los Angeles, March 1999. At best* ★★
**Warre** Bottled by Justerini & Brooks: palish, rosy hue; spirity, liquorice bouquet; medium-sweet, assertive, lots of grip, high acidity. Unusually, bottle with glass seal or button embossed '*Justerini/Warre/1922/Brooks*'. At a Rodenstock dinner at Arlberg, Austria, Sept 1993 ★★★

OTHER 1922S, OLD NOTES **Bom Retiro, Qta do** taste of crystallised violets. *1955* ★★★; **Croft** several notes, pale tawny, drying out and spirity but complete. *1968–1975* ★★; **Gould Campbell** madeira-like acidity. *1972* ★; **Taylor** dried-out, woody. *1973*; **Tuke Holdsworth** impressive, fine flavour. *Two good bottlings tasted in 1970* ★★★; and several 'shippers unknown' variable, often acidic. *At best* ★★

# 1923 ★★

A bigger crop than 1922 and good quality wine made. Despite this – probably for commercial reasons – not declared. However, **Offley**, who had started to ship their single-quinta wine in good but undeclared vintages, a practice more recently adopted by other shippers, put their **Boa Vista** on the market. It was light, somewhat ethereal, though very pleasant when tasted in the mid-1950s and in the late 1970s.

## 1924 ★★★★

Good quality but production was below average. Eighteen shippers declared. The port market gaining strength.
**Dow** On Harvey's retail price lists between 1954 and 1956 it was listed at 35 shillings per bottle. I have a dozen notes from the mid-1950s: fragrant but variable. Most recently: quite good colour; nose somewhat unyielding; medium-sweet, quite good flavour but very sharp finish. *At the Dow bicentenary tasting, Oct 1998. At best* ★★★
**Taylor** Fifteen notes, starting in 1953, but only six made since 1980. Consistently good, though high-toned and perhaps lacking length. I had a good bottle in 1991 which was unusually sweet for Taylor and for its age. An immediacy about the bouquet, at best rich, mellow, ethereal, scented; very positive flavour, with the characteristic Taylor backbone, dry finish. Then, a malty, oxidised bottle in 1992. Most recently: a bottle 'believed to be Taylor '24' from the cellars of a former Taylor agent, yet it had a short unbranded cork. Lively colour; firm, hard, spirity nose; still sweet, crisp with good acidity. *Last tasted Feb 1995. At best* ★★★★
**Warre** My notes are mixed: spirity finish (1956), well constituted, elegant, very good (1972), and one fairly recent note: medium-deep tawny tinged with ruby; showing age on the nose but still fairly sweet, lean, whiff of acetone, dry slightly bitter finish. *Tasted blind at a remarkable British Airways high-flying Catering and Wine Conference dinner held at Michel Roux's Waterside Inn (not to be confused with the new BA HQ at Waterside near Heathrow!), Bray, Nov 1996. At best* ★★★

OTHER 1924S, OLD NOTES **Croft** variable. A very good Wm. Smith of Bishop's Stortford bottle, sweet, rich, powerful. *1970* ★★★; **Graham** six notes from the mid-1950s, all good, the most recent was warm, soft, delicious. *1983* ★★★★★ *should still be good*; **Gould Campbell** good wine, rich. *1968* ★★ *doubtless tiring now*; and **Rebello Valente** pleasant enough, passing its best by the early 1950s ★★

## 1925 ★

A year of pests and diseases. The poor summer was saved by good late harvest conditions. Not declared.
**Offley Boa Vista** First tasted in 1972, bottled by the Army & Navy Cooperative Society (the 'A and N' were renowned for their bottling) and again noted as 'ethereal' but in excellent condition in 1979. A month later, another bottling: attractive tawny hue; nose still fruity but a bit 'dusty'; sweet, very pleasant, with a dry, lightly spirity finish. *Last tasted Nov 1979* ★★★

## 1926 ★

Almost the opposite, weather-wise, to 1925. It was too hot and dry and the yield was small. Not declared though I tasted several in the mid-1960s to mid-1970s, including **Qta das Lages**, bottled in 1928, spirity, aftertaste of olives; **Kopke**, twice, still sweet but fading and a special quarter cask of **Vargellas** specially shipped to a Lancashire wine merchant for one of his customers whose son was born in 1926. Interesting but spirity.

## 1927 ★★★★★

A great classic late vintage, the best between 1912 and 1935. Declared, at the top of the market, by a record 30 shippers. on the downward slope but, at best, superb.
**Cockburn** A huge production: 20,000 cases (dozens) of Cockburn's '27 vintage! The average retail price through the 1930s was around 60 shillings per dozen. On Harvey's lists in the mid-1950s the price rose from 30 to 35 shillings per bottle. A great classic.

I have tasted (and drunk) this vintage many times since 1959 and have never been disappointed. Of the four tasted in the mid- to late 1980s, the best bottled by Arnold Perret & Co of Gloucester, and consumed at my 60th birthday lunch in May 1987. A filmy crust, decanted clear and bright. Medium depth, lively, ruddy ruby hue; perfect bouquet, low-keyed and spirity at first but after 20 minutes opened up, spicy, nutty; medium-sweet, but fullish body, firm, lean, lissom, gloriously rich and spicy, silky tannin and acidity, marvellous length. It is always interesting to open a bottle for a client who believes his port is Cockburn, when his bin label merely indicated '1927'. The cork turned out to be reassuringly branded '*Cockburn vintage 1927 bottled 1929*'. The wine itself was a fully mature, warm amber; nose dusty, high-toned. Still sweet though, despite thinning. Good flavour, with the refinement of age (in 1994). Most recently two bottles: medium-tawny, very little red and with an overall brown tinge; sweet, meaty but low-keyed; nice texture, excellent condition, but drying out. *Last noted at the Cockburn 'Memories of a Century' tasting at the Travellers' Club, London, May 2002. At best* ★★★★★
**Croft** Many notes. Deliciously flavoury though spirity in the mid-1950s when I considered it at its peak. Two since: a rather unconvincing colour, and cloudy; sweet, creamy, high-toned; still sweet and fairly powerful, lean, alcoholic and a bit hard. Dry acidic finish. Classic but thinning. *Last tasted Dec 1989. At best* ★★★
**Dow** First tasted in 1955: soft, full, attractive. Excellent flavour but drying out in the early 1970s. Late 1980s: palish rosy-tinged tawny; light, spicy, high-toned, madeira-like bouquet; still fairly sweet, medium weight, faded though remnants of power, good length, acidity. Two bottles at the Dow bicentenary tasting. They were both paler than expected for a '27, the first showing its age, spirity, mushroomy; very hot, dry, old sercial-like finish, the other sweeter and rounder, less volatile. *Last tasted Oct 1998. At best* ★★★
**Fonseca** Also first tasted in 1955, full bodied, beautifully balanced; 'at peak'! Many good notes, the best, bottled by Grantham's of Sherborne, removed from a good private cellar in Dorset and tasted pre-sale in 1988. Most recently: fine colour, still fairly deep; extremely good, rich, classic liquorice 'Pontefract cakes' nose; still sweet, fullish, marvellous flavour, touch of eucalyptus, lots of bite and length. A great '27. *Last tasted Nov 1992* ★★★★★
**Graham** Three notes in the mid-1960s: very sweet, rich, chocolatey but brandy showing. A lovely chocolate-nosed, beautifully balanced bottle in Oporto in 1967 and, in 1971, showing full maturity with good, rich bouquet and flavour though drying out a little. An odd, hopefully unrepresentative bottle at a major tasting of '27s in 1989. Strange clear glass bottle. Malty and acidic nose; trace of aniseed. Most recently, slight bottle variation: sweet, chocolatey again, waxy, spirity; lovely texture and flavour. *Last noted at a Graham tasting, May 1991. At best* ★★★★

**Martinez** A dozen notes from the mid-1960s, some variable, one 'flabby cough mixture', but mainly good and, at best, excellent. Still fairly deep in colour; high-toned with brandy showing at first but mellowed in glass; medium-sweet, elegant, spicy. *Last tasted April 1992. At best* ★★★★

**Niepoort** Rolf Niepoort, like me, was born in 1927. His father kept a cask of this vintage and bottled off 360 bottles in 1941, all of which were recorked in 1978. Several of these very recognisable dumpy bottles were given to me, and drunk in the 1980s. Consistent notes: a rich, mahogany colour; well developed, very attractive, slightly raisiny, chocolatey, spicy old wax and liquorice nose; considerable sweetness balanced by crisp, slightly citrus components, touch of tar, high alcohol. A startling contrast to the English shippers' classic ports but extremely good in its way.† *Last tasted Dec 1989* ★★★★

**Noval, Qta do** Seven notes, first in 1972. One spoiled by a poor cork. Later some high acidity noted. But certainly not a 'shrinking violet'. Still fairly deep, richly coloured; massively impressive, penetrating bouquet, slightly medicinal but fragrant, rich, spicy vanilla, black treacle; medium-sweet – drying out slightly though fairly full-bodied. Intense, almost Taylor-like backbone and tannin. Firm fruit. Good length. Dry finish. *Last tasted Jan 1991* ★★★★

**Rebello Valente** It had '*REBELLO VALENTE PORT*' embossed on the capsule. The owner thought it was a '35 and the cork revealed all: clearly branded '1927'. Level top shoulder. A pale, warm amber, no red left; nose faint but sound; still very sweet on palate. Lightish, lean but flavoury. Acidity catching up. *Sept 1990* ★★

**Rosa, Qta de la** Bottled at the quinta. A pretty colour; forthcoming, ethereal nose showing age; medium-sweet, soft, strange flavour, dry finish. *Tasted Dec 1989* ★★

**Sandeman** First tasted in 1955 when I noted it as 'dull, lifeless' but good notes since, the best from a 'cock' or 'tregnum' (three-bottle bottle) from the Sandeman family cellars. Most recently: lovely colour with hint of cherry red and mature yellow rim; nutty-nosed, opened up in the glass; fairly sweet, now lightish, long, lean, spirity but elegant. Dry finish. *Last tasted Dec 1989* ★★★★

**Taylor** First tasted in 1954 and over 20 times since. Slight variations which would seem to depend partly on the bottler but mainly upon cellaring. One of the best was bottled by Justerini & Brooks, tasted in 1973. Another, from Earl Bathurst's cellars at Cirencester Park, a marvel in a half bottle, beautiful when first opened, rich, spicy, developing a strawberry-like nose five hours later. A bottle in 1989: fairly deep, lively ruby, lovely gradation of colour; very attractive classic 'British' liquorice bouquet; drying out, full-bodied, hot, high alcohol, fig-like fruit, good length, dry finish. A couple of years later rich, incredible depth and power; very sweet, mouthfilling, rounded, still tannic. Then in 1993 a memorable lunch at Christie's Paris office to celebrate the French edition of my *Great Vintage Wine Book*. I had double-decanted it before

### British and Portuguese styles of port

*Difficult to describe: it would much easier if we had a bottle of each to compare. Generally speaking, the British vintage ports, as typified by Dow, are less sweet, perhaps leaner, less exuberant. The Portuguese, as noted left (in Niepoort) are more raisiny, rich and chocolatey. Finesse versus fruit perhaps? It is perhaps significant that Niepoort appeals to the new port drinkers. Before American 'critics' discovered this wine the British trade and consumer considered it, if at all, as an outsider even though it was highly regarded and highly priced in some markets.*

leaving London. Magnificent. The bouquet lingered in our empty glasses. *Most recently a perfect bottle at a 'Last Friday Club' lunch at Raji's in Memphis, Dec 1997* ★★★★★

**Warre** I have several notes, all good, starting with 'soft, fat and fruity' in 1966. I had two superb bottlings in the 1970s by H & E Selby and that fine old firm, Stallard's of Worcester. Now palish but, like all the top '27s, it was lively-looking with ruby tinge; gentle, fragrant, classic bouquet of great depth; very sweet, full-bodied. High alcohol, extract, tannin and acidity.

Next, dining at Domaine de Chevalier in Bordeaux in 1998: a fully branded cork and wax seal embossed '*Muirhead*', probably a Scottish bottling. An attractive, medium, ruddy colour; most forthcoming liquorice-like bouquet; sweet, despite brandy showing through, a wine with great length and lean finish. Most recently, bottled by Cobbold & Co, Ipswich: fairly pale, no red left, open-rimmed; high-toned, whiff of amyl-acetate but still very sweet with a taste like squashed liquorice. *Last noted at the Symington family's tasting in London, May 2002. At best* ★★★★★

OTHER 1927s, OLD NOTES **Delaforce** seven consistently good notes between 1955 and 1965, 'magnificent', 'lively', 'lovely', 'well balanced'. *None tasted since 1965* ★★★★; **Krohn** soft, mature. *Mid-1970s* ★★★; and **Stormont Tait** lovely. *1977* ★★★

# 1928 ★★

A good vintage, but, at the time a declaration might have been considered, the economic slump was biting and the market for vintage port, then almost solely British, was sated with the abundantly shipped 1927 vintage.

# 1929 ★★

Small quantity, good quality but not declared for similar reasons to the 1928. **Offley Boa Vista** shipped: pungent, austere but flavoury in *1967*.

The end not just of a decade but of an era. It was another 30 years before the port trade really recovered.

# 1930—1949

The port trade was decimated by the great Depression, exacerbated by merchants and their customers awash with the stocks of the '27s. As a result, there was no market for the magnificent '31, for though some wine was made the vintage was not declared. Noval stands out like a lonely beacon.

As in France, the immediate post-World War Two period produced some exceptionally fine vintages, the small but widely 'declared' and still excellent '45, the very good '47 and the outstanding '48, neither of the latter being unanimously declared. There were several reasons: the remaining stocks of '27s, the prices of which were unchanged, had a dampening effect on what could be charged for the new vintages. Add to this post-war austerity and a perceived lessening of interest in 'the Englishman's Wine' and the curtain seemed to be coming down on port.

## Vintages at a Glance
**Outstanding ★★★★★**
1931, 1935, 1945
**Very Good ★★★★**
1934, 1944, 1947, 1948
**Good ★★★**
1933, 1942

## 1930

Unsettled weather. Intense heat damaged the grapes. Not declared. I have only tasted one, from a quarter cask of **Vargellas** shipped in 1932 by Taylor's to a Lancashire wine merchant to bottle for the Horridge's second son. Corks branded 'C.R.O.G.H. vintage 1930'. A collector's piece. Still sweet, lacking body, spirity but very pleasant. *From the original family cellar, pre-sale, March 1977* ★★

## 1931 ★★★★★

A splendid – nay great – vintage but, for reasons stated earlier, slump conditions and cellars still stocked with '27s, the British port houses, who at that time dominated the trade, decided not to declare. Though good wine was made, the towering reputation of this vintage rests on Noval, whose '31 Nacional I have long since considered as the 'Everest' of vintage ports.
**Noval, Qta do** I have been privileged to note this on no fewer than 18 occasions and at fairly regular intervals since 1962. A variety of bottlings, all good, some unstated on cork or capsule but including Justerini & Brooks and, perhaps the most superlatively typical, by Fearon, Block, Bridges, Routh, consumed in 1985. Also a rare post-prohibition American bottling, at a Wine and Food Society luncheon in Chicago in 1982, 'shipped by Averys and imported from Bristol, where it had been bottled in 1933 by Louis Glunz, Lincolnwood, Ill.: still very deep, opaque at the centre; huge, sweet, spirity bouquet that reminded me of caramelised raisins and then, as it opened up in the glass, of prunes and cloves. Still sweet but not overpoweringly so, full-bodied, an assertive prune-like flavour, hot, peppery, mouthfilling, still plump, with marvellous acidity. Three bottles more recently opened at the Hollywood Wine Society's 'Greatest Ports' tasting, two with rather suspiciously new red wax seals, one wine corked, the other jammy – not correct I thought. But an excellent example, the bottler's seal embossed '*Sandeman & Co, Glasgow, vintage 1931*': still very sweet, crisp, with good fruit and great length. *Last tasted March 1998* ★★★★★ *The best kept will continue to impress.*

**Noval Nacional** This, of course, is the supreme '31. Some of the above Novals might have been made from the 10% of the vineyard planted, ungrafted, with the traditional Nacional grape variety. Usually, however, *Nacional* appears somewhere on the bin label, wax seal and/or cork. A typical Noval Nacional was served by Tawfiq Khoury at a dinner in San Diego in 1982. I noted its amazing high-toned bouquet which reminded me of eau de cologne, armagnac and a sort of ultra-refined liquorice. Although only medium-sweet, it was incredibly full-bodied, a rich, bitter sweet wine, spicy, of great length. *Tasted in 1982* ★★★★★

### A glass of port after lunch

*Writing the note above reminded me of an event some years ago. I had met the gentleman (I think he was a retired brigadier) who was in charge of the Government Hospitality cellar at Lancaster House. Would I like to visit the cellar? A mutually convenient date, far in advance, was fixed.*

*When the day arrived, I was office-bound and frantic with auction deadlines. But it was only a few steps away from Christie's so I dutifully turned up at 12 noon and was shown round the cellars which, to my surprise, contained some real rarities, like Noval '31 and Ch Cheval Blanc '47. After the tour, the brigadier asked me if I had time for a spot of lunch. Initially I declined; I felt I had to get back. But he said I would have to have a bite to eat anyway, and his club was nearby. So, weakening, I joined him for lunch – with a glass of claret.*

*Then, 'How about a glass of port?' said my kind host. 'Really', I spluttered, 'I really have some terrible deadlines and a printer pressing for copy'. 'Have a glass of port', he insisted. Once, again, I feebly succumbed. I had a large glass of Graham's '55 which was not only a lovely drink but, miraculously, calmed my anxieties, sending me back to Christie's happy, my agitation evaporated, worries gone.*

*Since when I have never had a lily-livered attitude to a glass of port after lunch. It is as relaxing as it is pleasing.*

**Niepoort** Several notes: one clearly labelled '*bottled 1938 decanted (i.e. rebottled) 1979*' with a lovely sweet, fragrant bouquet; sweet on the palate. A charmer. Another, rather paler in colour with delicate grapey nose and fabulous sultana-like flavour. Yet another, very deep-coloured; a nose like syrup of figs, sweet, full, rich and rounded. All good to drink. All birthday presents from Rolf Niepoort, the most recent opened on my wife's birthday after a 1931 Domaine de la Romanée-Conti Richebourg (lovely) and Giacomo Borgogno's 1931

Barolo (charm vying with decay). The Niepoort was, unsurprisingly, better than both the reds: palish, amber, apple-green rim; sweet madeira-like nose, touch of bracken but overall a lovely scent; still sweet – like my wife – nice weight, lovely, slightly raisiny flavour, excellent finish. *Last noted at Daphne's birthday dinner held at Christie's, July 1996* ★★★★

OTHER NOTES Though the following are old tasting notes, I have listed them to demonstrate how many wines were made, though for a very limited market. **Bragão, Qta do Sandeman** just two pipes made. Oporto-bottled. Magnificent. 1971–1975 ★★★★; **Offley Boa Vista** bottled by Henekys, attractive, light, tangy. *1970* ★★★; **Burmester** deeply coloured, extraordinary flavour, 'warm', alcoholic grip and persistence. *1980* ★★★★; **Martinez** ethereal, delicate but complete. *1981* ★★★★; **'Pinhão'** spirity but lovely. *1967* ★★★★; **Rebello Valente,** Robertson's vintage *marque*: rich, high-toned, refined (1971), next rich, spirity. *1978* ★★★★; **Roncão, Qta do** a quinta also owned by Robertson. Bottled by the Wine Society: unusual style, powerful, distinctive. *1970* ★★★★; and **Warre** single-quinta: nice balance but not outstanding. *1960* ★★★

## 1932

Poor year, not declared.
**González Byass** Oporto-bottled. Rather dull, amber tawny; faded but sound. *Nov 1980* ★

## 1933 ★★★

Early flowering, heat-wave, early harvest. Not declared, for market reasons and because of the promise of the 1934s then, even more so, the 1935s.
**Cais, Qta do** I cannot remember where this odd half bottle came from. On the label was *'engarrafadem em 1988'*. Richly coloured for its age; equally surprisingly sweet, complete, firm, with good length and acidity. An attractive unknown. *At dinner at home, July 1997* ★★★

OTHER, OLDER NOTES **Cedovim,** a single-quinta, bottled by the Wine Society, pale, showing its age but firm and attractive. Four notes from 1965. *1972* ★★★; and **Niepoort,** Oporto-bottled 1936: pale old tawny; sweet, nutty bouquet; excellent flavour. *1988* ★★★★

## 1934 ★★★★

Once one of my favourite vintages. Fairly scarce as only 12 shippers declared. Worth looking out for.
**Dow** Picking began 24 September. Several good notes between 1960 and 1976. Most recently: pleasant colour, warm glow, curiously rich, malty nose; fairly sweet still, assertive, flavour combining meat and fruit. *Last noted at the Dow bicentenary tasting, Oct 1998. At best* ★★★
**Ramos-Pinto** Pale, bright, weak rim; sweet, chocolatey bouquet; excellent weight, flavour, condition. *A glass thrust into my hand at Prowein, Düsseldorf, March 2001* ★★★

OTHER, OLDER NOTES **Ferreira** pale but assertive. *1981* ★★★; **Fonseca** several excellent notes, 'perfection'. 1953–1983 ★★★★; **Foz, Qta da** showing age but pleasing. *1988* ★★★; **Martinez** several notes, deeply coloured in 1957, palish, fully mature, ageing gracefully when last tasted. *1987* ★★★; **Noval, Qta do**

several notes, dry, soft, very attractive in 1961, Wine Society bottling on gentle decline in 1973, lean, flavoury, lovely aftertaste. *1984* ★★★★; **Sandeman** nine notes, from deep, fat and smooth in 1956, perfect in 1967, less deep in colour, becoming spirity and rather dull. *1971. At best* ★★★★; and **Taylor** rich, lovely in 1966 and, strangely, bottled in 1977, a nutty flavoured old 'vintage tawny', drunk in Mexico City. *1980. At best* ★★★★

## 1935 ★★★★★

A classic vintage bottled in King George VI's Coronation year, 1937. Similar harvest conditions to 1934 but smaller crop. Market slowly recovering – 15 shippers. The best ports still superb, with many years of life ahead.
**Cockburn** My notes started in 1953, 'only' 18 years old then (the port, not me): 'full, fruity and spirity for a '35'. Perfect condition in 1966. By 1990, fully mature appearance, bouquet and palate. Sweet, gentle bouquet; medium-sweet, lightish and lean. Brandy and acidity a bit obtrusive. A 'Rick Sajbel selection' bought *circa* 1970, probably at Christie's, and the best port in Don Schliff's remarkable cellar: rosehip colour; gentle, harmonious bouquet; drying out but lovely, spicy, attenuated flavour (1999). My only remaining bottle decanted for a dinner party at our London flat in May 2000: a lovely palish rosehip colour; low-keyed at first but a beautiful sweet fragrance emerged. Still very sweet and powerful, combining softness and grip. Glorious. In November 2000 a bottle from Lenoir Josey's cellar: its classic 'waxy' bouquet, showing age but still sweet; perfect weight, thinning and fading, with ethereal, refined elegance. Most recent: two bottles, one with an aftertaste so terrible that I had to rinse my mouth before continuing. The other fragrant but with tarry nose and taste. *Both last noted at the Cockburn 'Memories of a Century' tasting, May 2002. At best* ★★★★★
**Delaforce** Good, sound nose; drying and thinning but attractive. *Nov 1992* ★★★
**Graham** Several notes since 1955. Perfection in 1979. At 30 years of age: good rich mature colour; marvellous bouquet, liquorice and prunes, some spirit now showing; fairly sweet, brandy sheathed in fleshy fruit, fragrant, perfect acidity, length. *Not tasted since Marvin Overton's 50th birthday dinner, Fort Worth, Feb 1985. At best* ★★★★★
**Taylor** Outstandingly the best 1935 and one of the greatest ports of this century. Tasted (and drunk) on 27 occasions since 1953. My notes describe its appearance as ranging from medium to very deep, but this might well result from variations of light in dining-rooms as well as different bottlings. The bouquet and taste more consistently marvellous: full, rich, spicy, touch of vanilla and liquorice, overall harmony, depth and power; still sweet, fairly full-bodied, almost chewy, with the inimitable Taylor backbone, great length and ethereal aftertaste. Perfection. A pair in 1991, Oporto-bottled and recorked in 1986. One was horrid: cod liver oil and malt, the other superb. Perfection, at peak, 6 stars, twice in 1992.

Three very recent notes: despite a rather smelly cork that broke, a superb wine, powerful, amazing length and flavour, at a dinner party at home June 2000. Another glorious bottle, losing depth of colour; nose slightly smoky, Spanish root; great length and residual power – dining in the Dairy, Waddesdon Manor, and, with classic bouquet, drying out a little but with inimitable Taylor backbone. Superb. *Last noted dining at Bill Baker's, Jan 2001. At best* ★★★★★ *but don't leave it another 20 years!*

OTHER, OLDER NOTES **Cálem** soft, gentle. *1974* ★★★; **Croft** three variable notes, one austere another delicate and delicious. *1975–1977. At best* ★★★★; **González Byass**, bottled 1938, mediocre, sickly sweet. *1980* ★; **Hooper** strange, unclassic, nice though. *1970–1971* ★★; **Martinez** light and thin. *1966* ★★; **Niepoort** Colheita orange amber; estery, refined. *1986* ★★★; **Offley Boa Vista** soft, sweet, strong yet mellow. *1959* ★★★; **Rebello Valente** unimpressive. Bitterness noted. *Mid-1950s* ★; **Sandeman** consistently good notes between *1970* and *1987*. Still sweet, fullish, classic ★★★★; and **Smith Woodhouse** sweet, gentle despite peppery finish. *1980* ★★★

## 1936 ★★

Good wines but not of vintage quality and, in any case, too soon to declare after the 1934s and 1935s.

## 1937 ★★

Sound, nice quality; not declared by British shippers.
**Poças Junior** Something of a rarity, bottled in 1974: a palish dusty tawny; madeira-like high acidity, medicinal old straw! Still sweet, however, lean and surprisingly drinkable. Daphne said the flavour reminded her of quince cheese; for me it had a singed muscatel taste. *At a 'Klassische Weindegustation' I conducted in Zurich, May 1994* ★★★ *(just)*.

OTHER WINES, OLDER NOTES **González Byass** bottled in 1940. Pale tawny; fruit, sweetness and flesh. *1980* ★★; **Hooper** bottled 1972. Rosehip colour; high-toned; medium-sweet, hot grapey flavour. Nice quality. *1988* ★★; **Noval, Qta do** matured in wood. Warm amber gold; nutty nose and flavour; medium-weight, on the lean side, very dry finish. *Sept 1988* ★; and **A J da Silva, Reserva** bottled *circa* 1980. Probably the same as Noval (da Silva was the trading company). Similar style. A bit more raisiny. *1987* ★

## 1938 ★★

Quite good wines made but, owing to wartime restrictions, not declared or shipped. None tasted recently though **Noval, Qta do** tawny-like, somewhat unbalanced. *1970* ★; and **Taylor** 'really rather nice'. *1956* ★★

## 1939

Small production, poor quantity and quality. Not declared.
**González Byass** Bottled 1942. Surprisingly attractive. Rich, fruity nose and taste, well balanced, dry finish. *One of a wide range of vintages from the González Byass lodge, pre-sale, Sept 1980* ★★★ *(Alas, not a very inspired set of wines.)*

## 1940 ★★

Small crop. Quite good wines. Not shipped.
**Niepoort** The firm — one has the impression that it is a one-man band, father followed by son, all indiosyncratic, quirky, but, in their own ways, brilliant. I have a note of two of their 1940s, one bottled in 1945, already an old tawny colour, flavoury but with high volatile acidity, the other put from wood into demijohns and bottled in 1970. Quite different. Little nose, but good firm fruit and acidity. *Both tasted in the late 1980s* ★★

**Taylor** Wax seal embossed '4xx Taylor' (Taylor's brand symbol), relabelled, cork fully branded. Recorked 1986. Medium, rosy-hued; rich, warm, stably; very sweet, fairly full, good rich flavour, excellent length and condition. *April 1991* ★★★

## 1941 ★

Moderate quality. Not declared.
**Dalva** Very odd: '*Porto Dalva, House Reserve, Matured in Wood*'. Doubtless a post-war shipment which found its way, cheaply, to a cut-price London retailer. A drab amber, cloudy — shaken not stirred! My host filtered it before decanting and the result was not displeasing. A wine for enquiring minds. *Dining at the Stanley-Clarks', Nov 1997* ★

ONLY ONE OTHER TASTED **Noval, Qta do** bottled 1944 and tasted ten years later, rich and luscious. Probably faded now. *1954. Then* ★★★

## 1942 ★★★

A good wartime year. Though declared and bottled in Oporto by ten shippers, very little actually shipped but just worth keeping an eye open for it.
**Graham** Noted as stylish but lacking usual plumpness in 1955 and 1971. Most recently: palish, rosy-hued tawny; low-keyed, old tawny nose; medium sweetness and body, sound, rich, stylish. From the colour and nose probably bottled in 1945. *Last tasted April 1990* ★★★
**Niepoort** Two very similar notes. First in 1985. Deep colour; sweet, forthcoming, vinous nose; very sweet, fairly full-bodied, soft, fleshy, slightly toasted flavour. *Last tasted April 1990* ★★★
**Noval, Qta do** Bottled in 1945. First tasted in 1955. Full, yet not the body for staying power. Most recently: palish, very mature appearance; nose harmonious but a bit dusty; medium sweetness and weight, nice fruit, stylish. Remarkably similar to the Graham but with higher acidity. *Last tasted April 1990* ★★★
**Taylor** Fairly pale tawny; rich, roasted, toasted nose; sweet, moderately full-bodied yet lightish in style. Good length. Still harbouring tannin and noticeable acidity. More recently, recorked by Taylor in 1986: amber; dusty then ethereal; elegant but drying out. *Last tasted April 1991* ★★

OTHER WINES, OLDER NOTES **Croft** full, sweet, the nicest of the '42s. *In the mid- to late 1950s* ★★★; **Morgan** big, flavoury. *1965* and *1968* ★★★; **González Byass** odd sort of wine, thin, unattractive. *1969*; and **Rebello Valente** blackcurrant-like fruit; lightish for a '42 in *1960*; more recently delicious, fully mature. *1980, at best* ★★★

## 1943 ★★

Not a bad harvest but not declared.

THREE NOTES TO GIVE AN INDICATION OF WHAT MIGHT HAVE BEEN **Dow** fairly deep, mature; waxy, liquorice nose; sweet, lightish, soft, with a very pleasant chocolatey flavour. Short though finished well. Good for a 40-year-old undeclared vintage. *1983* ★★★; **Eira Velha, Qta da** pale tawny; beautiful bouquet that expanded in the glass, fragrant, nutty; medium-sweet, lightish, elegant, nice texture, harmonious, lovely finish. *1986* ★★★★; and **Sandeman** light tawny; liquorice; some fruit but thinning out. *1964* ★★★

# 1944 ★★★★

Excellent quality but the majority of the shippers concentrated on the 1945. In any case, good wine was needed to boost stocks to meet anticipated demand. None tasted recently.

OLD NOTES **Delaforce** fat, full flavoured. *1964* ★★★; **Dow** not unlike a '34. Interesting. Long dry finish. 1959 and *1961* ★★★; and **Milieu, Qta do** bottled 1948 in Oporto by Guimaraens. Lightish, nice wine. *1969* ★★

# 1945 ★★★★★

The first end-of-war vintage was of superb quality, although, as in other European wine regions, the quantity was small. The growing season was perfect, although great heat at harvest time created some vinification problems resulting in some over-high volatile acidity. With rare exceptions all were Oporto-bottled. Twenty-two shippers, Cockburn the only major abstention. These tautly constructed, concentrated wines are still superb – if they have been well cellared.

**Butler Nephew** The least good '45 at the Hollywood Wine Society tasting in Florida: pale, very little red left; *garrafeira* (wood-aged), linoleum-like smell, faded; dried-out. Too much time in cask. *Feb 1989. Drink up.*

**Croft** Eighteen fairly consistent notes starting in the mid-1950s 'full yet good now' (on Harvey's lists at 24 shillings a bottle). Drinking perfectly in 1966, yet in 1971 I wrote 'Another 20 years life'. Then drying out a little by the early 1980s. A memorable bottle in October 1997 dining with Robin Reid and John Burnett and their wives, at Croft's lodge in Gaia. Good colour, lively, rosy-hued; delicate low-keyed but fragrant bouquet reminding me of Pontefract cakes, great depth; fairly sweet still, medium-weight, lean but firm, interesting leathery silky tannic texture, good quality, crisp dry finish. In 1999 at a dinner party at home: as the original label (Oporto-bottled) had disintegrated I broke the neck to extract the cork which, happily, was fully branded. The wine had a fairly solid 'crust' so it decanted clearly through my old silver sieve. Powerful nose; lean touch but lovely, spicy, warming flavour. Most recently; mocha and liquorice, rich, 'stably' bouquet; lean, attractive, with hot acidic finish. *Last noted at the Russian National Orchestra supporters' dinner at Spencer House, London, April 2002. At best* ★★★★ *Drink soon.*

**Dow** I have tasted this many times since 1959 when I noted it as sweet, full but not ready. Curiously, Dow bottled the wine in 1949. Only five pipes (each yielding approximately 55 dozen bottles) were shipped for bottling in England, virtually the only market at the time. One, by British Transport Hotels, tasted in 1989 showed considerable colour loss. It had a fruity, lean, liquorice nose, which after an hour or so became more and more fragrant. Surprisingly sweet for Dow, relatively light for the vintage, marvellous acidity, lean, dry finish. Another, bottled in October 1947 by Rigby & Evans with pre-war corks fully branded: no red left; lean, a touch of acetone on the nose and palate. Dry finish.

I have many more notes, eight since 1990. Three bottles opened at a Dow tasting in Aspen in the summer of 1994: one, Oporto-bottled, was acetic, whereas the two English-bottled were very good, sweet, fragrant. Four months later, a well-nigh perfect bottle at a *Dîner Classique* at one of my favourite hotels, the Baur au Lac in Zurich, and another surprisingly sweet (for Dow) and full-flavoured bottle the

following month at a Symington port tasting. Next, a disappointingly drab-looking Oporto-bottling though better on nose and palate at the Dow bicentenary tasting, somewhat made up for by another, deeper, sweeter and more fragrant served at the following lunch alongside an English-bottled jeroboam which, though attractive, was drying out a little. Palish, warm, rose-hip colour; light, spirity bouquet; lean, very dry finish. *Last noted at the Symington family's tasting at the Berkeley Hotel on my birthday, May 2002. At best* ★★★★

**Ferreira** Not ready in 1966, lovely in the mid-1970s and perfect in the early 1980s. In 1989 palish, fully mature, not much red left and a slightly weak tawny rim; crisp, peppery bouquet with a lot of bare brandy; more fruit and life on the palate than its colour suggested. A singed, sooty taste of scorched grapes, with end acidity and touch of bitterness. A powerful and interesting wine with some of the sweetness of Graham and backbone of Taylor. Good dry finish. Most recently at two Ferreira tastings for my son, Ferreira's US importer, one at the very smart Turnberry Club in Fort Lauderdale, the other five months later at Christie's in New York. Consistent notes, both fairly pale but with spicy, harmonious, bouquet, drying out but lovely. *Last tasted Sept 1997. At best* ★★★★ *Drink soon.*

**Fonseca** One note. A rather faded appearance, though healthy. Again, as with the Dow, the colour a bit misleading as the nose was richer and more positive than anticipated. A touch of singed caramel and a whiff of volatile acidity, the result of picking in great heat, developing in the glass a curious, explosive fragrance: hot, high-toned, fruit fading exposing spirit. Rather disappointing. *Feb 1989* ★★ *Drink up.*

**Graham** Bottled in London as well as in Oporto. Outstandingly the loveliest '45. First noted, 'undeveloped' in 1960 and in 1982 'at peak but 10–15 years of life'! Many consistently good notes. Deep-coloured, fairly intense, lively, attractive, long 'legs'; immediately forthcoming fragrance, spice, sweetness and fruit masking high alcoholic content; the sweetest of the eleven '45s tasted in Florida in 1989, and outstandingly the best (labelled '*Finest Reserve 1945 bottled in Oporto 1948 W & J Graham & Co*') at 'The World's Greatest Ports' tasting: a sweet-smelling, fragrant yet powerful wine, still tannic, profound. *Last tasted at yet another Hollywood Wine Society seminar, Florida, March 1998* ★★★★★

**Niepoort** Three very good notes in the mid- to late 1960s: a deep, powerful, attractive wine that I noted as being Oporto-bottled in March 1948. Five fairly recent notes: still fairly deep and intense; rich, idiosyncratic, prune-like nose, more like meat than fruit; sweet, full, chunky, velvety, good length and life ahead. The most recent, bottled in 1947, outstanding. *Last tasted dining with Dirk Niepoort, March 1996* ★★★★★

**Noval, Qta do** Tasted several times since 1956 though not recently; 'charm' noted fairly consistently. At the Hollywood Wine Society tasting of 1945s, Noval, bottled by Churtons of Liverpool, was palish but still had a youthful tinge; a fragrant, rich, harmonious bouquet; sweet, perfect weight, lovely fruit, good dry finish. A wine of feminine graciousness. More recently, with short cork and labelled '*da Silva*': rather unimpressive colour; unknit and spicy, orange blossom and candlewax bouquet; sweet, fullish, lean, intense, citrus-like acidity. *Last noted at the Noval tasting, Nov 1989. At best* ★★★★★ *Drink soon.*

**Rebello Valente** Overpowering in the late 1950s, lovely in mid-1960s. In the 1980s an attractive, lively rosy-hued appearance of some intensity; shy at first, lively, refreshing nose, spare but fruity; lean, flavoury, touch of liquorice, noticeable acidity. A crisp, lissom charmer. Most recently, with embossed lead capsule and body label, 'shipped by Robertson Bros & Co. Ltd.', the proprietors: lovely colour; classic liquorice nose and flavour. Lean. Attractive. *Last noted at a vinous Sunday lunch at Chippenham Lodge, Aug 1994 ★★★★ Drink soon.*

**Sandeman** Offered to the trade Oporto-bottled or for bottling in the UK. Several notes, including two good London bottlings. In the late 1960s and early 1970s chunky, 'needing another ten years', but after a further ten years mature-looking, rosehip-hued, nice gradation of colour; suave, silky, harmonious bouquet; drying out on palate, now on the light side, gentle, touch of vanilla, crisp, lacking length. Most recently, Oporto-bottled in a wartime green bottle, protruding cork and level into neck: fairly pale but lovely colour; sweet and equally lovely bouquet and flavour. Good length. Dry finish. *Last noted at a dinner party at home, Nov 2000 ★★★★*

**Taylor** Reputed from the start to be head and shoulders the best '45. A big strapping wine, totally unready in the mid-1960s, with magnificent depth and concentration in the late 1970s. Fairly consistent notes through the 1980s including plummy colour, sublime bouquet, laden with fruit and alcohol. Lovely colour; restrained but harmonious bouquet; sweet, perfect flavour, nutty, intense, great length, at Taylor's tercentenary tasting in 1991. (I recall much debate, the majority of tasters, including Jancis Robinson, Len Evans and Hugh Johnson, preferring the '45. I personally thought the '48 had the edge.) Then a memorable bottle at the 50th anniversary '1945 Vintage Dinner' hosted by Sir Christopher Mallaby, at the Embassy in Paris in December 1995. I noted 'powerful, assertive, years of life, impressive but not a joy'(!). Most recently noting good colour, positive fruit, length, and the Taylor backbone. Certainly good. Certainly impressive, but the '48 is finer. *Last tasted March 1998 ★★★★★ Plenty of life yet.*

**Warre** Variable notes, including one *framboise*-scented (in 1964), one woody. Showing marvellously well at the 1989 tasting of '45s in Florida: beautiful colour, lively, lovely gradation; very forthcoming, indeed, fairly forceful nose, brandy evident; a powerful wine with cockle-warming alcohol, crisp, lovely texture and elegance – for me the hallmark of Warre. Absolutely glorious; perfection. *Full marks at the Symington tasting in Nov 1994 ★★★★★ A splendid life ahead.*

OTHER, OLDER NOTES **Barros** Oporto-bottled. Surprisingly good. Sweet, rich, well balanced, lots of life. *Two notes in 1978 ★★★*; **Delaforce** full, sweet but unready in 1961; soft and velvety in 1968 but not tasted since ★★★★; **Eira Velha, Qta da** very fragrant, highish acidity. *1980 ★★★*; **Mackenzie** blackcurrant flavour, lacking body despite dark colour. *1956 ★★*; **Martinez** bottled in Oporto, some English-bottled in 1948. Fat, rich, sweet though austere finish in 1966. Not tasted since; **Offley Boa Vista** diverging opinions – but not tasted; **Quarles Harris** Oporto-bottled 1947: soft and rich in 1968, remarkably full and fruity, backbone and plenty of life in the *mid-1970s ★★★*; and **Smith Woodhouse** good wine. *1967 ★★★*

# 1946 ★

Uneven quality, not declared.

ONLY TWO NOTES **Sandeman** spirity, spicy, very pleasant. *1977 ★★*; and **Warre** bottled in Oporto, 1949: fully mature, light style, attractive. *1967 ★★*

# 1947 ★★★★

A very good vintage though only declared by 11 shippers. Certainly very attractive and popular in the wine-starved 1950s, which is why little remains, and why I have tasted so few recently. Good weather conditions: wet spring, long hot summer, a little rain before picking which began towards the end of September in excellent conditions.

**Cockburn** Small production. Considered a light vintage at the time. Up until this vintage, Cockburn were very sparing with the number of vintages they declared: '27, '35 – not the '45 – and then the '47. Several notes in the mid-1960s. Slightly variable, depending on bottler rather than condition. Attractive and ready in 1971; a somewhat odd, medicinal smell and taste with rather high, prickly acidity in 1980. A decade later despite crumbly cork, a good warm tawny colour, fairly heavy crust or sediment; soft barley-sugar nose which developed lovely powdery vanilla fragrance. Fairly sweet, nice weight, flesh, flavour and balance. Dry, liquorice finish. Attractive. Next, in 1999, with Cockburn label. Palish but lovely colour; fragrant bouquet; medium-sweet and correct weight and 'waxy' flavour. Good fruit though fading gracefully. Most recently: fairly pale, little red though pink/red highlights; pure liquorice, harmonious, well evolved; firm, good flavour and flesh, smooth texture, dry finish, delicious aftertaste. *Last noted at the Cockburn 'Memories of a Century' tasting, May 2002. At best ★★★*

**Delaforce** Only three notes. A palish, orange-tinged tawny; ethereal, fragrant but unknit; sweet, medium weight, a positive but rather estery flavour and highish acidity. *Last noted at a Delaforce tasting, April 1989 ★★ Drink up.*

**Sandeman** Variable. First tasted in 1958: 'typical' (of Sandeman and of Harvey's bottling). Ruby-coloured, a good 'officers' mess' port in the early 1960s. A lovely bottle in 1990: surprisingly deep, rich appearance; pronounced liquorice and vanilla bouquet; very sweet, pleasant weight and balance. More recently, considerable colour loss; lean, spirity; lacking flesh, fruit fading. *Last tasted March 1998. At best ★★★*

**Taylor's Special Qta** (bottled 1949) Although Taylor did not declare the '47 vintage, a limited quantity was shipped. Several notes, the most interesting with wax seal impressed '1947 SP Quinta Taylor, Dolamore Ltd London W1', presumably bottled by the latter. Good warm tawny colour with flash of red; rich, fragrant bouquet, a bit spirity, seemed very sweet, full-bodied, assertive flavour and Taylor backbone. Most recently, three bottles from different sources, the best a Corney & Barrow bottling. *Ending a 1947 vintage dinner given by Stephen Kaplan in Chicago, April 1997. At best ★★★★*

**Tuke Holdsworth** Several notes. Now rather pale, rosy-hued, weak-rimmed; faded. More like a '34. Most recently, from a half bottle with crumbling cork though good level. Tawny with warm gold highlights; drying out somewhat and showing age but a good flavour. Singed, spirity finish. *Last tasted at a family dinner, Dec 1997 ★★ Drink up.*

OLDER NOTES **Dow** hard and unready in 1958, still raw in 1964 but coming round in the later 1960s. In splendid form in *1972* but not tasted since ★★★★; **Noval, Qta do** ten notes starting with a good Harvey's bottling in 1958, 'well rounded' noted in the mid- to late 1960s, another excellent Berry Bros' bottling, soft but firm. Well balanced ★★★★; **Noval Nacional** remarkably youthful in the early 1970s: rich and rounded, one of the best '47s. Alas, not tasted since. *Should be magnificent ★★★★★*; **Smith Woodhouse** not taken too seriously in the late 1950s and early 1960s: pretty, flavoury, an early developer. Not tasted since. Probably well past best ★★; **Warre** a coarse Harvey's bottling in 1958, good notes in the mid-1980s, one, fined before bottling, had a twist of acidity (1972), but a superb Berry Bros' bottling, fully mature in *1982. At best* ★★★★

# 1948 ★★★★

A very good vintage but declared by only nine shippers which, in retrospect, was an unfortunate error of judgement as it turned out to be so successful. It was seven years before another vintage of real quality was declared.

The top three '48s: Taylor, Graham and Fonseca.

**Bomfim, Qta do** Palish, weak-looking; low-keyed, evolving ethereal fragrance; light style, rather lean and a bit sharp. *At the Dow bicentenary tasting, Oct 1998* ★★

**Fonseca** The third of the trio of great '48s. A dozen notes between 1958 and 1977, all good, 'fruity', 'perfect balance' etc. In November 1979, an impressively deep, rich J & B bottling (wax seal embossed *'Justerini & Brooks Bailey & Co. 1948'*) with a curious spicy taste and hot finish. Next, nine years later, the opening wine of the Hollywood Wine Society's 'The World's Greatest Vintage Ports' tasting. Much to our surprise it was in a magnum burgundy bottle. Quite genuine though. Presumably a post-war shortage of port magnums when Harvey's bottled the wine, with a fully branded cork, in 1950. Sweet, firm, well made but touch of corkiness, not entirely clean. The next month at a British Airways annual wine committee seminar at Mosimann's: mature but lively; fragrant – with a touch of mothballs; soft fleshy fruit, good backbone, peppery dry finish. *Good wine. Last tasted April 1998. At best* ★★★★ *Surviving half a century effortlessly.*

**Foz, Qta da** One of the most astonishing wines I have ever tasted. A bottle given to me by Joachim Cálem, then the owner of Cálem. It had a smallish faintly branded cork and a very heavy crust. The colour of the wine was very similar to the Ch Canon '85 I decanted at the same time. It also had a similar nose to the rather more youthful St-Émilion. Moreover, it was dry, very tannic and austere. I came to the conclusion that this must have been a red Douro table wine made at the quinta. But, just over two hours later, when the time came to serve it, the bouquet was unmistakably port-like, with a touch of Spanish root, and spirity. Even more

miraculously it had become sweet, with a lovely flavour and texture but finishing dry. *A Sunday lunch revelation, Nov 1997* ★★★ *It remains a great mystery.*

**Graham** First tasted ten years after the vintage when it was immensely deep and magnificent. I have made over 20 consistently good notes since then, including one of a fragrant Christopher's bottling, a bit lean and tannic for Graham. In 1990 one with almost Taylor-like strength and backbone. A glorious London-bottled wine warranting a very high mark at the Symington tasting in 1994, and again in 1995. In 1998 a pair, one was a very correct Graham Oporto bottling, the other, bottled by J & G Thompson of Leith, was better developed, full, fruity, more meaty bouquet. Dry finish. Most recently: warm, open and inviting rosehip colour; delicious fruit, fig, crisp, liquorice; fairly sweet, lean but lovely with hot finish. *Last noted at the Symington Family Port Companies' tasting at the Berkeley, London, May 2002. At best* ★★★★★

**Taylor** Tasted 21 times since 1958 when I noted it as 'fine, smooth. Fullest and darkest'. It has been invariably magnificent. Still fairly deep and intense; beautiful bouquet, lovely fruit, scented, citrus, vanilla; sweet, full-bodied, powerful yet perfect flavour and balance with glorious blackberry-like ripeness. The finest, loveliest of all the vintages at Taylor's tercentenary tasting in 1991. More recently, labelled *'Superior Vintage Port, bottled by John Harvey & Sons Ltd'*: fabulously fragrant; sweet, firm, spicy. Probably now the best-ever vintage of Taylor. One further comment: one of the finest ports ever made. *Last noted at the Hollywood Wine Society tasting, Florida, March 1998* ★★★★★

OTHER SHIPPERS, OLDER NOTES **Dow** Oporto-bottled but from a Danish cellar. Good chunky wine. *1970* ★★★★; **Mackenzie** two good notes. *1958* and *1970* ★★★; **Smith Woodhouse** fullish, fruity. *1965* ★★★; **Vargellas, Qta de** lovely flavour, slightly raisiny. *Lunch at Taylor's 1979* ★★★; **Warre** bottled 1951, variable, untypical Warre or '48. *1976. At best* ★★?

# 1949

Not declared. Freak weather conditions. Drought from the previous autumn until June, followed by a heatwave, 65°C and upwards, unprecedented even in Portugal. A little rain later, an early harvest, cooler. Reduced quantity.

# 1950—1969

The depth to which the port trade had sunk by 1950 will now be remembered only by those producers of my age who struggled to make ends meet in the first half of these two decades. I witnessed it first hand. My first visit to Oporto was in the early autumn of 1953. Armed with introductions from Tommy Layton at the end of my year's traineeship, I got a cheap passage on the *Seamew*, one of the small fleet of little more than coasters operated by the General Steam Navigation Company which, prior to container and road transport, shipped wine in casks from Bordeaux, Oporto and Cadiz (sherry) to the various British ports for bottling by wine merchants.

It is funny how, with a failing memory now, I can still remember clearly the name of the *Seamew's* Master, Captain Klemp, and my principal host, Christopher North, the manager of Hunt Roope, the port shipping arm of the Newman family whose vintage marque was Tuke Holdsworth (they still own the lovely old Quinta da Eira Velha). We had to wait at London docks for the tide to change; and, arriving on a warm sunny morning at the mouth of the Douro, had to wait again in order to cross the sandbar to moor mid-stream between the city of Oporto and Vila Nova de Gaia.

The view from the old British Club was splendid but not the surroundings. The poverty in Oporto was appalling, with barefoot children in rags. More to the point, most port shippers were on their last legs, some on the point of bankruptcy; also staying at the Club was a management consultant who was as glum as his clients across the river. The feeling we all had was that the port trade was on the verge of extinction. However, there were some good vintages in the 1950s (the '55 is still my favourite), though offered at what seem like ridiculously low prices, some quoted below; and a trio, three years apart, in the 1960s.

## Vintages at a Glance
**Outstanding ★★★★★**
1955, 1963, 1966
**Very Good ★★★★**
1960
**Good ★★★**
1954, 1958, 1961

# 1950 ★★

Interesting to note the prices following the declaration of the vintage. All F.O.B. (free on board. i.e. delivered to the ship, nowadays by truck or container), ex Oporto, *per pipe of* approximately 110 gallons, 55 dozen bottles: Dow, Offley's Boa Vista, Noval, Warre, Cockburn all £150, Croft, Quarles Harris and Sandeman £135. Seems unbelievable now. The producers were having a very hard time and customers benefitted. The '50s were on Harvey's lists in the mid-1950s for laying down at an average price of 17 shillings per bottle, of which customs and excise crippling duty took half (8 shillings and 4 pence).
**Crasto, Qta do** Still deep in colour; classic waxy, figgy bouquet; sweet, full and fruity, very vigorous for a 1950. *At dinner with the Roquette family, the owners of this charming and beautifully sited quinta overlooking the Douro, March 1996* ★★★
**Cockburn** Sixteen notes since 1959 and always found to be lean and spirity. Pale, fully mature, watery-rimmed; fragrant but reminiscent of an old Sercial madeira; medium-sweet, flavoury, dry finish. The most recent bottle rather undistinguished. *Last tasted May 1992. At best* ★★ *Drink up.*
**Croft** Four notes since a plummy Harvey's bottling in 1962, losing colour, very mature though still very sweet in the early 1970s. Now pale; old liquorice nose, yet surprisingly sweet and rich. *Last tasted Oct 1991. At best* ★★★ *Drink up.*
**Dow** Several notes. Once full and rich now variable, though an attractive bottle at the Dow bicentenary tasting: quite a good colour; glorious nose and delicious flavour. Very complete though perhaps lacking the length of a great vintage. Dry finish. *Last tasted Oct 1998. At best* ★★★★
**Ferreira** In 1981, when I first encountered it, it had an attractive scented fruitiness, but I recommended 'drink now'. In the spring of 1997 I reckoned it good advice, for the '50 at a Ferreira tasting was a touch sour and drying out. But a bottle opened a few months later at a pre-sale dinner in New York was a delightful surprise. It had a mature warmth, lovely nose, on the palate still very sweet though spirity. *Last tasted Sept 1997. At best* ★★★★ *just, but drink up.*
**Malvedos, Qta dos** Bottled 1952. Palish, orange-tinged; rich, sweaty, raisiny; medium sweetness and weight, chewy, sandy texture, dry acidic finish. *May 1991* ★
**Noval, Qta do** Five notes made between 1962 and 1970, all good except David Sandeman's (Glasgow): thin, nondescript, a light luncheon wine. Corney & Barrow's was lovely. Most recently, bottled by James Hawker, Plymouth: level upper mid-shoulder. Warm, chocolate-tawny colour; bouquet to match. Very sweet, nice weight, soft and agreeable. *Last tasted Nov 1988. At best* ★★★
**Noval Nacional** The best of all the '50s (in 1969) and a special bottling in 1957 for Queen Elizabeth II's visit to Oporto: amber tawny; rich, fine, nutty flavour and very dry finish. *Tasted in 1970* ★★★★
**Sandeman** Tasted more than any other '50. Fragrant, sweet but a bit spirity and acidic. *Last noted July 1986* ★★★ *Drink up.*
**Sandeman** A curiosity: a pipe (110 gallons) shipped in 1952 to a private customer in Wales but not bottled until 1985, after the owner's death. It had evaporated to 50 gallons and was bottled unfiltered. Though it had lost bulk it had gained strength. A lovely colour; rich, tangy, singed toffee, high-strength bouquet; sweet, full, very rich. Almost burning alcohol and acidity yet fat, smooth and velvety. *Tasted on two occasions, with David Sandeman, shortly after bottling, then, five months later, in Aug 1985* ★★★★

OTHER SHIPPERS, OLDER NOTES **Delaforce** good colour, good notes in the early 1960s, paler, touch of astringency. *Last tasted 1968, at best* ★★★; **Graham** smoky, drying out. *1978* ★★; **Morgan** palish and fully mature in 1976. Not bad ★★; **Offley Boa Vista** four variable notes, bland in 1962, a murky Smallwood's bottling in 1967, 'rich and powerful', 1970, 'not bad as '50s go'. *Last tasted in 1971. At best* ★★★; **Quarles Harris** Harvey's bottling was good, lovely to drink in 1958, a touch of pepperiness later. *Last noted 1969* ★★★; **Smith Woodhouse** fat when young, touch of astringency. *Last tasted 1968* ★★; **Tuke Holdsworth** which I helped bottle, on the pale side, severe, peppery. *1969–1970* ★★; and **Warre** a poor Harvey's bottling. Smell and taste of asbestos filter pads. *1962*

## 1951 ★

Not bad, but none declared. I have just one note.
**Malvedos, Qta dos** Palish, weak-rimmed; fragrant but unknit; medium sweetness and body, spirity, pungent, high acidity. *Magnum at a Graham's tasting, July 1986* ★

## 1952

Damp and dismal year. Not declared.

I HAVE FOUR OLD NOTES **Dow** Oporto-bottled, 1952, quite nice but still raw ★★; **Graham's Malvedos** from 1952 this was sold in undeclared vintages without the Quinta prefix. Deeper and more intense than the '51; unharmonious but interesting nose; sweet, full, soft, spirit and acidity uppermost. *Graham's tasting, July 1986* ★; **Niepoort** late-bottled in 1984. Pale tawny; sharp, estery volatile nose but sweet and nutty; drying out, light, some softness. *Aug, 1985* ★★; and **Ramos Pinto** rich, firm and fruity. Taste of cloves. *Aug 1979* ★★★

## 1953 ★★

Too dry, excessive heat in August. Better than the two preceding years but not up to vintage standard.

THREE OLD NOTES **Eira Velha, Qta da** very pale; rich, roasted; soft, very pleasant flavour, peppery finish. *Oct 1980* ★★★; **Graham's Malvedos** deeper than the '52. Taut, hard at first but bouquet unravelled pleasingly; sweet, fullish, soft, fleshy, nice fruit and finish. *At Graham's tasting, July 1986* ★★★; and **Sandeman** surprisingly delicate, gentle, flavoury, very sweet. *June, 1977* ★★

## 1954 ★★★

Excellent harvest but small yield. Coming after so many poor to middling vintages, some thought was given to declaring the '54, but the quantity available was insufficient (which would merely irritate potential buyers). Also by that time, the quality and quantity of the '55 was known – so there was no declaration. Rarely seen.
**Foz, Qta da** Tasted three times, first, surprisingly deep coloured, full bodied in 1975; in 1977, still deepish, ruddy-coloured; rather spirity nose; fairly sweet and characterful. *Last tasted March 1988* ★★★
**Graham's Malvedos** Rich and ruddy; gentle, fragrant, bouquet but something lacking; sweet, fullish, very good fruit, tannin and acidity. *At Graham's tasting, July 1986* ★★★★

OLDER NOTES **Offley Boa Vista** sample tasted in 1956 and preferred it to Graham. Five subsequent notes between 1967 and 1971, all good ★★★; **Dow** Oporto-bottled, from a Danish cellar. Very nice wine. *1970* ★★★; **Graham** fullish, fat, sweet, attractive in 1972. 'Perfect now.' *1979* ★★★★; and **Harvey's** sample of Graham tasted in 1956 and despite my misgivings was selected as Harvey's '54 (it was cheaper than Boa Vista: £120 per pipe as opposed to £150!). It was almost sickly sweet (1958) but when last tasted had settled down nicely. Rich, soft, firm. Lovely wine. *1968* ★★★

## 1955 ★★★★★

At last, a vintage of quality and quantity to meet an equally ripe and responding market. The best since 1948, the most widely declared – 26 shippers – since 1927.

Yet there were strange weather conditions with some excessive heat. Some still think that '54 was a better vintage. They were surely mistaken. Unquestionably '55 is my favourite vintage for drinking now.

Shippers F.O.B. prices to the trade were still low, ranging from £140 (Rebello), £150 Delaforce and Sandeman, to £170 for most of the rest. Harvey's of Bristol first listed the '55s for laying down in the autumn of 1958. Over 4000 dozen had been bought, the duty paid retail price for each of the 12 shippers listed being 20 shillings a bottle (except for Delaforce and Mackenzie, 19 shillings). Duty by then had been reduced to 6 shillings and 4 pence. (At that time, Harvey's still had considerable stocks of older vintages, back to 1927, the latter all at 36 shillings and 6 pence. I was in charge of Harvey's retail sales in Manchester at the time.) Those were the days – but not for the producers.
**Berry Bros' Own Selection** Sweet, soft, rich, peppery. *March 1989* ★★★
**Cockburn** I have been able to follow the progress of this port from cask (in 1956), pungent and purple, to maturity. At random: bottled by Hunter and Oliver, still deep and plummy in 1980; by the IECWS (The Wine Society), tasted in the early 1980s: good flavour and balance, and, more recently, by unknown bottlers: each medium-deep, with a warm glowing tawny rim; brandy showing on the nose; still fairly sweet, assertive, with good fruit, fair length but a bit hot and sharp. In 1990, lead capsule embossed and cork branded '*Cockburn's 1955 Vintage*' but bottler unknown: excellent level, beautiful colour,

---

### Saccone & Speed (1953–1955)

*I was a late starter. After spending a year as a trainee (cheap labour), with the brilliant but eccentric Tommy Layton, I visited Oporto and Jerez, ending up in Gibraltar to await a ship to take me back to England. There, by chance, I met the chairman of Saccone & Speed (these two original Gibraltarians had victualled the British Navy) who referred me to the London office, as a result of which I was offered my first proper job. In the autumn of 1953, aged 26, I reported for work in Sackville Street. Although Saccones were best known as major suppliers to the armed forces, they had acquired the old-established 'carriage trade' wine merchant, Hankey Bannister, and it was as number two on the private customer side (discreet office, not a bottle in sight) that I began my modestly paid wine merchanting career. I was doubly fortunate, for the wine buyer was the much respected Sir Guy Fison Bt, one of the earliest Masters of Wine (1954). He became my second mentor.*

beautiful gradation; soft, fragrant yet a touch of pepper and liquorice; sweet, medium full-bodied, lovely flavour, texture. Extended dry finish. Most recently: good colour; nose dusty at first, then creamy, opening up richly, fragrantly; lovely flavour, lean touch, but refined and flowery. Long, dry finish, fragrant aftertaste. *Last noted at Cockburn 'Memories of a Century' tasting, London, May 2002. At best ★★★★*

**Croft** A dozen notes. Slightly variable bottlings. 'Copybook' i.e., archetypal, in the mid-1960s, fully mature by the mid-1970s: firm yet fruity; fairly sweet, medium-weight, excellent flavour and balance. Dry, slightly spirity finish. Now fully mature; sweet, spicy, fleshy and as perfect as it will ever get. *Last noted at a nostalgic dinner at Croft's, Oporto, Oct 1997. At best ★★★★ Drink soon.*

**Delaforce** Deep, dense and unready in 1961. Curious elderflower whiff noted in mid-1960s, fruit well-developed by 1969. Now a warm mature appearance; low-keyed but harmonious fragrance; very sweet, lovely flavour, smooth flowery style. *Last tasted April 1989 ★★★★ Drink soon.*

**Dow** Countless good notes from the mid-1960s. Never very deep in colour though firm and flavoury. In June 1994 a couple of bottles at a Dow tasting in Aspen, a lovely London-bottled wine with a silkily tannic texture, the other very fragrant with a more peppery finish. Around this time some other bottles tending to dry out though very flavoury, with a lingering finish. Then vanilla and liquorice noted, and a touch of acidity creeping up. But a superb bottle at the bicentenary tasting. I could not fault it. *Last tasted Oct 1998 in top condition. At best ★★★★★ Worth seeking.*

**Ferreira** Several notes. Rich and powerful yet unready in the mid- to late 1960s. In the mid-1980s a rich and lovely wine. Then a sudden jump of 12 years: still an impressively rich appearance; fragrant, harmonious nose; perfect sweetness, weight and fruit. Dry finish. *Last noted at a Ferreira tasting at Christie's, Park Avenue, Sept 1997 ★★★★ Good now but no hurry.*

**Fonseca** Thirty years on and almost as deep and full as when first tasted in 1958. Lively-looking and rich; perfect, complete, harmonious bouquet with touch of tobacco and Spanish root; sweet, powerful – almost Taylor-like backbone, but shapely and fleshy. Harmonious, classic, at the 'The World's Greatest Vintage Ports' tasting in Florida in 1998. Most recently, mellow and mature-looking; 'liquorice' bouquet; still very sweet, crisp, lovely texture, length and finish. *Last tasted at a wine dinner at home, Jan 2000 ★★★★★ Will continue.*

**Gould Campbell** Lovely colour, bouquet and flavour. Still fairly deep; forthcoming bouquet, waxy, liquorice; sweet, full, soft, fleshy, good length, hot finish. *Last tasted Dec 1988 ★★★★*

**Graham** One of my all-time favourite ports. I have made nearly 30 notes since 1958, seven since 1990. A big wine that has evolved perfectly. A classic in 1991 bottled by Harvey's: mature but rosy-cheeked; glorious bouquet, a fabulous fragrance erupting out of its depths. Sweet, refined, silky, yet still tannic, fleshy yet firm. Showing well at a Gidleigh Park port tasting in the mid-1990s, fragrant, almost ethereal, lovely texture. Then a powerful magnum and four bottles in one month, each delectable. I noted the superb, black velvet-stained end of one of the corks, the unctuous 'tears' in the glass and the glowingly warm finish. In 1997, with Taylor's '55 at a Bacchus Society dinner in Coral Gables, ludicrously served alongside 'Autumn Pumpkin and Valrhona Chocolate Cake with Vanilla Ice Cream'. Ignoring the mismatch of food I thought I detected a reversal of roles, Graham having a more pronounced character than the Taylor. Most recently, decanted

at 6.20pm, fully mature; a light, spicy bouquet that opened up magnificently by 10.30. Still very sweet, delicious flavour, glorious length. Perfection. *Dinner at home, Oct 1999 ★★★★★*

**Noval, Qta do** Eleven notes, good but not great. Never very deep coloured and a relatively lightweight '55. Most recently palish, light-rimmed; low-keyed and delicate though with some depth, toasted liquorice; sweet, lean, spiky spicy flavour, good length, dry finish. *Last noted, Oporto-bottled, at the Noval tasting, Nov 1989 ★★★ Drink up.*

**Noval Nacional** An old note but a serious wine. At 25 years of age less intense than anticipated; very rich, liquorice nose; sweet, fullish, marvellous flavour and character. Spirity finish. *Nov 1980 ★★★★ Should be excellent now.*

**Taylor** Despite well over two dozen notes, not a wine I have yet come to grips with. An opaque blockbuster when young, astringent and unready up until the early 1980s. In the early 1990s still fairly deep-coloured; a vast, deep, high-toned, spicy nose; fairly sweet, full-bodied, packed with fruit, extract, tannin and acidity. Then, in April 1993, served at a state banquet at Buckingham Palace in honour of the President of Portugal (impressive: occasion and wine). In 1994, continuing my name dropping, a powerful spicy bottle dining with the Lloyd-Webbers in Eaton Square, followed by a full-of-bite bottle at a Christie's boardroom lunch. Most recently – yet again unsuitably served alongside 'Flavours of Chocolate, Hazelnut, Coffee and Pear, Essence of Cherries and Vanilla'. My misguided but generous host, a connoisseur in every other respect, should have known better. Naturally, I tasted the port before the dessert. It was beginning to lose its depth of colour and weight though retaining its backbone and a good classic bouquet and flavour. *Last noted at a dinner in Los Angeles, Feb 1998 ★★★★ (Possibly I am being ungenerous, for it is far from fading.)*

**Tuke Holdsworth** Two recent bottles, with fully embossed wax seals, long branded corks and Gough Bros' slip labels: medium, mature yet rich and lively-looking; bouquet of wax and liquorice; fairly sweet – one was drying out a little – medium-weight, good fruit but lean, with high alcohol and acid levels. Good drink though. *Last tasted April 1990 ★★★*

**Warre** Fifteen notes starting in 1966. Not a very deep-coloured wine but consistently noted as sweet, positive and attractive. Still somewhat unready in the late 1960s, even in the mid-1970s. In 1990 three notes, two superb, one a bit peppery and acidic; then a 'rave' note four years later at a Sunday wine lunch at Chippenham Lodge with my son and his wife, over from San Francisco, and two wine trade friends. An attractive, fully mature appearance; decanted just after noon, by 3pm it had developed a wonderful scent of cinnamon, liquorice, strawberry plus a refreshing citrus touch; sweet, the spiciness of pure ginger, with Warre elegance and length. Most recently: warm, open, rosehip colour; rich, fragrant, touch of liquorice; very sweet lovely flavour. Superb. *Last noted at the Symington Family Port Companies' tasting in London, May 2002 ★★★★★*

OLDER NOTES **Mackenzie** three notes, all Harvey's bottlings, in the mid-1960s. Slow to mature. Should be fine now ★★★; **Martinez** raw and leathery. One of the biggest '55s (1958). Slightly variable notes in late 1960s to early 1970s, various merchants' bottlings, Winterschladen's still powerful in 1977. *Last tasted 1977. At best ★★★*; **Niepoort** bottled in Oporto March 1958. Tasted twice in 1969, a fat, rich, well balanced wine. *1969 ★★★★*; **Offley Boa Vista** bottled by Harvey's in 1959 and tasted just after bottling. Ruby-coloured; light, dry-edged ★★★; **Rebello Valente** only one note: opaque yet soft in the mouth. *1969* ★★★ *worth looking out for;* **Sandeman** over a dozen notes, starting in 1958 deep, considerable bite, not great but consistently good notes through the 1960s and 1970s, softening, maturing. *Not tasted since 1978* ★★★; **Síbio, Qta do** bottled 1957. Rather dull, still immature and peppery in *1966*. Rarely seen ★★; and **Smith Woodhouse** 'plump little wine' in *1980. Should be delicious now* ★★★

# 1956

The worst weather conditions of the period. Snow followed by cold wet spring, summer and autumn. A washout.

# 1957

Irregular weather. Wine not up to vintage standard.
**Cálem** Bottled 1990. Medium-tawny; fairly high volatile acidity; sweet, fullish, rich, raisiny flavour. Very good in its way. *Dec 1990* ★★★
**Sandeman** Peppery; very flavoury, charming, nice fruit, dry finish. *Last tasted May 1991* ★★ *Ready.*

OTHER, OLDER NOTES **Cockburn** late-bottled. Unremarkable; **Noval, Qta do** awful, raw; and **Vargellas, Qta de** bottled 1960, skinny but flavoury. *All tasted in the mid-1960s to mid-1970s. Avoid.*

# 1958 ★★★

A pleasant enough vintage made in an unusually wet year. A light stop-gap vintage declared by 12 shippers, nice now but needs drinking. Many tasted but few recently.
**Delaforce** Nine notes. Never deeply coloured, nice enough in the mid-1960s. At best in mid-1970s but still pleasant, rosy-hued; slightly medicinal bouquet; medium-sweet, soft. *Last tasted March 1986* ★★ *Drink up.*
**Graham's Malvedos** Palish; a bit unyielding; quite attractive, short peppery finish. *Last tasted July 1992* ★★
**Harvey's** Disappointing, lean, lacking fruit. *Sadly, at the first Martin Bamford Memorial dinner at the Dorchester, Nov 1992* ★
**Noval, Qta do** Over 12 agreeable notes through the 1960s and 1970s. An easy, attractive wine. Most recently, bottled by Berry Bros: very sweet, good spicy flavour, but short. *Last tasted Nov 1989* ★★ *Drink up.*
**Noval Nacional** Rich, fabulous finish, at the quinta in 1969. Two slightly variable bottles in 1980: both very deep for a '58; one citrus-scented, one with quite an alcoholic kick. Each had wonderfully intense grapiness. Most recently, fairly deep; rich, meaty, mocha nose; very sweet, lovely but by no means a blockbuster Nacional. *Last noted at a Saintsbury Club dinner Oct 2000* ★★★★ *Now–2015.*
**Sandeman** Many notes from a soft, bland Harvey's bottling in 1966, sweet, rich and fruity through the late 1960s, 'nearing its peak' in 1978. A lean and edgy (raw, acidic) bottle in 1986 but ten years later, surprisingly sweet, drinking well at a Distillers' Court luncheon. *Last tasted June 1996* ★★★ *Drink up.*
**Tuke Holdsworth** Two notes, both Oporto-bottled by Hunt, Roope: palish, fully mature; singed, substantial bouquet; sweet, nice weight, rich, good fruit, plumper than expected. A very agreeable '58. *Last tasted Jan 1991* ★★★ *Drink soon.*
**Warre** The most often seen. Eighteen notes, all demonstrating that this has always been a sweet, lightish, soft and very agreeable wine. *Last tasted April 1992* ★★★ *Drink soon.*

OTHER '58s, OLDER NOTES **Butler Nephew** bottled 1961. Cardboard nose. Light. Not bad. *1980* ★; **Dow** big, severe, unready in *1969. Should be interesting now* ★★★?; **Feuerheerd** curiously sweet and fat. *1974* ★; **Guimaräes** refined but a bit 'mean'. *1966* and *1971* ★★; **Mackenzie** strong, velvety in the mid-1966s. *Not tasted since* ★★; **Martinez** many notes. Bigger than the other '58s from the start. Still a fine colour; fruity nose; sweet, full, spicy flavour in the *mid-1980s* ★★★; **Quarles Harris** good notes in the mid-1960s, 'lovely flavour, nice now' in *1969. Probably faded now* ★★★; **Royal Oporto** pale and Portuguese. Raisiny. *1972* ★; and **Vargellas, Qta de** nice wine in early *1970s* ★★ *Faded now?*

# 1959

The odd man out in Europe; the 1959 port harvest disappointing. Not declared. None tasted.

# 1960 ★★★★

An enthusiastically declared, and received, vintage, 24 shippers. The weather dictated the style of wine. A very hot summer.
Picking, which began in some areas as early as September 12th, and in a heatwave, ended in rain. The heat accounts for some noticeable acidity and, for those who picked late, a little weakness. Nevertheless agreeable, flavoury wines. More or less fully developed.
**Cálem Reserve** A sensationally good Colheita, bottled in 1995. I first drank this wine dining with Joachim Cálem and his wife at their home south of Oporto. Until then I had not been a great admirer of 'vintage tawnys' but I was persuaded that this was something special. Indeed it was. A pure, mature, palish tawny; nutty nose and a simply glorious flavour. Sweet, fleshy, perfection. This was in 1996. Joachim gave me one of

---

## Harvey's of Bristol (1955–1966)

*A very creative period for the company: wine under the benign influence of my third mentor, Harry Waugh, management under the dynamic chairman, George McWatters.*

*I left Saccone's in 1955 and, after an introductory stint in Bristol – where, in the ancient cellars beneath the offices, port, sherry and almost all other wines were bottled directly from the cask – I joined Harvey's London office, uncannily and coincidentally in King Street, a block away from Christie's. In 1957 I was posted to Manchester (on a 'set a thief to catch a thief' basis – I was practically a Mancunian by birth) to open up the retail business and serve as local director of this region. Harvey's had a fabulous list. All the classic wines in abundance. I became an MW in 1960 and the following year, at very short notice, I was transferred to Bristol where in the space of five years I was responsible for developing 'shops-within-shops' (from 2 to 19, in the UK), served on the wine-buying committee, most bizarrely was brand manager for Suchard's liqueur chocolates (they did not take kindly to my definition: the best liqueur chocolate is one which makes you drunk before you are sick); marketing – an unhappy time as the head of this new department knew nothing about wine or the wine trade; corporate design, acting as buffer between an opinionated Terence Conran and a philistine Group Board. Then, having reached the dizzy height of UK Sales Director, I thought it time to move on.*

*It had been a richly rewarding experience. And, at the age of 40, I was ripe for Christie's.*

his few remaining bottles which I eventually opened at a vinous dinner at Chippenham Lodge. I had rarely seen my wife make such a fuss about a dinner, worrying for days in advance, for one of our guests was Michel Roux (the Waterside Inn is closed on Mondays!). Anyway, this was the port I served. Bouquet like a sweet, honeyed Bual madeira; silky texture, nutty flavour, touch of liquorice. Languorous. *Last noted April 1997* ★★★★ *Drink now, but I doubt if you will ever find any!*

**Cockburn** Over 20 notes since 1966. Started losing its deep colour in the early 1980s. By the mid-1980s palish, mature and fully developed bouquet. Still fairly sweet, lean but elegant, dry, slightly acidic finish. *Last tasted Dec 1993* ★★★ *Drink soon.*

**Croft** Particularly impressive in the mid-1960s. Many notes, various bottlings, though few recently. For long a rather deep-coloured-ruby, retaining its colour in the 1980s. Now maturing. Stylish, attractive, sweet but lean, nice weight, firm dry finish. Drinking well but a wine of lesser breed than my noble host, (21st Earl) Mickey Suffolk. *Last noted dining at Charlton Park, Dec 1993* ★★★

**Dow** Nearly 30 notes mainly in the 1970s to mid-1980s recording normal colour loss, some with orange rim, all consistently noting the high-toned nose, fragrant but with a whiff of volatile acidity, lean but flavoury. (Michael Symington told me that several shippers' 1960s had high volatile acidity because of great heat during the vintage.) Then a quantum leap to a lovely bottle with an almost beetroot-like colour, fragrant as before but a sweeter impact, lovely flavour, complete, with dry finish. *Last noted at Dow's bicentenary tasting, Oct 1998. At best hovering around* ★★★★

**Ferreira** First tasted in 1981. Good colour. Lovely fruit. Sweet, fullish, crisp. Next, showing considerable evolution in March 1997 at Bartholomew's Ferreira trade tasting in Fort Lauderdale. A distinctly attractive wine, not deep, not too sweet, showing well. Then twice, six months later, drinking pleasantly at a boardroom luncheon at Christie's, New York, and acquitting itself fragrantly at a Ferreira tasting the same evening. Now palish, with a rosy hue, nice weight, lean, with dry finish. Fractionally past its best but very drinkable. *Last tasted Sept 1997* ★★★ *Drink now–2005.*

**Fonseca** Tasted many times over the past 30 years. Rain at the end of harvesting, so a lighter wine than usual. Not a great Fonseca and certainly not a patch on the 1963, yet it cannot help being attractive. Leaner and less structured than usual, a citrus-touch on the nose, drying out a little, but it made a most agreeable, if not wholly appropriate, end to a Commanderie de Bordeaux dinner in Bristol. *Last noted May 1995* ★★★ *Drink up.*

**Graham** Many notes. Lovely to drink from the start. 'Soft' noted fairly consistently from mid-1960s through the 1970s. Lively, attractive, sweet but lacking a little concentration. Two good Oporto-bottlings in 1991, fragrant but rather lean for Graham and two in the mid-1990s. Now fully mature with a lovely translucence; ethereal, delicate bouquet becoming rich and tangy. Still very sweet with good length and aftertaste. High alcohol content and an exquisite crystallised violet end flavour. *Last tasted Feb 1995* ★★★★ *Perfect now.*

**Martinez** Many notes, from deep, plummy and fruity in 1964. Maturing but quite a bite in the 1970s. Slightly variable bottlings but at best a good wine, lovely vinosity, fairly sweet, full-bodied, lean, hard, rather Taylor-like backbone, distinctive style. Spicy, drinking well. *Last noted lunching with David Carter in Gloucestershire, May 2001* ★★★★

**Noval, Qta do** 'Charm' appears in several of my 11 notes. Now palish, mature; tangy, attractive nose; still fairly sweet, medium weight, rather idiosyncratic spicy violets flavour. Acidity noticeable. *Last tasted Nov 1989* ★★★ *Drink soon.*

**Noval, Nacional** First tasted in 1969: a richly packed, flavoury wine; opaque, concentrated, unready in 1970. Next, in 1992: glorious scent; lovely fruit, flavour, length. Elegant, perfect. Most recently: a most explicitly identified bottle, original wax capsule embossed 1960 Nacional, labelled '*A J da Silva Ltd./Quinta do Noval 1960 vintage*', slip label '*Nacional Produced from Pre-Phylloxera Grapes*', and cork branded '*Nacional*'. Nothing could be clearer than that! (Sometimes it is hard to tell.) My only bottle, incidentally, carried on an early flight to Copenhagen and decanted at 11.35am in the offices of *Smag & Behag*, Denmark's leading wine and food journal, as a surprise lunchtime present for Henrik Oldenburg, the editor and a small group of local (and Swedish) wine buffs, all old friends of mine. The wine survived the journey: lovely colour, rich 'legs'; initially rather peppery, with dry Spanish root fragrance: fairly sweet, fairly full-bodied, rich, smooth and fleshy, with a lovely aftertaste. A beautiful port. *Last tasted Aug 1996* ★★★★★ *Drink now–2010, possibly beyond.*

**Sandeman** Tasted many times, mostly between 1966 and 1982. Good wine, with the high tone and leanness I associate with the '60s. Then a gap of ten years to 1999: a good Harvey's bottling taken from my own cellar to Brooks's, hosting a dinner for Ronald Holden, an enterprising wine tour organiser from Oregon. Now fully mature; a good classic nose; drying out a little, nice weight – not too alcoholically heavy, attractive flavour. Three months later, at home, an identical bottle: mellow, delicious. *Last tasted June 1999* ★★★ *Drink soon.*

**Smith Woodhouse** Just one note: medium, mature; dusty, peppery nose; medium-sweet, good fruit but quite a bite. *At a pre-sale tasting, Nov 1993* ★★★ *(just). Drink soon.*

**Taylor** 250 pipes shipped for UK bottling. Many notes, slight variation due mainly to different merchants' bottlings. Three bottles from the same London livery company's cellars tasted in the mid-1980s were variations on a theme. What I believe was Oporto-bottled looked the most mature; hefty, sweet, chocolatey on the nose; medium-sweet, fairly full-bodied. The Army & Navy Stores' bottling was deeper and plummier; a low-keyed but alcoholic nose; sweeter, fuller, with a better and longer flavour. The third, bottler unknown, less sweet, lean and uncompromising on the palate, good texture and end taste. More recently Oporto-bottled: still sweet, fleshy but 'hot' peppery and alcoholic. It will be interesting to see how this turns out. *Last tasted March 1992* ★★★(★) *Now–2015.*

**Tuke Holdsworth** A delicious creamy but crisp bottle with fruity tang in 1978. Two more recent, the first in 1989, both Oporto-bottled by Hunt, Roope, both fully mature, rosy-hued, the first had a rich raisiny nose, the second a scented almost ethereal bouquet. Both were medium-sweet, medium-light, with good length and dry, slightly acidic finish. *Last tasted Jan 1991* ★★★ *Drink up.*

**Warre** Also many notes, nearly 20 prior to 1981, different bottlings. Variable: one Oporto-bottled corked, another very flavoury. On average medium-deep, maturing appearance; a fairly sweet, classic and elegant wine, sometimes with twist of 1960 acidity. In 1990 a bottle with a lovely, slightly singed, almost muscatel aroma; very sweet, lovely flavour, texture and length. But two disappointing bottles at a Symington port tasting in 1994, both looking fully mature; both with rather high volatile acidity; drying out, crisp, with noticeable acid prickle. Most recently: nose still a bit hard; touch of leanness, good length, dry finish. Not a top Warre. *Last noted at the Symington Family Port Companies' tasting at the Berkeley, London, May 2002* ★★★

OTHER 1960s **Averys** rich, flavoury, forward. *1973* ★★★; **Burmester** bottled in Oporto, March 1962: fragrant, touch of liquorice on the nose, attractive, fresh and fruity. *Last tasted 1983* ★★★; **Delaforce** bottled by Harvey's. Ruddy-tinted; two-part nose, hard yet very forthcoming; sweet, lean, light style, touch of acid on the finish. *April 1989* ★★★; **Feuerheerd** quite good Harvey's bottlings. 1967 and *1972* ★★; **González Byass** curious, cheesy. *1972*; **Morgan** plummy colour, Spanish root nose and taste. *1976* ★; **Poças Junior** very sweet, easy, flavoury. *1981* ★★★; **Quarles Harris** attractive but short. *1972* ★★; **Rebello Valente** a deep-coloured '60, nice flavour, biting finish in mid- to late 1960s ★★★; **Serras** single-quinta port, quite nice, sweet, soft, fruity. *Oct 1986* ★★; and **Sibio, Qta de** sweet but hard. *1974* ★★★

## 1961 ★★★

Good wines made but vintage not declared. Too soon after the '60s and, by the time decisions were to be made, the high quality of the '63s was known. In a way a pity, as the '61 vintage was so brilliant elsewhere, in Bordeaux particularly, that there would have been a sales rub-off. However, this was the year when not only single-quinta wines began to show their paces but LBVs (late-bottled vintage ports) put in a major appearance, mainly for early consumption.

A SMALL SELECTION OF NOTES **Dow** bottled 1965. Very spirity; plummy fruit, a bit raw. *1984* ★; **Graham's Malvedos** bottled 1963. In 1971 I advised 'drink up'. This was a premature observation for in the mid-1980s and early 1990s it still had a deep, fairly intense look about it; fragrant, fruit and liquorice nose; very sweet, full-bodied, soft, fleshy, good length. *Last tasted May 1992* ★★★; and **Vargellas, Qta de** bottled in 1964. Fully mature; very sweet, rich, raisiny nose and taste. Soft. Attractive. *Feb 1995* ★★★

## 1962 ★★

Quite a good growing season, but, sandwiched between the much-shipped '60s and the important '63s, not declared. Some nice wines, still pleasant to drink. One classic: Noval Nacional.
**Graham's Malvedos** Bottled 1964. Soft ruby; crisp, flavoury in 1982. Three notes later. Now palish, very mature; light, spirity, sweet, rich, lovely texture, twist of lemon. *Last tasted May 1991* ★★ *Drink up.*
**Guimarães, Reserve** Palish, weak rim; estery, black treacle nose; very sweet, chewy, raisiny, pasty texture, slightly acidic. *Last tasted March 1991. Give it a miss.*
**Harvey's** Worth mentioning: an interesting blend of Cockburn and Martinez imported by Harvey's and bottled in Bristol. (Cork branded 'Harvey's 1962'.) Rather weak-rimmed; clove-like, singed, raisin nose; sweet, spicy, soft yet spirity. *Tasted twice in 1991* ★★ *Drink up.*
**Noval Nacional** This is a great wine, made from grapes grown in the 10% of the vineyards at the quinta planted with ungrafted local fruiting varieties. Six notes: 'black strap' in 1969, hardly any change in 1979 and, in 1989, still deep, thick and intense yet with a mature rim; an unusual bouquet,

peppery, old spice, dusty, alcoholic and with a distinct tea-like scent – a sign of quality. Sweet, full-bodied, powerful, concentrated, chocolatey, touch of black treacle, excellent acidity to bear it into the next century. Then, in January 1994, a deep, husky, slightly malty-nosed wine with magnificent richness and depth. Still peppery and spicy. Later that autumn, the oldest of 12 vintages at a possibly unprecedented Nacional tasting. I rated it second equal with the '82 after the perfect '63. Most recently: still virtually opaque with a strong tarry smell and taste like concentrated figs and liquorice. Powerful, impressive but lacking charm. *Last noted in the most unlikely setting, the famous Joe's Stone Crab Restaurant in Miami, at Bob Dickinson's opening Bacchus Society dinner, Oct 1997* ★★★★(★)
**Offley Boa Vista** Five notes – none recent. Rich and lovely in 1973. I thought it was a '58. At over 20 years of age, elegant, flavoury, nice weight. *Last tasted Oct 1985* ★★★ *Drink up.*

OTHER '62S AND OLDER NOTES **Dow** bottled 1966 low-keyed but attractive in late *1970s* ★★; **Niepoort** bottled 1985. A typically idiosyncratic but good Niepoort Colheita: orange tawny; high-toned, raisiny nose; sweet, good length, slightly acidic, caramelly finish. *Oct 1990* ★★; **Sandeman** nice enough in the mid-1970s, though not much future *Nov 1976* ★★; and **Warre** bottled 1966, palish, rosy-hued, hot spirity nose and taste. *Aug 1987* ★

## 1963 ★★★★★

A highly important vintage. Twenty-five shippers. Fairly favourable conditions, though a drought lasted from Whitsun through the summer months until September. There was a good harvest towards the end of that month. A large quantity of vintage port made, probably the biggest volume since 1927, and some very beautiful wines. The top: Dow, Warre, Fonseca, Graham and Taylor. Most are now fully mature and many are losing colour and living on their reputation.
**Averys** Waxy, Spanish root nose; sweet, very pleasant weight and flavour. John Avery informed us that it was a blend of Taylor, Fonseca and Sandeman, bottled in 1965. *At a Saintsbury Club dinner at Vintners' Hall, London, Oct 2001* ★★★
**Borges & Irmão** A pretty tough wine in the 1970s, typical Borges' fat and rich. Most recently, pale even for a mature '63. Lean, strange flavour and acidic finish. *Last noted at a pre-sale tasting in New York, Sept 1997. Avoid.*
**Cockburn** Many notes on a variety of English bottlings. Opaque, liquorice and raw brandy in 1965. Steady evolution through the 1970s and noted as complete and harmonious – at its best – in 1980. In 1985, lively-looking with ruby glow; interesting bouquet, tea, chocolate, liquorice, citrus. Never very sweet, lean, sinewy. But in the mid-1990s, quite a good colour. Its nose reminded me of burnt-out candle wax. Drying out. Most recently: palish, luminous; low-keyed at first but opened up fragrantly; lean dry finish but overall very appealing. Good length. *Showing well at Cockburn's 'Memories of a Century' tasting in London, May 2002* ★★★★
**Croft** Dozens of notes. First tasted in June 1965: lovely flavour, crystallised violets. Good throughout the 1970s and 1980s, though slight bottle and bottling variations. Three notes in the early to mid-1990s. Fairly consistently sweet and soft. A particularly agreeable bottle with bread and butter pudding at a Bacchus Society dinner at Brooks's; but then in 1995 a rather dusty, medicinal bottle, lean and drying out. Most recently, an Oporto-bottled magnum: medium-deep, suitably mature rim;

classic flowery bouquet; almost Graham-like sweetness though lean and fading a little. *Last noted dining with the Guises in Sherston, Jan 2002* ★★★ *Drink soon.*

**Delaforce** Eight notes since bottling in 1965 and much liked. Fragrant, sweet, elegant. Agreeable in its youth, perfect in the mid-1980s. Liquorice and tangerine flavour, good length in the early 1990s. Most recently, fully mature, rather lean but delicious. *Last noted just after midnight on arrival at a friend's cottage in Brittany, June 1999* ★★★★ *Perhaps the best-ever Delaforce.*

**Dow** Starting in 1965, I seem to have tasted an awful lot of Dow '63: 11 times up to the late 1970s, 20 times in the 1980s and well over a dozen in the 1990s. On the whole very good, though I recall one wormy-corked acetic disaster in the early days and a most unfortunate late-delivered, poorly decanted batch, hazy and bitter, at a livery company dinner in 1994. Bad handling can spoil a good port. There was a particularly fine magnum at the Dow bicentenary tasting: very deep colour, its rim somewhat indistinct, showing neither youth nor age; classic Spanish root bouquet; still sweet, rich, with marvellous fruit and flesh. The Symingtons told us that this was the last vintage of Dow foot-pressed in traditional open stone *lagares*. More recently, drying out at a 'hog-roast' Bar-B-Q in Memphis, Tennessee in September 1999, but perfect weight, flavour and balance at Vintners' Hall. *Last enjoyed at The One Hundred and Thirty-Eighth Meeting (dinner) of the Saintsbury Club, April 2001* ★★★★ *Drink now–2010.*

**Fonseca** From start (June 1965) to finish a consistently beautiful wine. One of the top '63s, and one of the best-ever Fonsecas. Half a dozen notes in the 1990s, but in the mid-decade losing colour though still lovely, and a fragrant, elegant Oporto-bottling in 1998 surviving 'Dark Chocolate and Hazelnut Praline' (oh dear! Why do these American gourmets do this?). Most recently, medium-deep, richly coloured; cinnamon and cress fragrance; still sweet, fairly assertive, tall, shapely, lissom. *Last tasted Dec 1998* ★★★★★ *Perfect now–2015.*

**Gould Campbell** Not tasted in its youth. Three dozen bought in the 1980s. Quite coincidentally, opened for dinner at Chippenham Lodge on New Year's Day in 1994 *and* 1995, and again that spring. All three bottles imported in cask by Clode & Baker, then the UK agent, and bottled in 1965 (branded on cork). Consistent notes: medium, warm mature appearance; distinctly sweet on nose and palate. Nutty. Citrus touch. *Last tasted April 1995* ★★★ *Drink soon.*

**Graham** Three dozen idyllic notes since 1965, no matter where or by whom bottled. For example, Danish-bottled and by Grants of St James's both similarly described (in 1975 and 1976) as huge, powerful and spirity. Among the most recent notes, a superb Corney & Barrow bottling, even with the bottling date on the cork, and an excellent Oporto-bottled wine: medium-deep, slightly plummy, maturing nicely; sweet, rich, compact, slightly chocolatey bouquet; very sweet compared to the '60 and '66, fairly full-bodied, chunky fruit, rich yet lissom, great power and penetration. Still with great potential for further development.

I have eight notes from the early to mid-1990s. Lovely bottles at the Christie's wine department's Christmas dinners in the boardroom in 1992 *and* 1993. 'Drinking perfectly' at the end of a Ch Mouton-Rothschild dinner at Brooks's Club the following spring and one of my highest rated ports at Symington tastings, 'very powerful' in 1994, and in 1995: a magnum, Oporto-bottled, which had, I thought, lost quite a bit of colour, 'delicious but fading'. *A lovely bottle last noted at home in July 1996* ★★★★★ *Drink now–2010.*

**Mackenzie** Just three notes: sweet, good flavour, shortly after bottling in June 1965, and two bottles at Christie's luncheons, drinking pleasantly enough. *Last tasted Nov 1992* ★★ *Drink up.*

**Martinez** Several consistent notes. Sweet, bland, rich in 1965. Good enough in the 1970s. Not particularly impressive but three perfectly adequate bottles at Christie's Boardroom luncheons between December 1994 and the New Year. Not very deep but sweet, nice weight, drinking well. *Last tasted Feb 1995* ★★ *Drink up.*

**Niepoort** Three notes since the mid-1980s. The first, though clearly a two-year bottling, had a rose-tawny hue, the most recent fairly deep and intense. But both were sweet, with a full fruity flavour and good length. *Last tasted Aug 1990* ★★★

**Niepoort** Bottled 1987. One of the many permutations of this small but high-quality family firm. A Colheita, what I call a 'vintage tawny', with characteristic pale amber colour, high-toned walnut bouquet; very sweet, crisp. *Aug 1990* ★★★

**Noval, Qta do** First tasted 1965. Even then soft and sweet. Many notes but only a few since the early 1980s. Good but not great. With the exception of a rather sharp Cockburn & Campbell bottling, fragrant, elegant, lean, and lightish in style, spicy and with slightly hot, spirity dry finish. Now fully mature; sweet bouquet, vanilla and liquorice; still sweet, lovely. *Last noted Sept 1993* ★★★ *Drink up.*

**Noval Nacional** As different as night and day: in 1989 a deep, intense-looking wine just striving to mature; immense, expansive, fig-like nose of great depth; medium-sweet but very full-bodied. An enormous, spicy wine with great length. My highest mark at a tasting of 12 Nacional vintages in 1994; glorious, uplifting, assertive. More recently at a Bacchus Society pre-dinner port tasting: robust, still youthful; tremendous bite and concentration. *Last noted in Miami, March 1998* ★★★★(★) *2010–2040.*

**Offley Boa Vista** Several very consistent notes. Impressively big wine in the mid-1960s. Medium, lively, mature; spicy, fragrant; fairly sweet, medium-weight, good length. A scent and flavour of singed raisins and liquorice. Crisp. Very flavoury. Nine notes in the last half of the 1990s, mainly at Christie's boardroom luncheons and always showing well, 'delicious', 'spicy'. Most recently six bottles at a Christie's wine tasting and dinner in Belgium. A combination of thoughtlessness and carelessness was nearly disastrous. Travelling on Eurostar, I placed the carton sideways on the rack not realising that a junior, after decanting, had put in the wrong stopper corks. Some bottles leaked. The carton was soggy and smelly – but we lost only one-third of a bottle, the rest survived: colour medium-deep; very good bouquet, touch of liquorice; sweet, nice weight, spicy. Enjoyed by all. *Last tasted at La Maison du Cygne, Brussels, March 1997* ★★★★ *Drink soon.*

**Rebello Valente** Two notes in the mid-1960s. Most recently: fully mature; sweet, delicious fruit on nose and palate. Lively, attractive. Slightly 'hot' acidic finish. *Last tasted Nov 1997* ★★★★ *Drink soon.*

**Sandeman** Eight mainly very good notes between 1965 and 1978, slightly variable notes since the early 1980s. Tasting rather peppery and spirity (touch of caramel and figs, my wife noted); not very sweet or full. I said 'lean'; my host said 'elegant' in 1989. Most recently, still a good colour, 'classic', flavoury, 'a pretty good '63'. *Last noted at a Russian National Orchestra dinner at Hatchlands, Surrey. (Torrential rain, we got lost in the dark, narrow cart track, ditched the car, long walk though mud to find farmer with tractor to pull us out. We were late.) Dec 2000* ★★★★ *Drink soon.*

**Taylor** Strangely, tasting this shortly after bottling in 1965 I noted it as being 'full, soft, forward'; then, later, fine but raw and unready during the late 1960s to early 1980s when it gained stature in my eyes. One, Oporto-bottled in 1966 and tasted in 1979, had already lost its youthful depth and the same bottling, noted in 1990, had also lost a lot of colour, retaining very little red though lively on the palate.

Dining at Saddlers' Hall in London in 1994, I noted it as lovely. It was certainly the best wine at the Saintsbury Club dinner in October 1996: 'perfect weight and flavour' (strangely delicious with the club's traditional Cox's Orange Pippin apples and wholemeal biscuits, perhaps less bizarre than the Americans' obsession with serving port with chocolate puddings!). Most recently, I noted a red-brown tawny; bouquet opening up beautifully; good flavour. And, of course, it had the customary Taylor backbone. *Last tasted in Miami, March 1998* ***** *Now–2020.*

**Warre** Despite a shaky start (in 1965) and a dozen slightly variable notes through the 1970s, for me this is now one of the best and most elegant of all the '63s. I have made a total of sixteen notes since the early 1980s when it emerged, fully fledged and totally delicious.

Only half a dozen noted in the 1990s, the most useful at the two Symington tastings, in 1994 and 1996, each time alongside the Graham and Dow. Warre looked the most mature of the three and had lost quite a bit of colour, particularly in magnum; very fragrant, harmonious, touch of spice, cloves, tangerine; stylish, beautifully balanced, gentle acidity. *Last noted, showing well at Hal Lewis's superb 'Mr Gourmet' dinner in Memphis, Tennessee, Sept 1999* **** *Now–2015.*

OTHER '63s, OLDER NOTES **Berry Bros' Selection** (reputed to have come from Taylor) Sweet, soft, lovely. *Last tasted March 1990* ****; **Burmester** bottled April 1965. Contrary notes: 'a bit feeble' in 1979. Very deep, rich, smell of sugared raisins; very sweet light style, flavoury in 1991. More recently: tawny colour; high tone; sweet, dry acidic finish. *Last tasted Aug 1993* *; **Cálem** deep; rich, plummy; very sweet, soft, fleshy. *March 1988* ****; **Feuerheerd** rich, still peppery in the mid-1970s. *** *rarely seen but should be drinking well;* **Hunt's** (Hunt, Roope) pale for a '63; mature; sweet, lightish, soft yet spicy. *July 1985* ***; **Krohn** orange tinge; figgy, mediocre. *Two notes Aug 1993, not recommended;* **Rosa, Qta de la** just down-river from Pinhão and only recently marketed as a single-quinta wine. Touch of ruby with tawny rim; soft sweet nose, touch of liquorice; a very sweet, powerful wine with loads of grip, tannin and acidity. *Nov 1988* ***(*); **Royal Oporto** very sweet, prune-like, fruity. *June 1987* **; and **Smith Woodhouse** just one recent note: medium, mature, slightly weak rim; attractive, high-toned, well-developed, citrus tinge; sweet entry, dry finish, crisp, still a bit hard. *Dec 1990* ***

# 1964 *

Severe winter, early drought, spring rains. A hot summer and very hot mid-September. Rain too late, picking a problem. Not an easy year, and not declared.

**Graham's Malvedos** Bottled in Oporto, 1966. Six notes. Deep colour in the early 1980s, now a very mature, orange-tinged appearance; very fragrant; medium-sweet, nice weight, flavour and style. Refreshing finish. *May 1991* *** *Drink up.*

**Noval Nacional** The least impressive of the 12 Nacional vintages, 1962–1987: comparatively weak, amber-brown colour; lean, spirity, nose and flavour. Dry finish. *Last tasted Sept 1994* * *Drink up.*

OTHER '64s, OLDER NOTES **Butler Nephew** firm, reasonably fruity. *Nov 1980* **; **González Byass** deep ruby, quite fat, nice fruit. *Nov 1980* **; **Guimaräes, Reserve** bottled 1966. First tasted shortly after bottling and still, in the mid-1980s, thick and plummy and very sweet. High-toned. *Last tasted Feb 1984* ***

# 1965 *

Some nice, ripe wines but, sandwiched between the '63s and '66s, a vintage not declared.

**Bomfim, Qta do** Only two vintage pipes were bottled. Attractive colour, medium ruby; surprisingly sweet nose and palate. Fragrant. Soft, fleshy, fruit. Delicious! *At Dow's bicentenary tasting, Oct 1998* *** *Drink soon.*

**Graham's Malvedos** Four notes: lovely, long flavour save one sharp and woody bottle. *Last tasted July 1986. At best* *** *Drink up.*

**Vargellas, Qta de** Bottled in the UK, 1968. Rich, attractive in 1973. Powerful Taylor backbone noticeable in the mid-1980s. Crisp, fruity, more maturity in late 1988s, now losing colour, weak rim; liquorice nose; lean, drying out. *Last tasted on the snail's pace train from Vargellas up in the Douro to Oporto, May 1997* ** *Drink up.*

OTHER '65s, OLDER NOTES **Borges & Irmão** 20 years in cask: amber, high volatile acidity, madeira-like. *May 1985;* **Cálem** bottled 1990: rosehip tawny; bouquet of oranges and cobnuts; sweet, soft, raisiny, attenuated. *Dec 1990* ***

---

### Visiting the Douro

*This is a must for all lovers of port. But be warned, there is no easy or speedy way. It must have been intolerable by coach and mule; it is still pretty excruciating by car, the more so the higher one drives upstream, and roads leading to individual quintas can be very narrow and tortuous. The most romantic – and tedious – way is by train, an infrequent service from Oporto with many, sometimes unaccountable, stops en route. But as a reward, there are incomparable views of the river and its vine-clad slopes. It is a must – if only once. My last train trip was from Quinta de Vargellas – they have their own stop, hardly a station – to Oporto. I seem to recall it took about seven hours, the tedium relieved by good wines, good company (fellow 'Distillers') and a special carriage complete with bar and waiter, laid on by our hosts, Taylors.*

*Now that the river, once tumultuous and dangerous, is canalised, tourist launches operate but I have no experience of these lock-hopping boat trips.*

*Although I first visited Oporto in 1953, I did not venture up river until the mid-1960s and I well recall the scene, hard to believe now, of abandoned terraces and vines uprooted, for the port trade was still at very low ebb. It is quite different now. Over the years a huge programme of replanting has taken place: it seems there is scarcely an inch to spare, the dangerously steep slopes bulldozed to create new terraces, and the rocky soil blasted to plant new vines. I hope they haven't overdone it.*

*Don't let me put you off: do go.*

# 1966 ★★★★★

A marvellous vintage declared by 20 shippers, Cockburn and Martinez being the odd-men out. Firm yet flexible wines with perfect weight and balance. Sinewy and long-lasting. Most will almost certainly outlast the '63s, and will probably turn out greater in the end. All this was due to a hot year which ripened but did not singe the grapes, and some rain at vintage time which reduced concentration. This vintage is still somewhat underestimated and undervalued.

**Berry Bros' Selection** A superbly balanced wine blended and bottled in Berry Bros' style and, of course, only available from No 3, St James's Street, London. Still deep, relatively youthful for its age; harmonious, waxy bouquet, fairly sweet, nice weight, elegant, well balanced. In short, delicious. (I have since learned that this was shipped via Percy Fox & Co, then Warre's agents.) *Several notes, last tasted Feb 1989* ★★★★★ *Ready.*

**Cálem** In 1988, deep, still ruby; lovely wine, long dry finish. Now fully mature. *Last tasted Aug 1993* ★★★ *Now–2010.*

**Cockburn** Though not declared I recently tasted a sample bottle. Attractive yet unsatisfactory. I noted 'sour cream' volatile acidity; lean, 'pinched' yet flavoury. Now I understand why Cockburn's did not ship their '66. *Noted Aug 1993.*

**Croft** In the mid-1980s: plummy; fruity; harmonious; good depth, nice weight. Now, noting a strange peppery nose; fairly sweet, touch of hardness. *Last tasted Aug 1993* ★★★ *Now–2010.*

**Delaforce** Rich, powerful, hefty tang in 1978. Eleven years later still surprisingly deep and immature; deep, firm, citrus touch; sweet, full, chunky for Delaforce, good length, alcohol and acidity. In 1993 sweeter and fuller bodied than the '63. Most recently: paler than expected; varnishy nose; very sweet, high-toned, spirity. *Last noted at Christie's, April 2002* ★★★ *Now–2010.*

**Dow** Several notes, several bottlings, all good. Some colour loss but rich and attractive. Only three notes since 1988, two in 1994, the first in Aspen, elegant, complete, lovely texture; fully developed, surprisingly sweet, then very good at a Symington tasting. At Dow's bicentenary tasting in 1998, a well-nigh perfect bottle, fragrant, very sweet yet with a Dow dry finish. Most recently: lovely, evolved, slightly spirity; very sweet for Dow, delicious, perfect now. *Last noted at the Symington families' tasting in London, May 2002* ★★★★★ *Now–2015.*

**Ferreira** Somewhat severe in 1978. A decade later: beautiful bouquet; fullish, firm, stylish and elegant. Two notes more recently: more forthcoming than the '63. Very sweet, soft, rich and rounded. Lovely. *Last tasted Aug 1993* ★★★★ *Now–2015.*

**Fonseca** Eight notes. Still opaque, rich and magnificent in the mid-1970s including a fine Justerini's bottling, and a deeply coloured yet delicate and flowery Harvey's bottling in 1980, a rich ripe Berry Bros' in 1985 and other equally lovely bottles either side. Then a glorious bottle in 1990, its fragrance lingering in the glass for five hours. The next two coincidentally at Saintsbury Club dinners, in 1994 and 1998. Both wines appeared quite deep for their age; both had a flawless bouquet, crisp, rich, classic. Both were sweet with lovely fleshy texture, fruit, flavour and finish. Might surpass even the '63. *Last noted Oct 1998* ★★★★★ *Now–2030.*

**Gould Campbell** Surprisingly deep, virtually opaque in the early 1980s, well-knit, plump and peppery. By 1990 medium, mature; very scented, slightly citrus-tinged bouquet; very sweet, rich, lovely texture. Three notes at comparative tastings in 1993, still impressively powerful yet elegant and lovely. *Last tasted Aug 1993* ★★★★ *Now–2020.*

**Graham** 250 pipes shipped for UK bottling. Another beauty, backed up with dozens of admiring notes (minus one woody bottle), starting with a lovely, full, fruity note in August 1968. Consistently sweet, and in the 1970s 'powerful'; 'fat'; 'superb' in the early 1980s. A mature, brown-tinged Oporto-bottled magnum with a fairly hefty nose and lovely, slightly muscatel-tinged taste at a Symington tasting in 1994; a harmonious UK-bottled wine at Gidleigh Park the following year, silkily clad, with wonderful shape and texture. Eleven bottles decanted and consumed at the great dinner to celebrate the 30th anniversary of Christie's wine department: sheer perfection. A superb, soft red-brown, long-'legged' Wine Society bottling at Christie's, Los Angeles, and later the same month before the first race at Ascot, still remarkably firm and lively – like my host and former managing director, Guy Hannen. Then (Nov 2000), in magnums, a lovely soft ruby colour; classic nose, liquorice, touch of tar; leaner than expected but lovely. Most recently: bottled 1968 by Christopher & Co: some colourless but superb bouquet, flavour and texture. *Last noted at a wine dinner at home, May 2001* ★★★★★ *Now–2030.*

**Niepoort** Bottled 1969. Deep, hot, highish acidity – needed plenty of time in decanter. Sweet. Good shape, weight, finish. *Last tasted Aug 1993* ★★★

**Noval, Qta do** Many notes between 1968 and 1980. Only one recently. In the early days somewhat beefy for Noval. Still very deep, with good 'legs'; good, figgy nose; very sweet, good flesh. An excellent Noval combining the sweetness of Graham and backbone of Taylor. Good flesh. Still tannic. *Last noted at a Corney & Barrow luncheon, Nov 1995* ★★★★ *Now–2015.*

**Noval Nacional** Not as deep as expected; nicely evolved, slightly spirity nose; medium-sweet, lean, very flavoury, good length. *Noted at a Nacional tasting, Sept 1994* ★★★★ *Now–2015.*

**Offley Boa Vista** Already losing depth of colour in the late 1970s but rich and fat with good fruit in the early 1980s. More recently, fully mature yet still rather hard fruit. Full-bodied. *Varied notes, last tasted Aug 1993* ★★★ *Now–2010.*

**Sandeman** Eight notes, four since the mid-1980s: sweet nose, vanilla, liquorice; lighter style, lean, elegant, nice balance, hot, dry, slightly acidic finish, yet delicious. *Last tasted Feb 1991* ★★★★ *Drink soon.*

**Smith Woodhouse** Medium, mature though ruddier than the Gould Campbell; rich fruit; very sweet, nice texture. Very good wine. *Dec 1990* ★★★★ *Drink soon.*

**Taylor** 250 pipes shipped for English bottling. Sixteen notes. Deep, rich, maturing; sweet, full-bodied, shapely, firm, good length, still tannic in the early 1990s. Losing colour and opening up in the mid-1990s, including a lovely bottle, nice weight, dry finish at Christie's wine department's Christmas dinner in 1996. Next at Christie's Tasting of the Century at Vinexpo – all 1966s, with Christopher Burr MW: substantial, mature-looking (Burr and the wine!), high-toned bouquet with touch of liquorice; sweet, lovely flavour, slightly hot finish. Most recently, surprisingly little red; rich fully evolved; good flesh and flavour. *Last tasted at the Fladgate Partnership tasting at Christie's, April 2002* ★★★★★ *But drink earlier than originally predicted, say now–2012.*

**Warre** Pleasing, flowery in the late 1970s. Firm and 'well filled' by the early 1980s. The most frequently noted recently seem to have been Oporto-bottled and consistently attractive and elegant. A wine with suppleness and a bit of a swagger. Several consistent notes over the past ten years. Now mature-looking, even a hint of orange; 'lovely' nose noted on three occasions; fairly, not very, sweet, perfect weight and flavour.

Most recently, similar notes, very good texture and flavour. 'What port is all about'. *Last noted at a Saintsbury Club dinner, April 2002* ★★★★★ *Now–2015*.

# 1967 ★★

The weather conditions were conducive to the making of good wine although the yield was small. I have, from the outset, thought that Cockburn and Martinez were unwise to buck the '66 trend and only declare the '67. It did not make a lot of marketing sense. Sandeman (who still regard this as one of the most underrated vintages) and Noval joined them, making four major declarations.

**Cockburn** Over 20 notes, mainly between 1972 and 1982; I was mainly unimpressed. Its initial depth of colour and richness sagged throughout the 1980s. Since 1985 palish and mature-looking; rather hard, pasty, spirity nose; drying out, medium weight, lean though some flesh and nice texture. Dry finish. Having said this, better than expected, lightish in weight and style and drinking fairly well. *Last noted after the Cockburn tasting, in London, May 2002* ★★★ *Drink soon*.

**Kopke** Bottled 1997. A real 'vintage tawny' in colour and character; high-toned, raisiny bouquet; sweet, delicious flavour. *Noted March 1999* ★★★★ *Drink soon*.

**Martinez** Bottled in Oporto and, I think, otherwise only by Harvey's in Bristol. The latter's was very good in 1980. Altogether a better colour, sweetness and weight than Cockburn. A curious, fragrant, spicy, pine-fresh bouquet; complex yet balanced. Opened up nicely. *Oct 1987* ★★★ *Drink soon*.

**Niepoort** A *garrafeira* 'vintage tawny', put into demijohns in 1971 for bottling as required. All very complicated, but the system works. Lovely garnet colour; walnuts and fruit; sweet, full, opulent, fig-like fragrance. Very good in its way. *Oct 1985* ★★★

**Noval, Qta do** When tasted still in cask in October 1970: prune-like. Destined to be late-bottled. More recently, lively ruby; evolved, rich, tangy nose with a whiff of grape skins; medium-sweet, lean, spicy, slightly short with a dry finish. *Jan 1991* ★★ *Drink soon*.

**Noval Nacional** Just two notes: in the late 1980s still very deep, intense; a hefty but slightly unknit nose fairly sweet, powerful yet with lean liquorice flavour and dry tannic finish. More recently medium-deep, more impressive than the '66, crisp fruit, still a bit hard. Scoring well. *Last noted at the Nacional tasting, Sept 1994* ★★★ *Now–2020*.

**Roêda, Qta da** Opaque, raw and spirity in 1969; flavoury but with some astringency in the 1970s. Five notes through the 1980s. Still deep; lean, spirity nose, some acidity showing. Sweet, fullish, surprisingly powerful, slightly raw but flavoury. Most recently, both at recent Christie's boardroom luncheons. Palishly mature; pleasantly soft, almost creamy, harmonious nose; fairly sweet, crisp fruit, drinking well. *Last tasted Oct 1998* ★★★ *Now–2010*.

**Sandeman** Deep and attractive in 1976, more recently maturing but rich; rather hard nose; very sweet, fullish, fleshy, attractive though I considered the 1966 fatter and better balanced. *Last tasted Oct 1988* ★★★ *Drink soon*.

**Taylor** Notes on an unusual tasting of three wines, made from different grapes, five years in cask in the Douro, five years in Gaia. Each had lost considerable colour, pale tawny, rather Verdelho-like appearance and nose. The best, sweet, fat and lovely, was made from a mixture of grapes including Nacional, Tinta Francesca, Bastardo, Sousão and Flor de Douro. *In Taylor's tasting room, Vila Nova de Gaia, Nov 1979*.

**Vargellas, Qta de** Several notes both Oporto-bottled and UK-bottled (in 1969). In the early to late 1970s opaque, rich, positive, though a hard dry finish. A decade later still fairly deep; a moderately sweet, very positive and attractive wine. Remains a bit hard. *Last tasted in July 1989* ★★★ *Drink now*.

# 1968 ★★

Later flowering; very dry and exceptionally hot summer, then an unsettled period though the weather improving in time for picking. Some nice wines made but not declared. A year for LBVs and single-quinta wines.

**Graham's Malvedos** Initially assertively hard, lacking Graham charm. A recent bottle seemed to be nutty and drying out but two others delicious, with fragrant, spicy nose like an old *garrafeira*; sweet, fullish, yet lean, expanding and expansive flavour. *Last tasted May 1992* ★★★ *Drink now*.

OTHER, OLDER NOTES **Croft** late-bottled, palish, pink-tinged; raisiny; pleasant light easy style in mid-*1980s*. ★★ *not for keeping*; **Guimarães, Reserve** deep, immature, full-bodied and tannic for the mid-1980s. Probably softened by now, *May 1985* ★★ *drink up*; **Noval, Qta do** opaque 'blackcurrant juice', sweet, full, fine, long ★★★; and **Noval Nacional** strangely the Nacional was less impressive ★★ *Both tasted at Noval's lodge just after bottling in October 1970*.

# 1969

Cold and wet from January to end of June. Hot July and August, then rain again. The grapes were unripe and the wines acidic. Not declared.

**Noval, Qta do** Deep purple; curious smell like brown sherry. High acidity. *From the cask in Gaia, Oct 1970*.

**Noval Nacional** Less deep; same smell; muscatel-like taste, very tart finish. Da Silva (the owners) did not know what to do with this wine as it was so poor.

**Vargellas, Qta de** Taylor's prime-site quinta, in the Upper Douro, managed to produce good enough grapes to make a deep, sweet and powerful wine tasted several times in the early to mid-1980s.

**Warre's LBV** Adequate: fairly deep, nice weight, refreshing. *Last tasted March 1986. Drink up*.

# 1970–1989

Difficult times were not yet over. One of the firms to go under in the 1970s was Graham's – their business was not just wine, they were also in textiles – and it was a considerable act of faith and financially risky for the Symington family to take Graham's on lock, stock and barrel, particularly as they already had a big portfolio of brands including Dow, Warre, Quarles Harris, Smith Woodhouse and Gould Campbell. I am sure they never regretted this, though when they took over port prices had still not taken off.

In 1970 the port producers unilaterally banned future shipping in cask. From then on all port was to be bottled in Oporto in the shippers' own lodges. I must confess, I was appalled by this one-sided decision; I felt it was another nail in the coffin of the traditional British merchants. But I had to cast off old-fashioned and romantic thoughts because the truth of the matter was that throughout the 1960s the skill, the art of handling and hand bottling, had been replaced by bottling lines, the red-nosed head cellarman being replaced by a production director. The producers themselves would now guarantee uniformity and quality.

As if to make up for a slight dearth of vintages declared in the 1970s, in the early 1980s three were declared in a row, some shippers preferring one or more but not all three vintages. To this day I cannot remember off hand who shipped the '81s, '82s and '83s: I have to refer to my notes.

But there was another surprising development: the growth of American interest in vintage port which, luckily for the shippers, was considered a 'first growth'. From a slow start in the early 1980s, thanks to this new image and active promotion, sales of port – and their prices – started to move up.

## *Vintages at a Glance*
**Outstanding ★★★★★**
1970, 1977
**Very Good ★★★★**
1983, 1985
**Good ★★★**
1980, 1982 (v), 1987 (v), 1989

## 1970 ★★★★★
Ideal growing and harvesting conditions. An outstanding vintage. Twenty-three shippers. It was also a turning point – after 1970 there were to be no more shipments in pipe for bottling by the British trade (see above).

I had not given the vintage much thought until Justerini & Brooks, in the mid-1980s, laid on a tasting of major shippers' '70s and '75s. It was a revelation. A much sturdier vintage than I had realised, confirmed by many subsequent tastings. This is classic port still on a seemingly limitless plateau of maturity.
**Borges & Irmão** One note: medium, weak-rimmed; open, figgy nose; not bad flavour. *Sept 1997* ★★
**Cachão, Qta do** Unusually interesting: made with grapes selected at the quinta by Belle and Barney Rhodes and made for them by Messias. Classic nose; excellent flavour with touch of vanilla and spice. *At the Rhodes' pre-sale dinner, Christie's, Park Avenue, Sept 1997* ★★★
**Cockburn** Correctly opaque at the time of bottling. At ten years of age still fairly deep though maturing; a hard, rather unyielding, cardboardy nose; medium-sweet, medium full-bodied. Its initial fieriness simmering down, but still hard. A good long lean tannic finish. Eleven notes since 1980. Rather unexciting. Most recent: sealing-wax and liquorice nose; sweet but not wholly knit and with curious methylated-spirity finish. *Last noted at Cockburn's 'Memories of a Century' tasting in London, May 2002* ★★★ just. Not a great Cockburn.

**Croft** Opening price to the UK trade in January 1972, Oporto-bottled: £9.25 per dozen! An impressive youth. Sweet, with good flavour, texture and length in the early to mid-1980s. Then medium-deep, a bit weak at the edges; high-toned citrus-like nose and flavour, with whiff of volatile acidity. Sweet, medium-weight, lean yet fleshy, good length. Next notes at two memorable dinners within five months: looking glorious by candlelight at the Factory House in Oporto, also drinking well at Croft's in October 1997: very attractive nose; sweet, good flavour, weight and finish. Showing well at the recent Fladgate tasting, sweet, very good flavour, touch of acidity on finish. *Last tasted May 2002. At best* ★★★★ *Now–2020*.
**Delaforce** First tasted in 1977: good wine. Several notes more recently, the most interesting at a Delaforce tasting in 1989, comparing a bottle and a magnum. The wine from the bottle had a very distinctive citrus (hint of mandarin) flavour whereas the magnum's appearance was distinctly deeper, plummier, less mature; a rather hard cheesy bouquet that developed richly. Both were fairly sweet, but the magnum packed greater power and length. In 1990 forthcoming, rich, high-toned bouquet; sweet, full-bodied, plenty of grip. In 1995, bottles donated by me in memory of my old friend 'Wog' Delaforce and consumed with Cox's Orange Pippins at a Saintsbury Club dinner. Someone noted the nose as 'sooty' and I thought it a touch austere. Could have been more fruity. More recently noted as 'correct', mature, drinking pleasantly. *Last tasted at another Saintsbury Club dinner in April 2000* ★★★ *Now–2010*.
**Dow** Nearly 30, well spread, slightly variable, notes. By the late 1980s still fairly deep and youthfully plum-coloured; excellent nose, fragrant, forthcoming, an almost Cabernet Sauvignon-like fruit, plus liquorice; full-bodied, nice texture, fleshy – as Dow goes. At two Symington tastings, in 1994 and 1996, alongside Graham and Warre, the first time not showing well, the next very much par for the course, though a different style. Uneven bottles in Aspen, one with high volatile acidity, but a good Oporto-bottling. Attractive and sweeter than

expected in 1997; rich, good 'grip' in 1998. Showing well at the definitive bicentenary tasting: maturing nicely; some fruit, fragrant, spicy bouquet and flavour. Hot dry finish. *Last tasted Oct 1998. At best ★★★★ Now–2020.*

**Feuerheerd** Just two notes. Opaque, purple; sweet, fruity, peppery nose and flavour in 1974. Most recently, medium-deep with a rather weak open rim, less sweet but with surprisingly good flavour and balance. *Last noted at the retirement dinner of Odette Ryan, for 30 years a pillar of Christie's wine department, Dec 2000 ★★★ for the port, ★★★★★ for Odette.*

**Fonseca** Virtually black when young and, in the early 1990s, still very deep, with the plumminess of maturity-in-waiting; restrained though fruity nose; initially very sweet, now merely sweet, full-bodied, rich, ripe, fleshy, with fruit and grip. A bottle decanted at home at 10.10am noted as very sweet and slightly chocolatey. At 3.45pm after my guests had departed, ripe, liquorice, high-toned. On the palate fairly sweet, rich, positive, lovely, with dry finish. Then, in magnums, at Christie's Port and Cigar dinner at Brooks's, October 2000. Next at Vintners' Hall in November 2001: not a big wine, but delicious. And two recent notes, the first in April (2002) at a Past Masters' dinner, disappointing, good flavour but lean, even thin. A month later low-keyed nose but 'very rich on palate'. *Last noted at the Fladgate tasting, May 2002. At best ★★★★*

**Foz, Qta da** Very impressive. Opaque; prune-like fruit; very sweet and full in the early 1980s. In 1990, still fairly deep though maturity showing at the rim. Extraordinary fruit, reminded me of figs. Full-bodied and fleshy. More recently, very full-bodied, loads of fruit, lovely texture. Lovely wine. *Last noted at Cálem's tasting at Christie's, Oct 1994 ★★★★ Now–2020.*

**González Byass** Plummy, spirity, better than expected in the early 1980s. Fully mature appearance; sweet, soft, quite pleasant. *At a Christie's boardroom lunch, July 1996 ★★ Drink up.*

**Gould Campbell** First tasted in 1973, deep, fine, rich. Three good notes in the mid-1980s, two bottled by the importer, Clode & Baker, slow to mature but good balance and length. Two notes in the early 1990s, one, possibly both, Oporto-bottled: medium-deep but, interestingly, with more of a youthful purple tinge than the '75. Very sweet, fruity nose, slightly high-toned, tea-like; fairly full on the palate, yet lean. Very flavoury. Most recently, one bottle unknit, slightly woody, the other sweet, attractive, light style. *Last noted at Fells' tasting, Oct 2000. At best ★★★ Drink soon.*

**Graham** The Graham family's last vintage. Originally (July 1972) opaque, still deep, plummy and fairly intense, showing rich extract; fragrant, high-toned yet harmonious bouquet though still a bit hard; very sweet, full-bodied, lots of fruit, grip, length, tannin and acidity. Chocolate and spice. Well over two dozen notes since 1982, all consistently good. In the mid-1990s, lovely, distinctive, very sweet. Equal top marks, Oporto-bottled, at Gidleigh Park, still with leathery tannins. Coping miraculously at a Zachys/Christie's charity dinner with chocolate soufflé. Showing well at the Primum Familiae Vini dinner at Vinopolis in November 2000. A superb bottle at a dinner party at home, May 2001. Most recently: soft tawny-red; gloriously fragrant and flowery; complete, excellent. *Last noted at the Symington tasting, May 2002 ★★★★★ Now–2020.*

**Martinez** Seven notes since 1977. Retaining most of its original depth of colour, sweetness and richness though bottlings have varied. For example, Gilbey Vintners' in 1988 was medium-deep and looking mature. More recently, bottler unknown (probably Harvey's), was opaque. 'Spirity' in relation to the nose recurs over the last 11 years. Unusual style, vinous,

fragrant. One bottle ruined by being served with unripe apples. *Last noted Feb 1991. At best ★★★ Drink soon.*

**Niepoort** 'Straight' vintage, two-year bottling and in their curiously attractive, stencilled, dumpy bottles. Two notes, first at a very extensive Niepoort tasting in 1985. Still deep, richly coloured; rather restrained nose, 'classic' noted then and more recently. Very sweet, fairly full-bodied, firm, fleshy, still a bit peppery. *Last tasted Aug 1990 ★★★★ Ready now.*

**Noval, Qta do** Many notes, nine since 1981. Not a big '70, a charmer, soft enough to drink even at the time of bottling in 1972. By the late 1980s medium, maturing; fairly sweet, middle-weight, a bit lean but soft and smooth, stylish and appealing. In 1991 tasted no fewer than ten times in different types of glass. More of a glass tasting than a port tasting, but Georg Riedel made a good point: the shape and size of glass does make a difference, to the perception of depth of colour, nose and taste. Showing well in the mid-1990s at an Inner Temple Bar guest night, guest of my daughter, Emma, and, more recently, at her 40th birthday dinner, same place, doubtless from the same stock prudently bought when it first came on the market. A most attractive wine. *Last noted at a III Form Club annual dinner, Jan 2002 ★★★★ Now–2015. Fully mature.*

**Noval Nacional** Three notes, first in 1989. Not as deep as the '67 Nacional but rich, displaying high extract; bouquet hard, with fig-like fruit and considerable depth; fairly sweet, full-bodied. Impressive. Showing well, with crisp, attractive flavour at the 1962–1987 Nacional tasting in 1994. Most recently, concentrated body, extract and flavour. Tannic finish. 'Needs 20 years.' *Last noted May 1999 ★★★(★★) 2020–2040?*

**Offley Boa Vista** Many notes. Originally very deep, its colour started to change to plummy after ten years and to show maturity around the mid-1980s. Now fully mature-looking, a medium-pale tawny. It has also softened, the bouquet fully evolved by the late 1980s. Still sweet but the originally lean, attenuated acidity noticeable throughout. Firm. Flavoury. *Last tasted Aug 1990 ★★★ Drink soon.*

**Rebello Valente** Never very deep, by the end of the 1980s it looked fully mature. Hard, spirity nose after five years in bottle. In 1990 rather smelly, on the verge of oxidation though it was very good on the palate. However a good, sweet, soft bottle at Hugh Johnson's in 1995. Next year, one with a horrid thick plastic capsule which put me off – I was doing a CD-ROM recording. Most recently, not bad, pleasant enough taste, dry finish. *Last tasted Dec 1998. At best ★★ Drink up.*

**Sandeman** Eleven notes, half between 1975 and 1979 and revealing bottling variations. One, bottled by Paten's of Peterborough with a short cork, looked fully mature in 1986 and was chunky with rather a sandy texture. Other bottlings tasted more recently: medium-deep but still a little immature-looking; sweet, harmonious bouquet with pleasing fruit masking a hard core and considerable depth. Sweet, fullish, good flavour, firm, with lots of tannin and acidity. Attractive wine. *Last tasted Aug 1990. At best ★★★★ Now–2015.*

**Smith Woodhouse** Six notes. After five years in bottle deep, hard-nosed, but very sweet, and ten years later little change. However, since 1987 some colour loss, now looking mature. Bouquet has opened up; mint, liquorice, fruit. Still fairly sweet, nice weight, flavoury, but tannin and acidity giving the wine a dry finish. *Last noted at Fells' tasting, Oct 2000 ★★★ Now–2010.*

**Taylor** First tasted in 1972, many notes, 18 since the early 1980s. Originally opaque, virtually black-purple, it remained plum-coloured for nearly 20 years and – with the exception of an unusually precocious Russell and McIver bottling in 1983 –

is still a vigorous ruby. Later several notes, slightly variable, particularly on the nose: whiff of mercaptan, rawness and volatility, at best harmonious though subdued. Certainly sweet, full-bodied, rich, good fruit, lovely mid-palate, still powerful, high alcoholic content, good length, tannin and acidity. Showing well at Saintsbury Club dinners in 1996 and 1999: very sweet, full flavoured though a trifle 'edgy'. Most recently, losing some colour; very good spicy bouquet; sweet enough, very good flavour. *Last tasted at the Swan Feast, Vintners' Hall, Nov 2001* ★★★★ *Lovely now.*

**Warre** Well over two dozen, all complimentary. By 1990, pristine purple easing a little, and starting to mature; lovely fruit, fragrance and vinosity. One bottle in 1994 packing a punch, lacking Warre elegance, another, later, 'elegance' re-instated. Later still the same year, at a big Symington tasting, firm flavour noted. Next year in Hong Kong, complete. And so forth. My notes range from medium-sweet to very sweet but, as so often, one's perception depends on the context in which the wine is tasted and drunk. Let's settle for sweet, full-bodied, rich, almost too rich, yet not overpowering, with the perfect weight and balance I expect from Warre at its best. *Last tasted Dec 1996* ★★★★★ *Now–2020.*

**Vargellas, Qta de** Well-nigh perfect with Stilton, sweet, rich, 'hot', alcoholic with dry finish. *At the Übersee Club, Hamburg, June 1997* ★★★★ *Drink soon.*

OTHER '70s THAT ONE MIGHT COME ACROSS, mainly last noted in the early 1990s: **Barros** ★★★★; **Berry Bros' Selection** (believed to be Warre) ★★★★; **Burmester** ★★★; **Butler Nephew** ★★; **Cabral** ★; **Cálem** ★★★; **Dalva** poor; **Feist** ★★★★; **Ferreira** ★★★; **Hutcheson** ★★★; **Krohn** ★★★; **Osborne** ★★; **Poças Junior** ★★★; **Rosa, Qta de la** ★★★; **Royal Oporto** ★★; **Saõ Luíz, Qta de** (Kopke) ★★★★; **Santos** ★★★; and **Souza** ★★★

## 1971 ★

Useful wines made for standard blends. Not declared.

## 1972 ★

Heat and drought sandwiched between heavy rain. Though some passable wines made, not generally declared.

**Dow** Modest but precocious in 1979. Most recently served at a boardroom luncheon. I now suspect, from my notes, that this was the late-bottled reserve for it had a rather weak-rimmed, rose tawny hue, surprisingly sweet though peppery. We all quite enjoyed it. *Last noted July 1994* ★ *Drink up.*

OTHER '72s **Cockburn's Crusted** hard nose and palate. Which reminds me of a luncheon in the early 1970s of the long defunct Wine Merchant's Union. A decanter of port was passed. My neighbour, 'Wog' Delaforce, greeted it with 'ha! Cockburn's Cloudy!'. The wine *was* cloudy and it turned out to be Cockburn's; **Eira Velha, Qta da** beautiful colour, very flavoury ★★★; and **Rebello Valente** fairly sweet, nice weight, soft, elegant, rather lean, good acidity. *Two notes in 1985* ★★★

## 1973

Weather pattern not unlike 1972. Not declared. Only one tasted: **Taylor's Crusted** sweet, very varnishy, hot finish. *At the Oxford and Cambridge University Club, April 2001* ★

## 1974 ★

Vintage marred by heavy rain. Abundant crop, but mostly of mediocre quality.

THREE WINES TASTED IN THE 1980S **Eira Velha, Qta da** very positive, quite nice; **Feist** charming; and **Rozes** pale amber, raisiny – yet attractive. *All rated* ★★★

## 1975 ★★

A modest vintage, with much to be modest about. An aberration declared by 17 major shippers and a rare example of a port vintage that has not lived up to the original cheerily optimistic expectations. Mild winter, warm spring, hot and dry summer. Rain in early and late September. Picking early October. I suspect that shippers declaring their '75s, despite the proximity of the excellent '77s, turned a blind eye to the heavy early autumn rain. The first mandatory bottling at source of a widely declared vintage did not get off to a good start. Having said that, the wines are flavoury and quite attractive but have no future. Drink soon.

**Cockburn** Opaque at the time of bottling but considerable colour loss by the mid-1980s. *Last tasted Dec 1993* ★★ *Drink up.*

**Croft** Well clad in the early 1980s. In the mid-1990s indecisive though flavoury. Most recently, palish, more like a 30-year-old, tawny, drying out but attractive. *Last noted at the end of an excellent dinner at the Jean Ramet restaurant in Bordeaux, Sept 1998* ★★★ *Drink soon.*

**Delaforce** No recent notes. Deep, rich though raw in October 1977. Pale, lean and raisiny in *1989* ★★ *Drink up.*

**Dow** Sixteen notes, deeply impressive shortly after bottling and consistently good throughout the 1980s. It seemed to me best after about ten years. Most recently at the Dow bicentenary tasting, palish, fully mature, drying out a little, lean but still an attractive wine. *Last noted Oct 1998* ★★★ *Drink soon.*

**Ferreira** Opaque, raw, powerful in 1977. Eleven years later medium-deep, still some red; very sweet, medium weight, quite flavoury. Fernando d'Almeida, the venerable blender, thought it not very good, rather like the '17, but 'will be best when it is very old'. *Last tasted March 1988* ★★★★ *Wait and see.*

**Fonseca** Initially huge, opaque, very sweet, in fact quite a big wine but starting to lose all three elements after a decade. Then four consistent notes all in the same year, medium-coloured, moderately sweet, though not a top Fonseca, still exhibiting style and texture. *A very pleasant end to our annual grouse dinner at Wiltons, Aug 1994* ★★★ *Drink soon.*

**Gould Campbell** Purple and pleasing in 1977, maturing nicely in the mid-1980s. By the early 1990s pale; nutty, medium-sweet with a rather original flavour. *Most recently a decent but unspectacular glass at The Boot & Flogger in Southwark, London, May 1999* ★★ *Drink up.*

**Graham** Impressively purple when young, but nearly 20 notes since 1983 indicate that it was probably at its best at 10–12 years of age. Yet, and yet, despite a loss of colour by the early 1990s, I found it a consistently pleasing drink. Rather strangely scented magnum noted in 1994. Most recently, a mature, fragrant, 'perfectly developed' bottle. One of the best of all the 1975s. *Last tasted dining with the Newalls (Sir Paul a recent Lord Mayor of London), July 1998* ★★★★ *Drink soon.*

**Noval, Qta do** Pleasantly mature; bouquet as evolved as it is ever likely to be; fairly sweet, flavour of walnuts, lightly clad. *Last tasted Nov 1989* ★★ *Drink soon.*

**Niepoort** Bottled 1979. Softly coloured; sweet, nutty, figgy nose with a touch of caramel and liquorice; sweet, lovely fruit and acidity. *At home, Dec 2001* ★★★

**Noval Nacional** Four notes. Fairly deep and rich colour, nose and flavour. Strange sweet fig-like nose; powerful, concentrated, tannic, unready in the mid- to late 1980s. At nearly 20 years of age, fully mature orange amber; distinctive, harmonious bouquet; very sweet, rather bland though with a hot finish. Similar notes most recently. Flavour more like an old tawny. Drying out, tannic. *Last noted at a wine dinner I hosted at the Hotel Louis C Jacob, Hamburg, March 2000* ★★★ *Drink now.*

**Quarles Harris** Deep purple and impressive in October 1977. High volatile acidity yet sweet and agreeable. *Last tasted Dec 1992* ★★ *Drink up.*

**Smith Woodhouse** Now pleasing but plummy; grapey, whiff of tangerine; sweet, surprisingly powerful yet soft and easy. Dry finish. *Last tasted Dec 1990* ★★★ *Drink soon.*

**Rebello Valente** Never very deep and full, now rather weak and watery with touch of malt and iron on the nose. Sweetish, fairly light. Dry finish. *Last tasted Nov 1988* ★ *Drink up.*

**Taylor** The best '75 by far. Immensely impressive in 1977 and, despite losing its concentration, with richness and sweetness in the early 1980s. In the early 1990s still relatively deep, youthfully plummy; hard, prune-like fruit; very sweet, quite powerful, stern, lean yet fleshy for a '75, with dry tannic finish. Showing some maturity though still hard. Lovely flavour. Taylor 'grip'. *Last noted Dec 1993* ★★★(★) *2005–2020.*

**Warre** More notes than any other, nearly 20 since 1980. One can trace its change in appearance from opaque in 1977, plummy in 1980, less deep but still fairly plummy in 1983, a touch of red in 1987 and in 1988 medium, mature, with a weak tawny rim. In parallel, the nose has changed from a youthfully stalky, spirity character, developing fragrance in the mid-1980s, and, latterly, a refreshing citrus, lean, fruity character. On the palate it has ranged from sweet, full and rich, through an elegant attractive ten-year stage to a touch of leanness, losing weight, still sweet, some elegance but lacking the body, finesse and length of a really good vintage. *Last tasted at dinner with the 'great and the good', April 2001* ★★★ *Now–2012*

**OTHER '75s Butler Nephew** unimpressive in the early 1980s; **Eira Velha, Qta da** at five years of age pale, mercaptan nose, high acidity. Admittedly only tasted once. *1980*; **Foz, Qta da** quite nice light luncheon port. *March 1988* ★★; **González Byass** ruby, sweet, fat, not bad in *1980* ★★; **Martinez** impressive in 1977, in *1986* evolving nicely, a lovely colour, a bit hard, lean and peppery. ★★★? *retaste?*; **Offley Boa Vista** full, fat and rich in 1977, attractive and just ready at ten years of age, medium-sweet, lightish and refreshing in *1987* ★★; **Poças Junior** weak rim; singed, raisiny nose and taste, very sweet, quite nice in the early *1980s, not tasted since* ★★; and **Rozes** high-toned, spirity, very sweet, full-flavoured, nice quality, cherry-like fruit *1980* ★★

## 1976 ★

The Douro Valley suffered a long drought from winter to the end of August. Heavy rains in late September. Not declared but some nice wines made, the best appearing as single-quinta wines or LBVs, for early drinking.

**Fonseca Guimaraens** Two notes, the 'club port'. Quite good colour nose and flavour. Sweet. Nice fruit. *Last noted at Brooks's, June 1997* ★★ *Drink up.*

**Graham's Malvedos** Several notes from the mid-1980s. Lively colour and character. Sweet, good flavour, nice texture. Refreshing, citrus-like elements, touch of tannic bitterness. *Last tasted Feb 1990* ★★ *Drink soon.*

**OTHER '76s Noval** late bottled, probably in 1980–1981. Deepish ruby, drinkable but unmemorable. Off the market now. Perhaps as well. *April 1982*; **Smith Woodhouse** bottled 1980. A lean, attractive LBV. *June 1988* ★★; and **Warre** bottled 1980. Quite assertive flavour. Crisp. Good length. *June 1988* ★★★

## 1977 ★★★★★

A serious vintage, well regarded and widely declared. Wet winter, cold spring and cool summer which delayed development. The weather changed for the better at the beginning of September and was followed by the hottest autumn since 1963. Declared between March and August (1979) by 20 shippers, notable exceptions being Martinez, Noval and Cockburn. The latter have admitted that this was an error of judgement; but it was a period of rather odd policy decisions. Whether this was due to the directors of Cockburn and Martinez on the spot or by their overlords in England I have not ascertained.

The major port shippers and their London agents held a tasting at Christie's in November 1979 shortly after the '77s were bottled and at which the majority of my first notes on the vintage were made. One or two opening prices to the trade were noted. They will come as a revelation – indeed a shock. But they were considered fairly high at the time. Prices were traditionally quoted F.O.B. (free on board).

**Croft** At the tasting of '77s at Christie's in 1979: dense black, prune-like, tangy, high acidity. Eight years later still fairly deep and relatively immature; nose restrained; sweet, full-bodied,

### LBV, crusted, colheita and single-quinta ports

*'LBV' stands for Late-Bottled Vintage, port of a stated vintage which matures for four to six years in wood before bottling. Less expensive than true vintage port, it is ready for drinking when first put on the market and, generally speaking, does not benefit from further bottle-ageing. LBVs have become commercially increasingly important. They have the advantage of a 'date' and are competitively priced. The downside is that many restaurants list an LBV under a vintage heading, the uninformed purchaser thinking that he is buying a classic, more expensive vintage port. Crusted port is a blend of more than one vintage bottled early to develop a 'crust' like vintage port.*

*'Colheita', a term the English usually find confusing (and difficult to pronounce) is a sort of extended LBV, a port of a stated vintage which spends its time in cask. I describe this sort of port as a 'vintage tawny' as it neither looks nor tastes like an LBV.*

*A single-quinta port is made in exactly the same way as vintage port but marketed under its own name rather than that of the Oporto-based producer. Apart from Noval, the best known of all the quintas of the Douro, up until recent times the brand-owning shipper would market his single-quinta port only in 'undeclared', i.e. lesser, vintages. Single-quinta ports are fashionable and demand has proliferated; it is also marketed in declared vintage years. The quality is dependable though the major port houses argue that the richness and subtlety of their top vintage wine is a result of blending the best grapes from different vineyards.*

elegant, good length, peppery alcohol, tannin and acidity. In 1999, starting to mature; bouquet opening up; rich, rather chocolatey flavour. At 20 years of age still a deep and youthful appearance. Sweet, good fruit, 'figgy'. In 1999 a beautifully evolved bouquet. Very flavoury. A not too ecstatic note at the Fladgate tasting but admit to tasting cursorily. *Last noted at Christie's, April 2002* ★★★★ *Now–2015.*

**Delaforce** Deceptively easy style in September and October 1979. Several notes ten years later. Still youthful; figs, liquorice and malt; sweet, full-flavoured, lots of tannin and acidity. Rich nose; surprisingly powerful. Dry finish. *Last tasted Oct 1999* ★★★(★)? *2004–2015.*

**Dow** In 1979 crisp, ruby purple; spirity, beef-tea nose; sweet, full yet fleshy. Loads of all the appropriate component parts. Over two dozen well-spaced notes, later illustrating the beginning of colour loss in mid-1980s, though still ruby, intense, translucent. The nose endlessly fascinating with sweet, fig-like fruit, a squeeze of tangerine, cognac-like spirit, tight-knit but developing fragrance. A decade later rich, intense, almost explosively assertive, with the grip of a good vintage and long lean dry finish. Attractive bottles in the late 1990s and, most recently, a very fragrantly scented magnum almost eau de cologne (we were informed that a very distinctive 'herbal' nose is common to all '77s). Unusual, high-toned, delicious. *Last noted at the Dow bicentenary tasting, Oct 1998* ★★★★(★) *Now–2020.*

**Ferreira** First noted in Nov 1979, just after bottling: a deep plummy purple; sweet but raw. Evolving nicely through the 1980s, lightish style but with noticeable tannins and acidity. Several consistent notes made at tastings in the USA organised by my son, Ferreira's North American importer. Now mature with distinctive liquorice-like fragrance. Fairly sweet, not a heavy weight. Drinking well. *Last noted at a charity port tasting at Raleigh Durham, Nov 1997* ★★★★ *Now–2010.*

**Fonseca** On 1 January 1980, the London agent invited orders for immediate shipment at £48 per dozen bottles F.O.B., in wooden cases with 'lead capsules, branded corks, labels and chalk marks'. Minimum order five cases. No free storage. 'Quantity small … excellent quality.' Very impressive at the opening tasting: deep purple; hard, spirity nose; powerful, well-balanced. At the end of the 1980s still fairly deep, plummy; classic, black cherry fruit nose; very sweet, fairly full-bodied, lovely texture. A great future predicted. However, like a lot of '77s beginning to lose colour by the mid-1990s, a bit spirity and lean but sweet, with delightful fruit. Showing well at Warren Winiarski's 30th anniversary dinner in the Napa Valley, March 1998. Most recently: sweet, glorious flavour, perfect now. *Last noted at the Grand Award banquet, New York, Oct 2001* ★★★★ *Now–2025.*

**Gould Campbell** Enormously impressive at two tastings in Nov 1979 and certainly one of my favourite '77s: very deep, red-black centre, purple rim. Despite appearance, a sweet, easy, attractive wine on nose and palate. Not tasted again until 1990 in the Symington tasting room at Vila Nova de Gaia. Still notably deep, purple, intense; low-keyed nose with a strange scent that reminded me of bacon rind. Very sweet, but lean with a dry finish. Only one bottle tasted since. Though still surprisingly youthful looking in its 20th year, less sweet and, I thought, lacking flesh. Still very deep with opaque core; muffled fruit, touch of honey; very sweet, attractive, piquant, dry finish. *Last tasted, two notes, in Nov 2000* ★★★★ *Now–2020.*

**Graham** A very good wine. Almost black in colour in 1979: a big, apple-nosed, very sweet, rich but angular wine. Gradual

colour loss through the 1980s but, as it matured, a wonderful *mélange* of fragrances developing: liquorice, strawberry, fig; fleshy, lovely fruit. Nearly 20, always admiring, notes. Showing well at a Gidleigh Park port tasting in 1995: medium-deep with red-brown rim; very rich, powerful bouquet opening up beautifully; sweet, good body and backbone, marvellous length, spicy finish. Most recently: delicious! *Last tasted Dec 1999* ★★★★(★) *Now–2030.*

**Offley Boa Vista** Firm, fruity but raw in November 1979, noticing a surprisingly short cork for a vintage needing bottle-ageing. I was less than rapturous. Five notes made in the mid-1990s in varying contexts have been consistent, 'showing well', good fruit, 'nice weight and balance'. *Last noted at a Christie's boardroom luncheon, Nov 1996* ★★★ *Now–2010.*

**Quarles Harris** One of the ubiquitous Symington's 'second XI'. I was impressed and noted it as massive, 'well stacked' in 1988. Seven somewhat uneven notes since. One looking more like a tired tawny, and a bit woody. The back up bottle was completely different, much better colour, crisp fruit (Boardroom lunch, 1997). In 1998, though losing fruit, delicious. But the company might have helped. Scent of chocolate and singed raisins. Most recently: weak-looking; dusty fruit, slightly wood nose and flavour though sweet and very rich on palate. *Last noted pre-sale, Dec 2001* ★★ *Drink up.*

**'Royal Jubilee'** Queen Elizabeth's Silver Jubilee year. Bottled 1979, corks branded '*Factory House 1977 Vintage Port*'. A blend of '77s contributed by the 12 (British) members of the Factory House, Oporto. Rich ruby, full of fruit in 1980 and, showing early evolution. *At the pre-sale tasting at Christie's, March 1981* ★★★★ *A rare collectors' wine.*

**Sandeman** At Christie's opening tasting: opaque russet purple; a bit lean and spirity, but with good potential. Five years later, delicious but unready. By the end of the 1980s, retaining its youthful looks, while evolving nicely. Only one note since: sweet, rather on the lean side and 'the best wine of the evening'. *Last tasted at a Circle of Wine Writers' 'Cyril Ray' Dinner, Nov 1996* ★★★ *Drink now–2010.*

**Smith Woodhouse** Opening price £37 per dozen F.O.B., £39.50 in bond, London. Bottled 1980 though a sample shown at the opening tasting in 1979: black, ruby-rimmed; prune and blackberry-like nose; voluptuous. Lively, fruity, pronounced flavour in 1983. In 1990 still relatively immature, sweet, rich, well-endowed with tannin and acidity and clearly with a good future. Still deeply coloured; attractive, flavoury, on the lean side, quite a bite. Needs time. *Last tasted Nov 2000* ★★(★★) *2005–2015.*

**Taylor** Black; harmonious but closed up; concentrated but reined-in at Christie's opening tasting in 1979. By 1991, at Taylor's tercentenary tasting, deep and fairly intense; equally deep and rich nose, sweet, full-bodied, powerful, packed with all the requisite components, vigorous, great length. In 1997 a disappointing bottle. Drying out. Unimpressive in 1999. Considerable colour loss, but still lovely, warm, and luminous; fragrant bouquet; almost Graham-like sweetness and uncharacteristically soft texture. Most recently: corky nose but much better on palate, fairly powerful, forthcoming, firm, good finish. *Last noted at the Fladgate tasting at Christie's, April 2002* ★★★★? *Must keep an eye on this.*

**Warre** Opening price to the trade £40 per case F.O.B. or £43 in bond, London, 25 case minimum order. Discounts thereafter. Very deep, hard, tea-leaf in 1979. Over 20 notes since showing a slow but gradual development. Fragrant, tea-like bouquet evolving; rich spicy, lovely by the end of the 1980s.

Consistently good through the 1990s including a well-nigh perfect bottle at a Symington tasting in 1994: typical Warre elegance, lissom and lovely. Then magnificent magnums, magnanimously donated by the Symingtons, at the Wine Trades' Benevolent Banquet in 1996. Drinking well at the Garrick in 1999. Most recently, at home. Now fully mature-looking; somewhat unknit; a hot dry finish. I preferred it after a day or two in the decanter but overall a bit disappointing. *Last tasted in May 2002. Now downgraded to* ★★★★ *Ready.*

OTHER '77s **Cálem** sweet, loaded with fruit. Impressive. *Oct 1986* ★★★★; **Diez** lovely gradation of colour; nose unforthcoming but some potential; sweet, full-bodied – notably high alcoholic content, rich, good length. *April 1990* ★★★; **Feuerheerd** pale and unimpressive. *July 1987*; **Foz, Qta da** very sweet, full of fruit, lovely. *March 1988* ★★★; **Poças Junior** plummy, very fruity, attractive. *Nov 1982* ★★★; **Rebello Valente** not seen since the opening tasting. Noted as very sweet, rich, forward. *Possibly* ★★★ *now*; and **Royal Oporto** sweet, raisiny, harmonious; prune-like flavour. *Feb 1986* ★(★★)

# 1978 ★★

Not an easy year. Cold wet winter, spring and early summer followed by drought from late June until early October. Great heat in September. Net result, a small crop of beefy wines. Noval, which did not declare the '77, did, for good reasons, ship the '78. But the year is notable for an increasing plethora of single-quinta wines.

**Cavadinha, Qta da** An old vineyard but the wine not previously marketed as single-quinta wine. The grapes are late maturing here. After eight years in bottle I found the nose a bit spirity and like wet cardboard. Very sweet, fullish, crisp, lean and attractive. Quite a lot of tannin still and citrus-like refreshing acidity. *June 1988* ★★(★)

**Côrte, Qta da** The first vintage marketed by Delaforce as a single-quinta wine. Tasted twice. Palish, pink tinge; 'warm' raisiny figgy nose; fairly sweet, easy, dry, slightly bitter finish. *Last tasted April 1988* ★★

**Dow** I do not normally include LBVs but this port, bottled in 1999, was – is – superb. Sweet but lean, good flavour and length. *On BA 001 (Concorde), Oct 1999* ★★★

**Eira Velha, Qta da** Bottled Jan 1981. This famous old quinta still belongs to the Newman family though the wine is matured and bottled by Cockburn and sold by Harvey's. When first tasted before bottling, exactly two years after the vintage, it was quite impressive, with a pleasing richness and balance. In the mid-1980s deep crisp ruby; bouquet holding back; medium sweetness and weight, a bit leaner than expected. A little strange. *Last tasted Oct 1986* ★★? *Must taste again.*

**Ferreira** Here is a real find, if you *can* find it. Probably the best 1978, first noted ten years after the vintage, a wine of considerable colour and power, full of fruit, tannin, acidity. Fleshy, lovely in the early 1990s and four good notes since. Now paler, mature; fragrant nose; very sweet, still fairly powerful, delicious crisp fruit. Dry finish. An archetypal vintage Ferreira. Since, noted 'very drinkable' (September 1999) and, most recently, good colour, mature edge; nice shape and texture. Good dry finish. *Last tasted in Bartholomew's office, San Francisco, Dec 2000* ★★★★ *Drink soon.*

**Fonseca Guimaraens** Luminous; medium-sweet, nice weight, dry finish. Extremely good. *With lunch at Taylor's, Oporto, a very wet day in May 1997* ★★★ *Drink soon.*

**Graham's Malvedos** Seven notes. Delicious. Good colour; very attractive nose, slightly raisiny, touch of liquorice; fairly sweet, medium weight, soft, fleshy. *Last tasted Nov 1992* ★★★(★) *Drink soon.*

**Noval, Qta do** At 11 years of age, mature; rather hard nose, whiff of tangerine; sweet, nice weight and style. *Not tasted since. Nov 1989* ★★ *Probably needs drinking.*

**Noval Nacional** In 1989: plum-coloured; rich, broad, very figgy nose of great depth; very sweet, full-bodied, rich, fat, concentrated, but less impressive at the tasting of 12 Nacional vintages five years later. More mature, very sweet, good flavour but lacking length. *Last noted Sept 1994* ★★★

**Vargellas, Qta de** In November 1979 I had an unusual opportunity to taste from the casks separate grape varieties grown in different parts of this renowned estate. Touriga Nacional was incredibly deep in colour, a crisply defined purple, sweet and firm. 'Roris' or Tinta Roriz, was also deep but less crisp. Nose and palate softer, more open-knit. 'Mistura' (mixture of varieties) the most forthcoming on the nose, sweet, with lovely fat and fruit. Clearly promising components. More recently, still youthful; fairly sweet, good though lean. *Last tasted at the annual Wine Trade's Benevolent Banquet in May 1992, the end of my stint as the Society's Chairman* ★★★ *Drink soon.*

OTHER '78s, OLDER NOTES **Kopke** another famous old name, but one relatively little known in Britain. I found their '78 very sweet but short. *Oct 1986* ★★; **Roêda, Qta da** a fine property, Croft's equivalent to Graham's Malvedos and Taylor's Vargellas. Palish, youthful, a bit feeble; slightly spirity, sweet, fair quality and length. *April 1988* ★★; **Rosa, Qta de la** surprisingly pale; immature nose, reminding me of an apple core; medium-sweet, fairly powerful, crisp fruit, still tannic. I assume colour was lost in cask at the quinta. *Nov 1988* ★★; **Royal Oporto** prolific producer, one of the biggest port houses. Somewhat looked down upon by the British (both here and there) but a big seller, on price, in America. Four notes in the mid-1980s. Fully mature-looking; the sweetness and richness of syrup of figs, soft and agreeable. *June 1987* ★★

---

## Decanter magazine

*Founded in 1977. Arising from the ashes of the legendary* Wine *magazine, for which I was a regular contributor in the 1960s with a column entitled 'Will you dine with a Master of Wine?'. (This was a very good series and hugely popular in America where they found our approach to food and wine pairing and description something of a novelty.)* Decanter *was brought to life by two robustly entertaining media types, Colin Parnell and the late Tony Lord.*

*My first monthly column, which later became a page, appeared in February 1978. The subject was port. Sitting in bed on Sunday mornings I write about the wines that I have tasted recently. It is a routine I'm loath to break, which causes some consternation to my editors who realise that if no word has reached their desks by Tuesday morning, they will have to hope the next Sunday is more productive. I believe I haven't missed an issue yet (my 300th column appeared in June 2002), though my handwriting has got worse over the years. The recent addition of a cut-out photograph, myself with my trusty Dutch bicycle, heading up the page has proved immensely effective. I visited a winery totally unknown to me in New Zealand in the autumn of 2000 and the young lady at reception promptly asked 'where have you left your bike?' This is most useful as now I know who reads my column!*

# 1979 ★★

Another summer of drought until heavy rain shortly before harvesting at the end of September. Abundant, above average quality but not declared. Some useful LBVs marketed. These should have been consumed by now.

**Dow's LBV** Appears to have been bottled over a period of three years: in 1983, and tasted soon after bottling, lusty but raw; bottled in 1984, pleasantly fruity in 1985; and bottled in 1985, a *mélange* on the nose, very sweet and soft with a grapey flavour, but short. *Tasted in 1986 and 1987. Variable.*

**Graham's Malvedos** Very nice sweet, fullish, crisp, fruity flavour. Refreshingly acidic finish. *Last tasted Jan 1993* ★★

# 1980 ★★★

A good vintage, very approachable now as the tannin levels are below the '83s. Useful to drink while waiting for the better vintages to mature. A particularly dry summer, picking started towards the end of September in fine dry weather. Cockburn, Martinez and Noval did not declare. Most of my earlier notes were made at a tasting organised by Tim Stanley-Clark at Christie's in June 1990. Out of interest, and to put prices into perspective, I mention some of the opening offers made soon after the declarations.

**Cálem** Medium, maturing nicely; very sweet, chocolatey, vanilla bouquet and flavour. Rich, figgy, soft, good length. Showing well. *June 1990* ★★★ *Drink soon.*

**Croft** No vintage but an LBV. Opaque, pruney, sweet, citrus cladding, hot acidic finish. *Last tasted Oct 2000* ★ *Drink soon.*

**Dow** First noted at a tasting in 1982 held by Michael Symington to launch the Dow 1980 vintage. Preceding the final blend were six lodge *lotes*, wines made from different grape varieties and grown in different districts, all of course of the 1980 vintage. For example 'BFQTA', a wine from two low-lying vineyards on the north bank of the Douro at Pinhão and made at Dow's Quinta do Bomfim: a tough bitter wine, unbalanced on its own but a vital part of the final blend. 'URT', a single-quinta wine from the upper Rio Torto. A high proportion of old vines: opaque, to me very classic. A similar tasting of individual '80s and the final blend was presented by Michael Symington the following September. After one year in bottle the definitive '80 was still hard and figgy on the nose, sweet, hot and spirity on the palate. Two years more in bottle and developing nicely, softer, revealing more flesh. Most recently still impressively deep and intense; rather stalky on the nose, touch of liquorice; very sweet, fullish, flavoury. Plenty of alcohol, tannin and acidity. Needs time. Showing well at a tasting of 13 vintages of Dow in Aspen in 1994, surprisingly sweet for Dow and full of fruit. Similar at a Symington port tasting later that month. A delightful half bottle at a Gidleigh Park wine weekend tasting 'fragrant, uplifting'. A bit overshadowed and drying out a little at the Dow bicentenary tasting – in fact 'dry finish' consistently noted. Firm, fragrant, 'floral', elegant with long dry finish at a Port Wine Institute vintage port tasting in 1999. *Drinking very pleasantly on several occasions with mature Cheddar (not Stilton) at Wilton's by the glass, the last in May 2002* ★★★★ *Now–2010.*

**Ferreira** A couple of notes, first in 1988. It seemed an agreeable early-maturing wine. Eight years later, though looking mature, fairly powerful on the palate. Pleasantly forthcoming, rather high-toned bouquet. Very sweet. *Last tasted in San Francisco, Dec 2000* ★★★ *Now–2010.*

**Fonseca** Opening offer to the UK wine trade, allocated 4500 cases, £55 per case F.O.B. From the outset a paler, lighter style of Fonseca though consistently sweet. Towards the end of the 1980s considerable maturity noticed though still peppery. Fully evolved by the mid-1990s, the consistency of notes upset by a glass at Pratts which I suspected had been in the decanter too long – one of the problems about ordering vintage port by the glass in a club or restaurant. Ask how long it has been decanted. Most recently – not by the glass – dining with one of my publishers. It looked almost like a 20-year-old tawny which was blushing a little. Lightweight in style but delightful. *Last noted at Segrave Foulkes, March 1997* ★★★ *Drink soon.*

**Foz, Qta da** Only two notes, both 'very sweet'. After four years in bottle soft, full and rich. More recently, light style, maturing nicely. *Last noted at a Cálem tasting at Christie's, Oct 1994* ★★★ *Drink soon.*

**Gould Campbell** First tasted in 1992: flavoury, good texture. Four recent notes. Showing pretty well at the big tasting in June and six months later. Virtually opaque, still a plummy immature purple; rich, figgy, harmonious nose; sweet, full of flavour and body, very rich, good fruit, fat for an '80, good length. *Last tasted Nov 2000* ★★★ *Now–2010.*

**Graham** Over a dozen admiring notes. Deep and intense in the mid- to late 1980s, touch of hardness, spicy. Four notes in the mid-1990s. Still plummily deep; good rich fig-like fruit; distinctly sweet, as one expects from Graham. Good length, somewhat tannic. More recently, nose of glorious richness; powerful, drinking well but time in hand. *Last tasted Oct 1998* ★★(★) *Now to 2015.*

**Niepoort** Four notes in the mid-1980s; singed walnuts and raisins; very sweet, rich, soft. Nice wine. Two recently: still deep and youthful; almost sickly sweet on the nose, ripe figs; medium full-bodied, very attractive fruit. Dry finish. *Last tasted Oct 1990* ★★★ *Drink soon.*

**Noval Nacional** Medium-deep, maturing; rich, singed, chocolatey nose; medium-sweet, lean and lively. *At the Nacional tasting, Sept 1994* ★★★ *Now–2015.*

**Offley Boa Vista** Somewhat uneven notes. Originally deep and lean. Certainly showing well at an extensive port tasting in Jackson, Mississippi. Still plummy, coloured, straightforward, lightish style, sweet, crisp. *Last noted at a trade association luncheon in Bristol, Feb 1999* ★★★ *(just). Drink soon.*

**Quarles Harris** Opening price £48 per case, F.O.B. At ten years of age plummy; sweet, slightly chocolatey, figgy nose and taste. Fragrant. Most recently, surprisingly deep though mature; strange but attractive bouquet, crystallised violets; rich but lean. Highish acidity. *Last tasted Nov 2000* ★★★ *(just). Now–2010.*

**Rebello Valente** Medium, maturing; sweet, classic, vanilla nose of some depth; sweet, medium weight, lean but shapely, lovely flavour, good length. *June 1990* ★★★ *Drink soon.*

**Sandeman** Impressive depth, weight and fruit before and just after bottling. Still deep, intense and immature-looking after six years in bottle; fairly full-bodied, flavoury, moderate length, tannin and refreshing acidity. After ten years, beginning to show some maturity; straightforward, rather spirity nose; nice weight, lean, flavoury. Most recently, very flavoury, attractive. *Last noted at a Distillers' Court lunch, Jan 1997* ★★★ *Drink soon.*

**Smith Woodhouse** Opening price £48 F.O.B. My highest rating of the 14 '80s tasted blind at Christie's in June 1990. Equally impressive at the line-up arranged by James Symington: notably deep, plummy; very forthcoming fruit on the nose, richness, almost malty; very sweet, full-bodied, lovely flavour, intensity and length. Coincidentally served at both the

Ch Margaux and Ch Lafite dinners at Brooks's Club in 2000, the 1980 acidity 'cutting' the Stilton well. *Last noted Nov 2000* ★★★★ *Now–2010.*

**Taylor** Decanted from four half-bottle shippers' samples for a Christie's wine course: opaque, purple; highly alcoholic but dumb; sweet, full-bodied, with bitter tannic finish in December 1982. Opening up pleasantly by the early 1990s but, alongside other '80s the least mature looking and still with that bitter tannic finish. Nevertheless, very attractive. Good length. Needs time. *Last noted at a Gidleigh Park port tasting, Devon, Feb 1995* ★★★(★) *2005–2020.*

**Warre** Opening price £52 F.O.B. Strangely, not tasted until 1990: rich, plummy, a quick developer. At two Symington tastings in the mid-1990s, alongside Dow and Graham, at the first I gave it higher marks, great length, superb; a year later found it looser knit and preferred the Graham. 'Best wine of the evening', unsurprisingly, at a Distillers' ladies banquet, and four interesting notes since. Still very deep; fragrant; extraordinarily dense, figgy flavour and impressive, very dry finish. *Last tasted Dec 1999* ★★★★ *Now–2010.*

**OTHER '80s, OLDER NOTES Barros** a very 'Portuguese' port as opposed to the British style, deep, intense; sweet full plummy chocolatey wine with a fragrant aftertaste. *Dec 1999* ★★★ *Drink soon;* **Hutcheson** (**Barros, Almeida**) deep, crisp, plummy; very sweet, spirity; sweet, rich, firm. Hard end. *Oct 1986* ★★★ *Should be ready now.*

# 1981

Not declared but noted for some reasonably successful LBV ports. The rest, of course, was used for standard blends. Not for cellaring.

**Niepoort** Bottled 1986. Two notes, first in 1990. Medium-deep, maturing; good fruit, reminded me of mincemeat (sweet mince pie!). Very sweet. Good fruit. Nice body and balance. Dry finish. *Last tasted at home, Jan 2002* ★★★

**Dow** Late bottled in 1986. Palish: unknit; very sweet, pleasant, easy, short. Dry acidic finish. *Oct 1990* ★★★

**TWO LBVs TASTED IN THE LATE 1980s** (date of bottling unknown) **Graham's** some depth, lively ★★; and **Taylor's** deep, sweet, vigorous ★★★ *Drink up.*

# 1982 ★★★ at best ★★★★

A confusing period, only a dozen major shippers declaring, Cockburn, Graham (except for their Malvedos) and Warre notably abstaining.

Interesting weather conditions: a very dry winter, refreshing spring rains, good flowering in May but an unusually hot and arid summer necessitating an unusually early harvest starting 8 September. Though light showers refreshed the grapes, fermentation took place at high temperatures. Some good wines drinking well, and seriously undervalued.

**Churchill Graham** The marriage of a scion of the Graham family to a Churchill justified the name of a new port brand – the first to start up for many years. (Unhappily the Symington's objected to the use of 'Graham'.) When first tasted, in 1984, it looked pretty impressive, with reasonable potential. Not showing well at a big tasting in 1990 but seems to have settled down. Now medium depth; crisp, fragrant nose; sweet, nice fruit. *Last tasted at Michael Le Marchant's, Oct 1998* ★★★ *Ready.*

**Croft** First tasted in 1985: broad, malty sultanas nose; sweet, full, nice flesh and fruit. Good length. A couple of notes five years later palish, rosy-hued, rather advanced for its age. Bouquet also very forthcoming, raisiny. Very sweet, almost chocolatey, full of flavour, stylish, silky tannins and lively acidity. More recently, good nose, remarkably attractive. *Last tasted Jan 1996* ★★★★ *Now–2010.*

**Delaforce** Their first declaration since 1977. Limited quantity. Two recent notes: medium-deep, attractive, quick-maturing; sweet, raisiny, slightly malty nose; sweet on the palate, fullish but lean, with crisp fruity flavour, tannin and highish acidity. *Last tasted June 1990* ★★(★) *Now–2010.*

**Dow** Just one note, three years after bottling: then still opaque, intense; sweet, full, rich, slightly short and with an edge of acidity. Also a surprisingly sweet and lovely Colheita. *Tasted at British Airways, April 2001* ★★★ *Now–2010.*

**Ferreira** One of the best 1982s judging by a quartet of notes made in 1988, 'packed with fruit', also in the mid-1990s. Colour a lovely, glowing deep ruby red, youthful for its age; very fragrant, high-toned bouquet; sweet, full-bodied – a lot to it. Dry finish. *Last noted and drinking well at the Knickerbocker Club's annual wine dinner, New York, Oct 1999* ★★(★) *Now–2015.*

**Foz, Qta da** In 1986, after two years in bottle: deep, crisp, intense; youthful, fruity, spirity. Most recently, still impressively deep, plummy; good fruit; very sweet, medium- to full-bodied. Delicious wine. *Last tasted June 1990* ★★★(★) *Now–2010.*

**Graham's Malvedos** A couple of notes, first in 1991: rich, plummy-coloured; curiously evolved nose of figs, raisins; very sweet, smooth, fleshily endowed with fruit, tannin and acidity. Next, very sweet, lovely flavour 'perfect now'. *Last tasted in March 1994* ★★★ *Drink soon.*

**Martinez** Under the same ownership, yet always playing second fiddle to the heavily promoted Cockburn. Usually excellent – as with this '82. Showing well at the big blind tasting in June and, more recently, at Cockburn's. Fairly deep, plummy, trying to make a start at maturing; very good, rich, intense, rather high-toned, figgy, raisiny nose; a big sweet wine, with a very attractive, slightly raisiny flavour, touch of leanness, otherwise excellent balance. *Last tasted Dec 1990* ★★★★ *Almost a 5-star future. Now–2015.*

**Niepoort** The standard two-year bottling. Five notes since the mid-1980s. Though an intense mulberry colour a year after bottling it seemed destined for early maturity. An unusual style, tasting of singed, stalky raisins, gingery, meaty. Attractive in its way. It went very well with strawberries in its fifth year but I thought it a bit hard and dull in a line-up of ten '82s. *Last tasted June 1990* ★★ *Drink soon.*

**Noval, Qta do** The first vintage declared by the new generation of the van Zeller family. Four admiring notes from the mid-1980s. Initially opaque, still fairly deep and very impressive, intense, youthful after five years in bottle; a lot to it: deep plummy fruit with a tannin smell like soft shoe leather, figs and walnuts. Sweet, full-bodied, rich, high extract, excellent length, tannin and acidity. Most recently, as described but beginning to show some maturity. Intense. Good potential. A top '82. *Last tasted June 1990* ★★★★ *2005–2015.*

**Noval Nacional** Bottled Feb 1985. Two notes, both at Nacional tastings, first in 1989. Consistent; deep, rich colour, maturing; equally rich spicy nose and flavour; sweet, full, glorious length and aftertaste. *Last tasted Sept 1994* ★★★★★ *2005–2025.*

**Offley Boa Vista** Three notes. In 1990 surprisingly deep in colour; nose consistently low-keyed but very sweet. Not ready then but more fully developed by 1996. Most recently a lovely ruby colour; lean; spirity nose; a somewhat hot, acidic finish coping well with cheese. *Last noted at home, Oct 2000* ★★ *Now–2010.*

**Ramos-Pinto** Two notes in 1990: still sweet but hard, with touch of mint and figs; crisp assertive fruit, powerful, lean yet shapely. Most recently: still youthfully plummy; very sweet, good figgy flavour. Coming round. *Last tasted at home, April 2002* ★★★

**'Rio Tinto'** An unnamed single-quinta wine from the Rio Tinto, a tributary of the Douro, imported by Eldridge Pope. An interesting district wine-marketing concept. Good colour, lovely fruit, good value. *July 1990* ★★★ *Drink soon.*

**Royal Oporto** My lowest rating in the blind tasting of '82s. Both bottles poor, one smelly, sulphide, the other oxidised. Both unclean. *June 1990.*

**Sandeman** Four notes. Opaque, huge, hard and peppery around the time of bottling. Still a youthful rich ruby after four years in bottle; strange nose, still hard, figs and brambles; distinctly sweet, fullish, a refreshing citrus touch, good length. Most recently, less deep, now plummy; straightforward, low-keyed, Spanish root nose. *Last tasted June 1990* ★★★ *Now–2010.*

**Seixo, Qta do** Deep, still youthful looking; sweet, good fruit and balance. *After dinner at Quinta Vâle de Meão at the top end of the Douro. I needed a second glass after a long and arduous drive. Oct 1997* ★★★ *Now–2010.*

**Warre** Colheita lissom, lovely, with exquisite, ethereal end taste. *April 2001* ★★★ *Drink soon.*

OTHER '82S, OLDER NOTES **Cruzeiro, Qta do** deep; warm, crusty nose; pleasing. *May 1985, then* ★★★ *drink soon*; and **Vargellas, Qta de** fairly well-developed even under three years of age. Sweet, soft, pleasing. *May 1985* ★★★ *drink soon.*

# 1983 ★★★★

A very attractive vintage. Superficially similar vintage to '82 but overshadowed by the appealing and more popular '85s. Roughly ten major shippers plus minor ones and LBVs. Good mid-term drinking.

A cold, wet May caused *desavinho (coulure)*. September was fine and sunny with average temperatures over 30°C almost throughout the month. The hot and dusty grapes were 'freshened up', to quote Michael Symington, by a few isolated rain storms during the last few days of September which merely interrupted the long, hot autumn. A good, but exceptionally late harvest in October, with high sugar readings.

I have quite a few notes, but the vintage was first put in perspective for me at a blind tasting of nine of the major '83s in Oporto in May 1985 and at the more extensive blind tasting at Christie's in June 1990 which included a dozen '83s.

Like the '82s, this vintage is currently underappreciated and seems destined to remain so. The wines are good value and drinking well.

**Cálem** Fairly deep, pleasant colour, maturing nicely; nose rather hard at first but developed and sweetened in the glass; very sweet, full-bodied, crisp, citrus-edged flavour, lean. Good. At this time still family-owned, traditional, rather British in style, very good. *June 1990* ★★★(★) *Now–2015.*

**Churchill** Churchill Graham were obliged to drop 'Graham' from the company name even though both Churchill and Graham were family names. Medium-sweet. Quite nice fruit. *March 1992* ★★★ *Drink soon.*

**Cockburn** Cockburn's first declaration since 1975, 'production small but of first-rate quality' (according to a director, Peter Cobb). Three notes made in summer 1985 confirmed its blackness of colour and exceptional sweetness and concentration, character, length and tannin – all harbingers of long life. The following November (1986) still intense with a hard immature spirity nose. Sweet, full-bodied, peppery (alcohol) and dry tannic finish. Two notes in 1990: still impressively deep and youthful-looking; sweet, scented, attractively piquant nose, still peppery. On both occasions noted as medium-sweet and medium- to full-bodied. In 1999 a leanish, long and tangy wine. Very flavoury. Now maturing. Showing well recently: surprisingly deep and intense; now not very clean cut, better on palate. Very sweet, flavoury, hot dry finish. *Last tasted May 2002* ★★★(★) *2005–2015.*

**Croft** Did not declare but produced an LBV. Three recent notes: still deep, plummy, fairly sweet, a bit lean and raw but quite flavoury. Easing now and pleasant. *May 1990* ★★ *Drink up.*

**Dow** Fifteen or so notes, starting with Michael Symington's tasting of a range of individual 'lodge *lotes*', all surprisingly different in colour and character, some lean, some fleshy, with a variety of herbaceous and fruit aromas, from which the final vintage blend was made, just as Cabernet Sauvignon, Cabernet Franc, Merlot and Petit Verdot are assembled to make a classed-growth Médoc. Even after two years in bottle, still opaque but starting to evolve nicely. In 1994, alongside Graham and Warre it was the least deep in colour, very forthcoming on the nose, sweet, slightly chocolatey. Four years later, thrown into a 'vertical' context at the Dow bicentenary tasting it was more open knit than the 1980, sweeter but also lightish in style. More recently, good flavour and balance. Dry finish. Drinking well. *Last noted Dec 1999* ★★★★ *Now–2010.*

**Ferreira** Just one note: medium-deep, plummy colour but maturing; sweet bouquet, touch of vanilla, spicy; medium-sweet but rich and full-bodied. Dry tannic finish. Delicious. *At a Sogrape tasting in Oporto, March 1996* ★★★ *Now–2010.*

**Fonseca** Nine notes. Predictably opaque in 1985; a lot of vinosity and flesh; sweet, full, fruity. In 1990 plummy; a hefty, rich bouquet and flavour of prunes and figs. Very sweet, fairly powerful, rather hard yet elegant. Wedged between the 1980 and 1985 at a Mentzendorf tasting it seemed to pursue a middle course in colour and sweetness. Now fully mature, lightish, open-rimmed, easy and pleasing. *Last noted at a book launch tasting in Germany, April 1998* ★★★★ *Drink now to 2010.*

**Gould Campbell** First noted in the Symington's tasting room in May 1985. It was as opaque as the Warre and fatter than Fonseca and Graham. Certainly rich and impressive. A couple of months later, noted a meaty almost malty richness on the nose, coupled with brandy. Also showing well at the blind tasting at Christie's: good grip, firm. In 1990, still impressively deep, immature; considerable depth of fruit; fairly sweet, flavoury, like a pretty child with an upturned nose. Two very recent notes: less deep in colour; attractive nose and taste. Crisp. Dry finish. *Last tasted Nov 2000* ★★★(★) *2005–2015.*

**Graham** Eleven notes. Black velvet in 1985 and 1986, fine wine, great length. In the early 1990s still impressively deep; rather muted nose, not unlike the '80. Rich, lean yet with good flesh. Distinctly, and typically, sweeter than its 'cousins' Dow and Warre at the valuable Symington tasting in 1994. A year later, still deep and intense; black cherry with purple rim; 'very Graham' nose, citrus-like fruit, attractive, still tannic. *A very good '83. Last noted at a Gidleigh Park tasting, Devon, Feb 1995* ★★★★ *Now–2020.*

**Niepoort** Deep purple in 1985 with curious malty, coffee-bean nose; soft yet highish acidity, good length. Showing well at the blind tasting of '83s (in 1990): fairly immature; good, peppery, fruity nose; very sweet, full of fruit, extract and flavour. Good length. Most recently, maturing colour, rich 'legs', smoky nose; full-bodied, raisiny flavour, quite a bite. An attractive wine. *Last tasted at home, Jan 2001* ★★★(★) *Now–2015.*

**Offley Boa Vista** Eight notes, most in the mid-1990s, first at Offley's in 1996, then memorably at lunch with Fernando Guedes at his historic Quinta Azevedo – torrential rain throughout the Distillers' Court visit in May 1997. Consistently very deep and still youthful looking (like our host), yet deliciously sweet and despite its fullness, flesh, and tannic bite. Most recently: fairly deep still; touch of liquorice; fairly sweet, still youthful and quite good fruit. *Last noted at a Distillers' dinner at Vintners' Hall, Feb 2002* ★★★

**Quarles Harris** A couple of notes: deep, intense, very flavoury in 1992. Most recently: better flavour than nose. *Last tasted Nov 2000* ★★ *Drink up.*

**Ramos-Pinto** Two notes in 1990: deep, plummy, starting to mature; nice nose, good fruit, slightly raisiny, figs, touch of stalkiness but inherently soft and harmonious. Distinctly sweet in the Portuguese style, medium- to full-bodied, assertively fruity, hard still yet fleshy. Needs time. Two recent notes: still fairly deep, youthful; very forthcoming, rustic yet fragrant bouquet; very sweet, figgy fruit. Attractive. *Last tasted out of magnums, Jan 2000* ★★★(★) *Now–2010.*

**Rebello Valente** Just one note: medium, showing considerable maturity; a fully evolved, broad, figgy nose and flavour with a whiff that reminded me of a raya sherry. Very sweet. Quite nice in its way but I am unenthusiastic. *June 1990* ★★ *Drink soon.*

**Roêda, Qta da** On the pale side, fully mature; fully evolved grapey, raisiny nose, very sweet, nice weight, pleasant flavour. *Noted at a Port Wine Institute single-quinta tasting, June 1998* ★★★ *Drink soon.*

**Royal Oporto** As with the '80 and '82, by far my lowest mark at the blind tasting at Christie's. Medium-deep, still rather immature; high volatile acidity on nose and palate. Sweetness and fruit but not recommended. *June 1990.*

**Smith Woodhouse** Seven notes. Showing well at the initial blind tasting in May 1985: rich, fat, attractive. Sweet, agreeable shortly after. Though impressively deep, intense and still youthful looking at Christie's, I found a stalkiness on nose and palate. In 1990, also in 1992, a much better note: very fruity on the nose; sweet, rich, lovely flavour. Most recently: fragrant, lean but flavoury. *Last tasted Nov 2000* ★★★(★) *Now–2015.*

**Taylor** Nine notes. In 1985, soon after bottling, opaque, spirity: richly flavoured. By 1990 noticeable loss of colour, the wine developing quicker than I expected. In 1996, 1997 and 1998 medium, open, mature appearance; sweet, soft, raisiny nose; medium-sweet, decent length, spicy, somewhat bitter finish. Frankly, less impressive than Taylor should be. *Last tasted, at home from a half bottle, Dec 1998* ★★(★)? *More time? I doubt.*

**Warre** Eleven notes. The usual classic appearance in 1985: opaque centre and violet rim. Very deep plummy purple by autumn 1986. In 1990 powerful yet restrained, almost chewable; sweet without being cloying, lovely flavour and texture, a bit lean but with characteristic Warre elegance and firm dry tannic finish. Texture and harmony noted at the Dow, Graham, Warre tasting in 1994 and its smooth 'elegance' and flesh in 1996. Now medium-deep, mature, drinking well. An attractive '83. *Last tasted Sept 1997* ★★★★ *Now–2015.*

**OTHER '83S, OLDER NOTES Cálem LBV** very good. *March 1988* ★★★; **Foz, Qta da** fine big classic wine. *Oct 1986* ★★★★; **Hutcheson** malty, peppery, figgy. *May 1989* ★★; **Quarles Harris** warm, soft, flavoury. *June 1985* ★★★; **Noval LBV** good, rich, flavoury. *Oct 1989* ★★★; **Seixo, Qta do** fabulously intense appearance; very powerful nose; sweet, fairly full, lovely citrus-edged fruit. *March 1988* ★★(★★)

# 1984 ★★

Not a 'declared' vintage year but, as is now customary, some single-quinta and late-bottled ports marketed.

**Côrte, Qta da** Rather pale and feeble appearance; Bovril (meat extract) nose and taste. Sweet but unimpressive. *Noted without particular enthusiasm, June 1998* ★ *Drink up or avoid.*

**Fonseca Guimaraens** The vintage blend as opposed to single-vineyard vintage. Just one note: at 13 years of age still youthful looking; low-keyed; lovely flavour more acidity and bite than the 1985. *Tasted at Taylor's, May 1997* ★★★ *Drink soon.*

**Graham's Malvedos** Bottled by Graham the regulation two years after the vintage. Plummy but maturing; very attractive classic port nose; very sweet, good flavour and reasonable length. Fragrant aftertaste. I liked it. *Last tasted Nov 1995* ★★★ *But drink soon.*

## British Airways tastings

*I was co-opted by British Airways in 1984 to select wines to accompany Michel Roux's menus for Concorde. Thereafter I was a regular member of BA's wine committee, my job being to see that 'justice is done' and that the right wines were selected for the airline's passengers. I was later joined by Hugh Johnson and Jancis Robinson. Peter Nixson, a former member of cabin staff, organiser of the tastings, is both amazingly efficient and extraordinarily knowledgeable. We would taste First Class and Concorde's wines together, and on other occasions Club World. I'm often asked whether wine tastes different at high altitude and if allowances have to be made for this. My main job was to look for wines with positive character, good colour and pronounced flavour; the aroma is not so important as it is not as detectable when flying. Between 30 and 50 wines would be tasted blind at each tasting, pulling out the six or so we liked best; only then was it revealed what the wines were. The tasting committee was disbanded in 2002.*

# 1985 ★★★★

A very attractive, vibrant vintage. The best since 1977. Twenty-six shippers declared. Very cold and long wet winter, damp spring, hot summer and excellent conditions for the harvest which began around 30 September. I tasted 20 '85s blind at a June 1990 tasting at Christie's arranged by Tim Stanley-Clark. At this, and at other tastings before and since, the quality and fine style of the vintage was apparent.

**Baron de Forrester** Although a colheita – what I always think of as a vintage tawny, matured for longer in cask than a standard two-year bottling – this wine is intriguing in several other respects. It is named after perhaps the greatest character to adorn a trade with more than its faire share of great characters.

Joseph James Forrester, a Yorkshireman born in 1809, joined the family firm Offley Forrester in 1831. A gifted amateur artist and cartographer – his portrait drawings of fellow notables hang in the British Club, Oporto – he was the first person to map the Douro Valley and was later created a Portuguese baron. In 1862 he was mysteriously and dramatically drowned travelling along the Douro by boat.

'Baron de Forrester' is now a brand name of Tuke Holdsworth, a former vintage marque owned by Ferreira (now Sogrape). Complicated! Anyway the wine itself is a mature, palish, orange colour; sweet of course, with a lovely silky texture and bitter finish. *Nov 1997* ★★

**Burmester** I particularly like Burmester's old tawnies so welcomed an invitation to visit and taste a further range of ports in their tasting room at Vila Nova de Gaia. In 1997 their '85 was starting to show some maturity; medium-sweet, leanish style. I am sorry to say that more recently I found its nose almost overpoweringly rich; too figgy, yet with touch of hardness. *Last at a Port Wine Institute's tasting, Oct 1999* ★★

**Cálem** Three notes in the summer and autumn of 1987. Good wine. At the Christie's tasting: still quite deep though about to elevate into its maturity curve; rich, fruity nose with the lively acidity noted on quite a lot of the '85s. Very sweet, full, glorious flavour. *Last tasted June 1990* ★★★★ *Now–2015.*

**Churchill** Intense and fragrant in July 1987. In 1990 opaque; high-toned, good fruit on nose and palate. Fairly sweet, full-bodied. Most recently: medium-deep; spicy; delicious flavour, firm tannins and acidity. Their best vintage to date. *Last noted Oct 1999* ★★★★ *Now–2015.*

**Cockburn** Opaque, intense; very distinctive – fish skin and iron – nose; fairly loaded, overall dry and volatile acidity noted at the blind tasting in June and in Cockburn's tasting room six months later. Still impressively deep and youthful; good fruit and a more evolved nose and palate than the '83. Very flavoury but a rather sharp attenuated finish. *Last tasted Dec 1990* ★★★ *Now–2010 (I must retaste).*

**Crasto, Qta do** I first visited this spectacularly sited old quinta in 1996: deep; classic nose; stylish, fragrant. The following year, blackberry-coloured; lovely fruit; sweet, fleshy – halfway between lissom and fat. Very attractive. *Last noted at a tasting in Jackson, Mississippi, April 1997* ★★★ *Now–2015. (They also make a good Douro red at Crasto.)*

**Croft** At just two years old: deep, thick, rich appearance; sweet, soft, malty nose; full, fat, nice texture. More recently (1990), though fairly deep and, of course, still immature, it gave me the impression of a wine likely to develop fairly quickly. Extremely good rich nose and fine flavour. Most recently: stylish, lovely. An attractive, well-balanced wine. *Last tasted Oct 1999* ★★★★ *Now–2015.*

**Dalva** Open, mature, forward; raisiny, almost feminine fragrance; powerful yet lean. Curious dry 'powdery' tannic finish. *Oct 1999* ★★ *Now–2010?*

**Delaforce** Five notes, the first two shortly after bottling: very deep purple; very sweet, plump and smooth. In the spring of 1989 and summer of 1990, still fairly youthful looking; a meaty, almost maltily rich nose; again markedly sweet. By the early 1990s, changed colour, maturing pleasantly, good flavour, body and balance. One of the best vintages of Delaforce I can recall. *Last tasted Nov 1992* ★★★★ *Now–2015.*

**Dow** Many notes. After bottling, vigorous, plenty of 'grip'; two years later still purple, with spicy fruit lurking beneath the brandy: intense, powerful. In 1990 I noted the leanness and acidity – its vibrant nervous system. By the mid-1990s, surprising sweetness, attractive fruit, elegance, soft, figgy nose, good texture. Most recently I recorded a dry finish but perfect ripeness. *Last tasted Dec 2001* ★★★★ *Lovely now–2015.*

**Ferreira** My equal top mark, with the '82, at a wide-ranging Ferreira tasting in Oporto in 1996, soft medium-deep ruby, maturing nicely; good fruit; very sweet, delicious flavour. Comments endorsed a year later at two later tastings in the USA. Most recently: delicious. *Last noted at the Distillers' Installation Dinner, Nov 2001* ★★★★ *Now–2010.*

**Fonseca** Showing great potential two years after the vintage and that first impression borne out by subsequent tastings. Still opaque and youthful-looking in the mid-1990s, fragrant, low-keyed, good flesh, glorious flavour. Four recent notes (1998–2000) in different places (London, Bruges, Chicago) and contexts (tastings, lectures, dinners) all but one full of praise, the exception being alongside Graham and Taylor. Most recently: still very deep; wonderfully relaxed, harmonious, forthcoming bouquet; excellent flavour and flesh. A lovely wine. *Last noted at Christie's, April 2002* ★★★★(★) *Now–2020.*

**Gilbert** Mature; fully developed nose; too figgy. Not that often seen, and one can see why. *Oct 1999* ★

**González Byass** Just one note: an office tasting before the sale of a large quantity at a very moderate price. Fairly mature looking; rich, raisiny nose; sweet, fleshy, ready. *Feb 1999* ★★★ *just. Drink soon.*

**Gould Campbell** Loaded with tannin, July 1987. Very high marks at the June 1990 tasting: deep, rich, velvety; good nose that seemed to expand richly in the glass over three hours; sweet, full-bodied, lots of fruit, life-preserving tannin and good acidity. Confirmation in 1990. A lovely deep rich wine. *Last tasted Nov 2000* ★★★★ *Drink now–2015.*

**Graham** Quite a few notes, all highly complimentary from initial tastings in April and July 1987, exhibiting its distinctive style. A gloriously velvety purple; harmonious from the start. Aged four, wonderfully complete. Superb at a Graham vertical in 1990, bouquet evolving well, lovely flavour and texture. In the mid-1990s, less deep, more plummy, simmering down a little, soft, delicious, at a dinner in the country. Three recent notes. Showing well at Stephen Kaplan's 1985 vintage dinner in April 2000: full, rich, fairly powerful. Now fully developed, perfectly balanced. *A perfect end to the millennium dinner of the worshipful Company of Distillers in the Painted Hall, Greenwich, May 2000* ★★★★★ *Now–2020.*

**Martinez** When first tasted (July 1987) I noted it as having a very curious nose and flavour, with a dry, rather acidic finish. Three years later, the citrus twist of acidity still noticeable but otherwise rated quite highly. Deep, rich, plummy colour; richness of fruit that so often calls to mind ripe figs; sweet, fullish body, hot fruity flavour. Most recently, better flavour than nose. *Last noted Oct 1999* ★★★ *Drink soon.*

**Niepoort** Sample half bottles tasted in April, May and Aug 1987 on the labels of which were notes made at fermentation time: natural 12.9% alcohol, 27.00 dry extract, total acidity 3.5, volatile acidity 0.52, and 6.2 iron. Not surprisingly opaque; rich, good fruit but with immature stalkiness and brandy; sweet, concentrated, spicy and fleshy. Then, showing well at the Christie's blind tasting: still opaque-centred with immature purple rim; high alcoholic content noted on the nose, plus figs, liquorice. Sweet, nice weight, good balance and fruit. *Last tasted June 1990* ★★★★ *Now–2015.*

**Noval, Qta do** Picking began on 27 September in excellent conditions. First tasted in July 1987. Exciting flavour. Lovely fruit. Two autumns later: powerful, figgy nose; very sweet, full-bodied, a fine shapely wine, good length. Showing well at Christie's tasting: attractive colour, starting to mature; deep, rich nose; touch of elegant leanness, long, dry, fruity-acid finish. A touch of spirit and leanness, very good acidity at a wine dinner at La Maison du Cygne, Brussels, 'disappointing' at a Sunday lunch (both in 1997), but a bottle I took over to Cordeillan Bages, Pauillac, 'showing well' the following September and at another Kaplan dinner in Chicago. Most recently, fully mature, beautifully evolved mocha-like bouquet, delicious, with power and length. *Last noted at III Form Club dinner, Jan 2002* ★★★★ *Drink now–2010.*

**Noval Nacional** At the Noval tasting in 1989 medium-deep, rich, starting to mature; harmonious though slightly subdued nose with whiff of walnuts; very sweet, immense, powerful, packed with fruit and vigour. Three notes since. Well developed at a major Nacional tasting in 1994, soft, singed, leaner than expected, also when sandwiched between the superb '82 and surprisingly good '87. Deep, powerful, with grip and great length. *Last noted at the Kaplan '1985' dinner in Chicago, April 2000* ★★★(★★) *2010–2030.*

**Offley Boa Vista** Good note July 1987, and exceptionally good, earning equal top marks tasted blind at Christie's. In 1990 still opaque, intense, immature; classic nose, with the rich, figgy, almost maltiness of very ripe grapes; very sweet, full-bodied, loaded with fruit, extract, tannin, acidity. Good length. Four good notes in the mid-1990s: showing some maturity; delicious, smooth and elegant. *The last three notes made at tastings in North Carolina, Nov 1997* ★★★★ *Now–2015.*

**Poças Junior** Opaque, full and figgy in 1987. Compared to its peers I found its figginess common and its texture coarse. *Last tasted Oct 1999* ★

**Quarles Harris** Three notes: starting to mature in 1990, well-evolved bouquet reminiscent of a late-harvest Zinfandel. Quite good. Similar in 1992. Most recently, a light ruby colour; jammy, rich but somehow unconvincing nose; very sweet but lacking length. *Last tasted Nov 2000* ★★ *Drink soon.*

**Ramos-Pinto** Two notes. At five years of age, deep, attractive, a clean-cut youthfulness; dusty and hard at first but rich underlying fruit; very sweet, fairly full-bodied, lovely flavour, soft and fleshy despite its tannin and acidity. Good length. *Last tasted Oct 1990* ★★★ *Now–2010.*

**Rebello Valente** A good opening note in July 1987. At the Christie's tasting: fairly deep, but though still purple looked to me like a quick developer; odd nose, like a wet blanket, hard, spirity, but fruit lurking. Much better on the palate: very sweet, full, with lovely spicy fruit, good length, hot finish. *Last tasted June 1990* ★★★ *(just). Drink soon.*

**Royal Oporto** Another questionable performance in the blind tasting of '85s at Christie's. One of the least deep and impressive. Plummy but a fairly weak rim. Nose unknit. After time in glass, sweaty, coarse. Better on the palate. A very sweet, powerful wine, full of fruit. *June 1990* ★★? *Drink up.*

**Sandeman** First tasted in July 1987: sweet and spicy. A year later, at a vertical of Sandeman vintages: very rich, meaty, malty, prunes and figs, slightly singed nose; sweet, full-bodied, loaded with tannin, acidity and alcohol, vanilla and spice. I gave it my highest mark, fractionally above the '77. At the Christie's tasting of '85s in 1990, still fairly deep, poised to start maturing; lots of fruit, pepper and high-toned acidity on the nose and palate. Very flavoury. Now fairly mature with fat and flesh. Drinking well. *Last noted at a Distillers' livery luncheon, Feb 2001* ★★★★ *Now–2010.*

**Smith Woodhouse** In July 1987: stylish, nicely put together. Showing well at a blind tasting in 1990: fairly deep, youthful but at the point of departure; lovely rich nose yet still with hard-edged immaturity; sweet, medium-full body, good fruit.

Now maturing, some colour loss; rich but unknit; lean, slightly ethereal, still tannic. *Last noted Nov 2000* ★★(★) *2005–2015.*

**Taylor** In July 1987 a predictably substantial wine. Tannic. Great length and aftertaste. Showing well at a horizontal of '85s in 1991. Tasted blind, one of the eight top-ranking wines. Impressively deep, intense, plummy; concentrated nose; full-bodied, rich, good length. Great potential. Showing well in the mid-1990s, far superior to the '83 when tasted at Taylor's in a torrentially rainy May (1997). Deep but bright; very fragrant, more spicy and powerful than Fonseca at a hotel school tasting in Bruges and the following spring, April 2000, in Chicago. Coffee-like flavour, with Taylor firmness and backbone. Time in hand. Most recently: fragrant, sweet, showing well at the Fladgate tasting. *At Christie's, April 2002* ★★★(★★) *2005–2025.*

**Warre** Nine notes since April 1987. A touch of toffee on the nose (malt, meat, toffee all reflecting the almost unctuous richness of the vintage, as is a thickness of colour). A dozen years later, still a fine deep red purple; extraordinary nose, whiff of wet oilskin, great vinosity, prunes, figs; sweet, fairly full-bodied, fleshy, elegant, beautifully balanced. 'An archetypal Warre.' High marks at an extensive Symington tasting in London in 1994 and, the following year, drinking beautifully high above Lake Toxaway, North Carolina. A still youthful, classic Warre at a Bär Bank/Christie's dinner in Vienna 1999. Most recently, in very good vintage company, fairly intense; 'classic' nose again; lovely flavour and texture. Very dry, fragrant finish. With Graham, my top '85. *Last tasted Dec 2001* ★★★★(★) *Now–2025.*

OTHER '85s, OLDER NOTES **Foz, Qta da** opaque, huge, opulent, very sweet, full but lean. *March 1988* ★★★(★); **Hooper** indistinct nose; sweet, full, fat, smooth but lacking length. *July 1987* ★★; **Hutcheson** plummy colour and nose; very sweet, fig-like flavour. *Sept 1989* ★★; **Kopke** medium colour; hard, lean, spirity; not very sweet, lean, crisp, nice length. *July 1987* ★★; **Messias** thick, plummy; sweet, smooth texture, a rather odd, slightly stalky flavour. *July 1987* ★★; and **Da Silva** very sweet, impressive. *July 1987* ★★★

# 1986 ★

Not a very propitious growing year. After three and a half months of virtually unbroken drought, the wind suddenly turned to the south and, during the second week of September, the Douro – indeed all Portugal – was inundated with rain, 5cm being recorded at Pinhão over the weekend of 13-14 September! Picking in the Upper Douro continued from 24 September under good, crisp, autumn conditions. Not declared. Mainly LBVs and single-quinta ports produced, all for early drinking.

**Bomfim, Qta do** Plummy; pleasant, fragrant; attractive wine. *June 1998* ★★

**Dow** Cask samples tasted in the spring after the vintage to compare two of the leading classic port grape varieties. Touriga Nacional, considered the best: extremely deep and intense; vast aroma of prunes and figs; fairly sweet, very full-bodied, very rich, severe. Touriga Francesa (renamed Touriga Franca in 2001), which makes useful blending wine: totally opaque; softer, more feminine, citrus nose and flavour; slightly less sweet, and lighter-bodied, leaner, very flavoury. The more I taste young ports, the more I admire the incredible stamina and experience of the 'noses', the master blenders, who are the lynchpins of all the great port houses.

**Fonseca Guimaraens** Tight knit, citrus-like nose; hot fragrant, surprising length, dry finish. *Oct 1999* ★★★

**Foz, Qta da** An intensely purple wine from a sample pipe. A sweet, gutsy yet lean wine. Impressive. *March 1988* ★★

**Graham's Malvedos** Opaque; sweet, rich, full in 1992. Still opaque; good fruit, a bit peppery. *Last tasted June 1998* ★★

**Niepoort** Bottled 1990. Deep, youthful; syrup of figs; very sweet, soft, fleshy, long, hot, slightly acidic end. *Oct 1990* ★★(★)

**Sandeman** Bottled 1990. Plummy; figgy; horrible; sweet, not liked. *Feb 1991*

**Vargellas, Qta de** Two notes in latter part of the 1990s. A fine colour, maturing nicely; very fragrant nose; sweet, glorious flavour, rather heady, dry tannic finish. Remarkably good. *Last noted Oct 1999* ★★★(★) *Now–2010.*

**Warre, Reserve** Mature; very good nutty nose and flavour; sweet, very good. *Nov 1999* ★★★★ *Drink soon.*

## 1987 ★★ to ★★★

Another uneven year. The early development of the vines was hampered by the previous winter's low rainfall. Then followed a long bout of hot weather, reaching a near record 38°C in Oporto in early August. There were intermittent violent storms in July and August. Heavily laden vines consisted of rather small, dried-up grapes which were picked in excessive heat (reaching 40°C in Pinhão) in mid-September, followed by rain. Nevertheless, some yields were above average and sugar readings of the early picked grapes were high, but there were considerable variations from district to district. Mainly wines for early drinking.

**Cavadinho, Qta da** Opaque, intense; rich figgy nose; fairly sweet, good flavour. Very dry tannic finish. Needs cheese! *June 1998* ★★(★)

**Croft** At ten years of age considerable colour loss, now a pure tawny in appearance, nose and taste. *At Croft's, May 1997* ★★

**Ferreira** Three notes: impressive colour and fruit at Ferreira's in 1996. Two years later in Palm Beach, sweet, soft, good finish and, later the same day, coping manfully with 'A Trio of Pastry du Chef: Blackberry Crème Brûlée, Cranberry Walnut Linzer, Frozen White Chocolate Soufflé' (sic – almost sick!). *Last noted inappropriately at A Taste of France, hosted by me at the Mar-a-Lago Club, Florida, Feb 1998* ★★★

**Foz, Qta da** Interesting samples from vineyards on the hot barren slopes of the excellent Cima Corgo district and the lower Baixa Corgo tasted in 1988, both opaque, the former with a hot, youthful, straw-like nose; full and lean, loaded with tannin and acidity, the latter more open-knit on nose and palate, slightly sweeter, less full-bodied. A decade later, good flesh and flavour. Nice wine. *Last tasted June 1998* ★★★

**Graham's Malvedos** Opaque, intense; very rich young fruit; sweet, raisiny yet lean. *May 1991* ★★★

**Martinez** Opaque, intense; rather hard, oaky nose with fig-like fruit and rather high acidity; medium-sweet, medium-full body, lean, dry finish. *Dec 1990* ★★(★)

**Niepoort** Rolf Niepoort suggested that I might try drinking young port with steak *au poivre*. I tried it in February 1990 with his '87, a thick-set, intense wine with an immature appearance; surprisingly fragrant only a few months after bottling; sweet, full-bodied, loads of fruit, tannin and acidity which all coped admirably with the pepper steak. In fact it seemed to hot-up even the pepper. More recently: as described, a good mouthful of a wine with an equally promising future. *Last tasted Oct 1990* ★★(★)

**Noval Nacional** Just one note. The youngest and one of the three top-rated vintages (with 1962 and 1982) at the remarkable vertical of 12 Nacionals. Still deep and immature of course; wonderfully sweet nose; very rich, full of fruit, extended finish. *Sept 1994* ★★★(★★) *2007–2030.*

**Offley Boa Vista** Very deep, sweet, soft texture. *At Offley's, March 1996* ★★★

**Tua, Qta do** Long owned by Cockburn but the first vintage to be marketed as a single-quinta. The grapes come entirely from this quinta which is just across a tributary of the Douro from Graham's Malvedos. An impressive, mouthfilling wine: opaque, intense; very good fruit; sweet, fairly full-bodied. A good start. *At Cockburn's, Dec 1990* ★★(★)

**Tuke Holdsworth** I noted (in March 1996) that Ferreira were buying in grapes for their Tuke marque. It was certainly quite different in character to Ferreira, tasted alongside. But it seemed mature and nice enough at ten years of age. *Last tasted at Ferreira's, May 1997* ★★ *Now–2010.*

**Warre** Colheita. Excellent flavour, lissom, lean, with exquisite finish. *April 2001* ★★★★ *Drink soon.*

## 1988 ★

After the abundance of recent years, relatively sparse budding was followed by three exceptionally damp and stormy months, causing mildew and *desavinho* (*coulure*). There was also hail damage. In early September, an intense heatwave caused some scorching of the grapes but also accelerated maturation. The harvest began towards the end of September. The crop was the smallest in memory. A financial disaster for the grape farmers and a serious shortfall for shippers.

**Bomfim, Qta do** Eight notes but none recent. At four years of age still opaque; delicious but very tannic. *Last tasted Oct 1992* ★★★? *Drink soon.*

**Graham's Malvedos** Four years after the vintage: black! Magnificent. Sweet, forthcoming aroma and taste. Leaner than '87. *Last tasted Oct 1996* ★★★★ *Now–2010.*

**Madalena, Qta da** Convincing colour; lightish style but fairly strong figgy flavour. *June 1998* ★★ *Drink soon.*

**Rosa, Qta de la** Fragrant; pleasant flavour, light style. *June 1998* ★★★ *Drink soon.*

**Warre** Colheita. Richly evolved nose; good flavour, hot finish. Slightly raw edge. *April 2001* ★★(★) *But not for keeping.*

## 1989 ★★★

Excessively dry winter, sporadic spring rain. Summer began early and was long and hot, though heavy rain in June. Harvest began some three weeks early and was completed in ideal conditions by early October. Though quality high, production below average. Following the shortfall of 1988s, shippers needed stock which ruled out a general vintage declaration.

**Burmester** Intense; strangely un-port-like; rich, powerful. *At Burmester's March 1996* ★★? *Drink soon.*

**Croft** Maturing fairly quickly. Rather raisiny nose. Just one all-too-brief note. *At Croft's, May 1997* ★★★? *Drink up.*

**Offley Boa Vista** Immensely deep; very full fruity wine laden with tannin. *At Offley's, March 1996* ★★★ *Now–2009.*

**Vesúvio, Qta de** Three notes: leaner than the '90 and '91 in 1994. Two years later, though still youthful in appearance, a marvellously forthcoming aroma, with full, figgy flavour to match. Most recently, less deep in colour; full, rich, very fleshy. *Last tasted June 1998* ★★★(★) *2006–2030.*

# 1990–1999

What has been very noticeable in the last decade or so is the shift of the market for vintage port, once the almost exclusive prerogative of the British, from my side of the Atlantic to the other. North American sales have been booming. In the USA it is considered a dessert wine, a perfect accompaniment for chocolate puddings! The Americans drink it young, uninhibited by convention and the image of elderly gentlemen in St James's clubs, passing the port, with Stilton cheese (I personally do not like Stilton with port, finding it generally too salty, too overpowering). Moreover, the drink-drive laws have undoubtedly reduced the consumption by our otherwise still fairly civilised society. Nevertheless, sales are flourishing, a far cry from the 1950s, but well below the shipments of the 1920s, not to mention the mid-18th century! France continues to be a major importer: by volume not vintage.

## Vintages at a Glance
**Outstanding** ★★★★★
None
**Very Good** ★★★★
1991, 1992 (v), 1994, 1997
**Good** ★★★
1990 (v), 1995, 1996, 1998 (v), 1999

## 1990 ★★ to ★★★

Good but not declared because of the recession in the two principal markets for vintage port, the UK and the USA.

Propitious conditions: successful budding and flowering; a big potential crop. However, searing heat late July into August 'burnt' the ripening grapes and dried up young vines. Heavy rain again mid- and end of the month swelled the grapes. A large crop, but instead of gloriously ripe fruit, the grapes had lower sugar and higher acidity levels than anticipated. Final yields were surprisingly high. Problems arose mid-harvest by an unforeseen brandy shortage; then, paradoxically, official permits were issued for quantities in excess of the original authorisation. As in the case of the 1989s, shippers needed the 1990s for their main stock-in-trade, the wood ports.
**Croft LBV** Very deep in colour. Fairly sweet. Good grip. *April 1997* ★★ *Drink up.*
**Graham** Tasting of wine made from grapes vinified separately. Tinta Barroca grown at Malvedos: opaque, purple; raw stalky nose; sweet, lean, swingeingly tannic. Tinta Roriz, also from Malvedos, softer yet with quite a kick. Touriga Nacional, even more intense, figgy fruit; less sweet, full-bodied, firm, classic. Tinta Francesca: incredible aroma, violets; fabulous flavour and length. *Tasted May 1991.*
**Graham's Malvedos** Ten notes, none recently. Initially opaque; fragrant, spirity; sweet, lively. *Last noted Oct 1992* ★★★
**Vesúvio, Qta do** The first vintage made by the Symingtons after they purchased this famous old quinta from Ferreira. Many notes made in 1992 while touring the USA with my son, Bartholomew, at that time President of Premium Port Wines, Symington's American import company†. Then, powerful yet harmonious, fleshy, lovely flavour. More recently less deep, a full rich flavour with promise of fairly early development. *Last tasted Nov 1994* ★★★ *Now–2010.*

† In 1996, after 9 years promoting Symington's major port and madeira brands, my son founded his own import company, 'Broadbent Selections' based in San Francisco, representing Ferreira and a portfolio of their wines.

## 1991 ★★★★

A very good year. Following a very wet new year and spring, there was a successful flowering in May but a hot, dry summer reduced the flesh and thickened the skins of the grapes. Deep-coloured wines of considerable promise. A widely declared vintage though notable absentees included Taylor and Fonseca.

Most of my early notes were made briefly and swiftly at the 1991 Port Declaration tasting at the East India and Sports Club, conveniently across the street from my office at Christie's, in June 1993. All the wines at this stage had a deep purple colour but were, of course, very tannic.
**Burmester** Noted good flavour at the MW 1991 port tasting in April 1995. Impressively deep; forthcoming nose; fairly sweet, some softness yet enough 'grip'. Dry finish. *Last noted at Burmester's, Vila Nova de Gaia, March 1996* ★★★ *Now–2010.*
**Churchill** Deep, rich, velvety; dumb but distinctive, classic; sweet, full, rich, well constructed, tannic, impressive. Good future. *At the MW tasting, April 1995* ★★★(★) *2005–2025.*
**Cockburn** Rich appearance, straightforward, good length in 1993. Two years later: good texture, rich, figgy flavour. It will be interesting to see how this develops. *Last noted at the MW tasting, April 1995* ★★★ *Now–2010.*
**Croft** Noticeably sweet, lovely flesh, good texture in 1993. I gave it a high mark at the MW tasting in 1995: intense; rich; very good flavour. Two years later, still opaque; harmonious; elegant. *Last noted at Croft's, May 1997* ★★★(★) *2003–2020.*
**Dow** Five consistently good notes. First in 1993, very distinctive. Next at a Dow vertical in Aspen in June 1994, then a very high mark at a Symington tasting that autumn and at the MW tasting in 1995. Initially an intense mulberry colour, still deep, velvety; powerful yet harmonious nose, rich, figgy; very sweet, crisp, good flesh and fruit. *Last noted at the Dow bicentenary tasting, Oct 1998* ★★★★(★) *2005–2025.*
**Ferreira** Hard, slightly stalky, peppery in 1993. Then two notes in the mid-1990s. Considerable depth of nose and flavour. Very much the Portuguese style. Very sweet, assertive. *Last tasted March 1996* ★★★(★) *Now–2015.*
**Fonseca Guimaraens** Fonseca did not declare the 1991. Distinctive depth, touch of leanness, very elegant even in its youth (1993). Then at four years of age, opaque; very distinctive, spicy, shapely, good length, peppery tannic finish. *Last noted April 1995* ★★★(★) *2003–2015.*
**Foz, Qta da** Just after bottling: aroma of figs and prunes; fairly hefty. Still raw. Cálem tends to be underestimated. I like their 'British' style. It should make a good bottle. *Last tasted with Jeremy Bull, then Cálem's manager, at Christie's, Oct 1994* ★★★(★) *2005–2025.*

**Gould Campbell** To be frank, mixed reviews. Lean yet very sweet and fruity in 1993. Then lean and disappointing at the MW tasting, but altogether richer and more positive at the recent Fells tasting. Fragrant, very sweet, dry finish. *Last noted November 2000 ★★★ Now–2015.*

**Graham** Outstanding in 1993. Then two good notes in the mid-1990s. Characteristically very sweet, very rich, full of fruit, complete, good length. *Last tasted April 1995 ★★★★ Now–2020.*

**Hutcheson** Nose of figs and prunes. As unmemorable as its name in the port firmament. *Tasted April 1995 ★ Drink soon.*

**Martinez** Stalky, lean but fruity in 1993. At four years of age deep but surprisingly evolved appearance; somewhat coarse texture. Not very impressed. *Noted April 1995 ★? Drink soon.*

**Niepoort** Showing well in 1993. A very distinctive style of wine. Rich, peppery, lean, tannic. *Last noted April 1995 ★★★(★) Drink now–2015.*

**Noval, Qta do** Rich, forthcoming, fleshy. Impressive. *Not tasted since June 1993 ★★★★? Now–2015*

**Poças Junior** Good enough. *Not tasted since June 1993 ★★★?*

**Quarles Harris** Intense fruit, rich, piquant acidity in 1993 and very high marks at the MW tasting in 1995, svelte, lovely texture, citrus touch to end taste. More recently soft, agreeable but slightly less enthusiastic. *Last noted at the Fells tasting, November 2000 ★★★ Now–2015.*

**Ramos-Pinto** A Portuguese house that deserves to be better known in British circles. Attractive. Touch of muscatel-like grapiness. A wine to drink, not to lay down for years. *April 1995 ★★ Drink soon.*

**Rozes** Very deep; high-toned; very sweet, 'svelte' noted again, pleasant flavour. *April 1995 ★★ Drink soon.*

**Smith Woodhouse** Lean, shapely, showing well in 1993. Distinctive style, touch of grapiness noted in 1995. Most recently, impressively deep, opaque core; nose opened up richly in glass; good fruit, touch of leanness, good 'grip'. *Last tasted November 2000 ★★★(★) 2004–2015.*

**Souza** Stencilled bottle: *Vieira de Souza.* Almost sickly sweet nose; malty, raw texture. *Noted April 1995. Uninteresting.*

**Vargellas, Qta de** Bottled by Taylor's in 1993 and first tasted shortly after bottling. I was enormously impressed and was intrigued by its violets-like fragrance and crisp fruit. Apparently it was not to be released for ten years but I persuaded them to sell me, through their agents, Mentzendorf, two cases. Also showing well at the MW tasting in 1995, lean and elegant with a zestful citrus touch. Five months later I was tempted to try it again. A most original flavour, refreshing but completely unready. Most recently, to see how it is progressing, delicious but needs yet more time. *Last tasted May 2001 ★★(★★★) 2006–2015.*

**Vesúvio, Qta do** Slight whiff of volatile acidity but sweet and soft despite life-supporting tannins in May 1993. Very highly rated at the Symington tasting in November 1994: opaque, full-bodied, lean and powerful. Much the same the following spring: very sweet, good flesh and length. *Last noted April 1995 ★★★(★) 2005–2020.*

**Warre** I like the style of Warre – there is always a touch of elegance. Dense; silky tannic texture, long hot finish in 1993. Two notes in the mid-1990s. Lovely flavour, fruity, crisp. Good future. *Last tasted April 1995 ★★★(★) 2003–2020.*

## 1992 ★★★ to ★★★★

A curious year both for the growing season and declarations. First of all, the north of Portugal suffered the worst winter drought since records began with no rain for six months. Early summer was very hot and dry with welcome rain to revive and swell the grapes in time for a cool and showery harvest, late pickers being the most successful. Fonseca and Taylor declared, the latter said to prefer their '92 to the '91 (though I found their Vargellas '91 superb). However, bear in mind also that Taylor's celebrated their tercentenary in 1992.

**Burmester** The '92 tasted only once, from their Qta de Nossa Señora do Carmo: totally different style to their '91. Crisp fruit. Nice wine. *At Burmester, March 1996 ★★★ Now–2012.*

**Croft** Two notes, one at Croft's in May 1997 and the other on a British Airways flight from Los Angeles. Starting to mature. Delicious. *Last tasted March 1999 ★★★ Drink now–2010.*

**Delaforce** First tasted in April 1995. Muffled, meaty, very sweet. Most recently: maturing nicely; singed, chocolatey nose; very good flesh and length. *Last tasted at the Fladgate tasting at Christie's, April 2002 ★★★ Now–2012.*

**Fonseca** Once again, rising to the occasion. Intensely deep yet despite its youthfulness, a deep, complete, harmonious nose and flavour. Very sweet, with grip and length. *Noted at a port declarations tasting April 1995 ★★★★ Now–2015.*

**Foz, Qta da** One note soon after bottling. Fairly hefty, figgy fruit, raw tannins. Should be good. *Oct 1994 ★★★ Now–2010.*

**Niepoort** At three years of age, opaque; curious nose; sweet, full, very good flavour. Tannic of course. *April 1995 ★★★ Now–2015.*

**Taylor** Very deep, still youthful; very sweet, jammy nose. Only tasted quickly but not very impressed. Rhône-like flavour. *At the Fladgate tasting at Christie's, April 2002 ★★(★)? Retaste.*

**Vesúvio, Qta do** Three notes from the mid-1990s. Immensely deep; fragrant, rich, slightly raisiny nose; full, fruity, stylish, lots of grip – in fact one noted as 'swingeingly tannic'. *Last tasted April 1995 (★★★★) 2005–2020.*

## 1993

Not declared. One of the poorest years in living memory. Following an exceptionally wet autumn in 1992 and winter, when heavy rain caused some terraces of vines to collapse, spring was dry, but the crucial flowering was inhibited by damp weather in May. The summer was cooler than usual and followed by very unsettled weather. The late pickers were delayed by continuous rain.

**Cockburn** Served, somewhat prematurely, at the 112th annual banquet of the Wine & Spirit Trades' Benevolent Society. Deep ruby; rather figgy; medium sweetness and body. Went well with the *Reblochon* cheese and speeches. *May 1998 ★*

**Ramos-Pinto** Medium-deep; 'warm' raisiny nose and flavour. Pleasant wine. *At a trade tasting, Jan 1997 ★★*

## 1994 ★★★★

Widely declared. Overall this was a very good vintage and particularly welcome after the disastrous '93s, despite a fairly dismal start: very wet spring and damp, humid conditions which hampered flowering. The summer was more satisfactory though an exceptionally hot week in August, with temperatures up to 40°C, caused some alarm. Harvest conditions from early to mid-September were satisfactory, though the volume was not high.

**Broadbent** In case the reader thinks this is an ego trip, let me hastily explain that this is a Niepoort wine bottled in 1997 and shipped for my son's import business in the USA. It has been a great success. I first tasted a sample bottle brought by Bartholomew to the Florida Winefest in April 1997, a full, soft, plummy wine with good length. One or two bottles tasted since. In April 2001 a bottle I intended to give to my château proprietor host in Bordeaux; she was absent, so I opened and polished off the bottle with two fellow wine writers. Still very deep; very sweet, plums and figs, powerful, touch of tar. It enlivened a dreary dinner. Most recently: showing well – thank goodness – at my 75th birthday dinner in May 2002. *Last tasted at Vintners' Hall, London, May 2002* ★★★(★) *Now–2012.*

**Burmester** Two notes, the first at Burmester in March 1996: vividly purple; crisp, tannic, attractive. The second eight months later at Georg Riedel's experimental port glass tasting. It had an aroma of syrup of figs – which I well recall as a young boy; very sweet, rich, good flesh. Good wine. Needs time. *Last noted November 1996* ★(★★★) *2003–2025.*

**Cockburn** 'A perfect year … *circa* 6000 cases of vintage.' Deep, fine, still plummy-coloured; a thick, rich figgy, fruitiness. Full, flavoury, very attractive. *Last tasted at Cockburn's 'Memories of a Century', London, May 2002* ★★(★★) *2005–2020.*

**Crasto, Qta do** Deep, plummy-coloured; very sweet, soft, attractive fruit, good texture. *At Bartholomew's port tasting in Jackson, Mississippi, April 1997* ★★(★) *Now–2015.*

**Croft** Unenthusiastic, at Croft's in 1997, preferring the '91. But opening up well: very sweet, figgy, caramelly nose; sweet, fleshy, attractive. *Last tasted at Christie's, April 2002* ★★★ *Now–2012.*

**Dow** The Symingtons, at their tasting in March 1996, informed us that they started picking at Quinta do Bomfim on 16 September, which is pretty early, and that the wine had the 'violets aroma of a great year'. It was certainly impressive, with a sort of waxy fruit, not at all spirity despite its youthfulness. More recently, still opaque; complete, opulent; laden with fruit and flesh, very dry finish. Very good future. *Last noted at Dow's bicentenary tasting, Oct 1998* ★(★★★★) *2006–2030.*

**Eira Velha, Qta da** Rich, excellent texture. *At Walter Siegel's centenary tasting, March 1997* ★★(★★) *Now–2020.*

**Ervamoira, Qta da** Sweet, fleshy, good fruit. *At the Port Wine Institute's single-quinta tasting, June 1998* ★★★ *Now–2015.*

**Ferreira** Four notes, the first two touring with my son in the USA, in April 1997. An impressive, powerful wine. The following month at Ferreira's, noting luscious, figgy fruit, richness and depth. Most recently, delicious wine with marvellous length and finish. *Last noted at 'A Porto Tasting' conducted with Bartholomew in Seattle, November 1998* ★★★(★★) *2005–2025.*

**Fonseca** Two cask samples each labelled '*Fonseca Guimaraens*', April and July 1996: thick, high extract, intensity, yet smooth. At the Wine Experience 'top 10' tasting in New York, 1998: opaque, intense, with long shapely 'legs'; very rich nose, sweet of course, full body and fruit, lovely velvety texture. With Taylor (see below), the *Wine Spectator*'s joint No 1 '100-point' wine. Most recently: similarly noted. An immensely impressive wine. *Last noted at the Fladgate tasting at Christie's, April 2002* ★(★★★★) *2006–2025.*

**Gould Campbell** Two somewhat inconsistent notes: rich, slightly toasted nose, quite stylish at the Symington tasting in April 1996. More recently, still opaque, plummy. A strange nose, hard, peppery, bitter mocha; sweet, distinctive, loads of grip, verging on coarse. Time will tell. *At the Fells tasting, November 2000* ★★? *2005–2010?*

**Graham** Wonderful wine, its richness masking its 20% brandy at the Symington tasting in April 1996. I also noted an excellent '94 bottled in 1999 on a British Airways flight to New York in September 1999. Great wine. *Last tasted Sept 1999* ★(★★★★) *2006–2030.*

**Offley Boa Vista** Two notes. Undeveloped but stylish at Offley's in March 1996. A year later opening up and showing well: crisp fruit, lovely flavour – delicious. *In Jackson, Mississippi, March 1997* ★★(★★)? *2004–2020.*

**Quarles Harris** Surprisingly forthcoming yet unknit nose and loose-knit but delicious flavour in April 1996. More recently, a convincing colour, a curiously hefty character; very sweet, plump, figgy, rich. *Last noted at a Fells tasting of Symington's '2nd eleven', November 2000* ★★★(★)? *Now–2015.*

**Smith Woodhouse** Noted at the same two tastings as Gould Campbell and Quarles Harris. Attractive colour; distinctive Pontefract cakes nose, more refined than Gould. A complete, lovely wine. *Last noted November 2000* ★★★(★★) *2004–2020.*

**Taylor** Labelled Taylor Fladgate, part of the original firm's title Taylor, Fladgate and Yeatman, but always shipped as 'Taylor's' to the UK. First noted as cask samples in June and July 1996. 'A heck of a bite', bitter (tannic) finish, and hard, spirity, full of fruit and great length. In other words a classic immature Taylor. With Fonseca (see above), the *Wine Spectator*'s joint No 1 '100-point' wine and certainly demonstrating its qualities. Still opaque and intense; nose more sublimated than Fonseca, but crisp, lovely fruit; sweeter though, with all the component parts for a splendid future. *Last tasted at the Wine Experience in New York, Dec 1998* (★★★★★) *2010–2040.*

**Vesúvio, Qta do** 40% Touriga Francesa (10% other varieties), 20% Touriga Nacional, 30% Tinta Barroca. First noted in April 1996: totally different in style to the main Symington brands, with its delicious, touch of uplifting citrus aromas; not as sweet, but glorious fruit. Still opaque; extraordinary, most distinctive, great potential. *Last noted at the Symington Family Port Companies' tasting in London, May 2002* (★★★★★) *2008–2030.*

**Warre** Said to have a 'typical cistus nose' i.e. resinous. Anyway, the most intensely dark of all the Symington's '94s. Very sweet, lovely flavour, perfect balance, good length. *Noted April 1996. Great future* (★★★★★) *2006–2026.*

# 1995 ★★★

Despite the quality, not generally declared as it was so hard on the heels of the much-hyped – and shipped – '94s. Reasonably good weather conditions during the growing and maturing season: a mild spring, early bud break, satisfactory flowering but a very hot, dry, stressful – for the vines – July. An early harvest was blessed with ideal conditions. Yields made up for the shortfalls of 1994 and 1993.

**Bomfim, Qta do** Showing well. Very dry finish. *At the Port Wine Institute single-quinta tasting, June 1998* ★★★ *Now–2010.*

**Broadbent** A sample from Niepoort tasted but not shipped. Less sweet, crisper than the '94. Good fruit though, and impressive. *May 1997* ★★★

**Canais, Qta dos** Cockburn's 150-ha vineyard opposite Vesúvio. Very sweet, figgy nose; good flavour, easy, attractive. *May 2002* ★(★★) *2005–2012.*

**Cavadinha, Qta da** Opaque (at four years of age); typical Warre fragrance; attractive character. *June 1998* ★★★ *Now–2010.*

**Crasto, Qta do** Previously virtually unheard of despite being one of the oldest – and most picturesque – quintas in the

Douro. The '95 made a great impression at the London Wine Trade Fair in May 1997. Deep, velvety, intense; lovely flavour, very attractive fruit, good flesh, clove-like finish. *Last noted at 'A Porto Tasting' in Seattle, November 1998. Worth looking out for* ★★(★) *2004–2015.*

**Croft, LBV** I do not normally take much notice of these very commercial LBVs but this was excellent: very deep; good nose and incredibly sweet without any specious figginess. *On BA 285 London to San Francisco, Feb 2002* ★★★ *Drink soon.*

**Eira Velha, Qta da** Cask sample at the Siegel tasting, March 1997, curiously rustic. Showing better at the single-quinta tasting, crisp, tangy, quite a bite. *Last tasted, June 1998* ★★?

**Ferreira** First noted in September 1997 at a Ferreira tasting at Christie's in New York, then, showing well, in North Carolina, crisp, peppery. A year later still almost black with ruby rim; rich, good fruit and length, with a wonderfully dry finish. *Last tasted in Seattle, November 1998* ★(★★), *possibly* ★(★★★) *2005–2020.*

**Fonseca Guimaraens** Only one note. Lovely wine. *May 1997* ★★★ *Now to 2010.*

**Foz, Qta da** Attractive, singed nose; dry, crisp, good fruit. *June 1998* ★★(★) *2003–2015.*

**Madalena, Qta da** Figgy; citrus touch, teeth-gripping acidity. *June 1998* (★★)? *Drink soon.*

**Offley Boa Vista** Four notes, all at my son's 'Broadbent Selections' tastings in the USA. Powerful appearance; fragrant; assertive, fig-like taste, good flesh, crisp fruit. Tannic bitterness. Needs time. *Last tasted November 1998* (★★★) *2005–2015?*

**Roêda, Qta da** No new wood used now, and more large wooden vats than traditional 'pipes'. A crisp, very fruity wine. *At Croft's, May 1997* ★(★★) *Now–2012.*

**Vargellas, Qta da** Firm, lean, not unlike 1991. Very tannic. *May 1997* (★★★) *2005–2020.*

**Tuke Holdsworth** Three notes, touring the USA. Impressively deep, more fruit and power than its 'cousin' Ferreira. *Last noted in Charlotte, North Carolina, November 1997* (★★★) *2003–2015.*

**Vale da Mina, Qta** Two notes. Christiano van Zeller's new vineyard next to Crasto. Rich looking. Firm yet with luscious fruit, crisp finish. Interesting. *Last tasted at 'A Porto Tasting' in Seattle, November 1998* ★★(★)? *Now–2012.*

---

### Staying at quintas

*Our first occasion was at vintage time in 1970, as the guests of the delightful Fernando van Zeller (whose appearance reminded me of the great comedian of classic French cinema, Fernandel); sitting on the terrace at Noval in the early evening, nibbling fresh almonds, sipping chilled white port and almost overcome by the scale and grandeur of the hills and of the valley below.*

*In 1988, a weekend with the Symington family at Malvedos, memories of much rain and, even more, of irresistible old tawny and how much one could consume, seemingly without ill effects; of sketching the quinta from all directions to produce for them a composite watercolour; between showers, venturing up the single track railway line, a short cut to Tua, and encountering a dark-eyed local beauty walking the other way. She stopped and patiently sat on a rock while I sketched her – fully clothed of course (both of us!).*

*More recently (1996), with the delightful Roquette family at Crasto, a quaint old quinta perched on a spur with panoramic views over the precarious terraces of vines and the river below.*

*In the Douro valley, time stands still.*

**Vesúvio, Qta do** One youthful note. Distinctive and impressive. I wonder whether Ferreira ever regretted selling Vesúvio, one of the greatest Douro quintas, to the ubiquitous Symington family? *At the single-quinta tasting, London, June 1998* ★(★★★) *2005–2020.*

## 1996 ★★★

Large crop, good quality but not declared. Following a very wet winter, with flooding and vineyard damage, the spring was mild and flowering satisfactory. However, the complete lack of rain from June through August delayed ripening, resulting in a late harvest, the best grapes being brought in towards the end of September and early October. Nevertheless, the overall production was usefully above average.

**Croft** Cask sample. Opaque; attractive. Hard to judge. *At Croft's, May 1997.*

**Vesúvio, Qta do** Bottled April 1998. Rich but not very deep; unknit but very attractive; lovely fruit and flavour. *July 1998* (★★★) *Say 2005–2010.*

## 1997 ★★★★

A very good, widely declared and high-priced vintage. Unusual growing conditions: unseasonably warm spring, flowering a month earlier than normal, yet a cool June and July slowed development. This was compounded by rain and humidity though fortunately the opposite occurred towards the end of August, continuing into September for a fine start to the harvest on the 15th, which, because of the irregularities, was a small though high-quality crop.

The sort of vintage that American port lovers will start drinking long before the wines reach full maturity.

**Barros** Medium-deep; muffled nose, walnuts; raspberry-like fruit. Attractive. *At the first MW tasting of '97s at the Reform Club, London, June 1999* (★★★) *2003–2012.*

**Broadbent** Purple rim; low-keyed, touch of liquorice; lissom, good length, spicy and attractive aftertaste. *In Bartholomew's tasting room, San Francisco, Dec 2000. Should make a good wine* (★★★★) *2004–2020.*

**Burmester** Very figgy; sweet, pleasant flavour, good tannin and acidity. *June 1999* (★★★) *2003–2015.*

**Cálem** Opaque core; rich, singed, fig-like fruit; crisp, hint of blackberry, attractive. *June 1999* (★★★★) *2005–2020.*

**Churchill** Distinctive, wet straw; crisp, lean, hot finish. Retaste. *June 1999* (★★)?

**Cockburn** Very deep; two-part, unknit; sweet, hot finish. *June 1999? Must taste again.*

**Côrte, Qta da** In June 1999: deep, velvety; scent of wet straw with raspberry-like fruit. Acidic. Recently: figgy, sweet, rich. *April 2002* ★(★★) *2003–2010.*

**Crasto, Qta do** Mixed notes: syrup of figs and chocolate; very fruity, lovely flavour, excellent finish at the MW tasting. Unquestionably full and rich but somehow didn't like it. *Last tasted, a glass after lunch, November 1999. Retaste.*

**Delaforce** Taut fruit; medium sweetness and body. Unready. *At Vinopolis Cantina, London, November 1999* (★★★) *2004–2015.*

**Dow** At their bicentenary tasting October 1998: black bramble colour; gorgeous, floral; very appealing, good fruit and grip – 'possible vintage declaration'. Showing well, classic, at the MW tasting. *June 1999* ★(★★★) *2007–2025.*

**Eira Velha, Qta da** Very fragrant; lissom, delicious flavour. *June 1999* ★(★★★) *2005–2020.*

**Fonseca** Distinctive, figgy but fragrant; beautiful flavour and length. Classic. *June 1999* (★★★★★) *2007–2025.*

**Gould Campbell** At the MW tasting: high-toned, slightly singed and chocolatey; good flavour, lean finish; straightforward. Nothing special. *Last noted at the Fells tasting of Symington 'second XIs', November 2000* ★(★★) *2004–2015.*

**Graham** Opaque; hefty, forthcoming aroma; rich, full flavoured, great length. Potentially a great classic. *June 1999* (★★★★★) *2007–2030.*

**Kopke** Low-keyed; more positive on palate. Attractive flavour. *June 1999* ★(★★) *2004–2015.*

**Martinez** Maturing quickly, appley-straw-like nose and flavour. *June 1999* (★★)? *Need to retaste.*

**Niepoort** Deep, velvety; very sweet, rich, good texture, hot finish. *June 1999* (★★★★) *2004–2020.*

**Noval, Qta do** Very attractive, very Noval. *June 1999* ★(★★★) *2003–2015.*

**Offley Boa Vista** Not deep; light style, but attractive. *June 1999* (★★★) *2003–2015.*

**Quarles Harris** Plummy, forthcoming at the MW tasting. Noted a distinctive, unusual nose and flavour, rich yet dry acidic finish. *Last noted at the Fells tasting of Symington 'second XIs', November 2000* (★★★)?

**Ramos-Pinto** 'Finest grapes from own Quinta, traditionally foot-crushed in stone *lagar*.' Deep royal purple; extraordinary scented pear juice nose and flavour noted at the MW tasting. More recently, a less eccentric note: brambly, peppery, delicious fruit. *Last noted at the Maisons Marques & Domaines tasting, Jan 2000* (★★★) *2005–2020.*

**Roêda, Qta da** Distinctive, slightly singed; lean, citrus touch on finish. *June 1999* ★(★★) *2004–2015.*

**Sandeman 'Vau'** This is a new brand, not a second wine, and made for early consumption. Despite this, it had the deep opacity of a straight vintage marque; classic nose; very sweet, good flavour. *June 1999* (★★★) *2006–2025.*

**Smith Woodhouse** Top-class. Showing well at the MW tasting and then very high marks at Fells' tasting. Interesting nose, touch of tar and liquorice, whiff of honeycomb; lean yet fleshy, very good flavour and finish. *Last noted November 2000* (★★★★) *2006–2025.*

**Taylor** In June 1999: opaque; low-keyed yet distinctive, rich, complex, great depth; a powerful wine, with dry finish. Classic.

Most recently, impressive, good future. *Last tasted at Christie's, April 2002* (★★★★★) *2010–2030.*

**Warre** Richly scented; elegant, excellent finish. *June 1999* (★★★★★) *2007–2025.*

## 1998 variable, up to ★★★

The second smallest vintage of the decade. Not generally declared but quality suitable for single-quinta wines and LBVs. To date, I have tasted only one vintage wine. It will probably sink without trace.

Weather and growing conditions were far from ideal. Following a wet winter it was hot and dry in February, more like spring, which advanced the vegetation, but rain returned in April and continued for two months seriously affecting flowering, fruit set and eventual crop. June was warm, hot and dry, and similar conditions in July and August continued into September, but at the end of that month the weather broke, dashing the hopes of an excellent harvest.

**Senhora da Ribera, Qta** Opaque; rich, figgy; sweet, full of fruit, very attractive flavour. Good acidity. Not too tannic. *July 2001* ★(★★) *Probably best 2003–2008.*

## 1999 ★★★

A vintage that almost made it, depending on when the grapes were picked and pressed — early or late. Upstaged, however, by the 2000.

Exceptionally cold and dry winter delayed budding. April and May were very wet, but flowering in excellent conditions in early June ensured a good size crop. The rest of June and July was warm with bouts of excessively high temperatures. Some beneficial rain in August and useful rain in September swelled the berries. However, not for the first time, towards the end of September the weather broke, becoming cool and unsettled with 12 days of rain at a critical period which made harvesting difficult. Those who picked either side of the rain made better wine. Only one tasted.

**Canais, Qta dos** Opaque, intense; immature but rich; fairly sweet, full flavoured, dry finish. Very attractive. *At Cockburn's 'Memories of a Century' tasting in London, May 2002* (★★★★) *2009–2018.*

---

### A list of the more important quintas referred to in the text, with their current owners

| | | | |
|---|---|---|---|
| **Boa Vista, Qta da** | Offley (Forrester) | **Milieu, Qta do** | The Real Companhia Velha |
| **Bomfim, Qta do** | Dow (Symington) | **Noval, Qta do** | AXA Millésimes |
| **Bom Retiro, Qta do** | Ramos-Pinto | **Passadouro, Qta do** | Niepoort |
| **Cachão, Qta do** | Messias | **Porto, Qta do** | Ferreira (Sogrape) |
| **Canais, Qta dos** | Cockburn (Allied Domecq) | **Roeda, Qta da** | Croft (Fladgate Partnership) |
| **Cavadinha, Qta da** | Warre (Symington) | **Roncão, Qta de** | Sandeman (Sogrape) |
| **Côrte, Qta da** | marketed by Delaforce | **Roriz, Qta de** | Van Zeller and Symington |
| **Crasto, Qta do** | Roquette family | **Rosa, Qta de la** | Bergquist family |
| **Cruzeiro, Qta do** | (Fonseca) Fladgate Partnership | **São Luiz, Qta de** | Barros, Almeida |
| **Eira Velha, Qta da** | The Newman family. Now marketed by Martinez | **Seixo, Qta do** | Ferreira (Sogrape) |
| | | **Senhora da Ribera, Qta** | Symington |
| **Ervamoira, Qta da** | Ramos-Pinto | **Sibio, Qta do** | Real Companhia Velha |
| **Foz, Qta da** | Cálem | **Terra Feita, Qta da** | Fladgate Partnership |
| **Lages, Qta da** | Ribero family (sells to Graham) | **Tua, Qta do** | Cockburn (Allied Domecq) |
| **Loureiro, Qta de** | Costa Seixas family | **Vale da Mina, Qta do** | Cristiano van Zeller |
| **Madalena, Qta da** | Symington | **Vargellas, Qta de** | Fladgate Partnership |
| **Malvedos, Qtas dos** | Graham (Symington) | **Vesúvio, Qta do** | Symington |

# 2000

The port market looks bright, a situation totally unpredictable half a century ago.

Following amalgamations, some quite recent, the vintage port market is dominated by two groups, both British, both still family-owned. The Symingtons have no outside shareholders, their main brands being Dow, Graham and Warre, their '*deuxième crus*' all made quite separately, being Gould Campbell, Quarles Harris and Smith Woodhouse. In addition to Vesúvio and Malvedos, they now have a half share, with João van Zeller, of the famous old Quinta da Roriz. What is now known as 'the Fladgate Partnership' is owned by three long-established port families, the Robertsons, the Bowers and Guimaraens. Their main brands are Taylor and Fonseca, a second brand, Fonseca Guimaraens, with the more recent acquisitions, Croft and Delaforce. Their flagship quinta is Vargellas. Another famous old name, still British-owned, is Cockburn; and Noval belongs to the AXA insurance group. Ferreira, the biggest selling port in Portugal, together with Offley Forrester, the brand Tuke Holdsworth and the recently acquired Sandeman are all part of the ubiquitous Guedes' Sogrape group.

## 2000 (★★★★★)

A combination of good weather conditions and an expectant market makes this a must. All major shippers declared the vintage in the spring of 2002, and in April and May I attended the London presentations by Cockburn, a seated tasting at the Travellers' Club, the 'Fladgate Partnership' at Christie's (a quick walk round affair), 'The Symington Family Port Companies' at the Berkeley and a speedy look at the other tasting of 2000s. My brief, and by no means 'definitive' notes follow.

First though the weather. The winter was mild and exceptionally dry, so dry that some producers began to lobby the government – not for the first time – to authorise irrigation in the Douro vineyards. However, after an early bud burst, cool and wet weather set in during April. Six weeks of almost uninterrupted rain, with three times the average in May, slowed down the vine development and delayed flowering, which took place under the most adverse conditions (to quote the Symingtons) with the certainty of a much reduced crop (up to 20% was predicted). Another major problem was that rain and humid conditions attracted mildew, obliging growers to spray frequently.

Despite an improvement in the weather, *veraison* was delayed, being completed at the end of July. There was some refreshing rain in August followed by very hot weather up to the vintage, which speeded up the maturity of the grapes that were picked towards the end of September. At Graham's Malvedos the fruit was excellent and fully ripe with high sugar readings and very low yields – all indicative of quality.

The appearance of young port is, virtually without exception, very deep, opaque at the centre and with a vivid purple rim that varies only slightly in intensity. So I see no point in repeating the colour description in my notes, unless there is an exception. Do not be deterred by the almost succulent fruit of the wines of this vintage. The 'big guns' have the components to last well into the middle of the current century. Many are mid-term, say 2010–2020. Some will undoubtedly be drunk too young, but with enjoyment.

THE 5-STAR WINES OF THE 2000 VINTAGE
**Dow** The 25th vintage declared since 1900. Great potential.
**Fonseca** Two notes: opaque; very fragrant, whiff of crystallised violets; an almost earthy richness. Stylish. One of my favourites.

**Graham** Two notes. Velvety intensity; remarkably sweet as always, floral scents, glorious flavour, richness masking tannin. Great wine.
**Noval Nacional** Colour of black treacle; concentrated; yet lean. Extra dimensions. Great length.
**Roriz, Qta do** Symington's second vintage since acquiring a half share in 1999. Very powerful. Great wine.
**Taylor** Two notes. Impressive in every way: opacity, power, richness, length. The flagship of the Fladgate Partnership.
**Vesúvio, Qta do** Nothing shy or retiring here. Superbly forthcoming fragrance and fruit; crisp, concentration, length.
**Warre** Two notes. Brambly, peppery nose; lovely flavour, great length, texture, style. Gilt edged.

THE 4-STAR WINES OF THE 2000 VINTAGE
**Cockburn** Something of a renaissance. Impressive, good flavour and flesh. Doubtless bolstered by their excellent Quinta dos Canais.
**Croft** Now under the Fladgate umbrella. Good flesh and grip.
**Delaforce** Also Fladgate. Good wine.
**Ferreira** Classic, substantial Portuguese style. Full of fruit. Delicious. Will develop fairly quickly but keep well.
**Gould Campbell** Dependable Symington 'second XI'. Good texture. Dry finish.
**Martinez** Nice style and weight. Floral.
**Niepoort** Another Dirk Niepoort virtuoso wine. Glorious colour; delicious grapey fruit and aftertaste.
**Noval, Qta do** Attractive fruit, delicious flavour. Mid-term.
**Offley Boa Vista** Crisp fruit, notably tannic.
**Smith Woodhouse** In my opinion top of the Symington's 'second XI'. Dry finish.

OF THE LESSER-KNOWN SHIPPERS, BRANDS AND QUINTAS
**Broadbent** Made to my son's specification for his US market. A superb Niepoort wine.
**Burmester** Rich, figgy, very sweet. Medium term.
**Crasto, Qta do** Intriguing, medium-sweet, good grip.
**Eira Velha, Qta da** Distinctive. Powerful.
**Passadouro, Qta do** Another Niepoort wine. Very deep; lean, flavoury, delicious.
**Ramos Pinto** I found this rather strange but attractive in its way. I must retaste.
**Rosa, Qta de la** Lean, but good sweet fruit and length. For mid-term drinking.

# Madeira

Madeira has always been one of my favourite wines. My wife and I drink it frequently, and for over a quarter of a century, when I was head of Christie's wine department, I kept a bottle of Verdelho for clients and friends, usually synonymous, who called mid-morning – so much better than office coffee – and Bual for the afternoon, so much more delicious than tea. Moreover, with unfailing regularity I am asked which is my favourite wine (after all these years where do I start?). I fall back on old madeira. And, to take with me if stranded on a desert island, I can be very specific: H M Borges 1862 Terrantez, or failing that the 1846. Apart from the glorious, indescribable perfume and taste, madeira is the one wine which is able to survive the heat and which can be dipped into at leisure. It doesn't go off after drawing the cork.

Well, what is madeira? It is a fortified (with brandy) wine made on the Portuguese-owned island of Madeira, situated in the Atlantic Ocean some 650km to the west of north Africa. The island has a wonderful year-round climate and its wines, named after specific grape varieties (see box page 502) are versatile, ranging from dry to very sweet, from aperitif to dessert. The wine is stable due to a unique heating process during its production and can survive hot climates. The best can claim – with Tokaji – to be the longest lasting of all wines.†

Fine old madeiras have been regarded as something of an acquired taste, but have always been much sought after and collected. During my years with Christie's we handled many collections, several from the private cellars of old families on the island – Acciaioly, Henriques, Lomelino and Blandy come to mind – but also from English connoisseurs, long since deceased – Stephen Gazelee, Harry Johnson (an anglophile American) and Ronald Avery. One of the earliest buyers of old madeira at Christie's was Dr Robert Maliner, later to become the organiser of the Hollywood Wine Society (Hollywood, Florida); unquestionably the best ever madeira tasting was held by him in 1995 (see box page 497).

Incidentally, there is a fine dividing line between vintage and solera madeira (see box page 503); it is usually far from clear which is which from the label or from the stencilled lettering on the bottle. Even true vintage madeira might well have been topped up, refreshed, at some time during its maturation in cask. So my rule at Christie's was for us to state in the catalogue precisely what was on the label, 'vintage' if vintage, 'solera' if solera; and if no clear indication just a dash: 'Bual – 1934', for example. In the following notes I have stated 'vintage' or 'solera' where known.

Following in the footsteps of tawny port, madeira is mainly sold blended, ready for drinking, does not need decanting and, a great boon, keeps well once opened. An inexpensive, 5-year-old 'medium-sweet' will probably be a Tinta Negra Mole 'Verdelho look-alike', whereas a 10-year-old Verdelho – my favourite – will be just that, and usually remarkably good. And, I am glad to say, vintage madeira is making a comeback.

† For more detailed information on this delightfully complicated wine I recommend *Madeira* by Alex Lidelland, if you can find a copy, the late Noël Cossart's *Madeira, the Island Vineyard*.

# 17th–19th centuries

Although wine had been made on the island since the 15th century, Charles II's Act of 1665 gave an impetus to the trade in Madeira. Enterprising British merchants established themselves in the early 18th century, particularly to take advantage of the island's facilities as a victualling port for shipping destined for the East and West Indies. By 1780 there were over 70 British trading houses on the island, exports of wine reaching some 15–17,000 'pipes' (each of approximately 110 gallons). It was around the middle of the 18th century that brandy was used to fortify and stabilise the wine for shipment to England and the colonies.

It is precisely because it is almost indestructible that the wine was so popular and so successful in the hot and humid American Colonies, in the British West Indies and with the garrisons and merchants in India. Cossart Gordon, founded in 1745, alone supplied over a hundred British regiments stationed in India. In American post-colonial times, until the Civil War, madeira was consumed in huge quantities. To this day, the Madeira Club in Savannah perpetuates the love of fine madeira, and private American collectors have acquired many of the finest wines.

'Fine old Maderia' (*sic*) featured in James Christie's first sale in December 1766. In 1768 Christie's auctioned 'a pipe of very fine old high-flavoured madeira' for a gentleman posted as governor to Madras. This was the year that Lieutenant (later Captain) Cook's ship HMS *Endeavour* called in at Funchal, the capital of Madeira, to pick up 3032 gallons of madeira for his two and a half year voyage – not just as a nourishing drink but to prevent scurvy!

## Vintages at a Glance
**Outstanding ★★★★★**
1793, 1795, 1798, 1802, 1808, 1822, 1830, 1836, 1846, 1862, 1868
**Very Good ★★★★**
1789, 1792, 1821, 1826, 1827, 1834, 1837, 1839, 1850, 1860, 1863, 1870, 1875, 1893, 1895, 1898, 1899
**Good ★★★**
1811, 1815, 1832, 1845, 1864, 1877, 1879, 1891, 1892

## Circa 1680

**Madeira or Canary Sack** The main interest here was the wine's impeccable provenance: the original cellar of the house of the Master Gunner of England in the City of London, destroyed or pulled down in 1682, and revealed during very recent excavations. Just on the edge of the City, the house would have survived the Great Fire of 1666.

The cellar was found to have a stock of 17th-century, short-necked, onion-shaped bottles, still sealed and containing wine. The bottles were X-rayed to reveal short corks, then one of them had a needle inserted so that a small quantity of the contents could be removed for a detailed chemical analysis. Essentially it was found that the alcoholic content was 6.5% by volume, roughly the same strength as beer. Acidity totalled a very normal 6g/l, and there was fairly high glycerol and some rather nasty fusel oils.

Two bottles were opened with great ceremony at the Museum of London (one of the least known and one of the most interesting of all London museums) and I was privileged to taste – more privilege than pleasure – the ancient liquid. Well, it was wine. A light table wine with a spicy, clove-like nose, a whiff of volatile acidity and other strange smells lurking in the wings. Dry, sharp, tangy. Probably madeira which, in England and the colonies, was used as table wine. The second bottle had a nasty, sharp smell, and one sniff and sip was enough. *Opened and tasted, with much ceremony (and television coverage), Dec 1999. A rare experience.*

## 1789 ★★★★
**Gran Cama de Lobos** Palish amber with apple-green rim; full, vivid, high-toned, spirity, yet refined old bouquet; fairly sweet, powerful, yet with a surprisingly smooth texture, leading to a somewhat austere, slightly varnishy, dry finish. *The oldest wine at Bill Baker's madeira tasting in Somerset, April 1994* ★★★★

## 1792 ★★★★
Though not tasted since the mid-1980s, two of the bottles, with the unmistakable remains of the original (1840) labels, and from a good provenance, were still in Lenoir Josey's Houston cellar when I took stock in the summer of 2000. **Madeira, Vintage 1792 Bottled by Blandy, 1840** HMS *Northumberland* called for provisions in Funchal on 7 August 1815 with Napoleon on board en route to his exile on St Helena, following his defeat at Waterloo a few months earlier. A pipe of madeira of the 1792 vintage was purchased, but neither paid for nor broached. After Napoleon's death, the cask was returned to Madeira and bottled by Blandy. Though a good, rich, amber colour, the wine had dried out but the flavour was still intriguing and the wine very drinkable. *Tasted at the Madeira Wine Association's (Blandy and associated companies) 'Wine Library' in Funchal, Dec 1983* ★★★

## 1793 ★★★★★
**Moscatel** Fairly deep amber; glorious tangy nose; still very sweet, deliciously rich but an easy style and weight. Perfect acidity. *With my old friend, Manuela de Freitas and her son, Riccardo, of Barbeito, at the Estalgém Quinta Bella Vista (my favourite hotel on Madeira, owned by Dr Roberto Ornelas Montero who collects 18th-century English furniture), Jan 1994* ★★★★★

## 1795 ★★★★★
**Madeira, Vintage 1795 Island bottled** Provenance unknown. A lovely, glowing amber, lime-rimmed, shot with orange gold;

high volatile acidity, caramelly, unknit; still some sweetness, acidic, short. *The oldest wine in an excellent madeira seminar at the Hollywood Wine Society's wine weekend, March 1995, ★★ for surviving exactly two centuries.*

**Terrantez Barbeito** Almost certainly solera, not straight vintage. Provenance was the Vasconcellas family via the de Freitas, owners of Barbeito. Barbeito have a reputation for their stocks of rare madeira but are diffident about putting them on the market. Several bottles of this 1895 have appeared at Christie's over the years and I have more than six notes. Most recently: palish amber; sweet, lovely, ethereal, crystallised violets bouquet; medium-sweet, concentrated yet not heavy, penetrating flavour, rapier-like acidity. Superb. *Last noted at a Hollywood Wine Society tasting, March 1998 ★★★★★*

**Terrantez Lomelino** Chocolatey; sweet, rich, soft, fleshy. *April 1993 ★★★★★*

## 1798 ★★★★★

**Terrantez Garrafeira Particular/Engarrafado por Vinhos Barbeito** Another old Terrantez wine from Barbeito (see above). Warm amber; crystallised violets; medium-sweetness and body, lovely ethereal flavour, good length, high acidity. *Produced after midnight at the close of Len Evans' 'Single Bottle Club' dinner in the Hunter Valley, Sept 2000 ★★★★★*

## 1802 ★★★★★

**Terrantez Acciaioly** Labelled '*Special Reserve 1802, Produced, bottled and guaranteed by Oscar Acciaioly*'. The oldest of a magnificent range of old madeira brought to Christie's for sale in 1989. First noted prior to cataloguing and the next not long after: medium-deep amber with a very pronounced apple-green rim; refined, with my favourite ethereal 'crystallised violets' scent; sweet, typically (for Terrantez) full-bodied but beautifully balanced, its power and richness coping well with its high acidity. *Bought at Christie's by Robert Maliner and last tasted at the Hollywood Wine Society's outstanding Terrantez seminar, January 1990 ★★★★★*

---

### Acciaioly

*One of the oldest Madeira families and descended from Simon Acciaioly (or Acciaioli) who left Florence to settle on the island in 1525. I confess I was totally unaware of the family and their wine until Michael, one of the two surviving sons, came to Christie's and showed me a list of the family's remarkable wines. As virtually the entire Madeira trade had been monopolised by British firms since the 18th century, the Acciaioly business concentrated on Scandinavia, being 'by appointment to the HM King Gustav Adolf VI of Sweden'. Sample bottles of the wine were pre-tasted for cataloguing and a substantial quantity sold at Christie's in 1989. (See 1802, 1832, 1836, 1837 and 1839.)*

---

## 1808 ★★★★★

Great vintage.

**Malmsey, Solera** According to Noël Cossart the 'best ever known'. I have three notes: very rich tawny brown; gloriously harmonious bouquet, caramel, coffee, 'ethereal' fragrance; still very sweet, characteristically high acidity balanced by its richness and power. *Last tasted Oct 1984 ★★★★★*

### Hollywood (Florida) Wine Society

*One of our early clients at Christie's, Dr Robert Maliner (a plastic surgeon), had the clever idea of hosting wine weekends for people who didn't know much about wine. This was sparked off in the early 1970s by my being invited to discuss with his friends a range of 1953 clarets. The Society's meetings were exceptionally well organised, with outside speakers. I was invited to host – 'moderate' – several annual events, reported on in the text.*

*Outstandingly the best were a session devoted to Terrantez and Bastardo in 1990 and another 'Great Madeiras' tasting in 1995.*

---

## 1811 ★★★

The renowned 'comet' vintage.

**Solera Blandy** Said to include vintages back to 1788, blended in 1961: warm amber; rich, 'thick', high volatile acidity; still very sweet, rich, good 'ethereal' mid-palate, excellent acidity. *At Bill Baker's rare madeira tasting at his mill house in Somerset, April 1993 ★★★★*

## 1815 ★★★

The 'Waterloo' vintage. Bual was particularly successful.

**'Waterloo' Bual, Solera Cossart Gordon** Wax seal. Labelled. Bottled in Funchal, shipped by Evans Marshall, London W1, Cossart's agents, probably in the 1950s. Lovely colour, warm amber, touch of orange-gold; sweet, caramel and honey; ethereal; medium-sweet, rich, slightly spirity, elegant, good length and the usual acidity. *Ending Manfred Wagner's dinner in Pfäffikon, near Zurich, Nov 2000 ★★★★*

## 1821 ★★★★

Excellent vintage. Several notes, none since the late 1970s.

## 1822 ★★★★★

**Verdelho Cossart Gordon** First noted in 1993 at a Madeira Wine Company tasting at the Portuguese Embassy in London: slight bottle variation. Palish amber; glorious bouquet with my favourite ethereal crystallised violets – not unlike a refined old cognac; medium-sweet, lovely flavour, great length and excellent acidity. The second more chocolatey. The following year, noting its apple-green rim and exquisite bouquet, at a tasting at Christie's for a Blandy's Madeira video (payment: a bottle of 10-year-old Malmsey!). *Last tasted Jan 1994 ★★★★*

## 1826 ★★★★

**Boal Solera Blandy** Amber brown; bouquet like horses' pee – fabulous!; full, rich, tangy. *At Bill Baker's madeira tasting, April 1993 ★★★★*

## 1827 ★★★★

**Bual, Qta do Serrado, Vintage** Straight vintage, in cask for 108 years, then in demijohn and finally bottled in 1988. From an Henriques family estate in Câmara de Lobos (understood to be Antonio Eduardo Henriques), in 1990. I first noted it at the pre-sale tasting and have tasted it six times since. Part of a very large stock, including the 1830 Malmsey sold by Christie's over two years. A fabulous wine, with all the great, old-vintage attributes, concentration yet finesse, length, fragrance. Most recently, very rich amber; sweet, mouth-tantalising, very high acidity. Superb. *Last noted at Maliner's great madeira tasting, March 1995* ★★★★★

## 1830 ★★★★★

**Malmsey** Another Henriques family wine, aged for 105 years in oak, then preserved in demijohns, bottled in 1988, shortly before shipment to London. With the 1827 Bual, the quantities were immense, roughly 100 dozen bottles of each wine, spaced through several sales. The 1830 vintage was the best. I have a total of eight notes: a deep, rich, glowing *oloroso*-coloured amber; chocolatey, sweet nose with fabulous, penetrating yet ethereal crystallised violets flavour and aftertaste. *Last tasted, a bottle from Hugh Johnson's cellar, at the Hallwag press conference, Frankfurt, Sept 1994* ★★★★★ *Quite a few bottles still around. Look out for it at auction.*
**Malmsey Reserve** Bottled from a demijohn by Harvey's of Bristol circa 1959: amber; crystallised violets; still sweet, perfect acidity. Superb. *April 1992* ★★★★★

## 1832 ★★★

**'Bismark' Madeira 'Brown Madère Impériale'** Nicolas (of Paris) label. Amber, faint lime rim; exquisite bouquet, to use my favourite description: like ethereal crystallised violets; initially seemed medium-sweet but its swingeing acidity giving it the overall effect of dryness. A rare experience. *Enjoyed after Ch Yquem 1847 at Rodenstock's dinner, March 2001* ★★★
**Terrantez 'Special Reserve, Medium-Sweet' Acciaioly** Rich amber; tangy, distinctive Terrantez character, austere, acidic. *April 1989* ★★★

## 1834 ★★★★

**Terrantez, Vintage Barbeito** First noted at Robert Maliner's Terrantez tasting in 1990: it was magnificent. I tasted it again five years later: very richly coloured, lime rim; a powerhouse of bouquet surging out of the glass; very sweet for Terrantez, rich, concentrated, great length; 'its acidity leaving the mouth high and dry'. *Last noted at the Hollywood Wine Society's madeira seminar, March 1995* ★★★★★

## 1836 ★★★★★

**Malmsey 'Special Reserve, Sweet' Acciaioly** Deep amber, harmonious; very sweet, smooth, rich texture, fabulous finish. *Pre-sale, April 1989* ★★★★★
**Sercial Cossart Gordon** Medium amber; gloriously rich tangy nose and flavour; sweeter and less acidic than most old Sercials, cognac-like finish. *Dec 1994* ★★★★★

## 1837 ★★★★

A very successful period for madeira, both vintages and trade being at a high level.
**Bual 'Special Reserve, Medium-Sweet' Acciaioly** Cork branded *Oscar Acciaioly*. Amber-gold; high-toned, refined; exquisite flavour and great length. *One of my favourites of the Acciaioly range I tasted prior to cataloguing, April 1989* ★★★★★

## 1839 ★★★★

**Verdelho 'Special Reserve, Medium-Sweet' Acciaioly** Three notes. First tasted in 1986 and then again three years later: amber; singed coffee and cognac-like bouquet; certainly sweeter than 'dry', except for its extended finish. Fragrant. Lovely. Most recently, a bottle bought at Christie's, exhibiting the inimitable refinement. *Last tasted in Don Schliff's remarkable cellar at Glendale, California, March 1999* ★★★★★

## 1845 ★★★

'Generally very fine, especially Bual' (according to Cossart).
**Bual, Solera Cossart Gordon** The firm's 'Centenary Solera'. Some, bottled in 1975, tasted several times, and variable. Showing well at a madeira tasting I conducted in Aspen in 1994: glowing amber; high-toned, harmonious, very nutty nose; medium-sweet, immensely powerful, hot finish. In 1995: amber brown; chocolatey, spirity; sweet, rich, well-balanced. Most recently, after 85 years in American oak, then in demijohns and finally bottled November 1988: its strength 21% alcohol, acidity 8.7g/l and residual sugar 117g/l. Frankly disappointing. Muffled, indistinctive nose and taste. *The oldest wine in a MW madeira seminar I chaired at Painters' Hall, London, Jan 1999. At best* ★★★

## 1846 ★★★★★

**Campanario Blandy** Old, dumpy, three-part moulded bottle stencilled '*Campanario 1846 Blandy's Madeira*'. Lovely warm amber with bright yellow rim; high volatile acidity, yet delicate and very fragrant; sweet, smooth texture, very rich, dry finish and exquisite aftertaste. *At Bill Baker's old madeira tasting, April 1994* ★★★★★
**Terrantez Blandy** Two bottles at the Madeira Wine Company tasting at the Portuguese Embassy in London. The first rather rich, thick and chocolatey on the nose, with a powerful flavour and finish; the second a warmer amber with exquisite crystallised violet bouquet, better length and finish. *Tasted Dec 1993. At best* ★★★★★
**Terrantez H M Borges** Several notes. First in 1973. The best bottled in 1900. Magnificent: orange-tinged; the acme of refinement yet amazingly powerful. What great madeira is all about. *Last noted at the Terrantez tasting I conducted for Robert Maliner, Jan 1990* ★★★★ *I gave my last bottle to Jaeger after his Domaine de la Romanée-Conti tasting, Feb 2002. A great sacrifice!*

## 1850 ★★★★

The second-to-last successful vintage before the devastating scourge, oidium, laid waste Madeira's vineyards and destroyed the livelihood of a large number of growers and merchants.
**Verdelho Pereira d'Oliveira** In oak 130 years, finally bottled in 1980. Fabulous colour, bouquet and flavour. *At the MADAS tasting in Bruges, May 1990* ★★★★

## 1860 ★★★★

Good growing season. Slight recovery but production small.
**Sercial, Solera Cossart Gordon** Stencilled and labelled. Two notes, first at a pre-sale tasting in 1994: medium amber; the much-liked 'cognac and crystallised violets', the latter I am now putting down to the effect of impregnated American old

oak. I might be wrong. Dry, as Sercial should be, firm, fine, perfect. More recently, a sweet, more singed and meaty nose; sweeter on palate too, but lovely flavour, good length and acidity. A different bottling? *Last noted at one of Pat Grubb's tastings in London, May 1997. At best ★★★★ ('Pat Grubb Selections' specialises in fine old madeira. Recommended.)*

**Sercial, Solera Leacock** 65 years in American oak, finally bottled in December 1988. Nose like 'calf's foot jelly', slightly meaty-malty; medium-sweet, 74g/l and typically high Sercial acidity: 12g/l. *At the MW seminar in London, Jan 1999 ★★*

## 1862 ★★★★★

Vineyards beginning to recover from oidium. Small production. Terrantez was the best ever made.

**Terrantez H M Borges** Bottles stencilled '*Terrantez HMB 1862*'. This firm, founded in 1877, built up a great collection of old madeira, acquiring this Terrantez from T T de Camara Lomelino. I have been privileged to taste this, for me, greatest of all madeiras, on five occasions, four in the 1980s, one more recently. My description would mirror much of what has appeared in my notes of some earlier vintages, except that this '62 has extra dimensions: warm amber which should be seen either by candlelight or by a window, catching the last rays of sunlight; an almost overwhelming bouquet and flavour, high toned, tangy, scented, power and delicacy magically combined. The most recent bottle, with an '*Esquin Imports*' (San Francisco) slip label, probably brought by fellow guest and great connoisseur, Barney Rhodes. Sweeter than some Terrantez, with slight touch of singed caramel and chocolate. Took to air like a fish to water. *One of the three top wines at Bill Baker's madeira tasting, April 1994. At best ★★★★★★ (6 stars!)*

**Terrantez Cossart Gordon** Two bottles noted at the Madeira Wine Company tasting at the Portuguese Embassy in London. Warm amber; tangy, sharp-edged, meaty, like a grilled lamb chop; medium-sweet leading to a superfine, extended, rapier-like, dry, acidic finish. Impressive but lacking the brilliance of the H M Borges wine above. *Dec 1998 ★★★★*

## 1863 ★★★★

**Boal** (*sic*) **Barbeito** Amber brown, pronounced apple-green rim; medium-sweet, full-bodied, very rich, long, dry, acidic finish. *Tasted at Reid's Hotel, Funchal, Jan 1994 ★★★★*

**Malmsey, Solera Blandy** I have 16 notes, all consistent. Most recently: impressively deep; beautiful bouquet, very sweet, soft, rich. Perfection. *Last noted at Robert Maliner's great madeira seminar, March 1995 ★★★★★*

---

### Oidium tuckerii

*The arrival of oidium or 'powdery mildew', native to the United States, on Madeira in 1851 proved to be a major turning point in the island's history. Its vineyards were almost completely wiped out over a period of just three years. Fine, cobwebby growth literally smothers the vine and prevents the berries from ripening fully; the fungal spores which spread the disease are easily wind-borne and thus very infectious. Although a cure was found – dusting the vine leaves with sulphur – the subsequent arrival of phylloxera on Madeira knocked the economy seriously, and only with the planting of resistant American rootstocks a few years later were the vineyards able to recover at all.*

## 1864 ★★★

Still *entre deux* calamities: oidium, then later, phylloxera. Small crop but good wines.

**Cama de Lobos** Believed **Blandy**. Rich amber; touch of chocolate, whiff of crystallised violets; sweet, full, rich. After supper at Christopher Burr's. Its style suited his viola playing which I had been accompanying for a delightful but exhausting two hours. *Aug 1998 ★★★*

**Sercial Blandy** Two bottles, the first amber; sharp volatile acidity; dry, rapier-like, the second paler, more chocolatey on the nose, with a smell I associate with cheap sherry, and distinctly sweeter. *At the Madeira Wine Company tasting at the Portuguese Embassy, London, Dec 1993. At best ★★*

**Verdelho, Gran Cama de Lobos Blandy** I suspect this is the same wine as the Cama de Lobos noted above. Tasted over half a dozen times and variable, presumably bottled at different times. At best, and as last tasted, a lovely tangy, almost tarry but refined bouquet and fabulous flavour. Fairly sweet, soft, well balanced. *Last noted at Maliner's tasting, March 1995. At best ★★★★*

## 1868 ★★★★★

**Boal, Very Old 'EBH' Cossart Gordon** Translucent, ethereal, herbaceous; full, rich, lovely texture, great length. *At Bill Baker's madeira tasting, April 1993 ★★★★★ (The stencilled initials are those of Doña Eugenia Bianchi Henriques, granddaughter of Carlo de Bianchi, owner of vineyards at Câmara de Lobos. A famous wine, surpassed only by the 1862 Terrantez.)*

## 1870 ★★★★

The last of the small post-oidium vintages and, of course, unbeknownst to both growers and merchants, also the last major vintage before phylloxera which arrived on the island with devastating consequences two years later.

**Bastardo** Unknown shipper. Bottle stencilled '*Bastardo 1870*' and imported by Esquin. Rather dull appearance; sickly, sweaty, unclean nose; yet very sweet, rich, rounded, with a good finish. *At Bill Baker's second madeira tasting, April 1994 ★★*

**Terrantez Blandy** Butter and caramel nose; harsh, disappointing. *At Bill Baker's madeira tasting, April 1993 ★*

**Verdelho, Solera Blandy** Labelled and stencilled. Rich but slightly cloudy (shaken not stirred); chocolatey; sweet, rich, acidic finish. *Tasted at Pat Grubb Selections, May 1997 ★★*

## 1874 ★★

Very small production but some good wines made from vineyards still not fully blighted by the phylloxera louse.

**Malmsey Blandy** Meaty, slightly malty; an original flavour, sweet but with a lean touch. Considerable length. *At the Madeira Wine Company tasting, London, Dec 1993 ★★★*

## 1875 ★★★★⁻

Tiny crop but some outstanding wines.

**Bastardo Cossart Gordon** Made from grapes grown at Quinta do Satão in Câmara de Lobos. First tasted at Maliner's unprecedented tasting of old Terrantez and Bastardo vintages in 1990 for the Hollywood Wine Society. An exquisite wine. Most recently, a bottle I bought at Christie's in June 1992 and decanted and tasted prior to leaving for Bill Baker's: medium-pale amber, touch of orange and apple-green rim. A slight powdery sediment; lovely, fragrant – oh dear, again 'crystallised violets'; medium-sweet, not as hefty and also leaner than Terrantez, hint of caramel, very dry finish. On arrival, I noted a more refined, Sercial-like, scent; rapier-like, lemon-tinged acidity. Three hours later, the bouquet was fully evolved. A charmer. My equal top mark (with the 1898 Terrantez) at the tasting. *Last noted April 1994* ★★★★★

## 1877 ★★★

**Sercial Blandy** Deeper colour than expected, more like Bual; exquisite, refined, ethereal old-cognac fragrance; also sweeter than expected, rich, tangy, lovely flavour, refined. *Dinner at Lou Skinner's in Coral Gables, March 1995* ★★★★★
**Terrantez H M Borges & Sucrs** Stencilled '*T 1877*'. First tasted in 1990: good nose; impressive. Very dry, twist of lime finish. Next, at Bill Baker's: fragrant though slightly varnishy and caramelly; powerful, assertive – very much a Terrantez character – rich, meaty, tangy, with short, clove-like, highly acidic finish. *Last tasted April 1994* ★★★

## 1879 ★★★

**Verdelho, Torre Bella** One of several wines from this famous estate in Câmara de Lobos, recorked in 1987, and shipped to England from the family's *frasqueira* by one of the owner's descendants, Captain Fairlie, for sale at Christie's. I have two notes. Lovely wine; ethereal, rose-cachou bouquet; fairly sweet, long, strong and characteristically acidic. *Last tasted in June 1988* ★★★★★

## 1880

**Terrantez, Reserva Pereira d'Oliveira** First tasted in 1990, 'over 100 years matured in oak cask'. Not very bright; sulphury, volcanic nose; swingeing acidity, fixed and volatile. I liked it no better at Pat Grubb's tasting: smelly nose, better on the palate. Dry. Short. *Last tasted May 1997.*

## 1887 ★

**São Felipe, Vintage Torre Bella** Shipped by Captain Fairlie for sale at Christie's but the quantity was too small to warrant my opening a bottle for the pre-sale tasting. Happily, purchased by that irrepressible enthusiast, Bob Maliner, and presented at a seminar I conducted for his Hollywood Wine Society: a really beautiful rich amber; vanilla, caramel and high volatile acidity – too high. *March 1995* ★

## 1890 ★★

The five years prior to 1890 marked the lowest period ever for growers and trade, both suffering from the results of the phylloxera blight and many going out of business. A small amount of wine produced.
**Malvazia Dr Manuel José Vieira** Fairly deep amber; very rich chocolatey nose; equally rich and assertive. Good length and aftertaste. *With the de Freitas family at Quinta Bella Vista, Funchal, Jan 1994* ★★★★
**Verdelho Pereira d'Oliveira** In cask 96 years. Finally bottled 1986. Alcohol (20%) predominant; rather pasty flavour and bitter finish. *At the MADAS tasting in Bruges, May 1990* ★

## 1891 ★★★

**Cama de Lobos** Bottled in 1897, recorked 1953, rebottled 1960. Three notes, all from stock previously stored in Santana, on the north coast of the island. Most recently, a bottle given to me by Richard Blandy and opened in its centenary year in the wine department at Christie's. Its scent filled my office. Rich, tangy, good length. *Jan 1991* ★★★★

## 1892 ★★★

Small crop. Some interesting wines.
**Sercial Barbeito** This might be the same wine that I had noted in 1980, as having exquisite flavour and ravishing acidity. More recently, produced as a sort of nightcap after an exhausting, fascinating, but very late Breuer dinner tasting in Rüdesheim, in the Rheingau: very tangy nose; good but austere, lethally long and acidic. *Nov 1996* ★★

## 1893 ★★★★

Although phylloxera was still a problem on the island, this was the first major vintage since it took hold in the early 1870s.
**Malmsey Cossart Gordon** This might well have been the anonymous stencilled bottle produced at a Yalumba 'museum tasting' in the Barossa Valley in 1985: magnificent, intensely fragrant, superfine, 5-star wine. More recently, at the Madeira Wine Company tasting in London, very rich, tangy bouquet and flavour. Good length. *Last tasted Dec 1993* ★★★★

## 1895 ★★★★

**Malmsey Pereira d'Oliveira** In oak for 92 years. Bottled 1987. Deep, rich, fullish, refined. Long acidic finish. *Tasted in Bruges, May 1990* ★★★★

## 1898 ★★★★

The most successful vintage since the pre-phylloxera period.
**Sercial, Solera Henriques & Henriques** Very good nose; great length and exquisite aftertaste. *At Maliner's madeira seminar, March 1995* ★★★★
**Verdelho, Solera Henriques & Henriques** A drab bottle in 1990. More recently: intense amber rim; ethereal, exquisite bouquet, lovely flavour, good length and delicious aftertaste. *Last noted at Maliner's madeira seminar, March 1995. At best* ★★★★
**Terrantez Cossart Gordon** Stencilled '*Terrantez 1890*', lead capsule embossed '*Cossart Gordon*'. Slightly paler than I expected but a lovely warm amber; a glorious, almost explosive yet superfine bouquet with all the hallmarks of greatness frequently described in relation to earlier vintages; very sweet yet lean and shapely, exquisite flavour and length. Rich, 'warm', perfect acidity and finish. *My top mark at Bill Baker's old madeira tasting in Somerset, April 1994* ★★★★★

## 1899 ★★★★

**Terrantez Blandy** Stencilled '*AO-SM*'. A glorious wine. Very acidic. *At Maliner's 'Great Wine' seminar, Jan 1990* ★★★★
**Terrantez Cossart Gordon** Richly coloured; hefty, touch of tar; sweet, flavour rather figgy, port-like. Very powerful wine with teeth-gripping acidity. *At the Madeira Wine Company tasting at the Portuguese Embassy, London, Dec 1993* ★★★

# 1900–1969

Call me an unredeemable romantic, but I have to confess that I feel that some of the lustre and wonder of madeira got lost during the 20th century. To be realistic, sales of madeira had plummeted in the latter part of the 19th century, partly, I suspect, because the producers and trade had been so badly hit by the outbreak of phylloxera. But the consumer was already losing interest. Of course, these remarks apply to the commercial, less expensive, blends. Happily, as will be seen, some superb vintage and solera madeiras continued to be produced, albeit in relatively small quantities for an equally small but nonetheless informed and appreciative market.

The other important point to make is that most madeira was not made to be cellared: it was an everyday wine to be consumed; and like Ch Lafite in Bordeaux, it was only the highest quality wine which could survive as a rare collectible. I well remember one of the greatest disappointments of my early Christie's career when I travelled to Scotland to inspect the cellars of the Marquis of Tweeddale at his grand house south of Edinburgh. Bin after bin of wine contained only madeira, a hundred or so dozens, all unlabelled, anonymous, purchased for drinking prior to World War One. I tried sample bottles from each bin. All were hopelessly oxidised. I left empty-handed.

## Vintages at a Glance
**Outstanding ★★★★★**
1900, 1901, 1910, 1936
**Very Good ★★★★**
1908, 1911, 1914, 1920, 1926, 1934, 1939, 1940, 1941, 1954, 1957, 1966, 1968
**Good ★★★**
1903, 1905, 1907, 1912, 1913, 1915, 1916, 1927, 1933, 1935, 1945, 1952, 1958, 1960, 1964

## 1900 ★★★★★

As it happens, the opening of the 20th century was as splendidly successful in Madeira as it was in other classic wine regions of Europe, not to mention Madeira's mother country – we, or some of us anyway, tend to forget – Portugal and, in particular, vintage port.
**Malmsey Rutherford & Miles** Deep, rich in colour, on nose and palate. Sweet, very powerful, great length. *At the Madeira Wine Company tasting at the Portuguese Embassy, London, Dec 1993* ★★★★
**Malvazia** (sic) **Barbeito** Opaque, amber brown; sweet, very rich, chocolatey nose and flavour yet with a refined, ethereal finish. Although there has been a long tradition of serving madeira with soup, usually with turtle soup, before roast beef at Lord Mayors' banquets, the correct wine should be Sercial or Verdelho. This Malvazia was too sweet, so I kept mine until after the port. *At the annual III Form Club dinner at Boodle's, London, Jan 2000* ★★★★
**Moscatel, Vintage Leacock** Strangely attractive nose, not grapey as expected; sweet, intense, beautiful flavour, lovely acidity but showing its age with a slightly bitter finish. *The oldest vintage at the madeira tasting conducted for my son, Bartholomew, in Aspen, Colorado, Jan 1994* ★★★
**Moscatel Pereira d'Oliveira** Two notes, first in 1980. Next at the MADAS madeira tasting in Bruges: 87 years in oak, bottled 1987, and the sweetest of the range (6.8° Baumé). A tremendous uplift of flavour yet, after such richness, leaving the mouth clean and dry. *Last noted May 1990* ★★★★
**Moscatel Power Drury** In oak 60 years, bottled 1985, at 19.6%, a full 1% lower than the d'Oliveira above; and only

5.4° Baumé. Good wine, but the anticipated grapey flavour did not materialise. It was madeira! *Also Bruges, May 1990* ★★★★
**Verdelho Blandy** Lively, intriguing, 'fishy', tangy; medium-dry, lean, attenuated dry finish. *At the Madeira Wine Company tasting at the Portuguese Embassy, London, Dec 1993* ★★★

## 1901 ★★★★★

**Malmsey Rutherford & Miles** Sweet, assertive, powerful, high acidity, great length. *Dec 1993* ★★★★★

## 1903 ★★★

Small but of good quality.
**Bual, Reserva Pereira d'Oliveira** Richly coloured; curious singed nose; far better on palate, sweet, fat, swingeing acidity. *Pat Grubb Selections, May 1992* ★★★

## 1905 ★★★

**Verdelho, Noguero** A vineyard on the Torre Bella estate in Câmara de Lobos. Surprisingly sweet, rich, chocolatey. Excellent acidity. From Captain Fairlie's stock shipped in error to Christie's via San Francisco. *Tasted pre-sale, Nov 1988* ★★★

**Verdelho, Torre** Another vineyard on the same estate at Câmara de Lobos: totally different, more of a Sercial-like piquancy. Dry. Taste of damp cardboard – but somehow exquisite. *Also tasted pre-sale, Nov 1988* ★★★★

## 1906 ★★

Another small crop but good Malmseys.
One old note (1980): a superlative **Leacock's Malvazia**.

## 1907 ★★★

**Bual, Vintage Blandy** Three notes in the late 1980s, a superb, mouthfilling wine, powerful yet refined. More recently, glowing amber; glorious bouquet and flavour, sweet, tangy. *Brought by some generous guest to a BYOB dinner at the Tribeca grill, New York, Feb 1996* ★★★★

**Malvazia, Reserva Pereira d'Oliveira** Deep; incredibly sweet, lacking refinement. *May 1990* ★★

## 1908 ★★★★

**Bual Blandy** Unknit nose, touch of mint and mocha; fairly sweet, fat, powerful. *At the Madeira Wine Company tasting at the Portuguese Embassy, London, Dec 1993* ★★★

**Bual Cossart Gordon** After 77 years in American oak, the wine was bottled in 1985. High acidity 14g/l and residual sugar 130g/l. Fabulous flavour. *At the Madeira Wine Association tasting, London, Jan 1999* ★★★★

## 1910 ★★★★★

Great vintage for all the different madeira grape varieties and the best all-round vintage of the period.

**Bual Cossart Gordon** Lovely wine. *Dec 1990* ★★★★

**Malvasia, Vintage Blandy** Very sweet, full-bodied, fat, smooth, soft yet powerful, masking acidity. *Aspen, June 1994* ★★★

**Sercial Cossart Gordon** Most unusual nose, slightly meaty, violets; equally distinctive flavour, good length, high acidity. *At the Madeira Wine Company tasting at the Portuguese Embassy, London, Dec 1993* ★★★

## 1911 ★★★★

**Bual Blandy** Glorious colour and bouquet; rich but with an almost Sercial-like leanness. *June 1990* ★★★★

## 1912 ★★★

**Malmsey Cossart Gordon** Rich amber; marvellous bouquet, crystallised violets through to lovely aftertaste. *Nov 1983* ★★★★

## 1913 ★★★

**Verdelho MWA** Amber gold; refined bouquet like old cognac; equally refined taste and long, rapier-like acidity. One bottle oxidised *Dec 1984. At best* ★★★

---

### Madeira's grapes

*Sercial, Verdelho, Bual (Boal) and Malmsey (or Malvazia) are the four major top-quality or 'noble' grape varieties, all white and planted in fairly small quantities. Traditionally, each one makes a different style of madeira, ranging from dry to sweet and for vintage madeira the grape varieties are not blended. Typically all have high, tangy acidity; Sercial is dry, Verdelho a versatile medium-dry, Bual is richer and medium-sweet and Malvasia (better known in English as Malmsey) makes a very sweet dark, rich dessert wine. After phylloxera ravaged the island in the 1870s, however, they took a back seat to the dull, local red Tinta Negra Mole, which, being more robust in constitution, soon succeeded as the island's principal grape variety.*

*Tinta Negra Mole is a 'chameleon' producer, turning out near-exact copies of each of the four madeira styles. In truth, it lacks the quality of the traditional grapes, which are now, thanks to recent European laws, back in their rightful place. Three other traditional varieties are Moscatel, Terrantez and Bastardo — the last two, both difficult, shy-bearing and prone to disease, only narrowly missed extinction following phylloxera.*

## 1914 ★★★★

Small crop. Noted for its Bual.

**Bual Rutherford & Miles** Superb bouquet; very rich, tangy, vanillin; sweet, full, rich, great persistence of flavour and aftertaste. *Brought down to earth with French onion soup at a Saintsbury Club dinner, London, April 1996* ★★★★★

## 1915 ★★★

Overall, a successful year.

**Bual, Solera Cossart Gordon** Fabulous, high-toned, elegant in 1981 ★★★★. More recently, curiously described as Colheita, meaning in respect of port, 'of the vintage but late-bottled'. Sharp nose; medium-sweet but lean, with rapier-like acidity. *Last noted at the Madeira Wine Company tasting at the Portuguese Embassy in London, Dec 1993* ★?

## 1916 ★★★

Some traditional suppliers of sweet wine to the Russian royalty and nobility lost a lot of business at the time, **Acciaioly** in particular. Only one tasted, **Cossart's Malmsey** believed to have been destined for the Imperial Russian Court but diverted: a lovely sweet, tangy wine. *Oct 1979* ★★★

## 1920 ★★★★

A superb post-war vintage.

**Bual Blandy** Probably three different bottlers: one, 30 years in wood, relatively low sugar content, 2.9° Baumé, a nose like the crust of *crème brûlée*, fragrant. *May 1990* ★★★★; a second, amber brown; toasted, tangy; sweet, full and rich. *Dec 1990* ★★★★; the third, malty, chocolatey though lovely flavour and excellent acidity. *Aspen, June 1994* ★★★★

**Malmsey, Vintage Cossart** Made from the last Malvasia Candida vines from the Faja dos Padres vineyard. Tasted on eight occasions and it is always sheer perfection. More recently, at Maliner's in 1995 and at Pat Grubb's tasting two years later. To summarise: medium-deep, rich amber, gold highlights; highly scented, floral, almost strawberry-like fruit, or *grande champagne* cognac; fairly sweet, fleshy yet not of this world, richness countering the customary acidity. Perfect balance. Fabulous flavour. *Last tasted May 1997* ★★★★★ *(I have just one bottle left!)*

## 1926 ★★★★

Magnificent vintage.

JUST ONE OLD NOTE **Cossart's Malmsey, Vintage** made like port by muting fermentation with the addition of brandy to retain the residual sugar, nothing added and not heated in the *estufa* system. In cask 40 years, in demijohns for ten years, bottled and tasted in 1976. Glorious wine. *Oct 1976* ★★★★

## 1927 ★★★

Good vintage, as on mainland Portugal.

**Bastardo** (An unfortunate grape name for my birth year) **Leacock** Rare, shy-bearing and difficult (perhaps it *was* me). Ah! Refined, evolving marvellously. Sweet. Rich. Thick. Tangy. *Jan 1990* ★★★★

## 1931 ★

Poor vintage. Trade at low ebb.
**Verdelho** Bottled 1979. From John Blandy's private cellar. Two notes: rich, malty, touch of acetone; sweet for Verdelho, extended acidic finish. *June 1990* ★★

## 1932 ★★

Quite good vintage but there was no market.
**Verdelho Blandy** Violet scented; fleshy and fat. Matching its dry finish. *June 1989* ★★★

## 1933 ★★★

Better quality but trade was still slow.
**Bual Blandy** Bottled in 1979. Scents of 'lime and linoleum', mint and chocolate; very sweet, good length, fragrant aftertaste. *Last tasted Jan 1990. At best* ★★★★
**Malmsey Justino Henriques** Several notes. First, stencilled 'VJH', in 1995 from a private cellar: high acidity, touch of fat, rich, fleshy and again, pre-sale in 1996. Next on my first visit to Justino's in 1997 to taste on behalf of my son, who was planning to import the wine: sweet, concentrated, perfectly balanced. Next, on Christmas Day 1997, very appropriate in front of the log fire at Saintsburyhill Farm, in my son-in-law's constituency. Lastly, now with the 'Broadbent Selections' label in my son's office in San Francisco to see how it – and sales – were shaping up. Ethereal, delicious; sales more substantial. *Last tasted Dec 1998* ★★★★

## 1934 ★★★★

Very good year for all wines.
**Bual Leacock** Classic, rarified, full flavoured. *Dec 1990* ★★★★★
**Verdelho, Vintage Cossart Gordon** First noted at the Madeira Wine Company tasting in 1993: tangy; nice flesh and richness. Then the following summer at the Winefest in Aspen: warm amber; honeyed, chocolatey; medium-sweet, well-balanced. *Last tasted in Colorado, June 1994* ★★★
**Verdelho, 'VJH' Justino Henriques** First in 1995: very high acidity, tangy, depth, fairly sweet, touch of fat. Next (1996), at a pre-sale auction tasting: softer, more chocolatey. Similarly at Pat Grubb's (1997). Later that autumn tasted at Justino's, noting marvellous length and concentration and destined for my son's 'Broadbent Selections' range. *Last tasted Oct 1997* ★★★★

## 1935 ★★★

**Bual H M Borges** Surprisingly chocolatey; refreshing citrus touch. Nice wine. *'Pat Grubb Selections', May 1997* ★★★

## 1936 ★★★★★

Excellent vintage. 'Sercial the finest this century' (according to Cossart) but, alas, not tasted. However **Blandy**'s **Cama de Lobos** with fully branded cork, magnificent. *1986* ★★★★★

## 1937 ★★

**Sercial Pereira d'Oliveira** Amber brown; heavy, chocolatey d'Oliveira style; better flavour than nose. Rich, tangy. Too sweet for Sercial but dry acidic finish. *March 1999* ★★★ *(just).*

### Vintage and solera

*Vintage madeira is the product of a single harvest, and will have aged in cask for a minimum of 20 years – a duration that certainly guarantees its stability. Many madeiras mature for longer than this before bottling, and finish off their maturation in glass carboys or demijohns to avoid prolonged contact with oak. Strictly speaking, a solera begins its life in the stated year but is refreshed with younger wines of the same grape and quality from time to time. In practice very little of, say, the '1864' will be found in the final bottle. Though 'vintage' has its appeal, soleras are often better, and less expensive.*

*Despite their rarity, old madeiras can be bought at auction or from specialist wine merchants such as 'Pat Grubb Selections', prices ranging upwards of £40 a bottle.*

*But to get the taste of madeira I highly recommend the fairly widely available 10-year-old blends of Sercial, Verdelho, Bual and Malmsey shipped by Blandy, Broadbent (in USA) and Cossart.*

## 1939 ★★★★

**Calheta** (A village on the island's south coast.) From John Blandy's cellar. Aged in wood, bottled 1979. Rich amber; glorious bouquet; medium-dry yet rich and full-flavoured. *June 1990* ★★★★★

## 1940 ★★★★

Very good vintage. Noted for its Sercial (according to Cossart).
**Sercial, Vintage Blandy** High-toned, pungent but magnificent in its highly acidic way. *At Aspen, June 1994* ★★★★
**Sercial, Vintage Cossart Gordon** Palish amber; tangy, ethereal; rich, acidic. *Hollywood Wine Society, March 1995* ★★★★
**Sercial 'VJH' Justino Henriques** Very high tangy acidity, good flavour (pre-auction 1995). The following year at Justino's: similar note, adding sharp, aromatic. *Last tasted Dec 1996* ★★★
**Sercial Broadbent, produced and bottled by Justino**'s The driest and most rarified of my son's range of madeiras: pale yellow, green-tinged with crisp, high, catarrh-clearing acidity; dryish but rich, tangy acidity. *Presented by my son and me at the Willow Park Liquor Store in Calgary, Jan 1999* ★★★ (This shop is reputed to have the most comprehensive range of wines in Canada.)
**Sercial Leacock** Tangy, lovely flavour, ethereal aftertaste. *Pat Grubb's tasting, May 1997* ★★★

## 1941 ★★★★

Particularly good for Bual and Malmsey.
**Bual, 'CDGC' Cossart Gordon** A rare, straight, unblended vintage made by Noël Cossart to celebrate the birth of his son David who was later to become a MW while working in Christie's wine department. An exquisite wine first tasted in 1984, and a decade later, bottled July 1976, at a pre-sale tasting. Soft yet ethereal bouquet; flavour reminding me of delicate violet cachous. Great wine. *Last noted May 1994* ★★★★★

## 1945 ★★★

**Bual, Solera Cossart Gordon** Knowing my liking for madeira my host, Tom Groffils, produced this at dinner before a tasting for alumni of Belgium's major hotel/restaurant college: deep amber; bouquet a cross between mocha and a thoroughbred racing stable; rich and tangy. *In Bruges, Nov 1999* ★★★

## 1948 ★★

**Verdelho Barbeito** Chocolate and 'raya' (a coarser sherry); better on palate. Dry finish. *At Pat Grubb's, May 1997* ★★

## 1950 ★★

**Sercial Cossart Gordon** Sweet, good; very powerful, very austere. *At a pre-sale tasting, March 1994* ★★★; **Leacock** not dissimilar. *1989* ★★★

## 1952 ★★★

Good vintage, Malmsey and Verdelho particularly notable.
**Malvasia Rutherford & Miles** Glorious bouquet; touch of caramel on palate. *At the Madeira Wine Company tasting at the Portuguese Embassy in London, Dec 1993* ★★★
**Verdelho, 'Jubilee Selection' Power Drury** Meaty, chocolatey; excellent flavour and attenuated length. *At Pat Grubb's, May 1997* ★★★★

## 1954 ★★★★

One of the most successful post-war vintages. Many notes.
**Bual Blandy** Very rich, powerful (at the 1993 Madeira Wine Company tasting). Next, labelled 'vintage', bottled in 1984: muffled, 'dry apricots' nose; tangy, high acidity (April 1994); lovely colour, medium-sweet, great length. *Last tasted at Robert Maliner's madeira seminar for the Hollywood Wine Society, March 1995* ★★★★
**Malmsey Henriques & Henriques** Tawny; high volatile acidity; very sweet, good length. *At Len Evans' 'Single-Bottle Club' dinner in the Hunter Valley, Sept 2000* ★★★★
**Negra Mole, Reserva Velho J-M Vieira Pereira** It is not often one sees madeira being sold with the ubiquitous and chameleon-like Tinta Negra Mole grape on the label. This bottle was given to me by Dr Montero of the Quinta Bella Vista in Funchal, and consumed with his Madeira cake on my return home. High acidity, whiff of my favourite crystallised violets; very rich, Bual style. *Teatime at Chippenham Lodge, Oct 1997* ★★★★
**Verdelho 'VJH' Justino Henriques** Rich, chocolatey, tawny (1995), and at Justino's (1996), good texture. *Last tasted under the 'Broadbent Selections' label, June 1999* ★★★★
**Verdelho, Vintage Rutherford & Miles** Amber tawny; honeyed, singed; very good flavour. *At Pat Grubb's tasting, May 1997* ★★★

## 1957 ★★★★

**Boal** (*sic*) **Rutherford & Miles** Beautiful, rarified. *Dec 1990* ★★★★
**Bual, Vintage Henriques & Henriques** The name Henriques sounds Portuguese but, in fact, it is a British-owned firm with John Cossart at the helm. Too chocolatey. Rather common taste. *Noted at Pat Grubb's, May 1997.*

## 1958 ★★★

**Bual Cossart Gordon** 37 years in American oak. Bottled June 1995. Ethereal; glorious flavour, length, finesse. *At the MW seminar in London, Jan 1999* ★★★★

## 1960 ★★★

**Terrantez, Vintage Leacock** Uplifting, sweet, slightly tarry; rich, intense. *At Pat Grubb's, May 1997* ★★★★

## 1964 ★★★

Good vintage. Many notes.
**Bual, Vintage Blandy** Bottled in 1985. Exquisite bouquet, ethereal, burnished and baked, crystallised violets; fairly sweet, glorious flavour, refined acidity. *My highest mark of ten top madeiras in Aspen, Jan 1994* ★★★★★
**Bual** possibly **Solera Blandy** Very pleasant but not in same league as the 'vintage'. *Tasted Dec, 1993* ★★★
**Bual 'VJH' Justino Henriques** Rich, ethereal nose and taste (1995). Next, at Justino's, seemed more malty, better on palate (1996). Revisiting Justino's to taste for Bartholomew's range: very deep amber; malty, concentrated nose and flavour, rich, well balanced (1997) and again that autumn. Most recently, my favourite of the 'Broadbent Selections' range: rich, meaty. *Last noted in New York, Dec 1998* ★★★★
**Malmsey Justino Henriques** Powerful. *1998* ★★★
**Malmsey, Vintage Blandy** Two notes, first in 1995: very good; rich, lean touch, length and acidity. *Most recently at Pat Grubb's, May 1997* ★★★

## 1966 ★★★★

**Bual Leacock** The looks, smell and taste of a much older, very fine, wine: apple-green rim; tangy, ethereal; rich, intense, racy acidity. *Aug 1994* ★★★★

## 1968 ★★★★

**Verdelho Blandy** 26 years in American oak. Bottled in May 1994. Palish amber; high-toned, fragrant; very tangy, good length, high acidity (9g/l). *At the MW seminar at Painters' Hall, London, Jan 1999* ★★★★

## 1969

**Bastardo, Vintage Cossart Gordon** Glad to see this rare old grape variety resurrected. Richly coloured; medium-sweet, tangy, good length. *At Pat Grubb's, May 1999* ★★★
**Sercial Rutherford & Miles** First noted at the Madeira Wine Company's tasting (1993): pale; a bit too chocolatey on the nose but correctly dry and tangy. The next year, deeper in colour with excellent nose and distinctly sweet for Sercial. *At a Distillers' dinner, London, Nov 1994. A bit of a lottery* ★★★★

# 1970–1999

$T$he moment of truth: when Portugal joined the European Community in 1986, EC rules insisted that the names of the noble grape varieties should not be used for wines made with the conveniently amenable Tinta Negra Mole though it was, I believe, not until 1993 that the new regulations were enforced. For years, in an effort to lower costs, partly to compete with the perceived competitor, sherry, and partly to sell madeira at all, this versatile and, strangely, red (all the others are white) grape was used. It was claimed that if Tinta Negra Mole was grown at maximum height in the higher vineyards, it made a Sercial-style wine, and if grown on the lower slopes on the island's south coast, near the sea, it would make a passable Malmsey. Henceforward, Sercial, Bual, Verdelho and Malmsey would have to be made entirely from the noble grapes of those same names. Even so, I have to admit that I have tasted several falsely named wines made from Tinta Negra Mole which have been remarkably good and virtually indistinguishable from the real thing. In the final analysis, it is the taste that counts.

## Vintages at a Glance
**Outstanding ★★★★★**
None
**Very Good ★★★★**
1995
**Good ★★★**
1971

## 1971 ★★★

**Bual Cossart Gordon** Twist of lemon; medium-sweet; rich, delicious, good length and finish. *At the Madeira Wine Company tasting at the Portuguese Embassy, London, Dec 1993* ★★★★
**Bual, Vintage Blandy** Something of a mixture, refined, acidic, chocolatey yet ethereal. *At Pat Grubb Selections, May 1997. On balance* ★★★
**Malmsey, Vintage Rutherford & Miles** Moderately good. *May 1997* ★★
**Sercial** Believed to be **Blandy** 24 years in oak, bottled 1995: palish yellow amber; fairly dry (residual sugar 48g/l), average strength (20% alcohol), swingeingly acidic (10g/l). Classic flavour and shape. *At the MW seminar, Jan 1999* ★★★★

## 1972–1980 variable

I tasted a wide range of wines at the Madeira Wine Association in Funchal in December 1983. From all the major grape varieties – Malvazia varying from remarkably high alcoholic content (23.1%) to an unusually low 17.2%; several including Sercial and, interestingly, Bual, nil Baumé, dry; Bual with Boal Surdo, unfermented must. All of these wines were in various stages of production and irrelevant to try to describe in detail.

## 1990

My wife and I spent Christmas 1990 at Reid's Hotel in Funchal and took advantage of more tastings of the new vintage at the Madeira Wine Association. They were surprisingly delicious even at that early stage.

## 1994

**Malmsey, Harvest (Vintage) Blandy** The first of a new wave, following the now well-established five- and ten-year old madeiras, a straight, young vintage marketed in 2000. First tasted, a sample bottle from Blandy's, tasted pre-theatre, Nov 2000: medium-deep amber; very good, classic, tangy nose; sweet, pleasing flavour, correct acidity. Most recently, a similar note. *Last tasted April 2001* ★★★

## 1995 ★★★★

**Broadbent Madeira, Colheita Justino Henriques** The first legal Colheita (the equivalent to what I always refer to as a vintage tawny port, see box page 479). First noted in unusual circumstances, at the end of a 'France in Your Glass' dinner at Eugénie-les-Bains. Most recently: for mid-morning elevenses at Chippenham Lodge. Warm amber; meaty, slightly scented, tangerine, raisiny; fairly sweet, rich, very tangy, good length and typical acidic finish. *Last tasted Jan 2002* ★★★★

# 2000 and the future

$M$adeira is one of those wines that most people would not dream of tasting, but once they have had a taste, they like it. I have first-hand experience of this because, as mentioned previously, I used to keep madeira in my office at Christie's to offer to visitors, and over the past handful of years have accompanied my son, Bartholomew, who imports the wine, on tours of parts of the United States and Canada, presenting the wines to wine societies, tasting groups and to retail customers – we perform a sort of double act. I am usually the stooge. But always, the reactions to the wine are positive. It is nice to see more than a glimmering of a revival in America, a traditional madeira market.

# The Americas

Originally, the expression 'New World' applied to the 'Americas', the 'Old World' to Europe. However, meanings have gradually changed. In vinous terms, not all that long ago, the 'New World' was applied to California and later embraced Australia, New Zealand and – rather bizarrely – to South Africa. Nowadays, 'New World' has a far broader meaning, less geographical and more to do with the styles of wine.

All the world seems to be making wine today and as not enough people are actually drinking it, there are bound to be problems. However, I shall, as usual, confine my discussions to those wines that have proved themselves over the years and are capable of and benefit from ageing. So I shall not dwell on the well-established wines of Chile or Argentina, let alone newcomer Uruguay. In Canada Ontario has emerged from the vinous wilderness (at one time vying for the most horrible wine I have ever tasted, was a Gewurztraminer from a now famous icewine producer, and a Chardonnay from the same area in Ontario). British Columbia and the Okanagan Valley, too, has made its name, despite problems en route, with icewine. Which brings me to the United States. There is scarcely a state in that Union which does not produce wine; nevertheless, I propose, rather unfairly, to bypass most of these, including the increasingly important Washington State and Oregon, with its very successful Pinot Noir, and deal just with California.

This might be the place to follow the migration of vines, for with the exception of the native North American species *Vitis labrusca* and *Vitis rupestris* mainly used for root stocks, wine grapes are of the species *Vitis vinifera* which have their origins in Europe. The Spanish conquistadors and missionaries brought, planted and propagated their own vine stock. Chile in the 19th century imported French vines and, because of their beneficial climate, hemmed in by the Pacific Ocean to the west and the impregnable barrier provided by the Andes all along its eastern boarder, they can still boast of their phylloxera-free vines.

The first and lasting success has been the Cabernet Sauvignon from Bordeaux. Here was a vine that could be identified with a style of wine of international repute. Pioneer, mainly Napa, wineries and the pundits of the University of California at Davis were the principal instigators. I recall that even as late as the mid-1960s, Robert Mondavi, with his enquiring mind and inexhaustible energy, paid his first visit to Europe, to see what made Bordeaux and Burgundy tick: it was first, and foremost, the distinctive grape varieties of each region. Paradoxically, this was something that the Europeans, the British at any rate, either took for granted or were totally ignorant of; after all, apart from Alsace, the grape variety did not appear on the label. The grape variety was almost subliminal. Claret was claret and that was that!

Bob and the rest of California were right. And happily Cabernet Sauvignon took to the West coast soils and climate like a duck to water, except that the result was a plumper duck. It was, I suppose, inevitable that other Bordeaux varieties would follow suit: Merlot, Cabernet Franc and, more surprisingly Petit Verdot. But it is the fleshy Merlot, encapsulating all the obvious virtues of deep colour and full fruit, that has hit the button.

Pinot Noir has been the biggest surprise. Thirty years ago it was considered a difficult grape to grow well. Now growers have got the hang of it. Though Oregan now seems to be its natural home, California also produces excellent examples, often with a very pure varietal character. But whoever would have thought that Syrah and even Viognier would take root; even Chenin Blanc (I recently enjoyed an excellent example from Carmel). All, please note, classic French varieties. The only major vine varieties not to transplant successfully are Gewurztraminer varieties and Riesling, except for late-harvest styles.

I am all in favour of variety; big fruity wines, oaky and obvious, light wines with elegance and finesse. Red, white, pink and fizzy. Horses for courses!

# California

$M$y preamble referred to the expression 'New World' which, in many eyes, particularly European, applied exclusively to the wines of California. Nowadays, 'New World' is an inappropriate way to describe a region of such towering importance. So, leaving aside mentions of Spanish missionaries, in at the start of California's vinous history, I shall abandon this outdated term and henceforth think of California wine as *nouvelle vague*, new wave – actually, almost a 'tsunami'. The endless striving for quality, the innovation, the sheer panache, have made the wines and wine people of California an enormous influence in the world of wine.

On a personal note, I have had the good fortune, initially through my close friendship with Harry Waugh, to have met the most cultured of all wine ambassadors, Belle and Barney Rhodes who, in the late 1950s and 1960s, visited London regularly, bringing with them superb wines, the early Chardonnays and Cabernet Sauvignons. Back in California they were of considerable influence, as I once wrote, 'flitting from winery to winery like bees, pollinating ideas and enthusiasm' – also investing in vineyards and major wineries. I am also indebted to their close friends, Dottie and (Dr) Bob Adamson. Thirty years ago, Bob took time off from his busy practice to conduct me round the Napa Valley, introducing me to Louis Martini, Fred McCrea at Stonyhill, a Chardonnay pioneer, and other leading lights.

Through my association with Heublein's and their highly influential annual Rare Wine Auctions which I helped organise and conduct for 13 years from 1969, I regularly tasted old vintages of Inglenook and Beaulieu Vineyard, and, taking part in their regular events in California, was able to visit other producers, south as well as north of San Francisco Bay, meeting the doyen André Tchelistcheff, the somewhat irascible Joe Heitz and, of course, Bob Mondavi for whom the word 'dynamic' must have been coined; also Maynard Amerine, Professor of Enology at University of California, Davis, who initially viewed me as something of an irrelevant amateur though we became close friends in due course. And others. It is to my regret that over the past few years (almost as long as my son has been living in San Francisco, which makes it doubly unforgivable) I have had fewer occasions to spend time on the West Coast though I have taken advantage of Marvin Shanken's annual California Wine Experience events, not only to taste a range of new classics but to meet many growers (for six years, from his first event – in New York – in 1981, at which Maynard Amerine shared double billing – I conducted Marvin's major tasting seminars). Last, but certainly not least, the annual Napa Valley Wine Auctions that, from 1981, I advised upon and conducted for several years; they afforded me unrivalled opportunities to meet the growers, all of whom struck me, as they still do, as being the most open, dedicated and enthusiastic of their breed.

Finally, despite the unwisdom of making excuses and apologies, I must explain that the following tasting notes relate to wines that have happily come my way. I have never regarded it as my main occupation to seek out the new, explore fully the old, or to produce a gazetteer of California wines. Too late anyway. They are now so many and so varied that the task would be impossible even if I lived there and did nothing else. So bear with me. Instead, what I have striven to achieve is an overview, tracing quality and styles of vintages, what they were like and the current state of play.

## 1936–1979

$E$xciting times. A crucial period of development following the end of prohibition. After a prolonged, enforced rest, wine in California suddenly sprang to life. A fresh start, attracting wine makers of genius such as André Tchelistcheff and, well into the post-war era, enology and viticulture being greatly influenced by Maynard Amerine and his professional colleagues at the University of California at Davis. The half dozen or so major wineries in the Napa valley in the 1950s were augmented by an influx of committed outsiders setting new standards, the decade of the 1960s seeing further incursions, further major developments throughout 'the golden state'. It comes as a surprise for me to recall that Robert Mondavi established his winery as recently as 1966; and that a decade later I was further surprised to see Joe Heitz's cellar door price for his 1970 Cabernet Sauvignon: $40, the exact equivalent of 1970 Château Latour. What presumption!

And that was only the start.

## Vintages at a Glance

**Outstanding** ★★★★★
1941, 1946, 1951, 1958, 1965, 1968, 1969 (v), 1974
**Very Good** ★★★★
1942, 1947, 1956, 1959, 1963, 1964, 1966, 1970, 1973, 1978
**Good** ★★★
1944, 1949, 1955, 1960, 1961, 1967, 1971, 1972 (v), 1975, 1976, 1979

## 1936 ★★

**Beaulieu Vineyard, Georges de Latour Cabernet Sauvignon** An older vintage in the 'Beaulieu Vineyard Centenary Tasting' at Vinopolis, London: medium-deep, with fine rich mahogany rim; touch of oxidation, Virol (malt) and pungent old stables; slightly sweet, faded fruit, slightly sour and yeasty finish. Of academic interest only. *Tasted at Vinopolis, London, July 1999.*

## 1939 ★★

**Beaulieu Vineyard, Georges de Latour Cabernet Sauvignon** First tasted in 1970, drying out but still a good drink. Most recently, bottle variation: both with a fine, rich, deep colour, but one malty, oxidised, the other meaty, peppery nose; soft texture, mellowed components, sound. *Last noted at Vinopolis, London, July 1999.*

## 1941 ★★★★★

**Beaulieu Vineyard, Georges de Latour Cabernet Sauvignon** Sugar 23.5 Balling. First tasted at a Heublein pre-auction tasting in 1972: deep, rich, extended finish. Most recently, slight bottle variation: now far less deep, tinge of orange; ripe, overripe really, meaty nose then a whiff of bananas and horrible taste. The other nose better behaved; sweeter, softer yet assertive and very tannic. *Last noted at Vinopolis, July 1999* ★★

## 1942 ★★★★

**Beaulieu Vineyard, Georges de Latour Cabernet Sauvignon** Very deep, almost opaque; first bottle, considerable extract, tea-like; medium-sweet, rich, soft, bricky Cabernet taste, dried-out. The second bottle better fruit. *Noted at Vinopolis, London, July 1999. At best* ★★

---

### Beaulieu Vineyards ('BV')

*Old established, originally the 'blue blood' of the Napa, whose reputation was established in the 1940s, 1950s and 1960s by the brilliant Russian-born winemaker André Tchelistcheff. Tchelistcheff came over from France in 1938, his skills as a winemaker being in demand for the restoration of this property post-Prohibition. Restore it he did, spurred on perhaps by an intense rivalry with near neighbour Inglenook, both on prime Napa territory, the Rutherford Bench, and both champions of the Cabernet grape, in their different ways. BV is particularly noted for its 100% Cabernet Sauvignon 'Georges de Latour Private Reserve'. A full range of vintages was noted at the Heublein pre-sale tastings and at their 25th and 50th anniversary celebrations.*

## 1943

**Beaulieu Vineyard, Georges de Latour Cabernet Sauvignon** Very deep, opaque core, brown rim. One bottle oxidised. The other rich, cheesy, meaty – reminded me of a not very good old Terrantez (madeira) flavour and finish. Interesting, mouthfilling, tarry. *Noted at Vinopolis, London, July 1999* ★

## 1944 ★★★

**Beaulieu Vineyard, Georges de Latour Cabernet Sauvignon** Not tasted since 1972: silky, rich, well balanced. I doubt if it will have survived.
**Charles Krug, Cabernet Sauvignon** The oldest vintage in the historic vertical tasting I was honoured to moderate at the Mondavi winery in 1985: I needed consummate tact since this was the first time the Mondavi brothers, Peter (of Krug) and Bob had met since Bob left Krug in 1964! ★★★★
**Beaulieu Vineyard, Georges de Latour Cabernet Sauvignon** Very deep, too brown; mocha nose, considerable depth of fruit, singed; sweet, soft, full, flavoury, surprising teeth gripping tannin. Second bottle 'ok'. *Noted at Vinopolis, London, July 1999* ★★★

## 1946 ★★★★★

**Beaulieu Vineyard, Georges de Latour Cabernet Sauvignon** Very attractive colour, rich, open maturity; slight bottle variation, old bouquet reminding me of Ausone or even Haut-Brion, leafy, tangy, rich, medium-sweet soft entry leading to a dry finish. The second bottle more elegant, delicious. *July 1999 At best* ★★★
**Beaulieu Vineyard, Pinot Noir** An old note but memorable. On my first visit to the Napa in May 1970 I was privileged to meet, at Beaulieu Vineyard, André Tchelistcheff, on his way to become the doyen of California winemakers. He kindly opened his '45, '46, '47 and '48 Pinot Noirs of which this '46 was – by any standards – a very great wine. Perhaps Tchelistcheff's greatest masterpiece. Still magnificent seven years later. *Last tasted May 1977* ★★★★★ *(Unhappily, I was not able to stay on to retaste this wine after the Beaulieu Vineyard tasting at Vinopolis in London in 1999. My loss.)*
**Charles Krug, Cabernet Sauvignon** Mentioned again because the tasting was particularly interesting: every vintage of Peter Mondavi's Krug from 1944 to 1965, followed by every Robert Mondavi vintage from 1966 to a barrel sample of the '82 in June 1985. The consistency of style and quality of the Krug very noticeable.

## 1947 ★★★★

**Beaulieu Vineyard, Georges de Latour Cabernet Sauvignon** (This was the very first vintage that 'Georges de Latour, Private Reserve', actually appeared on the label.) First tasted in 1972 and noted at the time as the first really top class Napa Cabernet Sauvignon I had ever tasted. Noted again in 1972 and 1977: incredibly deep, impressive, fruit-laden. 'Will last for years'. Well, one of the two bottles 22 years later lived up to that last statement. Now medium-deep; good, fragrant, autumnal bouquet; very interesting and very attractive, soft entry, dry finish. The second bottle, browner, gingery, with whiff of vinegar. *Last tasted at Vinopolis, July 1999. At best* ★★★★★

# 1948 ★

**Beaulieu Vineyard, Georges de Latour Cabernet Sauvignon** First tasted with Tchelistcheff in 1970, then at Heublein tastings in 1972: even then on the pale side, nose of cold tea – *à point* – quite ready. Most recently: one bottle brown, murky, oxidised, the other strange, unknit; soft, easy, just drinkable. *Last tasted at Vinopolis, London, July 1999* ★

# 1949 ★★★

**Beaulieu Vineyard, Georges de Latour Cabernet Sauvignon** Fine colour, mature rim; first bottle low-keyed, slightly medicinal; good fruit, texture and length though a touch of astringency. The other bottle very fragrant on the nose but palate cracking up. *Last tasted at Vinopolis, London, July 1999. At best* ★★★

# 1950 ★★

**Beaulieu Vineyard, Georges de Latour Cabernet Sauvignon** The '50 Private Reserve opened 'flight' 2 of the Beaulieu Vineyard centenary tasting at Vinopolis. Both bottles hopelessly oxidised, like overripe banana skins. *At Vinopolis, London, July 1999.*

# 1951 ★★★★★

The first of the great California vintages in a year considered execrable in Bordeaux, the same applied to 1956, 1965 and 1968 – which merely reminds us that climatically the Napa and the Médoc are totally different.
**Beaulieu Vineyard, Georges de Latour Cabernet Sauvignon** First tasted in 1971, and at 20 years of age as perfect as any wine could be. My third note was in 1984: an equally fabulous appearance; bouquet clasped tight, slow to emerge; sweet, fleshy, vast, velvety – noted at the time as an amalgam of '55 Ch Latour and '59 Cheval-Blanc. Praise indeed. Then a leap of 15 years : still very deep ; initially tight, low-keyed, old spice, sound ; rich, fullish fruit, astringent finish. The second bottle sweeter and softer. *Last noted at Vinopolis, London, July 1999. As a 20-year old* ★★★★★, *now, at best* ★★★

# 1952 ★★

**Beaulieu Vineyard, Georges de Latour Cabernet Sauvignon** Medium–deep, attractive open appearance; first bottle slightly oxidised, but sweet and quite good on the palate, rich fruit and grip. The second, a better nose, similar palate. *At Vinopolis, London, July 1999. At best* ★★

# 1953 ★★

**Beaulieu Vineyard, Georges de Latour Cabernet Sauvignon** Rich, attractive, open, mature; curious scent and taste, tea-like, privet, dusty tar. The second bottle like an old-ivy Lafite, sweet with tarry taste. *At Vinopolis, July 1999* ★★

# 1954 ★★

**Beaulieu Vineyard, Georges de Latour Cabernet Sauvignon** Big bottle variation, the first dark, drab brown, oxidised 'milk chocolate' nose. Tart. The second healthier appearance and nose, sweet, quite good flavour. Some elegance. *At Vinopolis, London, July 1999. At best* ★★★
**Inglenook, Cask Res J-3 Cabernet Sauvignon** The only other '54 I have tasted (on two occasions, the first in 1978). Lovely and at peak. *Last tasted May 1979* ★★★★

# 1955 ★★★

**Beaulieu Vineyard, Georges de Latour Cabernet Sauvignon** Palish; light, sweet, showing its age on nose and palate. Decent length though. Second bottle was paler; richer, singed nose but soft and drab on palate. *At Vinopolis, London, July 1999. At best* ★

# 1956 ★★★★

**Beaulieu Vineyard, Georges de Latour Cabernet Sauvignon** First tasted in 1970: deep; distinct Cabernet aroma, almost burgundy-like character. Most recently very disappointing: odd, cold, singed, mocha; sweet, soft, lacking. *Last noted at Vinopolis, London, July 1999. In 1970* ★★★, *now* ★
**Charles Krug, Cabernet Sauvignon Vintage Selection** An older note but demonstrating the superb quality, very Bordeaux-like in weight and character. Fleshy excellent fruit, and balance, length and finish. Outstanding 29-year-old. *Last tasted at the Krug/Mondavi vertical tasting, June 1985. Then* ★★★★★ *Probably still superb.*

# 1957

**Beaulieu Vineyard, Georges de Latour Cabernet Sauvignon** Drab colour, nose and taste. An unhealthy sweetness on palate and very unpleasant, astringent end. *At Vinopolis, London, July 1999.*

# 1958 ★★★★★

**Beaulieu Vineyard, Georges de Latour Cabernet Sauvignon** First noted in 1967 and impressive. At just over 20 years old: fine, mature; bouquet complete and contented; ripe, mellow sweetness. Probably at its best. Ten years later still impressively deep; glorious bouquet emerging from its depth; a trifle lean and lissom for Beaulieu Vineyard. Life-supporting acidity. Another decade passed: though deep, a touch too brown; attractive, fulsome, slightly varnishy, eucalyptus; splendid mouthfilling spicy fruit. Exciting. The second bottle with a touch of orange, less forthcoming and lacking punch. Most recently medium–deep, still surprisingly youthful; showing its age, *gibier*, slightly malty; losing fruit but an exciting gamey wine, with liplicking tannin and marked acidity, (my wife said 'wonderful', Hugh Johnson 'superb'). *Last tasted in the Dairy at Waddesdon Manor, Buckinghamshire, Oct 2000. In its prime* ★★★★★ *Now* ★★★★ *(just).*

OTHER EXCELLENT '58s
**Inglenook Cask F 10, Cabernet Sauvignon** Half a dozen noted from 1967. Most recently: powerful and a bit stalky. *Last tasted dining with Maynard Amerine in 1986* ★★★★
**Charles Krug, Cabernet Sauvignon Vintage Selection** Opaque; Latour-like depth and substance. Great. *1985* ★★★★★
**Louis Martini, Special Selection Cabernet Sauvignon** Perfect fruit, weight, balance, flavour. I was always an admirer of Louis' understated wines. *At peak in 1981. Then* ★★★★★

# 1959 ★★★★

**Beaulieu Vineyard, Georges de Latour Cabernet Sauvignon** Two recent bottles differing in a perplexing way: the one which was too brown and looked clearly oxidised had by far the best nose and flavour, hefty, interesting, opening up with vanilla and raspberry scent, sweet and rich on the palate, while the healthier-looking wine, with crisper, better fruit on the nose, was terrible on the palate. *At Vinopolis, London, July 1999. At best ★★★, but which?*

**OLDER NOTES ON OTHER '59s Heitz, Cabernet Sauvignon** fragrant. *1985 ★★★★*; **Inglenook, Cabernet Sauvignon** huge, fleshy, delicious. *1986 ★★★★*; **Charles Krug, Cabernet Sauvignon Vintage Selection 'Lot B'** magnificent though over oaked. *1985 ★★★★★ doubtless still good*; and **Louis Martini, 'California Mountain' Cabernet Sauvignon** understated but perfect. *1982 ★★★★*

# 1960 ★★★

**Beaulieu Vineyard, Georges de Latour Cabernet Sauvignon** First tasted in 1967, with the vinous cultural ambassadors of the Napa, Belle and Barney Rhodes (see box below). The wine was fragrant and attractive. In 1981 it was full, ripe and velvety, probably at its best having 'achieved its majority, aged 21'. Seemed more jammy and malty in 1986. Most recently, two bottles, one almost silky sweet on nose and palate, rich but showing its age, the other more fragrant, dryer and spicy. They could have been totally different wines. Indeed organoleptically, they were. *Last tasted at Vinopolis, London, July 1999. Now risky.*

# 1961 ★★★

**Beaulieu Vineyard, Georges de Latour Cabernet Sauvignon** Not tasted in its youth and heyday. Recently, two bottles: both low-keyed, smelly, hollow, short. *July 1999.*
**Charles Krug, Cabernet Sauvignon Vintage Selection** Glorious. *Tasted in 1985 ★★★★ Probably still good.*

# 1962 ★★

**Beaulieu Vineyard, Georges de Latour Cabernet Sauvignon** Pale, open, rose-like hue; sweet, fragrant Muscat and walnuts. More like port. Yeasty, oxidised finish. *Tasted at Vinopolis, London, July 1999.*

---

### Doctor and Mrs Bernard L Rhodes

*Affectionately known as Barney and Belle. Barney, enormously influential in the formative years of the Napa Valley, California. Belle, a tremendous organizer and cook. They planted Martha's Vineyard, then Bella Oaks, financed some major winemakers, and generally proceeded to get things started in the 1960s and 1970s. He was like a honey bee, pollinating ideas and know-how throughout the Napa and Sonoma valleys. He also pioneered the appreciation of California wines in the UK, and while on this side of the Atlantic, he was one of Christie's earliest wine clients, amassing a magnificent cellar during his visits here. A great man of wine and indeed, in my opinion, an unmatched 'palate'; the most knowledgeable yet most modest of all tasters.*

---

# 1963 ★★★★

**Beaulieu Vineyard, Georges de Latour Cabernet Sauvignon** Both bottles drab, a touch acidic, Oh dear! *At Vinopolis, London, July 1999.*

**OLDER NOTES Inglenook, Cabernet Sauvignon** *1982 ★★★★*; and **Charles Krug, Cabernet Sauvignon** perfectly balanced. *1985 ★★★★*

# 1964 ★★★★

**Beaulieu Vineyard, Georges de Latour Cabernet Sauvignon** Very high sugars. A huge, austere wine, quite unready in 1970 but by the end of that decade developing agreeably. However, still a bit unyielding, Médoc-like at Christie's pre-sale tasting in 1986. Most recently, fairly deep, richly coloured; bouquet to match, high-toned; sweet, malty fruit and not to my taste. The second bottle crisper. I had the impression that to counter its original mammoth richness the wine had been acidified. *Last tasted at Vinopolis, London, July 1999. Originally ★★★★, now uneven and should be avoided.*

# 1965 ★★★★★

**Beaulieu Vineyard, Georges de Latour Cabernet Sauvignon** Lovely at five years of age, maturing nicely at 10; perfection at the end of the 1970s, fully evolved by 1983, yet 'lots of life left' in 1989. A decade later, one bottle oxidised, the other rich, with quite an attractive flavour and grip. *Last tasted at Vinopolis, London, July 1999. Once ★★★★★, now at best ★★★*

**OLDER NOTE, Charles Krug, Cabernet Sauvignon** Magnificent. *1985 ★★★★★ might have survived.*

# 1966 ★★★★

**Beaulieu Vineyard, Georges de Latour Cabernet Sauvignon** Another good, ripe, early vintage. First tasted in 1972, well balanced but unready. At the tasting in the gardens at Beaulieu Vineyard to celebrate the 50th anniversary of Private Reserve wines, its nose reminded me of port and, though still tannic, lacked the length of a major vintage wine. Most recently both bottles showing quite well, still deeply coloured; spicy, attractive, fragrant and forthcoming bouquet. Sweet, rich, good fruit. One slightly astringent. *Last tasted at Vinopolis, London, July 1999 ★★★★*

**SOME OTHER '66s LAST TASTED IN THE 1980s**
**Robert Mondavi, Cabernet Sauvignon** Memorable because this was Bob Mondavi's first vintage at his own winery. It was better in magnum but though attractive, faded. *Last tasted in 1985. At best ★★★*
**Martin Ray, Cabernet Sauvignon** Incredibly deep; very powerful but with odd, smelly, peppery nose; horrible acidity. Undrinkable. *Tasted in San Diego, Nov 1986.*

# 1967 ★★★

**Beaulieu Vineyard, Georges de Latour Cabernet Sauvignon** Slight bottle variation, one not very clear, the other with a lovely colour, attractive fruit and weight. *April 1999 ★★★*

## 1968 ★★★★★

Great vintage.

**Beaulieu Vineyard, Georges de Latour Cabernet Sauvignon** Classic, many notes though not in its extreme youth. At the end of the 1970s it was showing 'Napa at its best'. In the early 1980s it had all the virtues and components in abundance. Showing well, rich, attractive at a pre-sale 'Finest and Rarest' in New York in 1997, and again at a BYOB dinner in 1999. Most recently: two interesting bottles, one deep and still youthful; good nose; very sweet, assertive, packed with fruit, good length, the other thick, hefty, rich. *Last tasted at Vinopolis, London, July 1999. At best still ★★★★★*

**Nathan Fay's, 'Homemade' Cabernet Sauvignon** The oldest vintage at the 'Red' Adams tasting at the Meadowood Resort in the Napa. 'Red' was winner of the Stag's Leap Wine Cellars lot at the Napa Valley Wine auction, June 1997: a tasting of Winiarski's wines and a dinner at his home. The wine had a healthy, mature colour; fragrant nose; nice weight, good dry finish. A lovely wine, holding well. *March 1998 ★★★★*

**Ridge, Monte Bello Cabernet Sauvignon** Curious background: a jeroboam from a barrel bought by Rick Sajbel's syndicate and bottled – not very well – by Rick himself. The wine was very deep, still youthful looking; spicy, peppery, high volatile acidity; dry, crisp, but raw, with high acidity. *Boldly served by Bob Dickinson at one of his Bacchus dinners in Coral Gables, Nov 1997 ★★*

SEVERAL OTHER VERY GOOD '68S TASTED IN THE 1980S the best being: **Heitz, Cabernet Sauvignon** in 1979, described as a cross between Ch Pétrus and Mouton-Rothschild! Deep, fabulous, spicy, fruit-packed and tannic. *1986 ★★★★★ should still be excellent*; **Inglenook, Cabernet Sauvignon** *1985 ★★★★*; **Louis Martini, Mountain Cabernet Sauvignon** glorious. *1987 ★★★*; and **Robert Mondavi, Cabernet Sauvignon** (which included 8% Cabernet Franc) rich, firm, tannic. *Last tasted in 1988 ★★★★*

## 1969 ★★ to ★★★★★

**Beaulieu Vineyard, Georges de Latour Cabernet Sauvignon** First tasted at the 50th anniversary tasting at Beaulieu Vineyard in 1985: still ruby; crisp, fragrant, finely balanced Cabernet, Bordeaux-like in style, weight, tannin and acidity. Most recently, two bottles, slight variation but both very good: medium-deep, attractive; minty, tea-like aromas soared out of the glass; full, rich, good length, tannin and acidity. The second bottle more eucalyptus, astonishingly like Martha's Vineyard, elegant, teeth-gripping finish. *Last tasted at Vinopolis, London, July 1999. At best ★★★★★*

**Heitz, Martha's Vineyard Cabernet Sauvignon** Bottled in September 1973 and I first tasted it in 1981. Then, and in 1985: rich, ruby-centred; great aromas, unmistakably spicy, pine, cinnamon and – though Joe Heitz hated the word – eucalyptus. (I used to stay with Martha and Tom May and their vineyard was surrounded by eucalyptus trees which scented the air.) A big wine, high extract, fruit packed yet elegant.

More recently, at a monumental fine wine dinner hosted by Bill Gates at The Bistro, Buckland, Atlanta: still deep, velvety; immediately forthcoming nose, almost a caricature of itself; glorious flavour with lean and gingery fruit, good length. Vibrant. *Last tasted Oct 1992 ★★★★★ Will still be magnificent.*

### Robert Mondavi

*A good friend for over 30 years. Having parted from his brother Peter at Charles Krug, Bob started from scratch in 1966, the year I joined Christie's. He was then 52. Ahead of him lay the creation of one of the largest and most dynamic wineries in the US, but such was (and is) his drive and energy. An inexhaustible experimenter he is now rightly regarded as the doyen not just of the Napa Valley but of California wine. Now in his late eighties, still bursting with enthusiasm and ideas, he continues to travel widely with his talented artist wife, Margrit. His sons Tim and Michael 'stay at home' and run the Robert Mondavi winery in his semi-retirement.*

JUST ONE OF THE SEVERAL '69S NOTED IN THE MID- 1980S **Robert Mondavi, Cabernet Sauvignon** (Including 15% Cabernet Franc and 3% Merlot.) A bit like a shooting star. Impressive, opened up well, then sagged a little. His unfined more ruby, more peppery, spicy, piquant. Bob, having started his own winery only three years earlier was into experimenting with the winemaking, especially oak, with varying success. This was very evident to me when I was commenting on his section of the two brothers' tasting. *Tasted in a boiling hot marquee at Robert Mondavi's winery, June 1985 ★★★*

## 1970 ★★★★

Small crop, one third of normal, the result of 28 nights of frost and an excessively hot summer.

**Beaulieu Vineyard, Georges de Latour Cabernet Sauvignon** I first went to the Napa Valley in the early 1970s, and thereafter I visited regularly, mainly in connection with Heublein pre-sale tastings (see box page 216). This was the first Beaulieu Vineyard I tasted in cask (100% oak), in 1972: deep purple, full of fruit, stalky. I was able to follow its progress over the years.

By the end of the 1970s though deep and tannic, it was rich and harmonious. By 1985 it was still struggling to get out of its shell, concentrated, tarry, 'silky' (texture), 'yet leathery' (tannins). I have half a dozen notes since: intense, meaty (1997), and two years later no fewer than five: at a trial dinner, then at the big Beaulieu Vineyard vertical tasting: by now it was medium-deep, crisp, fragrant, very sweet on the palate, rich but with very dry, edgy finish, but showing well at the first dinner to be held at Vinopolis, appropriately the *Decanter* magazine millennium dinner. Like all red wines of this ilk, the Beaulieu Vineyard '70 proved a perfect accompaniment to 'Confit of Duck'. Not long after that, served by Hal Lewis at his 'Mr Gourmet' installation dinner in Memphis, Tennessee. *Last noted Sept 1999 ★★★★*

SOME OTHER '70S TASTED IN THE MID-1980S **Chappellet Cabernet Sauvignon** not fully appreciated, fragrant, full bodied yet soft and velvety. *1982 ★★★*; **Inglenook Cabernet Sauvignon** opaque, full, fleshy *1986 ★★★★*; **Heitz, Martha's Vineyard Cabernet Sauvignon**, bottled August 1974. Opaque core; extract fruity, spicy. A glorious mouthful. *1985 ★★★★*; **Mayacamas Cabernet Sauvignon** rich, 'loaded' (*1982 ★★★*); **Robert Mondavi, Cabernet Sauvignon** (80%), unfined, more massive than the unfiltered 83% Cabernet Sauvignon, excellent flavour. *Both tasted June, 1985 ★★★★*; and **Ridge Fulton Zinfandel** nice weight, lovely texture, elegant. Paul Draper fully into his unmatched stride.

## 1971 ★★★

**Beaulieu Vineyard, Georges de Latour Cabernet Sauvignon** Medium, mature; fragrant, 'bricky'; sweet, full, rich, good fruit, touch of pungency. *Two bottles, July 1995* ★★★
**Ridge, Monte Bello Cabernet Sauvignon** Bottled October 1973, alcohol a modest 12.2%, First tasted at home in 1984: still youthful looking; lean yet concentrated. Noticeable iron on nose and palate. Next tasted the following year in my first visit to the century-old winery. I had not arranged my visit in advance and was lucky to find Paul Draper there. Just as well, as it is a long, hot, winding drive up to his winery on a hill top 2300 feet high, south of San Francisco Bay. The wines' very distinctive character are due to the vineyard's height, its 'island' of limestone, the concept of picking when the grapes are fully mature, added to the genius of Draper. Seven years later in magnums, boldly preceding '71 Ch Cheval Blanc and acquitting itself well with *Filet de Boeuf en Croûte*. My notes were brief as I was nervously waiting to give the annual oration. *Last tasted at the Saintsbury Club dinner, Oct 1992* ★★★★

---

### Paul Draper/Ridge

*One of the most consistently highly regarded winemakers of California – the craftsman behind Ridge Monte Bello, spectacular (but not overblown) Zinfandels and powerful but elegant Cabernets. All Paul's wines are in the elegant 'Old World' mould rather than the opulent, indulgent, point-scoring 'blockbuster' camp, which is why I admire them. Paul is a modest but determined man, who sees great importance in the role of terroir in his wines. Ridge Monte Bello 1971 was one of the Californian Cabernets that was mistaken for top-class Bordeaux in Steven Spurrier's famous Paris tasting of 1976.*

---

## 1972 ★★★ to ★★★★

**Beaulieu Vineyard, Georges de Latour Cabernet Sauvignon** Fairly deep; rich, fragrant, gingery, herbaceous; very sweet, full-bodied, high extract, still tannic – needed food. *Two bottles, July 1999* ★★★

OTHER '72S TASTED IN THE MID-1980S **Mayacamas, Late Harvest Zinfandel** (alcohol 17.5%) a quirky classic, not as deeply coloured, sweet or hefty as expected; fragrant fruit, plums, damsons. Delicious with Stilton. *1985* ★★★★; **Mount Eden, Pinot Noir** 'released' in 1975. Six years later: incredibly rich, harmonious; fabulous fruit, opulent. *1981* ★★★★; and **Ridge, Monte Bello Cabernet Sauvignon** deep; 'volcanic' nose. Stylish. *1985* ★★★★

## 1973 ★★★★

A very good vintage.
**Beaulieu Vineyard, Georges de Latour Cabernet Sauvignon** Two very disappointing bottles: cheesy, slightly sour nose and flavour. *Tasted at Vinopolis, London, July 1999.*
**Stag's Leap Wine Cellars, Cabernet Sauvignon 'SLV'** (Stag's Leap Vineyards) A famous wine (the French said notorious) for it was the outright winner of the Paris tasting (see box facing page). What is extraordinary is that Warren Winiarski, the genius behind the wine, had only planted the vines three years earlier. I first tasted the wine in Chicago in

1985, by which time it was maturing attractively. Most recently, at 'Red' Adams' tasting (see 1968). After 25 years it retained a very fragrant, spicy bouquet; was sweet though the tannins were still raw. The very same young vines that had such winning ways in 1976 were 'unsustaining', lacking the maturity to carry the wine for a lengthy period. But, for its age, it was still pretty good. *At Meadowood, March 1998* ★★★

AMONG THE MANY GOOD '73S TASTED IN THE MID- TO LATE 1980S, THE FOLLOWING WERE OUTSTANDING **Forman, Cabernet Sauvignon 'Grand Vin'** made by Ric Forman from a 2-acre/0.8-ha vineyard in Grass Valley leading up to Lake Tahoe. Amazing fruit. *1982* ★★★★; **Heitz, Cabernet Sauvignon** *1989* ★★★★; and their **Martha's Vineyard** bottled 1981. Superb. *1989* ★★★★★; **Robert Mondavi, Cabernet Sauvignon** glorious. *1985* ★★★★ and his **Reserve Cabernet Sauvignon** initially immense. Developed well. *Delicious in 1988* ★★★★

## 1974 ★★★★★

A great vintage. A long, cool growing season and very hot harvest weather. I have listed the most recent notes first.
**Beaulieu Vineyard, Georges de Latour Cabernet Sauvignon** Purple, tannic, great potential noted in 1979 and 1981, but within 10 years it had lost quite a bit of colour, still rich but mature. A rather malty-medicinal bottle in 1989, and an unfortunately oxidised bottle in New York, May 1999. Happily two bottles brought by Beaulieu Vineyard to their 'Centenary tasting' two months later earned high marks, particularly on the palate: very sweet, full of fruit, perfect flavour and weight. Putting paid to the frequently asked question, 'Will the '74 Cabs last?' The answer is, if well kept, yes. *Last tasted at Vinopolis, London, July 1999* ★★★★, *on the fringe of 5 star. But I suggest drinking it soon.*
**Conn Creek, Cabernet Sauvignon** Grapes grown in the Napa by Barbara and Milton Eisele (great friends of the Rhodes and Harry Waugh) harvested 17 October at 24° Brix, slow cool fermentation, 68°F, caused by cold nights. Aged in 60-gallon Nevers oak *barriques*, bottled February 1977. At 16 years of age, still plummy and almost opaque; very pronounced iron, medicinal, very Bordeaux-like sea breeze scent; ripe, fleshy, velvety texture, silky tannins, firm, dry finish. *Tasted alongside the '74 Phelps (see right), May 1991* ★★★★★
**Hanzell, Pinot Noir** Unusual, old-fashioned. The oldest of eight vintages from the cellar of a member of the family, introduced by my ex-Harvey's MW friends Hicks and Don. Medium-deep, red brown, rich 'legs'; sweet, perfectly harmonious bouquet that developed beautifully in the glass; sweet on palate, attractive flavour, crisp tannin and taste. A remarkable 19-year-old. *At Christie's, May 1993* ★★★★★
**Heitz, Angelica** From Central Valley grapes: warm amber; nose like Muscat de Beaumes-de-Venise with a whiff of madeira and old straw; an interesting dessert wine, with a dry finish. *In New York, May 1997* ★★★, *for interest.*
**Heitz, Martha's Vineyard Cabernet Sauvignon** One of California's greatest classics. First tasted, as just Cabernet Sauvignon, at the winery in 1979: spicy, magnificent. In 1982 a superb magnum, opaque, fragrant but unready. In 1991 a superb bottle given to me by Belle and Barney Rhodes. By now with a shade of orange at the rim with an amazingly scented bouquet. Fabulous mouthful but showing its age. Three more notes since. In 1997: holding back, spicy, excellent,

and a jeroboam, very eucalyptus. Next, a superb magnum in January 2000, and nine months later faultless bottles: still deep, fairly intense; unmistakable eucalyptus nose; crisp, high extract, excellent flavour and length. Great wine. *Last noted at a dinner hosted by Lord Rothschild in the Dairy at Waddesdon Manor, Oct 2000* ★★★★★

**Robert Mondavi, Reserve Cabernet Sauvignon** Flowery, very drinkable, maturing nicely in its tenth year. Alongside the 'regular' Cabernet Sauvignon it was deeper, more intense; beautifully evolved bouquet; packed with fruit. Rich, drinking well in 1988. A decade later, a bottle brought by Christa and Bob Paul and drunk with them at Brooks's: excellent, ripe bouquet and flavour, holding well and drinking well. Flawless taste and balance. *Last tasted Oct 1998* ★★★★★

**Joseph Phelps, Insignia** Cabernet Sauvignon 94% and Merlot 6%. Sweet and multi-layered in 1985. Six years later: deep, velvety ruby; fragrant, despite the *cépages* not remotely Bordeaux in style. High extract; alcohol 13.8%, glorious fruit and flesh, almost too sweet with food but delicious by itself. *At Chippenham Lodge with Belle and Barney Rhodes, May 1991* ★★★★★ *Should still be good.*

**Stag's Leap Wine Cellars, Cabernet Sauvignon 'SLV'** Immensely impressive when first tasted in 1976 and in 1979, still opaque, perfectly balanced, great future. At the Wine Experience 10-year tasting, richly coloured, very pronounced though somewhat idiosyncratic character. More recently, two notes in New York, first a pre-tasting of Tawfiq Khoury's wines: deep, velvety, mature; good, slightly singed fruit; sweet, distinctive, delicious, and later that evening at a BYOB at Christie's. *Last tasted Feb 1997* ★★★★

SOME OTHER '74S, LAST TASTED IN THE MID- TO LATE 1980S Caymus, Cabernet Sauvignon beautifully made, elegant. *1984* ★★★★★; **Chateau Montelena, Cabernet Sauvignon** herbaceous. *1986* ★★★; **Clos du Val, Cabernet Sauvignon** Lean for a '74 but elegant. *1986* ★★★★★; **Freemark Abbey, Cabernet Sauvignon** which came second in the class after '61 Ch Trotanoy at the Gault-Millau 'Olympiade' in Paris in 1979. Still rich, assertive. *1984* ★★★★ and their **Bosché Cabernet Sauvignon** *1986* ★★★★★; **Inglenook, Cabernet Sauvignon, Cask A9** beautiful. *1984* ★★★★★; **Charles Krug, Cabernet Sauvignon Vintage Selection Lot F1** mixed notes. Very ripe, rustic character, flavoury, stylish. *1986. At best* ★★★; **Mayacamas, Mountain Cabernet Sauvignon** immense, tannic. *1989* ★★★★; **Ridge, Monte Bello Cabernet Sauvignon** tremendous potential. *Last tasted in 1980* ★★★★★; and **Sterling, Reserve Cabernet Sauvignon** full, rich, ripe. *1989* ★★★★

## 1975 ★★★

Cold season and the vines retarded. Variable quality.
**Beaulieu Vineyard, Georges de Latour Cabernet Sauvignon** Two poor bottles at the Centenary tasting, one badly oxidised, the other acidic. *At Vinopolis, London, July 1999.*
**Hanzell, Pinot Noir** Lovely flavour, texture and acidity. *May 1993* ★★★★

OF THE MANY '75S TASTED IN THE MID- TO LATE 1980S, most hovered around 3 stars, the best of the 4 stars follow: **Freemark Abbey, Bosché Cabernet Sauvignon** (Cabernet from the Bosché family vineyard) sweet, harmonious, full, ripe, soft, fruity. *1986* ★★★★; **Heitz, Martha's**

Vineyard Cabernet Sauvignon bottled in 1979. Opaque, spicy, massive. *1985* ★★★★; and **Robert Mondavi, Reserve Cabernet Sauvignon** (including 10% Cabernet Franc and 5% Merlot), 33 months in cask and 24% new oak. Dry, lean, elegant. Good with food. *1983* ★★★★

## 1976 ★★★

Drought year. Stressed vines and a small crop. Drink up.
**Beaulieu Vineyard, Georges de Latour Cabernet Sauvignon** Two notes, first at the 50th anniversary tasting in 1985 at Beaulieu Vineyard: harmonious but closed ; very sweet, immense, packed with fruit and silky tannins. It is a pity that so many of the Beaulieu Vineyard wines brought to London for the centenary tasting were in such poor condition. The two '76s were simply not good enough, one on the verge though rich. In fact too sweet, malty. The other better on the nose but with an edge of acidity. *Last tasted at Vinopolis, London, July 1999. Should be better than this.*
**Hanzell, Pinot Noir** Vegetal nose; sweet, earthy, massive. (alcohol 15.1%). Another impressive wine in the Hicks and Don vertical tasting. *May 1993* ★★★★
**Stag's Leap Wine Cellars, Cabernet Sauvignon 'SLV'** Deep with browning edge; sweet, meaty, slightly medicinal nose; earthy, 'brown leaves' character, raw finish. *March 1998* ★

---

### Stag's Leap Wine Cellars

*Warren Winiarski's landmark winery. His Cask 23 is one of the Napa's first growths. It sprung to the world stage in 1976 after the now famous Paris tasting organised by Steven Spurrier (California Cabernet versus red Bordeaux), at which Cask 23, tasted blind alongside the Bordeaux greats by a team of illustrious tasters, came out top of the heap. A surprise to all but Warren maybe — since then he has never looked back. He is a passionate and 'professorial' believer in terroir first and foremost, and in Cabernet Sauvignon on his particular patch of it, on Napa Valley's Silverado Trail.*

---

OTHER INTERESTING '76S TASTED IN THE 1980S **Chapellet, Cabernet Sauvignon** deep, rich, fragrant. *1985* ★★★; **Chateau Montelena, Cabernet Sauvignon** big wine, flavoury. *1985* ★★★★; **Conn Creek, Cabernet Sauvignon** fleshy, lovely fruit. *1984* ★★★★; **Cuvaison, Cabernet Sauvignon** *1986* ★★★★; **Heitz, Bella Oaks Cabernet Sauvignon** raw but stylish. *1984* ★★★; **Jordan, Cabernet Sauvignon** another fine vintage and an overnight success. First tasted immediately after its release. Impressive. *1986* ★★★; **Louis Martini, Special Selection Cabernet Sauvignon** very pleasant mouthful. *1989* ★★★; **Robert Mondavi, Cabernet Sauvignon** shapely, attractive. *1986* ★★★★ and their **Cabernet Sauvignon Reserve** very rich. *1985* ★★★★; and **Ridge, Monte Bello Cabernet Sauvignon** characteristically fragrant, high quality. *1985* ★★★★

## 1977 ★★

Drought year.
**Beaulieu Vineyard, Georges de Latour Cabernet Sauvignon** In 1984 intense ruby ; full, velvety, silky, tannins. Most recently: rich, pleasant but rather static nose; very sweet, good fruit, attractive, a lot to it, tannic. *Two bottles tasted at Vinopolis, London, July 1999* ★★★

Heitz, Bella Oaks Cabernet Sauvignon Lovely colour, fruit, length and grip. *Last tasted March 1992* ★★★★
Jordan, Cabernet Sauvignon Rich, delicious. *Last tasted Feb 1993* ★★★
Ridge, Monte Bello Cabernet Sauvignon (3% Merlot) At 12 years of age: an amazing scent, crystallised violets, distinctive, lean. At 20 years old: deep, crisp ruby; sweet spicy, oaky bouquet; crisp fruit, alcoholic content strangely similar to Ch Rausan-Ségla '33: 11.7%, lovely flavour, tannin and acidity. *Last tasted March 1997* ★★★★ *Will be even better now*
Stag's Leap Wine Cellars, Cabernet Sauvignon Fay Vineyard Fragrant, fullish, mature, forthcoming, biscuity; dried-out, taste of tea leaves. *March 1998* ★★

SOME OTHER '77S TASTED IN THE 1980S Burgess, Vintage Selection Cabernet Sauvignon fruity, tannic. *1984* ★★★; Firestone, Vintage Reserve Cabernet Sauvignon well structured. *1984* ★★★★; Robert Mondavi, Cabernet Sauvignon *1985* ★★★ and their Reserve intense, fleshy, lovely *1987* ★★★★; Silver Oak, Cabernet Sauvignon well made. *1985* ★★★; and Trefethen, Cabernet Sauvignon spicy, lean, elegant. *1984* ★★★

## 1978 ★★★★

A very good, substantial and late vintage.
Beaulieu Vineyard, Georges de Latour Cabernet Sauvignon Still opaque in the mid-1980s, needing bottle age; by 1989 sweet, fragrant but excessively tannic. Most recently: medium-deep, rich 'legs'; sweet, attractive and a certain delicacy; delicious flavour, crisp fruit, body, extract and charm. *One of the best of the entire range of Beaulieu Vineyard wines tasted at Vinopolis, London, July 1999* ★★★★★
Chateau Montelena, Cabernet Sauvignon Super-ripe grapes, 10 days on skins, 2 years in barrel. The first estate-bottled vintage and the oldest at a Montelena seminar at the Wine Experience in New York. Still fairly deep, good colour, mature; wonderful fruit, evolving interestingly, stably, vinous, then, after 25 minutes, spearmint; sweet, lovely flavour, balance, length and finish. *New York, Oct 2000* ★★★★★
Hanzell, Pinot Noir Another impressively sweet, full, rich wine with good length and finish. *May 1993* ★★★★★
Robert Mondavi, Reserve Cabernet Sauvignon A dozen notes, first in 1983 and, with the exception of one oxidised bottle, all adulatory. Most recently: medium-deep, cherry red; good bouquet; sweet, fullish, very attractive and individual flavour, crisp fruit. *Last tasted at a Rodenstock weekend, Oct 1992* ★★★★
Stag's Leap Wine Cellars, Cabernet Sauvignon Lot 2 My top wine in a tasting of '78s in 1982. By the mid-1980s it was round, fleshy, full-flavoured. Needs finishing off. *Last tasted Sept 1984. Then* ★★(★★) *Doubtless at peak now.*
Stag's Leap Wine Cellars, Cask 23 A magnum at the 'Red' Adams tasting: opaque core; low-keyed nose; distinctive, curious earthy, meaty, oyster shell taste, an amalgam of Ch Lafite and Haut-Brion. Very impressive. Holding well. *Last tasted at Meadowood Resort and Country Club, Napa Valley, March 1998* ★★★★★ *Still developing.*

MANY GOOD '78S NOTED IN THE MID- TO LATE 1980S, the best being at least 4 stars: Diamond Creek, Red Rock Terrace Cabernet Sauvignon An impressive debut at the first Napa Valley Wine Auction I conducted in 1981. Al

Brounstein broke all my charity auction rules by insisting on a high reserve price – which, luckily, was well exceeded. Since when we have been very good friends! Still powerful and tannic. *1988* ★★★★; and his Volcanic Hill Cabernet Sauvignon from the other side of his small valley, with different soil and a different character: rich, crisp, flavoury. *1989* ★★★★; Freemark Abbey, Bosché Cabernet Sauvignon one of the best I can recall. *1985* ★★★★; Heitz, Martha's Vineyard Cabernet Sauvignon superb. *1984* ★★★★; Jordan, Cabernet Sauvignon Ch Latour-like dimensions. *1985* ★★★★; Charles Krug, Bosché Cabernet Sauvignon a most beautiful wine, lunching with Maynard Amerine in San Francisco. *1983* ★★★★; Louis Martini, Cabernet Sauvignon unaggressive, lovely flavour and texture. *1984* ★★★★; Joseph Phelps, Cabernet Sauvignon elegant. *1985* ★★★; Ridge, York Creek Cabernet Sauvignon Deep, sweet, full-bodied, good length. Lovely. *1988* ★★★★★; and Silver Oak, Cabernet Sauvignon Bordeaux-like. *1984* ★★★★

## 1979 ★★★

Cool vintage. Useful wines.
Beaulieu Vineyard, Georges de Latour Cabernet Sauvignon In 1990: deep, velvety; very rich fruit; chunky, flavoury. Four years later, magnums at a Rodenstock dinner: ruby, still youthful; minty; very dry, crisp, tannic, unready – but guinea fowl sweetened it up. Most recently, below-standard bottles at the extensive Beaulieu Vineyard vertical at Vinopolis in London: sour cheese, peppery; better on the palate, rich and full, but edgy. *Last tasted July 1999. Should be* ★★★ *at least.*
Chateau Montelena, Cabernet Sauvignon The second vintage and a great success at the Paris tasting in 1976. Recently: rich, mature; low-keyed, 'bricky' nose that evolved and held well in the glass; overall dry, high-toned somewhat volatile finish, still tannic, a touch of astringency. *At the Montelena seminar in New York, Oct 2000* ★★★
Hanzell, Pinot Noir Earthy. High acidity. *May 1993* ★★
Jordan, Cabernet Sauvignon First in cask: high-toned, 'whole fruit' character as if macerated. Showing well in 1985, tannic, bell-pepper flavour. Next, a magnum in Houston in 1992: still very deep, black cherry colour; excellent fruit, perfect balance, fleshy, lovely. *Last tasted Jan 1993* ★★★★
Stag's Leap Wine Cellars, Cask 23 At the 'Celebration' tasting in 1998; medium-deep, slightly to brown; pleasant, harmonious nose, light style, drying out. Most recently, a jeroboam presented by Warren Winiarski and served with *Pigeon aux Mais*: quite different to the bottles just described: deep, opaque core, nose uneven, slightly raw and peppery; dry, full-bodied, tannic like the '79 Médocs. *Last noted at the Dairy, Waddesdon Manor, Buckinghamshire, Oct 2000* ★★?

OTHER '79S WERE DISTINCTLY VARIABLE. Most interesting were: Acacia, Pinot Noir excellent Pinot character. *1983* ★★★★; Chalone, Pinnacles Pinot Noir also fine Pinot character. *1983* ★★★★; Opus One the first vintage of the Mondavi/Rothschild joint venture. First noted in 1984: very tannic. Seemed more fragrant a year later at the Krug/Mondavi tasting, its flavour filling out. *Showing well at a vertical in Sept 1988* ★★★; Ridge, York Creek Zinfandel (including 12% Petite Sirah) bottled May 1981. Lovely, rim, very fruity, iron, firm end acidity. *1987* ★★★★; and Shafer, Cabernet Sauvignon an early success for seven-year-old vines: huge, spicy. *1985* ★★★★

# 1980–1999

This was a period of considerable growth. In a matter of ten years the Napa Valley vineyards had grown from something like half a dozen well established wineries to dozens and then finally hundreds, the valley floor and sides almost literally carpeted with vines and architect-designed wineries. Although there was also expansion in Sonoma and from south of San Francisco Bay along the Central Coast to north of Santa Barbara, Napa was – frankly still is – the focal point. The profusion of vines, the enthusiasm and increasing skills of California winemakers and, most recently, the concentration on the quality of the grapes – for this is where it all starts – is inestimable. What I always noticed was the openness and friendliness of the winery owners and staff, competitive of course, but sharing information to solve problems. It has been an exhilarating period for producers and drinkers alike. The 1990s saw variable quality but some very impressive wines too and there was an unprecedented range of new 'cult' wines.

## Vintages at a Glance
**Outstanding ★★★★★**
1985, 1991, 1994 (v), 1997, 1999
**Very Good ★★★★**
1980, 1982, 1989 (v), 1990, 1992, 1993 (v), 1995 (v)
**Good ★★★**
1981 (v), 1984, 1988, 1996, 1998 (v)

## 1980 ★★★★

A good vintage following a long cool summer with almost daily fog rolling over the hills from the Pacific; a warm September ended with a heatwave which sent the sugar levels soaring. Wines of power rather than elegance. I have tasted many 1980s but few within the past decade.

**Beaulieu Vineyard, Georges de Latour Cabernet Sauvignon** First noted at the 50th anniversary tasting at Beaulieu Vineyard in 1990: opaque, red-rimmed; dumb and dusty, but with good fruit lurking beneath; powerful, good teeth-gripping tannin. Most recently, at the Beaulieu Vineyard Centenary tasting at Vinopolis: now medium-deep, rich 'legs', mature rim; nose developing a strange, slightly sour straw scent but this quickly settled down, with a pleasant mulberry-like fruitiness; sweet, rich, very flavoury, touch of peppercorns. Fully mature. *Last tasted July 1999 ★★★★ But drink soon.*

**Hanzell, Pinot Noir** Very much an odd man out. They produced some creditable if somewhat old-fashioned Pinot Noirs (and hefty Chardonnays). In the mid-1980s this reminded me of a good, mature Côtes du Rhône. More recently: a floral, elderberry nose; lovely piquant flavour but lacking length. *Last tasted May 1993 ★★★*

**Heitz, Bella Oaks Cabernet Sauvignon** Medium-deep, with incredibly long shapely 'legs'; touch of woodiness but sweet and fleshy; rich, powerful, slightly malty. Coping with 'Seared Rare Filet Mignon and Fois Gras' at a Bacchus Society dinner in honour of Belle Rhodes featuring no fewer than 80 wines from vineyards she and Barney owned or were closely associated with. *In Boston, March 1992 ★★★*

**Jordan, Cabernet Sauvignon** A lovely, full, rich wine, still tannic. *Jan 1993 ★★★(★) Doubtless fully mature now.*

SOME '80S NOTED BETWEEN 1988 AND 1990
**Kalin Cellars, Pinot Noir Cuvée DD** Lively; smoky, peaty varietal aroma; high strength, very good fruit, hard tannic finish. *Jan 1990 ★★★(★)*

**Mayacamas, Pinot Noir** Already mature, and rich, earthy, scented nose; some sweetness, nice weight, silky tannins. A delight. *Nov 1988 ★★★★ Despite its already evolved appearance, it is probably still delicious.*

**Opus One** (Cabernet Sauvignon and 4% Merlot) Seven notes. First tasted in 1984 and still opaque and immature at the Krug/Mondavi tasting the following year, but noted as 'dry, lean, sinewy like a fine '66 Médoc'. Most recently, in magnums: ruby; a low-keyed charmer, showing well. *Last noted at a Rodenstock wine weekend, Sept 1988 ★★★*

**Joseph Phelps, Insignia** (A Cabernet-dominated blend) Sweet yet tannic in the mid-1980s. More recently: a fine deep ruby; good fruit, fragrant blackcurrant; full-bodied (alcohol 13.8%), lovely flavour, balance and refreshing acidity. *A double magnum from Robert Charpie's cellar at a Wine & Food Society council meeting in London, August 1989 ★★★(★)*

THE BEST OF THE '80S TASTED IN THE MID-1980S
**Caymus, Cabernet Sauvignon from the Grace Family Vineyards** ★★(★★); **Chalone, Pinot Noir** ★★★★; **Clos du Bois, Pinot Noir** ★★★; **Clos du Val, Cabernet Sauvignon** ★★(★★); **Conn Creek, Cabernet Sauvignon** ★★(★★); **Cuvaison, Cabernet Sauvignon** (including 8% Merlot) ★(★★); **Robert Mondavi, Reserve Cabernet Sauvignon** ★★★; **Ridge, York Creek Cabernet Sauvignon** (including 15% Merlot) ★★(★★); **St Clement, Cabernet Sauvignon** ★★(★★); **Simi, Cabernet Sauvignon** (including 10% Merlot) ★★★(★); and **Stag's Leap Wine Cellars, Cask 23** ★★★(★)

## 1981 at best ★★★

Hot growing season with the earliest harvest – mid-August – in living memory. Fleshy reds, moderate quality. I tasted a wide range between 1987 and 1989, but only eight wines since then.

**Beaulieu Vineyard, Georges de Latour Cabernet Sauvignon** Three bottles, one corked at the Beaulieu Vineyard Centenary tasting, the other two raw, edgy, horrid. *Tasted at Vinopolis, London, July 1999.*

**Chalone, Pinot Noir** Mature; lovely nose and very good varietal flavour, but very tannic. *In New York, March 1997 ★★★(★)*

**Diamond Creek, Volcanic Hill Cabernet Sauvignon** Diamond Creek's three adjacent vineyards are all 100% Cabernet Sauvignon. The oldest vintage poured at a delightful picnic lunch under the trees: very fragrant: excellent, dry finish. *With Boots and Al Brounstein, June 2001 ★★★★*

## The Napa Valley Wine Auction

*Inspired by the annual Hospices de Beaune auctions, the Napa Valley Vintners' Association decided to follow suit, to raise money for local hospitals – and to stimulate a bit of publicity at the same time. Both objects have been achieved, beyond all expectations. My connection started with a telephone call from Bob Mondavi asking me whether I would be interested in helping organise and conduct a charity wine auction in the Napa. Of course I said yes.*

*So on a boiling hot 'Fathers' Day', a Sunday in June 1981, I conducted the first Napa Valley Wine Auction, a two-session all-day sale: 596 lots, 5 hours in a large tent, the temperature 110°F in the shade. A good start, it raised a very satisfactory $334,142. I then went on to take the next five annual sales and, during each week, managed to visit a large number of wineries and taste a wide range of wines.*

*I was invited back to conduct the 10th and was 'guest auctioneer' at the 20th, with my old friend Bob Mondavi and his wife Margrit in the chair. It now takes a team of three Christie's auctioneers 5½ hours to conduct under 60 live-auction lots – but the prices are breathtaking. In June 2000 the grand total for the day was around $9 million benefiting three lucky (teetotal) Napa Valley hospitals and other local good causes. It is now simply the biggest, most successful, charity auction in the world.*

---

**Hanzell, Cabernet Sauvignon** Rich, chocolatey, Cabernet nose; sweet, nice weight, good crisp flavour. *May 1993* ★★★
**Hanzell, Pinot Noir** 'Warm', rich, earthy; fairly sweet, attractive, good acidity. More recently, the youngest vintage in the Hanzell Pinot Noir line up. A similar note. Lovely wine. Fully mature. A classic period for a winery famed for its very powerful wines. *Last tasted May 1993* ★★★★
**Heitz, Bella Oaks Cabernet Sauvignon** Medium-deep, lovely colour: fabulous scent; fairly sweet, delicate fruit, delicious. *A bottle given to me by the Rhodes ages ago and served at a dinner at home, May 2000* ★★★★
**Jordan, Cabernet Sauvignon** Only its fifth vintage and ploughing on making pretty impressive Bordeaux-style wines, like this '81 I first tasted in the mid 1980s. At 12 years of age: mature yet tannic, very good flavour. *Last tasted June 1993* ★★(★★) *Doubtless in fine form now.*
**Opus One** Two notes in 1985: good fruit and flesh, spicy but acidic. Three years later, curious stalky nose, dry and too tart. At 18 years of age not holding up though only just missing: still a deep, rich colour, full, mature, with slight bead at the rim; a nose like an old claret, singed, cheesy, interesting; dry, fullish, but overall a touch of sourness, certainly on the finish. *Last tasted at lunch at Chippenham Lodge 1999* ★★ *We almost didn't succeed in tasting this, though, as it was very nearly impossible to extract the hard cork.*

OTHER '81s SHOWING WELL IN THE MID- TO LATE 1980s, all rated ★★★ unless otherwise indicated: **Caymus, Cabernet Sauvignon**; **Clos du Bois, Briarcrest** 100% Cabernet Sauvignon; and **Marlstone** (Cabernet Sauvignon 55%, Merlot 40% and Cabernet Franc 5%); **Clos du Val, Cabernet Sauvignon**; **Gundlach Bundschu** (what a name); **Kalin Cellars, Pinot Noir**; **Joseph Phelps Cabernet Sauvignon** ★★★★; **Ridge, Monte Bello Cabernet Sauvignon** (includes Merlot 8%) ★★★★; **Simi, Reserve Cabernet Sauvignon** and **Trefethen, Valley Floor Cabernet Sauvignon**.

## 1982 ★★★★

In many ways this was as successful as the Bordeaux '82s. Long cool summer, temperatures picking up in August and September, though interrupted by heavy localised rains and a tropical storm, 23–25 September. Moderately large crop of good grapes producing some very ripe wines. I have probably more notes on the '82s than any other vintage prior to 1985.
**Beaulieu Vineyard, Georges de Latour Cabernet Sauvignon** Grapes picked at optimum maturity. Showing well at a major blind tasting in 1986: excellent flavour, easy to comprehend. Five years later at the 50th anniversary tasting, still very deep; very sweet on nose and palate; rich-bodied, with silky-leathery tannins 'enfolding marvellous fruit'. Well, after too many duds – though with slight bottle variations – still a deeply impressive appearance; nose at the very edge of decrepitude though miraculously fruity, forthcoming, with a touch of raisins and, in its perverse way, undeniably attractive; very sweet on the palate, its high alcohol and extract masking the tannin. To conclude, I liked neither the weight nor the style. *Last noted at Vinopolis, London, July 1999* ★★★
**Carneros Creek, Fay Vineyard Cabernet Sauvignon** One bottle flawed, the other with good sweet fruit, soft, attractive. *At Stag's Leap Wine Cellars, March 1998* ★★
**Grace Family Vineyards, Cabernet Sauvignon** First tasted in 1988: an excellent chunky wine. Most recently; level right into the neck, medium, mature, light sediment; some sweetness, curious flavour, crisp fruit, quite a bite. Not as impressive as it should have been. *Dinner at 88 Rosebank with the Khourys, June 1999* ★★★
**Dunn, Howell Mountain Cabernet Sauvignon** I had never heard of Dunn until I came across it in a blind tasting of top '82 California and Bordeaux wines in 1986. It was sandwiched between Ch Haut-Brion and La Mission, in a 'flight' which included Ch Lafite, Ch Latour, Mondavi, Beaulieu Vineyard and Martha's Vineyard. I thought it was the best wine of the entire tasting! It was still showing well six years later. Most recently, my remaining bottle opened at a lunch party at Chippenham Lodge: still deep, rich and velvety; sweet, 'thick', brambly bouquet which held well; a touch of ripe sweetness, good fruit, perfect weight (alcohol 13%) but a very hot, dry, tannic finish. *Last tasted Nov 1997* ★★★★ *Will doubtless continue.*

---

## Marvin Shanken

*Number one 'mover and shaker' in North America, publisher of the influential* Wine Spectator *and the only person I know who could launch a hugely successful cigar magazine at a time when smoking had become – well, frowned upon, then banned in public places.*

*Marvin is the sort of man one doesn't say 'no' to. I first discovered this in 1981 when he insisted, against my wishes, that I should be a speaker at his first 'Wine Experience', a one-day event in New York. Persuasion eventually took the form of a return Concorde ticket, out Friday, back Sunday. The renowned Maynard Amerine, Professor of Enology at the University of California at Davis, addressed the morning seminar; I was the light relief (?) in the afternoon. Since when the Wine Experience, with top flight seminars and 'grand tastings', has become the most important annual event in America's wine calendar. His scholarship fund has raised millions of dollars for wine education and research. Inexhaustible; quite a chap.*

OF THE MANY OTHER VERY GOOD '82S TASTED BETWEEN 1986 AND 1991 the best were: **Beringer, Knights Valley Cabernet Sauvignon** I was in agreement with a myriad of fellow tasters at the California Wine Experience seminar of '82s I conducted in 1986, giving this high marks; it also showed well against the Bordeaux the following day. Mouthfilling and tannic, the latter (if I am allowed to requote from my notes) 'smelling like the armpit of a healthy, clean-living youth after exercise'. Two subsequent notes. *1987* ★★★★; **Caymus Vineyards, Special Selection Cabernet Sauvignon** here, I and the thousand or so in the audience disagreed. The majority voted this second out of the eight top California '82s, I rated it 8th. A bit over the top, speciously spicy. Like strawberry jam in the mouth. *1986* ★★★; **Chateau Montelena, Cabernet Sauvignon** ripe, good length. *1986* ★(★★★); **Diamond Creek, Red Rock Terrace Cabernet Sauvignon** fragrant, great impact, lean, tannic. *1986* ★★(★★); **Douglas Vineyards, Cabernet Sauvignon** (new to me) bottled by Zaca Mesa. Delicious. *1991* ★★★(★); **Groth, Cabernet Sauvignon** good wine. *1989* ★★★(★)); **Heitz, Martha's Vineyard Cabernet Sauvignon** spicy, packed with fruit. *1986* ★★★(★★); **William Hill, Cabernet Sauvignon** Pomerol-like, good texture, elegant. *1986* ★★★; **Inglenook, Cabernet Sauvignon Reserve Cask** extraordinary bouquet and flavour. *1986* ★★★★; **Jordan, Cabernet Sauvignon** (Merlot 15.5%) ripe, lovely. Length? *1986* ★★★; **Robert Mondavi, Reserve Cabernet Sauvignon** fragrant, ready. *1988* ★★★; and **Opus One** bottle variation as early as 1985. The first woody and raw. Next, a fragrant, flavoury charmer. Most recently in magnum and bottle: cherry red, good fruit and length. *1988* ★★★

FURTHER WINES, AT LEAST 3 STARS **David Bruce, Pinot Noir**; **Chateau Bouchaine, Cabernet Sauvignon**; **Clos du Bois, Briarcrest Cabernet Sauvignon**; **Clos du Val, Merlot**; **Cuvaison, Cabernet Sauvignon**; **Duckhorn, Merlot**; **Dry Creek Vineyards, Dry Creek Valley Cabernet Sauvignon**; **Mayacamas, Cabernet Sauvignon**; **Ridge, Monte Bello and York Creek**; **Saintsbury, Carneros Pinot Noir**; **Shafer, Hillside Select Cabernet Sauvignon**; **Simi, Reserve Cabernet Sauvignon** silky texture; and **Sterling Vineyards, Merlot**.

## 1983 ★★

The wettest winter on record. The summer was more like spring and there was heavy rain in mid-August. I mainly tasted these wines between 1985 and 1987. Few tasted since.
**Beaulieu Vineyard, Georges de Latour Cabernet Sauvignon** Medium-deep, very rich 'legs'; initially indistinct but quite fragrant fruit; sweet, soft, good fruit and flavour. Drying tannin. *Tasted at Vinopolis, London, July 1999* ★★★
**Jordan, Cabernet Sauvignon** Good fruit and length. Very tannic. *Last tasted Jan 1993* ★★(★)
**Stag's Leap Wine Cellars, Cask 23** A magnum at the 'Red' Adams tasting: very deep; good fruit, complete; sweet, excellent body and balance. *March 1998* ★★★★

OF THE OTHER '83S TASTED IN THE LATE 1980S TO EARLY 1990S **Clos du Val Pinot Noir** powerful, spicy. *1987* ★★★ and their **Zinfandel** a charmer. *1987* ★★★; **Duckhorn Merlot** 'Pétrus without flesh'. *1988* ★★?; **Kalin Cellars, Pinot Noir Cuvee DD** rich, good flavour noticeable

acidity. *1991* ★★★; **Charles Krug, Cabernet Sauvignon** fruit like Ch Lynch-Bages. Heavenly fruit. *1987* ★★★; **Robert Mondavi, Cabernet Sauvignon** several notes. Harmonious fruit, elegant. *1988* ★★★; **Opus One** bellpepper nose, good texture, lean and dry. *1988* ★★★; and **Ridge, Paso Robles Zinfandel** flavoury, great length. *1987* ★★★★

## 1984 ★★★

A moderately good vintage. There was a long dry period from early spring to the end of the harvest with record high temperatures in May. I have few recent notes.
**Beaulieu Vineyard, Georges de Latour Cabernet Sauvignon** Medium-deep, mature rim, rich 'legs'; straightforward, low-keyed but fragrant nose; medium-sweet, agreeable flavour, texture and balance – if anything a bit four-square. Also an attenuated sharp finish. *Tasted at Vinopolis, London, July 1999* ★★★ *(just)*.
**Caymus Vineyards, Special Selection Cabernet Sauvignon** Aged four years in 60-gallon Limousin and Nevers oak barrels. Fairly deep soft ruby; high-toned; dry, firm, crisp fruit, dry finish. *Dining with Spencer and Bartholomew in San Francisco, Nov 1998* ★★★
**Chateau Chevalier, Napa Pinot Noir** Rather ordinary. On AA 362, First Class, Honolulu to Los Angeles after tastings with my son and charity events in Hawaii. *Sept 1992* ★
**Dominus** (Cabernet Sauvignon 75%, Merlot 25%) The second vintage produced by the John Daniel Society (named after the founder of Inglenook) in a joint venture with Christian Moueix from Pomerol and first tasted in 1988: fairly intensive black cherry colour; good sweet fruit and spice; full-bodied, fleshy, good length and acidity. A most attractive wine for mid-term drinking. *August 1988, then* ★★(★★) *At peak now.*
**Groth, Cabernet Sauvignon** Attractive colour; sweet, appealing; soft fruit, rich weight (alcohol 12.5%), easy drinking. *At dinner with my son and daughter-in-law in San Francisco, Christmas Eve, Dec 2000* ★★★

ONE OR TWO MORE '84S TASTED BETWEEN 1988 AND 1991 **Acacia, Iund Vineyard Pinot Noir** fragrant, rich, prune-like fruit; excellent flavour. *June 1988* ★★★; **Calera, Jensen Vineyard Pinot Noir** singed Pinot; powerful, flavoury. *June 1988* ★★★ and their **Selleck Vineyard Pinot Noir** very fragrant, sweet, appealing. *June 1988* ★★★; **Clos du Bois, Briarcrest Cabernet Sauvignon** ★★★; **Cuvaison, Merlot** ★★★; **Freemark Abbey, Cabernet Sauvignon** good nose, nice weight, good flavour. *Sept 1988* ★★★; **Hess Collection, Cabernet Sauvignon** deep, sweet, full, impressive. *May 1999* ★★★; **Inglenook, Cabernet Sauvignon** ★★★; **Opus One** muffled fruit; good body and length, but tart. *Sept 1988* ★★?; **Ridge, Geyserville Zinfandel** A most extraordinary nose: figs, prunes and tar; loads of grip and spice. Fabulous – in its own way. ★★★★; and their **Monte Bello Cabernet Sauvignon** ★★★★; and **Sanford, Pinot Noir** scented aromas; sweet, rich, ripe Pinot flavour, tannic. *Sept 1988* ★★★

## 1985 ★★★★★

An extremely good vintage, one of my favourites. A fine, dry, fairly cool summer, apart from a heatwave in June – I well recall it as I was there to conduct the fifth Napa Valley Wine Auction. Heavy rain in September stopped the harvest, continuing afterwards in short, cool spells. However, the sun returned at the end of the month to complete the ripening.

By now the sheer number of very many good producers in California was making life difficult for an out-of-reach Englishman to put their efforts into perspective. My good friend Robert Paul, with around 100 California red wines in his cellar, selected 55 of the best Cabernets for me to taste blind in January 1991. It was an eye-opener. There is no space here to list them all, so I am starting with those wines for which I have a more recent note.

**Beaulieu Vineyard, Georges de Latour Cabernet Sauvignon** First tasted in 1991 at the blind tasting mentioned above: deep, richly coloured, maturing; attractive fruit; very flavoury but with a rather piquant, acidic finish. Most recently, at the Beaulieu Vineyard centenary tasting in London: now medium-deep, still with good, rich 'legs'; fruit low-keyed; good fruit, complete. Very good though not sensational. *Tasted at Vinopolis, London, July 1999* ★★★★ *Probably at best now.*

**Caymus Special Selection Cabernet Sauvignon** In 1991, plummy colour; lovely, crisp, oaky, spicy nose that opened up sensationally in the glass; fairly sweet, nice weight (alcohol 13%); full of fruit and flavour. A lovely wine. *Last noted dining at my son's in San Francisco, Sept 1992* ★★★★ *Should be perfect now.*

**Chateau Montelena, Cabernet Sauvignon** In 1991: deeply impressive; fragrant, spicy; full-bodied (alcohol 13.5%), very good fruit and flavour. More recently: richly coloured; velvety yet tannic. *Tasted pre-sale in New York, Sept 1997* ★★★★ *Ready now.*

**Dominus** Neither the grape varieties nor, as far as I could see, the alcoholic strength was mentioned on the label. In 1991: deep, ruby; fragrant but with unintegrated weedy fruit and cheesy tannins; dry, loads of fruit and grip. More recently: still ruby; very strange nose, rich, hefty, toasted; dry, tannic, still raw. *Noted at a pre-sale tasting, Sept 1997* ★★(★)

**Groth, Reserve Cabernet Sauvignon** I shall never forget this. At the 1991 tasting Bob Paul said this was a wine 'people kill for', meaning, of course, that it was very hard to get hold of (though Bob never had much of a problem). Tasting it blind, I liked it but would certainly not kill for it. Two years later, it appeared in another blind tasting, this time at Arne

## Robert (Bob) Paul

*International lawyer based in Miami, who started his interest in wine in the mid-1970s and now has a cellar of 30,000 bottles. Wine enthusiast par excellence with many honours and awards including the French Mérite Agricole, Bob is also a member of many wine societies and fraternities, not to mention a wine writer and giver of major tastings. These last are attended by châteaux proprietors and wine enthusiasts (professional and amateur), at least two of which I have 'moderated' (chaired): in 1988, 60 grand cru classé châteaux of the 1978 vintage; in 1989, 90 grand cru classés of Saint-Emilion and Pomerol. I was once ticked off by Bipin Desai who said 'The trouble with you Michael is that once you've finished speaking, there's nothing else for anyone to say!' So with Bob Paul I was very careful to let everyone else speak first. Bob also — privately, and entirely for my benefit — generously produced from his cellar 50 of the top California Cabernets of the 1985 vintage. For some years, he and Christa spent New Year with us and we regularly enjoyed our favourite stone crabs with them while travelling to and from our annual holiday in Saint Barts.*

Berger and Arnold Zabert's Weinprobe 'Parker 100' — an array of eight wines which had been awarded, at some time or other, 100 points by the eminent Robert Parker. Well, I confess — the Groth '85 probably warranted it: opaque, intense (an appearance much favoured by Parker); low-keyed, soft, mulberry fruit; sweet, full flavour and extract (another plus point), chewy, good fruit, flavour and length, touch of iron with aftertaste hinting of toffee. *At Le Canard restaurant, Hamburg, Sept 1993* ★★★★★

**Heitz, Bella Oaks Cabernet Sauvignon** In 1991 deep, immature: lovely, rich, figgy nose; sweet, full of fruit extract, tannin and acidity. Just 12 months later: deep, brilliant, intense colour with very rich 'legs'; nose, however, distinctly woody; better on the palate, very full, rich, very dry, tannic — the touch of wood confirmed. *Last noted at a Bacchus Society dinner, March 1992* ★★★★?

**Heitz, Martha's Vineyard Cabernet Sauvignon** Tasted blind in 1991, its eucalyptus nose a giveaway; full, sweet, meaty. Most recently — alas — a corked bottle at Kaplan's 1985 vintage event. *Last sniffed, disappointedly, April 2000. At best* ★★★★ *Should be perfect, even 5-star now.*

**Kendall-Jackson, Cardinale** One of my top three wines at Bob Paul's 1985 vintage blind tasting in 1991: deep plummy purple; excellent, crisp Cabernet aroma which opened up gloriously; dry, fullish but lean, excellent fruit, length and aftertaste. More recently, my one and only bottle consumed at a Sunday lunch at Chippenham Lodge: now, a soft dark cherry red; deep, blackberry-like nose and flavour. Full of fruit and spice. Lovely wine. *Last noted Aug 1994* ★★★★★ *Doubtless still very good.*

**Opus One** (no longer 100% Cabernet Sauvignon) Four good notes. Another of the top wines in Bob Paul's blind tasting in 1991. Impressively deep, with 'legs' like gothic arches; lovely, rich, spicy and fruity nose; full of soft fruit, good flesh, agreeably light (alcohol 12.1%), yet supremely well balanced. *Last tasted in New York, Feb 1992* ★★★★★

**Ridge, York Creek Cabernet Sauvignon** (including 10% Merlot and 2% Cabernet Franc). Bottled May 1987. Fairly deep, mature; showing age; very strange nose and fishy, 'seaweed', metallic, iron taste, coincidentally the same strength as Opus One (12.1%). Not sure what to make of this. *With my son and daughter-in-law on Christmas Day 2000, at 1915 Pierce Street, San Francisco.*

**Stag's Leap Wine Cellars, Cask 23** Also right at the top of the 55 Cabernet wines tasted with Bob Paul in 1991: fabulous appearance; fruit-laden, full-bodied (alcohol 13.8%), with a rich, ripe, Médoc-medicinal flavour. In 1997 I noted an equally fabulous bottle, more than holding its own between Marchese di Grésy's '85 Barbaresco Gaiun Martinenga and the blissful '85 Ch Cheval Blanc, at a modest Sunday lunch at Chippenham Lodge.

The following year, dining at the Winiarskis after the 'Red' Adams tasting: deep, still youthful, rich, with power and length. Most recently, a jeroboam brought by Warren Winiarski to the Russian National Orchestra's fundraising dinner at Waddesdon Manor: still very deep, opaque core but showing some maturity; a lovely, ripe, harmonious bouquet; sweet, beautiful flavour, perfect balance. *Last tasted Oct 2000* ★★★★★ *At its sublime peak.*

**Stag's Leap Wine Cellars, Cabernet Sauvignon 'SLV'** Fine, deeply coloured, still youthful; crisp, berry-like aroma and taste. Perfect tannin and acidity. *Dining at the Winiarskis, March 1998* ★★★★

**OF THE OTHER 45 '85 REDS TASTED BLIND AT BOB PAUL'S IN 1991**, the following I rated as 5-star: **Mayacamas, Cabernet Sauvignon** soft yet penetrating nose; lissom, lean, fruity, tannic; **Joseph Phelps, Insigna** (Cabernet Sauvignon 60%, Merlot 25%, Cabernet Franc 15%) an extraordinary scent, bellpeppers, whiff of spearmint then lime blossom; very distinctive flavour, tannic; **Rutherford Hill, 'XVS' Napa Cabernet Sauvignon** impressively deep; very fragrant; wonderful fruit and other components to match.

**OF THE OTHER 45 '85 REDS TASTED BLIND AT BOB PAUL'S IN 1991**, the following were close to the top, say 4-star plus: **Beringer, Knights Valley Proprietor's Growth Cabernet Sauvignon**; **Buena Vista, Private Reserve Carneros Cabernet Sauvignon**; **Diamond Creek, Red Rock Terrace and Volcanic Hill**; **Grgich Hills, Napa Cabernet Sauvignon**; **Hess Collection, Cabernet Sauvignon**; **Robert Mondavi, Reserve Cabernet Sauvignon**; **Joseph Phelps, Insignia, Auction Reserve**; **Shafer, Hillside Select Cabernet Sauvignon**; **Silver Oak, Alexander Valley Cabernet Sauvignon**; **Simi, Alexander Valley Reserve Cabernet Sauvignon**; and **Sterling, Reserve**.

## 1986 *variable*

'One long spring'. A protracted harvest, the final crop of Cabernets being picked in early October.

**Beaulieu Vineyard, Georges de Latour Cabernet Sauvignon** At the 50th anniversary in 1990, the youngest vintage in the line-up: opaque, purple; green, immature Cabernet aroma, 'moth balls'; moderate length, totally undrinkable. Nine years later, still a fine, deep colour; nose opened up with attractive fig-like fruit; some sweetness, good fruit, crisp but dry, very tannic and touch of edgy acidity. *Last tasted at Vinopolis, London, July 1999* ★★★

**Chateau Montelena, Cabernet Sauvignon** Very deep, rich, maturing; fragrant, berry-like, rich development; rich, powerful, alcoholic, masculine, loaded with tannin. *At the 'California Wine Experience' Montelena presentation, Oct 2000* ★★★(★) *For those who like to chew and spit out, or to keep.*

**Calera, Selleck Vineyard Pinot Noir** Very fragrant Pinot varietal aroma and flavour. Medium sweetness and weight (alcohol 13%), lovely texture and flavour. *At a Gidleigh Park wine weekend dinner, Devon, Feb 1994* ★★★★★

**Diamond Creek, Gravelly Meadow Cabernet Sauvignon** Very tannic ★★(★★)

**Diamond Creek, Red Rock Terrace Cabernet Sauvignon** Youthful ruby; amenable, lighter in style ★★★

**Diamond Creek, Volcanic Hill Cabernet Sauvignon** distinctly sweet yet also very tannic ★★(★★) *All three Diamond Creek wines tasted at a BYOB dinner in New York, Feb 1996. Drink, say, now–2012.*

**Opus One** (Cabernet Sauvignon 86.5%, Cabernet Franc 9.6%, Merlot 3.9%) The oldest vintage in a Christie's Opus One masterclass. I always make – or rather, Daphne always notes – detailed descriptions at these sessions, too long to re-state at length. Briefly, dark cherry; very Bordeaux-like fruit, smooth, leather and honey, an hour or so later, fragrant, tea leaves; sweet entry, nice weight (alcohol 12.5%), ripe, 'very pleasant to drink now'. *Dec 1997* ★★★★

**Stag's Leap Wine Cellars, Cabernet Sauvignon 'SLV'** Magnum at the 'Red' Adams tasting at Meadowood: deep;

distinct whiff of coffee-mocha – like walking past a coffee shop. Sweet, flavour to match. Black cherry fruit. *Celebrating the winery's 25th anniversary, March 1998* ★★★

**I HAVE TASTED SURPRISINGLY FEW '86 CABERNET SAUVIGNONS.** I tasted the following between 1989 and 1992.
**Forman, Cabernet Sauvignon** (including Merlot 15%, Cabernet Franc 10% and a fraction of Petit Verdot – one of the earliest vintages I can recall where this late-ripening Bordeaux varietal was used). Lovely scent, spicy; crisp, very fragrant. *Feb 1989* ★★(★★) *Probably at peak now.*
**Hess Collection, Cabernet Sauvignon** Good but very tannic. *May 1991* (★★★)
**Mount Veeder, Cabernet Sauvignon** Nose like fresh peas; sweet, full-bodied (13.8%), rich, masked tannin. Plausibly attractive. *Nov 1992* ★★★
**Sequoia Grove, Cabernet Sauvignon** Soft, fleshy, attractive. *June 1990* ★★(★)

**CONVERSELY, I HAVE TASTED A FAIRLY WIDE RANGE OF '86 PINOT NOIRS** The following were showing well in their youth: **Acacia, St Clair Vineyard** ★★★★; **Calera, Jensen** ★★★; **Carneros Creek, Loath's** ★★★; **Bouchaine, Carneros Napa** ★★★; **Saintsbury, Carneros** ★★★; **Sanford, Sanford & Benedict** a La Tâche look-alike! ★★★★; **Sterling, Winery Lake** ★★★; and **Zaca Mesa, Reserve** ★★★★

## 1987 ★★

Moderate quality. There was a mild winter and a frost-free spring. The potential crop was affected by a series of heatwaves in May. There was a dry summer, a cool September, then rain and excessive heat. There was an early harvest, the smallest in California for five years.

**Beaulieu Vineyard, Georges de Latour Cabernet Sauvignon** Three years in American oak. At ten years of age: medium deep, maturing; touch of cheese and stalkiness; better on palate. Nice weight. Good flavour. Touch of iron. Two years later: smelly stewed cabbage nose, then soft leather, sweet, pungent fruit. *Last noted at the Beaulieu Vineyard Centenary tasting, Vinopolis, London, July 1999. Avoid.*

**Chateau Montelena, Cabernet Sauvignon** Deep, rich, a tight, mature rim; very good, crisp, berry-like nose; sweet, full, rich, lovely. *At the Montelena seminar in New York, Oct 2000* ★★★★

**Dominus** (Cabernet Sauvignon 80% and the rest of the blend Cabernet Franc and Merlot) Attractive; good fruit. Very dry finish. *Briefly noted at a J-P Moueix tasting in London, March 1993* ★★(★)

**Robert Mondavi, Reserve Pinot Noir** Very good, ripe Pinot aroma: excellent. *At the Houston Grand Opera Wine Classic and Auction, Oct 1992* ★★★★

**Opus One** (Cabernet Sauvignon 95%, Cabernet Franc 3%, Merlot 2%) First tasted in 1991 at Philippe de Rothschild's London office: very deep, 'thick', high extract; hefty, rich fruit; excellent flavour and components. Next, at the Opus One masterclass in 1997: deep, intense; Bordeaux-like nose; sweet, good fruit, dry finish. Most recently and coincidentally noted as 'very Bordeaux-like'! Good flavour and flesh. *Last noted dining at Ch Mouton-Rothschild, Sept 1998* ★★★★

**Joseph Phelps, Insignia** Medium-deep; harmonious, excellent. *Briefly noted in between lots at the Houston Grand Opera Wine Classic dinner and auction, Oct 1992* ★★★★

FEW OTHER '87S TASTED. The following were of some interest in the early 1990s: **Beaulieu Vineyard, Carneros Pinot Noir** true to type ★★★; **Hess Collection, Cabernet Sauvignon** a really good food wine ★★★; **Saintsbury 'Garnet' Carneros Pinot Noir** very good varietal charmer and flavour ★★★★; and **Shafer Merlot** flesh but severely tannic ★★(★★)

## 1988 ★★★

A difficult year and another small yield. I have an equally small number of notes I am sorry to say. But then even from my few notes, it was clearly a good vintage.

**Beaulieu Vineyard, Georges de Latour Cabernet Sauvignon** Medium-deep, long, rich 'legs'; nice fruit, fragrant; remarkably soft, sweet, velvety entry, delicious flavour, slightly bitter, tannic finish. *At the Centenary tasting, Vinopolis, London, July 1999* ★★★★

**Beringer Knights Valley Cabernet Sauvignon** Odd, tight, unyielding nose and taste. Raw tannins. *Tasted blind, April 1992* (★★)

**Carmenet** (Cabernet Sauvignon 85%, Cabernet Franc 9%, Merlot 6%) New to me; part of the Chalone Group. Very deep; lovely, jammy, almost classic nose; fully loaded with all the component parts. Magnificent. *At a British Airways (blind) tasting for First Class, April 1992* ★★★(★)

**Dominus** (Cabernet Sauvignon 86%, Cabernet Franc 11%, Merlot 3%) Deep, very Bordeaux-like, good flesh, fruit and spice. Good future. *March 1992* (★★★★)

**Opus One** Only tasted in its youth: deep; good young fruit and oak; sweet, crisp fruit, lightish style, tannic finish. *Nov 1991* (★★★)

**Robert Mondavi, Reserve Cabernet Sauvignon** Unfiltered opaque core; rather singed, Italianate fruit; lovely sweetness and fruit, fairly powerful, spicy, crisp, very tannic. *At a 'Gala Abend' wine dinner in Mainz (fellow speaker was August Winkler), Sept 1992* (★★★)

**Saintsbury Carneros Pinot Noir** First noted in 1994: a cosily, warm Pinot-in-old-socks aroma; agreeable sweetness and beetroot (varietal) flavour and hot, dry finish. Next, most unusually, at a Saintsbury Club dinner: deep; meaty; sweet, good flavour but swingeing finish. *Last tasted Oct 1996* ★(★)

**Stag's Leap Wine Cellars Cabernet Sauvignon 'SLV'** Deep, rich, high extract; very good nose; lovely fragrance and oaky flavour. *At Warren Winiarski's stand at the Wine Experience 'Grand Tastings' in New York, Oct 1991* (★★★★) *Should have turned out well.*

## 1989 ★★ to ★★★★

Third year of drought was eased by spring rains. Summer was cool but pleasant. Early harvest interrupted by heavy rains, cold, and fog, rot affecting remaining grapes. Then an earthquake! Who said that California enjoyed perfect weather every year? Sonoma fared best.

Happily I have more notes than for the '88s, and more recent ones. A selection follows to give the feeling of the vintage, which, on the whole, I found attractive. Most are perfect for drinking now.

**Au Bon Climat, Benedict Vineyard Pinot Noir** Fairly intense; very pronounced 'beetroot' varietal aroma; very rich, lovely texture, flavour and acidity. A most dependable and true Pinot. *At Gidleigh Park, Devon, Feb 1994* ★★★★

**Beaulieu Vineyard, Georges de Latour Cabernet Sauvignon** Using a new generation of American oak for ageing: deep, plummy; broad, open, slightly mint leaf scent, then opening up with attractive, ripe fruit on nose and palate. Sweet, fairly hefty, very tannic. *At the centenary tasting at Vinopolis, London, July 1999* ★★★(★)

**Diamond Creek, Volcanic Hill Cabernet Sauvignon** Marvellous fruit on nose and palate; soft yet with grip. *On Al Brounstein's 'Grand Tastings' stand, Oct 1991* (★★★★) *Great potential.*

**Dominus** (Cabernet Sauvignon 89%, Merlot 10%, Petit Verdot 1%) Deep; dry, touch of iron. Sipped during my 'auction talk' with Christian Moueix. The wine sweetened up as our duologue progressed. *At Christie's, Park Avenue, Feb 1997* ★★(★)

**Freemark Abbey, Bosché Cabernet Sauvignon** Opaque; very forthcoming fruit; sweet, interesting flavour and tang. *Tasted blind May 1995* ★★(★) *Good potential.*

**Heitz Martha's Vineyard Cabernet Sauvignon** Intense ruby; crisp, spicy, blackberry-like aroma; sweet, marvellous fruit, very tannic. Very good indeed but not ready for drinking. *At the James Beard Foundation dinner at Christie's, New York, May 1995* ★★(★★)

**Kendall-Jackson Cabernet Sauvignon** Soft, easy fruit. Very attractive. *April 1992* ★★(★★)? *Should be at peak now.*

**Peter Michael, 'Les Pavots'** The Les Pavots vineyard is named after the poppies (*pavots* in French) that bloom in the spring on the mountain slopes above the appropriately, coincidentally, named Knights Valley (Sir Peter Michael, a very successful businessman, with wide-ranging interests – including wine – received his knighthood in this vintage year 1984.) Also, coincidentally, a rather floral nose; sweeter than expected, good fruit, silky, leathery tannins. *Dining at Chippenham Lodge, Nov 1993* ★★★(★)

**Robert Mondavi, Reserve Pinot Noir** Strange but attractive scent, cherry, privet and mint; medium-sweet, good crisp flavour. Craftily inserted in a blind tasting of top quality burgundies; in fact next to Méo-Camuzet's '89 Richebourg. It acquitted itself well. *At Rodenstock's 13th 'Raritäten Weinprobe', at the Hotel Schloss Reinhartshausen, Oct 1992* ★★★

**Sanford, Santa Barbara Pinot Noir** Rich, singed, 'beetroot' varietal aroma; rather jammy but fragrant. Bitter tannin finish, iodine and iron. Needs time. *At Gidleigh Park, Devon, Sept 1994* ★(★★)?

**Stag's Leap Wine Cellars Cabernet Sauvignon 'SLV' Fay Vineyard** First noted in 1993 at the annual 'Wines of the Californias' in London: spicy, soft; lovely flavour – by far the best Cabernet. Five years later, more mature of course; slightly vegetal nose; easy, stylish, elegant. Dry finish. *At the 'Red' Adams tasting, Winiarski's 25th anniversary, tasting, March 1998* ★★★

## 1990 ★★★★

Smaller crop than 1989 but harvested in near-perfect conditions, particularly in the Napa. A splendid vintage, most drinking well now but the best wines have yet more to come.

**Au Bon Climat, Pinot Noir** Looking round, as always, to find typical varietal character, Steven Spurrier selected this for Christie's wine course introductory sessions which I generally conduct. I therefore have several notes. However, I first tasted it in 1992 after a charity tasting I gave in Charlottesville, Virginia (after my pilgrimage to Monticello, Jefferson's grand home). Too young but with a good crisp flavour. Its slightly bitter tannin, helped by the beef on the first occasion, was more apparent at the tasting. Good wine though. Typical Pinot aroma of black truffles and beetroot. *Several notes, mainly at Christie's wine courses in 1993–94* ★★★

**Beaulieu Vineyard, Georges de Latour Cabernet Sauvignon** Several notes, first in 1996, showing moderately well against stiff competition: 144 of the world's finest reds. Next, in 1997, at the Winemakers' dinner at the Winefest, Sarasota: complete, fragrant; extremely good fruit, weight and balance. 'Lovely but will keep.' Most recently: soft fruit, opening up fragrantly; lovely crisp fruit, sweet mid-palate, dry, refreshing finish. *Last tasted at Vinopolis, London, July 1999* ★★★★

**Calera Jensen Vineyard Pinot Noir** Rich, powerful, concentrated, impressive. *At a Gidleigh Park wine dinner, Devon, Feb 1994* ★★★★(★)

**Caymus Vineyards, Special Selection Cabernet Sauvignon** (100%) First noted at Eigensatz's monumental world '90s horizontal in Luzern: deep, fairly intense; jammy, fragrant; good fruit and flavour. Tasted blind in the Cabernet 'flight', I rated it only half a point below Ch Haut-Brion and slightly higher than Ch Margaux, Ch La Mission Haut-Brion and Dunn. Most recently, the oldest of the five-vintage vertical at an 'Extraordinary California Wines' tasting at Waddesdon Manor: substantial, but very fragrant and stylish. *Last tasted Dec 2000* ★★★(★)

**Dalla Valle, 'Maya'** (Cabernet Sauvignon 55%, Cabernet Franc 45%) One of the California cult wines, the oldest of a five vintage vertical at Waddesdon: opaque; an extraordinary scent, strange, slightly varnishy; very dry, raw texture, tannic. I did not take to this or any of the other Dalla Valles except the '93. Daphne observed that they were all 'Parker wines'. *Over the top. Dec 2000* (★★)

**Dominus** (Cabernet Sauvignon 83%, Cabernet Franc 8%, Merlot 7%, Petit Verdot 2%) In 1996 an average mark in the second 'flight' at the 144 of the world's finest reds tasting. A strange, forthcoming, muffled mocha nose; moderate fruit. Tasted blind I thought it had a Merlot flavour and texture and must be a Pomerol. *In Luzern, June 1996* ★★★

**Groth Cabernet Sauvignon** Lovely ruby; uninhibited, strawberry-like; full of fruit but too self-conscious, with overpowering fragrance. Trying too hard yet, in its way, succeeding. *In New York, Oct 1996* ★★★★

**Jade Mountain Syrah** Opaque; deep, fig-like varietal aroma; loaded with fruit, alcohol, extract and tannin. A massive wine. *Nov 1993. Then* ★★(★★★) *Should be at peak now.*

**Robert Mondavi, Reserve Cabernet Sauvignon** Several notes. First, accompanying venison, in 1994: full of fruit; needed time. Next, in 1996, at the blind tasting of '90s in Luzern. Outclassed. Also I noticed a slightly tinny, beery, 'blown' nose with a touch of *ordure*; sweet, chunky, slightly astringent. Most recently, at the Vintners' gala dinner at Meadowood; still very deep and intense; full, fruity, very tannic. As I was at Bob Mondavi's table, I did not tell him that I thought it had a 'veritable farmyard and hen droppings' nose'. But so do certain well-known châteaux in the Médoc. *Last noted June 2001* ★★★ *in its way.*

**Olivet Lane, Russian River Pinot Noir** A winery new to me. Sweet, distinctive Pinot aroma and flavour. Rich. Tannic. Excellent. *Feb 1993* ★★(★★)

**Opus One** (Cabernet Sauvignon 87%, Cabernet Franc 10%, Merlot 3%) Several notes, first at a Diners' Club 'Vintage Evening' at the Waterside Inn. I was there to speak about the wines. Unhappily, this deep, spicy, full-bodied and still youthful wine dominated the *Bressole de Perdreau Poëlée*. It didn't work with the *Tête à tête de Fromage* either. Ch d'Yquem 1986 had been matched with, but would have been totally destroyed by Michael Roux's out-of-this-world *crème brûlée*, so I suggested abandoning the Opus after the partridge, tasting the Yquem with the cheese, then by itself, then – to prove a point – after a mouthful of *crème brûlée*. Naturally I did all this in the most tactful way. (It was hard work, though.) The next '90 Opus was in Luzern and one of the top wines in the flight: delicious fruit, complete (1996). The following year showing magnificently well at the Opus One masterclass; velvety fruit; very sweet, mouthfilling and beautifully constructed. *Last tasted Dec 1997* ★★★★(★)

**Joseph Phelps, Insignia** Impressively deep; brambly fruit and oak; positive, good fruit, overall crisp and dry. Good wine. *Holding its own against stiff competition in Luzern, June 1996* ★★★★

**Ridge, Monte Bello Cabernet Sauvignon** Keeping up the pace, tasted blind in Luzern (1996): deeper and richer-looking than most in its Cabernet flight; nose very sweet, almost malty, really over the top; good, chunky fruit. Most recently, the oldest of six vintages at Waddesdon Manor: still very deep; nose harmonious, elegant, berry-like; fairly sweet, fullish, good fruit, flavour and balance. *Last tasted Dec 2000* ★★★★

**Saintsbury, Reserve Pinot Noir** Most unusual to serve any, let alone two California wines at a Saintsbury Club dinner. Sweet, rich, good length, an upturned, bitter, iron finish. Unready. *Oct 1996* ★(★★)

**Sanford, Pinot Noir** Good flavour though still hard. One of my favourite California Pinots. *Feb 1993* ★★(★★) *Should be delicious now.*

**Sanford and Benedict Vineyard Barrel Select Pinot Noir** Deep; lively Pinot aroma; dry, crisp, spicy, very good. *Feb 1993* ★★(★★★)

**Shafer Hillside Select Cabernet Sauvignon** First tasted in 1993: lovely fruit; soft, full, fleshy; a bit too sweet with food. Next, at the world's best '90s tasting in 1996: opaque; sweet, rather low score (1996). Most recently, malty and overpriced. *In San Francisco, Nov 1998* ★★

**Shafer Merlot** Soft, slightly jammy, but good. *Feb 1993* ★★★

**Stag's Leap Wine Cellars, Cask 23** Several notes, identical marks to Opus One at the blind tasting of '90s in 1996: fragrant, lovely; very sweet, perfect weight, delicious flavour. Wonderful vinosity, balance and grip at the 'Red' Adams tasting (1998) and the best of a Cask 23 quartet at Waddesdon Manor: deep, but maturing; well-developed nose, rich, touch of mocha; sweet, complete, richness masking tannins. *Dec 2000* ★★★★★

**Stag's Leap Wine Cellars, Cabernet Sauvignon 'SLV'** Deep, rich, velvety; full- flavoured, lovely texture, with tannic grip, and **Fay Vineyard** the least mature-looking of the three '90s; fragrant, herbaceous; good fruit, grip and length. *Both at the 'Red' Adams tasting, March 1998* ★★★

## 1991 ★★★★★

Excellent vintage. Cool spring followed by successful flowering promising an abundant harvest, but the summer was also cool by Californian standards. Leaves were removed and crops thinned to encourage concentration and maturation. An unbroken Indian summer brought the grapes to full maturity. The net result was intensity of colour; good natural degrees of acidity thanks to the extended cool summer conditions and levels of alcohol conducive to finesse rather than massive structure. One cloud on the horizon was the spread of phylloxera, particularly in the Napa, where it was devastating whole blocks of vines on the valley floor.

In short, there are some lovely wines.

**Araujo, Eisele Vineyard Cabernet Sauvignon** The first of the 'cult wines' at a tasting of 'Extraordinary California Wines' … ' vintages 1990–1997', held in The Dairy at Waddesdon Manor. I confess that I had hardly heard of Araujo, let alone tasted any of its wine, so this – and much else at this literally beyond-price tasting – was both novel and salutary. The '91, the first of five vintages: medium-deep, still with youthful rim; very Bordeaux-like 'cheese' and berries, spicy, minty, opening up well; medium dryness and body, lean, good flavour and an interesting opening shot. *Dec 2000* ★★★(★)

**Beaulieu Vineyard, Georges de Latour Cabernet Sauvignon** Deep; low-keyed, spicy, opening up with whiff of mulberry, then more fig-like; sweet from start to finish, masking substantial tannins. *At the centenary tasting, Vinopolis, London, July 1999* ★★★(★)

**Caymus Vineyards, Special Selection Cabernet Sauvignon** (100%) Medium-deep ruby; well-developed, crisp fruit, opening up spicily; dryish, stylish, marked tannin and acidity. *At Waddesdon Manor, Buckinghamshire, Dec 2000* ★★(★★)

**Chateau Montelena, Montelena Estate** 'Cool vintage, high acid year'. Heavy sediment noted. Still fairly youthful; a bit of bottle stink soon cleared, soft, harmonious; very attractive, spicy, lean, elegant, Bordeaux-like, dry finish. *At the Montelena seminar, New York, Oct 2000* ★★★(★)

**Dalla Valle, 'Maya'** (Cabernet Sauvignon 55%, Cabernet Franc 45%) Opaque; minty, the Cabernet Franc crisp aroma distinguishable, holding harmoniously; medium-sweet, good texture, mature fruit, marked, rather harsh tannin. Preferred to all, except the '93. *At Waddesdon Manor, Buckinghamshire, Dec 2000* ★★★(★★)

**Diamond Creek, Red Rock Terrace Cabernet Sauvignon** Medium-deep; fragrant; crisp, dry, more acidity than tannin. *Tasted al fresco with Al Brounstein, June 2001* ★★★

**Dominus, Napanook Vineyard** (Cabernet Sauvignon 90%, Cabernet Franc 9%, Petit Verdot 1%) Opaque, intense; very sweet, ripe, full-bodied (alcohol 13.5%), good fruit. *In New York, Feb 1997* ★★★(★)

**Harlan Estate** The first of five consecutive vintages tasted at Waddesdon Manor, December 2000. Very deep, intense; substantial fruit, after 50 minutes nose thick, rich; dry, spicy, tannic. Frankly I didn't much take to it. Daphne was positively rude. Next, tasted at the Vintners' gala dinner at Meadowood: swingeingly tannic and, frankly, undrinkable. *Last tasted June 2001.*

**Robert Mondavi, Reserve Cabernet Sauvignon** Opaque core though showing some maturity; sweet, full (alcohol 13.5%), a touch of iron. *At the Napa Valley Auction Chairman's dinner, at the Mondavis' hilltop home, June 2001* ★★★(★)

**Robert Mondavi, Woodbridge Zinfandel** Woodbridge is Mondavi's more modestly priced range. Sweet, soft, fruity, attractive. Good value. *Dec 1993* ★★★ *Early drinking.*

**Opus One** (Cabernet Sauvignon 88%, Cabernet Franc 6%, Merlot 5%, Malbec 1%) Deep, velvety, 'legs' like Romanesque arches; crisp, fruity, mouthwatering, very sweet, fairly full-bodied (13.5%), tolerable tannin, good acidity. *At Christie's Opus One masterclass, Dec 1997* ★★★(★)

**Qupé, Syrah** Good, deep ruby; considerable depth of fruit, sweet, rich, delicious. What marvellous, relatively new to

California varieties now being produced. *Brought to taste by Ursula Hermacinski, Christie's star auctioneer, Feb 1994* ★★★★

**Ridge, Monte Bello** The second of five consecutive vintages served with Ludgershall beef: very deep, rich; elegant, harmonious, crisp berries; more meaty than the '90; medium sweetness and body, rich, lovely flavour. A class act. *At Waddesdon Manor, Dec 2000* ★★★★★

**Shafer Merlot** Full, soft, fleshy, rounded. Better by itself than with food. *Nov 1993* ★★★★ *Should be perfect now.*

**Stag's Leap Wine Cellars, Cask 23** Medium-deep; low-keyed, fragrant, whiff of vanilla; sweet, rich extract, tannin and acidity. *At the 'Red' Adams tasting, March 1998* ★★★

**Stag's Leap Wine Cellars, Cabernet Sauvignon Fay Vineyard** Lovely colour, still youthful; sweet, slightly singed fragrance and taste. *March 1998* ★★★

# 1992 ★★★★

For the first time in six years there was adequate winter rainfall to ease drought conditions. Flowering was early and successful. The early summer was somewhat unsettled but by mid-July the warmth had returned, with a crescendo of heat in August. Warm days and cool nights returned resulting in an early and well-nigh perfect harvest.

**Araujo, Eisele Vineyard Cabernet Sauvignon** The second of five consecutive vintages: fairly deep; sweeter, richer, more harmonious than the '91 with a rich, tarry uplift after 30 minutes in the glass; chewy, fullish, vaguely Ch Latour-like, good fruit and discreet oak. *At the tasting of 'Extraordinary American Wines' in The Dairy at Waddesdon Manor, Buckinghamshire, Dec 2000* ★★★★(★)

**Au Bon Climat, Arroyo Grande Valley Pinot Noir** Another successful vine 'transplant' and used at Christie's wine course seminars to demonstrate the varietal character: correct 'burgundian' colour, palish, soft, warm red brown with open rim; earthy, vegetal Pinot aroma; sweet, nice weight, though I noticed alcohol 13.6% on the main label, 12.5% on the back label. Who cares? Good varietal flavour and somewhat bitter tannic finish. Needs food. *Last tasted Nov 1995* ★★(★★)

**Beaulieu Vineyard, Georges de Latour Cabernet Sauvignon** Rich 'legs', nose and taste. Scents of vanilla, raspberry; very sweet, full, chewy, good fruit and balance. *At the Centenary tasting at Vinopolis, London, July 1999* ★★★(★)

**Caymus Vineyards, Special Selection Cabernet Sauvignon** The third vintage in the Caymus vertical. Very deep though hint of maturity; nose restrained but with good fruit and whiff of eucalyptus, opening up crisply; medium-sweet, lovely flavour, fragrant, more oaky than the '91. Very good with the quail. *At the Cult wine lunch at Waddesdon Manor, Dec 2000* ★★★★(★)

**Colgin, Herb Lamb Vineyard Cabernet Sauvignon** A cult wine made by the cult producer Helen Turley, the first of four consecutive vintages served at a Colgin dinner at Christie's, Park Avenue. The cost I noted: $300 a bottle. Fairly deep, rich 'legs'; fairly high volatile acidity; concentrated, spicy. Impressive, but scarcely a food wine. *Dec 1998* (★★★★★) *for those who like this sort of wine.*

**Dalla Valle, 'Maya'** (Cabernet Sauvignon 55% and Cabernet Franc 45%) Fairly deep; low-keyed though deep; dry, lean, somewhat raw tannin and acidity. Not for me. *At Waddesdon Manor, Dec 2000* (★★)?

**Dominus, Napanook Vineyard** (Cabernet Sauvignon 64%, Cabernet Franc 15%, Merlot 19%, Petit Verdot 2%)

Produced and bottled by the John Daniel Society, St Helena. Fairly deep, velvety, mature rim, rich, initially vegetal, sweetened in the glass, harmonious, soft toffee, finally lovely fruit; sweet, soft. Good fruit yet slightly raw finish. The oldest of six vintages kindly supplied by Christian Moueix, who was in the Napa Valley, for me to taste. *In San Francisco, March 2002* ★★★ *This ten-year-old is neither young and fruity nor 'sear and yellow'.*

**Harlan Estate** Medium-deep; good fruit, rich, touch of tar; very dry, like a supercharged Médoc. I found it tiring to the palate. *At Waddesdon Manor, Dec 2000* ★★(★)

**Opus One** (Cabernet Sauvignon 90%, Cabernet Franc 8%, Merlot 2%) Good colour; very fragrant, crisper than the '91 with a sort of dancing fruitiness; intriguing flavour, cherry-like fruit, though full-bodied (alcohol 13.9%), not heavy. Marvellous acidity. *At Christie's Opus One masterclass, Dec 1997* ★★★★(★)

**Qupé, Syrah** Used at the Christie's wine course introductory sessions to demonstrate varietal character. Deep, impressive, fairly intense, just starting to mature; a very good, wholesome, 'warm *terroir*' smell, an almost exaggerated Syrah nose, more like syrup of figs, the old-fashioned medicine for those suffering from constipation; rich, full-flavoured, rich but not alcoholic (in fact a surprisingly modest 12.5%); lovely fruit, peppery, tannic finish. *Last noted at Christie's, Nov 1995* ★★★(★)

**Ridge, Monte Bello** What Paul Draper's well-established classic was doing at this tasting amid the cult wines I do not know, though I suppose that, in a way, he does have a cult following. Impressively deep but by no means hefty. Medium-sweet, agreeable weight and flavour. *At Waddesdon Manor, Dec 2000* ★★★★(★)

**Screaming Eagle, Cabernet Sauvignon** 'The cult of cults'! Made from a small parcel of wines in a bigger vineyard owned by Jean Phillips and production is limited to 175–200 cases per vintage. In 1992, just 170 cases were made and sold for a phenomenal price on allocation. Fairly deep, mature; decent nose; medium sweetness and weight, crisp fruit. Unquestionably good. A very agreeable wine – for collectors only. *At Waddesdon Manor, Dec 2000* ★★★★★

**Shafer, Hillside Select Cabernet Sauvignon** Opaque core; very meaty-malty character; sweet, hefty, crisp, spicy with 'interesting tannins!' Doug Shafer, an old friend whom I much admire, told me that he aimed to have a minimum alcoholic strength of 14% for all his wines, including Chardonnay. Unsurprisingly they are heady. *Dining at Shafer, June 2001* ★★(★★) *Top of the class.*

**Stag's Leap Wine Cellars, Cask 23** First noted in 1998 at the 'Red' Adams tasting at Meadowood: deep, still youthful; good depth of fruit, texture and grip. Next, at the 'Extraordinary California Wines' tasting at Waddesdon Manor: medium-deep, bright garnet; nose very rich but not sweet, touch of mocha and smell of the barrel cellar; sweet, fullish, very attractive. *Last tasted Dec 2000* ★★★(★) *Possibly 5 stars when fully developed.*

**Stag's Leap Wine Cellars, Cabernet Sauvignon Fay Vineyard** (We were informed by Warren Winiarski that he used the best vats from the Fay vineyard for his Cask 23 blend.) Medium-deep, open rimmed; very fragrant, herbaceous, lively. *At Meadowood, March 1998* ★★★(★)

**Stag's Leap Wine Cellars, Cabernet Sauvignon 'SLV'** Attractive colour; a wet dog, slightly sweaty (tannic) nose; sweet, more powerful than the '92 Cabernet Fay Vineyard Good grip. *At the 'Red' Adams tasting at Meadowood, March 1998* ★★(★★)

# 1993 ★★ to ★★★★

Extremely variable quality and an overall loss of about 10% of the crop due to bizarre, erratic, and totally unpredictable weather conditions from spring to harvest time. Unusually cold and rainy in the early summer followed by heatwaves alternating with cold spells into October.

**Araujo, Eisele Vineyard Cabernet Sauvignon** Very deep, intense, rich 'legs'; minty and meaty developing fruit and spice; medium-sweet, full-bodied, amply supplied with fruit and spice. Very tannic. Needs food. *At the 'Extraordinary California Wines' hosted by friends of the Russian National Orchestra and Lord Rothschild, at a tasting dinner in the Dairy, Waddesdon Manor, Dec 2000* ★★(★★★) *The RNO tasting, noted here and either side of this vintage, afforded a unique opportunity to put the so-called cult wines into perspective.*

**Beaulieu Vineyard, Georges de Latour Cabernet Sauvignon** Cabernet Sauvignon 100%, 50-50 American and French oak: first noted in 1997 at the Winefest in Sarasota: black cherry; low-keyed nose and taste. Full-bodied. Good wine, unready. More recently, similar appearance but much more forthcoming on the nose, a great whoosh of high-toned, minty fragrance, then green olives; very sweet, full-bodied, chewy, brambly fruit, rather raw texture. *Last noted at the Beaulieu Vineyard centenary tasting at Vinopolis, London, July 1999* ★★(★★) *2003–2010.*

**Beaulieu Vineyard 'Tapestry' Reserve** A move from the 100% Cabernet Sauvignon to 75%, with Merlot 16%, Cabernet Franc 8%, Malbec 1%. Medium-deep; fleshy, well made but very tannic. *At the Florida Winefest trade tastings, April 1997* ★(★★)

**Philip Togni, Ca' Togni** A rather bizarre wine and title which, once you know about the peripatetic Phillip Togni, is unsurprising – British Army, Geology at Imperial College, London; then with Shell; then to Montpellier, Chile, Algeria, Bordeaux (Ch Lascombes and enology under Professor Peynaud) and California (Mayacamus, Gallo, Chappelet and Cuvaison). A rather drab tawny red; singed muscatel nose; cool, sweet, figgy, grapey taste. Good acidity. *At a wine dinner at Gidleigh Park, Devon, March 1997* ★★?

**Colgin, Herb Lamb Vineyard Cabernet Sauvignon** (In the lower Howell Mountain, the north-east corner of the Napa Valley.) Made by Helen Turley. I first tasted it when it was brought by a generous guest to a BYOB dinner in New York: very deep, velvety, immature; full of fruit; extremely flavoury and fragrant. An original flavour. Next at a wine department lunch in 1996 at Christie's, Park Avenue – appropriately, for Ann Colgin used to work for Christie's before she later struck out as a wine auctioneer. Deep ruby; good fruit; rich, easy to drink but less good as a 'food wine' – which is one of the problems with these overstrung cult wines. More recently, still deep, with opaque core; very fleshy, crystallised violets scent; sweet, very rich and spicy. A bit of a show off. *Last tasted Dec 1998* ★★★ *Impressive, but this is not my style of wine.*

**Dalla Valle, 'Maya'** Only 300 cases made. Fairly deep; very good, rich, meaty nose which sweetened in the glass; good body, fruit, extract. For me the best of their '90–'94 range. *At Waddesdon Manor, Dec 2000* ★★★(★★)

**Harlan Estate** Deep; good fruit and oak, opened up richly, both 'thick' and spirity – hard to explain; good fruit and spice, full-bodied. Not wholly convinced. *At Waddesdon Manor, Dec 2000* ★(★★)?

**Opus One** (Cabernet Sauvignon 89%, Cabernet Franc 7%, Merlot 4%) Good colour, still a rim of purple; beautiful, good depth, complete – a most attractive wine, spicy with a powerful finish. Needs time. *At the Opus One masterclass at Christie's, Dec 1997* ★★(★★★) *2003–2012?*

**Qupé, Syrah** Following the success of the '92, selected to represent the Syrah grape variety at Christie's wine course introductory class. Deep, intense, immature; 'hot', fig-like fruit, sweet, rich; superficially sweet; substantial, good extract, length, tannin and acidity. In short, all the component parts. *Jan 1996* ★★(★) *Now–2008.*

**Ridge, Monte Bello** Deep, full-flavoured and tannic. Both classic and idiosyncratic at the same time. *At Waddesdon Manor, Dec 2000* ★★(★★)

**Screaming Eagle, Cabernet Sauvignon** The second of four vintages: deep, intense; rich bouquet and flavour. Sweet, attractive, blackcurrant fruit, citrus-touch, tannin. *At Waddesdon Manor, Dec 2000* ★★★★(★) *Now–2010?*

**Shafer, Hillside Select Cabernet Sauvignon** Dry, lean, crisp, good acidity (difficult to taste in Shafer's extended *cave* which still smelled of new concrete). *Before dinner, June 2001* ★(★★★) *I trust.*

**Stag's Leap Wine Cellars, Cask 23** Slight bottle variation. Fairly deep, intense; complete, good fruit, attenuated and acidic. *At the 'Red' Adams tasting, March 1998* ★★(★) *Drink soon–2010.*

**Stag's Leap Wine Cellars, Cabernet Sauvignon 'SLV'** Medium-deep, mature; most distinctive, violet-scented, fully evolved; sweet, soft, loose knit yet some grip. *March 1998* ★★★ *Drink soon.*

# 1994 variable, up to ★★★★★

Too much rain; cool conditions – not our idea of California. Generally uneven and mediocre though Napa and Sonoma reds better than most and an excellent year for Cabernet Sauvignon. I have tasted a wide range and the best – or at least for me the most interesting – are listed below:

**Araujo, Eisele Vineyard Cabernet Sauvignon** (including Cabernet Franc 4% and Petit Verdot 3%) Daphne and Bart Araujo bought the well-established Eisele vineyard in 1990. First tasted at the Wine Experience 'Top Ten Tasting', November 1998, which included four '94 California wines, one white: predictably opaque and so intense that the colour seemed to pressurise the sides of the glass; lovely, spicy eucalyptus; sweet, rich fruit, silky tannins. Then at Waddesdon: still very deep; very good, spicy nose and flavour. Tannic. New oak finish. *Last tasted Dec 2000* ★★(★★★)

**Au Bon Climat, Pinot Noir** Correct, very pale violet tinge, open rim; 'warm', harmonious, vegetal nose, settling down contentedly in the glass, lovely, suave; sweetish, fairly substantial (as with the '92, different alcoholic strengths on labels: front 13%, back 12.5%). Good flavour and fruit. Adequate tannin and acidity. *At Christie's wine course, Jan 1996* ★★★(★)

**Beaulieu Vineyard, Signet Collection Ensemble** (Southern French varieties: Syrah, Grenache and others) Medium, soft cherry red; crisp, berry-like nose: good flavour but bitter tannins. *With beef Wellington at the Winemakers' dinner, Sarasota's Winefest, April 1997* ★★) *This annual wine fair is held in the grounds of the Long Boat Key hotel and country club. It is combined with a charity wine auction conducted by my colleague David Elswood and, as on this occasion, by myself.*

**Beaulieu Vineyard, Reserve Pinot Noir** From Carneros. Ten months in French oak. Deep, velvety; 'toasted beetroot', forthcoming, rich, deep, spicy; full, rich, fruity. *Very good in its way, Sarasota, April 1997* ★★★

**Beaulieu Vineyard, Georges de Latour Cabernet Sauvignon** Fairly deep, rich; plummy, figgy fruit; like a young Bordeaux; very sweet, rich fruit. All front end and middle. New clones we were told. *At the Beaulieu Vineyard centenary tasting, Vinopolis, London, July 1979* (★★★)? *Hard to know quite where this is going.*

**Beringer, Cabernet Sauvignon** A fixture at Christie's introductory wine courses. Eight good notes from October 1997. Well made and totally satisfactory. Maturing over this period. Very good fruit. Delicious. *Last tasted Jan 1999* ★★★(★)

**Caymus Vineyards, Napa Valley Cabernet Sauvignon** ('Regular' not Special Selection: 80% of the grapes bought from local growers). Also first noted at the *Wine Spectator's* 'Top Ten Tasting' in 1998: very deep, velvety; low-keyed, tarry'; lovely flavour, great length, stylish but very tannic, with bitter finish. More recently: very similar description. Very fragrant, totally different to the preceding '92. Delicious to drink by itself. *Last noted at Waddesdon Manor, Dec 2000* ★★★★★

**Chateau Montelena, Montelena Estate** Starting to mature; deliciously sweet nose and taste, rich, with edgy tannin and acid finish. We were informed that the wine had 'long chain tannins' and that it had not yet lost its puppy-stage fruit. *At the Wine Experience, New York, Oct 2000* ★★(★★)

**Colgin, Herb Lamb Vineyard Cabernet Sauvignon** Deep, rich; gushing scent, crystallised violets and taste. Unquestionably dashing and flavoury. Very tannic. *At Christie's Colgin dinner in New York, Dec 1998* ★★★★ *I cannot resist seduction.*

**Dalla Valle, Maya** (Maya is Gustav Dalla Valle's daughter who took over after he died.) The youngest of five consecutive vintages: opaque, immature; low keyed nose, oak, meaty then minty; full of fruit, good length but a swingeingly tannic finish. *At Waddesdon Manor, Dec 2000* ★★(★★★) *Hugely impressive but simply not the wine for me.*

**Diamond Creek, Volcanic Hill Cabernet Sauvignon** (100% Cabernet Sauvignon) Immature mauve, rich 'legs'; dry, very crisp. *At an al fresco picnic, June 2001* (★★★)

---

### Christie's wine courses

*Started up by Steven Spurrier and myself in 1982 and held throughout the year ever since. Each course comprises five sessions, each covering a different type of wine. Initially it was devoted to the wines of France. Then I persuaded Steven to put in at least one decent German Riesling. Now, this introductory session usually has 'new world' wines to illustrate the character of old-world varietals. Times have changed. There are also masterclasses on fine and rare wines. (I stick to talking about Bordeaux, in truth because then I don't need to do any homework!) At one time I was stressing the importance of 'balance' in a wine, of having all the right components in harmony. 'An unbalanced wine', I said, 'can be like a chap with one leg!' This got me into trouble because, when the tasting finished, out hopped a man with one leg. It was most embarrassing.*

*Daphne has sat in on every single one of my sessions: she sits next to me, takes notes and tells me to either hurry up and get on with it, or reminds me if I've forgotten something. She's heard every one of my stories dozens of times but I think she comes in case I get up to mischief afterwards – like the way she collects me after every wine dinner!*

**Dominus, Napanook Vineyard** (Cabernet Sauvignon 72%, the lowest percentage used between 1983, the first vintage, and 2000, Cabernet Franc 11%, Merlot 12% and Petit Verdot 5%). Now labelled '*Produced and bottled by Dominus Estate Corporation*': deep; extraordinary scents of tar and citrus fruit; very sweet, delicious flavour, leathery tannins. After two hours a raw feel to it. *At 1915 Pierce Street, San Francisco, March 2002* ★★★★★ *Probably best to drink soon after opening or decanting.*

**Harlan Estate** Very deep; initially fruity, meaty, oak, but I liked it less and less (Daphne, outspoken as always, said it reminded her of Fernet Branca). Better on the palate: good texture; power, flesh and fruit. Dry finish. *At Waddesdon Manor, Dec 2000* ★★★(★★) *for those who like this sort of wine.*

**Niebaum-Coppola, Rubicon** (Cabernet Sauvignon and Merlot) Deep, youthful, brambly, spicy, lovely; fullish (alcohol 14.1%), long, dry finish. *At a memorable lunch hosted by Ferdinand de Metz, President of the CIA (not at Langley; the Culinary Institute of America), after a tour of their immensely impressive facilities at Hyde Park, NY State, Dec 1998* ★★★★

**Opus One** (Cabernet Sauvignon 93%, Cabernet Franc 4%, Merlot 2%, Malbec 1%) Heaven knows – or perhaps the winemaker does – what the Malbec adds. Good, deep, impressive appearance; Bordeaux-like cedar nose, sweet, very scented; a powerhouse, far too immature even to taste. Overall dry, crisp, fruit dominant, long trajectory. *The youngest vintage in the Opus One masterclass at Christie's, Dec 1997* ★(★★★)? *I presume a long life.*

**Joseph Phelps, Insignia** (Cabernet Sauvignon 88%, Merlot 10%, Cabernet Franc 2%) Mainly from vineyards on the Rutherford Bench and Stags Leap area of the Napa. The winemaker, Fred Williams, introducing this wine, informed us that there was a severe thunderstorm in October at which time 80% of the Cabernet Sauvignon was still on the vine but it managed to ripen further thereafter. Opaque core, intense, very rich 'legs'; 'classic', touch of smokiness; sweet, tarry fruit – not unlike Ch Pontet-Canet in certain vintages – well made, rich, tannic. *At the* Wine Spectator*'s 'Top Ten Tasting', chaired by Jim Gordon, the Managing Editor, New York, Nov 1998* ★★★(★★)

**Qupé, Syrah** Very deep, velvety, opaque; unyielding, touch of iron; immature, severe, crisp fruit, tannic. Lacking length. Disappointing. *At Gidleigh Park, Devon, April 2001* (★★★)

**Ridge, Monte Bello** Very deep; glorious fruit, flavoury and spicy nose and palate very tannic. *At Waddesdon, Dec 2000* ★★(★★★) *A long laster.*

**Saintsbury, Carneros Pinot Noir** Mellow; very good varietal aroma, with warmth and depth; pleasant sweetness, crisp fruit, soft tannins. *At my 'Introduction to Wine and Wine Tasting' on the luxurious* Seabourn Spirit *somewhere off Sumatra, Jan 1998* ★★★

**Screaming Eagle, Cabernet Sauvignon** (see also the '92). Rich appearance, nose and taste. Most attractive. *At Waddesdon Manor, Dec 2000* ★★★★★ *Lovely now. I suspect most will either have been consumed or hoarded by rich collectors. Few will have an opportunity of actually drinking it.*

**Shafer, Hillside Select Cabernet Sauvignon** In 1999 very deep, velvety; fairly sweet, very full and fruity. Far too hefty (alcohol 14.5%) but impressive. Most recently, sweet, delicious to taste but not my idea of an ideal food wine. Still, I mustn't complain. *In Shafer's cave, June 2001* ★★★★

**Stag's Leap Wine Cellars, Cask 23** First noted at the 'Red' Adams tasting in 1998: still youthful; low-keyed nose, marvellous fruit, complete. More recently: fairly deep, brown rimmed; vegetal; some sweetness, full-bodied, drinking pretty

well (Daphne thought it the best of the 'flight'. As usual, I dithered). *In the Dairy at Waddesdon Manor, Dec 2000* ★★★(★) *Ready now but will keep.*

# 1995 ★★ to ★★★★

Another difficult year with varying results. Flooded vineyards were a problem and cold weather prolonged flowering and had the knock-on effect of delaying the eventual harvest for two to four weeks. Some delicious wines were made.

**Araujo, Eisele Vineyard Cabernet Sauvignon** Deep, fairly intense; low-keyed at first but opening up fragrantly; medium sweetness and body, delicious flavour, crisp fruit, good tannin and acidity. The fifth consecutive vintage which led me to the conclusion that Araujo deserved its cult followers. *At Waddesdon Manor, Dec 2000* ★★(★★★)

**Beaulieu Vineyard, Georges de Latour Cabernet Sauvignon** The current release at the time of tasting, though still looking immature; almost ridiculously sweet aroma of raspberry and scented vanilla; full, rich fruit, curious toasty flavour, soft and spicy. A thoroughly specious wine, pandering, I thought, to the popular taste. By the time we had ploughed through the '96, '97 and '98, I was exasperated and made myself very unpopular by suggesting to our Beaulieu Vineyard hosts that they should go downstairs and put their noses into two of the wine scent dispensers: one labelled oak – all vanilla; the other, I think, Cabernet – pure raspberry. *At the Beaulieu Vineyard Centenary tasting at Vinopolis, London, July 1999. No further comment.*

**Caymus Vineyards, Special Selection Cabernet Sauvignon** Very deep; meaty, well developed nose, deliciously emerging Cabernet aroma; well constituted. Rather oaky. *At Waddesdon Manor, Dec 2000* ★★★(★)

**Colgin, Herb Lamb Vineyard Cabernet Sauvignon** The last of the four consecutive vintages – value well over $1000 – at lunch in Christie's New York boardroom; opaque; nose not as exaggerated as the '93 and '94; complete, impressive, even enjoyable. *Last tasted Dec 1998* ★★★(★) *I shall not try to predict its future.*

**Diamond Creek, Volcanic Hill Cabernet Sauvignon** (Cabernet Sauvignon 100%) Al Brounstein's 8-acre/3.2-ha vineyard (Red Rock Terrace is 3 acres/1.2ha and Gravelly Meadows 5 acres/2ha), and a tribute to his foresight in spotting these contrasting soils in the tiny Diamond Mountain valley in 1968, and his energy and expertise in producing one of the most consistently fine Napa Cabernets; the sweet and spicy '95 no exception. *Two notes, one in 1998 and the other picnicking by his lake, June 2001* ★★★★

**Dominus, Napanook Vineyard** (Cabernet Sauvignon 80%, Cabernet Franc 10%, Merlot 6%, Petit Verdot 4%). Dark cherry, still youthful; extraordinarily scented, rich, spicy, mocha; very sweet, full-bodied (alcohol 14.1%) soft entry and mid-palate, good length, rich, soft tannins, touch of iron. *At 1915 Pierce Street, San Francisco, March 2002* ★★★(★★)

**Harlan Estate** The last of five consecutive vintages. Spicy, oaky nose which opened up fairly spectacularly; good fruit and all the component parts were correct, but noticeably tannic. Frankly, I found Harlan uneven. Their first vintage was the 1990 which now sells for up to $1000 per bottle. Annual production up to 2000 cases and released – on allocation – at $160 a bottle. *At Waddesdon Manor, Dec 2000* ★★★(★)

**Robert Mondavi, Reserve Cabernet Sauvignon** (including Merlot 4% and Cabernet Franc 4%) Three notes within three days, one at the trial dinner, the next at a press and VIP tasting I chaired prior to the *Decanter* Millennium dinner, and the third, presented by Marcia Mondavi, at the dinner itself. Rich cherry red, still youthful; rather muffled fruit, spicy; touch of sweetness, crisp, but in each instance I noted a bitter tannic finish somewhat ameliorated by the mushroom dish served. *At Vinopolis, London, July 1999* ★★(★)

**Opus One** (Cabernet Sauvignon 86%, Cabernet Franc 7%, Merlot 5%, Malbec 2%. Skin contact 39 days, 18 months in new French oak). The first of three vintages kindly supplied for me to taste and brought to my son's house in San Francisco: medium depth and intensity; bright, fragrant, crisp fruit and oak, its bouquet developing sweetly; rich fruit, good flavour, fair length, touch of tar and tannin. *March 2002* ★★★(★★)

**PlumpJack, Reserve Cabernet Sauvignon** After a fairly protracted lunch tasting (34 'Extraordinary California Wines') I and fellow guests were treated to a blind tasting. This was the fourth of the six-wine line-up: impressively deep, youthful; very fragrant, the most Bordeaux-like nose of the day; excellent flavour and balance. I added 'classic'. It turned out to be from a winery belonging to one of our hosts, Gordon Getty, in whose private plane the entire American contingent had crossed the Atlantic. *At Waddesdon Manor, Dec 2000* ★★★★

**Qupé, Syrah** Dark cherry; harmonious, fig-like varietal aroma, lovely fruit, spicy – like herbs from Provence; full of character, complete. A lovely wine. *At a Christie's wine course session, Jan 1997* ★★★★

**Ridge, Monte Bello** The youngest of five consecutive vintages. Dry, firm, very good. *At Waddesdon Manor, Dec 2000* ★★★(★)

**Screaming Eagle, Cabernet Sauvignon** The last of four consecutive vintages. I confess I had been prepared to pooh-pooh this cult of cults; I equally confess I thought all four wines were delicious. Naturally, because of its name, fabled reputation and tiny production, it commands a price that makes Romanée-Conti look like a bargain. Do I think that these prices are ridiculous? Of course, but – as with Le Pin and other cult wines – they bear no relation to reality and I think that other more classic producers should just shrug their shoulders and get on with life. *At Waddesdon Manor, Dec 2000* ★★★★(★)

**Stag's Leap Wine Cellars, Cabernet Sauvignon Fay Vineyard** Delicious, crisp, tannic. *Nov 1998* ★★★(★)

**Shafer, Hillside Select Cabernet Sauvignon** Opaque, velvety; impossible to smell in a cellar which combined young wine and wet concrete; fairly dry and full-bodied, crisp fruit. *At a quick walk-around tasting at Shafer, June 2001* ★★(★★)

# 1996 ★★★

A variable year. Cool spring, but one of the earliest bud breaks; rain in May caused vines to 'shatter' during flowering. Heatwaves in July and August, then abruptly cooling in the Napa and delaying ripening. The increased 'hang time' is supposed to add complexity. Cabernet Sauvignon and Merlot were the least affected.

**Arietta** The first vintage of the new partnership of Kongsgaard and Hatton, named after a famous piece by Beethoven. First tasted, with difficulty because of noise and distraction, during the charity auction dinner Fritz Hatton and I were involved with in San Juan: deep ruby; dry, crisp fruit, bitter tannin and iron finish. Most recently, the oldest of a six-vintage vertical brought by Fritz Hatton for me to taste: still

youthful and vigorous, like its progenitor: an unusual two-part, very scented tangerine and oak nose and taste, the citrus-like Cabernet Franc apparent. Very good. Still a bit raw. *Last tasted March 2002* ★★★(★)

**Beaulieu Vineyard, Georges de Latour Cabernet Sauvignon** Bottled October 1998. Exaggerated raspberry and vanilla, similar to the '95, also, I thought, a trace of excess volatile acidity. Overall dry and astringent. The trouble is, Beaulieu Vineyards customers will have been drinking this soon after its release in November 1999. *At Beaulieu Vineyards centenary tasting at Vinopolis, London, July 1999.*

**Chateau Montelena, Montelena Estate** Very deep; nicely evolved, soft, rich, 'hot vintage' scent; sweet, full, masked tannins. *At the Montelena seminar, New York, Oct 2000* ★★★(★)

**Diamond Creek, Red Rock Terrace Cabernet Sauvignon** Fine, deep, velvety; very good fruit and flesh. Complete. Tannic. At a charity tasting of wines from the Napa Valley, introduced by Jancis Robinson and conducted by Hugo Rose MW, of Lay & Wheeler, in aid of Parkinson's disease. Al Brounstein who founded Diamond Creek in the late 1960s is severely afflicted by Parkinson's but it has not diminished his enthusiasm, expertise – or business sense. This '96 has a UK price tag of £61.50 per bottle. *Tasted Nov 1999* ★★★★

**Dominus, Napanook Vineyard** (Cabernet Sauvignon 82%, Cabernet Franc 10%, Merlot 4%, Petit Verdot 4%). Deep, rich, maturing; fragrant, citrus-like, opening up into soft brown sugar, then, after an hour, extraordinarily full and harmonious; sweet, soft, delicious fruit, crystallised violets. Outstanding. *At 1915 Pierce Street, San Francisco, March 2002* ★★★★★

**Groth, Napa Cabernet Sauvignon** Plummy; sweet, thick, attractive, blackberry-like fragrance and flavour. Drinking well. *On board the* Crystal Symphony, *Sept 1999* ★★★

**Kongsgaard, Napa Valley Syrah** Said to be 100% Syrah but included 3% Viognier! First tasted in 1998 with difficulty, at the dinner auction in San Juan: deep, velvety; its smell just like a Player's Navy Cut cigarette packet; dry, still raw. Next, tasted with John Kongsgaard: now more like wine, harmonious, rich fruit, developing a whiff of strawberry; sweeter though lean and astringent. Blackberry-like fruit. *At 1915 Pierce Street, San Francisco, March 2002* ★★(★★)

**Opus One** (Cabernet Sauvignon 86%, Cabernet Franc 8%, Merlot 3%, Malbec 3%. Small crop, picked mid-September, 37 days skin contact, 19 months in new French oak.) One of *Wine Spectator*'s 'Top Ten' wines, presented in October 2000 by Philippe Sereys de Rothschild, Baroness Philippine's son: peppery, spicy eucalyptus scent; sweet, attractive fruit, a ripe almost Bordeaux-like character but more advanced. Most recently, deep, floral, vegetal nose, fruit and oak; attractive spicy flavour, fullish body (alcohol 13.5%) a lean touch and very tannic. *In San Francisco, March 2002* ★★(★★)

**Peter Michael, Les Pavots** Founded in 1987, higher elevation, cool climate. Virtually opaque; complete; sweet, rich, full of fruit, reasonably masked tannins. *Also one of the 'Top Ten' wines in the* Wine Spectator *seminar, New York, Oct 2000* ★★★(★)

**Robert Mondavi, Special Reserve Cabernet Sauvignon** (including Cabernet Franc 3%, Merlot 2%). First noted in November 1998, bottled specially for the Wine Experience gala dinner in San Francisco. Good fruit but far too young. Next, featured in the *Wine Spectator*'s 'Top Ten' seminar: very good nose, forthcoming, slightly scented; good fruit, body and length. *Last noted Oct 2000* ★★(★★)

**Robert Mondavi, Barrel-Aged Reserve Cabernet Sauvignon** Lovely colour; crisp; good fruit, very dry finish. *In* the Cabernet 'flight' at the 'Club 50' tasting in Düsseldorf, March 2000 ★★(★)

**Robert Mondavi, Oakville District Cabernet Sauvignon** A perfectly decent, not very expressive wine served with rack of lamb, after the 'Club 50' tasting. I had to leave early to catch a plane back to London. A happy event even so, in the company of Angelo Gaja (who dashed back even earlier) and organised by a good PR friend, Dorli Muhr of Wine & Partners, Vienna. *March 2000* ★★★

**Shafer, Hillside Select Cabernet Sauvignon** Deep purple, violet edge; sweet, chewy, lovely fruit, extract masking tannin. *In Shafer's cave, June 2001* (★★★★)

**Shafer, Merlot** Deep, plummy; hefty, meaty fruit; sweet, fleshy, hefty, delicious in its way. *Dining at Shafer, June 2001* ★★★★

# 1997 ★★★★★

After a run of small vintages, a bumper crop with yields up by 24% compared to 1996, though there was some unevenness due to tropical storms in Sonoma and Napa in August and September. The high proportion of premium wines helped to relieve price inflation.

**Acacia, Carneros Pinot Noir** Correct colour; rich singed Pinot nose; sweet, complete (alcohol 13%), quite a bite. As always at home, I taste and make notes prior to serving. In this case, I preferred it when freshly opened, and less and less as the dinner progressed. *At home, Sept 1999* ★★★ *But drink up.*

**Arietta Kongsgaard and Hatton** – Cabernet Franc 81%, Merlot 19%, from the Hudson vineyards planted in 1980. First tasted in July 1999. Good fruit, quite a bite. Most recently: deep, rich, velvety; crisp fruit, floral, developing an extremely sweet pineapple scent; sweet, rich, lovely texture and flavour. Spicy. Tannic. *Last tasted in San Francisco, March 2002* ★★★★(★)

**Beaulieu Vineyard, Georges de Latour Cabernet Sauvignon Reserve** Blended for bottling (1999); opaque, intense; a re-run of exotic raspberry and vanilla; sweet, strong raspberry flavour. More fruit than wine. It must be clear by now that I did not take to this new style. *At the Beaulieu Vineyard centenary tasting, Vinopolis, London, July 1999.*

**Cain, Cain Five** Cabernet Sauvignon 87%, Cabernet Franc 11%, Petit Verdot 1%, Malbec 1%. Fairly deep, plummy; crisp, berry-like fruit; medium sweetness and weight, full of fruit, dry finish. *During a Decanter 'Live Chat', Dec 2001* ★★★

**Chateau Montelena, Montelena Estate** Dark cherry; good, young fruit, developing well, sweet, rich, a good mouthful. The youngest of a nine-vintage Montelena line-up. *At the 'California Wine Experience', New York, Oct 2000* ★★(★★)

**Dominus, Napanook Vineyard** Cabernet Sauvignon 86.5%, Cabernet Franc 9%, Merlot 4.5%. Very deep, rich, velvety and less mature looking than the '96 Opus One tasted alongside; a rich, two-part, as yet unknit nose, muffled fruit; sweet on the palate too with a soft entry, good mid-palate fruit but very tannic, astringent finish. *At 1915 Pierce Street, San Francisco, March 2002* (★★★★)

**Kendall-Jackson, Reserve Cabernet Sauvignon** Sweet, pleasant, flying well. *A good 'Club World' red, on BA 175 to New York, Oct 2001* ★★★ *(just).*

**Robert Mondavi, Reserve Cabernet Sauvignon** In November 2000: very good flavour and length. Next: similar note but a touch of leanness and refreshing acidity. Needs time. *Last noted at the Vintners' gala dinner, Meadowood, June 2001* ★★(★★)

**Opus One** Cabernet Sauvignon 84%, Cabernet Franc 10%, Malbec 4%, Petit Verdot 2%. Early harvest. Largest crop of the decade thinned to the lowest per-acre yield. An exuberant fountain of full, rich Cabernet aroma, a touch of coffee, mocha and malt. Simmered down after an hour in the glass. Sweet, very attractive citrus and spice flavour. Very tannic. *At 1915 Pierce Street, San Francisco, March 2002* ★★(★★)

**PlumpJack, Reserve Cabernet Sauvignon** The first of six Cabernets (including a Bordeaux Supérieur) tasted blind. We were all fooled, except the eucalyptus nose led one to the Napa. A spicy attractive wine. Still very tannic. Gordon Getty was pleased by our reactions. *At Waddesdon Manor, Dec 2000* ★★(★★)

**Saintsbury, Carneros Pinot Noir** One of my most-liked Pinot Noirs used to demonstrate the varietal at our Christie's wine course introductory sessions. Typically 'burgundian', not deep, but soft, with open rim; mellow character developing in the glass, ripe rich fruit; sweet, nice texture, good flavour and weight (alcohol 13.5%). Dry finish. *Last tasted at Christie's, Nov 1999* ★★(★) *Probably at its best now.*

**Shafer, Hillside Select Cabernet Sauvignon** Deep, plummy; dry, crisp, well stacked, certainly interesting, with spicy aftertaste. The youngest vintage tasted in the cellars before dinner. Much as I admire Doug Shafer (and his son) – they make an entertaining double act talking about their wine, as I hope Bartholomew and I do, about his wine when on tour – I do find his wines too alcoholic; none, by choice, is less than 14%. Much has to do with the super-ripeness of his grapes, and doubtless American taste, which is why the leaner, less overtly powerful red Bordeaux are, in my opinion, far superior as food wines but, equally, not as obviously appealing as these domestic premium reds. Horses for courses, I say. *At Shafer's, June 2001* ★(★★★)

**Stag's Leap Wine Cellars, Cask 23** The youngest vintage at Winiarski's 'Red' Adams and the 25th anniversary tasting at Meadowood. Deep, of course; very vegetal, Bordeaux-like, sweaty tannin; too sweet and somewhat coarse. I trust time will tell (I was tempted to say 'turn a pig's ear into a silk purse', but won't). *Dec 2000* ★(★★)?

# 1998 ★★★?

Unquestionably a difficult year for the growers: February the worst on record, a cool and wet spring, unsuitable weather during flowering. Short, erratic bouts of intense heat in the summer and by mid-September hardly a single grape picked. The latest harvest in living memory, ending mid-November.

What with that and the attendant diseases and pests – the phylloxera endemic, having necessitated much replanting – not an easy time. Yet, thanks to more efficient vini- and viticultural practices, some very good wine made.

Alas, there is no way I can give the reader even a synopsis, but will let one or two significant wineries give an indication.

**Arietta, Merlot** 400 cases produced. Good but as yet unknit nose, arboreal, touch of citrus fruit, opening up and settling down nicely; sweet, fleshy, delicious. *With John and Fritz at 1915 Pierce Street, San Francisco, March 2002* ★★★★

**Arietta, Napa Valley** (Cabernet Franc 60%, Merlot 40%) 500 cases produced. Deep, crisp fruit, floral scents, opening up richly, mocha and oak; the sweetest of the 'flight' ('96 to '99) with a lovely flavour, spicy, dry, slightly astringent finish. *With John Kongsgaard and Fritz Hatton at 1915 Pierce Street, San Francisco, March 2002* ★★(★★)

**Beaulieu Vineyard, Georges de Latour Cabernet Sauvignon** Possibly the final blend brought over for the Beaulieu Vineyard centenary tasting in London, July 1999. I preferred it to the vanilla and raspberry '95s, '96s and '97s. Dare I say it, very Bordeaux-like with fresh, youthful, slightly scented Cabernet Sauvignon aroma; sweet, very oaky, clove-like spiciness with accompanying taste of freshly sawn wood. Then the briefest of notes on the Beaulieu Vineyard stand at the 'Wine Experience Grand tastings' in New York, merely 'very deep, big and hard' which is not, I agree, very helpful. As always, time will tell. *Last tasted Oct 2001* (★★★)?

**Diamond Creek, Volcanic Hill Cabernet Sauvignon** Opaque core, purple rim; lovely, intense fruit on nose and palate. Alas, no opportunity to taste the wines of Al's two other vineyards but judging from this, and knowing him, they will be good. *Picnicking at the winery, June 2001* ★★(★★★)?

**Dominus, Napanook Vineyard** (Cabernet Sauvignon 73%, Cabernet Franc 15%, Merlot 6%, Petit Verdot 6%.) Tasted with Christian Moueix at the 'California Wine Experience Grand tastings'. Only Marvin Shanken is capable of inducing the most important producers, growers and estate owners to man a meagre stand at the hot and crowded two long days of tastings every year. But of course it is useful 'exposure' for them and provides a rare opportunity for people to meet the great names behind the great wines. Dominus '98 was pretty impressive. Very tannic of course. *Oct 2001* (★★★★)?

**Kongsgaard, Napa Valley Syrah** (100%, planted 1980. Only 80 cases produced). Extremely good nose; sweet, leafy, oaky, touch of tangerine, developed well; some flavour, overall dry, somewhat astringent. Needs further bottle age. *At 1915 Pierce Street, San Francisco, March 2002.*

**Marimar Torres, Don Miguel Pinot Noir** An old friend, the sister of Miguel Torres, long resident and winemaker in the Napa. We exchange correspondence fairly frequently and she kindly sends me her Pinot Noirs and Chardonnays to taste. But this was tasted blind at Walter Eigensatz's great red wine event, 'The very best of Miguel Torres' session. His sister's wine was sweet, chewy, delicious. *At Bad Schwalbach, Nov 2000* ★★★★

# 1999 ★★★★★

One of the longest, coolest ripening periods supercharged by an almost week-long burst of heat at the end of September leading into November, one of the latest-ever harvests. Small crop and the major red varieties were very successful.

**Arietta, Merlot Kongsgaard and Hatton** (950 cases, priced at $75 per bottle). Very deep; intense, immature; sweet, floral, curiously toffee-like; medium-sweet, good fruit but harsh, oaky, teeth-gripping tannins. *Tasted with John Kongsgaard and Fritz Hatton at my son's house in San Francisco, March 2002* (★★★)?

**Arietta, Napa Valley Kongsgaard and Hatton** (Cabernet Franc 60%, Merlot 40%, only 300 cases produced, price $75 a bottle). Opaque, velvety; good crisp fruit, rich, 'singed' nose and flavour. Sweet, spicy, dry, tannic, oaky aftertaste. Lovely wine. *San Francisco, March 2002* ★★(★★★)

**Au Bon Climat Bien Nacido Pinot Noir** Selected to represent the grape variety at Christie's recent wine courses: soft, cherry-tinted; sweet, harmonious, very well made. *Last tasted Sept 2001* ★(★★★)

**Dominus, Napanook Vineyard** (Cabernet Sauvignon 75%, Cabernet Franc 13%, Merlot 9%, Petit Verdot 3% – not using new oak). Dark cherry; very attractive nose, developed sweetly, rather jammy; sweet, soft and firm, delicious, richness masking tannin. *San Francisco, March 2002* ★★★(★★) *Will make an excellent bottle.*

**Marimar Torres, Don Miguel Vineyard Pinot Noir** Good, scented, varietal aroma; delicious flavour, very oaky/spicy finish. *At home, Oct 2001* ★★★(★)

**Kongsgaard, Napa Valley Syrah** (100%, in 50% new burgundian oak. Just (at time of tasting) released only 100 cases at $125 per bottle): impressively deep; very sweet, oaky/spicy nose of great depth, brambly fruit; sweet, fleshy fruit, very spicy, tannic. I thought too oaky. *San Francisco, March 2002* ★(★★★) *(I had not met John Kongsgaard since 1986 when he was winemaker at Newton in the Napa Valley so I was delighted he had teamed up with my former Christie's colleague and fellow auctioneer, Fritz Hatton.)*

## 2000–2001

Americans as a whole, wine producers in particular, are optimistic and enthusiastic by nature, despite vicissitudes. Unquestionably, a whole new raft of seriously good wines are emerging from California. Growers know more about vine management than their predecessors, winemaking can scarcely be improved. Whether the market, already saturated, can sustain the plethora of relatively new wineries remains to be seen. It is likely that there will be a polarisation: the big, well-established companies with good distribution at one end, and the boutique wineries selling on allocation to connoisseurs and collectors at the other end. (Perhaps just worth mentioning a recent – 2002 – report by a leading wine research group that there are 5200 California wines on the market – not to mention competition from France, Italy, Australia and Chile!).

## 2000 (★★★★)

An outstanding growing season. Bud break, flowering and *veraison* all ahead of schedule. Then a long cool ripening period resulted in a prolonged harvest ending in early November. Apart from competition, premium wine prices are too high and the US dollar too strong, encouraging imports, discouraging exports.

## 2001 (★★★★★)

An outstanding vintage, certainly in Napa and Sonoma. Despite an uneasy start, with a too-easy bud break being hit by frost, there was the worst spring frost in 20 years. The summer, however, was well-nigh perfect, leading to an early harvest with Cabernet Sauvignon grapes, in particular, being smaller, with thick skins and concentrated flesh.

# Australia

A vast continent, the epitome of the New World. Though vines were planted and wines made nearly two centuries ago, Australia only really cast aside its beer swilling image and began to see wine as an enlightened beverage in the 1950s and 1960s, and to take wine really seriously in the 1970s. Australian wine is now set, in volume, to dominate the international market. However, this is not the first time that British imports from Australia have overtaken those from France; it happened between the late 1920s, and mid-1930s, thanks to 'Empire preference' duty rates. But what wine! Rough Australian reds bottled in England, and sold mainly as cheap 'red biddy' or, heaven forbid, for 'restorative' purposes. I certainly remember in the post-war period flagons, like Franconian *bocksbeutels*, of hearty 'burgundy', full of iron, reminding me that the principal object of the pioneer winemakers of New South Wales was to provide nourishment and to prevent scurvy in the penal colonies. These worthy-minded early winemakers tended to be doctors; Seppelt, the name of a major producer today, being just one.

For three quarters of the 20th century, the only wines exported to their principal market, England, managed to combine — at one and the same time — 'plonk' for the great unwashed and an invigorating iron tonic for the medically disabled. In fact, not unlike the Cape wines, the most successful Australian wines were fortified port styles (the liqueur Muscats made in North-East Victoria are still superb, see page 533). Idiosyncratic perhaps, raisiny but pretty good. They also kept well. The table wine pioneers had a hard time.

Scouring my tasting books I have, to my surprise, found a very large number of notes on Australian wines. I have visited that continent several times, first in 1977 to organise and conduct the first Christie's wine auction in association with Len Evans, who, warmhearted and generous fellow that he is, accompanied me to the Hunter Valley, where he still lives, to Melbourne and north-east Victoria, and to Adelaide and the Barossa. Although I have visited Australia subsequently, I have never been to Western Australia, the most recent of the major wine regions, or, for that matter, Tasmania.

As a measure of how recent the development of wines we now associate strongly with Australia has been, I well recall, in February 1977, perching on a couch in Dr Max Lake's very small consulting room in Sydney, and tasting his (and one of Australia's) first Chardonnays made at Lake's Folly in the Hunter Valley.

Thanks not only to many winery visits, but also to my attendance at some important wine shows, I have managed to taste a very wide range of wines; also, thanks to Len and his friends, many old classics and, on a couple of occasions, rarities from the Yalumba Wine Museum, both at the winery in Barossa Valley and in London.

Because of the sheer impossibility of covering the subject adequately, not to mention the irrelevance of young wines first tasted and consumed long ago, I am dividing the chapter into three sections: first Grange — the well-established collectors' classic, next a brief look back, followed by a hint of some recent greats and a postscript.

# Grange

'The Grange' is the name of a small cottage in a vineyard at Magill on the slopes overlooking the city of Adelaide, where, in 1844, Dr Rawson Penfold settled to make wine 'for his patients' health'. Little did he know that what over a century later would be known as 'Penfolds Grange Hermitage Claret', now just 'Grange', would become the single most renowned wine in Australia.

**1900 'Dr Penfold, Grange'** A possibly unique bottle bought at Christie's by Hardy Rodenstock and opened at one of his rare wine tastings. Additionally described as 'Burgundy', it had been shipped in cask and bottled in London in a screwtop *bocksbeutel* flagon, typical of the hearty, invigorating Australian reds, which were popular in Britain well into the middle of the 20th century. Although fairly deeply coloured, it had no red left but, to my surprise, was sound – indeed faultless – on nose and palate. Dry yet rich, some loss of body. *Tasted Sept 1987* ★★★

**1951 Grange Hermitage** Half a century later, and a very different sort of wine, the creation of Max Schubert, who, on his return from Bordeaux, was inspired to make a top class wine 'to last 20 years'. Using mainly Hermitage (Shiraz or Syrah) grapes grown in the Grange vineyard, fermented and matured in new oak casks, his first vintage, made in a very unfamiliar style, was not appreciated. Seppelt's wanted to shelve the idea but Schubert carried on experimenting.

**1955 Grange Hermitage** Made from 100% Shiraz 'from Magill and Kalimna [vineyards] enhanced with just a dash of Cabernet Sauvignon, eight months in new American oak hogsheads, and bottled in 1956. Once again, this didn't go down too well. In 1957 it was decided that costs were too high and production was discontinued. But in 1962, ignoring the rebuff, Schubert entered the '55 for the Sydney Wine Show where it was awarded a gold medal, an award said to have been repeated at wine shows over 170 times since. 'Since when', as they say, 'he, and what is now known just as 'Grange', have never looked back.'
  I first tasted the '55 Grange at Yalumba, in the Barossa, in 1985. At 30 years of age, it was remarkably like a mature Bordeaux. Five years later: medium-deep; fully evolved bouquet which sagged after 20 minutes; fairly sweet, toasted Graves-like flavour and good length. Next, at Seppelt's vertical in 1994, showing its age but harmonious and somewhat chocolatey. Most recently, the best of the pre-1960 reds at the Yalumba Museum tasting in London: warm amber colour; caramelly nose; still very sweet, soft textured. *Last tasted May 1999* ★★★★★ *for its original quality and for history. Now* ★★★

**1960** One old note but one of my first. Very rich, showing well. *Tasted blind at John Avery's in April 1973* ★★★

**1962** This was my first exposure to Grange, in 1972, when the ever-explorative Hugh Johnson brought a bottle to Christie's for me to taste. He said it was the Latour of Australia. Next, and the most memorable, tasted in the vineyard. A wonderful wine. *March 1977* ★★★★

**1963** With '**Bin 95**' on the label. Still 100% Shiraz. First tasted with Len Evans in 1985: opaque; a wine of vast

dimensions, still more to come. Next, at a remarkable MW 21-wine comparative tasting of Grange and Jaboulet's Hermitage La Chapelle in May 1992: black treacle colour; strange nose and taste, showing its age. Full, rich, slightly malty. Over the top but fascinating. Next, in 1993: singed, slightly madeira-like tang; as before, a touch of rusticity, still powerful. More recently: still deep and fairly intense; fabulously rich, sweet bouquet and flavour, massively supported. Still tannic. *The oldest of a 14-vintage horizontal at a Grange seminar with the Hollywood Wine Society, March 1995* ★★★★(★)

**1965** Shiraz 95%, Cabernet Sauvignon 5%, the Cabernet from vineyards in Magill, Kalimna, Southern Vales and the Barossa; 18 months in new American oak. Only one note: deep, rich, mature; lean, brick dust and liquorice; sweet, raw texture, loads of tannin. *At Bob Berenson's in New York, Oct 1990* ★★

**1966** A drought year. Including Cabernet Sauvignon 12%. First tasted in 1977: opaque, vast and velvety. Next, in 1990, less deep, now sweet, elegant and harmonious; losing weight but lovely, with silky, tannic texture. I rated it equal top with the '71. Two years later, though sweet, soft and cheesy, I felt it was losing its grip. Next, in 1994: mahogany tinge; lively, tea-like, good vinosity, harmonious; very smooth texture, dry finish. In 1995: fragrant, showing well. *Last noted at Christie's 'Tasting of the Century' (all 1966s), a bottle reconditioned by Penfold's. At Vinexpo, June 1999. At best* ★★★★

**1967** Including Cabernet Sauvignon 6%, 16 months in new American oak. First tasted in 1990: black cherry; good, ripe fruit, touch of coffee; nice wine. Five years later: showing some maturity; crisp, vanillin; sweet, rich, good texture and length. Delicious. *Last noted at the Hollywood tasting, March 1995* ★★★★

**1968** Cabernet Sauvignon 5%, 20 months in new American oak. First noted in 1990: well-developed; mature, with wonderful ginger biscuits scent as it opened up; sweet, pleasant weight, texture and acidity. Five years later: fully mature; singed, rich, almost Bual-like nose; more power than met the eye but this time I noted raw tannin. *Last tasted at the Hollywood Wine Society vertical tasting, March 1995* ★★

**1970** Cabernet Sauvignon 10%, 18 months in oak. One note at 20 years of age: medium-deep, mature appearance; rich, forthcoming nose, a bit toffee-like; an agreeable wine though I felt something was missing. *At Berenson's tasting, Oct 1990* ★★

**1971 'Bin 95'** Very high percentage of Cabernet Sauvignon, 13%. Several notes, first dining with Len Evans on my first visit to Australia in February 1977. Immensely impressive: opaque, packed, peppery – I even suggested it was a cross between Latour and Pétrus. In 1982 and 1985 still intense and tannic. In 1989 inappropriately served at a 'French Banquet' in

Singapore: huge, impressive. Showing well in 1990: high extract, good fruit, great depth. This time 'like a mature Latour'. Great wine. Two years later: medium-deep, lovely colour with a distinct orange tinge to its maturity; gloriously rich bouquet, perfect harmony, great depth; palate to match, lovely texture and fruit. Richness masking perfect tannin and acidity. 'Perfection'. Five months later, in Atlanta: ripe, 'sweaty saddle' Syrah nose; powerful yet suave. Great wine. Next in 1994: mature orange rim; 'sweet brown paper', fragrant; glorious richness and fullness, still tannic. The following year: still magnificent. Arguably the finest Grange. *Last noted at the Hollywood vertical, March 1995* ★★★★★

**1973 'Bin 95'** First tasted at Doug Crittenden's in Melbourne, April 1985: rich, immense, concentrated. A decade later: fully mature; singed, chocolatey, mocha nose; sweet, showing a bit of age and a bit hollow. *Last noted at the Hollywood Wine Society vertical, March 1995* ★★

**1975 'Bin 95'** Two noted in 1984: at Christie's first 'New World' pre-sale tasting, the next at a Rodenstock wine weekend. At nine years of age magnificent but undrinkable; massive, peppery, astringent. A decade later: deep, rich, lively; spicy, 'medicinal'; still rather austere. The following year, still opaque and relatively immature; fruit noted as 'bramble seedless'. Very sweet, soft, yet tannic. *Last noted at Nils Sternby's birthday tasting of '75s, April 1995* ★★★★

**1976 Grange's 25th vintage** Cabernet Sauvignon 11%, big production. First noted in 1990: vegetal nose, bramble, tar, black treacle evolving fragrantly over an hour in the glass; fairly sweet, with a wide-open chocolate flavour and 'strange drying finish'. Next, still very deep, opaque core, rich 'legs'; gloriously evolved bouquet, sweet, scented; very sweet, full-bodied, singed fruit with a rich, soft, tannic finish. Two years later: rich ruby; sensational nose, glorious fruit, loads of life. Faultless. Most recently: still opaque though showing maturity; cedary, harmonious bouquet of great depth; very sweet, lovely flavour, complete, chunky tannin. Magnificent. *Last noted at the Hollywood Wine Society vertical tasting, March 1995* ★★★★★

**1977** Cabernet Sauvignon 9%. In 1992: dark cherry; crisp, black-fruit character, opening up fragrantly; sweet, with Pomerol-like silky tannins yet with a refreshingly acidic finish. Two years later: still fairly intense; floral, fragrant yet slightly varnishy; lean after the '76, very austere. This time less silky, more sandpapery. *Last noted at Searcy's, May 1994* ★★(★) *It will never be great but its rough edges might be smoother by now.*

**1978** Cabernet Sauvignon 10%. By 1990 showing maturity; bouquet at first reluctant but opened up richly; sweet, pleasant weight, leathery tannin. Next at the MW tasting in 1992: similar note, rich, chewy, slightly short. Two years later: lovely colour; fully evolved, fragrant, slightly port-like nose; lean but lissom. Tannic. Most recently; deep, rich but maturing; fabulous, fully evolved, medicinal 'Pauillac' bouquet, like Lafite! Sweet yet tannic. Most attractive. *Last noted at the Hollywood Wine Society vertical tasting, March 1995* ★★★★

**1979** Cabernet Sauvignon 13%. First at Berenson's in 1992: lovely colour, rich, maturing; as usual, the nose opening up fragrantly; medium-sweetness and body, soft tannins. Elegant. More recently: with a sort of '82 Bordeaux richness;

explosively sweet bouquet; almost too sweet and rich, spicy and tannic. *Last noted May 1994* ★★★★

**1980** Cabernet Sauvignon only 4%. Acidified, unfined and bottled in 1982. First noted in 1990: dark cherry; fig-like — very Rhône Syrah character — full, lean, tannic. Next, in 1992, already brown-rimmed; low-keyed, spicy but harmonious nose; touch of bitterness and lacking length. Two years later: still deep and lively; rich fruit, eucalyptus; fragrant, spicy, dry finish. More recently: slightly cedary, 'medicinal'; chunky fruit, leathery tannin. *Last noted March 1995* ★★

**1981** Cabernet Sauvignon 11%. First tasted in 1988: lively bouquet, extraordinary flavour, very tannic. Next, in 1992: noting a strange, appley, Côtes-du-Rhône sort of nose. Gritty texture. Too tannic. More recently: brown-rimmed; raspberry jam and volatile acidity; dry, rasping tannin. The least good at both Berenson's and Seppelt's verticals. *Last tasted May 1994.*

**1982** Cabernet Sauvignon 6%. The usual 18 months in American oak hogsheads. In 1987: opaque, jam-packed with fruit, marvellous vinosity. Showing well in 1990. Two years later, less deep, now maturing nicely; soft, earthy, with blackberry-like fruit; well-developed, soft and sweet, but with a touch of bitterness on its tannic finish. In 1994: a hot, very sweet, malty though fruity bouquet; full, rich, oaky and massive fruit. The following year: open-rimmed but rich; sweet, chewy, chunky fruit. Next, in 1996: full, soft, rich, excellent. Most recently: opulent, figgy Syrah nose and flavour, full body, fruit, concentration. Hugely impressive but not exciting. *Last tasted at Bob Dickinson's Bacchus dinner, Coral Gables, Nov 1997* ★★★★★ *Will last for ages.*

**1983** Cabernet Sauvignon 6%. In 1990, dry, lean, raw and unimpressive. A totally contrasting note in 1992: deep, velvety; lovely, rich, bramble-like fruit; fairly sweet, full of fruit, fleshy though with bitter tannins. In 1994: still very deep, intense; hefty Rhône-like, singed character; lots of grip, impressive. The following year: a similar note, rich, brambly, still peppery, attractive. *Last noted at the Hollywood vertical, March 1995* ★★★★

**1984** Cabernet Sauvignon 5%. In 1992: deep; peppery, good fruit; sweet, full-bodied, but abrupt, like a '43 Bordeaux. More recently: rich, harmonious; smooth, elegant. Dry finish. *Last tasted May 1994* ★★★ *Drink up.*

**1985** Unusually, almost all Shiraz, Cabernet Sauvignon only 1%. First tasted in 1990: harmonious, stylish, elegant. 'A quick developer?' Then in 1992: deep; extraordinarily spicy, like powdered cinnamon, opening up beautifully; a full, fleshy, lovely wine. In 1994: deep yet mature looking; far less impressed by its nose, finding it sickly (sweet); decent texture, dry finish. Poor bottle? Most recently: still deep; its raspberry-like nose reminding me of Cabernet Franc; on the palate blackberry-like, slightly malty. Not showing all that well in the company of Kaplan's great '85s. *Last tasted in Chicago, April 2000* ★★★

**1986** High Cabernet Sauvignon, 13%. Ungrafted, low yielding vines. Excellent growing conditions. Cool, dry summer with one of the driest and latest-ever harvests. First in 1990: nose holding back; very sweet, immense, packed with soft, ripe fruit, high extract masking high tannins. Next in 1992, the youngest vintage at the MW vertical: still, of course, youthful looking; initially a green stemmy nose that after 30 minutes opened up fabulously; full, rich, stemmy fruit, a 'hot' dry, slightly bitter finish. In May 1994: ruby; unknit initially but then untangled and evolved fragrantly; very sweet, good fruit queried its length. The following spring: still opaque; spicy, berry-like fruit. *Last tasted at the Hollywood vertical, March 1995* ★★★★★

1987 Just one note: deep, rich; fully evolved, almost sickly sweet, raspberry-like nose. Palate a total contrast, somewhat raw and with a very dry tannic finish. *At Searcy's, May 1994* ★★

1988 Good colour; meaty, almost malty but with attractive, mulberry-rich fruit. Sweet, full-bodied. *At Searcy's, May 1994* ★★★★

1989 In May 1994: my highest mark at Seppelt's 20-vintage vertical, 1955–1990. Deep, rich-coloured; astonishing fruit; touch of eucalyptus; very sweet, full-bodied, glorious, mouthfilling, Pétrus-like richness. The following spring: fruit, flesh, fragrance. *Last noted at the Hollywood Wine Society vertical tasting, March 1995* ★★★(★★) *Magnificent.*

1990 Opaque, intense, with a slight prickle at the rim; at four years of age, scarcely developed. Medium-dry. Straightforward. 'An interesting future'. The following year: little changed though its nose opened up gloriously, with raspberry, bramble-like fruit; lovely wine, spicy, good length. In 1996: showing well among the 144 greatest reds of the 1990

vintage: similar notes, fig-like, Shiraz fruit; opulent, fleshy, impressive. It got the second highest number of votes in its flight (of 12) but, tasted blind, I had written 'excellent but not my sort of drink'. Most recently: presented by Hugh Johnson at *Decanter's* 'Man of the Year' tasting at Vinopolis: extraordinary bouquet, mint, hint of raspberry; very sweet, reminding me of a Beaulieu Vineyard Cabernet Sauvignon at its best. *Last tasted July 1999* ★★★★(★)

1992 One note: opaque, intense, plummy rim; lovely, rich, tarry nose, sweet molasses; very sweet, concentrated, very good fruit, tannin and acidity. *At the IWFS Syrah tasting, Singapore, Jan 1998* ★★(★★) *Considerable future.*

No recent releases tasted but the '98 'will be sensational' according to my 'pen pal' Len Evans AO, OBE, SA.

---

### Len Evans

*Unstinting ambassador of Australian wine, originally from Wales, and originally (like myself) an architect, Len is not only a highly skilled taster, opinionated show judge and accomplished raconteur on the subject of wine, but also a man whom I am proud to call a friend. One of his first achievements was to convince Australians that 'real men' could drink table wine, and not just beer. He later set up the highly successful Rothbury estate in the Hunter Valley, and hasn't looked back since. Modest, shy, retiring? I think not. Len is gregarious, witty, and very much larger than life.*

---

# A look back, 1930s–1980s

THE 1930S Unsurprisingly, few have survived. One of the earliest was a 1932 **Yalumba 'Sauternes'** (*1995* ★★★) and the only red tasted recently, a 1937 **'Sydney'** claret from the Hunter Valley. Not bad, a bit 'edgy' (but so are most '37 Médocs) *Yalumba Museum tasting, May 1999* ★★

THE 1940S two O'Shea classics, the 1942 **Mount Pleasant, 'T.Y.' Hermitage**: two bottles, one smelly, the other tolerable (*Yalumba tasting, May 1999*) and his 1943 **Hunter Valley 'Burgundy'**, malty and medicinal (*May 1985*). Alas, O'Shea's legendary reputation outlives his wine.

THE 1950S some improvement but the 1955 **Grange** (see page 530) well ahead of **Hardy**'s St Thomas 'multi-regional 'Burgundy' and **Yalumba**'s Galway Vintage Claret (*all three '55s tasted May 1999*).

THE 1960S There was a considerable improvement in quality and ageing ability. **Penfolds**' 1962 **'Bin 60A'**, another Max Schubert success (see page 530): a wine of legendary reputation, Cabernet Sauvignon from Coonawarra and Shiraz from Kalimna (South Australia). It was delicious (*last tasted May 1999*). The 1963 **Mildara** Cabernet Sauvignon 'known affectionately as Peppermint Patty', the first and most famous varietal produced by Mildara at Coonawarra was lovely, with a very distinctive eucalyptus nose (*last tasted May 1999*).

**Lindemans**' 1965 **Hunter Burgundy 'Bin 3110'** from the renowned Ben Ean vineyard was showing well (*May 1999*), 1966, 1967 and 1968 were all good vintages but apart from Grange, I have tasted few of these wines since the 1980s.

THE 1970S
1971 unquestionably the best (see Grange page 530), 1975 and 1976 both very good. **Henschke**'s 1978 **Hill of Grace**, a label established in the 1930s, was the first wine made by Stephen Henschke from the century-old Eden Valley Shiraz vineyards: good fruit though its finish a bit rasping (*at the Yalumba Museum tasting, May 1999*). Now, of course, one of Australia's first growth wines by any standards.

THE 1980S **Vasse Felix**'s 1980 **Cabernet Sauvignon** was one of the earliest vintages from the first vineyard established at Margaret River in Western Australia. Felix rapidly established a reputation for quality and integrity at the May 1999 Yalumba Museum tasting: it was very mature, of course, but sweet with good fruit and grip (the **Vasse Felix** 1999 **Cabernet Sauvignon** showed well at the Australian Day tasting, Jan 2002). Both 1984 and 1985 were very good vintages. I have tasted many wines but none recently. 1986 was excellent, **O'Callaghan**'s 1986 **Rockford Basket Press Shiraz** still very sweet, jammy, complete (*May 1999* ★★★) Can a wine be described as 'rustic' and 'refined'?

# Modern notables and old liqueurs

Quite apart from their unquestionably successful assault on the world's markets, with well made, still good value reds (and whites), Australia has equally unquestionably produced some outstanding wines which have already demonstrated their maturing capabilities and future.

But, as in the case of California, how great can they get? They grow top-quality grapes, the winemaking is faultless, there is now a consciousness of what the French call *terroir*. The horizon would appear to be limitless.

First of all, some notes made at Walter Eigensatz's monumental tasting of the best 1990 reds of the world in 1996. Of the 144 wines in 12 flights, all tasted blind, there were nine Australian reds including the Grange (see page 532).
IN FLIGHT ONE **Yarra Yering**'s **No 1 Cabernet Sauvignon** dark, intense cherry; very attractive fruit, crisp, blackberry, concentrated, on the verge of exotic; very sweet, full, rich, fruit-laden, tannic ★★★★; IN FLIGHT 2 **Taltarni**'s **Cabernet Sauvignon** an old favourite of mine: medium-deep; touch of resin, Cabernet and oak; pleasant flavour, weight and silky tannins ★★★★; IN FLIGHT 5 **Jim Barry**'s **Armagh Syrah** opaque, rather tinny fragrance; full of fruit but raw ★★★; **Wendouree**'s **Syrah** new to me. Impressive appearance; dumb, brambly; very attractive flavour ★★★★; IN FLIGHT 6 **Wynns**' **'John Riddoch' Cabernet Sauvignon** opaque, intense, still youthful; an astonishing concentration of fruit and oak, blackberry, mulberry; sweet, full, velvety. Great wine ★★★★★ (best of flight – blind – against Opus One, Pichon Lalande, Stag's Leap Cask 23, La Jota and others; half a point ahead of the next wine); **Rockford**'s **Basket Press Syrah** very fragrant, harmonious; very sweet, full, rich, chunky tannins, glorious ★★★★★; IN FLIGHT 7 **Coriole**'s **'Lloyd Reserve' Syrah** best of flight despite formidable opposition: deliciously ripe fruit on nose and palate. Almost too sweet, soft tannins, excellent for tasting, but not for me at table ★★★★; IN FLIGHT 8 **Chapel Hill**'s **Syrah Reserve** impressively deep; over-oaked, over-scented but speciously attractive; full of fruit. I noted that it received 8 votes for power but only 3 votes for elegance ★★★★. IN THE FINAL FLIGHT, 12, **Clarendon Hills**' **Syrah** opaque; vivid, floral, spicy oak, fabulous, crystallised fruit, fragrance and flavour. Too sweet and 'over the top'. Hugely impressive but not a table wine ★★★★

IN ADDITION to the 1990s showing well at the Eigensatz tasting, I have admired the following (with a notable vintage in brackets): **Henschke**'s **Hill of Grace Shiraz** (1991); **Leeuwin Estate**'s **Cabernet Sauvignon** (1991); **Mount Mary**'s **Quintet Cabernets** (1991); and **St Hallett**'s **Old Block Shiraz** (1990, and the 1999 particularly).

I HAVE MANY NOTES ON **Penfolds**' **Bin 707** and also, quite recently, their **Bin 128 Coonawarra Shiraz**.

AND OF VERY RECENT VINTAGES (1998 to 2000) I have particularly admired **Cape Mentelle**'s **Cabernet-Merlot**;

## Australian liqueur Muscats and 'Port'

*Some astonishingly good fortified wines are produced in Australia including much sought-after and extremely high priced 'Para Liqueur Port' and the somewhat neglected but, for me, delectable liqueur Muscats from Rutherglen and Glenrowan in North-East Victoria which I visited for the first time in March 1977.*

*I have several notes of the 'Para' including 'Seppelt' bottling No 112': ruddy colour, very intriguing, spirity chocolate raisin nose and 'singed muscatel' flavour with a touch of liquorice. The oldest, both tasted in 1993, were the 1878 and 1893: both opaque with an intense amber rim; the first with high-toned chocolate and black treacle bouquet, full-flavoured, very tangy, the century-old wine being much sweeter, soft and velvety. Really lovely.*

*But my favourites, and one can still buy them – Chambers ship three qualities – are the liqueur Muscats from Rutherglen. What they do not export are the old casks in which the wine has been left to evaporate and concentrate. Bill Chambers showed me some as old as his Rosewood winery, one containing unblended, unfortified wine from pre-phylloxera (pre-1910) Muscat grapes: opaque, so viscous that it was difficult to pour – and sensationally lovely. Another great character, Mick Morris, had also hoarded casks of the same age: opaque, more spirity, immensely powerful. This was, indeed, another world.*

**Chapel Hill**'s **The Vicar**; **Jim Barry**'s **Clare Valley Cabernet Sauvignon**; **Hollick**'s **Ravenswood Cabernet Sauvignon**; **Mount Langi Ghiran**'s **Shiraz**; and, definitely a cult wine: **Wild Duck Creek**'s **Late Harvest Shiraz**.

POSTSCRIPT What is encouraging is that the really big commercial companies also produce quality wines. I have long admired, Hardys, Lindemans, Penfolds, Rosemount, McWilliams, Wynns and the pioneers of the 1970s and 1980s, Leeuwin, Peter Lehmann, Petaluma, Rothbury and Tyrrell's. What is more, their expertise, as well as their wine is exported, in the form of 'the flying winemaker'.

My number one first-draft reader, my wife, said 'what about the white wine?' I admire them and drink them, particularly the Hunter Chardonnays and the South Australian Rieslings. But these are wines for drinking young. However good, they are rarely wines of contemplation, for learned discussion, for long cellaring or further pages in an already long vintage wine book.

# New Zealand

A 'New World' wine country par excellence. Once noted mainly for lamb and butter, New Zealand has only relatively recently sprung into prominence as a major wine producer. Quite apart from the wine itself, it has been helped – certainly in English eyes – by its image: distinctly 'un-foreign', and, though far away, comfortably familiar. It has also been extraordinarily well promoted, the New Zealand Wine Institute being a model of its kind. More importantly, the wine they produce hits the button, the whites in particular appeal to the modern taste, to the extent that there is scarcely a merchant or restaurant in the United Kingdom who does not list an New Zealand Sauvignon Blanc or Chardonnay. The wines are produced, shipped, sold and consumed quickly and in substantial quantities. But, however important commercially, these popular white wines have no place in a book about vintages. Why? Does anyone take note of the vintage when picking up a bottle of Sauvignon Blanc in a wine shop, or ordering an New Zealand Chardonnay from a restaurant wine list? These are wines for drinking, not keeping; for quaffing and not for pontificating about.

As for the reds, with one or two exceptions – some of the Hawkes Bay Cabernets or Martinborough and South Island Pinot Noirs, for example – they have insufficient track record, despite their high quality, which is hardly surprising because, like the dry whites, they are consumed more or less as soon as they come on the market.

If New Zealand was as near to Europe as the Canary Islands, it would be inundated with tourists and totally ruined, its beauty and charm irrevocably tarnished. My wife and I have only been once. Thanks to a bit of homework, advice from good friends (in particular, Margaret Harvey, a London-based New Zealander, and Rosemary George, the author of *The Wines of New Zealand*, both also Masters of Wine), and the organisation of the NZ Wine Institute, we were able in seven days to visit 21 major wineries in almost all the widespread wine districts. I was impressed. Courteous, efficient, informal (a tie-salesman's grave).

SELECTED BORDEAUX VARIETALS (TASTED IN NEW ZEALAND, OCT 2000)

**1991 Esk Valley 'Terraces'** (Hawkes Bay which is one New Zealand's best areas for Cabernet blends). Both this and the '95 had delicious fruit and flavour, the '91 only 12% alcohol, the '95 13.5%, and with a $60 price tag! Both ★★★★

**1991 Te Mata 'Coleraine'** (Hawkes Bay) Cabernet Sauvignon plus 16% Cabernet Franc. Drinking perfectly ★★★★, and just to prove his pedigree, John Buck produced at dinner his 1982: soft, smooth, still with leathery tannins ★★★

**1998 Alpha Domus 'The Aviator'** (Hawkes Bay) From the four main red Bordeaux varieties: opaque, intense; impressive, substantial, spicy, eucalyptus – too much new oak I suspect. Dry but good fruit ★★(★★)?

**1998 Delegat's** (Hawkes Bay) 100% 'hand-harvested' Merlot. Of their range I ranked this highly with its deep velvety core and rich, fleshy fruit. Good length. Tannic ★★★(★)

**1998 Matariki 'Anthology'** (Hawkes Bay) Merlot 49%, Cabernet Sauvignon 30%, Franc 8% and Syrah 13%. An ingenious and, I thought, successful blend: good fruit on nose and palate. Moderate alcohol (12.9%) and good finish ★★★★

**1998 Sileni Estates EV** (Exceptional vintage – a long hot summer and some of the richest and ripest grapes in Hawkes Bay). 'Right Bank' varietals: Merlot 80%, Cabernet Franc 20%. Impressive, but if anything, too sweet and jammy though with an astringent finish ★★(★)?

**1999 Matua Valley** (Hawkes Bay) Cabernet Sauvignon-Merlot. Attractive but rather jammy fruit ★★★

SELECTED PINOT NOIRS (TASTED IN NEW ZEALAND, OCT 2000)

**1998 Matua Valley** (Grapes from Martinborough) Rich, complex; pleasant sweetness, rich, ripe, very fruity. ★★★(★★)

**1998 Omihi Hills** (Waipara) The versatile and intellectual Daniel Schuster is a consultant to Ornellaia in Tuscany. His Pinot Noir is harmonious, rich yet unobtrusive ★★★★. The '96 had more varietal character, good length, still tannic★★(★)

**1998 Pegasus Bay 'Prima Donna'** (Waipara) Gold capsule. Best barrels, 100% Pinot Noir, unfiltered. Elegant, excellent flavour, silky tannins ★★★(★)

**1999 Mount Difficulty** (Central Otago, a South Island region to watch out for.) Pure varietal aroma and very distinctive flavour ★★★(★★)

**1999 Quarts Reef** (Central Otago) Almost identical note to Mount Difficulty. ★★★(★★)

**1999 Seresin** (Marlborough) Very varietal nose and flavour. Lovely ★★★★ The '98 was chewy, chunky – perhaps it was too hot a year for Pinot Noir ★★★

**1999 Vavasour** (Marlborough) Scent of beetroot and box (hedge); good body and flavour ★★★(★)

**1999 Wither Hills** (Marlborough) Fragrant Pinot, violet-cachou; rich and delicious ★★★(★★)

# South Africa

In historical terms, South African wines are not 'New World' at all, vines having been planted by the Dutch colonists in the mid- to late 17th century. Many of the lovely, traditional Cape Dutch homesteads date from the 18th century. Moreover, Cape wines, the famed Constantia in particular, were immensely fashionable and expensive from the second half of that century until well into the next. However, during the first half of the 20th century, Cape wines might as well not have existed, at least as far as exports were concerned.

When I entered the wine trade in the mid-1950s, the market was almost exclusively devoted to wines marketed by SAWFA (South African Wine Farmers' Association), deservedly well known for their surprisingly good, and good value, 'sherry'. Nederburg, in Paarl, gained a reputation for its excellent sweet wine, Edelkeur, long a favourite of mine, a botrytised Chenin Blanc. By the time of my first visit to the Cape in 1977 with fellow MWs, things were on the move, though exports were hampered by strong anti-Apartheid sentiments. Thanks to experimentation with cultivars (vine varieties), technical innovation, considerable new investment and the political scene change following the release of Nelson Mandela in 1990, attitudes and wines have improved out of all recognition.

Old-established family estates in the Paarl and Stellenbosch areas have long produced top class reds and whites, my favourites (both vinous and architectural) being Rustenberg and Meerlust. In the newer, cooler, coastal region to the south, excellent Pinot Noir and Chardonnay have been pioneered by Tim Hamilton-Russell and, latterly, Bouchard Finlayson. In the Eigensatz tasting (1996) of the world's best red wines of the 1990 vintage, the three selected South African wines acquitted themselves well: Kanonkop Paul Sauer, Thelema Cabernet Sauvignon and, in particular, Glen Carlou Merlot, one of my highest marks.

**1995 Beyerskloof, Cabernet Sauvignon** At Christie's wine course to represent this ubiquitous varietal: impressively deep and velvety; a good if hefty and rather meaty varietal aroma; good fruit, rich, with mouth-drying tannins. *Nov 1999* ★★(★)? *Should be drinking well now.*

**1995 Meerlust, Rubicon** One of Cape's classics, and the most beautiful 'Cape Dutch' homestead occupied by the Myburgh family for nearly 300 years. Matured in 80% new wood for 18 months. Good fruit, lovely flavour and remarkably good value. *At Maisons Marques & Domaines' tasting in London, Jan 2000. Then* ★★★(★) *Should be well-nigh perfect now.*

**1996 Bouchard Finlayson, Galpin Peak Pinot Noir** Soft centred Pinot colour; correct varietal aroma which opened up beautifully in the glass; overall dry, good fruit. *Wine Course, June 1999* ★★★ The 1997 'Tête de Cuvée' had a scented Pinot Aroma; rather Italianate flavour with good soft tannins. *At a British Airways Wine Committee dinner, June 2001* ★★★★

**1997 Kanonkop, Cabernet Sauvignon** Unusually deep, impressive, youthful; a very complete, harmonious wine; good, fresh and rather strawberry-like fruit. Very tannic. *To demonstrate the varietal, Christie's wine courses, autumn 2001* ★★(★★)

**1997 Saxenburg, Private Collection Shiraz** Immensely deep; very pleasant, slightly jammy fruit on nose and palate. Still very tannic. *At Berry Bros, London, Sept 2000* ★★(★)

**1998 Klein Constantia, Vin de Constance** I am familiar with Klein Constantia's wines – all good, though I find Sauvignon Blanc at 14% alcohol rather heady. This is fairly convincing, late 18th-century Constantia look-alike, even in the old Dutch half bottle shape: palish gold; most distinctive, unusual, and delicious minty-spearmint bouquet and flavour, fairly sweet. *Tasted in Geneva, May 1999* ★★★★

**1998 Sejana Merlot** In July 1999: soft young ruby; good fruit but with sweaty smell; sweet, fleshy, but questionable finish. Also retasted the following year: interesting scent, oaky; rich, figgy, some flesh, substantial alcohol (14%) and price, but spoiled by a strange tannic/iron finish. *Last tasted April 2000.* The 1999 as before started off quite well: full, soft and fleshy but with this omnipresent and unpleasant end taste. *Sept 2000.*

**1998 Steenberg Merlot** This had been awarded the R & R Fredericksburg Trophy for the best Merlot and the David Hughes' Trophy for the South African red. David should know, so I took it seriously. It was well clad with Merlot fleshiness and a pronounced spicy eucalyptus nose and taste. Certainly impressive. *At the Wine Challenge Grand Awards Dinner at the Guildhall, London, Oct 2000* ★★(★★)

**1999 Hamilton Russell, Chardonnay** As their excellent Pinot Noirs are more familiar to me, a brief comment on a classic white varietal: unusually pale for a new world style wine, good flavour but laden with new oak. *At a Distillers' Installation Dinner, Nov 2001* ★★★ The 1998 had more colour, a youthful pineappley nose and very scented strawberry-like flavour and end taste of vanilla. Attractive but, I thought, too sweet. *At lunch, July 2000* ★★★

**1999 Kloovenburg, Shiraz** 14 months in American oak. A very old estate producing very modern mouthfilling Shiraz. Alcohol 14%. Full of fruit and very oaky. *Nov 2001* ★★★

# Appendices

## People, organisations and events mentioned in the text

Please note that this is not a complete list. I am indebted also to many other individual hosts in whose company I have enjoyed and noted so many fine wines.

**Aalholm** The Raben-Levetzau family castle in Denmark with a fine cellar: much Danish-bottled claret from the cellar was sold at Christie's.

**Académie du Vin de Bordeaux** See box page 46.

**Adams, 'Red'** Purchaser of a Napa Valley Wine Auction lot: major vertical tasting and dinner donated by Stag's Leap Wine Cellars to mark their 25th anniversary.

**Adamson, Dr Bob** And wife 'Dottie', grape growers and generous hosts. Bob took me on my memorable first tour of Napa wineries.

*Alles über Wein* Germany's best wine magazine.

**d'Ambrumenil, David** In insurance and shipping.

**Amerine, Maynard A** Professor Emeritus of Enology at University of California, Davis, co-author with Professor Edward Roessler of *Sensory Evaluation of Wine* (1976 and 1980). Maynard was a highly influential figure from the post-Prohibition period until well into the 1970s. Initially, I think, he was scornful of my amateurish approach (and I finding his almost unintelligible); we subsequently became great friends.

**Antinori, Piero, Marchese** Distinguished head of old-established Italian wine producers. See box page 402.

**Arvay, Jànos** Tokaji producer who recently gave me an excellent tasting and tour of the area (see also Christian Sauska).

**Averys** Prominent Bristol wine merchants. The late Ronald Avery was one of the great characters of the British trade. His son John is 'a chip off the old block', Master of Wine, Chairman of the IWFS (q.v.), international judge and promoter of southern hemisphere wines.

**AXA Millésimes** The French insurance group, one of the world's largest, owns Bordeaux châteaux Pichon-Longueville, Pibran, Cantenac-Brown, Franc-Mayne and Suduiraut; Domaine de l'Arlot in Burgundy; Quinta do Noval in the Douro and Disznókö in Tokaji.

**Bacchus Society of America, The** Each year members elect a 'Mr Gourmet' who hosts a major two to three day wine and food event. See also Bob Dickinson and Hal Lewis and box page 65.

**Baker, Bill** Old friend, wine merchant and consultant. I have attended several old madeira tastings at his Mill House in Somerset.

**Bär Bank** Private Zürich bank headed by Thomas Bär. I conducted a tasting/dinner for the bank's VIP clients in 1998. He also owns the Podere Gaglione in Chianti which we visited in 1999. His wife Monika told me that they were not buying much art at Christie's because their spare cash was being swallowed up by the vineyard and winery!

**Barolet, Dr** The late Arthur Barolet took over an extensive Burgundy business founded by his father. The cellar, two stories deep, contained many thousands of dozens of wines from vintages dating back to 1911, a wide range of which I entitled the 'Collection du Dr Barolet' and sold at Christie's in December 1969.

**Barton, Anthony** Owner of Ch Léoville and Langoa-Barton in St-Julien. See box page 118.

**Beaulieu Vineyard** Known as 'BV'. Major old-established Napa winery. Top Cabernet Sauvignon is known as 'Private Reserve, Georges de Latour' (named after the founder). See box page 508.

**de Beaumont family, The** Former owners of Ch Latour. The cellars (vintages of Latour) of the Comtesse de Beaumont in Brittany and the Marquis de Beaumont at his castle in the Loire were packed by my wife and family over two Easter holidays. Subsequently we hired a self-drive van to pick the wine up for sale at Christie's in 1969 and 1975 respectively.

**Benson, Jeffrey** Wine dealer, compulsive collector – including walking sticks.

**Berger, Arne-Curt** Client, collector and organiser in Hamburg of 'Parker 100' tastings and wine dinners.

**Berenson, Bob** New York, in advertising. He hosted a memorable Grange Hermitage tasting in 1990.

**Berkmann, Joseph** Austrian-born restaurateur and UK wine importer. Pioneered some great wine dinners in the early 1970s. See box page 82.

**Bernard, Olivier** Owner of Domaine de Chevalier in Pessac-Léognan. I have enjoyed many tastings at the Domaine, and also dinner parties at which all the wines had vintages ending with the same number.

**Berry, Anthony** Former Chairman, now President of Berry Bros & Rudd and for long the Hon. 'Cellarer' of The Saintsbury Club (q.v.).

**Berry Bros & Rudd** 3 St James's Street, London. Old but surprisingly go-ahead wine merchant founded as a coffee house in 1698. See box page 37.

**Bettane, Michel** France's leading wine critic and taster. We meet regularly at Union des Grands Crus (q.v.) tastings in Bordeaux. He also attended Hardy Rodenstock's (q.v.) Ch d'Yquem marathon in 1998. See box page 87.

**Binaud family, The** Henry (an anglophile, hence Henry not Henri) married the daughter of the owner of Ch Cantemerle. They are very old Bordeaux friends of mine. Mme Binaud and her three daughters inherited fine cellars of old wine, subsequently sold at Christie's, including quantities of Ch La Tour de Mons as well as Ch Cantemerle.

**Bize-Leroy, Madame** 'Lalou' to her friends, once co-owner of the Domaine de la Romanée-Conti (q.v.), now concentrates on her own Domaine Leroy. Dynamic, forceful and a skilled mountain climber.

**Bjürkland, Johann** Swedish wine merchant resident in New York with offices in London and Burgundy.

**Black, Tom** American. Wines from his cellar were generously provided for the California 'cult' wine tasting at Waddesdon Manor, Buckinghamshire and Ch Cheval-Blanc at Spencer House, London. See also Russian National Orchestra.

**Bock, Dieter** German businessman and patron of the arts.

**Bohmrich, Roger** One of the first American Masters of Wine (q.v.). Conducted several Hollywood Wine Society (q.v.) seminars.

**Bordeaux Club** Six members share their best bottles at wine dinners. See box page 47.

**Borie family, The** The late and much respected Jean-Eugène Borie's two sons, Xavier and Bruno, own three major Bordeaux châteaux, Ducru-Beaucaillou, Haut-Batailley and Grand-Puy-Lacoste. Xavier runs the estates and Bruno owns Lillet, *the* Bordeaux apéritif.

**Breuer, Bernhard** Brilliant, sometimes controversial. He and his brother produce the Rheingau's best dry wines (Weingut Georg Breur). I have also attended several of his Rare Wine tasting dinners in Rüdesheim and at the dinner of 'The '9s' at Christie's.

**British Airways Wine Committee** Now disbanded. Remarkable tastings for the past 16 years. See box page 485.

**Broadbent family** My wife Daphne, daughter Emma, son Bartholomew all helped pack up old wines during family holidays! Bartholomew (married to Spencer) is now an enterprising wine importer based in San Francisco.

**Brooks's** One of the oldest gentlemen's clubs in London, founded in 1764. Some descendants of the original members still belong.

**Burr, Christopher** MW. For a time head of Christie's Wine Department.

**Carter, David** Fine cellar. His wife, Clare, is a cordon bleu cook.

**Cazes, Jean-Michel** Dynamic owner of Ch Lynch-Bages in Pauillac and until recently in charge of AXA's (q.v.) wine interests.

**Chaîne des Rôtisseurs** Wine and food society, particularly active in America. I am not a member but have conducted tastings for them.

**Champagne Academy** Annual week-long educational courses in Champagne organised by the leading *grande marque* houses for younger members of the UK trade. I attended the second, in 1957, then two weeks' long, and have missed only one annual dinner (in London) since.

**Charpie, Robert** Early Christie's client and one time robust chairman of the IWFS (q.v.).

**Christie's** The world's oldest fine art *and* wine auctioneers, founded in 1766. Two centuries later I became head of the first ever auction department devoted to wine. See box page 524.

**Christie's Wine Course** Founded by Steven Spurrier and myself in 1982. Regular sessions are held throughout the year.

**Chevaliers du Tastevin** A Burgundian *confrérie* or fraternity. See box page 242.

**Chippenham Lodge, 'CL'** Our two-hundred-year-old weekend hideaway near Bath.

**Cock, Frans de** See box page 227.

**Commanderie de Bordeaux** Founded in 1960 to promote the wines of Bordeaux. See box page 109.

**Cordier** From the 1920s important Bordeaux *négociants* and châteaux proprietors (Gruaud-Larose, Talbot, Lafaurie-Peyraguey and Meyney). Following Jean Cordier's death, Ch Talbot has been jointly owned – and effectively promoted – by his two daughters, Mme Bignon and Mme Rustmann.

**Crittenden, Doug** Prominent member of the Australian wine trade, now retired. Major tastings of old wines.

**Cruse family, The** Once the most important of Bordeaux's patrician *négociants* or 'merchant princes' and still socially prominent.

**Culinary Institute of America, The** The *other* 'CIA'. An impressive campus in upper New York State which I visited recently. Also now with a base in the Napa Valley.

*Decanter* As its oldest regular contributor (my 300th monthly article appeared in the June 2002 issue), I am bound to say it is the best British wine magazine! See box page 481.

**Delmas, Jean-Bernard** 'Delmas' and Ch Haut-Brion are virtually synonymous. Long a highly esteemed director of that château (also of La Mission) and a pioneer of clonal selection.

**Delon, Michel** Ch Léoville-Las-Cases was firmly on the map when the late Michel Delon took over from his father in the late 1970s. Efficient and shrewd, Michel created a 'super second' but was not the easiest of men. Even so, I learned a lot about tasting in his *chai*.

**Desai, Bipin** Masterly organiser of great tastings. See box page 108.

**Diel, Armin** Wine producer in the Nahe (Schlossgut Diel) and leading German wine critic.

**Dickinson, Bob** Miami, President of Carnival Cruise Lines and 'Mr Gourmet' 1997. See box page 65.

**Dillon family and cellars, The** Prominent American banking family. Clarence Dillon bought Ch Haut-Brion in 1935. His son, Douglas, one time US Ambassador in Paris, sold his magnificent cellar of wine at Christie's and his daughter Joan, first married to HRH Prince Charles of Luxembourg, on his death in 1977 married the Duc de Mouchy. Both the Duc and Duchesse are actively involved with Haut-Brion and the neighbouring La Mission. Joan's son, Comte Robert de Luxembourg is now managing director.

**Distillers' Company** The Worshipful Company of Distillers, a traditional London livery company of which I was Master, 1990–91.

**Domaine de la Romanée-Conti, 'DRC'.** See box page 223.

**Draper, Paul** One of California's most respected and consistent winemakers, of Ridge Vineyards. See box page 512.

**DRC** Domaine de la Romanée-Conti. See box page 223.

**Edmunds, Richard** In 1966 Dick became secretary of Boodle's Club in St James's Street and I joined Christie's. In 1996 we shared our 30th anniversary dinner.

**Eigensatz, Walter** Swiss German. Collector, generous host and superb organiser of memorable tastings. See box page 130.

**Eugénie-Les-Bains** Tiny village between Bordeaux and Pau dominated by Christine and Michel Guérard's (q.v.) hotel/restaurant Les Prés d'Eugénie, site of many wine weekends.

**Evans, Len** SA, OBE: larger than life Welsh-born Australian, winery owner, founder of Rothbury in the Hunter Valley, writer, raconteur, senior wine show judge, connoisseur, gregarious and generous in the extreme. See box page 532.

**Farr Vintners** London wine brokers. See box page 139.

**Fasque** The Gladstone family house in Scotland with a magnificent cellar. See box page 451.

**Flatt, Lloyd** Great tastings of Ch Mouton-Rothschild, Ausone and Lafite in New Orleans. See box page 11.

**Florida Weinfest** An over-ambitious 'international' wine show in Palm Beach, at which I was a speaker in 1998.

**Foulkes, Chris** and **Carrie** Book publishers.

**Freitas, Maria Manuela de** Of the distinguished Vasconcelos family. Owner of Barbeito (Madeira), now run by her son Riccardo.

**Frericks, Hans Peter** Munich businessman noted for his memorable Ch Pétrus tasting in 1986 at which Christian Mouiex and I tucked into lashings of beluga caviar with his '80 (see page 98).

**Friedrich, Jacqueline** American, living in Paris and the Loire, author of a helpful book on that region, *A Wine & Food Guide to the Loire*.

**Frost, David** From satirical review to TV guru. First encountered on his show in New York. See box page 451.

**Gaetani d'Aragona Lovatelli, Gelasio (Count)** Scion of a patrician Roman family, appearance of a Messiah, fiendish driver and immensely good company. And helpful – he knows everybody. His former wife now owns Argiano in Montalcino.

**Gagey, André** and **Pierre-Henry** André Gagey was the *gérant* at L Jadot, one of Burgundy's most dependable merchants and now American-owned. He is now retired but still keeps an eye on his son, Pierre-Henry who has succeeded him.

**Gaja, Angelo** Italian, from Barbaresco in Piedmont. A larger than life character. See box page 399.

*Gault-Millau* Long-established French wine and food magazine which made its name for fearless criticism. Organiser of two *Olympiade Mondiale* blind tastings in Paris.

**Geisel family, The** Owners of the excellent Hotel Königshof in Munich, the setting for several Rodenstock (q.v.) wine events; also a branch of the family owns the Hotel Victoria, Bad Mergentheim on the well-named Romantische Strasse near Würzburg (where I attended a Willsberger Bruno Giacosa tasting in 2002).

**Gidleigh Park Hotel** In Devon. I have hosted many wine weekends at the hotel. See box page 319.

**Glamis Castle** In Scotland. Birthplace of the late HM Queen Elizabeth, the Queen Mother. One of the great cellars including the 1870 Ch Lafite magnums sold at Christie's in 1971 (see page 16).

**Grosser Ring** Association of leading Mosel-Saar-Ruwer estates. Active organisers of tastings and the important annual wine auctions in Trier.

**Grubb, Pat** MW, very old wine trade friend, former head of Sotheby's wine department. Now a consultant, and wine merchant whose 'Pat Grubb Selections' list is strong on old madeiras.

**Gryn, Jo** Belgian wine journalist and *Gault-Millau* correspondent. We meet annually at the Union des Grands Crus (q.v.) tastings in Bordeaux, taste blind together and compare notes.

**Guérard, Michel** Legendary chef-owner of the Michelin 3-star hotel/restaurant Les Prés d'Eugénie at Eugénie-Les-Bains (q.v.) in south-west France.

**Guise, Carol** and **Jamie** Neighbours in the country. Produces excellent wines for excellent dinners. His father was the late Sir Anselme Guise Bt. of Elmore Court (see 1867 Ch d'Yquem page 173).

**Guntrum, Hanns Joachim (Hajo)** Joint owner of Weingut Louis Guntrum in the Rheinhessen which produces good wine lurking behind coloured bottles and fancy labels. He is an old friend; my son sells his wine by the container load.

**Halliday, James** One time lawyer, successful winemaker. Now the most highly regarded Australian wine writer and author.

**Hallwag** Successful Swiss/German publishers of my *Weinnotizen* and *Weine Prüfen Geniessen*.

**Hanson, Anthony** MW and Burgundy specialist, author of *Burgundy*, consultant to Haynes, Hanson & Clark and now 'senior director' of Christie's wine department.

**Hanson, Matts** Swedish man of wine with whom I have conducted wine tastings.

**Harris, Colin** Chelsea-domiciled and owner of a fine cellar.

**Harvey's of Bristol** Wine merchants. See box page 469.

**Hawkins, Charles** UK wine merchant/importer.

**Hébrard, Jacques** Long associated with Ch Cheval-Blanc, until recently owned by his wife and her two sisters. Many meetings, many tastings.

**Heublein** Major US wine importers, my association being solely as auctioneer at their highly successful annual wine auctions. See box page 216.

**Holden, Ronald** American organiser of high quality France in Your Glass wine tours of which I have hosted several at Eugénie-Les-Bains (q.v.), Georges Blanc's at Vonnas, Ch de Bagnols and elsewhere.

**Hollywood Wine Society** Florida. See box page 497.

**Homage à Ch d'Yquem und Schloss Johannisberg** An unprecedented, unique, comparative tasting co-hosted by Comte Alexandre de Lur Saluces and Paul Alfons, Fürst von Metternich-Winneburg at Schloss Johannisberg in 1984.

**Hood, Jim** Retired Bristol wine merchant.

**Hugel family, The** For over 350 years wine producers in Riquewihr, Alsace. References in the book particularly to Jean, son 'Johnny' and the latter's nephew Étienne.

**Ichinose, Ben** Major California collector.

**Incisi della Rocchetta, Niccolò (Marchese)** See box page 395.

**International Wine and Food Society, 'IWFS'** Founded by André Simon in England in 1933. See box page 76.

**Jacob, Louis C** Excellent hotel/restaurant on the outskirts of Hamburg, Germany. Memorable wine weekend in 2000.

**Jaeger, Wilfred** Venture capitalist and owner of a magnificent wine cellar in California. DRC and pre-phylloxera tastings. See box page 12.

**Jaffé, Professor Michael** The late distinguished art historian and member of the family formerly owning the Aschrott estate in Hochheim, Rheingau.

**Jefferson, Thomas** American President. See box page 171.

**Johnson, Hugh** The world's most successful wine author. Also an authority on trees. See also boxes page 47 and 424.

**Jorissen, Hans** Belgian. Old Christie's client. Memorable tastings, including Tokaji.

**Josey III, Lenoir** Collector from Houston, Texas. See box page 43.

**Kahn, Donald** See Russian National Orchestra.

**Kaplan, Stephen A** Chicago. Philanthropist and organiser of great tastings, dinners. See box page 425.

**Kesseler, August** Brilliant winemaker from Assmannshausen in the Rheingau. Makes Germany's best red wines.

**Khoury, Tawfiq** San Diego and Honolulu. Owner of one of the most extensive high quality cellars, part of which sold for record prices at Christie's in New York in 1997.

**Klatt, Michel** Industrialist and modest owner of a fine cellar.

**Knickerbocker Club** Fifth Avenue, New York. Gentlemen's club with convenient reciprocal arrangements with Brooks's in St James's. I have hosted two of their annual wine dinners.

**Kramer, Matt** American wine writer and brilliant conductor of 'Wine Experience' (q.v.) tasting seminars in New York.

**Kuhlmann, Magnus Freiherr von** Of Schloss Ramholz, a vast German 'Victorian' mansion and estate, his excellent cellar packed up by my wife, Brian Ebbeson, a wine department colleague, and myself. One of those hard-working fun jobs!

**Laidlaw, Sir Christophor** and **Nina**, his wife. Perfect hosts.
**Lake, Max** Sydney hand surgeon, pioneer Chardonnay and Cabernet winemaker (Lake's Folly, Hunter Valley).
**Latner, Joshua** Canadian. Hosted an excellent dinner at the Lanesborough Hotel in London.
**Lawther, James** MW living in Bordeaux.
**Lawton, Pierre** Scion of one of the oldest wine families in Bordeaux. Very successful young *négociant*, brilliant taster.
**Lawton, Mme**, née Lalande. Magnificent Bordeaux cellar, particularly of Ch Léoville-Poyferré.
**Lawton, Tastet et** Leading Bordeaux *courtiers*. Unique records since the 18th century.
**Laytons/Layton Tommy** See boxes page 54 and 350.
**Lebègue** Major UK wine importer headed by influential Guy Prince. Famous annual trade tastings.
**Lencquesaing, May de** Indefatigable owner of Ch Pichon-Longueville, Comtesse de Lalande in Pauillac.
**Leroy** See Bize-Leroy.
**Lever, Stuart** Magnificent cellar in Oxfordshire barn. Wine luncheon on lawn in rare summer heat in 1996.
**Lewis, Hal** 'Mr Gourmet' 1999 (see Bacchus Society). Hosted a splendid wine event in Memphis, Tennessee. Son-in-law of the late Arthur Hallé, an old friend with a great cellar.
**Lichine, Alexis** American of Russian extraction, monumental ego and charm to match. His *Wines of France* was the first wine book I read. Alexis promoted wines in the USA in the late 1940s and bought Ch Prieuré in Margaux. For a time this was my home-from-home in Bordeaux.
**Lloyd-Webber, Andrew (Lord)** Genius of musicals, collector of the finest Victorian paintings and wine lover. See box page 94.
**Loosen, Ernst, 'Ernie'** Dynamic head of leading Mosel producer, Dr Loosen.
**Loubat, Mme** Formidable widow, previous owner of Ch Pétrus and Libourne hotel/restaurant Loubat.
**Löwenstein, Prince Rupert** Management consultant with beautiful house and fine wine cellar in Surrey.
**Lundberg, Stig** Norwegian wine writer and pianist.
**Lur Saluces, Comte Alexandre de** For over two centuries his family owned Ch d'Yquem. Alexandre now manages the estate. Also President of the Académie du Vin de Bordeaux. See box page 46.
**Lurton family, The** The family owns more châteaux than any other in Bordeaux. My closest connections are with the indefatigable André, recent recipient of the *Légion d'Honneur*, his niece Bérénice Lurton-Thomas of Ch Climens, and Pierre Lurton, director of Ch Cheval-Blanc.
**Luze, Baron Geoffroy de** My oldest French friend. A trainee at Saccone & Speed (q.v.). Now retired and living at the exquisite Ch Paveil, in Soussans, Bordeaux.
**LVMH** French luxury goods group Louis Vuitton-Moët Hennessy owns champagne houses Moët & Chandon, Krug, Canard-Duchêne, Mercier, Ruinart, Pommery and Veuve Clicquot; as well as Ch d'Yquem in Bordeaux and numerous wineries in Australia, New Zealand, California and Argentina.
**Lyford Cay** An exclusive private estate in the Bahamas where the seriously rich have houses. I conducted annual tastings at the Lyford Cay Club in exchange for relaxing days by the pool.
**Lyons, Jonathan** Businessman. Former owner of London wine merchants.

**Mackenzie, Alastair** Schoolmaster, wine writer and author of *Château Mas de Daumas Gassac, the birth of a grand cru*.
**MADAS** A company in Bruges, Belgium, specialising in old madeira.
**Madeira Club, Savannah** Organises regular madeira tastings and dinners in historic Savannah, Georgia whose prosperous cotton and madeira trade was destroyed by the Civil War.
**MWA, MWC** Madeira Wine Association, then Company, in Funchal, incorporating Blandy, Cossart Gordon, Leacock and Rutherford madeira brands, now part owned by the Symington family of Oporto.
**Maliner, Dr Robert** Organiser of superb wine weekends in Florida. See box page 497.
**Manoncourt, Thierry** Owner of Ch Figeac in St-Émilion. He and his wife Marie-France are delightful hosts.
**Marchant, Michael le** Dealer in fine art and sculpture, with farmhouse and fine cellar in Somerset.
**Masters of Wine, Institute of** Originated as a UK trade examination, now open to candidates of high potential elsewhere, with MWs now in France, Switzerland, Australia, New Zealand and the United States. See box page 154.
**Mentzelopoulos family** (Ch Margaux) See box page 91.
**Metternich** Distinguished family presented with the ancient Schloss Johannisberg estate in the Rheingau by a grateful Emperor of Austria in the early 19th century. The widow of the last Prinz, Tatiana Prinzessin von Metternich-Winneburg lives at the Schloss and hosted Schloss Johannisberg's 900th anniversary tasting and dinner there in 2000.
**Metz, Ferdinand de** Director of the Culinary Institute of America (q.v.).
**Meyrick, Sir George, Bt** Magnificent cellars of old claret from Hinton Admiral, Hampshire and Bodorgan, Anglesey, sold at Christie's in 1970.
**Mondavi, Robert (Bob)** See box page 511.
**Mosimann, Anton** Renowned chef of Mosimann's, a dining club, formerly The Belfry, in Belgravia, London. Scene of many tastings and dinners.
**Moueix, Jean-Pierre** and **Christian** Lords of Pomerol. See box page 44.
**Mouchy, Duc** and **Duchesse de** See Dillon.
**Müller, Egon** Of Scharzhof in the Saar Valley. See box page 358.

**Napa Valley Wine Auction** See box page 516.
**Neipperg, Stefan Graf von** Successful German owner of Ch Canon-La-Gaffelière in St-Émilion. His brother runs the family wine estate, Schlossgut Graf von Neipperg in Württemberg, Germany.

**Okabayashi, Matsuo** Japanese long-term client of Christie's, collector and dealer in rare wines.
**Orr, David** With Harvey's (q.v.) in Jerez and Oporto, one-time managing director of Ch Latour and latterly of Ch Rauzan-Ségla and Ch Canon.
**Overton, Dr Marvin** American pioneer of brilliant themed tastings. See box page 89.

**Palumbo, Peter (Lord)** British. Buyer of Lot One of Christie's new wine department's first sale, 11 Oct 1966, and at all our subsequent major sales. See box page 452. True wine connoisseur and man of great taste.
**Parker, Robert (Bob)** American. The single most influential wine critic. See box page 104.

**Paul, Robert (Bob)** Coral Gables, Miami. Owner of a comprehensive collection of wine and giver of many major tastings with which I have collaborated as 'moderator'.

**Payne, Kerry** American entrepreneur. Organiser of an early Ch Latour tasting and host of major wine dinners.

**Penning-Rowsell, Edmund (Eddie)** The late dean of Bordeaux wine writers. See box page 77.

**Peppercorn, David** MW and old wine trade family, Bordeaux expert. Married to Serena Sutcliffe (q.v.).

**Peynaud, Professor Emile** Bordeaux's most influential enologist and wine adviser. See box page 50.

**Phillips, Barry** Former owner of The White Horse inn in Chilgrove, Sussex, famed for its cellar.

**Pigott, Stuart** British wine writer living in Berlin. Fearless critic of German wines.

**Plumb, Professor Sir John (Jack)** The late famed historian, Master of Christ's College, Cambridge and keeper of its, and his, famous cellar. See box page 47.

**Pol Roger, Danielle** and **Christian** With the de Billy family, presenting the charming and civilised face of champagne.

**Pong, Paolo** Hong Kong connoisseur. See box page 305.

**Pontallier, Paul** The articulate and inspirational director of Ch Margaux. Involved in other wine enterprises, notably with Bruno Prats (q.v.) in Chile.

**Prats, Bruno** Linked firmly with Ch Cos d'Estournel, now sold but run by his son Jean-Guillaume. His daughter Michèle was one of the speakers at a Hollywood Wine Society (q.v.) seminar in 1990.

**Price, Freddie** One of my oldest friends in the trade. For long with the wine merchant Dolamores. Importer of fine German wine. His wife Janet is a wine photographer.

**Primum Familiae Vinum, 'PFV'** Initiated in 1992, an association of some of the world's finest wine-producing families, complementary not competing. Their wines are well represented in my notes.

**Prince, Guy** See Lebègue.

**Prüm, J J** From Wehlen in the Mosel. See box page 346.

**Puisais, Jacques** One of France's leading wine tasters, president of the Union Nationale des Oenologues, the Union Internationale des Oenologues, the Institut Français du Goût, and so forth.


**Raben-Levetzau, Baron** See Aalholm.

**Renaud, Maurice** French. Dealer in fine and rare wine.

**Réserve, La** London wine merchant. Organises tasting seminars.

**Rhodes, Belle** and **Barney** For long influential players in the California wine scene. See box page 510.

**Ricard, Claude** He had to decide whether to become a concert pianist or run the small but high quality wine estate in the Graves, Dom de Chevalier. Well-liked, he did both well.

**Ribereau-Gayon, The Professors** Jean was the pioneering head of the Bordeaux's Institut d'Oenologie, now succeeded by his son Pascal.

**Riccardi, Riccardo (Count)** Not Italian but Piedmontese! Tall, gaunt, uncompromising; taught me about Italian quality wine. Past President of the Académie Internationale du Vin.

**Riedel, Georg** The man who put wine glasses on the international map. Superb quality, design – and marketing.

**Robinson, Jancis** Wine writer, author. See box page 201.

**Rodenstock, Hardy** Organiser of tasting events unmatched for range and quality of wines. See boxes page 110 and 211.

**Rolland, Michel** Based in Bordeaux. Wine consultant with a major influence on international style of (mainly) red wine.

**Rosebank** Our flat and my office overlooking the Thames near Hammersmith. Setting for many wine dinners.

**Rosebery, Lord** 5th Earl. See box page 422.

**Rothschild, Baron Eric de** Debonair head of the Domaines Barons de Rothschild (Ch Lafite, Duhart-Milon, Rieussec, L'Evangile – and in Chile and Portugal).

**Rothschild, Baron Philippe de** See box page 32.

**Rothschild, Baroness Philippine de** Baron Philippe's daughter and vivacious head of the Baron Philippe de Rothschild group, majority shareholder of Ch Mouton-Rothschild, Clerc-Milon, d'Armailhac. all in Pauillac, and of the biggest selling Bordeaux brand, Mouton Cadet. Also co-owner of Opus One in the Napa Valley.

**Roux bothers, The** Michel of the Waterside Inn, Bray, Albert and now Michel junior of Le Gavroche, Mayfair. Hugely influential chefs.

**Rush, Norman** Of Jackson, Mississippi. Wine distributor for whom I have conducted tastings and, on one occasion, as a tour guide of Bordeaux.

**Russell, Rudolf (Lord)** Younger son of the Duke of Bedford, a keen and knowledgeable taster.

**Russian National Orchestra** Highly regarded, unsubsidised, supported mainly by wealthy Americans including Gordon Getty. Fund-raising events have included recent great tastings and dinners in London, at Waddesdon Manor and Hatchlands, all hosted by Donald Kahn.

**Rutherfords, The** Prominent British wine trade family, David, an old friend now retired, succeeded his father Jack, a renowned connoisseur of claret, as the Hon. 'Cellarer' of The Saintsbury Club (q.v.).


**Saccone & Speed** Wine merchants, London and Gibraltar. See box page 467.

**Saintsbury Club, The** See box page 85.

**Salm-Salm, Michael Prinz zu** President of the VDP and runs 800-year family estate, Prinz zu Salm-Dalberg, in the Nahe. See box page 385.

**Sauska, Christian** Hungarian-born American helping in the revival of Tokaji.

**Schliff, Don** Client and collector with immaculately ordered underground cellar at his home in Glendale, California. Tasted madeira and old ports, and witnessed his ingenious method of heating port tongs for removing corks.

**Schubert, Max** Australian creator of Grange Hermitage.

**Shanken, Marvin** New York wine publisher (the *Wine Spectator* q.v.) and entrepreneur. See box page 516.

**Sichels, The** See box page 58. Allan Sichel was a founder member of the Bordeaux Club (q.v.).

**Simon, André L** French national, lived in England almost all his life. Educator, author, founder of the IWFS (q.v.). Great man, 'the Churchill of Wine and Food'.

**Skinner, Louis C (Lou)** See box page 67.

*Smag & Behag* The leading Danish food and wine magazine.

**Spurrier, Steven** Taught the French about wine at his *Académie du Vin* in Paris. Organised the famous French v. California blind tasting in 1976. Co-founder with me of Christie's wine courses (q.v.) in 1982.

**Sternby, Professor Nils** Of Malmöe, Sweden. Much travelled and leading member of the IWFS (q.v.).

**Stevenson, Tom** Champagne specialist, author of Christie's *World Encyclopedia of Champagne and sparkling wine.*

**Suckling, James** American, based in Italy, wine critic and European bureau chief of the *Wine Spectator*.

**Suffolk, 'Micky'** The 21st Earl. Keen wine buff, entertaining host.

**Sutcliffe, Serena** MW. Married to David Peppercorn (q.v.). Head of Sotheby's wine department.

**Sveass, Christan** Major Norwegian collector and host.

**Szepsy, Istvàn** Influential producer of Tokaji.

**Taams, Dr John** Dutch. See box page 66.

**Tchelistcheff, André** The late Beaulieu Vineyard genius. Doyen of California winemakers. See box page 22.

**Teysonneau, Mme** Great Bordeaux cellar. See box page 24.

**Thienpont family, The** Belgian wine merchants, owning Bordeaux châteaux, Vieux Ch Certan, Labegorce-Zédé and Le Pin.

**Third (III) Form Club** UK wine trade tasting club started by a group of (then) young men who, returning after the war, had joined or rejoined the trade. See box page 76.

**Thomson, Taylor** Canadian. Major collector.

**Torres, Miguel** Spanish. The unflamboyant dynamo behind the Torres family wine business in Penèdes, Spain, also in Chile. Brother of Marimar, wine producer in California.

**Union des Grands Crus** Large group of top Bordeaux châteaux from all the major appellations, excluding first growths and some 'super seconds'. See box page 103.

**Vandermeulen** Renowned Belgian wine bottler. It is said that the Belgian interest in burgundy was triggered by Philip the Bold (1363–1404) who married a Flemish wife and moved his court and capital from Dijon to Brussels. The Barolet (q.v.) business was mainly with Belgian customers.

**VDP Rheingau** Association of the top estates in the Rheingau. I conduct their fine and rare wine auctions. See page 385.

**Veronelli, Luigi** Italian journalist and publisher who fights fearlessly for quality.

**Villaine, Aubert de** Principal owner and manager (co-*gérant*) of the Domaine de la Romanée-Conti (q.v.). See box page 223.

**Vinexpo** Biennial trade fair. See box page 115.

**Vinopolis** 'City of Wine'. An impressive site on London's South Bank. Permanent exhibition with visitor tastings; trade tastings and large corporate events.

*Vinum* Swiss wine magazine for which I have conducted tastings.

**Wagner, Manfred** Swiss host of major tastings. See box page 225.

**Wassermann, Becky** American. Respected *courtier* (broker) working in Burgundy.

**Waugh, Harry** The late former director of Harvey's of Bristol (q.v.) and Ch Latour. Great taster. See box page 25.

**Weil, Weingut Robert** Major Rheingau estate. See box page 379.

**Weinart** See box page 155.

**Weiser, Ron** Prominent member of the Bacchus Society of America (q.v.). Now US Ambassador to Slovakia.

**Wheeler, John** We first met in Bordeaux in 1955. Involved with a serious non-trade tasting club.

**Wile, Julius** A highly respected and long retired member of the American wine trade but actively engaged in IWFS (q.v.)

activities, charitable work and the Culinary Institute of America (q.v.).

**Willsberger, Johann** Worldclass photographer of food, largely responsible for the design and illustrations of superbly produced German hardback magazine *Gourmet*; wine collector and organiser of a recent Bruno Giacomo tasting.

**Wilson, 'Barney'** Wheelchair-bound yet always cheerful English lawyer, with his wife Jane hosting top-class wine dinners.

**Wine Experience, The** Held in New York, occasionally alternating with San Francisco. A major event in the American wine calendar, started by Marvin Shanken (q.v.) of the *Wine Spectator* (q.v.) in 1981. Major seminars, over 1000 participants at seated tastings and a gala dinner at which the *Wine Spectator*'s annual distinguished Service Award is presented (I was honoured to receive this in 1991) and a series of awards for the best restaurant wine lists. See box page 516.

**Wine & Food Society, The** See IWFS.

**Wine Magazine** Started by Tommy Layton (q.v.) in the late 1940s. Revamped, and under the editorship of Kathleen Bourke, was successful and highly regarded by the mid-1960s. Some time after it ceased publication it was resuscitated as *Decanter* (q.v.). Confusingly but understandably there is another British magazine called *Wine*, founded in 1984.

**Wine Society, The** Short for the International Exhibition Wine Society, IECWS, founded in 1874. A British membership-owned wine retailer of high repute.

*Wine Spectator* The leading US wine journal. See also Marvin Shanken.

**Wine weekends** I believe that the wine weekend concept was started by the Castle Hotel, Taunton and shortly thereafter by Studley Priory near Oxford, at which I hosted a number. Gidleigh Park (q.v.), a Relais & Châteaux hotel on the edge of Dartmoor, has long organised some of the highest quality and most successful of these weekends, hosted by the likes of Jancis Robinson, Bill Baker and, until recently, myself.

**Winiarksi, Warren** Highly regarded owner of Stag's Leap Wine Cellars in the Napa Valley, his top wine the famous Cask 23. I have paid several visits to the winery and conducted tastings on his behalf, the most recent for 'Red' Adams. See box page 513.

**Winkeler, August** German wine writer living in Austria and in great demand at a speaker at major wine events. We meet frequently and I always address him as 'September'. The joke is wearing a bit thin.

**Wolf, Karl-Heinz** See box page 155.

**Woltners, The** Legendary owners of Ch La Mission Haut-Brion. See box page 53.

**Woodperry House** Sir John Thompson's great cellar. See box page 17.

**Yapp, Robin** Pioneer importer and retailer of the wines of the Loire and Rhône, now including other lesser known French wine regions like Madiran. His lists are informative.

**Yong, N K** 'Mr Wine' of South-East Asia. See box page 292.

**Zachys** Important retailer owned by Don Zacharia. Until recently Christie's wine auction partner in New York.

**Ziegler, Peter** German. Organiser of two of the greatest wine tastings I have ever attended. See box page 367.

**Zur Traube** Dieter Kaufman's enchanting riverside hotel restaurant at Grevenbroich near Düsseldorf, Germany. Site of the Bacchus Society (q.v.) dinner in May 2000.

# Glossary of words and expressions used in the tasting notes

**acid, acidity** Acidity is a vital component of all wine (tartaric acid is the main grape acid). For me it represents the wine's nervous system, adding zest and life. Wine with low acidity will be flabby and will not keep well; wine with too much will be sharp and tart. See also Volatile acidity.

**alcohol** An essential component of wine produced by the fermentation of natural grape sugars; 'light' or table wines usually vary between 11.5 and 13.5% (by weight or by volume); heavier table wines, particularly Sauternes, are 14 or 14.5%; sweet German wines from around 7 to 11.5%. Alcohol adds a certain sweetness as well as strength and, for me, represents the bone structure of wine. Fortified wines have grape or neutral spirit added at some stage in their production. Brandy added to port and madeira will bring them up to 20%, whereas sherry will range from 15.5 (*fino*) to 19%.

*allerfeinste* (German) The very finest.

*amoroso* A soft, sweet *oloroso* sherry.

*appellation contrôlée* French system of classifying and controlling wines from specific areas/regions.

*assemblage* The process of assembling wines from different lots or *cuves*, and, in Bordeaux, from different *cépages* (q.v.), to make up the final blend.

*Aszú* Sweet Tokaji wine, measured in *puttonyos* (q.v.).

*Auslese* (German) The third level in the QmP quality wine scale. See page 343.

**Balling** Measure of grape sugar before fermentation. Brix (q.v.) is similar.

*ban de vendanges* (French) Official declaration of the start of harvest.

**barley sugar** A British boiled sweet (candy) made from sugar and egg white.

**Baumé** Principal European measure of grape sugar.

*barrique* (French) Standard Bordeaux barrel with a capacity of 225l (25 dozen bottles).

*Beerenauslese (BA)* (German) The fourth level in the QmP quality wine scale. See page 343.

**bin, binned** Traditional British term for a shelf or rack in a cellar for storing and maturing wine.

**'blackstrap'** A wine with substance and 'grip' (q.v.). Usually port.

**bleeding** Reducing the water content of the grape juice before fermentation (*saignée* in French), usually done only after poor, rainy season.

**blind tasting** Glasses presented anonymously, with the name of the wine revealed after tasting, to avoid bias.

**body** Usually refers to the weight – extract and alcohol. Varies according to the type of wine.

**botrytis** See box page 173.

**bottle stink** Stale air between cork and wine. Usually dissipates quickly.

**bready** See box page 432.

**BYOB** Bring Your Own Bottle, usually without 'corkage' charge.

**Brix** Measurement of sugar content of grapes. Balling (q.v.) is similar.

*brut* Dry. See box page 423.

*cave* (French) Cellar.

*cépage* (French) Grape variety; (South Africa) cultivar.

*chai* (French) Cellar or winemaking facility.

**chaptalisation** Permitted addition of sugar to grape must prior to fermentation in years when natural sugar is deficient, to increase the alcoholic strength. Chaptalised wines can be very attractive when young but do not keep well.

*chef de culture* (French) Vineyard manager.

**claret** Traditional British name for red Bordeaux.

*climat* (French) A specifically defined vineyard site.

*clos* (Burgundy) A walled vineyard.

**cochylis** Pest that damages vines.

**colheita** (Portuguese) Style of port and madeira, the wine of a given vintage matured in cask. See box page 479.

**corked** Faulty cork that has a deleterious effect, spoiling the smell and taste of wine due, it has been discovered, to trichloranisole. An increasing problem; less frequent in the days of hand-corking machines where the cellarmen could inspect each cork. The introduction of bottling lines in the 1960s put paid to such close inspection.

**corky** Describes the smell of an old, poor, soft or disintegrating cork, varying in its effect. Sometimes the smell wears off.

*corsé* (French) Full-bodied.

*coulure* A condition whereby grape bunches fail to set properly. See box page 445.

*courtier* (French) Broker. *Kommissar* in German. Both act as a go-between between producer and merchant.

**crust** Firm sediment in the bottle of a well-matured vintage port.

**crusted** Style of port. See box page 479.

**cryoextraction** Freezing of must to replicate conditions necessary for an Eiswein/icewine.

**declaration** The announcement by a port producer (the brand owner), usually made in the second spring after the harvest, that the quality of wine is high enough for it to be shipped as 'vintage'.

*dégorgement* (French) A method of removing sediment from a champagne bottle.

**Denominazione di Origine Controllata (DOC)** Italian quality wine classification for wines of controlled origin, grape types and style.

**Denominazione di Origine Controllata e Garantita (DOCG)** Top Italian quality wine classification meant to be one step up from DOC (q.v.).

*dosage* Part of the champagne process. See box page 436.

**double-cross tasting** Tasting where the wines can be compared both horizontally (different wines from the same vintage) and vertically (the same wine from different vintages).

*Edelbeerenauslese* (German) Classification category for wine from selected super-ripe single berries, a level up from Beerenauslese (q.v. ).

*Edelfäule* (German) Botrytis or noble rot. See box page 343.

*Eiswein* (German) Wine from grapes frozen on the vine which concentrates the grape sugar. Always sweet. Icewine is the Canadian equivalent. See box page 353.

*élevage, élevé* (French) See box page 265.

*en primeur* (French) Wine purchased before bottling, often the spring after the vintage, mainly Bordeaux. Not a new practice but a largely speculative activity that intensified around 1970 and was revived by the 1982 vintage and since.

**Erstes Gewächs** (German) First growth vineyard/wine. See page 343.

**Eszencia** Intensely sweet Tokaji from botrytis-affected grapes. See box page 411.

**extract** Richness from components other than the basic elements of wine, i.e. sugar, water, alcohol (q.v.) and acidity (q.v.).

*faisandé* (French) High, gamey bouquet and taste.

*feine, feinste* (German) Fine, finest.

*fermier* (French) Farm, farmyard smell, rustic character.

**'flight'** A (usually) small group of wines, part of a larger tasting.

**F.O.B.** Free On Board. The producer or merchant delivers to the port of embarkation. The purchaser is responsible for freight, insurance and taxes thereafter.

*fruchtig* (German) Fruity, medium-sweet to sweet, as opposed to trocken (dry) wines.

**fruit gum** A fruit-flavoured, gelatine-based sweet (candy).

*Fuder* (German) Barrel, cask.

**full-bodied** Describes a mouthfilling table wine, high in extract (q.v.) and alcohol (q.v.), or a robust port or madeira.

*garrafeira* (Portuguese) A reserva (q.v.) quality wine.

*gérant, gérante* (French) Manager.

*gibier* (French) Game, gamey somewhat akin to *faisandé*.

**GL (Gay Lussac)** French measure of alcoholic strength.

*Goldkapsel* (German) Gold capsule, indicating a superior quality wine (prior to 1971 the prefix *feine* or *feinste* used).

*grand cru* See boxes page 234 and 331.

*grand format* (French) A large bottle.

*grand vin* (French) An important wine; the principal wine of a property.

**'green'** Unripe, acidic, raw wine.

**'green harvest'** The thinning out of bunches to concentrate the vines' nourishment; practised by those who put quality before quantity.

**'grip'** Positive firmness.

**Gripfix** A brand of glue paste with a distinctive marzipan-like smell.

**high-toned** ethereal, zestful acidity, mainly associated with madeira.

**horizontal tasting** Different wines of the same vintage.

**Jelly baby** A British candy.

*Kabinett* (German) The first level in QmP quality wine scale. See page 343. Sometimes in the past spelled 'Cabinet'.

*Kommissar* (German) A broker.

*lange* (German) Long. Indicates superior quality, as in *lange Goldkapsel*.

**LBV** Late Bottled Vintage port. See box page 479.

**laying down** Traditional British expression: binning (often storing in original cases) wine for maturation. A wine for laying down is one which

needs, and will benefit from, bottle ageing. One does not 'lay down' everyday wines for quick consumption.

**'legs'** or **'tears'** The globules which, after swirling, ooze down the sides of the glass; generally indicative of a rich wine.

**length** One of the hallmarks of quality is the length of time the flavour takes to cross the palate. In French, *persistance*.

**lodge** (port) See box page 456.

**maderised** A degree of oxidation tolerable in some old wines. Indicated by a drab brown tinge and flat taste.

*maître de chai* (French, mainly Bordeaux) Cellar master with major responsibilities from the delivery of grapes to vinification and *élevage* (q.v.).

*marque* (French) Brand. *Grande marque* champagnes are the major brands.

**mature** A mature wine is one in which all the component parts have, over a period of time (varying according to the type of wine), combined harmoniously. Perfect maturity is elusive; it should be the ultimate expression of the wine. It is essential that the initial elements should be well balanced and the wine cellared properly for time to effect the translation from immature, unready, to mature, perfect to drink. In essence this is what this book is all about.

**mercaptan** An unpleasant rubbery smell due to the breakdown of sulphur dioxide.

**microclimate** A widely and sensibly misused term by the trade, even by producers, and one that I adhere to. I use it to refer to the climate of one specific area or vineyard. However, in academic horti- and viticultural circles, a macroclimate embraces the climate of a region, a mesoclimate is the climate of a specific area, be it one vineyard or a valley, and a microclimate is the immediate physical environment of a vine.

**millerandage** Imperfect fruit set due to adverse weather conditions. Reduces the potential crop.

*moelleux* (French) Mellow. Usually medium-sweet.

**must** Grape juice before it is fermented into wine.

*monopole* (Burgundy) A solely owned vineyard.

*négociant* (French) Merchant. A *négociant-éleveur* buys wine for *élevage* (q.v.) in his own cellar.

**oak** The wood preferred by coopers (*tonneliers,* q.v.), used for centuries for maturing and transporting wine. New

oak *barriques* (q.v.) from seasoned wood from the vast forests of France and elsewhere, can be both well-used and abused. New oak imparts a clove- or cinnamon-like spiciness which is, alas, a fashionable taste and which, without adequate fruit and extract (q.v.), can dominate the smell and taste of wine, both red and white. Correctly used, oak adds complexity, flavour and, to a lesser extent, tannin (q.v.), and launches the wine into its path of maturity. Shortcuts can be, and are, taken by simply adding oak chips - like making tea with a cheap tea bag.

*Oechsle* A measure of grape sugar ripeness widely used in Germany.

**oidium** Common fungal disease. See box page 499.

**oxidised** A certain amount of oxidation is normal, even desirable (it comes through the staves of casks and through the cork, even though it is covered with a capsule) but the term oxidised refers to a wine – red or white – which has been over-exposed to air. Its colour will take on a drab brown tinge, rather like a cut apple, its nose and taste will be flat, often with a grubby, yeasty finish. An ullaged bottle, with level of wine mid or low shoulder, is an indication of cork failure and, unless the air is benign, the wine will not be fit to drink. (In the case of old champagne, the ullage, q.v., might just be carbon dioxide out of solution. All depends on the cork.)

*passerillage* (French) An expression used in sweet wine to indicate the use of shrivelled grapes not affected by botrytis but with enhanced sugar content.

**peppery** The effect of a young wine high in alcohol, notably vintage port.

*pétillant* (French) Slightly sparkling.

**phylloxera** A deadly aphid which attacks vine roots.

**'pinched'** Mean, thin on the palate.

**pipe** A traditional port and madeira cask, the size depending on use for maturing or shipping, but larger than a *barrique* (q.v.), contents roughly 475-525l (105 to 115 gallons).

**Pontefract cakes** Flat discs of liquorice made in Pontefract, Yorkshire. This is very much a personal association. Pontefract was the centre of production. The liquorice fields no longer exist.

*premier cru* (French) Literally, first growth. See box page 234.

**pricked** A British trade expression meaning acidic, over-tart, verging on vinegar.

**prickly** Touch of sharpness.

*puttonyos* (**putts**) A measure of concentrated grape juice added to Tokaji wines. See box page 411.

**QbA** German wine classification. See page 343.
**QmP** German wine classification. See page 343.
**quinta** (**Qta**) (Portuguese) A wine farm, equivalent to château in Bordeaux. A single-quinta wine (see box page 479) is a port made at a named quinta.

**raya** A lesser quality *oloroso* sherry used for blending. I use the word in a derogatory sense, implying a dull, common, straw-like smell.
**reconditioning** Topping up and recorking.
**RD** See box page 429.
*régisseur* (French) Manager, director.
*rendement* (French) Yield. An important term expressed in hl/ha (hectolitres per hectare). A small yield is usually of higher quality than a large yield.
**Reserva** (Spanish, Portuguese), **Réserve** (French), **Riserva** (Italian) all indicate a higher quality, whether or not specifically and officially defined.
*robe* (French) Appearance and colour of the wine.
**ruby** Used in this book simply to describe a colour, not a port style.

*saignée* See bleeding.
**'Second' wines** Wines made from young vines and/or from *cuves* or vats deemed of not high enough quality to be marketed as the *grand vin* (q.v.); usually associated with the bigger and more important Médoc châteaux. Expensive for the château proprietor: for example at Ch Lafite in 1999, only 40% of the crop was used for the *grand vin*. 'Second' wines are usually good and relatively good value.
*Sélection de Grains Nobles* Mainly in Alsace, France. See box page 327.
**shipper** The term has two meanings. A British shipper is a wine importer, London shippers often being the agent for an overseas producer. However, when it comes to port, a shipper is the producer, the Oporto-based brand owner.
**single-quinta** Style of port. See box page 479.
*sous bois* Reminiscent of damp, earthy undergrowth.
*sous-marque* A secondary brand of a large champagne house.
**Spanish root** A liquorice-tasting root for chewing.

*Spätlese* (German) The second level in the QmP quality wine scale. See page 343.
**spritz, spritzig** A refreshing prickle of carbonic acid gas, induced or occurring naturally in a young acidic wine.

**t & a** Abbreviations used in my tasting note books. This stands for tannin (q.v.) and acidity (q.v.).
**tannate of iron** A rusty taste.
**tannin** An important element in all red wine and often misunderstood or taken for granted, tannin is an anti-oxidant extracted mainly from grape skins but also from the staves of casks. Tannin acts as a preservative. It also – virtually all doctors now agree – helps keep one's arteries clear – in short, it is good for the heart. There are hard tannins and soft ripe tannins, the former having a mouth-puckering astringency and a bitter effect in the mouth, the latter usually considered more desirable, less harsh. Tannin precipitates colouring matter during the course of maturation, first in cask, then in bottle – which is why it is desirable to decant old wine. Finally, tannin leaves the mouth clean and dry between mouthfuls of food and aids the digestion. As you can see, I am a great fan of tannin and deplore the tendency to prefer soft, full, easy-to-taste wines which, though often gold medal winners, are not as good with food.
*tastevin* (French) A shallow cup, usually of silver or silver plated, used for tasting wine in dark Burgundian cellars; the circular indentations reflect the candlelight and reveal the clarity of the wine. Also used more pretentiously with ribbons of office and, inappropriately, by restaurant sommeliers. Worse still, used as ashtrays!
**tawny** The colour of very mature port. See box page 449.
**'tears'** See 'legs'.
**terroir** (French) An expression as widely misunderstood as it is widely used. An all-embracing term which covers every aspect of the natural environment of a vineyard site including soil, subsoil, exposure (to sun, wind, frosts) and microclimate (q.v.).
*tête de cuvée* (French) Generally implies wine from the best or top *cuve*, vat, or cask, similar to Reserva/Réserve (q.v.).
*tonneau* (French) Historically the traditional unit of sale in Bordeaux, the price being per *tonneau*; one *tonneau* equalled four *barriques* (q.v.), totalling approximately 100 dozen bottles.
*tonnelier, tonnellerie* (French) cooper,

cooperage; specialist(s) in the making of barrels. Some châteaux, Haut-Brion for example, employ their own coopers.
*trie* A 'pass'. See box page 194.
**trocken** (German) Dry (wine); not to be confused with TBA, below.
*Trockenbeerenauslese* (**TBA**) (German) The highest level in the QmP quality wine scale. See page 343.
**'tutored' tasting** Usually a seated tasting, with a lecturer discussing and comparing each wine. I hate the expression; but it is a good way to teach and to learn.

**ullage** The space between the cork and the wine. If abnormal, i.e. the wine does not reach into the neck of the bottle, the level is described in wine auction catalogues, and in my notes, as high fill, mid-shoulder etc. or measured in inches or centimetres. The lower the level, the greater the likelihood of oxidation. See facing page.

*Vendange Tardive* (French) Late harvest. See box page 327.
*véraison* (French) The stage of ripening when (in the summer) the grapes change colour.
**vertical tasting** A comparative tasting of different vintages of the same wine.
*vigneron* (French) Wine grower. Curiously, a term used more in Burgundy than in Bordeaux.
*vignoble* (French) Vineyard.
*vin de garde* (French) A quality wine which is suitable for laying down (q.v.).
**vintage** Relates to wine made in a single year, also loosely used for grape harvest, the time of picking. Also a style of port. See box page 449.
**Virol** An old-fashioned tonic for anaemia with a malty smell and taste.
**volatile acidity** A normal but usually very small component of wine. Some wines, madeira for example, have naturally high volatile acidity compensated for by the richness of the wine. Excess volatile acidity due to poor winemaking or poor storage conditions and oxidation can be detected by its vinegary smell and sharp taste.

**weight** The heaviness or lightness of a wine, depending on its component parts, particularly body (q.v.), extract (q.v.) and alcohol (q.v.).
**wood port** See box page 449.
**woody** An undesirable smell or taste, imparted, usually, by old or defective casks. Not to be confused with oak/oaky (q.v.).

# Level/Ullage Descriptions and Interpretations

The original drawing and Bordeaux definitions were devised for Christie's wine catalogues and then first published in the first sale of the 1987–88 auction season, a Claret Sale of 17 September 1987; the Burgundy definitions appeared in the Fine Wine Sale of 29 October. A pity that Christie's did not copyright all this as the diagrams and definitions have been widely copied by all and sundry since then!

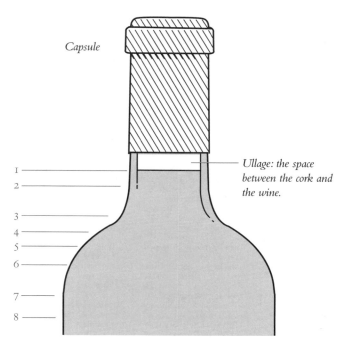

*Capsule*

*Ullage: the space between the cork and the wine.*

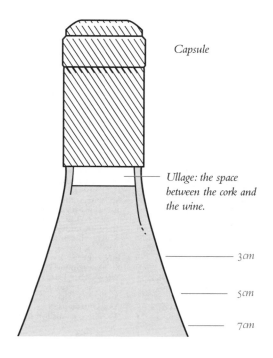

*Capsule*

*Ullage: the space between the cork and the wine.*

3 cm

5 cm

7 cm

## BORDEAUX

*1 high fill*: Normal fill, level of young wines (often the level of bottles of older vintages recorked at the châteaux).

*2 into neck*: Perfectly good for any age of wine. Outstandingly good for a wine of 10 years in bottle, or longer.

*3 top shoulder*: Normal for any red Bordeaux 15 years or older.

*4 upper-shoulder*: Slight natural reduction through the easing of the cork and evaporation through cork and capsule. Usually no problem. Acceptable for any wine over 20 years old. Exceptional for pre-1950 wines.

*5 mid-shoulder*: Probably some weakening of the cork and some risk. Not abnormal for wines 30-40 years of age. Pre-auction estimates usually take this into account.

*6 mid-low shoulder*: Some risk. Catalogue estimates will be low.

*7 low shoulder*: Risky and usually only accepted for sale if wine or label exceptionally rare or interesting. Always offered with low estimate.

*8 below low-shoulder*: Wine will usually be undrinkable and not acceptable for sale unless a rare sort of bottle.

## BURGUNDY

Because of the slope of shoulder it is impractical to describe levels as mid-shoulder, etc. Wherever appropriate the level between cork and wine will be measured and catalogued in centimetres. The condition and drinkability of burgundy is less affected by ullage than its equivalent from Bordeaux. For example, a 5- to 7-cm ullage in a 50-year-old burgundy can be considered normal, indeed good for its age, 3.5 to 4cm excellent for its age and even 7cm is rarely a risk.

| BOTTLE SIZES | | |
|---|---|---|
| Magnum | 2 bottles | 1.5 litre |
| Marie-Jeanne | 3 regular bottles | 2.25 litres |
| Tregnum (p) | 3 bottles | 2.25 litres |
| Jeroboam (bu, ch) | 4 bottles | 3 litres |
| Double magnum (bu,ch) | 4 regular bottles | 3 litres |
| Jeroboam (bo) | 6 regular bottles | 4.5 (or 5 litres) |
| Rehoboam | 6 regular bottles | 4.5 litres |
| Impériale | 8 regular bottles | 6 litres |
| Methuselah (bu) | 8 regular bottles | 6 litres |
| Salmanazar | 12 regular bottles | 9 litres |
| Balthazar (ch) | 16 bottles | 12 litres |
| port (p) burgundy (bu) bordeaux (bo) champagne (ch) | | |
| 1 regular bottle = 75 cl | | |

# Index of Wines

Wine names are listed in alphabetical order with vintage and page number. Please note there are many inconsistencies of spelling. For example, Burgundy (domaines and vineyards); Madeira grape names (Boal and Bual); and German wine names (Berncasteler/Bernkasteler, Doctor/Doktor). Vineyards in Burgundy, the Rhône, Alsace, the Loire, Germany and Madeira can have several owners who choose to use different versions of the name for their wines. To avoid duplication, domaine and estates have been omitted from the index so refer to the relevant page for details of the producer. In California the winery or producer name comes first.

## A

Acacia
Carneros Pinot Noir 1997 *527*; Iund Vineyard Pinot Noir 1984 *517*; Pinot Noir 1979 *514*; St Clair Vineyard Pinot Noir 1986 *519*
Agassac, Ch d' 2000 *168*
Aile d'Argent 1999 *213*
Aloxe-Corton 1916 *218*, 1920 *219*, 1980 *246*; Brunettes 1929 *221*; Vercot 2000 *272*; Vieilles Vignes 1964 *233*
Alpha Domus 'The Aviator' 1998 *534*
Angélus, Ch 1998 *158*, 1999 *161*, 2000 *165*; see also Angélus, Ch L' for wines before 1998
Angélus, Ch L' 1934 *38*, 1952 *54*, 1964 *70*, 1966 *74*, 1970 *82*, 1981 *101*, 1983 *107*, 1992 *137*, 1993 *140*, 1994 *145*, 1995 *147*, 1996 *151*, 1997 *155*; see also Angélus, Ch for wines after 1997
Angludet, Ch d' 1964 *70*, 1970 *82*, 1979 *96*, 1983 *110*, 1985 *116*, 1988 *124*, 1989 *128*, 1990 *134*, 1992 *137*, 1993 *139*, 1995 *149*, 1996 *153*, 1997 *155*, 1998 *158*, 1999 *161*, 2000 *165*
Anheuser Riesling 'Classic', Paul 2000 *390*
Anjou, Rablay 1928 *316*
Araujo, Eisele Vineyard Cabernet Sauvignon 1991, 1992 *522*, 1993 *523*, 1994 *524*, 1995 *525*
Arche, Ch d' 1876 *174*, 1900, 1906 *176*, 1923 *179*, 1936 *182*, 1975 *195*, 1986 *201*, 1987 *202*, 1989 *204*, 1990 *206*, 1996 *209*, 1998 *212*
Arche-Pugneau, Cru d' 1923 *179*
Arcins, Ch d' 1995 *149*
Arietta 1996 *526*, 1997 *527*; Merlot 1998 *527*, 1999 *528*; Napa Valley 1998 *527*, 1999 *528*
Armagh Syrah 1990 *533*
Armailhac, Ch d' 1989 *128*, 1990 *131*, 1992 *137*, 1993 *139*, 1994 *145*, 1995 *147*, 1996 *151*, 1997 *155*, 1998 *158*, 1999 *161*, 2000 *165*; see also Mouton d'Armailhacq, Mouton-Baron-Philippe, and Mouton-Baronne-Philippe
Arrosée, Ch L' 1985 *116*
Assmannshäuser Hinterkirch Spätburgunder Kabinett 1959 *351*; Höllenberg Riesling Spätburgunder

1943 *348*; Höllenberg Riesling Spätburgunder Kabinett 1946 *349*; Höllenberg Rot-Weiss Riesling Auslese 1938 *347*; Höllenberg Spätburgunder 1921 *346*; Höllenberg Spätburgunder Kabinett trocken 1986 *369*; Höllenberg Spätburgunder Spätlese '★★★' 1993 *377*; Höllenberg Spätburgunder Weissherbst Auslese 1975 *360*; Höllenberg Spätburgunder Weissherbst BA 1994 *379*; Höllenberg Spätburgunder Weissherbst Eiswein BA 1977 *363*; Höllenberg Spätburgunder Weissherbst Spätlese '★★★' 1994 *378-9*; Höllenberg Spätburgunder Weissherbst TBA 1994 *379*; Spätburgunder Auslese 1893 *344*; Assmannshäuser Weissherbst Auslese 1989 *370*
Aszú see Tokaji
Au Bon Climat Arroyo Grande Valley Pinot Noir 1992 *522*; Benedict Vineyard Pinot Noir 1989 *520*; Bien Nacido Pinot Noir 1999 *528*; Pinot Noir 1990 *520-1*, 1994 *524*
Ausone, Ch 1849 *13*, 1874, 1877 *18*, 1879 *19*, 1894 *22*, 1899 *23*, 1900, 1902 *25*, 1906 *26*, 1911 *27*, 1912, 1913, 1914, 1916 *28*, 1918 *29*, 1921 *31*, 1925 *33*, 1926 *34*, 1928 *35*, 1934 *38*, 1936 *39*, 1937 *40*, 1942 *41*, 1943 *42*, 1945 *44*, 1947 *46*, 1949 *50*, 1950 *52*, 1952 *54*, 1953 *55*, 1954 *57*, 1957 *59*, 1958 *60*, 1959 *61*, 1961 *65*, 1962 *68*, 1964 *70*, 1966 *72*, 1967 *75*, 1969 *77*, 1970 *80*, 1971 *83*, 1972 *84*, 1973 *85*, 1974 *86*, 1975 *87*, 1976 *90*, 1977 *91*, 1978 *92*, 1979 *95*, 1980 *98*, 1981 *99*, 1982 *102*, 1983 *107*, 1985 *113*, 1987 *120*, 1988 *121*, 1989 *125-6*, 1990 *130*, 1995 *146*, 1996 *150*, 1997 *155*, 2000 *165*
Auxey-Duresses 2000 *272*
Avelsbacher Hammerstein Riesling Auslese 1983 *366*
Averys (port) 1922 *457*, 1960 *471*, 1963 *471*
Ayala 1964 *431*, 1989 *445*, 1990 *446*

Azay-le-Rideau 1990 *321*, 1997 *323*

## B

Balestard-La-Tonnelle, Ch 1996 *153*, 1997 *155*, 2000 *168*
Barbaresco 1958 *394*, 1961 *394-5*, 1964 *395*, 1971 *396*, 1978 *397*, 1982 *398-9*, 1985 *400*, 1986, 1988 *401*, 1989 *402*, 1991 *404*, 1996 *405*, 1997 *406*; Asili 1988 *401*, 1990 *403*; Camp Gros 1985 *400*, 1997 *406*; 1978 *397*, 1990 *403*, 1996 *405*; Gaiun 1985 *400*, 1990 *403*; Gallina di Neive 1979 *397*; Martinenga 1997 *406*; Martinenga, Gaiun 1996 *405*; Monprivato 1982 *399*; Riserva 1962 *395*; Santo Stefano di Neive d'Alba 1969 *395*; Santo Stefano, Riserva Speciale 1974 *396*, 1978 *397*, 1985 *400*, 1988 *401*, 1990 *403*; Sorì San Lorenzo 1982 *399*, 1985 *400*, 1990 *403*, 1996 *405*; Sorì Tildin 1978 *397*, 1983 *399*, 1985 *400*, 1996 *405*; Vanotù 1982 *399*, 1990 *403*
Barbera d'Alba 1978 *397*
Barbera d'Asti 1996 *405*; La Court 1997 *406*, 1998, 1999 *408*; Quorum 1997 *406*; Cipressi della Court 1999 *408*, 2000 *409*
Barca Velha 1978, 1983, 1985, 1989, 1990, 1991, 1992, 1994, 1995 *418*
Baret, Ch 1946 *46*
Barolo 1952, 1958, 1959 *394*, 1978 *397*, 1980 *398*, 1982 *399*, 1985 *400*, 1990 *403*, 1991 *404*; Arborina 1990 *403*; Bric del Fiasc 1990 *403*; Bricco Boschis, Vigna San Guiseppe 1989 *402*; Brunate 1990 *403*; Bussia 1997 *406*; Bussia Riserva Speciale 1974, 1975 *396*, 1979 *397*; Bussia Roche 1997 *407*; Ca' d'Morissio 1997 *406*; Cannubi 1982 *399*, 1990 *403*, 1997 *406*; Cannubi Boschis 1990 *403*, 1997 *406*; Cascina Francia 1997 *407*; Cerequio 1982 *399*, 1990 *403*, 1996 *405*, 1997 *406*, 1998 *408*; Ciabot Manzoni 1997 *407*; Ciabot Mentin Ginestra 1982 *399*, 1990 *403*; Cicala 1997 *407*; Classico 1949 *394*, 1961 *395*; Colonello 1997 *407*; Costa Grimaldi 1997 *406*; Enrico VI 1997 *406*; Falletto 1997 *397*, 1986, 1988 *401*, 1997 *406*; Falletto

(White Label) 1982 *399*; Falletto, Riserva Speciale 1985 *400*; Gran Bussia 1982 *399*, 1990 *403*; Marcenasco 1978 *397*, 1997 *406*; Monfortino 1955 *394*, 1964 *395*, 1990 *403*; Monprivato 1982 *399*; Monprivato, Ca' d'Morissio, Riserva 1995 *405*; Monprivato, Riserva 1997 *406*; Nei Cannubi 1997 *406*; Ornato 1990 *403*; Parafada 1997 *407*; Rionda 1967 *395*, 1969 *396*; Rionda, Riserva Speciale 1978 *397*, 1982 *399*, 1990 *403*; Riserva 1937, 1944 *393*, 1947, 1954, 1957 *394*, 1961, 1962, 1967 *395*, 1970, 1971 *396*, 1978 *397*; Riserva Bricco Boschis 1985 *400*; Riserva Speciale 1951 *393*, 1959 *394*, 1967 *395*, 1970, 1971 *396*; Riserva Speciale (Red Label) Colline Rionda de Serralunga 1967 *395*, see also Barolo, Rionda above; Riserva, Villero 1989 *402*; Rocche dell'Annunziata 1990 *403*; Serralunga Riserva 1978 *397*; Sperss 1989 *402*, 1990 *403*, 1995 *405*; Vigna dei Pola 1997 *406*; Vigna Rionda 1997 *407*; Vigna La Rosa 1997 *407*; Le Vigne 1997 *406*; (White Label) 1974 *396*
Baron de Forrester 1985 *485-6*
Barros 1945 *464*, 1970 *478*, 1980 *483*, 1997 *492*
Barry, Jim, Clare Valley Cabernet Sauvignon *533*
Bastardo 1870 *499*, 1875 *499-500*, 1927 *502*; Vintage 1969 *504*
Bastor-Lamontagne, Ch 1929 *186*, 1968 *189*, 1970 *192*, 1976 *196*, 1989 *203*, 1990 *206*, 1996 *209*, 1997 *210-11*, 1998 *212*, 1999 *213*, 2000 *214*
Batailley, Ch 1924 *33*, 1945 *44*, 1947 *47*, 1955 *58*, 1959 *62*, 1961 *65*, 1966 *68*, 1966 *72*, 1969 *77*, 1970 *80*, 1971 *84*, 1973 *85*, 1975 *88*, 1976 *90*, 1979 *96*, 1982 *102*, 1983 *107*, 1985 *113*, 1986 *117*, 1989 *126*, 1990 *131*, 1993 *139*, 1994 *145*, 1995 *147*, 1996 *151*, 1997 *155*, 1998 *158*, 1999 *161*
Bâtard-Montrachet 1929 *274*, 1945 *275*, 1957 *276*, 1964 *277*, 1970 *278*, 1976, 1978 *279*, 1978, 1979 *280*, 1982, 1983 *282*, 1986 *285*, 1988 *287*, 1989 *288*, 1990 *289*, 1991 *290*, 1992 *291*, 1993 *293*, 1995 *295*, 1996

*296*, 1997 *297*, 1998 *298*, 1999 *299*, 2000 *300*; Cuvée Exceptionnelle 1947 *275*
Beaulieu Vineyard Carneros Pinot Noir 1987 *520*; Georges de Latour Cabernet Sauvignon 1936, 1939, 1941, 1942, 1943, 1944, 1946, 1947 *508*, 1948, 1949, 1950, 1951, 1952, 1953, 1954, 1955, 1956, 1957, 1958 *509*, 1959, 1960, 1961, 1962, 1963, 1964, 1965, 1966, 1967 *510*, 1968, 1969, 1970 *511*, 1971, 1972, 1973, 1974 *512*, 1975, 1976, 1977 *513*, 1978, 1979 *514*, 1980, 1981 *515*, 1982 *516*, 1983, 1984 *517*, 1985 *518*, 1986, 1987 *519*, 1988, 1989 *520*, 1990 *521*, 1991, 1992 *522*, 1993 *523*, 1994 *524*, 1995 *525*, 1996 *526*, 1997 *527*, 1998 *528*; Pinot Noir 1946 *508*; Reserve Pinot Noir 1994 *524*; Signet Collection Ensemble 1994 *524*; 'Tapestry' Reserve 1993 *523*
Beaune 1923 *220*; (blanc) 1996 *296*; 1er Cru, Cuvée Famille Chanson 1996 *265*; Clos des Avaux 1917 *218*, 1919 *218-19*; Belissand 1997 *267*; Boucherottes 1985 *252*, 1999 *270*; Bressandes 1985 *253*; Cent Vignes 1978 *244*, 1999 *270*; Clos de la Chaume, Gauffroy 1989 *257*; Chouacheux 1988 *255*; Cras 1997 *267*; Clos des Epenottes 1989 *257*, 1998 *268*; Clos des Fèves 1988 *255*, 1997 *267*; Clos des Fèves (blanc) 1997 *297*; Grèves 1943 *225*, 1947 *226*, 1979 *246*, 1986 *254*, 1995 *265*, 1998 *269*, 2000 *272*; Grèves, Vigne de l'Enfant Jésus 1961 *232*, 1971 *240*, 1976 *243*, 1984 *251*, 1986, 1987 *254*, 1991 *260*, 1992 *261*, 1997 *267*, 1998 *268*; Hospices de 1919 *219*; Hospices, Clos des Avaux 1964 *234*, 1969 *237*; Hospices, Cuvée Brunet 1971 *240*; Hospices, Cuvée Domaines Hospitaliers 1990 *258*; Hospices, Cuvée Dr Peste 1984 *251*; Hospices, Cuvée Hugues et L Bétault 1986 *253*; Hospices, Cuvée Maurice Drouhin 1962 *233*, 1986 *253*; Hospices, Cuvée Nicolas Rolin 1959 *231*, 1971 *240-1*; Hospices,

Cuvée Rousseau-
Deslandes 1946 226, 1959
231; Marconnets 1947 227,
1991 260; Mignotte 1985
252; Montremenots 1986
254; Montrevenots 1988
255; Clos des Mouches
1930 222, 1979 246, 1980
246, 1981 247, 1982 248,
1983 250, 1984 251, 1985,
1986 253, 1987 254, 1988
256, 1989 257, 1990 258,
1991 260, 1992 261, 1993
263, 1994, 1995 264, 1996
266, 1997 267, 1998 269,
1999 270, 2000 272; Clos
des Mouches (blanc) 1979
280, 1980, 1981 281, 1982,
1983 282, 1984 283, 1985
284, 1986 285, 1987 286,
1988 287, 1990 289, 1991
290, 1992 291, 1993 293,
1994 294, 1995 295, 1996
296, 1997 297, 1998 298,
2000 300; Clos de la
Mousse 1864 216, 1943 225;
Première Cuvée, Grizot
1865 216; Clos du Roi 1929
221, 1947 226, 1978 245,
1992 262; Teurons 1982
248, 1986 253, 1999 270;
Theurons 1973 241;
Toussaints 1983 250, 1988
255; Clos des Ursules 1979
246, 1982 248, 1983 250,
1985, 1986 253, 1988 255,
1989 257, 1990 258, 1991
260, 1992 262, 1993 263,
1994, 1995 264, 1996 266,
1997 267, 1998 269, 1999
270; Vignes Franches 1933
222, 1960 231, 1988 256,
1997 267
Beauregard, Ch 1981 101,
1982 102, 1983 110, 1985
116, 1992 137, 1993 142,
1996 151, 1997 155, 1998
158, 2000 168
Beauséjour, Ch 1962 68
Beauséjour-Bécot, Ch
1970 80, 1971 83, 1975 88,
1988 122, 1990 131, 1996
151, 1997 155, 1998 158,
1999 161, 2000 165
Beauséjour-Duffau-
Lagarosse, Ch 1983 107,
1985 116, 1991 136, 1995 149
Bel-Air-Marquis d'Aligre,
Ch c1848 13
Belair, Ch 1962 68, 1970 80,
1975 88, 1983 110, 1996 153,
2000 165
Belgrave, Ch 1961 67, 1982
102, 1996 153, 1997 156
Bell Rannie (port) 1875 453
Beringer
Cabernet Sauvignon 1994
524; Knights Valley
Cabernet Sauvignon 1982
517, 1988 520; Knights
Valley Proprietor's
Growth Cabernet
Sauvignon 1985 519
Bernadotte, Ch 1996 151,
1997 156, 1999 161, 2000 168
Berncasteler
Doctor Riesling 1915 345;
Doctor Riesling Auslese
1976 361, 1983 366; Doctor
Riesling feine Auslese
1959 351; Hintergraben
Riesling 1915 345

Bernkasteler
Badstube Riesling
Auslese 1976 363;
Badstube Riesling
Auslese Fuder 9 1964 354;
Badstube Riesling
Kabinett 1988 369;
Badstube Riesling
Spätlese 1988 370; Doctor
und Graben Riesling
Auslese 1971 357; Doctor
Riesling Auslese 1979 364;
Doctor Riesling Auslese
Christ-Eiswein 1990 373;
Doctor Riesling Auslese
lange Goldkapsel 1996
382; Doctor Riesling
Spätlese 1964, 1966 354;
Doktor Riesling Auslese
1989 372, 1999 387;
Johannisbrünnchen
Müller-Thurgau BA 1975
360; Johannisbrünnchen
Riesling Eiswein 1990 373
Berry Bros' (Own)
Selection 1955 467; 1963
473, 1966 474, 1970 478
Beychevelle, Ch 1899 23,
1922 31, 1929 36, 1934 38,
1937 40, 1943 42, 1948 48,
1949 51, 1950 53, 1952 54,
1953 55, 1955 58, 1957 59,
1958 60, 1959 61, 1960 63,
1961 65, 1962 68, 1964 70,
1966 72, 1967 75, 1968 76,
1969 77, 1970 80, 1971 83,
1972 84, 1973 85, 1974 86,
1975 88, 1976 90, 1977 91,
1978 92, 1979 95, 1981 101,
1982 102, 1983 107, 1984
111, 1985 113, 1986 117,
1987 120, 1988 122, 1989
126, 1990 131, 1991 136,
1992 137, 1993 139, 1994
143, 1995 147, 1996 151,
1997 156, 1998 158, 1999
161, 2000 165
Beyerskloof, Cabernet
Sauvignon 1995 535
Bienvenues-Bâtard-
Montrachet 1974 278, 1978
279, 1979 280, 1983 282,
1984 283, 1985 284, 1986
285, 1987 286, 1991 290,
1992 291, 1999 299, 2000 300
Billecart-Salmon 1982 438,
1985 442; Blanc de Blancs
1966 431, 1995 447; Cuvée
N F Billecart 1966 431,
1985 441, 1986 442
Binet, Blanc de Blancs
1985 442
Binger Scharlachberg
Riesling TBA 1967 355
Bischoffinger
Rosenkranz Ruländer
TBA 1992 376; Steinbuck
Ruländer TBA 1976 361,
1989 371
'Bismark' 'Brown Madère
Impériale' 1832 498
Blauer Spätburgunder 'SJ'
Karl 1996 382
Boal 1863 499, 1957 504;
Solera 1826 497; Very Old
'EBH' 1868 499; see also
Bual
Bollinger 1914 423, 1929,
1934 426, 1947 427, 1952
428, 1959, 1961 429, 1964,
1966 431, 1975, 1976 435,
1979 437, 1985 441; Grande

Année 1982, 1983 440,
1988, 1989 444, 1990 445,
1992 446; RD 1955, 1961
429, 1964 430-1, 1966 431,
1970 432, 1973 433, 1975
434, 1979 436, 1982 438-9,
1985 441; Vieilles Vignes
Françaises 1970 432, 1985
441
Bom Retiro, Qta do 1922
457
Bomfim, Qta do 1948 465,
1965 473, 1986 487, 1988
488, 1995 491
Bon-Pasteur, Ch 1985 116,
1989 128
Bonnes-Mares 1898 216,
1915 218, 1933 222, 1949 227,
1955 230, 1961 232, 1962
233, 1964 234, 1966 235,
1967 236, 1969 237, 1970
239, 1971 240, 241, 1972 241,
1976 243, 1978 245, 1982
248, 1985 252, 253, 1986 253,
1988 256, 1989 257, 1990
260, 1991 261, 1997 267,
1999 270, 2000 271; Vieilles
Vignes 1971 240
Bonnet, Ch 1978 92, 1989
126
Bonnezeaux 1959 317, 1964,
1966, 1969 318, 1989 320,
1996, 1997 323; Cuvée
Mathilde 1993 322; La
Montagne 1989 320
Borges & Irmão 1963 471,
1965 473, 1970 476
Bosq, Ch du 1995 149
Bouchaine see Chateau
Bouchaine
Bouchard Finlayson,
Galpin Peak Pinot Noir
1996 535
Bourgueil 1988 320; Cuvée
Ploquin, Dom du Chêne
Arrault 1976 319; Dom
Chesnaies 2000 325
Bouscaut, Ch 1928 36, 1975
89, 1989 128, 1996 153, 1998
158, 1999 161, 2000 165;
(blanc) 1937 182, 1999 213
Boyd-Cantenac, Ch 1961
67, 1966 74, 1975 88, 1978
94, 1979 95, 1982 102, 1983
110, 1996 153
Bragão, Qta do 1931 461
Branaire, Ch 1997 156, 1998
158, 1999 161, 2000 165; see
also Branaire-Ducru, Ch for
wines before 1997
Branaire-Ducru, Ch 1878
19, 1900 25, 1961 67, 1966
74, 1969 77, 1970 80, 1971
83, 1973 85, 1975 88, 1978
92, 1979 96, 1981 101, 1982
102, 1983 107, 1984 111,
1985 113, 1986 117, 1988
122, 1989 126, 1990 134,
1991 136, 1992 137, 1993
141, 1994 143, 1995 147,
1996 151; see also Branaire,
Ch for wines after 1996
Branaire-Ducru-Sarget,
Ch 1920 31
Branaire-Duluc-Ducru,
Ch 1877 18, 1924 33
Brane-Cantenac, Ch 1893
21, 1896 22, 1898, 1899 23,
1900 25, 1904, 1905, 1906
26, 1920 30, 1928 35, 1945
45, 1959 61, 1961 67, 1962
68, 1966 74, 1967 75, 1970

80, 1971 83, 1973 85, 1974
86, 1975 88, 1978 92, 1979
96, 1980 98, 1981 99, 1982
102, 1983 107, 1985 113,
1986 119, 1988 124, 1990
134, 1991 136, 1992 137,
1993 141, 1994 145, 1995
149, 1996 151, 1997 156,
1998 158, 1999 161, 2000 165
Branne-Mouton, Ch 1787
11; see also Mouton-
Rothschild, Ch
Brauneberger
Juffer Riesling Auslese
1975 360, 1990 373; Juffer
Riesling Auslese lange
Goldkapsel 1996 382;
Juffer-Sonnenuhr
Riesling Auslese 1937 347,
1983 366, 1989 371, 1990
373, 1992 376, 1994 379,
1995 380; Juffer-
Sonnenuhr Riesling
Auslese Goldkapsel 1979
364, 1985 368, 1999 387;
Juffer-Sonnenuhr
Riesling BA 1993 377, 1994
379; Juffer-Sonnenuhr
Riesling Kabinett 1999
387; Juffer-Sonnenuhr
Riesling Spätlese 1985 368,
1988 370, 1999 387; Juffer-
Sonnenuhr Riesling TBA
1976 361; Sonnenuhr
Riesling Auslese
Goldkapsel 1996 382;
Brauneberger Sonnenuhr
Riesling Auslese lange
Goldkapsel 1996 382
Breuil, Ch de 1945 316
Bricco della Bigotta 1987
401
Bricco dell'Uccellone
1986, 1988 401, 1992 404
Bricout, Grand Cru,
Arthur Bricout 1985 441
Broadbent (port) 1994
490-1, 1995 491, 1997 492,
2000 494; Madeira,
Colheita 1995 505
Broustet, Ch 1970 192, 1986
202, 1989 204, 1990 206,
1993, 1994 207, 1995 208,
1996 209, 1997 211, 1998
212, 1999 213, 2000 214
Bruce, David, Pinot Noir
1982 517
Brunello di Montalcino
1968 395, 1975, 1978 397,
1985 400, 1988 401, 402,
1990 403, 1995 400; Annata
1985 400; Castelgiocondo
1975 397, 1985 400;
Castelgiocondo Riserva
1990 403; Montosoli 1990
403; Pian delle Vigne 1995
405; Podere Pian di
Conte 1988 401; Riserva
1945, 1955 394, 1964, 1967,
1968 395, 1969, 1970 1971,
1975 396, 1981 398, 1982,
1983 399, 1985 400, 1987
401, 1988 401, 402, 1990 403;
Riserva Quercione 1990
403; Sopozific 1985 400;
'Sugarille' 1985 400;
'Sugarille' 1985 400;
Tenuta Greppo 1988 402;
Tenuta Greppo Riserva
1988 402
Brüssele
Kleinbottwarer
Lemberger Kabinett

trocken 1983 366;
Kleinbottwarer Riesling
Eiswein 1985 368;
Lemberger Auslese 1959
351-2
Bual 1908, 1910, 1911, 1914,
1920 502, 1933, 1934, 1935
503, 1954, 1958, 1966 504,
1971 505; 'CDGC' 1941
503; Qta do Serrado
(Vintage) 1827 497-8;
Reserva 1903 501; Solera
1815 497, 1845 498, 1915 502,
1945 503, 1964 504; 'Special
Reserve, Medium Sweet'
1837 498; Vintage 1907 501,
1957, 1964 504, 1971 505;
'VJH' 1964 504; see also
Boal
Buçaco 1927, 1940, 1953,
1959, 1960, 1963, 1982,
1983 418; Reserva 1951 418;
Reserva Especial 1945 418
Buena Vista, Private
Reserve Carneros
Cabernet Sauvignon 1985
519
Burg Ravensburger Dicker
Franz Schwarzriesling
Spätlese trocken 1990 373
Burgess, Vintage Selection
Cabernet Sauvignon 1977
514
Burghornberger
Wallmauer Traminer
Auslese 1976 361
Burmester 1931 461, 1960
471, 1963 473, 1970 478,
1985 486, 1989 488, 1991
489, 1992 490, 1994 491,
1997 492, 2000 494
Butler Nephew 1945 463,
1958 469, 1964 473, 1970
478, 1975 479

## C

Cabanne, Ch La 1961 67,
1975 89, 1985 116, 1996 153,
1997 156
Cabral 1970 478
Cachão, Qta do 1970 476
Caillou, Ch 1914 171, 1928
180, 1973 194, 1986 202,
1996 209, 1997 211, 1998
212, 1999 213
Cain, Cain Five 1997 527
Cais, Qta do 1933 461
Cálem 1935 462, 1957 469,
1963, 1965 473, 1966 474,
1970 478, 1977 481, 1980
482, 1983 484, 1985 486,
1997 492; LBV 1983 485;
Reserve 1960 469-70
Calera
Jensen Vineyard Pinot
Noir 1984 517, 1986 519,
1990 521; Selleck Vineyard
Pinot Noir 1984 517, 1986
519
Calheta (madeira) 1939 503
Calon-Ségur, Ch 1918 29,
1925 33, 1926 34, 1928 35,
1929 36, 1938 40, 1940 41,
1945 44, 1947 47, 1948 48,
1949 50, 1953 55-6, 1955 58,
1959 61, 1961 65, 1962 68,
1966 72, 1967 75, 1970 80,
1971 83, 1972 84, 1973 85,
1974 86, 1975 88, 1976 90,
1979 96, 1980 98, 1981 101,
1982 102, 1983 107, 1985

113, 1988 122, 1990 134, 1992 137, 1994 145, 1996 151, 1997 156

Cama de Lobos 1864 499, 1891 500, 1936 503

Camensac, Ch de 1975 89, 1982 105, 1985 113, 1986 119, 1996 153, 1999 161

Campanario 1846 498

Canais, Qta dos 1995 491, 1999 493

Canon, Ch 1892 21, 1937 39, 1959 62, 1961 65, 1962 68, 1964 70, 1966 74, 1970 80, 1971 83, 1975 88, 1978 94, 1979 96, 1981 99, 1982 102, 1983 107, 1985 113, 1986 117, 1988 122, 1989 126, 1990 134, 1992 137, 1993 141, 1994 145, 1995 149, 1996 151, 1997 156, 1998 158, 1999 161, 2000 165

Canon-La-Gaffelière, Ch 1952 54, 1964 70, 1966 74, 1970 82, 1978 94, 1979 96, 1981 101, 1985 113, 1986 119, 1988 122, 1989 128, 1990 131, 1993 142, 1994 145, 1995 149, 1996 151, 1997 156, 1998 158, 1999 161, 2000 165

Cantemerle, Ch 1904 26, 1916 28, 1920 30, 1921 31, 1926 34, 1928 35, 1929 36, 1934 38, 1945 44-5, 1948 49, 1949 50, 1952 54, 1961 67, 1964 70, 1966 74, 1967 75, 1969 77, 1970 80, 1971 83, 1972 84, 1974 86, 1975 88, 1976 90, 1978 94, 1979 96, 1982 103, 1983 107, 1985 113-14, 1986 119, 1987 120, 1989 126, 1990 134, 1992 137, 1993 142, 1994 143, 1995 149, 1996 151, 1997 156, 1998 159, 1999 161, 2000 165

Cantenac-Brown, Ch 1881 19, 1899 23, 1966 74, 1970 80, 1975 88, 1976 90, 1978 93, 1981 101, 1982 103, 105, 1989 126, 1990 131, 1991 136, 1992 137, 1993 139, 1994 145, 1995 149, 1996 151, 1997 156, 1998 159, 1999 161, 2000 165

Canzemer Altenberg Riesling Auslese 1975 361

Cap de Mourlin, Ch 1943 42, 1996 153, 1997 156, 1998 159, 2000 168

Capbern-Gasqueton, Ch 1982 105

Cape Mentelle, Cabernet Merlot 533

Carbonnieux, Ch 1928 35, 1970 80, 1975 88, 1988 122, 1993 142, 1994 145, 1996 153, 1997 156, 1998 159, 2000 165; (blanc) 1978 196-7, 1986 202

Cardonne, Ch La 1985 116

Carmenet 1988 520

Carmes-Haut-Brion, Ch Les 1996 151, 2000 165

Carmignano Capezzana 1986 401; Riserva 1930 393

Carneros Creek Fay Vineyard Cabernet

Sauvignon 1982 516; Loath's Pinot Noir 1986 519

Carruades de Ch Lafite 1869 16, 1902 25, 1923 32, 1934 38, 1937 40, 1953 56, 1955 58, 1959 62, 1962 68-9, 1966 74, 1987 120, 1988 122, 1996 153, 1997 156, 1999 161, 2000 165

Carruades de Mouton-Rothschild 1927 34

Castel Schwanberg Cabernet 1990 404

Castellane, de 1988 444

Casteller Bausch Mariensteiner Eiswein 1985 368; Feuerbach Domina Kabinett 1983 366; Hohnart Silvaner Natur 1967 355; Kugelspiel Rieslaner Auslese 1989 372; Kugelspiel Rieslaner BA 1989 371; Kugelspiel Rieslaner Spätlese 1982 365; Kugelspiel Silvaner Riesling Auslese 1992 376; Schlossberg Rieslaner Spätlese 1963 353; Trautberg Silvaner Riesling TBA 1971 357; Trautberg Silvaner TBA 1971 357

Cavadinha, Qta da 1978 481, 1987 488, 1995 491

Caymus Vineyards Cabernet Sauvignon 1974 513, 1980 515, 1981 516; Napa Valley Cabernet Sauvignon 1994 524; Special Selection Cabernet Sauvignon 1982, 1984 517, 1985 518, 1990 521, 1991, 1992 522, 1995 525

Cedovim 1933 461

Cepparello 1983 399, 1988 402, 1990 403, 1997 407

Certan, Ch 1920 31, 1949 51

Certan-de-May, Ch 1953 56, 1971 83, 1978 94, 1980 98, 1982 103, 1985 116, 1990 131, 1993 142, 1994 143, 1995 149

Certan 'Mme Demay', Ch 1918 29

Certan-Guiraud, Ch 1995 149; see also Hosanna for wines from 2000

Certan-Marzelle, Ch 2000 165

Chablis 1988 287, 1993 293, 1997 297, 1998 298, 1999 299; Blanchots 1998 298; Bougros 1992 291, 1993 293, 1998 298, 1999 299; Bougros, 'Côte de Bougerots' 1998 298; Les Clos 1992 291, 1996 296, 1998 298; Côte de Lechet 1999 299; Fourchaume 1997 297; Grenouilles 1993 293, 1998 298, 1999 299, 2000 300; Mont de Milieu 1992 291, 1998 298; Montée de Tonnerre 1993 293, 1998 298; Montmains 1988 287, 1998 298, 1999 299; Montmains, Vieille Vignes 1997 297; Preuses 1945 275, 1993 293, 1995

295, 1998 298, 2000 300; Vaillons 1996 296, 1998 298, 1999 299; Vaillons, Vieille Vignes 1997 297; Valmur 1992 291, 1995 295, 1996 296, 1998 298; Vaudésir 1993 293, 1998 298, 1999 299; Vaulignot 1995 295; Vaulorent 1992 291; Vieille Vignes 1998 298

Chalone Pinot Noir 1979 514, 1980, 1981 515

Chambertin 1904 217, 1925 220, 1929 221, 1945, 1946 226, 1949 227, 1953, 1955 229, 1959 231, 1961 232, 1962 233, 1964 234, 1966 235, 1967 236, 1969 237, 1976 243, 1983 250, 1985 252, 1988 256, 1992 261, 1995 264-5, 2000 271; Clos de Bèze 1906 217, 1911 218, 1933 222, 1947 226, 1955 230, 1961 232, 1971, 1972 241, 1974 242, 1980 246, 1982 248, 1983 250, 1985 252, 1987 254-5, 1988 255, 256, 1989 257, 1990 258-9, 1992 261, 1992 263, 1995 265, 1999 270, 2000 271; Héritiers (Latour) 1920 219, 1929 221, 1979 246, 1983 250, 1985 253, 1989 257; Tête de Cuvée 1900 217, 1940 224; Vieille Vignes 1988 256; Vieux Cépages 1915 218

Chambertin-Ruchottes 1942 225

Chambolle-Musigny 1919 219, 1920 219, 1934 223, 1941 224, 1945 226, 1951 228, 1953 229, 1955 230, 1959 231, 1966 235, 1967 236, 1971 240, 1986 254, 1987 255, 1990 259, 1991 261, 1999 270; 1er Cru 1943 225; Amoureuses 1929 221, 1934 223, 1964 234, 1970 239, 1971 241, 1986 254, 1989 257, 2000 272; Aux Beaux Bruns 1992 262; Baudes 1988 256; Charmes 1918 218, 1931 222, 1934 223, 1949 227, 1978 245, 1979 246, 1983 250, 1992 262; Fuées 1986 254, 1992 262, 1995 265, 1999 270, 2000 272; Hauts Doix 1988 256, 1989 257; Sentiers 1987 255, 1997 267; Véroilles 1985 265, 2000 272; Vieilles Vignes 1995 265; Clos du Village 1988 256

Chamisso 1858 451

Chantegrive, Ch 1996 153-4; (blanc) 1998 212

Chapel Hill, Syrah Reserve 1990 533

Chapelle-Chambertin 1964 233, 234, 1970 239, 1982 248, 1984 251

Chappellet, Cabernet Sauvignon 1970 511, 1976 513

Charbaut Certificate 1979 437; Cuvée de Reserve 1985 442

Charmes-Chambertin 1920, 1921 219, 1949 227,

1957 230, 1971 240, 241, 1981 247, 1983 250, 1988 255, 1996 266, 1997 267, 1999 270

Chartreuse, Ch de la 1994 207

Chassagne-Montrachet 1947 226, 1979 246; (blanc) 1947, 1949 275, 1966 277, 1982, 1983 282, 1984 283, 1987 286, 1988 287, 1989 288, 1989 289, 1991 290, 1994 294, 1998 298, 1999 299; 1er Cru 1987 255; Benoites 1999 299; Clos de la Boudriotte 1981 247, 1990 259; Boudriotte (blanc) 1978 280, 1988 287, 1989 288, 1991 290, 1993 293; Caillerets 1989 288, 1991 290, 1995 295, 1996 296, 1998 298, 2000 300; Champs-Gain 1998 298; Chaumées 1989 288, 1995 295; Chaumes, Clos de la Truffière 2000 300; Chevenottes 1988 287, 1992 291, 1995 295, 1997 297, 1998 298; Embrazées 1995 295; En Rémilly 1995 295; 'Grand-Montagne' 1993 293; Grandes Rouchottes 2000 300; Maltroie 1997 297; Clos de la Maltroye 1992 291, 1998 298, 1999 299, 2000 300; Morgeot 1984 283, 1987 286, 1991 290, 1995 295, 1998 298; Morgeot, Clos de la Chapelle 1991 290; Morgeot, Vignes Blanches 2000 300; Première Cuvée 1981 281; Romanée 1976 279; Clos St-Jean 1999 270; Clos St-Jean (blanc) 1992 292; Vergers 1985 284, 1993 293, 1994 294, 1995 295; Vieilles Vignes 1996 266; Virondot 1994 294

Chasse-Spleen, Ch 1924 33, 1948 49, 1961 67, 1970 80, 1975 89, 1976 90, 1977 91, 1978 93, 1979 96, 1981 99, 1982 103, 1983 110, 1985 114, 1986 117, 1988 124, 1989 126, 1992 137, 1993 141, 1996 151, 1997 156, 1998 159, 1999 162, 2000 168

Chateau Bouchaine Cabernet Sauvignon 1982 517; Carneros Napa Pinot Noir 1986 519

Chateau Chevalier, Napa Pinot Noir 1984 517

Chateau Montelena Cabernet Sauvignon 1974 513, 1976 513, 1978, 1979 514, 1982 517, 1985 518, 1986, 1987 519; Montelena Estate 1991 522, 1994 524, 1996 526, 1997 527

Chateau Musar 1956, 1959, 1961, 1964, 1966, 1967, 1969, 1970, 1972, 1975, 1977 419, 1978, 1979, 1981, 1983, 1985, 1986, 1988, 1989, 1993, 1994, 1995, 1996, 1997, 1998, 1999 420

Châteauneuf-du-Pape 1947 303, 1971, 1975 304, 1978 305, 1979, 1981 306,

1983-1985 307, 1987-1988 308, 1989 309, 1990 309-10, 1991 310, 1992, 1993, 1994 311, 1995, 1996 312, 1997, 1998, 1999 313, 2000 314; Dom de Beaurenard 1988 308; Bernadine 1985 307, 1989 309; Bosquet des Papes 1985 307; Clos de Brusquières 1988 308; Cailloux 1996 312; Cèdres 1984, 1985 307, 1989 309; 'Le Crau' 1997 313; 'Homage à Jacques Perrin' 1990 310, 1994, 1995 311, 1998 313; Dom de Marcoux 1984 307; Dom de Mont Redon 1987, 1988 308; Clos des Papes 1971 304; Petit Cuvée 1988 308; Ch de Vaudieu 1988 308; Dom du Vieux Télégraphe 1982 306

Chaume 1949, 1955 317

Chénas 1991 261

Cheval Blanc, Ch 1893 21, 1904 26, 1908, 1909, 1911 27, 1920 30, 1921 31, 1923 32, 1924 33, 1926 34, 1928 35, 1929 36, 1933 37, 1934 38, 1936, 1937 39, 1938 40, 1940, 1942 41, 1943 42, 1945 44, 1947 46-7, 1948 48, 1949 50, 1950 52, 1952 54, 1953 55, 1955 57, 1957 59, 1958 60, 1959 61, 1960 63, 1961 65, 1962 68, 1964 70, 1966 72, 1967 75, 1969 77, 1970 80, 1971 83, 1972 84, 1973 85, 1974 86, 1975 87-8, 1976 90, 1977 91, 1978 92, 1979 95, 1980 98, 1981 99, 1982 102, 1983 107, 1984 110-11, 1985 113, 1986 117, 1987 120, 1988 121, 1989 126, 1990 130, 1992 136, 1993 138, 1994 143, 1995 146, 1996 150, 1997 155, 1998 158, 1999 161, 2000 165

Chevalier, Chateau see Chateau Chevalier

Chevalier, Dom de 1928 35, 1929 36, 1934 38, 1935, 1937 39, 1945 45, 1947 47, 1948 49, 1952 54, 1954 57, 1957 59, 1959 61, 1961 65, 1964 70, 1966 74, 1967 75, 1968 76, 1970 80, 1971 83, 1975 88, 1978 93, 1979 96, 1980 98, 1981 99, 1983 107, 1984 111, 1985 114, 1987 120, 1988 124, 1989 128, 1990 131, 1993 141, 1994 145, 1995 149, 1996 151, 1997 156, 1998 159, 1999 162, 2000 165; (blanc) 1967 191, 1970, 1971 193, 1976 196, 1978 197, 1981 198, 1982 199, 1984 200, 1985 201, 1987 202, 1988 203, 1989 204, 1990 206, 1992 207, 1995 208, 1996 210, 1997 211, 1998 212, 1999 213, 2000 214

Chevalier-Montrachet 1948 275, 1962 277, 1971, 1974 278, 1976 279, 1978, 1979 280, 1982, 1983 282, 1985 284, 1986 285, 1987 286, 1988 287, 1990 289, 1991 290, 1992 292, 1993

293, 1994 294, 1995 295, 1997 297, 1999 299;
Desmoiselles 1973 278, 1983 282, 1985 284, 1986 285, 1990 289, 1991 291, 2000 300
Chianti Classico 1981 398, 1983 399, 1985 400, 1990 403, 1992 404, 1994 405, 1996 406, 1997 407, 1998, 1999 408; Brolio 1997 407; Castello di Brolio 1997 407; La Casuccia 1990 403; Pèppoli 1997 407; Poggio 1985 400; Riserva 1967 395, 1973 396, 1980, 1981 398, 1983 399, 1985 400, 1990 403, 1995 405, 1997 407, 1999 408; Riserva Badia a Passignano 1997 407; Riserva Brolio 1967 395; Riserva Ducale 1969 396, 1994 405; Riserva di Fizzano 1985 400; Riserva Millennio 1985 400; Riserva Prima 1981 398; Riserva, Tenute Marchese Antinori 1997 407; La Selvanella Riserva 1983 399; Ser Lapo 1985 400
Chianti, Colli Senesi 2000 409
Chianti, Nozzole 1980 398
Chianti Rufina 1947 394; Nipozzano 1970 396, 1978 397; Riserva Montesodi 1981 398; Riserva Villa di Vetrice 1990 403
Chinon
Clos de L'Olive 1955 317; Jeunes Vignes 1999 324; Churchill 1983 484, 1985 486, 1991 489, 1997 492
Churchill Graham 1982 483
Chusio, Il 1992 404
Cincinnato 1999 408
Cissac, Ch 1957 59, 1959 61, 1970 80, 1976 90, 1982 103, 1995 149
Citran, Ch 1970 82, 1992 137, 1996 154, 1997 156, 1998 159, 1999 162
Clarendon Hills, Syrah 1990 533
Clarke, Ch 1978 93, 1982 103, 1993 142, 1996 154, 1997 156, 1998 159, 2000 168
Clerc-Milon, Ch 1970 82, 1978 94, 1982 103, 1985 116, 1986 119, 1988 122, 1989 128, 1990 131, 1993 139, 1994 145, 1995 147, 1996 151, 1997 156, 1998 159, 1999 162, 2000 165
Clicquot see Veuve Clicquot
Climens, Ch 1918 177, 1921 178, 1924, 1926 179, 1927, 1928, 1929 180, 1937 182, 1943 183, 1947, 1948, 1949 184, 1950, 1952 185, 1953, 1955 186, 1959 187, 1961, 1962 188, 1964, 1966 189, 1967 190, 1969 191, 1970 192, 1971, 1972 193, 1973, 1974, 1975 194, 1976 195, 1977, 1978 196, 1979, 1980 197, 1981, 1982 198, 1983 199, 1984, 1985 200, 1986 201, 1987 202, 1988 202-3, 1989 203, 1990 205, 1991 206-7, 1992, 1994 207, 1995 208, 1996 209, 1997 210,

1998 211-12, 1999 212-13, 2000, 2001 214
Clinet, Ch 1961 67, 1988 122, 1989 126, 1990 131, 1992 137, 1993 139, 1994 145, 1995 149, 1996 154, 1997 156, 1998 159, 1999 162, 2000 165
Clocher, Clos du 1985 116
Clos for French wines beginning with Clos see under main name
Clos du Bois
Briarcrest Cabernet Sauvignon 1981 516, 1982 517; Marlstone 1981 516; Pinot Noir 1980 515
Clos du Val
Cabernet Sauvignon 1974 513, 1980 515, 1981 516; Merlot 1982 517; Pinot Noir 1983 517; Zinfandel 1983 517
Cockburn 1870 452, 1878, 1884, 1887, 1890 453, 1896 454, 1900, 1904, 1908 455, 1912 456, 1927 458, 1935 461, 1947 464, 1950 466, 1955 467-8, 1957 469, 1960 470, 1963 471, 1966 474, 1967 475, 1970 476, 1975 478, 1983 484, 1985 486, 1991 489, 1993 490, 1994 491, 1997 492, 2000 494; Crusted 1972 478
Colgin, Herb Lamb Vineyard Cabernet Sauvignon 1992 522, 1993 523, 1994 524, 1995 525
Conn Creek, Cabernet Sauvignon 1974 512, 1976 513, 1980 515
Conseillante, Ch La 1945 44, 1949 51, 1953 56, 1959 61, 1962 69, 1966 72, 1970 82, 1974 86, 1975 88, 1978 93, 1982 103, 1985 114, 1987 120, 1989 126, 1990 131, 1993 142, 1994 145, 1996 151, 1997 156, 1998 159, 1999 162, 2000 165-6
Cornas 1983, 1985 307, 1990 310, 1992 311; La Geynale 1985 307; La Louvée 1995 312; Dom de Rochepertuis 2000 314; Les Ruchets 1990, 1991 310, 1993 311, 1995 312; St-Pierre 1992 310, 2000 314
Cortaccio, Villa Cafaggio 1998 408
Côrte, Qta da 1978 481, 1984 485, 1997 492
Corton 1937, 1938, 1941 224, 1947 226, 227, 1949 227, 1959 231, 1961 232, 1962 233, 1966 235, 1970 239, 1976 243, 1985 252, 1986 253, 1987 254, 1988 255, 1990 259, 1992 261, 1993 263, 1994 264, 1995 265, 2000 271; Dom du Ch de Beaune 1985 253, 1989 257; Bressandes 1959 231, 1964 234, 1966 235, 236, 1976 243, 1982 248, 1987 255, 1988 256, 1989 257, 1990 259, 1995 265, 1998 269, 2000 271-2; Clos du Chapitre 1926 220; Clos des Cortons 1979 246, 1985 252, 1987 255, 1993 263,

1998 269; Clos Fiètres 1969 237, 1971 240, 1998 269; 'Grande Famille des Domaines' 1996 266; Hospices, Cuvée Charlotte Dumay 1964 233, 1976 243, 1983 250; Hospices, Cuvée Domaines Hospitaliers 1990 259; Hospices, Cuvée Dr Peste 1976 243, 1983 250, 1984 251, 1990 259; Maréchaudes 1970 239, 1985 252, 1988 256; Perrières 1978 245; Pougets 1970 239, 1988 256, 1994 264, 1999 270; Clos Rognet 1990 259; Clos du Roi 1858 216, 1933 222, 1970 239, 1976 243, 1986 253, 1988 256, 1989 257; Clos du Roy 1911 218; Clos de la Vigne au Saint 1926 220, 1966 235, 1982 248
Corton-Charlemagne 1929 274, 1947, 1949 275, 1952, 1955 276, 1961, 1962 277, 1970, 1971, 1973, 1975 278, 1976, 1977, 1978 279-80, 1979 280, 1981 281, 1982 282, 1983 283, 1985 284, 1986 285-6, 1988 287, 1989 288, 1990 289, 1991 291, 1992 292, 1993 293, 1994 294, 1995 295, 1996, 1997 297, 1998 299, 1999 299, 2000 300; Fourget 1987 286; Hospices, Cuvée François de Salins 1982 282
Corton-Grancey, Ch 1926 220, 1945 225, 1950, 1959 231, 1961 232, 1964 233, 1969 237, 1972 241, 1976 243, 1978 245, 1979 246, 1982 248, 1983 250, 1985 252, 1988 256, 1989 257, 1990 259, 1992 261, 1993 263, 1995 265, 1996 266, 1997 267
Corvo Duca Enrico 1984 400
Cos d'Estournel, Ch 1870 17, 1878 19, 1893 21, 1905 26, 1911 28, 1926 34, 1928 35, 1934 38-9, 1943 42, 1945 45, 1949 51, 1953 56, 1959 61, 1962 69, 1966 73, 1967 75, 1969 77, 1970 80, 1971 83, 1973 85, 1975 88, 1976 90, 1978 93, 1979 96, 1981 99, 1982 103, 1983 107, 1984 111, 1985 114, 1986 117, 1987 120, 1988 122, 1989 126, 1990 131, 1992 137, 1993 141, 1994 143, 1995 147, 1996 151, 1997 156, 2000 166
Cos Labory, Ch 1961 67, 1986 119, 1993 142, 1996 154, 1997 156, 1998 159, 2000 166
Côte-Rôtie 1985, 1987 308, 1990 310, 1993, 1994 311, 1995, 1996 312, 2000 314; Ch d'Ampuis 1985, 1987 308, 1997 313; Brune et Blonde 1978 305, 1979 306, 1984, 1985 307, 1993 311, 1995 312, 1998 313; Chantillonne 1985 308; Les Jumelles 1967 303,

1971, 1972, 1973 304, 1978 305, 1979, 1982 306, 1984 307, 1985, 1986 308, 1989 309, 1997 313, 2000 314; La Landonne 1978 305, 1985, 1986 308, 1988 309, 1998, 1999 313; La Mouline 1978, 1979, 1981 306, 1985, 1986 308, 1988 309, 1989 309, 1991 310, 1998, 1999 313; La Turque 1985, 1986 308, 1988 309, 1990, 1991 310, 1995 312, 1998, 1999 313
Coteaux du Layon 1945 316, 1964 318, 1989 320; Beaulieu 1996 323; Beaulieu, Clos des Ortinières 1989 320; Dom Pierre Blanche 1996 323; Le Clos du Bois 1997 324; Chaume 1959 317, 1985 319, 1997 324; Chaume, Les Aunis 1996 323, 1997 324, 1998 324; Chaume, Les Aunis, Cuvée Louis 1990 320; Chaume, Les Julines 1996 323; Les Clos 1999 324; Les Omnis, Dom des Forges 1996 323; La Roche 1992, 1993 322; Clos Ste-Cathérine 1989 320; Sélection de Grains Nobles 1994 322; Ch La Tomaze 1995 322; Ch La Tomaze, Cuvée Les Lys 1990 321
Côtes-du-Rhone 1997 313; Coudoulet de Beaucastel 1996 312, 1997, 1998 313
Coufran, Ch 1970 82, 1975 88, 1978 93, 1982 105, 1983 110, 1986 119, 1992 137, 1993 142, 1996 154, 1997 156, 1998 159, 1999 162
Coutet, Ch 1868 173, 1876 174, 1899 175, 1904 176, 1921 178, 1923 179, 1934 181, 1937 182, 1943 183, 1947, 1948, 1949 184, 1950, 1952 185, 1953, 1955 186, 1957, 1958 187, 1961, 1962 188, 1967 190, 1969 191, 1970 192, 1971 193, 1973, 1974, 1975 194, 1976 195, 1978 196, 1979 197, 1981 198, 1983 199, 1986 201, 1988 203, 1989 204, 1990 205, 1995 208, 1996 209, 1997 210, 1998 212; Cuvée Madame 1971 193
Couvent des Jacobins, Ch 1998 159
Crasto, Qta do 1950 466, 1985 486, 1994 491, 1995 491-2, 1997 492, 2000 494
Criots-Bâtard-Montrachet 1973 278, 2000 300
Crock, Ch Le 1975 89, 1994 145
Croft 1881 453, 1896 454, 1900 455, 1908 456, 1917, 1920, 1922 457, 1924, 1927 458, 1935, 1942 462, 1945 463, 1950 466, 1955 468, 1960 470, 1963 471-2, 1966 474, 1968 475, 1970 476, 1975 478, 1977 479-80, 1980 482, 1982 483, 1983 484, 1985 486, 1987, 1989 488, 1991 489, 1992 490, 1994 491, 1996 492, 2000 494; LBV 1990 489, 1995 492

Croix, Ch La 1975 88
Croix du Casse, Ch La 1981 99, 1983 107, 1995 149
Croix-de-Gay, Ch La 1947 47, 1966 75, 1979 96, 1985 116, 1988 122-3, 1996 152, 1997 156, 2000 166
Croix-Toulifaut, Ch La 1985 116
Croizet-Bages, Ch 1945 45, 1962 69, 1964 71, 1966 74, 1970 80, 1973 85, 1979 96, 1980 98, 1981 101, 1986 119, 1992 137, 1994 145, 1996 154, 1997 156, 1998 159, 2000 166
Crozes-Hermitage
Les Armandiers 2000 314; Dom de Thalabert 1972 304, 1979 306, 1983 307, 1988, 1989 309, 1990 310, 1995, 1996 312, 2000 314; 'Famille 2000' 1996 312; Guiraude 1988 309, 1990 310, 1994 311; Les Jalets 2000 314; Les Launes 1990 310; La Petite Ruche 1988 309; Réserve 1997 313
Cruzeau, Ch de 1989 126
Cruzeiro, Qta do 1982 484
Curé-Bon-La-Madeleine, Ch Le 1898 22-3, 1899 23
Cuvaison
Cabernet Sauvignon 1976 513, 1980 515, 1982 517; Merlot 1984 517
Cuvée for French wines beginning with Cuvée see under main name

**D**

Dalberger Schlossberg Riesling Spätlese 1989 372
Dalla Valle, 'Maya' 1990 521, 1991, 1992 522, 1993 523, 1994 524
Dalva 1941 462, 1970 478, 1985 486
Darmagi 1983 399, 1985 400, 1988, 1989 402, 1991 404
Dassault, Ch 1979 96, 1996 154, 1997 156, 1999 162, 2000 166
Dauphine, Ch La 1992 137, 1995 147
Dauzac, Ch 1893 21, 1924 33, 1926 34, 1969 77, 1982 105, 1983 110, 1991 136, 1992 137, 1993 142, 1995 147, 1996 154, 1999 162, 2000 166
Deidesheimer
Herrgottsacker Riesling Auslese 1976 363; Hohenmorgen Riesling Auslese 1996 382; Hohenrain Riesling TBA 1927 346; Kieselberg Riesling Auslese 1943 348; Kieselberg Riesling BA 1945 348; Kränzler Riesling BA 1945 348; Leinhölle Riesling TBA 1967 355; Paradiesgarten Riesling Kabinett 2000 390
Delaforce 1917 457, 1927 459, 1935 461, 1944 463, 1945, 1947 464, 1950 467, 1955 468, 1958 469, 1960 471, 1963 472, 1966 474, 1970 476, 1975 478, 1977

480, 1982 483, 1985 486, 1992 490, 1997 492, 2000 494
Delegat's Merlot 1998 534
Delamotte, Grand Cru, Blanc de Blancs 1990 446
Delbeck 1914 423, 1943 426, 1990 445
Delegat's Merlot 1998 534
Dernauer Pfarrwingert Spätburgunder Rotwein Auslese trocken 1997 385
Desmirail, Ch 1875 18, 1924 33, 1928 35, 1982 105, 1983 107, 1986 117-18, 1991 136, 1994 145, 1995 149, 1996 154
Deutz 1975 434; Blanc de Blancs 1985 442, 1993 447
Dhroner Hofberg Riesling Auslese 1979 364
Diamond Creek
  Gravelly Meadow Cabernet Sauvignon 1986 519; Red Rock Terrace Cabernet Sauvignon 1978 514, 1982 517, 1985, 1986 519, 1991 522, 1996 526; Volcanic Hill Cabernet Sauvignon 1978 514, 1981 515, 1985, 1986 519, 1989 520, 1994 524, 1995 525, 1998 528
Diez 1977 481
Doisy-Daëne, Ch 1929 180, 1945 183, 1947 184, 1953 186, 1959 187, 1962 189, 1971 193, 1976 196, 1983 199, 1985, 1986 201, 1989 204, 1990 206, 1996 209, 1997 211, 1998 212, 1999 213
Doisy-Dubroca, Ch 1920 178, 1973 194, 1986 202
Doisy-Védrines, Ch 1927 180, 1947, 1948 184, 1950 185, 1955 186, 1961, 1962 188, 1969 191, 1970 192, 1975 195, 1976 195, 1983 199, 1986 202, 1989 204, 1990 206, 1992, 1993, 1994 207, 1997 211, 1998 212, 1999 213, 2000 214
Dolcetto d'Alba 1993 404, 1999 408; Cascina Francia 1997 407; Fontanazza 1998 408; Monte Aribaldo 1988 402, 1998 408
Dom Pérignon 1955, 1959 429, 1961 429-30, 1962 430, 1964 431, 1969 432, 1970 432-3, 1971, 1973 433, 1975 434, 1976 435, 1980 438, 1982 439, 1983 440, 1985 441, 1988 443, 1990 445, 1992 446, 1993 447; Rosé 1978 436, 1982 439, 1985 441, 1988 443
Dom Ruinart 1982 439, 1993 447; Blanc de Blancs 1971, 1973 433, 1986 442, 1988 443, 1990 445; Rosé 1988 443
Dominique, Ch La 1945 45, 1948 49, 1971 83, 1976 90, 1989 128, 1993 139, 1994 145, 1996 154, 1997 156, 1998 159, 1999 162, 2000 166
Dominus 1984 517, 1985 518, 1987 519, 1988, 1989 520, 1990 521; Napanook Vineyard 1991 522, 1992 522-3, 1994, 1995 525, 1996 526, 1997 527, 1998, 1999 528

Dorsheimer
  Goldloch Riesling Auslese 1990 375, 1998 386; Pittermännchen Riesling Spätlese 2000 390
Douglas Vineyards, Cabernet Sauvignon 1982 517
Dow 1854 451, 1878, 1890, 1893 453, 1896 454, 1900 455, 1908 456, 1912 456-7, 1924, 1927 458, 1934 461, 1943 462, 1944, 1945 463, 1947 464, 1948 465, 1950 466, 1952, 1954 467, 1955 468, 1958 469, 1960 470, 1961, 1962 471, 1963 472, 1966 474, 1970 476-7, 1972, 1975 478, 1977 480, 1978 481, 1980 482, 1981, 1982 483, 1983 484, 1985 486, 1986 487, 1991 489, 1994 491, 1997 492, 2000 494; LBV 1979 482
Dragon, Ch du 1995 208
Drappier, Carte d'Or 1979 436, 1995 447
Dry Creek Vineyards, Dry Creek Valley Cabernet Sauvignon 1982 517
Duckhorn, Merlot 1982, 1983 517
Ducluzeau, Ch 1979 96, 1988 123
Ducru-Beaucaillou, Ch 1867 15, 1924 33, 1926, 1927 34, 1928 35, 1937 40, 1945 45, 1947 47, 1953 56, 1955 58, 1959 61, 1960 63, 1961 65-6, 1962 69, 1966 73, 1967 75, 1968 76, 1969 77, 1970 80, 1971 83, 1972 84, 1973 85, 1974 86, 1975 88, 1976 90, 1977 91, 1978 93, 1979 96, 1981 101, 1982 103, 1983 107-8, 1984 111, 1985 114, 1988 123, 1989 126, 1990 131, 1991 136, 1992 137, 1993 141, 1994 145, 1995 147, 1996 154, 1997 156, 1999 162
Duhart-Milon, Ch 1924 33, 1926 34, 1928 36, 1934 38, 1966 74, 1970 80, 1974 86, 1975 88, 1976 90, 1980 98, 1981 101, 1983 108, 1987 120, 1988 123, 1989 128, 1990 134, 1991 135, 1993 141, 1994 145, 1996 154, 1998 159, 1999 162, 2000 166
Dunn, Howell Mountain Cabernet Sauvignon 1982 516
Durbacher
  Plauelrain Riesling TBA 1985 368; Schlossberg Clevner Traminer 1955 351
Durfort-Vivens, Ch 1887 20, 1917 29, 1920 31, 1928 35, 1975 88, 1978 94, 1982 105, 1983 110, 1986 119, 1988 124, 1989 126-7, 1991 136, 1992 137, 1993 142, 1994 145, 1995 147, 1996 154, 1998 159, 1999 162

**E**

Echézeaux 1958 230, 1959 231, 1966 235, 1969 237, 1971 240, 241, 1975 242, 1976 243, 1978 245, 1981

247, 1982 249, 1983 249-50, 250, 1984 251, 1985 252-3, 1987 254, 1988 255, 256, 1989 257, 1990 259, 260, 1991 260, 261, 1992 261, 262, 1993 263, 1994 264, 1995 265, 1996 266, 1997 267, 1998 268, 1999 269, 270, 2000 272
Église, Clos L' 1945 45, 1947 47, 1961 66, 1975 88, 2000 166
Église, Dom de L' 1975 88, 1979 96, 1994 143, 1995 149
Église-Clinet, Ch L' 1921 31, 1947 47, 1959 61, 1966 73, 1971 83, 1975 88, 1976 90, 1978 93, 1981 99, 1982 103, 1983 108, 1985 114, 1986 118, 1987 120, 1988 123, 1989 127, 1990 131, 1991 135, 1992 137, 1993 139, 1994 143, 1995 147, 1996 152, 1997 156
Église-Clinet, Clos L' 1893 21, 1899 23, 1900 25, 1947 47, 1948 48, 1989 127
Eira Velha, Qta da 1896 454, 1943 462, 1945 464, 1953 467, 1972, 1974 478, 1975 479, 1978 481, 1994 491, 1995, 1997 492, 2000 494
Eitelsbacher
  Karthäuserhofberg Burgberg Riesling feinste Auslese 1953 350;
  Karthäuserhofberg Burgberg Riesling Spätlese 1976 363;
  Karthäuserhofberg Riesling Auslese 1989 372, 1994 379, 1999 387;
  Karthäuserhofberg Riesling Auslese Cask 22 1999 388;
  Karthäuserhofberg Riesling Auslese Cask 23 1990 374, 1999 388;
  Karthäuserhofberg Riesling Eiswein 1995 380;
  Karthäuserhofberg Riesling Kabinett 1989 372; Karthäuserhofberg Riesling Spätlese 1988 370, 1992 376;
  Karthäuserhofberg Riesling Spätlese trocken 1989 371;
  Karthäuserhofberg-Kronenberg Riesling feinste Auslese 1964 354; Marienholz Riesling Spätlese 1971 359
Eltviller
  Kalbspflicht Riesling 1969 356; Kalbspflicht Riesling Auslese 1990 375; Sandgrub Riesling 1947 349; Sonnenberg Riesling Auslese 1971 357, 1989 371; Sonnenberg Riesling BA 1971 357; Sonnenberg Riesling TBA 1985 368
Elysium 1989 371
Enclos, Ch L' 1929 36, 1945 45, 1971 83, 1985 116, 1994 145, 1995 147-8
Erbacher
  Bühl Riesling Auslese 1949 349; Herrenberg Riesling Auslese Cabinet

1953 350; Hohenrain Riesling Eiswein 1978 364, 1986 369, 1991 375; Hohenrain Riesling Erstes Gewächs 1998 386; Hohenrain Riesling Kabinett 1941 348; Hohenrain Riesling Spätlese 1934 347, 1971 357, 1976 361; Hohenrain Riesling Spätlese Cabinet 1964 354; Hohenrain Ruländer Spätlese 1971 357; Honigberg Riesling Auslese 1920 345, 1921 346; Langenwingert Riesling Kabinett 1966 354; Marcobrunn Riesling 1939 347, 1969 356; Marcobrunn Riesling Auslese 1929 346, 1945 348, 1971 357, 1976 361, 1983 366, 1989 371; Marcobrunn Riesling Auslese Cabinet 1915 345, 1959 352; Marcobrunn Riesling BA 1893 344, 1990 374, 1992 376; Marcobrunn Riesling Cabinet 1930 346; Marcobrunn Riesling Erstes Gewächs 1996 383, 1997 385; Marcobrunn Riesling Kabinett 1927 346; Marcobrunn Riesling Spätlese 1964 354, 1992 376, 1993 377, 1995 380, 1999 388; Marcobrunn Riesling Spätlese Blaukapsel 1990 374; Marcobrunn Riesling Spätlese Cabinet Fass Nr 59/24 1959 352; Marcobrunn Riesling Spätlese fruchtig 1999 388; Marcobrunn Riesling Spätlese trocken 1999 388; Marcobrunn Riesling TBA 1911 345, 1937 347, 1942 348, 1959 352, 1989 371, 1990 374; Michelmark Riesling BA Eiswein 1973 359; Michelmark Riesling Eiswein 1996 383; Michelmark Riesling TBA 1992 376; Rheinhell Riesling Auslese 1921 346; Rheinhell Riesling BA Strohwein 1970 356; Rheinhell Riesling Kabinett 1931 347, 1969 356; Rheinhell Weissburgunder und Chardonnay QbA trocken 1999 388, 2000 390; Schlossberg 'Erstes Gewächs' 1999 388; Schlossberg Riesling Auslese 1990 374, 1996 383; Schlossberg Riesling Kabinett trocken 1999 388, 2000 390; Schlossberg Ruländer TBA 1971 357; Siegelsberg 'Original' 1921 346; Siegelsberg Riesling Auslese 1975 360, 1996 383; Siegelsberg Riesling BA 2000 390; Siegelsberg Riesling Eiswein BA 1972 359; Siegelsberg Riesling Kabinett 1975 360; Siegelsberg Riesling

Kabinett fruchtig 2000 390; Siegelsberg Riesling Spätlese 1976 361; Siegelsberg Riesling TBA 1992 376; Siegelsberg Spätburgunder Weissherbst BA 1971 357; Siegelsberg Weissherbst TBA 1976 361; Steinmorgen Riesling Auslese 1985 368, 1994 379; Steinmorgen Riesling Eiswein 1979 364
Erdener
  Prälat Riesling Auslese 1988 370, 1989 371, 1994 379, 1996 383, 1999 388; Prälat Riesling Auslese Goldkapsel 1995 380, 1996 383, 1999 388; Prälat Riesling Auslese lange Goldkapsel 1996 383; Prälat Riesling feinste Auslese 1966 354; Prälat Riesling hochfeine Auslese 1966 354; Prälat Riesling Kabinett halbtrocken 1987 369; Prälat Riesling Spätlese 1987 369, 1989 371, 372; Treppchen Riesling Auslese 1989 371, 1994 379, 1995 381; Treppchen Riesling BA 1997 385; Treppchen Riesling feinste Auslese 1969 356; Treppchen Riesling Spätlese 1990 375
'Ermitage', Le Pavillon 1990 310
Ervamoira, Qta da 1994 491
Esk Valley 'Terraces' 1991 534
Essence see Tokaji Essence
Essencia see Tokaji Essencia
Essinger
  Osterberg Scheurebe Eiswein 1991 375; Rossberg Spätburgunder Weissherbst BA 1983 366; Ruländer TBA Eiswein 1976 363
Eszencia see Tokaji Eszencia
Étoile, Ch L' 1995 149
Évangile, Ch L' 1928 35, 1948 48, 1950 52, 1952 54, 1961 66, 1970 80, 1971 83, 1978 93, 1981 101, 1982 103, 1983 108, 1984 111, 1985 114, 1986 118, 1987 120, 1988 124, 1990 131, 1993 139, 1994 145, 1995 149, 1996 154, 1997 156

**F**

Farburet, Ch 1947 184
Fargues, Ch de 1967 190, 1971 193, 1975 195, 1976 196, 1979, 1980 197, 1984 200, 1987 202, 1988 203, 1990 205
Fay's, Nathan, 'Homemade' Cabernet Sauvignon 1968 511
Feist 1970, 1974 478
Ferrande, Ch de 1999 162
Ferreira 1815, 1836, 1834 450, 1840, 1847, 1851, 1854 451, 1858, 1863 452, 1877 453, 1900 455, 1908 456,

1912, 1917 *457*, 1934 *461*, 1945 *463*, 1950 *466*, 1955 *468*, 1960 *470*, 1966 *474*, 1970, 1975 *478*, 1977 *480*, 1978 *481*, 1980 *482*, 1982 *483*, 1983 *484*, 1985 *486*, 1987 *488*, 1991 *489*, 1994 *491*, 1995 *492*, 2000 *494*

Ferrière, Ch 1982 *105*, 1993 *142*, 1996 *154*, 1998 *159*, 2000 *166*

Fesles, Ch de 1933 *316*

Feuerheerd 1958 *469*, 1960 *471*, 1963 *473*, 1970 *477*, 1977 *481*

Feytit-Clinet, Ch 1982 *103*, 1985 *114*, 1993 *139*, 1995 *149*

Fieuzal, Ch de 1975 *89*, 1984 *111*, 1985 *114*, 1986 *118*, 1987 *120*, 1988 *123*, 1990 *131*, 1993 *141*, 1996 *152*, 1999 *162*, 2000 *166*

Figeac, Ch 1893 *21*, 1900 *25*, 1905, 1906 *26*, 1911 *28*, 1926 *34*, 1929 *36*, 1934 *39*, 1939 *40*, 1942, 1943 *42*, 1945 *45*, 1947 *47*, 1949 *50*, 1950 *53*, 1952 *54*, 1953 *56*, 1959 *61*, 1960 *63*, 1961 *66*, 1962 *68*, 1964 *70*, 1966 *73*, 1970 *80-1*, 1971 *83*, 1974 *86*, 1975 *88*, 1976 *90*, 1978 *94*, 1979 *96*, 1980 *98*, 1981 *99*, 1982 *103*, 1983 *108*, 1984 *111*, 1985 *114*, 1988 *123*, 1989 *127*, 1990 *131-2*, 1992 *138*, 1993 *141*, 1994 *145*, 1995 *148*, 1996 *154*, 1997 *156*, 1998 *159*, 1999 *162*, 2000 *166*

Filhot, Ch 1876, 1880 *174*, 1896, 1899 *175*, 1904 *176*, 1914 *177*, 1923, 1924, 1926 *179*, 1927, 1928, 1929 *180*, 1933, 1934 *181*, 1947 *184*, 1953, 1955 *186*, 1970 *192*, 1971 *193*, 1973 *194*, 1975 *195*, 1976 *196*, 1979 *197*, 1980, 1981 *198*, 1983 *199*, 1986 *201*, 1988 *203*, 1989 *204*, 1990 *206*, 1996 *209*, 1997 *211*, 1998 *212*, 2000 *214*

Filzener
Herrenberg Riesling BA 1996 *383*; Herrenberg Riesling Eiswein 1983 *366*

Firestone, Vintage Reserve Cabernet Sauvignon 1977 *514*

Fixin, Arvelets 1968 *236*

Fleur, Ch La 1947 *47*, 1948 *48*, 1949 *50*, 1950 *52-3*, 1952 *54*, 1955 *58*, 1961 *66*, 1964 *70*, 1966 *73, 75*, 1970 *81*, 1971 *83*, 1973 *85*, 1974 *86*, 1975 *88*, 1977 *91*, 1978 *93*, 1979 *96*, 1980 *98*, 1981 *99*, 1982 *103*, 1983 *109*, 1984 *111*, 1985 *114*, 1986 *118*, 1988 *123*, 1989 *127*, 1990 *132*, 1993 *139*, 1995 *149*

Fleur-de-Gay, Ch La 1991 *136*, 1996 *154*

Fleur-Gazin, Ch La 1945 *45*, 1979 *96*

Fleur-Pétrus, Ch La 1936 *39*, 1937 *40*, 1942 *42*, 1945 *45*, 1962 *69*, 1964 *70*, 1966 *75*, 1970 *81*, 1971 *83*, 1975 *88*, 1979 *96*, 1985 *114*, 1989 *127*, 1990 *134*, 1993 *139*, 1994 *145*, 1995 *148*, 1997 *156*, 2000 *166*

Fombrauge, Ch 1978 *93*, 1982 *106*, 1993 *139*

Fonplégade, Ch 2000 *166*

Fonréaud, Ch 1993 *142*, 1996 *154*, 2000 *168*

Fonroque, Ch 1997 *156*

Fonseca 1908 *456*, 1927 *458*, 1934 *461*, 1945 *463*, 1948 *465*, 1955 *468*, 1960 *470*, 1963 *472*, 1966 *474*, 1970 *477*, 1975 *478*, 1977 *480*, 1980 *482*, 1983 *484*, 1985 *486*, 1992 *490*, 1994 *491*, 1997 *493*, 2000 *494*

Fonseca Guimaraens 1976 *479*, 1978 *481*, 1984 *485*, 1991 *489*, 1995 *492*

Fontalloro 1986 *401*, 1990 *403*

Forman
Cabernet Sauvignon 1986 *519*; Cabernet Sauvignon 'Grand Vin' 1973 *512*

Forrester, Baron de 1985 *485-6*

Forster
Elster Riesling Spätlese 1977 *363-4*; Jesuitengarten Riesling Auslese 1976 *361*, 1994 *379*; Jesuitengarten Riesling BA 1992 *376*; Jesuitengarten Riesling Eiswein 1982 *366*; Kirchenstück Riesling Auslese 1971 *359*, 1976 *363*; Mariengarten Riesling Kabinett 1985 *368*; Mülweg Riesling Auslese 1962 *353*; Pechstein Riesling Auslese 1970 *356*; Pechstein Riesling BA 1990 *375*; Pechstein Riesling Eiswein 1989 *371*; Schnepfenflug an der Weinstrasse Ruländer Auslese 1975 *361*; Ungeheuer Riesling Auslese 1970 *345-6*; Ungeheuer Riesling Eiswein 1996 *383*; Ungeheuer Riesling Spätlese 1988 *370*; Ungeheuer Riesling TBA 1994 *379*

Forts de Latour 1970 *81*, 1971 *84*, 1974 *86*, 1975 *89*, 1978 *93*, 1979 *96*, 1980 *98*, 1981 *101*, 1991 *135*, 1996 *154*, 1997 *156*, 1998 *159*, 1999 *162*, 2000 *166*

Fourcas-Dupré, Ch 1985 *116*, 1993 *142*, 1996 *154*, 1998 *159*, 2000 *168*

Fourcas-Hosten, Ch 1961 *67*, 1985 *116*, 1992 *138*, 1993 *142*, 1996 *154*, 1997 *156*, 1998 *159*, 2000 *168*

Fourtet, Ch 1966 *74*, 1993 *142*, 1998 *159*

Fourtet, Clos 1924 *33*, 1929 *36*, 1957 *59*, 1961 *67*, 1970 *81*, 1981 *101*, 1982 *103*, 1983 *108*, 1985 *116*, 1989 *127*, 1992 *138*, 1996 *152*, 1997 *156*, 1999 *162*, 2000 *166*

Foz, Qta da 1934 *461*, 1948 *465*, 1954 *467*, 1970 *477*, 1975 *479*, 1977 *481*, 1980 *482*, 1982 *483*, 1983 *485*, 1985 *487*, 1986, 1987 *488*, 1991 *489*, 1992 *490*, 1995 *492*

Franc-Mayne, Ch 1993 *142*, 1996 *154*, 1997 *156-7*, 1998 *159*, 2000 *166*

France, Ch de 2000 *168*

Freemark Abbey
Bosché Cabernet Sauvignon 1974, 1975 *513*, 1978 *514*, 1989 *520*; Cabernet Sauvignon 1974 *513*, 1984 *517*

Freiherr v Fahrenberg Auslese 1949 *349*

Freinsheimer Musikantenbuchel Scheurebe Auslese 1995 *381*

'Frühlingswein' Riesling QbA trocken 2000 *390*

Fürst Spätburgunder Spätlese 1994 *379*

## G

Gaffelière, Ch La 1937 *40*, 1945 *45*, 1961 *67*, 1962 *69*, 1966 *74*, 1967 *75*, 1969 *77*, 1970 *81*, 1971 *84*, 1979 *96*, 1981 *101*, 1983 *110*, 1989 *128*, 1994 *145*, 1996 *154*, 1998 *159*, 1999 *162*, 2000 *166*

Gagliole 1996 *406*, 1997 *407*

Galway Vintage Claret 1955 *532*

Gay, Ch Le 1945 *45*, 1950 *53*, 1961 *67*, 1978 *94*, 1982 *103*, 1989 *127*, 1990 *132*

Gazin, Ch 1945 *44*, 1961 *67*, 1962 *69*, 1964 *71*, 1966 *73*, 1974 *86*, 1975 *88*, 1978 *94*, 1981 *101*, 1982 *106*, 1983 *110*, 1985 *114*, 1988 *124*, 1989 *127*, 1990 *132*, 1992 *138*, 1994 *145*, 1995 *149*, 1996 *154*, 1997 *157*, 1998 *159*, 1999 *162*, 2000 *166*

Geisenheimer
Kirchgrube Riesling feinste Auslese 1970 *356*; Kläuserweg Riesling Spätlese 1971 *357*; Mäuerchen Riesling BA 1904 *345*, 1976 *363*, 1994 *379*; Rothenberg Riesling Auslese 1996 *383*

Gevrey-Chambertin 1916 *218*, 1927 *220*, 1937 *224*, 1945 *226*, 1966 *236*, 1970 *239*, 1971 *240, 241*, 1976 *243*, 1981 *247*, 1982 *248*, 1984 *251*, 1988 *256*, 1993 *263*, 1995 *265*, 1997 *267-8*, 2000 *272*; Aux Echézeaux 1999 *270*; Cazetiers 1949 *227*, 1956 *230*, 1969 *237*, 1972 *241*, 1977 *244*, 1980 *246*, 1983 *250*, 250-1, 1986 *254*, 1988 *256*, 1995 *265*, 1999 *270*, 2000 *272*; Champeaux 1992 *262*; Combe aux Moines 1970 *239*, 1985 *252*, 1997 *267*; Combottes 1974 *242*, 1990 *259*; Estournelles St-Jacques 1980 *246*, 1997 *268*; Clos de la Justice 1967 *236*; Lavaux-St-Jacques 1972 *241*; Clos des Ruchottes 2000 *272*; Clos St-Jacques 1969 *237*, 1980 *246*, 1983 *250*, 1985 *252*, 1988 *256*, 1990 *259*, 1991 *261*, 1993 *263*, 1999 *270*, 2000 *272*; Varoilles

1976 *243*; Vieilles Vignes 1986 *254*, 1989 *257*, 1999 *270*

Gewurztraminer 1994 *334*, 1998 *336*, 2000 *337*; Cuvée 37 1959 *328*; Altenberg 1983 *330*; Cuvée Anne 1988 *331*, 1990 *333*; Brand Grand Cru 1989 *332*; Clos des Capucins, Clos St-Landelin 1985 *331*; Cuvée Christine 1989 *332*; Cuvée Exceptionelle 1961 *328*; Fronholz Ostertag 1990 *333*; Goldert Grand Cru 1988 *332*; Goldert Vendange Tardive 1994 *334*, 1998 *336*; Grand Cru Furstentum SGN 1995 *335*; Grand Cru Hengst 1998 *336*; Grand Cru Mamburg 1991 *333*; Gueberschwir Vendange Tardive 1983 *330*; Heimburg 1998 *336*; Heimburg SGN 1989 *332*; 'Jubilee' 1988 *332*, 1997 *335*; Kitterlé Grand Cru 1986 *331*; Cuvée Laurence 2000 *337*; Cuvée d'Or Quintessences de SGN 1994 *334*; Réserve 1989 *332*; Cuvée Seigneurs de Ribeaupierre 1983 *330*; SGN 1945 *327*, 1959, 1961, 1967 *328*, 1971 *329*, 1981, 1983 *330*, 1986 *331*, 1988 *332*, 1990 *333*, 1994 *334*, 1997 *335*; SGN 'S' 1989 *332*; Cuvée Théo 1989 *332*; Cuvée Tradition 1988 *332*; Vendange Tardive 1961, 1966 *328*, 1989 *332*, 1990 *333*, 1993 *334*, 1998 *336*; Vendange Tardive Réserve Exceptionnelle 1967 *328*; Vendange Tardive Réserve Exceptionnelle Auslese 1964 *328*; Vendange Tardive 'SGN par Jean Hugel', Fût 20 1976 *329*; Clos Windsbuhl 1988 *332*, 1998 *336*

Gigondas, Dom St-Gayon 1985 *308*

Gilbert (port) 1985 *486*

Gilbey (port) 1890 *453*

Gilette, Ch 1937 *182*, 1947 *184*, 1950 *185*, 1953, 1955 *186*, 1959 *187*, 1967 *190*

Giscours, Ch 1865 *15*, 1884 *20*, 1896 *22*, 1924 *33*, 1953 *56*, 1958 *60*, 1961 *67*, 1966 *74*, 1970 *81*, 1971 *84*, 1975 *88*, 1976 *90*, 1978 *93*, 1979 *96*, 1981 *99*, 1982 *103*, 1983 *108*, 1985 *114*, 1986 *118*, 1988 *124*, 1989 *127*, 1990 *134*, 1991 *136*, 1994 *143*, 1995 *148*, 1996 *152*, 1997 *157*, 1998 *159*, 1999 *162*, 2000 *166*

Gloria, Ch 1970 *81*, 1977 *91*, 1979 *96*, 1985 *116*

González Byass (port) 1903 *455*, 1910 *456*, 1932 *461*, 1935, 1937, 1939, 1942 *462*, 1960 *471*, 1964 *473*, 1970 *477*, 1975 *479*, 1985 *486*

Gosset 1952 *428*, 1959 *429*, 1961 *430*, 1964 *431*, 1973 *433-4*, 1976 *435*, 1982 *439*,

1988 *443*; Celebris 1988 *444*; Grand Millésime 1979 *437*, 1983 *440*, 1985 *441*, 1989 *445*

Gould Campbell 1908 *456*, 1922 *457*, 1924 *458*, 1955 *468*, 1963 *472*, 1966 *474*, 1970 *477*, 1975 *478*, 1977 *480*, 1980 *482*, 1983 *484*, 1985 *486*, 1991 *490*, 1994 *491*, 1997 *493*, 2000 *494*

Graacher
Domprobst Riesling Auslese 1971 *357*, 1976 *361*; Domprobst Riesling Auslese Goldkapsel 1996 *383*; Domprobst Riesling BA 1995 *381*; Domprobst Riesling Natur 1957 *351*; Himmelreich Riesling Auslese 1976 *361*, 1988 *370*, 1997 *385*; Himmelreich Riesling Auslese lange Goldkapsel 1976 *361*; Himmelreich Riesling BA 1970 *357*; Himmelreich Riesling Eiswein 1995 *381*; Himmelreich Riesling Eiswein BA 1971 *357*; Himmelreich Riesling Eiswein hochfeine Auslese 1969 *356*; Himmelreich Riesling Goldkapsel 1982 *366*; Himmelreich Riesling Kabinett 1979 *364*, 1998 *386*; Himmelreich Riesling Natur 1958 *351*; Himmelreich Riesling Spätlese 1982 *365*, 1988 *370*, 1997 *385*; Himmelreich TBA 1976 *363*; Humberg Riesling Natur 1951 *350*

Grace Family Vineyards, Cabernet Sauvignon 1980 *515*, 1982 *516*

Graham 1887 *453*, 1908 *456*, 1920 *457*, 1924, 1927 *458*, 1935 *461*, 1942 *462*, 1945 *463*, 1948 *465*, 1950, 1954 *467*, 1955 *468*, 1960 *470*, 1963 *472*, 1966 *474*, 1970 *477*, 1975 *478*, 1977 *480*, 1980 *482*, 1981 *483*, 1983 *484*, 1985 *486*, 1990 *489*, 1991 *490*, 1994 *491*, 1997 *493*, 2000 *494*; LBV 1981 *483*; Malvedos 1952, 1953, 1954 *467*, 1958 *469*, 1961, 1962 *471*, 1964, 1965 *473*, 1968 *475*, 1976 *479*, 1978 *481*, 1979 *482*, 1982 *483*, 1984 *485*, 1986, 1987, 1988 *488*, 1990 *489*

Gran Cama de Lobos 1789 *496*

Grand-Mayne, Ch 1992 *138*, 1993 *142*, 1996 *154*, 1998 *159*, 2000 *166*

Grand-Musigny 1904 *217*

Grand-Puy-Ducasse, Ch 1976 *91*, 1978 *94*, 1979 *96*, 1982 *106*, 1985 *114*, 1989 *127*, 1990 *134*, 1992 *138*, 1993 *142*, 1995 *149*, 1996 *154*, 1999 *162*, 2000 *166*

Grand-Puy-Lacoste, Ch 1945 *45*, 1949 *51*, 1953 *56*, 1959 *61*, 1961 *66*, 1962 *69*, 1964 *71*, 1966 *73*, 1970 *81*,

1971 *84*, 1973 *85*, 1975 *88*, 1976 *90*, 1978 *94*, 1979 *96*, 1980 *98*, 1981 *100*, 1982 *103-4*, 1983 *108*, 1984 *111*, 1985 *114*, 1986 *118*, 1987 *120*, 1988 *123*, 1989 *127*, 1990 *132*, 1991 *135*, 1992 *137*, 1993 *139*, 1994 *145*, 1995 *148*, 1996 *152*, 1997 *157*, 1999 *162*, 2000 *166*
Grande-Rue, La 1997 *268*
Grands-Echézeaux 1934 *222*, *223*, 1935 *223*, 1942 *225*, 1945 *226*, 1947 *227*, 1951 *228*, 1952, 1953 *229*, 1959 *231*, 1962 *233*, 1964 *233*, *234*, 1965 *234*, 1966 *235*, 1969 *236*, 1970 *238*, 1971 *240*, 1972, 1973 *241*, 1974, 1975 *242*, 1976 *243*, 1977, 1978 *244*, 1981 *247*, 1982 *248*, 1983 *249*, 1984 *251*, 1985 *252*, 1986 *253*, 1987 *254*, 1988 *255*, 1989 *257*, 1990 *260*, 1991 *260*, *261*, 1993 *262*, 1994 *264*, 1997 *267*, 1998 *268*, 1999 *269*, 2000 *272*; Tasteviné 1977 *244*
Grange (Hermitage) 1900, *530*, 1951, 1955 *530*, *532*, 1960, 1962, 1965-1968, 1970 *530*, 1977-1984 *531*, 1985 *531-2*, 1986-1990, 1992 *532*; Bin 95 1963 *530*, 1971 *530-1*, 1973, 1975 *531*; Grange's 25th Vintage, 1976 *531*
Gratien, Alfred 1969 *432*, 1982, 1983 *440*, 1985 *441*
Grave, Ch La 2000 *166*; see also Grave-Trigant-de-Boisset, Ch La for wines before 2000
Grave-Trigant-de-Boisset, Ch La 1971 *84*, 1974 *86*, 1975 *88*, 1979 *96*, 1981 *101*, 1989 *128*, 1990 *134*, 1996 *152*; see also Grave, Ch La for wines from 2000
Greysac, Ch 1998 *159*, 2000 *168*
Grgich Hills, Napa Cabernet Sauvignon 1985 *519*
Griottes-Chambertin 1990 *260*, 1999 *270*, 2000 *272*
Grosskarlbacher Burgweg Scheurebe Auslese 1990 *374*
Groth
Cabernet Sauvignon 1982, 1984 *517*, 1990 *521*; Napa Cabernet Sauvignon 1996 *526*; Reserve Cabernet Sauvignon 1985 *518*
Gruaud, Ch 1865 *15*
Gruaud-Larose, Ch 1825 *12*, 1865 *15*, 1870 *17*, 1874 *18*, 1878, 1881 *19*, 1887, 1888 *20*, 1893 *21*, 1899 *23*, 1900 *25*, 1905 *26*, 1911 *27*, 1914 *28*, 1917, 1918, 1919 *29*, 1920 *30*, 1921 *31*, 1924 *33*, 1928 *35*, 1929 *36*, 1934 *38*, 1943 *42*, 1945 *45*, 1947 *47*, 1953 *56*, 1955 *58*, 1957 *59*, 1959 *62*, 1961 *66*, 1962 *68*, 1964 *71*, 1966 *73*, 1968 *76*, 1969 *77*, 1970 *81*, 1971 *83*, 1972 *84*, 1973 *85*, 1974 *86*, 1975 *88*, 1976 *90*, 1977

*91*, 1978 *93*, 1979 *96*, 1981 *100*, 1982 *104*, 1983 *108*, 1985 *114-15*, 1986 *119*, 1987 *120*, 1988 *123*, 1989 *127*, 1990 *134*, 1991 *136*, 1992 *138*, 1993 *139-40*, 1994 *143*, 1995 *148*, 1996 *152*, 1997 *157*, 1998 *159*, 1999 *162*, 2000 *166*
Gruaud-Larose-Faure, Ch 1934 *38*
Guado al Tasso 1997 *407*
Guillot, Ch 1959 *62*
Guimarães 1958 *469*; Reserve 1962 *471*, 1964 *473*, 1968 *475*; see also Fonseca
Guiraud, Ch 1921 *178*, 1924 *179*, 1929 *180*, 1959 *187*, 1961, 1962 *188*, 1964, 1966 *189*, 1967 *190*, 1969 *191*, 1970 *192*, 1975 *194*, 1976 *195*, 1979 *197*, 1980, 1981 *198*, 1983 *200*, 1985, 1986 *201*, 1988 *203*, 1989 *204*, 1996 *209*, 1997 *210*, 1998 *212*, 1999 *213*
Guiteronde, Ch 1923, 1924 *179*, 1975 *195*
Gundlach Bundschu Cabernet Sauvignon 1981 *516*

## H

Haardter Bürgergarten Rieslaner Auslese 1996 *383*
Hallgartener Deutelsberg Riesling 1969 *356*; Jungfer Riesling Auslese 1968 *368*; Jungfer Riesling BA 1976 *361*; Schönhell Riesling BA 1994 *379*; Schönhell Riesling Eiswein 1983 *366*; Schönhell Riesling TBA 1959 *352*
Hamilton Russell, Chardonnay 1999 *535*
Hankey Bannister (port) 1853 *451*
Hanzell
Cabernet Sauvignon 1981 *516*; Pinot Noir 1974 *512*, 1975, 1976 *513*, 1978, 1979 *514*, 1980 *515*, 1981 *516*
Harlan Estate 1991 *522*, 1992 *523*, 1993 *523*, 1994, 1995 *525*
Harvey's (port) 1878 *453*, 1954 *467*, 1958 *469*, 1962 *471*
Hattenheimer
Engelmannsberg Riesling Auslese 1971 *357*, 1989 *371*; Engelmannsberg Riesling TBA 1971 *358*, 1976 *361*; Hassel Riesling BA 1949 *349*, 1967 *355*; Hassel Riesling Eiswein 1991 *375*; Hassel Riesling Kabinett 1970 *357*; Heiligenberg Riesling Auslese 1976 *361*; Mannberg Riesling 1948 *349*; Nussbrunnen Riesling Auslese 1971 *358*, 1976 *361*, 1989 *371*, 1993 *377*, 2000 *390*; Nussbrunnen Riesling BA 1971 *358*, 1976 *361*; Nussbrunnen Riesling Kabinett trocken 1999

*388*; Nussbrunnen Riesling Spätlese 2000 *390*; Nussbrunnen Riesling TBA 1983 *366*; Pfaffenberg Riesling Auslese 1995 *381*; Pfaffenberg Riesling BA 1971 *358*; Pfaffenberg Riesling Spätlese Goldkapsel 1996 *383*; Pfaffenberg Riesling TBA 1971 *358*; Schönhell Riesling Eiswein 1983 *366*; Schützenhaus Riesling Auslese 1967 *355*; Schützenhaus Riesling Goldkapsel 1996 *383*; Stabel Riesling Spätlese 1952 *350*; Wisselbrunnen Riesling Beerenauslese 1976 *363*; Wisselbrunnen Riesling Auslese 1976 *361*, 1990 *374*, 1992 *376*, 1998 *386*; Wisselbrunnen Riesling Auslese Goldkapsel 1992 *376*; Wisselbrunnen Riesling BA 1959 *352*, 1976 *363*, 1997 *385*; Wisselbrunnen Riesling Kabinett 1940 *348*, 1960 *353*; Wisselbrunnen Riesling Kabinett halbtrocken 1999 *388*, 2000 *390*; Wisselbrunnen Riesling Spätlese 1935 *347*, 1994 *379*; Wisselbrunnen Riesling TBA 1971 *358*
Haut-Bages-Averous, Ch 1991 *135*
Haut-Bages-Libéral, Ch 1985 *115*, 1996 *154*, 1997 *157*, 2000 *166*
Haut-Bages-Montpelou, Ch 1986 *119*
Haut-Bailly, Ch 1877 *18*, 1918 *29*, 1929 *36*, 1945 *45*, 1947 *47*, 1948 *49*, 1966 *74*, 1970 *81*, 1971 *84*, 1978 *93*, 94-5, 1979 *96*, 1981 *101*, 1982 *104*, 1983 *108*, 1985 *115*, 1986 *118*, 1988 *123*, 1989 *127*, 1990 *132*, 1993 *140*, 1994 *143*, 1995 *148*, 1996 *152*, 1997 *157*, 1998 *159*, 1999 *162*, 2000 *166*
Haut-Batailley, Ch 1961 *67*, 1962 *69*, 1966 *73*, 1970 *81*, 1971 *84*, 1978 *93*, 1979 *96*, 1982 *104*, 1983 *108*, 1985 *115*, 1988 *123*, 1989 *128*, 1990 *134*, 1992 *137*, 1994 *145*, 1996 *152*, 1997 *157*, 1999 *162*, 2000 *166*
Haut-Bergey, Ch 1993 *142*, 2000 *168*; (blanc) 1998 *212*
Haut-Brion, Ch 1875 *18*, 1906, 1907 *26*, 1909, 1910 *27*, 1919 *29*, 1920 *30*, 1921 *31*, 1923 *32*, 1926 *33-4*, 1928 *35*, 1929 *36*, 1931 *37*, 1934 *38*, 1937 *39*, 1940 *41*, 1943, 1944 *42*, 1945 *43-4*, 1947 *46*, 1948 *48*, 1949 *50*, 1950 *52*, 1952 *53-4*, 1953 *55*, 1955 *57*, 1957 *59*, 1958 *60*, 1959 *61*, 1960 *63*, 1961 *64-5*, 1962 *67-8*, 1964 *70*, 1965 *71*, 1966 *72*, 1968 *76*, 1969 *76-7*, 1970 *79*, 1971 *83*, 1972 *84*, 1973 *85*, 1974 *86*, 1975 *87*, 1976 *89-90*, 1977 *91*, 1978 *92*, 1979

95, 1980 *97-8*, 1981 *99*, 1982 *102*, 1983 *107*, 1984 *110*, 1985 *112*, 1986 *117*, 1987 *120*, 1988 *121*, 1989 *125*, 1990 *130*, 1992 *136*, 1993 *138*, 1995 *146*, 1996 *150*, 1997 *155*, 1998 *158*, 1999 *161*, 2000 *165*; (blanc) 1943 *183*, 1952 *185*, 1953, 1955 *186*, 1962 *189*, 1970 *193*, 1975 *195*, 1976, 1978 *196*, 1982 *199*, 1983 *200*, 1985 *201*, 1986 *202*, 1988 *203*, 1989 *204*, 1990 *206*, 1994, 1995 *208*, 1996 *210*, 1997 *211*, 1998 *212*, 1999 *213*, 2000 *214*
Haut-Brion-La Mission, Ch 1888 *20*
Haut-Peyraguey, (Ch) Clos 1893 *175*, 1959 *187*, 1975 *195*, 1983 *200*, 1986 *202*, 1990 *206*, 1993 *207*, 1996 *209*, 1997 *210*, 1998 *212*, 1999 *213*
Heidsieck 1907 *422*, 1923 *424*, 1928 *425*, 1934 *426*, 1945 *427*; Diamant Bleu 1982 *439*, 1985 *441*; Diamant Bleu, Rosé 1988 *444*
Heidsieck, Charles 1949 *428*, 1955 *429*, 1970 *433*, 1979 *437*, 1982, 1983 *440*, 1985 *441*, 1992 *446*, 1993, 1995 *447*; Blanc des Millénaires 1983 *440*, 1985 *441*; Champagne Charlie 1979 *437*, 1983 *440*, 1985 *441*
Heitz
Angelica 1974 *512*; Bella Oaks Cabernet Sauvignon 1976 *513*, 1977 *514*, 1980 *515*, 1981 *516*, 1985 *518*; Cabernet Sauvignon 1959 *510*, 1968 *511*, 1973 *512*; Martha's Vineyard Cabernet Sauvignon 1969, 1970 *511*, 1973 *512*, 1972-13, 1975 *513*, 1978 *514*, 1982 *517*, 1985 *518*, 1989 *520*
Henriot 1962 *430*, 1985 *442*, 1988 *443*, 1989 *444*
Hermitage 1952, 1961, 1969, 1970 *303*, 1971 *304*, 1978, 1979 *306*, 1982 *306-7*, 1984 *307*, 1985, 1987, 1988 *308*, 1989 *309*, 1990 *310*, 1992, 1993 *311*, 1996 *312*; La Chapelle 1949, 1961, 1966, 1969, 1970 *303*, 1971, 1972, 1976 *304*, 1978, 1979, 1981 *306*, 1982, 1983, 1984 *307*, 1985, 1986, 1987 *308*, 1988, 1989 *309*, 1990, 1991 *310*, 1995, 1996 *312*, 2000 *314*; Monnier de le Sizeranne 1990 *310*; Le Pied de la Côte 1990 *314*; Rochefine 1947 *303*; La Sizeranne 1978 *306*, 1983 *307*, 1985 *308*, 1991 *311*
Hess Collection, Cabernet Sauvignon 1984 *517*, 1985, 1986 *519*, 1987 *520*
Hill of Grace, Shiraz 1978 *532*, 1991 *533*
Hill, William, Cabernet Sauvignon 1982 *517*
Hochheimer
Domdechaney Kirchenstück Riesling

TBA 1990 *374*; Domdechaney Riesling Auslese 1950 *350*, 1990 *374*, 1994 *379*; Domdechaney Riesling Spätlese 1966 *354*, 1983 *366*, 1996 *383*; Engelmannberg Riesling TBA 1976 *362*; Hölle Riesling Auslese 1976 *362*, 1983 *366*, 1986 *369*, 1989 *371*, 1990 *374*; Hölle Riesling BA 1994 *379*, 1996 *383*; Hölle Riesling Eiswein 1987 *369*, 1997 *385*; Hölle Riesling Kabinett 1988 *370*; Hölle Riesling Spätlese halbtrocken 1997 *385*; Kirchenstück Gewürztraminer Auslese 1983 *367*; Kirchenstück Riesling Auslese 1983 *367*, 1986 *369*, 1990 *374*, 1991 *375*, 1992 *376*; Kirchenstück Riesling BA 1988 *370*; Kirchenstück Riesling Eiswein 1991 *375*; Kirchenstück Riesling Spätlese 1996 *383*, 1998 *386*, 2000 *391*; Kirchenstück Stielweg Riesling Auslese 1953 *350*; Königin Victoria Berg Riesling Auslese 1975 *361*; Königin Victoria Berg Riesling Spätlese 1983 *367*, 1988 *370*; Königin Victoria Berg Riesling TBA 1976 *363*, 1983 *367*; Reichestal Riesling Auslese 1992 *376*; Reichestal Riesling Eiswein 1989 *371*; Reichestal Riesling Kabinett 1999 *388*; Riesling TBA 1990 *374*; Stein Riesling TBA 1915 *345*; Stielweg Riesling Auslese trocken 1998 *386*; Stielweg Riesling Eiswein 1983 *367*; Stielweg Riesling Spätlese 1985 *368*; Stielweg Spätburgunder Weissherbst Eiswein 1992 *376*
Hohentweiler Olgaberg Traminer Auslese 1983 *367*
Hooper 1935, 1937 *462*, 1985 *487*
Hosanna 2000 *166*; see also Certan-Giraud, Ch for wines before 2000
Hunter & Oliver (port) 1896 *454*
Hunter Burgundy 'Bin 3110' 1965 *532*
Hunter Valley, 'Burgundy' 1943 *532*
Hunter Valley, 'Sydney' 1937 *532*
Hunt's (port) 1963 *473*
Hutcheson 1970 *478*, 1980 *483*, 1983 *485*, 1985 *487*, 1991 *490*

## I

Ihringer
Winklerberg Grauer

Burgunder Spätlese trocken '***' 1997 *385*; Winklerberg Spätburgunder Rotwein '***' Auslese 1997 *385*

Ingelheimer Schloss Westerhaus Riesling Eiswein 1985 *368*; Spätburgunder 1982 *366*

Inglenook Cabernet Sauvignon 1959, 1963 *510*, 1968, 1970 *511*, 1984 *517*; Cabernet Sauvignon Cask A9 1974 *513*; Cabernet Sauvignon Cask F10 1958 *509*; Cabernet Sauvignon Cask Res J-3 1954 *509*; Cabernet Sauvignon Reserve Cask 1982 *517*

Iphöfer Julius-Echter-Berg Huxelrebe Auslese 1988 *370*; Julius-Echter-Berg Riesling Spätlese trocken 'S' 2000 *391*; Julius-Echter-Berg Silvaner BA 1971 *359*; Julius-Echter-Berg Silvaner Spätlese trocken 2000 *391*; Kalb Ehrenfelser Eiswein 1997 *385*; Kalb Scheurebe TBA 1990 *375*; Kronsberg Rieslaner Spätlese 1998 *386*; Kronsberg Scheurebe Spätlese trocken 2000 *390*; Kronsberg Silvaner Spätlese 1999 *388*

Issan, Ch d' 1959 *62*, 1961 *67*, 1966 *73*, 1973 *85*, 1978 *95*, 1981 *101*, 1982 *106*, 1983 *108*, 1985 *115*, 1986 *118*, 1988 *123*, 1989 *128*, 1990 *134*, 1991 *136*, 1993 *142*, 1996 *154*, 2000 *166*

## J

J & C White & Co (port) 1844 *451*

Jacobins, Clos des 1975 *89*

Jacquart 1983 *440*, 1987 *443*; Cuvée Nominée 1985 *442*, 1988 *444*

Jacquesson 1975 *434*, 1976 *435*, 1990 *446*; Blanc de Blancs 1969 *432*; Perfection 1985 *442*; Rosé 1990 *446*; Signature 1985 *442*, 1989 *444*

Jade Mountain, Syrah 1990 *521*

Jasnières Dom de la Charrière, Sélection de Raisins Nobles 1996 *323*; Les Truffières 1989 *320*

'Johannisberg, Castle' 1870 *344*

Johannisberger Hölle Riesling Auslese 1964 *354*; Johannisberger Klaus Riesling Auslese 1975 *360*, 1982 *366*, 1989 *371*; Klaus Riesling TBA 1989 *371*, 1990 *374*; Mittelhöhle Riesling BA 1945 *348*; Vogelsang Riesling Auslese 1995 *381*

Johannisberg(er), Schloss Blaulack 1846 *344*;

Riesling Auslese 1937 *347*, 1949 *349*, 1967 *355*; Riesling Auslese Fass Nr 62 1945 *349*; Riesling BA 1971 *358*; Riesling BA Fass Nr 92 1943 *348*; Riesling Blaulack Eiswein 1991 *375*; Riesling Cabinet 1921 *346*; Riesling Cabinet Wein 1748 *344*; Riesling Dunkelblaulack 1934 *347*; Riesling Eiswein 1986 *369*; Riesling Eiswein Blaulack 1985 *368*; Riesling feine Spätlese 1959 *352*; Riesling Goldblaulack Auslese 1862 *344*; Riesling Goldlack 1893 *344*; Riesling Goldlack Auslese 1920 *346*; Riesling Goldlack BA 1943 *348*; Riesling Goldlack TBA 1862 *344*, 1947 *349*, 1967 *355*, 1976 *362*, 1999 *388*; Riesling Grünlack Spätlese trocken 2000 *391*; Riesling Rosagoldlack BA 1945 *349*, 1971 *358*, 1975 *360*; Riesling Rosalack Auslese 1963 *353*, 1971 *358*, 1996 *383*; Riesling Rosegold BA 1995 *381*; Riesling Rotlack Kabinett 1999 *388*, 2000 *391*; Riesling TBA 1967 *355*; Riesling TBA Fass Nr 163 1947 *349*; Riesling trocken 2000 *391*

Jordan, Cabernet Sauvignon 1976 *513*, 1977, 1978, 1979 *514*, 1980 *515*, 1981 *516*, 1982, 1983 *517*

Josephshöfer Riesling Auslese 1985 *368*

## K

Kalin Cellars Pinot Noir 1981 *516*; Pinot Noir Cuvée DD 1980 *515*, 1983 *517*

Kallstadter Kobnert Silvaner Kabinett 1976 *361*; Saumagen Huxelrebe TBA 1971 *358*; Saumagen Riesling Spätlese 1969 *356*

Kanonkop, Cabernet Sauvignon 1997 *535*

Kanzemer Altenberg Riesling 1979 *364*; Altenberg Riesling Auslese 1999 *388*; Altenberg Riesling Auslese Goldkapsel 1996 *383*, 1999 *388*; Altenberg Riesling Spätlese 1996 *383*

Kaseler Kehrnagel Riesling BA 1989 *371*

Kendall-Jackson Cabernet Sauvignon 1989 *520*; Cardinale 1985 *518*; Reserve Cabernet Sauvignon 1997 *527*

Kesseler August, Riesling Spätlese '**' 1994 *379*

Kiedricher Gräfenberg Riesling Auslese 1971 *358*, 1993 *377*, 1998 *386*; Gräfenberg

Riesling Auslese Goldkapsel 1990 *374*, 1992 *376*, 1996 *383*, 1997 *385*, 1998 *386*; Gräfenberg Riesling Auslese Nr 19 1995 *381*; Gräfenberg Riesling BA Goldkapsel 1992 *376*, 1993 *377-8*, 1996 *383*; Gräfenberg Riesling Spätlese 1927 *346*, 1976 *363*, 1996 *383*, 1997 *385*; Sandgrub Riesling Auslese 1990 *374*

Kirwan, Ch 1865 *15*, 1894 *22*, 1945 *45*, 1961 *67*, 1971 *83*, 1978 *93*, 1979 *96*, 1981 *100*, 1982 *106*, 1983 *108*, 1984 *111*, 1986 *118*, 1988 *123*, 1990 *134*, 1992 *138*, 1993 *140*, 1994 *145*, 1995 *149*, 1996 *152*, 1997 *157*, 1998 *159*, 1999 *162*, 2000 *166*

Klein Constantia, Vin de Constance 1998 *535*

Kloovenburg, Shiraz 1999 *535*

Kloster Eberbach Riesling BA 1989 *371*

Koch 1904 *422*

Kongsgaard, Napa Valley Syrah 1996 *526*, 1998, 1999 *528*

Königschaffhauser Steingrüble Spätburgunder Weissherbst Eiswein 1988 *370*; Steingrüble Spätburgunder Weissherbst TBA 1976 *363*

Kopke 1878 *453*, 1926 *458*, 1967 *475*, 1978 *481*, 1985 *487*, 1997 *493*

Kreuznacher Kahlenberg Riesling Auslese 1993 *378*; Krötenpfühl Riesling Auslese 1989 *371*; Krötenpfühl Riesling Eiswein 1983 *367*; Steinweg Riesling BA 1971 *358*

Krohn 1927 *459*, 1963 *473*, 1970 *478*

Krug (Champagne) 1928 *425*, 1952, 1953 *428*, 1955, 1959 *429*, 1961, 1962 *430*, 1964 *431*, 1969 *432*, 1971 *433*, 1973 *434*, 1975, 1976 *435*, 1979 *437*, 1981 *438*, 1982 *439*, 1985 *441*, 1988 *443*, 1989 *444*; Clos du Mesnil 1979 *437*, 1981 *438*, 1982 *439*, 1983 *440*, 1985 *441*, 1986 *442-3*; Collection 1966 *431*; Grande Cuvée *436*; Private Cuvée 1947 *427*; Rosé 1985 *441*

Krug, Charles (Napa) Bosché Cabernet Sauvignon 1978 *514*; Cabernet Sauvignon 1944, 1946 *508*, 1963, 1965 *510*, 1983 *517*; Cabernet Sauvignon Vintage Selection 1956 *509*, 1958 *509*, 1961 *510*; Cabernet Sauvignon Vintage Selection 'Lot B' 1959 *510*; Cabernet Sauvignon Vintage Selection Lot F1 1974 *513*

## L

Labégorce, Ch 1991 *135*, 1992 *138*, 2000 *168*

Labégorce-Zédé, Ch 1982 *106*, 1983 *108*, 1988 *124*, 1989 *128*, 1990 *132*, 1991 *135*, 1993 *140*, 1995 *148*, 1996 *152*

Lafaurie-Peyraguey, Ch 1906 *176*, 1909, 1912, 1913, 1914, 1918 *177*, 1920, 1921, 1922 *178*, 1924 *179*, 1927 *180*, 1933, 1934 *181*, 1937 *182*, 1945 *183*, 1947 *184*, 1955 *186*, 1959 *187*, 1961 *188*, 1964, 1966 *189*, 1967 *190*, 1969 *191*, 1970 *192*, 1971 *193*, 1975 *194*, 1976 *195*, 1979 *197*, 1981 *198*, 1982, 1983 *199*, 1986 *201*, 1988 *203*, 1989 *204*, 1990 *205*, 1992, 1993 *207*, 1994 *207-8*, 1995 *208*, 1996 *209*, 1997 *210*, 1998 *212*, 1999 *213*, 2000 *214*

Lafite, Ch 1799, 1803, 1806, 1811, 1814, 1825, 1832, 1844, 1846 *12*, 1848, 1858 *13*, 1864 *14*, 1865 *14-15*, 1868 *15*, 1869 *15-16*, 1870 *16*, 1871, 1872, 1874 *17*, 1875, 1876, 1877 *18*, 1878, 1879, 1880, 1881, 1882 *19*, 1883, 1886, 1887, 1888, 1889, 1890 *20*, 1891, 1892, 1893 *21*, 1894, 1895, 1896, 1897, 1898 *22*, 1899 *23*, 1900 *24*, 1902, 1903, 1904 *25*, 1905, 1906, 1907 *26*, 1908, 1909, 1910, 1911 *27*, 1912, 1913, 1914, 1916 *28*, 1917, 1918, 1919 *29*, 1920 *30*, 1921, 1922 *31*, 1923, 1924 *32*, 1925, 1926 *33*, 1928 *35*, 1929 *36*, 1931, 1933 *37*, 1934 *38*, 1937, 1938, 1939 *40*, 1940, 1941, 1942 *41*, 1943, 1944 *42*, 1945 *43*, 1946 *45-6*, 1947 *46*, 1948 *48*, 1949 *49*, 1950 *52*, 1951, 1952 *53*, 1953 *54*, 1954 *57*, 1956 *58-9*, 1957, 1958 *59*, 1959 *60*, 1960 *63*, 1961 *64*, 1962 *67*, 1963, 1964 *69*, 1965, 1966 *71*, 1967 *75*, 1968, 1969, 1970 *79*, 1971 *82*, 1972, 1973 *84*, 1974 *86*, 1975 *87*, 1976 *89*, 1977 *91*, 1978 *91-2*, 1979 *95*, 1980 *97*, 1981 *98*, 1982 *101*, 1983 *106*, 1984 *110*, 1985 *111-12*, 1986 *117*, 1987 *119-20*, 1988 *120-1*, 1989 *124-5*, 1990 *129*, 1991 *135*, 1992 *136*, 1993 *138*, 1994 *142*, 1995 *146*, 1996 *150*, 1997 *154-5*, 1998 *158*, 1999 *161*, 2000 *164*

'Lafite, Vin de' (blanc) 1934 *181*

Lafitte, Ch 1784 *10-11*, 1787 *11*

Lafon-Rochet, Ch 1960 *63*, 1961 *67*, 1964 *71*, 1966 *74*, 1981 *101*, 1983 *109*, 1985 *115*, 1986 *119*, 1988 *124*, 1990 *132*, 1992 *138*, 1993 *141*, 1994 *145*, 1995 *149*, 1996 *154*, 1997 *157*, 1998 *159*, 1999 *162*, 2000 *167*

Lages, Qta das 1926 *458*

Lagrange, Ch (Pomerol) 1978 *93*

Lagrange, Ch (St-Julien) 1955 *58*, 1961 *67*, 1978 *95*, 1979 *96*, 1982 *104*, 1983 *109*, 1986 *119*, 1989 *127*, 1990 *134*, 1991 *136*, 1993 *142*, 1994 *145*, 1995 *148*, 1996 *154*, 1997 *157*, 1998 *159*, 1999 *162*, 2000 *167*

Lagune, Ch La 1899 *23*, 1916 *28*, 1921 *31*, 1955 *58*, 1959 *62*, 1960 *63*, 1966 *73*, 1971, 1972 *84*, 1973 *85*, 1976 *90*, 1978 *93*, 1979 *96*, 1981 *101*, 1982 *104*, 1983 *109*, 1985 *115*, 1988 *124*, 1990 *132*, 1995 *148*, 1996 *152*, 1997 *157*, 1999 *162*, 2000 *167*

Lamarque, Ch 1992 *138*

Lambrays, Clos des 1934 *223*, 1937 *224*, 1945 *226*, 1951 *228*, 1981 *247*, 1985 *252*, 1988 *256*, 1995 *265*, 1999 *270*, 2000 *272*

Lamothe, Ch 1982 *199*, 1993 *207*, 1995 *208*, 1996 *209*, 1997 *211*, 1998 *212*, 1999 *213*

Lamothe-Despaljols, Ch 2000 *214*

Lamothe-Guignard, Ch 1986 *201*, 1988 *203*, 1989 *204*, 1990 *206*, 1993 *207*, 1996 *209*, 1997 *211*, 1998 *212*, 1999 *213*

Lanessan, Ch 1955 *58*, 1966 *74*, 1979 *96*, 1990 *132*

Lang-Biemont, Blanc de Blancs 1985 *442*

Langoa-Barton, Ch 1945 *45*, 1952 *54*, 1953 *56*, 1959 *62*, 1961 *67*, 1962 *69*, 1964 *71*, 1966 *74*, 1971 *84*, 1975 *88*, 1976 *90*, 1978 *93-4*, 1979 *96*, 1980 *98*, 1982 *104*, 1983 *109*, 1985 *115*, 1986 *118*, 1988 *124*, 1989 *128*, 1990 *134*, 1991 *136*, 1992 *138*, 1993 *140*, 1994 *145*, 1995 *149*, 1997 *157*, 1998 *159*, 1999 *162*, 2000 *167*

Lanson 1943 *426*, 1959 *429*, 1961 *430*, 1971 *433*, 1981 *438*, 1983 *440*, 1985 *442*, 1989 *444*, 1990 *446*; Blanc de Blancs 1983 *440*, 1989 *445*; Noble Cuvée 1979 *437*, 1985 *442*, 1988 *444*; Red Label 1975 *424*, 1976 *435-6*, 1979 *437*

Larcis-Ducasse, Ch 1967 *75*, 1970 *81*, 1983 *110*, 1985 *116*, 1990 *132*, 1994 *145*, 1996 *152*, 1997 *157*, 1998 *159*, 1999 *162*, 2000 *167*

Larmande, Ch 1985 *116*, 1993 *141*, 1994 *145*, 1995 *149*, 1997 *157*, 1998 *159*, 1999 *162*, 2000 *167*

Larose, Ch 1923 *32*, 1924 *33*

Laroze, Ch 1863 *14*, 1865 *15*

Larrivet-Haut-Brion, Ch 1993 *142*, 1996 *152*, 1997 *157*, 1998 *159*, 2000 *167*

Lascombes, Ch 1928 *36*, 1942 *42*, 1946 *46*, 1962 *69*, 1966 *73*, 1970 *81*, 1971 *83*, 1973 *85*, 1975 *88*, 1978 *95*, 1979 *96*, 1981 *101*, 1982 *106*, 1983 *109*, 1985 *115*, 1986 *118*, 1989 *127*, 1990 *132*, 1992 *137*, 1993 *142*, 1994 *143*, 1995 *148*, 1996 *152*, 1997 *157*, 1999 *162*, 2000 *167*

Latour, Ch 1861, 1863, 1864 14, 1865, 1868 15, 1870 16, 1874 17, 1875, 1877 18, 1878, 1881 19, 1887, 1888, 1890 20, 1892, 1893 21, 1897 22, 1898, 1899 23, 1900 24, 1901, 1903, 1904 25, 1905, 1906 26, 1908, 1911 27, 1912, 1913, 1916 28, 1917, 1918, 1919 29, 1920 30, 1921, 1922 31, 1923, 1924 32, 1925, 1926 33, 1927 34, 1928 34-5, 1929 36, 1930, 1931, 1932 37, 1933 37-8, 1934 38, 1935, 1936, 1937 39, 1938, 1939 40, 1940, 1941, 1942 41, 1943, 1944 42, 1945 43, 1946, 1947 46, 1948 48, 1949 49, 1950 52, 1952 53, 1953 54-5, 1954, 1955 57, 1956, 1957 59, 1958, 1959 60, 1960 63, 1961 64, 1962 67, 1964 69, 1965 71, 1966 71-2, 1967 75, 1968, 1969 76, 1970 79, 1971 82, 1972 84, 1973 85, 1974 86, 1975 87, 1976 89, 1977 91, 1978 92, 1979 95, 1980 97, 1981 98, 1982 101, 1983 106, 1984 110, 1985 112, 1986 117, 1987 120, 1988 121, 1989 125, 1990 129, 1991 135, 1992 136, 1993 138, 1994 142, 1995 146, 1996 150, 1997 155, 1998 158, 1999 161, 2000 164

Latour-Martillac, Ch 1978 95, 1996 154, 1997 157, 1998 159, 2000 167; (blanc) 1998 212

Latour-à-Pomerol, Ch 1921 31, 1947 47, 1948 48, 1959 62, 1961 67, 1966 75, 1970 82, 1971 84, 1975 88, 1976 90, 1979 96, 1981 100, 1982 104, 1989 128, 1990 132, 2000 167

Latricières-Chambertin 1955 229, 1964 234, 1966 236, 1985 252, 1988 256, 1993 263

Laubenheimer Karthäuser Riesling BA 1976 362

Laujac, Ch 1975 88

Laurent-Perrier 1955 429, 1985 441; Grande Siècle 1985 441, 1990 446; Grande Siècle, La Cuvée 1975 434-5, 1976, 1978 436; Millésime Rare 1973 434

Laville, Ch 1929 180

Laville Haut-Brion, Ch 1929 180, 1933, 1934 181, 1935, 1936, 1940, 1941 182, 1942, 1943, 1945 183, 1947, 1949 184, 1952 185, 1955 186, 1959 187, 1960, 1961 188, 1962, 1966 189, 1970, 1971 193, 1976, 1978 196, 1979 197, 1981 198, 1982 199, 1983 200, 1985 201, 1988 203, 1989 204, 1990 206, 1992, 1993 207, 1994 208, 1997 211, 1998 212, 1999 213, 2000 214; Crème de Tête 1982 199

Layer, Schloss Goldloch Riesling Edel BA 1967 355; Pittermännchen Riesling Cabinet TBA 1959 352

Lechère, Grand Cru,

Blanc de Blancs 1980 438
Léoville, Ch 1864 14, 1888 20, 1893 21
Léoville-Barton, Ch 1871 17, 1874 18, 1899 23, 1917 29, 1937 40, 1945 45, 1948 48, 1953 56, 1959 62, 1961 67, 1962 69, 1964 71, 1966 74, 1970 81, 1971 84, 1975 88, 1976 90, 1978 94, 1979 96, 1981 101, 1982 104, 1983 109, 1984 111, 1985 115, 1986 118, 1988 123, 1989 127, 1990 132, 1991 135, 1992 137, 1993 140, 1994 143-4, 1995 148, 1996 152, 1997 158, 1999 162, 2000 167

Léoville-Las-Cases, Ch 1871 17, 1900 25, 1909 27, 1920, 1921 31, 1924 33, 1928 35, 1929 36, 1945 45, 1948 49, 1949 50, 1952 54, 1953 56, 1957 59, 1959 62, 1961 66, 1962 68, 1964 71, 1966 73, 1967 75, 1970 81, 1971 83, 1973 85, 1975 88, 1976 90, 1978 94, 1979 96, 1980 98, 1981 100, 1982 104, 1983 109, 1984 111, 1985 115, 1986 119, 1987 120, 1988 123, 1989 127, 1990 132, 1991 135, 1992 137, 1993 141, 1994 144, 1995 148, 1997 157, 2000 167

Léoville-Poyferré, Ch 1874 18, 1890 20, 1891, 1893 21, 1899 23, 1909, 1911 27, 1916 28, 1918 29, 1920, 1921 31, 1926 34, 1929 36, 1945 45, 1952 54, 1959 62, 1961 67, 1962 69, 1964 71, 1970 81, 1973 85, 1974 86, 1975 88, 1976, 1977 91, 1978 94, 1979 96, 1980 98, 1981 101, 1982 104, 1983 109, 1985 115, 1986 119, 1989 127, 1990 132, 1992 138, 1993 141, 1994 144, 1995 148, 1996 152, 1997 157, 1998 159, 1999 162, 2000 167

Lepitre, Abel 1983 440

Leeuwin, Cabernet Sauvignon 1991 533

Liebfraumilch feinste Auslese 1921 346

Lieser Niederberg Helden Riesling Auslese 1993 378, 1994 379, 1999 388; Niederberg Helden Riesling Auslese ★★★ 1997 386; Niederberg Riesling Kabinett 1999 388; Niederberg Riesling Spätlese 1999 388

Lieserer Niederberg-Helden Riesling Auslese halbtrocken 1993 378

Liot, Ch 1955 186, 1975 195, 1976 196, 1980 197, 1986 201, 1988 203, 1989 204, 1994, 1995 208, 1996 209

Liversan, Ch 1984 111

'Lloyd Reserve' Syrah 1990 533

Lorcher Bodental-Steinberg Auslese 1976 362; Bodental-Steinberg Riesling BA 1976 362; Bodental-Steinberg

Riesling Spätlese 1971 358; Krone Riesling Auslese 1966 355; Pfaffenwies Riesling Auslese 1976 362
Loudenne, Ch 1990 134, 1992 138
Loureiro, Qta de 1871 452
Louvière, Ch La 1966 74, 1970 82, 1979 96, 1981 101, 1986 119, 1989 128, 1990 132, 1993 142, 1994 144, 1998 159, 2000 167; (blanc) 1933 181, 1967 191, 1998 212, 1999 213
Lupicaia 1993 404, 1998 408
Lynch-Bages, Ch 1928 35, 1945 45, 1948 49, 1949 51, 1953 56, 1957 59, 1959 62, 1961 66, 1962 69, 1966 73, 1967 75, 1970 81, 1971 84, 1973 85, 1974 86, 1975 89, 1976 90, 1978 94, 1979 96, 1980 98, 1981 100, 1982 104, 1983 109, 1984 111, 1985 115, 1986 118, 1987 120, 1988 123, 1989 128, 1990 132-3, 1991 135, 1992 138, 1993 140, 1994 144, 1995 149, 1996 152, 1997 157, 1998 159, 1999 162, 2000 167
Lynch-Moussas, Ch 1966 73, 1978 95, 1986 119, 1988 124, 1994 145, 1995 149, 1996 154, 1997 157, 1998 159, 1999 162, 2000 167

## M

Mackenzie (port) 1945 464, 1948 465, 1955 468, 1958 469, 1963 472
Mâcon-Azé, 'Chardonnay' 2000 300-1
Mâcon-Clessé, Dom de la Bon Gran 1995 295-6, 1996, 1997 297
Mâcon, Lugny 2000 301
Mâcon, Monbellet 'Wen en Pattes' 1998 298
Mâcon-Uchizy 1996 297
Mâcon-Viré 1996 297; Dom Gillet 1997 297; Cuvée Spéciale 1998 298
Madalena, Qta da 1988 488, 1995 492
Madeira 'Brown Madère Imperial', 'Bismark' 1832 498; Madeira or Canary Sack c1680 496; Madeira, Vintage 1792 496, 1795 496-7
Magdelaine, Ch 1962 68, 1966 74, 1969 77, 1970 81, 1971 84, 1975 88, 1976 91, 1979 96, 1982 104, 1989 128, 1990 134, 1993 142, 1995 149, 1997 157, 1998 159, 2000 167
Mailly, Cuvée des Echansons 1988 440; Grand Cru 1990 446
Malartic-Lagravière, Ch 1959 62, 1975 89, 1978 95, 1982 106, 1983 110, 1988 124, 1990 134, 1993 142, 1996 154, 2000 167
Malescasse, Ch 1993 142
Malescot-St-Exupéry, Ch 1904 25, 1945 45, 1948 49, 1959 62, 1961 66, 1962 68,

1966 74, 1967 75, 1971 84, 1973 85, 1974 86, 1975 89, 1978 94, 1982 104, 1983 109, 1986 119, 1990 134, 1992 138, 1993 142, 1994 144, 1996 154, 1998 159, 1999 163, 2000 167
Malle, Ch de 1975 194-5, 1979 197, 1981 198, 1983 199, 1985 201, 1988 203, 1989 204, 1990 205, 1994, 1995 208, 1996 209, 1997 211, 1998 212, 1999 213, 2000 214
Malmsey 1830 498, 1874 499, 1893, 1895 500, 1900, 1901 501, 1912, 1916 502, 1933 503, 1954, 1964 504; Harvest (Vintage) 1994 505; Reserve 1830 498; Solera 1808 497, 1863 499; 'Special Reserve, Sweet' 1836 498; Vintage 1920, 1926 502, 1964 504, 1971 505
Malvasia 1952 504; Vintage 1910 502
Malvazia 1890 500, 1900, 1906 501; Reserva 1907 502
Malvedos, Qta dos 1950 466, 1951 467
Marcobrunner Cabinet Riesling feinste Auslese 1893 344; Riesling edelbeeren Auslese 1967 355; Riesling feinste TBA 1945 349; see also Erbacher Marcobrunn
Margaux, Ch 1784, 1787, 1791 11, 1847, 1848 13, 1864 14, 1868 15, 1869, 1870 16, 1875 18, 1887, 1888, 1890 20, 1892, 1893 21, 1898 22, 1899 23, 1900 24, 1905, 1906, 1907 26, 1908, 1909, 1911 27, 1912, 1913, 1914 28, 1917, 1918, 1919 29, 1920 30, 1921 31, 1923, 1924 32, 1926 33, 1927 34, 1928 35, 1929 36, 1933 37, 1934 38, 1936 39, 1937 40, 1940, 1942 41, 1943 42, 1945 43, 1947 46, 1948 48, 1949 49, 1950 52, 1952 53, 1953 55, 1954, 1955 57, 1957 59, 1958, 1959 60, 1960 63, 1961 64, 1962 67, 1963, 1964 69, 1965 71, 1966 72, 1967 75, 1969 76, 1970 79, 1971 82-3, 1972 84, 1973 85, 1974 86, 1975 87, 1976 89, 1977 91, 1978 92, 1979 95, 1980 97, 1981 98, 1982 101, 1983 106, 1984 110, 1985 112, 1986 117, 1987 120, 1988 121, 1989 125, 1990 130, 1991 135, 1992 136, 1993 138, 1994 142-3, 1995 146, 1996 150, 1997 155, 1998 158, 1999 161, 2000 164-5; Deuxième Vin 1900 25, 1918 29
Marimar Torres, Don Miguel Pinot Noir 1998, 1999 528
Marquis, Clos du 2000 168
Marquis d'Alesme-Becker, Ch 1970 82, 1982 106, 1990 134, 1991 136
Marquis de Terme, Ch 1869 16, 1906 26, 1921 31, 1929 36, 1937 40, 1966 74, 1979 96, 1982 106, 1983 109,

1985 116, 1986 119, 1990 134, 1993 142, 1994 145, 1996 154, 1997 157, 1998 159, 2000 167
Marsan, Ch 1991 135
Martinez 1868 452, 1878 453, 1904 455, 1922 457, 1927 459, 1931, 1934 461, 1935 462, 1945 464, 1955 468, 1958 469, 1960 470, 1963 472, 1967 475, 1970 477, 1975 479, 1982 483, 1985 486, 1987 488, 1991 490, 1997 493, 2000 494
Martinho's Qta de São 1881 453
Martini, Louis Cabernet Sauvignon 1978 514; 'California Mountain' Cabernet Sauvignon 1959 510; Mountain Cabernet Sauvignon 1968 511; Special Selection Cabernet Sauvignon 1958 509, 1976 513
Mas de Daumas Gassac 1978-1979 338, 1980 338-9, 1981-1987 339, 1988 339-40, 1989-2001 340; Cuvée Emile Peynaud 2001 340; (blanc) 2001 341
Matariki 'Anthology' 1998 534
Matua Valley Cabernet Sauvignon-Merlot 1999 534; Pinot Noir 1998 534
Maucaillou, Ch 1993 142, 1999 163, 2000 168
Maugey, Ch 1998 159-60
Maximin Grünhäuser Abtsberg Riesling Auslese 1995 381; Abtsberg Riesling Kabinett 1988 370; Abtsberg Riesling Spätlese 1976 362, 1979 364, 1988 370, 1998 386, 1999 388; Herrenberg Riesling 1959 352; Herrenberg Riesling BA 1953 350; Riesling Kabinett 2000 391; Riesling Spätlese 1990 374, 2000 391
Mayacamas Cabernet Sauvignon 1970 511, 1982 517, 1985 519; Late Harvest Zinfandel 1972 512; Mountain Cabernet Sauvignon 1974 513; Pinot Noir 1980 513
Mazis-Chambertin 1937 224, 1947, 1949 227, 1953 229, 1959 231, 1962 233, 1964 234, 1967 236, 1972 241, 1978 245, 1985 252, 1986 254, 1990 260, 1991 261, 1992 262, 1993 263, 2000 272; Hospices, Cuvée Madeleine-Collignon 1984 251, 1985 252
Meerlust, Rubicon 1995 535
Menetou-Salon 1999 324, 2000 325
Menota, Ch 1976 196
Messias 1985 487
Meursault 1865, 1934, 1937 274, 1966 277, 1969 278, 1982 282, 1986 286, 1988

287, 1994 *294*, 1999 *299*;
Clos de la Barre 1982 *282*,
1990 *289*; Blagny 1982 *282*;
Ch de Blagny 1993 *293*;
Charmes 1865, 1934 *274*,
1941, 1947 *275*, 1969 *278*,
1983, 1984 *283*, 1985 *285*,
1986, 1987 *286*, 1988 *287*,
1989 *288*, 1990 *290*, 1991
*291*, 1992 *292*, 1999 *299*,
2000 *301*; Charmes,
Hospices, Bahèzres de
Lanlay 1983 *283*, 1997 *297*;
Charmes, Hospices,
Cuvée Albert Grivault
1979 *280*, 1986 *286*;
Charmes, Hospices,
Philippe le Bon 1971 *278*;
Chevaliers 1983 *283*;
Chevalières 1983 *283*; Clos
du Cromin 1986 *286*, 1993
*293*; 'Desirée' 1990 *290*;
Genevrières 1961 *277*,
1978 *280*, 1981 *281*, 1982
*282*, 1985 *285*, 1989 *288*,
1990 *290*, 1995 *296*, 1997
*297*, 1999 *299*; Genevrières,
Hospices, Cuvée Baudot
1988 *287*; Genevrières,
Tasteviné 1997 *297*;
Grands Charrons 1983
*283*, 1993 *293*; Hospices,
Cuvée Jean Humblot
1945 *275*; Ch de
Meursault 1979 *280*, 1982
*282*; Narvaux 1973 *278*,
1976 *279*, 1985 *285*, 1995
*296*; Ormeau 1992 *292*;
Perrières 1945, 1947 *275*,
1971 *278*, 1977 *279*, 1985
*284*, 1989 *288*, 1990 *290*,
1994 *294*, 1995 *296*; Clos
Les Perrières 1995 *296*;
Perrières, Réserve
Personnelle 1979 *280*;
Poruzots 1973 *278*, 1983
*283*, 1988 *287*; Cuvée
Réservée au Restaurant
Les Fevriers 1928 *274*;
Clos St-Felix 1993 *293*;
Sous la Velle 1993 *293*;
Tasteviné 1979 *280*; Tillets
1983 *283*
Meyer 1873 *452*
Meyney, Ch 1975 *89*
Michael, Peter, Les Pavots
1989 *520*, 1996 *526*
Mildara, Cabernet
Sauvignon 1963 *532*
Milieu, Qta do 1944 *463*
Millet, Ch 1990 *134*
Mission Haut-Brion, Ch
La 1878 *19*, 1895 *22*, 1900,
1904 *25*, 1911 *27*, 1914, 1916
*28*, 1918, 1919 *29*, 1920 *30*,
1921 *31*, 1924 *33*, 1926 *34*,
1928 *35*, 1929 *36*, 1931, 1933
*37*, 1934 *38*, 1935, 1936,
1937 *39*, 1938, 1939 *40*,
1940, 1941, 1942 *41*, 1943,
1944 *42*, 1945 *44*, 1946 *46*,
1947 *47*, 1948 *48-9*, 1949 *50-
1*, 1950 *53*, 1952 *54*, 1953 *56*,
1954 *57*, 1955 *58*, 1956, 1957
*59*, 1958 *60*, 1959 *62*, 1961
*66*, 1962 *68*, 1964 *70*, 1965
*71*, 1966 *73-4*, 1967 *75*, 1968
*76*, 1969 *77*, 1970 *81*, 1971
*84*, 1975 *85*, 1975 *88-9*, 1976
*90*, 1977 *91*, 1978 *94*, 1980
*98*, 1981 *100*, 1982 *104*, 1983
*109*, 1984 *111*, 1985 *115*,

1986 *119*, 1987 *120*, 1988
*124*, 1989 *128*, 1990 *133*,
1994 *145*, 1995 *149*, 1996
*154*, 1997 *157*, 1998 *160*,
1999 *163*, 2000 *167*
Mittelheimer Edelmann
Riesling Auslese 1948 *349*,
1973 *359*
Moët & Chandon 1904 *422*,
1911, 1914, 1915 *423*, 1923,
1926, 1928 *425*, 1943 *426*,
1959 *429*, 1961 *430*, 1964
*431*, 1976 *436*, 1982, 1983
*440*, 1985 *441*, 1986 *442*,
1988 *443*, 1990, 1992 *446*;
see also Dom Pérignon
Monbousquet, Ch 1982
*104-5*, 1997 *157*, 2000 *167*
Monbrison, Ch 1992 *138*,
1996 *154*, 1998 *160*, 2000 *167*
Mondavi, Robert
Barrel-Aged Reserve
Cabernet Sauvignon
1996 *526-7*; Cabernet
Sauvignon 1966 *510*, 1968,
1969, 1970 *511*, 1973 *512*,
1976 *513*, 1977 *514*, 1983
*517*; Oakville District
Cabernet Sauvignon
1996 *527*; Reserve
Cabernet Sauvignon
1973 *512*, 1974, 1975, 1976
*513*, 1977, 1978 *514*, 1980
*515*, 1982 *517*, 1985 *519*,
1988 *520*, 1990 *521*, 1991
*522*, 1995 *525*, 1996 *526*,
1997 *527*; Reserve Pinot
Noir 1987 *519*, 1989 *520*;
Woodbridge, Zinfandel
1991 *522*
Mondotte, Ch La 1997 *157*
Monferrato 'Countaci!'
1997 *407*, 1998, 1999 *408*
Montelena see Chateau
Montelena
Montlouis, Grains Nobles
1990 *321*; Vieilles Vignes
1998 *324*
Montrachet 1864, 1899,
1906, 1923 *274*, 1947, 1949
*275*, 1950 *276*, 1964, 1966,
1969 *277*, 1970, 1973, 1974
*278*, 1976-78 *279*, 1978, 1979
*280*, 1980, 1981 *281*, 1982
*281-2*, 1983 *282*, 1984 *283*,
1985 *284*, 1986 *285*, 1987,
1988 *286*, 1989 *287-8*, 1990
*289*, 1991 *290*, 1992 *291*,
1993 *292*, 1994 *293-4*, 1995
*294-5*, 1996 *296*, 1997 *297*,
1999 *299*, 2000 *300*
Montrose, Ch 1869 *16*, 1870
*17*, 1893 *21*, 1896 *22*, 1921
*31*, 1928 *35*, 1937 *40*, 1945
*45*, 1949 *51*, 1952 *54*, 1959
*62*, 1961 *67*, 1962 *69*, 1964,
1965 *71*, 1966 *74*, 1967 *75*,
1969 *77*, 1970 *81*, 1971, 1972
*84*, 1973 *85*, 1974 *86*, 1975
*89*, 1976 *90*, 1978 *94*, 1979
*96*, 1981 *100*, 1982 *105*, 1983
*109*, 1984 *111*, 1985 *116*,
1986 *119*, 1988 *124*, 1989
*128*, 1990 *133*, 1992 *138*,
1993 *142*, 1994 *144*, 1995
*149*, 1996 *152-3*, 1997 *157*
Monzinger
Frühlingsplätzchen
Riesling Auslese
Goldkapsel 1994 *379*
Morey St-Denis 1930 *222*,
1939 *224*, 1970 *239*, 1971

*240*, 1976 *243*, 1981 *247*,
1990 *259*, 2000 *272*; Clos
Bussière 1977 *244*; En la
Rue de Vergy 1991 *261*;
Clos des Ormes 1987 *255*;
Villages 2000 *272*
Morgan 1942 *462*, 1950 *467*,
1960 *471*
Moscatel 1793 *496*, 1900 *501*;
Vintage 1900 *501*
Moulin-à-Vent, Vieilles
Vignes 1964 *233*
Moulin-Riche, Ch 1899 *23*,
1904 *26*
Moulin-Touchais 1928,
1933, 1937, 1945, 1947 *316*,
1949, 1955, 1959 *317*, 1961,
1962, 1964, 1969 *318*, 1975,
1983 *319*
Moulinet, Ch 1964 *70*, 1985
*116*, 1989 *128*
Moulinet-Lassere, Ch 1975
*89*
Mount Difficulty, Pinot
Noir 1999 *534*
Mount Eden, Pinot Noir
1972 *512*
Mount Langi Ghiran
Shiraz 1994 *533*
Mount Mary, Quintet
Cabernets 1991 *533*
Mount Pleasant, 'T.Y.'
Hermitage 1942 *532*
Mount Veeder, Cabernet
Sauvignon 1986 *519*
Mouton d'Armailhacq,
Ch 1878 *19*, 1900 *25*, 1928
*35*, 1937 *39*, 1945 *45*, 1947
*47*, 1953 *56*, 1955 *58*; see also
Armailhac, Mouton-Baron-
Philippe and Mouton-
Baronne-Philippe
Mouton-Baron-Philippe,
Ch 1961 *67*, 1962 *69*, 1966
*74*, 1970 *81*; see also
Armailhac, Mouton-
d'Armailhacq and Mouton-
Baronne-Philippe
Mouton-Baronne-
Philippe, Ch 1975 *89*, 1978
*95*, 1979 *96*, 1980 *98*, 1981
*101*, 1982 *105*, 1983 *109*,
1985 *116*, 1986 *119*, 1988
*123*, 1989 *128*; see also
Armailhac, Mouton-
d'Armailhacq and Mouton-
Baron-Philippe
Mouton-Rothschild, Ch
1858 *13*, 1864 *14*, 1867 *15*,
1869 *16*, 1870 *16-17*, 1874
*17-18*, 1875 *18*, 1878, 1880,
1881 *19*, 1886, 1888, 1889
*20*, 1893 *21*, 1898, 1899 *23*,
1900 *25*, 1905, 1906, 1907
*26*, 1908, 1909, 1911 *27*,
1912, 1914, 1916 *28*, 1918
*29*, 1920 *30*, 1921 *31*, 1924
*32-3*, 1925, 1926 *33*, 1928 *35*,
1929 *36*, 1933, 1934 *38*, 1936
*39*, 1937, 1938, 1939 *40*,
1940, 1942 *41*, 1943, 1944
*42*, 1945 *43*, 1946, 1947 *46*,
1948 *48*, 1949 *49*, 1950 *52*,
1951, 1952 *53*, 1953 *55*,
1954, 1955 *57*, 1957 *59*, 1958
*60*, 1959 *60-1*, 1960 *63*, 1961
*64*, 1962 *67*, 1963 *69*, 1964
*70*, 1965 *71*, 1966 *72*, 1967
*75*, 1969 *76*, 1970 *79*, 1971
*83*, 1972 *84*, 1973 *85*, 1974
*86*, 1975 *87*, 1976 *89*, 1977
*91*, 1978 *92*, 1979 *95*, 1980

*97*, 1981 *99*, 1982 *101-2*,
1983 *106-7*, 1984 *110*, 1985
*112*, 1986 *117*, 1987 *120*,
1988 *121*, 1989 *125*, 1990
*130*, 1991 *135*, 1992 *136*,
1993 *138*, 1994 *143*, 1995
*146*, 1996 *150*, 1997 *155*,
1998 *158*, 1999 *161*, 2000 *165*
Mülheimer
Helenenkloster Riesling
Eiswein 1983 *367*, 1989 *371*,
1996 *383-4*;
Helenenkloster Riesling
Eiswein-Christwein 1986
*369*
Mumm 1982 *439*; Cordon
Rouge 1929 *425*, 1937 *426*,
1985 *442*, 1987 *443*, 1989
*445*; Crémant de
Cramant 1989 *445*; Grand
Cordon 1985 *441*; Mumm
de Mumm 1985 *441-2*;
René Lalou 1979 *437*, 1982
*439*, 1985 *442*, 1989 *445*
Münsterer
Dautenpflänzer Riesling
Auslese 1971 *359*;
Königsschloss Scheurebe
TBA 1989 *371*;
Pittersberg Riesling
Auslese 1998 *386*
Münzinger 'Antigua'
Kapellenberg Spätlese
Weissherbst Eiswein 1996
*384*
Musar see Chateau Musar
Muscadet 1999 *324*
Muscadet de Sèvre-et-
Maine, Dom de Noë
1999 *325*
Muscat 1989 *332*; Rangen
1985 *331*; Réserve 1989
*332*; Rothenberg
Vendange Tardive 1985
*331*
Musigny 1915 *218*, 1919 *219*,
1923 *220*, 1934 *223*, 1945
*226*, 1947, 1949 *227*, 1952
*229*, 1957 *230*, 1959 *231*,
1964 *233*, *234*, 1967 *236*,
1970 *239*, 1971 *240*, 1976
*243*, 1978 *245*, 1980 *246*,
1981 *247*, 1982 *248*, 1984
*251*, 1985 *253*, 1986 *254*,
1988 *256*, 1989 *257*, 1991
*261*, 1993 *263*, 2000 *272*;
(blanc) 1964 *277*, 1977 *279*,
1981 *281*, 1983 *283*, 1985
*285*; Tasteviné 1959 *231*;
Tête de Cuvée 1915 *218*;
Vieilles Vignes 1945 *226*,
1959 *231*, 1961 *232*, 1962
*233*, 1964 *233-4*, *234*, 1966
*235*, 1969 *237*, 1970 *239*,
1971, 1972 *241*, 1978 *245*,
1982 *248*, 1985 *252*
Mussbacher Eselshaut
Rieslaner Auslese 1992
*376*
Myrat, Ch de 1922 *178*,
1993 *207*, 1997 *211*, 1998
*212*, 1999 *213*

# N

Nackenheimer
Rothenberg Riesling
Auslese 1993 *378*, 1996 *384*,
1998 *387*; Rothenberg
Riesling Spätlese 1998
*387*; Rothenberg Riesling
TBA Naturrein 1921 *346*

Nairac, Ch 1973 *194*, 1975
*195*, 1976 *196*, 1982 *198*,
1983 *199*, 1986 *201-2*, 1988
*203*, 1989 *204*, 1990 *206*,
1991, 1992, 1993 *207*, 1994
*208*, 1996 *209*, 1997 *211*,
1998 *212*, 1999 *213*
Nebbiolo d'Alba 1997 *407*
Nebbiolo Passito, Nepas
1998 *408*
Negra Mole, Reserva
Velho 1954 *504*
Neipperger
Schlossberg Riesling
Auslese 1976 *362*
Nenin, Ch 1924 *33*, 1928 *35*,
1945 *45*, 1947 *47*, 1948 *49*,
1966 *74*, 1975 *89*, 1981 *101*,
1993 *142*, 1996 *154*
Neumagener Nusswingert
Riesling Spätlese 1996 *384*
Niebaum-Coppola,
Rubicon 1990 *525*
Niederhäuser
Hermannsberg Riesling
TBA 1994 *380*;
Hermannshöhle Riesling
Auslese 1992 *376*, 1994 *380*,
1998 *387*, 1999 *388*;
Hermannshöhle Riesling
Spätlese 1996 *384*
Niepoort 1887 *453*, 1895
*454*, 1900 *455*, 1927 *459*,
1931 *460-1*, 1933 *461*, 1935,
1940, 1942 *462*, 1945 *463*,
1952 *467*, 1955 *468*, 1962
*471*, 1963 *472*, 1966 *474*,
1967 *475*, 1970 *477*, 1975
*479*, 1980 *482*, 1981, 1982
*483*, 1983 *485*, 1985 *486*,
1986, 1987 *488*, 1991, 1992
*490*, 1997 *493*, 2000 *494*
Nierstein Riesling 1929 *346*
Niersteiner
Auflangen Riesling
Auslese 1921 *346*;
Auflangen Scheurebe
TBA 1976 *363*; Auflangen
Silvaner BA Eiswein 1979
*364*; Hipping und
Rehbach Riesling TBA
1964 *354*; Hipping
Riesling Auslese 1996 *384*;
Hipping Riesling
Spätlese 1990 *375*; Hölle
Gewürztraminer BA
1976 *362*; Klostergarten
Riesling TBA 1975 *361*;
Ober Rehbach Riesling
BA 1949 *349*, 1953 *350*;
Oelberg Riesling Eiswein
1996 *384*; Orbel Silvaner
Riesling Auslese 1947 *349*;
Pettenthal Riesling
Auslese 1971 *359*;
Pettental und Auflangen
Riesling TBA 1934 *347*;
Rehbach Riesling BA
1953 *350*; Spiegelberg
Silvaner TBA 1971 *359*
Noval, Qta do 1875 *452*,
1900 *455*, 1917 *457*, 1927
*459*, 1931 *460*, 1934 *461*,
1937, 1938, 1941, 1942 *462*,
1945 *463*, 1947 *464*, 1950
*466*, 1955 *468*, 1957, 1958
*469*, 1960 *470*, 1963 *472*,
1966 *474*, 1967, 1968, 1969
*475*, 1970 *477*, 1975 *478*,
1978 *481*, 1982 *483*, 1985
*486-7*, 1991 *490*, 1997 *493*,
2000 *494*; LBV 1976 *479*,

1983 *485*; Nacional 1931
*460*, 1947 *464*, 1950 *466*,
1955 *468*, 1958 *469*, 1960
*470*, 1962 *471*, 1963 *472*,
1964 *473*, 1966 *474*, 1967,
1968, 1969 *475*, 1970 *477*,
1975 *479*, 1978 *481*, 1980
*482*, 1982 *483*, 1985 *487*,
1987 *488*, 2000 *494*
Nuits, Cailles 1915 *218*
Nuits-Calvet 1900 *217*
Nuits-Meurgers 1985 *252*
Nuits-St-Georges 1919 *219*,
1926 *220*, 1949 *227*, 1964
*234*, 1982 *248*, 1985 *252*,
1988 *256*, 1994 *264*, 1995
*265*; 1er Cru 1937 *224*,
1964 *234*; Argillières 1962
*233*, 1969 *237*; Clos des
Argillières 1985 *253*, 1990
*259*; Aux Murgers 1992
*262*; Boudots 1972 *241*,
1982 *248*, 1999 *270*; Cailles
1988 *256*, 1998 *269*, 2000
*272*; Chaignots 1988 *256*;
Chaines Carteaux 1999
*270*; Clos des Corvées
1964 *234*, 1972 *241*;
Corvées Pagets 2000 *272*;
Ch Gris 1959 *231*, 1990 *259*;
Clos le la Maréchale
1985 *253*, 1988 *256*, 1997
*267*; Perrières 2000 *272*;
Poirets 1985 *253*; Porets-
St-Georges 1995 *265*; Clos
des Porrets 1952 *229*;
Porrets-St-Georges 1964
*234*, 1985 *253*, 1986 *254*,
1988 *256*; Pruliers 1964 *234*,
1985 *253*, 1986 *254*, 1988
*256*, 1991 *261*; St-Georges
1966 *236*, 1985 *253*, 1986
*254*, 1995 *265*, 2000 *272*;
Vaucrains 1982 *248*, 1988
*256*, 1995 *265*; Vignes-
Rondes 1990 *259*

# O

Oberemmeler
Hütte Riesling Auslese
1988 *370*, 1993 *378*, 1994
*380*, 1999 *389*; Hütte
Riesling Auslese '★' 1999
*389*; Hütte Riesling
Eiswein 1988 *370*, 1995 *381*;
Hütte Riesling feinste
Auslese 1969 *356*; Hütte
Riesling Spätlese 1988 *370*
Oberhäuser
Brücke Riesling Auslese
1995 *381*, 1996 *384*; Brücke
Riesling BA 1989 *371*,
1995 *381*; Leistenberg
Riesling Kabinett 1999
*389*
Ockfener
Bockstein Riesling
Auslese 1994 *380*, 1995 *381*;
Bockstein Riesling
Auslese Goldkapsel 1983
*367*; Bockstein Riesling
BA 1990 *375*; Bockstein
Riesling Spätlese 1994
*380*; Bockstein Riesling
TBA 1976 *362*
Oestricher
Doosberg Riesling
Spätlese 1994 *380*;
Lenchen Riesling Auslese
1959 *352*, 1971 *358*, 1996
*384*; Lenchen Riesling

Auslese Eiswein 1975 *360*,
1979 *364*, 1983 *367*;
Lenchen Riesling BA
1971 *358*, 1976 *362*;
Lenchen Riesling
Eiswein 1988 *370*;
Lenchen Riesling
hochfeine Auslese 1959
*352*
Offley Boa Vista 1908 *456*,
1919 *457*, 1923 *457-8*, 1925
*458*, 1929 *459*, 1931 *461*,
1935 *462*, 1945 *464*, 1950,
1954 *467*, 1955 *468*, 1962
*471*, 1963 *472*, 1966 *474*,
1970 *477*, 1975 *479*, 1977
*480*, 1980 *482*, 1982 *483-4*,
1983 *485*, 1985 *487*, 1987,
1989 *488*, 1994 *491*, 1995
*492*, 1997 *493*, 2000 *494*
Old Block Shiraz 1990,
1999 *533*
Olivet Lane, Russian River
Pinot Noir 1990 *521*
Olivier, Ch 1920 *30*, 1926
*34*, 1990 *134*, 1996 *154*, 1997
*157*, 1998 *160*, 2000 *167*
Omihi Hills, Pinot Noir
1998 *534*
Oppenheimer
Herrenberg Riesling
Auslese 1993 *378*;
Herrenberg Scheurebe
TBA 1992 *377*;
Herrenberg Silvaner
Eiswein 1990 *374*; Kreuz
Silvaner Eiswein 1989
*372*; Sackträger
Gewürztraminer TBA
1992 *376-7*; Sackträger
Riesling BA 1976 *362*;
Sackträger Riesling TBA
1989 *372*; Sackträger
Silvaner Auslese 1989 *372*
Opus One 1979 *514*, 1980
*515*, 1981 *516*, 1982, 1983,
1984 *517*, 1985 *518*, 1986,
1987 *519*, 1988 *520*, 1990
*521*, 1991 *522*, 1992 *523*,
1993 *524*, 1994 *525*, 1995
*526*, 1996 *526*, 1997 *527*
Ormes-de-Pez, Ch Les
1975 *89*, 1982 *106*, 1986 *119*,
1990 *133*, 1992 *138*, 1993
*142*, 1997 *157*, 1998 *160*,
2000 *167*
Ornellaia 1990 *403*, 1991 *404*,
1995 *405*, 1997 *407*, 1998,
1999 *408*, 2000 *409*
Osborne (port) 1970 *478*
Östricher see Oestricher

# P

Paillard, Bruno 1985 *442*,
1989 *444*
Palmer, Ch 1909 *27*, 1920
*30-1*, 1921 *31*, 1924 *33*, 1934
*39*, 1937 *40*, 1940, 1942 *41*,
1945 *45*, 1948 *49*, 1949 *51*,
1953 *56-7*, 1955 *58*, 1959 *62*,
1961 *63-4*, 1962 *68*, 1964 *71*,
1966 *74*, 1967 *75*, 1970 *82*,
1971 *83*, 1972 *84*, 1973 *85*,
1975 *89*, 1976 *91*, 1978 *94*,
1979 *96*, 1980 *98*, 1981 *100*,
1982 *105*, 1983 *109*, 1985
*116*, 1986 *118*, 1987 *120*,
1988 *123*, 1989 *128*, 1990
*133*, 1991 *135-6*, 1992 *138*,
1993 *140*, 1994 *144*, 1995
*149*, 1996 *153*, 1997 *157*,

1998 *160*, 1999 *163*, 2000 *167*
'Panta Rhei' QbA trocken
2000 *391*
Pape, Clos du 1924 *179*
Pape-Clément, Ch 1893
*21*, 1900 *25*, 1924 *33*, 1948
*49*, 1959 *62*, 1961 *66*, 1962
*69*, 1964 *71*, 1966 *74*, 1970
*82*, 1971 *84*, 1975 *89*, 1976
*91*, 1979 *96*, 1981 *101*, 1982
*106*, 1987 *120*, 1988 *124*,
1989 *128*, 1990 *133*, 1993
*142*, 1994 *144*, 1996 *153*,
1997 *157*, 1998 *160*, 1999
*163*, 2000 *167*; (blanc) 2000
*214*
Parempuyre, Ch 1921 *31*
Passadouro, Qta do 2000
*494*
Patache d'Aux, Ch 1990
*134*
Paveil-de-Luze, Ch 1986
*118*, 1994 *145*
Pavie, Ch 1947 *47*, 1948 *49*,
1955 *58*, 1962 *69*, 1964 *70*,
1966 *74*, 1970 *82*, 1971 *84*,
1975 *89*, 1976 *90*, 1979 *96*,
1981 *101*, 1982 *105*, 1988
*123-4*, 1989 *128*, 1990 *134*,
1991 *136*, 1992 *138*, 1993
*140*, 1994 *144*, 1996 *154*,
1997 *157*, 1998 *160*, 1999
*163*, 2000 *167*
Pavie-Decesse, Ch 1978 *94*,
1979 *96*, 1988 *124*, 1993 *142*,
1994 *145*, 1996 *154*, 1997
*157*, 1998 *160*, 2000 *167*
Pavillon Blanc de Ch
Margaux 1928, 1929 *180*,
1961 *188*, 1978 *197*, 1981
*198*, 1983 *200*, 1985 *201*,
1989 *204*, 1990 *208*
Pavillon Rouge de Ch
Margaux 1979 *96*, 1982
*105*, 1999 *163*, 2000 *167*
Pegasus Bay 'Prima
Donna', Pinot Noir 1998
*534*
Penfolds
'Bin 60A' 1962 *532*; Bin
128 Coonawarra Shiraz
1988 *707 533*
'Penguin' Eiswein 1998 *387*
Pensées de La Fleur 1987
*120*
Percarlo 1990 *404*
Pergole Torte, Le 1990 *404*,
1992, 1993 *404*, 1994, 1995
*405*, 1996 *406*, 1997 *407*
Pernand-Vergelesses
Ile de Vergelesses 1995
*265*, 1998 *269*, 2000 *272*;
'Méthode ancienne' 1974
*242*
Perrier, Joseph, Cuvée
Royale 1982 *440*
Perrier-Jouët 1892 *422*, 1911
*423*, 1928 *425*, 1953 *428*,
1975 *435*, 1988 *444*, 1992
*446*; Belle Époque 1982
*439*, 1983 *440*, 1985 *442*,
1989 *445*, 1995 *447*
Petit-Village, Ch 1920 *31*,
1942 *42*, 1966 *75*, 1975 *89*,
1976 *90*, 1979 *96*, 1982 *105*,
1986 *118*, 1990 *134*, 1991
*136*, 1992 *138*, 1993 *142*,
1996 *154*, 1997 *157*, 1998
*160*, 2000 *167*
Pétrus, Ch 1893 *21*, 1900 *25*,
1908 *27*, 1917 *29*, 1921, 1922
*31*, 1923 *32*, 1926 *34*, 1928

*35*, 1929 *36*, 1934 *38*, 1937
*40*, 1945 *44*, 1947 *47*, 1948
*48*, 1949 *50*, 1950 *52*, 1952
*54*, 1953 *55*, 1955 *57-8*, 1957
*59*, 1958 *60*, 1959 *61*, 1961
*65*, 1962 *68*, 1964 *70*, 1966
*72*, 1967 *75*, 1968 *76*, 1969
*77*, 1970 *80*, 1971 *83*, 1972
*84*, 1973 *85*, 1974 *86*, 1975
*88*, 1976 *90*, 1977 *91*, 1978
*92*, 1979 *95*, 1980 *98*, 1981
*99*, 1982 *102*, 1983 *107*, 1984
*111*, 1985 *113*, 1986 *117*,
1987 *120*, 1988 *121-2*, 1989
*126*, 1990 *130*, 1991 *135*,
1992 *137*, 1994 *143*, 1995
*146-7*, 1997 *155*, 2000 *165*
Peyrabon, Ch 1878 *19*
Pez, Ch de 1948 *49*, 1975 *89*,
1988 *124*, 1989 *128*, 1990
*134*, 1998 *160*
Phélan-Ségur, Ch 1920 *31*,
1982 *106*, 1991 *136*, 1992
*138*, 1993 *142*, 1996 *154*,
1997 *157*, 2000 *167*
Phelps, Joseph
Cabernet Sauvignon
1978 *514*, 1981 *516*;
Insignia 1974 *513*, 1980 *515*,
1985, 1987 *519*, 1990 *521*,
1994 *525*; Insignia,
Auction Reserve 1985 *519*
Philipponnat, Grand
Blanc 1989 *444*
Pichon-Baron, Ch 1874 *18*,
1937 *40*, 1945 *45*, 1947 *47-8*,
1957 *59*, 1959 *62*, 1961 *66*,
1966 *74*, 1967 *75*, 1970 *82*,
1971 *84*, 1973 *85*, 1975 *89*,
1977 *91*, 1978 *94*, 1979 *96*,
1981 *100*, 1982 *105*, 1983
*110*, 1985 *116*, 1986 *119*,
1988 *124*, 1989 *128*, 1990
*133*, 1991 *136*, 1992 *138*,
1993 *140*, 1994 *144*, 1995
*149*, 1996 *153*, 1997 *157*,
1998 *160*, 1999 *163*, 2000 *168*
Pichon-Lalande, Ch 1875
*18*, 1893 *21*, 1900 *25*, 1920,
1921 *31*, 1924 *33*, 1928 *35*,
1931 *37*, 1937 *40*, 1945 *45*,
1947 *48*, 1953 *56*, 1955 *58*,
1959 *62*, 1961 *66*, 1962 *68*,
1964 *70-1*, 1966 *74*, 1969 *77*,
1970 *82*, 1971 *83*, 1975 *89*,
1976 *90*, 1978 *94*, 1979 *96*,
1980 *98*, 1981 *100*, 1982 *105*,
1983 *109*, 1984 *111*, 1985
*116*, 1986 *118*, 1988 *124*,
1989 *128*, 1990 *133*, 1991
*136*, 1992 *138*, 1993 *141*,
1994 *144*, 1995 *149*, 1996
*153*, 1997 *157*, 1998 *160*,
1999 *163*, 2000 *168*
Pichon-Longueville,
Baron, Ch see Pichon-
Baron
Pichon-Longueville,
Comtesse de Lalande,
Ch see Pichon-Lalande
Piesporter
Goldtröpfchen Riesling
Auslese 1934 *347*, 1971 *359*,
1990 *375*, 1993 *378*, 1996
*384*, 1999 *389*;
Goldtröpfchen Riesling
BA 1971 *359*, 1995 *381*;
Goldtröpfchen Riesling
Spätlese trocken 1998 *387*
Pin, Ch Le 1982 *105*, 1983
*110*, 1985 *116*, 1986 *119*,
1988 *124*, 1989 *128*, 1990

*134*, 1991 *136*
'Pinhão' 1931 *461*
Pinot Gris see (Tokay)-
Pinot Gris
Pinot Noir 1981 *330*; 'Les
Neveux' 1999 *336*
Piper-Heidsieck 1985 *442*,
1989 *445*, 1990 *446*; Florens
Louise 1975 *435*
Pique-Caillou, Ch 2000 *168*
Plince, Ch 1982 *106*, 1985
*116*, 1990 *134*
PlumpJack, Reserve
Cabernet Sauvignon
1995 *526*, 1997 *527*
Poças Junior 1937 *462*, 1960
*471*, 1970 *478*, 1975 *479*,
1977 *481*, 1985 *487*, 1991 *490*
Pointe, Ch La 1945 *45*, 1961
*67*, 1962 *69*, 1966 *74*, 1979
*96*, 1988 *124*, 1989 *128*, 1993
*142*, 1994 *145*, 1996 *154*,
1998 *160*, 2000 *168*
Poja, La 1985 *400*, 1990 *404*
Pol Roger 1911, 1914 *423*,
1921 *424*, 1923, 1926 *425*,
1934, 1943 *426*, 1945, 1947
*427*, 1952, 1955 *428*, 1959
*429*, 1961 *430*, 1964 *431*,
1973 *434*, 1975 *435*, 1976
*436*, 1979 *437*, 1982 *439*,
1983 *440*, 1985, 1986 *442*,
1988 *443*, 1990 *445*, 1993
*447*; Blanc de
Chardonnay 1979 *437*,
1982 *439*, 1986 *443*, 1988
*443*, 1990 *445*, 1993, 1995
*447*; Cuvée Sir Winston
Churchill 1975 *435*, 1979
*437*, 1982 *439*, 1985, 1986
*442*, 1988 *443*, 1990 *445*
Pommard 1893 *216*, 1920
*219*, 1983 *250*, 1985 *253*,
1990 *259*; Champans 1986
*254*; Chanlains 1996 *266*;
Clos des Epéneaux 1990
*259*; Epenots 1928 *220*,
1934 *223*, 1959 *231*, 1964
*234*, 1983 *251*, 1988 *256*;
Fremiers 1989 *257*; Grand
Epenots, Clos des
Citeaux 1952 *229*; Grands
Epenots 1947 *226*, 1988
*256*; Hospices, Cuvée
Billardet 1985 *253*;
Jarollières 1992 *262*; Clos
de la Platière 1974 *242*;
Ch de Pommard 1979
*246*; Rugiens 1929 *221*,
1934 *223*, 1945 *226*, 1990
*259*, 1996 *266*, 2000 *272*;
Rugiens, Tastévine 1972
*241*; Sausilles 1988 *256*;
Vignots 1978 *245*
Pommery (& Greno) 1923,
1926 *425*, 1929 *425*, 1937,
1941, 1942, 1943 *426*, 1945
*427*, 1949 *428*, 1955 *429*,
1961 *430*, 1982 *439*, 1983
*440*, 1985 *442*, 1987 *443*,
1991 *446*, 1992 *447*; Louise
1979 *437*, 1981 *438*, 1982
*439*, 1985 *442*, 1987 *443*,
1988 *443*, 1989 *444*; Louise,
Rosé 1980 *438*
Pontet-Canet, Ch 1878 *19*,
1929 *36*, 1937 *40*, 1944 *42*,
1945 *45*, 1947 *48*, 1959 *62*,
1961 *67*, 1962 *69*, 1970 *82*,
1975 *89*, 1978 *95*, 1980 *98*,
1981 *101*, 1982 *105*, 1983
*110*, 1985 *116*, 1986 *119*,

1987 120, 1989 128, 1990 133, 1992 138, 1993 142, 1994 145, 1996 154, 1997 157, 1998 160, 1999 163, 2000 168
Potensac, Ch 2000 168
Pouget, Ch 1982 106
Pouilly-Fuissé 1994 294; Tête de Cuvée 1997 298; Vieilles Vignes 1989 288-9, 1990 290, 1992 292, 1995 296, 1998 298
Pouilly-Fumé 1992 322, 1996 323, 1998 324, 2000 325; Dom Berthiers 1996 323; Les Griottes 1998 324; La Logères 1998 324; La Moynerie 1998 324; Ch de Tracy 1996 323
Poujeaux, Ch 1975 89, 2000 168
Prieuré-Lichine, Ch 1953 57, 1961 67, 1967 76, 1973 85, 1975 89, 1978 95, 1981 100, 1982 105, 1983 109, 1985 116, 1986 119, 1987 120, 1988 124, 1989 128, 1990 133, 1991 136, 1992 138, 1993 142, 1994 146, 1995 149, 1996 153, 1998 160, 1999 163, 2000 168
Puligny-Montrachet 1959 276, 1966 277, 1983, 1984 283, 1986 286, 1988 287, 1990 290, 1996 297, 1998 298, 1999 299; Clos du Cailleret 1991 291, 1992 292, 1997 298, 1998 299; Champs-Canet 1991 291; Champs-Gains 1991 291, 1992 292, 1994 294; Clavoillon 1979 280, 1990 290, 1991 291, 1992 292, 1993 293, 1994 294, 1995 296; Combettes 1937 274, 1974 278, 1979 280, 1981 281, 1995 296, 1998 299, 1999 299; Folatières 1981 281, 1983, 1984 283, 1985 284, 1986 286, 1988 287, 1990 290, 1991 291, 1992 292, 1993 293, 1995 296, 1999 299, 2000 301; Garenne 1988 287, 1995 296, 1998 299; Clos de la Garenne 2000 301; Grand Champs 1989 289; Clos de la Mouchère 1959 277, 1978 280, 1991 291; Perrières 1986 286, 1991 291, 1995 296; Pucelles 1976, 1978 279, 1979 280, 1981 281, 1982 282, 1988 287, 1989 289, 1993 293, 1994 294; Ch de Puligny-Montrachet 1991 291; Referts 1992 292, 1996 297, 2000 301; Sous les Puits 1992 292; Truffière 1995 296; Truffières 1985 285

## Q

Quarles Harris 1945 464, 1950 467, 1958 469, 1960 471, 1975 479, 1977 480, 1980 482, 1983 485, 1985 487, 1991 490, 1994 491, 1997 493
Quarts de Chaume 1971 318, 1973, 1975, 1986 319, 1989 320, 1990 321
Quarts Reef, Pinot Noir 1999 534
Quinault, Ch 1998 160, 2000 168
Quincy 1995 322, 1996 323, 2000 325; Les Belles Dames 2000 325; Les Victoires 2000 325
Qupé, Syrah 1991 522, 1992 523, 1993 524, 1994 525, 1995 526

## R

'R' de Ruinart 1995 447
Rabaud, Ch 1943 183
Rabaud-Promis, Ch 1924, 1926 179, 1939 182, 1975 195, 1983 200, 1986 202, 1988 203, 1989 204, 1993 207, 1995 208, 1996 209, 1997 210, 1998 212
Ramos-Pinto 1934 461, 1952 467, 1982 484, 1983 485, 1985 487, 1991, 1993 490, 1997 493, 2000 494
Randersackerer Marsberg Rieslaner TBA 1994 380; Pfülben Rieslaner TBA 1992 377; Pfülben Silvaner BA 1976 363
Rauenthaler Baiken Riesling Auslese 1964 354, 1971 358, 1976 362; Baiken Riesling Spätlese 1971 358, 359; Baiken Riesling TBA 1933, 1937 347, 1953 351, 1959 352; Berg Riesling Auslese 1971 358; Herrberg Riesling Auslese Cabinet 1967 355; Herrberg Riesling Spätlese 1959 352; Nonnenberg Riesling 1994 380; Nonnenberg Riesling Charta 1990 374; Nonnenberg Riesling Erstes Gewächs 1992 377, 1995 381; Pfaffenberg Riesling TBA 1953 351; Rothenberg Riesling BA 1971 358
Rausan-Ségla, Ch 1852 13, 1865, 1868 15, 1878 19, 1900 25, 1911 27, 1920 31, 1924 33, 1928 35, 1934 38, 1937, 1938 40, 1945 45, 1949 51, 1953 57, 1959 62, 1961 67, 1962 69, 1966 74, 1967 76, 1970 82, 1971 84, 1973 85, 1975 89, 1982 105, 1983 109, 1985 116, 1986 119, 1988 124, 1989 128, 1990 133, 1992 137, 1993 141; see also Rauzan-Ségla, Ch for wines after 1993
Rauzan, Ch 1847 13, 1858 13
Rauzan-Gassies, Ch 1920, 1921 31, 1926 34, 1928 35, 1929 36, 1945 45, 1953 57, 1961 67, 1962 68, 1964 71, 1978 95, 1982 105, 1983 110, 1985 116, 1991 136, 1992 138, 1993 142, 1994 146, 1995 149, 1996 154, 1997 157, 1998 160, 1999 163, 2000 168
Rauzan-Ségla, Ch 1994 144, 1995 149, 1996 153,

1997 157, 1998 160, 1999 163, 2000 168; see also Rausan-Ségla, Ch for wines before 1994
Ravenswood, Cabernet Sauvignon 533
Ray, Martin, Cabernet Sauvignon 1966 510
Raymond-Lafon, Ch 1979 197, 1982 198, 1988 203
Rayne-Vigneau, Ch de 1884 174, 1904 176, 1914 177, 1921, 1922 178, 1924, 1926 179, 1927 179-80, 1928 180, 1949 184, 1955 186, 1962 189, 1970 192, 1973 194, 1975 195, 1979 197, 1980, 1981 198, 1983 199-200, 1984 200, 1986 202, 1988 203, 1989 204, 1993 207, 1995 208, 1996 209, 1997 210, 1998 212, 1999 213, 2000 214
Rebello Valente 1900 455, 1917, 1921 457, 1924 458, 1927 459, 1931 461, 1935, 1942 462, 1945 463-4, 1955 468-9, 1960 471, 1963 472, 1970 477, 1972 478, 1975 479, 1977 481, 1980 482, 1983 485, 1985 487
Reggiano 'Concerto' Lambrusco Rubino Secco 1999 409
Reinhartshausen, Schloss Gutsriesling trocken 1999 389, 2000 391
René, Clos 1945 45, 1962 69, 1970 82, 1982 106, 1985 116, 1995 149
Respide, Ch 1998 160
Rheingau Chardonnay 2000 391
Rheingau Riesling trocken 2000 391
Ribera, Senhora da, Qta 1998 493
Ricaud, Ch de 1921 178, 1929 180, 1937 182
Richebourg 1904, 1906 217, 1919, 1921 219, 1931 222, 1937, 1940 224, 1943 225, 1945 226, 1947 226, 1948, 1949 227, 1952, 1953, 1954 229, 1959 230, 231, 1962 232-3, 1964 234, 1966 235, 1969 237, 1971 240, 1972, 1973 241, 1974, 1975 242, 1977 243, 1977 244, 1978 245, 1981 247, 1982 249, 1985 252, 253, 1986 253, 1987 254, 1988 255, 1989 257, 1990 259, 1991 260, 1992 262, 1993 262, 1994 264, 1996 266, 1997 267, 1998 268, 1999 269
Riddoch, John, Cabernet Sauvignon 1990 533
Ridge
  Fulton Zinfandel 1970 511; Geyserville Zinfandel 1984 517; Monte Bello 1990 521, 1991 522, 1992 523, 1993 524, 1994 525, 1995 526; Monte Bello Cabernet Sauvignon 1968 511, 1971, 1972 512, 1974, 1976 513, 1977 514, 1981 516, 1982, 1984 517; Paso Robles Zinfandel 1983 517; York Creek Cabernet

Sauvignon 1978 514, 1980 515, 1982 517, 1985 518; York Creek Zinfandel 1979 514
Riesling 1900 327; Brand Grand Cru 1989 332, 1998 336; Clos des Capucins, Cuvée Theo 1993 334; Comtes d'Eguisheim 1989 332; Cuvée Exceptionelle 1959, 1961 328; Cuvée Frédéric-Emile 1986 331, 1990 333, 1993 334; Grand Cru Jubilee 2000 337; Grand Cru Kirchberg de Barr 1993 334; Grand Cru Schlossberg 1993 334; Grand Cru Schlossberg Cuvée Ste-Catherine 'L'Inédit' 2000 337; Grand Cru Schlossberg II 1996 335; Grand Cru Schoenenbourg de Riquewihr 1995 335; Gueberschwihr 1998 336; Clos Hauserer 1998 336; Clos Heimbourg 1998 336; Herrenweg 1998 336; 'Hugel' 2000 337; 'Jubilee' 1979 330, 1981 330, 1988 332; Kabinett 'Charta' 1997 336; Kaefferkopf 1928 327; Mambourg, Cuvée Centenaire 1979 330; Mittelbergheim Stein 1934 327; Muhlforst 1995 335; Cuvée Particulière 1971 329; 'Les Princes Abbés' 1989 332, 1996 335; 'Quintessenses de Sélection des Grains Nobles' 1989 332; Rangen 1999 336; Rangen de Thann Clos St-Urbain 1997 335, 1998 336; Rangen Grand Cru 1981 330, 1985 331; Réserve Personnelle 1981 330, see also Riesling 'Jubilee'; Saering Grand Cru 1989 332, 1990 333; Cuvée Ste Catherine II 1996 335, 1997 336; Clos Ste-Hune 1975, 1976 329, 1978 329-30, 1979, 1983 330, 1986 331, 1993 334; Clos Ste-Hune Vendange Tardive 1989 332; Schloss 1989 332; Schoenenbourg 1981 330; Schoenenbourg Vendange Tardive 1998 336; Sélection Spéciale 'Cuvée 27 1959 328; Sélection Spéciale 'Cuvée 37 1959 328; SGN 1900 327, 1976 329, 1988 332; TBA 1985 331; 'Tradition' 2000 337; Turkheim 1991 333, 1998 336; Vendange Tardive 1935, 1945 327, 1953, 1959, 1961, 1966 328, 1971, 1976 329, 1981, 1983 330, 1985 331, 1988, 1989 332, 1990 333, 1995 335, 1996, 1997 335; Vendange Tardive, Cuvée Frédéric Emile 1983 330; Clos Windsbuhl SGN 1989 332;
Rieussec, Ch 1859 172,

1929 180, 1945 183, 1947 184, 1957, 1959 187, 1961 188, 1962 189, 1967 190, 1969 191, 1970 192, 1971 193, 1975 195, 1976, 1978 196, 1979 197, 1980, 1981 198, 1982 199, 1983 200, 1985 201, 1986 202, 1989 204, 1990 205, 1993 207, 1995 208, 1996 209, 1997 210, 1998 212, 1999 213, 2000 214
'Rio Tinto' 1982 484
Roc-des-Combes, Ch 1995 149
Rocca di Montegross' Riserva 1995 405
Roche, Clos de la 1921 219, 1961 232, 1962 233, 1964 234, 1969 237, 1972 241, 1974 242, 1978 245, 1979 246, 1983 250, 1985 253, 1987 255, 1988 256, 1989 257, 1990 259, 1991 261, 1993 263, 1994 264, 1997 267, 1999 270
Rochemorin, Ch 1982 105, 1989 126
Rockford, Basket Press Shiraz 1986 532, 1990 533
Roêda, Qta da 1967 475, 1978 481, 1983 485, 1995 492, 1997 493
Roederer 1928 425, 1941 426, 1945 427, 1955 428, 1967, 1969 432, 1971 433, 1982, 1983 440, 1988 443, 1993 447; Crémant 1971 433; Cristal 1964 431, 1974 434, 1975 435, 1977, 1978 436, 1979 437, 1981 438, 1982 439, 1983 440, 1985 442, 1989 444; Rosé 1986 443, 1991 446
Rol Valentin, Ch 1996 153
Roland, Ch 1994 208
Romanée, La 1865 216, 1949 227, 1959 231, 1972 241, 1989 257, 1990 259; 'Grande Cru Exclusivité' 1987 254
Romanée, La Tâche 1923 220
Romanée-Conti 1865 216, 1921 219, 1927, 1928 220, 1937 223-4, 1940 224, 1943, 1944 225, 1945 225-6, 1952 228, 229, 1953, 1954 229, 1956, 1959 230, 1961 231, 1962 232, 1964 233, 1966 235, 1968 236, 1971 239, 1972, 1973 241, 1975 242, 1976 242-3, 1978 244, 1979 245, 1981 247, 1982, 1983 249, 1985 251, 1987 254, 1988 255, 1986 253, 1991 260, 1993 262, 1994 263, 1997 266, 1998 268, 1999 269
Romanée-St-Vivant 1906, 1914 218, 1929 221, 1933 222, 1934 223, 1938 224, 1947 226, 1949 227, 1952 229, 1959 231, 1961 232, 1964 234, 1966 235, 236, 1967 236, 1969 237, 1971 240, 1972 241, 1975 242, 1976 243, 1978 244, 1979 245, 1980 246, 1981 247, 1982 247-8, 1983 249, 1984 251, 1985 252, 1986 253, 1987 254, 1988 255, 1989

257, 1990 258, 259, 1991
260, 1992 261, 1993 262,
1994, 1995 264, 1996 265,
1997 267, 1998 268, 1999
269, 2000 271, 272; Quatre
Journaux 1929 221, 1953
229, 1978 245, 1983 251,
1985 253, 1989 257
Romer du Hayot, Ch 1975
195, 1976 196, 1981 198,
1983 200, 1986 202, 1990
206, 1993 207, 1996 209,
1997 211, 1999 213
Romitorio di Santedame
Toscana 1997 407
Ronção, Qta do 1931 461
Roriz, Qta do 1834 450,
1870 452, 2000 494
Rosa, Qta de la 1927 459,
1963 473, 1970 478, 1978
481, 1988 488, 2000 494
Rosso di Montalcino 1989
402
Rosso di Toscano 1997 407
Rouget, Ch 1928 35, 1947
48, 1964 71
Roumieu, Ch 1950 185,
1953 186
Roumieu-Lacoste, Ch
1970 192
Roxheimer Höllenpfad
Riesling Auslese 1989 372
'Royal Jubilee' (port) 1977
480
Royal Oporto 1958 469,
1963 473, 1970 478, 1977,
1978 481, 1982 484, 1983
485, 1985 487
Rozes 1974 478, 1975 479,
1991 490
Rubesco Torgiano 1968
395, 1970, 1971 396
Ruchottes-Chambertin
1959 231, 1983 250, 1990
259
Rüdesheimer
Apostelwein 1727 343-4;
Berg Lay Riesling
Cabinet 1968 356; Berg
Mauerwein Riesling
Auslese 1963 353; Berg
Roseneck Riesling
Auslese 1976 363, 1986
369, 1995 381; Berg
Roseneck Riesling BA
1979 364; Berg Rottland
Riesling Auslese 1971 359,
1989 372; Berg Rottland
Riesling Kabinett 1971
358; Berg Rottland
Riesling TBA 1989 372,
1993 378; Berg
Schlossberg Riesling
Auslese 1976 362, 1989
372; Berg Schlossberg
Riesling BA 1989 372,
1995 381; Berg
Schlossberg Riesling
Spätlese 1996 384; Berg
Schlossberg
Spätburgunder 1993 378;
Berg Schlossberg
Spätburgunder Spätlese
1996 384; Bischofsberg
Riesling BA 1990 374, 375;
Bischofsberg Riesling
TBA 1993 378; Klosterlay
Riesling BA 1976 362;
Magdalenenkreuz
Riesling Kabinett 2000
391; Schlossberg Riesling
Auslese 1989 372

Ruinart 1945 427, 1985 442;
see also Dom Ruinart and
R de Ruinart
Ruppertsberger
Linsenbusch Ehrenfelser
Spätlese 1975 361;
Linsenbusch Scheurebe
Spätlese 1981 365;
Reiterpfad Riesling
Auslese 1994 380;
Reiterpfad Scheurebe
BA 1992 377; Reiterspfad
Scheurebe TBA 1994 380
Russelheimer Riesling
Spätlese 1953 351
Rutherford Hill, 'XVS'
Napa Cabernet
Sauvignon 1985 519

## S

Saarburger
Rausch Riesling Auslese
1971 359, 1999 389; Rausch
Riesling Auslese
Goldkapsel 1994 380, 1996
384; Rausch Riesling
Auslese lange Goldkapsel
1999 389; Rausch Riesling
BA 1994 380; Rausch
Riesling Eiswein 1995 381;
Rausch Riesling Spätlese
1994 380
Saarstein, Schloss
Riesling BA 1971 358;
Riesling Spätlese 1999 389
Saché 1937 316
St-Amand, Ch 1924, 1926
179, 1982 199
St Clement, Cabernet
Sauvignon 1980 515
St-Denis, Clos 1943 225,
1972 241
St-Joseph 1990 310, 1991,
1993 311, 2000 314; La
Grande Pompée 1994 311
St-Nicolas de Bourgueil
1998 324; 'Les Harquerets'
1989 320; Dom Les
Quarterons 1982 319;
Vignoble de la
Jarnoterie 1969 318
St-Pierre, Ch 1961 67, 1970
82, 1975 89, 1981 100, 1983
109, 1986 119, 1991 136,
1995 149
St-Pierre-Bontemps, Ch
1899 23; see also St Pierre,
Ch for later wines
St-Pierre-Sevaistre, Ch see
St-Pierre, Ch
St Thomas 'Burgundy'
1955 532
Saintsbury
Carneros Pinot Noir
1982 517, 1986 519, 1988
520, 1994 525, 1997 527;
'Garnet' Carneros Pinot
Noir 1987 520; Reserve
Pinot Noir 1990 521
Sales, Ch de 1962 69, 1964
71, 1966 75, 1970 82, 1975
89, 1976 90, 1981 100, 1986
119, 1995 149
Salm-Dalberg Riesling
BA 1989 372
Salon 1964 431, 1971 433,
1973 434, 1979 437, 1982
439, 1983 440, 1988 443,
1990 446
'Samarkand' Riesling
QbA 2000 391

Sammarco 1986 401
San Leonardo 1993 404
San Leone 1995 405
San Martino, Villa
Cafaggio 1998 408
Sancerre 1995 322, 2000 325;
La Chapelle, Ch de
Thauvenay 1999 325; La
Crois au Garde 2000 325;
'Edmund' 1999 325;
Cuvée François de
Montigny 1998 324; La
Grande Cuvée 1997 324;
La Grande Cuvée Rouge
1997 324; Dom la
Moussière 1998 324; Clos
La Néole 1995 322; Cuvée
Pierre 1995 322; La Porte
de Caillou 1996 323; Les
Roches 1995 322, 1998 324;
Rosé, Cuvée Moulin
Bèle 1999 325; Rouge 1999
325; Rouge, 'Génération
★★★' 1997 324; Clos du
Roy 1992 322; Les
Roysiers 1992 322; Cuvée
St-Francis 1992 322; Les
Tuilleries 1998 324
Sanctus 1998 160
Sandeman 1887 453, 1894,
1896, 1897 454, 1904 455,
1908, 1911 456, 1917 457,
1927 459, 1934 461, 1935,
1943 462, 1945, 1946, 1947
464, 1950 466, 1953 467,
1955, 1957, 1958 469, 1960
470, 1962 471, 1963 472,
1966 474, 1967 475, 1970
477, 1977 480, 1980 482,
1982 484, 1985 487, 1986
488; 'Vau' 1997 493; Val de
Mendiz 1908 456
Sanford
Pinot Noir 1984 517, 1986
519, 1990 521; Sanford and
Benedict Vineyard Pinot
Noir 1986 519; Sanford
and Benedict Vineyard
Barrel Select Pinot Noir
1990 521; Santa Barbara
Pinot Noir 1989 520
Sangiovese, Rosso di
Toscano 1999 409
Santa Cristina 1994 405
Santenay 1911 218, 1925
220; (blanc) 1994 294;
Comme 1997 268 Clos de
Malte 1996 266
Santenay-Volnay,
Hospices, Cuvée Gauvin
1923 219-20
Santos 1970 478
São Felipe, Vintage 1887
500
São Luíz, Qta do 1970 478
Sassicaia 1976, 1978, 1979
397, 1980, 1981 398, 1982,
1983 399, 1984 400, 1985,
1986 401, 1990 404, 1993,
1995 405, 1996 406, 1997
407, 1998 408, 1999 409
Saumur-Champigny 1984
319
'Sauternes, Ch' 1887 174
Savennières, Clos du
Papillon 1990 321
Savigny (Lès-Beaune) 1964
234, 1982 248, 1992 262,
1993 263; Dominode 1999
270, 2000 272; Guettes 1999
270; Haut-Jarrons 1995
265; Hospices, Cuvée

Fouquerand 1923 220,
1935 223; Hospices,
'Cyrot' 1935 223; Lavières
1985 253; Narbantons 1997
268; Pimentiers 1997 268;
Serpentières 1990 259;
Vergelesses 1995 265, 2000
272
Saxenburg, Private
Collection Shiraz 1997
535
Scasso dei Cesari 1998 408
Scharzhofberger
Riesling Auslese 1959 352,
1964 354, 1971 358-9, 1976
362, 363, 1983 367, 1988 370,
1989 372, 1995 381;
Riesling Auslese Eiswein
1973 360; Riesling Auslese
Goldkapsel 1976 362, 1991
375, 1994 380, 1995 381,
1996 384, 1999 389;
Riesling BA 1975 360,
1989 372, 1993 378, 1994
380, 1999 389; Riesling
Eiswein 1984 368, 1988 370;
Riesling Fass Nr 7, Dom
1964 354; Riesling
Kabinett 1975 360, 1976
362, 1983 367, 1989 372,
1999 389; Riesling
Spätlese 1975 360, 1976
362, 1989 372, 1990 374,
1994 380, 1999 389;
Riesling Spätlese Fuder
36 1999 389; Riesling TBA
1975 360, 1976 362
Schloss for Schloss see
under main name
Schlossböckelheimer
Felsenberg Riesling
Auslese 1994 380, 1995 381;
Felsenberg Riesling
Kabinett 1988 370;
Köningsfels Riesling
Kabinett 1988 370;
Kupfergrube Riesling
Auslese 1976 362;
Kupfergrube Riesling
Kabinett 1970 357
Schlossgut Diel
Riesling Auslese
Goldkapsel 1994 380, 1995
381; Riesling Eiswein 1995
381-2
Schönborn, Schloss
Riesling TBA 1993 378
Screaming Eagle,
Cabernet Sauvignon
1992 523, 1993 524, 1994
525, 1995 526
Seifile 1906 406
Seixo, Qta do 1982 484,
1983 485
Sejana Merlot 1998 535
Sénéjac, Ch 1990 133
Senhora da Ribera, Qta
1998 493
Sequoia Grove, Cabernet
Sauvignon 1986 519
Serafim Cabral 1871 452
Sercial 1836 498, 1864 499,
1877, 1892 500, 1910 502,
1937, 1940 503, 1950, 1969
504, 1971 505; Solera 1860
498-9, 1898 500; Vintage
1940 503; 'VJH' 1940 503
Seresin, Pinot Noir 1999
534
Serras 1960 471
Serriger
Schloss Saarsteiner

Riesling Auslese 1983 367;
Schloss Saarsteiner
Riesling Eiswein 1995 382;
Vogelsang Riesling TBA
1976 363; Würtzberg
Riesling Auslese 1975 360
Shafer
Cabernet Sauvignon
1979 514; Hillside Select
Cabernet Sauvignon
1982 517, 1985 519, 1990
521, 1992 523, 1993 524,
1994 525, 1995 526, 1996-
1997 527; Merlot 1987 520,
1990 521, 1991 522, 1996 527
Síbio, Qta do 1955 469,
1960 471
Siebeldinger im
Sonnenschein
Spätburgunder
Weissherbst Auslese 1983
367
Sigalas-Rabaud, Ch 1896
175, 1955 186, 1959 187,
1962 188, 1964, 1966 189,
1967 190, 1969 191, 1970
192, 1971 193, 1975 195,
1976, 1977, 1978 196, 1979
197, 1981 198, 1984 200,
1986 202, 1988 203, 1989
204, 1990 206, 1995 208,
1996 209, 1997 210, 1998
212, 1999 213, 2000 214
Sileni Estates EV 1998 534
Sillery 1857, 1870, 1874 422
Silva, da 1985 487
Silva, A J da, Reserva 1937
462
Silver Oak
Alexander Valley
Cabernet Sauvignon
1977, 1978 514, 1985 519
Simi
Alexander Valley Reserve
Cabernet Sauvignon 1985
519; Cabernet Sauvignon
1980 515; Reserve
Cabernet Sauvignon
1981 516, 1982 517
Simonelles 1992 322
Siran, Ch 1916 28, 1918,
1919 29, 1921, 1922 31, 1923
32, 1934 38, 1943 42, 1947
48, 1948 49, 1949 51, 1953
56, 1955 58, 1967 75, 1970
82, 1971 83, 1975 89, 1978
94, 1983 110, 1989 128, 1990
134, 1992 138, 1993 142,
1994 146, 1996 154, 1997
158, 1998 160, 2000 168
Skinner & Rook (port)
1896 454
Smith Woodhouse 1900,
1904 455, 1935 462, 1945
464, 1947 464-5, 1948 465,
1950 467, 1955 469, 1960
470, 1963 473, 1966 474,
1970 477, 1975, 1976 479,
1977 480, 1980 482-3, 1983
485, 1985 487, 1990 494,
1994 491, 1997 493, 2000 494
Smith-Haut-Lafitte, Ch
1961 67, 1962 69, 1973 85,
1974 86, 1975 89, 1986 119,
1990 133, 1993 141, 1994
144, 1995 149, 1996 153,
1997 158, 1998 160, 2000
168; (blanc) 1995 208, 1998
212, 1999 213, 2000 214
Sociando-Mallet, Ch 1982
105, 1986 119, 1990 133-4,
1994 146, 1996 153

Sodi di San Niccolò, I
1994 405
Solaia 1978 397, 1985 401,
1989 402, 1990 404, 1997 407
Solera (madeira) 1811 497
Souza 1970 478, 1991 490
Spätburgunder Rotwein
'***' Auslese 1997 386; BA
1992 377
Stag's Leap Wine Cellars
Cabernet Sauvignon
Lot 2 1978 514; Cabernet
Sauvignon 'SLV' 1973
512, 1974, 1976 513, 1985
518, 1986 519, 1988 520,
1990 521, 1992 523, 1993
524; Cabernet Sauvignon
'SLV' Fay Vineyard 1989
520; Cask 23 1978, 1979
514, 1980 515, 1985 517,
1985 518, 1990 521, 1991
522, 1992 523, 1993 524,
1994 525, 1997 527;
Cabernet Sauvignon
Fay Vineyard 1977 514,
1990 521, 1991 522, 1992
523, 1995 526
Steenberg Merlot 1998 535
Stein Auslese 1897 344
Steinberger
Riesling Auslese 1949
349, 1986 369, 1989 372,
1993 378; Riesling BA
1959 352, 1964 354;
Riesling Cabinet BA
1911 345; Riesling
Cabinet Wein 1897 344;
Riesling edel BA 1953
351; Riesling Eiswein
1992 377; Riesling
Eiswein Auslese 1971 359;
Riesling feine Spätlese
Kabinett 1964 354;
Riesling 'First Growth'
1995 382; Riesling
naturrein 1948 349, 1950
350; Riesling naturrein
Fass Nr 58 1946 349;
Riesling Spätlese 1971
359; Riesling Spätlese
naturrein 1953 351;
Riesling TBA 1937 347,
1959 352, 1964 354
Steingrüble
Spätburgunder
Weissherbst Eiswein 1988
370
Sterling Vineyards
Merlot 1982 517; Reserve
1985 519; Reserve
Cabernet Sauvignon
1974 513; Winery Lake
Pinot Noir 1986 519
Stibbart (port) 1851 451
Stormont Tait 1927 459
Suau, Ch 1943 183, 1975
195, 1985 201, 1986 202,
1996 209, 1997 211, 1998 212
Suduiraut, Ch 1893, 1899
175, 1921 178, 1928 180,
1937 182, 1947 184, 1955
186, 1957, 1958, 1959 187,
1962, 1965, 1966 189, 1967
190, 1969 191, 1970 192,
1971, 1972 193, 1975 195,
1976, 1978 196, 1979 197,
1980 198, 1982 199, 1983,
1984 200, 1985 201, 1986
202, 1988 203, 1989 204,
1990 205-6, 1994, 1995 208,
1996 209, 1997 210, 1998
212, 1999 213, 2000 214

T

Tâche, La 1934 222, 223,
1937, 1938, 1940, 1942 224,
1943 225, 1945, 1947 226,
1948, 1949 227, 1951 228,
1952, 1953, 1954 229, 1956,
1957, 1958 230, 1959 231,
1961, 1962 232, 1963 233,
1964, 1965 234, 1966 235,
1967, 1969 236, 1970 238,
1971 240, 1972, 1973 241,
1974, 1975 242, 1976 243,
1977, 1978 244, 1979 245,
1980 246, 1981, 1982 247,
1983 249, 1984 251, 1985
251-2, 1986 253, 1987 254,
1988 255, 1989 256-7, 1990
258, 1991 260, 1992 261,
1993 262, 1994 263-4, 1997
266, 1998 268, 1999 269
Taittinger 1983 440; Artists'
Series 1982 439; Comtes
de Champagne, Blanc
de Blancs 1975 435, 1976
436, 1981 438, 1983 440,
1985, 1986 442, 1988 443-4,
1989 444; Comtes de
Champagne, Rosé 1986
443; La Française 1979 437
Talbot, Ch 1928 35, 1934 39,
1945 45, 1949 51, 1953 56,
1955 58, 1959 62, 1961 66,
1962 68, 1966 74, 1970 82,
1971, 1972 84, 1973 85, 1974
86, 1975 89, 1976 90, 1978
94, 1981 100, 1982 105, 1983
109, 1985 116, 1986 118,
1988 124, 1989 128, 1990
134, 1991 136, 1992 138,
1993 140, 1994 144-5, 1995
149, 1996 153, 1997 158,
1998 160, 1999 163, 2000
168; Caillou Blanc, Ch
1997 211
Taltarni, Cabernet
Sauvignon 1990 533
Tart, Clos de 1911 218,
1921 219, 1928 220, 1957
230, 1974 242, 1976 243,
1978 245, 1979 246, 1982
248, 1983 250, 1985 253,
1986 254, 1988 256, 1989
257, 1990 260, 1993 263,
2000 272
Tassinaia 1999 409
Tastes, Ch des 1924 179,
1934 181, 1950 185
Taylor 1863, 1870 452, 1896
454, 1904 455, 1908 456,
1912, 1917, 1920, 1922 457,
1924 458, 1927 459, 1934,
1935 461, 1938, 1940, 1942
462, 1945 464, 1948 465,
1955 468, 1960 470, 1963
473, 1966 474, 1967 475,
1970 477-8, 1975 479, 1977
480, 1980, 1981 483, 1983
485, 1985 487, 1992 490,
1994 491, 1997 493, 2000
494; Crusted 1973 478;
LBV 1981 483; Special
Quinta 1947 464
Te Mata, 'Coleraine' 1991
534
Terra Feita, Qta da 1907
455, 1911 456
Terrantez 1795, 1798, 1802
497, 1846 498, 1862, 1870
499, 1877, 1898, 1899 500;
Reserva 1880 500;
'Special Reserve,

Medium Sweet' 1832 498;
Vintage 1834 498, 1960 504
Tertre, Ch du 1964 71, 1985
116, 1986 118, 1995 149
Tertre-Daugay, Ch 1900 25,
1924 33
Tertre-Roteboeuf, Ch
1983 109, 1985 116, 1989
128, 1990 134, 1992 137,
1995 149, 1997 158, 1998 160
Thienot, Alain 1985 442
Tignanello 1971 396, 1977,
1978 397, 1982 399, 1985,
1986 401, 1988 402, 1989
403, 1990 404, 1993 405,
1996 406, 1997 407
Togni, Philip, Ca' Togni
1993 523
Tokaji Aszú 1865 410
Tokaji Aszú 3 putts 1943
411, 1990, 1991 414, 1993
415; 3 putts, Deák 1998 416
Tokaji Aszú 4 putts 1917
411, 1952 412, 1990, 1991,
1992 414; 4 putts, Deák
1998 416
Tokaji Aszú 5 puttonos
Ausbruch
Trockenbeerenauslese
Cabinet 1961 412; 5 putts
1865 410, 1937, 1945 411,
1973, 1981, 1988 413, 1990,
1992 414, 1993, 1994, 1995
415; 5 putts Birsalmas
1990, 1991 414; 5 putts,
'Blue label' 1991 414;
5 putts Botja 1991 414;
5 putts, Nyulászó 1991
414; 5 putts, Szt. Tamas
1991 414
Tokaji Aszú, '5 or 6' putts
1996 416
Tokaji Aszú, 6 'buttig'
1972 413
Tokaji Aszú, 6 putts 1912,
1924, 1935, 1942 411, 1947,
1952, 1956 412, 1964, 1968,
1975, 1988 413, 1992 414,
1993, 1994, 1995 415, 1996,
1997 416; 6 putts, 'Blue
label' 1996 415; 6 putts,
Königsberg 1996 416;
6 putts, Nyulászó 1993
415; 6 putts, Szarvas 1973
413, 1991 414, 1994 415;
6 putts, Szt Tamas 1993
415
Tokaji Aszú-Essencia 1937
411, 1947, 1963 412, 1964,
1968, 1972, 1988 413, 1993,
1995 415
Tokaji Aszú-Esszencia
1957 412
Tokaji Aszú Esszenzcia
1991 414
Tokaji Aszúeszencia 1983
413
Tokaji 'Botrytis Selection'
Deák 1998 416
Tokaji Essence 1834 410,
1972 413
Tokaji Essencia 1889, 1924,
1945 411, 1947 412, 1993 415
Tokaji Eszencia 1972 413
Tokaji 'Imperial Tokay'
1885 410
Tokaji Muskotàlyos Aszú,
5 putts 1963 413
Tokaji Muskotàlyos Aszú,
6 putts 1963 412-13
Tokaji Natu-essenz
Eszencia 1999 416

Tokaji Szamorodni 1901
411
Tokaji Szamorodni Borsai
Miklos, Sweet 1904 411
Tokay d'Alsace 1865 327
Tokay Ausbruch 1900, 1906
411
(Tokay-)Pinot Gris 1989
332, 1991 333, 1993 334;
Tokay Pinot Gris 'A 360
P' 1991 333; Altenberg
Clos Jebsal 1988 332;
Comtes d'Eguisheim
1985 331; Heimbourg
1998 336; Clos Jebsal
SGN 1991 333-4, 1995 335;
'Jubilee' 1986 331, 1988
332, 1998 336, 2000 337;
Kitterlé Grand Cru 1989
332, 1992 334; Cuvée
Laurence 1995, 1997 335;
Patergarten 1991 333, 1992
334; Réserve Personnelle
1983 330; Rothenbourg
1998 336; Clos St-Urbain
1978 330; SGN 1976 329,
1983 330; Cuvée Tradition
1988 332; Vendange
Tardive 1981 330, 1985 331,
1988 332, 1990 333, 1995
335; Vendange Tardive,
Réserve Exceptionelle
1967 328; Vendange
Tardive, Sélection Jean
1983 330; Clos Windsbuhl
1998 336;
Tokayer Ausbruch, 1876
410
Torgiano, Riserva
Rubesco, Monticchio
1988 402
Tour-de-By, Ch La 1983
109, 1985 116, 1989 128,
1990 134, 1991 136, 1992
138, 1994 145, 1996 154,
1997 158, 1998 160, 2000 168
Tour de Mons, Ch La
1945 45, 1961 68, 1964 71,
1966 74, 1975 89
Tour-Blanche, Ch La 1869
173, 1876 174, 1899 175,
1904 176, 1921 178, 1927
180, 1939 182, 1947 184,
1950 185, 1959 187, 1961
188, 1966 189, 1967 190,
1970 192, 1975 195, 1986
202, 1988 203, 1989 204,
1990 206, 1994, 1995 208,
1996 209, 1997 210, 1998
212, 1999 213
Tour-Carnet, Ch La 1978
95, 1985 116, 1990 134, 1992
138, 1996 154, 1997 158,
1998 160
Tour-Figeac, Ch La 1985
116, 1993 142, 1995 149,
2000 168
Tour Haut-Brion, Ch La
1926 34, 1940 41, 1945 45,
1959 62, 1966 74, 1969 77,
1970 82, 1971, 1972 84, 1973
85, 1974 86, 1975 89, 1978
95, 1979 96, 1981 100, 1996
154, 1997 158, 1998 160,
2000 168
Traiser Rotenfels Riesling
Eiswein 1983 367
Traminer
Réserve Exceptionnelle
1934 327; Cuvée
Exceptionelle 1959 328

Trefethen
Cabernet Sauvignon
1977 514; Valley Floor
Cabernet Sauvignon
1981 516
Trierer Thiergarten
Unterm Kreuz Auslese,
Weihnachts-Eiswein-
Edelwein 1970 357
Trinoro 1997 407-8, 1999,
2000 409
Trittenheimer
Leiterchen Riesling
Auslese 1999 389;
Leiterchen Riesling
Auslese Goldkapsel 1996
384
Tronquoy-Lalande, Ch
1995 149-50
Troplong-Mondot, Ch
1976 91, 1990 134, 1992 138,
1995 150, 1997 158, 2000 168
Trotanoy, Ch 1928 35, 1937
40, 1945 45, 1959 62, 1961
67, 1964 71, 1966 74, 1970
82, 1971 83, 1975 89, 1976
91, 1978 94, 1979 96, 1982
105, 1985 116, 1993 140,
1994 146, 1995 150, 1996
153, 1997 158, 2000 168
Trottevieille, Ch 1953 56,
1982 106, 1990 134, 1996 153
Tua, Qta do 1987 488
Tuke Holdsworth 1896 454,
1922 457, 1947 464, 1950
467, 1955 468, 1958 469,
1960 470, 1987 488, 1995 492

U

Ungsteiner Bettelhaus
Rieslaner TBA 1992 377
Ürziger
Würzgarten Riesling
Auslese 1975 360;
Würzgarten Riesling
Auslese Goldkapsel 1996
384; Würzgarten Riesling
Auslese lange Goldkapsel
1996 384; Würzgarten
Riesling Eiswein 1995 382;
Würzgarten Riesling
Spätlese 1996 384

V

Val see Clos du Val
Valandraud, Ch de 1992
137
Vale da Mina, Qta 1995 492
Valpolicella Classico 1999
409; La Grola 1988 402
Vargellas, Qta de 1917 457,
1926 458, 1930 460, 1948
465, 1957, 1958 469, 1961
471, 1965 473, 1967, 1969
475, 1970 478, 1978 481,
1982 484, 1986 488, 1991
490, 1995 492
Vasse Felix, Cabernet
Sauvignon 1980 532, 1999
532
Vavasour, Pinot Noir 1999
534
Vega Sicilia, Único 1941,
1942, 1948, 1953, 1957,
1960, 1962, 1964, 1965,
1966, 1975, 1981, 1982,
1990 417; Reserva
Especial 417
Venoge, de 1985 442
Verdelho 1822 497, 1850 498,

1890 *500*, 1900 *501*, 1913 *502*, 1931, 1932 *503*, 1948, 1968 *504*; Gran Cama de Lobos 1864 *499*; 'Jubilee Selection' 1952 *504*; Noguero 1919 *501*; Solera 1870 *499*, 1898 *500*; 'Special Reserve, Medium Sweet' 1839 *498*; Torre 1905 *501*; Torre Bella 1879 *500*; Vintage 1934 *503*, 1954 *504*; 'VJH' 1934 *503*, 1954 *504*
Verrenberger Verrenberg Lemberger Spätlese trocken 1985 *368*
Vesúvio, Qta do 1815 *450*, 1989 *488*, 1990 *489*, 1991, 1992 *490*, 1994 *491*, 1995, 1996 *492*, 2000 *494*
Veuve Clicquot 1923, 1928, 1929 *425*, 1934, 1937, 1942, 1943 *426*, 1947 *427-8*, 1949, 1952, 1953 *428*, 1955 *428-9*, 1959 *429*, 1966 *431*, 1975 *435*, 1978 *436*, 1982 *439*, 1983 *440*, 1985 *442*, 1988, 1989 *444*, 1990 *446*; Carte d'Or 1982 *439*; Gold Label 1976 *436*; La Grande Dame 1979 *437*, 1985 *442*, 1989 *444*, 1990 *446*, 1993 *447*; Grande Dame, Rosé 1988 *444*, 1989 *445*; Rosé 1975 *435*, 1979 *437*, 1985 *442*, 1990 *446*
Vicar, The *533*
Vieux Ch Certan 1937 *40*, 1945 *45*, 1947 *48*, 1949 *51*, 1953 *57*, 1959 *62*, 1961 *67*, 1962 *69*, 1964 *71*, 1966 *75*, 1971 *84*, 1975 *89*, 1980 *98*, 1982 *105*, 1983 *109*, 1985 *116*, 1988 *124*, 1993 *141-2*, 1994 *145*, 1996 *153*, 1997 *158*, 1998 *160*, 1999 *163*, 2000 *168*
Villemaurine, Ch 1898 *23*, 1992 *138*
Vin de Paille du Jubilee 1988 *332*
Vinho do Porto 1893 *453*
Violette, Clos 1982 *105*
Voigny, Ch 1937 *182*
Volkacher Karthäuser Weisser Burgunder BA 1992 *377*
Vollrads, Schloss Riesling Eiswein Goldkapsel 1991 *375*; Riesling Kabinett 1945 *349*; Riesling Kabinett trocken 1997 *386*; Riesling TBA 1947 *349*, 1976 *362*
Volnay 1921 *219*, 1933 *222*, 1934 *223*, 1960 *231*, 1982 *248*, 1985 *253*; 1er Cru 1979 *246*, 1999 *270*; Clos des Angles 1983 *250*; Clos de la Barre 1999 *270*; Caillerets 1959 *231*, 1964 *234*, 1969 *237*, 1978 *245*; Caillerets, (Ancienne) Cuvée Carnot 1929 *221*, 1934 *223*, 1997 *268*; Caillerets, Clos des 60 Ouvrées 1982 *248*, 1996 *266*; Champans 1976 *243*, 1995 *265*, 1996 *266*, 1998 *269*, 2000 *272*; Clos au Ch des Ducs 1986 *254*; Clos des Chênes 1934 *223*, 1964 *234*, 1978 *245*, 1985 *253*,

1988 *256*, 1997 *268*, 1998 *269*, 1999 *270*, 2000 *272*; Clos des Ducs 1995 *265*, 1998 *269*, 2000 *272*; Fremiets, Clos de la Rougeotte 1919 *219*; Hospices, Cuvée Blondeau 1937 *224*; Hospices, Cuvée Général Muteau 1962 *233*, 1992 *262*; Hospices, Cuvée Jehan de Massol 1950 *228*, 1988 *256*; Pitures 1992 *262*; Santenots 1865 *216*, 1924 *220*, 1949 *227*, 1995 *265*; Cuvée Sélectionée 1996 *266*; Taillepieds 1971 *240*, 1976 *243*, 1990 *259*, 1998 *269*, 1999 *270*, 2000 *272*; Vendanges Sélectionnées 1992 *262*; Clos du Verseuil 1990 *259*
Volte, Le 1992 *404*
Vosne-Romanée 1928 *220*, 1943 *225*, 1947, 1949 *227*, 1967 *236*, 1971 *240*, 1983 *250*, 1984 *251*, 1987 *255*, 1990 *259*, 1993 *263*; 1er cru, Cuvée Duvault–Blochet 1999 *270*; Aux Brûlées 1972 *241*, 1979 *245*, 1992 *262*; Aux Brûlées, Vieilles Vignes 2000 *272*; Aux Réas 1996 *266*, 1999 *270*; Beaumonts 1929 *221*, 1968 *236*, 1978 *245*, 1988 *248*, 1990 *259*; Beaux-Monts 1990 *259*, 1994 *264*, 1999 *270*; Champs Perdrix 1987 *254*; Clos du Château 2000 *272*; Chaumes 1996 *266*, 1997 *267*, *268*; Cros Parantoux 1978 *245*, 1979 *246*, 1980 *246-7*, 1990 *259*, 1992 *262*, 1995 *265*, 1997 *267*; Grand-Rue 1962 *233*; Hautes Maizières 1997 *268*, 2000 *272*; Orveaux 1983 *251*; Suchots 1985 *253*; Tastevinée 1969 *236*
Vougeot 1997 *268*
Vougeot, Clos (de) 1865 *216*, 1911 *218*, 1928 *220*, 1929 *221*, 1947 *226*, 1949 *227*, 1959 *231*, 1961 *232*, 1967 *236*, 1969 *237*, 1971 *240*, 1978 *245*, 1982 *248*, 1985 *253*, 1987 *255*, 1988 *256*, 1990 *259*, 260, 1993 *263*, 1994 *264*, 1997 *268*, 2000 *272*; (blanc) 1919 *274*; Musigni (sic) 1986 *254*, 1990 *259*; Clos de la Perrière 1970 *239*, 1977 *244*; du Prieuré 1950 *228*, 1961 *232*; Tastevinée 1982 *248*; Tasteviné 1989 *257*; Ch de la Tour 1929 *221*, 1966 *236*, 1980 *247*
Vouvray 1947, 1955, 1959 *317*, 1964, 1969 *318*, 1980 *319*, 1989 *320*, 1992, 1993, 1995 *322*, 1996 *323*; Clos Baudoin 1934 *316*, 1989 *320*, 1990 *321*; Clos du Bourg 1971 *318-19*, 1989 *320*, 1995 *322*; Colnot 1947 *316-17*; Cuvée Constance 1989 *320*; Cuvée Florent 1989 *320*; La Gaudrelle Réserve Personnelle 1996 *323*; Le Haut-Lieu 1947

*317*, 1989 *320*; Le Mont 1953 *317*, 1998 *324*; Clos Naudin 1959 *317*, 1990 *321*, 1996 *323*; Trie des Grains Nobles 1990 *321*

## W

Wachenheimer Goldbächel-Gerümpel Riesling allerfeinste Goldbeeren TBA 1937 *347*; Luginsland Riesling BA 1971 *359*; Mandelgarten Natur 1937 *347*; Mandelgarten Scheurebe BA 1969 *356*; Mandelgarten Scheurebe Spätlese 1985 *368*; Rechbächel Riesling Cabinet 1963 *354*; Rechbächel Riesling TBA 1957 *355*, 1992 *377*
Wallhauser Johannisberg Riesling Auslese 1999 *389*; Mühlenberg Grauer Burgunder Eiswein 1973 *360*, 1990 *375*; Mühlenberg Riesling Eiswein 1983 *367*; Mühlenberg Ruländer Eiswein TBA 1973 *360*
Wallufer Walkenberg Riesling Auslese 1989 *372*; Walkenberg Riesling BA 1976 *362-3*; Walkenberg Riesling Kabinett 1979 *364*
Warre 1851 *451*, 1870 *452*, 1900 *455*, 1922 *457*, 1924 *458*, 1927 *459*, 1931 *461*, 1945, 1946 *464*, 1947, 1948 *465*, 1950 *467*, 1955 *468*, 1958 *469*, 1960 *470-1*, 1962 *471*, 1963 *473*, 1966 *474-5*, 1970 *478*, 1975, 1976 *479*, 1977 *480-1*, 1980 *483*, 1982 *484*, 1983 *485*, 1985 *487*, 1987, 1988 *488*, 1991 *490*, 1994 *491*, 1997 *493*, 2000 *494*; LBV 1969 *475*; Reserve 1986 *488*
'Waterloo' Bual, Solera 1815 *497*
Wawerner Herrenberger Riesling Eiswein 1989 *372*
Wehlener Abtei Riesling hochfeine Auslese naturrein 1969 *356*; Nonnenberg Natur 1950 *350*; Nonnenberg Riesling Auslese Goldkapsel 1993 *378*; Sonnenuhr Riesling Auslese 1921 *346*, 1949 *350*, 1966 *355*, 1976 *363*, 1979 *364*, 1982 *366*, 1985 *368*, 1988 *370*, 1989 *372*, 1990 *375*, 1992 *377*, 1993 *378*, 1994 *380*, 1995 *382*, 1996 *384*, 1997 *386*, 1998 *387*; Sonnenuhr Riesling Auslese Goldkapsel 1971 *359*, 1976 *363*, 1982 *366*, 1983 *367*, 1988 *370*, 1990 *375*, 1992 *377*, 1993 *378*, 1994 *380*, 1995 *382*, 1996 *384*, 1998 *387*; Sonnenuhr Riesling Auslese Goldkapsel Cask 29 1997 *386*; Sonnenuhr Riesling Auslese lange

Goldkapsel 1976 *363*, 1983 *367*, 1990 *375*, 1998 *387*; Sonnenuhr Riesling BA 1953, 1957 *351*, 1970 *357*, 1971 *359*, 1975 *360*, 1976 *363*, 1982 *366*, 1983 *367*, 1985 *369*, 1989 *372*, 1995 *382*; Sonnenuhr Riesling Eiswein 1981 *365*, 1983 *367*, 1969 *356*; Sonnenuhr Riesling feine Auslese 1949 *350*, 1962 *353*, 1969 *356*; Sonnenuhr Riesling feine Auslese Fuder 15 1964 *354*, 1967 *355*; Sonnenuhr Riesling feinste Auslese 1943 *348*, 1959 *352*, 1967 *355*, 1969 *356*; Sonnenuhr Riesling feinste Auslese Eiswein 1970 *357*; Sonnenuhr Riesling hochfeine Auslese 1969 *356*; Sonnenuhr Riesling Kabinett 1984 *368*, 1997 *386*, 1998 *387*; Sonnenuhr Riesling lange Goldkapsel 1975 *360*, 1982 *366*, 1985 *368-9*, 1988 *370*, 1993 *378*, 1995 *382*; Sonnenuhr Riesling lange Goldkapsel Auslese 1976 *363*; Sonnenuhr Riesling Spätlese 1959 *352*, 1964 *354*, 1971 *359*, 1975 *360*, 1979 *364*, 1982 *366*, 1987 *369*, 1988 *370*, 1989 *372*, 1990 *375*, 1992 *377*, 1993 *378*, 1994 *380*, 1995 *382*, 1996 *384*, 1997 *386*, 1998 *387*; Sonnenuhr Riesling TBA 1959 *352*, 1971 *359*, 1976 *363*, 1989 *372*
Weil, Robert Riesling Kabinett 2000 *391*; Riesling Kabinett trocken 2000 *391*; Riesling Spätlese trocken 2000 *391*
Weissburgunder und Chardonnay QbA trocken 2000 *391*
Wenceslaus de Souza Guimarães 1815 *450*
Wendouree Syrah 1990 *533*
White & Co, J & C 1844 *451*
Wild Duck Creek, Late Harvest Shiraz *533*
Wiltinger Braune Kupp Riesling Auslese 1990 *375*; Braune Kupp Riesling Auslese Goldkapsel 1996 *384*; Braune Kupp Riesling Auslese BA 1993 *378*; Braune Kupp Riesling Spätlese 1989 *372*; Hölle Riesling Auslese 1989 *372*; Hölle Riesling Spätlese 1989 *372*; Jesuitengarten Riesling Spätlese 1969 *356*; Kupp Riesling Auslese 1976 *363*
Winkeler Hasensprung Riesling Auslese 1989 *372*, 1995 *382*; Hasensprung Riesling Eiswein 1992 *377*, 1998 *387*; Hasensprung Riesling Spätlese trocken 1990 *374*; Hasensprung Riesling TBA 1971 *359*,

1976 *363*; Honigsberg Riesling Spätlese 1983 *367*; Jesuitengarten Riesling Auslese 1976 *363*, 1996 *384*; Jesuitengarten Riesling BA 1989 *372*; Jesuitengarten Riesling Spätlese 1969 *356*
Wither Hills, Pinot Noir 1999 *534*
Wollsteiner Äffchen Sämling Auslese Eiswein 1962 *353*; Ziffchen Optima Ruländer BA 1979 *364*
Würzburger Abstleite Muskat Eiswein 1994 *380*

## Y

Yalumba 'Sauternes' 1932 *532*
Yarra Yering, No 1 Cabernet Sauvignon 1990 *533*
Ygrec 1959 *188*, 1962 *189*, 1966 *189-90*, 1971 *193*, 1978 *197*, 1985 *201*, 1986 *202*, 1988 *203*
Yquem, Ch d' (d omitted 1789-1855) 1784, 1787 *170*, 1802, 1811, 1814, 1818, 1822, 1825, 1828, 1831, 1834, 1838 *171*, 1840, 1841, 1846, 1847, 1848, 1851 *172*, 1858, 1859, 1861, 1864 *172*, 1865 *172-3*, 1867, 1868, 1869, 1870, 1871, 1874, 1875 *173*, 1876, 1884, 1886, 1887, 1888, 1890, 1891, 1892, 1893 *174-5*, 1894, 1895, 1896, 1899 *175*, 1900, 1901, 1902, 1903, 1904, 1905, 1906, 1907, 1908 *176*, 1909, 1911, 1912, 1913, 1914, 1916, 1917, 1918, 1919 *177*, 1920, 1921, 1922 *178*, 1923, 1924, 1925, 1926, 1927 *179*, 1928, 1929 *180*, 1931, 1932, 1933, 1934 *181*, 1935, 1936, 1937, 1938, 1939, 1940, 1941 *182*, 1942, 1943, 1944, 1945 *183*, 1946 *183-4*, 1947, 1948, 1949 *184*, 1950, 1953 *185*, 1954, 1955 *186*, 1956 *186-7*, 1957, 1958, 1959 *187*, 1960, 1961, 1962 *188*, 1963, 1965, 1966 *189*, 1967 *190*, 1968, 1969 *191*, 1970 *192*, 1971 *193*, 1973 *193-4*, 1975 *194*, 1976 *195*, 1977, 1978 *196*, 1979, 1980 *197*, 1981, 1982 *198*, 1983 *199*, 1984, 1985 *200*, 1986 *201*, 1987, 1988 *202*, 1989 *203*, 1990 *205*, 1991 *206*, 1992 *207*, 1994 *207*, 1995 *208*, 1996 *209*, 1997 *210*, 1998 *211*, 2001 *214*

## Z

Zaca Mesa, Reserve Pinot Noir 1986 *519*
Zeltinger Schlossberg Riesling feine Auslese 1966 *355*; Sonnenuhr Riesling Auslese 1996 *385*